An Ocean Apart

An Ocean Apart

THE RELATIONSHIP BETWEEN BRITAIN AND AMERICA IN THE TWENTIETH CENTURY

David Dimbleby
& David Reynolds

BBC BOOKS
Hodder & Stoughton
LONDON SYDNEY AUCKLAND TORONTO

British Library Cataloguing in Publication Data

Dimbleby, David
An ocean apart: the relationship between Britain and America in the twentieth century.
1. Great Britain – Foreign relations – United States 2. United States – Foreign relations – Great Britain 3. Great Britain – Foreign relations – 20th century
4. United States – Foreign relations – 20th century
I. Title II. Reynolds, David
327.41073 E183.8.G7

ISBN 0-340-40666-6
ISBN 0-563-20591-1 BBC

 Printed in Great Britain for Hodder and Stoughton Limited, Mill Road, Dunton Green, Sevenoaks, Kent and BBC Books, a division of BBC Enterprises Limited, Woodlands, 80 Wood Lane, London W12 0TT by St Edmundsbury Press Limited, Bury St Edmunds, Suffolk. Photoset by Rowland Phototypesetting Limited, Bury St Edmunds, Suffolk. Hodder and Stoughton Editorial Office: 47 Bedford Square, London WC1B 3DP.

Contents

Illustrations

Maps

Cartoons

Acknowledgment is due to the following for cartoons and illustrations in the text:

Steve Bell, page 304; Clifford Berryman/Library of Congress, Washington DC, page 121; Daniel Bishop/*St Louis Star-Times*, page 128; British Airways, page 300; Cummings/*Daily Express*, page 191; Garland/*Daily Telegraph*/Cartoon Study Centre, University of Kent, page 251; Giles/*Daily Express*, page 159; Hoover plc, page 104; Jak/Mail Newspapers plc, page 318; London University Library, page 9; Low/Mail Newspapers plc, page 167 and 189; Peter Newark's Western Americana, page 44; *Private Eye*, page 327; (Reproduced by permission of) *Punch*, pages 17, 36, 72, 174, 233 and 299; *Stars and Stripes*, page 151; (Reproduced by permission of) Tribune Media Services, pages 67, 91 and 131; Universal Press Syndicate/Oliphant, page 255; Vicky/Mail Newspapers plc, page 238; *Washington Post*/Herbert Block/Creators Syndication, page 218.

The publishers apologise for any unintentional omission or oversight, and will be pleased to insert an appropriate acknowledgment in any subsequent edition of this book.

Acknowledgments

The idea for this book sprang from the BBC TV and KCET Los Angeles television series of the same name, which was presented by David Dimbleby, with David Reynolds acting as principal historical adviser. Although this is not 'the book of the film', many of the interviews conducted and the stories unearthed for the series have provided new insights which have strengthened the narrative.

The television project was conceived by Peter Pagnamenta, who, shortly after work began, was promoted to head the BBC's Current Affairs Department. His place as executive producer was taken by George Carey. The series producer was Adam Curtis, with Peter Salmon and Belinda Giles producing two of the seven films. Blaine Baggett was the producer for KCET. The authors are grateful to all of them for their many valuable contributions to this book. They would also like to thank everyone who played a part in putting together the film series: Linda Parker, production assistant; Nick Catliff, Leonie Jameson, Kerry Platman, Betty Scharf, researchers; Christine Whittaker, David Thaxton, Kevin Brown, film researchers; June Leech, picture researcher; Professor Warren F. Kimball, American adviser.

Our publishers at Hodder and Stoughton have coped stoically with text arriving at the last minute, inevitable in a project of this kind, and have been unfailingly helpful and encouraging under the pressure of producing a complex book at great speed. To our editors, Ion Trewin and Jane Osborn, to their staff, especially Christine Casley, to Paul Dowswell, who found many of the pictures and cartoons, to Alec Spark, who drew the maps, and to Douglas Matthews who compiled the index, we are deeply indebted. Our thanks also go to our agents Michael Sissons and Peter Matson.

David Dimbleby would particularly like to thank: Belinda Giles, who apart from producing one of the films, assisted him with the book, offering in generous quantities encouragement and criticism; and Carolyn Smith, who not only typed and retyped many drafts of the manuscript, thus allowing joint authorship to become a reality, but who did so with a patience and understanding which twenty years of working with him does not appear to have diminished.

David Reynolds is very grateful to his colleagues at Christ's College for allowing him to monopolise the Fellows' word processor, and to Cambridge friends Dr John Thompson and Dr David Cannadine, Professor Bernard Bailyn of Harvard University, and his wife Margaret Ray Reynolds, who all commented on chapters of his original draft.

Professor John Blum of Yale University generously read the final manuscript, and Dr John Baylis, Ms Diane Kunz, Professor Richard Neustadt and Professor Barry Supple were among those who helped with specialist advice.

Crown copyright documents are quoted by permission of the Controller of HM Stationery Office. For other special permissions the authors are grateful to: The National Maritime Museum, Greenwich; the British Library of Political and Economic Science; the University of Birmingham; the Borthwick Institute, York; and Yale University Library.

David Dimbleby
December 1987 David Reynolds

Introduction

'Where y'all from?' asked a teenage student in St Louis, Missouri.

'Britain.'

'Oh, ya.' A moment's hesitation, then: 'Isn't that that itsy-bitsy little country – near France?'

'What do you know about it?'

'Let me think. Buckingham. Buckingham something.'

Then, triumphantly: 'Buckingham Palace.'[1]

The decline of Britain, from the most powerful nation in the world to a small country that a young American from the midwest can barely identify, has been as swift as the rise of the United States to occupy the position Britain once held. The two processes were intimately connected. America's rise would have been slower but for Britain's decline.

At the turn of the century Britain ruled over the largest empire ever seen: one-fifth of the globe was under her control. With the empire came ownership of the natural resources needed for industrial manufacture, a monopoly over much of the trade that flowed from it, and mastery, of the sea-lanes which provided safe passage for her ships. As America's industry started to expand and seek markets beyond its shores, it inevitably came into conflict with this empire. Britain was not much loved. To the United States, which had but recently thrown off the British yoke, she seemed not only arrogant in her assumption of a natural right to supremacy, but tricky and devious too. This hostility was exacerbated by the conviction of all right-thinking Americans that Britain's wealth was immoral, since it was based on colonialism, which reduced millions to servitude.

Britain would not have recognised this picture of herself. In her eyes, she was keeping the peace across great tracts of the earth and raising ignorant peoples to understand and adopt British attitudes to the rule of law, fair government and individual liberty. In the process she had naturally been rewarded with the economic advantages that flowed from her benign rule. The United States was not a serious threat to her position, although it was occasionally an irritant. For the most part America was regarded with amused condescension, a country not yet civilised, in the European sense, but uncouth and raw.

It is remarkable that power has passed from one great nation to another in such a short time without a shot being fired in anger, still less a major war being fought between them. It was not just their own good sense or friendship but other conflicts which have ensured this. The world has been torn apart by war twice in this century. On each occasion Britain has been among the first to enter the fray. In each conflict, at the point of exhaustion, she has been saved by the United States, and each time, although undefeated, Britain's power has been diminished and her economy weakened.

The United States, on the other hand, emerged from both wars much stronger. As a neutral its economy profited from manufacturing the weapons of war for the belligerents, while itself remaining at peace. Even after joining the wars America was protected from the devastation that its allies suffered by the vast oceans that separated it from the fighting.

Britain's decline as a consequence of these two wars created the opportunities America sought. Power did not have to be wrested from Britain. It fell into America's hands as a result of her weakness, a transition fraught with misunderstandings, mutual suspicion and occasionally outright hostility. Yet Britain and America were also partners in the two great conflicts, helping to win the victory and impose the peace in ways that shaped our modern world.

Americans sometimes say that they envy Britain 'her history', forgetting that her history is their history. The Founding Fathers were British, citizens of British America, who inherited attitudes that left their mark on every aspect of American society. Many of the settlers had first crossed the Atlantic to the New World in order to revive the British tradition of liberty which they felt was being eroded in Britain. They fought against Britain and secured their independence in defence of those same liberties. Liberal values inspired them to create a country more open and more democratic than Britain and to denounce the British Empire long after they had freed themselves from it. But the fact that the two countries shared a liberal inheritance has been more important than their differences over how it should be applied. In this century they have been natural allies in the fight against the threats from Prussian militarism, fascist dictatorship and communist revolution, bound together by a common belief in liberal, capitalist democracy.

The other important element in their common heritage is that both countries speak English. Much is made of the misunderstandings that arise across 'the barrier of a common language'. Winston Churchill remembered a wartime conference which nearly came to blows because of the opposite meanings of the verb 'to table'.* But the advantages outweigh any disadvantage. Contact between Britons and Americans has always been easy at every level – military, diplomatic, political and personal. They have been able to establish intimate ties, to understand the other's attitudes, to develop complex relationships without recourse to dictionaries or interpreters. In literature and learning, in films and television, in science, technology and industry, they have affected each other more closely than any other countries in modern history.

In this book we trace how the complex relationship between Britain and America has evolved during this century and how it has influenced the world we live in now. To understand this process it is necessary to start at the beginning, with the origins of the United States, long before it became known as a superpower, long before anyone could call Britain 'an itsy-bitsy little country – near France'.

* In Britain 'to table' a motion is to put it on the table for discussion; in the USA it means to withdraw it from consideration.[2]

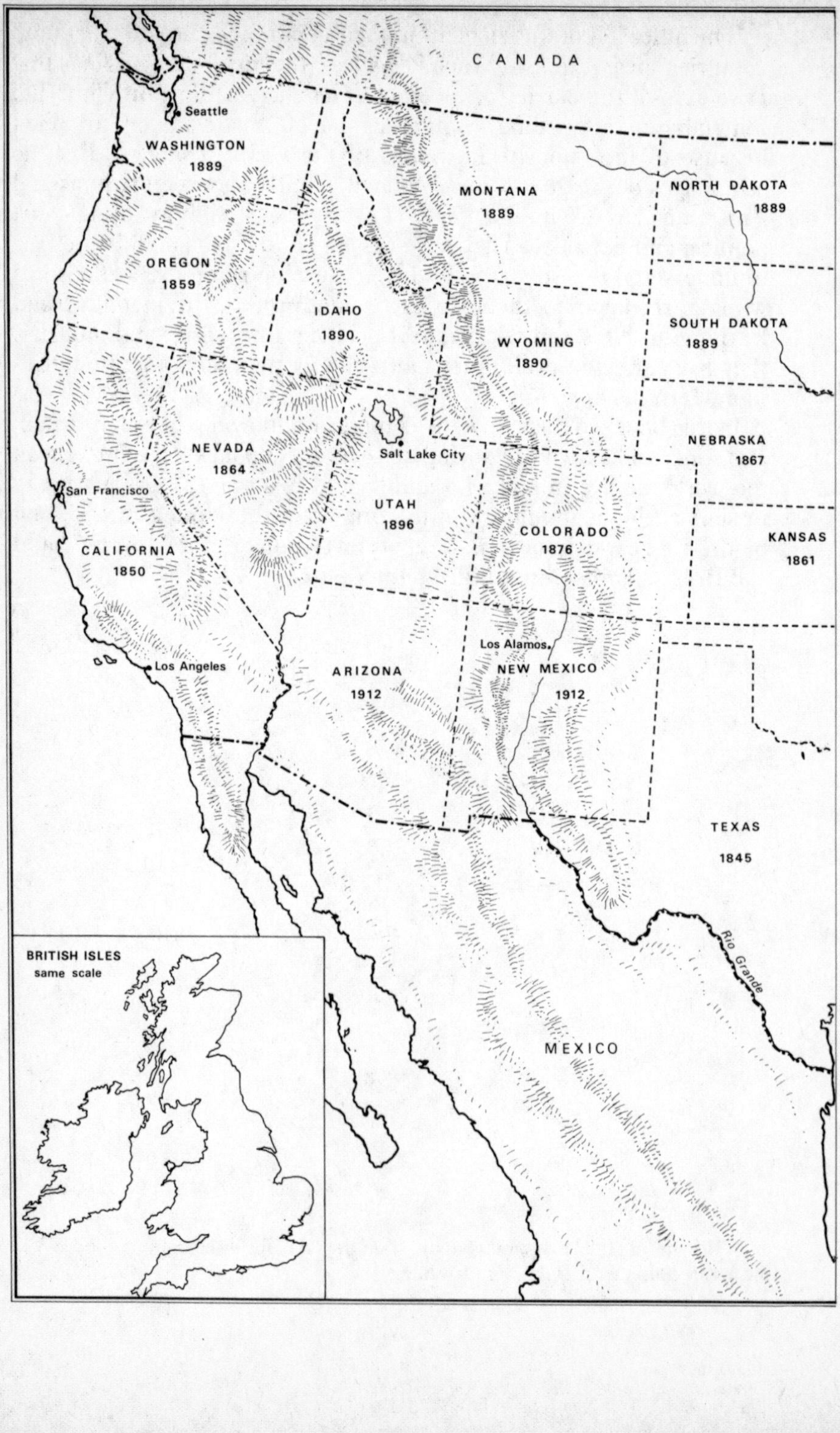
CANADA
Seattle
WASHINGTON
1889
MONTANA
1889
NORTH DAKOTA
1889
OREGON
1859
IDAHO
1890
SOUTH DAKOTA
1889
WYOMING
1890
NEBRASKA
1867
Salt Lake City
NEVADA
1864
San Francisco
UTAH
1896
COLORADO
1876
KANSAS
1861
CALIFORNIA
1850
Los Alamos
NEW MEXICO
1912
Los Angeles
ARIZONA
1912
TEXAS
1845
Rio Grande
MEXICO
BRITISH ISLES
same scale

THE UNITED STATES OF AMERICA
L SUPERIOR
L MICHIGAN
L HURON
L ONTARIO
L ERIE
St Lawrence
Quebec
MAINE
1820
MINNESOTA
1858
WISCONSIN
1848
MICHIGAN
1837
VERMONT
1791
NEW HAMPSHIRE
1788
NEW YORK
1788
Boston
MASS
1788
CONN
1788
RHODE IS
1790
Milwaukee
Detroit
New York
IOWA
1846
Chicago
PENNSYLVANIA
1787
Philadelphia
R Missouri
Omaha
OHIO
1803
NEW JERSEY
1787
ILLINOIS
1818
INDIANA
1816
MARYLAND
1788
Washington
DELAWARE
1787
WEST VIRGINIA
1863
R Ohio
Kansas City
St Louis
VIRGINIA
1788
MISSOURI
1821
KENTUCKY
1792
R Mississippi
NORTH CAROLINA
1789
TENNESSEE
1796
OKLAHOMA
1907
ARKANSAS
1836
Memphis
SOUTH CAROLINA
1788
Charleston
MISSISSIPPI
1817
GEORGIA
1788
ALABAMA
1819
Dallas
ATLANTIC
OCEAN
LOUISIANA
1812
New Orleans
FLORIDA
1845
BAHAMA
ISLANDS
GULF OF MEXICO
Miami
Dates indicate admission
to the Union as States
CUBA
0
400
Miles
0
500
Km

1

The Struggle for Independence

c. 1620–1865

The *Mayflower* hit the full force of an Atlantic storm a few weeks out from Plymouth. One of her main beams cracked and the tiny ship, less than 100 feet long, was forced to drift with the wind for days, tossed to and fro. As they lay in the dark below decks, nauseated by the movement and the stench, many of her 102 passengers must have wondered whether their decision to leave England was right. They were an ill-assorted bunch. Some were pilgrims, Puritans like William Bradford, whose determination to worship their God according to conscience and the Scriptures had led them from their homes in Nottinghamshire first to Holland and finally across the Atlantic. But others were 'strangers' to the pilgrim faith, men and women, mostly recruited by the London merchant adventurers financing the voyage, who were prompted by the depressed economy of England and the lack of opportunity to seek a better life across the ocean.

The Atlantic crossing took more than two months. As soon as they made their landfall on the scrubby sand dunes of Cape Cod on 11 November 1620, the free adult males solemnly pledged to 'Covenant and Combine ourselves together into a Civil Body Politic, for our better ordering and preservation'. But by the time they had found a place fit for habitation, with a good water supply and safe harbour, winter was already upon them and they did not begin work on the first house, a communal log cabin with thatched roof, until 25 December. Over the next three months, Bradford grimly recorded in his history of the colony, 'half of their company died, especially in January and February, being the depth of winter, and wanting houses and other comforts; being infected with the scurvy and other diseases which this long voyage and their inaccommodate condition had brought upon them'. Bradford's own wife, Dorothy, was one of the early fatalities. In April 1621 the *Mayflower*, which had wintered with them, set sail for England. Despite all their hardships, none of the settlers returned with her, but few could have watched the little ship turn down Plymouth Bay towards the open sea without their hearts sinking. They were now on their own. Behind them was what Bradford called 'a hideous and desolate wilderness, full of wild beasts and wild men'. And, on the other side, 'there was the mighty ocean which they had passed and was now as a main bar and gulf to separate them from all the civil parts of the world'.[1]

The founders of Plymouth colony were not the first Europeans to encounter the new continent and its Indian inhabitants. In South America, following Christopher Columbus's voyage of 1492, the Spanish and Portuguese carved out their own empires. They were lured by gold, justifying their cupidity in the name of God. Later, northern Europeans began to leave their mark on the eastern seaboard of North America. By the beginning of the seventeenth century trading posts were being established by the French on the St Lawrence river and by the Dutch at New Amsterdam at the mouth of the Hudson. But it was the English who mastered North America. Early settlements along the James river in Virginia (named for Elizabeth, the 'Virgin Queen') were followed by the establishment of Plymouth and by a steady influx of migrants during the 1630s and 1640s. Religious persecution, civil war and the collapse of the English cloth trade impelled many to make a leap of faith, hope or even desperation across the ocean into an unknown world. By 1660 Britain's mainland American colonists numbered 70,000.

These early settlers named their new settlements after the towns and villages they had left behind: Plymouth, Boston, Ipswich, Newbury, Gloucester. Granted land by a trading company or, later, by a colonial government, they divided it up in the manner they were used to back home. Many Massachusetts settlers had been accustomed to a degree of self-government in their remote villages in Yorkshire or the West Country. They re-created these patterns of life, with compact townships in the midst of open fields farmed in individual lots. There were town meetings, elected leaders and officers with familiar English names such as Town Constable and Surveyor of Highways. In Virginia and colonies further south the settlers followed practices typical of other parts of England, such as Suffolk and Essex, with separate farms at some distance from each other, organised by counties and governed through the county court by other familiar English officials, the Sheriffs and Justices of the Peace.

These first settlers were trying to reproduce the ways of life they had known in England, but free of the religious, political and economic constraints that had forced them to emigrate. They were Englishmen transplanted, and, in the process, transformed. The institutions they established, like the Virginia parish or the Massachusetts town meeting, proved very different from their English counterparts. There was no church hierarchy, with land, wealth and power, to keep the local parish in check. There was no rigid political structure of aristocratic landowners and royal government to regiment the life of local townships. Inevitably, some colonists became wealthier and more powerful than the rest, in southern colonies like Virginia establishing an élite of local gentry, and in ports like Boston and New York a class of wealthy merchants and lawyers. But life in all the colonies, though following English ways, remained freer and less structured than anything in England.

Politics also were English in outward form but different in practice. The constitutions of the colonies were based on the traditions of representative government in England, which had been wrested from the Crown over many generations, particularly at the time of the English Civil War of the 1640s. Each colony was self-governing, owing its allegiance ultimately to the Sovereign. A Governor usually represented the King, with an appointed Council and an elected Assembly taking the place of the two Houses of the British Parliament. As the lower houses expanded their powers throughout the colonies, they justified themselves by British precedent. The Massachusetts Assembly reminded its Governor in the 1760s, 'this house has the same inherent rights in this province as the House of Commons has in Great Britain'.[2]

The franchise followed the English pattern. Only males who were owners of freehold property could vote. In England this limited their numbers but in the colonies most settlers owned their land and so were entitled to vote. The result was a franchise more liberal than anywhere in Europe. Even those who travelled as indentured servants, with their sea-passage paid on condition they worked for a master for a period, were often given freehold property when their contracts expired after five or seven years. By 1750 between half and three-quarters of the white male colonists were enfranchised. In England, the most politically advanced European nation, the proportion was still only one in five.

In other ways British America was developing its own distinctive character as the eighteenth century progressed. A majority of colonists were still of English, Scottish or Welsh stock, but the first national census of 1790 revealed that already nearly a third of the white population was non-British, mainly Irish, German or Dutch. One-fifth of the total population was black, mostly slaves imported from West Africa to work on the tobacco and rice plantations of the South.

In 1775, less than two centuries after the first settlements, there were two and a half million people living in eighteen British colonies, which now stretched 1,600 miles down the Atlantic seaboard from the mist-clad Bay of Fundy to the steamy Florida swamps and had begun to push their way into the wild interior. The population of the colonies was already one-third the size of England and Wales.*

The seeds of independence had been sown. The American colonists were freer and more diverse in character than England, and they were growing in numbers and wealth. Yet most still thought of themselves as Englishmen. They certainly had little sense of any common identity as Americans. People's horizons were local, communications primitive. Loyalties hardly extended beyond the immediate community and there were bitter rivalries between individual colonies. New England colonies such as Massachusetts and Connecticut, influenced by their heritage of Puritanism and local self-government, differed in character from southern colonies like Virginia or South Carolina where the power of the Anglican church and the big landowners, or planters, predominated. On the edge of the British world, looking back across the ocean for their values and their identity, they were held together by the authority of the British Crown.

To begin with, the colonies were governed indulgently by the British Crown, not out of generosity but because its priorities lay elsewhere. As long as the American colonies caused no trouble and did not make demands on the British exchequer their relative independence was tolerated. In the first half of the eighteenth century Britain was more concerned with the struggle for empire between herself and her two arch European rivals, France and Spain.

While the British were colonising the eastern seaboard of America, the French were active further west. They were protecting their fur trade by a line of forts and by alliances with Indian tribes extending from the St Lawrence river to the Great Lakes, down the waterways of the Ohio and Mississippi rivers all the way to New Orleans. At the

* Of these eighteen colonies, thirteen declared their independence in 1776. Of the remainder, East Florida and West Florida were ceded by Britain to Spain in 1783 (and later acquired by the USA), while Quebec, Nova Scotia and Newfoundland formed the nucleus of the future Canada.

outbreak of the Seven Years War (1756–63) – or the French and Indian Wars as they are known in the United States – the British colonists played their part by attacking the French, who were preventing their expansion westwards. A succession of British victories, including General James Wolfe's at Quebec in 1759, secured all Canada and all the French possessions east of the Mississippi for Britain. The peace treaty, signed in Paris in 1763, made Britain the dominant power in North America, and ultimately guaranteed that it would be she, not France, who exerted the formative influence on the future USA.

Even at the time, the significance of Britain's victory was apparent. Four years after the war was over Edward Gibbon was embarking on his great history of *The Decline and Fall of the Roman Empire*. He planned to write in French, generally accepted as the language of civilisation. The Scottish philosopher David Hume dissuaded him: 'Let the French triumph in the present diffusion of their tongue. Our solid and increasing establishments in America . . . promise a superior stability and duration to the English language.'[3] In 1770 Ezra Stiles, a future president of Yale College, confidently predicted that English would 'become the vernacular tongue of more people than any one tongue on Earth, except the Chinese'.[4]

British successes in the Seven Years War were not confined to North America. France's navy had been destroyed and her colonies in India conquered. The British Empire had doubled in size, but the costs of its capture and subsequent administration were heavy burdens. The national debt had risen to nearly twice its pre-war level, at £130 million, and interest charges of over £4 million had to be found each year. There was no scope for further taxation in Britain and the government decided that the American colonies, until now virtually free of the burdens of taxation, should contribute to the cost of victory and of the army being maintained in America for the colonists' protection. The various forms of taxation proposed by Britain, whether stamp duties, taxes on sugar or tea, or levies on trade, were not onerous but they alarmed merchants, lawyers and tradesmen suffering from the post-war economic depression. These professional men argued that, since they were not represented in the British Parliament at Westminster, it had no right to tax them. Banding themselves into organisations called the 'Sons of Liberty' they incited mobs to attack the homes and sometimes the persons of the British administrators responsible for collecting the taxes.

The protesters were not looking for independence from Britain. As 'freeborn Englishmen' they wanted the principle of 'No taxation without Representation', a right won in Britain a century earlier, to be accepted in the colonies. Had wiser policies been pursued by successive British governments, the crisis might have been averted. But London reacted firmly to suppress dissent and restore its authority, by insisting that the taxes be paid and by refusing to consult the colonial assemblies. The colonists foresaw a grim future if Britain were successful. She would tap the increasing prosperity of America to finance her European wars and would do so without consent. By 1775 many were convinced that they faced an organised conspiracy to suppress their liberties. In the words of the young Alexander Hamilton, later to be the financial genius of the new republic, the British King, George III, now had 'a settled, fixed plan for *enslaving* the colonies'.[5]

After several months of protest, rioting and skirmishes with British troops, an entire British army of over 30,000 men landed near New York to restore order. It was 4 July 1776. On the same day, in Philadelphia, a Congress of the thirteen leading colonies approved a Declaration of Independence, largely written by the Virginian planter Thomas Jefferson. It described in clear, vivid words the nature of the contract between governor and governed, expressing this relationship in the most revolutionary form yet seen. The old political structure of Britain, with its authority derived from the Crown, was rejected in favour of a system in which men would decide for themselves how they would be governed. The traditional rights of freeborn Englishmen, to which the colonists had appealed in the past, were now rejected in favour of an appeal to the natural rights of all humanity:

> We hold these truths to be self-evident, that all men are created equal, that they are endowed by their Creator with certain unalienable Rights, that among these are Life, Liberty and the pursuit of Happiness. That to secure these rights, Governments are instituted among Men, deriving their just powers from the consent of the governed. That whenever any form of government becomes destructive of these ends, it is the Right of the People to alter or to abolish it and to institute new Government . . .

The Declaration went on to argue that George III's 'repeated injuries and usurpations' had imperilled the rights of his people, and concluded 'that these United Colonies are, and of Right ought to be, FREE AND INDEPENDENT STATES; that they are Absolved from all Allegiance to the British Crown'.[6]

The War for Independence lasted seven years from 1776 to 1783.

Britain suffered from her extended lines of supply across the Atlantic, from poor generalship, and from impenetrable terrain. Despite George Washington's stalwart leadership, the United States, as they now called themselves, were often short of resources and food, and lacked a clear strategy. But ultimately it was Britain's old enemies, France and Spain, who ensured her defeat by lending their support to the Revolution. France saw an opportunity for harrying Britain in the Caribbean and the Indian Ocean and threatened to invade England herself. By 1781 even the Dutch, Britain's old allies, were on the enemy side and the Royal Navy had lost control of the Atlantic. Britain's armies in America were cut off and, after the humiliating surrender of General Cornwallis's troops at Yorktown, were forced to cut their losses and sue for peace. The terms of the peace treaty in 1783 were generous to the new American nation. They acknowledged its independence and granted it borders up to the Great Lakes and the Mississippi.

America won independence as a loose alliance of separate states, but it soon became apparent that they would need a proper national government in order to survive. The Founding Fathers who met in Philadelphia in 1787 to draw up a new Constitution had no intention of replacing one form of tyranny with another, of setting up a powerful central government to dominate them as George III had done. They therefore chose a federal system: the national government was instituted mainly for defence, diplomacy and to meet basic economic needs such as the provision of a currency and a postal service. State governments retained authority over most areas of their daily life. The two houses of the US Congress were also structured to protect the rights of the states. In the House of Representatives populous states were allowed to elect more members, but in the upper house, the Senate, each state, regardless of size, was allowed two Senators, to protect the interests of minorities.

The new government was a republic. After their experience under George III the Americans were determined to prevent monarchy returning under another name. The President was allowed only limited authority as Head of State and Commander-in-Chief of the armed forces. To prevent the emergence of a British-style Prime Minister, whose control over the legislature gave him a relatively free hand to run affairs, neither the President nor any other member of the executive branch of government could be members of Congress. Congress and President were chosen separately, so that a President could never be sure that he would have sufficient support to do what he wanted. And the Congress was given substantial authority of its own, for example to approve senior executive appointments and, in the case of the Senate, to ratify treaties. This principle of separating the powers of government, ensuring checks and balances between the executive, the legislature and the judiciary, was a profound innovation, and one that would shape America's future history and its relations with Britain. As later British governments were to discover, Congress could prevent an American President delivering what he had promised.

In name the United States of America was now an independent nation with its own unique government. But in reality it would be many years before America could feel itself truly free of Britain. For the British acted swiftly to restore their control over the seas, temporarily lost in the 1780s. They imposed restrictions on the use of American ships on key sugar trade routes with her colonies in the Caribbean. Britain also retained control of all North America above the Great Lakes, and was slow to withdraw from the forts in the American north-west which she had conceded in 1783. The states of the new Union, impoverished by war, feared the possibility of a British campaign of reconquest.

The list of American grievances against the British grew when Britain and France renewed hostilities in the 1790s. Soon Britain was threatened with economic strangulation by Napoleon. She responded ruthlessly to her enemy's attempt to control the seas, claiming the right to board neutral ships and confiscate goods bound for enemy ports. American ship owners, who were prospering from the wartime trade, protested. They were even angrier when Britain claimed the right to seize British-born seamen from these ships, and impress them into the Royal Navy, regardless of whether or not they had taken up American citizenship. These irritations were compounded by the clamour from settlers in the American north-west to attack British Canada, and from Southerners to use the opportunity to push America's boundaries south into Florida, now controlled by Spain, who had become allied with Britain against Napoleon.

In June 1812 the Congress was asked by President James Madison whether Americans should 'continue passive under these progressive usurpations and these accumulating wrongs, or, opposing force to force in defense of their national rights, shall commit a just cause into the hands of the Almighty . . .'[7] Congress decided to declare war on Britain. It was a near disaster for the United States. The attempted invasion of Canada was a failure. The New England states, who had opposed the war, threatened to secede from the Union. In August 1814 British troops even sacked the American capital, Washington, and Madison and his wife barely had time to escape. The British commander, Admiral George Cockburn, found the table at the President's house set for dinner, with wine, in coolers of ice, ready to be served. After availing themselves of the Madisons' unintended hospitality, the British officers selected a few souvenirs, Cockburn taking one of the President's hats and a cushion from his wife's chair, and then left the house to be looted and fired by their soldiers. The new republic was humiliated, but this was just the way of war. The British were taking revenge for the burning of York (now Toronto), which was the capital of Canada.

The transatlantic conflict was a sideshow for Britain compared with the European war and, once Napoleon was defeated, she was ready to make peace. Despite subsequent crises, despite rivalry and suspicion, these two countries henceforth managed to settle their differences peacefully. Few great powers have been so successful. But the war of 1812 gave American nationalism a sharply anti-British edge. The President's house was painted white to cover the scorch marks, hence its future name, and subsequent British visitors, to this day, are firmly reminded of the reason. Out of the conflict also came a national anthem, 'The Star Spangled Banner', composed at a critical moment during the British siege of Baltimore.

The Napoleonic Wars had confirmed the extent of Britain's power. Putting the loss of her American colonies behind her, she carved out

American cartoonist Amos Doolittle (1813) sees the war as a chance for Jonathan (the USA) to teach John Bull a lesson.

a new empire in India, Australia and New Zealand. By the middle of the century she was producing forty per cent of the world's manufactured goods and importing over a third of the world's trade. Sterling was becoming as acceptable as gold and the City of London emerged as the main source of international investment. Meanwhile America remained a colony of Britain in economic terms. It had little industry of its own, mainly selling primary products to Britain and buying manufactured goods in return. Between 1820 and 1860 nearly half America's exports went to Britain, and forty per cent of American imports came from Britain. The trade was largely funded by great British banking houses, such as Barings, who also supplied much of the capital for developing America's transport system: roads, canals, bridges and above all the railroads that opened up the west.

Despite independence, then, the young United States lived in the shadow of Britain. America's military and economic weakness dictated a cautious foreign policy. President George Washington in his farewell address of 1796 had warned his fellow countrymen to beware of 'the insidious wiles of foreign influence'. Europe, he wrote, 'has a set of primary interests which to us have none or a very remote relation. Hence, she must be engaged in frequent controversies, the causes of which are essentially foreign to our concerns.' Washington did not suggest that America should sever trading connections with other countries. Nor did he rule out temporary alliances at times of crisis. But there should be no extension of these ties. 'Steer clear of permanent alliances with any portion of the foreign world,' he advised.[8] The policy was defined succinctly by Thomas Jefferson in 1801: 'peace, commerce, and honest friendship with all nations – entangling alliances with none'.[9]

The first serious test of these precepts came in 1823. In the 1810s Spain's colonies in South America were in revolt. To the delight of many Americans, who saw events there as the next stage of their own revolution of 1776, the Spanish were gradually forced out. But in 1823 there were fears that Spain, supported by France and Russia, might attempt reconquest. Britain, who had developed a profitable trade with these newly independent countries, was keen to prevent Spain's return. Foreign Secretary George Canning suggested to the American President, James Monroe, that they should form an alliance to resist the continental powers.

There followed a lively debate among America's leaders. Two former Presidents, Jefferson and Madison, swallowed their suspicions of Britain and urged acceptance of the offer. Jefferson advised that 'Great Britain is the nation which can do us the most harm of any

ll on earth, and with her on our side we need not fear the
rld'.[10] But John Quincy Adams, the Secretary of State, urged
ndent course. 'It would be more candid, as well as more
he told Monroe's Cabinet, 'to avow our principles explicitly
nd France, than to come in as a cock-boat in the wake of
man-of-war.'[11]

ce was accepted. America remained true to the principle
ling alliances, of acting alone. In December 1823, Monroe
ned Spain and her allies that 'we should consider any
heir part to extend their system to any portion of this
as dangerous to our peace and safety'. Although his
d not apply to 'the existing colonies or dependencies of
n power', he warned that interference with a state that
recognised as independent would be regarded as 'the
of an unfriendly disposition toward the United States'.
Doctrine, as it became known, was of immense import-
ture of American diplomacy. It laid claim to a special
on the American continent, both North and South, in
d States would brook no interference. It was a warning
l powers of Europe and to Britain to keep out, just
s promised not to 'interfere in the internal concerns'
[12]

of such a policy from the young nation seemed
ain and her allies had gone to war the United
e maintained the Monroe Doctrine without the
Navy. But Britain was gratified that, although
alliance, America had at least acted in parallel
Spain. Canning claimed later that he had 'called
istence to redress the balance of the Old'.[13]

American interests and values as the opposite
for a hypersensitive ex-colony. The Britain
d rebelled was depicted by them as the land
and privilege, of imperial oppression and
frivolity and corruption – in short as the
as Jefferson once called its inhabitants
ing, squibbling, carnivorous animals' and
olite, self-denying, feeling, hospitable,
erica.[14] American nationalists wanted
wn culture, to emphasise its separation.
mous dictionary, even called for a new
ation, our honor requires us to have
e as government.' He predicted that

in time North America would speak a language 'as different future language of England, as the modern Dutch, Da Swedish are from the German, or from one another'.[15]

All this was part of the process of building a separate defining its identity as a New World an ocean apart fror British visitors in the early nineteenth century often rema Americans' inveterate habit of boasting about their r and imagined achievements and deriding everything Bri Smith, the English writer and wit, tried to put them fi place in 1820:

> In the four quarters of the globe, who reads an Amer goes to an American play? or looks at an American pic What does the world yet owe to American physician: What new substances have their chemists discove old ones have they analyzed? What new constellati discovered by the telescopes of Americans? What in mathematics? Who drinks out of American glass American plates? or wears American coats or gov American blankets? Finally, under which of th governments of Europe is every sixth man a fellow-creatures may buy and sell and torture?

To such criticism Americans were acutely se novelist Fanny Trollope commented in 1832 have been called thin-skinned, but the citizen apparently, no skins at all; they wince if a bre unless it be tempered with adulation'.[17]

But, for all the rhetoric, American nationa their country was developing a distinctive cha century progressed. Even in the colonial pe non-English immigrants, and the flow b after Independence. Between 1815 and 1 migrated to the USA, of whom nearly tw and the German states, driven out by f were not Protestants but Roman Catho customs and religious practices. They se giving cities like New York and St character.

Equally unique was the rapid der Founding Fathers were mostly élitists should be kept in its place. But by th franchises had been abolished and nearly all white adult males had the vote. They were now able to elect not merely US Congressmen and members of their state assemblies but also their Head of State, the President. Elections were fiercely contested: in 1840 eighty per cent of the electorate voted in the contest for the presidency. And around them developed the razzmatazz of electioneering, with banners, slogans, parades and organised, grass-roots political parties. The idea that ordinary people should choose their government was an audacious experiment. It was another half-century or more before it began to take root in the monarchies of Europe.

But democracy was more than a system of government. Its egalitarian values permeated the whole of American society. Alexis de Tocqueville, author of the classic work *Democracy in America*, and the most perceptive European observer of the pre-Civil War era, considered 'the equality of conditions' to be 'the basic fact', the most striking 'novelty', about the United States.[18] De Tocqueville exaggerated. In the big cities of the north-east the top one per cent of the population owned about a quarter of the wealth in the 1820s. But he was broadly correct, especially about rural areas. Compared with Europe, America was more egalitarian, its social structure less ossified. There was no hereditary aristocracy, dominating national politics and social life. The greater availability of land enabled people to move around more easily and to shape their own fortunes. Even Americans entering what in Britain would be called domestic service retained their 'innate sentiment of independence', according to Thomas Grattan, the British traveller. 'They satisfy themselves that they are *helps*, not servants – that they are going to work with (not for) Mr so and so . . . they call him and his wife their *employers*, not their master and mistress.'[19]

By the 1830s American-style democracy was becoming an issue in British politics. The emerging middle classes cited the American example in their campaigns for the vote, free trade and a system of publicly-financed education. The United States, claimed John Stuart Mill, showed how a country could develop when the middle class was given free rein. He asked his readers in 1840 'whether, with the single difference of our remaining respect for aristocracy, the American people, both in their good qualities and in their defects, resemble anything so much as our own middle class?'[20] Radical democrats like the Chartists went further, claiming that 'what democracy is in practice, we are now able to show to the appalled aristocrats. Look across the Atlantic. There we see a great nation springing up as no other people ever did; there we see millions of contented and happy human beings . . . there we see representative self-government doing for the nation what no other government did or ever can do.'[21]

Conservatives countered by indicting America as a horrifying example of a society in which the principle of aristocracy, rule by the best, had been replaced by the pursuit of money and mob popularity. Thomas Hamilton, who toured America in 1830–1, wrote of its politics: 'No man can even enter public life without first truckling to the mob, and too often paltering with his conscience. He must profess – often falsely profess – to entertain all the prejudices of the ignorant men by whom he is elected. He goes to Congress with a halter round his neck.'[22] And Benjamin Disraeli, then Tory Chancellor of the Exchequer, but soon to become Prime Minister, warned in 1866: 'If a dominant multitude were to succeed in bringing the land of England into the condition of the land of America . . . England, from being a first-rate Kingdom, would become a third-rate Republic.'[23]

But, despite the growing British debate about democracy, America was still peripheral to Britain's vision of herself. And Americans were not, as yet, concerned to recast the outside world in their mould. They saw their destiny as lying not across the Atlantic but to the west, in the vast prairies, forests and mountain ranges of the hinterland. In 1800 this was still controlled by the European imperial powers, France, Spain and Britain, and by the original inhabitants, the American Indians. During the next half-century the new republic broke out of the eastern corridor in which it had been born, and established its authority from the Atlantic to the Pacific. The west, like Britain's empire, was won by bribery, intrigue and war, not to mention the gradual extermination of its Indian inhabitants. But that was not how most Americans saw it. To them it was America's 'manifest destiny to overspread and to possess the continent which Providence has given us for the development of the great experiment of Liberty'.[24]

France was the first to withdraw from America. In 1803, needing to finance the war with Britain, Napoleon sold Louisiana to the United States. The $11.25 million purchase price was, ironically, mainly raised through loans from British banks. The acquisition, far bigger than the present state of Louisiana, doubled the size of the United States at a stroke. Next, Spain was driven from Florida during the 1810s. Its Latin American empire also collapsed, leaving a vast, independent Mexican state along the United States' southern and western borders. This was quickly cut down to size by the aggressive expansionist policy of President James Polk. Texas broke away from Mexico and in 1845 was annexed to the United States. War with Mexico followed over border claims and by 1848 the modern southern

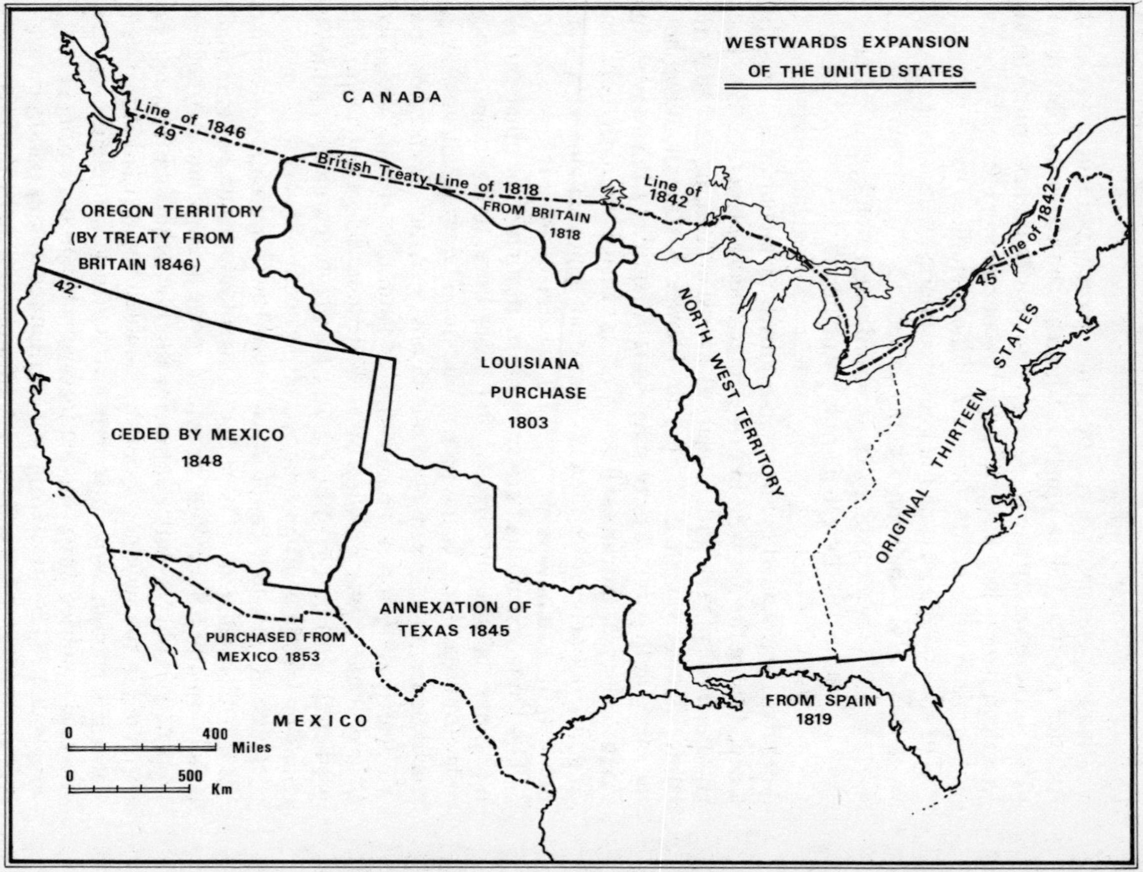

WESTWARDS EXPANSION
OF THE UNITED STATES
CANADA
Line of 1846
49°
British Treaty Line of 1818
FROM BRITAIN
1818
Line of
1842
Line of 1842
45°
OREGON TERRITORY
(BY TREATY FROM
BRITAIN 1846)
42°
LOUISIANA
PURCHASE
1803
NORTH WEST TERRITORY
ORIGINAL THIRTEEN STATES
CEDED BY MEXICO
1848
ANNEXATION OF
TEXAS 1845
PURCHASED FROM
MEXICO 1853
FROM SPAIN
1819
MEXICO
0
400
Miles
0
500
Km

boundaries of the United States had been virtually fixed. Territory that later became the US states of Arizona, Utah, Nevada, New Mexico and California, all previously part of Mexico, joined the Union.

Britain, alone of the former colonial powers, remained in North America, refusing to relinquish her hold on the Canadian territories. In 1839 there was a war scare over Canada's boundary with Maine. American nationalists sang:

> Britannia shall not rule the Maine,
> Nor shall she rule the water;
> They've sung that song full long enough,
> Much longer than they oughter.[25]

That issue was settled by negotiation in 1842, only to be followed by a new dispute further west in Oregon territory. Finally, in 1846, Polk and the British Foreign Secretary, Lord Aberdeen, agreed that the border between Canada and the United States should follow the forty-ninth parallel, forty-nine degrees latitude, all the way to the Pacific. Many Americans still resented any British presence in North America, but henceforth the Canadian border was no longer an issue between the two powers.

The United States had grown to nearly three million square miles, fifty times the size of England and Wales. It extended some 3,000 miles from coast to coast: on a map of Europe the equivalent journey would be from the Pyrenees to the Ural Mountains. Even before the Mexican war America's population of seventeen million exceeded Britain's and it was growing at a prodigious rate. De Tocqueville predicted that one day America and Russia would each 'hold in its hands the destinies of half the world'.[26]

But could this vast country hold together? Or would the United States tear itself apart? Those questions became central to American politics in the 1850s, for the great expansion to the Pacific had reopened an old and bitter argument about whether slavery would be permitted in the new territories of the west. The crisis led to a civil war which could have permanently divided the United States into two separate countries. It was not, at least initially, an issue of morality, a struggle for the rights of black people, but a battle for political power.

Slave owning, once widespread throughout America, was by 1850 confined to the Southern states, where it had become essential to the big cotton plantations on which the wealth of the Southern aristocracy depended. Few Northerners endorsed the rights of blacks to be free

"WHAT? YOU YOUNG YANKEE-NOODLE, STRIKE YOUR OWN FATHER!"

Punch ridicules America's impertinence in standing up to Britain over Oregon in 1846.

and equal citizens of the United States. On the contrary, many opponents of slavery, including Abraham Lincoln, thought the best solution to America's race problem would be to deport former slaves to Africa. Northerners were more concerned about what they called 'the slave power': slavery supported what seemed to them a fossilised social and political system. Its aristocratic, hierarchical nature seemed

THE LAND OF LIBERTY

A British cartoonist of the mid-nineteenth century scoffs at America's claim to moral superiority.

inimical to the egalitarian, democratic values that Northerners believed set America apart from Europe. A new 'Republican' Party emerged in the North in 1854 to champion these principles under the slogan 'free soil, free labor, free men'.

To allow slavery into the west would be an offence to Republican ideals. It would also compete with the opportunities there for white labour. New slave states would increase the support for aristocratic values in the US Senate, where each state had two Senators, regardless of size, and where the South would therefore be able to block the wishes of the Northern majority. Southerners, too, were concerned about the balance of power in Washington. If free states made up more than two-thirds of the Senate, slavery could be abolished by an amendment to the Constitution. Although three-quarters of white families in the South did not own slaves and therefore did not have a direct stake in the system, they were convinced that emancipation would mean racial violence and social revolution, sweeping away the rights of all whites. A Georgia newspaper called the Republican Party 'hideous, revolting, loathsome, a menace . . . to Society, to Liberty, and to Law . . . its decrees but the will of a wild mob'.[27]

By 1860 one Southern Senator commented that relations between Northerners and Southerners in Congress had virtually ceased to exist. 'No two nations on earth are or ever were more distinctly separated and hostile than we are here . . . How can the thing go on?'[28] In November 1860 the Republican Abraham Lincoln won the presidential election, almost entirely thanks to Northern votes. North and South were so estranged by now that many Southerners were convinced that this heralded the total abolition of slavery. Immediately the states of the Deep South announced their secession from the Union, claiming the same rights to form a government as their forefathers had asserted against Britain in 1776. When Lincoln used force against them in April 1861, the Upper South, led by Virginia, joined the rebellion. The 'Confederate States of America' was born.

Britain's role in the war that followed was denounced throughout the North. She began by declaring her neutrality, arguing that the ethical issues behind the war were unclear. In 1861 the Unionists did not claim to be conducting an anti-slavery crusade. Lincoln began his inaugural address with the pledge 'I have no purpose, directly or indirectly, to interfere with the institution of slavery in the States where it exists.'[29] Many English liberals, including Gladstone, saw the South's cause as a war for national liberation like the recent secession of the Italian states from Austria's Habsburg Empire. 'They are fighting not for SLAVERY but for INDEPENDENCE,' insisted William Squier, a Unitarian minister in Preston, England, an active supporter of the anti-slavery movement.[30]

There were also practical objections to Britain's supporting the North. Eighty per cent of British cotton, the raw material that kept Lancashire's mills at work and supported a textile industry employing four million people, came from the Southern states. In America Northerners scorned Britain's apparently mercenary motives. A New York magazine parodied her National Anthem:

God save me, great John Bull!
Long keep my pockets full!
Great John Bull!
Ever victorious,
Haughty, vainglorious,
Snobbish, censorious,
Great John Bull![31]

By the end of 1861 the two countries seemed close to war. A Northern warship, the *San Jacinto*, had stopped a British mail steamer, the *Trent*, off Cuba and seized two Confederate diplomats on their way to drum up support in Europe. The captain of the *San Jacinto*, Charles Wilkes, became an overnight hero in the North and was awarded a gold medal by Congress. But British opinion was incensed by this violation of international law and by the affront to Britain's naval supremacy. The Prime Minister, Lord Palmerston, began a Cabinet meeting by throwing his hat down on the table and telling his colleagues: 'I don't know whether you are going to stand this, but I'll be damned if I do.'[32] The British Government demanded an immediate apology from Washington and the release of the diplomats. As war fever mounted, British reinforcements were sent to Canada and plans were drawn up for an invasion south into Maine. The Union could ill afford a conflict with Britain as well as the Confederacy. Over Christmas 1861 Lincoln's Administration backed down. It released the two diplomats and offered an explanation (though not an apology) for Wilkes's action. Palmerston deemed that sufficient, but Northerners were raw at their humiliation.

Britain was now engaged in the same deadly game that America had played during the war with Napoleon. The British wanted to maintain normal commercial business, while the United States was determined to enforce the tightest possible blockade. Britain's continued trade with the Confederacy incensed the Union. They were particularly furious at the construction of warships for the South in British yards. The most notorious of these, the *Alabama*, was built by Laird's of Birkenhead in the winter of 1861–2. She sank nearly sixty Unionist vessels in less than two years before herself being destroyed.

A year later, in the summer of 1862, Britain turned from neutrality to covert support for the South. British opinion was appalled by the scale of the casualties in this first modern war, in which a seven-day battle in June had left 36,000 dead or injured. Palmerston, impressed by the South's survival, speculated publicly on whether this was 'the moment when it can be thought that a successful offer of mediation could be made to the two parties?'[33] Over the next two months his government explored the possibility of a joint approach with France and Russia to end the bloodbath and secure a negotiated peace, which would have led to two separate American states, the Union and the Confederacy.

But the tide now turned against the South. In September 1862, at the battle of Antietam, Robert E. Lee's army was forced to end its invasion of the North. In the same month Abraham Lincoln issued a proclamation emancipating all slaves. The practical advantage was the desertion of thousands of slaves from their plantations to join the Unionist armies as guides, spies, road builders and fighting soldiers.

With the South in retreat and the Northern cause assuming a moral superiority in the eyes of the world, no more was heard of British attempts at mediation. The war finally ended in April 1865 with large tracts of the South laid waste and the Confederate states under military occupation. The total death toll was 620,000, greater than America suffered in World Wars One and Two combined. The Union however had survived, its constitution intact, its republican values strengthened, its distrust of Britain confirmed. In 1864 the British Minister in Washington, Lord Lyons, believed that 'three-fourths of the American people are eagerly longing for a safe opportunity of making war with England . . .'[34] Northern resentment would take several decades to abate.

America had started life as a collection of English settlements, on the extremities of the British Empire. In less than two centuries it had broken away from British rule. Yet it took the new nation many decades after 1776 to establish true independence. Economically and culturally America remained almost a British colony. Britain and other European empires hedged it in to the north, west and south. Only with the winning of the west was America great enough to stand alone; only after the South's bid for independence had been crushed was it clear that this vast, prosperous, energetic country could remain united. Now Britain, the world's greatest power, had to face the fact that her errant offspring had grown to maturity. For parent, as for child, it was to prove a difficult process.

2

Learning to Live Together

c. 1865–1914

Nineteenth-century Englishmen tended to think of America as a version of their own country. As the Boston writer James Russell Lowell commented in 1869, to them the American was 'a kind of counterfeit Briton . . . a kind of inferior and deported Englishman'.[1] Americans, on the other hand, were prone to exaggerate the differences. 'The youth of America is their oldest tradition,' scoffed the playwright Oscar Wilde in 1893. 'It has been going on now for three hundred years.'[2]

The truth lay in between. America had established its identity as a nation by claiming to be a new country, quite unlike Britain. It did so self-consciously, often aggressively, as children react against their parents. Although the United States developed a distinctive character as the nineteenth century progressed – democratic, a mix of ethnic groups, with a weak central government – there were still obvious family resemblances to the mother country. America had more in common with Britain than with the countries of continental Europe, similarities which were to help the two countries build a closer, more equal relationship as the twentieth century dawned and which laid the basis for their co-operation in two world wars.

In spite of the increasing racial variety of America during the nineteenth century, with immigrants speaking most of the languages of western Europe, English remained the official language of the United States and newcomers were obliged to learn it. Until the 1890s the largest groups of immigrants were still English speakers, from Ireland, Canada and Australasia, as well as Britain. Every nineteenth-century President was of British stock, except Martin Van Buren (1837–41) whose Dutch family emigrated in 1631.

A common language and personal ties made possible a steady flow of people and ideas in both directions across the Atlantic, particularly when the steamship, introduced in the 1840s, reduced the voyage from two months to two weeks. Would-be reformers in Britain and America drew particularly close. When, after years of pressure in and outside Parliament, slavery had been brought to an end in the British Empire by 1833, the campaigners turned their attention to America. The dying Methodist leader John Wesley had urged William Wilberforce: 'Go on, in the Name of God and in the power of His might, till even American slavery, the vilest that ever saw the sun, shall vanish away before you.' Across the Atlantic their support was warmly welcomed by American abolitionists. The former slave, Frederick Douglass, observed that 'the growing intercourse between England and this country by means of steam-navigation ... gives us an opportunity to bring in the aid ... of those living on the other side of the Atlantic ... We entreat our British friends to continue to send in their remonstrances across the deep against slavery in this land.'[3]

Equally powerful were the bonds between peace crusaders in 1846, during the crisis between Britain and America over Oregon. Their inspiration was Elihu Burritt, the self-styled 'Learned Blacksmith' of Worcester, Massachusetts, who organised a grass-roots protest against the possibility of war. Within six months of its foundation his League of Universal Brotherhood had 30,000 members in England and 25,000 in America. Mass petitions, known as Friendly Addresses, were exchanged between British and American towns with similar names or similar industries. Replying to one from Manchester, England, 400 New York merchants wrote: 'As a matter of profit and loss, it would be infinitely better that the whole of Oregon should sink into the bottom of the ocean than that two such nations as Great Britain and the United States should go to war about it, to the disgrace of civilisation, Christianity, and rational freedom.'[4]

The tides of reform and philanthropy that ebbed and flowed across the Atlantic in the mid-nineteenth century showed that the ocean was not an insuperable barrier between the two countries. They were signs of a deeper current pulling America and Britain together in a turbulent world. For both countries increasingly stood out as examples of liberal values in an era when most civilised countries were still dominated by monarchy, aristocracy and a reactionary church. To be sure, British middle-class reformers had not turned their country into an American-style democracy, nor did they want to do so: even after the 1884 Reform Act only sixty per cent of adult men had the vote. But their campaigns to promote parliamentary reform, establish free trade and curb the powers of landowners and the Church of England had made Britain a strikingly liberal country by European standards.

America and Britain rooted their politics and law in the principle of individual liberty and the rights of private property, and the English common law remained basic to the legal systems of most American states. The liberty of the individual was also central to the economic life of both countries. The British and American industrial revolutions were not channelled by national governments to build up a powerful modern state, geared to the demands of war, as was happening in Germany, Russia and Japan. Instead they were inspired by individual businessmen, seizing opportunities for profit, creating their own industries, trade and investment within the framework of a free market.

Britain and America were also unusual in the power enjoyed by their legislatures. Although Victorian Britain remained a monarchy, it was a *constitutional* monarchy. The authority of the Queen was now tightly circumscribed by Parliament, particularly the House of Commons, whose MPs represented a majority of the male population. The powers of Parliament were admittedly less extensive than those of Congress over the President, but Britain was much closer to the American political system than to the autocratic monarchies of Europe like Germany, Russia or Austria-Hungary, where the legislatures were weak or represented only a privileged minority of the population.

In 1900 Great Britain seemed supreme. The scramble of the great powers for control of Africa had brought her Egypt, much of East Africa and a vast southern African domain carved out by Cecil Rhodes. At her Diamond Jubilee in 1897 the Queen Empress governed over a fifth of the globe. Her subjects were equal in number to the rival empires of France, Germany and Russia combined. A small European island, the size of Wyoming or Oregon, had become the greatest power the world had ever seen.

Britain's political power was matched by her economic strength. She accounted for three-quarters of the world's foreign investment and a fifth of world trade. Despite the extension of the franchise, the old social order remained remarkably tenacious. Aristocrats still dominated the political parties and absorbed the new commercial rich into the landed élite. And the monarchy, instead of declining in public esteem, won new popularity and affection as Victoria's reign neared its end. A puzzled American Ambassador marvelled in 1897 at the Diamond Jubilee celebrations:

> It was an explosion of loyalty that amazed John Bull himself. What a curious thing it is – that there has been no King in England since

> Elizabeth of special distinction – most of them far worse than mediocre – only the foreigner William III of any merit – and yet the monarchical religion has grown day by day, till the Queen is worshipped as more than mortal . . .[5]

Great Britain seemed secure at home as well as omnipotent abroad.

Behind the glittering façade, however, all was not well. Her dominance left Britain acutely vulnerable. On every side there were rivals, wanting to share in the pickings of imperialism. The most alarming threat came from the German Kaiser supported by his High Seas Fleet, but Britain was also at odds with France over North Africa, with Russia over the borders of her Asian empire in Persia and Afghanistan, and with the USA over their rival spheres of influence in the Americas. As Winston Churchill drily observed, 'our claim to be left in unmolested enjoyment of vast and splendid possessions, mainly acquired by violence, largely maintained by force, often seems less reasonable to others than to us'.[6]

Britain's diplomatic isolation was seriously exposed at the turn of the century. To protect her interests in South Africa she made war on the Boer, or Dutch, republics of the Orange Free State and the Transvaal, incurring the animosity of all Europe. Joseph Chamberlain, Colonial Secretary, described Britain as the 'weary Titan, staggering under the too vast orb of his own fate'.[7] It seemed only prudent to reduce the number of her potential enemies. The various disputes that existed between the United States and Britain were of relatively minor importance when set against London's worldwide problems, and the British chose to appease Washington's demands. This benefited America, changing the balance of power in the Western Hemisphere within a single decade and helping the United States to become a major force in the Caribbean and the Pacific.

In London, Anglo-American relations seemed of peripheral importance. Britain was not obsessed with America in the way she would become in the late twentieth century. In the United States, by contrast, relations with Britain were the main issue of foreign policy. It was as if America were trying to define itself in terms of its un-Britishness. Politicians of all persuasions enjoyed 'twisting the lion's tail'. To Northerners Britain's behaviour during the Civil War still rankled. Claims for compensation for the damage done to Union shipping by raiders like the *Alabama*, built in British shipyards, had been acrimoniously pursued. Gladstone finally accepted arbitration of the issue and in 1872 Britain agreed to pay $15.5 million in compensation, somewhat outweighing the benefits of having built the ships in the first place.

Americans were also infuriated by the continued British presence in North America. Canada had been given self-government in 1867, as a Dominion under the British Crown. But American politicians still talked of annexing the country. Successive Administrations turned a blind eye to Fenian raids across the border into Canada, intended by this Irish-American organisation as a way of provoking war between Britain and America which would help Ireland gain her independence.

There were frequent impassioned complaints about Britain's undue influence within the United States. Three-quarters of the foreign investment in the USA was British and the scale of Britain's holdings, particularly in railroads, mines and ranches, was a burning issue in the developing west. There were calls for tariffs to keep out British goods and protect infant American industries. One of the leading exponents of such a policy argued that this was 'the way to outdo England without fighting her'.[8] Farmers protested that the money and commodity markets of London and Liverpool were responsible for the decline of wheat, corn and cotton prices during the Depression of 1873–96. Ben Tillman, the ranting, one-eyed leader of the Populist movement in South Carolina, spluttered, 'America for Americans, and to hell with Britain and her Tories.'[9]

A clear indication that Britain was no longer going to challenge American interests came over an obscure boundary dispute in Venezuela – obscure, at least, in British eyes. For decades the Venezuelan Government had argued over the line of the jungle border with British Guiana. It appealed to the United States, citing the Monroe Doctrine, which had established as a basic tenet of American diplomacy the principle of non-interference in the Americas by European powers. In July 1895 President Grover Cleveland duly demanded that the British Government should submit the dispute to arbitration, adding provocatively 'to-day the United States is practically sovereign on this continent'.[10] Lord Salisbury, the British Prime Minister, believed the US note was bluster and he failed to reply for four months. When he did, he flatly rejected American interference, arguing that the Monroe Doctrine had no standing in international law.

Incensed at this dismissal of a sacred precept of American diplomacy, Cleveland sent a special message to Congress on 17 December 1895. America, he announced, would adjudicate the dispute itself. Thereafter, it would be 'the duty of the United States to resist by every means in its power as a willful aggression upon its rights and interests' any attempt by Britain to alter the border.[11]

For a few days America was in the grip of war fever. Republicans and Democrats backed the President. Some talked of invading

During the Venezuela crisis of 1895 *The New York World* showed Britain hogging the globe.

Canada, while Irish-Americans lined up as volunteers to fight the detested British. The British Ambassador told London that Cleveland's message 'had produced in Congress and among the Public a condition of mind which can only be described as hysterical'.[12] But then Wall Street panicked, and share prices plummeted. The churches spoke out against the talk of war and the Administration began to back down. In London the Cabinet, now preoccupied with the far graver crisis in Southern Africa, where the German Kaiser was sending messages of support to the Boers, was disinclined to pursue Salisbury's initially tough response to the USA. The principle of international arbitration of the dispute was reluctantly accepted.

It took three years for the results of the arbitration to be announced. The judgement accepted most of Britain's claims, but this was not the real significance of the Venezuelan crisis. What mattered was that it had altered the future conduct of Anglo-American relations. The confrontation and the threat of war concentrated minds on both sides of the Atlantic, and led to many resolutions, as over Oregon in 1846, insisting that war between Britain and America was inconceivable. One British petition, with several thousand signatures, summed up what had become an increasingly common sentiment in both countries: 'All English-speaking peoples united by race, language and religion, should regard war as the one absolutely intolerable mode of settling the domestic differences of the Anglo-American family.'[13]

In January 1897 the two governments signed a treaty agreeing in future to submit all major disputes to arbitration. It just failed to gain the two-thirds majority in the Senate required for ratification, but the widespread public support it received demonstrated the improvement in Anglo-American relations that had taken place.

The rapprochement was further enhanced by the extraordinary demonstration of pro-American feeling in Britain in 1898. In April of that year the United States had gone to war with Spain over her oppressive treatment of the Cubans and her slights to American interests on the island. In the face of almost universal European support for the Spanish cause Britain announced her neutrality and made her pro-American sympathies clear. Within hours of the news that the United States had declared war thousands of red, white and blue streamers decked buildings in London and the British press came out enthusiastically for the American side. American Independence Day, 4 July, was celebrated that year throughout Britain.

Just over a year later, the US Government returned the favour when Britain went to war in South Africa. American public opinion sided with the Boers in their attempt to defend their republics against the might of the British Empire. When the war was over the defeated Boer fighters toured the United States re-enacting their battles before enthusiastic audiences. The Administration, however, bent the rules of its official neutrality to allow an ill-prepared Britain to finance twenty per cent of the cost of the war on the US securities market. Hundreds of thousands of pairs of boots and nearly 200,000 pack mules were sent to ease shortages in the British army, while European attempts at mediation were deliberately ignored by the United States.

The United States traded on the atmosphere of goodwill to solve its other outstanding disputes with Britain. These were over the exact line of the border between Canada and Alaska and, quite separately, over the American proposal to build a canal through the Isthmus of Panama, connecting the Atlantic and Pacific oceans. The United States had agreed in a treaty of 1850 that the development of the

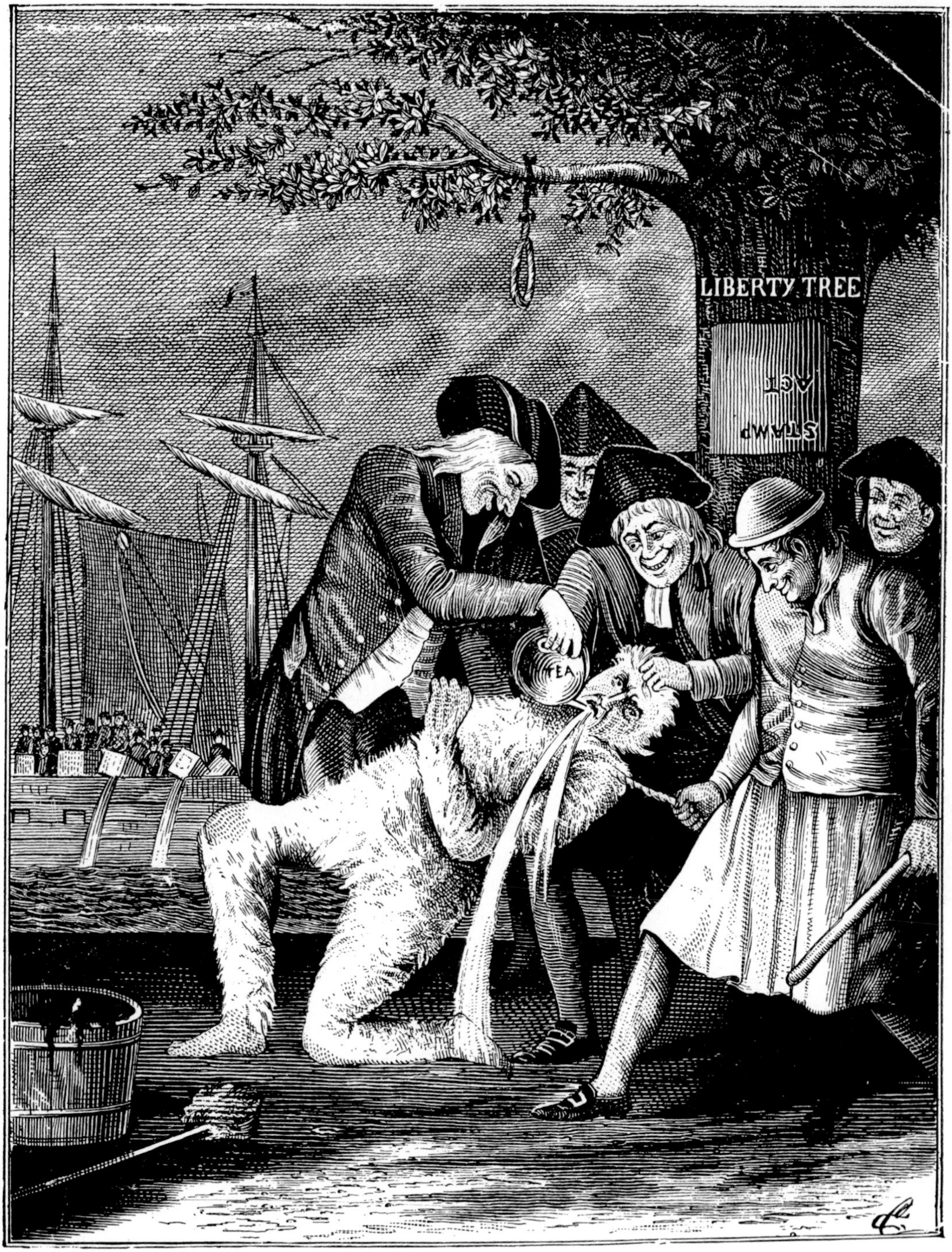

After the Boston Tea Party a British tax collector, tarred and feathered, is forced to drink British tea. Cartoon of 1774.

John Trumbull's impression of the signing of the Declaration of Independence. Jefferson in red waistcoat.

The beginning of Thomas Jefferson's rough draft of the Declaration of Independence.

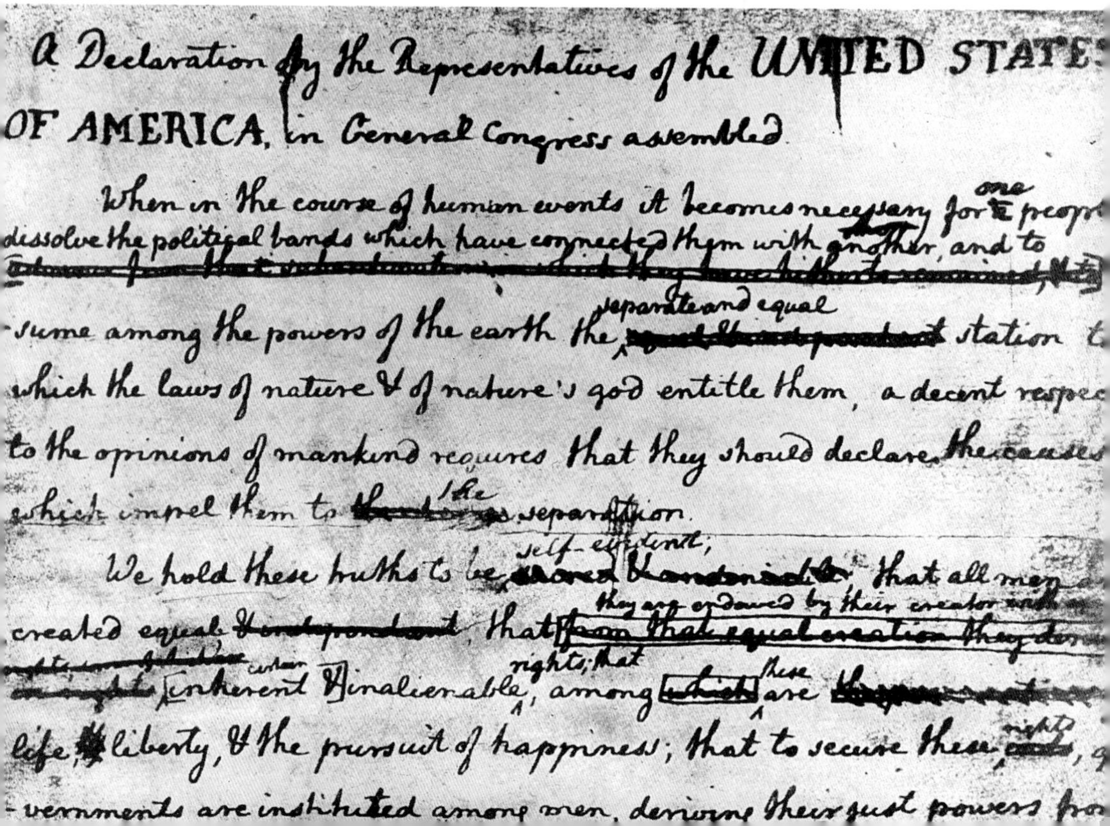

A Declaration by the Representatives of the UNITED STATE
OF AMERICA, in General Congress assembled.

When in the course of human events it becomes necessary for one peopl
dissolve the political bands which have connected them with another, and to
-sume among the powers of the earth the separate and equal station t
which the laws of nature & of nature's god entitle them, a decent respec
to the opinions of mankind requires that they should declare the causes
which impel them to the separation.

We hold these truths to be self-evident; that all men a
created equal, that they are endowed by their creator with
certain inherent & inalienable rights; that among these are
life, liberty, & the pursuit of happiness; that to secure these rights, g
-vernments are instituted among men, deriving their just powers fro

Quebec fell to the British in 1759. Canada stayed loyal to the Crown after 1776.

An artist's impression of the burning of Washington by the British in 1814.

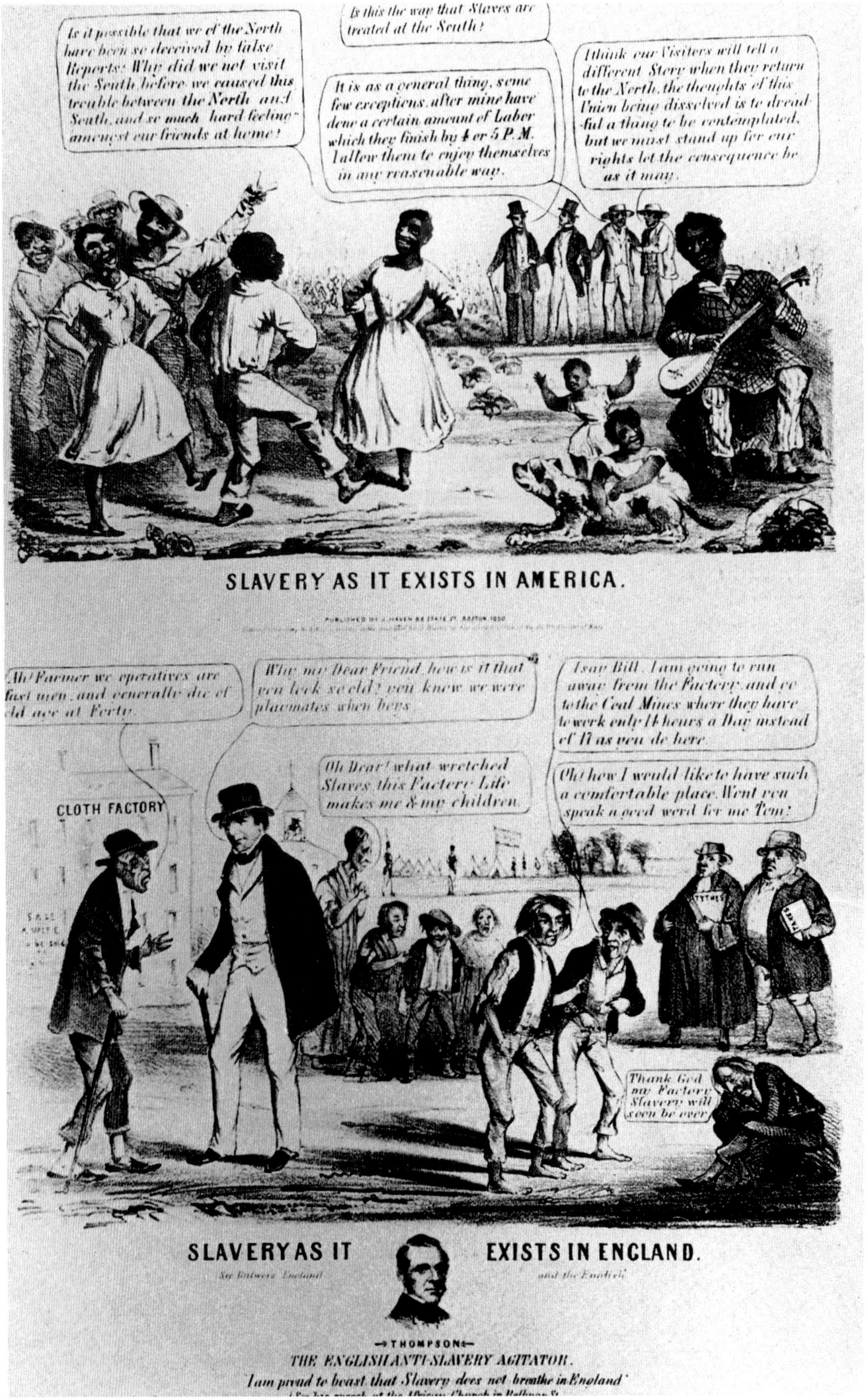

Defenders of slavery in the American South attack factory slavery in supposedly liberal England (1850).

Panama Canal would be a joint British and American venture. But America's emergence as a major Pacific power during the Spanish-American war made it essential for the US navy to move from its East to its West Coast ports, without making the long journey round South America via Cape Horn. Lord Salisbury was prepared to give up Britain's treaty rights but, under pressure from the Canadian Government, he made settlement of the disputed Alaskan-Canadian border a pre-condition.

It took several years to untangle this complicated diplomatic web. In 1899 in return for America's support in South Africa, Britain at last agreed to separate the issues. At this point the US President, Theodore Roosevelt, refused to allow the Alaskan dispute to go to arbitration, a reversal of America's previous insistence that arbitration should be accepted by Britain in the Venezuelan dispute. To Canada's chagrin, Britain now chose to put her own relationship with the United States first, and agreed that a judicial commission, composed of three American judges, two Canadian representatives and one British appointee should sit to decide the issue. Under pressure from London the British delegate consistently voted with the Americans against the Canadians, who understandably felt aggrieved that their country's interests were being sacrificed in the cause of Anglo-American friendship. The dispute was duly settled on American terms.

As for the canal, a new Anglo-American treaty was signed in February 1900 allowing America to go ahead with its construction on condition that the canal was a neutral zone and unfortified. Roosevelt and other enthusiastic supporters of America's growing naval might were unhappy at these restrictions. They forced the Secretary of State John Hay to re-negotiate the treaty. Eventually all the US demands for complete freedom of action were conceded and a new treaty was signed in November 1901. America was now free to build, operate and fortify a canal for use in peace and war. The only opposition was from Colombia, concerned that part of her territory was to be taken over by the United States. In a shady manoeuvre Roosevelt first promoted revolution in Colombia, then recognised the breakaway republic of Panama, in return for a treaty giving the United States *carte blanche* to build and run its canal. The Panama Canal was eventually opened in August 1914, a few days after war broke out in Europe.

The United States continued to berate Britain for her imperial aggression but by the turn of the century traces of imperialism were evident in American policy. Central America was becoming what would now be called an American 'sphere of influence', and Britain

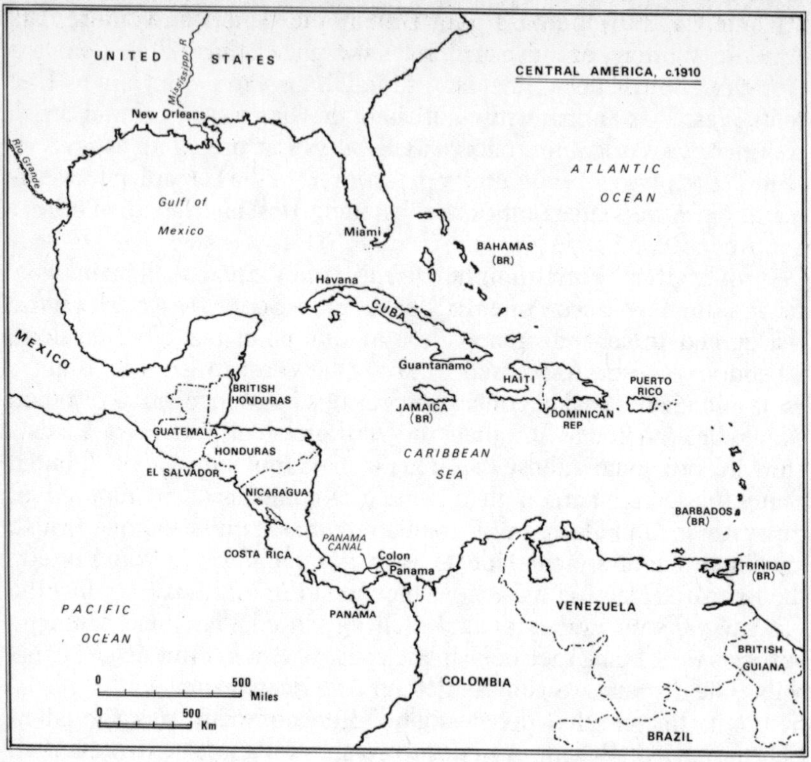

supported the USA's new role. When America took control of the Philippines from Spain in 1898 the London weekly, the *Spectator*, commented, patronisingly: 'She will govern them well enough, much better than any Power except ourselves, and we have more of the world's surface than we can well manage . . . It would be a relief if another English-speaking Power would take up a portion of our task . . .'[14] Cuba, in the wake of the Spanish-American war, had become effectively a protectorate of the United States, controlled by American interests and unable to conduct an independent foreign policy. Over the next few years the United States also intervened to protect its investments and maintain stability in Haiti, Honduras, Nicaragua, the Dominican Republic and Mexico.

In justification of this conduct President Theodore Roosevelt added a corollary to the Monroe Doctrine in 1904:

> Chronic wrongdoing, or an impotence which results in a general loosening of the ties of civilized society, may in America, as else-

where, ultimately require intervention by some civilized nation, and in the Western Hemisphere the adherence of the United States to the Monroe Doctrine may force the United States, however reluctantly, in flagrant cases of such wrongdoing or impotence, to the exercise of an international police power.[15]

As British influence in the area waned under the pressure of events in Europe, Asia and Africa, the United States was declaring its own 'Pax Americana'. For Britain the practical advantage of this growing Anglo-American accord was considerable. Many British politicians saw in it a proper recognition of the common background. Lord Salisbury, a tough, traditional Tory, had little time for sentiment in international affairs and considered America to be an upstart nation. But his Cabinet had in Joseph Chamberlain an exponent of the 'Anglo-Saxon race' theory. 'I refuse to speak or think of the United States as a foreign nation,' he told a Toronto audience in 1887. 'They are our flesh and blood.' In the euphoria of the Spanish-American war in 1898 he expressed the fervent hope that 'the Stars and Stripes and the Union Jack should wave together over an Anglo-Saxon alliance'.[16]

Darwin's descriptions of the survival of the fittest were cited in support of the theory. Britons and Americans, it was argued, shared unique racial characteristics of intelligence and industry which made them better than other peoples. They had inherited, from the Dark Age invaders of Britain, a capacity for self-government. It was their duty to spread these superior values, to bring enlightenment to primitive races and to vanquish the inferior Latin, Teutonic and Slavic peoples who were their rivals. Imperialism was considered not just a law of society, but a law of nature. Superior races must expand or die. In the words of the Ohio minister, Josiah Strong, one of America's leading exponents of this thesis:

> It seems to me that God, with infinite wisdom and skill, is training the Anglo-Saxon race for an hour sure to come in the world's future . . . when the pressure of population on the means of subsistence will be felt here as it is now felt in Europe and Asia. Then will the world enter on a new stage in its history – *the final competition of races, for which the Anglo-Saxon is being schooled* . . . And can any one doubt that the result of this competition of races will be the 'survival of the fittest'?[17]

In Britain, Lord Salisbury's successor as Prime Minister, A. J. Balfour (1902–5), was convinced that 'the two great co-heirs of

Advertisement in *Life* magazine, 28 July 1898.

Anglo-Saxon freedom and civilisation' had a common mission.[18] Americans were 'our kin beyond the sea' and the United States' growing influence in the Americas and the Pacific was desirable. 'The Monroe Doctrine,' Balfour stated, 'has no enemies in this country that I know of. We welcome any increase of the great influence of the United States upon the great Western Hemisphere.'[19]

It was a considerable relief to Britain no longer to count the United States among her potential foes. By 1906 Britain felt able to withdraw all her forces from Canada and the West Indies. The First Lord of the Admiralty wrote in 1905: 'There is no party in the United Kingdom nor even in the British Empire which does not contemplate a war with the United States of America as the greatest evil which could befall the British Empire in its foreign relations.'[20] With the territorial disputes settled, Britain no longer held the expanding US navy in her sights, though American admirals were still determined to outbuild Britain. For British leaders, war with the United States had been ruled out. It was, they said in the new cliché of the time, 'unthinkable'. Britain's reaction to a new power flexing its muscles was to accommodate it as long as there was no serious conflict with British interests, particularly since it seemed a country so close in values and kinship to her own. America's growing involvement in the Western Hemisphere was welcomed as an extension of Anglo-Saxon influence.

Britain was less comfortable, however, when that same power expanded economically and threatened to encroach directly on her commercial interests. As the United States' industrial and financial strength grew American goods flooded British markets and US capitalists, seeking to expand, started to buy up British companies. At the beginning of the twentieth century the British press was full of dire warnings about the 'American invasion' of Britain.

America's industrial revolution began much later than Britain's and did not take off until after the Civil War. With peace came reconstruction, and the railroad was its principal motive force. In 1865 most of America's 35,000 miles of track lay between the Atlantic and the Mississippi, but by 1900 the United States was served by 200,000 miles of track, more than in all of Europe put together. Much of the railroad boom had been financed by the City of London, but it had an immediate effect on America's coal, iron and steel production, leading to a fast indigenous development of those industries, where originally the materials had been imported from Britain. With the spread of the electric telegraph and, from the 1870s, the telephone the United States was becoming a huge national market. Remote farming areas were brought in reach of the big cities and the sea-ports.

American business was now ready to capitalise on the vast scale of the new country.

The industrial revolution in the United States not only outstripped Britain's, but took a very different course technologically. America's great innovation was to invent and develop the techniques of mass production, replacing the craftsman, who was responsible for every stage of manufacture, with the production line. Parts for machines, whether clocks, typewriters or sewing machines, were standardised and made interchangeable rather than being produced individually. By World War One, Henry Ford was applying these principles with dramatic success on his car 'assembly line' in Detroit.

The scale of modern production generated a voracious demand for new capital. Tycoons like John D. Rockefeller in the oil business or Andrew Carnegie in steel virtually ruled their industries, buying out their rivals and taking control of every stage of production from raw materials to retailing. They could not develop at the speed they required simply by ploughing back their profits, unlike the family firms that still dominated manufacturing in Britain. Specialist investment bankers grew up to meet the demand for cash and credit, pre-eminent among them the Wall Street banker J. P. Morgan. Rapacious for money, power and beautiful women, Morgan was chief banker to the giant conglomerate, US Steel, and the organiser of many of the great railroad mergers of the 1880s and 1890s. He arranged most of Britain's loans to pay for the Boer War and his firm was to play a crucial role in financing Britain's war effort in 1914–18.

By 1913 the United States had replaced Britain as the world's largest manufacturing nation, producing twice as much coal, three times as much pig-iron, and five times the quantity of steel. In the 1900s most of this was still absorbed by her domestic market. Britain was a far larger exporter sending forty per cent of her manufactured goods abroad, whereas America exported only five per cent. But America's new trusts, or big business combinations, already being criticised for their wealth and power, needed to expand beyond America's shores and many turned to Britain where there was no language barrier.

The first American business to set up on a permanent basis in Britain was Singer. The sewing-machine company opened a factory in Bridgeton near Glasgow in 1867. By 1900 there were seventy-five US subsidiaries or jointly-owned Anglo-American enterprises in Britain, funded by £10 million of American capital. By 1914 a further seventy companies had arrived. They included H. J. Heinz, introducing processed food to Britain, Henry Ford opening his first

British assembly plant at Trafford Park, near Manchester, in 1908, and F. W. Woolworth, beginning to revolutionise the retail trade with 'penny markets' in Liverpool, Manchester and Preston.[21]

Among the most prominent arrivals were the electrical industries, a new technology led by the United States. Britain's tramway systems were electrified mostly with American electrical equipment, as was the London underground railway system. This led to one of the first of a series of spectacular take-over battles that caught the public eye, as the buccaneers of US industry pitted their wits and strength against British companies.

In September 1900 the Charing Cross, Euston and Hampstead railway, one of London's many competing underground companies, was acquired by the owner of an empire of street-railways in Chicago, known as the Chicago Traction Tangle. Charles Tyson Yerkes's recipe for success was to 'buy up old junk, fix it up a little and unload it upon other fellows'.[22] His activities in Chicago had made him money but many enemies as well, and in 1899 he was forced to sell up there and move on. Yerkes's acquisition of a London underground railway company was the first round of a bruising battle to buy and electrify the entire system. Over the next two years he was locked in competition with another syndicate backed by J. P. Morgan who scented healthy profits to be made under, as well as in, the City of London. The cost of the plans eventually proved prohibitive, however, and after Parliament refused to authorise the necessary legislation both Yerkes and Morgan were forced to withdraw.

J. P. Morgan was also engaged in a struggle for control of shipping across the Atlantic, trying to wrest passenger and freight trade from British hands. In 1901 he began buying British shipping lines such as Leyland and White Star at inflated prices, until his syndicate threatened to dominate not only the shipping business but shipbuilding as well. Even Joseph Chamberlain, a great exponent of Anglo-American co-operation, called 'the Morgan Combination . . . a move in a great commercial war' which the British should be 'prepared to fight for all we are worth'.[23] When it seemed in 1902 that Cunard, the major British transatlantic carrier, might also sell out to Morgan's, Balfour's Cabinet came to the rescue. It agreed to loan Cunard £2.4 million for new vessels and to subsidise their operation. This kind of government support was anathema to many, but radical measures were considered essential to prevent Britain losing control of the North Atlantic.

Tobacco also became the object of take-over fever. In September 1901 James Buchanan Duke, the flamboyant president of the Ameri-

MAY 8, 1901.] PUNCH, OR THE LONDON CHARIVARI. 341
BRITISH
FANCY GOO
THEATRE ROYAL
LEYLAND
Bernard Partridge.
JONATHAN SHOPPING.
John Bull. "Now, my little man, what can I do for you?"
Master Jonathan. "Wal, guess I'll buy the whole store!"
["American millionaires agree to purchase the Leyland Line (Mediterranean, Portugal, Montreal and Antwerp) Fleets. A meeting of shareholders has been called in order to confirm the arrangements."—Vide "Daily News," May 1.]

Bernard Partridge in *Punch* (1901) on the Americans buying up Britain.

can Tobacco Company, bought up the Liverpool tobacco firm of Ogden's. He then announced that his company had set aside £6 million to capture the entire British and continental cigarette markets.

His approach was direct: 'Hello, boys,' he introduced himself to the staid and respectable Player brothers, 'I'm Duke from New York come to buy your business.'[24] Outraged, his prospective victims set up their own combine, 'Imperial Tobacco', which, after a bitter price and bonus war, forced 'Buck' Duke to concede defeat. American Tobacco agreed to stay out of Britain if Imperial Tobacco kept away from the USA. A joint company, 'British American Tobacco', would exploit sales in the rest of the world.

These take-over battles of 1901–2 provoked a response of near panic in Britain. The tobacco war in particular brought the 'American peril' to the attention of the man in the street. Newspapers and advertising hoardings warned, in lurid terms, of enslavement by American trusts and of the British working man being kidnapped by Uncle Sam. The journalist Frederick A. McKenzie, whose articles in the *Daily Mail* had alerted Britain to the American invasion, predicted

A BRITISH FACTORY
Employing over 2,000 British People.
Tobacco Industry in England,
Packing "GUINEA-GOLD" Cigarettes at OGDEN'S.

Patriotic British advertisement during the Anglo-American tobacco war.

the Americanisation of every aspect of British society. 'In the domestic life,' he wrote,

> we have almost got to this. The average citizen wakes in the morning at the sound of an American alarum clock; rises from his New England sheets, and shaves with his New York soap, and a Yankee safety razor. He pulls on a pair of Boston boots over his socks from West Carolina, fastens his Connecticut braces, slips his Waterbury watch into his pocket and sits down to breakfast . . . Rising from his breakfast table the citizen rushes out, catches an electric tram made in New York, to Shepherds Bush, where he gets into a Yankee elevator, which takes him on to the American-fitted railway to the city. At his office of course everything is American. He sits on a Nebraskan swivel chair, before a Michigan roll-top desk, writes his letters on a Syracuse typewriter, signing them with a New York fountain pen, and drying them with a blotting sheet from New England. The letter copies are put away in files manufactured in Grand Rapids.[25]

It was a journalistic fantasy. American goods and capital were still only a small proportion of the total British economy, but a general debate on the economic problems of Britain had been opened up, with the protagonists drawing indiscriminately on American evidence to support their theories. It was like the debate over American democracy in the mid-nineteenth century. Some employers, with the support of *The Times*, argued that 'the English disease' was caused by the restrictive practices of trade unions. Trade unionists themselves, on the other hand, and industrial reformers visited the USA and criticised the lack of incentives in Britain and the inadequacies of the education system. Technologists urged more mechanisation. Conservatives argued for protective tariffs, pointing to the American duties on imports which averaged more than fifty per cent. And the journalist W. T. Stead, who predicted in 1902 that the world would be Americanised in the twentieth century, argued that Britain's only hope was an Anglo-Saxon race union. 'Is there no Morgan,' he pleaded, 'who will undertake to bring about the greatest combination of all – a combination of the whole English-speaking race?'[26]

This theory was already being put into practice by the British upper classes who had discovered that the new American wealth was not averse to trading its money for social status. The pre-World War One generation saw over a hundred dynastic marriages between British and American families, propping up a faltering British aristocracy in the style to which it was accustomed. Sometimes both sides went too far. Consuelo Vanderbilt, heiress to the shipping and railroad fortune, had to be dragged to the altar in 1895 to marry the Duke of Marlborough, and the match ended bitterly in separation and divorce. The Duke's uncle had made a more propitious marriage to the vivacious daughter of a New York financier, Jennie Jerome. Their first child, born prematurely in November 1874, survived to be christened Winston Spencer Churchill. A later transatlantic marriage, that of a British publisher with the daughter of Dr Tarleton Belles of Spencer, Indiana, gave Britain another Conservative Prime Minister in Harold Macmillan who, like Churchill, made much of his American ancestry. And Joseph Chamberlain, the arch-proponent of Anglo-Saxon union, finally practised what he preached. His third wife was the daughter of President Cleveland's Secretary of War, Mary Endicott. The wealth that inspired many of these marriages was prodigious, far exceeding even the richest British families. By 1900 the Rockefellers, the Fords, the Mellons were dollar billionaires, twelve times as rich as British counterparts like the Duke of Westminster.[27]

There was an unsavoury side to America's rapid rise to industrial greatness. British newspapers began to report on political corruption, on violent strikes, and on the ruthlessness of money-making tycoons like Morgan and Rockefeller. Radicals who, in the previous century, had pointed admiringly to America's classless democracy were shocked by the new development. Plutocracy, rule by the rich, seemed to be at odds with Democracy. The Chartists and their fellow mid-nineteenth-century radicals had praised America as a paradise for the working man. By the 1900s the intellectuals and trade unionists responsible for creating the Labour Party saw a different society, which seemed to embody the very worst features of capitalism. William Clarke, a convert to socialism, wrote in the mid-1890s:

> A quarter of a century ago the American Republic was the guiding star of advanced English political thought. It is not so now: candour compels me to say that. It is not merely a question of machine politics, of political corruption, of the omnipotent party boss . . . Over and beyond this is the great fact of the division between rich and poor, millionaires at one end, tramps at the other, a growth of monopolies unparalleled, crises producing abject poverty just as in Europe.[28]

In future the United States would no longer be held up as an example of the promised New World by Britain's socialists but as the epitome of all that was wrong with the Old. For those disappointed idealists the dawn of the twentieth century marked an era of alienation rather than rapprochement in Anglo-American relations.

Across the ocean, however, America's élite welcomed the rapprochement. Alarmed that mass immigration was destroying the country's Anglo-Saxon character, it found previously unsuspected virtues in its English cousins. For at the turn of the century, the United States was facing an influx of newcomers unprecedented both in number and background. Twenty-three million entered the country between 1880 and 1914, by which time over one in seven of America's 105 million population had been born abroad. In the past, English-speaking immigrants had been in a majority, but by the 1900s only one in twenty came from England. Most were from eastern or south-eastern Europe. They dressed, ate and spoke in unfamiliar ways and were not in the main Protestants, but Roman Catholics, Orthodox or Jews. They settled in large numbers in the big cities so that by 1914 over one-third of the population of New York, Boston and Chicago was foreign-born. New York had more Germans than Hamburg, more Italians than Naples, twice the number of Irish in Dublin and a larger Jewish population than the whole of western Europe.[29]

The WASP Americans – White Anglo-Saxon Protestants – who had effectively run America, felt endangered. They were already disturbed by the growing political strength of the older immigrant groups from Germany and Ireland. The Irish, many of them emotionally involved in the cause of Irish independence, were bitterly opposed to the domination of American government by those of English origin. As they grew wealthier and more numerous, their political influence began to be felt. They campaigned not only for their own interests, but also represented the recent immigrants, using the advantage of being English-speaking to mediate between the newcomers and the WASP élite. Even more alarming to the WASPs were the German-Americans. They were fragmented by religion, dialect and politics, but nevertheless united on issues that affected their national identity. Encouraged by a German-language press that had adopted the Kaiser's views of Germany's innate superiority, many fought against assimilation and encouraged the growth of their culture in opposition to the English.

The WASP response was to draw instinctively closer to Britain and to campaign, in an attempt to maintain their supremacy, for restrictions on further immigration from Europe. Senator Henry Cabot Lodge of Massachusetts was a staunch American nationalist from a Boston family which traced its ancestry back to the era of the *Mayflower*. He had been brought up to be suspicious of Britain as a great power despite having many British friends, among them A. J. Balfour. In 1895 Lodge was arguing that Canada should be seized from Britain if war broke out over the Venezuela crisis, but by 1900 had changed his tune. He decided that Britain and America must now stand together in the struggle to preserve Anglo-Saxon supremacy in America and around the world. He wrote to Teddy Roosevelt about America's stance on the Anglo-Boer war. 'However much we sympathize with the Boers, the downfall of the British Empire is something no rational American could regard as anything but a misfortune to the United States.'[30] Lodge became a leading advocate of the restrictions on immigration.

'The one indispensable feature of our foreign policy,' declared the American Secretary of State, John Hay (1898–1905), 'should be a friendly understanding with England.' But this Yankee Republican, one of the principal architects of rapprochement, bridled when accused, as he often was, of being an anglophile. 'All I have ever done with England is to have wrung great concessions out of her with no compensation. And yet, these idiots say I'm not an American because I don't say, "To hell with the Queen," at every breath.'[31] Anglo-American co-operation, in other words, did not mean American submission to Britain's interests. It was America's interests that were being advanced. 'As long as England succeeds in keeping "the balance of power" in Europe, not only in principle, but in reality, well and good,' Theodore Roosevelt observed in 1910. 'Should she however for some reason or other fail in doing so, the United States would be obliged to step in at least temporarily, to restore the balance . . . In fact, we ourselves are becoming, owing to our strength and geographical situation, more and more the balance of power of the whole world.'[32] America was to be tested more quickly than he anticipated, for the balance of power in Europe was soon upset again, and this time Britain was unable to restore it alone.

At the beginning of the twentieth century Britain faced two principal rivals to her supremacy, Germany and the United States. With both she was locked in industrial competition and in a series of diplomatic disputes. Both were building fleets that threatened her traditional supremacy at sea. But her response to these two disturbing new powers was very different. As we have seen, with the United States she began to cultivate what would later be called a 'special relationship'. With Germany she drifted into a deep antagonism that led to two world wars.

America's challenge to Britain was remote, in the Western Hemisphere. Germany, on the other hand, was much closer to home, a potential menace to the Low Countries, the North Sea and the English Channel. Concern for national security was reinforced by the alien nature of German society, dominated by a Prussian aristocracy that extolled militarist values and denied popular liberties. Compared with the liberalism of Britain's Anglo-Saxon cousins across the ocean, Germany seemed a far greater threat. Henry Adams – Bostonian, historian, descendant of two American Presidents – described Germany as 'the grizzly terror which in twenty years effected what Adamses had tried for two hundred in vain – frightened England into America's arms'.[33]

The Kaiser saw no reason why Britain should be the world's supreme imperial power and he was determined to win Germany a place in the sun. As the German navy raced to outbuild Britain's, talk of war became commonplace. A crisis in the Balkans in 1914 brought the rivalry to a head. The assassination by Serbian nationalists of the heir to the Austro-Hungarian Empire, Germany's only ally, posed a fundamental threat to Germany's credibility. If nothing were done, the empire might disintegrate and Germany could be encircled and reduced to impotence by the increasingly powerful Triple Entente of Russia, Britain and France. By August 1914 Russia and France were at war with Germany and Austria, and Britain joined in after the German invasion of Belgium, whose neutrality Britain was bound by treaty to protect. Belgium provided the immediate cause and the moral indignation to overcome the anti-war feelings of many British Liberals. But the underlying issue was Britain's survival as a great power. In the words of one senior British diplomat, to say 'that England cannot engage in a big war means her abdication as an independent state'.[34] The British Lion now had to fight for its supremacy, in a battle for the survival of the fittest.

From Berlin to London, from Paris to the Russian capital of St Petersburg, the mood in August 1914 was one of relief, even euphoria. War would purify the soul, release the pent-up tensions of industrial life, and offer a golden opportunity for valour, patriotism and glory.

And everyone knew it would all be over by Christmas.

3

To Fight or Not to Fight?

1914–17

From the beginning President Woodrow Wilson made clear that this was not America's war. 'The United States must be neutral in fact as well as in name during these days that are to try men's souls,' he told his fellow countrymen two weeks after hostilities began. 'We must be impartial in thought as well as action, must put a curb upon our sentiments as well as upon every transaction that might be construed as a preference of one party to the struggle before another.'[1]

This stance of strict neutrality was to be much misunderstood in Britain, castigated as vacillation, moral insensitivity or even craven cowardice. But Wilson, like most Americans, could see no reason of morality or of national interest for the United States to enter Europe's war. Instead, Wilson believed, America's growing power and the influence that would stem from neutrality should be used in what he called 'the proper performance of our duty as the one great nation at peace, the one people holding itself ready to play a part of impartial mediation'.[2] Already the President was turning over in his mind ideas for a post-war world in which conquest would be outlawed by 'an association of nations, all bound together for the protection of the integrity of each'.[3]

Wilson was a man of deep, often self-righteous, moral conviction. He was a high-minded Christian, the son and grandson of Presbyterian ministers, and an academic who had previously been President of Princeton University. Personally his deepest instincts favoured Britain. His ancestry was English. He loved the English countryside, and spent several bicycling holidays touring it in his forties. His whole political

DON'T MIX IN A FAMILY QUARREL, UNCLE

Uncle Sam stands and watches while the Europeans – one big, happy royal family – fight it out.

thought was steeped in the English liberal tradition, with Gladstone as his great hero, and his first book had suggested that America adopt the British Cabinet system instead of its cumbersome separation of powers. But none of this blinded Wilson to the essential differences of values and interests between the two nations. Even in December 1914 he was sure that 'Germany is not alone responsible for the war',[4] and, as the conflict dragged on, his conviction grew that America offered the only salvation for a war-torn world.

But political prudence as well as moral conviction dictated Wilson's stance. As he said in his neutrality message, 'the people of the United States are drawn from many nations, and chiefly from the nations now at war'. He warned that Americans 'may become divided in camps of hostile opinion, hot against each other, involved in the war itself in impulse and opinion, if not in action'.[5] Wilson feared that America, already wracked by the cultural struggle between those of British stock and the rest, would now tear itself apart over the war.

German-Americans were the most numerous group of recent immigrants. Over eight million of America's 105 million population in 1914 had been born in Germany or had at least one German parent.

John Singer Sargent's portrait of Charles, ninth Duke of Marlborough, and his American wife, formerly Consuelo Vanderbilt.

J. Pierpont Morgan, Sr (1837-1913), founder of the great Wall Street banking firm.

Automobiles rolling off an early Ford assembly line.

VON TIRPITZ
LUSITANIA
Queenstown, 7. Mai 1915.
Der Cunarddampfer „Lusitania" ist torpediert worden und gesunken.

Admiral Tirpitz, founder of the German navy, celebrates the sinking of the *Lusitania* in this German postcard.

Some of the *Lusitania's* dead buried in Queenstown, Ireland (May 1915).

Some were indifferent to the war, others kept their heads down, but many eagerly championed the cause of the Fatherland. German-language papers celebrated the Kaiser's victories, while groups such as the 'National German-American Alliance', which boasted two million members in 1914, raised money for German war relief, bought the imperial government's war bonds and pressed the media to give the German case a fair hearing.

The Irish-Americans, some 4.5 million at the start of the war, also hoped that Britain would be taught a lesson. One, a boy at the time, remembers his family's reaction: 'They thought Britain was going to get whipped and they were happy about it . . . It was time they got it.'[6] In the small, mainly Irish mining town of Butte, Montana, the young men drilled secretly and learnt to use weapons in readiness for the day when they would be called back to Ireland to take part in the revolution. Patriotic societies in Butte and in the big Irish communities of cities like Boston and New York raised money for the Irish cause, sometimes working hand-in-glove with German agents. To them any foe of Britain was necessarily Ireland's friend.

Groups like the German-Americans and Irish-Americans may have been vociferous and organised, but pro-British feeling remained strong in the United States. A majority of Americans still traced their ancestry back to British roots and many of these were inclined to the Allied cause even though they had no intention of fighting for it. British sympathisers were to be found in high places. They included Colonel Edward House, the Texan adviser of the President, and Teddy Roosevelt, one of Wilson's opponents for the presidency in 1912. Pro-British feeling was particularly strong in Wall Street, where J. P. Morgan, Jr, son of the great financier and heir to his vast banking empire, was an ardent anglophile who spent half of each year in Britain. It was to Morgan's that the British Government turned in the early months of the war to handle its military purchases in the United States, to arrange contracts for rifles, shells and heavy guns, for food and vital raw materials such as oil, cotton and copper.

The British Government had not expected to need so much American assistance. Like most of the belligerents it had assumed that the war would be over before Christmas. But by 1915 the conflict had become a war of attrition, bogged down in the trenches of northern France and Flanders where thousands of lives and millions of shells were being expended in futile offensives. Morgan's were ideally placed to act as the channel for Britain's purchases in America. They were well connected in London through their partner house, Morgan Grenfell, and they also had contacts throughout American industry.

But, to begin with, J. P. Morgan moved cautiously. It seemed unwise to draw attention to Britain's growing dependence. Some of the companies he dealt with, his 'War Babies', never officially knew the ultimate destination of the goods they supplied to Morgan's. The President of the British Board of Trade, Walter Runciman, a friend of J. P. Morgan, attempted for instance to corner the market in American-produced electro-copper, to deny supplies to Germany. He and Morgan agreed that twenty different agents should be put on to the job, each apparently buying for a different client, and succeeded in securing three-quarters of America's output for Britain without attracting comment.

Despite his call at the outbreak of war for strict neutrality, there was little Wilson could do, or perhaps wanted to do, to prevent American supplies from being shipped to Britain. It was traditional American policy to trade freely with belligerent countries in time of war. But the Allies benefited more than Germany and the Central Powers from this stance, thanks to Britain's dominance of the seas, her financial reserves and her close links with Wall Street. America's exports to Britain and France rose from $750 million in 1914 to $2.75 billion in 1916, while exports to Germany dwindled in the same period from $345 million to a mere $2 million.

American 'neutrality' was clearly favouring the Allies. But to have restricted the war trade by law would have been a deliberate tilting of neutrality against the Allies in favour of Germany. Better, then, Wilson and his advisers believed, to let market forces take their course, especially when the war boom was helping pull America out of depression and opening up new markets around the world that Europeans were forced to abandon. The *New York American* gloated a few days after war broke out: 'TWO THOUSAND MILLIONS in trade is the prize which world conditions have set before the American people. Europe's tragic extremity becomes . . . America's golden opportunity.'[7] Few were as blunt, but the prediction was apt. As Thomas Jefferson had put it over a century before, 'the new world will fatten on the follies of the old'.[8]

There was, however, a price to be paid for sharing in this enviable feast. All the goods America manufactured and sold to Britain had to be shipped across the Atlantic. As a neutral the United States claimed the absolute right of freedom of the seas. But, as belligerents, neither Britain nor Germany conceded this right, especially with the war on land deadlocked, and it became essential for each side to try to strangle the other's economy. Each declared the waters around the other's coastline a war zone. Under international law belligerents could search neutral ships and seize their cargoes if these were destined for the enemy war effort. This assumed the ability to stop a ship at sea, board it, and examine the contents. The Royal Navy, with its superiority on the surface, had little difficulty in doing this and thus in conducting its ever-tightening blockade of Germany broadly within international law. The Germans relied on their new weapon, the U-boat, but this was extremely vulnerable once on the surface. Faced with Britain's policy of starving it into submission and America's growing trade with the Allies, the Kaiser's government abandoned the legal niceties of search and seizure and struck from underwater. On 4 February 1915 it announced that all enemy merchant vessels encountered within the war zone would be destroyed on sight. To avoid attack Britain had authorised her merchant ships to fly neutral flags. Consequently, the German declaration added, 'neutral vessels cannot always be prevented from suffering from the attacks intended for enemy ships'.[9]

At 2.10 p.m. GMT on 7 May 1915 the German submarine U-20 attacked the British Cunard liner *Lusitania* off the south coast of Ireland, near the end of her voyage from New York. Only one torpedo was fired at the 30,000-ton vessel, but the initial explosion was followed by a much louder one from within the hull. Fire spread rapidly, water flooded in, and within eighteen minutes the supposedly 'unsinkable' *Lusitania* had vanished beneath the surface of the waves. One thousand two hundred and one lives were lost, among them ninety-four children. One hundred and twenty-four of those who died were American citizens.

Germany claimed that the *Lusitania* was a legitimate target because she was entering the war zone and had been carrying ammunition to Britain. Morgan's, it later emerged, had shipped a consignment of 1,248 cases of shells, six million rounds of ammunition and eighteen cases of percussion fuses for the British army, and the second and fatal explosion had almost certainly been caused by detonation of this secret cargo. But American opinion was not assuaged. All but a few extreme German-Americans were consumed with horror and outrage. 'Wholesale murder on the high seas', the action of 'wild beasts', the New York *Nation* called it.[10] For anglophiles such as Teddy Roosevelt and Colonel House, the war was now clearly shown to be a moral contest between civilisation and barbarism. Roosevelt redoubled his efforts to persuade Wilson that America should rearm and protect its neutral rights by force.

The President tried to calm the hysteria. Speaking in Philadelphia three days after the sinking, he insisted:

> The example of America must be a special example. The example of America must be the example not merely of peace because it will not fight, but of peace because peace is the healing and elevating influence of the world, and strife is not. There is such a thing as a man being too proud to fight. There is such a thing as a nation being so right that it does not need to convince others by force that it is right.[11]

In Britain the President's remarks were greeted with contempt. 'Too proud to fight'? Or too scared? America's neutrality began to look more like cowardice than principle, moral blindness not visionary idealism. Music hall comedians mocked the President. In the trenches of France dud shells that failed to explode were nicknamed 'Wilsons'.

Despite his high-minded words, however, the President did not intend to turn the other cheek. Sitting at his typewriter, Wilson drafted a diplomatic note holding the German Government 'to a strict accountability' for any loss of American ships or lives within the war zone, and calling on it in the name of the 'sacred principles of justice and humanity' to abandon its indiscriminate U-boat campaign.[12]

Secretary of State William Jennings Bryan was deeply unhappy. He wanted the President to avoid the growing risk of war by forbidding American citizens to enter the war zone defined by Germany and by banning them from sailing on passenger vessels belonging to belligerent countries, such as the British Cunard liners. That might have been a prudent policy, but Wilson refused and Bryan resigned. The public demanded a tough line, and Bryan's counsel seemed inconsistent with America's honour and its rights as a neutral country. Wilson believed that he was standing up for all peace-loving countries, but in doing so he had made a fateful decision: if Germany did not back down, America might have to choose between peace and honour.

Thus began a year-long war of words between the American and German governments, punctuated by further sinkings of passenger liners and further American casualties. In September 1915 the German Ambassador to Washington publicly promised that 'liners will not be sunk by our submarines without warning and without safety of the lives of non-combatants'.[13] But enemy merchant vessels were still torpedoed on sight. After a Channel steamer, the *Sussex*, had been sunk in March 1916, with four Americans among the casualties, Wilson typed out a new note threatening to break off diplomatic relations unless *all* non-combatant ships, passenger or cargo, were given security against attack without warning. On 4 May the Kaiser's government reluctantly agreed. The so-called *Sussex* pledge was a major diplomatic victory for Wilson. It seemed that the typewriter had proved mightier than the sword.

While taking a tough line against the German U-boat, the Wilson Administration found itself increasingly unable to control America's economic entanglements with Britain. By mid-1915 Morgan's was spending millions each week to pay for Britain's war needs and, despite large sales of British investments in the USA, reserves were running low and sterling was under strain, driven down more than twenty cents from the official rate of $4.86. In September 1915 the British Government decided that a half-billion-dollar loan, raised through Morgan's, was the only way to keep financing Britain's vital American trade.

At the beginning of the war, Bryan, in line with his policy of strict neutrality, had announced with Wilson's consent that 'in the judgment of this Government loans by American bankers to any foreign nation which is at war is inconsistent with the true spirit of neutrality'.[14] But Bryan had resigned by September 1915 and Wilson's advisers insisted that such a policy was no longer tenable when the American economy was so dependent on the war trade with Britain. Robert Lansing, Bryan's anglophile successor as Secretary of State, warned that without loans Britain's trade would collapse, throwing the American economy into depression and distress. 'Can we afford,' he asked, 'to let a declaration as to our conception of the "true spirit of neutrality" made in the first days of the war stand in the way of our national interests which seem to be seriously threatened?'[15] Reluctantly Wilson agreed that henceforth the Administration would not discourage loans to belligerent governments. As with the war trade, so with finance, market forces would be left to dictate America's policy. Morgan's became Britain's fundraiser as well as her purchasing agent.

By the early months of 1916 America's neutrality was in practice, therefore, increasingly tilted towards Britain. The tough line on German submarine warfare, the permissive attitude to British supplies and loans, were all pushing America into the Allied camp. Yet Wilson now felt increasingly alienated from the British cause. He was particularly angry at London's failure to co-operate in his efforts to end the war.

In February 1916 Wilson's adviser, Colonel Edward House, had reached an understanding with the British Foreign Secretary, Sir Edward Grey: when Britain and France judged the moment to be opportune, Wilson would propose a conference to end the war. Should Germany refuse to participate or should it reject terms which both the President and the Allies considered reasonable, then, according to the House–Grey memorandum, 'the United States would probably enter the war against Germany'.[16] For Wilson this was an important first step towards the peace table. But in London more cynical views prevailed. Like most of his colleagues the Prime Minister, H. H. Asquith, considered the American proposal 'humbug and a mere manoeuvre of American politics',[17] aimed at strengthening Wilson's chances of re-election in November. The past twenty months had only hardened British resolve. The US Ambassador in London, Walter Hines Page, told House in May: 'The English do not see how there can be any mediation . . . this German military caste caused all the trouble and there can be no security in Europe as long as it lives in authority. That's the English view. It raped nuns in Belgium . . . it planned the destruction of the *Lusitania* . . . It'll do anything.'[18] Wilson's apparent indifference to the moral issues at stake seemed incredible and deeply offensive in London.

But the British failure to act on the House–Grey memorandum left Wilson equally angry and disillusioned. Britain seemed willing to pay any price for victory, a suspicion confirmed by the summer offensive on the Somme. On 1 July, after seven days of artillery bombardment in which 1.5 million shells were fired, thirteen British divisions climbed out of their trenches to attack the German line. Within two hours of their going over the top, 20,000 were dead. Even Ambassador Page in London, a staunch supporter of the British cause, was sickened at the carnage. He compared it to

> certain horrible, catastrophic, universal-ruin passages in Revelation – monsters swallowing the universe, blood and fire and clouds and an eternal crash, rolling ruin enveloping all things – well, all that's come. There are, perhaps, ten million men dead of this war and, perhaps, one hundred million persons to whom death would be a blessing. Add to these many millions more whose views of life are so distorted that blank idiocy would be a better mental outlook, and you'll get a hint (and only a hint) of what the continent has already become – a bankrupt slaughter-house inhabited by unmated women.[19]

Britain's moral reputation in America suffered a further blow in 1916 from the brutal suppression of the Easter Rising in Dublin. The leaders were summarily tried and shot, while Sir Roger Casement was hanged for treason, despite a plea of clemency from the US Senate. The British pleaded national security – Casement had arrived in Ireland from Germany in a U-boat – but most Americans, not just those of Irish extraction, were outraged. 'I doubt if the Germans have ever been as hopelessly stupid,' wrote one of House's correspondents. 'Certainly everything for which British Liberalism has stood, as contrasted to Prussian Junkerism, has been brushed away.'[20]

But the most dangerous crisis in Anglo-American relations occurred in 1916 over Britain's blockade of Germany. The British had been able to enforce this by traditional methods, intercepting ships and inspecting their cargoes, thereby avoiding the U-boats' indiscriminate attacks on shipping. The British blockade none the less was seriously damaging to American commercial interests, and the State Department had lodged repeated protests. The cotton trade, employing some four million people, had been particularly hard hit in 1915.

In the summer of 1916 matters came to a head. After the *Sussex* pledge, ending unrestricted submarine warfare, Germany's blockade was much less emotive in America. At the same time the British tightened their own blockade even further, in a desperate effort to starve Germany into surrender. American mail passing through British ports was opened and inspected, and eighty-seven US firms figured on a new blacklist of companies suspected of trading with Germany, thus banning them from all commerce with Britain. The damage to American trade was infuriating, for the blacklist was a commercial death-sentence throughout much of the world, but even unaffected Americans were incensed at the idea that they sold goods or sent letters only with the approval of John Bull. In late July Wilson wrote to House, 'I am, I must admit, about at the end of my patience with Great Britain and the Allies. This black list business is the last straw . . . I am seriously considering asking Congress to authorize me to prohibit loans and restrict exports to the Allies.'[21]

Wilson was now more determined than ever to bring about a peace settlement. In November, buttressed by a narrow presidential election victory on the slogan 'He Kept Us Out of War', he was ready to act. This time he decided not to approach London first: the failure of the House–Grey understanding had shown the folly of that. Instead, he would treat both sides impartially, as befitted a true neutral. Colonel House was distinctly unhappy. He warned Wilson that if Germany went along with a peace proposal and the Allies did not, America might drift into war with Britain. But the President was defiant, House recorded. 'He went so far as to say that if the Allies wanted war with us we would not shrink from it.'[22]

As Wilson argued with his advisers, producing one draft after another on his typewriter, an opportunity emerged to soften up the Allies for his new peace effort. Britain's perilous financial position provided the key. She was now spending £5 million on the war effort every day, of which £2 million had to be found in America. Of this £800,000 was currently being raised daily by American loans, but, because of the rundown of Britain's gold and American securities, the figure would soon be £1.6 million. In short, American loans would soon have to cover a third of Britain's war costs.

From the British Treasury, economist John Maynard Keynes warned the Cabinet bluntly of its dependence on the United States. It must not merely avoid irritating the Wilson Administration, it must actively conciliate the American public who were now being invited to lend their savings on a scale far larger than America's own national debt in order to keep Britain going. Keynes added: 'Any feeling of irritation or lack of sympathy with this country or with its policy in the minds of the American public (and equally any lack of confidence in the military situation as interpreted by this public) would render it extremely difficult, if not impossible, to carry through financial operations on a scale adequate to our needs.'[23] Grimly the Chancellor of the Exchequer, Reginald McKenna, summed up the implications of Britain's financial crisis. 'If things go on as at present,' he warned the Cabinet on 24 October 1916, 'I venture to say with certainty that by next June or earlier the President of the American Republic will be in a position, if he wishes, to dictate his own terms to us.'[24]

The following month Morgan's tried to ease Britain's financial crisis by selling up to a billion dollars in short-term British Treasury bonds on the American market, but on 27 November the Federal Reserve Board issued a public warning to America's banks. It had been checked first with Wilson who had deliberately strengthened the wording. The Board cautioned the banks that it did 'not regard it in the interest of the country at this time that they invest in foreign Treasury bills of this character'.[25] The effect was immediate. The price of Allied bonds fell precipitously and the following day Morgan's spent some $20 million to support sterling. The British were soon aware that the warning had been issued on Wilson's authority. The Ambassador in Washington, Sir Cecil Spring-Rice, told the Foreign Office gravely that 'the object of course is to force us to accept the President's mediation by cutting off supplies'.[26]

Wilson's initiative followed swiftly. On 18 December 1916 the President despatched identical notes to the governments on both sides. Under pressure from House and Lansing, Wilson had toned down his language. The notes stressed that 'the President is not proposing peace; he is not even offering mediation'. But Wilson did urge the belligerents to state their peace terms clearly and fully, so that it would be possible to see whether there was common ground. For, he noted, 'the objects which the statesmen of the belligerents on both sides have in mind in this war are virtually the same, as stated in general terms'.[27] The British Government was infuriated by Wilson's gratuitous insult, his equation of its war aims with those of Germany. It was said that the King wept when he read the note.

The following month, January 1917, Wilson spelled out in detail the new world order he envisaged once the war was over. It would centre on a League of Nations, a 'concert of power which will make it virtually impossible that such a catastrophe should ever overwhelm us again'. America would play its part in keeping the peace, Wilson promised, but only if it were 'a peace without victory'. For 'victory would mean peace forced upon the loser . . . It would be accepted in humiliation, under duress, at an intolerable sacrifice, and would leave a sting, a resentment, a bitter memory upon which terms of peace would rest, not permanently, but only as upon quicksand. Only a peace between equals can last.' Wilson went on to outline other principles of a just peace, including the freedom of the seas, the reduction of armaments and the right of national self-determination, all of which challenged British as well as German interests. 'These,' he proclaimed, 'are American principles, American policies . . . And they are also the principles and policies of forward looking men and women everywhere . . . They are the principles of mankind and must prevail.'[28]

Wilson's appeals met with no response in Europe. In December 1916 the Asquith government fell and a new coalition was formed under the energetic leadership of David Lloyd George. For two years he had chafed at the inadequacies of Britain's war effort and he felt little sympathy for Grey's conciliatory attitude to the United States. To forestall a mediation attempt by Wilson in September 1916 he had insisted publicly that there could be no end to the war 'until the Prussian military despotism is broken beyond repair . . . It took England twenty years to defeat Napoleon,' he reminded Americans, adding, 'it will not take twenty years to win this war, but whatever time is required, it will be done . . . The fight must be to a finish – to a knock-out.'[29] Though less dismissive of Wilson's December note than the Germans, Lloyd George and his colleagues did not take it seriously. Nor were they enthusiastic about Wilson's talk of a League of Nations. The general British view was that planning for peace was irrelevant until 'the lawless Hun' had been crushed. As Ambassador Spring-Rice observed tartly from Washington: 'The Good Samaritan did not pass by on the other side and then propose to the authorities at Jericho a bill for the better security of the highroads.'[30]

Despite public bravado, the Allied position was now precarious. 'We are going to lose this war,' Lloyd George sighed in a moment of desperation.[31] The carnage of 1916 had been appalling but had achieved nothing. Four hundred and fifty thousand British casualties were sustained on the Somme, 540,000 Frenchmen had fallen defending Verdun, while, on the Eastern Front, the Czar's armies had lost more than a million. Financially, Britain could not maintain her American purchases much longer. Her gold was virtually exhausted, most of her American assets had been sold and the Federal Reserve was in effect blocking new loans. Admittedly, Wilson could not afford to pull the financial strings too hard, for America was now almost as dependent as Britain on the transatlantic trade. Exports were now more than eleven per cent of America's gross national product. Nor, for all his irritation with Britain, would the President have wanted to bring down the Allied cause if that meant an outright German victory. But Wilson did not realise the full extent of Britain's financial crisis. He did not know, for instance, that by February 1917 the British Treasury only had enough gold and securities to cover four more weeks' purchases in the USA.

Fortunately for Britain, the Germans were even more ignorant than Wilson about her financial predicament. On 9 January 1917 the Supreme Command, led by Hindenburg and Ludendorff, persuaded the Kaiser to resume unrestricted submarine warfare at the end of the month. All suspect shipping in the war zone around the British Isles would be liable to attack, whether belligerent or neutral, warship or merchantman. This broke all Germany's previous assurances to Wilson, including the *Sussex* pledge of May 1916, and made it almost inevitable that America would declare war. Apparently unaware that Britain might collapse from financial exhaustion within weeks, a desperate German leadership gambled that by mid-summer, long before America would be able to mobilise, the U-boat blockade of Britain would have forced her to surrender.

In a speech in Milwaukee, a German-American stronghold, the previous year, Wilson had warned: 'There may at any moment come a time when I cannot preserve both the honor and the peace of the United States. Do not exact of me an impossible and contradictory thing.'[32] On 3 February 1917 the President broke off diplomatic relations with Germany. Many of his advisers now considered war unavoidable, but Wilson, like most of his countrymen, was still looking for a way out. He hoped that a policy of arming US merchant vessels might suffice to protect American neutral rights. 'So he is not going to fight after all!' Lloyd George exclaimed contemptuously. 'He is awaiting another insult before he actually draws the sword!'[33]

Britain did her utmost to induce America to join her. On 16 January British Naval Intelligence intercepted a message from the German Foreign Minister, Arthur Zimmermann, to the government of Mexico. In Room 40 of the Old Admiralty Building the message was quickly decoded. Zimmermann had proposed that if America went to war, an alliance should be forged between Germany, Mexico and Japan. He promised 'that Mexico is to reconquer the lost territory in Texas, New Mexico and Arizona', which the United States had taken in the 1840s.[34] British intelligence was sure this telegram could secure America's entry into the war. A copy was given to the American Ambassador who communicated it to Wilson. The President's own attitude was not deeply affected, but when the telegram was published in the press on 1 March the public was at first incredulous and then incensed. Germany's atrocities in Belgium or even on the high seas were one thing; plotting, however ineptly, to conquer three American states was quite another.

The mood in America was hardening. The sinking of three American ships by German U-boats with the loss of fifteen crew finally forced Wilson to act. There could no longer be any doubt about German intentions. After a Cabinet meeting on 20 March an anguished Wilson decided to give up armed neutrality and take the final step.

On the evening of 2 April 1917 the President addressed a special session of the Congress and asked it formally to 'accept the status of belligerent which has thus been thrust upon it'. In words that must have brought sighs of relief in Whitehall he explained what war would mean. 'It will involve the utmost practicable co-operation in counsel and action with the governments now at war with Germany, and . . . the extension to those governments of the most liberal financial credits, in order that our resources may so far as possible be added to theirs.' But Wilson also made clear that America was still not identifying itself completely with the Allied cause. 'We have no selfish ends to serve. We desire no conquest, no dominion.' America would fight for the same goals that it had championed as a neutral, for 'liberty', 'peace' and 'the rights of mankind'. 'The world must be made safe for democracy.'[35] His wife Edith wrote in her diary: 'Through cheering multitudes we drove home in silence. The step had been taken. We were both overwhelmed.'[36]

Congress quickly approved the President's request, although six

Senators and fifty members of the House voted against. At 1.18 on the afternoon of Good Friday, 6 April 1917, the President signed the war resolution. No photographers were present: the occasion, Wilson felt, was far too solemn for that. After thirty-two months of uneasy neutrality, the United States was finally at war.

4

Victory Without Peace

1917–20

The United States, like Great Britain, was founded on liberal values. In nineteenth-century Britain there was no standing army, no military conscription. Economic life was left to the initiative of individual entrepreneurs. Freedom of speech and assembly were highly prized civil liberties. But by 1917 British liberalism was under siege. Conscription and tight censorship had been imposed, government controls applied to the economy, and a bitter hatred of Germany was fostered in the do-or-die war effort. The old Liberal Party had been split beyond repair, and Lloyd George, once a passionate civil libertarian and anti-militarist, was now lusting for victory at all costs.

As Woodrow Wilson had feared, America found it equally hard to maintain liberal values in an atmosphere of total war. Whole industries such as railroads and shipping were brought under government control. Official boards in Washington directed key areas of the economy. The Administration soon drew up its own blacklist of firms suspected of trading with the enemy, and in December 1917 the British Ambassador reported wryly to London: 'The blacklist is now published and is far more extensive than our own. The *New York Times* which railed against ours publishes the American list almost without comment.'[1]

But the most marked anti-liberal outburst was the backlash against everything German. In Pittsburgh Beethoven's music was banned, and the violinist Fritz Kreisler was ostracised from American concert halls. In scores of cities the German language was removed from school curricula. Hamburgers were renamed 'liberty steaks', sauerkraut 'liberty cabbage'. One patriotic doctor in Massachusetts decided that even diseases were too good for Germans and insisted on diagnosing 'liberty measles'.

Many Americans of German stock were loyal or at least discreet. A few made dramatic gestures of patriotism: the Germania Club of Jacksonville, Florida, turned over its new $100,000 clubhouse to the American Red Cross free of charge. But parts of America came close to civil war. Even today, older citizens of New Ulm, a small town in Minnesota, cannot forget the summer of 1917. Shortly after war was declared Wilson introduced the draft – conscription. Fearing that they would be sent to fight their own people in Europe, the strong German-American community in New Ulm organised a rally to contest the legality of the draft. On 25 July 1917 more than 5,000 people marched to the City Hall where they heard some speeches and then dispersed. It was hardly seditious, but within weeks the head of the new Public Safety Commission for Minnesota had removed the Mayor and several other officials from their posts. There was talk of burning New Ulm down and some leading German-Americans received death threats. Local banks, doing what they thought was their patriotic duty, insisted that their German-American customers should invest in US government war loans, the 'Liberty Bonds', even if they had to borrow to do so. The names of those who refused to buy leaked out and the mob painted their farms and houses yellow.[2]

Even the President's mood hardened. During the summer of 1917 he denounced the 'hyphenate' minority, those German-Americans who, he claimed, were doing the Kaiser's bidding. He became more reticent about his peace aims and spoke out so vigorously against a negotiated peace that liberals in America and Britain feared he had deserted them. His aim was now peace *through* victory, not the 'peace without victory' he had proclaimed only a few months before. But Wilson was still clear about the peace he eventually wanted to achieve.

America's declaration of war on Germany meant that it would co-operate with Britain but not that it would sign a treaty of alliance. Wilson explained to A. J. Balfour, Grey's successor as Foreign Secretary, in April 1917 that the United States would be an 'associate' power, remaining independent of the Allies and able to make peace on its own terms when it chose. Although they were on the same side for the moment, Wilson was convinced that the USA and the Allies had fundamentally different war aims: America wanted a just peace and a new world order in which imperialism, arms races and military alliances were a thing of the past, whereas the Allies wanted territorial gain, vengeance and reparation for the damage they had suffered. But he thought he could bring the Allies to heel. He wrote in July 1917:

'England and France *have not the same views with regard to peace that we have* by any means. When the war is over we can force them to our way of thinking, because by that time they will, among other things, be financially in our hands . . .'[3]

But in 1917 the end of the war seemed a long way off. Just as the German Supreme Command had expected, the United States was slow to mobilise. In April 1917 the regular army numbered a mere 110,000 and the President's call for the draft was a major break with tradition and a further blow to American liberal values. 'Good Lord!' exclaimed one Senator, 'you're not going to send soldiers over there, are you?'[4] Draft registration did not begin until June and by the end of 1917 only 175,000 American troops had crossed the Atlantic.

But few who made that journey ever forgot it. Many of the troop ships left from Hoboken pier, on the New Jersey shore opposite New York.

> We boarded the ship under cover of darkness and then pulled as unobtrusively as possible out into the roadstead . . . I had never seen the Statue of Liberty and I got to a porthole and I remember the thrill that I had, that has always stayed with me, when I saw the Statue of Liberty and realised that maybe I might not see it again. We had fifteen hundred men on board. We were stacked in there like sardines and it took us fourteen days to get across, and we had about eight days of storm. Most of us were sick. Many men actually wanted somebody to shoot them, get them out of their misery.[5]

When news that a troop convoy was arriving spread through Liverpool, children ran down to the docks to greet the strangers in the big boy-scout hats. 'It was fantastic,' recalls one of them, now in his seventies. 'All you could see was Hershey (chocolate) bars getting thrown as far as they could . . . We used to run alongside them asking for cents, or spearmints, anything at all . . . I thought they were cowboys. I really never thought they'd do any fighting.'[6]

The American 'doughboys' were bound for France. Most passed through Britain quickly, *en route* from Liverpool to Southampton. But those who did stay were intrigued at what they saw: buildings older than anything in the United States, children sometimes close to starvation because of the growing food shortages, a country apparently devoid of young men outside the military hospitals. And then there were the women. 'We were absolutely stunned by the pure peaches and cream complexions of the English girls. We had never seen anything like that. We were used to girls with deep tans in the West.

They gave us this impression that they were like porcelain dolls, they were so pretty.'[7]

The private soldiers may have been enjoying themselves, but Britain's leaders wanted action. Both on sea and land they were now desperate for support, yet the Americans seemed determined to fight the war in their own way and in their own good time.

Admiral William Benson, the US Chief of Naval Operations, wanted to keep his fleet in American waters as defence against U-boat attacks. It needed further training and Benson also feared that Britain might be defeated, leaving America to fight Germany alone. He was deeply suspicious of the British. According to Admiral William Sims, who was sent to London in April 1917 to liaise with the British Admiralty, Benson's parting words were: 'Don't let the British pull the wool over your eyes. It is none of our business pulling their chestnuts out of the fire. We would as soon fight the British as the Germans.'[8] It took all Sims's powers of persuasion to convince Washington that the U-boat campaign was nearly starving Britain into submission, with shipping losses of 600,000 tons in March and 900,000 in April. By July 1917 thirty-six of America's fifty-one operational destroyers had been moved to British ports. In an unprecedented gesture, Sims placed them under British command to combat the U-boat menace off the west coast of Britain and Ireland.

The American army proved less co-operative. In the spring of 1918 the Germans mounted a series of massive new offensives on the Western Front. The previous November Lenin and the Bolsheviks had seized power in Russia. Within weeks they had pulled their country out of the war, freeing Germany to concentrate all its resources in a final onslaught against the British and French. On 21 March Ludendorff's armies ripped through the unprepared British front on the Somme. The British lost as much ground in that one day as they had gained in 140 days of suicidal fighting in the great Somme battles of 1916. In April and late May the Germans mounted further hammer blows. The first nearly drove a wedge between the British and French; the second brought the Germans within forty miles of Paris.

Where were the Americans? Stateside the bands were trumpeting out 'The Yanks are Coming', but the British were getting impatient. One private in the Second Worcesters recalls the song: 'We did a bit of laughing about this because we thought it was typically Yank, you know, boasting. We thought they were just a boastful lot.' But the laughter was now grim: 'We realised we were getting to the end of our manpower resources . . . we knew there weren't many left in England to back us up.'[9] After the March disaster a panic-stricken

Cabinet started withdrawing men from essential industries such as munitions and the mines. It even contemplated extending conscription to Ireland, only to be told by the Chief Secretary for Ireland that it 'might as well recruit Germans'.[10] Vehemently Lloyd George and the British Commander-in-Chief, Sir Douglas Haig, demanded that the United States send over as many combat troops as possible, for immediate amalgamation in hard-pressed British and French units.

But the Commander of the American Expeditionary Force, General John J. Pershing, had no intention of using his troops as a replacement pool for the Allies. He interpreted his orders to mean that he should build up a separate American army in Europe, properly trained and supplied, to be used in action when American policy determined. Haig complained that Pershing 'did not seem to realise the urgency of the situation . . . He hankers after a "*great self contained American Army*" but . . . it is ridiculous to think such an Army could function unaided in less than two years time.'[11] Pershing, however, would not be rushed, nor diverted from his aim. By the time the fifth and last great German offensive of 1918 had petered out in the middle of July, 1.2 million American troops were in France but few of them had seen action.

Pershing's conduct was a graphic illustration of what America's 'associate' status really meant. The United States would use its own power in its own way, not at the Allies' behest. And in January 1918 President Wilson had issued a new reminder of America's independent approach to world affairs when he set out his 'Fourteen Points' for a just peace.

On seizing power in Russia Lenin and the Bolsheviks had ransacked the Czar's files. They published secret treaties which confirmed that, once Germany and the Central Powers were defeated, the Allies intended to divide up the spoils between them. France was to take parts of Germany and Italy pieces of Austria. The Turkish Empire would be dismembered, with Britain a major beneficiary. In response, Wilson insisted that America was above such Old World duplicity. His first five points were a direct challenge to Britain's global power. They called for an end to secret diplomacy and its replacement by 'open covenants of peace, openly arrived at'; for 'absolute freedom of navigation upon the seas'; for 'the removal, so far as possible, of all economic barriers'; for the maximum possible disarmament 'consistent with domestic safety'; and for 'a free, open-minded and absolutely impartial adjustment of all colonial claims' weighing 'the interests of the populations concerned' equally with the rights of the governing powers.[12] Clearly, Wilson had not abandoned his aim of reshaping the Old World in the image of the New. And it appeared, as 1918 wore on, that Pershing's army would be his chosen instrument.

In mid-July the Allied counter-offensive began. For the first time Pershing's divisions, now formed into the First US Army, saw action in large numbers, but the brunt of the fighting was still borne by the British and French. In London it seemed that the war would drag on into 1919 or 1920. The Cabinet was increasingly anxious that Britain would by then be exhausted and at the mercy of any terms that Wilson cared to impose. Some even used this as renewed argument for a negotiated peace. General Jan Smuts warned Lloyd George in August 1918: 'It may well be that, by the indefinite continuance of the war, we shall become a second or third-class Power, and the leadership, not only financially and militarily, but in every respect will have passed on to America and Japan.'[13] Lloyd George was particularly angry that while Britain had provided half the shipping needed to transport Pershing's recalcitrant army to Europe, the American merchant fleet, now grown to forty per cent of Britain's, had captured a quarter of world trade.

Then, suddenly, it was all over. Germany's allies, Bulgaria, Turkey and Austria-Hungary, collapsed in the early autumn. Germany was left alone, its reserves exhausted, aware now that, with the strong, well-fed Americans coming into the line in their thousands, the Allies could not be beaten. Germany's morale snapped. At the beginning of October 1918 a new government assumed power under Prince Max of Baden, and, as revolution smouldered in Germany, an end to hostilities was agreed. But Prince Max was not negotiating with the Allies. He appealed over their heads to Wilson, asking for an armistice on the basis of the President's Fourteen Points. The Germans believed that these offered them much more generous terms than anything available from the embittered British and French.

Wilson negotiated an armistice with the Germans. He then sent House over to Paris to inform the Allies of what their 'Associate' had decided. The Allied leaders were furious, but House stopped them short. If the Fourteen Points were not accepted as the basis for negotiation, he warned, Wilson would go to Congress and ask whether America should continue to fight for countries that did not share its war aims. This ended most of the debate, but Britain still refused to accept point two dealing with the freedom of the seas. The Admiralty saw it as a challenge to Britain's sea power and her right of blockade, an attack on 'the very source of our national life, the maintenance of which is an act of self-preservation'.[14] House warned that if agreement could not be reached, there would ensue an all-out race to build the most powerful navy in the world. 'The United States,' he said, 'had more resources, more men and more money than Great Britain and in a contest, Great Britain would lose.' Lloyd George replied 'that Great Britain would spend her last guinea to keep a navy superior to that of the United States or any other power, and that no Cabinet official could continue in the Government of England who took a different position'.[15]

In the end Lloyd George won that point. He would not accept the principle of freedom of the seas in advance, but agreed to discuss the issue at the peace conference. He also secured another reservation allowing the Allies to demand reparations from Germany. He decided that the rest of the Fourteen Points were 'wide enough to allow us to place our own interpretation upon them'.[16] Despite their dependence on American money and manpower, the British clearly still had some leverage of their own. But there was no denying on Armistice Day, 11 November 1918, that President Wilson had ended the war virtually on his own terms. It remained to be seen whether he could write the peace treaty as well.

Wilson left New York on board the SS *George Washington* on 4 December 1918. In today's world of summits and shuttle diplomacy it is worth remembering that he was the first American President to travel to Europe while in office. It was a controversial, eventually a fateful, decision. For Wilson was staking his whole personal reputation on the peace conference, convinced that he alone could guide the world to a just and lasting peace.

After a few days in France, the President reached Dover on 26 December. As he disembarked schoolgirls strewed rose petals in his path. The King's train took him on to London amid scenes of rejoicing and celebration. There he and his wife, Edith, stood on the balcony of Buckingham Palace with King George V and Queen Mary, acknowledging the cheers of a crowd who chanted 'We want Wilson'. A young English girl, Edith Sowerbutts, was among those watching. 'Everybody cheered and clapped. He spoke optimistically. The world was going to be safe for Democracy and there would be no more wars, which pleased everybody. We were all very young and we believed all we were told.'[17]

These were heady days for the President. During the war he had appealed to large sections of British radical opinion, Liberal and Labour, who were revolted by the slaughter and yearned for a new and better world. The ecstatic reception in Europe confirmed his belief that he alone spoke for 'the silent mass of mankind'. The economist John Maynard Keynes was one of the welcoming liberals.

Wilson 'enjoyed a prestige and a moral influence throughout the world unequalled in history', he wrote later. The President also controlled 'the realities of power', with Europe dependent on America for manpower, food and finance. 'Never,' judged Keynes, 'has a philosopher held such weapons wherewith to bind the princes of this world.'[18]

The President's sense of his own virtue was dramatically illustrated at the state banquet held in his honour at Buckingham Palace on 27 December. After the privations of wartime this was an opportunity for the leaders of triumphant Britain to celebrate in pomp and pageantry. Dr Cary Grayson, Wilson's physician, was dazzled by the scene in the great dining room. 'On the walls,' he wrote in his diary, 'are hundreds of pieces of solid gold decorations, plaques, shields and the like . . . All of the table service is of solid gold, bearing the royal arms. The value of the gold dishes is said to be approximately $15,000,000.'[19] The guests at the banquet represented all parts of Britain and her empire, resplendent in dress uniforms, medals, and jewellery. The display was all the more striking when one remembers that four rival imperial dynasties, the Romanovs, the Habsburgs, the Hohenzollerns and the Ottomans, had recently disintegrated in bloody chaos. Left alone in battered but solitary splendour was the House of Saxe-Coburg-Gotha, prudently renamed the House of Windsor in 1917.

Yet the guest of honour at this pageant of princes cut a very different figure. Wilson was dressed in an ordinary black suit without medal or braid. His speech of thanks was clipped and formal, making not even passing reference to the contribution of the British Empire to the defeat of Germany. Those listening were chilled. 'There was no glow of friendship or of gladness at meeting men who had been partners in a common enterprise,' Lloyd George recalled.[20] It was as if Wilson had been fighting his own private war. Later the President warned the King:

> You must not speak of us who come over here as cousins, still less as brothers; we are neither. Neither must you think of us as Anglo-Saxons, for that term can no longer be rightly applied to the people of the United States. Nor must too much importance in this connection be attached to the fact that English is our common language . . . No, there are only two things which can establish and maintain closer relations between your country and mine: they are community of ideals and of interests.[21]

In some ways British and American 'ideals' were not so far apart as Wilson often implied. Many of his cherished convictions, such as disarmament, anti-imperialism and free trade, were not distinctively American. They were the traditions of nineteenth-century British liberalism in which the President was rooted, the ideals of William Cobden, John Bright and Wilson's great hero, Gladstone. Even the idea of a League of Nations was as much British as American. The term itself was popularised by a Cambridge don, Lowes Dickinson, who had helped found 'The League of Nations Society' in Britain in 1915. Sir Edward Grey, the Liberal Foreign Secretary, had pressed the idea on Wilson in the early part of the war, and after Grey's fall Lord Robert Cecil had kept the idea alive in the British Cabinet. He and General Jan Smuts of South Africa prodded Whitehall into drawing up detailed proposals for a League during 1918. The British came to Paris better prepared on the issue than Wilson himself.

Nevertheless, Wilson was right to assert that he and the British were far apart. Lloyd George and his colleagues had deserted the old liberal traditions which Wilson still espoused. No one else in the Cabinet was as enthusiastic as Cecil about making the League of Nations the centrepiece of a new system of international security. Britain had too much at stake in the old order to welcome the creation of a new, as the argument about the Fourteen Points had shown. And after a long and bloody war, in which 750,000 Britons had died, the demand for vengeance was overwhelming, voiced especially by Lloyd George's powerful Conservative partners in the Coalition Government. In the election campaign of November 1918 Lloyd George had started out promising that 'we must relentlessly set our face against . . . squalid principles of either revenge or avarice'. But under pressure from an enraged public, orchestrated by the *Daily Mail* and other Northcliffe newspapers who wanted Germany squeezed 'until the pips squeak', he was soon calling for reparations from Germany 'up to the limit of her capacity', a sum estimated by the Treasury at £25 billion.[22]

While liberalism was dying in Britain, Woodrow Wilson gave it a new lease of life. The United States, of course, was not completely disinterested. Freer trade, for instance, would obviously benefit the world's most powerful economy. But America had far less at stake in the peace conference than any other belligerent, with no territorial claims and only 130,000 dead. 'Wilsonianism' was British liberalism transformed by America's crusading sense of mission and enforced by America's enormous new power. The values abandoned by the Old World were now being turned against it by the messiah from the New.

The peace conference formally opened in Paris on 18 January 1919. It was the most momentous international gathering since the Congress of Vienna a century before, which had determined the shape of Europe after Napoleon. But this was a far larger affair. Britain had fewer than twenty diplomats at Vienna, but in 1919 it required five hotels to accommodate her staff of over 200. The Americans had 1,300 in their delegation at its peak. There were also thirty other national delegations, each with a vested interest in the outcome of the conference, and a press corps of 500, including 150 Americans, all determined to make a reality of Wilson's call for 'open diplomacy'. Little wonder, then, that for many participants the conference seemed totally chaotic. The British diplomat, Harold Nicolson, likened it to a 'riot in a parrot house'.[23]

The first month of the conference was dominated by Wilson. His overriding aim was to keep the League of Nations at the top of the agenda until its foundations had been established. After intense debate, a draft agreement was reached. For the first time in history there would be an international assembly, led by the great powers but open to all, which pledged itself to maintain peace and stability. If the territory of any state was endangered, or its independence threatened, the other League members would come to its aid by applying economic sanctions or direct military force.

Lloyd George doubted the wisdom of this last provision. It seemed dangerously utopian and, if observed to the letter, would place impossible obligations on great powers like Britain to intervene in every dispute. Personally he would have preferred a looser League based on the Allied Supreme War Council he had set up in 1917. This would expedite consultation between the powers, without making their response to aggression pre-ordained. But Wilson believed that this automatic commitment, enshrined in Article Ten of the League's Covenant, was indispensable. Reluctantly the British Cabinet went along with his grand design. It seemed the price necessary to ensure the President's co-operation on issues they regarded as vital at the peace conference. As Australia's Prime Minister, Billy Hughes, put it: 'Give him a League of Nations and he will give us all the rest.'[24]

The President himself presented the Covenant to a full session of the conference on St Valentine's Day, 14 February 1919, his triumph, as he thought, complete. Immediately afterwards he left Paris for home to handle urgent domestic business. The outlines of the League had now been agreed, but the peace terms to be imposed on Germany still had to be decided.

Wilson's return to Washington showed clearly that he had misjudged the temper of Congress. Under the US Constitution any international treaty has to be approved by two-thirds of the Senate, and in the midterm elections of November 1918 the Republicans had won a majority in both Houses of Congress. This meant that Wilson's arch-enemy, Henry Cabot Lodge, would be chairman of the Senate Foreign Relations Committee, responsible for managing the hearings and the debate on the treaty.

INTERRUPTING THE CEREMONY

McCUTCHEON, CHICAGO TRIBUNE–NEW YORK NEWS SYNDICATE, INC.

Wilson scorned members of Congress: he regarded them for the most part as small-minded and parochial. He had taken no Republican politicians with him to Paris and assumed he could railroad the treaty through the Senate. But back in Washington in February he discovered the depths of the opposition. He was flouting the most hallowed precept of American diplomacy, dating back to George Washington, that America should avoid entangling alliances. He was apparently overriding the right of Congress to declare war, by committing the country to automatic action whenever the League's Covenant was violated. It also seemed that the Covenant denied the Monroe Doctrine, the United States' claim that it could rightfully intervene if any outside power tried to establish itself on the American continent.

Wilson felt sure of his position. He reported to House, still in Paris, that 'the people of the United States are undoubtedly in favor of the League of Nations by an overwhelming majority. I can say this with perfect confidence.'[25] But the Senate remained unimpressed by his explanations of the League and of how it squared with American rights and interests. 'I feel as if I had been wandering with "Alice in Wonderland" and had had tea with the Mad Hatter,' complained one frustrated Senator.[26] Wilson's liberal internationalism was not shared by the hard-headed nationalists in Congress.

When Wilson returned to Paris on 14 March he had lost the initiative. Previously he had based his case for the League on a position of purity and high-mindedness. He had argued that the new world order should be free of all taint of imperialism and 'balance of power' politics. But now the Senate had insisted that America's sphere of influence in Central and South America, as defined by the Monroe Doctrine, should be admitted as an exception. Such special pleading was acutely embarrassing. Worse still, it was tactically disastrous, for if America claimed a special right to pursue its own self-interest the Allies would naturally do the same.

The French seized the opportunity to press their demand for punitive reparations from Germany. They considered these essential to rebuild their ravaged country. France also wanted permanent control of the Rhineland to ensure their security against renewed German attack. Lloyd George's position was midway between that of America and France. Under intense pressure at home, he was forced to plead Britain's case for reparations. But he had no desire to build up French power in Europe and he opposed their demands for the Rhineland. He feared that if Germany lost too much of her homeland that would sow the seeds of future war and also accelerate the spread of Bolshevism. Unlike France, Britain's main interests lay outside

Europe. She wanted to destroy Germany as a world power: to strip her of her colonies, to take over her navy and merchant fleet, and to safeguard the position of the British Empire.

By April 1919 Wilson, Lloyd George and Clemenceau were evenly matched. Britain and France depended much less on America now that the fighting was over and Wilson's leverage greatly reduced. Lloyd George and Clemenceau were more in step than Wilson with opinion back home, which made their negotiating positions far stronger. The British premier, often nicknamed 'the Wizard', was also tactically astute. He shifted discussions into a small 'Council of Four', comprising the leaders of Britain, France, America and Italy. There, without advisers and secretaries, business could be accelerated in a way that benefited the Europeans, trained in the cut and thrust of parliamentary debate. Wilson's mind, though powerful, was slower, less subtle. In long, informal discussions in late March and early April 1919 the President's resistance was gradually worn down.

Compromise, after all, is the essence of diplomacy. And it was now imperative that agreement be reached and a peace treaty signed. For Europe seemed on the brink of anarchy and revolution. The defeated powers were in economic chaos, but a proper programme of feeding and recovery could not be mounted until the war had formally come to an end. On 22 March Colonel House noted in his diary: 'I am discouraged at the outlook. We are not moving as rapidly now. From the look of things the crisis will soon be here. Rumblings of discontent every day. The people want peace. Bolshevism is gaining ground everywhere. Hungary has just succumbed. We are sitting upon an open powder magazine and some day a spark may ignite it.'[27] Lloyd George and Wilson shared these fears of Bolshevik revolution. Pressure mounted in Paris to reach a rapid agreement, and it was the exhausted President, for a while seriously ill from the influenza epidemic that was sweeping the world, who now made most of the concessions.

To satisfy Britain and France, Wilson agreed that greater reparations should be exacted from Germany than had first been proposed. After another row with Lloyd George he stopped pressing Britain on the freedom of the seas. And to placate Clemenceau, Wilson and Lloyd George agreed to a temporary occupation of the Rhineland for fifteen years. They also offered him an Anglo-American guarantee of French security. If Germany attempted to invade France, Britain and America would come to her assistance. This marked a historic departure from both countries' traditional policy of avoiding entangling alliances with continental Europe. But it also opened up a vast breach in the League's principle of global, collective security. In return, the Allies accepted the Senate's modifications of the Covenant. The League could now start its work, which remained Wilson's overriding objective.

The final text of the treaty, some 200 pages, was published on 7 May 1919. Liberals on the British and American delegations, who had been excluded from the intense top-level negotiations of the last few weeks, were horrified at what they read. The ideals of the Fourteen Points seemed to have been totally abandoned. John Maynard Keynes resigned from the British delegation in protest. 'I've never been so miserable as for the last two or three weeks; the peace is outrageous and impossible,' he wrote. 'Certainly if I was in the Germans' place I'd rather die than sign such a peace.'[28]

It nearly came to that. The German delegation had been kept waiting while the peace terms were worked out by America and the Allies. Now they too were aghast at what they read, rejecting the draft treaty as a travesty of the terms on which they had originally accepted the Armistice. They had assumed that the Fourteen Points would be the basis of the eventual peace. Lloyd George, increasingly alarmed about the dangers of harsh terms, secured some minor changes, but Clemenceau was intransigent and an exhausted Wilson was in no mood for further alterations. Finally Germany was given twenty-four hours to accept the treaty or be invaded. On 28 June 1919, in Louis XIV's great Hall of Mirrors at Versailles, two quaking German delegates signed the treaty.

For the French, it was a moment to savour. Bismarck had imposed a humiliating peace treaty on them in the same place thirty-eight years before. Now the tables had been turned with a vengeance. Yet even those who had struck the deal had their doubts. After the signing Lloyd George commented: 'We shall have to do the whole thing over again in twenty-five years time at three times the cost.'[29] Germany was left weakened but not crushed. The treaty might well have been far harsher, given the grimness of the war, but it still left a legacy of deep and abiding bitterness. Before long an aggrieved Germany would once again demand the status of a world power, this time under a leadership of appalling depravity.

On 29 June 1919, the day after the Treaty of Versailles had been signed, Wilson set off for home. He had reached agreement with the Allies. Now he had to win over two-thirds of the US Senate, in which the Republicans, under the hostile Lodge, had a majority. Looking ahead to the presidential election of 1920 they saw political capital to be made out of the League. But many Senators were not isolationists, opposed to any American involvement in the affairs of Europe. Lodge himself favoured the Anglo-American guarantee of France. Most Senators in fact shared Lloyd George's outlook, welcoming a loose international organisation but opposing the automatic, unlimited, global commitments proposed by Wilson. Eventually Lodge offered fourteen reservations to the proposed League which would give the United States the right to choose its own course of action on any issue of national importance. America would not be committed automatically to defend another country's territorial integrity, to implement economic sanctions or to accept the League's decisions on disarmament. The right of the Congress to determine America's foreign policy would be safeguarded.

Among the most ardent opponents of the League were Irish-Americans. They had expected Wilson to put Irish freedom high on the agenda at Paris, and in March 1919, a resolution swept through the House of Representatives demanding that the peace conference, 'in passing on the rights of various peoples, will favorably consider the claims of Ireland to the right of self-determination'.[30] But Wilson had enough problems in Paris without adding Ireland to the list. The issue was hardly discussed, and angry Irish-Americans, backed by over $1 million from their 'Irish Victory Fund', campaigned against the League to get their own back on Wilson and the British. 'If the League of Nations goes into effect as now presented,' the *Philadelphia Irish Press* declared, 'Americans will be found to assist England in crushing any insurrection that might occur in Ireland.'[31]

Despite the mounting opposition, Wilson remained confident that he was right. He tried to go over the Senate's head and appeal to public opinion. In 1919, just before the age of radio, long before the era of regular air travel, that meant an arduous speaking tour around the vast American heartland, journeying by special train. Wherever he went the President's message to the American people was clear: the treaty and the Covenant had taken months of negotiation and could not now be changed. 'If we want a League of Nations,' he insisted in Portland, Oregon, 'we must take this League of Nations . . . We must leave it or take it.' In Sioux Falls, South Dakota, he declared that the whole world was waiting for America to join the League, because 'America is the only idealistic Nation in the world . . . If America goes back upon mankind, mankind has no other place to turn.' And, for those who 'do not want me to be too altruistic,' he told an audience in St Louis, 'let me be very practical. If we are partners, let me predict that we will be the senior partner. The financial leadership will be ours. The industrial primacy will be ours.

The commercial advantage will be ours. The other countries of the world are looking to us for leadership and direction.'[32]

In the first three weeks of September 1919, Wilson travelled 8,000 miles by train, giving nearly forty hour-long speeches, often without the help of any amplification, as well as innumerable informal conferences. Coming after months of travel and argument, to and fro across the Atlantic, the strain was too much for the sixty-three-year-old President. On 25 September, in a state of nervous and physical exhaustion, Wilson was forced to return to Washington. On 2 October he suffered a severe stroke. For two weeks he was close to death; for several months he lay virtually helpless and his wife, Edith, ran the White House.

It was now clear that Lodge could deny the President his two-thirds majority. But illness clouded Wilson's judgement and hardened his will. He still refused to make any fundamental compromise, despite the urging of Senate Democrats and of his wife. On 28 November 1919, the day before the Senators voted, he sent them a letter stating that to vote for Lodge's reservations would amount to 'the nullification of the treaty'.[33] Next day neither side could win the necessary two-thirds majority. Wilson's proposed League fell well short, but so did

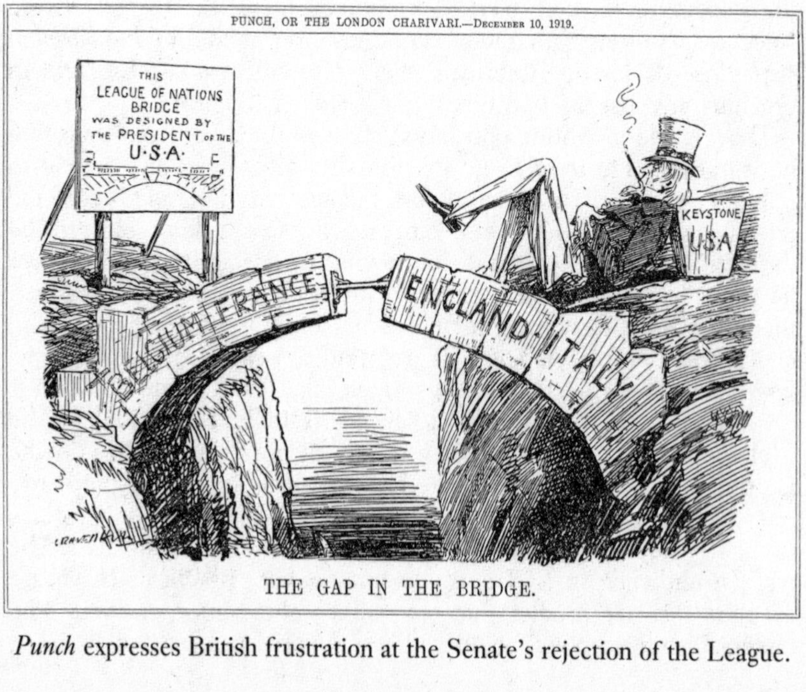

Punch expresses British frustration at the Senate's rejection of the League.

Lodge's League-with-reservations. In another vote in March 1920 an inflexible Wilson still retained the loyalty of enough Democrats to keep Lodge seven votes short. The United States would not be a member of the League of Nations, nor would it guarantee French security. One of the most momentous decisions that America had been asked to take was decided by stalemate.

Back in April 1917 Woodrow Wilson began a great crusade to make the world safe for democracy. American supplies sustained the Allied armies, its loans kept them fighting, its troops proved the last straw for the exhausted Germans. In October 1918 Wilson was able to dictate Armistice terms to friend and foe alike. But once Germany had collapsed, much of his leverage over the Allies disappeared. He was forced to compromise extensively at Paris to win European support for his League. Liberals felt the President had betrayed their trust. Worse, Wilson could not then secure approval in Washington for what had been agreed at Versailles. The League itself was betrayed by the country whose President had been its architect. 'America,' said Lloyd George, 'had been offered the leadership of the world, but the Senate had tossed the sceptre into the sea.'[34]

5

The Big Two

1921–35

The United States did not join the League of Nations, but, as Woodrow Wilson rightly pointed out, its place in the world had changed irrevocably. 'By the sheer genius of this people and the growth of our power we have become a determining factor in the history of mankind,' he declared in 1919, 'and after you have become a determining factor you cannot remain isolated, whether you want to or not.'[1] Although in the 1920s America maintained its cherished tradition of no entangling alliances with the Old World, the war had made it a major force in international affairs. Its fleet was nearly as large as the Royal Navy, it had the second biggest merchant marine in the world, and its vast loans to the Allies had transformed it from a debtor into a major creditor nation.

While the New World prospered, the Old World had destroyed itself. The Austro-Hungarian Empire had disappeared, splintered into small, chaotic rival states. Germany – defeated, disarmed and embittered – was now under a weak and unpopular republican regime. Russia had been torn apart by revolution and civil war, losing huge tracts of territory on its western frontier. And France, though a victor, had suffered 1.5 million killed, including over a tenth of its active male population. Seen from the vantage point of today, the Great War was a turning point in Europe's decline.

But one of the old European powers had come through the war much better than the rest. Great Britain had suffered 750,000 dead, the loss of fifteen per cent of her overseas assets and the collapse of many of her old industries. But she had not been invaded, and the main threat to British security, the German navy, lay rusting at the bottom of Scapa Flow. On the ruins of the old Turkish Empire she acquired vast mandates from the League of Nations in Palestine and

EUROPE AFTER WORLD WAR ONE
FINLAND
Petrograd
NORWAY
SWEDEN
ESTONIA
Pskov
LATVIA
USSR
LITHUANIA
DENMARK
Minsk
E PRUSSIA
Berlin
Warsaw
HOLLAND
POLAND
Kiev
GERMANY
BELGIUM
CZECHOSLOVAKIA
BESSARABIA
Paris
Vienna
Budapest
FRANCE
AUSTRIA
HUNGARY
ROUMANIA
SWITZERLAND
S TYROL
Bucharest
Belgrade
ITALY
YUGOSLAVIA
BULGARIA
Rome
ALBANIA
Salonika
TURKEY
GREECE
0
300
Miles
0
400
Km
INTERNATIONAL BOUNDARIES
TERRITORY LOST BY GERMANY
AUSTRO-HUNGARIAN EMPIRE UNTIL 1918
TERRITORY LOST BY RUSSIA

Mesopotamia (Iraq), becoming the major power in the oil-rich Middle East. The British Empire was now larger than it had been at Queen Victoria's death. 'England is the only real winner from this war,' wrote the German historian Erich Marks in 1920, 'England together with North America: one can see an Anglo-Saxon world dominion rising on the horizon.'[2]

Marks was not alone. To many in Germany and France it seemed that the era of 'the Anglo-Saxons' had dawned. Symbolically this could be seen in the language of the Paris peace conference, which, to the annoyance of France, had been conducted in English as much as French, previously the lingua franca of diplomacy and culture. The Big Three – Wilson, Lloyd George and Clemenceau – used English almost exclusively for their crucial discussions in March and April 1919. The substance as well as the language of diplomacy had changed. The League of Nations, as drafted in Paris, was basically a compromise between Woodrow Wilson and Robert Cecil: it was an Anglo-American plan, thrust on the rest of the world. Britain and America were the strongest financial powers, possessed the largest navies, and were relatively secure, stable and satisfied. During the 1920s they were to shape the post-war world.

Nevertheless, Britain was disconcerted by America's dramatic entrance on to the world stage. Few had anticipated how rapidly American power and influence would grow as a result of the war. No one in government had enjoyed the humiliation of being, in the words of the British press baron Lord Northcliffe in 1917, 'down on our knees to the Americans'.[3] In the wake of the Great War many British leaders decided that it was vital to maintain the closest co-operation with the Americans in order to safeguard British interests. As Cecil put it in 1917, 'If America accepts our point of view . . . it will mean the dominance of that point of view in all international affairs.' He was convinced that America could be guided by Britain, because it was new to the affairs of Europe and because, 'though the American people are very largely foreign, both in origin and in modes of thought, their rulers are almost exclusively Anglo-Saxons, and share our political ideals'.[4]

Henceforth the hope of a special relationship with America, the Old World discreetly managing the New, was to be at the centre of British policy. But the war had already shown that the relationship would not be easy to manipulate in the way Britain wanted. The Senate vote on the League dramatically illustrated the fact that an American President had much less freedom of action in foreign affairs than a British Prime Minister. Congress could easily upset the

President Woodrow Wilson *left*, and his close adviser, Colonel Edward House.

New York women campaign for Wilson's re-election (November 1916) on an anti-war platform.

2 April 1917: President Wilson asks Congress to declare war on Germany.

American troops in London, led by the band of the Welsh Guards (August 1917).

General John J. Persing *left centre* and King George V *right centre* review American troops.

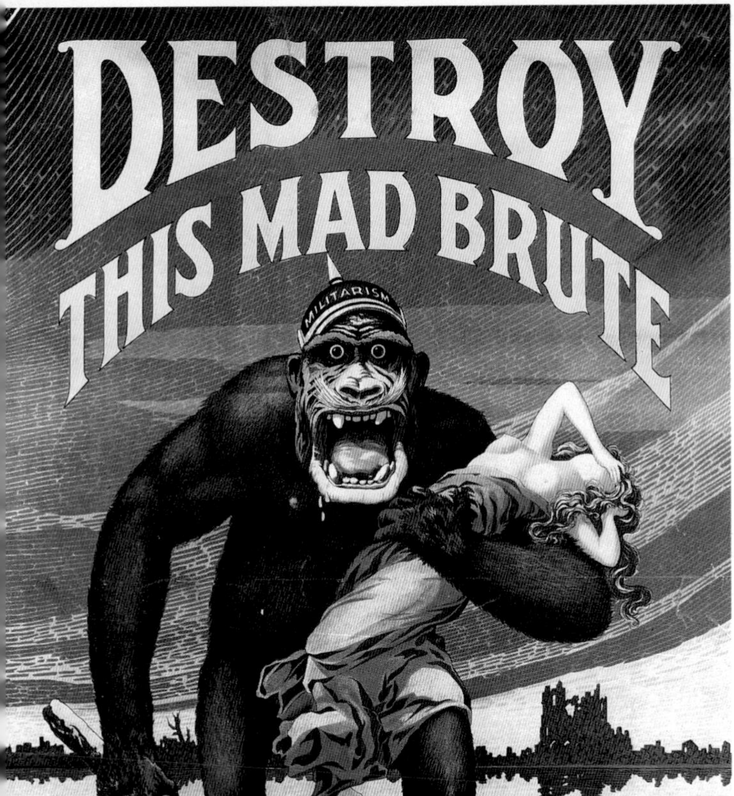

Once America entered the war in 1917 a propaganda campaign was mounted against all things German.

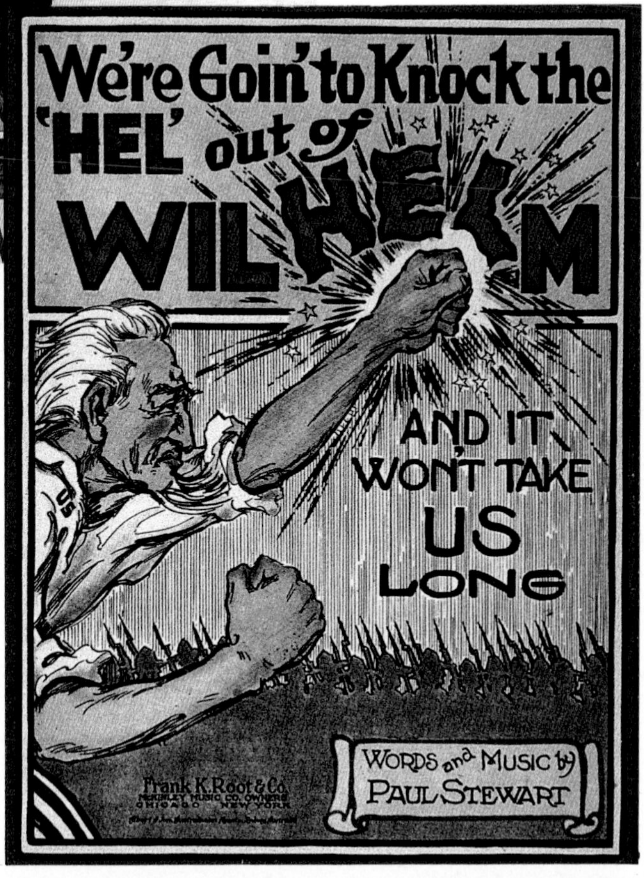

American patriotic songsheet of 1918.

The Old World welcomes the New: President Wilson at Dover, 26 December 1918.

President Wilson is driven through London's Trafalgar Square (December 1918).

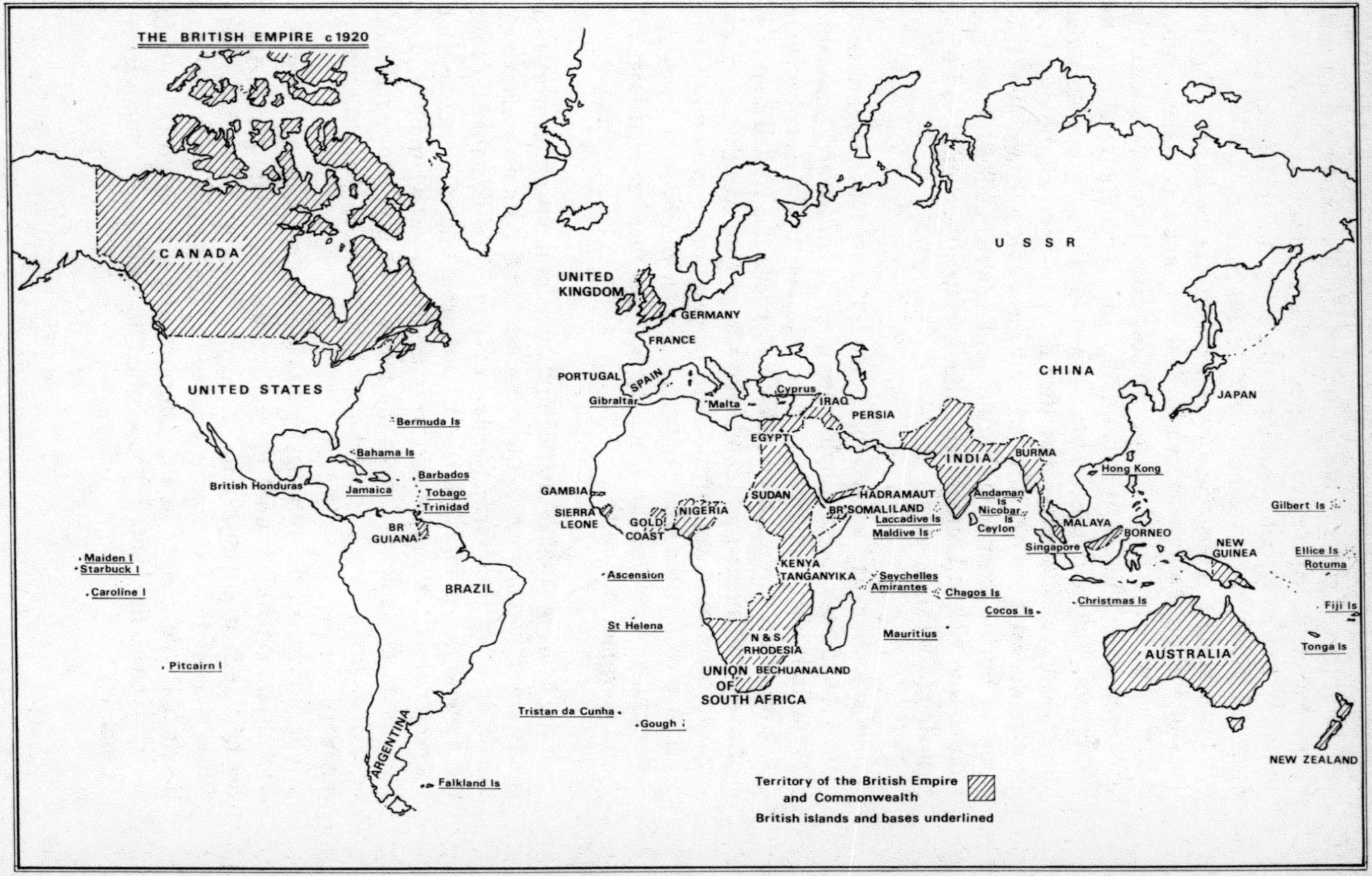
THE BRITISH EMPIRE c1920
CANADA
UNITED STATES
UNITED KINGDOM
GERMANY
FRANCE
PORTUGAL
SPAIN
Gibraltar
Malta
Cyprus
IRAQ
PERSIA
EGYPT
U S S R
CHINA
JAPAN
INDIA
BURMA
Hong Kong
Bermuda Is
Bahama Is
Barbados
Tobago
Trinidad
Jamaica
British Honduras
BR GUIANA
BRAZIL
ARGENTINA
Falkland Is
Maiden I
Starbuck I
Caroline I
Pitcairn I
GAMBIA
SIERRA LEONE
GOLD COAST
NIGERIA
SUDAN
HADRAMAUT
BR SOMALILAND
Laccadive Is
Maldive Is
Andaman Is
Nicobar Is
Ceylon
MALAYA
Singapore
BORNEO
NEW GUINEA
Gilbert Is
Ellice Is
Rotuma
Fiji Is
Tonga Is
Ascension
St Helena
KENYA
TANGANYIKA
Seychelles
Amirantes
Chagos Is
Cocos Is
Christmas Is
Mauritius
N & S RHODESIA
BECHUANALAND
UNION OF SOUTH AFRICA
AUSTRALIA
NEW ZEALAND
Tristan da Cunha
Gough
Territory of the British Empire and Commonwealth
British islands and bases underlined

best-laid plans of the diplomats. And, as Cecil's comments showed, British leaders were prone to exaggerate the 'Englishness' of America, despite Wilson's emphatic warning to the King at Buckingham Palace that the United States was no longer 'Anglo-Saxon'.

The most serious obstacle to co-operation was the fact that the Big Two of the post-war world were rivals as much as collaborators. Whatever the French suspected, 'Anglo-Saxon' unity was often only skin-deep. Sir William Wiseman, the British diplomat closest to Wilson and Colonel House, wrote at the time of the Armistice about 'the growing consciousness that after the war there will be only two great powers left – Great Britain and the United States. Which is going to be the greater, politically and commercially?'[5] Likewise, House, who visited London after the Treaty of Versailles had been signed, told Wilson:

> Almost as soon as I arrived in England, I sensed an antagonism to the United States. The English are quite as cordial and hospitable to the individual American as ever, but they dislike us collectively . . . While the British Empire vastly exceeds the United States in area and population and while their aggregate wealth is perhaps greater than ours, yet our position is much more favourable. It is because of this that the relations between the two countries are beginning to assume the same character as that between England and Germany before the war.[6]

At the heart of Anglo-American relations in the twenties were two issues: navies and finance. In these essential attributes of a great power Britain and America were in a class of their own. Together they set the framework within which lesser states would have to operate. But sea power and finance were also the issues around which their struggle for supremacy centred. Unlike the pre-war rivalry between Britain and Germany it was a peaceful struggle, but no less intense or important for that.

The strength of the rival navies was a continual source of hostility and misunderstanding until the early thirties. The mutual distrust reached such a pitch that in July 1927 Winston Churchill, then Chancellor of the Exchequer, told his Cabinet colleagues that 'no doubt it is quite right in the interests of peace to go on talking about war with the United States being "unthinkable"'. But, warned Churchill:

> everyone knows that this is not true. However foolish and disastrous such a war would be . . . we do not wish to put ourselves in the power of the United States. We cannot tell what they might do if at some future date they were in a position to give us orders about our policy, say, in India, or Egypt, or Canada, or on any other great matter behind which their electioneering forces were marshalled.[7]

It was a remarkably frank statement, and, coming from a British leader who was half American and a fervent apostle of Anglo-American friendship, it was a vivid demonstration of how low relations sank in this struggle over who should rule the waves.

The origins of the naval race are to be found in World War One. America's wartime programme of naval building had transformed it into a major sea power. Japan too had embarked on its own expansion and Britain's supremacy was under threat. In 1919 the Royal Navy still had forty-two capital ships (battleships and battle cruisers), compared with America's sixteen and Japan's fourteen. But by 1924, if current building programmes continued, Britain would have forty-three capital ships, America thirty-five and Japan twenty-two. The Admiralty was alarmed at the trend but in 1921 Lloyd George, still premier of a now shaky coalition government, was convinced that Britain could not afford a naval race with America. The country was facing a severe post-war recession and the government was desperately trying to reduce the National Debt, vastly inflated by the war, and to cut public spending.

The direct naval rivalry between Britain and America was complicated by the existence of the Anglo-Japanese alliance. First signed in 1902 to help protect British interests in China against Russia, it was about to expire in 1922. Although policy-makers in London were unhappy about Japanese encroachments into China during the war, most favoured continuing the alliance in some form to retain influence in Tokyo and to avoid the need for large naval forces in the China Seas. But many Americans were becoming concerned about what was called 'the Yellow Peril', including Japanese migration into the United States. The US navy viewed Japan as its main potential enemy in the Pacific and feared that, if war broke out between them, the Anglo-Japanese alliance could bring the Royal Navy in on the Japanese side. America and Britain had last been at war over a century earlier. Despite their bluster and their new-found power, American admirals like Benson had no desire to repeat the experience.

America had the wealth to outbuild Britain in a naval race. The US navy was determined to achieve parity with Britain and to destroy the Anglo-Japanese alliance. But Congress and the American public were not anxious for confrontation. In America as in Britain, there were growing demands for economy in 1921 as the post-war boom faded. And a powerful peace movement emerged, under the leadership of Senator William E. Borah of Idaho. Borah's bogeymen were the British and also the East Coast industrial and financial interests such as Morgan's, who, he believed, were starting the world on a new arms race. When Borah introduced a Senate resolution calling for an international conference to limit armaments, it passed through Congress with scant opposition. The new Republican Administration of President Warren G. Harding, originally sympathetic to the 'Big Navy' lobby, felt obliged to follow suit. It invited Britain, Japan, France and other sea powers to participate in a conference in Washington to limit armaments.

On 12 November 1921 the Washington conference formally opened. The delegates settled back in their seats, expecting the high-flown but hollow peace rhetoric characteristic of such grand occasions. Instead, the welcoming address from US Secretary of State Charles Evans Hughes included a 'bombshell' proposal for a ten-year 'holiday' in naval building, including the abandonment of America's ambitious expansion programmes. But in return Hughes wanted to establish a 5:5:3 ratio in capital ships between America, Britain and Japan. He went so far as to list the names of twenty-three ships that, he said, the Royal Navy must give up. The British delegation suddenly appreciated the gravity of what Hughes was saying. The reaction of an astounded Admiral Beatty, the First Sea Lord, was compared by one American journalist present to 'a bulldog, sleeping on a sunny doorstep, who had been poked in the stomach by the impudent foot of an itinerant soap canvasser'.[8]

Beatty and the Admiralty strenuously opposed the 'holiday' with its damaging effects on the Royal Navy's modernisation programmes. But Lloyd George overruled them. The British Government needed an agreement to stop a ruinous arms race. At Washington the British also agreed, in the face of American hostility, not to renew their alliance with Japan. It had not proved a successful conference for them. They had conceded equality at sea to the Americans, at least on paper, and they had terminated an important if shaky alliance, setting them on a path of growing confrontation with Japan. In 1921–2, however, none of this was considered disastrous. The ability of the great powers to prevent an arms race and resolve their differences peacefully seemed an encouraging improvement in international relations compared with the previous decade.

The Washington Treaty, signed in February 1922, covered only ships over 10,000 tons. It did not include cruisers, destroyers and submarines. In February 1927 President Calvin Coolidge, interested in controlling both armaments and defence budgets, invited the world's major sea powers to convene again, this time to discuss smaller ships. France and Italy, at loggerheads over the Mediterranean, refused, but Japan, Britain and the USA were again represented at the conference which opened in Geneva in June 1927. This time, however, Britain and America were openly at odds.

The US navy's General Board was still intent on acquiring a navy second to none. 'Equality with Great Britain is the sole basis on which a just treaty limitation can be imposed,' it stated categorically.[9] America's strategic planners were worried about the possibility of war against Japan, but Congress and the public were anxious to keep arms expenditure under control. Matching economy with strategy, the American delegation therefore demanded about thirty large cruisers, able to cruise at long range from base and with the heavy armament to deal with Japanese warships. The British, who were not particularly worried about Japan but were concerned about the protection of their global commerce, claimed the right to seventy cruisers, most of them smaller vessels suitable for protecting trade routes and patrolling Britain's sprawling empire. British and American interests differed fundamentally.

The chief American delegate described the talks at Geneva as not 'negotiations at all, but merely a form of hostilities'.[10] American shipbuilders lobbied intensively behind the scenes, helping create a hostile attitude towards arms control in the American press. The British delegation was increasingly overruled by anti-American sentiment in the Cabinet. Amid mutual recriminations the conference broke up in August. Such was the vehemence of American feeling that Prime Minister Stanley Baldwin cancelled plans for an official visit to the United States.

The Anglo-American dispute was only part of the complex web of arms control negotiations in the 1920s, involving armies as well as navies. Deadlocked with America, Britain turned to France, the principal land power and also a major force at sea, seeking a bilateral Anglo-French agreement that could then be enlarged to include America and other interested powers. During the summer of 1928 a compromise was reached which would leave the French free to build up their army and the British to construct the number of small cruisers they wanted. When garbled reports of this were leaked in the American press, there was an outcry against the way wily John Bull was apparently trying to fix up a deal behind Uncle Sam's back. One senior Congressman accused Britain of trying to 'retain domination of the high seas by subversive diplomacy', while the *Manchester Guardian*, a leading British newspaper, declared in November 1928 that 'not for many years have the Americans and the British been on terms as bad as they are now. There is ill-feeling, suspicion, misunderstanding and estrangement between the two nations.'[11] A frustrated Coolidge cited Britain as the main obstacle to arms control and threw his support behind a bill then going through Congress for fifteen new cruisers. It seemed like the start of a new arms race.

The detailed haggling about the size and number of cruisers was part of a larger problem. Britain remained adamant that in any future war she must be able to command the seas and blockade her enemies. Equally the United States insisted on its right as a potential neutral to unimpeded trade and travel. This was the old issue of the 'freedom of the seas' which had embittered relations in 1914–18. What gave the argument a new twist, the British Foreign Office believed, was the growth of the American navy, now approaching equality with Britain. In future it might well be able to force the British to accept the freedom of the seas. In the words of Robert Vansittart, head of the Foreign Office's American Department, 'America has in fact served notice on us that she will never again accept restrictions as existed between 1914 and 1917'.[12]

The Foreign Office believed that Britain must back down. She should promise that in a future war she would modify her strategy and no longer enforce the blockade with her traditional ferocity. America, it was argued, would then be less intransigent about the size of its navy. But after considerable debate in 1927–8 the Admiralty and the Cabinet refused to shift their position. They saw the blockade as a vital national interest and were prepared to call America's bluff, convinced that it would not retaliate. There was growing feeling that since 1919 Britain had appeased America too often for too little in return. Sir Maurice Hankey, the influential Secretary to the Cabinet, complained in October 1928: 'We played up to America over the Covenant of the League, abandonment of the Japanese Alliance, Washington Treaties, debt settlement, Irish settlement . . . always making concessions and always being told that the next step would change their attitude. Yet they are, as the result, more overbearing and suspicious against us than anyone else.'[13]

It took a change of government in both countries to break the deadlock. In March 1929 Herbert Hoover was sworn in as President, while Labour's Ramsay MacDonald became Prime Minister after elections in June. Unlike their predecessors, Coolidge and Baldwin, the new leaders took a keen, assertive interest in foreign affairs. In particular, they believed that disarmament was far too important to be left to the admirals. Geneva had shown the folly of that. Weeks of painstaking diplomacy that summer prepared the way for an eventual conference.

To improve relations MacDonald himself paid a very successful visit to the United States in October 1929. It was the first time that a British Prime Minister had visited the United States while in office – further evidence of America's new importance in world affairs. Highlights of MacDonald's trip included a ticker-tape parade through New York, several days of informal talks with Hoover and a moving address to the US Senate. The visit also helped improve Britain's image in the United States, for MacDonald did not fit the American stereotype of a British leader as aristocratic, languid and cunning. He was a Scot, a committed socialist and an outspoken opponent of the war in 1914, who convinced Americans of his sincere desire to end the arms race. The *New York Times* called the visit 'an overpowering success . . . On divers strings he has sounded the one clear note of a passion to secure established peace on earth through every reasonable and honorable means.'[14]

In January 1930 another naval conference opened in London. This time the ground had been properly prepared. Agreement was reached to extend what was sometimes called the 'Rolls-Royce: Rolls-Royce: Ford' formula. The ratio of 5:5:3 agreed at Washington in 1922 for American, British and Japanese capital ships would now apply to cruisers as well. The agreement was flexible enough to allow America to build more big cruisers and Britain more smaller cruisers. The US navy had been forced by Hoover to reduce the total number of cruisers it was allowed, but the biggest concession was made by the British. Under intense pressure from MacDonald the Admiralty accepted a ceiling of fifty cruisers instead of the seventy it had demanded in 1927. The Labour Government thus averted an Anglo-American arms race, but by making concessions to America of a kind deplored by many Tories. The US navy was still smaller than Britain's, but the British now acknowledged America's right, in theory at least, to a navy as large as their own.

But the London agreement of 1930 did not lead to real co-operation. Japan, the third member of the naval triumvirate, chafed at the restrictions imposed on her by the Big Two. She was anxious to become a great power in her own right. The easiest pickings lay in nearby China, a ruined empire fragmented by civil war, its economy dominated by foreign powers. In the winter of 1931–2 the Japanese army overran the Chinese province of Manchuria, in which it already had a foothold, and set up a puppet state. Manchuria's people and natural resources would strengthen the Japanese economy, and its vast spaces were attractive for colonisation by Japan's expanding population.

At the height of the war, early in 1932, fighting spread to the great Chinese port of Shanghai. Under a treaty signed in Washington ten years earlier the United States and Great Britain were the guarantors of China's integrity, but when the crisis came neither government was willing to become involved. America had too little at stake to risk war, and Britain far too much. She was not only the largest foreign investor in China but also kept close diplomatic and commercial links with Japan. Both Hoover and MacDonald therefore refused to countenance sanctions against the Japanese.

But Hoover's Secretary of State, Henry Stimson, wanted to make a moral protest. He enunciated the 'Stimson Doctrine', withholding diplomatic recognition of Japan's conquests. In February 1932 he also pressed Britain's Foreign Secretary, Sir John Simon, for a joint condemnation of Japan under the 1922 treaty. But Simon was evasive. He was trying to negotiate Japan's peaceful withdrawal from Shanghai and saw little point in provoking her gratuitously. He also believed, from past experience, that no real assistance would be forthcoming from the Americans, even if they talked big. Recalling Wilson's notorious speech of 1915 he noted, 'I am afraid America is "too proud to" do anything.' Stimson was piqued. Convinced that he had been betrayed by what he called the 'soft and pudgy' members of the British Cabinet, he became increasingly bitter about the whole affair.[15]

British policy was not wholly inert. Simon later pushed the non-recognition doctrine through the League of Nations, but Stimson developed his own account of the Manchurian crisis in writings during the 1930s and, despite British efforts, it became the orthodox version. The whole episode was so overblown that in 1939, for example, the eminent midwestern newspaperman, William Allen White, went so far as to claim that 'Munich became inevitable when England refused to join Stimson in the protest against the Japanese invasion of continental Asia'.[16] Stimson was an anglophile and White an ardent anti-Nazi. For Britain's natural sympathisers to be so suspicious of her is an indication of the tenuousness of Big Two co-operation.

By the early 1930s, therefore, after British concessions, America and Britain had reached an official agreement on sea power, but it did not herald any real co-operation between the two governments.

In finance, also, America's influence was increasingly apparent, and again the relations between the Big Two became severely strained.

In 1913 Britain had been the commercial and financial centre of the world. The City of London managed international money, and sterling was used as the main trading currency. The exchange rate of sterling, like other currencies, did not float but was set at a fixed price in terms of gold. This system, known as the 'gold standard', was meant to provide economic stability automatically because countries that allowed high inflation would price themselves out of foreign markets, run up a balance-of-payments deficit, and then be forced back into line through a drain on their gold reserves. In fact, the system depended for its successful operation largely on the economic leadership of Britain.

The war had destroyed the old order. The volume of world trade in 1920 was only about half that of 1913. Britain, after spending millions of pounds defending her exchange rate, was forced to abandon the gold standard in 1919, with most other countries except the United States. To pay for the war the Allies and their enemies had run up huge domestic and foreign debts. Eighty per cent of the war costs had been paid for by borrowing. The debts owed by the Allies to each other amounted to some $26.5 billion. In addition, under the Treaty of Versailles, the Allies were entitled to demand reparations from Germany. These were eventually adjudicated at $33 billion. The consequence of this huge increase in national and international debt was disastrous hyperinflation, above all in Germany.

Most bankers and politicians believed that a return to the gold standard was essential, but the debts and inflation were major obstacles in the way. In addition, Britain was no longer strong enough to take the lead alone. To help finance the war effort she had sold off most of her once vast American assets, and from 1916 the United States had become the Allies' main banker. The effect on the USA's international position was dramatic. In 1913 it had been a net debtor to the tune of $3.7 billion. By 1919 it was a net creditor of $3.7 billion. In the process New York had become a major world money market, with houses like J. P. Morgan's and the National City Bank developing expertise and influence as they mobilised American funds for investment overseas. Recreating the gold-standard economy could not therefore depend on the City of London alone. It required the combined resources and skills of the British and American financial communities.

At the centre of the story was Montagu Norman, Governor of the Bank of England from 1920 to 1944. Norman was a fastidious, secretive man, who cultivated an aura of mystery and power, going to abnormal lengths to avoid publicity. To one French banker he looked like someone 'out of a Van Dyck canvas: the long face, the pointed beard, the big hat . . .'[17] Norman's overriding goal was to maintain London as a major money market, which, he believed, could only be achieved through restoring Britain to gold. He realised this could not be done by Britain acting alone. He knew and liked America, having spent three years there as a young banker in the 1890s, and he developed a close relationship with his American counterpart, Benjamin Strong, the Governor of the Federal Reserve Bank of New York. Strong was an anglophile who shared Norman's dedication to getting the world back on gold. But America's financial system, like its central government, was weaker than that of Britain. Strong's powers were much less extensive than Norman's. So Norman worked with Strong but also relied on his ties with the Wall Street banks, of which Morgan's was the most co-operative and important.

The war debts were the chief obstacle to financial reconstruction. America had loaned $11.9 billion to the various Allied countries, of which $4.7 billion was owed by Britain alone. But the British had also lent a similar amount to their allies, some $11.1 billion. The British Government proposed that *all* war debts should simply be cancelled. To the Americans they argued that the proper equation was not dollars against dollars, but dollars against lives. British war deaths had been 750,000, America's 130,000. Some American policy-makers were sympathetic, but Congress and the American public took a different view. The money had been lent, not given, and if repayment were not made the whole burden would fall on the American taxpayer. The United States Government, it was pointed out, had spent more during the war years than in the whole of its previous history since 1789. A third of this had been loaned to the Allies and they had a duty to repay it. America's insistence was not popular in Britain. Uncle Sam gained the nickname 'Uncle Shylock'. It 'made the average Englishman think that the Americans are dirty swine', complained a senior Foreign Office man.[18]

Wilson's belief that Britain's financial dependence on America would give him *carte blanche* to determine the future of Europe had proved an illusion at the Paris peace conference, but the United States was still in a powerful position. Sir Auckland Geddes, the Ambassador in Washington, argued in 1921 that, if the American Congress was adamant about repayment of the loans, Britain must comply or risk being treated 'as a vassal State as long as the debt remains unpaid'.[19] Montagu Norman also believed that foreign confidence in London as a financial centre would collapse if Britain tried to avoid her obligations. In January 1923 he and Stanley Baldwin, the Conservative Chancellor of the Exchequer, spent ten days of tough negotiation in Washington. They eventually secured a package whereby Britain would repay in instalments, ten years at $161 million, then fifty years at $187 million. On that schedule Britain would be reimbursing America for its help during World War One until 1984.

The agreement was unpopular in Britain, but it did relieve transatlantic tension and restored Britain's international credit. An Englishman's word, it seemed, was still his bond. It also opened the way to deal with the vexed problem of German reparations to the Allies. Germany, in the throes of hyperinflation, had stopped its payments to France. In January 1923 French troops entered the Ruhr, as they were entitled under the Treaty of Versailles if Germany defaulted. Some French leaders saw the occupation as a way of gaining permanent control over the vital Rhineland: taking by force what the 'Anglo-Saxons' had denied them at the peace conference. The German Government responded by subsidising a campaign of passive resistance, which exacerbated its already spiralling inflation. By the time the campaign ended, with the German economy in ruins, France had gained only a hollow victory. For Germany was now in no position to repay anything. Without British and American help there would be no reparations and no recovery.

France having tried and failed to enforce the Treaty of Versailles, Britain and America combined to impose a new settlement on their terms. In April 1924 two committees of experts, chaired by the American and British bankers Charles Dawes and Reginald McKenna, recommended a reduction of Germany's reparations burden and a $200-million loan to support the German central bank. The City of London floated only a quarter of the loan, and half of it came from New York, a further indication of how financial power was shifting across the Atlantic.

The Dawes Plan boosted international confidence and encouraged the return of gold and foreign investment into Europe. The sterling-dollar exchange rate began to drift up towards the pre-war parity of $4.86 to the pound and Strong and Norman assisted the process in 1924–5 by informal co-operation in monetary policy: Strong relaxing US interest rates while Norman kept British rates high. By now most of Britain's trading partners were ready to return to the gold standard regardless of Britain. The new British Chancellor of the Exchequer, Winston Churchill, announced on 28 April 1925 that Britain would also return to gold. 'If we had not taken this action,' he confessed later, 'the whole of the rest of the British Empire would have taken it without us, and it would have come to a gold standard, not on the basis of the pound sterling, but of the dollar.'[20]

For a time in the mid-1920s the international economy seemed to be back on an even keel, with the leading roles now shared by Great Britain and the United States. But appearances were deceptive. By 1931, in the worldwide depression, America's economy collapsed and Britain was once again forced off the gold standard – a crisis which highlighted the widening gulf between the two great powers.

In the 1920s United States trade with the rest of the world had surged. America had become the world's largest exporter and, second only to Britain, its largest importer as well. Britain still had larger total foreign investments, but America had now become the world's principal source of *new* investment, lending $6.4 billion abroad between 1924 and 1929. This was nearly double Britain's contribution. Roughly half America's new investment was in Europe, particularly Germany, where it helped pay for reparations and for the funding of the Weimar Republic's welfare state. But most of it was lent short-term by private investors looking for new outlets for their surplus capital. The collapse of Wall Street from October 1929 and the deepening recession in America meant that many of the loans were withdrawn by investors who were being called upon to meet their obligations in the United States. The money had lubricated Europe's economy. Without it the system began to seize up.

In May 1931 the Credit Anstalt, Austria's leading bank, collapsed. By June the crisis had spread to Germany, and, in an attempt to stem the run on the Reichsmark, President Hoover called for a one-year moratorium on all debts and reparations payments. His action failed to stabilise the situation and in early July the German Government imposed exchange controls. That shifted the crisis to Britain, whose foreign lending was three or four times the size of her gold reserves. Investors, in huge numbers, sold sterling and the Bank of England was forced to spend large sums to support the $4.86 exchange rate for the pound. As in 1915 it turned to J. P. Morgan for help, but this time the situation, and the answer, were very different. The crisis that followed marked the end of Britain's post-war pretensions to match America's economic strength.

The Labour Government had done its best to counter the effects of the Slump in Britain. It had kept interest rates low and welfare payments high, but the result was a mounting budget deficit of over £100 million. An official committee, headed by Sir George May, recommended that the budget must be balanced, mainly by a twenty per cent cut in unemployment insurance. Montagu Norman and the City agreed, convinced that only this would revive foreign confidence. When asked about the chances of raising loans from American investors, Morgan said 'that before they could safely borrow in the USA, the Government would have to show at least some plan of restoration of financial stability and should at least have expressed the intention to reduce the expenditures to come within their means'.[21]

The Labour Cabinet wrestled with its dilemma during July and August as the sterling crisis worsened. Which was more important – Britain's position as a financial power or the well-being of its citizens? Norman believed that the latter depended on the former, but many of MacDonald's Cabinet were not so sure. By Friday 21 August the Treasury warned that without help from New York and Paris Britain's reserves would last only four more days. Over the weekend Cabinet members debated a compromise austerity package, including only a ten per cent cut in unemployment insurance, while awaiting a reply from New York. Eventually they were reduced to walking around the garden of Number Ten for over an hour on the Sunday evening until the message arrived. Morgan's put the ball back in the British court. 'Are we right in assuming that the programme under consideration will have the sincere approval and support of the Bank of England and the City generally and thus go a long way towards restoring internal confidence in Great Britain?' They also warned that 'of course our ability to do anything depends on the response of public opinion particularly in Great Britain to the Government's announcement of the programme' and on the willingness of the French to help as well.[22]

An anguished MacDonald admitted to his colleagues 'that the proposals as a whole represented the negation of everything that the Labour party stood for, and yet he was absolutely satisfied that it was necessary in the national interests to implement them if the country was to be secured'.[23] But nearly half his Cabinet disagreed and the Labour Government resigned on 24 August. MacDonald was persuaded by the King to form a National Government including Tories and Liberals. The new Cabinet adopted the cuts, and loans to support sterling were raised in America and France. But these failed to check the outflow of funds. Further requests were made to New York, but Morgan's had found the first loan hard enough to place at a time when America was sliding into Depression and, despite a direct appeal to the White House, a US government loan was out of the question. On 21 September 1931 the National Government gave up the struggle and Great Britain renounced the gold standard.

It was easy to blame the Americans for what had happened and many in the Labour movement did so. The day after the Labour Government resigned the *Daily Herald* denounced the 'virtual ultimatum from New York bankers' and claimed that they had been allowed 'to dictate, as the condition for a further credit to the Bank of England, the policy to be pursued in relation to unemployment benefit'.[24] But in reality Morgan and his colleagues were only echoing the judgement of the City and of financiers in Paris. Ultimately blame lay with British leaders of all parties for failing to come to terms with the harsh realities of the post-war world.

In the early 1920s the government and the City had been determined to rebuild London as a financial centre and they had returned to the gold standard at the pre-war rate. This decision was supported by all three political parties and nearly all economists. Yet it was an act of faith, even nostalgia, taken on the basis of only the most rudimentary economic analysis. As a result sterling was overvalued, probably by ten per cent, helping make British exports uncompetitive in world markets compared with those of America and of France, who undervalued the franc. By the late 1920s both these countries had much larger gold reserves than Britain and yet much smaller foreign obligations. The British were still trying to run the world financial system but without the resources they had before 1914. September 1931 made this clear. Douglas Dillon, a future US Treasury Secretary, started his career as a Wall Street banker the week Britain went off gold. He recalled later: 'we'd looked to the pound for years – everything I'd been brought up with – so when I started it was with the realization that we were coming into a new era and a new world . . . England was no longer commanding the world financial markets. They were just another player in the game.'[25]

But if Britain was unable to play her part in ensuring economic stability, America, the one country that could have helped limit the effects of the worldwide depression, also failed to act. Most Americans had not yet grasped their new dominant position and the responsibilities that came with it. The American investment in Europe was private capital, not government loans. The Hoover Administration could do nothing in 1930–1 as American investors withdrew funds from Europe just when the money was most needed to shore up the financial system. In other ways, too, America acted at odds with its new international role. Congress insisted on repayment of war debts, despite the burden this placed on Europe's already grave balance of payments, and the Administration encouraged the growth of protectionism. In 1930 American tariff rates on imports were raised to new

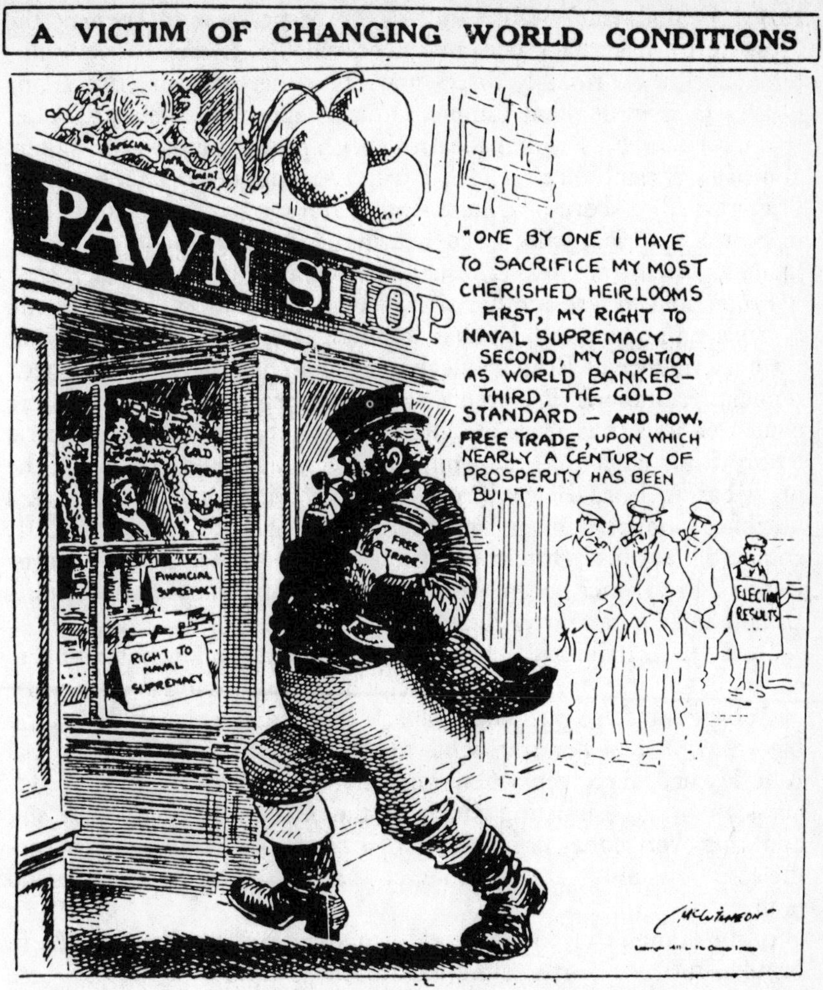

John T. McCutcheon, veteran cartoonist of the anglophobe *Chicago Tribune*, depicts John Bull giving up his world power (29 October 1931).

heights, shutting out foreign goods and raw materials from the vast American market and thereby intensifying the world depression.

America's new protectionism helped push Britain into a major shift in her own policy. Since the middle of the nineteenth century she had been a free-trade nation, encouraging world trade by minimising her tariffs against foreign imports. As the dominant economy of the Victorian era she could afford to do that. By the 1930s, however, she was increasingly challenged by industrial competitors who had grown strong behind tariff walls, and, as the depression deepened, the pressure to strike back became uncontrollable. In 1932 Britain imposed tariffs on roughly three-quarters of her imports. But at the Ottawa Conference that summer she also agreed to keep tariff rates lower for countries within the British Empire. This was the system known as 'Imperial Preference'. These advantages were later extended to more than a score of Britain's other trading partners, particularly in South America, who relied heavily on sterling and the City for financing their trade. An informal 'sterling area' began to emerge.

Protectionism was another sign of British weakness. Like the end of naval supremacy and the abandonment of the gold standard, it was further evidence of Britain's decline from a position of unchallenged dominance. Imperial Preference and the embryonic sterling area were conceived in part as a way of fighting off the challenge from America, by providing a secure base from which Britain could compete. The press baron, Lord Beaverbrook, owner of the *Daily Express*, was a notable exponent of this policy. And the United States was particularly vulnerable because Britain was the largest customer for its exports. Imperial Preference became one of the most rancorous issues dividing Britain and America over the next two decades.

By 1932 Britain had left the gold standard and was starting to consolidate her own economic bloc. The world economic system she had shaped and led was falling apart. In 1933 she also defaulted on the repayment of her war debts to the United States, arguing that America had made repayment virtually impossible at a time of depression by accumulating much of the world's gold reserves and imposing ever-higher tariffs against British goods. Americans, nevertheless, were bitter at what they considered Britain's lack of good faith.

In the summer of 1933 a world economic conference was held in London to try to sort out the mess. The prospects of success were never good: every country was now putting its short-term national interest first and adopting stringent protectionist measures. But the new American President, Franklin Roosevelt, brought discussions to an end by suddenly announcing in July 1933 that the United States would not support any permanent stabilisation of world currencies until the American economy was back on its feet. His 'bombshell' message strengthened British frustrations about the USA. Neville Chamberlain, Chancellor of the Exchequer, grumbled: 'I should think there has never been a case of a conference so completely smashed by one of the participants.'[26]

The rivalry of the Big Two and the conflict of their economic aims meant that the world had no effective leadership during its most acute economic crisis of the century. Britain was now too weak to stabilise the world economy unaided. Yet the United States was not ready to accept new responsibilities. Under a political system of 'checks and balances' the Administration lacked the power to override a nationalist Congress. Furthermore, American trade and foreign investment, though vital to the outside world, was of relatively little importance to the American economy itself, whose health still depended on the huge domestic market. America did not share Britain's self-interest in world prosperity. The economic historian, Charles Kindleberger, sums up the crisis of leadership starkly:

> The world economic system was unstable unless some country stabilized it, as Britain had done in the nineteenth century and up to 1913. In 1929, the British couldn't and the United States wouldn't. When every country turned to protect its national interest the world public interest went down the drain, and with it the private interests of all.[27]

By the early 1930s relations between America and Britain were marked by bitterness and recrimination. They had fought on the same side in one war and they were soon to fight in another, but in the years between, without a clear common enemy and in the throes of world depression, their own rivalry became intense. In the process long-standing suspicions of each other's society came to the surface.

At the end of the war British leaders had entertained extravagant hopes of a close relationship. Lloyd George asserted confidently in 1921: 'the people who govern America are our people. They are our kith and kin. The other breeds are not on top.'[28] By the time of the naval row in 1927 the Foreign Office had modified this Anglo-Saxonist theory, warning that 'we have treated them too much as blood relations, not sufficiently as a foreign country'.[29] And after the ravages of depression most British leaders were almost totally alienated. One crisis after another, from the League fiasco in 1919 to the London Economic Conference in 1933, had shown, they believed, that no faith could be placed in the United States, particularly when its Presidents had so little control over Congress.

In 1932 Baldwin summed up British conventional wisdom: 'You will get nothing from Americans but words, big words but only words.' In October 1933 this usually mild-mannered politician refused to dine with one of President Roosevelt's sons, because he 'says he has got to loathe the Americans so much that he hates meeting them'.[30]

Sir Robert Vansittart, now the top official at the Foreign Office and himself married to an American, had been preaching the appeasement of America in the naval crisis of 1927, but by 1934 he believed that 'we have been too tender, not to say subservient, with the US for a long time past. It is we who have made all the advances, and received nothing in return. It is still necessary, and I desire as much as ever, that we should get on well with this untrustworthy race. But,' he added, 'we shall never get very far; they will always let us down.'[31] This was the view of most British leaders in the 1930s.

Feelings were mutual. Across the Atlantic Americans were alienated not merely from Britain but from Europe as a whole. It was customary to blame the Depression on the failure of Britain and others to repay their war debts. There was a growing conviction that American involvement in the war had been a great mistake. By 1934 many argued that they had been sucked into war in 1917 by the so-called 'merchants of death', the big businessmen and financiers like J. P. Morgan. A Senate Committee chaired by the Republican Gerald P. Nye examined their activities in a long-running inquiry from September 1934 to February 1936. Morgan and his partners were interrogated at length amidst intense publicity about the firm's wartime activities as Britain's banker and arms buyer.

Nye's committee came up with little hard evidence to justify claims that Wall Street and the munitions manufacturers had dragged America into war, but their highly publicised hearings left a general impression that there was no smoke without fire. The influential American radio commentator, Raymond Gram Swing, claimed in May 1935 that 'it is almost a truism that the United States went into the World War in part to save from ruin the bankers who had strained themselves to the utmost to supply Great Britain and France with munitions and credits'.[32]

These ideas gained hold in 1935, just as Europe seemed on the brink of renewed war with the invasion of the African kingdom of Ethiopia by the Italian dictator, Benito Mussolini. In August Congress hastily passed a Neutrality Act which banned the export of arms to any belligerent country in time of war. It also gave the President powers to warn Americans against travelling on belligerent passenger vessels. In 1936 Congress added a ban on loans to belligerents. These were the kind of measures Secretary of State William Jennings Bryan had sought, in vain, in 1915. Next time, Congress was saying, there must be no *Lusitania*, no Morgan loans, to involve America emotionally and economically in Europe's war.

The Neutrality Acts symbolised a sharp reversal of US policies towards Europe. In the 1920s, although America had rejected political entanglements like the League, it had used its new economic strength to control the naval race and to help reconstruct Europe. But in the 1930s, disillusioned by the Depression and the dictators, America tried to insulate itself from any future conflict. The Neutrality Acts signalled that the United States would not exert its naval and economic power to save Europe from its follies, for fear of being dragged in itself. This was a far cry from Woodrow Wilson in 1918. Novelist Ernest Hemingway captured the prevailing mood in 1935: 'Of the hell broth that is brewing in Europe we have no need to drink. Europe has always fought: the intervals of peace are only armistices. We were fools to be sucked in once in a European war, and we shall never be sucked in again.'[33]

6

Americanisation

Business and society between the world wars

America in the 1920s seized the imagination of a new generation in Britain. For a decade, until the Depression of the 1930s, everything American seemed alluring, offering the prospect of escape from life in Britain which was drab by comparison. America was modern. America was rich. America was The Future.

The message was received in different ways. For some it was the new products that came on the market to end domestic drudgery: the vacuum cleaner, the refrigerator, the electric toaster. For others it was the style of America which excited, the patent-leather shoes worth queueing for in Oxford Street, the make-up advertised as 'Used by the Stars of Hollywood', and of course the new music of the Jazz Age. But for most people the Cinema was the Great Enchanter. Before television the main family outing for millions of people was the weekly visit to the movies. As the lights dimmed and the pictures flickered on to the screen, the humdrum was swept away. A new, bright, carefree world beckoned. It was, quite simply, what everyone longed for.

The impact of America was deplored by many of those who felt responsibility for the health of British society – teachers and politicians in particular. 'All America is Niagara,' moaned one Cambridge don. 'Force without direction, noise without significance, speed without accomplishment.'[1] But there was little critics could do to counter the effect. British people found the vigour, the originality and the verve of America appealing. These were not qualities acquired by chance. They sprang naturally from the innate strength and resources of the United States which had been demonstrated during World War One and were now free to exert themselves.

The United States came out of the war into a boom, quickly followed by a brief slump in 1920–1. But recovery was fast. From 1922 until the end of the decade unemployment was usually below five per cent and manufacturing output increased by nearly a third. It was a period of astonishing prosperity. America expanded into overseas markets, many of which Britain considered her own. The USA's share of world exports rose to sixteen per cent by 1929, as Britain's fell to twelve per cent. The British were no longer the world's largest exporters. All this was achieved by a country which only sold abroad a twentieth of what it produced, unlike Britain who, with her smaller population, needed to export a quarter of her national production to survive. For America, foreign trade was the icing on the cake; for Britain, a matter of economic survival.

When Britain's brief post-war boom burst in 1921 her economy went into a recession from which it was slow to recover. Throughout the twenties unemployment averaged ten to twelve per cent and demand was depressed. The root problem lay in the structure of British industry. She still relied on the old staple businesses – mining coal, making iron and steel, building ships, and weaving cloth. Where America was revolutionising business methods, mechanising her factories, and investing in research and development, much of Britain carried on as if nothing had changed. America developed new growth industries for the new world markets, based not on the use of coal and steam but on electricity and oil. The motor car and gadgets for the office and the home driven by electricity lent themselves to efficient production, with standardised parts, assembly lines, and aggressive marketing to produce enormous profits.

In much of the world during the 1920s the United States was able to erode Britain's dominance. In Japan and China, America replaced Britain as the main trading partner. In South America, where before the war the two had each sold a quarter of all the goods imported, America was better able to meet the new demand for cars, trucks, machinery and electrical goods and, by the end of the decade, its share of the region's imports had risen to thirty-eight per cent while Britain's fell to sixteen per cent. By the end of the twenties America had also surpassed Britain as the leading foreign investor in Canada and Latin America.

This natural rivalry was exacerbated by the American belief that Britain used unfair methods to protect her position. The British Empire, at the start of the 1920s, covered a quarter of the globe, and these possessions, whose subject status many Americans thought morally wrong, allowed Britain access to much of the world's supplies of raw materials such as rubber, tin and oil. Although her indigenous wealth was limited, she was able to control a far larger proportion of essential materials than America and after the economic losses of the war, which had cost fifteen per cent of her overseas wealth, she was determined to exploit her advantage to the full. British policy aroused intense hostility in the United States. In 1926 the US Ambassador in London warned Washington: 'Just as England built up a new prosperity after the Napoleonic Wars by using iron and coal, so, I think, she is planning to rebuild her fortunes and to obtain world leadership again by making use of her raw materials to be found in her tropical and sub-tropical possessions.'[2] American businessmen called for an 'Open-Door' policy of equal access to the world's markets and raw materials, battling to break down Britain's monopoly. In 1929 Prime Minister Stanley Baldwin warned his successor: 'The American money power is trying to get control of some of the natural resources of the Empire. They are working like beavers.'[3]

The battle over rubber was particularly acrimonious since its price directly affected the cost of motor-car tyres and thus hit a growing number of Americans where it hurt most – in their pockets. Harvey Firestone was angrier than anyone. He had begun his business life working for his uncle's Columbus Buggy Company. He suggested that these horse-drawn carts would ride more comfortably over the rough country roads if they were fitted with rubber tyres, but the idea was rejected. Firestone left to set up on his own and soon established a successful tyre company. Then, in his son's words, he met 'a man called Henry Ford, and he was starting some kind of a new fangled vehicle that would run without horses'.[4] Ford and Firestone agreed that pneumatic tyres should be produced to give the motor car a smooth ride and Ford ordered 2,000 sets. Firestone, with a factory in Akron, Ohio, soon became one of America's biggest tyre manufacturers, meeting a demand which increased every year as car production rose from under two million vehicles a year in 1920 to nearly four and a half million by 1929. By then one American in five had a car, compared with one Briton in fifty.

The automobile boom meant that America had become the world's leading importer of rubber, consuming over two-thirds of total production. And Britain, with plantations in Malaya and Ceylon, controlled about three-quarters of world supplies. She seemed to have a stranglehold on America. But the price of rubber started to fall in the early twenties. Too much was being produced and the costs, British rubber planters claimed, were no longer covered by the market price. The British Government set up an inquiry which resulted in the adoption in 1922 of the Stevenson Plan to reduce production to sixty per cent of its 1920 level. The enquiry found that while rubber cost twenty-two cents a pound to produce, it had sold in New York during 1921 for an average of 16.3 cents, and at times as low as twelve cents. Only by cutting output could the producers survive. But the effect of the cut was devastating for the United States. By 1925 the price of a pound of rubber, which had been intended to rise to about thirty cents, had soared to $1.21.

The American Secretary of Commerce for most of the 1920s was Herbert Hoover, the future Republican President. In 1925, encouraged by Firestone, he mounted a vigorous campaign against the Stevenson Plan, denouncing the price-fixing as a violation of Open-Door principles. In the war of words the British soon hit back, pointing out that America was prone to do exactly the same thing with cotton, manipulating output to keep prices up. One British diplomat pointed out: 'anything that increases the price of American cotton crop reacts at once upon the prosperity of our Lancashire textile districts'.[5]

The British also liked to remind Americans that, although they might talk about the Open Door with its equal opportunity in foreign markets, the USA had the highest tariffs in the world. A third of American imports were liable for duty and on these the average rate was forty per cent. Certain staple British exports such as steel, china and textiles, it was pointed out, were simply unsellable in the United States. Hoover would not listen. While denouncing the tariff barriers of other nations, he insisted on keeping American tariff barriers high, failing to see that eventually American trade would suffer because others would not be able to sell their goods and thus afford to buy from the United States. 'There is no practical force in the contention that we cannot have a protective tariff and a growing foreign trade. We have both today,' he asserted flatly in 1928, just before the boom collapsed.[6]

In the battle over rubber, conducted in the atmosphere of chauvinism and self-righteousness that pervades all trade wars, Hoover appealed to the gut American emotion of anglophobia. He promoted a rubber conservation campaign with the emotive slogan '1776–1925'. He toured the country agitating against Britain and encouraging the development of synthetic substitutes. In the end, however, market forces proved even more effective. American rubber manufacturers gradually shifted to Dutch suppliers in the East Indies, who had not joined the Stevenson scheme, and Britain's price and sales declined. By 1928 British planters controlled only about half the world's rubber supply and the Stevenson Plan was abandoned, much to the relief of the British Ambassador in Washington, 'since it removes a source of misunderstanding and continual bickering between the United States and ourselves'.[7] But in the process America had begun to adopt policies which it reviled when they were used by Britain, policies which in one case came uncomfortably close to setting up America's own colonial empire.

Harvey Firestone was the empire builder. Encouraged by Hoover he sent his experts round the world looking for suitable sites for rubber planting to break the British monopoly. He found an ideal spot in West Africa, in the state of Liberia, which had been founded in the mid-nineteenth century as a homeland for black slaves emancipated from the United States. Another American had also been interested in that land: Marcus Garvey, the militant black leader, who saw Liberia as an ideal base for his 'Back to Africa' movement. In the early 1920s the Liberian Government had encouraged his plans for settlement by American blacks. But they withdrew the offer in 1924 on learning of Garvey's secret intention to overthrow them because, as one Garvey adviser put it, the Americo-Liberian ruling élite was 'using the natives as slaves' and was 'the most despicable element in Liberia'.[8] It was land that Garvey had been planning to settle that Firestone's scouts chose as the ideal site for rubber planting.

Protracted negotiations followed. Liberia was in desperate need of new investment and of financial support for its shaky economy. Firestone offered both: a lease to develop one million acres as rubber plantations and a five-million-dollar loan to stabilise the country's finances. But the terms of the loan would leave Firestone virtually in control of Liberia's Treasury, under an American 'financial adviser' and his staff. The Liberian Government protested vehemently to the State Department at this challenge to its sovereignty. Officially the American Government claimed that it had nothing to do with economic negotiations by private American citizens, but, behind the scenes, informal pressure was applied. The Secretary of State warned his Liberian counterpart that 'obviously . . . it would be impossible to raise any loan in the United States on security which could be offered by Liberia unless there is to be the extensive development contemplated in the Firestone contracts . . . It is also clear that American bankers would insist on some supervision of the finances."[9]

The battle dragged on for much of 1925 and 1926. To satisfy the Liberian desire for independence, Firestone allowed them to borrow the $5 million from 'The Finance Corporation of America'. But, as one American commentator of the time pointed out, 'while the

Liberians may have believed that this is an independent organization, it is apparently an institution which Mr Firestone established and financed for the purpose of making this loan'.[10] The Liberians also tried to reduce the number and powers of American 'advisers' and to keep control of their fiscal policy. But eventually, with Harvey Firestone threatening to call the whole deal off, they signed an agreement largely on his terms.

Such tactics were hardly a novelty in the history of international business. The British Government had connived in this kind of commercial blackmail on numerous occasions in the past in Africa, South America and the Middle East. But America had always professed to be better than the Old World imperialists. As one of Marcus Garvey's followers ruefully comments: 'America did not and does not want the physical expansion of an Empire, as England, but they would close their eyes to industrial, commercial empires . . . wherever the American money is, there goes the flag.'[11] Or, as one American commentator on the trade war put it: 'We shall not make Britain's mistake. Too wise to govern the world, we shall merely own it.'[12]

In its search for bigger markets it was inevitable that American business would turn, as she had before the world war, to Britain. Here the flag could not follow, but the advantages of a common language, a stable government and a people who admired things American, even if their ruling class was dubious, made it a good risk. A new reason for investing in Britain was the need to get over British tariff barriers. It was not until the Ottawa Conference of 1932 that general tariffs were imposed in the surge of protectionism during the Depression, but vulnerable industries were already protected throughout the British Empire. Imported motor cars, for instance, attracted a thirty-three and a third per cent tax. Setting up in Britain meant not only that an American company could avoid the tariff barriers protecting the British market, but that it could take advantage of tariff-free exports to all the countries of the British Empire.

American car manufacturers found such a move essential. In 1920 Henry Ford's Model T took two-thirds of the British car market, but within a few years its lead had disappeared. To avoid the thirty-three and a third per cent duty Ford decided to set up a full-scale British operation. In 1928 he bought land at Dagenham, on the banks of the Thames east of London, and there built his largest plant outside the United States. Soon Dagenham was using the mass production methods pioneered in Detroit and producing cars for Britain, the British Empire and much of continental Europe. America's General Motors, likewise anxious to avoid the tariff, bought the Vauxhall car firm in 1927, and the big tyre companies, Goodrich, Goodyear and Firestone, also established British factories.

By 1929 there was nearly half a billion dollars of direct American investment in Britain. Only Canada, Cuba and Mexico had more. Many of the companies that arrived in Britain did so openly. Others, alarmed by the new wave of anti-Americanism that US investment was arousing, came surreptitiously. General Electric of America went to great lengths to disguise its ambition to buy up the whole British electrical manufacturing industry. GE already owned a subsidiary in Britain, British Thomson Houston, or BTH, which made everything from giant turbines to light bulbs. But GE's president, Gerard Swope, had his eyes on his main competitor in Britain, Metropolitan Vickers. In February 1928 he bought a controlling interest in Metrovick for £1.6 million. Once acquired, the shares were immediately transferred into the hands of a millionaire British industrialist, Dudley Docker, who had a reputation as a staunch defender of the principle that British industry should be in British hands. Officially he now owned Metropolitan Vickers. Swope gave Docker £50,000 in Metrovick shares, calling it 'a very inadequate compensation for all the assistance you have been'.[13] Privately Docker believed that co-operation with General Electric was now inevitable because everywhere 'the Americans were first in the field'.[14]

Despite Swope's subterfuge, rumours soon spread that the real purchaser of Metropolitan Vickers had been American, and, to end the speculation, an announcement was made. At the Annual General Meeting of Metropolitan Vickers on 29 March 1928 the chairman, Sir Philip Nash, stated 'Messrs Vickers Ltd sold the control of this Company to the International General Electric Company. It was at this stage that Mr F. Dudley Docker came into the transaction and the control now lies in his hands.'[15] Originally the statement was to say that Docker held 'voting control'. Since Swope owned eighty per cent of Metrovick voting shares, that would have been a bare-faced lie, and Docker insisted on the change. But even to say Docker had 'control' was to be economical with the truth. As the records of the company make clear, Swope was in full control. Docker was simply a convenient front.

Swope's ambitions did not stop with Metropolitan Vickers. He also acquired two other British electrical companies, but his real target was GE's British namesake and one remaining major European rival, British General Electric. He started to buy into this company and in September 1928 its chairman, Sir Hugo Hirst, took the extraordinary step of having all foreign shareholders disfranchised. But the Americans continued to buy, amassing sixty per cent of the stock by March 1929. Hirst then announced that new shares would be issued only to British citizens. Gerard Swope reacted with what the *New York Times* described as 'virtually an ultimatum in this financial war'.[16] If Hirst went ahead, he warned, American investors would boycott Britain. The point was not lost on the City of London and the British financial press who condemned Hirst's 'Bolshevistic' actions. He was forced to drop the proposed new British-only share issue, but the American shareholders remained disfranchised. Hirst made no apology for his '100 per cent British' campaign and drew public attention to the need to fight off the American invasion. Swope had to be satisfied with setting up the biggest electrical company in Britain comprising virtually everything but General Electric. In 1929 his four major companies were merged into Associated Electrical Industries (AEI).

American interests were also buying their way into the British electrical supply industry, at this time in the hands of a plethora of private generating companies. Two American entrepreneurs, Samuel Insull and Harley Clarke, began to acquire British power stations. By 1930 Clarke's Greater London and Counties Trust controlled fifty-four power companies from Oxfordshire to East Anglia. Its American ownership could not be kept secret. When it came out, Clarke appointed the distinguished British lawyer and politician Lord Birkenhead, a former Lord Chancellor, as chairman. Birkenhead announced, disingenuously, that 'the organisation with which I have decided to associate myself is British, although it is associated with the Clarke interests in the United States'.[17] The pretence that the Trust was simply making use of American capital while being under British control fooled no one, but no action was taken against it until 1936. By then its American ownership had become a liability. Profits from Britain were being siphoned back to America to support the ailing parent company. With government approval the Americans were bought out and the Trust became wholly British-owned.

It would be wrong to suggest that there was universal hostility to America's investment in Britain. When the British Cabinet discussed the electrical supply industry in May 1928, most ministers concluded that restrictions on foreign investment were 'undesirable and impossible'.[18] It was also clear that Britain had much to learn from American management, production methods and sales techniques. When Hoover, the vacuum-cleaner manufacturers,* set up in Britain

* Founded by the Ohio industrialist Herbert William Hoover, no relation of President Herbert Clark Hoover.

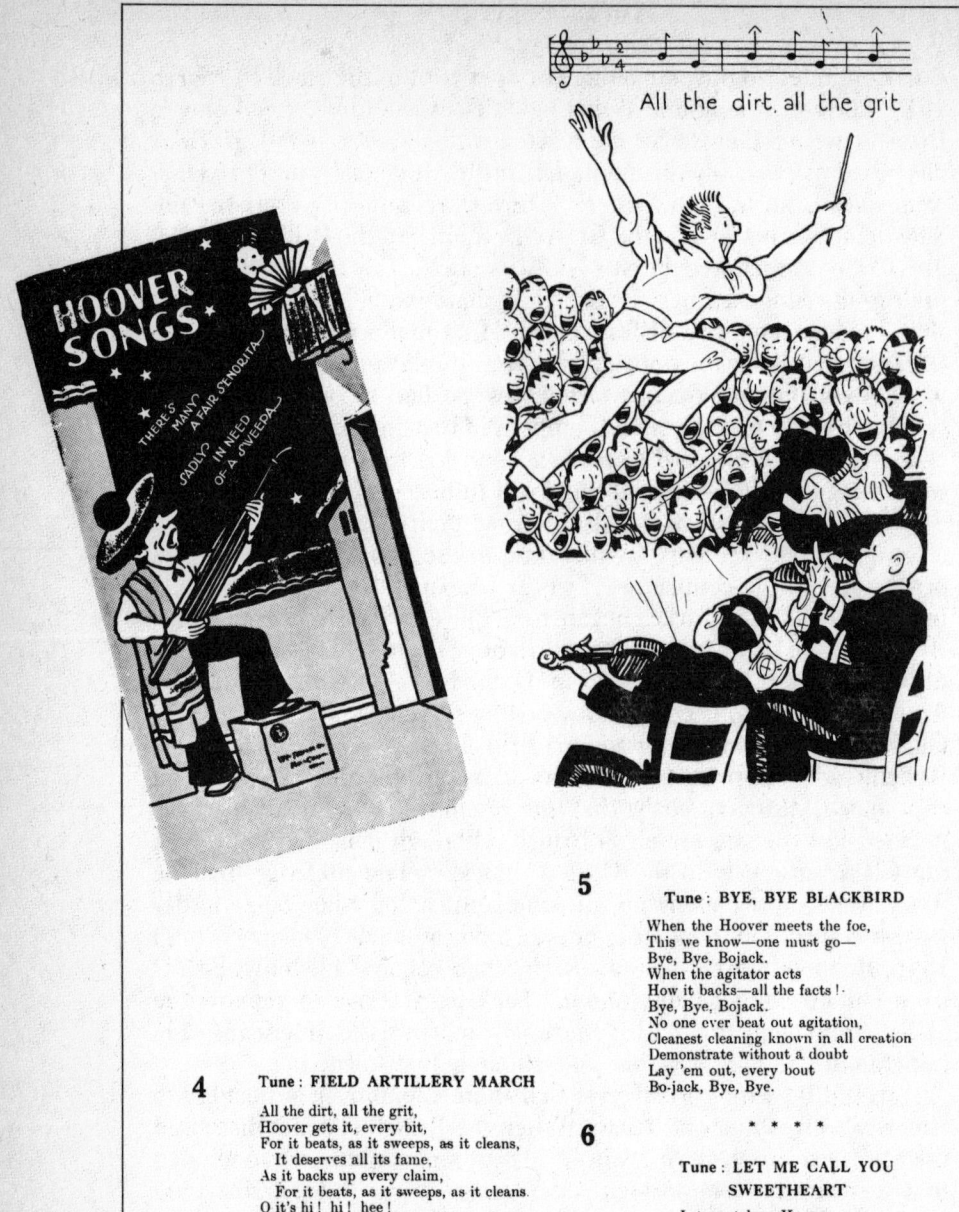

4 Tune: **FIELD ARTILLERY MARCH**

All the dirt, all the grit,
Hoover gets it, every bit,
For it beats, as it sweeps, as it cleans,
It deserves all its fame,
As it backs up every claim,
For it beats, as it sweeps, as it cleans.
O it's hi! hi! hee!
The kinds of dirt are three
We'll tell the world just what it means,
BING! BING! BING!
Spring or fall, the Hoover gets them all.
For it beats, as it sweeps, as it cleans.

* * * *

5 Tune: **BYE, BYE BLACKBIRD**

When the Hoover meets the foe,
This we know—one must go—
Bye, Bye, Bojack.
When the agitator acts
How it backs—all the facts!
Bye, Bye, Bojack.
No one ever beat out agitation,
Cleanest cleaning known in all creation
Demonstrate without a doubt
Lay 'em out, every bout
Bo-jack, Bye, Bye.

* * * *

6 Tune: **LET ME CALL YOU SWEETHEART**

Let me take a Hoover,
To your home at two.
Let me do some cleaning,—
Make your rugs like new.
All the dirt surrenders,
And the germs go too.
Not another cleaner
Does what it can do.

From a Hoover songbook of the early 1930s.

they sent some British sales managers to America to learn the extraordinary Hoover selling methods. Salesmen were taught to sing the Hoover songs, including the Hoover 'Field Artillery March': 'All the dirt, all the grit, Hoover gets it, every bit, For it beats, as it sweeps, as it cleans.' Salesmen were sent to conferences at British seaside holiday camps, dressed in a uniform of blazers and flannels with different coloured ties to represent the region of the country they came from. At the end of the course they were marched past a saluting stand and gave an 'eyes right' to the senior executives on the podium. Aggressive selling was required and the techniques used are legendary. The first hurdle was to get into the house to give a demonstration and then to find some way of wangling a down-payment from the housewife. One American salesman, according to legend, persuaded a widow to pawn the headstone from her husband's grave.

The main beneficiary of all this activity was the consumer. In 1923 there were only 5,000 electric cookers in service in Britain; in 1930 alone, 120,000 were installed. It was the vested interests who complained. Big business felt threatened by take-over and worried that Britain would become, in the words of one observer 'an appendage to the United States' unless she 'Americanised' her methods.[19] Less powerful interests were hostile too. By 1929 Woolworth's had 350 stores in all Britain's major towns and cities, with nothing priced above sixpence. Local traders were peeved and vented their anger on everything American. Winifred Davis's father owned a hardware shop in Sheffield. Woolworth's came to the town and began undercutting Davis's prices. A tin bath, which cost two shillings and eleven pence in the family store was sold by Woolworth's for only sixpence. She remembers the day her father took her to the British Empire Exhibition at Wembley in 1924 and complained about the American stand, with its simulation of Niagara Falls and the latest line in Kewpie dolls. 'They shouldn't be here,' he fumed. 'This is the *British Empire* Exhibition.'[20]

American culture, as well as American goods, was invading Britain. Jazz began to catch on among the fashionable in the 1920s. Black regimental bands such as the Seventy Black Devils had toured France with great success in 1918, playing rag and march tunes, and in 1919 a white group, the Original Dixieland Jazz Band, performed to wild acclaim in Britain. Other white bands followed. Gradually a market for American records developed and British dance bands began to give their music 'American' touches, with greater syncopation and the addition of drums, banjos and eventually saxophones. The Prince of Wales's well-known enthusiasm, particularly for drumming, helped give jazz a seal of approval. In night clubs he often joined the band and beat time on the drums, though, when asked what he thought of the Prince's abilities, virtuoso drummer Dave Tough replied discreetly that 'he might make a good King'.[21]

Businessmen grumbled at the American commercial invasion. Guardians of morality frowned disapprovingly on the values of the Jazz Age. But these expressions of hostility to Americanisation were as nothing compared with the reactions aroused by American domination of the film industry. In the Television Age it is hard to imagine the impact the cinema had, first the silent films and then the talkies. By the late 1930s more than twenty million admission tickets on average were sold every week, and what cinema-goers saw were almost always American films. The memory of one woman must have been the common experience of thousands. 'I lived in a mining village, a very dull dark sort of place . . . [In the cinema] you were in complete darkness, then all the screen would light up and you'd see all these marvellous film stars. Everything was bright. I just wanted to go there and be like them.'[22] Children in the street imitated American slang: 'OK, kid' and 'What are you doing tonight, babe?' It infuriated their parents and their teachers. By 1941 the Board of Education was mounting a campaign in schools 'to make children realise that Hollywood, hot music and slang are not the most important features of the life of the USA'.[23]

The girls imitated the looks of the stars by putting flour on their cheeks and soot on their eyelashes. Instead of lipstick, they dabbed their mouths with red tissue paper moistened with water. Their childhood longing to look like their movie idols led to the mass production of make-up for the first time. Until then it had been worn only in fashionable circles. Ordinary people did not use it. But the American make-up artist Max Factor discovered that the actresses he made up for the screen wanted to look the same when they were out in public as they did in their films. He invented pancake powder and soon realised its potential, not just for the stars, but for the fans who wanted to imitate them. He set up factories in Britain and America and sold 'The Make-Up of the Stars' to the women who had daubed flour on their cheeks as children.

The popular newspaper, the *Daily Express*, complained in 1927 that the bulk of picture-goers were being Americanised. 'They talk America, think America, and dream America. We have several million people, mostly women, who, to all intent and purpose, are temporary American citizens.'[24] The newspaper was not alone. Teachers, politicians and clergymen all complained that the films, apart from setting a bad example by showing a life either of crime or luxury, instilled too many American ideas. One Tory MP protested that the cinemas were 'booked up with masses of American rubbish forced on them by the monopoly of American interests'.[25]

In 1927 and again in 1937 Acts of Parliament were passed to try to limit the impact of the American movie industry on Britain. 'I want the world,' said the President of the Board of Trade in 1937, 'to be able to see British films true to British life, accepting British standards and spreading British ideals.'[26] In 1927 when the first Cinematograph Films Act was passed, only five per cent of films shown in Britain and throughout the empire were British-made. Britain's diplomats abroad complained that the flood of American movies was creating a demand for American rather than British products. The British press shared their alarm. 'The film is to America what the flag was once to Britain,' warned the *Morning Post*. 'By its means Uncle Sam may hope someday, if he be not checked in time, to Americanise the world.'[27]

The Films Acts were intended to protect the British film industry by requiring cinemas to show a quota of British films, to reach twenty per cent by 1936. In fact, by 1934 twenty-eight per cent of films shown in Britain were of British origin, but many of them were shoddy, cheap products, made solely to fulfil the quota. 'Quota Quickies', as they were contemptuously called, were often shot at night using sets which had been built for other films shot during the day. The actors and actresses arrived exhausted from productions on the West End stage and went through their lines in a perfunctory manner. To satisfy the law, the final product was sometimes seen only by the cinema's cleaning staff as they cleared up in the morning. No British audience would have paid to watch them.

In 1937 a new attempt was made to improve standards. This time the quotas were raised and a minimum financial outlay imposed. Hollywood, which depended on its overseas sales for its profits, was outraged by the British legislation. A third of its foreign income came from Britain. The State Department and Hollywood's trade organisation protested indignantly to the British Government. The State Department's standard line was: 'This government has adopted no restrictive regulations similar in any way to those enforced in certain foreign countries.'[28] That was strictly true, but then there was no need. In films as in commerce, the Americans demanded the Open Door abroad while keeping it tightly shut at home. By the late twenties the 'Big Five' American movie companies dominated the whole film industry in the USA. Because they made many of the major films, controlled the distribution network and owned most of the big movie theatres, even good British films had virtually no chance. Unable to remove the British quotas, the US giants, particularly MGM, adopted the same policy as Ford or Firestone towards British tariffs. They simply bought up British film companies and produced their own films in Britain.

It became clear that government action could not change public tastes. American films succeeded because they were slick and exciting, had high technical standards and good acting. No law could diminish their popularity. One cinema manager in the East End of London summed it all up. His audiences, he said, were very particular. 'They like good pictures, good American pictures, pictures of movement and action. They won't stand British pictures here at any price. When we have one in the Programme, many of our patrons come in late or early to avoid seeing the British picture.'[29]

The hostility and snobbery of Britain's élite were typified by the popular philosopher C. E. M. Joad. America, he wrote, was the epitome of 'modern civilisation'. It perverted the traditional pursuit of Truth, Beauty, and Goodness. Instead of Truth was the worship of the machine and 'the glorification of size, hustle and efficiency'. Films, slang and advertisements were all America could manage to take the place of great literature. Morality was reduced to the 'belief that all Americans are good and that all is therefore well with America'. God, sneered Joad, was seen 'as a glorified good American, receiving worship in return for His guaranteed support of all American enterprises'.[30]

The intelligentsia might carp at what author Harold Nicolson liked to call 'the eternal superficiality of the American race'.[31] But to millions of Britons the picture of America they saw in the cinema was a source of hope and encouragement. 'The skies were always blue, blue all the time, with a few white clouds . . . this wonderful dream of a land of unlimited opportunity where we could really become something different and better from what we were.'[32]

And America's intellectuals had no doubt that they were the wave of the future. 'God damn the continent of Europe,' exploded the novelist F. Scott Fitzgerald during a visit to London in 1921. 'It is of merely antiquarian interest.' Within twenty-five years, he predicted, New York would be the world's 'capital of culture' because 'culture follows money . . . We will be the Romans of the next generations as the English are now.'[33]

Britain was not alone in its love–hate reaction to the United States. In the 1920s ordinary people throughout much of Europe flocked to see American movies and buy American products. Many European governments imposed restrictions on American films and tried to

Versailles, 28 June 1919: the Big Three – Georges Clemenceau, Woodrow Wilson and David Lloyd George.

Allied officers try to see the signing of the peace treaty with Germany in the Hall of Mirrors.

Montagu Norman, Stanley Baldwin and Sir Auckland Geddes in Washington to negotiate a settlement of Britain's war debt to the USA (January 1923).

Confrontation between Senator Gerald P. Nye and J.P. Morgan during Senate hearings on the munitions industry (February 1936).

prevent American take-overs of their companies. But there was general agreement that the business methods of Americans such as Henry Ford were the key to survival in the modern age. Even in introverted Russia *Fordizatsia* was all the rage. The new Soviet leaders, desperately trying to industrialise their backward economy, recognised the need for Western skills and technology, especially from the United States. Once Russia had acquired them, Trotsky predicted, then 'Americanised Bolshevism will defeat and crush imperialist Americanism'. For 'Bolshevism has no enemy more fundamental and irreconcilable than American capitalism'. He called them 'the two basic and antagonistic forces of our age'.[34]

For many Americans, Bolshevik communism was the lurking enemy. The anxieties of Colonel House at Paris in 1919 were shared in America itself, where the wartime backlash against foreigners and political radicals mushroomed into a full-scale 'Red Scare'. Alarmed by a few anarchist bombings, Attorney General A. Mitchell Palmer hounded and imprisoned the political left. He warned that 'the blaze of revolution was sweeping over every American institution of law and order . . . licking at the altars of the churches . . . crawling into the sacred corners of American homes . . . burning up the foundations of society'.[35]

The war and the Red Scare broke America's socialist movement, which had won nearly a million votes in the presidential election of 1912. From now on the USA would be unique among Western nations in having no viable socialist or left-of-centre political party. In 1924 the British Labour Party, backed by the trade unions, formed a government for the first time and quickly opened diplomatic relations with the USSR, which the USA did not recognise until 1933. America's union movement, far weaker than Britain's, was staunchly apolitical. In 1931 Secretary of State Henry Stimson called it 'our chief barrier against communism'.[36] American workers saw little attraction in socialism, let alone communism. For most of them, particularly the immigrants from Europe, American capitalism seemed to work. They and their children were far better off than in the Old World. In the rueful words of one socialist commentator: 'On the reefs of roast beef and apple pie socialistic Utopias of every sort are sent to their doom.'[37]

America's boom in the 1920s was therefore more than simply an advertisement for its business methods. For Americans, and for many in Europe, it was vindication of the whole American way of life. Capitalism, not Bolshevism, seemed the ideology for the modern world. Americanisation was the dream and the coming reality.

But in October 1929 the dream ended and the nightmare began. For more than a year American investors had been borrowing feverishly to buy shares as Wall Street's big bull market climbed upwards. General Motors shares, for instance, had more than doubled in value in three years. But then the market broke. At times on 24 October 1929 there were stocks on sale that no one would buy at any price. Experts thought the fall might be temporary and bankers, led by J. P. Morgan, bought heavily to try to hold the market steady. But then on Black Tuesday, 29 October, sixteen million shares changed hands and within a month the stocks listed on Wall Street had fallen forty per cent in value.

The Great Crash of 1929 heralded the longest and deepest recession in American history. The market for cars, houses and consumer goods was saturated. Farmers were hit by the worldwide collapse of prices. Banks, who had lent too much against the now useless security of share values, were forced to call in loans to protect their liquidity. The American banking system, with hundreds of small independent banks set up with inadequate assets, was used to seeing banks fail even in normal years. Now they closed in unprecedented numbers – 6,000 between 1929 and 1932.

It took two years for the full effect to be felt. By 1932 the value of shares, and so of many people's savings, had fallen to one-tenth of their value at the peak of 1929. Starved of cash, businesses laid off workers. Unemployment rose from three per cent to twenty-five per cent by 1933. Output fell by a third. The effect was devastating. Laid-off coal miners shivered in tents through a West Virginia winter; below Riverside Drive in New York an encampment of destitute squatters lined the banks of the Hudson River for forty blocks; and between one and two million young people 'rode the rails' in search of work. 'There is not a garbage dump in Chicago,' the writer Edmund Wilson reported in 1933, 'which is not diligently harvested by the hungry . . . falling on the heap of refuse as soon as the truck had pulled out and digging in it with sticks and hands.'[38]

America had lost confidence in itself. In March 1929 Herbert Hoover had been inaugurated President, proclaiming a 'New Era' and assuring Americans, 'I have no fears for the future of our country. It is bright with hope.'[39] By 1932 Hoover, once the epitome of technocratic America, had become a synonym for disaster. The shanty towns of squatters that sprang up all over the country were nicknamed 'Hoovervilles'. America, so recently the envy of the world, now attracted mostly pity. Some natives in the Cameroons, an impoverished French colony in Africa, had a collection and sent the city of New

York three dollars and seventy-seven cents. It was, they explained, relief for the 'starving'.[40]

America's next President, Franklin Roosevelt, tried to rekindle faith in the great American dream. 'First of all,' he said in his inaugural address of March 1933, 'let me assert my firm belief that the only thing we have to fear is fear itself – nameless, unreasoning, unjustified terror.'[41] Almost by force of personality Roosevelt restored confidence in the banking system. His New Deal gave American unions new rights and set up a basic framework of social security. Vast programmes of 'public works', funded by the Federal Government, kept many in employment and gave American cities new parks, highways and airports. But even the jaunty Roosevelt could not end the Depression. In 1938 unemployment was still nearly twenty per cent and the level of investment was half that of 1929. America no longer seemed to be the example for the world.

Many people in Britain also suffered in the Depression. Old industries like coal and shipbuilding continued to decline and parts of Tyneside and South Wales saw twenty per cent unemployment. But Britain had grown used to such figures in the 1920s: they did not come out of the blue as in the USA. And the midlands and south-east recovered quickly from the Slump of 1929–32, experiencing the demand for houses, cars and consumer goods that had fuelled the American economy in the twenties. New British factories were built, living standards in the south improved, and Britain's industrial growth rate in the 1930s was one of the highest in the world.

The exaggerated fears of Americanisation receded as the flow of US investment in Britain slowed down. Some American firms, in trouble at home, pulled out completely. In 1931 Woolworth's sold almost half their English holdings and in 1933 Boots, the leading British chemists (drug-stores), was returned by United Drugs to British shareholders. Between 1933 and 1940 total US overseas investment fell, while Britain, despite her rival's rapid expansion in the newer industries around the world, remained the world's largest overseas investor.[42]

Some salutary lessons were learned by British industry from the American example. Henry Ford's Model T, which dominated the British motor-car market in 1920, had been overtaken by smaller British products. The motor manufacturer William Morris urged patriotic drivers to buy British with such success that by 1929 he controlled thirty-five per cent of the market. Another British company, Austin, was second with twenty-five per cent, and Ford trailed with only four per cent, partly because of its reluctance to find a modern replacement for the Model T which could challenge British products like the Austin Seven and the Morris Oxford. 'We have been defeated and licked in England,' groaned a top Ford executive in Detroit.[43] Partly recovering in the 1930s, with new models to break into the small-car market, Ford nevertheless remained in third place in 1938.

In other industries successful attempts were made to fight off the challenge of the American and German conglomerates. In chemicals the British Imperial Chemical Industries (ICI) was formed in 1926, followed in 1929 by the Anglo-Dutch Unilever, making soap and fats. One company, Courtaulds, a family textile firm from Essex, broke with particular success into the American market through its subsidiary, the American Viscose Corporation. In 1928 this produced sixty per cent of US rayon and contributed half of Courtaulds' gross income. *Fortune* magazine described it as 'a phenomenon comparable to Standard Oil or the automobile empire of Henry Ford'.[44]

British ideas as well as British business seemed to be having an effect on thirties America. Some of Roosevelt's New Deal reforms borrowed from British precedents. The Securities Act of 1933, to tighten up the regulation of Wall Street and prevent another crash, was modelled on the British Companies Act. The Guffey Coal Act of 1935 was influenced by the British Coal Mines Act of 1930 which, in the words of one Congressman, 'had saved the British coal industry'.[45] Roosevelt himself told an English friend that social security was the most important part of his domestic programme and 'said that he was really following in the pre-war footsteps of the Liberal party in that respect'.[46]

A few British economists and political reformers believed that the New Deal could teach Britain some lessons in return. The Next Five Years Group, including the young Tory MP Harold Macmillan, announced in its 1934 manifesto that 'dire poverty in the midst of plenty presents the sort of challenge to capacity for national organisation which President Roosevelt has accepted, but our own Government has declined'.[47] The following year Lloyd George, still bidding for a political comeback, called for a British New Deal with a massive programme of public works. Piecemeal responses to the Slump were not enough, he warned. 'You have to think out your problem anew exactly as they are doing in America.'[48]

But these were isolated voices. The British left, arguing that the Depression proved the bankruptcy of American capitalism, looked to the Soviet Union as their example. And Whitehall regained its habitual condescending tone about America. Roosevelt's New Deal was seen as a confused and belated attempt to bring America's economic and political institutions out of the age of liberal individualism into the twentieth century. The British Embassy in Washington frequently referred to the 'obsolescence of American institutions'.[49] In 1938 a Foreign Office report circulated to the Cabinet claimed that 'the glad, confident, boastful America has passed away; in its place is left a country – we cannot yet say a nation – that has lost its old landmarks, and seems to be staggering forward, leaderless, into an uncertain future'.[50]

The problem was that most British people had little informed knowledge of the United States against which to judge the sporadic reports in the media. Virtually no US history or literature was taught in British schools, and the press paid little attention to 'serious' American news. Even in the 'quality' papers, one survey estimated in 1936–7, the United States rarely received more than a sixth of the space devoted to foreign news and of this more than a third was given over to sensation, sex and crime.[51] There was, then, little to correct the stereotypes of America seen on the movies: cowboys out on the range, girls in satin negligées lounging in luxurious Manhattan apartments, drunks in the doorways of the Bowery, and trilby-hatted crooks with sub-machine guns tucked under their arms. American politics were corrupt, violence paid, and sex was a commodity. When Joseph Kennedy arrived as Ambassador to Britain in 1938 he was horrified at the way Britons seemed to believe that America 'was typified by motion pictures'. In vain he called for better press coverage of the USA 'so that people would believe that something happened there besides gangster shootings, rapes and kidnappings'.[52]

The American media paid greater attention to Britain. America's major newspapers contained far more serious news about British politics than the British press carried about America and in 1922 it was reckoned that nearly one in eight American pupils had a year of English history at some time during their high-school careers. But the history they were taught, no less than the films shown in Britain, often projected a distorted, unflattering image. For American history teaching was intensely nationalistic, a way of fusing a disparate collection of ethnic groups into a proud nation. Britain, particularly the Britain of the American Revolution, served as a convenient whipping boy. One concerned US historian asserted that 'Americans are taught from childhood to hate Britishers by the study of American history'.[53]

These impressions of Britain as a repressive, class-dominated, imperialist society were reinforced by Hollywood's own portrayals of the British. The 1930s saw a rash of American films based on books by Dickens and Kipling. Some were enormous box-office successes, such as *Lives of a Bengal Lancer*, starring Gary Cooper. Other money-spinners in America, like *A Yank at Oxford* and *Goodbye, Mr Chips* (both made by MGM in Britain to get round the quota), gave stereotyped portraits of the English university and public school. But the British monarchy was the biggest hit in America. One of the few British films of the 1930s to succeed there, grossing more than \$2½ million, was *The Private Life of Henry VIII* starring Charles Laughton as England's most notorious king.

For Americans, the monarchy also provided the most fascinating real-life British story of the decade – King Edward VIII's liaison with the American divorcée, Mrs Wallis Simpson. American press cuttings about the affair ran to half a million items and it was one of the top three American news stories of the decade. The handsome young prince had long been a trend-setter in Anglo-American relations. His taste in clothes had set fashions in New York after his visit there in 1924, grey flannel trousers and blue shirts with soft collars becoming all the rage. And in Britain he took a particular liking to things American, such as jazz, perhaps in reaction to the stuffy atmosphere of his father's court. When he succeeded George V in January 1936 his affair with Mrs Simpson became a matter of intense interest in the United States. Newspapers that summer were full of pictures of them cruising in the Mediterranean.

In Britain, however, the press kept a remarkable silence, in deference to the King's wishes, even though the affair was common gossip in London society. American interest reached fever pitch when Mrs Simpson secured a divorce at the end of October 1936. To minimise London publicity the case was heard in Ipswich, by unhappy coincidence the birthplace of Cardinal Wolsey who had managed Henry VIII's momentous divorce 400 years before. 'KING'S MOLL RENO'D IN WOLSEY'S HOME TOWN' ran the most ingenious of the American headlines.[54] The way now seemed clear for a royal wedding, just before the coronation. One of William Randolph Hearst's newspapers stated categorically 'KING WILL WED WALLY'. It claimed that Edward VIII believed that 'the most important thing for the peace and welfare of world is an intimate understanding and relationship between England and America, and that his marriage with this very gifted lady may help to bring about that beneficial co-operation between English-speaking nations.'[55]

At last Prime Minister Stanley Baldwin stepped in. The American press speculation was now felt to be seriously damaging Britain's image abroad, particularly in the British Dominions where, as Baldwin put it later, the Crown was 'the last link of Empire that is left'.[56]

Backed by most leading politicians except Churchill, he insisted that if the King made this match no political party would form a government to support him. In December Edward VIII was asked to choose. He could have his throne or his wife, but not both. He chose the woman he loved.

Despite London society gibes about 'Queen Wallis' and some protests in the US press, Mrs Simpson's 'Americanness' was not the basic objection, nor even her status, or lack of it, as a commoner. At issue was the fitness of a twice-divorced woman, with both husbands still alive, to be spouse of a King pledged as Defender of the Faith in a Church which still insisted that the sacrament of marriage was indissoluble. Mrs Simpson's American background prevented her appreciating what most Englishwomen would have known instinctively. Contrary to her movie-world image of royalty, the King of England could not have his way in everything.

It was a love story perfectly designed to satisfy America's fascination with monarchy, while vindicating its pride in republican institutions. Not even Hollywood's 'dream factory' could have done better. Except, that is, for the ending. Despite William Randolph Hearst's predictions, no royal marriage consummated a new Anglo-American alliance. It would take the worst crisis in either country's modern history to bridge the gulf caused by isolationism, rivalry and misperception and bring Britain and America closer than ever before, or ever again.

7

Britain Alone

1935–41

It is a commonplace that if Britain and America had stood up to the dictators in the 1930s World War Two would never have happened. Winston Churchill dubbed it 'the unnecessary war' and the first volume of his war memoirs took as its theme 'how the English-speaking Peoples, through their unwisdom, carelessness and good nature, allowed the wicked to rearm'.[1] With hindsight it is easy to castigate the leaders of both countries for their blindness to the dangers that threatened them and for a complacency that at times seems almost supine. It is harder to step back, to see the threats as they saw them at the time, and to understand the constraints that made effective Anglo-American co-operation so difficult.

By the early 1930s the world economy had collapsed into depression and threats to peace were already apparent. In 1931 an expansionist Japan took Manchuria, on the Asian mainland, from China, with only ineffectual protest from the League of Nations. After Hitler came to power in January 1933, he rapidly rearmed Germany and planned a vast Aryan empire in Europe and beyond. The Italian dictator, Mussolini, emboldened by Hitler's success, invaded Ethiopia virtually unchallenged in 1935, and from 1936 both dictators intervened on the side of Franco and the fascists in the Spanish Civil War.

Britain and America watched these events from the sidelines. Both countries were preoccupied by recovery from the Depression. Both were inhibited by a popular backlash against the slaughter of the Great War. They both shared a suspicion of the motives of the armaments industry and a reluctance to become entangled again in the continent of Europe. Rearmament was therefore slow, diplomacy hesitant and indecisive.

President Franklin D. Roosevelt, who succeeded Herbert Hoover in 1933, wanted to break the isolationist mould. Although he had lost faith in the League of Nations, having originally supported it when a junior member of the Wilson Administration, Roosevelt still believed that the United States should use its influence in the cause of world peace. That was not only a moral duty, he believed, but also a matter of self-interest. In 1937 he compared war to an infectious disease whose spread could only be prevented by putting the aggressors in 'quarantine' through diplomatic isolation or economic sanctions.

Practical politics, however, made it difficult to implement any such remedies. The Congress was isolationist by conviction, not wanting to involve America in another war or even to take action entailing the risk of war. The Neutrality Act of 1935 was designed to prevent the economic entanglements of trade and loans that had helped drag America into the Great War. Roosevelt himself shared these anxieties. 'I have seen war . . . I hate war,' he insisted in 1936.[2] He was also acutely sensitive to political realities, having watched the disintegration of Wilson's policies in the confrontation with Congress in 1919. For Roosevelt diplomacy had to be tailored to the public mood. His political posture was cruelly caricatured by Congresswoman Clare Boothe Luce as an index finger wetted and held up in the air.[3]

In the 1930s it was understandable for Americans to display little interest in world affairs. Three thousand miles of Atlantic Ocean seemed ample protection against Hitler's Germany, while the expansion of Italy or Japan was of limited concern to a country with few overseas possessions and little dependence on foreign trade. Britain, however, could not afford to take such a detached view. The English Channel, her moat in the past, was no barrier to the growing German air force, and British power and wealth depended on the survival of the empire and the protection of vulnerable trade routes. The First Sea Lord, Admiral Chatfield, summed up British thinking in 1934: 'We are in the remarkable position of not wanting to quarrel with anybody because we have got most of the world already, or the best parts of it, and we only want to keep what we have got and prevent others from taking it away from us.'[4]

Britain therefore had to maintain a delicate balance. Her interests lay in preventing not just renewed war but also the further erosion of her power. She wanted peace, but not at any price. The problem was that she lacked the means for a firm policy that would deter worldwide aggression. Rearmament was not popular with the British electorate, nor with the Treasury, who feared that it would damage economic recovery and so undermine foreign confidence in sterling. In particular Britain's navy, the main instrument for protecting her trade and empire, was inadequate for her responsibilities, after the reductions of the 1920s and successive arms control agreements.

By the mid-thirties Britain could no longer respond to a crisis in one part of the world while retaining sufficient ships to deal with a threat elsewhere. If the Royal Navy were needed in the Far East, the Mediterranean Fleet would have to sail for Singapore, denuding the Suez Canal and the Middle East. In 1934 the Treasury opposed a firm line against Japan, using this weakness as justification. In 1935–6 the Cabinet rejected oil sanctions against Mussolini over Ethiopia, on the grounds that the possibility of war with Japan made tough action against Italy imprudent.

Since a policy of deterrence seemed impossible, British leaders adopted a policy of appeasement. The attempt to buy off potential foes, often denigrated as short-sighted and even cowardly, was really a calculated gamble by Britain to negotiate her way out of danger. The aim was to reduce the number of enemies by satisfying their grievances in return for guarantees of peace and disarmament. Appeasement was the policy of the Tory-dominated National Government throughout the 1930s, but it was adopted with particular enthusiasm by Neville Chamberlain, who became Prime Minister in May 1937.

Chamberlain effectively seized control of foreign policy, trying to reach personal agreements with Hitler and Mussolini. He and most of his colleagues underestimated Hitler's long-term ambitions and exaggerated Germany's immediate military strength. Fearful of being plunged into a war on three fronts simultaneously they were unwilling to risk calling Germany's bluff, or Italy's or Japan's. Chamberlain was also pessimistic about the chances of effective help. The British Dominions were isolationist, France was in turmoil, and Russia was engulfed in Stalin's bloody purges. Like most of his colleagues, Chamberlain was particularly sceptical about the United States after the bitter experiences of the 1920s and early 1930s. 'It is always best and safest,' he once observed, 'to count on *nothing* from the Americans except words.'[5]

As the crisis worsened Roosevelt wanted to reinforce Britain's efforts to reduce international tension, but his plans were often frustrated by rifts between the two governments.

Trade was a major issue. America was becoming increasingly irritated by British discrimination against US products. In 1937 sixteen per cent of all the goods America exported went to Britain, making her America's most valuable trading partner, but their importance to Britain, expanding her trade with the empire, was declining. By 1937 only eleven per cent of British imports came from America whereas thirty-nine per cent came from the empire.[6] Roosevelt's Secretary of State, Cordell Hull, was alarmed at the effects on American farmers and manufacturers of this trend. He put the blame on Britain's policy of Imperial Preference which imposed lower tariffs on imports from the empire than on those from other nations. Hull felt the discrimination was unfair and was convinced that trade barriers and economic nationalism were the root causes of war. The British took a different view. Building up the empire's trade seemed the best way out of the Depression, and they were not willing to reduce Imperial Preferences until America offered drastic cuts in its own tariffs. Negotiations on lowering trade barriers between the two dragged on from 1934 to 1938.

The political damage of this stalemate was considerable. It became a State Department axiom that there could be no co-operation on other matters with Britain until a trade agreement had been reached. 'At present,' a senior US diplomat complained in 1936, 'she [Britain] thinks she can count on our help politically and yet hit us below the belt commercially all over the world.'[7]

The lack of co-operation was particularly apparent in East Asia. In 1937 Japan, encouraged by the lack of any effective reaction to her invasion of Manchuria, once again attacked China, in violation of the 1922 treaty. Instead of co-ordinating their actions against Japan, Britain and America acted independently and ineffectually.

President Roosevelt restated the sanctity of the treaties Japan had signed and refused to approve her infringements of Chinese territory, but he took no real action. Verbal protests and a gradual rebuilding of America's naval strength to the size allowed by the treaties was the limit of the White House response. Britain was equally hesitant. Since 1922 she had had no alliance with Japan. Her interests in China were now under threat, but she felt that her resources would only allow her to act in concert with the United States. For a brief moment in December 1937, after a Japanese attack on British and American vessels in the Yangtze river, it seemed possible that Roosevelt would agree to a blockade of Japan, but, before it could be considered, Japan had apologised for the incident and the crisis receded.

Early in 1938 Roosevelt turned his attention to the ominous situation in Europe. He put forward a proposal suggested by his Under-Secretary of State, Sumner Welles, for a peace conference to be held under the auspices of the United States. He hoped it would establish basic principles for the conduct of international relations, reduce the level of armaments and open up world trade. Roosevelt secretly asked for Chamberlain's support, urging him to reply within a week, but the Prime Minister was not impressed. 'The plan appeared to me fantastic,' he wrote in his diary, 'and likely to excite the derision of Germany and Italy. They might even use it to postpone conversations with us.'[8]

Without consulting his Foreign Secretary, Anthony Eden, who was on a brief holiday in France, Chamberlain sent Roosevelt a cool reply, outlining his own plans for talks with Mussolini and Hitler and asking the President to hold off for the moment. Lord Home, then Chamberlain's parliamentary private secretary, now thinks the reply was a mistake: 'It was the first indication that America was beginning to take some interest in the terrible situation that was developing in Germany. Chamberlain ought not to have turned it down.'[9]

On hearing the news Eden was furious. He disliked Chamberlain's personal diplomacy and wanted to encourage closer co-operation between Britain and the United States. 'What we have to choose between,' he argued, 'is Anglo-American co-operation in an attempt to ensure world peace and a piecemeal settlement approached by way of a problematical agreement with Mussolini.'[10] However naïve an American initiative might seem, he was sure it should be encouraged not rebuffed. Hurrying back to London he persuaded the Cabinet to react positively to Roosevelt's suggestion, and Chamberlain duly proposed that the President continue to explore his plan for an international conference while Britain tried direct negotiation with the dictators. But it was too late. By now Roosevelt's enthusiasm for the idea had cooled, and he was willing to let Chamberlain act alone.

'The loss of the last frail chance to save the world from tyranny otherwise than by war,' was Churchill's description of the failure of the Roosevelt initiative.[11] In fact it hardly seemed to deserve such a portentous epitaph. Roosevelt's ideas were vague and utopian, standing even less chance of success than Chamberlain's own appeasement. Perhaps the sad story is better seen as yet one more episode in the chronicle of misunderstandings between Britain and America in the 1930s.

For the rest of 1938 and 1939, until the outbreak of war with Germany, Chamberlain conducted increasingly fruitless negotiations with Hitler and Mussolini. Such sympathy as there had been in Britain for Germany's expansion had now abated. When Hitler entered the Rhineland in 1936 Lord Lothian had commented that the Germans were simply walking into 'their own back garden'.[12] He was not alone in thinking that Germany had been treated vindictively at Versailles and was entitled to some redress. But during 1938 Hitler invaded Austria and then threatened Czechoslovakia. By September war

Uncle Sam entangled in isolationism. Clifford Berryman's 1938 version of the famous Greek sculpture.

seemed inevitable. In London air-raid sirens were tested, trenches were dug in the parks, and millions of anti-gas masks were made ready for distribution. In a last effort to maintain the peace Chamberlain flew to Munich and made an agreement which gave Hitler half Czechoslovakia in exchange for pledges that he would make no further territorial demands and that Britain and Germany would never fight each other again.

Roosevelt, who had been watching from the sidelines since the failure of his peace initiative, was relieved that war had been averted and hopeful of a lasting peace. After Munich he cabled Chamberlain: 'I fully share your hope and belief that there exists today the greatest opportunity in years for a new order based on justice and law.'[13] Privately, however, he became increasingly doubtful during the winter that any agreement with Hitler would stick, and began pressing for American rearmament. Yet he still believed it was the responsibility of the democracies in western Europe to mount their own defence. America would back them up but not take the lead. 'What the British need today,' he wrote in February 1939, 'is a good stiff grog, inducing not only the desire to save civilization but the continued belief that they can do it. In such an event they will have a lot more support from their American cousins . . .'[14]

Relations between the two governments improved during 1939. The British were encouraged by Roosevelt's plans for rearmament and his condemnation of totalitarianism. The Americans applauded Britain's decision to end appeasement after Hitler took the remainder of Czechoslovakia in March 1939. A historic event that summer symbolised the new cordiality. King George VI became the first reigning British sovereign to set foot on the soil of the former colony. It was a brief visit, a four-day whirlwind tour that took the King and Queen Elizabeth, as guests of the President, to Washington, New York, and to the Roosevelt family home at Hyde Park on the Hudson river north of New York.

Everywhere the royal couple went they were greeted by enthusiastic crowds. Instead of a pompous, stuffy visit, the American press and newsreels showed a friendly and informal pair who lunched at Hyde Park not on caviar and champagne but on beer and hot dogs. The King discussed the signs of impending war with Roosevelt and gained the impression that the President would do everything in his power to help. The Foreign Office was delighted at the discreet courtship conducted during the royal tour, but it was hard-headed enough to know that, while the visit had warmed American hearts, only events would change American policy.

On the night of 31 August 1939 Hitler invaded Poland, ignoring Britain's ultimatum, and three days later Britain and France declared war. Unlike Wilson in 1914, Roosevelt at once made clear that American sympathies lay with the Allies. In a 'fireside chat' radio broadcast he said: 'I cannot ask that every American remain neutral in thought. Even a neutral cannot be asked to close his mind or conscience.'[15]

But neutrality was still America's official policy. The Neutrality Act had been amended in 1937 to permit Americans to trade with belligerent nations, except in armaments. To avoid the country being dragged into war by attacks on her ships and by foreign loans, as had happened in World War One, all these goods had to be collected by the buyer and paid for at the time of purchase, a system called 'cash and carry'. Within two months of the outbreak of war Roosevelt persuaded Congress to modify the act further. Britain needed supplies of armaments which she had been ordering in increasing quantities from America as war loomed, but at the outbreak of hostilities, in keeping with the Neutrality Act, these supplies had been halted.

THINK – AMERICANS – THINK

"Against the insidious wiles of foreign influence, I conjure you to believe me, fellow citizens, the jealousy of a free people ought to be constantly awake; since history and experience prove that foreign influence is one of the most baneful foes of Republican Government. 'Tis our true policy to steer clear of permanent alliances with any portion of the foreign world."
(George Washington)

TODAY:

The King and Queen of England, are on our Border; en route to the United States.

WHY ARE THEY COMIMG?
WHAT IS THE MOTIVE?

Is this a vacation tour? OR purely a propaganda mission?

THINK – AMERICANS – THINK

As the result of English propaganda we were involved in a world war. No one questions this.

Why should America officially extend the hand of welcome to England's crowned heads, when Americans groan under the burden of billions of dollars of defaulted payments on loans. Loans made as the result of propaganda during that war.

A DEBT THEY NEVER INTEND TO PAY

Have you read "England expects every American to do his duty" by Quincy Howe. You Should.

Are we to again pull English chestnuts out of the fire –
"On Tick" – Why cater to welchers.

THINK – AMERICANS – THINK

(Sponsored and distributed by a committee of Americans who believe in a revival of the spirit of "76")

60

Warnings printed for an Irish-American club and dropped by aircraft over Detroit when King George VI was just across the Canadian border (June 1939).

American munitions factories fell idle. By early November, arguing that it was in America's own economic interest to supply Britain, Roosevelt secured the repeal of the arms embargo. Britain could now buy whatever she wanted, as long as she paid cash and arranged delivery.

For the British the revised Neutrality Act was a welcome improvement. As in the Great War they could now draw on the vast industrial resources of the USA. But the ban on loans was worrying, and the inconvenient 'carry' clauses drove the two countries to subterfuge. Aeroplanes, for instance, could not be flown directly from factories in America to Canada and so on to Britain. Some were dismantled and shipped in crates by sea. Lockheeds in California, a small company that was expanding with orders from Britain, found an original solution that kept strictly within the terms of the Neutrality Act. The company bought a stretch of flat land in the far north of North Dakota, on the Canadian border. Lockheed pilots flew the planes to the grass airstrip. The engines were turned off and the pilots disembarked. A local farmer hitched a team of horses to the front undercarriage and drew the machines a few yards across the border into Canada thus ensuring that the planes had not left the USA under their own power. British or Canadian pilots then went aboard, restarted the engines, and took off for Britain.

For seven months after war was declared there was little fighting. Poland was swiftly dismembered by Germany and Russia, with whom Hitler had signed a non-aggression pact. There then followed the period of inactivity known as the phoney war. During it a last attempt was made by Roosevelt to explore the chances of peace. Sumner Welles was sent to Europe on a special mission. Chamberlain wrote scathingly of the intervention: 'Heaven knows I don't want the Americans to fight for us – we should have to pay too dearly for that if they had a right to be in on the peace terms – but if they are so sympathetic they might at least refrain from hampering our efforts and comforting our foes.'[16]

In April 1940 the phoney war came to an abrupt end. Germany invaded Scandinavia. A British expeditionary force arrived in Norway too late and was soon forced to withdraw. On 10 May the German army invaded the Netherlands, Belgium, Luxembourg and northern France. The Allied forces were soon in headlong retreat. At six o'clock that night the British Prime Minister resigned, having lost a vote of confidence over Norway in the House of Commons. His successor was Winston Churchill.

Although a diehard Tory, Churchill had been out of office for most of the 1930s when he had been an outspoken advocate of rearmament and a frequent critic of appeasement. Ed Murrow, head of CBS operations in Europe, reported to American radio listeners that eve-

A Firestone rubber plantation in Liberia.

The Hoover factory on London's Western Avenue at Perivale, built in 1931.

The British image of America: Edward G. Robinson in the gangster movie *Little Caesar* (1930).

The American image of Britain: Robert Taylor in *A Yank at Oxford* (1938).

Edward VIII and Mrs Simpson, sightseeing in Yugoslavia in the summer of 1936.

Pro-Nazi rally in New York's Madison Square Garden in 1934.

King George VI and President Franklin D. Roosevelt outside the President's church at Hyde Park, New York (June 1939).

ning that Churchill 'enters office with the tremendous advantage of being the man who was right . . . Mr Churchill can inspire confidence. And he can preach a doctrine of hate that is acceptable to the majority of this country.'[17] Unlike Chamberlain, Churchill was also an ardent champion of co-operation among what he liked to call 'the English-speaking peoples'. He had an American mother, knew the United States well and, on his appointment as First Lord of the Admiralty in September 1939, had responded eagerly to Roosevelt's secret request for regular information on naval matters. After his appointment as Prime Minister their correspondence was to develop into the most important channel of communication between the two governments. Between May 1940 and April 1945 Churchill sent Roosevelt a message, on average, once every thirty-six hours. 'No lover,' he said after the war, 'ever studied the whims of his mistress as I did those of President Roosevelt.'[18]

But all this was in the future in May 1940. When Churchill assumed office there were many in Washington who were wary. His belligerent stance on naval disarmament in the 1920s had not been forgotten. He was also suspected of erratic judgement and an excessive fondness for alcohol. When news of his appointment reached Washington Roosevelt commented drily that he 'supposed Churchill was the best man that England had, even if he was drunk half of his time'.[19]

It was the disastrous course of the war itself as much as the change of leaders that transformed Anglo-American relations. Within two weeks of Churchill's assumption of office the German army had reached the Channel coast. Three hundred and thirty thousand British and French troops, miraculously evacuated from Dunkirk, reached Britain bedraggled and without most of their weapons and equipment. By the middle of June France had surrendered. Britain stood alone with an army wholly inadequate for the task of defending her shores from the attack that seemed imminent. In the House of Commons Churchill rallied his countrymen: 'We shall never surrender; and even if, which I do not for a moment believe, this Island or a large part of it were subjugated and starving, then our Empire beyond the seas, armed and guarded by the British Fleet, would carry on the struggle until, in God's good time, the New World, with all its power and might, steps forth to the rescue and the liberation of the Old.'[20]

As Churchill's rhetoric acknowledged, Britain now had nowhere to turn but to America. Doubts about American reliability still lingered. Chamberlain and others had not forgotten World War One and the price extracted then for American military help. But, under Churchill's guidance, the British Government came to accept that without the

United States Britain was lost. Disregarding the dangerously low level of her gold and dollar reserves, which could not, as in World War One, be covered by US loans, Britain placed huge orders for munitions. When the money ran out the government hoped that supplies would continue to flow. But new orders could not meet the current crisis. Ships and planes would take months to build and by then Britain might have been overrun. Churchill begged Roosevelt for immediate practical help. On the East Coast of the United States were fifty Great War destroyers, 'mothballed' in their dockyards. If these could be recommissioned and lent to Britain they could be used to help repel a German invasion and to protect the sea lanes, with their vital supplies of food, from German submarines.

'Not a day should be lost,' Churchill cabled Roosevelt, emphasising the urgency of his request. Roosevelt's reply, one that Churchill would become used to receiving, was that he wanted to help but that Congress was unlikely to allow it. Again Churchill cabled: 'We must ask . . . as a matter of life or death to be reinforced with these destroyers.' Roosevelt did not reply and for two months after the fall of France sent no messages at all. Finally, in desperation, Churchill cabled on 31 July: 'Mr President, with great respect I must tell you that in the long history of the world, this is a thing to do now.'[21]

Roosevelt's reluctance to meet Churchill's appeal was partly political. Cautious as ever, he was unwilling to abandon formal neutrality before Congress was ready. But there was also the fear fostered, among others, by the American Ambassador in London, Joseph Kennedy, that Britain was on the verge of collapse. 'If we had to fight to protect our own lives,' Kennedy advised, 'we would do better fighting in our own backyard.'[22] Roosevelt himself assessed Britain's chances of survival in early July 1940 as no better than one in three. Offering destroyers, which America itself would need if Britain fell, could be a futile, even suicidal, gesture.

The President's military advisers were particularly reluctant to see too much given away. Although America was an industrial giant, its military strength was puny. In April 1940 the USA ranked twentieth among the world's military powers. The Dutch were nineteenth.[23] A country with an army of 250,000 men with outdated equipment and a navy only adequate to defend either the Pacific or the Atlantic, not both, simply did not have the resources to spare. After Dunkirk 500,000 US rifles were sold cheaply to the British army, but this was still a commercial arrangement, paid for from Britain's dwindling foreign exchange. Lending fifty destroyers was a very different matter.

By the middle of August, however, Roosevelt felt able to act.

Intelligence reports reaching Washington suggested that Britain might, after all, survive into 1941. Equally important was legal advice to the President that he need not go to Congress for special legislation but could act independently, under his authority as Commander-in-Chief. At last Roosevelt put a proposal to Churchill. Britain could have the destroyers, but she would have to offer something in return. The President wanted ninety-nine-year leases on eight British possessions in the Americas, stretching from Newfoundland to the Caribbean, on which the United States could build air and naval bases to strengthen its own defences. Roosevelt also requested a pledge from Churchill that if Britain fell the Royal Navy would not be surrendered but would carry on the fight from ports in the British Empire. The bases and the promises, Roosevelt explained, were 'molasses' to sweeten the pill in America.

When the British Cabinet received the proposal, its first reaction was to refuse. The secret War Cabinet minutes read: 'The view of the War Cabinet was that a formal bargain on the lines proposed was out of the question.'[24] Even Churchill was against giving what he called 'a blank cheque on the whole of our transatlantic possessions'.[25] But Britain no longer called the tune: she had little choice but to accept aid on whatever terms America proposed. Eventually a compromise was reached: two of the leases were designated a 'gift' from the British Government, the rest were made part of the formal deal that Roosevelt needed in order to persuade Americans that they were not, once again, being taken as suckers by the wily British. Even at a moment of world crisis, old suspicions died hard.

On 2 September 1940 the 'Destroyers for Bases' deal was signed. It was of symbolic as well as practical importance. The United States was formally neutral and yet, with this unneutral act, it had effectively pledged support for Britain as America's own front line of defence. When the destroyers finally arrived in Britain they came with a moving display of American sympathy. Immense care had been taken in fitting them out. There were bars of soap and clean towels, cocktail cabinets fully stocked, toys left for the children of the sailors who would take them over, and everywhere messages of encouragement scrawled on the walls and bulkheads: 'Sock 'em Hell' and 'Kill the Bastards'.[26]

Roosevelt's caution during this early part of the war, though unwelcome to Britain, was understandable. The presidential election was due in November 1940. Roosevelt had decided to run for a third term of office, an unprecedented and controversial decision. He had secured the endorsement of the Democratic Party in July but did not want to do anything during the campaign that would give credence to Republican charges that he was a 'war-monger'.

The President was, however, encouraged by the growing public support for Britain in the United States. In May 1940 a 'Committee to Defend America by Aiding the Allies' had been formed by a Kansas newspaper editor, William Allen White. The White Committee soon established chapters across the country which agitated for every help to be given to Britain, short of declaring war. One of its leading

BISHOP, *ST. LOUIS STAR-TIMES*

Pro-intervention: the Lilliputians tie down the sleeping Uncle Sam as the Nazi monster wades across the Atlantic.

members was the film star Douglas Fairbanks, Jr, who joined to warn America of the dangers of isolationism. He recalls Roosevelt telling him that as President he 'had to be like the captain in front of his troops. If he got too far ahead in expressing his own sympathies and opinion, then he would lose the people behind. He could only be a little ahead . . . and it was *our* job to push public opinion.'[27]

At times it took some pushing. Only two days after the 'Destroyers for Bases' agreement there was a sharp backlash. A new committee was formed to keep America out of the war. 'America First' was a direct rival of the White Committee, and drew its strongest support from the midwest, particularly around Chicago. This area had particularly large German populations, although opposition to entering the war did not just come from them or from the Italians, or from Britain's traditional opponents, the Irish. Among supporters of America First were many pacifists, those who did not believe the war was America's concern, and mothers who simply wanted to prevent their sons being sent as cannon-fodder to Europe. By December 1941 the organisation had 850,000 members. Its basic policy was to build up America's own defences and not to get entangled in Britain's war.

The figurehead of America First, always in demand at its rallies, was the aviator Charles Lindbergh, whom some suspected of fascist sympathies. Having toured German aircraft factories, he reported back to America the scale of German superiority to Britain in the air and warned about the folly of believing that Britain could win. Another supporter was the young Kingman Brewster, in later years to be President of Yale University and American Ambassador to Britain. He believes the movement reflected a broadly-based sentiment in the country. There were many who feared that total war could mean the destruction of American institutions, perhaps even democracy itself. In particular, America Firsters disputed the claim that Britain was the USA's front line. 'There was a feeling that Hitler could not invade us and we could not invade him. The Atlantic was just too big . . .' Looking back now Brewster concedes that for America to have followed the isolationists' cause 'would have been a disaster . . . But it wasn't because we thought Europe ought to go hang. It was because we didn't think America should hang in order to prevent that.'[28]

Roosevelt and those who believed America must do everything possible to help Britain had powerful allies among the American war correspondents stationed in London. During August and September the Battle of Britain was being fought out in the skies over southern England. Day after day the Luftwaffe came to attack Britain's airfields and bomb her cities, to meet with a daring and effective defence from

Britain's fighter squadrons. It was a dramatic battle for survival, watched and reported back each evening to America by radio.

Before the war began the Foreign Office had explored ways of persuading America to help Britain in the event of war. The British Embassy in Washington had advised that 'if America ever comes into an European war it will be some violent emotional impulse which will provide the last and decisive thrust. Nothing would be so effective as the bombing of London, translated by air to the homes of America.'[29] It was a shrewd prediction. The most distinguished of the American radio correspondents in London was Ed Murrow, CBS's bureau chief, who in the autumn of 1940 broadcast daily reports of the massive Luftwaffe onslaughts on the capital. 'The air raid is still on,' he whispered to American listeners on 11 September. 'I shall speak rather softly, because three or four people are sleeping on mattresses on the floor of this studio.'[30] On 24 September his quiet, tense voice was heard in America against the background sound of wailing air-raid sirens, the crump of bombs and the clatter of anti-aircraft fire. The impact on Americans living in safety 3,000 miles away was immeasurable. 'You burnt the city of London in our homes, and we felt the flames,' wrote the American poet Archibald MacLeish.[31]

By the autumn of 1940, with the presidential election only weeks away, the argument over America's response to the war was becoming bitter and sometimes violent. Fairbanks remembers abuse from the isolationist press, his films being banned or boycotted, his wife and children threatened with violence and kidnapping. He went to speak to a huge rally in Chicago. 'We were scared to death. My knees were cracking together like biscuits on the platform, but I got through it all right.'[32]

Roosevelt's opponent for the presidency was the Republican Wendell Willkie, a New York attorney and businessman with mid-western roots. Willkie sympathised with Britain and personally supported Roosevelt's policy of aid short of war, but as the campaign developed he began to slip behind in the polls and succumbed to pressure to attack Roosevelt on the war issue. He implied that the President had made secret commitments to the Allies and warned, 'if you re-elect him you may expect war in April 1941'. With two weeks of the campaign to go, Willkie was recovering and Roosevelt was forced to fight back. In Boston he gave an undertaking for which he was later much criticised: 'Your boys are not going to be sent into any foreign wars.' 'That hypocritical son of a bitch!' fumed Willkie. 'This is going to beat me!'[33] On 5 November 1940 Roosevelt was re-elected for a third term with 449 electoral votes to Willkie's eighty-two, a

Anti-intervention: McCutcheon reminds Americans of what happened the last time a US President campaigned on an anti-war platform (*Chicago Tribune*, 30 October 1940).

massive vote of confidence which gave the President more freedom of manoeuvre to conduct foreign policy.

The election over, Roosevelt went for a rest in the Caribbean. There, early in December 1940, he received a message from Churchill which was timed to catch him in a relaxed, responsive mood. Churchill later called this letter 'one of the most important I ever wrote'.[34] He followed the advice of the British Ambassador in Washington, Lord Lothian, by explaining Britain's predicament in detail. It was an alarming analysis. Britain urgently needed deliveries of munitions and aircraft. The worsening battle of the Atlantic was threatening to strangle her lifelines and starve her into surrender. Every ton of merchant shipping surplus to American requirements, Churchill argued, should be put at Britain's disposal, as should American naval escorts to accompany cargoes across the Atlantic. He also reminded the President that 'the moment approaches when we shall no longer be able to pay cash for shipping and other supplies'. The letter ended with a moving request that Roosevelt 'regard this letter not as an appeal for aid, but as a statement of the minimum action necessary to the achievement of our common purpose'.[35]

Roosevelt's reaction, unlike his response to the request for fifty destroyers earlier in the year, was swift and imaginative. On his return from his Caribbean holiday he gave a press conference in which he warned of Britain's imminent dollar crisis. 'The best immediate defense of the United States is the success of Great Britain in defending itself,' he insisted, and put forward a proposal not, as in World War One, for financial loans to be repaid after the war, but for America to lend Britain the goods she needed, leaving repayment or the return of the goods to be arranged later.

Roosevelt described his plan in terms which everyone could understand. 'Suppose my neighbor's home catches fire, and I have a length of garden hose four or five hundred feet away . . . Now what do I do? I don't say to him . . . "Neighbor, my garden hose cost me fifteen dollars; you have to pay me fifteen dollars for it." . . . I don't want fifteen dollars – I want my garden hose back after the fire is over.' And, added Roosevelt, if 'it gets smashed up – holes in it – during the fire, then the neighbor says, "All right, I will replace it."'[36]

On 10 January 1941 the Lend-Lease Bill was introduced into Congress and ran the gauntlet of committee hearings by both houses, at which members of the Administration and other witnesses were cross-examined in open session and with maximum publicity. The hearings provided a new forum for the debate about America's proper relationship with Britain.

Opponents of the scheme, the anti-interventionists like Congressman Hamilton Fish and Charles Lindbergh, concentrated their attack on two points: that the bill would give the President far too much power, making him a virtual dictator, and that it would suck America into the war. The counter argument, put by Senator Claude Pepper and others, was that the proponents of Lend-Lease were the true America Firsters, since helping Britain was the only realistic way of defending America. The bill itself was shrewdly entitled 'An Act to Promote the Defense of the United States'.

The debate was acrimonious. Pepper had long supported more help for the Allies and had spoken on the subject all over the country. For his pains he was hanged in effigy outside the Senate by a group of women protesting that he was trying to murder their sons. 'I was trying to explain to everyone that this was the only way we could stay out of the war. We could not afford to let Hitler become master of Europe and then maybe master of a large part of the world. We would have to fight him all over the world by ourselves.'[37]

The debate was not simply about the best means of defending America. It also reflected the deep-rooted American suspicions about Britain. The bill's opponents claimed that America was once more being taken for a ride by Britain, that cunning John Bull was inveigling a generous Uncle Sam into paying for a war that was not yet beyond his means. Many Americans found it hard to believe that Britain was short of cash when, as they saw it, she still owned a vast empire.

Roosevelt expected Churchill to make some gestures to help him with these political problems. These included releasing gold held in South Africa and selling one of Britain's major companies in the United States, American Viscose, the highly successful subsidiary of the textile giant Courtaulds. An American destroyer was sent to Cape Town to collect $50 million of gold, and American Viscose was compulsorily sold, only to be resold immediately at a much higher price by the consortium of American bankers who bought it – a profit which did not come back to Britain.

'Certain things were done,' Churchill wrote after the war, 'which seemed harsh and painful to us.'[38] At the time he drafted a telegram of complaint to Roosevelt. 'It is not fitting that any nation should put itself wholly in the hands of another, least of all a nation which is fighting under increasingly severe conditions for what is proclaimed to be a cause of general concern.'[39] But Churchill controlled his anger and the message was never sent. As with the Destroyers Deal, Britain was in no position to dictate the terms of American help.

It took Roosevelt two months to push Lend-Lease through Congress. On 11 March 1941 after votes which split on party lines – Democrats mainly for, Republicans mainly against – the bill was signed into law. The businessman Averell Harriman was despatched across the Atlantic to run the London end of Lend-Lease. His instructions from Roosevelt were blunt: 'Recommend everything that we can do, short of war, to keep the British Isles afloat.'[40]

Churchill later described Lend-Lease as 'the most unsordid act in history of any nation'.[41] It came as essential relief to a hard-pressed government and, compared with the arrangements for lending funds in World War One, it was as a generous and far-sighted gesture. Roosevelt was determined to avoid another disastrous row over war debts. Lend-Lease was not, however, pure altruism. Supporting Britain was seen as a way of defending America by keeping it out of the war. Claude Pepper admits that he saw Britain as 'a sort of mercenary' doing America's fighting for her.[42] Nor was Lend-Lease a gift. The terms had not been agreed, but repayment in some form was expected.

Churchill's overriding aim was still to persuade America to join forces with Britain. In 1917 President Wilson had finally declared war against Germany because of attacks on American shipping in the North Atlantic. In 1941 it seemed possible that this would happen again. German sinkings of merchant ships had reached new heights: 530,000 tons in March, 668,000 tons in April. At this rate, even allowing for new construction, Britain would have lost a quarter of her merchant fleet in a single year. Roosevelt issued secret orders that the American navy should be ready to escort Allied convoys across the North Atlantic from April, but at the last moment drew back in response to a renewed America First campaign against 'convoying'. Instead, to Churchill's dismay, he moved cautiously, extending US patrols to mid-Atlantic at the end of April, and in July taking over the garrisoning of Iceland from Britain.

The weary Prime Minister needed more than this. His government was demoralised by setbacks in Greece and North Africa. There were fears that once Hitler had achieved total dominance in the eastern Mediterranean he would turn once again to the invasion of Britain. For the first time since the desperate days of June 1940 Churchill now pleaded with Roosevelt to enter the war. On 4 May he cabled: 'Mr President, I am sure you will not misunderstand me if I speak to you exactly what is in my mind. The one decisive counterweight I can see . . . would be if the United States were immediately to range herself with us as a belligerent power . . . In this war every post is a winning post and how many more are we going to lose?'[43] In Washington many of Roosevelt's advisers agreed with Churchill's analysis but the President baulked at leading his people into war, convinced that it would only be possible when Hitler affronted American interests or honour in such a way that national unity would be guaranteed.

The two leaders had now been corresponding as heads of governments for over a year, but they had not yet met, except briefly in 1918. In the summer of 1941, however, the moment was opportune. Hitler's surprise attack on Russia in June 1941 and Russia's stout defence meant that the main thrust of the war was for the moment being pursued on the eastern European front, giving Churchill a breathing space. He took advantage of it by accepting Roosevelt's invitation to a full-scale conference, held in Placentia Bay, Newfoundland, in August. Churchill arrived aboard the battleship HMS *Prince of Wales*. He had rested on the voyage, taking exercise, striding the decks, and watching films in the wardroom at night. He was in high spirits, hopeful, like many in London, that Roosevelt now meant to call for a declaration of war. 'I do not think,' he had told the Queen before his departure, 'that our friend would have asked me to go so far for what must be a meeting of world-wide importance, unless he had in mind some further forward step.'[44]

The four-day meeting confirmed the friendship between the two leaders and created new links among their advisers. The emotional bonds between the two countries were symbolised by a service on the quarterdeck of the *Prince of Wales*. Churchill himself chose the hymns: 'For those in Peril on the Sea', 'Onward Christian Soldiers' and 'Oh God, Our Help in Ages Past'. The Union Jack and the Stars and Stripes were draped on the pulpit and the senior staffs of both governments, with the crews of the American and British ships, shared hymn-books and sang together. It was an inspiring occasion for all who took part.

The substance of the meetings was perhaps less to Churchill's taste, though he put on a bold front. Roosevelt resisted Churchill's call for a declaration of war. Instead he proposed a statement of joint war aims, which, while they confirmed America's determination to see Hitler defeated, exacted a price from Britain in the form of pledges that could imperil the continuance of her empire after the war.

It was not just opponents of Lend-Lease who suspected Britain's long-term motives. Elliott Roosevelt, the President's son, who was present at the conference, remembers his father also having doubts about Churchill. 'He felt that in the period following the war . . . Churchill believed that Great Britain would have a bigger Empire and greater influence, that he would take advantage of the help given by America, and that we would still be in a secondary role.'[45]

It was the same fear that Woodrow Wilson had expressed on America's entry into World War One. Wilson had put forward his Fourteen Points to establish that America's aims were not the same as the Allies'. Roosevelt used the Atlantic Charter, the agreement signed at the end of the Placentia Bay Conference, to try to bind Britain and America in common war aims that would satisfy the American people and embody America's distinctive vision of the post-war world.

Clause three of the charter stated that both countries 'respect the right of all peoples to choose the form of government under which they will live; and they wish to see sovereign rights and self-government restored to those who have been forcibly deprived of them'. Although these words were mainly aimed at the subject peoples of Hitler's Europe, they were soon seized on by politicians in Britain's empire and by American anti-colonialists to justify demands for independence. Clause four of the charter was also significant. It pledged both governments 'to further the enjoyment of all States, great or small, victor or vanquished, of access, on equal terms, to the trade and to the raw materials of the world'. This latest American attempt to break down Britain's Imperial Preference system was weakened by the saving condition, inserted at British insistence, of 'due respect for their existing obligations'.[46] Nevertheless, the Atlantic Charter served as a warning that the United States would use its leverage to try to force Britain to adopt policies in keeping with its own plans for the post-war world.

What mattered to Churchill though, in the heat of war, was not the future import of clauses three or four, but how to identify America firmly with Britain's cause. From that perspective the joint statement of war aims was invaluable. And although he failed to secure the American declaration of war he had hoped for, Churchill did obtain further promises of American naval help in the North Atlantic. The President had promised, he told the Cabinet on his return, to 'become more and more provocative' in the Atlantic. 'Everything was to be done to force an "incident" . . . which would justify him in opening hostilities.'[47]

On 4 September such an incident occurred. A U-boat attacked the US destroyer *Greer*, and Roosevelt used the opportunity to announce a state of virtual, though still undeclared, naval war. American warships now began escorting British and Canadian convoys, laden with vital military supplies and food, through 'American defensive waters', which were defined as longitude ten degrees west, or roughly three-quarters of the way across the Atlantic. The relief for Britain was immense. German vessels were warned that they would enter the area at their peril. In November these 'shoot on sight' orders were strengthened by the repeal of further sections of the Neutrality Act. Roosevelt could now arm American merchant ships and send them direct to Britain. He could also use the US navy to escort convoys all the way to British ports. But he did not rush to do so, aware of the strength of anti-war feeling in the country and in Congress. According to a Gallup poll on 22 October, for instance, only seventeen per cent of the American people favoured a declaration of war on Germany.[48]

The incident Roosevelt was waiting for, the affront which would unite the people behind him, was finally delivered not by Germany but by Japan. Germany's surprise attack on Russia removed Japanese fears that Stalin would be able to resist their expansion in Asia. Britain was unable to spare forces for Singapore and Malaya or ships to patrol the China Seas. Only the Americans with their main fleet at Pearl Harbor, Hawaii, offered any deterrent.

In July 1941 Japan overran the remainder of Indo-China. The Americans reacted by imposing an oil embargo and strengthening their forces in the Philippines. By December it was expected that Japan would mount an attack on British and Dutch possessions in south-east Asia. But the attack on Pearl Harbor took everyone by surprise. On the morning of Sunday 7 December Japanese planes bombed the American base, sinking or immobilising eight American battleships and leaving 2,400 dead. It was the most humiliating military disaster in American history.

The shock was palpable. An English visitor arrived by train in Chicago later the same day. 'We got out at the Union Terminal . . . a huge concourse of glass and iron and steel, silent as the grave, silent as a cathedral in the middle of the night, everybody not speaking, silent. Even the people sitting at the eating places, the restaurants, not speaking to each other and looking into the dim distance, absolutely stunned. It was like visiting a drugged nation.'[49]

At first some members of America First thought the news was a hoax, or some clever trick of Roosevelt's. But when the appalling truth dawned they abandoned their campaign and joined forces behind the President. On the eve of Pearl Harbor the Chairman of the New York chapter of America First had sent a long critical letter to Roosevelt. The Monday following the attack he wrote again: 'Please consider the contents of our letter, dated December 6, 1941, null and void.'[50]

America declared war on Japan, and Hitler, in turn, declared war on America. Roosevelt cabled Churchill, 'Today all of us are in the same boat with you and the people of the Empire, and it is a ship which will not and can not be sunk.'[51] The Prime Minister was jubilant. After nineteen months of lonely leadership Britain was now assured of survival and victory. On the night of Pearl Harbor, he recalled later, 'I went to bed and slept the sleep of the saved and thankful.'[52]

8

Mixed Up Together

1941–5

The day after America's entry into the war one of the British Chiefs of Staff questioned the forthright language being used in a request to the United States and urged that a more deferential tone be adopted. Winston Churchill replied with a wicked leer: 'Oh! that is the way we talked to her while we were wooing her; now that she is in the harem, we talk to her quite differently.'[1]

Churchill's first reaction to Pearl Harbor was relief that he now had a powerful ally on Britain's side. His next thought was to go immediately to Washington. He was worried lest America, in its fury with Japan, abandon the priority confirmed at the Atlantic Conference in 1941, of defeating Germany first. The attack on Pearl Harbor was only the prelude to successful Japanese assaults on the Philippines, Malaya, Singapore, Burma and the Dutch East Indies – victories that tipped the balance of power in the Pacific as profoundly as Hitler's Blitzkrieg had done in Europe in 1940. Powerful voices, particularly in the American navy, urged Roosevelt to concentrate on the Pacific and leave the Atlantic to Britain. Throughout the war these tensions persisted. Even today the British instinctively think of World War Two as primarily a European war, with the Pacific as a sideshow, while the Americans give more weight to MacArthur's and Nimitz's battles against the Japanese. The Russians, for their part, single out their defeat of Hitler on the Eastern Front as the event that won the war.

Churchill arrived in Washington in time for Christmas 1941, appearing with Roosevelt on the steps of the White House to turn on the Christmas lights. He stayed there for three weeks, often closeted with Roosevelt for hours on end, and his capacity for drinking and talking into the early hours of the morning worried Eleanor Roosevelt, who feared her husband would be exhausted. Although the two leaders had engaged in an intense correspondence, their wartime meetings had so far consisted only of the four days aboard ship in Placentia Bay which had led to the Atlantic Charter. At 'Arcadia', the code-name given to this second wartime meeting, acquaintance ripened into genuine friendship. Harry Hopkins, Roosevelt's special adviser, liked to tell of Roosevelt being wheeled one day into his guest's room only to find the Prime Minister emerging wet, glowing and completely naked from the bath. Apologising, Roosevelt began to withdraw, but Churchill beckoned him back. 'The Prime Minister of Great Britain,' he announced, 'has nothing to conceal from the President of the United States.'[2]

During 1942 the Churchill–Roosevelt 'special relationship' was at its closest. 'Trust me to the bitter end,'[3] were Roosevelt's parting words at the end of Arcadia, and, after he had received cordial birthday greetings from the Prime Minister in late January, he cabled back: 'It is fun to be in the same decade with you.'[4] Warm, private messages like this mingle with weighty strategic memoranda and quick-fire diplomatic salvos in their remarkable correspondence. Churchill recalled later in his memoirs: 'My relations with the President gradually became so close that the chief business between our two countries was virtually conducted by these personal exchanges between him and me.'[5] He told Foreign Secretary Anthony Eden in November 1942: 'My whole system is based upon partnership with Roosevelt.'[6]

The intimacy of the two leaders was reinforced by other friendships. Harry Hopkins, nicknamed 'Lord Root of the Matter' by Churchill, and Averell Harriman, both trusted Roosevelt advisers, had already earned British confidence and served as mediators between the two governments. In Washington General George C. Marshall, the US army Chief of Staff, was a close friend of Field-Marshal Sir John Dill, head of the British Joint Staff Mission. Their mutual trust helped resolve numerous disputes between the two governments over strategy. When Dill died in November 1944 Marshall wrote to his widow: 'officially the United States has suffered a heavy loss, and I personally have lost a dear friend, unique in my lifetime, and never to be out of my mind'.[7]

At all levels of the British and US bureaucracies personal contact made Anglo-American co-operation easier. In 1939 the British Embassy in Washington had fewer than twenty diplomats. During the war the official British presence in Washington swelled to a peak of 9,000, as almost every ministry from Whitehall established its own staff in the city. The same happened in London, with the old US

Embassy at 1 Grosvenor Square soon proving inadequate and the Americans taking over much of Mayfair, including part of the famous Oxford Street department store, Selfridge's.

In World War One America had refused to merge its war effort with Britain and France, jealously preserving its independence as an 'associate' power. But at the Arcadia Conference Marshall, who had witnessed the earlier squabbles at first hand as a member of Pershing's staff, successfully pressed for an unprecedented unified command. In each theatre of operations there was to be a single commander for all British and American forces – air, sea and ground. Thus General Alexander, a Briton, was later to command in Italy and General Eisenhower, an American, in France. At the top the Combined Chiefs of Staff would resolve problems of strategy and logistics under the direction of President and Prime Minister.

Other combined bodies were created to handle the assignment of munitions, shipping, raw materials, food and production. A full exchange of intelligence information was also agreed, ranging from evidence about the Axis troop movements to information on the enemy's economy and morale. Back in August 1940 Churchill had predicted with cautious understatement that Britain and America would become 'somewhat mixed up together in some of their affairs for mutual and general advantage'.[8] What ensued far exceeded even his most optimistic expectations. The alliance of World War Two was a far cry from the arm's-length 'association' of 1917–18, let alone the aloof suspicion of the 1930s. As Marshall said later, it was 'the most complete unification of military effort ever achieved by two Allied nations'.[9]

Churchill returned to Britain in January 1942 well pleased with his achievements at Arcadia. The conference re-affirmed that, 'notwithstanding the entry of Japan into the War, our view remains that Germany is still the prime enemy and her defeat is the key to victory. Once Germany is defeated, the collapse of Italy and the defeat of Japan must follow.'[10] A decision on where to commit American troops to battle had not yet been taken but Roosevelt, to stress his commitment, despatched the first GIs to the British Isles within weeks. Churchill told the King on his return from Washington that, after months of 'walking out' together, Britain and America were now 'married'.[11]

But the new warmth of the relationship could not disguise basic differences of interest. Throughout the war there was a fundamental disagreement between Britain and America over the best strategy for defeating Hitler. To the Americans, and to Stalin, Churchill seemed

To avoid breaching America's Neutrality Act, US-made bombers are dragged across the Canadian border by horse, *en route* to Britain (winter 1939-40).

King George VI inspects one of the Hudson aircraft built by Lockheed for the RAF.

American, British and Canadian radio commentators plan a joint outside broadcast *'Round London After Dark'* during the blitz (August 1940). Ed Murrow is to the left of the lamp.

unduly cautious about getting back on to the continent of Europe. They were suspicious of his motives, believing his aim was not simply to beat Hitler, but to do so in a manner that allowed the British Empire to remain intact, with Britain still controlling the main sea routes and the world's resources.

The American Joint Chiefs of Staff were impatient for a cross-Channel invasion at the first opportunity. In April 1942 General Marshall arrived in London secretly with their plans. They envisaged a massive build-up of Allied troops in Britain, including an American army of one million by April 1943, backed by airfields, supply depots and other support facilities. The aim was a full-scale Anglo-American invasion of France the following summer (code-named 'Round-Up'). Marshall also wanted cross-Channel raids throughout 1942 and entertained the possibility of an emergency invasion that year ('Sledgehammer'), if either Russia or Germany seemed on the verge of collapse. The Americans insisted that this was the crucial theatre in Europe. 'In no other area can we attain the overwhelming air superiority vital to successful land attack; while here and here only can the bulk of the British air and ground forces be employed. In this area the United States can concentrate and maintain a larger force than it can in any other.' Marshall's message was clear: 'Through France passes our shortest route to the heart of Germany.'[12]

Churchill and the British Chiefs of Staff pored over Marshall's plans. Sir Alan Brooke, Chief of the Imperial General Staff, told the Americans 'that we were all completely in agreement as regards 1943 but if we were forced this year to undertake an operation on the Continent it could only be on a small scale'.[13] The United States had virtually no battle-ready troops and British forces, who would therefore have to bear the brunt of any fighting, were already tied down in North Africa and the Far East. Privately Brooke, a veteran of Dunkirk, was even more sceptical about Marshall's 'castles in the air'.[14] The Americans seemed to have little idea of the immense logistical problems of the build-up or the difficulties of any break-out from the beachhead.

Brooke none the less agreed with Churchill that they could not afford an outright row with the Americans at such a desperate moment in the war. In a personal letter Roosevelt had made clear to the Prime Minister that Marshall's plan 'has my heart and *mind* in it'. Brooke's doubts were therefore swept under the carpet and Churchill cabled the President: 'I am in entire agreement in principle with all you propose, and so are the Chiefs of Staff.'[15] But General Marshall was not deceived. In the flying boat on the way back to Washington he turned to his senior army planner, Colonel Albert Wedemeyer, and said, 'I think the British have bought your plan, but I think they did so with their tongues in their cheek.'[16]

By June 1942, confirming Marshall's suspicions, Churchill was back in Washington persuading Roosevelt that no cross-Channel assault could be mounted that year. The British Chiefs of Staff had now studied the implications and 'unanimously agreed that operation "Sledgehammer" offered no hope of success and would merely ruin all prospects of "Round-Up" in 1943'.[17] But Roosevelt, like Churchill, felt it essential to open a second front somewhere in Europe during 1942. He had promised as much to the hard-pressed Russians and he was also concerned that, without action across the Atlantic, the American public would demand an all-out effort in the Pacific. Opinion polls indicated that most Americans wanted revenge on Japan for Pearl Harbor but up to thirty per cent favoured a compromise peace with Germany. 'I can see why we are fighting the Japanese,' commented one respondent to a Gallup poll, 'but I can't see why we are fighting the Germans.'[18]

Determined to give Americans the will to fight in Europe, Roosevelt went along with Churchill's plan for an invasion of Algeria and Tunisia (operation 'Torch'). British troops had their backs to the wall in Egypt; this would relieve the pressure and give the Allies their first taste of victory. General Marshall was appalled. He was sure that if the Allies diverted their resources to the Mediterranean it would make it impossible to invade France in 1943. But Roosevelt overruled his own Joint Chiefs of Staff. Torch would be mounted that autumn. Bitterly Wedemeyer told Marshall that British plans 'have been designed to maintain the integrity of the British Empire' and would lead to the Allies' total defeat in Europe and Asia.[19] General Dwight D. Eisenhower, recently arrived in England to prepare for the invasion of France, predicted that it could well be the 'blackest day in history'.[20]

A fundamental divide in strategy was now opening up between the two allies. Churchill, prompted by Brooke, inclined towards a step-by-step approach to defeating Germany. After victory in North Africa, the Allies should strike at Italy, the 'soft underbelly' of the Axis. This would weaken Hitler and make him vulnerable to a subsequent invasion of France, mounted only when the chances of success were high. The Pentagon became convinced that Churchill's principal purpose was to keep the Suez Canal secure for Britain and maintain her traditional influence in the Middle East. The US Secretary of War, Henry Stimson, agreed: 'The British . . . are

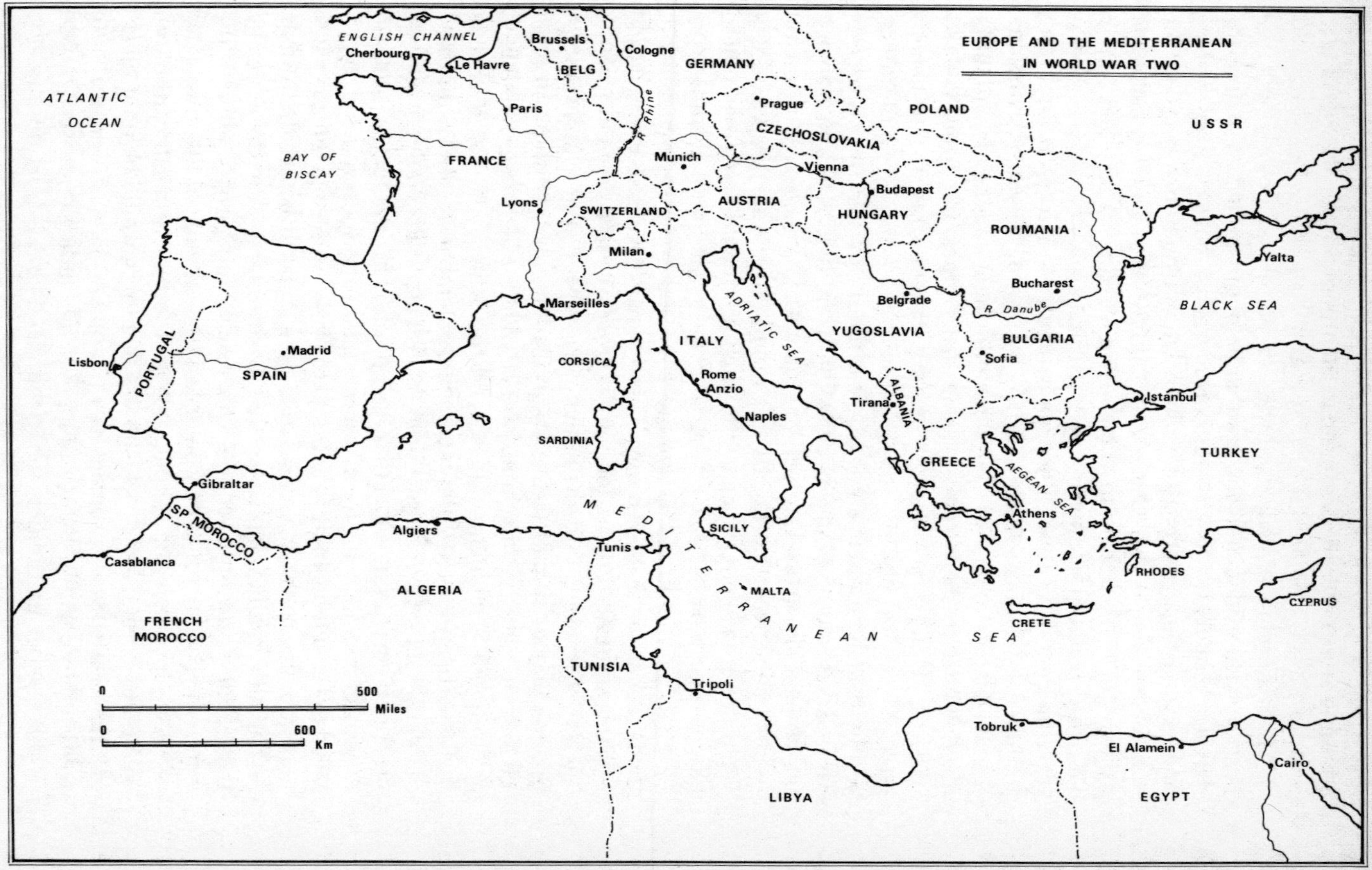
EUROPE AND THE MEDITERRANEAN
IN WORLD WAR TWO
ATLANTIC OCEAN
ENGLISH CHANNEL
Cherbourg
Le Havre
Brussels
BELG
Cologne
GERMANY
Paris
R Rhine
Prague
POLAND
USSR
CZECHOSLOVAKIA
BAY OF BISCAY
FRANCE
Munich
Vienna
Budapest
Lyons
SWITZERLAND
AUSTRIA
HUNGARY
ROUMANIA
Milan
Yalta
Bucharest
Belgrade
R Danube
BLACK SEA
Marseilles
ADRIATIC SEA
YUGOSLAVIA
BULGARIA
Madrid
ITALY
Sofia
Lisbon
PORTUGAL
SPAIN
CORSICA
Rome
Anzio
Istanbul
Tirana
ALBANIA
Naples
SARDINIA
TURKEY
GREECE
AEGEAN SEA
Gibraltar
Athens
MEDITERRANEAN SEA
SP MOROCCO
Algiers
SICILY
Tunis
Casablanca
RHODES
ALGERIA
MALTA
CYPRUS
CRETE
FRENCH MOROCCO
TUNISIA
0 500 Miles
Tripoli
0 600 Km
Tobruk
El Alamein
Cairo
LIBYA
EGYPT

straining every nerve to lay a foundation throughout the Mediterranean area for their own empire once the war is over.'[21]

That Churchill was obsessed with the empire is beyond doubt, but there is scant evidence to suggest that he put its protection before the defeat of Hitler. It was a major consideration, but not an overriding one. The British were also influenced by their memories of the slaughter in World War One, of the Somme and Passchendaele, and by two years of defeats in the present conflict. They knew, from Dunkirk, the peril of an army perched precariously with one foot on the continent of Europe. They knew that the English Channel, with its fierce tides and sudden storms, could not be treated with the disdain that its mere twenty-mile width might suggest. It had, after all, defended Britain from invasion many times and would as dispassionately act as a protector of the German army on the French coast.

The British preference was to 'close the ring' on Germany, picking off its allies and bombing its cities into ruin, before the final assault on Hitler's 'Fortress Europe' was mounted. Many in Washington became convinced that the British would only invade the Continent when there was no resistance left, when they could march in 'behind a Scotch bagpipe band', as Admiral Ernest King put it scathingly.[22]

What also irked the Pentagon in 1942 and 1943 was the ability of the British to get their own way. This was partly because Britain could call the strategic tune as long as its forces were doing most of the fighting in Europe. But the Americans were also at a disadvantage because of poor administrative co-ordination. The British by now had a tightly-run strategic machine. Brooke and his colleagues often fumed at Churchill's 'midnight follies', and the army, navy and RAF had their own deep-rooted differences, but agreement was always thrashed out in committee meetings and the British arrived at conferences with the Americans having concerted their position in advance. By contrast, American methods in 1942 were haphazard. Roosevelt frequently failed to consult his Joint Chiefs and the latter were sometimes unable to resolve their own differences and argued openly before the British.

The most vivid example was the Pacific strategy. Admiral King and the US navy saw little scope for themselves in Europe, whereas the war in the Pacific would be won or lost by command of the seas. They pressed repeatedly for supplies to be diverted to that theatre, and, when the decision for Torch showed that there would be no invasion of France in 1942 or probably 1943, a bitter Marshall was unable to resist their demands. Planes, shipping and landing craft were moved to the Pacific. In London Churchill was peeved. 'Just because the

Americans can't have a massacre in France this year, they want to sulk and bathe in the Pacific,' he complained privately.[23] But, having had his own way over the Mediterranean, he was in no position to resist.

By January 1943, when Churchill, Roosevelt and their staffs met at Casablanca, they had to face the full implications of their previous strategic decisions. Fighting a truly world war, against Germany, Italy and Japan, with major fronts already operating in the Pacific and the Mediterranean, they simply did not have enough men, supplies and above all ships to open up a new front across the English Channel. In the circumstances the Americans had little alternative but to accept British strategy to capitalise on their victories in North Africa and use them as a springboard into Sicily and then Italy.

Even so, the conduct of the negotiations at Casablanca further confirmed Britain's reputation for cunning. With Marshall and King now openly at odds over the 'Germany First' strategy, Roosevelt warned that the British would come with a plan and stick to it. He was right. Once again the Americans arrived with divided counsel, and paid dearly for it. They were outnumbered and outmanoeuvred. Wedemeyer, assisting Marshall with the presentation of the American proposals, found the British armed with a host of statistics and logistical projections to show that the American invasion plans would fail. 'The British descended on me like locusts,' Wedemeyer cabled back to Washington, and at the end of the conference, admitting defeat, he summed up: 'We came, we saw, we were conquered.'[24]

The plans for an invasion of northern Europe were shelved for another year, to the relief of Churchill's staff. 'I said at the end of the Casablanca Conference,' recalls Sir Ian Jacob, Military Assistant Secretary to the British War Cabinet, 'that if I had written the report I had wanted beforehand, it would have been the one I wrote at the end.'[25]

On his way to Casablanca President Roosevelt's plane had to re-fuel in the Gambia, a British colony on the west coast of Africa. Driving through the streets the President was appalled at what he saw. 'The natives were just getting to work. In rags . . . glum-looking.' He was told that the prevailing wage was the equivalent of fifty cents a day, plus half a cup of rice. He asked about the average life expectancy and was told twenty-six years. 'Those people are treated worse than the live-stock,' he exploded to his son. 'Their cattle live longer.'[26] It was said by the British at the conference that this visit confirmed his worst suspicions. Here was clear evidence of a poor country sucked dry by colonialism. The President wanted the British, French and

Dutch to hold their empires as 'trusteeships' of the United Nations and to set firm timetables for independence.

Many Americans shared his deep hostility to European imperialism. That, after all, was part of their heritage, dating back to 1776. *Life* magazine, one of America's most widely-read weeklies, published an 'Open Letter' addressed to 'the People of England' in October 1942. Americans might disagree amongst themselves on war aims, it said, but 'one thing we are sure we are *not* fighting for is to hold the British Empire together. We don't like to put the matter so bluntly, but we don't want you to have any illusions. If your strategists are planning a war to hold the British Empire together they will sooner or later find themselves strategizing all alone.'[27] Churchill's reply a month later was equally frank: 'We mean to hold our own. I have not become the King's First Minister in order to preside over the liquidation of the British Empire.'[28]

These disagreements had come to a head over India, the largest part of Britain's empire and by 1942 the last bastion against Japanese expansion westwards. By March the whole of south-east Asia, including the British colonies of Malaya, Singapore and Hong Kong and the American-dominated Philippines had fallen to Japan. Australia and India were now the Allied front line in the Pacific War and the Roosevelt Administration was concerned that Britain's repressive behaviour in India would undermine the Indian war effort.

In 1939 the British Viceroy had declared war on India's behalf, and put almost two million of her men under arms, without consulting India's political leaders. It led to a campaign of civil disobedience which disrupted the war effort. Roosevelt urged Churchill to announce that India would be given independence and to set up an interim government. 'Why should India defend a freedom she hasn't got?' asked one State Department official.[29] Many of the British Cabinet agreed that concessions were essential. Reluctantly, Churchill sent a Labour member of his government, Sir Stafford Cripps, to negotiate with the leaders of the Indian Congress Party about independence within the British Commonwealth once the war was over. To Churchill's intense irritation Roosevelt despatched an American envoy, Louis Johnson, to use his good offices.

Cripps's mission was not successful. Gandhi, for Congress, believed too little was being offered too late, and objected to the proposal to allow Muslims a state of their own. The talks broke down. Roosevelt was not satisfied and urged Churchill to re-open negotiations, arguing that American public opinion would blame Britain for their failure. Churchill usually did his best to fall in with Roosevelt's wishes,

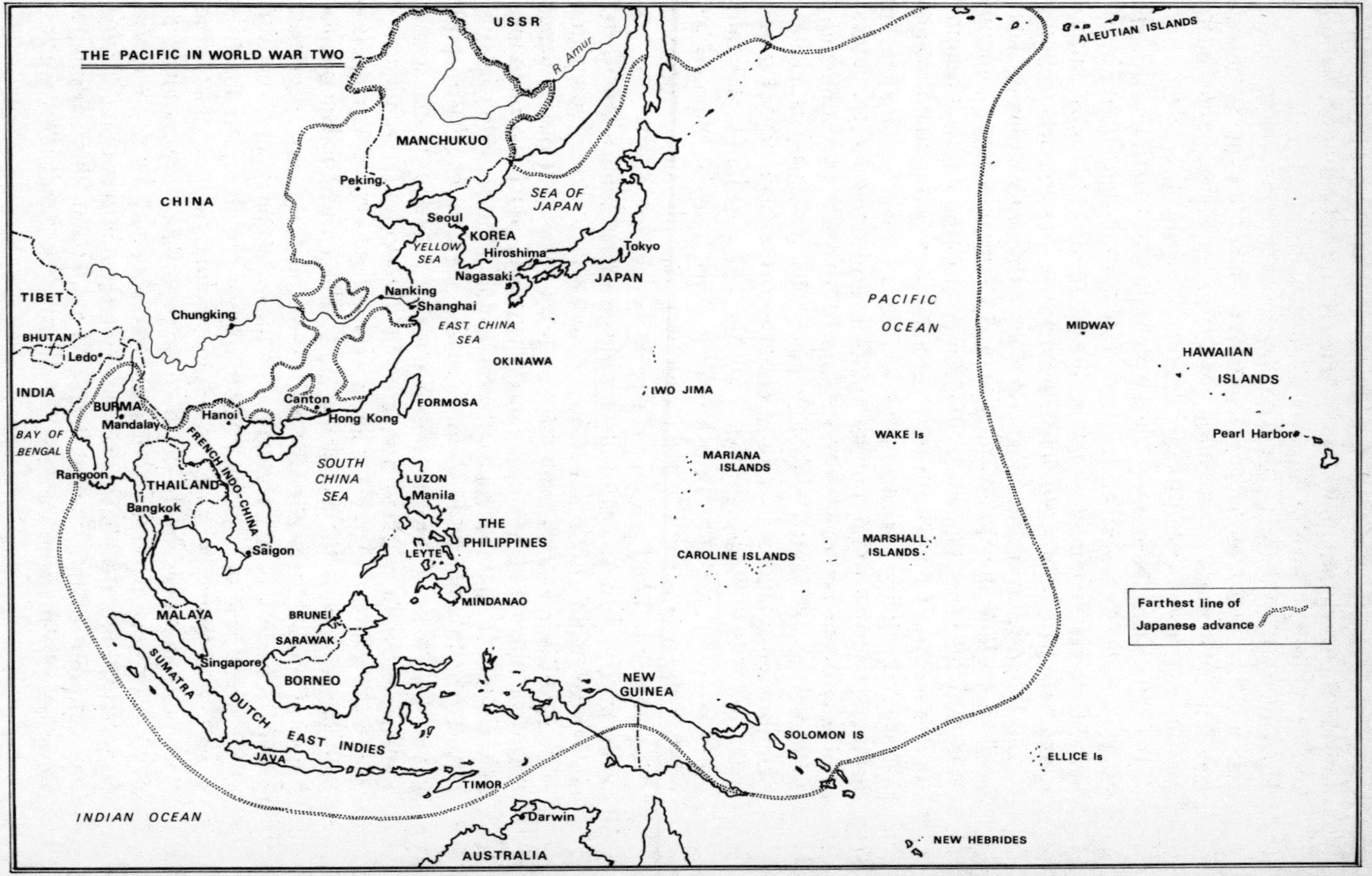

THE PACIFIC IN WORLD WAR TWO

considering co-operation with the United States to be the cornerstone of British policy. But the empire was not negotiable. He told Harry Hopkins, then in London, that if Roosevelt pushed the issue he would resign. According to Hopkins's vivid account, 'the string of cuss words lasted for two hours in the middle of the night'.[30] Roosevelt got the message. He never urged Indian independence again.

But the debate about imperialism would not go away. It particularly bedevilled the Anglo-American war effort in south-east Asia. Divergent strategies stemmed from divergent interests. In 1943 Britain wanted to drive south through Burma to recover her lost colonial territories in Malaya and Singapore. The Americans wanted to go north-east along the 'Ledo Road' to assist China, whom they were trying to cultivate as a new ally. The American deputy commander of south-east Asia Command (SEAC), General 'Vinegar Joe' Stilwell, was scathing about his British superior, Lord Louis Mountbatten. In his diaries he referred to him as 'childish Louis', the 'Glamour Boy' who was intent on 'playing the "Empah" Game'. The Americans soon nicknamed SEAC 'Save England's Asiatic Colonies', and the deteriorating relationship was summed up in a ditty: 'The Limeys make the policy, Yank fights the Jap, And one gets its Empire, and one takes the rap.'[31] The British were furious. They were providing most of the troops in SEAC and there was particular resentment in 1944 when the Allied victories in Burma were represented by the US media as almost an American show, with barely a reference to General Sir William Slim's 'forgotten' Fourteenth Army.

In these disputes it was easy for America to pose as the disinterested idealist. Unlike Britain, still nominally ruling nearly a quarter of the globe, the USA had few colonies, and its major one, the Philippines, was slated for independence once the war had ended. But anti-imperialism was also a matter of self-interest. American businessmen wanted access to markets protected by Imperial Preference. The American military cast covetous eyes on Japanese islands in the mid-Pacific, such as the Marshalls and Carolines, which they wanted for naval and air bases after the war. And Roosevelt's insistence that Chiang Kai-shek's corrupt regime in China must be regarded as one of the great powers, a claim regarded by Churchill as 'an absolute farce',[32] was largely intended to ensure support for US aims in the wartime conferences. In short, American professions of pure idealism were disingenuous. General Eisenhower summed up the position fairly: 'Britishers instinctively approach every military problem from the viewpoint of the Empire, just as we approach them from the viewpoint of American interests.'[33]

It was therefore with some satisfaction that the British were able to take America to task for its treatment of blacks in the United States. The American army was still segregated during World War Two, with the black regiments doing the more menial tasks such as cooking and truck driving rather than fighting in the front line. In deference to black pressure groups, however, the Pentagon agreed that some black troops would be sent overseas, and by D-Day over 100,000 were in Britain. In general, they were given a good reception by the British public, many of whom had never seen a non-white before. Black GIs were liked for their humour and courtesy (which often compared favourably with the brashness of white GIs), and their musical skill, especially in choirs and jazz bands, was much in demand. Joseph Curtis, a black schoolteacher from Washington, DC, was pleasantly surprised to discover that the English were not the 'stiff-necked racists' he had expected. While in Cornwall in 1944 he became close friends with the Barnes family of Chacewater, considering 'Mom' and 'Pop' Barnes his second parents. He recalls with pleasure the little birthday cake they baked for him from their meagre rations, covered in icing made without sugar.[34]

Unlike the American Deep South, where many of the blacks lived, Britain was not a segregated country. Blacks could enter pubs, shops, dance halls and other public facilities. But the US army authorities in Britain were sure that this would lead to trouble. White GIs were used to travelling, drinking and dating girls without coming into contact with blacks. The army therefore practised its own form of discreet segregation by giving black and white units leave-passes on different days of the week. Towns near American bases were 'black' one night and 'white' the next, and American military police (generally white) were heavy-handed with troublemakers.

Officially the British Government turned a blind eye to these practices. If the US army wanted to adopt them, British policemen were told, that was its own concern. But, behind the scenes, the British authorities went further. Despite the welcome shown by many Britons to the black GIs, the British attitude was often patronising, and contact between the blacks and white women was frowned upon. The British War Office went so far as to propose a special campaign among British troops to 'educate them to adopt towards the U.S.A. coloured troops the attitude of the U.S.A. Army authorities'.[35] The Colonial Office warned that this would cause uproar in the British Empire, and the War Office moderated its line. After debate, the Cabinet agreed in the autumn of 1942 that British troops should only be told to 'respect' the white American attitude and to avoid arguments about race relations. But some specific guidelines were laid down: 'For a white woman to go about in the company of a Negro American is likely to lead to controversy and ill-feeling,' and, while it was acceptable to offer 'friendly hospitality' to the GIs, 'care should be taken not to invite white and coloured American troops at the same time'.[36]

In general, trouble was confined to fights between black and white GIs, which the British, if they were wise, avoided. John Wilson, an English air-crew man, was travelling by train from Cardiff to York. 'The train was crowded but there was room next to me for another one. There was a coloured soldier outside [in the corridor]. I opened the door and said "Hey Jack, there's a seat here." The others in the compartment, except two of us, were all American soldiers. As soon as this coloured man sat down this other big chap got up and said "Get out you goddam nigger." I told him to belt up, and he came for me. My teeth were knocked right through my tongue.'[37]

The high commands on both sides of the Atlantic were keen to foster a good relationship between the GIs and British troops and civilians. Unlike World War One, when most of the US troops had passed quickly through Britain *en route* to France, World War Two witnessed the greatest single encounter between ordinary Americans and ordinary Britons, as hundreds of thousands of GIs trained in Britain in readiness for D-Day or manned the air bases used to bomb Hitler's Europe. By June 1944 one and three-quarter million Americans were in Britain. The Foreign Office pointed out that they would 'return to the United States with an impression of this country which will be an important, possibly the most important, factor in colouring, for many years to come, American opinion of us and our ways'.[38] Good relations between the GIs and the British people could help cement the alliance at the bottom as well as the top.

In general the relationship did work well, despite the prejudices of the history books and the fantasies of countless Hollywood feature films, which led some Americans to expect a country populated by stuffy aristocrats in cold country mansions, and some British to expect all Americans to be cowboys with the looks of Gregory Peck or gangsters in the mould of Al Capone. The authorities tried to overcome such misconceptions by commissioning a special film to be shown to all GIs arriving in Britain. *A Welcome to Britain*, made in 1943, starred American actor Burgess Meredith in the role of an ordinary GI. He took his fellow soldiers through the strange customs of the host country, teaching them how to avoid offending the natives. His advice was direct: don't laugh at them, don't tease the Scots about

Cartoon from *Stars and Stripes*, the US servicemen's newspaper.

their kilts, don't flirt with barmaids, and, if you are invited into their homes, don't eat them out of house and home. One good American meal might clean them out of a week's rations. Above all remember that these people have had a rough time in the war, and they, unlike us, have been fighting since 1939. Don't just come in and flash your money around and expect everyone to welcome you as a conquering hero.

These were timely warnings. It was easy for the young GIs, many of whom had never left America before, to have their heads turned by their reception in Britain. They were paid on average three times as much as British soldiers, they had superior rations, and they were admired by the local girls for their smart uniforms and dashing manners. Margaret Whiting, an English teenager in Cambridge, remembers the stir they caused. 'To go to one of their bases was absolutely fantastic because there was no shortage of anything. Each base was a little America, with plenty of food and drink and fantastic great iced cakes. Every night you could, you were out. All the girls were doing it. It was a lovely atmosphere. At the dances they were really friendly. They'd just come up and say: "Cut a rug."'[39]

William Stock, a GI from Milwaukee, admits: 'We were cocky. We were Yankee. We took pride in that. A lot of the English girls thought the Yankees came from Hollywood. I told them I was from California. Did I know Clark Gable? Lived next door. It was foolish, but everybody was doing it.' British soldiers were resentful, often violent, at the GIs' success with the girls, but as airman John Wilson sadly admits: 'They could have looked like Quasimodo and it would have made no difference, as long as they were American.'[40] About 70,000 British girls did their bit to put the Anglo-American alliance on a permanent footing by marrying GIs and settling in the United States.

As the numbers of American troops in Britain mounted, the Combined Chiefs of Staff were planning the next stage of the war. The conference of Roosevelt, Stalin and Churchill, held in Tehran in November 1943, marked a turning point in the relationship between Britain and America.[41] Until now Britain had been the dominant partner, through her greater experience and her superior forces. At Casablanca, as in the conferences of 1942, it was Churchill's and Brooke's Mediterranean strategy that had held sway over the divided Americans. But during 1943 the US Joint Chiefs sorted out their differences, improved their co-ordination and secured the full support of the President. America's superior strength was now beginning to tell within the alliance. Britain still had more troops in action than the USA, but they were dependent on the continued flow of American supplies. Influenced by American pledges to continue Lend-Lease aid after Germany had been defeated, Churchill had finally agreed in August 1943 to invade France the following summer. At Tehran the Americans were determined to hold him to his promise. They now had the organisation and the muscle to do so.

The political relationship had also changed. Roosevelt had watched Russia's courageous stand against Hitler's invasion and her survival when collapse had been predicted. He recognised in Stalin not just a war leader who had played a major role in defeating Hitler, but a politician who would dominate the post-war world. The lesson was clear. America must come to terms with Russia on her own and not allow Britain to claim an equal role. Back in 1942 he told Churchill: 'I think I can personally handle Stalin better than either your Foreign Office or my State Department. Stalin hates the guts of all your top people. He thinks he likes me better, and I hope he will continue to do so.'[42] At this, the first meeting of the Big Three, Roosevelt was determined to prove his point.

At Tehran Roosevelt went out of his way to demonstrate to Stalin that Britain and America were not ganging up on the Russians. He refused to meet Churchill in private either before or after the conference, and at various times during the meetings and at dinner publicly teased and baited him. At one point Stalin had to persuade Churchill not to leave the room in a huff. Roosevelt, Averell Harriman observed, 'always enjoyed other people's discomfort. I think it fair to say that it never bothered him very much when other people were unhappy.'[43] Elliott Roosevelt, the President's son, defends FDR's conduct. 'It was most important for Father not to appear to have a close relationship with Churchill. It would have made Stalin furious that there was a gang-up between Churchill and Roosevelt against him and that he was fighting a lone battle. He [Roosevelt] wasn't able to say, "Look, Winston, I have to do this," because Winston would have smirked and acted as though he was in on the joke.'[44]

At Tehran, in fact, Roosevelt generally sided with Stalin, not Churchill, when there were disagreements. The decisions reached there bore the hallmarks of the new Russo-American axis. There would be tough treatment for Germany after the war, a minor role for France and sympathy for Russian demands for territory in East Asia and Poland. Above all, on grand strategy, Churchill was outvoted by Roosevelt and Stalin. 'Overlord', the invasion of France, would now be the military priority, with a date fixed for the summer and an American supreme commander appointed.

Tehran left Churchill drained and despondent. A heavy cold turned to pneumonia and he had to stay in North Africa for a month to recuperate. There he reflected gloomily on how the Anglo-American marriage of 1942 had become part of an eternal triangle. Like Roosevelt, he was anxious to forge a good relationship with Russia, which he could clearly see would be the greatest land power in the world after the defeat of Germany and Japan. But he believed that a lasting alliance between Britain and America was the key to world peace. He wrote: 'It is my deepest conviction that unless Britain and the United States are joined together in a special relationship, including the Combined Staff organisation and a wide measure of reciprocity in the use of bases – all within the ambit of a world organisation – another destructive war will come to pass.'[45]

His Military Assistant Secretary, Ian Jacob, who had exulted at the British triumph at Casablanca, recalls the very different mood after Tehran. 'Our strength was declining and the Russians were rising. Roosevelt wanted to be in a position where he could deal with Stalin by himself, not tied to anyone else. So he was going to keep the British at arms length. Increasingly, as the war went on, the Americans paid no attention to anything we said, unless it happened to coincide with something that they wanted to do.'[46]

This shifting balance of power within the alliance was most dramatically revealed by the story of the development of the atomic bomb. The outbreak of war in 1939 coincided with the discovery of nuclear fission. At that stage theory and practice were far apart. Few physicists thought that the discovery could be transformed into a weapon of war in time for it to be used in the conflict. But in 1940 two refugee physicists working at Birmingham University in England demonstrated that it was practicable. The Frisch-Peierls memorandum was studied intensively by a British Government committee and on their recommendation, in September 1941, Churchill gave approval for work on the development of an atomic bomb to proceed with urgency. The committee's findings were also made available by Britain to the United States, where work on an atomic bomb had been desultory and poorly-funded. Roosevelt was now convinced that America should follow suit and the US programme began in earnest.

At this early stage Roosevelt asked Churchill to set up a joint Anglo-American project. There were cogent arguments in favour. If Britain's theoretical lead could be harnessed to America's resources and skills it might be possible to produce an atomic bomb before Germany, who was presumed to be conducting her own research. There were practical arguments too. Britain was now under daily aerial bombardment and the laboratories used for the atomic research were constantly at risk. Churchill, however, demurred, suggesting that it was sufficient for the two countries to exchange information, rather than work together. British ministers were reluctant to give up a lead that could give her a disproportionate influence during and after the war. There was also an understandable reluctance to share such a potent weapon with a country that was still neutral.

The two programmes therefore went ahead independently, under their code-names: 'Tube Alloys' in Britain, and the 'Manhattan Project' in the United States. It did not take long for the British team to discover that, once decided on a course of action, Americans pursued it with prodigious energy and determination. By mid-1942 it was obvious that they were pulling ahead and it was Britain's turn to extol the advantages of co-operation. Sir John Anderson, the minister responsible for Tube Alloys, reported to Churchill that 'the Americans have been applying themselves with enthusiasm and a lavish expenditure, which we cannot rival . . . We must . . . face the fact that the pioneer work done in this country is a dwindling asset and that, unless we capitalise it quickly, we shall be rapidly outstripped. We now have a real contribution to make to a "merger". Soon we shall have little or none.'[47]

In the summer of 1942 Churchill believed he had secured Roosevelt's agreement for full co-operation. But those involved with the American programme stonewalled, resorting to the same arguments used against her by Britain the previous year. If America was ahead why should she share what she knew and so relinquish the influence her exclusive possession of the weapon would give her? As in Britain the argument for self-interest was supported by a suspicion that all-important security was best guaranteed by going it alone. There were also fears that what Britain really wanted was the industrial benefits of nuclear energy once the war was over, an ambition America saw no reason to advance, especially when, as Secretary of War Henry Stimson put it in October 1942, 'we were doing nine-tenths of the work'.[48]

These views were held particularly strongly by the director of the Manhattan Project, General Leslie Groves. Suspicious of British motives, he became a fierce guardian of America's discoveries. By early 1943 the flow of information to Britain had virtually dried up, with collaboration limited to specific aspects of the project where British research was of use to the Americans. No overall picture of what America was doing was allowed to emerge. Visiting British scientists were excluded from key research areas which did not directly concern them. Churchill badgered Roosevelt and Hopkins for seven months to renew full co-operation, writing plaintively, 'My whole understanding was that everything was on the basis of fully sharing the results as equal partners.'[49]

It was not until the two leaders met at Quebec in August 1943 that partnership was resumed. The agreement reached there called for 'full and effective collaboration between the two countries in bringing the project to fruition'.[50] Churchill, however, had to disclaim any interest in the industrial and commercial aspects of nuclear energy and agreed to leave it to Roosevelt to decide what information of this kind should be given to Britain.

With this top-level authorisation, the British team left for America to work at Los Alamos and the other research laboratories. On a personal level their leader, Professor James Chadwick, worked extremely well with Groves, but the Americans continued to deny the British access to information Groves thought they did not need. 'The salad,' observed a report from the British Embassy, 'is heaped in a bowl permanently smeared with the garlic of suspicion.'[51]

The Americans spent over $2 billion on developing the atomic bomb. Compared with their vast manpower and resources, in Groves's words, 'the contribution of the British was helpful but not vital. Their work at Los Alamos was of high quality but their numbers were too small to enable them to play a major role.' Nevertheless, Groves admitted that the initial British impetus in 1941 had been essential to get the American programme going and commented that 'Churchill was probably the best friend that the Manhattan Project ever had' because of his constant interest and support. The Americans could have developed the bomb themselves, but without the British it might not have been developed in time. 'I cannot escape the feeling,' wrote Groves, 'that without active and continuing British interest there probably would have been no atomic bomb to drop on Hiroshima.'[52]

But that contribution did not prevent her being treated as the junior partner in the enterprise once the Americans had established their lead. When the war was over, even the limited co-operation came to an abrupt halt, to the fury of the British Government and British scientists.

6 June 1944, D-Day, began the last act of the war in Europe. Up to the very first landings some British leaders, including Churchill and Brooke, feared that the invasion might be premature and that Hitler would slaughter the Allied troops or pin them down for months on the beachhead, as had happened at Anzio in Italy earlier in the year. As he waited edgily on the eve of D-Day Brooke wrote in his diary: 'I am very uneasy about the whole operation . . . it may well be the most ghastly disaster of the whole war.'[53]

Despite the carnage on 'Omaha' beach and the slowness of the breakout, Brooke's grimmest fears were not realised. Eisenhower's armies were soon sweeping across northern Europe and for some weeks that summer there was heady talk of victory by Christmas. But what also preyed on Brooke's spirits, and those of Churchill, was the recognition that henceforward this would be America's show. Italy was a theatre under overall British command in which British forces had dominated and American units had been employed at Britain's behest. But once fronts were opened up in northern and southern France, the Americans diverted their shipping and divisions from Italy. Churchill begged Roosevelt to relent. But the President, stiffened by his Joint Chiefs, was adamant: 'My interest and hopes center on defeating the Germans in front of Eisenhower and driving on into Germany, rather than limiting this action for the purpose of staging a full major effort in Italy.'[54] It was galling to the British, denied the chance of further advances towards the Alps and into Austria. But, having dictated strategy in the early part of the alliance, they had to accept that America now called the tune.

After D-Day the United States for the first time had more troops in combat than the British, and the GIs kept on coming. Britain and the Commonwealth had mobilised all their available manpower, but in America thousands of young men were still starting basic training ready to fight for Uncle Sam. America's army was now second only to Russia's, its navy three times the size of Britain's, while its industry, spurred on by the demand for war material and secure from Hitler's bombs, was producing three times the output of 1939. Churchill was acutely aware of Britain's waning influence. 'Our armies are only one-half the size of the American and will soon be little more than one-third,' he lamented in December 1944. 'It is not so easy as it used to be for me to get things done.'[55]

Churchill and his colleagues were particularly afraid that their relative weakness within the alliance would have serious diplomatic consequences in the long-term. The head of British publicity in America had warned back in 1942 that if Americans 'regard our contribution to victory as having been secondary, and second rate, they will consider our views on the peace settlement as of secondary importance'.[56] A British publicity campaign was mounted in the United States to demonstrate that Lend-Lease had not been the one-way street that many Americans believed. Although Britain had received £5 billion of aid, she put the cost of 'Reverse Lend-Lease', including supplies and services to the American troops training in Britain, at £1.2 billion, and, as a proportion of their national income, each country's aid to the other was about the same, at around five per cent. In June 1944 Whitehall mounted another campaign to explain the scale of Britain's involvement in D-Day. The Joint Staff Mission in Washington had announced sombrely that 'OVERLORD is the last chance we shall have to put across to the American public the magnitude of the British military effort.'[57]

But there was little that publicity could do to redress the overwhelming impression in America that this was now America's war. In August 1944 the anglophobe *Chicago Tribune*, which had earlier been a vociferous supporter of the America First campaign, spelt out the lesson of what was happening. 'We Americans are winning this war. We are doing all of the fighting in the Pacific and have made virtually all the advances in France . . . This is an American-made victory and the peace must be an American peace.'[58]

But Churchill was not deterred from attempting to play a full role in peace-making. Increasingly his thoughts centred on Russia. After Tehran he had been alarmed and depressed at the apparent scale of Stalin's territorial ambitions. But his moods were erratic. In January 1944 he wrote to Anthony Eden of 'the deep-seated changes which have taken place in the character of the Russian State and Government' in recent years, and of 'the new confidence which has grown in our hearts towards Stalin'.[59] By the summer of 1944, however, as the Red Army swept through Poland and south into the Balkans, his fears welled up anew. 'The Russians are drunk with victory,' he warned Eden, 'and there is no length they may not go.'[60] If Stalin could not now be stopped, perhaps his ambitions could be channelled?

Despite Roosevelt's disapproval, Churchill flew to Moscow in October for a private meeting with the Soviet leader at which they determined the relative influence of Britain and Russia in south-east Europe. Under their 'percentages agreement' Russia was to be the dominant foreign power in Roumania and Bulgaria, while Britain was accorded similar status in Greece. Stalin did not dispute Churchill's insistence that 'Britain must be the leading Mediterranean Power'.[61]

Publicly the Americans condemned such agreements as Old World power politics. American opinion was particularly critical of the British military intervention in the Greek civil war. But at their last Big Three conference, at Yalta in the Crimea in February 1945, Roosevelt, despite again keeping his distance from Churchill, actually followed much the same line. The Red Army now controlled Poland and most of the Balkans, and was driving on towards Berlin. The President privately acknowledged that 'the Russians had the power in Eastern Europe, that it was obviously impossible to have a break with them and that, therefore, the only practicable course was to use what influence we had to ameliorate the situation'.[62] At times in early 1945 Churchill was even more fatalistic. 'Make no mistake,' he told his private secretary two weeks before Yalta, 'all the Balkans, except Greece, are going to be Bolshevised; and there is nothing I can do to prevent it. There is nothing I can do for Poland either.'[63]

Top priority for Roosevelt, and even for the sceptical Churchill, was to keep the Big Three together. Only this, they believed, could ensure the defeat of Germany and Japan and guarantee international peace once the war was over. At Yalta the best they felt they could do for Poland was to secure a pledge from Stalin for a new government, broadening out the existing, Moscow-backed communist regime, and for 'free and unfettered elections as soon as possible'.[64]

These agreements depended on mutual trust. Most of the British and American participants left the conference hopeful that this had been achieved. Later Harry Hopkins recalled the mood: 'The Russians had proved that they could be reasonable and far-seeing and there wasn't any doubt in the minds of the President or any of us that we could live with them and get along with them peacefully for as far into the future as any of us could imagine.'[65] Even Churchill came back optimistic. He reported to his ministers on 23 February: 'Poor Neville Chamberlain believed he could trust Hitler. He was wrong. But I don't think I'm wrong about Stalin.'[66]

Churchill's optimism was short-lived. Over the treatment of Russia's old enemies, Poland, Roumania and Bulgaria, Stalin would brook no interference, and the hopes of free elections for Poland were quickly dashed. Churchill was soon urging tough Anglo-American diplomacy to hold the Russians to the Yalta agreements. Then, on 12 April, Roosevelt died suddenly from a cerebral haemorrhage. Churchill's own anguish was heart-felt. He cabled Mrs Roosevelt: 'I have lost a dear and cherished friendship which was forged in the fire of war.' He told the House of Commons that 'in Franklin Roosevelt there died the greatest friend we have ever known, and the greatest champion of freedom who has ever brought help and comfort from the New World to the Old'.[67]

Yet Churchill's grief and his foreboding about Russia could not sour the sweet taste of victory. On 7 May news broke of the German surrender. Next day was a national holiday in Britain, with festivities, services of thanksgiving, and, at night, a fairyland of lights to celebrate the end of years of blackout. In Whitehall Churchill was mobbed by ecstatic Londoners. 'It is you who have led, uplifted and inspired us through the worst days,' wrote Anthony Eden, one of his closest colleagues. 'Without you this day could not have been.'[68]

But the war was not yet over. Japan remained unconquered, and for many Americans this was the only war that mattered. From 1942

"I don't care if the war is nearly over—I'm not selling my cab for a fiver for a souvenir."

One of Giles's many digs at the rich Yanks and the cantankerous British.

the main Pacific theatre had been an American command, with General Douglas MacArthur grimly struggling back to the Philippines from Australia while Admiral Chester Nimitz's task forces worked their way across the Pacific islands from Pearl Harbor. The British had little say in this campaign. They even found it hard to hold on to the white parts of their empire in Australasia.

The crisis in the Pacific in 1941–2 had loosened Australia's ties with Britain. Traditionally reliant on the Royal Navy for their defence, Australians suddenly found themselves facing a possible Japanese onslaught with no British fleet anywhere near the Pacific. In a dramatic message at the end of December 1941 the Labour premier, John Curtin, declared that 'Australia looks to America, free of any pangs as to our traditional links or kinship with the United Kingdom'.[69] The Americans obliged and soon Australia became a major American base for the Pacific conflict. As the war progressed Australians began to chafe at American direction and by 1945 Commonwealth sentiment was reasserting itself. But, although the war did not mean a total break with Britain, it did start a new trend. Henceforth Australasia would look increasingly for its security to the USA, now unquestionably the major Western power in the Pacific. For Australia and New Zealand, like Canada a decade or so before, the war was dissolving even the strongest bonds of Britain's empire.

During 1944 US forces drove the Japanese at great cost from the Solomon Islands and New Guinea. The following winter MacArthur honoured his vow to return to the Philippines. Now America's B-29 bombers could pound Japan's cities with high explosive and incendiaries. Yet the Japanese fought on with ruthless ferocity, often employing suicidal kamikaze pilots against American warships. The Pentagon contemplated an invasion of Japan without relish. It might take another year after the defeat of Germany and cost up to one million American casualties. Staff officers in Tokyo urged that 'all able-bodied Japanese, regardless of sex, should be called upon to engage in battle . . . Each citizen was to be prepared to sacrifice his life in suicide attacks on enemy armored forces.'[70]

Little wonder that at Yalta Roosevelt was almost more concerned about the Pacific than about Europe. He was determined to ensure Russian entry into the war against Japan within three months of victory in Europe. In return he agreed to Russia's territorial demands in China. For General Marshall, Russia's pledge to declare war on Japan made it worth spending two weeks away from Washington. Even Yalta's bedbugs and cold water seemed endurable. 'For what we have gained here I would gladly have stayed a whole month,' he confessed afterwards.[71] In all these arrangements Britain had little say. Her day as the leading foreign power in East Asia had now passed.

Russia duly declared war on Japan on 8 August 1945, and thus helped force the Japanese to surrender. But the real 'winning weapon' proved to be the atomic bomb, dropped first on Hiroshima on 6 August and then on Nagasaki three days later. Under the terms of the Quebec agreement British approval to use the bomb was required. Churchill had readily agreed. But it was only a formality. The United States alone controlled the world's newest and most appalling weapon of mass destruction. On 14 August Japan surrendered. That night an estimated two million people thronged the area around Times Square in New York, cheering, dancing and drinking. Next day some 5,000 tons of ticker-tape, confetti and wastepaper was cleared from the streets of Manhattan. 'Ours is the supreme position,' exulted the *New York Herald Tribune*. 'The Great Republic has come into its own; it stands first among the peoples of the earth.'[72]

Victory had been won. The wartime alliance was over and the GIs were soon on their way home. Often it had been a tempestuous affair, with bitter arguments and mutual jealousy. But, as Churchill frequently observed, 'there is only one thing worse than fighting with allies, and that is fighting without them!'[73] Between 1941 and 1945 the two countries had indeed become 'somewhat mixed up together ... for mutual and general advantage'. It was the closest wartime alliance in modern history. The memories would not be forgotten but, as events were soon to show, the relationship would never be as close again.

9

Uniting Against Russia

1945–9

The troop ship glided into New York harbour early in the morning as the first rays of sun glinted on the Statue of Liberty. Donald Worby was on deck with hundreds of others straining for a glimpse of the Manhattan skyline. 'There was a lot of big tough guys there, and boy, we all had a lump in our throat as big as our fist.'

On the voyage back across the Atlantic memories of war had given way to thoughts of home. Worby knew he was coming back to an America that had become richer as a result of the war, where people expected as of right luxuries that were unimaginable in Europe. He admired the way the British had put up with hardship, no 'whining or complaining', and wondered whether 'the folks back home' would have accepted it as gracefully. Homecoming was not easy. It took time to adjust to a country that was largely unscathed. One day, shortly after his return, he overheard a woman in a bakery explaining to another customer how sorry she was that the war was over. If only it had lasted another year she and her husband could have paid off the loans on the four properties they had bought with their wartime earnings. 'The other lady,' Worby recalls, 'had a son in the marines who had been killed. She was very upset and angry. She slid a banana cream pie off the counter and went over to this woman and smashed it right into her face and said, "That's for my boy who got killed in World War Two."' Worby reached in his pocket and said, 'I'd sure like to pay for that pie!'[1]

The wartime boom laid the foundations for American prosperity for the next quarter of a century. As the 'arsenal of democracy' the

United States was producing forty per cent of the world's armaments by 1944. There had been little rationing, few shortages, no bombing, and, as a result, incomes and consumption had soared. The contrast with Britain was most vivid not for returning GIs but for the 70,000 British girls they brought home with them. Barbara Markus, one of these war brides, felt she had dropped into another world. There was an abundance of everything, 'a light airy feeling', whereas Britain seemed 'quite sombre, quite stark'. On her wedding day she went to a steak restaurant. 'We had filet mignon. It was a good seven years since I had seen a piece of meat this size. I was the first one served, as I was the bride. I thought the steak was to be shared between everybody. It was quite a surprise when I found we got one each.'[2]

Britain had come out of the war exhausted by her efforts. Over 400,000 had died, more than in America, with three times her population. She had been fighting longer than any of the Allies and had borne the brunt of German bombing. The centres of many of her major cities were piles of rubble. Everything was scarce, clothing as well as food. With manpower concentrating on the war effort and overseas markets hard to reach, her export trade by 1944 was running at only a third of its pre-war level. She had lost a quarter of her national wealth. It was apparent that recovery would be slow and painful.

At this moment in her history, instead of returning to the pre-war free enterprise system to revive her fortunes, Britain embarked on a wide-ranging programme of social and political reform. In 1942 a plan had been drawn up for the post-war years to provide everyone with a minimum standard of living, free health care, and better support when unemployed or retired. To implement the Beveridge Plan the electorate rejected Winston Churchill, a traditional Tory, as Prime Minister and chose instead Clement Attlee, leader of the Labour Party, who was elected in July 1945. Churchill had won the war, but he did not seem the man to win the peace. When the results were declared Churchill's wife tried to console him. 'It may well be a blessing in disguise,' she said. Churchill grunted: 'At the moment it seems quite effectively disguised.'[3]

The Labour Government embarked on a programme that included nationalisation of major industries, strict central control of resources and the construction of a welfare state. Taken on its own this was a heavy financial burden for an impoverished country, and one senior British diplomat feared 'a weak foreign policy, a private revolution at home and the reduction of England to a second-class power'.[4] But Attlee and his colleagues, while intent on social change, did not propose to give up Britain's place at the top table. Under the leadership of Ernest Bevin, the bluff former union leader who was now Foreign Secretary, they still acted on the assumption that Britain was 'one of the Powers most vital to the peace of the world', one of the 'Big 3 (or 2½!)'.[5] Lord Keynes, an Economic Adviser to the Treasury, sounded the alarm: 'The gay and successful fashion in which we undertake liabilities all over the world and slop money out to the importunate represents an over-playing of our hand.' He warned the Cabinet that it could lead to a 'financial Dunkirk'.[6]

The crisis came almost at once. Eight days after the war ended with Japan's surrender, President Truman cancelled Lend-Lease, the provision of food and weapons on credit. The British Food Mission, despatching tons of supplies from the United States, only learnt about it when one of their ships was refused permission to sail. Next day the official announcement was made.

The speed with which the decision was taken shocked the British. It was as though a close friend who had seen her through a crisis had turned away without saying goodbye. Senator Claude Pepper, the liberal Democrat who had been hanged in effigy for supporting Lend-Lease in 1941, understood Britain's sense of grievance. 'You don't suddenly stop when the horse passed the mark, but let it canter to the end.'[7] But Congress had authorised Lend-Lease strictly as a wartime measure and America's instinct was now to put the war behind it as fast as possible. 'Bring Daddy Home' clubs were formed in towns and cities across America to put pressure on the President to demobilise. Marion T. Bennett, a Congressman of the 1940s, recalls the instinctive American reaction to the war: 'We'd given our allies everything they asked for and more, and now people were sick and tired of it and didn't want to hear any more about it.'[8]

The British Government immediately sent Lord Keynes to Washington to explain the damage that cancellation of Lend-Lease would do and to ask for a grant to help Britain out of her crisis. On arrival he was told that a free gift was out of the question and that at best Britain might get an interest-bearing loan. Over the next three months there were complex and often heated negotiations, both about the loan and the method of repayment for Lend-Lease. The eventual terms for the latter, when compared with the arrangements for settling the World War One debts, were generous. Some £5 billion had been borrowed, but Britain had spent about £1.2 billion in 'Reverse Lend-Lease' aid to America. Of the outstanding balance of £3.8 billion, Britain was asked to repay only £162 million (or $650 million).

The generosity of the terms for the repayment of Lend-Lease was obscured by resentment felt in Britain when the credit terms for the loan were announced: $3.75 billion was to be lent at two per cent interest, repayable over fifty years from the end of 1951. To Britain, used to the easy credit of Lend-Lease, any interest payments seemed unduly harsh, given the circumstances in which she now found herself and the sacrifices she had made in 1939–41 while America was still neutral. In the United States, however, a less sentimental approach was adopted. Returning GIs were paying more than two per cent for their home loans. Why should Britain be offered better terms? One American businessman told the State Department that the easy terms were justified: 'If you succeed in doing away with the Empire preference and opening up the Empire to United States commerce, it may well be that we can afford to pay a couple of billion dollars for the privilege.'[9] That accorded with the prevailing mood in Washington. The real price for the loan and the generous settlement of Lend-Lease was to be Britain's endorsement of the agreements on a new world economy concluded at the New Hampshire mountain resort of Bretton Woods in July 1944.

Throughout the war economists on both sides of the Atlantic had been working on ways of creating a stable and prosperous post-war world. During the Depression of the 1930s the international economy had disintegrated into separate blocs, tied to the leading currencies – sterling, the dollar, the franc and the mark. Trade had been mainly within these areas rather than through the world at large. British and American leaders both wanted to see a new, open world economy, but they found it hard to agree on the appropriate means. The State Department favoured making currencies freely convertible, one into another, and eliminating discriminatory tariff barriers, particularly Britain's Imperial Preference. That would benefit American trade and would also, US leaders believed, promote world peace. 'Nations which act as enemies in the marketplace cannot long be friends at the council table,' warned Will Clayton of the State Department.[10] But the British were unwilling to surrender protection for Britain's weakened trade and currency until they were sure that America would assume the burdens it had rejected during the Depression for sustaining the world economy. Churchill was emphatic: 'No abandonment of Imperial Preference unless or until we are in presence of a vast scheme of reducing trade barriers in which the United States is taking the lead.'[11]

The crucial negotiations dealt with a new international monetary system. They were conducted for the British by Keynes and for the Americans by Harry Dexter White. Both were men of outstanding intellect, but with very different styles: Keynes, witty, arrogant, with a mind like quicksilver; White, blunt, more defensive and perhaps less deft in argument. But it was White, in the end, who won the day.

Keynes had wanted to put the onus of the new monetary system on the USA, the world's strongest economy. He proposed that America's payments surpluses and stocks of gold should provide much of the capital needed for helping poorer nations whose currencies were in difficulty. Generous overdrafts would be made available to them from an international fund of over $25 billion, much of which would be provided by the United States. But, as in most of the wartime negotiations, he who paid the piper called the tune. It was Harry White's plan which became the basis of the agreement reached in July 1944 at Bretton Woods. This was for a more modest fund of $8.8 billion, of which the USA would contribute only $3.2 billion. Countries in difficulties would receive help, but on a smaller scale than Keynes had envisaged and with tough conditions about putting their own economies in order. Also contrary to Keynes's wishes, the new system would be denominated in gold or dollars, the one being freely convertible into the other. The dollar was now the world's leading currency. Henry Morgenthau, Secretary of the US Treasury, confessed that his aim in office had been 'to move the financial center of the world from London and Wall Street to the United States Treasury'.[12] Bretton Woods marked the achievement of that aim.

In Britain, however, there was little enthusiasm and the government dragged its feet on the Bretton Woods agreements throughout 1944 and 1945. As a further condition of the loan the US Government therefore insisted that Britain must ratify the agreement before the end of December 1945 and agree to make sterling freely exchangeable within a year. Attlee hastily placed the loan agreement, the settlement of Lend-Lease and the Bretton Woods arrangements before an unprepared Parliament.

In the Commons the mood was shocked and angry. Critics on the Conservative benches objected to the provisions for freer trade, calling them a sell-out of the British Empire, 'an economic Munich'. On the left it was feared that the government had surrendered its power to direct the economy and ensure full employment. One Labour MP described the agreements as 'niggardly, barbaric, antediluvian'.[13] Underlying the economic issues was a sense of national humiliation. Once again, it seemed, Britain was begging for American aid and being told the terms. The British weekly, *The Economist*, usually well-disposed to the United States, was particularly bitter: 'It is aggravating to find that the reward for losing a quarter of our national

WHAT, NO HOOVES? NO TAIL? (Copyright in All Countries)

British cartoonist David Low uses Attlee's visit to Washington to mock America's phobia about socialism. *Evening Standard*, 15 November 1945.

wealth in the common cause is to pay tribute for half a century to those who have been enriched by the war.'[14] In the end the government won its majority, but 100 MPs voted against the loan agreement and 169 abstained, including Churchill and most of the Tories. Having imposed terms on others for two centuries, the British were discovering what it was like to be on the receiving end.

After all the difficulties in Britain were resolved, the loan agreement became bogged down in the US Congress. Americans were concerned about problems at home – strikes, inflation, high taxes. Why should the United States again have to bail out a decaying empire? Britain should sell the Crown Jewels or some of her vast imperial real estate. To these familiar complaints about empire and monarchy was added a new one – maybe American money would be used by the new Labour Government to turn Britain into virtually a communist state? One Congressman summed it up. The loan, he said, would 'promote too damned much Socialism at home and too much damned Imperialism abroad'.[15] For many months in 1946 Britain's desperately needed loan was held up in Congressional committee.

The row over the loan was not the only sign that the relationship between Britain and America was changing. Another casualty of America's new nationalism was the atomic partnership. Throughout the war, as we have seen, it had been a chequered affair, with suspicion on both sides, but in September 1944 Roosevelt and Churchill signed a new agreement at the President's home at Hyde Park, New York. Using the British code-word, Tube Alloys, this affirmed that 'full collaboration between the United States and the British Government in developing tube alloys for military and commercial purposes should continue after the defeat of Japan unless and until terminated by joint agreement'.[16] The American copy of the memo was lost in Roosevelt's papers, wrongly filed by his naval aide among documents dealing with submarine torpedo tubes. But Churchill sent Truman a photocopy in July 1945. The following November the new President signed another secret understanding 'for full and effective co-operation in the field of atomic energy between the United States, the United Kingdom and Canada'.[17]

These two agreements seemed to promise continued Anglo-American partnership in the weapon that was seen as the basis of post-war security. But during 1946 Truman had second thoughts. Despite much talk at the end of the war about international control of atomic energy, there was a growing feeling in Congress that America should keep something so valuable and dangerous to itself. In February 1946 that conviction was strengthened when news broke of a Soviet spy ring in Ottawa, implicating British atomic scientists. In August the President approved the McMahon Act which terminated virtually all communication with foreign states about atomic energy. Congressmen were unaware of the agreements made with Britain in 1944 and 1945 and the Administration made no effort to enlighten them.* Truman concluded that to carry out the agreements in the frenzied atmosphere of 1946, with Washington seething with rumours about atomic spies, would in Dean Acheson's words, 'blow the Administration out of the water'.[19] A bitter Labour Cabinet, cut off by the United States, decided in January 1947 that, for reasons of security and prestige, Britain must start work on its own atomic bomb. As

* The principal author of the act, Senator Brien McMahon, admitted to the British in 1949 'that, if he had been given all the information for which he asked the American authorities on the history of the co-operation with the United Kingdom and Canada, there would probably have been no need for his Act to have been passed or, at any rate, not on such restrictive lines'.[18]

Bevin observed with typical pungency: 'We have got to have this thing over here whatever it costs . . . We've got to have the bloody Union Jack flying on top of it.'[20]

There were other indications that the wartime alliance had broken down. The two governments were publicly at odds over Palestine because of Truman's support for increased Jewish immigration into Britain's strife-torn mandate. Bevin added fuel to the flames by suggesting that the President did so because Americans 'did not want too many Jews in New York'.[21] The President had also ordered abolition of all the combined committees by which the two countries had run the war effort, and it was only with great difficulty that the British kept the Combined Chiefs of Staff in existence.

Most disturbing of all for the British in 1945–6 was the American attitude towards the Soviet Union. Germany's defeat had brought Russia deeper into Europe than at any time since 1814. Losses of perhaps twenty million people had left her paranoid about future security and alert for opportunities to expand farther at little cost. The Yalta agreements of February 1945 were not honoured as Churchill and Roosevelt had hoped. In Poland, Roumania and Bulgaria, states regarded by Russia as buffers against renewed German aggression, pro-Soviet regimes were quickly installed with the backing of the Red Army. Stalin's insistence on vast reparations from Germany was a major obstacle to Allied agreement on a peace treaty. Pressure was applied on Turkey to secure access for the Soviet fleet through the Dardanelles, and in Iran the Soviets failed to withdraw their troops, as agreed, in early 1946. All these Soviet actions were regarded with growing alarm in Whitehall. By September 1945 Bevin was complaining that 'our relations with the Russians about the whole European problem were drifting into the same condition as that in which we had found ourselves with Hitler'.[22]

Bevin, like Churchill, wanted a firm Anglo-American front against Soviet expansion, but the Truman Administration would have none of it. When Britain had come to the aid of the royalists in Greece in their civil war against communist forces at the end of 1944, the State Department had been openly critical. Many Americans viewed the Greek and Turkish problems not as examples of Soviet expansion but as part of the traditional Anglo-Russian rivalry that had afflicted the eastern Mediterranean for more than a century. Over eastern Europe the State Department protested strenuously about Soviet behaviour, but it would do nothing in concert with the British, and eventually Truman's Secretary of State, Jimmy Byrnes, recognised the new governments with only cosmetic changes. All this time US troops were being withdrawn from Europe, the total falling from 3.5 million in June 1945 to 200,000 two years later.

Within months of victory, therefore, Britain seemed in a desperate position. The Big Three, regarded at Yalta as the basis of post-war security, was in ruins. Disowned by America, browbeaten by Russia, Britain seemed at the mercy of the superpowers – to quote the head of the Foreign Office like 'Lepidus in the triumvirate with Mark Antony and Augustus'.[23]* Another British diplomat observed: 'This is the opportunity for a power on the make to grab territory and stake out interests beyond the limits of war-time conquests . . . The Russians see that the war has left us financially and economically weak and dependent upon the United States. They also know the American phobia about the British Empire and calculate that we cannot count fully on American support when defending our Imperial interests.'[24]

Winston Churchill, now out of office, was deeply disturbed at America's inertia in the face of what he saw as a clear Soviet threat to Europe. In Harry Truman he found a supporter who, by January 1946, was also uneasy about the policy the State Department was pursuing. 'I'm tired [of] babying the Soviets,' the President complained.[25] In March, while on a private visit to America, Churchill travelled with him to Westminster College, in Fulton, Missouri, Truman's home state. The President had read Churchill's speech on the train, pronouncing it 'admirable . . . It would do nothing but good,' he said, 'though it would make a stir.'[26] Churchill's message was stark: 'From Stettin in the Baltic to Trieste in the Adriatic, an iron curtain has descended across the Continent.' He did 'not believe that Soviet Russia desires another war' but was 'convinced that there is nothing they admire so much as strength'. In other words the extent of Soviet expansion would depend on the West's response. Churchill called for 'a special relationship between the United States and the British Commonwealth', which would mean combined military staffs, shared bases, resources and weapons, and eventually, perhaps, common citizenship. This 'fraternal association of the English-speaking peoples' was, he insisted, the only hope for a 'haggard' world, in which all countries, except America and the British Commonwealth, were now confronted by the peril of communism.[27]

As Truman predicted, Churchill's speech did indeed 'make a stir'. His warnings about Soviet conduct were echoed in Washington. On

* A reference to Shakespeare's *Julius Caesar*, Act IV, Scene 1, where Antony describes Lepidus as '. . . a slight unmeritable man,/Meet to be sent on errands: is it fit,/The threefold world divided, he should stand/One of the three to share it?'

22 February George Kennan, US chargé d'affaires in Moscow, had sent Washington an immensely influential analysis summing up Soviet conduct on lines similar to Churchill. Although Russia, he argued, was 'committed fanatically to the belief that with US there can be no permanent *modus vivendi*', the Soviets were 'still by far the weaker force' and they could be contained 'without recourse to any general military conflict' provided the US ensured 'the cohesion, firmness and vigor' of the West.[28] In March the Joint Chiefs of Staff warned privately that 'the defeat or disintegration of the British Empire would eliminate from Eurasia the last bulwark of resistance between the United States and Soviet expansion . . . Militarily, our present position as a world power is of necessity closely interwoven with that of Great Britain.'[29]

But popular reaction to Churchill's speech was less enthusiastic. Although a poll in March 1946 indicated that seventy per cent of Americans disapproved of Soviet foreign policy, the idea of a 'fraternal association' with Britain had few public supporters. Americans had only recently been converted to the idea of a United Nations Organisation to maintain world peace and many feared that a special Anglo-American relationship would undermine its foundations. 'Winnie, Winnie, go away. UNO is here to stay,' chanted protesters in New York.[30] The *Wall Street Journal* commented that 'the country's reaction to Mr Churchill's Fulton speech must be convincing proof that the United States wants no alliance or anything that resembles an alliance with any other nation'.[31]

It was only gradually that opinions altered. The Soviet failure to withdraw from northern Iran hardened American attitudes. So too did the growth of communist parties in France and Italy. Mounting anxiety about Europe helped passage of the British loan through Congress in the summer of 1946. Joseph Kennedy, faint-hearted American Ambassador to Britain in 1940, was among its supporters. 'The British people and their way of life,' he said, 'form the last barrier in Europe against Communism; and we must help them hold that line.'[32] But there was little readiness in Congress or the country to do more, and no enthusiasm for the kind of special relationship Churchill believed essential. It was not until the following year that events on the continent of Europe led Americans to reconsider the transatlantic relationship and take urgent steps to rebuild the alliance they had precipitately abandoned in 1945.

In Britain the winter of early 1947 was the worst since 1881. For weeks villages were cut off by snow drifts as the country shivered in blizzards and sub-zero temperatures. Coal stocks ran down so fast that electricity had to be rationed. Factories closed, production plummeted and British industry, vital to the country's recovery, ground to a virtual halt. The fuel shortage was exacerbated by a shortage of coal miners, the result of Britain's slow demobilisation of its forces. Her commitments overseas were so heavy that in October 1946 conscription had been re-introduced, the first time that this had happened when Britain was at peace.

Pressed by the Treasury, the Cabinet accepted that the country was overstretched and in February 1947 decided to cut back on Britain's obligations. This would release manpower for industry and reduce Britain's overseas spending which was draining her reserves and using up the American loan at what the Treasury called 'a reckless, and ever-accelerating, speed'.[33] The Palestine mandate would be handed back to the UN. Britain would pull out of India by June 1948. And by the end of March 1947 she would end financial aid to Greece and Turkey. The last decision was of particular importance for Anglo-American relations. On 21 February the British Embassy delivered to the State Department notes explaining the new policy and stressing the vital importance of Greece and Turkey in the deepening Cold War. With Britain pulling out, 'His Majesty's Government trust that the United States Government may find it possible to afford financial assistance'.[34]

Britain's decision was not unexpected. The Truman Administration knew the situation in Greece and the state of British finances, and the State Department warned the President independently that only 'urgent and immediate support' for Greece would prevent a communist victory and the probable 'loss of the whole Near and Middle East'.[35] But the speed of Britain's withdrawal and the short notice were a shock. Truman's Democratic Administration had to mobilise public support rapidly at a time when Congress was under Republican control.

Truman summoned senior Congressmen to a meeting in the White House. They were unhappy both about the cost and about having to bail Britain out yet again. But Dean Acheson, an Under Secretary of State, warned that a collapse in Greece would carry the communist 'infection', like 'apples in a barrel infected by one rotten one', through Africa and Europe, with Italy and France the next victims.[36] The Congressmen were impressed by Acheson's grim appraisal. Senator Arthur Vandenberg advised Truman that to get public support he had to take this sort of line in 'a personal appearance before Congress and scare hell out of the country'.[37]

On 12 March 1947 the President duly addressed a joint session of

The Atlantic Conference, August 1941. The British and American delegations worship together on board HMS *Prince of Wales*.

Roosevelt and Churchill after the service, with General George C. Marshall behind them. Left of Roosevelt, standing with heads bowed, are Harry Hopkins and Averell Harriman.

US aid to Britain: the first flotilla of old US destroyers arrives at Devonport (28 September 1940).

US aid to Britain: GIs bear the Stars and Stripes through Trafalgar Square (30 March 1944).

In south-east Asia the Allies' Deputy Commander, General 'Vinegar Joe' Stilwell, and his British superior, Admiral Lord Louis Mountbatten, did not always see eye to eye.

Inside the American servicemen's club, Rainbow Corner, in Shaftesbury Avenue, near London's Piccadilly (27 January 1945).

200 London children are guests of American servicemen for a wartime Thanksgiving.

Congress, setting out what became known as the 'Truman Doctrine'. He first explained the problems of Greece and Turkey, the one wracked by civil war and facing a communist take-over, the other needing economic support to resist Russian pressure. But they were only part of a larger issue, for the world as a whole faced a choice between 'freedom' and 'totalitarianism'. Totalitarian regimes imposed on free peoples undermined 'the foundations of international peace and hence the security of the United States', Truman stated. It must therefore be 'the policy of the United States to support free people who are resisting attempted subjugation by armed minorities or by outside pressures'.[38]

Truman had couched the appeal for what he admitted was 'little more than one-tenth of one per cent' of America's investment in World War Two in deliberately apocalyptic terms, to overcome resistance in Congress. His speech, which persuaded legislators to approve $400 million in aid for Greece and Turkey, was to redefine American foreign policy. Its object was now expressed in global terms as the defence of all free peoples threatened by totalitarianism. A threat to any one of them was seen as a threat to America itself. Britain, in abdicating responsibility for Greece and Turkey, had acted as the catalyst for this change. Her inability, similarly, to cope with the growing problems of western Europe was to draw America fully into the Cold War.

The state of Europe in 1947 was desperate. After a tour of Europe, US Under-Secretary of State Will Clayton reported in May: 'it is now obvious that we grossly underestimated the destruction to the European economy by the war . . . Europe is steadily deteriorating,' he warned. 'Millions of people in the cities are slowly starving,' and the European governments, including Britain, would run out of reserves to pay for essential imports before the end of the year. 'Without further prompt and substantial aid from the United States, economic, social and political disintegration will overwhelm Europe.' And, unlike previous UN aid projects, he emphasised, '*the United States must run this show*'.[39]

The State Department was already concerned about the problem and Acheson had spoken publicly about it, but his speech made little impact. On 5 June 1947, however, Secretary of State, George C. Marshall, was due to address the graduation ceremony at Harvard University. He made the European crisis his central theme. Marshall spelled out the breakdown in Europe and the need for a co-ordinated recovery plan. Aware of Congress's resistance to foreign aid, he insisted that America would only help those who helped themselves.

THE TRUMAN LINE

Punch, 28 May 1947.

'It would be neither fitting nor efficacious for this government to undertake to draw up unilaterally a program designed to place Europe on its feet economically. This is the business of the Europeans. The initiative, I think, must come from Europe.'[40]

The State Department had made certain that the British had been alerted in advance about Marshall's ideas. On hearing reports of

Marshall's speech over the radio, Bevin moved fast. It was, he said later, 'like a life-line to sinking men'[41] and he grasped it with both hands. He quickly arranged a meeting with the French Foreign Minister, Georges Bidault, and together they approached the Russians to help draw up a European recovery programme. But, on discovering that membership would mean revealing Russia's own industrial strategy and allowing her new East European satellites to trade freely with the West, the Soviet Union withdrew, leaving the relieved Bevin and Bidault free to proceed. In July 1947, with Bevin in the chair, sixteen countries began work in Paris to list their needs. Throughout, American officials shared in the discussions, but, as one of them admitted, the Marshall Plan was still rather like 'a flying saucer – nobody knows what it looks like, how big it is, in what direction it is moving, or whether it really exists'.[42] Bevin played a leading part in bringing it down to earth.

The urgency of their work was dramatised by Britain's sterling crisis. On 15 July 1947, reluctantly honouring the terms of the 1946 American loan, Britain ended exchange controls and made sterling freely convertible. Holders of sterling seized the chance to convert into dollars, forcing the British Government to suspend convertibility within five weeks. By then Britain had lost nearly $900 million and had been forced to draw on another $450 million of the loan, which was now almost exhausted. The 'dollar gap' had to be bridged before Europe could recover.

In late September the committee in Paris completed its work and put its proposals to Truman for American loans totalling $29 billion. The President cut that to $17 billion, spread over four years, and sent it to Congress. The Administration prepared the ground well. Congressmen had been taken to Europe to see the devastation for themselves. They had been told that Marshall Aid would protect Europe from communism, revive America's economy, save spending more on armaments – in short anything they wished to hear. The bill was eventually approved by Congress in March 1948. But it took more than Truman's propaganda to get it past the tight-fisted Republican majority. It needed nothing less than fears that World War Three was imminent.

In February 1948 the communists seized power in Czechoslovakia and Foreign Minister Jan Masaryk, well known in America, was found dead in suspicious circumstances. There were reports of mounting Soviet pressure on Finland and Norway to sign 'security' pacts. Rumours were rife that Italy would go communist in the April elections. A crisis atmosphere pervaded Washington. Truman scribbled a note to Marshall on 5 March: 'Will Russia move first? Who pulls the trigger? Then where do we go?' The same day General Lucius Clay, US Commander in Germany, reported a subtle change in Soviet attitudes and warned that war 'may come with dramatic suddenness'.[43] After a direct appeal from the President, Congress approved both Marshall Aid and the restoration of the draft.

Bevin did not believe that the Soviets wanted to fight, but he too was deeply alarmed at their 'war of nerves' and the growing influence of communism in Europe, Asia and the Middle East. In March 1948 he told the Cabinet: 'It has really become a matter of the defence of western civilisation, or everything will be swamped by this Soviet method of infiltration.'[44] Economic aid was no longer enough. In the same month Britain, France, Belgium, Luxembourg and the Netherlands concluded the Brussels Defence Pact. Bevin, again, was its principal architect, but he knew that only American backing could ensure western Europe's defence. In the crisis atmosphere of March 1948 Washington was ready to respond. 'Please inform Mr Bevin,' Marshall told the British Ambassador on 12 March, 'that . . . we are prepared to proceed at once in the joint discussions on the establishment of an Atlantic security system.'[45] Their talks were soon being swept along by the momentum of a new crisis.

At the centre of the deepening Cold War was Germany. In 1945 it had been divided into four zones – Russian, American, British and French – with all four powers occupying parts of the city of Berlin, which lay in the Russian zone. They were supposed to draw up a peace treaty, set up a new democratic government and then withdraw. But the four powers could not agree on Germany's future. Russia wanted massive reparations. She and France, both of whom had suffered most from Germany in the past, wanted German economic recovery to be carefully controlled. But the British were using up scarce resources, including their American loan, to feed a starving German population. By 1947 they agreed with the Americans that Germany must be made self-sufficient again. And, as the Cold War intensified in 1948 and France came round to the Anglo-American view, these three powers prepared to create a new west German state out of their zones of occupation. The alternative, the State Department argued, would have been to 'accept stalemate without action and thus permit Germany to sink deeper into political and economic chaos, with the attendant threat to the general welfare and security'.[46]

Russia opposed any new German state until Soviet security was guaranteed. In June 1948 the Western allies introduced a new currency in their zones, a step towards economic stability as well as political unity. In response, on 24 June, the Russians imposed a total blockade of all routes into Berlin.

Washington was initially indecisive. 'No one was sure, as yet, how the Russian move could be countered or whether it could successfully be countered at all,' recalled George Kennan later.[47] Truman considered various options, including forcing a way through with tanks or with an armoured train. But Bevin successfully urged a subtler riposte, one less fraught with the risk of war: an Anglo-American airlift of supplies from western Germany into the Allied sectors of Berlin. On 30 June both Bevin and Marshall proclaimed their determination to stay in Berlin and to keep it supplied. Over the next year more than two million tons were flown into the beleaguered city, some in ramshackle aircraft manned by private entrepreneurs.

The crisis over Berlin found America militarily unprepared. Its air power, like its army, had been demobilised after the war. The US wartime bases in Britain had also been closed down, though a secret understanding had been reached between leading airmen in 1946 that some should be available again in an emergency. In June 1948 Marshall asked Bevin to allow US bombers to use British bases and a Cabinet committee gave rapid approval.

General Leon Johnson was stationed at Colorado Springs when he received an urgent summons to Washington. Arriving at the Pentagon, he was told: 'We want you in England on a permanent change of station.' 'How soon?' Johnson asked. 'Yesterday.' Johnson grinned: 'I don't think I can make it that quickly, but I'll make it rather soon.'[48]

On 18 July two B-29 bomber groups, sixty planes, flew into Britain. Their arrival was given wide publicity. Another group followed in August. The B-29s were known as 'atomic bombers' because they had dropped the first nuclear weapons on Japan, and it was officially hinted that the aircraft arriving in Britain were armed with nuclear weapons. Facing the possibility of war over Berlin, the Labour Government was relieved to see them, and no hard questions were asked about the terms of the new American military presence. In June 1949 General Johnson commented: 'Never before in history has one first-class Power gone into another first-class Power's country without an agreement. We were just told to come over and "we shall be pleased to have you".'[49] By the time the British Government tried to establish a clear agreement, the US air force had an unshakeable foothold on British soil. Secretary of Defense James Forrestal noted in his diary in July 1948 that the bombers' presence 'would accustom the British to the necessary habits and routines that go in the accommodation of an alien, even though an allied power'. He added that 'once sent they would become somewhat of an accepted fixture, whereas a deterioration of the situation in Europe might lead to a condition of mind under which the British would be compelled to reverse their present attitude'.[50]

Ironically, a few months before the B-29s arrived, the British Government had surrendered its veto over the American use of the atomic bomb, a right secured by Churchill in the Quebec agreement of August 1943. Given America's dominance of the atomic bomb programme, the power was largely nominal, and Churchill had quickly given his consent in July 1945 when asked to approve the use of the atomic bomb on Japan. But US Senators were appalled when they learned privately of the veto in April 1947. Vandenberg called it 'astounding' and 'unthinkable', while Senator Bourke Hickenlooper warned Marshall that he 'would be unable to support American economic aid to Britain unless the situation was rectified at once'.[51] Pressed by the Administration, the British agreed in the so-called *modus vivendi* of January 1948 to surrender their veto power in return for promises of a new exchange of technical information on atomic energy. These promises were largely unfulfilled. Even the official historian of the British atomic energy programme found it surprising that, 'in view of the potential issues of life and death that were involved, neither officials nor Ministers showed any concern or interest in the surrender of Britain's veto, or right to consultation on the use of the bomb'.[52] By the time the B-29s arrived in Britain, the British Government had no control over their use.

None of this was seen to matter, however, in the crisis atmosphere of mid-1948, when Europe seemed close to war. The Berlin blockade gave added urgency to the talks about an Atlantic security pact, which was now gaining support in Congress as well as the Administration. Some favoured a unilateral American pledge, akin to the Monroe Doctrine or Truman Doctrine, stating that an attack on western Europe would be regarded as an attack on the USA. But, as Bevin observed, that would leave people in Britain 'very doubtful as to whether they had incurred any reciprocal obligation',[53] and the Pentagon was determined to secure access to European bases in return for the offer of American support. So the negotiators worked on a mutual defence pact, in which each of the twelve signatories would regard an attack on one as an attack on all.

A draft was ready by late 1948, but it was toned down by leading Senators who feared that the USA 'was rushing into some kind of automatic commitment' to defend Europe in any crisis.[54] When the treaty was signed, on 4 April 1949, America agreed only to assist its

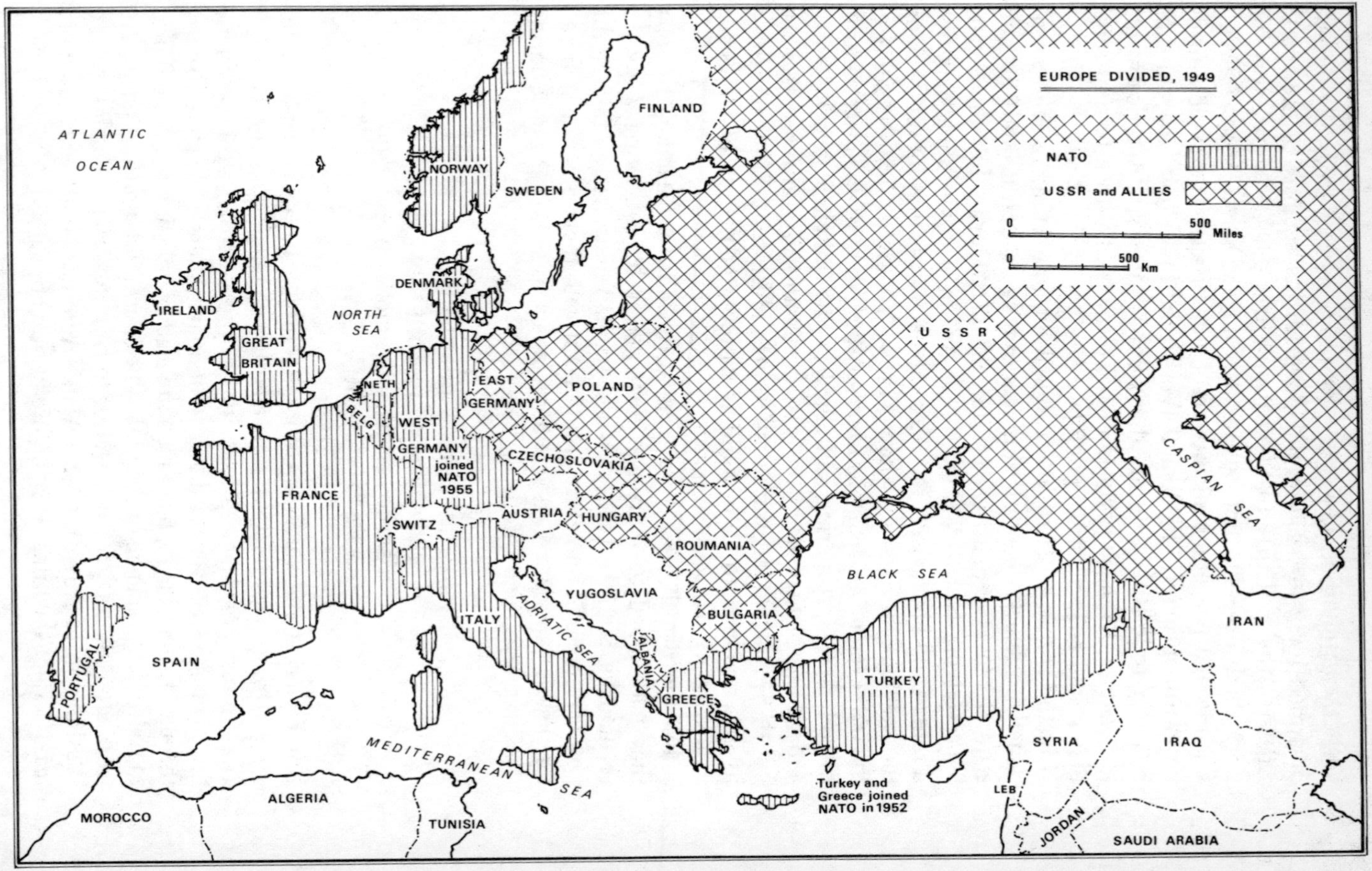
EUROPE DIVIDED, 1949
NATO
USSR and ALLIES
0
500 Miles
0
500 Km
ATLANTIC OCEAN
NORWAY
SWEDEN
FINLAND
IRELAND
GREAT BRITAIN
NORTH SEA
DENMARK
NETH
BELG
WEST GERMANY
joined NATO 1955
EAST GERMANY
POLAND
U S S R
CZECHOSLOVAKIA
FRANCE
SWITZ
AUSTRIA
HUNGARY
ROUMANIA
YUGOSLAVIA
BULGARIA
ALBANIA
GREECE
ITALY
ADRIATIC SEA
PORTUGAL
SPAIN
MEDITERRANEAN SEA
MOROCCO
ALGERIA
TUNISIA
BLACK SEA
TURKEY
Turkey and Greece joined NATO in 1952
CASPIAN SEA
IRAN
SYRIA
IRAQ
LEB
JORDAN
SAUDI ARABIA

allies by taking 'such action as it deems necessary, including the use of armed force, to restore and maintain the security of the North Atlantic area'.[55] Thirty years on from 1919, the US Senate was still wary about excessive entanglements. But the North Atlantic Treaty was the first peacetime alliance the United States had made outside its own hemisphere. If Donald Worby and his fellow GIs returning home in 1946 had been told that within three years America would have committed itself permanently to the security of western Europe, they would have been incredulous.

In the spring of 1949 international tension relaxed. Stalin abandoned his blockade of Berlin, acknowledging defeat, and the new state of West Germany came into existence. During July the Senate approved the North Atlantic Treaty by an overwhelming majority. Truman and his advisers felt deep satisfaction as they looked back on the previous four years. A new Europe had risen from the ruins of the old: even if one half was impoverished and under Soviet control, the other was prospering and allied to the United States. Recalling American isolationism in the past, Truman was convinced that the North Atlantic Treaty was 'a milestone in history . . . if it had existed in 1914 and in 1939 . . . it would have prevented the acts of aggression which led to two world wars'.[56]

For the British, too, there seemed cause for satisfaction. In 1945 they had hoped to remain a great power by cultivating a special relationship with the United States, seeing themselves as guiding the powerful but still immature young giant with their superior skill and diplomatic experience. As one anonymous verse-writer put it during the 1945 loan negotiations:

In Washington Lord Halifax
Once whispered to Lord Keynes:
'It's true *they* have the money bags
But *we* have all the brains.'[57]

But in 1945–6 the wartime partnership broke up, much as it had after 1918. Britain was left alone to face the Soviets, until the crises of 1947–9 brought America back into Europe with an aid programme for economic recovery and a revolutionary Atlantic alliance. Britain, through Ernest Bevin, had taken the lead in enlisting the New World to redress the balance of the Old. The special relationship seemed to work after all. As US Ambassador to Britain, Lewis Douglas, cabled Washington in August 1948, 'Anglo-American unity today is more firmly established than ever before in peacetime.'

But Douglas also noted an underlying problem: 'Britain has never before been in [a] position where her national security and economic fate are so completely dependent on and at [the] mercy of another country's decisions. Almost every day brings new evidence of her weakness and dependence on [the] US. This is a bitter pill for a country accustomed to full control of her national destiny.'[58] Over the next few years the truth of this contention was amply demonstrated.

10

Global Cold War

1949–54

On 24 June 1950 President Harry S. Truman was enjoying a brief respite from the burdens of office in his home town of Independence, Missouri, in the heartland of America on the outskirts of Kansas City. That evening, just after he had finished a quiet family dinner with his wife Bess and daughter Margaret, the telephone rang. It was a tense Dean Acheson, the Secretary of State, on the line from Washington. His message was blunt. 'Mr President, I have very serious news. The North Koreans have invaded South Korea.'[1] Truman flew back to Washington at once. It was the end of his much-needed vacation.

This was the beginning of a three-year conflict that shifted the Cold War from a European into a global arena and drew the United States into far-reaching commitments throughout Asia. It also brought Anglo-American relations, so recently restored by Marshall Aid and the North Atlantic Treaty, to a state of acrimony unmatched since the bitter rows between the two countries about the size of their navies in the 1920s.

Asia, unlike Europe, did not often make the headlines in the late 1940s. Yet vast changes were taking place beneath the surface of events. The United States had assumed control in Japan, leaving its allies with only a token say in the fate of their former enemy. Under General Douglas MacArthur's authoritarian leadership the Americans tried to reconstruct Japan as a democracy in America's image. On the mainland of Asia communism was on the march, challenging the French in Vietnam and the British in Malaya. Korea had been occupied by America and Russia in 1945, but, as in Germany, the two superpowers could not agree on the terms for a peace settlement. By 1948 two separate Korean states had emerged – the North tied to

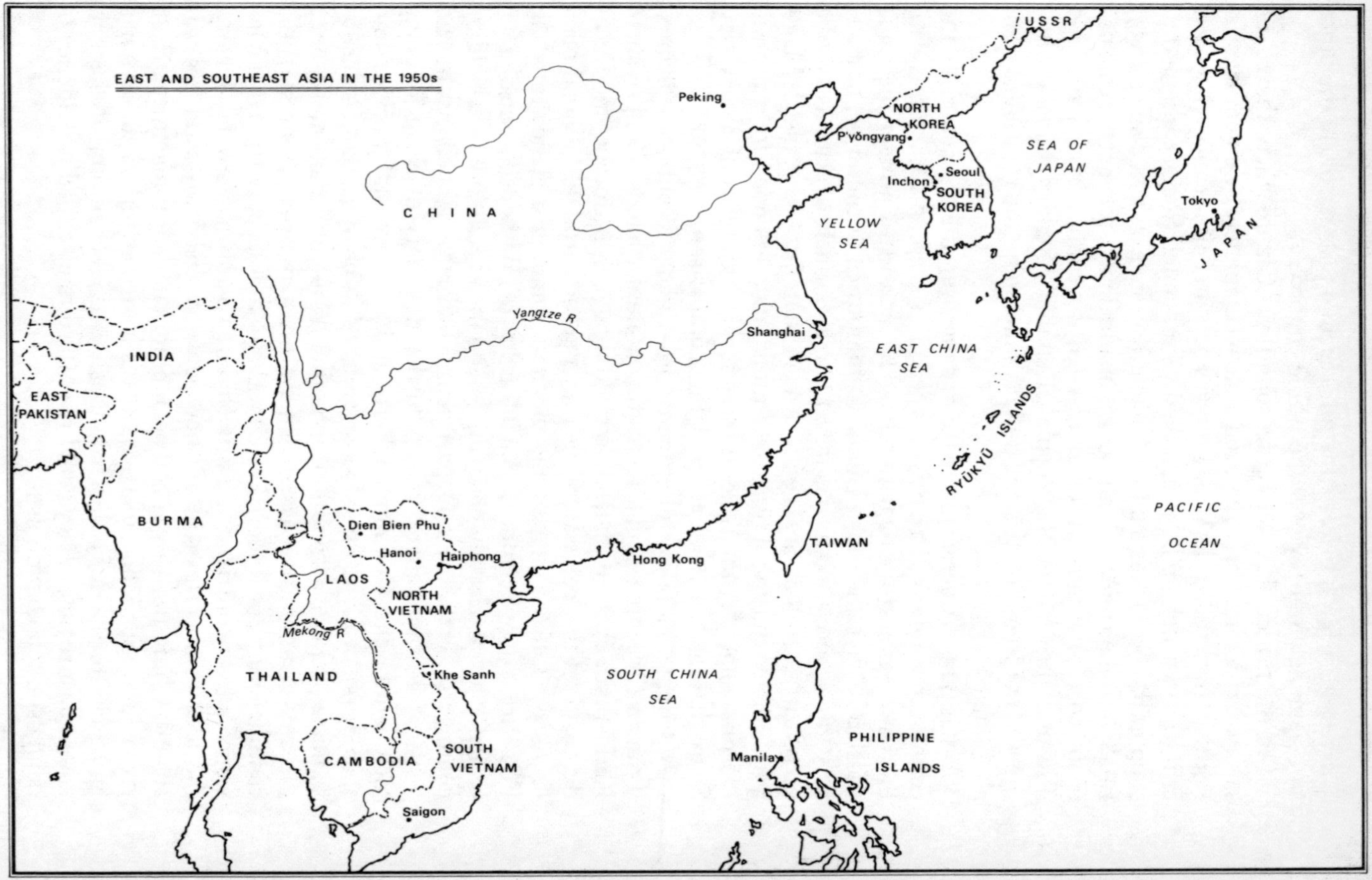

EAST AND SOUTHEAST ASIA IN THE 1950s

Moscow, the South to Washington – each bitterly hostile to the other and claiming authority over the whole country.

But the principal Asian battleground was China, where the 1940s saw American influence replaced almost completely by that of Russia. For the Chinese World War Two was only an episode in a thirty-year civil war in which millions had died. The United States continued to support the Nationalists under Chiang Kai-shek, as it had since 1937. But $3½ billion of American aid was insufficient to prevent the collapse of his corrupt regime. In October 1949 the communist leader, Mao Tse-tung, proclaimed the People's Republic of China. Chiang withdrew to the island of Taiwan, still claiming to be the rightful ruler of all China.

Britain and America parted company over their reaction to the Chinese revolution. The British needed to keep on good terms with the new regime to safeguard Hong Kong and to protect their still substantial investments in China. Commonwealth countries, particularly India, were also anxious for Britain to normalise relations as soon as possible. In January 1950 Britain therefore recognised Mao's government. But the Truman Administration intended to 'wait until the dust settled',[2] for America was now in the grip of a new Red Scare that made 1919 seem trivial by comparison.

In Congress a powerful group of pro-Chiang Republicans blamed Truman for letting China fall into communist hands. Congressman Karl Mundt claimed that, while building dykes in Europe, the President had let the 'red waters rush unchecked through the flood plain of Asia'.[3] Others jumped on the anti-communist bandwagon. In February 1950 Senator Joe McCarthy of Wisconsin, seeking an issue for his re-election campaign, denounced Acheson for shielding communists in the State Department. McCarthy claimed that he had a list of 205 diplomats 'known to the Secretary of State as being members of the Communist Party and who are still working and shaping policy in the State Department'.[4] His charges, though unsubstantiated, caused a sensation, and other dissident Republicans joined the anti-communist crusade, among them prospective presidential candidate Senator Robert Taft. It was also in February 1950 that Mao signed a treaty of friendship with Stalin. To anyone versed in history, the idea of a permanent alliance between their two countries was absurd: China and Russia had been bitter enemies for centuries. But, given America's mood in 1950, it was a further reason for Truman and Acheson to move very cautiously over recognition of the new communist regime. They could not afford to give further evidence of being 'soft' on communism.

When he received Acheson's call about the North Korean invasion of the South in June 1950 Truman therefore responded decisively. This was bare-faced aggression, sanctioned, he presumed, by Stalin, and it seemed vital to reassure Americans and the world that the defender of democracy would stand firm. Acheson told the British Government: 'Centrally directed Communist Imperialism has passed beyond subversion in seeking to conquer independent nations and is now resorting to armed aggression and war.'[5] With the Russians boycotting the UN Security Council because of Mao's exclusion, America was able to secure a resolution condemning North Korean aggression and committing a UN force to counter it.

Most of the UN troops were American, under the command of General MacArthur, recalled to active duty from his governorship in Japan. MacArthur stemmed the South Korean rout in September by his brilliant landing at the port of Inchon, 200 miles behind enemy lines. Now the North Koreans were in full retreat and a jubilant Truman Administration proclaimed that its goal was the reunification of the whole country under a democratic government. The Chinese warned that an American-dominated Korea, on their doorstep, would be unacceptable, but the Administration believed they were bluffing and allowed the rampaging MacArthur to press on to the Chinese border. On the night of 25–26 November some 300,000 Chinese troops attacked, driving the Americans in headlong retreat out of North Korea. MacArthur was blamed for his impetuosity, but Truman had approved his drive north, and it was Truman who soon caused an even greater ferment.

On 30 November, just after the Chinese invasion, the President gave a press conference. Convinced that a new world war was very close unless America demonstrated its resolve, he insisted that the United States would take 'whatever steps are necessary' in Korea. 'Will that include the atomic bomb?' asked one reporter. 'That includes every weapon we have,' the President replied. 'Does that mean that there is active consideration of the use of the atomic bomb?' 'There has always been consideration of its use.' Pressed about possible targets, Truman added: 'It's a matter that the military people will have to decide.'[6]

Paul Nitze, Director of Policy Planning at the State Department, heard the news in his fifth-floor office. 'For goodness sakes, Paul, get over here right away,' an agitated Truman aide told him. 'The President has just suggested in answer to a question that MacArthur had the authority to use atomic weapons if he determined they were necessary. What do we do about it?' Nitze raced over to the White

House and suggested that they simply 'change the record' of the news conference 'to say that General MacArthur did not have the authority to do it'. But he was too late. 'All the press of the world had it. It was already out on the wires so it couldn't be taken back.'[7]

In Britain Truman's ill-judged remarks caused consternation. In July 1950 the Cabinet, pressed hard by Washington, had agreed to send British troops to Korea. But there was growing concern about Washington's failure to consult with its allies and also alarm at the cost of the war, which had inflated world commodity prices and thus weakened the British economy. One senior member of the Foreign Office even warned that 'the American attitude may precipitate a general war in the Far East and thus World War'.[8] When news of Truman's press conference came through, Churchill and other Conservatives expressed their alarm and 100 Labour MPs signed a motion of criticism. Attlee was determined to reassure British opinion and to demonstrate to America and the world that this was a UN operation, not a purely American affair. When he told the Commons that he proposed to go immediately to Washington for talks with Truman, the House rang with cheers. It seemed like a dramatic reassertion of Britain's great power status and her special relationship with the United States.

Attlee knew that the press had blown Truman's remarks out of proportion, but his underlying concern was well founded. Whitehall was waking up to the fact that Britain had become, in George Orwell's words, America's 'Airstrip One'.[9] When the B-29s arrived during the Berlin crisis of 1948 they had used RAF bases in East Anglia. But in 1949 the US air force had asked to develop four airfields of its own in the Oxford area. This was a different issue. The Berlin crisis was over and Russia now had an atomic bomb, together with aircraft of sufficient range to drop it on Britain. The Ministry of Defence acknowledged that in all probability 'acceptance of the American proposals will involve the United States Air Force remaining in this country indefinitely'.[10] Bevin reminded the US Ambassador: 'What we had done was to allow the B-29 groups to be brought here as a protection during the difficult time arising out of the Berlin blockade. But there had never been a decision taken by the Cabinet regarding the permanent location of American bombers in this country; neither had we ever reported the question to Parliament.'[11]

Parliament was never consulted. Whitehall departments examined the matter secretly. The Foreign Office listed possible objections, including the effect on the local population of the base personnel with their high standard of living, the opportunity given Russian propaganda to suggest that Britain had become 'an occupied territory', and the fact that 'in allowing this island to become a forward base for American strategic bombing we increase the likelihood of becoming a primary target for any Russian atomic attack'. Despite these 'substantial objections', the Foreign Office believed that:

> the arguments on the other side appear, however, overwhelming. The primary aim of our Foreign Policy must be to keep the United States firmly committed in Europe. The presence of American troops in Germany is, of course, the main anchor which at present holds them, but . . . the establishment of secure air bases in this country . . . would certainly constitute an important additional tie . . . We must face the fact that this island is strategically well placed as an advanced air base and that we must accept this role.[12]

The Cabinet's Defence Committee decided to open negotiations with the United States, and in April 1950 agreement was reached on the development of four airfields at Fairford, Upper Heyford, Brize Norton and Greenham Common, with costs shared between the two governments. But these plans were soon superseded by the onset of the Korean War. With real fears of a Russian attack in Europe, additional air bases in Britain were required and the Pentagon now wanted to have the components of atomic weapons stockpiled there ready for any emergency. With Truman's approval planes were flown to Los Alamos and parked over a pit, where they were loaded in secret. The crews were never told exactly what they were carrying. When the bombers arrived in England they were taken away from the air-crew and moved to a classified area where a shroud was stretched round the fuselage to protect it from prying eyes. David Rolain, who flew on one of these B-29 'Silverplates', recalls that the British 'were strictly in the dark all the way round on this, but I think the RAF probably knew because we worked hand and foot with them'.[13]

Informally the British Government had given the nod, but they could not be consulted officially because the passing of atomic information to any foreign power was still forbidden under the McMahon Act of 1946. For the same reason the British were given few details about US war plans like 'Offtackle' which envisaged Britain as America's major base in any European war. The Chief of the Air Staff, Sir John Slessor, complained privately in July 1950 as the atomic bombs were brought to Britain: 'We know little about the United States Strategic Air Plan with reference to the part to be played by aircraft based in this country . . . In a matter like this, which was of life and death for the country and Western Europe, we were entitled not only to know the details of the plan but also to be consulted about them.'[14]

Little wonder that in December 1950, with Truman apparently threatening to use the bomb and Britain in the front line of Soviet retaliation, Attlee wanted, belatedly, to safeguard his country's position. He nearly succeeded. He was a shrewd politician, belying the mild manner that led Churchill to remark that 'there is less there than meets the eye'.* Attlee quietly took Truman aside during their White House meeting of 7 December to talk about the use of the atomic bomb. Returning to the conference table Truman informed his aides he had told Attlee 'that the Governments of the United Kingdom and the United States had always been partners in this matter and that he would not consider the use of the bomb without consulting with the United Kingdom'. Attlee 'asked whether this agreement should be put in writing, and the President replied no that it would not be in writing, that if a man's word wasn't any good it wasn't made any better by writing it down'.[16]

As Attlee, smiling quietly, expressed his thanks, Truman's advisers sat in horrified silence. Then Dean Acheson spoke. 'Let's adjourn the meeting for a few minutes, Mr President, we have something to talk to you about.' Gordon Arneson, Acheson's special assistant on atomic energy, went with them into a private room. He recalls that Truman 'was told in no uncertain terms, "You can't do that, Mr President. We can't do it. It's unconstitutional."'[17] Under the US Constitution, Acheson insisted, the President, as Commander-in-Chief, must be totally free to take actions he deemed necessary to defend the United States. Truman's promise was duly deleted from the official American record of the conference and the British were obliged to accept a much weaker passage in the final communiqué. This read: 'The President stated that it was his hope that world conditions would never call for the use of the atomic bomb. The President told the Prime Minister that it was also his desire to keep the Prime Minister at all times informed of developments which might bring about a change in the situation.'[18]

Keeping allies informed was not the same as joint consultation on the use of the bomb. A few months later, when Acheson was asked by Senator McMahon 'if any commitment had been made to any other

* To Truman, *en route* to Fulton in March 1946. The President defended Attlee: 'He seemed like a modest sort of fellow.' 'Yes,' muttered Churchill, 'he's got a lot to be modest about.'[15]

nation which might serve to delay the employment of US atomic weapons after the President had decided in his own mind that he wished to use them', he replied that 'no such commitment exists'.[19] Even the promise to keep Britain informed 'always has to be qualified by events', comments Lucius Battle, one of Acheson's key advisers at the time. He supports his interpretation with a telling example. During Attlee's visit a morning meeting was arranged at the White House. Not long before it was due to begin Dean Acheson was called by the number two at the Pentagon, Bob Lovett, and told that radar reports suggested that planes were attacking in strength from the north. Lovett said he would have to 'deal with it from an operational point of view'. Acheson explained that he was on his way to see Attlee. 'What shall I do? What shall I tell him?' Lovett replied: 'Explain it to him, but there's no way you can consult or ask him what to do.' After thirty minutes of panic at the State Department, the radar reflections proved to be not incoming Russian bombers but a flight of migrating geese.[20]

Attlee's visit to Washington exposed disagreements between the allies not just on the bomb but over other issues too: the danger of

David Low, *Daily Herald*, 12 January 1951.

America getting too involved in Asia, the degree to which China was a Soviet satellite, and the chances of an acceptable ceasefire and negotiated settlement in Korea. The final communiqué merely patched over the differences, and the following month the British Government was appalled when the United States proposed a UN resolution to brand China as the aggressor and impose punitive sanctions. On 25 January 1951 a majority of the Cabinet decided to vote against the US resolution, and only when the Americans watered it down was a public rift avoided.

Bevin was worried about the growing anti-American feeling. He reminded Attlee of the rationale of the special relationship: quiet persuasion not public confrontation was the way to change objectionable American policies. The British Commonwealth and western Europe, he wrote, were simply not 'strong enough, either economically or militarily, to hold out against the forces actively opposing them. The full participation of the United States is essential . . . Now is the time to build up the strength of the free world, morally, economically and militarily with the United States, and at the same time to exert sufficient control over the policy of the well-intentioned but inexperienced colossus on whose co-operation our safety depends . . . It can only be done by influencing the United States Government and people, not by opposing or discouraging them.'[21]

Bevin believed that British acquiescence in Asia was the price that had to be paid for American support in Europe. It was widely assumed that the Korean attack could be the prelude to a Russian offensive in Germany. The War Office advised the Cabinet in February 1951: 'War possible in 1951, probable in 1952.'[22] Previously the North Atlantic Treaty, for all its symbolic importance, had amounted to little more than a mutual defence pact. But in the crisis atmosphere of 1950–1 Washington began to 'put the "O" in NATO', to quote Averell Harriman, turning it from a paper commitment into an organised military alliance.[23] A proper command structure was established under the leadership of General Eisenhower and four new American combat divisions were sent to Europe, the first troop reinforcements since 1945. In return, Britain and France were persuaded to accept the principle of German rearmament and to boost their own defence spending. As America's main European partner, Britain increased the proportion of gross national product spent on defence from eight to fourteen per cent, second only to the USA.

The costs of rearmament provoked a sharp left-wing backlash against the American alliance. In 1945–7 the Labour left had called for an independent socialist foreign policy, denouncing the idea of

Britain as 'a pensioner of America . . . a junior partner in an American security system',[24] but they were silenced by the speed and generosity of Marshall Aid. Richard Crossman, a vociferous left-wing Member of Parliament, admitted in January 1948 that 'my own views about America have changed a great deal in the last six months. Many Members have had a similar experience.'[25] But dissent revived in April 1951, when a rearmament budget was introduced proposing Health Service charges for spectacles and dentures. Aneurin Bevan, the fiery Welsh ex-miner who had been the architect of the National Health Service, resigned from the Cabinet in protest, warning that the massive rearmament programme prompted by the Americans would undermine the economy. 'We have allowed ourselves to be dragged too far behind the wheels of American diplomacy,' he told the Commons.[26] According to Bevan the Soviet threat had been exaggerated, China was being driven into Stalin's hands by American conduct, and Britain's security and prosperity required a more independent line from the United States. One Conservative newspaper mocked that 'he would leave Britain confronting a perilous world, armed with false teeth'.[27]

Bevan had few followers in Parliament, but he caught the growing anti-American mood. In mid-1952 the Labour politician Hugh Gaitskell noted that 'hostility to America is fairly widespread in Britain today and has certainly increased since the outbreak of the Korean war'. The two main causes, he judged, were 'resentment at her wealth and power' and 'fear that she will involve us in war . . . The truth is that we have a dilemma. We do not like to admit our relative weakness, because we should then look much too like a satellite. But if we try and live up to a military standard we cannot afford, that means economic trouble. A poor relation who is driven to live beyond his means by his rich cousins will not feel well disposed to them.'[28]

America cannot win, says Cummings, *Daily Express*, 17 June 1952: condemned for deserting Europe, abused when coming to her aid.

By the time Gaitskell was writing, Labour was out of power. A new Conservative Government was elected in October 1951, headed by Winston Churchill, with Anthony Eden at the Foreign Office. This was the old wartime team that had managed the Grand Alliance of 1941–5. Churchill deprecated the growing friction between Britain and America and was determined to restore relations to the intimacy he had enjoyed with Roosevelt. But times had changed, though Churchill, nearing eighty, found that hard to accept. Evelyn Shuckburgh, Eden's private secretary, attended a meeting between Churchill and Truman in January 1952 at which the Prime Minister 'suddenly made an impassioned plea for Anglo-American co-operation in this great tradition we had had. And Truman said, "Thank you, Mr Prime Minister, we might pass that on to our advisers for further consideration." We felt very distressed by that,' Shuckburgh recalls.[29] Nor did Churchill enjoy greater success with Truman's Republican successor, Dwight D. Eisenhower. 'Ike' held his wartime leader in great esteem, but when they met in January 1953, soon after the President's inauguration, he concluded that 'Winston is trying to relive the days of World War II' and that he 'had developed an almost childlike faith that all of the answers are to be found merely in British-American partnership'.[30]

The limits of Churchill's influence became clear over the question of the atomic bomb. He had been furious at the way that, in his view, Labour had surrendered his wartime agreements with Roosevelt for atomic partnership and joint use of the bomb, at the time when 'by creating the American atomic base in East Anglia we have made ourselves the target, and perhaps the bull's eye of a Soviet attack'.[31] But in October 1951, just before the election, British diplomats had finally secured a formula from the Americans to cover the use of the bases in Britain. Privately Gordon Arneson of the State Department considered it 'quite thin' from the British point of view. But 'since the UK is prepared to accept it,' he told the Secretary of State, 'it would seem desirable to us to agree on the text as promptly as possible. If Churchill is returned to head the Government he will doubtless want to get a greater commitment from us. We would be in a better position to withstand his onslaught if this statement had already been agreed upon.'[32]

Arneson was right. On his visit to America in January 1952 Churchill had little choice but to accept the draft already agreed covering the US bases in Britain. The formula that he and Truman confirmed read: 'The use of these bases in an emergency would be a matter for joint decision by His Majesty's Government and the United States

Government in the light of the circumstances prevailing at the time.'[33] Each side was able to interpret this 'understanding' in its own way in public, Washington playing down any possible limitation on presidential power while Whitehall insisted that British interests were fully safeguarded. The words themselves seemed vague, but privately the British position on the bases was that 'there is naturally no question of their use in an emergency without our consent'. It seems from the available evidence that the Americans privately accepted this, although they urged the British to avoid saying so in public.[34] This Truman–Churchill 'understanding', backed by the secret interpretations, has remained the basis of the American presence in Britain ever since.

Despite this limited British success, the early 1950s had seen a marked shift in the tone of Anglo-American relations. Facing the threat of Soviet-backed communism in Europe in the 1940s the two countries had taken the lead in creating a unique Atlantic alliance. But, outside Europe, Britain and America had taken a very different view of the Chinese revolution, with the Americans becoming committed to an obsessive crusade against 'Red China'. By the end of 1950 the Cold War was global, and many, thinking back to the 1930s, feared that the sequence of crises would soon escalate into full-scale hostilities. The British Government had recovered some control over the use of US bases in Britain, but it had no other say on American use of the atomic bomb which, Truman and Eisenhower had both hinted, might be used to settle the Korean War.

The handling of the Cold War in Asia was not the only issue dividing the two allies. Equally contentious was their attitude to colonialism, which now assumed major importance as Britain tried to hold on to her position as a world power in the face of mounting anti-Western nationalism. In the past America's denunciation of imperialism had seemed to the British a way of picking up the spoils of empire for itself. Nowhere was the problem more acute than in the oil-rich Middle East, where the 1950s saw the last act of a drama that had been played out since World War One.

In the early twentieth century oil replaced coal as the essential fuel for modern industrial economies and for the navies and later the air forces of the world. America was blessed with large indigenous reserves, which satisfied most of its needs until World War Two, but Britain produced no oil of her own at this stage and, even before World War One, had used her dominant position in the Middle East to secure essential supplies. This was a costly business. Apart from the expense of exploitation, it was essential to protect pipelines and refineries and to agree with the rulers of the desert, under whose land

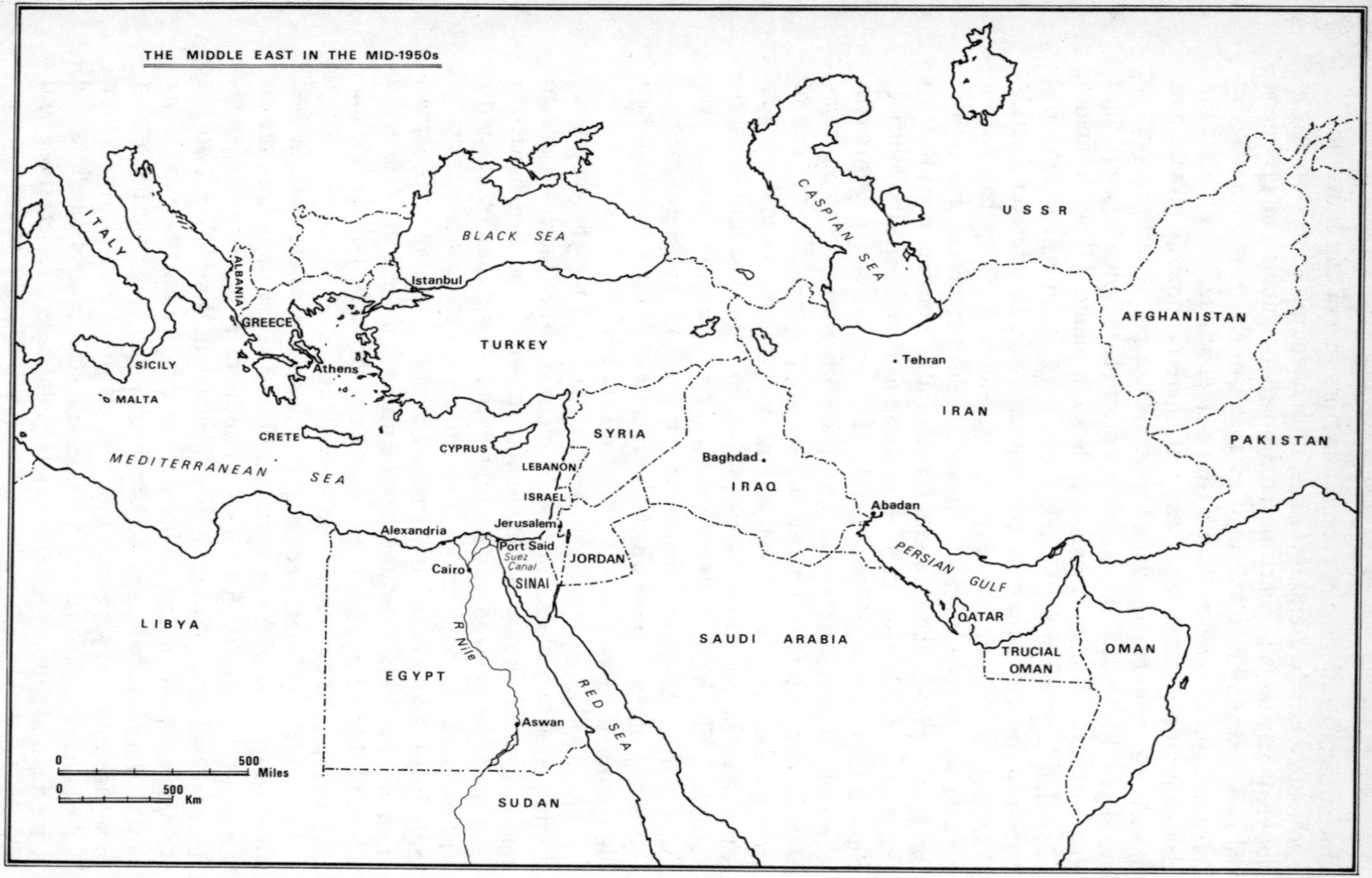
THE MIDDLE EAST IN THE MID-1950s
ITALY
SICILY
MALTA
ALBANIA
GREECE
Athens
CRETE
BLACK SEA
Istanbul
TURKEY
CYPRUS
MEDITERRANEAN SEA
CASPIAN SEA
USSR
AFGHANISTAN
Tehran
IRAN
PAKISTAN
SYRIA
LEBANON
ISRAEL
Jerusalem
Baghdad
IRAQ
Abadan
PERSIAN GULF
QATAR
TRUCIAL OMAN
OMAN
JORDAN
Port Said
Suez Canal
SINAI
Alexandria
Cairo
R Nile
LIBYA
EGYPT
Aswan
RED SEA
SAUDI ARABIA
SUDAN
0
500
Miles
0
500
Km

the oil lay, the terms on which drilling should take place and how the profits should be shared. So important was oil to Britain that the government took a majority shareholding in the Anglo-Persian Oil Company (forerunner of British Petroleum). Anglo-Persian, and Royal-Dutch Shell, in which British capital had a forty per cent share, were the major companies outside the United States.

Until the 1920s American oil companies concentrated almost entirely on exploiting domestic reserves, in states like Texas and Oklahoma. Unlike Anglo-Persian, they were private corporations with no government ownership, but the vital importance of oil meant that the US Government offered informal support for their activities. In the 1920s, motivated by the growing anxiety about America's access to raw materials, US companies started moving abroad, particularly in Central American countries like Venezuela, but also into the Middle East, which had previously been a British domain. In Persia British and American companies agreed to develop some concessions jointly: Standard Oil of New Jersey needed Anglo-Persian's transport and finance, while the British decided that the American presence helped prevent Russian expansion. 'Better Americans than Bolsheviks,' sniffed the head of the Foreign Office in 1921.[35] But despite these agreements, and a growing American presence in Saudi Arabia, Britain remained the predominant oil producer in the Middle East. In 1938 only about ten per cent of production in the region came from American-owned wells.

In oil, as in so many aspects of the relationship, World War Two marked a turning point. The conflict placed huge demands on American oil resources. Of the seven billion barrels produced for Allied use between December 1941 and August 1945, six billion came from the United States.[36] By 1943 the Roosevelt Administration could see that America's own reserves were no longer adequate and was determined to break Britain's stranglehold on the Middle East. Soon both governments were assiduously bribing local rulers, like Ibn Saud of Saudi Arabia, to keep them well-disposed and to secure oil concessions, while at the same time sending each other fulsome pledges of their good intentions. 'Please do accept my assurances,' Roosevelt cabled a suspicious Churchill in March 1944, 'that we are not making sheep's eyes at your oil fields in Iraq or Iran.' 'Let me reciprocate,' Churchill replied, 'by giving you the fullest assurance that we have no thought of trying to horn in upon your interests or property in Saudi Arabia.'[37]

It was not always a story of rivalry and suspicion. Often British and American oil companies made common cause against consumers and local rulers. But the underlying trend was clear. Gradually the British were being obliged to relinquish the dominant position in the Middle East that they had acquired, often by force, when there were few competitors and little local opposition. After World War Two they were fighting a losing battle against American and Russian oil expansion and against the mounting nationalist reaction to the hated foreign oil companies. The final struggle came in Iran (the new name for Persia).

The Anglo-Iranian Oil Company, as it was now known, had become a symbol of imperialist exploitation for the Iranians. Nationalisation of the oil fields and refineries became an increasingly popular demand, finally enacted by the Iranian Prime Minister, Dr Mohammed Mossadeq, in April 1951. The Labour Government was furious, despite its own record of nationalisation. By 1951 Iran was Britain's only non-dollar source of oil and a crucial bastion against Soviet expansion. Mossadeq's action was also a humiliation. The Foreign Secretary, Herbert Morrison, was among those advocating force to recover Anglo-Iranian's property, but it soon became apparent that Britain lacked the money and men to mount such a hazardous operation. Above all, the United States was opposed to it. The Cabinet agreed on 27 September that the American attitude was decisive. 'We could not afford to break with the United States on an issue of this kind.'[38]

The Truman Administration saw the matter in a fundamentally different light from the governments of Attlee and Churchill. The British regarded Mossadeq with contempt as a bald, runny-nosed little man, dressed in pyjamas and prone to fainting in public. The British Ambassador in Tehran regularly referred to him as a 'lunatic'.[39] The Americans, by contrast, considered Mossadeq to be a histrionic but rational nationalist, trying to recover for his own countrymen what decades of imperialist exploitation had denied them. Acheson believed that the crisis could have been averted if Anglo-Iranian had made timely concessions, instead of living in the nineteenth century when natives were seen and not heard. 'Never,' commented Acheson, 'had so few lost so much so stupidly and so fast.'[40] He held up as a model for the future the deal recently concluded by Aramco, the American oil giant, for a fifty-fifty profit-sharing arrangement with the Saudis. This, the Americans claimed, was the way to do business in a profitable but enlightened way.

Truman and Acheson did their best to mediate, pressing the British to accept nationalisation with adequate compensation. They were unsuccessful. Instead, British oil personnel were withdrawn from Iran, production was halted, and other major oil companies were persuaded not to buy Iranian oil until the dispute had been settled. Stalemate ensued, but gradually the Iranian economy was crumbling and with it the stability of the Shah's regime.

The new Republican Administration in January 1953 shifted American policy. Like Truman and Acheson, Eisenhower and his Secretary of State, John Foster Dulles, feared that the economic crisis might drive Mossadeq into communist hands. Unlike their predecessors they were prepared to act ruthlessly to prevent this. British intelligence judged that there was sufficient opposition to Mossadeq to mount a coup against him. Eden passed on the information to Washington and the British and American secret services concocted plan 'Ajax' to topple Mossadeq. 'So this is how we get rid of that madman,' Dulles chuckled when he was given a copy.[41] Led by Kim Roosevelt, Teddy's grandson and a cousin of FDR, the Central Intelligence Agency orchestrated anti-Mossadeq demonstrations and an army revolt in August 1953. The Shah, who had briefly fled the country, was restored and Mossadeq tried and imprisoned.

This was the first major 'covert operation' by the CIA, precursor of things to come – Guatemala in 1954 and Cuba in 1961. Eisenhower was much readier than Truman to use the CIA to achieve American ends in situations where public intervention would be impolitic. It was another sign that America was having to compromise its pristine moral principles when assuming the messy burdens of world power.

In Iran the oil crisis was settled with the new government. After tough bargaining a deal was arranged in 1954 which brought the British substantial compensation but broke their oil monopoly for good. Anglo-Iranian's share dropped to forty per cent and a consortium of American companies secured another forty per cent, leaving Dutch and French companies with the rest. As a result of the settlement, America's share of total Middle Eastern oil rose from forty-four per cent to fifty-eight per cent, while Britain's dropped from fifty-three per cent to twenty-four per cent.[42]

The Americans always denied that they had used the crisis to muscle in on British interests. George McGhee of the State Department, himself a former oilman, says, 'In Iran we came in your support, at your request. So I wouldn't call it flexing power.'[43] But the British were sceptical. The Ambassador in Washington, Sir Roger Makins, pointed out in 1954 that the United States was 'now firmly established as the paramount foreign influence in Turkey and in Saudi Arabia. They are gaining a similar ascendancy in Persia, and it now seems that Pakistan may to some extent be drawn into their orbit . . .

Are the Americans,' he asked, 'consciously trying to substitute their influence for ours in the Middle East?'[44]

In the early 1950s the global Cold War and the mounting opposition to colonialism saw America becoming a major influence in parts of the world it had previously ignored, while Britain found it ever harder to hold on to her great-power position. But it would be wrong to imply that Britain no longer mattered in the world. She was still the third strongest power. Much of her empire remained intact. She had substantial armed forces because she still retained conscription, and her industrial output vastly exceeded that of France or West Germany, let alone Japan. In 1952 she was the third country to test an atomic bomb, becoming the only other nuclear power apart from America and Russia.

Britain was therefore still America's most important ally in the struggle to contain the spread of communism around the world. British bases from Gibraltar to Singapore, from Alexandria to Simonstown, were invaluable supports for American ships and planes. Long-standing British contacts with native rulers could help shore up unstable governments teetering on the brink of revolution. Behind the scenes a secret worldwide alliance in the monitoring of signals intelligence had developed between America, Britain, Canada, Australia and New Zealand. Despite the Anglo-American rivalries and disagreement, therefore, the two had much in common, even in the depths of the Cold War. Privately American policy-makers like Paul Nitze used Churchill's phrase, 'a special relationship', to describe the alliance,[45] even though such language was rarely used in public because of the continued anglophobe feeling in the United States and the jealousy of America's other allies.*

Despite Britain's débâcle in Iran, the reality of her influence was displayed clearly during 1954 on the other side of the world, in Vietnam. When Mossadeq nationalised the Iranian oil fields in 1951, it was the Americans who restrained the British, discouraging the use of force and urging on them a negotiated settlement. In the Vietnam crisis in the spring of 1954, the boot was on the other foot, with Britain dissuading America from armed intervention and forcing through a negotiated settlement which, had it lasted, might have saved America from the quagmire of the 1960s.

* In May 1950 Secretary of State Dean Acheson discovered a memo written by his subordinates discussing the special relationship. He ordered all copies to be burned. Acheson did not dispute 'the genuineness of the special relationship', but 'in the hands of troublemakers,' he argued, the memo 'could stir no end of a hullabaloo, both domestic and international'.[46]

In 1954 Vietnam, with Laos and Cambodia, was still part of France's crumbling empire in Indo-China. For eight years the French, dominant in the south of Vietnam, had struggled against the Vietminh forces of the communist leader Ho Chi Minh. By March 1954 12,000 of France's crack troops were trapped in Dien Bien Phu, a remote northern village surrounded by hills packed with Vietminh insurgents. Like human ants the Vietminh carried the parts of heavy-artillery pieces up the steep slopes, from which, reassembled, they knocked out the French airfield, making resupply impossible. If Dien Bien Phu fell it was unlikely that the French public would be willing to carry on the unwinnable war.

The United States had welcomed the tide of decolonisation in Asia in the 1940s, even threatening the Dutch with termination of Marshall Aid if they did not pull out of Indonesia in 1949. But their tune began to change after the Chinese revolution, when it seemed that communist forces were exploiting the growing nationalist revolt to extend the influence of Moscow and Peking. At the end of 1949 the National Security Council warned Truman that the loss of south-east Asia to communism would be 'a major political rout the repercussions of which will be felt throughout the rest of the world'.[47] During the Korean War both America and China provided increasing support to the two sides in Vietnam, and by 1954 the United States was bearing nearly half the cost of the French war effort. Obsessed with the menace from 'Red China' the Americans had to decide in March 1954 whether to let Dien Bien Phu fall, and with it the French position in Vietnam, or to enter the war themselves. 'My God, we must not lose Asia,' Eisenhower exclaimed; 'we've got to look the thing right in the face.'[48]

Admiral Arthur Radford, chairman of the Joint Chiefs of Staff, favoured an air strike to relieve the French and even talked about using atomic weapons, but his colleagues, together with Dulles and Eisenhower, believed that this would lead to full-scale American intervention. Congressional leaders made it clear that they wanted 'no more Koreas', with America supplying most of the manpower, and they insisted that any American involvement, even air strikes, must be conditional on the support of America's allies, particularly Britain. Dulles set to work to build a common front in south-east Asia.

On 5 April 1954 Eisenhower sent an urgent appeal to Churchill. He asked for 'united action' to contain China, and played on their common wartime experience: 'we failed to halt Hirohito, Mussolini and Hitler by not acting in unity and in time . . . May it not be that our nations have learned something from that lesson?'[49] In March the British had agreed to talks about united action, but, fearful of the trend of American policy, Eden backtracked, much to Dulles's anger. The Foreign Secretary insisted that Britain would have nothing to do with military action or the American proposal for a south-east Asian equivalent of NATO, until the chances of a negotiated settlement had been fully explored. The British believed that the French were finished in Vietnam but they did not think this was disastrous, dismissing as grossly exaggerated Dulles's warnings that Indo-China was like the first in a row of dominoes whose fall would have 'a vital effect on Thailand, Malaya, and Indonesia' and could eventually 'lead to the loss of Japan'.[50] As in December 1950, the British feared that the Americans were bringing the world close to the brink of war by their visceral hatred of Mao's China.

American officials privately denounced the British as deceitful and 'weak-kneed',[51] but London's response proved decisive. The Eisenhower Administration sent no military support to the French; Dien Bien Phu fell and with it France's will to fight; and in the summer of 1954 the big powers convened in Geneva to negotiate – America, Britain, France, Russia, and, for the first time in a major conference, communist China.

Relations between Eden and Dulles were now close to breaking point. Eden fumed to his officials 'that all the Americans want to do is replace the French and run Indo-China themselves'. He went on: 'They want to replace us in Egypt too. They want to run the world.'[52] Without consulting Dulles he unveiled his own peace plan for Indo-China, involving independence for Cambodia and Laos and the partition of Vietnam, with the communists dominant in the North. For Dulles, the idea of the United States and Red China negotiating a 'sell-out' to communism was abhorrent. At Geneva he 'conducted himself with the pinched distaste of a puritan in a house of ill repute',[53] staying only briefly before turning matters over to his subordinates and publicly refusing to shake hands with Chou En-lai, a snub the Chinese never forgot. Dulles's principal expert on east Asia, Walter Robertson, insisted that they would have no dealings with the Chinese, official or social. 'You do not take a drink, when the court rises, with the criminal at the bar.'[54]

With the Americans sulking on the sidelines at Geneva, the initiative fell to Britain and Russia who both wanted a settlement. Even so, nothing would have been achieved without the French, whose new government was bent on ending the war. But Eden kept the negotiations going, and his partition plan formed the basis of the final settlement in July 1954. Vietnam would be divided in two, but unlike

Korea and Germany, it was intended that free elections in 1956 would pave the way for reunification of the country. The British privately had little doubt that Ho would win those elections, but they did not believe that this would be fatal for the West. The Americans, however, disagreed. They compared Eden's conduct at Geneva to Chamberlain's at Munich and refused to accept the Accords. It took an indefatigable Ho twenty years to achieve his aim, and in the process America experienced the worst defeat in its history. Whether the United States would have been better advised to have accepted the inevitable in 1954, much as Britain, with more at stake, had to do over Iran, is an intriguing conjecture.

In Britain Eden was widely praised for the Geneva settlement and credited with saving the world from war. After several years of resentment about American power, the British press relished the feeling that Britain was an independent actor on the world stage once more, and there was ill-disguised satisfaction at what the left-wing *New Statesman* called America's 'unmitigated defeat at Geneva'.[55] It seemed to confirm that the Anglo-American relationship was not a one-way street: Britain could still feel she had the brains to manage the sometimes irrational American brawn.

Eden enjoyed another diplomatic success in the autumn of 1954 over the vexed issue of German rearmament. Ever since the Korean War began the Americans had been pressing for this, arguing that western Europe would not otherwise be able to defend itself against Soviet attack. But it took several years to find a solution acceptable to the French, who still feared German aggression. In August 1954 the French Assembly finally vetoed the idea of a European Defence Community, which would have included a rearmed Germany. It did so in the face of a warning from Dulles that rejection 'would compel an agonizing reappraisal of basic United States policy'.[56]

Eden and his officials were alarmed. They feared that America, now embroiled in McCarthyism and preoccupied with Asia, might pull out of Europe and thus unravel the Atlantic alliance on which all British foreign policy was based. Eden himself toured European capitals to find a solution, arguing that 'this was a moment when Europe had to take the initiative to sort this essentially European problem out'.[57] Eden's approach indicated his desire for a more independent, though co-operative, relationship with the United States. At a conference in London in the autumn of 1954 he presented his proposals. Germany would rearm and join NATO but under suitable restrictions, including a pledge never to have nuclear weapons. Eden also made an unprecedented offer. For years the British had refused to commit troops permanently on the Continent, despite intense French efforts before both world wars. But on 30 September Eden told the conference that the British would keep four divisions and a tactical air force in Germany for as long as her allies desired. The conference was deeply moved. The French Ambassador wept openly, saying that 'for fifty years . . . French public opinion has waited for this announcement'.[58] With this new British commitment to reassure the French, the conference reached agreement and West Germany joined NATO in May 1955.

By the end of 1954 Britain could feel that she had redressed the balance of the Anglo-American alliance, which had seemed to have tipped so markedly against her in 1950–1. The British Government could claim credit for major diplomatic agreements over Vietnam and Germany. In the first she had restrained America and in the second led western Europe into a creative solution to its dilemma over German rearmament. Even over Iran, where Britain had been forced to share its oil monopoly with America, the Mossadeq regime had been toppled by Anglo-American action, and it was tempting to assume that in any future Middle Eastern crises America could eventually be brought round to the British position.

Few would have guessed at the end of 1954 that in less than two years not only the Anglo-American alliance but also Britain's position as a great power would be in ruins.

11

The Empire's Last Gasp

1955–6

The Suez crisis of 1956 saw the worst rift of the twentieth century between Britain and America. It reflected their contrasting attitudes to communism and colonialism, the different stake each had in the Middle East, and the growing disparity in power between the two countries. But Suez was also a tragedy of personalities, dramatically demonstrating how common language and even personal friendship could not prevent complete misunderstanding. Three main figures were involved: Anthony Eden, Britain's Prime Minister, President Dwight D. Eisenhower, and his Secretary of State, John Foster Dulles. But lurking behind Eden was Winston Churchill, from whose shadow Eden had been trying to escape for most of his political life and whose approach to Anglo-American relations was often at odds with his own.

Churchill was Prime Minister from October 1951 to April 1955. By this time he was a pale reflection of the war leader who had galvanised Whitehall and led his country through the darkest hours of her history. The old appetite for work had gone, he was often querulous and indecisive, and he found it hard to maintain concentration, particularly on unfamiliar problems. 'I have lived seventy-eight years without hearing of bloody places like Cambodia,' he complained in 1953.[1] But despite a serious stroke in June 1953, Churchill soldiered on, unable to contemplate political oblivion, but tantalising Eden, his heir-apparent, with repeated hints that he would soon resign.

Churchill reserved much of his limited energy for one foreign policy issue – the search for a great power summit to control nuclear weapons.

There is some irony in the Cold Warrior of Fulton becoming a leading apostle of détente, but Churchill was convinced that the vastly greater power of the hydrogen bomb (tested by America in 1952 and Russia in 1953) had transformed everything. He told his private secretary, Jock Colville, 'we're now as far from the atomic bomb as the atomic bomb was from the bow and arrow'.[2] He felt that it was his duty to guide the USA into 'world easement'. 'America is very powerful,' he remarked, 'but very clumsy.'[3]

In May 1953, after Stalin's death, the moment seemed propitious and Churchill called publicly for an informal great-power summit which, at the very least, he said, could help convince the participants 'that they might do something better than tear the human race, including themselves, into bits'.[4] But the Prime Minister's stroke dashed his hopes of a visit to Moscow, and his subsequent efforts to revive the project were frustrated by Eisenhower and Eden, who both regarded it as rash and premature. They did not share Churchill's belief that his wartime meetings with Roosevelt and Stalin demonstrated the wisdom of personal summitry.

With Churchill ailing, much of British diplomacy was left in the hands of his Foreign Secretary, Anthony Eden. Eden was a handsome, elegant man, who had made his name as a determined opponent of appeasement in the 1930s. His diplomatic experience was immense, having headed the Foreign Office in 1935–8 and 1940–5. Yet Eden was in some ways an undiplomatic personality: capable of great charm, but volatile in mood and often petulantly angry with events and people. He lacked Churchill's resilience of character, and his insecure vanity was legendary in Whitehall. 'He is like a sea anemone,' noted Evelyn Shuckburgh, his private secretary, 'covered with sensitive tentacles all recording currents of opinion around him. He quivers with sensitivity to opinion in the House [of Commons], the [Conservative] party, the newspapers.'[5]

Eden was very different from his American counterpart. John Foster Dulles evoked memories of his Princeton professor, Woodrow Wilson. Although more heavily built, there was the same gravity of manner, the same severe, bespectacled face. And, despite the fact that Dulles was a Republican not a Democrat, there was also a similar ideological approach to foreign affairs, grounded in Calvinist Christianity, and, in Dulles's case, animated by a burning hatred of communism. In the 1952 election campaign Dulles had achieved notoriety by his rhetoric about 'rolling back' communism and 'liberating' Russia's subject peoples. 'Why should we assume that what Soviet Communism can *do* in China, we cannot *undo*?' he asked a New Jersey audience in

How not to behave in Britain: *above* do not make fun of the money or *below* insult a Scotsman's kilt. Scenes from *A Welcome to Britain* (1943).

Planning the invasion of France: *(left to right)* Bradley, Ramsay, Tedder, Eisenhower, Montgomery, Leigh-Mallory and Bedell Smith (February 1944).

Yalta (February 1945). Behind Churchill, Roosevelt and Stalin are their Foreign Ministers: Eden, Stettinius and Molotov.

The Iron Curtain speech. Churchill at Westminster College, Fulton, Missouri, with President Truman behind (5 March 1946).

George C. Marshall and Ernest Bevin at a Thanksgiving luncheon in London (27 November 1947).

An American aircraft transporting supplies into the blockaded city of Berlin in 1948.

Inspection at a US air force base in Britain in 1952.

October 1952.[6] Much of the rhetoric was for domestic political consumption, to prove his credentials to a McCarthyite Republican Party. But he so alarmed the British that Eden and Churchill had even lobbied discreetly against Dulles's appointment as Secretary of State. They failed, but after seeing Eisenhower in Washington on 20 November 1952, Eden cabled Churchill: 'The new Secretary of State would not have been my choice. Ike was almost apologetic. We must do the best we can with him.'[7]

In private Dulles could be congenial company. But to most people he seemed ponderous and legalistic ('Dull, Duller, Dulles', in the words of one Washington joke). Trained as an international lawyer he often found Eden vague and imprecise, and Eden's languid habit of addressing colleagues as 'dear' was particularly disquieting. More important still, Dulles's legal ties had been with French and German leaders. He had no experience of the wartime partnership with Britain, which had shaped the outlook of other American policy-makers of the post-war period such as Marshall, Acheson and Eisenhower. At times Eden and Dulles worked well together, but the American never fully forgave Eden for his conduct over Vietnam in 1954 and relations between them were rarely good thereafter.

Eden's rifts with Dulles were, however, attributable to more than temperamental differences. Unlike Churchill, Eden was not convinced that co-operation with America should be the overriding priority of British policy. The half-American Churchill believed in the special relationship with almost religious fervour. 'My hope for the future,' he told Eisenhower in 1953, 'is founded on the increasing unity of the English-speaking world. If that holds all holds. If that fails no one can be sure of what will happen.'[8] Eden had no doubt that Anglo-American co-operation was important: that had been a major reason for his break with Neville Chamberlain in 1938. But he believed that Britain need not subordinate her foreign policy to every whim of Washington. His successes over Vietnam and Germany in 1954 strengthened these convictions, and when he finally became Prime Minister in April 1955 he was not willing to defer to the Americans if British interests seemed to dictate an independent line.

The search for disarmament was a striking example. In the spring of 1955 Eden suddenly saw great merits in the idea of a summit conference. Churchill commented with a sly smile, 'It is wonderful what difference it makes to your views about a top-level meeting when you get to the top.'[9] Although the Foreign Office still wished to concert policy on disarmament with the United States, Eden told his Cabinet that 'we should be unwise to wait too long upon the Americans in this matter: it might be some considerable time before they produced any views of their own. We should not hesitate to go forward with our own enquiries . . . and to bring forward suggestions of our own as soon as we were ready.'[10] When the summit conference, the first for ten years, was convened in Geneva in July 1955, Eden confidently expected to be the star, as he had been over Indo-China the previous year.

This comfortable assumption of continued European superiority was illustrated for the British by the conference cuisine. One day the Americans hosted lunch. According to Harold Macmillan, then Eden's Foreign Secretary, it was 'a disgusting meal, of large meat slices, hacked out . . . and served . . . with marmalade and jam'. When the French reciprocated, their guests were treated to 'a long series of exquisite courses with wines of equal distinction'. It was, Macmillan mused contentedly, 'a demonstration of the refinements of the Old World against the barbarism of the New, whether in East or West'.[11]

But the centre of attention at Geneva in 1955 was not Eden but Eisenhower, a man whom the British were prone to underestimate. Their recollections of him as Allied Supreme Commander in Europe during World War Two were pleasant but unflattering. 'In the war,' said Churchill in July 1953, 'he had a very genuine gift for friendship and for keeping the peace. But I decided in the States six months ago that he was really a Brigadier.' By the end of the year Churchill had concluded that 'everything is left to Dulles. It appears that the President is no more than a ventriloquist's doll.'[12] This was a common judgement in London: Sir Philip de Zulueta, Eden's private secretary at the time, feels that Eden never quite came to terms with Eisenhower's elevation from army officer to head of state.[13]

The British were therefore ill-prepared for the President's performance at the 1955 summit. Unlike at the Geneva Conference a year before, the Americans were serious participants and Ike surprised everyone, including the British, with his radical proposal on arms control. The President recognised that the central obstacle was verification, the need for each side, in the absence of mutual trust, to have an agreed method for reassuring itself that the other was not cheating. He therefore suggested an 'Open Skies' policy under which East and West would exchange maps showing the location of their military installations and would permit aerial photographic reconnaissance over their territory. Just as he finished his dramatic proposal there was a tremendous clap of thunder and all the lights in the conference hall went out. 'Well,' said Eisenhower, 'I expected to make a hit but not that much of one.'[14]

The President's plan did not, however, make a hit with the Russians, who rejected it as licensed espionage. But 'Open Skies' captured the headlines and was an indication of Ike's true role. Despite his easy-going manner, his verbal slips and the wide latitude he gave his subordinates, Eisenhower was the man who ultimately decided American foreign policy. Dulles understood that; the British did not – until it was too late.

Despite the shock to British pretensions at Geneva, Eden and his colleagues remained confident of their ability to play an independent role in the world. During 1955 the British made crucial decisions that left them outside the European Common Market when it came into being in 1958. It was a fateful step, taken against American advice, which would require a quarter of a century fully to correct, but which, at the time, seemed both right and inevitable.

The British had always been reluctant to throw in their lot with the countries across the 'English Channel', often using the word 'Europe' to exclude Britain and signify only the Continent. Back in 1930 Churchill had insisted: 'We are with Europe, but not of it. We are linked, but not compromised. We are interested and associated, but not absorbed . . . We belong to no single continent, but to all.'[15] Two world wars had modified that attitude but had not fundamentally altered it. In 1947–8, at a time when America seemed isolationist and Russia malevolent, Bevin talked of 'Western European Union' and instigated greater co-operation with France, Belgium, Holland and Luxembourg. But the British only favoured co-operation between governments; they did not intend to surrender national sovereignty to form a European federation. Nor would they accept the more limited idea, proposed by the French in 1950, for a European coal and steel community in which the industries of participating countries would be subject to a 'higher authority'.

In so far as proposals like the coal and steel community brought France and Germany together after years of strife, they were welcomed in London. But that did not mean Britain joining in. 'I meant it for them, not us,' remarked Churchill about the idea of a European army.[16] For Britain, still a world power, relations with continental Europe were not the top priority. France, West Germany and their neighbours were still struggling to recover from the defeat and devastation of the war. They hardly seemed fit allies for the victorious British whose empire, investments and commerce still girdled the globe. Ties of kinship were also important. Eden used to say 'that if you were to open the personal mail arriving from overseas in any post office in England you would find that ninety per cent of it came from beyond Europe, from Australia, Canada, India, Africa, anywhere, indeed, where British soldiers and administrators had served or British families settled'.[17] These countries meant much more to British people than France, Germany or Italy. Eden therefore spoke for Conservatives and Labour alike in 1952 when he called the suggestion that Britain should join:

> a federation on the continent of Europe . . . something which we know, in our bones, we cannot do . . . For Britain's story and her interests lie far beyond the continent of Europe. Our thoughts move across the seas to the many communities in which our people play their part, in every corner of the world. These are our family ties. That is our life: without it we should be no more than some millions of people living on an island off the coast of Europe, in which nobody wants to take any particular interest.[18]

Britain's instinctive feeling that she was not really European was incomprehensible to most Americans. During the Marshall Plan the Truman Administration had encouraged the British Government to accept the goal of a united, and ultimately federal, western Europe, which would help reduce the burdens on the United States. As Marshall Aid administrator, Paul Hoffman, observed, the aim was 'to get Europe on her feet and off our backs'.[19] Leadership of the 'new Europe' by Britain, America's closest ally, could ensure that it developed in a way that furthered American objectives. And, unlike the British, Americans were used to a continent-wide common market and a federal system of government. They believed that these had helped make America great and would, if implemented across the Atlantic, finally convert the mad, bad Old World from its obsessive rivalries and bloodshed. But constant American pressure on Britain was unavailing. The British were resentful that even close friends such as Averell Harriman entertained 'besetting fallacies . . . that Britain is a part of a Continental Europe that can be run as a single economic unit'.[20] They remained immune to American advice and eventually the two governments agreed to differ on this fundamental issue.

When, in the summer of 1955, the six members of the European Coal and Steel Community – France, West Germany, Italy, Belgium, the Netherlands and Luxembourg – met to plan a full-scale common market, the British Government only sent observers. They regarded the meeting as likely to create an inward-looking, protectionist organisation, at odds with Britain's trading interests around the world. Unable to steer the negotiations in the direction they desired, the

British left the Six to develop the Common Market without them. Nor were they interested in plans for a European atomic energy project. As the only country apart from the superpowers to hold nuclear weapons, Britain, it was felt, 'would have much to give but little to gain'.[21]

Within eighteen months, however, Britain's complacency was shattered. She was reduced to a point where the Foreign Office seriously considered abandoning its relationship with America and throwing in its lot with the Six.

The setting was Egypt. Since its construction by the British and French in 1869, the Suez Canal had been the main artery of the British Empire, connecting Britain with India and the Pacific. After India became independent in 1947 that function became less important, but, in the days before supertankers, it was still the route by which two-thirds of the oil produced in the Persian Gulf was shipped to the West, and therefore a sea route of immense strategic importance.

Britain had dominated Egypt since the 1880s, and the Canal Zone was the centre of her military presence in the eastern Mediterranean. This was a vast area of garrisons, airfields, supply depots and training grounds stretching from the canal almost to Cairo. It was as if the heart of England, from London to Birmingham, was under foreign military rule. For the Egyptians the Canal Zone was a visible reminder of the hated British occupation, and, after a military coup in 1952 which toppled the plump, sybaritic King Farouk, efforts to evict Britain were intensified. British personnel were attacked, mobs burned British property and Egyptians boycotted British employment, making it increasingly difficult to operate the Canal Zone.

Churchill and Eden, Prime Minister and Foreign Secretary, disagreed about the correct response. Both were determined to maintain Britain's position as a Middle Eastern power, but Eden argued that she had to adopt new methods in view of her diminished power and the growth of anti-colonial nationalism. He believed Britain should bow to the inevitable and evacuate the Canal Zone, while retaining the right of re-entry in an emergency. Churchill disliked what he called 'this policy of scuttle in Egypt',[22] and much of the Conservative Party agreed. Eden had to battle hard for many months. 'What we are trying to do in Egypt,' he told one critic, 'is not to run away from a regime which often says crude and hostile things, but rather to lay the foundations of security in the Middle East in the new and changed circumstances that now prevail there . . . It is a case of "new times, new methods".'[23] Gradually Eden won through, particularly when the beginning of the H-bomb age convinced Churchill and many of the military that sprawling conventional bases were now redundant. In 1954 the British agreed to withdraw all their troops from the Canal Zone by June 1956. The canal itself would continue to be operated by the Anglo-French company that owned it.

Eden hoped that the agreement had cleared the decks for a new relationship with Egypt, in which Colonel Gamal Abdel Nasser had now emerged as a leader. And, once the British presence had been terminated, the Americans were willing to step in with aid for Egypt. In late 1955 Britain and America agreed to provide Nasser with a loan of $70 million towards the Aswan High Dam, which would provide Egypt with electric power and better irrigation. But Nasser's ambition was not only the economic modernisation of his own country, but the political resurrection of the whole Arab world. His brand of socialist nationalism was not just anti-colonial but opposed to the exploitation of the Middle East by all the great powers. He set out to exploit the exploiters.

While accepting the loan from Britain and America, Nasser also ordered arms from the Soviet Union by way of Czechoslovakia. He tried to undermine the British-led Baghdad Pact, which Eden had hoped would be a Middle Eastern equivalent of NATO, and he dismissed the Anglo-American plan for a peace treaty with Israel. Eden 'compared Nasser with Mussolini and said his object was to be a Caesar from the Gulf to the Atlantic, and to kick us out of all of it'.[24] By March 1956 both the British and American governments had had enough. With the successful coup against Mossadeq in mind, the British prepared plans for covert operations against Egypt. Eden 'was quite emphatic that Nasser must be got rid of', Shuckburgh recorded on 12 March 1956. 'It is either him or us, don't forget that,' the Prime Minister said.[25]

The Americans were not yet ready to go that far, but the CIA started making contingency plans, and Dulles subjected the Dam project to renewed scrutiny. In Congress lobbies for Israel and US cotton were against it, and Nasser's recognition of communist China was a slap in the face for Dulles. On 19 July the Secretary of State summoned the Egyptian Ambassador, told him that the loan had been cancelled and issued a humiliating statement to the press casting doubt on Egypt's 'readiness and ability to concentrate its economic resources upon this vast construction program'.[26] The British were taken aback by the abruptness of Dulles's action, expecting the offer to be allowed simply 'to wither on the vine',[27] and Eisenhower also expressed disquiet at the way the Egyptians had been handled. Even Dulles had second thoughts. He normally walked straight out of his office with his hat on about seven-thirty each evening. But after work on 19 July he unexpectedly stopped and slumped down in a chair by the desk of one of his aides, Bill Macomber. 'Well,' he said, 'I hope we did the right thing.' Macomber tried to reassure him: 'I'm sure we did, sir.' 'Well,' said Dulles, 'I hope we did.' Then he put on his hat and walked out.[28]

The cancellation of the Aswan loan was the kind of dramatic gesture Nasser understood. A week later he more than matched it. On 26 July 1956, in a three-hour diatribe against the imperialists, he announced to an astonished world that he had nationalised the Suez Canal. In future it would be run by Egypt and the revenue would be used to finance the Aswan Dam. 'We shall build the High Dam,' Nasser proclaimed, 'on the skulls of 120,000 Egyptian workmen who died in building the Suez Canal.'[29] Eden was beside himself with rage. Fundamental British interests seemed in jeopardy, because a third of the ships using the canal were British and Britain only had oil reserves for six weeks. Eden's fury was fuelled by his sense of betrayal. He had gone out on a limb in 1954, arguing against strong Tory opposition that it was time to build a new, more trusting relationship with Egypt. Now his many critics were claiming that they had been totally vindicated.

Although the British started by imposing economic and political sanctions on Egypt, Eden was ready to use force. The Egypt Committee, set up by the British Cabinet to handle the crisis, noted on 30 July: 'While our ultimate purpose was to place the Canal under international control, our immediate objective was to bring about the downfall of the present Egyptian Government.'[30] Eden also made his attitude clear to Eisenhower. The day after nationalisation he cabled the President that, although currently exploring diplomatic measures, 'my colleagues and I are convinced that we must be ready, in the last resort, to use force to bring Nasser to his senses'.[31] A few days later he told Eisenhower again that 'the removal of Nasser and the installation in Egypt of a regime less hostile to the West' were major objectives, and he argued that 'I have never thought Nasser a Hitler . . . But the parallel with Mussolini is close. Neither of us can forget the lives and treasure he cost us before he was finally dealt with.'[32] At the height of the Dien Bien Phu crisis in Vietnam in 1954 Eisenhower had invoked the lessons of World War Two when he appealed to the British for help. Eden was trying the same tactic in reverse.

But Eisenhower was as unreceptive in 1956 as the British had been in 1954. His own Joint Chiefs of Staff favoured military action, but the President believed the British were 'out of date in thinking of this as a mode of action'.[33] It smacked of old-fashioned gunboat diplomacy, which would array the whole developing world against America. It would also outrage American anti-imperialist sensitivities.* Eisenhower was not indifferent to what had happened. He shared the growing alarm at Nasser's ambitions, and the Suez nationalisation had disturbing implications for America's control of the Panama Canal. But Suez was not a vital interest for America, as it was for Britain, and Eisenhower believed that the best way to react was through diplomacy. He sent Dulles to London at the beginning of August to persuade Eden to call a conference of those nations that used the canal. Eden was reluctant but finally agreed on the grounds that the delay while military action was prepared could be fruitfully used to harden international opinion against Nasser.

During August 1956 Britain mobilised her forces and called up some reservists. Parts of southern England looked as they had in World War Two, with long convoys of trucks and tanks, newly painted in brown and black desert camouflage, grinding through the country lanes on their way to the ports. The popular mood was bellicose, with shouts of 'Give 'em hell' sending the troops on their way to the Mediterranean.

Officially all this was a precaution, for diplomacy was still being tried. The Canal Users' Conference met in mid-August and proposed that an international body working under the United Nations should operate the canal. Nasser said no. Dulles then suggested that the users would operate the canal themselves. Eden went along with that, on, he believed, the clear understanding that the United States would back the scheme by force if Egypt resisted. But then in mid-September Dulles told a news conference that the United States would not shoot its way through the canal. On 2 October he confessed to the press that the Users' Association had 'no teeth' and explained that the United States wished to promote the peaceful transition from colonialism to independence 'without identifying itself 100 per cent either with the so-called colonial Powers or with the Powers which are primarily and uniquely concerned with the problem of getting their independence as rapidly as possible'. Suez, he added for good

* Back in December 1953 Eisenhower had got into an argument about colonialism with Jock Colville, Churchill's private secretary, who insisted hotly that 'India had been better governed by the Viceroy of India and the British Government of India than at present'. Eisenhower replied 'that as a matter of fact he thought so himself, but that to Americans liberty was more precious than good government'.[34]

measure, was an area outside America's obligations to her allies under the North Atlantic Treaty.[35]

Eden received news of Dulles's remarks while sitting in the Cabinet Room at Number Ten Downing Street. He was arguing with Anthony Nutting, a Foreign Office minister who opposed the use of force and was urging Eden to conciliate American opinion. Eden read the report, then threw it across the Cabinet table at Nutting, demanding contemptuously, 'Now what can you say for your American friends?'[36]

These were grim months for Anthony Eden. Sick from the recurrence of fevers caused by a badly-executed gall bladder operation, he faced an impossible dilemma. Two months had passed since Nasser's seizure of the canal, and during that time world opinion had clearly shown itself to be against the use of force, as had the Labour opposition at home. Worse still, the Egyptians were proving capable managers of the waterway and there was no disruption to shipping. Nevertheless Eden's convictions about Nasser had not changed and he was under intense pressure from his own party to recover the canal. He needed a pretext for reviving a crisis that was in danger of running down.

Salvation came from across the Channel. The French, co-owners of the canal, believed that escalating border raids in Sinai between Egypt and Israel signalled that another Arab–Israeli war was imminent. They were determined to exploit the opportunity. On 16 October Eden and his Foreign Secretary, Selwyn Lloyd, travelled secretly to Paris. The French proposed that Israel should be encouraged to invade Egypt and threaten the canal, thereby giving Britain and France a pretext for intervening to safeguard the waterway, their own property. Eden quickly agreed and at a further meeting on 24 October British diplomats confirmed the details in writing. The following day the British Cabinet was asked to approve contingency plans for a British response, should Israel attack Egypt, without being told of the collusion. The United States Government was told nothing at all.

Eden's neglect of America was consistent with his view that Britain could, if necessary, act on her own, without the assistance of the United States. Back in October 1955 he had told the Cabinet:

> Our interests in the Middle East were greater than those of the United States because of our dependence on Middle East oil, and our experience in the area was greater than theirs. We should not therefore allow ourselves to be restricted overmuch by reluctance to act without full American concurrence and support. We should frame our own policy in the light of our interests in the area and

get the Americans to support it to the extent we could induce them to do so.[37]

In planning the attack on Egypt Eden seemed to have decided that the Americans, though unhappy in principle, would go along with the operation or at least offer no serious opposition. That was certainly the view of the British Treasury as it prepared plans for the war. It was operating quite explicitly on only 'two hypotheses': 'full U.S., and general U.N. and Commonwealth support' or 'Go it alone with France – with only limited U.S., Commonwealth and other support'.[38] No one seems to have expected outright American hostility.

Yet that is what Britain soon faced. On 29 October the Israelis began their offensive into Sinai, with the agreed feint towards the canal. The following day London and Paris gave the belligerents twelve hours to pull back from the canal and allow British and French forces to occupy it. Israel accepted the ultimatum; the Egyptians rejected it, not surprisingly, since it would have meant that they retreated and the Israelis advanced about 100 miles. On the thirty-first British bombers went into action against Egyptian airfields, another action of dubious propriety since the two countries were not at war and Britain was claiming only to be trying to separate the Israeli and Egyptian forces.

Eisenhower's initial reaction was astonishment, then anger that the British should have reverted to gunboat diplomacy accompanied by glaring deception of their closest ally. 'I've just never seen great powers make such a complete *mess* and *botch* of things,' he exploded. 'Of course, there's just nobody, in a war, I'd rather have fighting alongside me than the British . . . But – *this* thing! My God!'[39] He telephoned Downing Street. The call was intercepted by Eden's press secretary, William Clark. 'Is that you, Anthony?' the angry voice inquired. 'Well, this is President Eisenhower, and I can only presume you have gone out of your mind.'[40]

There was more than a touch of hypocrisy in the American position. Eisenhower had no doubt about the threat posed by Nasser. On 6 October, less than a month before the Suez operation, he vetoed a CIA plan to 'topple Nasser' on the line of the plot against Mossadeq, but he did so on grounds not of principle but prudence. According to notes of the meeting, 'The President said that an action of this kind could not be taken when there is as much active hostility as at present. For a thing like this to be done without inflaming the Arab world, a time free from heated stress holding the world's attention as at present would have to be chosen.'[41] Eisenhower differed from Eden not on the goal of getting rid of Nasser, but on the appropriate issue and the method. The canal seemed a remnant of dated imperialism, and overt action to recover it would simply outrage the international community. As he told Eden in a letter on 3 September, 'American public opinion flatly rejects the thought of using force' to recover the canal. Likewise America's 'friends in the Middle East', though eager to 'see Nasser's deflation', were 'unanimous in feeling that Suez is not the issue on which to attempt to do this by force'.[42]

What made Britain's action even worse for Eisenhower was its timing. The President was standing for re-election on 6 November. His reputation rested on his ability to handle the world's diplomatic and military crises. He could not afford at this juncture to be humiliated by his closest allies. Ike's anger and that of Dulles were compounded by events in eastern Europe. In Hungary a new liberalising regime had briefly come to power, defying the Soviet Union and announcing the country's withdrawal from the Warsaw Pact. At the moment when Britain and France were bombing Egypt, Russian tanks rumbled into Budapest and the brutal suppression of the rising began.

Despite Dulles's campaign rhetoric about 'liberating' oppressed peoples, Washington had no intention of providing military assistance to the Hungarian rebels. But it hoped at least to present a united NATO front, deploring Russia's use of force and demonstrating to the Third World the West's moral superiority. The Suez operation tore that policy to shreds. Dulles told the National Security Council that if America wished to condemn 'Soviet colonialism in Eastern Europe' it would have to break with 'Anglo-French colonialism'. Otherwise 'all the independent countries will turn from us to the USSR. We will be looked upon as forever tied to British and French colonialist policies.'[43] Eisenhower was determined to go straight to the United Nations and ask for a resolution calling for a ceasefire and requiring all UN members to refrain from the use of force. He told a British diplomat: 'We plan to get there first thing in the morning – when the doors open – before the USSR gets there.'[44]

The Americans introduced their resolution in the Security Council on 30 October, where it was vetoed by Britain and France. On 1 November it was reintroduced by Dulles himself in the General Assembly. That same evening Eisenhower made his last speech of the election campaign in Philadelphia. Referring to the crisis he declared: 'We cannot subscribe to one law for the weak, another for the strong; one law for those opposing us, another for those allied with us. There can be only one law – or there shall be no peace.'[45]

America's unprecedented public stand against its closest allies won it unaccustomed acclaim from Asian and African nations. Even cleaners and typists at the UN building were congratulating American diplomats. The resolution was passed on 2 November by sixty-four votes to five. Only Australia and New Zealand sided with Britain, France and Israel. Canada was among the abstainers. In the 1980s denunciations of the West by the Third World in the United Nations were commonplace. In the 1950s they were rare. Britain, an architect of the UN, accustomed to instructing others about international morality, was now facing intense criticism from almost all the world, orchestrated by her principal ally. The shock was almost physical.

What followed was the humiliating collapse of the conspiracy, undermined by opposition at home and America's actions in the UN. At the time of the Assembly resolution the Anglo-French invasion force had not even reached the canal. Britain's nearest deep-water base to Egypt was Malta, almost a thousand miles away. To preserve the pretext that the force was acting in response to a threat to the canal, it could not set out from Malta until 31 October, after the Israelis had attacked and the Anglo-French ultimatum had been issued. By 4 November both Egypt and the Israelis, who had achieved their objectives in Sinai, were ready to accept a ceasefire, but the invasion force was still a day's sailing away. On 5 November British and French paratroopers were finally dropped around Port Said. But by this time the Soviets were threatening to intervene, Parliament and the country were bitterly divided, and there was serious talk of UN sanctions against Egypt's attackers. The operation had also lost all shreds of credibility. Eden and his Cabinet colleagues were exhausted from days of unrelenting criticism. On 6 November, according to the minutes, 'there was general agreement in the Cabinet that, in order to regain the initiative and to re-establish relations with those members of the United Nations who were fundamentally in sympathy with our aims, we should agree, subject to the concurrence of the French Government, to stop further military operations'.[46] Later that day Eden informed the French that Britain was accepting a ceasefire, just as the combined invasion force finally landed.

Even the Americans, who wanted a ceasefire, professed to be astonished at the timing of Eden's decision. Dulles asked Foreign Secretary Selwyn Lloyd on 17 November why, having started, the British did not 'go through with it and get Nasser down'?[47] But Eisenhower's principal reaction was relief that the conflict had ended before Russia had a chance to intervene. The ceasefire also coincided with news of his election victory. So, when Eden telephoned him on

7 November, Ike was in a buoyant and forgiving mood. He agreed that Eden should come to Washington, adding that the affair had been 'like a family spat'.[48]

Eden was delighted. He wanted to repair the breach and exploit Britain's position, with forces astride the canal, to ensure a satisfactory settlement. But Eisenhower's aides warned the President that an invitation to Eden would look as if America was conniving with Britain behind the back of the UN. So Eisenhower called back to say that the meeting was off. Subsequent telegrams from the President made it clear that there would be no contact until Britain and France had completely withdrawn their troops from Egypt and a UN peace-keeping force had been installed. 'Once these things are done,' Eisenhower told Eden, 'the ground will be favourable for our meeting.'[49]

Cold-shouldering the British was not Eisenhower's only weapon to evict them from Egypt. The crisis had started a heavy run on sterling and the Bank of England was digging deep into the reserves to preserve the value of the pound, a symbol of Britain's status in the world. Further loans from the United States became essential. The British Treasury had originally assumed that America would be co-operative or at least acquiescent during the Suez operation. Chancellor of the Exchequer Harold Macmillan returned home from a visit to Washington in late September convinced 'that the American Government, while publicly deploring our action, would be privately sympathetic, and thus content themselves with formal protests'.[50] But on 8 November the British Ambassador, Sir Harold Caccia, reported an alarming meeting with US Treasury Secretary George Humphrey, a vehement critic of Britain's conduct. Humphrey's line, Caccia warned London, was that 'for the United States to offer financial aid to the United Kingdom and France in the light of our actions in the last ten days would be totally unacceptable politically for some considerable time'.[51]

Britain's efforts to shift the Americans were unavailing. All would depend, they made it clear, on Britain showing that she was 'conforming to rather than defying the United Nations'.[52] The sterling crisis continued and during November Britain lost nearly $280 million, fifteen per cent of her reserves. On 28 November, Macmillan impressed on the Cabinet that to avoid financial disaster 'the good will of the United States Government was necessary; and it was evident that this good will could not be obtained without an immediate and unconditional undertaking to withdraw the Anglo-French force'.[53] Eden, now a sick man, was recuperating in Jamaica. In his absence

"Freezing to Death Isn't So Good Either"

From Herblock's *Special For Today* (Simon & Schuster, 1958).

the Cabinet capitulated and the last British troops were out of Port Said by Christmas.

As so often, Winston Churchill recognised the key issues. Pondering the débâcle later, he admitted that it was hard to know how he would have behaved had he still been Prime Minister. But he was clear on two points. 'I cannot understand why our troops were halted. To go so far and not go on was madness.' He was also 'certain' that he 'wouldn't have done anything without consulting the Americans'.[54] There in essence lay his differences with Eden.

The Suez crisis destroyed many of Britain's cherished illusions about the special relationship – about the community of interests between the two countries and the ability of Britain to manipulate American policy. Relations had been strained in the previous decade, of course, over China, Korea and Iran. But the disputes had generally been in private, and in the last analysis, British leaders believed, America could be induced to follow their lead. Suez exploded these assumptions: the divisions were fundamental, the row was public, and the Americans were unremitting in their opposition. Immediately afterwards there was an angry backlash against the United States, with some 120 Conservatives signing a Commons motion accusing America of 'gravely endangering the Atlantic Alliance'.[55]

Anti-American feeling was understandable, but what brought Eden down was not an American stab in the back: Britain's crisis was in reality self-induced. Until 1956 it remained the assumption in Britain, particularly among the general public, that the country was still a great power. India had been lost, but most of the other colonies and territories remained part of the British Empire, or the Commonwealth as it was now named, and British influence continued to pervade Asia, Africa and the Middle East. Suez exposed the extent of Britain's pretensions. Eden had tried to take an independent line in the Middle East, only to discover that Britain lacked the means to do so. Her armed forces were ill-prepared, she antagonised world opinion by her spurious cover-story, she lacked the bases and air transports needed for a swift operation, and her economy was vulnerable to American pressure. The outcome was the worst humiliation in Britain's twentieth-century history, beginning a long period of introspection and doubt, as the country tried to assimilate the lessons and rethink its role in the world.

Some members of the Foreign Office seized on the feelings of impotence and resentment in a memorandum submitted to the Cabinet in January 1957. 'Two great Powers, America and Russia, now immeasurably outstrip all the others,' the memo began bleakly. Britain had tried to keep up with them, but now, in the age of the hydrogen bomb, 'if we try to do so we shall bankrupt ourselves'. Instead, the Foreign Office advised, 'we should pool our resources with our European allies so that Western Europe as a whole might become a third nuclear power comparable with the United States and the Soviet Union'.[56]

Even at this grim moment the Cabinet was not willing to surrender Britain's status as an independent nuclear power. But there was general agreement that in non-nuclear matters a closer relationship with western Europe was desirable:

> the Suez crisis had made it plain that there must be some change in the basis of Anglo-American relations. It was doubtful whether the United States would now be willing to accord to us alone the special position which we had held as their principal ally during the war. We might therefore be better able to influence them if we were part of an association of Powers which had greater political, economic and military strength than we alone could command.[57]

For a decade Britain had kept her distance from the continent of Europe, sure that she remained a world power, confident of her special relationship with the United States. Suez seemed to have shattered both assumptions and opened up a new view of Britain's future role.

12

Dependence and Deterrence

1957–63

The Cabinet discussed Britain's relations with America and Europe on 8 January 1957. The following day Anthony Eden announced his resignation as Prime Minister on grounds of ill health. The man chosen to succeed him was Harold Macmillan, formerly Chancellor of the Exchequer. In foreign policy Macmillan wanted the best of both worlds: to bring Britain into a closer European partnership while also restoring relations with the United States. His six and a half years as Prime Minister would show whether the two policies were compatible.

Macmillan's appointment was in some ways an ironic choice, for he shared much of the blame for the Suez débâcle. In the early days of the crisis he had been a leading hawk in Cabinet, pressing Eden for military action, and urging collusion with Israel. In the autumn of 1956 his advice that 'Ike would lie doggo'[1] had helped lull his colleagues into unjustified complacency. By November, alarmed at the prospect of American economic sanctions, he had reversed his position to become a leading dove, urging the Cabinet to withdraw the troops and trying to open up private contacts with Eisenhower.

Of all the possible leaders of the Conservative Party Macmillan was the best suited to heal the transatlantic breach. Like Churchill he was the offspring of one of the Anglo-American marriages at the turn of the century and felt close ties with his mother's homeland. He had established a warm relationship with Eisenhower during the war as the British Minister Resident in Eisenhower's Mediterranean Allied Force Headquarters in 1943–4. Grappling with the political complexities of dealing with the Allies, Eisenhower had come to trust Macmillan's 'skill, his insight, his intelligence, his ability to handle complex issues and advise on them in a way in which Eisenhower had great confidence'.[2]

The attempt to resume normal relations, which both countries wanted, began awkwardly. The new British Ambassador, Sir Harold Caccia, was warned by Dulles not to visit the State Department too often, but to come instead to see him at his home in Washington at weekends to avoid attracting attention. But a formal invitation was soon issued to Macmillan to meet Eisenhower in March. Tactfully the President proposed Bermuda, British territory, rather than Washington as the venue, to save Macmillan from appearing to come begging to America. The atmosphere at the conference was frank, with blunt exchanges on Suez. Macmillan told Eisenhower that 'our Government and many of our people think that you were too hard on us – and rather let us down', a comment the President took up 'rather sharply', Macmillan recorded in his diary.[3] But the exchanges helped clear the air. The two leaders re-established top-level contacts between their governments, agreeing to write to each other regularly and informally as Roosevelt and Churchill had done during the war.

Evidence of the new rapport was an agreement reached at Bermuda which confounded Foreign Office sceptics about the Atlantic alliance and laid the basis of an Anglo-American nuclear relationship that has endured to the present day.

The British had never forgiven the Americans for reneging on the agreements reached in 1943–5 to develop nuclear weapons in partnership. The McMahon Act, which ruled out the exchange of nuclear secrets, rankled particularly with Churchill, leaving him, according to Sir Roger Makins, a senior diplomat of the period, in 'a bitter frame of mind'.[4] Denied access to American research, Britain had gone ahead with her own atomic programme, successfully testing an atomic device in October 1952 and a hydrogen bomb in May 1957. With America and Russia she was one of the world's three nuclear powers, but she had not yet devised a method for reliable delivery of the weapon apart from dropping them from increasingly vulnerable bombers.

Eisenhower felt that Britain had been treated 'unfairly and unjustly'.[5] He wanted to see her sharing with the United States in the nuclear deterrence strategy evolving within NATO. He told Churchill in 1953 that 'he had, in 1945 and 1946, used all his influence to prevent the McMahon Act and urged that good faith between the Allies, not the legal interpretations of documents, was required'. Shown a copy of Churchill's 1944 agreement with Roosevelt 'he seemed deeply impressed', Churchill noted. 'He had never seen it before.'[6] In 1954 Eisenhower had managed to achieve some minor amendments to the McMahon Act, despite a hostile Congress.

At Bermuda in March 1957 he went one step further. Agreement was reached there for sixty Thor missiles to be based in Britain. Thor was an intermediate-range missile, fitted with a nuclear warhead and capable of travelling 1,500 miles. The US Government wanted to deploy it within range of the Soviet Union and Britain was the obvious place, given the long-standing arrangements for American bases. In 1952 Churchill and Truman had agreed that 'the use of these bases in an emergency would be a matter for joint decision',[7] but the Thor agreement replaced joint decision with joint control. Macmillan informed the Commons that 'the rockets cannot be fired by any except British personnel, but the warhead will be in the control of the United States'.[8] This 'dual-key' system meant that each side held a veto over the use of the weapon, and each benefited from the deal. America had missiles within reach of Russia, and Britain shared in a missile deterrent long before she could develop her own. Bermuda, Eisenhower said, was 'by far the most successful international conference that I had attended since the close of World War II'.[9]

The nuclear relationship was further strengthened a few months later, this time as the direct result of a Soviet threat. On 4 October 1957 the Soviet Union launched the first man-made satellite, Sputnik, which circled the earth, passing across the United States as it did so. It came as little surprise to American experts who were preparing a similar satellite launch, but the reaction of the American public and press bordered on the hysterical, once the scale of the achievement had sunk in. Communist Russia, supposedly their technological inferior, had beaten them into space with a satellite reportedly eight times the weight of America's – a success followed within weeks by an even larger satellite carrying a live dog.

The military implications were alarming. In the past America, protected by vast oceans to the east and west, had felt almost invulnerable to direct attack. The air age and even the development of the atomic bomb did not seem to threaten the USA directly in the way it did countries in Europe. Russia had been slow to develop an intercontinental bomber with a range equivalent to the American B-52. But with the launch of Sputnik the Soviet Union proved it had a missile powerful enough to reach the United States in only thirty minutes. The Pentagon would not be ready to deploy its first Inter-Continental Ballistic Missiles (ICBMs), able to strike Russia directly from the United States, until the early 1960s. The Soviet leader Nikita Khrushchev crowed that the American B-52 belonged in a museum. Edward Teller, father of the US H-bomb project, called Sputnik a greater defeat for the United States than Pearl Harbor.[10]

Eisenhower rode out the storm. He used his authority as a former military Supreme Commander to ward off demands to put the country on a panic alert. Instead he seized the opportunity further to strengthen the nuclear relationship with Britain. It was no longer just because he wanted to right a perceived wrong, but because he needed allies as never before and only Britain had a nuclear capability. Within three weeks of the launch of Sputnik Macmillan was invited to Washington and on 24 October 1957 the British saw restored to them the nuclear co-operation they had been denied for so long. Special Anglo-American committees were set up to handle collaboration on nuclear weapons and Eisenhower promised to fight for further amendments to the McMahon Act in Congress. In July 1958 those revisions duly became law and the British and US governments signed a new agreement permitting a much fuller exchange of nuclear information, plant and materials. A further accord the following May allowed Britain to acquire nuclear weapons or nuclear weapon parts from the United States and to exchange nuclear fuels: British plutonium for American uranium. What Britain saw as the wrongs of 1945 had at last been righted.

The rapprochement between Britain and the United States was reinforced in the Middle East. Eisenhower was anxious to limit the damage caused to Western interests by Suez. He told Congressional leaders in January 1957 that 'the existing vacuum in the Middle East must be filled by the United States before it is filled by Russia'.[11] He later spelt out the 'Eisenhower Doctrine' which called for economic and military aid to nations in the area that were threatened by 'International Communism'. But it was Arab nationalism, rather than Khrushchev's manoeuvrings, which was the real threat. Early in 1958 Egypt and Syria merged to form the United Arab Republic. In July, as enthusiasm for Nasser swept the Arab world, the Iraqi monarchy and its government led by Nuri Said, Britain's leading ally in the region, were toppled in a bloody coup and Nuri's body was dragged naked through the streets of Baghdad to the delight of the mob. Fearful of a similar fate, the government of Lebanon, wracked by internal strife, called on America for help, and King Hussein of Jordan, who had been obliged to expel British forces from his country in 1956, appealed to Britain to come back and give assistance.

Eisenhower acted swiftly. He told Macmillan that US marines were going into the Lebanon. 'You are doing a Suez on me,' Macmillan protested.[12] Supported by the Sixth Fleet 10,000 US marines landed in Lebanon, to a friendly welcome from sunbathers on the beaches. Eisenhower did not want to give the impression of collusion between Britain and America, but when British paratroops flew into Jordan, American transports ferried in supplies while the Royal Navy made available its bases in Cyprus for US ships supporting the Lebanon operation. Khrushchev protested vociferously, doing his best to discredit the interventions in the United Nations. What mattered more to Britain was that Nasser had been rebuffed and, less than two years after Suez, she and America were again collaborating closely in the Middle East. At the end of the operation Eisenhower told Macmillan that they could 'take special satisfaction in the complete understanding and special co-operation which was evident between our two governments in these undertakings'. The Prime Minister replied that 'so long as your country and mine continue to act together in spirit and in deed, as we have over the last months, I am sure we can deal successfully with any eventuality'.[13]

The restoration of the relationship with America could not disguise the fact that Britain was now a poor relation, in straitened circumstances. It was most strikingly revealed in her inability to keep up with the superpowers in the arms race. Like the United States she had adopted nuclear deterrence as the main plank of national defence, but unlike America she had no effective modern method of delivering the bomb. The Americans relied on their B-52 bomber force, which, in spite of Khrushchev's scorn, remained unrivalled. Britain's much smaller V-bomber force was only coming into service in 1957–8, just as the dawn of the missile age made airborne deterrence obsolescent. Britain's reaction was to try to develop a nuclear missile of her own, Blue Streak.

Blue Streak was not as independent as was claimed. It relied on American technology for its rocket engine and guidance system, but, even so, by 1960 it had become clear that the missile was inadequate. The rocket was propelled by liquid fuel and took thirty minutes to prepare for launching. It operated from fixed sites and would therefore be vulnerable, like Thor, to a Soviet first strike. In February 1960 the British Cabinet's Defence Committee decided in principle that, rather than spend another £600 million on top of the £65 million already spent, it would scrap the missile. However, the final verdict would depend on whether the United States offered to help Britain acquire an alternative.

In Washington at the end of March 1960 Macmillan and Eisenhower agreed on a substitute, the new US Skybolt missile. Skybolt, which was still in the development stage, was an aircraft-launched missile and therefore particularly attractive to Britain because it could prolong the life of the V-bomber force. A jubilant Macmillan noted in his diary: 'This allows us to abandon Blue Streak ... without damage to our prospects of maintaining – in the late 60s and early 70s – our *independent* nuclear deterrent.'[14] The terms agreed were generous. Only the cost of the missiles she ordered would have to be met by Britain, with no contribution being made towards the research and development costs of the whole project. But there was a *quid pro quo*. In return for Skybolt Macmillan secretly agreed that US submarines, armed with the new Polaris missiles, would be offered the use of Holy Loch on the Clyde in Scotland as their forward base. Like the Thor deal, Holy Loch would allow the United States to strike at the Soviet Union from close range. Unlike Thor, however, these missiles were to be solely under US control, and when, in November, Macmillan announced details of the Polaris base he ran into a storm of criticism.

During 1960 the 'Ban the Bomb' movement had taken a firm hold on the British Labour Party. The marches of the Campaign for Nuclear Disarmament (CND), Britain's abandonment of Blue Streak and then the decision to buy Skybolt from America provoked a passionate debate about whether Britain should stay in the nuclear club. In April 1960 polls indicated that a third of the country favoured unilateral disarmament, in other words that Britain should abandon the bomb. Macmillan's talk of an 'independent nuclear deterrent' seemed fanciful in view of Britain's reliance on American missiles. Labour MP Denis Healey called nuclear independence 'the virility symbol of the atomic age ... Britain and France both clutched at it in the shock of having their military impotence exposed at Suez.'[15]

When on 1 November 1960 Macmillan announced in the Commons that the Americans would be given a base in Britain for the world's most advanced nuclear weapon, the protests from disarmers and Scottish nationalists were strident. John Rankin, a Labour MP from Glasgow, claimed that 'we are not really an ally of the United States; we are a satellite. We live on an expendable American base.'[16] Macmillan insisted that Holy Loch would be covered by an extension of the basing agreement reached in 1951–2 between Churchill and Truman. To avoid embarrassing the Americans, however, Macmillan was careful to speak only of:

> my understanding of the position reached. This is that we can be satisfied that the United States Government will not use these missiles anywhere in the world without the fullest possible previous consultation with us and our allies. I use the words 'fullest possible' consultation because consultation might obviously be impossible in circumstances of a sudden surprise attack upon the West. We would, indeed, not wish to insist on prior consultation in such circumstances, because it is the absolute certainty of retaliation which deters aggression.[17]

The Skybolt–Holy Loch arrangement was inspired by the same mixture of sentiment and self-interest as the wartime Destroyers for Bases deal of 1940. It cemented the nuclear relationship which Eisenhower and Macmillan had created, one enjoyed by no other ally of the United States. Britain, unable to afford to remain a member of the nuclear club on her own account, had persuaded America to pay the subscription for her. Macmillan argued that this strengthened deterrence; his critics claimed that he was keeping Britain in the bull's-eye of a Soviet attack.

Britain's three Conservative Prime Ministers in the 1950s all believed profoundly in the American alliance as the foundation of Britain's security, but each adopted a different approach towards it. Churchill, nostalgic for his wartime partnership with Roosevelt, tended to exaggerate Anglo-American harmony. Eden overestimated Britain's independent power and paid the price at Suez. Macmillan sought the middle ground. Unlike Eden, he was assiduous in consulting the Americans, but he was still ready to take an independent line when British interests dictated. Macmillan, no less than Eden, refused to be a lackey of Washington, but believed the lesson of Suez was clear: British initiatives had to be based on transatlantic trust. With trust restored, Macmillan tried, like his two predecessors, to use British influence to thaw the Cold War.

The urgency of the task was apparent. Late in 1958 a new crisis had blown up between the superpowers over the status of Berlin, a divided and occupied city since the end of World War Two. Khrushchev, in effect, was insisting that Berlin be incorporated into East Germany, a demand that Eisenhower was determined to reject. Macmillan agreed, anxious to show solidarity with the United States, but he feared that the crisis could escalate into uncontrollable confrontation. He decided to take up a long-standing Russian invitation to visit Moscow. Eisenhower, according to his Staff Secretary General Andrew Goodpaster, was 'concerned that Macmillan might be led into suggesting . . . concessions that went beyond what we were prepared to agree to'.[18]

In February 1959, theatrically adorned with a white fur hat, Macmillan arrived in Moscow, the first Western head of government to go there since the end of the war. The panache with which Macmillan conducted himself helped to create world-wide interest, as did his appearance on Russian television and photographs of him arm-in-arm with Russian milkmaids. The talks were tough and at one point Khrushchev snubbed Macmillan publicly by saying that he could not accompany the British visitors to Kiev because he was having a tooth filled. Nevertheless, Macmillan persuaded the Russians to show some flexibility. Khrushchev had set a six-month deadline for settling the Berlin crisis. This he now soft-pedalled, accepting instead a meeting of Foreign Ministers as the precursor to a full-dress summit. Eisenhower was reluctant to take part in a summit meeting until the ground had been thoroughly prepared but Macmillan kept up the pressure and in July the President agreed with Khrushchev to a joint exchange of visits to Washington and Moscow. At Camp David in September 1959 the two superpower leaders agreed in a private talk that, if Khrushchev would publicly drop the deadline for an agreement on Berlin, Eisenhower would consent to a Big Four summit in Paris in May 1960 involving America, Russia, Britain and France.

Fifteen days before the Paris summit was due to begin an American high-altitude U-2 reconnaissance plane was shot down over Russia. Since July 1956 there had been regular spy flights, each approved by the President. When Gary Powers's U-2 was shot down, the Eisenhower Administration at first issued a prepared cover-story about a weather research aircraft that had gone astray. To its embarrassment the Soviet authorities then put on display wreckage of the U-2 and paraded its pilot before the world's press. Khrushchev gave Eisenhower the opportunity to blame the Pentagon for the incident but the President refused to pass the buck, publicly defending the flights as essential to US security, though adding that there would be no more of them.

Khrushchev arrived in Paris in truculent mood. He had antagonised hawks in the Kremlin by his willingness to meet Eisenhower and was embarrassed by the U-2 incident which seemed to confirm their suspicions about America's intentions. He demanded American apologies and the punishment of those responsible, warning that the summit would have to be postponed until the atmosphere had cleared. With Eisenhower dismissing any idea 'that I'm going to crawl on my knees to Khrushchev',[19] the summit broke up on 16 May 1960 without any formal sessions being convened.

Macmillan remained publicly loyal, driving round Paris in an open car with the President, ostensibly sight-seeing, in reality displaying Anglo-American solidarity. Yet Sir Philip de Zulueta, the Prime Minister's private secretary, had 'never seen Harold Macmillan so depressed',[20] and in the Foreign Office there was 'amazement that the United States had not found a face-saving way out'. Khrushchev, it was believed, 'would have accepted almost any excuse. He even came to the British delegation in Paris to plead with the British to intervene with the U.S. and find some way out.'[21]

Though publicly unabashed, Eisenhower, too, was shaken by the collapse of the summit. The last months of his presidency were pervaded by a sense of regret and lost opportunity. On 10 November 1960, Macmillan wrote to Eisenhower recalling almost two decades of partnership. 'I can only assure you that I will try my best to keep our governments and our two countries on the same course. But,' he predicted dolefully, 'I cannot of course ever hope to have anything to replace the sort of relations that we have had.'[22] It was a sad end to a long and distinguished partnership.

'Let the word go forth from this time and place, to friend and foe alike, that the torch has been passed to a new generation of Americans, born in this century, tempered by war, disciplined by a hard and bitter peace . . .'[23] John F. Kennedy's words at his inauguration, with their implication that the older generation's days were over, gnawed at Macmillan. He had been born in the nineteenth century, Kennedy in the twentieth. There was a gap of twenty-three years between them, and Kennedy was only forty-three. How could Macmillan reproduce, for the benefit of Britain and the Western Alliance, the easy partnership he had enjoyed with Eisenhower, his old comrade-in-arms? He had known Kennedy's father, American Ambassador to Britain from 1938–40, as an appeaser and a defeatist. Macmillan, a prominent critic of Munich, could not easily forgive him. And the Kennedys were Catholics, of Irish descent, who had made their way in Boston Democratic politics, where to be anti-British was a badge of political respectability. The attractive new leader, with his polished Harvard manner, his photogenic wife and children, and an entourage said to contain the best and the brightest from business and the universities, was eager to break through a new frontier into the modern age. According to his private secretary, Sir Philip de Zulueta, Macmillan 'was afraid that he might be overtaken by this brilliant young man of a different generation and that he would not be relevant to Kennedy'.[24]

The relationship turned out better than Macmillan expected. Kennedy had lived in Britain during his father's ambassadorship and was intrigued by the patrician world of British high politics. He liked Macmillan's style, the deceptive 'Victorian languor' which concealed a shrewd, subtle politician.[25] He admired Macmillan's obvious commitment to arms control and to greater social justice. For his part Macmillan was flattered by Kennedy's charm and impressed by his sense of history. Both men shared a sharp, ironic sense of humour. After early disagreements over Kennedy's confrontational reaction to Soviet intransigence on Berlin and to communist insurgency in Laos, there developed, according to the President's aide, historian Arthur Schlesinger, 'Kennedy's closest personal relationship with a foreign leader'.[26]

The turning point came after Kennedy's first meeting with Khrushchev in Vienna in June 1961. Now that Eisenhower had broken the ice America no longer needed Britain to point the way to Moscow. Macmillan was unhappy about this development, particularly since the young President might prove no match for his wily and experienced opponent. When Kennedy and Khrushchev met, they disagreed on almost every world issue, particularly Berlin. 'I want peace,' said Khrushchev, 'but, if you want war, that is your problem.' Kennedy gave as good as he got: 'It is you, and not I, who wants to force a change.'[27] But the President was shaken by Khrushchev's intransigence. There seemed to be no meeting of minds, no hint of progress. Secretary of State Dean Rusk recalls that Kennedy was 'disturbed that Mr Khrushchev thought he could intimidate this new young President of the United States'.[28]

Next stop after Vienna was Paris. Kennedy could not speak French, unlike his glamorous wife Jacqueline, who stole the show, captivating even the stony heart of Charles de Gaulle, the French President. With a touch of bitter wit, Kennedy announced himself at a press luncheon as 'the man who accompanied Jacqueline Kennedy to Paris'.[29] When they arrived in London, their last European stop before returning home, the President was in low spirits and suffering acute pain from his weak back. He was under attack from the world's press as a young and callow leader who had bungled the Bay of Pigs invasion of Cuba in April and had now been worsted by Khrushchev in Vienna. The 'Jackie cult' had invaded England as well. People seemed more impressed with the First Lady than with the President. The Lord Chamberlain, in those days Britain's official censor, prohibited a satirical revue from including a sketch in which an actress portraying Mrs Kennedy sang:

While Jack fumbles with Russia, I use all my guile,
So the press and public won't guess for a while,
He is just like Ike dressed up Madison Avenue style.[30]

On 5 June 1961, tired and tense, Kennedy arrived at Number Ten Downing Street. Macmillan immediately saw that a formal conference, flanked by advisers, was inappropriate. With his habitual weary fling of the hand he said, 'Let's not have a meeting – the Foreign Office and all that. Why not have a peaceful drink and chat by ourselves?'[31] Gratefully Kennedy sat back and poured out his impressions of Khrushchev. He was not seeking advice on policy: America had long since followed its own road. He needed help on psychology, baffled at how to deal with a man who seemed unwilling to negotiate about anything. Macmillan spoke the same language, offering wisdom and sympathy, sharing confidences, helping Kennedy feel less alone in the burdens of world leadership. In the words of Macmillan's private secretary, the relationship became as 'uncle to nephew, or something like that'.[32]

The new friendship was reinforced by Macmillan's choice of British Ambassador to succeed Sir Harold Caccia. One of Kennedy's oldest British friends, David Ormsby Gore, was a Minister of State at the Foreign Office. Kennedy let Macmillan know that he was 'emphatic for David Gore'[33] and an unconventional but inspired appointment followed. Ormsby Gore was not a career diplomat but was of the same generation as Kennedy and operated on the President's wavelength. Soon he became almost a White House insider, mixing easily with the Kennedy clan and their staff, as ready to play touch football on Cape Cod as to discuss high policy in Washington.

In 1961 Britain therefore had a Prime Minister and an Ambassador who got on exceptionally well with Jack Kennedy. Macmillan hoped that these personal relationships could help advance the goals of British foreign policy. He had a clear idea of what this should be. There were three key elements. Britain should, first, maintain a special relationship with the United States, working for agreement on policy by using her influence and experience. She should also have an independent power base, an entitlement to the top table of world affairs, based on the possession of nuclear weapons. And lastly she should start to play a full part in the affairs of Europe, by joining the European Economic Community. These three ambitions, while in theory compatible, came into conflict in practice, and each, in its different way, was blighted in the few months between the autumn of 1962 and the spring of 1963.

First to be tested was the special relationship, on which Macmillan set so much store. In 1962 Khrushchev attempted to place nuclear missiles in Cuba, ninety miles from the United States. This led to a crisis which brought the United States and Russia nearer to nuclear war than ever before or since.

From the moment he gained power in Cuba in 1959 Fidel Castro had distanced himself from the United States, diminishing American economic domination and seizing American assets. Washington's growing enmity forced Castro into complete dependence on the Soviet bloc. The United States saw his actions as a threat to the Pax Americana in Central America. Following the example of Eisenhower's coup against a leftist regime in Guatemala in 1954, the CIA proposed to the newly-elected President Kennedy a similar strike against Cuba, which Eisenhower had already endorsed. A sceptical Kennedy gave his approval, but the subsequent Bay of Pigs invasion by Cuban exiles supported by the CIA, ended in disaster. Cubans stayed loyal to Castro, his forces hit back hard with their Russian equipment, and the invaders were pinned down on the beaches and forced to surrender. Wryly Kennedy observed that, under parliamentary government in Britain, he would have been obliged to resign, whereas in America failure had enhanced his charm. Shown a poll indicating eighty-two per cent backing for his Administration, he quipped: 'It's just like Eisenhower. The worse I do, the more popular I get.'[34]

But Kennedy paid a price for the Bay of Pigs fiasco, when, in the following year, Khrushchev decided to exploit Russia's newly dominant position in Cuba. The Soviet Union, in spite of Khrushchev's boasts in 1957 about a missile gap, had fallen behind in the nuclear-arms race. The United States was installing the new inter-continental Minuteman missiles, and already had ground-to-air missiles in Britain and, close to the Russian border, in Turkey. Khrushchev decided to counter these threats by installing Russian missiles in Cuba. It was a gambler's throw which, if successful, would humiliate President Kennedy, provide the missile advantage Khrushchev was seeking, and give him a dramatic propaganda victory over the West.

American U-2 spy planes detected the construction work taking place on Cuba. On 16 October the photographic intelligence was put before the President. All the missiles had not yet arrived but it was obvious that, if the United States was to react, it must do so fast. Amid deepest secrecy Kennedy convened a special crisis-management committee known as 'ExCom'. It agreed that the United States could

OVER THE GARDEN WALL

Punch voices British doubts early in the Cuban missile crisis of October 1962. Why should Kennedy be so exercised about Cuba when Khrushchev's Russia has long been overshadowed by US bases?

not accept Soviet missiles ninety miles off the coast of Florida. The options available were narrowed down to two. Most of the Joint Chiefs of Staff favoured an air strike to destroy the missile sites, which risked escalating the crisis and might not be successful. Kennedy, dubious of military advice after the failure of the Bay of Pigs, chose the alternative proposal. On Saturday afternoon, 20 October, he decided to blockade rather than bomb Cuba, a choice which would defer an immediate confrontation and give the Soviets time to retreat.

The crisis was kept secret. No allies were consulted or informed, so anxious was Kennedy not to give Russia prior warning of his plans. At lunchtime on Sunday, his decision already made, he summoned his friend, Ormsby Gore, the British Ambassador, to the White House. He explained the situation and outlined the two options that had been presented to him at ExCom, asking Gore which he favoured. The Ambassador, to Kennedy's satisfaction, plumped for the blockade. That evening Kennedy spoke to Macmillan in London and explained the decision and the background. On the following Monday, 22 October, the crisis was publicly revealed to the American people by television. The USA, the President announced, was imposing 'a strict quarantine on all offensive military equipment under shipment to Cuba'. Any nuclear missile launched from Cuba against any country in the Western Hemisphere would be regarded as a direct attack 'by the Soviet Union on the United States, requiring a full, retaliatory response upon the Soviet Union'.[35]

The reaction in London to Kennedy's announcement was not initially enthusiastic. Since 1959 Britain had disputed America's interpretation of the threat posed by Castro's Cuba, and had refused to bow to American pressure to cut off trade. In October 1962 Macmillan initially doubted whether the blockade was wise, unlike de Gaulle, who refused to look at the photographic evidence for the missile build-up, saying that America's word was good enough for him. In the British Parliament and in the press there were suspicions that the crisis was not genuine but another machination against Castro. It was asked why Kennedy had not resorted to the United Nations, as the Americans had been so keen to do over Suez, and it was even suggested by some on the left of the Labour Party that Kennedy, with Congressional elections imminent, was 'risking blowing the world to hell in order to sweep a few Democrats into office'.[36] Ormsby Gore was concerned at the scepticism being shown in Britain and he persuaded Kennedy to release the photographic evidence. Together the two men selected photographs that looked most convincing to the non-expert eye and when these were published the British press changed its tune.

Throughout the crisis Kennedy kept in close touch with Macmillan, speaking to him by telephone every evening. On some days there were several conversations. Kennedy brought Macmillan up to date with events and listened to his views. He wanted, according to George Ball, Under-Secretary of State, to maintain the unity of the West by keeping in close touch with Britain, but 'also wanted the sense of reassurance that he got from talking to an old experienced political leader for whom he had great respect'.[37] It was the same need that Macmillan had satisfied after Vienna in June 1961. But Britain was not consulted so much as informed about American policy. 'We did not ask London for guidance or advice,' explained Secretary of State Dean Rusk, 'because this was an issue primarily between ourselves and the Russians.'[38] The nearest Britain came to wielding any direct influence was the continual presence of Ormsby Gore at crisis meetings. He was responsible for persuading the President to reduce the area of the blockade from 800 to 500 miles to allow Khrushchev more time to decide how to respond.

In a state of apprehension bordering on terror, the world waited to see what effect Kennedy's ultimatum to Khrushchev would have. The news that the ships steaming towards the quarantine zone had turned back, with missiles clearly visible on their decks, was greeted with universal relief. On 28 October Khrushchev announced that the Soviet Union would withdraw all missile bases from Cuba. In return Moscow received an assurance that the United States would not again try to invade Cuba and that Jupiter missiles in Turkey, coming to the end of their natural life, would be withdrawn. The crisis had ended in triumph for the President.

Macmillan, in the House of Commons, insisted, 'It is not true that we in this country played an inactive role in this great trial of strength.'[39] But the reality was obvious. The world had been on the brink of disaster and Britain, like everyone else, had been entirely dependent on the conduct of the Big Two. The pretension that her membership of the nuclear club gave her any special influence had been shown to be a sham. Russia and America had been eyeball to eyeball, with Britain an almost impotent observer.

The euphoria in Washington over the successful outcome of the Cuba crisis was partly responsible for a dramatic confrontation between Britain and America in the last weeks of 1962. This was over Britain's possession of her own nuclear deterrent, the second element in Macmillan's strategy. Eisenhower's decision in March 1960 to offer Britain the air-to-ground missile Skybolt as her independent nuclear deterrent had not been universally approved in Washington. There was a powerful lobby inside the State Department which believed dogmatically that Britain should not be a nuclear power and that America was doing itself a disservice by providing the missile. The 'theologians', as they became known, were convinced that America should pay more attention to France and West Germany, both now revived and united within the European Community. America's unique nuclear partnership with Britain was, they believed, a major obstacle to good transatlantic relations at a time when France had just entered the nuclear club and West Germany was chafing at its exclusion. 'We must try to eliminate the privileged British status,' urged two of the 'theologians', Henry Owen and Henry Rowen, in April 1961. 'In matters nuclear, the road to Paris may well be through London.'[40] In the Pentagon there were others who wanted to 'de-nuclearise' Britain for different reasons. They believed that the world would be safer if only Russia and America had the bomb. Nuclear proliferation should be prevented. In June 1962 Kennedy's Defense Secretary, Robert McNamara, publicly criticised 'limited nuclear capacities operating independently' as 'dangerous, expensive, prone to obsolescence, and lacking in credibility as a deterrent'.[41]

The Europeanists in the State Department proposed an alternative to the British unilateral nuclear deterrent in the form of a Multilateral Force (MLF). This would be a naval force, crewed by members of all the NATO countries and carrying nuclear weapons. The United States would retain control over the actual decision to fire a nuclear missile but everyone, particularly the Germans, would feel more involved. It seems in retrospect a slightly absurd idea, a transparently political device which offered no substantial role to its non-American participants.

Macmillan would have none of it. Britain's nuclear capability was, he believed, an insurance policy against America failing to honour its nuclear guarantee of Europe. Now that the Soviets could strike directly at the USA, making any nuclear defence of Europe suicidal, this seemed a real possibility. He also argued, despite the evidence of the Cuban crisis, that membership of the nuclear club would give Britain a voice in world affairs that she would otherwise be denied. Suggestions by McNamara and others that America's allies should not have their own nuclear weapons were therefore deeply embarrassing to Macmillan. Pressed by Labour critics in the Commons in June 1962 as to whether Britain's nuclear forces were truly 'independent', he insisted that 'these forces, although we with our allies make joint plans, are constitutionally under the sovereignty of the Government of the day. That is the point, and in that sense they are independent.'[42] Labour was not impressed, particularly since Britain's nuclear force would soon be American missiles not British bombers, but for many Tories Britain's 'independent nuclear deterrent' had become an article of patriotic faith – symbol that she still remained a great power.

All might have been well had Skybolt proved a success. When it

President Truman greets the British Prime Minister, Clement Attlee, in Washington on 4 December 1950.

John Foster Dulles is welcomed by Anthony Eden on arrival in London on 11 April 1954.

Advice from Secretary of State John Foster Dulles to President Dwight D. Eisenhower (April 1954).

British paratroops soon after landing in Port Said (November 1956).

NO ENTRY
HI-PRESSURE
GAS TEST IN
OPERATION

A Thor missile being raised into the firing position at Feltwell, Norfolk (November 1958).

was offered to Britain by Eisenhower in 1960 it was in the development stage. The US air force was supporting it to keep the nuclear deterrent in their hands rather than see it transferred to the US navy with their new submarine-launched Polaris missiles. But by 1962 Skybolt was behind schedule. The tests were proving unsatisfactory and it failed the new criteria of 'cost-effectiveness' introduced by McNamara at the Pentagon. He saw it as a candidate for cancellation, but was reluctant to come clean to the British Government for fear that premature publicity would allow Skybolt's supporters in Congress to frustrate his plans. Hints were dropped to the British that all was not well, but Whitehall assumed that the US air force and its industrial allies would be a sufficiently powerful lobby to safeguard Skybolt. There was little understanding of Pentagon politics or the impact of McNamara's determination to cut unnecessary costs. Anyway, it was argued, Kennedy had assured Macmillan that there would be 'no publicity before decision and no decisions before consultation' with Britain.[43]

But, by the time McNamara visited London for talks on 11 December 1962, the likelihood of cancellation was being openly discussed in the British and American press. McNamara, at an airport press conference on his arrival, blithely announced that Skybolt's five tests had all ended in failure and went on to inform the British Government of the proposed cancellation. The British Minister of Defence, Peter Thorneycroft, was 'furious with this decision', according to Paul Nitze, who accompanied McNamara. The reaction, Nitze said, was 'stronger than expected', though he had not exactly anticipated 'hugs and kisses from the British'.[44]

Secretary of State Dean Rusk was taken aback by the furore in Britain. 'If I may say, with a smile, I think it is possible that the surprise in London was somewhat exaggerated as part of the bargaining position in order to get further nuclear co-operation from the United States.'[45] But if Whitehall was at fault for having failed to realise that Skybolt was in jeopardy, Kennedy's men seemed equally incapable of grasping how much Macmillan had invested politically in Skybolt. The Cuban crisis was behind them and, in their bullish confidence about having saved the world, they cared little for what seemed to be the minor details of an ally's defence spending. In the last weeks of 1962 with their eyes on other issues they allowed a crisis in the alliance to develop unchecked.

An Anglo-American summit had been arranged at Nassau, in the Bahamas, for the week before Christmas. This now became the venue for a showdown on the future of the nuclear special relationship.

Macmillan arrived tired and depressed. Anti-American sentiment was running high in London and, just before his departure, more than 100 Conservative MPs had signed a motion calling on him to safeguard the deterrent. Particularly striking was the reaction to a speech from Dean Acheson, the former Secretary of State, on 5 December, in which he commented that 'Great Britain has lost an Empire and has not yet found a role. The attempt to play a separate power role – that is, a role apart from Europe, a role based on a "special relationship" with the United States, a role based on being the head of a "Commonwealth" which has no political structure, or unity, or strength . . . – this role is about to be played out.'[46] Anger in Britain was intense. Acheson had touched a raw nerve. Macmillan let it be known publicly that in appearing 'to denigrate the resolution and will of Britain and the British people, Mr Acheson has fallen into an error which has been made by quite a lot of people in the course of the last four hundred years, including Philip of Spain, Louis XIV, Napoleon, the Kaiser and Hitler'.[47]

Many in London suspected that the speech had been inspired by the White House, but in fact Kennedy moved quickly to distance

"ER, COULD I BE THE HIND LEGS, PLEASE?"

Vicky, *Evening Standard*, 6 December 1962.

himself from Acheson. With the full authority of the President, White House aide McGeorge Bundy instructed the State Department to brief the press that 'US–UK relations are not based only on a power calculus, but also on deep community of purpose and long practice of close co-operation. Examples are legion . . . "Special relationship" may not be a perfect phrase, but sneers at Anglo-American reality would be equally foolish.'[48]

But the State Department 'theologians' were now ready to sever the relationship for good. George Ball, who, as Rusk's deputy, headed the State Department delegation at Nassau, believed that the cancellation of Skybolt offered an opportunity to terminate the nuclear alliance with Britain. He was against providing Polaris as an alternative. The advantage of Skybolt was that it would not last very long, but Polaris was another matter:

> It seemed to me we should avoid doing anything that would extend Britain's nuclear deterrent for another generation . . . I was very determined to have the British begin to get out of the feeling that they were a great power because they had an Empire, which they no longer had, and they had a nuclear weapon which the others didn't have, and they had a relationship with the United States which nobody else had. This seemed to me not very healthy even from the British point of view.[49]

But Macmillan still had no time for a mixed NATO Multilateral Force. He asked Ball disdainfully, 'You don't expect our chaps to share their grog with Turks, do you?'[50] The mood in the British camp at Nassau, according to veteran journalist Henry Brandon, writing soon afterwards, was 'resentment and suspicion of American intentions such as I have never experienced in all the Anglo-American conferences I have covered over the past twenty years'.[51]

Belatedly Kennedy grasped what was at stake for Macmillan. On the flight to Nassau he talked at length to the British Ambassador, Ormsby Gore, and studied the State Department's briefing book compiled by its British desk. This warned that 'the special Anglo-American relationship is threatened as it has not been since Suez by the cancellation of Skybolt . . . The Prime Minister needs a successful meeting for . . . political survival.'[52] At Nassau Kennedy offered Britain various choices. She could develop Skybolt herself on generous terms. Macmillan demurred. The missile was no longer credible, he told Kennedy. After all the public comment 'the virginity of the lady must now be regarded as doubtful'.[53] The offer of an alternative

American air-to-ground missile was also rejected: how, Macmillan asked, could he go back to the House of Commons and explain that Britain's much-vaunted independent deterrent would now be called 'Hound Dog'? Nor was the Prime Minister interested in an Anglo-American joint study to examine future options. There was only one thing he would accept, and that was Polaris.

The Macmillan who argued Britain's case at Nassau was a man President Kennedy had not seen before. His government was unpopular. It had just lost two by-elections, and was being mocked for its lack of influence over Cuba and the absurdity of its claim to own a nuclear deterrent that was at the mercy of the United States. He spoke with the skill and determination of a politician in mortal danger, convinced that his survival depended on the success of the conference. Movingly he outlined the vicissitudes of the nuclear relationship since the war, emphasising that Britain had kept her side of the agreements. He reminded Kennedy of the promises made by Roosevelt to Churchill, of the McMahon Act and of the bargain struck in 1960 with Eisenhower: Skybolt in return for Holy Loch. He hinted that if nothing were done to replace Skybolt there would be a grave anti-American backlash in Britain with the possibility of a neutralist government coming to power. In his own words he 'had to pull out all the stops'.[54] It was a formidable performance and by the end of the oration, according to de Zulueta, 'there wasn't a dry eye in the house, including mine . . . I think it swung the day.'[55]

Reluctantly Kennedy accepted that only Polaris would satisfy the British, but, responding to those like Ball who wanted to use the Skybolt crisis to bolster the MLF, he tried to mesh the Polaris deal into that policy. The final agreement reached at Nassau on 21 December 1962 was flexible but confusing. It offered Britain Polaris, but committed the weapon in principle to 'a NATO multilateral force' while reserving the right to the British Government to operate independently whenever it 'may decide that supreme national interests are at stake'.[56] Macmillan was delighted. He had obtained a nuclear deterrent superior to Skybolt which, being launched by submarine instead of bomber, would be far less vulnerable. He had also acquired it on favourable terms, with Britain obliged to make only a small contribution to research and development in addition to the price of each missile. A damaging clash with America had been avoided, and Britain could remain in the nuclear club. There was, however, as the European 'theologians' in the State Department anticipated, a price to pay. For the Polaris deal helped to undermine the third pillar of Macmillan's foreign policy – Britain's bid to enter the EEC.

In January 1958 France, West Germany, Italy, Belgium, the Netherlands and Luxembourg had formed themselves into the European Community. The British Government remained aloof, in line with the policy it had adopted towards the Schuman Plan of 1950 and the Messina Conference of 1955. It believed that Britain's economic future lay with the Commonwealth and the countries of the sterling area, and regarded the integration of western Europe mainly as a way of reconciling France and Germany and thus preventing a third European war. But by 1960 Germany was producing nearly a fifth of the world's manufacturing output and her economic miracle was transforming not just German society but also those of her European neighbours, as wealth began to flow freely across reduced tariff barriers. The British had been wrong-footed. They assumed that post-war prosperity would depend on rising prices for the world's raw materials, many of which they still controlled. They did not expect the rejuvenation of continental Europe, based on industries that started afresh after 1945. Germany, many Britons observed sourly, had lost the war but was winning the peace. And Britain, the German leader Konrad Adenauer joked in 1958, was like 'a rich man who has lost all his property but does not realise it'.[57]

Macmillan did realise what was happening. A convinced Europeanist, by 1960 he could see compelling economic reasons for Britain joining the EEC, even though the Labour Party was opposed and many Conservatives were distinctly unenthusiastic about the Community's long-term political objective of a united Europe. Yet Macmillan, like his predecessors Churchill and Eden, believed that Britain was not irreducibly European, that she must maintain her special links with the Commonwealth, the sterling area and the United States. In April 1961 Macmillan received an assurance from the Kennedy Administration, in line with long-standing American policy, that 'relations between the United States and the United Kingdom would be strengthened, not weakened, if the UK moved toward membership'.[58] The following August Macmillan formally applied for Britain to join.

By December 1962 the negotiations for British membership of the EEC were making progress, particularly on the special position to be given to Britain's trading partners in the Commonwealth. There were still substantial issues to be resolved and informed diplomats differed in their predictions of the outcome. But then French President Charles de Gaulle made his position brutally clear. At a meeting at Rambouillet in mid-December, just before the Nassau Conference, he told Macmillan that he did not consider Britain to be European and strongly implied that he would veto her application to join the Community. Fearful that this information would strengthen the hand of those in Washington who wanted to end Britain's special nuclear relationship with the United States, Macmillan did not reveal the news to Kennedy at Nassau.

De Gaulle's motives were no mystery. He did not want a rival power usurping France's leadership of the EEC. As one French minister put it to his British counterpart: 'It's very simple, my dear chap. At present in the Six there are five hens and one cock. If you join, with the other countries, there will be perhaps seven or eight hens. But there will be *two* cocks. Well – that's not so pleasant.'[59]

There was also a deeper reason for de Gaulle's opposition – his antipathy to the Anglo-American axis dating back to World War Two. As leader of the Free French forces he had been consistently snubbed by Roosevelt, who had no time for France and her imperial pretensions. For as long as possible FDR had blocked the Free French claim to be the provisional government of France and to share in the occupation of Germany. Although the British, particularly Eden, interceded where they could for France, Churchill generally sided with the Americans. In his memoirs de Gaulle recalled one bitter row on the eve of the D-Day landings, when Churchill finally exploded: 'This is something you ought to know: each time we have to choose between Europe and the open sea, we shall always choose the open sea. Each time I have to choose between you and Roosevelt, I shall always choose Roosevelt.'[60]

These were words de Gaulle did not forget when he regained office in 1958. Since the war France had seen a succession of weak ministries, unable to cope with economic stagnation and with the bitter wars in Indo-China and Algeria. De Gaulle produced a new constitution, which gave the President much greater power. He ended the Algerian conflict by granting the country independence and set about rebuilding France's position in Europe. This meant reducing America's influence. Americans, he believed, had not provided adequate help during France's colonial crises, and their strategic guarantee was dubious in the post-Sputnik era of *mutual* assured destruction. Britain's close relationship with the United States meant, in France's view, that she would be a Trojan horse in the EEC, guaranteeing continued American domination of western Europe.

De Gaulle had made up his mind long before Nassau. He had virtually given Macmillan his verdict at Rambouillet. But the Polaris deal provided him with a convenient additional justification, and he was not diverted by the belated American offer of a similar nuclear arrangement for France. In a magnificently staged press conference on 14 January 1963 the General vetoed the British application for membership. He dismissed Britain as not yet a true European: her economy and trading links were very different from those of the Six, and the result of her membership would, he said, probably be 'a colossal Atlantic Community under American dependence and leadership'.[61] Macmillan was near despair, noting in his diary that 'all our policies at home and abroad are in ruins'.[62]

For Macmillan in 1963, like his old friend Eisenhower in 1960, the last months in office were a sad anti-climax. His government was buffeted by security crises, particularly the sex scandal involving his War Minister, John Profumo, and the defection of Soviet agent, Kim Philby. The premier's patrician manner, once Super Mac's great asset, was now savagely lampooned by the satirists. He was often compared unfavourably with the vibrant Kennedy, who had become a hero among the liberal youth of Europe. That summer Macmillan's rating in the opinion polls was the lowest for any premier since Chamberlain, and his last meeting with Kennedy in June 1963 was not a success. After a triumphal visit to Berlin, the President found Macmillan jaded and devoid of new ideas. Gossip about his imminent resignation was rampant. It was a far cry from their meeting of minds after the Vienna summit only two years before.

There was one consolation for Macmillan during 1963: the signing of the first nuclear Test Ban Treaty by America, Russia and Britain. Since 1957 Macmillan had been arguing indefatigably for a ban, continually raising the issue with both Moscow and Washington, however unpropitious their moods. In the wake of the Cuban missile crisis Khrushchev finally decided that it was in Russia's interests to have an agreement with America. Macmillan also whittled away at the American demand for extensive inspections. One British diplomat recalled that 'we looked at Britain as being in the position of being able to bring the two sides together'.[63] Kennedy himself was deeply engaged but, on the admission of one leading American official, Macmillan deserved 'much of the credit for the . . . ultimately decisive step' in the negotiations – a joint proposal with Kennedy for high-level but not summit talks which was made in April 1963.[64] This broke the diplomatic impasse and paved the way for the eventual agreement signed the following August.

Although the treaty did not prohibit underground tests, it was the first major arms control agreement of the nuclear age. Macmillan viewed it as one of his greatest achievements, and in August Ormsby Gore told Kennedy that the Prime Minister was 'in such a state of euphoria that Alec [Douglas-Home, the Foreign Secretary] doubts whether he now has any intention of resigning'.[65] But the triumph was short-lived. In October 1963 sudden surgery forced Macmillan to give up and the Conservative leadership chose Douglas-Home as his successor.

In America, too, power changed hands in the autumn of 1963. On Friday 22 November President Kennedy was shot dead as his motorcade drove through Dallas. Americans were stunned, near panic, as rumours spread of a possible communist conspiracy. In Britain, too, the shock was palpable and unprecedented. Thousands waited to sign a book of condolence at the American Embassy, the Catholic Westminster Cathedral was packed to overflowing for a Requiem Mass, and Kennedy became only the third American President after Abraham Lincoln and Franklin Roosevelt to have a monument erected in his memory in London. Despite less than three years in office, his vivid personality and his martyr's death left an indelible impression on the British public.

With Kennedy's assassination and Macmillan's retirement an era in Anglo-American relations came to an end. Macmillan's close friendships, first with Eisenhower and then with Kennedy, had restored a relationship that had nearly been destroyed over Suez. He played an important role in helping thaw the Cold War, as intermediary between the superpowers. His premiership also left durable legacies, particularly the unique nuclear partnership between the United States and its transatlantic ally. Nevertheless, Macmillan's last year in office had demonstrated Britain's growing impotence in the superpower world, the Test Ban Treaty notwithstanding, and the special relationship had proved a major stumbling block to Britain's attempted entry into the 'New Europe'. For the next decade, as America became enmeshed in the most disastrous war of its history, Britain remained in suspense, contracting as a world power yet excluded from the EEC, in limbo 'between Europe and the open sea'.

13

Drifting Apart

1963–73

'For millions of Americans,' Lyndon Baines Johnson later recalled, 'I was . . . a pretender to the throne, an illegal usurper.'[1] Yet the Vice-President stepped into the dead Kennedy's shoes and, reassuring the country, led it through its mourning and into a new era of social reform. It was an impressive feat for which Johnson was rewarded by a landslide victory in the November 1964 elections, which secured the Democrats not only the presidency but a two to one majority in both houses of Congress. A month earlier Harold Wilson took office, Britain's first Labour Prime Minister since 1951. He had run what many commentators thought to be a presidential style campaign. 'What we are going to need,' Wilson declared in the summer of 1964, 'is something like what President Kennedy had after years of stagnation – a programme of a hundred days of dynamic action.'[2]

As in 1945 many in Washington found the prospect of dealing with a socialist government unappealing. Wilson had said during his campaign that he intended to renegotiate the Polaris agreement. His Tory opponents claimed that he would abandon control over Britain's nuclear weapons and 'surrender all our authority in world affairs'.[3] In America advocates of the NATO multilateral nuclear force, the MLF – 'zealots' according to Secretary of State Dean Rusk – were determined that Britain would agree to participate before the year was out. An early confrontation between the two newly elected leaders seemed likely.

In December 1964 Wilson and his senior colleagues arrived in Washington. Britain's new Minister of Defence, Denis Healey, had already decided that Polaris was too far advanced to be worth cancelling. The promised renegotiation of the Nassau agreement, therefore, amounted to no more than a cut in the number of submarines from five to four. Next on the agenda was the MLF. Healey was sceptical of the concept, which he mocked as 'artificial dissemination', a way of 'pretending to give Europe a voice in America's nuclear strategy without actually doing so'. According to Healey, American support for the MLF was a last attempt to produce a mechanism which could lead to a federated Europe, 'the grain of sand round which the pearl of European unity would develop'.[4]

For eighteen months an experimental MLF had been in operation on a US destroyer, the *Claude V. Ricketts.* The captain and executive officer were American, together with half the crew, but the rest were British, German, Dutch, Italians, Greeks and Turks. There were marked cultural differences to overcome. The British grumbled at going without their daily tot of rum, to conform with the US navy which had been dry since World War One. The Greeks did not welcome being served sweetcorn, an American favourite, which they considered 'something for chickens to eat'.[5] Discipline, according to the American skipper of the *Ricketts*, was the trickiest problem: it was not easy to persuade a foreigner to accept the austere American naval punishment of three days solitary, on bread and water, with only a Bible to read. The common language was English but a vocabulary of only 800 words, 'including some good old-fashioned Anglo-Saxon swear words', was apparently sufficient for most practical purposes.[6]

The experiment itself was a success, but the concept behind it a failure. 'It died a natural death,' Dean Rusk said, 'because our NATO allies, particularly Britain and Germany, could not agree on it.'[7] There was also opposition from Congress and a distinct lack of enthusiasm from President Johnson. Wilson offered Washington a substitute proposal, the ANF, or Atlantic Nuclear Force, an amalgam of existing national nuclear forces, with minimal mixed manning. 'We put it for the sake of courtesy,' said Denis Healey, 'after making a very strong case against the [MLF] proposal.' Johnson, relieved to be free of the MLF, agreed to explore the ANF idea and then allowed it to slip into oblivion during 1965. Healey did not think there was 'much weeping in Washington over it'.[8] America had now abandoned the attempt to restrict the nuclear power of its allies and resigned itself to the continued existence of both British and French nuclear forces.

Washington's first encounter with the new British Government had passed off well. Wilson gave the impression of being committed to Anglo-American co-operation while deriding Tory yearnings for the days of empire and transatlantic equality. At the White House dinner on 7 December 1964 he told Johnson: 'Some of those who talk about the special relationship, I think, are looking backwards and not looking forward. They talk about the nostalgia of our imperial age. We regard our relationship with you not as a *special* relationship, but as a *close* relationship, governed by the only things that matter, unity of purpose, and unity in our objectives.'[9]

But no personal rapport developed between the rough-spoken Texan President and the wily British Prime Minister, nothing like the relationship that had been built up by Macmillan with Eisenhower and Kennedy. George Ball, then Under-Secretary of State, recalls that 'LBJ had been impressed with Macmillan', but Wilson 'lacked Macmillan's consummate ability to deal on a friendly but slightly condescending basis. He wore no patrician armor, was too ordinary, too much like other politicians with whom LBJ had to deal, and Johnson took an almost instant dislike to him.'[10] In the Macmillan era cordial transatlantic friendships had cushioned the shock of conflicting policies and offset the decline of Britain's power. In the mid-1960s, a time of strained personal relations, the decline accelerated and the differences over policy became severe.

The foreign policy issue that eclipsed all others for America by the mid-1960s was the conflict in Vietnam. It spilled over into American domestic policies and fundamentally changed the perception of the United States in Britain. It demonstrated to America the limits of its power, and also the limits of its friendship with Britain, for in this long conflict Britain consistently failed to come up to Washington's expectations.

The partition of Vietnam, masterminded by Anthony Eden in 1954, had produced two rival states, the South under Ngo Dinh Diem and the North, under the communist Ho Chi Minh. The 1954 agreement had provided for elections throughout the country in 1956, but Diem refused to go along with this plan and the North–South divide continued. Ho had expected to win the elections and had no intention of allowing partition to become permanent, as it had in Korea. He insisted that the country must be reunited under communist rule and, in the late 1950s, he exploited Vietnamese opposition to Diem's corrupt government to create the Vietcong, a guerrilla force raised in the South but trained and controlled by the North.

Diem had been supported by America since 1954 as a bastion of democracy against the totalitarian regime in the North. Dulles had backed Diem's obstructionism, arguing that free elections were impossible in the areas controlled by the communists. He had never accepted the Geneva Accords of 1954 and told Eisenhower in February 1956 that 'our policy in Vietnam is directed toward . . . the continued strengthening of the position of Free Vietnam under President Diem . . . and . . . the eventual weakening of North Vietnam by political and psychological warfare'.[11] Faced with the threat from the Vietcong, Diem naturally asked America for further help and Kennedy agreed to provide it. Overt military intervention was rejected in favour of American 'advisers', whose job was to train Diem's men in counter-insurgency tactics and psychological warfare to defeat the Vietcong. At the time of Kennedy's death there were already 15,000 American advisers in Vietnam and the United States was bearing most of the cost of the war. Yet both militarily and politically the situation was deteriorating.

Kennedy believed that the fate of South Vietnam would decide America's influence in south-east Asia, and that its allies around the world would be watching to see how it discharged its responsibilities, but the lack of popular support for Diem was the weakness at the heart of the strategy. After attempts to encourage and enforce reform had proved ineffective, his Administration covertly supported Diem's overthrow in November 1963. Kennedy accepted that the military commitments America had now embarked upon were dangerous. If one stage failed, the next would be an escalation. 'It's like taking a drink,' he told one aide. 'The effect wears off, and you have to take another.'[12]

Johnson inherited the makings of a disaster. In the early days of his presidency, he gave little attention to Vietnam. He was ambitious for domestic reform, the field in which he had made his reputation in Congress. He wanted to take his place in history by introducing the welfare and civil rights programme known as 'the Great Society'. He was reluctant, he said later, to leave 'the woman I really loved – the Great Society – in order to get involved with that bitch of a war on the other side of the world'. But the war could not be ignored. Johnson was sensitive to Republican criticism that he, as a liberal Democrat, was soft on communism. If South Vietnam fell he feared there would be a national inquest far worse than the one after China went communist in 1949, which would 'shatter my Presidency . . . and damage our democracy'.[13] He accepted, as Kennedy had done, that Vietnam was a test case of America's credibility: pull out, he commented in 1965, and we 'might as well give up everywhere else – pull out of Berlin, Japan, South America'.[14] Under these pressures Johnson started to ignore the advice of State Department doves like George Ball who argued for a more cautious policy, and listened instead to the Joint Chiefs of Staff, who believed that direct American military intervention would bring the enemy to the negotiating table.

In January 1965 the deteriorating situation in South Vietnam led most of Johnson's inner circle of advisers to advocate selective bombing of the North. A new communist offensive, in early February, provided the pretext for a series of air attacks on specific targets, code-named 'Rolling Thunder'. By avoiding an outright declaration of war, Johnson was able to circumvent Congress. In July he took a further step, again on his own authority as Commander-in-Chief. He accepted the open-ended commitment of US combat troops. By the end of 1965 nearly 200,000 Americans were in South Vietnam.

Johnson did less than his military advisers wanted: 'enough, but not too much' was his motto.[15] He dared not risk all-out war with China, as had happened over Korea. So he escalated the war cautiously, behind the backs of the Congress. But Ho Chi Minh, skilfully exploiting the rivalry between Russia and China, and America's antagonism to both, was able to match each step Johnson took. During the next two years US restrictions on bombing targets were gradually lifted. From the spring of 1967 regular raids were mounted on targets in the cities of Hanoi and Haiphong, despite the danger of Russian or Chinese casualties, and the troop commitment rose to nearly half a million men. Johnson had become so deeply entangled that he could no longer extricate himself. As George Ball had warned in 1964, 'Once on the tiger's back we cannot be sure of picking the place to dismount.'[16] As long as Ho retained the support of Moscow and Peking he held the initiative. Simply by refusing to negotiate he could suck America deeper and deeper into the mire.

Throughout the war Johnson hoped for Britain's help. Increasingly beleaguered at home, he needed support from America's allies and, if possible, their military backing. He did not expect a major contingent from Britain, since she was already engaged in a counter-insurgency war against the forces of Sukarno's Indonesian Government, which were trying to infiltrate and destroy the Malaysian federation. But Wilson refused to send even a token force and earned Johnson's contempt for proffering advice from the sidelines and trying to act, in the Macmillan tradition, as mediator between the two sides in Vietnam.

When Wilson came to Washington for talks in December 1964 he was aware, according to William Bundy, one of Johnson's principal advisers on Vietnam, that American raids on North Vietnam were being planned. In his memoirs Wilson merely says that Johnson raised the question of British participation 'without excessive enthusiasm'.[17] On the night of 10–11 February 1965 Wilson called Johnson from London to express concern over the first bombing raids. He proposed coming to Washington to discuss the issue. Johnson retorted that unless he cared to send some British troops Wilson should mind his own business. 'I won't tell you how to run Malaysia, and you don't tell us how to run Vietnam.'[18] Bundy thinks Wilson 'overreacted and made out more surprised than he should have done. The time to have spoken was when he was in Washington in December, if he really felt the way he expressed himself in February.' In Bundy's view the incident affected Johnson's judgement of Wilson. He decided that the British Prime Minister did not really have his mind on the problem of ensuring stability and peace in south-east Asia, and showed that he was not 'what the French would call *un homme sérieux*'.[19]

The disagreements between Britain and America over south-east Asia had surfaced before, over the handling of the war in Korea in the 1950s. Asian communism was consistently perceived in Britain as less of a threat to world peace than it was in America. The British Government did not believe communism was monolithic, and thought that the Americans, by treating it as such, missed the opportunity of dividing Russia from China and thereby undermining Ho Chi Minh. But on Korea Britain had remonstrated with the Americans from the position of an ally, with her own troops fighting alongside the Americans. Over Vietnam she was standing on the sidelines.

To have sent troops to Vietnam would have been impossible for Wilson's government. Not only was there resistance in the Labour Party but also growing public hostility to the war. London witnessed some of the most violent demonstrations ever seen there. On 27 October 1968 thousands of young people battled with mounted police in Grosvenor Square. They broke the windows of the American Embassy and threatened to ransack it.

Wilson's solution to the dilemma was a typical compromise. He refused to condemn his ally outright, continuing to support American policy in general terms, but tried to assuage critics at home by criticising specific actions such as the bombing of Hanoi and Haiphong. Meanwhile he made repeated efforts to bring both sides to the peace table. In December 1965, for instance, he pressed Johnson to call a halt to the bombing of Vietnam as a test of Ho's goodwill. In July of the following year he flew to Moscow to urge the Kremlin to dissuade Hanoi from putting captured US bomber pilots on trial. But his most sustained effort at mediation came in February 1967, when the Soviet Premier Alexei Kosygin was visiting Britain.

Washington was in contact with Hanoi and had put forward a tentative proposal for a permanent halt to US bombing, in return for Hanoi's ending its troop infiltration of the South. Wilson told Kosygin of the plan and seemed to be winning his support, when Washington,

"O wad some pow'r the giftie gie us / To see oursels as others see us!"

World statesman or American stooge? Garland, in the *Daily Telegraph*, 19 July 1966, quotes Burns – a favourite of Kosygin – to mock Wilson.

without letting London know, abruptly changed the negotiating terms. Wilson cabled Johnson that he had been placed in a 'hell of a situation' with Kosygin,[20] and begged the President to give him a proper chance to enlist Soviet help. The bombing had just been halted as a gesture, for the duration of the Vietnamese holiday of Tet, and Wilson believed there was a chance of exploiting this pause to begin real negotiations.

Johnson and the National Security Council deliberated in Washington, as Kosygin spent Sunday evening, 12 February 1967, at a final meeting at Chequers, the Prime Minister's official country residence. Wilson talked on and on, about everything from high-tech to geology, in an effort to prevent the Russians from leaving. The American diplomat Chester Cooper sat in a garret with an open telephone line to the White House, waiting for Washington's response. Trying to force a decision, he held the telephone out of the window to prove that the Russian motorcade was revving up, ready to leave. But no reply came from Washington and a peeved Kosygin left Chequers to drive back to his London hotel. After his departure Washington abruptly agreed to suspend the bombing, if Hanoi would open negotiations before the Tet truce ended on the following day. Wilson rushed to Kosygin's hotel with the news at 1.00 a.m., but there was no time for a response from Hanoi within the deadline set by the Americans, and the fighting began again. An angry Wilson put a good face on it, assuring his Cabinet that he enjoyed the 'absolute confidence' of both Johnson and Kosygin and that they had been 'on the edge of peace'.[21]

Wilson had been let down by Johnson's failure to keep him informed and by the impossible final deadline, but, although the Russians showed more interest than before in the peace process, Hanoi remained unresponsive. The American Administration, for its part, never saw Wilson as a serious intermediary. It tolerated his involvement, as it did that of many others, somewhat sceptically. Bundy believed that Wilson was 'overwhelmingly minded to get into a negotiation at almost any cost, regardless of where that negotiation might lead and without having thought through how immensely difficult it was going to be'.[22] Many in Washington thought his main aim was to win the Nobel Peace Prize. In his memoirs LBJ remarked tartly: 'I have no doubt . . . that the British government's general approach to the war and to finding a peaceful solution would have been considerably different if a brigade of Her Majesty's forces had been stationed . . . in Vietnam.'[23]

Johnson's conception of politics was intensely personal: loyalty was the highest virtue, betrayal the deadliest sin. Wilson's failure to send troops was seen as dereliction of duty. It was also politically damaging to Johnson. Daily TV news reports from Vietnam showed America's headquarters in Saigon, in front of which flew the flags of her fellow-combatants, with the Union Jack conspicuously absent. Administration officials like Bundy argue that a British commitment 'would have made a considerable psychological difference . . . particularly in liberal circles, which was where the main criticism of the war came from'.[24] The Americans stressed that they only needed a token force. In Washington, in July 1966, LBJ told Wilson that 'a platoon of bagpipers would be sufficient, it was the British flag that was wanted'.[25] Dean Rusk also applied pressure. Rusk was an anglophile and former Rhodes scholar, who was deeply distressed by the British attitude. According to Louis Heren, a British correspondent in Washington, Rusk asked him at a cocktail party why the British couldn't manage 'just one battalion of the Black Watch'. Patiently Heren explained the British policy. Rusk glowered: 'When the Russians invade Sussex, don't expect us to come and help you.'[26]

Tangible evidence of British loyalty might have made Johnson more tolerant of Wilson's efforts to mediate in Vietnam but, even if British opinion had been supportive, it is unlikely that she could have played a significant role. Prime Minister Attlee's influence in Korea in 1950–1 was a reflection of Britain's strength as much as of her loyalty. In the early 1950s Britain was the world's third largest military power, with nearly a million men under arms. From 1954 four divisions and a tactical air force were committed to NATO in the defence of western

Europe. But a decade later the balance had shifted. West Germany overtook Britain's armed forces in 1964, with 430,000 men to her 425,000.[27] During the intervening years, as Britain brought conscription to an end, Germany had replaced her as the main military pillar of NATO in Europe. Although France had withdrawn her forces from NATO in 1966, discontented with America's leadership, Germany and France had developed close ties and were becoming the effective leaders of the European side of the Atlantic alliance.

The shift in military and political strength coincided with a similar shift in economic power. In 1953 Britain had the third strongest economy in the world, although it was only half as big as Russia's and one-eighth the size of the United States'. By 1963 Britain had fallen to fifth place, with Germany third and France fourth.[28] Her economic performance had suffered from her continued exclusion from the EEC. De Gaulle remained implacably opposed to her entry when, overcoming Labour opposition, Wilson investigated anew the possibility of membership in 1967.

Despite this relative decline, Wilson was determined to uphold a world role for Britain. Although she had given up most of her colonies, she still maintained bases and troops in Singapore, Aden and the Persian Gulf, which protected important pro-Western states and ensured access to vital European oil supplies. 'We are a world power, and a world influence, or we are nothing,' Wilson proclaimed in 1964, within a month of taking office.[29] Quick to deride the Tories as jingoists, he nevertheless believed Britain's ideals and interests were inextricably bound up with her presence in south-east Asia and the Middle East, and that the Commonwealth was still an effective instrument for British influence. The United States, heavily committed in Vietnam, welcomed British involvement East of Suez. In December 1964 Denis Healey, back from Washington, told the Cabinet that America wanted Britain 'to keep a foothold in Hong Kong, Malaya, the Persian Gulf, to enable us to do things for the alliance which they can't do. They think our forces are much more useful to the alliance outside Europe than in Germany.'[30] The following summer the Chancellor of the Exchequer, James Callaghan, was lectured on the dangers of excessive defence cuts during a visit to Washington. US Defense Secretary, Robert McNamara, told him that America was already over-committed in Asia and would certainly not assume additional commitments both there and in the Middle East if Britain pulled out. He insisted that 'the American Congress would not tolerate a situation in which the United States was the sole world policeman'.[31]

But the high cost of her commitments soon forced Britain to ignore America's wishes and re-examine her role overseas. Labour had come to power anxious to maintain the value of sterling which, still standing at the $2.80 level adopted in 1949, was now grossly overvalued. In the era of fixed exchange rates the level of the currency was seen as a status symbol, much as it had been when an earlier Labour Government under MacDonald had struggled with the consequences of too high a rate in the 1920s. In 1964 the result of its overvalued level, combined with a lack of competitiveness in Britain's economy, was persistent trade deficits and runs on the pound, as overseas investors lost confidence in sterling. Reductions in government spending became inevitable with overseas commitments a prime target.

Britain's role East of Suez, with its echoes of imperialism, was particularly unpopular among Labour's left wingers. In February 1966, as part of general reductions in defence spending, the Cabinet agreed to pull out of Aden in 1967–8. It reaffirmed, at the same time, its commitment to stay in the Gulf and in the Far East until the mid-seventies. More defence cuts followed in July 1967, but Wilson still refused to devalue sterling. One left-wing member of the Cabinet, Richard Crossman, was convinced that 'the decision not to devalue the pound and the East of Suez policy were very closely united'. Crossman felt that both were part of an essentially Tory foreign policy of maintaining Britain's world role and her credibility in Washington. 'It's my view,' he wrote, 'that this determination to cling to parity and keep Britain great has been the basic reason for all our economic troubles.'[32]

In the mid-1960s Britain defended the pound with the help of repeated credits from American banks and from the International Monetary Fund. James Callaghan denies that this help was given only in return for British support of American policy in Vietnam. 'Emphatically I must record that I encountered nothing said or implied to this effect.'[33] De Gaulle was trying to undermine America's financial hegemony and he regarded sterling as the dollar's first line of defence. It was therefore in America's financial interest, Callaghan claims, to protect the pound.

But the assistance was in vain. In the autumn of 1967 another devastating run on sterling finally forced Wilson to accept devaluation. New government spending cuts followed. Social policies close to Labour's heart, such as the provision of free drugs and medicines on the National Health Service, were affected and further defence cuts became politically unavoidable. The cost of Britain's presence in the Gulf was not a major part of total defence spending and the oil-rich

Gulf states, where British troops were stationed, indicated their willingness to bear the entire cost themselves. But, as *The Times* commented, 'the defence cuts are the *sine qua non* of a package which will involve the wholesale slaughter of sacred cows'.[34] Only Polaris and the British Army of the Rhine were sacrosanct as the Cabinet announced that Britain would withdraw from all its East of Suez bases, except Hong Kong, by March 1971.

The State Department was aghast. In February 1967 some middle-level officials in Washington had suggested offering Britain a multi-billion-dollar loan, or even gift, to fund her sterling debts and end for good the speculation against the pound. What they wanted in return was a firm British commitment to remain East of Suez – a demand Callaghan dismissed as 'unacceptable'.[35] When the British Foreign Secretary, George Brown, visited Washington in January 1968 to explain the withdrawal decision, one official pleaded: 'Be British, George, be British – how can you betray us?'[36] Johnson made a personal appeal to Wilson to reconsider his decision, and there were even hints of American economic retaliation, but to no avail. The Cabinet agreed to defer Britain's departure until December 1971, but no further.

The withdrawal could not have come at a worse time for Anglo-American relations. Johnson was facing the most devastating Vietcong assault so far in Vietnam and had no forces to spare to fill the vacuum

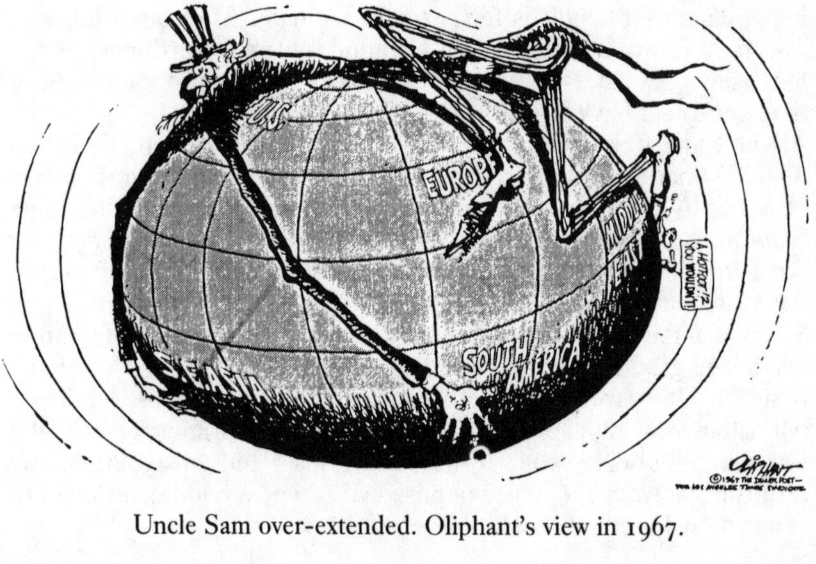

Uncle Sam over-extended. Oliphant's view in 1967.

in the Gulf. He was obliged to turn to Iran and Saudi Arabia to maintain the West's influence. Denis Healey, as the Minister of Defence responsible for implementing the British decision, had no doubt that it was right, arguing that it was too expensive to stay East of Suez and that, had she stayed, Britain would have become the target of nationalist opposition in the area. 'The Americans change their mind about Britain all the time. They spent the whole of the war trying to get us to give up the Empire everywhere and being very nasty to us when we didn't. Eisenhower and Dulles tried to torpedo the Anglo-French intervention in Suez, quite rightly in my opinion. Then they changed their position.'[37] Dean Rusk, Secretary of State, disagrees: 'I personally believe . . . that Britain over-reacted to the loss of Empire and has under-estimated its own position and influence in the world, its own ability to influence the course of events . . . In Washington we were disappointed, disturbed, regretful.'[38]

When Wilson visited the United States in February 1968, there was a sense that an era in British and world history had passed. Britain had withdrawn East of Suez and had devalued the pound. Such was the mood that the American press read a deliberate snub into the choice of songs for the White House dinner in Wilson's honour – 'On the Road to Mandalay' and 'I've Got Plenty of Nothing'. Johnson's wife, Lady Bird, called it 'the most ridiculous international furor so far' and Wilson brushed it off, claiming that the songs were his favourites. At the dinner Wilson once again played the role of world statesman, chatting easily with 'Lyndon' and 'Lady Bird' and discoursing at length on his plans for peace in Vietnam. Afterwards Johnson saw the Wilsons to their car, but his mind was on other things. As the limousine drew away, he ran up the stairs to his 'war room' saying 'I've got to get back to Khe Sanh.'[39]

Khe Sanh was in danger of becoming America's Dien Bien Phu. The US marines in this remote base near the Laotian border were besieged by two North Vietnamese divisions. LBJ insisted that Khe Sanh must be held at all costs, sending in reinforcements and laying waste to the surrounding countryside with bombs. As he did so the Vietcong launched devastating new offensives throughout South Vietnam at the end of the Tet holiday in January 1968. Film of fighting inside the grounds of the American Embassy in Saigon and of the besieged US marines in Khe Sanh was shown nightly on American television, providing proof that, despite Administration claims, the war was not being won. It was being lost, and in a particularly disturbing way, as though to oppose evil America had been forced to resort to evil methods itself.

Hearings by Senator William Fulbright's Foreign Relations Committee early in 1968 suggested Johnson had consistently deceived Congress about the nature of the war, the scale of American involvement, and the results of her efforts. Pictures shown around the world of the Saigon police chief summarily executing a Vietcong suspect on the street led many to wonder what kind of democracy the United States was really fighting for. In March these feelings surfaced during the first stage of the presidential election campaign, when Senator Eugene McCarthy, running on an anti-war ticket, came a strong second to the President in the New Hampshire Democratic primary, prompting John Kennedy's brother Robert to join the race against Johnson. America's premier newscaster, Walter Cronkite, back from his own tour of Vietnam, told viewers:

> It seems now more certain than ever that the bloody experience of Vietnam is to end in a stalemate. This summer's almost certain standoff will either end in real give-or-take negotiations or terrible escalation; and for every means we have to escalate the enemy can match us . . . And with each escalation, the world comes close to the brink of cosmic disaster.[40]

Spoken by the most trusted man in America, it was a staggering indictment of the Administration's policy.

The political challenges he faced at home prompted an extraordinary decision by President Johnson. McNamara, exhausted and disillusioned, had resigned as Defense Secretary and had been replaced by Clark Clifford, an adviser of Democratic Presidents since the Truman era. Clifford cast a fresh eye over US policy and persuaded Johnson that the war could not now be won on terms that would be acceptable to the American people. If he insisted on pursuing it and agreed to the request of the Joint Chiefs of Staff for another 200,000 troops to be drafted to Vietnam, he would split the Democratic Party and inflict terrible damage on the country. What was needed, Clifford advised, was 'not a war speech, but a peace speech'.[41] Johnson, the consummate politician, knew he was beaten. On 31 March he announced that nearly all air and ground operations against North Vietnam would be halted, that he would not seek re-election as President, and that his last months in office would be devoted to the search for peace. Some Americans half-wondered whether it was an early April fool, but the shattered President was in earnest.

Yet the summer of 1968 brought peace neither in Vietnam nor at home. Under the merciless eye of television it sometimes looked as if

American society itself was on the verge of collapse. Johnson had previously insisted that the war against poverty at home and the war against communism in Vietnam could be fought without increases in taxation. 'We are a rich Nation,' he told Congress in 1966, 'and can afford to make progress at home while meeting obligations abroad.'[42] But his fiscal policy proved irresponsible. Heavy government borrowing undermined confidence in the dollar abroad and fuelled roaring inflation at home. Soon the war in Vietnam was spilling its violence on to America's streets. A few days after Johnson's withdrawal from the presidential race the black civil rights leader Martin Luther King was assassinated, causing riots across the country, some of them only a few blocks from the White House and the Capitol. In June Bobby Kennedy, by now leading the Democratic race, was shot and killed in a San Francisco hotel. In August, at the Democratic Convention in Chicago, Mayor Daley's police force beat up peace protesters and innocent by-standers in full view of television cameras, and tear gas brought conference delegates running from their hotels. As horror succeeded horror America's reputation as the bastion of liberty, as a free and fair society, came under question. Only the brutal Russian invasion of Czechoslovakia in August reminded the world that the other superpower did not accept even the principle of civil liberty.

The election of Republican Richard Nixon in November 1968 led to a reassessment of the Vietnam War. With his National Security Adviser Henry Kissinger, a German-born Harvard professor, Nixon evolved a scheme for ending the war swiftly, with minimum protest at home, but without incurring an obvious military defeat. To mollify domestic opinion he began to withdraw American troops, substituting a policy of 'Vietnamisation', with the retraining of South Vietnam's own army. The air war, which caused few American casualties, was however, intensified. In an attempt to force Hanoi to the conference table North Vietnamese sanctuaries in Cambodia were bombed, bringing that country into the war directly for the first time, and raids on the North continued, including periodic saturation bombings of the cities of Hanoi and Haiphong. 'I can't believe,' Kissinger told his aides in 1969, 'that a fourth-rate power like North Vietnam doesn't have a breaking point.'[43] Nixon's efforts to secure 'peace with honor' included military strikes on the ground against Cambodia and Laos and the dropping on Indo-China of a greater tonnage of bombs than had fallen under Johnson, who had himself dropped more than America used in the whole of World War Two.[44]

Nixon and Kissinger did not intend to rely on brute force alone. America's crisis of the late 1960s prompted them to review the country's relations with the communist world, so clearing the way for a peace settlement in Vietnam. By the early 1960s Russia and China were openly at odds, contrary to America's image of communism as a global monolith. While Kennedy and Johnson failed to exploit the rift, Ho adroitly played off Moscow and Peking against each other and enlisted the aid of both against the United States. As long as he could continue to do so he would have the support he needed to fight the war. But Nixon, despite his history as a pro-McCarthy Cold Warrior, believed it was time for America to 'come . . . to grips with the reality of China' and stop pretending that Mao's regime did not exist.[45] China was now emerging from its Cultural Revolution and seeking new contacts with the West.

After secret diplomacy by Kissinger, Nixon struck a deal with Peking. In return for Chinese pressure on Hanoi, the United States would gradually extricate itself from support for Chiang Kai-shek on his outpost island of Taiwan. America was at last beginning to acknowledge that Mao, not Chiang, was the real ruler of China. To seal the bargain and demonstrate the thaw in relations, Nixon flew to Peking in February 1972 and was greeted at the airport by Premier Chou En-lai. Mindful of how Dulles had snubbed Chou by refusing to shake hands at the Geneva conference on Indo-China in 1954, Nixon walked down the steps of his aircraft with arm thrust forward. Later Chou said, 'Your handshake came over the vastest ocean in the world – twenty-five years of no communication.'[46]

Nixon also opened up a new relationship with Russia. Shocked by its rebuff in Cuba in 1962, the Soviet Union had built up its stock of nuclear missiles to near parity with America. An arms-control agreement now seemed attractive to the United States, and Russia, for its part, was keen to acquire American goods and technology for its backward economy. In May 1972, less than three months after his historic trip to Peking, Nixon became the first US President to visit Moscow. There he and the Soviet leader Leonid Brezhnev signed the Strategic Arms Limitation Treaty, SALT I, which froze existing missile systems at their current levels. A related agreement restricted the deployment of Anti-Ballistic Missile defences. Moscow, too, would be encouraged to distance itself from North Vietnam.

By this combination of brute force and subtle diplomacy Nixon and Kissinger wore down Hanoi's resistance at the peace talks in Paris. Finally in January 1973 an agreement was reached which could be called 'peace with honor', even though few thought it would last, as long as Hanoi yearned for a united country. Under the settlement American troops were withdrawn, but air and naval forces were kept in the region to prevent any North Vietnamese movement into the South. South Vietnam was to be protected by America from a distance, while funds were provided for internal reconstruction. The policy was not given long to work. Congress, in the wake of the Watergate scandal, halved US aid to Saigon, and passed the War Powers Act to curtail the President's power to wage limited war without Congressional approval. In 1975 a new Vietcong offensive began and on May Day victorious Vietcong troops swept into Saigon. The last that was seen of the Americans was a desperate scramble for helicopters lifting them and a few of their luckier Vietnamese supporters from the roof of the US Embassy. Fifty-five thousand Americans had died, apparently to no avail. Shaken and embittered, the United States was ready to turn in on itself, to lick its wounds, and to ask hard questions about its many other responsibilities around the world.

Nixon, like Johnson, had been destroyed by the war. To implement his Vietnam policy he had adopted obsessive secrecy as a protection against domestic opposition. The State Department was by-passed, Democrats were subjected to dirty-tricks campaigns and leaks of information were plugged by illegal means. When the activities of the White House 'plumbers', burgling opponents on behalf of the President, were revealed, Nixon sacked his own Attorney General in an effort to conceal the evidence on tape recordings of White House conversations. When these were finally made public, the President, abandoned by his party and facing impeachment, was forced to resign in August 1974.

The manner of Nixon's departure, reduced to a tearful rambling eulogy of his mother on worldwide television, belied the significance of his presidency. In three historic months in 1972 he had broken the frozen grip of the Cold War by being the first US President to visit Peking and Moscow, capitals of the communist world. The United States was finally beginning to acknowledge the legitimacy of these two alien regimes. It was also conceding to the Soviet Union equal status as a military power.

In the agreements with China and Russia, unlike the moves towards détente in the 1950s or the Test Ban Treaty of 1963, Great Britain played no part. Finished as a world power, she had slipped out of the major league and was now in search of a new relationship with the continent of Europe.

The Labour Government of Harold Wilson had decided that for commercial reasons Britain should join the European Community, even though the party remained suspicious of being tied too tightly to Europe. As long as General de Gaulle remained in power, however, he vetoed the application. His retirement in 1969 allowed negotiations to begin in earnest, conducted by a new Conservative Government, led by Edward Heath, which came to office in 1970. Heath was unique among Britain's post-war Prime Ministers, in being deeply sceptical of Britain's obsession with America. He had been an ardent pro-Marketeer for many years, cutting his diplomatic teeth as Macmillan's chief negotiator in 1961–3. In 1970 he returned with relish to the task of preparing for Britain's entry, convinced that her destiny lay in Europe, and that Europe's destiny was to develop as a continent friendly to America, but separate from it. In October 1971 he was rewarded with a House of Commons majority in favour of entry on the terms he had negotiated. The treaty was signed with much ceremony, and took effect on New Year's Day 1973. Denmark and Ireland joined as well. The 'Six' became the 'Nine'.

America's attitude to the enlarged EEC had changed in the years since it first hoped to see a federal Europe emerge from the ruins of World War Two. In 1945 it produced half the world's manufactured goods; in 1970 less than a third. During the 1960s the EEC had emerged as a serious economic rival. As America's share of world production and of exports fell, Europe's rose, until, by 1970, although still producing only half the output of the United States, the Six accounted for twenty-nine per cent of world exports against America's fourteen per cent. EEC tariff barriers were keeping out American farm produce; her internal subsidies helped European steel and other products undercut America in world markets. Together with Japan she was posing a serious challenge to American economic supremacy.

The loss of trade affected America's financial standing too. It had grown used to the position of dominance assumed after World War Two. US trade surpluses, based on the production of essential goods and raw materials, had been reinvested outside America in economic aid and military expenditure. The rest of the world was driven by the great dynamo of the American economy. America benefited in return by bolstering friendly countries as bastions against communism. But as the world recovered from World War Two America's share of total international reserves fell from fifty per cent in 1950 to only sixteen per cent twenty years later. By the late 1960s the United States could no longer afford the role of world leader.

As America's reserves fell and the competitiveness of its products declined, the dollar became overvalued. The costs of the Vietnam War and the inflation it spawned increased the pressure on the dollar but, since fixed exchange rates were still the international trading norm, there was no easy way of making the necessary adjustment. In

August 1971 Nixon unilaterally decided that the dollar would be floated – left to find its own level against other currencies instead of being fixed in terms of the price of gold. At the same time he imposed a temporary ten per cent surcharge on all foreign imports. Over the next eighteen months successive currency crises resulted in most major world currencies floating too, as central banks tried to adjust to the new era. Bretton Woods had served the post-war world well, but after twenty-five years it no longer fitted the new distribution of economic power. Just as the gold standard had depended on British supremacy, so Bretton Woods had rested on the hegemony of the dollar.

The United States remained the most powerful nation on earth but it was no longer impregnable. Economically it was being challenged by the newly enlarged EEC and by Japan. Militarily, with SALT I, it had conceded parity with the Soviet Union. Diplomatically an atmosphere of détente with Russia and the new links with China seemed to signal, if not the end of the Cold War, at least a marked thaw. Nixon propounded the argument that the language of two superpowers, of East versus West, no longer served to describe international relations. 'It would be a safer world and better world,' he said in 1972, 'if we have a strong, healthy United States, Europe, Soviet Union, China, Japan; each balancing the other, not playing one against the other, an even balance.'[47]

Logically this new philosophy demanded a reassessment of America's relationship with Europe, which had barely been examined since the establishment of NATO after the war. If Europe was back on her feet again, and even challenging the United States, it made sense to ask whether she should not take more responsibility for her own defence. Senator Mike Mansfield had focused attention on the point ever since 1966, when he first put down a resolution calling for reductions in American troops in Europe. He asked in 1970 why

> the 250 million people of Western Europe, with tremendous industrial resources and long military experience, are unable to organise an effective military coalition to defend themselves against 200 million Russians who are contending at the same time with 800 million Chinese, but must continue after 20 years to depend upon 200 million Americans for their defence.[48]

With the war in Vietnam coming to an end, Nixon, encouraged by his Secretary of State Henry Kissinger, decided to turn his attention to Europe. The initiative was ill fated from the start. Kissinger announced that 1973 would be the 'Year of Europe'. The very title stuck in the craw of many Europeans, suggesting that having sorted out Vietnam and the two communist giants, Washington wanted to sort out Europe, and thought it could all be done in twelve months. To the leaders of Europe that seemed a presumptuous and arrogant approach. The British Foreign Secretary, Sir Alec Douglas-Home, did not even hear about the proposal from Kissinger or the State Department, but read it on the news-agency tapes, and rang the French Foreign Minister to see if he could throw any light on it, but he knew nothing either.

The news tape Douglas-Home read was a report of a keynote speech given by Kissinger in New York on 23 April. It called for negotiations leading by the end of the year to 'a new Atlantic charter' between the United States and its European allies. The aim was to reduce economic rivalry, negotiate a more equitable sharing of defence burdens, and at the same time reassure the Europeans that their interests would not be overlooked in America's moves towards détente with the Soviet Union. Remembering the European condemnation of the Christmas bombing of Hanoi a few months earlier, Kissinger drew a contrast between the post-colonial countries of western Europe and their superpower ally: 'the United States has global interests and responsibilities. Our European allies have regional interests.' The time had come for a comprehensive stock-taking. America 'must strike a new balance between self-interest and the common interest'.[49]

The inauspicious start should have warned Kissinger that all was not well. He admits now that although the idea was 'based on a correct analysis' it 'misfired'. He concedes that it was put forward in 'too dramatic a form' and was unfortunately proposed two weeks after the Watergate scandal broke. 'I think that the desire of European leaders to be seen at a summit with President Nixon was not as great as it would have been two months earlier.' But he blames the European allies, and in particular Heath, for not simply saying to Washington 'for God's sake let's drop this for six months . . . but nobody said "no" and nobody said "yes"'.[50]

In past transatlantic misunderstandings, Britain had often adopted the role of go-between, interpreting America to Europe and moderating US policy. But this did not happen in 1973. Kissinger believes that, with Britain just entering the EEC, Heath did not want to be stigmatised as an American agent or a Trojan horse. Contrary to Kissinger's expectations, Heath refused to discuss the American proposals privately with Washington before they were put to the other European partners. Heath's view is that the US initiative was misguided. Kissinger was publicly trying to make out that there should now be one Europe to whom he could talk, while privately he 'sometimes still tried to play one [country] off against the other. None of us were prepared to play that game.'[51] On 25 July 1973 Heath cabled Nixon that all discussions must be conducted with the nine members of the EEC as a single group. Kissinger was furious. He believed that close consultation between Britain and America was invaluable. He told Sir Burke Trend, the influential Secretary to the Cabinet, that 'Atlantic – and especially Anglo-American – relations had thrived on intangibles of trust and communication' and warned that if Britain's current Europeanist tendencies continued, 'we were at a turning point in Atlantic relations'.[52]

The other countries of the EEC were no warmer towards Kissinger's proposals than Britain. Led by the French, they resented being dismissed as purely regional powers and rejected the link, implicit in Kissinger's speech, between continued American military commitments to Europe and European economic concessions to America. Reluctantly the Europeans started negotiating, but progress was slow, and, against Kissinger's wishes, economic and military questions were kept separate.

The talks were finally killed by a new outbreak of war in the Middle East, which served further to deepen the Atlantic divide. On 6 October 1973, the sacred Jewish holiday of Yom Kippur, Egypt and Syria mounted simultaneous attacks on Israel to avenge their defeat of 1967. Faced with what looked like the imminent destruction of an ill-prepared Israel, one of America's key client states, a round-the-clock airlift of supplies was mounted by Washington. America's European allies were asked if their NATO bases could be used to help the operation. All but the Netherlands and Portugal refused. German objections were overridden. Depending heavily on Arab oil supplies, the Europeans argued that the war was a non-NATO affair, 'out of area' in the jargon, and that they could not provide help.

Britain, unlike Greece and Turkey, did not announce her decision publicly, but quietly intimated to Washington that a request to use British bases would be unwelcome. Reports that Britain had refused the use of the RAF base at Akrotiri in Cyprus for reconnaissance flights could thus be 'staunchly denied' by Whitehall.[53] As Kissinger observes, 'there was never a formal refusal on the airlift because it had been made plain that we should not ask'.[54] He adds: 'we took it publicly more or less stoically' but we 'cursed to each other'.[55] Heath believes that it was not necessary for the Americans to involve Britain in the first place. They could perfectly well have used their own facilities all the time. Their motive was simply 'that they wanted to have someone else with them in doing what they wanted to do'. British policy was to be 'even handed' between Israel and the Arab states and it was not in her interest, according to Heath, 'to lean more to one side than the other'.[56]

Worse was to come for transatlantic relations. Israel recovered from its initial surprise and gradually drove the Egyptian armies back across Sinai. By late October, faced with Egypt's virtual destruction, Moscow seemed to be threatening direct military intervention. On 24 October 1973 Nixon and Kissinger decided that the Russians must be warned off. At 11.41 p.m. all US military commands around the world were placed on DefCon III alert – in Kissinger's words 'the highest state of readiness for essentially peacetime conditions'.[57] The next 'Defence Condition', DefCon II, covers a situation in which attack is imminent. DefCon I means war.

The object was to send an unambiguous warning to Moscow. The Administration did not want to dilute the effect by telling its allies in advance, since the information would almost inevitably leak out. But, as in 1962 over Cuba, Washington did accord the British special treatment. Just after 1.00 a.m. on 25 October Kissinger informed the British Ambassador, Lord Cromer, of the alert and of Nixon's latest letter to Moscow. He hoped that Britain would use her influence on the NATO allies when the latter were told of the American action a few hours later. Heath's reluctance to do so again infuriated Kissinger.

From London's point of view the fact that it had been 'informed' but not 'consulted' about the alert revived anxiety about the status of American bases in Britain. In a stormy House of Commons, Douglas-Home was left arguing that 'if the bases were to be *used* for any purpose, there would be consultation. But the Americans must be allowed to *alert* their forces the world over, just as we might in certain circumstances.'[58] This distinction between the actual use of the bases in war and simply putting them on alert – the first requiring British consent under the 1952 agreement, the second not – seemed a little tenuous in the worst superpower crisis since Cuba. Heath believes America should have consulted Britain in advance. It was 'mythology' that, with modern intelligence devices and satellites, there was no warning of the build up, and in any case 'we didn't feel that the situation required a nuclear alert'.[59] Kissinger is adamant that there was no time to 'wait for British approval' but hints at another explanation, 'after all the Europeans had disassociated themselves from us . . . all through the crisis'.[60]

Faced with America's warning the Soviet Union backed down and a ceasefire was arranged. But the crisis left its mark on Anglo-American relations, reinforcing fears in Britain that the United States thought it could treat Britain and Europe as pawns in its game of superpower politics. For Secretary of State Kissinger the lesson was different. 'I objected then, and I object today, wherever allies try to turn the alliance into a unilateral American guarantee of what they consider to be their vital interests without reciprocity.'[61] NATO, he believed, could not survive as a one-way street.

In the rapidly changing world of the early 1970s Britain and America seemed further apart than at any time since the end of World War Two. It was perhaps a consequence of both countries trying to redefine their roles in the world and discovering that the old relationship no longer seemed suitable to their changed circumstances. Britain was finally coming to terms with the end of her era of world power. In seeking a new future inside Europe, the Heath government was prepared for a hard-headed re-examination of the old special relationship. The United States, for its part, was also adjusting to a relative decline in its economic and military superiority. After a quarter of a century of struggle against Russia and China there was a new, if tentative, acceptance of their right to exist as major communist states. And America's defeated enemies of 1945, Germany and Japan, were now economic rivals. As power became diffused it seemed fair to redistribute the burdens of global security more equitably with America's allies, an ambition that Britain, along with her European allies, appeared to have thwarted.

By 1973, in short, there were many signs that America and Britain were drifting apart diplomatically. The special relationship seemed to be a thing of the past. But the Anglo-American connection has always been more than diplomacy, greater than a few transatlantic links between politicians, soldiers and bureaucrats. By the 1960s the tides of economic and cultural change were ebbing to and fro across the Atlantic with unprecedented intensity, bringing the two peoples, if not the two governments, into closer contact than ever before.

14

Living in the American Age

Business and society from the 1940s to the 1970s

No account of American life in the nineteenth century can avoid frequent references to Britain – the role of British products, investments and ideas in the expansion and development of the United States. By the end of the century America was in turn making its mark on the industrial and cultural life of Britain, but even in the 1920s and 1930s influences remained two-way. After 1945, however, the current ran strongly from west to east – a flow of commerce, capital and culture that led to a new British furore in the 1960s about an American 'invasion'. While American firms penetrated deep into British industrial life, a new generation of Britons, dismayed by the cautious, sedate and stuffy mood of the Establishment, took their cue from their counterparts across the ocean. Their spirits were lifted by the new wave of popular music and their rebelliousness nurtured by the American example. But what they believed to be the norms of modern American life had only recently been established. The United States had itself been transformed in two decades after 1945.

The post-war world saw the greatest sustained improvement in living standards ever experienced. In the United States, the richest country on earth, the wartime boom began a remarkable expansion in the economy and in personal wealth. There were periodic setbacks: growth was sluggish in the late 1940s and late 1950s, and in the 1970s recession bit hard. But in 1956 – when Eisenhower's election slogan was 'Everything's booming but the guns' – the income of the average

American was fifty per cent higher in real terms than in 1929. By 1960 it was thirty-five per cent more than in the war-boom year of 1945.

The growth was largely fuelled by consumer demand: America's population grew from 131 million in 1940 to 226 million forty years later. Its purchasing power was revolutionised by the expansion of personal credit, such as easy-instalment plans and the ubiquitous credit card. Much of the 1950s' growth was based on the needs of the modern home, particularly for electrical goods. By 1953 two-thirds of American families had a TV set; by 1960 ninety-eight per cent of homes with electrical wiring had a refrigerator. In the 1960s teenagers sustained the boom, wanting clothes, soft drinks, transistors and records. Much of the economy became geared to satisfying the tastes of this new consumer culture, and to shaping those tastes through multi-million dollar advertising that spread the gospel of happiness through possessions, satisfaction from novelty.

To produce these new, sophisticated goods required massive and expensive investment in research and development. As a result America moved farther away from the small-scale, individualist values espoused by nineteenth-century liberals. In key industries such as automobiles, chemicals, aerospace and electronics, size was everything. 'The proportion of total corporate assets owned by the 200 leading manufacturing concerns increased from 47.2 per cent in 1947 to 60.9 per cent in 1968.'[1] The consumer culture was also the corporate culture. Charles E. Wilson, the president of General Motors who became Eisenhower's Defense Secretary, provided the classic statement about the identity of interests: 'What's good for our country's good for General Motors, and vice versa.'[2]

Industrial consolidation was not the only sign that the age of economic individualism was over. Even the biggest companies could not sustain unaided the vast costs of research and development. But the US Government, pursuing its Cold War strategy, was ready to spend an unprecedented amount on defence and related areas such as electronics and computers. At its peak the Korean War had pushed defence spending to nearly fourteen per cent of GNP and sixty-six per cent of the total expenditure of the Federal Government. After the shock of Russia winning the race into space with Sputnik in 1957 the impetus was maintained by the missile programme and by Kennedy's pledge in 1961 to put a man on the moon before the end of the decade. Technical resources and skilled manpower were mobilised for the project. Lyndon Johnson explained America's motivation: 'Failure to master space means being second-best in the

Balmoral Castle (29 August 1959). Prince Philip, Princess Anne, President Eisenhower, Queen Elizabeth, Prince Charles.

John F. Kennedy and Harold Macmillan at Birch Grove, Macmillan's Sussex home (30 June 1963).

The Polaris-equipped submarine USS *Patrick Henry* and its support ship, the *Proteus*, in Holy Loch on the Clyde (8 March 1961).

Inset: an anti-nuclear protester perched on the tail-fin of the *Patrick Henry* (27 March 1961).

crucial arena of our Cold War world. In the eyes of the world, first in space means first, period; second in space is second in everything.'[3] On 20 July 1969 an estimated one billion TV viewers all over the world watched Neil Armstrong become the first man on the moon. It was a triumph of American skill and determination, but testimony also to the expanding role of government in the economy. By the mid-1960s the Federal Government was funding eighty per cent of all R and D in the USA, and all but ten per cent of that funding came from the Defense Department, the National Aeronautical and Space Agency and the Atomic Energy Commission.

Not everyone benefited from the boom in the economy created by government and the consumer. As for much of the twentieth century, the lowest fifth of America's population received only about one-twentieth of the national income. The poorest of the poor were mainly black, and the 1960s saw their belated effort to gain for themselves what whites had long denied them. Led by Martin Luther King, the civil rights movement, through its marches and protests in the early 1960s, helped eliminate much of the formal segregation that had existed in the South since the late nineteenth century, including separate toilets, eating places and seating on public transport. In 1965 it also won federal protection for blacks' right to vote. But by 1960 only half the black population was still in the South and three-quarters lived in urban areas. In Northern cities they organised for action and glimpsed, in the neighbouring white suburbs, what American society offered its favoured beneficiaries. But they could do little through marches and protests to deal with the underlying urban problems of discrimination in employment, housing and education. The big-city riots each summer from 1964 to 1968 were the result of their pent-up anger and frustration.

The civil rights movement provided the model and the inspiration for other agitation in the 1960s. Women began to organise, pressing for an end to sex discrimination and demanding an amendment to the Constitution guaranteeing equal rights. Even more potent were the youth protests, centred on the Vietnam War but expressing a more general reaction against the values of the consumer society. The emphasis was on personal fulfilment through sexual freedom, the use of drugs and experiments with various forms of Eastern mysticism, new values that were spread by the popular music of the day.

Already in the 1950s the revolt of the young against the lifestyle of their parents had been symbolised by rock 'n roll. This was a shrewdly marketed adaptation of black rhythm and blues, with white singers shouting out their lyrics against a continuous band accompaniment and an insistent beat. Parents of the fifties, accustomed to the decorous swing music of the Big Band era, were often alarmed or outraged, while their children responded with wild enthusiasm. The pioneers of this new era in popular music and culture were Bill Haley and the Comets, but they were quickly outshone by Elvis Presley, the farmboy from Mississippi, who had a vocal talent and sexual charisma that Haley lacked. Elvis, with his gyrating pelvis and greased-down hair, became the cult figure of the late fifties and early sixties. The leadership in American popular music was then taken over by the more politicised folk-rock of Joan Baez and Bob Dylan, both of whom were closely associated with the protest movement against the Vietnam War. By the mid-sixties a significant British influence was making itself felt. With the Beatles and the Rolling Stones popular music became the symbol of an international youth culture.

The protest movements, whether political or musical, did not seriously challenge the dominant consumer culture. Women and blacks sought not its elimination but the extension of its benefits. By global standards even America's poor were 'staggeringly well off'. The per capita income of Harlem, New York's black ghetto, 'ranked with that of the top five nations in the world',[4] and the most disadvantaged families often had telephones, cars and televisions. Even the young of the mammoth Woodstock music festival in 1969 or the Haight-Ashbury hippy colony of San Francisco ('Hashbury') depended on the affluent society for their wealth, leisure and lifestyle. Furthermore, the main focus of youth protest was the university campus – itself testimony to the success of the American way. By 1970 forty per cent of eighteen to twenty-one-year-olds were attending college or university (compared with sixteen per cent in 1940). The counter-culture was 'contemptuous of this world's goods as only people who take them for granted can be'.[5]

The Federal Government's response to poverty and protest also exhibited distinctively American characteristics. Socialism, let alone communism, remained a minority movement. In post-war America there was nothing comparable to the nationalisation programmes seen in Britain and much of western Europe, and the idea of a national health service remained anathema to most Americans. In the United States health care continued to be the concern of the individual through private insurance schemes. Nevertheless, just as the US Government had become more involved in the economy in the 1940s and 1950s, so the 1960s saw a vast increase in government welfare provisions. LBJ's 'Great Society' introduced such programmes as food stamps, Medicare (funded health insurance for the aged), and

Medicaid (medical help for those in particular need). The consequences of this 'welfare revolution' were profound. By 1974 welfare payments were consuming sixteen per cent of GNP and their share of the Federal Government's budget, over forty per cent, had outstripped defence.

The welfare state of the 1960s reinforced the impact of the warfare state created in the 1940s and 1950s. Both depended on a vast increase in government expenditure and on the revolutionary assumption that such expenditure was both moral and essential for a healthy economy and society. In short, Keynesianism was taking root in America.

John Maynard Keynes, the British economist and government adviser, was one of the most influential thinkers of the twentieth century. His ideas about the role of government investment in promoting economic growth and full employment and his criticism of the dogma of balanced budgets had found their American advocates since the New Deal. They had been practised intermittently since the 1930s – Roosevelt's reluctant deficit spending during the Depression, the arms booms of World War Two and Korea, and Eisenhower's fuelling of the 'military-industrial complex'. But Roosevelt, Truman and Eisenhower were all instinctively fiscal conservatives who regarded unbalanced budgets as temporary aberrations, occasional necessary evils, and Keynes was distrusted by many American businessmen and economists as a dangerous left-winger.

It was not until the 1960s that policy caught up with practice. By this time Keynes's thought had been widely disseminated in economic circles and popularised through textbooks like the best-seller by Professor Paul Samuelson, which had sold over two million copies by 1965. Kennedy's Council of Economic Advisers was staffed by Keynesians led by Walter Heller. They persuaded him to embark on a programme of tax cuts which, the President assured business leaders in a major speech in December 1962, was not intended 'to incur a budget deficit, but to achieve the more prosperous, expanding economy which can bring a budget surplus'. Afterwards Kennedy called the speech 'straight Keynes and Heller', adding 'they loved it'.[6] In 1965, with Kennedy's tax cuts and Johnson's wage and price restraint, the US economy grew by five per cent in real terms. Personal incomes rose seven per cent, corporate profits were up twenty-one per cent, and unemployment was only four per cent. With Keynesianism it now seemed possible to manage the economy to ensure long-term prosperity. Johnson's Budget Director, Charles Schultze, said: 'We can't prevent every little wiggle in the economy, but we now can prevent a major slide.' Even Milton Friedman, America's leading conservative economist, admitted: 'We are all Keynesians now.'[7]

Kennedy and Johnson were Democrats, more inclined than the Republicans to permit heavy government spending. At the end of the decade Richard Nixon tried to dampen inflation by a return to Republican fiscal orthodoxy, but his attempts to balance the budget helped create a recession which led him to adopt deficit spending in 1971. Acknowledging this U-turn, Nixon, too, confessed his conversion: 'I am now a Keynesian.'[8]

Although Keynesianism was more than, and often very different from, what Keynes intended, it was perhaps Britain's most important intellectual export to America in the post-war era. This economic philosophy served to legitimise the vastly increased role of government in the economic life of the country – a process that has helped transform America more profoundly in the last forty years than in the previous two hundred.

For Britain the post-war story was in some respects similar to the American. The British population also experienced a dramatic improvement in living standards so that in 1959 Macmillan could justly campaign on the slogan 'You've never had it so good'. And yet Britain's 'age of affluence' was different in that it occurred during a period of decline in the competitiveness of the national economy compared with those of her rivals. In both affluence and decline the hand of America was very evident.

It took Britain years to shake off the austerity of war. Thanks to her foreign exchange problems and the Korean conflict, rationing continued well into the 1950s, with meat not being fully derationed until 1956. But from the mid-1950s Britain began to cultivate a taste for American living. With the easing of exchange controls from 1958, American goods flowed into Britain and British manufacturers geared up to satisfy the growing demand. By 1971 two-thirds of British homes had refrigerators and washing machines and ninety-one per cent had televisions, whereas two decades before all these consumer goods had been rarities. Household appliances helped revolutionise the lives of women, while television transmitted into every home previously unimagined attitudes and lifestyles. The growth in consumer demand was sustained by a credit explosion emulating the USA – 'hire purchase' and later 'plastic money'. In this, as in much else, Britain was following America, a decade or so behind.

The most striking feature of the American invasion was popular music – the decisive influence in shaping the new British teenage culture. In the year of Suez Jimmy Porter, in John Osborne's play *Look Back in Anger*, grumbled: 'I must say it's pretty dreary living in the American Age – unless you're an American of course. Perhaps all our children will be Americans. That's a thought isn't it?'[9]

It was a prophecy that already seemed to be coming true. In September of the same year, 1956, Bill Haley's film *Rock Around the Clock* took Britain by storm. The *New York Times* reported that 'Britons are puzzled by the riotous behavior of the teen-agers who have been moved by rock 'n' roll music to sing and dance wildly in the streets, to slug inoffensive Bobbies and in general to behave in a most un-British fashion.'[10] The relentless music provoked the young audiences to dance in the aisles of cinemas and to jive and sing their way in groups through the centre of British towns, often clashing with the police in the process. Many cities banned the film from being shown, including Birmingham, Liverpool, Bristol and Belfast. Sometimes it sparked off blatant hooliganism. When it was shown in the Gaiety Cinema in Manchester, fifty youths threw light bulbs and lighted cigarettes down from the gallery and turned fire extinguishers on members of the audience. A magistrate told those arrested: 'It would be very much better if the police were allowed to deal with you in the way which would give you something to rock and roll about for a bit.'[11]

While the courts passed down stiff sentences, guardians of high culture scoffed at the new youth heroes. *The Times* mocked Elvis Presley for his 'combination of a hill-billy style of wailing with bodily contortions that are supposed to suggest the "fundamental human drive" . . . Mr Presley, now the proud owner of three Cadillacs and hundreds of the violent sports shirts he affects, says: "I don't want no regular spot on no TV programme. I love to act. I don't care nothing whatsoever about singing in no movie."' *The Times* commented: 'Mr Presley adds, by way of illustration, that English was what he liked best at school.'[12]

But Establishment contempt had no effect. The following year Bill Haley and the Comets, already burning out in the States, had a spectacularly successful tour of Britain, travelling around in a special train. Rock 'n roll caught on as the reaction of the young to their parents – in most extreme form through the adoption by Teddy boys of the Comets' dress code. British teenagers now tuned in to the ever-changing, high-decibel sounds of the American music scene. It led to an explosion in the British record industry, as it had in the United States from the early fifties. By 1973 the UK came fifth in the world league table of record and tape sales – spending the equivalent of $38 million or $6.86 for every person in the country. (The USA headed the list with retail sales of over two billion dollars, or $9.70

per head.)[13] Capitalising on the pop music craze was a whole array of leisure industries, particularly clothing, often modelled on American fashions such as blue jeans.

In other ways the loosening up of British life owed much to the American example: the development of commercial television in the mid-fifties, the spread of drugs in the 1960s, and the proliferation in the 1970s of pressure groups using American techniques of protest and lobbying. The American civil rights movement provided a particularly influential model, most of all for the Catholic minority in Northern Ireland. From 1968 they began to protest openly against decades of discrimination by Protestant Unionists, who dominated Ulster and who were determined to keep it part of the United Kingdom. The new sectarian violence, encouraging and encouraged by the Irish Republican Army (IRA), reopened an unsolved problem which successive British governments had chosen to ignore since the 1920s. It also reintroduced the Irish dimension into Anglo-American relations as US politicians with Irish-American constituencies, such as Edward Kennedy and Tip O'Neill, repeatedly raised the issue of Northern Ireland on Capitol Hill. Combating Irish-American agitation became a major concern of British diplomats in the United States in the 1970s.

Parts of Britain were also being shaped by the presence of American servicemen. Since the arrival of the B-29 bombers during the Berlin crisis in 1948, US military bases had become a small but significant reminder that Britain now sheltered under the Eagle's wing. The greatest concentration of American servicemen was in East Anglia. Many of the professional airmen had been there already in World War Two. Some had married East Anglian women, whom they brought back with them in the fifties, while many of the locals had friends or relatives in the United States. It was almost 'an American community', recalls Donald Griffiths of USAF Counter-Intelligence: 'You could go into a pub and have ice in your drink which you couldn't get anywhere else in England at the time . . . We used to call it the 49th state.'[14]

Despite periodic incidents, East Anglia became relatively used to the Americans – many of whom were married and therefore lived more stable lives than the 'over-sexed, over-paid' bachelor GIs of World War Two. Much more intrusive and controversial was the US Polaris submarine base established at Holy Loch on the Clyde from March 1961. The news was sprung on the inhabitants without consultation or warning – feeding Scottish nationalist anger, arousing widespread fears about radiation dangers. For the first year or so the local resort town of Dunoon attracted hundreds of CND anti-nuclear demonstrators who conducted American-style sit-ins around the base. Some locals, more alienated by the beatnik protesters than by the Americans, sported posters reading 'Go Home Weirdies',[15] and local business anticipated an economic boom from the sailors. But others were disturbed at the nuclear presence and upset by the conduct of some of the bachelor sailors from the depot ship who vented their frustrations at the boring work and long, dark winters by roisterous behaviour in town, causing a sharp increase in the local statistics for VD and illegitimacy.

The American command, facing problems that were familiar around the military bases of every nation, quickly imposed a curfew for their men and mounted an intensive campaign to promote good community relations. Senior officers wined and dined local community leaders, while their wives entertained local women's groups with slide shows about the United States. In dealing with protesters the policy was to 'out Gandhi Gandhi', in the words of the first base commander, Captain Richard Laning. On one occasion a CND protester paddled his canoe up to one of the submarines and climbed aboard. Instead of provoking an incident in front of eager ranks of press photographers Laning let him sit on the submarine's tail-fin until he got 'blue and shivering'. He was then taken to the quarter deck of the depot ship, where he was given 'not the third-degree treatment he expected but hot cocoa and a blanket, before being allowed to go'.[16]

But the US military presence in Britain was small compared with that of World War Two. It usually averaged between 60,000 and 70,000 base personnel and dependants from the early 1960s onwards.[17] Furthermore, Pentagon policy was generally to minimise contact with the local population by creating an all-American environment on base.

More pervasive in its effects on Britain was the new 'invasion' of American capital. The initial impetus was Britain's post-war dollar shortage, which limited her ability to import direct from the United States and therefore encouraged American firms to set up in Britain. But the real growth in US investment came after exchange controls were eased in 1958. American companies were quick to exploit the consumer boom and envisaged Britain, with its shared language, as an easily accessible entry-point into the EEC. By 1966 there were more than 1,600 American subsidiaries or Anglo-American-financed firms in the UK, with a total investment stake of nearly $6 billion – about one-tenth of all US corporate investment overseas. Only Canada had more. In 1965 these companies employed six per cent of the labour force in British manufacturing industry and produced ten per cent of the total goods made in British factories. Two-fifths of all the American investment was in five big companies: Esso (the tenth largest firm in Britain), Ford, Woolworth's, Vauxhall Motors and the tobacco giant, Gallahers.[18]

There was little US investment in Britain's declining industries such as textiles, steel and shipbuilding. Nor were many dollars seen in the north, with the significant exception of Scotland. Most American money was concentrated in the new consumer-goods industries and in those linked with advanced technology such as computers. These 1,600 companies produced more than half the cars, cosmetics, office machinery and vacuum cleaners purchased in Britain and nearly half the drugs sold to the National Health Service, while IBM supplied two-fifths of the British computer market. American companies such as Hoover, Heinz and Kodak had become household names in Britain. Ideas borrowed from America, ranging from TV dinners to opinion polls, from barbecues to frozen vegetables, were revolutionising daily life.

The statistics about US investment and particularly the well-publicised American take-overs of British household names such as Smith's Crisps, Gallahers and Rootes, one of the 'big three' car manufacturers, gave rise in the 1960s to a rash of polemics about 'the American invasion', reminiscent of those in the early 1900s and late 1920s. One such book asked: 'Need alliance involve occupation? Must we become Americans to save Western civilisation?'[19] Another, *The American Take-Over of Britain*, set out the British predicament with dramatic starkness: 'From the moment an English baby is weaned on American-owned baby food, until he is carted away in an American-owned funeral car, he is, to that extent, American-orientated from the cradle to the grave. Must it now be universal? Is it to be "all the way with LBJ"?'[20]

Some commentators emphasised the beneficial effects of American investment. Britain was gaining an infusion of new capital, technology and marketing skills, and many of the companies concerned, such as Ford, were high exporters who helped ease the British balance of payments problem. American-owned companies accounted for over seventeen per cent of Britain's manufacturing exports in 1966. Against this, critics stressed the loss of national control over key sectors of the economy. The American parent company would inevitably decide future strategy in the light of its worldwide interests, not those of local workers or of the British economy. The car industry was a prime example. Chrysler's take-over of Rootes in 1967 meant that each of

America's 'big three' automobile manufacturers owned a subsidiary or plant in Britain as well as one on the Continent. Chrysler had Rootes, plus Simca in France; GM controlled Vauxhall together with Opel in Germany; and Ford had major plants in Dagenham and Cologne. They soon began to 'rationalise' operations at Britain's expense, taking account of the country's peripheral geographical position and the labour problems in her car industry.

While American capital moved east, it seemed that British talent was going west. The so-called 'brain drain' of engineers and scientists to the United States became a lively topic of public debate in mid-1960s Britain. A special government inquiry reported that in 1966 Britain lost 4,200 engineers and technologists, half of them to North America. This represented over forty per cent of the 'new supply' of engineers and technologists leaving higher education three years before. Two thousand scientists also emigrated, equivalent to nearly a quarter of the 'new supply' three years earlier. Even allowing for immigration from the Commonwealth and the return of some of those who had worked in North America, Britain experienced a net loss of 2,700 engineers, technologists and scientists in 1966.[21]

Politicians and pundits debated the causes of the brain drain. Tory politician Quintin Hogg fulminated that 'the richest country in the world has been plundering the educational systems of Western Europe', because, he explained 'in such a way as to cause the maximum offence . . . the American high school system is not sufficiently good to produce high-class graduates on the scale required by American industry, American universities and the American Government'.[22] US Defense Secretary Robert McNamara put it differently, suggesting that 'brains on the whole are like hearts – they go where they are appreciated'.[23] He was referring not merely to American salary levels, up to three times those of young engineers in Britain, but to the availability of challenging work and the higher status accorded to industrial researchers in the United States. In the words of one British aeronautical engineer, exiled with dozens of colleagues in the Pacific north-west of America: 'This is a cultural wilderness. Deep down we all prefer England, its way of life, its people.' But, he went on, 'to be an engineer in England is to live on the edge of existence', treated as 'just a factory worker. The poor image of the engineer in England results in poor pay . . . In America we [the engineers] are on more equal terms with the other professions . . . An engineer is respected in America.'[24]

At root, the brain drain reflected the far greater expenditure on research and development in the United States compared with western

Europe – $24 billion as against $6 billion in 1966, according to one estimate[25] – despite the rough equivalence in total population. The most voracious appetites were in defence-related industries, particularly those connected with the space programme. Commentators warned that, if unmatched, America's concentration of resources and skills in these high-tech areas would open an unbridgeable gap between the United States and its competitors. Prime Minister Harold Wilson feared that Britain and Europe could be 'left in industrial terms as the hewers of wood and the drawers of water' while the Americans came to monopolise advanced technology.[26]

At the heart of the debate about America's economic challenge in the 1960s was British aircraft manufacture. This was a key national industry, central to Britain's defence interests and to her export drive. It also produced a high-tech 'fall-out' for the civilian economy in technologies such as electronics, computers and metallurgy. It was extremely expensive, requiring vast government support to remain competitive, but it was America's major rival in the Western world. The aircraft industry epitomised Britain's increasingly complex relationship with the United States.

By the early 1960s the industry seemed in reasonable shape to meet the American challenge. The Tories had forced it to consolidate from the extravagance of the twenty airframe companies that existed in 1958. By 1963 only two major groups were left, the British Aircraft Corporation (BAC) and Hawker Siddeley, while Westland became the main helicopter manufacturer. Hawker had RAF orders to develop the P-1154 supersonic fighter and the HS-681 transport, and BAC were working on the TSR-2 high-speed, low-level strike aircraft with its sophisticated computer guidance system. The P-1154 and HS-681 were still on the drawing-board but the TSR-2, despite technical problems and severe cost overruns, was ready ahead of its American rival, the F-111, and its first test flight took place in September 1964.

Within six months, however, all three aircraft had been abandoned, the prototypes of the TSR-2 ending up as scrap or gunnery targets for the army. In their place the new Labour Government had committed itself to buying more than a billion dollars' worth of American planes. After the Tories had 'gone American' over strategic missiles in 1960 and 1962, it seemed that Labour was now selling out the British aircraft industry to the United States.

The abrupt change of policy was caused partly by the usual inter-service rivalry. The Royal Navy, ruthlessly backed by Lord Mountbatten, Chief of the Defence Staff, was determined to safeguard its own aircraft-carrier programme at the expense of the RAF's planes.

But the British Treasury had long believed that the aircraft industry drained too much public money for too little return. Complex modern aircraft were enormously costly and took a decade or more to produce. Until proven they depended largely on government subsidies and domestic orders to cover the vast R and D investment, and the Treasury judged that Britain simply could not compete with the USA in either respect. It therefore advised the government to purchase US aircraft where possible, preferably manufactured under licence in Britain to reduce dollar costs, and to concentrate British energies on aircraft-engine production by Rolls-Royce. When Labour came to power in October 1964, faced with a grave financial crisis and pledged to get 'value for money' in defence, it accepted this Treasury advice. It immediately axed the P-1154 and HS-681, substituting orders for American Phantoms and Hercules C-130 transports.

But simple cost may not have been the only factor. In addition there was Wilson's determination not to devalue the pound – because of the effect he feared on Britain's financial reputation and, it was said, on her relationship with the United States. Supporters of the TSR-2 allege that the plane's cancellation was the price America extracted in return for an IMF loan to shore up sterling in December 1964. According to Julian Amery, the former Tory Aviation Minister, the Americans said, in effect, '"Look here – yes, we'll let you have the money but we don't see why we should subsidise prestige projects like the Concorde."' The government agreed to review the supersonic Concorde programme being carried out jointly by Britain and France but discovered that Amery had made it part of a treaty that would have been almost impossible to break. 'And it was at that point, as far as I understand it,' claims Amery, that 'the Americans said, "Well, what else could you cancel? You've got this very expensive TSR-2, which is much the same as our F-111 – why don't you cancel the TSR-2 and we'll let you have the F-111 fairly cheap?"'[27]

Such pressure would, of course, have been in line with standard IMF policy of dissuading debtors from what it regarded as inessential spending, but it would also have suited the interests of the US aircraft industry in eliminating major rivals. On the other hand, Labour's Defence Minister at the time, Denis Healey, dismisses allegations of American pressure as 'quite untrue'. While admitting that McNamara once 'not very seriously' suggested 'a disarmament agreement' whereby neither country produced a Concorde-style supersonic transport, he insists that 'there was never any pressure from the Americans on us so far as the TSR-2 was concerned' and says that the RAF was 'delighted' to have a cheap, secure source of planes from the USA.[28]

Nevertheless, the Americans appear to have heavily subsidised the price of the Hercules as an inducement to Britain: Australia paid nearly twice as much for the same aircraft. The F-111s, also attractively priced in the initial agreement, soon escalated dramatically in cost and were cancelled by the Labour Government, which had only just ordered them, in the post-devaluation cuts of 1967–8.

The benefits to Britain from the episode are far from clear, and any final judgement on the controversy must await the opening of the official British archives. But the determination to preserve the value of the pound, in part to help maintain Britain's world role and her influence in Washington, does seem to have made the country more dependent on the American-directed IMF and therefore more vulnerable to any American commercial pressure. The TSR-2 affair highlighted a growing tension between Britain's economic interests and the idea of a continuing special relationship with the USA. Was economic domination the price that had to be paid for the American alliance?

Initially Wilson had tried to match the Americans at their own game. He cultivated a technocratic, Kennedy-esque style, mocking Macmillan's Edwardian, grouse-moor image and the relevance of 'the fourteenth Earl of Home' in the swinging sixties. His first administration, 1964–6, saw the most determined effort of the post-war years to modernise the British economy – with a National Plan, a new Ministry of Technology to promote a high-tech revolution, and heavy government investment in industrial mergers, on the grounds that size made for competitiveness. But these attempted remedies fell foul of Britain's deepening economic crisis and Wilson's method of handling it.

Compared with its own past performance the British economy did not decline in the 1950s and 1960s. 'Between 1948 and 1968 real gross domestic product increased at an average annual rate of 2.7 per cent'[29] – a better performance than in the inter-war years or indeed the period before 1913. Even more striking was the unemployment rate which for a quarter-century from 1945 remained almost always below three per cent, compared with ten per cent or more in the inter-war years. In British terms, therefore, the post-war period saw impressive growth.

But relative to Britain's competitors, the picture looked very different. British GDP grew at roughly half the rate of most of the EEC, and by the late 1970s the country that had once been the richest in western Europe was nearly on a par with Italy in per capita output and income. At the heart of the problem was the collapse of Britain's share of world exports in manufactured goods, at a time when the consumer boom was sucking an ever-increasing flow of imports into the country. The result was a chronic payments deficit throughout the 1960s, which, in an era of fixed exchange rates, meant repeated runs on the pound.

Wilson could have devalued in 1964, as soon as he entered office, but he and his advisers refused to do so, convinced that they could support the pound and believing that the level of sterling was one of Britain's last status symbols as a world power. Wilson soon found, however, that the only alternative to devaluation was deflationary measures that directly conflicted with the need for investment and growth. Finally, after deflation at home and defence cuts abroad had both failed to save sterling, he was forced to devalue in November 1967 – when it was too late to save Britain's commercial competitiveness.

The failure of national economic policy made a joint European response to America's economic threat seem more attractive. Although Britain was particularly open to American economic penetration, not only because of its industrial weakness but because the common language made it easier for American companies to set up in the UK or to poach British talent, 'the American challenge' was a problem for most of western Europe. Jean-Jacques Servan-Schreiber, in his 1967 best-selling book with that title, was only the most prominent of commentators calling for a concerted response. He proposed Europe-wide companies, concentrating on high-tech industries, within a truly integrated Europe. 'This integration will be carried out by American big business if Europe does not do it herself,' he warned. 'Either we build a common European industrial policy, or American industry will continue taking over the Common Market.'[30]

By the mid-1960s even Labour, previously deeply suspicious of the EEC, was coming round to this point of view. After the aircraft cancellations of 1964–5, Healey turned to Anglo-French collaboration on a trainer/tactical strike aircraft and on swing-wing supersonic technology. The former resulted in the successful Jaguar, while the latter eventually became the Anglo-German-Italian Tornado developed in the 1970s.

More fundamentally, the American challenge and the failure of the British response were considerations that helped push Labour into applying for membership of the EEC in 1967. 'Let no one here doubt Britain's loyalty to NATO and the Atlantic Alliance,' Wilson told the Council of Europe in Strasbourg in January 1967. 'But . . . loyalty must never mean subservience. Still less must it mean an industrial helotry under which we in Europe produce only the conventional apparatus of a modern economy while becoming increasingly dependent on American business for the sophisticated apparatus which will call the industrial tune in the 70s and 80s.'[31] America's economic threat had proved more effective as an instrument of European integration than two decades of persuasive noises from Washington.

Like earlier scares, the sixties furore about the American invasion gradually abated. With the European media full of America's assassinations, protests and racial violence, many decided that 'poverty and peace in Britain were preferable to riches and riots in America',[32] and the brain drain soon became only a trickle. Britain's balance of payments improved after devaluation, and the belated success of Britain's EEC application between 1969 and 1972 gave a new and hopeful focus for British aspirations. It was also possible to gain some perspective on the extent of American economic penetration: even in 1966 the total investment by foreign companies in the UK was less than half that of British companies overseas, and British direct investment in the United States amounted to nearly half the American stake in Britain.[33] And it became clear that European countries experienced much less interference in their economic and political life from US companies than did developing states in South America, south-east Asia and the Middle East. In the 1950s Iran had been a particular target for British and American oil multinationals, but the most notorious example in the 1970s was the role of the American communications giant IT&T in Chile in 1973–4, when it helped to undermine the socialist government of Salvador Allende and encouraged General Pinochet's military coup. Nothing like that happened in Europe.

By the 1970s the anti-American reaction that had swept much of Europe during the previous decade, particularly on the political left, gave way to a more considered policy. No one followed Japan's long-standing practice of excluding virtually all foreign capital, but most developed countries tried to impose more stringent conditions on potential investors so as to minimise the costs and maximise the benefits. The 1970s also saw the beginnings of a significant reverse flow of investment, as multinationals from western Europe and Japan, particularly banks, started to set up on a large scale in the USA.

The world economy of the sixties and seventies, freed from many of the exchange and trade controls of the immediate post-war era and stimulated by the resurgence of Japan and western Europe, was demonstrating that the impetus for 'modernisation' no longer came predominantly from the United States. America led, but others followed. The modern age was no longer exclusively the American age.

The erosion of American leadership was most apparent in pop music, where the American invasion of Britain in the fifties by Bill Haley and Elvis Presley gave way to a British cultural invasion of America in the sixties. The most potent musical force of the decade was the Beatles, who developed from a Liverpool skiffle group to dominate the British popular music scene by 1962. When they arrived for the first time at Kennedy Airport, New York, in February 1964 they were greeted by more than 3,000 screaming girls, bearing posters reading 'Beatles, we love you'. Two hundred reporters and photographers turned the press conference into chaos as they scrambled for close-ups and quotes. One airport official shook his head in amazement: 'We've never seen anything like this before. Never. Not even for kings and queens.'[34]

Americans liked the group's distinctive accents, 'mop' haircuts and perky humour: asked at Kennedy Airport what he thought of Beethoven, Ringo Starr replied, 'I love him, especially his poems.' Even politicians jumped on the bandwagon. Sir Alec Douglas-Home, then the British Prime Minister, commended what the group was doing for Britain's balance of payments. 'They are my secret weapon,' he quipped.[35] Until their breakup in 1969 the group was probably the most important single influence in pop music not just in Britain and the USA but worldwide. In the 1970s the Rolling Stones took over the Beatles' mantle as the best-known British group in America.

As the United States became bogged down in the Vietnam War, with the draft or draft-dodging a major preoccupation of many young Americans, Britain seemed to offer the prospect of a freer, more civilised society. In reality what Americans saw was little more than a mirror image of what America had pioneered. By the mid-sixties England's capital was portrayed by the American media as a mecca for America's youth. *Time*, America's premier current-affairs weekly, featured 'London – The Swinging City' as its cover story in April 1966.[36] In the 1900s Vienna had been in the vanguard of culture, in the twenties Paris, in the forties New York. 'Today,' *Time* told its readers, 'it is London, a city steeped in tradition, seized by change, liberated by affluence . . . In a decade dominated by youth, London has burst into bloom. It swings, it is the scene.' This was the city of Beatles music, Mary Quant fashions, and Vidal Sassoon hairstyles, of mini-skirts, admen and biting satire.

Backing its analysis with eight pages of colour photos, largely taken around Carnaby Street, the centre of the youth fashion industry, *Time* insisted that 'today Britain is in the midst of a bloodless revolution. This time, those who are giving way are the old Tory-Liberal Establishment that ruled the Empire from the clubs along Pall Mall and St James's, the still-powerful City of London, the church and Oxbridge. In their stead is rising a new and surprising leadership community: economists, professors, actors, photographers, singers, admen, TV executives and writers – a swinging meritocracy . . . mostly under 40.' Symbolising the change, *Time* suggested, was Harold Wilson, at fifty Britain's youngest Prime Minister of the century, his Yorkshire tones a sign that 'it is no longer necessary to affect an Oxford accent to get ahead'.

Britain *was* changing in the sixties, but *Time*'s eulogy of swinging London, like British fears of American economic domination, was exaggerated. Much of British life proved resistant to the influence of the modern American age. Britain remained a country with its own distinctive attitude to work and a sceptical view of the American philosophy of hustle and bustle. It was accepted that Americans worked harder, but Britain's relative indolence was justified on the grounds that her quality of life was superior. The geographical mobility of labour, whether managers or shop-floor workers, which was essential to America's rapid economic growth, was not evident in Britain, where housing shortages and wide regional disparities in house prices made it harder for families to move, even if they had wanted to. Most Britons, however, put down deep roots in their local communities, preferring to accept lower rewards as the price of remaining with family and friends among whom they had grown up. White American society was much more homogeneous than Britain's, despite the vastly greater size of the United States. A Briton moving to another part of the country found himself among strangers, and disliked it. There was far greater difference between the ways of life in Conservative Cheltenham and the Labour-dominated Welsh mining town of Ebbw Vale, sixty miles away, than, say, between Wolfeboro, New Hampshire, and Wenatchee, Washington, 3,000 miles across America in the Pacific north-west.

In Britain 'class' remained a national obsession. To some extent the sixties did see the rise of the meritocracy, as a new and more prosperous generation exercised its economic power and political influence. Businesses and professions began to open up, accepting the products of expanding universities regardless of their social background. But at the top the country remained dominated by a small élite, linked if not by shared background at least by a common route to the top, through the public schools and the two ancient universities of Oxford and Cambridge. Their source of wealth was now more often industry or finance, instead of land; their origins were more

Prime Minister Harold Wilson and President Lyndon B. Johnson at the White House (December 1964).

Demonstration against the Vietnam War, near the US Embassy in Grosvenor Square, London (November 1968).

Queen Elizabeth, accompanied by Edward Heath, chats with President Richard Nixon and his wife, Pat, at Chequers (October 1970).

Bill Haley *(right, kneeling)* and the Comets (1957).

The Beatles during their American trip of August 1966.

Right: America's youth culture of the sixties invades Britain: hippy love-in in London's Hyde Park.

Below: British rock music goes West: A Rolling Stones concert in America.

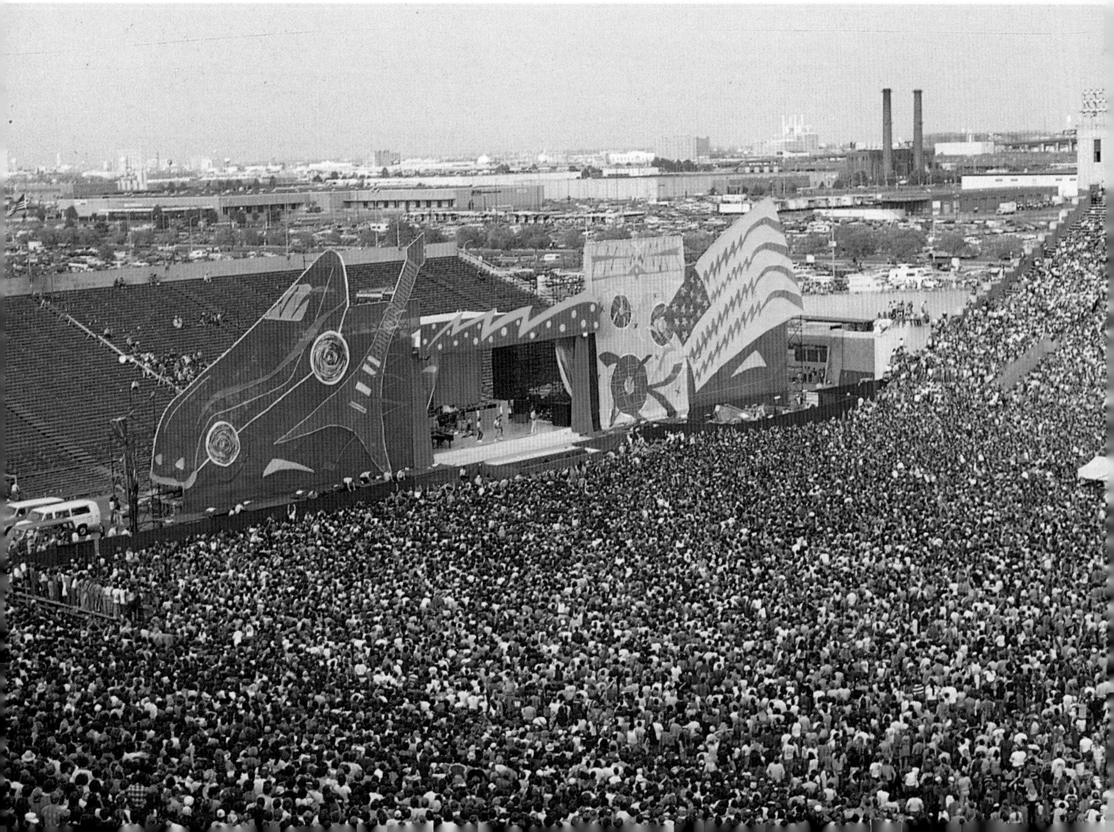

A British cultural export to America: BBC TV's *The First Churchills*.

Alistair Cooke, transatlantic interpreter.

An American cultural export to Britain: *Dallas*.

diverse than in earlier decades. But the British experience was still in marked contrast to that of America where élites were regional rather than national, and class was largely a matter of money instead of involving accent, education and manners as well. Lower down the social scale the British sense of class manifested itself in fraught industrial relations, riddled with demarcations of status and role, and in confrontation between management and unions, often centred on the use of new technology. American companies who tried to introduce their own methods of management often provoked conflict, as at Vauxhall in 1966, or, like Esso, found that it took years to reach a streamlined agreement on wages and conditions.

Perhaps the most striking survival of British tradition was the monarchy, which, despite periodic debate, went from strength to strength during the post-war years, making Britain the most celebrated exception in a predominantly republican world. Since 1910 the country has had only four monarchs, one of whom, Edward VIII, lasted less than a year. The other three – George V, George VI and Elizabeth II – could all be held up as paragons of morality and family values, while also displaying in full splendour the pomp and circumstance of Britain's past. Edward VIII was the great exception to this 'synthesis of private probity and public grandeur',[37] consorting with married women and scoffing at Court protocol. Significantly, the 'jazz age' prince was the most 'Americanised' member of the House of Windsor.

Ironically, it was radio and particularly television, usually the harbingers of change, which assisted in this consecration of 'the royal family' as the nation's symbol. Christmas messages from the monarch, the broadcasting of state occasions and the opening up of royalty's private life to the TV cameras – all this helped confirm the popularity of the Crown at a time when the rest of the landed aristocracy was declining rapidly in influence and prestige. Thirteen opinion polls (another American invention) taken between 1953 and 1976 suggested that on average only '11 per cent of the population was opposed to a monarchy throughout this period'.[38] For most British people their virtuous, politically neutral, long-lived monarchs came to symbolise the continuity of national values in an era of change and decay – despite the fact that the adulation of royalty was a relatively recent phenomenon.

Britain, then, remained at root resistant to the winds of change blowing across the Atlantic. The most controversial cultural influence on Britain in the 1960s was not America but the growing numbers of non-white migrants from the 'New Commonwealth'. By the end of the decade their presence had aroused a powerful political backlash of which the principal spokesman was Tory MP Enoch Powell. The proportion of non-whites in the population was only about 3.3 per cent by the mid-1970s, but in numerical terms the 1.8 million 'New Commonwealth' residents constituted a far larger coloured population than the 8,000 or so in Britain before World War Two, and many white Britons refused to accept the new immigrants and their offspring as members of the community. Yet by the 1970s forty per cent of non-whites had been born in Britain.[39] Talk of 'sending them home' ignored this simple fact.

The American race problem was repeating itself in Britain, albeit on a smaller scale, with non-white communities overwhelmingly concentrated in the decaying inner cities and increasingly alienated from the norms of a society of which they were members but not full beneficiaries. Yet, unlike American blacks, the British coloured population did not develop its own protest movement or political organisation. Resentment exploded in sporadic communal violence, often directed at the police. And, because the non-white population was located in a few urban areas, much of the country felt able to turn a deaf ear to its demands for equal treatment.

During the 1960s, at a time when the United States and Great Britain seemed to be drifting apart diplomatically, the American imprint on British life became more apparent than ever before – in industry, lifestyle and music. Britain's response was ambivalent, much as America's had been towards British influence on its own development in the nineteenth century: welcoming the material benefits but resenting the sense of dependence. Yet in the sixties, although living in the American age, Britain was not 'Americanised' – any more than the USA a century or two before had been 'Anglicised'. For the modern world was becoming a 'global village' in which the winds of change blew from many directions, not just one. And Britain retained its own distinctive social character, sometimes shaped by new forces such as racial diversity, usually drawing self-consciously on the legacy of the past. In the last analysis the fear of Americanisation was more pronounced than the reality, evidence of a country losing its power, pride and sense of direction in a new and unfamiliar world.

15

All at Sea

1973–80

From the 1970s onwards the story of Anglo-American relations no longer lies at the heart of world affairs. Britain and America, as allies or as rivals, had shaped the first half of the twentieth century, but, as America matured as a superpower, much of its diplomacy was conducted independently of the British influence that had helped direct its rise to world leadership. As Britain declined in global power, her foreign policy and her relations with the United States became peripheral to the vital issues of international affairs. Where Britain did matter, it was often as one of the western European states, as a member of NATO or the EEC, rather than by herself.

But Britain did not become completely European. If Edward Heath's vision of a Britain playing its full role in Europe had become a reality, the 1970s and 1980s would have been very different. Britain would have been integrated with her European neighbours, pursuing a coherent European foreign policy. There might have been little to say about America and Britain that could not equally have been said about America's relations with France or West Germany. But the vision of 1973 was deceptive, or perhaps premature. A united western Europe and a stable superpower détente were hard to achieve. The late seventies saw the world reverting to the patterns of the fifties and sixties, with Anglo-American relations restored, albeit diminished in importance, Britain still distant from continental Europe, and global politics dominated by hostile superpowers.

The last year of Edward Heath's Conservative Government had put the Anglo-American relationship under acute strain, first over Henry Kissinger's call for the 'Year of Europe' and then over Britain's refusal to support American policy during the Yom Kippur War. When Heath was defeated in the election of February 1974, Harold

Wilson's new Labour Government worked to restore ties with Washington. His Foreign Secretary, James Callaghan, recalls that 'Mr Heath's deep and lasting commitment to Europe had weakened our relations with the United States, and as a strong believer in the Atlantic Alliance, I was determined that these must be strengthened.'[1] In his first major statement of policy Callaghan criticised 'anti-American tinges' in European opinion and urged that Europe should engage in the 'fullest and most intimate' co-operation with the United States, adding that 'we repudiate the view that Europe will emerge only after a process of struggle against America'.[2]

Behind the scenes the two governments continued to foster the close defence ties that had characterised the Anglo-American relationship since the 1950s. Although Labour was officially pledged not to develop a new generation of nuclear weapons, Wilson and Callaghan renewed the agreements originally made with Eisenhower in 1958–9 for the exchange of nuclear information and materials. They also secretly continued the Tories' expensive modernisation programme for Polaris. Wilson told his Cabinet that nuclear weapons amounted to only two per cent of Britain's defence budget, that they gave her 'a unique entrée to US thinking' and that it was important for Britain's diplomatic influence to remain a nuclear power.[3]

The habits of close consultation between London and Washington were also resumed. Wilson visited Washington in February 1975, meeting Nixon's successor, Gerald Ford. One of Wilson's Cabinet ministers, Barbara Castle, noted in her diary afterwards that 'he could not resist a little touch of the old self-satisfaction at the way he had been received by President Ford. Relations with the US, he said, were "as good as they have ever been", adding typically, "The ceremonies of welcome went far beyond anything I have had before."'[4] Callaghan succeeded Wilson as premier in March 1976 and soon established a particularly good rapport with Jimmy Carter, who became President in January 1977. When Carter visited Britain that spring, Callaghan deliberately took him away from London and the south to see Newcastle and the industrial north-east of England. Carter visited Washington Old Hall, the ancestral home of the first President of the United States, and delighted the Newcastle crowds by shouting the local rallying cry, 'Haaway the Lads' in a passable Geordie accent. Carter and his UN Ambassador, Andrew Young, worked closely with Callaghan's government in its efforts to find a settlement in Rhodesia.

Although Britain no longer played a major global role, many American leaders considered these close contacts to be invaluable. The common language made communication easy, and the breadth of

Britain's international connections and experience still enabled her to offer authoritative advice. Henry Kissinger, who believed that this 'consultative relationship' was particularly useful to the United States, went so far as to say of his years as National Security Adviser in the White House: 'I kept the British Foreign Office better informed and more closely engaged than I did the American State Department.'[5]

Heath had been cold towards America, passionate about Europe. The Labour Government's greater warmth towards the United States reflected its coolness to the EEC. Michel Jobert, the French Foreign Minister, remarked that while Heath was 'a man of the Rhine', Wilson was 'a man of the Scilly Isles'.[6] On the EEC, as on most issues, Labour was divided, and, to secure party unity, Wilson campaigned in 1974 on a commitment to renegotiate the terms of Britain's entry and to submit the result to a national referendum. As with Labour's earlier pledge in the 1964 campaign to 'renegotiate' the Polaris agreement, the performance did not live up to the promise. Britain's partners offered only limited concessions and Wilson's Cabinet was still divided, but he went ahead with the referendum. His own ministers were free to campaign as they liked, and Britain was treated to the extraordinary spectacle of senior Cabinet colleagues arguing in public for and against membership. Barbara Castle commented in March 1975: 'Cabinet government barely exists any more and is certainly broadly in abeyance until the referendum is over.'[7] On 5 June 1975 two-thirds of the electorate voted and, by a majority of two to one, indicated its desire to stay within the European Community. Wilson announced that 'fourteen years of national argument are over'.[8]

Membership of the Common Market did not mean, however, that the British public thought of itself as European. In June 1979 interest in the new direct elections to the European Parliament was lukewarm. Nor was there much enthusiasm for the idea of a federal Europe which the United States had envisaged at the time of the Marshall Plan and which had been the dream of the EEC's founding fathers. As the decade progressed public attitudes towards the Community became, if anything, more antagonistic. Britain had joined at a bad moment. The long post-war European boom had ended and, in the recession that followed, the economic benefits promised by pro-Marketeers were slow to materialise. The British were also paying the price for joining after the Community's institutions had been created. The common agricultural policy, designed to protect the Continent's many small farmers, was an expensive burden for Britain, whose agricultural sector was less significant and relatively efficient.

Hopes that Europe would prove a new force in world affairs were also dashed. Since late 1972 the heads of government of the Community countries had developed the practice of regular summit meetings to co-ordinate policy and in 1973 Kissinger's call for a new Atlantic Charter had united western Europe against him. But when the Arabs quadrupled the price of oil after the Yom Kippur War the EEC's common front disintegrated. At their summit in Copenhagen in February 1974 the Community leaders bickered openly, unable to agree on whether to negotiate with the Arabs and whether to co-operate with the United States in an effort to stabilise oil prices. The result was 'a kind of *sauve-qui-peut*, a scurrying for advantage through bilateral negotiations with this or that oil-producing country'.[9] Ironically, only under Kissinger's leadership was Europe eventually able to establish some kind of joint oil policy. Unity on monetary policy proved equally elusive. In 1977 France and Germany developed a European Monetary System, designed to keep national currency and interest rates in harmony in Europe at a time when the Americans were allowing the dollar to slide. But Britain refused to join.

The vision of a united and influential European Community, which had inspired many in the early 1970s, had soon faded. The other new powers envisaged in the early 1970s, China and Japan, also failed to develop political and military strength to match their population and industrial resources. The two superpowers still dominated world affairs. They remained the only nuclear giants and arms limitation talks were a matter for them alone. And, by the end of the 1970s, the détente that seemed so hopeful a few years before had degenerated into renewed confrontation between America and Russia.

Jimmy Carter was one of the best-educated men to occupy the White House since World War Two. He was hard-working, experienced in business and trained as a nuclear engineer. Yet he was a Washington outsider, who remained naïve in the ways of political management and often failed to translate his almost visionary idealism into viable policies. Starting from the assumption that détente would continue, the President was anxious to shift the focus of American foreign policy away from superpower rivalry to issues that he thought had been neglected: human rights, Third-World development and nuclear non-proliferation. After the brutality of Vietnam, after the corruption of Watergate, he wanted the United States to behave in a more principled way.

Carter's inauguration dramatically symbolised his approach to the presidency. He saw himself in the mould of Woodrow Wilson, as the moral leader of his country. In his address, on the steps of the Capitol, he expressed the hope that he could build 'a lasting peace, based not on weapons of war but on international policies which reflect our own most precious values'. Carter and his family were driven back towards the White House in a motorcade of long black limousines, but suddenly the cars stopped in the middle of Pennsylvania Avenue, the Carters jumped out and, amid gasps and then cheers from the crowd, walked the rest of the way to the White House, the President and his wife hand in hand. He wrote later: 'I felt a simple walk would be a tangible indication of some reduction in the imperial status of the President and his family.'[10]

Carter soon began to act on his belief that the United States should stop behaving like a militaristic superpower. Despite protests from conservatives, he imposed a brake on the modernisation of America's strategic forces. The B-1 bomber was cancelled, naval spending reduced and the MX missile programme slowed down. He tried to increase the momentum of arms control talks. The 1972 SALT I treaty was only a temporary freeze on missile launchers. A comprehensive agreement had been drafted under Ford, but its approval was delayed because Carter wanted deeper cuts.

The President also tried to improve America's image among developing countries. In 1903 the United States had pressured the new Panamanian Republic to be allowed to build a canal through the isthmus and to exercise perpetual sovereignty over it. America's position in Panama had long been deeply resented in Central America, much as Britain and France had been in Egypt over the Suez Canal. Carter believed it essential to right an injustice and dispose of the criticism that America was an imperialist power. In 1977 he concluded a treaty with Panama, pledging US withdrawal at the end of the century with rights of return in an emergency. Despite the opposition of the Republican right, led by Ronald Reagan, who had repeatedly insisted that 'we built it, we paid for it, it's ours and . . . we are going to keep it',[11] Carter forced the canal treaty through the Senate in a long and bitter battle.

The Panama Canal treaty was Carter's principal diplomatic success. He soon found his foreign policy undermined because of the breakdown of détente.

By the time the SALT II arms limitation treaty was signed by Carter and Leonid Brezhnev in Vienna in June 1979, détente had become a dirty word in the United States. Many Americans had assumed that Moscow would now behave as the United States wanted. But the Soviets saw détente not as an end to rivalry but as competition by other means. They continued their efforts to gain parity with the global power and influence of the United States, shifting the focus away from Europe and nuclear weapons to the Third World. The seventies saw a rapid growth of Soviet influence in Africa, using Cuban troops in countries like Angola, and the expansion of the Soviet navy into the Pacific and Indian Oceans. Russia had now become not merely a major land power but, for the first time, a global sea power as well. Carter's National Security Adviser, Zbigniew Brzezinski, warned the President that he was underestimating the Soviet threat and argued from US history that a foreign policy of moral principle could only work if there was prior respect for American power. 'You first have to be a Truman before you are a Wilson,' he told the President.[12]

Carter's conversion occurred at Christmas 1979. On 27 December the President cut short his holiday and returned to the White House because of reports that the Soviet Union was airlifting troops and supplies into Afghanistan, over 200 flights in the previous twenty-four hours. The Russians had invaded to shore up their Marxist client regime on the USSR's southern borders. After a tense meeting with his advisers on 28 December Carter sent Brezhnev on the hot line what he considers 'the sharpest message of my Presidency', warning the Russian leader that the invasion was 'a clear threat to the peace' and that it 'could mark a fundamental and long-lasting turning point in our relations'.[13]

In public Carter was equally blunt. Under attack at home over his management of the economy, he struck out at Russia, calling this 'the greatest threat to peace since World War II' and claiming that it had 'made a more dramatic change in my own opinion of what the Soviets' ultimate goals are than anything they've done in the previous time I've been in office'.[14] With Afghanistan's neighbour, Iran, in turmoil following the fall of the Shah, there seemed a real Russian threat to the Persian Gulf, which was vital for the West's oil supplies. Carter quickly imposed sanctions on Russia, including an embargo on grain sales and a ban on American participation in the Moscow Olympics. More seriously, he also withdrew the SALT II treaty from Congress. Even before Afghanistan it faced strong opposition; after the invasion there was no hope of ratification. By 1980 the talk was not of détente but of a new Cold War.

America's European allies watched the twists and turns of US policy with disquiet. In the mid-1970s the economic friction between the United States and the EEC had intensified. The Americans protested that European subsidies and tariffs were undercutting key sectors of their economy. In 1977–8 the Europeans resented the decline of the dollar, which was encouraged by the Administration to make US exports more competitive, but which damaged their own trade. Western European governments were even more disturbed about arms control. As the SALT talks progressed during the 1970s, there were fears in European capitals that a deal might be reached over their heads. This could leave them outnumbered by the Warsaw Pact's conventional forces and outclassed by the newly-modernised Soviet intermediate nuclear missiles. These fears were acute in West Germany, which would be the battleground if the bluff of deterrence was called and conventional war broke out again.

After long negotiations the NATO allies therefore announced on 12 December 1979 that new American intermediate-range nuclear weapons would be deployed in western Europe: 108 Pershing II missiles in West Germany and 464 ground-launched Cruise missiles, 160 of which would be based in Britain. This was not a US initiative, forced on Europe, but Washington's response to the fears of European governments, particularly Bonn. Brzezinski commented later: 'I was personally never persuaded that we needed [the new weapons] for military reasons. I was persuaded reluctantly that we needed [them] to obtain European support for SALT.'[15]

Yet the European governments, again with the Germans in the lead, did not seek renewed confrontation with the Russians. They lived in closer proximity than the Americans to the Soviet Union and, as countries with few remaining global interests, they were less concerned than the United States about superpower rivalries in Africa or Asia. They wished to maintain the momentum of détente as long as their security was assured. So, on 12 December 1979, NATO also affirmed its determination to negotiate substantial reductions in nuclear forces on both sides in Europe. NATO policy, therefore, was 'dual-track': deploying new missiles while seeking long-term arms reductions. The idea was negotiation from a position of security.

A few weeks later came Afghanistan and Carter's withdrawal of SALT II from the Senate. America's sudden shift into renewed confrontation with Russia was profoundly unsettling for western Europe. There was little enthusiasm for sanctions and a widespread suspicion that Carter was exaggerating the threat to peace in order to strengthen his chances of re-election. Helmut Schmidt, the West German Chancellor, was particularly critical of what he called Carter's 'deadly game', even suggesting that Germany and France might serve as 'interpreters' between the two superpowers in an effort to maintain détente.[16]

But Carter and America were in no mood to listen. By 1980 they were preoccupied by a single diplomatic crisis that showed more vividly than any words of Carter, the limits of American power. Early in 1979 the Shah of Iran, America's bulwark in the Persian Gulf since the British withdrawal, was overthrown and a fundamentalist Islamic regime installed. That autumn Carter admitted the Shah into the United States for medical treatment. Incensed, Iranian 'students' took over the US Embassy in Tehran on 4 November 1979. Some of its inmates were later released but fifty-two were held hostage for 444 days, victims of visceral anti-American feeling welling up after years of forced Westernisation imposed, with Washington's backing, by the Shah's regime. Negotiations for the hostages' release failed, as did an attempted rescue mission in April 1980.

Carter, the media and the public were mesmerised by these fifty-two Americans. Their prospects were analysed on every news bulletin, their memory perpetuated by ubiquitous yellow ribbons. It was testimony to the high value placed by Americans on the security and freedom of their citizens. But few other countries would have become so obsessed. By defining foreign policy almost exclusively in terms of this one issue, Carter had allowed America itself to be taken hostage. The rest of his presidency was overwhelmed by the crisis, and the growing mood of frustration at American impotence was a major reason for Carter's defeat in the November 1980 election.

Both American and British diplomacy displayed a similar lack of direction in the later 1970s, appearing all at sea in unfamiliar waters – sometimes following old bearings, sometimes setting course anew. Britain looked to Europe, then to America; the United States explored détente, then swung back to Cold War confrontation. But the source of their confusion was not simply the unsettled state of the world. It was also due to the collapse of the Western economic boom which had lasted for most of the period since 1945. Both countries were shaken by the recession, and its larger ramifications helped to push them farther apart in the late 1970s.

The experience of virtually continuous economic growth had been a feature of life in much of the developed world in the quarter-century after 1945. A generation had grown up which took for granted prosperity, full employment and government largesse. Few were therefore prepared for the economic recession of the 1970s, which began to bite in 1973–4 when the Arab oil producers quadrupled oil prices and struck at one of the foundations of the post-war boom: cheap, secure energy supplies. The developed world soon faced an unprecedented problem, 'stagflation' – a combination of stagnant growth and roaring inflation which Keynesian orthodoxy seemed incapable of explaining, let alone of curing.

The US economy still grew in the 1970s and the living standards of Americans improved by nearly a quarter. But unemployment climbed to over six per cent, with blacks disproportionately hit, and prices more than doubled during the decade – four times as large an increase as in the fifties and sixties.[17] America was now less able than in the past to insulate itself from the ups and downs of the world economy. For much of the century, foreign trade had been of little importance to the US economy as a whole, but during the 1970s it grew to over one-fifth of Gross Domestic Product. Exports alone constituted nearly thirteen per cent of total GDP by 1981.[18] Key industries such as cars, steel, textiles and electronics were therefore vulnerable to competition from Europe, Japan and developing Pacific nations like South Korea. The 'national mood' was introspective and uncertain. Economic sluggishness, the energy crisis and the growth of foreign competition all suggested that the era of American abundance and supremacy might be coming to an end.

The recession of the mid-1970s also exposed a fundamental shift of power within the United States, which had been developing since World War Two. By 1980 one-tenth of Americans lived in California, which had overtaken New York during the 1960s as the most populous state, while Texas now came third, having nearly doubled in numbers during the previous thirty years. The 'Sunbelt' of states from Florida to California was the location of much of the new high-tech and defence-related industries, in contrast with the 'Rustbelt' of the north-east and midwest where many of the older, less competitive industries such as steel and automobiles were concentrated. The collapse of these industries, in the seventies recession, accelerated the migration south and west – away from the Atlantic seaboard, the area most shaped by European and particularly British influences and connections, towards the Pacific where America's new trading partners and rivals, notably Japan, were to be found.

The changing ethnic balance of America reinforced this shift in its economic geography. New leaders were challenging the old White Anglo-Saxon Protestant leadership, with its natural affinity for Britain. The great waves of immigrants from eastern and southern Europe which had crossed the Atlantic in the early twentieth century had gradually been assimilated into American society. They became a force, first in the politics of big northern cities such as Boston and Chicago, and then in the Democratic Party, from the New Deal onwards. After the war they left their mark on Washington itself, including its diplomacy. By the seventies American foreign policy was being made by men with names such as Kissinger and Brzezinski. Much had changed since the era of Marshall and Acheson, whose view of Britain had been influenced by their British ancestry and experiences of the wartime alliance.

Yet the assimilation of the European-Americans did not mean that the United States was no longer a nation of immigrants. It was just that the influx from across the Atlantic, which had shaped America in earlier centuries, had now dried up. In the 1970s over six per cent of Americans had been born abroad, a marked increase on each of the previous two decades. Forty per cent of them came from Asia, from countries such as Vietnam and South Korea, and another forty per cent from the Spanish-speaking countries of Central and South America. The Hispanic-Americans were the fastest-growing minority group in the United States. Officially they were calculated at 6.5 per cent of the population, but that was probably a considerable underestimate because the USA had a 1,500-mile border with Mexico, largely uncontrolled, which enabled thousands to slip in illegally.[19] By 1970 one in six Americans claimed to have a mother tongue that was not English. Nearly a quarter of these spoke Spanish and they had now overtaken German-speakers as the most numerous group with a non-English mother tongue.[20]

Many Hispanics and blacks did not want to assimilate completely into American life: they sought its economic and social benefits while retaining their cultural distinctiveness. This new pride in ethnic diversity was a spin-off from the civil rights movement of the 1960s, from slogans such as 'Black is Beautiful'. The America these minorities wanted was a pluralist one in which different ethnic groups lived together, not fusing their identity in the WASP culture. Their ideal was 'the salad bowl' not 'the melting pot'.

For Hispanics, in particular, language was a vital part of their effort to retain their cultural identity. In the 1960s the Federal Government had enacted legislation intended to improve minority groups' proficiency in English by teaching it to them in their mother tongue. In the 1970s this was often exploited by local Hispanic communities to promote Spanish as the primary teaching language in schools. In the past the United States had survived as a unified country because of its insistence that all newcomers must accept a common national language – English. Back in the early twentieth century German-Americans had battled against the dominant English-speaking culture: the draft protest in New Ulm in 1917 had been one example. In the 1970s, assisted by much broader legal recognition for minority rights, the growing Hispanic population posed a new challenge to the 'Anglo' ethos of America. These new Americans felt no special affinities with Britain.

Even those Americans who naturally looked across the Atlantic felt little but dismay at the state of Britain during the seventies. The country seemed incapable of grappling with the problems that it had been facing for several decades. They were easy to describe but hard to cure: declining old industries, lack of new investment, bad management, poor productivity, embattled labour relations and the absence of incentives. Growth in the rest of the world was sluggish; in Britain it was non-existent. In the mid-seventies, British living standards fell for the first time since 1945 and inflation was running at twenty-five per cent in 1975.

Although the economy failed to grow, the demands of its beneficiaries increased. Welfare payments and government subsidies to industry took an increasing proportion of national income, while labour unions competed in self-defeating wage claims which only fuelled inflation. Twice governments were brought down after conflict with the unions. In 1974 the Conservatives lost the election after Heath confronted the miners on the issue of pay restraint. Labour returned to power, but its Social Contract with the unions eventually collapsed in the Winter of Discontent of 1978–9. Americans had believed Britain, for all its failings, to be one of the world's most civilised societies. Now the media showed a country in which, it seemed, the dead lay unburied, the sick were turned away from hospitals and the refuse was piled high in the streets.

Not only was the United Kingdom hard to govern, it seemed to be breaking apart. The escalating sectarian violence in Northern Ireland forced Westminster to replace provincial government with direct rule from 1972, but no solution could be found. Tit-for-tat shootings increased and the British army, hated by the Catholics and distrusted by Loyalist Protestants, was drawn into an apparently unending commitment. In Wales and Scotland nationalist political parties were on the march, albeit more peacefully. They demanded a devolution of powers from London and won increasing support among voters. Labour, with a slim parliamentary majority, was reliant on their backing to keep itself in power in the mid-1970s and it eventually conceded referenda on Welsh and Scottish devolution in 1979.

To many Americans the United Kingdom seemed disorderly and disunited. Commentator Eric Sevareid, who had lauded Britain's defiance of Hitler in 1940, told television viewers in May 1975 that 'Britain is drifting towards a condition of ungovernability'. Economist

Milton Friedman insisted in November 1976 that a military coup, like that of General Pinochet in Chile, was 'the only outcome that is conceivable'.[21] Others claimed that Britain had 'become the latest version of the Sick Man of Europe',[22] a humiliating comparison with the old Turkish Empire before World War One. Many American conservatives pointed to Britain as an indictment of socialism, Keynesianism and the welfare state – vices to which, they judged, America itself had become dangerously attached.

Britain had become used to America no longer taking her seriously as a world power. But it was deeply distressing to realise that she was also losing her reputation for political sagacity. In the late nineteenth century Woodrow Wilson had praised the British system of Cabinet government as superior to America's separation of powers, which often made it hard for President and Congress to reach agreement on policy. In the 1950s American liberals had argued that in Britain the tighter party discipline and deference to political leaders would prevent grass-roots paranoia like McCarthyism. The author of an American textbook on British politics published in 1965 wrote: 'Just as Alexis de Tocqueville travelled to America in 1831 to seek the secrets of democracy, so today we might travel to England in search of the secrets of stable representative government.'[23]

But the turmoil of the seventies cast Britain in a different light. 'As it once showed the way to democratic success,' wrote one Harvard professor, 'today it blazes the trail towards democratic failure.'[24] Britain's institutions seemed incapable of coping with the demands of the seventies: vested interests apparently blocking industrial regeneration, pressure groups demanding greater shares of a diminishing national cake. Across the Atlantic, Americans, with Watergate and Vietnam behind them, regained faith in the wisdom of their own political institutions. An unfettered press and an independent legislature seemed essential to check the 'imperial presidency', exposing the iniquities of the Nixon Administration and reining in the President's power to wage war behind Congress's back. The comment of Woodrow Wyatt, a British political columnist and former MP – 'Don't think a Watergate couldn't happen here. You just wouldn't hear about it' – was noted with approval in America.[25]

By the mid-1970s Britain no longer mattered, even to anglophile Americans, as a world power or as a political example. It was her past not her present that now seemed attractive and in the seventies more and more Americans were ready to cross the ocean to sample, for a few weeks, the world they were glad to have lost.

Crossing the Atlantic by sea had always been the preserve of a few,

"*Say—it's really great to be invited into a typical English home.*"

The illusions of American tourists, according to *Punch*, 1 March 1972.

mostly the rich or the migrants. The start of commercial air travel did little initially to change that. But during the 1960s, with greater affluence and more competitive fares, transatlantic travel began to come within the reach of ordinary people. In 1965 Britain and France had each drawn about 670,000 American visitors. But thereafter Britain became the principal attraction. In 1970 1.4 million Americans visited the country, a figure that had doubled by 1984. Even more striking were the economic benefits. In 1960 Britain earned about $120 million from American tourists, in 1971 $344 million, and by the early 1980s over a billion dollars.[26]

Americans showed little interest in modern Britain, struggling to emerge from the ruins of the old. They came not to see new towns and new factories but to visit the relics of Britain's past: ancient cities, country houses, literary haunts. Above all tourists were fascinated by the monarchy, Britain's most distinctive national symbol, which had been given additional appeal through Queen Elizabeth II's Silver Jubilee in 1977 and the media's obsession with the lives and loves of

Britain's Churchillian past becomes copy for the admen: British Airways 'Poundstretcher' promotion for transatlantic flights.

her children. The marketing of Britain as a tourist attraction, an increasingly slick business operation, deliberately concentrated on these past glories. One of Britain's most successful promoters in the USA during the 1970s was actor Robert Morley, in advertisements for British Airways. His blimpish but genial Briton seemed like a parody of Churchill. Later the airline adopted Bulldog Winston as one of its marketing emblems. For 'post-industrial' Britain, tourism had developed into a major service industry. The country's past was becoming its future.

MEET WINSTON
Winston is the Poundstretcher 'mascot' and he's as British as the Union Jack he wears. Winston is your friend and he's around to make sure all your travel arrangements meet his most exacting demands in value-for-money flights and holidays. Winston is strong, faithful, tenacious, appealing. He's everything that Poundstretcher is and stands for.

Television reinforced these impressions. In the 1930s British news bulked large on the pages of serious American newspapers. By the 1970s Britain was rarely mentioned at all by the American media, with the exception of the royal family. But upmarket American television was keenly interested in things British. Many historical series produced by British television were bought up by American public

President Jimmy Carter with Prime Minister James Callaghan in Newcastle (May 1977).

London's Leicester Square during the Winter of Discontent (1978-9).

Secretary of State Alexander Haig at London's Heathrow Airport during the Falklands crisis (April 1982).

Prime Minister Margaret Thatcher and President Ronald Reagan at Camp David.

(that is, non-commercial) stations – *The Forsyte Saga*, *The First Churchills* or *Upstairs, Downstairs*. They were shown under the umbrella of 'Masterpiece Theater', hosted by the transplanted English journalist, Alistair Cooke, who explained the essential historical background to puzzled American viewers, much as he had edified a generation of British radio listeners with his *Letter from America*. In the 1970s 'Masterpiece Theater' was conveying the same archaic impressions of Britain as had movies of the 1930s such as *The Private Life of Henry VIII* or *A Yank at Oxford*. Television, like the tourism industry, perpetuated the image of Britain as a country that relished being behind the times, not one desperately trying to keep up with them.

The portrait of the United States presented on British television was no more flattering. British TV acquired action series from the United States: Westerns such as *The Lone Ranger* or *Laramie*, crime stories like *Perry Mason* and *Cagney and Lacey*, and those grotesque flauntings of American materialism – *Dallas* and *Dynasty*. These programmes played on familiar British stereotypes of America: a country of vice, violence and conspicuous wealth. This was the America that Britons loved – or loved to hate. As with the cinema of the 1930s, whose pernicious effects Ambassador Joseph Kennedy had castigated in 1939, so with television: a generation in Britain derived their main impressions of the United States from 'the box', unbalanced by any awareness of the real Americans whose lifestyle was almost as far removed from the movie image as was their own.

In the 1970s tourism and television helped to bridge the Atlantic divide. They offered ordinary Britons and ordinary Americans an unprecedented opportunity to get acquainted with the other country. But they could do little to counter Americans' sense that Britain was now irrelevant to the modern world; on the contrary they often reinforced it. Stripped of her empire and her wealth, torn by strife and dissension, Britain seemed at best a living museum. One Labour Member of Parliament, Andrew Faulds, envisaged her in the future as 'a sort of Switzerland with monuments in place of mountains . . . to provide the haven, heavy with history, for those millions . . . who will come seeking peace in a place away from the pulsating pressures and the grit and grievances of their own industrial societies'.[27]

But, despite the shocks of the seventies, not everyone in Britain was ready to write her off. In May 1979 conservative Britain elected her first woman Prime Minister, at a time when no American woman had even been a candidate for President or Vice-President. Margaret Thatcher did not accept that decline was irreversible. She set out to regenerate Britain at home and rebuild British influence abroad. In doing so, she looked across the Atlantic for support, to a new American President whose ideals were similar to her own and who was equally determined to restore his country's power and pride. Together they established one of the closest personal bonds in the history of Anglo-American co-operation and breathed new life into the special relationship.

16

A Relationship Renewed

1981–7

At noon on Tuesday 20 January 1981 Ronald Reagan was inaugurated as the fortieth President of the United States. Forty minutes later news came through that the fifty-two American hostages had left Tehran airport after 444 days of captivity. Carter's efforts to secure their release had finally borne fruit, aided by Algerian diplomacy and by a large financial settlement. But he was no longer in office to welcome them home. Reagan reaped the benefits of the mood of national rejoicing and capitalised on a widespread feeling that America must not be humiliated again. The new President was determined that his country should 'walk tall' once more, after the drift and self-doubt of the 1970s.

Reagan's inauguration marked a turning point not only for the United States but also for Anglo-American relations. He found a natural ally in Margaret Thatcher, Britain's Prime Minister since May 1979, despite their marked differences of temperament. Mrs Thatcher, although often hesitant and cautious about her political judgements, adopted in public a defiant tone. In the face of opposition her instinct was to respond not with discussion but with a forceful restatement of her views, as though repetition would be enough to reveal their self-evident truth. She prided herself on being a 'conviction' politician, a stance which was novel and appealing to many in an electorate that had become so accustomed to compromise that it had almost ceased to believe that a radical attempt to solve Britain's problems could succeed.

Mrs Thatcher had a quick mind and brisk manner. Her energy was indefatigable, her appetite for work voracious. Ronald Reagan was very different. With his friendly, informal style of conversation, his short attention span, his occasional slips of the tongue and lapses of memory, he gave the impression of an easy-going leader, content to lay down the guidelines of policy and leave others to sort out the details. While Mrs Thatcher bullied and cajoled her advisers into agreement, insisting that she 'could not waste time having any internal arguments',[1] President Reagan was protected by his aides from the press and public, except in carefully controlled circumstances. If he muddled two countries or forgot his facts, he would shrug his shoulders, grin amiably and leave it to a staff member to explain what he had really meant. It was not an attitude Mrs Thatcher would have tolerated in her own Cabinet. Responding to a speech she gave in Washington in February 1981, the President joked: 'You are a hard act to follow.'[2]

For all his insouciance, however, the President was a man of tenacity and courage, displayed within months of his inauguration when he was the target of attempted assassination. He knew what he wanted and how to get his way, winning the affection and respect of the American people to a degree unknown since Franklin Roosevelt. Both he and Margaret Thatcher had won high office in the face of snobbish contempt. Reagan, a former movie actor, was mocked for his presumption in even seeking the presidency. Mrs Thatcher, as a woman, had to endure the condescension of politicians within her own party as well as outside. Both had triumphed over these attempts to humiliate them and believed that they had made it to the top through their own efforts. Once in power they were determined to put their principles into practice.

For both leaders the central tenet of their faith was 'freedom',

British cartoonist Steve Bell satirises President Reagan's (and America's) view of the world.

which, they believed, was endangered at home and abroad. The enemy within was seen as big-spending, Keynesian government which throttled enterprise and stifled self-reliance. They wanted the freedom of the individual increased at the expense of the encroaching state. Abroad, they believed that communist Russia posed a threat to freedom and that the West, deluded by détente, had become complacent about the danger. They doubted that an accommodation could be reached with the Soviet Union on the basis of mutual self-interest and argued that negotiation could only take place from a position of much greater military strength.

Their aims, though seeming conservative, were radical – to resurrect the principles of the past in order to reshape the present. Both were trying to turn back the tides of recent history, to reverse the policies of Keynesianism and détente, to rekindle national pride, to check the sense of impotence and decline afflicting both their countries. Facing intense opposition at home, they leaned on each other for support. 'It is widely known that I share many of your ideals and beliefs, Prime Minister Thatcher,' the President observed two months after he had assumed office.[3] No previous President and Prime Minister had coincided so closely in their political philosophies, certainly not the anti-colonial Franklin Roosevelt and the diehard imperialist Winston Churchill, nor even the liberal John Kennedy and the progressive Harold Macmillan.

Their economic policies were commonly described as 'monetarist', but neither leader was a serious disciple of theory. They were practical politicians, using the language of economics to justify gut instincts, derived from personal experience, about how to make their countries prosperous again. As Mrs Thatcher observed, 'Economics are the method; the object is to change the heart and soul . . . of the nation.'[4] Both denounced Keynesian solutions, in particular increased government spending, as a counter to the recession of the early 1980s. But their priorities were different. For Reagan, the prime aim was to reduce taxes. So-called 'supply-side' economists predicted that this would stimulate growth, thereby generating greater tax revenues which the United States could spend on modernising its armed forces against the Soviet Union. For Thatcher, rampant inflation was the principal danger and her immediate goal was therefore to control government borrowing. The Prime Minister also wanted to curb the power of the big unions, whose wage claims, she believed, had fuelled inflation and brought the country to its knees in 1979. More fundamentally, she wanted to reverse the march of socialism. 'Each time you go further along the Socialist road,' she warned in 1977, 'nearer and nearer to the Communist State, then the consequences of the Communist State will follow.'[5]

The 'Thatcher Revolution' proved more radical than the 'Reagan Revolution'. No President can serve more than eight years and Reagan's own authority diminished rapidly from January 1987 when he lost effective control of Congress to the Democrats and was undermined by the Iran–Contra scandal. Mrs Thatcher, by contrast, secured re-election in 1983 and 1987, each time with healthy working majorities in Parliament, which enabled her to push through her policies in a way President Reagan must often have envied.

In Britain, inflation was running at twenty-one per cent in 1979; by 1987 it had stabilised at between four and five per cent. The government had reduced Britain's nationalised sector by half, raising £25 billion in the process and greatly widening the spread of share ownership, though without breaking up the existing monopolies to more competition. It had also weakened the union movement, by legislation and, in 1984–5, by defeating the strike by the National Union of Mineworkers, who had brought down the previous Conservative Government of Edward Heath a decade before. This victory and the recession helped force a more flexible union attitude to pay claims and new technology, not just in coal mining but in other industries such as cars and newspapers. By 1987 the government could point to four per cent growth and rapidly increasing productivity. The British economy, boasted Chancellor of the Exchequer Nigel Lawson, was 'on top of the world'.[6]

The price some Britons paid for this revolution was high. Unemployment soared from six per cent of the work force in 1979, when Mrs Thatcher took office, to thirteen per cent by 1983 – the worst level for half a century. And industrial production fell even more sharply in 1979–81 than it did in the Slump of 1929–32.[7] The world recession was partly to blame but so was the government's policy of keeping interest rates high to control inflation, thereby raising the value of the pound and pricing British manufactures out of many foreign markets. Under Mrs Thatcher, the apostle of business enterprise, the progressive 'de-industrialisation' of Britain spread to affect not just long-declining areas like the north-east but also previously prosperous regions such as the west midlands. Critics pointed to a widening gap between the 'two nations' – a thriving south-east and a decaying north.

Britain's underlying economic problems remained. After the 1987 election, Mrs Thatcher made the rejuvenation of the inner cities and the older industrial areas primary objectives, together with increased spending on education and health. Yet the government could expect less income in the future, now that most marketable nationalised industries had been sold off, and North Sea oil, which had fuelled government spending and covered Britain's worsening trade balance in the 1970s and 1980s, was beginning to dry up. Mrs Thatcher had changed Britain more than any Prime Minister since the 1940s; whether she had achieved a long-term reversal of the country's economic decline was not yet clear.

In America, the Reagan Revolution saw different successes and failures. The centrepiece of the President's programme was a dramatic cut in income tax, a tax which he believed to be a fundamental evil. Back in the 1960s he had claimed that 'we have received this progressive tax direct from Karl Marx', who intended it 'to tax the middle class out of existence, because you can't have socialism where you have a strong middle class'.[8] By 1987 the top rate of federal income tax was reduced to twenty-eight per cent, only one per cent above the *lowest* rate then obtaining in Britain. The highest British rate, even after the Thatcher Government's cuts, was sixty per cent.

But, as in Britain, government spending was not so easy to curb. Retirement pensions and Medicare (health care for the over-sixty-fives) were left largely intact, despite the fact that their ever-increasing costs took up nearly two-thirds of the welfare budget. It was hard to reduce them against the wishes of so many of Reagan's Republican supporters. In America, as in Britain, spending cuts tended to fall on those in society without organisation and influence – the low-income families and ethnic minorities, particularly in the inner cities, who bore the brunt of the recession. And the Reagan Revolution did little to confront America's underlying economic problem: its lack of competitiveness internationally. The nation that had given the world Ford, Hoover and Coca-Cola was now buying its consumer goods – cars, televisions and computers – from Japan and other Pacific industrial nations. Imports exceeded exports for the first time in the twentieth century and in 1986 the US trade deficit was about $160 billion.

But the gravest consequence of 'Reaganomics' was the soaring budget deficit. On the face of it a policy of tax cuts and increased defence spending seemed to guarantee an unbalanced budget, but the President believed the assurances of supply-side economists that big tax cuts would boost the economy so dramatically that it would soon generate the extra tax revenue needed to balance the books. Nothing of the sort happened. Supply-side theory proved utopian; the beneficiaries of government spending and their Congressional spokesmen blocked significant spending cuts; and Budget Director David Stockman made serious blunders in his haste to get the economic reforms through Congress while Reagan's post-election influence was at its peak in early 1981. Looking back he admits that 'designing a comprehensive plan to bring about a sweeping change in national economic governance in forty days is a preposterous, wantonly reckless notion', but he 'reckoned that the "window" for successfully launching sweeping change in national economic policy would be exceedingly brief'.[9]

The worst muddle was the defence budget. At 7.30 p.m. on Friday 30 January 1981 Stockman met Defense Secretary Caspar Weinberger and his aides in the Pentagon. There they agreed the outlines of the defence budget, Stockman doing the arithmetic on his pocket calculator. The meeting lasted less than half an hour. When they had finished, Weinberger looked at his watch, yawned and said: 'I call this a good night's work.' Stockman, whose day had begun at 4.30 a.m. and would not end until midnight, rushed off to his next engagement. Only when the figures were processed by the Budget Office computer a few weeks later did he realise that he had let the Pentagon get away with a defence budget of one and a half trillion dollars over five years. This meant a ten per cent increase in defence spending in real terms, double even Reagan's campaign promise.[10]

By the time this and other errors were appreciated, little could be done. The budget had to be ready for Congress by mid-February and Reagan was not interested in the details. Faced with problems or disagreements amongst his advisers, he would smile and say, 'Okay, you fellas work it out.' It was a far cry from Mrs Thatcher's interventionist style of leadership. As predictions of the future government deficit poured out of the Budget Office computer, they were fudged by what became known as the 'magic asterisk' – 'Future savings to be identified'.[11]

When savings were not made and, as predicted, the budget deficit soared, the President refused to curb defence spending, despite reports of extravagance and waste among the Pentagon's contractors. Nor would he abandon his cherished tax cuts, let alone increase income-tax rates to generate the necessary revenue. With the White House abdicating responsibility, Congress stepped in with a programme of mandatory spending cuts if the deficit exceeded specified limits. Even so the budget deficit was running at an unprecedented $220 billion per annum by July 1986. Reagan, America's most conservative President for decades, had piled up a national debt three times as large as that accumulated by all his thirty-nine predecessors.

The consequences for the rest of the world were profound. Since

World War Two American capital in the form of foreign investment, economic aid and military commitments had helped sustain the world economy. Now the process had gone into reverse. Because the US Government could not pay for its spending through tax revenue, it had to borrow. By 1985 the inflow of funds, particularly from Japan, to cover the budget and trade deficits had, for the first time since World War One, turned the United States into a net debtor nation, borrowing more than it lent. One of the world's most powerful economies was importing capital rather than exporting it.

The relationship between American and British business was also being reversed. British firms started taking over American companies on a large scale, a transatlantic invasion in the opposite direction from that of the 1960s. In the early 1980s many British businesses made large profits and were looking for new areas in which to invest. In 1979 the Thatcher Government had ended all exchange controls, allowing British capital to move freely abroad. With a favourable pound-dollar exchange rate and growing expertise in the City of London about American opportunities, British capital began to flow across the Atlantic. In 1985 British companies spent over $5 billion in take-overs in the USA; the following year the figure nearly trebled. Among the US corporations acquired were Moosehead Beer, J. Walter Thompson, the advertising giant, and Smith and Wesson, makers of the guns that won the West. In Britain, some asked whether the money should not have been spent at home, revitalising the depressed north, but by the mid-1980s, with capital free to choose its destination, Britain was the top direct foreign investor in the United States, owning about as much in America as the US owned in Britain.

Critics in America and Europe nevertheless warned that the eventual consequences of America's trade and budget deficits would be disastrous, but little was done in Washington. The economy seemed strong, the stock market was booming. Most Americans paid little attention to the effects of US policy on the rest of the world. Some of Mrs Thatcher's ministers added their voices to the criticism, but the Prime Minister was not among them. For her the special relationship was an article of faith. To rebuke America in public went against all her natural instincts. Sir Anthony Parsons, Mrs Thatcher's special adviser on foreign affairs in 1982–3, thinks she

> believes very strongly that the United States is absolutely vital to us, and that obviously one of the cardinal planks of our policy must be the best possible relations with the United States. By the same token, I think she believes that we can only hope to influence the

United States in private and affect their judgements over various issues where we may disagree, if the basic relationship is extremely good.[12]

Margaret Thatcher stood in marked contrast to her Conservative predecessor, Edward Heath. Although no anti-Marketeer, she showed little enthusiasm for the European Community. Her early years in office were spent demanding a rebate on Britain's excessive budget contribution – 'I cannot play Sister Bountiful to the Community'; 'We want our money'.[13] Whereas Heath had espoused the ideal of a united Europe, it seemed to Helmut Schmidt that Mrs Thatcher 'saw her main European mission as reducing as close to zero as possible Britain's net contribution to the financing of the European Community'.[14] The lack of affection was mutual. Mrs Thatcher had little time for the continental leaders, many of them socialists, with whom she had to deal. Born in 1925, reaching maturity in the era of the wartime Anglo-American alliance and the Cold War, she had no doubt that Britain's closest ties still lay with America – English-speaking, free enterprise, fervently anti-communist. By comparison Europe seemed disunited, left-wing and irredeemably foreign.

At the heart of the Thatcher foreign policy was the renewal of Britain's nuclear special relationship, established by Macmillan two decades before. By the late 1970s the Polaris submarine-launched deterrent was nearing the end of its useful life. Labour had been ready to modernise Polaris but not to acquire a new generation of strategic missiles, although Callaghan secretly opened negotiations with Carter in February 1979. Mrs Thatcher had no such inhibitions. She was determined that Britain should remain a nuclear power into the twenty-first century. In July 1980 it was announced that Britain would purchase Trident C-4 missiles from the USA for its new fleet of submarines, an agreement made with Jimmy Carter. When Reagan decided to upgrade the Trident programme and develop the more powerful D-5 missiles, the Thatcher Government, fearful of another Skybolt fiasco, quickly arranged an agreement for these instead. This was concluded in an exchange of letters between the two leaders in March 1982.

On the face of it Britain had secured an exceptional bargain. Unlike Polaris, Trident missiles would be installed and serviced in the United States. Britain was given the use of them at little more than cost price. Under the Polaris and Trident I agreements the British Government had agreed to pay five per cent of the total research and development costs of the programmes. For Trident II it was simply asked to pay a fixed R and D charge of $116 million (at 1982 prices) and to man the

Rapier air defence system around the US air force bases in Britain. And, as with Polaris, Mrs Thatcher promised that the Trident force would be assigned to NATO 'except where the United Kingdom Government may decide that supreme national interests are at stake'.[15] Again Britain would get the fruits of American technology for its own use and at minimum cost. No other country was allowed these benefits.

The uniqueness of these arrangements and the generosity of the terms indicated the Reagan Administration's urgent desire to strengthen NATO's defences. In the 1960s and for most of the 1970s, Washington had been lukewarm at best about Britain having its own nuclear force. But in his letter to Mrs Thatcher, the President observed that 'the United States readiness to provide these systems is a demonstration of the great importance which the United States Government attach to the maintenance by the United Kingdom of an independent nuclear deterrent capability'.[16]

Yet the special relationship was being used to provide a weapon that would probably be employed, if at all, only when that relationship had broken down. The ultimate justification for Britain having its own strategic deterrent lay in doubts about American reliability: was the United States likely to honour its guarantee of European security by launching its own missiles when it would be faced in return with the threat of devastating Soviet retaliation on American cities? The British Ministry of Defence preferred to pose the dilemma less bluntly, professing 'great confidence in the depth of resolve underlying the United States commitment'. But, it suggested, a Soviet Government, 'perhaps much changed in character from today's, perhaps also operating amid the pressures of turbulent internal or external circumstances, might believe that it could impose its will on Europe by military force without becoming involved in strategic nuclear war with the United States.'[17] The government insisted that Britain's modernised nuclear force, using missiles sold and serviced by the United States, provided an independent insurance.

The Trident decision was sharply attacked by the Opposition in Parliament. They argued that no British nuclear deterrent could ever be credible since its use would invite instant obliteration of a small and densely-populated island. To remain a nuclear power simply showed, they claimed, that Mrs Thatcher harboured delusions of past grandeur. Labour MP Robin Cook commented: 'It is time that we adjusted ourselves to the fact that we are a declining medium-range power and looked first and foremost at how we use our desperately scarce industrial resources to commercial advantage rather than on grandiose projects which we have inherited from the past.'[18]

Others attacked the cost of Trident, which had soared by 1985 to about £10 billion. The government argued that, spread over the total duration of the programme, Trident would only represent about six per cent of Britain's defence equipment budget, but the Commons Defence Committee claimed the proportion would be more than twelve per cent in the peak years of expenditure in the late 1980s.[19] Given Britain's underlying economic problems, the government's determination to cut borrowing and expenditure, and its commitment, reaffirmed as part of the Trident II deal, to increase spending on conventional forces in Europe, many defence analysts predicted a looming crisis in the defence budget if Trident went ahead. There was not enough money for all these defence commitments. Britain, they argued, could not afford to stay in the nuclear club, even with America paying so much of the bill.

Even those who believed in nuclear deterrence had their doubts about Trident. Trident I had double the range and four times the warheads of Polaris. Yet Trident II had nearly five times the 'yield', or explosive power, of Trident I and was even more accurate, perhaps to within 400 feet.[20] This might suit America's need for a weapon that could travel from the USA to Russia and could there penetrate hardened Soviet missile silos. But Britain, whose targets were Soviet cities and who was much closer to Russia, did not need such power, range and pinpoint accuracy. Because she was reliant on American technology, however, Britain had to take whatever the United States had in stock – Skybolt, Polaris, Trident I, Trident II – regardless of her specific needs. France, by contrast, had developed her own nuclear deterrent, tailored to French needs. Critics such as the then Social Democrat leader, David Owen, urged that Britain's nuclear future lay in collaboration with France on a deterrent appropriate to European needs, rather than being tied to the vagaries of Pentagon policy.

Within weeks of the Trident II deal, however, the benefits of a close military relationship with America seemed amply demonstrated. In April 1982 the repressive Argentine military junta, faced with growing domestic unrest, decided to divert attention to Argentina's long-standing grievance, the British occupation of the Falklands. The ownership of these remote South Atlantic islands, with their 1,800 British settlers, had been in dispute for a century and a half. In late 1980 the Thatcher Government, then in the process of negotiating an agreement to give Hong Kong back to China, had been talking to the Argentines about a similar scheme whereby they would be given freehold to the islands, which would then be leased back to the inhabitants for a period of time. But the minister responsible, Nicholas Ridley, was howled down by MPs of all parties in the House of Commons. Later, angry and shaken, he told one critic: 'If we don't do something, they will invade.'[21] No further negotiations followed, but meanwhile, to save money for Trident, the Defence Minister, John Nott, had been cutting hard at the Royal Navy's surface fleet. One of the casualties was HMS *Endurance*, a small patrol ship deployed in the South Atlantic as a symbol of Britain's commitment to the Falklands. The Foreign Office protested, but in vain: Nott had the backing of the Prime Minister.

General Leopoldo Galtieri's Government read these moves as signals that, although Britain refused to talk, she would not resist an Argentine take-over. It was a grave miscalculation. The Argentine invasion of the islands, protected only by a small garrison of marines, on 2 April 1982, provoked a wave of patriotic fury in Britain. MPs of all parties attacked Mrs Thatcher's Government for incompetence and the Foreign Secretary, Lord Carrington, felt obliged to resign. Incensed at the humiliation to Britain's pride and with her own political survival in jeopardy, the Prime Minister immediately despatched a Royal Navy Task Force to the South Atlantic. At its head were Britain's two aircraft carriers, *Hermes* and *Invincible*, which, until recently, had been high on Mr Nott's list for disposal. When the Task Force, packed with soldiers, supplies and aircraft, started on its long journey southward, there were still hopes that a demonstration of military force might be enough to persuade the Argentines to back down. But during April 1982 repeated attempts to secure a peace formula failed and it became clear that Britain faced a war to recover the islands.

Publicly the United States was slow to support Britain. Between the Argentine invasion and the start of full-scale hostilities, Washington sat on the fence. 'We're friends with both of the countries engaged in the dispute,' the President observed in his first comments on the crisis. Asked if America would act as 'honest broker', he said: 'If we can be of help in doing that, yes, anything that would bring about a peaceful solution to what seems to be an unnecessary disagreement.'[22] London was dismayed and angry, but the Reagan Administration faced a genuine conflict of loyalties. The Argentine junta was the linchpin of its anti-communist strategy in Latin America. President Carter's arms embargo had been lifted and General Galtieri assured of American backing. Faced with a conflict between its main supporter in South America and its closest NATO ally, the United States was in an impossible position. As former Secretary of State Henry

Kissinger observed: 'Sometimes you come up against a situation where you can't win.'[23]

The Thatcher Government had no sympathy for America's dilemma. In its view fundamental issues of principle were at stake – British sovereignty, the rights of the islanders, the illegal use of force. Particular wrath was reserved for Jeane Kirkpatrick, US Ambassador to the United Nations, who wanted to avoid alienating Argentina. 'The Argentinians have been claiming for 200 years that they own those islands,' she declared. 'If they own those islands, then moving troops into them is not armed aggression.'[24] Meanwhile Secretary of State Alexander Haig, sympathetic to Britain, engaged in intensive shuttle diplomacy between Washington, New York, London and Buenos Aires, travelling 33,000 miles in twelve days in search of a peaceful settlement. For their efforts, his team was denounced by Mrs Kirkpatrick as 'Brits in American clothes'. She asked: 'Why not disband the State Department and have the British Foreign Office make our policy?'[25] It was not until fighting started at the end of April that the United States sided publicly with Britain. On 30 April the President noted that 'the aggression was on the part of Argentina in this dispute . . . and I think the principle that all of us must abide by is, armed aggression of that kind must not be allowed to succeed'.[26]

But although it took Washington all April to come out publicly against Argentina, behind the scenes the Pentagon had been backing Britain from the start and its aid increased dramatically once America came off the fence. Directed by Caspar Weinberger, the anglophile Defense Secretary, the United States provided Britain's ill-equipped and over-extended forces with crucial help at a speed rarely achieved by the Pentagon's cumbersome bureaucracy. Weinberger set up a central clearing house, with direct access to his office. Fifteen stages were eliminated from the supply authorisation process and materiel was transferred from inventories in twenty-four hours instead of the normal two weeks. The assistance provided included ammunition, equipment, twelve million gallons of aviation fuel and 200 of the latest Sidewinder air-to-air missiles. Most useful of all, Britain was given vital military intelligence from intercepted signals and from one of America's surveillance satellites, specially moved away from its orbit over Russia for the purpose.[27]

This help was given without any special permission being sought. Dr John Lehman, US Secretary of the Navy at the time, explains: 'One has to understand the relationship of the United States Navy and the Royal Navy – there's no other relationship, I think, like it in the world between two military services.' Channels had existed since World War Two for regular naval exercises, exchanges of personnel, sharing of equipment, weapons and intelligence. 'There was no need to establish a new relationship . . . it was really just turning up the volume . . . almost a case of not being told to stop rather than crossing a threshold to start.'[28] Britain was reaping the benefits of agreements dating back over decades, including the UK–USA intelligence treaty of 1947. The President himself hinted at this. 'There are no new agreements that have come out of this at all,' he remarked in late May 1982. 'There are certain bilateral agreements and our relationship in the North Atlantic Alliance that we fulfill regardless of what's going on.'[29]

But there was more to the relationship than formal agreements. The Americans would probably not have done as much for any other NATO ally. John Lehman, who confesses, 'I had travelled to England twenty times before I got west of the Mississippi,' observes that 'the special relationship is very special indeed. There are not those channels with other countries that are operating day to day where you pick up the phone to call somebody at the other end and he's been at your home and you've been at his home, and you know him by his first name and you know his children's names and that kind of thing. I mean it's a different kind of a relationship.' And Lehman believes that the relationship was decisive for Britain. Without American help, he says, 'I think that Britain would have had to have withdrawn from the Falklands.'[30]

Although American help was crucial for Britain's success, victory was won by the skill and courage of her own forces, who, at the cost of 255 lives, retrieved the mistakes made by politicians and civil servants. On 14 June 1982, six weeks after the first British landings on the Falklands, the Argentines surrendered. Most of the American public cheered the British victory. Three to one they supported Britain against the dictatorial Argentine junta and made no secret of their admiration for the way the operation had been conducted. Americans were also surprised at the outpouring of patriotic fervour from the supposedly phlegmatic British and many revised their seventies' judgements about Britain going the same way as Chile. 'Great Britain is great again,' Mrs Thatcher proclaimed.[31] The war also resuscitated her own reputation, previously in the doldrums. Those closely involved all agreed: 'It was Mrs Thatcher's war. She held us to it. She never seemed to flinch from her conviction about its course. She took the risks on her shoulders and she won.'[32] In Britain and America, among her critics as well as her friends, Mrs Thatcher was confirmed as 'the iron lady', one of the West's most decisive leaders.

America was not blindly supporting Britain, however. Once the fighting was over and Galtieri had been shown that force did not pay, the Administration assumed that Britain would return to the negotiating table. But British blood had been spilt and Mrs Thatcher was not about to give away what had been so expensively recovered, particularly when the 'Falklands Factor' had played a part in her political recovery. She now insisted that the wishes of the islanders were paramount and that Britain would not relinquish sovereignty. She embarked on a costly 'Fortress Falklands' policy, developing the airport and providing a permanent garrison for the islands. Washington was concerned at this diversion of Britain's limited resources from her main commitments to NATO, and it was sure that Britain's colonial claims could not be sustained indefinitely.

For all the rhetoric about 'alliance' and 'friendship', America had not been consulted over Britain's policy in the spring of 1982. Under extreme duress Mrs Thatcher simply acted and President Reagan was left to respond in a way that minimised the damage to the United States. In October 1983 a similar tension between British and American interests arose, but this time it was the Americans who acted on their own – in Grenada.

Washington anticipated a Marxist take-over in this nearby Caribbean island. It was also concerned about the welfare of 600 Americans, fearing another Iran-style hostage crisis. Critics of the operation suspected that the Administration was even more anxious to divert public attention from the recent horrific terrorist attack on the US Marine barracks in Beirut in which 241 died. And so, with token military support from other Caribbean states, US troops were sent in to take control. Grenada was a former British colony and member of the Commonwealth. Its head of state was Queen Elizabeth II. Yet British Government objections were ignored, despite last-minute representations by Mrs Thatcher. According to Langhorn Motley, the State Department official handling the operation, 'there were two telephone calls to Mrs Thatcher from President Reagan', one before the final decision was taken, the other soon after. In both, he says, 'I am told that the majority of the talking was done by Mrs Thatcher . . . It was vintage Mrs Thatcher. Forceful!' But in neither case was the Prime Minister able to change the President's mind, and, Motley judged, Reagan was 'surprised and a little disappointed' at her reaction. Motley adds that some members of the Administration resented her lack of support after the help she had received over the Falklands. 'When she needed us we were there . . . we just didn't understand,

and I still don't understand to this day, this strong feeling that we shouldn't have done this.'[33]

It was a bitter humiliation for the Prime Minister, suggesting that she had little influence in Washington, and her critics made the most of it. Denis Healey, Labour's shadow Foreign Secretary, claimed that she 'had made something of a cult of her special relationship with the American President, at the expense of British interests, of her relations with our European partners and our relations with the Commonwealth'. Lambasting her 'servility to the American President', he dubbed her Reagan's 'obedient poodle'.[34]

Trident, the Falklands and Grenada together summed up the complex state of Anglo-American relations in the early 1980s. The special defence ties remained extremely close and the British could still exert considerable leverage on American policy in a major crisis such as the Falklands. But both the Falklands and Grenada also illustrated the growing importance to the United States of relations outside the Atlantic alliance, particularly in Latin America, and the fact that, ever since World War Two, the Anglo-American relationship had been asymmetrical: America mattered far more to the British than Britain did to the United States. 'An enduring alliance with the United States is fundamental to our beliefs and our objectives,' Mrs Thatcher declared in 1981.[35] For President Reagan, however, ties with Britain were only one facet of his diplomacy. Despite his warm regard for Mrs Thatcher, her country was no longer a decisive force in world affairs and only one of several allies with whom he kept in close touch. The underlying question was whether Mrs Thatcher was leaving Britain too dependent on the United States and too remote from her European partners, who, collectively, might help keep the transatlantic relationship in balance. This issue came to a head in the new Cold War between America and Russia.

Like Margaret Thatcher, Ronald Reagan came into office determined to restore his country's power and prestige after what he considered the drift of the 1970s. He quickly reinstated the MX missile and the B-1 bomber, both suspended by Carter, and promised substantial funds for the US navy to help it face the expanded Soviet fleet. The President took a much harder line than Carter on arms control. 'So far détente's been a one-way street that the Soviet Union has used to pursue its own aims,' the President observed in January 1981.[36] He condemned the SALT treaties concluded in the 1970s and showed no hurry to get back to the negotiating table until American defences were stronger. Meanwhile he denounced the Soviet Union in language not heard from the White House since the depths of the

Cold War. 'The Soviet Union underlies all the unrest that is going on,' he claimed in 1980. 'If they weren't engaged in this game of dominoes, there wouldn't be any hot spots in the world.'[37]

In 1981 the President's anti-Soviet rhetoric helped get his defence budget through Congress, but it aroused alarm at home and abroad. In the United States anti-nuclear groups proliferated, demanding a freeze on the weapons systems of both sides, and an estimated half-million people attended a rally in Central Park, New York, in June 1982. In western Europe there was a similar grass-roots revolt against government policies. In the détente of the 1970s the European allies had been fearful that the USA would leave them defenceless. The December 1979 decision to deploy Cruise and Pershing missiles had been NATO's answer. From 1982 European public opinion woke up to what had happened, just at the time when Reagan's Cold War rhetoric suggested that the United States had no interest in arms control negotiations – the other part of the 'dual-track' decision in December 1979. Anti-nuclear protests spread across western Europe.

"Farewell, Sir Ronald, and jolly good luck on the crusade!"

Off on the Holy War against the communists. JAK in *The Standard*, 10 June 1982.

In Britain, the decisions to deploy Cruise and buy Trident revived the Campaign for Nuclear Disarmament (CND), which had lain dormant since the 1960s. At the American base of Greenham Common, one of the sites for Cruise missiles, a permanent camp of women protesters was established. Nuclear weapons were not the only issue. There was also intense anti-American feeling, fostered by Britain's growing inferiority complex towards the USA and by the doubts about American reliability. Even supporters of Cruise were critical of the government's decision, on grounds of cost, not to install a 'dual-key' mechanism, like that on the Thor missiles of twenty years before. This, critics argued, would have been an insurance against a trigger-happy US President. Instead the government reaffirmed the old Churchill–Truman 'joint decision' agreement of 1952, insisting that this was a sufficient safeguard for British interests. The government's unspoken anxiety, reflected in its desire for Trident, was that America might renege on its commitments. Many of the British public feared that 'Rambo' Reagan was all too ready to honour those commitments – and blow Europe to pieces in the process.

In the British election of 1983 the Labour Party campaigned for a non-nuclear Britain – stripped of US bases and of her own nuclear force. It also repudiated NATO's 'dual-track' decision of 1979, being, in the words of its leader, Michael Foot, 'absolutely opposed to . . . the deployment of cruise missiles'.[38] Labour insisted that these would be matters for negotiation and that de-nuclearisation would help pay for a stronger British conventional role in NATO. But in Washington, recalls Richard Perle, then Assistant Secretary of Defense, 'no one believed that it was the intention of the Labour party to increase defence spending on conventional forces'. And 'no one could see a way that Europe could be defended only with conventional forces, even at greatly increased levels, which were unlikely, and therefore you had a major party, in . . . perhaps the key country of the alliance, off on an excursion that led to no coherent Western strategy'.[39] General Bernard Rogers, the American Supreme Commander of NATO's forces in Europe at this time, anticipated a U-turn if Labour took office, as had happened over Polaris in 1964. But he claims that if the non-nuclear policy had been implemented 'the United States would have withdrawn its forces completely from Western Europe . . . it would have unravelled the Alliance'.[40]

Both Perle and Rogers, like Mrs Thatcher, believed that a non-nuclear defence of Europe was impossible. Despite its economic resurgence, western Europe remained incapable of defending itself. That was not true, of course, in the crude sense sometimes expressed in the United States, where there was mounting public irritation at European 'free-riding'. The western Europeans *did* contribute substantially to their own security – providing between eighty and ninety per cent of NATO's manpower and conventional equipment. But, insists General Rogers, 'the real world was and is that NATO's conventional forces have always been out of balance with those of the Warsaw Pact, even for an alliance whose mission . . . is deterrence . . . Within days after a conventional attack by the Soviet Union,' Rogers argues, he would have had 'no option but to request the release of nuclear weapons, and that would come in less than two weeks.'[41] The only nuclear deterrent of sufficient size was American: the small nuclear forces of Britain and France were inadequate by themselves.

If the western Europeans desired a greater say in their own security, they had two options. Either they had to develop their own nuclear force, as the Foreign Office had urged dramatically in 1957 after Suez, or they had to make non-nuclear defence a real possibility by vastly increasing the size and sophistication of their conventional forces. Each course would require higher defence spending and far greater political unity than the western Europeans had shown to date. Without such a change of policy, they were left impotently waiting for the latest swings of US policy – alternately fearing desertion or domination, American isolationism or renewed Cold War.

By the summer of 1983 the Cruise and Pershing furore was abating. Mrs Thatcher's re-election in Britain and the victory of Helmut Kohl's Christian Democrats in West Germany ensured that the weapons were deployed. But then a new American initiative left its allies wrong-footed once again, and posed a fundamental challenge to the theory of extended deterrence upon which NATO strategy rested.

In March 1983 the President outlined the idea of a space-based defensive shield against nuclear missiles – the so-called Strategic Defense Initiative (SDI), popularly known as 'Star Wars'. This would marshal the latest laser technology to destroy nuclear missiles in space before they reached their targets. Instead of protecting America by threatening to obliterate Russia – the strategy of deterrence – the President was proposing a defence against Soviet missiles, which, he said, would eventually 'render these nuclear weapons impotent and obsolete'.[42] He even suggested that the technology might be shared with the Soviet Union. The Administration quickly mounted an advertising campaign about an astrodome defence under which American children could sleep soundly at night.

SDI proved a shrewd tactic for undercutting the American 'freeze' campaigners: the President was presenting himself as more peace-loving than them because he wanted total disarmament and not just a halt to the arms race. Reagan himself believed passionately in the idea of complete defence, but a majority of American scientists did not take it seriously. Two-thirds considered it 'improbable' or 'very unlikely' that SDI could be comprehensive enough to defend American cities from Soviet attack.[43] Many defence experts believed that deterrence was more sensible, because neither side dared attack and risk the other unleashing nuclear retaliation. If, they argued, America felt secure and Russia did not, a dangerous instability would have been introduced.

Few Pentagon officials believed in the President's vision of total defence. They saw SDI mainly as a way of protecting America's own offensive missiles: 'the defense of America's capacity to retaliate', in the words of Richard Perle.[44] For them the 'astrodome' imagery was largely public relations – an effective way to get money from a tight-fisted Congress for protracted and costly research into new generations of weapons. This work on lasers, optics, satellites and computers might well have valuable commercial spinoffs. For America's high-tech industries, dependent on Federal Government funds for research and development, SDI therefore seemed an ideal successor to the lucrative Apollo moon programme of the 1960s. Senator William Proxmire remarked that big corporations like Boeing, Rockwell and Lockheed 'look at SDI as an insurance policy that will maintain their prosperity for the next two decades'.[45]

Though shrewd politics for the Reagan Administration, SDI had little attraction for western Europe. If the President were right, the United States could become totally secure. This risked 'decoupling' America from Europe, no longer treating the defence of America and the defence of western Europe as indivisible. Europe might then be threatened by Soviet conventional forces and short-range nuclear missiles without America stepping in. Alternatively, if SDI only resulted, as the Pentagon expected, in America's anti-missile defences being strengthened, the arms race might spiral, with Russia increasing its nuclear arsenal and trying to match America in space-based defences. This could breach the 1972 Anti-Ballistic Missile Treaty, one of the main guarantees of mutual assured destruction, on which deterrence rested. Equally alarming for Europe were the commercial implications of SDI. Persuaded by the President's vision, Congress began to allocate billions of dollars to research. If the United States alone developed the programme it might open up a new Atlantic technological divide and start a brain drain far worse than that of the 1960s.

Mrs Thatcher's response demonstrated again her faith in the Anglo-American relationship. Publicly she welcomed SDI as a prudent hedge against similar Soviet research, but in private she tried to influence the direction of the project to protect British interests. On 22 December 1984, during a visit to the President at Camp David, she secured a joint statement on SDI. Against the wishes of the Pentagon, both leaders pledged that any attempt to move from SDI research to the deployment of new systems 'would, in view of treaty obligations, have to be a matter for negotiation'.[46] It was the first major American statement setting the SDI programme in the context of arms control. In December 1985 Britain became the first European state formally to join the SDI project. British support gave the Reagan Administration useful leverage in getting money out of Congress, while the Thatcher Government hoped to be rewarded with a substantial slice of the high-tech work.

Mrs Thatcher's approach to SDI was a classic example of the British conception of the special relationship – trying to influence America discreetly in private rather than carping noisily in public. It was the opposite approach to that of the French Government, which in 1983 had publicly questioned the American project and proposed a rival European scheme, Eureka. Britain eventually did participate in Eureka, but its commitment to SDI, and similar support from West Germany, undermined whatever chance the French project had of becoming the focus for a major European high-tech initiative. Whether Mrs Thatcher's approach was more prudent is unclear. The Pentagon had never liked the Camp David guidelines and its efforts to accelerate the SDI programme were frustrated not by British diplomacy but by Congress's unwillingness to vote the funds. Nor did Britain gain the substantial commercial benefits for which she had hoped. By February 1987 British SDI contracts amounted to only £24 million – a far cry from the £1 billion predicted by the Ministry of Defence when Britain joined the project.[47]

In Britain the Europe versus America debate was given a vivid focus by the Westland affair. At the end of 1985 Westland, Britain's only helicopter firm, was on the verge of collapse. Its continental rivals were unwilling to come to the rescue, until an American competitor, the multinational United Technologies which owned Sikorsky helicopters, put forward a bid. Britain's Minister of Defence, Michael Heseltine, was particularly concerned. He had helped cement Britain's new American connections, implementing the Cruise deployment and negotiating the SDI collaboration. But he had long believed in the need for European co-operation in defence projects, to counterbalance American technological dominance, and in 1985 he played a major part in securing five-nation agreement to build a European fighter aircraft. His anxieties about the American offer were shared by other senior Cabinet ministers, including Norman Tebbit, the Prime Minister's closest adviser. With Heseltine's encouragement, a European bid for Westland was hastily put together by a Franco-Italian-British consortium.

But the Westland Board supported Sikorsky and Mrs Thatcher agreed. Asked to choose, as she saw it, between a dynamic US enterprise and an eleventh-hour salvage operation by a collection of Continentals, she had no doubts. Her Cabinet fell into line, except for Michael Heseltine. A bitter political row followed, with the policy differences reinforced by a clash of strong personalities. Heseltine refused to accept her judgement and backed the European offer with flamboyant defiance, using all his skills with the media. She, equally determinedly, tried to undermine his arguments and silence his public opposition, employing every technique at the disposal of a Prime Minister. 'We'll take care of Heseltine,' she is reported to have told Westland.[48] The Defence Secretary was forced to resign and the Sikorsky offer was eventually accepted.

The most dramatic example of Mrs Thatcher's identification with America rather than Europe came later in 1986. Both President and Prime Minister had vigorously denounced international terrorism, particularly when connected with the Palestinian question, and Reagan had repeatedly identified the Libyan leader, Muammar el-Qaddafi, as its ultimate source. Just after Christmas 1985 sixteen passengers were killed in Palestinian terrorist attacks on Rome and Vienna airports. On 2 April 1986 four died when a bomb exploded on a TWA flight from Rome to Athens, and on 5 April another explosion wrecked a discotheque in West Berlin frequented by American servicemen and their families. One American died and sixty were injured.

Qaddafi denied involvement in all these atrocities but Reagan claimed that evidence of Libyan complicity was irrefutable. Over the previous few months he had imposed economic sanctions on Libya, moved the US Sixth Fleet close to the Libyan coast, and fed the media with diatribes against Qaddafi. After the April bombings the Administration was under mounting domestic pressure to take military action. The country was incensed at these atrocities and its 'can-do' spirit had also been buffeted by the loss of the space shuttle Challenger a few weeks before. The Administration prepared plans for air strikes against targets in Libya, and European leaders were secretly asked for support.

Only three months earlier, on 10 January 1986, Mrs Thatcher had spoken out emphatically against American talk of military action against Libya. 'I must warn you that I do not believe in retaliatory strikes that are against international law,' she told American journalists in London. A British policewoman had been killed by shots from the Libyan Embassy in London and the country had suffered over 2,000 deaths as a result of IRA terrorism, but, she said, there had never been any question of Britain making 'retaliatory strikes' or going in 'hot pursuit'. 'Once you start to go across borders,' she said, 'then I do not see an end to it. And I uphold international law very firmly.'[49]

Three months later Mrs Thatcher took a different line. On the night of 14–15 April she gave the US air force permission to use F-111s from its British bases to attack Tripoli. Simultaneously the US navy's A-6 attack aircraft from the nearby Sixth Fleet bombed Benghazi. American opinion overwhelmingly supported the President and Mrs Thatcher was applauded by the American media as America's only loyal European ally. France, who had refused America the use of its air space, was roundly condemned, as was the European Community, which had spent days arguing about sanctions when America wanted immediate action.

John Hughes, Press and Information Officer at the British Embassy in Washington, was overwhelmed by the American reaction. On the morning after the raid 'we received so many telephone calls that our switchboard was sort of jammed . . . In my time at the Embassy, and I think in most people's time at the Embassy, we've never seen quite anything like it . . . Overall, not just Washington but our Consulates right across the country, we had in the week after the Libyan bombing raid four thousand telephone calls, about ninety-eight per cent of which were favourable to the action taken by the British Government.' Some of those phoning added, 'I'll be calling your French colleague immediately after this telephone call and delivering a rather different message.'[50]

The official reason given in America and Britain for the use of the F-111s was that their superior accuracy was essential for the success of the raid. Some Pentagon sources were soon admitting, however, that President Reagan mainly wanted political support in Europe.[51] Mrs Thatcher justified her decision in the House of Commons in language rather different from that she had used in January: 'The United States has hundreds of thousands of forces in Europe to defend the liberty of Europe. In that capacity they have been subject to terrorist attack. It was inconceivable to me that we should refuse United States aircraft and pilots the opportunity to defend their people.'[52] As compelling, perhaps, was the obligation to repay President Reagan for his support over the Falklands, so important to her government four years before, particularly since he had felt let down by her over Grenada.

But Mrs Thatcher knew she would pay a price at home for her loyalty to the President. General Vernon Walters was sent to brief her about the operation at 10 Downing Street. At the end of their meeting he said: 'You know, Prime Minister, my normal job is United States representative to the United Nations, and when I go back there I'm going into the eye of the storm.' Mrs Thatcher replied: 'General, when I go back to the British electorate I'm going into the eye of the storm.'[53]

Mrs Thatcher was right. Opinion polls suggested that over two-thirds of the public condemned her involvement in the raid. Labour leader Neil Kinnock called the Prime Minister 'supine in her support for the American President', asserting 'she has not acted in the interests of Britain'.[54] Her supporters noted that, after the raids, little more was heard from Qaddafi, but opponents were able to add to her embarrassment when it was revealed at the end of 1986 that, despite his calls for a tough line on terrorism, the President had agreed to covert arms sales to Iran in an attempt to effect the release of American hostages held by pro-Iranian Arab terrorists in the Lebanon. Ronald Reagan seemed to be operating a double standard on terrorism: negotiating with some, bombing others. So, critics asked, why should Britain be dragged in?

Mrs Thatcher's reaction in 1986 was in striking contrast to that of Edward Heath in 1973. Faced with a similar request from President Nixon to use British bases during the Yom Kippur War, the Heath Government had demurred. It was judged to be an operation outside the NATO area and at odds with British policy. In 1986 Mrs Thatcher could also have refused the American request. But to have done so, she said, would have been inconceivable. Her commitment to the American alliance, her regard for the President and her debts to him over the Falklands were too strong. The two crises dramatised the differences between a Prime Minister whose instincts were European and one who was an Atlanticist.

Behind the scenes in Whitehall 'Europeanist' ideas were gaining favour by 1987. Even the Treasury had deserted Mrs Thatcher in her rearguard action against Britain's joining the European Monetary System. Civil servants in the Foreign Office and Ministry of Defence

Special relationship or Her Master's Voice? *Private Eye* after the Libyan raid.

were strengthening political and military links with France and West Germany and even looking ahead to the possibility of a joint Anglo-French nuclear deterrent in the twenty-first century, when Trident was finished. In public Foreign Secretary Sir Geoffrey Howe noted the pressures on the US defence budget and the shift in American interests towards the Pacific among 'trends in American thinking which might diminish our security – perhaps not today or tomorrow, but possibly in the longer term' and suggested 'a greater responsibility on the part of Europeans for the defence of Western Europe'.[55]

But the problem for those such as Germany's Helmut Schmidt who criticised Mrs Thatcher for failing to support European initiatives was that 'Europe' was still being created. Prone to bickering and indecision, unable to reform even its own wasteful agricultural policy, the European Community showed little capacity to organise its own defence. As Schmidt himself admitted, to expect Mrs Thatcher to use her rapport with President Reagan to advance European political and security interests 'would presuppose that the Europeans had a common analysis of their interests in these fields which obviously they lack right now'.[56]

Yet the problems of transatlantic relations would not go away. In the early 1980s, when Margaret Thatcher and Ronald Reagan were new to office, the world seemed to be returning to the patterns of the 1940s and 1950s – with two hostile superpowers dominating the stage and Britain throwing in her lot with America rather than Europe. By 1987 it was clear that, although both leaders had restored their countries' pride and established a remarkable personal alliance, they had not answered the fundamental questions about the future which had been raised in the early 1970s during the era of détente and Britain's entry into Europe.

By the mid-1980s a second phase of détente was developing. Having walked out of arms control negotiations at the end of 1983, the Russians started talking again two years later. Part of the reason was a new, energetic leader, Mikhail Gorbachev, who was anxious to reduce the defence burden on the inefficient Russian economy. President Reagan was also keen for an agreement before he left office. And he and Mrs Thatcher could also plausibly point to the Cruise and Pershing deployment and to the threat of SDI in forcing the Soviets back to the negotiating table. In November 1985 Reagan and Gorbachev were chatting like old friends around the fireside in Geneva.

The momentum of arms control faltered a year later at Reykjavik when Soviet opposition to Reagan's SDI programme proved a major obstacle to agreement. Government officials in America and Europe were alarmed at the President's apparently invincible belief that the elimination of nuclear weapons was an achievable goal, which would ensure a safer world. Mrs Thatcher invited herself to the United States after Reykjavik to try to modify the President's stance, much as she had done over SDI two years before. Their statement 'confirmed that NATO's strategy . . . would continue to require effective nuclear deterrents' and that 'reductions in nuclear weapons would increase the importance of eliminating conventional disparities'. And, whatever was agreed between the superpowers on strategic arms limitation, the President 'confirmed his full support for the arrangements made to modernise Britain's independent nuclear deterrent with Trident'.[57]

Richard Perle, one of Reagan's principal arms negotiators at Reykjavik, was relieved that, as before, Mrs Thatcher was prepared to challenge the President's non-nuclear creed. 'Some of us, learning that Mrs Thatcher was coming, were rather pleased at the prospect that some of the more intemperate and visionary views of the President might be modified, as indeed they were. So many of us regarded her as a voice of calm reason, and a much needed one, in particular on this issue of a world without nuclear weapons, which is dangerous nonsense. The President gives expression to it too frequently, but never in close proximity with a visit from Mrs Thatcher. So we get a brief respite from that rubbish when she comes.'[58]

Although SDI destroyed the Reykjavik summit, it did not prove an insuperable barrier to arms control. Quiet negotiation behind the scenes laid the ground for further progress. By the end of 1987 Gorbachev had visited the United States and an agreement had been reached on eliminating from Europe all intermediate-range missiles, including Cruise, Pershings and the Russian SS–20s. Prospects for a strategic arms treaty between the superpowers seemed good, though, as always, the attitude of the US Senate could not be taken for granted.

But the détente of the late 1980s raised the same problems as the first era of détente fifteen years before. NATO had introduced the intermediate-range missiles at Europe's request, responding to fears, particularly in West Germany, that, as America came to terms with Russia, Europe would be left vulnerable against Soviet conventional strength. Once the missiles were removed, the same problem would re-emerge. General Bernard Rogers, recently retired as NATO's Supreme Commander and a vigorous critic of the INF agreement, believes that 'what we're doing is making Western Europe safe for conventional war again. And that's exactly what the Soviets want.'[59]

So, although European leaders publicly welcomed the INF accord between America and Russia, behind the scenes there was much anxiety about NATO's European strategy for the future. Should Europe strengthen its own nuclear forces or develop a more effective conventional defence? How long could it safely shelter under the American umbrella?

The second phase of détente, like the first, also coincided with new doubts about America's ability to bear all the global burdens it had accumulated since World War Two. No longer supreme economically, the United States was still trying in the 1980s to persuade Japan and Germany to assume more responsibility for the health of the world economy, much as Britain had tried, in vain, to influence American policy in the 1920s and 1930s. And by 1987 the budget deficit, reduced since 1986 but still running at over $150 billion, had finally sparked off an economic crisis at home as Americans lost confidence in the President's powers of leadership. On Black Monday, 19 October, share values on the Dow Jones Industrial Average dropped by twenty-three per cent, nearly twice the size of the record one-day fall during the Great Crash of 1929. As further falls followed and shock waves spread around the financial markets of the world, Congress and President finally started to address the budget crisis, talking seriously about cutting spending and, against all Ronald Reagan's instincts, of increasing taxes. But, whatever curbs were imposed, the deficit would not vanish overnight and America's belt-tightening, as in the early 1970s, raised the question of why the USA was still undertaking so many overseas commitments while its economic rivals – Japan, Germany and western Europe as a whole – got away with so little defence spending in proportion to their now substantial wealth. There was renewed talk of reducing America's 300,000 troops in Europe.

Ronald Reagan and Margaret Thatcher had effected remarkable changes in the character of their countries and in their national self-esteem. But the underlying problems they had inherited still remained. Was the United States contracting as a superpower? How long would it feel able to honour its nuclear and conventional commitments to Europe? Was Britain still wise to rely so heavily on the United States? Should she be seeking to build a stronger Europe, capable of doing more for its own defence, or was western Europe incapable of managing its own affairs without American direction? Despite the upheavals of the seventies and eighties the questions for the future remained essentially the same and the answers equally elusive.

Conclusion

The rise of the United States to become the world's leading superpower was predictable. Once the country had won its independence, had spread west to the Pacific and had sealed its unity in the blood of civil war, its pre-eminence was assured. Size, population and abundant resources guaranteed America's supremacy. Britain's rapid decline was less easy to predict. A small European island, her world power depended on control of her empire, trade and investments. No one at the beginning of this century expected her to retain that position indefinitely, but few anticipated how quickly her grip on the world would slacken.

Two great wars accelerated this process of rise and decline. Britain faced a variety of foes, eager to take a share of her power and prosperity, and against Germany, twice in a quarter-century, she had to fight for her empire and for her very survival. From both of these wars she emerged on the winning side. But she lost a sixth of her wealth in World War One and a quarter of what remained in World War Two. The United States, on the other hand, emerged from the first as a creditor nation rather than a debtor and from the second as the producer of half the world's manufactured goods.

Yet America had not intended to embroil itself in either of these conflicts, hoping at the outset of each to remain insulated from European quarrels. The connections with Britain – economic, ideological and cultural – helped make this impossible, drawing the United States into commitments it would not otherwise have undertaken. And the power that accrued to America in the course of World War Two ruled out a return to isolationism, however desirable this might have seemed to some. In the 1940s America's new strength could have been mainly asserted in the Pacific, against Japan, but once again the British connection helped draw it into Europe, culminating in the North Atlantic Treaty of 1949.

These involvements were not simply attributable to ties of sentiment, language and common heritage, important though they were for some Americans. There was no automatic Anglo-Saxon alliance.

The United States had established its independence at Britain's expense, defining many of its values in antithesis to those of the monarchical, aristocratic, imperialist mother country. It remained suspicious of Britain's motives even in the period of their greatest intimacy during World War Two, and tried to break apart Britain's commercial and financial empire. Britain never willingly relinquished power or influence, but her position was so exposed, her resources so inadequate, that she had no choice but to treat the least menacing of her foes as a potential friend.

In these great crises of the twentieth century Britain had to accept whatever help the Americans were willing to offer, on the terms they proposed. If that meant trading the right to build bases on Caribbean islands for some old destroyers, or sacrificing Imperial Preference for financial aid, so be it. From the 1940s onwards Britain was living beyond her means, while still desperately trying to remain a great power. She stayed at the top table only by virtue of American assistance, ranging from dollar loans to the provision of nuclear missiles.

Although this was a hard-headed relationship, it was also remarkably close, particularly between 1941 and 1945. No modern allies have fused their war efforts so successfully. The ties of language and culture, though they could not eliminate friction, at least acted as emollients, allowing deep personal friendships to develop whose importance lasted well after 1945. And in both world wars the liberal values that the two countries shared seemed more important than the different interpretations sometimes put on them. Personal freedom, private property, government under the law – these were liberties established long before in Britain, inherited by America, and then championed by both countries in the twentieth century against autocrats, fascists and communists alike.

This relationship with the United States has inevitably complicated Britain's recent adjustment to her destiny as a middle-ranking European power. The contrast with France is striking. After 1945 the French faced many of the same problems as the British – imperial decline, industrial stagnation, the search for a European identity. Both relied on America for economic and military help. Yet, despite sheltering under the Eagle's wing, modern France developed much more self-consciously than Britain in opposition to the United States and things American. Under de Gaulle the French created a truly independent nuclear deterrent, not one using missiles bought from and serviced by the United States. They pulled out of an alliance that they deemed too heavily dominated by America, while working energetically to promote a Franco-German axis that is now the linchpin of the European Community. They also struggled to preserve the integrity of their culture, purging their language of Americanisms and trying to promote a francophone community around the world.

The divergent experiences of France and Britain in World War Two are part of the explanation for the different courses they have taken after 1945. In the war France was humiliated and occupied, while Britain emerged victorious in alliance with the Americans and her 'kin across the seas'. These seemed her natural allies for a generation. But at a deeper level the British find it hard to identify with the continent of Europe. Everything that makes the transatlantic relationship seem natural makes links with the Continent seem unnatural. Britain and America share the same tongue, and, because of their combined influence around the world, English has become the premier international language of the twentieth century – the lingua franca of science, technology and culture, used by perhaps a fifth of the world's population as their first or second tongue. Although Britain is particularly affected, language and related cultural differences are barriers between all the nations of western Europe, reinforced by lingering animosities from so many centuries of war. Scorn for a disunited European Community has led many, including Mrs Thatcher, to believe that Britain's interests are best served by maintaining her ties with the United States at almost any cost.

But, to survive, a relationship has to be two-way. In the past Britain mattered to America as its front line of defence, its entry-point to the continent of Europe and its ally in the containment of communism around the world. But Britain's power has waned, America's interests are shifting, and the relationship has become less important to the United States. America, reflecting its changing economic interests and ethnic balance, is again concentrating attention on Japan and the Pacific basin rather than Europe. Its transatlantic commitment after World War Two sprang directly from its hostility to the Soviet Union. The decision to defend western Europe against Russia was taken to ensure American, not European, security, for fear that the resources of one of the most important economic regions of the world would fall under Soviet control or influence. Out of it have come NATO, for ever in crisis but still the most durable peacetime alliance in modern history, and a tight bond with Britain, which serves as a vital base for air, submarine and missile defence, as well as for sophisticated intelligence gathering.

This role of 'unsinkable' aircraft carrier, which Britain has played for so long, could change if the process of détente with the Soviet Union continues and America's budget and trade crises are not solved.

Brits out of Ireland: pro-IRA demonstration in America (July 1983).

Yanks out of Britain: British demonstration against the raid on Libya (April 1986).

Hands across the Ocean: simultaneous rock concerts in Britain and America, linked by television, raise money for Ethiopian famine relief.

Mixed up together: American football comes to London's Hyde Park.

In future strategic arms negotiations Britain's American-made nuclear deterrent, at present guaranteed by both the British and US Governments, may be in jeopardy. Demands from American Congressmen and public opinion for withdrawal of the 300,000 troops in Europe could lead to major reductions and new doubts about the reliability of the American guarantee of European security. This would force western Europe into taking more responsibility for its own defence – by strengthening conventional forces, developing its own nuclear capability, or negotiating its own arms reduction agreements with the Soviet Union and eastern Europe.

None of this may happen – pundits have written NATO's obituary many times before – but it would be short-sighted to assume that the transatlantic alliance is the same now as it was in the 1940s. It would also be unwise to assume that the relationship between Britain and America will continue indefinitely in its present form. Close personal friendships alone will not insulate traditional policies against changing international realities. In the 1980s the rapport between Ronald Reagan and Margaret Thatcher has been as close as any in Anglo-American history, but it cannot conceal the signs, apparent since the early 1970s, that the interests of the two countries are growing further apart and the imbalance in their power is becoming more pronounced.

Today America is painfully adapting to the loss of its economic supremacy and, at the same time, establishing a more structured if still adversarial relationship with the Soviet Union as the Cold War appears to thaw. Britain is slowly facing up to the loss of her world power and to her reversion after three centuries to a largely European role. If America reduces its foreign burdens and tilts towards the Pacific, becoming less willing to help defend Europe and more aggressive in protecting its struggling economy, then Britain's future, some politicians argue, may lie in closer relations with her European partners. It will not be easy to turn a fractious, wasteful Economic Community into a united political force, let alone an alliance largely responsible for its own security. But in the twenty-first century the links with continental Europe may come to seem as appropriate to new generations of Britons as those with the United States seemed to Britain's leaders after World War Two.

Britain will always have a special relationship with the United States. The bonds of history, culture and language are too strong for it to be otherwise, and they have been strengthened in recent years by the impact of tourism and television. But in the past cultural values have pulled in the same direction as national interest, tying Britain and America in a double bond. In the future, Britain's feeling of cultural affinity with America may have to be balanced against a growing sense of common political and economic interest with the rest of Europe. These need not be incompatible. The United States has itself often expressed the hope that Britain would play a significant part in building a more united Europe. Greater western European co-operation, particularly in defence, could relieve America of some of its burdens. America's latest economic problems and the second phase of détente confirm trends apparent since the early 1970s and will give new impetus to the difficult search for greater European unity. But that lies in the future – apparently easier for the United States to confront than for Britain, a country accustomed to celebrating the triumphs of its past. For the generation of Britons who have lived through World War Two and the Cold War, it is not surprising that the Atlantic Ocean often seems narrower and less forbidding than the English Channel.

Notes and Further Reading

This book draws on the many scholarly studies of Anglo-American relations published in recent years, on original research in archives on both sides of the Atlantic and on interviews conducted for the BBC Television series of the same title. These notes give sources for quotations and important statistics, together with guidance for further reading. We hope this will help to make the book a survey that will prove of long-term use to students of the relationship.

Introduction

1 Dimbleby, conversation in St Louis, Missouri.
2 Winston S. Churchill, *The Second World War* (6 vols, London, Cassell, 1948-54), vol. III, p. 609.

BACKGROUND READING

1) *General surveys*

H. C. Allen, *Great Britain and the United States, 1783-1952* (London: Odhams, 1954). Still the best overview, but it does not cover recent events and has proved too sanguine about Britain's continuing power and the harmony of her relationship with the USA.

H. G. Nicholas, *The United States and Britain* (Chicago: University of Chicago Press, 1975). Readable and more up-to-date but brief.

David Frost and Michael Shea, *The Rich Tide: Men, Women, Ideas and their Transatlantic Impact* (London: Collins, 1986). The stories of people who shaped the economic, cultural and social life of the two countries, particularly in the eighteenth and nineteenth centuries.

2) *Surveys of the twentieth century*

Basil Collier, *The Lion and the Eagle: British and Anglo-American Strategy, 1900-1950* (London: Macdonald, 1972). The scope is indicated by the subtitle.

Bruce M. Russett, *Community and Contention: Britain and America in the Twentieth Century* (Cambridge, Mass.: MIT Press, 1963). A distinctive analysis of cultural and economic relations by a political scientist, seeking to determine the 'mutual responsiveness' of the two societies.

D. Cameron Watt, *Succeeding John Bull: America in Britain's Place, 1900-1975 – A Study of the Anglo-American Relationship and World Politics in the Context of British and American Foreign-Policy-Making in the Twentieth Century* (Cambridge: Cambridge University Press, 1984). A work of enormous scholarship, synthesising virtually all the recent monographs, but primarily a study of foreign-policy élites and not a history of Anglo-American relations as a whole.

3) *General interpretations of the 'special relationship'*

Max Beloff, 'The Special Relationship: An Anglo-American Myth', in Martin Gilbert, ed., *A Century of Conflict, 1850-1950: Essays for A. J. P. Taylor* (London: Hamish Hamilton, 1966), pp. 151-71. Sees it as a myth developed by the British élite to help cope with the decline of British power.

A. E. Campbell, 'The United States and Great Britain: Uneasy Allies', in John Braeman, Robert H. Bremner and David Brody, eds, *Twentieth-Century American Foreign Policy* (Columbus, Ohio: Ohio State University Press, 1971), pp. 471-501. A relationship founded on a common interest in the maintenance of peace, which lasted as long as Britain remained a great power.

Coral Bell, 'The "Special Relationship"', in Michael Leifer, ed., *Constraints and Adjustments in British Foreign Policy* (London: George Allen and Unwin, 1972), pp. 103-19. Stressing the capacity to discern common interests.

Alastair Buchan, 'Mothers and Daughters (or Greeks and Romans)', *Foreign Affairs*, vol. 54 (1976), pp. 645-69. A superb survey of the previous two hundred years and the shifting balance of the relationship.

Chapter 1 The Struggle for Independence, *c.* 1620–1865

1. William Bradford, *Of Plymouth Plantation, 1620–1647*, ed. Samuel E. Morison (New York: The Modern Library, 1952), quotations respectively from pp. 76, 77 and 62. This account also draws on the annotated passenger list in the older two-volume edition of Bradford's *History* (New York: Russell and Russell, 1912), pp. 399–412 and George D. Langdon, *Pilgrim Colony: A History of New Plymouth, 1620–1691* (New Haven: Yale University Press, 1966), esp. chs 1–2.
2. Michael Heale, *The Making of American Politics, 1750–1850* (London: Longman, 1977), p. 23.
3. John Kenyon, *The History Men: The Historical Profession in England since the Renaissance* (London: Weidenfeld and Nicolson, 1983), pp. 51–2.
4. James A. Henretta, *The Evolution of American Society, 1700–1815* (Lexington, Mass.: D.C. Heath, 1973), p. 9.
5. Hamilton (1774) in Bernard Bailyn, ed., *Pamphlets of the American Revolution*, vol. I (Cambridge, Mass.: Harvard University Press, 1965), p. 74.
6. J. R. Pole, ed., *The Revolution in America, 1754–1788: Documents and Commentaries* (London: Macmillan, 1970), pp. 36–9.
7. Madison's message to Congress, 1 June 1812, in James D. Richardson, ed., *A Compilation of the Messages and Papers of the Presidents, 1789–1897* (10 vols, Washington: Government Printing Office, 1896–1899), vol. I, p. 504.
8. Washington's Farewell Address, 17 Sept. 1796, in Richardson, ed., *Messages and Papers of the Presidents*, vol. I, pp. 222–3.
9. Jefferson's Inaugural Address, 4 March 1801, in Richardson, ed., *Messages and Papers of the Presidents*, vol. I, p. 323.
10. Jefferson to Monroe, 24 Oct. 1823, in Dexter Perkins, *The Monroe Doctrine, 1823–1826* (Cambridge, Mass.: Harvard University Press, 1927), p. 91.
11. Adams in Cabinet, 7 Nov. 1823 – Ernest R. May, *The Making of the Monroe Doctrine* (Cambridge, Mass.: Harvard University Press, 1975), p. 199.

12. Monroe's Annual Message, 2 Dec. 1823, in Richardson, ed., *Messages and Papers of the Presidents*, vol. II, pp. 218–19.
13. Canning's speech of 12 Dec. 1826, in Harold Temperley, *The Foreign Policy of Canning, 1822–1827: England, the Neo-Holy Alliance and the New World* (London: Frank Cass, 1966 ed.), p. 154.
14. Jefferson to Abigail Adams, 21 June 1785, in Lester J. Cappon, ed., *The Adams–Jefferson Letters* (2 vols, Chapel Hill: University of North Carolina Press, 1959), vol. I, pp. 33–4.
15. Noah Webster, *Dissertations on the English Language* (Boston: Isaiah Thomas, 1789), pp. 20, 22–3.
16. Sydney Smith in *Edinburgh Review*, vol. 65 (Jan. 1820), pp. 79–80.
17. Frances Trollope, *Domestic Manners of the Americans* (1832), ed. Richard Mullen (Oxford: Oxford University Press, 1984), p. 314.
18. Alexis de Tocqueville, *Democracy in America*, ed. J. P. Mayer (New York: Anchor Books, 1969), p. 9.
19. Thomas Colley Grattan (1859), in Walter Allen, ed., *Transatlantic Crossing: American Visitors to Britain and British Visitors to America in the Nineteenth Century* (London: Heinemann, 1971), p. 270.
20. J. S. Mill in *Edinburgh Review*, vol. 72 (Oct. 1840), p. 40.
21. The Chartist newspaper, *Weekly Chronicle*, 12 March 1837, in G. D. Lillibridge, *Beacon of Liberty: The Impact of American Democracy upon Great Britain, 1830–1870* (Philadelphia: University of Pennsylvania Press, 1954), p. 31.
22. Thomas Hamilton to Dugald Bannatyne, 15 Feb. 1831, in Hamilton's *Men and Manners in America* (1843 ed.), quoted in David P. Crook, *American Democracy in English Politics, 1815–1850* (Oxford: Clarendon Press, 1965), p. 127.
23. *Hansard's Parliamentary Debates*, 3rd series, vol. 183, columns 103–4, 27 April 1866.
24. John L. O'Sullivan, New York *Morning News*, 27 Dec. 1845, in Albert K. Weinberg, *Manifest Destiny: A Study of Nationalist Expansionism in American History* (Baltimore: Johns Hopkins Press, 1935), p. 145.
25. 1839 'Maine Battle Song' quoted in Thomas G. Paterson, J. Garry Clifford and Kenneth J. Hagan, *American Foreign Policy: A History to 1914* (Lexington, Mass.: D. C. Heath, 1983), p. 101.
26. de Tocqueville, *Democracy in America*, p. 413.
27. Augusta *Chronicle and Sentinel*, quoted in Michael F. Holt, *The Political Crisis of the 1850s* (New York: John Wiley, 1978), p. 241.
28. Senator James H. Hammond (South Carolina) to M. C. M. Hammond, 22 April 1860, in William R. Brock, *Conflict and Transformation: The United States, 1844–1877* (Harmondsworth: Penguin Books, 1973), p. 173.

29. Lincoln's Inaugural address, 4 March 1861, in Richardson, ed., *Messages and Papers of the Presidents*, vol. VI, p. 5.
30. Rev. William Croke Squier, in Mary Ellison, *Support for Secession: Lancashire and the American Civil War* (Chicago: University of Chicago Press, 1972), p. 38.
31. *Harper's Weekly*, 16 Nov. 1861, in Carl Sandburg, *Abraham Lincoln: The War Years* (4 vols, New York: Harcourt, Brace and Co., 1939), vol. I, p. 363.
32. According to his private secretary. See Kenneth Bourne, *Britain and the Balance of Power in North America, 1815–1908* (London: Longmans, 1967), p. 219.
33. Palmerston in House of Commons, 18 July 1862, in D. P. Crook, *The North, the South, and the Powers, 1861–1865* (New York: John Wiley, 1974), p. 216.
34. Lyons to Russell, 19 April 1864, in Charles S. Campbell, *From Revolution to Rapprochement: The United States and Great Britain, 1783–1900* (New York: John Wiley, 1974), p. 110.

BACKGROUND READING

1 General

W. A. Speck, *British America, 1607–1763* (London: British Association for American Studies, 1985) is a useful little pamphlet, comparing British and colonial societies.

R. C. Simmons, *The American Colonies: From Settlement to Independence* (London: Longman, 1976). A thorough, informed and readable survey.

David G. Allen, *In English Ways: The Movement of Societies and the Transferal of English Local Law and Custom to Massachusetts Bay in the Seventeenth Century* (Chapel Hill: University of North Carolina Press, 1981). A meticulous case study of five New England communities and their Old England antecedents.

2 Surveys of Anglo-American relations after Independence

Charles S. Campbell, *From Revolution to Rapprochement: The United States and Great Britain, 1783–1900* (New York: John Wiley, 1974). The best overview of the relationship in this period.

R. B. Mowat, *The Diplomatic Relations of Great Britain and the United States up to 1913* (London: Edward Arnold, 1925). A much older book, concentrating on diplomacy, but still useful.

Frank Thistlethwaite, *The Anglo-American Connection in the Early Nineteenth*

Century (Philadelphia: University of Pennsylvania Press, 1959). Still the best study of economic, social and cultural relations in the first half of the century.

Chapter 2 Learning to Live Together, *c*. 1865–1914

1. James Russell Lowell, 'On a Certain Condescension in Foreigners', *The Atlantic Monthly*, Jan. 1869, p. 94.
2. Lord Illingworth in 'A Woman of No Importance', *The Complete Works of Oscar Wilde* (London: Collins, 1968), p. 436.
3. Quotations from Wesley and Douglass in Frank Thistlethwaite, *The Anglo-American Connection in the Early Nineteenth Century* (Philadelphia: University of Pennsylvania Press, 1959), pp. 108–9.
4. Quoted in Merle Curti, *The American Peace Crusade, 1815–1860* (Durham, NC: Duke University Press, 1929), p. 116.
5. John Hay to Henry Adams, 7 July 1897, Hay Papers, vol. 3 (Library of Congress, Washington, DC).
6. Quoted in Paul M. Kennedy, *The Rise of the Anglo-German Antagonism, 1860–1914* (London: George Allen and Unwin, 1980), p. 467.
7. Quoted in Michael Howard, *The Continental Commitment: The Dilemma of British Defence Policy in the Era of the Two World Wars* (Harmondsworth: Pelican Books, 1974), p. 11.
8. Henry Carey, *The Way to Outdo England without Fighting Her: Letters to the Hon. Schuyler Colfax* (Philadelphia: H. C. Baird, 1865).
9. Quoted in Edward P. Crapol, *America for Americans: Economic Nationalism and Anglophobia in the late Nineteenth Century* (London: Greenwood Press, 1973), p. 4.
10. Note of 20 July 1895, in US Dept. of State, *Foreign Relations of the United States, 1895* (Washington: Government Printing Office, 1896), part I, p. 558.
11. Quoted in J. A. S. Grenville, *Lord Salisbury and Foreign Policy at the Close of the Nineteenth Century* (London: Athlone Press, 1970), p. 66.
12. Sir Julian Pauncefote to Lord Salisbury, 24 Dec. 1895, Foreign Office correspondence, FO 80/364, f. 269 (Public Record Office, London).
13. Quoted in Charles S. Campbell, *From Revolution to Rapprochement: The United States and Great Britain, 1783–1900* (New York: John Wiley, 1974), p. 183.
14. *Spectator*, 7 May 1898, quoted in A. E. Campbell, *Great Britain and the United States, 1898–1905* (London: Longmans, 1960), p. 152.
15. Annual Message, 6 Dec. 1904, in Fred L. Israel, ed., *The State of the Union Messages of the Presidents, 1790–1966* (3 vols, New York: Chelsea House/Robert Hector, 1966), vol. II, p. 2134.

16. J. L. Garvin, *The Life of Joseph Chamberlain* (3 vols, London: Macmillan, 1932–4), vol. 2, p. 334 and vol. 3, p. 302.
17. Quoted from Josiah Strong, *Our Country* (1885), in Stuart Anderson, *Race and Rapprochement: Anglo-Saxonism and Anglo-American Relations, 1895–1904* (London: Associated Universities Press, 1981), p. 34.
18. A. J. Balfour to Joseph H. Choate, 1 June 1905, Choate papers, box 11 (Library of Congress).
19. Balfour (1903) in Charles S. Campbell, *Anglo-American Understanding, 1898–1903* (Baltimore: Johns Hopkins Press, 1957), p. 299.
20. Lord Selborne, memo of 24 Feb. 1905, in Kenneth Bourne, *Britain and the Balance of Power in North America, 1815–1908* (London: Longmans, 1967), p. 381.
21. See John H. Dunning, *American Investment in British Manufacturing Industry* (London: George Allen and Unwin, 1958), esp. ch. 1.
22. T. C. Barker and Michael Robbins, *A History of London Transport*, vol. II (London: George Allen and Unwin, 1976), p. 61.
23. Joseph Chamberlain to the Duke of Devonshire, 22 Sept. 1902, in Vivian Vale, *The American Peril: Challenge to Britain on the North Atlantic, 1901–1904* (Manchester: Manchester University Press, 1984), p. 191.
24. B. W. E. Alford, *W.D. & H.O. Wills and the Development of the U.K. Tobacco Industry, 1786–1965* (London: Methuen, 1973), p. 258.
25. F. A. McKenzie, *The American Invaders* (London: Grant Richards, 1902), pp. 142–3.
26. W. T. Stead, *The Americanisation of the World* (London: Review of Reviews, 1902), p. 13.
27. W. D. Rubinstein, ed., *Wealth and the Wealthy in the Modern World* (London: Croom Helm, 1980), pp. 18–19.
28. Henry Pelling, *America and the British Left: From Bright to Bevan* (London: A. and C. Black, 1956), p. 65.
29. The standard study remains Maldwyn A. Jones, *American Immigration* (Chicago: University of Chicago Press, 1960). See also Stephan Thernstrom, ed., *Harvard Encyclopedia of American Ethnic Groups* (Cambridge, Mass.: Harvard University Press, 1980).
30. Lodge to Theodore Roosevelt, 2 Feb. 1900, Roosevelt papers, series I (Library of Congress, Washington).
31. Quotations from Hay to Henry White, 24 Sept. 1899, and Hay to J. W. Foster, 23 June 1900, in William Roscoe Thayer, *The Life and Letters of John Hay* (2 vols, London: Constable, 1915), vol. II, pp. 221, 234–5.
32. Howard K. Beale, *Theodore Roosevelt and the Rise of America to World Power* (Baltimore: Johns Hopkins Press, 1956), p. 447.
33. *The Education of Henry Adams: An Autobiography* (Boston: Houghton, Mifflin Co. ed., 1961), p. 363. (The book was written in 1905.)

34. Sir Eyre Crowe, memo of 31 July 1914, in Zara S. Steiner, *Britain and the Origins of the First World War* (London: Macmillan, 1977), p. 228.

BACKGROUND READING

See also the reading for ch. 1, especially C. S. Campbell and Mowat.

Bradford Perkins, *The Great Rapprochement: England and the United States, 1895–1914* (New York: Atheneum, 1968). This remains the basic survey of this period, concentrating on diplomacy.

A. E. Campbell, *Great Britain and the United States, 1898–1905* (London: Longmans, 1960). Case studies of British policy, with perceptive analysis of the underlying interests and ideology.

Richard H. Heindel, *The American Impact on Great Britain, 1898–1914* (Philadelphia: University of Pennsylvania Press, 1940). An old book, but full of fascinating detail on the economic and social contacts.

Chapter 3 To Fight or Not to Fight? 1914–17

1. 'An Appeal to the American People', 18 Aug. 1914, *The Papers of Woodrow Wilson*, ed. Arthur S. Link, *et al.* (Multi-volume edition, still in progress, Princeton: Princeton University Press, 1966–), vol. I, pp. 393–4.
2. Appeal, 18 Aug. 1914.
3. Arthur S. Link, *Wilson: The Struggle for Neutrality, 1914–1915* (Princeton: Princeton University Press, 1960), p. 56.
4. Link, *Wilson, 1914–15*, p. 53.
5. Appeal, 18 Aug. 1914.
6. Dimbleby, BBC 1 interview with Sonny Powers.
7. *New York American*, 8 Aug. 1914, in Jeffrey J. Safford, *Wilsonian Maritime Diplomacy, 1913–1921* (New Brunswick: Rutgers University Press, 1978), p. 38.
8. Jefferson to Edward Rutledge, 4 July 1790, *The Papers of Thomas Jefferson*, ed. Julian P. Boyd, vol. 16 (Princeton: Princeton University Press, 1961), p. 601.
9. Patrick Devlin, *Too Proud to Fight: Woodrow Wilson's Neutrality* (London: Oxford University Press, 1974), p. 200.
10. New York *Nation*, 13 May 1915, in Link, *Wilson, 1914–15*, p. 373.

11. Address in Philadelphia, 10 May 1915, Wilson, *Papers*, vol. 33, p. 149.
12. First *Lusitania* note, 12 May 1915, Wilson, *Papers*, vol. 33, pp. 174–8.
13. Devlin, *Too Proud to Fight*, p. 325.
14. Statement of 15 Aug. 1914, in Link, *Wilson, 1914–15*, p. 64.
15. Lansing to Wilson, 6 Sept. 1915, in US Dept. of State, *Foreign Relations of the United States: The Lansing Papers, 1914–20* (Washington: Government Printing Office, 1939), vol. I, p. 146.
16. House-Grey memorandum, 22 Feb. 1916, in Devlin, *Too Proud to Fight*, p. 437.
17. Quoted by C. M. Mason, 'Anglo-American Relations: Mediation and "Permanent Peace"', in F.H. Hinsley, ed., *British Foreign Policy under Sir Edward Grey* (Cambridge: Cambridge University Press, 1977), p. 479.
18. Walter Hines Page to Col. E. M. House, 23 May 1916, in Charles Seymour, *The Intimate Papers of Colonel House* (4 vols, London: Ernest Benn, 1926–8), vol. II, p. 256.
19. Page to Edwin A. Alderman, 22 June 1916, in Burton J. Hendrick, *The Life and Letters of Walter H. Page, 1855–1918*, vol. II (Garden City, NY: Garden City Publishing Co., 1927), p. 143.
20. Arthur Bullard to Col. E. M. House, 23 May 1916, in Arthur S. Link, *Wilson: Campaigns for Progressivism and Peace, 1916–1917* (Princeton: Princeton University Press, 1965), p. 13.
21. Wilson to House, 23 July 1916, Wilson, *Papers*, vol. 37, p. 467.
22. House diary, 15 Nov. 1916, Wilson, *Papers*, vol. 38, p. 658.
23. Keynes, 'The Financial Dependence of the United Kingdom on the United States of America', 10 Oct. 1916, FO 371/2796, 205593 (Public Record Office, London).
24. McKenna, 'Our Financial Position in America', 24 Oct. 1916, CAB 24/2, G–87 (PRO).
25. FRB statement of 27 Nov. 1916, Link, *Wilson, 1916–17*, p. 202.
26. Sir Cecil Spring-Rice to FO, 3 Dec. 1916, in Wilson, *Papers*, vol. 40, p. 137.
27. Note of 18 Dec. 1916, Wilson, *Papers*, vol. 40, pp. 273–6.
28. Address to the Senate, 22 Jan. 1917, Wilson, *Papers*, vol. 40, pp. 533–9.
29. Interview with Roy Howard, published 28 Sept. 1916, in John Grigg, *Lloyd George: From Peace to War, 1912–1916* (London: Methuen, 1985), pp. 424–8.
30. Sir Cecil Spring-Rice to Sir Eric Drummond, 13 Oct. 1916, FO 800/242, f. 253 (PRO).
31. Lord Hankey, *The Supreme Command* (2 vols, London: George Allen and Unwin, 1961), vol. II, p. 557, diary entry for 9 Nov. 1916.
32. Address in Milwaukee, 31 Jan. 1916, Wilson, *Papers*, vol. 36, p. 57.

33. *Lord Riddell's War Diary, 1914–1918* (London: Ivor Nicholson and Watson, 1933), 4 Feb. 1917, p. 238.
34. Patrick Beesly, *Room 40: British Naval Intelligence, 1914–1918* (Oxford: Oxford University Press, 1984), p. 216, text of complete copy of telegram obtained by Room 40 on 19 Feb. 1917.
35. Address to Joint Session of Congress, 2 April 1917, Wilson, *Papers*, vol. 41, pp. 519–27.
36. *Memoirs of Mrs Woodrow Wilson* (London: Putnam, 1939), p. 159.

BACKGROUND READING

1 General

Keith Robbins, *The First World War* (Oxford: OPUS, 1985). A succinct but comprehensive study of war, diplomacy, attitudes and social change.

James L. Stokesbury, *A Short History of World War I* (London: Robert Hale, 1981). Concentrates on battles and diplomacy.

Trevor Wilson, *The Myriad Faces of War: Britain and the Great War, 1914–1918* (Cambridge: Polity Press, 1986). A massive study of the battlefronts and the home front, of origins, impact and consequences.

Daniel M. Smith, *The Great Departure: The United States and World War I, 1914–1920* (New York: John Wiley, 1965). Still a good overview of the whole period of US neutrality, war and peace-making.

Ross Gregory, *The Origins of American Intervention in the First World War* (New York: W. W. Norton, 1971). A useful introduction on 1914–17.

2 Biographical studies

Kenneth O. Morgan, *Lloyd George* (London: Weidenfeld and Nicolson, 1974). A short, readable biography. (The detailed studies of Lloyd George's life and foreign policy, respectively by John Grigg and Michael Fry, have not yet reached his premiership.)

Arthur S. Link, *Woodrow Wilson: War, Revolution and Peace* (Arlington Heights, Illinois: AHM, 1979). The best short account, by Wilson's principal biographer.

J. A. Thompson, 'Woodrow Wilson and World War I: A Reappraisal', *Journal of American Studies*, vol. 19 (1985), pp. 325–48. A stimulating survey, arguing that Wilson was not a rigid idealist but did his best to match foreign policy to domestic constraints.

3 Some studies of the Anglo-American relationship

Ernest R. May, *The World War and American Isolation* (Cambridge, Mass.: Harvard University Press, 1959). This remains an outstanding account, integrating American, British and German policy.

Patrick Devlin, *Too Proud to Fight: Woodrow Wilson's Neutrality* (London: Oxford University Press, 1974). A vast book, stressing Wilson's idealism, but also including much detail on British policy and Anglo-American relations. Particularly good on neutral rights and the law of blockade.

John M. Cooper, Jr, 'The Command of Gold Reversed: American Loans to Britain, 1915–1917', *Pacific Historical Review*, vol. 45 (1976), pp. 209–30. Detailed yet dramatic on Britain's financial dependence.

Kathleen Burk, *Britain, America and the Sinews of War, 1914–1918* (London: George Allen and Unwin, 1985). A study of munitions and finance, using British and American sources, and emphasising the shift of economic power across the Atlantic.

Chapter 4 Victory Without Peace, 1917–20

1. Spring-Rice to Balfour, 7Dec. 1917, in Robert H. Ferrell, *Woodrow Wilson and World War I, 1917–1921* (New York: Harper and Row, 1985), p. 46.
2. Dimbleby, BBC 1 interviews in New Ulm. See also Frederick C. Luebke, *Bonds of Loyalty: German–Americans and World War I* (De Kalb, Illinois: Northern Illinois University Press, 1974), esp. ch. 8.
3. Wilson to House, 21 July 1917, *The Papers of Woodrow Wilson*, ed. Arthur S. Link, *et al.* (Multi-volume edition, still in progress, Princeton: Princeton University Press, 1966–), vol. 43, p. 238.
4. Senator Thomas S. Martin, in David M. Kennedy, *Over Here: The First World War and American Society* (New York: Oxford University Press, 1980), p. 144.
5. Dimbleby, BBC 1 interview with Winston Roche.
6. Dimbleby, BBC 1 interview with William Bruder.
7. Dimbleby – Roche interview.
8. David F. Trask, *Captains and Cabinets: Anglo-American Naval Relations, 1917–1918* (Columbia, Missouri: University of Missouri Press, 1972), p. 55.
9. Dimbleby, BBC 1 interview with 'Tanky' Taylor.

10. David R. Woodward, 'Did Lloyd George Starve the British Army of Men Prior to the German Offensive of 21 March 1918?', *The Historical Journal*, vol. 27 (1984), p. 250.
11. Robert Blake, ed., *The Private Papers of Douglas Haig, 1914–1918* (London: Eyre and Spottiswood, 1952), p. 307, diary for 1 May 1918.
12. Fourteen Points, 8 Jan. 1918, Wilson, *Papers*, vol. 45, pp. 534–9.
13. Smuts in Imperial War Cabinet, 14 Aug. 1918, David R. Woodward, *Lloyd George and the Generals* (Newark, Delaware: University of Delaware Press, 1983), p. 328.
14. Admiralty memo for War Cabinet, Dec. 1918, in V. H. Rothwell, *British War Aims and Peace Diplomacy, 1914–1918* (Oxford: Clarendon Press, 1971), p. 258.
15. House, diary, 4 Nov. 1918, Col. Edward M. House papers (Sterling Library, Yale University).
16. Remarks on 29 Oct. 1918, in Sterling Kernek, *Distractions of Peace during War: The Lloyd George Government's Reactions to Woodrow Wilson, December 1916 to November 1918* (Philadelphia: American Philosophical Society Transactions, 1975), p. 104.
17. Dimbleby, BBC 1 interview with Edith Sowerbutts.
18. John Maynard Keynes, *The Economic Consequences of the Peace* (1919) in *The Collected Writings of John Maynard Keynes*, vol. II (London: Macmillan, 1971), p. 24.
19. Dr Cary Grayson, diary, 27 Dec. 1918, in Wilson, *Papers*, vol. 53, p. 521.
20. David Lloyd George, *The Truth about the Peace Treaties* (London: Victor Gollancz, 1938), vol. I, p. 181.
21. Quoted in Lloyd C. Gardner, *Safe for Democracy: The Anglo-American Response to Revolution, 1913–1923* (New York: Oxford University Press, 1984), pp. 2–3.
22. A. Lentin, *Lloyd George, Woodrow Wilson and the Guilt of Germany: An Essay in the Pre-History of Appeasement* (Leicester: Leicester University Press, 1984), pp. 16–29.
23. Harold Nicolson, *Peacemaking, 1919* (London: Constable, 1933), p. 152.
24. Michael L. Dockrill and J. Douglas Goold, *Peace without Promise: Britain and the Paris Peace Conferences, 1919–23* (London: Batsford, 1981), p. 59.
25. Wilson to House, 3 March 1919, in Wilson, *Papers*, vol. 55, p. 392.
26. Sen. Frank Brandegee, in Ralph Stone, *The Irreconcilables: The Fight against the League of Nations* (New York: W. W. Norton, 1973), p. 63.
27. Charles Seymour, *The Intimate Papers of Colonel House* (4 vols, London: Ernest Benn, 1926–8), vol. 4, p. 405.
28. J. M. Keynes to Florence Keynes, 14 May 1919, *The Collected Writings*

of John Maynard Keynes, ed. Elizabeth Johnson, vol. XVI (London: Macmillan, 1971), p. 458.

29. Peter Rowland, *Lloyd George* (London: Barrie and Jenkins, 1975), p. 495.
30. Alan J. Ward, *Ireland and Anglo-American Relations, 1899–1921* (London: Weidenfeld and Nicolson, 1969), p. 176.
31. *Philadelphia Irish Press*, 24 May 1919, in Joseph P. O'Grady, ed., *The Immigrants' Influence on Wilson's Peace Policies* (Lexington: University of Kentucky Press, 1967), p. 77.
32. Woodrow Wilson, *War and Peace: Presidential Messages, Addresses, and Public Papers, 1917–1924*, eds Ray Stannard Baker and William E. Dodd (2 vols, New York: Harper and Brothers, 1927), vol. I, p. 640 (St Louis, 5 Sept. 1919), vol. II, pp. 52 (Sioux Falls, 8 Sept.) and 212 (Portland, 15 Sept.).
33. Thomas A. Bailey, *Woodrow Wilson and the Great Betrayal* (Chicago: Quadrangle Books, 1945), p. 185.
34. George W. Egerton, 'Britain and the "Great Betrayal": Anglo-American Relations and the Struggle for United States Ratification of the Treaty of Versailles, 1919–1920', *The Historical Journal*, vol. 21 (1978), p. 911.

BACKGROUND READING

See also the reading for chapter 3. Some books overlap both chapters.

1 General

Robert H. Ferrell, *Woodrow Wilson and World War I, 1917–1921* (New York: Harper and Row, 1985). A good, recent survey of war, diplomacy and the home front.

Charles L. Mee, Jr, *The End of Order: Versailles, 1919* (London: Secker and Warburg, 1981). A vivid, readable account of the Paris peace conference.

2 Some studies of the Anglo-American relationship

Sterling Kernek, *Distractions of Peace during War: The Lloyd George Government's Reactions to Woodrow Wilson, December 1916 to November 1918* (Philadelphia: American Philosophical Society Transactions, 1975). The debates about rival peace plans.

Wilton B. Fowler, *British-American Relations, 1917–1918: The Role of Sir William Wiseman* (Princeton: Princeton University Press, 1969). Based on the Wiseman papers, but providing good insights into British and US policy on finance, war aims and the use of US troops.

Edward B. Parsons, *Wilsonian Diplomacy: Allied-American Rivalries in War and Peace* (St Louis: Forum Press, 1978). Covers 1916–18. Trade, shipping and what to do with Pershing's army.

George W. Egerton, *Great Britain and the Creation of the League of Nations: Strategy, Politics, and International Organization, 1914–1919* (Chapel Hill: University of North Carolina Press, 1979). The Anglo-American negotiations about the League.

Lloyd C. Gardner, *Safe for Democracy: The Anglo-American Response to Revolution, 1913–1923* (New York: Oxford University Press, 1984). The attempts of Wilson and Lloyd George to find an ordered liberal alternative to revolution. Concentrates on policy towards Russia and China from 1917.

Chapter 5 The Big Two, 1921–35

1. Speech in Des Moines, Iowa, 6 Sept. 1919, in Woodrow Wilson, *War and Peace: Presidential Messages, Addresses, and Public Papers, 1917–1924*, eds Ray Stannard Baker and William E. Dodd (2 vols, New York: Harper and Brothers, 1927), vol. II, p. 18.
2. Klaus Hildebrand, '"British Interests" und "Pax Britannica": Grundfragen englischer Aussenpolitik im 19. und 20. Jahrhundert', *Historische Zeitschrift*, 221 (1975), p. 625.
3. Lord Northcliffe to Geoffrey Robinson, 1 July 1917, quoted in Kathleen Burk, 'Great Britain in the United States, 1917–1918: The Turning Point', *International History Review*, vol. 1 (1979), p. 228.
4. Cecil, memo for War Cabinet, 18 Sept. 1917, CAB 24/26, doc. 2074 (Public Record Office, London).
5. Wiseman, memo on US attitudes to the peace conference, c. 20 Oct. 1918, Wiseman papers, I/9/213 (Sir William Sterling Library, Yale University).
6. House to Wilson, 30 July 1919, in Charles Seymour, *The Intimate Papers of Colonel House* (4 vols, London: Ernest Benn, 1926–8), vol. IV, p. 510.
7. Memorandum for the Cabinet, 20 July 1927, in Martin Gilbert, *Winston S. Churchill*, vol. V, Companion Part I (London: Heinemann, 1979), p. 1033.
8. Mark Sullivan, quoted in Thomas H. Buckley, *The United States and the Washington Naval Conference, 1921–22* (Knoxville: University of Tennessee Press, 1970), p. 72.

9. US Navy General Board report, 21 April 1927, in Stephen Roskill, *Naval Policy between the Wars*, vol. I (London: Collins, 1968), p. 502.
10. Hugh Gibson to William Castle, 30 Sept. 1928, in Frank C. Costigliola, *Awkward Dominion: American Political, Economic, and Cultural Relations with Europe, 1919–1933* (Ithaca, NY: Cornell University Press, 1984), p. 189.
11. Christopher Hall, *Britain, America and Arms Control, 1921–1937* (London: Macmillan, 1987), p. 58. The Congressman was Fred Britten, Chairman of the House Naval Affairs Committee.
12. Vansittart, minute, 19 Oct. 1927, FO 371/12040, A6057/133/45 (Public Record Office, London).
13. Hankey to Thomas Jones (Prime Minister Baldwin's private secretary), 11 Oct. 1928, in Thomas Jones, *Whitehall Diary, vol. II, 1926–30* (London: Oxford University Press, 1969), pp. 147–8.
14. *New York Times*, 13 Oct. 1929, quoted in David Marquand, *Ramsay MacDonald* (London: Jonathan Cape, 1977), p. 508.
15. Christopher Thorne, *The Limits of Foreign Policy: The West, the League and the Far Eastern Crisis of 1931–1933* (London: Heinemann, 1972), quoting respectively from pp. 262, 260.
16. William Allen White to Lord Lothian, 16 March 1939, Lothian papers, GD 40/17/387 (Scottish Record Office, Edinburgh).
17. Emile Moreau, Governor of the Bank of France, in Andrew Boyle, *Montagu Norman* (London: Cassell, 1967), p. 198.
18. Sir Cecil Hirst, 12 Oct. 1925, in D. Cameron Watt, *Succeeding John Bull: America in Britain's Place, 1900–1975* (Cambridge: Cambridge University Press, 1984), p. 57.
19. Frank C. Costigliola, 'Anglo-American Financial Rivalry in the 1920s', *Journal of Economic History*, vol. 37 (1977), p. 913.
20. Speech of 5 Aug. 1925, in *Winston S. Churchill: His Complete Speeches, 1897–1963*, ed. Robert Rhodes James, vol. IV (New York: Chelsea House, 1974), p. 3742.
21. Diane B. Kunz, *The Battle for Britain's Gold Standard in 1931* (London: Croom Helm, 1987), p. 82.
22. Message of 23 Aug. 1931 in CAB 23/67, f. 365 (PRO). Apparently this was described to the Cabinet as a message from Benjamin Harrison and the Federal Reserve, perhaps because MacDonald feared that to mention the name of Morgan's would only further incense his critics. See Kunz, *Battle for Britain's Gold Standard*, p. 105.
23. Cabinet meeting, Cab. 46 (31), 23 Aug. 1931, CAB 23/67, f. 360 (PRO).
24. R. Bassett, *Nineteen Thirty-One: Political Crisis* (London: Macmillan, 1958), pp. 175, 173.
25. Dimbleby, BBC 1 interview with C. Douglas Dillon.

26. Neville Chamberlain to Ida Chamberlain, 15 July 1933, Neville Chamberlain papers, NC 18/1/836 (Birmingham University Library).
27. Charles P. Kindleberger, *The World in Depression, 1929–1939* (Berkeley: University of California Press, 1973), p. 292.
28. Quoted in W. Roger Louis, *British Strategy in the Far East, 1919–1939* (Oxford: Clarendon Press, 1971), p. 77.
29. Memo of Nov. 1927, in B. J. C. McKercher, *The Second Baldwin Government and the United States, 1924–1929* (Cambridge: Cambridge University Press, 1984), p. 1.
30. Both Baldwin quotations in Keith Middlemas and John Barnes, *Baldwin: A Biography* (London: Weidenfeld and Nicolson, 1969), p. 729.
31. Minute of 5 Feb. 1934, in Norman Rose, *Vansittart: Study of a Diplomat* (London: Heinemann, 1978), pp. 126–7.
32. John E. Wiltz, *In Search of Peace: The Senate Munitions Inquiry, 1934–1936* (Baton Rouge: Louisiana State University Press, 1963), p. 15.
33. Quoted in Cushing Strout, *The American Image of the Old World* (New York: Harper and Row, 1963), p. 205.

BACKGROUND READING

1 General

Graham Ross, *The Great Powers and the Decline of the European States System, 1914–1945* (London: Longman, 1983). A succinct if dry introduction to the diplomacy of the period.

Arnold A. Offner, *The Origins of the Second World War: American Foreign Policy and World Politics, 1917–1941* (New York: Krieger reprint, 1986). First published in 1975, but still a good overview of US policy.

F. S. Northedge, *The Troubled Giant: Britain among the Great Powers, 1916–1939* (London: G. Bell, 1966). Still a useful survey.

Derek H. Aldcroft, *From Versailles to Wall Street, 1919–1929* (London: Allen Lane, 1977). A good introduction to the economic history of the 1920s.

2 Some studies of the Anglo-American relationship: navies

Roger Dingman, *Power in the Pacific: The Origins of Naval Arms Limitation, 1914–1922* (Chicago: University of Chicago Press, 1976). Thorough study of British, American and Japanese naval policy.

B. J. C. McKercher, *The Second Baldwin Government and the United States, 1924–1929* (Cambridge: Cambridge University Press, 1984). Mainly on the naval race and freedom of the seas before and after the Geneva conference of 1927.

Christopher Hall, *Britain, America and Arms Control, 1921–1937* (London: Macmillan, 1987). A lucid account, concentrating on the naval conferences between 1927 and 1935.

3 Some studies of the Anglo-American relationship: finance

Jon Jacobson, 'Is there a new international history of the 1920s?', *American Historical Review*, vol. 88 (1983), pp. 617–45. A good introduction to the new literature on Europe in the 1920s and the American role.

Stephen V. O. Clarke, *Central Bank Co-operation, 1924–1931* (New York: Federal Reserve Bank of NY, 1967). Still the basic study of British and US policy, although it pre-dates the opening of the British archives.

D. E. Moggridge, *British Monetary Policy, 1924–1931: The Norman Conquest of $4.86* (Cambridge: Cambridge University Press, 1972). Basic study of British financial policy during the period of the return to Gold.

Frank C. Costigliola, 'Anglo-American Financial Rivalry in the 1920s', *Journal of Economic History*, vol. 37 (1977), pp. 911–34. A succinct survey, based on British and American archives.

Diane B. Kunz, *The Battle for Britain's Gold Standard in 1931* (London: Croom Helm, 1987). This is the best study of the financial diplomacy of the crisis, using British and American archives.

Chapter 6 Americanisation: business and society between the world wars

1. G. Lowes Dickinson, *Appearances: Being Notes of Travel* (London: J. M. Dent, 1914), p. 160.
2. Alanson Houghton to Owen Young, 13 Feb. 1926, in Frank C. Costigliola, *Awkward Dominion: American Political, Economic, and Cultural Relations with Europe, 1919–1933* (Ithaca, NY: Cornell University Press, 1984), p. 144.
3. Thomas Jones, *Whitehall Diary*, ed. Keith Middlemas, vol. II (London: Oxford University Press, 1969), p. 177, entry for 8 March 1929.
4. BBC 1 interview with Raymond Firestone.
5. Sir Arthur Willert, *Aspects of British Foreign Policy* (New Haven: Yale University Press, 1928), p. 15 – lecture given by Willert, the Head of

the Foreign Office News Dept., in Williamstown, Mass., in July 1927.

6. Joan Hoff Wilson, *Herbert Hoover: Forgotten Progressive* (Boston: Little, Brown and Co., 1975), p. 177.
7. Sir Esme Howard to Sir Austen Chamberlain, 26 April 1928, in Michael J. Hogan, *Informal Entente: The Private Structure of Cooperation in Anglo-American Economic Diplomacy, 1918–1928* (Columbia, Missouri: University of Missouri Press, 1977), p. 208.
8. Elie Garcia report, Aug. 1920, in E. David Cronon, *Black Moses: The Story of Marcus Garvey and the Universal Negro Improvement Association* (Madison: University of Wisconsin Press, 1969), p. 124.
9. Telegram of 22 May 1925, in US Department of State, *Foreign Relations of the United States, 1925* (Washington: Government Printing Office, 1940), vol. II, p. 432.
10. Raymond L. Buell, *The Native Problem in Africa* (2 vols, New York: Macmillan, 1928), vol. II, p. 837.
11. BBC 1 interview with Charles L. James, former assistant to Garvey.
12. Ludwell Denny, *America Conquers Britain: A Record of Economic War* (New York: Alfred A. Knopf, 1930), p. 407.
13. Swope to Docker, 16 Feb. 1928, in Robert Jones and Oliver Marriott, *Anatomy of a Merger: A History of G.E.C., A.E.I. and English Electric* (London: Jonathan Cape, 1970), p. 98.
14. R. P. T. Davenport-Hines, *Dudley Docker: The Life and Times of a Trade Warrior* (Cambridge: Cambridge University Press, 1984), p. 179.
15. Jones and Marriott, *Anatomy of a Merger*, p. 99.
16. *New York Times*, 31 March 1929, in Denny, *America Conquers Britain*, p. 142.
17. *Manchester Guardian*, 15 Feb. 1929, p. 11.
18. Leslie Hannah, *Electricity before Nationalisation: A Study of the Development of the Electrical Supply Industry in Britain to 1948* (London: Macmillan, 1979), p. 229.
19. J. Ellis Barker, *America's Secret: The Causes of Her Economic Success* (London: John Murray, 1927), p. 412.
20. BBC 1 interview with Winifred Davis.
21. Chris Goddard, *Jazz Away From Home* (New York: Paddington Press, 1979), p. 219.
22. BBC 1 interview with Doreen Evans.
23. Board of Education memo, July 1941, in David Reynolds, 'Whitehall, Washington and the Promotion of American Studies in Britain during World War Two', *Journal of American Studies*, vol. 16 (1982), p. 174.
24. *Daily Express*, 18 March 1927, p. 6.
25. Herbert Williams, in House of Commons, *Debates*, 16 March 1927, vol. 203, col. 2086.

26. Oliver Stanley, in House of Commons, *Debates*, 4 Nov. 1937, vol. 328, col. 1173.
27. *Morning Post* (1923), quoted in Edward G. Lowry, 'Trade Follows the Film', *Saturday Evening Post*, 7 Nov. 1925, p. 12.
28. Quoted by Thomas H. Guback, 'Hollywood's International Market', in Tino Balio, ed., *The American Film Industry* (Madison: University of Wisconsin Press, 1976), p. 394.
29. Quoted in Peter Stead, 'Hollywood's Message for the World: The British Response in the Nineteen Thirties', *Historical Journal of Film, Radio and Television*, vol. 1 (1981), p. 22.
30. C. E. M. Joad, *The Babbitt Warren* (London: Kegan, French, Trubner, 1926), esp. pp. xii, 4, 188, 190–1.
31. Nicolson to Vita Sackville-West, 17 Nov. 1934, in Harold Nicolson, *Diaries and Letters, 1930–1939*, ed. Nigel Nicolson (London: Collins, 1966), p. 189.
32. BBC 1 interview with John Carberry.
33. Fitzgerald to Edmund Wilson, May 1921, in Andrew Turnbull, ed., *The Letters of F. Scott Fitzgerald* (London: Bodley Head, 1964), p. 326.
34. Quotations from *Europa und Amerika* (1926) in Isaac Deutscher, *The Prophet Unarmed: Trotsky, 1921–1929* (London: Oxford University Press, 1959), p. 215.
35. Robert H. Ferrell, *Woodrow Wilson and World War I, 1917–1921* (New York: Harper and Row, 1985), p. 210.
36. John L. Gaddis, *Russia, the Soviet Union and the United States: An Interpretive History* (New York: Alfred A. Knopf, 1978), p. 113.
37. Werner Sombart, in Daniel Bell, *Marxian Socialism in the United States* (Princeton: Princeton University Press, 1967), p. 4.
38. Article of Feb. 1933, in Frank Freidel, *Franklin D. Roosevelt: Launching the New Deal* (Boston: Little, Brown and Co., 1973), p. 12.
39. Arthur M. Schlesinger, Jr, *The Age of Roosevelt: The Crisis of the Old Order, 1919–1933* (Boston: Houghton Mifflin, 1957), p. 155.
40. William E. Leuchtenburg, *Franklin D. Roosevelt and the New Deal, 1932–1940* (New York: Harper & Row, 1963), p. 28, recounting a story from the spring of 1931.
41. James MacGregor Burns, *Roosevelt: The Lion and the Fox* (New York: Harcourt, Brace and World, 1956), p. 163.
42. In 1930 total British long-term foreign investment (direct and portfolio) was estimated at $18.2 billion; American at between $14.7 billion and $15.4 billion. See Mira Wilkins, *The Maturing of Multinational Enterprise: American Business Abroad from 1914 to 1970* (Cambridge, Mass.: Harvard University Press, 1974), p. 156, note.
43. Comment of 1926 in Roy Church and Michael Miller, '"The Big

Three": Competition, Management and Marketing in the British Motor Industry, 1922–1939', in Barry Supple, ed., *Essays in British Business History* (Oxford: Clarendon Press, 1977), p. 169.

44. *Fortune*, July 1937 in D. C. Coleman, *Courtaulds: An Economic and Social History*, vol. II (Oxford: Clarendon Press, 1969), pp. 384–5.
45. Freidel, *Launching the New Deal*, p. 346 (Securities Act); Barry Supple, 'The Political Economy of Demoralization: The State and the Coalmining Industry in America and Britain between the Wars', n. 116, *Economic History Review*, forthcoming, 1988.
46. Sir Arthur Willert, memo of conversations with FDR in Jan. and March 1936, 14 April 1936, Willert papers, box 14, folder 59 (Yale University).
47. Henry Pelling, *America and the British Left: From Bright to Bevan* (London: A. and C. Black, 1956), p. 136.
48. Comments of Dec. 1934 in Peter Rowland, *Lloyd George* (London: Barrie and Jenkins, 1975), p. 713.
49. E.g. Sir Ronald Lindsay to Lord Halifax, despatch 360, April 1937, FO 371/21546, A 3440/1202/45 (Public Record Office, London).
50. Frank Ashton-Gwatkin, report on US economic situation in May 1938, CAB 24/277, CP 161 (38) (PRO).
51. Richard H. Heindel, *The American Impact on Great Britain, 1898–1914* (Philadelphia: University of Pennsylvania, 1940), pp. 15–18. He surveyed the press in 1936–7 and concluded that there had not been much change in quantity or quality since World War One.
52. *The Times*, 19 May 1939, p. 18.
53. H. Morse Stephens (1916) in Bruce M. Russett, *Community and Contention: Britain and America in the Twentieth Century* (Cambridge, Mass.: MIT Press, 1963), p. 133.
54. Frances Donaldson, *Edward VIII* (London: Weidenfeld and Nicolson, 1974), p. 232.
55. *New York Journal*, 26 Oct. 1936, in Brian Inglis, *Abdication* (London: Hodder and Stoughton, 1966), pp. 193–4.
56. House of Commons, *Debates*, vol. 318, col. 2179, 10 Dec. 1936.

BACKGROUND READING

1 General histories of Anglo-American economic relations

Philip S. Bagwell and G. E. Mingay, *Britain and America: A Study of Economic Change, 1850–1939* (London: Routledge and Kegan Paul, 1970).

Graeme M. Holmes, *Britain and America: A Comparative Economic History, 1850–1939* (New York: Barnes and Noble, 1976).

2 Studies of Anglo-American economic relations in the inter-war period

See also background reading for chapter 5.

Michael J. Hogan, *Informal Entente: The Private Structure of Co-operation in Anglo-American Economic Diplomacy, 1918–1928* (Columbia, Missouri: University of Missouri Press, 1977). Analyses policy on finance, oil, cables and radio, possibly exaggerating the ententes achieved.

Michael D. Goldberg, 'Anglo-American Economic Competition, 1920–1930', *Economy and History*, vol. XVI (1973), pp. 15–36. Surveys the global competition, with full statistical detail, but not official policy.

3 The American impact on British society

John Dizikes, *Britain, Roosevelt and the New Deal: British Public Opinion, 1932–1938* (New York: Garland, 1979). Reprint of 1964 Harvard PhD, based on books and newspaper sources.

Jeffrey Richards, *The Age of the Dream Palace: Cinema and Society in Britain, 1930–1939* (London: Routledge and Kegan Paul, 1984). The best study, with much discussion of American films and Americanisation.

George H. Knoles, *The Jazz Age Revisited: British Criticism of American Civilization during the 1920s* (Stanford: Stanford University Press, 1955). A detailed survey of British comment.

John H. Dunning, *American Investment in British Manufacturing Industry* (London: George Allen and Unwin, 1958). Concentrates on the 1950s, but with good background on earlier decades.

Chapter 7 Britain Alone, 1935–41

1. Winston S. Churchill, *The Second World War* (6 vols, London: Cassell, 1948–54), vol. I, pp. viii–ix.
2. Speech of 14 Aug. 1936, in Edgar B. Nixon, ed., *Franklin D. Roosevelt and Foreign Affairs*, vol. III (Cambridge, Mass.: Harvard University Press, 1969), p. 380.
3. James M. Burns, *Roosevelt: The Soldier of Freedom, 1940–1945* (New York: Harcourt, Brace, Jovanovich, 1970), p. 606.
4. Admiral Sir Ernle Chatfield to Sir Warren Fisher, 4 June 1934, Chatfield papers, CHT/3/1 (National Maritime Museum, Greenwich).
5. Neville Chamberlain to Hilda Chamberlain, 17 Dec. 1937, Chamberlain papers, NC 18/1/1032 (Birmingham University Library).

6. Richard N. Kottman, *Reciprocity and the North Atlantic Triangle, 1932–1938* (Ithaca, NY: Cornell University Press, 1968), p. 117.
7. Jay Pierrepont Moffat to Norman Davis, 7 Oct. 1936, Davis papers, box 41 (Library of Congress, Washington, DC).
8. Chamberlain, diary, 19 Feb. 1938, NC 2/24A.
9. Dimbleby, BBC 1 interview with Lord Home.
10. Eden to Chamberlain, draft, 18 Jan. 1938, Foreign Office correspondence, FO 371/21526, A 2127/64/45 (Public Record Office, London).
11. Churchill, *Second World War*, vol. I, p. 199.
12. J. R. M. Butler, *Lord Lothian* (London: Macmillan, 1960), p. 213.
13. Roosevelt to Chamberlain, 5 Oct. 1938, in William L. Langer and S. Everett Gleason, *The Challenge to Isolation, 1937–40* (New York: Council on Foreign Relations, 1952), p. 138.
14. Roosevelt to Roger B. Merriman, 15 Feb. 1939, President's Secretary's File, PSF 46: 'Great Britain' (Roosevelt Library, Hyde Park, New York).
15. Robert Dallek, *Franklin D. Roosevelt and American Foreign Policy, 1932–1945* (New York: Oxford University Press, 1979), p. 199.
16. Neville Chamberlain to Ida Chamberlain, 27 Jan. 1940, Chamberlain papers, NC 18/1/1140.
17. Broadcast of 10 May 1940 in Edward Bliss, Jr, ed., *In Search of Light: The Broadcasts of Edward R. Murrow, 1938–61* (London: Macmillan, 1968), p. 22.
18. Dimbleby, BBC 1 interview with Sir John Colville.
19. Harold L. Ickes, diary, 12 May 1940 (Library of Congress, Washington, DC).
20. Speech of 4 June 1940 in Robert Rhodes James, ed., *Winston S. Churchill: His Complete Speeches, 1897–1963* (New York: Chelsea House, 1974), vol. VI, p. 6231.
21. Warren F. Kimball, ed., *Churchill and Roosevelt: The Complete Correspondence* (3 vols, Princeton: Princeton University Press, 1984), vol. I, pp. 43, 51, 57, messages of 11, 15 June and 31 July 1940.
22. Kennedy to Roosevelt, 15 May 1940, State Dept. records, RG 59, 740.0011 EW 1939/2952 (National Archives, Washington, DC).
23. Christopher Thorne, *The Far Eastern War: States and Societies, 1941–1945* (London: Unwin Paperbacks, 1986), pp. 211–12.
24. War Cabinet minutes, 21 Aug. 1940, CAB 65/8, WM 231 (40) 1 (PRO).
25. Churchill to Roosevelt, 25 Aug. 1940, Kimball, *Correspondence*, vol. I, p. 65.
26. Dimbleby, BBC 1 interview with Graham Hutton.
27. Dimbleby, BBC 1 interview with Douglas Fairbanks, Jr.
28. Dimbleby, BBC 1 interview with Kingman Brewster.

29. Sir Ronald Lindsay to Rex Leeper, 17 March 1939, FO 395/648b, pp. 569–70 (PRO).
30. Edward R. Murrow, *This is London*, ed. Elmer Davis (New York: Simon and Schuster, 1941), p. 167.
31. Frank Gillard, 'Goodnight, and good luck', *The Listener*, 1 May 1975, p. 565.
32. Dimbleby – Fairbanks interview.
33. Quotations in this paragraph from Robert Divine, *Foreign Policy and US Presidential Elections* (New York: New Viewpoints, 1974), vol. I, pp. 80, 82–3.
34. Churchill, *Second World War*, vol. II, p. 501.
35. Kimball, ed., *Correspondence*, vol. I, pp. 101–9.
36. Quotations in this and the previous paragraph from press conference of 17 Dec. 1940, in Samuel Rosenman, ed., *The Public Papers and Addresses of Franklin D. Roosevelt, 1940* (New York: Macmillan, 1941), esp. pp. 604 and 607.
37. Dimbleby, BBC 1 interview with Claude Pepper.
38. Churchill, *Second World War*, vol. II, p. 506.
39. Draft of 28 Dec. 1940, Prime Minister's Papers, PREM 4/17/1 (PRO).
40. W. Averell Harriman and Elie Abel, *Special Envoy to Churchill and Stalin, 1941–1946* (New York: Random House, 1975), p. 19.
41. Churchill, *Second World War*, vol. II, p. 503.
42. Dimbleby – Pepper interview.
43. Churchill to Roosevelt, 4 May 1941, Kimball, *Correspondence*, vol. I, p. 182.
44. Churchill to Queen Elizabeth, 3 Aug. 1941, PREM 3/485/6, p. 16 (PRO).
45. Dimbleby, BBC 1 interview with Elliott Roosevelt.
46. USA, Dept. of State, *Foreign Relations of the United States, 1941* (Washington: Government Printing Office, 1958), vol. I, p. 368.
47. War Cabinet Minutes, 19 Aug. 1941, CAB 65/19, WM 84 (41)1, Confidential Annex (PRO).
48. Hadley Cantril, ed., *Public Opinion, 1935–1946* (Princeton: Princeton University Press, 1951), p. 977.
49. Dimbleby – Hutton interview.
50. Letters from Leonard N. Conrad, in Susan Winslow, ed., *Brother, Can You Spare a Dime?* (New York: Paddington Press, 1976), p. 159.
51. Roosevelt to Churchill, 8 Dec. 1941, in Kimball, ed., *Correspondence*, vol. I, p. 283.
52. Churchill, *Second World War*, vol. III, p. 540.

BACKGROUND READING

1 *General*

William Carr, *Poland to Pearl Harbor: The Making of the Second World War* (London: Edward Arnold, 1985). A genuinely global study, taking Asia as seriously as Europe. Strongest on 1939–41.

Robert A. Divine, *The Reluctant Belligerent: American Entry into World War II* (New York: Alfred A. Knopf, 2nd ed., 1979). The best survey of American policy.

Roy Douglas, *In the Year of Munich* (London: Macmillan, 1977), *The Advent of War, 1939–1940* (1978), and *New Alliances, 1940–1941* (1982). Offer good summaries of British policy based on the official documents.

2 *Biographical studies*

Robert Dallek, *Franklin D. Roosevelt and American Foreign Policy, 1932–1945* (New York: Oxford University Press, 1979). The basic text on FDR's foreign policy.

Martin Gilbert, *Finest Hour: Winston S. Churchill, 1939–1941* (London: Heinemann, 1983). The pertinent volume of the vast official biography.

Joseph Lash, *Roosevelt and Churchill, 1939–1941: The Partnership that Saved the West* (New York: W.W. Norton, 1976). A vivid account of their relationship, based on British and American archives.

3 *Studies of the Anglo-American relationship*

C. A. MacDonald, *The United States, Britain and Appeasement, 1936–1939* (London: Macmillan, 1980). A good, short analysis, based on British and US archives, emphasising the economic rivalries.

Ritchie Ovendale, *Appeasement and the English-Speaking World: Britain, the United States, the Dominions and the Policy of 'Appeasement', 1937–1939* (Cardiff: University of Wales Press, 1975). British policy towards the USA and Commonwealth. More sympathetic to Chamberlain, to British policy and to the idea of an 'English-speaking world' than most recent studies.

James R. Leutze, *Bargaining for Supremacy: Anglo-American Naval Relations, 1937–1941* (Chapel Hill: University of North Carolina Press, 1977). Naval rivalry, especially in 1940–1.

Malcolm H. Murfett, *Fool-Proof Relations: The Search for Anglo-American Naval Co-operation during the Chamberlain Years, 1937–40* (Singapore: Singapore University Press, 1984). Fuller on British side than Leutze, and, like Ovendale, sympathetic to Chamberlain.

David Reynolds, *The Creation of the Anglo-American Alliance, 1937–1941: A Study in Competitive Co-operation* (London: Europa Publications, 1981). Survey of the whole relationship: diplomatic, military and economic. Used as the foundation for this chapter.

Chapter 8 Mixed Up Together, 1941–5

1. Arthur Bryant, *The Turn of the Tide: A Study based on the Diaries and Autobiographical Notes of Field Marshal the Viscount Alanbrooke, KG, OM* (London: Collins, 1957), p. 282.
2. Robert E. Sherwood, *Roosevelt and Hopkins: An Intimate History* (New York: Harper and Brothers, 1948), p. 442.
3. War Cabinet minutes, WM 8 (42) 1, 17 Jan. 1942, CAB 65/25 (Public Record Office, London).
4. Roosevelt to Churchill, 30 Jan. 1942, in Warren F. Kimball, ed., *Churchill and Roosevelt: Their Complete Correspondence* (3 vols, Princeton: Princeton University Press, 1984), vol. I, p. 337.
5. Winston S. Churchill, *The Second World War* (6 vols, London: Cassell, 1948–54), vol. II, p. 22.
6. Churchill to Eden, 5 Nov. 1942, Prime Minister's Correspondence, PREM 4/27/1 (PRO).
7. Alex Danchev, *Very Special Relationship: Field Marshal Sir John Dill and the Anglo-American Alliance, 1941–1944* (London: Brassey's Defence Publishers, 1986), p. 3.
8. House of Commons, *Debates*, vol. 364, col. 1171, 20 Aug. 1940.
9. H. Duncan Hall, *North American Supply* (London: HMSO, 1955), p. 353.
10. Joint memo, 'American and British Strategy', WW1 (Final), 20 Jan. 1942, Annex I, CAB 80/33 (PRO).
11. Martin Gilbert, *Road to Victory: Winston S. Churchill, 1941–1945* (London: Heinemann, 1986), p. 44.
12. Marshall's memo in J. R. M. Butler, *Grand Strategy*, vol. III, part 2 of *History of the Second World War: UK Military Series* (London: HMSO, 1964), p. 675.
13. Meeting with Marshall, 14 April 1942, CAB 79/56 (PRO).
14. Bryant, *Turn of the Tide*, p. 357.
15. Roosevelt to Churchill, 3 April 1942, and Churchill to Roosevelt, 12

April 1942, in Kimball, ed., *Correspondence*, vol. II, pp. 441, 448.
16. Dimbleby, BBC 1 interview with General Albert C. Wedemeyer.
17. Chiefs of Staff 65th (42) (O) meeting, 6 July 1942, CAB 79/56 (PRO).
18. Richard W. Steele, 'American Popular Opinion and the War against Germany: The Issue of a Negotiated Peace', *Journal of American History*, vol. 65 (1978), p. 708.
19. Mark A. Stoler, *The Politics of the Second Front: American Military Planning and Diplomacy in Coalition Warfare, 1941–1943* (Westport, Conn.: Greenwood Press, 1977), p. 58.
20. Harry C. Butcher, *My Three Years with Eisenhower* (New York: Simon and Schuster, 1946), p. 29, diary entry for 23 July 1942.
21. Henry L. Stimson, diary, vol. 43, 1 June 1943 (Sterling Library, Yale University).
22. Stoler, *Politics of the Second Front*, p. 55.
23. Earl of Halifax, 'Secret Diary', 15 July 1942, Hickleton Papers, A 7.8.19 (Borthwick Institute, York).
24. Dimbleby, BBC 1 interview with General Wedemeyer.
25. Dimbleby, BBC 1 interview with Sir Ian Jacob.
26. Wm. Roger Louis, *Imperialism at Bay, 1941–1945: The United States and the Decolonization of the British Empire* (Oxford: Clarendon Press, 1977), p. 226.
27. *Life*, 12 Oct. 1942, in Louis, *Imperialism at Bay*, p. 198.
28. Churchill, *Complete Speeches*, vol. VI, p. 6695, 10 Nov. 1942.
29. Adolf A. Berle, diary, VIII.2.109, memo, 28 Feb. 1942 (Franklin D. Roosevelt Library, Hyde Park, New York).
30. Kimball, ed., *Churchill and Roosevelt: Correspondence*, vol. I, p. 447.
31. Christopher Thorne, *Allies of a Kind: The United States, Britain, and the War against Japan, 1941–1945* (London: Hamish Hamilton, 1977), pp. 337, 453.
32. Churchill to Eden, 25 Aug. 1944, PREM 4/30/11 (PRO).
33. Eisenhower to General Thomas T. Handy, 28 Jan. 1943, in Alfred D. Chandler, Jr, ed., *The Papers of Dwight David Eisenhower: The War Years, 1941–1945* (5 vols, Baltimore: Johns Hopkins University Press, 1970), vol. 2, p. 928.
34. Dimbleby, BBC 1 interview with Joseph Curtis.
35. David Reynolds, 'The Churchill Government and the Black American Troops in Britain during World War II', *Transactions of the Royal Historical Society*, 5th series, vol. 35 (1985), p. 121.
36. Memo, 'United States Negro Troops in the United Kingdom', 17 Oct. 1942, WP (42) 473, CAB 66/30 (PRO).
37. Dimbleby, BBC 1 interview with John Wilson.
38. Foreign Office memo, 10 July 1943, in David Reynolds, 'GI and Tommy

in Wartime Britain: The Army "Inter-Attachment" Scheme of 1943–4', *Journal of Strategic Studies*, vol. 7 (1984), p. 412.
39. Dimbleby, BBC 1 interview with Margaret Whiting.
40. Dimbleby, BBC 1 interviews with William Stock and John Wilson.
41. See Keith Sainsbury, *The Turning Point: Roosevelt, Stalin, Churchill, and Chiang-Kai-Shek, 1943. The Moscow, Cairo, and Teheran Conferences* (Oxford: Oxford University Press, 1985).
42. Roosevelt to Churchill, 18 March 1942, in Kimball, *Correspondence*, vol. I, p. 421.
43. John Grigg, *1943: The Victory That Never Was* (London: Methuen, paperback ed., 1985), p. 79.
44. Dimbleby, BBC 1 interview with Elliott Roosevelt.
45. Churchill to Richard Law, 17 Feb. 1944, PREM 4/27/10 (PRO).
46. Dimbleby, BBC 1 interview with Sir Ian Jacob.
47. Anderson to Churchill, 30 July 1942, PREM 3/139/8A (PRO).
48. Stimson to Roosevelt, 29 Oct. 1942, in Martin J. Sherwin, *A World Destroyed: The Atomic Bomb and the Grand Alliance* (New York: Vintage Books, 1977), p. 72.
49. Churchill to Hopkins, 27 Feb. 1943, PREM 3/139/8A (PRO).
50. Margaret Gowing, *Britain and Atomic Energy, 1939–1945* (London: Macmillan, 1964), p. 439.
51. Sir Ronald Campbell to Sir John Anderson, 29 Jan. 1945, quoted by Margaret Gowing, 'Nuclear Weapons and the "Special Relationship"', in Wm. Roger Louis and Hedley Bull, eds, *The 'Special Relationship': Anglo-American Relations since 1945* (Oxford: Clarendon Press, 1986), p. 120.
52. Leslie R. Groves, *Now It Can Be Told: The Story of the Manhattan Project* (New York: Da Capo ed., 1983), p. 408.
53. Arthur Bryant, *Triumph in the West, 1943–1946: Based on the Autobiographical Notes of Field Marshal the Viscount Alanbrooke, KG, OM* (London: Collins, 1957), pp. 205–6.
54. Roosevelt to Churchill, 29 June 1944, in Kimball, ed., *Correspondence*, vol. III, p. 222.
55. Churchill to Smuts, 3 Dec. 1944, in Gilbert, *Road to Victory*, p. 1081.
56. Memo by H. B. Butler, 15 May 1942, WP (42) 208, CAB 66/24 (PRO).
57. Joint Staff Mission to AMSSO, tel. 96, June 1944, FO 371/38696, AN 2423/2113/45 (PRO).
58. *Chicago Tribune*, 2 Aug. 1944, in Thorne, *Allies of a Kind*, p. 392.
59. Churchill to Eden, 16 Jan. 1944, PREM 3/399/6 (PRO).
60. Churchill to Eden, 8 May 1944, FO 954/20 (PRO).
61. Memorandum of Kremlin meeting, 9 Oct. 1944, in Graham Ross, ed., *The Foreign Office and the Kremlin: British Documents on Anglo-Soviet*

Relations, 1941–45 (Cambridge: Cambridge University Press, 1984), p. 174.

62. FDR's meeting with Senators, Jan. 1945, in Robert Dallek, *Franklin D. Roosevelt and American Foreign Policy, 1932–1945* (New York: Oxford University Press, 1979), pp. 507–8.
63. Sir John Colville, *The Fringes of Power: Downing Street Diaries, 1939–1955* (London: Hodder and Stoughton, 1985), p. 555, entry for 23 Jan. 1945.
64. Diane Shaver Clemens, *Yalta* (New York: Oxford University Press, 1970), p. 306.
65. Sherwood, *Roosevelt and Hopkins*, p. 870.
66. Hugh Dalton, diary, vol. 32, p. 28, 23 Feb. 1945 (British Library of Political and Economic Science, London).
67. Churchill, *Second World War*, vol. VI, pp. 413 and 417.
68. Eden to Churchill, 8 May 1945, in Gilbert, *Road to Victory*, p. 1351.
69. Appeal of 27 Dec. 1941, in R. J. Bell, *Unequal Allies: Australian-American Relations and the Pacific War* (Melbourne: Melbourne University Press, 1977), p. 47.
70. Ronald H. Spector, *Eagle Against the Sun: The American War with Japan* (New York: Vintage Books, 1985), p. 544.
71. Recalled by Alger Hiss in Michael Charlton, *The Eagle and the Small Birds. Crisis in the Soviet Empire: From Yalta to Solidarity* (London: BBC Publications, 1984), p. 46.
72. *New York Herald Tribune*, 15 Aug. 1945, in Thorne, *Allies of a Kind*, p. 503. Understandably the debate on the use of the bomb rumbles on – were the Japanese about to surrender? how far did the USA have Russia in mind? For the 'revisionist' case see Gar Alperovitz, *Atomic Diplomacy: The Use of the Atomic Bomb and the American Confrontation with Soviet Power* (New York: 2nd ed., Penguin books, 1985).
73. Brooke diary, 1 April 1945, in Bryant, *Triumph in the West*, p. 455.

BACKGROUND READING

1 General

James L. Stokesbury, *A Short History of World War II* (New York: William Morrow, 1980). A lively narrative.

Peter Calvocoressi and Guy Wint, *Total War: Causes and Courses of the Second World War* (Harmondsworth: Penguin, 1974). A big yet vivid book, as strong on Asia as on Europe.

Henry Pelling, *Britain and the Second World War* (London: Fontana, 1970). An excellent short study of the war at home and abroad.

Gaddis Smith, *American Diplomacy during the Second World War, 1941–1945* (New York: John Wiley, 2nd ed., 1985). A useful survey.

2 Biographical

James MacGregor Burns, *Roosevelt: The Soldier of Freedom, 1940–1945* (New York: Harcourt, Brace, Jovanovich, 1970). Still the best biography of FDR in this period. (See also Dallek, cited in reading to chapter 7.)

Martin Gilbert, *Road to Victory: Winston S. Churchill, 1941–1945* (London: Heinemann, 1986). Day-by-day account of Churchill's war, with extensive quotation from his papers.

3 Studies of the Anglo-American relationship

David Reynolds, 'Roosevelt, Churchill, and the Wartime Anglo-American Alliance, 1939–1945: Towards a New Synthesis', in Wm. Roger Louis and Hedley Bull, eds, *The 'Special Relationship': Anglo-American Relations since 1945* (Oxford: Clarendon Press, 1986), pp. 17–41. A survey of the relationship in its various facets, synthesising recent scholarship.

Christopher Thorne, *Allies of a Kind: The United States, Britain, and the War Against Japan, 1941–1945* (London: Hamish Hamilton, 1977). Vast yet incisive analysis of how the two allies conducted the Pacific war, with particular attention to China, India, south-east Asia and Australasia.

Wm. Roger Louis, *Imperialism at Bay, 1941–1945: The United States and the Decolonization of the British Empire* (Oxford: Clarendon Press, 1977). Detailed study of the debates about colonies, trusteeship, etc.

Alan P. Dobson, *US Wartime Aid to Britain, 1940–1946* (London: Croom Helm, 1986). Monograph on the tangled diplomacy of Lend-Lease.

Norman Longmate, *The G.I.s: The Americans in Britain, 1942–1945* (London: Hutchinson, 1975). Readable account, based on oral history and some British archives.

Chapter 9 Uniting Against Russia, 1945–9

1. Dimbleby, BBC 1 interview with Donald Worby.
2. Dimbleby, BBC 1 interview with Barbara Markus.
3. Winston S. Churchill, *The Second World War* (6 vols, London: Cassell, 1948–54), vol. VI, p. 583.

4. Sir Orme Sargent, soon to become Permanent Under-Secretary at the Foreign Office, quoted in Kenneth O. Morgan, *Labour in Power, 1945–1951* (Oxford: Oxford University Press, 1985), p. 42.
5. Quotations from Bevin, in Commons, *Debates*, vol. 437, col. 1965, 16 May 1947, and from David Dilks, ed., *The Diaries of Sir Alexander Cadogan, OM, 1938–1945* (London: Cassell, 1971), 2 Aug. 1945, p. 778.
6. Treasury memo, 14 Aug. 1945, CP (45) 112, CAB 129/1 (Public Record Office, London).
7. Dimbleby, BBC 1 interview with Claude Pepper.
8. Dimbleby, BBC 1 interview with Marion T. Bennett (Republican Congressman from Missouri, 1943–9).
9. Gen. Robert E. Wood to Will Clayton, 26 Nov. 1945, in Richard N. Gardner, *Sterling–Dollar Diplomacy in Current Perspective* (New York: Columbia University Press, 1980), p. 197.
10. Speech to businessmen in Detroit, 21 May 1945, in Robert A. Pollard, *Economic Security and the Origins of the Cold War, 1945–1950* (New York: Columbia University Press, 1985), p. 2.
11. Armand van Dormael, *Bretton Woods: Birth of a Monetary System* (London: Macmillan, 1978), p. 133.
12. *New York Herald Tribune*, 31 March 1946, in David Rees, *Harry Dexter White: A Study in Paradox* (New York: Macmillan, 1973), p. 138.
13. Quotations from Robert Boothby and Jennie Lee, 12 and 13 Dec. 1945, in House of Commons, *Debates*, vol. 417, cols 468 and 669.
14. *The Economist*, 15 Dec. 1945, p. 850.
15. Rep. Emmanuel Celler, in Gardner, *Sterling–Dollar Diplomacy*, p. 237.
16. Memo of 19 Sept. 1944, in Margaret Gowing, *Britain and Atomic Energy, 1939–1945* (London: Macmillan, 1964), p. 447.
17. Agreement of 15 Nov. 1945, in Margaret Gowing, assisted by Lorna Arnold, *Independence and Deterrence: Britain and Atomic Energy, 1945–1952* (2 vols, London: Macmillan, 1974), vol. I, p. 76.
18. A. V. Alexander, memo of 12 Oct. 1949 on meeting with Senator McMahon, 8 Oct., PREM 8/1097 (PRO).
19. Acheson memo of March 1946, in Gregg Herken, *The Winning Weapon: the Atomic Bomb in the Cold War, 1945–1950* (New York: Vintage Books, 1982), p. 145.
20. Bevin, 26 Oct. 1946, as recalled by Sir Michael Perrin, in Alan Bullock, *Ernest Bevin: Foreign Secretary, 1945–1951* (London: Heinemann, 1983), p. 352.
21. Speech in June 1946, in Wm. Roger Louis, *The British Empire in the Middle East, 1945–51* (Oxford: Clarendon Press, 1984), p. 428.
22. Bevin, in conversation with Molotov, 23 Sept. 1945. Faced with Molo-

tov's indignation, he later retracted, but the remark shows his state of mind. Bullock, *Bevin*, p. 132.

23. Sir Orme Sargent, minute, 1 Oct. 1945, FO 371/44557, AN 2560/22/45 (PRO).
24. Pierson Dixon, minute, 24 Sept. 1945, in Graham Ross, ed., *The Foreign Office and the Kremlin: British Documents on Anglo-Soviet Relations, 1941–45* (Cambridge: Cambridge University Press, 1984), p. 252.
25. Memo-letter of 5 Jan. 1946, in Robert L. Messer, *The End of an Alliance: James F. Byrnes, Roosevelt, Truman, and the Origins of the Cold War* (Chapel Hill: University of North Carolina, 1982), p. 158. Truman said in his memoirs that he read out this passage as a stinging rebuke to Byrnes, a claim Messer convincingly refutes. But Messer acknowledges that the memo did broadly represent Truman's thinking by early 1946.
26. Churchill to Attlee, 7 March 1946, in Fraser J. Harbutt, *The Iron Curtain: Churchill, America, and the Origins of the Cold War* (New York: Oxford University Press, 1986), p. 180.
27. Robert Rhodes James, ed., *Winston S. Churchill: His Complete Speeches* (New York: Chelsea House, 1974), vol. VII, pp. 7285–93.
28. Thomas H. Etzold and John L. Gaddis, eds, *Containment: Documents on American Policy and Strategy, 1945–1950* (New York: Columbia University Press, 1978), pp. 50–63.
29. JCS 1641/3, 13 March 1946, in Richard A. Best, Jr, *'Co-operation with Like-Minded Peoples': British Influences on American Security Policy, 1945–1949* (New York: Greenwood Press, 1986), p. 121.
30. John L. Gaddis, *The United States and the Origins of the Cold War, 1941–1947* (New York: Columbia University Press, 1972), p. 309.
31. *Wall Street Journal*, 19 March 1946, in Robin Edmonds, *Setting the Mould: The United States and Britain, 1945–1950* (Oxford: Clarendon Press, 1986), p. 6.
32. Kennedy (March 1946), in Gardner, *Sterling–Dollar Diplomacy*, p. 250.
33. Memo by Chancellor of the Exchequer, 21 March 1947, in Sir Richard Clarke, *Anglo-American Economic Collaboration in War and Peace, 1942–1949* (Oxford: Clarendon Press, 1982), p. 156.
34. British Embassy to State Dept., 21 Feb. 1947, in Terry H. Anderson, *The United States, Great Britain, and the Cold War, 1944–1947* (Columbia, Missouri: University of Columbia Press, 1981), p. 169.
35. Memo of 21 Feb. 1947, in Lawrence S. Wittner, *American Intervention in Greece, 1943–1949* (New York: Columbia University Press, 1982), p. 67.
36. Recollection of meeting of 27 Feb. 1947, in Dean Acheson, *Present at the Creation: My Years in the State Department* (London: Hamish Hamilton, 1970), p. 219.

37. Quoted in Best, *'Co-operation between Like-Minded Peoples'*, p. 134.
38. *Public Papers of the Presidents of the United States: Harry S. Truman, 1947* (Washington: Government Printing Office, 1963), pp. 176–80.
39. Clayton, memo, 27 May 1947, in US Dept. of State, *Foreign Relations of the United States, 1947* (Washington: Government Printing Office, 1972), vol. III, pp. 230–2.
40. Speech of 5 June 1947, in *Foreign Relations, 1947*, vol. III, p. 239.
41. Speech in Washington, 1 April 1949, in Bullock, *Bevin*, p. 405. For US priming see Walter Lipgens, *A History of European Integration, vol. i, 1945–7* (Oxford: Clarendon Press, 1982), p. 507.
42. Ben T. Moore to Clair Wilcox, 28 July 1947, in *Foreign Relations, 1947*, vol. III, p. 239.
43. Quotations from Truman and Clay in Robert J. Donovan, *Conflict and Crisis: The Presidency of Harry S. Truman, 1945–1948* (New York: W. W. Norton, 1977), pp. 359–60.
44. Bevin, memo, 'The Threat to Western Civilisation', 3 March 1948, CP (48) 72, CAB 129/25 (PRO).
45. Marshall to Lord Inverchapel, 12 March 1948, in US Dept. of State, *Foreign Relations of the United States, 1948* (Washington: Government Printing Office, 1974), vol. III, p. 48.
46. Internal State Dept. policy statement, 26 Aug. 1948, in Etzold and Gaddis, eds, *Containment*, p. 130.
47. Quoted in Avi Shlaim, *The United States and the Berlin Blockade, 1948–1949* (Berkeley: University of California Press, 1983), pp. 195–6.
48. Dimbleby, BBC 1 interview with Gen. Leon Johnson.
49. Quoted in *The World Today*, vol. 16 (Aug. 1960), p. 320.
50. Walter Millis, ed., *The Forrestal Diaries* (London: Cassell, 1952), 15 July 1948, pp. 429–30.
51. Simon Duke, *US Defence Bases in the United Kingdom: A Matter for Joint Decision?* (London: Macmillan, 1987), p. 40.
52. Except Vice-Chief of the Air Staff, Sir William Dickson. Gowing, *Independence and Deterrence*, vol. I, pp. 250–1.
53. Bevin to State Dept., 9 April 1948, in Alan K. Henrikson, 'The Creation of the North Atlantic Alliance, 1948–1952', *US Naval War College Review*, vol. 32 (May–June 1980), p. 15.
54. Acheson, quoted in Timothy P. Ireland, *Creating the Entangling Alliance: The Origins of the North Atlantic Treaty Organization* (New York: Greenwood Press, 1981), p. 110.
55. North Atlantic Treaty, 4 April 1949, article 5, in US Dept. of State, *Foreign Relations of the United States, 1949* (Washington: Government Printing Office, 1975), vol. IV, p. 282.
56. Remarks on 4 April 1949 in *Public Papers of the Presidents of the United*

States: Harry S. Truman, 1949 (Washington: Government Printing Office, 1964), pp. 196–8.

57. Gardner, *Sterling–Dollar Diplomacy*, p. xiii.
58. Douglas to Sec. State, 11 Aug. 1948, in US Dept. of State, *Foreign Relations of the United States, 1948* (Washington: Government Printing Office, 1974), vol. III, p. 1113.

BACKGROUND READING

1 General books on the origins of the Cold War

Martin McCauley, *The Origins of the Cold War* (London: Longman, 1983). A brief introduction, with documents, concentrating on the years 1941–8.

Thomas G. Paterson, *On Every Front: The Making of the Cold War* (New York: W. W. Norton, 1979). A short, readable analysis of US policy, 1945–50.

Elisabeth Barker, *The British between the Superpowers, 1945–50* (London: Macmillan, 1983). Useful narrative based on official British archives.

2 *General surveys of Anglo-American relations since 1945* (Useful background for this and subsequent chapters.)

John Baylis, *Anglo-American Defence Relations, 1939–1984* (London: Macmillan, 1984). The best survey of military matters.

Wm. Roger Louis and Hedley Bull, eds, *The 'Special Relationship': Anglo-American Relations since 1945* (Oxford: Clarendon Press, 1986). A wide range of essays on all aspects of the relationship – by historical period and theme (military, economic and in the Third World).

Jeffrey T. Richelson and Desmond Ball, *The Ties that Bind: Intelligence Co-operation between the UKUSA Countries* (London: Allen and Unwin, 1985). Recent study of the vital intelligence relationship; full of detail, but not always very revealing.

David Reynolds, 'A "special relationship"?: America, Britain and the International Order since World War Two', *International Affairs*, vol. 62 (winter 1985/6), pp. 1–20. An interpretative survey.

3 Studies of Anglo-American relations

Robin Edmonds, *Setting the Mould: The United States and Britain, 1945–1950* (Oxford: Clarendon Press, 1986). The best survey, synthesising recent scholarship.

Robert M. Hathaway, *Ambiguous Partnership: Britain and America, 1944–1947* (New York: Columbia University Press, 1981). Covers the general relationship from the autumn of 1944 to the spring of 1947.

Terry H. Anderson, *The United States, Great Britain, and the Cold War, 1944–1947* (Columbia, Missouri: University of Columbia Press, 1981). Covers a similar period but concentrates on British influence on US policy towards Russia.

Henry B. Ryan, *The Vision of Anglo-America: The US–UK Alliance and the Emerging Cold War, 1943–1946* (Cambridge: Cambridge University Press, 1987). British policy towards the USA in the Greek and Polish crises.

Fraser J. Harbutt, *The Iron Curtain: Churchill, America, and the Origins of the Cold War* (New York: Oxford University Press, 1986). An incisive account, focusing on the winter of 1945–6, but probably exaggerating Churchill's impact on US diplomacy.

Richard A. Best, Jr, *'Co-operation with Like-Minded Peoples': British Influences on American Security Policy, 1945–1949* (New York: Greenwood Press, 1986). Examines US strategic planning; also probably overstating British influence.

Michael J. Hogan, *The Marshall Plan: America, Britain and the Reconstruction of Western Europe, 1947–1952* (New York: Cambridge University Press, 1987). A major new assessment of the origins and impact of the plan.

Chapter 10 Global Cold War, 1949–54

1. Robert J. Donovan, *Tumultuous Years: The Presidency of Harry S. Truman, 1949–1953* (New York: W. W. Norton, 1982), p. 191.
2. Acheson remarks of 24 Feb. 1949, in Ritchie Ovendale, *The English-Speaking Alliance: Britain, the United States, the Dominions and the Cold War, 1945–51* (London: George Allen and Unwin, 1985), p. 187.
3. Mundt, speech of 18 April 1949, in Justus D. Doenecke, *Not to the Swift: The Old Isolationists in the Cold War Era* (London: Associated Universities Press, 1979), p. 179.
4. Wheeling speech, 9 Feb. 1950, in Thomas C. Reeves, *The Life and Times of Joe McCarthy: A Biography* (New York: Stein and Day, 1982), pp. 224–7.
5. Acheson to Douglas for British Govt., 27 June 1950, in Peter Lowe, *The Origins of the Korean War* (London: Longman, 1986), p. 162.
6. Press conference, 30 Nov. 1950, in *The Public Papers of the Presidents:*

Harry S. Truman, 1950 (Washington: Government Printing Office, 1965), p. 727.
7. Dimbleby, BBC 1 interview with Paul Nitze.
8. Pierson Dixon, minute, 12 July 1950, in M. L. Dockrill, 'The Foreign Office, Anglo-American Relations and the Korean War, June 1950–June 1951', in *International Affairs*, vol. 62 (1986), p. 462.
9. George Orwell, *Nineteen Eighty-Four* (London: Secker and Warburg, 1949), p. 7.
10. MOD, brief for Defence Commt. meeting of 31 Jan. 1950, in DEFE 7/516 (PRO).
11. Bevin, draft despatch to Washington, 26 Nov. 1949, in DEFE 7/516.
12. C. A. E. Shuckburgh, draft FO memo, 'United States Air Force Groups in the United Kingdom', 4 Jan. 1950, in DEFE 7/516.
13. Dimbleby, BBC 1 interview with David Rolain.
14. Comments in Chiefs of Staff meeting, 27 July 1950, in N. J. Wheeler, 'British nuclear weapons and Anglo-American relations', *International Affairs*, vol. 62 (winter 1985–6), p. 74.
15. Dimbleby, BBC1 interview with Clark Clifford.
16. Philip Jessup, memorandum for the record, 7 Dec. 1950, in US Dept. of State, *Foreign Relations of the United States, 1950* (Washington: Government Printing Office, 1976), vol. VII, p. 1462.
17. Dimbleby, BBC 1 interview with Gordon Arneson.
18. Copy of communiqué, 8 Dec. 1950, in PREM 8/1200 (PRO).
19. Exchange of 7 March 1951, in John Baylis, 'American Bases in Britain: The "Truman–Attlee" Understandings', *The World Today*, vol. 42 (Aug./Sept. 1986), p. 156.
20. Dimbleby, BBC 1 interview with Lucius Battle.
21. Bevin to Attlee, 12 Jan. 1951, PREM 8/1439 (PRO).
22. Ben Pimlott, ed., *The Political Diary of Hugh Dalton, 1918–40, 1945–60* (London: Jonathan Cape, 1986), p. 505.
23. Quoted in Dean Acheson, *Present at the Creation: My Years in the State Department* (London: Hamish Hamilton, 1969), p. 399.
24. Geoffrey Bing, *et al.*, *Keep Left* (London: *New Statesman*, May 1947), pp. 33, 42. The authors included Richard Crossman and Michael Foot.
25. House of Commons, *Debates*, 23 Jan. 1948, vol. 446, col. 566.
26. House of Commons, *Debates*, 23 April 1951, vol. 487, col. 38.
27. *Daily Sketch*, quoted in Michael Foot, *Aneurin Bevan: A Biography*, vol. II (London: Davis–Poynter, 1973), p. 339.
28. Memo of June or July 1952, in Philip M. Williams, ed., *The Diary of Hugh Gaitskell, 1945–1956* (London: Jonathan Cape, 1983), pp. 316–17.
29. Dimbleby, BBC 1 interview with Sir Evelyn Shuckburgh.

30. Robert Ferrell, ed., *The Eisenhower Diaries* (New York: W. W. Norton, 1981), 6 Jan. 1953, p. 223.
31. House of Commons, *Debates*, 15 Feb. 1951, vol. 484, col. 630.
32. Arneson to Secretary of State, 18 Oct. 1951, in Baylis, 'American Bases in Britain', p. 158.
33. Statement of 9 Jan. 1952, in FO 371/97592, AU 1051/12 (PRO).
34. Arneson, memo on proposed UK statement, 17 Oct. 1951, in Baylis, 'American Bases in Britain', p. 157. The Foreign Office, for instance, was telling peace groups in 1955 that, as a result of the statement, 'it would be impossible for the Americans in this country to take any military action without the consent of Her Majesty's Government'. R. P. Pinsent to Mrs E. F. Ineson, 2 Mar. 1955, FO 371/114415, AU 11917/2 (PRO).
35. Sir Eyre Crowe, quoted in Michael J. Hogan, *Informal Entente: The Private Structure of Co-operation in Anglo-American Economic Diplomacy, 1918–1928* (Columbia, Missouri: University of Missouri Press, 1977), p. 172.
36. Michael B. Stoff, *Oil, War, and American Security: The Search for a National Policy on Foreign Oil, 1941–1947* (New Haven: Yale University Press, 1980), p. 209.
37. Roosevelt to Churchill, 3 March 1944, and Churchill to Roosevelt, 4 March 1944, in Warren F. Kimball, ed., *Churchill and Roosevelt: The Complete Correspondence* (3 vols, Princeton: Princeton University Press, 1984), vol. III, pp. 14, 17.
38. CM 60 (51) 6, CAB 128/20 (PRO).
39. Sir Francis Shepherd, in Wm. Roger Louis, *The British Empire in the Middle East, 1945–51: Arab Nationalism, the United States and Postwar Imperialism* (Oxford: Clarendon Press, 1984), p. 651.
40. Acheson, *Present at the Creation*, p. 503.
41. Stephen Ambrose, with Richard Immerman, *Ike's Spies: Eisenhower and the Espionage Establishment* (New York: Doubleday, 1981), p. 200.
42. Ritchie Ovendale, *The Origins of the Arab-Israeli Wars* (London: Longman, 1984), p. 136.
43. Dimbleby, BBC 1 interview with George McGhee.
44. Sir Roger Makins, memo, 25 Jan. 1954, quoted in Wm. Roger Louis, 'American Anti-Colonialism and the Dissolution of the British Empire', in Wm. Roger Louis and Hedley Bull, eds, *The 'Special Relationship': Anglo-American Relations since 1945* (Oxford: Clarendon Press, 1986), p. 260.
45. Record of JCS-State Dept. meeting, 21 Nov. 1951, in US Dept. of State, *Foreign Relations of the United States, 1951* (Washington: Government Printing Office, 1983), vol. IV, p. 985.
46. Acheson, *Present at the Creation*, pp. 387–8.

47. NSC 48/1, 23 Dec. 1949, in Thomas H. Etzold and John L. Gaddis, eds, *Containment: Documents on American Policy and Strategy, 1945–1950* (New York: Columbia University Press, 1978), p. 259.
48. Eisenhower, 7 Feb. 1954, in George C. Herring and Richard H. Immerman, 'Eisenhower, Dulles and Dienbienphu: "The Day We Didn't Go to War" Revisited', *Journal of American History*, vol. 71 (1984), p. 346.
49. Eisenhower to Churchill, 5 April 1954, PREM 11/1074 (PRO).
50. Dulles-Eden memcon, 25 April 1954, in US Dept. of State, *Foreign Relations of the United States, 1952–4* (Washington: Government Printing Office, 1981), vol. XVI, p. 555.
51. George C. Herring, *America's Longest War: The United States and Vietnam, 1950–1975* (New York: John Wiley, 1979), p. 34.
52. Evelyn Shuckburgh, *Descent into Suez: Diaries, 1951–56* (London: Weidenfeld and Nicolson, 1986), p. 187, diary for 2 May 1954.
53. The comment of biographer Townsend Hoopes, *The Devil and John Foster Dulles* (London: André Deutsch, 1974), p. 222.
54. Shuckburgh, *Descent into Suez*, p. 164, diary entry for 12 April 1954.
55. *New Statesman*, 24 July 1954, in James Cable, *The Geneva Conference of 1954 on Indochina* (London: Macmillan, 1986), p. 128.
56. Dulles, statement to North Atlantic Council, 14 Dec. 1953, in US Dept. of State, *Foreign Relations of the United States, 1952–4* (Washington: Government Printing Office, 1983), vol. V, p. 868.
57. Butterworth to State Dept., 8 Sept. 1954, in *Foreign Relations of the United States, 1952–4*, vol. V, p. 1154.
58. Edward Fursdon, *The European Defence Community: A History* (London: Macmillan, 1980), pp. 321–2.

BACKGROUND READING

1 Studies of Anglo-American relations

We are now entering the no-man's-land between memoir and history, when the archives are either not yet opened or their materials still undigested in book form. But two studies are already available:

Ritchie Ovendale, *The English-Speaking Alliance: Britain, the United States, the Dominions and the Cold War, 1945–51* (London: George Allen and Unwin, 1985). From a British perspective examines the Anglo-American relationship over such issues as China, Korea and the Middle East.

Simon Duke, *US Defence Bases in the United Kingdom: A Matter for Joint*

Decision? (London: Macmillan, 1987). Covers the whole post-war period, though fullest on the years 1948–54.

See also background reading for chapter 9, especially:

Wm. Roger Louis and Hedley Bull, eds, *The 'Special Relationship': Anglo-American Relations since 1945* (Oxford: Clarendon Press, 1986) – essays by Bradford Perkins on the Truman era and D. Cameron Watt on the Eisenhower era.

2 *Biographies*

Stephen Ambrose, *Eisenhower: The President* (New York: Simon and Schuster, 1984). The best recent one-volume survey of his presidency.

Townsend Hoopes, *The Devil and John Foster Dulles* (London: André Deutsch, 1974). A detailed and critical evaluation of his diplomacy.

David Carlton, *Anthony Eden: A Biography* (London: Allen Lane, 1981). A recent account, often very critical of Eden.

Robert Rhodes James, *Anthony Eden* (London: Weidenfeld and Nicolson, 1986). The more sympathetic official biography, based largely on Eden's papers.

Chapter 11 The Empire's Last Gasp, 1955–6

1. Lord Moran, *Winston Churchill: The Struggle for Survival, 1940–1965* (London: Sphere Books, 1968), 28 April 1953, p. 428.
2. Dimbleby, BBC 1 interview with Sir John Colville.
3. Moran, *Churchill*, 25 June 1953, p. 433.
4. Speech in the Commons, 11 May 1953, in Anthony Seldon, *Churchill's Indian Summer: The Conservative Government, 1951–1955* (London: Hodder and Stoughton, 1981), p. 400.
5. Evelyn Shuckburgh, *Descent to Suez: Diaries, 1951–56* (London: Weidenfeld and Nicolson, 1986), p. 147, entry for 15 March 1954.
6. Speech in Bloomfield, NJ, 10 Oct. 1952, in Townsend Hoopes, *The Devil and John Foster Dulles* (London: André Deutsch, 1974), p. 131.
7. Eden to Churchill, 21 Nov. 1952, PREM 11/323 (Public Record Office, London).
8. Churchill to Eisenhower, 5 April 1953, PREM 11/1074 (PRO).
9. Shuckburgh, *Descent to Suez*, p. 277, entry for 31 Aug. 1955, recording Harold Macmillan on a conversation with Churchill in June.

10. CM 28 (55) 10, 15 Aug. 1955, CAB 128/29 (PRO).
11. Harold Macmillan, *Tides of Fortune, 1945–1955* (London: Macmillan, 1969), pp. 616, 621.
12. Moran, *Churchill*, pp. 462, 536, entries for 19 July and 7 Dec. 1953.
13. Dimbleby, BBC 1 interview with Sir Philip de Zulueta.
14. Stephen E. Ambrose, *Eisenhower the President* (New York: Simon and Schuster, 1984), p. 265.
15. Article on 'The United States of Europe', 15 Feb. 1930, in Michael Wolff, ed., *The Collected Essays of Sir Winston Churchill* (4 vols, London: Library of Imperial History, 1976), vol. II, pp. 184–5.
16. Recalled by Sir Anthony Nutting in Edward Fursdon, *The European Defence Community: A History* (London: Macmillan, 1980), p. 77.
17. Shuckburgh, *Descent to Suez*, p. 18.
18. Speech at Columbia University, New York, 11 Jan. 1952, in David Carlton, *Anthony Eden: A Biography* (London: Allen Lane, 1981), p. 311.
19. Peter Foot, 'Defence Burden-Sharing in the Atlantic Community, 1945–1954', *Aberdeen Studies in Defence Economics*, vol. 20 (summer 1981), p. 13.
20. E. G. Compton (HM Treasury), brief for Churchill, 15 Dec. 1951, in PREM 11/313 (PRO).
21. 'Report by Officials' for Cabinet, CP (55) 55, 29 June 1955, CAB 129/76 (PRO).
22. Moran, *Churchill*, p. 504, entry for 10 Oct. 1953.
23. Eden to Lord Hankey (a director of the Suez Canal Company), Feb. 1953, copy in PREM 11/636 (PRO).
24. Shuckburgh, *Descent to Suez*, p. 327, entry for 29 Jan. 1956.
25. Shuckburgh, *Descent to Suez*, p. 346, entry for 12 March 1956.
26. William J. Burns, *Economic Aid and American Policy toward Egypt, 1955–1981* (Albany, NY: SUNY Press, 1985), Appendix 2, p. 214.
27. Selwyn Lloyd, *Suez, 1956: A Personal Account* (London: Jonathan Cape, 1978), p. 69.
28. Dimbleby, BBC 1 interview with William Macomber.
29. *Keesing's Contemporary Archives*, p. 15001.
30. Egypt Committee, EC (56) 3rd mtg., 30 July 1956, CAB 134/1216 (PRO).
31. Eden to Eisenhower, 27 July 1956, PREM 11/1177 (PRO).
32. Eden to Eisenhower, 5 Aug. 1956, PREM 11/1177 (PRO).
33. Eisenhower, meeting of 31 July 1956, in Ambrose, *Eisenhower: The President*, p. 331.
34. John Colville, *Footprints in Time: Downing Street Diaries, 1939–1955* (London: Hodder and Stoughton, 1985), p. 686, entry for 6 Dec. 1953.
35. Washington Embassy to Foreign Office, telegram 2046, 2 Oct. 1956,

PREM 11/1174 (PRO). Dulles later apologised, calling the press conference 'a really bad blunder' (tel. 2052, 3 Oct. 1956), but Eden never forgave him.

36. Dimbleby, BBC 1 interview with Sir Anthony Nutting.
37. CM 34 (55) 8, 4 Oct. 1955, CAB 128/29 (PRO).
38. Sir Leslie Rowan, note on 'Economic and financial measures in the event of war with Egypt', 11 Sept. 1956, Treasury records, T 236/4188 (PRO).
39. Emmett John Hughes, *The Ordeal of Power: A Political Memoir of the Eisenhower Years* (London: Macmillan, 1963), p. 217, diary entry for 30 Oct. 1956.
40. Dimbleby, interview with William Clark. Clark told this story often – it may well have become exaggerated over time. See Robert Rhodes James, *Anthony Eden* (London: Weidenfeld and Nicolson, 1986), p. 568.
41. Staff notes, 6 Oct. 1956, in Stephen Ambrose, with Richard Immerman, *Ike's Spies: Eisenhower and the Espionage Establishment* (New York: Doubleday, 1981), p. 240.
42. Eisenhower to Eden, 3 Sept. 1956, PREM 11/1177 (PRO).
43. Dulles at NSC, 1 Nov. 1956, in Wm. Roger Louis, 'American Anti-Colonialism and the Dissolution of the British Empire', in Wm. Roger Louis and Hedley Bull, eds, *The 'Special Relationship': Anglo-American Relations since 1945* (Oxford: Clarendon Press, 1986), p. 277.
44. Meeting with J. E. Coulson, 29 Oct. 1956, in Ambrose, *Eisenhower: The President*, p. 359.
45. Ambrose, *Eisenhower: The President*, p. 364.
46. CM 80 (56), 6 Nov. 1956, CAB 128/30 (PRO).
47. Lloyd, *Suez*, p. 219, also pp. 257–8.
48. Dwight D. Eisenhower, *The White House Years: Waging Peace, 1956–1961* (London: Heinemann, 1966), p. 93.
49. Eisenhower to Eden, 7 Nov. 1956, PREM 11/1137 (PRO).
50. Harold Macmillan, *Riding the Storm, 1956–1959* (London: Macmillan, 1971), p. 149. After talking to Eisenhower Macmillan recorded in his diary: 'On Suez, he was sure that we must get Nasser down' (p. 134).
51. Sir Harold Caccia to Foreign Office, tel. 2272, 9 Nov. 1956, T 236/4189 (PRO).
52. Caccia to FO, 27 Nov. 1956, tel. 2352, T 236/4190 (PRO).
53. CM 90 (56), 28 Nov. 1956, CAB 128/30 (PRO).
54. Moran, *Churchill*, pp. 743–4, entries for 26 Nov. and 6 Dec. 1956.
55. House of Commons, *Debates*, vol. 562, col. 1094, 18 Dec. 1956.
56. '"The Grand Design" (Co-operation with Western Europe)', CP (57) 6, 5 Jan. 1957, CAB 129/84 (PRO).
57. Cabinet minutes, CM (57) 3, 8 Jan. 1957, CAB 128/30 (PRO).

BACKGROUND READING

See also general reading cited in chapter 9 and the biographies listed in chapter 10. Rhodes James's biography of Eden is the first non-memoir to use the British Cabinet documents extensively.

Studies of Suez (all before the archives were opened)

Hugh Thomas, *The Suez Affair* (London: Weidenfeld and Nicolson, 3rd ed., 1986). Originally published in 1966 and based on extensive interviews, this remains a very good account.

Richard E. Neustadt, *Alliance Politics* (New York: Columbia University Press, 1970). Suez as a case study in Anglo-American misperceptions.

Selwyn Lloyd, *Suez, 1956: A Personal Account* (London: Jonathan Cape, 1978). Posthumous apology, glossing over the full extent of collusion.

Donald Neff, *Warriors at Suez: Eisenhower takes America into the Middle East* (New York: The Linden Press/Simon and Schuster, 1981). A full account from an American perspective.

Chapter 12 Dependence and Deterrence, 1957–63

1. Richard E. Neustadt, *Alliance Politics* (New York: Columbia University Press, 1970), p. 21.
2. Dimbleby, BBC 1 interview with General Andrew Goodpaster [Eisenhower's Staff Secretary and closest foreign policy aide].
3. Harold Macmillan, *Riding the Storm, 1956–1959* (London: Macmillan, 1971), pp. 253–4, record for 21 March 1957.
4. Makins, quoted in Douglas MacArthur II, memo, 2 Dec. 1953, in *Foreign Relations of the United States, 1952–4* (Washington: Government Printing Office, 1983), vol. V, p. 1726.
5. Dimbleby – Goodpaster interview.
6. Churchill to Eden, tel. T2/53, 6 Jan. 1953, PREM 11/373 (PRO).
7. Understanding of 9 Jan. 1952, FO 371/97592, AU 1051/12 (PRO). See also above, chapter 10.
8. House of Commons, *Debates*, 1 April 1957, vol. 568, col. 56.
9. Dwight D. Eisenhower, *The White House Years: Waging Peace, 1956–1961* (London: Heinemann, 1966), p. 124.
10. Robert A. Divine, *Blowing on the Wind: The Nuclear Test Ban Debate, 1954–1960* (New York: Oxford University Press, 1978), p. 170.

11. Comments of 1 Jan. 1957, in Robert A. Divine, *Eisenhower and the Cold War* (Oxford: Oxford University Press, 1981), p. 90.
12. Stephen E. Ambrose, *Eisenhower: The President* (New York: Simon and Schuster, 1984), p. 471.
13. Quoted in Macmillan, *Riding the Storm*, p. 534.
14. Harold Macmillan, *Pointing the Way, 1959–1961* (London: Macmillan, 1972), p. 252, diary entry for 29 March 1960.
15. Denis Healey, article in *Commentary*, May 1961, quoted in Philip M. Williams, *Hugh Gaitskell* (Oxford: Oxford University Press, 1982), p. 341.
16. House of Commons, *Debates*, 1 Nov. 1960, vol. 629, col. 122.
17. Commons, *Debates*, 8 Nov. 1960, vol. 629, col. 831.
18. Dimbleby – Goodpaster interview.
19. Michael R. Beschloss, *MAYDAY: Eisenhower, Khrushchev and the U–2 Affair* (New York: Harper and Row, 1986), p. 278.
20. Dimbleby, BBC 1 interview with Sir Philip de Zulueta.
21. Robert H. Estabrook, interview with John Russell of FO, 18 Oct. 1961, Estabrook papers (John F. Kennedy Library, Boston).
22. Macmillan to Ike, 10 Nov. 1960, in Macmillan, *Pointing the Way*, p. 284.
23. Quotations from Kennedy inaugural, 21 Jan. 1961, in Theodore C. Sorensen, *Kennedy* (London: Hodder and Stoughton, 1965), pp. 245–8.
24. Dimbleby – de Zulueta interview.
25. The phrase comes from David Bruce, Kennedy's Ambassador to Britain. See Bruce to State Dept., telegram 2295, 12 Dec. 1961, National Security File, NSF 170/12 (Kennedy Library).
26. Arthur M. Schlesinger, Jr, *A Thousand Days: John F. Kennedy in the White House* (New York: Fawcett Books, 1971), p. 350.
27. Schlesinger, *Thousand Days*, p. 348.
28. Dimbleby, BBC 1 interview with Dean Rusk.
29. Herbert S. Parmet, *JFK: The Presidency of John F. Kennedy* (Harmondsworth: Penguin Books, 1984), p. 187.
30. *New York Times*, 6 June 1961, p. 14.
31. Schlesinger, *Thousand Days*, p. 350.
32. Dimbleby – de Zulueta interview.
33. Macmillan, *Pointing the Way*, p. 339.
34. Schlesinger, *Thousand Days*, p. 273.
35. Robert F. Kennedy, *Thirteen Days: The Cuban Missile Crisis* (London: Pan, 1969), pp. 134–5.
36. *Tribune*, quoted in David Nunnerley, *President Kennedy and Britain* (London: Bodley Head, 1972), p. 73.
37. Dimbleby, BBC 1 interview with George Ball.

38. Dimbleby – Rusk interview.
39. House of Commons, *Debates*, 30 Oct. 1962, vol. 666, col. 34.
40. Henry Owen (State Dept.) and Henry Rowen (Defense Dept.), draft memo, 'A New Approach to France', 21 April 1961, NSF 70 (Kennedy Library).
41. Speech at Ann Arbor, Michigan, 16 June 1962, in John D. Steinbruner, *The Cybernetic Theory of Decision: New Dimensions of Political Analysis* (Princeton: Princeton University Press, 1974), p. 206. The title conceals a very useful study of the MLF idea in American policy-making.
42. House of Commons, *Debates*, 26 June 1962, vol. 661, col. 957.
43. Richard E. Neustadt, report to the President, 15 Nov. 1963, 'Skybolt and Nassau', p. 52, NSF 322 (Kennedy Library). This is a 'sanitised' version of Neustadt's post-mortem on the crisis, but it reveals considerably more than the published account in Richard E. Neustadt, *Alliance Politics* (New York: Columbia University Press, 1970), although that remains the best published source. The interpretation offered here has also benefited greatly from Professor Neustadt's conversations with David Reynolds in Washington and at Harvard in May 1985.
44. Dimbleby, BBC 1 interview with Paul Nitze.
45. Dimbleby – Rusk interview.
46. Acheson's speech, West Point, 5 Dec. 1962, in Ian S. McDonald, ed., *Anglo-American Relations since the Second World War* (New York: St Martin's Press, 1974), pp. 181–2.
47. Published letter to Lord Chandos, 7 Dec. 1962, in Harold Macmillan, *At the End of the Day, 1961–1963* (London: Macmillan, 1973), p. 339.
48. McGeorge Bundy to Robert J. Manning, 7 Dec. 1962, NSF 170A/34 (Kennedy Library).
49. Dimbleby – Ball interview.
50. George W. Ball, *The Past Has Another Pattern: Memoirs* (New York: W. W. Norton, 1982), p. 267.
51. Henry Brandon, 'SKYBOLT: The Full Inside Story of How a Missile Nearly Split the West', *Sunday Times*, 8 Dec. 1963, pp. 29–31.
52. State Dept., British desk, 'Current Political Scene in the UK', 13 Dec. 1962, NSF 238: Nassau (Kennedy Library).
53. Macmillan, *At the End of the Day*, p. 358.
54. Macmillan, *At the End of the Day*, p. 360.
55. Dimbleby – de Zulueta interview.
56. Joint statement, 21 Dec. 1962, in *Public Papers of the Presidents of the United States: John F. Kennedy, 1962* (Washington: Government Printing Office, 1963), p. 909.
57. Richard J. Barnet, *Allies: America, Europe and Japan since the War* (London: Jonathan Cape, 1983), p. 181.

58. Assurance to Macmillan recorded in McGeorge Bundy, memo for the President, 7 April 1961, NSF 170/2 (Kennedy Library).
59. French agriculture minister, in Macmillan, *At the End of the Day*, p. 365, diary entry for 12 Jan. 1963.
60. Charles de Gaulle, *War Memoirs: Unity, 1942–1944*, trans. Richard Howard (London: Weidenfeld, 1956), p. 227.
61. De Gaulle's press statement, 14 Jan. 1963, official French translation, p. 7, NSF 73 (Kennedy Library).
62. Macmillan, *At the End of the Day*, p. 367, diary entry for 28 Jan. 1963.
63. Sir Michael Wright, in Nunnerley, *President Kennedy and Britain*, p. 109.
64. Glenn T. Seaborg, with Benjamin S. Loeb, *Kennedy, Khrushchev and the Test Ban* (Berkeley: University of California Press, 1981), p. 208. Seaborg was Chairman of the US Atomic Energy Commission.
65. Gore to Kennedy, 2 Aug. 1963, President's Office File, POF 31 (Kennedy Library).

BACKGROUND READING

1 Biographies

The official biography of Macmillan is still being written by Alistair Horne, but Macmillan's memoirs provide a good deal of useful material: *Riding the Storm, 1955–1959* (London: Macmillan, 1971); *Pointing the Way, 1959–1961* (1972); and *At the End of the Day, 1961–1963* (1973).

On Eisenhower see the memoirs, Dwight D. Eisenhower, *The White House Years: Waging Peace, 1956–1961*, (London: Heinemann, 1966) and Stephen Ambrose's biography cited in chapter 10.

On Kennedy, the study originally published by insider-historian Arthur M. Schlesinger, in 1965, *A Thousand Days: John F. Kennedy in the White House* (New York: Fawcett ed., 1971), remains essential reading, but see also Herbert S. Parmet, *JFK: The Presidency of John F. Kennedy* (Harmondsworth: Penguin, 1984).

2 Studies of Anglo-American relations

David Nunnerley, *President Kennedy and Britain* (London: Bodley Head, 1972). An excellent study of Anglo-American relations, 1961–3, based on extensive interviews, which still holds up well.

Andrew J. Pierre, *Nuclear Politics: The British Experience with an Independent Strategic Force, 1939–1970* (London: Oxford University Press, 1972). Written by a former US diplomat, much involved in nuclear negotiations of the 1960s, this is a detailed study with many penetrating insights into the Anglo-American relationship.

On nuclear relations see also the studies by John Baylis and Simon Duke (cited respectively in the reading for chapters 9 and 10).

Chapter 13 Drifting Apart, 1963–73

1. Doris Kearns, *Lyndon Johnson and the American Dream* (New York: Signet, 1976), p. 177.
2. Broadcast of 17 July 1964 in D. E. Butler and Anthony King, *The General Election of 1964* (London: Macmillan, 1964), p. 26, note 1. See also pp. 75 and 149.
3. Sir Alec Douglas-Home in Andrew J. Pierre, *Nuclear Politics: The British Experience with an Independent Strategic Force, 1939–1970* (London: Oxford University Press, 1972), p. 256.
4. Dimbleby, BBC 1 interview with Denis Healey.
5. Dimbleby, BBC 1 interview with Capt. Robert Dibble, RN.
6. Dimbleby, BBC 1 interview with Capt. Fortson, USN.
7. Dimbleby, BBC 1 interview with Dean Rusk.
8. Dimbleby interview with Denis Healey.
9. Harold Wilson, *The Labour Government, 1964–1970: A Personal Record* (London: Weidenfeld and Nicolson, and Michael Joseph, 1971), p. 50.
10. George W. Ball, *The Past Has Another Pattern: Memoirs* (New York: W. W. Norton, 1982), p. 336.
11. Dulles to Eisenhower, memo, 10 Feb. 1956, in US Dept. of State, *Foreign Relations of the United States, 1955–1957* (Washington: Government Printing Office, 1985), vol. I, pp. 641–2.
12. Comments of Nov. 1961 in Arthur M. Schlesinger, Jr, *A Thousand Days: John F. Kennedy in the White House* (New York: Fawcett Books, 1971), p. 505.
13. This quotation and 'bitch of a war' from Kearns, *Johnson*, pp. 263–4.
14. Comments of June 1965 in George C. Herring, *America's Longest War: The United States and Vietnam, 1950–1975* (New York: John Wiley, 1979), p. 143.
15. Herring, *America's Longest War*, p. 143.
16. Leslie H. Gelb, with Richard K. Betts, *The Irony of Vietnam: The System Worked* (Washington, DC: The Brookings Institution, 1979), p. 111.
17. Wilson, *Labour Government*, p. 48.
18. Wilson, *Labour Government*, p. 80.

19. Dimbleby, BBC 1 interview with William Bundy.
20. George C. Herring, ed., *The Secret Diplomacy of the Vietnam War: The Negotiating Volumes of the Pentagon Papers* (Austin, Texas: University of Texas Press, 1983), p. 460.
21. Richard Crossman, *The Diaries of a Cabinet Minister* (3 vols, London: Hamish Hamilton and Jonathan Cape, 1975–7), vol. 2, pp. 237–8, entry for 14 Feb. 1967.
22. Dimbleby – Bundy interview.
23. Lyndon B. Johnson, *The Vantage Point: Perspectives of the Presidency, 1963–1969* (London: Weidenfeld and Nicolson, 1971), p. 255.
24. Dimbleby – Bundy interview.
25. Wilson, *Labour Government*, p. 264.
26. Dimbleby, BBC 1 interview with Louis Heren.
27. International Institute of Strategic Studies (IISS), *The Strategic Balance, 1964–5* (1964), pp. 17–18, 22–4.
28. IISS, *Strategic Balance, 1972–3* (1972), p. 73.
29. *The Times*, 17 Nov. 1964, p. 6, quoting his Guildhall speech the previous evening.
30. Crossman, *Diaries*, vol. 1, p. 95, entry for 11 Dec. 1964.
31. James Callaghan, *Time and Chance* (London: Collins, 1987), p. 187.
32. Crossman, *Diaries*, vol. 2, pp. 181–2, entry for 1 Jan. 1967.
33. Callaghan, *Time and Chance*, p. 176, cf. p. 189.
34. Quoted in F. Gregory Gause, 'British and American Policies in the Persian Gulf, 1968–1973', *Review of International Studies*, vol. 11 (1985), p. 252.
35. Callaghan, *Time and Chance*, p. 211.
36. Crossman, *Diaries*, vol. 2, p. 646.
37. Dimbleby – Healey interview.
38. Dimbleby – Rusk interview.
39. Lady Bird Johnson, *A White House Diary* (London: Weidenfeld and Nicolson, 1970), pp. 629–32, entry for 8 Feb. 1968.
40. Kathleen J. Turner, *Lyndon Johnson's Dual War: Vietnam and the Press* (Chicago: University of Chicago Press, 1985), p. 231.
41. Townsend Hoopes, *The Limits of Intervention* (New York: David McKay Co., 1969), p. 219.
42. LBJ to Congress in 1966, in Herbert Y. Schandler, *The Unmaking of a President: Lyndon Johnson and Vietnam* (Princeton: Princeton University Press, 1977), p. 225.
43. Roger Morris, *Uncertain Greatness: Henry Kissinger and American Foreign Policy* (London: Quartet Books, 1977), p. 164.
44. Herring, *America's Longest War*, pp. 146, 250.
45. Article in *Foreign Affairs*, Oct. 1967, in Robert S. Litwak, *Détente and*

the Nixon Doctrine: American Foreign Policy and the Pursuit of Stability, 1969–1976 (Cambridge: Cambridge University Press, 1984), p. 55.

46. *The Memoirs of Richard Nixon* (London: Arrow Books, 1978), p. 560.
47. Interview in *Time*, 3 Jan. 1972, quoted in Seyom Brown, *The Faces of Power: Constancy and Change in United States Foreign Policy from Truman to Reagan* (New York: Columbia University Press, 1983), pp. 328–9.
48. Speech of 23 Jan. 1970, in Phil Williams, *The Senate and US Troops in Europe* (London: Macmillan, 1985), pp. 163–4.
49. 'Year of Europe' speech, 23 April 1973, in Henry A. Kissinger, *American Foreign Policy* (New York: W. W. Norton, 1974), pp. 165-77.
50. Dimbleby, BBC 1 interview with Henry Kissinger.
51. Dimbleby, BBC 1 interview with Edward Heath.
52. Henry Kissinger, *Years of Upheaval* (London: Weidenfeld and Nicolson, and Michael Joseph, 1982), p. 191.
53. *The Times*, 29 Oct. 1973, p. 6.
54. Kissinger, *Years of Upheaval*, p. 709.
55. Dimbleby – Kissinger interview.
56. Dimbleby – Heath interview.
57. Kissinger, *Years of Upheaval*, p. 588.
58. House of Commons, *Debates*, vol. 863, col. 969, 7 Nov. 1963 (emphasis added). Heath had made a similar distinction on 30 Oct. (see col. 36). This appears to be in line with a policy articulated back in July 1960 when the US Defense Secretary assured the British Minister of Defence that 'I should be happy to ensure that you are notified of any decision to alert US forces in the UK.' In other words, this would be an act of good neighbourliness, but not one required under the Truman–Churchill understanding about the use of bases. See Simon Duke, *US Defence Bases in the United Kingdom* (London: Macmillan, 1987), pp. 164–5.
59. Dimbleby – Heath interview.
60. Dimbleby – Kissinger interview.
61. Dimbleby – Kissinger interview.

BACKGROUND READING

It is indicative of the declining importance of the Anglo-American relationship by this period, as well as the paucity of primary sources, that there are few studies specifically on Anglo-American relations in the later 1960s and 1970s. Baylis, *Anglo-American Defence Relations* and Louis and Bull, eds, *The 'Special Relationship'* (both cited in reading to chapter 9) remain useful.

Alfred Grosser, *The Western Alliance: European-American Relations since 1945*

(London: Macmillan, 1980). A good general study of transatlantic connections up to about 1973 – diplomatic, military, economic and cultural – though stronger on France and Germany than on Britain.

Richard J. Barnet, *Allies: America, Europe and Japan since the War* (London: Jonathan Cape, 1983) is a more recent survey, covering the 1970s and stronger than Grosser on US policy.

Henry Kissinger, *The White House Years* and *Years of Upheaval* (London: Weidenfeld and Nicolson, and Michael Joseph, 1979, 1982) are essential sources on US policy – a mix of memoir, apologia and history.

Chapter 14 Living in the American Age: Business and society from the 1940s to the 1970s

1. Maldwyn A. Jones, *The Growth of Liberty: American History, 1607-1980* (Oxford: Oxford University Press, 1983), p. 578.
2. William E. Leuchtenburg, *A Troubled Feast: American Society since 1945*, (Boston: Little, Brown, 1973), p. 88.
3. Quoted in Walter A. McDougall, *The Heavens and the Earth: A Political History of the Space Age* (New York: Basic Books, 1985), p. 320.
4. Quotations from James T. Patterson, *America's Struggle against Poverty, 1900-1930* (Cambridge, Mass.: Harvard University Press, 1981), p. 80.
5. David Pichaske, *A Generation in Motion: Popular Music and Culture in the Sixties* (New York: Schirmer Books, 1979), p. xvi.
6. Robert M. Collins, *The Business Response to Keynes, 1929-1964* (New York: Columbia University Press, 1981), pp. 184-5.
7. *Time*, 31 Dec. 1965, pp. 46-7.
8. Michael Stewart, *Keynes and After* (Harmondsworth: Penguin, 1972), p. 287.
9. John Osborne, *Look Back In Anger* (London: Faber and Faber, 1957), p. 17.
10. Quoted in Mike Jahn, *Rock: From Elvis Presley to the Rolling Stones* (New York: Quadrangle/The New York Times Book Co., 1973), p. 42.
11. *The Times*, 12 Sept. 1956, p. 4.
12. *The Times*, 15 Sept. 1956, p. 4.
13. Steve Chapple and Reebee Carofalo, *Rock 'n' Roll Is Here to Pay: The History and Politics of the Music Industry* (Chicago: Nelson-Hall, 1977), p. 187.
14. Dimbleby, BBC 1 interview with Donald Griffiths.

15. George G. Giarchi, *Between McAlpine and Polaris* (London: Routledge and Kegan Paul, 1984), p. 115.
16. Dimbleby, BBC 1 interview with Richard Laning.
17. Simon Duke, *US Defence Bases in the United Kingdom: A Matter for Joint Decision?* (London: Macmillan, 1987), Table A2.2, p. 199. During the 1950s the figure was around 80,000. (These figures tend to overstate the American presence because they include some British citizens employed by the US forces.)
18. For details in this paragraph see John H. Dunning, 'The Role of American Investment in the British Economy', *PEP Broadsheet*, 507 (Feb. 1969), esp. pp. 119, 126.
19. Francis Williams, *The American Invasion* (London: Anthony Blond, 1962), p. 11.
20. James McMillan and Bernard Harris, *The American Take-Over of Britain* (London: Leslie Frewin, 1968), p. 6.
21. *The Brain Drain: Report of the Working Group on Migration*, Cmnd. 3417, Oct. 1967 (London: HMSO, 1967), pp. 8, 10 and 13.
22. House of Commons, *Debates*, 13 Feb. 1967, vol. 741, cols 125–6.
23. Quoted in *The Times*, 27 Feb. 1967, p. 2.
24. *The Brain Drain*, p. 98.
25. Charles Iffland and Henri Reuben, 'The Multilateral Aspects: The U.S., Europe, and the "Poorer" Economies', in Walter Adams, ed., *The Brain Drain* (New York: Macmillan, 1968), p. 63. ('Western Europe' here signifies the Six plus the UK.)
26. Speech of 13 Nov. 1967 in Jack N. Behrman, *National Interests and the Multinational Enterprise: Tensions among the North Atlantic Countries* (Englewood Cliffs, NJ: Prentice Hall, 1970), p. 56, note 1.
27. Dimbleby, BBC 1 interview with Julian Amery. For similar claims see Sir Stephen Hastings, *The Murder of TSR2* (London: MacDonald, 1966), pp. 110–11; Bruce Reed and Geoffrey Williams, *Denis Healey and the Policies of Power* (London: Sidgwick and Jackson, 1971), pp. 171–2; Charles Gardner, *British Aircraft Corporation: A History* (London: B. T. Batsford, 1981), pp. 108–9.
28. Dimbleby, BBC 1 interview with Denis Healey.
29. L. J. Williams, *Britain and the World Economy, 1919–1970* (London: Fontana, 1971), p. 126.
30. J. J. Servan-Schreiber, *The American Challenge* (New York: Avon, 1969), pp. 148–9.
31. *The Times*, 24 Jan. 1967, p. 8, quoting Wilson's speech of the previous day.
32. Anthony Sampson, *The New Anatomy of Britain* (London: Hodder and Stoughton, 1971), p. 326.

33. Dunning, 'The Role of American Investment', pp. 140–1.
34. *New York Times*, 8 Feb. 1964, p. 25. Also source for the following Starr quotation.
35. *New York Times*, 16 Feb. 1964, p. 3.
36. This and subsequent quotations from *Time*, 15 April 1966, pp. 32–42.
37. David Cannadine, 'The Context, Performance and Meaning of Ritual: The British Monarchy and the "Invention of Tradition", c. 1820–1977', in Eric Hobsbawm and Terence Ranger, *The Invention of Tradition* (Cambridge: Cambridge University Press, 1983), p. 155.
38. Philip Ziegler, *Crown and People* (London: Collins, 1978), p. 127.
39. Statistics from James Walvin, *Passage to Britain: Immigration in British History and Politics* (Harmondsworth: Penguin Books, 1984), pp. 199–200.

BACKGROUND READING

For surveys of American and British social history since World War Two see William E. Leuchtenburg, *A Troubled Feast: American Society since 1945* (Boston: Little, Brown, 1979); and Arthur Marwick, *British Society since 1945* (Harmondsworth: Penguin, 1982).

An attempt to examine the social interrelationships is Daniel Snowman, *Britain and America: An Interpretation of their Culture, 1945–1975* (New York: Harper Torchbooks, 1977).

Chapter 15 All at Sea, 1973–80

1. James Callaghan, *Time and Chance* (London: Collins, 1978), p. 295.
2. *New York Times*, 20 March 1974, pp. 1, 6.
3. Barbara Castle, *The Castle Diaries, 1974–1976* (London: Weidenfeld and Nicolson, 1980), p. 227, entry on Cabinet meeting of 20 Nov. 1974.
4. *The Castle Diaries*, p. 305, entry for 6 Feb. 1975.
5. Henry A. Kissinger, 'Reflections on a Partnership: British and American Attitudes to Postwar Foreign Policy', *International Affairs*, vol. 58 (1982), p. 577.
6. Haig Simonian, *The Privileged Partnership: Franco-German Relations in the European Community, 1969–1984* (Oxford: Clarendon Press, 1985), p. 266.
7. *The Castle Diaries*, p. 357, entry for 27 March 1975.

8. Harold Wilson, *Final Term: The Labour Government, 1974–1976* (London: Weidenfeld and Nicolson and Michael Joseph, 1979), p. 108.
9. Alfred Grosser, *The Western Alliance: European-American Relations since 1945* (London: Macmillan, 1980), p. 277.
10. Jimmy Carter, *Keeping Faith: Memoirs of a President* (New York: Bantam Books, 1982), quoting respectively from pp. 22 and 18.
11. Jules Witcover, *Marathon: The Pursuit of the Presidency, 1972–1976* (New York: Viking Press, 1977), p. 402.
12. Zbigniew Brzezinski, *Power and Principle: Memoirs of the National Security Adviser, 1977–1981* (London: Weidenfeld and Nicolson, 1983), p. 520.
13. Carter, *Keeping Faith*, p. 472.
14. Raymond L. Garthoff, *Détente and Confrontation: American-Soviet Relations from Nixon to Reagan* (Washington: Brookings Institution, 1985), quoting respectively from pp. 967–8 and 950.
15. Quoted in Strobe Talbott, *Deadly Gambits: The Reagan Administration and the Stalemate in Nuclear Arms Control* (New York: Vintage Books, 1985), p. 33.
16. Richard J. Barnet, *Allies: America, Europe and Japan since the War* (London: Jonathan Cape, 1984), pp. 408–9.
17. John L. Palmer and Isabel V. Sawhill, eds, *The Reagan Experiment: An Examination of Economic and Social Policies under the Reagan Administration* (Washington: The Urban Institute Press, 1982), pp. 33–4.
18. Phil Williams, 'The United States' Commitment to Western Europe: Strategic Ambiguity and Political Disintegration?', *International Affairs*, vol. 59 (1983), p. 200.
19. See David Reynolds, 'A "special relationship"?: America, Britain and the International Order since the Second World War', *International Affairs*, vol. 62 (1986), p. 17.
20. Dorothy Waggoner, 'Statistics on Language Use', in Charles A. Ferguson and Shirley Brice Heath, eds, *Language in the USA* (Cambridge: Cambridge University Press, 1981), pp. 490–1.
21. Sevareid and Friedman quoted in Bernard D. Nossiter, *Britain: A Future That Works* (London: André Deutsch, 1978), pp. 12–13.
22. R. Emmett Tyrrell, Jr, ed., *The Future That Doesn't Work: Social Democracy's Failure in Britain* (Garden City, NY: Doubleday, 1977), p. 2.
23. Richard Rose, *Politics in England*, quoted in Dennis Kavanagh, 'An American Science of British Politics', *Political Studies*, vol. 22 (1974), pp. 251–2: a very useful article on which much of the previous paragraph is based.
24. Samuel H. Beer, *Britain Against Itself: The Contradictions of Collectivism* (London: Faber and Faber, 1982), p. xv.

25. Arthur M. Schlesinger, Jr, *The Imperial Presidency* (New York: Popular Library, 1974), p. 462.
26. Statistics from British Tourist Authority Market Guide, *USA, 1986/7* (London: BTA, 1986), esp. pp. 12–13.
27. Andrew Faulds, article in *The Times*, 19 Jan. 1976, quoted in David Lowenthal, *The Past is a Foreign Country* (Cambridge: Cambridge University Press, 1985), p. 402.

BACKGROUND READING

Richard J. Barnet, *Allies: America, Europe and Japan since the War* (London: Jonathan Cape, 1983), surveys transatlantic relations during the period, though, significantly, with little reference to Britain.

R. Emmett Tyrrell, Jr, ed., *The Future That Doesn't Work: Social Democracy's Failure in Britain* (Garden City, NY: Doubleday, 1977) provides a sample of American criticism of Britain in the seventies.

M. Glenn Abernathy, Dilys M. Hill and Phil Williams, eds, *The Carter Years: The President and Policy Making* (London: Frances Pinter, 1984). An early but useful scholarly attempt to evaluate the Carter presidency.

Chapter 16 A Relationship Renewed, 1981–7

1. *Observer*, 25 Feb. 1979, in Denis Kavanagh, *Thatcherism and British Politics: The End of Consensus?* (Oxford: Oxford University Press, 1987), p. 253.
2. Remarks at British Embassy dinner, 27 Feb. 1981, in *Public Papers of the Presidents of the United States: Ronald Reagan, 1981* (Washington: Government Printing Office, 1982), p. 174.
3. Speech at White House dinner, 26 Feb. 1981, in Reagan, *Public Papers, 1981*, p. 168.
4. *Sunday Times*, 3 May 1981, in Martin Holmes, *The First Thatcher Government, 1979–1983: Contemporary Conservatism and Economic Change* (Brighton: Wheatsheaf Books, 1985), p. 209.
5. BBC 1, 'Panorama', 11 July 1977, in Bernard D. Nossiter, *Britain: A Future That Works* (London: André Deutsch, 1978), p. 42.
6. *The Economist*, 7 Nov. 1987, p. 15.
7. Peter Holmes, 'The Thatcher Government's Overall Economic Perform-

ance', in David S. Bell, ed., *The Conservative Government, 1979–1984: An Interim Report* (London: Croom Helm, 1985), esp. pp. 22–6.

8. Ronnie Dugger, *On Reagan: The Man and His Presidency* (New York: McGraw-Hill, 1983), p. 102.
9. David A. Stockman, *The Triumph of Politics: The Inside Story of the Reagan Revolution* (New York: Avon Books, 1986), pp. 88, 92.
10. Stockman, *Triumph of Politics*, pp. 116–18.
11. Stockman, *Triumph of Politics,* pp. 119, 135.
12. Hugo Young and Anne Sloman, *The Thatcher Phenomenon* (London: BBC Publications, 1986), p. 110.
13. Kavanagh, *Thatcherism*, p. 250.
14. Helmut Schmidt, 'Saving the Western Alliance', *New York Review of Books*, 31 May 1984, p. 25.
15. Thatcher to Reagan, 11 March 1982, in John Baylis, *Anglo-American Defence Relations, 1939–1984: The Special Relationship* (London: Macmillan, 1984), p. 202.
16. Reagan to Thatcher, 11 March 1982, in Baylis, *Anglo-American Defence Relations*, p. 203.
17. Ministry of Defence, 'The Future United Kingdom Strategic Nuclear Deterrent Force', Defence Open Government Document 80/23 (July 1980), paragraph 5.
18. In the House of Commons, 24 Jan. 1980, quoted in Lawrence Freedman, *Britain and Nuclear Weapons* (London: Macmillan, 1980), p. 140.
19. Timothy Garton Ash, 'The Trouble with Trident', *Spectator*, 12 April 1986, p. 12.
20. Peter Clausen, Allan Krass and Robert Zirkle, *In Search of Stability: An Assessment of New U.S. Nuclear Forces* (Cambridge, Mass.: Union of Concerned Scientists, 1986), ch. 3.
21. Paul Eddy and Magnus Linklater, with Peter Gillman, *The Falklands War* (London: Sphere Books, 1982), p. 53.
22. Reagan, *Public Papers, 1982* (1983), remarks to reporters, 5 April 1982, pp. 428, 431.
23. Quoted in *Time*, 17 May 1982, p. 22.
24. Alexander M. Haig, Jr, *Caveat: Realism, Reagan, and Foreign Policy* (London: Weidenfeld and Nicolson, 1984), p. 269.
25. Max Hastings and Simon Jenkins, *The Battle for the Falklands* (London: Pan Books, 1983), p. 295.
26. Reagan, *Public Papers, 1982* (1983), remarks to reporters, 30 April 1982, p. 540.
27. See 'America's Falklands War', *The Economist*, 3 March 1984, pp. 23–5.
28. Dimbleby, BBC 1 interview with Dr John Lehman.

29. Reagan, *Public Papers, 1982* (1983), remarks to reporters, 24 May 1982, p. 669.
30. Dimbleby – Lehman interview.
31. Eddy, Linklater and Gillman, *The Falklands War*, p. 262.
32. Hastings and Jenkins, *The Battle for the Falklands*, p. 379.
33. Dimbleby, BBC 1 interview with Langhorn Motley.
34. House of Commons, *Debates*, 6th series, vol. 47, col. 294, 26 Oct. 1983.
35. Speech at White House dinner, 26 Feb. 1981, in Reagan, *Public Papers, 1981*, p. 170.
36. Reagan, *Public Papers, 1981*, p. 57, press conference of 29 Jan. 1981.
37. Robert Dallek, *Ronald Reagan: The Politics of Symbolism* (Cambridge, Mass.: Harvard University Press, 1984), p. 141.
38. BBC 1 'Panorama' interview with Sir Robin Day, 6 June 1983, in Michael Foot, *Another Heart and Other Pulses: The Alternative to the Thatcher Society* (London: Collins, 1984), p. 199.
39. Dimbleby, BBC 1 interview with Richard Perle.
40. Dimbleby, BBC 1 interview with General Bernard Rogers.
41. Dimbleby – Rogers interview.
42. Reagan, *Public Papers, 1983* (1984), p. 443, address of 23 March 1983.
43. Union of Concerned Scientists, *Star Wars: Myth and Reality* (Washington: Union of Concerned Scientists, 1986), p. 27, citing poll of March 1986.
44. *Time*, 23 June 1986, p. 6.
45. *New York Times*, 5 Nov. 1985, quoted in Frank Barnaby, *What on Earth is Star Wars?: A Guide to the Strategic Defense Initiative* (London: Fourth Estate, 1986), p. 157.
46. Foreign and Commonwealth Office, *Arms Control and Disarmament Newsletter*, no. 22 (Oct.–Dec. 1984), p. 31.
47. *Daily Telegraph*, 14 Feb. 1987, p. 1; *The Times*, 14 Feb. 1987, p. 1.
48. Magnus Linklater and David Leigh, with Ian Mather, *Not With Honour: The Inside Story of the Westland Scandal* (London: Sphere Books, 1986), p. 90, quoting 'a note on the Whitehall files'.
49. *New York Times*, 11 Jan. 1986, p. 1.
50. Dimbleby, BBC 1 interview with John Hughes.
51. Cf. Simon Duke, *US Defence Bases in the United Kingdom: A Matter for Joint Decision?* (London: Macmillan, 1987), pp. xvii–xx.
52. House of Commons, *Debates*, 15 April 1986, vol. 95, col. 726.
53. Dimbleby, BBC 1 interview with General Vernon Walters.
54. *Observer*, 20 April 1986, p. 12.
55. Speech in Brussels, 16 March 1987, in Sir Geoffrey Howe, *East–West Relations* (London: Central Office of Information, 1987), pp. 20–1.
56. Young and Sloman, *The Thatcher Phenomenon*, p. 111.

57. Statement of 15 Nov. 1986, in Foreign and Commonwealth Office, *Arms Control and Disarmament: Quarterly Review*, no. 4 (Jan. 1987), p. 3.
58. Dimbleby – Perle interview.
59. Dimbleby – Rogers interview.

BACKGROUND READING

Joel Krieger, *Reagan, Thatcher, and the Politics of Decline* (Cambridge: Polity Press, 1986). A rare attempt to compare the two leaders' policies and to place them in the context of an interpretation of recent history.

Index

Contents

W. W. Norton & Company has been independent since its founding in 1923, when William Warder Norton and Mary D. Herter Norton first published lectures delivered at the People's Institute, the adult education division of New York City's Cooper Union. The Nortons soon expanded their program beyond the Institute, publishing books by celebrated academics from America and abroad. By mid-century, the two major pillars of Norton's publishing program—trade books and college texts—were firmly established. In the 1950s, the Norton family transferred control of the company to its employees, and today—with a staff of four hundred and a comparable number of trade, college, and professional titles published each year—W. W. Norton & Company stands as the largest and oldest publishing house owned wholly by its employees.

Editor: Julia Reidhead
Managing Editor, College: Marian Johnson
Developmental Editor: Kurt Wildermuth
Electronic Media Editor: Eileen Connell
Production Manager: Diane O'Connor
Associate Editor: Erin Granville
Copy Editors: Alice Falk, Katharine Ings, Candace Levy, Alan Shaw, Ann Tappert
Permissions Managers: Nancy Rodwan and Katrina Washington
Editorial Assistant: Catherine Spencer
Text Design: Antonina Krass
Art Research: Neil Ryder Hoos

Composition by Binghamton Valley Composition
Manufacturing by RR Donnelley

ISBN 0-393-92830-6 (pbk.)

W. W. Norton & Company, Inc., 500 Fifth Avenue, New York, N.Y. 10110
www.wwnorton.com

W. W. Norton & Company Ltd., Castle House, 75/76 Wells Street, London W1T 3QT

1 2 3 4 5 6 7 8 9 0

The Norton Anthology of English Literature

EIGHTH EDITION

THE MAJOR AUTHORS

VOLUME A

The Middle Ages through The Restoration and the Eighteenth Century

Stephen Greenblatt, *General Editor*
COGAN UNIVERSITY PROFESSOR OF THE HUMANITIES,
HARVARD UNIVERSITY

M. H. Abrams, *Founding Editor Emeritus*
CLASS OF 1916 PROFESSOR OF ENGLISH EMERITUS,
CORNELL UNIVERSITY

W • W • NORTON & COMPANY • *New York* • *London*

Carol T. Christ
PROFESSOR EMERITUS OF ENGLISH, UNIVERSITY OF CALIFORNIA, BERKELEY
PRESIDENT, SMITH COLLEGE

Alfred David
PROFESSOR OF ENGLISH EMERITUS, INDIANA UNIVERSITY

Barbara K. Lewalski
WILLIAM R. KENAN PROFESSOR OF ENGLISH AND OF HISTORY AND LITERATURE, HARVARD UNIVERSITY

Lawrence Lipking
PROFESSOR OF ENGLISH AND CHESTER D. TRIPP PROFESSOR OF HUMANITIES, NORTHWESTERN UNIVERSITY

George M. Logan
JAMES CAPPON PROFESSOR OF ENGLISH, QUEEN'S UNIVERSITY

Deidre Shauna Lynch
ASSOCIATE PROFESSOR OF ENGLISH, INDIANA UNIVERSITY

Katharine Eisaman Maus
JAMES BRANCH CABELL PROFESSOR OF ENGLISH, UNIVERSITY OF VIRGINIA

James Noggle
ASSOCIATE PROFESSOR OF ENGLISH AND WHITEHEAD ASSOCIATE PROFESSOR OF CRITICAL THOUGHT, WELLESLEY COLLEGE

Jahan Ramazani
EDGAR F. SHANNON PROFESSOR OF ENGLISH, UNIVERSITY OF VIRGINIA

Catherine Robson
ASSOCIATE PROFESSOR OF ENGLISH AND CHANCELLOR'S FELLOW, UNIVERSITY OF CALIFORNIA, DAVIS

James Simpson
PROFESSOR OF ENGLISH AND AMERICAN LITERATURE, HARVARD UNIVERSITY

Jon Stallworthy
PROFESSOR OF ENGLISH LITERATURE, OXFORD UNIVERSITY

Jack Stillinger
CENTER FOR ADVANCED STUDY PROFESSOR OF ENGLISH, UNIVERSITY OF ILLINOIS

Editors Emeriti

E. Talbot Donaldson, LATE OF INDIANA UNIVERSITY • Hallett Smith, LATE OF THE HUNTINGTON LIBRARY • Robert M. Adams, LATE OF THE UNIVERSITY OF CALIFORNIA, LOS ANGELES • Samuel Holt Monk, LATE OF THE UNIVERSITY OF MINNESOTA • George H. Ford, LATE OF THE UNIVERSITY OF ROCHESTER • David Daiches, LATE OF THE INSTITUTE OF ADVANCED STUDIES, UNIVERSITY OF EDINBURGH

The Norton Anthology of English Literature

EIGHTH EDITION
THE MAJOR AUTHORS

VOLUME A

THE MIDDLE AGES THROUGH THE RESTORATION AND THE EIGHTEENTH CENTURY

SALT Hand Book

SALT Hand Book

Key Documents and Issues 1972–1979

Edited by Roger P. Labrie

American Enterprise Institute for Public Policy Research
Washington, D.C.

Roger P. Labrie is a research associate specializing in defense policy at the American Enterprise Institute.

For the sake of clarity and consistency, the following general criteria have been used in editing the material reprinted in this volume. Punctuation and capitalization of acronyms and weapon system designations have been altered to conform with the style used in Department of Defense publications. All treaties and agreements are reprinted in their entirety; material unrelated to SALT has been deleted from some communiqués. Deletion of substantive material is marked by either a series of periods (for extraneous dialogue or for part of a paragraph) or by asterisks (for longer passages). In some instances, obvious errors of grammar have been corrected, and where an individual clearly misspoke, the editor has taken the liberty of inserting the intended word.

The editor wishes to thank Robert J. Pranger, director of foreign and defense policy studies at AEI, for his counsel and support in the preparation of this book.

Library of Congress Cataloging in Publication Data

Main entry under title:
SALT handbook.

(AEI studies ; 214)
Bibliography: p.
Includes index.
1. Strategic Arms Limitation Talks. 2. Arms control.
I. Labrie, Roger P. II. Series: American Enterprise
Institute for Public Policy Research. AEI studies ; 214.
JX1974.75.S16 327'.174 78-32175
ISBN 0-8447-3316-4

AEI Studies 214

Printed in the United States of America

THE AEI PUBLIC POLICY PROJECT ON NATIONAL DEFENSE

The American Enterprise Institute, as part of its foreign policy and related defense policy study program, decided in 1976 to establish a defense project in order to focus public debate on the array of vital defense issues. The project sponsors research into strategy, threat, force structure, defense economics, civil-military relations, and other areas and presents the results in publications such as this one and the unique *AEI Foreign Policy and Defense Review* series. In additon it sponsors forums, debates, and conferences, some of which are televised nationally.

The project is chaired by Melvin R. Laird, former congressman, secretary of defense, domestic counsellor to the President, and now senior counsellor of *Reader's Digest*. The twenty-two member advisory council represents a broad range of defense viewpoints. The project director is Robert J. Pranger, head of AEI's foreign and defense policy studies program.

Views expressed are those of the authors and do not necessarily reflect the views either of the advisory council and others associated with the project or of the advisory panels, staff, officers, and trustees of AEI.

CONTENTS

PART TWO
The SALT II Negotiations

PART THREE
A New Approach to SALT

FOREWORD

Few diplomatic undertakings have attracted as much public attention, or elicited as emotional a response from both policy makers and nongovernmental observers, as have the Strategic Arms Limitation Talks (SALT). Since November 17, 1969, the United States and the Soviet Union have been engaged in a series of negotiations whose consequences may well determine the course of superpower relations and the prospects for peace into the next century.

SALT is an attempt to achieve greater understanding and political control over the most destructive weapons ever devised by man. The existence of strategic nuclear arsenals capable of destroying entire nations constitutes not only a radical departure from previous conceptions of national military power but also a profound challenge to the political institutions of all societies, whatever their ideologies. As the usefulness of nuclear weapons has become increasingly uncertain, political leaders in both the United States and the Soviet Union have sought through SALT other means of protecting their national interests. Greater security has been sought from mutual agreement to slow the momentum of their respective nuclear weapon programs.

The euphoria that greeted the first SALT agreements in 1972 has dampened considerably in recent years. While virtually all its critics and supporters agree that SALT should not be viewed as an end in itself but rather as one of a number of policy options for the enhancement of national security, much of the controversy surrounding the negotiations stems from different conceptions of what the United States should seek to achieve in SALT. Our experience to date seems to confirm the proposition that, in and of itself, SALT cannot eliminate the threat of nuclear war. The international political objectives of nations, together with the means governments employ in implementing policies, play a major role in determining whether we will live in peace or war. By its very exist-

ence, SALT can encourage decision makers on both sides to be more critically aware of the implications of each country's weapon policies so that efforts in the political realm can establish greater stability in the relations among nations. Paradoxically, controversies over SALT also may exacerbate relations between the superpowers.

In addition, SALT is unique as a reflection of the enduring quality of the motives that led both superpowers to commence the talks in 1969. The fiscal constraints both governments confronted then are perhaps even more acute today, and it has become evident that the goal of enhancing national security cannot be realized simply by expanding nuclear arsenals on both sides. The mutual vulnerability of Soviet and American societies has become accepted as a fact of life today, and the belief in a technological salvation from a predicament that technology played no small role in creating (although still held in some quarters) is being seriously questioned by a growing number of scientists and political leaders. Finally, the opportunities for U.S.–Soviet détente may be more limited than originally conceived, but they continue to compete with opportunities for unilateral advantage in the policy-making circles of both nations.

This volume is designed to provide the interested public with easy access to the agreements and major policy declarations associated with the Strategic Arms Limitation Talks—in short, a history of the negotiations and an exposition of objectives as stated by those government officials most intimately involved in SALT. Only information from official government publications has been used; for the views and analyses of individuals not serving in government, the reader is encouraged to consult those parts of the volumes of congressional hearings not reprinted here, and the annotated bibliographies that follow each part of this handbook. The historical overviews by Roger P. Labrie that precede each section are an attempt to place the events of SALT in the broad context of U.S.–Soviet relations.

ROBERT J. PRANGER
Director of Foreign and Defense Policy Studies
American Enterprise Institute

PART ONE

The SALT I Agreements

Overview

Roger P. Labrie

Nations enter into negotiations for a variety of reasons. Since the United States and the Soviet Union have as their objective in SALT mutual restraint of strategic nuclear arsenals, it is appropriate to examine those aspects of the arms competition that convinced these superpowers of the wisdom of such a course. SALT, like all previous attempts at negotiating limitations on nuclear weapons, stemmed from the interaction of new weapon programs with prevailing strategic concepts. Innovations in weapon technology have often been perceived as threatening the stability assumed by theories of deterrence.

SALT should be viewed as a political process whereby governments bargain within themselves and with each other over proposals that would deny them certain opportunities. These proposals may vary from merely limiting to existing levels the number of weapon systems each nation has deployed to more ambitiously proscribing new technologies and actually reducing existing levels of arms. Ultimately, countries will accept and implement such proposals only when they are convinced their security will best be served by doing so. The perceived consequences for the national security of the United States and the Soviet Union of agreeing or failing to agree to constrain their arms competition will determine the success of SALT.

The Johnson Administration

In the nuclear age numerous attempts have been made to limit the expansion of nuclear arsenals. Most prominent among them is SALT, the genesis of which can be traced to a series of decisions dating from the latter half of 1966. In the wake of the Cuban missile crisis, it was apparent that the Soviet Union had embarked on a massive program to enlarge its nuclear arsenal. In addition, the first evidence that the

Soviets were deploying an ABM (antiballistic missile) system reached officials in Washington at that time. Meanwhile, the expansion of the U.S. strategic arsenal begun during the Kennedy administration was approaching completion.

President Lyndon Johnson and Secretary of Defense Robert McNamara, under mounting political pressure to respond to the Soviet build-up, decided not to increase the planned deployment of 1,000 Minuteman ICBMs but instead to accelerate programs for qualitatively improving existing missiles. McNamara's strategic concepts prevailed: security and stability were to be achieved, not by deploying additional weapons, but by maintaining an invulnerable retaliatory capability sufficient to assure the destruction of the Soviet Union. In addition, McNamara believed a stable deterrence relationship required the United States to take no action that could be perceived by the Soviet Union as threatening its ability to destroy us in retaliation.

Mutual vulnerability and assured destruction were concepts that failed to gain the acceptance of all who were involved in setting American defense policy. Indeed, there were signs that even some high-level officials in the Johnson administration had misgivings about these precepts. Presidents Kennedy and Johnson had accepted McNamara's judgment that assured destruction required an ability to destroy 20 to 25 percent of the Soviet population and 50 percent of its industrial capacity in a retaliatory strike.[1] The idea that the United States in turn must be susceptible to similar devastation was difficult to accept, given the unambiguous strategic superiority America had enjoyed since the beginning of the nuclear age.

In addition, the moral implications of a doctrine that called for targeting Soviet cities had become increasingly uncomfortable. In a speech at the University of Michigan in Ann Arbor, on 16 June 1962, McNamara had questioned the credibility of such a targeting doctrine and proposed instead one that would place greater emphasis on the destruction of Soviet military forces in a retaliatory strike.[2] Both of these concerns—the vulnerability of the United States to a Soviet nuclear attack and the credibility of a countercity targeting doctrine—were to become central motivating factors in the early efforts to begin negotiations with Moscow on the limitation of strategic arms.

ABM and MIRV: Contending Concepts. The nuclear age has not been immune to the dynamic interaction of offense and defense evident

---

[1] Alain C. Enthoven and K. Wayne Smith, *How Much Is Enough? Shaping The Defense Program, 1961–1969* (New York: Harper & Row, 1971), p. 175.

[2] See "Defense Arrangements of the North Atlantic Community," in *Department of State Bulletin*, 9 July 1962, pp. 64–69.

throughout military history, despite the unprecedented destructive capacity of nuclear weapons. The early history of SALT was dominated to a large extent by this interaction, with two weapon systems, ABM and MIRV (multiple independently targetable reentry vehicles), exemplifying contending strategic concepts. Eventually, these systems were to be seen as threatening the two pillars of stability McNamara had postulated, namely, assured destruction and mutual vulnerability.

Research and development for an American ABM system had begun in earnest in the mid-1950s with Nike-Zeus, and by 1959 the military was urging nationwide deployment of such a system as a means of protecting the United States from Soviet attack. The MIRV program was begun in 1961–1962, and acquired greater support within the defense community as a consequence of the Ann Arbor speech. McNamara's suggestion of a new countermilitary doctrine had the effect of increasing the number of targets against which the U.S. arsenal would have to be committed, relative to the target base of the existing predominantly countercity doctrine. Such a change in strategic doctrine was seized upon by some defense planners as a rationale for MIRVing missiles. It soon became apparent to some strategists that ABMS and MIRVS might be complementary systems, each serving a defensive purpose: MIRVS could be employed against Soviet offensive forces to blunt the impact of a retaliatory strike, while ABMS could serve as a more proximate defense for the territory and population of the United States. The Soviet Union, on the other hand, might view such a combination of weapons as constituting a disarming first-strike threat.

Similar weapon programs were being studied by the Soviet military. In 1965 the United States discovered evidence of a deployment of ABMS around Moscow. Known as Galosh, this ABM system aroused much anxiety in Washington; together with a new air defense missile system which had first appeared near the Estonian capital of Tallinn in 1962, it provided much impetus to the U.S. ABM and MIRV programs. Galosh was seen by many as the base for a nationwide Soviet ABM deployment; the potential of the Tallinn SA-5 antiaircraft missile for being upgraded to a ballistic missile interceptor became the subject of a protracted controversy within the Washington bureaucracy.

One consequence of the Galosh deployment was a decision made by the Johnson administration in 1965 to authorize development of MIRVS for both the Minuteman III ICBM and the new Poseidon SLBM. McNamara later justified this decision by pointing to Galosh and arguing that MIRV would increase the number of warheads that could be launched against the Soviet Union, thereby saturating the enemy's defenses. Multiplication of offensive warheads was deemed to be a less expensive and less destabilizing response than a counterdeployment of

ABMS by the United States. McNamara believed that an American deployment of ABMS would merely trigger an increase in Soviet offensive missiles while extending the arms race into the new realm of defensive weapons.

Meanwhile, popular support in the United States for an ABM system had been gathering momentum. In 1966 Congress voted more funds for ABM development than the administration had requested. In a series of meetings in November and December 1966, President Johnson, Secretary McNamara, and the Joint Chiefs of Staff reached major decisions on ABM and strategic arms control. McNamara's announcement to the public on 10 November that the Soviets had begun deploying Galosh was followed on 6 December by President Johnson's decisions to request from Congress authority to procure long lead-time components for an ABM system and to defer its deployment pending the outcome of efforts to negotiate limitations on ABMS.

Opening Negotiations. The Soviet response to the Johnson administration's proposal to begin talks on limiting strategic arms was noncommittal. While expressing a general interest in negotiations, Moscow refused to agree on a time and place for the talks and expressed greater willingness to discuss offensive than defensive arms limitations (a preference that would be reversed when SALT eventually got underway in 1969). In all likelihood the Soviets were unprepared to begin SALT in 1967 and were suspicious of American motives. Given its lead in ABMS, Moscow may well have seen the talks as a ploy by Washington to preserve its numerical advantage in offensive arms while limiting Galosh.[3]

An opportunity to determine Soviet willingness to negotiate actual arms limitations presented itself on 23 and 25 June 1967. President Johnson and Secretary McNamara met with Soviet Prime Minister Alexei Kosygin in Glassboro, New Jersey, and sought to convince him of the urgency of negotiations. Kosygin was unimpressed by McNamara's lecture on the destabilizing consequences of ABM deployments and refused to commit his government to negotiations. The failure of the Glassboro summit, together with the unanticipated detonation of a hydrogen device by the People's Republic of China in the summer of 1967, set the stage for President Johnson's decision to order deployment of the Sentinel ABM system.

Believing that deployment of ABM was now inevitable,[4] McNamara sought to minimize what he perceived to be its destabilizing potential

[3] Raymond L. Garthoff, "SALT and the Soviet Military," in *Problems of Communism*, vol. 24, no. 1 (January–February 1975), p. 22.

[4] In addition to congressional and military support for ABM, a number of civilian agencies within the Pentagon most concerned with the technical proficiency of the system now favored its deployment. President Johnson was concerned about the

by urging the President to eschew the "heavy" nationwide system espoused by military and congressional leaders. Such a system, he reasoned, would be interpreted in Moscow as an effort to blunt the Soviet Union's retaliatory capability and therefore would stimulate an acceleration of that country's current offensive arms build-up. President Johnson, though sympathetic to McNamara's reasoning, in effect opted for a compromise deployment. In a speech in San Francisco on 18 September 1967, McNamara unveiled the Chinese-oriented nationwide Sentinel ABM system.[5]

McNamara's speech was noteworthy for reasons other than the Sentinel decision. In it the secretary of defense provided a list of arguments against ABM deployment and expounded at length on what he saw to be its destabilizing implications. Reaffirming his belief that deterrence "means the certainty of suicide to the aggressor," McNamara told his audience that the current U.S. inventory of nuclear warheads was "both greater than we had originally planned and in fact more than we require." This was because strategic planners "must prepare for the worst plausible case" in their assessments of Soviet weapon programs. Since the consequences of miscalculation could be catastrophic, McNamara saw such "worst case" assessments as both inevitable and the cornerstone of what he called the "action-reaction phenomenon that fuels an arms race."

McNamara proceeded to explain that the United States could not avoid destruction even with the best ABM technology then foreseeable. Recognizing the growing political support for a nationwide ABM system directed at the Soviet Union, he warned against deployment of such a system, noting that it would certainly contribute to the action-reaction phenomenon that had come to characterize the strategic competition between the two countries. "Were we to deploy a heavy ABM system throughout the United States, the Soviets would clearly be strongly motivated to so increase their offensive capability as to cancel out our defensive advantage." Then the secretary presented some of the reasoning behind the administration's decision to deploy a "light" Sentinel

---

impact a decision not to deploy ABM would have on his prospects for reelection in 1968. Charges that he had allowed an "ABM gap" to arise could be anticipated. See Morton H. Halperin, *Bureaucratic Politics and Foreign Policy* (Washington, D.C.: Brookings Institution, 1974), pp. 297–298. It should be noted, however, that Moscow's Galosh ABM was not yet operational after two years of construction and that the system was encountering technical difficulties. Indeed, in 1967 the Soviets decided to cut back the number of ABM launchers originally planned for the Moscow site from ninety-six to sixty-four, even though this meant abandoning some construction already started. See Garthoff, "SALT and the Soviet Military," pp. 29–30.

[5] Secretary McNamara's speech was delivered to the annual convention of United Press International editors and publishers. See "The Dynamics of Nuclear Strategy," in *Department of State Bulletin*, 9 October 1967, pp. 443–451.

system, noting its possible value in case of accidental or "irrational" attack and against a possible Chinese threat in the next decade. Even the latter reason was not really persuasive for McNamara, who added that the "grounds for concluding that a light deployment . . . against this [Chinese] possibility is prudent" were only "marginal." He did note, however, that such a system "would enable us to add—as a concurrent benefit—a further defense of our Minuteman sites against Soviet attack."

In conclusion McNamara issued this warning: "There is a kind of mad momentum intrinsic to the development of all new nuclear weaponry. If a weapon system works—and works well—there is strong pressure from many directions to procure and deploy the weapon out of all proportion to the prudent level required." This, he said, was a danger inherent in the administration's decision to deploy the Sentinel system: "Pressures will develop to expand it into a heavy Soviet-oriented ABM system. We must resist that temptation firmly."

It would appear that the decision to deploy Sentinel was as pivotal in Soviet assessments of the desirability of negotiating arms restraint as the deployment of Galosh had been for similar American assessments a year earlier. Congress strongly supported Sentinel; in fact, many of the system's proponents, both on Capitol Hill and in the Pentagon, publicly portrayed Sentinel as merely a base for an eventual "heavy" nationwide defense against Soviet attack. On 24 June 1968 the Senate defeated an amendment to deny funds for Sentinel's deployment, and three days later Soviet Foreign Minister Andrei Gromyko announced in Moscow that his government was ready to begin negotiations with the United States to limit offensive and defensive arms. On 1 July, during a signing ceremony for the nuclear Nonproliferation Treaty, President Johnson announced that both countries had agreed to start the talks.

Negotiations were not to begin for over a year, however. Plans had been made for President Johnson and Prime Minister Kosygin to meet in Leningrad on 30 September for the start of SALT. On 20 August, the day before the summit meeting was to be announced, Soviet and Warsaw Pact armies invaded Czechoslovakia, and Washington postponed the announcement and the summit. The Johnson administration would later attempt to reschedule the meeting, but time and domestic political support for such an undertaking had run out. A new president had been elected.

The Nixon Administration

The Nixon administration's approach to SALT differed considerably from that of its predecessor. Although the strategic considerations that led

President Johnson to seek negotiated restraint of nuclear weapons were not lost on President Nixon and his advisers, the latter came to view SALT as a political instrument to be employed for advantage in other areas (particularly Vietnam and the Middle East) where the interests of the United States and the Soviet Union intersected. This approach, together with West Germany's Ostpolitik and secret negotiations between Washington and Peking, would eventually set the parameters of détente.

In the final months of the Johnson administration, the arms competition continued unabated. On 16 August 1968, the United States began flight testing MIRVs on Minuteman III ICBMs and Poseidon SLBMs. The first test of a Soviet multiple reentry vehicle (MRV) was conducted with the SS-9 ICBM on 28 August. Both nations also were proceeding with their ABM programs, the United States making advanced preparations for a fourteen-site deployment of Sentinel, the Soviet Union proceeding with Galosh. In addition, Moscow was still expanding its ICBM and SLBM forces.

Upon entering office in January 1969, President Nixon ordered a series of studies that would prepare his administration for SALT. Aside from the usual assessments of the global military balance and the status of U.S. strategic forces, these studies dealt with the previous administration's preparations for SALT and options for ABM deployment.

The Safeguard System. One result of these studies was made public on 14 March 1969, when President Nixon announced he would ask Congress to authorize deployment of the Safeguard ABM system. Safeguard would be deployed at twelve sites throughout the United States; unlike Sentinel, however, Safeguard would have as its primary objective the defense of America's land-based missiles. The main reason for adopting this new strategic doctrine for ABM was the administration's concern over the potential first-strike capability of the Soviet Union's SS-9 ICBM, especially in light of that country's advances in multiple warhead technology. Defense of the U.S. main retaliatory force was seen as enhancing the ability of the United States to deter attack from the Soviet Union without threatening the latter's retaliatory capability.[6]

President Nixon did not, however, abandon the rationales for Sen-

---

[6] Domestic political considerations also were evident in the decision to shift the primary focus of ABM away from defense of cities. Opposition to any ABM deployment was becoming more vocal not only within the scientific community but also on Capitol Hill. In addition, a number of citizens groups in Boston and Chicago opposed deployment of the system around their cities, fearing such an action would serve to attract Soviet warheads in a nuclear exchange. See John Newhouse, *Cold Dawn: The Story of SALT* (New York: Holt, Rinehart and Winston, 1973), p. 150; and *The Safeguard ABM System* (Washington, D.C.: American Enterprise Institute, 1970), p. 9.

tinel that McNamara had articulated in 1967. Safeguard would be deployed in two phases, the first devoted to ICBM defense, the second to defense of cities against a Chinese attack. The Soviet reaction to Sentinel had not gone unnoticed, and it was hoped that concern over a future nationwide ballistic missile defense for the United States would sustain Moscow's interest in SALT. That this was indeed the case became apparent when, on 10 July, Foreign Minister Gromyko delivered a speech to the Supreme Soviet reminiscent of McNamara's remarks in San Francisco almost two years earlier. In his speech, Gromyko drew particular attention to the cost of the arms race and the difficulty of controlling nuclear weapons.

No other issue, aside from Vietnam, would so preoccupy Congress over the next two years as Safeguard. The Senate Foreign Relations and Armed Services Committees each held extensive public hearings on ABM during the summer of 1969. Opposition to the administration's program focused on the impact Safeguard would have on an already bloated defense budget, the technical integrity of a system that would employ for missile defense technology originally developed for Sentinel's city-defense mission, and Safeguard's implications for both the arms race and SALT. Alternatives to ballistic missile defense also were considered, such as a launch-on-warning doctrine and placing a greater proportion of offensive missiles on less vulnerable submarines. In the end, by a margin of one vote, the Senate authorized deployment of Safeguard at two ICBM fields. At a minimum, the ABM debate had put the administration on notice that its plans for a future defense of cities would face serious opposition from Congress.

Commencing SALT. By early fall 1969, both the United States and the Soviet Union were prepared for SALT. Moscow had made known its concern over Safeguard, and, following the outbreak of fighting between Soviet and Chinese troops along the Ussuri River in March of that year, a number of officials in Washington began to suspect that deployment of Galosh would be confined to the Soviet capital to defend against an attack from China. When, on 25 October, the United States and the Soviet Union announced that SALT would begin on 17 November in Helsinki, both nations believed they were entering the negotiations from a position of strength. The United States saw Safeguard as a technically superior system with a growth potential that would provide leverage for achieving a limitation on ABMS as well as on offensive weapons; the Soviets, on the other hand, clearly had more momentum in the offensive arms competition.

The accompanying table illustrates the strategic offensive force levels of the United States and the Soviet Union on three occasions in

U.S. and Soviet Strategic Offensive Forces

	January 1967	September 1968	November 1969
United States			
ICBMS	1,054	1,054	1,054
SLBMS	576	656	656
Bombers	650	565	525
Total	2,280	2,275	2,235
U.S.S.R.			
ICBMS	500	875	1,140
SLBMS	100	110	185
Bombers	150	150	145
Total	750[a]	1,135[b]	1,470[c]

[a] Does not include 450 ICBMs and SLBMs under construction.
[b] Does not include 515 ICBMs and SLBMs under construction.
[c] Does not include 380 ICBMs and SLBMs under construction.
Source: Raymond L. Garthoff, "SALT and the Soviet Military," in *Problems of Communism*, vol. 24, no. 1 (January–February 1975), pp. 22–24.

the early history of SALT: when the Johnson administration first proposed negotiations in January 1967, at the time the negotiations were first scheduled to begin in September 1968, and when the talks finally got underway in November 1969.

The first round of the Strategic Arms Limitation Talks, SALT I, lasted two and a half years and consisted of seven negotiating sessions alternating between Helsinki and Vienna. Both the American and Soviet delegations included representatives of civilian and military agencies responsible for each country's nuclear weapon programs. Ambassador Gerard C. Smith led the U.S. negotiating team; Ambassador Vladimir S. Semenov headed the Soviet delegation. During the first session of SALT the delegations confined their efforts to a general exposition of their objectives in the negotiations. For Moscow, the main goal was a limitation on ABMS, a significant reversal of its original objective in 1967. Washington, while agreeing to restrain competition in defensive arms, also stated its intention to achieve agreement on limiting offensive delivery systems.

Although the Soviet Union had agreed before the start of SALT to discuss offensive arms limitations, it resisted American efforts to that end for well over a year. One of the Soviet delegation's techniques was to insist that any agreement on offensive systems take into account American forward-based systems (FBS), nuclear weapons deployed on land and water in Europe and the Far East. The Nixon administration

successfully opposed this Soviet position by arguing that FBS were theater weapons deployed to offset over 600 Soviet intermediate- and medium-range missiles pointed at Western Europe, and that such systems were outside the purview of negotiations on strategic arms.

Two other weapon systems were discussed during early sessions of SALT: MIRV and ABM. President Nixon had come under increasing, though unsuccessful, congressional pressure in 1969 to suspend MIRV tests pending the outcome of efforts to negotiate a ban on this system. At the start of the second session of the talks, in April 1970, the U.S. delegation offered a proposal that would ban testing and deployment of MIRVs, with on-site inspection to verify compliance. It is unlikely the Soviets would have accepted such a proposal even without the provision for on-site inspection, since Moscow now recognized a clear advantage in MIRVing its larger-payload missiles in the future. ABM, however, was a subject more amenable to resolution. In April 1970 the Soviets accepted an American proposal to limit deployment of ABMs to the capitals of both nations. Later, the Nixon administration would back away from this NCA (National Command Authority) formula because of its concern over congressional support for a Washington ABM deployment. Indeed, such concern was justified, as the Senate that summer deleted funds requested by the administration to initiate construction of Safeguard around Washington and three other cities. In addition, Moscow's Galosh was now seen as providing protection for approximately 300 ICBMs deployed within its operational radius.

The First Breakthrough. Throughout much of the latter half of 1970 the talks remained in stalemate, with Moscow pressing for an early agreement covering only ABMs and Washington insisting that such an agreement could only accompany limitations on offensive arms. In June the United States began deploying MIRVs on Minuteman III ICBMs; deployment of MIRVs or Poseidon SLBMs would follow within a year. The suspicions and distrust each nation harbored toward the other were not allayed by confrontations over Jordan in September and Soviet construction of a base for missile-carrying submarines in Cuba the following month.

In May 1971 the SALT deadlock was finally resolved with an exchange of letters between President Nixon and Prime Minister Kosygin after extensive "back channel" negotiations in Washington between Henry Kissinger, the President's national security adviser, and Soviet Ambassador Anatoly Dobrynin. On 20 May the breakthrough was announced in a joint statement. The United States and the Soviet Union would "concentrate this year on working out an agreement for the limitation of the deployment of antiballistic missile systems (ABMs).

They have also agreed that, together with concluding an agreement to limit ABMS, they will agree on certain measures with respect to the limitation of offensive strategic weapons."[7] Left unresolved in the "back channel" discussions were the specific limitations to be placed on offensive arms.

Throughout the remaining months of 1971 the delegations worked to fill in the details of the framework announced on 20 May. Shortly after the signing of the Quadripartite Agreement on Berlin on 3 September 1971, President Nixon disclosed he would be traveling to Moscow the following May. Although détente was now yielding progress on a number of fronts, there was little certainty a SALT agreement could be completed in time for signing at the summit.

The pace of diplomacy in early 1972 was intense. President Nixon visited Peking in February, and in April Kissinger went to Moscow for secret negotiations to break a new SALT deadlock and prepare an agenda for the upcoming summit. In meetings with General Secretary Leonid Brezhnev, agreement was reached to limit ABM deployments to two sites (NCA and an ICBM field) in each country and to include SLBMS in an interim agreement on offensive weapons. The latter provision was accepted by the Soviets after they had received assurances that they would be allowed to continue the expansion of their SLBM force in exchange for phasing out older ICBMS and SLBMS. The stage appeared set for the Moscow summit when, on 8 May, President Nixon ordered American forces to mine Haiphong and other ports in North Vietnam and bomb the rail lines carrying supplies from China to fuel Hanoi's spring offensive in the south. Despite this action the Soviet Union decided not to cancel the summit, and on 22 May the President arrived in Moscow.

Four days of hectic negotiations followed, during which the two countries resolved the remaining critical issues standing in the way of a SALT agreement.[8] Most of the terms of the ABM treaty already had been settled by the delegations in Helsinki. Ultimately, the success of the summit hinged on the provision limiting SLBMS. It had been agreed in April that deployments of ICBMS, SLBMS, and missile-carrying submarines were to be frozen at existing levels in the interim agreement. At issue were the numbers of SLBMS and submarines the Soviets had operational or under construction in May 1972—freeze levels from which they would be authorized to deploy additional missiles and submarines under the provisions of a protocol to the interim agreement.

[7] *Documents on Disarmament, 1971*, Publication 66 (Washington, D.C.: U.S. Arms Control and Disarmament Agency, 1973), p. 298.

[8] For a detailed account of the negotiations in Moscow, see Newhouse, *Cold Dawn*, pp. 249–260.

The protocol would allow the Soviet Union to increase the number of its SLBMS to 950 on sixty-two submarines provided it dismantle one older ICBM for each SLBM deployed beyond the number it had at the time of the summit. In other words, Moscow could not deploy additional missiles beyond the sum of the May 1972 freeze levels for ICBMS and SLBMS, but it could increase the number of submarine-launched missiles to 950 at the expense of an equal number of older land-based missiles.

In claiming it had 768 SLBMS on forty-eight submarines, Moscow sought to minimize the number of older missiles it would have to dismantle to reach the protocol's authorized ceiling. Washington asserted that the Soviets had between forty-one and forty-three submarines and approximately 640 SLBMS. In the end, 740 SLBMS on forty-three submarines were agreed to as compromise figures for the Soviet freeze levels, and on the evening of 26 May President Nixon and General Secretary Brezhnev signed the ABM treaty and interim agreement of SALT I.

1
The Moscow Summit, May 1972

Treaty on Anti-Ballistic Missile Systems, 26 May 1972

The United States of America and the Union of Soviet Socialist Republics, hereinafter referred to as the Parties,

Proceeding from the premise that nuclear war would have devastating consequences for all mankind,

Considering that effective measures to limit anti-ballistic missile systems would be a substantial factor in curbing the race in strategic offensive arms and would lead to a decrease in the risk of outbreak of war involving nuclear weapons,

Proceeding from the premise that the limitation of anti-ballistic missile systems, as well as certain agreed measures with respect to the limitation of strategic offensive arms, would contribute to the creation of more favorable conditions for further negotiations on limiting strategic arms,

Mindful of their obligations under Article VI of the Treaty on the Non-Proliferation of Nuclear Weapons,

Declaring their intention to achieve at the earliest possible date the cessation of the nuclear arms race and to take effective measures toward reductions in strategic arms, nuclear disarmament, and general and complete disarmament,

Desiring to contribute to the relaxation of international tension and the strengthening of trust between States,

Have agreed as follows:

Article I

1. Each Party undertakes to limit anti-ballistic missile (ABM) systems and to adopt other measures in accordance with the provisions of this Treaty.

SOURCE: Treaty between the United States of America and the Union of Soviet Socialist Republics on the Limitation of Anti-Ballistic Missile Systems. *Department of State Bulletin,* 26 June 1972, pp. 918–920.

2. Each Party undertakes not to deploy ABM systems for a defense of the territory of its country and not to provide a base for such a defense, and not to deploy ABM systems for defense of an individual region except as provided for in Article III of this Treaty.

Article II

1. For the purposes of this Treaty an ABM system is a system to counter strategic ballistic missiles or their elements in flight trajectory, currently consisting of:

(a) ABM interceptor missiles, which are interceptor missiles constructed and deployed for an ABM role, or of a type tested in an ABM mode;

(b) ABM launchers, which are launchers constructed and deployed for launching ABM interceptor missiles; and

(c) ABM radars, which are radars constructed and deployed for an ABM role, or of a type tested in an ABM mode.

2. The ABM system components listed in paragraph 1 of this Article include those which are:

(a) operational;
(b) under construction;
(c) undergoing testing;
(d) undergoing overhaul, repair or conversion; or
(e) mothballed.

Article III

Each Party undertakes not to deploy ABM systems or their components except that:

(a) within one ABM system deployment area having a radius of one hundred and fifty kilometers and centered on the Party's national capital, a Party may deploy: (1) no more than one hundred ABM launchers and no more than one hundred ABM interceptor missiles at launch sites, and (2) ABM radars within no more than six ABM radar complexes, the area of each complex being circular and having a diameter of no more than three kilometers; and

(b) within one ABM system deployment area having a radius of one hundred and fifty kilometers and containing ICBM silo launchers, a Party may deploy: (1) no more than one hundred ABM launchers and no more than one hundred ABM interceptor missiles at launch sites, (2) two large phased-array ABM radars comparable in potential to corresponding ABM radars operational or under construction on the date of signature of the Treaty in an ABM system deployment area containing ICBM silo

launchers, and (3) no more than eighteen ABM radars each having a potential less than the potential of the smaller of the above-mentioned two large phased-array ABM radars.

Article IV

The limitations provided for in Article III shall not apply to ABM systems or their components used for development or testing, and located within current or additionally agreed test ranges. Each Party may have no more than a total of fifteen ABM launchers at test ranges.

Article V

1. Each Party undertakes not to develop, test, or deploy ABM systems or components which are sea-based, air-based, space-based, or mobile land-based.

2. Each Party undertakes not to develop, test, or deploy ABM launchers for launching more than one ABM interceptor missile at a time from each launcher, nor to modify deployed launchers to provide them with such a capability, nor to develop, test, or deploy automatic or semiautomatic or other similar systems for rapid reload of ABM launchers.

Article VI

To enhance assurance of the effectiveness of the limitations on ABM systems and their components provided by this Treaty, each Party undertakes:

(a) not to give missiles, launchers, or radars, other than ABM interceptor missiles, ABM launchers, or ABM radars, capabilities to counter strategic ballistic missiles or their elements in flight trajectory, and not to test them in an ABM mode; and

(b) not to deploy in the future radars for early warning of strategic ballistic missile attack except at locations along the periphery of its national territory and oriented outward.

Article VII

Subject to the provisions of this Treaty, modernization and replacement of ABM systems or their components may be carried out.

Article VIII

ABM systems or their components in excess of the numbers or outside the areas specified in this Treaty, as well as ABM systems or their components prohibited by this Treaty, shall be destroyed or dismantled under agreed procedures within the shortest possible agreed period of time.

Article IX

To assure the viability and effectiveness of this Treaty, each Party undertakes not to transfer to other States, and not to deploy outside its national territory, ABM systems or their components limited by this Treaty.

Article X

Each Party undertakes not to assume any international obligations which would conflict with this Treaty.

Article XI

The Parties undertake to continue active negotiations for limitations on strategic offensive arms.

Article XII

1. For the purpose of providing assurance of compliance with the provisions of this Treaty, each Party shall use national technical means of verification at its disposal in a manner consistent with generally recognized principles of international law.

2. Each Party undertakes not to interfere with the national technical means of verification of the other Party operating in accordance with paragraph 1 of this Article.

3. Each Party undertakes not to use deliberate concealment measures which impede verification by national technical means of compliance with the provisions of this Treaty. This obligation shall not require changes in current construction, assembly, conversion, or overhaul practices.

Article XIII

1. To promote the objectives and implementation of the provisions of this Treaty, the Parties shall establish promptly a Standing Consultative Commission, within the framework of which they will:

(a) consider questions concerning compliance with the obligations assumed and related situations which may be considered ambiguous;

(b) provide on a voluntary basis such information as either Party considers necessary to assure confidence in compliance with the obligations assumed;

(c) consider questions involving unintended interference with national technical means of verification;

(d) consider possible changes in the strategic situation which have a bearing on the provisions of this Treaty;

(e) agree upon procedures and dates for destruction or dismantling of ABM systems or their components in cases provided for by the provisions of this Treaty;

(f) consider, as appropriate, possible proposals for further increasing the viability of this Treaty, including proposals for amendments in accordance with the provisions of this Treaty;

(g) consider, as appropriate, proposals for further measures aimed at limiting strategic arms.

2. The Parties through consultation shall establish, and may amend as appropriate, Regulations for the Standing Consultative Commission governing procedures, composition and other relevant matters.

Article XIV

1. Each Party may propose amendments to this Treaty. Agreed amendments shall enter into force in accordance with the procedures governing the entry into force of this Treaty.

2. Five years after entry into force of this Treaty, and at five year intervals thereafter, the Parties shall together conduct a review of this Treaty.

Article XV

1. This Treaty shall be of unlimited duration.

2. Each Party shall, in exercising its national sovereignty, have the right to withdraw from this Treaty if it decides that extraordinary events related to the subject matter of this Treaty have jeopardized its supreme interests. It shall give notice of its decision to the other Party six months prior to withdrawal from the Treaty. Such notice shall include a statement of the extraordinary events the notifying Party regards as having jeopardized its supreme interests.

Article XVI

1. This Treaty shall be subject to ratification in accordance with the constitutional procedures of each Party. The Treaty shall enter into force on the day of the exchange of instruments of ratification.

2. This Treaty shall be registered pursuant to Article 102 of the Charter of the United Nations.

Done at Moscow on May 26, 1972, in two copies, each in the English and Russian languages, both texts being equally authentic.

For the United States of America:

Richard Nixon

President of the United States of America

For the Union of Soviet Socialist Republics:

Leonid I. Brezhnev

General Secretary of the Central Committee of the CPSU

Interim Agreement on the Limitation of Strategic Offensive Arms, 26 May 1972

The United States of America and the Union of Soviet Socialist Republics, hereinafter referred to as the Parties,

Convinced that the Treaty on the Limitation of Anti-Ballistic Missile Systems and this Interim Agreement on Certain Measures with Respect to the Limitation of Strategic Offensive Arms will contribute to the creation of more favorable conditions for active negotiations on limiting strategic arms as well as to the relaxation of international tension and the strengthening of trust between States,

Taking into account the relationship between strategic offensive and defensive arms,

Mindful of their obligations under Article VI of the Treaty on the Non-Proliferation of Nuclear Weapons,

Have agreed as follows:

Article I

The Parties undertake not to start construction of additional fixed land-based intercontinental ballistic missile (ICBM) launchers after July 1, 1972.

Article II

The Parties undertake not to convert land-based launchers for light ICBMs, or for ICBMs of older types deployed prior to 1964, into land-based launchers for heavy ICBMs of types deployed after that time.

Article III

The Parties undertake to limit submarine-launched ballistic missile (SLBM) launchers and modern ballistic missile submarines to the numbers operational and under construction on the date of signature of this Interim Agreement, and in addition to launchers and submarines constructed under procedures established by the Parties as replacements for an equal number of ICBM launchers of older types deployed prior to 1964 or for launchers on older submarines.

Article IV

Subject to the provisions of this Interim Agreement, modernization and replacement of strategic offensive ballistic missiles and launchers covered by this Interim Agreement may be undertaken.

SOURCE: Interim Agreement between the United States of America and the Union of Soviet Socialist Republics on Certain Measures with Respect to the Limitation of Strategic Offensive Arms. *Department of State Bulletin*, 26 June 1972, pp. 920–921.

Article V

1. For the purpose of providing assurance of compliance with the provisions of this Interim Agreement, each Party shall use national technical means of verification at its disposal in a manner consistent with generally recognized principles of international law.

2. Each Party undertakes not to interfere with the national technical means of verification of the other Party operating in accordance with paragraph 1 of this Article.

3. Each Party undertakes not to use deliberate concealment measures which impede verification by national technical means of compliance with the provisions of this Interim Agreement. This obligation shall not require changes in current construction, assembly, conversion, or overhaul practices.

Article VI

To promote the objectives and implementation of the provisions of this Interim Agreement, the Parties shall use the Standing Consultative Commission established under Article XIII of the Treaty on the Limitation of Anti-Ballistic Missile Systems in accordance with the provisions of that Article.

Article VII

The Parties undertake to continue active negotiations for limitations on strategic offensive arms. The obligations provided for in this Interim Agreement shall not prejudice the scope or terms of the limitations on strategic offensive arms which may be worked out in the course of further negotiations.

Article VIII

1. This Interim Agreement shall enter into force upon exchange of written notices of acceptance by each Party, which exchange shall take place simultaneously with the exchange of instruments of ratification of the Treaty on the Limitation of Anti-Ballistic Missile Systems.

2. This Interim Agreement shall remain in force for a period of five years unless replaced earlier by an agreement on more complete measures limiting strategic offensive arms. It is the objective of the Parties to conduct active follow-on negotiations with the aim of concluding such an agreement as soon as possible.

3. Each Party shall, in exercising its national sovereignty, have the right to withdraw from this Interim Agreement if it decides that extraordinary events related to the subject matter of this Interim Agreement have jeopardized its supreme interests. It shall give notice of its decision to the other Party six months prior to withdrawal from this Interim

Agreement. Such notice shall include a statement of the extraordinary events the notifying Party regards as having jeopardized its supreme interests.

DONE at Moscow on May 26, 1972, in two copies, each in the English and Russian languages, both texts being equally authentic.

For the United States of America:

RICHARD NIXON

President of the United States of America

For the Union of Soviet Socialist Republics:

LEONID I. BREZHNEV

General Secretary of the Central Committee of the CPSU

Protocol to the Interim Agreement, 26 May 1972

The United States of America and the Union of Soviet Socialist Republics, hereinafter referred to as the Parties,

Having agreed on certain limitations relating to submarine-launched ballistic missile launchers and modern ballistic missile submarines, and to replacement procedures, in the Interim Agreement,

Have agreed as follows:

The Parties understand that, under Article III of the Interim Agreement, for the period during which that Agreement remains in force:

The US may have no more than 710 ballistic missile launchers on submarines (SLBMS) and no more than 44 modern ballistic missile submarines. The Soviet Union may have no more than 950 ballistic missile launchers on submarines and no more than 62 modern ballistic missile submarines.

Additional ballistic missile launchers on submarines up to the above-mentioned levels, in the U.S.—over 656 ballistic missile launchers on nuclear-powered submarines, and in the U.S.S.R.—over 740 ballistic missile launchers on nuclear-powered submarines, operational and under construction, may become operational as replacements for equal numbers of ballistic missile launchers of older types deployed prior to 1964 or of ballistic missile launchers on older submarines.

The deployment of modern SLBMS on any submarine, regardless of type, will be counted against the total level of SLBMS permitted for the U.S. and the U.S.S.R.

This Protocol shall be considered an integral part of the Interim Agreement.

DONE at Moscow this 26th day of May, 1972.

For the United States of America

RICHARD NIXON

President of the United States of America

For the Union of Soviet Socialist Republics

LEONID I. BREZHNEV

General Secretary of the Central Committee of the CPSU

SOURCE: Protocol to the Interim Agreement between the United States of America and the Union of Soviet Socialist Republics on Certain Measures with Respect to the Limitation of Strategic Offensive Arms. *Department of State Bulletin*, 26 June 1972, p. 921.

Agreed Interpretations and Unilateral Statements

Agreed Interpretations

(a) Initialed Statements.

The texts of the statements set out below were agreed upon and initialed by the Heads of the Delegations on May 26, 1972.

ABM Treaty

[A]

The Parties understand that, in addition to the ABM radars which may be deployed in accordance with subparagraph (a) of Article III of the Treaty, those non-phased-array ABM radars operational on the date of signature of the Treaty within the ABM system deployment area for defense of the national capital may be retained.

[B]

The Parties understand that the potential (the product of mean emitted power in watts and antenna area in square meters) of the smaller of the two large phased-array ABM radars referred to in subparagraph (b) of Article III of the Treaty is considered for purposes of the Treaty to be three million.

[C]

The Parties understand that the center of the ABM system deployment area centered on the national capital and the center of the ABM system deployment area containing ICBM silo launchers for each Party shall be separated by no less than thirteen hundred kilometers.

[D]

The Parties agree not to deploy phased-array radars having a potential (the product of mean emitted power in watts and antenna area in square meters) exceeding three million, except as provided for in Articles III, IV and VI of the Treaty, or except for the purposes of tracking objects in outer space or for use as national technical means of verification.

[E]

In order to insure fulfillment of the obligation not to deploy ABM systems and their components except as provided in Article III of the

SOURCE: *Department of State Bulletin*, 3 July 1972, pp. 11–14.

Treaty, the Parties agree that in the event ABM systems based on other physical principles and including components capable of substituting for the ABM interceptor missiles, ABM launchers, or ABM radars are created in the future, specific limitations on such systems and their components would be subject to discussion in accordance with Article XIII and agreement in accordance with Article XIV of the Treaty.

[F]

The Parties understand that Article V of the Treaty includes obligations not to develop, test or deploy ABM interceptor missiles for the delivery by each ABM interceptor missile of more than one independently guided warhead.

[G]

The Parties understand that Article IX of the Treaty includes the obligation of the US and the USSR not to provide to other States technical descriptions or blueprints specially worked out for the construction of ABM systems and their components limited by the Treaty.

Interim Agreement

[H]

The Parties understand that land-based ICBM launchers referred to in the Interim Agreement are understood to be launchers for strategic ballistic missiles capable of ranges in excess of the shortest distance between the northeastern border of the continental U.S. and the northwestern border of the continental USSR.

[I]

The Parties understand that fixed land-based ICBM launchers under active construction as of the date of signature of the Interim Agreement may be completed.

[J]

The Parties understand that in the process of modernization and replacement the dimensions of land-based ICBM silo launchers will not be significantly increased.

[K]

The Parties understand that dismantling or destruction of ICBM launchers of older types deployed prior to 1964 and ballistic missile launchers on older submarines being replaced by new SLBM launchers on modern submarines will be initiated at the time of the beginning of sea trials of a replacement submarine, and will be completed in the shortest possible

agreed period of time. Such dismantling or destruction, and timely notification thereof, will be accomplished under procedures to be agreed in the Standing Consultative Commission.

[L]

The Parties understand that during the period of the Interim Agreement there shall be no significant increase in the number of ICBM or SLBM test and training launchers, or in the number of such launchers for modern land-based heavy ICBMS. The Parties further understand that construction or conversion of ICBM launchers at test ranges shall be undertaken only for purposes of testing and training.

(b) COMMON UNDERSTANDINGS.

Common understanding of the Parties on the following matters was reached during the negotiations:

A. *Increase in ICBM Silo Dimensions*

Ambassador Smith made the following statement on May 26, 1972: "The Parties agree that the term 'significantly increased' means that an increase will not be greater than 10–15 percent of the present dimensions of land-based ICBM silo launchers."

Minister Semenov replied that this statement corresponded to the Soviet understanding.

B. *Location of ICBM Defenses*

The U.S. Delegation made the following statement on May 26, 1972: "Article III of the ABM Treaty provides for each side one ABM system deployment area centered on its national capital and one ABM system deployment area containing ICBM silo launchers. The two sides have registered agreement on the following statement: 'The Parties understand that the center of the ABM system deployment area centered on the national capital and the center of the ABM system deployment area containing ICBM silo launchers for each Party shall be separated by no less than thirteen hundred kilometers.' In this connection, the U.S. side notes that its ABM system deployment area for defense of ICBM silo launchers, located west of the Mississippi River, will be centered in the Grand Forks ICBM silo launcher deployment area." (See Initialed Statement [C].)

C. *ABM Test Ranges*

The U.S. Delegation made the following statement on April 26, 1972: "Article IV of the ABM Treaty provides that 'the limitations provided for in Article III shall not apply to ABM systems or their components used for development or testing, and located within current or

additionally agreed test ranges.' We believe it would be useful to assure that there is no misunderstanding as to current ABM test ranges. It is our understanding that ABM test ranges encompass the area within which ABM components are located for test purposes. The current U.S. ABM test ranges are at White Sands, New Mexico, and at Kwajalein Atoll, and the current Soviet ABM test range is near Sary Shagan in Kazakhstan. We consider that non-phased array radars of types used for range safety or instrumentation purposes may be located outside of ABM test ranges. We interpret the reference in Article IV to 'additionally agreed test ranges' to mean that ABM components will not be located at any other test ranges without prior agreement between our Governments that there will be such additional ABM test ranges."

On May 5, 1972, the Soviet Delegation stated that there was a common understanding on what ABM test ranges were, that the use of the types of non-ABM radars for range safety or instrumentation was not limited under the Treaty, that the reference in Article IV to "additionally agreed" test ranges was sufficiently clear, and that national means permitted identifying current test ranges.

D. *Mobile ABM Systems*

On January 28, 1972, the U.S. Delegation made the following statement: "Article V(1) of the Joint Draft Text of the ABM Treaty includes an undertaking not to develop, test, or deploy mobile land-based ABM systems and their components. On May 5, 1971, the U.S. side indicated that, in its view, a prohibition on deployment of mobile ABM systems and components would rule out the deployment of ABM launchers and radars which were not permanent fixed types. At that time, we asked for the Soviet view of this interpretation. Does the Soviet side agree with the U.S. side's interpretation put forward on May 5, 1971?"

On April 13, 1972, the Soviet Delegation said there is a general common understanding on this matter.

E. *Standing Consultative Commission*

Ambassador Smith made the following statement on May 24, 1972: "The United States proposes that the sides agree that, with regard to initial implementation of the ABM Treaty's Article XIII on the Standing Consultative Commission (SCC) and of the consultation Articles to the Interim Agreement on offensive arms and the Accidents Agreement,[1] agreement establishing the SCC will be worked out early in the follow-on SALT negotiations; until that is completed, the following

[1] See Article 7 of Agreement to Reduce the Risk of Outbreak of Nuclear War Between the United States of America and the Union of Soviet Socialist Republics, signed September 30, 1971. [Footnote in original; for text of the agreement, see *Department of State Bulletin* of 18 October 1971, p. 400.]

arrangements will prevail: when SALT is in session, any consultation desired by either side under these Articles can be carried out by the two SALT Delegations; when SALT is not in session, *ad hoc* arrangements for any desired consultations under these Articles may be made through diplomatic channels."

Minister Semenov replied that, on an *ad referendum* basis, he could agree that the U.S. statement corresponded to the Soviet understanding.

F. *Standstill*

On May 6, 1972, Minister Semenov made the following statement: "In an effort to accommodate the wishes of the U.S. side, the Soviet Delegation is prepared to proceed on the basis that the two sides will in fact observe the obligations of both the Interim Agreement and the ABM Treaty beginning from the date of signatures of these two documents."

In reply, the U.S. Delegation made the following statement on May 20, 1972: "The U.S. agrees in principle with the Soviet statement made on May 6 concerning observance of obligations beginning from date of signature but we would like to make clear our understanding that this means that, pending ratification and acceptance, neither side would take any action prohibited by the agreements after they had entered into force. This understanding would continue to apply in the absence of notification by either signatory of its intention not to proceed with ratification or approval."

The Soviet Delegation indicated agreement with the U.S. statement.

Unilateral Statements

(a) The following noteworthy unilateral statements were made during the negotiations by the United States Delegation:

A. *Withdrawal from the ABM Treaty*

On May 9, 1972, Ambassador Smith made the following statement: "The U.S. Delegation has stressed the importance the U.S. Government attaches to achieving agreement on more complete limitations on strategic offensive arms, following agreement on an ABM Treaty and on an Interim Agreement on certain measures with respect to the limitation of strategic offensive arms. The U.S. Delegation believes that an objective of the follow-on negotiations should be to constrain and reduce on a long-term basis threats to the survivability of our respective strategic retaliatory forces. The USSR Delegation has also indicated that the objectives of SALT would remain unfulfilled without the

achievement of an agreement providing for more complete limitations on strategic offensive arms. Both sides recognize that the initial agreements would be steps toward the achievement of more complete limitations on strategic arms. If an agreement providing for more complete strategic offensive arms limitations were not achieved within five years, U.S. supreme interests could be jeopardized. Should that occur, it would constitute a basis for withdrawal from the ABM Treaty. The U.S. does not wish to see such a situation occur, nor do we believe that the USSR does. It is because we wish to prevent such a situation that we emphasize the importance the U.S. Government attaches to achievement of more complete limitations on strategic offensive arms. The U.S. Executive will inform the Congress, in connection with Congressional consideration of the ABM Treaty and the Interim Agreement of this statement of the U.S. position."

B. *Land-Mobile ICBM Launchers*

The U.S. Delegation made the following statement on May 20, 1972: "In connection with the important subject of land-mobile ICBM launchers, in the interest of concluding the Interim Agreement the U.S. Delegation now withdraws its proposal that Article I or an agreed statement explicitly prohibit the deployment of mobile land-based ICBM launchers. I have been instructed to inform you that, while agreeing to defer the question of limitation of operational land-mobile ICBM launchers to the subsequent negotiations on more complete limitations on strategic offensive arms, the U.S. would consider the deployment of operational land-mobile ICBM launchers during the period of the Interim Agreement as inconsistent with the objectives of that Agreement."

C. *Covered Facilities*

The U.S. Delegation made the following statement on May 20, 1972: "I wish to emphasize the importance that the United States attaches to the provisions of Article V, including in particular their application to fitting out or berthing submarines."

D. *"Heavy" ICBMs*

The U.S. Delegation made the following statement on May 26, 1972: "The U.S. Delegation regrets that the Soviet Delegation has not been willing to agree on a common definition of a heavy missile. Under these circumstances, the U.S. Delegation believes it necessary to state the following: The United States would consider any ICBM having a volume significantly greater than that of the largest light ICBM now operational on either side to be a heavy ICBM. The U.S. proceeds on the premise that the Soviet side will give due account to this consideration."

E. Tested in ABM Mode

On April 7, 1972, the U.S. Delegation made the following statement: "Article II of the Joint Draft Text uses the term 'tested in an ABM mode,' in defining ABM components, and Article VI includes certain obligations concerning such testing. We believe that the sides should have a common understanding of this phrase. First, we would note that the testing provisions of the ABM Treaty are intended to apply to testing which occurs after the date of signature of the Treaty, and not to any testing which may have occurred in the past. Next, we would amplify the remarks we have made on this subject during the previous Helsinki phase by setting forth the objectives which govern the U.S. view on the subject, namely, while prohibiting testing of non-ABM components for ABM purposes: not to prevent testing of ABM components, and not to prevent testing of non-ABM components for non-ABM purposes. To clarify our interpretation of 'tested in an ABM mode,' we note that we would consider a launcher, missile or radar to be 'tested in an ABM mode' if, for example, any of the following events occur: (1) a launcher is used to launch an ABM interceptor missile, (2) an interceptor missile is flight tested against a target vehicle which has a flight trajectory with characteristics of a strategic ballistic missile flight trajectory, or is flight tested in conjunction with the test of an ABM interceptor missile or an ABM radar at the same test range, or is flight tested to an altitude inconsistent with interception of targets against which air defenses are deployed, (3) a radar makes measurements on a cooperative target vehicle of the kind referred to in item (2) above during the reentry portion of its trajectory or makes measurements in conjunction with the test of an ABM interceptor missile or an ABM radar at the same test range. Radars used for purposes such as range safety or instrumentation would be exempt from application of these criteria."

F. No-Transfer Article of ABM Treaty

On April 18, 1972, the U.S. Delegation made the following statement: "In regard to this Article [IX], I have a brief and I believe self-explanatory statement to make. The U.S. side wishes to make clear that the provisions of this Article do not set a precedent for whatever provision may be considered for a Treaty on Limiting Strategic Offensive Arms. The question of transfer of strategic offensive arms is a far more complex issue, which may require a different solution."

G. No Increase in Defense of Early Warning Radars

On July 28, 1970, the U.S. Delegation made the following statement: "Since Hen House radars [Soviet ballistic missile early warning

radars] can detect and track ballistic missile warheads at great distances, they have a significant ABM potential. Accordingly, the U.S. would regard any increase in the defenses of such radars by surface-to-air missiles as inconsistent with an agreement."

* * * * *

(b) The following noteworthy unilateral statement was made by the Delegation of the U.S.S.R. and is shown here with the U.S. reply:

On May 17, 1972, Minister Semenov made the following unilateral "Statement of the Soviet Side:" "Taking into account that modern ballistic missile submarines are presently in the possession of not only the U.S., but also of its NATO allies, the Soviet Union agrees that for the period of effectiveness of the Interim 'Freeze' Agreement the U.S. and its NATO allies have up to 50 such submarines with a total of up to 800 ballistic missile launchers thereon (including 41 U.S. submarines with 656 ballistic missile launchers). However, if during the period of effectiveness of the Agreement U.S. allies in NATO should increase the number of their modern submarines to exceed the numbers of submarines they would have operational or under construction on the date of signature of the Agreement, the Soviet Union will have the right to a corresponding increase in the number of its submarines. In the opinion of the Soviet side, the solution of the question of modern ballistic missile submarines provided for in the Interim Agreement only partially compensates for the strategic imbalance in the deployment of the nuclear-powered missile submarines of the USSR and the U.S. Therefore, the Soviet side believes that this whole question, and above all the question of liquidating the American missile submarine bases outside the U.S., will be appropriately resolved in the course of follow-on negotiations."

On May 24, Ambassador Smith made the following reply to Minister Semenov: "The United States side has studied the 'statement made by the Soviet side' of May 17 concerning compensation for submarine basing and SLBM submarines belonging to third countries. The United States does not accept the validity of the considerations in that statement."

On May 26 Minister Semenov repeated the unilateral statement made on May 17. Ambassador Smith also repeated the U.S. rejection on May 26.

Kissinger and Smith Outline the SALT I Agreements, 26 and 27 May 1972

Moscow, 26 May 1972*

Dr. Kissinger. Gentlemen, I thought that the most useful thing I could do was to give you a general background of these negotiations and of the President's view of the treaty, and Ambassador Smith, of course, who has conducted the negotiations and brought them to this conclusion, is in the best position to go through the details of the agreement. . . .

Nothing that this administration has done has seemed to it more important for the future of the world than to make an important first step in the limitation of strategic arms. All of us have been profoundly convinced that to arrest the arms race is one of the overriding concerns of this period. Now it is a subject of enormous technical complexity, and for the two great nuclear powers to make a beginning in putting their armaments under some restraint required political decisions and an enormous amount of technical work.

It is a process that has continued for many years. It started with extensive technical studies in Washington. It went through two and a half years of negotiations alternating between Helsinki and Vienna. It has been brought to a conclusion because both governments decided that in an agreement of this kind the stakes were larger than the simple technical issues; that what was at stake was a major step toward international stability, confidence among nations, and a turn in the pattern of postwar relationships.

This is why at various crucial moments in these negotiations there had been direct contacts between the President and Soviet leaders, which led by mutual agreement to breakthroughs—the first on May 20 of 1971, in which there was an agreement that broke the deadlock that had developed between the Soviet insistence that an agreement cover antiballistic missile systems only and our view that an agreement involved as well the offensive weapons. The compromise was that the initial treaty would deal with ABMs and that this would be accompanied by a freeze on certain categories of offensive weapons.

---

*Source: Press conference of Dr. Henry A. Kissinger, Assistant to the President for National Security Affairs, and Ambassador Gerald C. Smith. Office of the White House Press Secretary, 26 May 1972, as reprinted in U.S., Congress, Senate, Committee on Armed Services, *Military Implications of the Treaty on the Limitations of Anti-Ballistic Missile Systems and the Interim Agreement on Limitation of Strategic Offensive Arms*, 92d Cong., 2 Sess., 1972, pp. 97–103.

The next deadlock developed over the issue of what offensive weapons should be included, whether it should be confined to intercontinental ballistic missiles or whether submarine-launched ballistic missile systems should also be involved. The answer—this deadlock was broken at the end of April and in large part by direct contact between the Soviet leaders and the President—has finally resulted in the present agreement which Ambassador Smith has just brought back from Helsinki and which will be signed at eleven o'clock. Ambassador Smith is in the best position to explain the provisions of this agreement, but I wanted to make a few general observations about its significance and how it should be looked at.

The first point to make is that in an agreement that involves the central armaments on both sides it is foolish or shortsighted to approach the negotiations from the point of view of gaining a unilateral advantage. Neither nation will possibly put its security and its survival at the hazard of its opponent, and no agreement that brings disadvantage to either side can possibly last and can possibly bring about anything other than a new circle of insecurity. Therefore, the temptation that is ever present when agreements of this kind are analyzed as to who won is exceptionally inappropriate. We have approached these negotiations from the very beginning with the attitude that a wise proposal is one that is conceived by each side to be in the mutual interest, and we believe that if this agreement does what we hope it will, that the future will record that both sides won.

Secondly, let me make a few observations with respect to the freeze of offensive weapons, which has perhaps some of the more complicated provisions and the anticipation of which has aroused some comments in the United States.

First, the freeze concerns only two categories of offensive weapons; that is to say, intercontinental ballistic missiles and submarine-launched ballistic missiles. It does not include the number of warheads, nor does it include bombers, nor does it include, obviously, other systems based elsewhere than at sea or in the territory of each country.

Secondly, in assessing the significance of the freeze, it is not useful to analyze whether the freeze reflects a gap between the forces that are being frozen. In the two categories that are being frozen, that is to say, ICBMS and submarine-launched ballistic missiles, the facts are these: The Soviet Union has more intercontinental ballistic missiles than the United States. The Soviet Union has been building intercontinental ballistic missiles; the United States has not and has no such program at the moment. The Soviet Union has been building submarine-launched ballistic missiles at the rate of eight submarines a year. The United States has at this moment no submarines under construction.

Therefore, the question to ask in assessing the freeze is not what situation it perpetuates but what situation it prevents. The question is where we would be without the freeze. And if you project the existing building programs of the Soviet Union into the future, as against the absence of building programs over the period of the freeze in either of the categories that are being frozen, you will get a more correct clue to why we believe that there is a good agreement and why we believe that it has made a significant contribution to arresting the arms race.

The weapons are frozen, as we pointed out, in categories in which we have no ongoing programs. Now, having said this, however, I am not implying that we gained a unilateral advantage, because it is perhaps true that in the ABM field we had the more dynamic program, which is being arrested as a result of these developments.

* * *

Ambassador [Gerard C.] SMITH . . . First, let me say perhaps the obvious, that these documents are the product of long, careful, complex, and exhaustive negotiations. As a matter of fact, we were not finished with the last detail after we got on the airplane this evening in Helsinki. . . . I invited some of the Soviet delegation, including the chief of the delegation, Minister Semenov, to join us, and we continued to work on our way here to Moscow. So, this is about the freshest treaty that I have ever talked about.

I think that in sum these documents, when you look at them carefully, will demonstrate a solid, concrete, yet first step in the problem of controlling strategic arms. They are not the end of the road by any means, but I think that they are a very solid step forward.

You know, we have an obligation that sometimes people forget under the Nonproliferation Treaty of some years ago to get on with trying to limit strategic arms and get on with disarmament. I think as a general proposition these documents will show that we are not lax in that respect. We are conscious of our responsibilities.

Now, as Henry said, there are two basic documents here, the ABM treaty and the interim agreement, which, in effect, is a negotiating freeze arrangement to hold the situation to permit us to, hopefully, negotiate a treaty to match in the offensive field the treaty that we have succeeded in negotiating in the defensive field.

In the defensive field, I would urge you to look very carefully at the language of Article I, which looks very general but to my mind is a most significant step forward in relations between two great powers. In effect, it says that neither side is going to try to defend its nationwide territory. This is an admission of tremendous psychological significance, I believe—recognition that the deterrent forces of both sides are not going to be challenged.

When you think of the concerns that we have had for the last twenty-five years about first strike and counterforce, it seems to me a general recognition by both countries that they are not going to field a nationwide system is of first importance, politically, psychologically, and militarily.

In addition to that, the countries are going to agree not to lay the base for such a nationwide system. That got us into all sorts of radar problems which some of you people perhaps felt we took too long in solving, but much of the time we have spent was in trying to wrestle with this radar problem to prevent the possibility of a nationwide system arising.

In addition to that, the two nations have made commitments not to even try for a thick or regional defense in one part of the country except as specifically permitted under the agreement; that is, to defend one's capital or to defend a relatively small number of ICBM silos. So, although Article I looks like sort of a general statement, to my mind it is one of the most significant articles in the whole agreement.

Now, Article II defines what we are talking about and has a very important bearing on the whole question of what we call future ABM systems. This treaty has as a most significant aspect that it not only limits the present situation but has a choking-off effect on future systems which, under the terms of the treaty as we have reached understandings, will not be deployable unless this treaty is amended.

Article III is the heart of the treaty and deserves a great deal of study. I think we spent more time trying to wrestle with Article III than any other part of the treaty. I will go into details later if you like, but it says both sides can have two sites with no more than 100 launchers at each site, with radar sharply limited; one site for the defensive capital and one for the ICBMs. The Soviets will agree to deploy the ICBM site well away from the capital site, so the possibility for a base of a nationwide system is very poor.

In addition to the numbers, we have had to work out problems involving test ranges, numbers of test launchers, the question of modernization, the question of how you verify this treaty, and one of the significant conclusions that we have reached is that this treaty can safely be verified by national means of verification; that is, without onsite inspection. This is largely a limitation on numbers of relatively large objects which we are confident can be monitored, if you will, without onsite inspection. As a matter of fact, if I had my druthers and could have onsite inspection instead of our present national means, there would be no question in my mind that we would be much better off with national means of verification.

In addition to that, we will have commitments from the Soviets not to interfere with those national means of verification and not to

take measures to conceal their operation so as to prevent the workings of national means of verification. . . .

We are going to set up a Joint Consultative Commission which will, in effect, act as a surveying agent that will watch over the operation of the agreement, to which ambiguous situations can be referred, which will be a forum for further discussion of the possible amendments to see how this treaty is working, and to make sure that it stays viable over the years.

This treaty will have indefinite duration, but if it doesn't work, if our supreme interests are jeopardized, there is a provision that on short notice either side can escape from the binding obligations under the treaty.

Turn, now, for a minute to the offensive side. As Henry said, what we are trying to do is to set up a useful device that will hold the situation while we negotiate, hopefully, a matching treaty; that is, to match the treaty in the ABM defense field. I think that the measures that we have succeeded in spelling out in this interim agreement with the Russians will do just that. There will be a commitment on their part not to build any more of these ICBMs that have concerned us over the years. That commitment will extend to not building such things as SS-9s, and there will be provisions that if the sides want to increase their submarine missiles—which, if you can say so, are a more benign form of weapons system than ICBMs—they may do so, but only at the price of a substantial reduction program in other weapons systems.

Keep this in mind when you think about the possibility of increasing SLBMs: it is not for free. It is at a very substantial price in terms of reductions of other weapons systems. Reductions have never before been successfully negotiated, so I think this ought to be considered a great accomplishment.

I think I had better stop at that, since I am going to have a chance to go into specifics. I understand that there are to be some questions at this point.

Q. Mr. Smith, could you answer just a couple of basic things? On the question of the radar, could you give us an estimate of what percentage of the national territory will be protected by the ABM radar on each side? Secondly, on the offensive side, the submarines, there are no figures in the Fact Sheet, and the phrasing there seems to be a little ambiguous. Could you give us what you consider to be, in terms of numbers, the current levels of submarines on each side?

Ambassador SMITH. On the question of radar, I cannot give you a precise percentage. The radar coverage, of course, is not the essential consideration. No reentry vehicle was ever killed by a radar. It takes a lot of interceptors, in addition to radar, to do a defensive job. The radar

coverage, however, will be minute, and especially in the case of radar around ICBM fields, where there will be quantitative limitations as well as qualitative limitations, so only a relatively few radars will be permitted in these ICBM fields. We are quite confident that a radar base for a nationwide or thick regional defense is not possible under the terms of this treaty.

Now, in terms of numbers of submarines, I would like to reserve that until I can go into it more specifically.

* * *

Q. Do the Russians complete their construction of submarines presently under construction? They have seventeen operational and twenty-five presumably at some stage of construction. Will they be allowed to complete those before the freeze becomes effective?

Ambassador SMITH. Under the interim arrangement, they will be permitted to finish construction of submarines, yes. . . .

Q. Would you clear up the withdrawal rights from the treaty "if supreme interests are jeopardized and on six months' notice"? Is that "and/or" or must both conditions be prevalent, a supreme interest endangered; does this then require six month's notice of withdrawal?

Ambassador SMITH. That is correct. That is the same condition as in previous arms control treaties, such as the Nonproliferation Treaty.

Q. Does this Commission decide whether or not supreme interests are involved?

Ambassador SMITH. No. That is a unilateral decision for both countries.

Q. Doesn't this allow them to protect all of their ICBMs while we protect some of ours?

Ambassador SMITH. No. This will permit them to protect a smaller percentage of their ICBMs than ours, since they have substantially more than we have.

Q. If after five years there is no comprehensive offensive agreement, does the interim agreement lapse?

Ambassador SMITH. If the five years is past and the negotiations look fruitless, I would think we would not want to continue it. If the negotiations look as if they might still bear fruit, if both sides agree to extend the five-year arrangement, that is certainly in our field of vision.

* * *

Q. What about the submarines, the question of figures? Is this figure of forty-two Y-class submarines an accurate one that they will be allowed to complete, and we with forty-one?

Ambassador SMITH. I don't know about this figure of forty-two sub-

marines. I have seen all sorts of speculations about Soviet submarines, but it is perfectly clear that under this agreement if the Soviets want to pay the price of scrapping a substantial number of other important strategic weapons systems they can build additional submarines.
Q. What submarines do they have under construction now? I think you are evading the point on the number of submarines they will be frozen at under this treaty.
Ambassador SMITH. I am purposely evading the point because that is an intelligence estimate that I am not in a position to give out.

* * *

Dr. KISSINGER. Since I am not quite as constrained or don't feel as constrained as Ambassador Smith, lest we build up a profound atmosphere of mystery about the submarine issue, I will straighten it out as best I can. The base number of Soviet submarines is in dispute. It has been in dispute in our intelligence estimate exactly how much it is, though our intelligence estimates are in the range that was suggested.
Q. Forty-one to forty-three?
Dr. KISSINGER. I am not going to go beyond what I have said. It is in that general range. The Soviet estimate of their program is slightly more exhaustive. They, of course, have the advantage that they know what it is precisely. [Laughter.]

Now the provisions of the agreement, as I understand it, are that the Soviet Union can convert land-based missiles of a category of which we estimate that they have 210, plus 30-odd missiles on older nuclear submarines, into submarines or submarine-based launchers. This, then, would give them a figure of submarines and launchers substantially about the level that is now estimated as being under construction. This level has an upper ceiling.

Now, there are two things to be said. One, they can reach this level only at the sacrifice of existing weapons systems and, therefore, it would represent the first reduction of one category of weapons. Second, in the absence of this agreement, the Soviet Union was building submarines at the rate of eight or nine a year in any event, and their decision to build these submarines at that rate seems to have been fixed for some time.

Therefore, the ceiling on submarines has to be seen in terms of two factors. Factor one, where would the Soviet Union be without that ceiling? And without that ceiling the Soviet Union would be some 50 percent higher over the period of time if it exercised its full capacity of production. Second, in order to reach that ceiling, the Soviet Union will have to trade in heavy land-based missiles and/or submarine-based missiles of older types. So that in addition to arresting the momentum

of the submarine construction program, there is also a reduction of weapons that would under other circumstances not have been reduced.

The next question that can be asked then: Well, perhaps the best way to deal with this Soviet submarine program would have been to build more submarines of our own. I think those of you who followed defense matters know that the United States has no plan at this moment—and for that matter had no plan before this agreement—to build submarines over the five-year period of the freeze that this agreement was lasting. So we have to remember that we were prepared to live with a condition without an agreement that was significantly worse than it is with the agreement; and, secondly, that the freeze is purchased by the reduction of several hundred—if the Soviets exercise all their rights—land-based missiles and another category of sea-based missiles.

This is the context in which the submarine decision has to be seen.

* * *

Q. . . . Does the treaty permit the Soviets to complete their present submarine construction without penalty?

Dr. KISSINGER. Yes.

Q. Will these Tridents replace old Polaris submarines in that case?

Dr. KISSINGER. No ULMS submarines will be operational until after the freeze is over. There will be provisions in the treaty for when an existing weapon has to be scrapped in terms of the constructions of the follow-on program. If, in the development of ULMS, such a point should be reached before the end of the freeze, and if the treaty has not been extended by agreement, then of course those scrapping provisions would go into effect. Otherwise the ULMS would be a follow-on system to the existing one.

MOSCOW, 27 MAY 1972*

[Press Secretary Ronald L.] ZIEGLER. Let's continue now with the session we began over at the embassy earlier tonight. Dr. Kissinger's remarks will be on the record. . . .

Q. Henry, for factual purposes, I think it would help a great deal here, since we do not have the figures available, could you go into the existing figures that are available? In the public domain there are figures.

Dr. KISSINGER. In what category?

---

*SOURCE: Press conference of Dr. Henry A. Kissinger, Assistant to the President for National Security Affairs. *Department of State Bulletin*, 26 June 1972, pp. 871–879.

Q. Well, I think because this does cut across the whole range and one will be looking at the total figures of offensive weapons, even the bomber-delivered weapons would have relevance here.

Dr. Kissinger. First, the current figures are that in the field of ICBMs the United States has 1,054 and the Soviet Union has about 1,600. In the submarine field, the United States has about 656 and the Soviet Union has, again depending on what missiles you count, something between 680 and 700-plus. I will go into those figures in a minute when I explain the submarine agreement.

The Soviet Union has been building missiles at the rate of something like 250 a year. If I get arrested here for espionage, gentlemen, we will know who is to blame.

Q. What kind of missiles? Do you mean intercontinental?

Dr. Kissinger. I am talking about intercontinental, and it has been building submarine missiles at the rate of 128 a year. So, this is the backdrop against which you have to assess the agreement.

Therefore, on any day you would have picked over the last year, over the last two years, and on any day you are going to pick in the future, you will be able to demonstrate a Soviet numerical advantage. Moreover, it was a numerical advantage that was growing, because in the ICBM field we have, as you know, no ongoing program.

In the submarine field, as the question indicated to which I responded earlier, we also have no program for missiles that will be operational. In the submarine field we have now no submarine under construction. The first submarine that we have that would become operational would do so early in 1979 or late in 1978.

Therefore, any time over the next five years we were confronting a numerical margin that was growing, and a margin, moreover, which we could do nothing to reverse in that five-year period. Therefore, the question of whether the freeze perpetuates a Soviet numerical superiority is beside the point.

The question is: What would this margin have been without the freeze? That is the justification for the margin.

Second: Now, then, what are the figures going to be? The Soviet intercontinental ballistic missiles, gross or net—in other words, they will not grow beyond 1,618.

With respect to the submarines, we have developed a very complicated formula, and I have to spend some time in explaining it to you. It may also explain why there were so many night sessions this week here in Moscow, first between the President and Brezhnev and then between me and the Soviet Deputy Prime Minister Smirnov and Foreign Minister Gromyko.

Basically, the Soviet submarines are frozen at the level they now

have. Beyond that, however, since they had an ongoing program of eight submarines a year, they are permitted to trade in old missiles and old submarines for new submarines up to a total level of either sixty-two submarines or 950 missiles.

Q. May I ask a question here? When you say they are frozen at the level, you mean operational and under construction?

Dr. KISSINGER. Operational and under construction.

Q. Which is?

Dr. KISSINGER. Which is in dispute, first between our intelligence agencies, and second between us and the Soviets. Our intelligence agencies give us a certain range. Over a period of a year, this always comes out right, because you can see them. But at any given moment you cannot be absolutely sure. There is always a spread of two or three. At any rate, it is in the range that was discussed at the briefing.

When it was asked at the briefing, those figures were not far off. The Soviets claim that they have more than that. As I said at the briefing, the Soviets may not tell us exactly what they have, but they are in a better position to know than we, painful as this is to admit.

Let me finish going through these numbers. Under the formula that we have adopted, the Soviet Union can convert 210 old ICBMS and 30 old submarine-launched missiles into new submarine-launched missiles. In other words, in order to get more submarines they have to give up 240 old missiles—older missiles, still useful, but older missiles. That, in effect, is the rough formula.

Now, the formula is somewhat complicated by the fact that they have two types of Soviet boats, one with twelve and the other with sixteen missiles. So, the Soviets have to make a choice of sixty-two of fewer missiles, or lesser boats of more missiles, but that is a refinement into which we do not have to get in detail.

This is the submarine formula. It is, in short, that the Soviets are frozen at a level of what is currently operational or under construction. That level had to be somewhat arbitrarily established as between their claims and our assessments. At any rate, beyond that level they have to trade in all old missiles for new submarines up to a total ceiling that cannot exceed sixty-two submarines for 950 missiles. Again, I ask you to remember that that level of sixty-two submarines over the period of the freeze must be compared with the level of eighty to ninety submarines that would have been achieved without the freeze, in which circumstances there would not have been the retirement of the 240 older missiles on top of it. . . .

Q. I had a question on that. What is the definition of the words "under construction"?

Dr. KISSINGER. Well, some of the more profound minds in the bureau-

cracy, which is not necessarily saying a great deal [laughter], have addressed this question, and I believe that the definition of "under construction" that has been adopted is when the hull sections move into the shed where they are assembled into a submarine. . . . And this may account for the difference in our assessments of what the Soviets have under construction and what the Soviets tell us they have under construction. That is to say, they may count the hull sections and we count them only when they enter the shed. . . .

Q. Can you tell us what the arbitrary compromise line was you established with them between these two? Was it forty-five or something like that?

Dr. KISSINGER. Because of the difficulty of the fact that some of the Soviet boats have 12 missiles and some have 16 missiles, the Soviet argument was that they had 48 submarines under construction with 768 missiles. Our assessment was less. The figure we adopted is 710 if you consider new missiles and 740 if you add in the 30 of the older missiles that they have on submarines.

In either event, if they want to get up to the ceiling of 950 modern submarine-launched missiles, they have to retire 30 of the old submarine-launched missiles plus 210 of the ICBMS.

Q. That are included in the 1,618, is that correct?

Dr. KISSINGER. That are included in the 1,618. . . .

Q. And the other number [of SLBMS] would be 950?

Dr. KISSINGER. Yes. But, actually, if you do the arithmetic, you can't get up to exactly 950 by any combination of 16- and 12-class boats. I think the maximum they can get is 944, but that is a refinement we don't have to get into.

Q. Well, they could keep some of the thirty?

Dr. KISSINGER. They can keep some of the 30. They can piece together the 950, but then they have to keep the old missiles. They cannot come up with 950 new missiles from where they are now under any new assessment.

Q. Dr. Kissinger, isn't there a global figure of missiles that both of us are now operating under, and we can have any mix we choose?

Dr. KISSINGER. No, we cannot have any mix we choose. We can have a mix up to a certain ceiling in submarines, and we can retire only the older missiles. It is not permitted under this agreement to take new missiles and turn them into submarine missiles.

In other words, they cannot simply shift SS-11s into submarines any more than we can turn Minutemen into submarines. Under this agreement we have the right to convert fifty-four Titans into three submarines. The missiles built before 1964 can be converted into submarines, which gives us three and it gives them a larger number, but in

any event there is a global figure. You are quite right. There is a global figure with a certain freedom to mix, not a total freedom to mix but a certain freedom to mix.

Q. Dr. KISSINGER, how many of our submarine missiles are being MIRVed, and how many of the Minutemen are being MIRVed?

Dr. KISSINGER. I don't know exactly what the number of Minutemen is that is being MIRVed. Of the submarines, my trouble is I know the number, but I don't know whether it is classified or not.

Q. It is not.

Dr. KISSINGER. It is not? What is it then?

Q. You have deployed eight.

Dr. KISSINGER. But you don't know how many we are converting.

Q. You are converting thirty-one. [Laughter.]

Dr. KISSINGER. I thought all my former staff members joined candidates. [Laughter.]

That is essentially correct, but whether the submarine is MIRVed or not has nothing to do with whether it counts against the total. What counts against the total is the number of launchers, not the number of warheads on each launcher.

Q. What I am trying to get at is the number of warheads available to both sides.

Dr. KISSINGER. I didn't finish the answer to Murrey's question, because he also asked me about bombers.

Q. Also about bombers; and, Henry, [Defense] Secretary Laird's posture statement for the current year does give a figure on warheads. I don't happen to have it with me.

Dr. KISSINGER. I will give you a rough figure. Everything here is on the basis of reciprocity. Since I have given out the Soviet figures, I might as well give out the American figures. [Laughter.]

We have now 460 bombers, and we expect to have 450 bombers at the end of the freeze period. Our assessment is that the Soviets have about 140 comparable bombers. So, in terms of the total delivery vehicles on both sides during the freeze, if you count our overseas base forces, they are roughly equal. They are roughly about 2,500.

This is not the best test by itself, because if you compare megatonnage, the Soviet Union has about three times as much. If you count warheads, we have about three times as much during the whole period of the freeze. . . .

Q. Dr. Kissinger, would you say that the Soviets would be increasing their strategic advantage if they were to exercise their options and convert these various ICBMS and others to submarines?

Dr. KISSINGER. . . . The first thing one has to say is that the freeze, even without the conversion, is desired. With the conversion, it retires 240

Soviet launchers. On the other hand, I have to answer your question fairly: The 240 launchers that are being retired are less modern than the 240 launchers by which they are replaced.

The only thing you have to keep in mind is that it was not in our power to stop those 240 new launchers in any event. They are not being built as a result of the freeze. They were being built anyway.

Q. A technical question: Of the old launchers, the ICBMS they retired would be SS-7 and -8?

Dr. KISSINGER. That is correct.

Q. And the submarines, if they decided to retire the old ones, would replace what?

Dr. KISSINGER. Thirty to thirty-six missiles on the H-class submarines.

Q. How about the G-class?

Dr. KISSINGER. The G-class submarines can be retired. If they are modernized, they are counted against the 950. Do you see what I mean? They don't have to retire them. They do have to retire the H-class submarines if they want to go up to 950. They do not have to retire the G-class submarines, but if they modernize them they are counted against the 950.

First of all, the G-class submarines are diesel. Second, the range of their missiles is between 300 and 700 miles, so they are more comparable to our forward-based systems than they are to strategic systems. Third, if these missiles are modernized, if they have a more modern missile on the G-class submarine than the one there now, then that missile is counted against the 950 total and reduces their ability to build nuclear-powered submarines. It seems to us highly unreasonable to take this step, so we think that the G-class submarines are bound to get retired simply because they wear out. They are the oldest missile-carrying submarine they have.

Q. May I ask a nontechnical question? On defensive missiles, which they wanted, a treaty was signed to limit the number. On offensive, where we wanted a limitation, there was only a temporary agreement. Doesn't that seem as if we came out on the short end of the stick?

Dr. KISSINGER. Not at all, because, first of all, the temporary agreement is linked to the continuation of the defensive treaty, because we have made it clear that the continuation of the defensive treaty depends importantly on there being a follow-on agreement on offensive weapons. Second, with respect to these offensive weapons, the situation was so complex, there were so many weapons in the process of production, that it was an inevitable first step to get an end of the production for a while before one could make a rational agreement on the permanent arrangement. So, we have not come out on the short end of the stick. If the

offensive agreement lapses, we doubt seriously that the defensive agreement will continue.

Q. On the question of warheads, since that seems to be an important part of the total number of ICBMS, you mentioned the fact that the number of warheads is not affected. Can you then talk about numbers of warheads we have and they have?

Dr. KISSINGER. It is in the posture statement. Why don't you look it up? In the assessment we now have, it is about two and a half times as many warheads, and we expect at the end of the freeze period we will have about three times as many warheads.

Q. What is the prospect of their developing a MIRV?

Dr. KISSINGER. You would have to assume that anything we can do, they can do, with perhaps some time.

Q. How many years?

Dr. KISSINGER. I don't want to speculate on it, but I think it is reasonable to assume that they will develop a MIRV during the freeze period.

* * *

Q. Does this prohibit them from further testing of antisatellite systems?

Dr. KISSINGER. No, it doesn't prohibit them from testing, but interference with national means of detection would be considered contrary to the treaty, and there is a provision to that effect in the treaty.

Q. But if they continue to develop them—we know they have been—what happens then?

Dr. KISSINGER. It is not contrary to the treaty. What is contrary to the treaty is to use an antisatellite system, and that would be the issue. There is no way they could use an antisatellite system without, in effect, causing us to abrogate the treaty. I mean, if they did it on a substantial scale—I don't want to speak of every individual case.

Q. Could you say what was the last hangup that was settled today?

Dr. KISSINGER. As I told you when I met with you in Salzburg, there were four or five issues that had been unsettled. The President took those up with Mr. Brezhnev on Tuesday. As you remember, there were two sessions lasting well into the night. That settled two of them. There were then two other issues that remained to be settled. One was a somewhat esoteric technical one. It was esoterically technical on one level, but it had some significant implications. The second one had to do with the calculation from which we derived the point at which the trade-in of old missiles had to occur, what the number was that had to be traded in to get up to the ceiling, and how you handle the problem of the G-class submarines.

Q. When were those settled?

Dr. KISSINGER. There was one session that lasted until four o'clock on Wednesday. There was another session that lasted until three o'clock last night. This morning at 11:30, at a meeting, those two issues were settled. So at three o'clock it looked as if we would have to do at least another day or two of work on these two problems, but then this morning we had a meeting at 11:30, and it began to break. By noon I called Ron [Zeigler] and told him that it was beginning to break, and at one o'clock we had it settled.

Then the problem was to get the agreement drafted, and I think it was the first time in the history of Soviet-American relations that joint instructions were sent to two delegations, so that no misunderstandings could occur, and where we were kept informed by the Soviet side about meetings going on in the Soviet delegation in order to speed up the drafting process.

Then the delegation flew here in the American delegation's plane and arrived about nine o'clock with the treaty draft in their hands, because the decisions that were made at one o'clock still had to be put into treaty language.

All we did this morning was to arrive at the general framework. The delegations then had to put it into language that will be put before you soon.

So, a tremendous amount of work was done by the delegation, and it showed how rapidly things could move in diplomacy when both sides want to move.

* * *

Q. One clarifying question on the submarine. I believe the public record shows it was the United States who pressed publicly for the inclusion of the submarines—

Dr. KISSINGER. That is correct.

Q. Secretary Laird said he wouldn't favor a treaty unless submarines were included.

Dr. KISSINGER. That is correct.

Q. So, therefore, the idea that the United States got stuck with a submarine deal—

Dr. KISSINGER. That is an absurdity. It is a total absurdity. It was the United States which insisted that the submarines be included. The United States was in a rather complex position to recommend a submarine deal, since we were not building any and the Soviets were building eight or nine a year, which isn't the most brilliant bargaining position I would recommend people to find themselves in.

Therefore, we developed a formula by which the Soviets could

trade in some of their older missiles for submarines as long as they agreed to put a ceiling on the total construction of submarines. We discussed the issue with the Joint Chiefs of Staff, both in terms of what could be done with a rapid American submarine program and in terms of the complete proposal that emerged. The Joint Chiefs of Staff have supported this proposal, and I do not think they are the most dove-ish members of the American establishment. . . .

Q. What manner of verification can be effective against submarine numbers?

Dr. KISSINGER. As some of you know, we started this whole process of negotiation, to the dismay of some of you, very slowly, because we spent six months within the government making the most painstaking study of the possibilities of verification, and before we agreed to formulate any proposition, we wanted to make sure what the possibilities of verification were, what the margin of error was, what countermeasures we could take if we detected violations, and what risks we were running at each level.

We are confident that we have adequate means of verification. That does not mean that one or two submarines might not slip through, although we don't think so. What it does mean is, I would say it is extremely unlikely that the Soviet Union could build submarines of a number sufficient to upset the strategic balance in violation of this agreement without our knowing it and particularly if you consider what the risks of detection would represent for the Soviet Union.

So, we are confident that we can do this by national means of detection. But I must say also that I can't conceive of a country entering an agreement of freeze in order to cheat, given present national means of detection.

Q. Are you confident that this agreement can be sold to the Senate, and have you been giving some consultation to people like [Chairman of the Senate Armed Services Committee] John Stennis and others?

Dr. KISSINGER. Yes, we have been consulting with key senators. We believe that the overwhelming majority of the Senate, once it recognizes the nature of the agreement, the long-range implications of the agreement, and its character, will vote for it. I do not deny that the initial reaction of some people will be to look at the gap in numbers. But once they understand the consideration I put before you, that is to say, what the gap would be without this agreement, and the fact that this agreement for the first time brings agreed reductions in the missile forces of another country, I believe that many of those who express some hesitation will come around. We expect overwhelming passage.

Q. May I follow by asking: Are the Joint Chiefs unanimously in support of it?

Dr. Kissinger. The Joint Chiefs of Staff have unanimously supported the proposal we put forward last night and which was accepted this morning.

* * *

Q. Dr. Kissinger, Ambassador Smith raised the point of this being the first time where each side has acknowledged or deliberately allowed itself to remain vulnerable to attack by the other side and talked about psychological and political ramifications. I wonder if you could address yourself to that.

Dr. Kissinger. Well, to the extent that neither side is building a territorial defense, it is, of course, vulnerable, and to the extent that neither side can destroy the retaliatory force of its opponent enough to prevent a counterattack on its population, it remains vulnerable.

The implications of this are what they have always been over the last five years, because both sides are now vulnerable to each other, and therefore, the simplistic notion of the early 1960s which measured deterrent by the amount of civilian carnage that could be inflicted by one side on the other were always wrong. Hence, to consider the mass use of nuclear weapons in terms of the destruction of civilian populations, one faces a political impossibility, not to speak of a moral impossibility. But this has been a fact now for five or six years.

Q. Will the SALT machinery be kept in place for continuing negotiations, and if not, what will be the case?

Dr. Kissinger. Of course, we have now developed what we believe to be a rather good system for conducting these negotiations. . . . Over the last two years, when the negotiations have reached a deadlock, we have used the mechanism of presidential exchanges with the Soviet leaders to break the deadlock, in each case by compromise that turned out to be fair to both sides; and I think, having done this now—and I must say again that the experience of this week confirms it—that we can talk to each other now in a way that would have been inconceivable five years ago. . . .

* * *

Q. Dr. Kissinger, on the MIRV, aren't we really, by deploying MIRVs ourselves so rapidly, kind of forcing them or encouraging them into the MIRV business?

Dr. Kissinger. This is a debate that has been going on for the entire postwar period; namely, whether our technological change compels the Soviet technological change or whether the two technological changes are not occurring somewhat in parallel; and on the whole, the Soviet Union will do what it is technologically capable of doing.

You remember the debate about the hydrogen bomb in the early 1950s in which one argument against the hydrogen bomb was that if we developed it, the Soviet Union would be forced into following suit. As matters developed, we exploded our bomb six months before the Soviet Union did, making it obvious that we did not lead them but that they were pursuing a parallel evolution.

I think it is safe to say that the Soviet Union has been engaged in the first step toward MIRV at a time when we have not yet deployed MIRV, and I would not, therefore, accept the proposition.

Basic Principles of U.S.–Soviet Relations, 29 May 1972

The United States of America and the Union of Soviet Socialist Republics,

Guided by their obligations under the Charter of the United Nations and by a desire to strengthen peaceful relations with each other and to place these relations on the firmest possible basis,

Aware of the need to make every effort to remove the threat of war and to create conditions which promote the reduction of tensions in the world and the strengthening of universal security and international cooperation,

Believing that the improvement of US–Soviet relations and their mutually advantageous development in such areas as economics, science and culture, will meet these objectives and contribute to better mutual understanding and business-like cooperation, without in any way prejudicing the interests of third countries,

Conscious that these objectives reflect the interests of the peoples of both countries,

Have agreed as follows:

First. They will proceed from the common determination that in the nuclear age there is no alternative to conducting their mutual relations on the basis of peaceful coexistence. Differences in ideology and in the social systems of the USA and the USSR are not obstacles to the bilateral development of normal relations based on the principles of sovereignty, equality, non-interference in internal affairs and mutual advantage.

Second. The USA and the USSR attach major importance to preventing the development of situations capable of causing a dangerous exacerbation of their relations. Therefore, they will do their utmost to avoid military confrontations and to prevent the outbreak of nuclear war. They will always exercise restraint in their mutual relations, and will be prepared to negotiate and settle differences by peaceful means. Discussions and negotiations on outstanding issues will be conducted in a spirit of reciprocity, mutual accommodation and mutual benefit.

Both sides recognize that efforts to obtain unilateral advantage at the expense of the other, directly or indirectly, are inconsistent with these objectives. The prerequisites for maintaining and strengthening peaceful relations between the USA and the USSR are the recognition

---

SOURCE: Basic Principles of Relations between the United States of America and the Union of Soviet Socialist Republics. *Department of State Bulletin,* 26 June 1972, pp. 898–899.

of the security interests of the Parties based on the principle of equality and the renunciation of the use or threat of force.

Third. The USA and the USSR have a special responsibility, as do other countries which are permanent members of the United Nations Security Council, to do everything in their power so that conflicts or situations will not arise which would serve to increase international tensions. Accordingly, they will seek to promote conditions in which all countries will live in peace and security and will not be subject to outside interference in their internal affairs.

Fourth. The USA and the USSR intend to widen the juridical basis of their mutual relations and to exert the necessary efforts so that bilateral agreements which they have concluded and multilateral treaties and agreements to which they are jointly parties are faithfully implemented.

Fifth. The USA and the USSR reaffirm their readiness to continue the practice of exchanging views on problems of mutual interest and, when necessary, to conduct such exchanges at the highest level, including meetings between leaders of the two countries.

The two governments welcome and will facilitate an increase in productive contacts between representatives of the legislative bodies of the two countries.

Sixth. The Parties will continue their efforts to limit armaments on a bilateral as well as on a multilateral basis. They will continue to make special efforts to limit strategic armaments. Whenever possible, they will conclude concrete agreements aimed at achieving these purposes.

The USA and the USSR regard as the ultimate objective of their efforts the achievement of general and complete disarmament and the establishment of an effective system of international security in accordance with the purposes and principles of the United Nations.

Seventh. The USA and the USSR regard commercial and economic ties as an important and necessary element in the strengthening of their bilateral relations and thus will actively promote the growth of such ties. They will facilitate cooperation between the relevant organizations and enterprises of the two countries and the conclusion of appropriate agreements and contracts, including long-term ones.

The two countries will contribute to the improvement of maritime and air communications between them.

Eighth. The two sides consider it timely and useful to develop mutual contacts and cooperation in the fields of science and technology. Where suitable, the USA and the USSR will conclude appropriate agreements dealing with concrete cooperation in these fields.

Ninth. The two sides reaffirm their intention to deepen cultural

ties with one another and to encourage fuller familiarization with each other's cultural values. They will promote improved conditions for cultural exchanges and tourism.

Tenth. The USA and the USSR will seek to ensure that their ties and cooperation in all the above-mentioned fields and in any others in their mutual interest are built on a firm and long-term basis. To give a permanent character to these efforts, they will establish in all fields where this is feasible joint commissions or other joint bodies.

Eleventh. The USA and the USSR make no claim for themselves and would not recognize the claims of anyone else to any special rights or advantages in world affairs. They recognize the sovereign equality of all states.

The development of US–Soviet relations is not directed against third countries and their interests.

Twelfth. The basic principles set forth in this document do not affect any obligations with respect to other countries earlier assumed by the USA and the USSR.

Moscow, *May 29, 1972*

For the United States of America

RICHARD NIXON

President of the United States of America

For the Union of Soviet Socialist Republics

LEONID I. BREZHNEV

General Secretary of the Central Committee, CPSU

2
Congressional Action on SALT I

Rogers Report on the SALT I Agreements, 10 June 1972

ABM Treaty

In broad outline, the ABM Treaty, signed on May 26, 1972, provides that:

—A nationwide ABM deployment, and a base for such deployment, are prohibited;

—An ABM deployment for defense of an individual region is prohibited, except as specifically permitted;

—Permitted ABM deployments will be limited to two widely separated deployment areas in each country—one for defense of the national capital, and the other for the defense of ICBMS;

—For these purposes no more than 100 ABM launchers and no more than 100 ABM interceptor missiles at launch sites may be deployed within each 150-kilometer radius ABM deployment area, for a total of 200 deployed ABM interceptors and 200 deployed ABM launchers for each Party;

—ABM radars will be strictly controlled; radars to support the ABM defense of the national capital may be deployed only in a specified number of small radar complexes within the ABM deployment area; radars to support the ICBM defense will be limited to a specified number within the ABM deployment area and will also be subject to qualitative constraint.

In order to assure the effectiveness of these basic provisions of the Treaty, a number of detailed corollary provisions were also agreed:

—Development, testing and deployment of ABM systems or ABM

SOURCE: Report of Secretary of State William P. Rogers to President Nixon on the SALT I Agreements, 10 June 1972. *Department of State Bulletin*, 3 July 1972, pp. 3–11. Secretary Rogers' report, together with the texts of the ABM treaty and interim agreement (see Chapter 1), were submitted to the Senate and House of Representatives on 13 June 1972.

components that are sea-based, air-based, space-based or mobile land-based are prohibited;

—Deployment of ABM systems involving new types of basic components to perform the current functions of ABM launchers, interceptors or radars is prohibited;

—The conversion or testing of other systems, such as air defense systems, or components thereof to perform an ABM role is prohibited.

The Treaty also contains certain general provisions relating to the verification and implementation of the Treaty and to further negotiations:

—Each side will use national technical means for verification and the Parties agree not to interfere with such means and not to take deliberate concealment measures;

—A Standing Consultative Commission will be established to facilitate implementation of the Treaty and consider questions arising thereunder;

—The Parties will continue active negotiations for limitations on strategic offensive arms.

* * *

A. Limitations on ABM Systems

(1) *Deployment*

Article I(2) prohibits the deployment of ABM systems which would provide defense covering substantially the whole of the territory of a Party. ABM defenses of individual regions are also prohibited except as specifically set forth in Article III. . . .

Article I(2) also includes an undertaking not to provide a "base" for a nationwide ABM defense. This would, for example, prohibit the construction and deployment of ABM radars, or even ABM-capable radars deployed for other purposes, that could provide a base for a nationwide ABM system. (Articles III, IV, V and VI contain specific constraints that reinforce this prohibition.) The Treaty does not restrict air defense, space tracking, intelligence or other non-ABM systems *per se*. However, it does prohibit the testing or conversion of such systems or their components to perform an ABM role; moreover, the Parties have agreed not to deploy any phased-array radars over a certain size except as otherwise provided in the Treaty and except for the purpose of tracking objects in outer space or for use as national technical means of verification. This would prevent the possible use of such radars as a base for a nationwide ABM defense.

Article II defines an ABM system as "a system to counter strategic

ballistic missiles or their elements in flight trajectory." It indicates that such systems currently consist of ABM interceptor missiles, ABM launchers and ABM radars. ABM interceptor missiles are interceptor missiles constructed and deployed for an ABM role, or of a type hereafter tested in an ABM mode. ABM launchers are launchers constructed and deployed for launching ABM interceptor missiles. (A launcher associated with an interceptor missile that is hereafter tested in an ABM mode falls within the definition of an ABM launcher.) ABM radars are radars constructed and deployed for an ABM role (including target tracking or missile control, but not early warning), or of a type hereafter tested in an ABM mode.

* * *

Article III prohibits the deployment of any ABM systems or their components except as provided therein. Under Article III, the Parties may deploy only systems consisting of ABM interceptor missiles, ABM launchers and ABM radars. The limited deployment of such systems described in the next two paragraphs below is permitted only (a) within one deployment area centered on the nation's capital and having a radius of 150 kilometers, and (b) within one other deployment area having the same radius and containing ICBM silo launchers. The centers of the two deployment areas will be separated by no less than 1,300 kilometers.

In each of these deployment areas a Party may deploy no more than 100 ABM launchers and no more than 100 ABM interceptor missiles at launch sites. These totals would include any deployments within such areas for training purposes and, as indicated in Article II(2), would not be confined to those in operational status. In view of Article V(1), discussed below, only fixed, land-based ABM components may be deployed.

The restrictions on ABM radars cover radars of both existing types: phased-array radars (a modern type which scans by electronic means, a capability especially useful for ABM purposes) and mechanical-scan radars (an older type). These restrictions are as follows:

(i) Within the 150-kilometer radius deployment area centered on the nation's capital, no qualitative or quantitative constraints on radars are imposed, but location is circumscribed as follows: a Party may have ABM radars within no more than 6 ABM radar complexes, the permitted area of each complex being circular and having a diameter of no more than 3 kilometers. Phased-array ABM radars may not be located outside such complexes, regardless of when they become operational. Mechanical-scan ABM radars that become operational after May 26, 1972 are similarly constrained. The Parties understand that in addition

to the ABM radars which may be deployed in accordance with this provision, the Soviet mechanical-scan ABM radars operational on May 26, 1972 within the deployment area for defense of its capital may be retained.

(ii) Within the 150-kilometer radius deployment area for defense of ICBM silo launchers, the location of radars is not circumscribed, but qualitative and quantitative constraints are imposed. A Party may have:

—2 large phased-array ABM radars comparable in potential to corresponding ABM radars operational or under construction on the date of signature of the Treaty in such a deployment area; and

—no more than 18 ABM radars each having a potential less than that of the smaller of the 2 large phased-array ABM radars referred to above.

The only two large phased-array ABM radars operational or under construction in such a deployment area on the date of signature were the Perimeter Acquisition Radar (PAR) and Missile Site Radar (MSR) under construction near Grand Forks Air Force Base, North Dakota. The Parties understand that the potential—the product of mean emitted power in watts and antenna area in square meters—of the smaller of these two radars (the MSR) is considered for purposes of the Treaty to be three million.

* * *

The United States has not started construction at a deployment area centered on its national capital, and the Soviet Union has not started construction at a deployment area for defense of ICBM silo launchers.

(2) *Development, Testing, and Other Limitations*

Article IV provides that the limitations in Article III shall not apply to ABM systems or ABM components used for development or testing, and located within current or additionally agreed test ranges. It is understood that ABM test ranges encompass the area within which ABM components are located for test purposes, and that non-phased-array radars of types used for range safety or instrumentation purposes may be located outside of ABM test ranges. Article IV further provides that each Party may have no more than a total of 15 ABM launchers at test ranges. The current United States test ranges for ABM systems are located at White Sands, New Mexico and Kwajalein Atoll in the Pacific. The current Soviet test range for ABM systems is located near Sary Shagan, Kazakhstan SSR. ABM components are not to be deployed at any other test ranges without prior agreement between the Parties.

Article V limits development and testing, as well as deployment, of certain types of ABM systems and components. Paragraph V(1) limits such activities to fixed, land-based ABM systems and components by prohibiting the development, testing or deployment of ABM systems or components which are sea-based, air-based, space-based, or mobile land-based. . . .

Paragraph V(2) prohibits the development, testing or deployment of ABM launchers for launching more than one ABM interceptor missile at a time from each launcher; modification of deployed launchers to provide them with such a capability; and the development, testing or deployment of automatic or semi-automatic or other similar systems for rapid reload of ABM launchers. The Parties agree that this Article includes an obligation not to develop, test, or deploy ABM interceptor missiles with more than one independently guided warhead.

(3) *Future ABM Systems*

A potential problem dealt with by the Treaty is that which would be created if an ABM system were developed in the future which did not consist of interceptor missiles, launchers and radars. The Treaty would not permit the deployment of such a system or of components thereof capable of substituting for ABM interceptor missiles, launchers, or radars: Article II(1) defines an ABM system in terms of its function as "a system to counter strategic ballistic missiles or their elements in flight trajectory," noting that such systems "currently" consist of ABM interceptor missiles, ABM launchers and ABM radars. Article III contains a prohibition on the deployment of ABM systems or their components except as specified therein, and it permits deployment only of ABM interceptor missiles, ABM launchers, and ABM radars. Devices other than ABM interceptor missiles, ABM launchers, or ABM radars could be used as adjuncts to an ABM system, provided that such devices were not capable of substituting for one or more of these components. Finally, in the course of the negotiations, the Parties specified that "In order to insure fulfillment of the obligation not to deploy ABM systems and their components except as provided in Article III of the Treaty, the Parties agree that in the event ABM systems based on other physical principles and including components capable of substituting for ABM interceptor missiles, ABM launchers, or ABM radars are created in the future, specific limitations on such systems and their components would be subject to discussion in accordance with Article XIII and agreement in accordance with Article XIV of the Treaty." (As explained below, Article XIII calls for establishment of a Standing Consultative Commission, and Article XIV deals with amendments to the Treaty.)

(4) *Modernization and Replacement*

Article VII provides that, subject to the provisions of this Treaty, modernization and replacement of ABM systems or their components may be carried out. Modernization or replacement of present ABM systems or components is constrained by the various limitations and prohibitions in the Treaty. (See paragraph 2 of Article I, Article III, Article V, and Article VI.)

(5) *Destruction and Dismantling*

Article VIII provides that ABM systems or their components in excess of the numbers or outside the areas specified in the Treaty, as well as ABM systems or components prohibited by the Treaty, shall be destroyed or dismantled under agreed procedures within the shortest possible agreed period of time. Since no more than one ABM system deployment area for defense of ICBM silo launchers is permitted by Article III, this Article will apply, when the Treaty enters into force, to the ABM components previously under construction in the vicinity of Malmstrom Air Force Base in Montana.

B. Other Related Measures

(1) *Constraints on Non-ABM Systems or Components*

Article VI is designed to enhance assurance of the effectiveness of the basic limitations on ABM systems and their components provided by the Treaty. To this end, each Party undertakes in this Article (a) not to give missiles, launchers or radars, other than ABM interceptor missiles, ABM launchers and ABM radars, capabilities to counter strategic ballistic missiles or their elements in flight trajectory; (b) not to test such non-ABM missiles, launchers and radars "in an ABM mode" and (c) not to deploy in the future radars for early warning of strategic ballistic missile attack except at locations along the periphery of its national territory and oriented outward.

The first of these undertakings would, for example, prohibit the modification of air-defense missiles (SAMS) to give them a capability against strategic ballistic missiles.

* * *

In recognition of the fact that phased-array radars with more than a certain potential, though deployed for non-ABM missions such as air defense or air traffic control, would have an inherent capacity for ABM use, the Parties agreed not to deploy phased-array radars having a po-

tential exceeding three million watt-square meters, except as provided in Articles III, IV and VI of the Treaty and except for the purpose of tracking objects in outer space or for use as national technical means of verification. Deployment of non-ABM radars currently planned by the United States would not be affected.

(2) *International Transfers*

Article IX provides that, to assure the viability and effectiveness of the Treaty, each Party undertakes not to transfer to other States, and not to deploy outside its national territory, ABM systems or their components limited by the Treaty. The Parties understand that the first undertaking includes an obligation not to provide to other states technical descriptions or blueprints specially worked out for the construction of ABM systems and their components limited by the Treaty. In addition, the United States Delegation made clear that the provisions of this Article do not set a precedent for whatever provisions may be considered for a treaty on limiting strategic offensive arms, noting that the question of transfer of strategic offensive arms is a far more complex issue, which may require a different solution.

* * *

C. Verification and Consultation

(1) *Verification*

Article XII relates to verification of compliance with the Treaty's provisions, which is to be accomplished by national technical means. Paragraph 1 states that each Party will use national technical means of verification at its disposal in a manner consistent with generally recognized principles of international law for purposes of providing assurance of compliance with provisions of the Treaty. It does not require changes from current operating practices and procedures with respect to systems which will be used as national technical means of verification.

The second paragraph of this Article provides that each Party agrees not to interfere with the national technical means of verification of the other which are operating in accordance with paragraph 1 of the Article. This provision would, for example, prohibit interference with a satellite in orbit used for verification of the Treaty.

Paragraph 3 contains an agreement not to use deliberate concealment measures which impede verification by national technical means. This paragraph expressly permits continuation of current construction, assembly, conversion and overhaul practices.

(2) *Standing Consultative Commission*

Article XIII provides that the Parties shall establish promptly a Standing Consultative Commission (hereafter referred to as the Commission) to promote the objectives and to facilitate the implementation of the ABM Treaty. The Parties have further agreed to use the Commission to promote the objectives and implementation of the Interim Agreement. (See Article VI of the Interim Agreement.) The Commission will provide a consulting framework within which the Parties may consider various matters relating to the Treaty and the Interim Agreement. The Parties may also consider these matters in other channels.

A principal function of the Commission will be to consider questions of compliance with the obligations assumed under this Treaty and the Interim Agreement and also related situations which may be considered ambiguous. Each Party may voluntarily provide through the Commission information it considers necessary to assure confidence in compliance. Thus one Party might raise a question of compliance based on information gathered by national technical means of verification and the other Party could provide information to clarify the matter.

Attention was called above to the provisions in Article XII prohibiting intentional interference with national technical means of verification operating in accordance with its provisions. The Commission is charged by Article XIII with the responsibility to consider any questions of interference with such means. The Commission may also consider questions of concealment impeding verification by national means. The Commission may consider changes in the general strategic situation which have a bearing on the provisions of the Treaty. Related to this is the Commission's authority to consider proposals to further increase the viability of the Treaty—such as agreed interpretations after the Treaty has entered into force—and to consider proposals for amendment of the Treaty. (Amendments to the Treaty would have to be ratified pursuant to Articles XIV and XVI.) The Commission may also consider other appropriate measures, not specifically enumerated in Article XIII, aimed at further limiting strategic arms. Finally, through the Commission the Parties are to agree on procedures and dates for the implementation of Article VIII concerning destruction or dismantling of ABM systems or ABM components. . . .

The second paragraph of Article XIII provides for the establishment of regulations for the Commission governing procedures, composition and other relevant matters. Such matters can be worked out early in the follow-on negotiations. Meanwhile, any consultation desired by either side under these Articles can be carried out by the Dele-

gations during such negotiations or, when they are not in session, through other diplomatic channels.

The Commission is intended as a means to facilitate the implementation of the agreements and would not replace follow-on negotiations or use of other diplomatic channels.

D. Duration, Withdrawal and Further Negotiations

Article XV provides that the Treaty shall be of unlimited duration, but contains a withdrawal clause of the type that has become standard in post-war arms control treaties. This clause provides that each Party, in exercising its national sovereignty, shall have the right to withdraw from the Treaty if it decides that extraordinary events related to the subject matter of the Treaty have jeopardized its supreme interests. Notice of such decision is to be given to the other Party six months prior to withdrawal from the Treaty. Such notice is required to include a statement of the extraordinary events involved.

In this connection, the United States has stressed the unique relationship between limitations on offensive and defensive strategic arms. This interrelationship lends extraordinary importance to the undertaking in Article XI "to continue active negotiations for limitations on strategic offensive arms."

The special importance we attach to this relationship was reflected in the following formal statement relating to Article XI, which was made by the Head of the United States Delegation on May 9, 1972:

> The US Delegation has stressed the importance the US Government attaches to achieving agreement on more complete limitations on strategic offensive arms, following agreement on an ABM Treaty and on an Interim Agreement on certain measures with respect to the limitation of strategic offensive arms. The US Delegation believes that an objective of the follow-on negotiations should be to constrain and reduce on a long-term basis threats to the survivability of our respective strategic retaliatory forces. The USSR Delegation has also indicated that the objectives of SALT would remain unfulfilled without the achievement of an agreement providing for more complete limitations on strategic offensive arms. Both sides recognize that the initial agreements would be steps toward the achievement of more complete limitations on strategic arms. If an agreement providing for more complete strategic offensive arms limitations were not achieved within five years, US supreme interests could be jeopardized. Should that occur, it would constitute a basis for withdrawal from the ABM Treaty. The US does not wish to see such a situation

occur, nor do we believe that the USSR does. It is because we wish to prevent such a situation that we emphasize the importance the US Government attaches to achievement of more complete limitations on strategic offensive arms. The US Executive will inform the Congress, in connection with Congressional consideration of the ABM Treaty and the Interim Agreement, of this statement of the US position.

E. Other Provisions

Article XIV deals with amendments and review. Paragraph 1 provides that the Parties may propose amendments to the Treaty. Agreed amendments shall enter into force upon exchange of instruments of ratification. The second paragraph of Article XIV provides for formal review of the Treaty by the Parties at five year intervals. Paragraph 2 does not preclude agreement on proposed amendments of the Treaty during the first five years, or between formal reviews thereafter; it simply reflects recognition of the possibility of changes in the strategic relationship and the development of new strategic systems. These questions are also within the purview of the Standing Consultative Commission.

*   *   *

Interim Agreement and Protocol

The Interim Agreement between the United States of America and the Union of Soviet Socialist Republics on Certain Measures with Respect to the Limitation of Strategic Offensive Arms (Interim Agreement), including a Protocol which is integral thereto, was signed on May 26, 1972. The Interim Agreement consists of a preamble and eight operative articles. In the course of the negotiations, agreement was reached on a number of interpretive matters related to the Interim Agreement. . . .

This Agreement provides for a restriction of five years on strategic offensive missile launcher deployments pending negotiation of more complete limitations on strategic offensive arms. The main effects of the Interim Agreement will be that:

—the aggregate number of fixed, land-based ICBM launchers and SLBM launchers will be limited;

—starting construction of additional fixed, land-based ICBM launchers is prohibited;

—the number of launchers for modern heavy ICBMs, such as the Soviet SS–9, will be limited to that number currently operational and under construction;

—ceilings will be placed on the number of SLBM launchers and modern ballistic missile submarines operational on each side; and

—up to the agreed ceilings, deployment of additional SLBM launchers above a specified number for each Party requires an offsetting reduction of ICBM launchers of older types or SLBM launchers on older ballistic missile submarines.

* * *

A. ICBM Launchers

Article I of the Interim Agreement prohibits starting construction of additional fixed land-based ICBM launchers. While the text of Article I prescribes July 1, 1972 as the freeze date, the United States and the Soviet Union understand that, pending ratification and acceptance of the agreements, neither will take any action that will be prohibited thereby, in the absence of notification by either signatory of its intention not to proceed with ratification or approval.

This construction freeze covers all fixed land-based ICBM launchers, both silo and soft-pad, but does not include test and training ICBM launchers or mobile land-based ICBM launchers. Test and training launchers are, however, subject to other constraints. The United States has made clear to the Soviets that we would consider the deployment of operational land-mobile ICBM launchers during the period of the Interim Agreement to be inconsistent with the objectives of the Agreement. The Parties have agreed that the term ICBM includes any land-based strategic ballistic missile capable of ranges in excess of the shortest distance between the northeastern border of the continental United States and the northwestern border of the continental Soviet Union. Launchers for fractional orbital bombardment systems are considered to be ICBM launchers.

On May 26, 1972, the United States had 1,054 operational, land-based ICBM launchers and none under construction; on that date, the Soviet Union had a total of land-based ICBM launchers operational and under active construction estimated to be about 1,618. (ICBM launchers for testing and training purposes are excluded in each case.) Under the freeze, the Soviet Union may complete construction of ICBM launchers under active construction on May 26, 1972. While the Interim Agreement remains in effect, neither Party may start new construction (nor resume previously suspended construction) of fixed ICBM launchers except test and training launchers.

B. Heavy ICBM Launchers

Article II provides that the Parties shall not convert land-based launchers for light, or older heavy, ICBMs into land-based launchers for

modern heavy ICBMs, such as the Soviet SS–9. All currently operational ICBMs other than the SS–9 are either "light" (the United States Minuteman and the Soviet SS–11 and SS–13) or "older" ICBM launchers of types first deployed prior to 1964 (the United States Titan and the Soviet SS–7 and SS–8).

Article II would thus prohibit the conversion of a launcher for an SS–7, SS–8, SS–11 or SS–13 ICBM into a launcher for an SS–9 or any new modern heavy ICBM, and would similarly prohibit the conversion of a launcher for a Minuteman or Titan into a launcher for a modern heavy ICBM. The Parties agree that in the process of modernization and replacement the dimensions of land-based ICBM silo launchers will not be significantly increased, and that this means that any increase will not be greater than 10–15 percent of the present dimensions. The United States has also made clear that it would consider any ICBM having a volume significantly greater than that of the largest light ICBM now operational on either side (which is the Soviet SS–11) to be a heavy ICBM.

C. SLBM Launchers and Modern Ballistic Missile Submarines

Article III limits SLBM launchers and modern ballistic missile submarines to the numbers operational and under construction on May 26, 1972.

In addition, Article III and the Protocol permit launchers and submarines beyond 740 SLBM launchers on nuclear-powered submarines for the Soviet Union and 656 SLBM launchers on nuclear-powered submarines for the United States, subject to two constraints. First, additional SLBM launchers may become operational only as replacements for an equal number of ICBM launchers of types first deployed prior to 1964, or for launchers on older nuclear-powered submarines or for modern SLBM launchers on any type of submarine. Second, such substitution may not result in:

—the Soviet Union having operational more than 62 modern ballistic missile submarines or more than 950 SLBM launchers, including all SLBM launchers on nuclear-powered submarines and all modern SLBM launchers on any type of submarine;

—the United States having operational more than 44 modern ballistic missile submarines or more than 710 SLBM launchers.

Construction of replacement SLBM launchers up to the limits under the Protocol would require the dismantling or destruction, under agreed procedures, of an equal number of ICBM launchers of older types or of SLBM launchers on nuclear-powered submarines. Moreover, modern SLBM launchers deployed on any type of submarine would count against

the total ceiling on SLBM launchers. Dismantling or destruction would be required to commence no later than the date on which sea trials of a replacement ballistic missile submarine begin and to be completed in the shortest possible agreed period of time. Thus the Soviets will have to begin dismantling older ICBM or SLBM launchers no later than when the 741st SLBM launcher on a nuclear-powered submarine enters sea trials. Dismantling or destruction, as well as timely notification thereof, are to be carried out in accordance with procedures to be agreed upon in the Standing Consultative Commission.

D. Test and Training Launchers

The Parties agree that the number of test and training launchers for ICBMS and SLBMS, including "modern heavy" ICBMS, shall not be increased significantly above the current number of test and training launchers for such missiles. It is understood that construction or conversion of ICBM launchers at test ranges shall be undertaken only for the purposes of testing and training. It is also understood that ICBM launchers for test and training purposes may be constructed at operational sites.

E. Modernization and Replacement

Article IV provides that, subject to the provisions of the Interim Agreement, modernization and replacement of strategic ballistic missiles and launchers covered by the Interim Agreement may be undertaken. The conversion of current United States ICBM launchers to handle Minuteman III missiles, the conversion of current submarine launchers to handle Poseidon missiles, and the construction of new submarines as replacements for older submarines, are not prohibited by the Agreement.

F. Other Provisions

Article V of the Interim Agreement contains the same provisions on verification as appear in Article XII of the ABM Treaty. Verification will be carried out by national technical means operating in accordance with generally recognized principles of international law. Interference with, or deliberate concealment from, such means is prohibited. Neither Party is required to change its current practices of construction, assembly, conversion, or overhaul.

Article VI provides that in order to promote the objectives and implementation of the Interim Agreement, the Parties shall use the Standing Consultative Commission to be established pursuant to Article XIII of the ABM Treaty.

In Article VII the Parties agree to continue active negotiation for

limitations on strategic offensive arms. This Article also provides that the terms of this Interim Agreement will not prejudice the scope and terms of the limitations on strategic offensive arms which may be worked out in the subsequent negotiations. It is expected that these subsequent negotiations will start in the near future.

The first paragraph of Article VIII of the Interim Agreement provides that it shall enter into force upon the exchange of written notices of acceptance, simultaneously with the exchange of instruments of ratification of the ABM Treaty.

Paragraph 2 of Article VIII provides that the Interim Agreement shall remain in effect for five years, unless earlier replaced by agreement on more complete measures limiting strategic offensive arms.

The third paragraph of this Article provides each Party with a right, parallel to that contained in paragraph 2 of Article XV of the ABM Treaty, to withdraw upon six months' notice if such Party decides its supreme interests have been jeopardized by extraordinary events related to the subject matter of the Interim Agreement.

Senate Foreign Relations Committee Hearings on SALT I, June 1972

19 June 1972

The Chairman [Senator J. W. Fulbright]. The Committee on Foreign Relations is very pleased to welcome this morning the Secretary of State, Mr. William P. Rogers, and the Chief American Negotiator and Director of the Arms Control and Disarmament Agency, Dr. Gerard Smith.

It would have been better for the security of the world had we been able to hold this hearing some time ago.

Many years of intricate negotiations, both tentative and formal, have passed to bring us to this point. The committee has before it now the proposed treaty on the limitation of anti-ballistic missiles and the interim agreement on offensive missiles.

Now we have before us the prospect of further negotiations. The results, when added to the treaty and agreement before us, should at last bring the two superpowers and the rest of the world to a point at which worldwide destruction can be a more remote prospect.

Giving up the anti-ballistic missile, with the exception of the option on each side of the two sites, may be the most significant commitment made by the United States and the Soviet Union to the principle of coexistence. Insofar as each side is willing to abandon the effort to make itself invulnerable to attack or retaliation by the other, it also commits itself to peace and to the survival of the other.

We must ask ourselves, however, whether we are not in danger of having our actions belie our words. Already there have been sounds of alarm and cries to abandon any euphoria. Some say we must have an accelerated program for the development of a new type of missile submarine called Trident and of a new supersonic bomber to replace our B-52 fleet, as well as other offensive weapons not covered by the Moscow agreements.

Can we in good conscience and good sense engage the Russians in an accelerated arms race at the same time we have each conceded the survival of each other's position and political system?

As we all realize, no one can be invulnerable in the world now. Indeed, we are in a situation of mutual vulnerability. The anti-ballistic

---

Source: U.S., Congress, Senate, Committee on Foreign Relations, *Strategic Arms Limitation Agreements*, 92d Cong., 2d sess., 1972.

missile treaty before us has in it the central fact that the United States and the Soviet Union are indeed each other's hostage for reasonable behavior in a nuclear era.

More force, greater spending and additional weapons will not make either side more secure. More can only lead to a deepening of the balance of terror which has enslaved this world for more than a decade. A further drive for more to achieve a shifting parity can only heighten the possibilities of a holocaust which neither side should consider thinkable.

* * *

Secretary ROGERS. Mr. Chairman, I am pleased to appear before you in support of the treaty on the limitation of ABM systems and the interim agreement on the limitation of strategic offensive arms.

In his letter to the Senate of June 13 transmitting my report and its enclosures, the President urged your support so that the two agreements can be brought into force as soon as practicable. These agreements are important not just for our people; they are important for all people. They are important not only for the achievements they represent, but also for the opportunities they present. Strategic arms limitation is not a one-time effort but a continuing process.

These agreements are a significant achievement. They constitute an unprecedented step in controlling strategic arms. They are tangible evidence that both sides are moving into an era of negotiation. The two sides now have an important investment in cooperation which they are not likely to risk lightly. The United States and the Soviet Union have thus indicated a recognition that their relations can be improved by cooperation in some areas even though there remain important differences in others.

This success in SALT recognizes that global security is interdependent, and that unconstrained weapons competition is contrary to the interests of the nuclear powers and of the world.

During the SALT negotiations over the last two and a half years, we have kept in mind the need for wide support, both nationally and internationally, for any agreements reached. To that end the administration has closely consulted the Congress. We have also regularly consulted with our allies. . . .

Let me place the SALT agreements in perspective. When this administration entered office early in 1969, we faced a strategic situation in which the U.S.S.R. was engaged in a broad and dynamic buildup of its strategic offensive missile launchers. It was clear that a rough balance in strategic forces between the United States and the Soviet Union

was approaching. However, there was not then—and there is not now—any question that the United States could and would maintain strategic forces adequate to meet its security requirements, forces second to none. As President Nixon stated in this Foreign Policy Report of February, 1971, "Both sides would almost surely commit the necessary resources to maintain a balance." The President further noted that any Soviet attempt to obtain a large advantage would spark an arms race which would, in the end, prove pointless.

Through negotiation—rather than competition—we had an opportunity to achieve a more stable strategic relationship with the U.S.S.R. and to seek—over time—to create a situation in which both sides could use more of their resources for purposes other than building more strategic weapons.

* * *

Let me say . . . that in both agreements the U.S. has sought, where necessary, to set forth detailed obligations in the text of the agreements themselves. Where one of the sides preferred to put clarifying material or elaboration in agreed interpretations, and where this was sufficient, that approach was used. These agreed interpretations have been transmitted to the Congress; they include initialed statements and other common understandings. In certain cases where agreement could not be reached, U.S. views were stated formally in unilateral statements. Those, too, have been transmitted to the Congress. There are no secret agreements.

I would like to address first the ABM treaty. Under this treaty, both sides make a commitment not to build a nationwide ABM defense. This is a general undertaking of utmost significance. Without a nationwide ABM defense, there can be no shield against retaliation. Both great nuclear powers have recognized, and in effect agreed to maintain, mutual deterrence. Therefore, I am convinced beyond doubt that the possibility of nuclear war has been dramatically reduced by this treaty.

A major objective of SALT has been to reduce the tensions, uncertainties, and high costs which flow from the upward spiral of strategic arms competition. While the cost savings from these first SALT agreements will be limited initially, over the long term we will save the tens of billions of dollars which might otherwise have been required for a nationwide ABM defense.

Furthermore, with an interim limitation on offensive weapons—which we hope will lead to a more comprehensive and permanent limitation—there will be a break in the pattern of action and reaction under which each side reacts to what the other is doing, or may do, in an

open-ended situation. This cycle until now has been a major factor in driving the strategic arms race.

* * *

The CHAIRMAN. . . . Mr. Secretary, is it correct to say that this treaty assures the Russians that we will not attempt to prevent the effectiveness of their intercontinental ballistic missiles and we will not interfere with their intelligence gathering by satellite—what is generally called national means—and, of course, that the Russians assume the same obligation? In effect the lives of the people of each country are hostage to the other and there can scarcely be a more effective guarantee of each nation's restraint in the use of nuclear weapons.

Secretary ROGERS. Yes, I think that is an accurate statement, Mr. Chairman, and I think it is of great importance to realize the effect of this treaty for the reasons that you have mentioned; and that is why I say that I am of the conviction that it dramatically reduces the possibility of a nuclear war between these major nations.

The CHAIRMAN. If each side lives up to it, I think that is correct. It reminds me of the argument made during the very long hearings on the ABM. ABM was considered by many of the witnesses at that time as a destabilizing development. If it were permitted to proceed, it would contribute to the arms race rather than otherwise. Is that not correct, too? . . .

Secretary ROGERS. Yes, sir, I think with both sides agreeing as they have under this treaty that is a correct conclusion, Mr. Chairman.

The CHAIRMAN. While the option is given to have two ABM complexes, there is no requirement that each side proceed with that. They have the option of doing it if they like. If they both decide this system of defense is not an effective one, there is nothing to prohibit them from agreeing to have none at all; is that right?

Secretary ROGERS. That is right; but I think the assumption was in the discussions that probably both sides would proceed with—

The CHAIRMAN. That depends upon the development of the degree of confidence between the countries; doesn't it? If, as nothing upsets or disturbs either country as to the goodwill or intentions of the other, this is a possibility at least.

Secretary ROGERS. Well, let me say, Mr. Chairman, the statement that you have made initially is correct, that there is nothing in this treaty that requires either side to construct the additional site—

The CHAIRMAN. That is a limitation only.

Secretary ROGERS. It is a limitation only. But, as I say, I think the negotiations did clearly indicate that each side was going to continue, and I think that the Soviet Union felt that because we had an ICBM site pro-

tected, that they felt for obvious reasons they wanted to have one of their ICBM sites protected.

The CHAIRMAN. That is true. It assumes, of course, that an ABM system is an effective one. If either side decides that after all was the wrong project and it wasn't really an effective one, it could easily be overcome. They are free to decide not to proceed. That is the only point I wished to make.

Secretary ROGERS. Yes; I think it is quite clear that neither side would proceed if they thought the system was ineffective. I don't think either one would build an ABM system—an additional site—if they thought it was not going to be effective.

The CHAIRMAN. If this is the real meaning of the treaty, which to me is the most significant part of it all, I am unable to understand the insistence of the Secretary of Defense that we must go forward immediately with a very large accelerated program of offensive weapons beginning with the Trident, one of the most expensive, B-1 and F-14, and various other weapons systems. If this treaty is adopted, which I certainly expect it could be and I shall certainly support it, it seems that we ought to have a little time for each side to evaluate its effectiveness and to evaluate the attitude of the other side. To put it another way, when I read Mr. Laird's statement, as it was published, immediately it occurred to me that it raises the question of the sincerity of our undertakings. If this agreement is to be used as an excuse for a greatly increased arms race, it seems to me it raises serious questions of the seriousness with which we regard this agreement. I am still puzzled by that and worried about it. . . .

Secretary ROGERS. We think that one of the reasons that we were able to achieve these agreements was because we maintained our strength and that we proceeded with an ABM system, and we were able to negotiate from a position of strength.

Secondly, the proposals that have been made in the defense budget are not new proposals, they are proposals that the administration submitted before these agreements were completed. We think they are essential to our national security and should be supported by the Congress.

Third, we think at this time when we know perfectly well, particularly we know from the conversations between the President and General Secretary Brezhnev, that the Soviet Union plans to continue to build up its systems within the limitations imposed by these agreements, particularly the interim agreement—and he said so in no uncertain terms, made it perfectly clear to the President they were going to do that—so there was no misconception on our part that we should continue to have a defense posture that is strong and provides for our

national security. We think any change in that course now would make the possibilities of negotiation in the second phase of SALT much more difficult.

Now, I don't personally state it in precisely linkage terms. I say we present these agreements to the Congress because we believe they are significant and we are pleased that the Congress appears to support them, and we also submit the defense budget believing that it is in our national interest and our strength as a nation requires expenditures in that order of magnitude, and we think it is particularly important at this time that we not indicate to the Soviet Union we are all of a sudden going to undertake unilateral disarmament which makes the second phase of SALT unnecessary. . . .

The CHAIRMAN. . . . This is a quote from the Secretary of Defense's statement after testimony before the Armed Services Committee. . . . It reads as follows: On June 6th, Secretary Laird said before that committee, "I could not support the agreements if the Congress fails to act on the movement forward of the Trident system, on the B–1 bomber, and on the other programs that we have outlined to improve our strategic offensive systems during this five year period." I think that is accurate.

If we were considering only the interim agreement, I think there would be some logic in proceeding with these weapons systems. But if what I stated in the beginning is the real significance of the treaty, which I rate much more important than the interim agreement, which is supplementary and temporary in nature and subject to change, as you have stated, and if we are in good faith about the treaty, then it makes the interim agreement of a very different character. In that case, to proceed in the normal traditional manner of an arms race seems to me to be out of phase with the treaty itself. There is an inherent inconsistency in that approach because there is no doubt that if there is no effective defense the existing weapons are quite sufficient to destroy and to mutilate irreparably each country. . . . You say that you presume the Russians will proceed. It may well be, of course, that they will feel compelled to if we proceed. It is a case of tit for tat, as we always have. . . .

Secretary ROGERS. Mr. Chairman, I would like to make a couple of brief comments. As far as Mr. Laird's statement is concerned, the statement that you read, of course, is the accurate one, where he said "some movement forward," I think are the words he used. Some of the reporting, particularly the headlines, did not carry out that thought. But I think that Secretary Laird was expressing the same thought that the President was expressing in the letter of transmittal. We think now is

certainly the wrong time to unilaterally disarm. We have just demonstrated—

The CHAIRMAN. Nobody is proposing unilateral disarmament. That is a red herring. We are not proposing unilateral disarmament at all. It is a question of going forward with a vastly increased thing. Each of these Trident submarines is twice as big as existing ones and much longer range, and it costs really ten times as much. It isn't unilateral disarmament not to go forward with that kind of weapon. I am not saying we should unilaterally disarm and no one else is.

Secretary ROGERS. Mr. Chairman, as I said, when you say we think or we conjecture that the Soviet Union may proceed, the fact is they say so, they told us—let me finish. Chairman Brezhnev told the President they were going to proceed with their programs within the limitations imposed by the interim agreement and he wanted to make it clear there was no doubt about that so we weren't misled. . . . He explained to us that the Soviet Union was going to proceed within the limitations of the interim agreement, and we on our part should proceed with our programs. These are not what you suggested, greatly enlarged programs; they are programs that we submitted before these agreements were signed. So we do believe they are important. We believe they are important not only to the security of the United States but . . . to the successful negotiations in the second phase of SALT; and when I said unilateral disarmament, I meant that if we unilaterally decided not to proceed with offensive weapons systems that we had planned, based on these agreements, we would be making a mistake, because the Soviet Union is not going to, and we are prepared to work out mutual arrangements on limitations, further limitations of a permanent nature on offensive weapons. But partly because we had programs, ongoing programs, particularly because we had an ABM program, we were able to succeed in these negotiations.

The CHAIRMAN. I don't want to belabor, but at the briefing on Thursday this question was asked of Mr. Kissinger and he does not link these two together. This to me is a very significant difference. When he was speaking for the President at the White House at a public meeting. As you know, I asked him and he said they are not linked. He did not put it this way. Mr. Laird says he could not support the agreement if Congress fails to act. Mr. Kissinger said that these two stand on their own feet. . . .

Secretary ROGERS. My view is each of these stands, each of the two—I am speaking about the agreements on the one hand and the question of weapons on the other—stands on its own two feet. I think they should be judged on their merits.

Now, secondly, I think, Mr. Chairman, when you said that Secretary Laird said he won't favor ratification unless we get everything we want, that is not what he said. He said some forward movement on the programs.

*　　*　　*

Senator AIKEN. I have been reading lately in several places about the effectiveness of the laser-guided bombs in wiping out SAMS in North Vietnam. If a laser can be used in wiping out the SAMS, could the laser also be effective in the ABM system?. . . .

Secretary ROGERS. Under the agreement we provide that exotic ABM systems may not be deployed and that would include, of course, ABM systems based on the laser principle. . . .

Senator AIKEN. Is the ABM system getting obsolete? If the lasers can be used to knock out the SAMS, wouldn't they be effective against other types of missiles also?

[Ambassador Gerard C.] SMITH. Senator Aiken, I think it is an entirely different problem with respect to the use of lasers to help guide offensive missiles and from their use to guide defensive missiles, but we have covered this concern of yours in this treaty by prohibiting the deployment of future-type technology. Unless the treaty is amended, both sides can only deploy launchers and interceptors and radars. There are no inhibitions on modernizing this type of technology except that it cannot be deployed in mobile land-based or space-based or sea-based or air-based configurations. But the laser concern was considered and both sides have agreed that they will not deploy future-type ABM technology unless the treaty is amended.

*　　*　　*

Senator PELL. I was struck by the excellence of the President's word "sufficiency" in moving into these negotiations. Some years ago we used to talk about negotiating from strength. Then as we studied the problem more we became aware that if we are dealing with pretty much a man of equal strength we must accept parity or, as President Nixon put it, sufficiency. Now I find a turning around of the cycle. I was curious if it is semantic or if there is some thought we must retain the old idea of nuclear superiority, a position second to none, because you in your own testimony earlier referred to negotiating from strength, and the preamble of the agreement before us talks about a position second to none. . . .

Secretary ROGERS. . . . When we use the word sufficiency we mean a strong national defense capability second to none. Now, there have been some tendencies on the part of some to give the word sufficiency

the meaning that somehow we are prepared to be a little bit inferior or considerably inferior because we will show our good faith. We want to make it quite clear when we use the word sufficiency we mean a strong national security second to none. We don't claim it has to be anything except that, second to none, and it should be sufficient for purposes of our national defense; and we think that that kind of a posture, one of sufficiency, second to none, strong, will give us the best negotiating position in the second round of the SALT talks.

Senator PELL. But the possibility of retaliation and with devastating results on the second round would not be considered sufficiency in itself?

Secretary ROGERS. No.

* * *

Senator PELL. I think probably Ambassador Smith would best be able to answer this question. If the Soviets do what is allowed in land- and submarine-based forward movement on their side, what are the implications for us? If the Kremlin or Pentagon move ahead on the same basis and expand as much as they can within the framework of the agreement, would that put us in the very inferior position after a few years?

Mr. SMITH. I think one of the keys to the answer to your question is your last few words, "after a few years." Now, one cannot tell how long this interim freeze will last. People shorthandedly say this is a five-year agreement. I hope it won't be. It may be a one-year agreement; it may be a two-year agreement, depending on when we succeed in the follow-on negotiations.

Now, it is our calculation that nothing that the Soviets can do even if it went the full term of five years could upset the strategic balance. We will be going ahead, as you know, with substantial programs in the Poseidon and Minuteman field and in other strategic areas, so that it is our confident calculation that the strategic balance will remain firm during that period.

Senator PELL. Basically what you are saying is that both sides really told each other we are going to go full steam ahead within the terms of the agreement. Would that be correct?

Mr. SMITH. I think "full steam ahead" is much too strong a term. Certainly as far as any programs I know of, if we wanted, we could go much further and much faster. For instance, in such programs as the MIRV programs, you could step that up if you wanted to. There are a number of ways that the United States could produce more launchers rather quickly if it wanted to. So I don't see this as a full steam ahead situation, but it is our understanding that the Soviets are not going to be hesitating and reducing their programs because of the fact that a pre-

liminary SALT offensive agreement has been reached. It is by no means a completed agreement.

* * *

Senator COOPER. Reference has been made to the President's statement that the Soviet Union intends to build up its offensive missiles strength. Agreement has been reached upon the number of land-based missiles, submarine-launched missiles, protection against upgrading of SAM to the anti-ballistic area. What are the things that you expect the Soviet Union to continue to do, Ambassador Smith?

Mr. SMITH. Well, I think, Senator Cooper, the Soviet Union throughout this negotiation made it very clear that their modernization process should not be interfered with in connection with this first agreement and we, in general, agreed with that proposition. This is to a considerable extent a numerical limitation although there are some qualitative limitations in these arrangements. I think that what the Soviets had in mind is that they want to keep their missile systems up to date. Their missiles are not as efficient as ours. They want to have the opportunity too of having more modern missiles. A lot of their missiles are liquid fueled. They want to probably make them solid fueled. They want to have them more efficient and that is why we had a good deal of discussion about what could be done within the numerical restraints. For instance, one of the questions was, could you increase the size of launchers for an ICBM, and it was agreed that you could not increase the dimensions "significantly." It was subsequently agreed that "significantly increased" meant more than 10 or 15 percent. So I would expect that the Soviets will be engaged in programs which would involve some increase in the dimensions of their silo launchers.

In addition to that, the whole submarine program I look on as a modernization program. They apparently are willing to modernize their strategic forces by building more submarines at the price of phasing out ICBMS. I would anticipate we will see that modernization phenomenon continue in their forces just as we continue to modernize our forces by improving the warhead situation in our MIRV program, by hardening our silos and otherwise.

* * *

Senator MCGEE. . . . Was there agreement on the meaning of the term "heavy missile," or did the United States simply file its interpretation of what it meant to us?

Mr. SMITH. Senator McGee, there is good agreement. This was reflected in the exchanges, going back quite a bit, as to what is a heavy missile and what is a light missile at the present time.

There is no doubt that the SS-7s and the SS-8s and the SS-9s are heavy missiles, and the SS-11s and the SS-13s are light missiles, and that the Titan on the American side is a heavy missile and the Minuteman is a light missile. The question came up as to the future. Supposing some sort of a missile is developed that is in between? There we tried to get a specific definition of future missiles that would qualify for that term "heavy," and the Soviets were loath to get pinned down to a specific number. One of the arguments was, if you have a specific number and you are just over that in volume by one cubic meter, there would be a violation, and how can one be so precise about the future as to know exactly what technology would require?

The best that we were able to do was to make a unilateral statement that if the Soviets deployed a missile significantly larger than the SS-11, we would consider that a heavy missile and we expected the Soviets to take our point of view into consideration. They replied, saying that the record showed we had been unable to reach a specific agreement on the definition of "heavy" and that the executive agreement should stand as it was written.

I think that there is no doubt about the state of consensus as to the present. There is some possibility that in the future there may be a discussion between us as to whether a new class of missiles would be light or heavy, and we have a Standing Consultative Commission that we will set up and it is that sort of problem, I believe, that will be referred to that commission.

Senator McGEE. Is there no uncertainty or equivocation in your judgment as it affects the SS-9? I single that out because that is a straightforward statement. One of our very distinguished colleagues in the Senate on this matter said that the ambiguity led to no agreement and thus it leaves the SS-9 and its status in sort of quiet limbo.

Mr. SMITH. I think the record is clear that the SS-9 is accepted by both sides as a heavy missile.

Senator McGEE. A second statement has been made by one of our colleagues, and I read this because it was lifted out of a printed record, *News Day* I think. He says that the agreement gives the Soviets more of everything, more light ICBMS, more heavy ICBMS, more submarines, more submarine-launched missiles, more payload, even more ABM radar. In no area covered by the agreement "is the United States permitted to maintain parity with the Soviet Union."

Mr. SMITH. Well, I think that this is a straight, simple statement on the numbers of launchers. The present situation is that the Soviets have more ICBMS and they have more SLBMS under construction and operational. The recitation of the present numerical situation does not affect the value of these agreements.

It is our position, which is supported by our military authorities, that we have a position of sufficiency, that we have advantages in a number of other respects. We have a very substantial advantage in the number of warheads; we have doubled the number of warheads in our arsenal in the last three years. They are programed to be again doubled in the next two or three years. The quality of our forces is substantially better than the Soviets'. We have a bomber force that is something like three times the size of theirs, and there is no comparison between the efficiency of our bomber forces. We have a capability to add new armaments to our bomber force and we have them programed. So I think that there is no question that this agreement does not result in any inequality for the United States.

*   *   *

The CHAIRMAN. Mr. Secretary, I don't believe anybody has mentioned this. I have a few odds and ends. Article XIII provides for the establishment, in the first paragraph, of a Standing Consultative Commission—"to promote the objectives and implementation of the provisions of this treaty, the parties shall establish promptly a Standing Consultative Commission, within the framework of which they will . . ."—and there are several things. Would you say a word about that commission, either you or Mr. Smith, about what you anticipate its setup will be and how it will function?

Mr. SMITH. Mr. Chairman, we have in mind as a priority item in the follow-on SALT negotiations to draw up a charter for this organization. This is unprecedented in Soviet-American relations; so I can only speculate and say that personally I see, at least in the early days and the early years, a rather simple structure, perhaps four or five individuals only, both sides, meeting periodically, perhaps three or four times a year, largely dependent. It will have no decisional authority. It will be a straight consultative body to look into the questions that are recited in the subparagraphs of Article XIII.

The CHAIRMAN. Do you anticipate it being purely military or will it be civilian?

Mr. SMITH. I think it will be both. I would think that it will be headed up by the civilian side certainly for the United States and I think there will be high-level military and technical advisers. . . . We look on it as a very serious piece of machinery that recognizes that in this field you cannot for the indefinite future foresee how the evolution of the strategic relationship is going to go, and this is a good piece of machinery, we think, to oversee the operations of this new relationship.

*   *   *

The CHAIRMAN. There was one other thing raised, and maybe this is the proper time to raise the question, especially with Mr. Smith.

As you know, some members of the Senate, and maybe others, have raised the question that this treaty will result in a great advantage to the Soviets. They also mentioned the disparity in the megatonnage. There is an interesting piece in the *Times*, and, Mr. Smith, I think it is a good opportunity for you to clarify this. I will read it for you for your comment:

> But the number and size of missiles is less important than the destruction they can inflict. One large nuclear weapon cannot destroy as large an area as several small weapons. Two one-megaton bombs can destroy an area as large as one four-megaton bomb. The measuring rod used by the Pentagon in its secret studies to obtain a single figure for the total destructive capability of nuclear weapons of varied sizes is known as "equivalent megatonnage." A Soviet sixteen-megaton bomb would seem to give Russia a four-fold advantage over four one-megaton American bombs. But in floor area of destruction both amount to four "equivalent megatons" or parity.

This argument especially I think Senator Jackson has raised. He thinks and believes the Russians have 16- or 20- or 56-megaton bombs. I think this would be a good opportunity for you to clarify this. Is that statement approximately accurate?

Mr. SMITH. Well, I would like to have an opportunity to study the statement carefully, Mr. Chairman. But as a general matter, it is correct that the amount of destruction does not go up as you go up in numbers in megatonnage. To put it very simply, if you have a bomb that can destroy New York City, a bomb that is twice the size and yield is not a very valuable instrument, as far as we can see, and it won't destroy twice as much as a bomb that has half the megatonnage.

Now, we long ago made a decision that just to increase megatonnage was not the best way to approach an efficient strategic weapons system. A number of secretaries of defense considered this question, I think at least three, and they decided against going to weapons that had higher megatonnage. . . . We concluded long ago that it was much more appropriate to have a number of accurate and smaller-yield weapons rather than to have very large-yield weapons. One of the reasons, I think, you see an apparent or numerical discrepancy now is that the Soviets went in for the opposite philosophy. . . .

One of the advantages that has been overlooked in talking about this submarine arrangement, for instance, is that if the Soviets go up to their permitted levels in submarines, they will have to destroy, scrap, the SS-7s and SS-8s, which are very high-yield weapons in terms of this

megatonnage question. If they convert those into submarines, their total megatonnage will be substantially reduced.

We don't think that megatonnage differentials are useful ways of determining whether one side or the other has an advantage.

The CHAIRMAN. I think it is important for you to state that.

I think I recall recently one of the principal complaints about this treaty is that it allows them to retain over 300 SS-9s. These are described as the weapons that could destroy practically everything, and I think you explained that.

* * *

The CHAIRMAN. . . . Was a proposal ever made to have no ABM? Was it ever considered that both sides would relinquish any ABM sites?

Mr. SMITH. There were exchanges about that. We proposed the possibility of a complete ban on ABM in connection with a comprehensive agreement whereby there would be a treaty that would cover all strategic offensive weapons as well as defensive.

The CHAIRMAN. The committee has had, during the last several years, testimony that the large system around Moscow was very questionable. They started it out, I think, to be 120 [ABM launchers] and stopped around 50 or 60 and didn't proceed. We got the impression it was because they had serious doubts about its effectiveness. Now, they are not proceeding, as far as you know, with the alternative sites comparable to Grand Forks, are they?

Mr. SMITH. We do not see any comparable site. We do understand that they are developing ABM systems for the purpose of defending ICBM.

The CHAIRMAN. Would it be feasible to consider, at least in the ongoing negotiations, if the Russians would agree to give up theirs around Moscow if we give up ours around Grand Forks and neither one have to go through the rather futile extravagance? Is that clear out of the ballpark, or is there something that could be considered in your new negotiations that may take place this fall?

Mr. SMITH. I think if you ask us is it feasible, is it in the ballpark, I would think the answer would be yes. On the other hand, the administration has faced up to this question about possible deferral and has concluded it would be in our interest not to do so and to proceed with the second option permitted under the treaty. Both the Soviets and ourselves understand that we are free to proceed.

The CHAIRMAN. I understand the present situation. You can tell from what has been said by several members that there is certainly no unanimity among the Congress about putting one around Washington. . . .

Secretary Rogers. I think that, in answer to your question, Ambas-

sador Smith says he thinks it is feasible. Of course it is feasible to propose it. I do not think it is feasible to expect it will be successful.

The CHAIRMAN. What if you are faced with the situation that Congress won't appropriate the money for one around Washington? Wouldn't you be better off to go back and say, why don't we get rid of all of them? If we did that would you be content to allow them to have Moscow protected and we have Grand Forks protected? Would you be content with that?

Secretary ROGERS. I think we ought to stand on the treaty as it has been completed, and—

The CHAIRMAN. You have already said it doesn't force us to do it. You said we have the option to do it. You said that a moment ago. I am trying to explore it a little. Mr. Smith says a proposal was made by someone, whether the U.S. or Russia, to consider no ABM at all.

Secretary ROGERS. That was part of a comprehensive agreement, though.

The CHAIRMAN. But at that time it wasn't utterly unthinkable both countries would relinquish. Is that not true?

Secretary ROGERS. It is not unthinkable, that is correct.

* * *

The CHAIRMAN. . . . We would not be failing to support the treaty, as I understand it, if we do not go forward with ABM around Washington. That isn't a serious defection from the treaty. Russia wouldn't regard it as a violation of the treaty, would they?

Secretary ROGERS. No.

The CHAIRMAN. So no member could be accused of running out on the treaty or not supporting the treaty if he didn't support an ABM around Washington. Is that not correct?

Secretary ROGERS. It is not accurate. What the treaty does is limit the number of ABM deployments that can be—

The CHAIRMAN. If we chose to do it?

Secretary ROGERS. Yes, sir.

The CHAIRMAN. We don't undertake to do it. We don't undertake to create deployments?

Secretary ROGERS. That is correct.

The CHAIRMAN. I want to make it clear.

Secretary ROGERS. You have made it clear.

Mr. SMITH. I think, Mr. Chairman, if I may throw in a thought, when you consider the value or lack of value of a capital defense, you should keep in mind that the Soviets apparently put a very high value on having such a defense. That is to me some evidence of its importance.

The CHAIRMAN. I don't know. You have said they put a high value on big megatons. We think that is foolish. You don't think they are infallible. They make foolish mistakes, as we do, and thank goodness. If they hadn't been that way, we would have been in bad shape. They have matched pretty near every mistake of ours with one of their own.

21 JUNE 1972 (MORNING SESSION)

The CHAIRMAN [Senator Fulbright]. . . . We are very pleased this morning to have the Secretary of Defense [Melvin R. Laird] and the Chairman of the Joint Chiefs of Staff, Admiral [Thomas] Moorer.

*   *   *

Secretary LAIRD. . . . It is my view that what we are considering is a triple play for peace. We must take into account at the same time all three elements of this triple play: first, the ABM treaty; second, the interim agreement on offensive weapons; and third, the President's national security budget as presented to this Congress. . . .

The President has asked me to concentrate on the relationship of the agreements to the security of the United States, with appropriate emphasis on the critical importance of proposed U.S. strategic programs to the viability of the agreements already reached, and those we hope to reach in the follow-on talks that could begin this October.

I believe the ABM treaty and the interim agreement on offensive weapons now before the Congress are in the interest of America and the world. They enhance our security. They permit us to maintain needed strength. They help us to maintain confidence in the effectiveness and realism of our strategic deterrent. I am confident they can be verified by national means. But by themselves they do not automatically guarantee these national security gains.

In my view, the national security requirements of the United States make it equally urgent that (1) the Senate ratify the ABM treaty; (2) the Congress approve the interim agreement on offensive weapons; and (3) the House and the Senate reinforce these initiatives for arms limitation with strong support for the President's budget requests for the Department of Defense.

As the President has made clear, the merits of each case—the agreements and our pending strategic programs—require affirmative congressional action in both cases. Security, the basis of a peace, cannot be bought cheaply. The opportunities for enhanced security embodied in the SALT agreements would be nullified and our national security jeopardized unless there is continued strong support for an adequate

defense budget. The success of SALT and prospects for ultimate peace depend on sustained strength.

If we do not maintain this strength by going forward with the strategic programs we are recommending, we will face problems similar to those we had to face in SALT I: an onrushing and unchecked Soviet momentum in development and deployment reflected by the addition of ballistic missiles at the rate of some 250 per year for the past five years; a reluctance on the part of the Soviet Union to accept limitations on certain ongoing programs and other developmental programs; and, with the exception of Safeguard, no major U.S. deployment programs, but rather qualitative improvements in existing systems.

Only by intense negotiations were we successful in achieving the limitations contained in the interim agreement. Wishful thinking about what we might want the other side to do has no place in successful negotiations; nor does it have a place in planning our national security. As you know from your briefings on the agreements, limitations advocated by some were the subject of discussion and negotiation, but we could not reach agreement in all areas. I am, of course, referring to MIRV limitations, among other things.

In short, the agreements reached were dictated by the strategic balance and ongoing programs. They reflect what could be obtained through negotiations, not what some might have advocated as more desirable.

The programs that we are recommending are designed not to jockey for some unilateral advantage within the bounds of these agreements but in full recognition of the fact that they are necessary for our national security. . . . The defense programs that are before the Congress are needed to preserve the effectiveness of our deterrent, both with and without SALT. Without the current agreements before you, we would be taking further measures to protect our deterrent capability. With the agreements, we can continue our programs in prudent fashion as we move into follow-on negotiations, hopefully in October.

Let me briefly summarize the major programs we have proposed in the 1973 budget and the 1973 defense report, which was submitted to this Congress in February.

We need Trident, formerly called the underseas long-range missile system, at the earliest possible date. Last year we made the decision to accelerate Trident as the most appropriate new strategic initiative to preserve the sufficiency of our deterrent for the future. We should move forward to be in a position to deploy the first submarine on schedule.

It should be noted that our program will not get the first Trident

submarine into operation until after the scheduled expiration date of this interim agreement. Even though an increase from the present forty-one to forty-four boats is permitted, the U.S. total number of operational ballistic missile submarines will not increase during the period of this agreement. As you know, Trident is also presently planned as a replacement system. This request is contained in our 1973 budget estimate, which is currently being considered by the Congress. . . .

Similarly, the B–1 bomber development program must be kept on schedule. It is designed to provide us an option to deploy the first aircraft in the late 1970s.

With regard to the NCA defense contemplated in the ABM treaty, we can fund the NCA defense in fiscal year 1973 and still reduce, as a result of this treaty, the ABM budget request for fiscal year 1973 by $650 million from the amounts included in the 1973 budget submitted by the President. As I have reported to you, system components originally slated for defense of Minuteman sites will be continued with the objective of using these components at Washington. During fiscal year 1973 we propose to continue studies of NCA defense, continue advanced site preparation, and keep open options for specific national capital authority defense configuration. . . .

The site defense prototype development program, which is permitted by the treaty, preserves the option to deploy a terminal defense of U.S. ICBMS should that ever become necessary. The pending site defense program will provide for earlier availability of developmental hardware, earlier development of software, and earlier test and demonstration.

The revised satellite basing program will provide more rapid movement of our strategic bomber force to inland United States bases and, in addition, makes provision for reducing the time required to get them airborne.

The development of the submarine-launched cruise missile—SLCM—system is necessary to assure availability of future U.S.options for additional U.S. strength, if needed. This particular research and development program was included in the 1972 supplemental request submitted by the administration earlier this year. A decision was made by the Armed Services Committee to consider this supplemental request in conjunction with the 1973 budget. . . . The funding we are proposing will allow accelerated study of the SLCM system and initiate development of critical technology components such as propulsion and guidance. . . . The Soviets, as you know, now have significant numbers of submarine-launched cruise missiles deployed on nuclear boats, and they have ongoing an active production program in this area.

The SALT agreements, in my view, underscore the importance of effective command, control and communications—C^3. That is why we are recommending additional funding in the 1973 budget to improve secure communication with the airborne command post, advance our satellite technology, improve survivability of future computer data systems, and conduct system engineering studies of the world-wide military command and control system. We are also requesting in the 1973 Department of Defense budget request moderate increases in funding to move forward with work on improved reentry vehicles for our ballistic missiles. Clearly, adequate and effective verification capabilities are necessary. We have such capabilities now and are proposing moderate increases in funding to assure that verification of these agreements by national means will remain adequate in the future.

We must continue to preserve our security and to negotiate from a position of strength. . . . We enter these agreements with the following interdependent strong convictions:

- Our security will be enhanced.
- We have applied brakes to the momentum of Soviet strategic missile deployments.
- We have adequate means of verification.
- Congress will support the strategic programs we have proposed in the 1973 budget.
- We have taken the initial steps and have laid a solid foundation for further arms limitation and potential arms reductions in the future.

In summary, Mr. Chairman and members of the Foreign Relations Committee, the agreements are good, but we should not overlook the fact that the negotiations will continue, since we have only an interim agreement on offensive limitations.

We will realize significant savings in strategic expenditures through these agreements that could be about $5 billion over the next five years, even with approval of our ongoing program and proposed programs contained in the 1973 budget request as submitted by the President.

We can and must take those further steps to insure continued security while at the same time enhancing prospects for successful follow-on negotiations. This is the way to move toward future benefits with respect both to our security and to our defense expenditures. But we are not in this position yet.

*　　*　　*

Admiral MOORER. Mr. Chairman, members of the Committee: I am grateful for the opportunity to discuss with you today the SALT agreements and their interrelationship to our strategic force posture. . . .

Our strategic nuclear weapons have but one essential purpose—to deter conflict. The real objective is that these weapons never be used. Arms control agreements, to be either enduring or effective, must mutually enhance the security of both parties. We must, in order to survive as a nation, retain the power needed to deter aggression, not as a symbol of national aggrandizement, but as an essential shield for the preservation of our security. It is in this context that the treaty, the agreement, and the United States' strategic posture must be viewed.

The Joint Chiefs of Staff were officially represented on the SALT delegation and were consulted prior to signature. If we press forward vigorously with our programs designed to protect against a degradation in national security posture, the Joint Chiefs of Staff believe that the deterrent capability of our strategic forces will not be impaired, that the peace of the world may be enhanced, and that the undertakings will be in the best interests of the United States.

There are two essential ingredients in any analysis of the strategic consequences of these undertakings: first, the relative balance between the U.S.S.R. and U.S. projected over the life of the agreement; and second, drawing upon that analysis, a discussion of the essential continuing steps we must take to preserve U.S. security and the stability of international order as we move into the future.

It is necessary that we examine a little of the past in order to understand the present and to put the future in perspective. In discussing the FY 1971 budget with the Congress, Mr. Laird and I both said that the United States no longer had clear superiority in strategic nuclear weapons. In the course of considering our relative military posture during the FY 1972 budget hearings, I reported that the balance is tenuous. This year my report to the Congress reflected that the balance is turning against us in quantitative terms and that, short of an effective agreement on strategic arms limitations, the momentum of the Soviet strategic force buildup would likely carry Soviet forces well beyond the level planned for our forces in the mid- or late-1970s. This momentum resulted from the fact that the U.S.S.R. has had an active ICBM and SLBM construction and deployment program since the mid-sixties, while in a quantitative sense, the United States remained static—concentrating instead on qualitative improvements. We therefore must examine the impact of these agreements on the basis not only of what they freeze, but also upon what they forestall.

I would like now to briefly analyze the strategic military balance

and project it into the future in order to describe how the strategic arms limitation undertakings affect that balance. I will address specifically those forces affected by the undertakings: ICBMS, SLBMS, and ABMS. In addition, the three general quantitative measures which have been used to summarize the overall strategic military balance between the United States and the Soviet Union—numbers of delivery vehicles, megatons, and warheads—will be discussed.

Turning now to the numbers of U.S. and Soviet ICBM launchers, the U.S.S.R. is expected to have approximately 1,550 ICBMS on launchers by 1 July of this year. They have been deploying ICBMS at the rate of about 250 per year. Thus, if unconstrained, they could have had by midyear 1977 well over 2,000 such missiles on launchers. The number of ICBM launchers projected for the Soviets under SALT is between 1,600 and 1,400, depending on how many they choose to convert to SLBMS. In the SALT environment, we actually consider the lower number of ICBM launchers to be the more severe threat. The reason for this apparent anomaly is that a lower number of ICBM launchers reflects the phaseout and replacement of older missiles with modern SLBMS. It should be noted, however, that the maximum numbers of ICBMS and SLBMS that the Soviets could have had without the constraints of the undertakings were much in excess of those permitted by the agreement. U.S. ICBMS as projected in our five-year defense program would not have increased beyond the current level of 1,054.

SLBM launchers are the next item of interest. The U.S.S.R. is estimated to have about 580 operational SLBMS and is building at the rate of about 128 per year. They were, therefore, capable of operating about 1,200 SLBMS by 1977. A Soviet maximum of 950 modern launchers is all they are permitted by the undertakings. The U.S. SLBM launcher level will remain constant through 1977 at 656. Although under the agreement we are permitted to build up to 710 SLBM launchers by converting our 54 Titans to SLBM launchers, we cannot deploy our first new Trident submarine until 1978 and thus add to our SLBM launcher force.

The total number of intercontinental delivery vehicles projected for the United States and the Soviet Union should now be considered. The 140 U.S.S.R. and 457 U.S. bombers must now be added to the numbers of intercontinental delivery vehicles previously discussed. They are unaffected by the agreement. Approximately 2,100 deployable vehicles are now available to each party. The Soviet Union was expected to overtake us in this measure by mid-1972 and to have over 3,000 delivery vehicles operational by 1977. Under the terms of the undertaking, our best estimates reflect a level of 2,167 U.S. and 2,499 U.S.S.R. delivery vehicles. This factor, more than any other, points out

the significance of interrupting Soviet momentum. Granted, we have a freeze at a ratio of about 2,499 to 2,167 in favor of the Soviet Union, but we have forestalled a 1977 ratio of about three to two in their favor.

The U.S.S.R. was already far superior to us in total intercontinental strategic offensive megatonnage. Only in the numbers of strategic offensive warheads was the United States projected to maintain a lead over the Soviet Union during the next five years. Even here, the U.S.S.R. has the potential to overtake us. Given the technology which we have every reason to believe the Soviet Union either has or is acquiring, it is anticipated that they will move vigorously into MIRVs, both in their ICBMs and SLBMs. The considerably greater throw-weight or payload capacity of the Soviet missile force, particularly the SS-9–type missile, is especially adaptable to this task. It is still anticipated that they will considerably narrow our lead in terms of numbers of warheads by the late 1970s. However, the restraint on their deploying more than the 313 SS-9–type missiles now operational or under construction will impact upon this growth. Here we benefit from both what we freeze and what we forestall.

As I have noted on several prior occasions, an objective evaluation of the overall strategic balance between the United States and the Soviet Union requires consideration of all the factors in the strategic equation—delivery vehicles, megatons, and warheads—in an appropriate combination, together with pre-launch survivability, reliability, accuracy, range, and penetrability of enemy defensive systems.

* * *

Now, I would like to discuss the strategic defensive balance with regard to the ABM treaty. Both sides are limited to a maximum of two sites, with 100 launchers at each site. The U.S.S.R. currently has one site deployed around Moscow, with a total of 64 launchers. We have one site under construction at Grand Forks, North Dakota, which is about 90 percent complete at this time. The Soviet Union is limited to one additional site at an ICBM field, and we are limited to an additional 100-launcher site around Washington, D.C., for defense of our national command and control mechanism. As far as ABM launchers are concerned, therefore, both sides can have a comparable defense. This defense will protect our decision-making process and command and control facilities and provide additional time to implement appropriate retaliatory measures. The perception of assured response by those who would be our adversaries reduces the potential for attack. Further, the undertakings are structured to provide a degree of strategic equality and balance. Our failure to construct the Washington site to balance off the Soviet capability would leave an undesirable asymmetrical rela-

tionship which could be destabilizing and weaken our overall deterrent posture.

No discussion of these undertakings would be complete without consideration of the future. We must look beyond the five-year period of the interim agreement and consider the actions required now to preserve an appropriate strategic equilibrium should follow-on negotiations fail. The relaxation of tensions evidenced by the mutual determination to agree, reflected by these undertakings, reduces the probability of war. There is, however, no guarantee that successive arms-limiting steps can be taken so that a more permanent solution will be reached. The present undertakings, if properly pursued, should assist us in achieving a substantial diminution in tension and lead to peaceful progress. In the meantime, however, we must continue taking those essential military steps designed to maintain our deterrent. If we fail to follow the legitimate dictates of our own security, the leadership of the U.S.S.R. will chalk it up not to goodwill, but to a failure of will; not to our confidence, but to our weakness. They thus might be encouraged to engage in acts which could threaten the peace and security of the world. The Joint Chiefs of Staff, therefore, believe that action to achieve the following assurances must be taken now if the United States is to guard against a degradation of its national security posture:

Assurance I: A broad range of intelligence capabilities and operations to verify Soviet compliance in a strategic arms limitation environment.

- Provide high-confidence monitoring of Soviet compliance with the terms of the ABM treaty and the interim offensive agreement.
- Provide information on Soviet strategic activity, capabilities, and achievements as insurance against both technological and strategic surprise and for use in follow-on arms limitation negotiations.

Assurance II: Aggressive improvements and modernization programs.

- Maximize strategic capabilities within the constraints established by the ABM treaty and the interim offensive agreement.
- Plan for rapid augmentation of strategic forces beyond the constraints of the treaty and agreement to be made in the event of abrogation, withdrawal, or collapse of negotiations.

Assurance III: Vigorous research and development programs.

- Maintain weapons systems technological superiority.
- Continue testing to insure the effectiveness of new and existing nuclear weapons systems.

The Secretary of Defense has already outlined, in his statement, the major programs designed to provide the assurances that I have enumerated above. It is the conviction of the Joint Chiefs of Staff that these programs are essential in order not to jeopardize the future security of the United States. Furthermore, these programs will:

- Firstly, place the United States in a position to negotiate further acceptable limitations on offensive systems,
- Secondly, prevent the United States from being placed in a position of strategic inferiority in the years ahead, and
- Finally, provide positive evidence to our allies of our intention to maintain our strategic deterrent power, so necessary to their security within the SALT environment. . . .

The Joint Chiefs of Staff are in accord with the undertakings that are before you today, provided they are properly safeguarded, as discussed earlier. They may well constitute the essential first step toward an era of negotiation and a generation of peace.

* * *

The CHAIRMAN. You refer to an adequate defense budget, which is really the question. What is adequate is the question with regard to the ABM treaty.

If the treaty is lived up to, if both sides take it seriously—you have stated and other witnesses have stated that we have adequate means of verification, that there could be no serious cheating on this agreement. [CIA Director Richard] Helms is very positive about it, and I take it from your testimony you feel we have adequate means of verification. If that is so, and if each side has given up the idea of an effective defense against strategic weapons, it seems to me this has a very important bearing on what is adequate because it is acknowledged, I think, by everyone that the existing weapons now in being are quite adequate to destroy effectively each country. We have sufficient weapons, if their delivery is not thwarted, to destroy them, and the same on the other side. Therefore, it strikes me this has a very important bearing upon what is adequate. If you insist upon these enormously increased weapons with enormous costs, you will force them to respond in kind. All you are doing is continuing the arms race. The whole purpose of the ABM treaty, we thought, was to stop the arms race. There is, to me, an inherent inconsistency in these two positions. . . .

Secretary LAIRD. Mr. Chairman, as you know, the numbers that are contained in the offensive agreement, which is a first step toward follow-on negotiations in the offensive field, do give a numerical advantage to the Soviet Union.

The CHAIRMAN. Well, numerically—

Secretary LAIRD. I do not feel that this is a difficulty. It does not present a problem for the realism of our deterrent because we have technology which is, I believe, from eighteen to twenty-four months ahead of the Soviet Union. . . . But I am aware of the fact that the Soviet Union has stated that it is going forward with programs permitted under the agreement. And not only have they stated this, but they are also going forward with very effective test programs. I believe that they have the MIRV technology. They have done tests in this particular area and they will, I believe, flight test this MIRV technology within the next six to nine months.

The question of sufficiency is one that involves a judgment factor. I personally believe that we have a realistic deterrent today. I believe that our friends and allies—as well as the Soviet Union and the world—understand that. But I do not believe that we can take action today that does not permit us to carry forward with these programs for maintaining our technology and maintaining our replacement capabilities until we have achieved an adequate follow-on agreement.

* * *

The CHAIRMAN. The point comes back to this. It will destroy the whole spirit of these agreements if you persist or if our government persists in seeking an advantage, and a clear advantage, in any of these fields. The basis of the agreements is a high degree of parity. The numbers are not so significant if there is no defense against them. If the weapons are more than adequate and they can't defend against them, the fact that you have 100 or 500 more missiles doesn't make any appreciable difference. In addition, you have already stated you believe we have superiority in technology. . . . If we go forward with your proposals we will upset that balance, and I think we are likely to destroy the effectiveness of the treaty itself, and that is what we wish to protect. I think the issue about the adequate defense in view of the ABM agreement is the very crux of the matter and I don't quite think you have addressed yourself directly to that question.

* * *

Secretary LAIRD. . . . We are coming to Congress with a reduction in the 1973 budget, as a result of the ABM treaty, of some $650 million. We are projecting a five-year savings as a result of the ABM treaty of up to $5 billion. We are projecting a saving through 1981, as far as the ABM treaty is concerned over the period, of some $8.6 billion. I think that these things should be pointed out; and an amendment is coming forward to the 1973 budget which in part reflects the impact of these par-

ticular agreements, although it does not affect the B–1 or the Trident requests which we have before the Congress. There were some people, it seems to me, who were reading into these agreements the assumption that a reduction could be made in these ongoing offensive weapon programs which we have asked the Congress to continue. That is a point that I think is sometimes overlooked.

* * *

Senator COOPER. . . . The question I want to address myself to is, What are our security needs for the next five years? Now, it has been admitted that the Soviets could, under this treaty, interim agreement, have superiority in numbers of launchers and megatonnage. They could, if we do nothing and they go all out, have superiority in warheads if they deployed MIRV on all their systems, ICBMS and SLBMS. That is correct?

Secretary LAIRD. That is correct.

Senator COOPER. Do you anticipate in the next five years, or have any reason to believe, that they would try to achieve superiority in warheads or could achieve superiority in warheads?

Secretary LAIRD. Senator Cooper, it is very difficult—

Senator COOPER. We have now superiority of two to one in deliverable warheads, don't we?

Secretary LAIRD. It is very difficult for me to give you a projection on Soviet intentions. I believe they have the technology and the capability to move forward in this area because of the tremendous throw-weight that they have with their systems.

Now, when you asked me to interpret their intentions, I know they are going forward with test programs. Since the President left Moscow, very important tests have been conducted with their ICBMS and with other offensive systems. I cannot project the intentions of the Soviet Union other than to say they stated quite categorically that they would be going forward during the five-year period with all of the programs permitted in the offensive area.

Senator COOPER. With regard to the SLBM system you stated they could have a numerical superiority within a five-year period, if they go ahead with it. But I would like to ask you, Admiral Moorer, isn't it correct that the U.S. Poseidon-Polaris fleet, with its launchers, with its MIRVS, is superior in present capabilities and effectiveness to the Russian marine missile fleet?

Secretary LAIRD. There is no question about that. At the present time we not only have more modern operational submarines in the Polaris and Poseidon area, we have a greater number operational. They, however, have operational and under construction a greater number than the United States, and they are building at the rate of eight to nine a

year. We do not have a capability of bringing any new ballistic missile submarines to operational status during the period of this agreement. They, without the agreement, could have gone up to ninety if they had continued their current momentum. At the end of five years they could have had up to ninety and we would still have been at forty-one.

Senator Cooper. Now, considering the fact of this superiority not only in numbers of launchers, deliverable warheads, but also the range of our missiles and the ability to stay on station close to the Soviet Union, would you say there is any possibility of the Soviet Union attaining superiority over our SLBM fleet in two years?

Secretary Laird. In a period of two years, I would say no. I would like Admiral Moorer to comment on that question as Chairman of the Joint Chiefs of Staff; but I think if you limit it to two years, the answer would be no. Of course, for us to build a submarine would take at least five years from the time that we went forward, but I would like the Chairman to comment on that question.

Admiral Moorer. Senator Cooper, Secretary Laird and I have repeatedly said that we are confident we have adequate deterrence for today. What we are really talking about in proposing these programs is the future. I don't think that the people at large, the American public as a whole, recognize the very long lead-time involved in developing any modern weapon systems. We are concerned about slipping back into a state of obsolescence, and consequently we must move ahead now in order to maintain modern systems and maintain this deterrence that we are talking about.

Senator Cooper. I understand your argument. Secretary Laird said just a few minutes ago that he couldn't state that within five years that the Soviet Union would be superior to us in warheads. My question now goes to the question whether we should exercise restraint for two years and see what we can do to achieve nuclear offensive missile system reductions or move into a big new weapons program. You said flatly that you don't think that for two years we would be in danger. Admiral Moorer said that unequivocally.

Now, I will ask you this: The history of the arms race with the Soviet Union is that we first got the atomic bomb; they wouldn't agree to any restraint until later when they came up with it. We obtained superiority in numbers of ICBMS; they wouldn't agree to restraints until they deployed over 1,000 ICBMS. They agreed to restraints on ABMS, ICBMS, and SLBMS only when they deployed them in similar numbers.

Are the Soviets really bargaining from strength or are they just saying, "You have this system of weapons, so we will not agree to any limitations until we come up on a level with you"? The fundamental question is, if it is correct that for almost thirty years every deployment

we have made has been matched by an equivalent deployment and the only agreements we have reached have been on the basis of parity, why shouldn't we show restraint for two years instead of this demonstrably futile "bargaining from strength" so they will not do what they have done, it seems to me, in the past thirty years, "to not agree on any limitations until we get up to you"? If we build up in two years, they will undoubtedly do the same and the arms race will go on.

Secretary LAIRD. Mr. Chairman, and Senator Cooper, I think we have shown that restraint. When you talk about the position we will be in in two years, what I am really talking about and what the President has submitted to this Congress for the B–1 and the Trident systems are programs that will place us in a position where we can have this sufficiency, this parity of systems, during the period of the 1980s.

Now, the Soviet Union, if we were to stop research and development on a unilateral basis in these offensive areas, if we were to stop building a capability to go forward with these systems—and there we are talking about the period of 1978 and beyond—if we were to do that for a period of two years, I believe the safety and the security of our country would be jeopardized.

* * *

Senator JAVITS. Now, do you or do you not subscribe to the following proposition, again what we understand to be stated as administration doctrine, and I quote again from [Dr. Kissinger's] briefing which we had: "As long as it lasts, offensive missile forces have in effect a free ride to their targets. Beyond a certain level of sufficiency, differences in numbers are therefore not conclusive." . . .

Secretary LAIRD. . . . The question of deterrence is a question of what the potential adversaries or our allies think is a sufficient deterrent. I believe we have that sufficient deterrent today, and I believe our allies and our adversaries recognize that fact.

The important thing about deterrence is to prevent the use of nuclear weapons at any time, and that is what these programs are all about. We would hope that the money spent on these programs would be completely wasted in the sense the weapons would never be used; then deterrence has been completely successful. But as far as the numbers are concerned in this agreement that I am testifying on today, I believe, because of the technological lead that we have in this area, that we have a sufficient deterrent and it will prevent the use of nuclear weapons. That is the important thing for us to be considering.

Senate Armed Services Committee Hearings on SALT I, June–July 1972

20 June 1972 (Morning Session)

The Chairman [Senator John C. Stennis]. . . . I will call the names of our witnesses first: Secretary Laird, Admiral Moorer, Mr. Paul Nitze, assistant to the Secretary of Defense for SALT, and Lt. Gen. Royal B. Allison, assistant to the Chairman of the Joint Chiefs for SALT.

* * *

The Chairman. I believe that, in many ways, the decision to commit the United States to these agreements has been the most momentous decision of the nuclear age. I personally believe that this is the most important issue on which I have had to pass judgment since I came to the Senate. The Senate, and in the case of the interim agreement, the entire Congress, owes it to the nation to be more than a passive jury with respect to these agreements. It is important that all members of the Congress work hard to understand them, take an active part in the debate and discussions of them, and make an informed judgment. Closely connected with the question of whether to approve the agreements themselves is the question of what type of military program to approve for the Department of Defense. . . . As I have said often in the past, I believe these agreements are only a beginning, but it is time that we made a beginning in this important area. The issues about which I want to examine these witnesses today center around the following three questions:

- What are our capabilities to deter nuclear war today? In the judgment of these witnesses, do we have sufficient nuclear weapons for this most vital purpose?
- What would our capability be to deter nuclear war over the next several years in the absence of any agreement?
- Finally, what will our capability be—how will it be improved and how will it be limited—because of the agreement?

I believe those are the three primary questions overall that the American people are interested in.

* * *

Source: U.S., Congress, Senate, Committee on Armed Services, *Military Implications of the Treaty on the Limitations of Anti-Ballistic Missile Systems and the Interim Agreement on Limitation of Strategic Offensive Arms*, 92d Cong., 2d sess., 1972.

The CHAIRMAN. . . . Under this agreement will any of the United States' planned deployment programs for offensive missiles be affected?
Secretary LAIRD. They are not. During the period of this interim agreement one of the major systems which we have coming forward is, of course, the Trident submarine program, which is the follow-on to the Polaris/Poseidon program. Even on this schedule that was approved last year, and the research-development program proposed to the Congress in the acceleration last year, the first of these particular submarines would not be completed until the end of 1978. This is after the end of the period of this interim agreement. The B–1, of course, would not come in until the latter part of the 1970s and would be available early in the 1980s. Bombers, of course, are not affected under the terms of this agreement. . . .

The programs for the MIRV systems on the Minuteman III and the Poseidon conversions are not affected by this particular agreement. Although this agreement provides for as many as forty-four ballistic missile submarines, the United States would not be in a position to add these submarines during the period of this interim agreement. Three submarines are provided for that we could go forward with under this agreement, but with the schedule for the Trident system, those submarines would not be ready for deployment during the period of the agreement.
The CHAIRMAN. That is another illustration of our not giving up anything; but I want to continue in this same general question now as to what the pluses are. What about the tactical weapons?
Secretary LAIRD. They are not covered by the agreement.
The CHAIRMAN. Directly, was the threat of Soviet intermediate missiles targeted on Europe lessened in any way by this agreement?
Secretary LAIRD. No.
The CHAIRMAN. Was either Soviet or American ability to test and deploy MIRVs affected?
Secretary LAIRD. No, it has not been affected. As I testified earlier, the capability of the Soviet Union in this area was of concern and is of concern to us because of the thrust that the Soviets' systems do possess. This is true particularly of the SS-9 systems and the follow-on system to the SS–9 which is currently under development; but we believe that we have a technological capability and a superiority in the MIRV area which is from eighteen to twenty-four months ahead of the Soviet Union. . . . We know that they are testing MIRV technology at the present time, and I would believe that they would flight test this new MIRV technology of theirs within the next six to nine months.
The CHAIRMAN. So you are expecting them to MIRV their weapons?
Secretary LAIRD. Yes. . . .

The CHAIRMAN. I have one other question. On this same overall question of what the agreement does not do, what are the minuses here, so far as our position is concerned? How do the restrictions on ABM deployment adversely affect our ability to have Minuteman and our bombers survive a Soviet first strike?

Secretary LAIRD. As Secretary of Defense, I have supported the twelve-site ABM program. I felt the twelve-site ABM program would give protection to our deterrent force. It would give the kind of protection to our retaliatory force which would increase the overall realism that was behind our deterrent. There is no question that cutting back from the twelve-site program takes away that protection . . . but I believe that in order to achieve the agreement, certainly the United States had to give up something. The United States gave up the twelve-site program in order to stop the Soviet momentum in deploying offensive systems. Without the approval of this Congress for the ABM program, I do not believe either of these agreements would have been possible.

The CHAIRMAN. But you do have the same ceiling for each party so far as ABM is concerned.

Secretary LAIRD. We had an ongoing program with momentum in the ABM field. The Congress had approved deployment or advanced preparation at four sites, so the momentum in the antiballistic missile area was on the side of the United States and it was not on the side of the Soviet Union.

Senator SMITH. Mr. Secretary, do you have the number of Russian operational ICBMs?

Secretary LAIRD. Yes. . . . They are approximately 1,500. This is based upon the best intelligence information which is available to me as Secretary of Defense, and those figures have been made available to the committee.

Senator SMITH. That was my next question, Mr. Chairman. Were there any numbers disclosed during the discussions leading up to this agreement?

Secretary LAIRD. Disclosed by the Soviets?

Senator SMITH. Yes.

Secretary LAIRD. Numbers were discussed as far as submarine-launched ballistic missiles were concerned, because a firm limitation had to be established on them because construction was going forward in that area. As far as the ICBMs are concerned, the agreement provides that no new fixed ICBM launchers be constructed, so there is no need for a firm figure on the number. In the submarine area, there is a variation that is allowed by the Soviets' doing away with SS–7s and SS–8s, so they can make trade-offs in that area and the number of modern submarine-launched ballistic missile launchers can increase.

The total in the limitation is that the Soviet Union can have 2,359 missiles launchers. If they phase out the SS–7s and SS–8s, this would include 950 submarine-launched ballistic missiles, 1,096 light ICBMS of the so-called SS–11 class, and 313 of the modern large missile launchers. The verification of these numbers would, of course, have to be carried on by the national means of the United States.

Senator SMITH. Mr. Secretary, what I was trying to get for the record is just what number we have from the Russians' own words rather than our own means of detection. From your statement I would say what we had was from your own means of detection. Is that correct?

Secretary LAIRD. That is correct, as far as the ICBMS are concerned.

Senator SMITH. Mr. Secretary, will you withdraw your support if Congress does not provide all that is requested in the weapons systems?

Secretary LAIRD. I do not know what difference it would make if I withdrew my support. I support this agreement and this treaty, and I support the requests for strategic weapons systems which are carried in the President's budget. I do not believe that these three items are separable. My recommendation is that you approve the ABM treaty and agreement on offensive weapons, phase down our ABM program from a twelve-site program to a two-site program, and go forward with a follow-on submarine and B–1 bomber.

The Soviet Union will be able to go forward with its submarine construction programs. They will continue to turn out submarines from their shipyards. We should have that capability and should be developing that capability, and I could not be in a position as Secretary of Defense, or as a private citizen, of supporting any of these agreements without the assurance that these follow-on programs would go forward. I would certainly recommend, as my own opinion and recommendation, that we not go forward with this agreement or this treaty if we are going to abandon the programs that have been outlined in the strategic weapons field by the President of the United States and submitted to this Congress in his budget.

Senator SMITH. Thank you, Mr. Secretary. Admiral Moorer, would you be willing to answer that?

Admiral MOORER. Yes, Senator. I think it is important to recognize that as of today the total number of delivery vehicles is about equal, Senator Smith. What we are talking about . . . is what could happen if the Soviets take full advantage of all of what is allowed in the proposed agreement. I personally feel that it is most important that we go ahead with these programs; otherwise, we will fall back into obsolescence, whereas they will move forward with modernization and improvement.

* * *

Senator SYMINGTON. With respect to your argument that ULMS—Trident—is a bargaining chip for SALT II—

Secretary LAIRD. I do not make that argument. I have never referred to the submarine construction program as a bargaining chip.

Senator SYMINGTON. All right. In that the Soviets are apparently deploying their new submarine-launched ballistic missile with longer range in a new modified version of their Yankee-class submarines, why will not the deployment of our ULMS I longer-range missile in a modified Polaris/Poseidon be a sufficient counter to what the Soviets are doing with respect [to SALT]?

Secretary LAIRD. First, Senator Symington, I believe we should use the best technology we have as far as submarines are concerned in a follow-on submarine program.

I sponsored the amendments in the 1950s to accelerate the Polaris program in the House of Representatives, and it was decided in 1958 that we would have a forty-one boat program as far as Polaris is concerned. The first ten of our Polaris submarines cannot be economically converted to the Poseidon-type systems.

[Secretary Laird inserted the following information into the record.]

> In reaching the decision on the Trident program we considered modified Poseidon submarines to carry more launch tubes and the ULMS I missile. The Trident program was selected because Trident has the best prospect for maintaining a high degree of pre-launch survivability over the long term.
>
> In addition, the Trident submarine provides growth potential in the launch tubes to carry a larger ULMS II missile. This missile would permit even larger operating areas than ULMS I, or more payload, if either of these attributes should become necessary.

* * *

Senator DOMINICK. Mr. Secretary, the only real question that I have at this point deals with the question of our ability to back up our international policy in other areas. I gather that with or without the SALT agreements that we are far from a position that we were in 1962 at the time of the Cuban crisis, in terms of relative power of the Soviet Union and ourselves.

Secretary LAIRD. That is correct; there was no question that in that period the United States had a four- or five-to-one superiority over the Soviet Union in the strategic offensive weapons area. That was certainly true as far as numbers were concerned at that time.

Senator DOMINICK. From the point of view of the security of the coun-

try, then, the approval of the strategic offensive weaponry agreement and the treaty with the SALT talks would have no appreciable effect on our power position relative to the Soviet Union in terms of cutting us down or in terms of enlarging their relative superiority?

Secretary LAIRD. Yes, it does, because it does apply brakes to the momentum that the Soviet Union has gone forward with since 1965. I think the decision probably was made in 1962, but the first real evidence of the increased activity in the offensive area was not really brought to public attention or to the attention of our committees here in the Congress until about 1965. That momentum has gone forward. They had the capability of constructing eight to nine of these Y-class submarines a year. Without this agreement, and assuming that momentum continued, they could have eighty to ninety submarines by the end of the period of this particular offensive agreement. This limits them to sixty-two modern submarines. . . .

Senator DOMINICK. Conversely, it does not downgrade our relative position at the present time?

Secretary LAIRD. It does so by placing a halt on the momentum of the United States on ABMS. . . . I think that you have to bear that in mind in appraisal of both of these agreements. They must be considered together, just as our strategic offensive budget requests must be considered along with this agreement and along with this treaty.

Senator DOMINICK. With respect to conventional forces, this agreement does not deal with them at all, as I understand it.

Secretary LAIRD. That is correct.

Senator DOMINICK. And to the extent that they have the momentum in that area you are suggesting in the budget that we continue our development work so that we can modernize and at least offset some of that momentum; is that correct?

Secretary LAIRD. That is correct. I believe that we are moving from a period of arms competition to a period of arms limitation. I believe that arms limitation will apply not only to strategic weapons systems but also later on to conventional weapon systems and force levels. It will also apply eventually to military assistance programs. So we have an opportunity through negotiations in all of these areas to make important agreements to limit conventional military assistance as well as strategic weapons and perhaps to reduce in these areas. But we cannot do that if we take unilateral action to reduce before negotiations start and before we actually conduct negotiations in all of these fields.

* * *

Senator JACKSON. Mr. Secretary, I think you will agree [with] the need to get as clear a picture of the levels of strategic strength permitted by

the two sides under the agreement—especially with all the numbers that have been floating around. . . .

I am aware, of course, that even the total number of ICBM missiles . . . represents a unilateral position on our part and does not represent a bilateral understanding with the Russians.

Secretary LAIRD. That is correct. Regarding missile sizes, as you know, the United States told the Soviets that we consider a "heavy" ICBM to be one having a volume significantly greater than the largest light ICBM now operational on either side, which we consider to be the SS–11. . . .

Senator JACKSON. What I want to get is our interpretation. If I do nothing else during all of these hearings, Mr. Secretary, I think it is important that the Congress and the American people know what our government understands the agreement with the Soviet Union to be.

In all of my experience, I must say that I have never heard of an agreement which involves such a serious substantive matter as the whole land-based strategic force not being set out in detail in the agreement. This kind of ambiguity can breed suspicion, and lead to an unstable situation rather than to a more stable one. So if I do nothing else, I am going to try to nail down, line by line, the exact meaning of these agreements.

We start from the premise that we have a bilateral clear-cut agreement as to the number of operational Y-class, Polaris-type submarines permitted. It is spelled out, it is specific. Yet nowhere can anyone find a bilateral understanding as to the number of land-based missiles that are permitted. I submit that starting out with this kind of confusion can lead only to future trouble. I can easily envision a situation where our intelligence people announce that we have discovered *x* number, while the Russians come back and say, "We're sorry, but there is nothing in the agreement that confines us to *x* number; that is just your version of it.". . .

Secretary LAIRD. . . . I believe we can tell you exactly what is agreed and what is not.

Senator JACKSON. You see, we have—

Secretary LAIRD. Violations or ambiguous situations would be immediately called to the attention of the Standing Consultative Commission.

Senator JACKSON. I know. But the trouble is that we have nothing but general language when we should have a genuine and accurate bill of particulars. . . .

Secretary LAIRD. Senator Jackson, there is no question that the problem that you point up is one that might solve the definition of the term "significant." I believe that any growth of light missiles, in either diameter or depth, that exceeds 10 to 15 percent would be a violation of the agreement. I believe that that is the manner in which those words

should be read by the United States. I would like to have Paul Nitze comment on that question. He was part of the negotiations. . . .
Mr. NITZE. I do not believe that there is ambiguity as to what is agreed by the two parties. Article 1 makes the most important obligation of both sides crystal clear, and that is that the parties undertake not to start construction of additional fixed land-based intercontinental ballistic launchers after July 1, 1972. Now that is the obligation—
Senator JACKSON. Can we start right there? Can you tell me what those words mean, what you mean by "start construction after July 1"? What constitutes "starting construction"?
Mr. NITZE. This constitutes constructing a silo or a launcher in the field.
Senator JACKSON. This is our version of it.
Mr. NITZE. I think that is—
Senator JACKSON. Where is the bilateral understanding of that? We are dealing with a bilateral agreement. What is so confusing is that on this point alone we have an area of potentially great argument.

I can see what might well happen after July 1. Suppose the Soviets start digging holes during this interim period between now and July, and suppose they have steam shovels out on a site. Does this make it possible for them to go ahead and complete the work? What understanding do we have with the Soviet Union about that?
Mr. NITZE. With respect to that we do have a crystal-clear understanding. It is that after the date of the agreement, of the signing of the agreement, no action would be taken by either side which is in conflict with the agreements.
Senator JACKSON. Yes, but we have no agreement—
Mr. NITZE. Therefore, that would make it improper and a violation for them—
Senator JACKSON. Secretary Nitze, what really constitutes "under construction," and what bilateral understanding do we have about that term?
Mr. NITZE. I think the essential point here is that one could, of course, have an infinite regression where one could say that the meaning of any term depends upon some other term and so forth, and so on.
Senator JACKSON. Yes, but—
Mr. NITZE. But I think that within any rules of clarity as to what the intent of agreement is, this has been done with extreme care.
Senator JACKSON. Let me ask you this. Suppose a constitutent writes to me and says, Senator, I have read through the agreements and I note that there is a specific limitation on the number of operational Y-class submarines permitted, up to sixty-two, and a maximum of forty-four for the United States. It is explicit, it is written right in the

agreement. But, Senator, I do not find anything in the agreement that specifies the number of land-based missiles permitted the Soviet Union as of July 1. How would you answer that letter?

Mr. NITZE. Answer it by saying that the agreement specified that there would be no start of additional numbers, but that it did not provide for a specific limit on the number of launchers. It said that there would be no starts after a date, that was the agreement.

Senator JACKSON. Obviously, if there are no new starts after July 1, there is a definite number of launchers that will be either operational or under construction as of that date. Why is that number not specified in the agreements?

Mr. NITZE. Your question, as I understand it, Mr. Senator, was whether or not there is ambiguity. I think there is no ambiguity even though the agreement does not specify a numerical ceiling.

Senator JACKSON. All you are saying is that there is no ambiguity about the fact that the number is not specified. That is not the point. Without a specific number, there is definitely uncertainty and ambiguity because the Soviets cannot be held to a specific number of ICBM launchers. We think they are limited to 1,618, but we have no formal understanding with them on this point. So you have still not helped me answer my constituent's question.

Secretary LAIRD. The problem that you propose in this letter from your constituent is one that I think can be answered very easily. There is a cutoff completely on the construction of fixed land-based ICBM launchers but there is no cutoff on the construction of the submarines. The reason why a limitation was placed on the submarines is that this is an ongoing program that will go forward, and it is going forward at the present time. At the present time the Soviet Union has in being or under construction approximately forty-three of the Y-class submarines. This particular agreement allows them to move up and to complete sixty-two. So the situation was somewhat different from the arrangement on . . . missiles. There had to be a limitation set here. It was not a cutoff at forty-three and that is the reason that the figures are specified within the agreement.

Senator JACKSON. There is no difference. They agreed to a cutoff of sixty-two on operational Y-class submarines. Why could you not get the Soviet Union to indicate the maximum number of land-based missiles—the cutoff point—that they are permitted under this agreement? . . . How do you answer that?

Secretary LAIRD. I think you answer it the way I have answered it, that we have stopped the construction on the ICBMs whereas there is no stop of construction on submarines. It was necessary to set a limitation on the submarines and this is—

Senator JACKSON. It is also necessary to set a limitation on land-based missiles. You are talking in terms of—
Secretary LAIRD. I am satisfied—
Senator JACKSON (continuing). Of numbers?
Secretary LAIRD (continuing). That we have adequate verification as far as land-based construction is concerned.
Senator JACKSON. What are those numbers? Are they constructing any now?
Secretary LAIRD. Yes, they are.
Senator JACKSON. Have they started any new ones?
Secretary LAIRD. Not for over a year. They have some new silos under construction which I have informed this committee of in numbers. . . .
Senator JACKSON. But, Mr. Secretary, you will agree there is a time lag here. You will not be able to tell this committee on July 1, will you, the exact number of land-based missiles that the Soviet Union has deployed or has under construction?
Secretary LAIRD. Yes, we will be able to give you a very confident estimate at that particular time, but it has to be an estimate. I am satisfied that that estimate will be very nearly exact. . . .

* * *

Senator THURMOND. . . . In 1969, I believe, you testified in support of the Safeguard ABM system and took the position that the Soviet Union, with its program of SS–9 missiles, including qualitative developments, could wipe out our Minuteman missiles in a first strike if they were left unprotected. The Safeguard ABM was contemplated as having at least twelve sites. Now, the question is: Do the 100 ABM launchers permitted by the treaty around one ICBM site provide realistic assurances of sufficient deterrence, in your opinion?
Secretary LAIRD. I believe that a massive attack by the Soviet Union could saturate the system.

I would like to point out that when we were discussing the SS–9 systems back in 1969, if the construction rate had gone forward and there had been no stop in Soviet momentum, you could get yourself in the position where they could have up to 400 or 500 of these large missile systems. That particular momentum is stopped by this agreement, and I think that is important. But I cannot give you the assurance that with 100 interceptors at the ABM site in North Dakota, which is now 90 percent complete, and without the full twelve-site program, you can have the kind of protection which I was talking about in 1969. That is why we are giving up something here. We are giving up the twelve-site program. We are stopping that momentum and we

are stopping the momentum of the Soviet Union in the offensive area at the same time. . . .

Senator THURMOND. Mr. Secretary, since ABM was intended to protect our retaliatory capability, is the treaty a return to what some have called a "balance of terror"?

Secretary LAIRD. Of course, the whole theory of realistic deterrence is to make the use of strategic nuclear weapons a choice that no one would ever make. We want to put the opportunity for making that choice beyond the reason of any country. I am sure that the Soviet Union looks at that particular problem the same way, and that is what we are trying to do here, we are trying to see that nuclear weapons not be used.

* * *

Senator THURMOND. Mr. Secretary, it has been said that the treaty and interim agreement allow the Soviets the advantage in number and the United States an advantage in quality. In light of the present Soviet advantage in payload capacity, is it possible that within five years the combination of improved accuracy and MIRVing would give the Soviets both a qualitative and quantitative advantage over the United States?

Secretary LAIRD. Yes, sir. . . . The situation you mention could only come about, of course, if the United States did not go forward with the programs that we have recommended.

20 JUNE 1972 (AFTERNOON SESSION)

Senator CANNON. Mr. Secretary, I want to pursue the line of questioning that Senator Jackson was having with you a little earlier. At the same time the treaty and the agreements were signed in May, how many land-based ICBMs did the Soviets have completed and how many were there under active construction?. . .

Secretary LAIRD. The total number in being was 1,527, and if you include the number under construction it is 1,618.

Senator CANNON. So the 1,618 includes all that were constructed and under construction?

Secretary LAIRD. That includes ninety-one that are under construction but where construction has not been completed.

Senator CANNON. All right. Have there been any started since May, and up to the present time? This cutoff point is July 1, which is next week.

Secretary LAIRD. We have no evidence of any construction starts since the date that you—

Senator CANNON. As we understand it, then, the numbers that we are talking about that would be limited by the agreement would be the approximate figure of 1,618, to include all of those actually operational as of July 1 and to include all of those that we believe are under construction at that date?

Secretary LAIRD. That is correct.

Senator CANNON. Was this figure explored with the Soviets and were they unwilling to agree? Perhaps I should address this to you, Secretary Nitze. . . .

Mr. NITZE. We had not proposed that to them, Senator. I think the point of the matter is that the Soviet system is quite different from ours. They do not have congressional hearings of this type, and they do not make figures as to their deployed systems available. We do. Therefore, the figures which were the basis of the discussion were basically U.S. figures.

Senator CANNON. But you had to be talking about something with them. You agreed with them, for example, on a figure of sixty-two Y-class submarines, and we know they don't have sixty-two Y-class submarines now, so you certainly had to be talking figures with them.

Mr. NITZE. As Secretary Laird explained earlier, the sixty-two submarines were a ceiling for the future and did not bear upon the number of submarines now operational on their side.

Senator CANNON. Isn't the ICBM agreement a ceiling for the future in that it means a ceiling on all those they have constructed now and all those on which they will have started construction on July 1, because they are not to start any after that time? Therefore, it is a ceiling for the future, isn't it?

Mr. NITZE. As I stated this morning, the interim agreement is specific in that it prohibits new starts after July 1 of fixed, land-based ICBM launchers; and I also explained that there is an understanding between the two sides, which is the documentation, that neither side would take any action contrary to the agreements subsequent to the date of the signing of the agreements.

Senator CANNON. Do the Soviets have any holes that have been dug that are not under active construction at the present time; and, if so, are they included in these totals that you gave?

Secretary LAIRD. These are the totals of those silos that have been constructed or where construction has started. Construction is going forward on every one of the ninety-one silos at the present time.

Senator CANNON. So that under the agreement they would, in your

opinion, be able to go ahead on all ninety-one because they have actually started all prior to July 1?

Secretary LAIRD. That is correct.

* * *

Senator CANNON. How many modern nuclear-powered Y-class submarines do the Soviets have now?

Secretary LAIRD. The estimate which I gave to this committee is . . . a range from forty-one to forty-three, and I come down on the high side of forty-three.

Senator CANNON. That was both under construction and in being?

Secretary LAIRD. That is correct.

Senator CANNON. And approximately how many of those are they building a year?

Secretary LAIRD. I stated in the defense report that they are building at the rate of between nine and ten.

Senator CANNON. So that if they continue at that rate the agreement would really not preempt them from building further Y-class submarines for a period of two and a half to three more years after the completion of these presently under construction?

Secretary LAIRD. Provided that they abide by the other sections of the agreement, that construction could go forward, and I would anticipate that it would. . . .

Senator CANNON. So that based on that continuance they would really only come to their limit under this shipbuilding program roughly about five years from now?

Secretary LAIRD. Without the agreement, I believe that with the momentum which they have going, they could have up to ninety Y-class submarines at the end of the five-year period.

Senator CANNON. They couldn't very well have ninety at the end of the five-year period. Doesn't the record disclose that they have about twenty-three to twenty-five now and about another twenty under construction?

Secretary LAIRD. I am talking about the number that they would have operational and under construction. . . .

Senator CANNON. I was talking about operational. In other words, I was saying that they would reach their operational limit about five years from now based upon your present forecast.

Secretary LAIRD. That is about right. That does not compare with the forty-three figure we used earlier in our exchange, and I wanted to make sure that was understood.

Senator CANNON. I understand that. The forty-three figure included those under construction as well as operational.
Secretary LAIRD. That is correct. And the ninety figure also includes that.
Senator CANNON. Right; and the operational figure at the present time would be roughly somewhere in the order of twenty to twenty-five; is that correct, Admiral?
Admiral MOORER. Yes, sir. . . .
Senator CANNON. So we really won't know anything about their intentions to live up to the agreement with respect to the submarines for a period of several years off in the future.
Secretary LAIRD. We would know as soon as construction started on the sixty-third submarine. I agree with you that they could move forward provided that they did follow the other restraints that are in the offensive agreement and that would have to do with the dismantling of other missile launchers.

* * *

The CHAIRMAN [Senator Stennis]. As much as you can in open session, give us your conclusion about this National Command Authority—not just your recommendation now, but your reasoning that led you to this recommendation. I think it would be good if you could discuss this [in] open session.
Admiral MOORER. The Joint Chiefs of Staff have always recommended that we construct an ABM system to protect the National Command Authority, because we think that the decision-making process which selects the action to be taken and transmits this action to the operating forces is a very vital part of the deterrence package. Also, we believe that if the other side feels that this is a vulnerable part of the overall deterrence package which contains the command and control system plus the executing forces, then that in itself weakens the deterrent.

We have confidence that the operating forces can carry out their mission provided they get the correct instructions in a timely manner. Consequently, we feel that the decision-making process must be survivable.
The CHAIRMAN. Even though you had recommended this ABM here in Washington before, I do not remember that you pressed forth so much. Does it have then an added significance in view of the fact that we are going to have this treaty? Does the treaty give added importance to this ABM?
Admiral MOORER. In my view, it does, sir, because here again I think that it is important to use the part of the ABM capability that is allowed

by the proposed treaty to provide protection to the decision-making process.

The CHAIRMAN. Something has been said to the effect that this was to protect the people here in Washington, including the Congress, as contrasted to those who live out in other areas of the country. I think I understand what you mean; you are not thinking in terms of individuals here, you are thinking about the command position and the responsible persons who have to make those commands. Is that right?

Admiral MOORER. That is right. . . .

The CHAIRMAN. And that judgment has to be exercised and the command has to be given by someone.

Admiral MOORER. And it must be exercised, sir, in a very short time, and consequently we must give it maximum survivability.

* * *

Senator SYMINGTON. . . . I have asked about a mobile ICBM, wasn't quite clear this morning what happened to our mobile ICBM. Are the Russians going to be allowed to produce as many mobile ICBMS as they want?. . .

Secretary LAIRD. We have stated unilaterally our position. We would not consider this as consistent with the objectives of the agreement. This, however, is the unilateral declaration which I read to you this morning.

Senator SYMINGTON. Mr. Secretary, the reason I ask—for years I have been emphasizing that instead of building these gigantic expensive fixed systems we could build some mobile ICBMS. What I have seen in the way of what the Soviets have been doing—pictures—makes me believe they have been moving this way. We can say unilaterally, but was there any agreement they could not build mobile ICBMS?—that is all I am asking.

Secretary LAIRD. No, there is not a bilateral agreement with the Soviet Union. . . .

* * *

Senator SYMINGTON. Admiral, I would ask, do you believe the Soviets—based on your knowledge and that assurance of Brezhnev, which is one of the chief reasons to ask for these billions more of the taxpayers' money—will pursue mobile ICBMS?

Admiral MOORER. They have experimented in the past, Senator Symington. At the moment we do not have any indications that they are moving forward in a program of this kind. As you know, they have made field-type missiles, which are much smaller and much lighter. I personally think a mobile ICBM—the weight and the size and so on—would be a difficult thing to move around undetected.

Senator SYMINGTON. You do not think they plan to do it?
Secretary LAIRD. Our recommendations to you—
Admiral MOORER. No.
Secretary LAIRD [continuing]. On the Trident and B–1 . . . are based upon their not going forward with the mobile ICBM system.
Senator SYMINGTON. Then what reason did they give you for not including a mobile ICBM?
Secretary LAIRD. They wanted to keep that option open.
Senator SYMINGTON. I am surprised neither you nor the Chairman of the Joint Chiefs believe they are going ahead with it. Why should they make the exception if they didn't intend to go ahead with it?
Secretary LAIRD. I think you will have to address that to the Soviet Union. It is possible they were concerned that a ban on mobile ICBMS might ultimately interfere with their mobile IRBM program.
Senator JACKSON. . . . Mr. Secretary, first of all I want to ask some questions here on the subject of Soviet momentum, which is the basic premise of the administration's position, as I understand it.

The basic position of the administration relates to the situation that allegedly we would have had to face during the five-year period of the offensive agreement. This situation is said to result from the momentum that the Soviets have built up in turning out both land-based and sea-based strategic missiles. You say you have applied a brake to this momentum in Soviet strategic missile deployments.

But, does this really apply to the Soviet Y-class submarines? Under the agreement, the Soviets can have sixty-two operational Y-class submarines. But without this agreement, within five years the Soviets probably would not have had more than about sixty-five such submarines operational. I base this on the twenty to twenty-five operational today, and the forty that they could build over the next five years, for a total of sixty-five. And I would also point out, as I understand it, that within the terms of the agreement, the Soviets could have additional Y-class submarines in the pipeline, that is, under construction though not operational. Is that permitted under the agreement? Secretary Nitze, would you want to comment?
Mr. NITZE. . . . The Soviets may have no more than sixty-two modern submarines operational. In order to reach that number, and the limit of 950 ballistic missile launchers on submarines, they must dismantle the existing 209 older ICBM launchers.
Senator JACKSON. My point is that with or without this agreement you could have a situation where the Soviets have sixty-two Y-class submarines operational, and still have an additional number in the pipeline, that is, at some stage of construction. So, I must question whether you have really slowed down Soviet submarine momentum, because the

total number operational at the end of five years seems to be about the same—somewhere between sixty-two and sixty-five—with or without the agreement.

Let me raise another point about Soviet momentum. If you assume—and it seems to be a valid assumption—that the Soviets will retrofit some of their land-based missile forces, particularly the SS–9s, with an even larger booster that we might call the SS–16—is that, incidentally, the appropriate designation for the new, larger missile?

Secretary LAIRD. We do not have an appropriate designation.

Senator JACKSON. This is just for purposes of discussion. We have observed twenty-five new silos which are apparently designed to house a follow-on to the SS–9, a new missile which I am referring to as the SS–16.

Secretary LAIRD. Quite frankly, we have not seen the missile deployed in any of those silos.

Senator JACKSON. But we have been observing some of the test areas. And we have seen twenty-five new silos; is that right?

Secretary LAIRD. Yes.

Senator JACKSON. It is 288 of the SS–9s plus this new development of twenty-five silos. That is where we get the 313 figure for heavy missiles we are kicking around, is it not? I think that is correct—288 SS–9s and twenty-five of the new silos. I have put an SS–16 designation on this new missile for convenience. In any case, if the Soviets are going to retrofit—and there is every indication they will—then it seems to me that the momentum here in terms of numbers is not what it appears in some of the administration testimony and statements that have been made. If the Soviets concentrate on retrofitting they can improve their land-based force without having more than 1,618 land-based missiles. Is that not correct?

Secretary LAIRD. Our national technical means have established that the Soviets have 288 modern heavy ICBMS operational and twenty-five under construction.

Senator JACKSON. I think this is a very important point. We have been told over and over again that the Soviets would have had many more submarines than they can have under this agreement as well as many more land-based missiles. But as I study this I am becoming convinced that this assertion doesn't stand up. I think that point needs to be made. I am delighted that you concur in this because I have not been able to find a justification for administration statements that projected, in the absence of an agreement, more than sixty-two operational Y-class submarines at the end of five years, and which have projected many more land-based launchers as well.

Secretary LAIRD. They can have 2,359 launchers.

Senator JACKSON. Of what kind?
Secretary LAIRD. They can go to 950 launchers on the submarines. That would limit them to 1,096 for light ICBM launchers that are not replaceable with SLBM launchers. It would also limit them to 313 large ballistic missile launchers, the operational and under construction. No bilateral limit on "heavy" missiles.
Senator JACKSON. Yes. But we will get to those other numbers later, because the 313 figure is our own and does not represent a bilateral understanding as to the limit on Soviet "heavy" ballistic missile launchers. Is that correct?
Secretary LAIRD. We can read the language that applies. . . .
Senator JACKSON. You would be safe in answering my question "yes," because I cannot find anyplace where there is a bilateral agreement that 313 is the number of heavy missiles allowed to the Soviets.

* * *

Mr. NITZE. The understanding is perfectly specific that Article 1 is agreed between the parties, and Article 1 is that there will be no new starts after a specific date.
Senator JACKSON. All right.
Mr. NITZE. That is the agreement. The agreement is not that there will not be more than 313.
Senator JACKSON. That does not answer my question.
Mr. NITZE. Three hundred and thirteen is our estimate of the number of large missiles which are today operational and under construction, which were operational and under construction as of the date of the agreement, and we do have confidence in our national means of verification.

I think the possibility of error in that is very small indeed and is not significant in the light of this agreement. So the issue is the degree of confidence we have in our national means of verification. I think that confidence is high.
Senator JACKSON. . . . I must say I am just a country lawyer, but there is an elementary rule of contract law that an agreement, to be valid between the parties, must be agreed to bilaterally and that there must be consideration.
Mr. NITZE. There is complete bilateral understanding as to the agreement. The agreement is that there will be no new starts.
Senator JACKSON. That answers one question: There is an agreement that there will be no new starts. You say there is no misunderstanding on that. I think I can understand that. But my question is, what about the number of missiles that have been started? What are the totals? . . .

Secretary LAIRD. Senator Jackson, I think that Secretary Nitze has answered that question as far as the agreement is concerned. It depends entirely on our verification capability. We feel that we have an adequate verification capability and we feel that we can police this agreement as far as no new starts are concerned in the ICBM field.
Senator JACKSON. Mr. Secretary, how are you going to enforce, by our own verification means, a number of 1,618, if you cannot point to any written document which says that the Russians have agreed to that number? What is your answer?
Secretary LAIRD. I am confident that that number is correct.
Senator JACKSON. It may be correct to us, sir, but is it correct to the Russians? That is what I am asking. It is that simple. What is your answer, yes or no?
Secretary LAIRD. As far as violation is concerned, it is sufficient as far as I am concerned.

* * *

The CHAIRMAN. . . . I made a memo to myself when Senator Jackson was asking some very good questions about the acceptance of your numbers about what you have learned with reference to the land-based missiles. Now, had you verified those numbers and found them to be the same or approximately the same?
Secretary LAIRD. That is correct.
The CHAIRMAN. All right. That brings me to my real question. If this treaty is adopted, you will keep making the verifications, of course.
Secretary LAIRD. That is correct.
The CHAIRMAN. If they had disclosed that they were not correct, or in this agreement they had not come clean with you about this matter, even though they did not give you any numbers, and you found it to be in error, would you consider the agreement abrogated?
Secretary LAIRD. The provisions of the agreement regarding violations would come into effect and the proper procedures would be followed by our government.
Senator JACKSON. What is that?
Secretary LAIRD. We would first make a complaint and put our evidence before the Standing Consultative Commission.
Senator JACKSON. Then we get into the numbers game again.
The CHAIRMAN. But, as I understand, you relied on your information you had through your own instruments, and did they know you relied on that?
Secretary LAIRD. Yes, they did.
The CHAIRMAN. Did they know the number that you had in mind?

Secretary LAIRD. Yes, they did.
The CHAIRMAN. So if you show a substantial discrepancy from that number now, you will consider them in violation?
Secretary LAIRD. That is right; I would.

22 JUNE 1972 (AFTERNOON SESSION)

The CHAIRMAN [Senator Stennis]. Dr. Foster, . . . talking about capabilities this morning, and what the United States has and what Russia has and what they may have five years from now, I just want to go back to a fundamental, overall picture. Will we have this second strike capability five years from now to the extent that we could destroy Russia, if that were thought to be necessary?
Dr. [John S.] FOSTER [Director, Defense Research and Engineering]. Mr. Chairman, it is Secretary Laird's view and certainly my view that in the face of the Soviet technological effort and the deployments that are still permitted under SALT, if the United States were not to continue with its strategic program as requested in the President's budget, and new programs that may be required in the future, we wouldn't have the capability.

* * *

Senator JACKSON. . . . What I can't, Mr. Chairman, understand is that, while obviously we don't know what the intentions of the Soviet Union happen to be at any one given time, I think one can ask questions about why this tremendous yield, if they are building only for a second strike.

As I understand the picture, any objective group of scientists in the nuclear field, looking at the Soviet stockpile and given certain accuracy capabilities, would have to say that today Minuteman is in peril, if they achieve an accuracy that would give them that ability to hit Minuteman, considering the numbers of warheads they have available; is that not correct?
Dr. FOSTER. Yes, sir.
Senator JACKSON. . . . Assuming the same stockpile right now, what kind of CEP would the Soviets have to achieve in order to threaten Minuteman? You know we went through this exercise on ABM. . . .
Dr. FOSTER. Today the Minuteman force can survive in sufficient numbers an all-out attack, in place, from land-based strategic forces of the Soviet Union.
Senator JACKSON. What kind of CEP are you giving them?
Dr. FOSTER. I am assuming that the SS–9s have accuracy between [deleted] that the SS–11s have something like perhaps [deleted]. That still

leaves a significant number of Minutemen adequate for the deterrent capability.

Senator JACKSON. But suppose we give them our accuracy, which is [deleted], then give us the result?

Dr. FOSTER. If the Soviets had the accuracy that we believe we have in Minuteman, then the Minuteman force would be at risk.

Senator JACKSON. You wouldn't really have a credible response capability in that set of circumstances?

Dr. FOSTER. That's correct.

Senator JACKSON. I am supposing that we give to them our accuracy; this is the exercise we ran before, you remember?

Dr. FOSTER. That is why I was very careful to point out a concern that the Department of Defense has, and that is that if the Soviets were simply to increase the accuracy of their present ICBM force to [deleted], then the number of surviving Minutemen would not constitute a deterrent capability to the Soviet Union. . . . So it has nothing to do with the MIRVing aspect. The addition of MIRV to the Soviet ICBM force would result in fewer ICBM launchers required to place the Minuteman force at risk.

* * *

Dr. FOSTER. . . . We do have a problem with regard to the survivability of the Minuteman force, and the options are more limited than they were before; but that is the price that we have chosen to pay in order to put an upper limit on the total raw strategic power in the Soviet ICBMS. Our situation is simply a consequence of the fact that since 1966 the U.S. momentum in strategic systems, in retrospect, appears to some to have been too low. Nevertheless, the United States consciously set it that way, and that has made it more difficult for our negotiators. Had they had more to trade, they perhaps could have gotten a better deal; but I believe with what they had available, the negotiators did a pretty good job for the United States.

* * *

Senator JACKSON. . . . I think we made a mistake in trying to constantly confine the meaning of nuclear weapons to action-reaction situations. That is not the real world. What I see is that in the situation that I have outlined here, that if the Soviets end up with an ability to end the credibility of Minuteman and of our bomber force, that leaves us only with the sea force. What would an American president do if he was told that the bomber force and the Minuteman force had been knocked out totally? Would an American president in that situation, with the Rus-

sians having 1,100 SS–11s available, would the American president then proceed to order the destruction of Soviet cities when he is told that you are going to wipe out human life in North America? I don't think so. . . . So, it seems to me that in our effort to provide for our security here we have to think in terms of what these weapons mean diplomatically in the kind of foreign policy the adversary is going to pursue.

28 JUNE 1972 (MORNING SESSION)

The CHAIRMAN [Senator Stennis]. . . . We are glad to have with us this morning the members of the U.S. SALT delegation who have done the negotiating over the last two and a half years at Helsinki and Vienna. The primary spokesman will be Ambassador Gerard C. Smith, whose statement we received last night. We are also glad to have with us Mr. Paul Nitze and Gen. Royal B. Allison, the members of the delegation from the Department of Defense, and Ambassador Graham J. Parsons, the State Department representative. Also present is Mr. Raymond Garthoff of the delegation staff.

* * *

Mr. SMITH. . . . In assessing the agreements, the basic question is: Would not the United States be better off with them than without them? This question requires comparing the strategic prospects under the agreements with the prospects that would exist in their absence. Another way of putting the question is to ask how these agreements meet the strategic concerns that have existed in this country in the past few years.

There were concerns about the dangers involved in a large, costly, destabilizing ABM competition. Under the terms of the ABM treaty, those concerns should be sharply reduced if not entirely eliminated.

There was concern about the threat to our nuclear deterrent's high assurance of capability to penetrate Soviet defenses in a retaliatory strike. This concern rested not only on the prospect of large-scale Soviet ABM deployments, but also on the possibility of upgrade of Soviet SAM systems to give them an ABM capability. Under the ABM treaty the Soviets will take commitments not to deploy a widespread ABM system and not to upgrade SAMS, and to have only 200 ABMS. U.S. penetration capability can thus be clearly assured.

There was concern about the continuing growth in the numbers of Soviet ICBMS, especially the SS–9. Under the interim agreement the U.S.S.R. is committed not to start any additional ICBMS and is limited to

a number of SS–9s well below levels which seemed likely several years ago.

There was concern about the overall growth of the aggregate number of Soviet strategic launchers, both land- and sea-based. The growth of that aggregate total will be stopped under the interim agreement.

There was concern that our national capabilities to keep informed about Soviet deployments might, by adversary action, be rendered ineffective. In the ABM treaty the Soviet Union has taken a landmark commitment not to interfere with our national means of verification.

These concerns have been met without any restrictions being placed on ongoing or programed U.S. strategic offensive programs.

Mr. Chairman, I urge this committee to give favorable consideration to these two agreements. I believe they are in the interest of the United States.

I have spoken of the strategic concerns that exist in this country that are met by these agreements. Those are achievements of no small magnitude. It does not lessen their importance to say that not every U.S. concern has been met. I can assure the members of this committee that it is clear from the negotiations that not every Soviet concern has been met. That is a principal reason why the interim agreement is temporary.

We are, however, better off with the interim agreement in force, while we negotiate a comprehensive offensive limitation agreement.

* * *

Senator SMITH. Ambassador Smith, you state in your statement that there will be greater deterrence at less cost. Would you elaborate a bit on that, under the terms of the treaty?

Mr. SMITH. Yes. To the extent, Senator Smith, that offensive missiles have a challenge in the form of ABM systems that they would have to penetrate, then you need many more, and perhaps more sophisticated, offensive weapons than if you are facing a future in which there is only a small ABM screen through which they have to penetrate. And I think it is clear that the value of each offensive missile has gone up because it does not have to go through a screen of defensive missiles. This is what Dr. Kissinger was referring to, I think, in a recent press conference where he said they would get a free ride.

* * *

Senator JACKSON. What is the maximum number of Y-class submarines that the Soviet Union is permitted to have at sea or operational on the last day of the five-year period of the interim agreement?

Mr. SMITH. Sixty-two.
Senator JACKSON. What is the maximum number of Y-class submarines that the Soviet Union is permitted to have under construction (as replacements for Y-class submarines produced earlier) on the last day of the five-year period of the interim agreement?
Mr. SMITH. There is no formal agreement on this, but all of them must be replacements when they enter their sea trials.
Senator JACKSON. Could they have, for example, seventeen?
Mr. SMITH. If they were for replacement under agreed procedures, yes.
Senator JACKSON. In the absence of a SALT agreement covering submarine production, and assuming that the Soviets continue their present deployment rate for the next five years, what is the maximum of Y-class submarines that they could have either operational or under construction?
Mr. SMITH. The calculations that I have done on that indicate that they could have sixty-eight operational and at least sixteen under construction, for a total of at least eighty-four.

I would point out, Senator, however, that your question says at the present rate of deployment. It seems to me that absent this agreement there would be nothing to stop them from increasing their rate.

* * *

General ALLISON. Senator, I was just going to observe to Ambassador Smith, and he has asked me to respond, my observation as relates to the answer in the previous question. The estimate of eighty-four, while certainly in the range of estimates, is not in my opinion necessarily the highest level one might see in the estimate. I think it may go as high as eighty-eight. That, of course, is four submarines' difference, and it is a considerable element of force. . . .
Senator JACKSON. It seems to me that we get back to the difference between the two figures, which leads me directly to my next question. Do you agree with the claim that the interim agreement halts the momentum of the Soviet SLBM construction program over the next five years?
Mr. SMITH. I think it does.
Senator JACKSON. I am talking about submarine construction. . . . I am asking whether there is anything in this agreement which is actually going to slow down the momentum of their construction. That is the key thing. And, if so, by how many boats?
Mr. SMITH. It certainly puts a limit on their construction. Now, we cannot assume that they would not have changed their construction rate. I think the figure I gave you at the start indicated they could have a higher rate, leading to a higher number than sixty-two.

Senator JACKSON. One of the main arguments of the administration is that Soviet momentum has been slowed. Obviously I am directing my questions to that point. By how much have you slowed it down?

Mr. SMITH. I do not think you can answer that because you do not know—

Senator JACKSON. If you do not know by how much their momentum has been slowed, how can you claim that it has been slowed at all?

Mr. SMITH. Because you know it is not going to go above a certain level, otherwise it could not—

Senator JACKSON. That is not an answer. You certainly have some estimates as to the difference in the situation with this agreement and without this agreement. . . .

Mr. SMITH. Until one can know what they actually would have done absent an agreement, I do not think you can get a specific answer to that question.

Senator JACKSON. What was your working estimate? You had one, surely?

Mr. SMITH. We were thinking in terms of eighty or ninety boats.

Senator JACKSON. Operational?

Mr. SMITH. Operational and under construction. . . .

Senator JACKSON. How does the no-agreement estimate at a total of eighty-four submarines, operational and under construction, compare with what the situation will be under the agreement?

Mr. SMITH. They can only have sixty-two operational, and those—

Senator JACKSON. How many can they have under construction?

Mr. SMITH (continuing). Boats with which they can replace those that are operational.

Senator JACKSON. I know, but there is no limit on what they can have under construction under the terms of the agreement, is that not correct?

Mr. SMITH. If they are for replacement under agreed procedures.

Senator JACKSON. That is what I am saying.

Mr. SMITH. There is no limit on the number we can have.

Senator JACKSON. How does what they do under this agreement differ from what they would have had in the absence of an agreement?

Mr. SMITH. I think, Senator, the question is, "Did you get a degree of certainty where you had an uncertainty before?" I think we did.

Senator JACKSON. That is not the same as stopping the momentum.

Mr. SMITH. I think it is.

Senator JACKSON. I am only addressing myself to the position taken by the administration. So far you have not shown that the numbers would be substantially different in 1977 because of this agreement. Under this agreement, constructing Y-class submarines beyond the sixty-two op-

erational is perfectly permissible, if the additional submarines are designated as replacements.

Mr. SMITH. Senator, you should also keep in mind the price that they will have to pay if they want to get up to these numbers; without the agreement they would not have to replace. Under the agreement they are going to have to go in for a substantial reduction program, if they want to build up to sixty-two.

* * *

Senator JACKSON. The Soviets are permitted, according to our understanding, 1,618 land-based ICBM silos under the interim agreement. How many of these are they permitted to retrofit under the terms of this agreement?

Mr. SMITH. Senator, under the terms of the agreement there is no permitted level. There is a commitment not to build any more. . . . There is no limitation on retrofitting of existing launchers if they do not in the process convert light missiles into heavy missiles or older missiles into modern missiles.

Senator JACKSON. But we do not have a bilateral understanding of the number of heavy missiles permitted. And is it not also the case that the Soviets can retrofit all 1,618 of their land-based ICBM launchers?

Mr. SMITH. They can and so can we. We can retrofit our missiles and we are in the process, as you know, of making a very substantial increase in our missiles. Both sides wanted to retain the right to modernize.

Senator JACKSON. The largest part of the Soviet land-based ICBM deployment consists of SS–11 silos. If the Soviets were to retrofit their SS–11 silos with a new missile, how much could they increase the volume of those silos?

Mr. SMITH. Senator, to give you a precise answer I would like to do this arithmetic and submit that for the record. I cannot do this calculation right now.

Senator JACKSON. General Allison, can you respond to that?

General ALLISON. I note that in the question, the word "volume" is used. I cannot respond precisely, but it seems to me that in the documentation provided by the President, the Secretary of State, the matter of increase in dimensions of silos is addressed.

Senator JACKSON. Well, is it not a fact that they could increase the volume of those silos by about 50 percent? You see, we use the 10 to 15 percent figure to refer to the dimensions—length and diameter—of the silo. But when the length and the diameter of a cylinder are increased by 15 percent, the volume is increased by about 50 percent, in fact, by 52 percent I believe. . . . Mr. Nitze, do you have any comment on it?

Mr. NITZE. . . . The understanding is that there will be no significant increase in the present dimensions of land-based ICBM silos. It was also agreed that significant means no greater than 10 to 15 percent. If one were to take the worst case, that [is,] if the diameter were increased by 15 percent and the depth were increased by 15 percent, why then certainly one approaches approximately 50 percent.

Senator JACKSON. I was trying to find out what is permitted. And it is around 50 percent?

Mr. NITZE. Yes, I think that is the worst case. Such arithmetic would be correct if both the depth and the diameter were increased by 15 percent. However, the background to the negotiations makes it clear that an increase of up to 15 percent would be permitted in only one dimension (or possibly a combination of two dimensions), not in both depth and diameter. . . . The interim agreement does not have a provision with respect to the volume of the missiles that are permitted, but we did enter into the record a unilateral statement in which we said that the United States would consider an increase in volume, any significant increase in the volume, of the largest light ICBM now operational on either side would convert such a missile from the category of light to heavy.

Senator JACKSON. Secretary Nitze, if the Soviets were to enlarge their silos in accordance with the permissible allowance, that is, by about 50 percent, could they not then put into those silos missiles with that increased volume?

Mr. NITZE. I think that is a rough rule of thumb that is probably correct. However, any such large increase in volume would conflict with the U.S. unilateral statement.

28 JUNE 1972 (AFTERNOON SESSION)

Senator JACKSON. Mr. Ambassador, . . . would you tell the committee how many ballistic missile-carrying diesel submarines the Soviets can build?

Mr. SMITH. I don't know.

Senator JACKSON. What does the interim agreement permit?

Mr. SMITH. The treaty does not limit the construction of their diesel boats or ours.

Senator JACKSON. The Soviets know that we are not going to build diesel-powered submarines, Mr. Ambassador.

Mr. SMITH. And I doubt that they will build diesel submarines in this day and age.

Senator JACKSON. [They] are completely omitted.

Mr. SMITH. Omitted unless a modern missile is put in them.

Senator JACKSON. What do you mean by "modern"? The G-class submarine carries a ballistic missile with a 700-mile range. That is permitted, isn't it?
Mr. SMITH. Yes, but if they put a missile of long range on a G boat, it would have to count—
Senator JACKSON. I didn't put it that way.
Mr. SMITH. I referred to a modern missile. I don't consider a 700- or 400-mile SLBM a modern missile.
Senator JACKSON. A ballistic missile with a 700-mile range can reach the population centers of the United States along our coast. Why isn't the production of additional missiles of this range prohibited?
Mr. SMITH. Why didn't we prohibit what, the new production?
Senator JACKSON. No. Restrict the production of such missiles and restrict the production of new G-class submarines. They have the option of trading in the G class or the SS-7s and -8s for new SLBMS, as I understand it.
Mr. SMITH. They cannot turn in a launcher on a G boat, unless it is a modern missile launcher.
Senator JACKSON. But in any event—
Mr. SMITH. I think that is probably to our interest that they would have to destroy SS-7s and -8s rather than use class G launchers as trade-ins.
Senator JACKSON. Why didn't we restrict the deployment of G-class subs?
Mr. SMITH. Senator, we are talking here about a freeze, a temporary freeze, and we are talking about central modern strategic systems. It seems to me your point is why didn't we prohibit deployment of a relatively old class of diesel boats? It is partially answered by the fact that they are not central strategic systems. I look on them more as—
Senator JACKSON. Isn't it a fact that this is one of the last things we caved in on? Now, we caved in on a lot of things, but isn't it a fact that this was one of the last? Unfortunately, the press was given a confused picture. The *New York Times* and *Time* magazine—even the majority leader of the Senate, for that matter—were given erroneous information on the number of Y-class submarines the Soviets were permitted under this agreement. The *New York Times* printed figures showing, I think, forty-three for the Soviet Union and forty-two for the United States. I believe those were the figures. And some of us had to work hard to point out that, in fact, the Soviets were entitled to as many as sixty-two operational Y-class submarines, plus a potentially unlimited number of the G-class submarines.
Mr. SMITH. The question of what would constitute the submarine freeze was decided at Moscow.

Senator JACKSON. And just before the signing, it was agreed to let the Soviets retain all their G-class submarines, in addition to the sixty-two Y-class submarines they might have operational. And, in effect, it was agreed to allow the Soviets the right to build an unlimited number of G-class submarines.

Mr. SMITH. I think the alternative, Senator, would have been to permit them to trade in an old G missile launcher for a modern Y missile, so I would say a good case could be made for that. It would be better—

Senator JACKSON. I don't understand your answer. Why did the U.S. negotiators cave in at the last minute and allow the Soviets these additional G-class submarines?

Mr. SMITH. I don't think the word "caved in" actually describes the negotiating process. I am merely suggesting—

Senator JACKSON. You had a target date, didn't you?

Mr. SMITH. I had no such target date, no.

Senator JACKSON. Perhaps you didn't. Did you negotiate the provisions regarding the Y-class and G-class submarines?

Mr. SMITH. There was negotiation about the subs at Helsinki. There was negotiation about them in Vienna. The final arrangement was negotiated in Moscow.

Senator JACKSON. Did you have a deadline in Moscow?

Mr. SMITH. No, sir. I was not in Moscow until the papers were signed.

Senator JACKSON. Well, did you negotiate the provisions having to do with the G-class submarines?

Mr. SMITH. No. I was consulted about it. I was not physically—

Senator JACKSON. Who negotiated that?

Mr. Smith. The people in the White House party.

* * *

Senator JACKSON. Does the interim agreement permit the United States to substitute submarine-launched ballistic missiles for Minuteman?

Mr. SMITH. No, sir.

Senator JACKSON. Does the agreement permit us to harden our Minuteman force by deploying it in hard-rock silos?

Mr. SMITH. It permits us to harden Minuteman but it does not permit relocation. We can harden them in place but not by relocating them.

Senator JACKSON. So the answer to my question specifically—the answer is "No"?

Mr. SMITH. That is right. It is very important, we felt, not to have relocation of ICBM silos permitted that would make the verification problem of going from light to heavy missiles more difficult.

Senator JACKSON. In October 1970, I asked you what options would be

open to the United States if the Soviets, without adding to their land-based missile force, improved it qualitatively so it threatened the survival of Minuteman, and you replied, and I quote, "You can harden to a certain extent. You can under the present proposal put in as many as 250 large missiles of any sort you like under any conditions of hardening you like. You can also become less vulnerable by switching to some form of seaborne missile systems."

Now, in view of the fact that the right to deploy credible hard point defenses was given up some time ago, and we later gave up the right to deploy 250 large hardened missiles or to deploy a seaborne missile system, or, by a unilateral declaration, to deploy land-mobile ICBMS, how are we to defend the Minuteman force from an upgraded Soviet offensive force?

Mr. SMITH. On that date, October 1970, I take it we were talking then about a comprehensive agreement, both offensive and defensive. Since then we, as you know, in May of 1971, changed the negotiating context and we have been negotiating for an ABM treaty and a freeze on certain offensive weapons.

It seems to me in the context of this freeze we can meet your point by hardening, which we are doing; we can deploy larger Minuteman, which we are doing; we can deploy them as large as an SS–11, for example, which is very substantially larger than the Minuteman III. This is a problem that we certainly will want to consider in the follow-on negotiations, which I hope will start soon. It seems to me one further solution, there may be others, is the possibility of reductions of ICBMS.

Senator JACKSON. My question was in the context of how to protect Minuteman. In fact, this is one of the major issues: whether, under the treaty and under the interim agreement, we can have a survivable and therefore a credible strategic deterrent. The survivability of Minuteman lies in one of three courses: (1) an active ABM defense; (2) a passive defense in the form of truly effective hardening [of] Minuteman silos; and (3) moving the force to sea.

Under these agreements, all three we have denied to us. Yet these were the alternatives you presented to me in October 1970, as ways of protecting Minuteman or its equivalent—especially the option of going to sea.

* * *

Mr. SMITH. I would suggest that the fact that the Minuteman would not have to penetrate anything but a very small number of ABMS sharply increases the value of each Minuteman; that in itself is a way of upgrading the survivable Minuteman force. In addition to that we

are hardening, as you know, Minuteman. In addition to that, if you want to add more MIRVs to Minuteman you make the value of each surviving missile greater. In addition to that, I suggested in a follow-on negotiation we could go in, hopefully, for a program of reductions. . . .

Senator JACKSON. Under this agreement, do you think that if the Soviets take maximum advantage of the provisions of the agreement, that the United States can retain a survivable Minuteman force against a first strike?

Mr. SMITH. In what time period?

Senator JACKSON. Within the agreement five-year time frame.

Mr. SMITH. I am quite sure of that, yes.

Senator JACKSON. General Allison, do you agree with that statement?

General ALLISON. I think a very meaningful percentage of Minuteman can survive, but I would like to expand on that if I may just slightly.

Senator JACKSON. Could you give me an indication of what you mean by meaningful?

General ALLISON. I would prefer not to attempt to put a numerical figure on it because I don't think it will improve my answer.

I do believe, Senator Jackson, that when one talks about survival of a deterrent one should not identify solely one element of the deterrent force. I think to talk about the vulnerability of Minuteman alone is not providing—

Senator JACKSON. Let's not stray from the subject. The administration can't have it both ways, General. You know the administration argument for ABM: simply put, 420 SS-9s with three warheads each, that is 1,260 warheads of five megatons each, with an accuracy [of a quarter of a mile]. Now, the administration argued that an ABM was needed, since 5 percent of Minuteman surviving would not constitute a credible force.

Is 5 percent of Minuteman a credible force? Do you subscribe to that formula or do you disagree with it?

General ALLISON. Fifty surviving MIRVed Minuteman can be a meaningful addition to the rest of the strategic force.

Senator JACKSON. Is it credible?

General ALLISON. Is our total deterrent posture credible? Is that the question?

Senator JACKSON. No. The question is whether 5 percent of the Minuteman surviving is credible. Now, if 5 percent of Minuteman is credible in 1972 when the administration is defending the SALT agreements, why was it not also credible in 1969 when the administration was defending ABM?

General ALLISON. Senator Jackson, I thought I was responding to your figure, and you asked me if it is a credible force. I was remarking that

I also thought you were talking about the deterrent posture of the United States, and that in addition to the other forces we have certainly increased the credibility of our deterrent.

* * *

Senator JACKSON. But you are telling this committee that within the five-year life of the interim agreement the Soviets will not have the ability to knock out 95 percent of the Minuteman force.

Mr. SMITH. That would be my personal judgment; yes.

Senator JACKSON. Within this five-year time frame. Do you concur in that, General Allison?

General ALLISON. Senator Jackson, to make an estimate of a percentage such as this without examining it very thoroughly, I find it extremely difficult. . . .

You are asking me to make a judgment as to how the Soviet strategist will apply his force; and implicit in the question, it seems to me, is the estimate that all the Soviet force is going to be focused on striking one element of our strategic force and thus making it a very vulnerable force. I, on the other hand, think that the Soviet would not devote his entire force to that kind of attack. That is an opinion, Senator, no more, no less. But I don't think his strategist would set out to do that with the force they have in the time period.

Senator JACKSON. Under this agreement must they use their entire ICBM force to attack our ICBM force? To knock out?

General ALLISON. Until they develop and deploy things they do not now have, yes, sir, they would.

Senator JACKSON. Do you think they are unable to deploy the things they do not now have within this five-year time frame? Surely you must have thought about this.

General ALLISON. Surely, yes, sir, I have thought about it. Yes, they can develop things they do not now have. It would be my estimate, however—my speculation—that they would not develop and deploy MIRVS on all their SS–9s and deploy new systems with the precise accuracies I think are inherent in your question, sir.

Senator JACKSON. Can you assure the committee that under the permissible limits, the Soviets will not be able to get a force capable of knocking out 95 percent of Minuteman? Obviously you had to consider this when you recommended approval of the agreements to the Joint Chiefs.

General ALLISON. It seems to me that the question is not simply of knocking out the Minuteman force but—if I may repeat—it is the question I thought I was answering; that is, the stability of the deterrent.

* * *

General ALLISON. I think there is a point I would like the committee to know my view on, and that is all of these things were certainly taken into account in my mind as I worked on these negotiations, and my views are well known to the Joint Chiefs of Staff; that is, that focusing attention on one element of the force—Minuteman—and focusing attention on the survivability or vulnerability of Minuteman is not a sound approach to a view of what we are doing in strategic arms or a view of strategy; and I wanted you to know, Senator Jackson, I have made that very statement to those I report to.

* * *

Senator JACKSON. What is your judgment as to the number of Minuteman that would have to survive, the numbers that have to survive in order to be credible?

Mr. NITZE. I don't believe it is possible to put a specific figure on that.

Senator JACKSON. I mean round figures.

Mr. NITZE. It is a continuing function. The more that survive the more credible it is.

Senator JACKSON. What is the minimum?

Mr. NITZE. I never heard anybody discuss a figure less than fifty.

Senator JACKSON. I have never even heard of fifty being considered credible.

Mr. NITZE. As a component of your overall surviving force.

Senator JACKSON. As you know, the ABM system was justified on the basis that we needed a surviving Minuteman force of 250 to 300.

* * *

Senator JACKSON. . . . Now let me ask why, in your view, did the Soviet Union insist on retaining four times the throw-weight (or payload potential) of the U.S. missile forces?

Mr. SMITH. Senator, what we are talking about here is a freeze, not a definitive limitation. In connection with a freeze . . . the question of getting into reduction in payload would have been a greatly complicating factor. They didn't insist on retaining a certain percentage of payload advantage. We were negotiating a numerical freeze, and we would hope to get into the questions that will affect the payload differentials in later negotiations. . . . This is just to hold the situation such as—

Senator JACKSON. We are not holding the situation. If the SS–11 can be replaced by a missile 50 percent greater in volume, Soviet throw-weight is not being held in place. Why didn't we negotiate a throw-weight freeze?

Mr. SMITH. One of the problems, I think, is going to be the verification aspect of negotiating a throw-weight freeze.

Senator JACKSON. Did you try to negotiate a throw-weight freeze?
Mr. SMITH. No, sir; but when we get into questions of limiting offensive missiles, the verification of throw-weight is, I think, going to be very difficult.
Senator JACKSON. We can certainly monitor the volume of a missile and from that extrapolate that missile's throw-weight. Isn't that right?
Mr. SMITH. Of course, one of the troubles with the throw-weight freeze is that it would have prevented us from finishing the Poseidon program and the Minuteman III program. That was urged, I know, abandoning the Minuteman III program, but I don't think that would have been good for us.
Senator JACKSON. Do you think that we could not have kept these programs when the Soviets had a four-to-one throw-weight advantage?
Mr. SMITH. Not if it was a freeze.

18 JULY 1972 (MORNING SESSION)

Senator JACKSON. . . . The overriding question facing the Senate [is] whether or not under this agreement we can have a survivable deterrent. Now, with particular reference to Minuteman, I would like to follow up the question I asked General Allison during the last session: What is the judgment of the delegation regarding the survivability of Minuteman in the context of the interim agreement and the treaty?. . .
Mr. SMITH. I can't put a number on that, Senator. I am persuaded that the overall retaliatory forces of the United States will keep their integrity in 1977, under these agreements. . . .
Senator JACKSON. . . . My question is directed not just to the overall survivability of our deterrent forces but specifically to the survivability of Minuteman. This is a matter that has occupied much of the time of the Senate. . . . If you don't have an opinion on it now, we can, of course, take it up with the Joint Chiefs.

Perhaps General Allison can comment on it. . . .
General ALLISON. . . . In my judgment, analytical studies which examine the number of Minuteman missiles which might survive an attack in isolation from the remainder of the U.S. strategic forces ignore the advantages that accrue to the United States from having the mutually supporting retaliatory forces which we have today; that is, ICBMS, SLBMS, and strategic bombers. Such studies may be useful as an aid along with other analyses in arriving at strategic judgments, but could not, in my view, produce specific meaningful numerical results in isolation.

Having made that observation, Senator Jackson, I would comment that certainly we know there have been a good many studies conducted

within the Department of Defense that have committed major portions of the Soviet ICBM force against the Minuteman force, and some of these studies committed a projected force of Soviet SS–9s against the Minuteman force.

The results of these studies, I would remark, are sensitive to the number, accuracy, and yield of the attacking missiles; to the hardness of the Minuteman silo; to projected reliability factors of the SS–9s themselves; to very complex factors such as a projected retargeting capability; and to the degree of effectiveness of an ABM defense. In each of the studies and analyses with which I have been concerned, the threats in the analyses were illustrative of possible Soviet forces or projected Soviet forces, and the number of surviving Minuteman was substantial. . . . The results of analyses depend on factors used, and factors can drive analyses. There is one factor that is particularly important to be understood in judging results, and that is something that I mentioned a moment ago, the very complex factor of retargeting; that is, missile reliability and retargeting for failures.

I think that care ought to be used, great care ought to be used, in the use of finite numerical findings, very precise numerical findings, which are based on the application of that complex factor of wartime retargeting. . . .

* * *

Senator JACKSON. You recall, of course, the basic argument that was made in the ABM debate. . . .

General ALLISON. I am aware, and, in fact, after our last appearance before this committee I reviewed testimony in 1969, and I am aware of the testimony that was given which postulated a situation in which some 95 percent of the force, as I recall, might be destroyed. I believe I have a copy of the testimony; and there is a very important last sentence in the paragraph of the testimony, and it was the testimony of the Secretary of Defense, Hon. Melvin Laird, and the last sentence of his testimony remarked on a 20 percent failure rate and a retargeting capability, a capability to retarget missiles to compensate for that failure rate.

Senator Jackson, that is a key point, and it is clear, of course, immediately that if you did not have a very sophisticated retargeting capability, the results of the study would change substantially.

Senator JACKSON. I know the retargeting argument; we go through that every year. But if the Soviets double the number of RVs [reentry vehicles]—which they can do under this agreement, especially since they have said that they will take advantage of every provision in it—

there isn't any question but that they will have more than enough RVS available to compensate for the retargeting problem. Isn't that correct?

General ALLISON. Are you referring, sir, to the number over and above what they have today?

Senator JACKSON. Yes, to the number they can acquire under this agreement.

General ALLISON. I can't—the studies that I am referring to were projections, Senator Jackson, and they projected a force which permitted the Soviets to have those RVS.

Senator JACKSON. At that time, it is true we [were] talking about the potential—that of 420 SS–9s given three warheads per SS–9. Even under the agreement there are still many things to be settled about the definition of a "heavy" missile. But, leaving all that aside, the Soviets can certainly have over 3,000 warheads by 1977. We have had testimony that the Soviets could install perhaps twenty RVS on each of their 313 heavy missiles. That alone is over 6,000 warheads.

That, I think, answers the question on retargeting. We are now talking about a number of Soviet RVS potentially greater than 6,000 instead of the 1,260 which we used in the ABM debates.

General ALLISON. My response at this moment was, of course, related to your earlier statistics, and the projections of what they might do in the time frame of this agreement would need to be examined, certainly.

Senator JACKSON. As I recall, when we talked about retargeting, retargeting made no more than a 5 percent difference in the number of Minuteman surviving.

My deep concern here, General, is the survivability of Minuteman under this interim agreement. We don't have the flexibility under this interim agreement to go to sea, so I want to get to the heart of the Minuteman survivability question. Your suggestion that Minuteman will be survivable will have to be spelled out very clearly and in great detail. This has not yet been done, and I think it should be. . . .

It seems to me, we are dealing not just with action-reaction in the strategic concept of balance, but with action-reaction in terms of diplomacy, especially diplomatic intentions on the part of the adversary. So I am not here trying to play games with numbers or anything of the kind. . . .

In these detailed discussions of strategic weaponry, we often lose sight of the major point. The main point is the meaning that an adversary may give to what comes out of these arms control negotiations. Certainly we have to take into consideration how the strategic balance will influence the risks an adversary is willing to undertake. I think a

more confident Soviet Union is a more dangerous Soviet Union. We have seen the risks that the Soviets have taken when they were in an inferior strategic position. It is in this context that one has to understand the importance of a survivable and credible strategic force.

* * *

Senator JACKSON. Why, in your view, did the Soviet Union insist on limiting the number of interceptors in the U.S. ABM system at Grand Forks to only 100?

Mr. SMITH. The Soviets did not insist on that. We proposed it and they accepted it. We never had any substantial difference in numbers. At one time there was a very slightly higher number suggested, but the figure that we were shooting for was a figure to keep ABM deployment to a low level. This seemed a reasonably low figure. It is about the level that was projected for the Grand Forks deployment and, therefore, this was not a Soviet proposal.

Senator JACKSON. Why did we propose such a low number when we knew or should have known that it would be totally inadequate for the defense of Minuteman? You see, I would have argued for zero ABM, instead of an ineffective ABM.

Mr. SMITH. I am glad to hear you say that, because I personally share your view about zero. It seems to me in the future that is not ruled out, and I hope I can count on your backing for such a proposal. But the conclusion was it would be better to have a small system at this time, while the offensive missiles were not under definitive limitation, than to have zero. The number 100 seemed to be a figure that was consistent with the concept of arms control. If we had proposed 500 or 600 or 1,000, I think it would have looked very unlike arms control but instead an arms buildup.

Senator JACKSON. It may be consistent with arms control, but every expert on the subject has said it is totally inconsistent with the defense of Minuteman. . . . So why did we propose a limitation of 100 which we knew or should have known was inadequate to protect Minuteman?

Mr. SMITH. I think, Senator, if you wanted to have a deployment that was adequate to protect the Minuteman force, you would be up into thousands of interceptors, and that seemed not consistent with trying to limit the strategic arms race; that would feed it.

* * *

Mr. SMITH. I don't think you can get a correct picture by just looking at the impact of the agreement on the United States. If we had agreed to have 1,000 or 2,000 [ABM interceptors], or whatever is needed to field

a defense of ICBMS, we would have had to face the prospect of the Soviets having the same thing.

* * *

Senator JACKSON. In Article V of the treaty, the term "develop" appears in connection with an undertaking not to "develop, test or deploy" certain ABM systems or components. How do you define the term "develop" as it is used in Article V?

Mr. SMITH. We have given a good deal of analysis to this question, and it is a technical question, and I would ask you if I could not submit to you in writing our interpretation of what that term means. I think we can do that very quickly.

[The information follows:]

> . . . The SALT negotiating history clearly supports the following interpretation. The obligation not to develop such systems, devices or warheads would be applicable only to that stage of development which follows laboratory development and testing. The prohibitions on development contained in the ABM treaty would start at that part of the development process where field testing is initiated on either a prototype or breadboard model. It was understood by both sides that the prohibition on "development" applies to activities involved after a component moves from the laboratory development and testing stage to the field testing stage, wherever performed. The fact that early stages of the development process, such as laboratory testing, would pose problems for verification by national technical means is an important consideration in reaching this definition. Exchanges with the Soviet Delegation made clear that this definition is also the Soviet interpretation of the term "development". . . .

* * *

Senator JACKSON. Do you have any reason to believe that the Soviets accept a simple doctrine of assured destruction?

Mr. SMITH. It is hard to find any group of human beings that will accept a simple doctrine. There are always people on one side of the doctrine and people on the other side of the doctrine.

I think that the Soviets, as a result of the SALT negotiations, have moved toward accepting the concept of assured destruction. I would say that I don't know. I have no way of judging whether their doctrine, their national doctrine, says that this is their national strategic concept. I just don't know.

Senator JACKSON. What evidence is there that would indicate that, espe-

cially when we find the Soviet Union deploying very heavy missiles with a capability of destroying hardened silos? . . . Can you give us a scenario that would lead you to believe—a scenario for the future under this agreement—that would lead you to believe the Soviets had moved away from a doctrine of building toward a first-strike capability and toward a doctrine of assured destruction?

Mr. SMITH. The best evidence that they are moving in that direction is their acceptance of these very low levels of ABMS, which in effect indicates that they do not calculate that they can make a first strike and then handle a ragged retaliatory strike and keep it at tolerable levels. That, to my mind, is one of the most important things about this ABM agreement.

* * *

Senator JACKSON. . . . It seems to me that they, under this agreement, will have an ability to knock out our land-based forces. Mr. Garthoff shakes his head. I think he ought to answer the question. Mr. Garthoff?

Mr. GARTHOFF. . . . I don't know why the Soviet Union developed the SS–9 or follow-on missile. It could be that they saw it as more suitable as a candidate for MIRVing than the other missiles they had since it has larger throw-weight; it would be easier to MIRV. But I would certainly agree with Ambassador Smith's observation that there is no clear and easy correlation between size, or indeed any other capability of a given weapon system, and its purpose. . . .

Senator JACKSON. I think Senator Ervin has an answer to your point. You catch a burglar with burglar tools; I think you have some evidence of intent. . . . Why did the Soviets ten years ago want to build a weapon system with a twenty-five megaton payload capacity if they were even remotely interested in an assured destruction doctrine? . . .

Mr. GARTHOFF. Senator, there is, and there has been, interest in both countries at different times in damage limitation as well as assured destruction, and the SS–9 is also an advance over other systems they had, in various respects. They probably weighed in cost-effective terms the much greater cost of the SS–9 as against the SS–11, which were the two new missiles they had to go forward with a few years ago, and they decided to build three times as many SS–11s as –9s, but I don't think one can infer anything from that . . . .

* * *

Senator JACKSON. These really get down to a political judgment that the president would have to make. I have asked this question before. Let me ask it again, and perhaps General Allison would want to com-

ment. I am talking now in the context of this five-year period, and this is the scenario: With its big land-based missiles the Soviet Union knocks out our Minuteman force. Our bombers are knocked out with the sea-based SLBMS that the Soviets are permitted under this agreement. So the president is advised that our two land-based deterrents are not available, but that he has left a part of our SLBM force, our Polaris force—not all of it, since he couldn't have all forty-one of them if there were a surprise attack because there wouldn't be forty-one on station. And he is advised that the Soviet Union has left all of its SS–11s.

He is told that if the Polaris is used, that is if the Polaris is used against the Russian cities, the Soviets will have the means of virtually wiping out all human life on the North American continent. So, let me put it this way: In your judgment would an American president, under that set of facts, order the firing of the missiles from the American submarines?

Mr. SMITH. This question has been asked, as you know, for the last fifteen years, and I don't think that it depends on the SALT agreement. This is not a new situation created by the SALT agreement. I think the scenario you hypothesize is highly unlikely, but I don't see that the SALT agreements make it worse and, as I understand it, the Secretary of Defense agrees and the Joint Chiefs agree. Now, I can't go out beyond their military judgment and give you a separate judgment.

Senator JACKSON. No, but you know, every time we talk about Minuteman we are always talking about the diversity of our deterrent. . . . General Allison takes the position that we rely on our other deterrents. Now, there is a school of thought which holds that all we need are a couple of Polaris submarine boats to deter the Soviet Union, but I am talking now, Mr. Chairman, about a situation in which an American president has to make the decision as commander-in-chief. This isn't a question that is purely military.

Mr. SMITH. If I could give you a quick answer, my arithmetic, following your question, indicates that in that scenario we would have 3,840 reentry vehicles left, and it seems to me that would be fairly adequate to do what any president wanted, if you had twenty-four boats left instead of forty-one, with 160 reentry vehicles in each one of them.

Senator JACKSON. So what you are saying is that you think that an American president under that set of circumstances would order the firing of those missiles, knowing, however, that the Soviets had many, many more RVs than we had which could wipe us out? . . .

Mr. SMITH. Obviously, I can't give you a definitive answer to what a president would do at some time in the future. I think if I were the

president and postulated that worst-case situation and calculated I would still have 3,840 reentry vehicles having three times the yield of Hiroshima—which could do about twenty-four times the explosive damage of all damage done during the last war, could hit twenty-four times as many targets as all the cities destroyed and bombed in the last world war—I would say I would be in pretty good shape to deter that sort of an attack.

Senator JACKSON. But if we have lost our bombers, if we have lost our Minuteman, you don't think the president would be deterred from retaliating with Polaris?

Mr. SMITH. I think if you had 3,840 reentry vehicles, you would be in pretty good shape to deter that sort of worst case.

Senator JACKSON. No, no. We are postulating that we are right down to the choice, Ambassador Smith, of having all of our people wiped out if we retaliate. If the president knew that was going to happen, would he retaliate?

Mr. SMITH. I don't see that SALT really affects this. I think we are going to face, if we want to, those scary-type, extreme-type scenarios; we are going to face them without SALT.

* * *

Senator JACKSON. What is the minimum surviving U.S. strategic force adequate to deter the Soviet Union from posing an unacceptable threat to the United States.

Mr. SMITH. I can't answer that question, Senator Jackson. I don't think anybody can. . . . We are going ahead into SALT II with programs that will generate something like 10,000 warheads; and when you raise the question—what is the minimal surviving force?—it seems to me we are so far from that that I don't see the relevance of it. I don't see how you can get a fix on that question because it involves the Soviet state of mind.

Senator JACKSON. I know; but as soon as you mention warheads the old business about overkill starts. You just can't take those numbers for granted. It is the numbers that you have left after a first strike. . . .

Would the present interim agreement be acceptable as a permanent agreement?

Mr. SMITH. Not to me.

Senator JACKSON. Do any of you disagree with that statement? Secretary Nitze?

Mr. NITZE. No.

Senator JACKSON. General Allison?

General ALLISON. No, sir; I do not disagree.

24 July 1972 (Afternoon Session)

Senator Jackson. . . . The President has stated that the agreement limits the Soviets to sixty-two Y-class submarines at the end of the five-year period. How many more could they have under construction, designated as replacements for early Y-class boats?
Secretary Laird. First, Mr. Chairman, I think at this point in the record we should quote from Article 3 of the interim agreement, which the Congress presently has before it:

> The Parties undertake to limit submarine-launched ballistic missile launchers and modern ballistic submarines to the numbers operational and under construction on the date of the signature of this agreement, and in addition to launchers and submarines constructed under procedures established by the Parties as replacements for an equal number of ICBM launchers of older types deployed prior to 1964 or for launchers on older submarines.

The protocol to the interim agreement, Mr. Chairman, specifies that the Soviet Union may have 950 SLBM launchers and not more than sixty-two modern ballistic missile submarines.

That protocol further stipulates that additional ballistic missile launchers—over 740 ballistic missile launchers on nuclear-powered submarines now operational and under construction—may become operational as replacements for equal numbers of ballistic missile launchers of older types deployed prior to 1964 or of ballastic missile launchers on older submarines. Mr. Chairman, this figure includes the ballistic missile launchers on all Y-class and H-class submarines now under construction or operational in the Soviet Union.

In addition, agreed interpretation K to the interim agreement specifies that dismantling or destruction of ICBM launchers of older types deployed prior to 1964, and of ballistic missile launchers on older submarines being replaced by new SLBM launchers on modern submarines, will be initiated at the time of beginning sea trials of the replacement submarines and will be completed in the shortest possible agreed period of time.

Such dismantling or destruction and timely notification, therefore, will be accomplished under the procedures which are agreed to in the Standing Consultative Commission.

Mr. Chairman, as far as this agreement is concerned, I think the intent is quite clear. It is limited to sixty-two submarines. Although some could interpret the language in different ways, I would consider it a violation of the intent of this agreement to go beyond sixty-two submarines of the Y class.

Senator JACKSON. Well, I am glad to hear you say that because there are ambiguities in this; this goes to my question of how many more the Soviets could have under construction designated as replacements for early Y-class boats. I take it that it is your judgment, and the view of the President and the administration, that any attempt to use this ambiguity to build up—especially towards the end of this five-year period—a pipeline of boats, Y-class boats, advanced Y-class boats, whatever they may be, under construction, as a technical means of getting around the limit of sixty-two operational submarines, would be in clear violation of what we understand to be the agreement.

Secretary LAIRD. I would, and that would also apply to the United States.

Mr. Chairman, the effects of these provisions is that in order to reach the permitted ceiling of 950 ballistic missile launchers on sixty-two modern ballistic missile submarines, the Soviets would have to destroy or dismantle all their ICBMs of the older types deployed prior to 1964. This would include the 210 SS–7s and SS–8s, and it would also include thirty ballistic missile launchers on nine H-class submarines which they now have operational.

In the event that during the period of the interim agreement they were to initiate construction of additional modern ballistic missile submarines beyond the number necessary to reach the total of sixty-two, this could be done only as replacements and this would be under the procedures as specified under Article 3 of the interim agreement. We would consider any new construction starts which were merely for the purpose of maintaining the momentum of the Soviet Union construction program to be contrary to the intent of the agreement. . . .

Senator JACKSON. This is the administration position?

Secretary LAIRD. That is correct.

Senator JACKSON. I believe, Mr. Secretary, in response to this one question, you have done more than anyone I know of to help clarify what has been a truly serious problem for some of us. This is the problem of trying to nail down what is in these agreements, so that we can avoid trouble in the future. Second, it relates specifically to the administration's main thesis of stopping Soviet momentum. I think you have addressed yourself squarely to the momentum point, when you said that the agreements are indeed directed to stopping the Soviet momentum. So if there were a loophole which would allow the Soviets to have all of these additional Y-class boats under construction, even down to having them in outfitting yards, that would violate the whole objective here; would it not?

Secretary LAIRD. There is no question about that; and these agreements have a degree of mutuality to them. We are stopping our momentum

in the ABM field; they are stopping their momentum in the offensive weapons area. They must be considered together, and the interpretation which I have given this offensive agreement is certainly the intent of that agreement and I would consider any other interpretation a violation of that intent.

* * *

Senator JACKSON. . . . I want to raise another very important point that should be clarified for the record.

The largest part of the Soviet land-based ICBM deployment is in the SS–11 silos. If the Soviets were to retrofit their SS–11 silos with a new missile, how much could they (*a*) increase the volume of those silos and (*b*) increase the volume of the missiles that go in those silos? Are you prepared to answer that?

Secretary LAIRD. I am prepared to address that particular question. I believe, like I testified, that I would not go along with the interpretation that some members of the Senate and House have given to that provision in which they read that the 10 to 15 percent increase in dimensions could allow an increase in both dimensions.

Senator JACKSON. Diameter and length?

Secretary LAIRD. Yes. I would consider that a violation of the agreement. In no case would it be possible for the Soviet Union to retrofit their SS–11 silos with a new, significantly larger missile, or would it permit them to install in the SS–11 silos the SS–9s or the follow-on missile system to the SS–9.

The major increase that would be possible under the agreement would be in any one silo dimension, and of course that would limit the total volume increase to no more than 30 percent. With such a limitation it would not be possible to install an SS-9–class missile in an SS–11 silo.

Senator JACKSON. I would have thought that what the parties had intended was actually a maximum of 15 percent increase in the total volume, but when you read it—

Secretary LAIRD. I believe that up to a 30 percent volume increase in one dimension could be possible, and I believe that anything over and above that would be a violation under the most liberal interpretations of the agreement. . . . That is the administration's position. . . .

Senator JACKSON. Also running through all of this is the fact that by these agreements, we have given up the ABM for all practical purposes.

Secretary LAIRD. We stopped our momentum in the ABM.

Senator JACKSON. That is right, supposedly in return for the Soviets' stopping the momentum on their offensive systems. Isn't that what it really boils down to?

Secretary LAIRD. That is correct.

Senator JACKSON. So any attempt by the Soviets to read into this agreement an opportunity to bring about a large increase in their throw-weight would go to the heart of what we were trying to achieve in the interim agreement; isn't that correct?

Secretary LAIRD. That is correct.

Senator JACKSON. It would run counter to the very thing we were trying to achieve?

Secretary LAIRD. That is absolutely correct, Mr. Chairman. I think the Soviets are very likely going to deploy a new missile as a follow-on to the SS–9. Under the terms of the interim agreement they are free to retrofit 313 heavy silos to accommodate this new missile.

Senator JACKSON. Retrofit the 288 SS–9 silos. Twenty-five additional silos are already capable of receiving the new missiles.

Secretary LAIRD. That is correct; but they would have to retrofit the present SS–9s, although the limitation would be at the 313, and I would consider any other action on the part of the Soviet Union a violation of the agreement.

Senator JACKSON. Are we going to accept in SALT II the numerical inferiority we accepted in SALT I? . . .

Secretary LAIRD. . . . I would hope that in these negotiations we could move in the direction of equality as far as numbers and also as far as some of the other important areas dealing with offensive strategic weapon systems. . . .

Senator SMITH. Mr. Secretary, if phase II fails to place a limitation on the offensive weapons, do you believe it will be necessary to abrogate the ABM treaty to protect our land-based missile force?

Secretary LAIRD. I certainly would. If we are not in a position where we can go forward and have these follow-on programs, I think that that would be the only option that would be available in order to protect the security and safety of our country.

Senator SMITH. Do you agree with that, Admiral?

Admiral MOORER. Yes.

* * *

Senator JACKSON. . . . Are you concerned at the prospect of a vulnerable Minuteman force, and do you have any proposals for SALT II that might reduce the vulnerability of the Minuteman force?

Secretary LAIRD. First, I am concerned, yes. Second, we have some proposals. . . . The Minuteman today is certainly survivable. Limiting the Soviets to about 300 SS–9s helps in maintaining this survivability. . . . If they continued their present construction program through the period of 1972, 1973, 1974, at the rate they were going, you would

come up with a large missile systems deployment figure much higher than 300, which would have a considerable effect upon the survivability of the Minuteman system.

* * *

Secretary LAIRD. There are some things that we can do, if necessary, within the interim agreement. We can deploy Minuteman and Poseidon within the terms of the agreement on ships, or large airplanes; by withdrawing our unilateral declarations, we could go forward and deploy mobile ICBMS. . . .

Senator JACKSON. You wouldn't hesitate to recommend the withdrawal of that declaration?

Secretary LAIRD. I would not. . . . If the survivability of the Minuteman were jeopardized to that extent, Senator Jackson, I would recommend that consideration at that time be given to withdrawing our unilateral declaration so that we could also deploy mobile ICBMS.

* * *

Senator JACKSON. . . . Would you agree that activity in connection with Soviet ABM deployment leading toward a base for a thick defense of the Moscow region would constitute a violation of the spirit of the agreement or, if you prefer, the intent of the agreement?

Secretary LAIRD. Of the intent, yes. . . . We are both restricted to 100 launchers. . . .

Senator JACKSON. The intent of the agreements is to enhance our security by enhancing the survivability of our deterrent. So you would view Soviet behavior that threatens the survivability of our deterrent as a violation of the intent of the agreements?

Secretary LAIRD. I would agree.

Senator JACKSON. If there is a pattern which threatens the survivability of our deterrent, you would treat that as a violation of the intent of the parties in making this agreement, would you not?

Secretary LAIRD. I certainly would.

Public Law 92-448 Approving the Interim Agreement, 30 September 1972[1]

Joint Resolution

Resolved by the Senate and House of Representatives of the United States of America in Congress assembled, That the Congress hereby endorses those portions of the Declaration of Basic Principles of Mutual Relations Between the United States of America and the Union of Soviet Socialist Republics signed by President Nixon and General Secretary Brezhnev at Moscow on May 29, 1972, which relate to the dangers of military confrontation and which read as follows:

"The United States of America and the Union of Soviet Socialist Republics attach major importance to preventing the development of situations capable of causing a dangerous exacerbation of their relations . . ." and "will do their utmost to avoid military confrontations and to prevent the outbreak of nuclear war" and "will always exercise restraint in their mutual relations," and "on outstanding issues will conduct" their discussions and negotiations "in a spirit of reciprocity, mutual accommodation and mutual benefit," and

"Both sides recognize that efforts to obtain unilateral advantage at the expense of the other, directly or indirectly, are inconsistent with these objectives," and

"The prerequisites for maintaining and strengthening peaceful relations between the United States of America and the Union of Soviet Socialist Republics are the recognition of the security interests of the parties based on the principle of equality and the renunciation of the use or threat of force."

SEC. 2. The President is hereby authorized to approve on behalf of the United States the interim agreement between the United States of America and the Union of Soviet Socialist Republics on certain measures with respect to the limitation of strategic offensive arms, and the protocol related thereto, signed at Moscow on May 26, 1972, by Richard Nixon, President of the United States of America and Leonid I. Brezhnev, General Secretary of the Central Committee of the Communist Party of the Soviet Union.

---

[1] Public Law 92-448, as amended by Senator Jackson, was approved by the House of Representatives on 25 September 1972, and by the Senate on 30 September 1972. The interim agreement on offensive arms entered into force on 3 October 1972.—Ed.

SEC. 3. The Government and the people of the United States ardently desire a stable international strategic balance that maintains peace and deters aggression. The Congress supports the stated policy of the United States that, were a more complete strategic offensive arms agreement not achieved within the five years of the interim agreement, and were the survivability of the strategic deterrent forces of the United States to be threatened as a result of such failure, this could jeopardize the supreme national interests of the United States; the Congress recognizes the difficulty of maintaining a stable strategic balance in a period of rapidly developing technology; the Congress recognizes the principle of United States–Soviet Union equality reflected in the antiballistic missile treaty, and urges and requests the President to seek a future treaty that, inter alia, would not limit the United States to levels of intercontinental strategic forces inferior to the limits provided for the Soviet Union; and the Congress considers that the success of these agreements and the attainment of more permanent and comprehensive agreements are dependent upon the maintenance under present world conditions of a vigorous research and development and modernization program as required by a prudent strategic posture.

SEC. 4. The Congress hereby commends the President for having successfully concluded agreements with the Soviet Union limiting the production and deployment of antiballistic missiles and certain strategic offensive armaments, and it supports the announced intention of the President to seek further limits on the production and deployment of strategic armaments at future Strategic Arms Limitation Talks. At the same time, the Senate takes cognizance of the fact that agreements to limit the further escalation of the arms race are only preliminary steps, however important, toward the attainment of world stability and national security. The Congress therefore urges the President to seek at the earliest practicable moment Strategic Arms Reduction Talks (SART) with the Soviet Union, the People's Republic of China, and other countries, and simultaneously to work toward reductions in conventional armaments, in order to bring about agreements for mutual decreases in the production and development of weapons of mass destruction so as to eliminate the threat of large-scale devastation and the ever-mounting costs of arms production and weapons modernization, thereby freeing world resources for constructive, peaceful use.

SEC. 5. Pursuant to paragraph six of the Declaration of Principles of Nixon and Brezhnev on May 29, 1972, which states that the United States and the Union of Soviet Socialist Republics: "will continue to make special efforts to limit strategic armaments. Whenever possible, they will conclude concrete agreements aimed at achieving these pur-

poses"; Congress considers that the success of the interim agreement and the attainment of more permanent and comprehensive agreements are dependent upon the preservation of longstanding United States policy that neither the Soviet Union nor the United States should seek unilateral advantage by developing a first strike potential.

Senate Debate on the Jackson Amendment to Public Law 92-448, August and September 1972

14 August 1972

Mr. Jackson. Mr. President, senators who share my view that the Senate ought to go on record in support of the policy of the United States to seek a follow-on agreement that limits the threat to the survivability of our deterrent forces will welcome my amendment. The first part does precisely that. It urges restraint on the part of the Soviet Union by indicating that a failure to achieve a threat-limiting agreement could jeopardize the supreme national interests of the United States. In so doing, the amendment takes account of the fact that while the interim agreement may have some slight effect on the rate of growth of the Soviet threat to the survivability of our deterrent, it does not halt it. Therefore, should the threat overtake the negotiation of a follow-on agreement at any time within the next five years, our supreme national interests could be jeopardized. I will be surprised, Mr. President, to learn that there is any substantial opposition to this view within the Senate.

Mr. President, I have elsewhere described the present agreement as providing the United States with "interim subparity." The agreement confers on the Soviets a 50 percent advantage in numbers of land- and sea-based launchers and a 400 percent advantage in throw-weight. Now, the argument is made that this enormous disparity in numbers of launchers and throw-weight is offset by superior technology and numbers of warheads on our side. There is a certain limited truth to this claim. It is not an enduring truth: for while numbers are limited under the agreement, technology is not. It stands to reason, therefore, that in the long run "superior" technology cannot be relied upon to offset inferior numbers.

The inability of technology to compensate for numbers is not only true in general but is, in the present case, true for specific reasons as well. The greatest part of our presumed technological advantage lies in our lead over the Soviets in the development and deployment of MIRV warheads on our missile forces.

This lead is not one that can be maintained at anything approaching our current margin. On the contrary, when the Soviets develop a MIRV capability—and they are expected to do so at "any moment"—the

Source: U.S., Congress, Senate, *Congressional Record*, 92d Cong., 2d sess., 1972, vol. 118, no. 130, pp. S13467–S13469; and vol. 118, no. 138, pp. S14280–S14283.

combination of that capability and their vastly superior throw-weight will give them, given time and effort on their part, superiority in numbers of warheads.

There is an enormous volume of misinformation on the subject of alleged U.S. advantages arising from technology and geography. There is no doubt that in the long run, technology will tend toward equalization. How well I remember those who argued that the Soviets would require a decade or more to catch up with the United States in developing hydrogen weapons. The same sort of scientists who today argue that we can rest comfortably with inferior numbers of launchers because of an unbridgeable advantage in technology miscalculated by about nine and a half out of ten years back in 1947. The Russians, of course, were only months behind us, and our scientists were behind the eight ball.

As to geography, I have heard it argued—the chairman of the Foreign Relations Committee made the case himself last week—that owing to our possession of forward bases for our submarine fleet we need fewer submarines than the Soviets in order to maintain on-station times equal to theirs. Now, sea-based strategic forces are assuming increasing importance; so it is essential that we be correct on this point. Despite some statements to the contrary, the geographical asymmetries favor the Soviet submarine fleet and not our own. With the increased range such as that of the Soviet SS-NX-8 submarine-launched missile, the importance of forward bases is greatly diminished. Russian submarines will be on station with respect to a large number of U.S. targets within one day's travel time from Murmansk or Petropavlovsk. This is not substantially different from the situation of our submarines operating out of their forward bases. What is more important, however, is that the Russians have a very large land mass between our submarines and their vulnerable points while we do not. Most of the U.S. points that are targets for Soviet submarine-launched missiles are coastal or near-coastal.

So there is little substance to the claim that we are in a favorable geographical situation.

The point I wish to make, Mr. President, is that, over the long run, there is no substitute for equal numbers of launchers, taking account of throw-weight differentials. I believe that the Senate should join with our negotiators and administration spokesmen in rejecting, for the future, the sort of disparities that we have agreed to, on an interim basis, in the present agreement. And in so doing I believe that we ought to insist that the principle that was applied in the case of the ABM treaty—the principle of equality on which the Russians insisted—ought to be applied to a treaty on offensive weapons.

I was concerned, Mr. President, that our consent to the interim agreement, containing, as it does, the wide disparities to which I have referred, might be misunderstood as reflecting on the acceptability of such disparities in a follow-on treaty. In order to make the record clear I asked a number of witnesses before the Armed Services Committee to comment on this issue.

On 18 July, I asked Ambassador Gerard Smith, the director of the Arms Control and Disarmament Agency and head of our SALT delegation, "Would the present interim agreement be acceptable as a permanent agreement?"

Ambassador Smith replied, "Not to me."

I then directed the same question to other members of the SALT delegation. The former deputy secretary of defense and now assistant to the secretary of defense for SALT, Mr. Paul Nitze, said "No." General Royal Allison, a member of the delegation and assistant to the chairman of the joint chiefs of staff for strategic arms negotiations, also said "No."

On 24 July, I directed a similar question to Secretary Laird, with respect to whether a SALT II agreement should continue the numerical relationships established in the interim agreement. Secretary Laird, speaking for the administration, said:

> I would hope that in these negotiations we could move in the direction of equality as far as numbers and also as far as some of the other important areas dealing with offensive strategic weapon systems. I feel that this should be a very important thrust of our negotiations because this is very basic to the continued support of the obligations that we have undertaken with our friends and allies throughout the world in order to prevent the possibility of a nuclear exchange in the future.

The chief of naval operations, Admiral Zumwalt, testified:

> It is my view that in SALT II, we must achieve an equality of numbers. Just as the Soviets insisted on symmetry with regard to the ABM treaty, if we are going to go into a permanent treaty on the strategic side, I think we absolutely must insist on symmetry.

I know of no one in a responsible position in the administration who is in disagreement with this widely expressed view.

My amendment provides the Senate with an opportunity to declare itself in favor of equality in a follow-on agreement; and I am certain that in view of the basic good sense of that position and the overwhelming testimony before us, we will act to affirm it.

Mr. President, the question of what is to be included in the compu-

tation of equal forces in a follow-on agreement is related to the difficult issue of our forward deployments in Europe which are dedicated to the defense of our European allies and which are at sea.

The intent of my amendment as it bears on this matter is, I believe, perfectly clear and straightforward. In stating that "the Congress recognizes the principle of United States–Soviet Union equality reflected in the antiballistic missile treaty" and that accordingly "the Congress requests the President to seek a future treaty that, *inter alia,* would not limit the United States to levels of intercontinental strategic forces inferior to the limits provided for the Soviet Union," it is unmistakably clear that so-called forward-based systems, which are not intercontinental, should not be included in that calculation of equality. It is my view, and the intent of the pending amendment, that any eventual treaty must recognize the necessity that the intercontinental strategic forces of the U.S. and the U.S.S.R.—by which I mean to include ICBMS, submarine-launched nuclear missiles, and intercontinental-range bombers of the two powers—should bear an equal relationship to one another. This says nothing about the eventual role of or disposition of the issue of forward-based systems.

With regard to the question of forward-based systems it has been my understanding, as clearly set forth by representatives of the administration in testimony before the Senate, that the United States has refused to negotiate the issue of forward-based systems in a bilateral U.S.–U.S.S.R. negotiation. I understand that this position was based on the entirely justifiable view that such systems are part and parcel of our alliance defense commitment and could not appropriately be considered without satisfactory alliance participation. I fully support the administration's view on this matter and there is nothing in my amendment which in any way contradicts that position.

My amendment, in its final sentences, simply points to the need for a vigorous program of research, development, and modernization leading to a prudent strategic posture. I wish to emphasize that adoption of this language is not intended to bear upon the wisdom of any particular procurement item. Decisions on procurement ought to be taken on a case-by-case basis. So while it is useful for the Senate to go on record to the effect that we must continue our efforts in the research, development, and modernization area, senators can rest assured that this does not constitute an endorsement of any particular weapons system or any particular research and development effort. I emphasize this, Mr. President, because I would not wish senators to gain the impression that in voting for my amendment they are committing themselves to any future action on procurement items.

Mr. President, I began my remarks by observing that international

agreements always involve unwritten hopes and expectations and reservations. Sometimes it helps to set them down. In the present case I hope, and I am sure my colleagues share this hope, that a follow-on agreement will limit the threat to the survivability of our strategic deterrent forces. It is, in my view, well to underline this hope by language that lets the Soviets know that a failure to achieve this result would jeopardize our supreme national interests. My amendment does that.

I fully expect that our negotiators at SALT II will insist upon equality just as the Soviets insisted upon equality in the ABM treaty. The issue of whether the present agreement adds up to equality is beside the point; and there will be differences of opinion on that. But what I am certain we can agree on is the necessity that we not accept in SALT II levels of intercontinental strategic weapons that are inferior to the levels of intercontinental forces permitted for the Soviet Union. My amendment does that.

Finally, I am confident that the Senate would wish to reaffirm its confidence in the importance of our research and development efforts.

Mr. President, the overriding hope and expectation of all of us is that the SALT deliberations will eventually produce a treaty that will assure the survivability, and therefore the credibility, of our deterrent posture. Such a treaty would be an enormous step toward world peace.

Mr. President, I want to see the Senate of the United States play a full and equal role in the effort to bring about such a treaty. The place to start is by giving our advice as well as our consent to the present agreement. We have an obligation to give direction to the future efforts of the government on SALT policy. I believe that direction must be toward survivable forces and toward equality. I am confident the Senate shares this view and that it will act to support my amendment.

*   *   *

7 SEPTEMBER 1972

Mr. FULBRIGHT. The senator from Washington stated . . . that he had over forty cosponsors. I think he raises a question that is very important. It is my belief that some of those cosponsors do not understand the way the senator from Washington uses the word "equality." In his statement here a moment ago to the Senate, and as he made it before, he used the word "equality" without qualification. He said all his amendment seeks to do in the future is to lay down guidelines that our negotiators should seek equality.

I think I would understand and I think many members in the pub-

lic would understand that to mean overall equality, and that is overall equality of nuclear weapons—equality of capacity to develop new ones, either offensive or defensive weapons. That is what I take the statement to mean.

I do not believe it is understood that what the senator from Washington is really saying is that—regardless of the degree of superiority we may have in the field of airplanes and the capacity to deliver nuclear weapons by airplanes or from forward bases, or our superiority in other areas—these are excluded from his concept of equality, and that all that the senator is contemplating when he uses the word "equality" is in numbers of intercontinental missiles.

I believe in view of that circumstance, and aside from others, that a thorough discussion of the significance of the senator from Washington's amendment is necessary if the Senate is to vote intelligently and with understanding on what is involved in this agreement.

Within the last few days there have been indications that this is the way at least the Russians understand the agreement. The article I referred to earlier in *Izvestia* makes clear the Russians believe this amendment is an effort to undermine the interim agreement, it is an indication of lack of desire on our part to proceed with significant restrictions on nuclear arsenals.

* * *

I emphasize that this interim agreement is not a routine matter in my opinion. It could be the most significant move by this Congress in many years, if it is properly implemented and if we accept it in the spirit in which it was intended at the time of the summit meeting. It, along with the ABM agreement, could be a landmark action by Congress and the country if it is carried through properly, and by that I mean if we accept genuine parity or sufficiency, to use the word of the President, in this area rather than trying to manipulate this whole matter to the point that we have superiority and continuing superiority.

We had superiority for a long time. But the clear fact is that if we insist upon superiority, there will be no further progress in the control of armaments. On the contrary, it would result in a vast increase in the acceleration of the arms race, in my opinion, because the reaction against the failure of phase II in the SALT agreements would be an increase in the arms race because of the disappointment, as well as because of suspicion that would arise then, on the part of both sides, that the other side was going for that myth of first-strike capability. I do not believe first-strike capability is a possibility under present conditions, or the foreseeable conditions, but it is a concept which has been

sold and much talked about and could be easily distorted into a justification for an unlimited arms race.

* * *

Mr. JACKSON. May I say I think it is amazing for the chairman of the Foreign Relations Committee to tell over forty members of the Senate that they do not know what equality in intercontinental strategic forces is about. . . . My amendment does not say intercontinental strategic missiles; it says intercontinental strategic forces. Read the amendment. That includes bombers. That includes missiles fired from land bases. It includes missiles fired from submarines.

Mr. FULBRIGHT. If that is true, why does the senator object to the words *overall strategic?*

Mr. JACKSON. For the obvious reason.

Mr. FULBRIGHT. What is the reason?

Mr. JACKSON. For the obvious reason that the addition of the term *overall* would of necessity mean more than my amendment intends. I have said repeatedly that the intercontinental strategic forces to be balanced on the basis of equality are ICBMS, SLBMS and intercontinental-range bomber forces. I am not including, for example, tactical weapons. Addition of the word *overall* could prejudice the position of our NATO partners and other allies who are not participating directly in the SALT negotiations.

Mr. FULBRIGHT. Of course, we are getting into the type of debate which is appropriate to the senator's amendment. I think that is quite proper. The only thing is, I think it would be more appropriate to make these arguments—and we shall make them—when and if the senator's amendment is offered. They are legitimate questions of our differences of view. But I do not think it is clear at all from the senator's amendment and what has been said in the press that he is talking about overall nuclear equality in strategic weapons. It is not only weapons in Europe that we have, but we have weapons all around the periphery of the Soviet Union. We have them in Turkey. We have control of when they are used. We have them in the Far East. We have them on aircraft carriers. We have fourteen of them commissioned now, and we soon will have sixteen, and the Russians have none. Are these intercontinental or not? If they fly off an aircraft carrier in the North Sea, I admit they are not from our continent, but they are the same kind of destructive weapon.

. . . I reiterate that when the senator presents his proposal that all he asks is equality—equality of intercontinental strategic forces—I say that the average person would be impressed. Certainly I would be included in the definition of an average person. If he came to me, I would

say, "Sure, I am for equality." Everybody is for equality. The interim agreement is for equality. The President says it gives equality—at least equality.

The argument can be made that the Russians have inferiority at the moment, and that is why the permission was given in the interim agreement to increase their numbers of submarines.

. . . I suspect a number of senators think the senator means overall equality, that he takes all the weapons systems, offensive, defensive, puts them up against the Russians', and that there is approximate equality. That is what the interim agreement actually provides for; but the senator is offering an amendment which does not say that at all, and it is clear that is not proposed. His amendment calls for numerical equality in intercontinental ballistic missile forces, and he ignores all the other areas of nuclear weaponry where we have advantages or superiority, including the weapons that we already have in place around the periphery of the Soviet Union, on our aircraft carriers, and in Europe.

The other members of the Armed Services Committee—he does not have to take my word about it; the senator from Missouri [Stuart Symington] has had considerable experience, and is a former secretary of the air force; he has said and will say that these weapons in Europe can be put on a fighter bomber and, with one refueling, delivered to Moscow. The weapon does not come from the United States, but a two- or three-kiloton weapon delivered on Moscow, coming from Germany, is just as destructive as one coming out of a submarine.

All of these factors were taken into consideration by the President. Dr. Kissinger, at the White House, described this, and answered all of the questions as to whether there was parity as well as sufficiency, and he said there was. He said in no uncertain terms that this was not an imprudent agreement which leaves the United States in an inferior position.

Inferiority is clearly the implication in the senator's amendment. It is very cleverly written. He says, "Strategic forces inferior to the limit provided for the Soviet Union." The implication is clear that we are inferior in our strategic forces.

Well, what does he mean by our strategic forces? Again he comes back; the only thing he can mean is ICBMS.

Nobody denies that there is a numerical inferiority. However, our country, years ago, deliberately rejected the idea of weapons such as the SS-9s and the Titans, big multi-megaton weapons. We deliberately chose the smaller, one-megaton Minuteman, because it is a more efficient way to use our capacity for destruction. . . .

Mr. JACKSON. Would the senator say that an SS-9 might be designed for

a first-strike capability, in order to knock out a hardened site? Otherwise, why would they want to have a twenty-five–megaton warhead capability? . . . The forces we sought were totally different. We never sought a first-strike capability to knock out hardened sites. That is the difference, and that is what is disturbing about the huge Soviet missiles and the still larger missiles they are now developing.

Mr. FULBRIGHT. The senator assumes all of this. I do not think he has any basis for that at all. He is trying to read the minds of the Russians.

The first effort we made was to develop a big one, bigger than we now have. We were far ahead in technology, and so on, and our own military people, looking at it, decided that it was less efficient to put ten or twenty or twenty-five megatons in one missile, less efficient than to put the same or less megatonnage in four or five missiles, for various reasons. First, there is flexibility; you can fire at more targets more easily. It is more accurate; and four megatons, in the calculations I have, which come from expert sources, four megatons properly delivered in a Minuteman will cause the equivalency, they call it, in destruction, of sixteen megatons, or about four to one. If you concentrate it all in one, it is not efficient.

We started out that way, and simply as a matter of sophistication and knowledge, we decided it was more efficient to go to the Minuteman.

I think that is true. Everything we have been doing is to that effect, that that is correct. We are not about to go back to the big one.

When you MIRV a weapon, you have fewer megatons, but they divided it up. Why did they divide it up? Because it is more efficient to put MIRVed missiles in submarines. They are still so destructive no one can withstand it. . . .

Mr. JACKSON. Did the senator want to leave the record as I understood he left it, that we had the choice of several warheads for Minuteman, and could deliver up to a total of four megatons? Is that what the senator said?

Mr. FULBRIGHT. No; four separate megatons, I mean four missiles, one megaton per missile, is a more efficient way to use it than one big missile. We decided that years ago, more efficient than one missile with ten or fifteen megatons in it. We made the decision that it was more efficient and more effective.

Mr. JACKSON. It is not a matter, I would say, of efficiency. I think it is a matter of strategic policy.

Mr. FULBRIGHT. I mean efficiency in destructive power, the deliverability of destructive power. . . .

Mr. CRANSTON. The senator from Washington, in colloquy with the senator from Arkansas, stated that the trouble with the word *overall*

was that nuclear tactical weapons would then be included. Would the senator accept the word *overall* if it was followed by the words *exclusive of nuclear tactical weapons?*

Mr. Jackson. What would it mean then? Can the senator explain what it would mean?

Mr. Cranston. It would mean that all relevant factors in measuring sufficiency of force would be considered but nuclear tactical weapons would not be considered.

Mr. Jackson. What relevant factors?

Mr. Cranston. There are many factors that we have gone over in this debate. The great ring of forward-position forces that are used on sea, in the air, and from the ground. You would consider more than simply the number of missiles and throw-weight.

Mr. Jackson. Well, I would just point out that obviously you have to consider the relative posture, as we are talking about it, first in intercontinental strategic terms, to determine whether or not you are going to have any basis of equality or parity.

When the Soviets get 1,618 land-based missiles, and we have 1,000, when the Soviets get 950 launching tubes for sixty-two Y-class submarines, and we have forty-four ballistic missile submarines with a total of 710 tubes, I think it is apparent to the people of this country and to members of the Senate that this is not equality; and when you add on top of that that they have a four-to-one advantage in throw-weight, that is, in the capacity of these items that we are talking about, it is clear that we have not achieved parity.

I remember in the arguments over the ABM that the contention against the ABM was that when the Soviet Union got around our number of land-based missiles, they would stop development of ICBMs at around a thousand. Here they are at 1,618 already.

You know, you have to ask, Why was not some determination made by those who constantly worry about U.S. forces to get the Russians to cut back and reduce theirs? There is a golden opportunity for the Russians to agree to a thousand land-based missiles and to the forty-two Y-class submarines they now have, or to forty-four. There is a golden opportunity, Madam President, to have a real arms limitation agreement that will save money and resources on both sides.

Mr. Fulbright. Madam President, this comes back, I submit to the senator from Washington, to the same argument as before. One reason the Russians thought they should have more ICBMs was that they had no capacity to put weapons around our borders, as we have around theirs in such places as Turkey, Korea, and elsewhere, as well as in aircraft carriers. They do not have a single aircraft carrier.

This is a matter of each country's decision as to how it looks after

its defense. Not having the capacity to do what we have done, to have in being 7,000 warheads in Europe and other large numbers on aircraft carriers, and so on, scattered around the world, how do they offset that to reach even a degree of equality? They cannot do that under the situation in which they operate.

The senator is taking one area—ICBMS. He talks about the submarines. We believe, and we have been told, that we have superior submarines. We already have superior submarines. They are beginning to develop a missile that can travel a couple of hundred miles more than ours, but we have underway the Trident submarine, and so forth. There is the ever-increasing sophistication.

I think that the way the senator presents his case is very deceptive. I would have thought the same thing. If I had no background on it and the senator approached me cold and said, "Aren't you for equality with the Russians on strategic missiles?" I would say, "Sure, I am."

He would say, "Would you cosponsor my bill?"

I would say, "Sure. I'm for equality."

But it never would have occurred to me that the kind of equality he is talking about is superiority—equality in one area, and we are clearly superior in the others.

It can mean nothing, in truth, but superiority if we accept the senator's idea that we must have 1,618 ICBMS and 740 submarine tubes, just what the Russians could have, and they all, of course, would have to be exactly of the same explosive power and length. The whole idea that this one category should be balanced off nicely so that each side has the same amount is absolutely irrelevant and is a wrong way to look at it.

When you consider the power of destruction of one-fourth of all these weapons on the other country, in view of the fact that we have already agreed to the ABM treaty, in which each country has said it is not going to proceed to develop a defense against these weapons, then we do not need 1,600.

Then comes into play what the President has called sufficiency. I submit that 400 on each side is sufficient, because the other side has said, "We do not propose to develop and we do not have a defense against intercontinental ballistic missiles or against submarine missiles." The only kind of defense either would have at the present time, I suppose, is some kind of defense against those missiles delivered by airplanes, because we both have antiaircraft defenses of some kind, but we have nothing that could deal with a submarine-launched missile or an intercontinental ballistic missile. So when you get above 400, which often has been used as a figure adequate to destroy three-fourths of each other's industrial capacity and kill 300 million people—that is

enough to completely demoralize and destroy the other country's society.

So in talking about this, the senator is confusing the issue by equating nuclear weapons with conventional weapons. It is true that there is considerable merit in saying, with respect to conventional weapons, that we ought to have so many .45s against their .45s, so many different guns. There is some relevance in that argument. But with nuclear weapons, if there is no defense against it, I submit that the senator is playing around with the numbers game of a thousand or sixteen hundred or two thousand, and it is utterly meaningless. It has no significance. The concept of equality under those circumstances is meaningless.

The idea of first-strike capability seems to me also to be meaningless, because there is literally no possibility of a straight first-strike capability on either side with weapons of this kind and deployed as they are, including submarine weapons. Assume, for example—and I do not think they could—that the Russians could destroy 1,000 Minutemen, which is a fantastic and ridiculous assumption; what are they going to do about the submarines? A first-strike capability means that the country attacked could not effectively retaliate. With 700 or 500 or even 400, they could render unacceptable damage to the other.

So I think the whole idea of equality, as submitted by the senator, is simply not a meaningful term under the circumstances, because it is not understood that way, and I would not have understood it that way. . . .

Mr. Jackson. The senator has dwelt at great length on the subject of the 7,000 warheads in Europe. Would the senator give the Senate the benefit of his views as to the number of bombs or warheads we could put on Soviet soil in connection with a move on our part and, second, how many we could put on Soviet soil in the event of a Soviet first strike against our forces in Europe?

Mr. Fulbright. This has been discussed, as I have said, at considerable length. The senator from Missouri discussed it the other day. He stated time and again that with one refueling, the fighter bombers, of which we have several hundred, could take a nuclear weapon of about 200 kilotons, I think he said—

Mr. Jackson. How many weapons?

Mr. Fulbright. To Moscow.

If the senator is asking how many they could shoot down, nobody knows how efficient they are, but if you send enough of them over, you can. . . . We have plenty of weapons.

PART ONE

Annotated Bibliography

Frye, Alton. *A Responsible Congress: The Politics of National Security.* New York: McGraw-Hill, 1975.

This volume examines the important role Congress has played in the formulation of recent national security policy. Of particular interest are the chapters dealing with the Sentinel and Safeguard ABM systems, MIRV, and SALT. Frye contends that the early congressional debates over Sentinel influenced the Nixon administration's decision to alter ABM doctrine for Safeguard; in addition, he cites the belated legislative concern over MIRV and the Jackson amendment to Public Law 92-448 as examples of how Congress can affect executive branch negotiations.

Garthoff, Raymond L. "Negotiating with the Russians: Some Lessons from SALT." *International Security,* vol. 1, no. 4 (Spring 1977).

Having served as the executive officer and senior State Department adviser on the SALT I delegation, Garthoff draws upon his experience to provide a critical assessment of American negotiating techniques in the first SALT talks. The author is especially critical of the Kissinger-Dobrynin backchannel discussions and the manner in which the link between ABM and offensive arms limitations was resolved in the 20 May 1971 agreement, as well as the way negotiations were conducted at the 1972 Moscow summit. The latter, in the author's opinion, "represented a model of how *not* to conduct negotiations."

Garthoff, Raymond L. "SALT and the Soviet Military." *Problems of Communism,* vol. 24, no. 1 (January-February 1975).

This article looks at the role of the Soviet military establishment in SALT I and the way military interests shaped Soviet negotiating objectives. Garthoff believes the first SALT talks contributed to a greater awareness and understanding on the part of Soviet military and political leaders of the implications of decisions concerning nuclear weapons and doctrine. SALT is seen by the author as a valuable forum for more serious exchanges of views between the military establishments of both superpowers. Such a dialogue can foster greater mutual understanding of national defense policies and enhance the prospects for arms control agreements.

Newhouse, John. *Cold Dawn: The Story of SALT*. New York: Holt, Rinehart and Winston, 1973.

This volume remains the most comprehensive history of the SALT I negotiations available. Beginning with the Johnson administration's preparations for SALT and ending with the May 1972 Moscow summit, Newhouse examines the arms control interests of various government agencies and describes the National Security Council–dominated bureaucratic bargaining process whereby conflicting interests were reconciled. The actual negotiations in Helsinki and Vienna, together with the contribution made by the Nixon-Kosygin/Kissinger-Dobrynin backchannel discussions, are also presented in detail.

Willrich, Mason, and John B. Rhinelander, eds. *SALT: The Moscow Agreements and Beyond*. New York: The Free Press, 1974.

This volume is a compilation of essays dealing with the major issues associated with SALT I. Among the topics examined are the history of post-1945 nuclear arms control efforts, American and Soviet strategic weapons arsenals, prospects for verification of various agreements, the provisions of the ABM treaty and interim agreement, the interests of third countries in the SALT process, and issues of concern to both superpowers as they negotiate a SALT II agreement.

PART TWO

The SALT II Negotiations

Overview

Roger P. Labrie

In November 1972, American and Soviet SALT negotiators reconvened in Geneva to begin a new round of talks aimed at achieving a permanent comprehensive treaty limiting strategic offensive arms. The congressional mandate to seek "more permanent and comprehensive agreements" that "would not limit the United States to levels of intercontinental strategic forces inferior to the limits provided for the Soviet Union," embodied in Public Law 92-448, together with the unrelenting pace of technological advances in weapon systems, provided the context for negotiation of a SALT II treaty.

The optimism that accompanied the start of negotiations proved to be short-lived. The new agreement many hoped could be ready for signature when General Secretary Brezhnev visited Washington in June 1973 foundered over technical issues. When President Nixon traveled to Moscow the following year, resolution of those same issues was further complicated by the atmosphere growing out of the Watergate scandal. After President Ford's meeting with Brezhnev at Vladivostok in November 1974, agreement on a SALT II treaty again proved elusive, this time because of the emergence of new weapon systems and increasing skepticism in this country as to the value of America's détente relationship with the Soviet Union.

The Washington Summit, 1973

Shortly after the SALT II negotiations began in Geneva, it became evident that the United States and the Soviet Union held very different conceptions of what a long-term comprehensive agreement should entail. The United States sought a treaty based on the principle of "essential equivalence," providing for overall equality in the aggregate number of "central" strategic delivery systems (ICBMS, SLBMS, and bombers)

each nation could deploy. In addition, an approximate equality in throw-weight was to be negotiated, taking into account the payload of bombers. Throw-weight also was to be used to limit MIRV deployments: the aggregate throw-weight of each country's MIRVed missiles would be set at equal levels. Finally, each nation would be allowed to deploy whatever number of ICBMS, SLBMS, and bombers it wished, provided their combined totals did not exceed the established aggregate ceiling on strategic delivery vehicles (the freedom-to-mix concept). In short, the numerical disparities in offensive arms sanctioned by the interim agreement of May 1972 would be eliminated.

The Soviet Union, however, rejected the American notion of parity. Soviet negotiators insisted that the numerical advantages in delivery vehicles and throw-weight they had won in the first SALT agreement had to be incorporated into any permanent comprehensive treaty. In addition, they argued that such an agreement had to take into account American forward-based systems (FBS) and British and French strategic forces; the numerical advantage for the Soviet Union in "central" strategic weapons was seen as compensation. As for MIRVS, Moscow rejected Washington's formula for limiting the throw-weight of missiles that could carry such devices and instead proposed a ceiling on the number of missiles that could be MIRVed. The Soviets also insisted that the B-1 bomber and the Trident missile-launching submarine system the United States was developing should be banned; the Backfire bomber, which the Soviet Union had begun producing in 1969, would be exempt from SALT II limitations.[1]

As it turned out, the FBS and MIRV issues would elude negotiated settlement for two years. MIRV limitations proved to be particularly contentious, since in November 1972 the Soviet Union had not yet begun to test such warheads and therefore resisted any formula that might inhibit plans for their eventual deployment. By April 1973 it was apparent that a comprehensive agreement could not be concluded in time for Brezhnev's upcoming visit to Washington. Consequently, when Kissinger traveled to Moscow in early May to prepare for the summit, his objective was to reach agreement on some basic principles that could guide the ongoing Geneva negotiations.

General Secretary Brezhnev arrived in Washington on 18 June for several days of talks. Among the agreements signed in the course of his discussions with President Nixon were the "Basic Principles of Negotiations on the Further Limitation of Strategic Offensive Arms"

[1] A presentation of the contrasting American and Soviet objectives in SALT II prior to the Vladivostok summit can be found in Thomas W. Wolfe, *The SALT Experience: Its Impact on U.S. and Soviet Strategic Policy and Decisionmaking* (Santa Monica, California: Rand Corporation, 1975), pp. 70–90.

and the "Agreement on the Prevention of Nuclear War." In the basic principles document both leaders reaffirmed their commitment to negotiate a permanent agreement limiting offensive arms and set as their objective the completion of negotiations by the end of 1974.

The agreement on basic principles and the personal political commitment of Nixon and Brezhnev to the success of SALT failed to provide the understandings on substantive issues needed to break the deadlock in the negotiations. The Soviets continued to insist on inclusion of FBS in any comprehensive agreement, and no progress was made on the difficult problem of arriving at a formula for limiting MIRVS.

A sense of urgency was injected into the negotiations by Secretary of Defense Schlesinger's disclosure in August 1973 that the Soviets had recently tested an ICBM equipped with MIRV. Whatever momentum the talks might have acquired by the announcement, however, was soon dispelled by the Egyptian and Syrian attack on Israel the following October. When Moscow threatened to send three airborne divisions to the aid of Egypt, President Nixon ordered a worldwide alert of U.S. nuclear and conventional forces to deter Soviet intervention. In the months following the imposition of a cease-fire between Israel and its Arab neighbors, most of Washington's attention was focused not on SALT but on efforts to mediate between the Middle East belligerents.

The significance of these developments during the latter half of 1973 became apparent early in the following year. Officials in Washington had been concerned for some time about the advantages Moscow could derive from MIRVing its land-based missiles (in early 1974 the Soviets had four new ICBMS in advanced stages of testing). Because these missiles had larger throw-weights than their American counterparts, Pentagon analysts feared the Soviet Union could deploy a greater number of warheads on each of their missiles, and, combining this with anticipated advances in accuracy, eventually pose a threat to the survival of the Minuteman force. In addition, the events of the October 1973 war had served to focus greater attention on the role of strategic nuclear weapons in supporting America's security commitments to its allies.

In January 1974 Secretary Schlesinger unveiled a new doctrine for strategic nuclear weapons. Whereas most nuclear options at the disposal of the President until that time had entailed large-scale attacks on urban centers, the Schlesinger doctrine called for the creation of additional options allowing for more limited strikes against a wider selection of targets. Greater emphasis was to be placed on counterforce targeting.

Although the primary objective of the change in targeting doctrine was to convince the Soviets of the U.S. ability and willingness to use

nuclear weapons in response to a broader range of threats, the failure of SALT to place constraints on throw-weight and future Soviet deployment of MIRVS also entered into Schlesinger's calculations. Coupled with his articulation of the new doctrine was a request that Congress fund research and development programs to increase the accuracy and yield of U.S. missiles, thereby increasing their lethality against Soviet silos and other hardened military targets. Stating that the pace of these new programs would be determined by that of similar Soviet programs, Schlesinger put Moscow on notice that Washington was prepared to do what was necessary to maintain essential equivalence in counterforce capabilities. It was hoped that Soviet negotiators, faced with this prospect, would become more amenable to SALT limitations on throw-weight and MIRVS.

The Moscow Summit, 1974

With another summit meeting scheduled for the end of June, Secretary of State Kissinger traveled to Moscow in March 1974 for a series of talks with General Secretary Brezhnev. During his three days in the Soviet capital, Kissinger searched for some formula that would provide a "conceptual breakthrough" on what had become the most pressing issue in SALT, the limitation of MIRVS.

Two options were put before the Soviet leader. The first one called for a temporary agreement restricting deployment of MIRVS to an equal aggregate of missile throw-weight for both countries, in conjunction with an extension of the interim agreement for two to three years beyond its expiration date of 3 October 1977. After Brezhnev rejected this proposal, Kissinger presented his second option: In addition to extending the interim agreement for two to three years, it would have allowed the United States to deploy MIRVS on more missiles than could the Soviet Union, while the latter would have been permitted to MIRV a larger aggregate of missile throw-weight.[2] This proposal too was rejected. In essence, the United States had abandoned its objective of a permanent comprehensive agreement on offensive arms in favor of a temporary agreement that would have limited the competition in counterforce capabilities that both countries were on the verge of embarking upon.

The failure of the March negotiations to resolve the MIRV issue

---

[2] These proposals, together with the one made by President Nixon during the June-July 1974 Moscow summit, can be found in Paul H. Nitze, "The Vladivostok Accord and SALT II," *Review of Politics*, vol. 37 (April 1975), p. 152.

presaged the outcome of the next Moscow summit. Prospects for a SALT treaty were further dampened by the erosion of domestic political support for President Nixon owing to the threat of impeachment, and by Senator Jackson's allegations on the eve of the summit that "secret deals" had been made with regard to certain provisions of the interim agreement. Jackson and other critics contended that a loophole in the 1972 agreement might allow the Soviets to deploy 70 SLBMS above the authorized ceiling of 950 set for such missiles, and that a subsequent secret understanding between Secretary Kissinger and Soviet Ambassador Dobrynin had failed to close it. In responding to Jackson's charges, Kissinger did admit that the text of his June 1972 understanding with Dobrynin reaffirming the 950 ceiling on SLBMS had not been submitted to Congress as part of the SALT I agreements. Kissinger went on to aver, however, that the terms of the secret understanding had been conveyed to the House and Senate in the testimony of administration witnesses in 1972.[3]

The second Moscow summit began on 25 June 1974 and ended on 3 July with the issue of MIRV limitations still unresolved. A new American proposal providing for unequal numerical limits favorable to the United States (to compensate for the Soviet advantage in throw-weight) on the number of missiles both countries could MIRV was unacceptable to the Soviet government. In rejecting this proposal, Brezhnev is said to have presented to the President a grim assessment of American strategic power, noting both the qualitative superiority of American missiles and the first-strike implications of the Schlesinger retargeting doctrine.[4] The summit meeting ended with both leaders abandoning their commitment of the previous year to conclude a permanent agreement on offensive arms by the end of 1974. In a joint communiqué issued on the final day of talks, Nixon and Brezhnev instead expressed their intention to redirect their governments' efforts toward concluding an eight-year agreement that would enter into force in 1977 on the expiration of the interim agreement. The two leaders also signed a protocol to the 1972 ABM treaty (further limiting ABM deployments to one site in each country) and a treaty prohibiting underground testing of nuclear weapons with yields greater than 150 kilotons.

Assessing the Moscow summit, Secretary Kissinger concluded his

---

[3] The alleged "loophole" in the Kissinger-Dobrynin understanding was finally closed by American and Soviet technical experts on 18 June 1974. For additional details, see Leslie H. Gelb, "Washington Dateline: The Story of a Flap," *Foreign Policy*, no. 16 (Fall 1974), pp. 165–181.

[4] Joseph Kraft, "Letter From Moscow," *New Yorker* (29 July 1974), p. 70, as cited in Wolfe, *The SALT Experience*, p. 82.

3 July press conference with a warning as to the consequences of failing to limit MIRVs in the near future. Such a failure, he stated, would lead to

> an explosion of technology and an explosion of numbers at the end of which we will be lucky if we have the present stability, in which it will be impossible to describe what strategic superiority means. . . . We will be living in a world which will be extraordinarily complex, in which opportunities for nuclear warfare exist that were unimaginable fifteen years ago at the beginning of the nuclear age, and that is what is driving our concern.[5]

The Vladivostok Summit, 1974

The MIRV issue was finally resolved on 24 November 1974. Following President Nixon's resignation on 9 August, the new Ford administration had concluded that political and military considerations warranted renewed efforts to achieve a SALT agreement that would constrain the deployment of new technologies threatening strategic stability and détente.

In the course of another visit to Moscow by Secretary Kissinger in late October, the Soviet Union and the United States accepted a compromise proposal establishing the principle of equal numerical ceilings for each country's central strategic delivery systems and MIRV deployments. After two days of summit negotiations in the Soviet city of Vladivostok in late November, General Secretary Brezhnev and President Ford reached agreement on the basic outline of a SALT II treaty to limit strategic offensive arms until 1985. Under the proposed treaty, each nation would be allowed to deploy 2,400 strategic delivery vehicles, of which 1,320 could be MIRVed. The Soviet Union dropped its demand that it be compensated for FBS and British and French nuclear forces, and the United States gave up on efforts to negotiate limitations on throw-weight. Although difficult issues remained to be resolved, the Vladivostok accord did succeed in establishing a framework for subsequent negotiations.

Once talks resumed at the delegation level in Geneva in January 1975, attention quickly focused on three issues: verification of the MIRV ceiling, cruise missiles, and the Backfire bomber. The two countries were sharply divided on each of these issues. The United States argued that cruise missiles should be exempt from the Vladivostok force ceilings, while Backfire bombers should not, and that all missiles of a type successfully tested with MIRVs had to be counted against the

[5] The text of Secretary Kissinger's 3 July 1974 press conference is among the documents reprinted in Chapter 5.

1,320 ceiling. The Soviet Union took the opposite view on cruise missiles and Backfire bombers. In addition, it asserted that since some of the missiles it was testing with MIRVs would be deployed with single warheads, the American proposal for MIRV verification could not be accepted.

Further complicating the negotiations was a series of events in early 1975 that served to intensify the debates in the United States over détente and America's future role in world affairs. In January Moscow bitterly renounced the trade agreement it had signed with Washington in 1972, after Congress passed legislation linking "most favored nation" trade status and Export-Import Bank credits to liberalization of Soviet emigration policies. Public distrust of Soviet intentions was further heightened by persistent allegations that the Soviet Union was violating provisions of the SALT I agreements. Then, in April 1975, South Vietnam fell to Communist forces backed by the Soviet Union and other Communist countries.

Secretary Kissinger met with Foreign Minister Gromyko in Vienna on 19 and 20 May 1975 to discuss the MIRV verification issue. Solving this problem had become a top priority after Moscow deployed its first MIRVed missile in January. Among the possible solutions considered in Vienna (and during another meeting between Kissinger and Gromyko in Geneva in July) was a provision that would have restricted deployment of MIRVed ICBMs to specified missile fields. Allegations that the Soviets had violated SALT I continued to be heard in Washington, however, making agreement on this solution all but impossible.[6] The Soviet Union finally accepted the original U.S. proposal for MIRV verification as a result of talks between President Ford and General Secretary Brezhnev during the final session of the Helsinki Conference on 30 July and 2 August 1975.

In late 1975 there were subtle signs that a compromise solution to the controversy over cruise missiles and Backfire bombers might

[6] Allegations of Soviet violations of the SALT I agreements were now being voiced by more authoritative sources. In the July 1975 issue of *Reader's Digest*, former Secretary of Defense Melvin Laird wrote that Moscow had "cheated" on both the ABM treaty and the interim agreement. Mr. Laird contended the Soviets had "conducted radar tests specifically forbidden by the treaty" and had "installed new missiles called the SS-19, 50 percent bigger than most of their previous rockets" in approximately fifty silos. (See Melvin R. Laird, "Is *This* Détente?" *Reader's Digest*, July 1975, pp. 54–57.) For additional information on these and other alleged Soviet violations, see Tad Szulc, "Have We Been Had?" *New Republic* (7 June 1975), pp. 11–15; Henry S. Bradsher, "Are the Russians Cheating on Weapons Agreements?" *Washington Star*, 7 July 1975; Walter Slocombe, "Learning from Experience: Verification Guidelines for SALT II," *Arms Control Today*, vol. 6, no. 2 (February 1976); and Melvin R. Laird, "Arms Control: The Russians Are Cheating!" *Reader's Digest*, December 1977, pp. 97–101.

also be within reach. Efforts to capitalize on this opportunity, however, were frustrated by events unfolding in Africa. The Soviet Union and Cuba had begun to supply arms and combat personnel to one of three factions vying for power in Angola. Following the rejection by Congress of President Ford's request for additional funds to aid the opposing factions in the Angolan civil war, Communist-backed forces succeeded in establishing a Marxist government in the former Portuguese colony.

With the first primary elections but a few months away, and facing a serious challenge from more conservative elements within his own party, President Ford sent Secretary Kissinger to Moscow in January 1976 to explore ways of breaking the cruise missile–Backfire bomber deadlock. In the course of Kissinger's meetings with Soviet officials, both countries presented similar compromise proposals entailing some limitations on the range of cruise missiles in exchange for collateral restraints on the deployment of Backfire bombers to provide assurances that they would not be used in a manner threatening to the United States.[7] The Soviet Union also proposed a modest reduction in the number of strategic delivery vehicles authorized in the Vladivostok accord.

Despite the progress registered during the January 1976 Moscow talks, no final solution to the Backfire bomber–cruise missile controversy ever was reached. Arms control had fallen victim to dissension within the Ford administration, the presidential election campaign, and the vicissitudes of détente. With 90 percent of the SALT II treaty reportedly complete, resolution of the remaining 10 percent would await the efforts of a new administration.

---

[7] Secretary Kissinger reportedly proposed that air-launched cruise missiles be limited to a range of 2,500 kilometers (1,550 nautical miles). In addition, aircraft armed with such missiles would be counted against the 1,320 MIRV ceiling set in Vladivostok. See Richard Burt, "The Scope and Limits of SALT," *Foreign Affairs*, vol. 56, no. 4 (July 1978), p. 754.

3
The Washington Summit, June 1973

Kissinger Discusses Prospects for SALT, 14 June 1973

Dr. Kissinger. I thought I would speak to you about our expectations with respect to the forthcoming summit between President Nixon and General Secretary Brezhnev, try to give you our preparations for it, what we expect to come out of it, and then I will take your questions on that or any other subject.

The President and the General Secretary agreed that there would be another summit about a year after the conclusion of the last one when they last met in Moscow in May of last year. They then discussed in general terms what the objectives should be and how we might go about realizing them.

Since then there has been a meeting between the President and Foreign Minister Gromyko, which was quite extensive, both here in Washington and continued at Camp David. There have been frequent exchanges between the General Secretary and the President. There have been exchanges in Washington between Ambassador Dobrynin and American officials.

So the meeting that will take place next week has been carefully prepared for a period of more than a year, and it follows in outline the direction that was established at the May summit in Moscow.

* * *

. . . In the nuclear age there is no alternative to peace between the great nuclear countries. Not only do they have an obligation to avoid conflict, but they have an obligation to exercise restraint in their relations to each other and their relations to third countries, and ultimately they should strive to move from the easing of tension to the achieve-

Source: Press conference of Dr. Henry A. Kissinger, Assistant to the President for National Security Affairs, Washington, D.C., 14 June 1973. *Weekly Compilation of Presidential Documents*, 18 June 1973, pp. 771–778.

ment of positive goals for the benefit of their peoples and the peoples everywhere. This process, which started hesitantly and slowly in 1971 over the negotiations on Berlin, accelerated in the second half of 1971, and culminated in the Moscow summit of May 1972. . . .

Since then, we have attempted to consolidate this progress, and this summit between the General Secretary and the President will be an opportunity to take stock and to attempt to see what further progress can be made, not just in the avoidance of war, but in the building of an international system in which the fear of war comes to play a less and less crucial role and in which the positive aspirations of mankind can become the central focus for the concerns of all the countries, and especially of those countries who have it in their power to bring such untold suffering to mankind.

* * *

The limitations agreed upon last year were quantitative. They concerned the numbers of weapons each side could have in specified categories, and in the case of offensive weapons, this agreement was limited to five years. Since then, negotiations for a permanent agreement on the limitation of strategic arms have started and have been in progress for about six months.

They are more complex than the negotiations that led to the SALT agreement last May on two counts. They are more complex because we are now talking about a permanent agreement that will affect, therefore, the security of ourselves and of those countries that depend on us for the indefinite future. They are more complex, also, because in the last year it has become ever more evident that the arms race now is fueled not so much by quantitative but by qualitative changes. Improvements in accuracy, changes in the number of warheads on individual missiles, and similar technological changes can have a more profound impact on the strategic balance than a mere change in numbers. We are, therefore, involved in extraordinarily complex negotiations. We do not expect—indeed, we do not aim for—a settlement of these questions at this meeting. We will not force the pace of any negotiation to fit a particular schedule that has been established.

What we do expect is that the President and the General Secretary will have very extensive discussions as to the nature of the problem and as to the direction in which a solution might be sought, discussions which might open the way to more harmonious instructions, for more compatible instructions, to the two negotiating teams in Geneva.

We expect that one result of this meeting will be an acceleration of the SALT negotiations, and we hope that this meeting will be seen in

retrospect as having marked a turning point in these negotiations, much as an earlier agreement in 1971 marked the turning point in SALT I.

* * *

Now, last year was the first summit meeting between the President and the Soviet leaders. We expect that these meetings will become regular features of international diplomacy, and, therefore, the breakthroughs that were achieved last year will, in this and future meetings, be consolidated by a series of concrete steps, but along a route now that we hope will become increasingly familiar and will be considered increasingly regular.

One of the principal goals of the President since he came into office has been to create a structure of peace based on the recognition by all countries that they have a stake in the preservation of the international order, that energies could be turned to the achievement of human aspirations, and the recognition that the two great nuclear powers, precisely because they have the capability of inflicting such untold damage, have a special obligation to their peoples and to history to make a special effort in this direction.

* * *

Q. Can you explain how commercial and economic questions are going to play a very important role, given the very strong and continuing opposition in Congress to granting both MFN [most favored nation trade status] and credit to the Soviet Union?

Dr. KISSINGER. Of course, the programs that are planned depend on congressional authority, especially with respect to MFN. We can discuss the goals that the two countries can reasonably set for themselves assuming congressional authority. And we can discuss the kind of projects that would be appropriate both in economic terms and also from the point of view of the impact of the commitment of both sides to a period of peace, if some parts of their economy become to some extent linked to each other.

. . . We believe that the Congress, as it becomes fully informed, and as it studies in detail the relationship of the economic discussions to the general structure of our foreign policy, that the Congress will come to see that it is an important contribution to the whole effort to bring about these—to grant this authority.

* * *

Q. Dr. Kissinger, are you at all concerned at the time Brezhnev is going to be here that the Watergate hearings are going to be in progress, and

especially that former counsel John Dean is going to be testifying that very week with disclosures or accusations that could be very serious in terms of the presidency?

Dr. KISSINGER. When the summit was planned, the domestic evolution was not considered. But at the same time, it was our view that we should proceed with a program that had evolved on the basis of careful negotiation over an extended period of time, that attempts to achieve a peace of benefit to all Americans, and the consequences of having it take place at the same time as the hearings I will leave to the others to judge. There was no reason for us to change the summit. . . .

Q. Dr. Kissinger, on disarmament, two points: Are we going to propose a mutual limit on MIRVS, and also is the time right to propose a total test ban?

Dr. KISSINGER. With respect to the total test ban, we are now undertaking extensive studies within the government which will not be completed by the time of the summit. With respect to the MIRV issue, we have made certain proposals in Geneva, which are now the subject of negotiation.

The MIRV issue is one of the most complex and one of the most baffling before governments, because of the different rate at which the development has proceeded in the two countries, the different philosophy that has underlaid the evolution of their strategic forces, and also because of the difficulty of defining what adequate control for any of these limitations might be.

We expect that the subject will be discussed, but that it is technically so complex that the leaders will be able to do no better than to give guidelines to their negotiators.

* * *

Q. You said that you had hoped that a turning point might be reached in SALT. Does that imply that the negotiations have been stalemated up to this point?

Dr. KISSINGER. If you look at the history of SALT negotiations, you will find that they inevitably go through certain phases. There is an initial phase in which both sides put forward what look like maximum positions, but whose real purpose is to put before each other their general considerations, because I think, it is safe to say that neither side in SALT I or in SALT II ever expected that the opening proposals would be the final ones. The opening proposals are really basic categories which permit a consideration of the various items.

There then comes a second phase in which a conscious effort is made to accommodate the point of view of the other, and to search for common ground. That, too, is very rarely the conclusive phase. We

are now in that second phase. It is a phase which requires very detailed and very thoughtful discussions, which then provides the raw material out of which a breakthrough can be fashioned.

So I think it is incorrect to say that there is a stalemate. I think we are at a relatively earlier phase of the negotiations on SALT II than we were at a comparable time before the summit in SALT I, but we believe that it is following a normal course and that, in fact, the total negotiation period of time for SALT II will be shorter than it was for SALT I.

* * *

Q. Dr. Kissinger, is the United States administration in favor of including strategic bombers and forward-based systems in negotiations in the SALT II talks?

Dr. KISSINGER. I really don't want to go into the details of the negotiations. Of course, strategic bombers are part of the central strategic systems. With respect to forward-based systems, our position has been that this involves the central concerns of our allies and that they are in a different category.

Agreement on Basic Principles of Negotiations on Strategic Arms Limitation, 21 June 1973

The President of the United States of America, Richard Nixon, and the General Secretary of the Central Committee of the CPSU, L. I. Brezhnev,

Having thoroughly considered the question of the further limitation of strategic arms, and the progress already achieved in the current negotiations,

Reaffirming their conviction that the earliest adoption of further limitations of strategic arms would be a major contribution in reducing the danger of an outbreak of nuclear war and in strengthening international peace and security,

Have agreed as follows:

First. The two Sides will continue active negotiations in order to work out a permanent agreement on more complete measures on the limitation of strategic offensive arms, as well as their subsequent reduction, proceeding from the Basic Principles of Relations between the United States of America and the Union of Soviet Socialist Republics signed in Moscow on May 29, 1972, and from the Interim Agreement between the United States of America and the Union of Soviet Socialist Republics of May 26, 1972 on Certain Measures with Respect to the Limitation of Strategic Offensive Arms.

Over the course of the next year the two Sides will make serious efforts to work out the provisions of the permanent agreement on more complete measures on the limitation of strategic offensive arms with the objective of signing it in 1974.

Second. New agreements on the limitation of strategic offensive armaments will be based on the principles of the American-Soviet documents adopted in Moscow in May 1972 and the agreements reached in Washington in June 1973; and in particular, both Sides will be guided by the recognition of each other's equal security interests and by the recognition that efforts to obtain unilateral advantage, directly or indirectly, would be inconsistent with the strengthening of peaceful relations between the United States of America and the Union of Soviet Socialist Republics.

Third. The limitations placed on strategic offensive weapons can apply both to their quantitative aspects as well as to their qualitative improvement.

SOURCE: Basic Principles of Negotiations on the Further Limitation of Strategic Offensive Arms. *Department of State Bulletin*, 23 July 1973, p. 158.

Fourth. Limitations on strategic offensive arms must be subject to adequate verification by national technical means.

Fifth. The modernization and replacement of strategic offensive arms would be permitted under conditions which will be formulated in the agreements to be concluded.

Sixth. Pending the completion of a permanent agreement on more complete measures of strategic offensive arms limitation, both Sides are prepared to reach agreements on separate measures to supplement the existing Interim Agreement of May 26, 1972.

Seventh. Each Side will continue to take necessary organizational and technical measures for preventing accidental or unauthorized use of nuclear weapons under its control in accordance with the Agreement of September 30, 1971 between the United States of America and the Union of Soviet Socialist Republics.

Washington, June 21, 1973

For the United States of America:

RICHARD NIXON

President of the United States of America

For the Union of Soviet Socialist Republics:

L. I. BREZHNEV

General Secretary of the Central Committee, CPSU

Kissinger Outlines the Basic Principles of Negotiations on Strategic Arms Limitation, 21 June 1973

Dr. Kissinger. . . . Let me first give you some background on the principles that have been agreed upon and what they are intended to achieve.

As you know, the second round of SALT started last November, and as you know also, our representative is Ambassador [U. Alexis] Johnson. . . . The objective of these talks has been to consider a permanent agreement limiting offensive weapons to replace the interim agreement that was signed in Moscow last May and which came into effect last October to run for five years.

Now, in negotiating a permanent agreement, one faces problems that are more complex than those in an interim agreement. The essence of the interim agreement was that both sides froze their offensive weapons at the levels they had achieved last May and, frankly, at the levels that were foreseeable over the terms of the interim agreement, for a period of five years. And as you know, we have always rejected the argument that we had agreed to a numerical inferiority in the interim agreement, precisely because there was no possibility of overcoming that numerical inferiority in the five years for which the interim agreement was designed.

On the other hand, when you are dealing with a permanent agreement you are affecting the long-term strategic interests of both countries, and therefore numbers that are acceptable in an interim agreement will have a different connotation in a permanent agreement, and safeguards will have to be looked at in a different context.

Secondly, with respect to a permanent agreement, we now face the situation that the numerical arms race, quantitative arms race, has been, in some respects, eclipsed in significance by the qualitative arms race.

Throughout the 1960s, it was considered that the buildup was the greatest threat to the stability of the arms race and hence to international peace. In this period we have to consider as well that the improvement—refinement—of arms in terms of accuracy, in terms of throw-weight, in terms of multiple warheads, can be profoundly unsettling to this strategic equation even when the numbers on both sides are kept fairly constant.

And thirdly, when one is talking about a permanent agreement,

Source: Press conference of Dr. Henry A. Kissinger, Assistant to the President for National Security Affairs, Washington, D.C., 21 June 1973. *Department of State Bulletin*, 23 July 1973, pp. 134–141.

one has to consider the question not only of limiting arms but the objective of reducing arms. It was in this context that the negotiations started last November and have been conducted for the last six months.

The negotiations went through the usual phase of some exploratory discussions, followed by some more concrete proposals by both sides. However, we faced the situation in April where it became clear that a comprehensive agreement of a permanent nature would require more time than the interval before the summit allowed; and therefore the President [and] General Secretary Brezhnev, in their communications with each other, decided that perhaps the approach of agreeing on some principles that could guide the negotiators, coupled with some full discussions while they were meeting in the United States, could give a new impetus to the talks on strategic arms limitation. This is what was done.

In the closest consultation with Ambassador Johnson and with the allies most concerned, we developed a set of principles on a preliminary basis, which we have further discussed since the General Secretary has arrived in the United States and which led to the agreement which we are releasing today.

* * *

The first principle substantially speaks for itself. It commits both sides to accelerate their efforts, and it commits both sides to make a major effort to achieve an agreement in 1974, or during the course of 1974. The two leaders would not have made this formal statement if they did not believe that this goal was within reach and was attainable.

Therefore it represents a commitment by both sides to bring about—to do their utmost to bring about—a permanent agreement on the limitation of strategic arms during the course of next year. This agreement is to be based on the basic principles of international relations that were established last year in Moscow and on the interim agreement. However, the U.S. position has been clear that the agreement has to be more comprehensive and that the numbers that last governed the interim agreement would not be the numbers of a permanent agreement.

The second principle . . . attempts to set out the basic guidelines in which the two sides will approach the negotiations. It makes it clear that neither side can attempt to achieve through these negotiations a unilateral advantage and, secondly, that we have always maintained the position that we did not separate our security interests from those of our allies.

I must mention one other point with respect to the first principle, which is to say that both sides have agreed that the negotiations should

include not only limitations on strategic arms but measures for the reduction of strategic arms.

The third principle . . . is one of the essential differences between SALT I and SALT II. SALT I concerned primarily exclusively the question of numerical limitation. SALT II will include, as well, qualitative restraint. That will involve discussions on MIRVS, on throw-weight, and issues introduced by the other side with respect to specific types of armaments; for example, on airplanes.

The fourth principle states: "Limitations on strategic offensive arms must be subject to adequate verification by national technical means." [This] is a familiar principle from the previous SALT discussions, and . . . the negotiating record makes it clear that we include also the imperative that both sides will maintain practices which facilitate monitoring the agreement.

The fifth principle applies to the modernization of arms. . . . The essence here is that on the one hand there will be some provision for modernization and replacement. On the other hand, it also makes clear that the modernization and replacement cannot take place except under agreed conditions that do not threaten the purposes of the agreement. . . .

The significance of [the sixth] principle is that with respect to some issues that are time-urgent, in which the interval between now and the time in 1974 when we expect the permanent agreement to be concluded . . . might have a major impact on the existing strategic situations, both sides have agreed that they would be prepared to negotiate supplementary or separate measures to the interim agreement which would probably be of shorter duration and which would of course be absorbed by the permanent agreement.

The seventh principle is a reaffirmation of the accidental war agreement. . . .

* * *

Now, these principles have to be seen also in terms of the negotiating record at Geneva, where both sides are now discussing concrete proposals and where it is therefore perfectly clear what both sides mean by such phrases as "qualitative changes" and other phrases.

It must also be seen in the light of the extensive discussions that took place yesterday between the President and the General Secretary, which dealt with how to give effect to these principles and how to move forward to these negotiations so that the timetable that has been set out in these principles can be realistically met.

These, then, are the principles which will guide our actions over the next year. We expect that they will be seen as a major step in de-

veloping a permament agreement on the limitation of offensive weapons—the ultimate reduction—as a move toward bringing under control not only the pace of the arms race but its nature, and therefore will contribute to long-term prospects of peace.

Now I will be glad to answer any questions.

Q. Dr. Kissinger, why do you find the need to provide for further interim agreements if you think you are going to have a permanent agreement within eighteen months?

Dr. Kissinger. This issue will of course be left in detail to the negotiators. The need could arise, for example, in the case of certain technological developments, where restraints on the pace of testing could affect the situation in the space over the next twelve to eighteen months. It would be applied to those issues which are sensitive to the time interval that has been outlined in this agreement. It would not, obviously, apply to such issues as the numbers of weapons to be deployed because that would not arise in the twelve- to eighteen-month period.

Q. Does the United States seek parity in numbers in the permanent agreement?

Dr. Kissinger. The issue of how you define equal security and no unilateral advantage is one of the most complex. As you know, with respect to the interim agreement, we believe that the larger number of our warheads compensated for the somewhat larger number of their missiles, and also the larger number of our airplanes. And we also concluded that in the five-year period of this agreement we were not going to increase the number of these weapons anyway.

With respect to a permanent ban, the limitations must be equitable; that is, they must take into account the numbers of weapons and the numbers of warheads. And we will certainly seek, and we will obtain, what we consider strategic parity.

Q. So you don't have to have exactly the same numbers in terms—

Dr. Kissinger. It depends what other limitations exist, and therefore it is very difficult to answer it in the abstract. In general, our objective will be equality, but how you calculate this equality, we have to leave open to the negotiators. In effect, though, the total compositions of the forces should be substantially equal. . . .

Q. . . . If you mean that [the agreement] will deal with qualitative matters, can you relate principle 4, on the use of national technical means of inspection, to the control of MIRVs? Are you announcing that the United States is prepared to use national technical means of inspection to verify any kind of MIRV agreement that might be forthcoming?

Dr. Kissinger. . . . I think I would put it another way. I would say any kind of MIRV agreement that may be reached will have to be one that can be verified by national technical means, and therefore that those

MIRV agreements that are not verifiable by national technical means would be difficult to reconcile with these provisions, and therefore the question depends on the nature of MIRV limitations that we are talking about. But as I have made clear, we consider the development of multiple independent warheads one of the major factors of concern in the arms race. And that is clearly understood by the other side.

* * *

Q. Dr. Kissinger, is there any understanding about whether forward-based systems will be considered in these negotiations?

Dr. KISSINGER. The basic position of the two sides has been elaborated in previous negotiations. We have left no doubt that we consider our security interests and those of our allies inseparable, and that we believe that the central strategic systems should be the principal concern of this phase of the negotiations; that is to say, the ICBMS, bombers, and submarine-launched ballistic missiles.

The Soviet Union has taken a different view in the past. It is a view that we managed to avoid having to address in the first phase of SALT, and it is something which we believe can be negotiated in the second phase of SALT.

But we can state now that with respect to forward-based systems, we will make no agreement that separates our security interests from those of our allies, and that we believe that in this phase the central strategic systems should be the principal focus of negotiations.

Q. What can you tell us of the changes the Soviets have made in the last year in their missile programs and whether they have been completely in accordance with the agreements reached in Moscow?

Dr. KISSINGER. The Soviet Union, to the best of my information, has pursued an active program within the terms of the agreement. If we should receive any information that is contrary to that, we will actively pursue it in the standing committee and in other channels. . . .

Q. What is new about the qualitative principle? I thought it was understood right along that SALT II would be qualitative as well as numerical. Are you saying here there is something in this that now permits the Soviet Union to place a freeze on MIRVS? Is that what is new here? If not, what is the change?

Dr. KISSINGER. I am saying this is the first time that there is a formal statement to this effect by both sides. . . .

Q. So it is that the Soviet Union has agreed to negotiate on MIRV?

Dr. KISSINGER. I don't want to speak to the Soviet position because qualitative can include many things in addition to MIRV.

Q. Dr. Kissinger, is the final agreement on SALT contingent on any agreement or understanding of any kind, and if not, what is all this talk

about SALT not being reachable if the Soviet Union does not get most favored nation treatment?

Dr. KISSINGER. The SALT agreement is independent of other agreements, but it is of course dependent on the general climate of U.S.–Soviet relations. We have always held the view that the relationship between the general political climate and progress in SALT was close. It is not, however, linked as a condition to progress in any other negotiation; it has not been stated as such by us.

Q. Dr. Kissinger, may I follow that up? In the event the Jackson amendment[1] is adopted, will SALT go down the drain?

Dr. KISSINGER. I would not speculate on any particular agreement. We have said that in the event that the Jackson amendment is adopted in its present form that it would have a serious impact on Soviet-American relations. What the particular impact will be on any specific negotiation, I would not want to go into.

Q. Dr. Kissinger, what can we say to our readers in the area of the prospects for reductions? Aren't you kind of dangling out the proposition here that the world can look forward to a reduction in the spending for nuclear armaments? What can we tell them the real prospects might be? When would it come, the lower number of missiles? Would it involve large amounts of savings on either side?

Dr. KISSINGER. I don't want to go into specific proposals that are being negotiated. I will only say that our proposals will be consistent with these principles and they will include proposals for initial limitations to be followed by ultimate reductions.

Q. Dr. Kissinger, the linkage was not stated by us, with any other agreements. Have the Soviets raised the question of a linkage?

Dr. KISSINGER. The Soviet Union also has not raised any particular linkage.

Q. Dr. Kissinger, you said the numbers in the temporary agreement would not be the numbers in the permanent agreement—

Dr. KISSINGER. Not necessarily.

Q. Is it our side's position that the Soviet Union's numbers will have to be decreased more than our numbers have to, to reduce or eliminate the apparent disparity between the numbers agreed upon in the temporary agreement, and if so, do they accept that as a general proposition?

Dr. KISSINGER. How you set these limits, and what weapons you include in these limits, is of course one of the key issues in the negotia-

[1] Senator Henry M. Jackson and Representative Charles A. Vanik sponsored amendments to the Trade Reform Act of 1974 which prohibited the extension of most favored nation duty treatment and government-backed trade credits to any Communist nation that failed to allow substantially free emigration for its citizens.—Ed.

tions. For example, if you include bombers in the limits, the inequality in total numbers is different than if you are only talking about missiles.

Therefore, at what figure you set the limit, whether you set it at one below both sides' current strength, at the strength of one side, or somewhere in between, that remains to be determined through the negotiations, and I don't want to speculate on that.

Q. Dr. Kissinger, can you tell us, sir, if an attempt was made to reach an agreement in principle here on a MIRV freeze but that was found to perhaps be too complex to achieve at this stage of the negotiations?

Dr. KISSINGER. I don't want to go into the details of any particular negotiation. I don't think that would be appropriate for me to do.

* * *

Q. I have a double question. The first is: The implication of your earlier comment about national means and MIRVs—does that mean you will have to have a limitation on flight tests, a test ban on MIRVs, and you cannot get into a production ban? And the second question: If the two leaders are confident enough to set a deadline for the negotiations, why couldn't the other principles be more specific on such questions as MIRV and the numbers than you have been able to be today?

Dr. KISSINGER. Because, first, with respect to the question of what sort of limitations are verifiable by national means, it is obvious that flight testing is more easily verifiable than production, and this has been an issue we have covered in previous discussions on MIRV.

With respect to the principles, our objective is to have the permanent agreement and not have a spectacular announcement. Many issues that can be agreed to in principle nevertheless leave a margin—a narrow margin, but nevertheless a margin—for subsequent discussion, such as numbers, such as the type of qualitative limitations, and such as the procedures to be followed in eliminating the remaining margins. And for that reason, it was thought to be best if we went no further, then, now. But there have been discussions on how to proceed from here to meet this objective with some confidence.

Q. Dr. Kissinger, when you talk of quality, are you including limitations on technical improvements of accuracy of warheads?

Dr. KISSINGER. When I speak of quality, these are all permissible issues to be raised. They have to be seen, however, in the context of verifiability. And the more esoteric the problem the more complex the problem of verification becomes. And it is not in the interests of either side to have agreements, particularly of a permanent nature, in which both sides feel they are at the mercy of developments that they cannot control.

So I would say, in principle, this is something that can be included

in these discussions probably by means of restrictions on testing. In practice, however, it is getting into the more esoteric areas.

Q. Can you express confidence that we will have some kind of limitation, particularly on land-based MIRVS, within the next eighteen months?

Dr. KISSINGER. I have confidence that we will achieve an agreement consistent with the principles enunciated.

Agreement on Prevention of Nuclear War, 22 June 1973

The United States of America and the Union of Soviet Socialist Republics, hereinafter referred to as the Parties,

Guided by the objectives of strengthening world peace and international security,

Conscious that nuclear war would have devastating consequences for mankind,

Proceeding from the desire to bring about conditions in which the danger of an outbreak of nuclear war anywhere in the world would be reduced and ultimately eliminated,

Proceeding from their obligation under the Charter of the United Nations regarding the maintenance of peace, refraining from the threat or use of force, and the avoidance of war, and in conformity with the agreements to which either Party has subscribed,

Proceeding from the Basic Principles of Relations between the United States of America and the Union of Soviet Socialist Republics signed in Moscow on May 29, 1972,

Reaffirming that the development of relations between the United States of America and the Union of Soviet Socialist Republics is not directed against other countries and their interests,

Have agreed as follows:

Article I

The United States and the Soviet Union agree that an objective of their policies is to remove the danger of nuclear war and of the use of nuclear weapons.

Accordingly, the Parties agree that they will act in such a manner as to prevent the development of situations capable of causing a dangerous exacerbation of their relations, as to avoid military confrontations, and as to exclude the outbreak of nuclear war between them and between either of the Parties and other countries.

Article II

The Parties agree, in accordance with Article I and to realize the objective stated in that Article, to proceed from the premise that each Party will refrain from the threat or use of force against the other Party, against the allies of the other Party and against other countries,

---

Source: Agreement between the United States of America and the Union of Soviet Socialist Republics on the Prevention of Nuclear War. *Department of State Bulletin*, 23 July 1973, pp. 160–161.

in circumstances which may endanger international peace and security. The Parties agree that they will be guided by these considerations in the formulation of their foreign policies and in their actions in the field of international relations.

Article III

The Parties undertake to develop their relations with each other and with other countries in a way consistent with the purposes of this Agreement.

Article IV

If at any time relations between the Parties or between either Party and other countries appear to involve the risk of a nuclear conflict, or if relations between countries not parties to this Agreement appear to involve the risk of nuclear war between the United States of America and the Union of Soviet Socialist Republics or between either Party and other countries, the United States and the Soviet Union, acting in accordance with the provisions of this Agreement, shall immediately enter into urgent consultations with each other and make every effort to avert this risk.

Article V

Each Party shall be free to inform the Security Council of the United Nations, the Secretary General of the United Nations and the Governments of allied or other countries of the progress and outcome of consultations initiated in accordance with Article IV of this Agreement.

Article VI

Nothing in this Agreement shall affect or impair:

(a) the inherent right of individual or collective self-defense as envisaged by Article 51 of the Charter of the United Nations.

(b) the provisions of the Charter of the United Nations, including those relating to the maintenance or restoration of international peace and security, and

(c) the obligations undertaken by either Party towards its allies or other countries in treaties, agreements, and other appropriate documents.

Article VII

This Agreement shall be of unlimited duration.

ARTICLE VIII

This Agreement shall enter into force upon signature.

DONE at Washington on June 22, 1973, in two copies, each in the English and Russian languages, both texts being equally authentic.

For the United States of America:

RICHARD NIXON

President of the United States of America

For the Union of Soviet Socialist Republics:

L. I. BREZHNEV

General Secretary of the Central Committee, CPSU

Kissinger Explains the Agreement on Prevention of Nuclear War, 22 June 1973

DR. KISSINGER. Ladies and gentlemen, let me put this agreement [on the prevention of nuclear war] first in its context, describe what it is seeking to achieve, and then go through its specific provisions, a little bit of its history, and then I will take your questions.

The principal goal of the foreign policy of this administration ever since 1969 has been to set up what the President has called a structure of peace, by which we mean an international system less geared to the management of crises, less conscious of constant eruptions of conflict, in which the principal participants operate with a consciousness of stability and permanence.

This requires that all of the nations operate with a sense of responsibility, and it puts a particular obligation on the two great nuclear powers that have the capacity to destroy mankind and whose conflicts have produced so many of the crises of the postwar period.

In achieving this objective, the United States has operated on many levels. We have always believed that it required adequate strength to deter aggression. But we also have believed that we have to move from the period of military confrontation to a period which is characterized more by restraints and, eventually, cooperation. In our dealings with the other great nuclear superpower, the President, from the day of his first inauguration, has emphasized that we wanted to move from confrontation to negotiation.

In those negotiations we have operated on many levels. We have attempted to remove specific causes of tension. We have attempted to forge specific instruments of cooperation. And finally, we have attempted to develop certain principles of conduct by which the two great nuclear countries could guide their expectations and by which, both in relations to each other and in their relations to third countries, they could calm the atmosphere and replace purely military measures by a new attitude of a cooperative international system.

It is in this spirit that last year in Moscow the United States and the Soviet Union signed certain principles of conduct which were described then as a roadmap on a road that no one was forced to travel but that if we wanted to travel it, it was there for the two major countries.

SOURCE: Press conference of Dr. Henry A. Kissinger, Assistant to the President for National Security Affairs, Washington, D.C., 22 June 1973. *Department of State Bulletin*, 23 July 1973, pp. 141–147.

I believe we have traveled on this road in the last year; and therefore it was decided to formalize some of these principles in an agreement, to extend them in some respects, particularly concerning consultation. The origin of the negotiation, as it turned out, was at the last session of the Moscow summit meeting when there were some general exchanges with respect to how to control nuclear weapons in a political and diplomatic sense, beyond the negotiations going on in strategic arms limitations. . . .

Throughout, the United States has held the view that any obligations with respect to international conduct that applied to the great nuclear powers also had to apply to their relations to other countries, and we have held the view, which was shared by the Soviet leaders, that the principal problem was how to prevent a war and not how to conduct a war.

Therefore this is an agreement which is designed to regulate the relations of the two nuclear powers to each other and to other countries in time of peace. It is an attempt to prevent the outbreak of nuclear war. And to the extent that it contributes to this task, it can be a significant landmark in the relationship of the United States to the Soviet Union and in the relationships of the two great nuclear countries toward all other countries of the world.

Now let me run through the articles, which are largely self-explanatory.

Article I states that it is an objective of both the policy of the United States and the policy of the Soviet Union to remove the danger of nuclear war and the use of nuclear weapons. This has been a consistent goal of American foreign policy and is a goal shared by all of mankind.

Article II applies this objective to the general conduct of both sides; that is to say, the prevention of nuclear war presupposes the avoidance of situations capable of an exacerbation of relations, avoidance of military confrontation, and it is in that context that the outbreak of nuclear war can be excluded. The second article states this more concretely by elaborating that the prevention of nuclear war presupposes the avoidance of force or the use or threat of force by the two nuclear countries toward each other and toward other countries.

Article III is a general article that simply states that the two nuclear countries have to develop their relations with each other and with third countries in a way consistent with the purposes of this agreement, and it makes it clear that while it is a bilateral agreement the obligations are multilateral.

Article IV states that in any situation in which the two great

nuclear countries might find themselves in a nuclear confrontation, or in which either as a result of their policies toward each other or as the result of developments elsewhere in the world there is a danger of a nuclear confrontation between them or between them or any other country, they are obligated to consult with each other in order to avoid this risk.

Article V permits the consultation—that these consultations be communicated to the United Nations and to other countries, a clause which we would of course apply to our allies.

Article VI makes clear that this agreement deals with the prevention of war and that if it fails, the existing obligations in existing documents, treaties, and alliances will be maintained.

So, we see the basic significance of this agreement as a step, a significant step, toward the prevention of nuclear war and the prevention of military conflict. It is a formal obligation that the two nuclear superpowers have taken toward each other and, equally importantly, toward all other countries to practice restraint in their diplomacy, to build a peace that is permanent, to pursue a policy whose dedication to stability and peace will become, as General Secretary Brezhnev said last night at the banquet, irreversible.

Of course, anyone who has studied the history of the last thirty years must recognize that agreements are not always maintained and that there is nothing self-enforcing about this document. However, if the two great nuclear countries continue to be animated by the spirit in which they have conducted their policy of the last two years, then this document could mark a landmark on the road toward the structure of peace of which the President has been speaking and can be seen as a step toward a new era of cooperation in the relations of all nations and of lifting from them increasingly the fear of nuclear war and of war in general.

* * *

Q. . . . It seems to me that we agreed on the desirability of motherhood here. I don't see why it took so long to reach this agreement and what the disputes were. I wonder if you could outline some of the negotiations that went on, and what were the issues in this discussion?

Dr. KISSINGER. Well, I don't agree, first of all, with your premise, because this agreement was made by two countries whose conflicts and confrontations have characterized the entire postwar period. For them to formalize these series of restraints, the willingness to consult, was a very major step.

Secondly, I don't think it is useful at the conclusion of the negotia-

tion to go through all of the debates and provide a scorecard. I have indicated the general approach that we took, which was to extend the applications to the international system in general and not just have them apply to the United States and to the Soviet Union, and to put the emphasis on the prevention of war rather than on how wars might be conducted. But I don't think any useful purpose is served by going through all of the complexities.

Q. I have a two-part question. According to Article II, would China be regarded as an ally of the Soviet Union? And secondly, to what degree would this document be conceived as an effort to forestall any kind of military action against China?

Dr. KISSINGER. What Article II says is that force and the threat of force cannot be used against the ally of another country; it doesn't say anything about one's own allies. But it also says force and the threat of force cannot be used against any other country, so clearly under this agreement the use of force against any country under circumstances that would have wide international repercussions would be precluded.

It was not conceived as a protection for any particular country, but I think its practical consequence is that if it were observed—as we of course expect it will be—it will have the practical consequences of applying both to the situation you described as well as to many other conceivable situations.

Q. May I follow that up, Dr. Kissinger, please? Did you have prior consultations when you met with the Chinese representatives several days ago about any form of this document? And would you at some point this year or next like to broaden the document to include China as a signatory?

Dr. KISSINGER. The United States consulted several countries prior to the completion of this document, but I don't want to go into an enumeration of which countries were consulted. I do not discuss my conversations with the head of the Chinese Liaison Office, but I have no particular reason to suppose that they will necessarily approve a bilateral agreement between the United States and the Soviet Union, whatever its consequences. I will let them speak for themselves.

Q. Dr. Kissinger, there is one qualifier in Article II, where it says that both parties will refrain from the use or threat of force in circumstances which may endanger international security. When the Soviets went into Czechoslovakia, they obviously thought it didn't endanger international peace, and when the United States went into North Vietnam, they felt it didn't endanger international peace. Isn't that a large hole for a truck to go through?

Dr. KISSINGER. If either of the two signatories wants to find an excuse

to go to war, it will find an excuse to go to war. This has been the history of the postwar period. We are talking here of restraint on significant military actions; and what endangers international peace and security is not determined by the unilateral declaration of the country going to war but also by the reactions of other members of the international system, because this is what produces the threat to international peace and security.

Therefore, again, I can only repeat, if any of the signatories deal with this like sharp lawyers pushing against the edges of the agreement, they will of course then find ways of doing so.

On the other hand, the movement into sovereign countries of large forces would not be in our view consistent with the spirit of this agreement; but I really do not want to go into a detailed analysis of every conceivable situation that could arise.

Q. Dr. Kissinger, while realizing you cannot go into specific circumstances, could you discuss in a general way what your expectations are for applying this principle, for example, to the Middle East area or Asia to reduce the dangers of nuclear war in either of those areas?

Dr. Kissinger. I really do not want to go into specific areas. Obviously, if we did not believe that this agreement could make a contribution to bringing about international restraint in areas which have been demonstrable sources of international tension, if we did not believe it could make a major contribution to this, we would not have agreed to proceed with it.

So, as a general answer to your question, I would say that it is our intention to proceed on the basis that the restraint foreseen by this agreement will become an increasingly vital factor in international affairs. . . .

Q. Dr. Kissinger, I have two questions. You have said it would be impossible to indicate in every situation what this might tend to prohibit or inhibit. Could you give us an example looking back over the past twenty or twenty-five years of any situation in which force has been applied which you think it would be inhibited in the future? That is the first question.

The second question is: This is the kind of agreement which the Russians have been inclined to sign with a number of countries, and I wonder whether or not it was they who were the ones who originally raised the idea back in Moscow last May?

Dr. Kissinger. As to the agreement as it has now emerged, it would be difficult to say who raised the particular nature of this agreement. When the discussions were first raised in Moscow last year, it was indeed by the Soviet Union, but in a different context. The original dis-

cussion that gave the impetus to this has been transformed into an agreement in which, I think, the contribution of both sides can be said to be equal—

Q. You are particularly talking about the broadening aspect to other countries?

Dr. KISSINGER. And the emphasis on the prevention of war in general. But again, on the approach, I think at this point it can be said that both parties made a substantially equal contribution to this agreement.

Now, secondly, with respect to situations that might be prevented, I can think of several crises in this administration, and I would have thought in previous periods—the Cuban missile crisis would be one example. Several Berlin crises that we have had would be other examples that would have been avoided. I can think of some in this administration, but again, when we are talking about restraint we are talking about things that do not happen.

It is never very easy to demonstrate why something has not happened. I think it reflects the changes that have occurred in the international environment that such an agreement, which would have been inconceivable, say, on the visit fifteen years ago of Khrushchev, can now be described in one question as simply affirming motherhood—it is not the virtues of motherhood or desirability of motherhood.

Q. Dr. Kissinger, this agreement obviously will have a long-term effect within the United States and other countries. I wonder why this was not written in a treaty form so that the Senate could get a chance to discuss it in its entirety and question you about it. And two, has there really been discussion with the NATO allies? I know you didn't want to discuss that, but obviously in Europe there will be concern about the American credibility in case of large-scale conventional attacks in central Europe.

Dr. KISSINGER. There can be no concern, because Article VI fully covers existing NATO obligations, and because if war is not prevented there is no particular restraint then about how it is conducted. Secondly, several NATO allies were closely consulted over an extended period of time, but I don't want to go into details.

Q. As to the first part of the question, on the treaty?

Dr. KISSINGER. Excuse me. With respect to why it was not made in treaty form, it does not involve any particular positive actions that the United States has to take and it is a general statement of policy. The President, however, is meeting with the congressional leaders at 11:30, and he will discuss with them ways in which the Congress can register its support if it wishes to do so.

*   *   *

Q. Dr. Kissinger, do you interpret this document as one that supersedes the so-called Brezhnev doctrine?

Dr. Kissinger. This document makes no distinction in its application between the domestic structure of various forms of countries.

Q. Dr. Kissinger, is this document a renunciation of atomic war, and if not, why not?

Dr. Kissinger. . . .This document is designed to prevent the outbreak of nuclear war by imposing restraints on the major countries with respect to nuclear war and with respect to the use of force in general. Therefore it does not address the question of what happens if war cannot be prevented, because that is not its purpose. Its purpose is to prevent wars. It is not a renunciation of a particular form of war if war cannot be prevented, but we hope that it will make a major contribution to the prevention of war. . . .

Q. Did you discuss the concept of not using nuclear force first against each other, and why wasn't that included? . . .

Dr. Kissinger. There are two ways you can look at how to prevent nuclear war. One is by preventing war, and the second is by imposing on yourselves specific restraints with respect to particular categories of weapons if war cannot be avoided.

We choose to go the road of attempting to prevent war, and thereby nuclear war, because many other countries depend upon what actions will be taken in case an aggression occurs. Therefore, we did not believe it would contribute to peace if we made particular distinctions as to categories of weapons in case of war.

The overriding problem is to preserve the peace and to prevent war.

Q. Dr. Kissinger, does Article IV oblige the United States to act as sort of an arbiter or mediator of the Sino-Soviet conflict if it should get worse?

Dr. Kissinger. No. What Article IV provides is that if either of the countries contemplates nuclear war with any other country, or of course with the other nuclear country, it has an obligation to consult the other signatory with the purpose of avoiding the situation that would produce such a war.

We have no intention of being an arbiter between the Soviet Union and the People's Republic of China, and we look at this consultation as a mutual restraint rather than as one that creates a right of intervention all over the world.

Joint U.S.-U.S.S.R. Communiqué, 24 June 1973

At the invitation of the President of the United States, Richard Nixon, extended during his official visit to the USSR in May 1972, and in accordance with a subsequent agreement, General Secretary of the Central Committee of the Communist Party of the Soviet Union, Mr. Leonid I. Brezhnev, paid an official visit to the United States from June 18 to June 25. . . .

President Nixon and General Secretary Brezhnev held thorough and constructive discussions on the progress achieved in the development of US-Soviet relations and on a number of major international problems of mutual interest. . . .

I. The General State of US–Soviet Relations

Both Sides expressed their mutual satisfaction with the fact that the American-Soviet summit meeting in Moscow in May 1972 and the joint decisions taken there have resulted in a substantial advance in the strengthening of peaceful relations between the USA and the USSR and have created the basis for the further development of broad and mutually beneficial cooperation in various fields of mutual interest to the peoples of both countries and in the interests of all mankind. They noted their satisfaction with the mutual effort to implement strictly and fully the treaties and agreements concluded between the USA and the USSR, and to expand areas of cooperation.

They agreed that the process of reshaping relations between the USA and the USSR on the basis of peaceful coexistence and equal security as set forth in the Basic Principles of Relations Between the USA and the USSR signed in Moscow on May 29, 1972 is progressing in an encouraging manner. They emphasized the great importance that each Side attaches to these Basic Principles. They reaffirmed their commitment to the continued scrupulous implementation and to the enhancement of the effectiveness of each of the provisions of that document.

Both Sides noted with satisfaction that the outcome of the US-Soviet meeting in Moscow in May 1972 was welcomed by other States and by world opinion as an important contribution to strengthening peace and international security, to curbing the arms race and to developing businesslike cooperation among States with different social systems.

Both Sides viewed the return visit to the USA of the General Secre-

Source: *Department of State Bulletin*, 23 July 1973, pp. 130–134.

tary of the Central Committee of the CPSU, L. I. Brezhnev, and the talks held during the visit as an expression of their mutual determination to continue the course toward a major improvement in US-Soviet relations.

Both Sides are convinced that the discussions they have just held represent a further milestone in the constructive development of their relations.

Convinced that such a development of American-Soviet relations serves the interests of both of their peoples and all of mankind, it was decided to take further major steps to give these relations maximum stability and to turn the development of friendship and cooperation between their peoples into a permanent factor for worldwide peace.

II. The Prevention of Nuclear War and the Limitation of Strategic Armaments

Issues related to the maintenance and strengthening of international peace were a central point of the talks between President Nixon and General Secretary Brezhnev.

Conscious of the exceptional importance for all mankind of taking effective measures to that end, they discussed ways in which both Sides could work toward removing the danger of war, and especially nuclear war, between the USA and the USSR and between either party and other countries. Consequently, in accordance with the Charter of the United Nations and the Basic Principles of Relations of May 29, 1972, it was decided to conclude an Agreement Between the USA and the USSR on the Prevention of Nuclear War. That Agreement was signed by the President and the General Secretary on June 22, 1973. The text has been published separately.

The President and the General Secretary, in appraising this Agreement, believe that it constitutes a historical landmark in Soviet-American relations and substantially strengthens the foundations of international security as a whole. The United States and the Soviet Union state their readiness to consider additional ways of strengthening peace and removing forever the danger of war, and particularly nuclear war.

In the course of the meetings, intensive discussions were held on questions of strategic arms limitation. In this connection both Sides emphasized the fundamental importance of the Treaty on the Limitation of Anti-Ballistic Missile Systems and the Interim Agreement on Certain Measures with Respect to the Limitation of Strategic Offensive Arms signed between the USA and the USSR in May 1972 which, for the first time in history, place actual limits on the most modern and most formidable types of armaments.

Having exchanged views on the progress in the implementation of these agreements, both Sides reaffirmed their intention to carry them out and their readiness to move ahead jointly toward an agreement on the further limitation of strategic arms.

Both Sides noted that progress has been made in the negotiations that resumed in November 1972, and that the prospects for reaching a permanent agreement on more complete measures limiting strategic offensive armaments are favorable.

Both Sides agreed that the progress made in the limitation of strategic armaments is an exceedingly important contribution to the strengthening of US-Soviet relations and to world peace.

On the basis of their discussions, the President and the General Secretary signed on June 21, 1973, Basic Principles of Negotiations on the Further Limitation of Strategic Offensive Arms. The text has been published separately.

The USA and the USSR attach great importance to joining with all States in the cause of strengthening peace, reducing the burden of armaments, and reaching agreements on arms limitation and disarmament measures.

Considering the important role which an effective international agreement with respect to chemical weapons would play, the two Sides agreed to continue their efforts to conclude such an agreement in cooperation with other countries.

The two Sides agree to make every effort to facilitate the work of the Committee on Disarmament which has been meeting in Geneva. They will actively participate in negotiations aimed at working out new measures to curb and end the arms race. They reaffirm that the ultimate objective is general and complete disarmament, including nuclear disarmament, under strict international control. A world disarmament conference could play a role in this process at an appropriate time.

* * *

Both Sides believe that the talks at the highest level, which were held in a frank and constructive spirit, were very valuable and made an important contribution to developing mutually advantageous relations between the USA and the USSR. In the view of both Sides, these talks will have a favorable impact on international relations.

They noted that the success of the discussions in the United States was facilitated by the continuing consultation and contacts as agreed in May 1972. They reaffirmed that the practice of consultation should continue. They agreed that further meetings at the highest level should be held regularly.

Having expressed his appreciation to President Nixon for the hospitality extended during the visit to the United States, General Secretary Brezhnev invited the President to visit the USSR in 1974. The invitation was accepted.

June 24, 1973

RICHARD NIXON
President of the United States of America

LEONID I. BREZHNEV
General Secretary of the Central Committee, CPSU

4
Nuclear Strategy and SALT

Schlesinger Announces a Change in Nuclear Targeting, 10 January 1974

Q. What is the status of what has been described as a very difficult problem of coordinating the administration's position on a new approach to the SALT talks? And, if you can, what do you foresee in the next round of the SALT talks?
Secretary SCHLESINGER. I'm not sure that there is that great a difficulty in arriving at a position save to point out that the achievement of a strategic balance is an immensely complicated subject, in that one has to trade off numbers, throw-weight and the like.

Our objective is to obtain what we have referred to as essential equivalence. I think that I should underscore the fact, therefore, [that] we are prepared to reduce, stay level, or, if need be, increase our level of strategic arms, and that level will be determined by the policies and the decisions of the Soviet Union. If the Soviet Union is prepared to reduce arms, we can accommodate them. If the Soviet Union insists on moving ahead with a new set of deployments, we will be forced to match them. Therefore, as long as it is understood what our ultimate objective is, I think that by and large we have only the standard difficulties in agreeing on details within the administration. Now there's some question about timing, tactics, and the like, but I don't think that there's any disagreement within the administration with regard to the objectives.

I think it is important to point out an additional distinction. There is in prospect—or there has taken place, to be more precise—a change in the strategies of the United States with regard to the hypothetical employment of central strategic forces. A change in target-

SOURCE: Remarks of Secretary of Defense James R. Schlesinger before the Overseas Writers Association, Washington, 10 January 1974. Department of Defense, Public Affairs.

ing strategy as it were. This intersects with the issue [of] our position at SALT, but it is quite distinct from that position.

In order to bring about alterations in our targeting strategies, we do not have to increase the numbers or the throw-weight of what we have in our strategic arsenal. The sizing of the strategic arsenal will depend upon SALT and will depend upon the position taken by the Soviets at SALT. As I've indicated, we must be in a position in which the Soviets fully understand that if they insist on racing that we are prepared to match them, but that it is better by far, for both sides, to agree on essential equivalence. Consequently, the sizing of our strategic forces depends on SALT. The change in targeting doctrine is separable from that and does not impact necessarily on the sizing of our strategic forces.

Q. Could you amplify on the change in targeting strategy?

Secretary SCHLESINGER. I think that this has been discussed over the years; that to a large extent the American doctrinal position has been wrapped around something called "assured destruction," which implies a tendency to target Soviet cities initially and massively, and that this is the principal option that the president of the United States or the National Command Authorities would have in the event of a possible recourse to strategic weapons. It is our intention that this not be the only option and possibly not the principal option open to the National Command Authorities. . . .

Q. Could you put it in language so that a layman can understand what you're driving at?

Secretary SCHLESINGER. The main point that should be understood is that both sides now have, and will continue to have, invulnerable second-strike forces, and that with those invulnerable second-strike forces it is inevitable, or virtually inevitable, that the employment by one side of its forces against the cities of the other side in an all-out strike will immediately bring a counterstrike against its own cities. Consequently, the range of circumstances in which an all-out strike against an opponent's cities can be contemplated has narrowed considerably, and one wishes to have alternatives for the employment of strategic forces other than what would be for the party initiating a suicidal strike against the cities of the other side.

Q. Are you not saying, sir, that we would be shifting our targets to Soviet weapons rather than Soviet cities, and we will be perhaps improving the accuracy of our missiles so that we can knock out the Soviet missile sites if we have to, rather than going for the Soviet cities? Is that what you're saying?

Secretary SCHLESINGER. No. I think parts of that are quite appropriate, but not entirely. As I indicated a moment ago, the forces on both

sides are now so large and so secure that both sides have invulnerable second-strike capabilities, and therefore it is not possible to achieve a disarming first strike, which I think you were referring to.

Now, what I was referring to is a set of selective options against different sets of targets. We would not necessarily specify any particular set of targets. Military targets, whether silos or other military targets, are, of course, one of the possible target sets. But it is necessary to maintain a set of options which goes beyond the inherent attack—all-out attack—against enemy cities in the event of nuclear exchanges.

Q. Are you going to try to permit the improvement of nuclear accuracy?

Secretary SCHLESINGER. Yes.

Q. When was that decision made? How recently?

Secretary SCHLESINGER. I'm not sure what you mean by that. To what extent have I felt this way? I have felt that way—

Q. When was the decision made to improve the accuracy of nuclear targeting?

Secretary SCHLESINGER. To the extent that I have been involved with the Department of Defense, it has been since I've been at the Department of Defense.

Q. There have been some constraints [inaudible] to develop [inaudible]. Are you really saying we're going to go for more accuracy, which the military has not been permitted to do? I'm trying to decide at what point in time. . . .

Secretary SCHLESINGER. The answer to that, and I have no desire whatsoever to equivocate, is that there is no single point in time at which such a decision can be described as having taken place. I have discussed these matters with the Joint Chiefs over a period of months and, consequently, at any point in time they were fully cognizant of my position. Now, if you are referring to when a piece of paper went forward, I believe that the pieces of paper went forward last summer.

Q. Was there not a commitment by the President in a letter to Senator [Edward W.] Brooke[1] that the government would not [inaudible]?

Secretary SCHLESINGER. No, I don't believe so. I think that the government has indicated that it is not seeking a first-strike disarming capability. As I've indicated before, that capability is not within our grasp.

---

[1] In response to Senator Brooke's 5 December 1969 letter expressing concern over the implications of the MIRV program for a potential counterforce capability, President Nixon wrote to the Senator on 29 December that "the purpose of our strategic program is to maintain our deterrent, not to threaten any nation with a first strike. . . . There is no current U.S. program to develop a so-called 'hard-target' MIRV capability." See Alton Frye, *A Responsible Congress: The Politics of National Security* (New York: McGraw-Hill, 1975), p. 70.—Ed.

Q. Can we get at this in another way in terms of increased accuracy; development of new systems, for instance, cruise missiles? Is that what you're talking about?—in order to get this increased accuracy you go forward with the development of cruise missiles, mobile missiles maybe?

Secretary SCHLESINGER. No. I think that those are related primarily to the maintenance of invulnerability in second-strike forces, as well as the question of the gross sizing of the forces, which is a SALT-related issue rather than a targeting doctrine–related issue. Certainly, some of these forces might be employed in the kinds of hypothetical strikes to which I had referred.

Q. Does the MIRVing of the—going beyond MIRVing of the 550 Minutemen that the administration has initiated, and I guess almost completed, is that necessary or is that part of what you're talking about?

Secretary SCHLESINGER. No, sir. Absolutely not. Not necessary, and as has been indicated earlier, that refers to the total sizing of the forces and the total capabilities of the forces primarily in quantitative terms which are being determined at the SALT discussions. To the extent that the Soviets are agreeable, we are in a position to hold down the total size of our nuclear forces.

Q. How can we be assured, or how can the Russians be assured, that we are not seeking a first-strike capability when you enunciate this new targeting doctrine? How can they differentiate? Doesn't this have a momentum of its own?

Secretary SCHLESINGER. The answer to that, I think, is quite clear. In the first place, I referred to a disarming capability, and the Soviets are allowed under the interim agreement sixty-two submarines and 950 submarine-launched ballistic missiles. In addition, they have other forces. Any calculation would demonstrate, I believe, that it is not possible for us even to begin to eliminate the city-destruction capabilities embodied in their ICBM forces alone. So that, as I've indicated earlier, the attaining of a full disarming capability is not an option that is open either to the United States or to the Soviet Union.

Now, with regard to the development of these kinds of capabilities, what we are saying at the present time is that the overall power represented by our arsenal must be a match for the overall power represented by the Soviet strategic arsenal.

The Soviets have had in recent years a highly vigorous research and development effort. They have four new ICBMS in development, as you are aware. Three of those ICBMS have now been tested with MIRVS, and it is quite plausible to believe that the fourth will also be tested with MIRV. They have three submarine programs in operation—three fleet ballistic missile submarine programs. Therefore, their pro-

gram shows a great deal of vigor in the R&D stage. They have an immense amount of throw-weight presently coupled with technology inferior to that possessed by the United States. Our concern is that if they marry the technologies that are now emerging in their R&D program to the throw-weight and numbers that they have been allowed under the interim agreement, that they would develop a capability that was preponderant relative to that of the United States. This is impermissible from the standpoint of the American government so long as we bear the obligation to carry the nuclear shield not only for ourselves but our allies.

If the Soviets were able to develop these improved technologies presently available to the United States in the forms of guidance, MIRVs, warhead technology, at some point around 1980 or beyond they would be in a position in which they had a major counterforce option against the United States, and we would lack a similar option. Consequently, in the pursuit of symmetry, meaningful symmetry, for the two forces—and by meaningful symmetry, I do not mean symmetry in every respect—we cannot allow the Soviets unilaterally to obtain a counterforce option which we ourselves lack. We must have a symmetrical balancing of the strategic forces on both sides.

I think that you can say that the kinds of forces that we might put in the R&D stage are in anticipation of the possibility of Soviet deployments of the type that I have described, and that if SALT eventuates in an agreement which at a lower level does not require the introduction of these improved categories of equipment, that we would not feel obligated to introduce them. But we cannot be in a position, given the worldwide responsibilities of the United States and the need to maintain a worldwide balance, we cannot be in a position in which a major option is open to the Soviet Union which we, through a self-denying ordinance, have precluded for the United States. . . .

I think that one must also recognize with regard to the strategic forces that if both sides are operating intelligently and perceptively, that the likelihood of the employment of strategic forces is very low, approaching zero, and that probability will remain very low provided that we have the symmetry that I mentioned on both sides. Consequently, if there are hostilities, those hostilities will take place employing primarily conventional forces. . . .

This is not to say that nuclear forces are irrelevant. One might even say that all wars since 1945 have not been nuclear wars because they have been fought within a framework in which the threat of the employment of nuclear power remained in the background. So nuclear forces, strategic forces, provide the framework within which, hopefully, wars will remain conventional. . . .

Q. . . . You didn't mention it specifically, but I think it's a fact that for a long time both sides have had vast capability of overkill. You have mentioned and emphasized today that both sides are invulnerable as to second-strike capabilities. Given those two facts, why is it necessary for us to match the Soviets on every front of expansion, which to me, again as a layman, looks like spiraling increase in armaments rather than balance?

Secretary SCHLESINGER. It is not necessary to match on every specific front. I think that it is important, one, to maintain an invulnerable second-strike force. Secondly, that there should be symmetry in the pressures that could be brought to bear by the threat of the employment of nuclear forces—and this refers back to what I said earlier, that we cannot permit the other side to have a relatively credible counterforce capability if we lack the same. And thirdly, in view of the importance of strategic forces in establishing a framework within which conflicts may take place at a lower level, and the U.S. role in maintaining the worldwide balance, that there must be perceived equality between the forces of the Soviet Union and the United States. Perceived equality, not only to ourselves, not only to the Russians, but to third audiences—the Japanese, Europeans and Chinese.

The earlier part of your question referred to overkill capabilities and what I said earlier. Overkill is an expression which is part and parcel of the belief that the only objective—the only target—for nuclear forces should be the populations, the industry, and the cities on the other side. That refers back to a point of view about the hypothetical employment of strategic forces which has known various names over the years—assured destruction, massive retaliation, and the like. If one is thinking only in terms of the ability to bash the cities and the other side, we have more than enough forces. There are, however, target sets far more numerous than that and far more difficult to destroy selectively. What I have suggested is that if there are two classes of targets or many classes of targets, that to put ourselves in a position as upholders of the nuclear umbrella for most of the free world in which one's hypothetical opponent is in a position to attack all target classes and that we are restricted to attacking only one limited, destructive, and suicidal target class, [that] is not maintenance of essential equivalence.

Q. I ran off the trolley near the end, because it seems to me . . . that the targets now are not cities, are not mass destruction, but revised targets. If one side had the capability to do all these targets, whereas we had to restrict ourselves, is it not true that that represents in itself [inaudible] actually started to fire at these targets would involve a hell

of a lot of people, and doesn't that get back to a slightly broader definition of overkill?

Secretary SCHLESINGER. I don't think so, but I think that that's quite a complicated question, and [it] would take a fair amount of time to grapple with it. The point that I'm making is that it requires that one does not necessarily have to go after a large set of targets; one must be in a position so that one can respond in the event, in the hypothetical event, of aggression, with the strategic forces, preferably in a way that limits damage to both sides—to all sides—rather than in a way that hopefully reduces the possibility of that outcome by flamboyant advertising of the destructiveness of such a war.

* * *

Q. Mr. Secretary, earlier you said that we have more than enough forces to bash the Soviet cities, if that is our desired strategy. Does it not follow from that, therefore, that we already have a counterforce capability, and if so, what is it that you are seeking that we don't already have?

Secretary SCHLESINGER. No, that does not follow that we have a counterforce capability if one is able to destroy countervalue targets in that way. It depends upon the kinds of military targets that you may be referring to. It is evident, for example, that this large number of weapons in our stockpile provides us with the discriminating ability to go after certain classes of military targets—airfields and the like. We are also perfectly content to put a lid on the total quantity of nuclear forces at our present level or below, should we be able to persuade the Soviet Union to agree.

Now, what is it that we want? We have a sufficient amount of force now. We are not in difficulty in 1974, and if there was a willingness on the other side, a readiness on the other side, to put a lid on at this level, that would be quite satisfactory to the United States—or to put a lid on at a lower level, that would be satisfactory to the United States. What we must preserve is what I referred to before as "essential equivalence." We cannot be in a position of inferiority with regard to the strategic options that might be employed against the United States or its allies, and consequently we must be prepared—eager as we may be to put a lid on at the present level or at a lower level—we must be prepared for the possibility of an improvement and expansion of Soviet forces for which there has been some recent intelligence evidence, and that we must be prepared to match them so that there is no asymmetrical advantage with regard to those options that the Soviets have.

As I mentioned before, if the Soviets employed their present amount of throw-weight with the improved technologies, they could have on the order of 7,000 one-megaton weapons in their ICBM force, as opposed to a much smaller number of much, much lower-yield weapons in our own forces. . . . In the event of any conflict of wills, in which the forces available to both sides must be assessed, . . . the hypothetical leaders of the West under those circumstances would have to have much tougher wills than would their opponents, given the asymmetry of forces.

Now, this I think is quite consistent with the objective of the SALT I agreements in Moscow in 1972, in which both sides fully endorsed the proposition that neither side should seek strategic advantage. So what we are seeking, if I may put it this way, is to forestall the development of an asymmetrical situation that would be beneficial to the Soviet Union. If we can forestall it through SALT negotiations and avoid the major expenditures, that is desirable from the standpoint of the United States.

Iklé Discusses SALT and the New Targeting Doctrine, 8 May 1974

The CHAIRMAN [Mr. Charles Wilson]. . . . Many members of the Committee on Armed Services and the Congress at large have expressed concern with the lack of substantive information available on disarmament negotiations, particularly as they impact on our national defense posture. I personally have felt somewhat disadvantaged as a member of the Committee on Armed Services, in voting on personnel and weapons authorizations, by the dearth of clear evidence on how these negotiations will affect our defense requirements, and likewise how our decisions will impact on the conduct of sensitive negotiations. Such information will be increasingly important to all members of Congress this year, and therefore I believe the appointment of this subcommittee is most timely.

* * *

The CHAIRMAN. . . . The interim agreement and the protocol were defended in part as being necessary to curtail or halt the momentum of the large-scale Soviet buildup in offensive weapons. We were told that agreement would limit their progress but not the progress of current U.S. programs. Now, can you tell us whether this has in fact occurred?

Dr. IKLÉ. . . . The Soviets did have a continuing vigorous program deploying additional land-based missiles, ICBMS, in the late sixties—long after we stopped building additional Minuteman missiles—throughout the SALT I negotiations. Indeed, with the interim agreement and in accordance with the provision of that agreement, this continuing deployment came to a halt.

The protocol, which is related to the agreement fixing the numbers of ICBMS, does permit additional SLBM launchers and submarines to be built by the Soviet Union, up to the specific limits.

The interim agreement as a whole, as was made clear in congressional testimony, does not deal with the so-called qualitative aspects of strategic arms, such as MIRVS.

The CHAIRMAN. Has the Soviet progress been controlled in any way as a result of this agreement?

SOURCE: Testimony of Arms Control and Disarmament Agency Director Fred C. Iklé. U.S., Congress, House, Committee on Armed Services, Special Subcommittee on Arms Control and Disarmament, *Review of Arms Control and Disarmament Activities*, 93d Cong., 2d sess., 1974.

Dr. IKLÉ. On the dimensions which are fixed or limited by the agreement, indeed the progress has been stopped as to further deployment. There are other dimensions, other developments, some of which cannot be covered by an arms control agreement because of verification problems, such as accuracy. There are problems such as additional MIRV deployment, which are a major issue in the current SALT negotiations, which are not covered in the interim agreement.
The CHAIRMAN. In 1972, the consensus was that we had a two-year lead in technology over the Soviets in strategic offensive weapons. Do we still have the same relative advantage today?
Dr. IKLÉ. I would be hesitant, Mr. Chairman, to give a specific number on the different levels of development in technology. There are aspects, such as accuracy, which are hard to verify. There are questions of numbers of warheads where we do have a lead. There are questions of throw-weight where we do not have a lead. There are questions of submarines and other areas where it is difficult to assess the differential in technology between us and the Soviet Union. This would require more detailed treatment, perhaps in an executive session.
The CHAIRMAN. In your opinion, are we approaching the SALT II negotiations from a position of strength, as we have approached past negotiations?
Dr. IKLÉ. If I may just make a broad statement and respond to it in a personal fashion more than taking a formal position. It is my view that our strength in these negotiations and our ability to bring them toward a successful conclusion really depend on our own determination and our own self-assurance, our ability to convey to the Soviet military that we are able to compete if they force us, that we are willing to limit and stop the competition through agreement, and indeed willing to move toward mutual reductions. I think it is this determination which decides and will govern our strength in these negotiations.
The CHAIRMAN. Would you give us your opinion on the assertion that arms control agreements and discussions have the collateral effect of lulling the Congress and the U.S. citizens into an attitude of lassitude insofar as need for defense requirements are concerned?
Dr. IKLÉ. Again responding in a broader way, it is important to keep three problems in mind. The overriding one is that arms control negotiations dealing with important types of arms are hazardous and entail certain dangers. At the same time, given the destructive potential of nuclear arms in particular, and given the economic burden of conventional arms, it is even more dangerous to try to chart the future without making a serious attempt to reach constructive arms control agreements.

In essence, there are perhaps two dangers in arms control negotia-

tions—one to which you referred, namely . . . that they may give a sense of false confidence if not properly understood, that they may lull us into believing we have limited something which we have not limited, that we can verify something we cannot verify, that we are controlling something that perhaps is not controlled. To overcome that danger we have to carefully analyze what the agreements are. The executive branch has to work with Congress on these issues.

There is another danger on the opposite side, in that prolonged hard bargaining, such as we get into in some of these negotiations, may create a new form of competition—that all kinds of asymmetry in arms which both sides were perhaps able to live with before, gain new importance—that instead of reducing or limiting armaments, arms control negotiations, if not properly conducted and guided, might stimulate competition. We have to guard against both of these dangers and try to steer a course in the middle so we can really enhance our national security.

* * *

Mr. SPENCE. . . . My recollection is that we were more or less in this country forced into these agreements in SALT I because of the present rate of construction and looking at what we would do and what the Russians were doing from the standpoint of building submarines. They would have had ninety submarines in a few years and we would have had forty-one. Therefore, as I understand it, we were forced into these agreements because of our present pace versus their present pace in this area. Is that the way you understand it?

Dr. IKLÉ. Congressman Spence, I think it is fair to say that these numbers do reflect the differences in actual deployment and potential deployment which prevailed at the time in 1972.

Mr. SPENCE. As a matter of fact, you mentioned a while ago something about the outcome of these talks. You referred to our determination as a nation and that it would have considerable to do regarding the outcome. Back there we had the same problem. Our determination was not there, and they would outbuild us. We slipped into a fall-back position when we agreed to these numbers. That is my own opinion.

Dr. IKLÉ. I think one has to keep in mind, however, that we decided to stop building additional launchers in part because we felt this was not a desirable route to go in building deterrent forces; in part because we envisaged reaching agreement on essential parity with the Soviet Union. We did continue to MIRV our missile systems and thus increase the number of warheads.

Mr. SPENCE. Do you think the reason we agreed to being locked in on

smaller numbers in all of these areas was because of our MIRV capability at that time?

Dr. IKLÉ. I would think it was the overall picture—these differences in deployment rates you mentioned, our capability in MIRVing missiles, and our numbers of warheads, and also the fact that we were entering here into an interim agreement of limited duration which would give us time to negotiate the more permanent agreement, which is the process in which we are now involved in SALT II.

Mr. SPENCE. In other words, there were reasons—technology, MIRV, interim agreement—all of these things. Those were the reasons we agreed as we did.

Now, inasmuch as we have word that Russia also has a MIRV capability, this changes the whole picture; does it not?

Dr. IKLÉ. This makes it very important for us, and I would argue for both sides, to reach agreement on limiting the MIRV deployment process. Otherwise, it would merely be shifting the competition from one domain into another domain.

Mr. SPENCE. Inasmuch as they have more numbers of missiles, greater throw-weight, they can therefore put more separate warheads on their missiles and they really increase their advantage over us from the standpoint of numbers of warheads. Is that not correct?

Dr. IKLÉ. Potentially they could if there were a competition in which we felt restrained from building larger missiles and they exploited their larger missiles. You have to examine the ground rules for this competition and keep in mind the overriding purpose of not just our arms control negotiations but our foreign policy, to avoid competition which would not increase the security of either side.

If you merely kept these numbers as they are and let competition run away in another dimension, it could move down a very undesirable road. Clearly this is not our intention.

Mr. SPENCE. I asked Secretary Schlesinger, with the situation being as it is relative to their recent MIRV development, what we should do in our SALT II talks. He suggested we either start building bigger missiles—replacing our existing ICBMS with missiles with larger throw-weight—improve our technology, or attempt to get the other side to put a limit on their MIRV capability. Do you have any comment to make on that solution to the problem?

Dr. IKLÉ. I would think clearly our national preference ought to be the last direction, to get a limit on the MIRV capability. We do not want to start a competition which may even add a vulnerable weapons system on both sides.

Mr. SPENCE. There is the problem. In other words, if we are not successful in getting the other side to agree to limit their MIRVing capa-

bility so that we can keep some kind of a balance, what is our alternative except being forced into competition, spending more money, building bigger missiles, and, as you said, proliferating the situation in that way?

Dr. IKLÉ. If we unhappily should be forced into that competition—and we must expend every effort to prevent that—it would be important not to create a mirror image of what our antagonists would be doing in such a process, but to improve and strengthen the invulnerability of our strategic forces and to get the military capability we need to prevent nuclear war.

Mr. SPENCE. I was trying to make the point that this question, as far as I am concerned, is perhaps the biggest single question we will be dealing with in the foreseeable future in this country. Everything depends on the success of these negotiations. An alternative might have to be, if they do not agree to limiting their MIRVing capability, if we do not get into another arms race and remake our existing capability, we could always just drop out of the SALT I agreement. We have the option of getting out before the five years are up.

Dr. IKLÉ. There is a clause in the ABM treaty as well as the interim agreement that in the event the supreme national interest were jeopardized, either side could give notice to withdraw from the treaties. I think more important is the fact of the limited duration of the interim agreement and the process of negotiation in which we are now engaged.

Mr. SPENCE. These options we have. I want to show the various options we would have in our negotiations.

Dr. IKLÉ. That is right, Congressman. However, for the duration of the interim agreement, given the numbers, the deployment, and even including the MIRV deployment, there is no threat to our strategic capability threatening its functions. It is beyond its duration that we have to look and try to work out new arrangements.

Mr. SPENCE. In other words, you feel pretty good about the situation as it exists right now, even in view of their MIRV capability?

Dr. IKLÉ. Our present strategic capability is very reassuring. It serves the purpose to deter nuclear war or nuclear coercion. The problem in our arms control negotiation talks is to look into the future and to avoid this kind of unsatisfactory competition while at the same time to convey the determination that we cannot permit the other side to develop a significant superiority which could be used against us and our allies in the more distant future.

* * *

Mr. ASPIN. To back up a little bit on the question of the sufficiency of our deterrent, it is true, of course, that no matter how many warheads

on ICBMs the Soviets have or we have, the submarine-launched ballistic force is still invulnerable. Is that right?

Dr. IKLÉ. The submarine-launched forces are the least vulnerable part of our forces. Our main concern is to keep it that way.

Mr. ASPIN. That is really the backbone of this, so even if they did get more numbers of warheads, and if they have more numbers of launchers, the submarine launchers are still invulnerable.

The number of warheads we have is really substantially greater than the number the Soviet Union has. Indeed, during this five-year agreement the number of warheads will increase, and our disparity, in other words our advantage, will be greater. The unclassified numbers state that when the interim agreement was signed the United States had 5,000 to 6,000 warheads. The Soviet Union had 2,200.

Today, according to the Secretary of Defense, we have 7,100 and they have 2,300. By 1977, which is at the end of the five-year agreement, we will have 10,000 and they will have 4,000. Therefore, the number is actually increasing during that time, so we have a quantity advantage in terms of numbers of warheads during this interim agreement.

Of course, it is a five-year agreement because we recognized in the long run, the 1980s and 1990s, their advantage might be considerable. By that time the interim agreement will have ended and we will have negotiated something else.

I don't know whether those numbers are correct, but those are the unclassified numbers we get kicked around here. Perhaps you would like to put in more refined numbers in the classified version.

Dr. IKLÉ. We would be pleased to do that. The question as to the ratio of warheads—which is now to our advantage, very much so, and will remain to our advantage for some time—how precisely the ratio will move depends on the deployment rates on both sides. If the Soviet Union is intent on deploying their MIRV missiles fast, then their numbers would go up more rapidly.

Mr. ASPIN. Let me drop that and go to something else. We are perhaps not together, but we have been at many conferences where counterforce is argued. We don't want to go through that again. However, I would like to talk a little bit about some of the aspects of this. In particular, our defense forces were based upon an assured destruction theory. It seems in SALT I we got the Russians to agree to an assured destruction as their basis, in the sense that after SALT I both sides were mutually vulnerable to an attack from the other side in the sense we did away with the possibility of damage limitation through ABM.

Since then the Secretary of Defense has changed our doctrine and

announced the new doctrine of counterforce, and would like the United States to buy new higher-yield and more accurate weapons to pursue this. I am wondering why that is necessary, inasmuch as we did achieve an agreement with the Russians on an understanding of assured destruction. Why is it that assured destruction is not sufficient?

Dr. IKLÉ. As suggested, we could discuss these details at great length. I can give only a very sketchy response to your important question.

One, there is an uncertainty as to the extent to which the Soviet military planners embrace our strategic views, whether we call them assured destruction or mutual deterrence or whatever name you give it. That uncertainty is highlighted by the fact that they are building larger missiles which really do not fit into an assured destruction objective. From the point of view of assured destruction, one would want to emphasize the least vulnerable part of the force, such as SLBMS, as you mentioned yourself.

Second, there is a question of what the shift in our strategic doctrine is, and, more important, what it should devolve into.

As you know from other conversations we have had on strategic doctrine, keeping in mind that the overriding emphasis is to prevent nuclear war and to use deterrence as the main means to that end, we should not move in the direction of acquiring a first-strike or disarming capability. If that is what is meant by counterforce, that would be the wrong direction.

At the same time, we want to dissuade military planners from trying to get a counterforce capability against us which might stimulate them to launch into large programs and thus would undercut SALT. We want to close any gap in the spectrum of deterrence. We want to be able to deter possible military plans on the other side to use nuclear weapons in a limited way.

I think the important thing to keep in mind is not what may be a somewhat outlandish or bizarre idea of overall attack on our Minuteman missiles as a limited attack—that kind of attack is not a limited attack—but a use of nuclear weapons in a local theater, perhaps against our forces or against our allies. It is worth recalling that our own military thinking in the 1950s with regard to what we called tactical nuclear weapons envisaged such limited use. I think it is desirable for the future, in order to maintain world peace, that neither side become interested in that direction again. Therefore, we have to close this gap.

Mr. ASPIN. Let me ask a further question. We have certainly a great deal of capability to do many of the things we are talking about. For example, you talk about a limited attack, that we should be able to respond in a limited way. Don't we have that kind of capability right now to a very great extent? If the assured destruction calculations are

correct, we need only about 400 nuclear warheads for assured destruction. We have 7,100, which leaves quite a number.

Part of the Secretary's program is retargeting. I would like to separate the retargeting question, which is valid and good and ought to be done, from the procurement question. Why can't all of the reasons that you gave for counterforce be acquired just through retargeting and without buying the increased accuracy and increased yield?

Dr. IKLÉ. To a large extent I think the objectives can be met by these organizational changes and by changes in command and control procedures. As I understand it, this is what the Secretary of Defense and other representatives of the military are pursuing and recommending.

As I understand it, increases in accuracy would, for one, permit us to threaten military targets in a way which would not be killing as many innocent bystanders as if you had large inaccurate weapons.

Mr. ASPIN. A number of the military targets you might want to hit are near civilian population centers, which would inevitably result in civilian casualties. The people who advocate this kind of thing usually associate increased accuracy with reduced yields. That is how you get a weapon which does not kill civilians.

The Secretary wants increased accuracy and bigger yields. Put those together and you kill more civilians. I don't see anything that cannot be done as far as any of the things that need to be done which can't be done through retargeting; and why would we have to do this with procurement? This only costs several millions now but might cost more in the long run. How much will this cost down the road if we go to this increased accuracy and greater yield route? What will it cost for our strategic forces now? The number kicked around is $7 billion to $10 billion. Does that sound right to you?

Dr. IKLÉ. It sounds terribly large and would envisage a world where we really have not succeeded in our effort to get arms control agreements. It would be precisely this kind of situation, where we have this untrammeled competition, that we want to avoid.

Mr. ASPIN. Aren't we starting untrammeled competition with this kind of procurement?

Dr. IKLÉ. It is perhaps more appropriate for me to comment on the arms control implications of these questions rather than the detailed budget projections and military purposes. Witnesses from the Defense Department should answer that.

As a general remark, while a certain reform in our strategic doctrine is getting wide support and can be supported from the arms control point of view and from a military point of view, like any reform it can be driven to excesses and, therefore, no longer meet the purpose.

It is important in this reform that it not be driven to excesses. For instance, there is a danger that people may be misled into believing that limited nuclear wars are somehow safe, and an extension of our military capability.

Witnesses from the Defense Department have said that we are fully aware of the great dangers of any use of nuclear weapons and nobody should be misled into believing there are so-called safe, limited nuclear wars. There is a danger that procurement may be driven in directions which are not productive.

Having said all this, we have to recognize that we are involved in very hard bargaining situations with the Russians on SALT.

A little while ago questions were raised about differences in numbers, how we got into these differences in numbers. And it was observed: "Of course, the Russians had a program and we did not, and this led to a situation where it was in our interest in the end to settle, on these particular dimensions, for inferior numbers which were compensated for by other dimensions of our strategic forces not controlled by the agreement."

You might say that people who are anxious to show a capability to develop certain arms had this experience in mind, in a desire to signal to the other side that in our effort to limit and to reduce strategic arms we cannot be overtaken if the other side unhappily should choose to go toward competition. We want to dissuade them from wild competition.

Mr. ASPIN. I think by doing this we are going for competition and we are encouraging them to go into competition. What we have now is a situation where the Soviet Union has not developed a counterforce capability. Right now we have more counterforce capability than the Soviets because we have greater accuracy and more warheads. All we see in the Soviet Union is big missiles, which means in the long run they could develop a counterforce capability if they MIRVed and if they continued with their accuracy development.

However, if we start now with a counterforce capability, it is certain they will go for a counterforce capability with that increased capability they are building. You are fueling the arms race.

* * *

Mr. ASPIN. Let's talk about the effect of counterforce on SALT. In some sense the Secretary seems to be implying that this is a kind of bargaining chip. He says in his posture statement if they stop we stop.

Do you look on it as a bargaining chip? It does not seem to me to be a good bargaining chip. One of the qualifications for a good

bargaining chip is that it has to be verifiable. Accuracy is not verifiable. These kinds of things, qualitative improvements on missiles, are not verifiable. I don't think it will help us in SALT at all.

Dr. IKLÉ. To the extent that some of these technological developments are not verifiable, we cannot observe what the other side is doing. We therefore would have no basis to assume that they are practicing self-restraint if we do.

Mr. ASPIN. How does counterforce help us in SALT, then?

Dr. IKLÉ. One of the important problems we face in the SALT negotiations is this vigorous development program of larger land-based missiles on the Soviet side. It is not clear what the motivations are. . . . But strictly from an arms control point of view, the fixed land-based missiles are not the ideal types of weapons because of their potential vulnerability. The more apparent this becomes to both sides, the easier it will be to negotiate limitations on these missiles and subsequent reductions.

Mr. ASPIN. So we are developing a counterforce, their missile is more vulnerable, and we can negotiate it away?

Dr. IKLÉ. I don't think witnesses of the Defense Department would agree to develop counterforce in the sense of developing a first-strike capability.

Mr. ASPIN. An ability to strike their ICBMS.

Dr. IKLÉ. There is a problem of misunderstanding.

Mr. ASPIN. Let me give a couple more problems. One of the reasons we have trouble getting arms control negotiations, of course we have to negotiate first within our own government, and that is always a terrible problem because what are we going to give up?

If you develop war-fighting capability on ICBMS, it will be much tougher to get the military to give them up. The Air Force would have something else they would like to play with and therefore they will not be willing to give it up. One of the criteria for a bargaining chip is that we have to be willing to give it up. Developing a war-fighting capability on the ICBMS makes it tougher to convince the Air Force and consequently the Pentagon we should give up the thing.

The other thing is that once we develop war-fighting capability on the ICBMS, and they have war-fighting capability on their own ICBMS, reducing the number of ICBMS will be tougher, because the large numbers of them means there is some possibility some will survive. But if we reduce the number and you've got counterforce capability on both sides, then there will be vulnerability; so it means you will have to make the jump from very large numbers of ICBMS right down to zero. I think that will be a very difficult thing to negotiate.

I just don't think this helps solve it at all. It complicates the thing. It fuels the arms race and does not help with anything.

As another proposal, why don't we take something—and this is the question maybe I don't know whether you can answer in this open session or not—but it is clear what we would like the Soviet Union to stop. We would like them to stop those big missiles, big warheads, those enormous big missiles. What are we going to do?

So the question is, What have we got that the Soviet Union is afraid of that we can negotiate away? In other words, for us to get them to stop what we want them to stop, they have to want us to stop something. What have we got?

Dr. Iklé. Let me try to touch on all three points you made. You are right, of course, that there can develop an institutional attachment to particular weapons systems. In that sense it is harder to give it up. I think this administration, as well as previous administrations, have shown that when a bargain can be struck which is in the national interest we are willing to give up things. We gave up the ABM—

Mr. Aspin. The only reason we gave it up is that Congress was about to take it away, anyway.

Dr. Iklé. I remarked earlier that the cooperation of Congress and the executive branch is of importance. There has to be continuing interaction.

It was in this area where we had an ongoing development and where we gave up something which enabled us to arrive at a well-balanced treaty. It was in the area of missile launchers, where we did not have a program, that we have an interim agreement with numbers which raise the kinds of questions we discussed earlier.

As to the point on reductions becoming harder if missiles become more accurate, that is a correct analysis if we look at something sometimes referred to as the "duels" of missile forces, which I would consider a totally outlandish and bizarre way of looking at this terrible decision of launching an attack with nuclear arms. If you deal with a completely insane group in control of nuclear weapons you don't have deterrence, anyhow. If you deal with a moderately prudent group, clearly they cannot just look at the fixed land-based missiles; and the accuracy, as you have said yourself, does not affect bombers and SLBMS. Hence we could envisage reductions even though they have become more accurate.

Indeed, missile forces have become more accurate on both sides, certainly on our side, since 1960. In the late fifty's we had tentative plans for building a larger number of Minuteman missiles. Then we leveled off. Now it is our position that we are willing to reduce.

Thus, as accuracy increased, the willingness to reduce has gone up.

Mr. Aspin. . . . What do we have now that we can negotiate? Is counterforce that thing? Clearly in the SALT I agreement the thing the Soviet Union wanted us to stop was the ABM for whatever reason. They were afraid of it and they wanted us to stop it.

The Chairman. That is a question I was going to ask somewhat differently. What incentive is there for the Soviets to come to SALT II, and what do they want from it?

Mr. Aspin. Counterforce does not provide that incentive. What in your view do they want?

Dr. Iklé. It is hard to know exactly. They probably look at the whole spectrum of our programs, more importantly our R&D capability and potential intention in the future. It is a composite assessment they make of their capability should there be an intent on the other side to outstrip us in an arms race as against our capability.

Let me emphasize again: The overriding importance for world security, for our national security, is to avoid such an arms race. To do that we have to try to prevent even the ambition from developing on the other side.

I think our various research and development programs, including accuracy, including perhaps even larger yield—which is a very undesirable direction to go and we can elaborate on that—this overall capability is a very important incentive for them to agree with us to limitations and reductions, as against trying to compete with us in an arms race. Which particular item it is in the composite picture is hard to say.

Mr. Aspin. Counterforce itself is not the bargaining chip, but you are improving the ICBM so you can negotiate on the total composite of the ICBM? Counterforce itself is not verifiable by national means, so I guess what you are saying is that we are upgrading the capability of our ICBMS so we can negotiate in numbers of ICBMS with the Soviet Union in case they get their ICBMS to be of high quality. Is that the position?

Dr. Iklé. I think the Soviet military assessment as to the importance of a larger ICBM force is a very important factor in their willingness to agree to limitations. The risks we have to consider are not so much this kind of attack and retaliatory ability but the possibility that a military doctrine may develop, of which we obviously see beginnings, which would be similar to a doctrine held in the past in this country, hence not something so outlandish; namely, nuclear weapons can be used in theater conflicts.

Mr. Aspin. Let me just state the position I take and offer one more

suggestion. It seems to me that we are running a risk, by this counterforce, of starting something. We now have the ability to do this counterforce and by doing it will encourage the Russians into another missile race with their developing the counterforce. If we are afraid of their large ICBMS and their capability to develop a counterforce out of those large ICBMS, with MIRVS and other things, we should take something other than the counterforce. In other words, we should not think of negotiating just in terms of the two systems like ABM versus ABM, but perhaps their ICBMS versus foreign-based systems or something. They seem to be worried about foreign-based systems. Rather than developing counterforce, maybe we should think in terms —I know how complicated it is—think in terms of getting foreign-based systems.

Dr. IKLÉ. Your position is correct. There need not be exact matching. These other issues are part and parcel of our SALT negotiations. There is no objection in principle to having asymmetric relationships develop which would be to the advantage of both sides.

However, something can be said about the drive that institutions may attach to certain weapons systems. What may have helped in reaching the balanced ABM agreement was a mixture of both our own program and a technological realization that the capability of ABMS is really rather limited. Realization that the advantages of an indefinite proliferation of fixed land-based missiles is doubtful depends on the realization that the systems are vulnerable, and this depends in part on accuracy.

If technological developments are one-sided, then the realization as to the technological shortcomings may not be brought to bear on the Soviet military planners as they give their advice on SALT.

* * *

The CHAIRMAN. I wonder whether you can assess the impact in the SALT II negotiations of a congressional decision to cut production of the B–1 or the Trident.

Dr. IKLÉ. Since both of these programs are designed to improve the invulnerability of very essential components of our deterrent forces, the intercontinental bomber and the submarine-launched ballistic missiles, they play a key role in maintaining our strategic deterrence, but they also play a role in the competition in which we are unfortunately engaged regarding numbers, limitations, and the possibility of reductions.

If these programs were stopped, one would fear that this might put us into a situation similar to the one we were in during the late sixties and in 1972, when the Soviets had an ongoing program. As

you know, they had an ongoing program of building submarines and we did not.

What kind of submarine system and what kind of bomber we should have is not an arms control question but more appropriate for Defense Department witnesses to respond to.

Mr. ASPIN. Do you see B–1 or Trident being bargaining chips in SALT II?

Dr. IKLÉ. If we make substantial progress on limitations and reductions in central strategic systems, it is conceivable that with or without bargaining we would not want to add additional forces. We may want—

Mr. ASPIN. We were told they were bargaining chips. That was brought out with regard to Trident. Are we seriously going to bargain about them?

Dr. IKLÉ. If you envisage an overall limitation of essential equality, where SLBMS, ICBMS, and bombers would be limited, then we would certainly not increase the numbers. If we have reduction provisions, we would reduce them. Then the question would be essentially up to us as to whether we want to institute the more modern submarine for an older one. That would not necessarily be an arms control question.

The effect on the bargaining enters if there should be an unhappy tendency, which we try to avoid by all means, on the side of the Soviet military to outstrip us in numbers. If there are people on the other side who argue for such a course, and if they could point to the fact that the United States cannot come forth with additional numbers of submarines or bombers, then their argument might carry more weight in their internal deliberations. That is what we want to avoid, and that is where the bargaining chip comes in.

5

The Moscow Summit, June–July 1974

Kissinger Discusses SALT and Allegations of "Secret Agreements," March and June 1974

Washington, 21 March 1974*

Q. Mr. Secretary, there is one more element, I think, in your [forthcoming] Moscow talks [1] which was mentioned by Mr. Vest [George S. Vest, Special Assistant to the Secretary for Press Relations], which was that you would talk about the progress in the SALT talks in preparation for the President's visit. Now, he has said that he expected to have an agreement in 1974. The way things are going, is this going to be a hard, specific agreement or just an agreement on generalities in the way of principles?

Secretary Kissinger. We already have an agreement on generalities which we made last summer. All the SALT negotiations and, indeed, all the disarmament negotiations have gone through three phases. There is an initial phase of an exchange of technical information which usually takes place during a stalemate in the negotiating process; that is to say, the negotiating positions do not approach each other, but the technical comprehension of the issues is clarified.

Then—this is essentially what has been going on in Geneva up to now—then a point is reached where there has to be a conceptual breakthrough; that is to say, where the two sides have to agree on what it is they are trying to accomplish. And after that there has to be the hard negotiation on giving concrete content to this conceptual breakthrough.

We are now at the phase where I would say we are at the end of the phase of technical exchanges and of elaboration of positions, and

---

* Source: Press conference of Secretary of State Henry A. Kissinger, *Department of State Bulletin*, 8 April 1974, pp. 353–361.

[1] Secretary Kissinger was in Moscow from 24 to 28 March 1974.—Ed.

we are at a point where we should be making, or should be attempting, a conceptual breakthrough.

Therefore, I would expect that if there is a SALT agreement this year it will have an adequate concreteness and it will not be simply general principles. Now, how many areas it will cover and its relationship to a comprehensive permanent agreement—those are issues that have yet to be decided.

Q. I suppose by generalities, what I meant was an agreement, I think that you talked about as conceptual breakthroughs. In other words, you get an agreement on just exactly what you are going at and how you are going at it. Is that what you mean by conceptual?

Secretary KISSINGER. Well, we have had, really, three types of agreement in SALT.

We have had the agreement, such as the one of last summer, which simply stated general principles and their route of march.

Then we have had the agreement, like the one of May 20, 1971, which rather specifically stated the limits of the negotiation; which is to say, from that occasion we decided on the relationship between an agreement on defensive weapons and an agreement on offensive weapons.

Thirdly, there is the agreement such as was concluded in May 1972 in Moscow, which in very great detail worked out the limitations on defensive, and some interim limitations on offensive, weapons.

My guess would be that we can attempt something between the May 20, 1971, and the May 1972 agreement, but I'll be able to give you a better estimate after my talks in Moscow.

Q. Mr. Secretary, just to follow up on that, you just used the phrase "if there is going to be an agreement this year." Now, are you suggesting that there is a possibility now that there might not be? Because, as I understood it at least, the agreement that was signed last year at San Clemente stated that the two parties had agreed that there would be an agreement this year. Now, you have used the word "if," and I wonder if some doubts have developed in your mind?

Secretary KISSINGER. I don't have the text of the agreement, of the statement of principles, of last year. I think the phrase was something like that they would aim for an agreement this year. But regardless of what the exact phraseology is, you cannot make that a binding commitment. This expresses an aspiration and, backed by the two heads of government, a rather firm desire. I hope, and we will work very hard, to have an agreement this year.

I think the prospects are reasonably good, but I can make a better estimate after my visit to Moscow, because up to now we have been in the exploratory phase and neither side has up to now had to face

the issue of concrete agreement that might emerge this year. But it is clearly one of the principal topics for discussion in Moscow.

* * *

Q. Mr. Secretary, do you have the feeling of some observers that the atmosphere in Soviet-American relations this time is much chillier than it was on your previous trips to the Soviet Union, that somehow the movement toward détente has sort of slowed down or even suffered setbacks as a result of friction over the Middle East and over the inability of the United States to get this most favored nation treatment?

Secretary KISSINGER. The trip to the Soviet Union comes at a very important time. If one looks at the debate on détente in the United States, it is interesting how some of the terms of reference have changed. When there was a great deal of tension and constant confrontation, the end of tension and the diminishing of confrontation was in itself considered an achievement. Today there is a tendency to take it for granted and to go beyond it to seek more ambitious objectives. The whole debate on the Soviet domestic structure would have been essentially inconceivable five years ago, and it has added a new dimension to Soviet-American relations.

It is also true that the difficulties in the passage of MFN legislation and the threats to the credits raise some questions about understandings—that the Soviet Union had every reason to believe were valid—of what our purposes were or what the United States would contribute for its side of the détente. And there are frictions in the Middle East. And in SALT we have come up against the problems that have been described before—that qualitative change is much more difficult to control than quantitative change.

All of this is true. At the same time, the necessities that produced the policy of relaxation of tension remain. As I have often pointed out, any administration will sooner or later pursue them. Our attempt will be to work out with the Soviet Union the moderate course in foreign policy on which peace in the world depends and perhaps the survival of humanity will depend. I agree we are going there at a more difficult period than at some previous visits, but I'm going there with hope and with the confidence that the overriding reality that I have described will determine the decisions.

Q. Mr. Secretary, on a related question, you were speaking a bit earlier about the pressures in each society on both sides of the Atlantic, and now we are talking here about, in effect, the pressures in each society in American-Soviet relations. I recognize your remark earlier that it is the U.S. position that domestic policy should be separate from foreign policy. But in this complex here, with these pressures in

the Atlantic alliance, in American-Soviet relations, and in domestic pressures, doesn't this make an extraordinary complex of issues as you head into these talks in the Soviet Union?

Secretary KISSINGER. It does make an extraordinary complex of issues, many of which inevitably had to arise. As Europe gained greater strength, greater identity, and therefore greater autonomy, it was inevitable that the relationship with the United States had to be reexamined. As weapons of ever greater destructiveness spread to both sides, it was inevitable that the strategic relationship had to be studied and also that the security problems within the alliance were in need of reexamination.

So, in part, the difficulties, which you have correctly listed, are the result partly of the success of previous policies, partly the result of technological evolution, and partly the result of domestic developments in all countries. And they are the raw material from which decisions have to be made.

I agree that we are in a complex period. Its complexity consists of the fact that a new international system is painfully being formed, that the system that was created in the fifties is in fundamental flux, and that the seventies will be seen in retrospect as a period of an emerging new relationship among most of the power centers. We've been trying to point this out for several years, and many of these tendencies are now coming to a head simultaneously.

* * *

Q. Mr. Secretary, given the relative delicate nature of the Soviet-U.S. relations at the moment, do you think that the discussion in Washington on the need for accelerating certain weapons programs, coupled with the discussion on possible counterforce targeting, contributes to the prospects for a SALT agreement?

Secretary KISSINGER. I think the press corps isn't satisfied when I'm embroiled only with allies. I have to be embroiled with colleagues as well. [Laughter.]

On the first of these questions—the acceleration of our weapons programs—this has to be seen in the context of existing Soviet weapons programs; and at a time when the Soviet Union is developing four types of intercontinental weapons, it would be irresponsible for us not to continue with our own programs. We have, however, repeatedly stated that we are prepared and eager to submit our programs to discussion as a part of the Strategic Arms Limitation Talks.

Now, with respect to the counterforce strategy that you mentioned, as I understood Secretary Schlesinger's point of view and objective, he is seeking an ability to bring about discriminating targeting

of the American nuclear forces. This in itself is a problem separate from counterforce strategy, which implies the ability to wipe out the Soviet retaliatory force in a first strike. The necessity for discriminating targeting is imposed on us by the enormous destructiveness of modern weapons, in which a spasm type of response in which all the forces are used more or less simultaneously would bring about casualties to all of mankind, and especially to the Soviet and American societies, which neither of them could survive.

Therefore it is a moral, political, and military obligation as long as these forces exist to use them in a manner—if they are to be used at all—or at least to have the ability to use them in the most discriminating manner possible.

This is my understanding of the retargeting capability.

The problem of counterforce strategy is a different issue, which depends on the ability to launch a great many missiles simultaneously, confidence in the ability to do this, and on the accuracy. And that is a separate issue, which I do not believe has been raised explicitly.

WASHINGTON, 24 JUNE 1974*

Secretary KISSINGER. I thought I would begin with some observations on the forthcoming summit before we go to your questions.

In many respects the relationship between the Soviet Union and the United States is the most crucial toward the maintenance of peace in the world. The United States and the Soviet Union are the only two countries that have the capability of a general nuclear war and therefore the only countries that can end civilized life as we know it.

Moreover, the interests of the United States and of the Soviet Union intersect in many parts of the globe. There is therefore always a possibility that misunderstandings may lead to confrontation, and the confrontation could escalate into conflict.

A principle objective of the United States, therefore, has to be to make sure that relations between the United States and the Soviet Union are based on deliberate decisions and that misunderstanding is reduced to a minimum; and, secondly, to try to bring about a set of constructive and, where possible, cooperative relationships that give both sides an incentive in maintaining the peace.

This is the basic purpose of the summit. The summit will therefore have three principal parts.

One, a general exchange between the President and the Soviet

* SOURCE: Press conference of Secretary of State Henry A. Kissinger. *Department of State Bulletin*, 22 July 1974, pp. 133–145.

leadership which will review the international situation, try to identify areas of possible disagreement, and attempt to minimize the consequences of these disagreements, as well as to identify areas of possible cooperative action and work out the means of this cooperation.

Secondly, to deal with the most complex and in many respects the most serious problem of the modern period, which is the control of the nuclear arms race. Never before have political leaders had the capacity to destroy human life as a result of a unilateral decision—and to do it in a matter of days. Never before has technology been so at odds with the human capacity to comprehend it. Never before has technology developed a momentum of its own in such a manner that it becomes increasingly difficult to control it.

Our objectives with respect to the control of arms are as follows:

- Obviously, neither side should have a military advantage as the result of any agreement that may be made;
- Secondly, neither side should be able to have a political advantage as a result of any agreements that might be made;
- Thirdly, neither side should believe that such an advantage exists, even if in reality it does not exist, because the perception is more important in many respects than the reality; and
- Finally, neither side—no ally nor other interested country of either side—should have such a perception.

To achieve this is very complicated because the forces of both sides have been developed on the basis of different principles. There are asymmetries that were deliberately designed in the kind of forces both sides have built, in the way they are based, in the technology they represent.

But for the United States not to make a major effort in this field is something that no future generation could possibly understand; and the danger we see—and that we are trying to prevent—is to keep technology from driving policy, and to prevent a situation from arising in which the inertia of technological decisions brings about a qualitative change—first in the nature of military, and secondly in the nature of political, relations.

Secondly, it is not a minor decision to engage in an unrestricted arms race—not only because of the military consequences of such an arms race, but also because the justifications that would have to be made on either side to sustain such an effort might, in time, become incompatible with a policy of relaxation of tensions and might in themselves be a factor introducing confrontation.

I say this so that you understand what our motivations are; and

of course we recognize that serious people will differ with what weight is to be given to particular schemes. And of course any agreement we would make would be submitted to full congressional scrutiny. But this is the area of our concern, and it is one in which we plan to have serious, extensive, and searching talks in the Soviet Union.

The third area with which we will deal in the Soviet Union is an attempt to give a more positive structure to our relationships; that is to say, as in every previous summit, we will discuss a series of cooperative arrangements in the fields of economics, scientific exchange, and other matters of mutual concern. The purpose of these agreements or arrangements or discussions, or whatever the case may be, will be to draw both societies into a more civilized relationship, to give each side a stake in the maintenance of an orderly and increasingly humane international system, and thereby to contribute to the peace of the world.

This, then, is the purpose of the summit: to maintain a dialogue, to contain the danger of nuclear confrontation, and to create positive incentives for a peaceful world. . . .

Q. With respect to the—I think it was your second one, on the nuclear —"To contain the danger of the nuclear confrontation"—there has been a great deal of discussion, a good part of it uninformed, I think, about what agreements that you and Mr. Dobrynin may have made or not, which went beyond the '72 Moscow agreement. As you said at another point, the perception of things is much more important sometimes, psychologically, than the "things." Now, I realize your spokesman has denied such an agreement. Can you put this thing simply and bluntly for us?

Secretary Kissinger. I can put it bluntly. I don't think I can put it simply. [Laughter.]

There have been two points made. Point one is that as a result of a secret agreement between the administration and the Soviet Union, the Soviet Union has been permitted to modernize 70 missiles on the G-class submarines and that therefore the total number of modern submarine-launched missiles permitted to the Soviet Union is 1,020, and not 950 as the administration has publicly stated and as was represented to Congress.

The second argument is that the interim agreement permits the United States to build 710 submarine-launched missiles but in fact the United States is intending to maintain only 656 submarine-launched missiles, and that therefore the total for the United States is 54 less than has been represented to the Congress and to the public. So that the total change in the Soviet Union's favor is of 124 missiles —brought about as the result of secret agreements made between the United States and the Soviet Union.

Those arguments are totally false in every detail. They have no merit whatsoever, and I shall now explain why.

First, let me deal with the G-class submarine. At the time the interim agreement was signed, the Soviet Union was permitted a total of 950 modern ballistic missiles on nuclear submarines. That figure of 950 was to be achieved by—or it could be achieved only by—the replacement of older Soviet missiles for any modern missile that was deployed on submarines beyond the figure of 740. In other words, the Soviet Union would have to retire 210 older missiles in order to reach the total of 950.

This raised the issue of what missiles the Soviet Union would have to retire in order to reach the permitted total of 950. The United States had an interest that the 210 missiles that would be retired would be ICBMS—missiles of a range of 5,000 miles and of warheads in the six-megaton range—that is to say, the SS–7 and SS–8 missiles. We wanted to prevent the Soviet Union from trading in obsolescent missiles that in our judgment they would have to retire anyway; namely, the missiles that are on the G-class submarines.

On the G-class submarine, the Soviet Union possesses, we believe, twenty operational ones. Eleven of them have missiles of a range of 700 miles, and nine have missiles of a range of 300 miles. No G-class submarine has been on station on the Atlantic coast of the United States since 1967, and no G-class submarine has been on station off the Pacific coast of the United States since 1969.

The G-class submarine is a diesel-powered submarine that can stay under water for only two to three days, that is extremely noisy and therefore extremely vulnerable. And moreover, the 300-mile-range missile—which is, as I pointed out, on nine of these submarines—can be fired only if the submarine surfaces; it cannot be fired from under water.

Therefore it seemed to us extremely improbable that the Soviet Union would maintain in its force a weapon which it would have to carry 4,000 miles so that it could fire it the remaining 300 miles, when it already possessed 1,400 weapons that it could fire over a range of 1,500 miles.

We wanted to prevent the Soviet Union from trading in a weapon which we were certain they would have to retire in any event for a modern weapon. Or to put it another way, we wanted the Soviet Union to trade in ICBMS for the modern weapon. And frankly, we considered it a negotiating achievement when, in Moscow, the Soviet Union agreed that the replacement for the 210 modern submarine missiles could not come from the G-class submarines but would have to come either from the ICBMS or from other more modern forces that were built after 1965.

In my press conference on the night of May 26 to May 27 [1972], I explained this provision in great detail. I stated specifically—and if I may spend a minute in reading it to you—I was asked: "How about the G class?" My answer was:

> . . . If they are modernized, they are counted against the 950. . . . They don't have to retire them. They do have to retire the H-class submarines if they want to go up to 950. They do not have to retire the G-class submarines, but if they modernize them they are counted against the 950.

In other words, the Soviet Union had two choices. If they kept the G-class submarine in their force, they had that option. But if they put a modern missile on the old submarine, it would be counted in the 950. But they could not retire the obsolescent missiles on the G-class and trade them in for modern missiles.

So this is what I said on May 26. On June 5 [1972] there was a meeting of the Verification Panel—on which all agencies were represented—in which this provision was fully explained and received the unanimous support of those present. The only requirement that was made was to make sure we would tie down the Soviet Union by means of an interpretive statement to a provision which we considered entirely in our interest.

On June 15, I sent the following guidance to the Secretary of State, the Secretary of Defense, the Director of Central Intelligence, the Director of the Arms Control and Disarmament Agency, the Chairman of the Atomic Energy Commission, and the Chairman of the Joint Chiefs of Staff. I will now read this. It says:

> Enclosed for your use in the SALT hearings is the interpretation of the offensive agreement with regard to the SLBM limitations and replacement provisions. You should follow this guidance in preparing testimony and in responding to questions.

I will now read from this guidance:

> To reach 950 SLBMS on Y-class submarines will require the Soviets to retire H-class launchers. They will also have to retire SS-7 and -8 ICBMS. They cannot build launchers on Y-class boats to replace launchers on G-class boats unless the launchers on such boats have been deployed with modern SLBMS. G-class boats are outside the agreement unless they are modernized by equipping them with modern SLBM launchers. Any modern SLBM operationally deployed on G-class will be counted within the 950 ceiling and above the 740 baseline must be accompanied by corresponding destruction or dis-

> mantling of SS-7s and -8s or older nuclear-powered submarines.

It is obvious our concern was to make sure that the ICBMs with the large warheads would be dismantled.

This was the guidance we gave to the bureaucracy and which we asked them to tell congressional committees. This was also what Ambassador Smith testified before the Jackson subcommittee in July 1972.

When in carrying out the understanding with the Verification Panel that we would give an interpretive statement to the Soviet Union of what I had already said in the press conference—namely, that G-class boats would count only if modern missiles were put on them or, conversely, that they could not trade in G-class missiles for modern launchers—when we handed this interpretive statement to the Soviet Union, they disputed our interpretation and insisted that they should have the right to trade in these obsolescent missiles for new missiles.

And this led to a month of exchanges between us and the Soviet Union. And it then seemed to us that, since it was an election year, since there might be a change in administration, and since there could be a change of personnel even if there was no change of administration, that our successors should not find themselves in the same position as we did and that they should not have to go through the record and reconstruct the understanding. And, therefore, we asked the Soviet Ambassador to sign the interpretive statement that we had made—which I will now read—and which is almost verbatim what I had already said publicly in the press conference on May 26, the night the agreement was signed, and which we had, moreover, told every agency of the government should be our public position.

Let me read this so-called "understanding" which has been so much in the press:

> In clarification of interpretation of the provisions of the Protocol to the Interim Agreement With Respect to the Limitation of Strategic Offensive Arms signed on May 26, the United States understands that: One, the aggregate level of ballistic missile launchers on submarines established by the protocol for the United States and the USSR, 950 for the USSR and 710 for the United States, includes ballistic missile launchers on all nuclear-powered submarines and launchers for modern ballistic missiles which may be deployed on diesel-powered submarines.

There is therefore no basis whatever for saying that we authorized the modernization of missiles on diesel-powered submarines.

> Secondly, launchers for older ballistic missiles on diesel-powered submarines are not included in the above-mentioned levels and, therefore, cannot be used for purposes of replacement as defined in the protocol.

In other words, they had to get rid of ICBMS.

> Three, a modern ballistic missile on a submarine is a missile of the type which is deployed on nuclear-powered submarines commissioned in the USSR since 1965.

The Soviet side has indicated its agreement with this interpretation.

In other words, the so-called "secret agreement" is nothing other than a statement by the United States of what we had already stated publicly on May 26, of what we had told our bureaucracy on June 5, of what we had sent out in guidance to every agency on June 15. It does not permit the Soviet Union to build one additional modern ballistic missile on submarines above the level of 950 that we agreed upon. And therefore the figure given publicly and before congressional committees is correct. And what we are dealing with here is an attempt to tie down a provision of the agreement that was considered to the advantage of the United States, serving our purposes that we insisted on—and on that the Soviet Union resisted in putting into this form for six weeks.

Now, let me turn to the second point—the fact that the United States, again allegedly as a result of a secret understanding, agreed not to build up to the total permitted level of 710 submarine-launched missiles on submarines.

For this I have to explain the submarine issue. Before going to Moscow—indeed, before agreeing to specifying any submarine levels—at the request of the President, I consulted both the Chief of Naval Operations and the Chairman of the Joint Chiefs of Staff with respect to our building programs. Both told me that they did not wish to build additional submarines, missile-carrying submarines, of the type that it was then possible to build—substantially the existing Poseidon boats—and that they preferred to wait with the building of new submarines, until what was then called ULMS [undersea long-range missile system] and is now called Trident, would be operational—after 1977.

Therefore we knew that we had no intention of building any additional submarines until after the expiration of the interim agreement. Nevertheless we put into the interim agreement a provision according to which we could convert fifty-four of our older ICBMS to submarine-launched missiles. We put it into the interim agreement, quite frankly,

for the third and fourth reasons which I gave with respect to our general strategic policy—the perception of other countries of the American position.

We did not think it was desirable to put into an agreement a Soviet right to convert old missiles into submarine-launched missiles without maintaining an American right to convert old missiles into submarine-launched missiles. And therefore, to maintain the formal symmetry of the agreement, we put into the agreement a right which we had no intention to exercise.

Since we knew that upon return to the United States we would testify on behalf of the Trident—what is now called the Trident program—since while we were in Moscow there had been articles in our newspapers about the possibility that the United States might launch a big program for Trident boats, the President thought it desirable that on the last day of the summit conference of 1972 to tell the Soviet Union what would become apparent within a matter of weeks anyway; namely, that we had no intention of exercising the conversion right from Titan missiles to submarines during the period of the interim agreement.

This, again, did not change the total figures. We testified that the United States was entitled to have 1,710 missiles. It did not—I repeat—change the total figure. It meant that we would maintain 1,054 ICBMS and 656 submarine missiles. This was not a concession the United States made to the Soviet Union. It was a relatively minor gesture designed to retain general confidence.

. . . When I spoke to the assembled congressional leaders in the East Room of the White House on June 15, explaining our program, I said, and I quote: the interim agreement "will not prohibit the United States from continuing current and planned strategic offensive programs, since neither the multiple-warhead conversion nor the B–1 is within the purview of the freeze, and since the ULMS (that is, what is now called Trident) submarine system is not, nor ever was, planned for deployment until after 1977." In every five-year projection which we have submitted to the Congress, we have shown that we planned on forty-one boats and 1,054 missiles.

To sum up, the totals for the Soviet side which were submitted to the Congress, and which were publicly stated, have not been changed by any agreement, understanding, or clarification—public or private. The totals for the United States that were submitted to the Congress and stated publicly have not been altered by any agreement or understanding—public or private. The figures are exactly those that have been represented—exactly those that have been agreed to—and all of

the disputes arise over esoteric aspects of replacement provisions, and not about the substance of the agreement. . . .

Q. One loose end. You presented your interpretation to the Russians. They resisted it. I assume they finally signed it.

Secretary KISSINGER. They signed it, yes.

Q. Mr. Secretary, perhaps another loose end. This interpretative statement on the Soviet sea missiles—to what extent was Congress informed of this interpretative statement? And, secondly, if I may, why in your judgment is this now becoming a matter of dispute?

Secretary KISSINGER. The interpretative statement as such was not submitted to the Congress, but the interpretation was submitted to the Congress. The interpretative statement was not submitted because it was in the channel of the General Secretary to the President, and because there was some question about whether it really was proper to make the Soviet Union sign an American interpretation—involving the general question of faith.

I think, however, that that sort of issue, whether that sort of statement should be submitted, is easily soluble—and we will not insist on retaining [it] within presidential channels.

The major point is, however, that the substance of it—the fact of our interpretation and the fact that we would act accordingly—was submitted to the Congress both in public statements on our part and in testimony of administration witnesses.

Why is this becoming an issue now? I can only assume that there was a misunderstanding on the part of some of the witnesses or on the part of some of the senators who heard testimony about what they were being told.

Q. May I follow on that? I wonder if you saw in it any effort to harass the team this close to the summit? Is this coming from the same sort of people who have doubts about going to the summit on SALT now?

Secretary KISSINGER. I don't really want to speculate about motives. I think it is important that on issues of such importance, that we can discuss them calmly and in the long-term national interest, and I have no reason to doubt the sincerity of those who made these charges.

* * *

Q. Mr. Secretary, doesn't the dispute that you have just addressed yourself to at considerable length concerning the 124 missiles, and the fact that the President will be going to Moscow with the impeachment challenge hanging over him—doesn't that raise a strong likelihood that anything agreed on the nuclear field in Moscow will likely be highly contentious in the United States; and if so, how do you intend to deal with the problem?

Secretary KISSINGER. The urgency of dealing with the nuclear problem is produced by the pace of technology. Time and again, in the nuclear period, the pace of technology has outstripped the capacity of man to deal with it.

With respect to several aspects of the current nuclear arms race, there is a very definite time pressure. What we will do is to negotiate according to our best conception of the national interest. It is clear that any agreement that may be made will be subject to a rather contentious debate. This debate is, in any event, apparently unavoidable. And we can only hope that it will be conducted with realization on both sides that it involves fundamental questions of national survival and the future of humanity, that the good faith of the participants on either side is not at issue. And on that basis, I think such a debate would contribute to the national understanding.

Q. Mr. Secretary, two questions on SALT. The first one concerns your reading of the memo of understanding with Ambassador Dobrynin. If I heard your point three right, you said that a modern missile is defined as a missile on a submarine—of the type deployed on a nuclear-powered submarine—commissioned in the U.S.S.R. since 1965. Is that correct?

Secretary KISSINGER. That is correct.

Q. Is it not so that if the Soviets chose to develop a missile not commissioned since 1965, and not deployed on either the Delta-class or the Yankee-class submarine, that if they were willing to go to that expense, they could have added seventy modern missiles to the old diesel submarines?

Secretary KISSINGER. No, because it was also made clear that if a modern missile is put on the G-class submarine, then it will be counted in the total of 950.

Q. But that is not clear by the definition of these modern missile submarines. Because it says, in effect, that it is not commissioned since '65. If they are willing to develop a variation, they can put seventy new ones in, as long as it is not the same as is already in there.

Secretary KISSINGER. Well, in the context of all the exchanges that have taken place, in the context of all of our public statements, this is a sort of legalism that would be totally rejected by the United States.

First of all, it is an absurdity to assume that the Soviet Union would develop a special missile for a submarine that is in itself obsolescent.

Secondly, in the context of all of the exchanges that have taken place, it is perfectly clear that if a modern missile is put on a G-class submarine, we will insist on counting it as part of the 950. And while perhaps this hairsplitting interpretation is possible, it is totally inconsistent with the negotiating record—it is totally inconsistent with all

the exchanges that took place previously. It would be absolutely rejected by the United States. There is, moreover, no evidence whatsoever that any such missile is being developed and deployed by the Soviet Union on any vehicle, let alone on the G-class submarine.

Q. Mr. Secretary, as you go off to Moscow, does the U.S. government now have a unified position regarding the SALT negotiation?

Secretary KISSINGER. We do not have before us a Soviet proposal which requires a formal American position. We have a general agreement on the philosophy of our approach. I do not doubt that if we wanted to translate this philosophy into numbers, disagreements would emerge. But this is not the issue we now face. And in any event, it is the responsibility of the President, which I don't doubt he will exercise, to resolve disagreements, if disagreements should still exist, if we ever do arrive at numbers.

Q. Is it likely that you would then come up with some kind of SALT agreement during the summit meeting?

Secretary KISSINGER. I do not expect that we will get a completed SALT agreement at the summit. But you can't exclude the possibility of substantial progress.

Q. Mr. Secretary, would you address yourself to the underground threshold test ban probability, sir?

Secretary KISSINGER. We are, as has been publicly stated, discussing at this time the feasibility not of a complete underground test ban but of an underground test ban at a certain threshold. There are discussions among experts to determine the level at which such a threshold should be put, the kinds of verification that would be desirable, and the time at which such a test ban should go into effect—all of which will of course affect the strategic calculations and positions of both sides. We think that progress in this field is possible.

* * *

Q. Mr. Secretary, I just want to pin down—do you expect that there will be an agreement announced at the summit on underground nuclear testing? Secondly, what is the likelihood of a limited agreement on SALT pertaining to limitations of MIRV? And thirdly, as you know, the mood of Congress toward economic agreements with the Soviet Union is rather lukewarm, to say the best. There have been reports that the administration has worked out with the Soviet Union a ten-year trade agreement. Is this so? And what else can you tell us about the trade package?

Secretary KISSINGER. With respect to the limited underground test ban, it is difficult to predict what will come out of the summit because the experts' talks are still going on. I think it is possible that there could be

an agreement in principle, and an agreement on some of the criteria that will be used in the follow-on negotiations, and an agreement on certain levels like thresholds. I say it is possible. It is not certain. The details of verification, exchange of information, of geological data and so forth, would have to be worked out at a subsequent meeting.

With respect to SALT, in March, when I was there, the Soviet Union made a proposal which in concept was worth looking at, though its numbers have not proved acceptable to us.

Now, I think it is imperative that the strategic situation be fully reviewed by Mr. Brezhnev and the President. Whether on the basis of this review they feel capable of giving detailed instructions to their negotiating teams, or whether they will feel that further exchanges are necessary before detailed instructions can be given to their negotiating teams, cannot be decided until these talks have taken place.

On the economic agreements, there is a possibility of an economic agreement that does not require the expenditure of public funds but would, rather, reflect an exchange of information and the facilitating of economic exchanges. . . .

Our problem is that we have to continue the course which we believe is in the interests of world peace, subject to the fullest consultation with Congress, and to engage in the fullest public debate. But it is not a trivial matter whether, on the one hand, the arms race is continued without restriction, with all the justifications that that will entail; and secondly, whether every positive incentive for restrained conduct is systematically closed off. And that cannot be analyzed simply in terms of one or two situations but in terms of the ability and willingness of the United States and our allies to sustain it over the decade or so of confrontations which such a course would entail.

So as a responsible administration—as the administration responsible for the conduct of foreign policy—we must continue on our best judgment which we will put fully before the committees of Congress. I understand that the Senate Foreign Relations Committee is starting at the end of July a full set of public hearings on the direction of East-West relations, a course of action which I strongly support. And we will put the basic direction of our policy before the public for full discussion.

Q. Mr. Secretary, as far as the partial underground test ban is concerned, what will be the practical consequences of it in terms of the technological advances we have been talking of—what kind of testing would it preclude, in terms of MIRV, for example?

Secretary KISSINGER. What it would preclude is the testing of higher-yield weapons. And it would probably not affect the current generation of MIRVS. And it would make more difficult the combination of im-

proved accuracies and larger yields, which may again bring about a situation in which a premium will be put on a first strike. And I want to emphasize that many of the proposals that are being made to improve the strategic capability improve first-strike capabilities and do not improve the vulnerability of the weapons concerned, and it has always been understood that the greatest danger to stability is a growing gap between first- and second-strike capabilities. So this would have a somewhat inhibiting effect on larger yields in the next generation of MIRVS.

BRUSSELS, 26 JUNE 1974*

Secretary KISSINGER. . . . We believe that the first SALT agreement was in the interest of the United States and in the interest of world peace. It at least limited the quantitative race at levels that had been achieved at that time and with which both sides seemed to be comfortable even in the absence of an agreement.

Since then there has been an explosion with respect to technology. How to control technology and how to relate technological change to quantitative limits is one of the major problems of our period; and if we express concern about this, and if we believe that it is in the national interest to pursue this subject, it is not only because of the inherent quality of the arms race, it is also because of the kind of justification that will have to be used to sustain an unlimited arms race.

We are prepared to continue in the arms race as long as we must, and we will never accept a strategic disadvantage for the United States. But we do believe that we have an obligation to make a serious effort to explore how the technological explosion can be moderated and how to prevent the pace of deployment from driving the pace of diplomacy.

These are our purposes, and how well we will fulfill them depends of course on the outcome of the negotiations, which, as I have pointed out before, will certainly not be completed in the form of any permanent agreement on this visit. . . .

Q. Mr. Secretary, as we approach the summit, does either side have a military advantage, or as you have engaged in discussions prior to the summit, does either side think it has a military advantage—where do we stand now?

Secretary KISSINGER. Where we stand now is that the Soviet Union has a numerical advantage in missiles. This numerical advantage in missiles is substantially made up if you add to it the 450 long-range

---

* SOURCE: Press conference of Secretary of State Henry A. Kissinger. *Department of State Bulletin*, 29 July 1974, pp. 196–205.

bombers we possess; and if you look at it from the strategic point of view and not the negotiating point of view, you will have to add to it also the fact that we possess weapons deployed elsewhere that would certainly be used in a general nuclear war.

Therefore, whether you count numbers of vehicles that can reach each other's countries or warheads that are deployed, the United States still has a substantial numerical advantage.

If you look only at the throw-weight of missiles, then you will have to argue that the Soviet Union has an advantage in missile throw-weight, though it is less clear what they can do with it. If you add to it the throw-weight of our bombers, then you are again at a level of substantial equality.

I would say that these comparisons can be used for almost any purpose, but we are convinced that the United States probably has an advantage, but one that is not politically of any decisive importance, and it is our basic conviction that if the arms race is continued for another ten years, it will not yield either a strategic or a political advantage for either side but that it may well complicate the political relationships.

Q. Mr. Secretary, you refer to the fact that you don't expect an agreement in the form of a permanent final agreement. Will the President and Mr. Brezhnev be going for a conceptual breakthrough of the kind you went for in March—a statement of principles in an effort to resolve the MIRV issue, with a set of directives to the negotiators? Will you be trying for that, and do you expect it?

Secretary Kissinger. I generally try to avoid making the same mistake twice. [Laughter.] But basically, there are two ways of going at the problem.

The Soviet Union gave us an approach when we were in Moscow in March which, if the numbers were changed, could be considered a conceptual breakthrough. We did not reject the approach; we reject the numbers in which they expressed it. That is one way of going at it.

The other way of going at it is to conclude that that particular approach cannot be translated into appropriate numbers and to attempt therefore to find a new approach that then might perhaps deserve the label you gave them.

Q. Mr. Secretary, since you last spoke to us in Washington at the press conference, what progress has been made toward an underground test ban pact?

Secretary Kissinger. The experts' discussions have been suspended pending our arrival; and where we stand now is, they have gone as far as they can get. We still have to settle the threshold. There are still a number of issues that have to be settled—the level of the threshold,

there are differences between us and the Soviet Union both with respect to what is permitted below the threshold and what is permitted above the threshold. So there is a great deal that remains to be done in Moscow.

Q. I didn't understand that, Mr. Secretary. What do you mean by what would be permitted above?

Secretary KISSINGER. Well, there is one argument that below the threshold there should also be a limitation on the number of tests that are permitted. Above the threshold there is the question of peaceful nuclear explosions, whether they should be extended.

Q. Could you define the differences you have with Secretary Schlesinger on this matter and also explain what he means by rhetorical flourishes?

Secretary KISSINGER. I didn't see his press conference, and that is such an inconceivable idea as applied to me that I am sure he was misquoted. [Laughter.]

I read about those differences in the newspapers. I am not conscious of differences when we meet. I have expressed my view on counterforce strategy and on first-strike capabilities. I have never been led to believe that he differs from these views, so I will be glad to express my view on certain strategic issues.

I do not believe that a country can rely politically or militarily on a first-strike capability and I do not believe that a country can achieve a first-strike capability, and I believe that the effort to do so will raise profound political issues; but I understand that he has also said that he doesn't believe this is possible. But this is a view that I have held.

* * *

Q. Mr. Secretary, in light of the fact that the United States and the Soviet Union have been unable to find the basis for a new SALT agreement, do you think it is now inevitable that the Soviets will deploy the MIRV, and if so, when, and how serious is that in terms of the arms race?

Secretary KISSINGER. We think that on some categories of missiles, the Soviet Union is nearly ready to deploy MIRVs. At what rate they will deploy them it is not yet fully possible to foretell. We have estimates of what the rate will be, with an upper and lower limit; and obviously it would be our intention, if an arms control agreement were to be meaningful, to have a ceiling that is lower than the estimate of what we think they are going to build—otherwise, the ceiling will not have any meaning.

But I would say we have about a year and a half altogether before the decisions will be irrevocable, but it becomes harder with every passing six-month period.

Q. Is it inevitable now that they will do it?
Secretary KISSINGER. It is inevitable that some MIRVs will be deployed. The rate of deployment is still subject to negotiation.

*   *   *

Q. It was announced today that the Judiciary Committee will release all of its impeachment evidence, starting early next week. My question is: Might that create a problem in the negotiations if it is being released while you are still in Moscow?
Secretary KISSINGER. I am not familiar with the evidence, and foreign policy has had to be conducted in this atmosphere continuously, so I don't want to pass any judgment on this. I just don't know enough of the—
Q. Mr. Secretary, on that point, how inhibited will the President be in negotiating because of his domestic weakness, and will this summit produce less because of his domestic problems and possible Soviet doubt about his future?
Secretary KISSINGER. The President will not be inhibited. He will negotiate in what he considers to be the national interest. It is obvious that in the most important areas any possible result will produce controversy, and that certainly will not help the domestic situation.

So, the decisions will not be on the basis of domestic necessities, but on the basis of our judgment that the pace of technology will not wait for our domestic situation to clarify. But I have also given you my judgment of the probable outcome. Now, what more could have been achieved, no one will ever know.

*   *   *

Q. Mr. Secretary, if a permanent agreement on nuclear arms control cannot occur in the Moscow summit, should we anticipate an extension of the interim agreement of 1972?
Secretary KISSINGER. It is impossible that there will be an extension of the interim agreement unless it is tied to some substantial agreement on multiple warheads, and that probably will also not be fully achieved at the summit.

Joint U.S.–Soviet Communiqué, 3 July 1974

In accordance with the agreement to hold regular US-Soviet meetings at the highest level and at the invitation, extended during the visit of General Secretary of the Central Committee of the Communist Party of the Soviet Union L. I. Brezhnev to the USA in June 1973, the President of the United States of America and Mrs. Richard Nixon paid an official visit to the Soviet Union from June 27 to July 3, 1974.

During this stay President Nixon visited, in addition to Moscow, Minsk and the Southern Coast of the Crimea.

The President of the United States and the Soviet leaders held a thorough and useful exchange of views on major aspects of relations between the USA and the USSR and on the present international situation.

* * *

The talks were held in a most businesslike and constructive atmosphere and were marked by a mutual desire of both Sides to continue to strengthen understanding, confidence and peaceful cooperation between them and to contribute to the strengthening of international security and world peace.

I. Progress in Improving US–Soviet Relations

Having considered in detail the development of relations between the USA and the USSR since the US-Soviet summit meeting in May 1972, both Sides noted with satisfaction that through their vigorous joint efforts they have brought about over this short period a fundamental turn toward peaceful relations and broad, mutually beneficial cooperation in the interests of the peoples of both countries and of all mankind.

They emphasized the special importance for the favorable development of relations between the USA and the USSR of meetings of their leaders at the highest level, which are becoming established practice. These meetings provide opportunities for effective and responsible discussion, for the solution of fundamental and important bilateral questions, and for mutual contributions to the settlement of international problems affecting the interests of both countries.

Both Sides welcome the establishment of official contacts between the Congress of the US and the Supreme Soviet of the USSR. They

Source: *Department of State Bulletin*, 29 July 1974, pp. 185–191.

will encourage a further development of such contacts, believing that they can play an important role.

Both Sides confirmed their mutual determination to continue actively to reshape US-Soviet relations on the basis of peaceful coexistence and equal security, in strict conformity with the spirit and the letter of the agreements achieved between the two countries and their obligations under these agreements. In this connection they noted once again the fundamental importance of the joint documents adopted as a result of the summit meetings in 1972 and 1973, especially of the Basic Principles of Relations Between the USA and the USSR, the Agreement on the Prevention of Nuclear War, the Treaty on the Limitation of Anti-Ballistic Missile Systems, and the Interim Agreement on Certain Measures with Respect to the Limitation of Strategic Offensive Arms.

Both Sides are deeply convinced of the imperative necessity of making the process of improving US-Soviet relations irreversible. They believe that, as a result of their efforts, a real possibility has been created to achieve this goal. This will open new vistas for broad mutually beneficial cooperation, and for strengthening friendship between the American and Soviet peoples, and will thus contribute to the solution of many urgent problems facing the world.

Guided by these worthy goals, both Sides decided to continue steadfastly to apply their joint efforts—in cooperation with other countries concerned, as appropriate—first of all in such important fields as:

—removing the danger of war, including particularly war involving nuclear and other mass-destruction weapons;

—limiting and eventually ending the arms race especially in strategic weapons, having in mind as the ultimate objective the achievement of general and complete disarmament under appropriate international control;

—contributing to the elimination of sources of international tension and military conflict;

—strengthening and extending the process of relaxation of tensions throughout the world;

—developing broad, mutually beneficial cooperation in commercial and economic, scientific-technical and cultural fields on the basis of the principles of sovereignty, equality and non-interference in internal affairs with a view to promoting increased understanding and confidence between the peoples of both countries.

Accordingly, in the course of this summit meeting both Sides considered it possible to take new constructive steps which, they believe, will not only advance further the development of US-Soviet relations

but will also make a substantial contribution to strengthening world peace and expanding international cooperation.

II. Further Limitation of Strategic Arms and Other Disarmament Issues

Both Sides again carefully analyzed the entire range of their mutual relations connected with the prevention of nuclear war and limitation of strategic armaments. They arrived at the common view that the fundamental agreements concluded between them in this sphere continue to be effective instruments of the general improvement of US-Soviet relations and the international situation as a whole. The USA and the USSR will continue strictly to fulfill the obligations undertaken in those agreements.

In the course of the talks, the two Sides had a thorough review of all aspects of the problem of limitation of strategic arms. They concluded that the Interim Agreement on offensive strategic weapons should be followed by a new agreement between the United States and the Soviet Union on the limitation of strategic arms. They agreed that such an agreement should cover the period until 1985 and deal with both quantitative and qualitative limitations. They agreed that such an agreement should be completed at the earliest possible date, before the expiration of the Interim Agreement.

They hold the common view that such a new agreement would serve not only the interests of the United States and the Soviet Union but also those of a further relaxation of international tensions and of world peace.

Their delegations will reconvene in Geneva in the immediate future on the basis of instructions growing out of the summit.

Taking into consideration the interrelationship between the development of offensive and defensive types of strategic arms and noting the successful implementaton of the Treaty on the Limitation of Anti-Ballistic Missile Systems concluded between them in May 1972, both Sides considered it desirable to adopt additional limitations on the deployment of such systems. To that end they concluded a protocol providing for the limitation of each Side to a single deployment area for ABM Systems instead of two such areas as permitted to each Side by the Treaty.

At the same time, two protocols were signed entitled "Procedures Governing Replacement, Dismantling or Destruction and Notification Thereof, for Strategic Offensive Arms" and "Procedures Governing Replacement, Dismantling or Destruction, and Notification Thereof for ABM Systems and Their Components." These protocols were worked out by the Standing Consultative Commission which was established

to promote the objectives and implementation of the provisions of the Treaty and the Interim Agreement signed on May 26, 1972.

The two Sides emphasized the serious importance which the US and USSR also attach to the realization of other possible measures—both on a bilateral and on a multilateral basis—in the field of arms limitation and disarmament.

Having noted the historic significance of the Treaty Banning Nuclear Weapon Tests in the Atmosphere, in Outer Space and Under Water, concluded in Moscow in 1963, to which the United States and the Soviet Union are parties, both Sides expressed themselves in favor of making the cessation of nuclear weapon tests comprehensive. Desiring to contribute to the achievement of this goal the USA and the USSR concluded, as an important step in this direction, the Treaty on the Limitation of Underground Nuclear Weapon Tests providing for the complete cessation, starting from March 31, 1976, of the tests of such weapons above an appropriate yield threshold, and for confining other underground tests to a minimum.

The Parties emphasized the fundamental importance of the Treaty on the Non-Proliferation of Nuclear Weapons. Having reaffirmed their mutual intention to observe the obligations assumed by them under that Treaty, including Article VI thereof, they expressed themselves in favor of increasing its effectiveness.

A joint statement was also signed in which the US and USSR advocate the most effective measures possible to overcome the dangers of the use of environmental modification techniques for military purposes.

Both Sides reaffirmed their interest in an effective international agreement which would exclude from the arsenals of States such dangerous instruments of mass destruction as chemical weapons. Desiring to contribute to early progress in this direction, the USA and the USSR agreed to consider a joint initiative in the Conference of the Committee on Disarmament with respect to the conclusion, as a first step, of an international Convention dealing with the most dangerous, lethal means of chemical warfare.

Both Sides are convinced that the new important steps which they have taken and intend to take in the field of arms limitation as well as further efforts toward disarmament will facilitate the relaxation of international tensions and constitute a tangible contribution to the fulfillment of the historic task of excluding war from the life of human society and thereby of ensuring world peace. The US and the USSR reaffirmed that a world disarmament conference at an appropriate time can play a positive role in this process.

*　　*　　*

Both Sides highly appreciate the frank and constructive atmosphere and fruitful results of the talks held between them in the course of the present meeting. They are convinced that the results represent a new and important milestone along the road of improving relations between the USA and the USSR to the benefit of the peoples of both countries, and a significant contribution to their efforts aimed at strengthening world peace and security.

Having again noted in this connection the exceptional importance and great practical usefulness of US-Soviet summit meetings, both Sides reaffirmed their agreement to hold such meetings regularly and when considered necessary for the discussion and solution of urgent questions. Both Sides also expressed their readiness to continue their active and close contacts and consultations.

The President extended an invitation to General Secretary of the Central Committee of the CPSU, L. I. Brezhnev, to pay an official visit to the United States in 1975. This invitation was accepted with pleasure.

July 3, 1974

For the United States of America:

RICHARD NIXON

President of the United States of America

For the Union of Soviet Socialist Republics:

L. BREZHNEV

General Secretary of the Central Committee of the CPSU

Protocol to the Treaty on Anti-Ballistic Missile Systems, 3 July 1974

The United States of America and the Union of Soviet Socialist Republics, hereinafter referred to as the Parties,

Proceeding from the Basic Principles of Relations between the United States of America and the Union of Soviet Socialist Republics signed on May 29, 1972,

Desiring to further the objectives of the Treaty between the United States of America and the Union of Soviet Socialist Republics on the Limitation of Anti-Ballistic Missile Systems signed on May 26, 1972, hereinafter referred to as the Treaty,

Reaffirming their conviction that the adoption of further measures for the limitation of strategic arms would contribute to strengthening international peace and security,

Proceeding from the premise that further limitation of anti-ballistic missile systems will create more favorable conditions for the completion of work on a permanent agreement on more complete measures for the limitation of strategic offensive arms,

Have agreed as follows:

Article I

1. Each Party shall be limited at any one time to a single area out of the two provided in Article III of the Treaty for deployment of anti-ballistic missile (ABM) systems or their components and accordingly shall not exercise its right to deploy an ABM system or its components in the second of the two ABM system deployment areas permitted by Article III of the Treaty, except as an exchange of one permitted area for the other in accordance with Article II of this Protocol.

2. Accordingly, except as permitted by Article II of this Protocol: the United States of America shall not deploy an ABM system or its components in the area centered on its capital, as permitted by Article III (a) of the Treaty, and the Soviet Union shall not deploy an ABM system or its components in the deployment area of intercontinental

Source: Protocol to the Treaty between the United States of America and the Union of Soviet Socialist Republics on the Limitation of Anti-Ballistic Missile Systems. *Department of State Bulletin*, 29 July 1974, pp. 216–217. The protocol to the ABM treaty entered into force on 24 May 1976.—Ed.

ballistic missile (ICBM) silo launchers as permitted by Article III (b) of the Treaty.

ARTICLE II

1. Each Party shall have the right to dismantle or destroy its ABM system and the components thereof in the area where they are presently deployed and to deploy an ABM system or its components in the alternative area permitted by Article III of the Treaty, provided that prior to initiation of construction, notification is given in accord with the procedure agreed to in the Standing Consultative Commission, during the year beginning October 3, 1977 and ending October 2, 1978, or during any year which commences at five year intervals thereafter, those being the years for periodic review of the Treaty, as provided in Article XIV of the Treaty. This right may be exercised only once.

2. Accordingly, in the event of such notice, the United States would have the right to dismantle or destroy the ABM system and its components in the deployment area of ICBM silo launchers and to deploy an ABM system or its components in an area centered on its capital, as permitted by Article III (a) of the Treaty, and the Soviet Union would have the right to dismantle or destroy the ABM system and its components in the area centered on its capital and to deploy an ABM system or its components in an area containing ICBM silo launchers, as permitted by Article III (b) of the Treaty.

3. Dismantling or destruction and deployment of ABM systems or their components and the notification thereof shall be carried out in accordance with Article VIII of the ABM Treaty and procedures agreed to in the Standing Consultative Commission.

ARTICLE III

The rights and obligations established by the Treaty remain in force and shall be complied with by the Parties except to the extent modified by this Protocol. In particular, the deployment of an ABM system or its components within the area selected shall remain limited by the levels and other requirements established by the Treaty.

ARTICLE IV

This Protocol shall be subject to ratification in accordance with the constitutional procedures of each Party. It shall enter into force on the day of the exchange of instruments of ratification and shall thereafter be considered an integral part of the Treaty.

DONE at Moscow on July 3, 1974, in duplicate, in the English and Russian languages, both texts being equally authentic.

For the United States of America:

RICHARD NIXON
President of the United States of America

For the Union of Soviet Socialist Republics:

L. BREZHNEV
General Secretary of the Central Committee of the CPSU

Treaty on the Limitation of Underground Nuclear Weapon Tests, 3 July 1974

The United States of America and the Union of Soviet Socialist Republics, hereinafter referred to as the Parties,

Declaring their intention to achieve at the earliest possible date the cessation of the nuclear arms race and to take effective measures toward reductions in strategic arms, nuclear disarmament, and general and complete disarmament under strict and effective international control,

Recalling the determination expressed by the Parties to the 1963 Treaty Banning Nuclear Weapon Tests in the Atmosphere, in Outer Space and Under Water in its Preamble to seek to achieve the discontinuance of all test explosions of nuclear weapons for all time, and to continue negotiations to this end,

Noting that the adoption of measures for the further limitation of underground nuclear weapon tests would contribute to the achievement of these objectives and would meet the interests of strengthening peace and the further relaxation of international tension,

Reaffirming their adherence to the objectives and principles of the Treaty Banning Nuclear Weapon Tests in the Atmosphere, in Outer Space and Under Water and of the Treaty on the Non-Proliferation of Nuclear Weapons,

Have agreed as follows:

Article I

1. Each Party undertakes to prohibit, to prevent, and not to carry out any underground nuclear weapon test having a yield exceeding 150 kilotons at any place under its jurisdiction or control, beginning March 31, 1976.

2. Each Party shall limit the number of its underground nuclear weapon tests to a minimum.

3. The Parties shall continue their negotiations with a view toward achieving a solution to the problem of the cessation of all underground nuclear weapon tests.

Source: Treaty between the United States of America and the Union of Soviet Socialist Republics on the Limitation of Underground Nuclear Weapon Tests. *Department of State Bulletin*, 29 July 1974, pp. 217–218. The Treaty on Underground Nuclear Weapon Tests has not been ratified by the Senate.—Ed.

ARTICLE II

1. For the purpose of providing assurance of compliance with the provisions of this Treaty, each Party shall use national technical means of verification at its disposal in a manner consistent with the generally recognized principles of international law.

2. Each Party undertakes not to interfere with the national technical means of verification of the other Party operating in accordance with paragraph 1 of this Article.

3. To promote the objectives and implementation of the provisions of this Treaty the Parties shall, as necessary, consult with each other, make inquiries and furnish information in response to such inquiries.

ARTICLE III

The provisions of this Treaty do not extend to underground nuclear explosions carried out by the Parties for peaceful purposes. Underground nuclear explosions for peaceful purposes shall be governed by an agreement which is to be negotiated and concluded by the Parties at the earliest possible time.[1]

ARTICLE IV

This Treaty shall be subject to ratification in accordance with the constitutional procedures of each Party. This Treaty shall enter into force on the day of the exchange of instruments of ratification.

ARTICLE V

1. This Treaty shall remain in force for a period of five years. Unless replaced earlier by an agreement in implementation of the objectives specified in paragraph 3 of Article I of this Treaty, it shall be extended for successive five-year periods unless either Party notifies the other of its termination no later than six months prior to the expiration of the Treaty. Before the expiration of this period the Parties may, as necessary, hold consultations to consider the situation relevant to the substance of this Treaty and to introduce possible amendments to the text of the Treaty.

2. Each Party shall, in exercising its national sovereignty, have the right to withdraw from this Treaty if it decides that extraordinary events related to the subject matter of this Treaty have jeopardized its supreme interests. It shall give notice of its decision to the other Party

[1] The Treaty on Underground Nuclear Explosions for Peaceful Purposes, limiting tests to yields no greater than 150 kilotons, was signed by President Ford and General Secretary Brezhnev in Washington and Moscow on 28 May 1976. It has not been ratified by the Senate.—Ed.

six months prior to withdrawal from this Treaty. Such notice shall include a statement of the extraordinary events the notifying Party regards as having jeopardized its supreme interests.

3. This Treaty shall be registered pursuant to Article 102 of the Charter of the United Nations.

DONE at Moscow on July 3, 1974, in duplicate, in the English and Russian languages, both texts being equally authentic.

For the United States of America:

RICHARD NIXON

President of the United States of America

For the Union of Soviet Socialist Republics:

L. BREZHNEV

General Secretary of the Central Committee of the CPSU

Protocol to the Treaty on the Limitation of Underground Nuclear Weapon Tests, 3 July 1974

The United States of America and the Union of Soviet Socialist Republics, hereinafter referred to as the Parties,

Having agreed to limit underground nuclear weapon tests,

Have agreed as follows:

1. For the purpose of ensuring verification of compliance with the obligations of the Parties under the Treaty by national technical means, the Parties shall, on the basis of reciprocity, exchange the following data:

a. The geographic coordinates of the boundaries of each test site and of the boundaries of the geophysically distinct testing areas therein.

b. Information on the geology of the testing areas of the sites (the rock characteristics of geological formations and the basic physical properties of the rock, i.e., density, seismic velocity, water saturation, porosity and depth of water table).

c. The geographic coordinates of underground nuclear weapon tests, after they have been conducted.

d. Yield, date, time, depth and coordinates for two nuclear weapon tests for calibration purposes from each geophysically distinct testing area where underground nuclear weapon tests have been and are to be conducted. In this connection the yield of such explosions for calibration purposes should be as near as possible to the limit defined in Article I of the Treaty and not less than one-tenth of that limit. In the case of testing areas where data are not available on two tests for calibration purposes, the data pertaining to one such test shall be exchanged, if available, and the data pertaining to the second test shall be exchanged as soon as possible after a second test having a yield in the above-mentioned range. The provisions of this Protocol shall not require the Parties to conduct tests solely for calibration purposes.

2. The Parties agree that the exchange of data pursuant to subparagraphs a, b, and d of paragraph 1 shall be carried out simultaneously with the exchange of instruments of ratification of the Treaty, as provided in Article IV of the Treaty, having in mind that the Par-

---

SOURCE: Protocol to the Treaty between the United States of America and the Union of Soviet Socialist Republics on the Limitation of Underground Nuclear Weapon Tests. *Department of State Bulletin*, 29 July 1974, p. 218.

ties shall, on the basis of reciprocity, afford each other the opportunity to familiarize themselves with these data before the exchange of instruments of ratification.

3. Should a Party specify a new test site or testing area after the entry into force of the Treaty, the data called for by subparagraphs a and b of paragraph 1 shall be transmitted to the other Party in advance of use of that site or area. The data called for by subparagraph d of paragraph 1 shall also be transmitted in advance of use of that site or area if they are available; if they are not available, they shall be transmitted as soon as possible after they have been obtained by the transmitting Party.

4. The Parties agree that the test sites of each Party shall be located at places under its jurisdiction or control and that all nuclear weapon tests shall be conducted solely within the testing areas specified in accordance with paragraph 1.

5. For the purposes of the Treaty, all underground nuclear explosions at the specified test sites shall be considered nuclear weapon tests and shall be subject to all the provisions of the Treaty relating to nuclear weapon tests. The provisions of Article III of the Treaty apply to all underground nuclear explosions conducted outside of the specified test sites, and only to such explosions.

This Protocol shall be considered an integral part of the Treaty.

DONE at Moscow on July 3, 1974.

For the United States of America:

RICHARD NIXON

President of the United States of America

For the Union of Soviet Socialist Republics:

L. BREZHNEV

General Secretary of the Central Committee of the CPSU

Kissinger Assesses the Moscow Summit and the Arms Race, 3 July 1974

Secretary KISSINGER. I thought I would give you a brief summary of the summit as we see it, and I think the best way to start is to look at it in terms of the [24 July] press conference in which I tried to explain the purposes of the meeting.

I pointed out that there are three fundamental purposes in these summit meetings; one, for the leaders of the Soviet Union and the United States to exchange ideas and to check assessments about international affairs in general. The necessity for this arises because, as the two nations capable of destroying humanity, they have a special obligation to prevent conflicts caused by inadvertence, by miscalculation, by misassessment of each other's motives, examples of which history is replete. The second is to see whether they can, by meeting the needs of their peoples and of mankind, construct a network of positive relationships that will provide an incentive for moderation and for a beneficial and humane conduct of foreign policy.

The second large objective is to prevent the nuclear arms race and the arms race in general from dominating international affairs, and I want to stress again that this objective is no mean goal and one that will occupy American administrations in the absence of comprehensive agreements for as far into the future as we can see. It is not only the complexity of the weapons and their destructiveness; it is also the justifications that will have to be used in each country to sustain large armament programs that will, over a period of time, present a major obstacle to the humane or even safe conduct of foreign policy.

And the third general goal is to identify those areas of common interests, either produced by the nonmilitary aspects of technology or by others or by the nature of modern life, in which the Soviet Union and the United States can cooperate and thereby create a perspective on world affairs that recognizes the interdependence of events and the fact that isolation and confrontation are, over a period of time, inimical to progress and inconsistent with human aspirations.

Now, in terms of these three objectives, a great deal of time was spent by the two leaders in reviewing the international situation. . . . They were the most extensive discussions at that level of the arms race that have ever taken place, and with a frankness that would have

---

SOURCE: Press conference of Secretary of State Henry A. Kissinger, Moscow, 3 July 1974. *Department of State Bulletin*, 29 July 1974, pp. 205–215.

been considered inconceivable two years ago, indeed with an amount of detail that would have been considered violating intelligence codes in previous periods.

So, on the issue of SALT, for example, on which I will have more to say in a few minutes, the words of the communiqué, that far-reaching and deep conversations took place, are of very profound significance. And in the next phase of discussions, difficulties cannot be caused by misapprehensions about each other's general intentions and general perceptions of the nature of the strategic environment.

And thirdly, there were a series of agreements, about most of which you have already been briefed, in the field of cooperative relationships.

Now, let me speak for myself about the two areas of arms control and the general review of the international situation.

With respect to arms control, let me cover first the agreements that have been made and then let me talk about the strategic arms limitation talks.

With respect to the agreements that have been made, there are three: the agreement that neither side will build the second ABM site, the agreement on the limited threshold test ban, and thirdly, the agreement to begin negotiations on environmental warfare.

With respect to the first agreement, in which both sides forgo the second ABM site, you remember that the permanent agreement on defensive weapons signed in Moscow in 1972 permitted each of the two countries to maintain two ABM sites, one to defend its capital, the second to defend an ICBM field, provided that field was no closer than 1,300 kilometers to the capital. The United States at that time opted for a defense of an ICBM field. The Soviet Union opted for a defense of its capital. . . .

The United States and the Soviet Union have now decided to forgo that second ABM site and to maintain only the one ABM site that each currently has, which is Moscow for the Soviet Union and an ICBM field for the United States. However, because it was thought desirable to keep some flexibility with respect to which area could be defended, each side is permitted at one time during the course of the agreement, and once in a five-year period, to alter its original decision.

In other words, if the United States should decide that it would prefer to defend Washington rather than the ICBM site, we have the option once in a five-year period to move from the ICBM site to Washington, and equally the Soviet Union has the option of moving once in that five-year period from Moscow to an ICBM site. That option, having once been exercised, cannot be exercised the second time. In other words, countries cannot shuttle their ABM sites back and forth

between the capital and an ICBM field. Each side, in short, has the option once to reverse its original decision, and it may do so in any five-year period when the treaty comes up for automatic review.

The significance of this agreement is that it reinforces the original decision implicit in 1972—in fact, explicit in 1972—that neither side would maintain ABM defenses. It makes it even more difficult, if not impossible, to break out of the agreement rapidly, and in turn, the decision to forgo ABM defenses has profound strategic consequences which are sometimes lost sight of.

You must remember that the original impetus for the multiple warheads derived from the desire or the necessity to overcome ABM defenses and to make sure that the required number of missiles would get through. In the absence of ABM defenses, the extraordinary number of foreseeable multiple warheads will create a situation in which such terms as "superiority" should not be lightly thrown around because they may be devoid of any operational meaning.

The notion of nuclear sufficiency, of what is necessary under conditions of no ABM defenses, requires careful correlation with the number of available warheads. For present purposes, I want to say that any idea that any country can easily achieve strategic superiority is almost devoid, under these conditions, of any operational significance and can only have a numerical significance. The ABM agreement reinforces the element of strategic stability that was inherent in the original ABM agreement made in 1972.

The second agreement, on the threshold test ban, prohibits underground nuclear explosions above 150 kilotons and will therefore have the tendency to concentrate competition in the ranges of the lower-yield weapons. The date for its going into effect has been put into the future because a number of additional agreements remain to be worked out.

There remains to have an agreement on the peaceful uses of nuclear explosions, in which adequate assurance will be given that they will not be used to circumvent the intention of the agreement; and there is an agreement in principle that the inspection of peaceful nuclear explosions, among other things, will involve prior notification, precise definition of the time and place, and the presence of observers, which is a major step forward in our discussions. The second subject that will require further discussion is the exchange of geological information which is needed for the adequate verification of this threshold test ban.

The third area in which an agreement was reached was to begin discussions on the dangers of environmental warfare from the point

of view of overcoming these dangers. This is a form of warfare that is in its infancy, the nature of which is not properly understood, and which obviously, by definition, can have profound consequences for the future of mankind. The United States and the Soviet Union, in the near future, will open discussions on this problem of environmental warfare.

In addition to these three agreements, two protocols will be signed on the Standing Consultative Commission, and we will certainly make diplomatic history, because it will be the first time that secret agreements are publicly signed. The agreements are being kept secret at the request of the Soviet Union, because they involve dismantling procedures for replacement missiles under the interim agreement and the ABM agreement. However, they will be submitted to the appropriate congressional committees upon our return to the United States.

Let me say a word about the Standing Consultative Commission. The Standing Consultative Commission was created in the 1972 [ABM treaty] in order to implement the provisions for replacement or destruction of weapons under the two agreements on defensive and offensive weapons.

There is a protocol for defensive weapons because the United States will have to dismantle some deployments that have taken place at a site which under the agreement we can no longer maintain, and the Soviet Union will have to dismantle fifteen ABM launchers and associated radars on their test ranges.

Secondly, there is a protocol for offensive weapons, which discusses dismantling and replacement procedure under the provisions of the interim agreement where land-based missiles can be traded in for modern sea-based missiles and where older submarine-launched nuclear missiles can be traded in for newer submarine-launched sea-based missiles. These are the two protocols that have been the subject of an illuminating exchange that took place just before I left the United States.

It must be understood that it was the assignment from the beginning of the Standing Consultative Commission to work out precise provisions for replacement and dismantling; that for that purpose they had to go into greater technical detail than was the case in the agreement; and that two protocols will be signed—one to implement the defensive provisions, the other to implement the offensive provisions.

They break no new ground, they change no provisions. If I may say so, they close no loopholes, they deal only with the technical implementation of agreements previously reached. They will be submitted to congressional committees. They are not policy documents.

They are technical documents in implementation of the 1972 agreement, and they are being signed now as a result of work extending over a period of eighteen months, because it is only now that the replacement provisions are becoming effective due to the fact that the missiles, the ICBMS, did not have to be dismantled until the submarines containing the 741st missile on the Soviet side underwent sea trial. . . .

Now let me say a word about strategic arms limitation talks. As I pointed out prior to our coming here, the administration considers the problem of strategic arms limitation one of the central issues of our time. It is one of the central issues, because if it runs unchecked, the number of warheads will reach proportions astronomical compared to the time—when Armageddon seemed near—when there were something less than 1,000 warheads on both sides.

It is important because a perception may grow that these warheads will provide a capability which will not be sustained by any systematic analysis, but because in any event they bring about a gap between the perceived first- and second-strike capabilities which in itself will fuel a constantly accelerating arms race.

Now, the problem we face in these discussions is that under the interim agreement the Soviet Union possesses more missiles—though if you add together the total number of launchers, that is to say, strategic bombers, there is no significant gap; and after all, it was not the Soviet Union that made us build bombers, that was our own decision—and therefore an attempt has been made to establish a correlation between the number of MIRV missiles and the numbers of launchers, in which perhaps to some extent the larger numbers of missiles on one side can be offset by a larger number of MIRVS on the other.

The difficulty with this approach has been the limited time frame within which it was attempted to be implemented, so that during the maximum deployment period it would not be clear whether any of these limitations would not simply be to provide a base for a breakout when the agreement lapsed.

Therefore the two leaders have decided that the principal focus of the discussions would not be on a brief extension of the interim agreement tied to an equally brief MIRV agreement, but to see whether the three factors—time, quantity of launchers, and quantity of warheads—cannot be related in a more constructive and stabilizing fashion over a longer period of time; that is to say, by 1985. And in that context, some of the difficulty of relating the various asymmetries in number can be taken care of and a stability can be perhaps achieved in deployment rates that would remove, to a considerable extent, the insecurities inherent in an unchecked arms race.

As the communiqué says, the two sides will reconvene their delegations in Geneva on the basis of this approach and on the basis of instructions growing out of the summit meeting.

* * *

Q. Dr. Kissinger, two questions. One, how did you arrive at the date 1985 on the SALT business as a concluding date or terminating date?

Secretary KISSINGER. Because we couldn't pick 1984. [Laughter.]

Q. That is what I thought, but I know you will give a more serious answer in a minute. And secondly, what is the nature of the instruction that will be going out to the delegations that will reconvene in Geneva, and approximately when will they start?

Secretary KISSINGER. We would expect them to start around August 1, give or take two weeks. The date 1985 was picked for the following reasons.

We had been thinking in terms of extending the interim agreement by perhaps two or three years and at the same time coupling with it some MIRV limitations. This presented a number of extraordinarily difficult problems because we would be pressed in terms of quantity, since a number of our new programs, such as Trident, are going to be deployed starting around 1978, 1979; and on the other hand, the Soviet Union would be pressed in terms of quality because their deployment of MIRVs is only now starting. And the difficulty of making an agreement with a cutoff date of 1979 is, when you have gone through all the agony, you have not put a cap on the rate of deployment, most of which will be occurring after 1978, 1979.

So it seemed to us that by picking a period of 1985, one could take into account the projected programs and put on limitations that would have some operational significance and which, in any event, would introduce some stability into deployment rates in such a way that it was not each side's perception of the other that would be driving it into an ever-accelerating spiral.

As we were discussing on Sunday the various ways of tackling the problem, it became apparent that one of the big obstacles was the short time frame which we were considering, and that for what we had in mind it was really necessary to look at it in a longer time frame.

On the other hand, when you talk of a permanent agreement, you get yourself frozen into situations in which the technology is so unpredictable that it is very difficult to make reasonable judgments, and this is why the period 1985 was chosen.

It was chosen in the hope, not the assurance, that if such an agreement were reached next year, we would be talking of a ten-year agreement. This is one of the factors.

Q. Could I follow that, because it seems important. You talked about the technological explosion in Brussels, I think. Does this not suggest that in the period between now and 1985 you will have one hell of an arms race going on?

Secretary KISSINGER. No. It depends when the agreement is made. As I said in Brussels, and I maintain, that we have about eighteen months to gain control of the multiple warheads—control not in the sense of eliminating them, but by introducing some stability into the rate and nature of their deployment.

If an agreement is reached within that time frame, more or less—that doesn't mean down to the last month—then it can make a major contribution to turning down the arms race, to including the problem of reduction to which we attach importance, and to bringing stability into the strategic equation.

With every six-month period that it is delayed, the problem becomes more complicated; but the point is precisely to avoid what you called the "hell of an arms race." And the difficulty, as you analyze the problem with cutoff dates of 1978, 1979, is that both sides will be preparing for the break of the agreement while they are negotiating the agreement; and it became clear that one of the obstacles was that both sides, while negotiating limitations, were also putting themselves into the position of the agreement lapsing and therefore having to develop programs that would be pressing against limits of the agreement at the edge of its time period, and for that very reason have another vested interest not to have an agreement.

Q. Dr. Kissinger, General Secretary Brezhnev said last night that these accords could have been still broader than they were. First, I would like your comments on that and also whether it is not correct then from your interpretation that one could not say there are agreed guidelines on the MIRV warhead negotiations. Secondly, on the question of the underground nuclear test ban, could you clarify with some figures what I believe is a fact—that the limit of 150 kilotons would permit all continuing underground testing of MIRVs currently conducted by the United States, which are considerably below that range—and would that not allow the continuance even beyond the target date here of all the projectable multiple warheads likely to be produced by both sides?

Secretary KISSINGER. First, the degree of cooperation between the Soviet Union and the United States has not yet reached the point where the General Secretary shows me the text of his speeches before he makes them. [Laughter.] And therefore I am not the best witness of what he may have had in mind.

My impression from what I have observed is that both sides have

to convince their military establishments of the benefits of restraint, and that is not a thought that comes naturally to military people on either side.

Now, by definition, the limitations could have been broader. On the one hand, as you know, the Soviet Union has been proposing a complete test ban, but under provisions that are unverifiable and with escape clauses which would make it directed clearly against other countries. And therefore we have deferred a further discussion of the test ban, which we are not rejecting in principle—which, indeed, we are accepting in principle—for a later occasion. So I am assuming this is one thing the General Secretary had in mind.

The second is, from my description of the SALT discussions, obviously a broader agreement is conceivable. With respect to your question—are there agreed guidelines for Geneva?—the idea of extending the time frame arose really only on Monday, and it wasn't possible to work out detailed agreed guidelines in the interval.

On the other hand, certain basic principles do exist, and I believe we have made a major step forward in the approach to the problem.

With respect to the testing, it is not true that all the projected MIRV developments are in the category below 150 [kilotons]. Indeed, the enthusiasm seems to run more in the categories above 150, coupled with improved accuracies, but whenever I link these two I get a rebuttal. So I must be cautious. So if we are concerned that one of the threats to stability is the combination of accuracy and higher yields, then in the next phase of the MIRV warhead race this ban will make a major contribution.

Clearly, for the existing multiple warheads, the testing has been substantially completed on both sides. We are concerned with the next generation of warheads—not this generation of warheads—and with respect to those, it will play a very significant role.

Q. On this question of the 150 threshold, just if you can get a little more specific, what will it prevent us from doing that we had planned to do, planned to test, and what will it prevent the Soviets from doing that we know they had planned to test?

Secretary KISSINGER. . . . I cannot, obviously, go into what we were planning to do and what the Soviet Union was planning to do. It is obvious that, if one of the concerns is the elaboration of strategies that rely on first strikes, and if, to put it another way, the concern of each side is that the proliferation of warheads might make it subject to a first strike, then it stands to reason that with the hardening of silos, it is the increase in the explosive power of warheads together with improved accuracy that becomes of greatest concern; and therefore, to the extent those strategies become possible, conceivable, or dominant

on each side, whatever its previous approach, each side will be driven toward the elaboration of larger warheads on its MIRVS.

So I repeat, this is addressed to the next generation of warheads, not to the present generation of warheads.

Q. What I was getting at there, as I understood it—and I could be wrong—we test in miniature, or do to some extent. Wouldn't that put us well below 150, below 100 in fact, and do the Soviets do the same kind of testing in miniature or not?

Secretary KISSINGER. I don't think this is the place—nor can I think of many more convenient places [laughter]—to go in detail into our methods of testing or what we know about the Soviet methods of testing.

It is my understanding that miniature testing is very rarely done, never done with operational weapons, and the concern that has been expressed to us, as we were discussing this within our government, was precisely the necessity of full-scale tests of those categories of weapons of principal significance.

Q. Dr. Kissinger, will they be able to test MIRVS on the SS–9 under that 150-kiloton limitation?

Secretary KISSINGER. . . . It is our understanding that no MIRVS are being put on SS–9s, that they are developing a missile of comparable size which will have a MIRV capability. I am not making a hairsplitting point. The warhead of that missile which we call the SS–18—and on which our judgment is that the testing of the MIRVS is in its very early stage—those warheads, in our judgment, would be considerably larger than 150 kilotons and, indeed, if those warheads could be driven below 150 kilotons, we would consider it a considerable success.

Q. Do you interpret this limitation as in effect preventing them from MIRVing SS–9s or SS–18s?

Secretary KISSINGER. As I said, they are not MIRVing the SS–9s. In order to get MIRVS on a large missile, they would have to replace the SS–9 with an SS–18, but that is just a refinement.

Quite honestly, I believe they have probably tested the warheads they would want to put on the SS–18 already. However, these have always to be calculated in terms of weight-to-yield ratio; that is to say, at the present state of their technology, there may be a limit to the number of warheads of large yield they can put on the SS–18, while with continued testing, the number of warheads could be multiplied very considerably and still maintain the same explosive power; but I don't want to go beyond that. But you have to look at it both in terms of numbers of warheads that can be carried on an individual missile as well as in terms of the explosive power of each warhead, and both of them are a function of testing, because testing determines the

packaging, which is to say the size of the warhead, as well as the yield of the warhead.

Q. Mr. Secretary, will you be presenting to members of the Congress any indications of a lessening of tensions and the problems with respect to emigration and harassment, and have you found any further understanding and receptivity on the part of the Soviet leaders in this field?

Secretary KISSINGER. There was a discussion of the subject—and I will have to maintain the position that we have previously, which is to say that we believe that the objective which we think we share with those who have other approaches can, in our judgment, be realized more effectively without making it a public government-to-government confrontation.

* * *

Q. Dr. Kissinger, you sound as though you have, at least for the time being, given up hope for getting a comprehensive SALT agreement with the Soviet Union. Is that correct?

Secretary KISSINGER. Not a comprehensive, but a permanent, and this is not a question of giving up hope, it is a question of looking at the realities of how to move matters forward. We have been operating up to now within the constraint of either a very short-term or a sort of permanent agreement.

Now, permanent would have to have review clauses every five to ten years anyway. So when you talk of 1985, that is about as permanent as you can realistically become under present circumstances.

* * *

Q. I am kind of puzzled how you can take what happened here on SALT as anything less than a setback. If you have changed from searching for a permanent agreement to searching for one in a finite time period, and you postponed the time you have given yourself, or you have put back the time you have given yourself to find that agreement, it seems to me there are two setbacks there, and I don't see how you can say this hasn't been a failure at the summit.

Secretary KISSINGER. If you approach it in a formalistic way, then these are valid arguments. If you approach it from the point of view of what will in fact contribute to slowing down the arms race, then I believe that we have found an approach in which the factors that have inhibited progress can be hopefully overcome.

The difficulty with the previous negotiations has been that it has proved extremely difficult to reconcile the various asymmetries that exist in the design of the forces, in the locations of the forces, and in

the relative deployment rates of the forces. And the time limits we have been talking about until this visit created a situation in which both sides would be pressing against the limits of the agreement at the precise moment of its expiration date—the Soviet Union from the point of view of quality, the United States from the point of view of quantity—and therefore there was a great danger that the mere expiration date might fuel, especially in its final phases, a race.

And as a result of the discussion that took place Sunday, where for the first time, I believe, at least where the concerns and the perceptions of both sides were put before each other in what I considered an unusually frank way, and in which it turned out that the perception by each side of the other really was remarkably close—the only difference being that each side of course has to take the worst case of what the other one might do; I think this was the major gap that existed—it became apparent that the time pressure was a greater factor than had been commonly understood by either side.

So I don't want to do this in terms of setback. We are not running a race with ourselves. This is a problem which, I have been stressing, will be with us for a long time, and it shouldn't be seen in terms of hitting a home run on any one occasion.

Q. You, at the Brussels briefing, said there were only eighteen months before their decisions were irrevocable and each six months made it worse in terms of the rate of deployments.

Secretary KISSINGER. That is right, and I have reaffirmed that here.

Q. But what I mean is you introduced the time pressure, as you call it.

Secretary KISSINGER. There are two time factors, the time factor available for negotiation and the time factor involved in the length of the agreement. I have reaffirmed here that, in my judgment, the time frame in which the problems that I have identified can be constructively settled is in the eighteen-month range—twenty-four months, eighteen months, in that range—and one of the reasons for 1985 is that if this agreement were to be concluded in 1975, it would then take care of the next decade. This was one of the reasons behind it. So that time factor still exists, and that time factor will press on us and must press on us, if we are serious.

Q. Can I follow that up, sir? What would you envision will happen then, if the interim agreement expires or is allowed to expire in 1977 but you have not yet reached a replacement agreement—what will happen between 1977 and 1985 in terms of the arms race psychology?

Secretary KISSINGER. If we have not reached an agreement well before 1977, then I believe you will see an explosion of technology and an explosion of numbers at the end of which we will be lucky if we have the present stability, in which it will be impossible to describe what

strategic superiority means. And one of the questions which we have to ask ourselves as a country is: What in the name of God is strategic superiority? What is the significance of it, politically, militarily, operationally, at these levels of numbers? What do you do with it?

But my prediction would be that if we do not solve this problem well before, in my judgment, the end of the expiration of the agreement, we will be living in a world which will be extraordinarily complex, in which opportunities for nuclear warfare exist that were unimaginable fifteen years ago at the beginning of the nuclear age, and that is what is driving our concern. . . .

6
The Vladivostok Summit, November 1974

Kissinger Statement on Détente and SALT, 19 September 1974

The CHAIRMAN [Senator J. W. Fulbright]. The Foreign Relations Committee today resumes its hearings on U.S. relations with Communist countries. Although these hearings had been planned for some time, they were conceived as well as a response to suggestions that the nation would benefit from a broad debate on the advantages of what is called "détente," or what I would prefer to call simply the normalization of our relations with Communist countries.

The heart and core of the policy of détente—and the central purpose of our current policy, as I understand it—is the lessening of the danger of nuclear war. With an objective so basic and essential, it is hardly possible for us to give up on arms control or trade, no matter how discouraging the prospects may seem at any given time. We are not at liberty to give up on détente as an unpromising venture of no great consequence for the simple reason that the lessening of tensions among the great powers is an endeavor of the greatest consequence, to which there is no rational alternative. The alternative to SALT agreements is the arms race; the alternative to trade is one degree or another of economic boycott; the alternative to normal relations is the cold war, and the everpresent threat of hot war.

* * *

Secretary KISSINGER. Since the dawn of the nuclear age, the world's fears of holocaust and its hopes for peace have turned on the relationship between the United States and the Soviet Union.

Throughout history men have sought peace but suffered war; all

---

SOURCE: Testimony of Secretary of State Henry A. Kissinger in Hearings before the Senate Foreign Relations Committee, 19 September 1974. U.S., Congress, Senate, Committee on Foreign Relations, *Détente*, 93d Cong., 2d sess., 1975.

too often, deliberate decisions or miscalculations have brought violence and destruction to a world yearning for tranquillity. Tragic as the consequences of violence may have been in the past, the issue of peace and war takes on unprecedented urgency when, for the first time in history, two nations have the capacity to destroy mankind. In the nuclear age, as President Eisenhower pointed out two decades ago, "there is no longer any alternative to peace."

The destructiveness of modern weapons defines the necessity of the task; deep differences in philosophy and interests between the United States and the Soviet Union point up its difficulty. These differences do not spring from misunderstanding or personalities or transitory factors:

- They are rooted in history and in the way the two countries have developed.
- They are nourished by conflicting values and opposing ideologies.
- They are expressed in diverging national interests that produce political and military competition.
- They are influenced by allies and friends whose association we value and whose interests we will not sacrifice.

Paradox confuses our perception of the problem of peaceful coexistence: if peace is pursued to the exclusion of any other goal, other values will be compromised and perhaps lost; but if unconstrained rivalry leads to nuclear conflict, these values, along with everything else, will be destroyed in the resulting holocaust. However competitive they may be at some levels of their relationship, both major nuclear powers must base their policies on the premise that neither can expect to impose its will on the other without running an intolerable risk. The challenge of our time is to reconcile the reality of competition with the imperative of coexistence.

There can be no peaceful international order without a constructive relationship between the United States and the Soviet Union. There will be no international stability unless both the Soviet Union and the United States conduct themselves with restraint and unless they use their enormous power for the benefit of mankind.

Thus we must be clear at the outset on what the term "détente" entails. It is the search for a more constructive relationship with the Soviet Union reflecting the realities I have outlined. It is a continuing process, not a final condition that has been or can be realized at any one specific point in time. And it has been pursued by successive

American leaders, though the means have varied as have world conditions.

Some fundamental principles guide this policy:

- The United States cannot base its policy solely on Moscow's good intentions. But neither can we insist that all forward movement must await a convergence of American and Soviet purposes. We seek, regardless of Soviet intentions, to serve peace through a systematic resistance to pressure and conciliatory responses to moderate behavior.
- We must oppose aggressive actions and irresponsible behavior. But we must not seek confrontations lightly.
- We must maintain a strong national defense while recognizing that in the nuclear age the relationship between military strength and politically usable power is the most complex in all history.
- Where the age-old antagonism between freedom and tyranny is concerned, we are not neutral. But other imperatives impose limits on our ability to produce internal changes in foreign countries. Consciousness of our limits is recognition of the necessity of peace—not moral callousness. The preservation of human life and human society are moral values, too.
- We must be mature enough to recognize that to be stable, a relationship must provide advantages to both sides, and that the most constructive international relationships are those in which both parties perceive an element of gain. Moscow will benefit from certain measures, just as we will from others. The balance cannot be struck on each issue every day, but only over the whole range of relations and over a period of time.

* * *

Most Americans perceive relations between states as either friendly or hostile, both defined in nearly absolute terms. Soviet foreign policy, by comparison, is conducted in a gray area heavily influenced by the Soviet conception of the balance of forces. Thus Soviet diplomacy is never free of tactical pressures or adjustments, and it is never determined in isolation from the prevailing military balance. For Moscow, East-West contacts and negotiations are in part designed to promote Soviet influence abroad—especially in Western Europe—and to gain formal acceptance of those elements of the status quo most agreeable to Moscow.

The issue, however, is not whether peace and stability serve Soviet purposes, but whether they serve our own. Indeed, to the extent that

our attention focuses largely on Soviet intentions, we create a latent vulnerability. If détente can be justified only by a basic change in Soviet motivation, the temptation becomes overwhelming to base U.S.-Soviet relations not on realistic appraisal but on tenuous hopes: a change in Soviet tone is taken as a sign of a basic change of philosophy. Atmosphere is confused with substance. Policy oscillates between poles of suspicion and euphoria.

Neither extreme is realistic, and both are dangerous. The hopeful view ignores that we and the Soviets are bound to compete for the foreseeable future. The pessimistic view ignores that we have some parallel interests and that we are compelled to coexist. Détente encourages an environment in which competitors can regulate and restrain their differences and ultimately move from competition to cooperation.

*   *   *

Our approach proceeds from the conviction that, in moving forward across a wide spectrum of negotiations, progress in one area adds momentum to progress in other areas. If we succeed, then no agreement stands alone as an isolated accomplishment vulnerable to the next crisis. We did not invent the interrelationship between issues expressed in the so-called linkage concept; it was a reality because of the range of problems and areas in which the interests of the United States and the Soviet Union impinge on each other. We have looked for progress in a series of agreements settling specific political issues, and we have sought to relate these to a new standard of international conduct appropriate to the dangers of the nuclear age. By acquiring a stake in this network of relationships with the West, the Soviet Union may become more conscious of what it would lose by a return to confrontation. Indeed, it is our hope that it will develop a self-interest in fostering the entire process of relaxation of tensions.

*   *   *

By the end of the 1960s . . . it was clear that the international structure formed in the immediate postwar period was in fundamental flux, and that a new international system was emerging. America's historic opportunity was to help shape a new set of international relationships—more pluralistic, less dominated by military power, less susceptible to confrontation, more open to genuine cooperation among the free and diverse elements of the globe. This new, more positive international environment is possible only if all the major powers—and especially the world's strongest nuclear powers—anchor their

policies in the principles of moderation and restraint. They no longer have the power to dominate; they do have the capacity to thwart. They cannot build the new international structure alone; they can make its realization impossible by their rivalry.

* * *

The course of détente has not been smooth or even. As late as 1969, Soviet-American relations were ambiguous and uncertain. To be sure, negotiations on Berlin and SALT had begun. But the tendency toward confrontation appeared dominant.

We were challenged by Soviet conduct in the Middle East cease-fire of August 1970, during the Syrian invasion of Jordan in September 1970, on the question of a possible Soviet submarine base in Cuba, in actions around Berlin, and during the Indo-Pakistani war. Soviet policy seemed directed toward fashioning a détente in bilateral relations with our Western European allies, while challenging the United States.

We demonstrated then, and stand ready to do so again, that America will not yield to pressure or the threat of force. We made clear then, as we do today, that détente cannot be pursued selectively in one area or toward one group of countries only. For us détente is indivisible.

Finally, a breakthrough was made in 1971 on several fronts—in the Berlin settlement, in the SALT talks, in other arms control negotiations—that generated the process of détente. It consists of these elements: an elaboration of principles; political discussions to solve outstanding issues and to reach cooperative agreements; economic relations; and arms control negotiations, particularly those concerning strategic arms.

* * *

We cannot expect to relax international tensions or achieve a more stable international system should the two strongest nuclear powers conduct an unrestrained stategic arms race. Thus, perhaps the single most important component of our policy toward the Soviet Union is the effort to limit strategic weapons competition.

The competition in which we now find ourselves is historically unique:

- Each side has the capacity to destroy civilization as we know it.
- Failure to maintain equivalence could jeopardize not only our freedom but our very survival.

- The lead time for technological innovation is so long, yet the pace of change so relentless, that the arms race and strategic policy itself are in danger of being driven by technological necessity.
- When nuclear arsenals reach levels involving thousands of launchers and over 10,000 warheads, and when the characteristics of the weapons of the two sides are so incommensurable, it becomes difficult to determine what combination of numbers of strategic weapons and performance capabilities would give one side a militarily and politically useful superiority. At a minimum, clear changes in the strategic balance can be achieved only by efforts so enormous and by increments so large that the very attempt would be highly destabilizing.
- The prospect of a decisive military advantage, even if theoretically possible, is politically intolerable; neither side will passively permit a massive shift in the nuclear balance. Therefore the probable outcome of each succeeding round of competition is the restoration of a strategic equilibrium, but at increasingly higher levels of forces.
- The arms race is driven by political as well as military factors. While a decisive advantage is hard to calculate, the *appearance* of inferiority—whatever its actual significance—can have serious political consequences. With weapons that are unlikely to be used and for which there is no operational experience, the psychological impact can be crucial. Thus each side has a high incentive to achieve not only the reality but the appearance of equality. In a very real sense each side shapes the military establishment of the other.

If we are driven to it, the United States will sustain an arms race. Indeed, it is likely that the United States would emerge from such a competition with an edge over the Soviet Union in most significant categories of strategic arms. But the political or military benefit which would flow from such a situation would remain elusive. Indeed, after such an evolution it might well be that *both* sides would be worse off than before the race began. The enormous destructiveness of weapons and the uncertainties regarding their effects combine to make the massive use of such weapons increasingly incredible.

The Soviet Union must realize that the overall relationship with the United States will be less stable if strategic balance is sought through unrestrained competitive programs. Sustaining the buildup requires exhortations by both sides that in time may prove incompatible with restrained international conduct. The very fact of a strategic arms

race has a high potential for feeding attitudes of hostility and suspicion on both sides, transforming the fears of those who demand more weapons into self-fulfilling prophecies.

The American people can be asked to bear the cost and political instability of a race which is doomed to stalemate only if it is clear that every effort has been made to prevent it. That is why every president since Eisenhower has pursued negotiations for the limitation of strategic arms while maintaining the military programs essential to strategic balance.

There are more subtle strategic reasons for our interest in SALT. Our supreme strategic purpose is the prevention of nuclear conflict through the maintenance of sufficient political and strategic power. Estimates of what constitutes "sufficiency" have been contentious. Our judgments have changed with our experience in deploying these weapons and as the Soviets expanded their own nuclear forces. When in the late 1960s it became apparent that the Soviet Union, for practical purposes, had achieved a kind of rough parity with the United States, we adopted the current strategic doctrine.

We determined that stability required strategic forces invulnerable to attack, thus removing the incentive on either side to strike first. Reality reinforced doctrine. As technology advanced, it become apparent that neither side *could* realistically expect to develop a credible disarming capability against the other except through efforts so gigantic as to represent a major threat to political stability.

One result of our doctrine was basing our strategic planning on the assumption that in the unlikely event of nuclear attack, the president should have a wide range of options available in deciding at what level and against what targets to respond. We designed our strategic forces with a substantial measure of flexibility, so that the U.S. response need not include an attack on the aggressor's cities—thus inviting the destruction of our own—but could instead hit other targets. Translating this capability into a coherent system of planning became a novel, and as yet uncompleted, task of great complexity; but progress has been made. In our view such flexibility enhances the certainty of retaliation and thereby makes an attack less likely. Above all, it preserves the capability for human decision even in the ultimate crisis.

Another, at first seemingly paradoxical, result was a growing commitment to negotiated agreements on strategic arms. SALT became one means by which we and the Soviet Union could enhance stability by setting mutual constraints on our respective forces and by gradually reaching an understanding of the doctrinal considerations that underlie the deployment of nuclear weapons. Through SALT the two sides can

reduce the suspicions and fears which fuel strategic competition. SALT, in the American conception, is a means to achieve strategic stability by methods other than the arms race.

Our specific objectives have been:

1. To break the momentum of ever-increasing levels of armaments;
2. To control certain qualitative aspects—particularly MIRVS;
3. To moderate the pace of new deployments; and
4. Ultimately, to achieve reductions in force levels.

The SALT agreements already signed represent a major contribution to strategic stability and a significant first step toward a longer-term and possibly broader agreement.

* * *

Numerical balance is no longer enough. To achieve stability, it will be necessary to consider as well the impact of technological change in such areas as missile throw-weight, multiple reentry vehicles, and missile accuracy. The difficulty is that we are dealing not only with disparate levels of forces but with disparate capabilities, MIRV technology being a conspicuous example. The rate of increase of warheads is surging far ahead of the increase in delivery vehicles. This is why the United States considers MIRV limitation an essential component of the next phase of the SALT negotiations. If we fail, the rate of technology will outstrip our capacity to design effective limitations; constantly proliferating warheads of increasing accuracy will overwhelm fixed launchers. An arms race will be virtually inevitable.

* * *

Finally, a ten-year program gives us a chance to negotiate reductions. Reductions have occasionally been proposed as an alternative to ceilings; they are often seen as more desirable or at least easier to negotiate. In fact, it is a far more complicated problem. Reductions in launchers, for example, if not accompanied by restrictions on the number of warheads, will only magnify vulnerability. The fewer the aim points, the simpler it would be to calculate an attack. At the same time, reductions will have to proceed from some baseline and must therefore be preceded by agreed ceilings—if only of an interim nature. But a ten-year program should permit the negotiation of stable ceilings resulting from the start of a process of reductions.

Détente is admittedly far from a modern equivalent to the kind of stable peace that characterized most of the nineteenth century. But it is a long step away from the bitter and aggressive spirit that has characterized so much of the postwar period. When linked to such broad and unprecedented projects as SALT, détente takes on added meaning and opens prospects of a more stable peace. SALT agreements should be seen as steps in a process leading to progressively greater stability. It is in that light that SALT and related projects will be judged by history.

Kissinger Discusses Prospects for SALT II, 24 November 1974

Q. Dr. Kissinger, was there a specific proposal that was put forward by one side or the other?

Secretary KISSINGER. The sequence of events has been as follows: In October, in Moscow, the Soviet Union made a proposal, or advanced considerations, that I considered, that we have described, as constructive. Building on these considerations, the United States made some counterproposals which will be before the Soviet leaders when we meet today.

The Soviet leaders, in turn, advanced some considerations of their own to which the President, in turn, responded today; so it is a process in which the views of the two sides are being brought closer without as yet being identical, but we are in the same general ball park. We are talking about the same thing, on the same principles, and each exchange refines the issues more clearly and brings them closer.

Q. Mr. Secretary, are you talking about MIRVS? Can you give us any specifics of what area you are talking about?

Secretary KISSINGER. We are talking about comprehensive limitations including numbers as well as MIRVS. . . .

Q. Do you think now that you have come closer to your goal in 1975 on an agreement?

Secretary KISSINGER. Well, I think we have come closer to our goal of having an agreement in 1975.

Q. Dr. Kissinger, when you say overall numbers, as well as MIRVS, you are talking about total delivery systems or are you talking about total warheads or what?

Secretary KISSINGER. Well, this is one of the issues that is being discussed. But generally speaking, we are talking about total delivery systems.

Q. Has this been one of the subjects of discussion, how to define the number that you then will make known?

Secretary KISSINGER. Well, obviously, when you discuss strategic limitations, you discuss what sort of numbers would be considered appropriate as well as how you would then define them, and this is part of the discussion.

SOURCE: Press conference of Secretary of State Henry A. Kissinger, Vladivostok, 24 November 1974. *Department of State Bulletin*, 23 December 1974, pp. 893–897.

Q. . . . As I understand the events as you described them, the sequence, today the Soviets came forward with a proposal modifying their views on what we had given them earlier?
Secretary KISSINGER. Today the Soviets responded to what we put before them, which in turn was the response to what they had put before us in October. That is correct.
Q. And when was it that we gave this response to them?
Secretary KISSINGER. Oh, let's see. I guess on the Tuesday or Wednesday, whenever I had lunch with Ambassador Dobrynin. I guess on Wednesday before we left on the trip. . . .
Q. Dr. Kissinger, in connection with this meeting, are you optimistic?
Secretary KISSINGER. I am optimistic about this meeting, yes.

* * *

Q. Was the absence of the Watergate ever—
Secretary KISSINGER. Well, it is a different atmosphere from the one in July for many reasons.
Q. How so?
Secretary KISSINGER. Well, in any event, President Nixon was a lame-duck president, leaving Watergate aside. President Ford has announced that he is running for reelection in 1976, so he is not a lame-duck president.

In July, for a variety of reasons, things were not ripe for an agreement. I think now—I am not saying things are ripe for an agreement here, but I think both sides are making a very serious effort to come to an agreement during 1975.

* * *

Q. Has the progress been such that some sort of agreement will be signed here, and is there any change in our plans to leave tomorrow?
Secretary KISSINGER. No. I am certain that we will leave tomorrow. It may be a few hours later in the day than had been tentatively planned.

There is no possibility of signing a SALT agreement here. Whatever is provisionally agreed to here will have to be spelled out in very detailed negotiations which are going to be extremely complicated and which can easily fail. What we can do here is reach orders of magnitude, of directions in which to go, relationships of various categories to each other. That sort of thing can be done here.

Spelling this out, what it means, what restraints are necessary, what inspection, what requirements there are for this, there is not enough technical expertise here, and in any event it is inconceivable

that an agreement will be signed here. How the guidelines will be given, that remains to be seen after the session tomorrow morning.

* * *

Q. Mr. Secretary, would you please speculate on what considerations, political or otherwise, may have prompted the Russians to move in this direction and come this far and show this much progress?

Secretary KISSINGER. Don't go overboard yet on progress. I am trying to give you a sense of movement. I have always stressed that this is a very difficult subject, and it is quite possible that when we resume tomorrow it will turn out that we will not go further than where we have reached tonight. I think both sides have realized, and I think the Soviet side has also realized, that at some point we will be so deeply involved on both sides in the next round of weapons development and procurement that that cycle will become irreversible. The cycles can really be mastered only at certain strategic intervals, and once they have gone a certain time, whatever that particular cycle is will tend to be completed, and one has to wait for the next one to come around.

I think that realization that we have been stressing for a year, I think it is now accepted by both sides. And it is obvious that if the race continues that the United States will have to enter certain areas of weapons development that it would prefer not to have to do. I think it was a combination of factors like this that has accounted for the progress of the discussions of recent months.

Joint U.S.-Soviet Statement, 24 November 1974

During their working meeting in the area of Vladivostok on November 23–24, 1974, the President of the USA Gerald R. Ford and General Secretary of the Central Committee of the CPSU L. I. Brezhnev discussed in detail the question of further limitations of strategic offensive arms.

They reaffirmed the great significance that both the United States and the USSR attach to the limitation of strategic offensive arms. They are convinced that a long-term agreement on this question would be a significant contribution to improving relations between the US and the USSR, to reducing the danger of war and to enhancing world peace. Having noted the value of previous agreements on this question, including the Interim Agreement of May 26, 1972, they reaffirm the intention to conclude a new agreement on the limitation of strategic offensive arms, to last through 1985.

As a result of the exchange of views on the substance of such a new agreement, the President of the United States of America and the General Secretary of the Central Committee of the CPSU concluded that favorable prospects exist for completing the work on this agreement in 1975.

Agreement was reached that further negotiations will be based on the following provisions.

1. The new agreement will incorporate the relevant provisions of the Interim Agreement of May 26, 1972, which will remain in force until October 1977.

2. The new agreement will cover the period from October 1977 through December 31, 1985.

3. Based on the principle of equality and equal security, the new agreement will include the following limitations:

   a. Both sides will be entitled to have a certain agreed aggregate number of strategic delivery vehicles;

   b. Both sides will be entitled to have a certain agreed aggregate number of ICBMS and SLBMS [intercontinental ballistic missiles; submarine-launched ballistic missiles] equipped with multiple independently targetable warheads (MIRVS).

4. The new agreement will include a provision for further negotiations beginning no later than 1980–1981 on the question of further

SOURCE: *Department of State Bulletin*, 23 December 1974, p. 879.

limitations and possible reductions of strategic arms in the period after 1985.

5. Negotiations between the delegations of the US and USSR to work out the new agreement incorporating the foregoing points will resume in Geneva in January 1975.

November 24, 1974.

Joint U.S.-Soviet Communiqué, 24 November 1974

In accordance with the previously announced agreement, a working meeting between the President of the United States of America Gerald R. Ford and the General Secretary of the Central Committee of the Communist Party of the Soviet Union L. I. Brezhnev took place in the area of Vladivostok on November 23 and 24, 1974. Taking part in the talks were the Secretary of State of the United States of America and Assistant to the President for National Security Affairs, Henry A. Kissinger and Member of the Politburo of the Central Committee of the CPSU, Minister of Foreign Affairs of the USSR, A. A. Gromyko.

They discussed a broad range of questions dealing with American-Soviet relations and the current international situation.

*　　*　　*

I

The United States of America and the Soviet Union reaffirmed their determination to develop further their relations in the direction defined by the fundamental joint decisions and basic treaties and agreements concluded between the two States in recent years.

They are convinced that the course of American-Soviet relations, directed towards strengthening world peace, deepening the relaxation of international tensions and expanding mutually beneficial cooperation of states with different social systems meets the vital interests of the peoples of both States and other peoples.

Both Sides consider that based on the agreements reached between them important results have been achieved in fundamentally reshaping American-Soviet relations on the basis of peaceful coexistence and equal security. These results are a solid foundation for progress in reshaping Soviet-American relations.

Accordingly, they intend to continue, without a loss in momentum, to expand the scale and intensity of their cooperative efforts in all spheres as set forth in the agreements they have signed so that the process of improving relations between the US and the USSR will continue without interruption and will become irreversible.

Mutual determination was expressed to carry out strictly and fully the mutual obligations undertaken by the US and the USSR in accordance with the treaties and agreements concluded between them.

SOURCE: *Department of State Bulletin*, 23 December 1974, pp. 879–881.

II

Special consideration was given in the course of the talks to a pivotal aspect of Soviet-American relations: measures to eliminate the threat of war and to halt the arms race.

Both sides reaffirm that the Agreements reached betwen the US and the USSR on the prevention of nuclear war and the limitation of strategic arms are a good beginning in the process of creating guarantees against the outbreak of nuclear conflict and war in general. They expressed their deep belief in the necessity of promoting this process and expressed their hope that other states would contribute to it as well. For their part the US and the USSR will continue to exert vigorous efforts to achieve this historic task.

A joint statement on the question of limiting strategic offensive arms is being released separately.

Both sides stressed once again the importance and necessity of a serious effort aimed at preventing the dangers connected with the spread of nuclear weapons in the world. In this connection they stressed the importance of increasing the effectiveness of the Treaty on the Non-Proliferation of Nuclear Weapons.

It was noted that, in accordance with previous agreements, initial contacts were established between representatives of the US and of the USSR on questions related to underground nuclear explosions for peaceful purposes, to measures to overcome the dangers of the use of environmental modification techniques for military purposes, as well as measures dealing with the most dangerous lethal means of chemical warfare. It was agreed to continue an active search for mutually acceptable solutions of these questions.

* * *

IV

The state of relations was reviewed in the field of commercial, economic, scientific and technical ties between the USA and the USSR. Both Sides confirmed the great importance which further progress in these fields would have for Soviet-American relations, and expressed their firm intention to continue the broadening and deepening of mutually advantageous cooperation.

The two Sides emphasized the special importance accorded by them to the development on a long term basis of commercial and economic cooperation, including mutually beneficial large-scale projects. They believe that such commercial and economic cooperation will serve the cause of increasing the stability of Soviet-American relations.

Both Sides noted with satisfaction the progress in the implementation of agreements and in the development of ties and cooperation between the US and the USSR in the fields of science, technology and culture. They are convinced that the continued expansion of such cooperation will benefit the peoples of both countries and will be an important contribution to the solution of world-wide scientific and technical problems.

The talks were held in an atmosphere of frankness and mutual understanding, reflecting the constructive desire of both Sides to strengthen and develop further the peaceful cooperative relationship between the USA and the USSR, and to ensure progress in the solution of outstanding international problems in the interests of preserving and strengthening peace.

The results of the talks provided a convincing demonstration of the practical value of Soviet-American summit meetings and their exceptional importance in the shaping of a new relationship between the United States of America and the Soviet Union.

President Ford reaffirmed the invitation to L. I. Brezhnev to pay an official visit to the United States in 1975. The exact date of the visit will be agreed upon later.

For the United States of America:

GERALD R. FORD

President of the United States of America

For the Union of Soviet Socialist Republics:

L. I. BREZHNEV

General Secretary of the Central Committee of the CPSU

November 24, 1974

Kissinger Assesses the Vladivostok Summit, 24 November 1974

Secretary KISSINGER. The joint statement, in our judgment, marks the breakthrough with the SALT negotiations that we have sought to achieve in recent years and produces a very strong possibility of agreement, to be signed in 1975.

* * *

President Ford and the General Secretary, in the course of these discussions, agreed that a number of the issues that had been standing in the way of progress should be resolved and that guidelines should be issued to the negotiators in Geneva, which we expect to reconvene in early January.

They agreed that obviously, as the joint statement says, the new agreement will cover a period of ten years; that for the first two years of that period, the provisions of the interim agreement will remain in force, as was foreseen in the interim agreement; that after the lapse of the interim agreement, both sides could have equal numbers of strategic vehicles; and President Ford and General Secretary Brezhnev agreed substantially on the definition of strategic delivery vehicles.

During the ten-year period of this agreement, they would also have equal numbers of weapons with multiple independent reentry vehicles, and that number is substantially less than the total number of strategic vehicles.

There is no compensation for forward-based systems and no other compensations. In other words, we are talking about equal numbers on both sides for both MIRVS and for strategic delivery vehicles, and these numbers have been agreed to and will be discussed with congressional leaders after the President returns.

The negotiations will have to go into the details of verification, of what restraints will be necessary, how one can define and verify missiles which are independently targeted. But we believe that with good will on both sides it should be possible to conclude a ten-year agreement by the time that the General Secretary visits the United States at the summit; and at any rate, we will make a major effort in that direction.

As I said, the negotiations could be difficult and will have many

SOURCE: Press conference of Secretary of State Henry A. Kissinger, Vladivostok, 24 November 1974. *Department of State Bulletin*, 23 December 1974, pp. 898–905.

technical complexities, but we believe that the target is achievable. If it is achieved, it will mean that a cap has been put on the arms race for a period of ten years; that this cap is substantially below the capabilities of either side; that the element of insecurity inherent in an arms race in which both sides are attempting to anticipate not only the actual programs but the capabilities of the other side will be substantially reduced with levels achieved over a ten-year period by agreement.

The negotiations for reductions can take place in a better atmosphere, and therefore we hope that we will be able to look back to this occasion here as the period of—as the turning point that led to putting a cap on the arms race and was the first step to a reduction of arms. . . .

Q. Mr. Secretary, . . . are bombers under "a"?

Secretary KISSINGER. Yes.

Q. Bombers are included. When you say no compensation, you mean what we have in Europe counts against ourselves?

Secretary KISSINGER. No. What I mean is forward bases, which are not included in these totals.

Q. They don't count in this?

Secretary KISSINGER. Strategic bombers are included. Forward-based systems are not included.

Q. My question follows on that. What are the advantages for the Russians in agreeing on the numbers of MIRVs being equal, that they would not raise questions about compensating for our forward-based systems?

Secretary KISSINGER. Well, I think that we should ask the General Secretary for an explanation of why he—I can explain to you our point of view on these matters, but I believe that both sides face this problem.

The arms race has an impetus from at least three sources: one, political tension; second, the strategic plans of each side; and third, the intent of each side to anticipate what the other side might do. The most volatile of those in a period of exploding technology is the last one.

There is an element that is driving the arms race of insuring one's self against the potentialities of the other side that accelerates it in each passing year. I would suppose that the General Secretary has come to the same conclusion that we have, that whatever level you put for a ceiling, it is enough to destroy humanity several times over, so that the actual level of the ceiling is not as decisive as the fact that a ceiling has been put on it and that the element of your self-fulfilling prophecy that is inherent in the arms race is substantially reduced.

I would assume that it was considerations such as these that induced the General Secretary to do this.

Q. My question derives from the fact that no bargainer would put himself at a disadvantage, and I am just wondering what, from our standpoint, would be the net advantage of maintaining our forward bases without the Soviets complaining that there is some imbalance or some inequality or inequation in the overall purpose?

Secretary KISSINGER. Well, as you know, the Soviet Union had maintained that forward-based systems should be included in the totals, and this was one of the big obstacles to an agreement previously. The progress that has been made in recent months is that the Soviet Union gradually gave up asking for compensation for the forward-based systems partly because most of the forward-based systems, or I would say all of them, are not suitable for a significant attack on the Soviet Union. At any rate, this is an element that has disappeared from the negotiation in recent months.

Q. Secretary Kissinger, have you reached agreement on the number of MIRV vehicles or the number of MIRV warheads?

Secretary KISSINGER. The number of MIRVed vehicles. The number of warheads could differ, and of course there are some differentials in the throw-weight of individual missiles at any given period, though there is nothing in the agreement that prevents the United States, if it wishes to, from closing the throw-weight gap. We are not going to do it just to do it.

* * *

Q. Mr. Secretary, one last question, please. Would you address yourself to the question of good faith on this? This is very important and will be a very important agreement to the security of the people of both nations. What will you say as a statement of faith and a guarantee?

Secretary KISSINGER. When the security of both countries is involved and the national survival of both countries is involved, you cannot make an agreement which depends primarily on the good faith of either side. And what has to be done in the negotiations that are now starting is to assure adequate verification of the provisions of the agreement. We think that this is no problem, or no significant problem, with respect to the total numbers of strategic vehicles. It may be a problem with respect to determining what is a MIRVed vehicle. Nevertheless we believe that that, too, is soluble, though with greater difficulty than determining the total numbers.

Good faith is involved in not pressing against the legal limits of the agreements in a way that creates again an element of the insecurity that one has attempted to remove by fixing the ceiling or, to put it another way, by putting a cap on the arms race. But I think that the agreement will be very viable, and that the element of good faith is not the principal ingredient in releasing the agreement, though it was an important element in producing the agreement.

Kissinger Briefings on the Vladivostok Accord, November and December 1974

EN ROUTE TO PEKING, 25 NOVEMBER, 1974*

Q. What is the definition of a delivery vehicle?
Secretary KISSINGER. A delivery vehicle is anything that has international range. Any missile—submarine-launched and land-based—and any bomber.

Now, there is one special problem of bomber armament. Until these things are published, I can't be precise. On bomber armaments only those things that can plausibly be considered attacking weapons from a long distance, that can attack the Soviet Union outside the range of the air defense system and a long distance, would be considered. In other words, not those weapons which are used to attack the air defense system.

Q. How about a missile shot from an airplane?
Secretary KISSINGER. It depends what range it has.
Q. Well, the long range, for example?
Secretary KISSINGER. We don't have any like this. But if there were one, yes.
Q. The B–1?
Secretary KISSINGER. None of the weapons on the B–1 would be considered delivery systems. The B–1 is one delivery vehicle. It is not counted as a MIRV, even though you could make a case that it carries more than one bomb. The missiles on the B–1 are not counted as a delivery vehicle.

* * *

Q. How are you going to take care of the throw-weight problem?
Secretary KISSINGER. The throw-weight problem, in my judgment, and on a deep background basis, is a bit of a phony, because nobody asked us to design small missiles; that was our choice. We can't ask the Soviets to pay us compensation for the fact that we decided to build small missiles and they decided to build large missiles.

What I'm saying to you is this: If we decide to solve the throw-weight problem, if the President decides he wants to close the throw-weight gap, it is within his decision to do it. We are not going to do

* SOURCE: Background briefing of Secretary of State Henry A. Kissinger, 25 November 1974. Department of State, Bureau of Public Affairs. Reporters' questions in this briefing are paraphrased; Secretary Kissinger's replies are verbatim.—Ed.

it just to be doing it, because if you analyze what you are going to use it for, if you do it not demagogically but strategically, if you ask yourself what are you going to use the warheads for, against what targets, it may well be that we will decide that we do not have to deal with the throw-weight problem. But if we decide to deal with it, we can substantially close the gap; and if you add the bombers to it, there is no throw-weight gap. But that argument which I am making on our side is also phony, because missile throw-weight and bomber throw-weight are not exactly comparable.

What you are worried about in missile throw-weight is an attack on land-based systems. Over a ten-year period, no matter what you do, land-based systems are going to become highly vulnerable. There is no escaping it. And over a ten-year period I think the composition of our force, in our judgment, is a safer one than the Soviets', even though the Soviets have a throw-weight advantage, because we have a much smaller percentage of our throw-weight in fixed, land-based missiles. At a certain level of accuracy, which we are within sight of, no silo can survive against even the weapons we have. So you ask yourself what do you want more for.

Q. (Inaudible)

Secretary Kissinger. By the time the Soviets have enough MIRVs to threaten our land-based missiles, which cannot be for five to six years, we will have so much increased the accuracy and yield of our present weapons that we can threaten their missiles, on top of which by that time we could have a bigger missile, which is not precluded by the agreement.

We are not going to build weapons just to match every large thing the Soviets have. We are going to build weapons for our purposes, not for an exact competition. We are going to look at a larger missile, and we have a program which you know about—the MX missile which is being looked at. But we have many options. We can build a larger missile to put into silos. We can put a missile on airplanes. We have just begun the Trident development, on which we can get much larger throw-weight. So we are not in bad shape over a ten-year period, and we must not confuse what may happen. There is no way the Soviets can threaten our land-based missiles even theoretically for four to five years, depending at what rate they are deploying their MIRVs.

Even then, at the levels of MIRVs that are permitted under the agreement, it is just one hell of a risk. And look at the calculation an aggressor would have to make. We have, I don't want to go into precise figures, but we have much less than half of our throw-weight in land-based missiles, much less than half. For the Soviet Union to threaten us, somebody would have to convince Brezhnev or his succes-

sor—there has to be a successor because it could not happen before 1980—that they are capable of firing some four to five hundred missiles simultaneously (they have never fired more than three simultaneously); that all their MIRVS would work the way they are planned; that going in a north-south direction they are going to have the same accuracy as in an east-west direction, which is the way they were tested; that we would not fire on warning when we see several thousand warheads coming; and that after all of this has been done, they would only have got much less than half our total throw-weight. They would have to be crazy to do this. What would they achieve with this?

WASHINGTON, 3 DECEMBER 1974 *

Secretary KISSINGER. Let me sum up what can be said about the agreement. The President stated yesterday that the ceiling on strategic delivery vehicles is 2,400; the ceiling on MIRVS is 1,320. The number of land-based silos will remain constant, though they are subject to the same modifications that are permitted in the interim agreement—which is to say that their dimensions can be increased by 15 percent, and that airborne missiles of a range of more than 600 [kilometers] will be counted as individual missiles, though not as MIRVS.

I think these are the essential elements of the agreement—which means that each side is free to compose these 2,400 in any way it wishes, except that it cannot add land-based silos. It can add land-based mobiles; it can move land-based missiles to sea.

The numerical limitations of the interim agreement with respect to submarines, as well as to the total numbers of submarine-based missiles, will not be in effect. The only number of the interim agreement that will remain in effect is that of the land-based silos; and those are, of course, the most vulnerable part of the strategic forces. Those are the essential elements of the agreement.

* * *

Q. Mr. Secretary, do the silos remain so that they're limited to 15 percent in size, even though there's not anything specifically said?

Secretary KISSINGER. Well, that does not happen to be exactly true, because the United States, either because of great foresight—as the Russians believe—or for other reasons—as some others believe—designed its silos in such a way that they can take a considerably larger missile than is presently in them, so that it is within our capa-

* SOURCE: Background briefing of Secretary of State Henry A. Kissinger, 3 December 1974. Department of State, Bureau of Public Affairs.

bility, even without increasing the size of the silo substantially, to reduce Soviet throw-weight advantage; and, if we increase the silos by 15 percent, to come close to eliminating Soviet throw-weight advantage—if that's the decision that we want to take.

But . . . I believe that the throw-weight issue has been vastly overstated, and the decision of whether we will attempt to close the throw-weight will be taken by us for our reasons and not simply because the Soviet Union has heavier missiles than we do.

Q. Mr. Secretary, since the Soviet Union has not deployed any MIRV missiles and since the United States does not plan as many as 1,320 MIRV missiles, why couldn't you get a lower MIRV figure?

Secretary KISSINGER. We could have probably gotten a slightly lower MIRV figure: 1,320 is slightly above the American MIRV plan and therefore gives us some degree of flexibility. We could have gotten a slightly lower MIRV figure; it wouldn't have made any real difference.

Q. Where did you get the 1,320? How did you arrive at that figure?

Secretary KISSINGER. We arrived at the figure of 1,320 by taking some of the planned programs and, in effect, adding to them the Trident force.

* * *

Secretary KISSINGER. Let me make a general statement of what the significance of this agreement is before we get lost in a lot of technicalities.

First, in terms of the negotiating history of this agreement, there were the following items throughout the negotiations:

(1) Total aggregates.

(2) Limitations on MIRVS—for which the code name was "qualitative restraint."

(3) There was the issue of forward bases.

(4) There was the issue of the British and French nuclear forces.

(5) There was the fact that the Soviet Union claimed compensation for a more vulnerable geographic position—the fact that some potential enemies were geographically closer to it than to us—or, to put it into less complicated language, that China would have nuclear weapons aimed at the Soviet Union.

Therefore, these were the parameters of the negotiations as they had been going on for several years until this summer.

What we attempted to do is approve immediately a comprehensive agreement that would take care of all of the issues simultaneously. Therefore, until this summer we attempted to bring about an extension of the interim agreement, in which the Soviet Union had a differential in missiles and for which we wanted to compensate by obtaining

a differential in MIRV vehicles. Even though we were prepared to give them a differential in total missiles until the end of 1979, the differential in missiles for which we asked was not to be negotiable during the time of the summit [meeting between President Nixon and Secretary Brezhnev in July 1974].

Secondly, as we analyzed the problem at the time of the summit, it became clear that this was really a very precarious agreement—that you extended the interim agreement for a number of years at a time when the production program of both sides of MIRVs would reach a certain peak—that, therefore, the breakout potential was very substantial—and where the Soviet Union, or we, simply by deferring the deployment of one year's production, would have a massive breakout potential at the precise moment that the agreement ended.

Therefore, it was decided at the summit meeting . . . that we would, in July, aim for a ten-year agreement, in which it would be easier to catch several cycles of the program and to attempt to bring about a negotiation in this manner.

As far as the United States is concerned, we had a number of preparatory Verification Panel meetings, out of which emerged five to eight options which were presented to the President and to the NSC meeting which took place in October. . . .

These options range from some that were extraordinarily simple to others of great esoteric complexity. Out of these options, the President chose not one of the options but a combination of two of the simpler ones and asked me to present those in Moscow when I was there in October.

We had two days of very difficult and very inconclusive meetings, which then led to a meeting of the Politburo on the last day that I was in Moscow . . . at which, apparently, some fundamental decisions were taken by the Soviet Union, because that evening they made a proposition to us, which I made clear afterwards brought the issue within negotiating range.

Now, what brought it within negotiating range was the Soviet Union accepted then the principle of equal aggregate at some stage of the ten-year problem. They nevertheless still insisted on compensation for the British and French nuclear forces and some compensation for forward-based missiles.

The reason why equal aggregates become more important in a ten-year agreement than a five-year agreement was that if we gave up on the principle of equal aggregates in a ten-year agreement following [the] five-year [interim agreement], it would mean that [in] the period of 1972 through 1985 the United States would have accepted a position of numerical inferiority in strategic delivery vehicles, which whatever it

actually invites strategically—which I never thought was much—nevertheless, symbolically, could have had some political impact on the potential of other countries. This was the situation when I left the Soviet Union at the end of October.

On the basis of the proposal that the Soviet Union made to us in October—which they also put in writing to us—we formulated a counterproposal, in which equal aggregates were to be achieved earlier, sometime during the 1975 to 1985 period; and in the interval before the United States achieved total equal aggregate, there would be a MIRV differential in our favor.

. . . This, more or less, was the situation in Vladivostok. I brought it out only to make clear that there was not a precooked agreement that was simply ratified in Vladivostok. The negotiations were, roughly, as I had described them to you upon our arrival in Vladivostok.

Saturday evening we had an extended negotiation on what differentials in total numbers and what differentials in MIRV numbers for what period of time might be acceptable, and this is where it stood about midnight, when we adjourned.

It was the next morning that General Secretary Brezhnev made his proposal on moving to equal aggregates immediately—not asking for compensation for the British and French nuclear forces. And out of this developed a more extended discussion having to do with bomber armament and the position of heavy missiles—the limitation of heavy missiles, the agreement which we have discussed. . . .

I have heard it said that the United States gave the Soviet Union rather large figures. Now, I think the fact of the matter is quite the contrary. The overall total is below the figures which the Soviet Union has today. . . . We hope that the Soviet Union will be forced to reduce numbers to achieve the agreed level by 1977.

Secondly, before we went to Vladivostok—and not necessarily connected with Vladivostok—we asked the intelligence community to give us three projections of Soviet development, both in the MIRV field and in the missile field and in the total strategic delivery field. Those estimates were made by people who had no idea of the figures that we were debating.

The intelligence estimates were made in three estimates—a low estimate, a medium estimate, and a high estimate.

All three estimates . . . [were] considerably above the figures [finally agreed upon for] both the MIRVs and the delivery systems. . . .

So with all due respect, it is total nonsense to say that the United States gave the Soviet Union figures that were granted to them by us.

The United States agreed with the Soviet Union on figures below their present figures in total numbers of missiles, and well below our

estimate of where they would be—well below their lowest estimate of where they would be without an agreement—and substantially below our estimate, our most likely estimate, of where they would be without an agreement. And all of this was done without counting the British and French nuclear forces, without counting the forward-based systems, and without any of the other frills. . . .

The second argument, [that] all we are doing is continuing the race . . . is not true. If the Soviet Union had built to the level that was what our intelligence estimate predicted—and I repeat that our intelligence estimate projected without any knowledge of the figures we were discussing with the Soviet Union—if the Soviet Union had built up to those figures, we would have been faced with the following problem: We would have been faced with the problem of whether we wanted to match all those or exceed all those figures, or whether we were going to permit, as a result of an arms race, a gap to exist, which many in our country considered intolerable, though it was ratified as part of a SALT agreement.

In other words, the gap which we had permitted to arise without an agreement before 1972—which we had frozen as a result of the interim agreement—would have grown against us as of 1977.

Therefore, the only way the United States could have responded is either to let the gap grow or to make a massive effort in order to close it. So our expenditures on the strategic forces would have had to go up rapidly, and would have had to go up now.

Now, if we had permitted the gap to grow—in other words, if we had kept our strategic expenditures down—our capability of bringing the arms race under control would have declined substantially, because what arguments could we have used against the Soviet Union in order to induce them to accept figures even roughly comparable to the ones we have accepted? If we had gone into an arms race of our own, the consequences would have been quite unpredictable.

We had constantly felt that one of the primary objectives of these negotiations would be not to bring about a level in which the destruction of human life was not possible—that is beyond our ability—but rather to get the perceptions of both sides into a framework in which they are not a series of self-fulfilling prophecies—a fuel-wasting arms race which can be sustained only by the argument of "an imminent surprise attack" which, in turn, then makes political accommodations more and more difficult.

Now whether the level of forces is 2,400, 2,200, or 2,000 has some financial difference. But in terms of the capacity to destroy human life, it is almost irrelevant.

Therefore, the arguments that the levels before us are not unin-

teresting, but they do not go to the center of the issues—to reduce the strategic forces to a level where they cannot destroy human life—the reductions would have had to be to levels that are inconceivable today.

Now I would like you all to remember that in 1962, at the time of the Cuban missile crisis, the United States was at something like 1,500 warheads, maybe 2,000 warheads. The Soviet Union possessed something like 70 ICBM warheads.

But in the records of the deliberations at that time, the policy makers had the perception to see that the delivery of even a fraction of those Soviet warheads on the United States would present quite unmanageable problems for the United States.

We are now in a period where, with MIRVs and with the proliferation of strategic nuclear weapons, the level at which human life—or at least civilized life as we now know it—could be substantially reduced is not affected by whether the total ceiling is 2,400, 2,200, 2,000, or any of the ceilings that anyone has talked about.

In fact . . . you can make the argument that at certain levels of MIRV, the fewer the aimpoints the more precarious the situation becomes. . . .

The significance of this agreement is that a ceiling has been put on the total number for a ten-year period, so that the argument can no longer be made that the other side is racing into newer and newer fields.

In this respect, incidentally, the argument that this isn't saving any money is also incorrect, because if the Soviet Union had built to our expectations of its program . . . we would have had to expend a substantial additional sum to that which we now face. . . .

Now let me say a word about throw-weight. I believe, as I have said before, that throw-weight is not an important part of the issue, because throw-weight is not an entity in itself. Throw-weight is a means to an end. Throw-weight is significant if it is translated into numbers of warheads and accuracy—and that, in turn, matters if you have specific targets against which to use them. . . .

The Soviet Union has 85 percent of its throw-weight in the most vulnerable target, that is to say, in its land-based missile. The United States has only about 25 percent of its throw-weight in its most vulnerable targets—that is, our land-based missiles.

In the 1980s the greater flexibility of our force, and the greater vulnerability of their force, is very likely to bring about a situation in which the threat to their forces is likely to be much greater than the threat to our total force—regardless of what the weight of the individual warhead is.

So we believe that this agreement has, for the first time in the nuclear age, established a ceiling—for the first time in the nuclear age,

enabled both sides to plan without the fear of an escalating numerical arms race in both the overall numbers and the numbers of those vehicles which have multiple warheads. For the first time, it gives us the base from which to negotiate for our reduction, and it has eliminated from the negotiations those items that were most divisive within the [NATO] alliance.

So if we are worried about the arms race, not only about the numbers, but about the self-fulfilling prophecies about the perceptions by each side of the other—and about the arguments that will have to be used to continue this—then I believe that the achievements of this ceiling will turn out to have been of considerable historical importance.

* * *

Q. If I have the content of this straight, if I understand it correctly, on the basis of generally understood publications, we have had about 800 deployed MIRVS. We have had publicly announced plans for something in the neighborhood of 1,000. And this agreement sets a level of 1,320. The Soviets, at this point, as far as we know, don't have any MIRVS.

Secretary KISSINGER. That is right.

Q. So the agreement in ten years would permit them to build up to this 1,320. And each one of these missiles would have a certain number of warheads.

Now, the thing that I'm having difficulty with here is, obviously, it would cost billions of dollars for them to build up to the level where we are now, and it would take a great period of time to do it, too. And this is a catch-up for them, as far as the MIRVS are concerned.

Secretary KISSINGER. Yes.

Q. And what you are saying is that we have set this number "high," if I understand correctly—or the number has been set high—or we have been satisfied with the number set this high—because of our fears that they might have wanted to go way beyond where we are now. Is that right?

Secretary KISSINGER. Way beyond—

Q. 1,320?

Secretary KISSINGER. Way beyond the 1,320, that is right.

Q. So we actually believe that they not only were prepared to spend the billions of dollars to catch up with us, but to go way beyond?

Secretary KISSINGER. That we believe that this might well be the case, yes.

Q. How long have you had that conception? About a year and a half?

Secretary KISSINGER. I think any of you who have heard me speak about this problem have heard me speak with a great sense of urgency,

that if the MIRV development were not brought under control, that it would drive both sides in a direction which would become unmanageable.

And it was based on these intelligence estimates plus the fact that if the Soviet Union had decided, after the expiration of the interim agreement, to put its MIRVS into new holes rather than into the old holes—then if you assumed that they were aiming to give any number—1,500 missiles—1,500 MIRVS—we might have faced a missile force of 4,000 rather than 2,400, if that had been their decision. I am not saying it would have been their decision, but it was certainly their option.

Now, it is not true that our [MIRV] program was only 1,000. Our program was well above 1,000.

Q. Our program is publicly announced.

Secretary KISSINGER. Well, our program is publicly announced, whatever it is—we have set the level at roughly our program.

Q. It speaks—the intention of our program was about 1,320.

Secretary KISSINGER. Give or take. . . . You add the Tridents, the Poseidon, the Minutemen, and you will come to the figure [of 1,320].

Q. Mr. Secretary, on the same question, how does one logically reconcile the fact that the Soviet Union, which you say was going to be far beyond any of these projections, last October or last June was talking with us about a figure half the size of the 1,320? What is the logical rationale there?

Secretary KISSINGER. First of all, the Soviet Union did not accept the figure—which was a little higher than half—for a five-year period. Here we are talking about a ten-year period. Since the Soviet Union did not accept the figure, which was somewhat larger than half of what we settled for for a five-year period, which was the beginning of their MIRV program, you have a rather good estimate that in the second five-year period they would have done at least as much again, and, therefore, in a ten-year period you would have been well above 1,320.

Q. Who wanted the 1,320? Is that the Russian figure or the American figure?

Secretary KISSINGER. It's substantially our figure. I'm not saying we couldn't have had a hundred less.

Q. Mr. Secretary, we could have had three or four hundred less, wouldn't you say?

Secretary KISSINGER. I doubt it.

* * *

Q. As you look back at it now are you sorry you went ahead with the MIRV?

Secretary KISSINGER. Well, that's a good question. And I think this is the same question that people faced when the hydrogen bomb was developed. And it raises the issue whether your development of MIRVS or of a weapon produces the development on the other side, or whether by not going ahead you then simply give an advantage to the other side.

I would say in retrospect that I wish I had thought through the implications of a MIRVed world more thoughtfully in 1969 and 1970 than I did. What conclusion I would then have come to I don't know. . . .

Q. I wanted to ask about what appears to be a conflict between what you and the President are saying about putting a cap on the growth of weapons development, and what this agreement actually provides to the extent that I understand it.

Secretary KISSINGER. It puts a ceiling on the numbers of weapons in certain categories.

Q. Right. And you have always said, if I understood correctly, that warheads are in many respects a key figure simply because one is killed by warheads and not by vehicles.

Secretary KISSINGER. That is true.

Q. Now, since numbers of warheads are not limited and throw-weight is not limited—indeed, we have said that we maintain the option to build up our throw-weight—isn't it misleading to say that a ceiling has been put on the numbers of weapons?

Secretary KISSINGER. In the sense that you argue that the number of warheads can be increased.

Q. Yes.

Secretary KISSINGER. Well, we have a good estimate—in fact, we have a certain estimate—of the number of warheads that the Soviet Union had deployed on their present missiles because we have some idea of their testing program. And they are not likely to deploy a warhead that they hadn't tested. That's axiomatic. So to all practical purposes we have an estimate of the total number of warheads that are going to be deployed at that period. And they have a rather good estimate of the total number of warheads that we are likely to deploy in that period.

Now, it is, of course, possible that the two sides, within the total limit of 1,320, could develop . . . MIRVS which have [a] larger number of total warheads on them than the MIRVS that are presently designed. The question will soon have to be raised. In fact, it is a question that will have to be raised now: What is the advantage in multiplying the number of warheads beyond a certain point? As all of you know, I have never taken the view of numerical equality as seriously as some other people.

First of all, our estimate is that in the number of warheads, we will remain ahead in this ten-year period, for a variety of reasons, including the greater sophistication of our MIRVs. But in any event, we will reach a total number in which whether we build more warheads or not, it seems extremely unlikely to give us a decisive, or even significant, superiority. We have that theoretical capability within the 1,320 limit.

And, moreover, I would like to point out that we intend as soon as this agreement is ratified and begins to operate to begin negotiations on the reduction.

Q. Does this agreement as it now stands commit both sides to enter into negotiation for reduction at some point, and if so, at what point?

Secretary KISSINGER. It permits both sides to enter into negotiations for reduction no later than 1980.

Q. As I read it, you are not committing yourself to begin the negotiations before December of 1981.

Secretary KISSINGER. In 1980 or 1981.

Q. Right, but it could begin as late as December 1980, as I read the agreement. The question really is, realistically do you have any expectation that such arms reduction talks will begin seriously long before that?

Secretary KISSINGER. That will be our effort. And I think that once proposals on both sides have stabilized—you see, the Soviet Union will have to reduce their forces to get to the level of 2,400. If they deploy some of their new forces, some of the land-based mobiles that people are talking about, they will have to reduce even more forces. I think once the equal aggregates have been reached—or to put it another way, once the Soviets have gone down to the level that is required—I think we will certainly urge the beginning of talks on reduction. And I have great hopes that we will succeed.

Q. How long will it take them to MIRV up to a point where they will be willing to enter into arms reduction talks?

Secretary KISSINGER. Well, supposing the arms reduction brings about a reduction in the number of MIRVs and they haven't yet reached that level. So what? Then they would just not build up to the [number] presently permitted and only build up to the newly permitted levels. I think it will be easier to have reduction talks once you are not in an open-ended arms race in which both sides are watching production programs of the other, whose scope they cannot assess.

Q. Mr. Secretary, you described here, if I get it correctly, a process over these last months in which the Soviet Union point by point gave in to us while we resolutely held our ground. I guess I have two questions. What did we give up to them? And if you did not yield at some

point in the last month anything to them, what's your reasoning on why this came about?

Secretary KISSINGER. I believe that one of the difficulties of the previous negotiations was the uncertainty of our domestic situation. Conversely, I think that they confronted a new president as an individual with whom they might have to deal for a six-year period. Secondly, they dealt with a president unencumbered by past history, who therefore, if he failed to get an agreement, could go back to his original defense orientation and really pick up the arms race. Thirdly, I believe that they probably attempted to vindicate the significance of détente by getting off on the right foot with a new president or with a new administration.

I think it was a combination of all, plus, fourthly, they probably analyzed what I believe any thoughtful analyst of the strategic situation would have to do—that in the field of strategic forces superiority is an illusive concept. And I think it was a combination of all of these factors that produced rather significant movement between July and December—and I must tell you quite candidly, rather unexpectedly.

Q. How many warheads do you foresee on each side in 1985?

Secretary KISSINGER. Well, I would expect us to have somewhat above 10,000, and I would expect the Soviets to have less.

Q. Do your figures work out to about 11,000, Mr. Secretary?

Secretary KISSINGER. That sounds reasonable to me. I haven't multiplied it out. I expect the Soviets to be below that.

Q. Somewhat less?

Secretary KISSINGER. Maybe 9,000. It depends how many warheads—

Q. Mr. Secretary, you say the Soviets would have to reduce their force level—

Secretary KISSINGER. Could we put all the figures on deep background? All the figures I give I would like to put on deep background so that you multiply it out.

Q. You mentioned the Soviets would have to reduce their forces. You mean the forces they actually have deployed?

Secretary KISSINGER. The Soviet Union under SALT I is permitted, and would reach, something like 950 [SLBMS] plus 1,401 [ICBMS]. [That equals] 2,350.

Q. But they are not at that level now?

Secretary KISSINGER. Well, it depends. If you count the SS–7, they are at that level now, because what they are doing now is to trade in SS–7s and –8s for submarine-launched missiles. So if you count the 210 SS–7s and –8s, they are in the area between 2,300 and 2,400. And if you add the 150 bombers that they have, they are about at a total level

of 2,500 right now. So they will have to give up probably their bomber force.

Q. Mr. Secretary, what's your estimate of the Chinese nuclear capacity five years from now, at a time when the reduction talks are supposed to start between here and Moscow?

Secretary KISSINGER. Insignificant.

* * *

Q. Dr. Kissinger, just on the subject of throw-weight again, you conceded here this afternoon that, at least theoretically, the Soviets have the potential of increasing the number of warheads that a given missile could deliver, given their greater throw-weight, theoretically.

Secretary KISSINGER. So do we. We could increase the number of warheads on our missiles at least as fast as the Soviet Union could, because you have to assume that the Soviet Union is going to deploy the warheads which they have recently tested. You cannot assume that they are going to deploy a larger number of warheads than those they have tested. Therefore, you have to assume that this generation of Soviet MIRVS is going to use the number of warheads that they have tested. That number is comparable to the number of warheads that we carry on smaller missiles because of our superior technology. . . .

We could, if we wanted to, put more warheads even on our existing missiles. We have the additional option, if we wanted to, to design a larger missile to put into the existing holes which could carry many more warheads. So if you are asking about who could expand the number of his warheads more rapidly, the Soviet Union or we, I would say that over the period of the agreement I would bet on us.

Q. What I was really asking is, what is to prevent there being, in effect, another arms race in that given area?

Secretary KISSINGER. The fact that it doesn't make a great deal of sense to increase the number.

Q. Yes, but you have frequently told us that what is important is the perception that each side has of the other. And I can easily see this becoming a political football in this country.

Secretary KISSINGER. The capacity of this country to develop political footballs seems to me to be unlimited. [Laughter.] But I'll tell you what my recommendation to the President would be. It would be that we would not go into wild multiplication until we see the Soviets actually testing something.

Q. On this question of policing the MIRVS, Mr. Secretary, would you dwell briefly on that? Isn't that an area we are going to have to go into now, and isn't it tough and intricate, a major issue?

Secretary KISSINGER. The major issue in the negotiations now is going to be the verification issue. And it is because of an accident of Soviet design luckily not as difficult as it might easily be. Let me explain.

The Soviets have developed missiles to carry their MIRVS which do not fit into the existing silos—in other words, which require extensive modifications of the existing silos. Therefore, we will assume that any silo that is being substantially modified will be carrying a MIRV missile. Therefore, we will be able to count the number of their missiles by the number of silo modifications of that type, with which we are very familiar and which are undisputed.

Or to put it in another way, any missile that has been tested in a MIRV mode successfully will be counted by us as being MIRVed. In other words, we will not permit the Soviet Union to claim that they are deploying an SS–17 or –19 with the argument that it will only have a single warhead, since we believe that the [MIRV] testing program on the SS–17 and –19 has been substantially successfully concluded. Any silo that we see modified to take an SS–17 or –19 we would count as being MIRVed.

This is one of the issues that will have to be discussed in the verification. Otherwise, there is almost no other way of verifying, because you could not accept the unsupported statement of the Soviet Union that certain silos have only single warheads.

* * *

Q. Might we not have to go to on-site inspection to make certain that they are obeying the limit?

Secretary KISSINGER. No. There may have to be certain collateral restraints, into which I do not want to go now. But I believe that it is quite possible—we have gone over this in the Verification Panel on innumerable occasions—that if we can obtain the position that any silo that accepts a SS–17 or –19 missile—and we have already told the Soviets that this is going to be our definition—and after the SS–18 program is completed, which it is not yet, any silo that accepts SS–18 missiles will be treated as MIRVed. I think we have a largely foolproof method of inspection, with a few collateral restraints.

On submarines, the problem is going to be somewhat more complicated because we have not yet seen any [MIRV] tests of their submarine-based missiles. Therefore, we don't know what the characteristics will be. But on the whole we would have to again assume that any submarine capable of carrying a MIRVed missile, once the missile has been tested, likely will have to be counted as MIRVed, just as all of our submarines will have to be counted as MIRVed.

Q. Well, could they have SS–17s and –19s in silos that haven't been modified?

Secretary Kissinger. No.

Q. All those that have the new missiles have been modified?

Secretary Kissinger. That's right. And on that we have no question. And they have never rejected it. They've also never accepted it. But it's the only possible—if that is rejected, I see no other basis for inspection. When you talk of on-site inspection, we went through that drill in '69 and '70 when we didn't understand the MIRV problem well enough and thought you could simply screw a MIRV warhead on an existing missile. And actually, on-site inspection wouldn't help you very much because you would have to have a random inspection, you couldn't inspect every missile every day. With the time delays that would be involved until you get to the site, they could easily take off the MIRV warhead and put on a single warhead, have a MIRV storage, and when you leave put the MIRV back on the missile.

* * *

Q. Would it be fair to say that if they rejected the verification formula there is no deal?

Secretary Kissinger. If they reject the verification formula, unless there is enormous ingenuity in which we come up with another one, I really wouldn't know where to begin. I think if they reject verification it will be very hard to conceive how there can be a deal.

Q. What is your feeling? Do you think they will accept it?

Secretary Kissinger. I think they will accept it. I cannot conceive that they have gone this far in order to blow up the agreement now when verification is used, when it was very easy to blow it up on numbers.

Q. Unless they are buying time.

Secretary Kissinger. What time are they buying? Maybe one cycle of the defense budget. If we find out by next April that they are stalling on verification, and if they are worried about us going into a bigger defense program, I think we would have a much better chance with Congress having in good faith accepted these numbers and then finding that the numbers evaporate because they won't agree to really the only reasonable inspection system that can be designed. And there is no alternative to this inspection.

* * *

Q. Mr. Secretary, given the psychology of the arms race up to now, why do you think that pressures won't develop to keep improving the weapons that are agreed on?

Secretary KISSINGER. Well, but to say that you haven't got anything because you haven't got everything is a very dangerous course.

Q. I'm saying for the future; spending, for example.

Secretary KISSINGER. Well, whether you are improving weapons within an accepted ceiling or whether you are driving the ceiling while you are improving the weapons seems to me two different problems. It's quite possible that some improvements within the existing weapons [ceilings] would be possible. Again you have to distinguish two categories. The improvements in the Soviet force after they reach their ceiling will be composed of 1,320 MIRVs and 1,080 unMIRVed vehicles. My guess is that most of them will be ICBMs. The improvements that you can make in single-warhead weapons in relation to the strategic utility are relatively marginal. We have greater flexibility making improvements because our force is going to be composed of bombers and other elements. Now, the area of improvement is likely to be, therefore, in MIRVs. Now, you can improve accuracy, and you can improve yield. Then you have to ask yourself again, why?

The strategically unsettling effect of improvement in accuracy and yield is not as large when it is constricted within fixed numerical limits as it is when it is also driven by larger numbers. I find it conceptually very hard to see how you could get a decisive advantage by technological innovations that are now foreseeable in the offensive forces over the period of this agreement. I may be wrong, but I think that by limiting the numbers of both the qualitatively worrisome and the overall figures you have put some very significant constrictions on the arms race.

* * *

Q. Mr. Secretary, is it fair to say at this stage that the agreement in Vladivostok rules out the possibility that either side could achieve in the next ten years a first-strike capability?

Secretary KISSINGER. I would say that, yes. With the limitation you can say that there is a first-strike capability against certain categories of weapons. I would think that the land-based missiles on both sides are going to become increasingly vulnerable. And that is in any case going to happen, with or without this agreement. Then it is up to each side to compose its forces so that the land-based forces are not the most significant element in its force. And this I must say is a bigger problem for the Soviets than for us, because over that ten-year period our land-based force is not going to be the most significant element in our force.

Q. How are we going to verify that there is not an increase in their land-based mobiles?

Secretary Kissinger. The factor of confidence we have with respect to land-based mobiles is, of course, much less than it is with respect to land-based fixed. In land-based fixed, we have almost 100 percent confidence. In land-based mobile, we could be off by some 25 percent.

You have to remember now that any land-based mobile of any quantity will have to come out of either the submarines or the land-based fixed. . . .

* * *

Q. Mr. Secretary, can I go back to the reduction thing just once because of the importance that Senator Jackson, amongst others, at least professes to attach? From what level, at what point, do we hope again to negotiate reductions?

Secretary Kissinger. From the level agreed in these numbers.

Q. Before they are attained?

Secretary Kissinger. We are perfectly prepared to discuss them before they are attained.

I must say [something about the argument] that this agreement is inadequate because it doesn't reduce defense spending, and that what we should have done was to get lower numbers. The only way we could have even talked about lower numbers was to drastically increase defense spending and to hold the increase for a larger number of years—long enough to convince the Soviets that we were going to drive the race through the ceiling with them. At that point, getting the vested interests in this country to accept even the figures that we were going to talk about seems to me an argument that I find very difficult to deal with. . . .

If we had gone back to Geneva, when obviously the Soviets attach great symbolic importance to the first meeting between Brezhnev and President Ford in light of all the pressures that had existed against détente, and if this agreement in which the Soviet Union made very major concessions should suffer the fate of some other negotiations, then we must ask ourselves whether on the other side the whole process of détente may not have been drawn into the most serious question. Because here they met every point that all the critics of détente had consistently made—actually quite unexpectedly—in which equality is achieved in all significant categories, in which the arms race in terms of numbers is at least limited, and even qualitative improvements will have to be affected by the fact that they cannot be translated into quantity. I believe that, really, as a country we should not denigrate this thing.

7
Domestic Reaction to SALT

Congressional Report on SALT, 10 December 1974

IV. Climate Surrounding Current Arms Negotiations

While from one perspective future problems should be highlighted, it is important to note that immense strides in the area of arms controls have occurred in the past few years. From an academic toy for contemplation, the subject has become one for continued relevant exchange between the two superpowers. Events of immense significance have occurred in this field, specifically the ABM treaty and the interim agreement (SALT I). Exchanges on this subject have been developed in a manner which has successfully avoided many of the traditional political themes which usually adorn discussions between the superpowers. This is a significant achievement in itself, and great credit should be accorded the individuals responsible.

It should be noted that after the subcommittee had completed its hearings, the administration agreed to guidelines in Vladivostok preparatory to a formal agreement on further strategic arms limitations.

V. Subcommittee Observations

A. DÉTENTE

As exhilarating as can be the potential for arms control through negotiations and the seemingly frank exchanges with the Soviet Union which have occurred, there are three specific collateral considerations which accrue from these negotiations which should be understood.

First, it is increasingly obvious that the euphoria which develops and prematurely anticipates success from ongoing arms control nego-

---

SOURCE: U.S., Congress, House, Committee on Armed Services, Special Subcommittee on Arms Control and Disarmament, *Review of Arms Control and Disarmament Activities*, 93d Cong., 2d sess., 1974.

tiations has resulted in an unrealistic (and even irresponsible on the part of some of our leaders) feeling of security not justified by the facts. It is the nature of our country, which has a history of inherent goodwill on the part of its people, to transfer similar motives to other nations and their representatives. This, plus the optimistic visions conjured by the mention of arms control negotiations, create a degree of complacency in assessing international threats. The tendency toward this defense malaise, while unsettling, is certainly not justification to abandon negotiations, but rather reason for cautious expression on the part of governmental representatives in on-going assessments of the negotiations.

A second consideration which must be appreciated to maintain an objective perception of these negotiations comes from an expressed but not publicized view of history held by the Soviets. In simple terms, they perceive the correlation of forces, which encompasses economic, social, political, psychological, and other forces, as evolving in their favor vis-à-vis the United States. With this viewpoint as a base, their willingness to grant the U.S. major concessions in negotiations of such long-term significance is slight. There are, of course, other factors which influence their interest in concluding agreements; yet the very existence of this belief must skew their vision of acceptable solutions considerably.

Third, détente, or rather more appropriately, relative stability and candor in our relations with the Soviet Union, exists only because its existence is in our mutual interest. Our current military strength and the perquisites which accrue from it restrict the national aims and foreign policy goals of the Soviet Union in a manner which necessitates the tailoring of their approach to accommodate the existence of this factor. If our military strength erodes, so commensurately will the Soviets' interest in accommodation. No responsible reading of current history, and more specifically the interplay in the SALT negotiations, could reach any other conclusion. Dealing from strength is more than a pleasant phrase, it is an imperative for successful SALT negotiations.

B. NEGOTIATING STRUCTURE

Although a full and detailed treatment of the issues involved in negotiations as pregnant as are those in SALT and MBFR would be inappropriate in a public report such as this, there are some matters which the subcommittee became cognizant of involving the structure and composition of our government's negotiating process which should be aired and remedied. It is not melodramatic nor inaccurate to class negotiating as an art form in and of itself. However, to view it as art to be admired from afar yet without practical significance seriously

misreads its character because its practical impact on the outcome of any given set of negotiations is prodigious.

As was proven in the SALT I agreement, when the negotiations were against a set deadline (the summit conference), 35 percent of the substance of any agreement will be settled in the last thirty minutes of the negotiations. This is one example of a negotiating technique that is utilized all too well by the Soviets, and not appreciated appropriately by the U.S. government. It should be made clear, however, that this situation is institutional in nature, because the caliber of the individuals representing the U.S. in these delegations with whom the subcommittee conferred is absolutely superior. Institutionally, however, our system is given to fluctuation in its personnel over a period. The Soviets, on the other hand, in essence train negotiators who are steeped in techniques of negotiations, are dedicated to negotiating as a career, and are taught to see it not as a problem-solving technique, but rather a means to gain advantage. As a consequence, the Soviets appear, for example, to appreciate to a far higher degree than does the U.S. the real advantages of conducting negotiations on your home ground where all of the nation's technical expertise is available to be consulted when certain points are in issue, while the guest must rely on stretched-out communication systems to obtain such assistance.

Reminiscent of techniques studied in undergraduate logic courses familiar in the U.S., the Soviets also put to good use *agreements ad referendum* in which preliminary assurances are arrived at and concessions made by both sides, yet made subject on the Soviet side to approval by a higher authority. Of course, the next step is for the authority to then indicate a lack of enthusiasm for the agreement, requiring further concessions in order to gain approval. These are apparently only a few of the devices used to great effect by the Soviets, and which it appears our negotiators might utilize effectively given the flexibility to do so.

There is another situation that became evident, as the subcommittee inquired into the negotiating structure, that is troubling in concept. It appears that in formulating its position to present to the Soviets, the U.S. government intentionally arrives at a negotiating position which represents the outcome we expect will be arrived at, balancing the interests of *both sides*. On the other hand, the Soviet positions are more classically structured for the negotiating situation. Their positions are heavily weighted to their advantage in anticipation of a certain amount of brokering at the bargaining table and the arrival at a final agreement midway between the sides. The U.S. position does not have this flexibility inherent, and thus either we are forced to make no concessions, which is not conducive to a successful outcome

in such bargaining, or else we must concede in areas where concessions will be painful. This unfortunate situation apparently is endemic to our system, in which policies are formulated balancing the interests of a great many disparate government agencies, yet not oriented to appropriately appreciate the peculiarities of the negotiating table. This is another example of an institutional defect in our structure. Regardless of the basis for its existence, its effect is to undercut our negotiating position and the efficacy of our negotiators to the potential detriment of our national interests.

These comments are not meant to denigrate in any manner the negotiators and those working here in Washington; rather, they are intended as constructive suggestions from an outside source, aimed at pointing up what appear to be inherent defects in our institutional approach to arms negotiations. To set the subcommittee up as experts on the issues in the negotiations or the negotiation process would be presumptuous after this limited review, for the issues and technical problems are extremely complex. They are made more difficult by the differences between the two societies involved—our open society, where a considerable amount of discussion of relevant issues occurs in public, versus the Soviet "closed" system.

There is a remarkable example of how their closed society impacts on the negotiations. In the day-to-day conduct of the SALT negotiations, there are inevitable and innumerable discussions on each side's various strategic weapons. To this day, the Soviets have never revealed in any manner whatsoever, even through their negotiators in private sessions, their own national designations for, or the characteristics of, their strategic weaponry. Incredibly, all discussions are carried out using our own internal classifications of their armaments, with the Soviets never having once, throughout the course of these extended talks, ever referred to their own equipment in their own generic terminology for it. That discipline in their negotiators typifies some of the problems we encounter in attempting with any confidence to arrive at appropriate balances of weapons, and is representative of the type of obstacles our negotiators must face in dealing with the Soviets.

C. THE SECRETARY OF STATE

An obvious factor throughout the SALT negotiations primarily has been the ubiquitousness of the Secretary of State, Mr. Kissinger. Without doubt his efforts have been, in large part, responsible for many of the successes in this series of negotiations. Although one is inclined to voice criticism of such success reluctantly, there are aspects of the Secretary's envelopment of these negotiations which appear to be counterproductive.

(1) Control

The subcommittee was struck by the amount of restraint exercised by the Secretary over all players in these negotiations. On several occasions, the subcommittee was confronted with situations where active participants in the SALT policy framework made it clear that they could only speak candidly to the subcommittee on the negotiations in private. While it is not unusual nor even improper for members of the executive branch to shy from expressing opinions different or contrary from the official line, the subcommittee was concerned by the degree of restraint apparent over responsible officials. The subcommittee is concerned in this regard that varied input into the policy-making process may likewise be stifled by this control, for many of the matters which were expressed in this veiled manner were totally responsible and reasonable concerns which ought to be aired in a full and frank discussion on such significant policy matters.

(2) Continuing Character of Negotiations

In another area, the Secretary's administration of this negotiation process deserves critical comment. A problem first suggested to the subcommittee by Paul Nitze, a recently resigned member of the SALT negotiating team, and buttressed by other evidence as the subcommittee's hearings proceeded, is that the U.S. negotiating process has become—almost inextricably—intertwined in the personality of the current Secretary of State.

The subcommittee is cognizant of the fact that the Secretary of State has been an indispensable catalyst in the success of recent arms control, as well as other international agreements. It appears, though, that the essential element provided by the Secretary in these negotiations—that of the force of his own personality centered on the issue and directing the U.S. input—while successful to date, has also the potential for problems in the future when the current Secretary leaves office, as he inevitably will in our system, and these negotiations continue. An example of the problems of this control was presented recently when the Secretary's preoccupation with the Middle East forced him to be, to a degree, inattentive to the SALT issues, a fact which resulted in the absolute grinding to a halt of the negotiations.

(3) Front Channel–Back Channel

The situation which causes concern can be illustrated by a curious relationship that currently exists in the SALT negotiations and has been characterized in terms of the "front channel" and the "back channel" of the negotiations. The front channel is that represented by the forum in which the U.S. and Soviet negotiating teams meet to formally present proposals and work toward an agreement. The back

channel is the personal negotiating that takes place between Secretary Kissinger himself and the Soviet Foreign Minister, Mr. Gromyko, or even Secretary Brezhnev.

Of late, and including a large part of the negotiations that resulted in the interim agreement, the back channel has produced all movements of substance in the negotiations, with the front channel fleshing out the details after the fact. The obvious danger from such a system is that when Mr. Kissinger leaves his post, the U.S. government will be left a series of personal relationships which govern the progress and success of such negotiations, but which Mr. Kissinger's successor may well not be able to energize. This could be unfortunate for the U.S. long-term interests as it is apparent that the duration of these negotiations and the critical questions they consider will remain for an indeterminate time in the future. The subcommittee is concerned that the current arrangement may well inure to the detriment of our system. Although this problem is not one suited to legislative solution, it is certainly suited for congressional concern. For this reason, the subcommittee recommends that special care be exercised to prevent negotiations of this significance and probable length from becoming private orchestrations of one personality, no matter how effective the results in the short run. Efforts to invest the institutional framework with authority seem necessary.

D. DEFENSE DEPARTMENT INPUT INTO ESTABLISHMENT OF ADMINISTRATION POLICIES ON ARMS CONTROL NEGOTIATIONS

One aspect of the subcommittee's commission was to examine the adequacy of the Defense Department's input into arms control policy decisions, and its ability, if necessary, to reclama these decisions to the highest executive branch levels. Questions to this effect were asked of appropriate officials representing the Department of Defense as well as other agencies. In every case, the responses in open session to these questions stated that appropriate opportunities for input and sufficient avenues for reclama exist. The Deputy Secretary of Defense and the Chairman of the Joint Chiefs of Staff sit on the Verification Panel where arms control issues are developed and alternatives sharpened for presentation to the President in National Security Council sessions, on which the Secretary of Defense and the Chairman of the Joint Chiefs of Staff are statutory members. This formal structure appears adequate; however, the subcommittee believes that further study of this question is warranted before any firm conclusions can be drawn.

IV. Impact of Congressional Decisions

Dr. Iklé, in his testimony before the subcommittee, made the following statement:

> It is my view that our strength in these negotiations and our ability to bring them toward a successful conclusion really depend on our own determination and our own self-assurance, our ability to convey to the Soviet military that we are able to compete if they force us, that we are willing to limit and stop the competition through agreement, and indeed willing to move toward mutual reductions. I think it is this determination which decides and will govern our strength in these negotiations.

This is a very enlightening statement on the critical factor in these negotiations—determination. The mood of the U.S. is most accurately expressed under most circumstances by its elected representatives in the Congress, and for this reason, along with its control of the purse strings, the actions of the Congress will have, quite properly, a great impact on the outcome of such negotiations.

In this regard, the subcommittee was impressed by the obvious impact on the negotiations of congressional decisions during the authorization and appropriations proceedings. The Congress can assist in the creation of a climate conducive to negotiating by exhibiting the strength and resolve to compete with our adversaries if they approach these negotiations frivolously, while demonstrating enough flexibility to support initiatives available for mutual reductions. Congress is a visible representation of the determination and mood of the American people, which the Soviets consider so important in their analysis of the "correlation of forces."

Responsible action in our current nuclear environment is neither the advocation of disarmament nor a blind commitment to an all-out arms race, but rather a willingness to back serious negotiations while at the same time making clear our determination that we will not accept a result—through negotiations or other means—that weakens American security.

This determination requires, above all, an active, continuing interest and complete, up-to-date information on the problems and progress of negotiations. A number of congressional committees must necessarily be involved in this continuing review. In fulfilling its responsibility, it must be recognized that Congress can only provide the support required by our negotiators if the executive branch is candid with us in supplying information.

Schlesinger Discusses Soviet Compliance with SALT I, 6 March 1975

The CHAIRMAN [Senator Henry Jackson]. . . . Our hearing today is the second in a series devoted to the controversy surrounding Soviet compliance with certain provisions of the 1972 SALT I agreements—the interim agreement on offensive weapons and the ABM treaty. The Secretary of Defense is in a crucial and perhaps unique position to assist the subcommittee in evaluating the indications we have that the spirit, and perhaps even the letter, of these agreements is being circumvented by the Soviet Union.

Of particular concern are: reports that certain components associated with air defenses have been tested in a manner prohibited by the ABM treaty; the conversion of launchers for "light" missiles into launchers for "heavy" missiles; interference with national technical means of verification; the use of techniques of concealment and deception; and the deployment of new silos beyond the number agreed to in 1972, whose purpose is unclear and perhaps subject to rapid change. These are serious matters; it will be our purpose to establish the facts in each case.

In my judgment it is essential that we insist on precise implementation of the SALT I accords. Confidence in the process of arms control cannot survive in an atmosphere in which agreements previously entered into are subject to multiple instances of ambiguous behavior even as new agreements are being negotiated.

The problems of verification of a SALT II agreement are very much more difficult than those involved in the SALT I agreements—and the administration is only now beginning to discover the complexity of the verification issues that arise out of the 1972 agreements.

I wish to emphasize that a significant part of the problem we face in assessing whether the Soviets are in compliance with the 1972 agreements is of our government's own making. By resorting to so-called unilateral statements as a device for building into the 1972 agreements limitations that could not be negotiated, the Nixon administration set the stage for the current drama of ambiguity and confusion.

Moreover, the administration made certain commitments to the

SOURCE: Testimony of Secretary of Defense James R. Schlesinger. U.S., Congress, Senate, Committee on Armed Services, Subcommittee on Arms Control, *Soviet Compliance With Certain Provisions of the 1972 SALT I Agreements*, 94th Cong., 1st sess., 1975.

Congress concerning the standard it would insist upon as it related to our unilateral statements. It will be among our purposes today to ask whether the commitment of the administration to the Congress and the American people is being kept or whether it is being dissipated in a cloud of ambiguity.

We are very pleased to have the Secretary of Defense here, Secretary Schlesinger, and of course, the Chairman of the Joint Chiefs of Staff, General Brown. . . .

Secretary SCHLESINGER. Mr. Chairman, you have asked me today to address three related SALT issues: Soviet compliance with the 1972 SALT agreements, verification issues arising out of turning the Vladivostok aide-memoire into a formal agreement, and our experience of monitoring the SALT I agreements and what we have learned to form a basis for verification provisions of a follow-on SALT agreement. . . .

On the question of Soviet compliance with the SALT agreements, President Ford indicated [deleted] that the United States was not aware of any violations, but there were some ambiguities which needed to be resolved. We believe that the Soviet Union has been, and today is, in compliance with the terms of the SALT agreements. There are, however, some ambiguities in certain activities currently underway in the Soviet Union which need clarification. . . .

1. The United States is concerned that there are new large silos, that is, III–X silos, under construction in the western U.S.S.R. which could be used for launching ICBMS. Though the intelligence community believes that the intended purpose of these new silo-type facilities is for launch control, the United States is concerned that these silos may have the capability to launch ICBMS.

2. Examples of the type of concealment measures which concern the United States were provided to the Soviet side. These involved activities at the ballistic missile test ranges at [deleted] and at [deleted] shipyards. [Deleted] our primary concern in this regard is with the expanding pattern of concealment measures being undertaken in the U.S.S.R. which would impede or lessen the confidence we currently have in verifying the provisions of the two current SALT agreements.

3. You will recall that in one of its unilateral statements, the United States declared that it would consider any ICBM having a volume significantly greater than that of the largest light ICBM then operational on either side—that is, the SS–11—to be a heavy ICBM. In 1972, former Secretary of Defense Melvin Laird expressed his view during the hearings on SALT agreements that he would interpret this statement such that an increase of more than 30 percent in volume would be significant. The United States has considered the issue of agreement to the definition of a heavy ICBM. Its concern stemmed from the fact that

the volume of a new Soviet ICBM, the SS–19, is about 50 percent greater than the volume of the currently deployed SS–11. . . .

4. The fourth ambiguous activity is the possible Soviet testing of an air defense radar, [deleted] in an ABM mode. There are at least three possible explanations for this radar testing: (1) use of the radar in an instrumentation role to collect diagnostic data on reentry vehicles; (2) collection of data for use in modifying the SA–5 system to achieve an ABM intercept capability; or (3) collection of data for use in developing a new, perhaps dual-role SAM and ABM system. [Deleted.]

In general: We should strive for more specificity in the provisions and more comprehensive collateral constraints, and we should not make unilateral statements in association with future agreements.

Let me turn now to the more important verification issues arising from the Vladivostok accord. The provisions of the Vladivostok aide-memoire are familiar to members of the subcommittee.

Both sides are to be limited to no more than 1,320 ICBMS and SLBMS equipped with MIRVS. Under this provision, it will be necessary to agree to definitions and counting rules for ballistic missiles equipped with MIRVS.

The MIRV provisions pose a special verification problem as a result of the following uncertainties:

- Is it possible to verify which version of a particular missile is deployed when such missile has been tested with both a single RV and MIRVed payloads?
- Is it possible to verify which SLBM launchers in a particular SSBN class contain MIRVed missiles when there exist both MIRVed and unMIRVed missiles compatible with these launchers?
- Is it possible to verify whether a particular ICBM or SLBM launcher contains a MIRVed missile if it has been modified, for example, through changes to length or diameter and therefore made compatible with a known MIRVed missile?
- Is it possible to determine whether a launcher which once contained a MIRVed missile, and has been converted to an unMIRVed launcher, no longer contains MIRVS?

Although we will probably have difficulty in negotiating provisions which give us 100 percent certainty that the Soviets are in compliance with the MIRV limits, I do believe that provisions which result in acceptable uncertainty are realizable.

Finally, turning to the last point [deleted], it is premature to draw a firm conclusion on how our experience in monitoring SALT I agreements should affect our approach to the verification provisions of any follow-on SALT agreement. One could expect the Soviets to tread at

the limits of the provisions of the SALT agreements. If unchallenged, we then should expect them to overstep and go beyond the limits. If such activities are challenged as they occur, the strategic risk might be regarded as acceptable.

It is important to note that in the general area of verification there is an asymmetry favoring the Soviet Union—the United States is an open society with weapons systems subject to constant public scrutiny from their R&D phase to actual deployment. The Soviet Union should therefore have higher confidence in American compliance with the SALT agreements without insisting on measures additional to national technical means to adequately assure compliance. As a result, in the negotiations, the United States carries the main burden of pressing for agreement for such additional verification provisions.

Mr. Chairman, I think that a very critical issue is raised by the third paragraph of your initial remarks, in which you say, "Confidence in the process of arms control cannot survive in an atmosphere in which agreements previously entered into are subject to multiple instances of ambiguous behavior even as new agreements are being negotiated."

I think that there are two points that I would make here. First, that there are different classes of ambiguities, one of which I will call inherently ambiguous situations. I think the III–X silo may fall in this category, that there are things that are just not understood. On the other hand, there might be another category of ambiguity which we will call questionable ambiguity. And I think that your statement goes to the latter kind of ambiguity, in which one discerns that one's negotiating partner may be deliberately pressing the limits in order to create ambiguities as opposed to these circumstances in which ambiguities naturally arise.

The second observation that I would make is that we take some care in our own thoughts not to pitch our expectations too high. I say this for two reasons. First, the Soviet Union has a particular style. It has a long history over time of not precisely abiding by agreements, and in fact at many points breaking agreements. And that makes the Soviet Union a difficult partner to work with in these agreements.

Moreover, there is the fact that it is going to become increasingly difficult to verify, as we go beyond a fairly simple silo-counting operation to more complex phenomena, which might include possible missiles, and which will include MIRVed missiles. These are more difficult problems. [Deleted.]

I would observe, Mr. Chairman, that I do not enter these negotiations with an ingenuous view about the Soviet Union. I would say that I expect the Soviets to press to the limit in many areas, and that if one

starts with a pessimistic interpretation regarding the Soviets, there has been a degree of compliance which is at least to date reasonably reassuring.

The CHAIRMAN. . . . I will ask you this general question at the outset. In your judgment, is it important that, in reaching an agreement with the Soviets, we delineate very carefully and precisely the specifics of what we want included or excluded?

Secretary SCHLESINGER. Yes, sir, Mr. Chairman. The Soviets may be expected to push into any gray area, and they have indicated in past conversations with us that anything that is not precluded they are prepared to explore or to do. And for that reason, if we want to preclude their doing something, we have to be fairly precise. I think the issue of the deployment of the heavier throw-weight missiles replacing the SS–11 is an issue of this sort. If one reads the words of the agreement, the Soviets are doing something that is not precluded. It is inconsistent, quite clearly, I think, with our understanding of our own unilateral statement. But the Soviets do not feel bound by that unilateral statement. That is an area that calls for much greater precision in the future.

The CHAIRMAN. As a matter of fact, it is inconsistent with the assurances given to the Congress. I am sure you are aware of the testimony two years ago—three years this summer—on light and heavy missiles. And Secretary Laird, who testified then, has subsequently said that if the information as we now know it is true, then the current Soviet replacement program is a clear violation of that understanding.

Secretary SCHLESINGER. It is a clear violation, Mr. Chairman, of our unilateral statement.

The CHAIRMAN. That is what I mean. And you agree with that, don't you?

Secretary SCHLESINGER. Yes, sir. I think that what one must say is that the Soviets failed to agree with that unilateral statement because they intended to deploy the missiles that they have started to deploy. They agreed to the 15 percent increase on the dimension of the silos because that was an action that they could take without violating the treaty.

The CHAIRMAN. But this committee pointed out, in the process of interrogation, that there was a big loophole here, and that they could do what we now know they are doing. And we were assured by Dr. Kissinger and others that that was not the case. [Deleted.]

* * *

The CHAIRMAN. Just to run through [deleted] of these areas; first, on the conversion of the silos from light to heavy—we are talking about

the substitution of SS–17 and SS–19 missiles for the SS–11—what is the Soviet view of that?

Secretary SCHLESINGER. [Deleted.] They argue that the definition problem was "solved" [deleted] in SALT I, [deleted] that the only constraint on the throw-weight of missiles is the constraint on modern large ballistic missiles, and unless they change the light missiles into what were then called modern large ballistic missiles, they are in compliance. And they are perfectly happy with the leeway that affords them.

The CHAIRMAN. And of course they are addressing themselves solely to the bilateral aspects of the documents?

Secretary SCHLESINGER. Yes, sir.

The CHAIRMAN. And ignoring completely the unilateral statements that our people made?

Secretary SCHLESINGER. Yes, sir.

The CHAIRMAN. The III–X silo issue of course has been with us now for quite some time, and apparently [deleted] there has been nothing new in the way of assurances from the Soviets with regard to this matter; is that not correct?

Secretary SCHLESINGER. As of this moment, Mr. Chairman, there is nothing new. [Deleted.] So this is one of those things that I think in the process of time is an ambiguity that does get resolved. I would say some of the other issues that lie before us do not lend themselves to that inherent unraveling.

The CHAIRMAN. At the last briefing, of course, Mr. Colby [William E. Colby, Director, Central Intelligence Agency] gave us information regarding [deleted] concealment, the use of just ordinary plain concealment, which is prohibited clearly by the interim agreement. [Deleted.] And Mr. Colby was quite definite about the impact.

Secretary SCHLESINGER. This is an area that I think is of deeper concern to me, Mr. Chairman, because I think that the concealment issue may gradually erode and confuse our ability to monitor.

The CHAIRMAN. I would agree with you. When it is open and direct and fairly unequivocal, it does raise questions as to what else is going on, does it not, when it is that direct? [Deleted.] And in the area that we spent a lot of time over, the issue of the SS–11, the light-heavy missile issue, what I predicted was going to happen has happened. And yet we were assured positively that we would take action if that happened.

And that raises a question: How is the administration going to handle this with the Congress, based on the legislative history of the agreements? I was convinced—I am just a country lawyer, but I took one look at this, and it was very clear to me that the agreements were very carelessly drafted.

Senator McIntyre. What are you looking at?

The Chairman. I am talking specifically about our unilateral statement with reference to what constitutes a heavy missile. And we pointed out that the bilateral agreement does not reflect the interpretation that the administration made at the time. We pointed out that they could, under the bilateral terms, [deleted] go from a throw-weight then, I think it was around [deleted] pounds, to about three times as much. And they have done so; in my judgment they are now up to about [deleted] pounds.

Secretary Schlesinger. Seven thousand pounds of throw-weight. The constraint, Mr. Chairman, applies to the volume of the missile. And I think they have gone from 67 cubic meters to over 100. So it is about a 50 percent increase in the volume of the missile. And that, of course, permits greater throw-weight, as you indicate.

The Chairman. The reason I raise this issue is that in the President's message to the Congress at the time—I am reading from President Nixon's message to the Congress in transmitting the treaty and the interim agreement, June 13, 1972. And I quote: "The United States has also made clear that it would consider any ICBM having a volume significantly greater than that of the largest light ICBM now operational on either side, which is the SS–11, to be a heavy ICBM." Now, where does that leave us today in the light of that statement? This was the administration's assurance to Congress.

Secretary Schlesinger. By the definition you have cited, Mr. Chairman, all of the –19s, at least, would be defined as heavy.

The Chairman. When you say –19s, to keep the record straight, that is the follow-on to the SS–11?

Secretary Schlesinger. And the point is, we can say there is violation in our interpretation of our unilateral statement, but I am not sure what binding force that has on the Soviets.

The Chairman. But Congress has to rely on the statements, Mr. Secretary, that are submitted by the administration. And this is a part of the document, part of the understanding with the Congress. And I think it is quite clear that based on the message, and based on the unilateral statement, that the administration's understanding with the Congress on this point is not being carried out.

Secretary Schlesinger. I think it is clear from your observations, Mr. Chairman, that the expectations that the administration had went unfulfilled. But that is not a violation by the Soviet Union.

[Deleted.]

The Chairman. I want to say too, that at the time—to further nail this one down—I don't want to see these things occuring and recurring —in testimony before the committee at the time Mr. [Richard] Helms,

then head of the CIA, stated as follows: "It also was made quite clear to the Soviets that the SS–11 was the largest light ICBM being referred to. The SS–11 has a volume of about sixty-five cubic meters, and the U.S. indicated that a missile over seventy cubic meters in volume would be considered significantly greater in size." . . .

Secretary SCHLESINGER. We were all clear in our understanding of the issue in Washington, D.C., but did not convey that successfully to the Soviets.

The CHAIRMAN. Isn't that the worst possible way to start out an arms limitation agreement, Mr. Secretary, in all candor?

Secretary SCHLESINGER. Yes, sir. [Deleted.]

The CHAIRMAN. This isn't of course just a minor matter, because the SS–11 silos represent their largest single land-based missile force, does it not? What is it, about 1,100 launchers?

Secretary SCHLESINGER. Yes, sir.

The CHAIRMAN. And so with this kind of volumetric change, it makes quite a difference in terms of throw-weight when you can go from [deleted] odd pounds up to [deleted]. And we are talking about a much greater capability in terms of MIRVing the yield that goes with it.

Secretary SCHLESINGER. Yes, sir.

Senator SYMINGTON. . . . In your statement I remember you said that the Soviets have broken some agreements. Would you supply for the record—

Secretary SCHLESINGER. Excuse me, Senator Symington. What I indicated was that we have not confirmed evidence that the Soviets are in violation of the agreement.

Senator SYMINGTON. I see, In other words, they have taken advantage of any ambiguities?

Secretary SCHLESINGER. Yes, sir; they are pressing in certain gray areas, but as yet we have [deleted] no confirmed evidence that gives us the degree of confidence to say this is a violation.

Senator SYMINGTON. Thank you. Now, one other aspect that worries me. We made a lot about the test ban treaty, with a 150-kiloton limitation. Fundamentally, that whole thing was sort of a farce, wasn't it, from the standpoint of *(a)* up to, for "peaceful" purposes, 150 kilotons, and you would never know whether it was a military explosion or not; and *(b)* inasmuch as 150 kilotons is over ten times the actual strength of Hiroshima, wasn't that sort of silly?

Secretary SCHLESINGER. I think that if one can work out the details, that that does constrain somewhat future developments of weapons. I think it is important, as you indicate, not to exaggerate the significance of that kind of an agreement.

Senator SYMINGTON. For the life of me I can't understand how, with a

150-kiloton limitation, you could constrain anything. Could you explain that? . . .

Secretary SCHLESINGER. I think that the critical question, Senator Symington, does not deal with the ability to demolish urban centers; that one can do very handily with the weapons already available to both sides. The question of the yield-to-weight ratios for higher-yield weapons goes to the ability to destroy silos with high confidence. And in that area the continued progress of the development of high-yield weapons can cause greater concern. Consequently a constraint in that area can lead to some stabilization. But I reiterate what I said earlier, that the thrust of your comment, that one should not exaggerate the accomplishments, is well taken.

*   *   *

Senator BYRD. . . . In regard to unilateral statements, as I recall, you mentioned in some of your comments that that was probably regarded by our people as a tough procedure. What did you mean by that?

Secretary SCHLESINGER. I think that probably at that time the belief existed that if we asserted firmly enough that we believed that something or other should not take place, that the Soviets would be persuaded that they ran too high a risk to allow that activity to take place. I think that belief turned out to be inflated and erroneous. And, therefore, we had a propensity to indulge in fairly strong statements on the premise that that would put us in a position of seeming very firm, and in fact it probably turns out to indicate the reverse.

Senator BYRD. . . . Could it be considered self-serving on our part in the sense that our officials then could come before the Congress and say, "This is what has been done"?

Secretary SCHLESINGER. It could be in logic considered that way, Senator Byrd. But I don't think that that was the psychology. I think that this was an unwarranted degree of faith in those statements at that time. And I think that subsequent events very clearly indicate that the evaporation of those beliefs is far more costly than any advantages gained if they were intended to be self-serving statements at that time.

Senator BYRD. In your formal statement you said that you felt that the United States should avoid unilateral statements. Is that assertion on your part being taken to heart by the SALT II negotiatiors?

Secretary SCHLESINGER. I believe so. I should say that I do not want absolutely to preclude unilateral statements. They may serve some purpose in some very special circumstance. But I think that the history shows that unilateral statements are likely to backfire, and for that reason unless there is a very compelling argument in some spe-

cific circumstance, that they ought to avoid them. And I believe we probably will avoid them in the future.

Senator BYRD. It seems logical, as you pointed out, that you can't necessarily avoid all unilateral statements. But do you feel that there has been a change in strategy or in viewpoint in regard to that, not only from the point of view of those who represent your thinking, but from those who represent the State Department?

Secretary SCHLESINGER. I think so, Senator. I think it is universally evident around Washington, D.C., that those unilateral statements did us no good in the long run, and in some respect tended to undermine our position over the long run. And they were nonproductive.

*　　*　　*

The CHAIRMAN. Let us take the III–X silo. I recall when they first discovered this, and talked to the agency people about it, there was great concern. Initially at least, the real purpose of these facilities could not be determined. Now, have the Russians given us any clues or any assurances or any means by which we can really come to some conclusions regarding the problem?

Secretary SCHLESINGER. In the case of the III–X silo, Mr. Chairman, I believe that [deleted].

The CHAIRMAN. They said that two years ago.

Secretary SCHLESINGER. And in this particular case I think that the problem [deleted]. I do not talk about the other problems. I think we should continue to press the Soviets on the III–X issue, because I think we should press them on all of these areas until they can give us a clarification. We are pressing them with regard to making design changes that would clearly prevent the facilities from being used to circumvent the agreement.

The CHAIRMAN. But the initial design, as I understood it from by briefings. . . . is identical to that on a missile launching silo.

Secretary SCHLESINGER. Yes, sir.

The CHAIRMAN. What I am concerned about, Mr. Secretary, is that we are going into the details or the provisions regarding the Vladivostok agreement. That agreement was announced without a written document being in existence at the time, is that not correct?

Secretary SCHLESINGER. That is, Mr. Chairman.

The CHAIRMAN. And some weeks occurred before an aide-memoire was put together. And I would think that our lesson here is quite clear; it is hard enough when we have what we think is a precise bilateral agreement with the Russians to rely on it with some confidence, but when we start out having to reconstruct what took place verbally, that

is fraught with all sorts of future trouble and disagreements. Finally, the public is going to lose confidence in the ability of governments to reach an understanding which really they can rely on. And I think these are some rather harsh lessons that I thought maybe we had learned, but I am not so sure that we have learned those lessons. And if we are going down the road of more and more ambiguities and confusion, I think with the other troubles that we have had with the Soviets, we are just going to compound the problem.

That is all I wanted to say.

Hearing on the Vladivostok Accord, 8 July 1975

Mr. IKLÉ [Fred C. Iklé, Director of A.C.D.A.]. Let me try to clarify the basic issues that face us as we seek to work out an agreement based on the Vladivostok accord. The major points and difficulties that have come up can be grouped under three broad questions:

(1) Are we getting the right kind of arms control—that is, agreements that will genuinely limit arms, that will increase rather than decrease stability, that will provide a good basis for further reductions?

(2) Are we maintaining the strategic balance with the Soviet Union?

(3) Are the key limitations adequately verifiable?

No agreement can be devised to include and exclude things precisely the way each party would like. In negotiations, one cannot obtain the optimum on every score. We must balance the pluses and minuses among these three areas of basic objectives.

Take, for example, the question of the mobile missiles. In SALT I the United States sought to prohibit the deployment of mobile land-based ICBM launchers—a proposal on which we failed to reach agreement. We felt at that time the land-mobile ICBMS were undesirable from the point of view of verification. On the other hand, from the point of view of stability, experts point out that mobility of missiles is desirable because it can help reduce vulnerability. Which of these objectives should take priority, verification or invulnerability?

Similar trade-offs are required for MIRVS, new bomber aircraft, cruise missiles, and various potential qualitative developments; that is to say, trade-offs between (1) arms control objectives in the narrow sense, such as stability or lessened competition; (2) a proper United States-Soviet strategic balance; and (3) verifiability. Many criticisms of the Vladivostok accord overlook this fact of these trade-offs.

Now, let me make another point regarding the evaluation of SALT agreements. It would be a mistake to look at a SALT II agreement as if it was meant to settle the strategic relationship and competition between the United States and the Soviet Union once and for all. Strategic arms control negotiations must be seen as a continuing process. The avenues for future developments of arms are too diverse, too unpredictable to be circumscribed in a single agreement for all time.

SOURCE: U.S., Congress, House, Committee on International Relations, Subcommittee on International Security and Scientific Affairs, *The Vladivostok Accord: Implications To U.S. Security, Arms Control, And World Peace*, 94th Cong., 1st sess., 1975.

Moreover, the more we try to cram into a single agreement, the longer it will take to negotiate; and the more drawn out the negotiations, the greater the risks of exacerbating the very competition we seek to avoid. On the other hand, the thinner the agreement, the larger the gap through which arms competition will flow unchecked.

There has been criticism that the SALT II agreement might not limit all the possible areas of strategic competition. Of course it will not. If, since the beginning of SALT, we had tried to cover everything in one grand agreement, we would still be a long way from the ABM treaty, let alone have some limits on offensive arms. An important test of SALT agreements is not so much how comprehensive they are, but how they will alter the future competition and future negotiations about nuclear arms.

One great advantage of the Vladivostok limits is that they provide a simple, clear-cut benchmark of equality, and thus a basis from which future reductions and further limitations can more easily be negotiated. Major asymmetries tend to slow down negotiations on arms limitations and reductions, whereas an equal starting point tends to facilitate such negotiations. . . .

Viewing SALT as a continuing process helps us to focus on another important aspect. The very fact that such negotiations are going on forces the political leadership in the Soviet Union to pay attention to the purposes of their strategic armaments and to weigh arms control objectives against other political or military objectives. In the long run, this indirect impact of arms control through changing attitudes could be more beneficial than specific arms limitations. The SALT Standing Consultative Commission provides a forum to maintain continuity on a technical level. It has proven to be an effective, continuing link between strategic experts on both sides.

We need a long-term view, also, to do justice to the stubborn problem of verification. The overarching reason why verification has been such a formidable obstacle to arms control is that we have to monitor armaments in a closed society. The more openness, the easier it is to collect and corroborate the indicators needed for verification; and the more openness, the less the psychological or political needs for verification to begin with.

As matters now stand, monitoring an expanding array of arms control agreements levies increasing burdens of scope and complexity on our intelligence organizations. And it lies in the nature of this work that much has to proceed under the protection of secrecy. Unrestrained publicity about our monitoring methods provides a potential violator with a road map for deception or countermeasures, thus making the verification methods ineffective. We cannot inform the party whose

conduct we wish to verify of each and every step we take to check its compliance. Mr. Chairman, today the legal protection of our verification capability is inadequate. Appropriate legislation is needed. This subcommittee, with its keen and constructive interest in arms control, I am sure is sympathetic to this problem.

Another requirement regarding verification emerges apart from the necessary protection for our intelligence organizations. In the years to come, when the scope of arms control will—hopefully—expand, Congress, in my view, may have to assume a continuing and active role in verification. The question of compliance or violation may often depend on a complex pattern of evidence combining technical and political judgment. In the end, verification may be more like a jury verdict than a simple litmus test. And for jury verdicts to be viable, the people have to trust the jury. The appropriate congressional committees, in full cooperation with the executive branch, will have to act as guardians of this trust.

* * *

The CHAIRMAN [Clement J. Zablocki]. Was there any reason that an agreement was not reached at Vladivostok on the definition of a heavy bomber? . . .

Mr. IKLÉ. The purpose of the Vladivostok accord, Mr. Chairman, was to get an overall framework for further negotiations that would have to deal with definitions and with the question of what is to be included or excluded under strategic delivery vehicles. These by necessity are detailed questions which require the technical negotiating teams to work for many weeks or perhaps months to sort out. At Vladivostok we were dealing with a summit meeting that couldn't in these few hours or days available settle all the outstanding issues.

The CHAIRMAN. But isn't that the very nub of the problem; that if there isn't any clear-cut understanding or definition, that it will cause problems in the future because they have a different interpretation from ours? Besides, there's the language problem, how they interpret a phrase.

Mr. IKLÉ. Definitely, Mr. Chairman. For the agreement to be complete, these definitions have to be worked out with great care and great precision and great clarity. Ambiguity very often leads to disappointment. But things have to be taken in steps and stages. It was not possible at the summit meeting at Vladivostok to settle all these issues. That is not to say that the issues aren't important and don't have to be settled. That is precisely what the negotiators are now trying to do in Geneva.

The CHAIRMAN. On page 5 of your prepared statement, Dr. Iklé, if I may ask you to elaborate on the paragraph beginning, "Viewing SALT"

—in the second sentence you say, "The very fact that such negotiations are going on forces the political leadership in the Soviet Union to pay attention to the purposes of their strategic armaments and to weigh arms control objectives against other political or military objectives."

Would you care to elaborate? Is there any such evidence?

Mr. Iklé. The fact that the numbers of Soviet missiles, their throw-weight, and the number of Soviet armaments are being discussed at the highest level between the top leadership of the U.S.S.R. and the President on our side makes it necessary for the Soviet political leadership to become conversant with these issues, and to inquire from their military authorities why certain things are needed. To the extent that the Soviet leadership is interested in reaching agreements with the United States, and there is indication they certainly are, and to the extent that certain military authorities might stand in the way of such an agreement, they might have to ask questions of their military leaders which they would not be driven to ask if it weren't for the SALT talks. They might also ask questions as to what their military proposed for economic reasons because things cost so much in their overall budget. Here, however, we have an additional reason—the arms control reason—that is now being propelled to the attention of the top level officials.

* * *

Mr. Findley. The Senate amendment on MARV [maneuverable reentry vehicle] is somewhat restrictive. Do you think that amendment is in the public interest and a satisfactory way to deal with the MARV question?

Mr. Iklé. Well, the concern here is that MARV would be a destabilizing technical development and that it would increase the vulnerability of fixed land-based missiles by providing higher accuracy. The idea is that MARV's development, if it is to be stopped, is to be stopped before they test it because testing enhances verification. To the extent that MARVS are to be avoided, agreeing not to test might be the most feasible way to do it. We have learned with MIRV, the idea of MIRV limitations, that verification becomes far more difficult once the thing has been tested.

Mr. Findley. So you are not dissatisfied with the position taken by the Senate on that point?

Mr. Iklé. I think I made a narrower point. If one wants to avoid MARV developments altogether, the way to go about it is to try to limit testing, since we have a way to verify the cancellation of that kind of a development.

Mr. Findley. On page 4 you said that "an important test of SALT agreements is not so much how comprehensive they are, but how they will

alter the future competition and future negotiations. . . ." Just applying that premise this way in the emerging SALT II agreement, if cruise missiles are not included and if the Soviet Backfire bomber is not included, and if we don't have some effective verification of Soviet MIRVing, what effect will this combination have on future negotiations?

Mr. IKLÉ. From the point of view of constraining arms it means we have a much narrower agreement than one would wish, and we have to be very careful not to exacerbate competition of Backfire versus cruise missile and on MIRV levels. There will also be a greater burden on the follow-on negotiations to come to grips with these developments. Ideally one would want to cover as much as possible of this deleterious competition, but in some areas we may not be able to work out the verification arrangements or may not be able to work out the tradeoffs in the agreement, since one side wants to develop one thing and the other side wants to develop something else.

It is not self-evident that every unrestrained potential technological development will lead to competition. There are many instances where development didn't take place or was turned off because it didn't seem worthwhile even without any agreement.

* * *

Mr. LAGOMARSINO. You urge, and I think correctly so, that we view SALT as a continuing process, and you also say that you think we must not try to cover everything in one grand agreement, which obviously would be impossible in any event.

How much does ever evolving technology—and we used a lot of terms here this morning that are certainly new within the last few years, MIRV, MARV, and so on—how does this keep on, you might say, just a treadmill, just something that goes on? Someone invents a new process or a new development comes forward and we have to have a new agreement on that? . . .

Mr. IKLÉ. That is a fair question. The question is whether we can catch up and impose constructive restraints and limitations, or whether there will always be more new developments than the negotiators can catch up with.

Not all new technology is deleterious from the point of view of arms control. Some of it can be beneficial. Technology that makes strategic arms less vulnerable can be a good development. Technology that helps verification obviously can be a good development. Technology to reduce the risk of accidents certainly is desirable.

One has to take a differentiated view regarding technological development. Some of it can be very counterproductive, just leading to competition for competition's sake, because these items may become

items of political prestige; and if it is possible to throttle them or to cut them back, both sides will be much better off.

The CHAIRMAN. Dr. Iklé, on page 3 you pose a very interesting question. You list certain possibilities of negotiations and then you end the first paragraph with the question, "Which of these objectives should take priority: verification or invulnerability?" In your opinion, which should take priority?

Mr. IKLÉ. I hate to give a categorical answer to this question since it really depends on the type of arms that you are considering. Arms control agreements and negotiations could become counterproductive if, for the sake of having a verifiable agreement, we started prohibiting the very types of strategic arms that are the least vulnerable. For example, if it would be very difficult or impossible to verify submarine-launched ballistic missiles, which are considered rather invulnerable, it probably would still be a mistake to prohibit them just because they cannot be verified.

I mentioned the example of land-mobile missiles to some extent engendering delays. I think once you have a complete case you have to make an assessment as to the degree to which your verification capability may be degraded by permitting certain types of arms, and the degree to which the invulnerability of your forces might be degraded by prohibiting them, and reach judgment based on as much quantitative information as you can collect. We have done this in internal studies on the question of land-mobile missiles, for instance.

* * *

EXECUTIVE SESSION

The CHAIRMAN. Dr. Iklé, . . . there are repeated complaints that the [Vladivostok] aide-memoire has not been made public, although most of what is contained therein is public. Is there any reason? I think the other day you said that the Vladivostok accords were made public.

Mr. IKLÉ. The general idea of not making them public is that it facilitates ongoing negotiations. Our tactical moves are private while the negotiations are still in flux. I think it is just this general basic attitude which led to the decision not to make this public.

The CHAIRMAN. Is another reason perchance the fact that the aide-memoire may reveal that there was a lack of clarification within some of the agreements as far as definition, and this is what the executive branch doesn't want misinterpreted?

Mr. IKLÉ. A great many issues were not clarified at Vladivostok, which as I said in the open session is understandable, given that these were summit meetings under time pressure; and maybe the initial publicity

at the time of Vladivostok was a bit unfortunate in conveying the impression that all was settled, whereas in fact we have a great many unresolved important issues that Dr. Wade's testimony will get into.

* * *

Mr. BINGHAM. . . . One other thing; perhaps Dr. Wade or you could comment on this. I also asked you about the degree to which testing had been carried on with MARVS, and to what extent that prejudices the possibility of prohibiting the testing of strategic MARV.

Mr. WADE. [Director, Defense Department SALT Task Force]. Let me back up and comment on our early interest in MARV, going back perhaps ten years ago. The early interest in MARV, the maneuvering reentry vehicle, was to enhance our capability to penetrate Soviet ABM systems. In addition, there was interest to minimize any possible capability that Soviet SAM systems had for deployment in an ABM mode.

There has been some testing with MARVS in past years, primarily for basic research. But our interest today is even higher than it was in the past; namely, that the Soviets today have a large and significant ABM R&D program underway. This program has not diminished as a result of the ABM SALT agreements. The Soviet R&D program is a substantial one. They have a follow-on system [security deletion]. If we want to maintain Soviet interest in adhering to the ABM treaty over the long term, we must demonstrate to them that if they abrogate the treaty, once they achieve the technology that may provide the incentive for them to break the treaty, that we will have or can respond with a force structure that can negate the relative effectiveness of any new follow-on Soviet ABM deployment.

The second point, which is just as important, is that in the future the new technology that is required to make ABM systems viable will result in deployed technology that makes the distinction between SAM systems and ABM systems more and more gray. We should keep pressure on the Soviets not to get too confident in their ability to take a new SAM system and be able to employ it in an ABM mode. The MARV program has application for this role, that is, for evading defensive missiles. SAMS should be technically infeasible for use against a maneuvering RV. The confidence in our penetration system will go up accordingly. Therefore we believe the MARV program is a R&D program of major importance, as far as the Department of Defense is concerned.

In reference to the other application of the MARV, for improving overall missile-system accuracy, the Department of Defense believes that improving the accuracy of our missile systems improves the total spectrum of deterrence. You will note that the Soviets are well underway with their follow-on systems. They are improving the accuracy of

their new systems, and if we stand still and stop our own accuracy improvement programs, while the Soviets press forward with their new ICBMs with a significant weapons counterforce potential, there could develop a major asymmetry between the two sides. We believe this would be intolerable because we wouldn't be able to deter across the conflict spectrum with as high a confidence as the Soviets could have achieved. Those are the two basic reasons we believe the MARV program is of significant importance.

Mr. BINGHAM. You didn't answer my question about the testing.

Mr. WADE. If you want to present to the Soviets a meaningful deterrent R&D program, then minimize the possibility of their reaching a position in which they believe it would be to their benefit to abrogate the treaty, we should maintain the main R&D program. I believe stopping that program, sir, would hurt such a posture.

Mr. BINGHAM. I am sorry, but my question had to do with the degree to which the testing of evasive MARV—which I gather is a different weapon—to what extent has that prejudiced the possibility, if it were decided that it were desirable, to stop the testing of strategic MARV? To what extent are those tests indistinguishable? That is what I am saying.

Mr. WADE. The evasive MARV and the accuracy MARV are strategic MARVS. Which application of the MARV are you referring to? I am not quite sure I understand the question.

Mr. BINGHAM. I am referring to statements made in part in this subcommittee by Congressman Leggett, who said that there had been testing of what he referred to as an evasive MARV, which I understood to be a defensive-type weapon quite different from the kind of MARV that we are talking about that would have counterforce capabilities.

Mr. WADE. The first point to be made is that the evasive and the so-called high accurate MARV are both strategic weapon systems. Second, I think that area of distinction has been a little bit fuzzy. When you talk about an evasive MARV, accuracy is also inherent in that system. The primary rationale for the system, of course, is to penetrate future ABM or SAM systems. When you start maneuvering an RV, whether for evasive purposes or for high accuracy, basically it is the same type system.

In effect, if you try to distinguish between the two and stop any MARV program that has as its objective improved accuracy, you do stop the other part of the program too.

Mr. BINGHAM. Let me phrase the question this way: To what extent has MARV been tested by the United States?

Mr. WADE. I will check that for the record. As I recall there have been some test flights looking at the aerodynamics for basic research purposes.

[The following information was subsequently submitted by the Department of Defense:]

> MARVS have two applications: one, such as the Navy Mk–500, for evading defensive missiles, the other for improving overall missile systems' accuracy, such as the ABRES Precision-Guided Reentry Vehicle (PGRV). The Mk–500 Program is in advanced development, with two successful flight tests in FY 1975. [Security deletion.] The PGRV Program is limited at present to design studies with flight tests planned for some later date.

Mr. LAGOMARSINO. Doctor, very briefly, what is our current position in SALT II on verifying Soviet MIRVS?

Mr. IKLÉ. Our proposal was that a type of missile that has been tested with MIRVS should be counted as MIRVed when deployed, and it is on that proposal that we have reached an impasse in that the Soviets have so far not accepted it. This raises a question: Is there any substitute? Is there any way of distinguishing between a MIRVed, say, Soviet SS–18, the large missile, and an unMIRVed one, with our present verification [security deletion] means that we use? Nothing has turned up. . . .

Mr. LAGOMARSINO. Will the Soviet Backfire be included in the agreement?

Mr. IKLÉ. We hope it will be, because of its capability, but again that is an issue on which we have not reached a consensus yet.

* * *

Mr. WADE. . . . In formulating an approach to SALT, the Department of Defense works against the background of ensuring that a credible deterrent posture is maintained and that strategic stability is preserved. We have identified some rather specific requirements for maintaining credible deterrence and stability and I would like to review those requirements here.

The first requirement is essential equivalence in those basic factors that together determine the relative effectiveness of our strategic forces. [Security deletion.] I will have some additional comments on these factors later in my statement.

The second requirement is for highly survivable forces. Under all circumstances, we must have the capacity to effectively retaliate after

a first or preemptive strike by an adversary. Meeting this criterion requires us to ensure the prelaunch survivability of our strategic forces and the capability of those forces to successfully penetrate enemy defenses and deliver weapons on target.

The third requirement is for flexible response options, that is, for sufficient flexibility in our employment plans so that we can respond to any level of initial Soviet attack.

The fourth requirement is for a high degree of consistency between our actual capabilities and how those capabilities might be assessed by others. We all know from our personal experience that perceptions do not always conform to reality, and in our strategic planning we must insure against the possibility of serious misperception which could lead to miscalculation, confrontation, and crisis.

The Vladivostok understanding is consistent with our efforts with respect to the above requirements. The understanding does not hinder us in maintaining our retaliatory or flexible response capability because it permits options to continue deployment of our strategic forces in alternative deployment modes, which is important to the continued survivability and penetration capability of our strategic forces. In those areas where we may eventually have to adopt measures to maintain essential equivalence, the understanding permits us the necessary freedom of action. The understanding also allows us to follow through in our efforts to develop a flexible strategic employment policy.

A relatively high degree of arms balance exists at this point. This is not to say, however, that we can entrust ourselves to the status quo—the strategic environment is dynamic, and historically, few balances have been maintained for long periods of time. Strategic stability is not self-equilibrating but requires a great deal of sustained dynamic national effort. The Soviets are pursuing a number of strategic programs which have the potential for a serious destabilizing influence on the strategic balance. . . .

Notwithstanding the balance sought in the Vladivostok understanding, there are disturbing signs that the Soviets are not committed to strategic stability. This is shown in general terms in Secretary Schlesinger's report to Congress in February. He noted there that the Soviets devote more resources than the United States in most of the significant categories of defense:

20 percent more in overall research and development;
20 percent more in general purpose forces;
25 percent more in procurement; and
60 percent more in strategic nuclear offensive forces.

In the context of strategic nuclear offensive forces, the Soviets are now bringing to completion an unprecedented ICBM program. Four new types of ICBMs have either reached operational deployment status or will shortly do so. [Security deletion.]

The Soviets are also making headway with their SLBM program. The new model of the D-class submarine is now under construction. [Security deletion.]

The newest addition to the Soviet strategic bomber program is the Backfire. [Security deletion.]

The dynamic thrust of Soviet strategic force developments provides disturbing evidence of a Soviet lack of interest in restraint. Consequently, we must be prepared to pursue our own strategic initiatives if we are to assure our national security.

* * *

Mr. WADE. Chart no. 3 [security deletion] shows current and projected U.S. forces based on our current planning projections. The Vladivostok understanding places a cap on those two dimensions of the strategic arms competition. You will note on the chart on the left that I have included the FB–111 as part of our strategic force. As far as SALT is concerned the FB–111 is not considered a heavy bomber and to date has not been discussed under the aggregate limitation. . . .

Requirements for modernizing our strategic nuclear forces will in part be a result of force aging. We try to stretch the lifetime of our strategic forces as best we can, but weapon systems are no exception to the rule that time has an effect on utility. . . .

The full scope and pace of modernization will depend essentially on whether the Soviets are prepared in the future development of their strategic programs to forgo deployments permitted them under their agreements with us. As indicated earlier, the evidence we have at this time is not reassuring. Should this evidence continue to accumulate, we would be required to reevaluate the adequacy of our current plans. Chart no. 6 shows the modernization programs available to us at this time.

You will notice I have on chart no. 6 questions. These programs are basically under review at this time and are open as far as what the direction of the Department of Defense will be.

Finally, Soviet interest in further controlling the strategic arms competition will be put to the test in the third round of SALT negotiations. [Security deletion.] It is important, however, to understand that reductions alone are not necessarily the way to improve stability in

Chart 6

STRATEGIC FORCE MODERNIZATION

MIRVed MISSILES		
MM-III	⟶	M-X
POSEIDON	⟶	TRIDENT I & II
UnMIRVed MISSILES		
MM-II/TITAN II	⟶	?
POLARIS	⟶	?
STRATEGIC SUBMARINES		
POLARIS/POSEIDON	⟶	TRIDENT
STRATEGIC AIRCRAFT		
B-52	⟶	CRUISE MISSILES AND B-1
KC-135	⟶	ADVANCED TANKER/CARGO AIRCRAFT OR KC-135 MODIFICATIONS
TECHNOLOGY	⟶	IMPROVED RE-ENTRY SYSTEMS SSBN TECHNOLOGY SLCMs

the force relationship of the two sides. Reductions must focus on particular weapon systems—those of a kind that inherently lead to strategic instability.

* * *

The Chairman. Doctor, on page 5 of your statement you state, "In those areas where we may eventually have to adopt measures to maintain essential equivalence, the understanding permits us the necessary freedom of action." A similar understanding on the part of [the] Soviets permits necessary freedom of action. Is that true?

Mr. Wade. Yes, sir.

The Chairman. So then the question is how effective it really is, the Vladivostok agreement. If on a one-sided determination the Soviet Union or the United States determines that we are unable to maintain essential equivalence, that we then are free to take other armaments and the Soviet Union can do likewise, to me it doesn't appear that the Vladivostok agreement then is really binding.

Mr. Wade. No, sir; I don't believe that is quite true. The point behind that sentence is that now there is symmetry accorded both sides by the terms of the agreement. There is symmetry in the 2,400 limita-

tions on aggregate launchers. There is a symmetry in the 1,320 limitation on MIRV launchers. Therefore, both sides are allowed to deploy and maintain up to that level of forces. If there is a major asymmetry—as, for example, in missile throw-weight, which there is today between the two sides—and if you are interested in reducing that missile force asymmetry to equal and lower levels for the two sides (which I believe would be an important future goal for SALT), and if the Soviets would agree to such a measure or provision, this would be one (and certainly the preferred option) way to reach equal levels in this important area.

However, failing that, if you can't get a Soviet agreement for further limitation and reduction in missile throw-weight, you then have the second option, namely, of adding to your force to provide the necessary balance in that area if you think that particular area is important to be balanced.

The CHAIRMAN. Once the limition is set.

Mr. WADE. Yes, sir. SALT II is a positive first step. It provides a cap on total MIRV launchers and total aggregate launchers. It is not a panacea. As far as those measures that address specifically long-term stability, there is a lot to be desired in the Vladivostok accord.

Ford and Kissinger Discuss the Backfire Bomber–Cruise Missile Controversy and SALT, 9 and 10 November 1975

WASHINGTON, 9 NOVEMBER 1975*

Q. Mr. President, on the matter of relations with the Soviet Union, SALT II seems to have been stalled. . . . There is a sharp difference of opinion and considerable confusion in this country about the meaning and intention of détente with the Soviet Union. Will you give us your definition of détente, tell us what it means to you and what it should mean to the American people?

President FORD. I am not sure that is the best word, but that is the word that is being used. Détente means to me that two superpowers who are strong militarily and economically, who represent differing political and governmental views, instead of confronting one another can consult one another on a wide variety of areas of potential dispute, whether it is trade, whether it is military potential conflict, whether it is a number of other things.

Now, détente is not always going to mean that we solve every problem, because some of them are very complex and very controversial. It does mean it is a mechanism for the relaxation of tensions so that instead of glaring at one another and opening the potential of conflict, you can sit down and discuss differences of opinion and hope to accomplish a relaxation and progress without military conflict.

* * *

Q. Mr. President, the Vladivostok agreement limits the U.S. and the Soviet Union each to 2,400 strategic vehicles. That includes missiles and bombers. Studies done within our government indicate that the Soviet Union's Backfire bombers are capable of taking off from Soviet bases and bombing U.S. cities. Is it your firm position that each Soviet Backfire bomber should be counted against that Soviet total of 2,400?

President FORD. I don't believe I should discuss one of the most controversial issues in the negotiations with the Soviet Union. The Backfire is a weapons system that has a potential, although there is a difference of opinion as to whether or not its primary mission is one of intercontinental bombing. It is a very difficult decision among

* SOURCE: Remarks of President Gerald R. Ford on NBC television's "Meet the Press." *Weekly Compilation of Presidential Documents*, 17 November 1975, pp. 1255–1263.

several others. And I don't believe that with the importance of those negotiations that I should make a categorical statement on this program as to how we might handle the problem of the Backfire.
Q. Is it a fair inference, from the fact that you won't take a firm position on that, that that is a position we are willing to negotiate away?
President FORD. There are a number of other issues of equal importance where there might be some trade-off—I am not saying there will be—but there are some very complicated problems, and the Backfire is one of them. But for me to make a decision here and to make an announcement on this program, I think, would not be the proper way for a President to handle these very sensitive negotiations.
Q. Just to follow on that, Mr. President, are SALT negotiations in a state that you have had to give up your hope of having a summit meeting with Mr. Brezhnev this year?
President FORD. There is far less likelihood that we will have a summit meeting this year. We are continuously negotiating here and with the group of technicians. But the timetable doesn't look encouraging for 1975. I don't think that is necessarily bad. Under no circumstances do I feel under pressure to get an agreement at a certain date. I want a good agreement rather than to be pressured into having an agreement by a precise date. And it seems to me that we are making headway slowly....

We have to work at it because a SALT II agreement is in the best interest of this country and the Soviet Union and the world at large. But we are not going to be pressured to get a bad agreement by a certain date.

WASHINGTON, 10 NOVEMBER 1975*

Q. Mr. Secretary, the President said yesterday [on NBC's "Meet the Press"] that growing tensions in the Cabinet led to the dismissal of Secretary Schlesinger and the other shakeups. Can you explain what led to those tensions, and what was your responsibility for the shakeup?
Secretary KISSINGER. The President has pointed out repeatedly that he made the decision for the shakeup and that the decision was his. There were differences between Secretary Schlesinger and myself, as you would expect between two individuals of strong minds. I consider Secretary Schlesinger a man of outstanding ability and one of the best analysts of defense matters with whom I have dealt, and whom I have known for over a decade. The differences are partly due to the differ-

* SOURCE: Press conference of Secretary of State Henry A. Kissinger. *Department of State Bulletin*, 1 December 1975, pp. 776–784.

ence in perspective between the Department of Defense and the Department of State, and they will always exist. Some concern certain technical matters, usually having to do with the SALT negotiations. None were as sweeping as I have seen described in the press. And no question, there were some personality disputes which neither of us handled with the elegance and wisdom that perhaps was necessary.

Q. Mr. Secretary, where does the shakeup and the Soviet rejection of the latest American SALT proposal leave the negotiations now?[1]

Secretary KISSINGER. Well, as far as the shakeup is concerned and its impact on foreign policy, SALT and otherwise, the foreign policy of the United States is not conducted on the basis of personality. It is related to the permanent interests and values of the United States. And while it is absolutely inevitable that senior advisers of the President will disagree from time to time, we have the machinery by which decisions can be made, and those decisions should not be seen in terms of the prevalence of a particular individual or be conducted in terms of personalities. . . .

Q. Is it now up to the United States to come up with a new proposal to present to the Soviets?

Secretary KISSINGER. We don't believe that the mere fact that the Soviet Union has rejected an American proposal requires us to come forward with another one. We still are expecting some sort of reasoned response to our last proposal, and we cannot make a new decision until we see some modification in the Soviet position.

* * *

Q. . . . The summit with Mr. Brezhnev appears deferred until next year at least. And in an election year there is some doubt about getting an arms control agreement at all with the Russians. Where does that leave the whole structure of foreign policy today?

Secretary KISSINGER. . . . With respect to arms control agreements with the Soviet Union, I do not believe that they should be accelerated because of elections, nor should they be delayed because of elections. We will make those agreements that we consider in the national interest of the United States and without regard to the electoral process. . . .

Q. Mr. Secretary, will you discuss with us in some detail the nature and volume of the involvement of the Soviet Union and Cuba in An-

[1] On 21 September 1975 the United States proposed to the Soviet Union that an equal number of Backfire bombers and cruise missiles be allowed above the ceiling of 2,400 strategic delivery vehicles for each country agreed to in Vladivostok. The Soviet Union rejected this proposal in October. See David M. Maxfield, "Disputes Over New Weapons Imperil Arms Pact," *Congressional Quarterly Weekly Report*, vol. 33, no. 48 (29 November 1975), pp. 2583–2588.—Ed.

gola? . . . You mentioned this at a hearing the other day, and I would like to know if it is in manpower, dollars, et cetera—what you can tell us about it.

Secretary Kissinger. Well, I don't have the figures here, and I cannot go much beyond what I stated the other day, which is that the Soviet Union earlier this year introduced a substantial amount of military equipment into Angola—substantial in relation to the balance of forces that then existed—that Cuba has also participated in the form of advisers, and of military equipment.

We consider both of these steps by extracontinental powers a serious matter and really, as far as the Soviet Union is concerned, not compatible with the spirit of relaxation of tensions.

Q. Sir, we are also an extraterritorial power. What are we doing there?

Secretary Kissinger. Our interest in Angola, which is related to the fact that the access to the sea of surrounding countries goes through Angola, was basically generated by the intervention of other countries. The United States has no other interest except the territorial integrity and independence of Angola. We strongly support the call of the Organization of African Unity for a cease-fire and for negotiation among the three factions that are involved there to form a coalition government, and we have no U.S. interest to pursue in Angola.

* * *

Q. Mr. Secretary, your responses on SALT suggest that there is a large chasm between our position and the Soviets'—so large, in fact, that we can't make another proposal until they modify their rejection. Could you elaborate for us exactly what went wrong? And wouldn't you agree that détente and SALT is in some crisis now?

Secretary Kissinger. No. I have said previously that I believe that 90 percent of the SALT agreement is substantially—or of the SALT negotiation—is substantially agreed to. The remaining 10 percent is of course of considerable significance. Now, it doesn't mean that the chasm is very wide or is unbridgeable. What it does mean is that when we make a serious proposal without getting a substantive response, we cannot establish the principle that all the other side has to do is to reject an American proposal in order to elicit another proposal.

I believe that the differences between us and the Soviet Union on SALT are bridgeable. I believe that an agreement on strategic arms limitations is in the national interest and is in the world interest, especially if you compare it with the alternatives that the nation will face and that the world will face if an arms race continues unchecked. So I am confident that, with a serious effort on both sides, these differences can be bridged.

As far as détente is concerned, I can only emphasize again what I have said repeatedly in public statements. Détente is not a favor we grant to the Soviet Union. Détente reflects an assesment of the basic national positions—in which strategic arsenals exist on both sides capable of destroying humanity; in which the United States must be able to demonstrate to its own people that if a confrontation occurs we will have done everything on our side to preserve the peace; in which if we look ahead at the problem historically, we do not want to be in a position where millions of people get killed in a war and afterward no one will be able to explain exactly what produced it except mock rhetoric.

If the Soviet Union threatens our national interests or the national interests of any of our allies, the United States will resist. The United States will not hold still for any hegemonial aspirations, but the United States will also make an effort to transcend the conflicts and the controversies of the cold war in order to build a better future for the people of this country and for the people of the world. That policy will continue.

As it stands now, on the Strategic Arms Limitation Talks, there is the stagnation that I have described. It is a stagnation which we are prepared to break. We are prepared to look for an honorable compromise. But it is up to the Soviet Union to be prepared also to make a compromise.

Q. Mr. Secretary, if I may follow back that point, the President yesterday seemed to be hinting that he might be prepared to accept some sort of a compromise involving the Russian Backfire bomber. Would you discuss that, please?

Secretary KISSINGER. The issue of the Backfire is a rather complicated technical issue which raises a number of questions. There is no dispute that the Backfire, on one-way missions, flying subsonically, can reach the United States from the Soviet Union. It is also a fact that the United States possesses many planes that are not being counted that on one-way missions can reach the Soviet Union. And therefore the problem concerns what categories—it falls into the issue of what categories of weapons should be counted, especially when we get into what one really has to call "hybrid" systems that are designed for one mission but are also capable of carrying out another mission.

That is an important subject that has existed in the negotiations in which we are trying to find a solution and are prepared to listen to reasonable proposals.

* * *

Q. Mr. Secretary . . . you've said that—and the Soviets seem to agree—there should not be a summit without a SALT agreement in sight. On the other hand, President Ford is apparently going to China without any real substantive matters to be decided. Can you discuss why the President is going to China, and why not have a less dramatic summit agreement between Brezhnev and Ford, just to discuss world issues?

Secretary KISSINGER. Well, we have—by mutual agreement incidentally—both sides have linked a visit by Brezhnev to the United States to an imminent SALT agreement, partly because one did not want to have it associated with the failure of a specific negotiation.

If a meeting between the General Secretary and the President would appear desirable, we are not going to make an issue of principle out of this at some point. It has not been discussed, and there is no such plan—no such plan exists at the moment—but I don't want to exclude it for all time.

With respect to our relationships with the People's Republic of China, those relationships have really concerned basically the orientation of both countries toward international affairs. We do not have that much bilateral business with the People's Republic of China that we must link visits or high-level meetings with the People's Republic of China to specific progress on specific issues.

It is important for us, however, to exchange views on fundamental issues of international events in order to see where our national interest coincides and where a certain parallelism in our policies exists. This makes it necessary to have occasional meetings at a very high level with Chinese leaders. This is why once a year I have gone to the People's Republic of China and why the President is visiting—for the first time in four years that an American President has been in Peking.

* * *

Q. Mr. Secretary, there have been a number of press reports that you do not favor counting the Backfire bomber as a strategic weapon because it needs to be refueled in order to make a 6,000-mile run. Do you favor placing limits, above the 2,400 that were placed at Vladivostok on strategic delivery systems, on both the U.S. cruise missile and the Soviet Backfire bomber?

Secretary KISSINGER. I have read a number of reports about the alleged positions of both myself and Secretary Schlesinger, and I have seen, I would say, almost none that is accurate.

The last position that has been put before the Soviet Union, which included a provision regarding Backfires, was jointly worked out by Secretary Schlesinger and myself. It represented our joint position,

and that is the only governmental position that exists, to which of course I subscribed and I have every reason to believe that Secretary Schlesinger subscribed.

* * *

Q. Mr. Secretary, could you clear up the reports of a distortion in—that there is a difference between the State Department and the Pentagon on Soviet strength and of Soviet compliance with the arms control agreement? You have alluded a couple of times to differences.

Secretary Kissinger. There is no disagreement between the State Department and the Defense Department about estimates with respect to Soviet strength. All of those are developed on an interagency basis, and a common position exists with all of them.

With respect to compliance issues, the only minor difference that existed months ago was the manner in which they should be brought to the Soviet attention. That has been resolved for nearly a year. There has been a united position in which the compliance issues have been brought to the attention of the Soviet Union in the Standing Consultative Commission. Many of the issues have been resolved. Some of the issues still remain to be resolved, but they do not exist between the State and the Defense Departments; they exist between the U.S. government and the Soviet Union.

Kissinger Discusses U.S. Response to Allegations of Soviet SALT Violations, 9 December 1975

Secretary Kissinger. Ladies and gentlemen, before I go to your questions I thought it would be helpful to review some of the SALT issues that have been raised. . . . I will not deal with specific testimony that may have been given except to note that no opportunity was presented to any member of the administration to present the truth. What I would like to do is to deal with categories of assertions that have been made and then to explain the real state of affairs with respect to them.

The assertions have been made that there have been massive Soviet violations, that the administration colluded with the Soviet Union in masking these violations, that the administration has not pursued the issue of violations diplomatically, and that senior officials, especially the President, have not been kept informed about the facts with respect to these violations.

I would like to discuss with you the procedures that the government is following with respect to SALT compliance and illustrate them with one or two examples.

First of all it is important to keep in mind that with respect to SALT, or with respect to the strategic forces on both sides, we are dealing with military establishments of great technical complexity that are constantly engaged in military activities. These military establishments, moreover, on both sides are in the process of constant change, so that there is great fluidity in what one observes. We are not dealing with a static situation; we are dealing with a fluid situation. Therefore, too, the information that is obtained has to go through various stages of analysis.

The first information about any event is usually extraordinarily illusive and ambiguous, and one part of the process of the government is to refine the information until we reach a point at which senior officials can make a reasonable decision. I believe it is a good working hypothesis to assume that government is not run by conspiracy but by serious people trying to come to serious conclusions about difficult topics, especially when the charge of a violation of a formal agreement is not a minor matter to be introduced into the diplomatic discourse.

Now, first of all, what is meant by a violation? There are several meanings that can be attached to the notion of violation that are being used interchangeably in the current debate.

Source: Press conference of Secretary of State Henry A. Kissinger, Washington, D.C., 9 December 1975. *Department of State Bulletin*, 5 January 1976, pp. 1–12.

A violation can be a deliberate violation of a SALT limitation, aimed at increasing the Soviet strategic capability in ways which the agreement was intended to preclude.

Second, a violation can be an action inconsistent with the sense or the spirit of the agreement and tending to undermine its viability even though it is not prohibited by the agreement. There can be borderline situations where a technical violation cannot be established but where the activity strains the interpretation of particular provisions.

Third, there can be unintended violations, occurring, for example, through negligence of higher officials responsible for ensuring compliance by their subordinate organizations.

Fourth, there can be actions not banned by an agreement but which complicate verification of the agreement.

Fifth, there can be ambiguous activities resulting from differing interpretations of the provisions of the agreements.

Sixth, there can be activities that are assessed as ambiguous due to inadequate information or misinterpretation of information which suggests a violation where in fact none exists.

I want to repeat that many compliance issues will arise initially as ambiguous activities which could apply to any of these categories. Our policy is to seek clarification of ambiguous situations as soon as there is a tangible basis for doing so, and to resolve ambiguities as quickly as possible in order to preclude development of a more serious situation.

Now to go to the procedures for handling allegations of violations. Any one of these categories would be initially reported in intelligence channels, either from the Central Intelligence Agency or from the Department of Defense. The Department of State and the White House have no independent means of acquiring any of this information.

There is no instance in which a reported violation was not immediately—an alleged violation—was not immediately reported to the President. And we have searched all the files of all the incidents. . . .

In order to deal with the problem of compliance, there are four institutions. There is a special intelligence committee, which was established by the Director of the Central Intelligence Agency in the summer of 1973. This committee makes a quarterly report on the problem of SALT compliance . . . and all of its reports have gone directly to the President as well as to every senior member of the administration that is dealing with the problem of strategic arms. In addition, there are three other bodies. There is the Verification Panel of the NSC. There is the Verification Panel's Working Group. And there is, of course, the NSC itself.

The Verification Panel Working Group of the NSC has met on SALT matters eleven times since the middle of 1973. The Verification Panel has met four times on SALT matters—has met four times on compliance issues exclusively—since 1973. But in addition, it has met forty times on SALT matters since 1973. Each of these meetings, each of these forty meetings, is preceded by a CIA briefing that includes all compliance issues. So that, in addition to the four formal meetings, there were forty meetings of the Verification Panel where whatever compliance issues existed at the time were brought to the attention of the Verification Panel.

The President has been briefed on compliance matters ten times since the middle of 1973, six times in the administration of President Ford. There has been one NSC meeting solely devoted to compliance issues, and parts of others.

The procedure is that the working group will attempt to determine what is going on and will devise either options or recommendations for consideration by the Verification Panel. The Verification Panel then reviews it and makes a recommendation or defines options.

In all the meetings that I have described of the Verification Panel, there was never a split decision. The allegation that individuals or departments have held up consideration of compliance issues, have obscured consideration of compliance issues, have refused to deal with compliance issues, is a total falsehood. All the decisions of the Verification Panel with respect to compliance have been unanimous. That is to say, they were agreed to by the Department of Defense, by the Chiefs of Staff, by the Arms Control and Disarmament Agency, by the Central Intelligence Agency, and by the State Department.

There is no doubt that there may have been differences of opinion in the working group as these papers were being considered. I am not familiar with these disagreements, because unless they are passed on to the Verification Panel there would be no particular reason for me to deal with them.

Let me now turn to the handling of intelligence. First of all, I think it is important to understand how the flow of information to the President is handled, because it is a rather grave matter if it can be alleged that information is being kept from the President of the United States.

The flow of information to the President is handled in the following way. The President receives daily, unabbreviated and without a covering summary, the President's daily brief and the daily intelligence bulletin of the Central Intelligence Agency. These are placed on his desk together with separate notes from various departments every morning and waiting for him when he comes to his office.

In the period of the presidency of President Ford he has had, until recently, the practice of reading those two intelligence summaries in the presence not of a member of the National Security Council staff, but in the presence of a representative of the Central Intelligence Agency. Therefore any intelligence item that would deal with compliance would come to his immediate attention. And in compiling a list of the various compliance issues, it is apparent that the President's daily bulletin would reflect the information of the Central Intelligence Agency, as you would expect, within no more than two weeks of its first appearance on a technical level.

Secondly, any memorandum from a cabinet member or from the head of an agency is transmitted to the President, usually in those cases with a summary by the NSC staff on top of it. But never is the summary alone sent to the President. Therefore, any cabinet member, any member of the Joint Chiefs, the Chairman of the Joint Chiefs, the Director of the Central Intelligence Agency, all have the opportunity, and know they have the opportunity, to address the President directly. Never has the Assistant to the President held up any memorandum from any of these individuals or any other memorandum addressed to the President by the head of an agency.

However, there is no memorandum in the files by any of these individuals, by any chief of staff of any of the services, by any head of any department, raising any of the issues that have been alleged in recent testimony. There is nobody who has claimed that the issue of compliance was not being adequately pursued. There is nobody who has objected to the handling of the information. There has been no reclama of any of the decisions of the Verification Panel, except in one case where one department that had first recommended one course of action—that course of action being not to protest a seeming issue of noncompliance because it wanted to protect its sources of intelligence—later changed its mind and recommended that the issue be raised in the Standing Consultative Commission. When that department changed its mind, the President agreed with that new position, and the decision of the Verification Panel was changed.

The reason there have been so few NSC meetings on the subject is because the decisions of the Verification Panel have always been unanimous and because no member of the panel has ever appealed to the President with a contrary view.

With respect to the handling of intelligence, all intelligence concerning alleged noncompliance was immediately distributed to all the members of the Verification Panel and by them to those of their senior members that were concerned with SALT.

For the period that a preliminary investigation was going on, the

intelligence was not distributed in the technical publications that were addressed to those whose primary responsibility was not concerned with SALT at a level below the cabinet level. The longest time this ever took place was a period of two months, and usually the so-called hold has been for a period of about a week or two to permit the refinement of intelligence. There has been no case in which the intelligence was not distributed in the quarterly intelligence publication that was concerned with the question of SALT monitoring. And in no case was intelligence kept from members of the Verification Panel.

Even during the period that this refinement was going on, the United States did not feel itself precluded from taking diplomatic action. For example, in one instance, which I will get into in a minute in greater detail, in one instance there were reports of unidentified construction in Soviet missile fields. We received this report on June 20 [1973] at a time when Brezhnev was in the United States. It seemed improbable that the Soviet Union would violate the agreement by blatantly building additional missile silos, and therefore a further study of the subject was ordered.

Nevertheless, on June 26 the United States sent a note to the Soviet Union in the presidential channel raising the issue of that construction, even before we had begun our detailed examination of the issue. In that case the distribution of that information was kept out of those journals that went to individuals not concerned with SALT matters until August 8, when it was generally distributed. In that interval two American notes had been sent to the Soviet Union in the presidential channel raising that issue. . . .

But let us take the case of these missile silos. There appeared in the summer of 1973 in a number of Soviet missile fields the beginning of some construction that clearly looked like additional silos. If these had been converted into missile silos, there was no question that they would have represented a clear violation of the [interim] agreement.

The construction of a silo generally takes two years to complete. And it is important for you to keep in mind in any event that almost any of these noncompliance events extend over a time span that, to be significant, is months and usually years, so that those of us who are engaged in policy making, and not rhetoric, must have an opportunity to study the problem before we draw any final conclusions, and we do have this opportunity.

Now, when we approached the Soviet Union within six days of receiving that information in the White House, we were told that these would be command and control silos and that as the construction proceeded it would become increasingly evident that they would be command and control silos. This, incidentally, was also the judgment of our

intelligence community. . . . The question being raised was whether, at some later time, they could be converted into missile silos.

It is also fair to point out that the Soviet Union in reply raised certain questions about certain ambiguities in American practices which we were not excessively anxious to have publicized and which accounted for the fact that these exchanges were conducted in a rather less dramatic manner than some people might have thought appropriate.

There were six exchanges in this channel of increasing specificity, in which we began to advance criteria which could be met in order to assure us that these silos were in fact intended for command and control. This extended over a period of a year. At that point in 1974, we moved the discussion from the presidential channel to the Standing Consultative Commission and made formal representations building on the previous exchanges.

We have since received assurances, and I believe it is the unanimous opinion of all agencies, that we are dealing with command and control silos. We have been given criteria which seem to us for the time being adequate; and there is no agency that today disputes that this issue is for the time being quiescent, though we will be vigilant in making certain that any unusual construction activity at these silos would raise profound questions.

For a variety of reasons, including the fact that the information about alleged noncompliance inevitably involves sensitive intelligence, I cannot go through all of the allegations that have been made; though I would perhaps mention one other, which is the most serious one and which comes closest to the borderline of a possible violation, which has to do with the testing of certain antiaircraft radars in what might be considered an ABM mode.

The issue is complicated by the fact that, at American insistence, the ABM treaty includes a provision that antiaircraft radar could be used—could be tested—in a manner in space for range-instrumentation purposes. I might point out that this was our idea, and if we had not included that, that issue of the SA–5 radar could have been more rapidly resolved.

We received information that some testing was going on with respect to the SA–5 radar in 1973. At that time it was routinely distributed, and nobody paid any attention to it because it was not put into connection with a possible ABM testing program. Between April and June 1974 some more tests took place which at least raised the problem that the radar might be tracking incoming missiles. That clearly is not permitted by the treaty, though it raises an ambiguity with respect to whether this is done for range-instrumentation purposes.

In any event, several meetings of the working group and the Verification Panel took place. The first decision in December 1974 was, on the recommendation of the Defense Department and the Central Intelligence Agency, that this issue not be raised because we did not wish to reveal the source of our intelligence.

In January 1975 the Defense Department reversed itself and recommended that the issue be raised. As a result, the issue was raised in February 1975. Since then—within a seventeen-day period after we had raised the issue—this activity has stopped [and] has not since been resumed. It was at the borderline of violation, but it has now stopped.

There are other issues, some having to do with unilateral American statements which the Soviet Union specifically disavowed. I think it is at least open to question whether the United States can hold the Soviet Union responsible for its own statements when the Soviet Union has asserted that it does not accept that interpretation.

Therefore the issue of SALT compliance has been handled in a serious manner. It stands to reason that no responsible U.S. official could wish to make an agreement with the Soviet Union and permit the Soviet Union to violate it with impunity. It stands to reason that the United States would not accept noncompliance with an agreement that had any conceivable impact on the strategic equation.

I would, in fact, suggest that this debate of the allegation in which some violations are invented, and in which the lack of vigilance of the administration is asserted, may tempt the very noncompliance which it claims to seek to avoid, because it may create the impression that the U.S. government would make a serious agreement on a matter affecting the survival of the United States and that its senior officials would then collude in a violation of this agreement. Let no foreign government believe that this is conceivable. And I think the time has come that we deal with each other more seriously.

* * *

Q. Mr. Secretary, to what extent is politics interfering today with your attempts to work out a new SALT agreement? And do you see a deadline beyond which it would be, because of the political campaigns, impossible to make any real progress on a treaty?

Secretary KISSINGER. As Secretary of State it is my obligation to recommend to the President what I believe to be in the national interest. My recommendations are not affected by the political situation; and I have, so far, seen no evidence that his decisions are affected by the political situation.

I cannot say that the debate that is going on greatly enhances the atmosphere of confidence in the country, but our recommendations are

not affected by the political situation. We are not operating against a deadline.

* * *

Q. . . . Do you have any evidence today that the Soviet Union is prepared to offer, in your own words, a reasonable and serious counterproposal to the last American proposal that was made to the Russians?
Secretary KISSINGER. The exchanges which we have had with the Soviet Union since November indicate that the Soviet Union realizes that no settlement is possible on the basis of its present proposal, and that it is willing to negotiate on the basis of the proposition that it must modify its position, and that we are then also prepared to look at our position. And it is on this basis that a trip by me to Moscow has been discussed.
Q. Are there plans for such a trip in the immediate future?
Secretary KISSINGER. I would expect such a trip to take place within the next four to five weeks.

* * *

Q. Mr. Secretary, you mentioned, among the possible violations, Soviet interference with national means of inspection. Have they interfered with our—
Secretary KISSINGER. No, I have listed that as a—
Q. A possibility, yes. Have they interfered, or are they now attempting to interfere, with our national means of inspection? . . .
Secretary KISSINGER. . . . There has been a Soviet program from the middle—it dates back from the middle of the 1960s—to make photography and other means of detection more complicated. There have been some actions since the SALT agreement in that category. Several of those have been raised with the Soviet Union. Some of those that have been raised have been ended. None of those, up to now, have fundamentally interfered with our national means of detection.
Q. Are they currently trying to interfere?
Secretary KISSINGER. Well, you know there are so many separate things going on, there is always an effort. We have several things before them at this moment. I have said that, up to now, nothing has decisively interfered with our national means of detection.

* * *

Q. Mr. Secretary, . . . the charge that the Soviets have perhaps built another ABM test site at Kamchatka; can you address this?
Secretary KISSINGER. This is an issue that is now under discussion with the Soviet Union, and I simply want to explain the issue. It is one of these technical issues.

There is no dispute that the radar in Kamchatka faces the Soviet Union, and not the United States. And therefore we are dealing with a test radar. The ABM treaty requires that ABM testing could take place only at agreed test ranges, and we listed ours. The Soviet Union didn't list theirs.

Q. You listed one for them.

Secretary KISSINGER. We unilaterally listed one for them, and the Soviet Union gave an ambiguous reply to that, saying what their test ranges were was generally known; but they would not confirm or deny the one we gave for them. And I think we claimed two for ourselves.

If the Soviet Union had claimed the Kamchatka range for itself at that time, there would be no problem. If the Soviet Union told us today that the Kamchatka range is an ABM test range, then—supposing we were satisfied about the characteristics of the radar—there would be no significant problem.

So here we are dealing with a technical issue of what an agreed test range is—since there is no disagreement that the radar in Kamchatka faces into the Soviet Union and therefore must be used for some sort of internal tracking.

* * *

Q. Mr. Kissinger, on the subject of Angola, you and the President have made some accusations. A protest has been made to the Soviet Union about alleged intervention. There's comments about Cuban intervention there. Isn't it about time that you told us roughly what the United States has done in the way of helping forces in Angola, and since when?

Secretary KISSINGER. I have said that the United States has tried to be helpful to some neighboring countries. Whatever we have done has started long after massive Soviet involvement became evident. So this is not a case that really lends itself to great dispute on that subject, because the Soviet Union has been active there in this manner since March. But I would rather not go any further until we see what can be done in the present diplomatic effort.

Kissinger Discusses Angola, the Backfire Bomber–Cruise Missile Controversy, and Prospects for SALT, January, July, and October 1976

WASHINGTON, 14 JANUARY 1976*

Secretary KISSINGER. I have . . . [a] statement [which] deals with the U.S. attitude toward Soviet actions in Angola and toward the SALT negotiations.

The United States holds the view that the essence of the U.S.-Soviet relationship, if it is to proceed toward a genuine easing of tensions, is that neither side will seek to obtain unilateral advantage vis-à-vis the other, that restraint will govern our respective policies, and that nothing will be done that could escalate tense situations into confrontation between our two countries.

It is the U.S. view that these principles of mutual relations are not simply a matter of abstract good will. They are at the very heart of how two responsible great powers must conduct their relations in the nuclear era.

It must be clear that when one great power attempts to obtain a special position of influence based on military intervention and irrespective of original motives, the other power will sooner or later act to offset this advantage. But this will inevitably lead to a chain of action and reaction typical of other historic eras in which great powers maneuvered for advantage only to find themselves sooner or later embroiled in major crises and, indeed, in open conflict.

It is precisely this pattern that must be broken if a lasting easing of tensions is to be achieved.

Whatever justification in real or alleged requests for assistance the Soviet Union may consider to have had in intervening and in actively supporting the totally unwarranted Cuban introduction of an expeditionary force into Angola, the fact remains that there has never been any historic Soviet or Russian interest in that part of the world. It is precisely because the United States is prepared to accept principles of restraint for itself that it considers the Soviet move in Angola as running counter to the crucial principles of avoidance of unilateral advantage and scrupulous concern for the interests of others which we have jointly enunciated.

The United States considers such actions incompatible with a

* SOURCE: Press conference of Secretary of State Henry A. Kissinger. *Department of State Bulletin*, 2 February 1976, pp. 125–132.

genuine relaxation of tensions. We believe that this is a wholly unnecessary setback to the constructive trends in U.S.-Soviet relations which we cannot believe is ultimately in the Soviet or the world interest.

The question arises whether, in the light of Angola and its implications for Soviet-American relations, it is consistent with our policy to go to Moscow and to negotiate on SALT. There are two points that need to be made in this context.

First, we have never considered the limitation of strategic arms as a favor we grant to the Soviet Union, to be turned on and off according to the ebb and flow of our relations. It is clear that the continuation of an unrestrained strategic arms race will lead to neither a strategic nor a political advantage. If this race continues, it will have profound consequences for the well-being of all of humanity.

Limitation of strategic arms is therefore a permanent and global problem that cannot be subordinated to the day-to-day changes in Soviet-American relations. At the same time, it must be understood on both sides that if tensions increase over a period of time, the general relationship will deteriorate, and therefore the SALT negotiations will also be affected.

Second, we must consider the long-term consequences of a failure of the SALT negotiations. If the interim agreement lapses, the Soviets will be free of several severe restraints. They can add heavy ICBMS without restrictions. They can build more submarines without dismantling old ICBMS. There will be no equal ceiling of 2,400. The immediate impact would be that the numerical gap frozen in SALT I, and equalized in Vladivostok, would again become a factor, facing us with the choice of either large expenditures in a strategically and politically unproductive area or a perceived inequality with its political implications.

Of course we will not negotiate any agreement that does not achieve strategic equality for the United States and that we cannot defend as being in the national interest. Nor does it mean that Angola or similar situations will, if continued, not impinge on SALT as well as the general relationship. But it does mean that the general objective of a more orderly and stable nuclear relationship is in the interests of the United States and in the interests of the world and cannot be easily abandoned. This is why the President has decided that I should go to Moscow to negotiate on SALT, and we expect that the talks will be conducted in the same spirit by the Soviet side.

Q. Mr. Secretary, does the fact that you are going to Moscow now mean that you have forwarded a new proposal to the Kremlin on SALT?

Secretary KISSINGER. We have not yet forwarded a new proposal to Moscow on SALT, but we expect to do so before I go there, within the next day or two.

Q. Mr. Secretary, what is standing in the way of a compromise that would point the way to a treaty at this point?

Secretary KISSINGER. The obstacle to an agreement results primarily from issues that could not be considered fully at Vladivostok because the technology was not yet developed at that time. Primarily the issues concern how to deal with the Soviet Backfire bomber and how to deal with the American cruise missiles; whether and how to count them; whether and what restraints to accept. These are fundamentally the outstanding issues. Most other issues have either been settled in principle or in detail.

Q. Excuse me, if I may follow up. But that was the case several months ago, and you didn't go to Moscow. Now you are going. Does this mean that at least these two outstanding issues are pretty much settled?

Secretary KISSINGER. There has been no discussion with the Soviets except that the Soviets have assured us that they are prepared to modify their last position; and on that basis we hope to be able to work out some solution.

Q. Mr. Secretary, are you saying that you are making Soviet restraint in Angola a quid pro quo for any successful conclusion to the SALT treaty, or are you not saying that?

Secretary KISSINGER. . . . I am saying that Soviet actions in Angola, if continued, are bound to affect the general relationship with the United States; that a substantial deterioration of that relationship can also, over time, affect the strategic arms talks. . . .

Q. To follow up, if there is no change in the Soviet position on Angola, would you then expect that there could be a successful SALT II negotiation later on?

Secretary KISSINGER. We would have to face this in the light of the circumstances that may exist later.

Q. Mr. Secretary, you have been sending this message—you and the President have been sending this message to Moscow now for several weeks. Have you had any indication whatsoever that the Soviets might be interested in a diplomatic solution to Angola? And secondly, are you willing to discuss this with the Soviets when you go to Moscow?

Secretary KISSINGER. It is a close race between the messages we send and the deterioration of our domestic position; and messages that are not backed up at home lose a fair amount of their credibility.

We are prepared to discuss Angola, and we have had some ex-

changes with the Soviet Union on Angola in recent weeks which we will have to clarify.

* * *

Q. Mr. Secretary, is it your expectation that if things go as you anticipate that you will be able to conclude an agreement in Moscow? Will you set out for us what you are aiming at? Are you aiming at an agreement in principle?

Secretary KISSINGER. No, there cannot be a final agreement in Moscow. The most that is achievable in Moscow is an agreement in principle similar to the Vladivostok agreement but covering the outstanding issues such as Backfire and cruise missiles and to relate them to Vladivostok. And then there will have to be technical discussions at Geneva to work out the detailed provisions. And that, under the best of circumstances, would take another two to three months.

Q. Mr. Secretary, I am curious as to how you are going to conduct these parallel negotiations with the Soviets. On the one hand, you are indicating that the success of SALT may hinge on Soviet activities in Angola. On the other hand, you are going to Moscow in a few days presumably to conclude an agreement in principle. How can you do that without knowing what the Soviet reaction in Angola is?

Secretary KISSINGER. I have made clear in my statement that the regulation of nuclear arms in the strategic field between the United States and the Soviet Union is not a benefit we confer on the Soviet Union. It is a generic problem of world order that must be settled at some point and for which conditions are propitious now because of a long record of negotiation and because technology is at a point where it is possible to accept certain restraints now which might then have to wait for another cycle of technology before they can be made effective.

The point I am making is that if there is a general deterioration in our relationship, it could affect SALT. In any event, whatever is agreed in Moscow will take several months to negotiate in greater detail.

Q. . . . In other words, you are not saying, then, that if there is not some Soviet pullback in Angola before the termination of your trip to Moscow, that that is going to have an adverse effect on SALT.

Secretary KISSINGER. That is correct.

Q. Mr. Secretary, you said that messages not backed up at home lose certain credibility, I think. We are now entering a presidential election year. Isn't it likely that those messages will continue not to be backed up, and what impact will that have on foreign policy in general?

Secretary KISSINGER. I have always believed very strongly that the foreign policy of the United States must reflect the permanent values

and interests of the United States. It is not a partisan foreign policy. And to the best of my ability, I have attempted to conduct this office in a manner that can make it achieve bipartisan support.

It would therefore be a tragedy if during this election year we did not find some means to put some restraint on our domestic debates in the field of foreign policy and to find some means of common action.

As soon as the Congress returns I will talk to several of the leaders to see what cooperation is possible to put at least some restraint on partisan controversy, because the penalties we will pay for lack of unity will have to be paid for many years.

But it is a problem. I agree with you.

* * *

Q. Mr. Secretary, two questions. I am not sure I have this exactly right, but didn't you say at a previous press conference that the United States would not table another SALT proposal unless the Russians tabled another one first? And secondly, have all the members of the NSC and the Verification Panel signed off on this new proposal that we plan to offer in Moscow?

Secretary KISSINGER. With respect to the first question, I said that the United States cannot table a new proposal simply because the Soviets had rejected the old one. We have been given a clear promise that there would be a significant modification in the Soviet position. Under these conditions, we are prepared to put forward a modification of our position, because we would prefer to negotiate from our position rather than from some other.

We have made clear—and I can repeat it here—that if the Soviets do not modify their last position, there can be no agreement. And the position which we will forward to them will be substantially different from the last Soviet position. So it will require—

Q. Substantially different from their last position?

Secretary KISSINGER. It will also be somewhat different from our position. It is an honest attempt to find a solution that takes into account the real concerns of all sides.

With respect to our internal discussions . . . my impression is that there is unanimity on the course that we are pursuing. We have had very good meetings. We have had two Verification Panel meetings, two NSC meetings. There will probably be another NSC meeting before I go, just to review the bidding. And I would say that the government is operating . . . with complete unanimity.

Q. Mr. Secretary, the Joint Chiefs of Staff don't provide much drama for you, but are they signing on to this proposal?

Secretary KISSINGER. The Joint Chiefs of Staff are signing on to this proposal, yes.
Q. Mr. Secretary, would you recommend conclusion of a new SALT agreement with the Soviets if Soviet and Cuban forces are still in Angola?
Secretary KISSINGER. I am going to Moscow in order to see whether the deadlock in these negotiations can be broken. We should not play with the strategic arms limitation negotiations. It is a matter that is of profound concern for the long-term future. It is in an area in which no significant advantages can be achieved by either side but in which the momentum of events can lead to consequences that could be very serious. And therefore we will not use it lightly for bargaining purposes in other areas.

On the other hand, obviously if the general relationship deteriorates, then it could over a period of time even affect the Strategic Arms Limitation Talks. But I think we should make every effort to avoid that.

* * *

Q. Mr. Secretary, given the congressional attitudes on foreign affairs in general, do you intend to talk to any leaders of Congress before you go to Moscow to negotiate further, and is there any danger that a repudiation by Congress of a SALT agreement might be counterproductive to the very objectives you're seeking for the long term?
Secretary KISSINGER. I have been briefing congressional leaders on SALT negotiations consistently. There has been no significant new development in the negotiating process, but I will no doubt be in touch with some of the senior members of the Senate.

As far as repudiation of an agreement is concerned, it would of course be a very serious matter since, in any event, one of the biggest foreign policy problems we now face is the question from other countries of who speaks for the United States. Somebody has to speak for the United States, and there can be no foreign policy without authority.

So if an agreement were repudiated, it would accelerate this very dangerous tendency; but we do not have an agreement yet.

BRUSSELS, 23 JANUARY 1976*

Q. Mr. Secretary, there are reports that you have come back from Moscow with a Russian suggestion for lowering the Vladivostok ceil-

*SOURCE: Press conference of Secretary of State Henry A. Kissinger. *Department of State Bulletin*, 16 February 1976, pp. 165–168.

ing by some amount, and I wonder if you could confirm that and expand on it?

Secretary KISSINGER. I cannot go into the details of the negotiations here. The possibility in certain contexts together with other arrangements of lowering the ceiling was discussed, but I would like to stress that this is in the context of agreement on several other issues, and I cannot go any further into it.

Q. Mr. Secretary, what are the major unresolved issues now holding up agreement?

Secretary KISSINGER. First of all, as I said at the Moscow airport, a number of issues were resolved and were passed on to Geneva for technical implementation. Progress of some significance was made on other issues, and some other issues still remain to be resolved. The general category of problems connected with Backfire and certain aspects of cruise missiles still requires further study, though progress has been made with respect to some aspects of it.

*   *   *

Q. Would you give us your appraisal of the current state of U.S. détente relationships—what you have learned as a result of your meeting and your current assessment?

Secretary KISSINGER. Our impression is that the Soviet leaders are interested in continuing the détente relationship and to strengthen it. We believe that the negotiations with respect to strategic arms limitations made a positive contribution to that end. At the same time we have repeatedly expressed our view that Soviet and Cuban actions in Angola are not helpful to the détente relationship.

So I would have to call attention to both the pluses and the minuses.

*   *   *

Q. Mr. Secretary, is it your expectation that a SALT agreement could be reached with the Soviet Union this year?

Secretary KISSINGER. I believe that a SALT agreement with the Soviet Union this year is possible.

Q. Mr. Secretary, is it possible that the new Soviet proposal to reduce the Vladivostok ceiling might serve as a way of breaking the deadlock over the cruise–Backfire bomber dilemma?

Secretary KISSINGER. I would like to make clear that the prospect of reduction is in the context of several other elements of the agreement, and it may or may not be included in the final agreement. We will now study carefully the specific Soviet proposals to see whether they lend

themselves to adaptation or a response that can bridge the remaining differences.

WASHINGTON, 10 JULY 1976*

Q. The Strategic Arms Limitation Talks have been a cornerstone of your and the President's policy. A number of months have passed now with no apparent sign of progress. Could you give us some indication of where we are on this matter?

Secretary KISSINGER. The Strategic Arms Limitation Talks have settled a large percentage of the outstanding problems. There are two major issues that remain—whether Backfires should be counted in the total, and how cruise missiles should be either counted or limited.

On these two issues there has not been a final resolution. We have put forward an approach. The Soviet Union has put forward a different approach, and it has, up to now, not been possible to settle, to reconcile, those two approaches.

On the other hand, in Geneva, the teams have continued to negotiate on the very considerable area on which agreement has already been reached, working out the technical implementation of the agreements in principle that have been achieved, so that whenever those two issues of the cruise missile and the Backfire are finally resolved, it ought to be possible to make—when they are conceptually resolved—it ought to be possible to make fairly rapid progress toward a solution.

Q. Is there active negotiation on those two outstanding issues at this point?

Secretary KISSINGER. On those two issues we are studying the Soviet position. They are studying our position. And these two issues are still open, and there is no immediate negotiation going on until we have restudied our position on those two limited—on those two issues.

HARTFORD, CONN., 27 OCTOBER 1976†

Q. Mr. Secretary, . . . the major foreign policy issues in this campaign appear to have been the President's mistake on Eastern Europe and Jimmy Carter's reluctance to send troops to Yugoslavia. In view of the fact that there are some very important foreign policy questions —I think you have SALT, what to do next in the Middle East, what to

*SOURCE: Press conference of Secretary of State Henry A. Kissinger. *Department of State Bulletin*, 2 August 1976, pp. 164–172.

† SOURCE: Press conference of Secretary of State Henry A. Kissinger. *Department of State Bulletin*, 22 November 1976, pp. 640–647.

do next in China, questions which will face any new administration—what is your feeling about the quality of the foreign policy debate in this campaign?

Secretary KISSINGER. Of course, since I believe we have been correct in the foreign policy we've carried out, I'm assuming that the absence of more fundamental criticisms would tend to support this.

As I pointed out before, I really do not think that foreign policy should lend itself to a detailed partisan debate. And therefore I think it is in the interest of the United States that at least major tactical questions not become the subject of foreign policy disputes.

Q. Dr. Kissinger, I'd just like to follow up and mention the SALT talks. In view of the fact in the last ten years the U.S.S.R. has spent $10 billion on civil defense and military armaments, isn't it a waste of time—the SALT talks, that is?

Secretary KISSINGER. The SALT talks on the limitation of strategic armaments derive from the fact that both sides are developing nuclear weapons of enormous destructiveness and that both sides, the Soviet Union and the United States, for the first time in history face a situation in which two countries could destroy all of humanity. That is an unprecedented situation that leaders of no country in the world have ever had to face before.

What we're attempting to do in these talks is to put a ceiling on the strategic armaments of both sides—whatever they may have spent in the past, to put a ceiling on these strategic armaments—and then to use that ceiling as a point of departure from which to make reductions in these strategic armaments. We have a preliminary agreement to establish a ceiling that will be equal for both sides, and we are now negotiating what categories of weapons fall under each ceiling. This is what has held up the conclusion of the negotiations. I would think that the negotiations are about 85 to 90 percent concluded, that there are two issues that still remain to be settled. But whatever one thinks of what either country may have done in the field of armaments, it is in the interest of humanity that a ceiling be put on these weapons and that then they be reduced.

Iklé Reports on the Status of the SALT II Negotiations, 14 January 1977

Senator Percy. Now, looking back in perspective, . . . certainly news accounts of our most recent estimate of the strategic balance—and the reference is made to the very strong statements as recently as last Wednesday in the State of the Union message by President Ford—suggest that there may be the possibility of a basic change in Soviet intentions. Whereas earlier estimates have considered the Soviet objective to be one of rough weapons parity with the United States, the most recent estimates reportedly state that the Soviets are seeking superiority.

Another disturbing factor is the indication that our intelligence estimators have consistently underestimated Soviet capabilities and intentions. This indicates a condition in the strategic balance which calls into question the underlying premise on which we built our current strategic force, entered into negotiations for the limitation of Soviet and American weapons, and based our weapons research and development programs.

If we should lose or appear to lose our second-strike capability, our entire deterrence policy would be invalidated. The hearings which we undertake today will provide a forum for consideration of the national security and foreign policy implications of our strategic force structure and thus contribute to policy development and better public understanding of the complex issues involved.

* * *

Senator Percy. The components of the Triad, are aging and require change or upgrading. It is possible, if the new administration finds the latest estimate of Soviet intentions to be persuasive, that we may be asked to consider an entire new policy of strategic deterrence. We may be asked to consider a new treaty further limiting strategic arms development and deployment.

Our judgment on those important issues cannot unduly emphasize the cost or environmental and energy factors. The first consideration must be the strategic requirements of national security. Nevertheless, we must be careful not to be stampeded into decisions which go beyond the best estimated requirements of national security. Imprudent

Source: Testimony of Arms Control and Disarmament Agency Director Fred C. Iklé. U.S., Congress, Senate, Committee on Foreign Relations, *United States/Soviet Strategic Options*, 95th Cong., 1st sess., 1977.

investment in defense could itself be destabilizing by giving potential adversaries reason to doubt our peaceful intentions in the arms race, adding fuel to domestic inflation, and certainly adding to our mounting federal debt.

We cannot ignore the urgent call of our strategic planners for force modernization, continued research and development efforts, and improved early warning of possible attack against the United States. But we must weigh each of those decisions in the light of our national policy to reduce international tensions.

On the one hand, we must be fully cognizant of the threat posed to national security, and on the other, be mindful of the dangers of the new rounds of weapons-development competition. While there is general agreement on the facts of Soviet advances in air defense, improved payload for their ICBMs, and the potential of their new Backfire bomber, there is honest and strongly felt disagreement on Soviet intentions. . . .

Senator CLARK. I wonder if Senator Percy would yield for a comment? I may have misunderstood what you said.

I was under the impression that you were indicating that the recent national intelligence estimate suggests that the Soviet Union may well be seeking superiority. It is my impression that the recent national intelligence estimate concludes that the Soviet Union is not trying to reach superiority, but that was the conclusion of the so-called Team B. . . . The national intelligence community estimate, even though it is much gloomier than at any previous time, still does not make that assumption, but it is rather the Team B group that has come to that conclusion; that is my understanding. I am just wondering if I misunderstood what you said or if I am interpreting you correctly.

Senator PERCY. I think during the course of our questioning we will try to determine that.

* * *

[Dr. Iklé's prepared statement follows]

. . . Strategic arms limitations and strategic forces are shaped by developments that reach far back into the past, and what is decided now will reach far into the future. Strategic arms may take ten years to build and deploy, and once deployed may be kept in service for twenty years or more. Strategic arms control agreements require five years or so to conceive and negotiate and are then supposed to last for decades. So in fact, our strategic forces today are in large part the result of decisions taken in the 1950s; likewise, key elements of our approach to SALT were decided in the 1960s. During such a time span senior officials in the executive branch come and go, so it remains for Congress, and

the interaction between Congress and the executive branch, to contribute the continuity and long-term perspectives that are so essential....

Today I would like to describe for you what I see as a mixed picture marked by both substantial progress and continuing difficulty.

First, the good news. Substantial progress has been made in 1976 in drafting treaty language, article by article, to flesh out the Vladivostok accord. Without such a detailed and specific text, we could not know what we have agreed on, and this would leave room for evasion and foster future disputes....

The fact that such a solid treaty structure could be built attests to President Ford's accomplishment in reaching the Vladivostok accord. The agreed provisions for limiting ballistic missiles—the weapons which most threaten strategic stability—are about complete. Also, agreement has been reached on the need for future reductions.

The major issues that remain unsettled concern "gray area" systems which may have both strategic and tactical uses, namely the Soviet Backfire bomber and medium-range cruise missiles. The United States has long been ready to resolve these issues in an equitable way that will not undermine the Vladivostok accord and yet will preserve the agreed principle that SALT limitations must be verifiable.

Despite this record, we have often heard the accusation that the Ford administration, or more specifically, alleged dissension within the administration, is responsible for the fact that some important issues in SALT are still unsettled. This administration has been flexible in SALT where flexibility was warranted, and firm where firmness was needed. For example, at Vladivostok President Ford held onto the principle of equality and came back with an agreement reconfirming it. On the controversial issue of cruise missiles and the new Soviet bomber, we offered five different solutions within as many months. Yet the Soviet Union failed to make any effort to come up with counterproposals of its own which could help to resolve these issues. In retrospect, perhaps we took too many initiatives, giving our adversaries the impression that they could wait us out. Had the Soviets shown only some of this flexibility, an agreement might long since have been reached. We must keep in mind that the SALT process cannot function without a disposition to reasonable compromise on both sides.

As we look back on the compromise formulas which the present administration developed, and forward to the positions which the new one may take, it is clear that the possibilities are nearly endless and that we need some rough principles to apply as a test of a good agreement. Any successful formula will of course have to be a compromise—the important point is that it must be a balanced compromise.

The most notorious attempt to obtain a one-sided advantage in SALT was the Soviet claim, during an earlier period of the negotiations, that they should be permitted a larger number of strategic forces to compensate for U.S. nuclear systems deployed in defense of our allies overseas—the so-called forward-based systems. This claim was one-sided because it ignored the at least equal, if not larger number of opposing medium-range systems on the Soviet side confronting our European and Asian allies. The weakness of their position was most apparent in the claim that French and British missiles which threaten Moscow should be limited, while intermediate-range Soviet missiles which threaten London and Paris should not.

President Ford successfully resisted this claim, and in the end the Soviets accepted, in November 1974 at Vladivostok, the principle that a SALT agreement should limit our two countries to equal numbers of strategic offensive arms. However, it is important to recall this earlier history because we continue to hear suggestions that the United States must in some sense pay the Soviets off for dropping these demands by accepting Soviet terms for resolving the cruise missile and Backfire issues. This notion would establish the curious principle that by making unwarranted claims, and then dropping them, one becomes entitled to other concessions. The U.S. should, of course, continue to be willing to accept balanced limitations on weapons that are in the gray area between clearly tactical and clearly strategic systems. If U.S. tactical systems are to be limited because they also have some strategic capability, then so should Soviet systems. On the other hand, if Soviet systems such as their Backfire bomber are to be treated as tactical even though they have some strategic potential, such U.S. systems as intermediate-range cruise missiles should be treated in the same way.

Such an approach is necessary if the agreements are to provide a stable military balance. It is also necessary, if we hope to make progress in future negotiations, to extend the reach of arms control limits. For if we grant concessions now that belong in later negotiations, it will be difficult later to get the Soviet Union to accept new and more comprehensive agreements which would require that they give up these advantages prematurely conceded by us.

Mr. Chairman, in the midst of such unavoidable complications, it is important that we not become frustrated or overanxious. If we are to succeed in making the world a safer place through arms control, we must be careful not to overdramatize SALT. Too many seem to believe that if we don't reach an agreement right away, then all restraints will be off, all arms control will end, and a final go-for-broke arms race will occur which could quickly take us to war. Such prophecies have little historical foundation, but they do have a risk of becoming self-fulfilling.

Equally dangerous is the other side of the coin: the belief that if we do have a SALT agreement, then the arms competition will be ended, and we can cease to worry about the effectiveness and vulnerability of our strategic forces. This belief could undermine the stability of the agreements we do achieve.

We are of course trying as hard as we know how to negotiate an agreement that will be as comprehensive as possible. But we should not rest on the expectation that all arms competition will stop. Within the framework of a SALT agreement, and outside that framework, competition in both the quality and quantity of military hardware will probably continue. One sometimes hears the mistaken view that cruise missile development could be stopped if the U.S. were simply to accept the Soviet proposals to ban all cruise missiles with ranges greater than 600 kilometers. Even if this range restriction is scrupulously obeyed—and our ability to verify it is tenuous at best—there is no reason to think the Soviet Union would not vigorously continue to develop cruise missiles below this range on the many Soviet submarines, surface ships, and heavy bombers which today carry such systems. And while it might be desirable, on balance, to stop new cruise missile technology, there is virtually no part of that technology which the Russians could not develop using cruise missiles of this permitted range.

I would like to turn now, Mr. Chairman, to one persistent criticism of our strategic policy that combines a partial truth with a larger measure of misleading inaccuracy: the view that U.S. strategic programs drive the arms race, and the Soviets merely respond. The actual record strongly refutes this charge. If Soviet programs were merely a reaction to ours, their strategic budget would have declined over the last fifteen years, because that is what ours did; they would have stopped deploying ICBMs when they reached 1,000 instead of building up to 1,600, because we stopped at 1,000; they would have stopped at 710 ballistic sea-launched missiles, as we did, instead of building up to 950.

A similar pattern appears among the great many nuclear systems which exist outside of SALT. Thus, when we dismantled our intermediate-range ballistic missiles and bombers, the Soviets did not follow suit. On the contrary, they are modernizing those forces and substantially upgrading them with the new SS–20 missile and Backfire bomber. Indeed, contrary to what some people have argued, the United States does not have an advantage in these arms outside of SALT. Today, the Soviet Union has some 600 medium bombers (we have 60), some 600 medium-range ballistic missiles (we have none), and a larger number of nuclear-capable aircraft than the United States and its NATO allies together. The Soviets have also deployed large numbers of air-launched and sea-launched cruise missiles, even though the U.S. until recently

had taken very little interest in equipping its own forces with these systems.

This is not to say that we never set a competitive example which the Soviets seek to match—our development of MIRVs is sometimes said to be one such case—but unfortunately it is not the U.S. which drives the strategic competition. If we were in the driver's seat, our cutbacks in the past and our unilateral restraint would have put on the brakes.

However we debate among ourselves whether it is the United States or the Soviet Union which is to blame for some particular increase in armaments, we must address a more fundamental question. We have to ask whether our long-term objectives for arms control and disarmament are shared by the Soviet leadership, and to the extent they are not, how differing Soviet perceptions and goals are likely to affect the opportunities for arms control agreements.

We need a healthy sense of realism on this question. On the one hand, we could dangerously deceive ourselves if we took for granted that the Soviet military and political elite share our premises regarding the prevention of war—that is, that they seek a "stable" or mutually deterring balance the same way we do, and that this consensus will safely override disparities in armaments and differences in political philosophy.

On the other hand, we must reject the view that because of these differences in outlook serious progress in arms control is impossible. As long as we are careful to preserve two important principles, I am very confident that we can have effective arms control agreements even with so difficult an adversary as the Soviet Union.

First, we must continue to apply the test that agreements we enter have adequate provisions for verification. The readiness of each side to allow and even promote adequate verification is its pledge that, though our objectives and doctrines may differ, the terms of a SALT treaty will be observed. And the capability for timely detection of violations is essential for ensuring that our security is not jeopardized by our reliance on agreements.

Second, we must retain the technological capability and political will to respond appropriately to violations, if they should occur, with actions which preserve U.S. security. Our ability to do so can be a powerful deterrent against violations ever occurring.

On the basis of these two realistic principles, arms control efforts can truly flourish and move us toward a safer world.

In concluding, let me mention several considerations which I believe should be part of our thinking, not only about strategic arms control but about our strategic posture in general.

First of all, we need an appreciation of the vast uncertainties that confront us—we need a sense of modesty. All our calculations about missile attacks and the effects of nuclear destruction rest on many untested assumptions. We cannot validate our formulas and figures by trial and error. We simply do not know—and as long as we are successful in averting nuclear war, we cannot know—the complex interactions of nuclear weapons systems, the cascading effects on people and hardware from very many nuclear explosions. In nuclear deterrence there can be no full-scale experiments, no real learning.

Second, when we talk about "deterrence," "stability," or "unacceptable damage," we are not talking about physical realities. We are talking about ideas—our ideas—which may or may not influence the actions of the adversaries we wish to influence. Averting nuclear war depends not so much on how we see the vulnerability of our nuclear forces but on how Soviet military planners see it. We must pay more attention to the direction and thrust of Soviet military programs and to the ideas expressed in Soviet military doctrine. The Soviet government has never formally accepted the American concept of mutual deterrence. What ideas guide their buildup and use of military power? We must design our defenses to meet threats that actually face us, not simply threats we devise from our own logic of deterrence.

Third, we should refrain from hasty judgments about the possibility or impossibility of so-called limited nuclear war. If nuclear weapons should ever be used in a conflict between the superpowers, both governments would have a compelling obligation to their people to limit the fighting before it totally destroyed their countries. At the same time, however, the course of any such war would be highly unpredictable; and no one could be sure how it might be brought to an end. Given the hair-triggered missile systems, given the vulnerabilities of command and control, given the unpredictable effects of nuclear explosions on communications and on the functioning of governments, the risk of escalation would be enormous. So no responsible leader would pretend to himself that a limited nuclear war could be safely controlled. On the other hand, no responsible person should want to rig nuclear deterrent forces in such a way as to make it impossible to limit or cut short a nuclear war. The United States must not, in the face of any nuclear attack, no matter how restrained, be forced by doctrine or weapons to choose only between surrender or destruction of most of the civilized world.

Clearly, there is wide agreement in this country and among our allies that our capability for a limited nuclear response does serve deterrence. This consensus is made explicit in the U.S. position that we

might possibly use nuclear weapons first in the face of massive conventional attack that could not be turned back by our non-nuclear forces—for example, in Central Europe.

Mr. Chairman, I would like to conclude with one final consideration which, in a sense, towers above and pervades all others. It is too often left out because it is not easy to discuss in a few words. This is the question of morality.

Some people hold that the key to deterrence is the ability to kill people—men, women, and children, not soldiers; deliberately, not as a spill-over from attacks on military targets as happened in Vietnam and other wars. And these tens of millions of people, of course, would have had no influence whatsoever on the chain of events that brought the attack about. Indeed, the attack might have been unleashed by accident—a danger made serious by the fact that Soviet and U.S. missiles can be launched with cataclysmic speed.

We should not conduct arms control policy with a stunted moral conscience. It is with these considerations in mind that I share so strongly in President-elect Carter's hope to accomplish a substantial reduction in dependence upon atomic weapons as an instrument for international relations. Hopefully, we can take a step along that road by concluding a SALT II agreement that formalizes a relationship of strategic parity and reduces the political importance of strategic competition. Such a step should be followed, as quickly as possible, by efforts to reduce the destructive power of strategic forces, particularly of fixed ICBMS, and to extend the reach of arms control to include all nuclear weapons, not only strategic ones.

The general goals of reliable nuclear arms control are in fact moral goals: to prevent war, and to prevent as much suffering and damage as possible if war should occur. We must be realistic in our efforts to achieve these goals, but we must not forget that specific plans and actions are finally to be judged in moral terms.

* * *

Senator CHURCH. . . . Would you give us an estimate of the Soviet civilian defense program and its impact upon our effort to bring the nuclear arms race under control?

Mr. IKLÉ. . . . It seems to be true that a serious civilian effort is underway. It may have been underestimated by us and in some ways is puzzling, if not disturbing, going counter to what we thought the solution was with the ABM treaty and SALT.

On the other hand, we cannot be so positive about the possible effectiveness of civil defense with the enormous uncertainty of all our

experts about what nuclear weapons would do to man and society, to the ecology, to the food supplies, what have you.

It is possible that the civil defense program does reflect a difference in doctrines between us and the Soviet Union. Maybe—it is likely —you have to find a way of reaching arms control agreements that take into account different doctrines. Also, as I remarked earlier, there is a question of judgment—whether we ought to rely so much on the threat of killing people as a deterrent.

Concerns have been raised in this connection that the Soviet planners might plan an attack, reducing our nuclear forces or destroying most of them, and then count on recuperating from the damage that we could still inflict. Is the answer to that for us to try to kill more civilians? Or isn't the answer, rather, for us to try to get safer nuclear forces an enemy couldn't destroy, but which would maintain a continuing threat and which would, hence, take away from these imaginary planners the possibility of recuperating again? I would certainly lean to the second conclusion.

Senator CHURCH. I certainly agree with you in that. There are those who say with increasing certainty of assertion that the strategic forces of the Soviet Union, even within the agreements that we have heretofore reached, the SALT I agreement and the Vladivostok accords, have grown to a point where the Soviet Union has already achieved what is often called a meaningful strategic superiority over the United States; therefore, any further attempts to achieve a SALT II accord would make permanent this strategic superiority and thus work to the disadvantage of the security of this country. What do you have to say about this argument?

Mr. IKLÉ. I think, first, we should try to agree on the facts of the past. I don't think there is a disagreement on that. Over the last ten or fifteen years, there has been a massive deterioration in our capability in relationship to the Soviet capability. There has been a massive, revolutionary change. But we cannot conclude from that that the Russians are number one, we are number two, or vice versa. I think we shouldn't look at this like a ballgame where there is a score, where one is number one, the other number two. There are many balances we have to consider for different contingencies.

We have always been behind in some areas. Back in the 1950s, we regarded ourselves as being behind in conventional arms. In the past, we regarded our strategic nuclear arms as compensating for this imbalance in other areas. So as we move toward a more or less stable balance in nuclear arms, of course, we have to pay at little more attention to the conventional balance or imbalance that may exist.

Also, I think we cannot really, I feel as a personal judgment, that we shouldn't go around and ask ourselves are the Russians planning superiority? Are they planning a first strike? We don't know what they are planning in their innermost minds; but I think it is an uncertainty in their minds as well as ours, in their planning process.

What we do to restrain them, to induce them to move in the right path, will make the difference. If we just back out, then indeed they may rush forward and take over; but if we hold up our side, they would change their plans, I would hope.

* * *

Senator PELL. Why is it that we say it is OK not to be covered by arms limitations and not to have included in the SALT talks our own bombers in Europe which can reach the Soviet Union, but it is not OK for the Soviets to have their Backfire bombers which are incapable of reaching the United States on a round trip? I don't see the logic there.

Mr. IKLÉ. If you want to bring in regional weapons, medium bombers, you begin to look at a new and different balance where the numbers in most of these categories are larger on the Soviet side, like the 600 medium bombers. They have 600 medium-range ballistic missiles which we gave up in 1963. We wouldn't want to build one again. We don't want to get into new competition in these arms. But to the extent that new Soviet systems are being deployed, such as the Backfire, or ballistic missile, we have to consider what will balance this development; how we can maintain stability in a region which may be more important than the intercontinental stability.

If we don't want to be driven into building new medium bombers, new intermediate-range ballistic missiles, maybe we have to hold on, until we get some further arms control agreements, to things which are cheaper and easier. This may be an area where a cruise missile might have to play a role.

* * *

Senator PERCY. Dr. Iklé, you have warned about the dangers of a new round in the arms race, both in testimony before the Congress and in public statements. Yet this concern over Soviet intentions could actually spark a U.S. desire to accelerate Trident deployment, B–1 development, and the MX follow-on to the ICBM. This could also speed development of both the air-launched cruise missile and the submarine-launched cruise missile.

In your view, should we proceed at an accelerated pace with these weapons systems?

Mr. IKLÉ. We don't want to drive up our effort so much that we make it harder even to reach SALT agreements. This next SALT agreement is a follow-on agreement, so we want to proceed at a moderate pace.

I was involved when the current proposal was put together by President Ford on these programs. We had a consensus that this was the right path, taking into account the arms control side as well as the more unilateral security concerns that we have.

Senator PERCY. Should we increase our research and development funding for weapons development in an effort to insure against either a destruction capability or a technological edge on the part of the Soviet Union?

Mr. IKLÉ. In some areas I think we should, because this gives us the kind of constant monitoring, the potential enforcement of our arms control agreements; that we would have the technological capability in the very unfortunate event that agreements broke down, we could not compete and restore the balance.

For example, one thing that maintains the viability of the ABM treaty is that Soviet planners cannot and should not be able to count on developing a massive lead in research and technology which would then tempt them to give up the treaty at some point.

Senator PERCY. In the past, certainly all through the ABM debate, we talked about bargaining chips. Would the previously mentioned actions then—acceleration of new programs and research and development funding—further complicate negotiations or would they increase the incentive for the Soviets to negotiate?

Mr. IKLÉ. The systems you mentioned—Trident, B-1, MX—really are not affected by the SALT terms as envisioned under the Vladivostok accord. They are consistent with that outcome. That is why we decided to go ahead with it. That should make for a balanced position from which to negotiate, maybe reducing substantially the missile forces.

It has been said, in 1972, that we couldn't get equal numbers or lower numbers because we didn't have a program of our own. So we had no incentive for the Russians to agree to a different outcome. This is what you have to think about, without wasting money, of course.

PART TWO
Annotated Bibliography

Greenwood, Ted. "Reconnaissance and Arms Control." *Scientific American,* vol. 228, no. 2 (February 1973).

This article examines recent technical advances in photoreconnaissance satellite capabilities and concludes that existing U.S. national technical means of verification are adequate to monitor Soviet compliance with the SALT I agreements. The ABM treaty and interim agreement entailed primarily numerical limitations; the former, however, also placed limits on the testing of ABM components. Because SALT II will include restrictions on qualitative aspects of weapon systems and perhaps the testing of missiles, information derived from various land- and sea-based radars and sensors, as well as early-warning satellites, will have to supplement photoreconnaissance technology to assure adequate levels of verification.

Kahan, Jerome H. *Security in the Nuclear Age: Developing U.S. Strategic Arms Policy.* Washington, D.C.: Brookings Institution, 1975.

This volume provides a concise historical analysis of the development of U.S. nuclear strategy and weapon policies from 1953 to 1974. Kahan describes how policymakers came to accept the concepts of deterrence and invulnerability of retaliatory forces as central to American nuclear policy. Within these broad parameters, the evolution of doctrines governing the potential use of nuclear arms and weapon procurement are examined: "massive retaliation" under President Eisenhower, "assured destruction" (and a renewed emphasis on conventional means of defense) under Presidents Kennedy and Johnson, and "sufficiency" and the acceptance of parity under President Nixon. The author concludes by presenting an analysis of particular issues in the "great debate" of the 1970s over "the need to balance the important goal of seeking mutually stabilizing measures that can reduce nuclear costs and risks against the equally important objective of retaining the freedom and flexibility to pursue a national strategic policy consistent with our national objectives, alliance commitments, and worldwide political interests."

Lodal, Jan M. "Assuring Strategic Stability: An Alternate View." *Foreign Affairs*, vol. 54, no. 3 (April 1976).
Jan Lodal deals with many of the arguments put forth by Paul Nitze in the January 1976 issue of *Foreign Affairs* (below). Lodal writes that under the terms of the Vladivostok accord the United States would be free to increase the throw-weight of its missiles, deploy mobile ICBMS, and continue other force improvement programs. "Thus, as was the case with SALT I, the agreement probably imposes some real, although modest, limits on the Soviet strategic program, but imposes no operational limits on the U.S. program when compared with what we would have done without the agreement." While agreeing with Nitze that the Vladivostok accord will not reduce the threat to fixed land-based missiles, Lodal contends that threat stems not so much from missile throw-weight as from the increasing accuracy of warheads. Other options besides deploying mobile ICBMS are seen by the author as being more practical and less costly and less harmful to SALT.

Nitze, Paul H. "Assuring Strategic Stability in an Era of Détente." *Foreign Affairs*, vol. 54, no. 2 (January 1976).
The author, formerly the Defense Department representative on the SALT delegation, believes the Soviet Union is pursuing "a nuclear superiority that is not merely quantitative but designed to produce a theoretical war-winning capability." A treaty limiting offensive arms that incorporates the force levels of the Vladivostok accord would not, according to Nitze, address the most important measure of strategic power, namely, missile throw-weight. Soviet superiority in throw-weight, if exploited by improved accuracy and MIRVS, could eventually provide a theoretical war-winning capability to the Soviet Union. The author concludes that the United States should adopt a multiple launch-point system for deployment of more accurate mobile ICBMS in order to alleviate the threat to its main retaliatory force.

Pfaltzgraff, Robert L., Jr., and Jacquelyn K. Davis. *SALT II: Promise or Precipice?* Coral Gables, Florida: Center for Advanced International Studies, University of Miami, 1976.
The authors of this monograph provide a critical assessment of American negotiating objectives in SALT II. Of particular concern to Pfaltzgraff and Davis is the growing Soviet potential for launching a first strike against the Minuteman ICBM force. In addition to proposing various SALT provisions and unilateral actions the United States could take to alleviate the threat to Minuteman, the authors also examine the Backfire bomber–cruise missile controversy. Details of the January 1976 U.S. and Soviet compromise proposals to resolve this dispute are provided, together with an analysis of their implications for the strategic balance.

Pranger, Robert J., and Roger P. Labrie, eds. *Nuclear Strategy and National Security: Points of View.* Washington, D.C.: American Enterprise Institute, 1977.
This book of readings brings together official policy statements, congressional hearings, and analytical articles pertaining to the change in strategic nuclear targeting doctrine announced by Secretary of Defense James Schlesinger in January 1974. Among the topics covered are defense and foreign policy rationales for the change in doctrine, the vulnerability of fixed land-

based missiles, NATO's theater nuclear force posture, and civil defense. The implications of doctrine and strategy for weapon programs and SALT are also examined.

Wolfe, Thomas W. *The SALT Experience: Its Impact on U.S. and Soviet Strategic Policy and Decisionmaking.* Santa Monica, Calif.: Rand Corporation (R-1686-PR), September 1975.

This volume provides a comprehensive overview of the SALT negotiations from 1972 to 1975. Wolfe examines in detail the organizational arrangements of the U.S. and Soviet governments for dealing with SALT and related issues, as well as the institutions endemic to SALT, such as the delegations and the Standing Consultative Commission. The critical issues that arose in SALT II also are treated, together with the successes and failures of various summit meetings and back-channel negotiations. Wolfe concludes his study with an assessment of the Vladivostok accord and the impact of SALT on the nuclear arsenals and strategic doctrines of the two superpowers. With regard to doctrine, Wolfe writes: "If there has been any notable conceptual shift since SALT began, one might argue that it is to be found in revived U.S. interest in a counterforce doctrine, rather than in Soviet embrace of the mutual assured destruction rationale."

PART THREE

A New Approach to SALT

Overview

Roger P. Labrie

"We will move this year a step toward our ultimate goal—the elimination of all nuclear weapons from this earth." These words, spoken by President Jimmy Carter in his inaugural address on 20 January 1977, conveyed to the world the ambitious objective that would guide U.S. SALT policy under the new administration.

President Carter and many of his key advisers were dissatisfied with the negotiating history they inherited from the previous administration. Their new approach to SALT, unveiled during Secretary of State Vance's first trip to Moscow in March 1977, was predicated on different assumptions from those that had guided the policies of their predecessors. These assumptions concerned the contribution of arms control agreements to national security, the nature of U.S.-Soviet détente, and the role of nuclear weapons in the conduct of diplomacy and war. Presidents Nixon and Ford had valued SALT primarily for its political significance—namely, as a symbol of, and a contribution to, a broader policy of accommodation between East and West. President Carter, on the other hand, saw the SALT II negotiations as a historic opportunity to come to grips with the technological and doctrinal dynamics of the arms race. The new President's enthusiasm for SALT also reflected his concern over the pace and direction of technological advances in the years following the Vladivostok summit of 1974, as well as his deep-seated personal convictions about the moral and strategic implications of the nuclear arms race.

The architects of the Nixon-Ford approach had assumed that the early stages of the SALT process would yield few arms control dividends. With the exception of the ABM treaty in 1972, neither SALT I nor the Vladivostok accord had greatly constrained either country's

plans to deploy strategic arms.[1] Significant arms control agreements, according to this approach, would have to await a further lessening of mutual suspicions on the part of Washington and Moscow, and more positive signs that each was committed to a policy of peaceful accommodation in their many disputes.

Carter, on the other hand, believed that the trend toward ever more destabilizing weapon systems was outpacing, and perhaps even frustrating, the efforts of both countries to strengthen détente. In addition, the President viewed the potential contribution of arms control to national security as too important to be left a hostage to conflicting American and Soviet domestic and foreign policies. Even though relations between the two nuclear superpowers would continue to be characterized by competition as well as cooperation, the new President assumed that both countries could recognize an immediate mutual interest in limiting and even reducing the size and capabilities of their nuclear arsenals. A more aggressive approach to SALT, it was hoped, could minimize the chances that a clash of American and Soviet interests in some part of the world might escalate to nuclear war and, in addition, ease the path to bilateral cooperation on a broader range of issues.[2]

The new administration's approach to defense planning, especially for strategic arms, also showed signs of innovation. The strategic policy of the Ford administration had been to maintain a nuclear arsenal essentially equivalent to that of the Soviet Union, in terms of both the quantity of arms and their capabilities. Under a condition of essential equivalence, it was believed, neither country would perceive an advantage in using its nuclear weapons first in a crisis. Thus, ac-

---

[1] Recent assessments of the SALT I agreements can be found in David S. Sullivan, "The Legacy of SALT I: Soviet Deception and U.S. Retreat," *Strategic Review*, vol. 7, no. 1 (Winter 1979), pp. 26–41; and Raymond L. Garthoff, "SALT I: An Evaluation," *World Politics*, vol. 31, no. 1 (October 1978), pp. 1–25.

[2] Soviet attitudes toward, and objectives in, SALT remain the subjects of highly contentious debate. One view holds that the Soviets see SALT as the primary vehicle for establishing a status of parity with the United States in military power and maintaining a condition of stable mutual deterrence. Another school of thought claims that the Soviets have used SALT to neutralize or eliminate the most threatening strategic advantages of the United States while pursuing their own strategic programs—and gaining the resulting political benefits—within the "letter" of the agreements. The ABM treaty is often cited in support of both views. For the more benign viewpoint, see John Newhouse, *Cold Dawn: The Story of SALT* (New York: Holt, Rinehart and Winston, 1973); and Raymond L. Garthoff, "Mutual Deterrence and Strategic Arms Limitation in Soviet Policy," *International Security*, vol. 3, no. 1 (Summer 1978), pp. 112–147. A different point of view can be found in Colin S. Gray, "Détente, Arms Control and Strategy: Perspectives on SALT," *American Political Science Review*, vol. 70, no. 4 (December 1976), pp. 1242–1256; and Paul H. Nitze, "Assuring Strategic Stability in an Era of Détente," *Foreign Affairs*, vol. 54, no. 2 (January 1976), pp. 207–232.

cording to the Schlesinger strategy and former Secretary of Defense Donald Rumsfeld's subsequent elaboration, should SALT fail to constrain the emerging Soviet hard-target counterforce threat to the Minuteman ICBM force, the United States would have to acquire a similar capability against Soviet silo-based missiles. The Ford administration believed that this approach to SALT and strategic nuclear weapon planning would strengthen deterrence and reduce the potential for Soviet diplomatic coercion. In the event that deterrence failed and nuclear war occurred, the policy of essential equivalence called for targeting military and industrial facilities in order to prevent the Soviet Union from recovering more rapidly than the United States.[3]

President Carter's initial approach to SALT and defense planning reflected a somewhat different view of the role nuclear weapons should play in world politics and military strategy. The new administration was less certain of the political and military utility of nuclear arms than was its predecessor. Carter's defense and foreign policy spokesmen publicly questioned whether the Soviet Union could derive a diplomatic advantage from a theoretical capability to destroy a significant portion of the Minuteman force. They argued that, so long as the United States maintained a survivable retaliatory capability with sufficient flexibility and effectiveness against military and civilian targets, no rational Soviet leader would see any benefit in attacking the United States or its allies. While numerical essential equivalence was seen as politically desirable and obtainable through SALT, the new administration at first did not believe it necessary to match the Soviet Union's emerging hard-target counterforce capability in order to fulfill its basic policy of deterrence.[4]

[3] Major policy statements on the Schlesinger-Rumsfeld strategy can be found in Robert J. Pranger and Roger P. Labrie, eds., *Nuclear Strategy and National Security: Points of View* (Washington, D.C.: American Enterprise Institute, 1977).

[4] The Carter administration's approach to strategic weapon planning can be found in Harold Brown, *Department of Defense Annual Report, Fiscal Year 1979* (Washington, D.C., 2 February 1978), pp. 53–66; Harold Brown, *Department of Defense Annual Report, Fiscal Year 1980* (Washington, D.C., 25 January 1979), pp. 74–81; remarks of Secretary Brown before the Council on Foreign Relations and the Foreign Policy Association, New York, 5 April 1979, reprinted in Chapter 11; and Secretary Brown's commencement address at the U.S. Naval Academy, Annapolis, Maryland, 30 May 1979 (Office of the Assistant Secretary of Defense [Public Affairs], News Release No. 273-79). By early 1979, the administration's approach to nuclear weapon planning had undergone considerable change. Because of the failure of the SALT process to provide an adequate constraint on the Soviet hard-target counterforce threat, President Carter was faced with the decision of whether to deploy two new missile systems, MX and Trident II—each with improved capabilities for destroying Soviet silos—as replacements for a portion of the vulnerable Minuteman force. See George C. Wilson, " 'Counterforce' Arms Attract U.S., Soviets," *Washington Post*, 1 June 1979.

President Carter's new approach to SALT was to have a profound impact on the course of the negotiations. On the one hand, it was largely responsible for delaying, perhaps for as much as two years, the completion of a SALT II agreement. On the other hand, the treaty that was eventually signed proved to be more comprehensive, in terms of both its quantitative and its qualitative limitations, than the agreement nearing completion in early 1976. Similarly, the nuclear strategy and force posture of the United States will undergo significant changes in the years ahead as the administration's strategic planning concepts are translated into new weapon systems and operational doctrine.

The Moscow Talks, March 1977

The first attempt by the new administration to break the stalemate in the SALT negotiations came during Secretary of State Vance's first trip to Moscow in March 1977. Over the next twenty-seven months, eight additional high-level meetings and numerous backchannel negotiating sessions would be required before President Carter and General Secretary Brezhnev could meet in Vienna to sign the second strategic arms limitation treaty.

Vance put forth two new proposals during his first day of talks with Brezhnev and Foreign Minister Gromyko on 28 March. The first, and the one preferred by the United States, was called the "comprehensive" option. Under this proposal, both countries would reduce their strategic arsenals below the levels permitted by the Vladivostok accord (2,400 launchers, of which 1,320 could be MIRVed). In addition, the scope of the SALT II agreement would be broadened to include restrictions on qualitative improvements in strategic arms and specific limitations on those weapons of particular concern to the United States (Soviet heavy and MIRVED ICBMS) and the Soviet Union (American cruise missiles and the MX mobile ICBM). Vance's second proposal, known as the "deferral" option, called for completion of a much simpler treaty incorporating the Vladivostok force ceilings while deferring resolution of the contentious Backfire bomber–cruise missile issue for later negotiations. Brezhnev and Gromyko, on the other hand, urged that the negotiations continue within the framework established in Vladivostok and during subsequent talks with former Secretary of State Kissinger in January 1976.

Uppermost in the minds of the policy makers who drafted the comprehensive option was the projected vulnerability of the Minuteman force to the Soviet Union's increasingly accurate MIRVed ICBMS. A number of the option's provisions were specifically designed to alleviate this destabilizing threat. The most important of these were

a 50 percent reduction (from 308 to 150) in the number of modern heavy ICBMs the Soviets had been allowed to deploy under the SALT I interim agreement and the Vladivostok understanding, and a ceiling of 550 on each country's MIRVed ICBMs. This ceiling corresponded to the limit the United States had set for its own MIRVed Minuteman III force. In effect, these two provisions signified a return to the Nixon administration's original objective in SALT II of limiting the throw-weight and MIRV potential of Soviet land-based missiles. Under the comprehensive option, the U.S. land-based missile force would be left intact, while Soviet ICBM programs would be scaled back.

In order to impede the qualitative arms competition, the comprehensive option included limitations on the number of ICBM and SLBM test flights, together with a ban on modernization of existing ballistic missiles and deployment of new ones. The ban on new missiles would have prohibited deployment of mobile ICBMs such as the MX and the Soviet SS-16 then under development. The comprehensive option also included a range limit of 2,500 kilometers for all variations of cruise missiles, together with a provision for counting aircraft armed with long-range, air-launched cruise missiles (ALCMs) as MIRVed launchers. The Backfire bomber, on the other hand, would be exempt from the numerical limitations of the treaty provided the Soviets accepted certain restrictions on that aircraft's capabilities. All of these provisions would be included in a treaty limiting each country's strategic arsenal to an aggregate ceiling of no more than 1,800 to 2,000 launchers, 1,100 to 1,200 of which could be MIRVed.[5]

Neither the comprehensive nor the deferral option proved acceptable to the Soviet leadership, and Brezhnev and Gromyko offered no specific counterproposal as a basis for further bargaining. In a rare press conference following the conclusion of the talks, Gromyko characterized the comprehensive option as one-sided and detrimental to Soviet security. He also alleged that the United States was attempting to cast aside the Vladivostok accord in order to establish a new framework for SALT II. As for the deferral option, Gromyko

[5] Details of the March 1977 proposals can be found in Dr. Zbigniew Brzezinski's 1 April 1977 press conference and Secretary of Defense Harold Brown's 13 April 1977 remarks in Rochester, New York, both reprinted in Chapter 8. Even the far-reaching provisions of the comprehensive option may not have been sufficient to ensure the survivability of the Minuteman force. Secretary Brown has stated that "In our comprehensive SALT proposal . . . it was not the limits on numbers of launchers, but those on modifications, replacements, and total numbers of flight tests that offered the prospect of extending the survivability of Minuteman—and, even with that proposal, there would have been some question of the survivability of Minuteman. In short, Minuteman vulnerability was not a problem created by SALT, nor is it a problem we can solve with a SALT II agreement." See Brown, *Annual Report, Fiscal Year 1979*, p. 63.

maintained that it would have permitted unrestrained competition in cruise missiles, a competition, he claimed, that had been foreclosed by Presidents Ford and Brezhnev in Vladivostok. The agreement reached in Vladivostok, together with the principles agreed to in subsequent discussions with the Ford administration, were the only basis for negotiations, according to Gromyko, and any attempt by the United States to alter that basis could lead to the reopening of the issue of American forward-based systems in Europe that had been resolved in Vladivostok. Gromyko concluded his press conference with a denunciation of President Carter's outspoken stance on human rights violations in the Soviet Union.[6]

Despite the sharp public exchange of views that followed the Moscow talks, Vance and Gromyko agreed to continue their discussions in Geneva the following May. Both sides also agreed to establish "working groups" to study a variety of other arms control issues, such as conventional arms transfers, naval deployments in the Indian Ocean, antisatellite weapons, and a comprehensive ban on nuclear testing.

The Geneva Talks, May 1977

By the time Vance and Gromyko met again on 18 May, the acrimonious atmosphere that characterized their first encounter in Moscow had dissipated. The two-month interval between the talks had given both governments an opportunity to reexamine their last proposals and prepare new approaches. Despite President Carter's pledge following the Moscow talks to "hang tough" on his comprehensive and deferral options, and the Soviet government's equally adamant rejection of the new American proposals, Vance and Gromyko arrived in Geneva intent on reaching a compromise solution to the SALT stalemate.

After three days of discussions notably free of public diplomacy, Vance announced that an agreement had been reached on a new framework for the negotiations. In accordance with this framework—

[6] Foreign Minister Gromyko's press conference of 31 March 1977 is reprinted in Chapter 8. Apart from Moscow's unwillingness to accept any significant limitations on the hard-target counterforce potential of its ICBM force, another explanation for its rejection of the comprehensive option may be found in the rigidities of the Soviet bureaucracy and planned economy. In March 1977 the Soviet Union was well into a new Five Year Plan (1976–1980) whose strategic nuclear weapon programs "had been predicated on the levels allowed by the bilateral 'commitment'—as the Soviets saw it—under the 1974 Vladivostok accord." See Garthoff, "SALT I: An Evaluation," pp. 15–16. The provision in the comprehensive option banning deployment of new ballistic missiles also may have run into initial opposition from the Soviet Union's four missile design bureaus. See Walter Pincus, "SALT Missile Loophole," *Washington Post*, 7 January 1979.

the product of an American proposal—the SALT II agreement would consist of three "tiers," each incorporating some aspects of the Vladivostok understanding and the March comprehensive option. The first tier, a treaty lasting through the end of 1985, would include the aggregate launcher ceiling and MIRV limit established in Vladivostok. In addition, Vance proposed 10 percent reductions in the Vladivostok limits—from 2,400 to 2,160 for strategic launchers, and from 1,320 to 1,200 for MIRVs. Although Gromyko agreed to discuss a reduction of the aggregate launcher ceiling during the life of the treaty, he refused to consider any reduction of the MIRV limit or the ceiling of 308 on his country's heavy ICBMS. The second tier of the new agreement, a three-year protocol to the treaty, would include limitations on particular weapon systems (such as cruise missiles and mobile ICBMS), missile modernization, and new types of missiles. The third tier would be a joint statement of principles establishing a framework for future negotiations leading to a SALT III agreement. It was the Carter administration's hope that those elements of the comprehensive option that could not be included in the SALT II treaty and protocol would be subjects for discussion in SALT III.

With a framework for SALT II now in hand, Soviet and American negotiators resumed their meetings at the delegation level in Geneva and set about the task of filling in the details of the new package. While the delegations grappled with secondary issues related primarily to verification, policy makers in Washington and Moscow searched for new proposals to present at the next round of Vance-Gromyko talks scheduled for September. Officials in the Carter administration were still intent on finding some formula that would limit the size of each country's MIRVed missile force and, in particular, Soviet MIRVed ICBMS that posed the greatest threat to Minuteman. Another American objective was to inhibit improvements to the Soviet missile force.

Meanwhile, the administration announced two decisions concerning the strategic force posture of the United States. The first, made earlier in the year, was to upgrade the NS-20 guidance system on all 550 Minuteman IIIs and to deploy on 300 of them MK-12A reentry vehicles with new and more powerful warheads. These improvements to the Minuteman force would double the probability of each new warhead destroying a Soviet missile silo.[7] The second decision, an-

[7] See Bernard Weinraub, "Deployment of New U.S. Warhead Viewed as Major Step in Arms Race," *New York Times*, 1 June 1979. Each new warhead will have a yield of approximately 350 kilotons (as compared with 170 kilotons for current Minuteman III warheads) and an accuracy of 0.1 nautical mile (600 feet) CEP. See K. M. Tsipis, "The MX Missile: A Look Beyond the Obvious," *Technology Review*, May 1979.

nounced by the President on 30 June, was to cancel production of the B-1 bomber and to accelerate development of air-launched cruise missiles for deployment on B-52 bombers.

The B-1 decision generated a good deal of controversy on Capitol Hill. Extensive hearings were conducted by a number of congressional committees on the implications of the President's decision for SALT and the future of the Triad. Out of these hearings, a consensus emerged in Congress that a mixed force of penetrating bombers and cruise missile carriers should be maintained. Among the alternatives to the B-1 examined in those hearings were a "stretched" version of the FB-111 bomber and wide-body military transports or commercial aircraft to carry cruise missiles. Concern over the future viability of the "air-breathing" leg of the Triad also had the effect of focusing renewed attention on the growing vulnerability of the Minuteman force. On 15 September, Secretary of Defense Brown revealed that the Soviet Union was developing a new, fifth generation of ICBMS consisting of four missiles, in addition to its ongoing program for replacing older land-based missiles with MIRVed SS-17, SS-18, and SS-19 ICBMS. "Exactly why the Soviets are pushing so hard to improve their strategic nuclear capabilities is uncertain," said Brown. "What is certain is that we cannot ignore their efforts."[8]

The Washington Talks, September 1977

By the time Foreign Minister Gromyko visited Washington in late September for the third round of high-level talks, three issues had become of critical importance to the United States: range limitations on cruise missiles, restrictions on modernization of existing ballistic missiles and deployment of new ones, and the extent to which SALT II could alleviate the growing threat to silo-based missiles. Adding a sense of urgency to the negotiations was the scheduled expiration of the SALT I interim agreement on 3 October.

Gromyko's meetings with President Carter and Secretary Vance on 23 and 27 September produced another breakthrough. The United States resubmitted its earlier proposal to reduce the Vladivostok aggregate launcher ceiling from 2,400 to 2,160 prior to 1986 and, in addition, accepted the ceiling of 1,320 for all MIRVed launchers (including heavy bombers equipped with cruise missiles having a range exceeding 600 kilometers), provided Moscow would accept a subceiling of 1,200 for MIRVed ICBMS and SLBMS. Carter and Vance also

[8] Remarks of Secretary of Defense Harold Brown before the National Security Industrial Association, Washington, D.C., 15 September 1977. Office of the Assistant Secretary of Defense (Public Affairs), News Release No. 430-77.

proposed another subceiling of 800 for MIRVed ICBMS. Gromyko in turn proposed an aggregate launcher ceiling of 2,250 and a subceiling of 1,250 on MIRVed missiles. He also for the first time accepted the idea of an additional subceiling on MIRVed ICBMS, but proposed that the limit be set at 820. The United States then agreed to the subceiling of 820 and dropped an earlier proposal to limit Soviet modern heavy ICBMS (SS-9s and SS-18s) to 220. Thus, Moscow could retain its 308 heavy ICBMS allowed under the SALT I interim agreement and the Vladivostok accord while the United States, having no modern heavy missiles, would be prohibited from deploying any under the treaty.

Gromyko also gave his government's approval to an American plan for verifying compliance with the numerical limitations on MIRVed missile launchers. Under this three-part counting rule, all missiles of a type tested with MIRVS would be considered MIRVed missiles, regardless whether they were actually deployed with multiple warheads; all launchers of a type that housed a MIRVed missile would be counted as MIRVed launchers, regardless of the type of missile they contained; and certain launchers that resemble MIRVed launchers would be counted as MIRVed launchers. The third part of the counting rule applied specifically to 180 "look-alike" silos containing single-warhead SS-11 and MIRVed SS-19 ICBMS deployed together in two missile fields in the Ukraine. Because of the great difficulty in distinguishing between the two types of silos by satellite observation, Moscow agreed to count all 180 silos as MIRVed launchers. Both countries also agreed to ban rapid-reload ICBM launchers.

The Washington talks also yielded progress on a number of provisions in the SALT II protocol. Tentative agreements were reached on the following: a range limit of 2,500 kilometers for ALCMS; a range limit of 600 kilometers for deployed ground- and sea-launched cruise missiles (GLCMS and SLCMS); and a ban on testing and deployment of "new types" of ICBMS and SLBMS, with certain exemptions. The Soviets had originally wanted the range limits on cruise missiles in the treaty. In addition, Gromyko preferred a ban only on new types of MIRVed missiles, while Carter and Vance proposed banning new types of single- and multiple-warhead missiles. Both sides agreed that testing and deployment of ICBMS on mobile launchers would be proscribed for the duration of the protocol.

Lastly, major steps were taken toward resolving the Backfire bomber issue. The United States conditionally conceded that the Backfire would not be counted as a heavy bomber under the SALT II treaty unless it were equipped with long-range cruise missiles. In return, Gromyko submitted a draft letter stating that the capabilities

of the Backfire bomber would not be upgraded to those of a heavy bomber, and that the production rate of Backfires would not be increased. Although the United States considered the letter inadequate, the concessions made by both sides on this difficult issue were critical to the ultimate success of the negotiations.[9]

Despite this considerable progress, a number of important issues still remained unresolved. Among these were additional rules on verification, limitations on modernization of existing ballistic missiles, the number of exemptions that would be allowed in the ban on deployment of new types of missiles, restrictions on the transfer to third countries of technology limited by the treaty and protocol, and the creation of a common data base detailing the number of weapons in each country's strategic arsenal.

The success of the Washington talks generated considerable optimism that the SALT II agreement would be completed by the end of the year. An improved atmosphere now seemed to characterize Soviet-American relations, reflecting the progress in the SALT talks and in the negotiations with the Soviet Union and Britain on a comprehensive nuclear test ban treaty, as well as forward movement on other issues of mutual interest. At the end of September, Washington and Moscow announced that they would continue to abide by the terms of the soon-to-expire interim agreement on offensive arms while negotiations continued on the new treaty. Also, a U.S.-Soviet statement of principles, signed on 1 October, augured closer cooperation between the two countries on the problems of the Middle East.

The Negotiations Continue, 1978–1979

The Carter administration's philosophy toward arms control and defense planning, already evident in its March 1977 comprehensive SALT proposals and its decision to cancel the B-1 bomber, found further expression in the fiscal year 1979 defense budget. Although the administration did seek funding for most of the strategic weapon programs it inherited from the Ford administration—such as the improvements to the Minuteman force, the Trident submarine and SLBM, and cruise missiles—it postponed a decision to accelerate de-

[9] Additional information on the agreements reached during the Washington talks can be found in the following articles: Richard Burt, "Major Concessions By U.S. and Soviet on Arms Reported," *New York Times*, 11 October 1977; Murrey Marder, "A Compromise on SALT," *Washington Post*, 12 October 1977; Richard Burt, "Major Concessions on Cruise Missiles by Soviet Reported," *New York Times*, 18 November 1977; Strobe Talbott, "Who Conceded What to Whom," *Time*, 21 May 1979, p. 30; and Secretary of State Vance's briefing on 20 October 1977, in U.S. Congress, House of Representatives, Committee on International Relations, *Strategic Arms Limitation Talks*, 95th Cong., 1979, pp. 3–6.

velopment of the MX mobile ICBM, a weapon system favored by its predecessor and closely tied to SALT and the future of the Triad.

The suspended judgment on the MX reflected the administration's difficulties in translating its new approach to nuclear weapon planning into a coherent policy. The President's defense advisers were wrestling with a number of conflicting pressures. On the one hand, the SALT process had not succeeded in arresting the trend toward more destabilizing counterforce weapons in the American and Soviet strategic arsenals. Next, there was deep concern on the part of some administration officials over the projected vulnerability of the Minuteman force, with its unique capabilities for prompt and controlled responses against a wide range of targets. Finally, a growing number of Democrats and Republicans alike were calling for deployment of the MX without further delay, and for a more vigorous pursuit of the objectives embodied in the March 1977 comprehensive SALT proposals. Arrayed against these pressures were the improved hard-target counterforce capability of the MX, its more survivable yet less verifiable mobile basing modes, and its potentially adverse impact on the arms race. Moscow might respond by increasing the number of warheads on its missiles, thereby making ineffective any economically feasible mobile basing scheme.

In his annual report to Congress for fiscal year 1979, Secretary of Defense Brown acknowledged the dilemma facing the administration. Only "a small percentage" of U.S. silo-based missiles could be confidently expected to survive a Soviet first strike by the early- to mid-1980s, according to Brown.[10] The United States, therefore, had either to deploy the MX—in existing silos or in a mobile basing scheme—or to allow the growing vulnerability of the Minuteman force to degrade the retaliatory capability of the ICBM leg of the Triad. A decision to deploy the MX would require additional choices on the degree of mobility of the missile and its effectiveness against Soviet silos. Complicating these choices were a variety of other issues, rang-

[10] Brown, *Annual Report, Fiscal Year 1979*, p. 106. Increasingly pessimistic estimates of the vulnerability of the Minuteman force reflected recent improvements in Soviet missile accuracy. Flight tests of the SS-18 and SS-19 ICBMs in late 1977 and early 1978 revealed potential accuracies approaching 0.1 nautical mile (600 feet) CEPs. Achievement of such accuracies by these fourth generation ICBMS was reported to be three to five years ahead of previous Pentagon estimates. SS-18s and SS-19s currently deployed, however, are not equipped with the new post-boost vehicles used in these recent tests. U.S. intelligence projects that if they are so equipped, 90 percent of the Minuteman force could be vulnerable to destruction by only one-third to one-fourth of the Soviet Union's ICBM warhead inventory by 1982. See Clarence A. Robinson, Jr., "Soviets Boost ICBM Accuracy," *Aviation Week & Space Technology*, 3 April 1978, pp.14–16; and William Beecher, "Report on the National Scene: Excruciating SALT Options," *Astronautics and Aeronautics*, 8 October 1978, p. 8.

ing from the environmental impact of different mobile basing schemes to their compatibility with a verifiable SALT agreement. The latter issue pointed to an additional dilemma: a mobile deployment of the MX might lead to a similar decision on the part of the Soviets, with no guarantee that Moscow's mobile missile would lend itself to verification. Although Secretary Brown left open the possibility that the MX might enter full-scale engineering development later in the year, it was clear that he valued the new missile program more for its contribution to the survival of the ICBM force than for its ability to destroy Soviet silos.[11]

Moscow, April 1978. Prospects for an early completion of the SALT II agreement were dashed in the closing months of 1977 because of the technical and political complexities of the remaining issues. In the early months of 1978, new strains in U.S.-Soviet relations further complicated the negotiations. A Soviet airlift of arms and Cuban troops into Ethiopia, begun in November 1977 to aid that country in its war against invading forces from neighboring Somalia, by February had come to be viewed in Washington as a threat not only to peace in a strategically important region of the world but also to SALT. In scenes reminiscent of the Angola situation two years earlier, American officials publicly expressed concern over Communist intervention in third world disputes and at the same time struggled to insulate SALT from a new public debate over the value of détente. Critics of the administration's SALT policy had become increasingly outspoken since the last round of talks in September; with a potential crisis brewing on the Horn of Africa, some now advocated a suspension of the negotiations. Despite these mounting pressures, President Carter sent Secretary Vance to Moscow for another round of talks.

Vance's discussions with Brezhnev and Gromyko on 20–22 April touched on Africa but focused mainly on SALT. One of the issues on

[11] Brown, *Annual Report, Fiscal Year 1979*, pp. 106–107. The Ford administration recommended accelerating engineering development of the MX in its fiscal year 1978 budget. Former Secretary of Defense Rumsfeld was quite explicit in his application of the policy of essential equivalence to the land-based missile force: "Projections of Soviet ICBM capability indicate that a serious imbalance in missile hard target kill capability could develop in the mid-1980s if we fail to improve U.S. forces. . . . Deployment of MX in a more survivable mode would prevent the development of such an asymmetry." Rumsfeld added that "the United States should not accept a strategic relationship in which we must bear the heavier costs of alternative basing while the Soviets are allowed the luxury of retaining their fixed ICBMs. Since high accuracies can be built into mobile as well as fixed systems, the Soviet leadership should be aware that if the United States moves toward mobility, the Soviets will have strong incentives to go mobile as well." See Donald H. Rumsfeld, *Annual Defense Department Report, Fiscal Year 1978*, 17 January 1977, pp. 130 and 72.

which progress was made concerned the treaty's force ceilings. Both countries had agreed to lower the Vladivostok aggregate launcher ceiling during their last negotiating session in Washington. At that time, Gromyko had proposed a new ceiling of 2,250; President Carter had asked for a 10 percent reduction, from 2,400 to 2,160. In addition, the President had proposed a subceiling of 1,200 for MIRVed ICBM and SLBM launchers, while Gromyko had preferred 1,250. In Moscow, a compromise was reached whereby the aggregate launcher ceiling would be reduced to 2,250 on a date to be determined, while the subceiling on MIRVed missile launchers was set at 1,200.

Other issues proved less susceptible to solution. Since May 1977, Washington and Moscow had been exchanging ideas on a ban on testing and deployment of "new types" of ICBMs and SLBMs during the period of the protocol. Gromyko continued to press for a ban covering only MIRVed missiles. In effect, this could have impeded the MX program while allowing the Soviets to deploy a new solid-fuel, single-warhead replacement for their SS-11 ICBM. Vance rejected the proposal and informed Gromyko that, if there were to be any exemptions to the ban on new missiles, the United States must be allowed to deploy the MX with multiple warheads. Although no solution to this issue was reached, both sides did agree to permit one exemption to the ban on new SLBMs in the protocol. (New types of SLBMs were later exempted altogether from SALT II restrictions, except for a limit on warheads.) The "new types" issue was further complicated by a disagreement over the extent to which existing missiles could be modernized without being counted as new types.

A definition of cruise missile range also eluded agreement. Vance proposed that the definition allow for the zigzag flight path of the missile. Gromyko repeated his government's objection to the allowance. However, the foreign minister dropped his earlier objection to deployment of long-range ALCMs on aircraft other than heavy bombers.

Closely related to the limitations on cruise missiles was the issue of "noncircumvention." For months the Soviets had maintained that the treaty should explicitly prohibit the transfer of strategic nuclear weapons technology to third countries. Such a provision might prevent the United States from sharing cruise missile technology with its NATO allies and also interfere with American-British cooperation on delivery systems for nuclear weapons. During the talks in Moscow, Gromyko accepted a less restrictive provision barring both countries from taking any action that would circumvent the limitations of the treaty and protocol.

The last issue to be discussed in Moscow was the Backfire

bomber. Vance proposed that the Soviets include in their letter of assurance the following pledges: that the production rate of the bomber not be increased above its current level, that Backfires not be based in certain "forward" regions of the Soviet Union within easy striking distance of U.S. targets, and that the bombers not take part in training exercises simulating intercontinental missions. Gromyko rejected parts of Vance's proposal.[12]

New York and Washington, May 1978. Despite the controversy over the Horn of Africa, the Moscow talks had yielded some modest progress. There was forward movement on other arms control issues as well. A new compromise proposal on Mutual and Balanced Force Reduction (MBFR) in Europe, offered by the Western nations on 19 April, was matched by a counter-proposal from the Warsaw Pact on 8 June that took into account many of the West's demands. In early May, Washington announced that Moscow had agreed to commence negotiations on limiting conventional arms transfers, and that preliminary discussions with the Soviets on banning antisatellite weapons also would begin in Helsinki on 8 June.

SALT, however, continued to be plagued by events extraneous to the negotiations throughout the spring and summer of 1978. New frictions between Washington and Moscow were created by a rebel invasion of Zaire's Shaba province in early May and later by a string of arrests and trials in the United States and the Soviet Union. Washington began accusing Cuba, and indirectly the Soviet Union, of complicity in the Angola-based Katangan rebel invasion of Shaba, while Moscow denied the charges and in turn accused the United States of interference by supplying military transports to ferry French and Belgian troops into Zaire. Later in the month, FBI agents in New Jersey arrested two Russian employees of the United Nations on charges of attempting to buy secret information on U.S. antisubmarine warfare capabilities. The Soviets retaliated on 12 June by arresting an American businessman in Moscow for alleged currency violations. Later that same month, a Soviet television editor filed slander charges against two American journalists for their articles on Soviet dissidents.

---

[12] American and Soviet negotiating positions can be found in: Clarence A. Robinson, Jr., "SALT Stance Allows New Missiles," *Aviation Week & Space Technology*, 24 April 1978, pp. 16–19; Oswald Johnson, "Moscow Said to Yield Slightly in Arms Talks," *International Herald Tribune*, 25 April 1978; Richard Burt, "U.S. Accepts Plan By Soviet To Limit Planes and Missiles," *New York Times*, 4 May 1978; Murrey Marder, "Missile, Bomber Limit Accord Tentatively Reached," *Washington Post*, 5 May 1978; George C. Wilson, "Soviets Ease Up On Missile Role for U.S. Jets," *Washington Post*, 7 May 1978; and Richard Burt, "U.S. Offers To Alter Planes Carrying Cruise Missiles," *New York Times*, 8 May 1978.

Then, on 10 July, two days before Vance and Gromyko were to meet in Geneva for more talks on SALT, Soviet authorities put on trial two prominent dissidents—Anatoli Shcharanskiy, on charges of treason, and Alexander Ginzburg, for alleged anti-Soviet agitation and propaganda.[13]

In the midst of these controversies, Vance and Gromyko resumed their negotiations in New York on 25 May. Limitations on qualitative improvements of ICBMS and the ban on new types of ballistic missiles were at the heart of their discussions. Vance proposed a freeze on the fractionation of missile throw-weight. Under the proposal, an existing ICBM could not be tested or deployed with more warheads than the largest number previously tested on that type of missile. Thus, Soviet SS-17s, SS-18s, and SS-19s would be limited to four, ten, and six warheads respectively, while Minuteman IIIs would be frozen at seven (even though they were deployed with only three warheads). American negotiators believed such a freeze would prevent the Soviets from taking maximum advantage of the superior throw-weight of their ICBMS, thereby limiting the number of warheads that could be targeted against the Minuteman force or its successor.

Although Gromyko was noncommittal on the proposed freeze, he put on the table two similar proposals for cruise missiles. The first one would limit to twenty the number of ALCMS that could be carried by bombers, with a proviso that additional cruise missiles could be deployed on such aircraft if the latter were counted as more than one MIRVed launcher. Gromyko's second proposal was to prohibit cruise missiles armed with multiple warheads.

Two days later, the foreign minister met with President Carter at the White House and presented two proposals for banning new types of ICBMS. One would have allowed each country one exemption for a single-warhead missile and would have placed this provision in either the treaty or the protocol. The other option called for a ban without exemptions in the treaty. Under this second proposal, Moscow was offering not to test or deploy its planned single-warhead replacement for the SS-11 until 1986, in return for a similar commitment on the MX. Brushing aside both proposals, Carter lectured Gromyko on the adverse consequences for détente of the Cuban presence in Angola. As Gromyko left the White House, he told reporters that the President was misinformed about the role Cuba was alleged to have played in the Shaba invasion.

---

[13] Additional information on these events and their impact on SALT can be found in Joseph Kraft, "Letter From Moscow," *New Yorker*, 16 October 1978, pp. 110–139.

Vance formally rejected Gromyko's proposals to limit new types of ICBMs when they met again in New York the following week. While the United States was willing to consider a complete ban on deployment of new types under the treaty, it would not accept a ban that would prevent testing of the MX through 1985. American officials also were dismayed by the weak controls on missile modernization in Gromyko's proposals, since they would have done little to inhibit the Soviet Union's ongoing programs to improve the hard-target counterforce capabilities of its existing ICBMS.[14]

It was now evident that relations with the Soviet Union had deteriorated to a very low level, and, as a consequence, progress in SALT was being impeded. In remarks during an interview on 28 May, National Security Adviser Brzezinski cited examples of recent Soviet misconduct in Europe, the Middle East, Asia, and Africa to support his contention that Moscow was violating the "code of détente." The President's aide asserted that such a course of action should not be "cost-free." Brzezinski then went on to say that the United States and the Soviet Union were "close, very close, and in some ways quite far away" from successfully concluding the SALT negotiations. If Moscow were to accept the latest American proposals, he added, "we could have agreement within days. If they are not accepted, we will wait until they are accepted."[15]

Geneva, July 1978. The next round of talks between Vance and Gromyko took place in Geneva on 12 and 13 July. These negotiations were noteworthy not only because of the progress that was achieved but also because they occurred despite Moscow's decision to put on

---

[14] Accounts of the Vance-Gromyko talks, and the meeting with President Carter, can be found in: Richard Burt, "U.S. Says Soviet Snags Arms Talks by Demand on Cruise-Missile Curb," *New York Times*, 27 May 1978; Murrey Marder, "Carter, Gromyko Disagree Sharply On Africa Policy," *Washington Post*, 28 May 1978; Walter Pincus and Robert G. Kaiser, "U.S. Is Said to Reject Gromyko SALT Proposal," *Washington Post*, 3 June 1978; Richard Burt, "Vance and Gromyko Seek to Set New Arms Talks," *New York Times*, 6 July 1978; Kraft, "Letter From Moscow," p. 122; and Don Oberdorfer, "SALT Twist: Curb Qualitative Race," *Washington Post*, 12 May 1979.

[15] "Interview: National Security Adviser Brzezinski on 'Meet the Press,'" *Department of State Bulletin*, July 1978, p. 27. Excerpts from this interview are reprinted in Chapter 11. As if to confirm the impression that Brzezinski's remarks reflected administration policy, the *Washington Post* reported on 2 June that the administration had decided, for reasons of domestic politics and foreign policy, to delay any further progress in the SALT talks. See the article by Robert G. Kaiser and Walter Pincus entitled "White House Imposing Freeze on Strategic Arms Talks." For the text of President Carter's personal response to the *Post's* report, see "President: 'This Story . . . Is Totally Inaccurate,'" *Washington Post*, 3 June 1978.

trial Shcharanskiy and Ginzburg and the two American journalists just prior to the start of the talks.

The ban on new types of ICBMS was again the dominant issue in the negotiations. Vance suggested that both countries limit themselves to testing, but not deploying, one new MIRVed or single-warhead ICBM during the life of the treaty. This proposal would not have interfered with Washington's plans for the MX, since that missile was not expected to be ready for deployment until 1986 at the earliest. However, it would have blocked early deployment of Moscow's replacement for the SS-11. Gromyko rejected Vance's proposal and, in a reversal of the position he had taken during his meeting with President Carter on 27 May, said his government now was willing to accept an earlier American proposal to permit each country to test and deploy one new type of ICBM (with either single or multiple warheads) under the treaty. Vance and his aides viewed this as another breakthrough, even though Gromyko linked his new offer to Washington's acceptance of other Soviet proposals.

With a solution to the ban on new types of ICBMS now at hand, the negotiators turned to other matters. Gromyko offered another compromise: he would accept a freeze on the number of warheads on existing ICBMS if Vance would accept a limit of twenty ALCMS per bomber. Although the United States did not intend to deploy more than twenty ALCMS on its B-52s, Vance held out for a larger allotment in order to retain greater flexibility in designing a future fleet of cruise missile carriers.

Vance also informed Gromyko that the United States interpreted the draft text of the treaty as permitting deployment of ICBMS in a more survivable basing mode. What Vance had in mind was the multiple aimpoint (MAP) basing system the air force was considering for the MX. Under the MAP scheme, approximately 200 missiles would be enclosed in launch canisters and deployed in random "shell-game" fashion among 4,500 concrete-lined holes called vertical shelters. The Pentagon maintained that a missile deployed in the MAP system would be a mobile ICBM permitted under the treaty, albeit proscribed by the three-year protocol. While not rejecting this interpretation of the treaty, Gromyko expressed reservations about both the verifiability of the proposed deployment scheme and its compliance with the treaty's ban on construction of new, fixed, land-based missile launchers.

As the talks broke up on 13 July, Vance and Gromyko announced that their discussions had provided a basis for additional compromises on the remaining issues and that both sides should now reflect on the new ideas that had been presented. The two negotiators

also reaffirmed their determination to complete the treaty by the end of the year and said they would meet again in September.[16]

New York and Washington, September–October 1978. Prospects for completion of a SALT II treaty began to improve in late summer. The controversies over the invasion of Zaire and the trials in the Soviet Union were ebbing, and it seemed that the groundwork was in place for resolving the remaining arms issues.

In September, President Carter decided to encourage further progress in the talks for a comprehensive nuclear test ban treaty by modifying the U.S. negotiating position. The President instructed his negotiators to seek a three-year ban on nuclear testing rather than the five-year accord he had proposed in May. The five-year ban had encountered serious opposition on Capitol Hill, in the Pentagon, and in the Department of Energy's nuclear weapon labs, on the grounds that an agreement of that duration could put the reliability of existing nuclear warheads in doubt. A breakthrough in the talks was achieved earlier in the year when the United States, Britain, and the Soviet Union agreed in principle to allow seismic monitoring devices to be placed on each country's territory to facilitate verification.[17]

Before the next round of Vance-Gromyko talks, Arms Control and Disarmament Agency Director Warnke visited Moscow to give Soviet officials a preview of some new American proposals. One of these was an idea on how to resolve the dispute over the number of ALCMS to be allowed on bombers. Under this approach, an average number of cruise missiles would be permitted per bomber, with each aircraft counting as one MIRVed launcher. Warnke also explored the possibility of a ban on testing SLBMS capable of depressed trajectory flight, but the Soviets showed little interest. Such a ban could protect ICBMS from being "pinned down" by submarine-launched missiles and also enhance the survivability of bomber bases and early-warning radar stations located in coastal regions.

---

[16] Additional information on the July 1978 Geneva talks is contained in the following articles: William Beecher, "Abroad: A Proposal on SALT," *Boston Globe*, 13 July 1978; Bernard Gwertzman, "Vance and Gromyko Unable to Resolve Arms-Accord Issues," *New York Times*, 14 July 1978; Richard Burt, "Carter Deal Said to Win Military Over to Arms Treaty," *New York Times*, 14 July 1978; William Beecher, "Moscow Makes Offer on Missile," *Boston Globe*, 16 July 1978; and Richard Burt, "Soviet Objects to U.S. Missile Plan, Complicating Talks on Arms Pact," *New York Times*, 24 July 1978.

[17] See Don Oberdorfer, "U.S. Seeks A-Test Treaty of Three Years, Not Five," *Washington Post*, 5 October 1978. Moscow agreed in January 1979 to allow ten seismic monitoring stations on its territory. The negotiators still disagreed, however, on the type of stations that would be allowed and how they would be operated. See "Arms-Pact Concession Disclosed," *New York Times*, 26 January 1979.

Vance and Gromyko resumed their discussions in New York on 27 September, shortly after the conclusion of the Camp David Middle East summit. They focused on three issues: cruise missiles, new types of ICBMs and SLBMs, and Backfire bombers. At a White House meeting with President Carter on 30 September, Gromyko made a major concession on cruise missiles. In a surprise move, he withdrew his government's long-standing demand for a range limit of 2,500 kilometers on ALCMs, even though the United States had agreed in principle to such a limitation a year earlier. In place of the ALCM range limit, Gromyko submitted a new proposal on cruise missiles and reaffirmed two other proposals. The new proposal called for extending the duration of the 600 kilometer range limit on deployed GLCMs and SLCMs until 1986 by transferring this limitation from the protocol to the treaty. The other proposals were to subject cruise missiles armed with conventional warheads to the same range limitations and counting rules that would regulate nuclear-armed cruise missiles, and to apply a strict definition to cruise missile range with no allowance for the missile's irregular flight path. Vance replied that the United States would accept Moscow's range definition if Gromyko in turn agreed that the treaty would limit only nuclear-armed ALCMs. Washington was prepared, however, to accept range limitations on conventionally armed GLCMs and SLCMs in the protocol. The reasons behind this American approach were twofold: to avoid setting a precedent in the treaty for limiting nonnuclear weapons under SALT, and to preserve the option of deploying conventionally armed cruise missiles in Europe without any constraints after the protocol expired.

Progress was made on other issues. After much disagreement over whether submarine-launched ballistic missiles under development should be exempt from the ban on new types, both countries decided not to limit new SLBMs under the treaty. However, Gromyko accepted in principle an American proposal to limit the number of warheads that could be placed atop new types of ICBMs and SLBMs. A solution to the Backfire issue also seemed near when Moscow agreed not to increase the bomber's production rate and payload capacity; for its part, Washington declared that it would reserve the right to deploy a penetrating bomber of its own—comparable to Backfire—outside the treaty's aggregate launcher ceiling.

A number of other issues still stood in the way of a completed agreement. These included the schedule for dismantling Soviet launchers in excess of the reduced aggregate ceiling of 2,250, the duration of the protocol, and, most important of all, the limits on modernizing existing ICBMs under the new types provision. On this last issue, Vance and Gromyko continued to exchange ideas on a

formula that would require new or modernized existing ICBMS to be classified as new types if their basic characteristics (length, diameter, launch-weight, and throw-weight) were significantly different from ICBMS previously tested.

After the conclusion of the talks on 1 October, Vance told reporters that both sides now viewed the remaining major issues as parts of a package. "Until you reach agreement on all items," said Vance, "you don't have an agreement." The secretary of state also announced that he would be traveling to Moscow later in the month "to pick up the discussions there and see if we can conclude an agreement."[18]

Moscow, October 1978. The Moscow talks yielded less progress than Washington had anticipated. In fact, on one key issue there was actually a setback. While the Soviets now were willing to accept the averaging formula Warnke had proposed for resolving the cruise missile carrier aircraft issue (namely, permitting an average number of ALCMS per plane—the precise number was still in dispute), they withdrew their consent to the fractionation freeze on existing ICBMS. Gromyko pointed out that his earlier concession on the warhead freeze had been contingent on Vance agreeing to a fixed number of ALCMS per aircraft. More definite progress was made on another issue. Gromyko accepted an American proposal setting limits of ten and fourteen warheads respectively on new ICBMS and SLBMS. These limits corresponded to the largest number of warheads tested by either country on those kinds of missiles. Vance's delegation saw this as an important achievement, since it allowed the United States to deploy its new ICBM with as many warheads as the Soviets had on the SS-18, the largest of their heavy missiles.

Three other issues were discussed in Moscow. In order to comply with the reduced aggregate launcher ceiling in the treaty, the Soviets would have to dismantle approximately 250 strategic launch-

[18] Details of the September 1978 talks can be found in: Clarence A. Robinson, Jr., "U.S. Weighs New SALT Offer to Soviets," *Aviation Week & Space Technology*, 4 September 1978, pp. 24–26; Charles W. Corddry, "U.S. Brings Up New Issue for SALT II Talks," Baltimore *Sun*, 16 September 1978; Bernard Gwertzman, " 'Now-or-Never' Session of SALT Talks Approaches," *Washington Star*, 24 September 1978; Bernard Gwertzman, "U.S. Aides Clearly Pleased By Progress in SALT Talks," *Washington Star*, 2 October 1978; Robert G. Kaiser and Don Oberdorfer, "U.S. and Soviets Reported on Verge of SALT II Pact," *Washington Post*, 6 October 1978; Henry S. Bradsher, "SALT Narrows Down to a Few Sticky Issues," *Washington Star*, 15 October 1978; William Beecher, "Russians Offer New Proposal For SALT Pact," *Boston Globe*, 18 October 1978; and Don Oberdorfer, "Small but Mighty Missiles Cast Long Shadow on Negotiations," *Washington Post*, 13 May 1979.

ers. About 100 of these were to be dismantled in the first months of the treaty to comply with the initial ceiling of 2,400. At issue was the deadline for dismantling the remaining 150 launchers to reach the new ceiling of 2,250. Complicating this issue was the related question of the protocol's duration. As envisioned in May 1977, when the three-tier framework had been established, the protocol was to last for three years. However, because the negotiations were consuming more time than had been anticipated, the United States now preferred a shorter period for the protocol. Washington proposed that the protocol's expiration date and the deadline for Soviet compliance with the reduced aggregate launcher ceiling be on the same day, 31 December 1980. On the other hand, Moscow continued to press for a protocol lasting three years from the day the treaty was ratified. Moscow also preferred a deadline of mid-1982 for the dismantling of its excess launchers.

Lastly, a new problem had arisen on the sensitive issue of verification. On 29 July, the Soviets tested an SS-18 ICBM and encrypted the telemetry beamed from the missile and its "bus," from which warheads are released. Moscow had begun encrypting telemetry in 1974 but had terminated the practice following protests from Washington. Both countries intercepted telemetry from each other's missiles in order to determine their launch-weight, throw-weight, and other performance characteristics. Fearing that telemetry encryption could prevent the United States from monitoring Soviet missile tests to verify compliance with the limitations on new types of ICBMs and missile modernization, the intelligence community in Washington argued for a total ban on encryption. The Carter administration, however, decided to seek a less comprehensive prohibition since not all telemetry was related to performance characteristics limited by the treaty. During the talks in Moscow, Vance tried to get Gromyko to agree that some telemetry encryption could interfere with verification and should be banned by the treaty. Gromyko refused to be drawn into a detailed discussion of the issue.[19]

Geneva, December 1978. Disappointed by the little progress achieved in the Moscow talks, the Carter administration made it known that Vance and Gromyko would not meet again until the prospects for

[19] Information on the October 1978 Moscow talks can be found in: Don Oberdorfer, "U.S. Team Cautious on Arms Pact," *Washington Post*, 21 October 1978; Don Oberdorfer, "Moscow Talks Begin With Four Issues Pending," *Washington Post*, 22 October 1978; Richard Burt, "Hopes for Early Arms Accord Fade in Washington," *New York Times*, 7 November 1978; William Beecher, "U.S. Considers Plan to Monitor SALT," *Boston Globe*, 5 December 1978; and Talbott, "Who Conceded What to Whom," p. 31.

resolving the remaining issues had improved. In early December, Vance and Soviet Ambassador Dobrynin opened their own channel of negotiations in Washington and laid the groundwork for compromise solutions to several of the major outstanding issues. Confident that another round of high-level talks now might wrap up the treaty, the United States and the Soviet Union announced that their foreign ministers would meet again in Geneva on 21 and 22 December.

A week before the talks, Washington and Peking issued a surprise announcement that they would establish diplomatic relations on 1 January 1979. Believing that this action would not adversely affect the negotiations in Geneva, President Carter expressed his hope that the SALT summit could be held prior to the start of Chinese Vice Premier Deng Xiaoping's visit to the United States at the end of January. After receiving on 19 December what he described as a "very positive" message from Brezhnev, the President told the American people that "I can say without any doubt that our new relationship with China will not put any additional obstacles in the way of a successful SALT agreement."[20]

On arriving in Geneva, Gromyko sought to dampen speculation that he and Vance were on the verge of completing the treaty. "We do not foresee the conclusion of the agreement here," said the foreign minister. "We are here to contribute to the preparation of the conclusion."[21] Vance's arrival statement echoed Gromyko's caution. The secretary of state said that the purpose of the talks was to "find a mutually acceptable basis for a very early agreement." Vance added that, while he did not expect to initial a final text in Geneva, he did hope that this meeting would be his last with Gromyko on SALT II.[22]

A commentary from Tass, on 21 December, added another cloud of uncertainty over the talks. The Soviet news agency took issue with Carter's positive characterization of Brezhnev's letter of 19 December on normalization of American-Chinese relations. Tass reported that Brezhnev's letters also had included a warning that the Soviet Union "will most closely follow what the development of American-Chinese relations will be in practice and from this draw appropriate conclusions for Soviet policy."[23]

Despite these notes of caution, Vance's negotiating team was optimistic. In large part, this attitude stemmed from recent progress

---

[20] *Weekly Compilation of Presidential Documents*, 25 December 1978, p. 2276.

[21] See "Gromyko Doubts Talks Will Yield Arms Pact," *New York Times*, 21 December 1978.

[22] Department of State, Press Release No. 462, 21 December 1978.

[23] See David K. Shipler, "Soviet, Citing Its Note to Carter, Indicates Concern on China Ties," *New York Times*, 22 December 1978.

in the talks with Dobrynin and at the delegation level. Also, just a few weeks earlier, American negotiators had informed their Soviet counterparts that Washington was dropping its demand that conventionally armed cruise missiles be exempt from limitations in the treaty. Verification was the driving force behind this concession. The Pentagon, which previously advocated the exemption, had recently observed tests of ALCMS on Backfire bombers. The military now was concerned that the Soviet Union might take advantage of the exemption in the future and argue that the cruise missiles deployed on its Backfire bombers were not armed with nuclear warheads; consequently, the Backfires would not have to be counted as strategic launchers in the treaty. However, because the United States earlier had linked its acceptance of Moscow's strict definition of cruise missile range to Soviet acceptance of the treaty exemption for conventionally armed cruise missiles, the American concession on the exemption also meant that Washington now accepted the Soviet range definition.

More progress was made during the first two days of the Geneva talks. Gromyko gave Moscow's final approval to the fractionation freeze limiting the number of warheads on existing ICBMS. The Soviets, however, objected to allowing Minuteman III missiles to be deployed with up to seven warheads, the largest number tested on that type of missile. Since the Minuteman III had never been deployed with more than three warheads, the Soviets argued, the fractionation freeze for that missile should be set at three. Although Vance did not accept this argument, the issue was not seen as a serious impediment to completion of the treaty.

Vance and Gromyko then resumed their bargaining over cruise missiles and succeeded in narrowing their differences over the average number of ALCMS that would be allowed on bombers. Gromyko also raised two other issues. First, he asked that unarmed cruise missiles used for reconnaissance purposes be subject to the same limitations that applied to armed cruise missiles. The reason for this proposal was the difficulty in distinguishing between the two types of missile by national technical means of verification. Vance rejected the proposal. The second issue was one Vance considered already resolved: a ban on cruise missiles armed with multiple warheads. American negotiators had provided assurance earlier in the talks that the United States had no plans for deploying such systems during the period covered by the treaty. After discussing several other minor technical issues, Vance and Gromyko turned to the two remaining critical issues: missile modernization and telemetry encryption.

Limiting qualitative improvements on existing missiles had been a key feature of the Carter administration's March 1977 comprehen-

sive option. Serious negotiations on this issue, however, had not begun until April 1978, when Vance proposed that limits be placed on modifications of basic characteristics of ballistic missiles. According to the formula he proposed, any enlargement or reduction of an existing missile's physical dimensions, launch-weight, or throw-weight beyond 5 percent would require that missile to be classified as a "new type." Likewise, only new missiles with basic characteristics that differed by more than 5 percent from those on missiles previously tested would be counted as new types. A change in the number of stages on a missile's booster or any change of propellant, also would make a missile a new type. Gromyko had expressed reservations about some of the missile characteristics singled out by Vance during their meeting in April, but had agreed to them in principle—along with the 5 percent limits—during the next round of talks in May.

By the time Vance and Gromyko met in December, however, the tentative agreement on modernization had broken down. Earlier in the month, the Soviets had reaffirmed their acceptance of the 5 percent limit on enlarging missile characteristics but had withdrawn Gromyko's earlier approval of the 5 percent limit on "downsizing" in favor of no constraints on reducing characteristics. During the talks on 21–22 December, Gromyko offered still another proposal, this one calling for a limit of 20 percent on "downsizing." Vance continued to press for a 5 percent limit on reductions.

The encryption issue did not pose as serious a problem, at least to start with. Vance and Gromyko delegated to the heads of the SALT delegations the task of drafting a "common understanding" that would prohibit the use of encryption or any other techniques to conceal missile telemetry bearing on the limitations in the treaty. Vance supplemented this written understanding on 22 December with a statement referring to the SS-18 test the Soviets had encrypted in July. With the encryption issue apparently resolved and the completion of the treaty now within reach, Vance and Gromyko decided to extend their talks an additional day so they could receive further guidance from their governments on the remaining issues. Meanwhile, the White House alerted American television networks that an announcement of the completion of the SALT II negotiations might be forthcoming the next day.

When the talks resumed on 23 December, it quickly became evident that the treaty would not be completed. Both sides still could not agree on limits for missile modernization (Gromyko continued to insist on an allowance of 20 percent on "downsizing") and on the average number of ALCMs that could be deployed on bombers. In addition, the "common understanding" on encryption had failed to

win the complete approval of the intelligence community in Washington. Two days earlier, the Soviets had encrypted another test of their SS-18, and President Carter and his top advisers now feared the common understanding might not be sufficient to preclude future misunderstandings on this issue. Overnight, Vance had been instructed to deliver an amplifying statement explicitly identifying the July 1978 encryption incident as an example of the type of practice the United States would consider a violation of the treaty. Gromyko refused to accept the statement and informed Vance that the Kremlin would not complete plans for a SALT summit—which both governments had tentatively scheduled for mid-January—until all remaining issues had been resolved. With no quick solutions in sight, the Geneva talks came to an end.[24]

Weapons and Strategy. Prior to the resumption of high-level negotiations in February 1979, Secretary Brown presented to Congress the administration's fiscal year 1980 defense budget. In his annual report of 25 January accompanying the budget, Brown listed a number of Soviet strategic weapon programs underway, including deployment of MIRVed SS-17, SS-18, and SS-19 ICBMS at the rate of 125 a year; deployment of the new MIRVed SS-N-18 SLBM on Delta-class submarines; development of four new ICBMS and a new long-range bomber; and continued production of the Backfire bomber. (A week later, it was revealed that the Soviet Union had tested ALCMS with ranges up to 1,200 kilometers from a Backfire bomber.) The administration's new budget contained funding requests for continued development of the MX missile, improvements to the Minuteman III and B-52 bomber forces, an additional Trident submarine and missiles, antisatellite weapons, and a series of studies for a new bomber.

As in the previous year's budget, the administration postponed a decision on whether to proceed with full-scale development of the MX even though funds for such development were included in a supplemental request for the fiscal year 1979 budget. Ostensibly, the key factor in the delay was the absence of a suitable basing mode for the new missile. It was unclear to what extent the delay could be

[24] Information on the Geneva talks can be found in the following articles: Don Oberdorfer, "U.S. Soviet Agreement Is Seen on Arms Pact," *Washington Post*, 23 December 1978; Don Oberdorfer, "New Issues Bar SALT Agreement," *Washington Post*, 24 December 1978; Don Oberdorfer, "Unexpected Issues Dashed SALT Hopes," *Washington Post*, 25 December 1978; Kenneth H. Bacon, "Some Officials Think Soviets Are Stalling On SALT To Ponder U.S.-China Relations," *Wall Street Journal*, 26 December 1978; Richard Burt, "Arms Snag Linked to Demands By Soviet on New U.S. Missiles," *New York Times*, 28 December 1978; Pincus, "SALT Missile Loophole"; Don Oberdorfer, "The Heart of the Matter," *Washington Post*, 10 May 1979; and Talbott, "Who Conceded What to Whom," p. 34.

attributed to debate within the administration over the need for a missile with improved hard-target counterforce capabilities. The controversy over the basing mode, however, was directly related to verification of SALT.

In May 1978, the Pentagon's Defense Science Board had concluded that the best technical solution to the Minuteman vulnerability problem was to deploy the MX in the multiple aimpoint basing scheme, later renamed multiple protective structures (MPS). A White House advisory panel, however, subsequently recommended against MPS and in favor of an air-mobile basing concept utilizing special transport aircraft. In December, Secretary Brown instructed the air force to review its basing options and, in particular, restudy the cost and feasibility of an air-launched intercontinental ballistic missile. When the air force submitted its new recommendations at the end of March 1979, MPS was still its preferred basing mode. In a series of White House meetings in May, two additional options emerged for the President's consideration: a "hybrid" trench, mobile basing scheme (with up to 8,000 hardened launch points) for the MX; and deployment of a smaller common MX/Trident II missile in some existing Minuteman III silos and on Trident submarines. The hybrid trench would combine features of the MPS scheme (a multiplicity of hardened launchpoints and random dispersal) with others from the previously disfavored buried trench (simplicity and ease of verification). The common missile option, on the other hand, would entail greater reliance on the sea-based deterrent.[25]

Brown also used his fiscal year 1980 report to unveil a new "countervailing strategy" for America's strategic nuclear arsenal. The essential features of the strategy were identified as

> forces in sufficient numbers and quality so that they can: (1) survive a well-executed surprise attack; (2) react with the timing needed, both as to promptness and endurance, to assure the deliberation and control deemed necessary by the National Command Authorities (NCA); (3) penetrate any enemy defenses; and (4) destroy their designated targets.

In order to accomplish these objectives, Brown said that America's strategic force posture would require "redundancy and diversity . . . to

[25] See Richard Burt, "U.S. Weighs Halting MX Missile, Shifting to a Submarine Weapon," *New York Times*, 6 May 1979; Clarence A. Robinson, Jr., "Acceptable Basing Mode for MX Sought," *Aviation Week & Space Technology*, 21 May 1979, pp. 14–16; Richard Burt, "President Defends Mobile Missile Plan," *New York Times*, 30 May 1979; Wilson, "'Counterforce' Arms Attract U.S., Soviets"; and Norman Kempster, "Nuclear Missile Force Options Narrowed," *Los Angeles Times*, 1 June 1979.

ensure against the failure of any one component of the capability, to permit the cross targeting of key enemy facilities, and to complicate the enemy's defenses as well as his attack." The secretary of defense also noted that "survivable command-control-communications are equally essential if we are to respond appropriately to an enemy attack and have some chance of limiting the exchange." To support the latter objective, the new strategy called for weapons with high accuracy and reduced nuclear warhead yields, along with some civil defense protection for populations located near strategic weapon deployment sites.

Brown's report also examined some implications of the countervailing strategy for targeting doctrine and weapon capabilities. "To have a true countervailing strategy," said Brown, "our forces must be capable of covering, and being withheld from, a substantial list of targets." Although cities should not be excluded from such a list, he conceded that a strategy based on the assured destruction of Soviet urban centers "no longer is wholly credible." As a yardstick for judging the adequacy of U.S. hard-target destruction potential, Brown suggested an ability to "cover hard targets with at least one reliable warhead with substantial capability to destroy the target," together with "the retargeting capability necessary to permit reallocation of these warheads either to a smaller number of crucial hard targets, or to other targets on the list. Even with slow-reacting capabilities such as cruise missiles," Brown continued, "this would ensure that an enemy's silos are not a kind of sanctuary from which he can shoot with impunity." In addition to silos, Soviet general purpose forces deployed against NATO, command-control facilities, war reserve stocks, lines of communication, as well as war-related industries would be included as potential targets. "The strategy behind such a list is essentially defensive in nature," said Brown. The secretary concluded that current U.S. forces were "adequate" to fulfill the requirements of the new strategy.[26]

The Vance-Dobrynin Channel. At the conclusion of their last meeting in Geneva, Secretary of State Vance and Foreign Minister Gromyko

[26] Brown, *Annual Report, Fiscal Year 1980*, pp. 74–81. Secretary Brown elaborated on the countervailing strategy in his commencement address at the U.S. Naval Academy on 30 May 1979. After stating that a Soviet counterforce attack on the Minuteman force and other U.S. strategic bases "would kill millions of Americans," he added: "The Soviets would have to expect that we would retaliate accordingly. . . . We would not be limited to a massive attack on Soviet cities, we could retaliate against military targets." Implicit in these remarks, and in the annual report, is the requirement for a survivable second-strike counterforce capability.

had agreed that resolution of the issues still blocking completion of SALT II should be accomplished through regular diplomatic channels. Shortly thereafter, negotiations resumed at the delegation level in the Swiss capital. While modest progress was recorded in those talks, discussion of the major outstanding issues—the definition of new types of ICBMS and telemetry encryption—was reserved for Vance and Soviet Ambassador Dobrynin in Washington. It was not until Chinese Vice Premier Deng Xiaoping had concluded his talks with President Carter at the end of January 1979, however, that the Vance-Dobrynin channel was reopened.[27]

Vance and Dobrynin held their first negotiating session on 1 February at the State Department. The Soviet diplomat began the meeting with a statement expressing his government's displeasure over the use of the term "hegemony," a codeword for Soviet aggressive designs, in the Joint Press Communiqué issued by the United States and China earlier in the day. After Dobrynin was reassured that Washington would follow an even-handed policy toward the two Communist countries, he and Vance engaged in a general discussion of SALT.

The first substantive negotiation on major arms issues came on 13 February. Vance offered Dobrynin a deal on the definition of new types of ICBMS: if Moscow would accept the long-standing American proposal for a 5 percent limit on reductions of basic characteristics of missiles, Washington would agree to a ban on multiple warheads on cruise missiles. The Soviets had yet to budge from the position Gromyko had taken on new types during the Geneva talks of the previous December—Moscow could agree to limit increases in missile characteristics to 5 percent, but would not accept a similar limitation on "downsizing." Instead, it proposed a 20 percent limit on reductions of characteristics.

An event potentially disruptive to the negotiations occured on 17 February. On that day, Chinese armed forces launched a month-long border incursion into Vietnam, an ally of the Soviet Union. Peking announced that the purpose of the action was to "teach a lesson" to the Vietnamese, who had just concluded their own invasion

---

[27] Information on the negotiations at the delegation level and in the Vance-Dobrynin channel can be found in the following: Kevin Klose, "Soviets Ask U.S. to Clarify China Policy," *Washington Post*, 2 February 1979; Robert G. Kaiser, "Soviets Take Significant SALT Step," *Washington Post*, 2 March 1979; Don Oberdorfer, "Reds vs. Reds in Indochina: A New, Confusing Kind of War," *Washington Post* (Outlook), 1 April 1979; Don Oberdorfer, "Dobrynin Confers With Vance, Says SALT Very Close," *Washington Post*, 8 April 1979; Oberdorfer, "The Heart of the Matter"; "SALT II: And Now For the Battle," *Newsweek*, 21 May 1979, p. 36; and Talbott, "Who Conceded What to Whom," p. 35.

of Cambodia to overthrow that country's Chinese-backed government. When Dobrynin and Vance held another scheduled meeting on the 19th, the ambassador brought no response to Vance's latest proposal on new types. With the Soviet press alleging that the United States had acquiesced to the Chinese attack during Deng Xiaoping's visit to Washington, American officials began to fear that Moscow might stall the SALT talks until Peking's forces were withdrawn from Vietnam.

President Carter delivered his strongest endorsement yet of the emerging SALT II treaty in a speech at Georgia Tech the following day. The President made a special effort to convince the Kremlin, as well as his own domestic critics, that SALT was too important to be delayed on account of the war in Asia and a revolution in Iran. Many in the United States believed that the Soviet Union was encouraging turmoil in the Persian Gulf. In his speech, Carter declared:

> I cannot and I will not let the pressure of inevitable competition [with the Soviet Union] overwhelm possibilities for cooperation, any more than I will let cooperation blind us to the realities of competition, which we are fully prepared to meet. Because this carefully negotiated and responsible arms control agreement will make the world safer and more secure, it is in our national interest to pursue it, even as we continue competition with the Soviet Union elsewhere in the world. Therefore, I will seek both to conclude this new SALT agreement and to respond to any Soviet behavior which adversely affects our interests.[28]

The Soviet response to the President's speech came a week later. On 27 February, Dobrynin met again with Vance and this time the ambassador presented his government's first compromise proposal on a major issue in over two months. Dobrynin said he now could accept a limit of 10 percent on "downsizing" of ICBM characteristics. Although Vance rejected the new offer, it was seen by American officials as a sign that the Soviet leadership agreed with President Carter that the rivalry between the two countries should not interfere with SALT. Confirmation of this Soviet attitude came a few days later when General Secretary Brezhnev presented his own defense of the nearly completed treaty. Brezhnev told a Moscow audience that he looked forward to signing the treaty "during my meeting with President Carter, hopefully in the near future."[29]

---

[28] The text of President Carter's address at Georgia Tech on 20 February 1979 is reprinted in Chapter 11.

[29] Excerpts from General Secretary Brezhnev's speech are reprinted in Chapter 11.

The negotiations continued to yield progress during the first half of March. It was agreed that the expiration of the protocol and compliance with the treaty's reduced aggregate ceiling of 2,250 for all strategic launchers would take place on the same day—31 December 1981. In addition, Dobrynin informed Vance that the Backfire issue could be resolved on the basis of a letter Brezhnev would give to Carter when the two leaders met at the summit to sign the treaty. That letter was to contain assurances that the production rate of the Backfire would not be increased beyond its current level—thirty per year—and that the bomber would not be upgraded to perform the mission of a heavy bomber. Vance and Dobrynin also agreed that no more than twenty ALCMS could be deployed on each existing heavy bomber, while other aircraft would be permitted to carry an average of twenty-eight cruise missiles.

The pace of the negotiations quickened even as Washington and Moscow continued to compete for influence in the Middle East. In early March, the United States dispatched military aid to North Yemen after Communist-backed South Yemen staged a series of border raids. Moscow, meanwhile, joined with radical Arab nations in denouncing the Egyptian-Israeli peace treaty that had just been completed with the help of President Carter's personal mediation. Despite this continuing rivalry, the Vance-Dobrynin channel remained open, with the negotiators at times meeting on a daily basis. On 18 March, Vance confidently announced that "the bitter end" of the negotiations was at hand and that he and Dobrynin were "very close to completing" the treaty.[30]

Vance's prediction proved to be premature. The disputes over a definition of new types of ICBMS and telemetry encryption still had not been settled. Verification of any solution to these issues had become a more complex and serious problem for the United States. In January, American technicians had begun dismantling most of their electronic monitoring stations in Iran after it became apparent that the shah would succumb to revolutionary forces. The stations were important links in a vast network of intelligence-gathering facilities that monitored Soviet military activities.

Two stations were kept in operation after the shah was deposed in mid-January. Known as Detachment 5 and Kabkan, these installations were important primarily for their unique locations for monitoring Soviet compliance with existing and future SALT agreements. Kabkan was geographically situated for "line-of-sight" observation of the Soviet Union's main ICBM test facility at Tyuratam, 800 miles to

[30] "Interview on 'Face the Nation,'" *Department of State Bulletin*, May 1979, p. 41.

the north. Telemetry from the early states of a missile's flight was recorded at Kabkan and provided important data for assessing Soviet compliance with the limitations on new types of ICBMs and telemetry encryption. Other monitoring stations in Iran could observe Soviet cruise missile and intermediate-range ballistic missile tests in the region between Kapustin Yar and Sary Shagan farther to the north.

By the beginning of March, all American monitoring stations in Iran had been either dismantled or abandoned. Compounding the concern over the loss of these stations was the compromise of another link in the verification chain, the KH-11 photoreconnaissance satellite. In early 1978, a technical manual detailing the capabilities of the KH-11 had fallen into the hands of Soviet agents. To compensate for these intelligence setbacks, the Carter administration began planning to equip U-2 spy planes with special antennas to monitor Soviet activities while flying over Turkey, where other American listening posts are located. Other plans called for reprogramming an existing satellite and a radar station in Norway to intercept telemetry from Soviet missiles; a new satellite to perform this function could be available by the mid-1980s.[31]

The "new types" and encryption issues were finally resolved in early April. The solution to the telemetry issue resulted from an exchange of letters between Carter and Brezhnev. The correspondence was intended to establish a common understanding on the types of telemetry that should not be encrypted because of their bearing on limitations in the treaty. In his first letter, the President specifically cited two cases where telemetry from SS-18 test flights had been encrypted—on 29 July and 21 December 1978. Carter told the Soviet leader that a repetition of the extensive encryption used on those tests would be considered a violation of the treaty's ban on deliberate concealment measures. Brezhnev's response was ambiguous; while not rejecting the President's position, Brezhnev objected to the reference to specific missile tests in the letter. He also challenged Carter to state specifically which channels of telemetry the United States

[31] On the location and functions of Detachment 5 and Kabkan, see Charles W. Corddry, "U.S. Intelligence Is Set Back by Loss of Last Iran Spy Site," Baltimore *Sun*, 2 March 1979; and John K. Cooley, "US 'Ears' in Iran Were Vital to Arms Limits," *Christian Science Monitor*, 5 March 1979. For contrasting views on the importance of the bases in Iran for SALT verification, see Hedrick Smith, "U.S. Aides Say Loss of Post in Iran Impairs Missile-Monitoring Ability," *New York Times*, 2 March 1979; and Herbert Scoville, Jr., "SALT Verification and Iran," *Arms Control Today*, vol. 9, no. 2 (February 1979). On plans to compensate for the bases in Iran, see Richard Burt, "U.S. May Use Modified U-2 Plane to Monitor Soviet Missile Testing," *New York Times*, 4 April 1979; Philip J. Klass, "U.S. Monitoring Capability Impaired," *Aviation Week & Space Technology*, 14 May 1979, p. 18; and Richard Burt, "U.S. Plans New Way to Check Soviet Missile Tests," *New York Times*, 29 June 1979.

thought should be free of encryption. On 29 March, Vance handed Dobrynin another letter from the President, along with a separate note that again cited the July and December tests. Vance also restated the American position on the definition of new types of ICBMS.

Carter's second letter and the side note were successful. On 7 April, Dobrynin returned to the State Department and informed Vance that the Soviet government considered the encryption issue resolved on the basis of the written exchanges between the two heads of state. During that same meeting, Dobrynin also accepted the 5 percent limit on "downsizing." Thus, any ICBM with basic characteristics that differed from those of existing missiles by more than 5 percent, or with a different number of stages or a different propellant, would be classified as a "new type." In accordance with an earlier agreement, neither country would be allowed to deploy more than one new type of ICBM prior to 1986. At the conclusion of his meeting with Vance, Dobrynin told reporters that the treaty now was "very close" to completion.

The controversy over the loss of the monitoring stations in Iran grew more acute in mid-April after secret congressional testimony by CIA Director Stansfield Turner was leaked to the press. According to the *New York Times*, Turner told the Senate Intelligence Committee that the monitoring capability lost in Iran could not be fully restored until 1984. Secretary of Defense Brown immediately sought to clarify Turner's testimony. Brown told the press that the United States would be capable of "regaining enough" of the monitoring capability that had been lost to "adequately" verify Soviet compliance with SALT II in "about a year." President Carter also tried to allay concern over the adequacy of American monitoring capability when he told a press conference on 30 April that "I would not sign nor present to the Congress or to the American people any treaty which in my opinion could not be adequately verified from the first day it's effective." Carter also stated that he "would do all I could, monitoring very closely Soviet activities, to comply with the basic agreements reached" even if the Senate failed to ratify the new treaty.[32]

The final details of the treaty were resolved during the first week of May. Again, the most serious problem centered on procedures used by the Soviets in testing their missiles. During two tests of the SS-18—on 21 and 26 December 1978—warhead dispensing mechanisms were observed to have performed more than ten release maneuv-

[32] For Turner's testimony, see Hedrick Smith, "Turner Sees Delay on Monitoring Sites," *New York Times*, 17 April 1979. The text of Secretary Brown's statement can be found in Bernard Gwertzman, "Brown Sees Pact To Curtail Arms Verifiable by '80," *New York Times*, 18 April 1979. For Carter's remarks, see *Weekly Compilation of Presidential Documents*, 7 May 1979, pp. 749–750.

ers. Under the fractionation freeze agreed to in December 1978, the SS-18 was to be prohibited from carrying more than ten warheads. Although no more than ten dummy warheads had been released during the tests in question, intelligence officials in Washington suspected that the additional maneuvers might allow the Soviets to violate the warhead freeze once the treaty was in effect. To add to the sensitivity of the issue, the United States had employed similar procedures for testing decoy warheads on some of its own missiles.

Following a series of intensive discussions, Vance and Dobrynin arrived at an agreement. Additional release maneuvers beyond the maximum number of warheads allowed on a missile type would be permitted provided they were clearly distinguishable as releases for decoys. As an added precaution, significant reductions in the weight of warheads already tested would be prohibited. This would safeguard against surreptitious deployment of additional warheads without having to increase the throw-weight of the missile.

Only one issue of consequence now remained. Moscow wanted a formal statement that the United States would not deploy more than three warheads on its Minuteman III ICBM. Because that missile had been tested with seven warheads, that many could legally be deployed under the fractionation freeze. Even though American negotiators had assured the Soviets that there were no plans to increase the number of warheads on the missile, Dobrynin continued to press for a formal statement on the question. Vance finally agreed to provide the statement during their twenty-fifth meeting of the year on 7 May. Two days later, Vance announced the conclusion of the negotiations, and on 11 May the White House and the Kremiln announced that President Carter and General Secretary Brezhnev would meet in Vienna the following month to sign the SALT II agreements.

Strategy and the MX Missile. Following a series of meetings during the last part of May and the first week of June, during which President Carter and his top national security advisers assessed the trends in the strategic relationship with the Soviet Union, the White House announced on 8 June the President's decision to proceed with full-scale development of the MX missile. Carter's action set in motion a plan to deploy 200 of the new missiles in a land-mobile basing mode at a cost of approximately $30 billion. Following the completion of the testing program for the MX—which could not begin until the protocol ban on testing mobile ICBM systems expired at the end of 1981—deployment of the missile would begin in 1986 and be completed by the end of the decade. Although no final decision was made on exactly how the MX would be deployed, it seemed likely that the

President would accept the Pentagon's plan for the "hybrid" trench basing mode. This scheme was seen as more compatible with the requirements for SALT verification than other basing modes considered, such as MPS.[33]

The MX decision actually was part of a broader plan to improve the capability of U.S. strategic forces to destroy hardened military and industrial targets. Along with the MX, the United States was pursuing other counterforce weapon programs. These included more powerful warheads and improved accuracy for the majority of the Minuteman III force, cruise missiles, and the Trident II SLBM.[34] After more than two years of analysis and SALT negotiations, it seemed the Carter administration had returned to the strategic force planning concepts of the Ford administration.

President Carter had defended the option of deploying the MX during a press conference on 29 May. Carter stated that "the most destablizing thing that we could have in our strategic relationship with the Soviets would be acknowledged inferiority or a vulnerable strategic deployment of missiles." Despite the modest success of the SALT negotiations in limiting the growth of strategic arsenals, the President had concluded that, in addition to maintaining "an adequate level of armaments . . . we must maintain the security from attack of the armaments we have. So when we do deploy new types of missiles to stay current and to keep our equivalency with the Soviet Union, that, in my opinion contributes to peace."[35]

Secretary of Defense Brown provided a more detailed rationale for the MX in a speech at the U.S. Naval Academy, in Annapolis, Maryland, the following day. Brown stated that the driving forces behind mobile basing of strategic arms lay in the progression of offensive weapons technology and a conscious strategic policy on the part of the Soviet Union. "As early as 1962–1963," said Brown, "the Soviets had a policy of building forces for preemptive attack of U.S. ICBMS." Because of the direction both countries were imposing on technology, "we and the Soviet Union are reaching a period in which

---

[33] On how the MX decision was made, see Vernon A. Guidry, Jr., "Next Missile Step Is Deployment," *Washington Star*, 26 June 1979; and Vernon A. Guidry, Jr., "Decision on MX Set Up a New Hard Choice," *Washington Star*, 27 June 1979. An analysis of the cost and feasibility of various mobile basing modes for ICBMS, and of the missile options considered by the Carter administration, can be found in Congressional Budget Office, *The MX Missile and Multiple Protective Structure Basing: Long-Term Budgetary Implications*, Budget Issue Paper for Fiscal Year 1980 (June 1979).

[34] See George C. Wilson, "U.S. Missile Accuracy Predicted High by 1990s," *Washington Post*, 22 June 1979.

[35] *Weekly Compilation of Presidential Documents*, 4 June 1979, p. 966.

each can successfully target the other's hardened fixed systems more cheaply than either can further harden its systems to make them survivable. It is this reality that drives us to non-fixed ballistic missile basing." Another rationale for the MX program, linked to the next round of SALT, also was discernible in Brown's remarks: "Future reductions of Soviet forces . . . will require us to have force expansion options of our own. This will provide the Soviets an incentive for mutual reductions through negotiations—negotiations in which we too will have to forgo something. Our phasing of new systems, then, must reflect how further balanced reductions of strategic weaponry may occur."[36] Implicit in the secretary of defense's statement was that the size of the MX deployment could be reduced if Moscow would agree to more drastic reductions in its strategic arsenal in SALT III.

The Vienna Summit, June 1979

The SALT agreements that were signed by President Carter and General Secretary Brezhnev were the result of over six and one-half years of negotiations. Three successive American administrations had labored to produce a set of documents that was remarkable in its breadth and detail. As the two leaders arrived in the Austrian capital for the first summit meeting in almost four years between the heads of state of the most powerful nations on earth, it appeared that all of the many issues that composed SALT II had been resolved. The summit itself seemed anticlimactic.

In the interval between Vance's announcement of the conclusion of the negotiations on 9 May and the start of the summit on 16 June, the Soviet and American SALT delegations meeting in Geneva had worked hard to translate into treaty language the agreements that had been reached in the Vance-Dobrynin channel. Other technical details also were resolved by the two delegations. One issue, however, led to intensive discussions.[37]

---

[36] Office of the Assistant Secretary of Defense (Public Affairs), News Release No. 273-79, 30 May 1979.

[37] Accounts of the final negotiations at the delegation level and at the Vienna summit can be found in the following: Vernon A. Guidry, Jr., "Single Issue Stands in Way of Wrapping Up SALT Treaty," *Washington Star*, 8 June 1979; Don Oberdorfer, "U.S., Soviets Argue About Arms Budgets," *Washington Post*, 17 June 1979; Vernon A. Guidry, Jr., "Next SALT Round Outlook Cloudy," *Washington Star*, 18 June 1979; Press briefing by Press Secretary Jody Powell, Ambassador Ralph Earle, and others, 18 June 1979 (Office of the White House Press Secretary); Don Oberdorfer, "Vienna Summit: More an Exploration of Positions Than a Meeting of the Minds," *Washington Post*, 23 June 1979; and Martin Schram, "Vienna: Bomber Issue Gave Carter His Baptism in Summitry," *Washington Post*, 24 June 1979.

Soviet negotiators asked for an exception to the 5 percent limit on "downsizing" of the launch-weight and throw-weight of ICBMS so that missiles could be tested with fewer warheads than the maximum numbers permitted by the fractionation freeze. Some American officials saw this request as a potential loophole in the provision limiting new types of ICBMS. The United States eventually accepted the Soviet request since it had already conducted such tests with some of its own missiles and might want to do so again in the future. Both sides agreed that any decrease in the launch-weight or throw-weight of an ICBM must result solely from a reduction in the number of warheads tested. On 14 June, Ralph Earle and Victor Karpov, the chairmen of the American and Soviet SALT delegations, initialed the texts of the treaty and associated documents and brought them to Vienna.

The first day of formal talks at the Vienna summit, 16 June, was devoted to SALT and an overview of the global situation. The two leaders reviewed a number of provisions in the treaty and protocol, and restated some of the key understandings that had been reached in the negotiations. Carter reaffirmed that the protocol would expire on 31 December 1981 and that it should not be considered a precedent for future limitations on the weapons it covered. Brezhnev warned the President that any basing mode for the MX missile that did not lend itself to verification by national technical means would seriously jeopardize future SALT negotiations. While the discussion of these issues produced no surprises, the exchange of views on the Backfire bomber did not go as planned.

According to the agenda both sides had agreed to prior to the summit, Brezhnev was to have given the President a written statement containing assurances that the production rate of the Backfire bomber would not be increased above its current level. Carter then was to have handed the Soviet leader another written statement saying that it was the understanding of the United States that the current production rate was thirty per year. Brezhnev was to have concluded the exchange by confirming the American understanding.

When the two leaders met on the afternoon of 16 June, Carter decided not to give to Brezhnev the written American statement. Instead, the President conveyed orally the contents of the statement, and Brezhnev in turn gave Carter the written Soviet statement. Only after the meeting ended did the American delegation realize that Brezhnev had not confirmed the U.S. understanding on the Backfire's current production rate.

Carter and Brezhnev spent most of their second day of talks exchanging ideas on possible topics for SALT III. Carter expressed his

desire for more drastic numerical reductions and qualitative limitations of strategic arsenals. He also suggested that methods of verification be broadened to include additional cooperative measures and possibly on-site inspection. Future limits on air defense systems, civil defense, and depressed trajectory SLBMS were other topics discussed by the President. The creation of "safe havens" for ballistic missile submarines, to assure the invulnerability of these weapons, was another issue mentioned by Carter. As an inducement to continued progress in the SALT talks, the President also told Brezhnev that the United States was prepared to discuss further reductions in the numerical ceilings in SALT II prior to the expiration of the treaty. The Soviet leader, for his part, stressed the need for limitations on long-range, theater nuclear delivery systems in Europe—including American forward-based systems—in the next SALT treaty.

Carter returned to the Backfire issue later in the day. The President reminded Brezhnev that it had been agreed before the summit that he would confirm the American understanding on the Backfire's production rate. Following what was described as an "interesting and lively discussion," Brezhnev told Carter that the Backfire bomber was currently being produced at the rate of thirty per year.

The SALT II treaty was finally signed on 18 June 1979. "In signing this treaty," said Brezhnev, "we are helping to defend the most sacred right of every individual—the right to live." President Carter responded by noting that the Strategic Arms Limitation Talks, which had begun nearly ten years earlier, had not yet brought to an end the nuclear arms race between the two superpowers. Without SALT II, Carter declared, "an unrestrained competition would tempt fate in the future and would insult our intelligence and threaten the very existence of humanity. This prospect is a challenge to our courage and to our creativity. If we cannot control the power to destroy," the President concluded, "we can neither guide our fate nor preserve our own future."[38]

---

[38] Exchange of remarks between President Carter and General Secretary Brezhnev upon signing the SALT II treaty, 18 June 1979 (Office of the White House Press Secretary).

8

The Moscow Talks, March 1977

Carter Discusses SALT and Human Rights, February and March 1977

WASHINGTON, 8 FEBRUARY 1977*

Q. Mr. President, . . . could you tell us, sir, do you believe that there should be a rough parity between the nuclear forces of the Soviet Union and the United States? Do you think we ought to, in the arms negotiations, strive for superior force, or do you believe that as long as we have the ability to inflict horrendous damage on them that it really doesn't matter which side has the most bombs?

President CARTER. At the present time, my judgment is that we have superior nuclear capability. The Soviet Union has more throw-weight, larger missiles, larger warheads; we have more missiles, a much higher degree of accuracy, and also, we have three different mechanisms which are each independently adequate to deliver atomic weapons—airplanes, submarines, and intercontinental ballistic missiles. I think that we are roughly equivalent, even though I think we are superior, in that either the Soviet Union or we could destroy a major part of the other nation if a major attack was made, with losses in the neighborhood of fifty to one hundred million people if a large exchange was initiated.

We have the capability, as do the Soviets, to detect the launching of opposing missiles, and then I, as President, and the leaders in Russia would have to be faced with the question of how much of a retaliatory attack to make. But in the exchange, tens of millions of people would be killed. And the threat of this kind of holocaust is what makes it important that we do keep an adequate deterrent capability. And it also is crucial for all of us to remember that it is necessary to have drastic reduction in dependence on atomic weapons.

---

* SOURCE: Press conference of President Jimmy Carter. *Weekly Compilation of Presidential Documents,* 14 February 1977, pp. 155–160.

Almost every major speech that I have made since I have been involved in national politics, I expressed—committed, first, to stabilize the situation; second, to have demonstrable reductions in dependence upon atomic weapons and set as our committed long-range goal complete elimination of nuclear weapons from the earth....

If we and the Soviet Union can demonstrate an ability to stop the present growth and then to have substantial reductions, I believe, then, we can go to the French, British, the Chinese, and others and say, "Would you join us in stopping testing and in moving in clearly monitorable ways to reduce dependence on atomic weapons?"

Q. . . . You said that you thought that each of the two countries, ourselves and the Soviets, might have to take some initiatives. Now, I am trying to translate that into some of the problems that we face. Is the United States today prepared to take the initiative perhaps in restraining the development of the cruise missile in order to get something going in the SALT talks?

President CARTER. I wouldn't want to single out one particular weapon which is still in the development stage, but I will give you a couple of examples that are symbolic in nature, not too profound.

One is that I've suggested to the Soviet Union that they let us know and that we let them know before we launch any kind of intercontinental ballistic missile in a test phase. We launch our missiles from Vandenberg Air Force Base—we don't launch them from the standard silos. The Soviet Union does launch missiles from their standard operating silos for test purposes. I think a prior notice that this launch was going to take place—twenty-four hours or forty-eight hours—would help a great deal.

I've called on the Soviet Union to join us in a comprehensive test ban, to stop all nuclear testing for at least an extended period of time—two years, three years, four years. The Soviets are interested in using nuclear explosives to divert the course of a river in northern Russia. I don't think they need to test any more. If they want to put that as a proviso in the agreement, that they would like to go ahead and divert that river, I think that would be something that we could negotiate and let us have observers there to learn from them and vice versa. But I think that the initiation of proposals that might be mutually acceptable of this kind is very, very important.

Now, we have two unresolved questions derived from the Vladivostok agreement called SALT II, and that is the cruise missile and the Backfire bomber. I would be willing to go ahead with the Soviet Union, conclude a quick agreement, if they think it advisable, and omit the Backfire bomber and the cruise missile from the negotiations at this

stage. And then in a SALT III talk, if necessary, put those two items back in for further discussion.

But I think it is important for us, without any pressure on me to proceed too hastily, in a very careful and methodical way to demonstrate to the world that we are sincere.

Q. . . . Would you consider saying to the Soviets, say the B–1 or any other weapons system, we are not going to develop it for six months, we'd like to see something from you in the way of reciprocity?

President CARTER. Let me avoid reference to a particular weapons system on our side. Let me refer to a weapons system on their side. The Soviets have a missile with limited range—it is not intercontinental in nature—called the SS–20. They have begun to install those missiles in mobile installations where they can move them in a concealed way from one part of an area to another. It makes it very difficult to pinpoint their exact location.

I would like to see the Soviets cease deployment of the mobile missile, even though it is not of intercontinental type. It is very difficult to distinguish it from the intercontinental missile called the SS–16. But if they would agree to a cessation of the use or deployment of the mobile-type missiles, for instance, . . . that would be a very important point for us to join them in a mutual agreement. It would mean we would not then perhaps spend the large amounts of money to develop our own mobile missile. But if the Soviets should move to a development of an intercontinental missile that can be moved from one place to another undetected, and its location cannot be pinpointed, then that would put a great pressure on us to develop a mobile missile of our own.

So, I think on both sides there has to be some initiation. But as individual weapons systems are restrained, using initiative, you have got to be sure that the overall balance of deterrent is not disturbed.

* * *

Q. Mr. President, there have been a series of actions taken in recent days by the Soviet Union, including the expulsion of American journalists and the arrest of Alexander Ginsburg, actions that we have taken issue with in one form or another. How concerned are you that by being outspoken on issues of human rights that we may jeopardize possibly our relations with the Soviet Union on other matters?

President CARTER. Well, this brings up the question that is referred to as linkage. I think we come out better in dealing with the Soviet Union if I am consistently and completely dedicated to the enhancement of human rights, not only as it deals with the Soviet Union but all other

countries. I think this can legitimately be severed from our inclination to work with the Soviet Union, for instance, in reducing dependence upon atomic weapons and also in seeking mutual and balanced force reductions in Europe.

I don't want the two to be tied together. I think the previous administration, under Secretary Kissinger, thought that there ought to be this linkage—that if you mentioned human rights . . . you might endanger the progress of the SALT talks. I don't feel that way. I think it ought to be clear, and I have made clear directly in communication to Mr. Brezhnev and in my meeting with Ambassador Dobrynin, that I was reserving the right to speak out strong and forcefully whenever human rights are threatened, not every instance, but when I think it is advisable. This is not intended as a public relations attack on the Soviet Union, and I would hope that their leaders could recognize the American people's deep concern about human rights.

WASHINGTON, 9 MARCH 1977*

Q. What effect, in your mind, if any, is the extent of debate in the Senate over Mr. Warnke's qualifications to be the chief SALT negotiator going to have eventually on our negotiating position?

President CARTER. I don't believe that the exact vote in the Senate on Mr. Warnke's confirmation will have a major effect on future negotiations with the Soviet Union on SALT.

The obvious impression that concerns me is a demonstration of lack of confidence of the Senate in my own ability and attitudes as a chief negotiator. Obviously, as President, any decisions made with the Russians on reduction of atomic weapons would have to be approved by me.

I have promised the Joint Chiefs of Staff, who in the past perhaps have been by-passed in the process, that they will always know ahead of time what our position will be at the negotiating table. I've not promised the Joint Chiefs of Staff that they would have the right to approve or disapprove every individual item in negotiations.

But I hope that the Senate will give Mr. Warnke a strong vote.[1] I think many of the people that oppose Mr. Warnke just do not want to see any substantial reductions in atomic weapons, even though they

* SOURCE: Press conference of President Jimmy Carter. *Weekly Compilation of Presidential Documents*, 14 March 1977, pp. 328–334.

[1] On 9 March 1977 the Senate voted 58 to 40 to confirm Mr. Warnke as chief U.S. SALT negotiator. By a vote of 70 to 29, Mr. Warnke also was confirmed as Director of the Arms Control and Disarmament Agency.—Ed.

are agreed to mutually by us and the Soviet Union or even if they are designed to reduce the threat of nuclear destruction of the world.

I feel very deeply that we ought to pursue with every possible means an agreement with the Soviet Union for substantial reductions in atomic weapons. I think Mr. Warnke agrees; most of the Senators agree.

* * *

Q. On several occasions, Mr. President, you have spoken in terms of the U.S. being ready to move to a quick SALT agreement, omitting cruise missiles, Backfire bombers, if necessary. I'm wondering, sir, have you had any indication yet of Russian intentions on this subject?

President CARTER. The Soviet Union, so far as I know, still would like to include the cruise missile question in the present negotiations. They don't want to discuss the Backfire bomber at all. And my hope has been and is that by the exclusion of both those controversial items, which will require long and tedious negotiations, that we might move to a rapid agreement at SALT II and immediately begin to discuss, for instance, the Backfire bombers, the cruise missiles in subsequent negotiations. But I do not have any indication yet that the Soviets have changed their position on that issue.

Q. Mr. President, what about nuclear reductions?

President CARTER. Again, I think you have two approaches to the question.

I have proposed both directly and indirectly to the Soviet Union, publicly and privately, that we try to identify those items on which there is relatively close agreement—not completely yet, because details are very difficult on occasion. But I have, for instance, suggested that we forgo the opportunity to arm satellite bodies and also to forgo the opportunity to destroy observation satellites.

We've also proposed that the Indian Ocean be completely demilitarized, that a comprehensive test ban be put into effect, that prior notification of test missile launchings be exchanged. And I would like to see any of these items on which the Soviets will agree quickly, be concluded, and then get down to the much more difficult negotiations on much more drastic overall commitments to atomic weapons, leading ultimately to the complete elimination of atomic weapons from the face of the earth.

This is going to be a long, slow, tedious process. But I think if we and the Soviets could agree on the easier items—and none of them are very easy—quickly, it would show good faith. I think it would let the world know that we are serious in stopping once and for all what has

been a continuous and rapid escalation in atomic weapon capabilities since they were first evolved.

WASHINGTON, 24 MARCH 1977*

Q. Mr. President, in terms of bringing the American people in on the dialogue, you spoke of arms reduction. Does that mean that Vance will take a new set of proposals on SALT? And two, you spoke of the cooperative attitude of the Soviets. Does that mean that you don't think that any of Brezhnev's statements in the past week will have any bearing, in terms of your human rights stand, on the SALT negotiations?

President CARTER. Well, I think the first question is easily answered. Yes, we will take new proposals to the Soviet Union. We are not abandoning the agreements made in the Vladivostok agreement. As you know, all previous SALT agreements have been, in effect, limitations that were so high that they were, in effect, just ground rules for intensified competition and a continued massive arms growth in nuclear weapons.

We hope to bring not only limitations . . . but also actual substantial reduction [if] the Soviets will agree. That will be our first proposal. I spelled this out briefly in my United Nations speech.[1]

And the second fall-back position will be, in effect, to ratify Vladivostok and to wait until later to solve some of the most difficult and contentious issues. We hope that the Soviets will agree to the substantial reduction. . . .

I study Mr. Brezhnev's speeches in their entirety. And I think the speech made this past week to their General Trade Union Conference and one made previously at Tula—I consider them to be very constructive.

There was a delineation in his speech between human rights—which he equates with intrusion into their own internal affairs, and I don't agree with that assessment—that has been divided in his speeches from the subject of peace and arms limitation, including nuclear arms. So I have nothing that I have heard directly or indirectly from Mr. Brezhnev that would indicate that he is not very eager to see substantial progress made in arms limitations.

Q. Mr. President . . . you said you thought it was a good thing for you to speak out on negotiation details, but you didn't say why. As I understand the criticism, sir, it is that it impedes negotiations when you put

---

* SOURCE: Press conference of President Jimmy Carter. *Weekly Compilation of Presidential Documents*, 28 March 1977, pp. 439–445.

[1] The text of President Carter's 17 March 1977 address to the United Nations General Assembly can be found in *Department of State Bulletin*, 11 April 1977, pp. 329–333.—Ed.

out on the table, just in a range of thought, things that the parties haven't privately been able to work out. Why do you think it does not impede negotiations?

President CARTER. Well, I think if anyone would analyze the details of the statements that I have made so far, they are not so narrowly defined or specific that they would prevent both parties to a dispute from negotiating in good faith with a fairly clean slate ahead of them. . . .

I think, in many instances, the propositions that I have promulgated publicly are generally conceded to be very important and legitimate, but the public expression of those matters has not been made to the American people over a period of years. . . . And I believe that it is very important for the American people to know the framework within which discussions might take place and to give me, through their own approval, strength, as a party to some of the resolutions of disputes, and also to make sure that when I do speak, I don't speak with a hollow voice, but that the rest of the world knows that on my stand —for instance, on human rights—that I am not just speaking as a lonely voice, but that I am strongly supported by the Congress and the people of the country.

Vance Outlines Plans for the Moscow Talks, 26 March 1977

Q. Mr. Secretary, what are your minimum and maximum goals for this trip to Moscow?
Secretary VANCE. . . . Our goal is to see if we can, in these discussions with the Soviets, reach agreement on a framework which would guide the negotiations which will have to follow in Geneva for a SALT II agreement. In essence we will be presenting two alternative packages to the Soviets, with the hope that we will be able to reach agreement with them as to one of the two packages and thus provide the framework which I have referred to.
Q. Mr. Secretary, do you expect the Soviet reply during these three days, or do you think there will be a request on their part to study it before they actually give you a formal reply?
Secretary VANCE. I would expect that they would give us a formal reply during the period we are in Moscow.
Q. Do you and the party seem very optimistic? A sense, a feeling of optimism of coming away with something?
Secretary VANCE. No, I've never said I was very optimistic, but the President has said that we have high hopes that we would be able to reach agreement with the Soviets. I don't want to characterize ourselves as very optimistic. We will be hopeful and thus hope to achieve the objective which I mentioned to you a minute ago.

* * *

Q. Mr. Secretary, when you indicate you have two packages—one is a large comprehensive one and one is [inaudible] package—aren't you automatically saying that what you are really going to be talking about here is the [inaudible] package?
Secretary VANCE. I hope not. No, I hope very much that we will spend our time talking about the comprehensive package. That clearly in my view is the preferred package. It is a package that really gets to the heart of arms control, and this is the one which we clearly prefer and thus hope that it can be the central piece of our discussion.

* * *

Q. Mr. Secretary, does the fact that we are bringing two proposals to the Russians mean that we would not consider any third proposal?

SOURCE: Press briefing of Secretary of State Cyrus R. Vance, en route to Brussels, 26 March 1977. Department of State, Press Release No. 130, 28 March 1977.

Secretary VANCE. We are open and will always listen to whatever the Soviets have to say, and if it seems fair and equitable, of course we would take that into consideration in our negotiations with them.
Q. [Inaudible.]
Secretary VANCE. The essentials are, but there may be minor aspects upon which we would be willing to discuss variations. But not the essentials.
Q. Not the essentials of the comprehensive package?
Secretary VANCE. No, the essentials of the comprehensive package we think are fundamental and—
Q. And not subject to [inaudible]?
Secretary VANCE. Not subject to.

* * *

Q. Mr. Secretary, the Soviets feel that the United States is coming at them with a totally new proposal which the Soviets maintain is unwarranted and wipes out the years of effort spent on negotiation [inaudible] Vladivostok. What is your actual view as to how far you can possibly get in a matter of a few days on such a fundamental issue?
Secretary VANCE. As I indicated, what we are trying to reach is an agreement on a framework. We think the fundamental package provides that framework. The details obviously cannot be negotiated in a few days; but if we can agree that that is the framework, then we can go to Geneva and there negotiate on the details.
Q. The other part of that question is: How does the United States respond to the question or the contention that the Soviet Union has not been bargaining with Henry Kissinger or Jerry Ford but with the United States? [That] the United States is now proposing a fundamental change in what was agreed upon at Vladivostok?
Secretary VANCE. The objective of SALT is to reduce the arms race and to make real progress in cutting back on the number of nuclear weapons on both sides, thus ending up with rough parity on both sides. We believe that the so-called comprehensive package does just that, and therefore the sooner we can get on to making real progress the better off both sides are.

Vance and Carter Assess the Moscow Talks, 30 March 1977

MOSCOW, 30 MARCH 1977*

Secretary VANCE. . . . We met this afternoon with General Secretary Brezhnev and Foreign Minister Gromyko and other officials. At that meeting the Soviets told us that they had examined our two proposals and did not find either acceptable. They proposed nothing new on their side.

Let me give you a brief outline . . . on the nature of the two proposals which we put forward.

The first proposed what we had called our deferral proposal. Under this proposal we suggested the deferral of consideration of the cruise missile and the Backfire bomber issues, and that we resolve all other remaining issues under the Vladivostok accord and sign a new treaty. The proposal is only consistent with the agreement reached at Vladivostok, as you know, and there was no agreement reached at Vladivostok with respect to either cruise missiles or the Backfire bomber and therefore they have been and are open issues. So, in essence, our proposal was: Let's sign up what has been agreed at Vladivostok and put aside the cruise missile and get on with SALT III.

As an alternative, and what we have referred to as the comprehensive proposal—the one that we preferred and urged that they give serious consideration to—was a proposal which would have really made substantive progress toward true arms control. It had in it four elements—or has in it four elements. Let me run through them briefly with you.

The first deals with aggregates. We proposed that there be a substantial reduction in the overall aggregate of strategic delivery vehicles.

Second, we proposed that there be a reduction in the number of what are called modern large ballistic missile launchers.

Third, we proposed that there be a reduction in the MIRV launcher aggregate.

And fourth, we proposed that there be a limit on the launchers of ICBMs equipped with MIRVs. In other words, we proposed a sublimit in that area.

Going on to ICBM restrictions, we proposed that there continue to be a ban on construction of new ICBM launchers. We proposed in ad-

* SOURCE: Press conference of Secretary of State Cyrus R. Vance. *Department of State Bulletin*, 25 April 1977, pp. 400–404.

dition a ban on modification of existing ICBMs. In addition to that, we proposed a limit on the number of flight tests for existing ICBMs. We proposed in addition a ban on the development, the testing, and deployment of new ICBMs. In addition to that, we proposed a ban on the development, testing, and deployment of mobile ICBM launchers.

With respect to the cruise missiles, we proposed a ban on the development, testing, and deployment of all cruise missiles, whether nuclear-armed or conventionally-armed, of intercontinental range. In other words, we set a [range] limit. I'm not going to give you that precise number, but there was a specific number over which they would be banned, and that limit was the limit between intercontinental and nonintercontinental.

Finally, with respect to the Backfire bomber, we indicated that we want them to provide us with a list of measures to assure that the Backfire bomber would not be used as a strategic bomber.

That, in essence, is the comprehensive package which we put forward.

We agreed to continue discussions in the future. Foreign Minister Gromyko and I will be meeting in May to discuss the Middle East and other items, including strategic arms limitation. In addition to that, we have agreed to set up a number of working groups in various areas to follow up on the discussions which we have had here in Moscow.

Let me give you a list of the areas in which we will have these follow-on working groups. They include the area of comprehensive test bans; the area of chemical weapons; the area of prior notification of missile test-firing; the area of antisatellite weapons; the area of civil defense; the area of possible military limitations in the Indian Ocean; the area of radiological weapons; the area of conventional weapons; and we agreed to set up a regular schedule of meetings to deal with the whole question of proliferation.

That is the summary of where we are at this point.

Q. Mr. Secretary, what effect do you think the outcome of these negotiations will have on U.S.-Soviet relations?

Secretary VANCE. I think we made progress in these negotiations and they were useful. I think that U.S.-Soviet relations will continue to be good. I hope in the future we can strengthen those relations.

Needless to say, I am disappointed that we have failed to make progress in what I consider to be the most essential of all these areas, namely, the area of strategic nuclear arms. But I think that our relationships will continue. We will certainly do everything we can to continue to try and strengthen relations.

* * *

Q. Mr. Secretary, did the Soviet side give you any reason to hope that there may be some further negotiation on your proposal and on their proposal so that you might find a bridge between the two?
Secretary VANCE. Yes. We agreed that we would continue discussions. That is all.
Q. To what extent do you think the issue of human rights might have played a role in the failure of these discussions?
Secretary VANCE. Well, human rights did not come up after the first day. We never discussed it again.
Q. You don't think it in any way affected their thinking on your proposals?
Secretary VANCE. I do not believe it did. No, I think it stood on its own feet; but you will have to ask them.
Q. I'm not clear what happens next. Is one side supposed to come up with a new proposal, or where do we go from here? Specifically?
Secretary VANCE. Where we go from here is that I am hoping that they would consider the proposals which we have made. We think that they provide a reasonable basis for further discussions.

We will be meeting again. I hope by that time there will be something to put on the table which will permit us to make progress.
Q. Did they give you some indication that they think this is a basis, that your proposals are a basis, for further negotiations?
Secretary VANCE. All they gave us today was that they said they did not find it acceptable.

* * *

Q. Is it still possible, sir, to think to replace SALT I by October, when it expires?
Secretary VANCE. Yes, I think it is still possible. I would come back to the point that the deferral proposal is a proposal which is based upon what was agreed to at Vladivostok and simply puts aside the very difficult issues of Backfire and the cruise missile, and one could sign that and move immediately on to the more complex problems which are contained in the comprehensive proposal. . . .
Q. Mr. Secretary, did they then give you an indication that the deferral proposal might be a better basis for further talks than the comprehensive proposal? Did they make a distinction between the two rejected proposals?
Secretary VANCE. They did not make a distinction between the two.

* * *

Q. Mr. Secretary, you told us two days ago that the Soviets had put on the table a slightly modified version of the January 1976 proposal. Is that still on the table—

Secretary VANCE. Yes.
Q. We have two American proposals and a Soviet proposal?
Secretary VANCE. That is right.

* * *

Q. Mr. Secretary, what was the central reason . . . that the Soviets gave you for their rejection for both proposals that the United States put forth?
Secretary VANCE. It was their view that the deferral proposal did not accord with Vladivostok. It is our very clear view that it does accord with Vladivostok because Backfire and cruise missiles were not included in the Vladivostok accord and they remained unsettled issues—so that there is a difference of view between the Soviets and ourselves on that matter.
Q. Was there a central dispute, sir, on the difference between the two aide-memoires out of Vladivostok, the one on ballistic missiles—the American version mentioning ballistic missiles and the Soviet version mentioning just missiles?
Secretary VANCE. There was discussion of the aide-memoire, yes.
Q. Could you tell us, sir, what their reason was for rejecting the comprehensive package?
Secretary VANCE. They really should speak on this themselves, but I will tell you that their indication is that they do not feel that, as they put it, that it is an equitable package. We believe that it is equitable and it does attack the central questions which are involved in seeking a real arms control agreement.
Q. Is that proposal still on the table and negotiable?
Secretary VANCE. It is. All proposals are still on the table.

* * *

Q. Mr. Secretary, did you formally tell the Soviets that we also found their proposal unacceptable? And could you tell us why we do find their proposal unacceptable?
Secretary VANCE. The reason that we have found their proposal unacceptable is that it does not deal properly with the cruise missile issue.
Q. Did you discuss the possibility of extending the SALT I agreement beyond the end of October?
Secretary VANCE. We did not discuss that, no.

WASHINGTON, 30 MARCH 1977*

Q. Mr. President, . . . do you still believe that the Soviets in no way linked your human rights crusade with arms control negotiations?

* SOURCE: Remarks to the press by President Jimmy Carter. *Weekly Compilation of Presidential Documents*, 4 April 1977, pp. 469–473.

President CARTER. I can't certify to you that there is no linkage in the Soviets' minds between the human rights effort and the SALT limitations. We have no evidence that this was the case. Secretary Vance thought it was quite significant, for instance, that when General Secretary Brezhnev presented a prepared statement on the human rights issue that it was done in a different meeting entirely from the meeting in which the SALT negotiations occurred.

So our assessment is that there was no linkage, but I can't certify that there is no linkage in the Soviets' minds.

Q. Mr. President, you've said that the Soviets contend that Secretary Kissinger and your predecessors had promised that we would not deploy, I believe, the cruise missile.

President CARTER. Yes.

Q. Just where and how do they contend that this promise was given, and have you checked with them to see if in fact it was?

President CARTER. Yes. Both President Ford and Secretary Kissinger have maintained publicly, and to me privately, that there was never any agreement on the part of the United States to contain or to prohibit the deployment or development of cruise missiles.

The language that was used in the early Vladivostok agreement, which, as you know, has not yet been ratified, was a prohibition against air-launched missiles. Secretary Kissinger's position has been—and he is much better able to speak than I am to speak for him—that that meant ballistic missiles, which was a subject of the Vladivostok talks.

Two and a half years ago or so, when these talks took place, the cruise missile capability was not well understood, and there was no detailed discussion at all of the cruise missile. The Soviets claim that when they did discuss air-launched missiles that they were talking about cruise missiles. Secretary Kissinger said that he was not talking about cruise missiles.

Q. Sir . . . they are not contending that there was any secret understanding or discussion or anything?

President CARTER. No.

Q. They're talking about the language that was in the Vladivostok agreement?

President CARTER. Exactly.

Q. Did the Russians have a counterproposal on SALT that they offered us, or were they content simply to listen to our proposals?

President CARTER. They listened to our two proposals. Of course, their proposal has been to ratify their understanding of the Vladivostok agreement, which includes their capability of developing the Backfire bomber and our incapability of developing cruise missiles. That's an

agreement that we never understood to be part of the Vladivostok agreement.

Q. Mr. Carter, if necessary to achieve any progress, are you willing to modify your human rights statements or will you continue to speak out?

President CARTER. No. I will not modify my human rights statements. . . .

* * *

Q. Mr. President, how would you characterize what happened today? How serious a setback is this? Did we expect that the Soviets might be more receptive to our positions?

President CARTER. We had no indications either in direct or indirect communications with Brezhnev that they were ready to accept our positions. We carefully prepared over a period of five or six weeks what we thought was a balanced and what we still think is a balanced proposal with drastic reductions.

I might say that there is a unanimous agreement among the key members of Congress, the State Department, my own staff, the Secretary of Defense, the Joint Chiefs, that this is a good and fair proposal. I have hopes that the substance of our proposal will be accepted by the Soviet Union in the future, because it's to their advantage and ours to do so. . . .

Q. Mr. President, would it be fair to say that the talks broke down because the United States is now not prepared to accept restrictions on cruise missiles?

President CARTER. No.

Q. Isn't that the heart of it?

President CARTER. That is not the heart of it at all. We are prepared to accept restrictions on the cruise missile if it's part of an overall and balanced package. We are not prepared to accept a unilateral prohibition against the development or deployment of the cruise missile absent some equivalent response from the Soviet Union, including the Backfire bomber. But we put together a package which was fair and balanced. But we are not prepared unilaterally to forgo an opportunity, unless it's equivalent to a Soviet response.

Q. Yes, sir, I didn't mean unilaterally; but on the January 1976 trip by Secretary Kissinger to the Soviet Union, there was active negotiation regarding a balanced reduction involving some limitations on cruise missiles. So when you say, sir, that the Soviets say we agreed to restrict cruise missiles, aren't they referring to 1976 and not to Vladivostok, when indeed the cruise missile was on the drawing board and not a real thing?

President Carter. I don't believe that—I don't want to get myself into the position of speaking for Secretary Kissinger. I don't think there has ever been any insinuation of an American agreement that the Soviets could build and deploy the Backfire bomber without limitation while we limited cruise missiles. And that's the position that the Soviets adopted as the Vladivostok agreement.

* * *

Q. Mr. President, Senator [Howard] Baker, just outside a few moments ago, said that during your briefing of the congressional leadership you said you intended to "hang tough." Did you say that, and what did you mean by that?

President Carter. Yes. I do. I think that it's important for us to take advantage of an opportunity this year to negotiate not just a superficial ratification of rules by which we can continue the arms race, but to have a freeze on deployment and development of new missiles and an actual reduction in launchers and MIRVed missiles below what was agreed to previously. And on those items, I intend to remain very strong in my position.

I don't think it's to our nation's advantage to put forward in piecemeal fashion additional proposals. Our experience in the past has been that the Soviet Union extracts from those comprehensive proposals those items that are favorable to them and want to continue to negotiate the other parts of the proposals that might not be so favorable to them.

* * *

Q. Has the breakdown of these talks in any way influenced your thinking on development of future U.S. weaponry? That is, will you be now more inclined to go for full production of the B–1 or any other advanced weapon systems?

President Carter. Obviously, if we feel at the conclusion of next month's discussions that the Soviets are not acting in good faith with us and that an agreement is unlikely, then I would be forced to consider a much more deep commitment to the development and deployment of additional weapons. But I would like to forgo that decision until I'm convinced the Soviets are not acting in good faith. I hope they will.

Gromyko Assesses the Moscow Talks, 31 March 1977

Foreign Minister GROMYKO. In connection with the visit of U.S. Secretary of State Cyrus Vance in Moscow, rumors appeared abroad, chiefly in the United States, as well as all sorts of versions in regard to the outcome of the talks held. It will be recalled that U.S. President Carter also made a statement without even waiting for the Secretary of State's arrival in Washington.

I must say that the rumors do not accord with the actual state of affairs. What is more, some of them distort the actual situation, and that is why there is need for appropriate explanations and clarifications from our side.

One of the main questions discussed during the talks held by Leonid Brezhnev with U.S. Secretary of State Cyrus Vance, and also during my own meetings with the Secretary of State, was the question of concluding a new agreement on the limitation of strategic arms, since the agreement now in force expires in October of this year.

What is the essence of the Vladivostok accord? For example, what is the essence of the main question which was considered? It would not be out of place to recall this.

Way back in Vladivostok an accord was reached that the Soviet Union and the United States will each have 2,400 strategic arms carriers, including 1,320 MIRVs. This is the main content of the Vladivostok accord.

You know that there were many reports—both official and semiofficial—saying that there was progress after Vladivostok. There were also more moderate reports. But, in general, it is true that quite a few steps forward have been made. There were opportunities to bring things to completion. This, however, did not happen. Then all of a sudden the question arose of the so-called cruise missiles. What does this mean? There is hardly need to dwell on the technical aspect of the matter. They tried to prove that the Vladivostok accord did not refer to the cruise missiles, that these missiles . . . are generally not subject to any limitations and that the Vladivostok accord concerns ballistic missiles only. We resolutely objected to this attempt. At Vladivostok the question was posed differently. No green light was given there to the cruise missiles. The question was posed thus: to achieve such an agreement that would shut off all channels of the strategic arms race and reduce the threat of nuclear war.

SOURCE: Remarks to the press by Foreign Minister Andrei Gromyko, Moscow, 31 March 1977. *News and Views From the U.S.S.R.*, Soviet Embassy Information Department, Washington, D.C.

The United States of America and the Soviet Union exchanged relevant official documents which sealed the Vladivostok accords. Everything, it seemed, was clear, and it remained to carry the matter forward to the signing of an agreement. Working on some of the questions, including the juridical wording of the agreement, were the delegations of the U.S.S.R. and the U.S.A. at Geneva. At first, things were moving. But all of a sudden, a wall had risen and everything was frozen. Apparently somebody, some influential forces in the U.S., found all this not to their liking. And you know that great difficulties arose and these difficulties have not been removed. If one is to speak frankly, of late these difficulties have increased. What should we call this situation and this kind of position, which certain people in the United States began taking after Vladivostok? This is the line of revision, a line of revising the commitments taken in Vladivostok.

We are categorically opposed to this. We are all for the edifice that was built by such hard work in Vladivostok—an edifice on which such intellectual and other resources were spent—not only to be preserved, but that things should be brought to a conclusion and a new agreement on limiting strategic arms should be concluded between the U.S.S.R. and the U.S.A.

We were told, and it was said to us even in the last days when the talks were on in Moscow, that one of the obstacles is the Soviet Union's possession of a certain type of bomber (it is called Backfire in the United States) which, it was said, can be used as a strategic weapon, and that this plane absolutely must be taken into consideration in the agreement. We categorically rejected it and continue rejecting such attempts. Time and again, Leonid Brezhnev personally explained to President Ford, specifically during the meeting in Helsinki [during the European Security Conference, 30 July to 1 August 1975], and later to President Carter, that it concerns a medium-range bomber and not a strategic bomber. Nevertheless, this question was tossed at us once again. Somebody evidently needs to artificially create this additional obstacle. It is better known to the Americans at what level these obstacles are being created. We note that this question is being artificially introduced to complicate the situation along the road of concluding an agreement. . . .

Throughout the talks here in Moscow, our side emphasized the main idea that the foundation for a new agreement that has been built up should not be destroyed, but that it should be preserved at all cost. And truly, what will happen if the arrival of a new leadership in some country will scrap all the constructive things that were achieved in relations with other countries? What stability in relations with other countries can be talked about in such a case? What stability can be

talked about in relations between the U.S.A. and the U.S.S.R. in this case? We, our side, would like to see precisely stability in our relations, and that these relations should be as good as possible and based on the principles of peaceful coexistence and, even better, that they should be friendly. This is our stand and we would like to see similar actions in reply from the other side, that is, the United States of America.

A version is now being circulated in the U.S.A. alleging that the U.S. representatives at the Moscow talks proposed some broad program for disarmament, but that the Soviet leadership did not accept this program. I must say that this version does not accord with reality. This version is essentially false. Nobody proposed such a program to us.

I am dwelling on some facts from which you, certainly, will draw for yourselves some conclusions. For example, it is proposed to us now to reduce the total number of strategic arms carriers to 2,000 or even to 1,800 units, and MIRVs to 1,200–1,100. What is more, it is simultaneously proposed to liquidate half of those rockets in our possession which are simply disliked by somebody in the United States. They are described differently: sometimes "too heavy" or "excessively effective." They dislike these rockets and that is why the Soviet Union must be deprived of half of these weapons. So the question is whether such a unilateral way of putting the question is a way to agreement. No; it only damages the Vladivostok accord, breaks the balance of limitations concerning which agreement was reached in Vladivostok. What changed after Vladivostok? Nothing; absolutely nothing changed. Call this as you like, but this is no way of solving problems.

* * *

Next, in the talks with Cyrus Vance it was suggested that we revise the right of the two sides to modernize existing missiles as laid down in the present agreement, just as in the Vladivostok accord. This was taken for granted. No problems arose here. But no, it is now proposed to break up the agreement also in this respect, and to do so in a way that would give advantages to the United States, with the Soviet Union finding itself in a worse position. Clearly, we shall not depart from the principle of equality also in this respect. And to put forward such demands is a dubious if not a cheap move.

One more fact. It was proposed to us to include in the agreement a clause prohibiting the development of new types of weapons. At a first glance, it would seem that there is nothing wrong with this. But I would like to recall that the Soviet Union itself has long ago made the proposal on banning the manufacture of new types and new systems of weapons of mass extermination. Moreover, we have submitted to the

United Nations a draft of the relevant international treaty. And what was the response? Maybe the U.S. government supported this treaty? No, it did not say a single word in support of this treaty.

Indeed, at the Moscow talks too, only the most general words were uttered to the effect that such a clause should be included into the agreement, in a "package" at that, or geared to other obviously unacceptable proposals. All this made a very dubious impression. If there is a serious intention in this matter then, as I have already said, there is a concrete proposal. . . .

It seems to us that in international affairs in general, including relations between the U.S.A. and the Soviet Union, it would be better to examine relevant problems on a more realistic, on an honest basis. The more attempts there are to play a game in this matter, to tread on the foot of the partner, the more difficulties there will be. This will not promote an improvement in Soviet-American relations, the cause of détente, consolidation of peace. This should be said especially in connection with recent statements appearing in the United States in newspapers and, unfortunately, not only in newspapers.

I should like to add a few more words. If the U.S.A. is prepared to ban new types of weapons, why then is the need to produce the B-1 strategic bomber, so beloved by some people in the U.S.A., defended all that much? The same is true of the manufacture of the Trident atomic submarine. Leonid Brezhnev spoke of these new American weapons systems both in his public speeches and in his remarks during the official negotiations with the American side, and did so repeatedly. So what we have is that certain declarations by the American side do not tally with the actual readiness to ban new types of weapons of mass extermination.

One would rather not speak on this theme, but one has to. In his last statement, the President of the United States used the word "sincerity" when referring to the Soviet leadership's attitude to questions of strategic arms limitation. I would like to say: We do not lack sincerity. We have plenty of it. It is on this basis that we are building all our policy and would want all to build their policies on the same basis, so that the deeds would not differ from the words.

U.S. representative Cyrus Vance described his proposals as the basis for a broad and all-encompassing agreement. But it is easy, after an objective study of these proposals, to draw the conclusion that they pursue the aim of getting unilateral advantages for the U.S.A. to the detriment of the Soviet Union, its security and the security of its friends and allies. The Soviet Union will never be able to agree to this. This was openly said by Leonid Brezhnev to the U.S. Secretary of State

during the first talk. He said the same during the last talk which was held yesterday.

Reading some of the statements made in the U.S.A. you probably noticed that not only what some people call all-encompassing proposals, but also an alternative "narrow proposal" has been made to us. But what is the essence of this "narrow proposal?" Here it is: We are simply told, let us conclude an agreement that will concern ballistic missiles and strategic bombers. At the same time, it is proposed to leave aside the cruise missiles and the Soviet bomber referred to as Backfire which, as I have already mentioned, is not strategic at all. It looks as if a concession is being made to us, but this is an extremely strange concession. We are offered what does not belong to the United States. A nonstrategic aircraft was named a strategic one, and then they say: We are ready not to include this bomber in the agreement now, if the Soviet Union consents to give a green light for the manufacture and deployment of the U.S. cruise missiles. So according to this narrower agreement, the cruise missiles would be totally excluded from an agreement. Such a decision would mean that, while plugging one gap—the ballistic missiles—a new gap, maybe an even wider and deeper one, would be simultaneously opening—nuclear weapons carriers.

I stress nuclear weapons carriers. But it is our objective to prevent an outbreak of a nuclear war, to deliver mankind from nuclear war. Is it not the same for a human being to die of a weapon from a cruise missile, as from a weapon from a ballistic missile? The result is the same. Apart from it, the manufacture of cruise missiles will swallow up no less funds, dollars, pounds sterling, rubles, francs, lire, et cetera. Do people stand to gain from it? One cannot help asking what such an agreement will give for security. And is it going to be security in general? No, it will not be security, which peoples sincerely want. It will not even be a semblance of security. That is why we rejected, frankly speaking, this so-called narrow agreement too. We declared that it does not present a solution to the problem and does not even come close to solving this problem. This is what the U.S. Secretary of State took back when he left Moscow.

We do not know how all this will be presented to public opinion in the U.S.A. Judging by the first symptoms, the actual state of things is distorted. The results of the exchange of opinions and the statements that were made to the U.S. Secretary of State were also distorted. Leonid Brezhnev's statements were distorted too.

All this does not help towards a productive solution of problems, though we would sincerely wish so. But we are ready to continue talks

on all these problems. The Soviet leaders have enough patience. We would like the discussions, regardless of where they are held—here in Moscow, in Washington or in other places—to finally come to a favorable conclusion.

Leonid Brezhnev strongly emphasized: We firmly stand for good relations with the United States just as with other countries in the world. We stand for relations based on the principles of peaceful coexistence, for friendly relations. And the possibilities for it are far from having been exhausted. They have not been exhausted because the point at issue is the United States and the Soviet Union.

We do not intend to belittle the substantial differences that now exist between the stands of the U.S.A. and the Soviet Union. The Secretary of State was told about it frankly. But does this mean that there are insurmountable obstacles? No, it does not. We would like to express the hope that the leadership of the United States will take up a more realistic stand, that it will give greater consideration to the interests of the security of the Soviet Union and its allies and will not strive for unilateral advantages.

* * *

I shall touch on two more questions. Some people pretend that they are not directly concerned with the problem that was discussed as the basic one during the stay of the U.S. Secretary of State in Moscow. But it is far from being so.

I would like to formulate the first question thus. This is the question of not handing strategic weapons over to third countries and of taking no actions whatever to evade the agreement, the signing of which we are now concerned. On this question we formulated a concrete proposal. It was discussed. At any rate, we put it forward in Geneva in the course of the talks between the U.S. and Soviet delegations. But our representatives as a matter of fact received no substantive reply. We attach no small importance to the solution of this matter.

The second question is about the advance deployment of U.S. nuclear weapons in Europe, around Europe and in other areas, from where the Soviet territory is within reach. In concluding the first agreement on the limitation of strategic weapons we made official statements to the effect that we must return to this question. In the interests of reaching an agreement, we did not propose in Vladivostok that the provision of liquidation of U.S. nuclear weapons of advance deployment be included into an agreement as a compulsory term. But now we have a different view of this issue in the light of the latest U.S. proposals. This is a matter of our security and the security of our allies. We are entitled to pose the question of liquidating U.S. advance deployment

means. This concerns atomic powered submarines, bombers capable of carrying nuclear weapons, and aircraft carriers in the corresponding region of Europe. . . . Call it what you may—a toughening of position, a change of position. But I have to say it again: This question now faces us in connection with the latest U.S. proposals.

* * *

Q. What can you say about the statements from the White House that, in case of a failure of the talks on the limitation of strategic arms, the U.S.A. will create and deploy new strategic weapons?

Mr. GROMYKO. I can say only one thing: If anyone takes this road, he would assume the whole responsibility for the consequences of such actions. In our opinion, every effort must be made to curb the arms race, to achieve positive results in the talks.

* * *

Q. Does the line by the U.S. President on the question of "human rights" affect resolving of the strategic arms problem? Don't you think that the campaign being waged in the U.S.A. by certain circles on the far-fetched "human rights" question is a deliberate building up of tension?

Mr. GROMYKO. The second question helps me to answer the first one. I will not say that, in discussing any aspect of the problem of preparing a new agreement on the limitation of strategic arms, we talked about "rights." Of course not. But the thing is that all that is lately said in the U.S.A. about "human rights" . . . naturally poisons the atmosphere and aggravates the political climate. But does this help to solve other issues, including those related to strategic arms? No, it does not. On the contrary, it hinders it. And speaking on the essence of the matter, I would like to say as follows: We do not claim to be teachers of anybody, since the domestic affairs of states are concerned, and only the states themselves can decide on their domestic affairs. I stress "domestic affairs." But we will not allow anybody to assume the pose of teachers and decide how to solve our internal affairs—I stress "our internal affairs."

* * *

Q. Can you say what was, in your view, the use of the meeting with Secretary of State Vance, meaning the use for a better understanding between the U.S.S.R. and the U.S.A.?

Mr. GROMYKO. I would answer the question as follows: The visit of the Secretary of State was necessary and indeed useful because we must know each other well. I mean not a superficial acquaintance, but the

knowledge of positions, the knowledge of the policies of the countries on the problems concerned. We also diverge on questions, and important questions they are. I have already spoken about it and I don't think that there is a necessity to repeat it. Some agreement was reached to continue discussions of unsolved matters on which we could not find a common language with the U.S.A. An exchange of views may be held, not necessarily at a high level, but, say, at the level of experts, counsellors. Then we will be able to see where we stand. We hope that the U.S. side will show a serious attitude to these efforts. On our part we guarantee this.

Brzezinski Outlines the New American SALT Proposals, 1 April 1977

Mr. BRZEZINSKI. What I would like to do is essentially give you as much information as I legitimately can on the proposal that we made in Moscow. In so doing, I don't propose to engage in any recrimination, but would merely like to lay out for you the kind of proposal we made and the thinking that went into that proposal. For I believe that the thinking that the proposal reflected is almost as important as the proposal itself.

What we were trying to accomplish and what we intend to accomplish is to move forward to genuine disarmament. That is to say, to obtain a significant reduction in the level of the strategic confrontation. We believe that SALT agreements should not only set the framework for continued competition, but that they should indeed limit that competition, reduce its scope, introduce greater stability into our relationship.

Our proposals were thus designed to accomplish two basic purposes: to give both sides the political and the strategic parity to which each of them is entitled—and this means that there should be no self-evident advantage in the agreement which would be either of a strategic character or which would be susceptible to political perceptions as an advantage; and secondly, it was our basic purpose to seek an agreement which would provide to both sides again political and strategic stability. Parity in the first instance, stability in the second instance.

By this, I mean a proposal which would take into account the fact that if you only have certain kinds of limits but do not anticipate technological dynamics, what may seem stable in 1977 or 1978 could become very unstable in 1980 or 1985. It was therefore felt that genuine strategic arms limitations—indeed, a genuine strategic arms reductions agreement—ought to take both of these elements into account.

The proposal that we made was therefore very finely crafted. We attempted very deliberately to forgo those elements in our strategic posture which threaten the Soviets the most, and we made proposals to them that they forgo those elements in their strategic posture which threaten us the most. We felt particularly by concentrating on the land-based ICBMS that are MIRVed we would take into account the greatest sources of insecurity on both sides.

I truly believe that this proposal, if accepted, or when accepted,

---

SOURCE: Press conference of Dr. Zbigniew Brzezinski, Assistant to the President for National Security Affairs, Washington, D.C., 1 April 1977. Office of the White House Press Secretary, 1 April 1977.

could serve as a driving wedge, as a historical driving wedge, for a more stable and eventually more cooperative American and Soviet relationship. It is thus a proposal which is not only strategic but political in its character, and Secretary Vance, in his remarks in Moscow, placed a great deal of emphasis on the political significance of this proposal.

It was a proposal which has strategic as well as political intentions very much in mind. Because of that, it was also a proposal which was accompanied by a series of other proposals designed to place the American-Soviet relationship not only on a more stable basis, but to make the cooperative elements in that relationship more comprehensive. . . . All of that cumulatively was designed to produce greater mutual stability, to widen areas of cooperation, to indeed offset the competitive elements in our relationship by a widening pattern of cooperation. And we are encouraged by the fact that eight working groups were set up on the basis of these proposals, as well as some that the Soviets made, in order to move forward on these issues. . . .

It is in this context that we proposed a comprehensive package with negotiating flexibility inherent in it, in order to structure [a] rather different and more stable and more equitable U.S.-Soviet strategic relationship.

That package has two key elements in it.

First of all, it called for reductions which were of a greater scope than just symbolic. And the second equally important part of the package involved a proposal for a freeze, for a halt on the modernization of ICBMS. . . . You can well see how these two key fundamental elements are interrelated. We proposed the reduction so as to lower the level of the competition, and we proposed a freeze in order to halt it qualitatively and quantitatively. Thus, it is in many respects the first truly, genuinely disarmament-oriented proposal introduced into the Strategic Arms Limitations Talks.

We proposed more specifically that the present strategic aggregates which were set [at Vladivostok] at the high level of 2,400 for each side be reduced to a range between 1,800 and 2,000; and here again is a demonstration of the inherent flexibility of the package, because this is something which we were prepared to discuss.

We proposed, moreover, that within that framework the present level of MIRVS, which is set at 1,320, be reduced to something between 1,100 and 1,200. And we also suggested that in that context it would be desirable that the total number of the so-called Soviet modern large ballistic missiles, particularly the SS-9 and SS-18, be reduced because, within the framework of lowered aggregates, these large missiles with their potential for numerous MIRVing (indeed, the SS-18 can be

MIRVed up to eight to ten warheads) become increasingly significant and introduce an asymmetrical aspect into the relationship.

On that basis we proposed that both sides freeze the deployment of all of their ICBMS and ban modifications on existing ICBMS, and indeed limit the number of annual flight tests for ICBMS, thereby reducing the likelihood of significant modifications; and also ban the development, testing, and deployment of new types of ICBMS; and particularly ban the deployment, testing, and development of mobile ICBMS, a factor, again, which if not checked could introduce very major uncertainty into the U.S.-Soviet strategic relationship.

This more specifically meant that on the U.S. side we were prepared to freeze our Minuteman III deployment—that is to say, the MIRVed ICBM—at 550, which is where it is currently. And we would forgo further improvements in all U.S. ICBMS, and we would abandon the MX program, both for silo and mobile basing. And we would forgo any plans for any other ICBMS.

On the Soviet side we proposed that the Soviets freeze the number of their strategic ICBMS, the SS-17s, -18s, and -19s, at a number not in excess of 550—which actually means that they could still go up, because they are below that number—and these would be the Soviet MIRVed missiles. Given the size of some of them (this is an important point to bear in mind, for it raises the issue of equity), their total number of warheads eventually could be greater than our land-based ICBMS would provide. And we would expect that the MLBM, or the modern large ballistic missile component, within the context of the 550 would not be greater than 150. This is important because this would provide for a reduction.

Q. Could you repeat that?

Mr. BRZEZINSKI. We also proposed that the total number of the modern large ballistic missiles—which we would expect would be the SS-18s, because they are the most modern Soviet ballistic missiles that are large—would not be greater than 150, and that would be a reduction from the present total; but that will be an important element of stability because that large number of the modern large ballistic missiles introduces the destabilizing potential inherent in large throw-weight and many, many warheads.

Q. Do they currently have 320 [modern large ballistic missiles]?

Mr. BRZEZINSKI. Three hundred and eight. We would also expect the Soviets to abandon the development and deployment of the SS-16, which is their mobile ICBM, just as we would abandon the MX.

Q. How about the SS-20—would that also be abandoned?

Mr. BRZEZINSKI. The SS-20 in its precise configuration is not a strategic weapon. And we would want, in the course of the agreement, to

develop arrangements which would permit us to have the needed assurance that the SS-20 is not being upgraded into the equivalent of the SS-16 because, as some of you clearly know, the SS-20 with a third stage could be, in effect, the equivalent of the SS-16. We would therefore want to have some arrangements whereby we could clearly differentiate between the two.

Finally, we would propose to make an arrangement with regard to the Backfire which would give us some assurances that it would not be used as a strategic weapon by the Soviet Union, and this is something that would be negotiated more fully within this framework. We would propose to ban all strategic cruise missiles, and that, again, is something which would be negotiated. In that context, though, it is to be noted that the Soviet side has insisted that the Backfire is not a strategic weapon, though it has a radius of over 2,000 miles. We would presumably define the cruise missile as being strategic at the level lower than that in the context of our negotiations.

I would say that if one analyzes this proposal in detail, I think one is justified within the limits of human reason—within the confines of one's own background, tradition, and concerns, which necessarily confine our ability to be absolutely certain about our judgments—that this was a genuine effort at an equitable arrangement. We would constrain those aspects of our strategic programs which are threatening to the Soviets. We would want the Soviets to adjust similarly in those regards which are most threatening to us. We would cap the arms race, we would impose a limit on the numbers through a reduction, significant reduction, and we would impose restraints of a qualitative type on offensive systems. Thus, we would both take a giant step forward.

I see a certain analogy between the situation in which we find ourselves today and the late 1960s. At that time, some of you might recall, we proposed to the Soviets that ABMS be banned because ABMS introduce an inherent element of instability into the relationship. The first Soviet reaction to that proposal by Prime Minister Kosygin was very negative, given their backgrounds, their traditions, their ways of looking at the strategic relationship. Yet, over time, through a continuing discourse, the Soviet side came to recognize the fact that indeed, in the age of highly advanced strategic systems, the introduction of the ABM element into the equation was truly destabilizing; and the most important accomplishment of SALT I was precisely that which the Soviets earlier had so indignantly rejected, namely, a ban on the ABM systems.

We are thus in the first phase of an ambitious and far-reaching search for a significant American-Soviet accommodation. We believe in some respects we are in the earlier educational part of the process

in which both sides have to think through the implications both of an unchecked arms race and of the benefits of reductions and a freeze. We are going to continue these talks with the Soviets. . . . We are hopeful that the search for something truly significant will bear fruit.

* * *

Q. Would you please clarify two points? Your definition of the American definition of the strategic cruise, and would you go over again . . . the MIRV idea? Were you talking simply about MIRV equivalency or was this—

Mr. BRZEZINSKI. In regard to the cruise missile, our position is that a cruise missile which is not capable of employment either in a transcontinental operation or which doesn't have a range in excess of weapons systems that are typically considered to be strategic, is nonstrategic. And since there has been an ongoing discussion with the Soviets as to what is and is not a strategic weapon, we would want to reach a more precise definition of that in the course of the negotiations, banning those cruise missiles which have as themselves a strategic range, and retain for both sides flexibility for those that are not.

I should add also that if any of the cruise missiles that would be retained by both sides were to be placed, for example, on the bombers, these bombers would then count as a MIRV weapon and would therefore be counted within the MIRV aggregate.

Specifically talking about the MIRVS, our proposal is to freeze the land-based ICBMS that can be MIRVed at 550 and to reduce [to 150] particularly the number of those very large Soviet ICBMS which can be MIRVed into very numerous warheads, given their throw-weight, because that, in the long run, could introduce an element of instability for both sides.

We would, at the same time, in that context, forgo those systems which are particularly threatening to the Soviet land-based ICBM force. It is to be remembered in this context that, at least for the time being, the Soviet strategic forces are heavily dependent on their land-based ICBMS. Those American systems which could threaten these land-based ICBMS are naturally and understandably particularly threatening to the Soviets. . . .

Q. Doctor, you didn't talk about the so-called data base. . . .

Mr. BRZEZINSKI. I don't want to go into too many specifics . . . but, specifically with regard to the data base, let me limit myself to this observation. . . .

I would hope and we would expect that in a symmetrical strategic relationship, which it has now become, the Soviet Union would provide us with all of the necessary data, just as we provided them with the

necessary data, and we would each have and retain the needed means for verifying the accuracy of that data.

Q. How?

Mr. Brzezinski. For one thing, through satellites, which are very important sources of information; but beyond that, with regard to the cruise missile, we would have to perhaps explore some additional ways of verification. I don't want to be too specific, because that is something which again would have to be negotiated, but let me merely note the difficulty with which, again, many of you are familiar.

It is very difficult to differentiate between the cruise missiles which are strategic and nonstrategic—their sizes, dimensions, are the same. It is very difficult to differentiate between a cruise missile which has a nuclear warhead and those which do not. So we would have to have some additional, more comprehensive arrangements to give both sides the assurance that they need to have on this issue.

Q. I am really not asking for details, but is this an on-site inspection proposal, basically?

Mr. Brzezinski. I don't think we have yet reached the stage in which direct on-site examination of all weapons systems is feasible. But certainly, if the Soviet side were prepared to accept some on-site verification, it would be a giant step towards mutual confidence, and we would certainly welcome on-site Soviet inspection of some of our weapons systems. . . . And I would hope that as Soviet confidence grows, as Soviet preoccupation with secrecy declines, that they will find this idea less and less abhorrent.

Q. You talked about the Soviet concern for their land-based weapons, and there has always been a lack of symmetry between their perception of their defense needs and the U.S., which is why they came up with a freedom of choice within their weapons systems.

Your proposal, the American proposal—according to what you say—would appear to take away a lot of their freedom of choice, and, at the same time, it doesn't say anything about sea-based missiles, which also are a threat, or the Soviets perceive them as a threat to their land-based systems. Therefore, can you explain why, in your perception, this is equivalent? A third thing [is] that they have to cut back from 308 to 150 in their super-launch missiles, and we don't have to cut back any land-based.

Mr. Brzezinski. First of all, as far as the freedom to mix is concerned, that would still be retained by both sides, though there would be upper limits set on what you can do, particularly in regards to land-based [MIRVed] ICBMs. That limit indeed would be set at 550. But each side, or one of the sides, could decide that it prefers to have fewer of these

and more sea-based. So, in that sense, there is some freedom to mix, no doubt about it.

As far as the Soviet throw-weight or large ballistic missiles are concerned, their reduction is a necessary concomitant of mutual stability, because if they are not reduced in numbers, then by MIRVing them the Soviet Union would gain, particularly within these lower aggregates, a very significant advantage.

I think one has to recognize the fact that if you have fewer total numbers, then any asymmetry becomes increasingly significant, and the Soviets do have that asymmetry to their advantage in the possession of the large ballistic missiles which can be MIRVed up to eight or ten warheads.

In addition to that, there is this other problem, which I don't want to exaggerate, but which has to be taken into account when we think of equity at the lower aggregates: namely, the Backfire. We were prepared to consider special arrangements for the Backfire. But again, the Backfire—however one defines it, whether it is a strategic or nonstrategic weapon—becomes more significant if you have lower aggregates than if you have higher aggregates. If these aggregates are high, then you can say, well, it is more marginal, but if you go down at 1,800, then the introduction of the Backfire, at some number which is in excess of 100, becomes a factor. And yet we are prepared to accommodate on that, too.

I am not going to argue . . . that this was an infallible package which has to be taken in toto. All I am going to say is that we made the damnedest effort to produce a package which, within the limits of our own intelligence—and by intelligence, I not only mean information, I also mean what is in our heads—we could say was reasonably equitable for both sides. We did our best to define it that way and will be glad to discuss it, and we intend to discuss it. We would like to find out what aspects of this are particularly troubling to the Soviets, because that is what negotiations are about, and conceivably, if the case is persuasive, this or that adjustment could be made in return for this or that adjustment.

Q. What was the Soviet reaction to the package in the general sense? Did they reject it out of hand or say that certain things were difficult?

Mr. BRZEZINSKI. To say that the Soviets rejected it out of hand gives it a dramatic and categorical quality which I really do not think the circumstances justify.

The sequence was essentially as follows. Prior to the Vance mission, we did indicate to the Soviets that we will be making proposals for significant reduction. We did that deliberately because we wanted the Politburo to think about these issues.

As you know, the Soviets do not have an arms control agency. The Soviets do not have influential groups in their society that are concerned with arms control. Arms control proposals are assessed in the Soviet Defense Ministry, which has certain interesting implications, and we felt it would not be particularly constructive to send in a detailed proposal which then is staffed out in the Soviet Defense Ministry and goes up to the Soviet Politburo with a categorical critique. We wanted the top Soviet leaders to focus on this issue.

Therefore, we drew their attention to the fact that we will be making proposals that call for reductions that we think would have a significant impact on the broader nature of our relationship. And then Secretary Vance presented that and, as I said earlier, not only in its strategic setting but also in its political context, when he made his opening statement to the Soviets.

The Soviet leadership then expressed a preference for the discussion of other issues . . . and then in the final or the pre-final session, I forget which, Secretary Brezhnev informed Secretary Vance that this proposal was not acceptable to the Soviet Union. But he coupled it, at the same time, with a clearcut indication that it is the Soviet expectation, which is matched by us, that these talks, including the SALT aspects, will continue, and that, indeed, the Gromyko-Vance meeting will be resumed directly in Geneva in May.

So, it is in this context that I think one ought to assess where we are; and, again, I would like to draw your attention to the analogy that I made before, namely, to the initial reaction by Prime Minister Kosygin when, for the first time, he was confronted at the top level, and not through bureaucratic channels, with the arguments why an ABM is mutually destabilizing. This was a new argument for him. It was not a convincing argument initially, even though it was made very persuasively when he met in Glassboro with President Johnson and Secretary McNamara. And then subsequently it became clear that such an arrangement was indeed in mutual interest.

Q. Dr. Brzezinski, in Mr. Vance's news conference in Moscow he alluded to a Soviet counterproposal based on the 1976 discussions with Dr. Kissinger. I am interested in why that counterproposal was not negotiable.

Mr. BRZEZINSKI. I don't want to engage here in a critique of the Soviet position because, as I said at the beginning of my remarks, I am really not going to engage in recriminations or a kind of side dialogue on their proposals versus our proposals, but really to try to explain the rationale and the content of ours.

Let me limit myself, therefore, to one comment. It is our broad feeling that, twenty-seven years after the beginning of the nuclear race,

the time is right in our relations for doing something more than just creating frameworks for continued competition. It is our feeling that the framework defined by Vladivostok is so high in its numbers, so open-ended in its consequences, so susceptible to quantitative as well as qualitative improvements, that in some respects it comes close to a misstatement to call any such arrangement arms limitations. All it is, really, is an arrangement for continued arms competition, and we have gone to the Soviets with a proposal which we crafted as best we could in order to convince them that maybe the time is right to take a significant step toward reductions.

We gave them ranges so they could pick either the more ambitious or the less ambitious part of it, depending on their estimate of the strategic consequences of cuts. They have very good analysts. They should be able, and I am sure they are able, to assess whether 2,000 is better for them, or 1,800, whether 1,200 MIRVs is better for them, or 1,100, and so forth. So we weren't very categorical about it.

Q. Dr. Brzezinski, you placed heavy stress at the beginning on the political aspect of this, as well as this strategic aspect of the proposal. You said that no one expected them to accept it out of hand, but neither was there widespread expectation of the kind of fierce reaction from the Russians, including the press conference yesterday by Mr. Gromyko. Politically speaking, do you feel that the reception of the proposal and what has happened has set back Soviet-American relations, or were you surprised at what happened; and, if you weren't, was this a miscalculation?

Mr. BRZEZINSKI. If I wasn't, then it couldn't be a miscalculation. It would be a miscalculation if I was.

No, we did not expect the Soviets to accept this total framework on the basis of three days' talks. We expected them to consider it. Our judgment . . . was that the discussions were generally conducted in business-like fashion, that the Soviets' side, through little gestures, went out of its way to indicate that this is an ongoing relationship. They did not hide the fact that they took a negative view of this proposal, and they were quite explicit on it, but there were no nasty polemics in the meeting.

You are absolutely right in saying that some of the statements, maybe even some of the gestures that were made in the press conference by the Soviet minister, were of a more assertive type. But I would describe that perhaps as a reaction to the political perception that indeed the United States has come up with a proposal which, if accepted, would have a significant contribution to disarmament.

The Soviets, over the years, have prided themselves on being in the forefront of the disarmament proposals, and perhaps there was

just a tiny touch of defensiveness, therefore, in some of these gestures and some of these comments. I don't think that these gestures and these comments are really that important. What is important is that the relationship involves continued negotiations, that agreements were read in Moscow to develop working groups on a large number of highly sensitive issues . . . and that, therefore, the negotiating process continues. And in the negotiating process you expect to be turned down, to be pressed, to be asked to make accommodations and concessions, but that is part of the game.

Q. Doctor, what did we offer to forgo that they would have found most threatening to their land-based missiles? I am not clear on that.

Mr. Brzezinski. Particularly the MX, which in its consequences—given its accuracy and so forth—by the early eighties could be extremely, extremely threatening to them; and in that sense, I think that in itself would [be] a source of considerable assurance to them.

Beyond that, if we were to limit the cruise missiles merely to tactical cruise missiles, this too, in the longer run, would be a significant assurance to them. Beyond that, we would have to make some accommodations, given the total numbers in Minutemen I and II and in the Poseidons.

Basically, what it would give them is the sense of security that the United States is forgoing, as a basic strategic option, the acquisition of first-strike capability against their land-based systems.

Brown Discusses SALT and Defense Planning, 13 April 1977

Today, two weeks after Secretary Vance's visit to Moscow, let me begin by suggesting two propositions that may appear to constitute a paradox. The first is that, as Secretary of Defense, I consider equitable arms control agreements to be a help—not a hindrance—in strategic nuclear planning. The second proposition is that, despite this conviction, I strongly favor the continuation of a substantial, diversified, modernized U.S. strategic nuclear force. I think that is what is required to maintain a stable balance of forces and an effective deterrent.

Let me explain why I regard these two propositions as complementary halves of a policy aimed at peace and security.

For better or worse, strategic nuclear forces remain fundamental to the security of the United States and its allies. We must assume they seem similarly fundamental to the leaders of the Soviet Union. It is undeniable that these forces involve destructive power unprecedented in history. It was this situation that led Winston Churchill to speculate that, in the atomic age, safety would become "the sturdy child of terror, and survival the twin brother of annihilation."

To deal with this situation, the United States in its strategic planning has sought three major objectives: deterrence, stability, and equivalence. We believe that if either side approached the capability for a knockout first-strike blow, relations between the United States and the Soviet Union would become extremely volatile and much more hazardous. We recognize that if our second-strike deterrent is to be stable, as well as secure, the Soviet deterrent must be secure as well. We have forgone the quest for a first-strike superiority over the Soviet Union. But this does not mean we accept inferiority—we insist on equality, and nothing less.

Recognize, however, that when we talk about "equality" between the U.S. and U.S.S.R. in nuclear weapons, we are not talking about a single delicately calibrated point. Equality does not require identity. Rather, it is a condition met by a broad band of possible force structures on the two sides. Within that band the two sides' forces—judged on a variety of measures, including present and projected technologies as well as potential scenarios for a nuclear exchange—are

SOURCE: Remarks of Secretary of Defense Harold Brown at the University of Rochester (New York), 13 April 1977. Office of the Assistant Secretary of Defense (Public Affairs), News Release No. 161–77, 13 April 1977.

roughly equivalent overall. We and the Soviets are now, in fact, in such a position of rough equivalence.

* * *

Unfortunately, however, the strategic relationship is not self-stabilizing. The very process of continued deployments and developments has dangers. Three paths are open to the United States and the Soviet Union as each decides what part of its resources to devote in the future to strategic nuclear forces. We can go up, we can go down, or we can remain essentially level in numbers and types of weapons. To note that these are the choices in one sense states the obvious. But the point is not trivial, for there are both costs and risks to the courses that involve intensified competition on both sides.

I cannot be sure what the Soviets will do. But I do know this: If they choose the upward path and continue to increase the size and effectiveness of their strategic forces, this country beyond question will respond to ensure that our forces continue to provide a deterrence that is credible, is stable, and produces perceived equivalence. The United States can achieve its objectives of deterrence, stability, and equivalence in the face of Soviet strategic force improvements. We can do so, if necessary, without a strategic arms limitation agreement, although less surely and at a great price to both sides in resources. Our resource base is large enough to ensure that the Soviets cannot gain political and military advantages over us. On the other hand, I hope the Soviets realize that it is in the interest of both nations to forgo the upward path, to avoid tipping the strategic balance.

To date, the ABM treaty and the numerical limits of the SALT I interim agreement on strategic offensive forces have contributed somewhat to easing the uncertainties which face defense planners. In particular, the ABM treaty removed one major concern. But technology has been moving more rapidly than have our mutual efforts to moderate the competition. MIRVs, increased accuracy, and the Soviet installation of larger ICBMs in existing silos have largely undermined the constraints on offensive weapons imposed by SALT I.

In these circumstances, we have had no alternative but to follow two complementary courses of action. The first is to ensure, within SALT constraints, that our strategic force remains capable of meeting our objectives despite the continuing Soviet strategic buildup—a buildup, I should note, which has also taken place within SALT constraints. That course . . . has entailed maintaining the strategic balance by means of a large, diversified, and modernized U.S. strategic

force posture. In doing so we are spending about one percent of our gross national product on strategic nuclear forces. Only modest increases are projected on our part as long as the Soviets do not substantially increase their strategic force posture.

The preferred path, of course, would be for both sides to reduce in number their strategic weapons, and then to slow down technological improvements which could lead to one side's acquiring advantage. In the competitive situation that is almost certain to persist between the U.S. and the Soviet Union, the two sides will compete within the limitations. But arms limitation measures, skillfully designed and verified, can make the task of planning easier and more efficient. They can help remove some complicating factors. They can, if equitable and sensible, ease concerns about the future which might otherwise stimulate force buildups which would be destabilizing.

The lack of substantial ballistic missile defenses to be penetrated, as a result of the ABM treaty, means that the two sides can plan their offensive forces without having to take into account attrition by even primitive ABM systems. And if fixed ICBMs in hard silos could be made secure for another ten years or more through controls to limit improvements of accuracy and through reductions in throw-weight, then the need for land-based mobile missile systems would become less urgent. Deterrence could then be achieved with higher confidence, fewer forces, more stability, and probably lower costs.

Arms control, thus, can make defense planning more effective and efficient in reaching national objectives. Equitable control and reductions of strategic arms should enhance the security of both the United States and the Soviet Union, and increase the stability of the strategic balance. The reduced nuclear force postures of the two nations need not be mirror images of each other, but they must be essentially equivalent in capability, and they must not cast doubt upon the survivability of the other side's retaliatory forces.

It is still too early to say how the current arms reduction effort will fare, although my analysis of the long-term interests which we share with the Soviet Union makes me optimistic for that long term. Their acceptance of either of the President's two proposals, presented by Secretary Vance in Moscow, would provide both sides with deterrence, stability, and essential equivalence.

* * *

The comprehensive option . . . is the first proposal made by either government which substantively spells out in detail a real and politically meaningful reduction in strategic nuclear forces. It would not just reduce forces in the aggregate. In addition, by establishing

restraints, it would enhance the survivability of both sides' ICBM forces now and in the future.

There are four basic elements to this option. First, it would reduce the aggregates. . . . The numerical limits are the same for the two sides except for one that continues a Soviet advantage in modern large ballistic missiles, though at a reduced level. Since the Soviets have more strategic nuclear delivery vehicles than we do, the reduction in vehicles would immediately affect them more than us. But on the other hand, we now have about three times as many MIRVed missiles as they do, so the MIRV limit would affect the U.S. before it would the Soviets. Finally, although the Soviets would have to give up more than half of their modern large ballistic missiles, they would keep the rest—and they could MIRV all they kept—while we would not be permitted to have any such large missiles in our arsenal, MIRVed or unMIRVed.

The second element in the comprehensive option is a prohibition on the introduction of new ICBM capabilities, thereby improving stability within the strategic balance by reducing the vulnerability of both ICBM forces. It would continue the ban on building new ICBM silos which was agreed to at Vladivostok. It would also prohibit the modification of existing ICBMs and ban the development, testing, and deployment of new types of ICBMs as well as mobile ICBMs.

At the present time, both sides are reasonably confident that the bulk of their ICBM forces would survive an attack. [Our] objective . . . is simply to keep it that way. In support of this objective, we propose to limit ICBM tests to six per year. This will make it far less likely that either side would become so confident in the accuracy of its ICBMs as to believe that it could knock out most of the other side's ICBMs. Although development of submarine-launched ballistic missiles could continue, testing of these also would be limited to six per year. That limit on testing would reduce the pace of SLBM development and hinder the attainment of high accuracy by both nations' SLBM forces.

In sum, this approach would enhance stability by delaying substantially the time when fixed ICBMs become vulnerable. And since the Soviets have a much larger portion of their strategic nuclear force in ICBMs than we have, I cannot see how anyone could claim that this arrangement would be inequitable to them.

A third element of the proposal is that it would ban cruise missiles with ranges greater than 2,500 km (about 1,550 miles). This range restriction would prevent us from substituting cruise missiles for SLBMs, thereby assuming significant independent strategic uses. The limitation would permit us to use cruise missiles as penetration aids for our bombers against the large and comprehensive Soviet air

defense system—a system the Soviets have never been willing to include in SALT discussions. It would not, however, interfere with the use of cruise missiles outside the SALT context, that is, in tactical or theater applications. In short, the cruise missile proposal limits strategic uses of cruise missiles, as is appropriate in a strategic arms limitation agreement. But it would not make us pay for a SALT agreement by limits on our nonstrategic ability to counter Soviet weapons that are controlled neither in SALT nor elsewhere.

The final element of the comprensive proposal provides that Soviet Backfire bombers will not be counted in the aggregate as long as they are not deployed as strategic weapons. The United States will insist on appropriate assurances that these bombers, which have a combat radius sufficient for some strategic uses, will not now or in the future perform strategic missions. There are a number of actions the Soviets could take to that end, and we are ready to consider what they propose. In short, this provision would accept the Soviet position that the Backfire is not a strategic weapon, and simply require them to provide us with acceptable and verifiable assurances that such will in fact be the case.

How would an agreement along these lines affect the future? Because such a treaty would last for perhaps eight or ten years, estimates of what the comparative strategic forces would be like at the end of that period are of course only projections, not hard facts. Soviet SLBM MIRV systems would have time to go through several generations, and the numbers of weapons a bomber can carry varies widely with circumstances. However, we can identify in approximate terms certain likely trends:

- The United States would retain its lead in the total number of warheads and bomber weapons added together.
- The Soviets would lead in ICBM warheads, whereas the United States would lead in SLBM warheads.
- The Soviets would retain their substantial lead in total missile throw-weight. Their ICBM warheads would continue to be larger as well as more numerous than our own. The United States, on the other hand, would continue to lead in bomber payload.

The comprehensive proposal thus would affect the diverse elements of the U.S. and Soviet strategic forces in different ways. It can be evaluated only in its totality in judging its equitability.

Our two proposals, particularly the comprehensive option, are far-reaching. They would have a real impact on U.S. and Soviet strategic weapons programs, and would provide us with a chance to

deal with a key source of instability—ICBM improvements. The proposals are also equitable. They would serve the interests of the Soviet Union no less than our own, by avoiding the costs and risks of increasing the numbers and sophistication of nuclear arms. Finally, the proposals are realistic. . . . They respond to the security concerns of both sides.

9
The Geneva Talks, May 1977

Vance Discusses the Upcoming Geneva Talks, 4 May 1977

Secretary VANCE. Let me give you a rundown on where we stand since we had our meetings in Moscow.

I have had several conversations with the Soviets here in Washington since we returned from Moscow. In those conversations we have discussed two matters.

The first has been to set up the procedures and dates for the working groups which, you know, we agreed to establish as a result of the Moscow meetings. . . . Secondly, we have reviewed the two proposals which we put on the table in Moscow and the longstanding Soviet proposal with respect to SALT which existed before we went to Moscow. We have put no new proposals on the table, nor have they. We have merely reviewed the existing proposals.

We will be discussing SALT with the Soviets when I go to Geneva to meet with the Foreign Minister. I do not want to predict at this time what may come out of those discussions. We will just have to wait and see what happens at the time.

* * *

Q. Can you explain what modifications, if any, were made in the American proposal while the delegation was in Moscow, specifically referring to this question of nonheavy bombers carrying cruise missiles?

Secretary VANCE. I would be glad to talk to that. This relates to the question of whether or not there should be a limitation on the range of missiles that could be carried by tactical aircraft.

One of the elements of the proposal which we made to the So-

SOURCE: Press conference of Secretary of State Cyrus R. Vance, Washington, D.C., 4 May 1977. *Department of State Bulletin*, 23 May 1977, pp. 513–520.

viets in Moscow was that any missile, air-launched cruise missile, with a range over 600—in other words, between 600 kilometers and 2,500 kilometers—could only be carried on heavy bombers. The reason for that was to meet the problem created by the Backfire bomber, which the Soviets maintain is an intermediate bomber. But if one were to be able to hang long-range missiles on it, it could, as you can obviously see, change the characteristics of that bomber.

Now, coming to the specifics of how that provision came into being, the provision with respect to tactical aircraft not being able to carry air-launched cruise missiles with ranges over 600 kilometers was first developed in 1975. When this administration came into office we reviewed those studies. In the discussions in the NSC subsequently, one of the options which was considered was that option. The reason for its consideration is as I have indicated. It is a very important aspect of limiting or constraining the Backfire so that it cannot become an intercontinental bomber. And it was determined in the NSC and approved by the President that this would be a provision.

That provision was not contained specifically in the very brief general instructions which I took with me to Moscow. But when we got to Moscow and put down on paper the specific proposal in all its detail, it was clear that that had to be spelled out so that there would be no ambiguity in dealing with the Soviet Union, and it was therefore included in the specific proposal which was put before the Soviets.

*　*　*

Q. Mr. Secretary, your comments about SALT suggest there is a deadlock; is that correct?
Secretary VANCE. Nobody has moved from their position at this point, but the parties are talking to each other. So you can draw your own conclusions, use whatever words you want. We are talking to each other, and I hope out of this process we will be able to make some progress.

*　*　*

Q. Sir, when you say there is no deadline on SALT, did you have in your mind that the interim agreement lapses in October? Isn't that a deadline of sorts?
Secretary VANCE. It is a fact that the interim agreement expires in October; but if we reach October and we have not had an agreement, we have two choices. We can either extend the agreement if the Soviets are willing to do so, or we can continue to proceed without an

agreement but on the assumption that we will continue as if there were a continuing agreement. And I am not saying that we won't reach agreement or that we will reach agreement by October. But I don't feel we are fighting any deadline that is going to cause us to take actions that are not wise and prudent.

Joint Communiqué, 21 May 1977

In the course of the discussions between Cyrus R. Vance, Secretary of State of the U.S.A., and L. I. Brezhnev, General Secretary of the Central Committee of the CPSU, and A. A. Gromyko, Member of the Politburo of the CPSU, Minister of Foreign Affairs of the U.S.S.R., held in Moscow at the end of March, 1977, Cyrus R. Vance and A. A. Gromyko met in Geneva on May 18–20.

They examined in detail the situation regarding the preparation of a new agreement on the limitation of strategic offensive arms based on the Vladivostok Accord and taking into account the results of subsequent discussions. Both sides agreed that the discussions in Geneva were necessary and useful and that progress had been made in developing a common framework for further negotiations. As a result of the exchange of views, the differences between the two sides on several of the previously unresolved questions have been narrowed. It is agreed that the discussions of all unresolved questions will be continued with the aim of an early conclusion of a new agreement that will replace the interim agreement on certain measures with respect to the limitation of strategic offensive armaments.

Cyrus R. Vance and A. A. Gromyko also had a thorough exchange of views on the problem of the settlement in the Middle East. . . .

SOURCE: *Department of State Bulletin,* 13 June 1977, p. 633.

Vance Outlines a New Framework for SALT II, 21 May 1977

Secretary VANCE. In our judgment the talks have been both necessary and useful and also constructive. Progress has been made.

We have reached general agreement on a common framework for the SALT II agreement. This consists of three elements: first, a treaty; second, a protocol to the treaty; and third, a statement of general principles which would govern the conduct of SALT III. All of these parts are interdependent, and I want to make that point very strongly. This is an interdependent whole made up of these different parts. The treaty would run until 1985; the protocol would be for a period of three years. . . . This framework provides a method of blending the three proposals which have been on the table since our discussions in Moscow.

Differences remain, substantial differences between the sides on a number of issues. They break down into several categories. One category is whether certain items should be included in the treaty or in the protocol. Another set of items raises questions as to whether they should be included at all in either the protocol or the treaty. And the third set is the precise nature of all of the items which would be included in a statement of general principles. . . .

Q. Mr. Secretary, you said that we reached general agreement on a common framework for a SALT treaty. The communiqué does not state that. The language of the communiqué falls short of stating that you have reached general agreement. Why is that?

Secretary VANCE. When I say general agreement, what I mean is that we have on the form of it—namely, treaty, protocol, and a statement of general principles—we have agreement. We do not have agreement [on] what comes within the various elements, as I have indicated to you. We have differences of opinion on that.

Q. Mr. Secretary, what happens now? Who will do the negotiating and when? Do you think you will have these three component parts by October?

Secretary VANCE. We are going to talk at three different levels. Some of the discussions will be had between the two delegations here in Geneva. Some of the discussions will probably be had at ambassadorial levels within the two capitals between the local ambassador

---

SOURCE: Press conference of Secretary of State Cyrus R. Vance, Geneva, 21 May 1977. *Department of State Bulletin*, 13 June 1977, pp. 628–633.

and the foreign minister. And Mr. Gromyko and I will be meeting again at a time to be set in the future. . . .

Q. And the second part of that question: Do you think you will have it by October?

Secretary VANCE. I really don't know. This is a long process, as I've said many, many times. It's one which requires patience. We are going to devote ourselves to carrying through on a continuing basis on this, but I don't want to make any predictions as to when we'll reach agreement.

Q. Mr. Secretary, would you elaborate on how the protocol would operate, as distinct from the treaty itself?

Secretary VANCE. Yes; the protocol would be limited to three years, whereas the treaty would run until 1985.

Q. Excuse me, three years starting when?

Secretary VANCE. Starting with the signing of the treaty and the protocol. It would run for three years and therefore would expire—assuming that one could be reached in the near future—well in advance of 1985.

Q. Why was this course taken? Can you—

Secretary VANCE. Because it helps provide a blending of the various elements.

Q. Mr. Secretary, on the blending, is it fair to say—since you are using the word blending—that the Soviets accept President Carter's deep-cuts proposal as one of the principles of the SALT agreement?

Secretary VANCE. Certainly one of the—let me say that SALT II and SALT III in our judgment are a continuum, and it is extremely important to set up the process so that this continuum can take place. Therefore, one of the portions of this framework is to provide the long-term goals which would be taken care of in SALT III and which, insofar as we are concerned, involve the comprehensive proposals. We have made clear to the Soviets our views with respect to what should be included in the statement of general principles. They will want to reflect on that and, I'm sure, give some views of their own as to what items should be included in such a statement of general principles, and that will be part of the ongoing talks.

Q. Mr. Secretary, is there an agreement on what you will do if you do not have a new treaty by the time the current treaty expires?

Secretary VANCE. No, we did not discuss that.

* * *

Q. What is the purpose of the protocol? Does it begin around the cruise missile question? It is still not clear why you would have a three-year protocol.

Secretary VANCE. There are some items which, in the judgment of the parties, do not fit in an agreement which lasts as long as 1985, and therefore there should be a shorter period of time to take care of those items.

Q. What kind of items are you talking about?

Secretary VANCE. I have indicated that because of the interdependence of these, I am not going to spell out what items go in what particular parts of the package.

Q. Is it all agreed which items you are going to—

Secretary VANCE. We have agreed on some; we have not agreed on others.

Q. Is there a definite list of the unresolved questions?

Secretary VANCE. We are not going to make available a list of that.

Q. Does it exist?

Secretary VANCE. Yes, we each understand what the unresolved issues are.

* * *

Q. How would you compare this framework in significance with the Vladivostok understanding of November 1974?

Secretary VANCE. As the communiqué indicates, the Vladivostok accords are part of this general framework. I would point out to you that insofar as the U.S. position is concerned, we have always believed that the Vladivostok accords were an appropriate part of the discussions. Our deferral proposal related specifically to the Vladivostok accords, and the principles of it were certainly included also in our comprehensive proposal as well. So that is nothing new.

Q. So when you talk about the Vladivostok accords, are you talking solely about 1974 or are you including Secretary Kissinger's discussion in 1976?

Secretary VANCE. The '76 discussions would be included within the overall framework we are talking about. When I use the word Vladivostok accords, I use it with a more restricted meaning than I think you are suggesting.

Q. Mr. Secretary, there was a great deal of talk before these discussions took place here of cooling, of freezing and deadlock of U.S.-Soviet relations. Do you feel that what has transpired here has set these two nations on a new course at all?

Secretary VANCE. Well, I said . . . that I thought these had been very constructive talks, and I believe the Soviets would share that view, and I think the atmosphere is better as a result of these talks.

Q. Mr. Secretary, do you give the continuation of these talks a good prospect of success in this year?

Secretary VANCE. On dates, I really don't want to speculate, because I think it is rather fruitless to speculate. There are serious issues that remain between us, and it's going to take a lot of discussion and negotiation before one can see whether or not these issues can be resolved.

Q. In face of what you negotiated so far, Mr. Secretary, do you exclude a view that envisions a summit conference this year?

Secretary VANCE. I don't exclude it.

* * *

Q. Mr. Secretary, at his press conference in Moscow, Mr. Gromyko said that the Soviet Union would raise the question of forward-basing of missiles in certain circumstances. Is that issue still on the table?

Secretary VANCE. It was one of the ones that was raised during our talks here, yes.

Q. Has it been resolved?

Secretary VANCE. Again I am not going to comment on specific items as to whether they have or have not been resolved.

Q. Mr. Secretary, when you arrived here was this framework what you had in mind? Are you leaving here with what you wanted to leave with?

Secretary VANCE. Let me say that such a framework was in mind when we arrived here.

Q. And you expected nothing more than that?

Secretary VANCE. I am pleased that this framework was basically agreed upon.

* * *

Q. . . . Is there real progress toward resolving the real dispute or is it just another jiggling around of the same disagreement? In other words, have you actually removed some of the basic disagreements from the table or are you just working out another framework but the same basic problems still exist?

Secretary VANCE. I would say two things. I think there has been some progress toward resolving some of the issues. But I would say, secondly, that serious differences remain between us which are going to have to be worked out and which will be difficult to work out.

Q. Mr. Secretary, from what you have said, it would appear that you do not have a clear commitment at this time from the Soviets to talk about deep cuts. Is that correct?

Secretary VANCE. I would put it this way, that if we achieve the total

package which I have talked about—in other words, the total framework—then there would be such a commitment in the overall result.

* * *

Q. Mr. Secretary [inaudible] to the Soviet demand for limitation of spread of cruise technology to the NATO allies?

Secretary VANCE. Our position with respect to forward-based systems is well known. We believe that those are not an appropriate subject for discussion in this bilateral forum, that that is a question for discussion in the multilateral forum. Our posititon on that is well known and has been for a long time.

Q. Mr. Secretary, did you discuss on-site inspection?

Secretary VANCE. Not as such. We decided to discuss the question of verification.

Q. Without going into the details, I wonder if you could give us a little more help on the concept of the protocol and what it is meant to do. One would speculate very rapidly that you can put constraints on the deployment of cruise and Backfire in the protocol for three years and then bargain in the meantime. Is that the general idea, or—

Secretary VANCE. Those kinds of items could be included in the protocol.

Q. Will the SALT II agreement be based on the figures of Vladivostok, and the reductions only envisioned in the next stage [inaudible]? Will it be at this 2,400 ceiling, and only in SALT III you will come to reductions?

Secretary VANCE. The answer to that is there may be reductions prior to SALT III. And that's as far as I want to go on that.

Carter Cancels Production of the B-1 Bomber, 30 June 1977

President CARTER. This has been one of the most difficult decisions that I have made since I've been in office. During the last few months, I've done my best to assess all the factors involving production of the B–1 bomber. My decision is that we should not continue with deployment of the B–1, and I am directing that we discontinue plans for production of this weapons system. The Secretary of Defense agrees that this is a preferable decision. . . .

The existing testing and development program now underway on the B–1 should continue to provide us with the needed technical base in the unlikely event that more cost-effective alternative systems should run into difficulty. Continued efforts at the research and development stage will give us better answers about the cost and effectiveness of the bomber and support systems, including electronic countermeasures techniques.

During the coming months, we will also be able to assess the progress toward agreements on strategic arms limitations in order to determine the need for any additional investments in nuclear weapons delivery systems. In the meantime, we should begin deployment of cruise missiles using air-launched platforms, such as our B–52s, modernized as necessary. Our Triad concept of retaining three basic delivery systems will be continued with submarine-launched ballistic missiles, intercontinental ballistic missiles, and a bomber fleet, including cruise missiles as one of its armaments. We will continue thereby to have an effective and flexible strategic force whose capability is fully sufficient for our national defense.

*   *   *

Q. Mr. President, what were the major factors that led to your decision against the B–1 bomber?

President CARTER. There are a number of factors. One is obviously the recent evolution of the cruise missile as an effective weapon itself. The tests of this system have been very successful so far.

Another one, of course, is the continued ability to use the B–52 bombers—particularly the Gs and Hs—up well into the 1980s, and the belief on my part that our defense capability using the submarine-launched missiles and intercontinental ballistic missiles combined with the B–52/cruise missile combination is adequate.

SOURCE: Press conference of President Jimmy Carter, Washington, D.C., 30 June 1977. *Weekly Compilation of Presidential Documents*, 4 July 1977, pp. 951–960.

We will also explore the possibility of cruise missile carriers, perhaps using existing airplanes or others as a standoff launching base.

But I think in toto the B–1, a very expensive weapons system basically conceived in the absence of the cruise missile factor, is not necessary. Those are the major reasons.

Q. Mr. President, the Soviet Union has shown great concern about the cruise missile capability of the United States. What limits are you ready to accept, if any, on air-launched cruise missiles so far as their range; and secondly, are you willing to accept the proposition that an airplane carrying cruise would be counted as a MIRV under the limits that you would set in a SALT agreement?

President CARTER. Those questions are being negotiated now. We have a fairly compatible position with the Soviets on maximum range of air-launched cruise missiles carried over from the Vladivostok discussions. I don't think there's any particular difference in that. It's an adequate range in my opinion for the cruise missiles to be launched as a standoff weapon without the carrying airplane having to encroach into Soviet territory. This, though, is a matter that has not yet been finally resolved.

Also, the definition of what is a MIRVed weapon is one that is still in dispute. We don't believe that a bomber equipped with cruise missiles as a weapon ought to be classified as a MIRVed weapon. But depending upon the Soviets' attitude in reaching an overall comprehensive settlement, those matters are still open for discussion.

* * *

Q. Mr. President, is this decision on your part not to go ahead with the B–1 intended as any kind of a signal to the Soviets that you are willing to—that you want to do something quickly in the strategic arms talks?

President CARTER. I can't deny that that's a potential factor. But that has not been a reason for my decision. I think if I had looked upon the B–1 as simply a bargaining chip for the Soviets, then my decision would have been to go ahead with the weapon. But I made my decision on my analysis that, within a given budgetary limit for the defense of our country, which I am sure will always be adequate, that we should have the optimum capability to defend ourselves.

But this is a matter that's of very great importance, and if at the end of a few years the relations with the Soviets should deteriorate drastically, which I don't anticipate, then it may be necessary for me to change my mind. But I don't expect that to occur.

Brown Discusses the Cancellation of the B-1 Bomber and SALT, 1 July 1977

Q. Can you tell us if this decision [not to build the B–1 bomber] obviates any further interest in controlling strategic cruise missiles in SALT; and what program have you got underway for defending America against Backfire-launched cruise missiles?

Secretary BROWN. The cruise missile remains a subject for negotiation and I would hope agreement in SALT. Clearly, because we are orienting our strategic nuclear capability more in the direction of cruise missiles, although we retain a Triad and we retain a penetrating bomber capability, we have to continue to assure that our position on the cruise missiles in SALT does not interfere in any serious way with our plans for the incorporation of cruise missiles into the strategic bomber force. That is one thing on which there have been discussions with the Soviets; our position in those discussions is such that what we plan for our cruise missiles on bombers is allowed.

Q. How about the defense against the Backfire-launched cruise missile?

Secretary BROWN. Yes, that is a different question, and it needs to be seen in the context of U.S. air defense generally. We can't, in any very effective way, because we have such minimal air defenses, defend against bombers that reach the U.S. without cruise missiles. We concluded some time ago that the defense against a massive bomber attack, especially in the era of intercontinental ballistic missiles, is not worth the money it costs.

The Soviets have not yet concluded that; it may be that these decisions will help persuade them to that same conclusion. But, so long as the situation is that we have no anti-ballistic missile defense and no substantial bomber defense, I see no great purpose in going after a cruise missile defense, which is even harder and less rewarding.

Q. I was confused by something the President said yesterday in discussing this. He said that the United States and the Soviet Union had come to a virtual agreement on a range of a cruise missile—Vladivostok range. Now, certainly you can't expect the B-52 to have a standoff capability off the U.S.S.R. with a 375-mile range, can you?

Secretary BROWN. There is no agreement, and in fact neither the U.S.

SOURCE: Press conference of Secretary of Defense Harold Brown, Washington, D.C., 1 July 1977. Office of the Assistant Secretary of Defense (Public Affairs).

nor the Soviet position is, that cruise missiles launched from bombers should be limited to 375 miles, 600 kilometers. In fact, you know, we have a position on cruise missiles from bombers; the Soviets also have a position. Those are not identical; there is considerable overlap, but neither of them spells out that limit.

I think that you may be interpreting the President's answer too narrowly. Vladivostok itself, of course, did not cover cruise missiles. It mentioned a 600-kilometer range. There have been subsequent discussions on quite different ranges for cruise missiles from bombers.

* * *

Q. This decision on the B–1—there is some thought that this was an attempt to influence the SALT negotiations, and perhaps influence the Russians into an agreement. Does it have anything to do with that?
Secretary Brown. The thought that it's either a bargaining chip that we should have kept or a bargaining chip that we should have offered up so as to get them to make decisions not to go ahead with systems of their own, did not really enter into this decision.

* * *

Q. . . . Has the Air Force priced itself out of the bomber market by going so expensive? . . .
Secretary Brown. The B–1 would have been a more attractive option, probably, had it been 30 percent less expensive, but I believe that the technology of cruise missile development played a larger part. The fact that cruise missile tests have shown that they really can fly very low, that the guidance system, the TERCOM—terrain contour mapping and update guidance system—works very accurately, provide a new technological alternative and a new operational alternative that really had to be compared with the B–1.

The B–1 is a good aircraft. There is no doubt in my mind that it could have been produced, and that it would have had performance capable of serving an effective strategic role. But, one is projecting ahead to Soviet defenses; and although I'm convinced that we could with the B–1 penetrate Soviet defenses, I'm even more convinced that we can do so with cruise missiles. That's what happened and that was the basis of my conclusion.

* * *

Q. Mr. Secretary, is this the last manned bomber which you believe we'll ever develop?
Secretary Brown. I don't know; I have no way of telling. I am con-

vinced that there are going to continue to be bombers that launch weapons. If we go ahead with a cruise missile carrier, that clearly will be in the category of a bomber. It just happens to have rather long trajectory to its terminal missile launch. Whether we will have a new penetrating bomber, one which is designed to go in virtually over the target, I don't know; but I am convinced that manned aircraft launching weapons—which I would therefore call bombers—will continue to be in the inventory of our strategic forces for the indefinite future.

* * *

Q. At the start of the press conference you said that the United States must make sure that its SALT position does not harm the plan to introduce cruise missiles into the force. How do you expect to obtain a SALT agreement restraining Soviet systems of concern to the United States if we're unwilling to accept restraints on U.S. systems of concern to the Soviets?

Secretary BROWN. I did not say that we would not accept any constraints; I said that the constraints we accept must not harm our strategic capability and—

Q. You said there's no agreement in the long-range cruise missiles.

Secretary BROWN. Everything we do or have preempts some condition.

Q. We proposed at the latest SALT talks an air-launched cruise missile of 1,500 miles—

Secretary BROWN. Yes.

Q. There's no agreement on it but now we're going ahead with it.

Secretary BROWN. I said of our position that it is sufficient to accommodate what we plan to do, and so I think you and I agree on what we say. . . .

Q. Is the 1,500-mile range an adequate range for this purpose, or do you have to go to a higher range than that?

Secretary BROWN. One thousand five hundred miles goes from well outside Soviet defenses, which in turn are outside their borders, to almost all of the target system, and all the main targets.

Q. Silos, sir, in the heartland of Russia?

Secretary BROWN. Those empty silos, or so they will be.

Q. Aren't they going to retain some of those missiles for a second strike? They're not going to shoot all their missiles off on a first strike, sir.

Secretary BROWN. We can reach those too. We needn't be able to—and I think we can reach those with enough different systems, including

some of these, so that we can take care of that problem. I think there are difficult problems in any strategic force, but that's not a main one.

* * *

Q. Were the proliferation implications taken into account in the President's decision? For example, are you now closer to giving the cruise missile to NATO allies, including West Germany; and to a later stage, what about in the Middle East?

Secretary BROWN. The decisions taken here have to do with air-launched cruise missiles. They do not affect our positions, our negotiations—which are still evolving, still underway—on cruise missiles launched from other sources, from other media. The effects of the cruise missile, its possibility both as an allied weapon in the European theater and as a Soviet weapon against NATO, are being examined closely with NATO. No conclusions have yet been reached on it.

It has some attractions, it also has some risks, and until those are fully evaluated, we can't reach a decision on what the proper relation of the cruise missile to NATO is, let alone affect anywhere else.

Carter Outlines American Policy Toward the Soviet Union, 21 July 1977

For decades the central problems of our foreign policy revolved around antagonism between two coalitions, one headed by the United States and the other headed by the Soviet Union.

Our national security was often defined almost exclusively in terms of military competition with the Soviet Union. This competition is still critical, because it does involve issues which could lead to war. But however important this relationship of military balance, it cannot be our sole preoccupation, to the exclusion of other world issues which also concern us both.

Even if we succeed in relaxing tensions with the U.S.S.R., we could still awake one day to find that nuclear weapons have been spread to dozens of other nations who may not be as responsible as are we. Or we could struggle to limit the conventional arsenals of our two nations to reduce the danger of war, only to undo our efforts by continuing without constraint to export armaments around the world.

As two industrial giants, we face long-term, world-wide energy crises. Whatever our political differences, both of us are compelled to begin conserving world energy and developing alternatives to oil and gas.

Despite deep and continuing differences in world outlook, both of us should accept the new responsibilities imposed on us by the changing nature of international relations. . . . Both the United States and the Soviet Union have learned that our countries and our people, in spite of great resources, are not all-powerful. We've learned that this world, no matter how technology has shrunk distances, is nevertheless too large and too varied to come under the sway of either one or two superpowers. And, what is perhaps most important of all, we have, for our part, learned, all of us, this fact, these facts, in a spirit not of increasing resignation but of increasing maturity. . . .

The whole history of Soviet-American relations teaches us that we will be misled if we base our long-range policies on the mood of the moment, whether that mood be euphoric or grim. All of us can remember times when relations seemed especially dangerous and other times when they seemed especially bright. We've crossed those

SOURCE: Remarks of President Jimmy Carter before the Southern Legislative Conference, Charleston, South Carolina, 21 July 1977. *Department of State Bulletin,* 15 August 1977, pp. 193–197.

peaks and valleys before. And we can see that, on balance, the trend in the last third of a century has been positive.

The profound differences in what our two governments believe about freedom and power and the inner lives of human beings—those differences are likely to remain, and so are other elements of competition between the United States and the Soviet Union. That competition is real and deeply rooted in the history and the values of our respective societies. But it's also true that our two countries share many important overlapping interests. Our job—my job, your job—is to explore those shared interests and use them to enlarge the areas of cooperation between us on a basis of equality and mutual respect.

As we negotiate with the Soviet Union, we will be guided by a vision—of a gentler, freer, and more bountiful world. But we will have no illusions about the nature of the world as it really is. The basis for complete mutual trust between us does not yet exist. Therefore, the agreements that we reach must be anchored on each side in enlightened self-interest—what's best for us, what's best for the Soviet Union. That's why we search for areas of agreement where our real interests and those of the Soviets coincide.

We want to see the Soviets further engaged in the growing pattern of international activities designed to deal with human problems—not only because they can be of real help, but because we both should be seeking for a greater stake in the creation of a constructive and peaceful world order.

When I took office, many Americans were growing disillusioned with détente—President Ford had even quit using the word—and, by extension, people were concerned with the whole course of our relations with the Soviet Union. Also, and perhaps more seriously, world respect for the essential rightness of American foreign policy had been shaken by the events of a decade—Vietnam, Cambodia, CIA, Watergate. At the same time, we were beginning to regain our sense of confidence and our purpose and unity as a nation.

In this situation, I decided that it was time for honest discussions about international issues with the American people. I felt that it was urgent to restore the moral bearings of American foreign policy. And I felt that it was important to put the U.S. and Soviet relationship, in particular, on a more reciprocal, realistic, and ultimately more productive basis for both nations. It is not a question of a "hard" policy or of a "soft" policy, but of a clear-eyed recognition of how most effectively to protect our own security and to create the kind of international order that I've just described. This is our goal.

We've looked at the problems in Soviet-American relations in a fresh way, and we've sought to deal with them boldly and construc-

tively with proposals intended to produce concrete results. I'd like to point out just a few of them.

- In the talks on strategic arms limitations—the SALT talks—we advanced a comprehensive proposal for genuine reductions, limitations, and a freeze on new technology which would maintain balanced strategic strength.
- We have urged a complete end of all nuclear tests, and these negotiations are now under way. Agreement here could be a milestone in U.S.-Soviet relations.
- We're working together toward a ban on chemical and biological warfare and the elimination of inventories of these destructive materials.
- We have proposed to curb the sales and transfers of conventional weapons to other countries, and we've asked France, Britain, and other countries to join with us in this effort.
- We're attempting to halt the threatening proliferation of nuclear weapons among the nations of the world which don't yet have the ability to set off nuclear explosives.
- We've undertaken serious negotiations on arms limitations in the Indian Ocean.
- We've encouraged the Soviets to sign, along with us, the treaty of Tlatelolco, which would ban the introduction of nuclear weapons into the southern part of the Western Hemisphere.
- We have begun regular consultations with the Soviet leaders, as cochairmen of the prospective Geneva conference, to promote peace in the Middle East.
- We and our allies are negotiating together with the Soviet Union and their allies in the Warsaw Pact nations to reduce the level of military forces in Europe.
- We've renewed the 1972 agreement for cooperation in science and technology, and a similar agreement for cooperation in outer space.
- We're seeking ways to cooperate in improving world health and in relieving world hunger.

In the Strategic Arms Limitation Talks—confirming and then building on Vladivostok accords—we need to make steady progress toward our long-term goals of genuine reductions and strict limita-

tions, while maintaining the basic strategic balance. We've outlined proposals incorporating significant new elements of arms control: deep reductions in the arsenals of both sides, freezing the deployment and technology, and restraining certain elements in the strategic posture of both sides that threaten to destabilize the balance which now exists.

The Vladivostok negotiations of 1974 left some issues unresolved and subject to honest differences of interpretation. Meanwhile, new developments in technology have created new concerns—the cruise missile, the very large intercontinental ballistic missiles of the Soviets.

The Soviets are worried about our cruise missiles, and we are concerned about the security of our own deterrent capability. Our cruise missiles are aimed at compensating for the growing threat to our deterrent represented by the buildup of strategic Soviet offensive weapons forces. If these threats can be controlled, and I believe they can, then we are prepared to limit our own strategic programs. But if an agreement cannot be reached, there should be no doubt that the United States can and will do what it must to protect our security and to insure the adequacy of our strategic posture.

Our new proposals go beyond those that have been made before. In many areas we are in fact addressing for the first time the tough, complex core of long-standing problems. We are trying for the first time to reach agreements that will not be overturned by the next technological breakthrough. We are trying, in a word, for genuine accommodation.

But none of these proposals that I've outlined to you involves the sacrifice of security. All of them are meant to increase the security of both sides. Our view is that a SALT agreement which just reflects the lowest common denominator that can be agreed upon easily will only create an illusion of progress and, eventually, a backlash against the entire arms control process. Our view is that genuine progress in SALT will not merely stabilize competition in weapons but can also provide a basis for improvement in political relations as well.

When I say that these efforts are intended to relax tensions, I'm not speaking only of military security. I mean as well the concern among our own individual citizens—Soviet and American—that comes from the knowledge which all of you have that the leaders of our two countries have the capacity to destroy human society through misunderstandings or mistakes. If we can relax this tension by reducing the nuclear threat, not only will we make the world a safer place but we'll also free ourselves to concentrate on constructive action to give the world a better life.

We've made some progress toward our goals, but to be frank,

we also hear some negative comments from the Soviet side about SALT and about our more general relations. If these comments are based on a misconception about our motives, then we will redouble our efforts to make our motives clear; but if the Soviets are merely making comments designed as propaganda to put pressure on us, let no one doubt that we will persevere.

What matters ultimately is whether we can create a relationship of cooperation that will be rooted in the national interests of both sides. We shape our own policies to accommodate a constantly changing world, and we hope the Soviets will do the same. Together we can give this change a positive direction.

* * *

Part of the Soviet Union leaders' current attitude may be due to their apparent—and incorrect—belief that our concern for human rights is aimed specifically at them or is an attack on their vital interests.

There are no hidden meanings in our commitment to human rights. We stand on what we have said on the subject of human rights. Our policy is exactly what it appears to be: the positive and sincere expression of our deepest beliefs as a people. It's addressed not to any particular people or area of the world but to all countries equally; yes, including our own country. And it's specifically not designed to heat up the arms race or bring back the cold war.

On the contrary, I believe that an atmosphere of peaceful cooperation is far more conducive to an increased respect for human rights than an atmosphere of belligerence or hatred or warlike confrontation. The experience of our own country this last century has proved this over and over again.

We have no illusions that the process will be quick or that change will come easily. But we are confident that if we do not abandon the struggle, the cause of personal freedom and human dignity will be enhanced in all nations of the world. We're going to do that.

In the past six months we've made clear our determination—both to give voice to Americans' fundamental beliefs and to obtain lasting solutions to East-West differences. If this chance to emphasize peace and cooperation instead of animosity and division is allowed to pass, it will not have been our choice.

* * *

Beyond all the disagreements between us—and beyond the cool calculations of mutual self-interest that our two countries bring to

the negotiating table—is the invisible human reality that must bring us closer together. I mean the yearning for peace, real peace, that is in the very bones of us all.

I'm absolutely certain that the people of the Soviet Union, who have suffered so grievously in war, feel this yearning for peace. And in this they are at one with the people of the United States. It's up to all of us to help make that unspoken passion into something more than just a dream—and that responsibility falls most heavily on those like you, of course, but particularly like President Brezhnev and me, who hold in our hands the terrible power conferred on us by the modern engines of war.

Mr. Brezhnev said something very interesting recently, and I quote from his speech: "It is our belief, our firm belief," he said, "that realism in politics and the will for détente and progress will ultimately triumph, and mankind will be able to step into the twenty-first century in conditions of peace stable as never before." I see no hidden meanings in that. I credit its sincerity. And I express the same hope and belief that Mr. Brezhnev expressed. With all the difficulties, all the conflicts, I believe that our planet must finally obey the Biblical injunction to "follow after the things which make for peace."

Warnke Discusses the Status of SALT, 27 July 1977

Morning Session

The Chairman [Melvin Price]. In connection with our review of strategic capabilities, and in light of the cancellation of the B–1, we asked Mr. Warnke to testify on proposals being put forth at the SALT negotiations so we can judge how these proposals relate to the future viability of our strategic forces. With the thought that it might be useful, we have placed before each member a memo prepared by the staff which merely summarizes in unclassified form the pending proposals on SALT II as we understand them. . . .

[The following are excerpts from the staff memo.]

Proposed treaty structure

It is proposed that a SALT II agreement will consist of a three-tier structure which will be:

A. An agreement consisting of a modified Vladivostok accord, to be ratified as the SALT II treaty. This treaty would continue in effect until 1985.

B. The second part of the proposed agreement is a protocol covering a number of weapons during the first three years the treaty comes into effect.

C. Finally, a statement of principles would conclude the agreement. This statement of principles would serve as the guidelines for the SALT III negotiations, and these negotiations would be intended to begin after the ratification of the SALT II treaty.

I. THE OVERALL CEILING

The present proposal would reduce the overall number of permitted strategic nuclear launchers to 2,250, down from the 2,400 level proposed at Vladivostok. Additionally, there would be a reduction in the number of MIRVs from the proposed Vladivostok level of 1,320 to 1,200.

II. B-1/CRUISE MISSILES

* * *

A. The treaty would ban the testing or deployment of cruise missiles with a range exceeding 2,500 kilometers (ap-

Source: Testimony of ACDA Director Paul C. Warnke. U.S., Congress, House of Representatives, Committee on Armed Services, *Hearings on H.R. 8390 and Review of the State of U.S. Strategic Forces*, 95th Cong., 1st sess., 1977.

proximately 1,500 miles). [Air-launched] cruise missiles presently could only be carried by "heavy bombers," namely the B–52.

B. The three-year protocol would not permit the testing or deployment of ground- or sea-launched cruise missiles with a range in excess of 600 kilometers.

C. The Soviets are insisting that the "heavy bombers" carrying ALCM be counted under the 1,320 MIRV ceiling.

III. NEW STRATEGIC MISSILES

The United States has proposed a ban on the testing or deployment of any new intercontinental ballistic missiles. This ban would also extend to the deployment of a mobile ICBM. These provisions would be covered under the three-year protocol.

IV. MODERN HEAVY ICBMS

SALT I permitted the Soviet Union to deploy some 300 modern heavy ICBMS (SS–9s); the U.S. has none. The U.S. has sought to reduce the deployment level of this Soviet weapon. In March the U.S. proposed that the Soviets cut the number of their modern heavy ICBMS by half; this proposal was rejected. The present proposal would permit the Soviets to keep these missiles, but over the three-year life of the protocol the United States is proposing that no more than 190 of these systems be converted to the SS–18 MIRV.

V. ICBM WEIGHT DEFINITIONS

The SS–9, with 12,000 pounds throw-weight, was defined as a heavy missile at SALT I. The definition for a light missile was the SS–11, with 1,500 pounds throw-weight. The new definitions, respectively, are the SS–18 with 16,000 pounds throw-weight, and the SS–19 with some 7,500 pounds throw-weight.

VI. SILO RELOAD CAPABILITY

U.S. defense planners have been concerned that the Soviet "cold-launch technique" would allow the Soviets to reload their silos with the extra missiles they are believed to build and store. (SALT I limits the number of launchers, defined as silos, not missiles.) In an effort to eliminate this "reload threat," the U.S. is proposing that the Soviets not be allowed to keep the extra missiles within a given proximity to the silo.

VII. SS-20

The U.S. proposal would ban mobile ICBMS, but not the Soviet intermediate-range missile, the SS–20. This weapon

poses a problem for U.S. planners because the SS–20 is made up of the first two stages of the SS–16, an ICBM. Under the U.S. proposal, "assurances" are being sought which would preclude the conversion of the SS–20 to an SS–16.

VIII. FLIGHT TEST RESTRICTION

The U.S. is proposing to limit the flight tests of ICBMS, probably to six a year. Underlying this proposal is the desire to slow down or restrict the Soviets from making improvements to their ICBM forces. Unless such improvements are stopped, the fear is that the large-sized Soviet warheads, with improved accuracy, would compromise the U.S. Minuteman ICBM force in the silo.

IX. THE BACKFIRE BOMBER

The Soviet Backfire bomber, under the current U.S. proposal, would not be counted in the overall number of strategic nuclear delivery vehicles. Thus, they would be allowed a number of Backfires in excess of the proposed 2,250 ceiling for strategic nuclear delivery vehicles. The U.S. is proposing that the Soviets limit their production number over the three-year life of the protocol, in addition to providing collateral constraints such as prohibiting Arctic deployment and limiting the number of deployed tankers.

Mr. WARNKE. You have asked me to testify with respect to the proposals now being advanced at the SALT talks. I would like to break those down into two categories.

One of them concerns the proposals currently being discussed by the delegations in Geneva. And the other is the proposals that have been discussed—that is, the ideas discussed—in meetings between Secretary of State Vance and Foreign Minister Gromyko.

As far as the SALT talks in Geneva are concerned, the delegations have been dealing exclusively with the issues that have been previously raised in the years since the Vladivostok accord of 1974. These are issues that are involved in developing what is referred to as the joint draft text.

The delegations have been confined basically to four issues. One of them has to do with the question of an agreed data base. . . . It has been our feeling with respect to SALT II that, since this will be a more complex agreement, it is necessary that we have an agreed data base. This means an exchange of figures between the United States and the Soviet Union with regard to the various categories of weapons that would be limited in a SALT II agreement. We have been discussing this concept with the Soviet delegation at Geneva. It has not as yet been resolved. We believe some progress is being made.

A second issue we have been discussing at Geneva has to do with the prohibition against deliberate concealment. . . . It is our belief that there must be in any SALT II agreement a prohibition against measures of deliberate concealment that could interfere with the monitoring of verification. . . .

A third issue which has been discussed in the talks . . . is the issue of MIRV verification. . . . [Deleted] it is necessary to develop some agreed-upon formula for determining what will count against the MIRVed missile total of 1,320. [Deleted.] We have made considerable progress with the Soviet delegation in reaching agreement with respect to that counting rule.

Then the fourth issue which has been discussed has to do with the Soviets' proposal for provisions against the circumvention of the agreement. . . .

As far as other SALT-related proposals are concerned, they have occurred at two meetings between Secretary of State Vance and Foreign Minister Gromyko. The first of these was in the last week of March, when, as you all know, we presented alternatives. One was our so-called comprehensive proposal, which would have involved genuinely effective constraints on the strategic arms competition. And the other was the so-called deferral proposal, which would have deferred for SALT III consideration of restraints on the Backfire bomber and the cruise missile.

Now, as you know, both proposals were rejected by the Soviet Union. Subsequently, there were informal discussions between Secretary Vance and Ambassador Dobrynin of the Soviet Union. And these were followed up at a meeting in Geneva—on May 18, 19, and 20—between Secretary of State Vance and Foreign Minister Gromyko. At that point, views were exchanged as to how to break the impasse with respect to SALT II.

An agreement was reached on a so-called framework for further negotiations. That framework consisted of three parts. . . . The ideas exchanged with respect to each of these categories were as follows:

With regard to the treaty, there seemed to be a consensus that, as specified in the Vladivostok accord, the treaty would last through 1985. And that treaty would set forth, first of all, the aggregates which had been agreed upon at Vladivostok, which is 2,400 for strategic nuclear delivery vehicles, of which 1,320 could be launchers of MIRVed missiles. [Deleted.] There also seemed to be agreement on the so-called joint draft text, which has been under negotiation in Geneva, to the extent it had been agreed upon on November 20, 1976, which was when the previous round of talks stopped. [Deleted.]

That would be essentially the first part, Mr. Chairman, of this

three-piece framework. It would basically be consistent with the Vladivostok accord, but would not deal with the more contentious, more troublesome weapons systems.

The second part would be a 3-year protocol. [Deleted.] . . .

[In] the ideas that were exchanged between Secretary Vance and Foreign Minister Gromyko back in May in Geneva . . . there seemed to be some similarity of views with respect to air-launched cruise missiles, except for two major differences. [Deleted.] There were also views expressed with respect to ground-launched cruise missiles and sea-launched cruise missiles. Again, there was considerable similarity with one major difference. [Deleted.]

* * *

What we had in mind [in terms of the statement of principles] was that, if we are unable to get a SALT II agreement covering every element of the comprehensive package we presented in Moscow in March, there still ought to be an agreement between the Soviet Union and the United States that these are issues which will be resolved in a SALT III agreement. And they are the kinds of propositions that would, in fact, make for more effective arms control.

This would include . . . further reductions. [Deleted.] In addition, we would put in our joint statement of principles restrictions on modernization and modification of existing intercontinental ballistic missiles. Further, there would be limits on flight tests, which would serve to reinforce and provide some sort of assurance with respect to the ban on both modification of present ICBMS and development of new ICBMS. Also, in the joint statement of principles, there would have to be included the subject of verification, and a commitment on the part of the Soviet Union that any SALT III agreement, just as any SALT II agreement, would have to be adequately verified.

That is the state of the play at the present time. There are plans, as I am sure the committee knows, for Secretary Vance and Foreign Minister Gromyko to meet again in September.

* * *

The CHAIRMAN. How would you verify a freeze on new technology, deployments, or follow-through improvements if forbidden by the SALT agreement?

Mr. WARNKE. I think it would be a combination of things, Mr. Chairman. Of course, there would be reliance to some extent on national technical means, but to have a genuinely effective and verifiable ban on modification and modernization of ICBMS, you would have to have

some constraints on testing practices. For example, limitations on the number of flight tests would be a valuable adjunct in that regard.

The CHAIRMAN. A moment ago in discussing the strategic balance concept, you used the expression "rough equivalence." Would such a definition accept the idea of U.S. inferiority in manned bombers, throw-weight, numbers of launchers, and warhead yield?

Mr. WARNKE. Well, we have, as I said, Mr. Chairman, a situation of rough equivalence at the present time because of a variety of things. We have it because of our technological lead and the fact that our warheads are far more numerous than those of the Soviet Union. [Deleted.] We also have a significant lead as far as manned bombers are concerned, and the throw-weight that exists in the bombs that are carried on those bombers. Adding everything together, we feel we are in a position in which the Soviet Union has no element of strategic superiority in the overall sense.

Mr. BOB WILSON. Mr. Warnke, in your initial discussions, since you have come aboard, has the B–1 been a part of such discussions or proposals?

Mr. WARNKE. No; it has not, Mr. Wilson. It has never been discussed by me or by my delegation with the Soviet Union.

Mr. BOB WILSON. But have you discussed it in your own group as perhaps one of the bargaining chips that would be used in connection, perhaps, with the Backfire bomber, or other elements?

Mr. WARNKE. No; we have not, Mr. Wilson. We have had no such discussions within my agency, nor have I had any such discussions with any other governmental agency.

Mr. BOB WILSON. In the limitation you put on the cruise missile of [deleted] has the Air Force indicated—do you know whether the Air Force has indicated that such a limitation would be detrimental to them as far as the targeting of certain targets within the Soviet Union?

Mr. WARNKE. I have had no such report, Mr. Wilson. No.

* * *

Mr. ASPIN. If we had decided, or if the President decided as he did decide, he did not want to proceed with the development of the B–1 bomber, the question arises: Why didn't we try and get something out of the Soviets at the time that we were going to decide we didn't want it? And one way, of course, would be to offer it up as a bargaining chip in terms of getting something from them. . . . Why wasn't it used as a bargaining chip? Or, did the Soviets not care enough about it at all and therefore we couldn't have gotten any-

thing for it? And if we couldn't have used it as a bargaining chip, could we have used it as some kind of a good will gesture?. . .
Mr. Warnke. . . . With regard to the question as to whether it could have been used as a bargaining chip, I would say that possibility still remains open. We are in a position where we can maintain that this represents an element of constraint on our part that ought to be matched.

The difficulty, however, with using it as a bargaining chip is that, as I understand the decision, it was a choice between alternatives, and the choice was made for the alternative which struck us as being preferable militarily. It is awfully hard to say we think it is a better system to have a standoff bomber with an air-launched cruise missile than the B–1, and still at the same time say because we made the militarily preferable choice you ought to give us something in return. I would say we have that kind of a dilemma.

*   *   *

Mr. Mitchell. . . .We learned the Soviet Union has a very fine civil defense effort, yet ours is in almost total disarray. . . . It seems to me if we have equivalence in strategic armaments and in conventional armaments but not in civil defense, the equation isn't completely balanced. . . . I understand Secretary Vance wanted to have civil defense included in the negotiations, but he was refused.

My questions are, do you feel that our lack of any good civil defense effort does unbalance that equation? And the second question, should it be included in the negotiations to really prevent war through maintaining this balance all the way along the line?
Mr. Warnke. Let me talk about that in terms of chronology.

At the present time I would certainly agree with the statements of Secretary Brown that, despite the greater Soviet civil defense efforts, there is no chance that either side could survive as a functioning society in the event of significant nuclear war.

That doesn't, of course, mean that we can ignore the greater Soviet civil defense effort. If they continue with that civil defense effort at the same time that we are controlling the strategic offensive arms, it could become a significant factor in the strategic balance.

For example, supposing we were able to get agreement on very, very drastic cuts in intercontinental ballistic missiles and submarine-launched ballistic missiles. At some point a significant defense effort could serve as an effective means of lessening the damage to Soviet society, and it would be a constraint on our ability to reduce strategic nuclear arms on a reciprocal basis.

Accordingly, it is something that ought to be taken into account.

It is something that has been raised by Secretary Vance with Foreign Minister Gromyko, and it is one of the items on which preliminary agreement was reached that there ought to be negotiations. So that those negotiations will take place. . . .

Mr. MITCHELL. . . . It seems to me since January we have been taking steps to weaken our defense effort. The President is talking about cutting the budget $5 to $7 billion. We canceled our big carriers. We are proposing troop withdrawals from Korea. We closed down the Minuteman III production line. We scrapped the B–1. We are closing bases all over the country.

My question is: Have you seen any weakening in the resolve of the Soviet Union? Have you observed that they are likely to cut back, or they have made any efforts softening their resolve, since we made our cutbacks? And no. 2, is this a sound policy, in your estimation, having dealt with the Soviets as extensively as you have? Does this unilateral weakening of our defense effort, while the Soviets are rapidly increasing their strength, encourage them in any way to eventually cut back, do you think?

Mr. WARNKE. I am afraid, Mr. Congressman, I couldn't accept your characterization of the decisions that have been made as weakening our defense capability. I think what they represent are choices among possible options, and we are, of course, going ahead with the cruise missile program. I have already mentioned to you the apprehension the Soviets expressed about the military potential of the cruise missile.

We are proceeding with our development of the so-called MX, which would be a new generation of ICBMS. That unquestionably will continue unless there are some arms control arrangements which make it prudent on our part to discontinue these programs. So that I don't believe we are weakening our defense capability.

I have seen, at the same time, no indication at all that the Soviet Union is cutting back on its defense effort. I think it is pretty clear that they spend substantially more money than we spend on defense. I think that they spend more because they don't do it as well as we do. But nonetheless, they are willing to assume a very, very significantly greater economic burden than we do.

Mr. BEARD. . . . Let me ask you this, Mr. Warnke: On the range capabilities of cruise missiles, there, of course, has been a great deal of discussion, and as you go forward there will be a great deal more discussion. Do you feel if we had SALT restrictions as to range we can verify them? Do we know how to verify range limitations?

Mr. WARNKE. I would say verification of cruise missile ranges at the present time would present a very, very difficult problem. [Deleted.]

But that is one of the issues that would have to be determined during the period of the protocol.

*   *   *

Mr. Beard. If we allow Minuteman to become vulnerable to the Soviets, would it be legitimate to say we are acting contrary to all deterrent principles? . . .

Mr. Warnke. I think it would be very, very unwise for the United States to allow a situation to develop in which our ICBM force could be attrited by a Soviet first strike.

We would certainly under those circumstances still retain the submarine-launched ballistic missiles. Now, that might be an adequate deterrent. But I don't believe that we ought to put ourselves in a position in which the Soviets, given some intense provocation or intense international situation which troubled them, by striking first could deprive us of an ICBM retaliatory force.

Mr. Beard. In other words, mobile ICBMs would enhance the strategic ability?

Mr. Warnke. If our fixed ICBM silos were to become vulnerable, certainly mobile ICBMs would increase our survivability.

Afternoon Session

Mr. Stratton. Mr. Warnke, has Secretary Brown approved the 2,500 kilometer limitation on the cruise missile?

Mr. Warnke. He did approve both the March proposal and the suggestions advanced in Geneva in May.

Mr. Stratton. They were advanced prior to the decision on the B–1 bomber, is that not correct?

Mr. Warnke. That is correct.

*   *   *

Mr. Ford [Committee Staff Director]. Mr. Warnke, first of all, could I ask you what the objective is that you propose to achieve [by] limiting flight tests of the ICBMs to [deleted] or so a year?

Mr. Warnke. The objective would be to reenforce any provision which would prevent modernization of existing ICBMs or the development of new types of ICBMs. In other words, what it would do would be to retard further development of new and improved ballistic missiles.

Mr. Ford. But, then, you are not maintaining that would prevent them from modernizing the missiles? Aren't there steps they could

take to achieve that modernization even with that flight test limitation?

Mr. WARNKE. The flight test limitation certainly would not prevent it entirely, no, particularly because if they wanted to they could devote all of the permitted flight tests to improve systems.

Mr. FORD. They could test several guidance systems at one time if they wanted to, in each of the flights?

Mr. WARNKE. I think that would be possible.

Mr. FORD. Or they could test them in space boosters?

Mr. WARNKE. That is correct.

Mr. FORD. They could test them in submarine-launched ballistic missiles?

Mr. WARNKE. That is right. It would not be the total answer in itself.

Mr. FORD. But are there other steps which are specifically designed to prevent the modernization, other than the flight tests?

Mr. WARNKE. In the comprehensive package, I believe that that would be the principal reenforcing method. And also, I think you have to recognize, Mr. Ford, that there are certain types of improvements which could not effectively be banned. I know of no way, for example, to verify changes in software as distinguished from hardware.

Mr. FORD. Now, you mentioned before the limitation on heavy and light ICBMS. [Deleted.] In SALT I, the limitations were 12,000 on the heavy ICBMS and 1,500 pounds on a light ICBM. I wondered what was the purpose in giving them this increase in throw-weight in the definition of light and heavy?

Mr. WARNKE. I don't believe, Mr. Ford, it was a question of giving them that increase in throw-weight. It is a problem of dealing with existing systems.

Now, regrettably, we have not been able to get effective strategic nuclear arms control in time to prevent the development of new systems. That is why there is some urgency in my mind in trying to get control. Otherwise you end up with an agreement which is less effective. If we had been able to get a SALT II comprehensive-type agreement back in 1972, we could have imposed restrictions which would have been more complete than is now possible.

Mr. FORD. Well, what you are saying, in effect, is that the limits now are dictated by what they have already got?

Mr. WARNKE. That is correct.

Mr. FORD. We are not really thinking of asking them to throw away anything?

Mr. WARNKE. Oh yes, we are. But we don't believe that we can get them to begin to discard systems until we can first get them to freeze.

Mr. FORD. OK. Now, could you tell us to what extent the SALT negotiations are related to the comprehensive test ban treaty, and whether you believe the comprehensive treaty could include provisions for peaceful nuclear explosions?

Mr. WARNKE. First, as far as there being any direct or organic link, there is none. You could have a SALT II agreement along the lines we are discussing without having the comprehensive test ban, and vice versa.

I believe, though, just as a limitation on flight tests would reenforce a ban on modification of new types of ICBMS, similarly a comprehensive test ban that prohibited all nuclear weapons testing would interfere substantially with efforts either to upgrade or introduce new systems.

As far as the question as to whether or not you could have a PNE [peaceful nuclear explosion] exception is concerned, our view is that, to have a genuinely comprehensive test ban, it should preclude all types of nuclear explosions.

10
The Washington Talks, September 1977

Communiqué, 24 September 1977

On September 22 and 23, 1977, talks were held in Washington between Jimmy Carter, President of the United States of America, and Cyrus Vance, Secretary of State of the United States of America, and Andrei A. Gromyko, Member of the Politburo of the Central Committee of the Communist Party of the Soviet Union and Minister of Foreign Affairs of the USSR.

A useful exchange of views took place on key questions of US-Soviet relations and on several international issues of interest to both sides.

Both sides expressed their desire for a constructive and stable development of relations between the United States and the Soviet Union, building on existing treaties and agreements. To this end, both sides consider it necessary to intensify their efforts to find mutually acceptable solutions to existing problems. Both sides agreed that such efforts, which can assure progress in various spheres of US-Soviet relations, serve the interests of their peoples as well as contributing to the strengthening of peace and the lessening of international tensions.

Both sides attach particular importance to the development and implementation of further measures aimed at the effective prevention of nuclear war and the limitation of armaments, thereby contributing to progress toward real disarmament.

In their discussions, the two sides focused on issues relating to the limitation of strategic arms, particularly those pertaining to the preparation of a new agreement on the limitation of strategic offensive arms. Progress was achieved in bringing closer together the positions of the

---

SOURCE: *Department of State Bulletin*, 7 November 1977, pp. 643–644.

two sides.[1] However, there are still issues requiring agreement. They have issued additional statements on this subject.

Other specific arms limitations issues which are the subject of negotiations between the US and the USSR were also discussed: negotiations for a comprehensive ban on nuclear testing; the non-proliferation of nuclear weapons; the prohibition of chemical weapons; the prohibition of radiological and other new types and systems of mass destruction weapons; and questions relating to the Indian Ocean. The two sides noted the utility of the negotiations on these issues that have so far taken place and expressed their intention of continuing their active efforts to achieve practical results.

Both sides emphasized the great importance they attach to achieving real progress in the negotiations on the mutual reduction of forces and armaments in Central Europe in accordance with the agreed principle of undiminished security for all parties. They expressed their intention to continue efforts to achieve agreement.

The two sides also expressed their intention to work for a successful and constructive Belgrade meeting of representatives of states parties to the Conference on Security and Cooperation in Europe.

Pursuant to their previous discussions, the two sides reviewed the situation in the Middle East. The US and the USSR affirmed that they will continue their determined efforts to convene the Geneva Conference by the end of this year at the latest.

---

[1] Information concerning the progress made during the Washington talks can be found in the Overview for Part Three of this volume, and in the testimony of Secretary Vance and ACDA Director Warnke before the Senate Foreign Relations Committee on 3 and 29 November 1977, reprinted elsewhere in this chapter.—Ed.

Joint Statement, 24 September 1977

In discussions between Secretary Vance and Minister Gromyko on the questions related to strategic arms, both sides—the Soviet Union and the United States of America—have reaffirmed their determination to conclude a new agreement limiting strategic offensive arms and have declared their intention to continue active negotiations with a view to completing within the near future the work on that agreement.

The United States and the Soviet Union agree that the Treaty on the Limitation of Anti-Ballistic Missile Systems, signed in Moscow in 1972 and amended in 1974, serves the security interests of both countries. They share the view that this treaty decreases the risk of nuclear war and facilitates progress in the further limitation and reduction of strategic offensive arms. Both sides also agree that the ABM treaty has operated effectively, thus demonstrating the mutual commitment of the U.S.S.R. and the U.S.A. to the goal of nuclear arms limitations and to the principle of equal security.

Accordingly, in connection with the 5-year review of the ABM treaty, the two sides reaffirm their commitment to the treaty. It is agreed that this review will be conducted in the Standing Consultative Committee after its regular fall meeting.

SOURCE: *Department of State Bulletin*, 7 November 1977, p. 644.

Warnke Informs Congress of the Expiration of the Interim Agreement, 26 September 1977

I appreciate the opportunity to appear before the committee today to discuss the expiration of the SALT I Interim Agreement on Certain Measures With Respect to the Limitation of Strategic Offensive Arms. The 1972 interim agreement expires on October 3, and it is clear that a SALT II agreement to replace it cannot be concluded by that date.

In recent days, there has been much discussion in the press about the administration's plans with respect to this matter. On September 23, Secretary Vance issued a statement to the effect that, in order to maintain a stable situation while the SALT II negotiations are being completed, the United States intends not to take any action inconsistent with the interim agreement or the goals of the ongoing negotiations, provided that the Soviet Union exercises similar restraint. The Soviets have now issued a policy statement along the lines of our statement.

It should be noted that U.S. defense plans would not cause us to exceed any of the interim agreement limits in the near future, while the Soviets are in a position to do so because of their active ongoing SLBM construction programs.

We carefully considered what action should be taken in view of the fact that the October 3 date would pass before the completion of negotiations on a new agreement. In our deliberations, we concluded, after consultation with a number of members of both the Senate and House, that an extension of the interim agreement would be inappropriate for two reasons. First, it would have reduced the pressure on the Soviets and on us to pursue a SALT II agreement based on equal aggregates of strategic offensive arms; and second, it would formally reaffirm acceptance of the disparity in numbers of strategic weapons established in the interim agreement.

Our policy statement is exactly what it says—a declaration of present intent. It is nonbinding and nonobligatory. The interim agreement will expire on October 3 and will not be extended; no agreement limiting strategic offensive arms will be in force after next Monday. The United States will be free to change the policy announced in its statement of September 23 at any time. Because our nonbinding statement is not part of an international agreement and does not impose any

---

SOURCE: Statement of ACDA Director Paul C. Warnke before the Senate Foreign Relations Committee. *Department of State Bulletin*, 7 November 1977, pp. 642–643; and Soviet Embassy Information Department, 26 September 1977.

obligation on the United States, we have not requested congressional approval for it.

We will carefully and continually monitor Soviet activities. If these activities or any other circumstances warrant, we will be free to take whatever actions are appropriate, irrespective of the provisions set forth in the interim agreement.

We will, of course, continue to consult closely with members of this committee and other members of Congress on the progress of SALT. We hope you will support our efforts in this regard.

STATEMENTS BY THE UNITED STATES AND THE SOVIET UNION WITH RESPECT TO THE EXPIRATION OF THE INTERIM AGREEMENT.

Statement by Secretary Vance, 23 September 1977:

> In order to maintain the status quo while SALT II negotiations are being completed, the United States declares its intention not to take any action inconsistent with the provisions of the Interim Agreement on Certain Measures With Respect to the Limitation of Strategic Offensive Arms which expires October 3, 1977, and with the goals of these ongoing negotiations provided that the Soviet Union exercises similar restraint.

Statement of the Soviet government, 25 September 1977:

> In accordance with the readiness expressed by both sides to complete within the near future the work on a new agreement limiting strategic offensive arms and in the interests of maintaining the status quo while the talks on the new agreement are being concluded, the Soviet Union expresses its intention to keep from any actions incompatible with the provisions of the Interim Agreement on Some Measures Pertaining to the Limitation of Strategic Offensive Arms which expires on October 3, 1977, and with the goals of the talks that are being conducted, provided that the United States of America shows the same restraint.

Vance and Warnke Discuss the Status of SALT, 3 and 29 November 1977

3 November 1977

Secretary Vance. . . . I think we all agree that the destructive power of each side is far in excess of what could rationally be required by either side to maintain strategic deterrence. Moreover, technology threatens to produce new weapons which could destabilize this balance by giving one side the illusion of a temporary advantage. Any SALT agreement should, therefore, lower the levels of strategic forces of both sides, and should also restrain those technological improvements which threaten the balance. This has been a goal which, until this prospective agreement, has eluded us in SALT.

Any SALT agreement must be consistent with our own security and that of our allies. This means that any agreement must leave us and our allies at least as strong relative to the Soviet Union as the situation which would exist in the absence of an agreement.

SALT cannot leave us or our allies in the position where we are vulnerable to nuclear coercion. This means, in my opinion, that in SALT we must preserve the principle of rough parity.

In addition to these fundamental objectives concerning our strategic and security relationships with the Soviets, the SALT process has an important political dimension with respect to United States-Soviet and overall East-West relations.

It would have been almost inconceivable ten years ago to imagine the situation which we have today, in which two adversaries discuss on a systematic and rational basis security interests of the utmost importance to both sides. This central fact has created the foundations for a political relationship with the Soviets that reduces the tensions of the cold war and sets some important boundaries to our ideological and political and military competition. Given that we preserve and protect our essential strategic and security interests in an agreement, the fact of the ongoing SALT process, then, serves this important policy objective.

SALT is a bargaining process. Certainly we don't agree with many of the concepts set forth by the Soviets. They, too, have a different view of our proposals. The aim of the negotiations is to reach a fair and

---

SOURCE: Testimony of Secretary of State Cyrus R. Vance and ACDA Director Paul C. Warnke. U.S., Congress, Senate, Committee on Foreign Relations, *Briefing on SALT Negotiations*, 95th Cong., 2nd sess., 1978.

equitable agreement, for without fairness and equity there can be no agreement.

Up to now we have been looking at SALT from our point of view, in terms of what is in our interest. Many of these ideas were carefully incorporated in our Moscow comprehensive proposal which represented the central core of what we would like in an agreement. Obviously the Soviets saw that proposal in a much different fashion and rejected it as an attempt to gain what they call "unilateral advantage."

We then entered into a process, as one normally does in negotiations, of seeking adjustments in the starting positions of both sides that would serve our purposes and move us toward our goals. In this process we have not abandoned the goals set forth in the Moscow proposal, and, in fact, have moved the Soviets a considerable distance toward accepting ideas in our Moscow proposals which they flatly rejected at that time.

As to the agreement, we have tried to reflect these broad concerns in a number of specific tasks for SALT. We believe our current proposals reflect those goals in a number of fundamental ways.

First and foremost, the agreement would establish equal aggregates between the sides and at lower levels than agreed to in SALT I or later at Vladivostok.

This agreement would reinforce the principle of overall strategic equivalence. It would place overall limits on Soviet forces through 1985. It would also put important limits on Soviet MIRVed ICBMS, precisely those forces which we see as potentially most upsetting to the strategic stability.

This agreement would require the Soviets to take down about 300 strategic delivery vehicles—actually to dismantle systems now targeted against the United States. In addition, the resultant Soviet force level would be well below our best estimate of their force level in the absence of a SALT agreement. Our programs, in contrast, could go forward as planned. [Deleted.]

Equally important is the fact that for the first time we are trying to reach an agreement with significant qualitative constraints on offensive weapons. [Deleted.]

We have heard a great deal about what the SALT agreement taking shape would do about the potential Soviet capacity to launch a strike against our Minuteman ICBM force. If we can achieve what we have proposed on qualitative restrictions, it would have the effect of slowing down the time by which the Soviets could hope to acquire such a capability.

We have sought to do what is possible to constrain the threat to our land-based ICBMS. We concluded that in terms of this objective, a

limit on all MIRVed ICBMs was at least as advantageous as a limit on modern large ballistic missiles, and could be more so.

More specifically, this agreement does go some way toward containing the potential threat to Minuteman in two ways. [Deleted.] It would also place a limit on the number of ICBMs that can carry MIRVs. In both respects, our proposal is an advance over the Vladivostok agreement, which called for no qualitative controls on ICBMs and set no separate ceiling on Soviet MIRVed ICBMs.

But, given a determined Soviet effort to improve the accuracies of their ICBM warheads, and the number of warheads that could be available to the Soviets under our proposed SALT agreement, I cannot say that the SALT II accord which is likely to emerge is going to prevent the Soviets from eventually acquiring such a capability. This observation does not mean that the proposed agreement has failed to do its job. Even an agreement with tighter qualitative controls may not be able to accomplish this task. What we need to do is to put the Minuteman survivability issue into perspective.

For one thing, I do not put much stock in a scenario in which Soviet leaders decide to launch a strike against our land-based forces, since it is difficult to imagine how the Soviet leadership would consider that the U.S.S.R. could escape devastating retaliation, given our ability to counter with a large, effective force against their major urban targets. Whatever the fate of our land-based forces, we would retain under the proposed SALT agreement a powerful sea-based missile force and bomber forces. And, we are keeping options open to deal with the Minuteman survivability problem, such as allowing R&D for mobile ICBMs. Finally, in the absence of a SALT agreement we would face a far more dangerous and unmanageable threat to our fixed land-based forces, since the Soviets would then be totally unrestrained from qualitative and quantitative improvements.

More generally, we have tried in our proposal to get a handle on the new technologies we now face, including mobile ICBMs and cruise missiles. [Deleted.]

Cruise missiles would be limited under the protocol. . . . This is an area of major Soviet concern. They have made it clear to us that from their point of view an agreement must take into account these systems. We have proposed a way in which our planned programs could go forward in the interim, while we and our allies study the utility of these new weapons. Our proposed cruise missile position would keep cruise missile options open for ourselves and for our allies after the protocol period.

We take the question of insuring adequate verification of a SALT

agreement seriously. It has been the subject of intensive discussions with the Soviet Union and significant studies within the administration.

It is important to recognize that we are moving into a realm of SALT limitations in which we cannot expect to be able to verify some of the limitations with precise accuracy. In this situation, we need to look at verification in the context of what constitutes an adequate level of verification capability in light of our basic strategic concerns.

For example, we expect to have a very high degree of confidence in our ability to verify with precision the proposed limitations of the overall numbers of strategic Soviet systems, MIRVed missiles, MIRVed ICBMS, et cetera. Verification of cruise missile restrictions, on the other hand, will be more difficult.

Nevertheless, we believe that we have constructed these limitations in such a manner that they can be adequately verified. In judging this adequacy, we weigh the impact of the resultant uncertainties on our overall security against the advantages which accrue from accepting such limitations. Thus, the key question is whether verification uncertainties for a particular limitation could be significant in endangering our security.

It is also important to recognize that great uncertainties would exist over Soviet weapons programs in the absence of a SALT agreement, and to assess our overall security situation under a SALT agreement in its entirety. From these perspectives, I believe we will be in acceptable shape in the verification area.

We sometimes take for granted the contribution which the SALT agreements and the SALT process make to our intelligence collection capability. National technical means are now accepted methods for collecting intelligence. Interference with national technical means is prohibited, as are deliberate concealment measures which impede verification.

As you know, we have proposed a set of principles for SALT III which would be an integral part of this agreement. In those principles we have incorporated many elements from our comprehensive proposal in an effort to obtain even greater reductions and tighter qualitative limits in a future agreement.

I think our proposal puts us on the right road for the first time. It is the first step toward reducing forces on both sides and getting an important grip on the question of future systems.

* * *

I cannot predict all the negative political consequences of a failure in SALT. Given the fact, however, that SALT is seen by both sides as a

barometer of our overall relations, a failure would have serious consequences on the broader East-West relations. I know that this view is shared by our European allies. Failure to reach a SALT agreement would be seen by many as a signal that both sides had abandoned their efforts to seek improved relations.

I am also concerned about the serious implications such an action would have on the thinking of the Soviet leadership in the future.

Finally, SALT is the prime example of a complex enterprise that drives to the very heart of our national security. It is filled with uncertainties and with dilemmas. There are no easy answers and no quick solutions. It requires sophisticated analysis and balanced judgments.

* * *

Senator JAVITS. In your statement you say: "But given a determined Soviet effort to improve the accuracies of their ICBM warheads and the numbers of warheads that would be available to the Soviets under our proposed SALT agreement, I can't say that the SALT II accord likely to emerge is going to prevent the Soviets from eventually acquiring such a capability"—to wit, to destroy our Minutemen.

Then you go on to say——

Secretary VANCE. Not to destroy, but in effect to damage very heavily.

Senator JAVITS. Then you go on to say: "More generally, we have tried in our proposal to get a handle on the new technologies we now face, including mobile ICBMS and cruise missiles." [Deleted.]

Now have those three restrictions been laid on top of the template, to wit, our need for new technologies to face what you recognize as a serious threat, to wit, R&D—Research and Development—on mobile ICBMS, and do they fit, and if so, why?

Secretary VANCE. The answer is yes, they have been laid on top of the template. The reason that those provisions have been put in the protocol rather than in the treaty is for the very reason that you raise.

Senator JAVITS. That is the three-year limitation?

Secretary VANCE. The three-year limitation, that is correct. During these three years, the United States will have under the treaty and protocol the right to test the mobile launcher capability and thus to develop that capability, which would then put the United States on an equal footing with the Soviets, who already have that capability.

In the meantime, we could continue with development, but not testing, of the MX missile itself.

* * *

Senator CASE. What are the reasons for your expression of confidence that adequate verification will exist for such things as how many MIRVS they put on their missiles?

Secretary VANCE. There are certain areas where we are going to have problems with respect to verification. As I indicated, insofar as the treaty is concerned, we think that we can satisfactorily verify the items in the treaty.

The problem areas arise in those matters which are dealt with in the protocol. [Deleted.] This may be one of those cases where one has to make a calculated determination whether or not, in the overall context, is it better to have a treaty with some elements not verifiable as compared to no treaty.

* * *

Senator GLENN. I know [verification] is the key to selling [SALT II] to me.... It is most difficult in the qualitative area, above all, as you mentioned [deleted]. How many MIRVS can they put on the top of a booster?...

Secretary VANCE. I think we will be able to check a great deal of this out through the testing route.

Senator GLENN. I would question that, and I will tell you why.

Let's say that we have a nest of [MIRVS] up here. I could send one of these things up. We could put on four or five, which would agree with our previous limit. It would go out and spray those four or five out. We would observe that test. But we would not know that the nest was set for fifty or seventy-five. So, I can see a testing program that once again is nonverifiable.

Secretary VANCE. But I think that one then gets to the question of what kind of targets are you trying to take out, and can you have the size vehicle that is going to do the kind of job that has to be done, and will one really take the risk of using a system which is not tested. That is a terribly big risk for anybody to take. So, all these kinds of calculations have to be woven in.

Senator GLENN. That is a big problem.

Secretary VANCE. Yes.

Senator GLENN. I think these qualitative areas [deleted] for instance are important.

We made some changes when we got new metallurgical capabilities in our engines. The specs go up, the fuel specs go up, the range increases, and those are things that I just do not see how we can verify. They are very vital because it changes the whole picture of what part of our country they can cover with what boosters and what they can do with their MIRVS. It is exceedingly difficult, it seems to me, to verify those by any NTM [national technical means] that we now have.

* * *

Senator STONE. Mr. Secretary, in your presentation you stated: "National technical means are now accepted methods for collecting intelligence. Interference with national technical means is prohibited, as are deliberate concealment measures which impede verification."

Secretary Brown announced a week or two ago that the Soviets have already or were about to perfect antisatellite weapons, that therefore in effect we were accelerating our search for the same types of systems, and that within a few years or less we would have our own systems. Isn't it logically indicated then, if in the search for verification we have to protect these NTMS, that we try to get a limit or prohibition on antisatellite weapons on the part of the Soviets and offer in return the same slowdown or prohibition on our part?

Secretary VANCE. The answer is yes. . . . We have been concerned from the very outset about the development of antisatellite capabilities. [Deleted.] I do think it is of extreme importance that we preserve the capability of using satellites.

I will put as a footnote, however, that if there were any attempts to destroy satellites, at that point we would really be in a war-type situation. The important point is not so much potential elimination of this capability in advance of an attack as it is the threat of blinding us once an actual war-type situation occurred. If they started shooting down our satellites, obviously this would create a situation of tension between our people which would put us very close to war.

Senator STONE. Mr. Secretary, are we convinced or persuaded that the Soviet Union is not developing a less obvious method than shooting down a satellite, which would technically interfere with or impede the work of a satellite?

Secretary VANCE. No, [deleted].

* * *

Senator CLARK. You will recall that in 1972, when the Senate was considering the SALT I agreement, Senator Jackson and a number of others sponsored legislation which is generally referred to as the Jackson amendment. This said, and I quote, "to request the President to seek a future treaty that would not limit the United States to levels of intercontinental strategic forces inferior to the limits provided for the Soviet Union."

Mr. Secretary, does every provision of your proposal of the eight-year treaty strictly comply with the Jackson amendment?

Secretary VANCE. Yes. What we end up with is equal aggregates, but there is a right to mix. So everybody has to make his own choices as to which he wants to put his emphasis on as among the various kinds of

systems. But we are essentially ending up with equal aggregates. So my feeling is that this is met.

* * *

Senator CLARK. Since the Soviets are apparently, or at least according to the best information that I have, not developing cruise missiles of the kind we are talking about in this case, it seems to me that it gives us a major advantage, at least under the proposal, in that we are permitted to proceed with cruise missile carriers, as I think we have determined is necessary in the absence of the B–1. Yet, while the Soviets are similarly permitted cruise missile carriers—and they have no intention of developing them—does this not in effect give us a very significant advantage in the sense of having a more versatile force?

Secretary VANCE. I think it does give us a more versatile force, and each one of the B–52s which would be included as a carrier could carry twenty air-launched cruise missiles. That gives you quite a formidable force.

Senator CLARK. Perhaps I am overstating this—and correct me if I am wrong—but if we are going to count cruise carriers as MIRVS, and in view of the fact that the Soviets are not developing cruise missiles, then in effect we have a different limit than they do, don't we? . . . Don't we, in effect, have a higher MIRV limit than they do? We don't in the treaty, obviously, but effectively we do.

Secretary VANCE. If they decide not to go that route.

Senator CLARK. At least for the next several years we will, anyway.

* * *

Senator KENNEDY. Could you tell us what the position of the administration is on the MX? Given the direction in which you are moving in SALT, what are you going to request in terms of the MX?

Senator MATHIAS. May I sharpen that question a bit? Would the MX be the price, the domestic price, for SALT?

Secretary VANCE. No, it would not. The MX option, however, is kept open in the agreement which we are negotiating in SALT. [Deleted.]

Insofar as MX is concerned, under the schedules which we have, there are no flight tests planned during this three-year period, so the only effect that would have would be on the Soviets.

Insofar as deployment is concerned, MX certainly is not going to be ready for deployment, if it is ever put into production, until the 1980s, and therefore that is not affected. But it would affect the Soviets, [deleted].

Now, at the end of the protocol period we will have the option still

open to us to go forward with MX, should that be, under all the circumstances, the course of action that our national security would require. But there is no determination at this point that that is the direction in which we ought to go. We simply don't know enough yet about what the general situation will be, what the state of development will show. Therefore there is no determination.

It is not the price, as you were suggesting, Senator Mathias.

29 NOVEMBER 1977

Senator PEARSON. Doesn't this effort to put limitations on the quantitative aspect of intercontinental missiles, strategic missiles, pull us away from the advantages of Vladivostok? You made the point that that treaty was good because it put absolute limits on everything.

Mr. WARNKE. That's right.

Senator PEARSON. Now, with the three-year protocol and with the development of the cruise missiles and the arguments that go around about the Backfire and so forth, don't we really pull out a little bit from that certainty of real number limits set at Vladivostok, even though they were very high limits? I am not arguing whether or not that is bad or good, but perhaps the circumstances and the issues make us do that.

Mr. WARNKE. Senator, I don't think that it pulls away from Vladivostok because the treaty itself, the treaty lasting through 1985, would set initially the Vladivostok ceilings, and then pull them down.

Senator PEARSON. Pull them down as much as you can?

Mr. WARNKE. Yes. What it would do would be to set the 2,400 figure for strategic nuclear delivery vehicles.

Senator PEARSON. Then in three years the limit would be off because no one knows what you are going to do with cruise missiles—is that it?

Mr. WARNKE. No; the limit would not be off at the end of three years. Those limits would remain through 1985.

Senator PEARSON. Yes; but what is included within the limits—everything?

Mr. WARNKE. Within the limits you would include the strategic nuclear delivery systems, yes. You would include the ICBM launchers, the SLBM launchers, the heavy bombers, the heavy bombers equipped with air-launched cruise missiles, and you would also include mobile missiles if they were ever deployed.

Senator PEARSON. Is the Backfire in it?

Mr. WARNKE. The Backfire would be handled separately. [Deleted.]

Senator PEARSON. Is that a key issue right now?

Mr. WARNKE. That is a key issue right now. [Deleted.]

Senator PEARSON. Is it the attitude of the administration and the negotiators to keep limits to the extent possible on the development of new weapons—

Mr. WARNKE. Absolutely.

Senator PEARSON [continuing]. And to maintain the theory and the purpose of the Vladivostok limits?

Mr. WARNKE. That is correct. It would not only keep the 2,400 limit initially, but over a period of about three years it would reduce that limit.

Senator PEARSON. Are you encouraged about the 2,160?

Mr. WARNKE. [Deleted.]

Senator PEARSON. Now what about verification?

Mr. WARNKE. Verification on the whole, Senator, fortunately is more than adequate. [Deleted.] As far as 2,400 is concerned, [deleted], we can have absolute—well, nothing in the world is absolute, I suppose—we can have far more than adequate assurance of compliance with those provisions. Our national technical means enable us to determine how many fixed silos there are for ICBMS.

Senator PEARSON. Does that include MIRVS?

Mr. WARNKE. It does, Senator Pearson, because we have been able to get the Soviets to agree to a very, very controlled system of MIRV counting. [Deleted.] What we propose is that any missile of a type that has ever been tested with a MIRVed warhead is counted as a MIRVed missile, regardless of whether or not it has a MIRVed warhead on it. In other words, it is a type rule. It applies to all missiles of a type that has ever been tested or deployed with a MIRV warhead. [Deleted.]. . . . In other words, we know that there are no more than that certain number of launchers of MIRVed missiles. There may be less; but nonetheless, we count the maximum number, and the Soviets have agreed to that.

* * *

Senator BAKER. I am trying to identify the dimensions of our risk. That is, what opportunity do the Soviets have to avoid the MIRV limitations in terms of our ability to independently ascertain and verify the situation? As I perceive it, it would be [deleted] that are not now MIRVed, and it is your contention that they would have to change the configuration of the silos before they could MIRV them, and we could detect that, and that would bring them under the rule.

Mr. WARNKE. That is correct.

Senator BAKER. But the real risk would be if they did not have to change the configuration of the silos, wouldn't it?

Mr. WARNKE. The risk, Senator, would exist if they were able to develop a new missile that would fit into a silo for an unMIRVed missile. [Deleted.]

Senator BAKER. But that is the risk—that they would devise a missile that could be MIRVed that would fit a silo of [an SS-] 7, 9, or 11.

Mr. WARNKE. We would know that if that should occur, Senator.

Senator BAKER. How would we know?

Mr. WARNKE. We would know because of our intelligence sources. They would enable us to determine what new missiles they are developing.

Senator BAKER. That is a key and crucial point. I won't go any further. I understand what you mean by "national technical means." But I don't understand what you mean by "our intelligence sources." Are you speaking of other than national technical means?

Mr. WARNKE. That includes primarily national technical means in this instance, because they are adequate for this purpose. [Deleted.]

Senator BAKER. Of course that debate is as old as the entire effort at strategic arms limitation; that is, what type of information do you require—on-site inspection? Do we require no verification beyond our own intelligence sources? Do we depend entirely on "national technical means?"

What you are saying is that by a combination of national technical means and other intelligence sources, and without any addition—such as on-site access and inspection—we could ascertain that the Soviets have designed and deployed a missile in [an SS-] 7, 9, or 11 silo that was MIRVed. Is that it?

Mr. WARNKE. That is correct, Senator.

Senator BAKER. That is also the dimension of the risk, isn't it?

Mr. WARNKE. It depends upon what you mean by "risk." I don't regard it as being a reasonable risk. I don't think that that risk exists.

Senator BAKER. What I mean by "risk" is, if we can tell for certain that something is MIRVed, there is no risk; if there is any chance that we can't, there is a risk.

Mr. WARNKE. That is right. But, in order to have a MIRVed missile that could fit in the silos that are not counted against the MIRV total, they would have to develop a new missile. The development of a new missile involves a whole variety of phenomena which are detectable by national technical means.

* * *

Senator CHURCH. I would like to get back to a point which Senator Case has raised.

There has been so much argument among those who have been

inclined to oppose SALT agreements in the past that somehow this agreement might theoretically put our ICBMs and our Minuteman system into some kind of jeopardy. I would like to examine that thesis.

First of all, if we did not have the agreement, then there would be no inhibition at all upon the Soviet Union to proceed to build as many MIRVed missiles as she is capable of building. In other words, the theoretical threat to our Minuteman systems would be obviously greater in the absence of an agreement than in an agreement that curtails the number of MIRVed missiles that even our own intelligence anticipates the Soviets would otherwise build. Is that correct?

Mr. WARNKE. That is correct.

Senator CASE. But no less.

Senator CHURCH. Right. But if our intelligence feels that in the absence of an agreement the Russians could build more MIRVed missiles than they agree to build under an agreement that we can verify, then clearly we have taken one step forward in reducing the possible theoretical risk to our Minuteman.

My second question is this: If under the protocol the Russians agree to build no new missiles or not to modify existing missiles [deleted] step that still further reduces the theoretical possibility of striking and destroying our Minutemen. Is that correct?

Mr. WARNKE. That is correct.

Senator CHURCH. My third question is this: Even a theoretical strike against our Minuteman system could be achieved only if the Soviets, having developed a sufficiently large force of sufficiently accurate missiles, would launch a strike against those missiles, and we left our missiles in their silos even though we would have approximately thirty minutes warning of the strike?

Mr. WARNKE. That is correct.

Senator CHURCH. So, even under the most optimum circumstances of this theoretical situation, assuming they had developed the capability, they could destroy our missile force only with our acquiescence?

Mr. WARNKE. I think that is an accurate way to put it, yes.

Senator CHURCH. So, what is the big argument about?

Mr. WARNKE. I think, Senator Church, it is an argument that has been going now for at least the past twelve years. I know that when I was in the Department of Defense back in the late 1960s there were scenarios then that were developed which would indicate a threat to our land-based ICBM force. This is no new discovery. It is not anything that has been the result of SALT.

As a matter of fact, SALT has, to some extent, reduced the theoretical risk by setting limits. A SALT II agreement along the lines that are now emerging would further limit the threat to Minuteman. But you

cannot totally dissipate the scenario which does indicate that the Minuteman force could be substantially attrited by a counterforce strike. The chances of that counterforce strike would require that a Soviet planner have sufficient confidence in the reliability and the accuracy of his missiles, have sufficient confidence that he can avoid the fratricide effects of having missiles come in after other missiles have exploded and thus interfere with the performance of the incoming missiles. And, as you point out, he should have the further assurance that the United States would sit there blandly for the twenty minutes warning that we would receive of the oncoming Soviet force and leave our missiles in those silos. But, nonetheless, we have to concede, I think, the fact that as land-based missiles become both more deadly and more vulnerable, that does, to some extent, destabilize the strategic balance. They become more of a threat, but at the same time they become no less vulnerable.

That is what we are trying to cope with, not because that necessarily destroys our deterrent—it doesn't—but because of the fact that we will have a more stable situation if people are not able to speculate about the possible vulnerability of Minuteman.

I think that in viewing the Minuteman vulnerability scenario against the issue of SALT versus no SALT, you have to figure out what the possibilities are, what will occur if we don't have a SALT II treaty. Well, instead of having something like [deleted] or less strategic nuclear delivery vehicles, our projections are that the Soviet Union will have in excess of [deleted]. As far as MIRVed missiles are concerned, instead of having something like [deleted] they will have something like [deleted]. Now, whether in those circumstances it becomes more feasible for a Soviet planner to contemplate a strike which would attrite our Minuteman force as he has more missiles that he could direct toward that purpose, I don't think that even then it would be a good gamble on the part of any sane man. But nonetheless, SALT II will, in fact, reduce the theoretical risk to Minuteman. SALT III, in my view, will do more along those lines.

Senator SARBANES. But once assuming we hold it constant, though—

Mr. WARNKE. Hold it constant in what way, Senator?

Senator SARBANES. If there is no limitation, you then assume the Soviets will do X, Y, and Z.

Mr. WARNKE. Right.

Senator SARBANES. But you then assume that against the United States not doing anything. If there are no limitations and the Soviets are going to do X, Y, and Z, then I assume that we are going to do A, B, and C to counter X, Y, and Z. Therefore this comparison would not hold.

Senator CHURCH. Then the numbers would just escalate on both sides.

Senator SARBANES. Yes, so I would assume; or there would be different weapons systems or something of that sort.

I understand the point. But I don't see how writing a scenario that in effect says if we don't get the agreement the Soviets will do this, and then set that off against a U.S. posture that does nothing, gets you the proper comparison.

Mr. WARNKE. I believe that it does, Senator Sarbanes, for the short range: that there would be, in fact, be a period of time in which the Soviet forces would have expanded by about 50 percent with very little expansion on our part because of the fact that they have the ongoing programs and we don't.

Senator CASE. They do have a momentum, don't they?

Mr. WARNKE. Yes; they do.

* * *

Senator CASE. Are we agreeing to other things that are troublesome?

Mr. WARNKE. There is certainly nothing which is under negotiation at the present time that would, in any respect whatsoever, increase the vulnerability of our strategic forces.

Senator CASE. Of our major strategic missile forces?

Mr. WARNKE. That's right. What we are trying to do instead is to restrict the threat to it.

Now, as Senator Sarbanes has pointed out, we would not stand still if the Soviets went ahead with a 50-percent buildup, but the things that we would do would not diminish the likelihood of the vulnerability of our Minuteman force. We would be doing other things. We have, of course, done those other things in the past.

I think it is very significant to take a look at the comparison between the two strategic force postures. The Soviet Union has something like 70 percent of its strategic forces in the land-based ICBMS. Because of concerns that have existed in this country for more than a decade, we have decided to have three separate strategic forces to reduce the vulnerability argument. So, we have approximately one-third in ICBMS, one-third in submarine-launched ballistic missiles, and one-third in strategic bombers. So, the counterforce threat impacts more heavily on the Soviet Union than it does on us.

Obviously, if they went ahead with their buildup, we would go ahead with a buildup, too. There is no question about that. We would do whatever is necessary to insure that our security remains. But in my view, the best way to preserve that security is to get an effective arms-control agreement so that you do not have the buildup which is going to increase the risks of counterforce. . . .That is why I pointed out. . .that in the absence of a SALT agreement their forces are

projected to go up something like 50 percent, and we would have to make an appropriate response. It still would not eliminate the vulnerability of Minuteman. The only way that could be eliminated is—well, I suppose there are alternate courses for both sides to put their strategic forces to sea and on strategic bombers, or to find some way in SALT agreements—not in this present one, but in follow-on SALT agreements—to further cut back on the counterforce potential of the MIRVed ICBM forces on each side. That would have to be a very, very substantial reduction in order to satisfy the proponents of the Minuteman vulnerability scenario, because obviously, if you are cutting back on forces on both sides, you are not only cutting back on the attacking forces, you are cutting back on the targets.

Senator PEARSON. I was concerned about something you said a few minutes ago when we were talking about the Backfire. You said something about a separate agreement on the development and deployment of Backfire. That triggered off in my mind a concern about unilateral statements or separate agreements or the reliance upon SALT III to solve problems that could conceivably be solved in SALT II.

If you send to the Senate a treaty that you well know has some unilateral agreements, statements, and other things, you know that you have created an added problem.

Mr. WARNKE. I can see that, Senator.

Senator PEARSON. That is what I want to ask you about.

Let's get back to the Backfire. Is it the intent to leave that out and to have a separate agreement somehow or other as to the development, deployment, and range limitations of that—outside the SALT II treaty?

Mr. WARNKE. The Backfire issue, Senator, has not been resolved at the present point.

* * *

Mr. WARNKE. There are basically two kinds of unilateral statements, Senator Pearson, one of which, in my view, is an acceptable method of getting agreement and one of which is not.

I think that the problem we have had with unilateral statements in the past is that we have made statements about what the Soviets would do. That obviously is a totally unsatisfactory kind of arrangement. I think for the United States to say what the Soviet Union is not going to do is of no value. What we need are statements by the Soviet Union as to what they commit themselves not to do.

In SALT I there were some unilateral statements of the former type. There were unilateral statements to the effect that the United States regarded it as being within the spirit of the agreement that mobile ICBMs would not be deployed. The Soviet Union refused to make that

statement, and as a consequence you could not say to them, "You can't go ahead with this development because you promised not to do it"—you committed yourself not to do it.

Now, a unilateral statement to the effect that the person making the statement commits himself obviously is something which is susceptible of enforcement. So, there are differences between those two kinds of unilateral statements.

Senator PEARSON. Outside the treaty provision?

Mr. WARNKE. There will probably be some things outside the treaty provision, I would think, yes. What they would be at the present point I am not sure.

* * *

Senator GLENN. . . . If we have an agreement that is nonverifiable, to me that is sort of the worst of both worlds, because we will live up to it, and if they don't, we have no means of verifying what they are doing. . . . Let me give a little detail on what I mean.

We are unable to distinguish now between the SS–20 and the SS–16 mobiles. They can convert without detection. We cannot really pinpoint which boosters are MIRVed and not MIRVed. We cannot tell whether the Backfire is going to be refueled or not because refueling probes can be internal. . . .

The most difficult area of all is qualitative upgrading. If they improve the accuracies of their systems with new guidance or new engines that give them a different range, we have absolutely no way that I am aware of of detecting that. The only thing that has even been said in counter to that is that they will have to test them and that we will observe the tests. But we don't know whether they have a brand new guidance system or whether they just lumped one in with their old guidance system with greater accuracy. . . .

We have no way of checking their reload capabilities on individual silos, repeater silos, where they can fire one and have it ready to go again shortly with another one, which gives them an expanded capability.

These are examples that I can think of this morning, just off the top of my head, without really going through any documents.

* * *

Mr. WARNKE. . . . I do not agree that we are negotiating provisions that are not verifiable. I think that we are negotiating provisions on which we will have a high order of confidence in their verifiability. That does not mean that problems will not remain. It does not mean that the problems won't get more acute as you get on to even more complicated

forms of arms control. But I will have no difficulty in assuring this committee that SALT II will be verifiable.

Senator GLENN. In all aspects?

Mr. WARNKE. In all aspects we will have adequate verification, yes.

Senator GLENN. You say that Backfire is now out of this area, right?

Mr. WARNKE. Backfire will be a part of the total package, but how it will be handled has not been settled at the present time.

Senator GLENN. How do we verify whether Backfire has refueling capability?

Mr. WARNKE. You will be able to verify whether or not the refueling capability of Backfire presents a strategic threat to the United States by a variety of means, [deleted]. . . . The Soviets at the present point have a very limited and very old tanker force. One possible means is to prevent any association of tankers with Backfire, any testing of tankers with Backfire. [Deleted.]

Senator GLENN. You are assuming that we can detect all tankers, then?

Mr. WARNKE. Yes. . . . We have a high degree of confidence, Senator Glenn, in our ability at the present point to determine which aircraft are tankers and which are not.

Senator GLENN. I don't know how you can do that when planes look like transport airplanes to begin with. Unless there is some means that I am not aware of, I don't see how you can verify which is and which is not a tanker. We have planes flying around here every day which are tankers and cannot be detected, or which can have tanks put in them on short notice and become tankers. I presume the Russians could do the same thing.

Mr. WARNKE. They could. But, as I said, at the present point we have a high degree of confidence as to which are tankers; and we would be able, in our opinion, to determine whether or not they were being used with Backfire in order to give Backfire a refueling capability.

Senator GLENN. I would contest your statement in the absence of any proof, because I don't think we have that means.

Mr. WARNKE. I cannot defend the Backfire constraints at the present point, Senator Glenn, because they have not been worked out.

Senator GLENN. Then we have no means at the moment.

Mr. WARNKE. We don't have the constraints.

* * *

Senator CHURCH. If they have developed and tested these antisatellite missiles, some successfully, what then is to prevent them from stockpiling a sufficient number of such missiles so that if they were ever to decide upon a preemptive strike, they could knock out our surveillance system first?

Mr. WARNKE. The tests, of course, are very obvious. Therefore we have been able to keep track of any tests up to this point. The tests up to this point have been very limited and [deleted].

As far as their taking a chance on trying antisatellite activity is concerned, that obviously would be the clearest indication of an attempt at a preemptive strike. It would clearly violate the SALT agreement. It would violate it in two respects.

Senator CHURCH. It would put us all on a Red Alert.

Mr. WARNKE. Yes, that is right. It would put us immediately on the kind of alert we would have if there were any sort of mass evacuation of Soviet cities. I think that as a consequence that would be tantamount to an announcement of an intent to launch a strike. If we were caught at that point by surprise, it would be a reflection on our common sense. But antisatellite activity is barred in SALT II. It would constitute interference with national technical means, which is prohibited. It would constitute an attempt at deliberate concealment, which is prohibited.

* * *

Mr. WARNKE. Senator Glenn has said, of course correctly, that no agreement could be 100 percent verifiable. I think we sometimes tend to look at verification just from the standpoint of the person who is worried about the other side cheating. We also have to look at it from the standpoint of the potential cheater.

What kind of a chance could a potential cheater afford to take? Suppose you have an agreement which is 80 percent verifiable, so that there were eight chances out of ten that he would be caught. He certainly could not afford to take that sort of chance. I think we ought to aim for something in that order of likelihood.

Warnke Discusses SALT and the Concerns of NATO Allies, 6 January 1978

Q. Mr. Warnke, during the [NATO] talks in Brussels last month, the West Germans in particular seemed to be making nervous sounds about their fears that SALT III would take up forward-based systems, and they seemed to be demanding, or asking in some form or other, for a real voice—it almost sounded like a veto—over further negotiations for SALT III. Can you say whether FBS will be included in SALT III or in the guidelines you're now drawing up, and if not, do you think this will be taken up at some future point? Should it be taken up at some future point?

Mr. WARNKE. Well, on that, no decision has been reached as yet as to what we would put into the statement of principles to guide SALT III; that's still in the position of formation at the present point. I believe that the President at Warsaw [on 30 December 1977] indicated his view that you should begin to talk about theater nuclear forces. That happens to be my own personal view too.

I think that I would not say that we would talk about forward-based systems, because that suggests that we only talk about American nuclear forces in Europe and the forces of the British and the French. Now, obviously, if we're going to discuss American forward-based systems, we would also insist on discussing restrictions on Soviet theater nuclear forces. And that's a question which, as I say, has not as yet been decided. It's a complicated one. We've endeavored to keep SALT bilateral—it's complicated enough to try and do it just between the two countries. If you have an MBFR sort of a forum, that necessarily injects an awful lot of complications.

At the same time, there is no question of the fact that we would not discuss what sometimes is referred to as the "gray area systems"—the longer-range theater nuclear forces—without doing it with the approval of our NATO allies and in close consultation with them. So that I don't think there's any question of fact that our allies would expect to have that sort of consultation. But I don't think they're apprehensive about our doing it without consultation, because they know we wouldn't do it. But if there's going to be any discussion of such things as theater nuclear forces, it would have to be done if not on a multi-

SOURCE: Remarks of ACDA Director Paul C. Warnke before the Overseas Writers Club, Washington, D.C., 6 January 1978. United States Arms Control and Disarmament Agency (Public Affairs).

lateral basis, at least with some sort of provision for continuing consultation.

* * *

Q. . . . Do you think, Mr. Warnke, that the United States will be able to keep the repeated promise that there will be nothing in SALT II prohibiting the United States to transfer technology concerning, for instance, intermediate-range cruise missiles to the NATO allies? Has that been decided yet?

Mr. WARNKE. Well, I believe that statements to that effect have been made both by Secretary Vance and Secretary Brown, and I agree with both of them.

Q. Is that still being talked about in SALT II, or is it off the table . . . that technology transfer will not be prohibited, will not be part of an agreement?

Mr. WARNKE. Well—a transfer of what? I mean, obviously, if a particular system is not restricted in a SALT treaty, then there would be no explicit or implicit prohibition against the transfer of its technology. At the same time, I think you have to recognize that if you have a treaty, that there is an implicit, if not an explicit representation that you're not going to circumvent the treaty. The United States won't enter into an international treaty and then run circles around it.

Q. Well, do these promises, . . . these secretarial statements, do they cover long-range cruise missile technology? Why should it be talked about if it's not part of the agreement, anyway?

Mr. WARNKE. Why should it be talked about by whom?

Q. By the Secretary of State.

Mr. WARNKE. Well, as I recall the statement of the Secretary of State, he said that there would be nothing that would prevent the transfer of cruise missile technology. Is that the statement to which you refer?

Q. Right.

Mr. WARNKE. Yeah. That's the statement he made. I agree with it.

Q. For any range cruise missile?

Mr. WARNKE. I didn't say that. I say, we'll have to wait until SALT II is completed to find out what the restrictions are on SALT II.

Q. I read where the administration has slowed MX work. If that's so, I wonder if that is in response, or in anticipation of any response of the Russians to slow down something on their side?

Mr. WARNKE. I'm not really familiar with the basis on which the decision was made. It was not made pursuant to anything in the negotiations.

Q. You mean, we're slowing down the rate of the program without—

Mr. WARNKE. I would suggest that you ask Secretary Brown. That's his field, not mine.

Q. Two questions. One, how does the decision of [French] President Giscard d'Estaing to go ahead with the cruise missile affect your negotiations? Secondly, you mentioned in your earlier speech that the fears of the Europeans were exaggerated in the press. Now, [West German] Chancellor Schmidt, in his [28 October 1977] Alastair Buchan lecture, probably summarized those fears more powerfully than anybody else. Would you react to that one, too?

Mr. WARNKE. Well, I've read Chancellor Schmidt's speech. I don't think that that reflects any alarm as far as the direction of SALT is concerned. I think he points out the fact that there is concern about the growing Soviet-Warsaw Pact buildup and that this is a matter which ought to be taken into consideration in arms control negotiations. Now, as I say, I don't regard this as being either a sign of panic or a sign of distrust.

Q. No, no—he says the essential argument is that, with a strategic balance between the two superpowers, West European security becomes doubtful.

Mr. WARNKE. This is nothing new, and this is not the result of SALT, so it certainly can be no indictment of SALT.

Strategic parity is the inevitable result of a continued nuclear arms competition—that where you've got a country with the resources and with the will and with the technology, you can see to it the other side does not obtain or continue any sort of nuclear superiority. Now, that happened a long time ago. It would be nice if we had nuclear superiority; it might make the Europeans more comfortable. But they're going to have to accept the fact that there is strategic parity and they're going to have to accept—and I think welcome—the fact that arms control will see to it that that strategic balance remains stable. And I think that you have to separate out the question of what you do about any sort of conventional imbalance. You're not going to be able to trade off a nonexistent strategic superiority in order to gain conventional parity, and I don't read Chancellor Schmidt's speech as suggesting that.

Q. But, you see, inherent in his argument is the reason for the Europeans to have something like cruise missiles, and that brings me back to my first question of why Giscard—

Mr. WARNKE. Well, as I say, the SALT negotiations have been exclusively bilateral, and SALT II, at least, will continue to be exclusively bilateral. And certainly nothing that we do would be designed in any way to inhibit any option that the French want to exercise by themselves. And I don't regard a decision on cruise missiles by the French as making SALT II infeasible.

Q. Mr. Warnke, have the Soviets [inaudible] the threat of China to bolster their negotiating positions in SALT? And if the Soviet Union and the United States are successful in reducing the level of their own nuclear weapons, how long will it be before we must include China in SALT talks?

Mr. WARNKE. Well, I must say that certainly there are references made by the Soviet negotiators to the threat of China, and explanations, for example, as to why it is that they're conducting such an extensive conventional buildup. But I don't think they've ever proposed to me, and I certainly would pay no attention to any sort of suggestion, that we ought to give them some sort of compensation in their forces because of the fact that they face a Chinese threat.

Now, with regard to the question as to whether we can afford to have restrictions on our strategic arms in view of the Chinese, certainly the disparity at the present point is so great that there is nothing that the Chinese can do within five, ten, fifteen, twenty—you name it—years which would in any way threaten the strategic retaliatory capability of the Soviet Union or of the United States.

Now, as a consequence, we have urged in the comprehensive test ban talks that the Soviet Union agree to a treaty which would enter into force without insisting that the Chinese and the French adhere to that treaty as a precondition to its effectiveness. We think that the best way to proceed is for the United Kingdom, the Soviet Union, and the United States to agree to a treaty, get as much international adherence as we can, and then hope that over a period of time the Chinese and the French will agree to the treaty. But certainly we can afford to do that. Our security is not jeopardized by the continued testing programs of the French and the Chinese.

Q. Have the Russians raised in the negotiations what they've raised with some people publicly in terms of the Chinese threat, that they're only willing to accept a three-year term for the comprehensive test ban because of a desire to see where the Chinese are in their testing program at the end of that period, thus in a sense saying at the end of that period you might discontinue the agreement?

Mr. WARNKE. I think we have to anticipate that in any comprehensive test ban treaty there will be a provision for review on a periodic basis so that you can see what developments have taken place and conclude whether or not it's possible for you to continue to adhere to the ban. I would expect a provision of that sort to exist in the treaty.

* * *

Q. I'd like to return to the question . . . of whether or not some of the restrictions within the life of the protocol might, in terms of political

dynamics, become more permanent. Clearly, this is a crucial question for some of the European countries that do have an interest in technology like the cruise missile.

If I understand some of the logic of the protocol, there is a linkage between American restraint on the cruise missile and Soviet restraint on the deployment of a new family of ICBMS. This leads to the possibility that, come 1980, while in principle or in theory one's options, as you pointed out, would be open to go ahead with the cruise missiles if that was thought to be necessary, at the same time you would be implicitly allowing the Soviets to decide the protocol would go by the boards, to go ahead with their new family of ballistic missile developments. I think that would make it very likely that a number of people in the arms control community would urge very strongly that the cruise missile, in fact, be included under a more permanent arrangement because of the implications of allowing the Soviets to go ahead with their developments. In that case, don't you think that there is at least a strong argument to suggest that the idea of leaving the options open is not as clear-cut as many people such as yourself have really argued?

Mr. WARNKE. You have exactly the same problem whether you've got these things in a protocol or not. I mean, you would still have the same question: What are you willing to give up, and in return for what? And you have to decide that on the basis of your best judgment as to where your net advantage lies.

Now, obviously, the conclusion could be reached that continuing restrictions on cruise missiles was worth it because of certain other things that you could get, but that question remains open. And the only way in which you would be prejudiced would be if you had an unbalanced protocol which somehow gave you less bargaining leverage than it gave the other side. I'm confident that the protocol will be such that our bargaining leverage will be at least as good as that of the Soviet side; and from that standpoint we will be able to make that decision based on all of the considerations, including the military utility—what would happen if both sides got the same technology—and whether or not you can get something for continuing to restrain it which is better for you than going ahead with the program. So from that standpoint, I am in fact confident the option does remain open.

Pravda Examines the Problems Obstructing a SALT Agreement, 11 February 1978

"International relations are now at a crossroads, as it were, which could lead either to a growth of trust and cooperation, or else to a growth of mutual fears, suspicion, and arms stockpiles—a crossroads leading, ultimately, either to lasting peace, or at best, to balancing on the brink of war. Détente offers the opportunity of choosing the road of peace. To miss this opportunity would be a crime. The most important, the most pressing task now is to halt the arms race which has engulfed the world," stresses the General Secretary of the Central Committee of the Communist Party of the Soviet Union, President of the Presidium of the U.S.S.R. Supreme Soviet, Leonid I. Brezhnev.

The problem of limiting strategic arms holds a special place in the attainment of this task. It is not by chance, therefore, that the talks on this matter conducted by the Soviet Union and the United States attract the interest of the entire international public. . . . The Vladivostok accord of 1974 signified a new stage in the solution of the problem, opening up possibilities for encompassing additional components of the strategic forces of the two countries, for limiting them both quantitatively and qualitatively.

It is known, however, that for reasons not depending on the U.S.S.R., work to draft this agreement has not been completed to this day. The Soviet Union consistently and constructively pursued a line of concluding this work in strict accordance with all that was agreed upon in Vladivostok, on the basis of strict observance of the principle of equality and undiminished security of the sides.

This, unfortunately, cannot be said about the American side. Without going into details, it should be recalled that the process of negotiations developed very unevenly, and, especially at the initial stages, was accompanied by serious difficulties. This was connected with the advancement by the American side of such proposals that, by their essence, were directed at overturning the Vladivostok accords and at giving the United States obvious advantages. It took time and big efforts—mostly in the course of the Soviet-American meetings in Moscow in March 1977 and in May of the same year in Geneva and in September in Washington—for a more sober and balanced line to start manifesting itself in the American approach. As a result, it proved

---

SOURCE: *Pravda* editorial, "The Task of Limiting Strategic Arms: Prospects and Problems," 11 February 1978. Reprinted in *News and Views from the U.S.S.R.*, Soviet Embassy Information Department, Washington, D.C.

possible to bring the talks back to the principled directions that were jointly defined in Vladivostok and made concrete in the course of subsequent discussions.

A certain advance in finding solutions to major still unresolved questions was achieved as a result of the conversations that the U.S.S.R. Foreign Minister had with the President and the Secretary of State of the United States in Washington last September. This became possible first of all owing to the consistently constructive line of the U.S.S.R. and also the elements of flexibility and realism shown by the American side. Both sides confirmed their resolve to conclude a new agreement and firmly stated their intention to continue vigorous talks so as to complete work on the agreement in the near future. . . .

Objectively, all this gave new important impulses for concluding the practical drafting of the texts of the relevant documents—a treaty with a period of operation up until 1985; a three-year protocol on certain interim measures, which is an inalienable part of the treaty; and also a possible joint statement on the main directions of further talks on new measures in the field of limiting and then cutting strategic armaments.

It would seem that a green light has finally been given to these big and important endeavors. Facts, however, show that such a development of events does not suit the forces in the United States which are against a positive development of Soviet-American relations and which constantly try to slow down and even frustrate totally the agreement on the limitation of strategic arms. They stubbornly strive to make this question a topic of sharp internal political struggle in the United States. The opponents of the agreement became especially active when prospects of its conclusion opened up.

These forces act in various ways. Some people—especially from among the retired high-placed military, "specialists-theoreticians" on questions of strategy, organizations of the type of the Committee on the Present Danger, some organs of the press that are direct advocates of the Pentagon and the military-industrial complex—openly oppose any agreements with the U.S.S.R. on the limitation of armaments and call for an intensification of military efforts and for ensuring military superiority over the U.S.S.R. Manipulating the thesis about protecting "the national security interests" of the United States, they impudently invent something like scripts for waging nuclear war. Waging war, but not preventing war. They count how many nuclear warheads and bombs will be needed to deliver a strike at some country. The nations of the world want peace and lasting détente, but these people keep thinking about what else to invent to destroy human beings. . . .

The historic course of development has long made untenable the

designs to ensure for the United States a military superiority over the U.S.S.R. The leaders of the United States themselves were compelled to officially recognize the state of military-strategic equilibrium between the two countries. There is no future in attempts to revive plans of achieving military superiority over the U.S.S.R. But they can lead to a new spiral of the arms race, to a greater danger of a nuclear-missile conflict, with all the ensuing consequences for all countries and peoples, including the United States. . . .

The arsenal of means of struggle used by the opponents of détente and measures to lessen military danger are not distinguished for being novelties. The main one of these means is the threadbare myth about the "Soviet military threat." This myth is being blown up again to undermine chances for the conclusion of an agreement on limiting strategic offensive weapons. The American public is being persistently told that the Soviet Union allegedly wants by means of such an agreement to acquire a strategic superiority over the United States, to create a possibility for it to deliver a "crippling nuclear-missile strike," et cetera.

By its entire consistent peace-loving policy the Soviet Union resolutely refutes the falsity and absurdity of such concoctions and their deliberate provocative intentions.

As it was stated by L. I. Brezhnev, "Our efforts are directed precisely at preventing any first and second strikes, at preventing nuclear war in general. Our approach to these questions can be formulated as follows: The defense potential of the Soviet Union should be sufficient to prevent anybody from risking to disrupt our peaceful life. Not a course of superiority in armaments, but a course of reducing them, of lessening military confrontation—such is our policy."

* * *

Along with the open opponents of the agreement on the limitation of strategic arms, there are such people in the United States who do not appear to directly oppose the agreement but in reality strive in every way to create ever-new obstacles on the road to its conclusion. This is done under the outwardly respectable pretext of trying to "amend" or "improve" the agreement. True, when they think that the government insufficiently heeds their arguments they throw off the mask and openly begin to accuse it of allegedly being excessively "soft" and "yielding" at the talks with the Soviet Union. And here vanishes even the outward distinction between them and overt opponents of the agreement.

They would like to "amend" the drafted agreement in such a way as to undermine the fundamental principle of equality and undiminished security of the sides, to ensure for the United States obvious

advantages to the detriment of the Soviet Union's security interests. If this cannot be achieved, they reason, at least it is possible to additionally procrastinate and complicate the attainment of agreement.

It was repeatedly stressed by the Soviet side that there should be no illusions about the U.S.S.R. accepting such limitations that would give the United States one-sided advantages. Those Americans who try to make the public think that it is possible to impose unacceptable terms of the agreement on the Soviet Union are doing their own people a great disservice. The agreement is needed equally by both sides, just as it is needed by all countries and peoples. The principle of equality and undiminished security as the only basis of agreement is not some artificial invention. It is organically connected with the very nature of modern weapons and the objectively existing equilibrium between the strategic forces of the U.S.S.R. and the United States.

Let us dwell in somewhat greater detail on questions used these days most frequently in the U.S. by those who would like to "amend" the agreement.

It is known that the talks have been at a standstill for a long time as a result of the U.S. position on the matter of the long-range cruise missiles. Yet, it was clear from the very outset that long-range cruise missiles, recognized as strategic weapons by the Americans themselves, are subject to limitation along with other strategic systems, such as intercontinental ballistic missiles, submarine-borne ballistic missiles, and heavy bombers. In the final analysis, the sides did agree that the "air-to-earth" type of cruise missiles with ranges from 600 to 2,500 kilometers ought to be limited. It was agreed that heavy bombers equipped with such missiles will be equal to strategic missiles with multiple independently targetable warheads, and that these bombers will be counted in the established quotas for such carriers—1,320 units on each side. As for "air-to-earth" cruise missiles with ranges in excess of 2,500 kilometers, these are subject to banning altogether.

Owing to the Soviet side's constructive position, the question of sea- and land-based cruise missiles with ranges in excess of 600 kilometers was also agreed upon. It is envisaged to ban their trials and deployment initially for a three-year period in order to give the sides additional time for finding a final solution.

It would seem that everything is clear, and that what looks like a basically technical task is all that remains to tackle—to put these decisions into appropriate treaty wording. Yet it is here that those who clamor for "amending" the treaty get into the action.

It turns out the limitations on cruise missiles do not suit them. On the one hand, they allege, this is an unwarranted "concession" in favor

of the U.S.S.R. in general. On the other, attempts are being made to practically emasculate the above-mentioned agreed limitations. For example, an argument is put forth to the effect that the U.S. must have the right to deploy "air-to-earth" cruise missles not only on heavy bombers subject to limitations, but actually on any type of aircraft, transports included. This would practically allow an unlimited and actually uncontrolled number of aircraft to appear, stuffed with scores of long-range cruise missiles and having the same destructive power as nuclear warheads of intercontinental missiles and submarine-borne missiles. What, then, one may ask, would be the worth of limitations contained in the treaty, and of the treaty altogether? It would be a scrap of paper, not an agreement aimed at averting nuclear war. The Soviet Union is not going to affix its signature to such a scrap of paper.

These people would like to exempt sea- and land-based cruise missiles from the limitations. Here we see an obvious striving to secure already today a free hand after the three-year protocol period in regard to the deployment of such missiles, for increasing their agreed range over 600 kilometers and, lastly, to reserve the possibility of deploying them outside U.S. territory—that is, as close as possible to the borders of the U.S.S.R. No comment, as they say, is needed. For it is clear that this is just another attempt to emasculate the essence of already agreed-upon limitations, to destroy the entire agreement.

One must especially stress the danger of attempts to leave loopholes whereby the cruise missiles could appear on the territories of other countries, first of all, the United States' NATO allies. This question is part of the overall problem, that the treaty being elaborated must completely exclude any possibility of the transfer of strategic armaments to third countries, or its obviation through the mediation of third countries. The sides must make unambiguous commitments on this score. Otherwise, the treaty's viability will again be reduced to naught. Those who are now trying in this way to "amend" the solution on the question of cruise missiles must realize how grave a responsibility they are taking upon themselves, both in regard to the treaty and from the viewpoint of the interests of the U.S. itself, since the Soviet Union, of course, will not remain passive if someone will try in this manner to upset the present balance of forces to the detriment of its security.

Another matter which is constantly being talked about by certain quarters in the U.S. in connection with the new treaty is controlling its observance. It is being asserted beforehand that the control system envisaged under the treaty is unreliable, and that there is no guarantee that the Soviet Union will not violate it. Actually this is an attempt to cast aspersions on U.S.S.R. policy, to bolster once again the tattered

myth about some ill intentions on the part of the Soviet Union. In particular, rumors are being spread alleging that the Soviet Union is developing means of destroying American observation satellites.

All these are ill-intentioned fabrications. When it signs an agreement, the Soviet Union strictly and unswervingly observes its commitments. . . . This kind of talk alleging that control is unreliable is aimed at questioning the system of control by the national technical means of each side, which has reliably justified itself. The realization of already existing accords in the sphere of strategic arms limitation convincingly proved that such means of control fully answer their purpose. This is fully applicable to the new treaty as well.

While stating that national technical control means are adequate, the Soviet Union, in the name of finding reciprocally acceptable solutions, has expressed its readiness, in principle, to agree that if a strategic missile of some type will be but once tested with multiple warheads, then all the missiles of this type will be counted in the quota of carriers with such warheads, as established under the treaty. This measure is aimed at raising the effectiveness of the treaty still more from the viewpoint of controls. . . . Thus, fabrications about the "unreliability" of controls are intended for uninformed people, and, what is more, are deliberately aimed at sowing doubt about the agreement as a whole.

We ought to dwell separately on the matter of new types of strategic armaments and the modernization of existing systems. Opponents of the treaty have raised a hue and cry around these questions, trying to present matters as if the American side is coming out here with far-reaching "radical" proposals, yet the Soviet Union, you see, is not ready for such a solution. The purpose is the same—to distort, to denigrate the Soviet position.

What, then, is the actual state of affairs? Let us note, first of all, that this thesis as such is by no means anything new. The American side had already put forth similar unacceptable proposals during the Moscow negotiations last March. At that time these proposals were given a principled evaluation. And it was convincingly shown that they are aimed at a revision of the Vladivostok accords, at undermining the principle of equality and the undiminished security of the sides.

Well known, at the same time, are the really constructive proposals set forth during the negotiations by the Soviet Union aimed at the reciprocal renunciation of the manufacture and deployment of new kinds of strategic weapons. In view of the discussions held, and taking into account the American position, the U.S.S.R. subsequently proposed a ban, for the period the three-year protocol is in force, on new types of intercontinental ballistic missiles with multiple warheads and sub-

marine-borne ballistic missiles with such warheads. Such a ban would in full measure meet the purposes of the treaty, since it is precisely these types of missiles that may render the main destabilizing effect on the prevailing strategic situation. At the same time, concerning both sides in equal measure, such a commitment fully corresponds to the principle of equality and undiminished security.

Yet the American side proposes to ban, for the period the protocol is in force, all new types of land-based intercontinental ballistic missiles in general, both with multiple warheads and without them. Now, this is just the proposal that is being depicted as going much further than the Soviet position. However, just as in a number of other cases, it is intended for naive and uniformed people. But what does it really mean?

By suggesting to ban all new types of intercontinental ballistic missiles, those who make this proposal at the same time omit all other kinds of strategic arms altogether—submarine-borne ballistic missiles, heavy bombers, cruise missiles—which means that new, more perfect, and more powerful types of such systems are allowed to be created, given only the limitation on land-based intercontinental ballistic missiles. If one also takes into account that, for different reasons, the two sides have by no means a similar composition of strategic forces, it becomes absolutely clear that the above-mentioned proposal is directly aimed against the principle of equality and undiminished security, that it is aimed at securing unilateral advantages at the expense of the Soviet Union. This is precisely the very essence of the United States' so-called radical approach!

The same goals underlie the U.S. stand on the matter of modernizing existing strategic armaments. There are some who would again like to "amend" the earlier agreed-upon clauses of the treaty so as to arbitrarily limit certain Soviet weapon systems, while giving the U.S. a free hand in regard to a whole range of components of strategic forces. The acceptance of such proposals would practically mean that, far from limiting a qualitative strategic arms race, the treaty would, on the contrary, give it a new big boost.

The one-sidedness of the American position is confirmed also by the practical actions of the U.S., leaving aside earlier examples doubtlessly testifying that it was precisely the American side which, at every stage, was the initiator of unleashing the strategic arms race by introducing newer systems of such weapons. . . . It is known, in particular, that at the time of the strategic arms limitation talks, when the first agreements were elaborated and accepted, the U.S. began deploying missiles with multiple nuclear warheads.

Recently created for Minuteman missiles is a new, much more powerful nuclear warhead, the MK-12A, and measures are being taken

to further increase the precision of these missiles. The Trident missiles complex is being developed for new submarines; the MX intercontinental missile is being developed, intended for use on mobile launchers; and long-range cruise missiles are being readied for serial production. Apart from those mentioned above, new, even more perfected weapons systems are in the stage of research and development. . . .

The thesis alleging the Soviet Union's unwillingness, as opposed to the U.S.A., to agree to a considerable reduction of strategic offensive weapons still figures among the inventions used by the treaty's opponents. The Soviet side has repeatedly outlined its position in this regard. The problem of balancing the interests of the sides, and the practical realization in the treaty of the principle of equality and undiminished security, is concentrated in this question perhaps more than in any other. The Soviet proposals proceed from the need to certainly take into account all the factors of the strategic situation, as it is at present and is likely to be in the future, in the period when the new treaty comes into force. This includes, in particular, such factors as the geographic position of the sides, the forward-based nuclear means available to the U.S.A. on territories of other countries in immediate proximity to the U.S.S.R., and the fact that some of its allies possess strategic weapons of their own. All these are rather tangible factors, and they must be taken into account. Nor can there be any different approach. Only in this case will substantial reductions of levels not destabilize the strategic situation nor result in advantages accruing to one side at the expense of the security interests of the other.

The Soviet Union by no means holds that the new agreement will be the ultimate stage in the efforts of the sides directed at restraining the nuclear arms race. The sides have already reached agreement that talks on further measures in the field of limiting strategic armaments will be started immediately after the conclusion of the current draft agreement. Moreover, there is an agreement in principle about the possibility of lowering the initially agreed-upon ceilings during the period of operation of the current draft agreement.

All have become sick and tired of the artificially created question of the Soviet plane called "Backfire" in the West, which has been artificially attached to the agreement. Clearly manifesting itself in this question are the obviously obstructionist tactics of the overt and covert opponents of the agreement, their striving to deliberately erect obstacles on the road to its conclusion.

The question is sufficiently well known. This plane is a medium-range bomber and, as such, has nothing to do at all with the subject matter of the negotiations because it does not belong to the class of strategic weapons. Nevertheless, consistently displaying a constructive

approach, the Soviet side found it possible to give all the necessary explanations concerning this plane. American specialists have a clear idea of the actual state of affairs. Nevertheless, this plane is the object of a continuing propaganda outcry. This is being done with the sole purpose of making this question another stumbling block at the talks. Despite obvious facts, concoctions are being constantly circulated about the danger that this plane might pose to the United States—for instance, if it is refueled in flight, or in some other contrived situation. But if we take to this road, then virtually any combat plane ought to fall under the limitations of the agreement that is being drafted. In any case, this would apply to all planes on aircraft carriers and all United States tactical planes situated at so-called advance bases, for instance in Europe, from which they might reach the territory of the U.S.S.R. even without refueling in flight. If we are to go further, we could recall the well-known facts about American fighter-bombers making transatlantic flights from the United States to Western Europe and refueling in mid-flight. So if anybody really has grounds to raise such questions, it is the Soviet side. But to raise all these questions now would mean not to advance along the road of the speediest achievement of the agreement but, on the contrary, to lead matters to a situation where there will be no agreement at all.

It appears that these are exactly the motivations of those who are continuing the clamor over the Backfire. But it takes a long time to understand that nobody will succeed in imposing unacceptable conditions on the Soviet side, be it in the question of the Backfire or in any other question.

Just as hopeless are the designs to scare the Soviet Union by talk that, if the relevant provisions of the agreement are not "amended" in favor of the United States, the American Senate will not ratify the treaty, which is required by law. Those who resort to such a maneuver are in fact trying to challenge not the Soviet Union but their own country, their own people, who are objectively interested in the same measure, and not one iota less than Soviet people, in putting an end to the strategic arms race. So, to bully the Soviet side by refusing to ratify the agreement is just pointless. For we too could pose the question in exactly the same manner.

Those who artificially retard the preparation of the treaty by returning again and again to questions about levels of strategic armaments, modernization, the Backfire aircraft, et cetera, should not forget or pretend to forget the presence, for example, of such a grave problem as the above-mentioned American forward-based nuclear means and the U.S. carrier-based aircraft—that is, weapons which by virtue of their location are capable of reaching Soviet territory. The Soviet

Union by no means forgets this, for it immediately involves its security: This means many hundreds of nuclear weapon carriers aimed at targets on U.S.S.R. territory. It is understandable, therefore, that the Soviet side comes out firmly for resolving this question in accordance with the principle of equality and undiminished security.

One should not forget that newer and newer mass annihilation weapons are being created in the U.S.A., including the neutron weapon. The Soviet Union has proposed a comprehensive ban on new kinds of mass annihilation weapons and new systems thereof, as well as the reciprocal renunciation of manufacturing the neutron weapon in particular. We shall resolutely work for the realization of these proposals. A really lasting peace and international security, as desired by all the peoples, can be ensured not by talk and declarations, but by concrete practical steps toward ending the arms race and toward disarmament. To do everything possible for this is the duty of all governments.

Carter Administration Report on Compliance with SALT I, 21 February 1978

I. Introduction

The purpose of this paper is to provide a brief account of the background, discussion, and status of those questions related to compliance with the SALT agreements of 1972—the ABM treaty and the interim agreement on strategic offensive arms—which have been raised by the U.S. and the U.S.S.R. It also provides a brief discussion of matters which have been mentioned in the press but which have not been raised with the U.S.S.R.

* * *

III. Questions Raised by the United States

* * *

C. *Modern Large Ballistic Missiles (SS–19 Issue)*

Article II of the interim agreement states: "The Parties undertake not to convert land-based launchers for light ICBMs, or for ICBMs of older types deployed prior to 1964, into land-based launchers for heavy ICBMs of types deployed after that time." This provision was sought by the U.S. as part of an effort to place limits on Soviet heavy ICBMs (SS–9 and follow-ons). We did not, however, obtain agreement on a quantitative definition of a heavy ICBM which would constrain increases in the size of Soviet light ICBMs (SS–11 and follow-ons). Thus, the U.S. side stated on the final day of SALT I negotiations:

> The U.S. Delegation regrets that the Soviet Delegation has not been willing to agree on a common definition of a heavy missile. Under these circumstances, the U.S. Delegation believes it necessary to state the following: The United States would consider any ICBM having a volume significantly greater than that of the largest light ICBM now operational on either side to be a heavy ICBM. The U.S. proceeds on the premise that the Soviet side will give due account to this consideration.

The U.S.S.R. delegation maintained the position throughout SALT I that an agreed definition of heavy ICBMs was not essential to the understanding reached by the sides in the interim agreement on the subject

---

Source: "Compliance with the SALT I Agreements." Administration report submitted by Secretary of State Cyrus R. Vance to the U.S. Senate, Committee on Foreign Relations; text made public on 28 February 1978.

of heavy ICBMS and made clear that they did not agree with the U.S. statement quoted above. When deployment of the SS–19 missile began, its size, though not a violation of the interim agreement provisions noted above, caused the U.S. to raise the issue with the Soviets in early 1975. Our purpose was to emphasize the importance the U.S. attached to the distinction made in the interim agreement between "light" and "heavy" ICBMS, as well as the continuing importance of that distinction in the context of the SALT II agreement under negotiation at the time. Following some discussion in the SCC [Standing Consultative Commission], further discussions of this question in that forum were deferred because it was under active consideration in the SALT II negotiations.

Since that time, the U.S. and U.S.S.R. delegations have agreed in the draft text of the SALT II agreement on a clear demarcation, in terms of missile launch-weight and throw-weight, between light and heavy ICBMS.

* * *

F. *Soviet ABM Radar on Kamchatka Peninsula*

Article IV of the ABM treaty states: "The limitations provided for in Article III [on deployment] shall not apply to ABM systems or their components used for development or testing, and located within current or additionally agreed test ranges. . . ." In October, 1975, a new radar was installed at the Kamchatka impact area of the Soviet ICBM test range. Since Article IV exempts from the limitations of Article III only those ABM components used for development or testing at current or additionally agreed ranges, location of this radar, which the U.S. identified as an ABM radar, on the Kamchatka Peninsula could have constituted establishment of a new Soviet ABM test range.

This situation, however, was made ambiguous by two facts: (1) Just prior to the conclusion of the SALT negotiations in 1972, the U.S. provided to the Soviet delegation a list of U.S. and Soviet ABM test ranges which did not include the Kamchatka impact area. The Soviet side neither confirmed nor denied the accuracy or completeness of the U.S. listing, and indicated that use of national technical means assured against misunderstanding of Article IV; and (2) The presence of an older-type ABM radar could be viewed as having established the Kamchatka impact area as an ABM test range at the time the ABM treaty was signed.

Though the location of a new ABM radar on Kamchatka was not strategically significant, it was decided that this matter should be raised with the Soviet side in order to set the record straight.

We brought the situation to the attention of the Soviet side. The

U.S.S.R. indicated that a range with a radar instrumentation complex existed on the Kamchatka Peninsula on the date of signature of the ABM treaty and that they would be prepared to consider the Kamchatka range a current test range within the meaning of Article IV of the ABM treaty. The U.S. continued the exchange to establish that Kamchatka is an ABM test range, that Sary Shagan and Kamchatka are the only ABM test ranges in the U.S.S.R., and that Article IV of the ABM treaty requires agreement concerning the establishment of additional test ranges.

The Soviet side has acknowledged that Kamchatka is an ABM test range and that it and Sary Shagan are the only ABM test ranges in the U.S.S.R. On the third point, discussions are continuing on how properly to satisfy the need for discussing and agreeing upon the establishment of an ABM test range. Agreement appears near on this matter.

G. *Soviet Dismantling or Destruction of Replaced ICBM Launchers*

Under the interim agreement and the protocol thereto of May 26, 1972, the U.S.S.R. was permitted to have no more than 950 SLBM launchers and 62 modern, nuclear-powered ballistic missile submarines. In addition, it was provided that Soviet SLBM launchers in excess of 740 might become operational only as replacements for older ICBM and SLBM launchers, which would be dismantled or destroyed under agreed procedures. Such procedures were developed in the SCC and became effective on July 3, 1974. The procedures include detailed requirements for the dismantling or destruction actions to be accomplished, their timing, and notification about them to the other party.

By early 1976, the Soviets had developed a requirement to dismantle fifty-one replaced launchers. It soon became apparent to the U.S. that the Soviets would probably not complete all the required dismantling actions on all of the launchers on time. Therefore, the U.S. decided to raise this question with the Soviets; but before we could do so, the notification concerning dismantling or destruction provided by the Soviet side in the SCC acknowledged that the dismantling of forty-one older ICBM launchers had not been completed in the required time period. The Soviet side explained the situation and predicted that all the dismantling actions would be completed by June 1, 1976, and agreed to the U.S. demand that no more submarines with replacement SLBM launchers begin sea trials before such completion. Both conditions were met. Since that time, although we have observed some minor procedural discrepancies at a number of those deactivated launch sites and at others as the replacement process continued, all the launchers have been in a condition that satisfied the essential substantive requirements, which are that they cannot be used to launch missiles and cannot

be reactivated in a short time. As necessary, we have pursued the question of complete and precise accomplishment of the detailed requirements of the agreed procedures.

H. *Concealment at Test Range*

Provisions of the interim agreement pertinent to this discussion are:

Article V.3: "Each Party undertakes not to use deliberate concealment measures which impede verification by national technical means of compliance with the provisions of this Interim Agreement. . . ."

Agreed statement concerning launcher dimensions: ". . . in the process of modernization and replacement, the dimensions of land-based ICBM silo launchers will not be significantly increased."

Agreed statement concerning test and training launchers: ". . . there shall be no significant increase in the number of ICBM and SLBM test and training launchers or in the number of such launchers for modern land-based heavy ICBMS . . . construction or conversion of ICBM launchers at test ranges shall be undertaken only for purposes of testing and training."

In early 1977, we observed the use of a large net covering over an ICBM test launcher undergoing conversion at a test range in the U.S.S.R.

There was agreement in the U.S. that this subject could be appropriate for discussion in SALT in the context of the ongoing discussions on the subject of deliberate concealment measures in connection with a SALT II agreement. The subject was initially raised in this context.

In addition, we also expressed our view that the use of a covering over an ICBM silo launcher concealed activities from national technical means of verification and could impede verification of compliance with provisions of the interim agreement, specifically, the provision which dealt with increases in dimensions of ICBM silo launchers as recorded in the agreed statement quoted above. The U.S. took the position that a covering which conceals activities at an ICBM silo from national technical means of verification could reduce the confidence and trust which are important to mutual efforts to establish and maintain strategic arms limitations.

It has been the Soviet position that the provisions of the interim agreement were not applicable to the activity in question. Nevertheless, they subsequently removed the net covering.

IV. QUESTIONS RAISED BY THE U.S.S.R.

A. *Shelters over Minuteman Silos*

Paragraph 3 of Article V of the interim agreement states: "Each Party undertakes not to use deliberate concealment measures which

impede verification by national technical means of compliance with the provisions of this Interim Agreement. This obligation shall not require changes in current construction, assembly, conversion, or overhaul practices."

The U.S. used shelters which were either 300 or 700 square feet in size over Minuteman ICBM silos to provide environmental protection during initial construction as well as modernization from 1962 through 1972. Beginning in 1973, in connection with modernization and silo-hardening work, prefabricated shelters of about 2,700 square feet were used. From four to twelve of these shelters were in place over silos at any given time, for from ten days to four weeks depending upon the severity of the weather.

The Soviets raised this subject, taking the position that the activity was inconsistent with Article V of the interim agreement since it could be classified as deliberate concealment, and that, therefore, it should cease. The U.S., based on the nature of the shelters and their use strictly for environmental purposes, not for concealment, believed that their use was consistent with Article V.

In early 1977, the U.S. decided to modify the use of environmental shelters over Minuteman ICBM silos based on explicit confirmation of the common view shared by us and the Soviets that neither side should use shelters over ICBM silos that impede verification by national technical means of compliance with the provisions of the interim agreement. Our use of shelters has recently been modified by reducing their size almost 50 percent in recognition of that understanding.

B. *Atlas and Titan I Launchers*

The "Protocol on Procedures Governing Replacement, Dismantling or Destruction, and Notification Thereof, for Strategic Offensive Arms," as noted above, provides detailed procedures for dismantling ICBM launchers and associated facilities, one principle of which is that reactivation of dismantled launchers should take substantially more time than construction of a new one.

There are 177 former launchers for the obsolete Atlas and Titan I ICBM systems at various locations across the continental United States. All these launchers were deactivated by the end of 1966.

The Soviet side apparently perceived an ambiguity with respect to the status and condition of these launchers, based on the amount of dismantling which had been done and its effect on their possible reactivation time. They raised this issue in early 1975.

The U.S. view was that these launchers were obsolete and deactivated prior to the interim agreement and were not subject to that agreement or to the accompanying procedures for dismantling or destruction.

However, we did provide some information on their condition illustrating that they could not be reactivated easily or quickly. The discussion on this question ceased in mid-1975.

C. *Radar on Shemya Island*

Article III of the ABM treaty states: "Each Party undertakes not to deploy ABM systems or their components except . . . within one ABM deployment area . . . centered on the Party's national capital . . . and within one deployment area . . . containing ICBM silo launchers. . . ."

In 1973, the United States began construction of a new phased-array radar on Shemya Island, Alaska, at the western end of the Aleutian Island chain. This radar is to be used for national technical means of verification, space track, and early warning.

The Soviets raised a question in 1975, suggesting that the radar was an ABM radar, which would not be permitted at this location.

The U.S. side discussed this matter with the Soviets and as a result, we believe, eliminated any concern about possible inconsistency with the provisions of the ABM treaty. The radar became operational in early 1977.

D. *Privacy of SCC Proceedings*

Paragraph 8 of the Regulations of the SCC states: "The proceedings of the Standing Consultative Commission shall be conducted in private. The Standing Consultative Commission may not make its proceedings public except with the express consent of both Commissioners."

Prior to the special SCC session held in early 1975 to discuss certain questions related to compliance, several articles appeared in various U.S. publications with wide circulation. These articles speculated about the possibility of certain Soviet "violations" of the SALT agreements which would be discussed, and tended to draw the conclusion that there were violations, based on what was purported to be accurate intelligence information.

The Soviets have expressed to us their concern about the importance of confidentiality in the work of the SCC, and about the publication of such items. They were apparently particularly concerned about press items that may appear to have official U.S. government sanction.

We have discussed with the Soviets the usefulness of maintaining the privacy of our negotiations and discussions and limiting speculation in the public media on SCC proceedings, as well as the need to keep the public adequately informed.

E. *Dismantling or Destruction of the ABM Radar under Construction at Malmstrom Air Force Base*

When the ABM treaty was signed on May 26, 1972, the U.S. had ABM defenses under construction in two deployment areas for the defense of ICBMS. Since the ABM treaty permitted each party only one such ABM system deployment area, the U.S. immediately halted the construction, which was in the early stages, at Malmstrom AFB, Montana. Specific procedures for the dismantling or destruction of the ABM facilities under construction at Malmstrom were negotiated as part of the Protocol on Procedures for ABM Systems and Their Components, signed on July 3, 1974.

Dismantling of the ABM facilities under construction at Malmstrom was completed by May 1, 1974.

In late 1974, we notified the U.S.S.R. in the SCC that dismantling activities at the Malmstrom site had been completed. Somewhat later, the Soviet side raised a question about one detailed aspect of the dismantling which they apparently felt had not been carried out in full accord with the agreed procedures.

We reviewed with the Soviet side the actions taken by the U.S. to dismantle the Malmstrom site, and also showed them some photographs of the before and after conditions there. The question was apparently resolved on the basis of that discussion.

V. Other Questions and Charges

. . . . Activities not raised with the U.S.S.R. as ambiguous or of possible concern have also been examined by the U.S. In those cases, analysis of the available intelligence information showed that they did not warrant discussion or categorization as inconsistent with the agreements. Generally, it has been the practice to avoid public discussions of these matters.

From time to time, articles have appeared in U.S. periodicals and newspapers alleging Soviet violations of the provisions of the SALT I agreements. As indicated earlier, these reports or commentaries have been generally speculative, and have concluded or implied that violations or "cheating" by the Soviets had taken place.

Among the subjects most recently or frequently mentioned are those listed below.

A. *"Blinding" of U.S. Satellites*

Soviet use of something like laser energy to "blind" certain U.S. satellites could be an activity inconsistent with the obligations in Article XII of the ABM treaty and Article V of the interim agreement "not to

interfere with" or "use deliberate concealment measures" which impede verification, by national technical means, of compliance with the provisions of those agreements. In 1975, information relevant to possible incidents of that nature was thoroughly analyzed, and it was determined that no questionable Soviet activity was involved and that our monitoring capabilities had not been affected by these events. The analysis indicated that the events had resulted from several large fires caused by breaks along natural gas pipelines in the U.S.S.R. Later, following several reports in the U.S. press alleging Soviet violations, and in response to questions about those reports, the U.S. press was informed of those facts by several U.S. officials.

B. *Mobile ABM*

From time to time it has been stated that the U.S.S.R., in contravention of Article V of the ABM treaty, has developed, tested, or deployed a mobile ABM system, or a mobile ABM radar, one of the three components of a mobile ABM system.

The U.S.S.R. does not have a mobile ABM system or components for such a system. Since 1971, the Soviets have installed at ABM test ranges several radars associated with an ABM system currently in development. One of the types of radars associated with this system can be erected in a matter of months, rather than requiring years to build as has been the case for ABM radars both sides have deployed in the past. Another type could be emplaced on prepared concrete foundations. This new system and its components can be installed more rapidly than previous ABM systems, but they are clearly not mobile in the sense of being able to be moved about readily or hidden. A single complete operational site would take about half a year to construct. A nationwide ABM system based on this new system under development would take a matter of years to build.

C. *ABM Testing of Air Defense Missiles*

Article VI of the treaty specifically prohibits the testing in an ABM mode of missiles which are not ABM interceptor missiles, or giving them ABM capabilities. Our close monitoring of activities in this field have not indicated that ABM tests or any tests against strategic ballistic missiles have been conducted with an air defense missile; specifically, we have not observed any such tests of the SA–5 air defense system missile, the one occasionally mentioned in this connection in the open press.

D. *Mobile ICBMs*

The development and testing of a mobile ICBM is not prohibited by the interim agreement, but the U.S. stated [in] SALT I that we would

consider deployment of such systems to be inconsistent with the objectives of the agreement. We do not believe the Soviets have deployed an ICBM in a mobile mode.

The possibility that the Soviet SS–20, which is a mobile intermediate-range ballistic missile system, has been given or could be given ICBM range capabilities has been discussed in the press. The SS–20 is being deployed to replace older medium- and intermediate-range missiles. It is judged to be capable of reaching the Aleutian Islands and western Alaska from its present and likely deployment areas in the eastern U.S.S.R.; however, it cannot reach the contiguous forty-eight states from any of its likely deployment areas in the Soviet Union. While the range capability of any missile system, including the SS–20, can be extended by reducing the total weight of its payload or adding another propulsion stage, there is no evidence that the Soviets have made any such modifications to the SS–20. We have confidence that we would detect the necessary intercontinental-range testing of such a modified system.

E. *Denial of Test Information*

It has been reported in some articles on SALT that the Soviets have violated the interim agreement by encoding missile-test telemetry, and that such activity is contrary to the provisions of Article V of the interim agreement which were noted in Section V.A above. Such activity would be inconsistent with those provisions of the interim agreement if it impeded verification of compliance with agreement provisions; it has not been considered to have done so. In the SALT II negotiations we have treated this subject in considerable detail, since such activity could affect verification of compliance with certain provisions of the agreement.

F. *ASAT*

It has been alleged that Soviet development of an antisatellite system is a violation of the obligation not to interfere with national technical means of verification of compliance with SALT provisions. Since development of such systems is not prohibited, this program does not call into question Soviet compliance with existing agreements. The actual use of an ASAT system against U.S. national technical means is prohibited, but this has not occurred.

Carter Administration Report on Verification of the Proposed SALT II Agreement, 23 February 1978

1. *Overall Assessment*

The anticipated SALT II agreement is adequately verifiable. This judgment is based on assessment of the verifiability of the individual provisions of the agreement and the agreement as a whole. Although the possibility of some undetected cheating in certain areas exists, such cheating would not alter the strategic balance in view of U.S. programs. Any cheating on a scale large enough to alter the strategic balance would be discovered in time to make an appropriate response. There will be areas of uncertainty, but they are not such as to permit the Soviets to produce a significant unanticipated threat to U.S. interests, and those uncertainties can, in any event, be compensated for with the flexibility inherent in our own programs.

2. *Description of the Proposed Agreement*

The proposed SALT II agreement has three principal elements:

- A treaty to last until 1985, embodying basically the Vladivostok accord with some reductions below the Vladivostok ceilings;
- A protocol to last until September 1980, temporarily limiting certain aspects of cruise missiles, new types of ballistic missiles, and mobile ICBMS; and
- Principles and guidelines for SALT III.

The proposed treaty includes the following major provisions:

- An initial overall aggregate level of 2,400 strategic systems, to be reduced to an agreed number between 2,160 and 2,250 during the term of the treaty.
- A 1,320 sublimit on MIRVed ICBM and SLBM launchers and aircraft equipped with long-range cruise missiles.
- A sublimit of an agreed number between 1,200 and 1,250 on MIRVed ballistic missiles.
- A sublimit of 820 on MIRVed ICBM launchers.

SOURCE: "Verification of the Proposed SALT II Agreement." Administration report submitted by ACDA Director Paul C. Warnke to the U.S. Senate, Committee on Foreign Relations; text made public on 24 February 1978.

The proposed protocol includes the following provisions:

- A ban on deployment of mobile ICBM launchers and on the flight testing of ICBMs from such launchers.
- Limitations on the flight testing and deployment of new types of ballistic missiles.
- A ban on the flight testing and deployment of cruise missiles capable of a range in excess of 2,500 km, and on the deployment of cruise missiles capable of a range in excess of 600 km on sea- or land-based launchers.

The agreement is still under active negotiation. Unless otherwise stated, the verification assessment for unresolved issues addresses only the U.S. position.

3. *Verification*

Verification is the process of determining, to the extent necessary to safeguard our national security, that the other side is complying with the SALT agreement. We must have high confidence in our ability to detect Soviet noncompliance before it could significantly affect our interests. This process of judging the adequacy of verification must take into account the capabilities of existing and future intelligence collection systems and the ability of the other side to evade detection if it should attempt to do so. Equally important is the U.S. ability to respond to Soviet cheating, should it occur. The U.S. technological base, its R&D programs, and the substantial capabilities of its strategic forces provide this hedge.

This process must also assess the political and military significance of potential violations and the costs, risks, and gains to the Soviets of cheating. It also takes into account the degree to which the advantages conferred on the U.S. by a particular provision outweigh the disadvantages caused by problems of verification. In such cases, we must consider the potential gains to the U.S. of being allowed the flexibility to take certain actions, even though allowing the Soviets the same options may complicate verification. Cruise missile limitations constitute a prime example of such a situation.

Assessing the adequate verifiability of the proposed SALT agreement is most heavily based on our confidence in U.S. monitoring capabilities. Such monitoring is carried out by the intelligence community and involves data collection and assessment of what the other side is doing or not doing. For the most part, the intelligence community has performed and would continue to perform these functions even in the absence of a SALT agreement. Many of the uncertainties that are dis-

cussed below would also exist in our intelligence assessments of Soviet strategic programs without an agreement.

Monitoring tasks in SALT can be divided into three categories: (1) counting numerically limited systems, such as ICBM and SLBM launchers and heavy bombers; (2) measuring limited quantities, such as the throw-weight of an ICBM; and (3) monitoring for evidence that a prohibited activity is being undertaken.

[Deleted.]

Our monitoring judgments assume the availability of present and programmed collection assets. However, these assessments are conservative in that they do not take into account the possibility of unusual or unpredictable intelligence successes or fortuitous blunders by the Soviets which could have the effect of enhancing verification.

We have had over five years' experience in monitoring Soviet compliance with the ABM treaty and the interim agreement. We have demonstrated our ability to verify compliance with the SALT I agreements with high confidence. This experience reinforces our assessment of the capabilities of U.S. national technical means to verify compliance with SALT agreements. The U.S. has promptly raised with the Soviets any unusual or ambiguous activities which gave rise to U.S. concern. Consequently, the Soviets are well aware that the U.S. will call them into account for any questionable activities related to their strategic programs and will expect satisfactory clarification or resolution of the problems involved.

Since monitoring will always be subject to some degree of uncertainty, we must also assess the likelihood that the Soviets would cheat, taking into account the benefits that would accrue to them from such cheating, as well as the risks of their being detected. As a matter of prudence, therefore, we analyze scenarios involving altered or covert Soviet practices that could adversely affect our confidence in Soviet compliance. The following considerations are some that the Soviets must take into account before making a decision to cheat or not to cheat: (1) their uncertainty about our overall capability to monitor and analyze their activities; (2) the potential U.S. reaction to discovered cheating; and (3) the possible strategic gains from cheating.

It must be stressed that, as noted previously, the U.S. does not rely on trust, on Soviet intentions, or on political incentives for the Soviets to comply in assessing whether verification of a SALT agreement is adequate. Such judgments must be based most heavily on our monitoring capabilities, especially with regard to potentially significant Soviet noncompliance, and on the U.S. ability to respond in a timely manner to possible Soviet cheating.

Finally, as with all aspects of a treaty, we must decide whether

particular provisions and the agreement as a whole represent a net gain for U.S. security compared to the absence of such provisions or to the no-treaty case. The projected higher levels of Soviet capability in the absence of a treaty would have to be matched or countered by expanded U.S. programs, probably with no net increase in U.S. security. So long as U.S. programs that may be required to hedge against lower monitoring confidence are not unduly restricted by the treaty, some uncertainties can be accepted in an overall agreement that serves U.S. security interests.

4. *Verifiability of Major Limitations*

As stated previously, the verification tasks of the anticipated SALT II agreement can be grouped into three categories: (1) counting; (2) measuring capability; and (3) other tasks which, in general, are bans on certain types of systems and conduct. The scope of these tasks are illustrated in the attached table [deleted]. Our judgment that the proposed agreement is adequately verifiable is based on an analysis of these tasks. The reasons for this judgment are reflected in the following discussion of the major verification tasks posed by the agreement.

5. *Overall Verifiability of Agreement*

In assessing the adequacy of verification of the agreement, it is important to consider its totality and not only particular provisions.

A consideration in determining whether the agreement as a whole is adequately verifiable has been whether the Soviets could exploit the monitoring uncertainties of several individual provisions, each of which is judged as adequately verifiable, in a way that would affect our national security interests. We have confidence that we can adequately verify compliance in such a context because the probability of detecting the fact of cheating increases markedly if the number of provisions being violated increases. Combined with the likelihood of detecting significant cheating on individual limitations, the ability to detect the fact of small cheating on a number of provisions enhances our monitoring confidence.

The Soviets cannot be sure of our overall capability to monitor a SALT II agreement. Thus, Soviet planners would be expected to make careful conservative assumptions regarding U.S. verification capabilities. For example, a slightly less than 50 percent chance of detection, which is considered "low confidence" in monitoring capability to the U.S., would probably appear as "high risk" to a Soviet planner contemplating cheating. Given U.S. R&D hedges and our greater industrial and technological base, the Soviets would not lightly undertake this risk and the attendant danger of U.S. abrogation.

In sum, although the possibility of some undetected cheating in certain areas exists, such cheating would not alter the strategic balance in view of U.S. programs. However, any cheating on a scale large enough to affect the strategic balance would be discovered in time to make an appropriate response. For these reasons, and others noted in this paper, we believe that the SALT II agreement, taken as a whole, is adequately verifiable.

11
The Negotiations Continue, 1978–1979

Brzezinski Examines Some Unresolved Issues, 1 March 1978

Mr. Brzezinski. When we made our initial offers about a year ago, we made two offers. Of course, most people forget that. We made an offer of a comprehensive settlement, which would involve a significant step-down in arms on both sides, restrictions of qualitative improvements; and then we made a modest proposal, to essentially agree [to] what we agree on and sign an agreement, and then go on to negotiate other things. That was rejected. It was a stalemate that lasted until September [1977].

During the Gromyko visit here, during September, a positive breakthrough was made on a number of controversial issues, most notably on the relationship of the air-launched cruise missile–carrying heavy bombers to MIRVs, and we made a major concession. We agreed for the first time to count the heavy bombers carrying ALCMs under the same limit as the MIRVs—the 1,320 limit for MIRVed ballistic missiles of all sorts plus the heavy bombers with ALCMs. That was a very major decision by us. In return for it, the Russians made a concession of limiting all of their land-based MIRVs to a number in the eight hundreds, most likely 820. Since then, the two delegations have been negotiating very steadily on specific issues, and there has been steady progress made, I would say almost on a weekly basis; but a number of major issues remain unresolved.

How are we talking, incidentally?

Vice President Mondale. On the record.

Mr. Brzezinski. I would say that essentially the issues that remain right now are the following. First of all, there is the question of the

---

Source: Remarks to the press by Dr. Zbigniew Brzezinski, Assistant to the President for National Security Affairs, Washington, D.C., 1 March 1978. Office of the Vice President's Press Secretary.

definition of the new types [of weapons] that are to be restricted. In other words, this is an issue which involves the nature of the qualitative improvements that are to be inhibited through SALT II. This is a complicated matter, in part because the generation of new weapons by the two sides is of a different type. We tend to move from one system to another system. The Russians tend to tinker and improve existing systems.

Therefore, how do you define what is a new type? It becomes rather difficult. Is the improvement of a marginal type, changing of the screws, a significant improvement or not? How about several improvements of this sort? How about the introduction of a new guidance system for an existing missile? At what point do minor improvements become major improvements? At what point do improvements become qualitative changes?

So the question of inhibition on modernization involves very difficult issues. This has become further complicated by the Soviet desire to have a specific exemption permitting them to introduce one new missile type, the new ICBM. And this, of course, would be a significant step. This would permit them to replace some of their more antiquated missiles—SS-11s. So that is one major issue to be resolved.

Q. Is that the SS-16?

Mr. BRZEZINSKI. The SS-11 they want to replace. The SS-16 already exists. It would be a totally new system. And that, of course, is a complication, to put it mildly.

Another issue which is yet to be resolved involves the issue of cruise missile range definition. Here again, to simplify the issue, I suppose most people would say if you are setting a limit on the range of cruise missiles, it is a limit from the place of launch to the place of target. The problem, however, is the cruise missile does not fly in a straight line at a certain altitude. It flies at different altitudes and it flies in a zigzag pattern. It has a terrain contour–oriented guidance system. It flies at different speeds. And thus you have to introduce into the range an allowance for the cruise missile to follow its flight pattern. How much of an allowance should you make? And that is an issue which is yet to be resolved.

Well, another issue which is yet to be worked out is, of course, the bothersome issue of the Backfire. What kind of restrictions on the Backfire can give us the assurance that it is not genuinely a strategic system? The Russians feel strongly this should be exempted altogether, [that] it is an intermediate-range system. They feel that their word on it suffices. Our position is, in addition to their word,

we would like to have explicit assurances, the effect of which will be to make it impossible for them to use the system as a strategic system.

There is still the issue of the aggregates. Our position is that the total limits imposed on all strategic systems should be reduced from the Vladivostok level of 2,400 to 2,160—that is to say, a flat 10 percent reduction. The Soviets would prefer a more modest reduction down to 2,250.

The second major issue is that the combined ALCM-MIRVed limit—you remember I said this was a major concession by us in September—of 1,320 should have a sublimit for it of 1,200 specifically for the MIRVS alone. I will repeat: The combined MIRVed-ALCM limit of 1,320 ought to have a specific MIRVed [ballistic missile] sublimit of only 1,200. You can readily see the effect of that. It permits us to have 120 heavy bombers with ALCMS without paying a price for it in MIRVS. The Russians insist that this limit be 1,250, which gives us only 70 such heavy bombers, after which we have to pay a price in MIRVS. We feel that we made such a major concession in accepting the ALCMS in a combined MIRV-ALCM limit that we cannot now accept a sublimit which is higher than 1,200. This is a very significant point for us.

I suppose another issue which is still to be resolved is the kind of principles of SALT III that SALT II will incorporate. It is our hope that when SALT II is signed, it will include targets for SALT III. And we would like to make these targets fairly explicit and fairly ambitious—significant reductions, further restraints on modernization.

There is still some negotiating going on on [the] data base. This is an exchange of data on both sides. In the past, much of SALT was negotiated on the basis of American data. We are now having an exchange of data. We are making good progress on that.

There is a question of MIRV verification. This is a highly complicated technical issue again, but we want certain assurances that missiles which are not MIRVed are not placed in launchers which are the same for MIRVS and nonMIRVS. This is an important issue for verification purposes. And you know the Senate will not approve a treaty which does not have reasonable chances of verification.

In the similar category, there is some question of how to distinguish different kinds of planes which are strategic but which are also used for nonstrategic missions—for example, heavy bombers used for anti-submarine warfare or [as] heavy tankers. Do you count them or not count them? If you don't count them, how do you distinguish them, and how do you make sure they are not easily transferable from one mode to the other?

Here in a nutshell is the package of issues. Why did I go into

this detail? Largely to indicate to you the problems in SALT which have necessitated a slow pace are real. They are not political. They are not artificial. They are genuinely complicated and difficult issues. And we have made reasonably good progress on them. But on some of these issues, I think an act of political will will be required to resolve them. And that, of course, is bound to be complicated by the overall international context.

Q. . . . The real question is, are you saying "act of political will"—does it mean taking a risk in terms of making concessions which have not yet been made?

Mr. BRZEZINSKI. Well, we have, I believe, made substantial adjustments in our position to make a treaty possible and to make a treaty that meets certain basic purposes. The first is maintenance of American security now and, let's say, by 1985, which is at least the minimum for which we have to be planning. And this treaty, I think, provides security for us, stable security; that is to say, a capacity to absorb a first strike, to respond, get, and to maintain [inaudible].

Secondly, it has to provide stability; that is to say, it must not be a treaty in which one side feels that the other side is gaining an asymmetrical advantage. We believe that these arrangements, if they are contrived along the positions that we have proposed, do not put the Soviets at a disadvantage but do not permit the Soviets to exercise an advantage over us.

The third requirement is verification. We can only agree to things we can verify in some fashion and to some degree.

These three requirements have to be met. And meeting these three requirements means that we can't make substantial accommodations beyond the ones we have already made.

Q. What would the act of political will consist of?

Mr. BRZEZINSKI. I think the act of political will would consist of, for example, decisions on the aggregates, on which I think one has to have foresight and willingness really to scale down the sums.

Q. Are you saying "act of political will" on their part or our part?

Mr. BRZEZINSKI. On their part.

Q. I see. You don't see any necessity for any further act of political will here?

Mr. BRZEZINSKI. I think we have already exercised that political will by making proposals which I think are constructive, which will precipitate some debate in the Senate. And you know this debate is going to be very intense. I think it is fair to say that if we make adjustments that are significant in their scope beyond the position which I have evolved, then the process of ratification will become very complicated.

Q. I would like to ask you one question about the act of political will in terms of restraint in the Horn of Africa. Is there any linkage in terms of SALT?

Mr. BRZEZINSKI. We are not imposing any linkage on it because we feel that SALT in itself is of benefit to the United States and to the Soviet Union—more or less equal benefits. At the same time, it is only a matter of realistic judgment to conclude that if tensions were to rise because of the unwarranted intrusion of Soviet power into a purely local conflict, then that will inevitably complicate the context not only of the negotiating process itself, but of any ratification that would follow the successful conclusion of the negotiations.

We are not imposing linkages, but linkages may be imposed by unwarranted exploitation of local conflict for larger international purposes.

Q. In other words, you are saying you don't have to worry about the administration, but may have to worry about the Senate?

Mr. BRZEZINSKI. I don't think the two can be cut apart that sharply. We are in very close contact with the concerned senators. We have had a large number of legislators over as participant observers in the SALT process. We have been meeting with them in this room, discussing our position. So I think we have on the whole a reasonably good mutual understanding. There are differences, and we know that some senators are critical of the position we have. But by and large, I think if an agreement is reached on these issues on a reasonable basis, that the Senate will ratify, provided the international situation is not unduly complicated by unwarranted efforts.

Q. It appears from the way you spelled out some of the remaining problems—such as cruise missiles that take variable directions and zigzag and so on, the matter of minor improvements which then blossom into major improvements—as you get into an area where this becomes all so sophisticated, sometimes it seems that the problems, the technical problems, increase as fast as you solve other problems. Does it seem that way to you?

Mr. BRZEZINSKI. There is no doubt about it. I think we are engaged in a historically significant race against technological momentum which infinitely complicates the patterns of political accommodation. If you look at SALT today and you compare the complexity of the issues with which we are grappling with the SALT of 1971–1972, the increasing complexity is quite staggering.

When one looks ahead and considers the kind of weapons both sides are likely to be able to introduce by the late-eighties, and considers what then the problems of structuring strategic stability would

be like, one gets very, very concerned and appalled. This is why there is genuine urgency in getting a reasonable SALT agreement, and this is why there is genuine importance in both sides eschewing actions which emotionalize and complicate the political contexts in which the negotiating process takes place.

This is why one has to be concerned about some developments that have transpired in recent months.

Brzezinski Discusses Africa, China, and SALT, 28 May 1978

Q. Castro says the Cubans were not involved in the invasion of Zaire. President Carter says they were. Foreign Minister Gromyko says that the President had bad information about Soviet and Cuban involvement in Africa.[1] The Senate Foreign Relations Committee would like to know what the evidence is of Cuban involvement in the Zaire invasion. What can you tell us about the evidence?

Mr. Brzezinski. First of all, I can assure you that what the President said was right. The invasion of Katanga or Shaba from Angola could not have taken place without the full knowledge of the Angolan government.

It could not have taken place without the invading parties having been armed and trained by the Cubans and, indeed, perhaps also the East Germans, and we have sufficient evidence to be quite confident in our conclusion that Cuba shares the political and the moral responsibility for the invasion; indeed, even for the outrages that were associated with it.

* * *

Q. Is the evidence clear and specific that the Cubans were directly involved in the invasion of Zaire, or is it, as some U.S. officials have suggested, ambiguous, open to several interpretations?

Mr. Brzezinski. I think there is a difference between direct involvement and responsibility. Direct involvement would mean direct participation—direct participation in the fighting, in command and control, [a] presence on the ground, and all of that.

We are talking about responsibility, responsibility for something which should not have taken place, which is a violation of territorial integrity, which in fact is a belligerent act. We believe that the evidence we have sustains the proposition—more than that, sustains the conclusion that the Cuban government and in some measure the Soviet government bear the responsibility for this transgression, and this is a serious matter. This is a matter which is not conducive to international stability nor to international accommodation.

Source: Remarks of Dr. Zbigniew Brzezinski, Assistant to the President for National Security Affairs, on NBC television's "Meet the Press," Washington, D.C., 28 May 1978. *Department of State Bulletin*, July 1978, pp. 26–28.

[1] Foreign Minister Gromyko made his remark on 27 May following a meeting with President Carter and Secretary of State Vance at the White House. Vance and Gromyko also discussed SALT in New York on 25 and 31 May 1978.—Ed.

Q. While you were in China,[2] did you encourage the Chinese to act any more openly to oppose Soviet ventures in the developing world?
Mr. Brzezinski. The foreign policy of the People's Republic of China I don't think is based on encouragement from abroad. It reflects a comprehensive Chinese view of the international situation.

I did note the fact that in the public statements, the Chinese have been very critical of the Soviet-Cuban intrusion into internal African affairs, and in my very comprehensive consultations with the Chinese leaders I did have the opportunity to discuss this issue.

Q. . . . You had expressed for some time interest in involving ourselves in Angola. Do you now see that that is a closed matter?
Mr. Brzezinski. I am not quite sure on what you base your assertion that I have expressed an interest in becoming involved in Angola.

I have held the view, and I do hold the view, that the Soviet-Cuban intrusion into African matters not only has the unfortunate effect of transforming difficult racial conflicts, [but] of transforming the struggle for majority rule into also a very complicated and dangerous international conflict, as well as an ideological conflict.

I do not believe that this kind of Soviet-Cuban involvement ought to be cost-free, and there are a variety of ways in which concerned countries can convince the Soviets and the Cubans that their involvement, their intrusion, is not only conducive to greater international instability but in fact carries with it consequences which may be inimical to them as well.

I believe this is the responsible and the right course of action to contemplate because, otherwise, we will be faced in the longer run with an increasingly difficult situation; and I think we know from history that it is wiser to contain a conflict at a time when it is still subject to containment through discussion, responsible negotiation, limited countermoves, than at the point at which it has already become a major conflagration.

* * *

Q. You just put part of the blame for what you call the transgression in Zaire on East Germany and the Soviet Union. Our Vice President was just at the United Nations criticizing the Russians for deploying the SS–20 missile against Western Europe. You have been quoted as ridiculing Soviet actions in Ethiopia as you stood on the Great Wall in China. Are we to read from all this that détente is dead?
Mr. Brzezinski. First of all, I really wasn't ridiculing Soviet actions as I stood on the Great Wall of China. I did make some reference to it in

[2] Mr. Brzezinski visited the People's Republic of China on 20–22 May 1978.—Ed.

the course of a casual conversation with a very charming Deputy Foreign Minister of the People's Republic of China.

As far as détente is concerned, I think it is terribly important for all of us to understand what it is and what it is not. There is a tendency to assume that détente is the equivalent of a comprehensive, indeed, total accommodation between the United States and the Soviet Union. That has never been the case.

Détente really is a process of trying to contain some of the competitive aspects in the relationship—competitive aspects which I believe still are predominant—and to widen the cooperative aspects. In that process, at one time or another, either the cooperative or the competitive aspects tend to be more predominant. I would say that today the competitive aspects have somewhat surfaced, and I would say categorically that this is due to the shortsighted Soviet conduct in the course of the last two or so years.

Q. Do you have any reason whatsoever to believe that Soviet conduct will cease to be shortsighted?

Mr. Brzezinski. I think that if the Soviet Union realizes that there are genuine rewards in accommodation and genuine costs in unilateral exploitation of the world's troubles, then the cooperative aspects will expand.

I am troubled by the fact that the Soviet Union has been engaged in a sustained and massive effort to build up its conventional forces, particularly in Europe, to strengthen the concentration of its forces on the frontiers of China, to maintain a vitriolic worldwide propaganda campaign against the United States, to encircle and penetrate the Middle East, to stir up racial difficulties in Africa, and to make more difficult a moderate solution of these difficulties, perhaps now to seek more direct access to the Indian Ocean.

This pattern of behavior I do not believe is compatible with what was once called the code of détente, and my hope is, through patient negotiations with us but also through demonstrated resolve on our part, we can induce the Soviet leaders to conclude that the benefits of accommodation are greater than the shortsighted attempt to exploit global difficulties.

Q. The President and the Secretary of State, you and Soviet Foreign Minister Gromyko, and others, have been talking about strategic arms limitations agreements. How close are we to some kind of agreement?

Mr. Brzezinski. We are close, very close, and in some ways quite far away. That is to say, it is within grasp, if reason prevails. We have made, it seems to me, very proper, balanced proposals. If they are

accepted, we could have agreement within days. If they are not accepted, we will wait until they are accepted.

* * *

Q. Reports from China indicate that you pleased Chinese leaders by making a number of anti-Soviet remarks but that your visit did not result in any change in our relationship with China, any particular progress in that area. Is that roughly accurate?

Mr. Brzezinski. No, I would say that is roughly inaccurate.

The purpose of my visit to China was threefold. The first was to engage in a comprehensive consultative review of our respective positions on international affairs. The second was to see whether, within the present context, our bilateral relationship can in some respects be further developed. The third was to reaffirm our commitment to normalization and perhaps to make a modest contribution of an indirect sort to it.

Both myself and the Chinese leaders agreed that the visit was beneficial; we agreed that it could be described as useful, important, and constructive. It focused largely on the long-term strategic nature of our relationship, the fact that we have certain common basic interests. And it stressed particularly the importance of mutual understanding of some of the key issues that confront respectively China and the United States.

Q. . . . Was there any specific change in our policy, any progress that resulted that you can put your finger on?

Mr. Brzezinski. If two major countries engage in detailed reviews of their respective policies regarding major issues—and in the course of my visit to China I spent some fourteen hours in sustained discussions not only with the Foreign Minister, who plays an important role in his own right, but with Vice Premier Ch'en Hsi-lien and Chairman Hua Kuo-feng, and this as of itself entails certain longer-range consequences.

The United States and the People's Republic of China do have parallel interests. In the pursuit of these parallel interests, we do undertake certain actions. If we understand each other better, this as of itself is of great significance.

Vance and Gromyko Meet in New York, 31 May 1978

Secretary VANCE. Good evening. Foreign Minister Gromyko and I, as you know, have met for some five hours.[1] We have spent most of our time discussing the remaining problems that exist in the SALT negotiations. We have examined, in great depth, the issues that are still before us. We have not completed our discussions, but I believe I can say that the discussions have been useful. The Foreign Minister and I will be checking our respective calendars, and at a mutually convenient date . . . we will be meeting again.

Foreign Minister GROMYKO. Generally speaking, I share the thoughts that have just been expressed by the Secretary of State. But since I too have to make a certain contribution to this meeting, I will say a few words in addition to what the Secretary has said.

We have indeed touched upon several questions in the course of this discussion—I guess something in the vicinity of half a dozen, including the question of the possibility of the conclusion of a new agreement on the limitation of strategic offensive arms. And our discussion on that question was useful. But I would not [inaudible]. I've said in the course of the talks before, that many of the questions are complex ones. They're difficult and tough questions, and some of them have been agreed upon; others not.

But there are still some outstanding questions. Well, if you asked me, I'd say how many? Two or maybe three which have not yet been finally resolved. I wouldn't go so far as to make a rigid statement and say that they have not been agreed on at all. I would simply say that they have not been finalized. And as the situation stands today, I guess we will still have some more meetings to have between representatives of the Soviet Union and of the United States on that question.

Another thing that it would be worthwhile saying is that both sides expressed their determination to bring their discussions to a conclusion. And if indeed the two sides do display that determination, the talks will be brought to a conclusion. And that is of exceptional importance to me.

We touched upon several other matters. And if I were to try and deny that we touched upon the questions of Africa, you probably

---

SOURCE: Remarks to the press by Secretary of State Cyrus R. Vance and Foreign Minister Andrei Gromyko, New York, 31 May 1978. Department of State, Public Affairs.

[1] Secretary of State Vance and Foreign Minister Gromyko also met in New York on 25 May and in Washington with President Carter on 27 May 1978.—Ed.

wouldn't believe me. So why should I deny it? If I were to try and deny that we also made some references to the general state of relationships between the Soviet Union and the United States and to the atmosphere that we see here, at least insofar as the press and other mass media are concerned, you probably wouldn't believe me. So why should I deny that? And so I would say that the discussion of these and certain other matters that we took up were also useful and expedient, and perhaps even necessary.

* * *

Q. Mr. Secretary, the state of relations between the United States and the Soviet Union is today openly worse than it has been for years. What effect has that had on the SALT talks and on the discussion of other problems outstanding between the two of you?

Secretary VANCE. The relationships between our two countries are in a state of tension; there is no question about that. On the other hand, we have been able to have, as both Mr. Gromyko and I have said, useful talks. I hope that the relationships between the two will be better. I think the fact that we were able to talk frankly about a whole variety of issues, including the general state of our bilateral relationships, is important and indeed, as Mr. Gromyko said, necessary. So that I would describe the general atmosphere of our talks as businesslike and useful.

Q. [Inaudible]. Mr. Secretary, that they were willing to cut down on their involvement in military affairs of Cubans in Africa? How about that issue?

Secretary VANCE. I really can't go into detail. You are going to have to ask him to speak for himself on that issue.

Q. Did you raise the issue?

Secretary VANCE. The issue was discussed, yes.

Q. Did you discuss President Carter's remarks that he made today in Washington about the buildup of the Soviet Union's conventional military forces in the European area?

Secretary VANCE. We discussed the question of conventional forces and the buildup of the Soviet conventional forces.

Q. Did you discuss the possible use of nuclear weapons by the United States to defend the NATO area?

Secretary VANCE. No, the use of nuclear weapons was not discussed, except strategic nuclear weapons.

Q. Mr. Secretary, did you come to any agreement on any of these subjects? Africa, weapons in Europe, or SALT?

Secretary VANCE. We came to no agreements. But I think we have a

clearer understanding of each other's positions, and we will both reflect on the results of the conversation. One more question.

Q. Is there any one issue in SALT that you can now check off as a result of today as basically settled?

Secretary VANCE. No. All I can say is that we examined in depth two or three of the remaining—the two principal remaining issues, which are very tough issues, as he said, and we've still got more work to do on them.

Brown Discusses SALT and Linkage, 4 June 1978

Q. Mr. Secretary . . . you have said that no matter what is likely to emerge from SALT II, the treaty that is being worked on now, the American Minuteman force will be vulnerable to Soviet attack by the early 1980s. The projected administration answer to this was to try to develop the mobile MX missile for a longer period of time—it would be available in a longer period. How then would you explain why Mr. Gromyko . . . in his [27 May 1978] visit to the White House, made a proposal that would in effect kill the American MX through 1985?

Secretary BROWN. I don't want to discuss specific proposals made by either side in the SALT talks so long as those SALT talks continue to be relatively confidential. I will, however, respond in general terms to your question.

Indeed, Minuteman, no matter what we do in the way of a SALT agreement, will be vulnerable in the early 1980s. Minuteman, of course, is not the only capability the United States has in the way of strategic forces: We've got bombers, many of them; we will have cruise missiles; we have submarine-launch ballistic missiles. But the land-based ICBM force is a valuable and important part of our forces. We therefore do have plans to modernize it, and one way to do that is with a new missile which could be based in a more survivable mode. Any agreement which prevents that from happening would, I think, have to carry with it on the other side a great many restrictions in order to constitute a fair trade. Something which simply keeps the Soviets from building one missile while allowing them to change and modernize a good many others is not a fair trade for our only planned new land-based missile.

* * *

Q. Mr. Secretary, would there be any linkage in any of these SALT agreements to African developments, to Soviet involvement in Africa? There seems to be some split in the Cabinet over that, Mr. Brzezinski feeling apparently that there should be some linkage, the President indicating that the Soviet actions in Africa might have some effect on negotiations now, SALT negotiations. Is that where we're drifting?

Secretary BROWN. I've expressed my concern about actions sponsored by the Soviets in Africa and carried out through their Cuban mer-

---

SOURCE: Remarks of Secretary of Defense Harold Brown on CBS television's "Face the Nation," Washington, D.C., 4 June 1978. Department of Defense, Public Affairs.

cenaries, proxies. I think that we need to resist that, I think the United States needs to resist that, and I think that we need to be able to show that such actions can't be carried out without incurring some penalty to those who do carry them out. But in selecting such responses, I think we must be very careful not to select things that we think will penalize the other side, but that will penalize us just as much. In SALT, I think we have something that . . . is in the common interest of the Soviet Union and the United States, with the proviso that it maintain essential equivalence in the strategic field and not undercut our strategic security. So I would not hold up a SALT agreement in order to demonstrate unhappiness with Soviet actions in Africa.

There is a separate issue, which is: What is the state of American public opinion, and what will congressional reactions be? And I think that inevitably African adventurism on the part of the Soviet Union would make it harder to get a SALT agreement approved by the Congress.

Q. Mr. Secretary, when I was asking you whether the American proposal in the SALT agreement was cast in concrete, as you undoubtedly guessed, I was thinking of what Mr. Brzezinski said on "Meet the Press" last Sunday. And he said in effect—well, let me see if I can't quote it exactly: "We have made very proper, balanced proposals. If they are accepted, we could have an agreement within days. If they are not accepted, we will wait until they are accepted." Now, has that been misinterpreted to mean that our proposals are cast in concrete, or are you and Mr. Brzezinski disagreeing over this?

Secretary BROWN. I think it is a misinterpretation to say that our proposals are cast in concrete, and I have said again that we have recast them a number of times and I would not bar recasting them again. At the same time, I think it should be said that the United States has made a substantial number of concessions in these negotiations. The Soviets have made some concessions too. I believe that for us to accept their overall position would be damaging to our security. I believe that our position, if the Soviets accept it, is acceptable in terms of both our security and Soviet security. There's some ground in between, but as you can see from the way I've expressed it, I don't think that we've got a great deal of negotiating room.

Carter Outlines the Elements of American Policy Toward the Soviet Union, 7 June 1978

The word "détente" can be simplistically defined as "the easing of tension between nations." The word is, in practice, however, further defined by experience, as those nations evolve new means by which they can live with each other in peace.

To be stable, to be supported by the American people, and to be a basis for widening the scope of cooperation, then détente must be broadly defined and truly reciprocal. Both nations must exercise restraint in troubled areas and in troubled times. Both must honor meticulously those agreements which have already been reached to widen cooperation, naturally and mutually limit nuclear arms production, permit the free movement of people and the expression of ideas, and to protect human rights.

Neither of us should entertain the notion that military supremacy can be attained, or that transient military advantage can be politically exploited.

Our principal goal is to help shape a world which is more responsive to the desire of people everywhere for economic well-being, social justice, political self-determination, and basic human rights.

We seek a world of peace. But such a world must accommodate diversity—social, political, and ideological. Only then can there be a genuine cooperation among nations and among cultures.

We desire to dominate no one. We will continue to widen our cooperation with the positive new forces in the world.

We want to increase our collaboration with the Soviet Union, but also with the emerging nations, with the nations of Eastern Europe, and with the People's Republic of China. We are particularly dedicated to genuine self-determination and majority rule in those areas of the world where these goals have not yet been attained.

Our long-term objective must be to convince the Soviet Union of the advantages of cooperation and of the costs of disruptive behavior.

We remember that the United States and the Soviet Union were allies in the Second World War. . . . In the agony of that massive conflict, 20 million Soviet lives were lost. Millions more who live in the Soviet Union still recall the horror and the hunger of that time.

Source: Remarks of President Jimmy Carter at the United States Naval Academy, Annapolis, Maryland, 7 June 1978. *Weekly Compilation of Presidential Documents*, 12 June 1978, pp. 1052–1057.

I'm convinced that the people of the Soviet Union want peace. I cannot believe that they could possibly want war.

Through the years, our nation has sought accommodation with the Soviet Union, as demonstrated by the Austrian Peace Treaty, the Quadripartite Agreement concerning Berlin, the termination of nuclear testing in the atmosphere, joint scientific explorations in space, trade agreements, the antiballistic missile treaty, the interim agreement on strategic offensive armaments, and the limited test ban agreement.

Efforts still continue with negotiations toward a SALT II agreement, a comprehensive test ban against nuclear explosives, reductions in conventional arms transfers to other countries, the prohibition against attacks on satellites in space, an agreement to stabilize the level of force deployment in the Indian Ocean, and increased trade and scientific and cultural exchange. We must be willing to explore such avenues of cooperation despite the basic issues which divide us. The risks of nuclear war alone propel us in this direction.

The numbers and destructive potential of nuclear weapons has been increasing at an alarming rate. That is why a SALT agreement which enhances the security of both nations is of fundamental importance. We and the Soviet Union are negotiating in good faith almost every day, because we both know that a failure to succeed would precipitate a resumption of a massive nuclear arms race.

I'm glad to report to you today that the prospects for a SALT II agreement are good.

Beyond this major effort, improved trade and technological and cultural exchange are among the immediate benefits of cooperation between our two countries. However, these efforts to cooperate do not erase the significant differences between us.

What are these differences?

To the Soviet Union, détente seems to mean a continuing aggressive struggle for political advantage and increased influence in a variety of ways. The Soviet Union apparently sees military power and military assistance as the best means of expanding their influence abroad. Obviously, areas of instability in the world provide a tempting target for this effort, and all too often they seem ready to exploit any such opportunity.

As became apparent in Korea, in Angola, and also, as you know, in Ethiopia more recently, the Soviets prefer to use proxy forces to achieve their purposes.

To other nations throughout the world, the Soviet military buildup appears to be excessive, far beyond any legitimate requirement to defend themselves or to defend their allies. For more than

fifteen years, they have maintained this program of military growth, investing almost 15 percent of their total gross national product in armaments, and this sustained growth continues.

The abuse of basic human rights in their own country, in violation of the agreement which was reached at Helsinki, has earned them the condemnation of people everywhere who love freedom. By their actions, they've demonstrated that the Soviet system cannot tolerate freely expressed ideas or notions of loyal opposition and the free movement of peoples.

The Soviet Union attempts to export a totalitarian and repressive form of government, resulting in a closed society. Some of these characteristics and goals create problems for the Soviet Union.

Outside a tightly controlled bloc, the Soviet Union has difficult political relations with other nations. Their cultural bonds with others are few and frayed. Their form of government is becoming increasingly unattractive to other nations, so that even Marxist-Leninist groups no longer look on the Soviet Union as a model to be imitated.

Many countries are becoming very concerned that the nonaligned movement is being subverted by Cuba, which is obviously closely aligned with the Soviet Union and dependent upon the Soviets for economic sustenance and for military and political guidance and direction.

Although the Soviet Union has the second largest economic system in the world, its growth is slowing greatly, and its standard of living does not compare favorably with that of other nations at the same equivalent stage of economic development.

Agricultural production still remains a serious problem for the Soviet Union, so that in times of average or certainly adverse conditions for crop production, they must turn to us or turn to other nations for food supplies.

We in our country are in a much more favorable position. Our industrial base and our productivity are unmatched. Our scientific and technological capability is superior to all others. Our alliances with other free nations are strong and growing stronger, and our military capability is now and will be second to none.

In contrast to the Soviet Union, we are surrounded by friendly neighbors and wide seas. Our societal structure is stable and cohesive, and our foreign policy enjoys bipartisan public support which gives it continuity.

We are also strong because of what we stand for as a nation: the realistic chance for every person to build a better life; protection by both law and custom from arbitrary exercise of government power; the right of every individual to speak out, to participate fully in

government, and to share political power. Our philosophy is based on personal freedom, the most powerful of all ideas, and our democratic way of life warrants the admiration and emulation by other people throughout the world.

Our work for human rights makes us part of an international tide, growing in force. We are strengthened by being part of it. . . .

Our analysis of American military strength also furnishes a basis for confidence. We know that neither the United States nor the Soviet Union can launch a nuclear assault on the other without suffering a devastating counterattack which could destroy the aggressor nation. Although the Soviet Union has more missile launchers, greater throw-weight, and more continental air defense capabilities, the United States has more warheads, generally greater accuracy, more heavy bombers, a more balanced nuclear force, better missile submarines, and superior antisubmarine warfare capability.

A successful SALT II agreement will give both nations equal but lower ceilings on missile launchers and also on missiles with multiple warheads. We envision in SALT III an even greater mutual reduction in nuclear weapons.

With essential nuclear equivalence, relative conventional force strength has now become more important. The fact is that the military capability of the United States and its allies is adequate to meet any foreseeable threat.

It is possible that each side tends to exaggerate the military capability of the other. Accurate analyses are important as a basis for making decisions for the future. False or excessive estimates of Soviet strength or American weakness contribute to the effectiveness of the Soviet propaganda effort. . . .

Let there be no doubt about our present and future strength.

This brief assessment which I've just made shows that we need not be overly concerned about our ability to compete, and to compete successfully. Certainly there is no cause for alarm. The healthy self-criticism and the free debate which are essential in a democracy should never be confused with weakness or despair or lack of purpose.

What are the principal elements of American foreign policy to the Soviet Union? Let me outline them very briefly.

We will continue to maintain equivalent nuclear strength, because we believe that in the absence of worldwide nuclear disarmament, such equivalency is the least threatening and the most stable situation for the world.

We will maintain a prudent and sustained level of military spending, keyed to a stronger NATO, more mobile forces, and undiminished presence in the Pacific. We and our allies must and will be able

to meet any foreseeable challenge to our security from either strategic nuclear forces or from conventional forces. America has the capability to honor this commitment without excessive sacrifice on the part of our citizens, and that commitment to military strength will be honored.

Looking beyond our alliances, we will support worldwide and regional organizations which are dedicated to enhancing international peace, like the United Nations, the Organization of American States, and the Organization for African Unity.

In Africa we and our African friends want to see a continent that is free of the dominance of outside powers, free of the bitterness of racial injustice, free of conflict, and free of the burdens of poverty and hunger and disease. We are convinced that the best way to work toward these objectives is through affirmative policies that recognize African realities and that recognize aspirations.

The persistent and increasing military involvement of the Soviet Union and Cuba in Africa could deny this hopeful vision. We are deeply concerned about the threat to regional peace and to the autonomy of countries within which these foreign troops seem permanently to be stationed. That is why I've spoken up on this subject today. And this is why I and the American people will support African efforts to contain such intrusion, as we have done recently in Zaire.

I urge again that all other powers join us in emphasizing works of peace rather than the weapons of war. In their assistance to Africa, let the Soviet Union now join us in seeking a peaceful and a speedy transition to majority rule in Rhodesia and in Namibia. Let us see efforts to resolve peacefully the disputes in Eritrea and in Angola. Let us all work, not to divide and to seek domination in Africa, but to help those nations to fulfill their great potential.

We will seek peace, better communication and understanding, cultural and scientific exchange, and increased trade with the Soviet Union and with other nations.

We will attempt to prevent the proliferation of nuclear weapons among those nations not now having this capability.

We will continue to negotiate constructively and persistently for a fair strategic arms limitation agreement. We know that no ideological victories can be won by either side by the use of nuclear weapons.

We have no desire to link this negotiation for a SALT agreement with other competitive relationships nor to impose other special conditions on the process. In a democratic society, however, where public opinion is an integral factor in the shaping and implementation of foreign policy, we do recognize that tensions, sharp disputes, or

threats to peace will complicate the quest for a successful agreement. This is not a matter of our preference but a simple recognition of fact.

The Soviet Union can choose either confrontation or cooperation. The United States is adequately prepared to meet either choice.

We would prefer cooperation through a détente that increasingly involves similar restraint for both sides; similar readiness to resolve disputes by negotiations, and not by violence; similar willingness to compete peacefully, and not militarily. Anything less than that is likely to undermine détente. And this is why I hope that no one will underestimate the concerns which I have expressed today.

A competition without restraint and without shared rules will escalate into graver tensions, and our relationship as a whole with the Soviet Union will suffer. I do not wish this to happen, and I do not believe that Mr. Brezhnev desires it. And this is why it is time for us to speak frankly and to face the problems squarely.

By a combination of adequate American strength, of quiet self-restraint in the use of it, of a refusal to believe in the inevitability of war, and of a patient and persistent development of all the peaceful alternatives, we hope eventually to lead international society into a more stable, more peaceful, and a more hopeful future.

Pravda Examines American Policy Toward the Soviet Union, 17 June 1978

Recent facts indicate that changes dangerous to the cause of peace are taking place in the policy of the USA. An acute struggle has been going on for quite some time now in the ruling circles of that country over questions of détente and relations with the Soviet Union and other socialist countries. And as times goes on, there are more and more signs that the representatives of groupings that would like to undermine détente and return the world to the cold war, to new confrontations and unrestrained military rivalry, are beginning to take the upper hand. This is testified to not only by speeches coming from the President and a number of other high-ranking U.S. officials, but also by Washington's concrete deeds.

Contrary to the aspirations of the peoples to put an end to the arms race, the U.S. is taking the course of whipping it up, is adopting new vast plans for building up its military power, even for decades ahead. At the same time, negotiations with the Soviet Union on strategic arms limitation are being deliberately slowed down.

The U.S. Government is also undertaking actions the purpose of which are difficult to evaluate in any other way than as the deliberate worsening of bilateral relations with the U.S.S.R. There is no end to attempts at interfering in our country's internal affairs. The ties and contacts between the two countries are being restricted by U.S. unilateral actions.

The opponents of good USA-U.S.S.R. relations are seeking a common language with the aggressive anti-Sovietism of the Chinese rulers who loudly proclaim détente and peace to be a fraud, and war the only real prospect.

The USA, lastly, has become the main inspirer of a new colonialism in Africa—of a policy of armed interventions and open interference in the affairs of African states, of suppressing the national liberation movements. . . .

Implementing a turn-about in politics on such a broad front is, of course, no simple matter. It has to be somehow "justified." For these purposes, attempts are being made again to blame the Soviet Union and other socialist countries for the worsening of the international situation. The makers of Washington's "new" policy are trying

---

SOURCE: *Pravda* article, "On the Present Policy of the U.S. Government." *News and Views From the U.S.S.R.*, Soviet Embassy Information Department, Washington, D.C.

to put it on some "theoretical" base, exaggerating in every way the elements of rivalry and belittling the importance of cooperation in U.S.S.R.-USA relations. Some members of the administration, for example, the presidential assistant, Zbigniew Brzezinski, did this so grossly and clumsily that they gave rise to a lot of confusion in the minds of both U.S. allies and their own compatriots.

An attempt to clarify things was made in President Jimmy Carter's recent speech at Annapolis. However the U.S. President obviously failed to introduce clarity into American policy, above all, into its policy in regard to the U.S.S.R. He failed for the simple reason that his speech was an attempt to reconcile the irreconcilable: assurances of loyalty to the ideas of détente and of improving Soviet-American relations, with unconcealed attacks addressed at the Soviet Union; expressions of respect for the peaceableness and staunchness of the Soviet people, who lost 20 million of their sons and daughters in the war against Hitler's aggression, with so preconceived and distorted a description of Soviet realities as one has not encountered even in the most ill-wishing American papers since the times of the cold war.

The U.S. President and his councillors may rest assured that this speech was read in the Soviet Union with attention and was objectively assessed. Nor were the positive remarks it contained left unnoticed, which indicate that the U.S. leaders cannot but take into account that détente enjoys sufficiently broad support in the country's political circles and among the American public.

But if this speech is to be taken for a "program," as it was preliminarily publicized, rather than dispelling, it increased the doubts about the course taken by the USA. Suffice it to recall President Carter's statement contained in it to the effect that the Soviet Union should "choose either confrontation or cooperation" and that the USA is prepared to meet either choice.

To put the matter this way is to address it wrongly. The Soviet Union long ago and unequivocally made its choice in favor of peace and cooperation. Yet, the way this question is posed by the U.S. President may only indicate that it is exactly the USA—to be more precise, the present American administration—which has not yet made the final choice, or rather, is trying to depart from the principles of relations worked out earlier with the U.S.S.R., which include the recognition of the fact that in a nuclear age there is no acceptable alternative to peaceful coexistence. It is apparently not fortuitous that, while enumerating in that same speech the United States' good works in favor of détente, the President omitted two very important documents: the principles of relationships between the U.S.S.R. and

the USA, and the agreement on averting nuclear war. Meanwhile, it is precisely in these documents that the two powers made their choice in favor of détente, and the mutual commitments stemming from it are stressed with special force.

* * *

Let us now turn to the Strategic Arms Limitation Talks. These talks, aimed at working out a new agreement on limiting strategic arms, have been going on, as is known, for many years, and agreement has already been reached on an overwhelming majority of questions. The Soviet Union is doing everything in its power for the successful finalization of the remaining questions on a reciprocally acceptable basis and for the earliest conclusion of the preparations for the agreement. For this purpose, it is constantly submitting concrete and constructive proposals.

Such proposals were submitted during the recent talks of Andrei Gromyko, the Foreign Minister of the U.S.S.R., with President Carter and Secretary of State Cyrus Vance. However, while verbally recognizing the importance of concluding an agreement, the American leadership did not actually display readiness to discuss concretely the still unresolved issues. In general, it did not submit any proposals of its own. Moreover, absurd statements were made which the American press, too, could not assess otherwise than unacceptable to the Soviet Union. The United States, you see, would wait until the U.S.S.R. accepted the American proposals.

Noteworthy also is another point. Much is being said now in the United States, in official circles among others, about the difficulties with which the ratification of a future agreement could meet in the Senate. But the government itself, obviously, does not hasten to assume a definite stand, to start upholding the agreement in Congress and before public opinion by denying the various falsehoods to which the arms limitation opponents resort in respect to the future agreement. On the contrary, in this complicated situation many government leaders are busy stirring up mistrust toward the Soviet Union, spreading lies about the "Soviet military threat." Is there anything surprising, therefore, in the fact that the atmosphere around the future agreement is not clearing, but rather becoming even more complicated?

Artificial complications are also being created in the other negotiations on disarmament. Despite official denials, a line is actually being pursued to link the disarmament negotiations with other absolutely unrelated questions. . . .

What grounds, in the light of all these facts, does the United

States have to sound the alarm about the Soviet Union's desire to achieve "military superiority?" What grounds? No, it is not these concocted dangers that the U.S. fears in reality, but equality, parity; it does not want its preservation, expecting to establish its own military superiority by means of new lunges ahead in the arms race and by putting a brake on the negotiations. It goes without saying that this runs counter to the initial principle of equality and equal security of sides agreed upon by the U.S.S.R. and the United States. The U.S.S.R. does not intend to violate it, but it will not allow this principle to be violated by others. Yes, it will not allow this to happen.

Along with stepped-up military preparations, the changes in the U.S. course find expression also in the transition to an openly interventionist, neocolonialist policy vis-à-vis the countries of Africa. This is borne out by the events in Zaire, the armed interference in the internal affairs of this country by several Western states under the political and military leadership of Washington, plans to include these or other African states in the sphere of NATO activities and attempts to knock together imperialist collective armed forces to suppress the liberation struggle on that continent. And, here again, concoctions about the "Soviet threat" to Africa, about "Soviet-Cuban interference" in its affairs, are resorted to as a diverting maneuver. Even the already refuted inventions on this score are being upheld as before without any shame.

In the meantime, Moscow learned about the events in Zaire from reports of Western news services. There are, in general, no Soviets or Cubans in any capacity whatsoever in Shaba. Just as there are no copper, cobalt or uranium mines belonging to the U.S.S.R. in that land. They are at the disposal of the Western nations, primarily the United States.

* * *

Particularly disastrous for mutual confidence are the attempts to interfere in the internal affairs of the other side. And such attempts have now been elevated in the United States to the level of state policy. Seemingly nice-sounding motives are being chosen for them: "human rights," "humanism," "defense of freedom." But actually we have here the same designs to undermine the socialist system that our people have had to encounter in this or that form since 1917. . . . Such actions engender new doubts about the true intentions of the leaders of the United States and certain nations allied to it, poison the political atmosphere, and complicate cooperation.

The latest intrigues—to be more exact, the "petty intrigues"—of Washington around China in no way serve to strengthen confidence.

The desire in itself to use the "Chinese card" in the global game is not at all new for American politicians. However, up until now the U.S. leaders, it appeared, realized that this card could not be used without creating dangers to the cause of peace and to themselves, for that matter, to the national interests of the United States.

However, certain leaders who hold high posts in Washington are so overwhelmed by anti-Soviet emotions that, judging by everything, they are now dismissing these dangers. Such leaders close their eyes to the fact that alignment with China on an anti-Soviet basis would rule out the possibility of cooperation with the Soviet Union in the matter of reducing the danger of a nuclear war and, of course, of limiting armaments. They forget also that the Chinese leaders are playing here a game of their own. If the United States and the NATO countries are not loathe to exploit in their own interests the difficulties which have arisen in Soviet-Chinese relations, the Peking leaders, for their part, have something quite different on their mind—namely, to aggravate to the limit the relations between the U.S.S.R. and the United States and to exploit this aggravation by no means in American, but in their own interests. Soviet-American confrontation and, still better, war—this is the cherished dream of Peking. Maybe Washington will give a thought to this matter without rashness, coolly.

* * *

It appears that the internal situation in the United States, too, is of considerable importance—the aggravation of the problems of inflation and unemployment, the poverty of millions of black and white citizens of the world's richest capitalist country, and widespread crime.

The aggravation of these problems—and there is such a great desire to divert attention from them by means of artificially exaggerated external alarms—the government's inability to cope with them, and the resultant accusations of it being "weak" and "soft," create for some American leaders an irresistible temptation to prove their "firmness." It is rather hard to display it, say, in the struggle against inflation or unemployment. But it seems to them that it is easier to transfer this "firmness," or at least to try to transfer it, into foreign policy. . . . A sort of competition has begun between some politicians: "Who will take a 'firmer' stand in international affairs? Who will be 'tougher' in talking to the Soviet Union?"

It seems that there are politicians in Washington who find this to be an acceptable tactic that can be replaced, as time passes, with other, more moderate and considered tactics. But, by far, not everything that one can get away with in American domestic politics is

acceptable in foreign politics. Here, as we see already today, the "tough line" has every chance to develop from a tactic into a dangerous and uncontrollable political course, acquire a force of inertia that it is difficult to overcome, and evoke in the world a corresponding counteraction. And payment for error in such a turn in events will be measured not simply by the drop of somebody's popularity: it threatens to take the form of new costly spirals of the arms race, political crises, the growth of the tax burden, and maybe even worse consequences, even for the people of the United States.

Of course, firmness and courage are qualities that any politician will find useful, but only when they are directed at good aims, are combined with political wisdom—with the ability to guide oneself by supreme interests and to separate them from petty, transient advantages—and with the ability and desire to peer into the future, to assess in advance the consequences of one's present-day actions. Likewise, courage in politics is by no means the equivalent of bravado or the readiness to resort to strong expressions or to wield a club. Political courage is different: it is in the ability to outline and consistently implement a principled political course as well as in the ability to control one's emotions, to display restraint without fearing the heckling of political opportunists and in not falling for the advice of adventurers.

The changes in Washington's policy are beginning to give rise to apprehensions in America itself and in the countries allied with it. What will be the consequences of the policy now pursued by President Carter? Where is he leading his country and the entire "Atlantic community," for that matter? These questions are appearing all the time on the pages of the Western press. Also expanding is criticism of Washington's foreign policy: the threats with which it is fraught, the danger of returning to the cold war and the aggravation of international tension give rise to mounting concern and alarm.

The world public is concerned also by the following question: How will the Soviet Union respond to the toughening of the American policy? This question acquires the greater topicality the more obvious the insufficiently considered and, at times, openly provocative nature of many actions undertaken by the United States becomes. . . .

The Soviet Union is not intending to assist the authors of such plans. Our people have seen too much and experienced too much to give in to pressure, to retreat before saber-rattling. We chose the road of peace and will not allow anyone to push us off this road. We are not accepting the invitation to join the funeral of détente and of the hopes of millions of people for a peaceful future, for a possibility of a life worthy of man and his children.

Détente and the struggle for peace and disarmament have proved their great vital force and have the broadest support of the peoples. The Soviet Union and the other countries of socialism are fully resolved to conduct a consistent and stubborn struggle for them along all directions and, first of all, along such a direction as the limitation and reduction of armaments. . . . In the situation complicated by the policy of the United States, the Soviet Union confirms again its course aimed at the relaxation of international tension and the development of good, mutually advantageous relations with the United States, given that the United States also wants this. . . .

It is impossible to press for such aims proclaimed by the United States President as strengthening peace, limiting armaments, and normal relations with the Soviet Union, and at the same time to whip up an anti-Soviet hysteria, to try by means of attacks on the U.S.S.R. to solve one's problems—both external, domestic, and even personal ones. The present course of the United States is fraught with serious dangers—dangers for the United States, for all countries interested in peace, and for the entire course of international relations. We hope for the speediest realization of this truth in Washington.

Vance and Gromyko Meet in Geneva, 10 and 13 July 1978

WASHINGTON, 10 JULY 1978*

Q. . . . Has the administration made a unilateral decision to go ahead with a mobile missile—call it "shell-game missile" or whatever? And if it has, isn't it obliged to negotiate that with the Soviet Union or at least tell them? Or do you feel, within terms of the SALT I and your negotiations so far, that one party has the right in its own self-defense to move its missiles around and build more silos?

Secretary VANCE. I don't want to go into the details of what may be discussed in the upcoming negotiations. I think I can, however, shed some light on the basic underlying questions which you raise.

Insofar as whether the United States has decided to go forward with a mobile missile, that decision simply has not been made yet, and that is a decision which will have to be made in the future. The options with respect to that, however, I would expect will be preserved, and, indeed, I would be confident that they would be preserved.

* * *

Q. Senator Jackson this morning—to return to this problem of the dissidents—said that your trip to Geneva is the wrong signal to the Soviets at the wrong time. He went on to say that by going to Geneva at the same time that these trials are taking place, the United States is, in effect, leaving Anatoli Shcharanskiy and some of the other dissidents mercy to whatever judgment the Soviets care to pass on them, including the possibility of a death sentence in the Shcharanskiy case.

Are there any limits, in our view, beyond which the Soviets cannot go in sentencing these people and the two American journalists who are scheduled for trial on July 18th?[1] Are there any limits at which point the United States will use either trade, transfer of Western technology, the number of Soviet journalists that are accredited in this country, to in some way respond to the Soviet moves in both these areas?

Secretary VANCE. Let me say that we have already taken two actions which you have seen—namely the cancellation of two trips, one by

---

*SOURCE: Press conference of Secretary of State Cyrus R. Vance. *Department of State Bulletin*, August 1978, pp. 16–20.

[1] Craig R. Whitney of the *New York Times* and Harold D. Piper of the Baltimore *Sun* were formally accused on 28 June 1978 by the Soviet government of having libeled Soviet state television.

Barbara Blum and the other by Frank Press and their respective delegations to the Soviet Union.[2] We have a number of other considerations before us as to actions that one might take. I don't want to speculate about what we might or might not do in the future.

However, let me say that I respectfully disagree with what Senator Jackson has said. . . . I think it is of the utmost importance, because of the unique nature of the SALT discussions, that we should proceed with those discussions.

We have made very clear our position with respect to the treatment of the dissidents. We indicated . . . that these trials violate fundamental principles of justice. I said that we deplore these events. I said that it will inevitably affect the climate of relations and impose obstacles to the building of confidence and cooperation between our two countries.

Therefore, I think we have made it very clear to the Soviet Union how seriously we view the actions which are being taken with respect to dissidents.

* * *

Q. . . . There was some speculation today that, as a result of the trials in Moscow, the President might have decided not to put forward specifically new proposals but to stand pat on the American proposals as they have been for the past two months and see whether the Russians come in with something new.

Secretary VANCE. If I were you, I wouldn't jump to any conclusions.

* * *

Q. Do you consider the timing of the announcement of the Shcharanskiy trial and the Ginzburg trial for today—[two] days before you sit down with Mr. Gromyko—a provocation? And, if not, could you speculate at all for us on your idea of the Soviet motivations for such timing?

Secretary VANCE. I honestly don't know what their motivations are, and I think it would be fruitless and unwise for me to speculate as to what their motivations are.

Let me say, however, that the actions which have been taken, whenever they are taken and whether they are taken now, a few days in advance of my meeting with Gromyko, or at any time in the past or in the future, would be matters of great concern to us, as to which

---

[2] Barbara Blum is Deputy Administrator of the Environmental Protection Agency, and Frank Press is Director of the Office of Science and Technology Policy in the Executive Office of the President.

we would speak out and indicate the depth of concern that we have about these matters.

Q. There seemed to be a number of reasons arguing for a delay, though not a complete breakdown, in the Geneva talks—the trials in the Soviet Union, the mood of Congress, and so on. What are the arguments for going to Geneva right now? What are the imperatives for going there at this moment?

Secretary VANCE. The imperatives for going to Geneva right now are that we are dealing with negotiations that, as I have said, affect the national security of our nation and the security and well-being of the world in general. It is a question which deals with prospects of mutual annihilation on either side, with the consequences that that could have not only for the two countries involved but for the world in general.

Therefore, we think that this issue must be treated differently from others and should be addressed on a continuing basis with the highest priority. We have indicated in the past that we would not link these discussions with other discussions. We continue to believe that is a correct and sound policy, and that is the policy we are following.

Q. In spite of the fact that there is not linkage, the President has said in the past that certain Soviet actions could affect the atmosphere in which the ratification process would take place. Would you say that that atmosphere has been seriously aggravated by the decision of the Russian government to take this action at this time?

Secretary VANCE. The answer is yes. I think that the general atmosphere clearly has been aggravated.

Q. Do you still believe that a SALT treaty will be ratified by the Senate given all of the things that have happened in the last five or six months, which you have conceded does aggravate the atmosphere?

Secretary VANCE. My answer is yes, I believe it will.

GENEVA, 13 JULY 1978*

Foreign Minister GROMYKO. During these two days [12 and 13 July] a thorough exchange of views was held on some questions of interest both to the Soviet Union and to the United States of America. Primary attention was given to the questions relating to the preparation of a new agreement on the limitation of strategic offensive arms. Both

*SOURCE: Remarks to the press by Secretary of State Cyrus R. Vance and Foreign Minister Andrei Gromyko. *Department of State Bulletin*, September 1978, pp. 31–32.

sides consider that the exchange of views on these questions was useful and provides a basis for further bringing the positions of the sides on the outstanding questions closer together. The discussion of these questions will be continued.

Among others, there were discussed the question of the complete and general ban on nuclear weapons tests, the problem of the Middle East settlement, and some questions of bilateral relations.

Secretary VANCE. As the Foreign Minister has indicated, new ideas were put forward by both sides. They were discussed at length between us. The conversations, as the Foreign Minister indicated, were useful and will serve as a basis for further narrowing the differences between us.

We also covered a number of other subjects, as he has indicated, and we look forward to continuing our discussions and will be keeping in touch with each other.

* * *

Q. Do you think there is a basis for making a SALT agreement, or completing one, during this year?

Secretary VANCE. We both hope that we can achieve a sound SALT agreement which would be in the interests of both our nations and in the interests of the world this year. And we will both strive—

Foreign Minister GROMYKO. The sooner the better.

Secretary VANCE. Right, the sooner the better.

Q. Would progress have been easier were there not this distraction of controversy over trials in the Soviet Union? Did it get in your way—that controversy?

Foreign Minister GROMYKO. That is a question which is within the internal competence of the Soviet Union. And I have no intention of discussing it with anyone, even with you. And I trust you will understand me correctly. I will take no offense.

* * *

Q. By saying that you've made some progress that is useful for providing a basis for narrowing the gap, does that mean it's a fact that of the remaining tough issues you still haven't resolved either of those?

Secretary VANCE. I would say the answer is yes. We have not resolved either; but I think what we said we have, by these conversations, provided [is] a basis for, hopefully, narrowing the remaining gap.

Q. Does the prospect for a treaty seem to be moving backward all the time? Are you still thinking of a three-year protocol or is that kind of blending into the life of the treaty at this point?

Secretary VANCE. I don't want to get into details. I have said all along that I am not going to get into details of any of these things which we are negotiating, and I am just going to adhere to that.

* * *

Q. Could you say you have narrowed the differences at all concerning the general atmosphere concerning the two countries—not specifically relating to SALT—but generally any improvement in the relations which could have been better in the last few months?
Secretary VANCE. There are still clearly differences between us on certain issues. I think always, though, it is useful to have a chance to sit down and have a face-to-face discussion on a variety of issues, including any which either of us wish to raise. I find it helpful and useful, and I hope that the Foreign Minister does too.
Foreign Minister GROMYKO. I would say, just by adding to what the Secretary has said, it is absolutely true that there are differences in our policies. But if there is a desire and the will to narrow down and eliminate those differences, there is a possibility to do so. And the building of peace and of further détente is certainly worth the effort expended on them.
Q. In that connection, did you discuss the possibility of a summit meeting, and can you comment on whether you think it's a good idea?
Foreign Minister GROMYKO. We did not discuss that question as such. But the statements that have been made by both the one and the other side on that score are well known. A meeting under certain conditions is possible. "Conditions" is too strong—under certain "circumstances."

* * *

Q. What progress was made on a comprehensive test ban?
Secretary VANCE. We reviewed the situation with regard to the comprehensive test ban with the heads of the two delegations and had a chance to put questions to the two sides. No specific new decisions or anything like that were taken as a result of our conversations, but it was helpful to have a chance to find out where the remaining differences are and what the possibilities are of resolving them.
Q. Is that treaty tied to the completion of the SALT II agreement so that it will not be finished before SALT II?
Foreign Minister GROMYKO. From our standpoint there is no direct tie between them, and we are, in fact, against such a position. Each of these questions should be considered on its merits, and I guess the Secretary can say what the U.S. position is.
Secretary VANCE. I have no difference on that.

Q. Have you made progress on a matter of atmospherics, or have you made substantive progress? I don't hear any talk of "brick-by-brick" this time. Have you laid any bricks? Are there any, even parts of issues that you can check off as completed?

Secretary VANCE. I said that new ideas were put forward by both sides, and I also said, as did the Foreign Minister, that we thought that as a result of those exchanges that we had had a useful session which provided a basis for narrowing the differences.

Foreign Minister GROMYKO. . . . Let me just, turning to SALT, say, and I trust the Secretary will agree, that on both sides there were some new ideas expressed. But sometimes to draw conclusions from such ideas it requires the sun to rise more than once—more than twice.

Q. I understand that new ideas were expressed but were any new ideas accepted? . . .

Foreign Minister GROMYKO. You know decisions are not taken with the suddenness of a cloudburst, and you know how much time has elapsed since Vladivostok, for instance. So some of these things take time before decisions can be made, but if there is interest in resolving the issue, if there is desire, it can be done.

Jones Discusses SALT and ICBM Vulnerability, 25 July 1978

Q. General, there have been reports that the Joint Chiefs of Staff have removed some of their reservations regarding the Backfire bomber, like its refueling capability, its basing mode, in order to strengthen the air defense of the United States and to go ahead with the F-111H, I guess it is called. Would you comment on those reports?
General JONES. After that was reported, Tom Ross [Assistant Secretary of Defense (Public Affairs)] put out word that it's incorrect. The Joint Chiefs of Staff continue to recommend that the Backfire be counted. We have discussed the Backfire in depth, and one thing we have been concerned about is that some of the restrictions that would be put on the Backfire would not be, in our judgment, realistic restrictions because they could be changed overnight. So we were basically saying that assurances didn't solve the Backfire problem. On the other hand, we continue to recommend that the Backfire be counted in SALT.

*　　　*　　　*

Q. General, I wonder . . . whether you consider the multiple aim point system as the leading, front-running candidate now to preserve the land base leg of the Triad? How do you stand on mobile missiles and the multiple aim point basing idea?
General JONES. . . . With or without a SALT agreement, the ICBM force will become vulnerable in the days ahead. We're not talking about vulnerability of the whole Triad, but the ICBM force will become vulnerable and we think it is important to do something about that vulnerability—that will create an unstable situation—and the solution to it isn't to abandon this one leg of the Triad.

To the issue of survivability, the best solution we see is a multiple aiming point. And to the Soviets I say: You have caused this problem by your large number of reentry vehicles, with increased accuracy, and we can solve it one of two ways. Either you do not have all of those RVS—reentry vehicles—with all that accuracy, or we have the option and the capability in this country to take the action to protect our ICBM force. And the MAP program looks the most attractive now.

SOURCE: Press conference of General David C. Jones, Chairman, Joint Chiefs of Staff, Washington, D.C., 25 July 1978. Department of Defense, Public Affairs.

Q. When you say MAP, just so we are on the same wave-length, you are talking about the above ground shell game concept with the vertical shelters, right? Is that what you have in mind?

General JONES. Shell game is your word. Multiple aiming point means that you can move it around from place to place, and at any one time the potential adversary may not know where it is. Just as a submarine, they don't know where a submarine is located.

Now, you've got various options. You've got some holes—they are not launch holes as with our Minuteman, but they provide some hardness, so they could be closer together. You could have them in shelters above ground, you can have trenches. All of these are still under consideration, and there are some other options. We sort of classify most of those under MAP, or multiple aiming point.

Q. But you are not leaning toward any one of those options?

General JONES. Well, as of now from a cost standpoint and from some other factors, what we call the vertical shelter appears to be most attractive. But we have not rejected the other concepts.

Q. Have you done enough analysis yet to be sure that, whatever form of MAP you use, it will be cost effective? In other words, you can dig a hole cheaper than they can build an RV?

General JONES. We are still working on the whole program. As of now, our conclusions are that it would be cheaper for us to proliferate the holes than the Soviets for the RVS, particularly if you are talking about their developing new systems to do it. So as of now it looks cost effective to us.

Q. Is it marginally cost effective or substantially cost effective?

General JONES. In our judgment, substantially cost effective, but you've got a lot of variables, you have some unknowns, and we have a full-scale development program that we are recommending for the MX program and you've got the three options and others as to where to go. So there are still some unknowns in this program, but we think it's important to proceed.

Q. General, do you consider the MAPS or ALPS [alternative launch-point system] a mobile system? Some, like Mr. Nitze [Paul Nitze, former Deputy Secretary of Defense and SALT negotiator], do not consider it mobile. And also, is it important enough that you would not accept a SALT treaty which did not include something of this kind of protection for your land-based missiles?

General JONES. Well, I'm not going to, on any subcategory, say whether I will accept or reject or support or not support a SALT treaty. I must say that I would have deep reservations about not being able to proceed with a survivable ICBM. And my interpretation is that the

MAP concept is the very end of the mobile. And therefore, I consider that mobiles are authorized and that therefore the MAP is authorized. And to me that is not a matter for discussion or negotiation.
Q. General, do you support the urgency that Mr. Nitze put out yesterday? He called for a crash program, this ALPS. In other words, going with, I guess it is the minimum type of system where you just expand on the Minuteman III fields by having alternate holes to fool the Soviets. He called for a crash program yesterday.
General Jones. What we advocate primarily is proceeding with an MX program because we have two problems: We've got vulnerability and we've got a great imbalance in throw-weight. And we need to address both of these.

So in an orderly but expedited way, I would proceed, and this is my personal view, with an MX program; and as a part of that, look at various ways in advance of the operational capability of the MX to use another missile such as the Minuteman in that MAP concept. So it is different than Mr. Nitze is talking about, but it is not inconsistent conceptually.
Q. On the Backfire bomber: If there was a SALT agreement without the Backfire being counted, what sort of programs on our side would you see as necessary to balance that? Or, on the other hand, what sort of other restrictions against the Russians would you feel were necessary?
General JONES. Well, I will preface it by saying, as I stated earlier, we continue to recommend that Backfire be counted in SALT. If it is not for some reason or other, programs have been discussed by many people as to what could be done. There are two considerations: One is to improve our air defenses to the point that it would not be reasonable to consider the Backfire as an effective system trying to penetrate the United States; the other one is for us to have an option for our own Backfire.

I wouldn't advocate this second option as just a "they have their Backfire, we have our Backfire." If we ever went in this direction, it should be because we would have a fundamental need for a system in this category. But this is all against the backdrop of a discussion that takes place after I state that we continue to recommend Backfire be counted.
Q. Do you feel that we have a fundamental need for a Backfire of our own?
General JONES. I believe that the manned bomber is required as far into the future as I can see. And it has some flexibility, some versatility. We are improving the B-52, and I am not talking about just

with a cruise missile. I would hope that some day we would have a new manned bomber in this country, and I'd hope to be able to persuade others. I am not talking about resurrecting the B-1.

* * *

Q. Do you think it is a good idea at this juncture of the relationships militarily between the Soviet Union and the United States to have a SALT agreement of any kind? If so, why? If not, why?

General JONES. It is very tempting, in view of what the Soviets are doing in human rights and in Africa and other areas of the world, to say, "let's stop all negotiations." But, you know, if you reflect on it, there is no area that is more important really to sit down and discuss, and that is strategic offensive weapons with millions of tons of destructive power and a tremendous buildup in the Soviet forces.

So I say, I resist the temptation to recommend that we suspend any talks, because it is such an important area. I also say we ought to hang tough on the negotiations.

Q. What is in it for a SALT agreement? What is good about a SALT agreement?

General JONES. If you can have a cap on strategic systems, if you can reduce them, if you can have opportunities for SALT III that may go further, it could be to the advantage of both sides. It won't solve all the problems. It is clear that the Minuteman will become vulnerable with or without the SALT agreement or any SALT agreement we would expect in the days ahead.

A concern that I would have is if we had a SALT agreement and people thought that that solved their problems, that now we can pay attention to something else, euphoria set in, that we don't have to look after our strategic programs. In my judgment we are going to have to spend more money in the strategic programs in the days ahead than we have in the recent past. That doesn't mean, though, that a SALT agreement couldn't be helpful, and I am hopeful that we can get a SALT agreement that can allow us the opportunity to maintain overall essential equivalence with the Soviet Union.

Q. But even so, it is more money, SALT agreement or not; is that what you are saying?

General JONES. In my judgment, depending on the agreement, we may end up spending less than without agreement. Without an agreement we would probably have to increase considerably more than with an agreement. I just want to dispell any idea that SALT is going to mean a reduction in the strategic force budget in the days ahead.

Q. So it is more money even with an agreement?

General JONES. Yes. But that can be substantially less than what may be required without an agreement. So there are good reasons to have an agreement, one that is fair, equitable and allows us to have essential equivalence, financial as well as just overall strategic balance.

Warnke and Brown Examine the Impact of SALT II on Strategic Forces, July–October 1978

HARTFORD, CONN., 25 JULY 1978*

For almost six years, in three administrations, two Republican and one Democratic, the United States has been negotiating a new strategic arms limitation agreement. That agreement is now reaching completion, and I'm happy to say that it will meet the goals that have been sought since the fall of 1972.

* * *

Turning first to the question of strategic stability, we have today a situation that fully meets that criterion. No Soviet military planner could possibly contemplate launching a nuclear strike against the United States because of the certainty that our retaliatory strike could devastate the Soviet Union and end its existence as a modern society. As a matter of fact, we could do more damage in response than they could do by striking first. Now that, I submit, is a situation of assured deterrence and of strategic stability. And the SALT agreement will protect and improve a stable strategic balance.

Because of the major breakthrough that was achieved by President Ford in his meeting with General Secretary Brezhnev in Vladivostok in 1974, SALT II will establish the principle of equal aggregates in intercontinental nuclear delivery vehicles. Each side will be entitled initially to a total of 2,400 and within that total there will be equal entitlement in the number of launchers of MIRVed missiles. . . . President Ford was able to achieve this understanding without giving the Soviet side any compensation for the fact that we have located in Europe the so-called forward-based systems that can strike Soviet targets. We have, for example, over 160 F-111s in the United Kingdom that can deliver nuclear bombs and nuclear missiles on Soviet targets. These have not been constrained by SALT II and will not be.

Strategic stability will be further improved by agreed upon reductions. As a consequence of these reductions, the Soviets will have to dismantle and destroy about 300 nuclear delivery systems. In the absence of SALT, our intelligence sources indicate that they would increase their present total by more than 600 nuclear delivery systems.

* SOURCE: Remarks of ACDA Director Paul C. Warnke before the Conference on U.S. Security and the Soviet Challenge. Department of State, Bureau of Public Affairs, *Current Policy* No. 27, August 1978.

So what SALT means is that there will be some 1,000 fewer strategic nuclear weapons directed against the territory of the United States. And on the other hand, because our present total is below the new ceiling, we will not have to make any cuts, but can actually add another 250 ballistic missile launchers or heavy bombers.

Reference has been made to the decision to cancel the B-1 bomber. I want to make it very clear that that was not an arms control decision. There is nothing in SALT that would prevent the United States from building B-1s. The halt in that program was decided by the Pentagon and by the President on the basis of cost effectiveness, the conclusion being reached that the cruise missiles on our existing B-52 bombers provided a more effective and surer way of penetrating Soviet defenses. But if we sign SALT II next month, we could begin immediately to build the full program of B-1s. It would not be stopped by SALT in any sense whatsoever. We have the slack of something like 250 additional systems, so that we could build a full program of 244 B-1s. I doubt that we'll do it, but that's not because of SALT.

. . . As the technological competition continues, the intercontinental ballistic missiles of each side are becoming at one and the same time both more deadly and more vulnerable, and that of course increases the risk that at a time of extreme international tension, one side might be tempted to use its intercontinental ballistic missiles first because of the fear that they wouldn't be there to be used in a second retaliatory strike. This tends to promote the adoption of such strategic doctrines as that of launch-on-warning which would mean, of course, a greatly increased risk of nuclear war at a time of international tension. . . . We have been able to work out certain sub-ceilings, and one of the sub-ceilings [is] related to intercontinental ballistic missiles with MIRVS. The Soviets have now agreed to set a ceiling which would mean 100 fewer launchers of this type of missile than they would otherwise have. Now, that's not enough of a cut in itself to eliminate all future risks to the survivability of our own ICBM forces. But it's a very desirable first step for bringing about a more durable situation of assured stability.

And then finally, as an attempt to strengthen strategic stability, we have been trying since March of 1977 to negotiate a ban on new types of intercontinental ballistic missiles. The kind of ban we have in mind would also prevent extensive modification of existing missiles. For example, one key objective is to prevent further fractionation of these missile warheads, to prevent the addition of additional reentry vehicles to the large Soviet missiles. It is well known that their missiles are bigger than ours. The decision not to build bigger

missiles was made consciously by the United States. Nonetheless, the result is a difference in the throw-weight of the missiles of the two sides. As a consequence, the very large Soviet missiles could be given at least twice as many reentry vehicles as those with which they are presently equipped. What we are negotiating is a freeze that would prevent that further fractionation of reentry vehicles and thus would reduce the number of nuclear weapons with which they could strike the United States. The Soviets have agreed in principle to that kind of a prohibition, depending on the resolution of other issues. This would for the first time begin to restrain the qualitative aspect of the nuclear arms competition. It will mean not just quantitative limits and reductions, but also actual qualitative controls.

The exact nature and scope of this limitation is one of the most important problems and remains fully to be resolved. When Secretary Vance and I met with Foreign Minister Gromyko, just about two weeks ago, this was discussed at length and both sides have made new proposals. I think that the distance between us is beginning to narrow, but nonetheless it does remain on the negotiating agenda. It's not hard to see why it remains. It's a particularly tough negotiating problem because of the asymmetry in the forces. The Soviet Union is more dependent upon ICBMs than we are. We've divided our forces about equally among the three parts of our deterrent Triad. We have something slightly in excess of 30 percent in manned bombers, the same in ballistic missile submarines and the same in the intercontinental ballistic missiles. The Soviet Union, on the other hand, has something like 70 percent of its strategic nuclear resources in the land-based ballistic missiles. Thus a restraint on ICBMs will affect them more than it will us.

* * *

It's interesting that, beginning immediately after the Vladivostok understanding in 1974, the Soviet Union tried to put constraints on our modernization of our heavy bomber force. What they wanted to do was to count a heavy bomber with long-range cruise missiles as if it were a MIRVed ballistic missile. Now at Vladivostok, as I mentioned, the overall total of strategic nuclear delivery vehicles was set at 2,400. There was a subtotal of 1,320 set for MIRVed ballistic missile launchers. What the Soviets had been insisting was that we should also count against that 1,320 any heavy bomber that was armed with long-range cruise missiles. It would have meant, in effect, a reduction in the number of MIRVed ballistic missile launchers that we could have as compared to the Soviet Union. We refused to accept that argument and proposed instead an approach whereby each side would have the

same entitlement for MIRVed ballistic missiles and then each could have, in addition, over 100 heavy bombers equipped with long-range cruise missiles. This formula is now agreed upon, and it fully accommodates the cruise missile program that the Pentagon has in mind. I might note that the Soviet Union is unlikely to have this kind of long-range cruise missile until many years after ours are deployed.

New Orleans, La., 22 August 1978*

In deciding just how many defense dollars we need, we have to start by looking at the military efforts and capabilities of the Soviet Union. I have examined those Soviet capabilities carefully, with the help and advice of the Joint Chiefs of Staff. . . . We find that the Soviets have been engaged in a substantial military buildup for nearly twenty years. Over that period they have increased their military expenditures by about 4 percent each year in real terms, compounded, year in and year out. And their buildup is continuing.

But that does not mean that we and our allies have been sitting on our hands, or that we have suddenly become inferior to the Warsaw Pact. We are not. And it does not mean that, as we continue to improve our forces, we should make them a carbon copy of the Soviet posture, or that we should plan forces simply to match certain Soviet capabilities.

The Soviets must wrestle with a number of problems that we do not now have, especially with respect to China. Their planning has to take into account a difficult geography and a harsh climate—though they do have the advantage of internal lines of communication. They lack willing and effective allies. Our planning should neither forget their burdens, nor assume we have the same problems; we have problems, but ours are different. Thus, simple comparisons of Soviet and American forces are only the beginning of understanding our military needs. In planning our forces, we need to be careful not to be misled by such comparisons.

Take the case of our strategic nuclear posture. With the warheads we already deploy, we can target all significant military objectives in the Soviet Union, even after undergoing a first strike by the Soviets. Our basic offensive strength, in other words, is adequate today. But as strategic forces have grown more sophisticated in both the Soviet Union and the United States, the requirements of deterrence have become more demanding: not necessarily in terms of mis-

* SOURCE: Remarks of Secretary of Defense Harold Brown before the Annual National Convention of the American Legion. Office of the Assistant Secretary of Defense (Public Affairs), News Release No. 437–78, 22 August 1978.

sile throw-weight, or megatonnage, or warheads—the sorts of measures one often hears about—but rather in other dimensions.

For example, control and the ability to withhold some offensive forces—to be able to attack some targets and spare others at a particular phase of combat—may be as important as rapid reaction against the entire enemy target system. As a consequence, our offense needs improved communications, command and control, even though such capability tends to be ignored in most simple comparisons of Soviet and American strategic capabilities.

Age also often is ignored in simple comparisons, and some of our offensive forces are growing old. Also, some—particularly the ICBM component—are becoming more vulnerable than is desirable from the standpoint of flexibility, even though we might decide to use those forces under attack before they were destroyed.

We have not been idle in the face of these needs. Aging of the force is being brought under control. The modernization of the submarine and bomber forces—with the Trident missile and with cruise missiles—is well under way. We are moving toward development of a new and more sophisticated ICBM. And we are continuing to examine possible replacements for our B-52 bombers.

We are giving equal priority to our other strategic force needs, even though they are less visible and do not lend themselves to simple numerical comparisons with Soviet capabilities:

- Our warning systems are being improved.
- We are developing increased accuracy for all our missiles—ballistic and cruise.
- We are upgrading our communications and ability to use those communications selectively.
- New warheads soon will be deployed, and advanced avionics systems for our bombers are being tested.

Right now, even after a Soviet surprise attack, we could deliver literally thousands of thermonuclear weapons to targets in the Soviet Union. Despite the improving Soviet offensive and defensive forces, that capability of ours is not going to decline in the future. It is going to increase.

In response to the potential threat new Soviet ICBMS pose to our ICBMS, I have asked the military services and the Joint Chiefs of Staff to consider a number of options to enhance the survivability of that leg of our nuclear deterrence Triad—a Triad which is composed of bombers and cruise missiles, submarine-launched ballistic missiles, and intercontinental land-based missiles. A number of mobile ICBM

basing concepts are being evaluated, including some involving alternate launch points for each missile. This concept envisions moving missiles and their launchers among multiple sites which might themselves be hardened, thus substantially complicating Soviet targeting of our deterrent.

No decision has been made whether or not to deploy mobile ICBM systems, like the alternate launch point system (or multiple aiming point [MAP] system, as it is sometimes called) that I just mentioned. Nor have we decided which particular concept we would implement, if we were to elect to deploy a mobile ICBM system. The current and projected capabilities of our strategic forces give us time to study thoroughly questions of technical feasibility, military effectiveness, and cost prior to making decisions about deploying mobile ICBMS.

Any mobile ICBM basing system would, of course, have to be fully consistent with all provisions—including verification provisions—of a strategic arms limitation agreement. The United States will not deploy a mobile ICBM system that would not permit adequate verification of the number of launchers deployed and other provisions of the agreement. You may be confident that we will insist that any Soviet system meet the same verification standards.

The parts of the joint draft text of the SALT II agreement that have already been agreed allow deployment of mobile ICBM systems of the types we are considering. The draft agreement explicitly permits deployment of mobile ICBM launchers during its term, after the expiration of an interim protocol period which would end well before mobile ICBM systems would be ready for deployment.

I know that some of you are concerned about SALT. I want to assure you that no SALT agreement will be signed unless it is in the interest of the United States to sign it. That means particularly that it must not undermine our military security. An acceptable strategic arms limitation agreement is not going to weaken the U.S. second-strike capability that I have described. We will retain our assurance—and the Soviets will know—that we can deliver such a devastating second-strike blow. And that will remain true despite the current Soviet civil defense program.

WASHINGTON, 30 OCTOBER 1978*

Q. Paul, SALT has been under negotiation now for six years, and you've been at it for two years. Those same issues have held it up for a long period of time now. Why is there no SALT?

* SOURCE: Press conference of ACDA Director Paul C. Warnke. U.S. Arms Control and Disarmament Agency, Office of Public Affairs, 1 November 1978.

Mr. WARNKE. . . . The process itself is a difficult one. It's awfully hard to reach meaningful arms control agreements. You could reach sort of a token agreement in a short period of time. But if you're trying genuinely to end up with something which is not only going to be good in itself but also lay the basis for later steps, it's going to go slowly.

Now, here, what we're trying to do is, unlike the SALT I interim agreement on offensive arms, to do more than just sort of ratify the arms competition. We are trying, actually, to interfere with programs that otherwise would be completed. And, as I say, that's an unnatural kind of an act on the part of any sovereign state. And, therefore, it's one which is taken with a great deal of resistance.

Q. To what extent have political factors in the last several months held up—on both our side and their side—either complicated or in any way delayed progress toward a treaty?

Mr. WARNKE. That's a difficult question to answer, and I don't think that you can answer it except by guessing.

As you know, I've been maintaining consistently that there should not be linkage between SALT and other elements in the relationship—that you can't use SALT as a reward, you can't use it as punishment. It has to stand on its own feet. At the same time, I think that you have to recognize that the general climate of relations does affect the negotiations. And I believe that had there been less strain in the relationship this year, there would have been more receptivity on both sides.

I think when you tend to feel that the other side is behaving in a fashion of which you disapprove, that you are not apt to be perhaps as responsive to their positions as you might otherwise be. But, as I say, it's an atmospheric thing rather than a logical thing. But it does have some effect.

* * *

Q. Your comments about the value of the protocol in not deciding these issues of cruise missiles and mobile missiles while we complete negotiations could be turned around and used to imply a criticism of the issues that are being decided in the heat of negotiations—and maybe the things that have ended up in the treaty are being decided too hastily. Is that—

Mr. WARNKE. No. I don't think that I would accept that.

Q. It amounts to what you were saying.

Mr. WARNKE. No. What I say is there are some items on which decisions are really not ready, and that the risk would be to decide those prematurely. They aren't ripe for decision.

Q. But have all those been saved for the protocol?

Mr. WARNKE. I would say that they have. Take, for example, the question of a ban on new types. Now, at one point, we considered that to be a protocol item. But we've been able to reach an agreement which preserves the options that we feel are important to preserve. And, therefore, you can move that into the treaty. Now, if you remember, at one point what we were proposing was no new type of ICBM. And we were willing to do that for the protocol period. But, with the understanding now that there will be one exception on each side, there's no reason to make that a protocol item. Because the only thing we are interested in for the entire treaty period is the possibility of one new ICBM.

Q. Was it a mistake, then, last—when was it, March or April [1977]—to propose wholesale cutbacks? The administration's first position would have required all sorts of major decisions. Did you lose time?

Mr. WARNKE. No.

Q. Because now you're in favor of—what you're saying now, and I don't know if you were in favor of it then—the limited measures, putting issues off—temporary measures—and yet you came out, if I remember, for a huge substantial slash—

Mr. WARNKE. Well, I think there are basically two answers to that. One of them is that I certainly don't maintain that you ought to put all issues off. You shouldn't. You ought to decide, on a long-term basis, as many of them as you are prepared to make a considered judgment on.

But what I've suggested is that there are always going to be a couple of items that aren't ripe for decision—just as the question of ground-launched cruise missiles or the question of mobile launchers of ICBMS are not now ripe for decision. After all, with regard to a mobile ICBM launcher, we haven't even been able to arrive at a concept which is satisfactory to us. So that's the sort of issue that ought to be put off. The issues such as drastic reductions are issues that we have been prepared to decide now. And we would have been happy if the Soviet Union had been prepared to decide on that point too.

Q. It was a long time ago, but do you think you've lost time?

Mr. WARNKE. It's hard to say.

Q. Are they punishing us for it?

Mr. WARNKE. No, I don't think that they're punishing us for it. And it seems to me that it's going to work out all right; that we're in a position in which, if you take a look at the two proposals of March 1977, where we're going to end up is in between, but in between much more on the side of the comprehensive proposal than on the side of the deferral proposal. . . .

Q. Was that a sensible way to proceed in March of 1977 or was that procedure dictated largely by the internal American domestic politics and the concerns of the right wing?

Mr. WARNKE. No. I would say that it was not the product of any concern about thunder on the right. It was an effort on the part of the President to see if we couldn't take a very substantial step forward in arms control. And it turned out to be a more ambitious step than the Soviets were prepared to contemplate. I think that was the sole motivation.

Whether it was a mistake or not is something that I think we can't determine as yet. I think that it did create the kind of atmosphere in which we have been able to go further with SALT II than if we had gone in immediately with a more modest approach. I think it did sort of raise the stakes, and that, as a consequence, we will get a better SALT II agreement. Now, on the other hand, we've had to pay the price perhaps in time. I think we're going to get a better agreement perhaps somewhat later than if we had gone in with a more modest approach. I think that's where I'd come out.

* * *

Q. [Inaudible—concerning SALT III.]

Mr. WARNKE. Well, as far as the timing of SALT III is concerned, I think that that's pretty much agreed by both sides that we will do that promptly after the completion of SALT II. And I think we should.

It's hard to see what kind of form SALT III will take. It will be very different from SALT II because you won't have to go through all of the basics. See, in SALT II you had to negotiate all of the boilerplate of a treaty—the definitions, the question of the verification rules, a lot of things that won't have to be renegotiated. So, in a sense, you could visualize SALT III as sort of a series of amendments of SALT II. You could take a particular package of amendments and try and negotiate them. But this is something, obviously, that we're going to have to feel our way toward.

. . . [The Soviets] have pushed for a long time, of course, to include our forward-based systems and the nuclear forces of allied states as part of SALT. Now that's the basic dichotomy between the definitions of strategic weapons, with our maintaining that strategic weapons are those that can be launched from one country and strike the other country, whereas they maintain that any weapons that can strike the territory of the other country ought to be counted as strategic.

Now, that's what they yielded in Vladivostok. That was the fundamental breakthrough that President Ford accomplished. But

they have made it very clear always that they would try and raise forward-based systems and the forces of the other side as part of SALT III. We have made it equally clear that we aren't prepared now to concede that these would be relevant to a SALT agreement. And if they were in fact to be involved—that is, the forward-based systems—then we would be prepared to discuss that issue only in conjunction with a discussion of theater nuclear forces on both sides.

We've also made it clear that, as far as we're concerned, SALT is bilateral, and, therefore, the forces of other countries aren't relevant to the issue. But I have no doubt that they will continue to push their position.

Vance and Gromyko Meet in Geneva, 23 December 1978

Secretary VANCE. In the course of our meetings over the past three days, Foreign Minister Gromyko and I have essentially reached agreement on most of the questions on which differences have existed. We will continue to work on those questions that have not yet been resolved through our regular diplomatic channels. Both sides will do their best in order that the preparation of an agreement for signing may be completed in the nearest future.

Let me anticipate a question that I know you are going to ask because you have asked it every other time and I have not yet commented on it. We are agreed in principle on the meeting of the heads of our two states. The question of timing of such a meeting will be a subject for careful consideration by both sides.

Foreign Minister GROMYKO. You have probably guessed that we talked with each other as to what we should tell you and therefore, without any difficulty, I subscribe to what the U.S. Secretary of State has just said.

A lot of work has indeed been done. We really can say that most of the questions on which there was no agreement before have essentially been agreed. But there is still some more work to be done to complete preparation of the treaty on strategic offensive arms.

I express my satisfaction on behalf of the Soviet Union at the fact that both sides are fully determined to complete their work and to ensure the conclusion of the agreement within the shortest possible time.

I think that the statements we have made are so clear that there will be no more questions.

Q. Will this require another meeting at the ministerial level?

Foreign Minister GROMYKO. We did not make any such arrangements. And I will go still further and say that we both, I think, express the hope that there will be no further need for such a meeting.

Q. Mr. Minister, do you think that the questions that remain to be solved are fundamental matters or are they more in the way of details that need to be wrapped up?

Foreign Minister GROMYKO. Well, some of them are important. Some of them are the matters of the second category but anyway, they have certain meaning. It is difficult sometimes to put matters on the

---

SOURCE: Remarks to the press by Secretary of State Cyrus R. Vance and Foreign Minister Andrei Gromyko, Geneva, 23 December 1978. Department of State, Press Release No. 467.

first shelf, then on the second shelf, then on the third shelf. Some of them, not many of them. Not many.

Q. Must they be completed before the summit conference takes place?

Foreign Minister GROMYKO. They must be completed.

Q. Are you confident that they will be completed rather shortly?

Foreign Minister GROMYKO. We expect what I said, that both sides determine to complete them soon.

Carter Discusses SALT and America's Role in the World, 20 February 1979

As the events of recent days have shown, peace remains a fragile thing, vulnerable to assaults from all sides.

Disturbances in Iran, the Western Indian Ocean, and Southeast Asia are a challenge to our determination and our leadership. They underscore the importance of strength in our national defenses, wisdom in our diplomacy, and steadfastness in the pursuit of arms control and peace.

I want to speak to you today about America's role and America's purpose in this world of change and turbulence.

* * *

Ever since the end of the Second World War, the United States has been the leader in moving our world closer to a stable peace and genuine security. We have the world's strongest economy; we have the world's strongest military forces; and we share burdens of mutual defense with friends abroad whose security and prosperity are as vital to us as to themselves.

With our strong allies, we have succeeded in preventing a global war for more than one-third of a century—the longest period of general peace in modern times. And as President of the United States, I am determined to keep our nation at peace.

We help to sustain a world trading and monetary system that has brought greater prosperity to more of the world's people than ever before in history. We are working to resolve conflicts among other nations so that each can develop its own future in independence and peace. And we've helped to maintain the conditions in which more than 100 new nations have come into being, and in which human hope—and its fulfillment—has taken a revolutionary leap forward.

In short, we in the United States provide the bedrock of global security and economic advance in a world of unprecedented change and conflict.

In such a world America has four fundamental security responsibilities: to provide for our own nation's strength and safety; to stand by our allies and our friends; to support national independence and integrity of other nations; and to work diligently for peace.

SOURCE: Remarks of President Jimmy Carter at the Georgia Institute of Technology, Atlanta, Georgia, 20 February 1979. *Weekly Compilation of Presidential Documents*, 26 February 1979, pp. 300–306.

We do not oppose change. Many of the political currents sweeping the world express a desire that we share—the desire for a world in which the legitimate aspirations of nations and individuals have a greater chance for fulfillment.

The United States cannot control events within other nations. A few years ago, we tried this and we failed. But we recognized as inevitable that the uncertainty and the turmoil that come with change can have its darker side as well. We saw this in a senseless act of violence last week in Afghanistan, when a brave and good man—Ambassador Adolph Dubs—gave his life in the performance of his duty as a representative of the United States. . . .

We also see the darker side of change when countries in turbulence provide opportunities for exploitation by outsiders who seek not to advance human aims, but rather to extend their own power and their own position at the expense of others.

As I speak to you today, the country of Iran—with which we have had close relations for the last thirty years—is in revolution. It's been our hope that Iran could modernize without deep internal conflicts, and we sought to encourage that effort by supporting its government, by urging internal change toward progress and democracy, and by helping to provide a background of regional stability.

The revolution in Iran is a product of deep social, political, religious, and economic factors growing out of the history of Iran itself. Those who argue that the United States should or could intervene directly to thwart these events are wrong about the realities of Iran. So, too, are those who spout propaganda that protecting our own citizens is tantamount to direct intervention.

We have not and we will not intervene in Iran, yet the future of Iran continues to be of deep concern to us and to our friends and allies. It's an important nation in a critical part of the world, an immediate neighbor of the Soviet Union, a major oil producer that also sits beside the principal artery for most of the world's trade in oil. And it is still a significant potential force for stability and progress in the region.

Iran is a proud nation with a long history—more than 2,000 years—of struggle to establish and to guarantee its own freedom. The independence of Iran is also in our own vital interest and in the interest of our closest allies—and we will support the independence of Iran.

* * *

But just as we respect Iran's independence and integrity, other nations must do so as well. If others interfere, directly or indirectly,

they are on notice that this will have serious consequences and will affect our broader relationships with them.

At the same time, we are intensifying our efforts to promote stability throughout the Middle East so that the security and the independence of the nations of that part of the world will be maintained.

* * *

For us in the United States, any crisis in the Middle East has the most immediate and serious consequences. But we are also deeply concerned by what is happening now in Southeast Asia. The same principles of American policy apply: We support the independence and integrity of the regional nations; we will stand by our friends; and we will continue as a nation to work for peace.

Just in the last few weeks we've seen a Vietnamese invasion of Cambodia and, as a result, a Chinese frontier penetration into Vietnam. Both actions threaten the stability of one of the world's most important and promising regions—Southeast Asia.

We have opposed both military actions. Let me outline very briefly the principles that govern our conduct.

First, we will not get involved in conflict between Asian Communist nations. Our national interests are not directly threatened, although we are concerned, of course, at the wider implications of what might happen in the future and what has been happening in the past.

We are using whatever diplomatic and political means are available to encourage restraint on all parties and to seek to prevent a wider war. While our influence is limited, because our involvement is limited, we remain the one great power in all the world which can have direct and frank discussions with all the parties concerned. For this reason, we have a useful and important role to play in the restoration of stability. We will continue our efforts, both directly with the countries involved and through the United Nations, to secure an end to the fighting in the region, to bring about a withdrawal of Vietnam forces from Cambodia, and of Chinese forces from Vietnam, and to gain the restoration of the independence and integrity of all nations involved.

At the same time, we are continuing to express our deep concern that this conflict may widen still further—with unforeseen and grave consequences for nations in the region and also beyond.

In any event, the United States is fully prepared to protect the vital interests of our people wherever they may be challenged.

* * *

As we face this immediate series of crises, we also look constantly to the broader needs of security. If we are to meet our responsibilities, we must continue to maintain the military forces we need for our defense and to contribute to the defense of our allies.

This year, I have proposed a substantial real increase in the defense budget. The events of recent weeks underscore the responsibility of the Congress to appropriate these funds in full. There must be no doubt that the people of the United States are fully prepared to meet our commitments and to back up those commitments with military strength.

Turmoil and crisis also underscore the vital need to work whereever possible to stabilize and to reduce competition in strategic nuclear weapons. This effort has the same ultimate goals as does our strong defense—the goals of security, stability, and peace. In pursuit of these goals, our nation faces no more important task this year than the successful conclusion of a strategic arms limitation agreement.

Just as we work to support national independence and to aid our friends and allies in times of trial, we must work to regulate nuclear arms capable of threatening life throughout this planet. For a SALT agreement is a fundamental element of strategic and political stability in a turbulent world—stability which can provide the necessary political basis for us to contain the kinds of crises that we face today, and to prevent their growing into a terrible nuclear confrontation.

After more than six years of negotiations—conducted by three different Presidents—agreement has now been reached on most of the major components of a sound and verifiable SALT II treaty.

The emerging agreement will establish for the first time equal numbers of strategic arms for both sides. It will thus reverse the Soviet's numerical advantage which was temporarily established in the SALT I treaty of 1972, when they had about a 40 percent built-in negotiated advantage.

To reach these new levels, the Soviets will be required to reduce their overall number of strategic arms. Over 250 Soviet missiles or bombers—almost 10 percent of their strategic forces—will have to be destroyed or dismantled. At the same time, because we are now well below the agreed ceiling, we could substantially increase our own operational strategic forces.

The SALT II agreement will also provide negotiated limits on building new types of weapons and limits on the improvement of existing ones—the so-called qualitative arms race can be controlled.

SALT II will limit the size of land-based missiles and the number of warheads that can be placed on them. Without these limits, the

Soviets could vastly increase the number of warheads on their large land-based missiles—with grave implications to the strategic balance. SALT II will therefore contribute to our ability to deal with the growing vulnerability of our land-based missiles. Without it, the Soviet Union could continue to increase the number of their warheads, tending to nullify our effort to protect our missiles.

The agreement will also permit us and our allies to pursue all the defense programs that we believe might eventually be needed—the MX missile; the Trident submarine and its missiles; air-, ground-, and sea-launched cruise missiles; cruise missile carrier aircraft; and a new penetrating bomber. These would be permitted.

Thus SALT II would allow our own prudent programs to move ahead and also will place important limits on what the Soviets might otherwise do. And this SALT II agreement will be a basis for further negotiations for additional substantial cuts in the level of nuclear armaments.

Without the SALT II agreement, the Soviet Union could have nearly one-third more strategic forces by 1985 than with SALT II. We would, of necessity, as a nation, match such a buildup. The costs would be enormous, the risks self-evident. And both nations would wind up less secure.

The stakes in SALT are too high to rely on trust. Any SALT II treaty that I sign will be adequately verifiable, using our own independent means of guaranteeing Soviet compliance with terms of the agreement.

SALT II will specifically forbid any interference that would impede our ability to verify compliance with the treaty. Any effort on the part of the Soviet Union to interfere with our verification activities would be a detectable violation of the agreement itself, and an early signal of any possible cheating.

Finally, let me put this agreement in the context of our overall relations with the Soviet Union and the turbulence that exists in many parts of the world. The question is not whether SALT can be divorced from this complicated context. It cannot. As I have often said, our relationship with the Soviet Union is a mixture of cooperation and competition. And as President of the United States, I have no more difficult and delicate task than to balance these two. I cannot and I will not let the pressures of inevitable competition overwhelm possibilities for cooperation, any more than I will let cooperation blind us to the realities of competition, which we are fully prepared to meet.

Because this carefully negotiated and responsible arms control agreement will make the world safer and more secure, it is in our national interest to pursue it, even as we continue competition with

the Soviet Union elsewhere in the world. Therefore, I will seek both to conclude this new SALT agreement and to respond to any Soviet behavior which adversely affects our interests.

To reject SALT II would mean that the inevitable competition in strategic nuclear arms would grow even more dangerous. Each crisis, each confrontation, each point of friction—as serious as it may be in its own right—would take on an added measure of significance and an added dimension of danger. For it would occur in an atmosphere of unbridled strategic competition and deteriorating strategic stability. It is precisely because we have fundamental differences with the Soviet Union that we are determined to bring this dangerous dimension of our military competition under control.

In today's world, it is vital to match the pursuit of ideals with the responsible use of force and of power. The United States is a source of both, ideals and power. Our ideals have inspired the world for more than two centuries; and for three generations, since World War II, our power has helped other nations to realize their own ideals.

The determination and strength of purpose of the American people are crucial for stability in a turbulent world. If we stand together in maintaining a steady course, America can protect its principles and interests and also be a force for peace.

Americans have always accepted the challenge of leadership. And I am confident that we will do so now.

Brezhnev Discusses SALT and Other Arms Control Issues, 2 March 1979

The ending of the arms race, the prevention of the danger of a world nuclear war have now become the most pressing, the most burning tasks for mankind. The Soviet Union, just as the other socialist countries, does not stint efforts in the struggle for these aims. . . .

One of the biggest tasks in this respect is undoubtedly the drafting of the new Soviet-American agreement on the limitation of strategic offensive arms. It appears that the work of more than six years is now close to completion. Of course, in some things the treaty, from our point of view, could have been better. Not everything in it fully accords with our wishes. But that is a reasonable compromise which takes into consideration the interests of both sides. On the whole, however, this is an important and good endeavor.

First, the new agreement, if it is signed, ratified, and enters into force, will create for several years—concerning a number of important points until 1985—a definite barrier in the way of the further stockpiling of the most destructive and costly types of arms. The principle of the equality and equal security of the sides will find expression in this agreement. It can be said definitely that its implementation will not inflict any damage to the security of the Soviet Union, or to the security of the United States for that matter. On the whole, I would say, it will be advantageous to both countries.

Second, the entry of the agreement into force will mean that the process of curbing the arms race, started on the initiative of the U.S.S.R., is continuing. The SALT I agreement was followed by SALT II. After the latter's entry into force, work will begin on the SALT III agreement. It should go still further, put a brake on the creation of new types of weapons, provide this time not only for a limitation on the growth of arms, but also for their reduction by both sides.

The present agreement will also probably help revive the other currently conducted talks; for instance, on the full prohibition of nuclear weapons tests, on restricting the sale of conventional arms and, we hope, also the talks on the reduction of armed forces and armaments in Central Europe.

Then, third, the conclusion of the SALT II agreement will undoubtedly have a beneficial effect on the international climate in general.

SOURCE: Remarks of President Leonid Brezhnev before the electorate of the Bauman electoral district, Moscow, 2 March 1979. *News and Views From the U.S.S.R.*, Soviet Embassy Information Department, Washington, D.C.

When its drafting is completed, the new agreement will probably be signed during my meeting with President Carter, hopefully in the near future. We intend to discuss also a number of questions of the further development of Soviet-American relations, of consolidating the relaxation of international tension and strengthening universal peace.

* * *

Of course, we are not playing down the difficulties standing in the way of strengthening peace and the security of peoples. To spread détente to the military sphere is today's priority task. This is particularly necessary because the NATO bloc is feverishly building up its armaments, complicating the situation in Europe. On our part, we are striving for agreement on real measures to lessen the level of military confrontation on the continent, which would strengthen the foundations of European peace. Unfortunately, there are so far no changes in this respect.

Take the negotiations in Vienna. At present, they have bogged down in the quagmire of dispute over the methods of counting the personnel of the sides' armed forces—right to the last cook or medical orderly. Frankly speaking, this is simply the Western countries' tactics, an attempt to evade agreement right at the time when the positions of the sides on the substance of the matter came considerably closer. After all, it is a fact that a general military equilibrium does exist in Europe, even if there are differences in the structure of the armed forces of each side. And it is from this fact that one should proceed.

The proposals of the socialist countries are known. I shall remind you that within the framework of these proposals the Soviet Union is prepared, to start with, to withdraw from Central Europe within a year 30,000 military personnel and a considerable amount of military equipment, including 1,000 tanks, on condition that the United States reduces, and on a lesser scale at that, its armed forces in this area. We are still waiting for a constructive reply to these proposals.

Reports are appearing ever more frequently lately that the Pentagon is pressuring the FRG [Federal Republic of Germany] in order to secure its consent to stationing in that country, in addition to the American forward-based weapons already present there, medium-range nuclear missile weapons aimed at the Soviet Union. It appears that voices of protest against this can be heard in the FRG.

This is quite understandable, for the implementation of these plans, just as of the plans of the American military in respect to

neutron weapons, would result only in a new growth of tension in Europe, in a new upsurge of the arms race and also in a drastic growth of the danger to the FRG itself.

As for the Soviet Union, it has already stated more than once that it stands not for building up, but for reducing nuclear missiles or other weapons through agreement of the sides on the basis of complete reciprocity. This also concerns medium-range weapons in Europe, but with due account, of course, for the existence there of American military bases as well. . . .

Another question. With the aim of strengthening mutual trust, participants in the European Conference have started to inform one another about military exercises conducted in the respective area, and to invite foreign observers to them. Perhaps we could now expand this practice and give advance notice not only about exercises, but also about all considerable troop movements in the framework of the area concerned, and also about major naval exercises when held near the waters of other participating countries of the European Conference.

We are prepared, of course, to also study other proposals directed at strengthening mutual trust.

In 1976, Warsaw Treaty member states proposed that all participating countries of the European Conference undertake not to be the first to use nuclear weapons against one another. In response, the West began to maintain that this would allegedly increase the probability of wars with the use of conventional weapons. If so, let us then reach agreement on not being the first to use either nuclear or conventional weapons. In other words, let us conclude something like a nonaggression pact between the participants in the European Conference. This, I believe, would fully conform to the spirit of Helsinki.

Brown Examines SALT II and Strategic Weapons Policy, 5 April 1979

Two concepts underlie U.S. strategic forces planning: deterrence and essential equivalence.

Deterrence of nuclear war is our most fundamental defense objective. A credible deterrent can be achieved only if we possess the military force necessary to persuade our enemies that, whatever the circumstances, if they start a course of action that could lead to war they will either:

- pay an unacceptable price to achieve their objective or;
- be frustrated in their effort to achieve that objective.

Our basic strategy requires us to be able to inflict such damage on a potential adversary that, regardless of the circumstances, the prospect of that damage will preclude his attack on the United States, our allies, or our vital interests. To achieve this we need, first of all, a survivable capability to devastate the industry and cities of the Soviet Union. Assured destruction capability—which is what I've just defined—is the bedrock of nuclear deterrence. It is not, however, in my judgment, sufficient in itself as a strategic doctrine. Massive retaliation may not be appropriate, nor will its prospect always be sufficiently credible, to deter the full range of actions we seek to prevent.

We need capabilities convincingly able to do, and sure to carry out, under any circumstances the *Soviets* consider realistic, whatever damage the Soviets consider will deter *them*. Put differently, the perceptions of those whom we seek to deter can determine what is needed for deterrence in various circumstances. For fully effective deterrence, we need to be able to respond at the level appropriate to the type and scale of a Soviet attack. Fully effective deterrence requires forces of sufficient size and flexibility to attack selectively a range of military and other targets, and to enable us to hold back a significant reserve.

This ability to provide measured retaliation in response to less-than-total attacks—and thus to prevent the Soviets from imagining that they can gain meaningful advantage at some level of nuclear conflict—is essential to credible deterrence. Moreover, whatever doubts one may have about whether a nuclear war could be kept limited—and I have

---

SOURCE: Remarks of Secretary of Defense Harold Brown before The Council on Foreign Relations and the Foreign Policy Association, New York, 5 April 1979. Office of the Assistant Secretary of Defense (Public Affairs), News Release No. 153–79, 5 April 1979.

severe ones—it would be the height of folly to put the United States in a position in which uncontrolled escalation would be the only course we could follow.

By any reasonable standard, we have a credible deterrent today and will have one for the foreseeable future. We have, and will continue to have, survivable forces capable of massive destruction of Soviet cities and industrial potential, even after an all-out surprise attack. We also have—and will have increasingly in the coming years—both the forces, and the targeting and employment policies, that allow for selective use of nuclear force to respond to more limited provocations. The rapid Soviet buildup in strategic forces over the past decade, as compared to our own more modestly paced improvements in forces, should not obscure the basic power and credibility of our deterrent.

Moreover, the problems we face—in particular the growing vulnerability of our fixed-silo ICBMs—will not force us to choose between all-out attacks on cities, on the one hand, and surrender, on the other. Our capacity to make selective strikes at military and other targets, while maintaining a reserve, is large now and will grow in the future, despite ICBM vulnerability.

Essential equivalence—our second broad objective—is somewhat different from credible deterrence. It is one possible criterion for such deterrence, particularly if we want our nuclear forces to have an effect that goes beyond deterrence of an all-out strategic surprise attack. The use of essential equivalence as an objective reflects the reality that nuclear forces—like other military forces—have a broader political role, not entirely determined by technical, static (force-counting) or even dynamic (war-gaming) calculations of military capability.

As long as our relationship with the Soviet Union is more competitive than cooperative—and this is clearly the case in military terms—maintaining essential equivalence of strategic nuclear forces is necessary to prevent the Soviets from gaining political advantage from a real or perceived strategic imbalance.

Essential equivalence thus demands that our forces not only be on a par with those of the Soviet Union, but be seen to be so. We need not—we should not—imitate Soviet forces in an inevitably futile, immensely costly, and potentially very dangerous effort to match or exceed the Soviets in every conceivable index of strategic power. To say, however, we can tolerate some "gaps" that are offset by U.S. advantages by other measures is not to say we can tolerate an overall imbalance, whether perceived or real.

Today, essential equivalence exists. While the Soviets have certain advantages, such as ICBM throw-weight and deliverable megatonnage,

we now have offsetting advantages in numbers of warheads, accuracy, and antisubmarine warfare capability.

Most importantly, while no one can assuredly predict the outcome of any nuclear exchange, neither we nor the Soviets would gain in any rational sense from such a conflict.

It's worth considering, for a moment, whether these objectives are ambitious enough:

- Ought we to be satisfied with equivalance and with preventing Soviet actions by deterrence?
- Ought we instead to seek to exploit our resources and our technology to attain strategic superiority?

In the first place, massive numerical superiority in strategic forces, even when we had it in the 50s and 60s, proved to be no panacea for our military needs, and still less for our diplomatic problems. We and our allies required strong conventional forces for our security.

The potential futility of any quest for superiority derives, I believe, from the realities of nuclear weaponry and bilateral superpower relations. Modern nuclear weapons technology is such that while equivalence is a realistic goal, superiority is not, *providing* that the other side is determined to prevent it. Each superpower can, by actions that are well within its technical and economic capability, prevent the other from gaining an overall advantage, much less supremacy.

The system is not self-equilibrating; neither equivalence nor even deterrence will be maintained automatically. Avoiding inferiority requires us to have the will and resolve to do the things that will enable us to maintain the strategic balance. For, if the Soviets ever were to achieve superiority, I am convinced they would make every effort to exploit it politically, and even militarily. I am confident that we will continue to show the will and resolve to prevent the Soviets from attaining superiority. But I think it would be equally wrong to suppose that the Soviets, challenged to a race for superiority, would passively yield such an advantage to us.

In brief, equivalence and deterrence are at one and the same time our maximum feasible—and our minimum tolerable—objectives. And at present, our forces meet those objectives.

But if the present balance is adequate in terms of our objectives of deterrence and equivalence, we face challenges for the future that we can ignore only at great peril. If today we are in a satisfactory relationship vis-à-vis the Soviet Union, what of tomorrow? Less rhetorically, what will the strategic balance be like during the planning horizons we can reasonably contemplate?

Some trends are of real concern. The Soviets are rapidly catching up to us in a number of key areas where we have led in the past, especially in the areas of accuracy and reentry vehicle numbers. Additionally, the improvements the Soviets have made in long-range theater nuclear forces may be of great significance as the central balance becomes more equal. Further, the growing vulnerability of our land-based missile force in the early 1980s could, if not corrected, contribute to a perception of U.S. strategic inferiority that would have severely adverse political—and could have potentially destabilizing military—consequences.

In reviewing the challenges the Soviets are posing in the strategic area, we should remember that the United States has not been idle. In the past 10 years, we have deployed more than a thousand MIRVed missiles, thereby increasing our missile warhead total nearly four-fold. SRAM (the Short-Range Attack Missile) has increased the capability of the B-52 force. Further, we have programs to improve each of the three elements of the U.S. Triad of strategic forces.

* * *

Without the SALT II agreement, the Soviet Union could have nearly one-third more strategic systems than with the agreement. And there would be corresponding effects on other measures. For example, instead of the 2,250 SNDVs of the treaty, they could have 3,000. Naturally, we do not know what the Soviets would do in the absence of a treaty, but these higher strategic system levels are well within their capability. And the history of the nuclear era is strewn with the wreckage of confident U.S. predictions that the Soviets would at some point or another cease to add to force levels that were already—according to the U.S. predictors—as large as the Kremlin could possibly want. In my view, it is probable that without SALT II we would enter into an era of greater uncertainty—in both military and political terms—that would result in increased strategic forces on both sides, as hedges against that uncertainty.

Faced with such a Soviet buildup, the U.S. could, and I am confident would, respond. Given our determination to maintain essential equivalence, and the demonstrated Soviet willingness to avoid strategic inferiority even at great cost, the net result of such a numbers race would be greater strategic force levels at vastly greater expense and at substantial risk to stability.

The United States does not have unlimited resources to spend on strategic weapons programs without significantly affecting other defense priorities—such as improvements in conventional forces—and other government programs, such as those required to combat inflation.

But we do need to spend enough, and what is enough depends in part on the actions of our adversaries.

SALT will not solve all our problems. Even with SALT we will need, and we will be permitted, to expand our strategic nuclear efforts above their present levels. Those levels, incidently, are about half, in constant dollar terms, what they were during the mid-1960s. But SALT will mean greater stability and predictability in the strategic challenges we face, and so the balance could be maintained at a substantially lower level of destructive power. Furthermore, with SALT, it would be significantly less expensive (perhaps as much as $30 billion less expensive over the next decade) for the United States to maintain that balance than without a SALT II agreement.

SALT II, while forestalling this pointless numbers race, will leave us the flexibility to carry out programs to deal with the challenges the treaty will not eliminate. We can develop, test, and deploy each of our planned programs—cruise missiles, Trident, MX—in the fashion, and on the schedule, that we have planned. Apart from putting some distinguishing features on our ALCMS and cruise missile carriers (to aid counting under SALT), we will not be forced by SALT II to alter our strategic programs which we need to balance Soviet programs that are allowed in SALT II and that are, in large measure, already in place.

In at least one important respect—Minuteman vulnerability—SALT II will make the solution of a problem easier than without an agreement. SALT II will limit, to well below previously projected levels, the number of Soviet MIRVed ICBMS, will freeze the number of warheads on existing ballistic missile launchers, and will limit the number of RVS allowed for new ICBMS. These restrictions sharply reduce the significance of the Soviet throw-weight advantage which, without limitation, would, for example, enable them to deploy 20 or perhaps even 40 warheads on their largest ICBMS.

The combination of limitations on missile launchers and numbers of warheads will ease somewhat the difficulty of maintaining the survivability of our land-based ICBMS. The deployment of a new mobile ICBM system, regardless of basing mode, will be more feasible because an upper bound will be placed on the number of warheads that can be targeted against the aim points represented by that deployment. SALT II becomes, then, an important element in ensuring ICBM survivability.

Equally important, SALT II will leave us free to pursue with our allies the important issues of modernization of NATO's TNF forces, and to consider arms control initiatives in this area.

SALT will serve U.S. interests. It enhances the stability of the deterrent and allows us the flexibility to embark on needed modernization of our strategic forces without triggering another expensive and poten-

tially destabilizing arms race. I do not doubt our economic or technical ability to compete successfully with the Soviets in strategic weapons. I do question whether such an effort is the best use of our national—or even defense—budget. And I do not believe that we would purchase increased security with that sort of effort.

Under the treaty, we can maintain flexible and credible deterrence, and assure essential equivalence.

Without the treaty, we could also do these things, but it would be more costly and less certain. I see the treaty as a valuable method of meeting our strategic goals—as a major component in our strategy along with our weapons programs. In my judgment, it is a very important component, although we must recognize that it will have to be accompanied by substantial U.S. defense programs—expanded ones in the strategic field.

Carter Examines the Benefits of SALT II for American Security, 25 April 1979

Each generation of Americans faces a choice that defines our national character, a choice that is also important for what it says about our own nation's outlook toward the world.

In the coming months, we will almost certainly be faced with such a choice—whether to accept or to reject a new strategic arms limitation treaty. The decision we make will profoundly affect our lives and the lives of people all over the world for years to come. We face this choice from a position of strength, as the strongest nation on earth economically, militarily, and politically.

* * *

But our noblest duty is to use our strength to serve our highest interest—the building of a secure, stable, and a peaceful world. We perform that duty in the spirit proclaimed by John F. Kennedy in 1963, the year he died. "Confident and unafraid," he said, "we labor on—not toward a strategy of annihilation, but toward a strategy of peace."

In our relations with the Soviet Union, the possibility of mutual annihilation makes a strategy of peace the only rational choice for both sides.

Because our values are so different, it is clear that the United States of America and the Soviet Union will be in competition as far ahead as we can imagine or see. Yet we have a common interest in survival, and we share a common recognition that our survival depends, in a real sense, on each other. The very competition between us makes it imperative that we bring under control its most dangerous aspect—the nuclear arms race. That is why the strategic arms limitation talks are so very important. This effort by two great nations to limit vital security forces is unique in human history; none have ever done this before.

As the Congress and the American people consider the SALT treaty, which is now nearly complete, the debate will center around four basic questions: Why do we need SALT? How is the treaty related to our overall defense strategy? Can Soviet compliance be verified? How does the treaty relate to Soviet activities which challenge us and challenge our interests? Let me address each question in turn.

SOURCE: Remarks of President Jimmy Carter before the Annual Convention of the American Newspaper Publishers Association, New York, 25 April 1979. *Weekly Compilation of Presidential Documents*, 30 April 1979, pp. 693–699.

First, why do we need a strategic arms limitation treaty? We need it because it will contribute to a more peaceful world—and to our own national security.

Today, we and the Soviet Union, with sharply different world outlooks and interests, both have the ominous destructive power literally to destroy each other as a functioning society, killing tens of millions of people in the process. And common sense tells us—as it tells the Soviet Union—that we must work to make our competition less dangerous, less burdensome, and less likely to bring the ultimate horror of nuclear war.

Indeed, the entire world has a vital interest in whether or not we control the strategic arms race. We have consulted closely with our allies, who count on us not only to maintain strong military forces to offset Soviet military power, but also, and equally important, to manage successfully a stable East-West relationship. SALT is at the heart of both these crucial efforts. That is why the leaders of France and Great Britain, Germany, Canada, and other nations have voiced their full support for the emerging treaty.

Some nations which have so far held back from building their own nuclear weapons—and at least a dozen other nations on earth now have that capability—will be strongly influenced in their decision by whether the two nuclear superpowers will restrain our weapons. Rejection of the new strategic arms limitation treaty would seriously undermine the effort to control proliferation of these deadly weapons. And nothing, nothing, would more surely damage our other critical efforts in arms control—from a ban on all nuclear testing to the prevention of dangerous satellite warfare in space; from equalizing NATO and Warsaw Pact forces to restraining the spread of sophisticated conventional weapons on earth.

Every President since the dawn of the nuclear age has pursued the effort to bring nuclear arms under control. And this must be a continuing process.

President Kennedy, building on the efforts of Presidents Truman and Eisenhower, signed the first agreement with the Soviet Union in 1963 to stop the poisonous testing of nuclear explosives in the atmosphere.

In 1968, five years later, under President Johnson, the United States and the Soviet Union joined other nations throughout the world in signing the Non-Proliferation Treaty, an important step in preventing the spread of nuclear explosives to other nations.

In 1972, under President Nixon, the SALT I agreement placed the first agreed limits on the number of offensive weapons, and the anti-

ballistic missile treaty, the ABM treaty, made an enduring contribution to our own security.

President Ford continued in negotiations at Helsinki and at Vladivostok. Each negotiation builds on the accomplishments of the last. Each agreement provides a foundation for further progress toward a more stable nuclear relationship.

Three Presidents have now spent more than six years negotiating the next step in this process—SALT II. We have all negotiated carefully and deliberately. Every step of the way, we've worked with our military leaders and other experts, and we've sought the advice and counsel of the members of Congress.

An overwhelming majority of the American people recognize the need for SALT II. Our people want and our people expect continued, step-by-step progress toward bringing nuclear weapons under control.

Americans will support a reasoned increase in our defense effort, but we do not want a wholly unnecessary return to the cold war and an all-out arms race, with its vastly greater risks and costs. Through strength, we want world peace.

Let me turn to the second question—how is SALT II related to our overall defense strategy?

The strategic forces of the United States and the Soviet Union today are essentially equivalent. They have larger and more numerous land-based missiles. We have a larger number of warheads and, as you know, significant technological and geographical advantages.

Each side has the will and the means to prevent the other from achieving superiority. Neither side is in a position to exploit its nuclear weapons for political purposes, nor to use strategic weapons without facing almost certain suicide.

What causes us concern is not the current balance but the momentum of the Soviet strategic buildup. Over the past decade, the Soviets have steadily increased their real defense spending, year by year, while our own defense spending over that decade has had a net decrease.

In areas not limited by SALT I, they have launched ambitious programs to strengthen their strategic forces. At some future point, the Soviet Union could achieve a strategic advantage, unless we alter these trends. That is exactly what I want to do—with the support of the American people and the bipartisan support of Congress.

We must move on two fronts at the same time. First, within mutually accepted limits, we must modernize our own strategic forces. Along with the strengthening of NATO, that is a central purpose of the increased defense budget that I've submitted to Congress—improvements which are necessary even in a time of fiscal restraint. And second, we

must place more stringent limits on the arms race than are presently imposed by SALT I. That is the purpose of the SALT II treaty.

The defense budget I've submitted will ensure that our nuclear force continues to be essentially equivalent to that of the Soviet Union. This year, we've begun to equip our submarines with new, more powerful, and longer range Trident I missiles. Next year, the first of our new, even more secure Trident submarines will be going to sea, and we are working on a more powerful and accurate Trident II missile for these submarines.

Our cruise missile program will greatly enhance the effectiveness of our long-range bomber force. These missiles will be able to penetrate any air defense system which the Soviet Union could build in the foreseeable future.

We are substantially improving the accuracy and the power of our land-based Minuteman missiles. But in the coming decade missiles of this type, based in fixed silos, will become increasingly vulnerable to surprise attack. The Soviets have three-quarters of their warheads in such fixed-based missiles, compared to only one-quarter of ours. Nevertheless, this is a very serious problem, and we must deal with it effectively and sensibly.

The Defense Department now has under consideration a number of options for responding to this problem, including making some of our own ICBMS mobile. I might add—and this is very important—that the options which we are evaluating would be far more costly—and we would have far less confidence of their effectiveness—in the absence of SALT II limits. For without these limits on the number of Soviet warheads, the Soviet Union could counter any effort we made simply by greatly increasing the number of warheads on their missiles.

Let me emphasize that the SALT II agreement preserves adequate flexibility for the United States in this important area.

Our strategic forces must be able to survive any attack and to counterattack military and civilian targets in the aggressor nation. And the aggressor nation must know that we have the ability and the will to exercise this option if they should attack us. We have had this capability—which is the essence of deterrence—in the past; we have it today; and SALT II, plus the defense programs that I've described, will ensure that we have it for the future.

The SALT II agreement will slow the growth of Soviet arms and limit the strategic competition, and by helping to define future threats that we might face, SALT II will make our defense planning much more effective.

* * *

Let me turn now to the third of the four questions—how can we know whether the Soviets are living up to their obligations under this SALT agreement?

No objective—no objective—has commanded more energy and attention in our negotiations. We have insisted that the SALT II agreement be made verifiable. We are confident that no significant violation of the treaty could take place without the United States detecting it.

Our confidence in the verifiability of the agreement derives from the size and the nature of activities we must monitor and the many effective and sophisticated intelligence collection systems which we in America possess. For example, nuclear submarines take several years to construct and assemble. Missile silos and their supporting equipment are large and quite visible. Intercontinental bombers are built at a few plants, and they need major airfields. Our photoreconnaissance satellites survey the entire Soviet Union on a regular basis, and they give us high confidence that we will be able to count accurately the numbers of all these systems.

But our independent verification capabilities are not limited only to observing these large-scale activities. We can determine not only how many systems there are, but what they can do. Our photographic satellites and other systems enable us to follow technological developments in Soviet strategic forces with great accuracy. There is no question that any cheating which might affect our national security would be discovered in time for us to respond fully.

For many years, we have monitored Soviet strategic forces and Soviet compliance with the SALT agreements with a high degree of confidence. The overall capability remains. It was certainly not lost with our observation stations in Iran, which was only one of many intelligence sources that we use to follow Soviet strategic activities. We are concerned with that loss, but we must keep it in perspective. This monitoring capability relates principally to the portion of the new agreement dealing with the modernization limits on ICBMS and to only a portion of such modernization restraints.

The sensitive intelligence techniques obviously cannot be disclosed in public, but the bottom line is that if there is an effort to cheat on the SALT agreement, including the limits on modernizing ICBMS, we will detect it, and we will do so in time fully to protect our security.

And we must also keep in mind that quite apart from SALT limits, our security is affected by the extent of our information about Soviet strategic forces. With this SALT II treaty, that vital information will be much more accessible to us. The agreement specifically forbids, for the first time, interference with the systems used for monitoring compliance and prohibits any deliberate concealment that would impede verifica-

tion. Any such concealment activity would itself be detectable, and a violation of this part of the agreement would be so serious as to give us grounds to cancel the treaty itself.

As I have said many times, the stakes are too high to rely on trust, or even on the Soviets' rational inclination to act in their own best interest. The treaty must—and the treaty will be—verifiable from the first day it is signed.

And finally, how does SALT II fit into the context of our overall relations with the Soviet Union?

Because SALT II will make the world safer and our own nation more secure, it is in our national interest to control nuclear weapons even as we compete with the Soviets elsewhere in the world.

A SALT II agreement in no way limits our ability to promote our interests or to answer Soviet threats to those interests. We will continue to support the independence of Third World nations who struggle to stay free. We will continue to promote the peaceful resolution of local and regional disputes and to oppose efforts by any others to inflame these disputes with outside force. And we will continue to work for human rights.

It's a delusion to believe that rejection of a SALT treaty would somehow induce the Soviet Union to exercise new restraints in troubled areas. The actual effect of rejecting such a treaty might be precisely the opposite. The most intransigent and hostile elements of a Soviet political power structure would certainly be encouraged and strengthened by our rejection of a SALT agreement. The Soviets might very well feel that they then have little to lose by creating new international tensions.

A rejection of SALT II would have significance far beyond the fate of a single treaty. It would mean a radical turning away from America's longtime policy of seeking world peace. We would no longer be identified as the peace-loving nation. It would turn us away from the control of nuclear weapons and from the easing of tensions between Americans and the Soviet people under the system of international law based on mutual interests.

* * *

For these reasons, we will not try to impose binding linkage between Soviet behavior and SALT, and we will not accept any Soviet attempts to link SALT with aspects of our own foreign policy of which they may disapprove.

Again, SALT II is not a favor we are doing for the Soviet Union; it's an agreement carefully negotiated in the national security interests of the United States of America.

* * *

As the national discussion takes place, let us be clear about what the issues are—and are not.

Americans are committed to maintaining a strong defense. That is not the issue.

We will continue to compete, and compete effectively, with the Soviet Union. That is not the issue.

The issue is whether we will move ahead with strategic arms control or resume a relentless nuclear weapons competition. That's the choice we face—between an imperfect world with a SALT agreement, or an imperfect and more dangerous world without a SALT agreement.

With SALT II, we will have significant reductions in Soviet strategic forces; far greater certainty in our defense planning and in the knowledge of the threats that we might face; flexibility to meet our own defense needs; the foundation for further controls on nuclear and conventional arms; and our own self-respect and the earned respect of the world for a United States demonstrably committed to the works of peace.

Without SALT, the Soviets will be unconstrained and capable, and probably committed to an enormous further buildup.

Without SALT, there would have to be a much sharper rise in our own defense spending, at the expense of other necessary programs for our people.

Without SALT, we would end up with thousands more strategic nuclear warheads on both sides, with far greater costs—and far less security—for our citizens.

Without SALT, we would see improved relations with the Soviet Union replaced by heightened tensions.

Without SALT, the long, slow process of arms control, so central to building a safer world, would be dealt a crippling and, perhaps, a fatal blow.

Without SALT, the world would be forced to conclude that America had chosen confrontation rather than cooperation and peace.

This is an inescapable choice we face. For the fact is that the alternative to this treaty is not some perfect agreement, drafted unilaterally by the United States in which we gain everything and the Soviets gain nothing; the alternative now, and in the foreseeable future, is no agreement at all.

I am convinced that the United States has a moral and a political will to control the relentless technology which could constantly devise new and more destructive weapons to kill human beings. We need not drift into a dark nightmare of unrestrained arms competition. We Americans have the wisdom to know that our security depends on more

than just maintaining our unsurpassed defense forces. Our security and that of our allies also depends on the strength of ideas and ideals, and on arms control measures that can stabilize and finally reverse a dangerous and a wasteful arms race which neither side can win. This is a path of wisdom. This is a path of peace.

12
The Vienna Summit, June 1979

Vance Discusses Prospects for the Vienna Summit, 13 June 1979

Q. Mr. Secretary, the Congress appears to have some very definite ideas about foreign policy that appear at some times to be in conflict with the administration. . . . You said that the SALT treaty is intertwined and that it doesn't bear meddling. But what are the limits, do you think, that the Congress could reach which would be tolerable? In other words, what could the Senate do, without sending you back to the negotiating table, in the way of reservations or amendments?
Secretary VANCE. I have said, and I repeat again today, that the SALT treaty is a very carefully drafted document. It is a balanced document. It is a document in which there have been, over a period of six-plus years, negotiations where steps were taken on each side which involved concessions, and therefore [it] is a delicate balance. I believe that any attempt to amend the treaty which would affect the substance of the treaty would create a situation in which the treaty's existence would be severely jeopardized, if not destroyed.

* * *

Q. Mr. Secretary, given the President's problems with the Congress on such issues as SALT, Panama, Rhodesia, is there any possibility that this could affect his power, his authority to negotiate with Soviet leader Brezhnev? And is there any risk that Brezhnev might see the President as someone who cannot deliver on foreign policy?
Secretary VANCE. No. I do not believe that he will see the President as someone who cannot deliver on foreign policy. I think if you take a look at the key votes that we had on foreign policy last year—one sees Panama, one sees the arms sales in the Middle East, one sees the lifting of the Turkish arms embargo—all of those, I think, are clear

---

SOURCE: Press conference of Secretary of State Cyrus R. Vance, Washington, D.C., 13 June 1979. Department of State, Press Release no. 154, 13 June 1979.

examples of strong leadership on the part of the President and strong leadership which carries the day in the Congress.

Q. To follow on that, Mr. Secretary, the President is perceived as somewhat weakened politically now—his standing in the polls is low. Mr. Brezhnev's health is poor. What do you expect to be able to achieve at this summit?

Secretary VANCE. We expect to achieve several things. First, the signing of the SALT treaty, which is a matter of paramount importance. In addition to that, I hope that we will be able to make further progress in giving impetus to other arms control matters and negotiations which have been ongoing. This would be another important step forward. Thirdly, it will give us a chance to discuss with the Soviets a number of issues on which we have different perspectives, different views; hopefully, out of this can come a better understanding of the views and positions of the two parties. And, fourthly, I believe it will give a very good opportunity for the two leaders of our two countries to meet with each other, to establish a channel of direct communications. This is terribly important, I believe, in the conduct of our foreign policy, particularly with two nations as great and powerful as the United States and the Soviet Union.

* * *

Q. Mr. Secretary, Senator Jackson [on 12 June 1979] said that he feared the administration and previous administrations might be following a policy of appeasement toward the Soviet Union. I wonder if you would like to comment on that?

Secretary VANCE. Yes, I would like very much to comment on that. First, let me say that the SALT treaty deserves serious and reasoned debate. I hope very much that we can conduct this debate responsibly and relatively free of emotionally charged rhetoric. I believe that is what the American people expect, and that is what we all want.

Now, to describe the policy of the administration and the policy pursued by President Nixon, President Ford, and Secretary Kissinger as appeasement is, in my judgment, misguided and simply wrong. We have no delusions about the fundamental differences which exist between ourselves and the Soviet Union; neither did the prior administrations.

We are maintaining and strengthening our military defense. We are engaged in a broad modernization of our strategic forces, and, with our NATO allies, we are vastly improving our NATO defense, and I think we have reversed the pattern as far as defense spending is concerned by going toward a 3 percent annual increase.

What I think Senator Jackson really is talking about is the whole

process of arms control, and he is questioning whether or not arms control makes sense.

Now, there is never going to be an agreement in which you are not going to have to have negotiations and bargaining. No one can get everything that one wants in a negotiation. The question is: At the end of the road during such a negotiation, what kind of an agreement or treaty is it?

I have no hesitation at all in saying that this is a good agreement. It is a sound agreement. It is an agreement which lessens the threat to the United States and enhances our security and the security of our allies. I think it is important for all of us to recognize in today's world that . . . it would be foolhardy for us to embark upon an all-out arms race.

Let me say, finally, that I believe that strength in our military forces and arms control are compatible. They are not in contradiction with each other.

*   *   *

Q. Mr. Secretary, what point do you most want to get across to them at the summit, to the Russians?

Secretary Vance. One of the important points is that détente is a two-way street and that we both must recognize it as such. Another is that it is essential that we find ways to regulate the arms competition, or potential arms competition between us, so that we can have a more stable and safer world.

Q. Mr. Secretary, you have been careful not to mention, it seems, the possibility of improving trade relations with the Soviets as a result of this summit. Is it the case that your negotiations with Ambassador Dobrynin have not produced a satisfactory resolution to the problem of the Jackson-Vanik Amendment?

Secretary Vance. Trade is important. We obviously will be discussing trade. What will come out of that discussion, I do not know. But I do not want to minimize at all the importance of trade. I hope very much that we will be able to expand trade with the Soviet Union in the same way that I hope we will be able to expand trade with the People's Republic of China. I think this will be good for our country and for those two countries, if we are able to make progress in those areas. But I cannot at this point predict what the result will be of our discussion in Vienna.

Q. Mr. Secretary, the Soviets seem to find the President's decision to go ahead with an MX missile at some variance with the idea of an arms control agreement, and they have said so in commentaries in the past several days. Do you expect the President or yourself to discuss

this matter and the rationale of it, and particularly the basing mode of a possible missile, with the Russians in Vienna?

Secretary VANCE. We would be very happy to discuss with the Soviets any questions like that which they would care to raise.

The President has made the decision to go ahead with the MX missile and he has indicated that its deployment will be in a mobile mode and a verifiable mode. The acquisition of that system, in my judgment, will lead to greater stability, contrary to what some are suggesting, because it will give us a more survivable leg of the Triad insofar as land-based systems are concerned.

So that I think that the step to move forward in that direction is a sound step; it is a step which is consistent with arms control; and it is also consistent with giving us a defense posture which is strong and survivable.

Treaty on the Limitation of Strategic Offensive Arms, 18 June 1979

The United States of America and the Union of Soviet Socialist Republics, hereinafter referred to as the Parties,

Conscious that nuclear war would have devastating consequences for all mankind,

Proceeding from the Basic Principles of Relations Between the United States of America and the Union of Soviet Socialist Republics of May 29, 1972,

Attaching particular significance to the limitation of strategic arms and determined to continue their efforts begun with the Treaty on the Limitation of Anti-Ballistic Missile Systems and the Interim Agreement on Certain Measures with Respect to the Limitation of Strategic Offensive Arms, of May 26, 1972,

Convinced that the additional measures limiting strategic offensive arms provided for in this Treaty will contribute to the improvement of relations between the Parties, help to reduce the risk of outbreak of nuclear war and strengthen international peace and security,

Mindful of their obligations under Article VI of the Treaty on the Non-Proliferation of Nuclear Weapons,

Guided by the principle of equality and equal security,

Recognizing that the strengthening of strategic stability meets the interests of the Parties and the interests of international security,

Reaffirming their desire to take measures for the further limitation and for the further reduction of strategic arms, having in mind the goal of achieving general and complete disarmament,

Declaring their intention to undertake in the near future negotia-

---

SOURCE: Treaty Between the United States of America and the Union of Soviet Socialist Republics on the Limitation of Strategic Offensive Arms. Department of State, 18 June 1979.

NOTE: The text of the SALT II Treaty and Protocol is accompanied by a set of Agreed Statements and Common Understandings, signed by President Carter and General Secretary Brezhnev on 18 June 1979, which are prefaced as follows:

"In connection with the Treaty Between the United States of America and the Union of Soviet Socialist Republics on the Limitation of Strategic Offensive Arms, the Parties have agreed on the following Agreed Statements and Common Understandings undertaken on behalf of the Government of the United States of America and the Government of the Union of Soviet Socialist Republics."

As an aid to the reader, the Agreed Statements and Common Understandings are presented immediately following the paragraph of the Treaty or Protocol to which they relate. For example, following Paragraph I of Article II of the Treaty are the Agreed Statements and the Common Understandings associated with that paragraph. The text of the Treaty and Protocol are in italics.

tions further to limit and further to reduce strategic offensive arms,
Have agreed as follows:

Article I

Each Party undertakes, in accordance with the provisions of this Treaty, to limit strategic offensive arms quantitatively and qualitatively, to exercise restraint in the development of new types of strategic offensive arms, and to adopt other measures provided for in this Treaty.

Article II

For the purposes of this Treaty:

1. Intercontinental ballistic missile (ICBM) launchers are land-based launchers of ballistic missiles capable of a range in excess of the shortest distance between the northeastern border of the continental part of the territory of the United States of America and the northwestern border of the continental part of the territory of the Union of Soviet Socialist Republics, that is, a range in excess of 5,500 kilometers.

First Agreed Statement. The term "intercontinental ballistic missile launchers," as defined in paragraph 1 of Article II of the Treaty, includes all launchers which have been developed and tested for launching ICBMS. If a launcher has been developed and tested for launching an ICBM, all launchers of that type shall be considered to have been developed and tested for launching ICBMS.

First Common Understanding. If a launcher contains or launches an ICBM, that launcher shall be considered to have been developed and tested for launching ICBMS.

Second Common Understanding. If a launcher has been developed and tested for launching an ICBM, all launchers of that type, except for ICBM test and training launchers, shall be included in the aggregate numbers of strategic offensive arms provided for in Article III of the Treaty, pursuant to the provisions of Article VI of the Treaty.

Third Common Understanding. The one hundred and seventy-seven former Atlas and Titan I ICBM launchers of the United States of America, which are no longer operational and are partially dismantled, shall not be considered as subject to the limitations provided for in the Treaty.

Second Agreed Statement. After the date on which the Protocol ceases to be in force, mobile ICBM launchers shall be subject to the relevant limitations provided for in the Treaty which are applicable to ICBM launchers, unless the Parties agree that mobile ICBM launchers shall not be deployed after that date.

2. Submarine-launched ballistic missile (SLBM) launchers are launchers of ballistic missiles installed on any nuclear-powered submarine or launchers of modern ballistic missiles installed on any submarine, regardless of its type.

Agreed Statement. Modern submarine-launched ballistic missiles are: for the United States of America, missiles installed in all nuclear-powered submarines; for the Union of Soviet Socialist Republics, missiles of the type installed in nuclear-powered submarines made operational since 1965; and for both Parties, submarine-launched ballistic missiles first flight-tested since 1965 and installed in any submarine, regardless of its type.

3. Heavy bombers are considered to be:

(a) currently, for the United States of America, bombers of the B-52 and B-1 types, and for the Union of Soviet Socialist Republics, bombers of the Tupolev-95 and Myasishchev types;

(b) in the future, types of bombers which can carry out the mission of a heavy bomber in a manner similar or superior to that of bombers listed in subparagraph (a) above;

(c) types of bombers equipped for cruise missiles capable of a range in excess of 600 kilometers; and

(d) types of bombers equipped for ASBMs.

First Agreed Statement. The term "bombers," as used in paragraph 3 of Article II and other provisions of the Treaty, means airplanes of types initially constructed to be equipped for bombs or missiles.

Second Agreed Statement. The Parties shall notify each other on a case-by-case basis in the Standing Consultative Commission of inclusion of types of bombers as heavy bombers pursuant to the provisions of paragraph 3 of Article II of the Treaty; in this connection the Parties shall hold consultations, as appropriate, consistent with the provisions of paragraph 2 of Article XVII of the Treaty.

Third Agreed Statement. The criteria the Parties shall use to make case-by-case determinations of which types of bombers in the future can carry out the mission of a heavy bomber in a manner similar or superior to that of current heavy bombers, as referred to in subparagraph 3(b) of Article II of the Treaty, shall be agreed upon in the Standing Consultative Commission.

Fourth Agreed Statement. Having agreed that every bomber of a type included in paragraph 3 of Article II of the Treaty is to be considered a heavy bomber, the Parties further agree that:

(a) airplanes which otherwise would be bombers of a heavy bomber type shall not be considered to be bombers of a heavy bomber

type if they have functionally related observable differences which indicate that they cannot perform the mission of a heavy bomber;

(b) airplanes which otherwise would be bombers of a type equipped for cruise missiles capable of a range in excess of 600 kilometers shall not be considered to be bombers of a type equipped for cruise missiles capable of a range in excess of 600 kilometers if they have functionally related observable differences which indicate that they cannot perform the mission of a bomber equipped for cruise missiles capable of a range in excess of 600 kilometers, except that heavy bombers of current types, as designated in subparagraph 3(a) of Article II of the Treaty, which otherwise would be of a type equipped for cruise missiles capable of a range in excess of 600 kilometers shall not be considered to be heavy bombers of a type equipped for cruise missiles capable of a range in excess of 600 kilometers if they are distinguishable on the basis of externally observable differences from heavy bombers of a type equipped for cruise missiles capable of a range in excess of 600 kilometers; and

(c) airplanes which otherwise would be bombers of a type equipped for ASBMS shall not be considered to be bombers of a type equipped for ASBMS if they have functionally related observable differences which indicate that they cannot perform the mission of a bomber equipped for ASBMS, except that heavy bombers of current types, as designated in subparagraph 3(a) of Article II of the Treaty, which otherwise would be of a type equipped for ASBMS shall not be considered to be heavy bombers of a type equipped for ASBMS if they are distinguishable on the basis of externally observable differences from heavy bombers of a type equipped for ASBMS.

First Common Understanding. Functionally related observable differences are differences in the observable features of airplanes which indicate whether or not these airplanes can perform the mission of a heavy bomber, or whether or not they can perform the mission of a bomber equipped for cruise missiles capable of a range in excess of 600 kilometers or whether or not they can perform the mission of a bomber equipped for ASBMS. Functionally related observable differences shall be verifiable by national technical means. To this end, the Parties may take, as appropriate, cooperative measures contributing to the effectiveness of verification by national technical means.

Fifth Agreed Statement. Tupolev-142 airplanes in their current configuration, that is, in the configuration for anti-submarine warfare, are considered to be airplanes of a type different from types of heavy bombers referred to in subparagraph 3(a) of Article II of the Treaty and not subject to the Fourth Agreed Statement to paragraph 3 of Article II of the Treaty. This Agreed Statement does not preclude

improvement of Tupolev-142 airplanes as an anti-submarine system, and does not prejudice or set a precedent for designation in the future of types of airplanes as heavy bombers pursuant to subparagraph 3(b) of Article II of the Treaty or for application of the Fourth Agreed Statement to paragraph 3 of Article II of the Treaty to such airplanes.

Second Common Understanding. Not later than six months after entry into force of the Treaty the Union of Soviet Socialist Republics will give its thirty-one Myasishchev airplanes used as tankers in existence as of the date of signature of the Treaty functionally related observable differences which indicate that they cannot perform the mission of a heavy bomber.

Third Common Understanding. The designations by the United States of America and by the Union of Soviet Socialist Republics for heavy bombers referred to in subparagraph 3(a) of Article II of the Treaty correspond in the following manner:

> Heavy bombers of the types designated by the United States of America as the B-52 and the B-1 are known to the Union of Soviet Socialist Republics by the same designations;
>
> Heavy bombers of the type designated by the Union of Soviet Socialist Republics as the Tupolev-95 are known to the United States of America as heavy bombers of the Bear type; and
>
> Heavy bombers of the type designated by the Union of Soviet Socialist Republics as the Myasishchev are known to the United States of America as heavy bombers of the Bison type.

4. Air-to-surface ballistic missiles (ASBMs) are any such missiles capable of a range in excess of 600 kilometers and installed in an aircraft or on its external mountings.

5. Launchers of ICBMs and SLBMs equipped with multiple independently targetable reentry vehicles (MIRVs) are launchers of the types developed and tested for launching ICBMs or SLBMs equipped with MIRVs.

First Agreed Statement. If a launcher has been developed and tested for launching an ICBM or an SLBM equipped with MIRVS, all launchers of that type shall be considered to have been developed and tested for launching ICBMS or SLBMS equipped with MIRVS.

First Common Understanding. If a launcher contains or launches an ICBM or an SLBM equipped with MIRVS, that launcher shall be considered to have been developed and tested for launching ICBMS or SLBMS equipped with MIRVS.

Second Common Understanding. If a launcher has been developed and tested for launching an ICBM or an SLBM equipped with MIRVS, all

launchers of that type, except for ICBM and SLBM test and training launchers, shall be included in the corresponding aggregate numbers provided for in Article V of the Treaty, pursuant to the provisions of Article VI of the Treaty.

Second Agreed Statement. ICBMS and SLBMS equipped with MIRVS are ICBMS and SLBMS of the types which have been flight-tested with two or more independently targetable reentry vehicles, regardless of whether or not they have also been flight-tested with a single reentry vehicle or with multiple reentry vehicles which are not independently targetable. As of the date of signature of the Treaty, such ICBMS and SLBMS are: for the United States of America, Minuteman III ICBMS, Poseidon C-3 SLBMS, and Trident C-4 SLBMS; and for the Union of Soviet Socialist Republics, RS-16, RS-18, RS-20 ICBMS and RSM-50 SLBMS.

Each Party will notify the other Party in the Standing Consultative Commission on a case-by-case basis of the designation of the one new type of light ICBM, if equipped with MIRVS, permitted pursuant to paragraph 9 of Article IV of the Treaty when first flight-tested; of designations of additional types of SLBMS equipped with MIRVS when first installed on a submarine; and of designations of types of ASBMS equipped with MIRVS when first flight-tested.

Third Common Understanding. The designations by the United States of America and by the Union of Soviet Socialist Republics for ICBMS and SLBMS equipped with MIRVS correspond in the following manner:

> Missiles of the type designated by the United States of America as the Minuteman III and known to the Union of Soviet Socialist Republics by the same designation, a light ICBM that has been flight-tested with multiple independently targetable reentry vehicles;
>
> Missiles of the type designated by the United States of America as the Poseidon C-3 and known to the Union of Soviet Socialist Republics by the same designation, an SLBM that was first flight-tested in 1968 and that has been flight-tested with multiple independently targetable reentry vehicles;
>
> Missiles of the type designated by the United States of America as the Trident C-4 and known to the Union of Soviet Socialist Republics by the same designation, an SLBM that was first flight-tested in 1977 and that has been flight-tested with multiple independently targetable reentry vehicles;
>
> Missiles of the type designated by the Union of Soviet Socialist Republics as the RS-16 and known to the United States of America as the SS-17, a light ICBM that has been flight-tested with

a single reentry vehicle and with multiple independently targetable reentry vehicles;

Missiles of the type designated by the Union of Soviet Socialist Republics as the RS-18 and known to the United States of America as the SS-19, the heaviest in terms of launch-weight and throw-weight of light ICBMs, which has been flight-tested with a single reentry vehicle and with multiple independently targetable reentry vehicles;

Missiles of the type designated by the Union of Soviet Socialist Republics as the RS-20 and known to the United States of America as the SS-18, the heaviest in terms of launch-weight and throw-weight of heavy ICBMs, which has been flight-tested with a single reentry vehicle and with multiple independently targetable reentry vehicles;

Missiles of the type designated by the Union of Soviet Socialist Republics as the RSM-50 and known to the United States of America as the SS-N-18, an SLBM that has been flight-tested with a single reentry vehicle and with multiple independently targetable reentry vehicles.

Third Agreed Statement. Reentry vehicles are independently targetable:

(a) if, after separation from the booster, maneuvering and targeting of the reentry vehicles to separate aim points along trajectories which are unrelated to each other are accomplished by means of devices which are installed in a self-contained dispensing mechanism or on the reentry vehicles, and which are based on the use of electronic or other computers in combination with devices using jet engines, including rocket engines, or aerodynamic systems;

(b) if maneuvering and targeting of the reentry vehicles to separate aim points along trajectories which are unrelated to each other are accomplished by means of other devices which may be developed in the future.

Fourth Common Understanding. For the purposes of this Treaty, all ICBM launchers in the Derazhnya and Pervomaysk areas in the Union of Soviet Socialist Republics are included in the aggregate numbers provided for in Article V of the Treaty.

Fifth Common Understanding. If ICBM or SLBM launchers are converted, constructed or undergo significant changes to their principal observable structural design features after entry into force of the Treaty, any such launchers which are launchers of missiles equipped with MIRVs shall be distinguishable from launchers of missiles not equipped with MIRVs, and any such launchers which are launchers of missiles not equipped with MIRVs shall be distinguishable from launch-

ers of missiles equipped with MIRVs, on the basis of externally observable design features of the launchers. Submarines with launchers of SLBMs equipped with MIRVs shall be distinguishable from submarines with launchers of SLBMs not equipped with MIRVs on the basis of externally observable design features of the submarines.

This Common Understanding does not require changes to launcher conversion or construction programs, or to programs including significant changes to the principal observable structural design features of launchers, underway as of the date of signature of the Treaty.

6. ASBMs equipped with MIRVs are ASBMs of the types which have been flight-tested with MIRVs.

First Agreed Statement. ASBMS of the types which have been flight-tested with MIRVS are all ASBMS of the types which have been flight-tested with two or more independently targetable reentry vehicles, regardless of whether or not they have also been flight-tested with a single reentry vehicle or with multiple reentry vehicles which are not independently targetable.

Second Agreed Statement. Reentry vehicles are independently targetable:

(a) if, after separation from the booster, maneuvering and targeting of the reentry vehicles to separate aim points along trajectories which are unrelated to each other are accomplished by means of devices which are installed in a self-contained dispensing mechanism or on the reentry vehicles, and which are based on the use of electronic or other computers in combination with devices using jet engines, including rocket engines, or aerodynamic systems;

(b) if maneuvering and targeting of the reentry vehicles to separate aim points along trajectories which are unrelated to each other are accomplished by means of other devices which may be developed in the future.

7. Heavy ICBMs are ICBMs which have a launch-weight greater or a throw-weight greater than that of the heaviest, in terms of either launch-weight or throw-weight, respectively, of the light ICBMs deployed by either Party as of the date of signature of this Treaty.

First Agreed Statement. The launch-weight of an ICBM is the weight of the fully loaded missile itself at the time of launch.

Second Agreed Statement. The throw-weight of an ICBM is the sum of the weight of:

(a) its reentry vehicle or reentry vehicles;

(b) any self-contained dispensing mechanisms or other appropriate devices for targeting one reentry vehicle, or for releasing or for dispensing and targeting two or more reentry vehicles; and

(c) its penetration aids, including devices for their release.

Common Understanding. The term "other appropriate devices," as used in the definition of the throw-weight of an ICBM in the Second Agreed Statement to paragraph 7 of Article II of the Treaty, means any devices for dispensing and targeting two or more reentry vehicles; and any devices for releasing two or more reentry vehicles or for targeting one reentry vehicle, which cannot provide their reentry vehicles or reentry vehicle with additional velocity of more than 1,000 meters per second.

8. Cruise missiles are unmanned, self-propelled, guided, weapon-delivery vehicles which sustain flight through the use of aerodynamic lift over most of their flight path and which are flight-tested from or deployed on aircraft, that is, air-launched cruise missiles, or such vehicles which are referred to as cruise missiles in subparagraph 1(b) of Article IX.

First Agreed Statement. If a cruise missile is capable of a range in excess of 600 kilometers, all cruise missiles of that type shall be considered to be cruise missiles capable of a range in excess of 600 kilometers.

First Common Understanding. If a cruise missile has been flight-tested to a range in excess of 600 kilometers, it shall be considered to be a cruise missile capable of a range in excess of 600 kilometers.

Second Common Understanding. Cruise missiles not capable of a range in excess of 600 kilometers shall not be considered to be of a type capable of a range in excess of 600 kilometers if they are distinguishable on the basis of externally observable design features from cruise missiles of types capable of a range in excess of 600 kilometers.

Second Agreed Statement. The range of which a cruise missile is capable is the maximum distance which can be covered by the missile in its standard design mode flying until fuel exhaustion, determined by projecting its flight path onto the Earth's sphere from the point of launch to the point of impact.

Third Agreed Statement. If an unmanned, self-propelled, guided vehicle which sustains flight through the use of aerodynamic lift over most of its flight path has been flight-tested or deployed for weapon

delivery, all vehicles of that type shall be considered to be weapon-delivery vehicles.

Third Common Understanding. Unmanned, self-propelled, guided vehicles which sustain flight through the use of aerodynamic lift over most of their flight path and are not weapon-delivery vehicles, that is, unarmed, pilotless, guided vehicles, shall not be considered to be cruise missiles if such vehicles are distinguishable from cruise missiles on the basis of externally observable design features.

Fourth Common Understanding. Neither Party shall convert unarmed, pilotless, guided vehicles into cruise missiles capable of a range in excess of 600 kilometers, nor shall either Party convert cruise missiles capable of a range in excess of 600 kilometers into unarmed, pilotless, guided vehicles.

Fifth Common Understanding. Neither Party has plans during the term of the Treaty to flight-test from or deploy on aircraft unarmed, pilotless, guided vehicles which are capable of a range in excess of 600 kilometers. In the future, should a Party have such plans, that Party will provide notification thereof to the other Party well in advance of such flight-testing or deployment. This Common Understanding does not apply to target drones.

Article III

1. Upon entry into force of this Treaty, each Party undertakes to limit ICBM launchers, SLBM launchers, heavy bombers, and ASBMs to an aggregate number not to exceed 2,400.

2. Each Party undertakes to limit, from January 1, 1981, strategic offensive arms referred to in paragraph 1 of this Article to an aggregate number not to exceed 2,250, and to initiate reductions of those arms which as of that date would be in excess of this aggregate number.

3. Within the aggregate numbers provided for in paragraphs 1 and 2 of this Article and subject to the provisions of this Treaty, each Party has the right to determine the composition of these aggregates.

4. For each bomber of a type equipped for ASBMs, the aggregate numbers provided for in paragraphs 1 and 2 of this Article shall include the maximum number of such missiles for which a bomber of that type is equipped for one operational mission.

5. A heavy bomber equipped only for ASBMs shall not itself be included in the aggregate numbers provided for in paragraphs 1 and 2 of this Article.

6. Reductions of the numbers of strategic offensive arms required to comply with the provisions of paragraphs 1 and 2 of this Article shall be carried out as provided for in Article XI.

Article IV

1. Each Party undertakes not to start construction of additional fixed ICBM launchers.

2. Each Party undertakes not to relocate fixed ICBM launchers.

3. Each Party undertakes not to convert launchers of light ICBMs, or of ICBMs of older types deployed prior to 1964, into launchers of heavy ICBMs of types deployed after that time.

4. Each Party undertakes in the process of modernization and replacement of ICBM silo launchers not to increase the original internal volume of an ICBM silo launcher by more than thirty-two percent. Within this limit each Party has the right to determine whether such an increase will be made through an increase in the original diameter or in the original depth of an ICBM silo launcher, or in both of these dimensions.

Agreed Statement. The word "original" in paragraph 4 of Article IV of the Treaty refers to the internal dimensions of an ICBM silo launcher, including its internal volume, as of May 26, 1972, or as of the date on which such launcher becomes operational, whichever is later.

Common Understanding. The obligations provided for in paragraph 4 of Article IV of the Treaty and in the Agreed Statement thereto mean that the original diameter or the original depth of an ICBM silo launcher may not be increased by an amount greater than that which would result in an increase in the original internal volume of the ICBM silo launcher by thirty-two percent solely through an increase in one of these dimensions.

5. Each Party undertakes:

(a) not to supply ICBM launcher deployment areas with intercontinental ballistic missiles in excess of a number consistent with normal deployment, maintenance, training, and replacement requirements;

(b) not to provide storage facilities for or to store ICBMs in excess of normal deployment requirements at launch sites of ICBM launchers;

(c) not to develop, test, or deploy systems for rapid reload of ICBM launchers.

Agreed Statement. The term "normal deployment requirements," as used in paragraph 5 of Article IV of the Treaty, means the deployment of one missile at each ICBM launcher.

6. Subject to the provisions of this Treaty, each Party undertakes not to have under construction at any time strategic offensive arms referred to in paragraph 1 of Article III in excess of numbers consistent with a normal construction schedule.

Common Understanding. A normal construction schedule, in paragraph 6 of Article IV of the Treaty, is understood to be one consistent with the past or present construction practices of each Party.

7. Each Party undertakes not to develop, test, or deploy ICBMs which have a launch-weight greater or a throw-weight greater than that of the heaviest, in terms of either launch-weight or throw-weight, respectively, of the heavy ICBMs deployed by either Party as of the date of signature of this Treaty.

First Agreed Statement. The launch-weight of an ICBM is the weight of the fully loaded missile itself at the time of launch.

Second Agreed Statement. The throw-weight of an ICBM is the sum of the weight of:

(a) its reentry vehicle or reentry vehicles;

(b) any self-contained dispensing mechanisms or other appropriate devices for targeting one reentry vehicle, or for releasing or for dispensing and targeting two or more reentry vehicles; and

(c) its penetration aids, including devices for their release.

Common Understanding. The term "other appropriate devices," as used in the definition of the throw-weight of an ICBM in the Second Agreed Statement to paragraph 7 of Article IV of the Treaty, means any devices for dispensing and targeting two or more reentry vehicles; and any devices for releasing two or more reentry vehicles or for targeting one reentry vehicle, which cannot provide their reentry vehicles or reentry vehicle with additional velocity of more than 1,000 meters per second.

8. Each Party undertakes not to convert land-based launchers of ballistic missiles which are not ICBMs into launchers for launching ICBMs, and not to test them for this purpose.

Common Understanding. During the term of the Treaty, the Union of Soviet Socialist Republics will not produce, test, or deploy ICBMs of the type designated by the Union of Soviet Socialist Republics as the RS-14 and known to the United States of America as the SS-16, a light ICBM first flight-tested after 1970 and flight-tested only

with a single reentry vehicle; this Common Understanding also means that the Union of Soviet Socialist Republics will not produce the third stage of that missile, the reentry vehicle of that missile, or the appropriate device for targeting the reentry vehicle of that missile.

9. Each Party undertakes not to flight-test or deploy new types of ICBMs, that is, types of ICBMs not flight-tested as of May 1, 1979, except that each Party may flight-test and deploy one new type of light ICBM.

First Agreed Statement. The term "new types of ICBMS," as used in paragraph 9 of Article IV of the Treaty, refers to any ICBM which is different from those ICBMS flight-tested as of May 1, 1979 in any one or more of the following respects:

(a) the number of stages, the length, the largest diameter, the launch-weight, or the throw-weight, of the missile;

(b) the type of propellant (that is, liquid or solid) of any of its stages.

First Common Understanding. As used in the First Agreed Statement to paragraph 9 of Article IV of the Treaty, the term "different," referring to the length, the diameter, the launch-weight, and the throw-weight, of the missile, means a difference in excess of five percent.

Second Agreed Statement. Every ICBM of the one new type of light ICBM permitted to each Party pursuant to paragraph 9 of Article IV of the Treaty shall have the same number of stages and the same type of propellant (that is, liquid or solid) of each stage as the first ICBM of the one new type of light ICBM launched by that Party. In addition, after the twenty-fifth launch of an ICBM of that type, or after the last launch before deployment begins of ICBMS of that type, whichever occurs earlier, ICBMS of the one new type of light ICBM permitted to that Party shall not be different in any one or more of the following respects: the length, the largest diameter, the launch-weight, or the throw-weight, of the missile.

A Party which launches ICBMS of the one new type of light ICBM permitted pursuant to paragraph 9 of Article IV of the Treaty shall promptly notify the other Party of the date of the first launch and of the date of either the twenty-fifth or the last launch before deployment begins of ICBMS of that type, whichever occurs earlier.

Second Common Understanding. As used in the Second Agreed Statement to paragraph 9 of Article IV of the Treaty, the term "different," referring to the length, the diameter, the launch-weight, and the throw-weight, of the missile, means a difference in excess of five per-

cent from the value established for each of the above parameters as of the twenty-fifth launch or as of the last launch before deployment begins, whichever occurs earlier. The values demonstrated in each of the above parameters during the last twelve of the twenty-five launches or during the last twelve launches before deployment begins, whichever twelve launches occur earlier, shall not vary by more than ten percent from any other of the corresponding values demonstrated during those twelve launches.

Third Common Understanding. The limitations with respect to launch-weight and throw-weight, provided for in the First Agreed Statement and the First Common Understanding to paragraph 9 of Article IV of the Treaty, do not preclude the flight-testing or the deployment of ICBMs with fewer reentry vehicles, or fewer penetration aids, or both, than the maximum number of reentry vehicles and the maximum number of penetration aids with which ICBMs of that type have been flight-tested as of May 1, 1979, even if this results in a decrease in launch-weight or in throw-weight in excess of five percent.

In addition to the aforementioned cases, those limitations do not preclude a decrease in launch-weight or in throw-weight in excess of five percent, in the case of the flight-testing or the deployment of ICBMs with a lesser quantity of propellant, including the propellant of a self-contained dispensing mechanism or other appropriate device, than the maximum quantity of propellant, including the propellant of a self-contained dispensing mechanism or other appropriate device, with which ICBMs of that type have been flight-tested as of May 1, 1979, provided that such an ICBM is at the same time flight-tested or deployed with fewer reentry vehicles, or fewer penetration aids, or both, than the maximum number of reentry vehicles and the maximum number of penetration aids with which ICBMs of that type have been flight-tested as of May 1, 1979, and the decrease in launch-weight and throw-weight in such cases results only from the reduction in the number of reentry vehicles, or penetration aids, or both, and the reduction in the quantity of propellant.

Fourth Common Understanding. The limitations with respect to launch-weight and throw-weight, provided for in the Second Agreed Statement and the Second Common Understanding to paragraph 9 of Article IV of the Treaty, do not preclude the flight-testing or the deployment of ICBMs of the one new type of light ICBM permitted to each Party pursuant to paragraph 9 of Article IV of the Treaty with fewer reentry vehicles, or fewer penetration aids, or both, than the maximum number of reentry vehicles and the maximum number of penetration aids with which ICBMs of that type have been flight-tested,

even if this results in a decrease in launch-weight or in throw-weight in excess of five percent.

In addition to the aforementioned cases, those limitations do not preclude a decrease in launch-weight or in throw-weight in excess of five percent, in the case of the flight-testing or the deployment of ICBMS of that type with a lesser quantity of propellant, including the propellant of a self-contained dispensing mechanism or other appropriate device, than the maximum quantity of propellant, including the propellant of a self-contained dispensing mechanism or other appropriate device, with which ICBMS of that type have been flight-tested, provided that such an ICBM is at the same time flight-tested or deployed with fewer reentry vehicles, or fewer penetration aids, or both, than the maximum number of reentry vehicles and the maximum number of penetration aids with which ICBMS of that type have been flight-tested, and the decrease in launch-weight and throw-weight in such cases results only from the reduction in the number of reentry vehicles, or penetration aids, or both, and the reduction in the quantity of propellant.

10. Each Party undertakes not to flight-test or deploy ICBMs of a type flight-tested as of May 1, 1979 with a number of reentry vehicles greater than the maximum number of reentry vehicles with which an ICBM of that type has been flight-tested as of that date.

First Agreed Statement. The following types of ICBMS and SLBMS equipped with MIRVS have been flight-tested with the maximum number of reentry vehicles set forth below:

For the United States of America

ICBMS of the Minuteman III type	—	seven reentry vehicles;
SLBMS of the Poseidon C-3 type	—	fourteen reentry vehicles;
SLBMS of the Trident C-4 type	—	seven reentry vehicles;

For the Union of Soviet Socialist Republics

ICBMS of the RS-16 type	—	four reentry vehicles;
ICBMS of the RS-18 type	—	six reentry vehicles;
ICBMS of the RS-20 type	—	ten reentry vehicles;
SLBMS of the RSM-50 type	—	seven reentry vehicles.

Common Understanding. Minuteman III ICBMS of the United States of America have been deployed with no more than three reentry vehicles. During the term of the Treaty, the United States of

America has no plans to and will not flight-test or deploy missiles of this type with more than three reentry vehicles.

Second Agreed Statement. During the flight-testing of any ICBM, SLBM, or ASBM after May 1, 1979 the number of procedures for releasing or for dispensing may not exceed the maximum number of reentry vehicles established for missiles of corresponding types as provided for in paragraphs 10, 11, 12, and 13 of Article IV of the Treaty. In this Agreed Statement "procedures for releasing or for dispensing" are understood to mean maneuvers of a missile associated with targeting and releasing or dispensing its reentry vehicles to aim points, whether or not a reentry vehicle is actually released or dispensed. Procedures for releasing anti-missile defense penetration aids will not be considered to be procedures for releasing or for dispensing a reentry vehicle so long as the procedures for releasing anti-missile defense penetration aids differ from those for releasing or for dispensing reentry vehicles.

Third Agreed Statement. Each Party undertakes:

(a) not to flight-test or deploy ICBMs equipped with multiple reentry vehicles, of a type flight-tested as of May 1, 1979, with reentry vehicles the weight of any of which is less than the weight of the lightest of those reentry vehicles with which an ICBM of that type has been flight-tested as of that date;

(b) not to flight-test or deploy ICBMs equipped with a single reentry vehicle and without an appropriate device for targeting a reentry vehicle, of a type flight-tested as of May 1, 1979, with a reentry vehicle the weight of which is less than the weight of the lightest reentry vehicle on an ICBM of a type equipped with MIRVs and flight-tested by that Party as of May 1, 1979; and

(c) not to flight-test or deploy ICBMs equipped with a single reentry vehicle and with an appropriate device for targeting a reentry vehicle, of a type flight-tested as of May 1, 1979, with a reentry vehicle the weight of which is less than fifty percent of the throw-weight of that ICBM.

11. Each Party undertakes not to flight-test or deploy ICBMs of the one new type permitted pursuant to paragraph 9 of this Article with a number of reentry vehicles greater than the maximum number of reentry vehicles with which an ICBM of either Party has been flight-tested as of May 1, 1979, that is, ten.

First Agreed Statement. Each Party undertakes not to flight-test or deploy the one new type of light ICBM permitted to each Party pursuant to paragraph 9 of Article IV of the Treaty with a number of

reentry vehicles greater than the maximum number of reentry vehicles with which an ICBM of that type has been flight-tested as of the twenty-fifth launch or the last launch before deployment begins of ICBMS of that type, whichever occurs earlier.

Second Agreed Statement. During the flight-testing of any ICBM, SLBM, or ASBM after May 1, 1979 the number of procedures for releasing or for dispensing may not exceed the maximum number of reentry vehicles established for missiles of corresponding types as provided for in paragraphs 10, 11, 12, and 13 of Article IV of the Treaty. In this Agreed Statement "procedures for releasing or for dispensing" are understood to mean maneuvers of a missile associated with targeting and releasing or dispensing its reentry vehicles to aim points, whether or not a reentry vehicle is actually released or dispensed. Procedures for releasing anti-missile defense penetration aids will not be considered to be procedures for releasing or for dispensing a reentry vehicle so long as the procedures for releasing anti-missile defense penetration aids differ from those for releasing or for dispensing reentry vehicles.

12. Each Party undertakes not to flight-test or deploy SLBMs with a number of reentry vehicles greater than the maximum number of reentry vehicles with which an SLBM of either Party has been flight-tested as of May 1, 1979, that is, fourteen.

First Agreed Statement. The following types of ICBMS and SLBMS equipped with MIRVS have been flight-tested with the maximum number of reentry vehicles set forth below:

For the United States of America

ICBMS of the Minuteman III type	—	seven reentry vehicles;
SLBMS of the Poseidon C-3 type	—	fourteen reentry vehicles;
SLBMS of the Trident C-4 type	—	seven reentry vehicles;

For the Union of Soviet Socialist Republics

ICBMS of the RS-16 type	—	four reentry vehicles;
ICBMS of the RS-18 type	—	six reentry vehicles;
ICBMS of the RS-20 type	—	ten reentry vehicles;
SLBMS of the RSM-50 type	—	seven reentry vehicles.

Second Agreed Statement. During the flight-testing of any ICBM, SLBM, or ASBM after May 1, 1979 the number of procedures for releasing or for dispensing may not exceed the maximum number of reentry vehicles established for missiles of corresponding types as provided for in paragraphs 10, 11, 12, and 13 of Article IV of the Treaty. In

this Agreed Statement "procedures for releasing or for dispensing" are understood to mean maneuvers of a missile associated with targeting and releasing or dispensing its reentry vehicles to aim points, whether or not a reentry vehicle is actually released or dispensed. Procedures for releasing anti-missile defense penetration aids will not be considered to be procedures for releasing or for dispensing a reentry vehicle so long as the procedures for releasing anti-missile defense penetration aids differ from those for releasing or for dispensing reentry vehicles.

13. Each Party undertakes not to flight-test or deploy ASBMs with a number of reentry vehicles greater than the maximum number of reentry vehicles with which an ICBM of either Party has been flight-tested as of May 1, 1979, that is, ten.

Agreed Statement. During the flight-testing of any ICBM, SLBM, or ASBM after May 1, 1979 the number of procedures for releasing or for dispensing may not exceed the maximum number of reentry vehicles established for missiles of corresponding types as provided for in paragraphs 10, 11, 12, and 13 of Article IV of the Treaty. In this Agreed Statement "procedures for releasing or for dispensing" are understood to mean maneuvers of a missile associated with targeting and releasing or dispensing its reentry vehicles to aim points, whether or not a reentry vehicle is actually released or dispensed. Procedures for releasing anti-missile defense penetration aids will not be considered to be procedures for releasing or for dispensing a reentry vehicle so long as the procedures for releasing anti-missile defense penetration aids differ from those for releasing or for dispensing reentry vehicles.

14. Each Party undertakes not to deploy at any one time on heavy bombers equipped for cruise missiles capable of a range in excess of 600 kilometers a number of such cruise missiles which exceeds the product of 28 and the number of such heavy bombers.

First Agreed Statement. For the purposes of the limitation provided for in paragraph 14 of Article IV of the Treaty, there shall be considered to be deployed on each heavy bomber of a type equipped for cruise missiles capable of a range in excess of 600 kilometers the maximum number of such missiles for which any bomber of that type is equipped for one operational mission.

Second Agreed Statement. During the term of the Treaty no bomber of the B-52 or B-1 types of the United States of America and

no bomber of the Tupolev-95 or Myasishchev types of the Union of Soviet Socialist Republics will be equipped for more than twenty cruise missiles capable of a range in excess of 600 kilometers.

Article V

1. Within the aggregate numbers provided for in paragraphs 1 and 2 of Article III, each Party undertakes to limit launchers of ICBMs and SLBMs equipped with MIRVs, ASBMs equipped with MIRVs, and heavy bombers equipped for cruise missiles capable of a range in excess of 600 kilometers to an aggregate number not to exceed 1,320.

2. Within the aggregate number provided for in paragraph 1 of this Article, each Party undertakes to limit launchers of ICBMs and SLBMs equipped with MIRVs, and ASBMs equipped with MIRVs to an aggregate number not to exceed 1,200.

3. Within the aggregate number provided for in paragraph 2 of this Article, each Party undertakes to limit launchers of ICBMs equipped with MIRVs to an aggregate number not to exceed 820.

4. For each bomber of a type equipped for ASBMs equipped with MIRVs, the aggregate numbers provided for in paragraphs 1 and 2 of this Article shall include the maximum number of ASBMs for which a bomber of that type is equipped for one operational mission.

Agreed Statement. If a bomber is equipped for ASBMS equipped with MIRVS, all bombers of that type shall be considered to be equipped for ASBMS equipped with MIRVS.

5. Within the aggregate numbers provided for in paragraphs 1, 2, and 3 of this Article and subject to the provisions of this Treaty, each Party has the right to determine the composition of these aggregates.

Article VI

1. The limitations provided for in this Treaty shall apply to those arms which are:

(a) operational;

(b) in the final stage of construction;

(c) in reserve, in storage, or mothballed;

(d) undergoing overhaul, repair, modernization, or conversion.

2. Those arms in the final stage of construction are:

(a) SLBM launchers on submarines which have begun sea trials;

(b) ASBMs after a bomber of a type equipped for such missiles has been brought out of the shop, plant, or other facility where its final assembly or conversion for the purpose of equipping it for such missiles has been performed;

(c) other strategic offensive arms which are finally assembled in a shop, plant, or other facility after they have been brought out of the shop, plant, or other facility where their final assembly has been performed.

3. ICBM and SLBM launchers of a type not subject to the limitation provided for in Article V, which undergo conversion into launchers of a type subject to that limitation, shall become subject to that limitation as follows:

(a) fixed ICBM launchers when work on their conversion reaches the stage which first definitely indicates that they are being so converted;

(b) SLBM launchers on a submarine when that submarine first goes to sea after their conversion has been performed.

Agreed Statement. The procedures referred to in paragraph 7 of Article VI of the Treaty shall include procedures determining the manner in which mobile ICBM launchers of a type not subject to the limitation provided for in Article V of the Treaty, which undergo conversion into launchers of a type subject to that limitation, shall become subject to that limitation, unless the Parties agree that mobile ICBM launchers shall not be deployed after the date on which the Protocol ceases to be in force.

4. ASBMs on a bomber which undergoes conversion from a bomber of a type equipped for ASBMs which are not subject to the limitation provided for in Article V into a bomber of a type equipped for ASBMs which are subject to that limitation shall become subject to that limitation when the bomber is brought out of the shop, plant, or other facility where such conversion has been performed.

5. A heavy bomber of a type not subject to the limitation provided for in paragraph 1 of Article V shall become subject to that limitation when it is brought out of the shop, plant, or other facility where it has been converted into a heavy bomber of a type equipped for cruise missiles capable of a range in excess of 600 kilometers. A bomber of a type not subject to the limitation provided for in paragraph 1 or 2 of Article III shall become subject to that limitation and to the limitation provided for in paragraph 1 of Article V when it is brought out of the shop, plant, or other facility where it has been converted into a bomber of a type equipped for cruise missiles capable of a range in excess of 600 kilometers.

6. The arms subject to the limitations provided for in this Treaty shall continue to be subject to these limitations until they are dis-

mantled, are destroyed, or otherwise cease to be subject to these limitations under procedures to be agreed upon.

Agreed Statement. The procedures for removal of strategic offensive arms from the aggregate numbers provided for in the Treaty, which are referred to in paragraph 6 of Article VI of the Treaty, and which are to be agreed upon in the Standing Consultative Commission, shall include:

(a) procedures for removal from the aggregate numbers, provided for in Article V of the Treaty, of ICBM and SLBM launchers which are being converted from launchers of a type subject to the limitation provided for in Article V of the Treaty, into launchers of a type not subject to that limitation;

(b) procedures for removal from the aggregate numbers, provided for in Articles III and V of the Treaty, of bombers which are being converted from bombers of a type subject to the limitations provided for in Article III of the Treaty or in Articles III and V of the Treaty into airplanes or bombers of a type not so subject.

Common Understanding. The procedures referred to in subparagraph (b) of the Agreed Statement to paragraph 6 of Article VI of the Treaty for removal of bombers from the aggregate numbers provided for in Articles III and V of the Treaty shall be based upon the existence of functionally related observable differences which indicate whether or not they can perform the mission of a heavy bomber, or whether or not they can perform the mission of a bomber equipped for cruise missiles capable of a range in excess of 600 kilometers.

7. In accordance with the provisions of Article XVII, the Parties will agree in the Standing Consultative Commission upon procedures to implement the provisions of this Article.

Article VII

1. The limitations provided for in Article III shall not apply to ICBM and SLBM test and training launchers or to space vehicle launchers for exploration and use of outer space. ICBM and SLBM test and training launchers are ICBM and SLBM launchers used only for testing or training.

Common Understanding. The term "testing," as used in Article VII of the Treaty, includes research and development.

2. The Parties agree that:

(a) there shall be no significant increase in the number of ICBM

or SLBM test and training launchers or in the number of such launchers of heavy ICBMs;

(b) construction or conversion of ICBM launchers at test ranges shall be undertaken only for purposes of testing and training;

(c) there shall be no conversion of ICBM test and training launchers or of space vehicle launchers into ICBM launchers subject to the limitations provided for in Article III.

First Agreed Statement. The term "significant increase," as used in subparagraph 2(a) of Article VII of the Treaty, means an increase of fifteen percent or more. Any new ICBM test and training launchers which replace ICBM test and training launchers at test ranges will be located only at test ranges.

Second Agreed Statement. Current test ranges where ICBMS are tested are located: for the United States of America, near Santa Maria, California, and at Cape Canaveral, Florida; and for the Union of Soviet Socialist Republics, in the areas of Tyura-Tam and Plesetskaya. In the future, each Party shall provide notification in the Standing Consultative Commission of the location of any other test range used by that Party to test ICBMS.

First Common Understanding. At test ranges where ICBMS are tested, other arms, including those not limited by the Treaty, may also be tested.

Second Common Understanding. Of the eighteen launchers of fractional orbital missiles at the test range where ICBMS are tested in the area of Tyura-Tam, twelve launchers shall be dismantled or destroyed and six launchers may be converted to launchers for testing missiles undergoing modernization.

Dismantling or destruction of the twelve launchers shall begin upon entry into force of the Treaty and shall be completed within eight months, under procedures for dismantling or destruction of these launchers to be agreed upon in the Standing Consultative Commission. These twelve launchers shall not be replaced.

Conversion of the six launchers may be carried out after entry into force of the Treaty. After entry into force of the Treaty, fractional orbital missiles shall be removed and shall be destroyed pursuant to the provisions of subparagraph 1(c) of Article IX and of Article XI of the Treaty and shall not be replaced by other missiles, except in the case of conversion of these six launchers for testing missiles undergoing modernization. After removal of the fractional orbital missiles, and prior to such conversion, any activities associated with these launchers shall be limited to normal maintenance requirements for launchers in which missiles are not deployed. These six

launchers shall be subject to the provisions of Article VII of the Treaty and, if converted, to the provisions of the Fifth Common Understanding to paragraph 5 of Article II of the Treaty.

Article VIII

1. Each Party undertakes not to flight-test cruise missiles capable of a range in excess of 600 kilometers or ASBMs from aircraft other than bombers or to convert such aircraft into aircraft equipped for such missiles.

Agreed Statement. For purposes of testing only, each Party has the right, through initial construction or, as an exception to the provisions of paragraph 1 of Article VIII of the Treaty, by conversion, to equip for cruise missiles capable of a range in excess of 600 kilometers or for ASBMS no more than sixteen airplanes, including airplanes which are prototypes of bombers equipped for such missiles. Each Party also has the right, as an exception to the provisions of paragraph 1 of Article VIII of the Treaty, to flight-test from such airplanes cruise missiles capable of a range in excess of 600 kilometers and, after the date on which the Protocol ceases to be in force, to flight-test ASBMS from such airplanes as well, unless the Parties agree that they will not flight-test ASBMS after that date. The limitations provided for in Article III of the Treaty shall not apply to such airplanes.

The aforementioned airplanes may include only:

(a) airplanes other than bombers which, as an exception to the provisions of paragraph 1 of Article VIII of the Treaty, have been converted into airplanes equipped for cruise missiles capable of a range in excess of 600 kilometers or for ASBMS;

(b) airplanes considered to be heavy bombers pursuant to subparagraph 3(c) or 3(d) of Article II of the Treaty; and

(c) airplanes other than heavy bombers which, prior to March 7, 1979, were used for testing cruise missiles capable of a range in excess of 600 kilometers.

The airplanes referred to in subparagraphs (a) and (b) of this Agreed Statement shall be distinguishable on the basis of functionally related observable differences from airplanes which otherwise would be of the same type but cannot perform the mission of a bomber equipped for cruise missiles capable of a range in excess of 600 kilometers or for ASBMS.

The airplanes referred to in subparagraph (c) of this Agreed Statement shall not be used for testing cruise missiles capable of a range in excess of 600 kilometers after the expiration of a six-month period from the date of entry into force of the Treaty, unless by the

expiration of that period they are distinguishable on the basis of functionally related observable differences from airplanes which otherwise would be of the same type but cannot perform the mission of a bomber equipped for cruise missiles capable of a range in excess of 600 kilometers.

First Common Understanding. The term "testing," as used in the Agreed Statement to paragraph 1 of Article VIII of the Treaty, includes research and development.

Second Common Understanding. The Parties shall notify each other in the Standing Consultative Commission of the number of airplanes, according to type, used for testing pursuant to the Agreed Statement to paragraph 1 of Article VIII of the Treaty. Such notification shall be provided at the first regular session of the Standing Consultative Commission held after an airplane has been used for such testing.

Third Common Understanding. None of the sixteen airplanes referred to in the Agreed Statement to paragraph 1 of Article VIII of the Treaty may be replaced, except in the event of the involuntary destruction of any such airplane or in the case of the dismantling or destruction of any such airplane. The procedures for such replacement and for removal of any such airplane from that number, in case of its conversion, shall be agreed upon in the Standing Consultative Commission.

2. Each Party undertakes not to convert aircraft other than bombers into aircraft which can carry out the mission of a heavy bomber as referred to in subparagraph 3(b) of Article II.

Article IX

1. Each Party undertakes not to develop, test, or deploy:

(a) ballistic missiles capable of a range in excess of 600 kilometers for installation on waterborne vehicles other than submarines, or launchers of such missiles;

Common Understanding to subparagraph (a). The obligations provided for in subparagraph 1(a) of Article IX of the Treaty do not affect current practices for transporting ballistic missiles.

(b) fixed ballistic or cruise missile launchers for emplacement on the ocean floor, on the seabed, or on the beds of internal waters and inland waters, or in the subsoil thereof, or mobile launchers of such missiles, which move only in contact with the ocean floor, the seabed, or the beds of internal waters and inland waters, or missiles for such launchers;

Agreed Statement to subparagraph (b). The obligations provided for in subparagraph 1(b) of Article IX of the Treaty shall apply to all areas of the ocean floor and the seabed, including the seabed zone referred to in Articles I and II of the 1971 Treaty on the Prohibition of the Emplacement of Nuclear Weapons and Other Weapons of Mass Destruction on the Seabed and the Ocean Floor and in the Subsoil Thereof.

(c) systems for placing into Earth orbit nuclear weapons or any other kind of weapons of mass destruction, including fractional orbital missiles;

Common Understanding to subparagraph (c). The provisions of subparagraph 1(c) of Article IX of the Treaty do not require the dismantling or destruction of any existing launchers of either Party.

(d) mobile launchers of heavy ICBMs;

(e) SLBMs which have a launch-weight greater or a throw-weight greater than that of the heaviest, in terms of either launch-weight or throw-weight, respectively, of the light ICBMs deployed by either Party as of the date of signature of this Treaty, or launchers of such SLBMs; or

(f) ASBMs which have a launch-weight greater or a throw-weight greater than that of the heaviest, in terms of either launch-weight or throw-weight, respectively, of the light ICBMs deployed by either Party as of the date of signature of this Treaty.

First Agreed Statement to subparagraphs (e) and (f). The launch-weight of an SLBM or of an ASBM is the weight of the fully loaded missile itself at the time of launch.

Second Agreed Statement to subparagraphs (e) and (f). The throw-weight of an SLBM or of an ASBM is the sum of the weight of:

(a) its reentry vehicle or reentry vehicles;

(b) any self-contained dispensing mechanisms or other appropriate devices for targeting one reentry vehicle, or for releasing or for dispensing and targeting two or more reentry vehicles; and

(c) its penetration aids, including devices for their release.

Common Understanding to subparagraphs (e) and (f). The term "other appropriate devices," as used in the definition of the throw-weight of an SLBM or of an ASBM in the Second Agreed Statement to subparagraphs 1(e) and 1(f) of Article IX of the Treaty, means any devices for dispensing and targeting two or more reentry vehicles; and any devices for releasing two or more reentry vehicles or for targeting one reentry vehicle, which cannot provide their reentry vehi-

cles or reentry vehicle with additional velocity of more than 1,000 meters per second.

2. Each Party undertakes not to flight-test from aircraft cruise missiles capable of a range in excess of 600 kilometers which are equipped with multiple independently targetable warheads and not to deploy such cruise missiles on aircraft.

Agreed Statement. Warheads of a cruise missile are independently targetable if maneuvering or targeting of the warheads to separate aim points along ballistic trajectories or any other flight paths, which are unrelated to each other, is accomplished during a flight of a cruise missile.

Article X

Subject to the provisions of this Treaty, modernization and replacement of strategic offensive arms may be carried out.

Article XI

1. Strategic offensive arms which would be in excess of the aggregate numbers provided for in this Treaty as well as strategic offensive arms prohibited by this Treaty shall be dismantled or destroyed under procedures to be agreed upon in the Standing Consultative Commission.

2. Dismantling or destruction of strategic offensive arms which would be in excess of the aggregate number provided for in paragraph 1 of Article III shall begin on the date of the entry into force of this Treaty and shall be completed within the following periods from that date: four months for ICBM launchers; six months for SLBM launchers; and three months for heavy bombers.

3. Dismantling or destruction of strategic offensive arms which would be in excess of the aggregate number provided for in paragraph 2 of Article III shall be initiated no later than January 1, 1981, shall be carried out throughout the ensuing twelve-month period, and shall be completed no later than December 31, 1981.

4. Dismantling or destruction of strategic offensive arms prohibited by this Treaty shall be completed within the shortest possible agreed period of time, but not later than six months after the entry into force of this Treaty.

Article XII

In order to ensure the viability and effectiveness of this Treaty, each Party undertakes not to circumvent the provisions of this Treaty, through any other state or states, or in any other manner.

Article XIII

Each Party undertakes not to assume any international obligations which would conflict with this Treaty.

Article XIV

The Parties undertake to begin, promptly after the entry into force of this Treaty, active negotiations with the objective of achieving, as soon as possible, agreement on further measures for the limitation and reduction of strategic arms. It is also the objective of the Parties to conclude well in advance of 1985 an agreement limiting strategic offensive arms to replace this Treaty upon its expiration.

Article XV

1. For the purpose of providing assurance of compliance with the provisions of this Treaty, each Party shall use national technical means of verification at its disposal in a manner consistent with generally recognized principles of international law.

2. Each Party undertakes not to interfere with the national technical means of verification of the other Party operating in accordance with paragraph 1 of this Article.

3. Each Party undertakes not to use deliberate concealment measures which impede verification by national technical means of compliance with the provisions of this Treaty. This obligation shall not require changes in current construction, assembly, conversion, or overhaul practices.

First Agreed Statement. Deliberate concealment measures, as referred to in paragraph 3 of Article XV of the Treaty, are measures carried out deliberately to hinder or deliberately to impede verification by national technical means of compliance with the provisions of the Treaty.

Second Agreed Statement. The obligation not to use deliberate concealment measures, provided for in paragraph 3 of Article XV of the Treaty, does not preclude the testing of anti-missile defense penetration aids.

First Common Understanding. The provisions of paragraph 3 of Article XV of the Treaty and the First Agreed Statement thereto apply to all provisions of the Treaty, including provisions associated with testing. In this connection, the obligation not to use deliberate concealment measures includes the obligation not to use deliberate concealment measures associated with testing, including those measures aimed at concealing the association between ICBMS and launchers during testing.

Second Common Understanding. Each Party is free to use various methods of transmitting telemetric information during testing, including its encryption, except that, in accordance with the provisions of paragraph 3 of Article XV of the Treaty, neither Party shall engage in deliberate denial of telemetric information, such as through the use of telemetry encryption, whenever such denial impedes verification of compliance with the provisions of the Treaty.

Third Common Understanding. In addition to the obligations provided for in paragraph 3 of Article XV of the Treaty, no shelters which impede verification by national technical means of compliance with the provisions of the Treaty shall be used over ICBM silo launchers.

Article XVI

1. Each Party undertakes, before conducting each planned ICBM launch, to notify the other Party well in advance on a case-by-case basis that such a launch will occur, except for single ICBM launches from test ranges or from ICBM launcher deployment areas, which are not planned to extend beyond its national territory.

First Common Understanding. ICBM launches to which the obligations provided for in Article XVI of the Treaty apply, include, among others, those ICBM launches for which advance notification is required pursuant to the provisions of the Agreement on Measures to Reduce the Risk of Outbreak of Nuclear War Between the United States of America and the Union of Soviet Socialist Republics, signed September 30, 1971, and the Agreement Between the Government of the United States of America and the Government of the Union of Soviet Socialist Republics on the Prevention of Incidents On and Over the High Seas, signed May 25, 1972. Nothing in Article XVI of the Treaty is intended to inhibit advance notification, on a voluntary basis, of any ICBM launches not subject to its provisions, the advance notification of which would enhance confidence between the Parties.

Second Common Understanding. A multiple ICBM launch conducted by a Party, as distinct from single ICBM launches referred to in Article XVI of the Treaty, is a launch which would result in two or more of its ICBMs being in flight at the same time.

Third Common Understanding. The test ranges referred to in Article XVI of the Treaty are those covered by the Second Agreed Statement to paragraph 2 of Article VII of the Treaty.

2. The Parties shall agree in the Standing Consultative Commission upon procedures to implement the provisions of this Article.

Article XVII

1. To promote the objectives and implementation of the provisions of this Treaty, the Parties shall use the Standing Consultative Commission established by the Memorandum of Understanding Between the Government of the United States of America and the Government of the Union of Soviet Socialist Republics Regarding the Establishment of a Standing Consultative Commission of December 21, 1972.

2. Within the framework of the Standing Consultative Commission, with respect to this Treaty, the Parties will:

(a) consider questions concerning compliance with the obligations assumed and related situations which may be considered ambiguous;

(b) provide on a voluntary basis such information as either Party considers necessary to assure confidence in compliance with the obligations assumed;

(c) consider questions involving unintended interference with national technical means of verification, and questions involving unintended impeding of verification by national technical means of compliance with the provisions of this Treaty;

(d) consider possible changes in the strategic situation which have a bearing on the provisions of this Treaty;

(e) agree upon procedures for replacement, conversion, and dismantling or destruction, of strategic offensive arms in cases provided for in the provisions of this Treaty and upon procedures for removal of such arms from the aggregate numbers when they otherwise cease to be subject to the limitations provided for in this Treaty, and at regular sessions of the Standing Consultative Commission, notify each other in accordance with the aforementioned procedures, at least twice annually, of actions completed and those in process;

(f) consider, as appropriate, possible proposals for further increasing the viability of this Treaty, including proposals for amendments in accordance with the provisions of this Treaty;

(g) consider, as appropriate, proposals for further measures limiting strategic offensive arms.

3. In the Standing Consultative Commission the Parties shall maintain by category the agreed data base on the numbers of strategic offensive arms established by the Memorandum of Understanding Between the United States of America and the Union of Soviet Socialist Republics Regarding the Establishment of a Data Base on the Numbers of Strategic Offensive Arms of June 18, 1979.

Agreed Statement. In order to maintain the agreed data base on the numbers of strategic offensive arms subject to the limitations pro-

vided for in the Treaty in accordance with paragraph 3 of Article XVII of the Treaty, at each regular session of the Standing Consultative Commission the Parties will notify each other of and consider changes in those numbers in the following categories: launchers of ICBMS; fixed launchers of ICBMS; launchers of ICBMS equipped with MIRVS; launchers of SLBMS; launchers of SLBMS equipped with MIRVS; heavy bombers; heavy bombers equipped for cruise missiles capable of a range in excess of 600 kilometers; heavy bombers equipped only for ASBMS; ASBMS; and ASBMS equipped with MIRVS.

Article XVIII

Each Party may propose amendments to this Treaty. Agreed amendments shall enter into force in accordance with the procedures governing the entry into force of this Treaty.

Article XIX

1. This Treaty shall be subject to ratification in accordance with the constitutional procedures of each Party. This Treaty shall enter into force on the day of the exchange of instruments of ratification and shall remain in force through December 31, 1985, unless replaced earlier by an agreement further limiting strategic offensive arms.

2. This Treaty shall be registered pursuant to Article 102 of the Charter of the United Nations.

3. Each Party shall, in exercising its national sovereignty, have the right to withdraw from this Treaty if it decides that extraordinary events related to the subject matter of this Treaty have jeopardized its supreme interests. It shall give notice of its decision to the other Party six months prior to withdrawal from the Treaty. Such notice shall include a statement of the extraordinary events the notifying Party regards as having jeopardized its supreme interests.

Done at Vienna on June 18, 1979, in two copies, each in the English and Russian languages, both texts being equally authentic.

FOR THE UNITED STATES OF AMERICA	FOR THE UNION OF SOVIET SOCIALIST REPUBLICS
JIMMY CARTER	L. BREZHNEV
President of the United States of America	General Secretary of the CPSU, Chairman of the Presidium of the Supreme Soviet of the U.S.S.R.

Protocol to the Treaty on the Limitation of Strategic Offensive Arms, 18 June 1979

The United States of America and the Union of Soviet Socialist Republics, hereinafter referred to as the Parties,

Having agreed on limitations on strategic offensive arms in the Treaty,

Have agreed on additional limitations for the period during which this Protocol remains in force, as follows:

Article I

Each Party undertakes not to deploy mobile ICBM launchers or to flight-test ICBMs from such launchers.

Article II

1. Each Party undertakes not to deploy cruise missiles capable of a range in excess of 600 kilometers on sea-based launchers or on land-based launchers.

2. Each Party undertakes not to flight-test cruise missiles capable of a range in excess of 600 kilometers which are equipped with multiple independently targetable warheads from sea-based launchers or from land-based launchers.

Agreed Statement. Warheads of a cruise missile are independently targetable if maneuvering or targeting of the warheads to separate aim points along ballistic trajectories or any other flight paths, which are unrelated to each other, is accomplished during a flight of a cruise missile.

SOURCE: Protocol to the Treaty Between the United States of America and the Union of Soviet Socialist Republics on the Limitation of Strategic Offensive Arms. Department of State, 18 June 1979.

NOTE: The text of the SALT II Treaty and Protocol is accompanied by a set of Agreed Statements and Common Understandings, signed by President Carter and General Secretary Brezhnev on 18 June 1979, which are prefaced as follows:

"In connection with the Treaty Between the United States of America and the Union of Soviet Socialist Republics on the Limitation of Strategic Offensive Arms, the Parties have agreed on the following Agreed Statements and Common Understandings undertaken on behalf of the Government of the United States of America and the Government of the Union of Soviet Socialist Republics."

As an aid to the reader, the Agreed Statements and Common Understandings are presented immediately following the paragraph of the Treaty or Protocol to which they relate. For example, following Paragraph 2 of Article II of the Protocol is the Agreed Statement associated with that paragraph. The text of the Treaty and Protocol are in italics.

3. For the purposes of this Protocol, cruise missiles are unmanned, self-propelled, guided, weapon-delivery vehicles which sustain flight through the use of aerodynamic lift over most of their flight path and which are flight-tested from or deployed on sea-based or land-based launchers, that is, sea-launched cruise missiles and ground-launched cruise missiles, respectively.

First Agreed Statement. If a cruise missile is capable of a range in excess of 600 kilometers, all cruise missiles of that type shall be considered to be cruise missiles capable of a range in excess of 600 kilometers.

First Common Understanding. If a cruise missile has been flight-tested to a range in excess of 600 kilometers, it shall be considered to be a cruise missile capable of a range in excess of 600 kilometers.

Second Common Understanding. Cruise missiles not capable of a range in excess of 600 kilometers shall not be considered to be of a type capable of a range in excess of 600 kilometers if they are distinguishable on the basis of externally observable design features from cruise missiles of types capable of a range in excess of 600 kilometers.

Second Agreed Statement. The range of which a cruise missile is capable is the maximum distance which can be covered by the missile in its standard design mode flying until fuel exhaustion, determined by projecting its flight path onto the Earth's sphere from the point of launch to the point of impact.

Third Agreed Statement. If an unmanned, self-propelled, guided vehicle which sustains flight through the use of aerodynamic lift over most of its flight path has been flight-tested or deployed for weapon delivery, all vehicles of that type shall be considered to be weapon-delivery vehicles.

Third Common Understanding. Unmanned, self-propelled, guided vehicles which sustain flight through the use of aerodynamic lift over most of their flight path and are not weapon-delivery vehicles, that is, unarmed, pilotless, guided vehicles, shall not be considered to be cruise missiles if such vehicles are distinguishable from cruise missiles on the basis of externally observable design features.

Fourth Common Understanding. Neither Party shall convert unarmed, pilotless, guided vehicles into cruise missiles capable of a range in excess of 600 kilometers, nor shall either Party convert cruise missiles capable of a range in excess of 600 kilometers into unarmed, pilotless, guided vehicles.

Fifth Common Understanding. Neither Party has plans during the term of the Protocol to flight-test from or deploy on sea-based or

land-based launchers unarmed, pilotless, guided vehicles which are capable of a range in excess of 600 kilometers. In the future, should a Party have such plans, that Party will provide notification thereof to the other Party well in advance of such flight-testing or deployment. This Common Understanding does not apply to target drones.

Article III

Each Party undertakes not to flight-test or deploy ASBMs.

Article IV

This Protocol shall be considered an integral part of the Treaty. It shall enter into force on the day of the entry into force of the Treaty and shall remain in force through December 31, 1981, unless replaced earlier by an agreement on further measures limiting strategic offensive arms.

Done at Vienna on June 18, 1979, in two copies, each in the English and Russian languages, both texts being equally authentic.

FOR THE UNITED STATES OF AMERICA	FOR THE UNION OF SOVIET SOCIALIST REPUBLICS
JIMMY CARTER	L. BREZHNEV
President of the United States of America	General Secretary of the CPSU, Chairman of the Presidium of the Supreme Soviet of the U.S.S.R.

Memorandum of Understanding Regarding the Establishment of a Data Base on the Numbers of Strategic Offensive Arms, 18 June 1979

For the purposes of the Treaty Between the United States of America and the Union of Soviet Socialist Republics on the Limitation of Strategic Offensive Arms, the Parties have considered data on numbers of strategic offensive arms and agree that as of November 1, 1978 there existed the following numbers of strategic offensive arms subject to the limitations provided for in the Treaty which is being signed today.

	U.S.A.	U.S.S.R.
Launchers of ICBMS	1,054	1,398
Fixed launchers of ICBMS	1,054	1,398
Launchers of ICBMS equipped with MIRVS	550	576
Launchers of SLBMS	656	950
Launchers of SLBMS equipped with MIRVS	496	128
Heavy bombers	574	156
Heavy bombers equipped for cruise missiles capable of a range in excess of 600 kilometers	0	0
Heavy bombers equipped only for ASBMS	0	0
ASBMS	0	0
ASBMS equipped with MIRVS	0	0

At the time of entry into force of the Treaty the Parties will update the above agreed data in the categories listed in this Memorandum.

SOURCE: Memorandum of Understanding Between the United States of America and the Union of Soviet Socialist Republics Regarding the Establishment of a Data Base on the Numbers of Strategic Offensive Arms. Department of State, 18 June 1979.

Done at Vienna on June 18, 1979, in two copies, each in the English and Russian languages, both texts being equally authentic.

FOR THE
UNITED STATES OF AMERICA

RALPH EARLE II

Chief of the United States
Delegation to the
Strategic Arms Limitation Talks

FOR THE
UNION OF SOVIET
SOCIALIST REPUBLICS

V. KARPOV

Chief of the U.S.S.R.
Delegation to the
Strategic Arms Limitation Talks

U.S. Statement of Data on the Numbers of Strategic Offensive Arms, 18 June 1979

The United States of America declares that as of June 18, 1979 it possesses the following numbers of strategic offensive arms subject to the limitations provided for in the Treaty which is being signed today:

Launchers of ICBMS	1,054
Fixed launchers of ICBMS	1,054
Launchers of ICBMS equipped with MIRVS	550
Launchers of SLBMS	656
Launchers of SLBMS equipped with MIRVS	496
Heavy bombers	573
Heavy bombers equipped for cruise missiles capable of a range in excess of 600 kilometers	3
Heavy bombers equipped only for ASBMS	0
ASBMS	0
ASBMS equipped with MIRVS	0

June 18, 1979

RALPH EARLE II

Chief of the United States Delegation to the Strategic Arms Limitation Talks

SOURCE: Statement of Data on the Numbers of Strategic Offensive Arms as of the Date of Signature of the Treaty. Department of State, 18 June 1979.

U.S.S.R. Statement of Data on the Numbers of Strategic Offensive Arms, 18 June 1979

The Union of Soviet Socialist Republics declares that as of June 18, 1979 it possesses the following numbers of strategic offensive arms subject to the limitations provided for in the Treaty which is being signed today:

Launchers of ICBMS	1,398
Fixed launchers of ICBMS	1,398
Launchers of ICBMS equipped with MIRVS	608
Launchers of SLBMS	950
Launchers of SLBMS equipped with MIRVS	144
Heavy bombers	156
Heavy bombers equipped for cruise missiles capable of a range in excess of 600 kilometers	0
Heavy bombers equipped only for ASBMS	0
ASBMS	0
ASBMS equipped with MIRVS	0

June 18, 1979

V. Karpov

Chief of the U.S.S.R.
Delegation to the Strategic
Arms Limitation Talks

Source: Statement of Data on the Numbers of Strategic Offensive Arms as of the Date of Signature of the Treaty. Department of State, 18 June 1979.

Joint Statement of Principles and Basic Guidelines for Subsequent Negotiations, 18 June 1979

The United States of America and the Union of Soviet Socialist Republics, hereinafter referred to as the Parties,

Having concluded the Treaty on the Limitation of Strategic Offensive Arms,

Reaffirming that the strengthening of strategic stability meets the interests of the Parties and the interests of international security,

Convinced that early agreement on the further limitation and further reduction of strategic arms would serve to strengthen international peace and security and to reduce the risk of outbreak of nuclear war,

Have agreed as follows:

First. The Parties will continue to pursue negotiations, in accordance with the principle of equality and equal security, on measures for the further limitation and reduction in the numbers of strategic arms, as well as for their further qualitative limitation.

In furtherance of existing agreements between the Parties on the limitation and reduction of strategic arms, the Parties will continue, for the purposes of reducing and averting the risk of outbreak of nuclear war, to seek measures to strengthen strategic stability by, among other things, limitations on strategic offensive arms most destabilizing to the strategic balance and by measures to reduce and to avert the risk of surprise attack.

Second. Further limitations and reductions of strategic arms must be subject to adequate verification by national technical means, using additionally, as appropriate, cooperative measures contributing to the effectiveness of verification by national technical means. The Parties will seek to strengthen verification and to perfect the operation of the Standing Consultative Commission in order to promote assurance of compliance with the obligations assumed by the Parties.

Third. The Parties shall pursue in the course of these negotiations, taking into consideration factors that determine the strategic situation, the following objectives:

1) significant and substantial reductions in the numbers of strategic offensive arms;

2) qualitative limitations on strategic offensive arms, including restrictions on the development, testing, and deployment of new

---

SOURCE: Joint Statement of Principles and Basic Guidelines for Subsequent Negotiations on the Limitation of Strategic Arms. Department of State, 18 June 1979.

types of strategic offensive arms and on the modernization of existing strategic offensive arms;

3) resolution of the issues included in the Protocol to the Treaty Between the United States of America and the Union of Soviet Socialist Republics on the Limitation of Strategic Offensive Arms in the context of the negotiations relating to the implementation of the principles and objectives set out herein.

Fourth. The Parties will consider other steps to ensure and enhance strategic stability, to ensure the equality and equal security of the Parties, and to implement the above principles and objectives. Each Party will be free to raise any issue relative to the further limitation of strategic arms. The Parties will also consider further joint measures, as appropriate, to strengthen international peace and security and to reduce the risk of outbreak of nuclear war.

Vienna, June 18, 1979

FOR THE
UNITED STATES OF AMERICA

JIMMY CARTER

President of the
United States of America

FOR THE
UNION OF SOVIET SOCIALIST REPUBLICS

L. BREZHNEV

General Secretary of the CPSU,
Chairman of the Presidium of
the Supreme Soviet of the U.S.S.R.

Soviet Backfire Statement

On June 16, 1979, President Brezhnev handed President Carter the following written statement:

"The Soviet side informs the US side that the Soviet 'Tu-22M' airplane, called 'Backfire' in the USA, is a medium-range bomber, and that it does not intend to give this airplane the capability of operating at intercontinental distances. In this connection, the Soviet side states that it will not increase the radius of action of this airplane in such a way as to enable it to strike targets on the territory of the USA. Nor does it intend to give it such a capability in any other manner, including by in-flight refueling. At the same time, the Soviet side states that it will not increase the production rate of this airplane as compared to the present rate."

* * *

President Brezhnev confirmed that the Soviet Backfire production rate would not exceed 30 per year.

President Carter stated that the United States enters into the SALT II Agreement on the basis of the commitments contained in the Soviet statement and that it considers the carrying out of these commitments to be essential to the obligations assumed under the Treaty.

CYRUS VANCE

SOURCE: Soviet Backfire Statement. Department of State, 18 June 1979. Asterisks in original.—Ed.

PART THREE
Annotated Bibliography

Aspin, Les. "The Verification of the SALT II Agreement." *Scientific American*, vol. 240, no. 2 (February 1979).

Aspin believes that U.S. national technical means of verification are "excellent" for detecting Soviet cheating in "all the areas in which major violations . . . could upset the present strategic 'balance of terror.' " The author's conclusions are drawn from an analysis of SALT II provisions based on three questions: How could the Soviets cheat, how could the United States detect Soviet cheating, and what could the Soviets gain (and the United States lose) by cheating? The best opportunity for monitoring Soviet compliance is in the testing phase of the development of new or modified weapon systems, according to Aspin. However, Soviet violations might not be detected in several areas: deployment of additional ICBMs on a "small scale," Backfire bomber performance, upgrading of the SS-20 IRBM, conversion of heavy bomber variants, and cruise missile range. Aspin concludes that technological advances in cruise missiles and other weapon systems will make verification of future SALT agreements less certain and "may well require a substantial lowering of the present standards of confidence for detecting violations."

Ermarth, Fritz W. "Contrasts in American and Soviet Strategic Thought." *International Security*, vol. 3, no. 2 (Fall 1978).

The author defines strategic doctrine as "a set of operative beliefs, values, and assertions that in a significant way guide official behavior with respect to strategic research and development (R&D), weapons choice, forces, operational plans, arms control, etc." In general, U.S. strategic doctrine is to deter nuclear war with low levels of arms, crisis stability, and the ultimate threat of destruction of the aggressor. Soviet doctrine, on the other hand, calls for forces and operational plans that are designed to enhance the prospects of survival as a nation and the defeat of the enemy should deterrence fail. U.S. strategic doctrine views the consequences of nuclear war as precluding any meaningful victory. In addition, American policy assumes deterrence to be the only meaningful objective of strategic arsenals. It also seeks to minimize instability caused by certain weapon technologies, defines strategic interests in terms of intercontinental distances, and is unclear as to the possibility of limiting nuclear conflict. In contrast, Soviet doctrine maintains that nuclear war can result in a meaningful outcome that serves national interests. According to

this policy, deterrence should extend beyond mere defense of the homeland to help secure foreign policy objectives. The Soviets view instability in strategic relationships as inevitable and believe that strategic interests begin at the nation's doorstep and that conflict limitation may be desirable. Ermarth concludes that the United States has misunderstood Soviet strategic doctrine and has followed policies in SALT and force planning that have allowed the Soviet Union to become more assertive in its foreign policy.

Garthoff, Raymond L. "Mutual Deterrence and Strategic Arms Limitation in Soviet Policy." *International Security*, vol. 3, no. 1 (Summer 1978).
Garthoff surveys the writings of Soviet military leaders and civilians to answer the following question: Do the Soviets accept the concept of mutual deterrence as the basis for strategic arms control with the United States? He concludes that, since the late 1960s, "the Soviet political and military leadership has recognized that under contemporary conditions there is a strategic balance between the two superpowers which provides mutual deterrence; that the nuclear strategic balance is basically stable, but requires continuing military efforts to assure its continuation; and that agreed strategic arms limitations can make a contribution, possibly a significant one, to reducing these otherwise necessary reciprocal military efforts." The war-fighting and war-winning character of Soviet doctrine and weapon programs is explained by the Marxist-Leninist tenet of the invincibility of socialism (even in nuclear war) and the natural proclivity of the military for larger defense budgets.

Gompert, David C., and others. *Nuclear Weapons and World Politics: Alternatives for the Future*. New York: McGraw-Hill Book Company, for the 1980s Project of the Council on Foreign Relations, 1977.
This volume contains essays describing four alternative nuclear "regimes" and the policies to achieve them. A regime is defined as "a system of international obligations (formal accords, tacit commitments, and informal understandings), national force structures (how many and what kinds of weapons), and doctrines (when, where, why, how, and which nuclear weapons ought to be used) that together govern the role of nuclear weapons in war, peace, and diplomacy." The first nuclear regime, described by Michael Mandelbaum, extends into the future the existing strategic relationship founded on deterrence by mutual assured destruction. Under Richard L. Garwin's second nuclear regime, the United States, either with the cooperation of the Soviet Union or unilaterally, would seek to reduce its dependence on nuclear weapons by confining their use solely to deterrence of nuclear attack and retaliation. The third regime, described by John H. Barton, sees a world in which nuclear arsenals are proscribed and the role of international organizations in preserving peace and security is enlarged. David C. Gompert examines the fourth regime, one where "strategic deterioration" may result from nuclear proliferation, the possession by the United States and the Soviet Union of first-strike capabilities, or the acquisition by one superpower of a significantly superior nuclear capability over the other. Each author prescribes military, diplomatic, and arms control policies to further the cause of a particular regime or to alleviate its destabilizing attributes.

Lodal, Jan M. "SALT II and American Security." *Foreign Affairs*, vol. 57, no. 2 (Winter 1978/79).
Lodal believes that "SALT is much more than either a political exercise or arms

control for its own sake. To be successful, SALT must improve our security by helping to stabilize the strategic balance between the United States and the Soviet Union." The author's analysis of the technical provisions of the SALT II agreements lead him to conclude that that objective has been met. For the future, the concerns of the Western European allies over the reliability of the U.S. nuclear umbrella must be addressed, perhaps with plans to deploy new theater nuclear forces as an inducement to Soviet agreement on reducing its comparable forces in SALT III. Rejection of the SALT II treaty "would lead the rest of the world to see the United States as hesitant, insecure, and incapable of mounting an effective political and military effort to establish a stable peace in the nuclear age."

Lord, Carnes. "Verification and the Future of Arms Control." *Strategic Review*, vol. 6, no. 2 (Spring 1978).
"If SALT has become the touchstone of U.S.-Soviet détente," writes the author, then "verification may be becoming the touchstone of SALT." Verification can no longer be viewed as simply a technical issue; under SALT I, it became "a source of impassioned political controversy" that bears not only on arms control but also on public perceptions of détente. The author believes that the United States has approached verification as a technical problem and has assumed that public confidence in the verifiability of SALT results from technical means for monitoring Soviet military activities. "The reality," he notes, "is that most controversies over questions of verifiability center not on technical facts but on the evaluation of those facts in the larger context of policy." Lord looks at several considerations that should enter into assessments of the adequacy of monitoring capabilities and suggests the need for "a radical rethinking" of the desirability of arms control limitations on weapon systems (such as cruise missiles) that do not lend themselves to technical monitoring. The author also examines the problems associated with determining whether a violation has taken place and whether or how the United States should respond to evidence of violations. "If any presumption should exist as to the requirements of response, it is that response should be active and vigorous."

Lowenthal, Mark M. *SALT Verification*. Washington, D.C.: Library of Congress, Congressional Research Service, Report no. 78-142F, 24 April 1979.
Lowenthal examines the organizational and technical issues associated with verification of the SALT II agreements. The report includes a detailed description of the U.S. "verification community" and a table illustrating the technical monitoring systems available for verifying Soviet compliance with the quantitative and qualitative limitations in the treaty and protocol. The verification process is described as consisting of six steps: (1) the negotiations, where the verifiability of proposed limitations are assessed; (2) monitoring of Soviet activities; (3) analysis of data; (4) reporting of data to political leaders; (5) deciding whether the data supports a conclusion that violations exist; and (6) resolution of the issue. The author briefly recounts the verification experience under SALT I, the Carter administration's reorganization of the verification community, and the various technical means for monitoring military activities. Lowenthal concludes that "verification remains a continuing source of contention rather than a means of building public confidence and support" for arms control.

Metzger, Robert, and Paul Doty. "Arms Control Enters the Gray Area." *International Security*, vol. 3, no. 3 (Winter 1978/1979).

The authors argue that continued progress in limiting the central strategic nuclear weapon systems of the United States and the Soviet Union "could be an illusion if at least a start is not made in bringing weapons of lesser range under control." The weapons that fall in the "gray area" not limited by SALT include the fighter bombers, medium bombers, carrier-based aircraft, IRBMS and MRBMS, and cruise missiles that the superpowers have deployed in Europe and the western regions of the U.S.S.R. Recent deployment of the Soviet SS-20 IRBMS and Backfire bombers targeted against Western Europe have heightened concern among the NATO allies about the shifting balance in long-range theater nuclear forces. In addition, SALT II may actually serve to focus the East-West arms competition more on the European theater. Geographic asymmetries, problems in defining gray area weapon systems, and a variety of other technical and political issues associated with negotiations to limit theater nuclear forces are also examined. The article includes detailed inventories of NATO and Warsaw Pact gray area systems.

Sienkiewicz, Stanley. "SALT and Soviet Nuclear Doctrine." *International Security*, vol. 2, no. 4 (Spring 1978).

Much of the euphoria that accompanied the ABM treaty in 1972 stemmed from the widespread belief that U.S. and Soviet strategic doctrine were in fundamental agreement. The trends in the strategic balance and in Soviet weapon procurement since then have lead to disillusionment with the SALT process. Sienkiewicz reviews the evolution of Soviet nuclear doctrine to show how the political struggles that preceded the coming to power of Khrushchev and Brezhnev conferred on the military greater independence in formulating defense policy. The American view that security in the nuclear age resides in a condition of mutual vulnerability is "at radical variance with all of the traditions and professional instincts of the Soviet defense establishment." The Soviet answer to security is a policy of damage limitation, whereby preemptive counterforce strikes, strong air defenses, and civil defense protect the political leadership and the country's civilian population and industry. Deterrence based on mutual assured destruction is a civilian concept that is strongly resisted by the military leaders in Moscow. Despite the differences in U.S. and Soviet doctrine, SALT has and can continue to produce meaningful results. In the ABM treaty the Soviets agreed to arms limitations that are inconsistent with their doctrine when the United States supplied the incentive in the form of its own weapon programs.

U.S., Congress, House of Representatives, Committee on Armed Services. *SALT II: An Interim Assessment.* Report of the Panel on the Strategic Arms Limitation Talks and the Comprehensive Test Ban Treaty, 95th Congress, 2nd session, 23 December 1978.

The report concludes that "When coupled with the realities and trends in the military force structures [of the two superpowers], SALT II could have profound and adverse effects upon the United States–Soviet strategic balance. Since SALT II will not constrain—in any militarily significant way—the Soviet Union's military power but will constrain several important U.S. strategic force options, SALT II will not prevent a destabilizing imbalance of power from emerging." Alleging that the United States "has exercised unilateral arms restraint" unmatched by the Soviet Union over the last decade, the panel

recommends that Washington proceed with a more survivable basing mode for existing ICBMS as well as the MX, the Trident submarine and missile programs, all variations of cruise missiles, and a new penetrating bomber. Among the panel's other findings: the 600-kilometer range limit for ground- and sea-launched cruise missiles render these weapons "useless"; "independent verification of several important aspects of SALT II will not be possible"; SALT II "does not respond to the policies expressed by Congress in Public Law 92-448"; Backfire bombers should be counted in the treaty's aggregate launcher ceiling; SALT II fails to constrain the Soviet threat to American ICBMS; and "arms control should not be the dominant element in U.S. national security policy." The report also includes the dissenting views of Representative Bob Carr.

U.S., Congress, Office of Technology Assessment. *The Effects of Nuclear War.* Washington, D.C., May 1979.

This study, done at the request of the Senate Foreign Relations Committee, examines the effects of nuclear war on the civilian populations, economies, and sociopolitical systems of the United States and the Soviet Union. A recurring theme is the uncertainties as to the extent of prompt and long-term casualties and destruction that would accompany any nuclear war. The study notes that "the extreme uncertainties about the effects of a nuclear attack, as well as the certainty that the minimum consequences would be enormous, both play a role in the deterrent effect of nuclear weapons." Among the topics discussed are the differences between the two countries in population distribution and proximity to potential targets, vulnerabilities of agricultural systems and urban centers, civil defense preparations, and strategic nuclear arsenals. Four hypothetical nuclear exchanges are used to illustrate the effects of nuclear war: attacks on Detroit and Leningrad; strikes against each country's oil refineries; counterforce attacks against missile fields and submarine and bomber bases; and large-scale attacks against U.S. and Soviet military and economic targets.

Appendix: The SALT II Debate

The debate over America's objectives in the SALT II negotiations began even as the SALT I agreements were being considered by Congress in the summer of 1972. During the next six and one-half years of negotiations, conducted by three successive administrations, the debate continued and seemed to intensify whenever a breakthrough in the talks was imminent or major new proposals were put forth by the United States. The Vladivostok accord of November 1974, the comprehensive proposals of March 1977, and the substantial progress recorded in the talks in September 1977 each provided greater substance to the debate and fuel to the controversy.

The selections that follow illustrate the divergent views of the major public organizations participating in the SALT II debate. The materials from the Committee on the Present Danger and the Coalition for Peace Through Strength were published prior to the completion of the treaty, while the selections from the Arms Control Association and the Center for Defense Information were released after the SALT II agreements were signed.—Ed.

Is SALT II a Fair Deal for the United States?

The President tells us, I believe correctly, that the issues surrounding SALT II are the most important facing this country. Those issues include the basic thrust and direction of our foreign policy, the evolving

SOURCE: Paul H. Nitze, *Is SALT II a Fair Deal for the United States?* (Washington, D.C.: Committee on the Present Danger, 16 May 1979), pp. 3–13.

conventional and nuclear military balance, our defense programs and budgets, and the relationship of SALT II to those issues. . . .

The Conventional and the Strategic Balance

At all times since World War II the Soviet Union has had superior conventional forces on the European central front and on its northern and southern flanks. This has been due, in part, to geography, the U.S.S.R. enjoying the central position and interior lines, and, in part, to the greater effort of the Warsaw Pact nations.

In the years up to the early 1950s this Soviet conventional superiority was offset by the U.S. nuclear monopoly. Later NATO's conventional deficiency was in large measure offset by U.S. theater nuclear weapons. Today the U.S. theater nuclear superiority has disappeared, and it has proved necessary to assign a number of our Poseidon submarines to cover targets of interest to European NATO. As the Soviets deploy increasing numbers of SS-20 MIRVed missiles, Backfire, and other high performance theater bombers, more of our surviving strategic nuclear forces will be needed for theater missions.

For most of the post–World War II era the U.S. Navy has enjoyed unchallenged control of the seas. This assured that we could project our power, wherever needed, on the periphery of the Eurasian landmass. The Soviet Union, together with its associates, is on the way to developing such a capability. Even now Soviet intermediate-range nuclear weapons, such as the SS-20s and the Backfires, provide an umbrella arching out some two to three thousand miles from the Soviet borders over Europe, the Middle East, South Asia, China, and the bordering seas.

The prudence, and therefore the likelihood, of either the Soviet Union or the United States using conventional or theater nuclear weapons, even in connection with an issue not directly involving the territory of the other, is importantly affected by the confidence it has in the quality of its strategic intercontinental nuclear forces relative to those of the other side.

The Soviet ruling group has a full understanding of the potential destructiveness of nuclear weapons. Otherwise, they would not have demanded such enormous sacrifices from their population to create their huge military machine. Nor would they have persisted year after year in a civil defense program twenty times as elaborate and costly as ours. The Soviet rulers do not want nuclear war. They believe the best way to avoid a nuclear war and still achieve their objectives is to have overwhelming superiority. As von Clausewitz, the famous mili-

tary strategist, put it, the aggressor never wants war; he would prefer to enter your country unopposed.

But the Soviet Union does propose that no important decisions be made in the world without its aims and ambitions being taken fully into account. And beyond that, much of what they say to internal audiences within Russia, and what they do, is consistent with an aspiration to world hegemony.

Soviet Global Strategy

For many years the focus of Soviet strategy has been on Western Europe. By achieving dominance over the Middle East, they aim to outflank Europe. They propose to outflank the Middle East by achieving controlling positions in Afghanistan, Iran, and Iraq on one side, South and North Yemen, Eritrea, Ethiopia, and Mozambique on the other, and by achieving the neutrality of Turkey to the north. Concurrently, they are attempting to encircle China by pressure on Pakistan and India, by alliance with Vietnam, and dominance over North Korea. The United States is the only power in a position potentially to frustrate these aims. It is therefore seen as the principal enemy.

In seeking each specific objective within their global policy, the Soviet rulers use the lowest level of pressure or of violence necessary and sufficient to achieve that objective. The purpose of their capabilities at the higher levels of potential violence, all the way up to intercontinental nuclear war, is to deter, and if necessary control, escalation by us to such higher levels.

It is a copybook principle in strategy that, in actual war, advantage tends to go to the side in a better position to raise the stakes by expanding the scope, duration, or destructive intensity of the conflict. By the same token, at junctures of high contention short of war, the side better able to cope with the potential consequences of raising the stakes has the advantage. The other side is the one under greater pressure to scramble for a peaceful way out. To have the advantage at the utmost level of violence helps at every lesser level. In the Korean war, the Berlin blockades, and the Cuban missile crisis the United States had the ultimate edge because of our superiority at the strategic nuclear level. That edge has slipped away.

These circumstances form a background for understanding the stakes in SALT II. In broad terms the U.S. aim has been to arrange a standoff so as to neutralize the strategic nuclear threat overhanging superpower rivalry. The Soviet Union's contrasting aim has been and

is to take over and nail down the advantage which the U.S. has appeared willing to relinquish.

What We Wanted in SALT II

Our aim, when we began the SALT II negotiations six years ago, was a treaty of indefinite duration, to parallel the ABM treaty, and with these objectives:

- Limits on offensive nuclear capabilities equal for both sides.
- Terms assuring "crisis stability," that is, a situation where, in a crisis threatening war, there would be no significant advantage to the side striking first, preempting, or launching from under indications of attack.
- Limits calling for, or consistent with, true reduction in offensive nuclear armaments and their capabilities and in related expenditures.
- The limits should be verifiable; they should meet the legitimate concerns of our allies; they should be low enough to be economically and politically feasible for the United States to attain.
- In sum, the agreements should be such as to reduce the risks of nuclear war and the weight of nuclear armaments on world politics.
- Finally, for there to be a valid agreement, the terms must be acceptable both to the Soviet leadership and to two-thirds of the United States Senate—the necessary requirement for a valid agreement.

For reasons to be considered below, the SALT II terms, now all but finally agreed, meet none of these original objectives, except perhaps the last.

U.S. Casualties in the Negotiations

The first negotiating casualty, abandoned in 1974, was the hope for a treaty of indefinite duration paralleling the ABM treaty. We settled in 1974 for a short-term pact to end in 1985—a time when the strategic relationship between the two sides is likely to be far less favorable to the United States than it was in 1974.

The second casualty was equality. Notwithstanding the equal limits of 2,400—and later 2,250—on strategic nuclear delivery vehicles, and of 820 on MIRVed ICBM launchers, neither the actuality of

equality nor the appearance, if one takes a second look, is preserved. To illustrate:

• Within the permitted number of ICBM launchers, the Soviet Union is permitted more than 300 very large ICBMS of the latest type. Our side none.

• It will be impossible for the U.S. to have more than 550 MIRVed ICBM launchers at the time the treaty lapses and probably fewer. The Soviet side almost certainly will have deployed its full 820 by 1985—probably by 1982.

• We will have no more than three warheads on each of our MIRVed ICBMS. The Soviet Union is permitted and is expected to have deployed four, six, and ten warheads on each of its SS-17s, -19s, and -18s, respectively. The U.S. will be permitted to test a new ICBM missile with up to ten warheads during the period of the treaty. However, we will almost certainly not be able to deploy such a missile within that time period.

• The Soviet Backfire bombers, and comparable U.S. bombers, will be exempt from the count of strategic launchers. The U.S.S.R. will have 300 to 400 Backfire bombers by 1985. Our side will have no similar planes by 1985; our FB-111s are less proficient and much less numerous.

The third casualty, and the most worrisome, is "crisis stability." Over the past fifteen years it would not have profited either side to attack first. It would have required the use of more ICBMS by the attacking side than the attack could have destroyed. By the early 1980s that situation will have changed. By that time, the Soviet Union will be in a position to destroy 90 percent of our ICBMS with an expenditure of a fifth to a third of its ICBMS. Even if one assumes the survival of most of our bombers on alert for sufficient time to launch an immediate response, and the survival of our submarines at sea for a much longer time, our remaining forces after a Soviet initial counterforce attack would be strategically outmatched by the Soviet Union's retained war-making capability.

The fourth casualty has been true reductions. Although the number of Soviet launchers will decline from around 2,500 to 2,250 during the term of the treaty, the more significant indices of nuclear power will rise dramatically on the Soviet side, and to a lesser extent on our side as well. From the beginning of 1978 to the end of 1985, the number of Soviet warheads will have doubled; ours will have

increased by a half. The area destructive capabilities of Soviet weapons will have increased by a half; ours by a quarter. The capability of their weapons to knock out hardened targets, such as missile silos, will have increased tenfold; even if our cruise missiles, still under development, fulfill present expectations, our capability will have increased fourfold.

By 1985, under the limits of SALT II and taking into account the current programs of the two sides, it will be virtually impossible for the United States to avoid a situation in which our prompt counterforce capability against hardened military targets (silos; command, control, and communications centers; storage depots; and shelters for leadership personnel; et cetera) will be an eighth that of the Soviet Union or even less. This will be compounded by the fact that they will have twice as many hard targets as we, and their targets will be, on average, twice as hard as ours.

SALT II: A Bad Bargain

Even the sponsors of SALT II do not anticipate that SALT II will warrant a reduction in our expenditures on nuclear forces, or that the Soviets will reduce theirs.

A bad agreement does not cease to be a bad agreement by being wholly verifiable. But SALT II is not only a bad agreement, it is also far from being verifiable. Even before the loss of our key monitoring facilities in Iran and the compromise of our KH-11 satellite through Soviet espionage, we did not have the ability to verify Soviet compliance with important provisions of the treaty. Now our ability has been significantly weakened. The problem of verification is further confounded by imprecise definitions used in the treaty and by the absence of definition with respect to certain important terms.

I believe SALT II, as now envisaged, will not reduce the risks of war. On the contrary, it can increase the risks of war if it reinforces the judgment that we are militarily stronger than the U.S.S.R. at a time when we are not. War and defeat can arise from just such gross misjudgments of relative military capabilities by the weaker of two opposing powers.

A more sober evaluation of the balance, at a time when it is too late to reverse trends, could result in forced accommodation to the Soviet Union leading to a situation of global retreat and Finlandization.

Our budgeted direct expenditures on strategic nuclear forces are now about $10 billion a year. In the six years from 1956–1962 they averaged approximately $30 billion a year in today's dollars. We

simply cannot reverse present adverse trends with currently projected programs and expenditures.

I hope the upcoming SALT debate will provide a much more solid basis of understanding in the public mind of what is happening to the political-military balance and what is necessary to reverse current trends. Only in light of such an understanding can the public and the Congress wisely judge what to do about SALT II.

* * *

SALT II does make a start at controlling offensive strategic nuclear arms. But is it a good start? It limits the wrong things. The limits are imprecisely defined. They are too high—they are so high as to have nothing to do with effective arms control. Even Senators McGovern, Hatfield, and Proxmire tell us they intend to vote against SALT II because it isn't arms control.

The reductions called for are in the number of deployed launchers, not in missiles or warheads or in their effectiveness. Under SALT II, as pointed out earlier, the capability of Soviet missiles to destroy hardened military targets is expected to rise by 1,000 percent. With such a precedent what should we expect from SALT III?

* * *

The SALT negotiations have now been going on for ten years. Therefore, it is possible to examine the historical record and have some judgment as to the nature of the process and the factors that drive the outcome.

Several points emerge. The first is a difference of approach to the negotiations. The purposes of the two sides were discrepant from the outset. We wished for equal limitations designed to diminish the impact of nuclear weapons upon world politics. The Soviet side viewed the negotiations as an engagement between adversaries. The Soviet task was to achieve the right to that nuclear predominance which we appeared willing to relinquish. . . .

Related to our discrepant purposes have been our discrepant programs. We thought it wise to exercise restraint in our nuclear programs, hoping that such restraint would demonstrate our good will and might lead to reciprocal restraint on the other side. Our restraint turned out to be unilateral.

Senator Tower went to Geneva to participate with our delegation in the negotiations for a few days. He arrived shortly after the President had announced his decision to cancel the B-1. Senator Tower asked Academician Shchukin, the most able and distingushed member of the Soviet delegation, what the Soviet side would do to reciprocate

for our cancellation of the B-1. Mr. Shchukin replied: "You misunderstand us. We are not pacifists nor are we philanthropists." I am sure Mr. Shchukin had in mind a third point but was too polite to make it. "Nor are we fools."

The result has been that the United States has only one new missile in engineering development, the Trident I missile. The Soviet Union has progressed with whole families of new ICBMS, SLBMS, and bombers. While our strategic weapons program has been shrinking, theirs has been rapidly expanding. As a result, the pressure has been heavy on the U.S. negotiators to make concessions to get an agreement promptly. Every delay meant a deterioration in our trading position. A delay of a few months or even years did not worry the Soviet side. They were confident that as time passed the strategic balance would move further in their favor and thus improve their underlying trading position. As Henry Kissinger put it, "our negotiating position was hardly brilliant."

These considerations bear upon the prospects for SALT III. Unless we promptly act to reverse current trends, the strategic power realities reflected in the SALT III negotiations will be even more unfavorable to us than those which have been reflected in the SALT II negotiations.

An Analysis of SALT II

Despite the fact that the SALT II agreement provides for equal aggregates in some classes of strategic offensive weapons and will obligate the Soviets to reduce the number of weapons now in their strategic inventory, SALT II has so many flaws in it which work to the disadvantage of the United States that it cannot be "saved" by a few minor amendments—even if one assumes that the Soviets would accept those amendments.

Technical Flaws

Among the more serious technical flaws are these:

First, the treaty formula is an illusion. It does not, in fact, provide for equal aggregates in all classes of strategic weapons. . . . The

SOURCE: *An Analysis of SALT II* (Boston, Virginia: Coalition for Peace Through Strength, May 1979), pp. 36–46.

Backfire bomber and the SS-20 (and the SS-16, in the sense that the number of those third stages that convert the SS-20 into the SS-16 are not known and that the same mobile launch vehicle which transports the SS-20 can also carry the SS-16) have been excluded from the SALT count, as have the Soviet sea-launched cruise missiles (submarine-launched and ship-launched—the SS-N-3 and SS-N-12). These special exclusions mean that even after the Soviets have reduced the number of their strategic weapons to the SALT ceiling of 2,250 by December 31, 1981, they will in fact have hundreds more strategic weapons than the U.S. And on that same date, the total United States strategic inventory will still be several hundred below the SALT II ceiling.

But, in contrast to the exclusions granted to the Soviets, the officials of this administration have found another way of doing a favor for the Soviets by making it appear that the U.S. is very nearly at the authorized ceiling. . . . U.S. officials have agreed to count B-52s now in the "bone yard" in the Arizona desert, along with the four experimental B-1s.

Within the aggregate of MIRVed ICBMS, there remains the problem of the heavy ICBM with its first-strike potential. Not only is the Soviet Union granted the right to have heavy ICBMS, but the U.S. is specifically restricted from deploying a similar weapon even if it wished to do so.

The unilateral grant of exclusion for the Backfire is totally illogical. Moreover, it serves to exaggerate the importance of the disparity in the U.S. and Soviet air defense systems.

Second, the ABM treaty, which carries over from SALT I, has not been modified in keeping with the changes that have been made in the SALT II treaty. The SALT I interim executive agreement covered only ICBMS and SLBMS—not heavy bombers. The related ABM treaty dealt with defensive systems against ICBMS and SLBMS. SALT II now includes heavy bombers among the strategic weapons, but the ABM treaty has not been expanded to include air defense systems.

According to Secretary of Defense Harold Brown's *Annual Report for FY 1980*, the U.S. has 309 interceptor aircraft and about 60 radars in its air defense system. It has no surface-to-air (SAM) missiles. In comparison, the Soviets have over 2,600 interceptor aircraft, 7,000 radars, and 12,000 SAMS on launchers. In addition, the Soviet civil defense system adds another dimension to their total strategic defense capability.

This disparity in defensive systems is utterly inconsistent both with the doctrine of Mutual Assured Destruction and the principle of equal aggregates.

Third, the new agreement will allow the Soviets to maintain their new "medium" ICBMS, the SS-17 and SS-19. A loosely written provision in the SALT I agreement dealing with the amount of increase in the size of ICBMS opened the door for the SS-17s and SS-19s. The former has a throw-weight of 6,000 pounds; the latter, 7,000 pounds. Their predecessors (SS-11s and SS-13s) had throw-weights of 2,000 pounds. The SS-17 is armed with four MIRVed warheads; the SS-19 with six MIRVed warheads. For purposes of comparison, the U.S. Minuteman missile has a throw-weight of 2,500 pounds and carries three MIRVed warheads.

The provision in SALT I limiting the permissible growth in the size of ICBMS to 15 percent was specifically inserted in the agreement to prevent the Soviets from being able to increase significantly the total throw-weight of their ICBM force. The Soviets insisted the 15 percent applied to the volume of the missiles, rather than to a specific measurement, such as diameter or length. Despite the Soviets' exploitation of that provision, U.S. SALT II negotiators sought no ways to correct the increased imbalance in ICBM throw-weight by restricting the numbers of Soviet missiles or providing for compensating privileges for the U.S.

Fourth, the increase in the throw-weight and accuracy of Soviet ICBMS along with the MIRVing of the SS-17, SS-18, and SS-19 warheads has undermined the credibility of the U.S. strategic deterrent because U.S. ICBMS may no longer be considered survivable. This condition is the direct result of the SALT I and SALT II agreements. The credibility of the U.S. strategic deterrent could have been maintained by the U.S. insisting on limiting the size of Soviet ICBMS or by insisting upon compensations for the United States.

The situation would not be quite as critical as it is if the United States had taken full advantage of the privileges granted to it under the SALT I formula. Instead, the Nixon, Ford, and Carter administrations have all contributed to the undermining of the U.S. strategic deterrence by restraining the development and deployment of new U.S. weapons. The number of U.S. strategic weapons is below the SALT II authorized ceiling because the U.S. has refused to build new weapons. The quality of some of its weapons is less than it could have been because the U.S. has not upgraded its weapons after designing better components. As an example, the U.S. has delayed installing the larger and more accurate MK-12A warhead in the Minuteman III.

Regardless of whether one wishes to blame the Soviets for taking undue advantage of the provisions of SALT I or the United States for failing to take full advantage of its rights, the net effect of the SALT

process has been to shift the balance of strategic power in favor of the Soviet Union and to place the United States in a position of military inferiority.

The question of concern at present is whether this administration will take the necessary steps to correct the imbalance in strategic power even if the Congress and the people demand that this be done. The recent declaration by the President, that he intends to abide by the terms of SALT II whether the Congress approves it or not, suggests that the President will not heed any calls for improving our strategic posture. And the new *Annual Report* to the Congress in support of the Fiscal Year 1980 defense budget by the Secretary of Defense contains no new plans for expanding or accelerating U.S. strategic programs.

Fifth, the SALT II agreement addresses loosely the issue of the unilateral advantage the Soviets enjoy in cold-launch technique. Of the new ICBMS now coming into the Soviet inventory, the SS-17s and SS-18s are launched by compressed gas, and their rocket motors do not ignite until the missiles are clear of the silos. Therefore, they do not burn up their silos in the launch process, as ours do in their "hot" launch. Backup Soviet missiles stored in warehouses could be brought rapidly to the operational site and lowered into refurbished silos, and they would be available for launch in a matter of a few hours. Thus the cold-launch technique provides the Soviets with the opportunity to circumvent the provisions of the SALT II treaty limiting the levels of permissible ICBM launchers—and by a sizable factor. It is important to note that the giant SS-18 is one of the cold-launch missiles.

It is utterly unreasonable to assume that the Soviets, having gone to the expense of developing and building silos for the cold launching of their missiles, would deny themselves the advantage of this technique in the event of a nuclear showdown.

Sixth, the means of verifying compliance with the terms of the new treaty are totally inadequate. The so-called "national technical means" of verification, meaning satellites and ground-based monitoring devices, offer even less assurance of verifying compliance with the complicated provisions of SALT II than they did with the simpler provisions of SALT I. In particular, there is absolutely no way that satellite photographs or the returns from ground-based sensors can be relied on to determine such detailed facts as: which missiles are armed with MIRVed warheads and how many warheads each missile carries; what are the ranges of the various kinds of cruise missiles; what bombers, surface ships, or submarines are armed with cruise missiles; how

many missiles are stored in warehouses close to launch sites; and how many mobile missiles are in the Soviet inventory.

The revolution in Iran has had the effect of denying us the right to use several monitoring posts which provided critical data about Soviet missile tests. Our "national technical means" of verification, therefore, have been seriously degraded by the loss of the Iranian monitoring posts. In addition, the Soviets have successfully tested satellites that could "kill" our intelligence satellites. The loss of those satellites would drastically reduce our ability to monitor Soviet compliance with SALT II. The question has to be asked: Why have the Soviets gone to the great expense of developing killer satellites unless their purpose was to deny the U.S. the means to monitor SALT II?

Even general verification with the terms of SALT II will require positive and cooperative action by the Soviets, such as placing "externally observable differences" (EOD) or "functionally related observable differences" (FROD) on those bombers or other aircraft armed with air-launched cruise missiles or air-launched ballistic missiles. Yet the same U.S. officials who boast that we can verify SALT II have felt it necessary to insist that the Soviets take affirmative steps to make up for the deficiencies of our means of verification.

It is of considerable interest that in recent months the Soviets have been encrypting or coding data being transmitted from their missiles during tests, making it extremely difficult for the U.S. to assess the characteristics of the weapons being tested. This action at a critical time in the negotiations indicates quite clearly the intent of the Soviets to restrict the U.S. in every way possible from being able to confirm Soviet compliance with the terms of the agreement.

Consistent with the method of pre-emptive compliance in other areas of the new agreement, the administration has simplified the problem of compliance for the Soviets by redefining the term "verification." That is, this administration has indicated that it feels no need to be able to determine absolute adherence by the Soviets with all terms of the agreement. To the contrary, the administration will be content if it can verify major violations, violations that could significantly alter the balance of power. Administration spokesmen have compounded this invitation to the Soviets to cheat by declaring that the U.S. could always take the necessary steps to offset any major Soviet violations. The fact is that there are no U.S. strategic programs, standing by patiently in the wings, that could be brought in swiftly to offset the advantage the Soviets would gain by a major violation.

Ours is an open society, and Soviet agents can easily acquire a great deal of information about our systems and strategic programs to

confirm the intelligence gained from reconnaissance satellites. But United States agents, on the other hand, have an exceedingly difficult time gaining information about Soviet systems in the closed and heavily policed Soviet society.

Finally, the point must be raised about the wisdom of entrusting our security to a diplomatic agreement with a nation that refuses to allow on-site inspection, and for years refused even to provide a count of the weapons in its inventory.

Seventh, the language in the SALT II agreement is imprecise on certain critical points. Terms like "heavy bomber" and "new" ICBM are not rigorously defined. By a simple declaration that a new weapon is a modification of an existing weapon, no matter what the improvements in capability, the Soviets will be able to circumvent the terms of the agreement, as they did in SALT I. Admittedly, the U.S. could also circumvent the terms of the agreement in exactly the same way, except that a closed society can engage in such deceptions easily, while breaches of the agreement by the U.S. would be all but impossible. In light of the difficulties resulting from the less-than-precise language in SALT I, one would have thought that U.S. negotiators this time would have demanded very explicit definitions of all key terms. To no small degree, the matter of verification rests on the definitions of terms in the agreement.

Eighth, the statement of principles was intended to be a blueprint for SALT III. But its terms are meaningless. This fact has serious implications.

One of the principal arguments used in support of SALT I, and one that is being used constantly by this administration to develop support for SALT II, is that SALT should be viewed as a process. The public, therefore, should not place undue emphasis on the weakness in any one agreement. Each new agreement, the contention goes, will solve additional problems. And, therefore, each new agreement in that process will move the two parties further along toward the goal of genuine arms reductions. The administration's SALT-sellers are holding up the prospect for lower levels of strategic arms in a SALT III as justification for approving SALT II. What this ploy amounts to is offering the hope for a better agreement in the future to divert attention from the flaws in the present agreement.

SALT II deserves endorsement by the Congress and the people only if it can be shown conclusively that it can in fact contribute to the security of the United States by providing a strategic relationship that enhances the security of the United States, without reference to SALT III.

SALT II must not only pass the immediate test in regard to the

balance of strategic power and mutual national security, it must also pass the test of international perception. If the Soviets and their allies and sympathizers worldwide perceive the agreement as an indication of the further deterioration of U.S. and Western resolve and determination to survive, then the Communist camp will be encouraged to expand and intensify all forms of "class struggle." If the Soviets alone perceive of the agreement as our acceptance of their strategic superiority, then we can assume that the Soviets will become militarily more adventuresome and daring as they seek to extend their political control. We can expect coercive diplomacy and nuclear blackmail.

Fundamental Flaws

In addition to the technical flaws in SALT II, the agreement can be faulted on more basic counts which raise the issue of whether the U.S. should have ever attempted to reach an arms control agreement with the Soviet Union.

Among the more serious fundamental flaws are these.

First, SALT II, like SALT I, is based on faulty military doctrine and policy. There are a number of examples that deserve to be cited.

The basic concept of parity as an acceptable strategic relationship is perpetuated in SALT II. The principle of "equal aggregates" is supposedly consistent with the objective of parity. But parity is a condition which not only cannot be precisely determined, it is a condition which places the United States at a significant disadvantage because of the differences in military strategy of the two nations. Because the U.S. adheres to a strategy of deterrence and retaliation, it must have more weapons and highly survivable weapons. Yet, we have fewer weapons and less survivable weapons than the Soviet Union.

The Soviets do not follow a strategy of deterrence and retaliation. In their doctrinal writing, they spell out their belief in a strategy of first strike, and their weapons have been designed with that use in mind. Therefore, in their case, a condition of parity plus their policy of strategic initiative gives them superiority.

* * *

The basic strategy of deterrence also remains in SALT II. It is essential to realize that deterrence rests on credibility. . . . In fact, the United States deterrent is no longer credible. The reason is that after a Soviet first strike, the Soviets would still have enough strategic nuclear forces to destroy sixty percent of all Americans if the United

States were to retaliate. On the other hand, the Soviets might lose no more than four percent of their population because of their active and civil defenses.

It is most unlikely that any U.S. president would retaliate after a Soviet first strike if the Soviet response would kill 100 million to 150 million Americans.

It is one of the special ironies of SALT II that the vulnerability of U.S. strategic weapons could force the U.S. to resort to a policy of launch on warning. Launch on warning demands that the National Command Authority make its decisions rapidly, with little or no time to consider options, let alone to seek to negotiate a halt in the conflict. Yet to fail to launch our weapons on warning of an attack would be to condemn the majority of them to destruction.

Present U.S. policy calls for "riding out" a first strike. And the White House has, understandably, been reluctant to adopt the high-risk policy of launch on warning. Yet adopting that policy is one of the few options available to restore credibility to the U.S. deterrent.

Still another basic military doctrine which remains in SALT II is that of Mutual Assured Destruction. . . . Because the United States has almost eliminated its defenses while the Soviets have increased theirs, SALT I and SALT II have increased the possibility of the assured destruction of the United States.

Finally, the United States continues to practice phased unilateral disarmament, even though parity was reached around 1969. Indeed, this administration is canceling and delaying U.S. strategic programs at a rate reminiscent of Secretary McNamara.

Second, as a result of the flaws in SALT II and the continuation of illogical or outmoded military doctrines during the SALT process, the United States is now in the most vulnerable condition in its history.

We will be locked into strategic inferiority and overall military inferiority as a result of SALT. The imbalance in both strategic and conventional military power has grown worse during the period of SALT.

SALT has not only failed to cap the arms race, as its proponents declared it would, it has also failed to deal at all with the possibility that the Soviets might attain a technological breakthrough which would totally outmode SALT and could, quite possibly, place the U.S. at the mercy of the Soviet Union. Such a technological circumvention of the provisions and limits of SALT is a genuine possibility.

The gigantic Soviet effort to develop a particle beam weapon is the most ominous of their several advanced R&D programs. If this weapon is developed, the Soviets will possess a genuine antiballistic

missile defense system, and the balance of power will shift dramatically in their favor.

By virtue of the constraints on the U.S. provided by SALT II, it will be exceedingly costly for the U.S. to offset current Soviet advantages by adding to the capabilities of its existing weapons or developing new ones not constrained by the new agreement. Contrary to statements by the administration, it would be much less expensive for the U.S. to restore an acceptable balance of strategic power outside the constraints of SALT II than within them.

For example, the U.S. is not allowed to have heavy ICBMS. Therefore, it must seek technological improvements to its lighter ICBMS. But the very smallness of our weapons constrains the improvements that can be made. Again, ground- and sea-launched cruise missiles are limited in their range by virtue of SALT, and the U.S. has agreed not to provide cruise missile technology to our NATO allies. The theater balance of power in NATO would be considerably improved if longer-range cruise missiles could be provided to NATO. Therefore, the U.S. will have to offset that constraint by developing a different weapon—a more expensive process.

The challenge for the United States is to restore a strategic balance—with particular emphasis on the credibility of our deterrence—whether SALT II is ratified or not. Even if the treaty is not ratified, the United States must take some exceedingly urgent steps between now and 1982, because the period 1982–1985 will be one in which the Soviets will enjoy a critical military advantage.

Third, one of the most serious flaws of the SALT process has been its effect on the NATO alliance. SALT has always been binational—the exclusive prerogative of the two nuclear superpowers. One cannot dispute the fact that the strategic arsenals of the United States and the Soviet Union are orders of magnitude greater than those of other nations in the "nuclear club." Nor can one argue the point that if a true rapprochement could be reached between the superpowers through détente diplomacy, all the nations of the world would benefit from the relaxation of tensions.

* * *

The national security interests of the United States are well served by its participation in NATO. It is, therefore, a striking irony of SALT—and one of potentially disastrous consequences—that the U.S. concentration on the SALT process has caused us to neglect the NATO alliance. In effect, the United States has sacrified positive and predictable gains it could have made from increased participation in NATO for highly uncertain gains from SALT. . . .

Today, NATO leaders are deeply concerned and distressed that the United States, which has provided the nuclear umbrella over the Atlantic Alliance, is considering a treaty that would lock NATO's only real nuclear power into a position of inferiority. Such a condition would greatly weaken NATO's deterrent and would provide added incentive for the Soviets to be adamant in future NATO–Warsaw Pact negotiations.

NATO leaders also resent the provisions in the protocol which forbid the installation of ground-launched cruise missiles in Western Europe for three years, and even deny NATO the right to benefit from U.S. cruise missile technology. The feeling in NATO is that such action violates the principle of allied equality and puts them in the position of second-class nations.

Many of the former advantages to both NATO and the U.S. have been sacrificed in the name of SALT. And, at present, NATO powers are concerned about what steps they should take to ensure their survival in the absence of the U.S. strategic umbrella. One of their options is accommodation with the Communist bloc.

Fourth, the SALT process, now into its tenth year, has failed basically to resolve the question of the fundamental differences in the political philosophies and the implication of those differences in regard to national security.

The proponents of SALT have argued that the philosophical differences between the two nations are not insurmountable, and that the benefits from détente and arms control would be of such magnitude that they would ensure bargaining in good faith. Moreover, the threat of a nuclear war is so great, the SALT proponents argue, that the two superpowers would seek to overcome whatever philosophical barriers stood between them. There is little to be gained by not trying. Such arguments have considerable appeal to Americans, raised within the framework of the Judeo-Greco-Christian tradition.

Many of our policymakers mirror-image the Soviets in that tradition and assume that the Soviets will see the identical advantages that we see in friendship and cooperation, versus hatred and class struggle. It remains inconceivable to most Americans that Communists actually see as much evil in the capitalist system as they claim to. Therefore, they assume the possibility that the philosophical differences can be overcome. They blank out of their minds the purges of Stalin and the political prison camps described by Solzhenitsyn in *Gulag Archipelago,* and see instead a basic human brotherhood between the American and Russian people. But nearly a decade of SALT and détente now proves that the Soviets have not decided in favor of friendship and cooperation.

Soviet leaders officially glory in the success of the war in Vietnam and in the economic difficulties that face the West. The cost in human life paid for the victory in Vietnam and the victories in Africa is of no consequence. The only just peace that Soviet officials ever refer to is one in which there will [be] no more military or political challenge from capitalist-imperialist states. They are willing to pay the necessary price in blood for *that* ultimate peace.

There is no evidence to support the position that Soviet leaders have forsaken Marxist-Leninist principles and the goal of the destruction of capitalism. Soviet leaders foresee America and capitalism, in the words of Brezhnev, as being "a system without a future." It is becoming increasingly difficult to support the benevolent theory that a merging or convergence of the two systems will take place in the course of time.

The Soviet rejection of President Carter's plea for a new understanding on human rights and its flagrant violations of the Helsinki human rights agreement of 1975 underscore strongly the philosophical gulf that remains between the Soviet Union and the United States. The violent treatment of dissidents within the Soviet Union serves to illustrate that the Soviets view human rights always in regard to the well-being of the collective society and never as something inalienable to the individual as a citizen.

The attitude of U.S. and Western diplomats toward the concept of stability is another indicator of the difference that persists between the two superpowers. Western diplomats equate stability with peace and normality, and seek it as an objective in their relations with all nations. Stability, in the Western mind, does not suggest a static condition, but rather one in which change takes place in an orderly fashion in keeping with established laws and customs.

But the doctrine of Marxism-Leninism does not see virtue in stability. That doctrine is based on historical laws of change in which violence is respected as the necessary agent of change. The Communist Party of the Soviet Union considers itself obligated to instigate violence in order to bring about a world Communist structure.

Soviet leaders continue to express their support of Marxism-Leninism in all their formal declarations. And they see their efforts as increasingly successful. They declare that the policy of détente was one the United States was forced to resort to as a result of the shift in the "correlation of forces" toward socialism and away from capitalism.

Soviet leaders have declared that they have gained military superiority and that they are now able to dictate the course of world events. The boldness with which Soviet leaders have interjected their military forces in Africa evidences their confidence in the total politi-

cal, economic, and military power of the socialist camp and the inability of the West to resist them.

The decade of détente and SALT has seen no shift by the Soviet Union away from its revolutionary doctrine. And it is excessively optimistic—indeed, irrational—to assume that negotiations with the Soviet Union aimed at arms limitation agreements can be mutually beneficial while the Soviet Union continues to hold to its revolutionary principles. The charitable interpretation placed on Soviet intentions by some U.S. SALT negotiators has failed to evoke a non-revolutionary approach to the negotiations from their Soviet counterparts.

The Soviet performance at the SALT negotiations demonstrates the Marxist-Leninist approach to diplomacy with the West, and forecasts the ultimate failure of détente and SALT.

Statement of the Board of Directors of the Arms Control Association on the SALT II Agreements

The Board of Directors of the Arms Control Association strongly supports the SALT II agreements and urges their ratification by the United States without substantive change. The Board takes this position despite its concern that the failure of the negotiating parties to achieve further reductions and constraints and their acceptance of the deployment of one new type of land-based missile for each side may endanger the future of strategic arms limitation.

The SALT II agreements represent a significant, if long overdue, achievement in defining and maintaining the strategic nuclear balance and in improving the predictability of military threats to American security. During more than six years of difficult negotiations in an era of rapid technological change, successive U.S. teams have effectively protected American strategic interests, while obtaining important concessions from the Soviet Union. Upon entry into force, the treaty would enhance Western and world security through 1985. Its effectiveness beyond 1985 will depend on force decisions under the terms of the SALT II agreements—such as the new U.S. MX missile and basing system and analogous Soviet developments—and the nature of subsequent limits toward which both parties have pledged continuing effort.

SOURCE: "Statement of the Board of Directors of the Arms Control Association on the SALT II Agreements," released on 18 June 1979.

A series of interlocking provisions, the agreements should be considered as a whole in relation to the total balance of strategic offensive nuclear forces, rather than in isolation. Through compromises and trade-offs among dissimilar offensive forces serving different strategic requirements, the agreements establish a comprehensive and equitable framework for balancing and constraining offensive strategic arsenals. This will enhance the stability of the strategic balance, help prevent dangerous inequalities, and provide a foundation for future limitations and reductions.

The four major accomplishments of the SALT II agreements are:

1. Establishing equal aggregate ceilings of 2,250 by the end of 1981 on the total number of all types of offensive strategic nuclear delivery vehicles (all intercontinental ballistic missile launchers and heavy bombers) each side may possess, as well as subceilings on specific types of multiple warhead launchers. These ceilings will slow the competition that would otherwise lead to increased numbers of strategic nuclear delivery vehicles.

2. Providing a lower subceiling of 820 on the number of land-based missile launchers for intercontinental ballistic missiles (ICBMS) with multiple independently targetable reentry vehicles (MIRVS), and limits on the number of warheads that each type of ICBM may carry. These are the systems regarded as most threatening to a stable strategic balance.

3. Establishing a series of important restrictions on improved or new types of intercontinental ballistic missiles.

4. Introducing a variety of special measures for verifying compliance with the agreements and increasing the predictability of an enemy threat.

The agreements would not by any means bring the strategic arms competition to an end and in several cases would leave undesirable opportunities for the deployment of weapons that could render the nuclear stand-off more fragile. Nevertheless, the SALT II agreements build on and complement the virtual prohibition of ballistic missile defenses contained in the antiballistic missile (ABM) treaty. They also substantially improve on the interim offensive weapons agreement of 1972 and the 1974 Vladivostok accords. Finally, they provide a firm and agreed starting point for further limitations.

The SALT II treaty is of historic importance because it is the first in the nuclear age to require the dismantling, without replacement, of deployed, offensive nuclear weapons. Of equal practical significance are the accompanying limits and constraints on improvements in weapons technology, which increasingly stimulates competition and threatens to upset the existing nuclear stand-off.

American Security

The SALT II agreements improve U.S. security most significantly by:

1. Preventing Soviet deployment by 1985 of an officially estimated minimum of 500 *additional* strategic offensive delivery systems (ICBM launchers, submarine ballistic missile launchers, and long-range aircraft) and requiring the dismantling of over 250 *existing* Soviet intercontinental delivery systems by December 31, 1981, with over 100 to be dismantled in the first six months after entry into force. This would not only reduce by over 250 the current number of modern Soviet delivery vehicles but would also prevent their replacement with improved models. The treaty would permit the Soviet Union to retain its 308 very large ICBMs, but it would prohibit the Soviet Union from increasing the size or number of these missiles, from building new ones, and from placing more than ten warheads on each.

2. Placing effective upper bounds on the total number of Soviet intercontinental ballistic missile warheads, by limiting the total number of launchers for missiles with MIRVs, by additionally limiting the number of land-based missiles with MIRVs, and by limiting the number of MIRVs placed on any given missile. Since the U.S.S.R. is presently below these limits, they would still be permitted to build up to these upper limits in warheads. However, these upper limits will provide a fixed basis for American defense planning.

3. Restricting the U.S.S.R., as well as the U.S., to a single, new type of ICBM, which, if deployed by the U.S.S.R., would have to replace existing weapons. This will prevent the past Soviet practice of testing and deploying as many as four new ICBM models at a time. The agreements will also severely limit modernization of existing ICBM types.

4. Prohibiting the Soviet Union from testing, deploying, or producing the potentially mobile SS-16 intercontinental missile and the components unique to it.

5. Providing American defense planners with improved information on Soviet strategic forces, permitting more realistic planning and diminishing the need for "worst case" estimates which have historically led to excessive nuclear forces.

The additional predictability in the strategic nuclear environment established by SALT II is particularly important in view of the impending change in Soviet leadership, which may reopen Soviet debate on defense issues. The SALT II limits would constrain the strategic force decisions made by any new Soviet leadership in ways favorable to nuclear stability.

The agreements permit the U.S. to:

1. Add to its overall number of strategic nuclear delivery vehicles by deploying the new Trident or other replacement submarine. The new Trident I missile is also permitted. The increased range of this missile allows Poseidon and Trident submarines to disperse over broader ocean areas, increasing their already high invulnerability to detection and attack.

2. Deploy 120 aircraft each equipped with an average of 28 air-launched cruise missiles of unlimited range (or more such aircraft, if the U.S. prefers to cut back on MIRVed missiles). This deployment will improve the future effectiveness of the airborne portion of the strategic deterrent.

3. Continue development and testing of long-range sea-launched and ground-launched cruise missiles at the rate currently envisioned in American development plans, thus keeping open the option for NATO deployment of such weapons should NATO deem them necessary after the protocol to the treaty expires at the end of 1981.

The SALT II agreements would *not* permit the United States to test or deploy very large land-based missiles, which historically American defense planners have not wanted to do. Yet they would permit the U.S. to deploy a new land-based missile with as many as ten warheads, which is the limit permitted for the Soviet very large missiles.

In a concession favorable to the United States, the Soviet Union has agreed to limit production of its medium-range Backfire bomber to the current level of thirty per year and to forgo any extension of its capabilities to an intercontinental range. At a production rate of thirty per year, the Backfire would add very little to Soviet coverage of *strategic* targets, while its use in a strategic role would reduce significantly Soviet ability to cover *theater* targets—the primary mission for which Backfire is designed.

U.S. negotiators were able to achieve these Backfire limits, a breach of which would be considered a breach of the SALT II treaty, without accepting any parallel limits on American forward-based delivery systems (aircraft based in Europe, in Asia, and at sea capable of delivering nuclear weapons on Soviet territory) or limits on French and British nuclear weapons targeted on the Soviet Union.

The range and payload limitations of Backfire and the inadequate number of Soviet tanker aircraft available for in-flight refueling make the Backfire a very poor weapon for intercontinental missions. The U.S. forward-based aircraft can reach the Soviet Union more easily than the Backfire could reach the U.S. Finally, should the Soviet Union equip Backfire bombers for long-range, air-launched cruise

missiles, these aircraft would automatically come under the aggregate SALT II limits and would require one-for-one reductions in the numbers of either Soviet ballistic missiles or bombers unequipped for cruise missiles.

International Security

The SALT II agreements will improve world security generally by constraining the competitive build-up in land-based, multiple-warhead missiles which fosters fears of surprise attack and may thus provoke a nuclear war, especially in a crisis. The agreements also contain a basis for, and a commitment to continue, the reduction in the superpower nuclear arsenals. Many nations have argued that they need nuclear weapons because the U.S. and the Soviet Union have failed to make good on earlier treaty pledges to limit and reduce their arsenals. The SALT II treaty will be an important step toward undercutting their arguments.

The completion of negotiations for a comprehensive ban on all nuclear testing is now stalled until SALT II is ratified. Such a ban, together with current and future SALT limits, would also reduce the incentives and arguments of other countries for acquiring nuclear weapons. If the spread of nuclear weapons to other nations is not checked, American and global security will be greatly complicated and threatened.

Similarly, while it is clear that the conclusion of SALT II will not necessarily stimulate progress on other arms control initiatives, such as the antisatellite warfare talks, it is equally clear that no progress will be made in these areas until SALT II is completed.

Arms Control Impact

While protecting essential security interests during the life of the treaty, the agreements would make important strides in both checking and, for the first time, reversing the offensive weapons rivalry in several crucial areas. SALT II would:

1. Require the unprecedented dismantling of operational offensive nuclear weapons, ban the development, testing, or deployment of certain new types of delivery systems, and commit both sides to work for limits on other new types not yet produced.

2. Limit the number of all operational MIRVed ballistic missile launchers on each side to 1,200, place a sublimit of 820 on operational, MIRVed, land-based ballistic missile launchers, and place a ceiling on the number of multiple, separately targetable warheads on each mis-

sile, thereby placing for the first time some controls on the two most dangerous features of the nuclear forces of both countries.

3. Prohibit the testing or deployment of land-based, intercontinental ballistic missiles from mobile launchers for the duration of the protocol.

4. Limit the testing and deployment of a new system of advanced land-based missiles for each country to a single type. If MIRVed, this new type must count against the lower ceiling of 820 allowed for MIRVed, land-based missiles. It cannot be a heavy or very large missile and must conform to the characteristics set forth in the treaty for the light class of weapons in terms of launcher and missile payload (or throw-weight), launcher and missile dimensions, and fuel. The treaty would not limit guidance systems, which determine missile accuracy.

5. Provide a framework for comparing and counting varied and complex offensive nuclear forces—an essential first step in achieving additional reductions and limitations.

6. Ensure that any deployment of aircraft equipped with long-range, air-launched cruise missiles by either side must be counted against the 2,250 total and the 1,320 subtotal allowed for strategic launchers, so that deployment would be at the expense of an equal number of land-based or sea-based ballistic missiles or standard, long-range, nuclear bombers. This will prevent unrestrained competition in this new type of weapon system.

Verification

The essential requirement of verification is the capacity to detect any activity in violation of the SALT II provisions before that activity could have a significant impact on U.S. security. Any activity important enough to affect U.S. security would have to affect the major dimensions of Soviet forces (numbers and types of weapons, numbers of warheads, new weapons, et cetera), where it would be detectable by American surveillance. The SALT II agreements contain numerous provisions which would enhance the already thorough monitoring capacity of the United States. To aid verification, the agreements provide for:

1. The initial exchange and subsequent updating of *agreed* data on numbers of weapons constrained by the agreements, providing for the first time information from the U.S.S.R. on its weapons. The accuracy of Soviet data is confirmed independently by the U.S. before being agreed to. The exchange of agreed data will improve U.S. abil-

ity to check and challenge apparent discrepancies and will reduce ambiguities about future Soviet activities.

2. Expanding and reinforcing the prohibitions in earlier agreements against deliberate concealment from and interference with "national technical means" of verification (reconnaissance satellites, et cetera) including a ban on encoding of missile performance data (telemetry) which impedes SALT verification.

3. Elaborate counting rules (for example, every missile would be counted as carrying the maximum warheads with which it has ever been tested; long-range cruise missiles would be counted as nuclear, whether or not equipped with nuclear warheads); associated rules requiring procedures for differentiating controlled systems from uncontrolled systems; and definitions of some of the weapons and improvements permitted by the treaty.

The treaty will also extend the mandate of the Standing Consultative Commission (SCC), established by SALT I, to resolve ambiguities related to compliance and to establish procedures for dismantling missile launchers. The SCC will play an important role in the implementation of the new agreements. All difficulties raised by either party in SALT I have been satisfactorily resolved through the SCC.

Confirmation of compliance with arms limitation agreements involves many of the same techniques employed to gather military intelligence. Verification of the specific terms of agreements, however, requires less information and less exacting standards of evaluation than are desired for general military intelligence. Therefore, notwithstanding the closing of U.S. intelligence facilities in Iran, the SALT II agreements can be verified well enough so that no Soviet action with significant potential impact on American defense interests could go undetected. Verification of the overall SALT II ceilings and restrictions on MIRVs is not significantly affected by the closing of the sites in Iran. These provisions can be verified satisfactorily by other means, such as reconnaissance satellites and U.S. monitoring facilities near the reentry end of Soviet missile test ranges. With less reliability, the limits on new weapons and on modernization of existing types can still be satisfactorily verified at present. Verifiability will be improved by additional U.S. monitoring programs before any significantly new missile could be produced. Certain provisions of the SALT II agreements can also be verified with a lesser probability of detection. But high confidence verification of these provisions is not essential to American security. Monitoring of these less significant provisions would, however, reinforce U.S. confidence in Soviet compliance with the crucial terms of the agreements. A material violation of even a

minor technical provision would provide the U.S. with grounds for a formal complaint to the Soviet Union, backed up by the sanction that, if no satisfaction were forthcoming, the U.S. could withdraw from the treaty or take other action on the grounds of the violation.

ICBM Vulnerability

Experts agree that a single, fixed, land-based missile silo could be destroyed by a reliable missile system which has a warhead with the necessary combination of accuracy and explosive power (yield). But the lack of experience with multiple missile firings means that no defense planner could have high confidence in the success of an essentially simultaneous, salvo attack involving up to two warheads aimed at each of more than 1,000 separate silos. An attack on ICBM silos would, in addition, invite devastating retaliation against the attacker from airborne and seaborne nuclear weapons, which are even more impervious to a successful, simultaneous attack, especially if on alert. Therefore, the problem of ICBM silo vulnerability is largely hypothetical from an operational standpoint. It nevertheless impairs the assurance of the superpowers in the survival of their land-based forces, in particular during a crisis.

The theoretical vulnerability of fixed, land-based missile silos is solvable by arms control agreements only if the reliable, land-based, MIRVed missiles capable of destroying silos are severely reduced or prohibited on both sides, an outcome not achieved in SALT II. The SALT II agreements are an improvement on the Vladivostok accords, constraining on both sides the numbers of land-based ICBMs and MIRVs with adequate accuracy and yield available to pose a potential threat of a barrage attack on the other party's silos. Yet the agreements do not limit these presumptive silo-destroying weapons sufficiently to eliminate fears of an attack.

Concerns

It is in the area of silo vulnerability that the SALT II agreements fail to meet the objective of improving American security by mutual and equitable limits on weapons which threaten or are believed to threaten the United States. The agreements do not bar the Soviet Union or the United States from a major increase in silo-destruction potential by increasing the accuracy of their missiles or expanding, in some cases up to ten apiece, the number of high-yield warheads on current or proposed ICBMs. The United States would be allowed to test and deploy its proposed new mobile, silo-destroying, land-based

Experimental Missile (MX) after the protocol expires in 1981. The Soviet Union would also be permitted to test and deploy a new, perhaps analogous, system. In the meantime, the U.S.S.R. can increase the accuracy and number of MIRVS in its existing ICBM force, especially its very large ICBMS. These developments could well create a climate of heightened mutual fear and uncertainty, especially in a crisis. The combination of MIRVS, accuracy, and yield permitted by the agreements could thereby undermine the continuation of nuclear deterrence and spur new rounds in weapons competition.

Deployment of more land-based, silo-destroying missiles will threaten nuclear stability and erode the basis of SALT still further if they are emplaced in mobile basing modes which multiply potential targets, forcing an adversary to program additional warheads for targets which, in fact, contain no missiles. No system of verification for mobile ICBMS has yet been devised that would clearly be acceptable to both sides and would permit the kind of high-confidence monitoring on which SALT is based. Moreover, if the United States deploys a silo-destroying missile, such as the MX, in a basing mode that is verifiable (a judgment that rests ultimately with the Soviet Union, not the United States), there is no guarantee that the Soviet Union would adopt a similar system because of the different characteristics of its ICBMS, particularly their use of liquid fuels. To protect their ICBMS against American MX missiles, the Soviets could develop very different and less verifiable mobile basing systems or they could develop an antiballistic missile system designed to guard ICBMS, thereby threatening the viability of the ABM treaty.

The deployment of silo-destroying mobile missiles and the difficulty of verifying the number of these missiles in deceptive basing modes could well induce fears propelling the superpowers into a competition that would proliferate mobile missile targets and silo-destroying warheads, with a decline in the security of both nations. The prospect of the developments could lead, as well, to an unwillingness to agree to further reductions in the next phase of SALT, to an unwillingness to renew the SALT II treaty in 1985, or to pressures to raise the SALT II ceilings on ICBMS and MIRVS. Since ICBMS form a far larger proportion of Soviet strategic forces, the future Soviet leadership will be under particularly strong pressures to resort to such remedies for Soviet silo vulnerability.

Ironically, however, a mobile, silo-destroying ICBM system (which could not be completely deployed in the U.S. until about 1990) would not be viable without the limitations of the SALT I and SALT II treaties. Without the ICBM and MIRV constraints in SALT II, missiles in the multiple-aim-point basing system proposed for the United States could

theoretically be pinned down or overwhelmed by additional Soviet MIRVed missiles. Without the constraints on ABM systems in SALT I, confidence in the effectiveness of silo-destroying missiles would be reduced. Hence, mobile, silo-destroying ICBMs threaten the continuation of the very arms limits on which their effective operation depends. These new, mobile systems could lead to the demise of the SALT process before their deployment is completed, making this a counterproductive approach to the theoretical problem of silo vulnerability. Land-based, mobile systems for silo-destroying missiles will pose a far greater danger to American security, and to the SALT process and its accomplishments, than does the current prospect of a hypothetical, Soviet attack on American land-based missiles.

A similar, but less critical, problem is presented by ground-launched and sea-launched cruise missiles which are difficult to verify and can achieve great accuracy. Deployment on both sides could seriously reduce the predictability of the strategic environment and undermine the basis of negotiated limits, since, once developed and tested, the deployment of these weapons may be difficult to verify.

Future Steps

The SALT II agreements do not oblige either party to increase its silo-threatening potential or to adopt mobile, deceptive basing systems. There are several options for increasing the survivability of strategic nuclear forces. Land-based, multiple-aim-point systems are the worst of these options in effectiveness, cost, and impact on the nuclear stand-off. The United States should therefore not commit itself in any irrevocable way to missiles, such as the MX, with increased silo destruction capability or to mobile, deceptive basing modes. In particular, it should not decide on a particular missile before a conclusive decision on its basing mode.

Further reductions in land-based, MIRVed ICBMs are a far safer and more effective solution to the technical problem of silo vulnerability than are new or improved weapons which will stimulate an intense and perilous competition in silo-destroying capability in the late 1980s, jeopardizing SALT and international security. The latter approach is inconsistent with fifteen years of American strategic policy of stabilizing the nuclear environment through arms limitation and maximizing investment in more survivable airborne and seaborne weapons.

While the SALT II agreements are imperfect and leave unresolved the critical problems of silo-destroying missiles and potentially unverifiable weapons, their achievements should not be minimized. If

ratified, the SALT II agreements will improve the strategic climate by reducing current risks and uncertainties; they will benefit U.S. security by ending until 1985 the numerical rivalry and by beginning to control the burdensome costs and dangerous risks of an unconstrained competition in offensive nuclear weapons.

These benefits for American security can only be fully and lastingly realized by advancing the step-by-step SALT process. Moreover, the pace of technological innovation continues to outrun the painstaking course of negotiations, creating new threats to U.S. security. Therefore, American defense interests are best served by quickly attaining the immediate and substantial advantages of SALT II and, on this foundation, moving rapidly to resolve the remaining problems in future talks.

The first priority in subsequent negotiations must be to achieve significantly lower numbers of MIRVed ICBMS and total numbers of warheads on both sides, to seek limitations on flight testing, and to close the self-defeating option for a concealed, mobile ICBM for both sides before the expiration of the protocol in 1981. The best means of negotiating further limits will be to seek a series of separate, limited modifications of the SALT II treaty, rather than through comprehensive negotiations, and by precluding new systems before they can be deployed.

On those who contend that American defense will benefit more from no SALT II agreements or from postponing still further their long-delayed conclusion rests an enormous burden of proof and responsibility. We do not believe it can be met.

SALT II: One Small Step for Mankind

Artificial Issues

The debate in the Senate and the country over SALT II will probably center on four issues raised by opponents of the treaty. These issues will be much argued over, but they are perhaps not as important as will be made out. Emotions are easily aroused over them and over-simplification (as well as over-complication) can blur the facts. These artificial

SOURCE: "SALT II: One Small Step for Mankind." *The Defense Monitor* (Washington, D.C.: Center For Defense Information, July 1979). Dr. Thomas H. Karas was the principal analyst for this issue of the *Monitor*.

issues may distract attention from the more fundamental question: How can we get control of the nuclear arms race?

Artificial Issue No. 1: "Does the treaty put the United States in a strategically inferior position to the Soviet Union?" Given the size and vast destructive power of the nuclear arsenals of the two sides, one has to define special, limited criteria of comparison to show that one side or the other is ahead or behind. Such manipulations of the facts are possible because the nuclear forces on the two sides are asymmetrical—they are composed of different kinds of weapons. The Soviets have more ICBMS than we do, but our SLBMS carry many more nuclear weapons. Their ICBMS are bigger, but ours are more accurate. Their missile accuracy is starting to catch up to ours, but we are about to acquire many even more accurate cruise missiles. Their weapons can deliver a greater total amount of explosive power than ours, but we have many more weapons that can be aimed at separate targets, thus spreading the damage much further.

The treaty itself does not limit the Soviet "Backfire" bomber which might, under some unlikely circumstances, be used to attack the United States (but the Soviets have undertaken commitments to limit the bomber which the State Department says have "the same legal force as the rest of the SALT II agreement"). Nor does the treaty limit 66 U.S. FB-111 bombers that most assuredly *would* be used against the Soviet Union in a nuclear war; nor does it limit the 500 or so U.S. aircraft in Europe that might be used to drop hundreds of nuclear weapons on the Soviet Union.

Such comparisons can go on and on. By the end of the period covered by SALT II, in 1985, the U.S. will have around 13,000 strategic nuclear weapons. The Soviets may have 10,000 strategic nuclear weapons. At these levels, the idea of superiority and inferiority makes little sense. The U.S. "advantage" of 3,000 nuclear weapons would not save the U.S. from destruction in a nuclear war. The Soviet "advantage" in megatons (total explosive energy) would not save them. Even thousands of nuclear weapons one way or the other are not going to make it possible to win a nuclear war.

If the number of strategic weapons and the total megatonnage were significant, the SALT II treaty would be militarily advantageous to the United States. The SALT II treaty will require the U.S. to refrain from deploying only 60 or so MIRVed nuclear delivery vehicles that it might otherwise have. All new weapons programs now planned will be able to move ahead (in testing or deployment) on schedule. The Soviets, on the other hand, will be required to restrain the already considerable momentum of their own weapons-building program. There are no plausible

grounds for the assertion that the treaty imposes some military disadvantage on the United States.

Artificial Issue No. 2: "Does the treaty do nothing to keep our ICBMS from becoming more vulnerable to Soviet attack?" This is the so-called "Minuteman vulnerability problem." By some calculations, it can be predicted that in a few years a Soviet surprise ICBM attack on our land-based missiles might destroy 90 percent or more of those missiles in their protective silos. It would have been desirable if the U.S. could have negotiated a treaty which cut Soviet weapons programs so far as to eliminate this risk, but the fact is that such an agreement was not possible.

Since the treaty does not reduce ICBM vulnerability, some opponents of the treaty feel that the treaty is thus giving the Soviets an unfair military advantage. This should not be accepted as a serious criticism of the treaty. If there were not a SALT II treaty at all, land-based ICBMS would still be vulnerable. The growing accuracy and numbers of Soviet nuclear weapons which threaten the ICBMS would not be constrained without a treaty. As the U.S. improves the accuracy and numbers of its nuclear weapons, the Soviet land-based ICBMS will also become more and more vulnerable.

Although the treaty does not reduce ICBM vulnerability, neither does it restrain any of the measures with which the U.S. might try to make the ICBMS less vulnerable. The treaty protocol permits the deployment of mobile land-based ICBMS after 1982. President Carter has let it be known that he is going along with the Pentagon's demand for the costly mobile MX, which the Air Force will try to hide among thousands of shelters to make it much harder for the Soviets to locate and destroy the two hundred missiles in the system. The Congressional Budget Office has pointed out that not only is this plan *allowed* by the SALT II treaty, but it *requires* the limits imposed by the treaty on the Soviets if it is to work as planned. Another option for dealing with the potenial vulnerability of ICBMS would be to do away with them altogether and to rely more on missiles in invulnerable submarines. This step would also be allowed under the treaty.

The third reason Minuteman vulnerability is not a significant issue for judging the SALT II treaty is that the potential vulnerability of our ICBMS does not in fact result in a serious military disadvantage for the United States. Those who assert that it does result in a disadvantage rest their case on a fanciful scenario of nuclear war in which the Soviets attack our land-based ICBMS and not our cities and bomber force. The U.S. would then supposedly be afraid to attack the Soviet Union for fear of causing the Soviets to attack our cities.

There are many reasons this postulated scenario should not be taken seriously:

- There are so many uncertainties involved in trying to carry out an attack on our entire ICBM force that Soviet leaders would have to be insane to try it.
- Such an attack, even though not aimed at cities, would kill millions of Americans and cause certain massive U.S. retaliation.
- A limited, controlled nuclear war involving only missiles against missiles is wildly implausible: escalation in nuclear war cannot be controlled once it starts.
- Even without ICBMs, the U.S. would have several thousand nuclear weapons on submarines and bombers that could destroy all Soviet cities, their industry and all military bases.

Artificial Issue No. 3: "Can we have foolproof verification of the treaty so the Soviets will not cheat?" Clearly we cannot. No methods of verification can be 100 percent certain, and the demand for foolproof verification of every aspect of weapon systems would obstruct *any* arms control agreements. Those who insist on 100 percent verifiability want to scuttle any treaty.

During the six years of the treaty, U.S. plans call for the addition of 3,000 nuclear weapons to get up to a total near 13,000. At these levels of nuclear weapons, even hundreds of nuclear weapons added or subtracted to either side would make little difference in the outcome of a nuclear war. Two significant terms of the treaty greatly facilitate verification. Both sides have agreed to furnish technical data on each other's systems which can then be monitored by satellites and radar. And both sides have agreed to stop encoding test information to enhance verification. With no treaty these elements would be lost and monitoring Soviet military programs would be greatly hampered. If the Soviets do cheat it will become obvious in time and we can then abrogate the treaty if we wish. But no amount of cheating will affect the outcome of a nuclear war.

Artificial Issue No. 4: "Why should we cooperate with the Soviet Union on SALT if they will not behave themselves in Africa and elsewhere?" This idea of "linkage" of SALT with other issues is based on the premise that a SALT treaty is a favor we do for the Russians. The people who want to link SALT with other areas of disagreement that we have with the Soviets argue that we should try to improve Soviet behavior by not "giving" them a SALT agreement until they shape up.

Both the premise and the conclusion of this argument are false.

SALT is not a favor we do for the Russians. It is instead a recognition of the mutual peril we face in the existence of nuclear weapons. The danger is so great that it overrides the importance of our disagreements on other issues. (As the SALT I negotiations neared completion in 1972, we were bombing the Soviets' ally, North Vietnam.) In fact, the very presence of our other conflicts makes it all the more important to agree on ways of preventing them from leading to nuclear war.

Strategic arms limitations are not a favor for the Soviets, but if they were, it is unlikely that we could use them to modify other aspects of Soviet behavior (such as the pace of emigration or support of Cuba) to meet our desires. On the contrary, a U.S. refusal to go ahead with SALT would probably reinforce in the Soviets the belief that the only way to feel secure is through unilateral action to improve their world power position. Rejecting SALT would result in more, not less, of the Soviet behavior that displeases us.

The SALT Process—Pro and Con

If the Senate were to reject the present SALT II treaty and demand that it be renegotiated, it is at least possible that the SALT process, the continuity of the Strategic Arms Limitations *Talks*, might be maintained. Alternatively, the Soviets might conclude that the U.S. government has become impossible to negotiate with seriously and they might refuse to carry the process further. What is the value of the SALT process? Are we better off with it or without it?

A number of positive things can be said in favor of SALT as a process. First, by engaging in SALT the two superpowers acknowledge that they are in the same boat: they live under the threat of nuclear catastrophe. Ongoing SALT keeps this fact before the attention of the leaders of both sides. It also helps to remind the press and the man in the street that the danger of nuclear war should not be ignored. In addition, the need to prepare for SALT may contribute to the development of governmental constituencies in favor of limiting arms. In the U.S., for example, the existence of SALT greatly increased the importance of the Arms Control and Disarmament Agency within the government.

A second benefit of the SALT process is to increase the understanding of each side of how the other side thinks about nuclear arms. Americans may have hoped to "educate" Soviet leaders in American concepts of arms control and strategic stability. If so, such conversion of the Soviets to American ways of thinking may have been too much to hope for. Even so, letting the Soviets know how we think about nuclear issues may help improve communication between the two sides. Such improved understanding might be important if a crisis occurred, but it

might also help restrain Soviet planners' worst-case analyses of what the U.S. is "up to."

American exposure to Soviet thinking might also improve American estimates of what the Soviets are up to. A better understanding of Soviet hopes and fears about nuclear weapons can contribute to American policies which may seem less threatening to the Soviet Union and, therefore, be less likely to provoke dangerous reactions.

Actual agreements coming out of the talks and sustained by the continuing process of consultation can contribute even more to stabilizing the competition between us and the Soviets. Defined limits on what the other side will do in the next few years permit planners on each side not to have to rely on "worst-case" projections of what the other side is liable to do. In this way we can avoid building forces that, in anticipating the worst from the other side, end up provoking them to it.

For many people, this kind of "arms control," which seems to amount to a regulated arms race, is not going to be good enough. The negative side of the SALT process is that the two superpowers seem to get together to legitimate the continuation of their arms race. While talking about arms limitations, what they are doing is collaborating to expand and refine their nuclear arsenals at an agreed-upon rate.

Not only does the SALT process legitimate the nuclear arms race, but it may even accelerate it. As a price for their support of the agreement, the military on each side demand high limits on what can be built and then they demand that all the weapons permitted by the agreement must be built. For the U.S. military and their allies in the government, the price of approval of SALT II seems to be the Air Force's MX missile.

SALT also focuses the attention of the Congress, the press, and the public on numerical comparisons of the strategic arms of the two sides. In deciding what weapons to buy, the most appropriate question is, "What do *we* expect to accomplish by using or threatening to use them?" The answer to this question is only indirectly related to the kinds and numbers of weapons the Soviets have. With the comparisons fostered by SALT, however, we ask instead: "Do we have more or fewer ICBMS (or SLBMS, or bombers, or megatons) than the Soviets?" Instead of deciding what weapons we need and building only those, we try to maintain a symbolic equality with the Russians by matching what they have. What is more, new weapons are proposed so that we will have something to bargain with at SALT.

SALT—Why Are the Results So Poor?

The actual arms limitations that have emerged from ten years of SALT are not encouraging. Why is this? That we have the talks at all is at

least a sign that the governments of the United States and the Soviet Union have begun to recognize that nuclear confrontation could lead to mutual disaster and that cooperative action to meet the common danger is desirable.

At the same time, the governments, and particularly the military bureaucracies of the two sides, still have not come fully to grips with the revolutionary implications of nuclear weapons for international relations. Among the leaders of both sides the idea lingers on that nuclear war could be conducted like previous wars. In their view, nuclear war would not be a war without winners: the side that is militarily better prepared will be the winner.

Each side acts only partly on the understanding that nuclear war is so unthinkable that we must put aside traditional military thinking and control nuclear weapons before they destroy us. Thus, the Soviet Union participates in SALT not only to achieve mutual restraint, but also to try to obtain certain advantages. SALT, for example, implies international recognition of the status of the Soviet Union as a great power on a par with the United States. The importance of Soviet world leadership is thereby confirmed and strengthened. More concretely, SALT may help the Soviets constrain U.S. military advantages, such as the U.S. technological lead. The first SALT treaty saved the Soviets from having to compete with the U.S. in a field where they were likely to lag behind: antiballistic missile technology.

American participation in SALT is also carried on with mixed motives. As long as the U.S. held a position of nuclear superiority over the Soviet Union, it did not show genuine interest in strategic arms limitations. When the Soviets began to catch up, the idea of SALT became more attractive.

Henry Kissinger recently said of SALT:

> . . . starting in 1970 our Defense Department was pleading with us to negotiate a freeze on the Soviets lest the disparity in numbers would continue to grow. We needed a freeze not only for arms control but for strategic reasons. . . . We froze a disparity in order to gain time to reverse the situation. And we did. . . . If there had been no agreement, we could have done no more; and we would have been worse off because the Soviets were in a position to add numbers immediately and we were not.

Both sides, then, have failed fully to accept the consequences of nuclear weapons for the traditional practice of international power politics. Each still seeks to acquire a feeling of security through unilateral measures of preparation for war. Arms control regulates the competition up to a point, but the rules of great power behavior do not change

significantly. Neither side fully acknowledges that nuclear weapons have placed it irrevocably at the mercy of the other's self-control. Neither side is quite convinced that cooperation for mutual safety has become the only rational course.

Given the persistence of these traditional attitudes toward military force and international power and prestige, the insufficiency of the SALT agreements is not surprising. The question is, will Senate rejection of the SALT II treaty accomplish something better?

If the Treaty Is Rejected

Some senators who have suggested that they might vote against the treaty seem to hold the view that nuclear weapons require us to move away from traditional attitudes about the utility of military power. For them, the treaty does not do much to control arms. What is more, they believe that in going ahead with new arms programs such as the MX, the Carter administration is paying too high a price to try to get the votes of the hardliners.

On the other hand, *most* of the Senators who apparently oppose the treaty do so because they think there is too much control of U.S. arms and not enough control of Soviet arms. These Senators are much more comfortable with the traditional pursuit of national power through military strength. If the SALT II treaty is not ratified, or if it is crippled with amendments or reservations not acceptable to the Soviet Union, the outcome may be the result of a coalition between the two kinds of Senators. In the aftermath, which group will get its way?

Both sets of senators would probably advise President Carter to go back to the Soviets and negotiate a "better" treaty (although they may have differing conceptions of what "better" would mean). Considering the difficulty over the last seven years in producing the present treaty, it is hard to see how more concessions can be wrested from the Soviets. On the contrary, they may well decide that it is impossible to negotiate in good faith with the Americans, who are obviously divided from within over SALT and cannot pursue a coherent position.

President Brezhnev brought three members of the Soviet Politburo, including the Minister of Defense, Ustinov, to the Vienna summit meeting. This gesture may have been intended to indicate the continuity of Brezhnev's policies. But if Brezhnev should lose power or die before the treaty is ratified, it is not at all certain that his successors will follow the course he has tried to set. It seems unlikely that they would want to save a treaty negotiated by Brezhnev by making further concessions to the United States.

President Carter has apparently indicated in one interview that if

SALT II were not ratified, he would nonetheless adhere to its provisions while he was President. However, if the treaty he has negotiated is rejected, he is not likely to remain President past 1980. In the meantime, most of the political pressures in the United States will not be for unilateral arms restraint. Rejection of the treaty is likely to vindicate those opponents of the treaty who say the U.S. military position is declining relative to that of the Soviets and that we need even more arms than are allowed by the treaty. There are a number of accelerations and additions to its strategic nuclear arms programs that the U.S. could make if the political climate allowed higher military expenditures. There are also steps the Soviet Union could take to keep up in the arms race.

The U.S. domestic political reaction to the failure of SALT II could lead to accelerated arms programs. The Soviet political system might react in the same way. Soviet hardliners could argue that the Brezhnev policy of negoiated arms regulation had been discredited and that only additional arms could bring a greater sense of security to the Soviet Union.

As the military competition took on renewed vigor, there would inevitably be international political repercussions. For example, strains in the NATO alliance might increase. Our allies could no longer look forward to the possibility that SALT III might limit the Soviet nuclear threat in Europe. At the same time, the policy of détente being pursued by our allies, especially Germany, would be endangered by the new atmosphere of hostility and military build-up. The negotiation of mutual force reductions in Europe would probably be impossible. Despite a renewed U.S. commitment to military deterrence, tensions between the U.S. and its allies might increase.

Moreover, given the inability of the President of the United States to carry out his policies because of Senate opposition, our allies may conclude that the U.S. cannot be relied on to provide coherent leadership in the alliance. Whatever impressions a new military toughness might make could be undercut by the image of U.S. indecisiveness and internal division. Our major allies have formally advocated ratification of SALT II; rejection could help erode their allegiance.

A renewed military build-up by the U.S. seems the most likely consequence of the nonratification of SALT II. Another possibility would be continuation of a Carter executive order keeping the U.S. within SALT II limits. During the period of a de facto SALT II agreement, perhaps a new SALT treaty could be negotiated. Ideally, such a new treaty would provide at least the following measures:

1. Significant reductions, not just freezes, on strategic nuclear weapons.
2. Tighter limits on the testing and development of new weapons.

3. Some kind of answer to the proposition that MIRVed Soviet ICBMS are threatening the survivability of U.S. ICBMS.

4. Reductions in the nuclear systems that can be launched from the Soviet Union into Western Europe and vice versa.

Presumably these will be goals for SALT III even if SALT II is ratified. But it is doubtful if the leaders of both the U.S. and the Soviet Union would be in a position to negotiate them successfully if the U.S. Senate rejects SALT II.

Another possible option for U.S. policy in the absence of a SALT treaty would be to stop measuring the adequacy of our own forces by the size of Soviet forces. Instead, we would decide on some minimum level of strategic nuclear weaponry that should be sufficient to deter a Soviet attack and then stick to that level whatever the Soviets do. We would, under this policy, no longer feel compelled (as under the SALT process) to match Soviet numbers or worry about "equivalance." If the Soviets wanted to match our unilateral restraints, fine. If not, we would not feel compelled by a SALT agreement to race them in arms build-up. While this is theoretically possible it is more likely in the absence of a SALT agreement that the pressures in both the U.S. and U.S.S.R. would be for increased armaments.

Glossary

ABM. *See* ANTIBALLISTIC MISSILE DEFENSE.

ACDA. Arms Control and Disarmament Agency.

AIR DEFENSE. All measures to intercept and destroy hostile aircraft and cruise missiles, or otherwise neutralize them. Equipment includes interceptor aircraft, surface-to-air missiles, surveillance devices, and ancillary installations.

AIR-LAUNCHED BALLISTIC MISSILE (ALBM). Any ballistic missile transported by and launched from land- or sea-based aircraft.

AIR-LAUNCHED CRUISE MISSILE (ALCM). A cruise missile designed to be launched from an aircraft. *See also* CRUISE MISSILE.

AIR-TO-SURFACE BALLISTIC MISSILE (ASBM). A ballistic missile launched from an airplane against a target on the earth's surface. For the purpose of SALT II, an ASBM is considered to be such a missile capable of a range in excess of 600 kilometers when carried by an aircraft. *See also* BALLISTIC MISSILE.

ALBM. *See* AIR-LAUNCHED BALLISTIC MISSILE.

ALCM. *See* AIR-LAUNCHED CRUISE MISSILE.

ANTIBALLISTIC MISSILE DEFENSE (ABM). All measures to intercept and destroy hostile ballistic missiles, or otherwise neutralize them.

SOURCE: Definitions have been adapted by the editor from U.S., Congress, House, Committee on International Relations, Subcommittee on International Security and Scientific Affairs, *The Vladivostok Accord: Implications to U.S. Security, Arms Control, and World Peace.* 94th Cong., 1st Sess. 1975, pp. 193–198; U.S. Arms Control and Disarmament Agency, *SALT Lexicon*, revised ed. (Washington, D.C.: July 1975); U.S. Arms and Control and Disarmament Agency, *SALT II Glossary of Terms* (Washington, D.C., no date); and other sources.

Equipment includes weapons, target acquisition, tracking and guidance radars, plus ancillary installations.

ANTISATELLITE SYSTEM (ASAT). All measures to intercept and destroy earth-orbiting navigation, communication, surveillance, or early-warning satellites. Equipment may include ground-based lasers or satellites.

ANTISUBMARINE WARFARE (ASW). All measures to reduce or nullify the effectiveness of hostile submarines. The term specifically concerns operations to detect, locate, track, and destroy submarines used for strategic nuclear and conventional purposes.

ASAT. *See* ANTISATELLITE SYSTEM.

ASBM. *See* AIR-TO-SURFACE BALLISTIC MISSILE.

ASW. *See* ANTISUBMARINE WARFARE.

BALLISTIC MISSILE. A pilotless projectile propelled into space by one or more rocket boosters. Thrust is terminated at some early stage, after which reentry vehicles follow trajectories that are governed mainly by gravity and aerodynamic drag. Midcourse corrections and terminal guidance permit only minor modifications to the flight path. *See also* REENTRY VEHICLE.

CEP. *See* CIRCULAR ERROR PROBABLE.

CIA. Central Intelligence Agency.

CIRCULAR ERROR PROBABLE (CEP). A measure of the delivery accuracy of a weapon system, used as a factor in determining probable damage to targets. It is the radius in nautical miles of a circle around a target within which a warhead has a 0.5 probability of falling.

COLD LAUNCH. A "pop up" technique that ejects ballistic missiles from silos or submarine launch tubes using power plants that are separate from the delivery vehicles. Primary ignition of the missiles is delayed until the projectiles are safely removed from the launchers.

COMMAND, CONTROL, COMMUNICATION (C^3). An arrangement of facilities, equipment, personnel, and procedures used to acquire, process, and disseminate information needed by decision makers in planning, directing, and controlling operations.

COUNTERFORCE STRIKE. The employment of strategic air and missile forces to destroy or render impotent the military capabilities of an

enemy. Bombers and their bases, ballistic missile submarines, ICBM silos, ABM and air defense installations, command, control, communication centers, and nuclear and conventional force stockpiles are typical counterforce targets.

COUNTERVALUE STRIKE. An attack aimed at an opponent's cities or industries.

CRUISE MISSILE. A guided missile that uses aerodynamic lift to offset gravity, and propulsion to counteract drag. *See also* AIR, SEA, AND GROUND-LAUNCHED CRUISE MISSILES.

DOD. Department of Defense.

DUAL-CAPABLE SYSTEM. A system capable of delivering either conventional or nuclear weapons.

ECM. *See* ELECTRONIC COUNTERMEASURES.

ELECTRONIC COUNTERMEASURES (ECM). A form of electronic warfare that prevents or degrades effective enemy use of the electromagnetic spectrum. Jamming is a typical tactic.

EMT. *See* EQUIVALENT MEGATONNAGE.

ENCRYPTION. The encoding of communications for the purpose of concealing information. In SALT II, this term has been applied to a practice whereby a side alters the manner by which it transmits telemetry from a weapon being tested rendering the information deliberately undecipherable. *See also* TELEMETRY.

EQUIVALENT MEGATONNAGE (EMT). A measure used to compare the destructive potential of different combinations of nuclear warhead yields and accuracies against countervalue targets.

FBS. *See* FORWARD-BASED SYSTEM.

FIRST STRIKE. The ability to eliminate effective retaliation by the opposition in a general nuclear war. *See also* SECOND STRIKE.

FLEXIBILITY. Capabilities that afford countries and weapon systems a range of options, and facilitate smooth adjustment when situations change.

FORWARD-BASED SYSTEM (FBS). U.S. delivery systems based in third countries or on aircraft carriers that are capable of delivering a nuclear strike against the territory of the U.S.S.R.

FRACTIONATION. The division of the payload of a missile into several warheads. The use of a MIRV payload is an example of fractionation. *See also* PAYLOAD.

FRATRICIDE. The destruction or neutralization of one nuclear weapon by another belonging to the same country. Blast, heat, and radiation all may contribute.

GLCM. *See* GROUND-LAUNCHED CRUISE MISSILE.

GROUND-LAUNCHED CRUISE MISSILE (GLCM). A cruise missile capable of being launched from a land-based launcher. *See also* CRUISE MISSILE.

HARDENING OF SILOS. Protection of a missile site with concrete and earth and other measures to withstand blast, heat, or radiation from a nuclear attack.

HARD TARGET. A target protected against the blast, heat, and radiation produced by nuclear explosions. There are many degrees of hardening. The Strategic Air Command underground command post, for example, is shielded against overpressures exerting only a few pounds per square inch. Ballistic missile silos, on the other hand, could withstand much greater assaults. *See also* SOFT TARGET.

HEAVY BOMBER. *See* STRATEGIC BOMBER.

ICBM. *See* INTERCONTINENTAL BALLISTIC MISSILE.

INTERCONTINENTAL BALLISTIC MISSILE (ICBM). A ballistic missile with a range of 3,000 nautical miles (5,500 kilometers) or more. *See also* BALLISTIC MISSILE.

INTERMEDIATE-RANGE BALLISTIC MISSILE (IRBM). A ballistic missile with a range of 1,500 to 3,000 nautical miles (2,800 to 5,500 kilometers). *See also* BALLISTIC MISSILE.

IRBM. *See* INTERMEDIATE-RANGE BALLISTIC MISSILE.

JCS. Joint Chiefs of Staff.

KILOTON (KT). A measure of the yield of a nuclear weapon equivalent to 1,000 tons of TNT.

KT. *See* KILOTON.

LAUNCHER. The equipment that launches a missile. ICBM launchers are land-based launchers that can be either fixed or mobile. SLBM launchers are the missile tubes on a ballistic missile submarine. An ASBM launcher is the carrier aircraft with associated equipment. Launchers for cruise missiles can be installed on aircraft, ships, or land-based vehicles or installations.

Launch-on-warning. A doctrine calling for the launch of ballistic missiles when a missile attack against them is detected and before the attacking warheads reach their targets.

Long-range cruise missile. An air-breathing missile with a range of 360 nautical miles (600 kilometers) or more.

LRCM. *See* Long-range cruise missile.

Maneuverable reentry vehicle (marv). A ballistic missile warhead or decoy whose accuracy can be improved by terminal guidance mechanisms.

MAP. Multiple aimpoint system. *See also* Multiple protective structures.

MARV. *See* Maneuverable reentry vehicle.

MBFR. *See* Mutual and balanced force reduction.

Medium bomber. A multi-engined aircraft that lacks intercontinental range without in-flight refueling but is suitable for strategic bombing under special circumstances. *See also* Strategic bomber.

Medium-range ballistic missile (mrbm). A ballistic missile with a range of 600 to 1,500 nautical miles (1,100 to 2,800 kilometers). *See also* Ballistic missile.

Megaton (mt). A measure of the yield of a nuclear weapon equivalent to 1 million tons of tnt (that is, 1,000 kilotons).

MIRV. *See* Multiple independently targetable reentry vehicle.

MLBM. *See* Modern large ballistic missile.

Mobile missile. Any ballistic missile that depends partly or entirely on mobility to ensure prelaunch survivability. Carriers may be aircraft, ships, or motor vehicles. *See also* Prelaunch survivability.

Modern large ballistic missile (mlbm). An intercontinental ballistic missile of a type deployed since 1964 and having a volume significantly greater than the largest light icbm (the Soviet SS–11) operational in 1972. Under the salt ii treaty, only Soviet SS–9 and SS–18 icbms are defined as modern large ballistic missiles.

MPS. *See* Multiple protective structures.

MRBM. *See* Medium-range ballistic missile.

MRV. *See* Multiple reentry vehicle.

MT. *See* Megaton

MULTIPLE AIMPOINT SYSTEM (MAP). *See* MULTIPLE PROTECTIVE STRUCTURES.

MULTIPLE INDEPENDENTLY TARGETABLE REENTRY VEHICLE (MIRV). A missile payload comprising two or more warheads that can engage separate targets. *See also* MULTIPLE REENTRY VEHICLE and REENTRY VEHICLE.

MULTIPLE PROTECTIVE STRUCTURES (MPS). A deployment mode for mobile ICBMS that would depend upon concealment for pre-launch survivability of its missiles. As envisioned by the U.S. Air Force, the MPS scheme calls for periodically moving approximately 200 ICBMS among up to 4,500 vertical shelters, with the objective of denying the enemy knowledge of the precise location of the missiles. This deployment mode was originally called the multiple aimpoint system (MAP). *See also* PRELAUNCH SURVIVABILITY.

MULTIPLE REENTRY VEHICLE (MRV). A missile payload comprising two or more warheads that engage the same target. *See also* MULTIPLE INDEPENDENTLY TARGETABLE REENTRY VEHICLE and REENTRY VEHICLE.

MUTUAL AND BALANCED FORCE REDUCTION (MBFR). A series of negotiations between certain members of NATO and the Warsaw Pact begun in Vienna in 1973. The negotiations seek to limit and reduce levels of arms and combat personnel in Central Europe.

NATIONAL COMMAND AUTHORITIES (NCA). The top national security decision makers of a country. In the United States, they are limited to the president, the secretary of defense, and their duly deputized alternates or successors.

NATIONAL TECHNICAL MEANS OF VERIFICATION (NTM). Techniques which are under national control for monitoring compliance with the provisions of an agreement; usually refers to satellite surveillance and ground- and sea-based radar systems.

NATO. North Atlantic Treaty Organization.

NCA. *See* NATIONAL COMMAND AUTHORITIES.

NSC. National Security Council.

NTM. *See* NATIONAL TECHNICAL MEANS OF VERIFICATION.

PAYLOAD. The ordnance delivered by any system, expressed in numbers of bombs, standoff weapons, or missile warheads, and/or in terms of yield (kilotons, megatons).

POSTLAUNCH SURVIVABILITY. The ability of any given delivery system to breach enemy defenses and attack designated targets. *See also* PRELAUNCH SURVIVABILITY.

PREEMPTIVE STRIKE. A nuclear attack initiated in anticipation of an opponent's decision to resort to nuclear war.

PRELAUNCH SURVIVABILITY. The ability of any given delivery system to survive a surprise first strike and retaliate. *See also* FIRST STRIKE and POSTLAUNCH SURVIVABILITY.

REENTRY VEHICLE (RV). That part of a ballistic missile designed to reenter the earth's atmosphere during terminal stages of its trajectory.

RV. *See* REENTRY VEHICLE.

SAC. Strategic Air Command.

SALT. *See* Strategic Arms Limitation Talks.

SAM. *See* SURFACE-TO-AIR MISSILE.

SATELLITE BASE. An operating base used routinely by strategic bombers to reduce congestion at main bases, and thus reduce vulnerabilities to nuclear attack.

SCC. *See* STANDING CONSULTATIVE COMMISSION.

SEA-LAUNCHED CRUISE MISSILE (SLCM). A cruise missile capable of being launched from a submerged or surfaced submarine or from a surface ship. *See also* CRUISE MISSILE.

SECOND STRIKE. Excludes preemptive and preventive actions before the onset of a war. After an aggressor initiates hostilities, the defender retaliates. In general nuclear war, this implies the ability to survive a surprise first strike and respond effectively. *See also* FIRST STRIKE.

SHORT-RANGE BALLISTIC MISSILE (SRBM). A ballistic missile with a range of less than 600 nautical miles (1,100 kilometers). *See also* BALLISTIC MISSILE.

SHORT-RANGE CRUISE MISSILE (SRCM). An air-breathing missile with a range of less than 360 nautical miles (600 kilometers). *See also* CRUISE MISSILE.

SILO. Underground facilities for a hard-site ballistic missile and/or crew, designed to provide prelaunch protection against the effects

of a nuclear weapon. High-yield, precision weapons are needed to destroy the most durable construction.

SINGLE INTEGRATED OPERATIONAL PLAN (SIOP). The U.S. plan for nuclear retaliation. If deterrence fails, it affords the president with many options, regardless of circumstances.

SIOP. *See* SINGLE INTEGRATED OPERATIONAL PLAN.

SLBM. *See* SUBMARINE-LAUNCHED BALLISTIC MISSILE.

SLCM. *See* SEA-LAUNCHED CRUISE MISSILE.

SNDV. Strategic nuclear delivery vehicle.

SOFT TARGET. A target not protected against the blast, heat, and radiation produced by nuclear explosions. There are many degrees of softness. Some missiles and aircraft, for example, are built in ways that ward off certain effects, but they are "soft" in comparison with hardened shelters and silos. *See also* HARD TARGET.

SRBM. *See* SHORT-RANGE BALLISTIC MISSILE.

SRCM. *See* SHORT-RANGE CRUISE MISSILE.

SSBN. A nuclear-powered ballistic missile submarine.

STANDING CONSULTATIVE COMMISSION (SCC). A permanent U.S.-Soviet commission established in accordance with the provisions of the ABM treaty. Its purpose is "to promote the objectives and implementation of the provisions" of the treaty and the SALT I interim agreement.

STANDOFF MISSILE. An air-to-surface missile used to suppress enemy air defenses or to strike primary targets. Such a missile would usually be launched outside of an enemy's territory, thereby reducing fuel requirements and limiting the danger to the launch aircraft and crew.

STRATEGIC ARMS LIMITATION TALKS. A series of negotiations between the United States and the Soviet Union that began in November 1969. The first round of talks, SALT I, concluded in May 1972 with the signing of a treaty limiting antiballistic missile systems and an interim agreement limiting certain strategic offensive arms. The second round of talks, SALT II, got underway in November 1972 and concluded in June 1979 with the signing of a treaty limiting strategic offensive arms, a protocol to the treaty, and other documents.

STRATEGIC BOMBER. A multi-engine aircraft with intercontinental range, designed specifically to engage targets whose destruction would reduce an enemy's capacity and/or will to wage war. *See also* MEDIUM BOMBER.

STRATEGIC FORCES. Commonly refers to U.S. nuclear weapons that can engage targets in the Soviet Union and China, and to Soviet and Chinese weapons that can strike the United States. Also includes antiballistic missile and air defense systems.

SUBMARINE-LAUNCHED BALLISTIC MISSILE (SLBM). Any ballistic missile transported by and launched from a submarine.

SURFACE-TO-AIR MISSILE (SAM). A surface-launched missile employed to counter airborne threats.

TELEMETRY. Data pertaining to the functions and performance of a weapon during the course of a test. The data is transmitted by radio. *See also* ENCRYPTION.

TERCOM. *See* TERRAIN CONTOUR MATCHING.

TERRAIN CONTOUR MATCHING (TERCOM). A system that correlates contour map data with terrain being overflown by ballistic or cruise missiles. The results provide position fixes at intervals. These can be used to correct inertial guidance errors, and thereby improve accuracy.

THROW-WEIGHT. The maximum useful weight which has been flight tested on the boost stages of a ballistic missile. Throw-weight includes the weight of the reentry vehicles and warheads, penetration aids, dispensing and release mechanisms, reentry shrouds, covers, buses, and propulsion devices with their propellants (but not the final boost stages) which are present at the end of the boost phase.

TNF. Theater nuclear forces.

TRIAD. The basic structure of the U.S. strategic deterrent force, comprising land-based ICBMS, the strategic bomber force, and the Polaris/Poseidon submarine fleet.

ULMS. *See* UNDERSEA LONG-RANGE MISSILE SYSTEM.

UNDERSEA LONG-RANGE MISSILE SYSTEM (ULMS). An advanced nuclear-powered ballistic missile submarine system proposed by the U.S. Navy in 1969. Subsequently modified, ULMS is now known as Trident.

VERIFICATION. The process of determining the degree to which parties to an agreement are complying with provisions of the agreement.

WARHEAD. That part of a ballistic or cruise missile which contains nuclear explosives.

YIELD. The force of a nuclear explosion expressed in terms of the number of tons of TNT that would have to be exploded to produce the same energy; usually expressed in kilotons or megatons.

INDEX

Cover Design: Stephen Kraft

Preface to the Eighth Edition

The outpouring of English literature overflows all boundaries, including the capacious boundaries of the Major Authors edition of *The Norton Anthology of English Literature*. But these pages manage to contain many of the most remarkable works written in English during centuries of restless creative effort. We have included epic poems and short lyrics; love songs and satires; tragedies and comedies written for performance on the commercial stage, and private meditations meant to be perused in silence; prayers, popular ballads, prophecies, ecstatic visions, erotic fantasies, sermons, short stories, letters in verse and prose, critical essays, polemical tracts, several entire novels, and a great deal more. Such works generally form the core of courses that are designed to introduce students to English literature, with its history not only of gradual development, continuity, and dense internal echoes, but also of sudden change and startling innovation.

One of the joys of literature in English is its spectacular abundance. Even within the geographical confines of England, Scotland, Wales, and Ireland, where the majority of texts brought together in this collection originated, one can find more than enough distinguished and exciting works to fill the pages of this anthology many times over. The abundance is all the greater if one takes, as the editors of this anthology do, a broad understanding of the term *literature*. The meaning of the term has in the course of several centuries shifted from the whole body of writing produced in a particular language to a subset of that writing consisting of works that claim special attention because of their unusual formal beauty or expressive power. Certain literary works, arousing enduring admiration, have achieved sufficient prominence to serve as widespread models for other writers and thus to constitute something approximating a canon. But just as there have never been in English-speaking countries academies empowered to regulate the use of language, so too there have never been firmly settled guidelines for canonizing particular texts. Any individual text's claim to attention is subject to constant debate and revision; established texts are jostled both by new arrivals and by previously neglected claimants; and the boundaries between the literary and whatever is thought to be "nonliterary" are constantly challenged and redrawn. The heart of this collection consists of poems, plays, and prose fiction, but, like the language in which they are written, these categories are themselves products of ongoing historical transformations, and we have included many texts that call into question any conception of literature as denoting only a limited set of particular kinds of writing. English literature as a field arouses not a sense of order but what Yeats calls "the emotion of multitude."

This anthology aims to enable its readers to gauge the achievement of the principal authors it represents by providing generous samplings of their most characteristic and brilliant work. We have tried, whenever possible, not to give a brief glimpse but rather to facilitate a satisfying, sustained engagement with each writer. But we have also included some individual works whose compelling interest merits their representation in these pages, even though the scope of this book does not permit a wider survey of the author's writings.

By the designation "major authors," the editors call attention to an unusual power to excite and reward close attention. Our grasp of this power—our notion of where to look for it, how to identify it, and what to do when we find it—does not stand still. The questions that we ask and the pleasures that we seek change over time, and with these changes the literary landscape is transformed. Hence there are twelve new writers in this Eighth Edition, six of whom are women. To cite a few examples: Margery Kempe, a medieval woman who had the temerity to insist loudly upon the importance of her own spiritual life and left behind a remarkable autobiographical memoir; John Wilmot, the Second Earl of Rochester, and Eliza Haywood, who scandalized their contemporaries, though for very different reasons, and produced fascinating, transgressive works of art; and John Clare, a poor agricultural laborer who became one of the great nature poets of the early nineteenth century. Several of the authors and works newly included—Robert Louis Stevenson's *The Strange Case of Dr. Jekyll and Mr. Hyde* and Rudyard Kipling's *The Man Who Would Be King*—have long thrilled readers (and inspired popular films), but their inclusion in this edition highlights the narrative cunning and imaginative intensity through which they achieve their effects. Other new offerings represent the flowering of major contemporary talents, such as two brilliant Canadian writers, Alice Munro and Anne Carson.

Where do we draw the boundaries? Following the lead of most college courses, we have separated off, on pragmatic grounds, English literature from American literature, but, in keeping with the multinational, multicultural, and hugely expansive character of the language, we have incorporated, particularly for the modern period, a substantial number of texts by authors from other countries. This border-crossing is not just a phenomenon of modernity. It is fitting that among the first works here is *Beowulf*, a powerful epic written in the Germanic language known as Old English about a singularly restless Scandinavian hero. *Beowulf*'s remarkable translator in *The Norton Anthology of English Literature*, Seamus Heaney, is one of the great contemporary masters of English literature—he was awarded the Nobel Prize for Literature in 1995—but it would be potentially misleading to call him an "English poet" for he was born in Northern Ireland and is not in fact English. It would be still more misleading to call him a "British poet," as if the British Empire were the most salient fact about the language he speaks and writes or the culture by which he was shaped. What does matter is that the language in which Heaney writes is English, and this fact links him powerfully with the authors in these volumes, a linguistic community that stubbornly refuses to fit comfortably within any firm geographical or ethnic or national boundaries. So too, to glance at other authors and writings in the anthology, in the sixteenth century William Tyndale, in exile in the Low Countries and inspired by German religious reformers, translated the New Testament from Greek and thereby changed the course of the English language; in the seventeenth century Aphra Behn deeply touched her readers with a story that moves from Africa, where its hero is born, to South America, where Behn herself may have witnessed some of the tragic events she describes; and early in the twentieth century Joseph Conrad, born in Ukraine of Polish parents, wrote in eloquent English a celebrated novella whose deeply ambivalent endorsement of European empire was trenchantly challenged at the century's end by such writers as Brian Friel (born in County Tyrone, Northern Ireland), J. M. Coetzee (born in Cape Town, South Africa), and Salman Rushdie (born in Bombay, India).

A vital literary culture is always on the move. This principle was the watchword of M. H. Abrams, the distinguished literary critic who first conceived *The Norton Anthology of English Literature,* brought together the original team of editors, and, with characteristic insight, diplomacy, and humor, oversaw seven editions and graciously offered counsel on this eighth edition. Abrams wisely understood that the dense continuities that underlie literary performance are perpetually challenged and revitalized by innovation. He understood too that scholarly discoveries and the shifting interests of readers constantly alter the landscape of literary history. Hence from the start he envisaged that, if the anthology were to be successful, it would have to undergo a process of periodic revision and reselection, an ambitious enterprise that would draw upon the energy and ideas of new editors brought in to work with the seasoned team.

The Eighth Edition of the Major Authors *Norton Anthology* represents the most thorough-going instance in its long publishing history of this generational renewal. Across the whole chronological breadth of the volumes, new editors joined forces with the existing editors in a spirit of close collaboration. The revitalized team has considered afresh each of the selections and rethought all the other myriad aspects of the anthology. In doing so, we have, as in past years, profited from a remarkable flow of voluntary corrections and suggestions proposed by students, as well as teachers, who view the anthology with a loyal but critical eye. Moreover, we have again solicited and received detailed information on the works actually assigned, proposals for deletions and additions, and suggestions for improving the editorial matter, from over two hundred reviewers from around the world, almost all of them teachers who use the book in a course. The active participation of an engaged and dedicated community of readers has been crucial as the editors of the *Norton Anthology* grapple with the task of strengthening the selection of more traditional texts even while adding many texts that reflect the transformation and expansion of the field of English studies. The great challenge (and therefore the interest) of the task is linked to the space constraints that even this hefty volume must observe. The virtually limitless resources of the Web site make at least some of the difficult choices less vexing, but the editorial team kept clearly in view the central importance in the classroom of the printed pages. The final decisions on what to include were made by the editors, but we were immeasurably assisted by our ongoing collaboration with teachers and students.

We have in this edition continued to expand the selection of writing by women in all of the historical periods. The sustained work of scholars in recent years has recovered dozens of significant authors who had been marginalized or neglected by a male-dominated literary tradition and has deepened our understanding of those women writers who had managed, against considerable odds, to claim a place in that tradition. The First Edition of the Major Authors *Norton Anthology* included no women writers; this Eighth Edition includes twenty-six, of whom six are newly added. Poets and dramatists whose names were scarcely mentioned even in the specialized literary histories of earlier generations—Aemilia Lanyer, Lady Mary Wroth, Margaret Cavendish, Anna Letitia Barbauld, Charlotte Smith, Letitia Elizabeth Landon, and many others—now appear in the company of their male contemporaries. There are in addition three complete long prose works by women—Aphra Behn's *Oroonoko*, Eliza Haywood's *Fantomina,* and Virginia Woolf's *A Room of One's Own*—along with new selections from such celebrated fiction writers as Jean Rhys and Alice Munro.

The novel is, of course, a stumbling block for an anthology. The length of many great novels defies their incorporation in any volume that hopes to include a broad spectrum of literature. At the same time it is difficult to excerpt representative passages from narratives whose power often depends upon amplitude or upon the slow development of character or upon the on-rushing urgency of the story. Therefore, better to represent the achievements of novelists, the publisher is making available the full list of 180 Norton Critical Editions, any one of which may be packaged for free with the Major Authors edition (one-volume paperbound, one-volume clothbound, or two-splits package).

Now, as in the past, cultures define themselves by the songs they sing and the stories they tell. But the central importance of visual media in contemporary culture has heightened our awareness of the ways in which songs and stories have always been closely linked to the images that societies have fashioned. The Major Authors edition of *The Norton Anthology of English Literature* features fifty-eight pages of color plates. In addition, black-and-white engravings and illustrations by Hogarth, Blake, and Dante Gabriel Rossetti provide compelling examples of the hybrid art of the "visual narrative." In selecting visual material—from the Sutton Hoo treasure of the seventh century to Anish Kapoor's immense *Marsyas* in the twenty-first century—the editors had several aims: to provide images that conjure up, whether directly or indirectly, the individual writers in each section; to provide images that relate specifically to works in the anthology; and to provide images that shape and illuminate the culture of a particular literary period. We have tried to choose visually striking images that will capture students' attention and provoke discussion, and our captions draw attention to important details and cross-reference related literary texts.

Period-by-Period Revisions

The scope of the extensive revisions we have undertaken can be conveyed more fully by a list of some of the principal texts and features that have been added to the present edition.

The Middle Ages. The period, edited by Alfred David and James Simpson, is divided into three sections: Anglo-Saxon Literature, Anglo-Norman Literature, and Middle English Literature of the Fourteenth and Fifteenth Centuries. The heart of the Anglo-Saxon section is the great epic *Beowulf,* in a translation, specially commissioned for *The Norton Anthology of English Literature,* by Seamus Heaney. Another acclaimed translation, Marie Borroff's modern rendering of *Sir Gawain and the Green Knight* is featured in the Middle English section. New selections from Langland's *Piers Plowman*, the female mystic Julian of Norwich, and the religious visionary Margery Kempe together form an important new topical cluster, "Christ's Humanity." Also in the cluster, and strengthening our representation of medieval drama, is the powerful *York Play of the Crucifixion*.

The Sixteenth Century. Two celebrated plays are at the core of this section: Marlowe's *Doctor Faustus* and Shakespeare's *Twelfth Night*, the latter included for the first time in the Major Authors edition. The editors, George Logan and Stephen Greenblatt, have strengthened the selection of poems with six additional sonnets by Shakespeare and a revealing verse exchange between Queen Elizabeth and her glittering courtier, Sir Walter Ralegh.

The Early Seventeenth Century. New to this section, edited by Barbara Lewalski and Katharine Eisaman Maus, are two powerful poems—John Donne's "Good Friday, 1613. Riding Westward" and Andrew Marvell's "An Horatian Ode"—along with the most famous chapter from Hobbes's *Leviathan*. A substantial selection from Milton's *Paradise Lost* remains the section's centerpiece. Complete longer works include John Donne's soul-searching *Satire* 3, Aemilia Lanyer's country-house poem "The Description of Cookham," and Milton's "Lycidas."

The Restoration and the Eighteenth Century. The editors, Lawrence Lipking and James Noggle, include for the first time a selection of poems by the scandalous libertine John Wilmot, second earl of Rochester, along with a wry yet touching poem of "imperfect enjoyment" by Aphra Behn. We introduce as well *Fantomina*, a novella of sexual role-playing by an author new to the *Norton Anthology*, Eliza Haywood. Other longer texts presented in complete form in this section include Dryden's satires "Absalom and Achitophel" and "Mac-Flecknoe," Aphra Behn's novel *Oroonoko*, Pope's *The Rape of the Lock* and "Epistle to Dr. Abuthnot," Hogarth's graphic satire "Marriage A-la-Mode," Johnson's *Vanity of Human Wishes* and *Rasselas*, and Gray's "Elegy Written in a Country Churchyard."

The Romantic Period. In addition to a new poem by Anna Letitia Barbauld, the period editors, Jack Stillinger and Deidre Shauna Lynch, introduce two new figures to the galaxy of Romantic poets. The first, Charlotte Smith, is represented by a number of her *Elegiac Sonnets*, poems that she published when she was in debtor's prison with her husband and children, and by a substantial selection from *The Emigrants*, her long poem about migrants who have fled revolutionary persection. The second, John Clare, was a poor farm laborer who became one of the most celebrated naturalists and poets of the age.

The Victorian Age. Among the significant additions to this section, edited by Carol Christ and Catherine Robson, are Robert Louis Stevenson's *The Strange Case of Dr. Jekyll and Mr. Hyde* and three works by Rudyard Kipling, including his novella *The Man Who Would Be King*. Both Stevenson and Kipling are new to the Major Authors edition. Also included for the first time are Elizabeth Barrett Browning's long poem "The Runaway Slave at Pilgrim's Point" and Alfred, Lord Tennyson's "Mariana." Complete longer works include Tennyson's *The Passing of Arthur*; Robert Browning's "Fra Lippo Lippi," " 'Childe Roland,' " "Andrea del Sarto," and "Caliban upon Setebos"; Matthew Arnold's "The Scholar Gypsy"; Christina Rossetti's *Goblin Market*; and Oscar Wilde's comedy *The Importance of Being Earnest*.

The Twentieth Century and After. Several new and reselected writers mark this major revision by the editors, Jon Stallworthy and Jahan Ramazani. The section features a brilliant play, Brian Friel's *Translations*, which has vital connections to literary and cultural issues that extend throughout the volume. Canadian writers—the poet Anne Carson and the prose writer Alice Munro—appear for the first time. There is a new story by Jean Rhys, a new selection from J. M. Coetzee's *Waiting for the Barbarians*, and new poems from Yeats, Auden, and Walcott. There is, as before, a remarkable array of complete longer texts, including Conrad's *Heart of Darkness*, Woolf's *A Room of One's Own*, Eliot's *The Waste Land*, Mansfield's "The Garden Party," and Beckett's *Endgame*. Seamus Heaney's works, to which two new poems have been added, provide the occasion to look back again to the beginning of this volume with Heaney's translation of *Beowulf*. This translation is a reminder that the most recent works can double back upon the distant past, and that words set down by men and women who have crumbled into dust can speak to us with astonishing directness.

Editorial Procedures

The Major Authors edition adheres to the core principles that have always characterized *The Norton Anthology of English Literature*. Period introductions, headnotes, and annotations are designed to give readers the information they need to understand each text, without imposing interpretations. The aim of these editorial materials is to make the anthology self-sufficient, so that it can be read anywhere—in a coffee bar, on a bus, or under a tree. Above all, we have tried to keep in mind the actual classroom situation. Teachability is central to every aspect of these volumes.

Our fidelity to a trusted and well-tried format may make it difficult for long-time users to take in, at first glance, how thorough-going the revisions of the Eighth Edition actually are. The editorial team undertook to rethink and update virtually everything in these pages, from the endpaper maps, scrutinized for accuracy by Catherine Robson and redrawn by cartographer Adrian Kitzinger, to the appendix on English money, which, thanks to James Noggle's clever chart, now provides answers to the perennial question, But what was money actually worth? Similarly, the appendix on "Religions in England," completely rewritten by Katharine Maus, and the one on "Geographic Nomenclature," revised by Jahan Ramazani, quickly illuminate what students have often found obscure. The anthology also includes a section, "Poems in Process," revised and expanded by Deidre Lynch, with the help of Alfred David and James Simpson. This section reproduces from manuscripts and printed texts the genesis and evolution of a number of poems whose final form is printed in the volume. And, thanks to James Simpson, we now have a freshly conceived and thoroughly rewritten appendix on "Literary Terminology," recast as a quick-reference alphabetical glossary, with examples from works in *The Norton Anthology of English Literature*.

Drawing upon the latest scholarship and upon their classroom experience, the editors have substantially rewritten the period introductions and headnotes. We have updated as well the Selected Bibliographies and have carefully revised the Texts/Contexts timelines. And, for the first time, we have provided in-text cross-references to the extensive *Norton Literature Online* Web site. With all aspects of the anthology's apparatus our intention is to facilitate direct and informed access to the extraordinary works of literature assembled here.

The Norton Anthology of English Literature prides itself on the scholarly accuracy and readability of its texts. To ease students' access, we have normalized spelling and capitalization in texts up to and including the Romantic period to follow the conventions of modern English; we leave unaltered, however, texts in which modernizing would change semantic or metrical qualities. From the Victorian period onward, we have restored the original spelling and punctuation to selections retained from the previous edition in the belief that the authors' choices, when they pose no difficulties for student readers, should be respected.

We continue other editorial procedures that have proved useful in the past. After each work, we cite (when known) the date of composition on the left and the date of first publication on the right; in some instances, the latter is followed by the date of a revised edition for which the author was responsible. We have used square brackets to indicate titles supplied by the editors for the convenience of readers. When a portion of a text has been omitted, we have indicated that omission with three asterisks. If the omitted portion is important for following the plot or argument, we have provided a brief summary within the text or in a footnote. Finally, we have reconsidered annotations throughout and increased the number of marginal glosses for archaic, dialect, or unfamiliar words.

Additional Resources

With the Eighth Edition of *The Norton Anthology of English Literature*, the publisher is proud to launch an extensive new online resource—Norton Literature Online (wwnorton.com/literature)—the gateway to all of the outstanding literature resources available from Norton. Students who activate the registration code included in each new copy of the *Norton Anthology* will find at Norton Literature Online a deep and broad array of general resources, among them a glossary of literary terms, advice on writing about literature and using MLA documentation style, study aids and quizzes, an author portrait gallery featuring 380 authors, more than 100 maps, and over 90 minutes of recorded readings and musical selections. To encourage students to explore Norton Literature Online, cross-references in the anthology draw attention to relevant materials, notably to the 27 topical clusters in the much-praised Norton Topics Online site. Prepared by the anthology editors, the topics include the editors' introductions, a gathering of annotated texts and images, and study questions and research links relevant to each topic. For use with the Eighth Edition, three entirely new Twentieth Century topics—"Imagining Ireland," "Modernist Experiment," and "Representing the Great War"—and a recast Romantic topic, "The Satanic and Byronic Hero," have been added, among other updates and improvements. Norton Literature Online is also the portal to the Online Archive (wwnorton.com/nael/noa), which offers more than 150 downloadable texts from the Middle Ages through the early Victorian period, as well as some 80 audio files. An ongoing project, the Online Archive is being expanded with all public-domain texts trimmed from *The Norton Anthology of English Literature* over seven editions. A new feature of the Archive, a Publication Chronology, lists over 1,000 texts and the edition in which each was introduced, dropped, and sometimes reintroduced. As such, the table and the archive of texts now being assembled (a massive project of a few years' duration) are a unique window on changing interests in the teaching of English literature over four decades.

Teaching with The Norton Anthology of English Literature: *A Guide for*

Instructors has been reconceived for ease of use and substantially rewritten by Sondra Archimedes, University of California, Santa Cruz; Elizabeth Fowler, University of Virginia; Laura Runge, University of South Florida; and Philip Schwyzer, University of Exeter. The Guide offers extensive help, from planning a course and developing a syllabus and course objectives to preparing exams. For authors and works, the Guide entries provide a "hook" to start a lively class discussion; a Quick Read section to refresh instructors on essential information about a text or author; Teaching Suggestions that call out interesting textual or contextual features; Teaching Clusters of suggested groups or pairs of texts; and Discussions Questions. Built into the *Guide for Instructors* is a Media Guide, by Philip Schwyzer, which offers specific suggestions for integrating the anthology's rich multimedia resources with the text and for incorporating them into traditional or distance-learning courses. Finally, the Norton Resource Library (www.wwnorton.com/nrl), by Philip Schwyzer, offers instructors brief period introductions and "class sessions" to facilitate close reading, art galleries and literary links, enhanced period timelines, essay assignments, sample syllabi, and instructions for customizing the material. These materials are compatible with WebCT and other course-management systems.

The editors are deeply grateful to the hundreds of teachers worldwide who have helped us to improve the Major Authors edition of *The Norton Anthology of English Literature*. A list of the advisors who prepared in-depth reviews and the instructors who replied to a detailed questionnaire follows on a separate page, under Acknowledgments. The editors would like to express appreciation for their assistance to Elizabeth Anker (University of Virginia), Sandie Byrne (Oxford University), Timothy Campbell (Indiana University), Sarita Cargas (Oxford University), Jason Coats (University of Virginia), Joseph W. Childers (University of California, Riverside), Daniel Cook (University of California, Davis), Linda David, William Flesch (Brandeis University), Robert Folkenflik (University of California, Irvine), Robert D. Fulk (Indiana University), Omaar Hena (University of Virginia), Tom Keirstead (Indiana University), Shayna Kessel (University of Southern California), Joanna Lipking (Northwestern University), Ian Little (Liverpool University), Tricia Lootens (University of Georgia), Erin Minear (Harvard University), Elaine Musgrave (University of California, Davis), J. Morgan Myers (University of Virginia), Kate Nash (University of Virginia), Ruth Perry (M.I.T.), Emily Peterson (Harvard University), Kate Pilson (Harvard University), Jane Potter (Oxford Brookes University), Leah Price (Harvard University), Angelique Richardson (Exeter University), Philip Schwyzer (Exeter University), and Ramie Targoff (Brandeis University). We especially thank John W. Sider (Westmont College) for his meticulous review of standing annotations and myriad suggestions for improvements. We also thank the many people at Norton who contributed to the Eighth Edition: Julia Reidhead, who served not only as the inhouse supervisor but also as an unfailingly wise and effective collaborator in every aspect of planning and accomplishing this Eighth Edition; Marian Johnson, Managing Editor, College, who kept the project moving forward with a remarkable blend of focused energy, intelligence, and common sense; Kurt Wildermuth, developmental and project editor; Alice Falk, Katharine Ings, Candace Levy, Alan Shaw, and Ann Tappert, manuscript editors; Eileen Connell, electronic media editor; Diane O'Connor, production manager; Nancy Rodwan and

Katrina Washington, permissions managers; Toni Krass, designer; Neil Ryder Hoos, art researcher; Erin Granville, associate editor; and Catherine Spencer, editorial assistant. All these friends provided the editors with indispensable help in meeting the challenge of representing the unparalleled range and variety of English literature.

We dedicate this Eighth Edition of *The Norton Anthology of English Literature* to our friend, mentor, and inspiring guide, M. H. Abrams. His shaping power over these volumes and the profession it serves will long endure.

Acknowledgments

Among our many critics, advisors, and friends, the following were of especial help toward the preparation of the Major Authors, Eighth Edition by providing either advice or critiques of particular periods of the anthology: Jesse Airaudi (Baylor University), Daniel Adams (St. John's University), Kenneth Alrutz (Miami University), David L. Anderson (Butler County Community College), Robert Anderson (Oakland University), Peter Auksi (University of Western Ontario), James E. Barcus (Baylor University), David Barnard (University of Regina), Ian Baucom (Duke University), Dr. Richard Beadle (St John's College, Cambridge University), Lance Bertelsen (University of Texas at Austin), Scott Boltwood (Emory and Henry College), James S. Brown (Charleston Southern University), James Bryant-Trerise (Clackamas Community College), Natalie B. Cole (Oakland University), David Collins (Westminster College), Sherry Covington (East Texas Baptist University), Valentine Cunningham (Oxford University), Richard Dolan, Jr. (Georgia State University), Deborah Dooley (Nazareth College), Timothy Drake (Queen's University), Ian Duncan (University of California, Berkeley), Robert Einarsson (Grant MacEwan College), Marilyn M. Ewing (Eastern Oregon University), Mary Elizabeth Ellzey (Shepherd College), Robert Forman (St. John's University), Patsy Fowler (Gonzaga University), Bill Franklin (North Central Texas College), Rosanne Gasse, (Brandon University), Teriann Gaston (University of Texas at Arlington), Vincent Gillespie (Oxford University), Cynthia Griffith (Danville Community College), John Gordon (Connecticut College), Robert Haight (Kalamazoo Valley Community College), Keith Hale (South Texas Community College), Kelly Hall (Florida State University), Shari Hammond (Southwest Virginia Community College), Elizabeth Hanson, (Queen's University), Alan F. Hickman (University of Arkansas at Pine Bluff), Karen R. Jacobs (Louisiana Tech University), Emrys Jones (Oxford University), Suzanne Keen (Washington and Lee University), Flo Keyes (Castleton State College), Kathleen Kincade (Indiana State University), Bruce King, Melisa Klimaszewski (Oakland University), Jonathan Kramnick (Rutgers University), David Kuijt (University of Maryland), Janice Lasseter (Samford University), Shawn Liang (Mohawk Valley Community College), Jane Lilienfeld (Lincoln University), Peter Lindenbaum (Indiana University), Oliver Lovesey (Okanagan University College), Scott Lucas (The Citadel), Jeanette Lynes (St. Francis Xavier University), Krista Lysack (University of Western Ontario), Father Germain Marc'hadour (Angers, France), Leah S. Marcus (Vanderbilt University), Wayne Martindale (Wheaton College), Brian May (Northern Illinois University), Laurence W. Mazzeno (Alvernia College), Michael L. McInturff (Birmingham-Southern College), James McWard (Johnson County Community College), Heather L. Meakin (Case Western Reserve University), Steve Michael (Wayland Baptist University), Clarence H. Miller (St. Louis University), Sandra Moore (Mississippi Delta Community College), Michael Moses (Duke University), Joanne

S. Norman (Bishop's University), Pat Panzarelth (St. Bonaventure University), David Phillips (Charleston Southern University), Adela Pinch (University of Michigan), Tison Pugh (University of Central Florida), James A. W. Rembert (The Citadel), Rick Simmons (Louisiana Tech University), Phillip Rogers (Queen's University), Mary Beth Rose (University of Illinois at Chicago), Heidi Sjostrom (Marquette University), Billy B. Smith (Ranger College), Malinda Snow (Georgia State University), Janet Sorensen (Indiana University), Michele Stanco (Università degli Studi di Napoli "Federico II"), Jackina Stark (Ozark Christian College), Ralph S. Stevens (Coppin State College), Marta Straznicky (Queen's University), Kennetha Stringer (Drury University), Barbara Sudol (St. John's University), James Sullivan (California State University at LA), Greg Underwood (Pearl River Community College), John Wall (North Carolina State University), Phillip Wedgeworth (Jones County Junior College), Laura White (University of Nebraska, Lincoln), John Wilson (College of the Ozarks), Johnny Wink (Ouachita Baptist University), and David Wyatt (University of Maryland).

The Norton Anthology of English Literature

EIGHTH EDITION

MAJOR AUTHORS

VOLUME A

THE MIDDLE AGES THROUGH THE RESTORATION AND THE EIGHTEENTH CENTURY

The Middle Ages to ca. 1485

43–ca. 420:	Roman invasion and occupation of Britain
ca. 450:	Anglo-Saxon Conquest
597:	St. Augustine arrives in Kent; beginning of Anglo-Saxon conversion to Christianity
871–899:	Reign of King Alfred
1066:	Norman Conquest
1154–1189:	Reign of Henry II
ca. 1200:	Beginnings of Middle English literature
1360–1400:	Geoffrey Chaucer; *Piers Plowman; Sir Gawain and the Green Knight*
1485:	William Caxton's printing of Sir Thomas Malory's *Morte Darthur*, one of the first books printed in England

The Middle Ages designates the time span roughly from the collapse of the Roman Empire to the Renaissance and Reformation. The adjective "medieval," coined from Latin *medium* (middle) and *aevum* (age), refers to whatever was made, written, or thought during the Middle Ages. The Renaissance was so named by nineteenth-century historians and critics because they associated it with an outburst of creativity attributed to a "rebirth" or revival of Latin and, especially, of Greek learning and literature. The word "Reformation" designates the powerful religious movement that began in the early sixteenth century and repudiated the supreme authority of the Roman Catholic Church. The Renaissance was seen as spreading from Italy in the fourteenth and fifteenth centuries to the rest of Europe, whereas the Reformation began in Germany and quickly affected all of Europe to a greater or lesser degree. The very idea of a Renaissance or rebirth, however, implies something dormant or lacking in the preceding era. More recently, there have been two non-exclusive tendencies in our understanding of the medieval period and what follows. Some scholars emphasize the continuities between the Middle Ages and the later time now often called the Early Modern Period. Others emphasize the ways in which sixteenth-century writers in some sense "created" the Middle Ages, in order to highlight what they saw as the brilliance of their own time. Medieval authors, of course, did not think of themselves as living in the "middle"; they sometimes expressed the idea that the world was growing old and that theirs was a declining age, close to the end of time. Yet art, literature, and science flourished during the Middle Ages, rooted in the Christian culture that preserved, transmitted, and transformed classical tradition.

Although the Roman Catholic Church provided continuity, the period was one of enormous historical, social, and linguistic change. To emphasize these changes and the events underlying them, we have divided the period into three primary sections: Anglo-Saxon Literature, Anglo-Norman Literature, and Middle English Literature in the Fourteenth and Fifteenth Centuries. The Anglo-Saxon invaders, who began their conquest of the southeastern part of Britain around 450, spoke an early form of the language we now call Old English. Old English displays its kinship with other Germanic languages (German or Dutch, for example) much more clearly than does contemporary British and American English, of which Old English is the ancestor. As late as the tenth century, part of an Old Saxon poem written on the Continent was transcribed and transliterated into the West Saxon dialect of Old English without presenting problems to its English readers. In form and content Old English literature also has much in common with other Germanic literatures with which it shared a body of heroic as well as Christian stories. The major characters in *Beowulf* are pagan Danes and Geats, and the only connection to England is an obscure allusion to the ancestor of one of the kings of the Angles.

The changes already in progress in the language and culture of Anglo-Saxon England were greatly accelerated by the Norman Conquest of 1066. The ascendancy of a French-speaking ruling class had the effect of adding a vast number of French loan words to the English vocabulary. The conquest resulted in new forms of political organization and administration, architecture, and literary expression. In the twelfth century, through the interest of the Anglo-Normans in British history before the Anglo-Saxon Conquest, not only England but all of Western Europe became fascinated with a legendary hero named Arthur who makes his earliest appearances in Celtic literature. King Arthur and his knights became a staple subject of medieval French, English, and German literature.

Literature in English was performed orally and written throughout the Middle Ages, but the awareness of and pride in a uniquely *English* literature does not actually exist before the late fourteenth century. In 1336 Edward III began a war to enforce his claims to the throne of France; the war continued intermittently for one hundred years until finally the English were driven from all their French territories except for the port of Calais. One result of the war and these losses was a keener sense on the part of England's nobility of their English heritage and identity. Toward the close of the fourteenth century English finally began to displace French as the language for conducting business in Parliament and much official correspondence. Although the high nobility continued to speak French by preference, they were certainly bilingual, whereas some of the earlier Norman kings had known no English at all. It was becoming possible to obtain patronage for literary achievement in English. The decision of Chaucer (d. 1400) to emulate French and Italian poetry in his own vernacular is an indication of the change taking place in the status of English, and Chaucer's works were greatly to enhance the prestige of English as a vehicle for literature of high ambition. He was acclaimed by fifteenth-century poets as the embellisher of the English tongue; later writers called him the English Homer and the father of English poetry. His friend John Gower (1330?–1408) wrote long poems in French and Latin before producing his last major work, the *Confessio Amantis* (The Lover's Confession), which in spite of its Latin title is composed in English.

The third and longest of the three primary sections, Middle English Literature in the Fourteenth and Fifteenth Centuries, is thus not only a chronological and linguistic division but implies a new sense of English as a literary medium that could compete with French and Latin in elegance and seriousness.

Book production throughout the medieval period was an expensive process. Until the invention of moveable type in the mid-fifteenth century (introduced into England by Caxton in 1476), medieval books were reproduced by hand in manuscript (literally "written by hand"). While paper became increasingly common for less expensive manuscripts in the fifteenth century, manuscripts were until then written on carefully prepared animal (usually calf or sheep) skin, known as parchment or vellum. More expensive books could be illuminated both by colored and calligraphic lettering, and by visual images.

The institutions of book production developed across the period. In the Anglo-Saxon period monasteries were the main centers of book production and storage. Until their dissolution in the 1530s, monastic and other religious houses continued to produce books, but from the early fourteenth century, particularly in London, commercial book-making enterprises came into being. These were loose organizations of various artisans such as parchmentmakers, scribes, flourishers, illuminators, and binders, who usually lived in the same neighborhoods in towns. A bookseller or dealer (usually a member of one of these trades) would coordinate the production of books to order for wealthy patrons, sometimes distributing the work of copying to different scribes, who would be responsible for different gatherings, or quires, of the same book. Such shops could call upon the services of professional scribes working in the bureaucracies of the royal court.

The market for books also changed across the period: while monasteries, other religious houses, and royal courts continued to fund the production of books, from the Anglo-Norman period books were also produced for (and sometimes by) noble and gentry households. From the fourteenth century the market was widened yet further, with wealthy urban patrons also ordering books. Some of these books were dedicated to single works, some largely to single genres; most were much more miscellaneous, containing texts of many kinds and (particularly in the Anglo-Norman period) written in different languages (especially Latin, French and English). Only a small proportion of medieval books survive; large numbers were destroyed at the time of the dissolution of the monasteries in the 1530s.

Texts in Old English, Early Middle English, the more difficult texts in later Middle English (*Sir Gawain and the Green Knight, Piers Plowman*), and those in other languages are given in translation. Chaucer and other Middle English works may be read in the original, even by the beginner, with the help of marginal glosses and notes. These texts have been spelled in a way that is intended to aid the reader. Analyses of the sounds and grammar of Middle English and of Old and Middle English prosody are presented on pages 15–21.

ANGLO-SAXON LITERATURE

From the first to the fifth century, England was a province of the Roman Empire and was named Britannia after its Celtic-speaking inhabitants, the Britons. The Britons adapted themselves to Roman civilization, of which the ruins survived to impress the poet of *The Wanderer*, who refers to them as "the old works of giants." The withdrawal of the Roman legions during the fifth century, in a vain attempt to protect Rome itself from the threat of Germanic conquest, left the island vulnerable to seafaring Germanic invaders. These belonged primarily to three related tribes, the Angles, the Saxons, and the Jutes. The name *English* derives from the Angles, and the names of the counties Essex, Sussex, and Wessex refer to the territories occupied by the East, South, and West Saxons.

The Anglo-Saxon occupation was no sudden conquest but extended over decades of fighting against the native Britons. The latter were, finally, largely confined to the mountainous region of Wales, where the modern form of their language is spoken alongside English to this day. The Britons had become Christians in the fourth century after the conversion of Emperor Constantine along with most of the rest of the Roman Empire, but for about 150 years after the beginning of the invasion, Christianity was maintained only in the remoter regions where the as yet pagan Anglo-Saxons failed to penetrate. In the year 597, however, a Benedictine monk (afterward St. Augustine of Canterbury) was sent by Pope Gregory as a missionary to King Ethelbert of Kent, the most southerly of the kingdoms into which England was then divided, and about the same time missionaries from Ireland began to preach Christianity in the north. Within 75 years the island was once more predominantly Christian. Before Christianity there had been no books. The impact of Christianity on literacy is evident from the fact that the first extended written specimen of the Old English (Anglo-Saxon) language is a code of laws promulgated by Ethelbert, the first English Christian king.

In the centuries that followed the conversion, England produced many distinguished churchmen. One of the earliest of these was Bede, whose Latin *Ecclesiastical History of the English People*, which tells the story of the conversion and of the English church, was completed in 731; this remains one of our most important sources of knowledge about the period. In the next generation Alcuin (735–804), a man of wide culture, became the friend and adviser of the Frankish emperor Charlemagne, whom he assisted in making the Frankish court a great center of learning; thus by the year 800 English culture had developed so richly that it overflowed its insular boundaries.

In the ninth century the Christian Anglo-Saxons were themselves subjected to new Germanic invasions by the Danes who in their longboats repeatedly ravaged the coast, sacking Bede's monastery among others. Such a raid late in the tenth century inspired *The Battle of Maldon*, the last of the Old English heroic poems. The Danes also occupied the northern part of the island, threatening to overrun the rest. They were stopped by Alfred, king of the West Saxons from 871 to 899, who for a time united all the kingdoms of southern England. This most active king was also an enthusiastic patron of literature. He himself translated various works from Latin, the most important of which was Boethius's *Consolation of Philosophy*, a sixth-century Roman work also translated in the fourteenth century by Chaucer. Alfred probably also instigated a translation of Bede's *History* and the beginning of the *Anglo-Saxon Chronicle*: this year-by-year record in Old English of important events in England was maintained at one monastery until the middle of the twelfth century. Practically all of Old English poetry is preserved in copies made in the West Saxon dialect after the reign of Alfred.

Old English Poetry

The Anglo-Saxon invaders brought with them a tradition of oral poetry. Because nothing was written down before the conversion to Christianity, we have only circumstantial evidence of what that poetry must have been like. Aside from a few short inscriptions on small artifacts, the earliest records in the English language are in manuscripts produced at monasteries and other religious establishments, beginning in the seventh century. Literacy was mainly restricted to servants of the church, and so it is natural that the bulk of Old English literature deals with religious subjects and is mostly drawn from Latin sources. Under the expensive conditions of manuscript production, few texts were written down that did not pertain directly to the work of the church. Most of Old English poetry is contained in just four manuscripts.

Germanic heroic poetry continued to be performed orally in alliterative verse and was at times used to describe current events. *The Battle of Brunaburh*, which celebrates an English victory over the Danes in traditional alliterative verse, is preserved in the *Anglo-Saxon Chronicle*. *The Battle of Maldon* commemorates a Viking victory in which the Christian English invoke the ancient code of honor that obliges a warrior to avenge his slain lord or to die beside him.

These poems show that the aristocratic heroic and kinship values of Germanic society continued to inspire both clergy and laity in the Christian era. As represented in the relatively small body of Anglo-Saxon heroic poetry that survives, this world shares many characteristics with the heroic world described by Homer. Nations are reckoned as groups of people related by kinship rather than by geographical areas, and kinship is the basis of the heroic code. The tribe is ruled by a chieftain who is called *king*, a word that has "kin" for its root. The *lord* (a word derived from Old English *hlaf*, "loaf," plus *weard*, "protector") surrounds himself with a band of retainers (many of them his blood kindred) who are members of his household. He leads his men in battle and rewards them with the spoils; royal generosity was one of the most important aspects of heroic behavior. In return, the retainers are obligated to fight for their lord to the death, and if he is slain, to avenge him or die in the attempt. Blood vengeance is regarded as a sacred duty, and in poetry, everlasting shame awaits those who fail to observe it.

Even though the heroic world of poetry could be invoked to rally resistance to the Viking invasions, it was already remote from the Christian world of Anglo-Saxon England. Nevertheless, Christian writers like the *Beowulf* poet were fascinated by the distant culture of their pagan ancestors and by the inherent conflict between the heroic code and a religion that teaches that we should "forgive those who trespass against us" and that "all they that take the sword shall perish with the sword." The *Beowulf* poet looks back on that ancient world with admiration for the courage of which it was capable and at the same time with elegiac sympathy for its inevitable doom.

For Anglo-Saxon poetry, it is difficult and probably futile to draw a line between "heroic" and "Christian," for the best poetry crosses that boundary. Much of the Christian poetry is also cast in the heroic mode: although the Anglo-Saxons adapted themselves readily to the ideals of Christianity, they did not do so without adapting Christianity to their own heroic ideal. Thus Moses and St. Andrew, Christ and God the Father are represented in the style of heroic verse. In the *Dream of the Rood*, the Cross speaks of Christ as "the young hero, . . . strong and stouthearted." In Cædmon's *Hymn* the creation of heaven and earth is seen as a mighty deed, an "establishment of wonders." Anglo-Saxon heroines, too, are portrayed in the heroic manner. St. Helena, who leads an expedition to the Holy Land to discover the true Cross, is described as a "battle-queen." The biblical narrative related in the Anglo-Saxon poem *Judith* is recast in the terms of Germanic heroic poetry. Christian and heroic ideals are poignantly blended in *The Wanderer*, which laments the separation from one's lord and kinsmen and the transience of all earthly treasures. Love between man and woman, as described by the female speaker of *The Wife's Lament*, is disrupted by separation, exile, and the malice of kinfolk.

The world of Old English poetry is often elegiac. Men are said to be cheerful in the mead hall, but even there they think of war, of possible triumph but more possible failure. Romantic love—one of the principal topics of later literature—appears hardly at all. Even so, at some of the bleakest moments, the poets powerfully recall the return of spring. The blade of the magic sword with which Beowulf has killed Grendel's mother in her sinister underwater lair begins to melt, "as ice melts / when the Father eases the fetters off the frost / and unravels the water ropes, He who wields power."

Poetic language is created out of a special vocabulary that contains a multiplicity of terms for *lord, warrior, spear, shield*, and so on. Synecdoche and metonymy are common figures of speech as when "keel" is used for *ship* or "iron," for *sword*. A particularly striking effect is achieved by the kenning, a compound of two words in place of another as when *sea* becomes "whale-road" or *body* is called "life-house." The figurative use of language finds playful expression in poetic riddles, of which about one hundred survive. Common (and sometimes uncommon) creatures, objects, or phenomena are described in an enigmatic passage of alliterative verse, and the reader must guess their identity. Sometimes they are personified and ask, "What is my name?"

Because special vocabulary and compounds are among the chief poetic effects, the verse is constructed in such a way as to show off such terms by creating a series of them in apposition. In the second sentence of Cædmon's *Hymn*, for example, God is referred to five times appositively as "he," "holy Creator," "mankind's Guardian," "eternal Lord," and "Master Almighty." This use of parallel and appositive expressions, known as *variation*, gives the verse a highly structured and musical quality.

The overall effect of the language is to formalize and elevate speech. Instead of being straightforward, it moves at a slow and stately pace with steady indirection. A favorite mode of this indirection is irony. A grim irony pervades heroic poetry even at the level of diction where *fighting* is called "battle-play." A favorite device, known by the rhetorical term *litotes*, is ironic understatement. After the monster Grendel has slaughtered the Danes in the great hall Heorot, it stands deserted. The poet observes, "It was easy then to meet with a man / shifting himself to a safer distance."

More than a figure of thought, irony is also a mode of perception in Old English poetry. In a famous passage, the Wanderer articulates the theme of *Ubi sunt?* (where are they now?): "Where has the horse gone? Where the young warrior? Where the giver of treasure? . . ." *Beowulf* is full of ironic balances and contrasts—between the aged Danish king and the youthful Beowulf, and between Beowulf, the high-spirited young warrior at the beginning, and Beowulf, the gray-haired king at the end, facing the dragon and death.

The formal and dignified speech of Old English poetry was always distant from the everyday language of the Anglo-Saxons, and this poetic idiom remained remarkably uniform for the roughly three hundred years before the Norman Conquest. This clinging to old forms—grammatical and orthographic as well as literary—by the Anglo-Saxon church and aristocracy conceals from us the enormous changes that were taking place in the English language and the diversity of its dialects. The dramatic changes between Old and Middle English did not happen overnight or over the course of a single century. The

Normans displaced the English ruling class with their own barons and clerics, whose native language was a dialect of Old French that we call Anglo-Norman. Without a ruling literate class to preserve English traditions, the custom of transcribing vernacular texts in an earlier form of the West-Saxon dialect was abandoned, and both language and literature were allowed to develop unchecked in new directions.

ANGLO-NORMAN LITERATURE

The Normans, who took possession of England after the decisive Battle of Hastings (1066), were, like the Anglo-Saxons, descendants of Germanic adventurers, who at the beginning of the tenth century had seized a wide part of northern France. Their name is actually a contraction of "Norsemen." A highly adaptable people, they had adopted the French language of the land they had settled in and its Christian religion. Both in Normandy and in Britain they were great builders of castles, with which they enforced their political dominance, and magnificent churches. Norman bishops, who held land and castles like the barons, wielded both political and spiritual authority. The earlier Norman kings of England, however, were often absentee rulers, as much concerned with defending their Continental possessions as with ruling over their English holdings. The English Crown's French territories were enormously increased in 1154 when Henry II, the first of England's Plantagenet kings, ascended the throne. Through his marriage with Eleanor of Aquitaine, the divorced wife of Louis VII of France, Henry had acquired vast provinces in the southwest of France.

The presence of a French-speaking ruling class in England created exceptional opportunities for linguistic and cultural exchange. Four languages coexisted in the realm of Anglo-Norman England: Latin, as it had been for Bede, remained the international language of learning, used for theology, science, and history. It was not by any means a written language only but also a lingua franca by which different nationalities communicated in the church and the newly founded universities. The Norman aristocracy for the most part spoke French, but intermarriage with the native English nobility and the business of daily life between masters and servants encouraged bilingualism. Different branches of the Celtic language group were spoken in Scotland, Ireland, Wales, Cornwall, and Brittany.

Inevitably, there was also literary intercourse among the different languages. The Latin Bible and Latin saints' lives provided subjects for a great deal of Old English as well as Old French poetry and prose. The first medieval drama in the vernacular, *The Play of Adam*, with elaborate stage directions in Latin and realistic dialogue in the Anglo-Norman dialect of French, was probably produced in England during the twelfth century.

The Anglo-Norman aristocracy was especially attracted to Celtic legends and tales that had been circulating orally for centuries. The twelfth-century poets Thomas of England, Marie de France and Chrétien de Troyes each claim to have obtained their narratives from Breton storytellers, who were probably bilingual performers of native tales for French audiences. "Breton" may indicate that they came from Brittany, or it may have been a generic term for a Celtic bard. Marie speaks respectfully of the storytellers, while Thomas expresses caution about their tendency to vary narratives; Chrétien accuses them of marring their material, which, he boasts, he has retold with an elegant fusion of form and meaning. Marie wrote a series of short romances, which she refers to as "lays" originally told by Bretons. Her versions are the most original and sophisticated examples of the genre that came to be known as the Breton lay, represented here by Marie's *Lanval*. It is very likely that Henry II is the "noble king" to whom she dedicated her lays and that they were written for his court. Thomas composed a moving, almost operatic version of the adulterous passion of Tristran and Isolt, very different from the powerful version of the same story by Beroul, also composed in the last half of the twelfth century. Chrétien is the principal creator of the romance of chivalry in which knightly adventures are a means of exploring psychological and ethical dilemmas that the knights must solve, in addition to displaying martial prowess in saving ladies from monsters, giants, and wicked knights. Chrétien, like Marie, is thought to have spent time in England at the court of Henry II.

Thomas, Marie, and Chrétien de Troyes were innovators of the genre that has become known as "romance." The word *roman* was initially applied in French to a work written in the French vernacular. Thus the thirteenth-century *Roman de Troie* is a long poem about the Trojan War in French. While this work deals mainly with the siege of Troy, it also includes stories about the love of Troilus for Cressida and of Achilles for the Trojan princess Polyxena. Eventually, "romance" acquired the generic associations it has for us as a story about love and adventure.

Romance was the principal narrative genre for late medieval readers. Insofar as it was centrally concerned with love, it developed ways of representing psychological interiority with great subtlety. That subtlety itself provoked a sub-genre of questions about love. Thus in the late twelfth century, Andreas Capellanus (Andrew the Chaplain) wrote a Latin treatise, the title of which may be translated *The Art of Loving Correctly* [*honeste*]. In one part, Eleanor of Aquitaine, her daughter, the countess Marie de Champagne, and other noble women are cited as a supreme court rendering decisions on difficult questions of love—for example, whether there is greater passion between lovers or between married couples. Whether such "courts of love" were purely imaginary or whether they represent some actual court entertainment, they imply that the literary taste and judgment of women had a significant role in fostering the rise of romance in France and Anglo-Norman England.

In Marie's *Lanval* and in Chrétien's romances, the court of King Arthur had already acquired for French audiences a reputation as the most famous center of chivalry. That eminence is owing in large measure to a remarkable book in Latin, *The History of the Kings of Britain*, completed by Geoffrey of Monmouth, ca. 1136–38. Geoffrey claimed to have based his "history" on a book in the British tongue (i.e., Welsh), but no one has ever found such a book. He drew on a few earlier Latin chronicles, but the bulk of his history was probably fabricated from Celtic oral tradition, his familiarity with Roman history and literature, and his own fertile imagination. The climax of the book is the reign of King Arthur, who defeats the Roman armies but is forced to turn back to Britain to counter the treachery of his nephew Mordred. In 1155 Geoffrey's Latin was rendered into French rhyme by an Anglo-Norman poet called Wace, and fifty or so years later Wace's poem was turned by Layamon, an English priest, into a much longer poem that combines English alliterative verse with sporadic rhyme.

Layamon's work is one of many instances where English receives new material directly through French sources, which may be drawn from Celtic or Latin sources. There are two Middle English versions of Marie's *Lanval*, and the English romance called *Yvain and Gawain* is a cruder version of Chrétien's *Le Chevalier au Lion* (The Knight of the Lion). There is a marvelous English lay, *Sir Orfeo*, a version of the Orpheus story in which Orpheus succeeds in rescuing his wife from the other world, for which a French original, if there was one, has never been found. Romance, stripped of its courtly, psychological, and ethical subtleties, had an immense popular appeal for English readers and listeners. Many of these romances are simplified adaptations of more aristocratic French poems and recount in a rollicking and rambling style the adventures of heroes like Guy of Warwick, a poor steward who must prove his knightly worth to win the love of Fair Phyllis. The ethos of many romances, aristocratic and popular alike, involves a knight proving his worthiness through nobility of character and brave deeds rather than through high birth. In this respect romances reflect the aspirations of a lower order of the nobility to rise in the world, as historically some of these nobles did. William the Marshall, for example, the fourth son of a baron of middle rank, used his talents in war and in tournaments to become tutor to the oldest son of Henry II and Eleanor of Aquitaine. He married a great heiress and became one of the most powerful nobles in England and the subject of a verse biography in French, which often reads like a romance.

Of course, not all writing in Early Middle English depends on French sources or intermediaries. The *Anglo-Saxon Chronicle* continued to be written at the monastery of Peterborough. It is an invaluable witness for the changes taking place in the English language and allows us to see Norman rule from an English point of view. *The Owl and the Nightingale* (?late twelfth century) is a witty and entertaining poem in which these two female birds engage in a fierce debate about the benefits their singing brings to humankind. The owl grimly reminds her rival of the sinfulness of the human condition, which her mournful song is intended to amend; the nightingale sings about the pleasures of life and love when lord and lady are in bed together. The poet, who was certainly a cleric, is well aware of the fashionable new romance literature; he specifically has the nightingale allude to Marie de France's lay *Laüstic*, the Breton word, she says, for "rossignol" in French and "nightingale" in English. The poet does not side with either bird; rather he has amusingly created the sort of dialectic between the discourses of religion and romance that is carried on throughout medieval literature.

There is also a body of Early Middle English religious prose aimed at women. Three saints' lives celebrate the heroic combats of virgin martyrs who suffer dismemberment and death; a tract entitled *Holy Maidenhead* paints the woes of marriage not from the point of view of the husband, as in standard medieval antifeminist writings, but from that of the wife. Related to these texts, named the Katherine Group after one of the virgin martyrs, is a religious work also written for women but in a very different spirit. The *Ancrene Riwle* (Anchoresses' Rule), or *Ancrene Wisse* (Anchoresses' Guide) as it is called in another manuscript, is one of the finest works of English religious prose in any period. It is a manual of instruction written at the request of three sisters who have chosen to live as religious recluses. The author, who may have been their personal confessor, addresses them with affection, and, at times, with kindness and humor. He is also profoundly serious in his analyses of sin, penance, and love.

MIDDLE ENGLISH LITERATURE IN THE FOURTEENTH AND FIFTEENTH CENTURIES

The styles of *The Owl and the Nightingale* and *Ancrene Riwle* show that around the year 1200 both poetry and prose were being written for sophisticated and well-educated readers whose primary language was English. Throughout the thirteenth and early fourteenth centuries, there are many kinds of evidence that, although French continued to be the principal language of Parliament, law, business, and high culture, English was gaining ground. Several authors of religious and didactic works in English state that they are writing for the benefit of those who do not understand Latin or French. Anthologies were made of miscellaneous works adapted from French for English readers and original pieces in English. Most of the nobility were by now bilingual, and the author of an English romance written early in the fourteenth century declares that he has seen many nobles who cannot speak French. Children of the nobility and the merchant class are now learning French as a second language. By the 1360s the linguistic, political, and cultural climate had been prepared for the flowering of Middle English literature in the writings of Chaucer, Gower, Langland, and the *Gawain* poet.

The Fourteenth Century

War and disease were prevalent throughout the Middle Ages but never more devastatingly than during the fourteenth century. In the wars against France, the gains of two spectacular English victories, at Crécy in 1346 and Poitiers in 1356, were gradually frittered away in futile campaigns that ravaged the French countryside without obtaining any clear advantage for the English. In 1348 the first and most virulent epidemic of the bubonic plague—the Black Death—swept Europe, wiping out a quarter to a third of the population. The toll was higher in crowded urban centers. Giovanni Boccaccio's description of the plague in Florence, with which he introduces the *Decameron*, vividly portrays its ravages: "So many corpses would arrive in front of a church every day and at every hour that the amount of holy ground for burials was certainly insufficient for the ancient custom of giving each body its individual place; when all the graves were full, huge trenches were dug in all of the cemeteries of the churches and into them the new arrivals were dumped by the hundreds; and they were packed in there with dirt, one on top of another, like a ship's cargo, until the trench was filled." The resulting scarcity of labor and a sudden expansion of the possibilities for social mobility fostered popular discontent. In 1381 attempts to enforce wage controls and to collect oppressive new taxes provoked a rural uprising in Essex and Kent that dealt a profound shock to the English ruling class. The participants were for the most part tenant farmers, day laborers, apprentices, and rural workers not attached to the big manors. A few of the lower clergy sided with the rebels against their wealthy church superiors; the priest John Ball was among the leaders. The movement was quickly suppressed, but not before sympathizers in London had admitted the rebels through two city gates, which had been barred against them. The insurgents burned down the palace of the hated duke of Lancaster, and they summarily beheaded the archbishop of Canterbury and the treasurer of England, who had taken refuge in the Tower of London. The church had become the target of popular resentment because it was among the greatest of the oppressive landowners and because of the wealth, worldliness, and venality of many of the higher clergy.

These calamities and upheavals nevertheless did not stem the growth of international trade and the influence of the merchant class. In the portrait of Geoffrey Chaucer's merchant, we see the budding of capitalism based on credit and interest. Cities like London ran their own affairs under politically powerful mayors and aldermen. Edward III, chronically in need of money to finance his wars, was obliged to negotiate for revenues with the Commons in the English Parliament, an institution that became a major political force during this period. A large part of the king's revenues depended on taxing the profitable export of English wool to the Continent. The Crown thus became involved in the country's economic affairs, and this involvement led to a need for capable administrators. These were no longer drawn mainly from the church, as in the past, but from a newly educated laity that occupied a rank somewhere between that of the lesser nobility and the upper bourgeoisie. The career of Chaucer, who served Edward III and his successor Richard II in a number of civil posts, is typical of this class—with the exception that Chaucer was also a great poet.

In the fourteenth century, a few poets and intellectuals achieved the status and respect formerly accorded only to the ancients. Marie de France and Chrétien de Troyes had dedicated their works to noble patrons and, in their role as narrators, address themselves as entertainers and sometimes as instructors to court audiences. Dante (1265–1321) made himself the protagonist of *The Divine Comedy*, the sacred poem, as he called it, in which he revealed the secrets of the afterlife. After his death, manuscripts of the work were provided with lengthy commentaries as though it were Scripture, and public readings and lectures were devoted to it. Francis Petrarch (1304–1374) won an international reputation as a man of letters. He wrote primarily in Latin and contrived to have himself crowned "poet laureate" in emulation of the Roman poets whose works he imitated, but his most famous work is the sonnet sequence he wrote in Italian. Giovanni Boccaccio (1313–1375) was among Petrarch's most ardent admirers and carried on a literary correspondence with him.

Chaucer read these authors along with the ancient Roman poets and drew on them in his own works. Chaucer's *Clerk's Tale* is based on a Latin version Petrarch made from the last tale in Boccaccio's *Decameron*; in his prologue, the Clerk refers to Petrarch as "lauriat poete" whose sweet rhetoric illuminated all Italy with his poetry. Yet in his own time, the English poet Chaucer never attained the kind of laurels that he and others accorded to Petrarch. In his earlier works, Chaucer portrayed himself comically as a diligent reader of old books, as an aspiring apprentice writer, and as an eager spectator on the fringe of a fashionable world of courtiers and poets. In *The House of Fame*, he relates a dream of being snatched up by a huge golden eagle (the eagle and many other things in this work were inspired by Dante), who transports him to the palace of the goddess Fame. There he gets to see phantoms, like the shades in Dante's poem, of all the famous authors of antiquity. At the end of his romance *Troilus and Criseyde*, Chaucer asks his "litel book" to kiss the footsteps where the great ancient poets had passed before. Like Dante and Petrarch, Chaucer had an ideal of great poetry and, in his *Troilus* at least, strove to emulate it. But in *The House of Fame* and in his final work, *The*

Canterbury Tales, he also views that ideal ironically and distances himself from it. The many surviving documents that record Geoffrey Chaucer's career as a civil servant do not contain a single word to show that he was also a poet. Only in the following centuries would he be canonized as the father of English poetry.

Chaucer is unlikely to have known his contemporary William Langland, who says in an autobiographical passage added to the third and last version of his great poem *Piers Plowman* that he lived in London on Cornhill (a poor area of the city) among "lollers." "Loller" was a slang term for the unemployed and transients; it was later applied to followers of the religious and social reformer John Wycliffe, some of whom were burned at the stake for heresy in the next century. Langland assailed corruption in church and state, but he was certainly no radical. It is thought that he may have written the third version of *Piers Plowman*, which tones down his attacks on the church, after the rebels of 1381 invoked Piers as one of their own. Although Langland does not condone rebellion and his religion is not revolutionary, he nevertheless presents the most clear-sighted vision of social and religious issues in the England of his day. *Piers Plowman* is also a painfully honest search for the right way that leads to salvation. Though learned himself, Langland and the dreamer who represents him in the poem arrive at the insight that learning can be one of the chief obstacles on that way.

Langland came from the west of England, and his poem belongs to the "Alliterative Revival," a final flowering in the late fourteenth century of the verse form that goes all the way back to Anglo-Saxon England. Anglo-Saxon traditions held out longest in the west and north, away from London, where Chaucer and his audience were more open to literary fashions from the Continent.

John Gower is a third major late fourteenth-century English poet. While his first and second large works are written in French and Latin verse respectively, his *Confessio Amantis* (1390) is written in English octosyllabic couplets. Gower's first two works are severe satires; the *Confessio*, by contrast, broaches political and ethical issues from an oblique angle. Its primary narrative concerns the treatment of a suffering lover. His therapy consists of listening to, and understanding, many other narratives, many of which are drawn from classical sources. Like Chaucer, Gower anglicizes and absorbs classical Latin literature.

Admiration for the poetry of both Chaucer and Gower and the controversial nature of Langland's writing assured the survival of their work in many manuscripts. The work of a fourth major fourteenth-century English poet, who remains anonymous, is known only through a single manuscript, which contains four poems all thought to be by a single author: *Cleanness* and *Patience*, two biblical narratives in alliterative verse; *Pearl*, a moving dream vision in which a grief-stricken father is visited and consoled by his dead child, who has been transformed into a queen in the kingdom of heaven; and *Sir Gawain and the Green Knight*, the finest of all English romances. The plot of *Gawain* involves a folklore motif of a challenge by a supernatural visitor, first found in an Old Irish tale. The poet has made this motif a challenge to King Arthur's court and has framed the tale with allusions at the beginning and end to the legends that link Arthur's reign with the Trojan War and the founding of Rome and of Britain. The poet has a sophisticated awareness of romance as a literary genre and plays a game with both the hero's and the reader's expectations of what is supposed to happen in a romance. One could say that the broader subject of *Sir Gawain and the Green Knight* is "romance" itself, and in this respect the poem resembles Chaucer's *Canterbury Tales* in its author's interest in literary form.

Julian of Norwich is a fifth major writer of this period. The first known woman writer in the English vernacular, the anchoress Julian participates in a Continental tradition of visionary writings, often by women. She spent a good deal of her life meditating and writing about a series of visions, which she called "showings," that she had received in 1373, when she was thirty years old. While very carefully negotiating the dangers of writing as a woman, and of writing sophisticated theology in the vernacular, Julian manages to produce visionary writing that is at once penetrating and serene.

The Fifteenth Century

In 1399 Henry Bolingbroke, the duke of Lancaster, deposed his cousin Richard II, who was murdered in prison. As Henry IV, he successfully defended his crown against several insurrections and passed it on to Henry V, who briefly united the country once more and achieved one last apparently decisive victory over the French at the Battle of Agincourt (1415). The premature death of Henry V in 1422, however, left England exposed to the civil wars known as the Wars of the Roses, the red rose being the emblem of the house of Lancaster; the white, of York. These wars did not end until 1485, when Henry Tudor defeated Richard III at Bosworth Field and acceded to the throne as Henry VII.

The most prolific poet of the fifteenth century was the monk John Lydgate (1371?–1449), who produced dream visions; a life of the Virgin; translations of French religious allegories; a *Troy Book; The Siege of Thebes*, which he framed as a "new" Canterbury tale; and a thirty-six-thousand-line poem called *The Fall of Princes*, a free translation of a French work, itself based on a Latin work by Boccaccio. The last illustrates the late medieval idea of tragedy, namely that emperors, kings, and other famous men enjoy power and fortune only to be cast down in misery. Lydgate shapes these tales as a "mirror" for princes, i.e., as object lessons to the powerful men of his own day, several of whom were his patrons. A self-styled imitator of Chaucer, Lydgate had a reputation almost equal to Chaucer's in the fifteenth century. The other significant poet of the first half of the fifteenth century is Thomas Hoccleve (1367?–1426). Like Lydgate, Hoccleve also wrote for powerful Lancastrian patrons, but his poetry is strikingly private, painfully concerned as it often is with his penury and mental instability.

Religious works of all kind continued to be produced in the fifteenth century, but under greater surveillance. The Lancastrian authorities responded to the reformist religious movement known as "Lollardy" in draconian ways. They introduced a statute for the burning of heretics (the first such statute) in 1401, and a series of measures designed to survey and censor theology in English in 1409. Despite this, many writers continued to produce religious works in the vernacular. Perhaps the most remarkable of these writers is Margery Kempe (who records her visit to Julian of Norwich in about 1413). Kempe made pilgrimages to the Holy Land, Rome, Santiago, and to shrines in Northern Europe. These she records, in the context of her often fraught and painful personal life, in her *Book of Margery Kempe*. Both Julian of Norwich and Margery Kempe, in highly individual ways, allow us to see the medieval church and its doctrines from female points of view.

Social, economic, and literary life continued as they had throughout all of the previously mentioned wars. The prosperity of the towns was shown by performances of the mystery plays—a sequence or "cycle" of plays based on the Bible and produced by the city guilds, the organizations representing the various trades and crafts. The cycles of several towns are lost, but those of York and Chester have been preserved, along with two other complete cycles, one possibly from Wakefield in Yorkshire, and the other titled the "N-Town" Cycle. Under the guise of dramatizing biblical history, playwrights such as the Wakefield Master manage to comment satirically on the social ills of the times. The century also saw the development of the morality play, in which personified vices and virtues struggle for the soul of "Mankind" or "Everyman." Performed by professional players, the morality plays were precursors of the professional theater in the reign of Elizabeth I.

The best of Chaucer's imitators was Robert Henryson, who, in the last quarter of the fifteenth century, wrote *The Testament of Cresseid*, a continuation of Chaucer's great poem *Troilus and Criseyde*. He also wrote the *Moral Fabilis of Esope*, among which *The Cock and the Fox* is a remake of Chaucer's *Nun's Priest's Tale*.

The works of Sir Thomas Malory (d. 1471) gave the definitive form in English to the legend of King Arthur and his knights. Malory spent years in prison Englishing a series of Arthurian romances that he translated and abridged chiefly from several enormously long thirteenth-century French prose romances. Malory was a passionate devotee of chivalry, which he personified in his hero Sir Lancelot. In the jealousies and rivalries that finally break up the round table and destroy Arthur's kingdom, Malory saw a distant image of the civil wars of his own time. A manuscript of Malory's works fell into the hands of William Caxton (1422?–1492), who had introduced the new art of printing by movable type to England in 1476. Caxton divided Malory's tales into the chapters and books of a single long work, as though it were a chronicle history, and gave it the title *Morte Darthur*, which has stuck to it ever since. Caxton also printed *The Canterbury Tales*, some of Chaucer's earlier works, and Gower's *Confessio Amantis*. Caxton himself translated many of the works he printed for English readers: a history of Troy, a book on chivalry, Aesop's fables, *The History of Reynard the Fox*, and *The Game and Playe of Chesse*. The new technology extended literacy and made books more easily accessible to new classes of readers. Printing made the production of literature a business and made possible the bitter political and doctrinal disputes that, in the sixteenth century, were waged in print as well as on the field of battle.

MEDIEVAL ENGLISH

The medieval works in this anthology were composed in different states of our language. Old English, the language that took shape among the Germanic settlers of England, preserved its integrity until the Norman Conquest radically altered English civilization. Middle English, the first records of which date from the early twelfth century, was continually changing. Shortly after the introduction of printing at the end of the fifteenth century, it attained the form designated as Early Modern English. Old English is a very heavily inflected language. (That is, the words change form to indicate changes in function, such as person, number, tense, case, mood, and so on. Most languages have some inflection—for example, the personal pronouns in Modern English have different forms when used as objects—but a "heavily inflected" language is one in which almost all classes of words undergo elaborate patterns of change.) The vocabulary of Old English is almost entirely Germanic. In Middle English, the inflectional system was weakened, and a large number of words were introduced into it from French, so that many of the older Anglo-Saxon words disappeared. Because of the difficulty of Old English, all selections from it in this book have been given in translation. The present discussion, then, is concerned primarily with the relatively late form of Middle English used by Chaucer and the East Midland dialect in which he wrote.

The chief difficulty with Middle English for the modern reader is caused not by its inflections so much as by its spelling, which may be described as a rough-and-ready phonetic system, and by the fact that it is not a single standardized language, but consists of a number of regional dialects, each with its own peculiarities of sound and its own systems for representing sounds in writing. The East Midland dialect—the dialect of London and of Chaucer, which is the ancestor of our own standard speech—differs greatly from the dialect spoken in the west of England (the original dialect of *Piers Plowman*), from that of the northwest (*Sir Gawain* and *the Green Knight*), and from that of the north (*The Second Shepherds' Play*). In this book, the long texts composed in the more difficult dialects have been translated or modernized, and those that—like Chaucer—appear in the original, have been re-spelled in a way that is designed to aid the reader. The remarks that follow apply chiefly to Chaucer's East Midland English, although certain non-Midland dialectal variations are noted if they occur in some of the other selections.

I. The Sounds of Middle English: General Rules

The following general analysis of the sounds of Middle English will enable the reader who does not have time for detailed study to read Middle English aloud and preserve some of its most essential characteristics, without, however, worrying too much about details. The next section, "Detailed Analysis," is designed for the reader who wishes to go more deeply into the pronunciation of Middle English. The best way of absorbing the sound of Middle English pronunciation is to listen to it; Norton Literature Online offers recordings of selections as an aid to this end.

Middle English differs from Modern English in three principal respects: (1) the pronunciation of the long vowels *a, e, i* (or *y*), *o*, and *u* (spelled *ou, ow*); (2) the fact that Middle English final *e* is often sounded; and (3) the fact that all Middle English consonants are sounded.

1. LONG VOWELS

Middle English vowels are long when they are doubled (*aa, ee, oo*) or when they are terminal (*he, to, holy*); *a, e,* and *o* are long when followed by a single consonant plus a vowel (*name, mete, note*). Middle English vowels are short when they are followed by two consonants.

Long *a* is sounded like the *a* in Modern English "father": *maken, madd.*

Long *e* may be sounded like the *a* in Modern English "name" (ignoring the distinction between the close and open vowel): *be, sweete.*

Long *i* (or *y*) is sounded like the *i* in Modern English "machine": *lif, whit; myn, holy*.

Long *o* may be sounded like the *o* in Modern English "note" (again ignoring the distinction between the close and open vowel): *do, soone*.

Long *u* (spelled *ou, ow*) is sounded like the *oo* in Modern English "goose": *hous, flowr*.

Note that in general Middle English long vowels are pronounced like long vowels in modern European languages other than English. Short vowels and diphthongs, however, may be pronounced as in Modern English.

2. FINAL E

In Middle English syllabic verse, final *e* is sounded like the *a* in "sofa" to provide a needed unstressed syllable: *Another Nonnë with hire haddë she*. But (cf. *hire* in the example) final *e* is suppressed when not needed for the meter. It is commonly silent before words beginning with a vowel or *h*.

3. CONSONANTS

Middle English consonants are pronounced separately in all combinations—*gnat: g-nat; knave: k-nave; write: w-rite; folk: fol-k*. In a simplified system of pronunciation the combination *gh* as in *night* or *thought* may be treated as if it were silent.

II. The Sounds of Middle English: Detailed Analysis

1. SIMPLE VOWELS

Sound	Pronunciation	Example
long *a* (spelled *a, aa*)	*a* in "father"	*maken, maad*
short *a*	*o* in "hot"	*cappe*
long *e* close (spelled *e, ee*)	*a* in "name"	*be, sweete*
long *e* open (spelled *e, ee*)	*e* in "there"	*mete, heeth*
short *e*	*e* in "set"	*setten*
final *e*	*a* in "sofa"	*large*
long *i* (spelled *i, y*)	*i* in "machine"	*lif, myn*
short *i*	*i* in "wit"	*wit*
long *o* close (spelled *o, oo*)	*o* in "note"	*do, soone*
long *o* open (spelled *o, oo*)	*oa* in "broad"	*go, goon*
short *o*	*o* in "oft"	*pot*
long *u* when spelled *ou, ow*	*oo* in "goose"	*hous, flowr*
long *u* when spelled *u*	*u* in "pure"	*vertu*
short *u* (spelled *u, o*)	*u* in "full"	*ful, love*

Doubled vowels and terminal vowels are always long, whereas single vowels before two consonants other than *th, ch* are always short. The vowels *a, e*, and *o* are long before a single consonant followed by a vowel: *nāmë, sēkë* (sick), *hōly*. In general, words that have descended into Modern English reflect their original Middle English quantity: *lĭven* (to live), but *līf* (life).

The close and open sounds of long *e* and long *o* may often be identified by the Modern English spellings of the words in which they appear. Original long close *e* is generally represented in Modern English by *ee*: "sweet," "knee," "teeth," "see" have close *e* in Middle English, but so does "be"; original long open *e* is generally represented in Modern English by *ea*: "meat," "heath," "sea," "great," "breath" have open *e* in Middle English. Similarly, original long close *o* is now generally represented by *oo*: "soon," "food," "good," but also "do," "to"; original long open *o* is represented either by *oa* or by *o*: "coat," "boat," "moan," but also "go," "bone," "foe," "home." Notice that original close *o* is now almost always pronounced like the *oo* in "goose," but that original open *o* is almost never so pronounced; thus it is often possible to identify the Middle English vowels through Modern English sounds.

The nonphonetic Middle English spelling of *o* for short *u* has been preserved in a number of Modern English words ("love," "son," "come"), but in others *u* has been restored: "sun" (*sonne*), "run" (*ronne*).

For the treatment of final *e*, see "General Rules," "Final *e*."

2. DIPHTHONGS

Sound	Pronunciation	Example
ai, ay, ei, ay	between *ai* in "aisle" and *ay* in "day"	*saide, day, veine, preye*
au, aw	*ou* in "out"	*chaunge, bawdy*
eu, ew	*ew* in "few"	*newe*
oi, oy	*oy* in "joy"	*joye, point*
ou, ow	*ou* in "thought"	*thought, lowe*

Note that in words with *ou, ow* that in Modern English are sounded with the *ou* of "about," the combination indicates not the diphthong but the simple vowel long *u* (see "Simple Vowels").

3. CONSONANTS

In general, all consonants except *h* were always sounded in Middle English, including consonants that have become silent in Modern English, such as the *g* in *gnaw*, the *k* in *knight*, the *l* in *folk*, and the *w* in *write*. In noninitial *gn*, however, the *g* was silent as in Modern English "sign." Initial *h* was silent in short common English words and in words borrowed from French and may have been almost silent in all words. The combination *gh* as in *night* or *thought* was sounded like the *ch* of German *ich* or *nach*. Note that Middle English *gg* represents both the hard sound of "dagger" and the soft sound of "bridge."

III. Parts of Speech and Grammar

1. NOUNS

The plural and possessive of nouns end in *es*, formed by adding *s* or *es* to the singular: *knight, knightes; roote, rootes*; a final consonant is frequently doubled before *es: bed, beddes*. A common irregular plural is *yën*, from *yë*, eye.

2. PRONOUNS

The chief comparisons with Modern English are as follows:

Modern English	East Midlands Middle English
I	*I, ich* (*ik* is a northern form)
you (singular)	*thou* (subjective); *thee* (objective)
her	*hir(e), her(e)*
its	*his*

you (plural)	*ye* (subjective); *you* (objective)
they	*they*
their	*hir* (*their* is a Northern form)
them	*hem* (*them* is a Northern form)

In formal speech, the second person plural is often used for the singular. The possessive adjectives *my, thy* take *n* before a word beginning with a vowel or *h: thyn yë, myn host.*

3. ADJECTIVES

Adjectives ending in a consonant add final *e* when they stand before the noun they modify and after another modifying word such as *the, this, that,* or nouns or pronouns in the possessive: *a good hors,* but *the (this, my, the kinges) goode hors.* They also generally add *e* when standing before and modifying a plural noun, a noun in the vocative, or any proper noun: *goode men, oh goode man, faire Venus.*

Adjectives are compared by adding *er(e)* for the comparative, *est(e)* for the superlative. Sometimes the stem vowel is shortened or altered in the process: *sweete, swettere, swettest; long, lenger, lengest.*

4. ADVERBS

Adverbs are formed from adjectives by adding *e, ly,* or *liche*; the adjective *fair* thus yields *faire, fairly, fairliche.*

5. VERBS

Middle English verbs, like Modern English verbs, are either "weak" or "strong." Weak verbs form their preterites and past participles with a *t* or *d* suffix and preserve the same stem vowel throughout their systems, although it is sometimes shortened in the preterite and past participle: *love, loved; bend, bent; hear, heard; meet, met.* Strong verbs do not use the *t* or *d* suffix, but vary their stem vowel in the preterite and past participle: *take, took, taken; begin, began, begun; find, found, found.*

The inflectional endings are the same for Middle English strong verbs and weak verbs except in the preterite singular and the imperative singular. In the following paradigms, the weak verbs *loven* (to love) and *heeren* (to hear), and the strong verbs *taken* (to take) and *ginnen* (to begin) serve as models.

	Present Indicative	Preterite Indicative
I	*love, heere*	*loved(e), herde*
	take, ginne	*took, gan*
thou	*lovest, heerest*	*lovedest, herdest*
	takest, ginnest	*tooke, gonne*
he, she, it	*loveth, heereth*	*loved(e), herde*
	taketh, ginneth	*took, gan*
we, ye, they	*love(n) (th), heere(n) (th)*	*loved(e) (en), herde(n)*
	take(n) (th), ginne(n) (th)	tooke(n), gonne(n)

The present plural ending *eth* is southern, whereas the *e(n)* ending is Midland and characteristic of Chaucer. In the north, *s* may appear as the ending of all persons of the present. In the weak preterite, when the ending *e* gave a verb three or more syllables, it was frequently dropped. Note that in certain strong verbs like *ginnen* there are two distinct stem vowels in the preterite; even in Chaucer's time, however, one of these had begun to replace the other, and Chaucer occasionally writes *gan* for all persons of the preterite.

	Present Subjunctive	Preterite Subjunctive
Singular	*love, heere*	*lovede, herde*
	take, ginne	*tooke, gonne*
Plural	*love(n), heere(n)*	*lovede(n), herde(n)*
	take(n), ginne(n)	*tooke(n), gonne(n)*

In verbs like *ginnen*, which have two stem vowels in the indicative preterite, it is the vowel of the plural and of the second person singular that is used for the preterite subjunctive.

The imperative singular of most weak verbs is *e: (thou) love*, but of some weak verbs and all strong verbs, the imperative singular is without termination: *(thou) heer, taak, gin*. The imperative plural of all verbs is either *e* or *eth: (ye) love(th), heere(th), take(th), ginne(th)*.

The infinitive of verbs is *e* or *en: love(n), heere(n), take(n), ginne(n)*.

The past participle of weak verbs is the same as the preterite without inflectional ending: *loved, herd*. In strong verbs the ending is either *e* or *en: take(n), gonne(n)*. The prefix *y* often appears on past participles: *yloved, yherd, ytake(n)*.

OLD AND MIDDLE ENGLISH PROSODY

All the poetry of Old English is in the same verse form. The verse unit is the single line, because rhyme was not used to link one line to another, except very occasionally in late Old English. The organizing device of the line is alliteration, the beginning of several words with the same sound ("Foemen fled"). The Old English alliterative line contains, on the average, four principal stresses and is divided into two half-lines of two stresses each by a strong medial caesura, or pause. These two half-lines are linked to each other by the alliteration; at least one of the two stressed words in the first half-line, and often both of them, begin with the same sound as the first stressed word of the second half-line (the second stressed word is generally nonalliterative). The fourth line of *Beowulf* is an example (*sc* has the value of modern *sh*; þ is a runic symbol with the value of modern *th*):

Oft Scyld Scefing   sceaþena þreatum.

It will be noticed that any vowel alliterates with any other vowel. In addition to the alliteration, the length of the unstressed syllables and their number and pattern is governed by a highly complex set of rules. When sung or intoned—as it was—to the rhythmic strumming of a harp, Old English poetry must have been wonderfully impressive in the dignified, highly formalized way that aptly fits both its subject matter and tone.

The majority of Middle English verse is either in alternately stressed rhyming verse, adapted from French after the conquest, or in alliterative verse that is descended from Old English. The latter preserves the caesura of Old English and in its purest form the same alliterative system, the two stressed words of the first half-line (or at least one of them) alliterating with the first stressed word in the second half-line. But most of the alliterative poets allowed themselves a number of deviations from the norm. All four stressed words may alliterate, as in the first line of *Piers Plowman:*

In a summer season   when soft was the sun.

Or the line may contain five, six, or even more stressed words, of which all or only the basic minimum may alliterate:

A *fair field full* of   *folk found* I there between.

There is no rule determining the number of unstressed syllables, and at times some poets seem to ignore alliteration entirely. As in Old English, any vowel may alliterate with any other vowel; furthermore, since initial *h* was silent or lightly pronounced in Middle English, words beginning with *h* are treated as though they began with the following vowel.

There are two general types of stressed verse with rhyme. In the more common, unstressed and stressed syllables alternate regularly as x X x X x X or, with two unstressed syllables intervening as x x X x x X x x X or a combination of the two as x x X x X x x X (of the reverse patterns, only X x X x X x is common in English). There is also a line that can only be defined as containing a predetermined number of stressed syllables but an irregular number and pattern of unstressed syllables. Much Middle English verse has to be read without expectation of regularity; some of this was evidently composed in the irregular meter, but some was probably originally composed according to a strict metrical system that has been obliterated by scribes careless of fine points. One receives the impression that many of the lyrics—as well as the *Second Shepherds' Play*—were at least composed with regular syllabic alternation. In the play *Everyman*, only the number of stresses is generally predetermined but not the number or placement of unstressed syllables.

In pre-Chaucerian verse the number of stresses, whether regularly or irregularly alternated, was most often four, although sometimes the number was three and rose in some poems to seven. Rhyme in Middle English (as in Modern English) may be either between adjacent or alternate lines, or may occur in more complex patterns. Most of the *Canterbury Tales* are in rhymed couplets, the line containing five stresses with regular alternation—technically known as iambic pentameter, the standard English poetic line, perhaps introduced into English by Chaucer. In reading Chaucer and much pre-Chaucerian verse, one must remember that the final *e*, which is silent in Modern English, could be pronounced at any time to provide a needed unstressed syllable. Evidence seems to indicate that it was also pronounced at the end of the line, even though it thus produced a line with eleven syllables. Although he was a very regular metricist, Chaucer used various conventional devices that are apt to make the reader stumble until he or she understands them. Final *e* is often not pronounced before a word beginning with a vowel or *h*, and may be suppressed whenever metrically convenient. The same medial and terminal syllables that are slurred in Modern English are apt to be suppressed in Chaucer's English: *Canterb'ry* for *Canterbury; ev'r* (perhaps *e'er*) for *evere*. The plural in *es* may either be syllabic or reduced to *s* as in Modern English. Despite these seeming irregularities, Chaucer's verse is not difficult to read if one constantly bears in mind the basic pattern of the iambic pentameter line.

Additional information about the Middle Ages, including primary texts and images, is available at Norton Literature Online (wwnorton.com/literature). Online topics are

- Medieval Estates and Orders
- King Arthur
- The First Crusade
- The Linguistic and Literary Contexts of *Beowulf*

THE MIDDLE AGES

TEXTS	CONTEXTS
	43–ca. 420 Romans conquer Britons; Brittania a province of the Roman Empire
	307–37 Reign of Constantine the Great leads to adoption of Christianity as official religion of the Roman Empire
ca. 405 St. Jerome completes *Vulgate,* Latin translation of the Bible that becomes standard for the Roman Catholic Church	
	432 St. Patrick begins mission to convert Ireland
	ca. 450 Anglo-Saxon conquest of Britons begins
523 Boethius, *Consolation of Philosophy* (Latin)	
	597 St. Augustine of Canterbury's mission to Kent begins conversion of Anglo-Saxons to Christianity
ca. 658–80 *Cædmon's Hymn,* earliest poem recorded in English	
731 Bede completes *Ecclesiastical History of the English People*	
? ca. 750 *Beowulf* composed	
	ca. 787 First Viking raids on England
871–99 Texts written or commissioned by Alfred	**871–99** Reign of King Alfred
ca. 1000 Unique manuscript of *Beowulf* and *Judith*	
	1066 Norman Conquest by William I establishes French-speaking ruling class in England
	1095–1221 Crusades
ca. 1135–38 Geoffrey of Monmouth's Latin *History of the Kings of Britain* gives pseudohistorical status to Arthurian and other legends	
	1152 Future Henry II marries Eleanor of Aquitaine, bringing vast French territories to the English crown
1154 End of *Peterborough Chronicle,* last branch of the *Anglo-Saxon Chronicle*	
? ca. 1165–80 Marie de France, *Lais* in Anglo-Norman French from Breton sources	
ca. 1170–91 Chrétien de Troyes, chivalric romances about knights of the Round Table	**1170** Archbishop Thomas Becket murdered in Canterbury Cathedral
	1182 Birth of St. Francis of Assisi
? ca. 1200 Layamon's *Brut*	
? ca. 1215–25 *Ancrene Riwle*	**1215** Fourth Lateran Council requires annual confession. English barons force King John to seal Magna Carta (the Great Charter) guaranteeing baronial rights
ca. 1304–21 Dante Alighieri writing *Divine Comedy*	

TEXTS	CONTEXTS
	ca. 1337–1453 Hundred Years' War
	1348 Black Death ravages Europe
	1362 English first used in law courts and Parliament
1368 Chaucer, *Book of the Duchess*	
	1372 Chaucer's first journey to Italy
1373–93 Julian of Norwich, *Book of Showings*	
ca. 1375–1400 *Sir Gawain and the Green Knight*	
	1376 Earliest record of performance of cycle drama at York
1377–79 William Langland, *Piers Plowman*(B-Text)	
ca. 1380 Followers of John Wycliffe begin first complete translation of the Bible into English	
	1381 People's uprising briefly takes control of London before being suppressed
ca. 1385–87 Chaucer, *Troilus and Criseyde*	
ca. 1387–89 Chaucer working on *The Canterbury Tales*	
ca. 1390–92 John Gower, *Confessio Amantis*	
	1399 Richard II deposed by his cousin, who succeeds him as Henry IV
	1400 Richard II murdered
	1401 Execution of William Sawtre, first Lollard burned at the stake under new law against heresy
ca. 1410–49 John Lydgate active	
	1415 Henry V defeats French at Agincourt
ca. 1425 *York Play of the Crucifixion*	
	1431 English burn Joan of Arc at Rouen
ca. 1432–38 Margery Kempe, *The Book of Margery Kempe*	
ca. 1450–75 Wakefield mystery cycle, *Second Shepherds' Play*	
	1455–85 Wars of the Roses
ca. 1470 Sir Thomas Malory in prison working on *Morte Darthur*	
ca. 1475 Robert Henryson active	
	1476 William Caxton sets up first printing press in England
1485 Caxton publishes *Morte Darthur*, one of the first books in English to be printed	**1485** The earl of Richmond defeats the Yorkist king, Richard III, at Bosworth Field and succeeds him as Henry VII, founder of the Tudor dynasty
ca. 1510 *Everyman*	
	1575 Last performance of mystery plays at Chester

Anglo-Saxon Literature

THE DREAM OF THE ROOD

The *Dream of the Rood* (i.e., of the Cross) is the finest of a rather large number of religious poems in Old English. Neither its author nor its date of composition is known. It appears in a late tenth-century manuscript located in Vercelli in northern Italy, a manuscript made up of Old English religious poems and sermons. The poem may antedate its manuscript, because some passages from the Rood's speech were carved, with some variations, in runes on a stone cross at some time after its construction early in the eighth century; this is the famous Ruthwell Cross, which is preserved near Dumfries in southern Scotland. The precise relation of the poem to this cross is, however, uncertain.

The experience of the Rood—its humiliation at the hands of those who changed it from tree to instrument of punishment for criminals, its humility when the young hero Christ mounts it, and its pride as the restored "tree of glory"—has a suggestive relevance to the condition of the sad, lonely, sin-stained Dreamer. His isolation and melancholy is typical of exile figures in Old English poetry. For the Rood, however, glory has replaced torment, and at the end, the Dreamer's description of Christ's triumphant entry into heaven with the souls He has liberated from hell reflects the Dreamer's response to the hope that has been brought to him. Christ and the Cross both act, paradoxically, in keeping with, and diametrically opposed to, a code of heroic action: Christ is heroic and passive, while the Cross is loyal to its lord, yet must participate in his death.

The Dream of the Rood[1]

Listen, I will speak of the best of dreams, of what I dreamed at midnight when men and their voices were at rest. It seemed to me that I saw a most rare tree reach high aloft, wound in light, brightest of beams. All that beacon[2] was covered with gold; gems stood fair where it met the ground, five were above about the crosspiece. Many hosts of angels gazed on it, fair in the form created for them. This was surely no felon's gallows, but holy spirits beheld it there, men upon earth, and all this glorious creation. Wonderful was the triumph-tree, and I stained with sins, wounded with wrongdoings. I saw the tree of glory shine splendidly, adorned with garments, decked with gold: jewels had worthily covered the Lord's tree. Yet through that gold I might perceive ancient agony of wretches, for now it began to bleed on the right side.[3] I was all afflicted with sorrows, I was afraid for that fair sight. I saw that bright beacon change in clothing and color: now it was wet with moisture, drenched with

1. This prose translation, by E. T. Donaldson, has been based in general on the edition of the poem by John C. Pope, *Eight Old English Poems*, 3rd ed., rev. by R. D. Fulk (2000).

2. The Old English word *beacen* also means token or sign and battle standard.

3. The wound Christ received on the Cross was supposed to have been on the right side.

flowing of blood, now adorned with treasure. Yet I, lying there a long while troubled, beheld the Saviour's tree until I heard it give voice: the best of trees began to speak words.

"It was long ago—I remember it still—that I was hewn down at the wood's edge, taken from my stump. Strong foes seized me there, hewed me to the shape they wished to see, commanded me to lift their criminals. Men carried me on their shoulders, then set me on a hill; foes enough fastened me there. Then I saw the Lord of mankind hasten with stout heart, for he would climb upon me. I dared not bow or break against God's word when I saw earth's surface tremble. I might have felled all foes, but I stood fast. Then the young Hero stripped himself—that was God Almighty—strong and stouthearted. He climbed on the high gallows, bold in the sight of many, when he would free mankind. I trembled when the Warrior embraced me, yet I dared not bow to earth, fall to the ground's surface; but I must stand fast. I was raised up, a cross; I lifted up the Mighty King, Lord of the Heavens: I dared not bend. They pierced me with dark nails: the wounds are seen on me, open gashes of hatred. Nor did I dare harm any of them. They mocked us both together. I was all wet with blood, drenched from the side of that Man after he had sent forth his spirit. I had endured many bitter happenings on that hill. I saw the God of Hosts cruelly racked. The shades of night had covered the Ruler's body with their mists, the bright splendor. Shadow came forth, dark beneath the clouds. All creation wept, bewailed the King's fall; Christ was on Cross.

"Yet from afar some came hastening to the Lord.[4] All that I beheld. I was sore afflicted with griefs, yet I bowed to the men's hands, meekly, eagerly. Then they took Almighty God, lifted him up from his heavy torment. The warriors left me standing, covered with blood. I was all wounded with arrows. They laid him down weary of limb, stood at the body's head, looked there upon Heaven's Lord; and he rested there a while, tired after the great struggle. Then warriors began to build him an earth-house in the sight of his slayer,[5] carved it out of bright stone; they set there the Wielder of Triumphs. Then they began to sing him a song of sorrow, desolate in the evening. Then they wished to turn back, weary, from the great Prince; he remained with small company.[6] Yet we[7] stood in our places a good while, weeping. The voice of the warriors departed. The body grew cold, fair house of the spirit. Then some began to fell us to earth—that was a fearful fate! Some buried us in a deep pit. Yet thanes[8] of the Lord, friends, learned of me there. . . . decked me in gold and silver.[9]

"Now you might understand, my beloved man, that I had endured the work of evildoers, grievous sorrows. Now the time has come that men far and wide upon earth honor me—and all this glorious creation—and pray to this beacon. On me God's Son suffered awhile; therefore I tower now glorious under the heavens, and I may heal every one of those who hold me in awe. Of old I became the hardest of torments, most loathed by men, before I opened the right road of life to those who have voices. Behold, the Lord of Glory honored

4. According to John 19.38–39, it was Joseph of Arimathea and Nicodemus who received Christ's body from the Cross.
5. I.e., the Cross.
6. I.e., alone (an understatement).
7. I.e., Christ's Cross and those on which the two thieves were crucified.
8. Members of the king's body of warriors.
9. A number of lines describing the finding of the Cross have apparently been lost here. According to the legend, St. Helen, the mother of Constantine the Great, the first Christian emperor, led a Roman expedition that discovered the true Cross in the 4th century.

me over all the trees of the wood, the Ruler of Heaven, just as also he honored his mother Mary, Almighty God for all men's sake, over all woman's kind.

"Now I command you, my beloved man, that you tell men of this vision. Disclose with your words that it is of the tree of glory on which Almighty God suffered for mankind's many sins and the deeds Adam did of old. He tasted death there; yet the Lord arose again to help mankind in his great might. Then he climbed to the heavens. He will come again hither on this earth to seek mankind on Doomsday, the Lord himself, Almighty God, and his angels with him, for then he will judge, he who has power to judge, each one just as in this brief life he has deserved. Nor may any one be unafraid of the word the Ruler will speak. Before his host he will ask where the man is who in the name of the Lord would taste bitter death as he did on the Cross. But then they will be afraid, and will think of little to begin to say to Christ. There need none be afraid who bears on his breast the best of tokens, but through the Cross shall the kingdom be sought by each soul on this earthly journey that thinks to dwell with the Lord."

Then I prayed to the tree, blithe-hearted, confident, there where I was alone with small company. My heart's thoughts were urged on the way hence. I endured many times of longing. Now is there hope of life for me, that I am permitted to seek the tree of triumph, more often than other men honor it well, alone. For it my heart's desire is great, and my hope of protection is directed to the Cross. I do not possess many powerful friends on earth, but they have gone hence from the delights of the world, sought for themselves the King of Glory. They live now in the heavens with the High Father, dwell in glory. And every day I look forward to when the Lord's Cross that I beheld here on earth will fetch me from this short life and bring me then where joy is great, delight in the heavens, where the Lord's folk are seated at the feast, where bliss is eternal. And then may it place me where thenceforth I may dwell in glory, fully enjoy bliss with the saints. May the Lord be my friend, who once here on earth suffered on the gallows-tree for man's sins: he freed us and granted us life, a heavenly home. Hope was renewed, with joys and with bliss, to those who endured fire.[1] The Son was victorious in that foray, mighty and successful. Then he came with his multitude, a host of spirits, into God's kingdom, the Almighty Ruler; and the angels and all the saints who dwelt then in glory rejoiced when their Ruler, Almighty God, came where his home was.

1. This and the following sentences refer to the Harrowing (i.e., pillaging) of Hell; after His death on the Cross, Christ descended into Hell, from which He released the souls of certain of the patriarchs and prophets, conducting them triumphantly to Heaven.

BEOWULF

Beowulf, the oldest of the great long poems written in English, may have been composed more than twelve hundred years ago, in the first half of the eighth century, although some scholars would place it as late as the tenth century. As is the case with most Old English poems, the title has been assigned by modern editors, for the manuscripts do not normally give any indication of title or authorship. Linguistic evidence shows that the poem was originally composed in the dialect of what was then Mercia, the Midlands of England today. But in the unique late-tenth-century manuscript preserving the poem, it has been converted into the West-Saxon dialect of the southwest in which most of Old English literature survives. In 1731, before any modern transcript of the text had been made, the manuscript was seriously damaged in a fire that destroyed the building in London that housed the extraordinary collection of medieval English manuscripts made by Sir Robert Bruce Cotton (1571–1631). As a result of the fire and subsequent deterioration, a number of lines and words have been lost from the poem.

It is possible that *Beowulf* may be the lone survivor of a genre of Old English long epics, but it must have been a remarkable and difficult work even in its own day. The poet was reviving the heroic language, style, and pagan world of ancient Germanic oral poetry, a world that was already remote for his contemporaries and that is stranger to the modern reader, in many respects, than the epic world of Homer and Virgil. With the help of *Beowulf* itself, a few shorter heroic poems in Old English, and later poetry and prose in Old Saxon, Old Icelandic, and Middle High German, we can only conjecture what Germanic oral epic must have been like when performed by the Germanic *scop*, or bard. The *Beowulf* poet himself imagines such oral performances by having King Hrothgar's court poet recite a heroic lay at a feast celebrating Beowulf's defeat of Grendel. Many of the words and formulaic expressions in *Beowulf* can be found in other Old English poems, but there are also an extraordinary number of what linguists call *hapax legomena*—that is, words recorded only once in a language. The poet may have found them elsewhere, but the high incidence of such words suggests that he was an original wordsmith in his own right.

Although the poem itself is English in language and origin, it deals not with native Englishmen but with their Germanic forebears, especially with two south Scandinavian tribes, the Danes and the Geats, who lived on the Danish island of Zealand and in southern Sweden. Thus the historical period the poem concerns—insofar as it may be said to refer to history at all—is some centuries before it was written—that is, a time after the initial invasion of England by Germanic tribes in the middle of the fifth century but before the Anglo-Saxon migration was completed. The one datable fact of history mentioned in the poem is a raid on the Franks in which Hygelac, the king of the Geats and Beowulf's lord, was killed, and this raid occurred in the year 520. Yet the poet's elliptical references to quasihistorical and legendary material show that his audience was still familiar with many old stories, the outlines of which we can only infer, sometimes with the help of later analogous tales in other Germanic languages. This knowledge was probably kept alive by other heroic poetry, of which little has been preserved in English, although much may once have existed.

It is now widely believed that *Beowulf* is the work of a single poet who was a Christian and that his poem reflects well-established Christian tradition. The conversion of the Germanic settlers in England had been largely completed during the seventh century. The Danish king Hrothgar's poet sings a song about the Creation (lines 87–98) reminiscent of Cædmon's *Hymn*. The monster Grendel is said to be a descendant of Cain. There are allusions to God's judgment and to fate (*wyrd*) but none to pagan deities. References to the New Testament are notably absent, but Hrothgar and Beowulf often speak of God as though their religion is monotheistic. With sadness the poet relates that, made desperate by Grendel's attacks, the Danes pray for help at heathen shrines—apparently backsliding as the children of Israel had sometimes lapsed into idolatry.

Although Hrothgar and Beowulf are portrayed as morally upright and enlightened pagans, they fully espouse and frequently affirm the values of Germanic heroic poetry. In the poetry depicting this warrior society, the most important of human relationships was that which existed between the warrior—the thane—and his lord, a relationship based less on subordination of one man's will to another's than on mutual trust and respect. When a warrior vowed loyalty to his lord, he became not so much his servant as his voluntary companion, one who would take pride in defending him and fighting in his wars. In return, the lord was expected to take care of his thanes and to reward them richly for their valor; a good king, one like Hrothgar or Beowulf, is referred to by such poetic epithets as "ring-giver" and as the "helmet" and "shield" of his people.

The relationship between kinsmen was also of deep significance to this society. If one of his kinsmen had been slain, a man had a moral obligation either to kill the slayer or to exact the payment of *wergild* (man-price) in compensation. Each rank of society was evaluated at a definite price, which had to be paid to the dead man's kin by the killer if he wished to avoid their vengeance—even if the killing had been an accident. In the absence of any legal code other than custom or any body of law enforcement, it was the duty of the family (often with the lord's support) to execute justice. The payment itself had less significance as wealth than as proof that the kinsmen had done what was right. The failure to take revenge or to exact compensation was considered shameful. Hrothgar's anguish over the murders committed by Grendel is not only for the loss of his men but also for the shame of his inability either to kill Grendel or to exact a "death-price" from the killer. "It is always better / to avenge dear ones than to indulge in mourning" (lines 1384–85), Beowulf says to Hrothgar, who has been thrown back into despair by the revenge-slaying of his old friend Aeschere by Grendel's mother.

Yet the young Beowulf's attempt to comfort the bereaved old king by invoking the code of vengeance may be one of several instances of the poet's ironic treatment of the tragic futility of the never-ending blood feuds. The most graphic example in the poem of that irony is the Finnsburg episode, the lay sung by Hrothgar's hall-poet. The Danish princess Hildeburh, married to the Frisian king Finn—probably to put an end to a feud between those peoples—loses both her brother and her son when a bloody fight breaks out in the hall between a visiting party of Danes and her husband's men. The bodies are cremated together on a huge funeral pyre: "The glutton element flamed and consumed / the dead of both sides. Their great days were gone" (lines 1124–25).

Such feuds, the staple subject of Germanic epic and saga, have only a peripheral place in the poem. Instead, the poem turns on Beowulf's three great fights against preternatural evil, which inhabits the dangerous and demonic space surrounding human society. He undertakes the fight against Grendel to save the Danes from the monster and to exact vengeance for the men Grendel has slain. Another motive is to demonstrate his strength and courage and thereby to enhance his personal glory. Hrothgar's magnificent gifts become the material emblems of that glory. Revenge and glory also motivate Beowulf's slaying of Grendel's mother. He undertakes his last battle against the dragon, however, only because there is no other way to save his own people.

A somber and dignified elegiac mood pervades *Beowulf*. The poem opens and closes with the description of a funeral and is filled with laments for the dead. Our first view of Beowulf is of an ambitious young hero. At the end, he has become an old king, facing the dragon and death. His people mourn him and praise him, as does the poet, for his nobility, generosity, courage, and, what is less common in Germanic heroes, kindness to his people. The poet's elegiac tone may be informed by something more than the duty to "praise a prince whom he holds dear / and cherish his memory when that moment comes / when he has to be convoyed from his bodily home" (lines 3175–77). The entire poem could be viewed as the poet's lament for heroes like Beowulf who went into the darkness without the light of the poet's own Christian faith.

The present verse translation is by the Irish poet Seamus Heaney, who received the Nobel Prize for literature in 1995. Selections from Heaney's own poems appear later in the anthology.

TRIBES AND GENEALOGIES

1. *The Danes (Bright-, Half-, Ring-, Spear-, North-, East-, South-, West-Danes; Shieldings, Honor-, Victor-, War-Shieldings; Ing's friends)*

Shield

Beow

Halfdane

Heorogar | Hrothgar *m.* Wealhtheow | Halga | Daughter *m.* Onela the Swede

Hrethric | Hrothmund | Freawaru *m.* Ingeld the Heatho-Bard | Hrothulf

2. *The Geats (Sea-, War-, Weather-Geats)*

Hrethel

Herebeald | Haethcyn | Hygelac *m.* Hygd | Daughter *m.* Ecgtheow

Heardred | Daughter* *m.* Eofor | Beowulf the Geat

3. *The Swedes*

Ongentheow

Ohthere | Onela *m.* Halfdane's Daughter

Eanmund | Eadgils

4. *Miscellaneous*

A. The Half-Danes (also called Shieldings) involved in the fight at Finnsburg may represent a different tribe from the Danes described above. Their king Hoc had a son, Hnaef, who succeeded him, and a daughter Hildeburh, who married Finn, king of the Jutes.

B. The Jutes or Frisians are represented as enemies of the Danes in the fight at Finnsburg and as allies of the Franks or Hugas at the time Hygelac the Geat made the attack in which he lost his life and from which Beowulf swam home. Also allied with the Franks at this time were the Hetware.

C. The Heatho-Bards (i.e., "Battle-Bards") are represented as inveterate enemies of the Danes. Their king Froda had been killed in an attack on the Danes, and Hrothgar's attempt to make peace with them by marrying his daughter Freawaru to Froda's son Ingeld failed when the latter attacked Heorot. The attack was repulsed, although Heorot was burned.

The Poet's Song in Heorot

To give the reader a sample of the language, style, and texture of *Beowulf* in the original we print the following passage, lines 90–98, in Old English with interlinear glosses. In Old English spelling, æ (line 90) is a vowel symbol that represents the vowel of Modern English *cat*; þ (line 90) and ð (line 92) both represent the sound *th*. The spelling *sc* (line 91) = *sh; c* (line 92) = *k*. The large space in the middle of the

* The daughter of Hygelac who was given to Eofor may have been born to him by a former wife, older than Hygd.

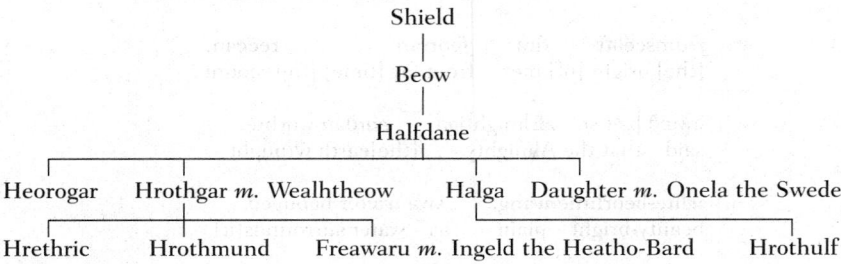

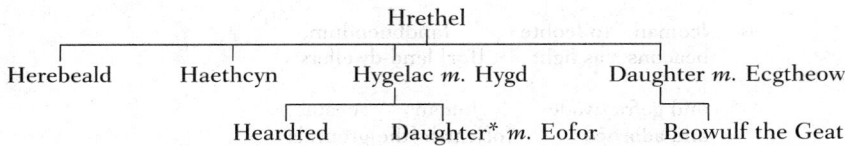

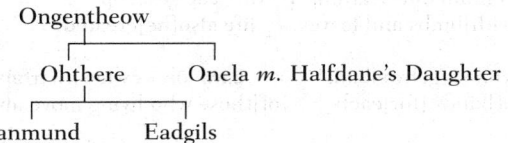

line indicates the caesura. The alliterating sounds that connect the half-lines are printed in bold italics.

Sægde se þe cuþe
Said he who knew [how]

frumsceaft ***f***ira ***f***eorran reccan,
[the] origin [of] men from far [time] [to]recount,

cwæð þæt se ***Æ***lmightiga ***eo***rðan worhte,
said that the Almighty [the]earth wrought

wlite-beorhtne ***w***ang, swa ***w***æter bebugeð,
beauty-bright plain as water surrounds[it]

gese***t***te ***s***ige-hreþig ***s***unnan ond monan,
set triumph-glorious sun and moon

leoman to ***l***eohte ***l***andbuendum,
beacons as light [for] land-dwellers

ond ge***f***rætwade ***f***oldan sceatas
and adorned [of]earth [the]grounds

leomum ond ***l***eafum, ***l***if eac gesceop
[with]limbs and leaves, life also[he]created

cynna gehwylcum* þara ðe ***c***wice hwyrfaþ.
[of]kinds [for]each [of]those who living move about

A NOTE ON NAMES

Old English, like Modern German, contained many compound words, most of which have been lost in Modern English. Most of the names in *Beowulf* are compounds. Hrothgar is a combination of words meaning "glory" and "spear"; the name of his older brother, Heorogar, comes from "army" and "spear"; Hrothgar's sons Hrethric and Hrothmund contain the first elements of their father's name combined, respectively, with *ric* (kingdom, empire; Modern German *Reich*) and *mund* (hand, protection). As in the case of the Danish dynasty, family names often alliterate. Masculine names of the warrior class have military associations. The importance of family and the demands of alliteration frequently lead to the designation of characters by formulas identifying them in terms of relationships. Thus Beowulf is referred to as "son of Ecgtheow" or "kinsman of Hygelac" (his uncle and lord).

The Old English spellings of names are mostly preserved in the translation. A few rules of pronunciation are worth keeping in mind. Initial *H* before *r* was sounded, and so Hrothgar's name alliterates with that of his brother Heorogar. The combination *cg* has the value of *dg* in words like "edge." The first element in the name of Beowulf's father "Ecgtheow" is the same word as "edge," and, by the figure of speech called synecdoche (a part of something stands for the whole), *ecg* stands for *sword* and Ecgtheow means "sword-servant."

* Modern syntax would be "for each of kinds." In Old English, the endings *-a* and *-um* indicate that *gewylcum* is an indirect object and *cynna*, a possessive plural.

For more information about *Beowulf*, see "The Linguistic and Literary Contexts of *Beowulf*," at Norton Literature Online.

Beowulf

[PROLOGUE: THE RISE OF THE DANISH NATION]

So. The Spear-Danes[1] in days gone by
and the kings who ruled them had courage and greatness.
We have heard of those princes' heroic campaigns.
There was Shield Sheafson,[2] scourge of many tribes,
a wrecker of mead-benches, rampaging among foes.
This terror of the hall-troops had come far.
A foundling to start with, he would flourish later on
as his powers waxed and his worth was proved.
In the end each clan on the outlying coasts
beyond the whale-road had to yield to him
and begin to pay tribute. That was one good king.
Afterward a boy-child was born to Shield,
a cub in the yard, a comfort sent
by God to that nation. He knew what they had tholed,[3]
the long times and troubles they'd come through
without a leader; so the Lord of Life,
the glorious Almighty, made this man renowned.
Shield had fathered a famous son:
Beow's name was known through the north.
And a young prince must be prudent like that,
giving freely while his father lives
so that afterward in age when fighting starts
steadfast companions will stand by him
and hold the line. Behavior that's admired
is the path to power among people everywhere.
Shield was still thriving when his time came
and he crossed over into the Lord's keeping.
His warrior band did what he bade them
when he laid down the law among the Danes:
they shouldered him out to the sea's flood,
the chief they revered who had long ruled them.
A ring-whorled prow rode in the harbor,
ice-clad, outbound, a craft for a prince.
They stretched their beloved lord in his boat,
laid out by the mast, amidships,
the great ring-giver. Far-fetched treasures
were piled upon him, and precious gear.

1. There are different compound names for tribes, often determined by alliteration in Old English poetry. Line 1 reads, *"Hwæt, we Gar-dena in gear-dagum,"* where alliteration falls on *Gar* (spear) and *gear* (year). Old English hard and soft *g* (spelled *y* in Modern English) alliterate. The compound *gear-dagum* derives from "year," used in the special sense of "long ago," and "days" and survives in the archaic expression "days of yore."

2. Shield is the name of the founder of the Danish royal line. Sheafson translates *Scefing*, i.e., *sheaf* + the patronymic suffix-*ing*. Because Sheaf was a "foundling" (line 7: *feasceaft funden*, i.e., found destitute) who arrived by sea (lines 45–46), it is likely that as a child Shield brought with him only a sheaf, a symbol of fruitfulness.

3. Suffered, endured.

I never heard before of a ship so well furbished
with battle-tackle, bladed weapons
and coats of mail. The massed treasure
was loaded on top of him: it would travel far
on out into the ocean's sway.
They decked his body no less bountifully
with offerings than those first ones did
who cast him away when he was a child
and launched him alone out over the waves.[4]
And they set a gold standard up
high above his head and let him drift
to wind and tide, bewailing him
and mourning their loss. No man can tell,
no wise man in hall or weathered veteran
knows for certain who salvaged that load.
  Then it fell to Beow to keep the forts.
He was well regarded and ruled the Danes
for a long time after his father took leave
of his life on earth. And then his heir,
the great Halfdane,[5] held sway
for as long as he lived, their elder and warlord.
He was four times a father, this fighter prince:
one by one they entered the world,
Heorogar, Hrothgar, the good Halga,
and a daughter, I have heard, who was Onela's queen,
a balm in bed to the battle-scarred Swede.
  The fortunes of war favored Hrothgar.
Friends and kinsmen flocked to his ranks,
young followers, a force that grew
to be a mighty army. So his mind turned
to hall-building: he handed down orders
for men to work on a great mead-hall
meant to be a wonder of the world forever;
it would be his throne-room and there he would dispense
his God-given goods to young and old—
but not the common land or people's lives.[6]
Far and wide through the world, I have heard,
orders for work to adorn that wallstead
were sent to many peoples. And soon it stood there
finished and ready, in full view,
the hall of halls. Heorot was the name[7]
he had settled on it, whose utterance was law.
Nor did he renege, but doled out rings
and torques at the table. The hall towered,
its gables wide and high and awaiting
a barbarous burning.[8] That doom abided,

4. See n. 2, above. Since Shield was found destitute, "no less bountifully" is litotes or understatement; the ironic reminder that he came with nothing (line 43) emphasizes the reversal of his fortunes.

5. Probably named so because, according to one source, his mother was a Swedish princess.

6. The king could not dispose of land used by all, such as a common pasture, or of slaves.

7. I.e., "Hart," from antlers fastened to the gables or because the crossed gable-ends resembled a stag's antlers; the hart was also an icon of royalty.

8. An allusion to the future destruction of Heorot by fire, probably in a raid by the Heatho-Bards.

but in time it would come: the killer instinct
unleashed among in-laws, the blood-lust rampant.[9]

[HEOROT IS ATTACKED]

Then a powerful demon,[1] a prowler through the dark,
nursed a hard grievance. It harrowed him
to hear the din of the loud banquet
every day in the hall, the harp being struck
and the clear song of a skilled poet
telling with mastery of man's beginnings,
how the Almighty had made the earth
a gleaming plain girdled with waters;
in His splendor He set the sun and the moon
to be earth's lamplight, lanterns for men,
and filled the broad lap of the world
with branches and leaves; and quickened life
in every other thing that moved.
So times were pleasant for the people there
until finally one, a fiend out of hell,
began to work his evil in the world.
Grendel was the name of this grim demon
haunting the marches, marauding round the heath
and the desolate fens; he had dwelt for a time
in misery among the banished monsters,
Cain's clan, whom the Creator had outlawed
and condemned as outcasts.[2] For the killing of Abel
the Eternal Lord had exacted a price:
Cain got no good from committing that murder
because the Almighty made him anathema
and out of the curse of his exile there sprang
ogres and elves and evil phantoms
and the giants too who strove with God
time and again until He gave them their reward.
So, after nightfall, Grendel set out
for the lofty house, to see how the Ring-Danes
were settling into it after their drink,
and there he came upon them, a company of the best
asleep from their feasting, insensible to pain
and human sorrow. Suddenly then
the God-cursed brute was creating havoc:
greedy and grim, he grabbed thirty men
from their resting places and rushed to his lair,
flushed up and inflamed from the raid,
blundering back with the butchered corpses.
Then as dawn brightened and the day broke,
Grendel's powers of destruction were plain:
their wassail was over, they wept to heaven
and mourned under morning. Their mighty prince,

9. As told later (lines 2020–69), Hrothgar plans to marry a daughter to Ingeld, chief of the Heatho-Bards, in hopes of resolving a long-standing feud. See previous note.

1. The poet withholds the name for several lines. He does the same with the name of the hero as well as others.

2. See Genesis 4.9–12.

the storied leader, sat stricken and helpless,
humiliated by the loss of his guard,
bewildered and stunned, staring aghast
at the demon's trail, in deep distress.
He was numb with grief, but got no respite
for one night later merciless Grendel
struck again with more gruesome murders.
Malignant by nature, he never showed remorse.
It was easy then to meet with a man
shifting himself to a safer distance
to bed in the bothies,[3] for who could be blind
to the evidence of his eyes, the obviousness
of the hall-watcher's hate? Whoever escaped
kept a weather-eye open and moved away.
So Grendel ruled in defiance of right,
one against all, until the greatest house
in the world stood empty, a deserted wallstead.
For twelve winters, seasons of woe,
the lord of the Shieldings[4] suffered under
his load of sorrow; and so, before long,
the news was known over the whole world.
Sad lays were sung about the beset king,
the vicious raids and ravages of Grendel,
his long and unrelenting feud,
nothing but war; how he would never
parley or make peace with any Dane
nor stop his death-dealing nor pay the death-price.[5]
No counselor could ever expect
fair reparation from those rabid hands.
All were endangered; young and old
were hunted down by that dark death-shadow
who lurked and swooped in the long nights
on the misty moors; nobody knows
where these reavers from hell roam on their errands.
So Grendel waged his lonely war,
inflicting constant cruelties on the people,
atrocious hurt. He took over Heorot,
haunted the glittering hall after dark,
but the throne itself, the treasure-seat,
he was kept from approaching; he was the Lord's outcast.
These were hard times, heartbreaking
for the prince of the Shieldings; powerful counselors,
the highest in the land, would lend advice,
plotting how best the bold defenders
might resist and beat off sudden attacks.
Sometimes at pagan shrines they vowed
offerings to idols, swore oaths
that the killer of souls[6] might come to their aid

3. Huts, outlying buildings. Evidently Grendel wants only to dominate the hall.
4. The descendants of Shield, another name for the Danes.
5. I.e., *wergild* (man-price); monetary compensation for the life of the slain man is the only way, according to Germanic law, to settle a feud peacefully.
6. I.e., the devil. Heathen gods were thought to be devils.

and save the people. That was their way,
their heathenish hope; deep in their hearts
they remembered hell. The Almighty Judge
of good deeds and bad, the Lord God,
Head of the Heavens and High King of the World,
was unknown to them. Oh, cursed is he
who in time of trouble has to thrust his soul
in the fire's embrace, forfeiting help;
he has nowhere to turn. But blessed is he
who after death can approach the Lord
and find friendship in the Father's embrace.

[THE HERO COMES TO HEOROT]

So that troubled time continued, woe
that never stopped, steady affliction
for Halfdane's son, too hard an ordeal.
There was panic after dark, people endured
raids in the night, riven by the terror.
When he heard about Grendel, Hygelac's thane
was on home ground, over in Geatland.
There was no one else like him alive.
In his day, he was the mightiest man on earth,
highborn and powerful. He ordered a boat
that would ply the waves. He announced his plan:
to sail the swan's road and seek out that king,
the famous prince who needed defenders.
Nobody tried to keep him from going,
no elder denied him, dear as he was to them.
Instead, they inspected omens and spurred
his ambition to go, whilst he moved about
like the leader he was, enlisting men,
the best he could find; with fourteen others
the warrior boarded the boat as captain,
a canny pilot along coast and currents.
Time went by, the boat was on water,
in close under the cliffs.
Men climbed eagerly up the gangplank,
sand churned in surf, warriors loaded
a cargo of weapons, shining war-gear
in the vessel's hold, then heaved out,
away with a will in their wood-wreathed ship.
Over the waves, with the wind behind her
and foam at her neck, she flew like a bird
until her curved prow had covered the distance,
and on the following day, at the due hour,
those seafarers sighted land,
sunlit cliffs, sheer crags
and looming headlands, the landfall they sought.
It was the end of their voyage and the Geats vaulted
over the side, out on to the sand,
and moored their ship. There was a clash of mail
and a thresh of gear. They thanked God

for that easy crossing on a calm sea.
When the watchman on the wall, the Shieldings' lookout
whose job it was to guard the sea-cliffs,
saw shields glittering on the gangplank
and battle-equipment being unloaded
he had to find out who and what
the arrivals were. So he rode to the shore,
this horseman of Hrothgar's, and challenged them
in formal terms, flourishing his spear:
"What kind of men are you who arrive
rigged out for combat in your coats of mail,
sailing here over the sea-lanes
in your steep-hulled boat? I have been stationed
as lookout on this coast for a long time.
My job is to watch the waves for raiders,
any danger to the Danish shore.
Never before has a force under arms
disembarked so openly—not bothering to ask
if the sentries allowed them safe passage
or the clan had consented. Nor have I seen
a mightier man-at-arms on this earth
than the one standing here: unless I am mistaken,
he is truly noble. This is no mere
hanger-on in a hero's armor.
So now, before you fare inland
as interlopers, I have to be informed
about who you are and where you hail from.
Outsiders from across the water,
I say it again: the sooner you tell
where you come from and why, the better."
The leader of the troop unlocked his word-hoard;
the distinguished one delivered this answer:
"We belong by birth to the Geat people
and owe allegiance to Lord Hygelac.
In his day, my father was a famous man,
a noble warrior-lord named Ecgtheow.
He outlasted many a long winter
and went on his way. All over the world
men wise in counsel continue to remember him.
We come in good faith to find your lord
and nation's shield, the son of Halfdane.
Give us the right advice and direction.
We have arrived here on a great errand
to the lord of the Danes, and I believe therefore
there should be nothing hidden or withheld between us.
So tell us if what we have heard is true
about this threat, whatever it is,
this danger abroad in the dark nights,
this corpse-maker mongering death
in the Shieldings' country. I come to proffer
my wholehearted help and counsel.
I can show the wise Hrothgar a way
to defeat his enemy and find respite—

if any respite is to reach him, ever.
I can calm the turmoil and terror in his mind.
Otherwise, he must endure woes
and live with grief for as long as his hall
stands at the horizon on its high ground."
  Undaunted, sitting astride his horse,
the coast-guard answered: "Anyone with gumption
and a sharp mind will take the measure
of two things: what's said and what's done.
I believe what you have told me, that you are a troop
loyal to our king. So come ahead
with your arms and your gear, and I will guide you.
What's more, I'll order my own comrades
on their word of honor to watch your boat
down there on the strand—keep her safe
in her fresh tar, until the time comes
for her curved prow to preen on the waves
and bear this hero back to Geatland.
May one so valiant and venturesome
come unharmed through the clash of battle."
  So they went on their way. The ship rode the water,
broad-beamed, bound by its hawser
and anchored fast. Boar-shapes[7] flashed
above their cheek-guards, the brightly forged
work of goldsmiths, watching over
those stern-faced men. They marched in step,
hurrying on till the timbered hall
rose before them, radiant with gold.
Nobody on earth knew of another
building like it. Majesty lodged there,
its light shone over many lands.
So their gallant escort guided them
to that dazzling stronghold and indicated
the shortest way to it; then the noble warrior
wheeled on his horse and spoke these words:
"It is time for me to go. May the Almighty
Father keep you and in His kindness
watch over your exploits. I'm away to the sea,
back on alert against enemy raiders."
  It was a paved track, a path that kept them
in marching order. Their mail-shirts glinted,
hard and hand-linked; the high-gloss iron
of their armor rang. So they duly arrived
in their grim war-graith[8] and gear at the hall,
and, weary from the sea, stacked wide shields
of the toughest hardwood against the wall,
then collapsed on the benches; battle-dress
and weapons clashed. They collected their spears
in a seafarers' stook, a stand of grayish
tapering ash. And the troops themselves

7. Carved images of boars were placed on helmets, probably as good luck charms to protect the warriors.

8. "Graith": archaic for apparel.

were as good as their weapons.
Then a proud warrior
questioned the men concerning their origins:
"Where do you come from, carrying these
decorated shields and shirts of mail,
these cheek-hinged helmets and javelins?
I am Hrothgar's herald and officer.
I have never seen so impressive or large
an assembly of strangers. Stoutness of heart,
bravery not banishment, must have brought you to Hrothgar."
The man whose name was known for courage,
the Geat leader, resolute in his helmet,
answered in return: "We are retainers
from Hygelac's band. Beowulf is my name.
If your lord and master, the most renowned
son of Halfdane, will hear me out
and graciously allow me to greet him in person,
I am ready and willing to report my errand."
Wulfgar replied, a Wendel chief
renowned as a warrior, well known for his wisdom
and the temper of his mind: "I will take this message,
in accordance with your wish, to our noble king,
our dear lord, friend of the Danes,
the giver of rings. I will go and ask him
about your coming here, then hurry back
with whatever reply it pleases him to give."
With that he turned to where Hrothgar sat,
an old man among retainers;
the valiant follower stood foursquare
in front of his king: he knew the courtesies.
Wulfgar addressed his dear lord:
"People from Geatland have put ashore.
They have sailed far over the wide sea.
They call the chief in charge of their band
by the name of Beowulf. They beg, my lord,
an audience with you, exchange of words
and formal greeting. Most gracious Hrothgar,
do not refuse them, but grant them a reply.
From their arms and appointment, they appear well born
and worthy of respect, especially the one
who has led them this far: he is formidable indeed."
Hrothgar, protector of Shieldings, replied:
"I used to know him when he was a young boy.
His father before him was called Ecgtheow.
Hrethel the Geat[9] gave Ecgtheow
his daughter in marriage. This man is their son,
here to follow up an old friendship.
A crew of seamen who sailed for me once
with a gift-cargo across to Geatland
returned with marvelous tales about him:
a thane, they declared, with the strength of thirty

9. Hygelac's father and Beowulf's grandfather.

in the grip of each hand. Now Holy God
has, in His goodness, guided him here
to the West-Danes, to defend us from Grendel.
This is my hope; and for his heroism
I will recompense him with a rich treasure.
Go immediately, bid him and the Geats
he has in attendance to assemble and enter.
Say, moreover, when you speak to them,
they are welcome to Denmark."
At the door of the hall,
Wulfgar duly delivered the message:
"My lord, the conquering king of the Danes,
bids me announce that he knows your ancestry;
also that he welcomes you here to Heorot
and salutes your arrival from across the sea.
You are free now to move forward
to meet Hrothgar in helmets and armor,
but shields must stay here and spears be stacked
until the outcome of the audience is clear."
The hero arose, surrounded closely
by his powerful thanes. A party remained
under orders to keep watch on the arms;
the rest proceeded, led by their prince
under Heorot's roof. And standing on the hearth
in webbed links that the smith had woven,
the fine-forged mesh of his gleaming mail-shirt,
resolute in his helmet, Beowulf spoke:
"Greetings to Hrothgar. I am Hygelac's kinsman,
one of his hall-troop. When I was younger,
I had great triumphs. Then news of Grendel,
hard to ignore, reached me at home:
sailors brought stories of the plight you suffer
in this legendary hall, how it lies deserted,
empty and useless once the evening light
hides itself under heaven's dome.
So every elder and experienced councilman
among my people supported my resolve
to come here to you, King Hrothgar,
because all knew of my awesome strength.
They had seen me boltered[1] in the blood of enemies
when I battled and bound five beasts,
raided a troll-nest and in the night-sea
slaughtered sea-brutes. I have suffered extremes
and avenged the Geats (their enemies brought it
upon themselves; I devastated them).
Now I mean to be a match for Grendel,
settle the outcome in single combat.
And so, my request, O king of Bright-Danes,
dear prince of the Shieldings, friend of the people
and their ring of defense, my one request
is that you won't refuse me, who have come this far,

1. Clotted, sticky.

the privilege of purifying Heorot,
with my own men to help me, and nobody else.
I have heard moreover that the monster scorns
in his reckless way to use weapons;
therefore, to heighten Hygelac's fame
and gladden his heart, I hereby renounce
sword and the shelter of the broad shield,
the heavy war-board: hand-to-hand
is how it will be, a life-and-death
fight with the fiend. Whichever one death fells
must deem it a just judgment by God.
If Grendel wins, it will be a gruesome day;
he will glut himself on the Geats in the war-hall,
swoop without fear on that flower of manhood
as on others before. Then my face won't be there
to be covered in death: he will carry me away
as he goes to ground, gorged and bloodied;
he will run gloating with my raw corpse
and feed on it alone, in a cruel frenzy
fouling his moor-nest. No need then
to lament for long or lay out my body:[2]
if the battle takes me, send back
this breast-webbing that Weland[3] fashioned
and Hrethel gave me, to Lord Hygelac.
Fate goes ever as fate must."
Hrothgar, the helmet of Shieldings, spoke:
"Beowulf, my friend, you have traveled here
to favor us with help and to fight for us.
There was a feud one time, begun by your father.
With his own hands he had killed Heatholaf
who was a Wulfing; so war was looming
and his people, in fear of it, forced him to leave.
He came away then over rolling waves
to the South-Danes here, the sons of honor.
I was then in the first flush of kingship,
establishing my sway over the rich strongholds
of this heroic land. Heorogar,
my older brother and the better man,
also a son of Halfdane's, had died.
Finally I healed the feud by paying:
I shipped a treasure-trove to the Wulfings,
and Ecgtheow acknowledged me with oaths of allegiance.
"It bothers me to have to burden anyone
with all the grief that Grendel has caused
and the havoc he has wreaked upon us in Heorot,
our humiliations. My household guard
are on the wane, fate sweeps them away
into Grendel's clutches—but God can easily
halt these raids and harrowing attacks!
"Time and again, when the goblets passed

2. I.e., for burial. Hrothgar will not need to give Beowulf an expensive funeral.

3. Famed blacksmith in Germanic legend.

and seasoned fighters got flushed with beer
they would pledge themselves to protect Heorot
and wait for Grendel with their whetted swords.
But when dawn broke and day crept in
over each empty, blood-spattered bench,
the floor of the mead-hall where they had feasted
would be slick with slaughter. And so they died,
faithful retainers, and my following dwindled.
Now take your place at the table, relish
the triumph of heroes to your heart's content."

[FEAST AT HEOROT]

Then a bench was cleared in that banquet hall
so the Geats could have room to be together
and the party sat, proud in their bearing,
strong and stalwart. An attendant stood by
with a decorated pitcher, pouring bright
helpings of mead. And the minstrel sang,
filling Heorot with his head-clearing voice,
gladdening that great rally of Geats and Danes.
From where he crouched at the king's feet,
Unferth, a son of Ecglaf's, spoke
contrary words. Beowulf's coming,
his sea-braving, made him sick with envy:
he could not brook or abide the fact
that anyone else alive under heaven
might enjoy greater regard than he did:
"Are you the Beowulf who took on Breca
in a swimming match on the open sea,
risking the water just to prove that you could win?
It was sheer vanity made you venture out
on the main deep. And no matter who tried,
friend or foe, to deflect the pair of you,
neither would back down: the sea-test obsessed you.
You waded in, embracing water,
taking its measure, mastering currents,
riding on the swell. The ocean swayed,
winter went wild in the waves, but you vied
for seven nights; and then he outswam you,
came ashore the stronger contender.
He was cast up safe and sound one morning
among the Heatho-Reams, then made his way
to where he belonged in Bronding country,
home again, sure of his ground
in strongroom and bawn.[4] So Breca made good
his boast upon you and was proved right.
No matter, therefore, how you may have fared
in every bout and battle until now,
this time you'll be worsted; no one has ever

4. Fortified outwork of a court or castle. The word was used by English planters in Ulster to describe fortified dwellings they erected on lands confiscated from the Irish [Translator's note].

outlasted an entire night against Grendel."
  Beowulf, Ecgtheow's son, replied:
"Well, friend Unferth, you have had your say
about Breca and me. But it was mostly beer
that was doing the talking. The truth is this:
when the going was heavy in those high waves,
I was the strongest swimmer of all.
We'd been children together and we grew up
daring ourselves to outdo each other,
boasting and urging each other to risk
our lives on the sea. And so it turned out.
Each of us swam holding a sword,
a naked, hard-proofed blade for protection
against the whale-beasts. But Breca could never
move out farther or faster from me
than I could manage to move from him.
Shoulder to shoulder, we struggled on
for five nights, until the long flow
and pitch of the waves, the perishing cold,
night falling and winds from the north
drove us apart. The deep boiled up
and its wallowing sent the sea-brutes wild.
My armor helped me to hold out;
my hard-ringed chain-mail, hand-forged and linked,
a fine, close-fitting filigree of gold,
kept me safe when some ocean creature
pulled me to the bottom. Pinioned fast
and swathed in its grip, I was granted one
final chance: my sword plunged
and the ordeal was over. Through my own hands,
the fury of battle had finished off the sea-beast.
  "Time and again, foul things attacked me,
lurking and stalking, but I lashed out,
gave as good as I got with my sword.
My flesh was not for feasting on,
there would be no monsters gnawing and gloating
over their banquet at the bottom of the sea.
Instead, in the morning, mangled and sleeping
the sleep of the sword, they slopped and floated
like the ocean's leavings. From now on
sailors would be safe, the deep-sea raids
were over for good. Light came from the east,
bright guarantee of God, and the waves
went quiet; I could see headlands
and buffeted cliffs. Often, for undaunted courage,
fate spares the man it has not already marked.
However it occurred, my sword had killed
nine sea-monsters. Such night dangers
and hard ordeals I have never heard of
nor of a man more desolate in surging waves.
But worn out as I was, I survived,
came through with my life. The ocean lifted
and laid me ashore, I landed safe

on the coast of Finland.
Now I cannot recall
any fight you entered, Unferth,
that bears comparison. I don't boast when I say
that neither you nor Breca were ever much
celebrated for swordsmanship
or for facing danger on the field of battle.
You killed your own kith and kin,
so for all your cleverness and quick tongue,
you will suffer damnation in the depths of hell.
The fact is, Unferth, if you were truly
as keen or courageous as you claim to be
Grendel would never have got away with
such unchecked atrocity, attacks on your king,
havoc in Heorot and horrors everywhere.
But he knows he need never be in dread
of your blade making a mizzle of his blood
or of vengeance arriving ever from this quarter—
from the Victory-Shieldings, the shoulderers of the spear.
He knows he can trample down you Danes
to his heart's content, humiliate and murder
without fear of reprisal. But he will find me different.
I will show him how Geats shape to kill
in the heat of battle. Then whoever wants to
may go bravely to mead, when the morning light,
scarfed in sun-dazzle, shines forth from the south
and brings another daybreak to the world."
Then the gray-haired treasure-giver was glad;
far-famed in battle, the prince of Bright-Danes
and keeper of his people counted on Beowulf,
on the warrior's steadfastness and his word.
So the laughter started, the din got louder
and the crowd was happy. Wealhtheow came in,
Hrothgar's queen, observing the courtesies.
Adorned in her gold, she graciously saluted
the men in the hall, then handed the cup
first to Hrothgar, their homeland's guardian,
urging him to drink deep and enjoy it
because he was dear to them. And he drank it down
like the warlord he was, with festive cheer.
So the Helming woman went on her rounds,
queenly and dignified, decked out in rings,
offering the goblet to all ranks,
treating the household and the assembled troop,
until it was Beowulf's turn to take it from her hand.
With measured words she welcomed the Geat
and thanked God for granting her wish
that a deliverer she could believe in would arrive
to ease their afflictions. He accepted the cup,
a daunting man, dangerous in action
and eager for it always. He addressed Wealhtheow;
Beowulf, son of Ecgtheow, said:
"I had a fixed purpose when I put to sea.

As I sat in the boat with my band of men,
I meant to perform to the uttermost
what your people wanted or perish in the attempt,
in the fiend's clutches. And I shall fulfill that purpose,
prove myself with a proud deed
or meet my death here in the mead-hall."
This formal boast by Beowulf the Geat
pleased the lady well and she went to sit
by Hrothgar, regal and arrayed with gold.
Then it was like old times in the echoing hall,
proud talk and the people happy,
loud and excited; until soon enough
Halfdane's heir had to be away
to his night's rest. He realized
that the demon was going to descend on the hall,
that he had plotted all day, from dawn light
until darkness gathered again over the world
and stealthy night-shapes came stealing forth
under the cloud-murk. The company stood
as the two leaders took leave of each other:
Hrothgar wished Beowulf health and good luck,
named him hall-warden and announced as follows:
"Never, since my hand could hold a shield
have I entrusted or given control
of the Danes' hall to anyone but you.
Ward and guard it, for it is the greatest of houses.
Be on your mettle now, keep in mind your fame,
beware of the enemy. There's nothing you wish for
that won't be yours if you win through alive."

[The Fight with Grendel]

Hrothgar departed then with his house-guard.
The lord of the Shieldings, their shelter in war,
left the mead-hall to lie with Wealhtheow,
his queen and bedmate. The King of Glory
(as people learned) had posted a lookout
who was a match for Grendel, a guard against monsters,
special protection to the Danish prince.
And the Geat placed complete trust
in his strength of limb and the Lord's favor.
He began to remove his iron breast-mail,
took off the helmet and handed his attendant
the patterned sword, a smith's masterpiece,
ordering him to keep the equipment guarded.
And before he bedded down, Beowulf,
that prince of goodness, proudly asserted:
"When it comes to fighting, I count myself
as dangerous any day as Grendel.
So it won't be a cutting edge I'll wield
to mow him down, easily as I might.
He has no idea of the arts of war,
of shield or sword-play, although he does possess

a wild strength. No weapons, therefore,
for either this night: unarmed he shall face me
if face me he dares. And may the Divine Lord
in His wisdom grant the glory of victory
to whichever side He sees fit."
  Then down the brave man lay with his bolster
under his head and his whole company
of sea-rovers at rest beside him.
None of them expected he would ever see
his homeland again or get back
to his native place and the people who reared him.
They knew too well the way it was before,
how often the Danes had fallen prey
to death in the mead-hall. But the Lord was weaving
a victory on His war-loom for the Weather-Geats.
Through the strength of one they all prevailed;
they would crush their enemy and come through
in triumph and gladness. The truth is clear:
Almighty God rules over mankind
and always has.
                    Then out of the night
came the shadow-stalker, stealthy and swift.
The hall-guards were slack, asleep at their posts,
all except one; it was widely understood
that as long as God disallowed it,
the fiend could not bear them to his shadow-bourne.
One man, however, was in fighting mood,
awake and on edge, spoiling for action.
  In off the moors, down through the mist-bands
God-cursed Grendel came greedily loping.
The bane of the race of men roamed forth,
hunting for a prey in the high hall.
Under the cloud-murk he moved toward it
until it shone above him, a sheer keep
of fortified gold. Nor was that the first time
he had scouted the grounds of Hrothgar's dwelling—
although never in his life, before or since,
did he find harder fortune or hall-defenders.
Spurned and joyless, he journeyed on ahead
and arrived at the bawn.[5] The iron-braced door
turned on its hinge when his hands touched it.
Then his rage boiled over, he ripped open
the mouth of the building, maddening for blood,
pacing the length of the patterned floor
with his loathsome tread, while a baleful light,
flame more than light, flared from his eyes.
He saw many men in the mansion, sleeping,
a ranked company of kinsmen and warriors
quartered together. And his glee was demonic,
picturing the mayhem: before morning
he would rip life from limb and devour them,

5. See p. 41, n. 4.

feed on their flesh; but his fate that night
was due to change, his days of ravening
had come to an end.
Mighty and canny,
Hygelac's kinsman was keenly watching
for the first move the monster would make.
Nor did the creature keep him waiting
but struck suddenly and started in;
he grabbed and mauled a man on his bench,
bit into his bone-lappings, bolted down his blood
and gorged on him in lumps, leaving the body
utterly lifeless, eaten up
hand and foot. Venturing closer,
his talon was raised to attack Beowulf
where he lay on the bed, he was bearing in
with open claw when the alert hero's
comeback and armlock forestalled him utterly.
The captain of evil discovered himself
in a handgrip harder than anything
he had ever encountered in any man
on the face of the earth. Every bone in his body
quailed and recoiled, but he could not escape.
He was desperate to flee to his den and hide
with the devil's litter, for in all his days
he had never been clamped or cornered like this.
Then Hygelac's trusty retainer recalled
his bedtime speech, sprang to his feet
and got a firm hold. Fingers were bursting,
the monster back-tracking, the man overpowering.
The dread of the land was desperate to escape,
to take a roundabout road and flee
to his lair in the fens. The latching power
in his fingers weakened; it was the worst trip
the terror-monger had taken to Heorot.
And now the timbers trembled and sang,
a hall-session[6] that harrowed every Dane
inside the stockade: stumbling in fury,
the two contenders crashed through the building.
The hall clattered and hammered, but somehow
survived the onslaught and kept standing:
it was handsomely structured, a sturdy frame
braced with the best of blacksmith's work
inside and out. The story goes
that as the pair struggled, mead-benches were smashed
and sprung off the floor, gold fittings and all.
Before then, no Shielding elder would believe
there was any power or person upon earth
capable of wrecking their horn-rigged hall
unless the burning embrace of a fire
engulf it in flame. Then an extraordinary

6. In Hiberno-English the word "session" (*seissiún* in Irish) can mean a gathering where musicians and singers perform for their own enjoyment [Translator's note].

wail arose, and bewildering fear
came over the Danes. Everyone felt it
who heard that cry as it echoed off the wall,
a God-cursed scream and strain of catastrophe,
the howl of the loser, the lament of the hell-serf
keening his wound. He was overwhelmed,
manacled tight by the man who of all men
was foremost and strongest in the days of this life.
But the earl-troop's leader was not inclined
to allow his caller to depart alive:
he did not consider that life of much account
to anyone anywhere. Time and again,
Beowulf's warriors worked to defend
their lord's life, laying about them
as best they could, with their ancestral blades.
Stalwart in action, they kept striking out
on every side, seeking to cut
straight to the soul. When they joined the struggle
there was something they could not have known at the time,
that no blade on earth, no blacksmith's art
could ever damage their demon opponent.
He had conjured the harm from the cutting edge
of every weapon.[7] But his going away
out of this world and the days of his life
would be agony to him, and his alien spirit
would travel far into fiends' keeping.
Then he who had harrowed the hearts of men
with pain and affliction in former times
and had given offense also to God
found that his bodily powers failed him.
Hygelac's kinsman kept him helplessly
locked in a handgrip. As long as either lived,
he was hateful to the other. The monster's whole
body was in pain; a tremendous wound
appeared on his shoulder. Sinews split
and the bone-lappings burst. Beowulf was granted
the glory of winning; Grendel was driven
under the fen-banks, fatally hurt,
to his desolate lair. His days were numbered,
the end of his life was coming over him,
he knew it for certain; and one bloody clash
had fulfilled the dearest wishes of the Danes.
The man who had lately landed among them,
proud and sure, had purged the hall,
kept it from harm; he was happy with his nightwork
and the courage he had shown. The Geat captain
had boldly fulfilled his boast to the Danes:
he had healed and relieved a huge distress,
unremitting humiliations,
the hard fate they'd been forced to undergo,
no small affliction. Clear proof of this

7. Grendel is protected by a charm against metals.

could be seen in the hand the hero displayed
high up near the roof: the whole of Grendel's
shoulder and arm, his awesome grasp.

[CELEBRATION AT HEOROT]

Then morning came and many a warrior
gathered, as I've heard, around the gift-hall,
clan-chiefs flocking from far and near
down wide-ranging roads, wondering greatly
at the monster's footprints. His fatal departure
was regretted by no one who witnessed his trail,
the ignominious marks of his flight
where he'd skulked away, exhausted in spirit
and beaten in battle, bloodying the path,
hauling his doom to the demons' mere.[8]
The bloodshot water wallowed and surged,
there were loathsome upthrows and overturnings
of waves and gore and wound-slurry.
With his death upon him, he had dived deep
into his marsh-den, drowned out his life
and his heathen soul: hell claimed him there.
Then away they rode, the old retainers
with many a young man following after,
a troop on horseback, in high spirits
on their bay steeds. Beowulf's doings
were praised over and over again.
Nowhere, they said, north or south
between the two seas or under the tall sky
on the broad earth was there anyone better
to raise a shield or to rule a kingdom.
Yet there was no laying of blame on their lord,
the noble Hrothgar; he was a good king.
At times the war-band broke into a gallop,
letting their chestnut horses race
wherever they found the going good
on those well-known tracks. Meanwhile, a thane
of the king's household, a carrier of tales,
a traditional singer deeply schooled
in the lore of the past, linked a new theme
to a strict meter.[9] The man started
to recite with skill, rehearsing Beowulf's
triumphs and feats in well-fashioned lines,
entwining his words.
He told what he'd heard
repeated in songs about Sigemund's exploits,[1]
all of those many feats and marvels,
the struggles and wanderings of Waels's son,[2]

8. A lake or pool, although we learn later that it has an outlet to the sea. Grendel's habitat.
9. I.e., an extemporaneous heroic poem in alliterative verse about Beowulf's deeds.
1. Tales about Sigemund, his nephew Sinfjotli (Fitela), and his son Sigurth are found in a 13th-century Old Icelandic collection of legends known as the *Volsung Saga*. Analogous stories must have been known to the poet and his audience, though details differ.
2. Waels is the father of Sigemund.

things unknown to anyone
except to Fitela, feuds and foul doings
confided by uncle to nephew when he felt
the urge to speak of them: always they had been
partners in the fight, friends in need.
They killed giants, their conquering swords
had brought them down.
After his death
Sigemund's glory grew and grew
because of his courage when he killed the dragon,
the guardian of the hoard. Under gray stone
he had dared to enter all by himself
to face the worst without Fitela.
But it came to pass that his sword plunged
right through those radiant scales
and drove into the wall. The dragon died of it.
His daring had given him total possession
of the treasure-hoard, his to dispose of
however he liked. He loaded a boat:
Waels's son weighted her hold
with dazzling spoils. The hot dragon melted.
Sigemund's name was known everywhere.
He was utterly valiant and venturesome,
a fence round his fighters and flourished therefore
after King Heremod's[3] prowess declined
and his campaigns slowed down. The king was betrayed,
ambushed in Jutland, overpowered
and done away with. The waves of his grief
had beaten him down, made him a burden,
a source of anxiety to his own nobles:
that expedition was often condemned
in those earlier times by experienced men,
men who relied on his lordship for redress,
who presumed that the part of a prince was to thrive
on his father's throne and defend the nation,
the Shielding land where they lived and belonged,
its holdings and strongholds. Such was Beowulf
in the affection of his friends and of everyone alive.
But evil entered into Heremod.
They kept racing each other, urging their mounts
down sandy lanes. The light of day
broke and kept brightening. Bands of retainers
galloped in excitement to the gabled hall
to see the marvel; and the king himself,
guardian of the ring-hoard, goodness in person,
walked in majesty from the women's quarters
with a numerous train, attended by his queen
and her crowd of maidens, across to the mead-hall.
When Hrothgar arrived at the hall, he spoke,
standing on the steps, under the steep eaves,

3. Heremod was a bad king, held up by the bard as the opposite of Beowulf, as Sigemund is held up as a heroic prototype of Beowulf.

gazing toward the roofwork and Grendel's talon:
"First and foremost, let the Almighty Father
be thanked for this sight. I suffered a long
harrowing by Grendel. But the Heavenly Shepherd
can work His wonders always and everywhere.
Not long since, it seemed I would never
be granted the slightest solace or relief
from any of my burdens: the best of houses
glittered and reeked and ran with blood.
This one worry outweighed all others—
a constant distress to counselors entrusted
with defending the people's forts from assault
by monsters and demons. But now a man,
with the Lord's assistance, has accomplished something
none of us could manage before now
for all our efforts. Whoever she was
who brought forth this flower of manhood,
if she is still alive, that woman can say
that in her labor the Lord of Ages
bestowed a grace on her. So now, Beowulf,
I adopt you in my heart as a dear son.
Nourish and maintain this new connection,
you noblest of men; there'll be nothing you'll want for,
no worldly goods that won't be yours.
I have often honored smaller achievements,
recognized warriors not nearly as worthy,
lavished rewards on the less deserving.
But you have made yourself immortal
by your glorious action. May the God of Ages
continue to keep and requite you well."
Beowulf, son of Ecgtheow, spoke:
"We have gone through with a glorious endeavor
and been much favored in this fight we dared
against the unknown. Nevertheless,
if you could have seen the monster himself
where he lay beaten, I would have been better pleased.
My plan was to pounce, pin him down
in a tight grip and grapple him to death—
have him panting for life, powerless and clasped
in my bare hands, his body in thrall.
But I couldn't stop him from slipping my hold.
The Lord allowed it, my lock on him
wasn't strong enough; he struggled fiercely
and broke and ran. Yet he bought his freedom
at a high price, for he left his hand
and arm and shoulder to show he had been here,
a cold comfort for having come among us.
And now he won't be long for this world.
He has done his worst but the wound will end him.
He is hasped and hooped and hirpling with pain,
limping and looped in it. Like a man outlawed
for wickedness, he must await
the mighty judgment of God in majesty."

There was less tampering and big talk then
from Unferth the boaster, less of his blather
as the hall-thanes eyed the awful proof
of the hero's prowess, the splayed hand
up under the eaves. Every nail,
claw-scale and spur, every spike
and welt on the hand of that heathen brute
was like barbed steel. Everybody said
there was no honed iron hard enough
to pierce him through, no time-proofed blade
that could cut his brutal, blood-caked claw.
Then the order was given for all hands
to help to refurbish Heorot immediately:
men and women thronging the wine-hall,
getting it ready. Gold thread shone
in the wall-hangings, woven scenes
that attracted and held the eye's attention.
But iron-braced as the inside of it had been,
that bright room lay in ruins now.
The very doors had been dragged from their hinges.
Only the roof remained unscathed
by the time the guilt-fouled fiend turned tail
in despair of his life. But death is not easily
escaped from by anyone:
all of us with souls, earth-dwellers
and children of men, must make our way
to a destination already ordained
where the body, after the banqueting,
sleeps on its deathbed.
Then the due time arrived
for Halfdane's son to proceed to the hall.
The king himself would sit down to feast.
No group ever gathered in greater numbers
or better order around their ring-giver.
The benches filled with famous men
who fell to with relish; round upon round
of mead was passed; those powerful kinsmen,
Hrothgar and Hrothulf, were in high spirits
in the raftered hall. Inside Heorot
there was nothing but friendship. The Shielding nation
was not yet familiar with feud and betrayal.[4]
Then Halfdane's son presented Beowulf
with a gold standard as a victory gift,
an embroidered banner; also breast-mail
and a helmet; and a sword carried high,
that was both precious object and token of honor.
So Beowulf drank his drink, at ease;
it was hardly a shame to be showered with such gifts
in front of the hall-troops. There haven't been many
moments, I am sure, when men exchanged

4. Probably an ironic allusion to the future usurpation of the throne from Hrothgar's sons by Hrothulf, although no such treachery is recorded of Hrothulf, who is the hero of other Germanic stories.

four such treasures at so friendly a sitting.
An embossed ridge, a band lapped with wire
arched over the helmet: head-protection
to keep the keen-ground cutting edge
from damaging it when danger threatened
and the man was battling behind his shield.
Next the king ordered eight horses
with gold bridles to be brought through the yard
into the hall. The harness of one
included a saddle of sumptuous design,
the battle-seat where the son of Halfdane
rode when he wished to join the sword-play:
wherever the killing and carnage were the worst,
he would be to the fore, fighting hard.
Then the Danish prince, descendant of Ing,
handed over both the arms and the horses,
urging Beowulf to use them well.
And so their leader, the lord and guard
of coffer and strongroom, with customary grace
bestowed upon Beowulf both sets of gifts.
A fair witness can see how well each one behaved.
The chieftain went on to reward the others:
each man on the bench who had sailed with Beowulf
and risked the voyage received a bounty,
some treasured possession. And compensation,
a price in gold, was settled for the Geat
Grendel had cruelly killed earlier—
as he would have killed more, had not mindful God
and one man's daring prevented that doom.
Past and present, God's will prevails.
Hence, understanding is always best
and a prudent mind. Whoever remains
for long here in this earthly life
will enjoy and endure more than enough.
They sang then and played to please the hero,
words and music for their warrior prince,
harp tunes and tales of adventure:
there were high times on the hall benches,
and the king's poet performed his part
with the saga of Finn and his sons, unfolding
the tale of the fierce attack in Friesland
where Hnaef, king of the Danes, met death.[5]

Hildeburh
had little cause

5. The bard's lay is known as the Finnsburg Episode. Its allusive style makes the tale obscure in many details, although some can be filled in from a fragmentary Old English lay, which modern editors have entitled *The Fight at Finnsburg*. Hildeburh, the daughter of the former Danish king Hoc, was married to Finn, king of Friesland, presumably to help end a feud between their peoples. As the episode opens, the feud has already broken out again when a visiting party of Danes, led by Hildeburh's brother Hnaef, who has succeeded their father, is attacked by a tribe called the Jutes. The Jutes are subject to Finn but may be a clan distinct from the Frisians, and Finn does not seem to have instigated the attack. In the ensuing battle, both Hnaef and the son of Hildeburh and Finn are killed, and both sides suffer heavy losses.

to credit the Jutes:
son and brother,
she lost them both
on the battlefield.
She, bereft
and blameless, they
foredoomed, cut down
and spear-gored. She,
the woman in shock,
waylaid by grief,
Hoc's daughter—
how could she not
lament her fate
when morning came
and the light broke
on her murdered dears?
And so farewell
delight on earth,
war carried away
Finn's troop of thanes
all but a few.
How then could Finn
hold the line
or fight on
to the end with Hengest,
how save
the rump of his force
from that enemy chief?
So a truce was offered
as follows:[6] first
separate quarters
to be cleared for the Danes,
hall and throne
to be shared with the Frisians.
Then, second:
every day
at the dole-out of gifts
Finn, son of Focwald,
should honor the Danes,
bestow with an even
hand to Hengest
and Hengest's men
the wrought-gold rings,
bounty to match
the measure he gave
his own Frisians—
to keep morale
in the beer-hall high.
Both sides then
sealed their agreement.
With oaths to Hengest

6. The truce was offered by Finn to Hengest, who succeeded Hnaef as leader of the Danes.

Finn swore
openly, solemnly,
that the battle survivors
would be guaranteed
honor and status.
No infringement
by word or deed,
no provocation
would be permitted.
Their own ring-giver
after all
was dead and gone,
they were leaderless,
in forced allegiance
to his murderer.
So if any Frisian
stirred up bad blood
with insinuations
or taunts about this,
the blade of the sword
would arbitrate it.
A funeral pyre
was then prepared,
effulgent gold
brought out from the hoard.
The pride and prince
of the Shieldings lay
awaiting the flame.
Everywhere
there were blood-plastered
coats of mail.
The pyre was heaped
with boar-shaped helmets
forged in gold,
with the gashed corpses
of wellborn Danes—
many had fallen.
Then Hildeburh
ordered her own
son's body
be burnt with Hnaef's,
the flesh on his bones
to sputter and blaze
beside his uncle's.
The woman wailed
and sang keens,
the warrior went up.[7]
Carcass flame
swirled and fumed,
they stood round the burial

7. The meaning may be that the warrior was placed up on the pyre, or went up in smoke. "Keens": lamentations or dirges for the dead.

mound and howled
as heads melted,
crusted gashes
spattered and ran
bloody matter.
The glutton element
flamed and consumed
the dead of both sides.
Their great days were gone.
Warriors scattered
to homes and forts
all over Friesland,
fewer now, feeling
loss of friends.
Hengest stayed,
lived out that whole
resentful, blood-sullen
winter with Finn,
homesick and helpless.
No ring-whorled prow
could up then
and away on the sea.
Wind and water
raged with storms,
wave and shingle
were shackled in ice
until another year
appeared in the yard
as it does to this day,
the seasons constant,
the wonder of light
coming over us.
Then winter was gone,
earth's lap grew lovely,
longing woke
in the cooped-up exile
for a voyage home—
but more for vengeance,
some way of bringing
things to a head:
his sword arm hankered
to greet the Jutes.
So he did not balk
once Hunlafing
placed on his lap
Dazzle-the-Duel,
the best sword of all,[8]
whose edges Jutes
knew only too well.
Thus blood was spilled,

8. Hunlafing may be the son of a Danish warrior called Hunlaf. The placing of the sword in Hengest's lap is a symbolic call for revenge.

the gallant Finn
slain in his home
after Guthlaf and Oslaf[9]
back from their voyage
made old accusation:
the brutal ambush,
the fate they had suffered,
all blamed on Finn.
The wildness in them
had to brim over.
The hall ran red
with blood of enemies.
Finn was cut down,
the queen brought away
and everything
the Shieldings could find
inside Finn's walls—
the Frisian king's
gold collars and gemstones—
swept off to the ship.
Over sea-lanes then
back to Daneland
the warrior troop
bore that lady home.

The poem was over,
the poet had performed, a pleasant murmur
started on the benches, stewards did the rounds
with wine in splendid jugs, and Wealhtheow came to sit
in her gold crown between two good men,
uncle and nephew, each one of whom
still trusted the other;[1] and the forthright Unferth,
admired by all for his mind and courage
although under a cloud for killing his brothers,
reclined near the king.
The queen spoke:
"Enjoy this drink, my most generous lord;
raise up your goblet, entertain the Geats
duly and gently, discourse with them,
be open-handed, happy and fond.
Relish their company, but recollect as well
all of the boons that have been bestowed on you.
The bright court of Heorot has been cleansed
and now the word is that you want to adopt
this warrior as a son. So, while you may,
bask in your fortune, and then bequeath
kingdom and nation to your kith and kin,
before your decease. I am certain of Hrothulf.
He is noble and will use the young ones well.

9. It is not clear whether the Danes have traveled home and then returned to Friesland with reinforcements, or whether the Danish survivors attack once the weather allows them to take ship.
1. See p. 51, n. 4.

He will not let you down. Should you die before him,
he will treat our children truly and fairly.
He will honor, I am sure, our two sons,
repay them in kind, when he recollects
all the good things we gave him once,
the favor and respect he found in his childhood."
She turned then to the bench where her boys sat,
Hrethric and Hrothmund, with other nobles' sons,
all the youth together; and that good man,
Beowulf the Geat, sat between the brothers.
The cup was carried to him, kind words
spoken in welcome and a wealth of wrought gold
graciously bestowed: two arm bangles,
a mail-shirt and rings, and the most resplendent
torque of gold I ever heard tell of
anywhere on earth or under heaven.
There was no hoard like it since Hama snatched
the Brosings' neck-chain and bore it away
with its gems and settings to his shining fort,
away from Eormenric's wiles and hatred,[2]
and thereby ensured his eternal reward.
Hygelac the Geat, grandson of Swerting,
wore this neck-ring on his last raid;[3]
at bay under his banner, he defended the booty,
treasure he had won. Fate swept him away
because of his proud need to provoke
a feud with the Frisians. He fell beneath his shield,
in the same gem-crusted, kingly gear
he had worn when he crossed the frothing wave-vat.
So the dead king fell into Frankish hands.
They took his breast-mail, also his neck-torque,
and punier warriors plundered the slain
when the carnage ended; Geat corpses
covered the field.
Applause filled the hall.
Then Wealhtheow pronounced in the presence of the company:
"Take delight in this torque, dear Beowulf,
wear it for luck and wear also this mail
from our people's armory: may you prosper in them!
Be acclaimed for strength, for kindly guidance
to these two boys, and your bounty will be sure.
You have won renown: you are known to all men
far and near, now and forever.
Your sway is wide as the wind's home,
as the sea around cliffs. And so, my prince,
I wish you a lifetime's luck and blessings
to enjoy this treasure. Treat my sons

2. The necklace presented to Beowulf is compared to one worn by the goddess Freya in Germanic mythology. In another story it was stolen by Hama from the Gothic king Eormenric, who is treated as a tyrant in Germanic legend, but how Eormenric came to possess it is not known.

3. Later we learn that Beowulf gave the necklace to Hygd, the queen of his lord Hygelac. Hygelac is here said to have been wearing it on his last expedition. This is the first of several allusions to Hygelac's death on a raid up the Rhine, the one incident in the poem that can be connected to a historical event documented elsewhere.

with tender care, be strong and kind.
Here each comrade is true to the other,
loyal to lord, loving in spirit.
The thanes have one purpose, the people are ready:
having drunk and pledged, the ranks do as I bid."
  She moved then to her place. Men were drinking wine
at that rare feast; how could they know fate,
the grim shape of things to come,
the threat looming over many thanes
as night approached and King Hrothgar prepared
to retire to his quarters? Retainers in great numbers
were posted on guard as so often in the past.
Benches were pushed back, bedding gear and bolsters
spread across the floor, and one man
lay down to his rest, already marked for death.
At their heads they placed their polished timber
battle-shields; and on the bench above them,
each man's kit was kept to hand:
a towering war-helmet, webbed mail-shirt
and great-shafted spear. It was their habit
always and everywhere to be ready for action,
at home or in the camp, in whatever case
and at whatever time the need arose
to rally round their lord. They were a right people.

[ANOTHER ATTACK]

  They went to sleep. And one paid dearly
for his night's ease, as had happened to them often,
ever since Grendel occupied the gold-hall,
committing evil until the end came,
death after his crimes. Then it became clear,
obvious to everyone once the fight was over,
that an avenger lurked and was still alive,
grimly biding time. Grendel's mother,
monstrous hell-bride, brooded on her wrongs.
She had been forced down into fearful waters,
the cold depths, after Cain had killed
his father's son, felled his own
brother with a sword. Branded an outlaw,
marked by having murdered, he moved into the wilds,
shunned company and joy. And from Cain there sprang
misbegotten spirits, among them Grendel,
the banished and accursed, due to come to grips
with that watcher in Heorot waiting to do battle.
The monster wrenched and wrestled with him,
but Beowulf was mindful of his mighty strength,
the wondrous gifts God had showered on him:
he relied for help on the Lord of All,
on His care and favor. So he overcame the foe,
brought down the hell-brute. Broken and bowed,
outcast from all sweetness, the enemy of mankind
made for his death-den. But now his mother

had sallied forth on a savage journey,
grief-racked and ravenous, desperate for revenge.
She came to Heorot. There, inside the hall,
Danes lay asleep, earls who would soon endure
a great reversal, once Grendel's mother
attacked and entered. Her onslaught was less
only by as much as an amazon warrior's
strength is less than an armed man's
when the hefted sword, its hammered edge
and gleaming blade slathered in blood,
razes the sturdy boar-ridge off a helmet.
Then in the hall, hard-honed swords
were grabbed from the bench, many a broad shield
lifted and braced; there was little thought of helmets
or woven mail when they woke in terror.
The hell-dam was in panic, desperate to get out,
in mortal terror the moment she was found.
She had pounced and taken one of the retainers
in a tight hold, then headed for the fen.
To Hrothgar, this man was the most beloved
of the friends he trusted between the two seas.
She had done away with a great warrior,
ambushed him at rest.
Beowulf was elsewhere.
Earlier, after the award of the treasure,
the Geat had been given another lodging.
There was uproar in Heorot. She had snatched their trophy,
Grendel's bloodied hand. It was a fresh blow
to the afflicted bawn. The bargain was hard,
both parties having to pay
with the lives of friends. And the old lord,
the gray-haired warrior, was heartsore and weary
when he heard the news: his highest-placed adviser,
his dearest companion, was dead and gone.
Beowulf was quickly brought to the chamber:
the winner of fights, the arch-warrior,
came first-footing in with his fellow troops
to where the king in his wisdom waited,
still wondering whether Almighty God
would ever turn the tide of his misfortunes.
So Beowulf entered with his band in attendance
and the wooden floorboards banged and rang
as he advanced, hurrying to address
the prince of the Ingwins, asking if he'd rested
since the urgent summons had come as a surprise.
Then Hrothgar, the Shieldings' helmet, spoke:
"Rest? What is rest? Sorrow has returned.
Alas for the Danes! Aeschere is dead.
He was Yrmenlaf's elder brother
and a soul-mate to me, a true mentor,
my right-hand man when the ranks clashed
and our boar-crests had to take a battering
in the line of action. Aeschere was everything

the world admires in a wise man and a friend.
Then this roaming killer came in a fury
and slaughtered him in Heorot. Where she is hiding,
glutting on the corpse and glorying in her escape,
I cannot tell; she has taken up the feud
because of last night, when you killed Grendel,
wrestled and racked him in ruinous combat
since for too long he had terrorized us
with his depredations. He died in battle,
paid with his life; and now this powerful
other one arrives, this force for evil
driven to avenge her kinsman's death.
Or so it seems to thanes in their grief,
in the anguish every thane endures
at the loss of a ring-giver, now that the hand
that bestowed so richly has been stilled in death.
"I have heard it said by my people in hall,
counselors who live in the upland country,
that they have seen two such creatures
prowling the moors, huge marauders
from some other world. One of these things,
as far as anyone ever can discern,
looks like a woman; the other, warped
in the shape of a man, moves beyond the pale
bigger than any man, an unnatural birth
called Grendel by the country people
in former days. They are fatherless creatures,
and their whole ancestry is hidden in a past
of demons and ghosts. They dwell apart
among wolves on the hills, on windswept crags
and treacherous keshes, where cold streams
pour down the mountain and disappear
under mist and moorland.
A few miles from here
a frost-stiffened wood waits and keeps watch
above a mere; the overhanging bank
is a maze of tree-roots mirrored in its surface.
At night there, something uncanny happens:
the water burns. And the mere bottom
has never been sounded by the sons of men.
On its bank, the heather-stepper halts:
the hart in flight from pursuing hounds
will turn to face them with firm-set horns
and die in the wood rather than dive
beneath its surface. That is no good place.
When wind blows up and stormy weather
makes clouds scud and the skies weep,
out of its depths a dirty surge
is pitched toward the heavens. Now help depends
again on you and on you alone.
The gap of danger where the demon waits
is still unknown to you. Seek it if you dare.
I will compensate you for settling the feud

as I did the last time with lavish wealth,
coffers of coiled gold, if you come back."

[BEOWULF FIGHTS GRENDEL'S MOTHER]

Beowulf, son of Ecgtheow, spoke:
"Wise sir, do not grieve. It is always better
to avenge dear ones than to indulge in mourning.
For every one of us, living in this world
means waiting for our end. Let whoever can
win glory before death. When a warrior is gone,
that will be his best and only bulwark.
So arise, my lord, and let us immediately
set forth on the trail of this troll-dam.
I guarantee you: she will not get away,
not to dens under ground nor upland groves
nor the ocean floor. She'll have nowhere to flee to.
Endure your troubles today. Bear up
and be the man I expect you to be."
With that the old lord sprang to his feet
and praised God for Beowulf's pledge.
Then a bit and halter were brought for his horse
with the plaited mane. The wise king mounted
the royal saddle and rode out in style
with a force of shield-bearers. The forest paths
were marked all over with the monster's tracks,
her trail on the ground wherever she had gone
across the dark moors, dragging away
the body of that thane, Hrothgar's best
counselor and overseer of the country.
So the noble prince proceeded undismayed
up fells and screes, along narrow footpaths
and ways where they were forced into single file,
ledges on cliffs above lairs of water-monsters.
He went in front with a few men,
good judges of the lie of the land,
and suddenly discovered the dismal wood,
mountain trees growing out at an angle
above gray stones: the bloodshot water
surged underneath. It was a sore blow
to all of the Danes, friends of the Shieldings,
a hurt to each and every one
of that noble company when they came upon
Aeschere's head at the foot of the cliff.
Everybody gazed as the hot gore
kept wallowing up and an urgent war-horn
repeated its notes: the whole party
sat down to watch. The water was infested
with all kinds of reptiles. There were writhing sea-dragons
and monsters slouching on slopes by the cliff,
serpents and wild things such as those that often
surface at dawn to roam the sail-road
and doom the voyage. Down they plunged,

lashing in anger at the loud call
of the battle-bugle. An arrow from the bow
of the Geat chief got one of them
as he surged to the surface: the seasoned shaft
stuck deep in his flank and his freedom in the water
got less and less. It was his last swim.
He was swiftly overwhelmed in the shallows,
prodded by barbed boar-spears,
cornered, beaten, pulled up on the bank,
a strange lake-birth, a loathsome catch
men gazed at in awe.
Beowulf got ready,
donned his war-gear, indifferent to death;
his mighty, hand-forged, fine-webbed mail
would soon meet with the menace underwater.
It would keep the bone-cage of his body safe:
no enemy's clasp could crush him in it,
no vicious armlock choke his life out.
To guard his head he had a glittering helmet
that was due to be muddied on the mere bottom
and blurred in the upswirl. It was of beaten gold,
princely headgear hooped and hasped
by a weapon-smith who had worked wonders
in days gone by and adorned it with boar-shapes;
since then it had resisted every sword.
And another item lent by Unferth
at that moment of need was of no small importance:
the brehon[4] handed him a hilted weapon,
a rare and ancient sword named Hrunting.
The iron blade with its ill-boding patterns
had been tempered in blood. It had never failed
the hand of anyone who hefted it in battle,
anyone who had fought and faced the worst
in the gap of danger. This was not the first time
it had been called to perform heroic feats.
When he lent that blade to the better swordsman,
Unferth, the strong-built son of Ecglaf,
could hardly have remembered the ranting speech
he had made in his cups. He was not man enough
to face the turmoil of a fight under water
and the risk to his life. So there he lost
fame and repute. It was different for the other
rigged out in his gear, ready to do battle.
Beowulf, son of Ecgtheow, spoke:
"Wisest of kings, now that I have come
to the point of action, I ask you to recall
what we said earlier: that you, son of Halfdane
and gold-friend to retainers, that you, if I should fall
and suffer death while serving your cause,
would act like a father to me afterward.

4. One of an ancient class of lawyers in Ireland [Translator's note]. The Old English word for Unferth's office, *thyle,* has been interpreted as "orator" and "spokesman."

If this combat kills me, take care
of my young company, my comrades in arms.
And be sure also, my beloved Hrothgar,
to send Hygelac the treasures I received.
Let the lord of the Geats gaze on that gold,
let Hrethel's son take note of it and see
that I found a ring-giver of rare magnificence
and enjoyed the good of his generosity.
And Unferth is to have what I inherited:
to that far-famed man I bequeath my own
sharp-honed, wave-sheened wonder-blade.
With Hrunting I shall gain glory or die."
After these words, the prince of the Weather-Geats
was impatient to be away and plunged suddenly:
without more ado, he dived into the heaving
depths of the lake. It was the best part of a day
before he could see the solid bottom.
Quickly the one who haunted those waters,
who had scavenged and gone her gluttonous rounds
for a hundred seasons, sensed a human
observing her outlandish lair from above.
So she lunged and clutched and managed to catch him
in her brutal grip; but his body, for all that,
remained unscathed: the mesh of the chain-mail
saved him on the outside. Her savage talons
failed to rip the web of his war-shirt.
Then once she touched bottom, that wolfish swimmer
carried the ring-mailed prince to her court
so that for all his courage he could never use
the weapons he carried; and a bewildering horde
came at him from the depths, droves of sea-beasts
who attacked with tusks and tore at his chain-mail
in a ghastly onslaught. The gallant man
could see he had entered some hellish turn-hole
and yet the water there did not work against him
because the hall-roofing held off
the force of the current; then he saw firelight,
a gleam and flare-up, a glimmer of brightness.
The hero observed that swamp-thing from hell,
the tarn-hag in all her terrible strength,
then heaved his war-sword and swung his arm:
the decorated blade came down ringing
and singing on her head. But he soon found
his battle-torch extinguished; the shining blade
refused to bite. It spared her and failed
the man in his need. It had gone through many
hand-to-hand fight, had hewed the armor
and helmets of the doomed, but here at last
the fabulous powers of that heirloom failed.
Hygelac's kinsman kept thinking about
his name and fame: he never lost heart.
Then, in a fury, he flung his sword away.
The keen, inlaid, worm-loop-patterned steel

was hurled to the ground: he would have to rely
on the might of his arm. So must a man do
who intends to gain enduring glory
in a combat. Life doesn't cost him a thought.
Then the prince of War-Geats, warming to this fight
with Grendel's mother, gripped her shoulder
and laid about him in a battle frenzy:
he pitched his killer opponent to the floor
but she rose quickly and retaliated,
grappled him tightly in her grim embrace.
The sure-footed fighter felt daunted,
the strongest of warriors stumbled and fell.
So she pounced upon him and pulled out
a broad, whetted knife: now she would avenge
her only child. But the mesh of chain-mail
on Beowulf's shoulder shielded his life,
turned the edge and tip of the blade.
The son of Ecgtheow would have surely perished
and the Geats lost their warrior under the wide earth
had the strong links and locks of his war-gear
not helped to save him: holy God
decided the victory. It was easy for the Lord,
the Ruler of Heaven, to redress the balance
once Beowulf got back up on his feet.

Then he saw a blade that boded well,
a sword in her armory, an ancient heirloom
from the days of the giants, an ideal weapon,
one that any warrior would envy,
but so huge and heavy of itself
only Beowulf could wield it in a battle.
So the Shieldings' hero hard-pressed and enraged,
took a firm hold of the hilt and swung
the blade in an arc, a resolute blow
that bit deep into her neck-bone
and severed it entirely, toppling the doomed
house of her flesh; she fell to the floor.
The sword dripped blood, the swordsman was elated.

A light appeared and the place brightened
the way the sky does when heaven's candle
is shining clearly. He inspected the vault:
with sword held high, its hilt raised
to guard and threaten, Hygelac's thane
scouted by the wall in Grendel's wake.
Now the weapon was to prove its worth.
The warrior determined to take revenge
for every gross act Grendel had committed—
and not only for that one occasion
when he'd come to slaughter the sleeping troops,
fifteen of Hrothgar's house-guards
surprised on their benches and ruthlessly devoured,
and as many again carried away,
a brutal plunder. Beowulf in his fury
now settled that score: he saw the monster

in his resting place, war-weary and wrecked,
a lifeless corpse, a casualty
of the battle in Heorot. The body gaped
at the stroke dealt to it after death:
Beowulf cut the corpse's head off.
Immediately the counselors keeping a lookout
with Hrothgar, watching the lake water,
saw a heave-up and surge of waves
and blood in the backwash. They bowed gray heads,
spoke in their sage, experienced way
about the good warrior, how they never again
expected to see that prince returning
in triumph to their king. It was clear to many
that the wolf of the deep had destroyed him forever.
The ninth hour of the day arrived.
The brave Shieldings abandoned the cliff-top
and the king went home; but sick at heart,
staring at the mere, the strangers held on.
They wished, without hope, to behold their lord,
Beowulf himself.
Meanwhile, the sword
began to wilt into gory icicles
to slather and thaw. It was a wonderful thing,
the way it all melted as ice melts
when the Father eases the fetters off the frost
and unravels the water-ropes, He who wields power
over time and tide: He is the true Lord.
The Geat captain saw treasure in abundance
but carried no spoils from those quarters
except for the head and the inlaid hilt
embossed with jewels; its blade had melted
and the scrollwork on it burned, so scalding was the blood
of the poisonous fiend who had perished there.
Then away he swam, the one who had survived
the fall of his enemies, flailing to the surface.
The wide water, the waves and pools,
were no longer infested once the wandering fiend
let go of her life and this unreliable world.
The seafarers' leader made for land,
resolutely swimming, delighted with his prize,
the mighty load he was lugging to the surface.
His thanes advanced in a troop to meet him,
thanking God and taking great delight
in seeing their prince back safe and sound.
Quickly the hero's helmet and mail-shirt
were loosed and unlaced. The lake settled,
clouds darkened above the bloodshot depths.
With high hearts they headed away
along footpaths and trails through the fields,
roads that they knew, each of them wrestling
with the head they were carrying from the lakeside cliff,
men kingly in their courage and capable
of difficult work. It was a task for four

to hoist Grendel's head on a spear
and bear it under strain to the bright hall.
But soon enough they neared the place,
fourteen Geats in fine fettle,
striding across the outlying ground
in a delighted throng around their leader.
In he came then, the thanes' commander,
the arch-warrior, to address Hrothgar:
his courage was proven, his glory was secure.
Grendel's head was hauled by the hair,
dragged across the floor where the people were drinking,
a horror for both queen and company to behold.
They stared in awe. It was an astonishing sight.

[another celebration at heorot]

Beowulf, son of Ecgtheow, spoke:
"So, son of Halfdane, prince of the Shieldings,
we are glad to bring this booty from the lake.
It is a token of triumph and we tender it to you.
I barely survived the battle under water.
It was hard-fought, a desperate affair
that could have gone badly; if God had not helped me,
the outcome would have been quick and fatal.
Although Hrunting is hard-edged,
I could never bring it to bear in battle.
But the Lord of Men allowed me to behold—
for He often helps the unbefriended—
an ancient sword shining on the wall,
a weapon made for giants, there for the wielding.
Then my moment came in the combat and I struck
the dwellers in that den. Next thing the damascened
sword blade melted; it bloated and it burned
in their rushing blood. I have wrested the hilt
from the enemies' hand, avenged the evil
done to the Danes; it is what was due.
And this I pledge, O prince of the Shieldings:
you can sleep secure with your company of troops
in Heorot Hall. Never need you fear
for a single thane of your sept or nation,
young warriors or old, that laying waste of life
that you and your people endured of yore."
Then the gold hilt was handed over
to the old lord, a relic from long ago
for the venerable ruler. That rare smithwork
was passed on to the prince of the Danes
when those devils perished; once death removed
that murdering, guilt-steeped, God-cursed fiend,
eliminating his unholy life
and his mother's as well, it was willed to that king
who of all the lavish gift-lords of the north
was the best regarded between the two seas.
Hrothgar spoke; he examined the hilt,

that relic of old times. It was engraved all over
and showed how war first came into the world
and the flood destroyed the tribe of giants.
They suffered a terrible severance from the Lord;
the Almighty made the waters rise,
drowned them in the deluge for retribution.
In pure gold inlay on the sword-guards
there were rune-markings correctly incised,
stating and recording for whom the sword
had been first made and ornamented
with its scrollworked hilt. Then everyone hushed
as the son of Halfdane spoke this wisdom:
"A protector of his people, pledged to uphold
truth and justice and to respect tradition,
is entitled to affirm that this man
was born to distinction. Beowulf, my friend,
your fame has gone far and wide,
you are known everywhere. In all things you are even-tempered,
prudent and resolute. So I stand firm by the promise of friendship
we exchanged before. Forever you will be
your people's mainstay and your own warriors'
helping hand.

Heremod was different,
the way he behaved to Ecgwela's sons.
His rise in the world brought little joy
to the Danish people, only death and destruction.
He vented his rage on men he caroused with,
killed his own comrades, a pariah king
who cut himself off from his own kind,
even though Almighty God had made him
eminent and powerful and marked him from the start
for a happy life. But a change happened,
he grew bloodthirsty, gave no more rings
to honor the Danes. He suffered in the end
for having plagued his people for so long:
his life lost happiness.

So learn from this
and understand true values. I who tell you
have wintered into wisdom.

It is a great wonder
how Almighty God in His magnificence
favors our race with rank and scope
and the gift of wisdom; His sway is wide.
Sometimes He allows the mind of a man
of distinguished birth to follow its bent,
grants him fulfillment and felicity on earth
and forts to command in his own country.
He permits him to lord it in many lands
until the man in his unthinkingness
forgets that it will ever end for him.
He indulges his desires; illness and old age
mean nothing to him; his mind is untroubled
by envy or malice or the thought of enemies

with their hate-honed swords. The whole world
conforms to his will, he is kept from the worst
until an element of overweening
enters him and takes hold
while the soul's guard, its sentry, drowses,
grown too distracted. A killer stalks him,
an archer who draws a deadly bow.
And then the man is hit in the heart,
the arrow flies beneath his defenses,
the devious promptings of the demon start.
His old possessions seem paltry to him now.
He covets and resents; dishonors custom
and bestows no gold; and because of good things
that the Heavenly Powers gave him in the past
he ignores the shape of things to come.
Then finally the end arrives
when the body he was lent collapses and falls
prey to its death; ancestral possessions
and the goods he hoarded are inherited by another
who lets them go with a liberal hand.

"O flower of warriors, beware of that trap.
Choose, dear Beowulf, the better part,
eternal rewards. Do not give way to pride.
For a brief while your strength is in bloom
but it fades quickly; and soon there will follow
illness or the sword to lay you low,
or a sudden fire or surge of water
or jabbing blade or javelin from the air
or repellent age. Your piercing eye
will dim and darken; and death will arrive,
dear warrior, to sweep you away.

"Just so I ruled the Ring-Danes' country
for fifty years, defended them in wartime
with spear and sword against constant assaults
by many tribes: I came to believe
my enemies had faded from the face of the earth.
Still, what happened was a hard reversal
from bliss to grief. Grendel struck
after lying in wait. He laid waste to the land
and from that moment my mind was in dread
of his depredations. So I praise God
in His heavenly glory that I lived to behold
this head dripping blood and that after such harrowing
I can look upon it in triumph at last.
Take your place, then, with pride and pleasure,
and move to the feast. Tomorrow morning
our treasure will be shared and showered upon you."

The Geat was elated and gladly obeyed
the old man's bidding; he sat on the bench.
And soon all was restored, the same as before.
Happiness came back, the hall was thronged,
and a banquet set forth; black night fell
and covered them in darkness.

Then the company rose
for the old campaigner: the gray-haired prince
was ready for bed. And a need for rest
came over the brave shield-bearing Geat.
He was a weary seafarer, far from home,
so immediately a house-guard guided him out,
one whose office entailed looking after
whatever a thane on the road in those days
might need or require. It was noble courtesy.

[BEOWULF RETURNS HOME]

That great heart rested. The hall towered,
gold-shingled and gabled, and the guest slept in it
until the black raven with raucous glee
announced heaven's joy, and a hurry of brightness
overran the shadows. Warriors rose quickly,
impatient to be off: their own country
was beckoning the nobles; and the bold voyager
longed to be aboard his distant boat.
Then that stalwart fighter ordered Hrunting
to be brought to Unferth, and bade Unferth
take the sword and thanked him for lending it.
He said he had found it a friend in battle
and a powerful help; he put no blame
on the blade's cutting edge. He was a considerate man.
And there the warriors stood in their war-gear,
eager to go, while their honored lord
approached the platform where the other sat.
The undaunted hero addressed Hrothgar.
Beowulf, son of Ecghteow, spoke:
"Now we who crossed the wide sea
have to inform you that we feel a desire
to return to Hygelac. Here we have been welcomed
and thoroughly entertained. You have treated us well.
If there is any favor on earth I can perform
beyond deeds of arms I have done already,
anything that would merit your affections more,
I shall act, my lord, with alacrity.
If ever I hear from across the ocean
that people on your borders are threatening battle
as attackers have done from time to time,
I shall land with a thousand thanes at my back
to help your cause. Hygelac may be young
to rule a nation, but this much I know
about the king of the Geats: he will come to my aid
and want to support me by word and action
in your hour of need, when honor dictates
that I raise a hedge of spears around you.
Then if Hrethric should think about traveling
as a king's son to the court of the Geats,
he will find many friends. Foreign places
yield more to one who is himself worth meeting."

Hrothgar spoke and answered him:
"The Lord in his wisdom sent you those words
and they came from the heart. I have never heard
so young a man make truer observations.
You are strong in body and mature in mind,
impressive in speech. If it should come to pass
that Hrethel's descendant dies beneath a spear,
if deadly battle or the sword blade or disease
fells the prince who guards your people
and you are still alive, then I firmly believe
the seafaring Geats won't find a man
worthier of acclaim as their king and defender
than you, if only you would undertake
the lordship of your homeland. My liking for you
deepens with time, dear Beowulf.
What you have done is to draw two peoples,
the Geat nation and us neighboring Danes,
into shared peace and a pact of friendship
in spite of hatreds we have harbored in the past.
For as long as I rule this far-flung land
treasures will change hands and each side will treat
the other with gifts; across the gannet's bath,
over the broad sea, whorled prows will bring
presents and tokens. I know your people
are beyond reproach in every respect,
steadfast in the old way with friend or foe."
Then the earls' defender furnished the hero
with twelve treasures and told him to set out,
sail with those gifts safely home
to the people he loved, but to return promptly.
And so the good and gray-haired Dane,
that highborn king, kissed Beowulf
and embraced his neck, then broke down
in sudden tears. Two forebodings
disturbed him in his wisdom, but one was stronger:
nevermore would they meet each other
face to face. And such was his affection
that he could not help being overcome:
his fondness for the man was so deep-founded,
it warmed his heart and wound the heartstrings
tight in his breast.
The embrace ended
and Beowulf, glorious in his gold regalia,
stepped the green earth. Straining at anchor
and ready for boarding, his boat awaited him.
So they went on their journey, and Hrothgar's generosity
was praised repeatedly. He was a peerless king
until old age sapped his strength and did him
mortal harm, as it has done so many.
Down to the waves then, dressed in the web
of their chain-mail and war-shirts the young men marched
in high spirits. The coast-guard spied them,
thanes setting forth, the same as before.

His salute this time from the top of the cliff
was far from unmannerly; he galloped to meet them
and as they took ship in their shining gear,
he said how welcome they would be in Geatland.
Then the broad hull was beached on the sand
to be cargoed with treasure, horses and war-gear.
The curved prow motioned; the mast stood high
above Hrothgar's riches in the loaded hold.
The guard who had watched the boat was given
a sword with gold fittings, and in future days
that present would make him a respected man
at his place on the mead-bench.
Then the keel plunged
and shook in the sea; and they sailed from Denmark.
Right away the mast was rigged with its sea-shawl;
sail-ropes were tightened, timbers drummed
and stiff winds kept the wave-crosser
skimming ahead; as she heaved forward,
her foamy neck was fleet and buoyant,
a lapped prow loping over currents,
until finally the Geats caught sight of coastline
and familiar cliffs. The keel reared up,
wind lifted it home, it hit on the land.
The harbor guard came hurrying out
to the rolling water: he had watched the offing
long and hard, on the lookout for those friends.
With the anchor cables, he moored their craft
right where it had beached, in case a backwash
might catch the hull and carry it away.
Then he ordered the prince's treasure-trove
to be carried ashore. It was a short step
from there to where Hrethel's son and heir,
Hygelac the gold-giver, makes his home
on a secure cliff, in the company of retainers.
The building was magnificent, the king majestic,
ensconced in his hall; and although Hygd, his queen,
was young, a few short years at court,
her mind was thoughtful and her manners sure.
Haereth's daughter behaved generously
and stinted nothing when she distributed
bounty to the Geats.
Great Queen Modthryth
perpetrated terrible wrongs.[5]
If any retainer ever made bold
to look her in the face, if an eye not her lord's[6]
stared at her directly during daylight,
the outcome was sealed: he was kept bound,

5. The story of Queen Modthryth's vices is abruptly introduced as a foil to Queen Hygd's virtues. A transitional passage may have been lost, but the poet's device is similar to that of using the earlier reference to the wickedness of King Heremod to contrast with the good qualities of Sigemund and Beowulf.

6. This could refer to her husband or her father before her marriage. The story resembles folktales about a proud princess whose unsuccessful suitors are all put to death, although the unfortunate victims in this case seem to be guilty only of looking at her.

in hand-tightened shackles, racked, tortured
until doom was pronounced—death by the sword,
slash of blade, blood-gush, and death-qualms
in an evil display. Even a queen
outstanding in beauty must not overstep like that.
A queen should weave peace, not punish the innocent
with loss of life for imagined insults.
But Hemming's kinsman[7] put a halt to her ways
and drinkers round the table had another tale:
she was less of a bane to people's lives,
less cruel-minded, after she was married
to the brave Offa, a bride arrayed
in her gold finery, given away
by a caring father, ferried to her young prince
over dim seas. In days to come
she would grace the throne and grow famous
for her good deeds and conduct of life,
her high devotion to the hero king
who was the best king, it has been said,
between the two seas or anywhere else
on the face of the earth. Offa was honored
far and wide for his generous ways,
his fighting spirit and his farseeing
defense of his homeland; from him there sprang Eomer,
Garmund's grandson, kinsman of Hemming,[8]
his warriors' mainstay and master of the field.
 Heroic Beowulf and his band of men
crossed the wide strand, striding along
the sandy foreshore; the sun shone,
the world's candle warmed them from the south
as they hastened to where, as they had heard,
the young king, Ongentheow's killer
and his people's protector,[9] was dispensing rings
inside his bawn. Beowulf's return
was reported to Hygelac as soon as possible,
news that the captain was now in the enclosure,
his battle-brother back from the fray
alive and well, walking to the hall.
Room was quickly made, on the king's orders,
and the troops filed across the cleared floor.
 After Hygelac had offered greetings
to his loyal thane in a lofty speech,
he and his kinsman, that hale survivor,
sat face to face. Haereth's daughter
moved about with the mead-jug in her hand,
taking care of the company, filling the cups

7. I.e., Offa I, a legendary king of the Angles. We know nothing about Hemming other than that Offa was related to him. Offa II (757–96) was king of Mercia, and although the story is about the second Offa's ancestor on the Continent, this is the only English connection in the poem and has been taken as evidence to date its origins to 8th-century Mercia.

8. I.e., Eomer, Offa's son. See previous note. Garmund was presumably the name of Offa's father.

9. I.e., Hygelac. Ongentheow was king of the Swedish people called the Shylfings. This is the first of the references to wars between the Geats and the Swedes. One of Hygelac's war party named Eofer was the actual slayer of Ongentheow.

that warriors held out. Then Hygelac began
to put courteous questions to his old comrade
in the high hall. He hankered to know
every tale the Sea-Geats had to tell:
"How did you fare on your foreign voyage,
dear Beowulf, when you abruptly decided
to sail away across the salt water
and fight at Heorot? Did you help Hrothgar
much in the end? Could you ease the prince
of his well-known troubles? Your undertaking
cast my spirits down, I dreaded the outcome
of your expedition and pleaded with you
long and hard to leave the killer be,
let the South-Danes settle their own
blood-feud with Grendel. So God be thanked
I am granted this sight of you, safe and sound."
  Beowulf, son of Ecgtheow, spoke:
"What happened, Lord Hygelac, is hardly a secret
any more among men in this world—
myself and Grendel coming to grips
on the very spot where he visited destruction
on the Victory-Shieldings and violated
life and limb, losses I avenged
so no earthly offspring of Grendel's
need ever boast of that bout before dawn,
no matter how long the last of his evil
family survives.
          When I first landed
I hastened to the ring-hall and saluted Hrothgar.
Once he discovered why I had come,
the son of Halfdane sent me immediately
to sit with his own sons on the bench.
It was a happy gathering. In my whole life
I have never seen mead enjoyed more
in any hall on earth. Sometimes the queen
herself appeared, peace-pledge between nations,
to hearten the young ones and hand out
a torque to a warrior, then take her place.
Sometimes Hrothgar's daughter distributed
ale to older ranks, in order on the benches:
I heard the company call her Freawaru
as she made her rounds, presenting men
with the gem-studded bowl, young bride-to-be
to the gracious Ingeld,[1] in her gold-trimmed attire.
The friend of the Shieldings favors her betrothal:
the guardian of the kingdom sees good in it
and hopes this woman will heal old wounds
and grievous feuds.
          But generally the spear
is prompt to retaliate when a prince is killed,
no matter how admirable the bride may be.

1. King of the Heatho-Bards; his father, Froda, was killed by the Danes.

"Think how the Heatho-Bards are bound to feel,
their lord, Ingeld, and his loyal thanes,
when he walks in with that woman to the feast:
Danes are at the table, being entertained,
honored guests in glittering regalia,
burnished ring-mail that was their hosts' birthright,
looted when the Heatho-Bards could no longer wield
their weapons in the shield-clash, when they went down
with their beloved comrades and forfeited their lives.
Then an old spearman will speak while they are drinking,
having glimpsed some heirloom that brings alive
memories of the massacre; his mood will darken
and heart-stricken, in the stress of his emotion,
he will begin to test a young man's temper
and stir up trouble, starting like this:
'Now, my friend, don't you recognize
your father's sword, his favorite weapon,
the one he wore when he went out in his war-mask
to face the Danes on that final day?
After Withergeld[2] died and his men were doomed,
the Shieldings quickly claimed the field;
and now here's a son of one or other
of those same killers coming through our hall
overbearing us, mouthing boasts,
and rigged in armor that by right is yours.'
And so he keeps on, recalling and accusing,
working things up with bitter words
until one of the lady's retainers lies
spattered in blood, split open
on his father's account.[3] The killer knows
the lie of the land and escapes with his life.
Then on both sides the oath-bound lords
will break the peace, a passionate hate
will build up in Ingeld, and love for his bride
will falter in him as the feud rankles.
I therefore suspect the good faith of the Heatho-Bards,
the truth of their friendship and the trustworthiness
of their alliance with the Danes.
But now, my lord,
I shall carry on with my account of Grendel,
the whole story of everything that happened
in the hand-to-hand fight.
After heaven's gem
had gone mildly to earth, that maddened spirit,
the terror of those twilights, came to attack us
where we stood guard, still safe inside the hall.
There deadly violence came down on Hondscio
and he fell as fate ordained, the first to perish,
rigged out for the combat. A comrade from our ranks

2. One of the Heatho-Bard leaders.
3. I.e., the young Danish attendant is killed because his father killed the father of the young Heatho-Bard who has been egged on by the old veteran of that campaign.

had come to grief in Grendel's maw:
he ate up the entire body.
There was blood on his teeth, he was bloated and dangerous,
all roused up, yet still unready
to leave the hall empty-handed;
renowned for his might, he matched himself against me,
wildly reaching. He had this roomy pouch,
a strange accoutrement, intricately strung
and hung at the ready, a rare patchwork
of devilishly fitted dragon-skins.
I had done him no wrong, yet the raging demon
wanted to cram me and many another
into this bag—but it was not to be
once I got to my feet in a blind fury.
It would take too long to tell how I repaid
the terror of the land for every life he took
and so won credit for you, my king,
and for all your people. And although he got away
to enjoy life's sweetness for a while longer,
his right hand stayed behind him in Heorot,
evidence of his miserable overthrow
as he dived into murk on the mere bottom.
"I got lavish rewards from the lord of the Danes
for my part in the battle, beaten gold
and much else, once morning came
and we took our places at the banquet table.
There was singing and excitement: an old reciter,
a carrier of stories, recalled the early days.
At times some hero made the timbered harp
tremble with sweetness, or related true
and tragic happenings; at times the king
gave the proper turn to some fantastic tale,
or a battle-scarred veteran, bowed with age,
would begin to remember the martial deeds
of his youth and prime and be overcome
as the past welled up in his wintry heart.
"We were happy there the whole day long
and enjoyed our time until another night
descended upon us. Then suddenly
the vehement mother avenged her son
and wreaked destruction. Death had robbed her,
Geats had slain Grendel, so his ghastly dam
struck back and with bare-faced defiance
laid a man low. Thus life departed
from the sage Aeschere, an elder wise in counsel.
But afterward, on the morning following,
the Danes could not burn the dead body
nor lay the remains of the man they loved
on his funeral pyre. She had fled with the corpse
and taken refuge beneath torrents on the mountain.
It was a hard blow for Hrothgar to bear,
harder than any he had undergone before.
And so the heartsore king beseeched me

in your royal name to take my chances
underwater, to win glory
and prove my worth. He promised me rewards.
Hence, as is well known, I went to my encounter
with the terror-monger at the bottom of the tarn.
For a while it was hand-to-hand between us,
then blood went curling along the currents
and I beheaded Grendel's mother in the hall
with a mighty sword. I barely managed
to escape with my life; my time had not yet come.
But Halfdane's heir, the shelter of those earls,
again endowed me with gifts in abundance.
"Thus the king acted with due custom.
I was paid and recompensed completely,
given full measure and the freedom to choose
from Hothgar's treasures by Hrothgar himself.
These, King Hygelac, I am happy to present
to you as gifts. It is still upon your grace
that all favor depends. I have few kinsmen
who are close, my king, except for your kind self."
Then he ordered the boar-framed standard to be brought,
the battle-topping helmet, the mail-shirt gray as hoar-frost,
and the precious war-sword; and proceeded with his speech:
"When Hrothgar presented this war-gear to me
he instructed me, my lord, to give you some account
of why it signifies his special favor.
He said it had belonged to his older brother,
King Heorogar, who had long kept it,
but that Heorogar had never bequeathed it
to his son Heoroward, that worthy scion,
loyal as he was. Enjoy it well."
I heard four horses were handed over next.
Beowulf bestowed four bay steeds
to go with the armor, swift gallopers,
all alike. So ought a kinsman act,
instead of plotting and planning in secret
to bring people to grief, or conspiring to arrange
the death of comrades. The warrior king
was uncle to Beowulf and honored by his nephew:
each was concerned for the other's good.
I heard he presented Hygd with a gorget,
the priceless torque that the prince's daughter,
Wealhtheow, had given him; and three horses,
supple creatures brilliantly saddled.
The bright necklace would be luminous on Hygd's breast.
Thus Beowulf bore himself with valor;
he was formidable in battle yet behaved with honor
and took no advantage; never cut down
a comrade who was drunk, kept his temper
and, warrior that he was, watched and controlled
his God-sent strength and his outstanding
natural powers. He had been poorly regarded
for a long time, was taken by the Geats

for less than he was worth:[4] and their lord too
had never much esteemed him in the mead-hall.
They firmly believed that he lacked force,
that the prince was a weakling; but presently
every affront to his deserving was reversed.
The battle-famed king, bulwark of his earls,
ordered a gold-chased heirloom of Hrethel's[5]
to be brought in; it was the best example
of a gem-studded sword in the Geat treasury.
This he laid on Beowulf's lap
and then rewarded him with land as well,
seven thousand hides; and a hall and a throne.
Both owned land by birth in that country,
ancestral grounds; but the greater right
and sway were inherited by the higher born.

[THE DRAGON WAKES]

A lot was to happen in later days
in the fury of battle. Hygelac fell
and the shelter of Heardred's shield proved useless
against the fierce aggression of the Shylfings:[6]
ruthless swordsmen, seasoned campaigners,
they came against him and his conquering nation,
and with cruel force cut him down
so that afterwards
the wide kingdom
reverted to Beowulf. He ruled it well
for fifty winters, grew old and wise
as warden of the land
until one began
to dominate the dark, a dragon on the prowl
from the steep vaults of a stone-roofed barrow
where he guarded a hoard; there was a hidden passage,
unknown to men, but someone[7] managed
to enter by it and interfere
with the heathen trove. He had handled and removed

4. There is no other mention of Beowulf's unpromising youth. This motif of the "Cinderella hero" and others, such as Grendel's magic pouch, are examples of folklore material, probably circulating orally, that made its way into the poem.
5. Hygelac's father and Beowulf's grandfather.
6. There are several references, some of them lengthy, to the wars between the Geats and the Swedes. Because these are highly allusive and not in chronological order, they are difficult to follow and keep straight. This outline, along with the Genealogies (p. 29), may serve as a guide. *Phase 1:* After the death of the Geat patriarch, King Hrethel (lines 2462–70), Ohthere and Onela, the sons of the Swedish king Ongentheow, invade Geat territory and inflict heavy casualties in a battle at Hreosnahill (lines 2472–78). *Phase 2:* The Geats invade Sweden under Haethcyn, King Hrethel's son who has succeeded him. At the battle of Ravenswood, the Geats capture Ongentheow's queen, but Ongentheow counterattacks, rescues the queen, and kills Haethcyn. Hygelac, Haethcyn's younger brother, arrives with reinforcements; Ongentheow is killed in savage combat with two of Hygelac's men; and the Swedes are routed (lines 2479–89 and 2922–90). *Phase 3:* Eanmund and Eadgils, the sons of Ohthere (presumably dead), are driven into exile by their uncle Onela, who is now king of the Swedes. They are given refuge by Hygelac's son Heardred, who has succeeded his father. Onela invades Geatland and kills Heardred; his retainer Weohstan kills Eanmund; and after the Swedes withdraw, Beowulf becomes king (lines 2204–8, which follow, and 2379–90). *Phase 4:* Eadgils, supported by Beowulf, invades Sweden and kills Onela (lines 2391–96).
7. The following section was damaged by fire. In lines 2215–31 entire words and phrases are missing or indicated by only a few letters. Editorial attempts to reconstruct the text are conjectural and often disagree.

a gem-studded goblet; it gained him nothing,
though with a thief's wiles he had outwitted
the sleeping dragon. That drove him into rage,
as the people of that country would soon discover.
The intruder who broached the dragon's treasure
and moved him to wrath had never meant to.
It was desperation on the part of a slave
fleeing the heavy hand of some master,
guilt-ridden and on the run,
going to ground. But he soon began
to shake with terror;[8] . . . . . . in shock
the wretch . . . .
. . . . panicked and ran
away with the precious . . . . . .
metalwork. There were many other
heirlooms heaped inside the earth-house,
because long ago, with deliberate care,
some forgotten person had deposited the whole
rich inheritance of a highborn race
in this ancient cache. Death had come
and taken them all in times gone by
and the only one left to tell their tale,
the last of their line, could look forward to nothing
but the same fate for himself: he foresaw that his joy
in the treasure would be brief.
A newly constructed
barrow stood waiting, on a wide headland
close to the waves, its entryway secured.
Into it the keeper of the hoard had carried
all the goods and golden ware
worth preserving. His words were few:
"Now, earth, hold what earls once held
and heroes can no more; it was mined from you first
by honorable men. My own people
have been ruined in war; one by one
they went down to death, looked their last
on sweet life in the hall. I am left with nobody
to bear a sword or to burnish plated goblets,
put a sheen on the cup. The companies have departed.
The hard helmet, hasped with gold,
will be stripped of its hoops; and the helmet-shiner
who should polish the metal of the war-mask sleeps;
the coat of mail that came through all fights,
through shield-collapse and cut of sword,
decays with the warrior. Nor may webbed mail
range far and wide on the warlord's back
beside his mustered troops. No trembling harp,
no tuned timber, no tumbling hawk
swerving through the hall, no swift horse
pawing the courtyard. Pillage and slaughter
have emptied the earth of entire peoples."

8. Lines 2227–30 are so damaged that they defy guesswork to reconstruct them.

And so he mourned as he moved about the world,
deserted and alone, lamenting his unhappiness
day and night, until death's flood
brimmed up in his heart.
Then an old harrower of the dark
happened to find the hoard open,
the burning one who hunts out barrows,
the slick-skinned dragon, threatening the night sky
with streamers of fire. People on the farms
are in dread of him. He is driven to hunt out
hoards under ground, to guard heathen gold
through age-long vigils, though to little avail.
For three centuries, this scourge of the people
had stood guard on that stoutly protected
underground treasury, until the intruder
unleashed its fury; he hurried to his lord
with the gold-plated cup and made his plea
to be reinstated. Then the vault was rifled,
the ring-hoard robbed, and the wretched man
had his request granted. His master gazed
on that find from the past for the first time.
When the dragon awoke, trouble flared again.
He rippled down the rock, writhing with anger
when he saw the footprints of the prowler who had stolen
too close to his dreaming head.
So may a man not marked by fate
easily escape exile and woe
by the grace of God.
The hoard-guardian
scorched the ground as he scoured and hunted
for the trespasser who had troubled his sleep.
Hot and savage, he kept circling and circling
the outside of the mound. No man appeared
in that desert waste, but he worked himself up
by imagining battle; then back in he'd go
in search of the cup, only to discover
signs that someone had stumbled upon
the golden treasures. So the guardian of the mound,
the hoard-watcher, waited for the gloaming
with fierce impatience; his pent-up fury
at the loss of the vessel made him long to hit back
and lash out in flames. Then, to his delight,
the day waned and he could wait no longer
behind the wall, but hurtled forth
in a fiery blaze. The first to suffer
were the people on the land, but before long
it was their treasure-giver who would come to grief.
The dragon began to belch out flames
and burn bright homesteads; there was a hot glow
that scared everyone, for the vile sky-winger
would leave nothing alive in his wake.
Everywhere the havoc he wrought was in evidence.
Far and near, the Geat nation

bore the brunt of his brutal assaults
and virulent hate. Then back to the hoard
he would dart before daybreak, to hide in his den.
He had swinged the land, swathed it in flame,
in fire and burning, and now he felt secure
in the vaults of his barrow; but his trust was unavailing.

Then Beowulf was given bad news,
the hard truth: his own home,
the best of buildings, had been burned to a cinder,
the throne-room of the Geats. It threw the hero
into deep anguish and darkened his mood:
the wise man thought he must have thwarted
ancient ordinance of the eternal Lord,
broken His commandment. His mind was in turmoil,
unaccustomed anxiety and gloom
confused his brain; the fire-dragon
had razed the coastal region and reduced
forts and earthworks to dust and ashes,
so the war-king planned and plotted his revenge.
The warriors' protector, prince of the hall-troop,
ordered a marvelous all-iron shield
from his smithy works. He well knew
that linden boards would let him down
and timber burn. After many trials,
he was destined to face the end of his days,
in this mortal world, as was the dragon,
for all his long leasehold on the treasure.

Yet the prince of the rings was too proud
to line up with a large army
against the sky-plague. He had scant regard
for the dragon as a threat, no dread at all
of its courage or strength, for he had kept going
often in the past, through perils and ordeals
of every sort, after he had purged
Hrothgar's hall, triumphed in Heorot
and beaten Grendel. He outgrappled the monster
and his evil kin.

One of his cruelest
hand-to-hand encounters had happened
when Hygelac, king of the Geats, was killed
in Friesland: the people's friend and lord,
Hrethel's son, slaked a swordblade's
thirst for blood. But Beowulf's prodigious
gifts as a swimmer guaranteed his safety:
he arrived at the shore, shouldering thirty
battle-dresses, the booty he had won.
There was little for the Hetware[9] to be happy about
as they shielded their faces and fighting on the ground
began in earnest. With Beowulf against them,
few could hope to return home.

Across the wide sea, desolate and alone,

9. A tribe of the Franks allied with the Frisians.

the son of Ecgtheow swam back to his people.
There Hygd offered him throne and authority
as lord of the ring-hoard: with Hygelac dead,
she had no belief in her son's ability
to defend their homeland against foreign invaders.
Yet there was no way the weakened nation
could get Beowulf to give in and agree
to be elevated over Heardred as his lord
or to undertake the office of kingship.
But he did provide support for the prince,
honored and minded him until he matured
as the ruler of Geatland.
Then over sea-roads
exiles arrived, sons of Ohthere.[1]
They had rebelled against the best of all
the sea-kings in Sweden, the one who held sway
in the Shylfing nation, their renowned prince,
lord of the mead-hall. That marked the end
for Hygelac's son: his hospitality
was mortally rewarded with wounds from a sword.
Heardred lay slaughtered and Onela returned
to the land of Sweden, leaving Beowulf
to ascend the throne, to sit in majesty
and rule over the Geats. He was a good king.
In days to come, he contrived to avenge
the fall of his prince; he befriended Eadgils
when Eadgils was friendless, aiding his cause
with weapons and warriors over the wide sea,
sending him men. The feud was settled
on a comfortless campaign when he killed Onela.
And so the son of Ecgtheow had survived
every extreme, excelling himself
in daring and in danger, until the day arrived
when he had to come face to face with the dragon.
The lord of the Geats took eleven comrades
and went in a rage to reconnoiter.
By then he had discovered the cause of the affliction
being visited on the people. The precious cup
had come to him from the hand of the finder,
the one who had started all this strife
and was now added as a thirteenth to their number.
They press-ganged and compelled this poor creature
to be their guide. Against his will
he led them to the earth-vault he alone knew,
an underground barrow near the sea-billows
and heaving waves, heaped inside
with exquisite metalwork. The one who stood guard
was dangerous and watchful, warden of the trove
buried under earth: no easy bargain
would be made in that place by any man.
The veteran king sat down on the cliff-top.

1. See p. 77, n. 6, Phases 3 and 4.

He wished good luck to the Geats who had shared
his hearth and his gold. He was sad at heart,
unsettled yet ready, sensing his death.
His fate hovered near, unknowable but certain:
it would soon claim his coffered soul,
part life from limb. Before long
the prince's spirit would spin free from his body.
Beowulf, son of Ecgtheow, spoke:
"Many a skirmish I survived when I was young
and many times of war: I remember them well.
At seven, I was fostered out by my father,
left in the charge of my people's lord.
King Hrethel kept me and took care of me,
was openhanded, behaved like a kinsman.
While I was his ward, he treated me no worse
as a wean[2] about the place than one of his own boys,
Herebeald and Haethcyn, or my own Hygelac.
For the eldest, Herebeald, an unexpected
deathbed was laid out, through a brother's doing,
when Haethcyn bent his horn-tipped bow
and loosed the arrow that destroyed his life.
He shot wide and buried a shaft
in the flesh and blood of his own brother.
That offense was beyond redress, a wrongfooting
of the heart's affections; for who could avenge
the prince's life or pay his death-price?
It was like the misery endured by an old man
who has lived to see his son's body
swing on the gallows. He begins to keen
and weep for his boy, watching the raven
gloat where he hangs: he can be of no help.
The wisdom of age is worthless to him.
Morning after morning, he wakes to remember
that his child is gone; he has no interest
in living on until another heir
is born in the hall, now that his first-born
has entered death's dominion forever.
He gazes sorrowfully at his son's dwelling,
the banquet hall bereft of all delight,
the windswept hearthstone; the horsemen are sleeping,
the warriors under ground; what was is no more.
No tunes from the harp, no cheer raised in the yard.
Alone with his longing, he lies down on his bed
and sings a lament; everything seems too large,
the steadings and the fields.
Such was the feeling
of loss endured by the lord of the Geats
after Herebeald's death. He was helplessly placed
to set to rights the wrong committed,
could not punish the killer in accordance with the law
of the blood-feud, although he felt no love for him.

2. A young child [Northern Ireland; Translator's note].

Heartsore, wearied, he turned away
from life's joys, chose God's light
and departed, leaving buildings and lands
to his sons, as a man of substance will.
"Then over the wide sea Swedes and Geats
battled and feuded and fought without quarter.
Hostilities broke out when Hrethel died.[3]
Ongentheow's sons were unrelenting,
refusing to make peace, campaigning violently
from coast to coast, constantly setting up
terrible ambushes around Hreosnahill.
My own kith and kin avenged
these evil events, as everybody knows,
but the price was high: one of them paid
with his life. Haethcyn, lord of the Geats,
met his fate there and fell in the battle.
Then, as I have heard, Hygelac's sword
was raised in the morning against Ongentheow,
his brother's killer. When Eofor cleft
the old Swede's helmet, halved it open,
he fell, death-pale: his feud-calloused hand
could not stave off the fatal stroke.
"The treasures that Hygelac lavished on me
I paid for when I fought, as fortune allowed me,
with my glittering sword. He gave me land
and the security land brings, so he had no call
to go looking for some lesser champion,
some mercenary from among the Gifthas
or the Spear-Danes or the men of Sweden.
I marched ahead of him, always there
at the front of the line; and I shall fight like that
for as long as I live, as long as this sword
shall last, which has stood me in good stead
late and soon, ever since I killed
Dayraven the Frank in front of the two armies.
He brought back no looted breastplate
to the Frisian king but fell in battle,
their standard-bearer, highborn and brave.
No sword blade sent him to his death:
my bare hands stilled his heartbeats
and wrecked the bone-house. Now blade and hand,
sword and sword-stroke, will assay the hoard."

[BEOWULF ATTACKS THE DRAGON]

Beowulf spoke, made a formal boast
for the last time: "I risked my life
often when I was young. Now I am old,
but as king of the people I shall pursue this fight
for the glory of winning, if the evil one will only
abandon his earth-fort and face me in the open."

3. See p. 77, n. 6, Phases 1 and 2.

Then he addressed each dear companion
one final time, those fighters in their helmets,
resolute and highborn: "I would rather not
use a weapon if I knew another way
to grapple with the dragon and make good my boast
as I did against Grendel in days gone by.
But I shall be meeting molten venom
in the fire he breathes, so I go forth
in mail-shirt and shield. I won't shift a foot
when I meet the cave-guard: what occurs on the wall
between the two of us will turn out as fate,
overseer of men, decides. I am resolved.
I scorn further words against this sky-borne foe.
"Men-at-arms, remain here on the barrow,
safe in your armor, to see which one of us
is better in the end at bearing wounds
in a deadly fray. This fight is not yours,
nor is it up to any man except me
to measure his strength against the monster
or to prove his worth. I shall win the gold
by my courage, or else mortal combat,
doom of battle, will bear your lord away."
Then he drew himself up beside his shield.
The fabled warrior in his war-shirt and helmet
trusted in his own strength entirely
and went under the crag. No coward path.
Hard by the rock-face that hale veteran,
a good man who had gone repeatedly
into combat and danger and come through,
saw a stone arch and a gushing stream
that burst from the barrow, blazing and wafting
a deadly heat. It would be hard to survive
unscathed near the hoard, to hold firm
against the dragon in those flaming depths.
Then he gave a shout. The lord of the Geats
unburdened his breast and broke out
in a storm of anger. Under gray stone
his voice challenged and resounded clearly.
Hate was ignited. The hoard-guard recognized
a human voice, the time was over
for peace and parleying. Pouring forth
in a hot battle-fume, the breath of the monster
burst from the rock. There was a rumble under ground.
Down there in the barrow, Beowulf the warrior
lifted his shield: the outlandish thing
writhed and convulsed and viciously
turned on the king, whose keen-edged sword,
an heirloom inherited by ancient right,
was already in his hand. Roused to a fury,
each antagonist struck terror in the other.
Unyielding, the lord of his people loomed
by his tall shield, sure of his ground,
while the serpent looped and unleashed itself.

Swaddled in flames, it came gliding and flexing
and racing toward its fate. Yet his shield defended
the renowned leader's life and limb
for a shorter time than he meant it to:
that final day was the first time
when Beowulf fought and fate denied him
glory in battle. So the king of the Geats
raised his hand and struck hard
at the enameled scales, but scarcely cut through:
the blade flashed and slashed yet the blow
was far less powerful than the hard-pressed king
had need of at that moment. The mound-keeper
went into a spasm and spouted deadly flames:
when he felt the stroke, battle-fire
billowed and spewed. Beowulf was foiled
of a glorious victory. The glittering sword,
infallible before that day,
failed when he unsheathed it, as it never should have.
For the son of Ecgtheow, it was no easy thing
to have to give ground like that and go
unwillingly to inhabit another home
in a place beyond; so every man must yield
the leasehold of his days.
Before long
the fierce contenders clashed again.
The hoard-guard took heart, inhaled and swelled up
and got a new wind; he who had once ruled
was furled in fire and had to face the worst.
No help or backing was to be had then
from his highborn comrades; that hand-picked troop
broke ranks and ran for their lives
to the safety of the wood. But within one heart
sorrow welled up: in a man of worth
the claims of kinship cannot be denied.

His name was Wiglaf, a son of Weohstan's,
a well-regarded Shylfing warrior
related to Aelfhere.[4] When he saw his lord
tormented by the heat of his scalding helmet,
he remembered the bountiful gifts bestowed on him,
how well he lived among the Waegmundings,
the freehold he inherited from his father[5] before him.
He could not hold back: one hand brandished
the yellow-timbered shield, the other drew his sword—
an ancient blade that was said to have belonged
to Eanmund, the son of Ohthere, the one
Weohstan had slain when he was an exile without friends.
He carried the arms to the victim's kinfolk,

4. Although Wiglaf is here said to be a Shylfing (i.e., a Swede), in line 2607 we are told his family are Waegmundings, a clan of the Geats, which is also Beowulf's family. It was possible for a family to owe allegiance to more than one nation and to shift sides as a result of feuds. Nothing is known of Aelfhere.

5. I.e., Weohstan, who, as explained below, was the slayer of Onela's nephew Eanmund. Possibly, Weohstan joined the Geats under Beowulf after Eanmund's brother, with Beowulf's help, avenged Eanmund's death on Onela and became king of the Shylfings. See p. 77, n. 6, Phase 2.

the burnished helmet, the webbed chain-mail
and that relic of the giants. But Onela returned
the weapons to him, rewarded Weohstan
with Eanmund's war-gear. He ignored the blood-feud,
the fact that Eanmund was his brother's son.[6]
Weohstan kept that war-gear for a lifetime,
the sword and the mail-shirt, until it was the son's turn
to follow his father and perform his part.
Then, in old age, at the end of his days
among the Weather-Geats, he bequeathed to Wiglaf
innumerable weapons.
And now the youth
was to enter the line of battle with his lord,
his first time to be tested as a fighter.
His spirit did not break and the ancestral blade
would keep its edge, as the dragon discovered
as soon as they came together in the combat.
Sad at heart, addressing his companions,
Wiglaf spoke wise and fluent words:
"I remember that time when mead was flowing,
how we pledged loyalty to our lord in the hall,
promised our ring-giver we would be worth our price,
make good the gift of the war-gear,
those swords and helmets, as and when
his need required it. He picked us out
from the army deliberately, honored us and judged us
fit for this action, made me these lavish gifts—
and all because he considered us the best
of his arms-bearing thanes. And now, although
he wanted this challenge to be one he'd face
by himself alone—the shepherd of our land,
a man unequaled in the quest for glory
and a name for daring—now the day has come
when this lord we serve needs sound men
to give him their support. Let us go to him,
help our leader through the hot flame
and dread of the fire. As God is my witness,
I would rather my body were robed in the same
burning blaze as my gold-giver's body
than go back home bearing arms.
That is unthinkable, unless we have first
slain the foe and defended the life
of the prince of the Weather-Geats. I well know
the things he has done for us deserve better.
Should he alone be left exposed
to fall in battle? We must bond together,
shield and helmet, mail-shirt and sword."
Then he waded the dangerous reek and went
under arms to his lord, saying only:
"Go on, dear Beowulf, do everything

6. An ironic comment: since Onela wanted to kill Eanmund, he rewarded Weohstan for killing his nephew instead of exacting compensation or revenge.

you said you would when you were still young
and vowed you would never let your name and fame
be dimmed while you lived. Your deeds are famous,
so stay resolute, my lord, defend your life now
with the whole of your strength. I shall stand by you."
After those words, a wildness rose
in the dragon again and drove it to attack,
heaving up fire, hunting for enemies,
the humans it loathed. Flames lapped the shield,
charred it to the boss, and the body armor
on the young warrior was useless to him.
But Wiglaf did well under the wide rim
Beowulf shared with him once his own had shattered
in sparks and ashes.
Inspired again
by the thought of glory, the war-king threw
his whole strength behind a sword stroke
and connected with the skull. And Naegling snapped.
Beowulf's ancient iron-gray sword
let him down in the fight. It was never his fortune
to be helped in combat by the cutting edge
of weapons made of iron. When he wielded a sword,
no matter how blooded and hard-edged the blade,
his hand was too strong, the stroke he dealt
(I have heard) would ruin it. He could reap no advantage.
Then the bane of that people, the fire-breathing dragon,
was mad to attack for a third time.
When a chance came, he caught the hero
in a rush of flame and clamped sharp fangs
into his neck. Beowulf's body
ran wet with his life-blood: it came welling out.
Next thing, they say, the noble son of Weohstan
saw the king in danger at his side
and displayed his inborn bravery and strength.
He left the head alone,[7] but his fighting hand
was burned when he came to his kinsman's aid.
He lunged at the enemy lower down
so that his decorated sword sank into its belly
and the flames grew weaker.
Once again the king
gathered his strength and drew a stabbing knife
he carried on his belt, sharpened for battle.
He stuck it deep in the dragon's flank.
Beowulf dealt it a deadly wound.
They had killed the enemy, courage quelled his life;
that pair of kinsmen, partners in nobility,
had destroyed the foe. So every man should act,
be at hand when needed; but now, for the king,
this would be the last of his many labors
and triumphs in the world.
Then the wound

7. I.e., he avoided the dragon's flame-breathing head.

dealt by the ground-burner earlier began
to scald and swell; Beowulf discovered
deadly poison suppurating inside him,
surges of nausea, and so, in his wisdom,
the prince realized his state and struggled
toward a seat on the rampart. He steadied his gaze
on those gigantic stones, saw how the earthwork
was braced with arches built over columns.
And now that thane unequaled for goodness
with his own hands washed his lord's wounds,
swabbed the weary prince with water,
bathed him clean, unbuckled his helmet.

Beowulf spoke: in spite of his wounds,
mortal wounds, he still spoke
for he well knew his days in the world
had been lived out to the end—his allotted time
was drawing to a close, death was very near.

"Now is the time when I would have wanted
to bestow this armor on my own son,
had it been my fortune to have fathered an heir
and live on in his flesh. For fifty years
I ruled this nation. No king
of any neighboring clan would dare
face me with troops, none had the power
to intimidate me. I took what came,
cared for and stood by things in my keeping,
never fomented quarrels, never
swore to a lie. All this consoles me,
doomed as I am and sickening for death;
because of my right ways, the Ruler of mankind
need never blame me when the breath leaves my body
for murder of kinsmen. Go now quickly,
dearest Wiglaf, under the gray stone
where the dragon is laid out, lost to his treasure;
hurry to feast your eyes on the hoard.
Away you go: I want to examine
that ancient gold, gaze my fill
on those garnered jewels; my going will be easier
for having seen the treasure, a less troubled letting-go
of the life and lordship I have long maintained."

And so, I have heard, the son of Weohstan
quickly obeyed the command of his languishing
war-weary lord; he went in his chain-mail
under the rock-piled roof of the barrow,
exulting in his triumph, and saw beyond the seat
a treasure-trove of astonishing richness,
wall-hangings that were a wonder to behold,
glittering gold spread across the ground,
the old dawn-scorching serpent's den
packed with goblets and vessels from the past,
tarnished and corroding. Rusty helmets
all eaten away. Armbands everywhere,
artfully wrought. How easily treasure

buried in the ground, gold hidden
however skillfully, can escape from any man!
  And he saw too a standard, entirely of gold,
hanging high over the hoard,
a masterpiece of filigree; it glowed with light
so he could make out the ground at his feet
and inspect the valuables. Of the dragon there was no
remaining sign: the sword had dispatched him.
Then, the story goes, a certain man
plundered the hoard in that immemorial howe,
filled his arms with flagons and plates,
anything he wanted; and took the standard also,
most brilliant of banners.
                                        Already the blade
of the old king's sharp killing-sword
had done its worst: the one who had for long
minded the hoard, hovering over gold,
unleashing fire, surging forth
midnight after midnight, had been mown down.
  Wiglaf went quickly, keen to get back,
excited by the treasure. Anxiety weighed
on his brave heart—he was hoping he would find
the leader of the Geats alive where he had left him
helpless, earlier, on the open ground.
  So he came to the place, carrying the treasure
and found his lord bleeding profusely,
his life at an end; again he began
to swab his body. The beginnings of an utterance
broke out from the king's breast-cage.
The old lord gazed sadly at the gold.
  "To the everlasting Lord of all,
to the King of Glory, I give thanks
that I behold this treasure here in front of me,
that I have been allowed to leave my people
so well endowed on the day I die.
Now that I have bartered my last breath
to own this fortune, it is up to you
to look after their needs. I can hold out no longer.
Order my troop to construct a barrow
on a headland on the coast, after my pyre has cooled.
It will loom on the horizon at Hronesness[8]
and be a reminder among my people—
so that in coming times crews under sail
will call it Beowulf's Barrow, as they steer
ships across the wide and shrouded waters."
  Then the king in his great-heartedness unclasped
the collar of gold from his neck and gave it
to the young thane, telling him to use
it and the war-shirt and gilded helmet well.
"You are the last of us, the only one left
of the Waegmundings. Fate swept us away,

8. A headland by the sea. The name means "Whalesness."

sent my whole brave highborn clan
to their final doom. Now I must follow them."
That was the warrior's last word.
He had no more to confide. The furious heat
of the pyre would assail him. His soul fled from his breast
to its destined place among the steadfast ones.

[BEOWULF'S FUNERAL]

It was hard then on the young hero,
having to watch the one he held so dear
there on the ground, going through
his death agony. The dragon from underearth,
his nightmarish destroyer, lay destroyed as well,
utterly without life. No longer would his snakefolds
ply themselves to safeguard hidden gold.
Hard-edged blades, hammered out
and keenly filed, had finished him
so that the sky-roamer lay there rigid,
brought low beside the treasure-lodge.
Never again would he glitter and glide
and show himself off in midnight air,
exulting in his riches: he fell to earth
through the battle-strength in Beowulf's arm.
There were few, indeed, as far as I have heard,
big and brave as they may have been,
few who would have held out if they had had to face
the outpourings of that poison-breather
or gone foraging on the ring-hall floor
and found the deep barrow-dweller
on guard and awake.
The treasure had been won,
bought and paid for by Beowulf's death.
Both had reached the end of the road
through the life they had been lent.
Before long
the battle-dodgers abandoned the wood,
the ones who had let down their lord earlier,
the tail-turners, ten of them together.
When he needed them most, they had made off.
Now they were ashamed and came behind shields,
in their battle-outfits, to where the old man lay.
They watched Wiglaf, sitting worn out,
a comrade shoulder to shoulder with his lord,
trying in vain to bring him round with water.
Much as he wanted to, there was no way
he could preserve his lord's life on earth
or alter in the least the Almighty's will.
What God judged right would rule what happened
to every man, as it does to this day.
Then a stern rebuke was bound to come
from the young warrior to the ones who had been cowards.
Wiglaf, son of Weohstan, spoke

disdainfully and in disappointment:
"Anyone ready to admit the truth
will surely realize that the lord of men
who showered you with gifts and gave you the armor
you are standing in—when he would distribute
helmets and mail-shirts to men on the mead-benches,
a prince treating his thanes in hall
to the best he could find, far or near—
was throwing weapons uselessly away.
It would be a sad waste when the war broke out.
Beowulf had little cause to brag
about his armed guard; yet God who ordains
who wins or loses allowed him to strike
with his own blade when bravery was needed.
There was little I could do to protect his life
in the heat of the fray, but I found new strength
welling up when I went to help him.
Then my sword connected and the deadly assaults
of our foe grew weaker, the fire coursed
less strongly from his head. But when the worst happened
too few rallied around the prince.
  "So it is good-bye now to all you know and love
on your home ground, the open-handedness,
the giving of war-swords. Every one of you
with freeholds of land, our whole nation,
will be dispossessed, once princes from beyond
get tidings of how you turned and fled
and disgraced yourselves. A warrior will sooner
die than live a life of shame."
  Then he ordered the outcome of the fight to be reported
to those camped on the ridge, that crowd of retainers
who had sat all morning, sad at heart,
shield-bearers wondering about
the man they loved: would this day be his last
or would he return? He told the truth
and did not balk, the rider who bore
news to the cliff-top. He addressed them all:
"Now the people's pride and love,
the lord of the Geats, is laid on his deathbed,
brought down by the dragon's attack.
Beside him lies the bane of his life,
dead from knife-wounds. There was no way
Beowulf could manage to get the better
of the monster with his sword. Wiglaf sits
at Beowulf's side, the son of Weohstan,
the living warrior watching by the dead,
keeping weary vigil, holding a wake
for the loved and the loathed.
                    Now war is looming
over our nation, soon it will be known
to Franks and Frisians, far and wide,
that the king is gone. Hostility has been great
among the Franks since Hygelac sailed forth

at the head of a war-fleet into Friesland:
there the Hetware harried and attacked
and overwhelmed him with great odds.
The leader in his war-gear was laid low,
fell among followers: that lord did not favor
his company with spoils. The Merovingian king
has been an enemy to us ever since.
"Nor do I expect peace or pact-keeping
of any sort from the Swedes. Remember:
at Ravenswood,[9] Ongentheow
slaughtered Haethcyn, Hrethel's son,
when the Geat people in their arrogance
first attacked the fierce Shylfings.
The return blow was quickly struck
by Ohthere's father.[1] Old and terrible,
he felled the sea-king and saved his own
aged wife, the mother of Onela
and of Ohthere, bereft of her gold rings.
Then he kept hard on the heels of the foe
and drove them, leaderless, lucky to get away
in a desperate rout into Ravenswood.
His army surrounded the weary remnant
where they nursed their wounds; all through the night
he howled threats at those huddled survivors,
promised to axe their bodies open
when dawn broke, dangle them from gallows
to feed the birds. But at first light
when their spirits were lowest, relief arrived.
They heard the sound of Hygelac's horn,
his trumpet calling as he came to find them,
the hero in pursuit, at hand with troops.
"The bloody swathe that Swedes and Geats
cut through each other was everywhere.
No one could miss their murderous feuding.
Then the old man made his move,
pulled back, barred his people in:
Ongentheow withdrew to higher ground.
Hygelac's pride and prowess as a fighter
were known to the earl; he had no confidence
that he could hold out against that horde of seamen,
defend his wife and the ones he loved
from the shock of the attack. He retreated for shelter
behind the earthwall. Then Hygelac swooped
on the Swedes at bay, his banners swarmed
into their refuge, his Geat forces
drove forward to destroy the camp.
There in his gray hairs, Ongentheow
was cornered, ringed around with swords.
And it came to pass that the king's fate

9. The messenger describes in greater detail the Battle of Ravenswood. See the outline of the Swedish wars on p. 77, n. 6.

1. I.e., Ongentheow.

was in Eofor's hands,[2] and in his alone.
Wulf, son of Wonred, went for him in anger,
split him open so that blood came spurting
from under his hair. The old hero
still did not flinch, but parried fast,
hit back with a harder stroke:
the king turned and took him on.
Then Wonred's son, the brave Wulf,
could land no blow against the aged lord.
Ongentheow divided his helmet
so that he buckled and bowed his bloodied head
and dropped to the ground. But his doom held off.
Though he was cut deep, he recovered again.
"With his brother down, the undaunted Eofor,
Hygelac's thane, hefted his sword
and smashed murderously at the massive helmet
past the lifted shield. And the king collapsed,
the shepherd of people was sheared of life.
Many then hurried to help Wulf,
bandaged and lifted him, now that they were left
masters of the blood-soaked battle-ground.
One warrior stripped the other,
looted Ongentheow's iron mail-coat,
his hard sword-hilt, his helmet too,
and carried the graith[3] to King Hygelac,
he accepted the prize, promised fairly
that reward would come, and kept his word.
For their bravery in action, when they arrived home,
Eofor and Wulf were overloaded
by Hrethel's son, Hygelac the Geat,
with gifts of land and linked rings
that were worth a fortune. They had won glory,
so there was no gainsaying his generosity.
And he gave Eofor his only daughter
to bide at home with him, an honor and a bond.
"So this bad blood between us and the Swedes,
this vicious feud, I am convinced,
is bound to revive; they will cross our borders
and attack in force when they find out
that Beowulf is dead. In days gone by
when our warriors fell and we were undefended,
he kept our coffers and our kingdom safe.
He worked for the people, but as well as that
he behaved like a hero.
We must hurry now
to take a last look at the king
and launch him, lord and lavisher of rings,
on the funeral road. His royal pyre
will melt no small amount of gold:

2. I.e., he was at Eofor's mercy. Eofor's slaying of Ongetheow was described in lines 2486–89, where no mention is made of his brother Wulf's part in the battle. They are the sons of Wonred. *Eofor* means boar; *Wulf* is the Old English spelling of wolf.

3. Possessions, apparel.

heaped there in a hoard, it was bought at heavy cost,
and that pile of rings he paid for at the end
with his own life will go up with the flame,
be furled in fire: treasure no follower
will wear in his memory, nor lovely woman
link and attach as a torque around her neck—
but often, repeatedly, in the path of exile
they shall walk bereft, bowed under woe,
now that their leader's laugh is silenced,
high spirits quenched. Many a spear
dawn-cold to the touch will be taken down
and waved on high; the swept harp
won't waken warriors, but the raven winging
darkly over the doomed will have news,
tidings for the eagle of how he hoked and ate,
how the wolf and he made short work of the dead."[4]
  Such was the drift of the dire report
that gallant man delivered. He got little wrong
in what he told and predicted.
                                        The whole troop
rose in tears, then took their way
to the uncanny scene under Earnaness.[5]
There, on the sand, where his soul had left him,
they found him at rest, their ring-giver
from days gone by. The great man
had breathed his last. Beowulf the king
had indeed met with a marvelous death.
  But what they saw first was far stranger:
the serpent on the ground, gruesome and vile,
lying facing him. The fire-dragon
was scaresomely burned, scorched all colors.
From head to tail, his entire length
was fifty feet. He had shimmered forth
on the night air once, then winged back
down to his den; but death owned him now,
he would never enter his earth-gallery again.
Beside him stood pitchers and piled-up dishes,
silent flagons, precious swords
eaten through with rust, ranged as they had been
while they waited their thousand winters under ground.
That huge cache, gold inherited
from an ancient race, was under a spell—
which meant no one was ever permitted
to enter the ring-hall unless God Himself,
mankind's Keeper, True King of Triumphs,
allowed some person pleasing to Him—
and in His eyes worthy—to open the hoard.
  What came about brought to nothing
the hopes of the one who had wrongly hidden

4. The raven, eagle, and wolf—the scavengers who will feed on the slain—are "the beasts of battle," a common motif in Germanic war poetry. "Hoked": rooted about [Northern Ireland, Translator's note].

5. The site of Beowulf's fight with the dragon. The name means "Eaglesness."

riches under the rock-face. First the dragon slew
that man among men, who in turn made fierce amends
and settled the feud. Famous for his deeds
a warrior may be, but it remains a mystery
where his life will end, when he may no longer
dwell in the mead-hall among his own.
So it was with Beowulf, when he faced the cruelty
and cunning of the mound-guard. He himself was ignorant
of how his departure from the world would happen.
The highborn chiefs who had buried the treasure
declared it until doomsday so accursed
that whoever robbed it would be guilty of wrong
and grimly punished for their transgression,
hasped in hell-bonds in heathen shrines.
Yet Beowulf's gaze at the gold treasure
when he first saw it had not been selfish.
  Wiglaf, son of Weohstan, spoke:
"Often when one man follows his own will
many are hurt. This happened to us.
Nothing we advised could ever convince
the prince we loved, our land's guardian,
not to vex the custodian of the gold,
let him lie where he was long accustomed,
lurk there under earth until the end of the world.
He held to his high destiny. The hoard is laid bare,
but at a grave cost; it was too cruel a fate
that forced the king to that encounter.
I have been inside and seen everything
amassed in the vault. I managed to enter
although no great welcome awaited me
under the earthwall. I quickly gathered up
a huge pile of the priceless treasures
handpicked from the hoard and carried them here
where the king could see them. He was still himself,
alive, aware, and in spite of his weakness
he had many requests. He wanted me to greet you
and order the building of a barrow that would crown
the site of his pyre, serve as his memorial,
in a commanding position, since of all men
to have lived and thrived and lorded it on earth
his worth and due as a warrior were the greatest.
Now let us again go quickly
and feast our eyes on that amazing fortune
heaped under the wall. I will show the way
and take you close to those coffers packed with rings
and bars of gold. Let a bier be made
and got ready quickly when we come out
and then let us bring the body of our lord,
the man we loved, to where he will lodge
for a long time in the care of the Almighty."
  Then Weohstan's son, stalwart to the end,
had orders given to owners of dwellings,
many people of importance in the land,

to fetch wood from far and wide
for the good man's pyre:
"Now shall flame consume
our leader in battle, the blaze darken
round him who stood his ground in the steel-hail,
when the arrow-storm shot from bowstrings
pelted the shield-wall. The shaft hit home.
Feather-fledged, it finned the barb in flight."
Next the wise son of Weohstan
called from among the king's thanes
a group of seven: he selected the best
and entered with them, the eighth of their number,
under the God-cursed roof; one raised
a lighted torch and led the way.
No lots were cast for who should loot the hoard
for it was obvious to them that every bit of it
lay unprotected within the vault,
there for the taking. It was no trouble
to hurry to work and haul out
the priceless store. They pitched the dragon
over the cliff-top, let tide's flow
and backwash take the treasure-minder.
Then coiled gold was loaded on a cart
in great abundance, and the gray-haired leader,
the prince on his bier, borne to Hronesness.
The Geat people built a pyre for Beowulf,
stacked and decked it until it stood foursquare,
hung with helmets, heavy war-shields
and shining armor, just as he had ordered.
Then his warriors laid him in the middle of it,
mourning a lord far-famed and beloved.
On a height they kindled the hugest of all
funeral fires; fumes of woodsmoke
billowed darkly up, the blaze roared
and drowned out their weeping, wind died down
and flames wrought havoc in the hot bone-house,
burning it to the core. They were disconsolate
and wailed aloud for their lord's decease.
A Geat woman too sang out in grief;
with hair bound up, she unburdened herself
of her worst fears, a wild litany
of nightmare and lament: her nation invaded,
enemies on the rampage, bodies in piles,
slavery and abasement. Heaven swallowed the smoke.
Then the Geat people began to construct
a mound on a headland, high and imposing,
a marker that sailors could see from far away,
and in ten days they had done the work.
It was their hero's memorial; what remained from the fire
they housed inside it, behind a wall
as worthy of him as their workmanship could make it.
And they buried torques in the barrow, and jewels
and a trove of such things as trespassing men

had once dared to drag from the hoard.
They let the ground keep that ancestral treasure,
gold under gravel, gone to earth,
as useless to men now as it ever was.
Then twelve warriors rode around the tomb,
chieftains' sons, champions in battle,
all of them distraught, chanting in dirges,
mourning his loss as a man and a king.
They extolled his heroic nature and exploits
and gave thanks for his greatness; which was the proper thing,
for a man should praise a prince whom he holds dear
and cherish his memory when that moment comes
when he has to be convoyed from his bodily home.
So the Geat people, his hearth-companions,
sorrowed for the lord who had been laid low.
They said that of all the kings upon earth
he was the man most gracious and fair-minded,
kindest to his people and keenest to win fame.

Anglo-Norman Literature

MARIE DE FRANCE

Much of twelfth-century French literature was composed in England in the Anglo-Norman dialect (see pp. 7–8). Prominent among the earliest poets writing in the French vernacular, who shaped the genres, themes, and styles of later medieval European poetry, is the author who, in an epilogue to her *Fables,* calls herself Marie de France. That signature tells us only that her given name was Marie and that she was born in France, but circumstantial evidence from her writings shows that she spent much of her life in England. A reference to her in a French poem written in England around 1180 speaks of "dame Marie" who wrote "lais" much loved and praised, read, and heard by counts, barons, and knights and indicates that her poems also appealed to ladies who listened to them gladly and joyfully.

Three works can be safely attributed to Marie, probably written in the following order: the *Lais* (English "lay" refers to a short narrative poem in verse), the *Fables*, and *St. Patrick's Purgatory*. Marie's twelve lays are short romances (they range from 118 to 1,184 lines), each of which deals with a single event or crisis in the affairs of noble lovers. In her prologue, Marie tells us that she had heard these *performed*, and in several of the lays she refers to the Breton language and Breton storytellers—that is, professional minstrels from the French province of Brittany or the Celtic parts of Great Britain. Because no sources of Marie's stories have survived, it is not possible to determine the exact nature of the materials she worked from, but they were probably oral and were presented with the accompaniment of a stringed instrument. Marie's lays provide the basis of the genre that came to be known as the "Breton lay." In the prologue Marie dedicates the work to a "noble king," who is most likely to have been Henry II of England, who reigned from 1154 to 1189.

The portrait of the author that emerges from the combination of these works is of a highly educated noblewoman, proficient in Latin and English as well as her native French, with ideas of her own and a strong commitment to writing. Scholars have proposed several Maries of the period who fit this description to identify the author. A likely candidate is Marie, abbess of Shaftesbury, an illegitimate daughter of Geoffrey of Anjou and thus half-sister of Henry II. Correct or not, such an identification points to the milieu in which Marie moved and to the kind of audience she was addressing.

Many of Marie's lays contain elements of magic and mystery. Medieval readers would recognize that *Lanval* is about a mortal lover and a fairy bride, although the word "fairy" is not used in the tale. In the Middle Ages fairies were not thought of as the small creatures they became in Elizabethan and later literature. Fairies are supernatural, sometimes dangerous, beings who possess magical powers and inhabit another world. Their realm in some respects resembles the human (fairies have kings and queens), and fairies generally keep to themselves and disappear when humans notice them. But the tales are often about crossovers between the human and fairy worlds. Chaucer's *Wife of Bath's Tale* is such a story. In *Lanval* the female fairy world eclipses King Arthur's chivalric court (which Marie had read about in Wace's *Roman de Brut*) in splendor, riches, and generosity.

Two Middle English versions of Marie's *Lanval* exist, but we prefer to offer a modern verse translation of the original. Marie wrote in eight-syllable couplets, which was the standard form of French narrative verse, employed also by Wace and Chrétien de Troyes. Here is what the beginning of Marie's prologue to the *Lais* says about her view of a writer's duty and, implicitly, of her own talent:

Ki Deu ad duné escïence	He to whom God has given knowledge
E de parler bon' eloquence	And the gift of speaking eloquently,
Ne s'en deit taisir ne celer,	Must not keep silent nor conceal the gift,
Ainz se deit volunters mustrer.	But he must willingly display it.

Lanval[1]

Another lay to you I'll tell,
Of the adventure that befell
A noble vassal whom they call
In the Breton tongue Lanval.
Arthur, the brave and courtly king,
At Carlisle was sojourning
Because the Scots and Picts allied
Were ravaging the countryside;
Of Logres they had crossed the border° *Arthur's kingdom*
Where often they caused great disorder.
He had come there with his host
That spring to hold the Pentecost.
He lavished ample patronage
On all his noble baronage—
That is the knights of the Round Table
(In all the world none are so able).
Wives and land he gave in fee
To knights who served in his meiny,° *household*
Except for one: that was Lanval,
Nor did his men like him at all.
They envied him his handsomeness,
His courage, prowess, and largesse.
There were a few who made a show
Of friendship, but in case some blow
Of fortune were to cause him pain
They'd have no reason to complain.
Although a king's son of great worth,
He was far from his place of birth.
As one of the king's company
He spent all of his property,
For he got nothing from the king
And would not ask for anything.
Now Lanval is much preoccupied,
Gloomy, seeing the darker side.
My lords, you should not think it rare,
A newcomer is full of care
When he comes to a foreign land
And finds no help from any hand.
The knight whose tale I want to tell,
Who served King Arthur very well,

1. The translation is by Alfred David and is based on *Marie de France: Lais*, edited by Alfred Ewert (1947).

Mounting upon his steed one day,
For pleasure's sake set on his way.
Outside the town he went to ride
Alone into the countryside.
He got off by a running brook,
But there his horse trembled and shook.[2]
He unlaced the saddle and moved away,
Left the horse in the meadow to roam and play.
He folded up his riding gown
To make a pillow and lay down.
He broods about his woeful plight;
Nothing can make his spirit light.
As he lies there ill at ease
He looks down to the bank and sees
Two maidens approaching on the green,
The fairest he had ever seen.
Their clothes were in expensive taste,
Close-fitting tunics, tightly laced,
Made of deep-dyed purple wool.
Their faces were most beautiful.
The older of the two conveyed
Gold washing basins, finely made,
The other, a towel—I won't fail
To tell the truth in each detail.[3]
The two of them went straightaway
Right to the spot where the knight lay.
Lanval, the soul of courtesy,
Rose to his feet immediately.
They greeted him first by his name
And told the reason why they came.
"My lady, Sir Lanval, who is so free,
Beautiful, wise, and praiseworthy,
Ordered us to come for you,
For she herself has come here, too.
We shall bring you safely to her:
See, her pavilion is over there."
The knight went with them; he paid no mind
To the horse in the meadow he left behind.
The tent to which they bring the knight
Was fairly pitched, a beauteous sight.
Not Queen Semiramis of yore,
Had she commanded even more
Wisdom, wealth, and power, nor
Octavian, the emperor,
Would have been rich enough to pay
For the right-hand flap of the entryway.
On top was set an eagle of gold,
The cost of which cannot be told,
Nor of the cords and poles which brace
That structure and hold it in place.

2. Animals are believed to have a sixth sense that detects the presence of otherworldly beings.
3. Cf. lines 174–75, where these articles are used. Washing one's hands before meals indicates aristocratic luxury and refinement. Marie makes a mock pretense that her listeners could hardly imagine these splendors of the other world.

No earthly king could own this tent
For any treasure that he spent.
Inside the tent the maiden was:
Not rose nor lily could surpass
Her beauty when they bloom in May.
The sumptuous bed on which she lay
Was beautiful. The drapes and tassel,
Sheets and pillows were worth a castle.
The single gown she wore was sheer
And made her shapely form appear.
She'd thrown, in order to keep warm,
An ermine stole over her arm,
White fur with the lining dyed
Alexandrian purple. But her side,
Her face, her neck, her bosom
Showed whiter than the hawthorn blossom.
  The knight moved toward the bed's head.
She asked him to sit down and said,
"Lanval, fair friend, for you I've come,
For you I've traveled far from home.
If you are brave and courteous,
You'll be more glad and prosperous
Than ever was emperor or king,
For I love you over everything."
Her loveliness transfixed his gaze.
Love pierced his eyes with its bright rays,
Set fire to and scorched his heart.
He gave fair answer on his part.
"Lady," he said, "if this should be
Your wish (and such joy meant for me),
To have me for your paramour,
There's no command, you may be sure,
Wise or foolish, what you will,
Which I don't promise to fulfill.
I'll follow only your behest.
For you I'll give up all the rest."
When the lady heard him say
That he would love her in this way,
She presented him her heart
And her body, every part.
Now Lanval has taken the right road!
This gift she afterwards bestowed:
Whatsoever thing he wanted
She promised him that she would grant it—
Money, as fast as he can spend it,
No matter how much, she will send it.
The more largesse he gives, the more
Gold and silver in his store.
Now Sir Lanval is harbored well.
To him then spoke the damoiselle:
"*Ami*,"[4] she said, "please understand,
I warn and pray you and command:

4. Literally "friend," but used as a term of endearment for a lover. The feminine form is *amie*.

You must never tell anyone
About the love that you have won.
The consequence I shall declare:
Should people learn of this affair,
You shall never again see me,
Nor have my body in your fee."
He promised her that he would do
Whatever thing she told him to.
He lay beside her on the bed:
Now is Lanval well bestead.
He stayed with her all afternoon
Until it would be evening soon
And gladly would have stayed all night
Had she consented that he might.
But she told him, "Rise up, *Ami*.
You may no longer stay with me.
Get on your way; I shall remain.
But one thing I will tell you plain:
When you would like to talk to me
At any rendezvous that's free
Of blame or of unseemliness,
Where one his true love may possess,
I shall attend you at your will
All your wishes to fulfill."
These words gave him great happiness.
He kissed her, then got up to dress.
The damsels who had brought him there
Gave him expensive clothes to wear.
This world has no such comely squire
As Lanval in his new attire.
He was no simpleton or knave.
Water to wash his hands they gave,
Also the towel with which he dried,
And next he was with food supplied.
His love ate supper with Lanval,
A thing he did not mind at all.
They served him with great courtesy,
Which he accepted with much glee.
There were many special dishes
That the knight found most delicious.
There was also an interval[5]
Which gave great pleasure to Lanval.
And many times the gallant knight
Kissed his love and held her tight.
  At last after the meal was cleared,
Lanval's horse again appeared.
It had been saddled with utmost care:
He found the service beyond compare.
He took his leave, mounted the horse,
Back toward town he held his course.

5. French *entremès*: a side dish served between main courses; an interlude between acts. Marie may well intend a double-entendre involving both meanings.

Often Lanval looks to his rear,
And he is very much in fear.
As he rides he thinks about
What happened and is assailed by doubt.
He can't be certain if or when
He'll ever see his love again.
Arrived back home, Sir Lanval sees
His men dressed in new liveries.
That night the lavish host he plays,
But no one knows from whence he pays.
There is no knight of any sort
In need of lodging or support
Whom Lanval doesn't make his guest
And serves him richly of the best.
Lanval gives expensive presents;
Lanval remits the captive's sentence;
Lanval puts minstrels in new dress;
Lanval does honors in excess.
There is no stranger or private friend
On whom Lanval does not spend.
He lives in joy and in delight,
Whether it be by day or night.
He sees his lady often and
Has all the world at his command.
  That same summer, I would say,
After the feast of St. John's Day,
Thirty knights made an excursion,
For the sake of their diversion,
To a garden beneath the tower
In which the queen had her bower.
Among that party was Gawain
And his cousin, the good Yvain.
Sir Gawain spoke, brave and sincere,
Whom everybody held so dear,
"By God, my lords, we've not done right
By our companion, that good knight—
Lanval, liberal in everything,
And his father is a wealthy king—
To leave that nobleman behind."
And straightway they turn back and find
Sir Lanval at his residence
And beg that they might take him thence.
  From a window with fine molding
The queen herself leaned out beholding
(Waited on by damsels three)
King Arthur's festive company.
She gazed at Lanval and knew him well.
She called out to one damoiselle
And sent her for her maids-in-waiting,
The fairest and most captivating.
With her into the garden then
They went to relax with the men.
Thirty she took along and more,

Down the stairs and out the door.
Rejoiced to have the ladies meet them,
The gentlemen advance to greet them.
Each girl by a knight's hand is led:
Such pleasant talk is not ill-bred.
Lanval goes off alone and turns
Aside from all the rest. He yearns
To hold his love within his arms,
To kiss, embrace, and feel her charms.
The joy of others is less pleasant
To him, his own not being present.
When she perceives him stand alone,
The queen straightway to him has gone
To sit beside him and reveals
All the passion that she feels:
"Lanval, I've honored you sincerely,
Have cherished you and loved you dearly.
All my love is at your disposal.
What do you say to my proposal?
Your mistress I consent to be;
You should receive much joy from me."
"Lady," he said, "hold me excused
Because your love must be refused.
I've served the king for many a day;
My faith to him I won't betray.
Never for love, and not for you,
Would I be to my lord untrue."
Made angry by these words, the queen
Insultingly expressed her spleen.
"Lanval," she said, "It's evident
That to such pleasures you have no bent.
Often I have heard men aver
That women are not what you prefer.
But you have many pretty boys
With whom you like to take your joys.
Faithless coward of low degree,
My lord was badly served when he
Suffered your person to come near.
For that he could lose God, I fear."
   Hearing this, Lanval was dismayed;
His answer was not long delayed.
With spite, as he was much upset,
He spoke what soon he would regret.
"My lady queen," was his retort,
"I know nothing about that sport.
But I love one, and she loves me;
From every woman I know of, she
Deserves to bear the prize away.
And one more thing I wish to say,
So that you may know it plain:
Each serving-maid in her domain,
The poorest of her household crew,
My lady, is worth more than you

In beauty of both figure and face,
In good breeding and bounteous grace."
In tears the queen at once repairs
Back to her chamber up the stairs.
Dolorous she is and mortified
To be by him thus villified.
She goes to bed where sick she lies,
Vowing never again to rise,
Unless the king grants her redress
For that which caused her such distress.
The king had come back from the wood
Cheerful because the day was good.
He entered the bedroom of the queen,
Who, seeing him, broke out in spleen.
Fallen at his feet, she cried, "*Merci!*[6]
Lanval has done me infamy."
To be her lover he had affected.
When his advances were rejected,
He had reviled her shamefully
And boasted he had an *amie*
So chic, noble, and proud, he said,
That even her lowliest chambermaid,
The poorest one that might be seen,
Was worthier than she—the queen.
The king grew marvelously wroth,
And solemnly he swore an oath:
Unless the knight proved what he'd boasted,
The king would have him hanged or roasted.
Leaving the chamber, the king then
Summoned three of his noblemen.
After Lanval they were to go,
Who, feeling enough of grief and woe,
Had gone back home, being well aware,
That he had spoiled the whole affair.
Since he had told of their *amour*,
He had lost his love for sure.
In his room alone he languished,
Melancholy and sorely anguished.
He calls his love time and again,
But all his pleadings are in vain.
Sighs he utters and complaints,
And from time to time he faints.
A hundred times he cries *merci*
And begs her speak to her *ami*.
He cursed his tongue like one demented;
It is a wonder what prevented
Him from committing suicide;
But though he beat himself and cried,
She would not show him any grace,
Even so much as show her face

6. An exclamation appealing for compassion and favor.

That he might see her once again.
Alas, how can he bear the pain?
The king's men have arrived to say
He must to court without delay.
The king had summoned him for this reason:
The queen had charged the knight with treason.
Lanval went with them very sadly.
Should he be killed, he'd bear it gladly.
The knight was brought before the king,
Grief-stricken, not saying anything,
Like someone in great misery.
The king spoke out indignantly:
"Vassal, you've played a churlish game
To do me injury and shame.
It was treason to demean
And speak slander to the queen
It was a foolish boast to call
Your love the noblest one of all,
And her servant—to declare her
Worthier than the queen and fairer."
Lanval protested, word for word,
Any dishonor done to his lord
Respecting the queen's accusation
Of a guilty solicitation.
But of his speech—to give her due—
He confessed that it was true.
The mistress he had boasted of
He mourned, for he had lost her love.
Regarding that, he said he'd do
Whatever the court told him to.
This put the king in a great fury.
He summoned his knights to act as jury
To tell how to proceed by law
So none might catch him in a flaw.[7]
All obey the royal will,
Whether it suits them well or ill.
They met together to consult
And deemed and judged with this result:
A court day set, Lanval goes free
But must find pledges to guarantee
His lord that judgment he'll abide,
Return to court and there be tried
By Arthur's entire baronage,
Not just the palace entourage.[8]
Back to the king the barons bring
The judgment of their parleying.
The king demands his sureties,
Thus putting Lanval ill at ease.

7. The trial of Lanval shows precise knowledge of twelfth-century legal procedure concerning the respective rights of the king and his barons.

8. The case is important enough to require judgment by all of Arthur's vassals, not just the immediate household. Hence the delay of the trial.

A foreigner, he felt chagrin
Since he had neither friend nor kin.
Gawain stepped forth and pledged that he
Would stand as Lanval's surety.
And his companions in succession
Each one made the same profession.
The king replied, "He is in your hands
At risk to forfeit all your lands
And fiefs, whatever they may be,
Which each of you obtained from me."
The pledges made, the court adjourned,
And Lanval to his place returned.
The knights escort him on his way.
They admonish him and say
To shun excessive melancholy;
And they lay curses on love's folly.
Worried about his mental state,
Each day they go investigate
Whether he takes nourishment
Or to himself is violent.
On the day that had been set,
All King Arthur's barons met.
Attending were the king and queen;
Pledges brought Lanval on the scene.
They were all sad on his account—
A hundred of them I could count
Who would have done their best to see
Him without trial go scot-free,
Since he was wrongfully arraigned.
On the charge, the king maintained,
And his response, he must be tried:
And now the barons must decide.
To the judgment they go next
Greatly worried and perplexed,
Since the noble foreign guest
In their midst is so hard-pressed.
Some were willing to condemn
To oblige their sovereign.
The Duke of Cornwall counseled thus:
"No fault shall be ascribed to us:
Though some show joy and some remorse,
Justice must take its lawful course.
A vassal by the king denounced,
Whose name—'Lanval'—I heard pronounced,
Has been accused of felony
And charged that mischievously he
To a mistress had pretended
And Madame the Queen offended.
By the faith I owe you duly,
In this case, should one speak truly,
The king being the sole adversary,
No defense were necessary—
Save with respect to his lord's name,

A man must never speak him shame.[9]
Sir Lanval by his oath must stand,
And the king quitclaim our land,
If the knight can guarantee
The coming here of his *amie*.
Should it prove true what he has claimed,
By which the queen felt so defamed,
Of that he'll be judged innocent,
Since he spoke without base intent.
But if he cannot prove it so,
In that case we must let him know,
All the king's service he must lose
And banished say his last adieus."
The knight was sent the court's decree
And informed by them that he
Must summon his *amie* and send her
To be his witness and defender.
The knight responded that he could not:
To his rescue come she would not.
To the judges they made report
That he looked for no support.
The king pressed them to make an ending
And not to keep the queen attending.
  When they came to enforce the law,
Two maidens from afar they saw
On two fine steeds, riding apace,
Who were extremely fair of face.
Of purple taffeta a sheath
They wore with nothing underneath.
The men took pleasure in these sights.
Sir Gawain and three of his knights
Went to Sir Lanval to report
And show the girls coming to court.
Happy, he asked him earnestly
If one of them were his *amie*.
He told them that he knew not who
They were, where from, or going to.
The damoiselles rode on withal
Upon their mounts into the hall,
And they got off before the dais
There where the king sat at his place.
Their features were of beauty rare;
Their form of speech was debonair:
"King, clear your chambers, if you please,
And hang them with silk draperies,
Where my lady may pause to rest,
For she wishes to be your guest.
The king gladly gave his consent.
Two of his courtiers he sent

9. Lanval's denial of the queen's accusation of improper advances (lines 369–72) is accepted, but he is nevertheless guilty of dishonoring his lord unless he can prove the claims about his mistress to which he has admitted.

To show them to their rooms upstairs.
No more was said of these affairs.
The king ordered his men at once
To give their sentence and response.
The long procrastination had,
He said, made him extremely mad.
"My lord," they answered, "we have acted.
But our attention was distracted
By those ladies we have seen.
But now the court shall reconvene."
They reassembled much perturbed,
By too much noise and strife disturbed.
While they engaged in this debate,
Two damoiselles of high estate—
In silks produced in Phrygia,
On mules from Andalusia—
Came riding up the street just then.
This gave great joy to Arthur's men,
Who told each other this must be
The worthy Lanval's remedy.
To him there hastened Sir Gawain
With his companions in his train.
"Sir knight," he said, "be of good cheer.
For God's sake speak to us! See here,
Two maidens are approaching us,
Most beautiful and decorous;
Surely one must be your *amie*."
Lanval made answer hastily.
He said that he recognized neither.
He didn't know or love them either.
Meanwhile the damoiselles had gone
And dismounted before the throne
Where the king was sitting on the dais.
From many there they won great praise
For figure, visage, and complexion.
They came much nearer to perfection
Than did the queen, so people said.
The elder was courteous and well bred.
She spoke her message with much flair:
"King, tell your household to prepare
A suite to lodge my lady, who
Is coming here to speak with you."
The king had them conducted where
His men had lodged the previous pair.
As soon as they were from him gone,
He told his barons to have done
And give their verdict right away.
There had been far too much delay;
The queen had found it most frustrating
That they so long had kept her waiting.
When they were just about to bring
Judgment, a girl was entering
The town, whose beauty, it was clear,

In all the world could have no peer.
She rode upon a milkwhite horse,
Which bore her gently down the course.
Its neck and head were shapeliest;
Of all creatures, it was the best.
Splendidly furnished was this mount:
Beneath the heavens, no king or count
Could have afforded gear so grand
Unless he sold or pawned his land.
And this is how she was arrayed:
A white linen shift displayed—
There where it was with laces tied—
Her slender flanks on either side.
Her figure shapely; hips tapered low;
Her neck, whiter than branch in snow;
Her eyes were gray; her face was bright;
Her mouth, lovely; nose, set just right;
Eyebrows black, forehead fair:
Blonde and curly was her hair.
Golden wire sheds no such ray
As did her locks against the day.
A mantle was around her drawn,
A cloak of deep-dyed purple lawn.
A falcon on her wrist sat still;
A greyhound followed her at will.
In town was neither high nor low,
Old man or child, who did not go
And line the streets along the way
To watch as she made her entrée.
As she passed by, and they gazed after;
Her beauty quieted jest and laughter.
She rode up to the castle slowly.
The judges, seeing her, were wholly
Astonished at that spectacle
And held it for a miracle.
The heart of every single knight
Among them warmed with sheer delight.
Those who loved Sir Lanval well
Quickly went to him to tell
About the maiden who perchance,
Please God, brought him deliverance:
"Comrade, another one draws nigh,
By no means dark of hair or eye;[1]
Among all women there can be
None fairer in this world than she."
Lanval heard and raised his eye;
He knew her well and gave a sigh.
The blood shot up into his cheeks,
And somewhat hastily he speaks:
"In faith," he said that's my *amie*!
Now I don't care if they kill me

1. Blonde hair and blue (or gray) eyes are considered the standard for beauty in romance.

If but her mercy is assured,
For when I see her, I am cured."
The maid rode through the palace door,
So fair came never there before.
In front of Arthur she got down
With the whole company looking on.
Softly she let her mantle fall,
The better to be seen by all.
King Arthur, who was most discreet,
To greet her got up on his feet.
In turn, to honor her the rest
Offered their service to the guest.
When they had satisfied their gaze
And greatly sung her beauty's praise,
She made her speech in such a way
As she did not intend to stay:
"King, I have loved one of your band—
It's Lanval, there you see him stand.
I would not have the man ill-used—
In your court he has been accused
Of lies he spoke. Listen to me,
The queen committed perjury;
He never asked her for her love.
As for the things he boasted of,
If I may be his warranty,
Your barons ought to speak him free."
The king agreed he would abide
By what they lawfully decide.
Among them there was no dissent;
Lanval was pronounced innocent.
The damoiselle set off again,
Though the king asked her to remain.
Outside there stood a marble rock
With steps to make a mounting block,
From which armed men would get astride
When they from court set out to ride.
Lanval climbed up on it before
The damoiselle rode out the door.
Swiftly he sprang the horse to straddle
And sat behind her on the saddle.
With him to Avalon she returned,
As from the Bretons we have learned,
An isle most beautiful, they say,
To which the youth was borne away.
No man has heard more of his fate.
I've nothing further to relate.

Middle English Literature in the Fourteenth and Fifteenth Centuries

SIR GAWAIN AND THE GREEN KNIGHT
ca. 1375–1400

The finest Arthurian romance in English survives in only one manuscript, which also contains three religious poems—*Pearl, Patience*, and *Purity*—generally believed to be by the same poet. Nothing is known about the author except what can be inferred from the works. The dialect of the poems locates them in a remote corner of the northwest midlands between Cheshire and Staffordshire, and details of Sir Gawain's journey north show that the author was familiar with the geography of that region. But if author and audience were provincials, *Sir Gawain* and the other poems in the manuscript reveal them to have been highly sophisticated and well acquainted both with the international culture of the high Middle Ages and with ancient insular traditions.

Sir Gawain belongs to the so-called Alliterative Revival. After the Norman Conquest, alliterative verse doubtless continued to be recited by oral poets. At the beginning, the *Gawain* poet pretends that this romance is an oral poem and asks the audience to "listen" to a story, which he has "heard." Alliterative verse also continued to appear in Early Middle English texts. Layamon's *Brut* is the outstanding example. During the late fourteenth century there was a renewed flowering of alliterative poetry, especially in the north and west of Britain, which includes *Piers Plowman* and a splendid poem known as *The Alliterative Morte Darthur*.

The *Gawain* poet's audience evidently valued the kind of alliterative verse that Chaucer's Parson caricatures as "Rum-Ram-Ruf by lettre" (see p. 265, line 43). They would also have understood archaic poetic diction surviving from Old English poetry such as *athel* (noble) and words of Scandinavian origin such as *skete* (quickly) and *skifted* (alternated). They were well acquainted with French Arthurian romances and the latest fashions in clothing, armor, and castle building. In making Sir Gawain, Arthur's sister's son, the preeminent knight of the Round Table, the poet was faithful to an older tradition. The thirteenth-century French romances, which in the next century became the main sources of Sir Thomas Malory, had made Sir Lancelot the best of Arthur's knights and Lancelot's adultery with Queen Guinevere the central event on which the fate of Arthur's kingdom turns. In *Sir Gawain* Lancelot is only one name in a list of Arthur's knights. Arthur is still a youth, and the court is in its springtime. Sir Gawain epitomizes this first blooming of Arthurian chivalry, and the reputation of the court rests upon his shoulders.

Ostensibly, Gawain's head is what is at stake. The main plot belongs to a type folklorists classify as the "Beheading Game," in which a supernatural challenger offers to let his head be cut off in exchange for a return blow. The earliest written occurrence of this motif is in the Middle Irish tale of *Bricriu's Feast*. The *Gawain* poet could have encountered it in several French romances as well as in oral tradition. But the outcome of the game here does not turn only on the champion's courage as it does in *Bricriu's Feast*. The *Gawain* poet has devised another series of tests for the hero that link the beheading with his truth, the emblem of which is the pentangle—a five-pointed star—displayed on Gawain's coat of arms and shield. The word *truth* in Middle English means not only what it still means now—a fact, belief, or idea held to be "true"—but what is conveyed by the old-fashioned variant from the same root: *troth*—that is, faith pledged by one's word and owed to a lord, a spouse, or anyone who puts someone else under an obligation. In this respect, Sir Gawain is being measured against a moral and Christian ideal of chivalry. Whether or not he succeeds in that contest is a question carefully left unresolved—perhaps as a challenge for the reader.

The poet has framed Gawain's adventure with references in the first and last stanzas to what are called the "Brutus books," the foundation stories that trace the origins of Rome and Britain back to the destruction of Troy. A cyclical sense of history as well as of the cycles of the seasons of the year, the generations of humankind, and of individual lives runs through *Sir Gawain and the Green Knight*.

The poem is written in stanzas that contain a group of alliterative lines (the number of lines in a stanza varies). The line is longer and does not contain a fixed number or pattern of stresses like the classical alliterative measure of Old English poetry. Each stanza closes with five short lines rhyming *a b a b a*. The first of these rhyming lines contains just one stress and is called the "bob"; the four three-stress lines that follow are called the "wheel." For details on alliterative verse, see "Old and Middle English Prosody" (pp. 19–21). The opening stanza is printed below in Middle English with an interlinear translation. The stressed alliterating sounds have been italicized.

Sithen the ***s***ege and the ***a***ssaut was ***s***esed at Troye,
After the siege and the assault was ceased at Troy,

The ***b***orgh ***b***rittened and ***b***rent to ***b***rondes and askes,
The city crumbled and burned to brands and ashes,

The ***t***ulk that the ***t***rammes of ***t***resoun ther wroght
The man who the plots of treason there wrought

Was ***t***ried for his ***t***richerie, the ***t***rewest on erthe.
Was tried for his treachery, the truest on earth.

Hit was ***E***nnias the ***a***thel and his highe kynde,
It was Aeneas the noble and his high race,

That sithen de***p***reced ***p***rovinces, and ***p***atrounes bicome
Who after subjugated provinces, and lords became

Welneghe of al the ***w***ele in the ***w***est iles.
Wellnigh of all the wealth in the west isles.

Fro ***r***iche ***R***omulus to ***R***ome ***r***icchis hym swythe,
Then noble Romulus to Rome proceeds quickly,

With gret ***b***obbaunce that ***b***urghe he ***b***iges upon fyrst
With great pride that city he builds at first

And ***n***evenes hit his aune ***n***ome, as hit ***n***ow hat;
And names it his own name, as it now is called;

Ticius to ***T***uskan and ***t***eldes bigynnes,
Ticius (goes) to Tuscany and houses begins,

Langaberde in ***L***umbardie ***l***yftes up homes,
Longbeard in Lombardy raises up homes,

And ***f***er over the ***F***rench ***fl***od, ***F***elix Brutus
And far over the English Channel, Felix Brutus

On mony ***b***onkkes ful ***b***rode ***B***retayn he settes
On many banks very broad Brittain he sets

Wyth ***w***ynne,
With joy,

Where ***w***erre and ***w***rake and ***w***onder
Where war and revenge and wondrous happenings

Bi sythes has wont therinne,
On occasions have dwelled therein

And oft bothe ***b***lysse and ***b***lunder
And often both joy and strife

Ful ***s***kete has ***s***kyfted ***s***ynne.
Very swiftly have alternated since.

Sir Gawain and the Green Knight[1]

Part 1

Since the siege and the assault was ceased at Troy,
The walls breached and burnt down to brands and ashes,
The knight that had knotted the nets of deceit
Was impeached for his perfidy, proven most true,[2]
It was high-born Aeneas and his haughty race
That since prevailed over provinces, and proudly reigned
Over well-nigh all the wealth of the West Isles.[3]
Great Romulus[4] to Rome repairs in haste;
With boast and with bravery builds he that city
And names it with his own name, that it now bears.
Ticius to Tuscany, and towers raises,
Langobard[5] in Lombardy lays out homes,
And far over the French Sea, Felix Brutus[6]
On many broad hills and high Britain he sets,
most fair.
Where war and wrack and wonder
By shifts have sojourned there,

1. The Modern English translation is by Marie Borroff (1967), who has reproduced the alliterative meter of the original as well as the "bob" and "wheel," the five-line rhyming group that concludes each of the long irregular stanzas.
2. The treacherous knight is Aeneas, who was a traitor to his city, Troy, according to medieval tradition, but Aeneas was actually tried ("impeached") by the Greeks for his refusal to hand over to them his sister Polyxena.
3. Perhaps Western Europe.
4. The legendary founder of Rome is here given Trojan ancestry, like Aeneas.
5. The reputed founder of Lombardy. "Ticius": not otherwise known.
6. Great-grandson of Aeneas and legendary founder of Britain; not elsewhere given the name Felix (Latin "happy").

And bliss by turns with blunder
In that land's lot had share.

And since this Britain was built by this baron great,
Bold boys bred there, in broils delighting,
That did in their day many a deed most dire.
More marvels have happened in this merry land
Than in any other I know, since that olden time,
But of those that here built, of British kings,
King Arthur was counted most courteous of all,
Wherefore an adventure I aim to unfold,
That a marvel of might some men think it,
And one unmatched among Arthur's wonders.
If you will listen to my lay but a little while,
As I heard it in hall, I shall hasten to tell
anew.
As it was fashioned featly
In tale of derring-do,
And linked in measures meetly
By letters tried and true.

This king lay at Camelot[7] at Christmastide;
Many good knights and gay his guests were there,
Arrayed of the Round Table[8] rightful brothers,
With feasting and fellowship and carefree mirth.
There true men contended in tournaments many,
Joined there in jousting these gentle knights,
Then came to the court for carol-dancing,
For the feast was in force full fifteen days,
With all the meat and the mirth that men could devise,
Such gaiety and glee, glorious to hear,
Brave din by day, dancing by night.
High were their hearts in halls and chambers,
These lords and these ladies, for life was sweet.
In peerless pleasures passed they their days,
The most noble knights known under Christ,
And the loveliest ladies that lived on earth ever,
And he the comeliest king, that that court holds,
For all this fair folk in their first age
were still.
Happiest of mortal kind,
King noblest famed of will;
You would now go far to find
So hardy a host on hill.

While the New Year was new, but yesternight come,
This fair folk at feast two-fold was served,
When the king and his company were come in together,
The chanting in chapel achieved and ended.

7. Capital of Arthur's kingdom, presumably located in southwest England or southern Wales.

8. According to legend, Merlin made the Round Table after a dispute broke out among Arthur's knights about precedence: it seated one hundred knights. The table described in the poem is not round.

Clerics and all the court acclaimed the glad season,
Cried Noel anew, good news to men;
Then gallants gather gaily, hand-gifts to make,
Called them out clearly, claimed them by hand,
Bickered long and busily about those gifts.
Ladies laughed aloud, though losers they were,
And he that won was not angered, as well you will know.[9]
All this mirth they made until meat was served;
When they had washed them worthily, they went to their seats,
The best seated above, as best it beseemed,
Guenevere the goodly queen gay in the midst
On a dais well-decked and duly arrayed
With costly silk curtains, a canopy over,
Of Toulouse and Turkestan tapestries rich,
All broidered and bordered with the best gems
Ever brought into Britain, with bright pennies
to pay.
Fair queen, without a flaw,
She glanced with eyes of grey.
A seemlier that once he saw,
In truth, no man could say.

But Arthur would not eat till all were served;
So light was his lordly heart, and a little boyish;
His life he liked lively—the less he cared
To be lying for long, or long to sit,
So busy his young blood, his brain so wild.
And also a point of pride pricked him in heart,
For he nobly had willed, he would never eat
On so high a holiday, till he had heard first
Of some fair feat or fray some far-borne tale,
Of some marvel of might, that he might trust,
By champions of chivalry achieved in arms,
Or some suppliant came seeking some single knight
To join with him in jousting, in jeopardy each
To lay life for life, and leave it to fortune
To afford him on field fair hap or other.
Such is the king's custom, when his court he holds
At each far-famed feast amid his fair host
so dear.
The stout king stands in state
Till a wonder shall appear;
He leads, with heart elate,
High mirth in the New Year.

So he stands there in state, the stout young king,
Talking before the high table of trifles fair.
There Gawain the good knight by Guenevere sits,
With Agravain à la dure main on his other side,
Both knights of renown, and nephews of the king.
Bishop Baldwin above begins the table,

9. The dispensing of New Year's gifts seems to have involved kissing.

And Yvain, son of Urien, ate with him there.
These few with the fair queen were fittingly served;
At the side-tables[1] sat many stalwart knights.
Then the first course comes, with clamor of trumpets
That were bravely bedecked with bannerets bright,
With noise of new drums and the noble pipes.
Wild were the warbles that wakened that day
In strains that stirred many strong men's hearts.
There dainties were dealt out, dishes rare,
Choice fare to choose, on chargers so many
That scarce was there space to set before the people
The service of silver, with sundry meats,
on cloth.
Each fair guest freely there
Partakes, and nothing loth;
Twelve dishes before each pair;
Good beer and bright wine both.

Of the service itself I need say no more,
For well you will know no tittle was wanting.
Another noise and a new was well-nigh at hand,
That the lord might have leave his life to nourish;
For scarce were the sweet strains still in the hall,
And the first course come to that company fair,
There hurtles in at the hall-door an unknown rider,
One the greatest on ground in growth of his frame:
From broad neck to buttocks so bulky and thick,
And his loins and his legs so long and so great,
Half a giant on earth I hold him to be,
But believe him no less than the largest of men,
And that the seemliest in his stature to see, as he rides,
For in back and in breast though his body was grim,
His waist in its width was worthily small,
And formed with every feature in fair accord
was he.
Great wonder grew in hall
At his hue most strange to see,
For man and gear and all
Were green as green could be.

And in guise all of green, the gear and the man:
A coat cut close, that clung to his sides,
And a mantle to match, made with a lining
Of furs cut and fitted—the fabric was noble,
Embellished all with ermine, and his hood beside,
That was loosed from his locks, and laid on his shoulders.
With trim hose and tight, the same tint of green,
His great calves were girt, and gold spurs under
He bore on silk bands that embellished his heels,
And footgear well-fashioned, for riding most fit.

1. The side tables are on the main floor and run along the walls at a right angle with the high table, which is on a dais.

And all his vesture verily was verdant green;
Both the bosses on his belt and other bright gems
That were richly ranged on his raiment noble
About himself and his saddle, set upon silk,
That to tell half the trifles would tax my wits,
The butterflies and birds embroidered thereon
In green of the gayest, with many a gold thread.
The pendants of the breast-band, the princely crupper,
And the bars of the bit were brightly enameled;
The stout stirrups were green, that steadied his feet,
And the bows of the saddle and the side-panels both,
That gleamed all and glinted with green gems about.
The steed he bestrides of that same green
so bright.
A green horse great and thick;
A headstrong steed of might;
In broidered bridle quick,
Mount matched man aright.

Gay was this goodly man in guise all of green,
And the hair of his head to his horse suited;
Fair flowing tresses enfold his shoulders;
A beard big as a bush on his breast hangs,
That with his heavy hair, that from his head falls,
Was evened all about above both his elbows,
That half his arms thereunder were hid in the fashion
Of a king's cap-à-dos,[2] that covers his throat.
The mane of that mighty horse much to it like,
Well curled and becombed, and cunningly knotted
With filaments of fine gold amid the fair green,
Here a strand of the hair, here one of gold;
His tail and his foretop twin in their hue,
And bound both with a band of a bright green
That was decked adown the dock with dazzling stones
And tied tight at the top with a triple knot
Where many bells well burnished rang bright and clear.
Such a mount in his might, nor man on him riding,
None had seen, I dare swear, with sight in that hall
so grand.
As lightning quick and light
He looked to all at hand;
It seemed that no man might
His deadly dints withstand.

Yet had he no helm, nor hauberk neither,
Nor plate, nor appurtenance appending to arms,
Nor shaft pointed sharp, nor shield for defense,
But in his one hand he had a holly bob
That is goodliest in green when groves are bare,

2. The word *capados* occurs in this form in Middle English only in *Gawain*, here and in line 572. The translator has interpreted it, as the poet apparently did also, as *cap-à-dos*, i.e., a garment covering its wearer "from head to back," on the model of *cap-à-pie*, "from head to foot," referring to armor.

And an ax in his other, a huge and immense,
A wicked piece of work in words to expound:
The head on its haft was an ell long;
The spike of green steel, resplendent with gold;
The blade burnished bright, with a broad edge,
As well shaped to shear as a sharp razor;
Stout was the stave in the strong man's gripe,
That was wound all with iron to the weapon's end,
With engravings in green of goodliest work.
A lace lightly about, that led to a knot,
Was looped in by lengths along the fair haft,
And tassels thereto attached in a row,
With buttons of bright green, brave to behold.
This horseman hurtles in, and the hall enters;
Riding to the high dais, recked he no danger;
Not a greeting he gave as the guests he o'erlooked,
Nor wasted his words, but "Where is," he said,
"The captain of this crowd? Keenly I wish
To see that sire with sight, and to himself say
my say."
He swaggered all about
To scan the host so gay;
He halted, as if in doubt
Who in that hall held sway.

There were stares on all sides as the stranger spoke,
For much did they marvel what it might mean
That a horseman and a horse should have such a hue,
Grow green as the grass, and greener, it seemed,
Than green fused on gold more glorious by far.
All the onlookers eyed him, and edged nearer,
And awaited in wonder what he would do,
For many sights had they seen, but such a one never,
So that phantom and faerie the folk there deemed it,
Therefore chary of answer was many a champion bold,
And stunned at his strong words stone-still they sat
In a swooning silence in the stately hall.
As all were slipped into sleep, so slackened their speech
apace.
Not all, I think, for dread,
But some of courteous grace
Let him who was their head
Be spokesman in that place.

Then Arthur before the high dais that entrance beholds,
And hailed him, as behooved, for he had no fear,
And said "Fellow, in faith you have found fair welcome;
The head of this hostelry Arthur am I;
Leap lightly down, and linger, I pray,
And the tale of your intent you shall tell us after."
"Nay, so help me," said the other, "He that on high sits,
To tarry here any time, 'twas not mine errand;
But as the praise of you, prince, is puffed up so high,

And your court and your company are counted the best,
Stoutest under steel-gear on steeds to ride,
Worthiest of their works the wide world over,
And peerless to prove in passages of arms,
And courtesy here is carried to its height,
And so at this season I have sought you out.
You may be certain by the branch that I bear in hand
That I pass here in peace, and would part friends,
For had I come to this court on combat bent,
I have a hauberk at home, and a helm beside,
A shield and a sharp spear, shining bright,
And other weapons to wield, I ween well, to boot,
But as I willed no war, I wore no metal.
But if you be so bold as all men believe,
You will graciously grant the game that I ask
by right."
Arthur answer gave
And said, "Sir courteous knight,
If contest bare you crave,
You shall not fail to fight."

"Nay, to fight, in good faith, is far from my thought;
There are about on these benches but beardless children,
Were I here in full arms on a haughty steed,
For measured against mine, their might is puny.
And so I call in this court for a Christmas game,
For 'tis Yule and New Year, and many young bloods about;
If any in this house such hardihood claims,
Be so bold in his blood, his brain so wild,
As stoutly to strike one stroke for another,
I shall give him as my gift this gisarme noble,
This ax, that is heavy enough, to handle as he likes,
And I shall bide the first blow, as bare as I sit.
If there be one so wilful my words to assay,
Let him leap hither lightly, lay hold of this weapon;
I quitclaim it forever, keep it as his own,
And I shall stand him a stroke, steady on this floor,
So you grant me the guerdon to give him another,
sans blame.
In a twelvemonth and a day
He shall have of me the same;
Now be it seen straightway
Who dares take up the game."

If he astonished them at first, stiller were then
All that household in hall, the high and the low;
The stranger on his green steed stirred in the saddle,
And roisterously his red eyes he rolled all about,
Bent his bristling brows, that were bright green,
Wagged his beard as he watched who would arise.
When the court kept its counsel he coughed aloud,
And cleared his throat coolly, the clearer to speak:
"What, is this Arthur's house," said that horseman then,

"Whose fame is so fair in far realms and wide?
Where is now your arrogance and your awesome deeds,
Your valor and your victories and your vaunting words?
Now are the revel and renown of the Round Table
Overwhelmed with a word of one man's speech,
For all cower and quake, and no cut felt!"
With this he laughs so loud that the lord grieved;
The blood for sheer shame shot to his face,
and pride.
With rage his face flushed red,
And so did all beside.
Then the king as bold man bred
Toward the stranger took a stride.

And said "Sir, now we see you will say but folly,
Which whoso has sought, it suits that he find.
No guest here is aghast of your great words.
Give to me your gisarme, in God's own name,
And the boon you have begged shall straight be granted."
He leaps to him lightly, lays hold of his weapon;
The green fellow on foot fiercely alights.
Now has Arthur his ax, and the haft grips,
And sternly stirs it about, on striking bent.
The stranger before him stood there erect,
Higher than any in the house by a head and more;
With stern look as he stood, he stroked his beard,
And with undaunted countenance drew down his coat,
No more moved nor dismayed for his mighty dints
Than any bold man on bench had brought him a drink
of wine.
Gawain by Guenevere
Toward the king doth now incline:
"I beseech, before all here,
That this melee may be mine."

"Would you grant me the grace," said Gawain to the king,
"To be gone from this bench and stand by you there,
If I without discourtesy might quit this board,
And if my liege lady misliked it not,
I would come to your counsel before your court noble.
For I find it not fit, as in faith it is known,
When such a boon is begged before all these knights,
Though you be tempted thereto, to take it on yourself
While so bold men about upon benches sit,
That no host under heaven is hardier of will,
Nor better brothers-in-arms where battle is joined;
I am the weakest, well I know, and of wit feeblest;
And the loss of my life would be least of any;
That I have you for uncle is my only praise;
My body, but for your blood, is barren of worth;
And for that this folly befits not a king,
And 'tis I that have asked it, it ought to be mine,
And if my claim be not comely let all this court judge,

in sight."
The court assays the claim,
And in counsel all unite
To give Gawain the game
And release the king outright.

Then the king called the knight to come to his side,
And he rose up readily, and reached him with speed,
Bows low to his lord, lays hold of the weapon,
And he releases it lightly, and lifts up his hand,
And gives him God's blessing, and graciously prays
That his heart and his hand may be hardy both.
"Keep, cousin," said the king, "what you cut with this day,
And if you rule it aright, then readily, I know,
You shall stand the stroke it will strike after."
Gawain goes to the guest with gisarme in hand,
And boldly he bides there, abashed not a whit.
Then hails he Sir Gawain, the horseman in green:
"Recount we our contract, ere you come further.
First I ask and adjure you, how you are called
That you tell me true, so that trust it I may."
"In good faith," said the good knight, "Gawain am I
Whose buffet befalls you, what'er betide after,
And at this time twelvemonth take from you another
With what weapon you will, and with no man else
alive."
The other nods assent:
"Sir Gawain, as I may thrive,
I am wondrous well content
That you this dint shall drive."

"Sir Gawain," said the Green Knight, "By God, I rejoice
That your fist shall fetch this favor I seek,
And you have readily rehearsed, and in right terms,
Each clause of my covenant with the king your lord,
Save that you shall assure me, sir, upon oath,
That you shall seek me yourself, wheresoever you deem
My lodgings may lie, and look for such wages
As you have offered me here before all this host."
"What is the way there?" said Gawain. "Where do you dwell?
I heard never of your house, by him that made me,
Nor I know you not, knight, your name nor your court.
But tell me truly thereof, and teach me your name,
And I shall fare forth to find you, so far as I may,
And this I say in good certain, and swear upon oath."
"That is enough in New Year, you need say no more,"
Said the knight in the green to Gawain the noble,
"If I tell you true, when I have taken your knock,
And if you handily have hit, you shall hear straightway
Of my house and my home and my own name;
Then follow in my footsteps by faithful accord.
And if I spend no speech, you shall speed the better:
You can feast with your friends, nor further trace

my tracks.
Now hold your grim tool steady
And show us how it hacks."
"Gladly, sir; all ready,"
Says Gawain; he strokes the ax.

The Green Knight upon ground girds him with care:
Bows a bit with his head, and bares his flesh:
His long lovely locks he laid over his crown,
Let the naked nape for the need be shown.
Gawain grips to his ax and gathers it aloft—
The left foot on the floor before him he set—
Brought it down deftly upon the bare neck,
That the shock of the sharp blow shivered the bones
And cut the flesh cleanly and clove it in twain,
That the blade of bright steel bit into the ground.
The head was hewn off and fell to the floor;
Many found it at their feet, as forth it rolled;
The blood gushed from the body, bright on the green,
Yet fell not the fellow, nor faltered a whit,
But stoutly he starts forth upon stiff shanks,
And as all stood staring he stretched forth his hand,
Laid hold of his head and heaved it aloft,
Then goes to the green steed, grasps the bridle,
Steps into the stirrup, bestrides his mount,
And his head by the hair in his hand holds,
And as steady he sits in the stately saddle
As he had met with no mishap, nor missing were
his head.
His bulk about he haled,
That fearsome body that bled;
There were many in the court that quailed
Before all his say was said.

For the head in his hand he holds right up;
Toward the first on the dais directs he the face,
And it lifted up its lids, and looked with wide eyes,
And said as much with its mouth as now you may hear:
"Sir Gawain, forget not to go as agreed,
And cease not to seek till me, sir, you find,
As you promised in the presence of these proud knights.
To the Green Chapel come, I charge you, to take
Such a dint as you have dealt—you have well deserved
That your neck should have a knock on New Year's morn.
The Knight of the Green Chapel I am well-known to many,
Wherefore you cannot fail to find me at last;
Therefore come, or be counted a recreant knight."
With a roisterous rush he flings round the reins,
Hurtles out at the hall-door, his head in his hand,
That the flint-fire flew from the flashing hooves.
Which way he went, not one of them knew
Nor whence he was come in the wide world
so fair.

The king and Gawain gay
Make game of the Green Knight there,
Yet all who saw it say
'Twas a wonder past compare.

Though high-born Arthur at heart had wonder,
He let no sign be seen, but said aloud
To the comely queen, with courteous speech,
"Dear dame, on this day dismay you no whit;
Such crafts are becoming at Christmastide,
Laughing at interludes, light songs and mirth,
Amid dancing of damsels with doughty knights.
Nevertheless of my meat now let me partake,
For I have met with a marvel, I may not deny."
He glanced at Sir Gawain, and gaily he said,
"Now, sir, hang up your ax,[3] that has hewn enough,"
And over the high dais it was hung on the wall
That men in amazement might on it look,
And tell in true terms the tale of the wonder.
Then they turned toward the table, these two together,
The good king and Gawain, and made great feast,
With all dainties double, dishes rare,
With all manner of meat and minstrelsy both,
Such happiness wholly had they that day
in hold.
Now take care, Sir Gawain,
That your courage wax not cold
When you must turn again
To your enterprise foretold.

Part 2

This adventure had Arthur of handsels[4] first
When young was the year, for he yearned to hear tales;
Though they wanted for words when they went to sup,
Now are fierce deeds to follow, their fists stuffed full.
Gawain was glad to begin those games in hall,
But if the end be harsher, hold it no wonder,
For though men are merry in mind after much drink,
A year passes apace, and proves ever new:
First things and final conform but seldom.
And so this Yule to the young year yielded place,
And each season ensued at its set time;
After Christmas there came the cold cheer of Lent,
When with fish and plainer fare our flesh we reprove;
But then the world's weather with winter contends:
The keen cold lessens, the low clouds lift;
Fresh falls the rain in fostering showers
On the face of the fields; flowers appear.
The ground and the groves wear gowns of green;

3. A colloquial expression equivalent to "bury the hatchet," but here with an appropriate literal sense also.
4. New Year's presents.

Birds build their nests, and blithely sing
That solace of all sorrow with summer comes
ere long.
And blossoms day by day
Bloom rich and rife in throng;
Then every grove so gay
Of the greenwood rings with song.

And then the season of summer with the soft winds,
When Zephyr sighs low over seeds and shoots;
Glad is the green plant growing abroad,
When the dew at dawn drops from the leaves,
To get a gracious glance from the golden sun.
But harvest with harsher winds follows hard after,
Warns him to ripen well ere winter comes;
Drives forth the dust in the droughty season,
From the face of the fields to fly high in air.
Wroth winds in the welkin wrestle with the sun,
The leaves launch from the linden and light on the ground,
And the grass turns to gray, that once grew green.
Then all ripens and rots that rose up at first,
And so the year moves on in yesterdays many,
And winter once more, by the world's law,
draws nigh.
At Michaelmas° the moon *September 29*
Hangs wintry pale in sky;
Sir Gawain girds him soon
For travails yet to try.

Till All-Hallows' Day[5] with Arthur he dwells,
And he held a high feast to honor that knight
With great revels and rich, of the Round Table.
Then ladies lovely and lords debonair
With sorrow for Sir Gawain were sore at heart;
Yet they covered their care with countenance glad:
Many a mournful man made mirth for his sake.
So after supper soberly he speaks to his uncle
Of the hard hour at hand, and openly says,
"Now, liege lord of my life, my leave I take;
The terms of this task too well you know—
To count the cost over concerns me nothing.
But I am bound forth betimes to bear a stroke
From the grim man in green, as God may direct."
Then the first and foremost came forth in throng:
Yvain and Eric and others of note,
Sir Dodinal le Sauvage, the Duke of Clarence,
Lionel and Lancelot and Lucan the good,
Sir Bors and Sir Bedivere, big men both,
And many manly knights more, with Mador de la Porte.
All this courtly company comes to the king
To counsel their comrade, with care in their hearts;

5. All Saints' Day, November 1.

There was much secret sorrow suffered that day
That one so good as Gawain must go in such wise
To bear a bitter blow, and his bright sword
lay by.
He said, "Why should I tarry?"
And smiled with tranquil eye;
"In destinies sad or merry,
True men can but try."

He dwelt there all that day, and dressed in the morning;
Asked early for his arms, and all were brought.
First a carpet of rare cost was cast on the floor
Where much goodly gear gleamed golden bright;
He takes his place promptly and picks up the steel,
Attired in a tight coat of Turkestan silk
And a kingly cap-à-dos, closed at the throat,
That was lavishly lined with a lustrous fur.
Then they set the steel shoes on his sturdy feet
And clad his calves about with comely greaves,
And plate well-polished protected his knees,
Affixed with fastenings of the finest gold.
Fair cuisses enclosed, that were cunningly wrought,
His thick-thewed thighs, with thongs bound fast,
And massy chain-mail of many a steel ring
He bore on his body, above the best cloth,
With brace burnished bright upon both his arms,
Good couters and gay, and gloves of plate,
And all the goodly gear to grace him well
that tide.
His surcoat blazoned bold;
Sharp spurs to prick with pride;
And a brave silk band to hold
The broadsword at his side.

When he had on his arms, his harness was rich,
The least latchet or loop laden with gold;
So armored as he was, he heard a mass,
Honored God humbly at the high altar.
Then he comes to the king and his comrades-in-arms,
Takes his leave at last of lords and ladies,
And they clasped and kissed him, commending him to Christ.
By then Gringolet was girt with a great saddle
That was gaily agleam with fine gilt fringe,
New-furbished for the need with nail-heads bright;
The bridle and the bars bedecked all with gold;
The breast-plate, the saddlebow, the side-panels both,
The caparison and the crupper accorded in hue,
And all ranged on the red the resplendent studs
That glittered and glowed like the glorious sun.
His helm now he holds up and hastily kisses,
Well-closed with iron clinches, and cushioned within;
It was high on his head, with a hasp behind,
And a covering of cloth to encase the visor,

All bound and embroidered with the best gems
On broad bands of silk, and bordered with birds,
Parrots and popinjays preening their wings,
Lovebirds and love-knots as lavishly wrought
As many women had worked seven winters thereon,
entire.
The diadem costlier yet
That crowned that comely sire,
With diamonds richly set,
That flashed as if on fire.

Then they showed forth the shield, that shone all red,
With the pentangle[6] portrayed in purest gold.
About his broad neck by the baldric he casts it,
That was meet for the man, and matched him well.
And why the pentangle is proper to that peerless prince
I intend now to tell, though detain me it must.
It is a sign by Solomon sagely devised
To be a token of truth, by its title of old,
For it is a figure formed of five points,
And each line is linked and locked with the next
For ever and ever, and hence it is called
In all England, as I hear, the endless knot.
And well may he wear it on his worthy arms,
For ever faithful five-fold in five-fold fashion
Was Gawain in good works, as gold unalloyed,
Devoid of all villainy, with virtues adorned
in sight.
On shield and coat in view
He bore that emblem bright,
As to his word most true
And in speech most courteous knight.

And first, he was faultless in his five senses,
Nor found ever to fail in his five fingers,
And all his fealty was fixed upon the five wounds
That Christ got on the cross, as the creed tells;
And wherever this man in melee took part,
His one thought was of this, past all things else,

6. A five-pointed star, formed by five lines that are drawn without lifting the pencil from the paper, supposed to have mystical significance; as Solomon's sign (line 625) it was enclosed in a circle.

That all his force was founded on the five joys[7]
That the high Queen of heaven had in her child.
And therefore, as I find, he fittingly had
On the inner part of his shield her image portrayed,
That when his look on it lighted, he never lost heart.
The fifth of the five fives followed by this knight
Were beneficence boundless and brotherly love
And pure mind and manners, that none might impeach,
And compassion most precious—these peerless five
Were forged and made fast in him, foremost of men.
Now all these five fives were confirmed in this knight,
And each linked in other, that end there was none,
And fixed to five points, whose force never failed,
Nor assembled all on a side, nor asunder either,
Nor anywhere at an end, but whole and entire
However the pattern proceeded or played out its course.
And so on his shining shield shaped was the knot
Royally in red gold against red gules,
That is the peerless pentangle, prized of old
in lore.
Now armed is Gawain gay,
And bears his lance before,
And soberly said good day,
He thought forevermore.

He struck his steed with the spurs and sped on his way
So fast that the flint-fire flashed from the stones.
When they saw him set forth they were sore aggrieved,
And all sighed softly, and said to each other,
Fearing for their fellow, "Ill fortune it is
That you, man, must be marred, that most are worthy!
His equal on this earth can hardly be found;
To have dealt more discreetly had done less harm,
And have dubbed him a duke, with all due honor.
A great leader of lords he was like to become,
And better so to have been than battered to bits,
Beheaded by an elf-man,° for empty pride! *supernatural being*
Who would credit that a king could be counseled so,
And caught in a cavil in a Christmas game?"
Many were the warm tears they wept from their eyes
When goodly Sir Gawain was gone from the court
that day.
No longer he abode,
But speedily went his way
Over many a wandering road,
As I heard my author say.

Now he rides in his array through the realm of Logres,[8]
Sir Gawain, God knows, though it gave him small joy!
All alone must he lodge through many a long night

7. Most commonly in Middle English literature, the Annunciation, Nativity, Resurrection, Ascension, and Assumption, although the list varies. These overlap but are not identical with the Five Joyful Mysteries of the Rosary, which were not formally established until the 16th century.
8. One of the names for Arthur's kingdom.

Where the food that he fancied was far from his plate;
He had no mate but his mount, over mountain and plain,
Nor man to say his mind to but almighty God,
Till he had wandered well-nigh into North Wales.
All the islands of Anglesey he holds on his left,
And follows, as he fares, the fords by the coast,
Comes over at Holy Head, and enters next
The Wilderness of Wirral[9]—few were within
That had great good will toward God or man.
And earnestly he asked of each mortal he met
If he had ever heard aught of a knight all green,
Or of a Green Chapel, on ground thereabouts,
And all said the same, and solemnly swore
They saw no such knight all solely green
in hue.
Over country wild and strange
The knight sets off anew;
Often his course must change
Ere the Chapel comes in view.

Many a cliff must he climb in country wild;
Far off from all his friends, forlorn must he ride;
At each strand or stream where the stalwart passed
'Twere a marvel if he met not some monstrous foe,
And that so fierce and forbidding that fight he must.
So many were the wonders he wandered among
That to tell but the tenth part would tax my wits.
Now with serpents he wars, now with savage wolves,
Now with wild men of the woods, that watched from the rocks,
Both with bulls and with bears, and with boars besides,
And giants that came gibbering from the jagged steeps.
Had he not borne himself bravely, and been on God's side,
He had met with many mishaps and mortal harms.
And if the wars were unwelcome, the winter was worse,
When the cold clear rains rushed from the clouds
And froze before they could fall to the frosty earth.
Near slain by the sleet he sleeps in his irons
More nights than enough, among naked rocks,
Where clattering from the crest the cold stream ran
And hung in hard icicles high overhead.
Thus in peril and pain and predicaments dire
He rides across country till Christmas Eve,
our knight.
And at that holy tide
He prays with all his might
That Mary may be his guide
Till a dwelling comes in sight.

By a mountain next morning he makes his way
Into a forest fastness, fearsome and wild;
High hills on either hand, with hoar woods below,

9. Gawain went from Camelot north to the northern coast of Wales, opposite the islands of Anglesey; there he turned east across the Dee to the forest of Wirral in Cheshire.

Oaks old and huge by the hundred together.
The hazel and the hawthorn were all intertwined
With rough raveled moss, that raggedly hung,
With many birds unblithe upon bare twigs
That peeped most piteously for pain of the cold.
The good knight on Gringolet glides thereunder
Through many a marsh and mire, a man all alone;
He feared for his default, should he fail to see
The service of that Sire that on that same night
Was born of a bright maid, to bring us his peace.
And therefore sighing he said, "I beseech of Thee, Lord,
And Mary, thou mildest mother so dear,
Some harborage where haply I might hear mass
And Thy matins tomorrow—meekly I ask it,
And thereto proffer and pray my pater and ave
and creed."
He said his prayer with sighs,
Lamenting his misdeed;
He crosses himself, and cries
On Christ in his great need.

No sooner had Sir Gawain signed himself thrice
Than he was ware, in the wood, of a wondrous dwelling,
Within a moat, on a mound, bright amid boughs
Of many a tree great of girth that grew by the water—
A castle as comely as a knight could own,
On grounds fair and green, in a goodly park
With a palisade of palings planted about
For two miles and more, round many a fair tree.
The stout knight stared at that stronghold great
As it shimmered and shone amid shining leaves,
Then with helmet in hand he offers his thanks
To Jesus and Saint Julian,[1] that are gentle both,
That in courteous accord had inclined to his prayer;
"Now fair harbor," said he, "I humbly beseech!"
Then he pricks his proud steed with the plated spurs,
And by chance he has chosen the chief path
That brought the bold knight to the bridge's end
in haste.
The bridge hung high in air;
The gates were bolted fast;
The walls well-framed to bear
The fury of the blast.

The man on his mount remained on the bank
Of the deep double moat that defended the place.
The wall went in the water wondrous deep,
And a long way aloft it loomed overhead.
It was built of stone blocks to the battlements' height,
With corbels under cornices in comeliest style;
Watch-towers trusty protected the gate,

1. Patron saint of hospitality.

With many a lean loophole, to look from within:
A better-made barbican the knight beheld never.
And behind it there hoved a great hall and fair:
Turrets rising in tiers, with tines° at their tops, *spikes*
Spires set beside them, splendidly long,
With finials° well-fashioned, as filigree fine. *gable ornaments*
Chalk-white chimneys over chambers high
Gleamed in gay array upon gables and roofs;
The pinnacles in panoply, pointing in air,
So vied there for his view that verily it seemed
A castle cut of paper for a king's feast.[2]
The good knight on Gringolet thought it great luck
If he could but contrive to come there within
To keep the Christmas feast in that castle fair
and bright.
There answered to his call
A porter most polite;
From his station on the wall
He greets the errant knight.

"Good sir," said Gawain, "Wouldst go to inquire
If your lord would allow me to lodge here a space?"
"Peter!" said the porter, "For my part, I think
So noble a knight will not want for a welcome!"
Then he bustles off briskly, and comes back straight,
And many servants beside, to receive him the better.
They let down the drawbridge and duly went forth
And kneeled down on their knees on the naked earth
To welcome this warrior as best they were able.
They proffered him passage—the portals stood wide—
And he beckoned them to rise, and rode over the bridge.
Men steadied his saddle as he stepped to the ground,
And there stabled his steed many stalwart folk.
Now come the knights and the noble squires
To bring him with bliss into the bright hall.
When his high helm was off, there hied forth a throng
Of attendants to take it, and see to its care;
They bore away his brand° and his blazoned shield; *sword*
Then graciously he greeted those gallants each one,
And many a noble drew near, to do the knight honor.
All in his armor into hall he was led,
Where fire on a fair hearth fiercely blazed.
And soon the lord himself descends from his chamber
To meet with good manners the man on his floor.
He said, "To this house you are heartily welcome:
What is here is wholly yours, to have in your power
and sway."
"Many thanks," said Sir Gawain;
"May Christ your pains repay!"
The two embrace amain
As men well met that day.

2. A common table decoration at feasts.

Gawain gazed on the host that greeted him there,
And a lusty fellow he looked, the lord of that place:
A man of massive mold, and of middle age;
Broad, bright was his beard, of a beaver's hue,
Strong, steady his stance, upon stalwart shanks,
His face fierce as fire, fair-spoken withal,
And well-suited he seemed in Sir Gawain's sight
To be a master of men in a mighty keep.
They pass into a parlor, where promptly the host
Has a servant assigned him to see to his needs,
And there came upon his call many courteous folk
That brought him to a bower where bedding was noble,
With heavy silk hangings hemmed all in gold,
Coverlets and counterpanes curiously wrought,
A canopy over the couch, clad all with fur,
Curtains running on cords, caught to gold rings,
Woven rugs on the walls of eastern work,
And the floor, under foot, well-furnished with the same.
Amid light talk and laughter they loosed from him then
His war-dress of weight and his worthy clothes.
Robes richly wrought they brought him right soon,
To change there in chamber and choose what he would.
When he had found one he fancied, and flung it about,
Well-fashioned for his frame, with flowing skirts,
His face fair and fresh as the flowers of spring,
All the good folk agreed, that gazed on him then,
His limbs arrayed royally in radiant hues,
That so comely a mortal never Christ made
as he.
Whatever his place of birth,
It seemed he well might be
Without a peer on earth
In martial rivalry.

A couch before the fire, where fresh coals burned,
They spread for Sir Gawain splendidly now
With quilts quaintly stitched, and cushions beside,
And then a costly cloak they cast on his shoulders
Of bright silk, embroidered on borders and hems,
With furs of the finest well-furnished within,
And bound about with ermine, both mantle and hood;
And he sat at that fireside in sumptuous estate
And warmed himself well, and soon he waxed merry.
Then attendants set a table upon trestles broad,
And lustrous white linen they laid thereupon,
A saltcellar of silver, spoons of the same.
He washed himself well and went to his place,
Men set his fare before him in fashion most fit.
There were soups of all sorts, seasoned with skill,
Double-sized servings, and sundry fish,
Some baked, some breaded, some broiled on the coals,
Some simmered, some in stews, steaming with spice,
And with sauces to sup that suited his taste.

He confesses it a feast with free words and fair;
They requite him as kindly with courteous jests,
well-sped.
"Tonight you fast[3] and pray;
Tomorrow we'll see you fed."
The knight grows wondrous gay
As the wine goes to his head.

Then at times and by turns, as at table he sat,
They questioned him quietly, with queries discreet,
And he courteously confessed that he comes from the court,
And owns him of the brotherhood of high-famed Arthur,
The right royal ruler of the Round Table,
And the guest by their fireside is Gawain himself,
Who has happened on their house at that holy feast.
When the name of the knight was made known to the lord,
Then loudly he laughed, so elated he was,
And the men in that household made haste with joy
To appear in his presence promptly that day,
That of courage ever-constant, and customs pure,
Is pattern and paragon, and praised without end:
Of all knights on earth most honored is he.
Each said solemnly aside to his brother,
"Now displays of deportment shall dazzle our eyes
And the polished pearls of impeccable speech;
The high art of eloquence is ours to pursue
Since the father of fine manners is found in our midst.
Great is God's grace, and goodly indeed,
That a guest such as Gawain he guides to us here
When men sit and sing of their Savior's birth
in view.
With command of manners pure
He shall each heart imbue;
Who shares his converse, sure,
Shall learn love's language true."

When the knight had done dining and duly arose,
The dark was drawing on; the day nigh ended.
Chaplains in chapels and churches about
Rang the bells aright, reminding all men
Of the holy evensong of the high feast.
The lord attends alone: his fair lady sits
In a comely closet, secluded from sight.
Gawain in gay attire goes thither soon;
The lord catches his coat, and calls him by name,
And has him sit beside him, and says in good faith
No guest on God's earth would he gladlier greet.
For that Gawain thanked him; the two then embraced
And sat together soberly the service through.

3. Gawain is said to be "fasting" because the meal, although elaborate, consisted only of fish dishes, appropriate to a fasting day.

Then the lady, that longed to look on the knight,
Came forth from her closet with her comely maids.
The fair hues of her flesh, her face and her hair
And her body and her bearing were beyond praise,
And excelled the queen herself, as Sir Gawain thought.
He goes forth to greet her with gracious intent;
Another lady led her by the left hand
That was older than she—an ancient, it seemed,
And held in high honor by all men about.
But unlike to look upon, those ladies were,
For if the one was fresh, the other was faded:
Bedecked in bright red was the body of one;
Flesh hung in folds on the face of the other;
On one a high headdress, hung all with pearls;
Her bright throat and bosom fair to behold,
Fresh as the first snow fallen upon hills;
A wimple the other one wore round her throat;
Her swart chin well swaddled, swathed all in white;
Her forehead enfolded in flounces of silk
That framed a fair fillet, of fashion ornate,
And nothing bare beneath save the black brows,
The two eyes and the nose, the naked lips,
And they unsightly to see, and sorrily bleared.
A beldame, by God, she may well be deemed,
of pride!
She was short and thick of waist,
Her buttocks round and wide;
More toothsome, to his taste,
Was the beauty by her side.

When Gawain had gazed on that gay lady,
With leave of her lord, he politely approached;
To the elder in homage he humbly bows;
The lovelier he salutes with a light embrace.
He claims a comely kiss, and courteously he speaks;
They welcome him warmly, and straightway he asks
To be received as their servant, if they so desire.
They take him between them; with talking they bring him
Beside a bright fire; bade then that spices
Be freely fetched forth, to refresh them the better,
And the good wine therewith, to warm their hearts.
The lord leaps about in light-hearted mood;
Contrives entertainments and timely sports;
Takes his hood from his head and hangs it on a spear,
And offers him openly the honor thereof
Who should promote the most mirth at that Christmas feast;
"And I shall try for it, trust me—contend with the best,
Ere I go without my headgear by grace of my friends!"
Thus with light talk and laughter the lord makes merry
To gladden the guest he had greeted in hall
that day.
At the last he called for light
The company to convey;

Gawain says goodnight
And retires to bed straightway.

On the morn when each man is mindful in heart
That God's son was sent down to suffer our death,
No household but is blithe for his blessed sake;
So was it there on that day, with many delights.
Both at larger meals and less they were lavishly served
By doughty lads on dais, with delicate fare;
The old ancient lady, highest she sits;
The lord at her left hand leaned, as I hear;
Sir Gawain in the center, beside the gay lady,
Where the food was brought first to that festive board,
And thence throughout the hall, as they held most fit,
To each man was offered in order of rank.
There was meat, there was mirth, there was much joy,
That to tell all the tale would tax my wits,
Though I pained me, perchance, to paint it with care;
But yet I know that our knight and the noble lady
Were accorded so closely in company there,
With the seemly solace of their secret words,
With speeches well-sped, spotless and pure,
That each prince's pastime their pleasures far
outshone.
Sweet pipes beguile their cares,
And the trumpet of martial tone;
Each tends his affairs
And those two tend their own.

That day and all the next, their disport was noble,
And the third day, I think, pleased them no less;
The joys of St. John's Day° were justly praised, *December 27*
And were the last of their like for those lords and ladies;
Then guests were to go in the gray morning,
Wherefore they whiled the night away with wine and with mirth,
Moved to the measures of many a blithe carol;
At last, when it was late, took leave of each other,
Each one of those worthies, to wend his way.
Gawain bids goodbye to his goodly host
Who brings him to his chamber, the chimney beside,
And detains him in talk, and tenders his thanks
And holds it an honor to him and his people
That he has harbored in his house at that holy time
And embellished his abode with his inborn grace.
"As long as I may live, my luck is the better
That Gawain was my guest at God's own feast!"
"Noble sir," said the knight, "I cannot but think
All the honor is your own—may heaven requite it!
And your man to command I account myself here
As I am bound and beholden, and shall be, come
what may."
The lord with all his might
Entreats his guest to stay;

Brief answer makes the knight:
Next morning he must away.

Then the lord of that land politely inquired
What dire affair had forced him, at that festive time,
So far from the king's court to fare forth alone
Ere the holidays wholly had ended in hall.
"In good faith," said Gawain, "you have guessed the truth:
On a high errand and urgent I hastened away,
For I am summoned by myself to seek for a place—
I would I knew whither, or where it might be!
Far rather would I find it before the New Year
Than own the land of Logres, so help me our Lord!
Wherefore, sir, in friendship this favor I ask,
That you say in sober earnest, if something you know
Of the Green Chapel, on ground far or near,
Or the lone knight that lives there, of like hue of green.
A certain day was set by assent of us both
To meet at that landmark, if I might last,
And from now to the New Year is nothing too long,
And I would greet the Green Knight there, would God but allow,
More gladly, by God's Son, than gain the world's wealth!
And I must set forth to search, as soon as I may;
To be about the business I have but three days
And would as soon sink down dead as desist from my errand."
Then smiling said the lord, "Your search, sir, is done,
For we shall see you to that site by the set time.
Let Gawain grieve no more over the Green Chapel;
You shall be in your own bed, in blissful ease,
All the forenoon, and fare forth the first of the year,
And make the goal by midmorn, to mind your affairs,
no fear!
Tarry till the fourth day
And ride on the first of the year.
We shall set you on your way;
It is not two miles from here."

Then Gawain was glad, and gleefully he laughed:
"Now I thank you for this, past all things else!
Now my goal is here at hand! With a glad heart I shall
Both tarry, and undertake any task you devise."
Then the host seized his arm and seated him there;
Let the ladies be brought, to delight them the better,
And in fellowship fair by the fireside they sit;
So gay waxed the good host, so giddy his words,
All waited in wonder what next he would say.
Then he stares on the stout knight, and sternly he speaks:
"You have bound yourself boldly my bidding to do—
Will you stand by that boast, and obey me this once?"
"I shall do so indeed," said the doughty knight;
"While I lie in your lodging, your laws will I follow."
"As you have had," said the host, "many hardships abroad
And little sleep of late, you are lacking, I judge,

Both in nourishment needful and nightly rest;
You shall lie abed late in your lofty chamber
Tomorrow until mass, and meet then to dine
When you will, with my wife, who will sit by your side
And talk with you at table, the better to cheer
our guest.
A-hunting I will go
While you lie late and rest."
The knight, inclining low,
Assents to each behest.

"And Gawain," said the good host, "agree now to this:
Whatever I win in the woods I will give you at eve,
And all you have earned you must offer to me;
Swear now, sweet friend, to swap as I say,
Whether hands, in the end, be empty or better."
"By God," said Sir Gawain, "I grant it forthwith!
If you find the game good, I shall gladly take part."
"Let the bright wine be brought, and our bargain is done,"
Said the lord of that land—the two laughed together.
Then they drank and they dallied and doffed all constraint,
These lords and these ladies, as late as they chose,
And then with gaiety and gallantries and graceful adieux
They talked in low tones, and tarried at parting.
With compliments comely they kiss at the last;
There were brisk lads about with blazing torches
To see them safe to bed, for soft repose
long due.
Their covenants, yet awhile,
They repeat, and pledge anew;
That lord could well beguile
Men's hearts, with mirth in view.

Part 3

Long before daylight they left their beds;
Guests that wished to go gave word to their grooms,
And they set about briskly to bind on saddles,
Tend to their tackle, tie up trunks.
The proud lords appear, appareled to ride,
Leap lightly astride, lay hold of their bridles,
Each one on his way to his worthy house.
The liege lord of the land was not the last
Arrayed there to ride, with retainers many;
He had a bite to eat when he had heard mass;
With horn to the hills he hastens amain.
By the dawn of that day over the dim earth,
Master and men were mounted and ready.
Then they harnessed in couples the keen-scented hounds,
Cast wide the kennel-door and called them forth,
Blew upon their bugles bold blasts three;
The dogs began to bay with a deafening din,
And they quieted them quickly and called them to heel,

A hundred brave huntsmen, as I have heard tell,
together.
Men at stations meet;
From the hounds they slip the tether;
The echoing horns repeat,
Clear in the merry weather.

At the clamor of the quest, the quarry trembled;
Deer dashed through the dale, dazed with dread;
Hastened to the high ground, only to be
Turned back by the beaters, who boldly shouted.
They harmed not the harts, with their high heads,
Let the bucks go by, with their broad antlers,
For it was counted a crime, in the close season,
If a man of that demesne should molest the male deer.
The hinds were headed up, with "Hey!" and "Ware!"
The does with great din were driven to the valleys.
Then you were ware, as they went, of the whistling of arrows;
At each bend under boughs the bright shafts flew
That tore the tawny hide with their tapered heads.
Ah! they bray and they bleed, on banks they die,
And ever the pack pell-mell comes panting behind;
Hunters with shrill horns hot on their heels—
Like the cracking of cliffs their cries resounded.
What game got away from the gallant archers
Was promptly picked off at the posts below
When they were harried on the heights and herded to the streams:
The watchers were so wary at the waiting-stations,
And the greyhounds so huge, that eagerly snatched,
And finished them off as fast as folk could see
with sight.
The lord, now here, now there,
Spurs forth in sheer delight.
And drives, with pleasures rare,
The day to the dark night.

So the lord in the linden-wood leads the hunt
And Gawain the good knight in gay bed lies,
Lingered late alone, till daylight gleamed,
Under coverlet costly, curtained about.
And as he slips into slumber, slyly there comes
A little din at his door, and the latch lifted,
And he holds up his heavy head out of the clothes;
A corner of the curtain he caught back a little
And waited there warily, to see what befell.
Lo! it was the lady, loveliest to behold,
That drew the door behind her deftly and still
And was bound for his bed—abashed was the knight,
And laid his head low again in likeness of sleep;
And she stepped stealthily, and stole to his bed,
Cast aside the curtain and came within,
And set herself softly on the bedside there,
And lingered at her leisure, to look on his waking.

The fair knight lay feigning for a long while,
Conning in his conscience what his case might
Mean or amount to—a marvel he thought it.
But yet he said within himself, "More seemly it were
To try her intent by talking a little."
So he started and stretched, as startled from sleep,
Lifts wide his lids in likeness of wonder,
And signs himself swiftly, as safer to be,
with art.
Sweetly does she speak
And kindling glances dart,
Blent white and red on cheek
And laughing lips apart.

"Good morning, Sir Gawain," said that gay lady,
"A slack sleeper you are, to let one slip in!
Now you are taken in a trice—a truce we must make,
Or I shall bind you in your bed, of that be assured."
Thus laughing lightly that lady jested.
"Good morning, good lady," said Gawain the blithe,
"Be it with me as you will; I am well content!
For I surrender myself, and sue for your grace,
And that is best, I believe, and behooves me now."
Thus jested in answer that gentle knight.
"But if, lovely lady, you misliked it not,
And were pleased to permit your prisoner to rise,
I should quit this couch and accoutre me better,
And be clad in more comfort for converse here."
"Nay, not so, sweet sir," said the smiling lady;
"You shall not rise from your bed; I direct you better:
I shall hem and hold you on either hand,
And keep company awhile with my captive knight.
For as certain as I sit here, Sir Gawain you are,
Whom all the world worships, whereso you ride;
Your honor, your courtesy are highest acclaimed
By lords and by ladies, by all living men;
And lo! we are alone here, and left to ourselves:
My lord and his liegemen are long departed,
The household asleep, my handmaids too,
The door drawn, and held by a well-driven bolt,
And since I have in this house him whom all love,
I shall while the time away with mirthful speech
at will.
My body is here at hand,
Your each wish to fulfill;
Your servant to command
I am, and shall be still."

"In good faith," said Gawain, "my gain is the greater,
Though I am not he of whom you have heard;
To arrive at such reverence as you recount here
I am one all unworthy, and well do I know it.
By heaven, I would hold me the happiest of men

If by word or by work I once might aspire
To the prize of your praise—'twere a pure joy!"
"In good faith, Sir Gawain," said that gay lady,
"The well-proven prowess that pleases all others,
Did I scant or scout it, 'twere scarce becoming.
But there are ladies, believe me, that had liefer far
Have thee here in their hold, as I have today,
To pass an hour in pastime with pleasant words,
Assuage all their sorrows and solace their hearts,
Than much of the goodly gems and gold they possess.
But laud be to the Lord of the lofty skies,
For here in my hands all hearts' desire
doth lie."
Great welcome got he there
From the lady who sat him by;
With fitting speech and fair
The good knight makes reply.

"Madame," said the merry man, "Mary reward you!
For in good faith, I find your beneficence noble.
And the fame of fair deeds runs far and wide,
But the praise you report pertains not to me,
But comes of your courtesy and kindness of heart."
"By the high Queen of heaven" (said she) "I count it not so,
For were I worth all the women in this world alive,
And all wealth and all worship were in my hands,
And I should hunt high and low, a husband to take,
For the nurture I have noted in thee, knight, here,
The comeliness and courtesies and courtly mirth—
And so I had ever heard, and now hold it true—
No other on this earth should have me for wife."
"You are bound to a better man," the bold knight said,
"Yet I prize the praise you have proffered me here,
And soberly your servant, my sovereign I hold you,
And acknowledge me your knight, in the name of Christ."
So they talked of this and that until 'twas nigh noon,
And ever the lady languishing in likeness of love.
With feat words and fair he framed his defense,
For were she never so winsome, the warrior had
The less will to woo, for the wound that his bane
must be.
He must bear the blinding blow,
For such is fate's decree:
The lady asks leave to go;
He grants it full and free.

Then she gaily said goodbye, and glanced at him, laughing,
And as she stood, she astonished him with a stern speech:
"Now may the Giver of all good words these glad hours repay!
But our guest is not Gawain—forgot is that thought."
"How so?" said the other, and asks in some haste,
For he feared he had been at fault in the forms of his speech.

But she held up her hand, and made answer thus:
"So good a knight as Gawain is given out to be,
And the model of fair demeanor and manners pure,
Had he lain so long at a lady's side,
Would have claimed a kiss, by his courtesy,
Through some touch or trick of phrase at some tale's end."
Said Gawain, "Good lady, I grant it at once!
I shall kiss at your command, as becomes a knight,
And more, lest you mislike, so let be, I pray."
With that she turns toward him, takes him in her arms,
Leans down her lovely head, and lo! he is kissed.
They commend each other to Christ with comely words,
He sees her forth safely, in silence they part,
And then he lies no later in his lofty bed,
But calls to his chamberlain, chooses his clothes,
Goes in those garments gladly to mass,
Then takes his way to table, where attendants wait,
And made merry all day, till the moon rose
in view.
Was never knight beset
'Twixt worthier ladies two:
The crone and the coquette;
Fair pastimes they pursue.

And the lord of the land rides late and long,
Hunting the barren hind over the broad heath.
He had slain such a sum, when the sun sank low,
Of does and other deer, as would dizzy one's wits.
Then they trooped in together in triumph at last,
And the count of the quarry quickly they take.
The lords lent a hand with their liegemen many,
Picked out the plumpest and put them together
And duly dressed the deer, as the deed requires.
Some were assigned the assay of the fat:
Two fingers' width fully they found on the leanest.
Then they slit the slot open and searched out the paunch,
Trimmed it with trencher-knives and tied it up tight.
They flayed the fair hide from the legs and trunk,
Then broke open the belly and laid bare the bowels,
Deftly detaching and drawing them forth.
And next at the neck they neatly parted
The weasand° from the windpipe, and cast away the guts. *esophagus*
At the shoulders with sharp blades they showed their skill,
Boning them from beneath, lest the sides be marred;
They breached the broad breast and broke it in twain,
And again at the gullet they begin with their knives,
Cleave down the carcass clear to the breach;
Two tender morsels they take from the throat,
Then round the inner ribs they rid off a layer
And carve out the kidney-fat, close to the spine,
Hewing down to the haunch, that all hung together,
And held it up whole, and hacked it free,

And this they named the numbles,[4] that knew such terms
of art.
They divide the crotch in two,
And straightway then they start
To cut the backbone through
And cleave the trunk apart.

With hard strokes they hewed off the head and the neck,
Then swiftly from the sides they severed the chine,
And the corbie's bone[5] they cast on a branch.
Then they pierced the plump sides, impaled either one
With the hock of the hind foot, and hung it aloft,
To each person his portion most proper and fit.
On a hide of a hind the hounds they fed
With the liver and the lights,° the leathery paunches, *lungs*
And bread soaked in blood well blended therewith.
High horns and shrill set hounds a-baying,
Then merrily with their meat they make their way home,
Blowing on their bugles many a brave blast.
Ere dark had descended, that doughty band
Was come within the walls where Gawain waits
at leisure.
Bliss and hearth-fire bright
Await the master's pleasure;
When the two men met that night,
Joy surpassed all measure.

Then the host in the hall his household assembles,
With the dames of high degree and their damsels fair.
In the presence of the people, a party he sends
To convey him his venison in view of the knight.
And in high good-humor he hails him then,
Counts over the kill, the cuts on the tallies,
Holds high the hewn ribs, heavy with fat.
"What think you, sir, of this? Have I thriven well?
Have I won with my woodcraft a worthy prize?"
"In good earnest," said Gawain, "this game is the finest
I have seen in seven years in the season of winter."
"And I give it to you, Gawain," said the goodly host,
"For according to our convenant, you claim it as your own."
"That is so," said Sir Gawain, "the same say I:
What I worthily have won within these fair walls,
Herewith I as willingly award it to you."
He embraces his broad neck with both his arms,
And confers on him a kiss in the comeliest style.
"Have here my profit, it proved no better;
Ungrudging do I grant it, were it greater far."
"Such a gift," said the good host, "I gladly accept—
Yet it might be all the better, would you but say
Where you won this same award, by your wits alone."

4. The other internal organs.
5. A bit of gristle assigned to the ravens ("corbies").

"That was no part of the pact; press me no further,
For you have had what behooves; all other claims
forbear."
With jest and compliment
They conversed, and cast off care;
To the table soon they went;
Fresh dainties wait them there.

And then by the chimney-side they chat at their ease;
The best wine was brought them, and bounteously served;
And after in their jesting they jointly accord
To do on the second day the deeds of the first:
That the two men should trade, betide as it may,
What each had taken in, at eve when they met.
They seal the pact solemnly in sight of the court;
Their cups were filled afresh to confirm the jest;
Then at last they took their leave, for late was the hour,
Each to his own bed hastening away.
Before the barnyard cock had crowed but thrice
The lord had leapt from his rest, his liegemen as well.
Both of mass and their meal they made short work:
By the dim light of dawn they were deep in the woods
away.
With huntsmen and with horns
Over plains they pass that day;
They release, amid the thorns,
Swift hounds that run and bay.

Soon some were on a scent by the side of a marsh;
When the hounds opened cry, the head of the hunt
Rallied them with rough words, raised a great noise.
The hounds that had heard it came hurrying straight
And followed along with their fellows, forty together.
Then such a clamor and cry of coursing hounds
Arose, that the rocks resounded again.
Hunters exhorted them with horn and with voice;
Then all in a body bore off together
Between a mere in the marsh and a menacing crag,
To a rise where the rock stood rugged and steep,
And boulders lay about, that blocked their approach.
Then the company in consort closed on their prey:
They surrounded the rise and the rocks both,
For well they were aware that it waited within,
The beast that the bloodhounds boldly proclaimed.
Then they beat on the bushes and bade him appear,
And he made a murderous rush in the midst of them all;
The best of all boars broke from his cover,
That had ranged long unrivaled, a renegade old,
For of tough-brawned boars he was biggest far,
Most grim when he grunted—then grieved were many,
For three at the first thrust he threw to the earth,
And dashed away at once without more damage.
With "Hi!" "Hi!" and "Hey!" "Hey!" the others followed,

Had horns at their lips, blew high and clear.
Merry was the music of men and of hounds
That were bound after this boar, his bloodthirsty heart
to quell.
Often he stands at bay,
Then scatters the pack pell-mell;
He hurts the hounds, and they
Most dolefully yowl and yell.

Men then with mighty bows moved in to shoot,
Aimed at him with their arrows and often hit,
But the points had no power to pierce through his hide,
And the barbs were brushed aside by his bristly brow;
Though the shank of the shaft shivered in pieces,
The head hopped away, wheresoever it struck.
But when their stubborn strokes had stung him at last,
Then, foaming in his frenzy, fiercely he charges,
Hies at them headlong that hindered his flight,
And many feared for their lives, and fell back a little.
But the lord on a lively horse leads the chase;
As a high-mettled huntsman his horn he blows;
He sounds the assembly and sweeps through the brush,
Pursuing this wild swine till the sunlight slanted.
All day with this deed they drive forth the time
While our lone knight so lovesome lies in his bed,
Sir Gawain safe at home, in silken bower
so gay.
The lady, with guile in heart,
Came early where he lay;
She was at him with all her art
To turn his mind her way.

She comes to the curtain and coyly peeps in;
Gawain thought it good to greet her at once,
And she richly repays him with her ready words,
Settles softly at his side, and suddenly she laughs,
And with a gracious glance, she begins on him thus:
"Sir, if you be Gawain, it seems a great wonder—
A man so well-meaning, and mannerly disposed,
And cannot act in company as courtesy bids,
And if one takes the trouble to teach him, 'tis all in vain.
That lesson learned lately is lightly forgot,
Though I painted it as plain as my poor wit allowed."
"What lesson, dear lady?" he asked all alarmed;
"I have been much to blame, if your story be true."
"Yet my counsel was of kissing," came her answer then,
"Where favor has been found, freely to claim
As accords with the conduct of courteous knights."
"My dear," said the doughty man, "dismiss that thought;
Such freedom, I fear, might offend you much;
It were rude to request if the right were denied."
"But none can deny you," said the noble dame,

"You are stout enough to constrain with strength, if you choose,
Were any so ungracious as to grudge you aught."
"By heaven," said he, "you have answered well,
But threats never throve among those of my land,
Nor any gift not freely given, good though it be.
I am yours to command, to kiss when you please;
You may lay on as you like, and leave off at will."
With this,
The lady lightly bends
And graciously gives him a kiss;
The two converse as friends
Of true love's trials and bliss.

"I should like, by your leave," said the lovely lady,
"If it did not annoy you, to know for what cause
So brisk and so bold a young blood as you,
And acclaimed for all courtesies becoming a knight—
And name what knight you will, they are noblest esteemed
For loyal faith in love, in life as in story;
For to tell the tribulations of these true hearts,
Why, 'tis the very title and text of their deeds,
How bold knights for beauty have braved many a foe,
Suffered heavy sorrows out of secret love,
And then valorously avenged them on villainous churls
And made happy ever after the hearts of their ladies.
And you are the noblest knight known in your time;
No household under heaven but has heard of your fame,
And here by your side I have sat for two days
Yet never has a fair phrase fallen from your lips
Of the language of love, not one little word!
And you, that with sweet vows sway women's hearts,
Should show your winsome ways, and woo a young thing,
And teach by some tokens the craft of true love.
How! are you artless, whom all men praise?
Or do you deem me so dull, or deaf to such words?
Fie! Fie!
In hope of pastimes new
I have come where none can spy;
Instruct me a little, do,
While my husband is not nearby."

"God love you, gracious lady!" said Gawain then;
"It is a pleasure surpassing, and a peerless joy,
That one so worthy as you would willingly come
And take the time and trouble to talk with your knight
And content you with his company—it comforts my heart.
But to take to myself the task of telling of love,
And touch upon its texts, and treat of its themes
To one that, I know well, wields more power
In that art, by a half, than a hundred such
As I am where I live, or am like to become,
It were folly, fair dame, in the first degree!

In all that I am able, my aim is to please,
As in honor behooves me, and am evermore
Your servant heart and soul, so save me our Lord!"
Thus she tested his temper and tried many a time,
Whatever her true intent, to entice him to sin,
But so fair was his defense that no fault appeared,
Nor evil on either hand, but only bliss
they knew.
They linger and laugh awhile;
She kisses the knight so true,
Takes leave in comeliest style
And departs without more ado.

Then he rose from his rest and made ready for mass,
And then a meal was set and served, in sumptuous style;
He dallied at home all day with the dear ladies,
But the lord lingered late at his lusty sport;
Pursued his sorry swine, that swerved as he fled,
And bit asunder the backs of the best of his hounds
When they brought him to bay, till the bowmen appeared
And soon forced him forth, though he fought for dear life,
So sharp were the shafts they shot at him there.
But yet the boldest drew back from his battering head,
Till at last he was so tired he could travel no more,
But in as much haste as he might, he makes his retreat
To a rise on rocky ground, by a rushing stream.
With the bank at his back he scrapes the bare earth,
The froth foams at his jaws, frightful to see.
He whets his white tusks—then weary were all
Those hunters so hardy that hoved round about
Of aiming from afar, but ever they mistrust
his mood.
He had hurt so many by then
That none had hardihood
To be torn by his tusks again,
That was brainsick, and out for blood.

Till the lord came at last on his lofty steed,
Beheld him there at bay before all his folk;
Lightly he leaps down, leaves his courser,
Bares his bright sword, and boldly advances;
Straight into the stream he strides towards his foe.
The wild thing was wary of weapon and man;
His hackles rose high; so hotly he snorts
That many watched with alarm, lest the worst befall.
The boar makes for the man with a mighty bound
So that he and his hunter came headlong together
Where the water ran wildest—the worse for the beast,
For the man, when they first met, marked him with care,
Sights well the slot, slips in the blade,
Shoves it home to the hilt, and the heart shattered,
And he falls in his fury and floats down the water,
ill-sped.

Hounds hasten by the score
To maul him, hide and head;
Men drag him in to shore
And dogs pronounce him dead.

With many a brave blast they boast of their prize,
All hallooed in high glee, that had their wind;
The hounds bayed their best, as the bold men bade
That were charged with chief rank in that chase of renown.
Then one wise in woodcraft, and worthily skilled,
Began to dress the boar in becoming style:
He severs the savage head and sets it aloft,
Then rends the body roughly right down the spine;
Takes the bowels from the belly, broils them on coals,
Blends them well with bread to bestow on the hounds.
Then he breaks out the brawn in fair broad flitches,
And the innards to be eaten in order he takes.
The two sides, attached to each other all whole,
He suspended from a spar that was springy and tough;
And so with this swine they set out for home;
The boar's head was borne before the same man
That had stabbed him in the stream with his strong arm,
right through.
He thought it long indeed
Till he had the knight in view;
At his call, he comes with speed
To claim his payment due.

The lord laughed aloud, with many a light word,
When he greeted Sir Gawain—with good cheer he speaks.
They fetch the fair dames and the folk of the house;
He brings forth the brawn, and begins the tale
Of the great length and girth, the grim rage as well,
Of the battle of the boar they beset in the wood.
The other man meetly commended his deeds
And praised well the prize of his princely sport,
For the brawn of that boar, the bold knight said,
And the sides of that swine surpassed all others.
Then they handled the huge head; he owns it a wonder,
And eyes it with abhorrence, to heighten his praise.
"Now, Gawain," said the good man, "this game becomes yours
By those fair terms we fixed, as you know full well."
"That is true," returned the knight, "and trust me, fair friend,
All my gains, as agreed, I shall give you forthwith."
He clasps him and kisses him in courteous style,
Then serves him with the same fare a second time.
"Now we are even," said he, "at this evening feast,
And clear is every claim incurred here to date,
and debt."
"By Saint Giles!" the host replies,
"You're the best I ever met!
If your profits are all this size,
We'll see you wealthy yet!"

Then attendants set tables on trestles about,
And laid them with linen; light shone forth,
Wakened along the walls in waxen torches.
The service was set and the supper brought;
Royal were the revels that rose then in hall
At that feast by the fire, with many fair sports:
Amid the meal and after, melody sweet,
Carol-dances comely and Christmas songs,
With all the mannerly mirth my tongue may describe.
And ever our gallant knight beside the gay lady;
So uncommonly kind and complaisant was she,
With sweet stolen glances, that stirred his stout heart,
That he was at his wits' end, and wondrous vexed;
But he could not rebuff her, for courtesy forbade,
Yet took pains to please her, though the plan might
go wrong.
When they to heart's delight
Had reveled there in throng,
To his chamber he calls the knight,
And thither they go along.

And there they dallied and drank, and deemed it good sport
To enact their play anew on New Year's Eve,
But Gawain asked again to go on the morrow,
For the time until his tryst was not two days.
The host hindered that, and urged him to stay,
And said, "On my honor, my oath here I take
That you shall get to the Green Chapel to begin your chores
By dawn on New Year's Day, if you so desire.
Wherefore lie at your leisure in your lofty bed,
And I shall hunt hereabouts, and hold to our terms,
And we shall trade winnings when once more we meet,
For I have tested you twice, and true have I found you;
Now think this tomorrow: the third pays for all;
Be we merry while we may, and mindful of joy,
For heaviness of heart can be had for the asking."
This is gravely agreed on and Gawain will stay.
They drink a last draught and with torches depart
to rest.
To bed Sir Gawain went:
His sleep was of the best;
The lord, on his craft intent,
Was early up and dressed.

After mass, with his men, a morsel he takes;
Clear and crisp the morning; he calls for his mount;
The folk that were to follow him afield that day
Were high astride their horses before the hall gates.
Wondrous fair were the fields, for the frost was light;
The sun rises red amid radiant clouds,
Sails into the sky, and sends forth his beams.
They let loose the hounds by a leafy wood;
The rocks all around re-echo to their horns;

Soon some have set off in pursuit of the fox,
Cast about with craft for a clearer scent;
A young dog yaps, and is yelled at in turn;
His fellows fall to sniffing, and follow his lead,
Running in a rabble on the right track,
And he scampers all before; they discover him soon,
And when they see him with sight they pursue him the faster,
Railing at him rudely with a wrathful din.
Often he reverses over rough terrain,
Or loops back to listen in the lee of a hedge;
At last, by a little ditch, he leaps over the brush,
Comes into a clearing at a cautious pace,
Then he thought through his wiles to have thrown off the hounds
Till he was ware, as he went, of a waiting-station
Where three athwart his path threatened him at once,
all gray.
Quick as a flash he wheels
And darts off in dismay;
With hard luck at his heels
He is off to the wood away.

Then it was heaven on earth to hark to the hounds
When they had come on their quarry, coursing together!
Such harsh cries and howls they hurled at his head
As all the cliffs with a crash had come down at once.
Here he was hailed, when huntsmen met him;
Yonder they yelled at him, yapping and snarling;
There they cried "Thief!" and threatened his life,
And ever the harriers at his heels, that he had no rest.
Often he was menaced when he made for the open,
And often rushed in again, for Reynard was wily;
And so he leads them a merry chase, the lord and his men,
In this manner on the mountains, till midday or near,
While our hero lies at home in wholesome sleep
Within the comely curtains on the cold morning.
But the lady, as love would allow her no rest,
And pursuing ever the purpose that pricked her heart,
Was awake with the dawn, and went to his chamber
In a fair flowing mantle that fell to the earth,
All edged and embellished with ermines fine;
No hood on her head, but heavy with gems
Were her fillet and the fret° that confined her tresses; *ornamental net*
Her face and her fair throat freely displayed;
Her bosom all but bare, and her back as well.
She comes in at the chamber-door, and closes it with care,
Throws wide a window—then waits no longer,
But hails him thus airily with her artful words,
with cheer:
"Ah, man, how can you sleep?
The morning is so clear!"
Though dreams have drowned him deep,
He cannot choose but hear.

Deep in his dreams he darkly mutters
As a man may that mourns, with many grim thoughts
Of that day when destiny shall deal him his doom
When he greets his grim host at the Green Chapel
And must bow to his buffet, bating all strife.
But when he sees her at his side he summons his wits,
Breaks from the black dreams, and blithely answers.
That lovely lady comes laughing sweet,
Sinks down at his side, and salutes him with a kiss.
He accords her fair welcome in courtliest style;
He sees her so glorious, so gaily attired,
So faultless her features, so fair and so bright,
His heart swelled swiftly with surging joys.
They melt into mirth with many a fond smile,
Nor was fair language lacking, to further that hour's
delight.
Good were their words of greeting;
Each joyed in other's sight;
Great peril attends that meeting
Should Mary forget her knight.

For that high-born beauty so hemmed him about,
Made so plain her meaning, the man must needs
Either take her tendered love or distastefully refuse.
His courtesy concerned him, lest crass he appear,
But more his soul's mischief, should he commit sin
And belie his loyal oath to the lord of that house.
"God forbid!" said the bold knight. "That shall not befall!"
With a little fond laughter he lightly let pass
All the words of special weight that were sped his way;
"I find you much at fault," the fair one said,
"Who can be cold toward a creature so close by your side,
Of all women in this world most wounded in heart,
Unless you have a sweetheart, one you hold dearer,
And allegiance to that lady so loyally knit
That you will never love another, as now I believe.
And, sir, if it be so, then say it, I beg you;
By all your heart holds dear, hide it no longer
with guile."
"Lady, by Saint John,"
He answers with a smile,
"Lover have I none,
Nor will have, yet awhile."

"Those words," said the woman, "are the worst of all,
But I have had my answer, and hard do I find it!
Kiss me now kindly: I can but go hence
To lament my life long like a maid lovelorn."
She inclines her head quickly and kisses the knight,
Then straightens with a sigh, and says as she stands,
"Now, dear, ere I depart, do me this pleasure:
Give me some little gift, your glove or the like,
That I may think on you, man, and mourn the less."

"Now by heavens," said he, "I wish I had here
My most precious possession, to put it in your hands,
For your deeds, beyond doubt, have often deserved
A repayment far passing my power to bestow.
But a love-token, lady, were of little avail;
It is not to your honor to have at this time
A glove as a guerdon from Gawain's hand,
And I am here on an errand in unknown realms
And have no bearers with baggage with becoming gifts,
Which distresses me, madame, for your dear sake.
A man must keep within his compass: account it neither grief
nor slight."
"Nay, noblest knight alive,"
Said that beauty of body white,
"Though you be loath to give,
Yet you shall take, by right."

She reached out a rich ring, wrought all of gold,
With a splendid stone displayed on the band
That flashed before his eyes like a fiery sun;
It was worth a king's wealth, you may well believe.
But he waved it away with these ready words:
"Before God, good lady, I forgo all gifts;
None have I to offer, nor any will I take."
And she urged it on him eagerly, and ever he refused,
And vowed in very earnest, prevail she would not.
And she sad to find it so, and said to him then,
"If my ring is refused for its rich cost—
You would not be my debtor for so dear a thing—
I shall give you my girdle; you gain less thereby."
She released a knot lightly, and loosened a belt
That was caught about her kirtle, the bright cloak beneath,
Of a gay green silk, with gold overwrought,
And the borders all bound with embroidery fine,
And this she presses upon him, and pleads with a smile,
Unworthy though it were, that it would not be scorned.
But the man still maintains that he means to accept
Neither gold nor any gift, till by God's grace
The fate that lay before him was fully achieved.
"And be not offended, fair lady, I beg,
And give over your offer, for ever I must
decline.
I am grateful for favor shown
Past all deserts of mine,
And ever shall be your own
True servant, rain or shine."

"Now does my present displease you," she promptly inquired,
"Because it seems in your sight so simple a thing?
And belike, as it is little, it is less to praise,
But if the virtue that invests it were verily known,
It would be held, I hope, in higher esteem.
For the man that possesses this piece of silk,

If he bore it on his body, belted about,
There is no hand under heaven that could hew him down,
For he could not be killed by any craft on earth."
Then the man began to muse, and mainly he thought
It was a pearl for his plight, the peril to come
When he gains the Green Chapel to get his reward:
Could he escape unscathed, the scheme were noble!
Then he bore with her words and withstood them no more,
And she repeated her petition and pleaded anew,
And he granted it, and gladly she gave him the belt,
And besought him for her sake to conceal it well,
Lest the noble lord should know—and, the knight agrees
That not a soul save themselves shall see it thenceforth
with sight.
He thanked her with fervent heart,
As often as ever he might;
Three times, before they part,
She has kissed the stalwart knight.

Then the lady took her leave, and left him there,
For more mirth with that man she might not have.
When she was gone, Sir Gawain got from his bed,
Arose and arrayed him in his rich attire;
Tucked away the token the temptress had left,
Laid it reliably where he looked for it after.
And then with good cheer to the chapel he goes,
Approached a priest in private, and prayed to be taught
To lead a better life and lift up his mind,
Lest he be among the lost when he must leave this world.
And shamefaced at shrift he showed his misdeeds
From the largest to the least, and asked the Lord's mercy,
And called on his confessor to cleanse his soul,
And he absolved him of his sins as safe and as clean
As if the dread Day of Doom were to dawn on the morrow.
And then he made merry amid the fine ladies
With deft-footed dances and dalliance light,
As never until now, while the afternoon wore
away.
He delighted all around him,
And all agreed, that day,
They never before had found him
So gracious and so gay.

Now peaceful be his pasture, and love play him fair!
The host is on horseback, hunting afield;
He has finished off this fox that he followed so long:
As he leapt a low hedge to look for the villain
Where he heard all the hounds in hot pursuit,
Reynard comes racing out of a rough thicket,
And all the rabble in a rush, right at his heels.
The man beholds the beast, and bides his time,
And bares his bright sword, and brings it down hard,
And he blenches from the blade, and backward he starts;

A hound hurries up and hinders that move,
And before the horse's feet they fell on him at once
And ripped the rascal's throat with a wrathful din.
The lord soon alighted and lifted him free,
Swiftly snatched him up from the snapping jaws,
Holds him over his head, halloos with a will,
And the dogs bayed the dirge, that had done him to death.
Hunters hastened thither with horns at their lips,
Sounding the assembly till they saw him at last.
When that comely company was come in together,
All that bore bugles blew them at once,
And the others all hallooed, that had no horns.
It was the merriest medley that ever a man heard,
The racket that they raised for Sir Reynard's soul
that died.
Their hounds they praised and fed,
Fondling their heads with pride,
And they took Reynard the Red
And stripped away his hide.

And then they headed homeward, for evening had come,
Blowing many a blast on their bugles bright.
The lord at long last alights at his house,
Finds fire on the hearth where the fair knight waits,
Sir Gawain the good, that was glad in heart.
With the ladies, that loved him, he lingered at ease;
He wore a rich robe of blue, that reached to the earth
And a surcoat lined softly with sumptuous furs;
A hood of the same hue hung on his shoulders;
With bands of bright ermine embellished were both.
He comes to meet the man amid all the folk,
And greets him good-humoredly, and gaily he says,
"I shall follow forthwith the form of our pledge
That we framed to good effect amid fresh-filled cups."
He clasps him accordingly and kisses him thrice,
As amiably and as earnestly as ever he could.
"By heaven," said the host, "you have had some luck
Since you took up this trade, if the terms were good."
"Never trouble about the terms," he returned at once,
"Since all that I owe here is openly paid."
"Marry!" said the other man, "mine is much less,
For I have hunted all day, and nought have I got
But this foul fox pelt, the fiend take the goods!
Which but poorly repays such precious things
That you have cordially conferred, such kisses three
so good."
"Enough!" said Sir Gawain;
"I thank you, by the rood!"
And how the fox was slain
He told him, as they stood.

With minstrelsy and mirth, with all manner of meats,
They made as much merriment as any men might

(Amid laughing of ladies and light hearted girls;
So gay grew Sir Gawain and the goodly host)
Unless they had been besotted, or brainless fools.
The knight joined in jesting with that joyous folk,
Until at last it was late; ere long they must part,
And be off to their beds, as behooved them each one.
Then politely his leave of the lord of the house
Our noble knight takes, and renews his thanks:
"The courtesies countless accorded me here,
Your kindness at this Christmas, may heaven's King repay!
Henceforth, if you will have me, I hold you my liege,
And so, as I have said, I must set forth tomorrow,
If I may take some trusty man to teach, as you promised,
The way to the Green Chapel, that as God allows
I shall see my fate fulfilled on the first of the year."
"In good faith," said the good man, "with a good will
Every promise on my part shall be fully performed."
He assigns him a servant to set him on the path,
To see him safe and sound over the snowy hills,
To follow the fastest way through forest green
and grove.
Gawain thanks him again,
So kind his favors prove,
And of the ladies then
He takes his leave, with love.

Courteously he kissed them, with care in his heart,
And often wished them well, with warmest thanks,
Which they for their part were prompt to repay.
They commend him to Christ with disconsolate sighs;
And then in that hall with the household he parts—
Each man that he met, he remembered to thank
For his deeds of devotion and diligent pains,
And the trouble he had taken to tend to his needs;
And each one as woeful, that watched him depart,
As he had lived with him loyally all his life long.
By lads bearing lights he was led to his chamber
And blithely brought to his bed, to be at his rest.
How soundly he slept, I presume not to say,
For there were matters of moment his thoughts might well
pursue.
Let him lie and wait;
He has little more to do,
Then listen, while I relate
How they kept their rendezvous.

Part 4

Now the New Year draws near, and the night passes,
The day dispels the dark, by the Lord's decree;
But wild weather awoke in the world without:
The clouds in the cold sky cast down their snow
With great gusts from the north, grievous to bear.

Sleet showered aslant upon shivering beasts;
The wind warbled wild as it whipped from aloft,
And drove the drifts deep in the dales below.
Long and well he listens, that lies in his bed;
Though he lifts not his eyelids, little he sleeps;
Each crow of the cock he counts without fail.
Readily from his rest he rose before dawn,
For a lamp had been left him, that lighted his chamber.
He called to his chamberlain, who quickly appeared,
And bade him get him his gear, and gird his good steed,
And he sets about briskly to bring in his arms,
And makes ready his master in manner most fit.
First he clad him in his clothes, to keep out the cold,
And then his other harness, made handsome anew,
His plate-armor of proof, polished with pains,
The rings of his rich mail rid of their rust,
And all was fresh as at first, and for this he gave thanks
indeed.
With pride he wears each piece,
New-furbished for his need:
No gayer from here to Greece;
He bids them bring his steed.

In his richest raiment he robed himself then:
His crested coat-armor, close-stitched with craft,
With stones of strange virtue on silk velvet set;
All bound with embroidery on borders and seams
And lined warmly and well with furs of the best.
Yet he left not his love-gift, the lady's girdle;
Gawain, for his own good, forgot not that:
When the bright sword was belted and bound on his haunches,
Then twice with that token he twined him about.
Sweetly did he swathe him in that swatch of silk,
That girdle of green so goodly to see,
That against the gay red showed gorgeous bright.
Yet he wore not for its wealth that wondrous girdle,
Nor pride in its pendants, though polished they were,
Though glittering gold gleamed at the end,
But to keep himself safe when consent he must
To endure a deadly dint, and all defense
denied.
And now the bold knight came
Into the courtyard wide;
That folk of worthy fame
He thanks on every side.

Then was Gringolet girt, that was great and huge,
And had sojourned safe and sound, and savored his fare;
He pawed the earth in his pride, that princely steed.
The good knight draws near him and notes well his look,
And says sagely to himself, and soberly swears,
"Here is a household in hall that upholds the right!
The man that maintains it, may happiness be his!

Likewise the dear lady, may love betide her!
If thus they in charity cherish a guest
That are honored here on earth, may they have his reward
That reigns high in heaven—and also you all;
And might I live in this land but a little while,
I should willingly reward you, and well, if I might."
Then he steps into the stirrup and bestrides his mount;
His shield is shown forth; on his shoulder he casts it;
Strikes the side of his steed with his steel spurs,
And he starts across the stones, nor stands any longer
to prance.
On horseback was the swain
That bore his spear and lance;
"May Christ this house maintain
And guard it from mischance!"

The bridge was brought down, and the road gates
Unbarred and carried back upon both sides;
He commended him to Christ, and crossed over the planks;
Praised the noble porter, who prayed on his knees
That God save Sir Gawain, and bade him good day,
And went on his way alone with the man
That was to lead him ere long to that luckless place
Where the dolorous dint must be dealt him at last.
Under bare boughs they ride, where steep banks rise,
Over high cliffs they climb, where cold snow clings;
The heavens held aloof, but heavy thereunder
Mist mantled the moors, moved on the slopes.
Each hill had a hat, a huge cape of cloud;
Brooks bubbled and broke over broken rocks,
Flashing in freshets that waterfalls fed.
Roundabout was the road that ran through the wood
Till the sun at that season was soon to rise,
that day.
They were on a hilltop high;
The white snow round them lay;
The man that rode nearby
Now bade his master stay.

"For I have seen you here safe at the set time,
And now you are not far from that notable place
That you have sought for so long with such special pains.
But this I say for certain, since I know you, sir knight,
And have your good at heart, and hold you dear—
Would you heed well my words, it were worth your while—
You are rushing into risks that you reck not of:
There is a villain in yon valley, the veriest on earth,
For he is rugged and rude, and ready with his fists,
And most immense in his mold of mortals alive,
And his body bigger than the best four
That are in Arthur's house, Hector[6] or any.

6. Either the Trojan hero or one of Arthur's knights.

He gets his grim way at the Green Chapel;
None passes by that place so proud in his arms
That he does not dash him down with his deadly blows,
For he is heartless wholly, and heedless of right,
For be it chaplain or churl that by the Chapel rides,
Monk or mass-priest or any man else,
He would as soon strike him dead as stand on two feet.
Wherefore I say, just as certain as you sit there astride,
You cannot but be killed, if his counsel holds,
For he would trounce you in a trice, had you twenty lives
for sale.
He has lived long in this land
And dealt out deadly bale;
Against his heavy hand
Your power cannot prevail.

"And so, good Sir Gawain, let the grim man be;
Go off by some other road, in God's own name!
Leave by some other land, for the love of Christ,
And I shall get me home again, and give you my word
That I shall swear by God's self and the saints above,
By heaven and by my halidom[7] and other oaths more,
To conceal this day's deed, nor say to a soul
That ever you fled for fear from any that I knew."
"Many thanks!" said the other man—and demurring he speaks—
"Fair fortune befall you for your friendly words!
And conceal this day's deed I doubt not you would,
But though you never told the tale, if I turned back now,
Forsook this place for fear, and fled, as you say,
I were a caitiff coward; I could not be excused.
But I must to the Chapel to chance my luck
And say to that same man such words as I please,
Befall what may befall through Fortune's will
or whim.
Though he be a quarrelsome knave
With a cudgel great and grim,
The Lord is strong to save:
His servants trust in him."

"Marry," said the man, "since you tell me so much,
And I see you are set to seek your own harm,
If you crave a quick death, let me keep you no longer!
Put your helm on your head, your hand on your lance,
And ride the narrow road down yon rocky slope
Till it brings you to the bottom of the broad valley.
Then look a little ahead, on your left hand,
And you will soon see before you that self-same Chapel,
And the man of great might that is master there.
Now goodbye in God's name, Gawain the noble!
For all the world's wealth I would not stay here,

7. Holiness or, more likely, patron saints.

Or go with you in this wood one footstep further!"
He tarried no more to talk, but turned his bridle,
Hit his horse with his heels as hard as he might,
Leaves the knight alone, and off like the wind
goes leaping.
"By God," said Gawain then,
"I shall not give way to weeping;
God's will be done, amen!
I commend me to his keeping."

He puts his heels to his horse, and picks up the path;
Goes in beside a grove where the ground is steep,
Rides down the rough slope right to the valley;
And then he looked a little about him—the landscape was wild,
And not a soul to be seen, nor sign of a dwelling,
But high banks on either hand hemmed it about,
With many a ragged rock and rough-hewn crag;
The skies seemed scored by the scowling peaks.
Then he halted his horse, and hoved there a space,
And sought on every side for a sight of the Chapel,
But no such place appeared, which puzzled him sore,
Yet he saw some way off what seemed like a mound,
A hillock high and broad, hard by the water,
Where the stream fell in foam down the face of the steep
And bubbled as if it boiled on its bed below.
The knight urges his horse, and heads for the knoll;
Leaps lightly to earth; loops well the rein
Of his steed to a stout branch, and stations him there.
He strides straight to the mound, and strolls all about,
Much wondering what it was, but no whit the wiser;
It had a hole at one end, and on either side,
And was covered with coarse grass in clumps all without,
And hollow all within, like some old cave,
Or a crevice of an old crag—he could not discern
aright.
"Can this be the Chapel Green?
Alack!" said the man, "here might
The devil himself be seen
Saying matins at black midnight!"

"Now by heaven," said he, "it is bleak hereabouts;
This prayer-house is hideous, half-covered with grass!
Well may the grim man mantled in green
Hold here his orisons, in hell's own style!
Now I feel it is the Fiend, in my five wits,
That has tempted me to this tryst, to take my life;
This is a Chapel of mischance, may the mischief take it!
As accursed a country church as I came upon ever!"
With his helm on his head, his lance in his hand,
He stalks toward the steep wall of that strange house.
Then he heard, on the hill, behind a hard rock,
Beyond the brook, from the bank, a most barbarous din:
Lord! it clattered in the cliff fit to cleave it in two,

As one upon a grindstone ground a great scythe!
Lord! it whirred like a mill-wheel whirling about!
Lord! it echoed loud and long, lamentable to hear!
Then "By heaven," said the bold knight, "that business up there
Is arranged for my arrival, or else I am much
misled.
Let God work! Ah me!
All hope of help has fled!
Forfeit my life may be
But noise I do not dread."

Then he listened no longer, but loudly he called,
"Who has power in this place, high parley to hold?
For none greets Sir Gawain, or gives him good day;
If any would a word with him, let him walk forth
And speak now or never, to speed his affairs."
"Abide," said one on the bank above over his head,
"And what I promised you once shall straightway be given."
Yet he stayed not his grindstone, nor stinted its noise,
But worked awhile at his whetting before he would rest,
And then he comes around a crag, from a cave in the rocks,
Hurtling out of hiding with a hateful weapon,
A Danish° ax devised for that day's deed, *i.e., long-bladed*
With a broad blade and bright, bent in a curve,
Filed to a fine edge—four feet it measured
By the length of the lace that was looped round the haft.
And in form as at first, the fellow all green,
His lordly face and his legs, his locks and his beard,
Save that firm upon two feet forward he strides,
Sets a hand on the ax-head, the haft to the earth;
When he came to the cold stream, and cared not to wade,
He vaults over on his ax, and advances amain
On a broad bank of snow, overbearing and brisk
of mood.
Little did the knight incline
When face to face they stood;
Said the other man, "Friend mine,
It seems your word holds good!"

"God love you, Sir Gawain!" said the Green Knight then,
"And well met this morning, man, at my place!
And you have followed me faithfully and found me betimes,
And on the business between us we both are agreed:
Twelve months ago today you took what was yours,
And you at this New Year must yield me the same.
And we have met in these mountains, remote from all eyes:
There is none here to halt us or hinder our sport;
Unhasp your high helm, and have here your wages;
Make no more demur than I did myself
When you hacked off my head with one hard blow."
"No, by God," said Sir Gawain, "that granted me life,
I shall grudge not the guerdon, grim though it prove;
Bestow but one stroke, and I shall stand still,

And you may lay on as you like till the last of my part
be paid."
He proffered, with good grace,
His bare neck to the blade,
And feigned a cheerful face:
He scorned to seem afraid.

Then the grim man in green gathers his strength,
Heaves high the heavy ax to hit him the blow.
With all the force in his frame he fetches it aloft,
With a grimace as grim as he would grind him to bits;
Had the blow he bestowed been as big as he threatened,
A good knight and gallant had gone to his grave.
But Gawain at the great ax glanced up aside
As down it descended with death-dealing force,
And his shoulders shrank a little from the sharp iron.
Abruptly the brawny man breaks off the stroke,
And then reproved with proud words that prince among knights.
"You are not Gawain the glorious," the green man said,
"That never fell back on field in the face of the foe,
And now you flee for fear, and have felt no harm:
Such news of that knight I never heard yet!
I moved not a muscle when you made to strike,
Nor caviled at the cut in King Arthur's house;
My head fell to my feet, yet steadfast I stood,
And you, all unharmed, are wholly dismayed—
Wherefore the better man I, by all odds,
must be."
Said Gawain, "Strike once more;
I shall neither flinch nor flee;
But if my head falls to the floor
There is no mending me!"

"But go on, man, in God's name, and get to the point!
Deliver me my destiny, and do it out of hand,
For I shall stand to the stroke and stir not an inch
Till your ax has hit home—on my honor I swear it!"
"Have at thee then!" said the other, and heaves it aloft,
And glares down as grimly as he had gone mad.
He made a mighty feint, but marred not his hide;
Withdrew the ax adroitly before it did damage.
Gawain gave no ground, nor glanced up aside,
But stood still as a stone, or else a stout stump
That is held in hard earth by a hundred roots.
Then merrily does he mock him, the man all in green:
"So now you have your nerve again, I needs must strike;
Uphold the high knighthood that Arthur bestowed,
And keep your neck-bone clear, if this cut allows!"
Then was Gawain gripped with rage, and grimly he said,
"Why, thrash away, tyrant, I tire of your threats;
You make such a scene, you must frighten yourself."
Said the green fellow, "In faith, so fiercely you speak
That I shall finish this affair, nor further grace

allow."
He stands prepared to strike
And scowls with both lip and brow;
No marvel if the man mislike
Who can hope no rescue now.

He gathered up the grim ax and guided it well:
Let the barb at the blade's end brush the bare throat;
He hammered down hard, yet harmed him no whit
Save a scratch on one side, that severed the skin;
The end of the hooked edge entered the flesh,
And a little blood lightly leapt to the earth.
And when the man beheld his own blood bright on the snow,
He sprang a spear's length with feet spread wide,
Seized his high helm, and set it on his head,
Shoved before his shoulders the shield at his back,
Bares his trusty blade, and boldly he speaks—
Not since he was a babe born of his mother
Was he once in this world one-half so blithe—
"Have done with your hacking—harry me no more!
I have borne, as behooved, one blow in this place;
If you make another move I shall meet it midway
And promptly, I promise you, pay back each blow
with brand.
One stroke acquits me here;
So did our covenant stand
In Arthur's court last year—
Wherefore, sir, hold your hand!"

He lowers the long ax and leans on it there,
Sets his arms on the head, the haft on the earth,
And beholds the bold knight that bides there afoot,
How he faces him fearless, fierce in full arms,
And plies him with proud words—it pleases him well.
Then once again gaily to Gawain he calls,
And in a loud voice and lusty, delivers these words:
"Bold fellow, on this field your anger forbear!
No man has made demands here in manner uncouth,
Nor done, save as duly determined at court.
I owed you a hit and you have it; be happy therewith!
The rest of my rights here I freely resign.
Had I been a bit busier, a buffet, perhaps,
I could have dealt more directly, and done you some harm.
First I flourished with a feint, in frolicsome mood,
And left your hide unhurt—and here I did well
By the fair terms we fixed on the first night;
And fully and faithfully you followed accord:
Gave over all your gains as a good man should.
A second feint, sir, I assigned for the morning
You kissed my comely wife—each kiss you restored.
For both of these there behooved two feigned blows
by right.
True men pay what they owe;

No danger then in sight.
You failed at the third throw,
So take my tap, sir knight.

"For that is my belt about you, that same braided girdle,
My wife it was that wore it; I know well the tale,
And the count of your kisses and your conduct too,
And the wooing of my wife—it was all my scheme!
She made trial of a man most faultless by far
Of all that ever walked over the wide earth;
As pearls to white peas, more precious and prized,
So is Gawain, in good faith, to other gay knights.
Yet you lacked, sir, a little in loyalty there,
But the cause was not cunning, nor courtship either,
But that you loved your own life; the less, then, to blame."
The other stout knight in a study stood a long while,
So gripped with grim rage that his great heart shook.
All the blood of his body burned in his face
As he shrank back in shame from the man's sharp speech.
The first words that fell from the fair knight's lips:
"Accursed be a cowardly and covetous heart!
In you is villainy and vice, and virtue laid low!"
Then he grasps the green girdle and lets go the knot,
Hands it over in haste, and hotly he says:
"Behold there my falsehood, ill hap betide it!
Your cut taught me cowardice, care for my life,
And coveting came after, contrary both
To largesse and loyalty belonging to knights.
Now am I faulty and false, that fearful was ever
Of disloyalty and lies, bad luck to them both!
and greed.
I confess, knight, in this place,
Most dire is my misdeed;
Let me gain back your good grace,
And thereafter I shall take heed."

Then the other laughed aloud, and lightly he said,
"Such harm as I have had, I hold it quite healed.
You are so fully confessed, your failings made known,
And bear the plain penance of the point of my blade,
I hold you polished as a pearl, as pure and as bright
As you had lived free of fault since first you were born.
And I give you, sir, this girdle that is gold-hemmed
And green as my garments, that, Gawain, you may
Be mindful of this meeting when you mingle in throng
With nobles of renown—and known by this token
How it chanced at the Green Chapel, to chivalrous knights.
And you shall in this New Year come yet again
And we shall finish out our feast in my fair hall,
with cheer."
He urged the knight to stay,
And said, "With my wife so dear

We shall see you friends this day,
Whose enmity touched you near."

"Indeed," said the doughty knight, and doffed his high helm,
And held it in his hands as he offered his thanks,
"I have lingered long enough—may good luck be yours,
And he reward you well that all worship bestows!
And commend me to that comely one, your courteous wife,
Both herself and that other, my honoured ladies,
That have trapped their true knight in their trammels so quaint.
But if a dullard should dote, deem it no wonder,
And through the wiles of a woman be wooed into sorrow,
For so was Adam by one, when the world began,
And Solomon by many more, and Samson the mighty—
Delilah was his doom, and David thereafter
Was beguiled by Bathsheba, and bore much distress;
Now these were vexed by their devices—'twere a very joy
Could one but learn to love, and believe them not.
For these were proud princes, most prosperous of old,
Past all lovers lucky, that languished under heaven,
bemused.
And one and all fell prey
To women that they had used;
If I be led astray,
Methinks I may be excused.

"But your girdle, God love you! I gladly shall take
And be pleased to possess, not for the pure gold,
Nor the bright belt itself, nor the beauteous pendants,
Nor for wealth, nor worldly state, nor workmanship fine,
But a sign of excess it shall seem oftentimes
When I ride in renown, and remember with shame
The faults and the frailty of the flesh perverse,
How its tenderness entices the foul taint of sin;
And so when praise and high prowess have pleased my heart,
A look at this love-lace will lower my pride.
But one thing would I learn, if you were not loath,
Since you are lord of yonder land where I have long sojourned
With honor in your house—may you have His reward
That upholds all the heavens, highest on throne!
How runs your right name?—and let the rest go."
"That shall I give you gladly," said the Green Knight then;
"Bertilak de Hautdesert, this barony I hold.
Through the might of Morgan le Faye,[8] that lodges at my house,
By subtleties of science and sorcerers' arts,
The mistress of Merlin,[9] she has caught many a man,
For sweet love in secret she shared sometime
With that wizard, that knows well each one of your knights
and you.

8. Arthur's half-sister, an enchantress who sometimes abetted him, sometimes made trouble for him.

9. The wise magician who had helped Arthur become king.

Morgan the Goddess, she,
So styled by title true;
None holds so high degree
That her arts cannot subdue.

"She guided me in this guise to your glorious hall,
To assay, if such it were, the surfeit of pride
That is rumored of the retinue of the Round Table.
She put this shape upon me to puzzle your wits,
To afflict the fair queen, and frighten her to death
With awe of that elvish man that eerily spoke
With his head in his hand before the high table.
She was with my wife at home, that old withered lady,
Your own aunt[1] is she, Arthur's half-sister,
The Duchess' daughter of Tintagel, that dear King Uther
Got Arthur on after, that honored is now.
And therefore, good friend, come feast with your aunt;
Make merry in my house; my men hold you dear,
And I wish you as well, sir, with all my heart,
As any man God ever made, for your great good faith."
But the knight said him nay, that he might by no means.
They clasped then and kissed, and commended each other
To the Prince of Paradise, and parted with one
assent.
Gawain sets out anew;
Toward the court his course is bent;
And the knight all green in hue,
Wheresoever he wished, he went.

Wild ways in the world our worthy knight rides
On Gringolet, that by grace had been granted his life.
He harbored often in houses, and often abroad,
And with many valiant adventures verily he met
That I shall not take time to tell in this story.
The hurt was whole that he had had in his neck,
And the bright green belt on his body he bore,
Oblique, like a baldric, bound at his side,
Below his left shoulder, laced in a knot,
In betokening of the blame he had borne for his fault;
And so to court in due course he comes safe and sound.
Bliss abounded in hall when the high-born heard
That good Gawain was come; glad tidings they thought it.
The king kisses the knight, and the queen as well,
And many a comrade came to clasp him in arms,
And eagerly they asked, and awesomely he told,
Confessed all his cares and discomfitures many,
How it chanced at the Chapel, what cheer made the knight,
The love of the lady, the green lace at last.
The nick on his neck he naked displayed
That he got in his disgrace at the Green Knight's hands,

1. Morgan was the daughter of Igraine, duchess of Tintagel, and her husband the duke; Igraine conceived Arthur when his father, Uther, lay with her through one of Merlin's trickeries.

alone.
With rage in heart he speaks,
And grieves with many a groan;
The blood burns in his cheeks
For shame at what must be shown.

"Behold, sir," said he, and handles the belt,
"This is the blazon of the blemish that I bear on my neck;
This is the sign of sore loss that I have suffered there
For the cowardice and coveting that I came to there;
This is the badge of false faith that I was found in there,
And I must bear it on my body till I breathe my last.
For one may keep a deed dark, but undo it no whit,
For where a fault is made fast, it is fixed evermore."
The king comforts the knight, and the court all together
Agree with gay laughter and gracious intent
That the lords and the ladies belonging to the Table,
Each brother of that band, a baldric should have,
A belt borne oblique, of a bright green,
To be worn with one accord for that worthy's sake.
So that was taken as a token by the Table Round,
And he honored that had it, evermore after,
As the best book of knighthood bids it be known.
In the old days of Arthur this happening befell;
The books of Brutus' deeds bear witness thereto
Since Brutus, the bold knight, embarked for this land
After the siege ceased at Troy and the city fared
amiss.
Many such, ere we were born,
Have befallen here, ere this.
May He that was crowned with thorn
Bring all men to His bliss! Amen.

Honi Soit Qui Mal Pense[2]

2. "Shame be to the man who has evil in his mind." This is the motto of the Order of the Garter, founded ca. 1350: apparently a copyist of the poem associated this order with the one founded to honor Gawain.

GEOFFREY CHAUCER
ca. 1343–1400

Medieval social theory held that society was made up of three "estates": the nobility, composed of a small hereditary aristocracy, whose mission on earth was to rule over and defend the body politic; the church, whose duty was to look after the spiritual welfare of that body; and everyone else, the large mass of commoners who were supposed to do the work that provided for its physical needs. By the late fourteenth century, however, these basic categories were layered into complex, interrelated, and unstable social strata among which birth, wealth, profession, and personal ability all played a part in determining one's status in a world that was rapidly changing economically, politically, and socially. Chaucer's life and his works, especially *The Canterbury Tales,* were profoundly influenced by these forces. A growing and prosperous middle class was beginning to play increasingly important roles in church and state, blurring the traditional class boundaries, and it was into this middle class that Chaucer was born.

Chaucer was the son of a prosperous wine merchant and probably spent his boyhood in the mercantile atmosphere of London's Vintry, where ships docked with wines from France and Spain. Here he would have mixed daily with people of all sorts, heard several languages spoken, become fluent in French, and received schooling in Latin. Instead of apprenticing Chaucer to the family business, however, his father was apparently able to place him, in his early teens, as a page in one of the great aristocratic households of England, that of the countess of Ulster who was married to Prince Lionel, the second son of Edward III. There Chaucer would have acquired the manners and skills required for a career in the service of the ruling class, not only in the role of personal attendant in royal households but in a series of administrative posts. (For Chaucer's portrait, see the color insert in this volume.)

We can trace Chaucer's official and personal life in a considerable number of surviving historical documents, beginning with a reference, in Elizabeth of Ulster's household accounts, to an outfit he received as a page (1357). He was captured by the French and ransomed in one of Edward III's campaigns during the Hundred Years War (1359). He was a member of King Edward's personal household (1367) and took part in several diplomatic missions to Spain (1366), France (1368), and Italy (1372). As controller of customs on wool, sheepskins, and leather for the port of London (1374–85), Chaucer audited and kept books on the export taxes, which were one of the Crown's main sources of revenue. During this period he was living in a rent-free apartment over one of the gates in the city wall, probably as a perquisite of the customs job. He served as a justice of the peace and knight of the shire (the title given to members of Parliament) for the county of Kent (1385–86) where he moved after giving up the controllership. As clerk of the king's works (1389–91), Chaucer was responsible for the maintenance of numerous royal residences, parks, and other holdings; his duties included supervision of the construction of the nave of Westminster Abbey and of stands and lists for a celebrated tournament staged by Richard II. While the records show Chaucer receiving many grants and annuities in addition to his salary for these services, they also show that at times he was being pressed by creditors and obliged to borrow money.

These activities brought Chaucer into association with the ruling nobility of the kingdom, with Prince Lionel and his younger brother John of Gaunt, duke of Lancaster, England's most powerful baron during much of Chaucer's lifetime; with their father, King Edward; and with Edward's grandson, who succeeded to the throne as Richard II. Near the end of his life Chaucer addressed a comic *Complaint to His Purse* to Henry IV—John of Gaunt's son, who had usurped the crown from his cousin Richard—as a reminder that the treasury owed Chaucer his annuity. Chaucer's wife, Philippa, served in the households of Edward's queen and of John of Gaunt's second wife, Constance, daughter of the king of Castile. A Thomas Chaucer, who was probably Chaucer's son, was an eminent man in the next generation, and Thomas's daughter Alice was married successively to the earl of Salisbury and the duke of Suffolk. The gap between the commoners and the aristocracy would thus have been bridged by Chaucer's family in the course of three generations.

None of these documents contains any hint that this hardworking civil servant wrote poetry, although poetry would certainly have been among the diversions cultivated at English courts in Chaucer's youth. That poetry, however, would have been in French, which still remained the fashionable language and literature of the English aristocracy, whose culture in many ways had more in common with that of the French nobles with whom they warred than with that of their English subjects. Chaucer's earliest models, works by Guillaume de Machaut (1300?–1377) and Jean Froissart

(1333?–1400?), the leading French poets of the day, were lyrics and narratives about courtly love, often cast in the form of a dream in which the poet acted as a protagonist or participant in some aristocratic love affair. The poetry of Machaut and Froissart derives from the thirteenth-century *Romance of the Rose,* a long dream allegory in which the dreamer suffers many agonies and trials for the love of a symbolic rosebud. Chaucer's apprentice work may well have been a partial translation of the twenty-one-thousand-line *Romance.* His first important original poem is *The Book of the Duchess,* an elegy in the form of a dream vision commemorating John of Gaunt's first wife, the young duchess of Lancaster, who died in 1368.

The diplomatic mission that sent Chaucer to Italy in 1372 was in all likelihood a milestone in his literary development. Although he may have acquired some knowledge of the language and literature from Italian merchants and bankers posted in London, this visit and a subsequent one to Florence (1378) brought him into direct contact with the Italian Renaissance. Probably he acquired manuscripts of works by Dante, Petrarch, and Boccaccio—the last two still alive at the time of Chaucer's visit, although he probably did not meet them. These writers provided him with models of new verse forms, new subject matter, and new modes of representation. *The House of Fame,* still a dream vision, takes the poet on a journey in the talons of a gigantic eagle to the celestial palace of the goddess Fame, a trip that at many points affectionately parodies Dante's journey in the *Divine Comedy.* In his dream vision *The Parliament of Fowls,* all the birds meet on St. Valentine's Day to choose their mates; their "parliament" humorously depicts the ways in which different classes in human society think and talk about love. Boccaccio provided sources for two of Chaucer's finest poems—although Chaucer never mentions his name. *The Knight's Tale,* the first of *The Canterbury Tales,* is based on Boccaccio's romance *Il Teseida* (The Story of Theseus). His longest completed poem, *Troilus and Criseyde* (ca. 1385), which tells the story of how Trojan Prince Troilus loved and finally lost Criseyde to the Greek warrior Diomede, is an adaptation of Boccaccio's *Il Filostrato* (The Love-Stricken). Chaucer reworked the latter into one of the greatest love poems in any language. Even if he had never written *The Canterbury Tales, Troilus* would have secured Chaucer a place among the major English poets.

A final dream vision provides the frame for Chaucer's first experiment with a series of tales, the unfinished *Legend of Good Women.* In the dream, Chaucer is accused of heresy and antifeminism by Cupid, the god of love himself, and ordered to do penance by writing a series of "legends," i.e., saints' lives, of Cupid's martyrs, women who were betrayed by false men and died for love. Perhaps a noble patron, possibly Queen Anne, asked the poet to write something to make up for telling about Criseyde's betrayal of Troilus.

Throughout his life Chaucer also wrote moral and religious works, chiefly translations. Besides French, which was a second language for him, and Italian, Chaucer also read Latin. He made a prose translation of the Latin *Consolation of Philosophy,* written by the sixth-century Roman statesman Boethius while in prison awaiting execution for crimes for which he had been unjustly condemned. The *Consolation* became a favorite book for the Middle Ages, providing inspiration and comfort through its lesson that worldly fortune is deceitful and ephemeral and through the platonic doctrine that the body itself is only a prison house for the soul that aspires to eternal things. The influence of Boethius is deeply ingrained in *The Knight's Tale* and *Troilus.* The ballade *Truth* compresses the Boethian and Christian teaching into three stanzas of homely moral advice.

Thus long before Chaucer conceived of *The Canterbury Tales,* his writings were many-faceted: they embrace prose and poetry; human and divine love; French, Italian, and Latin sources; secular and religious influences; comedy and philosophy. Moreover, different elements are likely to mix in the same work, often making it difficult to extract from Chaucer simple, direct, and certain meanings.

This Chaucerian complexity owes much to the wide range of Chaucer's learning and his exposure to new literary currents on the Continent but perhaps also to the special social position he occupied as a member of a new class of civil servants. Born into the urban middle class, Chaucer, through his association with the court and service of the Crown, had attained the rank of "esquire," roughly equivalent to what would later be termed a "gentleman." His career brought him into contact with overlapping bourgeois and aristocratic social worlds, without his being securely anchored in either. Although he was born a commoner and continued to associate with commoners in his official life, he did not live as a commoner; and although his training and service at court, his wife's connections, and probably his poetry brought him into contact with the nobility, he must always have been conscious of the fact that he did not really belong to that society of which birth alone could make one a true member. Situated at the intersection of these social worlds, Chaucer had the gift of being able to view with both sympathy and humor the behaviors, beliefs, and pretensions of the diverse people who comprised the levels of society. Chaucer's art of being at once involved in and detached from a given situation is peculiarly his own, but that art would have been appreciated by a small group of friends close to Chaucer's social position—men like Sir Philip de la Vache, to whom Chaucer addressed the humorous envoy to *Truth*. Chaucer belongs to an age when poetry was read aloud. A beautiful frontispiece to a manuscript of *Troilus* pictures the poet's public performance before a magnificently dressed royal audience, and he may well have been invited at times to read his poems at court. But besides addressing a listening audience, to whose allegedly superior taste and sensibility the poet often ironically defers (for example, *The General Prologue,* lines 745–48), Chaucer has in mind discriminating readers whom he might expect to share his sense of humor and his complex attitudes toward the company of "sondry folk" who make the pilgrimage to Canterbury.

The text given here is from E. T. Donaldson's *Chaucer's Poetry: An Anthology for the Modern Reader* (1958, 1975) with some modifications. For *The Canterbury Tales* the Hengwrt Manuscript has provided the textual basis. The spelling has been altered to improve consistency and has been modernized in so far as is possible without distorting the phonological values of the Middle English. A discussion of Middle English pronunciation, grammar, and prosody is included in the introduction to "The Middle Ages" (pp. 14–21).

The Canterbury Tales

Chaucer's original plan for *The Canterbury Tales*—if we assume it to be the same as that which the fictional Host proposes at the end of *The General Prologue*—projected about one hundred twenty stories, two for each pilgrim to tell on the way to Canterbury and two more on the way back. Chaucer actually completed only twenty-two and the beginnings of two others. He did write an ending, for the Host says to the Parson, who tells the last tale, that everyone except him has told "his tale." Indeed, the pilgrims never even get to Canterbury. The work was probably first conceived in 1386, when Chaucer was living in Greenwich, some miles east of London. From his house he might have been able to see the pilgrim road that led toward the shrine of the famous English saint, Thomas à Becket, the archbishop of Canterbury who was murdered in his cathedral in 1170. Medieval pilgrims were notorious tale tellers, and the sight and sound of the bands riding toward Canterbury may well have suggested to Chaucer the idea of using a fictitious pilgrimage as a framing device for a number of stories. Collections of stories linked by such a device were common in the later Middle Ages. Chaucer's contemporary John Gower had used one in his *Confessio Amantis*. The most famous medieval framing tale besides Chaucer's is Boccaccio's *Decameron,* in which ten different narrators each tell a tale a day for ten days. Chaucer could have known the *Decameron,* which contains tales with plots analogous to plots found also in *The Canterbury Tales,* but these stories were widespread, and there is no proof that Chaucer got them from Boccaccio.

Chaucer's artistic exploitation of the device is, in any case, altogether his own. Whereas in Gower a single speaker relates all the stories, and in Boccaccio the ten speakers—three young gentlemen and seven young ladies—all belong to the same sophisticated social elite, Chaucer's pilgrim narrators represent a wide spectrum of ranks and occupations. This device, however, should not be mistaken for "realism." It is highly unlikely that a group like Chaucer's pilgrims would ever have joined together and communicated on such seemingly equal terms. That is part of the fiction, as is the tacit assumption that a group so large could have ridden along listening to one another tell tales in verse. The variety of tellers is matched by the diversity of their tales: tales are assigned to appropriate narrators and juxtaposed to bring out contrasts in genre, style, tone, and values. Thus the Knight's courtly romance about the rivalry of two noble lovers for a lady is followed by the Miller's fabliau of the seduction of an old carpenter's young wife by a student. In several of *The Canterbury Tales* there is a fascinating accord between the narrators and their stories, so that the story takes on rich overtones from what we have learned of its teller in *The General Prologue* and elsewhere, and the character itself grows and is revealed by the story. Chaucer conducts two fictions simultaneously—that of the individual tale and that of the pilgrim to whom he has assigned it. He develops the second fiction not only through *The General Prologue* but also through the "links," the interchanges among pilgrims connecting the stories. These interchanges sometimes lead to quarrels. Thus *The Miller's Tale* offends the Reeve, who takes the figure of the Miller's foolish, cuckolded carpenter as directed personally at himself, and he retaliates with a story satirizing an arrogant miller very much like the pilgrim Miller. The antagonism of the two tellers provides comedy in the links and enhances the comedy of their tales. The links also offer interesting literary commentary on the tales by members of the pilgrim audience, especially the Host, whom the pilgrims have declared "governour" and "juge" of the storytelling. Further dramatic interest is created by the fact that several tales respond to topics taken up by previous tellers. The Wife of Bath's thesis that women should have sovereignty over men in marriage gets a reply from the Clerk, which in turn elicits responses from the Merchant and the Franklin. The tales have their own logic and interest quite apart from the framing fiction; no other medieval framing fiction, however, has such varied and lively interaction between the frame and the individual stories.

The composition of none of the tales can be accurately dated; most of them were written during the last fourteen years of Chaucer's life, although a few were probably written earlier and inserted into *The Canterbury Tales*. The popularity of the poem in late medieval England is attested by the number of surviving manuscripts: more than eighty, none from Chaucer's lifetime. It was also twice printed by William Caxton, who introduced printing to England in 1476, and often reprinted by Caxton's early successors. The manuscripts reflect the unfinished state of the poem—the fact that when he died Chaucer had not made up his mind about a number of details and hence left many inconsistencies. The poem appears in the manuscripts as nine or ten "fragments" or blocks of tales; the order of the poems within each fragment is generally the same, but the order of the fragments themselves varies widely. The fragment containing *The General Prologue;* the Knight's, Miller's, and Reeve's tales; and the Cook's unfinished tale, always comes first, and the fragment consisting of *The Parson's Tale* and *The Retraction* always comes last. But the others, such as that containing the Wife of Bath, the Friar, and the Summoner or that consisting of the Physician and Pardoner or the longest fragment, consisting of six tales concluding with the Nun's Priest's, are by no means stable in relation to one another. The order followed here, that of the Ellesmere manuscript, has been adopted as the most nearly satisfactory.

THE GENERAL PROLOGUE

Chaucer did not need to make a pilgrimage himself to meet the types of people that his fictitious pilgrimage includes, because most of them had long inhabited literature as well as life: the ideal Knight, who had taken part in all the major expeditions and battles of the crusades during the last half-century; his fashionably dressed son, the Squire, a typical young lover; the lady Prioress, the hunting Monk, and the flattering Friar, who practice the little vanities and larger vices for which such ecclesiastics were conventionally attacked; the prosperous Franklin; the fraudulent Doctor; the lusty and domineering Wife of Bath; the austere Parson; and so on down through the lower orders to that spellbinding preacher and mercenary, the Pardoner, peddling his paper indulgences and phony relics. One meets all these types throughout medieval literature, but particularly in a genre called estates satire, which sets out to expose and pillory typical examples of corruption at all levels of society. (For more information on estates satire, see "Medieval Estates and Orders" at Norton Literature Online.) A remarkable number of details in *The General Prologue* could have been taken straight out of books as well as drawn from life. Although it has been argued that some of the pilgrims are portraits of actual people, the impression that they are drawn from life is more likely to be a function of Chaucer's art, which is able to endow types with a reality we generally associate only with people we know. The salient features of each pilgrim leap out randomly at the reader, as they might to an observer concerned only with what meets the eye. This imitation of the way our minds actually perceive reality may make us fail to notice the care with which Chaucer has selected his details to give an integrated sketch of the person being described. Most of these details give something more than mere verisimilitude to the description. The pilgrims' facial features, the clothes they wear, the foods they like to eat, the things they say, the work they do are all clues not only to their social rank but to their moral and spiritual condition and, through the accumulation of detail, to the condition of late-medieval society, of which, collectively, they are representative. What uniquely distinguishes Chaucer's prologue from more conventional estates satire, such as the *Prologue* to *Piers Plowman*, is the suppression in all but a few flagrant instances of overt moral judgment. The narrator, in fact, seems to be expressing chiefly admiration and praise at the superlative skills and accomplishments of this particular group, even such dubious ones as the Friar's begging techniques or the Manciple's success in cheating the learned lawyers who employ him. The reader is left free to draw out the ironic implications of details presented with such seeming artlessness, even while falling in with the easygoing mood of "felaweship" that pervades Chaucer's prologue to the pilgrimage.

FROM THE CANTERBURY TALES

The General Prologue

Whan that April with his° showres soote° — *its / fresh*
The droughte of March hath perced to the roote,
And bathed every veine[1] in swich° licour,° — *such / liquid*
Of which vertu[2] engendred is the flowr;
Whan Zephyrus eek° with his sweete breeth — *also*
Inspired[3] hath in every holt° and heeth° — *grove / field*

1. I.e., in plants.
2. By the power of which.
3. Breathed into. "Zephyrus": the west wind.

The tendre croppes,° and the yonge sonne[4] *shoots*
Hath in the Ram his halve cours yronne,
And smale fowles° maken melodye *birds*
That sleepen al the night with open yë°— *eye*
So priketh hem° Nature in hir corages[5]— *them*
Thanne longen folk to goon° on pilgrimages, *go*
And palmeres for to seeken straunge strondes
To ferne halwes,[6] couthe° in sondry° londes; *known / various*
And specially from every shires ende
Of Engelond to Canterbury they wende,
The holy blisful martyr[7] for to seeke
That hem hath holpen° whan that they were seke.° *helped / sick*
  Bifel° that in that seson on a day, *It happened*
In Southwerk[8] at the Tabard as I lay,
Redy to wenden on my pilgrimage
To Canterbury with ful° devout corage, *very*
At night was come into that hostelrye
Wel nine and twenty in a compaignye
Of sondry folk, by aventure° yfalle *chance*
In felaweshipe, and pilgrimes were they alle
That toward Canterbury wolden° ride. *would*
The chambres and the stables weren wide,
And wel we weren esed° at the beste.[9] *accommodated*
And shortly,° whan the sonne was to reste,[1] *in brief*
So hadde I spoken with hem everichoon° *every one*
That I was of hir felaweshipe anoon,° *at once*
And made forward[2] erly for to rise,
To take oure way ther as[3] I you devise.° *describe*
  But nathelees,° whil I have time and space,[4] *nevertheless*
Er° that I ferther in this tale pace,° *before / proceed*
Me thinketh it accordant to resoun[5]
To telle you al the condicioun
Of eech of hem, so as it seemed me,
And whiche they were, and of what degree,° *social rank*
And eek° in what array that they were inne: *also*
And at a knight thanne° wol I first biginne. *then*
  A Knight ther was, and that a worthy man,
That fro the time that he first bigan
To riden out, he loved chivalrye,
Trouthe and honour, freedom and curteisye.[6]
Ful worthy was he in his lordes werre,° *war*
And therto hadde he riden, no man ferre,° *farther*
As wel in Cristendom as hethenesse,[7]

4. The sun is young because it has run only halfway through its course in Aries, the Ram—the first sign of the zodiac in the solar year.
5. Their hearts.
6. Far-off shrines. "Palmeres": palmers, wide-ranging pilgrims—especially those who sought out the "straunge strondes" (foreign shores) of the Holy Land.
7. St. Thomas à Becket, murdered in Canterbury Cathedral in 1170.
8. Southwark, site of the Tabard Inn, was then a suburb of London, south of the Thames River.
9. In the best possible way.
1. Had set.
2. I.e., (we) made an agreement.
3. Where.
4. I.e., opportunity.
5. It seems to me according to reason.
6. Courtesy. "Trouthe": integrity. "Freedom": generosity of spirit.
7. Heathen lands. "Cristendom" here designates specifically only crusades waged by the nations of Roman Catholic Western Europe in lands under other dispensations, primarily Arabic, Turkish, and

And[8] evere honoured for his worthinesse.
At Alisandre[9] he was whan it was wonne;
Ful ofte time he hadde the boord bigonne[1]
Aboven alle nacions in Pruce;
In Lettou had he reised,° and in Ruce, *campaigned*
No Cristen man so ofte of his degree;
In Gernade° at the sege eek hadde he be *Granada*
Of Algezir, and riden in Belmarye;
At Lyeis was he, and at Satalye,
Whan they were wonne; and in the Grete See° *Mediterranean*
At many a noble arivee° hadde he be. *military landing*
At mortal batailes[2] hadde he been fifteene,
And foughten for oure faith at Tramissene
In listes[3] thries,° and ay° slain his fo. *thrice / always*
This ilke° worthy Knight hadde been also *same*
Sometime with the lord of Palatye[4]
Again° another hethen in Turkye; *against*
And everemore he hadde a soverein pris.° *reputation*
And though that he were worthy, he was wis,[5]
And of his port° as meeke as is a maide. *demeanor*
He nevere yit no vilainye° ne saide *rudeness*
In al his lif unto no manere wight:[6]
He was a verray,° parfit,° gentil° knight. *true / perfect / noble*
But for to tellen you of his array,
His hors° were goode, but he was nat gay.[7] *horses*
Of fustian° he wered° a gipoun[8] *thick cloth / wore*
Al bismotered with his haubergeoun,[9]
For he was late° come from his viage,° *lately / expedition*
And wente for to doon his pilgrimage.
With him ther was his sone, a yong Squier,[1]
A lovere and a lusty bacheler,
With lokkes crulle° as° they were laid in presse. *curly / as if*
Of twenty yeer of age he was, I gesse.
Of his stature he was of evene° lengthe, *moderate*
And wonderly delivere,° and of greet° strengthe. *agile / great*
And he hadde been som time in chivachye[2]
In Flandres, in Artois, and Picardye,

Moorish Islam but also, as indicated in the list of the Knight's campaigns given below, the Christian Eastern Orthodox Church. Conspicuous by absence is any reference to major battles in the Hundred Years War, fought between French and English Catholics. For excerpts from Christian, Jewish, and Arabic texts on the First Crusade, go to Norton Literature Online.

8. I.e., and he was.

9. The capture of Alexandria in Egypt (1365) was considered a famous victory, although the Crusaders abandoned the city after a week of looting. Below: "Pruce" (Prussia), "Lettow" (Lithuania), and "Ruce" (Russia) refer to campaigns by the Teutonic Order of Knights on the shores of the Baltic Sea in northern Europe against the Eastern Orthodox Church, "Gernada" (Granada), "Algezir" (Algeciras), and "Belmarye" (Belmarin), to northern Spain and Morocco; "Lyeis" (Ayash, seaport near Antioch, modern Syria), "Satalye," "Palatye" (Antalya and Balat, modern Turkey), "Tramyssene" (Tlemcen, modern Algeria).

1. Sat in the seat of honor at military feasts.

2. Tournaments fought to the death.

3. Lists, tournament grounds.

4. A Moslem: alliances of convenience were often made during the Crusades between Christians and Moslems.

5. I.e., he was wise as well as bold.

6. Any sort of person. In Middle English, negatives are multiplied for emphasis, as in these two lines: "nevere," "no," "ne," "no."

7. I.e., gaily dressed.

8. Tunic worn underneath the coat of mail.

9. All rust-stained from his hauberk (coat of mail).

1. The vague term "Squier" (Squire) here seems to be the equivalent of "bacheler" (line 80), a young knight still in the service of an older one.

2. On cavalry expeditions. The places in the next line are sites of skirmishes in the constant warfare between the English and the French.

And born him wel as of so litel space,[3]
In hope to stonden in his lady° grace. *lady's*
Embrouded° was he as it were a mede,[4] *embroidered*
Al ful of fresshe flowres, white and rede;° *red*
Singing he was, or floiting,° al the day: *whistling*
He was as fressh as is the month of May.
Short was his gowne, with sleeves longe and wide.
Wel coude he sitte on hors, and faire ride;
He coude songes make, and wel endite,° *compose verse*
Juste[5] and eek° daunce, and wel portraye° and write. *also / sketch*
So hote° he loved that by nightertale[6] *hotly*
He slepte namore than dooth a nightingale.
Curteis he was, lowely,° and servisable, *humble*
And carf biforn his fader at the table.[7]
A Yeman hadde he[8] and servants namo° *no more*
At that time, for him liste[9] ride so;
And he[1] was clad in cote and hood of greene.
A sheef of pecok arwes,° bright and keene, *arrows*
Under his belt he bar° ful thriftily;° *bore / properly*
Wel coude he dresse° his takel° yemanly:[2] *tend to / gear*
His arwes drouped nought with fetheres lowe.
And in his hand he bar a mighty bowe.
A not-heed° hadde he with a brown visage. *close-cut head*
Of wodecraft wel coude° he al the usage. *knew*
Upon his arm he bar a gay bracer,[3]
And by his side a swerd° and a bokeler,[4] *sword*
And on that other side a gay daggere,
Harneised° wel and sharp as point of spere; *mounted*
A Cristophre[5] on his brest of silver sheene;° *bright*
An horn he bar, the baudrik[6] was of greene.
A forster° was he soothly,° as I gesse. *forester / truly*
Ther was also a Nonne, a Prioresse,
That of hir smiling was ful simple and coy.[7]
Hir gretteste ooth was but by sainte Loy!° *Eloi*
And she was cleped° Madame Eglantine. *named*
Ful wel she soong° the service divine, *sang*
Entuned° in hir nose ful semely;[8] *chanted*
And Frenssh she spak ful faire and fetisly,° *elegantly*
After the scole° of Stratford at the Bowe[9]— *school*
For Frenssh of Paris was to hire unknowe.
At mete° wel ytaught was she withalle:° *meals / besides*
She leet° no morsel from hir lippes falle, *let*
Ne wette hir fingres in hir sauce deepe;
Wel coude she carye a morsel, and wel keepe° *take care*

3. I.e., considering the little time he had been in service.
4. Mead, meadow.
5. Joust, fight in a tournament.
6. At night.
7. It was a squire's duty to carve his lord's meat.
8. I.e., the Knight. The "Yeman" (Yeoman) is an independent commoner who acts as the Knight's military servant.
9. It pleased him to.
1. I.e., the Yeoman.
2. In a workmanlike way.
3. Wrist guard for archers.
4. Buckler (a small shield).
5. St. Christopher medal.
6. Baldric (a supporting strap).
7. Sincere and shy. The Prioress is the mother superior of her nunnery.
8. In a seemly, proper manner.
9. The French learned in a convent school in Stratford-at-the-Bow, a suburb of London, was evidently not up to the Parisian standard.

That no drope ne fille° upon hir brest. *should fall*
In curteisye was set ful muchel hir lest.[1]
Hir over-lippe° wiped she so clene *upper lip*
That in hir coppe° ther was no ferthing° seene *cup / bit*
Of grece,° whan she dronken hadde hir draughte; *grease*
Ful semely after hir mete she raughte.° *reached*
And sikerly° she was of greet disport,[2] *certainly*
And ful plesant, and amiable of port,° *mien*
And pained hire to countrefete cheere[3]
Of court, and to been statlich° of manere, *dignified*
And to been holden digne[4] of reverence.
But, for to speken of hir conscience,
She was so charitable and so pitous° *merciful*
She wolde weepe if that she saw a mous
Caught in a trappe, if it were deed° or bledde. *dead*
Of[5] smale houndes hadde she that she fedde
With rosted flessh, or milk and wastelbreed;° *fine white bread*
But sore wepte she if oon of hem were deed,
Or if men smoot it with a yerde smerte;[6]
And al was conscience and tendre herte.
Ful semely hir wimpel° pinched° was, *headdress / pleated*
Hir nose tretis,° hir yën° greye as glas, *well-formed / eyes*
Hir mouth ful smal, and therto° softe and reed,° *moreover / red*
But sikerly° she hadde a fair forheed: *certainly*
It was almost a spanne brood,[7] I trowe,° *believe*
For hardily,° she was nat undergrowe. *assuredly*
Ful fetis° was hir cloke, as I was war;° *becoming / aware*
Of smal° coral aboute hir arm she bar *dainty*
A paire of bedes, gauded all with greene,[8]
And theron heeng° a brooch of gold ful sheene,° *hung / bright*
On which ther was first writen a crowned A,[9]
And after, *Amor vincit omnia.*[1]
  Another Nonne with hire hadde she
That was hir chapelaine,° and preestes three.[2] *secretary*
  A Monk ther was, a fair for the maistrye,[3]
An outridere[4] that loved venerye,° *hunting*
A manly man, to been an abbot able.° *worthy*
Ful many a daintee° hors hadde he in stable, *fine*
And whan he rood,° men mighte his bridel heere *rode*
Ginglen° in a whistling wind as clere *jingle*
And eek° as loude as dooth the chapel belle *also*
Ther as this lord was kepere of the celle.[5]
The rule of Saint Maure or of Saint Beneit,
By cause that it was old and somdeel strait[6]—

1. I.e., her chief delight lay in good manners.
2. Of great good cheer.
3. And took pains to imitate the behavior.
4. And to be considered worthy.
5. I.e., some.
6. If someone struck it with a rod sharply.
7. A handsbreadth wide.
8. Provided with green beads to mark certain prayers. "A paire": string (i.e., a rosary).
9. An A with an ornamental crown on it.

1. "Love conquers all."
2. The three get reduced to just one nun's priest.
3. I.e., a superlatively fine one.
4. A monk charged with supervising property distant from the monastery. Monasteries obtained income from large landholdings.
5. Prior of an outlying cell (branch) of the monastery.
6. Somewhat strict. St. Maurus and St. Benedict were authors of monastic rules.

This ilke° Monk leet olde thinges pace,° *same / pass away*
And heeld° after the newe world the space.° *held / course*
He yaf° nought of that text a pulled hen[7] *gave*
That saith that hunteres been° nought holy men, *are*
Ne that a monk, whan he is recchelees,[8]
Is likned til° a fissh that is waterlees— *to*
This is to sayn, a monk out of his cloistre;
But thilke° text heeld he nat worth an oystre. *that same*
And I saide his opinion was good:
What° sholde he studye and make himselven wood° *why / crazy*
Upon a book in cloistre alway to poure,° *pore*
Or swinke° with his handes and laboure, *work*
As Austin bit?[9] How shal the world be served?
Lat Austin have his swink to him reserved!
Therefore he was a prikasour° aright. *hard rider*
Grehoundes he hadde as swift as fowl in flight.
Of priking° and of hunting for the hare *riding*
Was al his lust,° for no cost wolde he spare. *pleasure*
I sawgh his sleeves purfiled° at the hand *fur lined*
With gris,° and that the fineste of a land; *gray fur*
And for to festne his hood under his chin
He hadde of gold wrought a ful curious[1] pin:
A love-knotte in the grettere° ende ther was. *greater*
His heed was balled,° that shoon as any glas, *bald*
And eek his face, as he hadde been anoint:
He was a lord ful fat and in good point;[2]
His yën steepe,° and rolling in his heed, *protruding*
That stemed as a furnais of a leed,[3]
His bootes souple,° his hors in greet estat° *supple / condition*
Now certainly he was a fair prelat.[4]
He was nat pale as a forpined° gost: *wasted away*
A fat swan loved he best of any rost.
His palfrey° was as brown as is a berye. *saddle horse*
  A Frere ther was, a wantoune° and a merye, *jovial*
A limitour,[5] a ful solempne° man. *ceremonious*
In alle the ordres foure is noon that can° *knows*
So muche of daliaunce° and fair langage: *sociability*
He hadde maad ful many a mariage
Of yonge wommen at his owene cost;
Unto his ordre he was a noble post.[6]
Ful wel biloved and familier was he
With frankelains over al[7] in his contree,
And with worthy wommen of the town—
For he hadde power of confessioun,
As saide himself, more than a curat,° *parish priest*

7. He didn't give a plucked hen for that text.
8. Reckless, careless of rule.
9. I.e., as St. Augustine bids. St. Augustine had written that monks should perform manual labor.
1. Of careful workmanship.
2. In good shape, plump.
3. That glowed like a furnace with a pot in it.
4. Prelate (an important churchman).
5. The "Frere" (Friar) is a member of one of the four religious orders whose members live by begging; as a "limitour" he has been granted by his order exclusive begging rights within a certain limited area.
6. I.e., pillar, a staunch supporter.
7. I.e., with franklins everywhere. Franklins were well-to-do country men.

For of° his ordre he was licenciat.[8] *by*
Ful swetely herde he confessioun,
And plesant was his absolucioun.
He was an esy man to yive penaunce
Ther as he wiste to have[9] a good pitaunce;° *donation*
For unto a poore ordre for to yive
Is signe that a man is wel yshrive,[1]
For if he yaf, he dorste make avaunt° *boast*
He wiste° that a man was repentaunt; *knew*
For many a man so hard is of his herte
He may nat weepe though him sore smerte:[2]
Therfore, in stede of weeping and prayeres,
Men mote° yive silver to the poore freres.[3] *may*
His tipet° was ay farsed° ful of knives *hood / stuffed*
And pinnes, for to yiven faire wives;
And certainly he hadde a merye note;
Wel coude he singe and playen on a rote;° *fiddle*
Of yeddinges he bar outrely the pris.[4]
His nekke whit was as the flowr-de-lis;° *lily*
Therto he strong was as a champioun.
He knew the tavernes wel in every town,
And every hostiler° and tappestere,° *innkeeper / barmaid*
Bet° than a lazar or a beggestere.[5] *better*
For unto swich a worthy man as he
Accorded nat, as by his facultee,[6]
To have with sike° lazars aquaintaunce: *sick*
It is nat honeste,° it may nought avaunce,° *dignified / profit*
For to delen with no swich poraile,[7]
But al with riche, and selleres of vitaile;° *foodstuffs*
And over al ther as[8] profit sholde arise,
Curteis he was, and lowely of servise.
Ther was no man nowher so vertuous:° *effective*
He was the beste beggere in his hous.° *friary*
And yaf a certain ferme for the graunt:[9]
Noon of his bretheren cam ther in his haunt.[1]
For though a widwe° hadde nought a sho,° *widow / shoe*
So plesant was his *In principio*[2]
Yit wolde he have a ferthing° er he wente; *small coin*
His purchas was wel bettre than his rente.[3]
And rage he coude as it were right a whelpe;[4]
In love-dayes[5] ther coude he muchel° helpe, *much*

8. I.e., licensed to hear confessions.
9. Where he knew he would have.
1. Shriven, absolved.
2. Although he is sorely grieved.
3. Before granting absolution, the confessor must be sure the sinner is contrite; moreover, the absolution is contingent on the sinner's performance of an act of satisfaction. In the case of Chaucer's Friar, a liberal contribution served both as proof of contrition and as satisfaction.
4. He absolutely took the prize for ballads.
5. "Beggestere": female beggar. "Lazar:" leper.
6. It was not suitable because of his position.
7. I.e., poor trash. The oldest order of friars had been founded by St. Francis to administer to the spiritual needs of precisely those classes the Friar avoids.
8. Everywhere.
9. And he paid a certain rent for the privilege of begging.
1. Assigned territory.
2. A friar's usual salutation: "In the beginning [was the Word]" (John 1.1).
3. I.e., the money he got through such activity was more than his proper income.
4. And he could flirt wantonly, as if he were a puppy.
5. Days appointed for the settlement of lawsuits out of court.

For ther he was nat lik a cloisterer,
With a thredbare cope, as is a poore scoler,
But he was lik a maister[6] or a pope.
Of double worstede was his semicope,° *short robe*
And rounded as a belle out of the presse.° *bell mold*
Somwhat he lipsed° for his wantounesse° *lisped / affectation*
To make his Englissh sweete upon his tonge;
And in his harping, whan he hadde songe,° *sung*
His yën twinkled in his heed aright
As doon the sterres° in the frosty night. *stars*
This worthy limitour was cleped Huberd.
  A Marchant was ther with a forked beerd,
In motelee,[7] and hye on hors he sat,
Upon his heed a Flandrissh° bevere hat, *Flemish*
His bootes clasped faire and fetisly.° *elegantly*
His resons° he spak ful solempnely, *opinions*
Souning° alway th' encrees of his winning.° *implying / profit*
He wolde the see were kept for any thing[8]
Bitwixen Middelburgh and Orewelle.
Wel coude he in eschaunge sheeldes[9] selle.
This worthy man ful wel his wit bisette:° *employed*
Ther wiste° no wight° that he was in dette, *knew / person*
So statly° was he of his governaunce,[1] *dignified*
With his bargaines,° and with his chevissaunce.° *bargainings / borrowing*
Forsoothe° he was a worthy man withalle; *in truth*
But, sooth to sayn, I noot° how men him calle. *don't know*
  A Clerk[2] ther was of Oxenforde also
That unto logik hadde longe ygo.[3]
As lene was his hors as is a rake,
And he was nought right fat, I undertake,
But looked holwe,° and therto sobrely. *hollow*
Ful thredbare was his overeste courtepy,
For he hadde geten him yit no benefice,[4]
Ne was so worldly for to have office.° *secular employment*
For him was levere[5] have at his beddes heed
Twenty bookes, clad in blak or reed,
Of Aristotle and his philosophye,
Than robes riche, or fithele,° or gay sautrye.[6] *fiddle*
But al be that he was a philosophre[7]
Yit hadde he but litel gold in cofre;° *coffer*
But al that he mighte of his freendes hente,° *take*
On bookes and on lerning he it spente,
And bisily gan for the soules praye
Of hem that yaf him wherwith to scoleye.° *study*

6. A man of recognized learning.
7. Motley, a cloth of mixed color.
8. I.e., he wished the sea to be guarded at all costs. The sea route between Middelburgh (in the Netherlands) and Orwell (in Suffolk) was vital to the Merchant's export and import of wool—the basis of England's chief trade at the time.
9. Shields were units of transfer in international credit, which he exchanged at a profit.
1. The management of his affairs.
2. The Clerk is a student at Oxford; to become a student, he would have had to signify his intention of becoming a cleric, but he was not bound to proceed to a position of responsibility in the church.
3. Who had long since matriculated in philosophy.
4. Ecclesiastical living, such as the income a parish priest receives. "Courtepy": outer cloak.
5. He would rather.
6. Psaltery (a kind of harp).
7. The word may also mean alchemist, someone who tries to turn base metals into gold. The Clerk's "philosophy" does not pay either way.

Of studye took he most cure° and most heede. *care*
Nought oo° word spak he more than was neede, *one*
And that was said in forme[8] and reverence,
And short and quik,° and ful of heigh sentence:[9] *lively*
Souning° in moral vertu was his speeche, *resounding*
And gladly wolde he lerne, and gladly teche.
  A Sergeant of the Lawe, war and wis,[1]
That often hadde been at the Parvis[2]
Ther was also, ful riche of excellence.
Discreet he was, and of greet reverence—
He seemed swich, his wordes weren so wise.
Justice he was ful often in assise° *circuit courts*
By patente[3] and by plein° commissioun. *full*
For his science° and for his heigh renown *knowledge*
Of fees and robes hadde he many oon.
So greet a purchasour° was nowher noon; *speculator in land*
Al was fee simple[4] to him in effect—
His purchasing mighte nat been infect.[5]
Nowher so bisy a man as he ther nas;° *was not*
And yit he seemed bisier than he was.
In termes hadde he caas and doomes[6] alle
That from the time of King William[7] were falle.
Therto he coude endite and make a thing,[8]
Ther coude no wight pinchen° at his writing; *cavil*
And every statut coude° he plein° by rote.[9] *knew / entire*
He rood but hoomly° in a medlee cote,[1] *unpretentiously*
Girt with a ceint° of silk, with barres[2] smale. *belt*
Of his array telle I no lenger tale.
  A Frankelain[3] was in his compaignye:
Whit was his beerd as is the dayesye;° *daisy*
Of his complexion he was sanguin.[4]
Wel loved he by the morwe a sop in win.[5]
To liven in delit° was evere his wone,° *sensual delight / wont*
For he was Epicurus[6] owene sone,
That heeld opinion that plein° delit *full*
Was verray° felicitee parfit.° *true / perfect*
An housholdere and that a greet was he:
Saint Julian[7] he was in his contree.
His breed, his ale, was always after oon;[8]

8. With decorum.
9. Elevated thought.
1. Wary and wise. The Sergeant is not only a practicing lawyer but one of the high justices of the nation.
2. The Paradise, the porch of St. Paul's Cathedral, a meeting place for lawyers and their clients.
3. Royal warrant.
4. Owned outright without legal impediments.
5. Invalidated on a legal technicality.
6. Law cases and decisions. "By termes": i.e., by heart.
7. I.e., the Conqueror (reigned 1066–87).
8. Compose and draw up a deed.
9. By heart.
1. A coat of mixed color.
2. Transverse stripes.
3. The "Frankelain" (Franklin) is a prosperous country man, whose lower-class ancestry is no impediment to the importance he has attained in his county.
4. A reference to the fact that the Franklin's temperament, "humor," is dominated by blood as well as to his red face (see p. 180, n. 8).
5. I.e., in the morning he was very fond of a piece of bread soaked in wine.
6. The Greek philosopher whose teaching is popularly believed to make pleasure the chief goal of life.
7. The patron saint of hospitality.
8. Always of the same high quality.

A bettre envined° man was nevere noon. *wine-stocked*
Withouten bake mete was nevere his hous,
Of fissh and flessh, and that so plentevous° *plenteous*
It snewed° in his hous of mete° and drinke, *owed / food*
Of alle daintees that men coude thinke.
After° the sondry sesons of the yeer *ding to*
So chaunged he his mete° and his soper.° *upper*
Ful many a fat partrich hadde he in mewe,° *age*
And many a breem,° and many a luce° in stewe.[9] *ke*
Wo was his cook but if his sauce were
Poinant° and sharp, and redy all his gere.
His table dormant in his halle alway
Stood redy covered all the longe day.[1]
At sessions ther was he lord and sire.
Ful ofte time he was Knight of the Shire.[2]
An anlaas° and a gipser° al of silk *dagger*
Heeng at his girdel,[3] whit as morne° milk. *mo*
A shirreve° hadde he been, and countour.[4] *sh*
Was nowhere swich a worthy vavasour.[5]
  An Haberdasshere and a Carpenter,
A Webbe,° a Dyere, and a Tapicer°— *weaver / tapestry mak*
And they were clothed alle in oo liveree[6]
Of a solempne and greet fraternitee.
Ful fresshe and newe hir gere apiked° was; *trimmed*
Hir knives were chaped° nought with bras, *mounted*
But al with silver; wrought ful clene and weel
Hir girdles and hir pouches everydeel.° *altogether*
Wel seemed eech of hem a fair burgeis° *burgher*
To sitten in a yeldehalle° on a dais. *guildhall*
Everich, for the wisdom that he can,[7]
Was shaply° for to been an alderman. *suitable*
For catel° hadde they ynough and rente,° *property / income*
And eek hir wives wolde it wel assente—
And elles certain were they to blame:
It is ful fair to been ycleped° "Madame," *called*
And goon to vigilies all bifore,[8]
And have a mantel royalliche ybore.[9]
  A Cook they hadde with hem for the nones,[1]
To boile the chiknes with the marybones,° *marrowbones*
And powdre-marchant tart and galingale.[2]
Wel coude he knowe° a draughte of London ale. *recognize*
He coude roste, and seethe,° and broile, and frye, *boil*
Maken mortreux,° and wel bake a pie. *stews*

9. *Fishpond.*
1. Tables were usually dismounted when not in use, but the Franklin kept his mounted and set ("covered"), hence "dormant."
2. County representative in Parliament. "Sessions": i.e., sessions of the justices of the peace.
3. Hung at his belt.
4. Auditor of county finances.
5. Feudal landholder of lowest rank; a provincial gentleman.
6. In one livery, i.e., the uniform of their "fraternitee" or guild, a partly religious, partly social organization.
7. Was capable of.
8. I.e., at the head of the procession. "Vigiles": feasts held on the eve of saints' days.
9. Royally carried.
1. For the occasion.
2. "Powdre-marchant" and "galingale" are flavoring materials.

But gr harn was it, as it thoughte° me, *seemed to*
That his shine a mormal° hadde he, *ulcer*
Fo nkmanger,[3] that made he with the beste.
hipman was ther, woning° fer by weste—° *dwelling / in the west*
ught I woot,° he was of Dertemouthe.[4] *know*
rood upon a rouncy° as he couthe,[5] *large nag*
a gowne of falding° to the knee. *heavy wool*
daggere hanging on a laas° hadde he *strap*
Aboute his nekke, under his arm adown.
The hote somer hadde maad his hewe° al brown; *color*
And certainly he was a good felawe.
Ful many a draughte of win hadde he drawe[6]
Fro Burdeuxward, whil that the chapman sleep:[7]
Of nice° conscience took he no keep;° *fastidious / heed*
If that he faught and hadde the hyer° hand, *upper*
By water he sente hem hoom to every land.[8]
But of his craft, to rekene wel his tides,
His stremes° and his daungers° him bisides,[9] *currents / hazards*
His herberwe° and his moone, his lodemenage,[1] *anchorage*
There was noon swich from Hulle to Cartage.[2]
Hardy he was and wis to undertake;[3]
With many a tempest hadde his beerd been shake;
He knew alle the havenes° as they were *harbors*
Fro Gotlond to the Cape of Finistere,[4]
And every crike° in Britaine° and in Spaine. *inlet / Brittany*
His barge ycleped was the Maudelaine.° *Magdalene*
With us ther was a Doctour of Physik:° *medicine*
In al this world ne was ther noon him lik
To speken of physik and of surgerye.
For° he was grounded in astronomye,° *because / astrology*
He kepte° his pacient a ful greet deel[5] *tended to*
In houres by his magik naturel.[6]
Wel coude he fortunen the ascendent
Of his images[7] for his pacient.
He knew the cause of every maladye,
Were it of hoot or cold or moiste or drye,
And where engendred and of what humour:[8]
He was a verray parfit praktisour.[9]
The cause yknowe,° and of his° harm the roote, *known / its*

3. A white stew or mousse.
4. Dartmouth, a port in the southwest of England.
5. As best he could.
6. Drawn, i.e., stolen.
7. Merchant slept. "Fro Burdeauxward": from Bordeaux; i.e., while carrying wine from Bordeaux (the wine center of France).
8. He drowned his prisoners.
9. Around him.
1. Pilotage, art of navigation.
2. From Hull (in northern England) to Cartagena (in Spain).
3. Shrewd in his undertakings.
4. From Gotland (an island in the Baltic) to Finisterre (the westernmost point in Spain).
5. Closely.
6. Natural—as opposed to black—magic. "In houres": i.e., the astrologically important hours (when conjunctions of the planets might help his recovery).
7. Assign the propitious time, according to the position of stars, for using talismanic images. Such images, representing either the patient himself or points in the zodiac, were thought to be influential on the course of the disease.
8. Diseases were thought to be caused by a disturbance of one or another of the four bodily "humors," each of which, like the four elements, was a compound of two of the elementary qualities mentioned in line 422: the melancholy humor, seated in the black bile, was cold and dry (like earth); the sanguine, seated in the blood, hot and moist (like air); the choleric, seated in the yellow bile, hot and dry (like fire); the phlegmatic, seated in the phlegm, cold and moist (like water).
9. True perfect practitioner.

Anoon he yaf the sike man his boote.° *remedy*
  Ful redy hadde he his apothecaries
To senden him drogges° and his letuaries,° *drugs / medicines*
For eech of hem made other for to winne:
Hir frendshipe was nought newe to biginne.
Wel knew he the olde Esculapius,[1]
And Deiscorides and eek Rufus,
Olde Ipocras, Hali, and Galien,
Serapion, Razis, and Avicen,
Averrois, Damascien, and Constantin,
Bernard, and Gatesden, and Gilbertin.
Of his diete mesurable° was he, *moderate*
For it was of no superfluitee,
But of greet norissing° and digestible. *nourishment*
His studye was but litel on the Bible.
In sanguin° and in pers° he clad was al, *blood red / blue*
Lined with taffata and with sendal;° *silk*
And yit he was but esy of dispence;° *expenditure*
He kepte that he wan in pestilence.[2]
For° gold in physik is a cordial,[3] *because*
Therfore he loved gold in special.
  A good Wif was ther of biside Bathe,
But she was somdeel deef,° and that was scathe.° *a bit deaf / a pity*
Of cloth-making she hadde swich an haunt,° *skill*
She passed° hem of Ypres and of Gaunt.[4] *surpassed*
In al the parissh wif ne was ther noon
That to the offring[5] bifore hire sholde goon,
And if ther dide, certain so wroth° was she *angry*
That she was out of alle charitee.
Hir coverchiefs° ful fine were of ground°— *headcovers / texture*
I dorste° swere they weyeden° ten pound *dare / weighed*
That on a Sonday weren° upon hir heed. *were*
Hir hosen° weren of fin scarlet reed,° *leggings / red*
Ful straite yteyd,[6] and shoes ful moiste° and newe. *supple*
Bold was hir face and fair and reed of hewe.
She was a worthy womman al hir live:
Housbondes at chirche dore[7] she hadde five,
Withouten° other compaignye in youthe— *not counting*
But therof needeth nought to speke as nouthe.° *now*
And thries hadde she been at Jerusalem;
She hadde passed many a straunge° streem; *foreign*
At Rome she hadde been, and at Boloigne,
In Galice at Saint Jame, and at Coloigne:[8]

1. The Doctor is familiar with the treatises that the Middle Ages attributed to the "great names" of medical history, whom Chaucer names: the purely legendary Greek demigod Aesculapius; the Greeks Dioscorides, Rufus, Hippocrates, Galen, and Serapion; the Persians Hali and Rhazes; the Arabians Avicenna and Averroës; the early Christians John (?) of Damascus and Constantine Afer; the Scotsman Bernard Gordon; the Englishmen John of Gatesden and Gilbert, the former an early contemporary of Chaucer.
2. He saved the money he made during the plague time.
3. A stimulant. Gold was thought to have some medicinal properties.
4. Ypres and Ghent ("Gaunt") were Flemish cloth-making centers.
5. The offering in church, when the congregation brought its gifts forward.
6. Tightly laced.
7. In medieval times, weddings were performed at the church door.
8. Rome, Boulogne (in France), St. James (of Compostella) in Galicia (Spain), and Cologne (in

She coude° muchel of wandring by the waye: *knew*
Gat-toothed[9] was she, soothly for to saye.
Upon an amblere[1] esily she sat,
Ywimpled° wel, and on hir heed an hat *veiled*
As brood as is a bokeler or a targe,[2]
A foot-mantel° aboute hir hipes large, *riding skirt*
And on hir feet a paire of spores° sharpe. *spurs*
In felaweshipe wel coude she laughe and carpe:° *talk*
Of remedies of love she knew parchaunce,° *as it happened*
For she coude of that art the olde daunce.[3]
  A good man was ther of religioun,
And was a poore Person° of a town, *parson*
But riche he was of holy thought and werk.
He was also a lerned man, a clerk,
That Cristes gospel trewely° wolde preche; *faithfully*
His parisshens° devoutly wolde he teche. *parishioners*
Benigne he was, and wonder° diligent, *wonderfully*
And in adversitee ful pacient,
And swich he was preved° ofte sithes.° *proved / times*
Ful loth were him to cursen for his tithes,[4]
But rather wolde he yiven, out of doute,[5]
Unto his poore parisshens aboute
Of his offring[6] and eek of his substaunce:° *property*
He coude in litel thing have suffisaunce.° *sufficiency*
Wid was his parissh, and houses fer asonder,
But he ne lafte° nought for rain ne thonder, *neglected*
In siknesse nor in meschief,° to visite *misfortune*
The ferreste° in his parissh, muche and lite,[7] *farthest*
Upon his feet, and in his hand a staf.
This noble ensample° to his sheep he yaf *example*
That first he wroughte,[8] and afterward he taughte.
Out of the Gospel he tho° wordes caughte,° *those / took*
And this figure° he added eek therto: *metaphor*
That if gold ruste, what shal iren do?
For if a preest be foul, on whom we truste,
No wonder is a lewed° man to ruste. *uneducated*
And shame it is, if a preest take keep,° *heed*
A shiten° shepherde and a clene sheep. *befouled*
Wel oughte a preest ensample for to yive
By his clennesse how that his sheep sholde live.
He sette nought his benefice[9] to hire
And leet° his sheep encombred in the mire *left*
And ran to London, unto Sainte Poules,[1]
To seeken him a chaunterye[2] for soules,

Germany) were all sites of shrines much visited by pilgrims.
9. Gap-toothed, thought to be a sign of amorousness.
1. Horse with an easy gait.
2. "Bokeler" and "targe": small shields.
3. I.e., she knew all the tricks of that trade.
4. He would be most reluctant to invoke excommunication in order to collect his tithes.
5. Without doubt.
6. The offering made by the congregation of his church was at the Parson's disposal.
7. Great and small.
8. I.e., he practiced what he preached.
9. I.e., his parish. A priest might rent his parish to another and take a more profitable position.
1. St. Paul's Cathedral.
2. Chantry, i.e., a foundation that employed priests for the sole duty of saying masses for the souls of wealthy deceased persons. St. Paul's had many of them.

Or with a bretherhede to been withholde,[3]
But dwelte at hoom and kepte wel his folde,
So that the wolf ne made it nought miscarye:
He was a shepherde and nought a mercenarye.
And though he holy were and vertuous,
He was to sinful men nought despitous,° — *scornful*
Ne of his speeche daungerous° ne digne,° — *disdainful / haughty*
But in his teching discreet and benigne,
To drawen folk to hevene by fairnesse
By good ensample—this was his bisinesse.
But it° were any persone obstinat, — *if there*
What so he were, of heigh or lowe estat,
Him wolde he snibben° sharply for the nones:[4] — *scold*
A bettre preest I trowe° ther nowher noon is. — *believe*
He waited after[5] no pompe and reverence,
Ne maked him a spiced conscience,[6]
But Cristes lore° and his Apostles twelve — *teaching*
He taughte, but first he folwed it himselve.
    With him ther was a Plowman, was his brother,
That hadde ylad° of dong° ful many a fother.[7] — *carried / dung*
A trewe swinkere° and a good was he, — *worker*
Living in pees° and parfit charitee. — *peace*
God loved he best with al his hoole° herte — *whole*
At alle times, though him gamed or smerte,[8]
And thanne his neighebor right as himselve.
He wolde thresshe, and therto dike° and delve,° — *work hard / dig*
For Cristes sake, for every poore wight,
Withouten hire, if it laye in his might.
His tithes payed he ful faire and wel,
Bothe of his propre swink[9] and his catel.° — *property*
In a tabard° he rood upon a mere.° — *workman's smock / mare*
    Ther was also a Reeve° and a Millere, — *estate manager*
A Somnour, and a Pardoner[1] also,
A Manciple,° and myself—ther were namo. — *steward*
    The Millere was a stout carl° for the nones. — *fellow*
Ful big he was of brawn° and eek of bones— — *muscle*
That preved[2] wel, for overal ther he cam
At wrastling he wolde have alway the ram.[3]
He was short-shuldred, brood,° a thikke knarre.[4] — *broad*
Ther was no dore that he nolde heve of harre,[5]
Or breke it at a renning° with his heed.° — *running / head*
His beerd as any sowe or fox was reed,° — *red*
And therto brood, as though it were a spade;
Upon the cop right[6] of his nose he hade

3. Or to be employed by a brotherhood; i.e., to take a lucrative and fairly easy position as chaplain with a parish guild (see p. 179, n. 6).
4. On the spot, promptly.
5. I.e., expected.
6. Nor did he assume an overfastidious conscience, a holier-than-thou attitude.
7. Load.
8. Whether he was pleased or grieved.
9. His own work.

1. "Somnour" (Summoner): server of summonses to the ecclesiastical court. "Pardoner": dispenser of papal pardons (see p. 185, n. 8, and p. 186, 2nd n. 5).
2. Proved, i.e., was evident.
3. A ram was frequently offered as the prize in wrestling, a village sport.
4. Sturdy fellow.
5. He would not heave off (its) hinge.
6. Right on the tip.

A werte,° and theron stood a tuft of heres, *wart*
Rede as the bristles of a sowes eres;° *ears*
His nosethirles° blake were and wide. *nostrils*
A swerd and a bokeler° bar° he by his side. *shield / bore*
His mouth as greet was as a greet furnais.° *furnace*
He was a janglere° and a Goliardais,[7] *chatterer*
And that was most of sinne and harlotries.° *obscenities*
Wel coude he stelen corn and tollen thries[8]—
And yit he hadde a thombe[9] of gold, pardee.° *by heaven*
A whit cote and a blew hood wered° he. *wore*
A baggepipe wel coude he blowe and soune,° *sound*
And therwithal° he broughte us out of towne. *therewith*
  A gentil Manciple[1] was ther of a temple,
Of which achatours° mighte take exemple *buyers of food*
For to been wise in bying of vitaile;° *victuals*
For wheither that he paide or took by taile,[2]
Algate he waited so in his achat[3]
That he was ay biforn and in good stat.[4]
  Now is nat that of God a ful fair grace
That swich a lewed° mannes wit shal pace° *uneducated / surpass*
The wisdom of an heep of lerned men?
Of maistres° hadde he mo than thries ten *masters*
That weren of lawe expert and curious,° *cunning*
Of whiche ther were a dozeine in that hous
Worthy to been stiwardes of rente° and lond *income*
Of any lord that is in Engelond,
To make him live by his propre good[5]
In honour dettelees but if he were wood,[6]
Or live as scarsly° as him list° desire, *economically / it pleases*
And able for to helpen al a shire
In any caas° that mighte falle° or happe, *event / befall*
And yit this Manciple sette hir aller cappe![7]
  The Reeve was a sclendre° colerik[8] man; *slender*
His beerd was shave as neigh° as evere he can; *close*
His heer was by his eres ful round yshorn;
His top was dokked[9] lik a preest biforn;° *in front*
Ful longe were his legges and ful lene,
Ylik a staf, ther was no calf yseene.° *visible*
Wel coude he keepe° a gerner° and a binne— *guard / granary*
Ther was noon auditour coude on him winne.[1]
Wel wiste° he by the droughte and by the rain *knew*
The yeelding of his seed and of his grain.
His lordes sheep, his neet,° his dayerye,° *cattle / dairy herd*
His swin, his hors, his stoor,° and his pultrye *stock*

7. Goliard, teller of ribald stories.
8. Take toll thrice—i.e., deduct from the grain far more than the lawful percentage.
9. Thumb. Ironic allusion to a proverb: "An honest miller has a golden thumb."
1. The Manciple is the business agent of a community of lawyers in London (a "temple").
2. By tally, i.e., on credit.
3. Always he was on the watch in his purchasing.
4. Financial condition. "Ay biforn": i.e., ahead of the game.
5. His own money.
6. Out of debt unless he were crazy.
7. This Manciple made fools of them all.
8. Choleric describes a person whose dominant humor is yellow bile (choler)—i.e., a hot-tempered person. The Reeve is the superintendent of a large farming estate.
9. Cut short; the clergy wore the head partially shaved.
1. I.e., find him in default.

Was hoolly° in this Reeves governinge, *wholly*
And by his covenant yaf[2] the rekeninge,
Sin° that his lord was twenty-yeer of age. *since*
There coude no man bringe him in arrerage.[3]
Ther nas baillif, hierde, nor other hine,
That he ne knew his sleighte and his covine[4]—
They were adrad° of him as of the deeth.° *afraid / plague*
His woning° was ful faire upon an heeth;° *dwelling / meadow*
With greene trees shadwed was his place.
He coude bettre than his lord purchace.° *acquire goods*
Ful riche he was astored° prively.° *stocked / secretly*
His lord wel coude he plesen subtilly,
To yive and lene° him of his owene good,° *lend / property*
And have a thank, and yit a cote and hood.
In youthe he hadde lerned a good mister:° *occupation*
He was a wel good wrighte, a carpenter.
This Reeve sat upon a ful good stot° *stallion*
That was a pomely° grey and highte° Scot. *dapple / was named*
A long surcote° of pers° upon he hade,[5] *overcoat / blue*
And by his side he bar° a rusty blade. *bore*
Of Northfolk was this Reeve of which I telle,
Biside a town men clepen Baldeswelle.° *Bawdswell*
Tukked[6] he was as is a frere aboute,
And evere he rood the hindreste of oure route.[7]
   A Somnour[8] was ther with us in that place
That hadde a fir-reed° cherubinnes[9] face, *fire-red*
For saucefleem° he was, with yën narwe, *pimply*
And hoot° he was, and lecherous as a sparwe,° *hot / sparrow*
With scaled° browes blake and piled[1] beerd: *scabby*
Of his visage children were aferd.° *afraid*
Ther nas quiksilver, litarge, ne brimstoon,
Boras, ceruce, ne oile of tartre noon,[2]
Ne oinement that wolde clense and bite,
That him mighte helpen of his whelkes° white, *pimples*
Nor of the knobbes° sitting on his cheekes. *lumps*
Wel loved he garlek, oinons, and eek leekes,
And for to drinke strong win reed as blood.
Thanne wolde he speke and crye as he were wood;° *mad*
And whan that he wel dronken hadde the win,
Thanne wolde he speke no word but Latin:
A fewe termes hadde he, two or three,
That he hadde lerned out of som decree;
No wonder is—he herde it al the day,
And eek ye knowe wel how that a jay° *parrot*

2. And according to his contract he gave.
3. Convict him of being in arrears financially.
4. There was no bailiff (i.e., foreman), shepherd, or other farm laborer whose craftiness and plots he didn't know.
5. He had on.
6. With clothing tucked up like a friar.
7. Hindmost of our group.
8. The "Somnour" (Summoner) is an employee of the ecclesiastical court, whose duty is to bring to court persons whom the archdeacon—the justice of the court—suspects of offenses against canon law. By this time, however, summoners had generally transformed themselves into corrupt detectives who spied out offenders and blackmailed them by threats of summonses.
9. Cherubs, often depicted in art with red faces.
1. Uneven, partly hairless.
2. These are all ointments for diseases affecting the skin, probably diseases of venereal origin.

Can clepen "Watte"[3] as wel as can the Pope—
But whoso coude in other thing him grope,° *examine*
Thanne hadde he spent all his philosophye;[4]
Ay *Questio quid juris*[5] wolde he crye.
He was a gentil harlot° and a kinde; *rascal*
A bettre felawe sholde men nought finde:
He wolde suffre,° for a quart of win, *permit*
A good felawe to have his concubin
A twelfmonth, and excusen him at the fulle;[6]
Ful prively° a finch eek coude he pulle.[7] *secretly*
And if he foond° owher° a good felawe *found / anywhere*
He wolde techen him to have noon awe
In swich caas of the Ercedekenes curs,[8]
But if[9] a mannes soule were in his purs,
For in his purs he sholde ypunisshed be.
"Purs is the Ercedekenes helle," saide he.
But wel I woot he lied right in deede:
Of cursing° oughte eech gilty man him drede, *excommunication*
For curs wol slee° right as assoiling° savith— *slay / absolution*
And also war him of a *significavit*.[1]
In daunger[2] hadde he at his owene gise° *disposal*
The yonge girles of the diocise,
And knew hir conseil,° and was al hir reed.[3] *secrets*
A gerland hadde he set upon his heed
As greet as it were for an ale-stake,[4]
A bokeler hadde he maad him of a cake.
With him ther rood a gentil Pardoner[5]
Of Rouncival, his freend and his compeer,° *comrade*
That straight was comen fro the Court of Rome.[6]
Ful loude he soong,° "Com hider, love, to me." *sang*
This Somnour bar to him a stif burdoun:[7]
Was nevere trompe° of half so greet a soun. *trumpet*
This Pardoner hadde heer as yelow as wex,
But smoothe it heeng° as dooth a strike° of flex;° *hung / hank / flax*
By ounces[8] heenge his lokkes that he hadde,
And therwith he his shuldres overspradde,° *overspread*
But thinne it lay, by colpons,° oon by oon; *strands*
But hood for jolitee° wered° he noon, *nonchalance / wore*
For it was trussed up in his walet:° *pack*
Him thoughte he rood al of the newe jet.° *fashion*

3. Call out: "Walter"—like modern parrots' "Polly."
4. I.e., learning.
5. "What point of law does this investigation involve?" A phrase frequently used in ecclesiastical courts.
6. Fully. Ecclesiastical courts had jurisdiction over many offenses that today would come under civil law, including sexual offenses.
7. "To pull a finch" (pluck a bird) is to have sexual relations with a woman.
8. Archdeacon's sentence of excommunication.
9. Unless.
1. And also one should be careful of a *significavit* (the writ that transferred the guilty offender from the ecclesiastical to the civil arm for punishment).
2. Under his domination.
3. Was their chief source of advice.
4. A tavern was signalized by a pole ("ale-stake"), rather like a modern flagpole, projecting from its front wall; on this hung a garland, or "bush."
5. A Pardoner dispensed papal pardon for sins to those who contributed to the charitable institution that he was licensed to represent; this Pardoner purported to be collecting for the hospital of Roncesvalles ("Rouncival") in Spain, which had a London branch.
6. The papal court.
7. I.e., provided him with a strong bass accompaniment.
8. I.e., thin strands.

Dischevelee° save his cappe he rood al bare. *with hair down*
Swiche glaring yën hadde he as an hare.
A vernicle[9] hadde he sowed upon his cappe,
His walet biforn him in his lappe,
Bretful° of pardon, come from Rome al hoot.° *brimful / hot*
A vois he hadde as smal° as hath a goot;° *high-pitched / goat*
No beerd hadde he, ne nevere sholde have;
As smoothe it was as it were late yshave:
I trowe° he were a gelding[1] or a mare. *believe*
But of his craft, fro Berwik into Ware,[2]
Ne was ther swich another pardoner;
For in his male° he hadde a pilwe-beer° *bag / pillowcase*
Which that he saide was Oure Lady veil;
He saide he hadde a gobet° of the sail *piece*
That Sainte Peter hadde whan that he wente
Upon the see, til Jesu Crist him hente.° *seized*
He hadde a crois° of laton,° ful of stones, *cross / brassy metal*
And in a glas he hadde pigges bones,
But with thise relikes[3] whan that he foond° *found*
A poore person° dwelling upon lond,[4] *parson*
Upon° a day he gat° him more moneye *in / got*
Than that the person gat in monthes twaye;
And thus with feined° flaterye and japes° *false / tricks*
He made the person and the peple his apes.° *dupes*
But trewely to tellen at the laste,
He was in chirche a noble ecclesiaste;
Wel coude he rede a lesson and a storye,° *liturgical narrative*
But alderbest° he soong an offertorye,[5] *best of all*
For wel he wiste° whan that song was songe, *knew*
He moste° preche and wel affile° his tonge *must / sharpen*
To winne silver, as he ful wel coude—
Therefore he soong the merierly° and loude. *more merrily*
Now have I told you soothly in a clause[6]
Th'estaat, th'array, the nombre, and eek the cause
Why that assembled was this compaignye
In Southwerk at this gentil hostelrye
That highte the Tabard, faste° by the Belle;[7] *close*
But now is time to you for to telle
How that we baren us[8] that ilke° night *same*
Whan we were in that hostelrye alight;
And after wol I telle of oure viage,° *trip*
And al the remenant of oure pilgrimage.
But first I praye you of youre curteisye
That ye n'arette it nought my vilainye[9]
Though that I plainly speke in this matere
To telle you hir wordes and hir cheere,° *behavior*

9. Portrait of Christ's face as it was said to have been impressed on St. Veronica's handkerchief, i.e., a souvenir reproduction of a famous relic in Rome.
1. A neutered stallion, i.e., a eunuch.
2. I.e., from one end of England to the other.
3. Relics, i.e., the pigs' bones that the Pardoner represented as saints' bones.
4. Upcountry.
5. Part of the mass sung before the offering of alms.
6. I.e., in a short space.
7. Another tavern in Southwark.
8. Bore ourselves.
9. That you do not attribute it to my boorishness.

Ne though I speke hir wordes proprely;° *accurately*
For this ye knowen also wel as I:
Who so shal telle a tale after a man
He moot° reherce,° as neigh as evere he can, *must / repeat*
Everich a word, if it be in his charge,° *responsibility*
Al speke he[1] nevere so rudeliche and large,° *broadly*
Or elles he moot telle his tale untrewe,
Or feine° thing, or finde° wordes newe; *make up / devise*
He may nought spare[2] although he were his brother:
He moot as wel saye oo word as another.
Crist spak himself ful brode° in Holy Writ, *broadly*
And wel ye woot no vilainye° is it; *rudeness*
Eek Plato saith, who so can him rede,
The wordes mote be cosin to the deede.
  Also I praye you to foryive it me
Al° have I nat set folk in hir degree *although*
Here in this tale as that they sholde stonde:
My wit is short, ye may wel understonde.
  Greet cheere made oure Host[3] us everichoon,
And to the soper sette he us anoon.° *at once*
He served us with vitaile° at the beste. *food*
Strong was the win, and wel to drinke us leste.° *it pleased*
A semely man oure Hoste was withalle
For to been a marchal[4] in an halle;
A large man he was, with yën steepe,° *prominent*
A fairer burgeis° was ther noon in Chepe[5]— *burgher*
Bold of his speeche, and wis, and wel ytaught,
And of manhood him lakkede right naught.
Eek therto he was right a merye man,
And after soper playen he bigan,
And spak of mirthe amonges othere thinges—
Whan that we hadde maad oure rekeninges[6]—
And saide thus, "Now, lordinges, trewely,
Ye been to me right welcome, hertely.° *heartily*
For by my trouthe, if that I shal nat lie,
I sawgh nat this yeer so merye a compaignye
At ones in this herberwe° as is now. *inn*
Fain° wolde I doon you mirthe, wiste I[7] how. *gladly*
And of a mirthe I am right now bithought,
To doon you ese, and it shal coste nought.
  "Ye goon to Canterbury—God you speede;
The blisful martyr quite you youre meede.[8]
And wel I woot as ye goon by the waye
Ye shapen you[9] to talen° and to playe, *converse*
For trewely, confort ne mirthe is noon
To ride by the waye domb as stoon;° *stone*
And therefore wol I maken you disport
As I saide erst,° and doon you som confort; *before*
And if you liketh alle, by oon assent,

1. Although he speak.
2. I.e., spare anyone.
3. The landlord of the Tabard Inn.
4. Marshal, one who was in charge of feasts.
5. Cheapside, business center of London.
6. Had paid our bills.
7. If I knew.
8. Pay you your reward.
9. Intend.

For to stonden at[1] my juggement,
And for to werken as I shall you saye,
Tomorwe whan ye riden by the waye—
Now by my fader° soule that is deed, *father's*
But° ye be merye I wol yive you myn heed!° *unless / head*
Holde up youre handes withouten more speeche."
  Oure counseil was nat longe for to seeche;° *seek*
Us thought it was not worth to make it wis,[2]
And graunted him withouten more avis,° *deliberation*
And bade him saye his voirdit° as him leste.[3] *verdict*
  "Lordinges," quod he, "now herkneth for the beste;
But taketh it nought, I praye you, in desdain.
This is the point, to speken short and plain,
That eech of you, to shorte° with oure waye *shorten*
In this viage, shal tellen tales twaye°— *two*
To Canterburyward, I mene it so,
And hoomward he shal tellen othere two,
Of aventures that whilom° have bifalle; *once upon a time*
And which of you that bereth him best of alle—
That is to sayn, that telleth in this cas
Tales of best sentence° and most solas°— *meaning / delight*
Shal have a soper at oure aller cost,[4]
Here in this place, sitting by this post,
Whan that we come again fro Canterbury.
And for to make you the more mury° *merry*
I wol myself goodly° with you ride— *kindly*
Right at myn owene cost—and be youre gide.
And who so wol my juggement withsaye° *contradict*
Shal paye al that we spende by the waye.
And if ye vouche sauf that it be so,
Telle me anoon, withouten wordes mo,° *more*
And I wol erly shape me[5] therefore."
  This thing was graunted and oure othes swore
With ful glad herte, and prayden[6] him also
That he wolde vouche sauf for to do so,
And that he wolde been oure governour,
And of oure tales juge and reportour,° *accountant*
And sette a soper at a certain pris,° *price*
And we wol ruled been at his devis,° *disposal*
In heigh and lowe; and thus by oon assent
We been accorded to his juggement.
And therupon the win was fet° anoon; *fetched*
We dronken and to reste wente eechoon° *each one*
Withouten any lenger° taryinge. *longer*
  Amorwe° whan that day bigan to springe *in the morning*
Up roos oure Host and was oure aller cok,[7]
And gadred us togidres in a flok,
And forth we riden, a litel more than pas,° *walking pace*
Unto the watering of Saint Thomas;[8]

1. Abide by.
2. We didn't think it worthwhile to make an issue of it.
3. It pleased.
4. At the cost of us all.
5. Prepare myself.
6. I.e., we prayed.
7. Was rooster for us all.
8. A watering place near Southwark.

And ther oure Host bigan his hors arreste,° *halt*
And saide, "Lordes, herkneth if you leste:° *it please*
  Ye woot youre forward° and it you recorde:[9] *agreement*
If evensong and morwesong° accorde,° *morning song / agree*
Lat see now who shal telle the firste tale.
As evere mote° I drinken win or ale, *may*
Who so be rebel to my juggement
Shal paye for al that by the way is spent.
Now draweth cut er that we ferrer twinne:[1]
He which that hath the shorteste shal biginne.
  "Sire Knight," quod he, "my maister and my lord,
Now draweth cut, for that is myn accord.° *will*
Cometh neer," quod he, "my lady Prioresse,
And ye, sire Clerk, lat be youre shamefastnesse°— *modesty*
Ne studieth nought. Lay hand to, every man!"
  Anoon to drawen every wight bigan,
And shortly for to tellen as it was
Were it by aventure, or sort, or cas,[2]
The soothe° is this, the cut fil° to the Knight; *truth / fell*
Of which ful blithe and glad was every wight,
And telle he moste° his tale, as was resoun, *must*
By forward and by composicioun,[3]
As ye han herd. What needeth wordes mo?
And whan this goode man sawgh that it was so,
As he that wis was and obedient
To keepe his forward by his free assent,
He saide, "Sin° I shal biginne the game, *since*
What, welcome be the cut, in Goddes name!
Now lat us ride, and herkneth what I saye."
And with that word we riden forth oure waye,
And he bigan with right a merye cheere° *countenance*
His tale anoon, and saide as ye may heere.

[*Summary* *The Knight's Tale* is a romance of 2,350 lines, which Chaucer had written before beginning *The Canterbury Tales*—one of several works assumed to be earlier that he inserted into the collection. It is probably the same story, with only minor revisions, that Chaucer referred to in *The Legend of Good Women* as "al the love of Palamon and Arcite." These are the names of the two heroes of *The Knight's Tale*, kinsmen and best friends who are taken prisoner at the siege and destruction of ancient Thebes by Theseus, the ruler of Athens. Gazing out from their prison cell in a tower, they fall in love at first sight and almost at the same moment with Theseus's sister-in-law, Emily, who is taking an early-morning walk in a garden below their window. After a bitter rivalry, they are at last reconciled through a tournament in which Emily is the prize. Arcite wins the tournament but, as he lies dying after being thrown by his horse, he makes a noble speech encouraging Palamon and Emily to marry. The tale is an ambitious combination of classical setting and mythology, romance plot, and themes of fortune and destiny.]

9. You recall it.
1. Go farther. "Draweth cut": i.e., draw straws.
2. Whether it was luck, fate, or chance.
3. By agreement and compact.

The Miller's Prologue and Tale

The Miller's Tale belongs to a genre known as the "fabliau": a short story in verse that deals satirically, often grossly and fantastically as well as hilariously, with intrigues and deceptions about sex or money (and often both these elements in the same story). These are the tales Chaucer is anticipating in *The General Prologue* when he warns his presumably genteel audience that they must expect some rude speaking (see lines 727–44). An even more pointed apology follows at the end of *The Miller's Prologue*. Fabliau tales exist everywhere in oral literature; as a literary form they flourished in France, especially in the thirteenth century. By having Robin the Miller tell a fabliau to "quit" (to requite or pay back) the Knight's aristocratic romance, Chaucer sets up a dialectic between classes, genres, and styles that he exploits throughout *The Canterbury Tales*.

The Prologue

Whan that the Knight hadde thus his tale ytold,
In al the route° nas° ther yong ne old *group / was not*
That he ne saide it was a noble storye,
And worthy for to drawen° to memorye, *recall*
And namely° the gentils everichoon. *especially*
Oure Hoste lough° and swoor, "So mote I goon,[1] *laughed*
This gooth aright: unbokeled is the male.° *pouch*
Lat see now who shal telle another tale.
For trewely the game is wel bigonne.
Now telleth ye, sire Monk, if that ye conne,° *can*
Somwhat to quite° with the Knightes tale." *repay*
The Millere, that for dronken[2] was al pale,
So that unnethe° upon his hors he sat, *with difficulty*
He nolde° avalen° neither hood ne hat, *would not / take off*
Ne abiden no man for his curteisye,
But in Pilates vois[3] he gan to crye,
And swoor, "By armes[4] and by blood and bones,
I can° a noble tale for the nones, *know*
With which I wol now quite the Knightes tale."
Oure Hoste sawgh that he was dronke of ale,
And saide, "Abide, Robin, leve° brother, *dear*
Som bettre man shal telle us first another.
Abide, and lat us werken thriftily."° *with propriety*
"By Goddes soule," quod he, "that wol nat I,
For I wol speke or elles go my way."
Oure Host answerde, "Tel on, a devele way![5]
Thou art a fool; thy wit is overcome."
"Now herkneth," quod the Millere, "alle and some.[6]
But first I make a protestacioun° *public affirmation*
That I am dronke: I knowe it by my soun.° *tone of voice*
And therfore if that I misspeke° or saye, *speak or say wrongly*
Wite it[7] the ale of Southwerk, I you praye;

1. So might I walk—an oath.
2. I.e., drunkenness.
3. The harsh voice usually associated with the character of Pontius Pilate in the mystery plays.
4. I.e., by God's arms, a blasphemous oath.
5. I.e., in the devil's name.
6. Each and every one.
7. Blame it on.

For I wol telle a legende° and a lif — *saint's life*
Bothe of a carpenter and of his wif,
How that a clerk hath set the wrightes cappe."[8]
  The Reeve answerde and saide, "Stint thy clappe![9]
Lat be thy lewed° dronken harlotrye.° — *ignorant / obscenity*
It is a sinne and eek° a greet folye — *also*
To apairen° any man or him defame, — *injure*
And eek to bringen wives in swich fame.° — *reputation*
Thou maist ynough of othere thinges sayn."
  This dronken Millere spak ful soone again,
And saide, "Leve° brother Osewold, — *dear*
Who hath no wif, he is no cokewold.° — *cuckold*
But I saye nat therfore that thou art oon.
Ther ben ful goode wives many oon,° — *a one*
And evere a thousand goode ayains oon badde.
That knowestou wel thyself but if thou madde.° — *rave*
Why artou angry with my tale now?
I have a wif, pardee,° as wel as thou, — *by God*
Yit nolde° I, for the oxen in my plough, — *would not*
Take upon me more than ynough° — *enough*
As deemen of myself that I were oon:[1]
I wol bileve wel that I am noon.
An housbonde shal nought been inquisitif
Of Goddes privetee,° nor of his wif. — *secrets*
So[2] he may finde Goddes foison° there, — *plenty*
Of the remenant° needeth nought enquere."° — *rest / inquire*
  What sholde I more sayn but this Millere
He nolde his wordes for no man forbere,
But tolde his cherles tale in his manere.
M'athinketh° that I shal reherce° it here, — *I regret / repeat*
And therefore every gentil wight I praye,
Deemeth nought, for Goddes love, that I saye
Of yvel entente, but for° I moot reherse — *because*
Hir tales alle, be they bet° or werse, — *better*
Or elles falsen° som of my matere. — *falsify*
And therfore, whoso list it nought yheere° — *hear*
Turne over the leef,° and chese° another tale, — *page / choose*
For he shal finde ynowe,° grete and smale, — *enough*
Of storial[3] thing that toucheth gentilesse,° — *gentility*
And eek moralitee and holinesse:
Blameth nought me if that ye chese amis.
The Millere is a cherl, ye knowe wel this,
So was the Reeve eek, and othere mo,
And harlotrye° they tolden bothe two. — *ribaldry*
Aviseth you,[4] and putte me out of blame:
And eek men shal nought maken ernest of game.

8. I.e., how a clerk made a fool of a carpenter.
9. Stop your chatter.
1. To think that I were one (a cuckold).
2. Provided that.
3. Historical, i.e., true.
4. Take heed.

The Tale

Whilom° ther was dwelling at Oxenforde — *once upon a time*
A riche gnof° that gestes heeld to boorde,[5] — *churl*
And of his craft he was a carpenter.
With him ther was dwelling a poore scoler,
Hadde lerned art,[6] but al his fantasye° — *desire*
Was turned for to lere° astrologye, — *learn*
And coude a certain of conclusiouns,
To deemen by interrogaciouns,[7]
If that men axed° him in certain houres — *asked*
Whan that men sholde have droughte or elles showres,
Or if men axed him what shal bifalle
Of every thing—I may nat rekene hem alle.
This clerk was cleped° hende[8] Nicholas. — *called*
Of derne love he coude, and of solas,[9]
And therto he was sly and ful privee,° — *secretive*
And lik a maide meeke for to see.
A chambre hadde he in that hostelrye
Allone, withouten any compaignye,
Ful fetisly ydight[1] with herbes swoote,° — *sweet*
And he himself as sweete as is the roote
Of licoris or any setewale.[2]
His *Almageste*[3] and bookes grete and smale,
His astrelabye, longing for[4] his art,
His augrim stones,[5] layen faire apart
On shelves couched° at his beddes heed; — *set*
His presse° ycovered with a falding reed;[6] — *storage chest*
And al above ther lay a gay sautrye,° — *psaltery (harp)*
On which he made a-nightes melodye
So swetely that al the chambre roong,° — *rang*
And *Angelus ad Virginem*[7] he soong,
And after that he soong the *Kinges Note*:[8]
Ful often blessed was his merye throte.
And thus this sweete clerk his time spente
After his freendes finding and his rente.[9]
This carpenter hadde wedded newe° a wif — *lately*
Which that he loved more than his lif.
Of eighteteene yeer she was of age;
Jalous he was, and heeld hire narwe in cage,
For she was wilde and yong, and he was old,
And deemed himself been lik a cokewold.[1]

5. I.e., took in boarders.
6. Who had completed the first stage of university education (the trivium).
7. I.e., and he knew a number of propositions on which to base astrological analyses (which would reveal the matters in the next three lines).
8. Courteous, handy, attractive.
9. I.e., he knew about secret love and pleasurable practices.
1. Elegantly furnished.
2. Setwall, a spice.
3. The 2nd-century treatise by Ptolemy, still the standard astronomy textbook.
4. Belonging to. "Astrelabye": astrolabe, an astronomical instrument.
5. Counters used in arithmetic.
6. Red coarse woolen cloth.
7. "The Angel to the Virgin," an Annunciation hymn.
8. Probably a popular song of the time.
9. In accordance with his friends' provision and his own income.
1. I.e., suspected of himself that he was like a cuckold.

He knew nat Caton,[2] for his wit was rude,
That bad men sholde wedde his similitude:[3]
Men sholde wedden after hir estat,[4]
For youthe and elde° is often at debat. *age*
But sith that he was fallen in the snare,
He moste endure, as other folk, his care.
  Fair was this yonge wif, and therwithal
As any wesele° hir body gent and smal.[5] *weasel*
A ceint she wered, barred[6] al of silk;
A barmcloth° as whit as morne° milk *apron / morning*
Upon hir lendes,° ful of many a gore;° *loins / flounce*
Whit was hir smok,° and broiden° al bifore *undergarment / embroidered*
And eek bihinde, on hir coler° aboute, *collar*
Of° col-blak silk, withinne and eek withoute; *with*
The tapes° of hir white voluper° *ribbons / cap*
Were of the same suite of[7] hir coler;
Hir filet° brood° of silk and set ful hye; *headband / broad*
And sikerly° she hadde a likerous° yë; *certainly / wanton*
Ful smale ypulled[8] were hir browes two,
And tho were bent,° and blake as any slo.° *arching / sloeberry*
She was ful more blisful on to see
Than is the newe perejonette° tree, *pear*
And softer than the wolle° is of a wether;° *wool / ram*
And by hir girdel° heeng° a purs of lether, *belt / hung*
Tasseled with silk and perled with latoun.[9]
In al this world, to seeken up and down,
Ther nis no man so wis that coude thenche° *imagine*
So gay a popelote° or swich° a wenche. *doll / such*
Ful brighter was the shining of hir hewe
Than in the Towr[1] the noble° yforged newe. *gold coin*
But of hir song, it was as loud and yerne° *lively*
As any swalwe° sitting on a berne.° *swallow / barn*
Therto she coude skippe and make game° *play*
As any kide or calf folwing his dame.° *mother*
Hir mouth was sweete as bragot or the meeth,[2]
Or hoord of apples laid in hay or heeth.° *heather*
Winsing° she was as is a joly° colt, *skittish / high-spirited*
Long as a mast, and upright° as a bolt.° *straight / arrow*
A brooch she bar upon hir lowe coler
As brood as is the boos° of a bokeler;° *boss / shield*
Hir shoes were laced on hir legges hye.
She was a primerole,° a piggesnye,[3] *primrose*
For any lord to leggen° in his bedde, *lay*
Or yit for any good yeman to wedde.
  Now sire, and eft° sire, so bifel the cas *again*
That on a day this hende Nicholas

2. Dionysius Cato, the supposed author of a book of maxims used in elementary education.
3. Commanded that one should wed his equal.
4. Men should marry according to their condition.
5. Slender and delicate.
6. A belt she wore, with transverse stripes.
7. The same kind as, i.e., black.
8. Delicately plucked.
9. I.e., with brassy spangles on it.
1. The Tower of London, the Mint.
2. "Bragot" and "meeth" are honey drinks.
3. A pig's eye, a name for a common flower.

Fil° with this yonge wif to rage° and playe, *happened / flirt*
Whil that hir housbonde was at Oseneye[4]
(As clerkes been ful subtil and ful quainte),° *clever*
And prively he caughte hire by the queinte,[5]
And saide, "Ywis,° but° if ich° have my wille, *truly / unless / I*
For derne° love of thee, lemman, I spille,"° *secret / die*
And heeld hire harde by the haunche-bones,° *thighs*
And saide, "Lemman,° love me al atones,[6] *sweetheart*
Or I wol dien, also° God me save." *so*
And she sproong° as a colt dooth in a trave,[7] *sprang*
And with hir heed she wried° faste away; *twisted*
She saide, "I wol nat kisse thee, by my fay.° *faith*
Why, lat be," quod she, "lat be, Nicholas!
Or I wol crye 'Out, harrow,° and allas!' *help*
Do way youre handes, for your curteisye!"
  This Nicholas gan mercy for to crye,
And spak so faire, and profred him so faste,[8]
That she hir love him graunted atte laste,
And swoor hir ooth by Saint Thomas of Kent[9]
That she wolde been at his comandement,
Whan that she may hir leiser[1] wel espye.
"Myn housbonde is so ful of jalousye
That but ye waite° wel and been privee *be on guard*
I woot right wel I nam but deed,"[2] quod she.
"Ye moste been ful derne° as in this cas." *secret*
"Nay, therof care thee nought," quod Nicholas.
"A clerk hadde litherly biset his while,[3]
But if he coude a carpenter bigile."
And thus they been accorded and ysworn
To waite° a time, as I have told biforn. *watch for*
Whan Nicholas hadde doon this everydeel,° *every bit*
And thakked° hire upon the lendes° weel, *patted / loins*
He kiste hire sweete, and taketh his sautrye,
And playeth faste, and maketh melodye.
  Thanne fil° it thus, that to the parissh chirche, *befell*
Cristes owene werkes for to wirche,° *perform*
This goode wif wente on an haliday:° *holy day*
Hir forheed shoon as bright as any day,
So was it wasshen whan she leet° hir werk. *left*
  Now was ther of that chirche a parissh clerk,[4]
The which that was ycleped° Absolon: *called*
Crul° was his heer, and as the gold it shoon, *curly*
And strouted° as a fanne[5] large and brode; *spread out*
Ful straight and evene lay his joly shode.[6]
His rode° was reed, his yën greye as goos.° *complexion / goose*

4. A town near Oxford.
5. Elegant (thing); a euphemism for the female genitals.
6. Right now.
7. Frame for holding a horse to be shod.
8. I.e., made such vigorous advances.
9. Thomas à Becket.
1. I.e., opportunity.
2. I am no more than dead, I am done for.
3. Poorly employed his time.
4. Assistant to the parish priest, not a cleric or student.
5. Wide-mouthed basket for separating grain from chaff.
6. Parting of the hair.

With Poules window corven[7] on his shoos,
In hoses° rede he wente fetisly.° *stockings / elegantly*
Yclad he was ful smale° and proprely, *finely*
Al in a kirtel° of a light waget°— *tunic / blue*
Ful faire and thikke been the pointes[8] set—
And therupon he hadde a gay surplis,° *surplice*
As whit as is the blosme upon the ris.° *bough*
A merye child° he was, so God me save. *young man*
Wel coude he laten blood, and clippe,[9] and shave,
And maken a chartre of land, or acquitaunce;[1]
In twenty manere° coude he trippe and daunce *ways*
After the scole of Oxenforde tho,° *then*
And with his legges casten° to and fro, *prance*
And playen songes on a smal rubible;° *fiddle*
Therto he soong somtime a loud quinible,[2]
And as wel coude he playe on a giterne:° *guitar*
In al the town nas brewhous ne taverne
That he ne visited with his solas,° *entertainment*
Ther any gailard tappestere[3] was.
But sooth to sayn, he was somdeel squaimous° *a bit squeamish*
Of° farting, and of speeche daungerous.[4] *about*
  This Absolon, that joly° was and gay, *pretty, amorous*
Gooth with a cencer° on the haliday, *incense burner*
Cencing the wives of the parissh faste,
And many a lovely look on hem he caste,
And namely° on this carpenteres wif: *especially*
To looke on hire him thoughte a merye lif.
She was so propre° and sweete and likerous,[5] *neat*
I dar wel sayn, if she hadde been a mous,
And he a cat, he wolde hire hente° anoon. *pounce on*
This parissh clerk, this joly Absolon,
Hath in his herte swich a love-longinge° *lovesickness*
That of no wif ne took he noon offringe—
For curteisye he saide he wolde noon.
The moone, whan it was night, ful brighte shoon,° *shone*
And Absolon his giterne° hath ytake— *guitar*
For paramours° he thoughte for to wake— *love*
And forth he gooth, jolif° and amorous, *pretty*
Til he cam to the carpenteres hous,
A litel after cokkes hadde ycrowe,
And dressed him up by a shot-windowe[6]
That was upon the carpenteres wal.
He singeth in his vois gentil and smal,° *dainty*
"Now dere lady, if thy wille be,
I praye you that ye wol rewe° on me," *have pity*
Ful wel accordant to his giterninge.[7]
This carpenter awook and herde him singe,

7. Carved with intricate designs, like the tracery in the windows of St. Paul's.
8. Laces for fastening the tunic and holding up the hose.
9. Let blood and give haircuts. Bleeding was a medical treatment performed by barbers.
1. Legal release. "Chartre": deed.
2. Part requiring a very high voice.
3. Gay barmaid.
4. Prudish about (vulgar) talk.
5. Wanton, appetizing.
6. Took his position by a hinged window.
7. In harmony with his guitar playing.

And spak unto his wif, and saide anoon,
"What, Alison, heerestou nought Absolon
That chaunteth thus under oure bowres° wal?" *bedroom's*
And she answerde hir housbonde therwithal,
"Yis, God woot, John, I heere it everydeel."° *every bit*
  This passeth forth. What wol ye bet than weel?[8]
Fro day to day this joly Absolon
So woweth° hire that him is wo-bigoon: *woos*
He waketh° al the night and al the day; *stays awake*
He kembed° his lokkes brode[9] and made him gay; *combed*
He woweth hire by menes and brocage,[1]
And swoor he wolde been hir owene page° *personal servant*
He singeth, brokking° as a nightingale; *trilling*
He sente hire piment,° meeth,° and spiced ale, *spiced wine / mead*
And wafres° piping hoot out of the gleede;° *pastries / coals*
And for she was of towne,[2] he profred meede°— *money*
For som folk wol be wonnen for richesse,
And som for strokes,° and som for gentilesse. *blows (force)*
Somtime to shewe his lightnesse and maistrye,[3]
He playeth Herodes[4] upon a scaffold° hye. *platform, stage*
But what availeth him as in this cas?
She loveth so this hende Nicholas
That Absolon may blowe the bukkes horn;[5]
He ne hadde for his labour but a scorn.
And thus she maketh Absolon hir ape,[6]
And al his ernest turneth til° a jape.° *to / joke*
Ful sooth is this proverbe, it is no lie;
Men saith right thus: "Alway the nye slye
Maketh the ferre leve to be loth."[7]
For though that Absolon be wood° or wroth, *furious*
By cause that he fer was from hir sighte,
This nye° Nicholas stood in his lighte. *nearby*
  Now beer° thee wel, thou hende Nicholas, *bear*
For Absolon may waile and singe allas.
  And so bifel it on a Saterday
This carpenter was goon til Oseney,
And hende Nicholas and Alisoun
Accorded been to this conclusioun,
That Nicholas shal shapen° hem a wile° *arrange / trick*
This sely[8] jalous housbonde to bigile,
And if so be this game wente aright,
She sholden sleepen in his arm al night—
For this was his desir and hire° also. *hers*
And right anoon, withouten wordes mo,
This Nicholas no lenger wolde tarye,
But dooth ful softe unto his chambre carye
Bothe mete and drinke for a day or twaye,

8. Better than well.
9. I.e., wide-spreading.
1. By go-betweens and agents.
2. Because she was a town woman.
3. Facility and virtuosity.
4. Herod, a role traditionally played as a bully in the mystery plays.
5. Blow the buck's horn, i.e., go whistle, waste his time.
6. I.e., thus she makes a monkey out of Absolon.
7. Always the sly man at hand makes the distant dear one hated.
8. Poor innocent.

And to hir housbonde bad hire for to saye,
If that he axed after Nicholas,
She sholde saye she niste° wher he was— *didn't know*
Of al that day she sawgh him nought with yë:
She trowed° that he was in maladye, *believed*
For for no cry hir maide coude him calle,
He nolde answere for no thing that mighte falle.° *happen*
This passeth forth al thilke° Saterday *this*
That Nicholas stille in his chambre lay,
And eet,° and sleep,° or dide what him leste,[9] *ate / slept*
Til Sonday that the sonne gooth to reste.
This sely carpenter hath greet mervaile
Of Nicholas, or what thing mighte him aile,
And saide, "I am adrad,° by Saint Thomas, *afraid*
It stondeth nat aright with Nicholas.
God shilde° that he deide sodeinly! *forbid*
This world is now ful tikel,° sikerly: *precarious*
I sawgh today a corps yborn to chirche
That now a° Monday last I sawgh him wirche.° *on / work*
Go up," quod he unto his knave° anoon, *manservant*
"Clepe° at his dore or knokke with a stoon.° *call / stone*
Looke how it is and tel me boldely."
This knave gooth him up ful sturdily,
And at the chambre dore whil that he stood
He cride and knokked as that he were wood,° *mad*
"What? How? What do ye, maister Nicholay?
How may ye sleepen al the longe day?"
But al for nought: he herde nat a word.
An hole he foond ful lowe upon a boord,
Ther as the cat was wont in for to creepe,
And at that hole he looked in ful deepe,
And atte laste he hadde of him a sighte.
This Nicholas sat evere caping° uprighte *gaping*
As he hadde kiked° on the newe moone. *gazed*
Adown he gooth and tolde his maister soone
In what array° he saw this ilke° man. *condition / same*
This carpenter to blessen him[1] bigan,
And saide, "Help us, Sainte Frideswide![2]
A man woot litel what him shal bitide.
This man is falle, with his astromye,° *astronomy*
In som woodnesse° or in som agonye. *madness*
I thoughte ay° wel how that it sholde be: *always*
Men sholde nought knowe of Goddes privetee.° *secrets*
Ye, blessed be alway a lewed° man *ignorant*
That nought but only his bileve° can.° *creed / knows*
So ferde° another clerk with astromye: *fared*
He walked in the feeldes for to prye° *gaze*
Upon the sterres,° what ther sholde bifalle, *stars*
Til he was in a marle-pit[3] yfalle—
He saw nat that. But yit, by Saint Thomas,

9. He wanted.
1. Cross himself.
2. Patron saint of Oxford.
3. Pit from which a fertilizing clay is dug.

Me reweth sore[4] for hende Nicholas.
He shal be rated of[5] his studying,
If that I may, by Jesus, hevene king!
Get me a staf that I may underspore,° *pry up*
Whil that thou, Robin, hevest° up the dore. *heave*
He shal[6] out of his studying, as I gesse."
And to the chambre dore he gan him dresse.[7]
His knave was a strong carl° for the nones,° *fellow / purpose*
And by the haspe he haaf° it up atones: *heaved*
Into° the floor the dore fil° anoon. *on / fell*
This Nicholas sat ay as stille as stoon,
And evere caped up into the air.
This carpenter wende° he were in despair, *thought*
And hente° him by the shuldres mightily, *seized*
And shook him harde, and cride spitously,° *vehemently*
"What, Nicholay, what, how! What! Looke adown!
Awaak and thenk on Cristes passioun![8]
I crouche[9] thee from elves and fro wightes."° *wicked creatures*
Therwith the nightspel saide he anoonrightes[1]
On foure halves° of the hous aboute, *sides*
And on the thresshfold° on the dore withoute: *threshold*
"Jesu Crist and Sainte Benedight,° *Benedict*
Blesse this hous from every wikked wight!
For nightes nerye the White Pater Noster.[2]
Where wentestou,° thou Sainte Petres soster?" *did you go / sister*
And at the laste this hende Nicholas
Gan for to sike° sore, and saide, "Allas, *sigh*
Shal al the world be lost eftsoones° now?" *again*
  This carpenter answerde, "What saistou?
What, thenk on God as we doon, men that swinke."° *work*
  This Nicholas answerde, "Fecche me drinke,
And after wol I speke in privetee
Of certain thing that toucheth me and thee.
I wol telle it noon other man, certain."
  This carpenter gooth down and comth again,
And broughte of mighty° ale a large quart, *strong*
And when that eech of hem hadde dronke his part,
This Nicholas his dore faste shette,° *shut*
And down the carpenter by him he sette,
And saide, "John, myn hoste lief° and dere, *beloved*
Thou shalt upon thy trouthe° swere me here *word of honor*
That to no wight thou shalt this conseil° wraye;° *secret / disclose*
For it is Cristes conseil that I saye,
And if thou telle it man,[3] thou art forlore,° *lost*
For this vengeance thou shalt have therfore,

4. I sorely pity.
5. Scolded for.
6. I.e., shall come.
7. Took his stand.
8. I.e., the Crucifixion.
9. Make the sign of the cross on.
1. The night-charm he said right away (to ward off evil spirits).
2. Pater Noster is Latin for "Our Father," the beginning of the Lord's Prayer. The line is obscure, but a conjectural reading would be, "May the White 'Our Father' (or 'Our White Father') [either a prayer or the personification of a protecting power] defend [*nerye*] (us) against nights." The "nightspel" is a jumble of Christian references and pagan superstition.
3. To anyone.

That if thou wraye me, thou shalt be wood."[4]
"Nay, Crist forbede it, for his holy blood,"
Quod tho this sely° man. "I nam no labbe,° *innocent / tell-tale*
And though I saye, I nam nat lief to gabbe.[5]
Say what thou wilt, I shal it nevere telle
To child ne wif, by him that harwed helle."[6]
"Now John," quod Nicholas, "I wol nought lie.
I have yfounde in myn astrologye,
As I have looked in the moone bright,
That now a Monday next, at quarter night,[7]
Shal falle a rain, and that so wilde and wood,° *furious*
That half so greet was nevere Noees° flood. *Noah's*
This world," he saide, "in lasse° than an hour *less*
Shal al be dreint,° so hidous is the showr. *drowned*
Thus shal mankinde drenche° and lese° hir lif." *drown / lose*
This carpenter answerde, "Allas, my wif!
And shal she drenche? Allas, myn Alisoun!"
For sorwe of this he fil almost[8] adown,
And saide, "Is there no remedye in this cas?"
"Why yis, for[9] Gode," quod hende Nicholas,
"If thou wolt werken after lore and reed[1]—
Thou maist nought werken after thyn owene heed;° *head*
For thus saith Salomon that was ful trewe,
'Werk al by conseil and thou shalt nought rewe.'° *be sorry*
And if thou werken wolt by good conseil,
I undertake, withouten mast or sail,
Yit shal I save hire and thee and me.
Hastou nat herd how saved was Noee
Whan that oure Lord hadde warned him biforn
That al the world with water sholde be lorn?"° *lost*
"Yis," quod this carpenter, "ful yore° ago." *long*
"Hastou nat herd," quod Nicholas, "also
The sorwe of Noee with his felaweshipe?
Er° that he mighte gete his wif to shipe, *before*
Him hadde levere,[2] I dar wel undertake,
At thilke time than alle his wetheres[3] blake
That she hadde had a ship hirself allone.[4]
And therfore woostou° what is best to doone? *do you know*
This axeth° haste, and of an hastif° thing *requires / urgent*
Men may nought preche or maken tarying.
Anoon go gete us faste into this in° *lodging*
A kneeding trough or elles a kimelin° *brewing tub*
For eech of us, but looke that they be large,° *wide*
In whiche we mowen swimme as in a barge,[5]
And han therinne vitaile suffisaunt[6]
But for a day—fy° on the remenaunt! *fie*

4. Go mad.
5. And though I say it myself, I don't like to gossip.
6. By Him that despoiled hell—i.e., Christ.
7. I.e., shortly before dawn.
8. Almost fell.
9. I.e., by.
1. Act according to learning and advice.
2. He had rather.
3. Rams. I.e., he'd have given all the black rams he had.
4. The reluctance of Noah's wife to board the ark is a traditional comic theme in the mystery plays.
5. In which we can float as in a vessel.
6. Sufficient food.

The water shal aslake° and goon away *diminish*
Aboute prime[7] upon the nexte day.
But Robin may nat wite° of this, thy knave, *know*
Ne eek thy maide Gille I may nat save.
Axe nought why, for though thou axe me,
I wol nought tellen Goddes privetee.° *secrets*
Suffiseth thee, but if thy wittes madde,° *go mad*
To han° as greet a grace as Noee hadde. *have*
Thy wif shal I wel saven, out of doute.
Go now thy way, and speed thee heraboute.
But whan thou hast for hire° and thee and me *her*
Ygeten us thise kneeding-tubbes three,
Thanne shaltou hangen hem in the roof ful hye,
That no man of oure purveyance° espye. *preparations*
And whan thou thus hast doon as I have said,
And hast oure vitaile faire in hem ylaid,
And eek an ax to smite the corde atwo,
Whan that the water comth that we may go,
And broke an hole an heigh[8] upon the gable
Unto the gardinward,[9] over the stable,
That we may freely passen forth oure way,
Whan that the grete showr is goon away,
Thanne shaltou swimme as merye, I undertake,
As dooth the white doke° after hir drake. *duck*
Thanne wol I clepe,° 'How, Alison? How, John? *call*
Be merye, for the flood wol passe anoon.'
And thou wolt sayn, 'Hail, maister Nicholay!
Good morwe, I see thee wel, for it is day!'
And thanne shal we be lordes al oure lif
Of al the world, as Noee and his wif.
But of oo thing I warne thee ful right:
Be wel avised° on that ilke night *warned*
That we been entred into shippes boord
That noon of us ne speke nought a word,
Ne clepe, ne crye, but been in his prayere,
For it is Goddes owene heeste dere.[1]
Thy wif and thou mote hange fer atwinne,[2]
For that bitwixe you shal be no sinne—
Namore in looking than ther shal in deede.
This ordinance is said: go, God thee speede.
Tomorwe at night whan men been alle asleepe,
Into oure kneeding-tubbes wol we creepe,
And sitten there, abiding Goddes grace.
Go now thy way, I have no lenger space° *time*
To make of this no lenger sermoning.
Men sayn thus: 'Send the wise and say no thing.'
Thou art so wis it needeth thee nat teche:
Go save oure lif, and that I thee biseeche."

7. 9 A.M.
8. On high.
9. Toward the garden.
1. Precious commandment.
2. Far apart.

This sely carpenter gooth forth his way:
Ful ofte he saide allas and wailaway,
And to his wif he tolde his privetee,
And she was war,° and knew it bet° than he, *aware / better*
What al this quainte cast was for to saye.[3]
But nathelees she ferde° as she wolde deye, *acted*
And saide, "Allas, go forth thy way anoon.
Help us to scape,° or we been dede eechoon. *escape*
I am thy trewe verray wedded wif:
Go, dere spouse, and help to save oure lif."
Lo, which a greet thing is affeccioun!° *emotion*
Men may dien of imaginacioun,
So deepe° may impression be take. *deeply*
This sely carpenter biginneth quake;
Him thinketh verrailiche° that he may see *truly*
Noees flood come walwing° as the see *rolling*
To drenchen° Alison, his hony dere. *drown*
He weepeth, waileth, maketh sory cheere;
He siketh° with ful many a sory swough,° *sighs / groan*
And gooth and geteth him a kneeding-trough,
And after a tubbe and a kimelin,
And prively he sente hem to his in,° *dwelling*
And heeng° hem in the roof in privetee; *hung*
His° owene hand he made laddres three, *with his*
To climben by the ronges° and the stalkes° *rungs / uprights*
Unto the tubbes hanging in the balkes,° *rafters*
And hem vitailed,° bothe trough and tubbe, *victualed*
With breed and cheese and good ale in a jubbe,° *jug*
Suffising right ynough as for a day.
But er° that he hadde maad al this array, *before*
He sente his knave, and eek his wenche also,
Upon his neede[4] to London for to go.
And on the Monday whan it drow to[5] nighte,
He shette° his dore withouten candel-lighte, *shut*
And dressed° alle thing as it sholde be, *arranged*
And shortly up they clomben° alle three. *climbed*
They seten° stille wel a furlong way.[6] *sat*
"Now, Pater Noster, clum,"[7] saide Nicholay,
And "Clum" quod John, and "Clum" saide Alisoun.
This carpenter saide his devocioun,
And stille he sit° and biddeth° his prayere, *sits / prays*
Awaiting on the rain, if he it heere.° *might hear*
The dede sleep, for wery bisinesse,
Fil° on this carpenter right as I gesse *fell*
Aboute corfew time,[8] or litel more.
For travailing of his gost[9] he groneth sore,
And eft° he routeth,° for his heed mislay.[1] *then / snores*
Down of the laddre stalketh Nicholay,

3. What all this clever plan meant.
4. On an errand for him.
5. Drew toward.
6. The time it takes to go a furlong (i.e., a few minutes).
7. Hush (?). "Pater Noster": Our Father.
8. Probably about 8 P.M.
9. Affliction of his spirit.
1. Lay in the wrong position.

And Alison ful softe adown she spedde:
Withouten wordes mo they goon to bedde
Ther as the carpenter is wont to lie.
Ther was the revel and the melodye,
And thus lith° Alison and Nicholas *lies*
In bisinesse of mirthe and of solas,° *pleasure*
Til that the belle of Laudes[2] gan to ringe,
And freres° in the chauncel° gonne singe. *friars / chancel*
  This parissh clerk, this amorous Absolon,
That is for love alway so wo-bigoon,
Upon the Monday was at Oseneye,
With compaignye him to disporte and playe,
And axed upon caas a cloisterer[3]
Ful prively after John the carpenter;
And he drow him apart out of the chirche,
And saide, "I noot:[4] I sawgh him here nought wirche° *work*
Sith Saterday. I trowe that he be went
For timber ther oure abbot hath him sent.
For he is wont for timber for to go,
And dwellen atte grange[5] a day or two.
Or elles he is at his hous, certain.
Where that he be I can nought soothly sayn."
  This Absolon ful jolif was and light,[6]
And thoughte, "Now is time to wake al night,
For sikerly,° I sawgh him nought stiringe *certainly*
Aboute his dore sin day bigan to springe.
So mote° I thrive, I shal at cokkes crowe *may*
Ful prively knokken at his windowe
That stant° ful lowe upon his bowres° wal. *stands / bedroom's*
To Alison now wol I tellen al
My love-longing,° for yet I shal nat misse *lovesickness*
That at the leeste way[7] I shal hire kisse.
Som manere confort shal I have, parfay.° *in faith*
My mouth hath icched al this longe day:
That is a signe of kissing at the leeste.
Al night me mette[8] eek I was at a feeste.
Therfore I wol go sleepe an hour or twaye,
And al the night thanne wol I wake and playe."
  Whan that the firste cok hath crowe, anoon
Up rist° this joly lovere Absolon, *rises*
And him arrayeth gay at point devis.[9]
But first he cheweth grain[1] and licoris,
To smellen sweete, er he hadde kembd° his heer. *combed*
Under his tonge a trewe-love[2] he beer,° *bore*
For therby wende° he to be gracious.° *supposed / pleasing*
He rometh° to the carpenteres hous, *strolls*
And stille he stant° under the shot-windowe— *stands*

2. The first church service of the day, before daybreak.
3. Here a member of the religious order of Osney Abbey. "Upon caas": by chance.
4. Don't know.
5. The outlying farm belonging to the abbey.
6. Was very amorous and cheerful.
7. I.e., at least.
8. I dreamed.
9. To perfection.
1. Grain of paradise; a spice.
2. Sprig of a cloverlike plant.

Unto his brest it raughte,° it was so lowe— *reached*
And ofte he cougheth with a semisoun.° *small sound*
"What do ye, hony-comb, sweete Alisoun,
My faire brid,[3] my sweete cinamome?° *cinnamon*
Awaketh, lemman° myn, and speketh to me. *sweetheart*
Wel litel thinken ye upon my wo
That for your love I swete° ther I go. *sweat*
No wonder is though that I swelte° and swete: *melt*
I moorne as doth a lamb after the tete.° *teat*
Ywis, lemman, I have swich love-longinge,
That lik a turtle° trewe is my moorninge: *dove*
I may nat ete namore than a maide."
  "Go fro the windowe, Jakke fool," she saide.
"As help me God, it wol nat be com-pa-me.° *come-kiss-me*
I love another, and elles I were to blame,
Wel bet° than thee, by Jesu, Absolon. *better*
Go forth thy way or I wol caste a stoon,
And lat me sleepe, a twenty devele way."[4]
  "Allas," quod Absolon, "and wailaway,
That trewe love was evere so yvele biset.[5]
Thanne kis me, sin that it may be no bet,
For Jesus love and for the love of me."
  "Woltou thanne go thy way therwith?" quod she.
  "Ye, certes, lemman," quod this Absolon.
  "Thanne maak thee redy," quod she. "I come anoon."
And unto Nicholas she saide stille,° *quietly*
"Now hust,° and thou shalt laughen al thy fille." *hush*
  This Absolon down sette him on his knees,
And said, "I am a lord at alle degrees,[6]
For after this I hope ther cometh more.
Lemman, thy grace, and sweete brid, thyn ore!"° *mercy*
  The windowe she undooth, and that in haste.
"Have do," quod she, "come of and speed thee faste,
Lest that oure neighebores thee espye."
  This Absolon gan wipe his mouth ful drye:
Derk was the night as pich or as the cole,
And at the windowe out she putte hir hole,
And Absolon, him fil no bet ne wers,[7]
But with his mouth he kiste hir naked ers,
Ful savourly,° er he were war of this. *with relish*
Abak he sterte,° and thoughte it was amis, *started*
For wel he wiste a womman hath no beerd.° *beard*
He felte a thing al rough and longe yherd,° *haired*
And saide, "Fy, allas, what have I do?"
  "Teehee," quod she, and clapte the windowe to.
And Absolon gooth forth a sory pas.[8]
  "A beerd, a beerd!"[9] quod hende Nicholas,
"By Goddes corpus,° this gooth faire and weel." *body*
  This sely Absolon herde everydeel,° *every bit*

3. Bird or bride.
4. In the name of twenty devils.
5. Ill-used.
6. In every way.
7. It befell him neither better nor worse.
8. I.e., walking sadly.
9. A trick (slang), but with a play on line 629.

And on his lippe he gan for anger bite,
And to himself he saide, "I shal thee quite."° *repay*
Who rubbeth now, who froteth° now his lippes *wipes*
With dust, with sond,° with straw, with cloth, with chippes, *sand*
But Absolon, that saith ful ofte allas?
"My soule bitake° I unto Satanas,° *commit / Satan*
But me were levere[1] than all this town," quod he,
"Of this despit° awroken° for to be. *insult / avenged*
Allas," quod he, "allas I ne hadde ybleint!"° *turned aside*
His hote love was cold and al yqueint,° *quenched*
For fro that time that he hadde kist hir ers
Of paramours he sette nought a kers,[2]
For he was heled° of his maladye. *cured*
Ful ofte paramours he gan defye,° *renounce*
And weep° as dooth a child that is ybete. *wept*
A softe paas[3] he wente over the streete
Until° a smith men clepen daun Gervais,[4] *to*
That in his forge smithed plough harneis:° *equipment*
He sharpeth shaar and cultour[5] bisily.
This Absolon knokketh al esily,° *quietly*
And saide, "Undo, Gervais, and that anoon."° *at once*
"What, who artou?" "It am I, Absolon."
"What, Absolon? What, Cristes sweete tree!° *cross*
Why rise ye so rathe?° Ey, benedicite,° *early / bless me*
What aileth you? Som gay girl, God it woot,
Hath brought you thus upon the viritoot.[6]
By Sainte Note, ye woot wel what I mene."
This Absolon ne roughte nat a bene[7]
Of al his play. No word again he yaf:
He hadde more tow on his distaf[8]
Than Gervais knew, and saide, "Freend so dere,
This hote cultour in the chimenee° here, *fireplace*
As lene[9] it me: I have therwith to doone.
I wol bringe it thee again ful soone."
Gervais answerde, "Certes, were it gold,
Or in a poke nobles alle untold,[1]
Thou sholdest have, as I am trewe smith.
Ey, Cristes fo,[2] what wol ye do therwith?"
"Therof," quod Absolon, "be as be may.
I shal wel telle it thee another day."
And caughte the cultour by the colde stele.° *handle*
Ful softe out at the dore he gan to stele,
And wente unto the carpenteres wal:
He cougheth first and knokketh therwithal
Upon the windowe, right as he dide er.° *before*
This Alison answerde, "Who is ther
That knokketh so? I warante[3] it a thief."

1. I had rather.
2. He didn't care a piece of cress for woman's love.
3. I.e., quiet walk.
4. Master Gervais.
5. He sharpens plowshare and coulter (the turf cutter on a plow).
6. I.e., on the prowl.
7. Didn't care a bean.
8. I.e., more on his mind.
9. I.e., please lend.
1. Or gold coins all uncounted in a bag.
2. Foe, i.e., Satan.
3. I.e., wager.

"Why, nay," quod he, "God woot, my sweete lief,° *dear*
I am thyn Absolon, my dereling.° *darling*
Of gold," quod he, "I have thee brought a ring—
My moder yaf it me, so God me save;
Ful fin it is and therto wel ygrave:° *engraved*
This wol I yiven thee if thou me kisse."
This Nicholas was risen for to pisse,
And thoughte he wolde amenden[4] al the jape:° *joke*
He sholde kisse his ers er that he scape.
And up the windowe dide he hastily,
And out his ers he putteth prively,
Over the buttok to the haunche-boon.
And therwith spak this clerk, this Absolon,
"Speek, sweete brid, I noot nought wher thou art."
This Nicholas anoon leet flee[5] a fart
As greet as it hadde been a thonder-dent° *thunderbolt*
That with the strook he was almost yblent,° *blinded*
And he was redy with his iren hoot,° *hot*
And Nicholas amidde the ers he smoot:° *smote*
Of° gooth the skin an hande-brede° aboute; *off / handsbreadth*
The hote cultour brende so his toute° *buttocks*
That for the smert° he wende for to[6] die; *pain*
As he were wood° for wo he gan to crye, *crazy*
"Help! Water! Water! Help, for Goddes herte!"
This carpenter out of his slomber sterte,
And herde oon cryen "Water!" as he were wood,
And thoughte, "Allas, now cometh Noweles[7] flood!"
He sette him up[8] withoute wordes mo,
And with his ax he smoot the corde atwo,
And down gooth al: he foond neither to selle
Ne breed ne ale til he cam to the celle,[9]
Upon the floor, and ther aswoune° he lay. *in a faint*
Up sterte hire[1] Alison and Nicholay,
And criden "Out" and "Harrow" in the streete.
The neighebores, bothe smale and grete,
In ronnen for to gauren° on this man *gape*
That aswoune lay bothe pale and wan,
For with the fal he brosten° hadde his arm; *broken*
But stonde he moste° unto his owene harm, *must*
For whan he spak he was anoon bore down[2]
With° hende Nicholas and Alisoun: *by*
They tolden every man that he was wood—
He was agast so of Noweles flood,
Thurgh fantasye, that of his vanitee° *folly*
He hadde ybought him kneeding-tubbes three,
And hadde hem hanged in the roof above,
And that he prayed hem, for Goddes love,
To sitten in the roof, *par compaignye*.[3]

4. Improve on.
5. Let fly.
6. Thought he would.
7. The carpenter is confusing Noah and Noel (Christmas).
8. Got up.
9. He found time to sell neither bread nor ale until he arrived at the foundation, i.e., he did not take time out.
1. Started.
2. Refuted.
3. For company's sake.

The folk gan laughen at his fantasye.
Into the roof they kiken° and they cape,° *peer / gape*
And turned al his harm unto a jape,° *joke*
For what so that this carpenter answerde,
It was for nought: no man his reson° herde; *argument*
With othes grete he was so sworn adown,
That he was holden° wood in al the town, *considered*
For every clerk anoonright heeld with other:
They saide, "The man was wood, my leve brother,"
And every wight gan laughen at this strif.° *fuss*
Thus swived[4] was the carpenteres wif
For al his keeping° and his jalousye, *guarding*
And Absolon hath kist hir nether° yë, *lower*
And Nicholas is scalded in the toute:
This tale is doon, and God save al the route!° *company*

The Wife of Bath's Prologue and Tale

In creating the Wife of Bath, Chaucer drew upon a centuries-old tradition of antifeminist writings that was particularly nurtured by the medieval church. In their conviction that the rational, intellectual, spiritual, and, therefore, higher side of human nature predominated in men, whereas the irrational, material, earthly, and, therefore, lower side of human nature predominated in women, St. Paul and the early Church fathers exalted celibacy and virginity above marriage, although they were also obliged to concede the necessity and sanctity of matrimony. In the fourth century, a monk called Jovinian wrote a tract in which he apparently presented marriage as a positive good rather than as a necessary evil. That tract is known only through St. Jerome's extreme attack upon it. Jerome's diatribe and other antifeminist and antimatrimonial literature provided Chaucer with a rich body of bookish male "auctoritee" (authority) against which the Wife of Bath asserts her female "experience" and defends her rights and justifies her life as a five-time married woman. In her polemical wars with medieval clerks and her matrimonial wars with her five husbands, the last of whom was once a clerk of Oxenford, the Wife of Bath seems ironically to confirm the accusations of the clerks, but at the same time she succeeds in satirizing the shallowness of the stereotypes of women and marriage in antifeminist writings and in demonstrating how much the largeness and complexity of her own character rise above that stereotype.

The Prologue

Experience, though noon auctoritee
Were in this world, is right ynough for me
To speke of wo that is in mariage:
For lordinges,° sith I twelf yeer was of age— *gentlemen*
Thanked be God that is eterne on live—
Housbondes at chirche dore[1] I have had five
(If I so ofte mighte han wedded be),
And alle were worthy men in hir degree.
But me was told, certain, nat longe agoon is,

4. The vulgar verb for having sexual intercourse.
1. The actual wedding ceremony was celebrated at the church door, not in the chancel.

That sith that Crist ne wente nevere but ones° *once*
To wedding in the Cane[2] of Galilee,
That by the same ensample° taughte he me *example*
That I ne sholde wedded be but ones.
Herke eek,° lo, which° a sharp word for the nones,[3] *also / what*
Biside a welle, Jesus, God and man,
Spak in repreve° of the Samaritan: *reproof*
"Thou hast yhad five housbondes," quod he,
"And that ilke° man that now hath thee *same*
Is nat thyn housbonde." Thus saide he certain.
What that he mente therby I can nat sayn,
But that I axe° why the fifthe man *ask*
Was noon housbonde to the Samaritan?[4]
How manye mighte she han in mariage?
Yit herde I nevere tellen in myn age
Upon this nombre diffinicioun.° *definition*
Men may divine° and glosen° up and down, *guess / interpret*
But wel I woot,° expres,° withouten lie, *know / expressly*
God bad us for to wexe[5] and multiplye:
That gentil text can I wel understonde.
  Eek wel I woot° he saide that myn housbonde *know*
Sholde lete° fader and moder and take to me,[6] *leave*
But of no nombre mencion made he—
Of bigamye or of octogamye:[7]
Why sholde men thanne speke of it vilainye?
  Lo, here the wise king daun° Salomon: *master*
I trowe° he hadde wives many oon,[8] *believe*
As wolde God it leveful° were to me *permissible*
To be refresshed half so ofte as he.
Which yifte[9] of God hadde he for alle his wives!
No man hath swich° that in this world alive is. *such*
God woot this noble king, as to my wit,° *knowledge*
The firste night hadde many a merye fit° *bout*
With eech of hem, so wel was him on live.[1]
Blessed be God that I have wedded five,
Of whiche I have piked out the beste,[2]
Bothe of hir nether purs[3] and of hir cheste.° *money box*
Diverse scoles maken parfit° clerkes, *perfect*
And diverse practikes[4] in sondry werkes
Maken the werkman parfit sikerly:° *certainly*
Of five housbondes scoleying° am I. *schooling*
Welcome the sixte whan that evere he shal![5]
For sith I wol nat kepe me chast in al,
Whan my housbonde is fro the world agoon,

2. Cana (see John 2.1).
3. To the purpose.
4. Christ was actually referring to a sixth man who was not married to the Samaritan woman (cf. John 4.6 ff.).
5. I.e., increase (see Genesis 1.28).
6. See Matthew 19.5.
7. I.e., of two or even eight marriages. The Wife of Bath is referring to successive, rather than simultaneous, marriages.
8. Solomon had seven hundred wives and three hundred concubines (1 Kings 11.3).
9. What a gift.
1. I.e., so pleasant a life he had.
2. Whom I have cleaned out of everything worthwhile.
3. Lower purse, i.e., testicles.
4. Practical experiences.
5. I.e., shall come along.

Som Cristen man shal wedde me anoon.° *right away*
For thanne th'Apostle[6] saith that I am free
To wedde, a Goddes half, where it liketh me.[7]
He saide that to be wedded is no sinne:
Bet is to be wedded than to brinne.[8]
What rekketh me[9] though folk saye vilainye
Of shrewed° Lamech[1] and his bigamye? *cursed*
I woot wel Abraham was an holy man,
And Jacob eek, as fer as evere I can,° *know*
And eech of hem hadde wives mo than two,
And many another holy man also.
  Where can ye saye in any manere age
That hye God defended° mariage *prohibited*
By expres word? I praye you, telleth me.
Or where comanded he virginitee?
I woot as wel as ye, it is no drede,° *doubt*
Th'Apostle, whan he speketh of maidenhede,° *virginity*
He saide that precept therof hadde he noon:
Men may conseile a womman to be oon,° *single*
But conseiling nis° no comandement. *is not*
He putte it in oure owene juggement.
For hadde God comanded maidenhede,
Thanne hadde he dampned° wedding with the deede;[2] *condemned*
And certes, if there were no seed ysowe,
Virginitee, thanne wherof sholde it growe?
Paul dorste nat comanden at the leeste
A thing of which his maister yaf° no heeste.° *gave / command*
The dart[3] is set up for virginitee:
Cacche whoso may, who renneth° best lat see. *runs*
But this word is nought take of[4] every wight,° *person*
But ther as[5] God list° yive it of his might. *it pleases*
I woot wel that th'Apostle was a maide,° *virgin*
But nathelees, though that he wroot and saide
He wolde that every wight were swich° as he, *such*
Al nis but conseil to virginitee;
And for to been a wif he yaf me leve
Of indulgence; so nis it no repreve° *disgrace*
To wedde me[6] if that my make° die, *mate*
Withouten excepcion of bigamye[7]—
Al° were it good no womman for to touche[8] *although*
(He mente as in his bed or in his couche,
For peril is bothe fir° and tow° t'assemble— *fire / flax*
Ye knowe what this ensample may resemble).[9]
This al and som,[1] he heeld virginitee

6. St. Paul.
7. I please. "A Goddes half": on God's behalf.
8. "It is better to marry than to burn" (1 Corinthians 7.9). Many of the Wife's citations of St. Paul are from this chapter, often secondhand from St. Jerome's tract *Against Jovinian*.
9. What do I care.
1. The first man whom the Bible mentions as having two wives (Genesis 4.19–24); he is cursed, however, not for his marriages but for murder.
2. I.e., at the same time.
3. I.e., prize in a race.
4. Understood for, i.e., applicable to.
5. Where.
6. For me to marry.
7. I.e., without there being any legal objection on the score of remarriage.
8. "It is good for a man not to touch a woman" (1 Corinthians 7.1).
9. I.e., what this metaphor may apply to.
1. This is all there is to it.

More parfit than wedding in freletee.° *frailty*
(Freletee clepe I but if[2] that he and she
Wolde leden al hir lif in chastitee.)
I graunte it wel, I have noon envye
Though maidenhede preferre° bigamye:° *excel / remarriage*
It liketh hem to be clene in body and gost.° *spirit*
Of myn estaat ne wol I make no boost;
For wel ye knowe, a lord in his houshold
Ne hath nat every vessel al of gold:
Some been of tree,° and doon hir lord servise. *wood*
God clepeth° folk to him in sondry wise, *calls*
And everich hath of God a propre[3] yifte,
Som this, som that, as him liketh shifte.° *ordain*
Virginitee is greet perfeccioun,
And continence eek with devocioun,
But Crist, that of perfeccion is welle,° *source*
Bad nat every wight he sholde go selle
Al that he hadde and yive it to the poore,
And in swich wise folwe him and his fore:°[4] *footsteps*
He spak to hem that wolde live parfitly°— *perfectly*
And lordinges, by youre leve, that am nat I.
I wol bistowe the flour of al myn age
In th'actes and in fruit of mariage.
  Telle me also, to what conclusioun° *end*
Were membres maad of generacioun
And of so parfit wis a wrighte ywrought?[5]
  Trusteth right wel, they were nat maad for nought.
Glose° whoso wol, and saye bothe up and down *interpret*
That they were maked for purgacioun
Of urine, and oure bothe thinges smale
Was eek° to knowe a femele from a male, *also*
And for noon other cause—saye ye no?
Th'experience woot it is nought so.
So that the clerkes be nat with me wrothe,
I saye this, that they been maad for bothe—
That is to sayn, for office° and for ese° *use / pleasure*
Of engendrure,° ther we nat God displese. *procreation*
Why sholde men elles in hir bookes sette
That man shal yeelde[6] to his wif hir dette?° *(marital) debt*
Now wherwith sholde he make his payement
If he ne used his sely° instrument? *innocent*
Thanne were they maad upon a creature
To purge urine, and eek for engendrure.
  But I saye nought that every wight is holde,° *bound*
That hath swich harneis° as I to you tolde, *equipment*
To goon and usen hem in engendrure:
Thanne sholde men take of chastitee no cure.° *heed*
Crist was a maide° and shapen as a man, *virgin*
And many a saint sith that the world bigan,

2. Frailty I call it unless.
3. I.e., his own.
4. Matthew 19.21.
5. And wrought by so perfectly wise a maker.
6. I.e., pay.

Yit lived they evere in parfit chastitee.
I nil° envye no virginitee: *will not*
Lat hem be breed° of pured° whete seed, *bread / refined*
And lat us wives hote° barly breed— *be called*
And yit with barly breed, Mark telle can,
Oure Lord Jesu refresshed many a man.[7]
In swich estaat as God hath cleped us
I wol persevere: I nam nat precious.° *fastidious*
In wifhood wol I use myn instrument
As freely° as my Makere hath it sent. *generously*
If I be daungerous[8], God yive me sorwe:
Myn housbonde shal it han both eve and morwe,° *morning*
Whan that him list[9] come forth and paye his dette.
An housbonde wol I have, I wol nat lette,[1]
Which shal be bothe my dettour° and my thral,° *debtor / slave*
And have his tribulacion withal° *as well*
Upon his flessh whil that I am his wif.
I have the power during al my lif
Upon his propre° body, and nat he: *own*
Right thus th'Apostle tolde it unto me,
And bad oure housbondes for to love us weel.
Al this sentence° me liketh everydeel.° *sense / entirely*

[AN INTERLUDE]

Up sterte° the Pardoner and that anoon: *started*
"Now dame," quod he, "by God and by Saint John,
Ye been a noble prechour in this cas.
I was aboute to wedde a wif: allas,
What° sholde I bye° it on my flessh so dere? *why / purchase*
Yit hadde I levere° wedde no wif toyere."° *rather / this year*
"Abid," quod she, "my tale is nat bigonne.
Nay, thou shalt drinken of another tonne,° *tun, barrel*
Er° that I go, shal savoure wors than ale. *before*
And whan that I have told thee forth my tale
Of tribulacion in mariage,
Of which I am expert in al myn age—
This is to saye, myself hath been the whippe—
Thanne maistou chese° wheither thou wolt sippe *choose*
Of thilke° tonne that I shal abroche;° *this same / open*
Be war of it, er thou too neigh approche,
For I shal telle ensamples mo than ten.
'Whoso that nil° be war by othere men, *will not*
By him shal othere men corrected be.'
Thise same wordes writeth Ptolomee:
Rede in his *Almageste* and take it there."[2]
"Dame, I wolde praye you if youre wil it were,"

7. In the descriptions of the miracle of the loaves and fishes, it is actually John, not Mark, who mentions barley bread (6.9).
8. In romance *dangerous* is a term for disdainfulness with which a woman rejects a lover. The Wife means she will not withhold sexual favors, in emulation of God's generosity (line 156).
9. When he wishes to.
1. I will not leave off, desist.
2. "He who will not be warned by the example of others shall become an example to others." The *Almagest*, an astronomical work by the Greek astronomer and mathematician Ptolemy (2nd century C.E.), contains no such aphorism.

Saide this Pardoner, "as ye bigan,
Telle forth youre tale; spareth for no man,
And teche us yonge men of youre practike."° *mode of operation*
"Gladly," quod she, "sith it may you like;° *please*
But that I praye to al this compaignye,
If that I speke after my fantasye,[3]
As taketh nat agrief° of that I saye, *amiss*
For myn entente nis but for to playe."

[THE WIFE CONTINUES]

Now sire, thanne wol I telle you forth my tale.
As evere mote I drinke win or ale,
I shal saye sooth: tho° housbondes that I hadde, *those*
As three of hem were goode, and two were badde.
The three men were goode, and riche, and olde;
Unnethe° mighte they the statut holde *scarcely*
In which they were bounden unto me—
Ye woot wel what I mene of this, pardee.
As help me God, I laughe whan I thinke
How pitously anight I made hem swinke;° *work*
And by my fay,° I tolde of it no stoor:[4] *faith*
They hadde me yiven hir land and hir tresor;
Me needed nat do lenger diligence
To winne hir love or doon hem reverence.
They loved me so wel, by God above,
That I ne tolde no daintee of[5] hir love.
A wis womman wol bisye hire evere in oon[6]
To gete hire love, ye, ther as she hath noon.
But sith I hadde hem hoolly in myn hand,
And sith that they hadde yiven me al hir land,
What° sholde I take keep° hem for to plese, *why / care*
But it were for my profit and myn ese?
I sette hem so awerke,° by my fay, *awork*
That many a night they songen° wailaway. *sang*
The bacon was nat fet° for hem, I trowe, *brought back*
That some men han in Essexe at Dunmowe.[7]
I governed hem so wel after° my lawe *according to*
That eech of hem ful blisful was and fawe° *glad*
To bringe me gaye thinges fro the faire;
They were ful glade whan I spak hem faire,
For God it woot, I chidde° hem spitously.° *chided / cruelly*
Now herkneth how I bar me[8] proprely:
Ye wise wives, that conne understonde,
Thus sholde ye speke and bere him wrong on honde[9]—
For half so boldely can ther no man
Swere and lie as a woman can.

3. If I speak according to my fancy.
4. I set no store by it.
5. Set no value on.
6. Busy herself constantly.
7. At Dunmow, a side of bacon was awarded to the couple who after a year of marriage could claim no quarrels, no regrets, and the desire, if freed, to remarry one another.
8. Bore myself, behaved.
9. Accuse him falsely.

I saye nat this by wives that been wise,
But if it be whan they hem misavise.[1]
A wis wif, if that she can hir good,[2]
Shal bere him on hande the cow is wood,[3]
And take witnesse of hir owene maide
Of hir assent.[4] But herkneth how I saide:
"Sire olde cainard,° is this thyn array?[5] *sluggard*
Why is my neighebores wif so gay?
She is honoured overal° ther she gooth: *wherever*
I sitte at hoom; I have no thrifty° cloth. *decent*
What doostou at my neighebores hous?
Is she so fair? Artou so amorous?
What roune° ye with oure maide, benedicite?[6] *whisper*
Sire olde lechour, lat thy japes° be. *tricks, intrigues*
And if I have a gossib° or a freend *confidant*
Withouten gilt, ye chiden as a feend,
If that I walke or playe unto his hous.
Thou comest hoom as dronken as a mous,
And prechest on thy bench, with yvel preef.[7]
Thou saist to me, it is a greet meschief° *misfortune*
To wedde a poore womman for costage.[8]
And if that she be riche, of heigh parage,° *descent*
Thanne saistou that it is a tormentrye
To suffre hir pride and hir malencolye.° *bad humor*
And if that she be fair, thou verray knave,
Thou saist that every holour° wol hire have: *lecher*
She may no while in chastitee abide
That is assailed upon eech a side.
"Thou saist som folk desiren us for richesse,
Som[9] for oure shap, and som for oure fairnesse,
And som for she can outher° singe or daunce, *either*
And som for gentilesse and daliaunce,° *flirtatiousness*
Som for hir handes and hir armes smale°— *slender*
Thus gooth al to the devel by thy tale![1]
Thou saist men may nat keepe[2] a castel wal,
It may so longe assailed been overal.° *everywhere*
And if that she be foul,° thou saist that she *ugly*
Coveiteth° every man that she may see; *desires*
For as a spaniel she wol on him lepe,
Til that she finde som man hire to chepe.° *bargain for*
Ne noon so grey goos gooth ther in the lake,
As, saistou, wol be withoute make;° *mate*
And saist it is an hard thing for to weelde° *possess*
A thing that no man wol, his thankes, heelde.[3]
Thus saistou, lorel,° whan thou goost to bedde, *wretch*

1. Unless it happens that they make a mistake.
2. If she knows what's good for her.
3. Shall persuade him the chough has gone crazy. The chough, a talking bird, was popularly supposed to tell husbands of their wives' infidelity.
4. And call as a witness her maid, who is on her side.
5. I.e., is this how you behave?
6. Bless me.
7. I.e., (may you have) bad luck.
8. Because of the expense.
9. "Som," in this and the following lines, means "one."
1. I.e., according to your story.
2. I.e., keep safe.
3. No man would willingly hold.

And that no wis man needeth for to wedde,
Ne no man that entendeth° unto hevene— *aims*
With wilde thonder-dint° and firy levene° *thunderbolt / lightning*
Mote thy welked nekke be tobroke![4]
Thou saist that dropping° houses and eek smoke *leaking*
And chiding wives maken men to flee
Out of hir owene hous: a, benedicite,
What aileth swich an old man for to chide?
Thou saist we wives wil oure vices hide
Til we be fast,[5] and thanne we wol hem shewe—
Wel may that be a proverbe of a shrewe!° *rascal*
Thou saist that oxen, asses, hors,° and houndes, *horses*
They been assayed° at diverse stoundes;° *tried out / times*
Bacins, lavours,° er that men hem bye,° *washbowls / buy*
Spoones, stooles, and al swich housbondrye,° *household goods*
And so be° pottes, clothes, and array°— *are / clothing*
But folk of wives maken noon assay
Til they be wedded—olde dotard shrewe!
And thanne, saistou, we wil oure vices shewe.
Thou saist also that it displeseth me
But if° that thou wolt praise my beautee, *unless*
And but thou poure° alway upon my face, *gaze*
And clepe me 'Faire Dame' in every place,
And but thou make a feeste on thilke day
That I was born, and make me fressh and gay,
And but thou do to my norice° honour, *nurse*
And to my chamberere within my bowr,[6]
And to my fadres folk, and his allies[7]—
Thus saistou, olde barel-ful of lies.
And yit of our apprentice Janekin,
For his crispe° heer, shining as gold so fin, *curly*
And for° he squiereth me bothe up and down, *because*
Yit hastou caught a fals suspecioun;
I wil° him nat though thou were deed° tomorwe. *want / dead*
"But tel me this, why hidestou with sorwe[8]
The keyes of thy cheste° away fro me? *money box*
It is my good° as wel as thyn, pardee. *property*
What, weenestou° make an idiot of oure dame?[9] *do you think to*
Now by that lord that called is Saint Jame,
Thou shalt nought bothe, though thou were wood,° *furious*
Be maister of my body and of my good:
That oon thou shalt forgo, maugree thine yën.[1]
"What helpeth it of me enquere° and spyen? *inquire*
I trowe thou woldest loke° me in thy cheste. *lock*
Thou sholdest saye, 'Wif, go wher thee leste.° *it may please*
Taak youre disport.[2] I nil leve° no tales: *believe*
I knowe you for a trewe wif, dame Alis.'
We love no man that taketh keep or charge[3]

4. May thy withered neck be broken!
5. I.e., married.
6. And to my chambermaid within my bedroom.
7. Relatives by marriage.
8. I.e., with sorrow to you.
9. I.e., me, the mistress of the house.
1. Despite your eyes, i.e., despite anything you can do about it.
2. Enjoy yourself.
3. Notice or interest.

Wher that we goon: we wol been at oure large.[4]
Of alle men yblessed mote he be
The wise astrologen° daun Ptolomee, *astronomer*
That saith this proverbe in his *Almageste*:
'Of alle men his wisdom is the hyeste
That rekketh° nat who hath the world in honde.'[5] *cares*
By this proverbe thou shalt understonde,
Have thou[6] ynough, what thar° thee rekke or care *need*
How merily that othere folkes fare?
For certes, olde dotard, by youre leve,
Ye shal han queinte[7] right ynough at eve:
He is too greet a nigard that wil werne° *refuse*
A man to lighte a candle at his lanterne;
He shal han nevere the lasse° lighte, pardee. *less*
Have thou ynough, thee thar nat plaine thee.[8]
"Thou saist also that if we make us gay
With clothing and with precious array,
That it is peril of oure chastitee,
And yit, with sorwe, thou moste enforce thee,[9]
And saye thise wordes in th' Apostles[1] name:
'In habit° maad with chastitee and shame *clothing*
Ye wommen shal apparaile you,' quod he,
'And nat in tressed heer[2] and gay perree,° *jewelry*
As perles, ne with gold ne clothes riche.'[3]
After thy text, ne after thy rubriche,[4]
I wol nat werke as muchel as a gnat.
Thou saidest this, that I was lik a cat:
For whoso wolde senge° a cattes skin, *singe*
Thanne wolde the cat wel dwellen in his in;° *lodging*
And if the cattes skin be slik° and gay, *sleek*
She wol nat dwelle in house half a day,
But forth she wol, er any day be dawed,[5]
To shewe her skin and goon a-caterwawed.° *caterwauling*
This is to saye, if I be gay, sire shrewe,
I wol renne° out, my borel° for to shewe. *run / clothing*
Sir olde fool, what helpeth[6] thee t'espyen?
Though thou praye Argus with his hundred yën[7]
To be my wardecors,° as he can best, *bodyguard*
In faith, he shal nat keepe° me but me lest:[8] *guard*
Yit coude I make his beerd,[9] so mote I thee.° *prosper*
"Thou saidest eek that ther been thinges three,
The whiche thinges troublen al this erthe,
And that no wight may endure the ferthe.° *fourth*
O leve° sire shrewe, Jesu shorte° thy lif! *dear / shorten*
Yit prechestou and saist an hateful wif

4. I.e., liberty.
5. Who rules the world.
6. If you have.
7. Elegant, pleasing thing; a euphemism for sexual enjoyment.
8. I.e., you need not complain.
9. Strengthen your position.
1. I.e., St. Paul's.
2. I.e., elaborate hairdo.
3. See I Timothy 2.9.
4. Rubric, i.e., direction.
5. Has dawned.
6. What does it help.
7. Argus was a monster whom Juno set to watch over one of Jupiter's mistresses. Mercury put all one hundred of his eyes to sleep and slew him.
8. Unless I please.
9. I.e., deceive him.

Yrekened° is for oon of thise meschaunces.[1] *is counted*
Been ther nat none othere resemblaunces
That ye may likne youre parables to,[2]
But if° a sely° wif be oon of tho? *unless / innocent*
"Thou liknest eek wommanes love to helle,
To bareine° land ther water may nat dwelle; *barren*
Thou liknest it also to wilde fir—
The more it brenneth,° the more it hath desir *burns*
To consumen every thing that brent° wol be; *burned*
Thou saist right° as wormes shende° a tree, *just / destroy*
Right so a wif destroyeth hir housbonde—
This knowen they that been to wives bonde."° *bound*
Lordinges, right thus, as ye han understonde,
Bar I stifly mine olde housbondes on honde[3]
That thus they saiden in hir dronkenesse—
And al was fals, but that I took witnesse
On Janekin and on my nece also.
O Lord, the paine I dide hem and the wo,
Ful giltelees, by Goddes sweete pine!° *suffering*
For as an hors I coude bite and whine;° *whinny*
I coude plaine° and° I was in the gilt, *complain / if*
Or elles often time I hadde been spilt.° *ruined*
Whoso that first to mille comth first grint.° *grinds*
I plained first: so was oure werre stint.[4]
They were ful glade to excusen hem ful blive° *quickly*
Of thing of which they nevere agilte hir live.[5]
Of wenches wolde I beren hem on honde,[6]
Whan that for sik[7] they mighte unnethe° stonde, *scarcely*
Yit tikled I his herte for that he
Wende° I hadde had of him so greet cheertee.° *thought / affection*
I swoor that al my walking out by nighte
Was for to espye wenches that he dighte.[8]
Under that colour[9] hadde I many a mirthe.
For al swich wit is yiven us in oure birthe:
Deceite, weeping, spinning God hath yive
To wommen kindely° whil they may live. *naturally*
And thus of oo thing I avaunte me:[1]
At ende I hadde the bet° in eech degree, *better*
By sleighte or force, or by som manere thing,
As by continuel murmur° or grucching;° *complaint / grumbling*
Namely° abedde hadden they meschaunce: *especially*
Ther wolde I chide and do hem no plesaunce;[2]
I wolde no lenger in the bed abide
If that I felte his arm over my side,
Til he hadde maad his raunson° unto me; *ransom*
Thanne wolde I suffre him do his nicetee.° *foolishness (sex)*
And therfore every man this tale I telle:

1. For the other three misfortunes see Proverbs 30.21–23.
2. Are there no other (appropriate) similitudes to which you might draw analogies?
3. I rigorously accused my old husbands.
4. Our war brought to an end.
5. Of which they were never guilty in their lives.
6. Falsely accuse them.
7. I.e., sickness.
8. Had intercourse with.
9. I.e., pretense.
1. Boast.
2. Give them no pleasure.

Winne whoso may, for al is for to selle;
With empty hand men may no hawkes lure.
For winning° wolde I al his lust endure, *profit*
And make me a feined° appetit— *pretended*
And yit in bacon[3] hadde I nevere delit.
That made me that evere I wolde hem chide;
For though the Pope hadde seten° hem biside, *sat*
I wolde nought spare hem at hir owene boord.° *table*
For by my trouthe, I quitte° hem word for word. *repaid*
As help me verray God omnipotent,
Though I right now sholde make my testament,
I ne owe hem nat a word that it nis quit.
I broughte it so aboute by my wit
That they moste yive it up as for the beste,
Or elles hadde we nevere been in reste;
For though he looked as a wood° leoun, *furious*
Yit sholde he faile of his conclusioun.° *object*
  Thanne wolde I saye, "Goodelief, taak keep,[4]
How mekely looketh Wilekin,[5] oure sheep!
Com neer my spouse, lat me ba° thy cheeke— *kiss*
Ye sholden be al pacient and meeke,
And han a sweete-spiced° conscience, *mild*
Sith ye so preche of Jobes pacience;
Suffreth alway, sin ye so wel can preche;
And but ye do, certain, we shal you teche
That it is fair to han a wif in pees.
Oon of us two moste bowen, doutelees,
And sith a man is more resonable
Than womman is, ye mosten been suffrable.° *patient*
What aileth you to grucche° thus and grone? *grumble*
Is it for ye wolde have my queinte° allone? *sexual organ*
Why, taak it al—lo, have it everydeel.° *all of it*
Peter,[6] I shrewe° you but ye° love it weel. *curse / if you don't*
For if I wolde selle my bele chose,[7]
I coude walke as fressh as is a rose;
But I wol keepe it for youre owene tooth.° *taste*
Ye be to blame. By God, I saye you sooth!"° *the truth*
Swiche manere° wordes hadde we on honde. *kind of*
Now wol I speke of my ferthe° housbonde. *fourth*
  My ferthe housbonde was a revelour° *reveler*
This is to sayn, he hadde a paramour° *mistress*
And I was yong and ful of ragerye,° *passion*
Stibourne° and strong and joly as a pie:° *untamable / magpie*
How coude I daunce to an harpe smale,° *gracefully*
And singe, ywis,° as any nightingale, *indeed*
Whan I hadde dronke a draughte of sweete win.
Metellius, the foule cherl, the swin,
That with a staf birafte° his wif hir lif *deprived*
For° she drank win, though I hadde been his wif, *because*

3. I.e., old meat.
4. Good friend, take notice.
5. I.e., Willie.
6. By St. Peter.
7. French for "beautiful thing"; a euphemism for sexual organs.

Ne sholde nat han daunted° me fro drinke; *frightened*
And after win on Venus moste° I thinke, *must*
For also siker° as cold engendreth hail, *sure*
A likerous° mouth moste han a likerous° tail: *greedy / lecherous*
In womman vinolent° is no defence— *who drinks*
This knowen lechours by experience.
But Lord Crist, whan that it remembreth me[8]
Upon my youthe and on my jolitee,
It tikleth me aboute myn herte roote—
Unto this day it dooth myn herte boote° *good*
That I have had my world as in my time.
But age, allas, that al wol envenime,° *poison*
Hath me biraft[9] my beautee and my pith°— *vigor*
Lat go, farewel, the devel go therwith!
The flour is goon, ther is namore to telle:
The bren° as I best can now moste I selle; *bran*
But yit to be right merye wol I fonde.° *strive*
Now wol I tellen of my ferthe housbonde.
I saye I hadde in herte greet despit
That he of any other hadde delit,
But he was quit,° by God and by Saint Joce: *paid back*
I made him of the same wode a croce[1]—
Nat of my body in no foul manere—
But, certainly, I made folk swich cheere[2]
That in his owene grece I made him frye,
For angre and for verray jalousye.
By God, in erthe I was his purgatorye,
For which I hope his soule be in glorye.
For God it woot, he sat ful ofte and soong° *sang*
Whan that his sho ful bitterly him wroong.° *pinched*
Ther was no wight save God and he that wiste° *knew*
In many wise how sore I him twiste.
He deide whan I cam fro Jerusalem,
And lith ygrave under the roode-beem,[3]
Al° is his tombe nought so curious[4] *although*
As was the sepulcre of him Darius,
Which that Apelles wroughte subtilly:[5]
It nis but wast to burye him preciously.° *expensively*
Lat him fare wel, God yive his soule reste;
He is now in his grave and in his cheste.° *coffin*
Now of my fifthe housbonde wol I telle—
God lete his soule nevere come in helle—
And yit he was to me the moste shrewe:[6]
That feele I on my ribbes al by rewe,[7]
And evere shal unto myn ending day.
But in oure bed he was so fressh and gay,
And therwithal so wel coulde he me glose° *flatter, coax*

8. When I look back.
9. Has taken away from me.
1. I made him a cross of the same wood. The proverb has much the same sense as the one quoted in line 493.
2. Pretended to be in love with others.
3. And lies buried under the rood beam (the crucifix beam running between nave and chancel).
4. Carefully wrought.
5. Accordingly to medieval legend, the artist Apelles decorated the tomb of Darius, king of the Persians.
6. Worst rascal.
7. In a row.

Whan that he wolde han my bele chose,
That though he hadde me bet° on every boon,° *beaten / bone*
He coude winne again my love anoon.° *immediately*
I trowe I loved him best for that he
Was of his love daungerous[8] to me.
We wommen han, if that I shal nat lie,
In this matere a quainte fantasye:[9]
Waite what[1] thing we may nat lightly° have, *easily*
Therafter wol we crye al day and crave;
Forbede us thing, and that desiren we;
Preesse on us faste, and thanne wol we flee.
With daunger oute we al oure chaffare:[2]
Greet prees° at market maketh dere° ware, *crowd / expensive*
And too greet chepe is holden at litel pris.[3]
This knoweth every womman that is wis.
  My fifthe housbonde—God his soule blesse!—
Which that I took for love and no richesse,
He somtime was a clerk at Oxenforde,
And hadde laft° scole and wente at hoom to boorde *left*
With my gossib,° dwelling in oure town *confidante*
God have hir soule!—hir name was Alisoun;
She knew myn herte and eek my privetee° *secrets*
Bet° than oure parissh preest, as mote I thee.° *better / prosper*
To hire biwrayed° I my conseil° al, *disclosed / secrets*
For hadde myn housbonde pissed on a wal,
Or doon a thing that sholde han cost his lif,
To hire,° and to another worthy wif, *her*
And to my nece which I loved weel,
I wolde han told his conseil everydeel;° *entirely*
And so I dide ful often, God it woot,
That made his face often reed° and hoot° *red / hot*
For verray shame, and blamed himself for he
Hadde told to me so greet a privetee.
  And so bifel that ones° in a Lente— *once*
So often times I to my gossib wente,
For evere yit I loved to be gay,
And for to walke in March, Averil, and May,
From hous to hous, to heere sondry tales—
That Janekin clerk and my gossib dame Alis
And I myself into the feeldes wente.
Myn housbonde was at London al that Lente:
I hadde the better leiser for to playe,
And for to see, and eek for to be seye° *seen*
Of lusty folk—what wiste I wher my grace° *luck*
Was shapen° for to be, or in what place? *destined*
Therfore I made my visitaciouns
To vigilies[4] and to processiouns,
To preching eek, and to thise pilgrimages,
To playes of miracles and to mariages,

8. I.e., he played hard to get.
9. Strange fancy.
1. Whatever.
2. (Meeting) with reserve, we spread out our merchandise.
3. Too good a bargain is held at little value.
4. Evening service before a religious holiday.

And wered upon[5] my gaye scarlet gites°— *gowns*
Thise wormes ne thise motthes ne thise mites,
Upon my peril,[6] frete° hem neveradeel: *ate*
And woostou why? For they were used weel.
 Now wol I tellen forth what happed me.
I saye that in the feeldes walked we,
Til trewely we hadde swich daliaunce,° *flirtation*
This clerk and I, that of my purveyaunce° *foresight*
I spak to him and saide him how that he,
If I were widwe, sholde wedde me.
For certainly, I saye for no bobaunce,° *boast*
Yit was I nevere withouten purveyaunce
Of mariage n'of othere thinges eek:
I holde a mouses herte nought worth a leek
That hath but oon hole for to sterte° to, *run*
And if that faile thanne is al ydo.[7]
I bar him on hand[8] he hadde enchaunted me
(My dame° taughte me that subtiltee); *mother*
And eek I saide I mette° of him al night: *dreamed*
He wolde han slain me as I lay upright,° *on my back*
And al my bed was ful of verray blood—
"But yit I hope that ye shul do me good;
For blood bitokeneth° gold, as me was taught." *signifies*
And al was fals, I dremed of it right naught,
But as I folwed ay my dames° lore° *mother's / teaching*
As wel of that as othere thinges more.
But now sire—lat me see, what shal I sayn?
Aha, by God, I have my tale again.
 Whan that my ferthe housbonde was on beere,° *funeral bier*
I weep,° algate,° and made sory cheere, *wept / anyhow*
As wives moten,° for it is usage,° *must / custom*
And with my coverchief covered my visage;
But for I was purveyed° of a make.° *provided / mate*
I wepte but smale, and that I undertake.° *guarantee*
 To chirche was myn housbonde born amorwe;[9]
With neighebores that for him maden sorwe,
And Janekin oure clerk was oon of tho.
As help me God, whan that I saw him go
After the beere, me thoughte he hadde a paire
Of legges and of feet so clene[1] and faire,
That al myn herte I yaf unto his hold.° *possession*
He was, I trowe,° twenty winter old, *believe*
And I was fourty, if I shal saye sooth—
But yit I hadde alway a coltes tooth:[2]
Gat-toothed[3] was I, and that bicam me weel;
I hadde the prente[4] of Sainte Venus seel.° *seal*
As help me God, I was a lusty oon,
And fair and riche and yong and wel-bigoon,° *well-situated*

5. Wore.
6. On peril (to my soul), an oath.
7. I.e., the game is up.
8. I pretended to him.
9. In the morning.
1. I.e., neat.
2. I.e., youthful appetites.
3. Gap-toothed women were considered to be amorous.
4. Print, i.e., a birthmark.

And trewely, as mine housbondes tolde me,
I hadde the beste quoniam[5] mighte be.
For certes I am al Venerien
In feeling, and myn herte is Marcien:[6]
Venus me yaf my lust, my likerousnesse,° *amorousness*
And Mars yaf me my sturdy hardinesse.
Myn ascendent was Taur[7] and Mars therinne—
Allas, allas, that evere love was sinne!
I folwed ay° my inclinacioun *ever*
By vertu of my constellacioun;[8]
That made me I coude nought withdrawe
My chambre of Venus from a good felawe.
Yit have I Martes° merk upon my face, *Mars's*
And also in another privee place.
For God so wis° be my savacioun,° *surely / salvation*
I loved nevere by no discrecioun,° *moderation*
But evere folwede myn appetit,
Al were he short or long or blak or whit;
I took no keep,° so that he liked° me, *heed / pleased*
How poore he was, ne eek of what degree.
What sholde I saye but at the monthes ende
This joly clerk Janekin that was so hende° *courteous, nice*
Hath wedded me with greet solempnitee,° *splendor*
And to him yaf I al the land and fee° *property*
That evere was me yiven therbifore—
But afterward repented me ful sore:
He nolde suffre no thing of my list.° *wish*
By God, he smoot° me ones on the list° *struck / ear*
For that I rente° out of his book a leef, *tore*
That of the strook° myn ere weex° al deef. *blow / grew*
Stibourne° I was as is a leonesse, *stubborn*
And of my tonge a verray jangleresse,° *chatterbox*
And walke I wolde, as I hadde doon biforn,
From hous to hous, although he hadde it[9] sworn;
For which he often times wolde preche,
And me of olde Romain geestes° teche, *stories*
How he Simplicius Gallus lafte° his wif, *left*
And hire forsook for terme of al his lif,
Nought but for open-heveded he hire sey[1]
Looking out at his dore upon a day.
  Another Romain tolde he me by name
That, for his wif was at a someres° game *summer's*
Withouten his witing,° he forsook hire eke; *knowledge*
And thanne wolde he upon his Bible seeke
That ilke proverbe of Ecclesiaste[2]
Where he comandeth and forbedeth faste° *strictly*
Man shal nat suffre his wif go roule° aboute; *roam*
Thanne wolde he saye right thus withouten doute:

5. Latin for "because"; another euphemism for a sexual organ.
6. Influenced by Mars. "Venerien": astrologically influenced by Venus.
7. My birth sign was the constellation Taurus, a sign in which Venus is dominant.
8. I.e., horoscope.
9. I.e., the contrary.
1. Just because he saw her bareheaded.
2. Ecclesiasticus (25.25).

"Whoso that buildeth his hous al of salwes,° *willow sticks*
And priketh° his blinde hors over the falwes,[3] *rides*
And suffreth° his wif to go seeken halwes,° *allows / shrines*
Is worthy to be hanged on the galwes."° *gallows*
But al for nought—I sette nought an hawe[4]
Of his proverbes n'of his olde sawe;
N' I wolde nat of him corrected be:
I hate him that my vices telleth me,
And so doon mo, God woot, of us than I.
This made him with me wood al outrely:° *entirely*
I nolde nought forbere° him in no cas. *submit to*
Now wol I saye you sooth, by Saint Thomas,
Why that I rente° out of his book a leef, *tore*
For which he smoot me so that I was deef.
He hadde a book that gladly night and day
For his disport° he wolde rede alway. *entertainment*
He cleped it *Valerie*[5] *and Theofraste,*
At which book he lough° alway ful faste; *laughed*
And eek ther was somtime a clerk at Rome,
A cardinal, that highte Saint Jerome,
That made a book[6] again° Jovinian; *against*
In which book eek ther was Tertulan,
Crysippus, Trotula, and Helouis,[7]
That was abbesse nat fer fro Paris;
And eek the Parables of Salomon,
Ovides *Art,*[8] and bookes many oon—
And alle thise were bounden in oo volume.
And every night and day was his custume,
Whan he hadde leiser and vacacioun° *free time*
From other worldly occupacioun,
To reden in this book of wikked wives.
He knew of hem mo legendes and lives
Than been of goode wives in the Bible.
For trusteth wel, it is an impossible° *impossibility*
That any clerk wol speke good of wives,
But if it be of holy saintes lives,
N'of noon other womman nevere the mo—
Who painted the leon, tel me who?[9]
By God, if wommen hadden writen stories,
As clerkes han within hir oratories,° *chapels*
They wolde han writen of men more wikkednesse
Than al the merk[1] of Adam may redresse.
The children of Mercurye and Venus[2]

3. Plowed land.
4. I did not rate at the value of a hawthorn berry.
5. "*Valerie*": i.e., the *Letter of Valerius Concerning Not Marrying,* by Walter Map; "*Theofraste*": Theophrastus's *Book Concerning Marriage.* Medieval manuscripts often contained a number of different works, sometimes, as here, dealing with the same subject.
6. St. Jerome's antifeminist *Against Jovinian.*
7. "Tertulan": i.e., Tertullian, author of treatises on sexual modesty. "Crysippus": mentioned by Jerome as an antifeminist. "Trotula": a female doctor whose presence here is unexplained. "Helouis": i.e., Eloise, whose love affair with the great scholar Abelard was a medieval scandal.
8. Ovid's *Art of Love.* "Parables of Salomon": the biblical Book of Proverbs.
9. In one of Aesop's fables, the lion, shown a picture of a man killing a lion, asked who painted the picture. Had a lion been the artist, of course, the roles would have been reversed.
1. Mark, sex.
2. I.e., clerks and women, astrologically ruled by Mercury and Venus, respectively.

Been in hir werking° ful contrarious:° *operation / opposed*
Mercurye loveth wisdom and science,
And Venus loveth riot° and dispence;° *revelry / spending*
And for hir diverse disposicioun
Each falleth in otheres exaltacioun,[3]
And thus, God woot, Mercurye is desolat
In Pisces wher Venus is exaltat,[4]
And Venus falleth ther Mercurye is raised:
Therfore no womman of no clerk is praised.
The clerk, whan he is old and may nought do
Of Venus werkes worth his olde sho,° *shoe*
Thanne sit° he down and writ° in his dotage *sits / writes*
That wommen can nat keepe hir mariage.
  But now to purpose why I tolde thee
That I was beten for a book, pardee:
Upon a night Janekin, that was our sire,[5]
Redde on his book as he sat by the fire
Of Eva first, that for hir wikkednesse
Was al mankinde brought to wrecchednesse,
For which that Jesu Crist himself was slain
That boughte° us with his herte blood again— *redeemed*
Lo, heer expres of wommen may ye finde
That womman was the los° of al mankinde.[6] *ruin*
  Tho° redde he me how Sampson loste his heres: *then*
Sleeping his lemman° kitte° it with hir sheres, *lover / cut*
Thurgh which treson loste he both his yën.
  Tho redde he me, if that I shal nat lien,
Of Ercules and of his Dianire,[7]
That caused him to sette himself afire.
No thing forgat he the sorwe and wo
That Socrates hadde with his wives two—
How Xantippa caste pisse upon his heed:
This sely° man sat stille as he were deed; *poor, hapless*
He wiped his heed, namore dorste° he sayn *dared*
But "Er that thonder stinte,° comth a rain." *stops*
  Of Pasipha[8] that was the queene of Crete—
For shrewednesse° him thoughte the tale sweete— *malice*
Fy, speek namore, it is a grisly thing
  Of hir horrible lust and hir liking.° *pleasure*
Of Clytermistra[9] for hir lecherye
That falsly made hir housbonde for to die,
He redde it with ful good devocioun.
  He tolde me eek for what occasioun
Amphiorax[1] at Thebes loste his lif:
Myn housbonde hadde a legende of his wif

3. Because of their contrary positions (as planets), each one descends (in the belt of the zodiac) as the other rises, hence one loses its power as the other becomes dominant.
4. I.e., Mercury is deprived of power in Pisces (the sign of the Fish), where Venus is most powerful.
5. My husband.
6. The stories of wicked women Chaucer drew mainly from St. Jerome and Walter Map.
7. Deianira unwittingly gave Hercules a poisoned shirt, which hurt him so much that he committed suicide by fire.
8. Pasiphaë, who had intercourse with a bull.
9. Clytemnestra, who, with her lover, Aegisthus, slew her husband, Agamemnon.
1. Amphiaraus, betrayed by his wife, Eriphyle, and forced to go to the war against Thebes.

Eriphylem, that for an ouche° of gold *trinket*
Hath prively unto the Greekes told
Wher that hir housbonde hidde him in a place,
For which he hadde at Thebes sory grace.
Of Livia tolde he me and of Lucie:[2]
They bothe made hir housbondes for to die,
That oon for love, that other was for hate;
Livia hir housbonde on an even late
Empoisoned hath for that she was his fo;
Lucia likerous° loved hir housbonde so *lecherous*
That for° he sholde alway upon hire thinke, *in order that*
She yaf him swich a manere love-drinke
That he was deed er it were by the morwe.[3]
And thus algates° housbondes han sorwe. *in every way*
Thanne tolde he me how oon Latumius
Complained unto his felawe Arrius
That in his garden growed swich a tree,
On which he saide how that his wives three
Hanged hemself for herte despitous.[4]
"O leve° brother," quod this Arrius, *dear*
"Yif me a plante of thilke blessed tree,
And in my gardin planted shal it be."
Of latter date of wives hath he red
That some han slain hir housbondes in hir bed
And lete hir lechour dighte[5] hire al the night,
Whan that the cors° lay in the floor upright;° *corpse / on his back*
And some han driven nailes in hir brain
Whil that they sleepe, and thus they han hem slain;
Some han hem yiven poison in hir drinke.
He spak more harm than herte may bithinke,° *imagine*
And therwithal he knew of mo proverbes
Than in this world ther growen gras or herbes:
"Bet° is," quod he, "thyn habitacioun *better*
Be with a leon or a foul dragoun
Than with a womman using° for to chide." *accustomed*
"Bet is," quod he, "hye in the roof abide
Than with an angry wif down in the hous:
They been so wikked° and contrarious, *perverse*
They haten that hir housbondes loveth ay."
He saide, "A womman cast° hir shame away *casts*
When she cast of° hir smok,"[6] and ferthermo, *off*
"A fair womman, but she be chast also,
Is like a gold ring in a sowes nose."
Who wolde weene,° or who wolde suppose *think*
The wo that in myn herte was and pine?° *suffering*
And whan I sawgh he wolde nevere fine° *end*
To reden on this cursed book al night,
Al sodeinly three leves have I plight° *snatched*

2. Livia murdered her husband in behalf of her lover, Sejanus. "Lucie": i.e., Lucilla, who was said to have poisoned her husband, the poet Lucretius, with a potion designed to keep him faithful.
3. He was dead before it was near morning.
4. For malice of heart.
5. Have intercourse with.
6. Undergarment.

Out of his book right as he redde, and eke
I with my fist so took[7] him on the cheeke
That in oure fir he fil° bakward adown. *fell*
And up he sterte as dooth a wood° leoun, *raging*
And with his fist he smoot me on the heed° *head*
That in the floor I lay as I were deed.° *dead*
And whan he sawgh how stille that I lay,
He was agast, and wolde have fled his way,
Til atte laste out of my swough° I braide:° *swoon / started*
"O hastou slain me, false thief?" I saide,
"And for my land thus hastou mordred° me? *murdered*
Er I be deed yit wol I kisse thee."
And neer he cam and kneeled faire adown,
And saide, "Dere suster Alisoun,
As help me God, I shal thee nevere smite.
That I have doon, it is thyself to wite.° *blame*
Foryif it me, and that I thee biseeke."° *beseech*
And yit eftsoones° I hitte him on the cheeke, *another time*
And saide, "Thief, thus muchel am I wreke.° *avenged*
Now wol I die: I may no lenger speke."
  But at the laste with muchel care and wo
We fille[8] accorded by us selven two.
He yaf me al the bridel° in myn hand, *bridle*
To han the governance of hous and land,
And of his tonge and his hand also;
And made[9] him brenne° his book anoonright tho. *burn*
And whan that I hadde geten unto me
By maistrye° al the sovereinetee,° *skill / dominion*
And that he saide, "Myn owene trewe wif,
Do as thee lust° the terme of al thy lif; *it pleases*
Keep thyn honour, and keep eek myn estat,"
After that day we hadde nevere debat.
God help me so, I was to him as kinde
As any wif from Denmark unto Inde,° *India*
And also trewe, and so was he to me.
I praye to God that sit° in majestee, *sits*
So blesse his soule for his mercy dere.
Now wol I saye my tale if ye wol heere.

[ANOTHER INTERRUPTION]

  The Frere lough° whan he hadde herd all this: *laughed*
"Now dame," quod he, "so have I joye or blis,
This is a long preamble of a tale."
And whan the Somnour herde the Frere gale,° *exclaim*
"Lo," quod the Somnour, "Goddes armes two,
A frere wol entremette him[1] everemo!
Lo, goode men, a flye and eek a frere
Wol falle in every dissh and eek matere.

7. I.e., hit.
8. I.e., became.
9. I.e., I made.
1. Intrude himself.

What spekestou of preambulacioun?
What, amble or trotte or pisse or go sitte down!
Thou lettest° oure disport in this manere." *hinder*
"Ye, woltou so, sire Somnour?" quod the Frere.
"Now by my faith, I shal er that I go
Telle of a somnour swich a tale or two
That al the folk shal laughen in this place."
"Now elles, Frere, I wol bishrewe° thy face," *curse*
Quod this Somnour, "and I bishrewe me,
But if I telle tales two or three
Of freres, er I come to Sidingborne,[2]
That I shal make thyn herte for to moorne°— *mourn*
For wel I woot thy pacience is goon."
Oure Hoste cride, "Pees, and that anoon!"
And saide, "Lat the womman telle hir tale:
Ye fare as folk that dronken been of ale.
Do, dame, tel forth youre tale, and that is best."
"Al redy, sire," quod she, "right as you lest°— *it pleases*
If I have licence of this worthy Frere."
"Yis, dame," quod he, "tel forth and I wol heere."

The Tale

Chaucer may have originally written the fabliau that became *The Shipman's Tale* for the Wife of Bath. If so, then he replaced it with a tale that is not simply appropriate to her character but that develops it even beyond the complexity already revealed in her *Prologue*. The story survives in two other versions in which the hero is Sir Gawain, whose courtesy contrasts sharply with the behavior of the knight in the Wife's tale. (For excerpts from *The Marriage of Sir Gawain and Dame Ragnell*, see "King Arthur" at Norton Literature Online.) As Chaucer has the Wife tell it, the tale expresses her views about the relations of the sexes, her wit and humor, and her fantasies. Like Marie de France's lay *Lanval* (see pp. 98–111), the Wife's tale is about a fairy bride who seeks out and tests a mortal lover.

In th'olde dayes of the King Arthour,
Of which that Britouns speken greet honour,
Al was this land fulfild of faïrye:[3]
The elf-queene° with hir joly compaignye *queen of the fairies*
Daunced ful ofte in many a greene mede°— *meadow*
This was the olde opinion as I rede;
I speke of many hundred yeres ago.
But now can no man see none elves mo,
For now the grete charitee and prayeres
Of limitours,[4] and othere holy freres,
That serchen every land and every streem,
As thikke as motes° in the sonne-beem, *dust particles*
Blessing halles, chambres, kichenes, bowres,
Citees, burghes,° castels, hye towres, *townships*
Thropes, bernes, shipnes,[5] dayeries—
This maketh that ther been no faïries.

2. Sittingbourne (a town forty miles from London).
3. I.e., filled full of supernatural creatures.
4. Friars licensed to beg in a certain territory.
5. Thorps (villages), barns, stables.

For ther as wont to walken was an elf
Ther walketh now the limitour himself,
In undermeles° and in morweninges,° *afternoons / mornings*
And saith his Matins and his holy thinges,
As he gooth in his limitacioun.[6]
Wommen may go saufly° up and down: *safely*
In every bussh or under every tree
Ther is noon other incubus[7] but he,
And he ne wol doon hem but[8] dishonour.
  And so bifel it that this King Arthour
Hadde in his hous a lusty bacheler,° *young knight*
That on a day cam riding fro river,[9]
And happed° that, allone as he was born, *it happened*
He sawgh a maide walking him biforn;
Of which maide anoon, maugree hir heed,[1]
By verray force he rafte° hir maidenheed; *deprived her of*
For which oppression° was swich clamour, *rape*
And swich pursuite° unto the King Arthour, *petitioning*
That dampned was this knight for to be deed[2]
By cours of lawe, and sholde han lost his heed—
Paraventure° swich was the statut tho— *perchance*
But that the queene and othere ladies mo
So longe prayeden the king of grace,
Til he his lif him graunted in the place,
And yaf him to the queene, al at hir wille,
To chese° wheither she wolde him save or spille.[3] *choose*
The queene thanked the king with al hir might,
And after this thus spak she to the knight,
Whan that she saw hir time upon a day:
"Thou standest yit," quod she, "in swich array° *condition*
That of thy lif yit hastou no suretee.° *guarantee*
I graunte thee lif if thou canst tellen me
What thing it is that wommen most desiren:
Be war and keep thy nekke boon° from iren. *bone*
And if thou canst nat tellen me anoon,° *right away*
Yit wol I yive thee leve for to goon
A twelfmonth and a day to seeche° and lere° *search / learn*
An answere suffisant° in this matere, *satisfactory*
And suretee wol I han er that thou pace,° *pass*
Thy body for to yeelden in this place."
  Wo was this knight, and sorwefully he siketh.° *sighs*
But what, he may nat doon al as him liketh,
And atte laste he chees° him for to wende, *chose*
And come again right at the yeres ende,
With swich answere as God wolde him purveye,° *provide*
And taketh his leve and wendeth forth his waye.
He seeketh every hous and every place
Wher as he hopeth for to finde grace,

6. I.e., the friar's assigned area. His "holy thinges" are prayers.
7. An evil spirit that seduces mortal women.
8. "Ne . . . but": only.
9. Hawking, usually carried out on the banks of a stream.
1. Despite her head, i.e., despite anything she could do.
2. This knight was condemned to death.
3. Put to death.

To lerne what thing wommen love most.
But he ne coude arriven in no coost[4]
Wher as he mighte finde in this matere
Two creatures according in fere.[5]
  Some saiden wommen loven best richesse;
Some saide honour, some saide jolinesse;° *pleasure*
Some riche array, some saiden lust abedde,
And ofte time to be widwe and wedde.
Some saide that oure herte is most esed
Whan that we been yflatered and yplesed—
He gooth ful neigh the soothe, I wol nat lie:
A man shal winne us best with flaterye,
And with attendance° and with bisinesse° *attention / solicitude*
Been we ylimed,° bothe more and lesse. *ensnared*
  And some sayen that we loven best
For to be free, and do right as us lest,° *it pleases*
And that no man repreve° us of oure vice, *reprove*
But saye that we be wise and no thing nice.° *foolish*
For trewely, ther is noon of us alle,
If any wight wol clawe° us on the galle,° *rub / sore spot*
That we nil kike° for° he saith us sooth: *kick / because*
Assaye° and he shal finde it that so dooth. *try*
For be we nevere so vicious withinne,
We wol be holden° wise and clene of sinne. *considered*
  And some sayn that greet delit han we
For to be holden stable and eek secree,[6]
And in oo° purpos stedefastly to dwelle, *one*
And nat biwraye° thing that men us telle— *disclose*
But that tale is nat worth a rake-stele.° *rake handle*
Pardee,° we wommen conne no thing hele:° *by God / conceal*
Witnesse on Mida.° Wol ye heere the tale? *Midas*
  Ovide, amonges othere thinges smale,
Saide Mida hadde under his longe heres,
Growing upon his heed, two asses eres,
The whiche vice° he hidde as he best mighte *defect*
Ful subtilly from every mannes sighte,
That save his wif ther wiste° of it namo. *knew*
He loved hire most and trusted hire also.
He prayed hire that to no creature
She sholde tellen of his disfigure.° *deformity*
  She swoor him nay, for al this world to winne,
She nolde do that vilainye or sinne
To make hir housbonde han so foul a name:
She nolde nat telle it for hir owene shame.
But nathelees, hir thoughte that she dyde° *would die*
That she so longe sholde a conseil° hide; *secret*
Hire thoughte it swal° so sore about hir herte *swelled*
That nedely som word hire moste asterte,[7]
And sith she dorste nat telle it to no man,
Down to a mareis° faste° by she ran— *marsh / close*

4. I.e., country.
5. Agreeing together.
6. Reliable and also closemouthed.
7. Of necessity some word must escape her.

Til she cam there hir herte was afire—
And as a bitore bombleth[8] in the mire,
She laide hir mouth unto the water down:
"Biwray° me nat, thou water, with thy soun,"° *betray / sound*
Quod she. "To thee I telle it and namo:° *to no one else*
Myn housbonde hath longe asses eres two.
Now is myn herte al hool,[9] now is it oute.
I mighte no lenger keep it, out of doute."
Here may ye see, though we a time abide,
Yit oute it moot:° we can no conseil hide. *must*
The remenant of the tale if ye wol heere,
Redeth Ovide, and ther ye may it lere.[1]
This knight of which my tale is specially,
Whan that he sawgh he mighte nat come thereby—
This is to saye what wommen loven most—
Within his brest ful sorweful was his gost,° *spirit*
But hoom he gooth, he mighte nat sojourne:° *delay*
The day was come that hoomward moste° he turne. *must*
And in his way it happed him to ride
In al this care under° a forest side, *by*
Wher as he sawgh upon a daunce go
Of ladies foure and twenty and yit mo;
Toward the whiche daunce he drow ful yerne,[2]
In hope that som wisdom sholde he lerne.
But certainly, er he cam fully there,
Vanisshed was this daunce, he niste° where. *knew not*
No creature sawgh he that bar° lif, *bore*
Save on the greene he sawgh sitting a wif°— *woman*
A fouler wight ther may no man devise.° *imagine*
Again[3] the knight this olde wif gan rise,
And saide, "Sire knight, heer forth lith° no way.° *lies / road*
Telle me what ye seeken, by youre fay.° *faith*
Paraventure it may the better be:
Thise olde folk conne° muchel thing," quod she. *know*
"My leve moder,"° quod this knight, "certain, *mother*
I nam but deed but if that I can sayn
What thing it is that wommen most desire.
Coude ye me wisse,° I wolde wel quite youre hire."[4] *teach*
"Plight° me thy trouthe here in myn hand," quod she, *pledge*
"The nexte thing that I requere° thee, *require of*
Thou shalt it do, if it lie in thy might,
And I wol telle it you er it be night."
"Have heer my trouthe," quod the knight. "I graunte."
"Thanne," quod she, "I dar me wel avaunte° *boast*
Thy lif is sauf,° for I wol stande therby. *safe*
Upon my lif the queene wol saye as I.
Lat see which is the pruddeste° of hem alle *proudest*
That wereth on[5] a coverchief or a calle° *headdress*

8. Makes a booming noise. "Bittore": bittern, a heron.
9. I.e., sound.
1. Learn. The reeds disclosed the secret by whispering *"aures aselli"* (ass's ears).
2. Drew very quickly.
3. I.e., to meet.
4. Repay your trouble.
5. That wears.

That dar saye nay of that I shal thee teche.
Lat us go forth withouten lenger speeche."
Tho rouned° she a pistel° in his ere, *whispered / message*
And bad him to be glad and have no fere.
  When they be comen to the court, this knight
Saide he hadde holde his day as he hadde hight,° *promised*
And redy was his answere, as he saide.
Ful many a noble wif, and many a maide,
And many a widwe—for that they been wise—
The queene hirself sitting as justise,
Assembled been this answere for to heere,
And afterward this knight was bode° appere. *bidden to*
To every wight comanded was silence,
And that the knight sholde telle in audience° *open hearing*
What thing that worldly wommen loven best.
This knight ne stood nat stille as dooth a best,° *beast*
But to his question anoon answerde
With manly vois that al the court it herde.
  "My lige° lady, generally," quod he, *liege*
"Wommen desire to have sovereinetee° *dominion*
As wel over hir housbonde as hir love,
And for to been in maistrye him above.
This is youre moste desir though ye me kille.
Dooth as you list:° I am here at youre wille." *please*
  In al the court ne was ther wif ne maide
Ne widwe that contraried° that he saide, *contradicted*
But saiden he was worthy han° his lif. *to have*
  And with that word up sterte° that olde wif, *started*
Which that the knight sawgh sitting on the greene;
"Mercy," quod she, "my soverein lady queene,
Er that youre court departe, do me right.
I taughte this answere unto the knight,
For which he plighte me his trouthe there
The firste thing I wolde him requere° *require*
He wolde it do, if it laye in his might.
Bifore the court thanne praye I thee, sire knight,"
Quod she, "that thou me take unto thy wif,
For wel thou woost that I have kept° thy lif. *saved*
If I saye fals, say nay, upon thy fay."
  This knight answerde, "Allas and wailaway,
I woot right wel that swich was my biheeste.° *promise*
For Goddes love, as chees° a newe requeste: *choose*
Taak al my good and lat my body go."
  "Nay thanne," quod she, "I shrewe° us bothe two. *curse*
For though that I be foul and old and poore,
I nolde for al the metal ne for ore
That under erthe is grave° or lith° above, *buried / lies*
But if thy wif I were and eek thy love."
  "My love," quod he. "Nay, my dampnacioun!° *damnation*
Allas, that any of my nacioun[6]
Sholde evere so foule disparaged° be." *degraded*

6. I.e., family.

But al for nought, th'ende is this, that he
Constrained was: he needes moste hire wedde,
And taketh his olde wif and gooth to bedde.
Now wolden some men saye, paraventure,
That for my necligence I do no cure[7]
To tellen you the joye and al th'array
That at the feeste was that ilke day.
To which thing shortly answere I shal:
I saye ther nas no joye ne feeste at al;
Ther nas but hevinesse and muche sorwe.
For prively he wedded hire on morwe,[8]
And al day after hidde him as an owle,
So wo was him, his wif looked so foule.
Greet was the wo the knight hadde in his thought:
Whan he was with his wif abedde brought,
He walweth° and he turneth to and fro. *tosses*
His olde wif lay smiling everemo,
And saide, "O dere housbonde, benedicite,° *bless me*
Fareth° every knight thus with his wif as ye? *behaves*
Is this the lawe of King Arthures hous?
Is every knight of his thus daungerous?° *standoffish*
I am youre owene love and youre wif;
I am she which that saved hath youre lif;
And certes yit ne dide I you nevere unright.
Why fare ye thus with me this firste night?
Ye faren like a man hadde lost his wit.
What is my gilt? For Goddes love, telle it,
And it shal been amended if I may."
"Amended!" quod this knight. "Allas, nay, nay,
It wol nat been amended neveremo.
Thou art so lothly° and so old also, *hideous*
And therto comen of so lowe a kinde,° *lineage*
That litel wonder is though I walwe and winde.° *turn*
So wolde God myn herte wolde breste!"° *break*
"Is this," quod she, "the cause of youre unreste?"
"Ye, certainly," quod he. "No wonder is."
"Now sire," quod she, "I coude amende al this,
If that me liste, er it were dayes three,
So° wel ye mighte bere you[9] unto me. *provided that*
"But for ye speken of swich gentilesse° *nobility*
As is descended out of old richesse—
That therfore sholden ye be gentilmen—
Swich arrogance is nat worth an hen.
Looke who that is most vertuous alway,
Privee and apert,[1] and most entendeth° ay° *tries / always*
To do the gentil deedes that he can,
Taak him for the gretteste° gentilman. *greatest*
Crist wol° we claime of him oure gentilesse, *desires that*
Nat of oure eldres for hir 'old richesse.'
For though they yive us al hir heritage,

7. I do not take the trouble.
8. In the morning.
9. Behave.
1. Privately and publicly.

For which we claime to been of heigh parage,° *descent*
Yit may they nat biquethe for no thing
To noon of us hir vertuous living,
That made hem gentilmen ycalled be,
And bad[2] us folwen hem in swich degree.
"Wel can the wise poete of Florence,
That highte Dant,[3] speken in this sentence;° *topic*
Lo, in swich manere rym is Dantes tale:
'Ful selde° up riseth by his braunches[4] smale *seldom*
Prowesse° of man, for God of his prowesse *excellence*
Wol that of him we claime oure gentilesse.'
For of oure eldres may we no thing claime
But temporel thing that man may hurte and maime.
Eek every wight woot this as wel as I,
If gentilesse were planted natureelly
Unto a certain linage down the line,
Privee and apert, thanne wolde they nevere fine° *cease*
To doon of gentilesse the faire office°— *function*
They mighte do no vilainye or vice.
"Taak fir and beer° it in the derkeste hous *bear*
Bitwixe this and the Mount of Caucasus,
And lat men shette° the dores and go thenne,° *shut / thence*
Yit wol the fir as faire lye° and brenne° *blaze / burn*
As twenty thousand men mighte it biholde:
His° office natureel ay wol it holde, *its*
Up° peril of my lif, til that it die. *upon*
Heer may ye see wel how that genterye° *gentility*
Is nat annexed° to possessioun,[5] *related*
Sith folk ne doon hir operacioun
Alway, as dooth the fir, lo, in his kinde.° *nature*
For God it woot, men may wel often finde
A lordes sone do shame and vilainye;
And he that wol han pris of his gentrye,[6]
For he was boren° of a gentil° hous, *born / noble*
And hadde his eldres noble and vertuous,
And nil himselven do no gentil deedes,
Ne folwen his gentil auncestre that deed° is, *dead*
He nis nat gentil, be he duc or erl—
For vilaines sinful deedes maken a cherl.
Thy gentilesse[7] nis but renomee° *renown*
Of thine auncestres for hir heigh bountee,° *magnanimity*
Which is a straunge° thing for thy persone. *external*
For gentilesse[8] cometh fro God allone.
Thanne comth oure verray gentilesse of grace:
It was no thing biquethe us with oure place.
Thenketh how noble, as saith Valerius,[9]
Was thilke Tullius Hostilius
That out of poverte° roos to heigh noblesse. *poverty*
Redeth Senek° and redeth eek Boece:° *Seneca / Boethius*

2. I.e., they bade.
3. Dante (see his *Convivio*).
4. I.e., by the branches of a man's family tree.
5. I.e., inheritable property.
6. Have credit for his noble birth.
7. I.e., the gentility you claim.
8. I.e., true gentility.
9. A Roman historian.

Ther shul ye seen expres that no drede° is *doubt*
That he is gentil that dooth gentil deedes.
And therfore, leve housbonde, I thus conclude:
Al° were it that mine auncestres weren rude,[1] *although*
Yit may the hye God—and so hope I—
Graunte me grace to liven vertuously.
Thanne am I gentil whan that I biginne
To liven vertuously and waive° sinne. *avoid*
"And ther as ye of poverte me repreve,° *reprove*
The hye God, on whom that we bileve,
In wilful° poverte chees° to live his lif; *voluntary / chose*
And certes every man, maiden, or wif
May understonde that Jesus, hevene king,
Ne wolde nat chese° a vicious living. *choose*
Glad poverte is an honeste° thing, certain; *honorable*
This wol Senek and othere clerkes sayn.
Whoso that halt him paid of[2] his poverte,
I holde him riche al hadde he nat a sherte.° *shirt*
He that coveiteth[3] is a poore wight,
For he wolde han that is nat in his might;
But he that nought hath, ne coveiteth° have, *desires to*
Is riche, although we holde him but a knave.
Verray° poverte it singeth proprely.° *true / appropriately*
Juvenal saith of poverte, 'Merily
The poore man, whan he gooth by the waye,
Biforn the theves he may singe and playe.'
Poverte is hateful good, and as I gesse,
A ful greet bringere out of bisinesse;[4]
A greet amendere eek of sapience° *wisdom*
To him that taketh it in pacience;
Poverte is thing, although it seeme elenge,° *wretched*
Possession that no wight wol chalenge;[5]
Poverte ful often, whan a man is lowe,
Maketh[6] his God and eek himself to knowe;
Poverte a spectacle° is, as thinketh me, *pair of spectacles*
Thurgh which he may his verray° freendes see. *true*
And therfore, sire, sin that I nought you greve,
Of my poverte namore ye me repreve.° *reproach*
"Now sire, of elde° ye repreve me: *old age*
And certes sire, though noon auctoritee
Were in no book, ye gentils of honour
Sayn that men sholde an old wight doon favour,
And clepe him fader for youre gentilesse—
And auctours[7] shal I finde, as I gesse.
"Now ther ye saye that I am foul and old:
Thanne drede you nought to been a cokewold,° *cuckold*
For filthe and elde, also mote I thee,[8]
Been grete wardeins° upon chastitee. *guardians*
But nathelees, sin I knowe your delit,

1. I.e., low born.
2. Considers himself satisfied with.
3. I.e., suffers desires.
4. I.e., remover of cares.
5. Claim as his property.
6. I.e., makes him.
7. I.e., authorities.
8. So may I prosper.

I shal fulfille youre worldly appetit.
"Chees° now," quod she, "oon of thise thinges twaye: *choose*
To han me foul and old til that I deye
And be to you a trewe humble wif,
And nevere you displese in al my lif,
Or elles ye wol han me yong and fair,
And take youre aventure° of the repair[9] *chance*
That shal be to youre hous by cause of me—
Or in some other place, wel may be.
Now chees youreselven wheither° that you liketh." *whichever*
This knight aviseth him[1] and sore siketh;° *sighs*
But atte laste he saide in this manere:
"My lady and my love, and wif so dere,
I putte me in youre wise governaunce:
Cheseth° youreself which may be most plesaunce° *choose / pleasure*
And most honour to you and me also.
I do no fors the wheither[2] of the two,
For as you liketh it suffiseth° me." *satisfies*
"Thanne have I gete° of you maistrye," quod she, *got*
"Sin I may chese and governe as me lest?"° *it pleases*
"Ye, certes, wif," quod he. "I holde it best."
"Kisse me," quod she. "We be no lenger wrothe.
For by my trouthe, I wol be to you bothe—
This is to sayn, ye, bothe fair and good.
I praye to God that I mote sterven wood,[3]
But° I to you be al so good and trewe *unless*
As evere was wif sin that the world was newe.
And but I be tomorn° as fair to seene *tomorrow morning*
As any lady, emperisse, or queene,
That is bitwixe the eest and eek the west,
Do with my lif and deeth right as you lest:
Caste up the curtin,[4] looke how that it is."
And whan the knight sawgh verraily al this,
That she so fair was and so yong therto,
For joye he hente° hire in his armes two; *took*
His herte bathed in a bath of blisse;
A thousand time arewe° he gan hire kisse, *in a row*
And she obeyed him in every thing
That mighte do him plesance or liking.° *pleasure*
And thus they live unto hir lives ende
In parfit° joye. And Jesu Crist us sende *perfect*
Housbondes meeke, yonge, and fresshe abedde—
And grace t'overbide° hem that we wedde. *outlive*
And eek I praye Jesu shorte° hir lives *shorten*
That nought wol be governed by hir wives,
And olde and angry nigardes of dispence°— *spending*
God sende hem soone a verray° pestilence! *veritable*

9. I.e., visits.
1. Considers.
2. I do not care whichever.
3. Die mad.
4. The curtain around the bed.

The Pardoner's Prologue and Tale

As with *The Wife of Bath's Prologue* and *Tale, The Pardoner's Prologue* and *Tale* develop in profound and surprising ways the portrait sketched in *The General Prologue*. In his *Prologue* the Pardoner boasts to his fellow pilgrims about his own depravity and the ingenuity with which he abuses his office and extracts money from poor and ignorant people.

The medieval pardoner's job was to collect money for the charitable enterprises, such as hospitals, supported by the church. In return for donations he was licensed by the pope to award token remission of sins that the donor should have repented and confessed. By canon law pardoners were permitted to work only in a prescribed area; within that area they might visit churches during Sunday service, briefly explain their mission, receive contributions, and in the pope's name issue indulgence, which was not considered to be a sale but a gift from the infinite treasury of Christ's mercy made in return for a gift of money. In practice, pardoners ignored the restrictions on their office, made their way into churches at will, preached emotional sermons, and claimed extraordinary power for their pardons.

The Pardoner's Tale is a bombastic sermon against gluttony, gambling, and swearing, which he preaches to the pilgrims to show off his professional skills. The sermon is framed by a narrative that is supposed to function as an *exemplum* (that is, an illustration) of the scriptural text, the one on which the Pardoner, as he tells the pilgrims, always preaches: "*Radix malorum est cupiditas*" (Avarice is the root of evil).

The Introduction

Oure Hoste gan to swere as he were wood° — *insane*
"Harrow,"° quod he, "by nailes and by blood,[1] — *help*
This was a fals cherl and a fals justise.[2]
As shameful deeth as herte may devise
Come to thise juges and hir advocats.
Algate° this sely° maide is slain, allas! — *at any rate / innocent*
Allas, too dere boughte she beautee!
Wherfore I saye alday° that men may see — *always*
The yiftes of Fortune and of Nature
Been cause of deeth to many a creature.
As bothe yiftes that I speke of now,
Men han ful ofte more for harm than prow.° — *benefit*
"But trewely, myn owene maister dere,
This is a pitous tale for to heere.
But nathelees, passe over, is no fors:[3]
I praye to God to save thy gentil cors,° — *body*
And eek thine urinals and thy jurdones,[4]
Thyn ipocras and eek thy galiones,[5]
And every boiste° ful of thy letuarye°— — *box / medicine*

1. I.e., God's nails and blood.
2. The Host has been affected by the Physicians's sad tale of the Roman maiden Virginia, whose great beauty caused a judge to attempt to obtain her person by means of a trumped-up lawsuit in which he connived with a "churl" who claimed her as his slave; in order to preserve her chastity, her father killed her.
3. I.e., never mind.
4. Jordans (chamber pots): the Host is somewhat confused in his endeavor to use technical medical terms. "Urinals": vessels for examining urine.
5. A medicine, probably invented on the spot by the Host, named after Galen. "Ipocras": a medicinal drink named after Hippocrates.

God blesse hem, and oure lady Sainte Marye.
So mote I theen,[6] thou art a propre man,
And lik a prelat, by Saint Ronian![7]
Saide I nat wel? I can nat speke in terme.[8]
But wel I woot, thou doost° myn herte to erme° *make / grieve*
That I almost have caught a cardinacle.[9]
By corpus bones,[1] but if° I have triacle,° *unless / medicine*
Or elles a draughte of moiste° and corny° ale, *fresh / malty*
Or but I here anoon° a merye tale, *at once*
Myn herte is lost for pitee of this maide.
"Thou bel ami,[2] thou Pardoner," he saide,
"Tel us som mirthe or japes° right anoon." *jokes*
"It shal be doon," quod he, "by Saint Ronion.
But first," quod he, "here at this ale-stake[3]
I wol bothe drinke and eten of a cake."° *flat loaf of bread*
And right anoon thise gentils gan to crye,
"Nay, lat him telle us of no ribaudye.° *ribaldry*
Tel us som moral thing that we may lere,° *learn*
Som wit,[4] and thanne wol we gladly heere."
"I graunte, ywis,"° quod he, "but I moot thinke *certainly*
Upon som honeste° thing whil that I drinke." *decent*

The Prologue

Lordinges—quod he—in chirches whan I preche,
I paine me[5] to han° an hautein° speeche, *have / loud*
And ringe it out as round as gooth a belle,
For I can al by rote[6] that I telle.
My theme is alway oon,[7] and evere was:
Radix malorum est cupiditas.[8]
First I pronounce whennes° that I come, *whence*
And thanne my bulles shewe I alle and some:[9]
Oure lige lordes seel on my patente,[1]
That shewe I first, my body to warente,° *keep safe*
That no man be so bold, ne preest ne clerk,
Me to destourbe of Cristes holy werk.
And after that thanne telle I forth my tales[2]—
Bulles of popes and of cardinales,
Of patriarkes and bisshopes I shewe,
And in Latin I speke a wordes fewe,
To saffron with[3] my predicacioun,° *preaching*
And for to stire hem to devocioun.
Thanne shewe I forth my longe crystal stones,° *jars*
Ycrammed ful of cloutes° and of bones *rags*

6. So might I prosper.
7. St. Ronan or St. Ninian, with a possible play on "runnion" (sexual organ).
8. Speak in technical idiom.
9. Apparently a cardiac condition, confused in the Host's mind with a cardinal.
1. An illiterate oath, mixing "God's bones" with *corpus dei* ("God's body").
2. Fair friend.
3. Sign of a tavern.
4. I.e., something with significance.
5. Take pains.
6. I know all by heart.
7. I.e., the same. "Theme": biblical text on which the sermon is based.
8. Avarice is the root of evil (1 Timothy 6.10).
9. Each and every one. "Bulles": papal bulls, official documents.
1. I.e., the pope's or bishop's seal on my papal license.
2. I go on with my yarn.
3. To add spice to.

Relikes been they, as weenen° they eechoon. *suppose*
Thanne have I in laton° a shulder-boon *brass*
Which that was of an holy Jewes sheep.
"Goode men," I saye, "take of my wordes keep:° *notice*
If that this boon be wasshe in any welle,
If cow, or calf, or sheep, or oxe swelle,
That any worm hath ete or worm ystonge,[4]
Take water of that welle and wassh his tonge,
And it is hool[5] anoon. And ferthermoor,
Of pokkes° and of scabbe and every soor° *pox, pustules / sore*
Shal every sheep be hool that of this welle
Drinketh a draughte. Take keep eek° that I telle: *also*
If that the goode man that the beestes oweth° *owns*
Wol every wike,° er° that the cok him croweth, *week / before*
Fasting drinken of this welle a draughte—
As thilke° holy Jew oure eldres taughte— *that same*
His beestes and his stoor° shal multiplye. *stock*
  "And sire, also it heleth jalousye:
For though a man be falle in jalous rage,
Lat maken with this water his potage,° *soup*
And nevere shal he more his wif mistriste,° *mistrust*
Though he the soothe of hir defaute wiste,[6]
Al hadde she[7] taken preestes two or three.
  "Here is a mitein° eek that ye may see: *mitten*
He that his hand wol putte in this mitein
He shal have multiplying of his grain,
Whan he hath sowen, be it whete or otes—
So that he offre pens or elles grotes.[8]
  "Goode men and wommen, oo thing warne I you:
If any wight be in this chirche now
That hath doon sinne horrible, that he
Dar nat for shame of it yshriven° be, *confessed*
Or any womman, be she yong or old,
That hath ymaked hir housbonde cokewold,° *cuckold*
Swich° folk shal have no power ne no grace *such*
To offren to[9] my relikes in this place;
And whoso findeth him out of swich blame,
He wol come up and offre in Goddes name,
And I assoile° him by the auctoritee *absolve*
Which that by bulle ygraunted was to me."
  By this gaude° have I wonne, yeer by yeer, *trick*
An hundred mark[1] sith° I was pardoner. *since*
I stonde lik a clerk in my pulpet,
And whan the lewed° peple is down yset, *ignorant*
I preche so as ye han herd bifore,
And telle an hundred false japes° more. *tricks*
Thanne paine I me[2] to strecche forth the nekke,
And eest and west upon the peple I bekke° *nod*

4. That has eaten any worm or been bitten by any snake.
5. I.e., sound.
6. Knew the truth of her infidelity.
7. Even if she had.
8. Pennies, groats, coins.
9. To make gifts in reverence of.
1. Marks (pecuniary units).
2. I take pains.

As dooth a douve,° sitting on a berne;° *dove / barn*
Mine handes and my tonge goon so yerne° *fast*
That it is joye to see my bisinesse.
Of avarice and of swich cursednesse° *sin*
Is al my preching, for to make hem free° *generous*
To yiven hir pens, and namely° unto me, *especially*
For myn entente is nat but for to winne,[3]
And no thing for correccion of sinne:
I rekke° nevere whan that they been beried° *care / buried*
Though that hir soules goon a-blakeberied.[4]
For certes, many a predicacioun° *sermon*
Comth ofte time of yvel entencioun:
Som for plesance of folk and flaterye,
To been avaunced° by ypocrisye, *promoted*
And som for vaine glorye, and som for hate;
For whan I dar noon otherways debate,° *fight*
Thanne wol I stinge him[5] with my tonge smerte° *sharply*
In preching, so that he shal nat asterte° *escape*
To been defamed falsly, if that he
Hath trespassed to my bretheren[6] or to me.
For though I telle nought his propre name,
Men shal wel knowe that it is the same
By signes and by othere circumstaunces.
Thus quite° I folk that doon us displesaunces;[7] *pay back*
Thus spete° I out my venim under hewe° *spit / false colors*
Of holinesse, to seeme holy and trewe.
But shortly myn entente I wol devise:° *explain*
I preche of no thing but for coveitise;° *covetousness*
Therfore my theme is yit and evere was
Radix malorum est cupiditas.
  Thus can I preche again that same vice
Which that I use, and that is avarice.
But though myself be gilty in that sinne,
Yit can I make other folk to twinne° *separate*
From avarice, and sore to repente—
But that is nat my principal entente:
I preche no thing but for coveitise.
Of this matere it oughte ynough suffise.
  Thanne telle I hem ensamples[8] many oon
Of olde stories longe time agoon,
For lewed° peple loven tales olde— *ignorant*
Swiche° thinges can they wel reporte and holde.[9] *such*
What, trowe° ye that whiles I may preche, *believe*
And winne gold and silver for° I teche, *because*
That I wol live in poverte wilfully?° *voluntarily*
Nay, nay, I thoughte° it nevere, trewely, *intended*
For I wol preche and begge in sondry landes;
I wol nat do no labour with mine handes,

3. My intent is only to make money.
4. Go blackberrying, i.e., go to hell.
5. An adversary critical of pardoners.
6. Injured my fellow pardoners.
7. Make trouble for us.
8. Exempla (stories illustrating moral principles).
9. Repeat and remember.

Ne make baskettes and live therby,
By cause I wol nat beggen idelly.[1]
I wol none of the Apostles countrefete:° *imitate*
I wol have moneye, wolle,° cheese, and whete, *wool*
Al were it[2] yiven of the pooreste page,
Or of the pooreste widwe in a village—
Al sholde hir children sterve[3] for famine.
Nay, I wol drinke licour of the vine
And have a joly wenche in every town.
But herkneth, lordinges, in conclusioun,
Youre liking° is that I shal telle a tale: *pleasure*
Now have I dronke a draughte of corny ale,
By God, I hope I shal you telle a thing
That shal by reson been at youre liking;
For though myself be a ful vicious man,
A moral tale yit I you telle can,
Which I am wont to preche for to winne.
Now holde youre pees, my tale I wol biginne.

The Tale

In Flandres whilom° was a compaignye *once*
Of yonge folk that haunteden° folye— *practiced*
As riot, hasard, stewes,[4] and tavernes,
Wher as with harpes, lutes, and giternes° *guitars*
They daunce and playen at dees° bothe day and night, *dice*
And ete also and drinke over hir might,[5]
Thurgh which they doon the devel sacrifise
Within that develes temple in cursed wise
By superfluitee° abhominable. *overindulgence*
Hir othes been so grete and so dampnable
That it is grisly for to heere hem swere:
Oure blessed Lordes body they totere[6]—
Hem thoughte that Jewes rente° him nought ynough. *tore*
And eech of hem at otheres sinne lough.° *laughed*
And right anoon thanne comen tombesteres,° *dancing girls*
Fetis° and smale,° and yonge frutesteres,[7] *shapely / slender*
Singeres with harpes, bawdes,° wafereres[8]— *pimps*
Whiche been the verray develes officeres,
To kindle and blowe the fir of lecherye
That is annexed unto glotonye:[9]
The Holy Writ take I to my witnesse
That luxure° is in win and dronkenesse. *lechery*
Lo, how that dronken Lot[1] unkindely° *unnaturally*
Lay by his doughtres two unwitingly:
So dronke he was he niste° what he wroughte.° *didn't know / did*

1. I.e., without profit.
2. Even though it were.
3. Even though her children should die.
4. Wild parties, gambling, brothels.
5. Beyond their capacity.
6. Tear apart (a reference to oaths sworn by parts of His body, such as "God's bones!" or "God's teeth!").
7. Fruit-selling girls.
8. Girl cake vendors.
9. I.e., closely related to gluttony.
1. See Genesis 19.30–36.

Herodes, who so wel the stories soughte,[2]
Whan he of win was repleet° at his feeste, *filled*
Right at his owene table he yaf his heeste° *command*
To sleen° the Baptist John, ful giltelees. *slay*
Senek[3] saith a good word doutelees:
He saith he can no difference finde
Bitwixe a man that is out of his minde
And a man which that is dronkelewe,° *drunken*
But that woodnesse, yfallen in a shrewe,[4]
Persevereth lenger than dooth dronkenesse.
O glotonye, ful of cursednesse!° *wickedness*
O cause first of oure confusioun!° *downfall*
O original of oure dampnacioun,° *damnation*
Til Crist hadde bought° us with his blood again! *redeemed*
Lo, how dere, shortly for to sayn,
Abought° was thilke° cursed vilainye; *paid for / that same*
Corrupt was al this world for glotonye:
Adam oure fader and his wif also
Fro Paradis to labour and to wo
Were driven for that vice, it is no drede.° *doubt*
For whil that Adam fasted, as I rede,
He was in Paradis; and whan that he
Eet° of the fruit defended° on a tree, *ate / forbidden*
Anoon he was out cast to wo and paine.
O glotonye, on thee wel oughte us plaine!° *complain*
O, wiste a man[5] how manye maladies
Folwen of excesse and of glotonies,
He wolde been the more mesurable° *moderate*
Of his diete, sitting at his table.
Allas, the shorte throte, the tendre mouth,
Maketh that eest and west and north and south,
In erthe, in air, in water, men to swinke,° *work*
To gete a gloton daintee mete° and drinke. *food*
Of this matere, O Paul, wel canstou trete:
"Mete unto wombe,° and wombe eek unto mete, *belly*
Shal God destroyen bothe," as Paulus saith.[6]
Allas, a foul thing is it, by my faith,
To saye this word, and fouler is the deede
Whan man so drinketh of the white and rede[7]
That of his throte he maketh his privee° *toilet*
Thurgh thilke cursed superfluitee.° *overindulgence*
The Apostle[8] weeping saith ful pitously,
"Ther walken manye of which you told have I—
I saye it now weeping with pitous vois—
They been enemies of Cristes crois,° *cross*
Of whiche the ende is deeth—wombe is hir god!"[9]
O wombe, O bely, O stinking cod,° *bag*
Fulfilled° of dong° and of corrupcioun! *filled full / dung*

2. For the story of Herod and St. John the Baptist, see Mark 6.17–29. "Who so . . . soughte": i.e., whoever looked it up in the Gospel would find.
3. Seneca, the Roman Stoic philosopher.
4. But that madness, occurring in a wicked man.
5. If a man knew.
6. See 1 Corinthians 6.13.
7. I.e., white and red wines.
8. I.e., St. Paul.
9. See Philippians 3.18.

At either ende of thee foul is the soun.° *sound*
How greet labour and cost is thee to finde!° *provide for*
Thise cookes, how they stampe° and straine and grinde, *pound*
And turnen substance into accident[1]
To fulfillen al thy likerous° talent!° *greedy / appetite*
Out of the harde bones knokke they
The mary,° for they caste nought away *marrow*
That may go thurgh the golet[2] softe and soote.° *sweetly*
Of spicerye° of leef and bark and roote *spices*
Shal been his sauce ymaked by delit,
To make him yit a newer appetit.
But certes, he that haunteth swiche delices° *pleasures*
Is deed° whil that he liveth in tho° vices. *dead / those*
  A lecherous thing is win, and dronkenesse
Is ful of striving° and of wrecchednesse. *quarreling*
O dronke man, disfigured is thy face!
Sour is thy breeth, foul artou to embrace!
And thurgh thy dronke nose seemeth the soun
As though thou saidest ay,° "Sampsoun, Sampsoun." *always*
And yit, God woot,° Sampson drank nevere win.[3] *knows*
Thou fallest as it were a stiked swin;° *stuck pig*
Thy tonge is lost, and al thyn honeste cure,[4]
For dronkenesse is verray sepulture° *burial*
Of mannes wit° and his discrecioun. *intelligence*
In whom that drinke hath dominacioun
He can no conseil° keepe, it is no drede.° *secrets / doubt*
Now keepe you fro the white and fro the rede—
And namely° fro the white win of Lepe[5] *particularly*
That is to selle in Fisshstreete or in Chepe:[6]
The win of Spaine creepeth subtilly
In othere wines growing faste° by, *close*
Of which ther riseth swich fumositee° *heady fumes*
That whan a man hath dronken draughtes three
And weeneth° that he be at hoom in Chepe, *supposes*
He is in Spaine, right at the town of Lepe,
Nat at The Rochele ne at Burdeux town;[7]
And thanne wol he sayn, "Sampsoun, Sampsoun."
  But herkneth, lordinges, oo° word I you praye, *one*
That alle the sovereín actes,[8] dar I saye,
Of victories in the Olde Testament,
Thurgh verray God that is omnipotent,
Were doon in abstinence and in prayere:
Looketh° the Bible and ther ye may it lere.° *behold / learn*
  Looke Attila, the grete conquerour,[9]
Deide° in his sleep with shame and dishonour, *died*

1. A philosophic joke, depending on the distinction between inner reality (substance) and outward appearance (accident).
2. Through the gullet.
3. Before Samson's birth an angel told his mother that he would be a Nazarite throughout his life; members of this sect took no strong drink.
4. Care for self-respect.
5. A town in Spain.
6. Fishstreet and Cheapside in the London market district.
7. The Pardoner is joking about the illegal custom of adulterating fine wines of Bordeaux and La Rochelle with strong Spanish wine.
8. Distinguished deeds.
9. Attila was the leader of the Huns who almost captured Rome in the 5th century.

Bleeding at his nose in dronkenesse:
A capitain sholde live in sobrenesse.
And overal this, aviseth you[1] right wel
What was comanded unto Lamuel[2]—
Nat Samuel, but Lamuel, saye I—
Redeth the Bible and finde it expresly,
Of win-yiving° to hem that han[3] justise: *wine-serving*
Namore of this, for it may wel suffise.
And now that I have spoken of glotonye,
Now wol I you defende° hasardrye:° *prohibit / gambling*
Hasard is verray moder° of lesinges,° *mother / lies*
And of deceite and cursed forsweringes,° *perjuries*
Blaspheme of Crist, manslaughtre, and wast° also *waste*
Of catel° and of time; and ferthermo, *property*
It is repreve° and contrarye of honour *disgrace*
For to been holden a commune hasardour,° *gambler*
And evere the hyer he is of estat
The more is he holden desolat.[4]
If that a prince useth hasardrye,
In alle governance and policye
He is, as by commune opinioun,
Yholde the lasse° in reputacioun. *less*
Stilbon, that was a wis embassadour,
Was sent to Corinthe in ful greet honour
Fro Lacedomye° to make hir alliaunce, *Sparta*
And whan he cam him happede° parchaunce *it happened*
That alle the gretteste° that were of that lond *greatest*
Playing at the hasard he hem foond,° *found*
For which as soone as it mighte be
He stal him[5] hoom again to his contree,
And saide, "Ther wol I nat lese° my name, *lose*
N'I wol nat take on me so greet defame° *dishonor*
You to allye unto none hasardours:
Sendeth othere wise embassadours,
For by my trouthe, me were levere[6] die
Than I you sholde to hasardours allye.
For ye that been so glorious in honours
Shal nat allye you with hasardours
As by my wil, ne as by my tretee."° *treaty*
This wise philosophre, thus saide he.
Looke eek that to the king Demetrius
The King of Parthes,° as the book[7] saith us, *Parthians*
Sente him a paire of dees° of gold in scorn, *dice*
For he hadde used hasard therbiforn,
For which he heeld his glorye or his renown
At no value or reputacioun.
Lordes may finden other manere play
Honeste° ynough to drive the day away. *honorable*

1. Consider.
2. Lemuel's mother told him that kings should not drink (Proverbs 31.4–5).
3. I.e., administer.
4. I.e. dissolute.
5. He stole away.
6. I had rather.
7. The book that relates this and the previous incident is the *Policraticus* of the 12th-century Latin writer John of Salisbury.

Now wol I speke of othes false and grete
A word or two, as olde bookes trete:
Greet swering is a thing abhominable,
And fals swering is yit more reprevable.° *reprehensible*
The hye God forbad swering at al—
Witnesse on Mathew.[8] But in special
Of swering saith the holy Jeremie,[9]
"Thou shalt swere sooth thine othes and nat lie,
And swere in doom° and eek in rightwisnesse,° *equity / righteousness*
But idel swering is a cursednesse."° *wickedness*
Biholde and see that in the firste Table[1]
Of hye Goddes heestes° honorable *commandments*
How that the seconde heeste of him is this:
"Take nat my name in idel or amis."
Lo, rather° he forbedeth swich swering *sooner*
Than homicide, or many a cursed thing.
I saye that as by ordre thus it stondeth—
This knoweth that[2] his heestes understondeth
How that the seconde heeste of God is that.
And fertherover,° I wol thee telle al plat° *moreover / plain*
That vengeance shal nat parten° from his hous *depart*
That of his othes is too outrageous.
"By Goddes precious herte!" and "By his nailes!"° *fingernails*
And "By the blood of Crist that is in Hailes,[3]
Sevene is my chaunce,° and thyn is cink and traye!"[4] *winning number*
"By Goddes armes, if thou falsly playe
This daggere shal thurghout thyn herte go!"
This fruit cometh of the bicche bones[5] two—
Forswering, ire, falsnesse, homicide.
Now for the love of Crist that for us dyde,° *died*
Lete° youre othes bothe grete and smale. *leave*
But sires, now wol I telle forth my tale.
Thise riotoures° three of whiche I telle, *revelers*
Longe erst er prime[6] ronge of any belle,
Were set hem in a taverne to drinke,
And as they sat they herde a belle clinke
Biforn a cors° was caried to his grave. *corpse*
That oon of hem gan callen to his knave:° *servant*
Go bet,"[7] quod he, "and axe° redily° *ask / promptly*
What cors is this that passeth heer forby,
And looke° that thou reporte his name weel."° *be sure / well*
"Sire," quod this boy, "it needeth neveradeel:[8]
It was me told er ye cam heer two houres.
He was, pardee,° an old felawe of youres, *by God*
And sodeinly he was yslain tonight,° *last night*
Fordronke° as he sat on his bench upright; *very drunk*
Ther cam a privee° thief men clepeth° Deeth, *stealthy / call*

8. "But I say unto you, Swear not at all" (Matthew 5.34).
9. Jeremiah 4.2.
1. I.e., the first three of the Ten Commandments.
2. I.e., he that.
3. An abbey in Gloucestershire supposed to possess some of Christ's blood.
4. Five and three.
5. I.e., damned dice.
6. Long before 9 A.M.
7. Better, i.e., quick.
8. It isn't a bit necessary.

That in this contree al the peple sleeth,° *slays*
And with his spere he smoot his herte atwo,
And wente his way withouten wordes mo.
He hath a thousand slain this° pestilence. *during this*
And maister, er ye come in his presence,
Me thinketh that it were necessarye
For to be war of swich an adversarye;
Beeth redy for to meete him everemore:
Thus taughte me my dame.° I saye namore." *mother*
"By Sainte Marye," saide this taverner,
"The child saith sooth, for he hath slain this yeer,
Henne° over a mile, within a greet village, *hence*
Bothe man and womman, child and hine[9] and page.
I trowe° his habitacion be there. *believe*
To been avised° greet wisdom it were *wary*
Er that he dide a man a dishonour."
"Ye, Goddes armes," quod this riotour,
"Is it swich peril with him for to meete?
I shal him seeke by way and eek by streete,[1]
I make avow to Goddes digne° bones. *worthy*
Herkneth, felawes, we three been alle ones:° *of one mind*
Lat eech of us holde up his hand to other
And eech of us bicome otheres brother,
And we wol sleen this false traitour Deeth.
He shal be slain, he that so manye sleeth,
By Goddes dignitee, er it be night."
Togidres han thise three hir trouthes plight[2]
To live and dien eech of hem with other,
As though he were his owene ybore° brother. *born*
And up they sterte,° al dronken in this rage, *started*
And forth they goon towardes that village
Of which the taverner hadde spoke biforn,
And many a grisly ooth thanne han they sworn,
And Cristes blessed body they torente:° *tore apart*
Deeth shal be deed° if that they may him hente.° *dead / catch*
Whan they han goon nat fully half a mile,
Right as they wolde han treden° over a stile, *stepped*
An old man and a poore with hem mette;
This olde man ful mekely hem grette,° *greeted*
And saide thus, "Now lordes, God you see."[3]
The pruddeste° of thise riotoures three *proudest*
Answerde again, "What, carl° with sory grace, *fellow*
Why artou al forwrapped° save thy face? *muffled up*
Why livestou so longe in so greet age?"
This olde man gan looke in his visage,
And saide thus, "For° I ne can nat finde *because*
A man, though that I walked into Inde,° *India*
Neither in citee ne in no village,
That wolde chaunge his youthe for myn age;
And therefore moot° I han myn age stille, *must*

9. Farm laborer.
1. By highway and byway.
2. Pledged their words of honor.
3. May God protect you.

As longe time as it is Goddes wille.
"Ne Deeth, allas, ne wol nat have my lif.
Thus walke I lik a restelees caitif,° *wretch*
And on the ground which is my modres° gate *mother's*
I knokke with my staf bothe erly and late,
And saye, 'Leve° moder, leet me in: *dear*
Lo, how I vanisshe, flessh and blood and skin.
Allas, whan shal my bones been at reste?
Moder, with you wolde I chaunge° my cheste[4] *exchange*
That in my chambre longe time hath be,
Ye, for an haire-clout[5] to wrappe me.'
But yit to me she wol nat do that grace,
For which ful pale and welked° is my face. *withered*
But sires, to you it is no curteisye
To speken to an old man vilainye,° *rudeness*
But° he trespasse° in word or elles in deede. *unless / offend*
In Holy Writ ye may yourself wel rede,
'Agains[6] an old man, hoor° upon his heed, *hoar*
Ye shall arise.'[7] Wherfore I yive you reed,° *advice*
Ne dooth unto an old man noon harm now,
Namore than that ye wolde men dide to you
In age, if that ye so longe abide.[8]
And God be with you wher ye go° or ride: *walk*
I moot go thider as I have to go."
"Nay, olde cherl, by God thou shalt nat so,"
Saide this other hasardour anoon.
"Thou partest nat so lightly,° by Saint John! *easily*
Thou speke° right now of thilke traitour Deeth, *spoke*
That in this contree alle oure freendes sleeth:
Have here my trouthe, as thou art his espye,° *spy*
Tel wher he is, or thou shalt it abye,° *pay for*
By God and by the holy sacrament!
For soothly thou art oon of his assent[9]
To sleen us yonge folk, thou false thief."
"Now sires," quod he, "if that ye be so lief° *anxious*
To finde Deeth, turne up this crooked way,
For in that grove I lafte° him, by my fay,° *left / faith*
Under a tree, and ther he wol abide:
Nat for youre boost° he wol him no thing hide. *boast*
See ye that ook?° Right ther ye shal him finde. *oak*
God save you, that boughte again[1] mankinde,
And you amende." Thus saide this olde man.
And everich of thise riotoures ran
Til he cam to that tree, and ther they founde
Of florins° fine of gold ycoined rounde *coins*
Wel neigh an eighte busshels as hem thoughte—
Ne lenger thanne after Deeth they soughte,
But eech of hem so glad was of the sighte,
For that the florins been so faire and brighte,

4. Chest for one's belongings, used here as the symbol for life—or perhaps a coffin.
5. Haircloth, for a winding sheet.
6. In the presence of.
7. Cf. Leviticus 19.32.
8. I.e., if you live so long.
9. I.e., one of his party.
1. Redeemed.

That down they sette hem by this precious hoord.
The worste of hem he spak the firste word:
"Bretheren," quod he, "take keep° what that I saye: *heed*
My wit is greet though that I bourde° and playe. *joke*
This tresor hath Fortune unto us yiven
In mirthe and jolitee oure lif to liven,
And lightly° as it cometh so wol we spende. *easily*
Ey, Goddes precious dignitee, who wende[2]
Today that we sholde han so fair a grace?
But mighte this gold be caried fro this place
Hoom to myn hous—or elles unto youres—
For wel ye woot that al this gold is oures—
Thanne were we in heigh felicitee.
But trewely, by daye it mighte nat be:
Men wolde sayn that we were theves stronge,° *flagrant*
And for oure owene tresor doon us honge.[3]
This tresor moste ycaried be by nighte,
As wisely and as slyly as it mighte.
Therefore I rede° that cut° amonges us alle *advise / straws*
Be drawe, and lat see wher the cut wol falle;
And he that hath the cut with herte blithe
Shal renne° to the town, and that ful swithe,° *run / quickly*
And bringe us breed and win ful prively;
And two of us shal keepen° subtilly *guard*
This tresor wel, and if he wol nat tarye,
Whan it is night we wol this tresor carye
By oon assent wher as us thinketh best."
That oon of hem the cut broughte in his fest° *fist*
And bad hem drawe and looke wher it wol falle;
And it fil° on the yongeste of hem alle, *fell*
And forth toward the town he wente anoon.
And also° soone as that he was agoon,° *as / gone away*
That oon of hem spak thus unto that other:
"Thou knowest wel thou art my sworen brother;
Thy profit wol I telle thee anoon:
Thou woost wel that oure felawe is agoon,
And here is gold, and that ful greet plentee,
That shall departed° been among us three. *divided*
But nathelees, if I can shape° it so *arrange*
That it departed were among us two,
Hadde I nat doon a freendes turn to thee?"
That other answerde, "I noot[4] how that may be:
He woot that the gold is with us twaye.
What shal we doon? What shal we to him saye?"
"Shal it be conseil?"[5] saide the firste shrewe.° *villain*
"And I shal telle in a wordes fewe
What we shul doon, and bringe it wel aboute."
"I graunte," quod that other, "out of doute,
That by my trouthe I wol thee nat biwraye."° *expose*
"Now," quod the firste, "thou woost wel we be twaye,
And two of us shal strenger° be than oon: *stronger*

2. Who would have supposed.
3. Have us hanged.
4. Don't know.
5. A secret.

Looke whan that he is set that right anoon
Aris as though thou woldest with him playe,
And I shal rive° him thurgh the sides twaye, *pierce*
Whil that thou strugelest with him as in game,
And with thy daggere looke thou do the same;
And thanne shal al this gold departed be,
My dere freend, bitwixe thee and me.
Thanne we may bothe oure lustes° al fulfille, *desires*
And playe at dees° right at oure owene wille." *dice*
And thus accorded been thise shrewes twaye
To sleen the thridde, as ye han herd me saye.
This yongeste, which that wente to the town,
Ful ofte in herte he rolleth up and down
The beautee of thise florins newe and brighte.
"O Lord," quod he, "if so were that I mighte
Have al this tresor to myself allone,
Ther is no man that liveth under the trone° *throne*
Of God that sholde live so merye as I."
And at the laste the feend oure enemy
Putte in his thought that he sholde poison beye,° *buy*
With which he mighte sleen his felawes twaye—
Forwhy° the feend° foond him in swich livinge *because / devil*
That he hadde leve° him to sorwe bringe:[6] *permission*
For this was outrely° his fulle entente, *plainly*
To sleen hem bothe, and nevere to repente.
And forth he gooth—no lenger wolde he tarye—
Into the town unto a pothecarye,° *apothecary*
And prayed him that he him wolde selle
Som poison that he mighte his rattes quelle,° *kill*
And eek ther was a polcat[7] in his hawe° *yard*
That, as he saide, his capons hadde yslawe,° *slain*
And fain he wolde wreke him[8] if he mighte
On vermin that destroyed him[9] by nighte.
The pothecarye answerde, "And thou shalt have
A thing that, also° God my soule save, *as*
In al this world there is no creature
That ete or dronke hath of this confiture° *mixture*
Nat but the mountance° of a corn° of whete— *amount / grain*
That he ne shal his lif anoon forlete.° *lose*
Ye, sterve° he shal, and that in lasse° while *die / less*
Than thou wolt goon a paas[1] nat but a mile,
The poison is so strong and violent."
This cursed man hath in his hand yhent° *taken*
This poison in a box and sith° he ran *then*
Into the nexte streete unto a man
And borwed of him large botels three,
And in the two his poison poured he—
The thridde he kepte clene for his drinke,
For al the night he shoop him[2] for to swinke° *work*
In carying of the gold out of that place.

6. Christian doctrine teaches that the devil may not tempt people except with God's permission.
7. A weasellike animal.
8. He would gladly avenge himself.
9. I.e., were ruining his farming.
1. Take a walk.
2. He was preparing.

And whan this riotour with sory grace
Hadde filled with win his grete botels three,
To his felawes again repaireth he.
    What needeth it to sermone of it more?
For right as they had cast° his deeth bifore, *plotted*
Right so they han him slain, and that anoon.
And whan that this was doon, thus spak that oon:
"Now lat us sitte and drinke and make us merye,
And afterward we wol his body berye."° *bury*
And with that word it happed him par cas[3]
To take the botel ther the poison was,
And drank, and yaf his felawe drinke also,
For which anoon they storven° bothe two. *died*
    But certes I suppose that Avicen
Wroot nevere in no canon ne in no *fen*[4]
Mo wonder signes[5] of empoisoning
Than hadde thise wrecches two er hir ending:
Thus ended been thise homicides two,
And eek the false empoisonere also.
    O cursed sinne of alle cursednesse!
O traitours homicide, O wikkednesse!
O glotonye, luxure,° and hasardrye! *lechery*
Thou blasphemour of Crist with vilainye
And othes grete of usage° and of pride! *habit*
Allas, mankinde, how may it bitide
That to thy Creatour which that thee wroughte,
And with his precious herte blood thee boughte,° *redeemed*
Thou art so fals and so unkinde,° allas? *unnatural*
    Now goode men, God foryive you youre trespas,
And ware° you fro the sinne of avarice: *guard*
Myn holy pardon may you alle warice°— *save*
So that ye offre nobles or sterlinges,[6]
Or elles silver brooches, spoones, ringes.
Boweth your heed under this holy bulle!
Cometh up, ye wives, offreth of youre wolle!° *wool*
Youre name I entre here in my rolle: anoon
Into the blisse of hevene shul ye goon.
I you assoile° by myn heigh power— *absolve*
Ye that wol offre—as clene and eek as cleer
As ye were born.—And lo, sires, thus I preche.
And Jesu Crist that is oure soules leeche° *physician*
So graunte you his pardon to receive,
For that is best—I wol you nat deceive.

The Epilogue

    "But sires, oo word forgat I in my tale:
I have relikes and pardon in my male° *bag*
As faire as any man in Engelond,

3. By chance.
4. The *Canon of Medicine*, by Avicenna, an 11th-century Arabic philosopher, was divided into sections called "fens."
5. More wonderful symptoms.
6. "Nobles" and "sterlinges" were valuable coins.

Whiche were me yiven by the Popes hond.
If any of you wol of devocioun
Offren and han myn absolucioun,
Come forth anoon, and kneeleth here adown,
And mekely receiveth my pardoun,
Or elles taketh pardon as ye wende,° *ride along*
Al newe and fressh at every miles ende—
So that ye offre alway newe and newe[7]
Nobles or pens whiche that be goode and trewe.
It is an honour to everich° that is heer *everyone*
That ye have a suffisant° pardoner *competent*
T'assoile you in contrees as ye ride,
For aventures° whiche that may bitide: *accidents*
Paraventure ther may falle oon or two
Down of his hors and breke his nekke atwo;
Looke which a suretee° is it to you alle *safeguard*
That I am in youre felaweshipe yfalle
That may assoile you, bothe more and lasse,[8]
Whan that the soule shal fro the body passe.
I rede° that oure Hoste shal biginne, *advise*
For he is most envoluped° in sinne. *involved*
Com forth, sire Host, and offre first anoon,
And thou shalt kisse the relikes everichoon,° *each one*
Ye, for a grote: unbokele° anoon thy purs." *unbuckle*
"Nay, nay," quod he, "thanne have I Cristes curs!
Lat be," quod he, "it shal nat be, so theech!° *may I prosper*
Thou woldest make me kisse thyn olde breech° *breeches*
And swere it were a relik of a saint,
Though it were with thy fundament° depeint.° *anus / stained*
But, by the crois which that Sainte Elaine foond,[9]
I wolde I hadde thy coilons° in myn hond, *testicles*
In stede of relikes or of saintuarye.° *relic-box*
Lat cutte hem of: I wol thee helpe hem carye.
They shal be shrined in an hogges tord."° *turd*
This Pardoner answerde nat a word:
So wroth he was no word ne wolde he saye.
"Now," quod oure Host, "I wol no lenger playe
With thee, ne with noon other angry man."
But right anoon the worthy Knight bigan,
Whan that he sawgh that al the peple lough,° *laughed*
"Namore of this, for it is right ynough.
Sire Pardoner, be glad and merye of cheere,
And ye, sire Host that been to me so dere,
I praye you that ye kisse the Pardoner,
And Pardoner, I praye thee, draw thee neer,
And as we diden lat us laughe and playe."
Anoon they kiste and riden forth hir waye.

7. Over and over.
8. Both high and low (i.e., everybody).
9. I.e., by the cross that St. Helena found. Helena, mother of Constantine the Great, was reputed to have found the cross on which Christ was crucified.

The Nun's Priest's Tale

In the framing story, *The Nun's Priest's Tale* is linked to a dramatic exchange that follows *The Monk's Tale*. The latter consists of brief tragedies, the common theme of which is the fall of famous men and one woman, most of whom are rulers, through the reversals of Fortune. Like *The Knight's Tale*, this was probably an earlier work of Chaucer's, one that he never finished. As the Monk's tragedies promise to go on and on monotonously, the Knight interrupts and politely tells the Monk that his tragedies are too painful. The Host chimes in to say that the tragedies are "nat worth a botterflye" and asks the Monk to try another subject, but the Monk is offended and refuses. The Host then turns to the Nun's Priest, that is, the priest who is accompanying the Prioress. The three priests said in *The General Prologue* to have been traveling with her have apparently been reduced to one.

The Nun's Priest's Tale is an example of the literary genre known as the "animal fable," familiar from the fables of Aesop in which animals, behaving like human beings, point a moral. In the Middle Ages fables often functioned as elementary texts to teach boys Latin. Marie de France's fables in French are the earliest known vernacular translations. This particular fable derives from an episode in the French *Roman de Renard*, a "beast epic," which satirically represents a feudal animal society ruled over by Noble the Lion. Reynard the Fox is a wily trickster hero who is constantly preying upon and outwitting the other animals, although sometimes Reynard himself is outwitted by one of his victims.

In *The Nun's Priest's Tale*, morals proliferate: both the priest-narrator and his hero, Chauntecleer the rooster, spout examples, learned allusions, proverbs, and sententious generalizations, often in highly inflated rhetoric. The simple beast fable is thus inflated into a delightful satire of learning and moralizing and of the pretentious rhetoric by which medieval writers sometimes sought to elevate their works. Among them, we may include Chaucer himself, who in this tale seems to be making affectionate fun of some of his own works, like the tragedies which became *The Monk's Tale*.

A poore widwe somdeel stape° in age — *advanced*
Was whilom° dwelling in a narwe[1] cotage, — *once upon a time*
Biside a grove, stonding in a dale:
This widwe of which I telle you my tale,
Sin thilke° day that she was last a wif, — *that same*
In pacience ladde° a ful simple lif. — *led*
For litel was hir catel° and hir rente,° — *property / income*
By housbondrye° of swich as God hire sente — *economy*
She foond° hirself and eek hir doughtren two. — *provided for*
Three large sowes hadde she and namo,
Three kin,° and eek a sheep that highte° Malle. — *cows / was called*
Ful sooty was hir bowr° and eek hir halle. — *bedroom*
In which she eet ful many a sclendre° meel; — *scanty*
Of poinant° sauce hire needed neveradeel:° — *pungent / not a bit*
No daintee morsel passed thurgh hir throte—
Hir diete was accordant to hir cote.° — *cottage*
Repleccioun° ne made hire nevere sik: — *overeating*
Attempre° diete was al hir physik,° — *moderate / medicine*
And exercise and hertes suffisaunce.° — *contentment*
The goute lette hire nothing for to daunce,[2]
N'apoplexye shente° nat hir heed.° — *hurt / head*
No win ne drank she, neither whit ne reed:° — *red*

1. I.e., small.
2. The gout didn't hinder her at all from dancing.

Hir boord° was served most with whit and blak,[3] *table*
Milk and brown breed, in which she foond no lak;[4]
Seind bacon, and somtime an ey° or twaye, *egg*
For she was as it were a manere daye.[5]
A yeerd° she hadde, enclosed al withoute *yard*
With stikkes, and a drye dich aboute,
In which she hadde a cok heet° Chauntecleer: *named*
In al the land of crowing nas° his peer. *was not*
His vois was merier than the merye orgon
On massedayes that in the chirche goon;[6]
Wel sikerer[7] was his crowing in his logge° *dwelling*
Than is a clok or an abbeye orlogge;° *timepiece*
By nature he knew eech ascensioun
Of th'equinoxial[8] in thilke town:
For whan degrees fifteene were ascended,
Thanne crew° he that it mighte nat been amended.° *crowed / improved*
His comb was redder than the fin coral,
And batailed° as it were a castel wal; *battlemented*
His bile° was blak, and as the jeet° it shoon; *bill / jet*
Like asure[9] were his legges and his toon;° *toes*
His nailes whitter° than the lilye flowr, *whiter*
And lik the burned° gold was his colour. *burnished*
This gentil° cok hadde in his governaunce *noble*
Sevene hennes for to doon al his plesaunce,° *pleasure*
Whiche were his sustres and his paramours,[1]
And wonder like to him as of colours;
Of whiche the faireste hewed° on hir throte *colored*
Was cleped° faire damoisele Pertelote: *called*
Curteis she was, discreet, and debonaire,° *meek*
And compaignable,° and bar° hirself so faire, *companionable / bore*
Sin thilke day that she was seven night old,
That trewely she hath the herte in hold
Of Chauntecleer, loken° in every lith.° *locked / limb*
He loved hire so that wel was him therwith.[2]
But swich a joye was it to heere hem singe,
Whan that the brighte sonne gan to springe,
In sweete accord *My Lief is Faren in Londe*[3]—
For thilke time, as I have understonde,
Beestes and briddes couden speke and singe.
  And so bifel that in a daweninge,
As Chauntecleer among his wives alle
Sat on his perche that was in the halle,
And next him sat this faire Pertelote,
This Chauntecleer gan gronen in his throte,
As man that in his dreem is drecched° sore. *troubled*
  And whan that Pertelote thus herde him rore,° *roar*

3. I.e., milk and bread.
4. Found no fault.
5. I.e., a kind of dairywoman. "Seind": scorched (i.e., broiled).
6. I.e., is played.
7. More reliable.
8. I.e., he knew by instinct each step in the progression of the celestial equator. The celestial equator was thought to make a 360° rotation around the earth every twenty-four hours; therefore, a progression of 15° would be equal to the passage of an hour (line 37).
9. Blue (lapis lazuli).
1. His sisters and his mistresses.
2. That he was well contented.
3. "My Love Has Gone Away," a popular song of the time.

She was agast, and saide, "Herte dere,
What aileth you to grone in this manere?
Ye been a verray slepere,[4] fy, for shame!"
  And he answerde and saide thus, "Madame,
I praye you that ye take it nat agrief.° *amiss*
By God, me mette I was in swich meschief[5]
Right now, that yit myn herte is sore afright.
Now God," quod he, "my swevene recche aright,[6]
And keepe my body out of foul prisoun!
Me mette° how that I romed up and down *dreamed*
Within oure yeerd, wher as I sawgh a beest,
Was lik an hound and wolde han maad arrest[7]
Upon my body, and han had me deed.[8]
His colour was bitwixe yelow and reed,
And tipped was his tail and bothe his eres
With blak, unlik the remenant° of his heres;° *rest / hairs*
His snoute smal, with glowing yën twaye.
Yit of his look for fere almost I deye:° *die*
This caused me my groning, doutelees."
  "Avoi,"° quod she, "fy on you, hertelees!° *fie / coward*
Allas," quod she, "for by that God above,
Now han ye lost myn herte and al my love!
I can nat love a coward, by my faith.
For certes, what so any womman saith,
We alle desiren, if it mighte be,
To han housbondes hardy, wise, and free,° *generous*
And secree,° and no nigard, ne no fool, *discreet*
Ne him that is agast of every tool,° *weapon*
Ne noon avauntour.° By that God above, *boaster*
How dorste° ye sayn for shame unto youre love *dare*
That any thing mighte make you aferd?
Have ye no mannes herte and han a beerd?° *beard*
Allas, and conne° ye been agast of swevenes?° *can / dreams*
No thing, God woot, but vanitee[9] in swevene is!
Swevenes engendren of replexiouns,[1]
And ofte of fume° and of complexiouns,° *gas / bodily humors*
Whan humours been too habundant in a wight.[2]
Certes, this dreem which ye han met° tonight *dreamed*
Comth of the grete superfluitee
Of youre rede colera,[3] pardee,
Which causeth folk to dreden° in hir dremes *fear*
Of arwes,° and of fir with rede lemes,° *arrows / flames*
Of rede beestes, that they wol hem bite,
Of contek,° and of whelpes grete and lite[4]— *strife*
Right° as the humour of malencolye[5] *just*
Causeth ful many a man in sleep to crye

4. Sound sleeper.
5. I dreamed that I was in such misfortune.
6. Interpret my dream correctly (i.e., in an auspicious manner).
7. Would have laid hold.
8. I.e., killed me.
9. I.e., empty illusion.
1. Dreams have their origin in overeating.
2. I.e., when humors (bodily fluids) are too abundant in a person. Pertelote's diagnosis is based on the familiar concept that an excess of one of the bodily humors in a person affected his or her temperament (see p. 180, n. 8).
3. Red bile.
4. And of big and little dogs.
5. I.e., black bile.

For fere of blake beres° or boles° blake, *bears / bulls*
Or elles blake develes wol hem take.
Of othere humours coude I tell also
That werken many a man in sleep ful wo,
But I wol passe as lightly° as I can. *quickly*
Lo, Caton,[6] which that was so wis a man,
Saide he nat thus? 'Ne do no fors of[7] dremes.'
Now, sire," quod she, "whan we flee fro the bemes,[8]
For Goddes love, as take som laxatif.
Up° peril of my soule and of my lif, *upon*
I conseile you the beste, I wol nat lie,
That bothe of colere and of malencolye
Ye purge you; and for° ye shal nat tarye, *in order that*
Though in this town is noon apothecarye,
I shal myself to herbes techen you,
That shal been for youre hele° and for youre prow,° *health / benefit*
And in oure yeerd tho° herbes shal I finde, *those*
The whiche han of hir propretee by kinde° *nature*
To purge you binethe and eek above.
Foryet° nat this, for Goddes owene love. *forget*
Ye been ful colerik° of complexioun; *bilious*
Ware° the sonne in his ascencioun *beware that*
Ne finde you nat repleet° of humours hote;° *filled / hot*
And if it do, I dar wel laye° a grote *bet*
That ye shul have a fevere terciane,[9]
Or an agu° that may be youre bane.° *ague / death*
A day or two ye shul han digestives
Of wormes, er° ye take youre laxatives *before*
Of lauriol, centaure, and fumetere,[1]
Or elles of ellebor° that groweth there, *hellebore*
Of catapuce, or of gaitres beries,[2]
Of herb-ive° growing in oure yeerd ther merye is[3]— *herb ivy*
Pekke hem right up as they growe and ete hem in.
Be merye, housbonde, for youre fader° kin! *father's*
Dredeth no dreem: I can saye you namore."
"Madame," quod he, "graunt mercy of youre lore,[4]
But nathelees, as touching daun° Catoun, *master*
That hath of wisdom swich a greet renown,
Though that he bad no dremes for to drede,
By God, men may in olde bookes rede
Of many a man more of auctoritee° *authority*
Than evere Caton was, so mote I thee,° *prosper*
That al the revers sayn of his sentence,° *opinion*
And han wel founden by experience
That dremes been significaciouns
As wel of joye as tribulaciouns
That folk enduren in this lif present.

6. Dionysius Cato, supposed author of a book of maxims used in elementary education.
7. Pay no attention to.
8. Fly down from the rafters.
9. Tertian (recurring every other day).
1. Of laureole, centaury, and fumitory. These, and the herbs mentioned in the next lines, were all common medieval medicines used as cathartics.
2. Of caper berry or of gaiter berry.
3. Where it is pleasant.
4. Many thanks for your instruction.

Ther needeth make of this noon argument:
The verray preve[5] sheweth it in deede.
"Oon of the gretteste auctour[6] that men rede
Saith thus, that whilom two felawes wente
On pilgrimage in a ful good entente,
And happed so they comen in a town,
Wher as ther was swich congregacioun
Of peple, and eek so strait of herbergage,[7]
That they ne founde as muche as oo cotage
In which they bothe mighte ylogged° be; *lodged*
Wherfore they mosten° of necessitee *must*
As for that night departe° compaignye. *part*
And eech of hem gooth to his hostelrye,
And took his logging as it wolde falle.° *befall*
That oon of hem was logged in a stalle,
Fer° in a yeerd, with oxen of the plough; *far away*
That other man was logged wel ynough,
As was his aventure° or his fortune, *lot*
That us governeth alle as in commune.
And so bifel that longe er it were day,
This man mette° in his bed, ther as he lay, *dreamed*
How that his felawe gan upon him calle,
And saide, 'Allas, for in an oxes stalle
This night I shal be mordred° ther I lie! *murdered*
Now help me, dere brother, or I die!
In alle haste com to me,' he saide.
"This man out of his sleep for fere abraide,° *started up*
But whan that he was wakened of his sleep,
He turned him and took of this no keep:° *heed*
Him thoughte his dreem nas but a vanitee.° *illusion*
Thus twies in his sleeping dremed he,
And atte thridde time yit his felawe
Cam, as him thoughte, and saide, 'I am now slawe:° *slain*
Bihold my bloody woundes deepe and wide.
Aris up erly in the morwe tide,[8]
And atte west gate of the town,' quod he,
'A carte ful of dong° ther shaltou see, *dung*
In which my body is hid ful prively:
Do thilke carte arresten boldely.[9]
My gold caused my mordre, sooth to sayn'
—And tolde him every point how he was slain,
With a ful pitous face, pale of hewe.
And truste wel, his dreem he foond° ful trewe, *found*
For on the morwe° as soone as it was day, *morning*
To his felawes in° he took the way, *lodging*
And whan that he cam to this oxes stalle,
After his felawe he bigan to calle.
"The hostiler° answerde him anoon, *innkeeper*
And saide, 'Sire, youre felawe is agoon:° *gone away*

5. Actual experience.
6. I.e., one of the greatest authors (perhaps Cicero or Valerius Maximus).
7. And also such a shortage of lodging.
8. In the morning.
9. Boldly have this same cart seized.

As soone as day he wente out of the town.'
"This man gan fallen in suspecioun,
Remembring on his dremes that he mette;° *dreamed*
And forth he gooth, no lenger wolde he lette,° *tarry*
Unto the west gate of the town, and foond
A dong carte, wente as it were to donge° lond, *put manure on*
That was arrayed in that same wise
As ye han herd the dede° man devise; *dead*
And with an hardy herte he gan to crye,
'Vengeance and justice of this felonye!
My felawe mordred is this same night,
And in this carte he lith° gaping upright!° *lies / on his back*
I crye out on the ministres,' quod he,
'That sholde keepe and rulen this citee.
Harrow,° allas, here lith my felawe slain!' *help*
What sholde I more unto this tale sayn?
The peple up sterte° and caste the carte to grounde, *started*
And in the middel of the dong they founde
The dede man that mordred was al newe.[1]
"O blisful God that art so just and trewe,
Lo, how that thou biwrayest° mordre alway! *disclose*
Mordre wol out, that see we day by day:
Mordre is so wlatsom° and abhominable *loathsome*
To God that is so just and resonable,
That he ne wol nat suffre it heled° be, *concealed*
Though it abide a yeer or two or three.
Mordre wol out: this my conclusioun.
And right anoon ministres of that town
Han hent° the cartere and so sore him pined,[2] *seized*
And eek the hostiler so sore engined,° *racked*
That they biknewe° hir wikkednesse anoon, *confessed*
And were anhanged° by the nekke boon. *hanged*
Here may men seen that dremes been to drede.[3]
"And certes, in the same book I rede—
Right in the nexte chapitre after this—
I gabbe° nat, so have I joye or blis— *lie*
Two men that wolde han passed over see
For certain cause into a fer contree,
If that the wind ne hadde been contrarye
That made hem in a citee for to tarye,
That stood ful merye upon an haven° side— *harbor's*
But on a day again° the even-tide *toward*
The wind gan chaunge, and blewe right as hem leste:[4]
Jolif° and glad they wenten unto reste, *merry*
And casten° hem ful erly for to saile. *determined*
"But to that oo man fil° a greet mervaile; *befell*
That oon of hem, in sleeping as he lay,
Him mette[5] a wonder dreem again the day:
Him thoughte a man stood by his beddes side,

1. Recently.
2. Tortured.
3. Worthy of being feared.
4. Just as they wished.
5. He dreamed.

And him comanded that he sholde abide,
And saide him thus, 'If thou tomorwe wende,
Thou shalt be dreint:° my tale is at an ende.' *drowned*
"He wook and tolde his felawe what he mette,
And prayed him his viage° to lette;° *voyage / delay*
As for that day he prayed him to bide.
"His felawe that lay by his beddes side
Gan for to laughe, and scorned him ful faste.° *hard*
'No dreem,' quod he, 'may so myn herte agaste° *terrify*
That I wol lette for to do my thinges.° *business*
I sette nat a straw by thy dreminges,[6]
For swevenes been but vanitees and japes:[7]
Men dreme alday° of owles or of apes,[8] *constantly*
And of many a maze° therwithal— *delusion*
Men dreme of thing that nevere was ne shal.[9]
But sith I see that thou wolt here abide,
And thus forsleuthen° wilfully thy tide,° *waste / time*
God woot, it reweth me;[1] and have good day.'
And thus he took his leve and wente his way.
But er that he hadde half his cours ysailed—
Noot I nat why ne what meschaunce it ailed—
But casuelly the shippes botme rente,[2]
And ship and man under the water wente,
In sighte of othere shippes it biside,
That with hem sailed at the same tide.
And therfore, faire Pertelote so dere,
By swiche ensamples olde maistou lere° *learn*
That no man sholde been too recchelees° *careless*
Of dremes, for I saye thee doutelees
That many a dreem ful sore is for to drede.
"Lo, in the lif of Saint Kenelm[3] I rede—
That was Kenulphus sone, the noble king
Of Mercenrike°—how Kenelm mette a thing *Mercia*
A lite° er he was mordred on a day. *little*
His mordre in his avision° he sey.° *dream / saw*
His norice° him expounded everydeel° *nurse / every bit*
His swevene, and bad him for to keepe him[4] weel
For traison, but he nas but seven yeer old,
And therfore litel tale hath he told
Of any dreem,[5] so holy was his herte.
By God, I hadde levere than my sherte[6]
That ye hadde rad° his legende as have I. *read*
"Dame Pertelote, I saye you trewely,
Macrobeus,[7] that writ the *Avisioun*
In Affrike of the worthy Scipioun,

6. I don't care a straw for your dreamings.
7. Dreams are but illusions and frauds.
8. I.e., of absurdities.
9. I.e., shall be.
1. I'm sorry.
2. I don't know why nor what was the trouble with it—but accidentally the ship's bottom split.
3. Kenelm succeeded his father as king of Mercia at the age of seven, but was slain by his aunt (in 821).
4. Guard himself.
5. Therefore he has set little store by any dream.
6. I.e., I'd give my shirt.
7. Macrobius wrote a famous commentary on Cicero's account in *De Republica* of the dream of Scipio Africanus Minor; the commentary came to be regarded as a standard authority on dream lore.

Affermeth° dremes, and saith that they been — *confirms*
Warning of thinges that men after seen.
"And ferthermore, I praye you looketh wel
In the Olde Testament of Daniel,
If he heeld° dremes any vanitee.[8] — *considered*
"Rede eek of Joseph[9] and ther shul ye see
Wher° dremes be somtime—I saye nat alle— — *whether*
Warning of thinges that shul after falle.
"Looke of Egypte the king daun Pharao,
His bakere and his botelere° also, — *butler*
Wher they ne felte noon effect in dremes.[1]
Whoso wol seeke actes of sondry remes° — *realms*
May rede of dremes many a wonder thing.
"Lo Cresus, which that was of Lyde° king, — *Lydia*
Mette° he nat that he sat upon a tree, — *dreamed*
Which signified he sholde anhanged° be? — *hanged*
"Lo here Andromacha, Ectores° wif, — *Hector's*
That day that Ector sholde lese° his lif, — *lose*
She dremed on the same night biforn
How that the lif of Ector sholde be lorn,° — *lost*
If thilke° day he wente into bataile; — *that same*
She warned him, but it mighte nat availe:° — *do any good*
He wente for to fighte natheless,
But he was slain anoon° of Achilles. — *right away*
But thilke tale is al too long to telle,
And eek it is neigh day, I may nat dwelle.
Shortly I saye, as for conclusioun,
That I shal han of this avisioun[2]
Adversitee, and I saye ferthermoor
That I ne telle of[3] laxatives no stoor,
For they been venimes,° I woot it weel: — *poisons*
I hem defye, I love hem neveradeel.° — *not a bit*
"Now lat us speke of mirthe and stinte° al this. — *stop*
Madame Pertelote, so have I blis,
Of oo thing God hath sente me large grace:
For whan I see the beautee of youre face—
Ye been so scarlet reed° aboute youre yën— — *red*
It maketh al my drede for to dien.
For also siker° as *In principio,*[4] — *certain*
Mulier est hominis confusio.[5]
Madame, the sentence° of this Latin is, — *meaning*
'Womman is mannes joye and al his blis.'
For whan I feele anight youre softe side—
Al be it that I may nat on you ride,
For that oure perche is maad so narwe, allas—
I am so ful of joye and of solas° — *delight*
That I defye bothe swevene and dreem."
And with that word he fleigh° down fro the beem, — *flew*

8. See Daniel 7.
9. See Genesis 37.
1. See Genesis 39–41.
2. Divinely inspired dream (as opposed to the more ordinary "swevene" or "dreem").
3. Set by.
4. Beginning of the Gospel of St. John that gives the essential premises of Christianity: "In the beginning was the Word."
5. Woman is man's ruination.

For it was day, and eek his hennes alle,
And with a "chuk" he gan hem for to calle,
For he hadde founde a corn lay in the yeerd.
Real° he was, he was namore aferd:° *regal / afraid*
He fethered[6] Pertelote twenty time,
And trad hire as ofte er it was prime.[7]
He looketh as it were a grim leoun,
And on his toes he rometh up and down:
Him deined[8] nat to sette his foot to grounde.
He chukketh whan he hath a corn yfounde,
And to him rennen° thanne his wives alle. *run*
Thus royal, as a prince is in his halle,
Leve I this Chauntecleer in his pasture,
And after wol I telle his aventure.
  Whan that the month in which the world bigan,
That highte° March, whan God first maked man, *is called*
Was compleet, and passed were also,
Sin March biran,° thritty days and two,[9] *passed by*
Bifel that Chauntecleer in al his pride,
His sevene wives walking him biside,
Caste up his yën to the brighte sonne,
That in the signe of Taurus hadde yronne
Twenty degrees and oon and somwhat more,
And knew by kinde,° and by noon other lore, *nature*
That it was prime, and crew with blisful stevene.° *voice*
"The sonne," he saide, "is clomben[1] up on hevene
Fourty degrees and oon and more, ywis.° *indeed*
Madame Pertelote, my worldes blis,
Herkneth thise blisful briddes° how they singe, *birds*
And see the fresshe flowers how they springe:
Ful is myn herte of revel and solas."
But sodeinly him fil° a sorweful cas,° *befell / chance*
For evere the latter ende of joye is wo—
God woot that worldly joye is soone ago,
And if a rethor° coude faire endite, *rhetorician*
He in a cronicle saufly° mighte it write, *safely*
As for a soverein notabilitee.[2]
Now every wis man lat him herkne me:
This storye is also° trewe, I undertake, *as*
As is the book of *Launcelot de Lake*,[3]
That wommen holde in ful greet reverence.
Now wol I turne again to my sentence.° *main point*
  A colfox[4] ful of sly iniquitee,
That in the grove hadde woned° yeres three, *dwelled*
By heigh imaginacion forncast,[5]
The same night thurghout the hegges° brast° *hedges / burst*
Into the yeerd ther Chauntecleer the faire
Was wont, and eek his wives, to repaire;

6. I.e., embraced.
7. 9 A.M. "Trad": trod, copulated with.
8. He deigned.
9. The rhetorical time telling yields May 3.
1. Has climbed.
2. Indisputable fact.
3. Romances of the courteous knight Lancelot of the Lake were very popular.
4. Fox with black markings.
5. Predestined by divine planning.

And in a bed of wortes° stille he lay *cabbages*
Til it was passed undren° of the day, *midmorning*
Waiting his time on Chauntecleer to falle,
As gladly doon thise homicides alle,
That in await liggen to mordre[6] men.
O false mordrour, lurking in thy den!
O newe Scariot! Newe Geniloun![7]
False dissimilour!° O Greek Sinoun,[8] *dissembler*
That broughtest Troye al outrely° to sorwe! *utterly*
O Chauntecleer, accursed be that morwe° *morning*
That thou into the yeerd flaugh° fro the bemes! *flew*
Thou were ful wel ywarned by thy dremes
That thilke day was perilous to thee;
But what that God forwoot° moot° needes be, *foreknows / must*
After° the opinion of certain clerkes: *according to*
Witnesse on him that any parfit° clerk is *perfect*
That in scole is greet altercacioun
In this matere, and greet disputisoun,° *disputation*
And hath been of an hundred thousand men.
But I ne can nat bulte it to the bren,[9]
As can the holy doctour Augustin,
Or Boece, or the bisshop Bradwardin[1]—
Wheither that Goddes worthy forwiting° *foreknowledge*
Straineth me nedely[2] for to doon a thing
("Nedely" clepe I simple necessitee),
Or elles if free chois be graunted me
To do that same thing or do it naught,
Though God forwoot° it er that I was wrought; *foreknew*
Or if his witing° straineth neveradeel, *knowledge*
But by necessitee condicionel[3]—
I wol nat han to do of swich matere:
My tale is of a cok, as ye may heere,
That took his conseil of his wif with sorwe,
To walken in the yeerd upon that morwe
That he hadde met° the dreem that I you tolde. *dreamed*
Wommenes conseils been ful ofte colde,[4]
Wommanes conseil broughte us first to wo,
And made Adam fro Paradis to go,
Ther as he was ful merye and wel at ese.
But for I noot° to whom it mighte displese *don't know*
If I conseil of wommen wolde blame,
Passe over, for I saide it in my game°— *sport*
Rede auctours where they trete of swich matere,
And what they sayn of wommen ye may heere—
Thise been the cokkes wordes and nat mine:

6. That lie in ambush to murder.
7. I.e., Ganelon, who betrayed Roland to the Saracens (in the medieval French epic *The Song of Roland*). "Scariot": Judas Iscariot.
8. Sinon, who persuaded the Trojans to take the Greeks' wooden horse into their city—with, of course, the result that the city was destroyed.
9. Sift it to the bran, i.e., get to the bottom of it.
1. St. Augustine, Boethius (6th-century Roman philosopher, whose *Consolation of Philosophy* was translated by Chaucer), and Thomas Bradwardine (archbishop of Canterbury, d. 1349) were all concerned with the interrelationship between people's free will and God's foreknowledge.
2. Constrains me necessarily.
3. Boethius's "conditional necessity" permitted a large measure of free will.
4. I.e., baneful.

I can noon harm of no womman divine.° *guess*
 Faire in the sond° to bathe hire merily *sand*
Lith° Pertelote, and alle hir sustres by, *lies*
Again° the sonne, and Chauntecleer so free° *in / noble*
Soong° merier than the mermaide in the see— *sang*
For Physiologus[5] saith sikerly
How that they singen wel and merily.
 And so bifel that as he caste his yë
Among the wortes on a boterflye,° *butterfly*
He was war of this fox that lay ful lowe.
No thing ne liste him[6] thanne for to crowe,
But cride anoon "Cok cok!" and up he sterte,° *started*
As man that[7] was affrayed in his herte—
For naturelly a beest desireth flee
Fro his contrarye[8] if he may it see,
Though he nevere erst° hadde seen it with his yë. *before*
This Chauntecleer, whan he gan him espye,
He wolde han fled, but that the fox anoon
Saide, "Gentil sire, allas, wher wol ye goon?
Be ye afraid of me that am youre freend?
Now certes, I were worse than a feend
If I to you wolde° harm or vilainye. *meant*
I am nat come youre conseil° for t'espye, *secrets*
But trewely the cause of my cominge
Was only for to herkne how ye singe:
For trewely, ye han as merye a stevene° *voice*
As any angel hath that is in hevene.
Therwith ye han in musik more feelinge
Than hadde Boece,[9] or any that can singe.
My lord your fader—God his soule blesse!—
And eek youre moder, of hir gentilesse,° *gentility*
Han in myn hous ybeen, to my grete ese.
And certes sire, ful fain° wolde I you plese. *gladly*
 "But for men speke of singing, I wol saye,
So mote I brouke[1] wel mine yën twaye,
Save ye, I herde nevere man to singe
As dide youre fader in the morweninge.
Certes, it was of herte° al that he soong.° *heartfelt / sang*
And for to make his vois the more strong,
He wolde so paine him[2] that with bothe his yën
He moste winke,[3] so loude wolde he cryen;
And stonden on his tiptoon therwithal,
And strecche forth his nekke long and smal;
And eek he was of swich discrecioun
That ther nas no man in no regioun
That him in song or wisdom mighte passe.
I have wel rad° in *Daun Burnel the Asse*[4] *read*

5. Supposed author of a bestiary, a book of moralized zoology describing both natural and supernatural animals (including mermaids).
6. He wished.
7. Like one who.
8. I.e., his natural enemy.
9. Boethius also wrote a treatise on music.
1. So might I enjoy the use of.
2. Take pains.
3. He had to shut his eyes.
4. Master Brunellus, a discontented donkey, was the hero of a 12th-century satirical poem by Nigel Wireker.

Among his vers how that ther was a cok,
For a preestes sone yaf him a knok[5]
Upon his leg whil he was yong and nice,° — *foolish*
He made him for to lese° his benefice.[6] — *lose*
But certain, ther nis no comparisoun
Bitwixe the wisdom and discrecioun
Of youre fader and of his subtiltee.[7]
Now singeth, sire, for sainte° charitee! — *holy*
Lat see, conne° ye youre fader countrefete?"° — *can / imitate*
  This Chauntecleer his winges gan to bete,
As man that coude his traison nat espye,
So was he ravisshed with his flaterye.
  Allas, ye lordes, many a fals flatour° — *flatterer*
Is in youre court, and many a losengeour° — *deceiver*
That plesen you wel more, by my faith,
Than he that soothfastnesse° unto you saith! — *truth*
Redeth Ecclesiaste[8] of flaterye.
Beeth war, ye lordes, of hir trecherye.
  This Chauntecleer stood hye upon his toos,
Strecching his nekke, and heeld his yën cloos,
And gan to crowe loude for the nones;° — *occasion*
And daun Russel the fox sterte° up atones, — *jumped*
And by the gargat° hente° Chauntecleer, — *throat / seized*
And on his bak toward the wode him beer,° — *bore*
For yit ne was ther no man that him sued.° — *followed*
  O destinee that maist nat been eschued!° — *eschewed*
Allas that Chauntecleer fleigh° fro the bemes! — *flew*
Allas his wif ne roughte nat of[9] dremes!
And on a Friday fil° al this meschaunce! — *befell*
  O Venus that art goddesse of plesaunce,
Sin that thy servant was this Chauntecleer,
And in thy service dide al his power—
More for delit than world[1] to multiplye—
Why woldestou suffre him on thy day[2] to die?
  O Gaufred,[3] dere maister soverein,
That, whan thy worthy king Richard was slain
With shot,[4] complainedest his deeth so sore,
Why ne hadde I now thy sentence and thy lore,[5]
The Friday for to chide as diden ye?
For on a Friday soothly slain was he.
Thanne wolde I shewe you how that I coude plaine° — *lament*
For Chauntecleres drede and for his paine.
  Certes, swich cry ne lamentacioun
Was nevere of ladies maad when Ilioun° — *Ilium, Troy*
Was wonne, and Pyrrus[6] with his straite° swerd, — *drawn*

5. Because a priest's son gave him a knock.
6. The offended cock neglected to crow so that his master, now grown to manhood, overslept, missing his ordination and losing his benefice.
7. His (the cock in the story) cleverness.
8. The Book of Ecclesiasticus, in the Apocrypha.
9. Didn't care for.
1. I.e., population.
2. Friday is Venus's day.
3. Geoffrey of Vinsauf, a famous medieval rhetorician, who wrote a lament on the death of Richard I in which he scolded Friday, the day on which the king died.
4. I.e., a missile.
5. Thy wisdom and thy learning.
6. Pyrrhus was the Greek who slew Priam, king of Troy.

Whan he hadde hent° King Priam by the beerd — *seized*
And slain him, as saith us *Eneidos*,[7]
As maden alle the hennes in the cloos,° — *yard*
Whan they hadde seen of Chauntecleer the sighte.
But sovereinly° Dame Pertelote shrighte° — *supremely / shrieked*
Ful louder than dide Hasdrubales[8] wif
Whan that hir housbonde hadde lost his lif,
And that the Romains hadden brend° Cartage: — *burned*
She was so ful of torment and of rage° — *madness*
That wilfully unto the fir she sterte,° — *jumped*
And brende hirselven with a stedefast herte.
O woful hennes, right so criden ye
As, whan that Nero brende the citee
Of Rome, criden senatoures wives
For that hir housbondes losten alle hir lives:[9]
Withouten gilt this Nero hath hem slain.
Now wol I turne to my tale again.
The sely° widwe and eek hir doughtres two — *innocent*
Herden thise hennes crye and maken wo,
And out at dores sterten° they anoon, — *leapt*
And sien° the fox toward the grove goon, — *saw*
And bar upon his bak the cok away,
And criden, "Out, harrow,° and wailaway, — *help*
Ha, ha, the fox," and after him they ran,
And eek with staves many another man;
Ran Colle oure dogge, and Talbot and Gerland,[1]
And Malkin with a distaf in hir hand,
Ran cow and calf, and eek the verray hogges,
Sore aferd° for berking of the dogges — *frightened*
And shouting of the men and wommen eke.
They ronne° so hem thoughte hir herte breke;[2] — *ran*
They yelleden as feendes doon in helle;
The dokes° criden as men wolde hem quelle;° — *ducks / kill*
The gees for fere flowen° over the trees; — *flew*
Out of the hive cam the swarm of bees;
So hidous was the noise, a, benedicite,° — *bless me*
Certes, he Jakke Straw[3] and his meinee° — *company*
Ne made nevere shoutes half so shrille
Whan that they wolden any Fleming kille,
As thilke day was maad upon the fox:
Of bras they broughten bemes° and of box,° — *trumpets / boxwood*
Of horn, of boon,° in whiche they blewe and pouped,° — *bone / tooted*
And therwithal they skriked° and they houped°— — *shrieked / whooped*
It seemed as that hevene sholde falle.
Now goode men, I praye you herkneth alle:
Lo, how Fortune turneth° sodeinly — *reverses, overturns*
The hope and pride eek of hir enemy.

7. As the *Aeneid* tells us.
8. Hasdrubal was king of Carthage when it was destroyed by the Romans.
9. According to the legend, Nero not only set fire to Rome (in 64 C.E.) but also put many senators to death.
1. Two other dogs.
2. Would break.
3. One of the leaders of the Uprising of 1381, which was partially directed against the Flemings living in London.

This cok that lay upon the foxes bak,
In al his drede unto the fox he spak,
And saide, "Sire, if that I were as ye,
Yit sholde I sayn, as wis° God helpe me, *surely*
'Turneth ayain, ye proude cherles alle!
A verray pestilence upon you falle!
Now am I come unto this wodes side,
Maugree your heed,[4] the cok shal here abide.
I wol him ete, in faith, and that anoon.'"
The fox answerde, "In faith, it shal be doon."
And as he spak that word, al sodeinly
The cok brak from his mouth deliverly,° *nimbly*
And hye upon a tree he fleigh° anoon. *flew*
And whan the fox sawgh that he was agoon,
"Allas," quod he, "O Chauntecleer, allas!
I have to you," quod he, "ydoon trespas,
In as muche as I maked you aferd
Whan I you hente° and broughte out of the yeerd. *seized*
But sire, I dide it in no wikke° entente: *wicked*
Come down, and I shal telle you what I mente.
I shal saye sooth to you, God help me so."
"Nay thanne," quod he, "I shrewe° us bothe two: *curse*
But first I shrewe myself, bothe blood and bones,
If thou bigile me ofter than ones;
Thou shalt namore thurgh thy flaterye
Do° me to singe and winken with myn yë. *cause*
For he that winketh whan he sholde see,
Al wilfully, God lat him nevere thee."° *prosper*
"Nay," quod the fox, "but God yive him meschaunce
That is so undiscreet of governaunce° *self-control*
That jangleth° whan he sholde holde his pees." *chatters*
Lo, swich it is for to be reccheless° *careless*
And necligent and truste on flaterye.
But ye that holden this tale a folye
As of a fox, or of a cok and hen,
Taketh the moralitee, goode men.
For Saint Paul saith that al that writen is
To oure doctrine it is ywrit, ywis:[5]
Taketh the fruit, and lat the chaf be stille.[6]
Now goode God, if that it be thy wille,
As saith my lord, so make us alle goode men,
And bringe us to his hye blisse. Amen.

Close of *Canterbury Tales*

At the end of *The Canterbury Tales,* Chaucer invokes a common allegorical theme, that life on earth is a pilgrimage. As Chaucer puts it in his moral ballade *Truth,* "Here in noon home . . . / Forth, pilgrim, forth!" In the final fragment, he makes explicit a metaphor that has been implicit all along

4. Despite your head—i.e., despite anything you can do.
5. See Romans 15.4.
6. The "fruit" refers to the kernel of moral or doctrinal meaning; the "chaf," or husk, is the narrative containing that meaning. The metaphor was commonly applied to scriptural interpretation.

in the journey to Canterbury. The pilgrims never arrive at the shrine of St. Thomas, but in *The Parson's Tale*, and in its short introduction and in the "Retraction" that follows it, Chaucer seems to be making an end for two pilgrimages that had become one, that of his fiction and that of his life.

In the introduction to the tale we find the twenty-nine pilgrims moving through a nameless little village as the sun sinks to within twenty-nine degrees of the horizon. The atmosphere contains something of both the chill and the urgency of a late autumn afternoon, and we are surprised to find that the pilgrimage is almost over, that there is need for haste to make that "good end" that every medieval Christian hoped for. This delicately suggestive passage, rich with allegorical overtones, introduces an extremely long penitential treatise, translated by Chaucer from Latin or French sources. Although often assumed to be an earlier work, it may well have been written by Chaucer to provide the ending for *The Canterbury Tales*.

In the "Retraction" that follows *The Parson's Tale*, Chaucer acknowledges, lists, revokes, and asks forgiveness for his "giltes" (that is, his sins), which consist of having written most of the works on which his reputation as a great poet depends. He thanks Christ and Mary for his religious and moral works. One need not take this as evidence of a spiritual crisis or conversion at the end of his life. The "Retraction" seems to have been written to appear at the end of *The Canterbury Tales*, without censoring any of the tales deemed to be sinful. At the same time, one need not question Chaucer's sincerity. A readiness to deny his own reality before the reality of his God is implicit in many of Chaucer's works, and the placement of the "Retraction" within or just outside the border of the fictional pilgrimage suggests that although Chaucer finally rejected his fictions, he recognized that he and they were inseparable.

From The Parson's Tale

The Introduction

By that[1] the Manciple hadde his tale al ended,
The sonne fro the south line[2] was descended
So lowe, that he has nat to my sighte
Degrees nine and twenty as in highte.
Four of the clokke it was, so as I gesse,
For elevene foot, or litel more or lesse,
My shadwe was at thilke time as there,
Of swich feet as° my lengthe parted° were — *as if / divided*
In sixe feet equal of proporcioun.[3]
Therwith the moones exaltacioun[4]—
I mene Libra—always gan ascende,
As we were entring at a thropes° ende. — *village's*
For which oure Host, as he was wont to gie° — *lead*
As in this caas oure joly compaignye,
Saide in this wise, "Lordinges everichoon,
Now lakketh us no tales mo than oon:
Fulfild is my sentence° and my decree; — *purpose*
I trowe° that we han herd of ech degree; — *believe*
Almost fulfild is al myn ordinaunce.
I praye to God, so yive him right good chaunce

1. By the time that.
2. I.e., the line that runs some 28° to the south of the celestial equator and parallel to it.
3. This detailed analysis merely says that the shadows are lengthening.
4. I.e., the astrological sign in which the moon's influence was dominant.

That telleth this tale to us lustily.
Sire preest," quod he, "artou a vicary,° *vicar*
Or arte a Person? Say sooth, by thy fay.° *faith*
Be what thou be, ne breek° thou nat oure play, *break*
For every man save thou hath told his tale.
Unbokele and shew us what is in thy male!° *bag*
For trewely, me thinketh by thy cheere° *expression*
Thou sholdest knitte up wel a greet matere.
Tel us a fable anoon, for cokkes bones!"[5]
This Person answerde al atones,° *immediately*
"Thou getest fable noon ytold for me,
For Paul, that writeth unto Timothee,
Repreveth° hem that waiven soothfastnesse,[6] *reproves*
And tellen fables and swich wrecchednesse.
Why sholde I sowen draf° out of my fest,° *chaff / fist*
Whan I may sowen whete if that me lest?[7]
For which I saye that if you list to heere
Moralitee and vertuous matere,
And thanne that ye wol yive me audience,
I wol ful fain,° at Cristes reverence, *gladly*
Do you plesance leveful° as I can. *lawful*
But trusteth wel, I am a southren man:
I can nat geeste Rum-Ram-Ruf by lettre[8]—
Ne, God woot, rym holde° I but litel bettre. *consider*
And therfore, if you list—I wol nat glose[9]—
I wol you telle a merye tale in prose
To knitte up al this feeste and make an ende.
And Jesu for his grace wit me sende
To shewe you the way in this viage° *journey*
Of thilke parfit glorious pilgrimage
That highte° Jerusalem celestial. *is called*
And if ye vouche sauf, anoon I shal
Biginne upon my tale, for which I praye
Telle youre avis:° I can no bettre saye. *opinion*
But nathelees, this meditacioun
I putte it ay under correccioun
Of clerkes, for I am nat textuel:[1]
I take but the sentence,° trusteth wel. *meaning*
Therefore I make protestacioun° *public acknowledgment*
That I wol stonde to correccioun."
Upon this word we han assented soone,
For, as it seemed, it was for to doone[2]
To enden in som vertuous sentence,° *doctrine*
And for to yive him space° and audience; *time*
And bede[3] oure Host he sholde to him saye
That alle we to telle his tale him praye.
Oure Hoste hadde the wordes for us alle:
"Sire preest," quod he, "now faire you bifalle:

5. Cock's bones, a euphemism for God's bones.
6. Depart from truth (see 1 Timothy 1.4).
7. It pleases me.
8. I.e., I cannot tell stories in the alliterative measure (without rhyme): this form of poetry was not common in southeastern England.
9. I.e., speak in order to please.
1. Literal, faithful to the letter.
2. Necessary to be done.
3. I.e., we bade.

Telleth," quod he, "youre meditacioun.
But hasteth you; the sonne wol adown.
Beeth fructuous,° and that in litel space,° *fruitful / time*
And to do wel God sende you his grace.
Saye what you list, and we wol gladly heere."
And with that word he saide in this manere.

Chaucer's Retraction

Here taketh the makere of this book his leve[4]

Now praye I to hem alle that herkne this litel tretis[5] or rede, that if ther be any thing in it that liketh[6] hem, that therof they thanken oure Lord Jesu Crist, of whom proceedeth al wit[7] and al goodnesse. And if ther be any thing that displese hem, I praye hem also that they arrette it to the defaute of myn unconning,[8] and nat to my wil, that wolde ful fain have said bettre if I hadde had conning. For oure book saith, "Al that is writen is writen for oure doctrine,"[9] and that is myn entente. Wherfore I biseeke[1] you mekely, for the mercy of God, that ye praye for me that Crist have mercy on me and foryive me my giltes, and namely of my translacions and enditinges[2] of worldly vanitees, the whiche I revoke in my retraccions: as is the *Book of Troilus;* the Book also of *Fame;* the *Book of the Five and Twenty Ladies;*[3] the *Book of the Duchesse;* the *Book of Saint Valentines Day of the Parlement of Briddes;* the *Tales of Canterbury,* thilke that sounen into[4] sinne; the *Book of the Leon;*[5] and many another book, if they were in my remembrance, and many a song and many a leccherous lay: that Crist for his grete mercy foryive me the sinne. But of the translacion of Boece[6] *De Consolatione,* and othere bookes of legendes of saintes, and omelies,[7] and moralitee, and devocion, that thanke I oure Lord Jesu Crist and his blisful Moder and alle the saintes of hevene, biseeking hem that they from hennes[8] forth unto my lives ende sende me grace to biwaile my giltes and to studye to the salvacion of my soule, and graunte me grace of verray penitence, confession, and satisfaccion to doon in this present lif, thurgh the benigne grace of him that is king of kinges and preest over alle preestes, that boughte[9] us with the precious blood of his herte, so that I may been oon of hem at the day of doom that shulle be saved. *Qui cum patre et Spiritu Sancto vivit et regnas Deus per omnia saecula.*[1] *Amen.*

1386–1400

4. "Chaucer's Retraction" is the title given to this passage by modern editors. The heading, "*Here . . . leve,*" which does appear in all manuscripts, may be by Chaucer himself or by a scribe.
5. Hear this little treatise, i.e., *The Parson's Tale.*
6. Pleases.
7. Understanding.
8. Ascribe it to the defect of my lack of skill.
9. Romans 15.4.
1. Beseech.
2. Compositions. "Namely": especially.
3. I.e., the *Legend of Good Women.*
4. Those that tend toward.
5. The *Book of the Lion* has not been preserved.
6. Boethius.
7. Homilies.
8. Hence.
9. Redeemed.
1. Who with the Father and the Holy Spirit livest and reignest God forever.

Christ's Humanity

The literary and visual representation of the godhead is necessarily, in any religion, a powerful index of religious culture. In some religions, indeed, visual representation of God is such a sensitive issue that it is forbidden altogether. Christian culture has experienced moments of severe hostility to visual representation (for example, in the Reformation period of the sixteenth century), but has, in general, permitted images of God (and especially of God-become-man, Christ). In the later Middle Ages in Europe the bodily representation of Christ became a central preoccupation for writers, readers, and visual artists.

In the late eleventh century St. Anselm of Canterbury (1033–1099) developed a new conception of the Atonement ("at-one-ment"), the act whereby humans are reconciled with God after the separation caused by Original Sin. An earlier theory had posited that the Atonement was the solution to a dispute between God and the Devil concerning property rights over Mankind. In his tract *Why Did Christ Become Man?* Anselm argued instead that the real center of the Atonement was Mankind's moral responsibility to pay God back. Humanity needed to repay God for the sin committed, but was unable to do so. Faced with this impasse, God could either simply abolish the debt, or else *become human*, in order to repay Himself, as it were. God chose this latter route, allowing Christ to suffer and die as a human in order to clear the debt.

Earlier representations of the Crucifixion had tended to place the accent on Christ as impassive King, standing erect on the Cross, come to claim His property of mankind. In the *Dream of the Rood* (see pp. 24–26), for example, Christ's suffering is for the most part absorbed by the Cross itself, while Christ is represented as a conquering, royal hero. Later medieval representations of Christ, by contrast, accentuate the suffering, sagging, lacerated body of a very human God. In this newly conceived theology, Christ's suffering humanity takes center stage. The artistic significance of this massively influential development was itself massive. Certainly the older tradition survived in vital form: compare, for example, the triumphalist lyric "What is He, this Lordling, that Cometh from the Fight?" with the quiet suffering of "Ye that Pasen by the Weye." Langland's Christ, too, comes to claim his property as a conquering hero. It was, nonetheless, the tradition of Christ suffering in His humanity that dominated literary and visual art from the thirteenth century until the Reformation initiated in 1517.

These theological developments had forceful artistic and stylistic consequences. Because the theology was best expressed through visual or verbal images, it fed readily into both painting and a highly pictorial literature. In both painting and literature, a humble style, focusing on the particularities of bodily pain and grief, became the bearer of high theological significance. The painting of Giotto (1266?–1337), for example, broke with a prior tradition of painting that represented an elegant Christ against a splendid gold background; Giotto's inelegant and crucified Christ suffers under the pull of his own weight. Spiritual experience was, in the first instance, something *seen* more than something *thought*. It was also a spirituality rooted in the dramatic present: as one saw Christ, one saw Him in the here and now. Thus works in this almost cinematic mode foreshorten historical and geographical distance: such texts encourage readers, that is, to imagine that they are physically and emotionally present at the crucial scenes of Christ's life. In some examples of the tradition, viewers are encouraged to imagine those around Christ (especially Romans and Jews) as wholly responsible for the infliction of pain; in others, viewers are made to realize that they are themselves responsible for the continued suffering of Christ.

As deployed by the Church, this movement discouraged abstract thought. It did nevertheless have the effect of widening access to spiritual experience, and, in ways unforeseen by official sponsors of such piety, could be the springboard for very sophisticated theology. As the Church attempted to deepen the spiritual literacy of its members from the late twelfth century, emphasis on Christ's humanity in art and literature opened powerful spiritual experience to a much wider audience of readers and viewers. To engage in this spirituality, a public did not need to be versed in detailed matters of doctrine. Instead, a reader or viewer had to develop the capacity for sympathetic response to physical suffering. Such spirituality gained official impetus though the foundation of the Franciscan order of friars (1223), who promoted earthly poverty in imitation of, and emotional response to, Christ's sufferings. The centrality of Christ's living presence in the liturgy was, furthermore, reaffirmed and extended with the establishment, throughout Christendom, of the Feast of Corpus Christi (the Feast of the Body of Christ), first proclaimed by the pope in 1264 and again in 1311. This feast celebrated the Eucharistic host, or wafer, as Christ's body. It grew steadily in popularity and came to involve outdoor processions depicting the biblical foreshadowings of the Eucharist, as a prelude to display of the Eucharist itself. In some medieval English cities this was the day also chosen for the performance of cycle plays, sometimes known as the plays of Corpus Christi.

Female readers in particular, who had been excluded from the Latin-based, textual traditions of theology, discovered fertile ground in this tradition of so-called "affective," or emotional, piety. Through such emotive imagining, one gained an apparently unmediated, and potentially authoritative, relation with Christ. Women working in this tradition did not necessarily remain, however, within its visual, imaginative terms: Julian of Norwich is, for example, capable of developing very subtle and abstract thought, holding the incarnate image in view all the while.

This powerfully emotional piety also provoked wider social applications of the Christian narrative. Whereas "The Parable of the Christ Knight" in the *Ancrene Riwle* presents a suffering Christ as an aristocratic lover for a very select spiritual elite of women, the Christ of Margery Kempe is very much the "homely" husband of a bourgeois woman. On a much larger scale, the mystery plays mark the moment in which urban institutions represent Christ for themselves. In this drama, both Old and New Testament narrative is inflected by the trials of domestic and urban experience (on the origins, civic sponsorship, and production of these plays, see the headnote to "The York Play of the Crucifixion," pp. 290–91).

WILLIAM LANGLAND
ca. 1330–1387

William Langland is agreed by most scholars to be the sole author of a long religious allegory in alliterative verse known as *The Vision of Piers Plowman* or more simply *Piers Plowman,* which survives in at least three distinct versions that scholars refer to as the A-, B-, and C-texts. The first, about twenty-four hundred lines long, breaks off at a rather inconclusive point in the action; the second is a revision of the first plus an extension of more than four thousand lines; and the third is a revision of the second. About Langland we know hardly anything except what can be inferred from the poem itself. He came from the west of England and was probably a native of the Malvern Hills area in which the opening of the poem is set. We can never identify the persona of the narrator of a medieval text positively or precisely with its author, especially when we are dealing with allegory. Nevertheless, a passage that was added to the C-text gives the strong impression of being at one and the same time an allegory in which the narrator represents willful Mankind and a poignantly ironic self-portrait of the stubborn-willed poet who occasionally plays on his own name: "I have lived in *land* . . . my name is *Long Will*" (15.152). In this new episode the narrator tries to defend his shiftless way of life against Conscience and Reason, presumably his own conscience and reason. Conscience dismisses his specious argument that a clerical education has left him no "tools" to support himself with except for his prayer book and the Psalms with which he prays for the souls of those from whom he begs alms. The entire work conforms well with the notion that its author was a man who was educated to enter the church but who, through marriage and lack of preferment, was reduced to poverty and may well have wandered in his youth like those "hermits" he scornfully describes in the prologue.

Piers Plowman has the form of a dream vision, a common medieval type in which the author presents the story under the guise of having dreamed it. The dream vision generally involves allegory, not only because one expects from a dream the unrealistic, the fanciful, but also because people have always suspected that dreams relate the truth in disguised form—that they are natural allegories. Through a series of such visions it traces the Dreamer-narrator's tough-minded, persistent, and passionate search for answers to his many questions, especially the question he puts early in the poem to Lady Holy Church: "How I may save my soul." Langland's theme is nothing less than the history of Christianity as it unfolds both in the world of the Old and New Testaments and in the life and heart of an individual fourteenth-century Christian—two seemingly distinct realms between which the poet's allegory moves with dizzying rapidity.

In the Prologue Langland's narrator falls asleep and witnesses a compact vision of the whole of late fourteenth-century English society. Poised between two stark and static possibilities of heaven and hell, an intensely active, mobile earthly life is concentrated into a "field full of folk." Some ideal practitioners of earthly occupations are surrounded and undermined by a much larger set of very energetic social types who exploit their occupations for entirely selfish ends. Langland practices an estates satire, which surveys and excoriates each worldly occupation (cf. Chaucer's very different example of estates satire in the *General Prologue* to the *Canterbury Tales*; for other examples, see "Medieval Estates and Orders" at Norton Literature Online). He reserves his especial anger for those who abuse ecclesiastical authority, and for the wealthy, pitiless laity (i.e. non-ecclesiastical figures).

Passus, Latin for "step," is the word used for the poem's basic divisions. *Passus 1* promises to give some intellectual and moral purchase on the teeming energies of the Prologue. Holy Church instructs the poem's narrator and dreamer Will in the proper relation of material wealth and spiritual health. In particular, she accentuates the value of the "best treasure," *truthe*, one of Langland's key words: *truthe* is the justice that flows from God; it manifests itself in the exercise of earthly justice and fidelity, and in the correlative poetic value of truth-telling. Will recognizes the force of Holy Church's sermon, but still needs to know it by an interior form of knowledge, grounded in the depths of the self.

It would seem that the rest of the poem is devoted to the discovery of that internalized truth. The first of the poem's large-scale narratives (*Passus 2–4*) represents the attempt of earthly justice to control the disruptive energies of the profit economy. That economy is represented by the personification "Lady Mede," meaning "reward beyond deserving." After this sequence concerning earthly justice, the poem then turns to the deeper, more personal mechanisms of spiritual justice. In *Passus 5*, accordingly, the seven Deadly Sins confess in turn, before the poem's ideal earthly representative of justice, Piers Plowman, offers to lead a spiritual pilgrimage to the shrine of *St. Truthe*.

The ideal of *truthe* takes a local habitation, then, in the model of society that Piers establishes for the conduct of his "pilgrimage." The truest form of pilgrimage is no pilgrimage at all; instead, all classes of society should stay at home and work harmoniously for the production of material food by agricultural workers, with knights helping plowmen and protecting the Church, while priests pray for both workers and knights. This ideal scene is pictured in *Passus 6*.

Langland's poem might seem, thus far, to be a deeply conservative one, whereby justice is manifest only in a manorial society, within which each person knows his or her place, and works harmoniously and obediently with the others. There is, however, a problem with this model: it collapses. In *Passus 6* the ideal society put into action by Piers fails entirely; workers simply refuse to work, abuse the authority of knights, and respond only to the terrible pressure of Hunger, a punishing, Gargantuan figure who graphically evokes the ravages of famine in the fourteenth century.

In *Passus* 7 the limitations of the *truthe* model become dramatically visible. A pardon sent from God as *Truthe* promises no pardon at all, but only retribution for those who fail to meet the standards of God's justice, and reward for those who do not so fail. As the plowing has demonstrated, however, all fail. Such a "pardon" promises nothing but universal damnation. In an exceptionally powerful, dramatic and enigmatic moment, Piers actually tears this pardon in two, as he disputes with a priest about its force. Earlier in the poem it had seemed that all Will had to do was to absorb Holy Church's understanding of *Truthe*; once Piers tears the pardon, however, we realize that the search for *Truthe* modifies the goal. We realize, that is, that *Truthe* cannot be the whole truth. The shortcomings of *Truthe* propel Will to a more urgent search for God's love and forgiveness, beyond justice, in the deepest resources of his own self. This search climaxes in the vision of Christ's Atonement (*Passus 18*, the selection here).

A large number of manuscripts and two sixteenth-century editions show that *Piers Plowman* was avidly read and studied by a great many people from the end of the fourteenth century to the reign of Elizabeth I. Some of these readers have left a record of their engagement with the poem in marginal comments. Almost from the first, it was a controversial text. Within four years of the writing of the second version—which scholars have good evidence to date 1377, the year of Edward III's death and Richard II's accession to the throne—it had become so well known that the leaders of of the Uprising of 1381 used phrases borrowed from it as part of the rhetoric of the rebellion (for an example of such rhetoric, see the letter by John Ball, "The Uprising of 1381," in "Medieval Estates and Orders" at Norton Literature Online). Langland's sympathy with the sufferings of the poor and his indignant satire of corruption in Church and State undoubtedly made his poem popular with the rebels. Although he may not have sympathized with the violence of the rebels and their leaders, he recognized that for the Church to be preserved, it needed profound reform. The passionate sympathy for the commoner, idealized in *Piers Plowman*, also appealed to reformers who felt that true religion was best represented not by the ecclesiastical hierarchy but by the humblest orders of society. Many persons reading his poem in the sixteenth century (it was first printed in 1550) saw in *Piers Plowman* a prophecy and forerunner of the English Reformation. Immersed as it is in thorny political and theological controversies of its own day, *Piers Plowman* is arguably the most difficult and, at times, even the most frustrating of Middle English texts, but its poetic, intellectual, and moral complexity and integrity also make it one of the most rewarding.

Passus 18

Passus 18 describes the central event of Christianity, the Crucifixion, followed by an account of Christ's descent into hell, traditionally called the "Harrowing of Hell." The Dreamer has come a long way in his personal search for truth, and this vision is the most immediate and fulfilling answer to the questions he addressed to Holy Church, although not a final answer, for in Langland's poem the search has no end in this life. Piers, who had assumed aspects of Adam, Moses, and the Good Samaritan (while never ceasing to be the ideal plowman), is now partially identified with Christ. The terms of this identification are rooted in material necessity of food: Christ has come to fetch the "fruit" of Piers Plowman (lines 31 and 34). The "food" that Christ seeks has now become the souls of the patriarchs and prophets, and of all mankind, which must be redeemed from the devil's power. And just as the earthly Piers becomes Christ-like, so too does Christ, in His bodily manifestation, become intensely human. He jousts in the arms (i.e., no arms at all, but the unprotected flesh) of Piers Plowman (line 24); He comes to earth precisely in order to *know* what being human is like (lines 229–32); and He does so precisely because of his co-natural, sympathetic kinship with suffering humanity (lines 408–10).

For all that, Langland does not focus here for long on the grievous suffering of Christ. On the contrary, he addresses the terms of the Atonement through intellectual debate, first through the Four Daughters of God (personifications taken from Psalm 85.10), and then through Christ's direct encounter with Lucifer. Against powerful legal and written evidence to the contrary, first Mercy and Peace and then Christ Himself reveal a divine curiosity and sympathy with imprisoned humanity. This mercy is anterior to, and more powerful than, the law of strict *Truthe* or justice, by which mankind appears to have been irredeemably damned. So far from being a wounded, suffering Christ, Langland's Christ is at once spiritually triumphant and a delighted trickster, by whose divine guile the devil has been fooled.

The Vision of Piers Plowman[1]

Passus 18

[THE CRUCIFIXION AND HARROWING OF HELL]

Wool-chafed[2] and wet-shoed I went forth after
Like a careless creature unconscious of woe,
And trudged forth like a tramp, all the time of my life,
Till I grew weary of the world and wished to sleep again,
And lay down till Lent, and slept a long time,
Rested there, snoring roundly, till *Ramis-Palmarum*.[3]
I dreamed chiefly of children and cheers of "*Gloria, laus*!"
And how old folk to an organ sang "*Hosanna*!"
And of Christ's passion and pain for the people he had reached for.
One resembling the Samaritan[4] and somewhat Piers the Plowman
Barefoot on an ass's back bootless came riding
Without spurs or spear: sprightly was his look,
As is the nature of a knight that draws near to be dubbed,
To get himself gilt spurs and engraved jousting shoes.
Then was Faith watching from a window and cried, "*A, fili David*!"
As does a herald of arms when armed men come to joust.
Old Jews of Jerusalem joyfully sang,
"*Blessed is he who cometh in the name of the Lord*."
And I asked Faith to reveal what all this affair meant,
And who was to joust in Jerusalem. "Jesus," he said,

1. The translation is by E. T. Donaldson (1990) and is based on *Piers Plowman: The B Version*, edited by George Kane and E. T. Donaldson (1975).
2. Scratchy wool was worn next to the body as an act of penance.
3. Palm Sunday (literally, "branches of palms"): the background of this part of the poem is the biblical account of Christ's entry into Jerusalem on this day, when the crowds greeted him crying, "Hosanna (line 8) to the son of David (line 15): Blessed is he that cometh in the name of the Lord (line 17a); Hosanna in the highest" (see Matthew 21.9). "*Gloria, laus*" (line 7) are the first words of an anthem, "Glory, praise, and honor," that was sung by children in medieval religious processions on Palm Sunday.
4. In the previous vision, the Dreamer has encountered Abraham, or Faith (mentioned in lines 15, 18, 28, and 92); Moses, or Hope; and the Good Samaritan, or Charity, who was riding toward a "jousting in Jerusalem" and who now appears as an aspect of Christ.

"And fetch what the Fiend claims, the fruit of Piers the Plowman."
"Is Piers in this place?" said I; and he pierced me with his look:
"This Jesus for his gentleness will joust in Piers's arms,
In his helmet and in his hauberk, *humana natura,*
So that Christ be not disclosed here as *consummatus Deus.*[5]
In the plate armor of Piers the Plowman this jouster will ride,
For no dint will do him injury as *in deitate Patris.*[6]
"Who shall joust with Jesus," said I, "Jews or Scribes?"[7]
"No," said Faith, "but the Fiend and False-Doom°-To-Die. *sentence*
Death says he will undo and drag down low
All that live or look upon land or water.
Life says that he lies, and lays his life in pledge
That for all that Death can do, within three days he'll walk
And fetch from the Fiend the fruit of Piers the Plowman,
And place it where he pleases, and put Lucifer in bonds,
And beat and bring down burning death forever.
O death, I will be thy death."[8]
Then Pilate came with many people, *sedens pro tribunali,*[9]
To see how doughtily Death should do, and judge the rights of both.
The Jews and the justice were joined against Jesus,
And all the court cried upon him, "*Crucifige*!"[1] loud.
Then a plaintiff appeared before Pilate and said,
"This Jesus made jokes about Jerusalem's temple,
To have it down in one day and in three days after
Put it up again all new—here he stands who said it—
And yet build it every bit as big in all dimensions,
As long and as broad both, above and below."
"*Crucifige!*" said a sergeant, "he knows sorcerer's tricks."
"*Tolle! tolle!*"[2] said another, and took sharp thorns
And began to make a garland out of green thorn,
And set it sorely on his head and spoke in hatred,
"*Ave, Rabbi,*" said that wretch, and shot reeds[3] at him;
They nailed him with three nails naked on a Cross,
And with a pole put a potion up to his lips
And bade him drink to delay his death and lengthen his days,
And said, "If you're subtle, let's see you help yourself.
If you are Christ and a king's son, come down from the Cross!
Then we'll believe that Life loves you and will not let you die."
"*Consummatum est,*"[4] said Christ and started to swoon,
Piteously and pale like a prisoner dying.
The Lord of Life and of Light then laid his eyelids together.
The day withdrew for dread and darkness covered the sun;
The wall wavered and split and the whole world quaked.
Dead men for that din came out of deep graves

5. The perfect (three-personed) God. "*Humana natura*": human nature, which Christ assumed in order to redeem humanity. "Hauberk": coat of mail.
6. In the godhead of the Father: as God, Christ could not suffer but as man, he could.
7. People who made a very strict, literal interpretation of the Old Law and hence rejected Christ's teaching of the New.
8. Cf. Hosea 13.14.
9. Sitting as a judge (cf. Matthew 27.19).
1. Crucify him! (John 19.15).
2. Away with him, away with him! (John 19.15).
3. Arrows, probably small ones intended to hurt rather than to kill. "*Ave, Rabbi*": "Hail, master" (Matthew 26.49): these are actually Judas's words when he kissed Christ in order to identify him to the arresting officers.
4. It is finished (John 19.30).

And spoke of why that storm lasted so long:
"For a bitter battle," the dead body said;
"Life and Death in this darkness, one destroys the other.
No one will surely know which shall have the victory
Before Sunday about sunrise"; and sank with that to earth.
Some said that he was God's son that died so fairly:
Truly this was the Son of God.[5]
And some said he was a sorcerer: "We should see first
Whether he's dead or not dead before we dare take him down."
Two thieves were there that suffered death that time
Upon crosses beside Christ; such was the common law.
A constable came forth and cracked both their legs
And the arms afterward of each of those thieves.
But no bastard was so bold as to touch God's body there;
Because he was a knight and a king's son, Nature decreed that time
That no knave should have the hardiness to lay hand on him.
But a knight with a sharp spear was sent forth there
Named Longeus[6] as the legend tells, who had long since lost his sight;
Before Pilate and the other people in that place he waited on his horse.
For all that he might demur, he was made that time
To joust with Jesus, that blind Jew Longeus.
For all who watched there were unwilling, whether mounted or afoot,
To touch him or tamper with him or take him down from the Cross,
Except this blind bachelor that bore him through the heart.
The blood sprang down the spear and unsparred[7] his eyes.
The knight knelt down on his knees and begged Jesus for mercy.
"It was against my will, Lord, to wound you so sorely."
He sighed and said, "Sorely I repent it.
For what I here have done, I ask only your grace.
Have mercy on me, rightful Jesu!" and thus lamenting wept.
Then Faith began fiercely to scorn the false Jews,[8]
Called them cowards, accursed forever.
"For this foul villainy, may vengeance fall on you!
To make the blind beat the dead, it was a bully's thought.
Cursed cowards, no kind of knighthood was it
To beat a dead body with any bright weapon.
Yet he's won the victory in the fight for all his vast wound,
For your champion jouster, the chief knight of you all,
Weeping admits himself worsted and at the will of Jesus.
For when this darkness is done, Death will be vanquished,
And you louts have lost, for Life shall have the victory;
And your unfettered freedom has fallen into servitude;
And you churls and your children shall achieve no prosperity,

5. Matthew 27.54.
6. Longeus (usually Longinus) appears in the apocryphal Gospel of Nicodemus, which provided Langland with the material for much of his account of Christ's despoiling of hell.
7. Opened; in the original there is a play on words with "spear." "Bachelor": knight.
8. The references in this passage (lines 92–110) and in lines 258–60 appear to reflect a blind anti-Semitism all too prevalent in late-medieval art and literature, brought out especially in portrayals of the Passion. Elsewhere Langland exhibits a more enlightened attitude—for instance, in a passage in which he holds up Jewish charity as an example to Christians. In the present passage he may intend a distinction between those who betrayed and condemned Jesus and the "old Jews of Jerusalem" who welcomed him in the Palm Sunday procession (lines 7–17).

Nor have lordship over land or have land to till,
But be all barren and live by usury,
Which is a life that every law of our Lord curses.
Now your good days are done as Daniel prophesied;
When Christ came their kingdom's crown should be lost:
When the Holy of Holies comes your anointing shall cease."[9]
What for fear of this adventure and of the false Jews
I withdrew in that darkness to *Descendit-ad-Inferna,*[1]
And there I saw surely *Secundum Scripturas*[2]
Where out of the west a wench,[3] as I thought,
Came walking on the way—she looked toward hell.
Mercy was that maid's name, a meek thing withal,
A most gracious girl, and goodly of speech.
Her sister as it seemed came softly walking
Out of the east, opposite, and she looked westward,
A comely creature and cleanly: Truth was her name.
Because of the virtue that followed her, she was afraid of nothing.
When these maidens met, Mercy and Truth,
Each of them asked the other about this great wonder,
And of the din and of the darkness, and how the day lowered,
And what a gleam and a glint glowed before hell.
"I marvel at this matter, by my faith," said Truth,
"And am coming to discover what this queer affair means."
"Do not marvel," said Mercy, "it means only mirth.
A maiden named Mary, and mother without touching
By any kind of creature, conceived through speech
And grace of the Holy Ghost; grew great with child;
With no blemish to her woman's body brought him into this world.
And that my tale is true, I take God to witness,
Since this baby was born it has been thirty winters,
Who died and suffered death this day about midday.
And that is the cause of this eclipse that is closing off the sun,
In meaning that man shall be removed from darkness
While this gleam and this glow go to blind Lucifer.
For patriarchs and prophets have preached of this often
That man shall save man through a maiden's help,
And what a tree took away a tree shall restore,[4]
And what Death brought down a death shall raise up."
"What you're telling," said Truth, "is just a tale of nonsense.
For Adam and Eve and Abraham and the rest,
Patriarchs and prophets imprisoned in pain,
Never believe that yonder light will lift them up,
Or have them out of hell—hold your tongue, Mercy!
Your talk is mere trifling. I, Truth, know the truth,
For whatever is once in hell, it comes out never.
Job the perfect patriarch disproves what you say:
Since in hell there is no redemption."[5]

9. Daniel 9.24.
1. He descended into hell (from the Apostles' Creed).
2. According to the Scriptures.
3. The word is Langland's and had much the same connotations in his time as it has in ours.
4. The first tree bore the fruit that Adam and Eve ate, thereby damning humankind; the second tree is the cross on which Christ was crucified, thereby redeeming humankind.
5. Cf. Job 7.9.

Then Mercy most mildly uttered these words:
"From observation," she said, "I suppose they shall be saved,
Because venom destroys venom, and in that I find evidence
That Adam and Eve shall have relief.
For of all venoms the foulest is the scorpion's:
No medicine may amend the place where it stings
Till it's dead and placed upon it—the poison is destroyed,
The first effect of the venom, through the virtue it possesses.
So shall this death destroy—I dare bet my life—
All that Death did first through the Devil's tempting.
And just as the beguiler with guile beguiled man first,
So shall grace that began everything make a good end
And beguile the beguiler—and that's a good trick:
A trick by which to trick trickery."[6]
"Now let's be silent," said Truth. "It seems to me I see
Out of the nip[7] of the north, not far from here,
Righteousness come running—let's wait right here,
For she knows far more than we—she was here before us both."
"That is so," said Mercy, "and I see here to the south
Where Peace clothed in patience[8] comes sportively this way.
Love has desired her long: I believe surely
That Love has sent her some letter, what this light means
That hangs over hell thus: she will tell us what it means."
When Peace clothed in patience approached near them both,
Righteousness did her reverence for her rich clothing
And prayed Peace to tell her to what place she was going,
And whom she was going to greet in her gay garments.
"My wish is to take my way," said she, "and welcome them all
Whom many a day I might not see for murk of sin.
Adam and Eve and the many others in hell,
Moses and many more will merrily sing,
And I shall dance to their song: sister, do the same.
Because Jesus jousted well, joy begins to dawn.
Weeping may endure for a night, but joy cometh in the morning.[9]
Love who is my lover sent letters to tell me
That my sister Mercy and I shall save mankind,
And that God has forgiven and granted me, Peace, and Mercy
To make bail for mankind for evermore after.
Look, here's the patent," said Peace: "*In pace in idipsum:*
And that this deed shall endure, *dormiam et requiescam.*"[1]
"What? You're raving," said Righteousness. "You must be really drunk.
Do you believe that yonder light might unlock hell
And save man's soul? Sister, don't suppose it.
At the beginning God gave the judgment himself
That Adam and Eve and all that followed them

6. From a medieval Latin hymn.
7. The word is Langland's and the sense obscure; it probably meant "coldness" to him, although an Old English word similar to *nip* meant "gloom."
8. What Langland envisioned clothes of patience to look like, aside from their "richness" (line 173), it is impossible to say; to him any abstraction could become a concrete allegory without visual identification.
9. Psalm 30.5.
1. The "patent" or "deed" is a document conferring authority: this one consists of phrases from Psalm 4.8: "In peace in the selfsame"; "I will sleep and find rest."

Should die downright and dwell in torment after
If they touched a tree and ate the tree's fruit.
Adam afterwards against his forbidding
Fed on that fruit and forsook as it were
The love of our Lord and his lore too,
And followed what the Fiend taught and his flesh's will
Against Reason. I, Righteousness, record this with Truth,
That their pain should be perpetual and no prayer should help them,
Therefore let them chew as they chose, and let us not chide, sisters,
For it's misery without amendment, the morsel they ate."
"And I shall prove," said Peace, "that their pain must end,
And in time trouble must turn into well-being;
For had they known no woe, they'd not have known well-being;
For no one knows what well-being is who was never in woe,
Nor what is hot hunger who has never lacked food.
If there were no night, no man, I believe,
Could be really well aware of what day means.
Never should a really rich man who lives in rest and ease
Know what woe is if it weren't for natural death.
So God, who began everything, of his good will
Became man by a maid for mankind's salvation
And allowed himself to be sold to see the sorrow of dying.
And that cures all care and is the first cause of rest,
For until we meet *modicum*,° I may well avow it, *small quantity*
No man knows, I suppose, what 'enough' means.
Therefore God of his goodness gave the first man Adam
A place of supreme ease and of perfect joy,
And then he suffered him to sin so that he might know sorrow,
And thus know what well-being is—to be aware of it naturally.
And afterward God offered himself, and took Adam's nature,
To see what he had suffered in three separate places,
Both in Heaven and on earth, and now he heads for hell,
To learn what all woe is like who has learned of all joy.
So it shall fare with these folk: their folly and their sin
Shall show them what sickness is—and succor from all pain.
No one knows what war is where peace prevails,
Nor what is true well-being till 'Woe, alas!' teaches him."
Then was there a wight with two broad eyes:
Book was that beaupere's[2] name, a bold man of speech.
"By God's body," said this Book, "I will bear witness
That when this baby was born there blazed a star
So that all the wise men in the world agreed with one opinion
That such a baby was born in Bethlehem city
Who should save man's soul and destroy sin.
And all the elements," said the Book, "hereof bore witness.
The sky first revealed that he was God who formed all things:
The hosts in Heaven took *stella comata*[3]
And tended her like a torch to reverence his birth.
The light followed the Lord into the low earth.
The water witnessed that he was God for he walked on it;

2. Fine fellow. The book's two broad eyes suggest the Old and New Testaments. "Wight": creature, person.
3. Hairy star, i.e., comet.

Peter the Apostle perceived his walking
And as he went on the water knew him well and said,
'Bid me come unto thee on the water.'[4]
And lo, how the sun locked her light in herself
When she saw him suffer that made sun and sea.
The earth for heavy heart because he would suffer
Quaked like a quick° thing and the rock cracked all to pieces. *living*
Lo, hell might not hold, but opened when God suffered,
And let out Simeon's sons[5] to see him hang on Cross.
And now shall Lucifer believe it, loath though he is,
For Jesus like a giant with an engine[6] comes yonder
To break and beat down all that may be against him,
And to have out of hell every one he pleases.
And I, Book, will be burnt unless Jesus rises to life
In all the mights of a man and brings his mother joy,
And comforts all his kin, and takes their cares away,
And all the joy of the Jews disjoins and disperses;
And unless they reverence his Rood and his resurrection
And believe on a new law be lost body and soul."
"Let's be silent," said Truth, "I hear and see both
A spirit speaks to hell and bids the portals be opened."
Lift up your gates.[7]
A voice loud in that light cried to Lucifer,
"Princes of this place, unpin and unlock,
For he comes here with crown who is King of Glory."
Then Satan[8] sighed and said to hell,
"Without our leave such a light fetched Lazarus away:[9]
Care and calamity have come upon us all.
If this King comes in he will carry off mankind
And lead it to where Lazarus is, and with small labor bind me.
Patriarchs and prophets have long prated of this,
That such a lord and a light should lead them all hence."
"Listen," said Lucifer, "for this lord is one I know;
Both this lord and this light, it's long ago I knew him.
No death may do this lord harm, nor any devil's trickery,
And his way is where he wishes—but let him beware of the perils.
If he bereaves me of my right he robs me by force.
For by right and by reason the race that is here
Body and soul belongs to me, both good and evil.
For he himself said it who is Sire of Heaven,
If Adam ate the apple, all should die
And dwell with us devils: the Lord laid down that threat.

4. Matthew 14.28.
5. Simeon, who was present at the presentation of the infant Jesus in the temple, had been told by the Holy Ghost that "he should not see death" before he had seen "the Lord's Christ" (Luke 2.26). The Apocryphal Gospel of Nicodemus echoes the incident in reporting that Simeon's sons were raised from death at the time of Jesus's crucifixion.
6. A device, probably thought of as a gigantic slingshot, although, of course, Christ needs nothing to break down his enemies but his own authority.
7. The first words of Psalm 24.9, which reads in the Latin version, "Lift up your gates, O princes, and be ye lift up, ye everlasting doors, and the King of Glory shall come in."
8. Langland, following a tradition also reflected in Milton's *Paradise Lost,* pictures hell as populated by a number of devils: Satan; Lucifer (line 273 ff.), who began the war in heaven and tempted Eve; Goblin (line 293); Belial (line 321); and Ashtoreth (line 404). Lucifer the rebel angel naturally became identified with Satan, a word that in the Old Testament had originally meant an evil adversary; many of the other devils are displaced gods of pagan religions.
9. For Christ's raising of Lazarus from the dead, cf. John 11.

And since he who is Truth himself said these words,
And since I've possessed them seven thousand winters,
I don't believe law will allow him the least of them."
"That is so," said Satan, "but I'm sore afraid
Because you took them by trickery and trespassed in his garden,
And in the semblance of a serpent sat upon the apple tree
And egged them to eat, Eve by herself,
And told her a tale with treasonous words;
And so you had them out, and hither at the last."
"It's an ill-gotten gain where guile is at the root,
For God will not be beguiled," said Goblin, "nor tricked.
We have no true title to them, for it was by treason they were damned."
"Certainly I fear," said the Fiend,[1] "lest Truth fetch them out.
These thirty winters, as I think, he's gone here and there and preached.
I've assailed him with sin, and sometimes asked
Whether he was God or God's son: he gave me short answer.
And thus he's traveled about like a true man these two and thirty winters.
And when I saw it was so, while she slept I went
To warn Pilate's wife what sort of man was Jesus,[2]
For some hated him and have put him to death.
I would have lengthened his life, for I believed if he died
That his soul would suffer no sin in his sight.
For the body, while it walked on its bones, was busy always
To save men from sin if they themselves wished.
And now I see where a soul comes descending hitherward
With glory and with great light; God it is, I'm sure.
My advice is we all flee," said the Fiend, "fast away from here.
For we had better not be at all than abide in his sight.
For your lies, Lucifer, we've lost all our prey.
Through you we fell first from Heaven so high:
Because we believed your lies we all leapt out.
And now for your latest lie we have lost Adam,
And all our lordship, I believe, on land and in hell."
Now shall the prince of this world be cast out.[3]
Again the light bade them unlock, and Lucifer answered,
"Who is that?[4]
What lord are you?" said Lucifer. The light at once replied,
"The King of Glory.
The Lord of might and of main and all manner of powers:
The Lord of Powers.
Dukes of this dim place, at once undo these gates
That Christ may come in, the Heaven-King's son."

1. Here and in line 309 "the Fiend" is presumably Lucifer's most articulate critic, Satan, whom Christ names as his tempter in Matthew 4.10.
2. In Matthew 27.19 Pilate's wife warns Pilate to "have nothing to do with that just man [Jesus]," for she has been troubled by a dream about him. Langland has the Fiend admit to having caused the dream so that Pilate's wife should persuade her husband not to harm Jesus and thus keep him safe on earth and not come to visit hell and despoil it.
3. John 12.31. "Prince of this world" is a title for the devil.
4. This and the next two phrases translated from the Latin are from Psalm 24.8, following immediately on the words quoted in line 262a.

And with that breath hell broke along with Belial's bars;
For° any warrior or watchman the gates wide opened. *in spite of*
Patriarchs and prophets, *populus in tenebris,*[5]
Sang Saint John's song, *Ecce agnus Dei.*[6]
Lucifer could not look, the light so blinded him.
And those that the Lord loved his light caught away,
And he said to Satan, "Lo, here's my soul in payment
For all sinful souls, to save those that are worthy.
Mine they are and of me—I may the better claim them.
Although Reason records, and right of myself,
That if they ate the apple all should die,
I did not hold out to them hell here forever.
For the deed that they did, your deceit caused it;
You got them with guile against all reason.
For in my palace Paradise, in the person of an adder,
You stole by stealth something I loved.
Thus like a lizard with a lady's face[7]
Falsely you filched from me; the Old Law confirms
That guilers be beguiled, and that is good logic:
A tooth for a tooth and an eye for an eye.[8]
Ergo[9] soul shall requite soul and sin revert to sin,
And all that man has done amiss, I, man, will amend.
Member for member was amends in the Old Law,
And life for life also, and by that law I claim
Adam and all his issue at my will hereafter.
And what Death destroyed in them, my death shall restore
And both quicken° and requite what was quenched through sin. *revitalize*
And that grace destroy guile is what good faith requires.
So don't believe it, Lucifer, against the law I fetch them,
But by right and by reason here ransom my liegemen.
I have not come to destroy the law but to fulfill it.[1]
You fetched mine in my place unmindful of all reason
Falsely and feloniously; good faith taught me
To recover them by reason and rely on nothing else.
So what you got with guile through grace is won back.
You, Lucifer, in likeness of a loathsome adder
Got by guile those whom God loved;
And I, in likeness of a mortal man, who am master of Heaven,
Have graciously requited your guile: let guile go against guile!
And as Adam and all died through a tree
Adam and all through a tree return to life,
And guile is beguiled and grief has come to his guile:
And he is fallen into the ditch which he made.[2]
And now your guile begins to turn against you,
And my grace to grow ever greater and wider.

5. "People in darkness," the phrase is from Matthew 4.16, citing Isaiah 9.2, "The people that walked in darkness have seen a great light."
6. Behold the Lamb of God (John 1.36).
7. In medieval art the devil tempting Eve was sometimes represented as a snake (see the "serpent" of line 288) and sometimes as a lizard with a female human face and standing upright.
8. See Matthew 5.38 citing Exodus 21.24.
9. Therefore. The Latin conjunction was used in formal debate to introduce the conclusion derived from a number of propositions.
1. See Matthew 5.17.
2. Psalm 7.15.

The bitterness that you have brewed, imbibe it yourself
Who are doctor[3] of death, the drink you made.
For I who am Lord of Life, love is my drink
And for that drink today I died upon earth.
I struggled so I'm thirsty still for man's soul's sake.
No drink may moisten me or slake my thirst
Till vintage time befall in the Vale of Jehoshaphat,[4]
When I shall drink really ripe wine, *Resurrectio mortuorum.*[5]
And then I shall come as a king crowned with angels
And have out of hell all men's souls.
Fiends and fiendkins shall stand before me
And be at my bidding, where best it pleases me.
But to be merciful to man then, my nature requires it.
For we are brothers of one blood, but not in baptism all.
And all that are both in blood and in baptism my whole brothers
Shall not be damned to the death that endures without end.
Against thee only have I sinned, etc.[6]
It is not the custom on earth to hang a felon
Oftener than once, even though he were a traitor.
And if the king of the kingdom comes at that time
When a felon should suffer death or other such punishment,
Law would he give him life if he looks upon him.[7]
And I who am King of Kings shall come in such a time
Where doom to death damns all wicked,
And if law wills I look on them, it lies in my grace
Whether they die or do not die because they did evil.
And if it be any bit paid for, the boldness of their sins,
I may grant mercy through my righteousness and all my true words;
And though Holy Writ wills that I wreak vengeance on those
that wrought evil,
No evil unpunished, etc.[8]
They shall be cleansed and made clear and cured of their sins,
In my prison purgatory till *Parce!*° says 'Stop!' *Spare!*
And my mercy shall be shown to many of my half-brothers,
For blood-kin may see blood-kin both hungry and cold,
But blood-kin may not see blood-kin bleed without his pity:
I heard unspeakable words which it is not lawful for a man to utter.[9]
But my righteousness and right shall rule all hell

3. The ironical use of the word carries the sense both of "physician" and of "one learned in a discipline."
4. On the evidence of Joel 3.2, 12, the site of the Last Judgment was thought to be the Vale of Jehoshaphat.
5. The resurrection of the dead (from the Nicene Creed).
6. Psalm 51.4. The psalm is understood to assign the sole power of judging the sinner to God, because it is only against God that the sinner has acted.
7. I.e., "Law dictates that the king pardon the felon if the king sees him."
8. [He is a just judge who leaves] no evil unpunished [and no good unrewarded]. Not from the Bible but from Pope Innocent III's tract *Of Contempt for the World* (1195).
9. In 2 Corinthians 12.4, St. Paul tells how in a vision he was snatched up to heaven where he heard things that may not be repeated among men. Langland is apparently invoking a similar mystic experience when he puts into Christ's mouth a promise to spare many of his half-brothers, the unbaptized. The orthodox theology of the time taught that all the unbaptized were irredeemably damned, a proposition Langland refused to accept: in his vision he has heard words to the contrary that might not be repeated among men, because they would be held heretical.

And mercy rule all mankind before me in Heaven.
For I'd be an unkind king unless I gave my kin help,
And particularly at such a time when help was truly needed.
Enter not into judgment with thy servant.[1]
Thus by law," said our Lord, "I will lead from here
Those I looked on with love who believed in my coming;
And for your lie, Lucifer, that you lied to Eve,
You shall buy it back in bitterness"—and bound him with chains.
Ashtoreth and all the gang hid themselves in corners;
They dared not look at our Lord, the least of them all,
But let him lead away what he liked and leave what he wished.
Many hundreds of angels harped and sang,
Flesh sins, flesh redeems, flesh reigns as God of God.[2]
Then Peace piped a note of poetry:
As a rule the sun is brighter after the biggest clouds; After hostilities love is brighter.
"After sharp showers," said Peace, "the sun shines brightest;
No weather is warmer than after watery clouds;
Nor any love lovelier, or more loving friends,
Than after war and woe when Love and peace are masters.
There was never war in this world nor wickedness so sharp
That Love, if he liked, might not make a laughing matter.
And peace through patience puts an end to all perils."
"Truce!" said Truth, "you tell the truth, by Jesus!
Let's kiss in covenant, and each of us clasp other."
"And let no people," said Peace, "perceive that we argued;
For nothing is impossible to him that is almighty."
"You speak the truth," said Righteousness, and reverently kissed her,
Peace, and Peace her, *per saecula saeculorum:*[3]
Mercy and Truth have met together; Righteousness and Peace have kissed each other.[4]
Truth sounded a trumpet then and sang *Te Deum Laudamus,*[5]
And then Love strummed a lute with a loud note:
Behold how good and how pleasant, etc.[6]
Till the day dawned these damsels caroled.
When bells rang for the Resurrection, and right then I awoke
And called Kit my wife and Calote my daughter:
"Arise and go reverence God's resurrection,
And creep to the Cross on knees, and kiss it as a jewel,
For God's blessed body it bore for our good,
And it frightens the Fiend, for such is its power
That no grisly ghost may glide in its shadow."

1. Psalm 143.2.
2. From a medieval Latin hymn. The source of the two Latin verses immediately below is Alain of Lille, a late 12th-century poet and philosopher.
3. For ever and ever (the liturgical formula).
4. Psalm 85.10.
5. We praise thee, O Lord.
6. Psalm 133.1. The verse continues, "it is for brothers to dwell together in unity."

JULIAN OF NORWICH
1342–ca. 1416

The "Showings," or "Revelations" as they are also called, were sixteen mystical visions received by the woman known as Julian of Norwich. The name may be one that she adopted when she became an anchoress in a cell attached to the church of St. Julian that still stands in that city in East Anglia, then one of the most important English cities. An anchorite (m.) or anchoress (f.) is a religious recluse confined to an enclosure, which he or she has vowed never to leave. At the time of such an enclosing the burial service was performed, signifying that the enclosed person was dead to the world and that the enclosure corresponded to a grave. The point of this confinement was, of course, to pursue more actively the contemplative or spiritual life.

Julian may well have belonged to a religious order at the time that her visions led her to choose the life of an anchoress. We know little about her except what she tells us in her writings. She is, however, very precise about the date of her visions. They occurred, she tells us, at the age of thirty and a half on May 13, 1373. Four extant wills bequeath sums for Julian's maintenance in her anchorage. The most important document witnessing her life is *The Book of Margery Kempe*. Kempe asked Julian whether there might be any deception in Kempe's own visions, "for the anchoress," she says, "was expert in such things." Kempe's description of Julian's conversation accords well with the doctrines and personality that emerge from Julian's own book.

A Book of Showings survives in a short and a long version. The longer text, from which the following excerpts are taken, was the product of fifteen and more years of meditation on the meaning of the visions in which much had been obscure to Julian. Apparently the mystical experiences were never repeated, but through constant study and contemplation the showings acquired a greater clarity, richness, and profundity as they continued to be turned over in a mind both gifted with spiritual insight and learned in theology. Her editors document her extensive use of the Bible and her familiarity with medieval religious writings in both English and Latin.

Julian's sixteen revelations are each treated in uneven numbers of Chapters; these groupings of chapters form an extended meditation on a given vision. Each vision is treated with an unpredictable combination of visual description of what Julian saw, the words she was offered, and the meanings she "saw." Her visions are, in her words, "ghostly" (that is, spiritual), "bodily," and subtle combinations of the two. They embrace powerful visual phenomena such as blood drops running from the crown of thorns and revelations that take place in pure mind. All are, nevertheless, "seen"; the spiritualized meanings do not render bodily sights redundant.

The selections here, Chapters 5 and 7, are from Julian's First Vision. This vision is provoked by Julian's own bodily approximation to the bodily pains of Christ, as she thinks she is dying. The crucifix offered for her comfort provokes a kinetic, fresh response, as it seems to move into life, bleeding and persuading Julian that the vision is God's unmediated gift to her. Julian moves well beyond this initial sight, however; she sees a sequence of created things: the Virgin Mary as the best creature that God made, and, lower down the scale, the entire world in her palm, "the quantity of an hazelnut." Such a vision might lead away from created things altogether, into a realm of pure essence; significantly, it does not, precisely because Julian never leaves the sight of the wounded, bodily Christ, whose very physical suffering is somehow simultaneous with these almost immaterial visions. Julian strains the tradition of affective piety to its limits, but ends by transforming rather than rejecting it.

The serene optimism Julian's visions express for the material, created world and for fallen creatures extends into the most daring and surprising realms of speculation. "Sin is behovely": these are (Julian's) Christ's own words. They are expressed in the Thirteenth Vision for the first time (Chapter 27), but only in the extended, daring meditation of the Fourteenth Vision (not included in the Shorter Version) are they given their deepest sense. At the heart of Julian's profoundly optimistic theology is a transformative understanding of Christ's Humanity. She develops, without ever mentioning it explicitly, the idea of the *felix culpa,* the notion that, given its happy consequence in Christ's redemption of mankind, Adam's sin, or *culpa*, was somehow "happy" (*felix*). Christ is so much a part of us, by Julian's account, that He is "the ground of our kind [natural/kind] making" (Chapter 59). He is our Mother, who strains and suffers as He gives birth to our salvation. Julian's concept of Jesus as mother has antecedents in both Old and New Testaments, in medieval theology, and in the writings of medieval mystics (both men and women), but nowhere else in Middle English writing is the concept so subtly and resonantly explored.

Julian was clearly aware of the dangers of expressing such high mysteries as a woman writer. She participates, it is true, in a late medieval tradition of visionary writing, often by women, such as the *Dialogue* of Catherine of Siena (translated into Middle English as the *Orchard of Syon*) and the *Revelations* of St. Bridget of Sweden (also translated into Middle English). Julian, however, does not refer to these figures; instead, she negotiates the difficulties and dangers of writing as a woman with enormous tact and shrewdness, both disclaiming and creating exceptional authority. Part of her strategy is to write with calm lucidity; part is to claim that the vision is not particular to her alone. Precisely by virtue of a common humanity, the visions are common property: "We are all one, and I am sure I saw it for the profit of many other."

From A Book of Showings to the Anchoress Julian of Norwich[1]

Chapter 5

[ALL CREATION AS A HAZELNUT]

In this same time that I saw this sight of the head bleeding, our good Lord showed a ghostly sight of his homely loving. I saw that he is to us all thing that is good and comfortable to our help. He is our clothing that for love wrappeth us and windeth us, halseth us[2] and all becloses us, hangeth about us for tender love that[3] he may never leave us. And so in this sight I saw that he is all thing that is good, as to my understanding.

And in this he showed a little thing, the quantity of an hazelnut, lying in the palm of my hand, as me seemed, and it was as round as a ball. I looked thereon with the eye of my understanding, and thought: What may this be? And it was answered generally thus: It is all that is made. I marvelled how it might last, for me thought it might suddenly have fallen to nought for[4] littleness. And I was answered in my understanding: It lasteth and ever shall, for God loveth it; and so hath all thing being by the love of God.

In this little thing I saw three properties. The first is that God made it, the second that God loveth it, the third that God keepeth[5] it. But what beheld I therein? Verily, the maker, the keeper, the lover. For till I am substantially united to him[6] I may never have full rest ne very[7] bliss; that is to say that I be so fastened to him that there be right nought that is made between my God and me.

1. The text is based on that given by Edmund Colledge, O.S.A., and James Walsh, S. J., for the Pontifical Institute of Mediaeval Studies, Toronto (1978), but it has been freely edited and modern spelling has been used where possible.
2. Envelops us and embraces us.
3. So that.
4. Because of.
5. Looks after.
6. Joined to him in "substance," which Julian regards as the eternal essence of being.
7. True.

This little thing that is made, me thought it might have fallen to nought for littleness. Of this needeth us to have knowledge, that us liketh nought all thing that is made, for to love and have God that is unmade.[8] For this is the cause why we be not all in ease of heart and of soul, for we seek here rest in this thing that is so little, where no rest is in, and we know not our God, that is almighty, all wise and all good, for he is very rest. God will be known, and him liketh that we rest us in him; for all that is beneath him suffiseth not to us. And this is the cause why that no soul is in rest till it is noughted of all things that is made.[9] When she is wilfully[1] noughted for love, to have him that is all, then is she able to receive ghostly rest.

And also our good Lord showed that it is full great pleasance to him that a sely[2] soul come to him naked, plainly and homely. For this is the kind[3] yearning of the soul by the touching of the Holy Ghost, as by the understanding that I have in this showing: God of thy goodness gave me thyself, for thou art enough to me, and I may ask nothing that is less that may be full worship to thee. And if I ask any thing that is less, ever me wanteth;[4] but only in thee I have all.

And these words of the goodness of God be full lovesome to the soul and full near touching the will of our Lord, for his goodness fulfilleth all his creatures and all his blessed works and overpasseth[5] without end. For he is the endlesshead and he made us only to himself and restored us by his precious passion, and ever keepeth us in his blessed love; and all this is of his goodness.

* * *

Chapter 7

[CHRIST AS HOMELY AND COURTEOUS]

And in all that time that he showed this that I have now said in ghostly sight, I saw the bodily sight lasting of the plenteous bleeding of the head. The great drops of blood fell down fro under the garland like pellets, seeming as it had come out of the veins. And in the coming out they were brown red, for the blood was full thick; and in the spreading abroad they were bright red. And when it came at the brows, there they vanished; and not withstanding the bleeding continued till many things were seen and understanded. Nevertheless the fairhead and livelihead continued in the same beauty and liveliness.

The plenteoushead is like to the drops of water that fall of the evesing[6] of an house after a great shower of rain, that fall so thick that no man may number them with no bodily wit.[7] And for the roundness they were like to the scale of herring in the spreading of the forehead.

These three things came to my mind in the time: pellets for the roundhead[8] in the coming out of the blood, the scale of the herring for the roundhead in the spreading, the drops of the evesing of a house for the plenteoushead unnumerable. This showing was quick[9] and lively and hideous and dreadful and sweet and lovely; and of all the sight that I saw this was most comfort to me, that our good Lord, that is so reverend and dreadful, is so homely and so

8. I.e., we need to know that we should not be attracted to earthly things, which are made, to love and possess God, who is not made, who exists eternally.
9. Emptied of (its attachment to) all created things.
1. Of its free will.
2. Innocent.
3. Natural.
4. I am forever lacking.
5. Surpasses.
6. Eaves.
7. Intelligence.
8. Roundness.
9. Vivid.

courteous, and this most fulfilled me with liking and sickerness[1] in soule.

And to the understanding of this he showed this open example. It is the most worship[2] that a solemn king or a great lord may do to a poor servant if he will be homely with him; and namely if he show it himself of a full true meaning[3] and with a glad cheer both in private and openly. Then thinketh this poor creature thus: "Lo, what might this noble lord do more worship and joy to me than to show to me that am so little this marvelous homeliness? Verily, it is more joy and liking to me than if he gave me great gifts and were himself strange in manner." This bodily example was showed so high that this man's heart might be ravished and almost forget himself for joy of this great homeliness.

Thus it fareth by our Lord Jesu and by us, for verily it is the most joy that may be, as to my sight, that he that is highest and mightiest, noblest and worthiest, is lowest and meekest, homeliest and courteousest. And truly and verily this marvelous joy shall be show us all when we shall see him. And this will our good Lord that we believe and trust, joy and like, comfort us and make solace as we may with his grace and with his help, into[4] the time that we see it verily. For the most fullhead of joy that we shall have, as to my sight, is this marvelous courtesy and homeliness of our fader, that is our maker, in our Lord Jesu Christ, that is our brother and oure saviour. But this marvelous homeliness may no man know in this life, but if he have it by special showing of our Lord, or of great plenty of grace inwardly given of the Holy Ghost. But faith and belief with charity deserve the meed,[5] and so it is had by grace. For in faith with hope and charity our life is grounded. The showing is made to whom that God will, plainly teacheth the same opened and declared, with many privy points belonging to our faith and belief which be worshipful to be known. And when the showing which is given for a time is passed and hid, then faith keepeth it by grace of the Holy Ghost into our life's end. And thus by the showing it is none other than the faith, ne less ne more, as it may be seen by our Lord's meaning in the same matter, by then[6] it come to the last end.

ca. 1390

1. Security.
2. Honor.
3. Intent.
4. Until.
5. Reward. "Charity": love. See 1 Corinthians 13.13.
6. By the time that.

MARGERY KEMPE
ca. 1373–1438

The Book of Margery Kempe is the spiritual autobiography of a medieval laywoman, telling of her struggles to carry out instructions for a holy life that she claimed to have received in personal visions from Christ and the Virgin Mary. The assertion of such a mission by a married woman, the mother of fourteen children, was in itself sufficient grounds for controversy; in addition, Kempe's outspoken defense of her visions as well as her highly emotional style of religious expression embroiled her with fellow citizens and pilgrims and with the Church, although she also won both lay and clerical supporters. Ordered by the archbishop of York to swear not to teach in his diocese, she courageously stood up for her freedom to speak her conscience.

Margery Kempe was the daughter of John Burnham, five-time mayor of King's Lynn, a thriving commercial town in Norfolk. At about the age of twenty she married John Kempe, a well-to-do fellow townsman. After the traumatic delivery of her first child—the rate of maternal mortality in childbirth was high—she sought to confess to a priest whose harsh, censorious response precipitated a mental breakdown, from which she eventually recovered through the first of her visions. Her subsequent conversion and strict religious observances generated a good deal of domestic strife, but she continued to share her husband's bed until, around the age of forty, she negotiated a vow of celibacy with him, which was confirmed before the bishop and left her free to undertake a pilgrimage to the Holy Land. There she experienced visions of Christ's passion and of the sufferings of the Virgin. These visions recurred during the rest of her life, and her noisy weeping at such times made her the object of much scorn and hostility. Her orthodoxy was several times examined, but her unquestioning acceptance of the Church's doctrines and authority, and perhaps also her status as a former mayor's daughter, shielded her against charges of heresy.

Kempe was unable to read or write, but acquired her command of Scripture and theology from sermons and other oral sources. Late in her life, she dictated her story in two parts to two different scribes; the latter of these was a priest who revised the whole text. Nevertheless, it seems likely that the work retains much of the characteristic form and expression of its author.

Kempe's text offers a perspective on the tradition of "affective piety" unlike any other: here that visionary tradition comes to life in the context of vividly realized, often painful psychological and bodily experience. Kempe's own marriage, and her often troubled worldly relations, inform and are informed by her "homely" and sometimes erotic spiritual relations. Her imitation of Christ moves her to travel vast distances to be present at the scenes of Christ's suffering, just as she sees Christ present in male babies or good-looking young men. She sees the living divine presence in the Eucharistic host. "Sir," she says to a skeptic, "His death is as fresh to me as He had died this same day." This form of intensely sympathetic vision has, however, its negative obverse. As in Chaucer's *Prioress's Tale*, where tender feeling for the Blessed Virgin is complemented by hatred for the "cursed Jewes," Christian pathos produces an anti-Semitic reflex (Book 1.79).

From The Book of Margery Kempe[1]

Book 1.35–36

[MARGERY'S MARRIAGE TO AND INTIMACY WITH CHRIST]

35. As this creature[2] was in the Apostles' Church at Rome on Saint Lateran's Day,[3] the Father of Heaven said to her, "Daughter, I am well pleased with thee inasmuch as thou believest in all the sacraments of Holy Church and in all faith that longeth[4] thereto, and especially for that thou believest in manhood of my Son and for the great compassion that thou hast of His bitter Passion." Also the Father said to this creature, "Daughter, I will have thee wedded to my Godhead, for I shall show thee my privities and my counsels,[5] for thou shall wonen[6] with me without end."

Then the creature kept silence in her soul and answered not thereto, for she was sore afraid of the Godhead and she could no skill[7] of the dalliance of

1. The text is based on the unique manuscript, first discovered in 1934, edited by Lynn Staley. Spelling and inflexional forms have in many cases been modernized.
2. Throughout the book Kempe refers to herself in the third person as "this creature," a standard way of saying "this person, a being created by God."
3. Saint John Lateran's Day, November 9.
4. Pertains.
5. Private deliberations.
6. Dwell.
7. "Could no skill": was ignorant of.

the Godhead, for all her love and all her affection was set in the manhood of Christ, and thereof could she good skill and she would for no thing have parted therefrom. She was so much affected to[8] the manhood of Christ that when she saw women in Rome bear children in their arms, if she might witen[9] that they were any menchildren, she should then cry, roar, and weep as though she had seen Christ in His childhood. And, if she might have had her will, oftentimes she would have taken the children out of the mothers' arms and have kissed them in the stead of Christ. And, if she saw a seemly[1] man, she had great pain to look on Him less than[2] she might have seen Him that was both God and Man. And therefore she cried many times and often when she met a seemly man and wept and sobbed full sore in the manhood of Christ as she went in the streets at Rome, that they that saw her wondered full much on her, for they knew not the cause.

And therefore it was no wonder if she were still[3] and answered not the Father of Heaven when He told her that she should be wedded to His Godhead. Then said the Second Person, Christ Jesu, whose manhood she loved so much, to her, "What sayst thou, Margery, daughter, to my Father of these words that He speaketh to thee? Art thou well pleased that it be so?" And then she would not answer the Second Person but wept wonder sore, desiring to have still Himself and in no wise to be departed from Him. Then the Second Person in Trinity answered to His Father for her and said, "Father, have her excused, for she is yet but young and not fully learned[4] how she should answer."

And then the Father took her by the hand in her soul before the Son and the Holy Ghost and the Mother of Jesu, and all the twelve apostles and Saint Katherine and Saint Margaret, and many other saints and holy virgins with great multitude of angels, saying to her soul, "I take thee, Margery, for my wedded wife, for fairer, for fouler, for richer, for poorer, so that[5] thou be buxom[6] and bonyr[7] to do what I bid thee do. For, daughter, there was never child so buxom to the mother as I shall be to thee both in well and in woe, to help thee and comfort thee. And thereto I make thee surety." And then the Mother of God and all the saints that were present in her soul prayed that they might have much joy together.

And then the creature with high devotion, with great plenty of tears, thanked God of this ghostly[8] comfort holding[9] herself in her own feeling right unworthy to any such grace as she felt, for she felt many great comforts, both ghostly comforts and bodily comforts. Sometimes she felt sweet smells with her nose; it were sweeter, her thought,[1] than ever was any sweet earthly thing that she smelled before, nor she might never tell how sweet it were, for her thought she might have lived thereby if they would have lasted. Sometimes she heard with her bodily ears such sounds and melodies that she might not well hear what a man said to her in that time less[2] he spoke the louder. These sounds and melodies had she heard nyhand[3] every day the term of twenty-five year when this book was written, and especially when she was in devout prayer, also many times while she was at Rome and in England both.

She saw with her bodily eyes many white things flying all about her on every

8. Drawn to.
9. Know.
1. Handsome.
2. Unless.
3. Silent.
4. Instructed.
5. As long as.
6. Obedient.
7. Submissive.
8. Spiritual.
9. Considering herself.
1. It seemed to her.
2. Unless.
3. Almost.

side as thick in a manner as motes[4] in the sun; it were right subtle and comfortable, and the brighter that the sun shined, the better she might see them. She saw them diverse times and in many diverse places, both in church and in her chamber, at her meat[5] and in her prayers, in field and in town, both going and sitting. And many times she was afraid what they might be, for she saw them as well on nights in darkness as on daylight. Then, when she was afraid of them, our Lord said unto her, "By this token, daughter, believe it is God that speaketh in thee, for whereso God is Heaven is, and where that God is there be many angels, and God is in thee and thou art in Him. And therefore be not afraid, daughter, for these betoken that thou hast many angels about thee to keep thee both day and night that no devil shall have power over thee nor none evil man to dere[6] thee." Then from that time forward she used to say when she saw them come, "*Benedictus qui venit in nomine domini.*"[7] Also our Lord gave her another token, the which endured about sixteen year and it increased ever more and more, and that was a flame of fire wonder hot and delectable and right comfortable, not wasting but ever increasing, of lowe,[8] for though the weather were never so cold, she felt the heat burning in her breast and at her heart, as verily as a man should feel the material fire if he put his hand or his finger therein.

When she felt first the fire of love burning in her breast, she was afraid thereof, and then our Lord answered to her mind and said, "Daughter, be not afraid, for this heat is the heat of the Holy Ghost, the which shall burn away all thy sins, for the fire of love quencheth[9] all sins. And thou shalt understand by this token the Holy Ghost is in thee, and thou wost[1] well wherethatever the Holy Ghost is there is the Father, and where the Father is there is the Son, and so thou hast fully in thy soul all the Holy Trinity. Therefore thou hast great cause to love me right well, and yet thou shalt have greater cause than ever thou haddest to love me, for thou shalt hear that[2] thou never heardest, and thou shalt see that thou never saw, and thou shalt feel that thou never feltest. For, daughter, thou art as sekyr[3] of the love of God as God is God. Thy soul is more sekyr of the love of God than of thine own body, for thy soul shall part[4] from thy body but God shall never part from thy soul, for they be[5] onyd[6] together without end. Therefore, daughter, thou hast as great cause to be merry as any lady in this world, and, if thou knew, daughter, how much thou pleasest me when thou suffrest me wilfully to speak in thee, thou shuldest never do otherwise, for in this is an holy life and the time is right well spent. For, daughter, this life pleaseth me more than wearing of habergeon[7] or of the hair[8] or fasting of bread and water, for if thou seydest every day a thousand Pater Noster,[9] thou shouldst not please me so well as thou dost when thou art in silence and sufferest me to speak in thy soul.

36. "Fasting, daughter, is good for young beginners and discrete[1] penance, namely[2] that their ghostly father giveth them or enjoineth[3] them for to do. And

4. Specks of dust.
5. Food.
6. Harm.
7. "Blessed is he who comes in the name of the Lord" (Matthew 21.9). A blessing used in the Mass as part of the consecration.
8. Flame.
9. Extinguishes.
1. Know.
2. That which.
3. Certain.
4. Separate.
5. Are.
6. United.
7. Sleeveless coat or jacket of chain mail.
8. Hair-shirt, worn by penitents.
9. "Our Father," i.e. the Lord's Prayer.
1. Circumspect.
2. Especially.
3. Imposes upon.

for to bid many beads[4] it is good to them that can no better do, and yet it is not perfect. But it is a good way to perfectionward. For I tell thee, daughter, they that are great fasters and great doers of penance they wold[5] that it should be held[6] the best life; also they that give themselves to say many devotions they wold have that the best life, and they that give much alms they wold that that were held the best life. And I have oftentimes, daughter, told thee that thinking, weeping, and high contemplation is the best life in earth. And thou shalt have more merit in heaven for one year of thinking in thy mind than for an hundred year of praying with thy mouth, and yet thou wilt not believe me, for thou wilt bid many beads whether I will or not.

"And yet, daughter, I will not be displeased with thee whether[7] thou think, say, or speak, for I am always pleased with thee. And, if I were in earth as bodily as I was ere I died on the cross, I should not be ashamed of thee as many other men be, for I should take thee by the hand among the people and make thee great cheer that they should well know that I loved thee right well. For it is convenient[8] the wife to be homely[9] with her husband. Be he never so great a lord and she so poor a woman when he weddeth her, yet they must lie together and rest together in joy and peace. Right so must it be between thee and me, for I take no heed what thou hast been but what thou woldest[1] be. And oftentimes have I told thee that I have clean forgiven thee all thy sins. Therefore must I needs be homely with thee and lie in thy bed with thee.

"Daughter, thou desirest greatly to see me, and thou mayst boldly, when thou art in thy bed, take me to thee as for thy wedded husband, as thy dearworthy darling, and as for thy sweet Son, for I will be loved as a son should be loved with the mother and will that thou love me, daughter, as a good wife ought to love her husband. And therefore thou mayst boldly take me in the arms of thy soul and kiss my mouth, my head, and my feet as sweetly as thou wilt. And, as oftentimes as thou thinkest on me ere thou woldest do any good deed to me, thou shalt have the same meed[2] in heaven as if thou didst it to mine own precious body which is in heaven, for I ask no more of thee but thine heart for to love, that loveth thee,[3] for my love is ever ready to thee." Then gave she thanking and praising to our Lord Jesu Christ for the high grace and mercy that He showed unto her unworthy wretch.

This creature had diverse tokens in her bodily hearing. One was a manner of sound as it had been a pair of bellows blowing in her ear. She, being abashed[4] thereof, was warned in her soul no fear to have for it was the sound of the Holy Ghost. And then our Lord turned that sound into the voice of a dove, and sithen[5] He turned it into the voice of a little bird which is called a redbreast that sang full merrily oftentimes in her right ear. And then should she evermore have great grace after that she heard such a token. And she had been used to such tokens about twenty-five year at the writing of this book. Then said our Lord Jesu Christ to His creature, "By these tokens mayst thou well witen[6] that I love thee, for thou art to me a very mother and to all the world, for that great charity that is in thee, and yet I am cause of that charity myself, and thou shalt have a great mede therefore in heaven."

1436–38

4. Prayers (the original sense of the word "bedes," applied by association to beads in a rosary).
5. Desire.
6. Considered.
7. Whatever.
8. Fitting.
9. Familiar.
1. Wish to.
2. Reward.
3. Referring back to Christ (i.e., "I, who love you, ask . . .").
4. Confounded.
5. Afterward.
6. Know.

THE YORK PLAY OF THE CRUCIFIXION
ca. 1425

The increasing prosperity and importance of the towns was shown by performances of the mystery plays—a sequence or "cycle" of plays based on the Bible and produced by the city guilds, the organizations representing the various trades and crafts. The cycles of several towns are lost, but those of York and Chester have been preserved along with two other complete cycles, one possibly from Wakefield in Yorkshire, and the other titled the "N-town cycle" (along with many other fragments).

Medieval mystery plays had an immensely confident reach in both space and time. In York, for example, the theatrical space and time of this urban, amateur drama was that of the entire city, lasting from sunrise throughout the entire long summer holiday. The time represented ran from the Fall of the Angels and the Creation of the World right through to the end of time, in the Last Judgment. Between these extremities of the beginning and end of time, each cycle presents key episodes of Old Testament narrative, such as the Fall and the Flood, before presenting a concentrated sequence of freely interpreted New Testament plays focused on the life and Passion of Christ.

The church had its own drama in Latin, dating back to the tenth century, which developed through the dramatization and elaboration of the liturgy—the regular service—for certain holidays, the Easter morning service in particular. The vernacular drama was once thought to have evolved from the liturgical, passing by stages from the church into the streets of the town. However, even though the vernacular plays at times echo their Latin counterparts and although their authors may have been clerics, the mysteries represent an old and largely independent tradition of vernacular religious drama. As early as the twelfth century a *Play of Adam* in Anglo-Norman French was performed in England, a dramatization of the Fall with highly sophisticated dialogue, characterization, and stagecraft.

During the late fourteenth and the fifteenth centuries, the great English mystery cycles were formed in provincial, yet increasingly powerful and independent cities. They were the production of the city itself, with particular responsibility for staging and performance devolving onto the city guilds. A guild was also known as a "mystery," from Latin *ministerium,* whence the phrase "mystery plays." A guild combined the functions of modern trade union, club, religious society, and political action group. The performance and staging required significant investments of time and money from amateur performers, the status of whose mystery might be at stake in the quality of their performance. Often the subject of the play corresponded to the function of the guild (thus the Pinners, or nail-makers, performed the York Crucifixion, for example).

Most of our knowledge of the plays, apart from the texts themselves, comes through municipal and guild records, which tell us a great deal about the evolution, staging and all aspects of the production of the cycles. In some of the cities each guild had a wagon that served as a stage. The wagon proceeded from one strategic point in the city to another, and the play would be performed a number of times on the same day. In other towns, plays were probably acted out in sequence on a platform erected at a single location such as the main city square.

The cycles were performed every year at the time of one of two great early summer festivals—Whitsuntide, the week following the seventh Sunday after Easter, or Corpus Christi, a week later (falling somewhere between May 21 and June 24). They served as both religious instruction and entertainment for wide audiences, including unlearned folk like the carpenter in *The Miller's Tale* (lines 405–74), who recalls from them the trouble Noah had getting his wife aboard the ark, but also educated laypeople and clerics, who besides enjoying the sometimes boisterous comedy would find the plays acting out traditional interpretations of Scripture such as the ark as a type, or prefiguration, of the church.

Thus the cycles were public spectacles watched by every layer of society, and they paved the way for the professional theater in the age of Elizabeth I. The rainbow in *Noah's Flood* (lines 356–71; for the text of *Noah's Flood*, go to Norton Literature Online) and the Angel's *Gloria* in the *Shepherds' Play*, with their messages of mercy and hope, unite actors and audience in a common faith. Yet the first shepherd's opening speech, complaining of taxation and the insolent exploitation of farmers by "gentlery-men," shows how the plays also served as vehicles of social criticism and reveal many of the rifts and tensions in the late-medieval social fabric.

The particular intersection of religious and civic institutions that made the cycles possible was put under strain from the beginning of the Reformation in England from the 1530s. Given the strength of civic institutions, the cycles survived into the reign of Elizabeth, but partly because they were identified with the Catholic Church, were suppressed by local ecclesiastical pressures in each city in the late 1560s and 1570s. The last performance of the York Cycle in 1569 is very nearly coincident with the opening of the first professional theater in Whitechapel (London) in 1567.

The climax of the mystery cycles is reached with a sequence of plays about the passion, or suffering, of Christ. Everything in each cycle leads up to the Crucifixion, the turning point in human history, when the original sin of Adam and Eve is paid for by Christ's suffering and death. No cycle has a more dramatic series of passion plays than that performed at York, the longest of the four extant English cycles. Records of the York mystery plays begin to appear in the last quarter of the fourteenth century when York was, next to London, England's most populous and prosperous city. Richard II came to see the cycle in 1397. Sometime after 1415 the plays of the passion sequence were extensively revised by a gifted playwright referred to by scholars as the York Realist. The *Crucifixion*, although not written in that author's distinctive alliterative style, has sometimes been attributed to him, and is, in any case, a powerful example of late medieval dramatic art. It is also an especially powerful example of the representation of Christ in his suffering humanity that was characteristic of late medieval spirituality.

The York plays leading up to the *Crucifixion* are especially cruel: a silent Jesus is vilified, scourged, crowned with thorns, and battered and mocked in a sadistic game of blind man's bluff. Much of the York *Crucifixion* revolves around the mechanical difficulties the soldiers encounter in nailing Jesus to the Cross. The play focuses on the soldiers; they are villains, to be sure, but ordinary men engaged in what they see as ordinary work. They are not monsters.

The gory details, part of the play's "realism," create a shudder, but the play has larger designs on its audience. While the soldiers are hard at work, the audience see only them, complaining of bad workmanship in those who bored the nail holes too far apart, necessitating the stretching of Christ's arms. Only when Christ is raised does the audience recognize the full extent to which both soldiers and audience have been immune from the pain inflicted by the soldiers' work. When the Cross is finally raised, the actor-Christ speaks to "All men that walk by way or street" (cf. the lyric "Ye that Pasen by the Weye," derived from Lamentations 1.12). He thereby addresses the spectators in the streets of York as though *they* were representing the crowd around the Cross on Calvary, directly involving and implicating them in the drama and its theme of salvation. The soldiers may concentrate on their "work" of nailing Christ to the Cross, but the audience is prompted to reflect on the relation between daily labor and the "works" of mercy incumbent upon each Christian. The meaning of Christ's words is, however, lost on the soldiers, who truly "know not what they do" and proceed to quarrel about possession of Christ's cloak.

The York Play of the Crucifixion

CAST OF CHARACTERS

JESUS FOUR SOLDIERS

[*Calvary*]

1ST SOLDIER. Sir knights, take heed hither in hie,° *haste*
This deed on dergh we may not draw.[1]
Ye woot° yourself as well as I *know*
How lords and leaders of our law
Has given doom that this dote° shall die. *fool*
2ND SOLDIER. Sir, all their counsel well we know.
Sen° we are comen to Calvary, *since*
Let ilk° man help now as him awe.° *each / ought*
3RD SOLDIER. We are all ready, lo,
This forward° to fulfill. *agreement*
4TH SOLDIER. Let hear how we shall do,
And go we tite theretill.[2]

1ST SOLDIER. It may not help here for to hone,° *delay*
If we shall any worship° win. *honor*
2ND SOLDIER. He must be dead needlings° by noon. *of necessity*
3RD SOLDIER. Then is good time that we begin.
4TH SOLDIER. Let ding° him down, then is he done: *strike*
He shall not dere° us with his din. *annoy*
1ST SOLDIER. He shall be set and learned soon[3]
With care° to him and all his kin. *sorrow*
2ND SOLDIER. The foulest dead° of all *death*
Shall he die for his deeds.
3RD SOLDIER. That means cross° him we shall. *crucify*
4TH SOLDIER. Behold, so right he reads.° *speaks*

1ST SOLDIER. Then to this work us must take heed,
So that our working be not wrang.° *wrong*
2ND SOLDIER. None other note to neven is need,[4]
But let us haste him for to hang.
3RD SOLDIER. And I have gone for gear good speed,[5]
Both hammers and nails large and lang.° *long*
4TH SOLDIER. Then may we boldly do this deed.
Come on, let kill this traitor strong.° *flagrant*
1ST SOLDIER. Fair might ye fall in fere[6]
That has wrought on this wise.
2ND SOLDIER. Us needs not for to lear° *learn*
Such faitours° to chastise. *fakers*

1. We may not delay the time of this deed.
2. And let's get to it quickly.
3. He'll be put in his place and taught quickly.
4. There is no need to mention any other business.
5. Quickly.
6. May you all have good luck together.

3RD SOLDIER. Sen ilk a thing is right arrayed,
The wiselier° now work may we. *more skillfully*
4TH SOLDIER. The cross on ground is goodly graid,° *prepared*
And bored[7] even as it ought to be.
1ST SOLDIER. Look that the lad on length be laid,
And made be fest° unto this tree.[8] *fastened*
2ND SOLDIER. For all his fare he shall be flayed:° *beaten*
That on assay[9] soon shall ye see.
3RD SOLDIER. Come forth, thou cursed knave,
Thy comfort soon shall keel.° *grow cold*
4TH SOLDIER. Thine hire here shall thou have.
1ST SOLDIER. Walk on, now work we weel.° *well*

JESUS Almighty God, my Father free,° *noble*
Let these matters be made in mind:
Thou bade that I should buxom° be, *obedient*
For Adam° plight for to be pined.° *Adam's / tortured*
Here to dead° I oblige me[1] *death*
Fro° that sin for to save mankind, *from*
And sovereignly beseek I thee,[2]
That they for me may favor find.
And from the Fiend them fend,° *defend*
So that their souls be safe,
In wealth° withouten end. *welfare*
I keep° nought else to crave. *care*

1ST SOLDIER. We,[3] hark, sir knights, for Mahound's blood.
Of Adam-kind° is all his thought! *mankind*
2ND SOLDIER. The warlock waxes worse than wood.[4]
This doleful dead° ne dreadeth he nought. *death*
3RD SOLDIER. Thou should have mind, with main and mood,[5]
Of wicked works that thou hast wrought.
4TH SOLDIER. I hope° that he had been as good° *think / well off*
Have ceased of saws that he up sought.[6]
1ST SOLDIER. Those saws° shall rue° him sore *sayings / repent*
For all his sauntering[7] soon.
2ND SOLDIER. I'll speed them that him spare[8]
Till he to dead° be done. *death*

3RD SOLDIER. Have done belive,° boy, and make thee boun° *at once / ready*
And bend thy back unto this tree.
[JESUS *lies down.*]

7. I.e., bored with holes for the nails, which were probably wooden.
8. I.e., the cross. "Fare": behavior.
9. I.e., in actual experience.
1. Render myself liable.
2. And above all I beseech thee.
3. "We": an exclamation of surprise or displeasure. "Mahound's": Muhammad's; the sacred figures of other religions were considered devils by Christians in the Middle Ages; the soldier is swearing by the Devil.
4. This devil grows worse than crazy.
5. You should think, with all your strength and wits.
6. I.e., to have ceased of the sayings that he thought up.
7. Behaving like a saint.
8. Bad luck to them that spare him.

4TH SOLDIER. Behold, himself has laid him down,
In length and breadth as he should be.
1ST SOLDIER. This traitor here tainted° of treasoun, *convicted*
Go fast and fetch him then, ye three.
And sen he claimeth kingdom with crown,
Even as a king here hang shall he.
2ND SOLDIER. Now certes I shall not fine° *stop*
Ere his right hand be fest.° *fastened*
3RD SOLDIER. The left hand then is mine:
Let see who bears him[9] best.

4TH SOLDIER. His limbs on length then shall I lead,° *stretch*
And even unto the bore° them bring. *hole*
1ST SOLDIER. Unto his head I shall take heed,
And with my hand help him to hing.° *hang*
2ND SOLDIER. Now sen we four shall do this deed,
And meddle° with this unthrifty° thing, *deal / unrewarding*
Let no man spare for special speed,[1]
Till that we have made ending.
3RD SOLDIER. This forward° may not fail, *agreement*
Now are we right arrayed.° *set up*
4TH SOLDIER. This boy here in our bail° *control*
Shall bide° full bitter braid.° *abide / treatment*

1ST SOLDIER. Sir knights, say, how work we now?
2ND SOLDIER. Yes, certes, I hope° I hold this hand. *think*
And to the bore I have it brought,
Full buxomly° withouten band.° *effortlessly / cord*
1ST SOLDIER. Strike on then hard, for him thee bought.[2]
2ND SOLDIER. Yes, here is a stub° will safely stand: *nail*
Through bones and sinews it shall be sought.° *driven*
This work is well, I will warrand.° *warrant*
1ST SOLDIER. Say, sir, how do we thore?° *there*
This bargain may not blin.[3]
3RD SOLDIER. It fails° a foot and more, *falls short*
The sinews are so gone in.° *shrunken*

4TH SOLDIER. I hope that mark° amiss be bored. *hole*
2ND SOLDIER. Then must he bide° in bitter bale.° *wait / woe*
3RD SOLDIER. In faith, it was over-scantly scored.[4]
That makes it foully° for to fail. *badly*
1ST SOLDIER. Why carp° ye so? Fast° on a cord *complain / fasten*
And tug him to, by top and tail.[5]
3RD SOLDIER. Yea, thou commands lightly° as a lord: *readily*
Come help to haul, with ill hail.[6]
1ST SOLDIER. Now certes° that shall I do *certainly*

9. Handles himself.
1. Let nobody slacken because of his own welfare.
2. Drive the nail in hard, for him who redeemed thee: a splendidly anachronistic oath.
3. This arrangement may not fail: the arrangement is of the four soldiers at the four ends of the cross.
4. It was overcarelessly bored.
5. And stretch him to it, head and toe.
6. With bad luck to you.

Full snelly° as a snail. — *quickly*
3RD SOLDIER. And I shall tach° him to — *attach*
Full nimbly with a nail.

This work will hold, that dare I heet,° — *promise*
For now are fest° fast both his hend.° — *fastened / hands*
4TH SOLDIER. Go we all four then to his feet:
So shall our space° be speedly° spend. — *time / well*
2ND SOLDIER. Let see, what bourd his bale might beet.[7]
Thereto my back now will I bend.
4TH SOLDIER. Ow! this work is all unmeet:° — *wrongly done*
This boring must be all amend.
1ST SOLDIER. Ah, peace, man, for Mahound,° — *Mohammed*
Let no man woot° that wonder, — *know*
A rope shall rug° him down, — *jerk*
If all his sinews go asunder.

2ND SOLDIER. That cord full kindly can I knit,° — *knot*
The comfort of this carl° to keel.° — *knave / cool*
1ST SOLDIER. Fest on then fast that all be fit.
It is no force° how fell° he feel. — *matter / badly*
2ND SOLDIER. Lug on, ye both, a little yit,° — *yet*
3RD SOLDIER. I shall not cease, as I have seel.[8]
4TH SOLDIER. And I shall fond° him for to hit. — *try*
2ND SOLDIER. Ow, hail!° — *pull*
4TH SOLDIER. Ho, now I hold° it weel.° — *think / well*
1ST SOLDIER. Have done, drive in that nail
So that no fault be found.
4TH SOLDIER. This working would not fail
If four bulls here were bound.

1ST SOLDIER. These cords have evil° increased his pains — *badly*
Ere° he were till° the borings brought. — *before / to*
2ND SOLDIER. Yea, asunder are both sinews and veins
On ilk a side, so have we sought.° — *afflicted*
3RD SOLDIER. Now all his gauds° nothing him gains: — *tricks*
His sauntering shall with bale be bought.[9]
4TH SOLDIER. I will go say to our sovereigns
Of all these works how we have wrought.
1ST SOLDIER. Nay, sirs, another thing
Falls first to you and me:[1]
They bade we should him hing° — *hang*
On height that men might see.

2ND SOLDIER. We woot well so their words were,
But sir, that deed will do us dere.° — *harm*
1ST SOLDIER. It may nought mend° for to moot° more: — *improve / argue*

7. Let's see, what trick could increase his suffering.
8. As I may have good luck.
9. His acting like a saint (?) shall be paid for with pain.
1. You and I must do first.

This harlot° must be hanged here. *rascal*
2ND SOLDIER. The mortise[2] is made fit° therefore. *ready*
3RD SOLDIER. Fast on your fingers then, in fere.[3]
4TH SOLDIER. I ween° it will never come there. *think*
We four raise it not right to°-year. *this*
1ST SOLDIER. Say, man, why carps thou so?
Thy lifting was but light.° *easy*
2ND SOLDIER. He means there must be mo° *more*
To heave him up on height.

3RD SOLDIER. Now certes I hope it shall not need
To call to us more company.
Methink we four should do this deed,
And bear him to yon hill on high.
1ST SOLDIER. It must be done withouten dread:° *doubt*
No more, but look ye be ready,
And this part shall I lift and lead.° *carry*
On length he shall no longer lie.
Therefore now make you boun:° *ready*
Let bear him to yon hill.
4TH SOLDIER. Then will I bear here down,
And tent his toes untill.[4]

2ND SOLDIER. We two shall see till either side,
For else this work will wry° all wrang.° *turn out / wrong*
3RD SOLDIER. We are ready.
4TH SOLDIER. Good sirs, abide,
And let me first his feet up fang.° *take*
2ND SOLDIER. Why tent ye so to tales this tide?[5]
1ST SOLDIER. Lift up!
[*All lift the cross together.*]
4TH SOLDIER. Let see!
2ND SOLDIER. Ow! Lift along!
3RD SOLDIER. From all this harm he should him hide° *protect*
And° he were God. *if*
4TH SOLDIER. The Devil him hang!
1ST SOLDIER. For great harm° I have hent:° *injury / received*
My shoulder is in sunder.
2ND SOLDIER. And certes I am near shent,° *ruined*
So long have I born under.[6]

3RD SOLDIER. This cross and I in two must twin°— *separate*
Else breaks my back in sunder soon.
4TH SOLDIER. Lay down again and leave° your din. *cease*
This deed for us will never be done.
[*They lay it down.*]
1ST SOLDIER. Assay,° sirs, let see if any gin° *try / trick*

2. A hole in the ground shaped to receive the cross.
3. Fasten your fingers on it, all together.
4. Then I'll carry the part down here and attend to his toes.
5. Why are you so intent on talking at a time like this?
6. So long have I borne it up.

May help him up, withouten hone.° *delay*
For here should wight° men worship win, *strong*
And not with gauds° all day to gone. *pranks*

2ND SOLDIER. More wighter° men than we *stronger*
Full few I hope° ye find. *think*

3RD SOLDIER. This bargain° will not be,° *arrangement / work*
For certes me wants wind.

4TH SOLDIER. So will° of work never we wore.° *at a loss / were*
I hope this carl some cautels cast.[7]

2ND SOLDIER. My burden sat° me wonder sore: *vexed*
Unto the hill I might not last.

1ST SOLDIER. Lift up and soon he shall be thore.° *there*
Therefore fest° on your fingers fast. *fasten*

3RD SOLDIER. Ow, lift!

1ST SOLDIER. We, lo!

4TH SOLDIER. A little more!

2ND SOLDIER. Hold then!

1ST SOLDIER. How now?

2ND SOLDIER. The worst is past.

3RD SOLDIER. He weighs a wicked weight.

2ND SOLDIER. So may we all four say,
Ere he was heaved on height
And raised on this array.° *way*

4TH SOLDIER. He made us stand as any stones,
So boistous° was he for to bear. *bulky*

1ST SOLDIER. Now raise him nimbly for the nones,[8]
And set him by this mortise here;
And let him fall in all at once,
For certes that pain shall have no peer.° *equal*

3RD SOLDIER. Heave up!

4TH SOLDIER. Let down, so all his bones
Are asunder now on sides sere.[9]
[*The cross is raised.*]

1ST SOLDIER. That falling was more fell° *cruel*
Than all the harms he had.
Now may a man well tell° *count*
The least lith° of this lad. *joint*

3RD SOLDIER. Methinketh this cross will not abide
Nor stand still in this mortise yit.° *yet*

4TH SOLDIER. At the first was it made overwide:
That makes it wave, thou may well wit.° *learn*

1ST SOLDIER. It shall be set on ilk a side,
So that it shall no further flit.° *move*
Good wedges shall we take this tide,° *time*
And fast° the foot, then is all fit. *fasten*

7. I think this knave cast some spells.
8. For the purpose.
9. Are pulled apart on every side.

2ND SOLDIER. Here are wedges arrayed° *prepared*
For that, both great and small.
3RD SOLDIER. Where are our hammers laid
That we should work withal?

4TH SOLDIER. We have them here even at our hand.
2ND SOLDIER. Give me this wedge, I shall it in drive.
4TH SOLDIER. Here is another yit ordand.° *ready*
3RD SOLDIER. Do take° it me hither belive.° *give / quickly*
1ST SOLDIER. Lay on then fast.
3RD SOLDIER. Yes. I warrand.° *guarantee*
I thring them sam, so mote I thrive.[1]
Now will this cross ful stably stand:
All if he rave they will not rive.[2]
1ST SOLDIER. Say, sir, how likes thou now
The work that we have wrought?
4TH SOLDIER. We pray you, say us how
Ye feel, or faint ye aught?[3]

JESUS All men that walk by way or street,
Take tent—ye shall no travail tine[4]—
Behold mine head, mine hands, my feet,
And fully feel now ere ye fine° *cease*
If any mourning may be meet
Or mischief° measured unto mine. *injury*
My Father, that all bales may bete,[5]
Forgive these men that do me pine.° *torment*
What they work woot° they nought: *know*
Therefore my Father I crave
Let never their sins be sought,° *searched*
But see their souls to save.

1ST SOLDIER. We, hark! he jangles like a jay.
2ND SOLDIER. Methink he patters like a pie.° *magpie*
3RD SOLDIER. He has been doand° all this day, *doing so*
And made great mening° of mercy. *talk*
4TH SOLDIER. Is this the same that gun° us say *did*
That he was God's son almighty?[6]
1ST SOLDIER. Therefore he feels full fell affray,[7]
And doomed this day was for to die.
2ND SOLDIER. Vath! *qui destruis templum!*[8]
3RD SOLDIER. His saws° were so, certain. *sayings*
4TH SOLDIER. And, sirs, he said to some
He might raise it again.

1ST SOLDIER. To muster° that he had no might, *exhibit*
For all the cautels° that he could cast; *charms*

1. I press them together, so may I thrive.
2. Even if he struggles, they will not budge.
3. Or do you feel somewhat faint?
4. Take heed, you shall not lose your labor.
5. My father, who may remedy all evils.
6. That he was the son of almighty God.
7. For that he suffers a full cruel assault.
8. In Faith thou who destroys the temple (cf. Mark 14.58, John 2.19).

All if he were in word so wight,[9]
For all his force now is he fast.
All Pilate deemed is done and dight:° *accomplished*
Therefore I read° that we go rest. *advise*
2ND SOLDIER. This race must be rehearsed right[1]
Through the world both east and west.
2ND SOLDIER. Yea, let him hang here still
And make mows on the moon.[2]
4TH SOLDIER. Then may we wend° at will. *go away*
1ST SOLDIER. Nay, good sirs, not so soon.

For certes us needs another note:[3]
This kirtle would I of you crave.
2ND SOLDIER. Nay, nay, sir, we will look° by lot *see*
Which of us four falls° it to have. *chances*
3RD SOLDIER. I read° we draw cut° for this coat. *advise / lots*
Lo, see now soon, all sides to save.[4]
4TH SOLDIER. The short cut° shall win, that well ye woot, *straw*
Whether it fall to knight or knave.
1ST SOLDIER. Fellows, ye thar not flite,[5]
For this mantle is mine.
2ND SOLDIER. Go we then hence tite,° *quickly*
This travail here we tine.[6]

9. Even though he was so clever in words.
1. This course of action must be repeated correctly.
2. And make faces at the moon.
3. For surely we have another piece of business to settle.
4. See now straightway, to protect all parties.
5. Fellows, you don't need to quarrel.
6. We're wasting our time here.

SIR THOMAS MALORY
ca. 1405–1471

Morte Darthur (Death of Arthur) is the title that William Caxton, the first English printer, gave to Malory's volume, which Caxton described more accurately in his Preface as "the noble histories of * * * King Arthur and of certain of his knights." The volume begins with the mythical story of Arthur's birth. King Uther Pendragon falls in love with the wife of one of his barons. Merlin's magic transforms Uther into the likeness of her husband, and Arthur is born of this union. The volume ends with the destruction of the Round Table and the deaths of Arthur, Queen Guinevere, and Sir Lancelot, who is Arthur's best knight and the queen's lover. The bulk of the work is taken up with the separate adventures of the knights of the Round Table.

During the thirteenth century the stories about Arthur and his knights had been turned into a series of enormously long prose romances in French, and it was these, as Caxton informed his readers, "Sir Thomas Malory did take out of certain books of French and reduced into English." For Caxton's Preface and excerpts from a modern translation of the French *Prose Vulgate Cycle* (Malory's "French books"), see "King Arthur" at Norton Literature Online.

Little was known about the author until the early twentieth century when scholars began to unearth the criminal record of a Sir Thomas Malory of Newbold Revell in

Warwickshire. In 1451 he was arrested for the first time to prevent his doing injury—presumably further injury—to a priory in Lincolnshire, and shortly thereafter he was accused of a number of criminal acts. These included escaping from prison after his first arrest, twice breaking into and plundering the Abbey of Coombe, extorting money from various persons, and committing rape. Malory pleaded innocent of all charges. The Wars of the Roses—in which Malory, like the formidable earl of Warwick (the "kingmaker"), whom he seems to have followed, switched sides from Lancaster to York and back again—may account for some of his troubles with the law. After a failed Lancastrian revolt, the Yorkist king, Edward IV, specifically excluded Malory from four amnesties he granted to the Lancastrians.

The identification of this Sir Thomas Malory (there is another candidate with the same name) as the author of the *Morte* was strengthened by the discovery in 1934 of a manuscript that differed from Caxton's text, the only version previously known. The manuscript contained eight separate romances. Caxton, in order to give the impression of a continuous narrative, had welded these together into twenty-one books, subdivided into short chapters with summary chapter headings. Caxton suppressed all but the last of the personal remarks the author had appended to individual tales in the manuscript. At the very end of the book Malory asks "all gentlemen and gentlewomen that readeth this book * * * pray for me while I am alive that God send me good deliverance." The discovery of the manuscript revealed that at the close of the first tale he had written: "this was drawyn by a knight presoner Sir Thomas Malleoré, that God sende him good recover." There is strong circumstantial evidence, therefore, that the book from which the Arthurian legends were passed on to future generations to be adapted in literature, art, and film was written in prison by a man whose violent career might seem at odds with the chivalric ideals he professes.

Such a contradiction—if it really is one—should not be surprising. Nostalgia for an ideal past that never truly existed is typical of much historical romance. Like the slave-owning plantation society of Margaret Mitchell's *Gone with the Wind*, whose southern gentlemen cultivate chivalrous manners and respect for gentlewomen, Malory's Arthurian world is a fiction. In our terms, it cannot even be labeled "historical," although the distinction between romance and history is not one that Malory would have made. Only rarely does he voice skepticism about the historicity of his tale; one such example is his questioning of the myth of Arthur's return. Much of the tragic power of his romance lies in his sense of the irretrievability of past glory in comparison with the sordidness of his own age.

The success of Malory's retelling owes much to his development of a terse and direct prose style, especially the naturalistic dialogue that keeps his narrative close to earth. And both he and many of his characters are masters of understatement who express themselves, in moments of great emotional tension, with a bare minimum of words.

In spite of its professed dedication to service of women, Malory's chivalry is primarily devoted to the fellowship and competitions of aristocratic men. Fighting consists mainly of single combats in tournaments, chance encounters, and battles, which Malory never tires of describing in professional detail. Commoners rarely come into view; when they do, the effect can be chilling—as when pillagers by moonlight plunder the corpses of the knights left on the field of Arthur's last battle. Above all, Malory cherishes an aristocratic male code of honor for which his favorite word is "worship." Men win or lose "worship" through their actions in war and love.

The most "worshipful" of Arthur's knights is Sir Lancelot, the "head of all Christian knights," as he is called in a moving eulogy by his brother, Sir Ector. But Lancelot is compromised by his fatal liaison with Arthur's queen and torn between the incompatible loyalties that bind him as an honorable knight, on the one hand, to his lord Arthur and, on the other, to his lady Guinevere. Malory loves his character Lancelot even to the point of indulging in the fleeting speculation, after Lancelot has been admitted to the queen's chamber, that their activities might have been innocent, "for love that time was not as love is nowadays." But when the jealousy and malice of two wicked knights forces the affair into the open, nothing can avert the breaking up of the fellowship of the Round Table and the death of Arthur himself, which Malory relates with somber magnificence as the passing of a great era.

From Morte Darthur[1]

[THE CONSPIRACY AGAINST LANCELOT AND GUINEVERE]

In May, when every lusty[2] heart flourisheth and burgeoneth, for as the season is lusty to behold and comfortable,[3] so man and woman rejoiceth and gladdeth of summer coming with his fresh flowers, for winter with his rough winds and blasts causeth lusty men and women to cower and to sit fast by the fire—so this season it befell in the month of May a great anger and unhap that stinted not[4] till the flower of chivalry of all the world was destroyed and slain. And all was long upon two unhappy[5] knights which were named Sir Agravain and Sir Mordred that were brethren unto Sir Gawain.[6] For this Sir Agravain and Sir Mordred had ever a privy[7] hate unto the Queen, Dame Guinevere, and to Sir Lancelot, and daily and nightly they ever watched upon Sir Lancelot.

So it misfortuned Sir Gawain and all his brethren were in King Arthur's chamber, and then Sir Agravain said thus openly, and not in no counsel,[8] that many knights might hear: "I marvel that we all be not ashamed both to see and to know how Sir Lancelot lieth daily and nightly by the Queen. And all we know well that it is so, and it is shamefully suffered of us all[9] that we should suffer so noble a king as King Arthur is to be shamed."

Then spoke Sir Gawain and said, "Brother, Sir Agravain, I pray you and charge you, move no such matters no more afore[1] me, for wit you well, I will not be of your counsel."[2]

"So God me help," said Sir Gaheris and Sir Gareth,[3] "we will not be known of your deeds."[4]

"Then will I!" said Sir Mordred.

"I lieve[5] you well," said Sir Gawain, "for ever unto all unhappiness, sir, ye will grant.[6] And I would that ye left all this and make you not so busy, for I know," said Sir Gawain, "what will fall of it."[7]

"Fall whatsoever fall may," said Sir Agravain, "I will disclose it to the King."

"Not by my counsel," said Sir Gawain, "for and[8] there arise war and wrack betwixt[9] Sir Lancelot and us, wit you well, brother, there will many kings and great lords hold with Sir Lancelot. Also, brother, Sir Agravain," said Sir

1. The selections here are from the section that Caxton called book 20, chaps. 1–4, 8–10, and book 21, chaps. 3–7, 10–12, with omissions. In the Winchester manuscript this section is titled "The Most Piteous Tale of the Morte Arthur Saunz Guerdon" (i.e., the death of Arthur without reward or compensation). The text is based on Winchester, with some readings introduced from the Caxton edition; spelling has been modernized and modern punctuation added.
2. Merry.
3. Pleasant.
4. Misfortune that ceased not.
5. On account of two ill-fated.
6. Gawain and Agravain are sons of King Lot of Orkney and his wife, Arthur's half-sister Morgause. Mordred is the illegitimate son of Arthur and Morgause.
7. Secret.
8. Secret manner.
9. Put up with by all of us.
1. Before. "Move": propose.
2. On your side. "Wit you well": know well, i.e., give you to understand.
3. Sons of King Lot and Gawain's brothers.
4. A party to your doings.
5. Believe.
6. You will consent to all mischief.
7. Come of it.
8. If.
9. Strife between.

Gawain, "ye must remember how often times Sir Lancelot hath rescued the King and the Queen. And the best of us all had been full cold at the heart-root[1] had not Sir Lancelot been better than we, and that has he proved himself full oft. And as for my part," said Sir Gawain, "I will never be against Sir Lancelot for[2] one day's deed, when he rescued me from King Carados of the Dolorous Tower and slew him and saved my life. Also, brother, Sir Agravain and Sir Mordred, in like wise Sir Lancelot rescued you both and three score and two[3] from Sir Tarquin. And therefore, brother, methinks such noble deeds and kindness should be remembered."

"Do as ye list,"[4] said Sir Agravain, "for I will layne[5] it no longer."

So with these words came in Sir Arthur.

"Now, brother," said Sir Gawain, "stint your noise."[6]

"That will I not," said Sir Agravain and Sir Mordred.

"Well, will ye so?" said Sir Gawain. "Then God speed you, for I will not hear of your tales, neither be of your counsel."

"No more will I," said Sir Gaheris.

"Neither I," said Sir Gareth, "for I shall never say evil by[7] that man that made me knight." And therewithal they three departed making great dole.[8]

"Alas!" said Sir Gawain and Sir Gareth, "now is this realm wholly destroyed and mischieved,[9] and the noble fellowship of the Round Table shall be disparbeled."[1]

So they departed, and then King Arthur asked them what noise they made. "My lord," said Sir Agravain, "I shall tell you, for I may keep[2] it no longer. Here is I and my brother Sir Mordred broke[3] unto my brother Sir Gawain, Sir Gaheris, and to Sir Gareth—for this is all, to make it short—how that we know all that Sir Lancelot holdeth your queen, and hath done long; and we be your sister[4] sons, we may suffer it no longer. And all we woot[5] that ye should be above Sir Lancelot, and ye are the king that made him knight, and therefore we will prove it that he is a traitor to your person."

"If it be so," said the King, "wit[6] you well, he is none other. But I would be loath to begin such a thing but[7] I might have proofs of it, for Sir Lancelot is an hardy knight, and all ye know that he is the best knight among us all. And but if he be taken with the deed,[8] he will fight with him that bringeth up the noise, and I know no knight that is able to match him. Therefore, and[9] it be sooth as ye say, I would that he were taken with the deed."

For, as the French book saith, the King was full loath that such a noise should be upon Sir Lancelot and his queen. For the King had a deeming[1] of it, but he would not hear of it, for Sir Lancelot had done so much for him and for the Queen so many times that, wit you well, the King loved him passingly[2] well.

"My lord," said Sir Agravain, "ye shall ride tomorn[3] on hunting, and doubt ye not, Sir Lancelot will not go with you. And so when it draweth toward night,

1. Would have been dead.
2. On account of.
3. I.e., sixty-two.
4. You please.
5. Conceal.
6. Stop making scandal.
7. About.
8. Lamentation.
9. Put to shame.
1. Dispersed.
2. Conceal.
3. Revealed.
4. Sister's.
5. Know.
6. Know.
7. Unless.
8. Unless he is caught in the act.
9. If.
1. Suspicion.
2. Exceedingly.
3. Tomorrow.

ye may send the Queen word that ye will lie out all that night, and so may ye send for your cooks. And then, upon pain of death, that night we shall take him with the Queen, and we shall bring him unto you, quick[4] or dead."

"I will well,"[5] said the King. "Then I counsel you to take with you sure fellowship."

"Sir," said Sir Agravain, "my brother, Sir Mordred, and I will take with us twelve knights of the Round Table."

"Beware," said King Arthur, "for I warn you, ye shall find him wight."[6]

"Let us deal!"[7] said Sir Agravain and Sir Mordred.

So on the morn King Arthur rode on hunting and sent word to the Queen that he would be out all that night. Then Sir Agravain and Sir Mordred got to them[8] twelve knights and hid themself in a chamber in the castle of Carlisle. And these were their names: Sir Colgrevance, Sir Mador de la Porte, Sir Guingalen, Sir Meliot de Logres, Sir Petipace of Winchelsea, Sir Galeron of Galway, Sir Melion de la Mountain, Sir Ascamore, Sir Gromore Somyr Jour, Sir Curselayne, Sir Florence, and Sir Lovell. So these twelve knights were with Sir Mordred and Sir Agravain, and all they were of Scotland, or else of Sir Gawain's kin, or well-willers[9] to his brother.

So when the night came, Sir Lancelot told Sir Bors[1] how he would go that night and speak with the Queen.

"Sir," said Sir Bors, "ye shall not go this night by my counsel."

"Why?" said Sir Lancelot.

"Sir," said Sir Bors, "I dread me[2] ever of Sir Agravain that waiteth upon[3] you daily to do you shame and us all. And never gave my heart against no going that ever ye went[4] to the queen so much as now, for I mistrust[5] that the King is out this night from the Queen because peradventure he hath lain[6] some watch for you and the Queen. Therefore, I dread me sore of some treason."

"Have ye no dread," said Sir Lancelot, "for I shall go and come again and make no tarrying."

"Sir," said Sir Bors, "that me repents,[7] for I dread me sore that your going this night shall wrath[8] us all."

"Fair nephew," said Sir Lancelot, "I marvel me much why ye say thus, sithen[9] the Queen hath sent for me. And wit you well, I will not be so much a coward, but she shall understand I will[1] see her good grace."

"God speed you well," said Sir Bors, "and send you sound and safe again!"

So Sir Lancelot departed and took his sword under his arm, and so he walked in his mantel,[2] that noble knight, and put himself in great jeopardy. And so he passed on till he came to the Queen's chamber, and so lightly he was had[3] into the chamber. And then, as the French book saith, the Queen and Sir Lancelot were together. And whether they were abed or at other manner of disports, me list[4] not thereof make no mention, for love that time[5] was not as love is nowadays.

4. Alive.
5. Readily agree.
6. Strong.
7. Leave it to us.
8. Gathered to themselves.
9. Partisans.
1. Nephew and confidant of Sir Lancelot.
2. I am afraid.
3. Lies in wait.
4. Never misgave my heart against any visit you made.
5. Suspect.
6. Perhaps he has set.
7. I regret.
8. Cause injury to.
9. Since.
1. Wish to.
2. Cloak. Lancelot goes without armor.
3. Quickly he was received.
4. I care. "Disports": pastimes.
5. At that time.

But thus as they were together there came Sir Agravain and Sir Mordred with twelve knights with them of the Round Table, and they said with great crying and scaring[6] voice: "Thou traitor, Sir Lancelot, now are thou taken!" And thus they cried with a loud voice that all the court might hear it. And these fourteen knights all were armed at all points, as[7] they should fight in a battle.

"Alas!" said Queen Guinevere, "now are we mischieved[8] both!"

"Madam," said Sir Lancelot, "is there here any armor within your chamber that I might cover my body withal? And if there be any, give it me, and I shall soon stint[9] their malice, by the grace of God!"

"Now, truly," said the Queen, "I have none armor neither helm, shield, sword, neither spear, wherefore I dread me sore our long love is come to a mischievous end. For I hear by their noise there be many noble knights, and well I woot they be surely[1] armed, and against them ye may make no resistance. Wherefore ye are likely to be slain, and then shall I be burned! For and[2] ye might escape them," said the Queen, "I would not doubt but that ye would rescue me in what danger that ever I stood in."

"Alas!" said Sir Lancelot, "in all my life thus was I never bestead[3] that I should be thus shamefully slain for lack of mine armor."

But ever in one[4] Sir Agravain and Sir Mordred cried: "Traitor knight, come out of the Queen's chamber! For wit thou well thou art beset so that thou shalt not escape."

"Ah, Jesu mercy!" said Sir Lancelot, "this shameful cry and noise I may not suffer, for better were death at once than thus to endure this pain." Then he took the Queen in his arms and kissed her and said, "Most noblest Christian queen, I beseech you, as ye have been ever my special good lady, and I at all times your poor knight and true unto[5] my power, and as I never failed you in right nor in wrong sithen the first day King Arthur made me knight, that ye will pray for my soul if that I be slain. For well I am assured that Sir Bors, my nephew, and all the remnant of my kin, with Sir Lavain and Sir Urry,[6] that they will not fail you to rescue you from the fire. And therefore, mine own lady, recomfort yourself,[7] whatsoever come of me, that ye go with Sir Bors, my nephew, and Sir Urry and they all will do you all the pleasure that they may, and ye shall live like a queen upon my lands."

"Nay, Sir Lancelot, nay!" said the Queen. "Wit thou well that I will not live long after thy days. But and[8] ye be slain I will take my death as meekly as ever did martyr take his death for Jesu Christ's sake."

"Well, Madam," said Sir Lancelot, "sith it is so that the day is come that our love must depart,[9] wit you well I shall sell my life as dear as I may. And a thousandfold," said Sir Lancelot, "I am more heavier[1] for you than for myself! And now I had liefer[2] than to be lord of all Christendom that I had sure armor upon me, that men might speak of my deeds ere ever I were slain."

"Truly," said the Queen, "and[3] it might please God, I would that they would take me and slay me and suffer[4] you to escape."

6. Terrifying.
7. Completely, as if.
8. Come to grief.
9. Stop.
1. Securely.
2. If.
3. Beset.
4. In unison.
5. To the utmost of.
6. The brother of Elaine, the Fair Maid of Astolat, and a knight miraculously healed of his wound by Sir Lancelot. "Remnant": rest.
7. Take heart again.
8. If.
9. Come to an end.
1. More grieved.
2. Rather.
3. If.
4. Allow.

"That shall never be," said Sir Lancelot. "God defend me from such a shame! But, Jesu Christ, be Thou my shield and mine armor!" And therewith Sir Lancelot wrapped his mantel about his arm well and surely; and by then they had gotten a great form[5] out of the hall, and therewith they all rushed at the door. "Now, fair lords," said Sir Lancelot, "leave[6] your noise and your rushing, and I shall set open this door, and then may ye do with me what it liketh you."[7]

"Come off,[8] then," said they all, "and do it, for it availeth thee not to strive against us all. And therefore let us into this chamber, and we shall save thy life until thou come to King Arthur."

Then Sir Lancelot unbarred the door, and with his left hand he held it open a little, that but one man might come in at once. And so there came striding a good knight, a much[9] man and a large, and his name was called Sir Colgrevance of Gore. And he with a sword struck at Sir Lancelot mightily. And he put aside[1] the stroke and gave him such a buffet[2] upon the helmet that he fell groveling dead within the chamber door. Then Sir Lancelot with great might drew the knight within[3] the chamber door. And then Sir Lancelot, with help of the Queen and her ladies, he was lightly[4] armed in Colgrevance's armor. And ever stood Sir Agravain and Sir Mordred, crying, "Traitor knight! Come forth out of the Queen's chamber!"

"Sirs, leave[5] your noise," said Sir Lancelot, "for wit you well, Sir Agravain, ye shall not prison me this night. And therefore, and[6] ye do by my counsel, go ye all from this chamber door and make you no such crying and such manner of slander as ye do. For I promise you by my knighthood, and ye will depart and make no more noise, I shall as tomorn appear afore you all and before the King, and then let it be seen which of you all, other else ye all,[7] that will deprove[8] me of treason. And there shall I answer you, as a knight should, that hither I came to the Queen for no manner of mal engine,[9] and that will I prove and make it good upon you with my hands."

"Fie upon thee, traitor," said Sir Agravain and Sir Mordred, "for we will have thee malgré thine head[1] and slay thee, and we list. For we let thee wit we have the choice of[2] King Arthur to save thee other slay thee."

"Ah, sirs," said Sir Lancelot, "is there none other grace with you? Then keep[3] yourself!" And then Sir Lancelot set all open the chamber door and mightily and knightly he strode in among them. And anon[4] at the first stroke he slew Sir Agravain, and after twelve of his fellows. Within a little while he had laid them down cold to the earth, for there was none of the twelve knights might stand Sir Lancelot one buffet.[5] And also he wounded Sir Mordred, and therewithal he fled with all his might.

And then Sir Lancelot returned again unto the Queen and said, "Madam, now wit you well, all our true love is brought to an end, for now will King Arthur ever be my foe. And therefore, Madam, and it like you[6] that I may have you with me, I shall save you from all manner adventurous[7] dangers."

"Sir, that is not best," said the Queen, "me seemeth, for[8] now ye have done

5. Bench.
6. Stop.
7. Pleases you.
8. Go ahead.
9. Big.
1. Fended off.
2. Blow.
3. Inside.
4. Quickly.
5. Stop.
6. If.
7. Or else all of you.
8. Accuse.
9. Evil design.
1. In spite of you.
2. From.
3. Defend.
4. Right away.
5. Withstand Sir Lancelot one blow.
6. If it please you.
7. Perilous.
8. Because.

so much harm, it will be best that ye hold you still with this. And if ye see that as tomorn they will put me unto death, then may ye rescue me as ye think best."

"I will well,"[9] said Sir Lancelot, "for have ye no doubt, while I am a man living I shall rescue you." And then he kissed her, and either of them gave other a ring, and so there he left the Queen and went until[1] his lodging.

[WAR BREAKS OUT BETWEEN ARTHUR AND LANCELOT][2]

Then said King Arthur unto Sir Gawain, "Dear nephew, I pray you make ready in your best armor with your brethren, Sir Gaheris and Sir Gareth, to bring my Queen to the fire, there to have her judgment and receive the death."

"Nay, my most noble king," said Sir Gawain, "that will I never do, for wit you well I will never be in that place where so noble a queen as is my lady Dame Guinevere shall take such a shameful end. For wit you well," said Sir Gawain, "my heart will not serve me for to see her die, and it shall never be said that ever I was of your counsel for her death."

"Then," said the King unto Sir Gawain, "suffer[3] your brethren Sir Gaheris and Sir Gareth to be there."

"My lord," said Sir Gawain, "wit you well they will be loath to be there present because of many adventures[4] that is like to fall, but they are young and full unable to say you nay."

Then spake Sir Gaheris and the good knight Sir Gareth unto King Arthur: "Sir, ye may well command us to be there, but wit you well it shall be sore against our will. But and[5] we be there by your strait commandment, ye shall plainly[6] hold us there excused—we will be there in peaceable wise and bear none harness of war upon us."

"In the name of God," said the King, "then make you ready, for she shall have soon[7] her judgment."

"Alas," said Sir Gawain, "that ever I should endure[8] to see this woeful day." So Sir Gawain turned him and wept heartily, and so he went into his chamber.

And then the Queen was led forth without[9] Carlisle, and anon she was dispoiled into[1] her smock. And then her ghostly father[2] was brought to her to be shriven of her misdeeds.[3] Then was there weeping and wailing and wringing of hands of many lords and ladies, but there were but few in comparison that would bear any armor for to strengthen[4] the death of the Queen.

Then was there one that Sir Lancelot had sent unto that place, which went to espy what time the Queen should go unto her death. And anon as[5] he saw the Queen dispoiled into her smock and shriven, then he gave Sir Lancelot warning. Then was there but spurring and plucking up[6] of horses, and right so they came unto the fire. And who[7] that stood against them, there were they slain—there might none withstand Sir Lancelot. So all that bore arms and

9. Agree.
1. To.
2. Lancelot and Sir Bors mobilize their friends for the rescue of Guinevere. In the morning Mordred reports the events of the night to Arthur who, against Gawain's strong opposition, condemns the queen to be burned, for "the law was such in those days that whatsoever they were, of what estate or degree, if they were found guilty of treason there should be none other remedy but death."
3. Allow.
4. Chance occurrences.
5. If.
6. Openly. "Straight": strict.
7. Right away.
8. Live.
9. Outside.
1. Undressed down to.
2. Spiritual father, i.e., her priest.
3. For her to be confessed of her sins.
4. Secure.
5. As soon as.
6. Urging forward.
7. Whoever.

withstood them, there were they slain, full many a noble knight. * * * And so in this rushing and hurling, as Sir Lancelot thrang[8] here and there, it misfortuned him[9] to slay Sir Gaheris and Sir Gareth, the noble knight, for they were unarmed and unwares.[1] As the French book saith, Sir Lancelot smote Sir Gaheris and Sir Gareth upon the brain-pans, wherethrough[2] that they were slain in the field, howbeit[3] Sir Lancelot saw them not. And so were they found dead among the thickest of the press.

Then when Sir Lancelot had thus done, and slain and put to flight all that would withstand him, then he rode straight unto Queen Guinevere and made a kirtle[4] and a gown to be cast upon her, and then he made her to be set behind him and prayed her to be of good cheer. Now wit you well the Queen was glad that she was escaped from death, and then she thanked God and Sir Lancelot.

And so he rode his way with the Queen, as the French book saith, unto Joyous Garde,[5] and there he kept her as a noble knight should. And many great lords and many good knights were sent him, and many full noble knights drew unto him. When they heard that King Arthur and Sir Lancelot were at debate,[6] many knights were glad, and many were sorry of their debate.

Now turn we again unto King Arthur, that when it was told him how and in what manner the Queen was taken away from the fire, and when he heard of the death of his noble knights, and in especial Sir Gaheris and Sir Gareth, then he swooned for very pure[7] sorrow. And when he awoke of his swoon, then he said: "Alas, that ever I bore crown upon my head! For now have I lost the fairest fellowship of noble knights that ever held Christian king[8] together. Alas, my good knights be slain and gone away from me. Now within these two days I have lost nigh forty knights and also the noble fellowship of Sir Lancelot and his blood,[9] for now I may nevermore hold them together with my worship.[1] Alas, that ever this war began!

"Now, fair fellows," said the King, "I charge you that no man tell Sir Gawain of the death of his two brethren, for I am sure," said the King, "when he heareth tell that Sir Gareth is dead, he will go nigh out of his mind. Mercy Jesu," said the King, "why slew he Sir Gaheris and Sir Gareth? For I dare say, as for Sir Gareth, he loved Sir Lancelot above all men earthly."[2]

"That is truth," said some knights, "but they were slain in the hurling,[3] as Sir Lancelot thrang in the thickest of the press. And as they were unarmed, he smote them and wist[4] not whom that he smote, and so unhappily[5] they were slain."

"Well," said Arthur, "the death of them will cause the greatest mortal war that ever was, for I am sure that when Sir Gawain knoweth hereof that Sir Gareth is slain, I shall never have rest of him[6] till I have destroyed Sir Lancelot's kin and himself both, other else he to destroy me. And therefore," said the King, "wit you well, my heart was never so heavy as it is now. And much more I am sorrier for my good knights' loss[7] than for the loss of my fair queen;

8. Pressed. "Hurling": turmoil.
9. He had the misfortune.
1. Unaware.
2. Through which.
3. Although.
4. Petticoat.
5. Lancelot's castle in England.
6. Strife.
7. Sheer.
8. That Christian king ever held.
9. Kin.
1. Glory.
2. Earthly men.
3. Turmoil.
4. Knew.
5. Unluckily.
6. He will never give me any peace.
7. The loss of my good knights.

for queens I might have enough, but such a fellowship of good knights shall never be together in no company. And now I dare say," said King Arthur, "there was never Christian king that ever held such a fellowship together. And alas, that ever Sir Lancelot and I should be at debate. Ah, Agravain, Agravain!" said the King, "Jesu forgive it thy soul, for thine evil will that thou and thy brother Sir Mordred haddest unto Sir Lancelot hath caused all this sorrow." And ever among these complaints the King wept and swooned.

Then came there one to Sir Gawain and told him how the Queen was led away with[8] Sir Lancelot, and nigh a four-and-twenty knights slain. "Ah, Jesu, save me my two brethren!" said Sir Gawain. "For full well wist I," said Sir Gawain, "that Sir Lancelot would rescue her, other else he would die in that field. And to say the truth he were not of worship but if he had[9] rescued the Queen, insomuch as she should have been burned for his sake. And as in that," said Sir Gawain, "he hath done but knightly, and as I would have done myself and I had stood in like case. But where are my brethren?" said Sir Gawain. "I marvel that I hear not of them."

Then said that man, "Truly, Sir Gaheris and Sir Gareth be slain."

"Jesu defend!"[1] said Sir Gawain. "For all this world I would not that they were slain, and in especial my good brother Sir Gareth."

"Sir," said the man, "he is slain, and that is great pity."

"Who slew him?" said Sir Gawain.

"Sir Lancelot," said the man, "slew them both."

"That may I not believe," said Sir Gawain, "that ever he slew my good brother Sir Gareth, for I dare say my brother loved him better than me and all his brethren and the King both. Also I dare say, an[2] Sir Lancelot had desired my brother Sir Gareth with him, he would have been with him against the King and us all. And therefore I may never believe that Sir Lancelot slew my brethren."

"Verily, sir," said the man, "it is noised[3] that he slew him."

"Alas," said Sir Gawain, "now is my joy gone." And then he fell down and swooned, and long he lay there as he had been dead. And when he arose out of his swoon, he cried out sorrowfully and said, "Alas!" And forthwith he ran unto the King, crying and weeping, and said, "Ah, mine uncle King Arthur! My good brother Sir Gareth is slain, and so is my brother Sir Gaheris, which were two noble knights."

Then the King wept and he both, and so they fell on swooning. And when they were revived, then spake Sir Gawain and said, "Sir, I will go and see my brother Sir Gareth."

"Sir, ye may not see him," said the King, "for I caused him to be interred and Sir Gaheris both, for I well understood that ye would make overmuch sorrow, and the sight of Sir Gareth should have caused your double sorrow."

"Alas, my lord," said Sir Gawain, "how slew he my brother Sir Gareth? Mine own good lord, I pray you tell me."

"Truly," said the King, "I shall tell you as it hath been told me—Sir Lancelot slew him and Sir Gaheris both."

"Alas," said Sir Gawain, "they bore none arms against him, neither of them both."

8. By.
9. Of honor if he had not.
1. Forbid.
2. If.
3. Reported.

"I woot not how it was," said the King, "but as it is said, Sir Lancelot slew them in the thickest of the press and knew them not. And therefore let us shape a remedy for to revenge their deaths."

"My king, my lord, and mine uncle," said Sir Gawain, "wit you well, now I shall make you a promise which I shall hold by my knighthood, that from this day forward I shall never fail[4] Sir Lancelot until that one of us have slain the other. And therefore I require you, my lord and king, dress[5] you unto the wars, for wit you well, I will be revenged upon Sir Lancelot; and therefore, as ye will have my service and my love, now haste you thereto and assay[6] your friends. For I promise unto God," said Sir Gawain, "for the death of my brother Sir Gareth I shall seek Sir Lancelot throughout seven kings' realms, but I shall slay him, other else he shall slay me."

"Sir, ye shall not need to seek him so far," said the King, "for as I hear say, Sir Lancelot will abide me and us all within the castle of Joyous Garde. And much people draweth unto him, as I hear say."

"That may I right well believe," said Sir Gawain, "but my lord," he said, "assay your friends and I will assay mine."

"It shall be done," said the King, "and as I suppose I shall be big[7] enough to drive him out of the biggest tower of his castle."

So then the King sent letters and writs throughout all England, both the length and the breadth, for to summon all his knights. And so unto King Arthur drew many knights, dukes, and earls, that he had a great host, and when they were assembled the King informed them how Sir Lancelot had bereft him his Queen. Then the King and all his host made them ready to lay siege about Sir Lancelot where he lay within Joyous Garde.

[THE DEATH OF ARTHUR][8]

So upon Trinity Sunday at night King Arthur dreamed a wonderful dream, and in his dream him seemed that he saw upon a chafflet[9] a chair, and the chair was fast to a wheel, and thereupon sat King Arthur in the richest cloth of gold that might be made. And the King thought there was under him, far from him, an hideous deep black water, and therein was all manner of serpents, and worms, and wild beasts, foul and horrible. And suddenly the King thought that the wheel turned upside down, and he fell among the serpents, and every beast took him by a limb. And then the King cried as he lay in his bed, "Help, help!"

And then knights, squires, and yeomen awaked the King, and then he was so amazed that he wist[1] not where he was. And then so he awaked[2] until it was nigh day, and then he fell on slumbering again, not sleeping nor thoroughly waking. So the King seemed[3] verily that there came Sir Gawain unto him with a number of fair ladies with him. So when King Arthur saw him, he said, "Welcome, my sister's son. I weened ye had been dead. And now I see

4. Give up the pursuit of.
5. Prepare.
6. Appeal to.
7. Strong.
8. The pope arranges a truce, Guinevere is returned to Arthur, and Lancelot and his kin leave England to become rulers of France. At Gawain's instigation Arthur invades France to resume the war against Lancelot. Word comes to the king that Mordred has seized the kingdom, and Arthur leads his forces back to England. Mordred attacks them upon their landing, and Gawain is mortally wounded and dies, although not before he has repented for having insisted that Arthur fight Lancelot and has written Lancelot to come to the aid of his former lord.
9. Scaffold. "Him seemed": it seemed to him.
1. Knew.
2. Lay awake.
3. It seemed to the king.

thee on-live, much am I beholden unto Almighty Jesu. Ah, fair nephew and my sister's son, what been these ladies that hither be come with you?"

"Sir," said Sir Gawain, "all these be ladies for whom I have foughten for when I was man living. And all these are tho[4] that I did battle for in righteous quarrels, and God hath given them that grace, at their great prayer, because I did battle for them for their right, that they should bring me hither unto you. Thus much hath given me leave God, for to warn you of your death. For and ye fight as tomorn[5] with Sir Mordred, as ye both have assigned,[6] doubt ye not ye must be slain, and the most party of your people on both parties. And for the great grace and goodness that Almighty Jesu hath unto you, and for pity of you and many mo other good men there[7] shall be slain, God hath sent me to you of his special grace to give you warning that in no wise ye do battle as tomorn, but that ye take a treatise for a month-day.[8] And proffer you largely,[9] so that tomorn ye put in a delay. For within a month shall come Sir Lancelot with all his noble knights and rescue you worshipfully and slay Sir Mordred and all that ever will hold with him."

Then Sir Gawain and all the ladies vanished. And anon the King called upon his knights, squires, and yeomen, and charged them wightly[1] to fetch his noble lords and wise bishops unto him. And when they were come the King told them of his avision,[2] that Sir Gawain had told him and warned him that, and he fought on the morn, he should be slain. Then the King commanded Sir Lucan the Butler[3] and his brother Sir Bedivere the Bold, with two bishops with them, and charged them in any wise to take a treatise for a month-day with Sir Mordred. "And spare not: proffer him lands and goods as much as ye think reasonable."

So then they departed and came to Sir Mordred where he had a grim host of an hundred thousand, and there they entreated[4] Sir Mordred long time. And at the last Sir Mordred was agreed for to have Cornwall and Kent by King Arthur's days,[5] and after that, all England, after the days of King Arthur.

Then were they condescended[6] that King Arthur and Sir Mordred should meet betwixt both their hosts, and everich[7] of them should bring fourteen persons. And so they came with this word unto Arthur. Then said he, "I am glad that this is done," and so he went into the field.

And when King Arthur should depart, he warned all his host that, and they see any sword drawn, "Look ye come on fiercely and slay that traitor Sir Mordred, for I in no wise trust him." In like wise Sir Mordred warned his host that "And ye see any manner of sword drawn, look that ye come on fiercely, and so slay all that ever before you standeth, for in no wise I will not trust for this treatise." And in the same wise said Sir Mordred unto his host, "For I know well my father will be avenged upon me."

And so they met as their pointment[8] was and were agreed and accorded thoroughly. And wine was fetched and they drank together. Right so came an

4. Those.
5. If you fight tomorrow.
6. Decided.
7. I.e., who there. "Mo": more.
8. For a month from today. "Treatise": treaty, truce.
9. Make generous offers.
1. Quickly.
2. Dream.
3. "Butler" here is probably only a title of high rank, although it was originally used to designate the officer who had charge of wine for the king's table.
4. Dealt with.
5. During King Arthur's lifetime.
6. Agreed.
7. Each.
8. Arrangement.

adder out of a little heath-bush, and it stung a knight in the foot. And so when the knight felt him so stung, he looked down and saw the adder. And anon he drew his sword to slay the adder, and thought[9] none other harm. And when the host on both parties saw that sword drawn, then they blew beams,[1] trumpets, and horns, and shouted grimly. And so both hosts dressed them[2] together. And King Arthur took his horse and said, "Alas, this unhappy day!" and so rode to his party, and Sir Mordred in like wise.

And never since was there never seen a more dolefuller battle in no Christian land, for there was but rushing and riding, foining[3] and striking; and many a grim word was there spoken of either to other, and many a deadly stroke. But ever King Arthur rode throughout the battle[4] of Sir Mordred many times and did full nobly, as a noble king should do, and at all times he fainted never. And Sir Mordred did his devoir[5] that day and put himself in great peril.

And thus they fought all the long day, and never stinted[6] till the noble knights were laid to the cold earth. And ever they fought still till it was near night, and by then was there an hundred thousand laid dead upon the down. Then was King Arthur wood-wroth[7] out of measure when he saw his people so slain from him. And so he looked about him and could see no mo[8] of all his host, and good knights left no mo on-live, but two knights: the t'one[9] was Sir Lucan the Butler and [the other] his brother Sir Bedivere. And yet they were full sore wounded.

"Jesu, mercy," said the King, "where are all my noble knights become?[1] Alas that ever I should see this doleful day! For now," said King Arthur, "I am come to mine end. But would to God," said he, "that I wist[2] now where were that traitor Sir Mordred that has caused all this mischief."

Then King Arthur looked about and was ware where stood Sir Mordred leaning upon his sword among a great heap of dead men.

"Now give me my spear," said King Arthur unto Sir Lucan, "for yonder I have espied the traitor that all this woe hath wrought."

"Sir, let him be," said Sir Lucan, "for he is unhappy.[3] And if ye pass this unhappy day ye shall be right well revenged upon him. And, good lord, remember ye of your night's dream, and what the spirit of Sir Gawain told you tonight, and yet God of his great goodness hath preserved you hitherto. And for God's sake, my lord, leave off by this,[4] for, blessed be God, ye have won the field: for yet we been here three on-live, and with Sir Mordred is not one on-live. And therefore if ye leave off now, this wicked day of destiny is past."

"Now, tide[5] me death, tide me life," said the King, "now I see him yonder alone, he shall never escape mine hands. For at a better avail[6] shall I never have him."

"God speed you well!" said Sir Bedivere.

Then the King got his spear in both his hands and ran toward Sir Mordred, crying and saying, "Traitor, now is thy deathday come!"

And when Sir Mordred saw King Arthur he ran until him with his sword

9. Meant.
1. A kind of trumpet.
2. Prepared to come.
3. Lunging.
4. Battalion.
5. Knightly duty.
6. Stopped.
7. Mad with rage.
8. Others.
9. That one, i.e., the first.
1. What has become of all my noble knights?
2. Knew.
3. I.e., unlucky for you.
4. I.e., with this much accomplished.
5. Betide.
6. Advantage.

drawn in his hand, and there King Arthur smote Sir Mordred under the shield, with a foin[7] of his spear, throughout the body more than a fathom.[8] And when Sir Mordred felt that he had his death's wound, he thrust himself with the might that he had up to the burr[9] of King Arthur's spear, and right so he smote his father King Arthur with his sword holden in both his hands, upon the side of the head, that the sword pierced the helmet and the tay[1] of the brain. And therewith Sir Mordred dashed down stark dead to the earth.

And noble King Arthur fell in a swough[2] to the earth, and there he swooned oftentimes, and Sir Lucan and Sir Bedivere ofttimes heaved him up. And so, weakly betwixt them, they led him to a little chapel not far from the seaside, and when the King was there, him thought him reasonably eased. Then heard they people cry in the field. "Now go thou, Sir Lucan," said the King, "and do me to wit[3] what betokens that noise in the field."

So Sir Lucan departed, for he was grievously wounded in many places. And so as he yede[4] he saw and harkened by the moonlight how that pillers[5] and robbers were come into the field to pill and to rob many a full noble knight of brooches and bees[6] and of many a good ring and many a rich jewel. And who that were not dead all out there they slew them for their harness[7] and their riches. When Sir Lucan understood this work, he came to the King as soon as he might and told him all what he had heard and seen. "Therefore by my read,"[8] said Sir Lucan, "it is best that we bring you to some town."

"I would it were so," said the King, "but I may not stand, my head works[9] so. Ah, Sir Lancelot," said King Arthur, "this day have I sore missed thee. And alas that ever I was against thee, for now have I my death, whereof Sir Gawain me warned in my dream."

Then Sir Lucan took up the King the t'one party[1] and Sir Bedivere the other party; and in the lifting up the King swooned and in the lifting Sir Lucan fell in a swoon that part of his guts fell out of his body, and therewith the noble knight's heart burst. And when the King awoke he beheld Sir Lucan how he lay foaming at the mouth and part of his guts lay at his feet.

"Alas," said the King, "this is to me a full heavy[2] sight to see this noble duke so die for my sake, for he would have holpen[3] me that had more need of help than I. Alas that he would not complain him for[4] his heart was so set to help me. Now Jesu have mercy upon his soul."

Then Sir Bedivere wept for the death of his brother.

"Now leave this mourning and weeping, gentle knight," said the King, "for all this will not avail me. For wit thou well, and[5] I might live myself, the death of Sir Lucan would grieve me evermore. But my time passeth on fast," said the King. "Therefore," said King Arthur unto Sir Bedivere, "take thou here Excalibur[6] my good sword and go with it to yonder water's side; and when thou comest there I charge thee throw my sword in that water and come again and tell me what thou sawest there."

7. Thrust.
8. I.e., six feet.
9. Hand guard.
1. Edge.
2. Swoon.
3. Let me know.
4. Walked.
5. Plunderers.
6. Bracelets.
7. Armor. "All out": entirely.
8. Advice.
9. Aches.
1. On one side.
2. Sorrowful.
3. Helped.
4. Because.
5. If.
6. The sword that Arthur had received as a young man from the Lady of the Lake; it is presumably she who catches it when Bedivere finally throws it into the water.

"My lord," said Sir Bedivere, "your commandment shall be done, and [I shall] lightly[7] bring you word again."

So Sir Bedivere departed. And by the way he beheld that noble sword, that the pommel and the haft[8] was all precious stones. And then he said to himself, "If I throw this rich sword in the water, thereof shall never come good, but harm and loss." And then Sir Bedivere hid Excalibur under a tree. And so, as soon as he might, he came again unto the King and said he had been at the water and had thrown the sword into the water.

"What saw thou there?" said the King.

"Sir," he said, "I saw nothing but waves and winds."

"That is untruly said of thee," said the King. "And therefore go thou lightly again and do my commandment; as thou art to me lief[9] and dear, spare not, but throw it in."

Then Sir Bedivere returned again and took the sword in his hand. And yet him thought[1] sin and shame to throw away that noble sword. And so eft[2] he hid the sword and returned again and told the King that he had been at the water and done his commandment.

"What sawest thou there?" said the King.

"Sir," he said, "I saw nothing but waters wap and waves wan."[3]

"Ah, traitor unto me and untrue," said King Arthur, "now hast thou betrayed me twice. Who would have weened that thou that has been to me so lief and dear, and thou art named a noble knight, and would betray me for the riches of this sword. But now go again lightly, for thy long tarrying putteth me in great jeopardy of my life, for I have taken cold. And but if thou do now as I bid thee, if ever I may see thee I shall slay thee mine[4] own hands, for thou wouldest for my rich sword see me dead."

Then Sir Bedivere departed and went to the sword and lightly took it up, and so he went to the water's side; and there he bound the girdle[5] about the hilts, and threw the sword as far into the water as he might. And there came an arm and an hand above the water and took it and clutched it, and shook it thrice and brandished; and then vanished away the hand with the sword into the water. So Sir Bedivere came again to the King and told him what he saw.

"Alas," said the King, "help me hence, for I dread me I have tarried overlong."

Then Sir Bedivere took the King upon his back and so went with him to that water's side. And when they were at the water's side, even fast[6] by the bank hoved[7] a little barge with many fair ladies in it; and among them all was a queen; and all they had black hoods, and all they wept and shrieked when they saw King Arthur.

"Now put me into that barge," said the King; and so he did softly. And there received him three ladies with great mourning, and so they set them[8] down. And in one of their laps King Arthur laid his head, and then the queen said, "Ah, my dear brother, why have ye tarried so long from me? Alas, this wound on your head hath caught overmuch cold." And anon they rowed fromward the land, and Sir Bedivere beheld all tho ladies go froward him.

7. Quickly.
8. Handle. "Pommel": rounded knob on the hilt.
9. Beloved.
1. It seemed to him.
2. Again.
3. The phrase seems to mean "waters wash the shore and waves grow dark."
4. I.e., with mine.
5. Sword belt.
6. Close.
7. Waited.
8. I.e., they sat.

Then Sir Bedivere cried and said, "Ah, my lord Arthur, what shall become of me, now ye go from me and leave me here alone among mine enemies?"

"Comfort thyself," said the King, "and do as well as thou mayest, for in me is no trust for to trust in. For I must into the vale of Avilion[9] to heal me of my grievous wound. And if thou hear nevermore of me, pray for my soul."

But ever the queen and ladies wept and shrieked that it was pity to hear. And as soon as Sir Bedivere had lost the sight of the barge he wept and wailed and so took the forest, and went[1] all that night. And in the morning he was ware betwixt two holts hoar[2] of a chapel and an hermitage.[3]

* * *

Thus of Arthur I find no more written in books that been authorized,[4] neither more of the very certainty of his death heard I never read,[5] but thus was he led away in a ship wherein were three queens: that one was King Arthur's sister, Queen Morgan la Fée, the t'other[6] was the Queen of North Wales, and the third was the Queen of the Waste Lands. * * *

Now more of the death of King Arthur could I never find but that these ladies brought him to his burials,[7] and such one was buried there that the hermit bore witness that sometime was Bishop of Canterbury.[8] But yet the hermit knew not in certain that he was verily the body of King Arthur, for this tale Sir Bedivere, a Knight of the Table Round, made it to be written. Yet some men say in many parts of England that King Arthur is not dead, but had by the will of our Lord Jesu into another place. And men say that he shall come again and he shall win the Holy Cross. Yet I will not say that it shall be so, but rather I will say, Here in this world he changed his life. And many men say that there is written upon his tomb this verse: *Hic iacet Arthurus, rex quondam, rexque futurus.*[9]

[THE DEATHS OF LANCELOT AND GUINEVERE][1]

And thus upon a night there came a vision to Sir Lancelot and charged him, in remission[2] of his sins, to haste him unto Amesbury: "And by then[3] thou come there, thou shalt find Queen Guinevere dead. And therefore take thy fellows with thee, and purvey them of an horse-bier,[4] and fetch thou the corse[5] of her, and bury her by her husband, the noble King Arthur. So this avision[6] came to Lancelot thrice in one night. Then Sir Lancelot rose up ere day and told the hermit.

"It were well done," said the hermit, "that ye made you ready and that ye disobey not the avision."

Then Sir Lancelot took his eight fellows with him, and on foot they yede[7]

9. A legendary island, sometimes identified with the earthly paradise.
1. Walked. "Took": took to.
2. Ancient copses.
3. In the passage here omitted, Sir Bedivere meets the former bishop of Canterbury, now a hermit, who describes how on the previous night a company of ladies had brought to the chapel a dead body, asking that it be buried. Sir Bedivere exclaims that the dead man must have been King Arthur and vows to spend the rest of his life there in the chapel as a hermit.
4. That have authority.
5. Tell.
6. The second.
7. Grave.
8. Of whom the hermit, who was formerly bishop of Canterbury, bore witness.
9. "Here lies Arthur, who was once king and king will be again."
1. Guinevere enters a convent at Amesbury where Lancelot, returned with his companions to England, visits her, but she commands him never to see her again. Emulating her example, Lancelot joins the bishop of Canterbury and Bedivere in their hermitage where he takes holy orders and is joined in turn by seven of his fellow knights.
2. For the remission.
3. By the time.
4. Provide them with a horse-drawn hearse.
5. Body.
6. Dream.
7. Went.

from Glastonbury to Amesbury, the which is little more than thirty mile, and thither they came within two days, for they were weak and feeble to go. And when Sir Lancelot was come to Amesbury within the nunnery, Queen Guinevere died but half an hour afore. And the ladies told Sir Lancelot that Queen Guinevere told them all ere she passed that Sir Lancelot had been priest near a twelve-month:[8] "and hither he cometh as fast as he may to fetch my corse, and beside my lord King Arthur he shall bury me." Wherefore the Queen said in hearing of them all, "I beseech Almighty God that I may never have power to see Sir Lancelot with my worldly eyes."

"And thus," said all the ladies, "was ever her prayer these two days till she was dead."

Then Sir Lancelot saw her visage, but he wept not greatly, but sighed. And so he did all the observance of the service himself, both the *dirige*[9] and on the morn he sang mass. And there was ordained[1] an horse-bier, and so with an hundred torches ever burning about the corse of the Queen, and ever Sir Lancelot with his eight fellows went about[2] the horse-bier, singing and reading many an holy orison,[3] and frankincense upon the corse incensed.[4]

Thus Sir Lancelot and his eight fellows went on foot from Amesbury unto Glastonbury, and when they were come to the chapel and the hermitage, there she had a *dirige* with great devotion.[5] And on the morn the hermit that sometime[6] was Bishop of Canterbury sang the mass of requiem with great devotion, and Sir Lancelot was the first that offered, and then als[7] his eight fellows. And then she was wrapped in cered cloth of Rennes, from the top[8] to the toe, in thirtyfold, and after she was put in a web[9] of lead, and then in a coffin of marble.

And when she was put in the earth Sir Lancelot swooned and lay long still, while[1] the hermit came and awaked him, and said, "Ye be to blame, for ye displease God with such manner of sorrow-making."

"Truly," said Sir Lancelot, "I trust I do not displease God, for He knoweth mine intent—for my sorrow was not, nor is not, for any rejoicing of sin, but my sorrow may never have end. For when I remember of her beaulté and of her noblesse[2] that was both with her king and with her,[3] so when I saw his corse and her corse so lie together, truly mine heart would not serve to sustain my careful[4] body. Also when I remember me how by my defaute and mine orgule[5] and my pride that they were both laid full low, that were peerless that ever was living of Christian people, wit you well," said Sir Lancelot, "this remembered, of their kindness and mine unkindness, sank so to mine heart that I might not sustain myself." So the French book maketh mention.

Then Sir Lancelot never after ate but little meat,[6] nor drank, till he was dead, for then he sickened more and more and dried and dwined[7] away. For the Bishop nor none of his fellows might not make him to eat, and little he drank, that he was waxen by a kibbet[8] shorter than he was, that the people could not know him. For evermore, day and night, he prayed, but sometime he slumbered a broken sleep. Ever he was lying groveling on the tomb of King

8. Nearly twelve months.
9. Funeral service.
1. Prepared.
2. Around.
3. Reciting many a prayer.
4. Burned frankincense over the body.
5. Solemnity.
6. Once.
7. Also. "Offered": made his donation.
8. Head. "Cloth of Rennes": A shroud made of fine linen smeared with wax, produced at Rennes.
9. Afterward she was put in a sheet.
1. Until.
2. Her beauty and nobility.
3. That she and her king both had.
4. Sorrowful.
5. My fault and my haughtiness.
6. Food.
7. Wasted.
8. Grown by a cubit.

Arthur and Queen Guinevere, and there was no comfort that the Bishop nor Sir Bors, nor none of his fellows could make him—it availed not.

So within six weeks after, Sir Lancelot fell sick and lay in his bed. And then he sent for the Bishop that there was hermit, and all his true fellows. Then Sir Lancelot said with dreary steven,[9] "Sir Bishop, I pray you give to me all my rights that longeth[1] to a Christian man."

"It shall not need you,"[2] said the hermit and all his fellows. "It is but heaviness of your blood. Ye shall be well mended by the grace of God tomorn."

"My fair lords," said Sir Lancelot, "wit you well my careful body will into the earth; I have warning more than now I will say. Therefore give me my rights."

So when he was houseled and annealed[3] and had all that a Christian man ought to have, he prayed the Bishop that his fellows might bear his body to Joyous Garde. (Some men say it was Alnwick, and some men say it was Bamborough.) "Howbeit," said Sir Lancelot, "me repenteth[4] sore, but I made mine avow sometime that in Joyous Garde I would be buried. And because of breaking[5] of mine avow, I pray you all, lead me thither." Then there was weeping and wringing of hands among his fellows.

So at a season of the night they all went to their beds, for they all lay in one chamber. And so after midnight, against[6] day, the Bishop that was hermit, as he lay in his bed asleep, he fell upon a great laughter. And therewith all the fellowship awoke and came to the Bishop and asked him what he ailed.[7]

"Ah, Jesu mercy," said the Bishop, "why did ye awake me? I was never in all my life so merry and so well at ease."

"Wherefore?" said Sir Bors.

"Truly," said the Bishop, "here was Sir Lancelot with me, with mo[8] angels than ever I saw men in one day. And I saw the angels heave[9] up Sir Lancelot unto heaven, and the gates of heaven opened against him."

"It is but dretching of swevens,"[1] said Sir Bors, "for I doubt not Sir Lancelot aileth nothing but good."[2]

"It may well be," said the Bishop. "Go ye to his bed and then shall ye prove the sooth."

So when Sir Bors and his fellows came to his bed, they found him stark dead. And he lay as he had smiled, and the sweetest savor[3] about him that ever they felt. Then was there weeping and wringing of hands, and the greatest dole they made that ever made men. And on the morn the Bishop did his mass of Requiem, and after the Bishop and all the nine knights put Sir Lancelot in the same horse-bier that Queen Guinevere was laid in tofore that she was buried. And so the Bishop and they all together went with the body of Sir Lancelot daily, till they came to Joyous Garde. And ever they had an hundred torches burning about him.

And so within fifteen days they came to Joyous Garde. And there they laid his corse in the body of the choir,[4] and sang and read many psalters[5] and

9. Sad voice.
1. Pertains. "Rights": last sacrament.
2. You shall not need it.
3. Given communion and extreme unction.
4. I am sorry.
5. In order not to break.
6. Toward.
7. Ailed him.
8. More.
9. Lift.
1. Illusion of dreams.
2. Has nothing wrong with him.
3. Odor. A sweet scent is a conventional sign in saints' lives of a sanctified death.
4. The center of the chancel, the place of honor.
5. Psalms.

prayers over him and about him. And ever his visage was laid open and naked, that all folks might behold him; for such was the custom in tho[6] days that all men of worship should so lie with open visage till that they were buried.

And right thus as they were at their service, there came Sir Ector de Maris that had seven year sought all England, Scotland, and Wales, seeking his brother, Sir Lancelot. And when Sir Ector heard such noise and light in the choir of Joyous Garde, he alight and put his horse from him and came into the choir. And there he saw men sing and weep, and all they knew Sir Ector, but he knew not them. Then went Sir Bors unto Sir Ector and told him how there lay his brother, Sir Lancelot, dead. And then Sir Ector threw his shield, sword, and helm from him, and when he beheld Sir Lancelot's visage, he fell down in a swoon. And when he waked, it were hard any tongue to tell the doleful complaints that he made for his brother.

"Ah, Lancelot!" he said, "thou were head of all Christian knights. And now I dare say," said Sir Ector, "thou Sir Lancelot, there thou liest, that thou were never matched of earthly knight's hand. And thou were the courteoust[7] knight that ever bore shield. And thou were the truest friend to thy lover that ever bestrode horse, and thou were the truest lover, of a sinful man,[8] that ever loved woman, and thou were the kindest man that ever struck with sword. And thou were the goodliest person that ever came among press of knights, and thou was the meekest man and the gentlest that ever ate in hall among ladies, and thou were the sternest knight to thy mortal foe that ever put spear in the rest."[9]

Then there was weeping and dolor out of measure.

Thus they kept Sir Lancelot's corse aloft fifteen days, and then they buried it with great devotion. And then at leisure they went all with the Bishop of Canterbury to his hermitage, and there they were together more than a month.

Then Sir Constantine that was Sir Cador's son of Cornwall was chosen king of England, and he was a full noble knight, and worshipfully he ruled this realm. And then this King Constantine sent for the Bishop of Canterbury, for he heard say where he was. And so he was restored unto his bishopric and left that hermitage, and Sir Bedivere was there ever still hermit to his life's end.

Then Sir Bors de Ganis, Sir Ector de Maris, Sir Gahalantine, Sir Galihud, Sir Galihodin, Sir Blamour, Sir Bleoberis, Sir Villiars le Valiant, Sir Clarrus of Clermount, all these knights drew them to their countries. Howbeit[1] King Constantine would have had them with him, but they would not abide in this realm. And there they all lived in their countries as holy men.

And some English books make mention that they went never out of England after the death of Sir Lancelot—but that was but favor of makers.[2] For the French book maketh mention—and is authorized—that Sir Bors, Sir Ector, Sir Blamour, and Sir Bleoberis went into the Holy Land, thereas Jesu Christ was quick[3] and dead, and anon as they had stablished their lands;[4] for the book saith so Sir Lancelot commanded them for to do ere ever he passed out of this world. There these four knights did many battles upon the miscreaunts,[5] or Turks, and there they died upon a Good Friday for God's sake.

6. Those.
7. Most courteous.
8. Of any man born in original sin.
9. Support for the butt of the lance.
1. However.
2. The authors' bias.
3. Living. "Thereas": where.
4. As soon as they had put their lands in order.
5. Infidels.

Here is the end of the whole book of King Arthur and of his noble knights of the Round Table, that when they were whole together there was ever an hundred and forty. And here is the end of *The Death of Arthur*.[6]

I pray you all gentlemen and gentlewomen that readeth this book of Arthur and his knights from the beginning to the ending, pray for me while I am alive that God send me good deliverance. And when I am dead, I pray you all pray for my soul.

For this book was ended the ninth year of the reign of King Edward the Fourth, by Sir Thomas Malory, knight, as Jesu help him for His great might, as he is the servant of Jesu both day and night.

1469–70 1485

6. By the "whole book" Malory refers to the entire work; the *Death of Arthur*, which Caxton made the title of the entire work, refers to the last part of Malory's book.

The Sixteenth Century 1485–1603

1485: Accession of Henry VII inaugurates Tudor dynasty
1509: Accession of Henry VIII
1517: Martin Luther's Wittenberg Theses; beginning of the Reformation
1534: Henry VIII declares himself head of the English church
1557: Publication of Tottel's *Songs and Sonnets,* containing poems by Sir Thomas Wyatt; Henry Howard, earl of Surrey; and others
1558: Accession of Elizabeth I
1576: Building of The Theater, the first permanent structure in England for the presentation of plays
1588: Defeat of the Spanish Armada
1603: Death of Elizabeth I and accession of James I, the first of the Stuart kings

The Ancient Roman poet Virgil characterized Britain as a wild, remote place set apart from all the world, and it must still have seemed so in the early sixteenth century to the cosmopolitan inhabitants of cities like Venice, Madrid, and Paris. To be sure, some venturesome travelers crossed the Channel and visited London, Oxford, or Cambridge, bringing home reports of bustling markets, impressive universities, and ambitious nobles vying for position at an increasingly powerful royal court. But these visitors were but a trickle compared with the flood of wealthy young Englishmen (and, to a lesser extent, Englishwomen) who embarked at the first opportunity for the Continent. English travelers were virtually obliged to learn some French, Italian, or Spanish, for they would encounter very few people who knew their language. On returning home, they would frequently wear foreign fashions—much to the disgust of moralists—and would pepper their speech with foreign phrases.

At the beginning of the sixteenth century, the English language had almost no prestige abroad, and there were those at home who doubted that it could serve as a suitable medium for serious, elevated, or elegant discourse. It is no accident that one of the most important works of early sixteenth-century literature, Thomas More's *Utopia,* was not written in English: More, who began his great book in 1515 when he was on a diplomatic mission in the Netherlands, was writing for an international intellectual community, and as such his language of choice was Latin. His work quickly became famous throughout Europe, but it was not translated into English until the 1550s. Evidently, neither More himself nor the London printers and booksellers thought it imperative to publish a vernacular *Utopia.* Yet by the century's end there were signs of a great increase in what we might call linguistic self-confidence, signs that at least some contemporary observers were aware that something extraordinary had happened to their language. Though in 1600 England still remained somewhat peripheral to the Continent, English had been fashioned into an immensely powerful expressive medium, one whose cadences in the works of Marlowe, Shakespeare, or the translators of the Bible continue after more than four centuries to thrill readers.

How did it come about that by the century's end so many remarkable poems, plays, and prose works were written in English? The answer lies in part in the spectacular creativity of a succession of brilliant writers, many of the best of whom are represented in these pages. Still, a vital literary culture is the product of a complex process, involving thousands of more modest, half-hidden creative acts sparked by a wide range of motives, some of which we will briefly explore.

THE COURT AND THE CITY

The development of the English language in the sixteenth century is linked at least indirectly to the consolidation and strengthening of the English state. Preoccupied by violent clashes between the thuggish feudal retainers of rival barons, England through most of the fifteenth century had rather limited time and inclination to cultivate rhetorical skills. The social and economic health of the nation had been severely damaged by the so-called Wars of the Roses, a vicious, decades-long struggle for royal power between the noble houses of York and Lancaster. The struggle was resolved by the establishment of the Tudor dynasty that ruled England from 1485 to 1603. The family name derives from Owen Tudor, an ambitious Welshman who himself had no claim to the throne but who married Catherine of Valois, widow of the Lancastrian king Henry V. Their grandson, the earl of Richmond, who also inherited Lancastrian blood on his mother's side, became the first Tudor monarch: he won the crown by leading the army that defeated and killed the reigning Yorkist king, Richard III, at the battle of Bosworth Field. The victorious Richmond, crowned King Henry VII in 1485, promptly consolidated his rather shaky claim to the throne by marrying Elizabeth of the house of York, hence effectively uniting the two rival factions.

England's barons, impoverished and divided by the dynastic wars, could not effectively oppose the new power of the Crown, and the leaders of the Church also generally supported the royal power. The wily Henry VII was therefore able to counter the multiple and competing power structures characteristic of feudal society and to impose a much stronger central authority and order on the nation. Initiated by the first Tudor sovereign, this consolidation progressed throughout the sixteenth century; by the reign of the last Tudor—Henry's granddaughter, Elizabeth I—though the ruler still needed the consent of Parliament on crucial matters (including the all-important one of levying taxes), the royal court had concentrated in itself much of the nation's power.

The court was a center of culture as well as power: court entertainments such as theater and masque (a sumptuous, elaborately costumed performance of dance, song, and poetry); court fashions in dress and speech; court tastes in painting, music, and poetry—all shaped the taste and the imagination of the country as a whole. Culture and power were not, in any case, easily separable in Tudor England. In a society with no freedom of speech as we understand it and with relatively limited means of mass communication, important public issues were often aired indirectly, through what we might now regard as entertainment, while lyrics that to us seem slight and nonchalant could serve as carefully crafted manifestations of rhetorical agility by aspiring courtiers.

Whereas late medieval noblemen had guarded their power by keeping their distance from London and the king, ruling over semi-independent fiefdoms, in the Tudor era the route to power lay in proximity to the royal body. (One of the coveted positions in the court of Henry VIII was Groom of the Stool, "close stool" being the Tudor term for toilet.) The monarch's chief ministers and favorites were the primary channels through which patronage was dispensed to courtiers who competed for offices in the court, the government bureaucracies, the royal household, the army, the church, and the universities, or who sought titles, grants of land, leases, or similar favors. But if proximity held out the promise of wealth and power, it also harbored danger. Festive evenings with the likes of the ruthless Henry VIII were not occasions for relaxation. The court fostered paranoia, and an attendant obsession with secrecy, spying, duplicity, and betrayal.

Tudor courtiers were torn between the need to protect themselves and the equally pressing need to display themselves. For lessons in the art of intrigue, many no doubt turned to Machiavelli's notorious *Il Principe* (The Prince), with its cool guidance on how power may be gained and kept. For advice on the cultivation and display of the self, they could resort to the still more influential *Il Cortegiano* (The Courtier) by Count Baldassare Castiglione. It was particularly important, Castiglione wrote, to conceal the effort that lay behind elegant accomplishments, so that they would seem natural. In this anxious atmosphere, courtiers became highly practiced at crafting and deciphering graceful words with double or triple meanings. Sixteenth-century poets had much to learn from courtiers, the Elizabethan critic George Puttenham observed; indeed many of the best poets in the period, Sir Thomas Wyatt, Sir Philip Sidney, Sir Walter Ralegh, and others, *were* courtiers.

If court culture fostered performances for a small coterie audience, other forces in Tudor England pulled toward a more public sphere. Markets expanded significantly, international trade flourished, and cities throughout the realm experienced a rapid surge in size and importance. London's population in particular soared, from 60,000 in 1520, to 120,000 in 1550, to 375,000 a century later, making it the largest and fastest-growing city not only in England but in all of Europe. Every year in the first half of the seventeenth century about 10,000 people migrated to London from other parts of England—wages in London tended to be around 50 percent higher than in the rest of the country—and it is estimated that one in eight English people lived in London at some point in their lives. Elderly Londoners in the 1590s could barely recognize the city of their childhood; London's boom was one factor among many contributing to the sense of a culture moving at increasing velocity away from its historical roots.

About a decade before Henry VII won his throne, the art of printing from movable metal type, a German invention, had been introduced into England by William Caxton (ca. 1422–1491), who had learned and practiced it in the Low Countries. Though reliable statistics are impossible to come by, literacy seems to have increased during the fifteenth century and still more during the sixteenth, when Protestantism encouraged a direct encounter with the Bible. Printing made books cheaper and more plentiful, providing more opportunity to read and more incentive to learn. The greater availability of books may also have reinforced the trend toward silent reading, a trend that gradually transformed what had been a communal experience into a more intimate encounter with a text.

Yet it would be a mistake to imagine these changes as sudden and dramatic. Manuscripts retained considerable prestige among the elite; throughout the sixteenth and well into the seventeenth centuries court poets in particular were wary of the "stigma of print" that might mark their verse as less exclusive. Although Caxton, who was an author and translator as well as a printer, introduced printed books, he attempted to cater to courtly tastes by translating works whose tone was more medieval than modern. The fascination with the old chivalric code of behavior is reflected as well in the jousts and tournaments that continued at court for a century, long after gunpowder had rendered them obsolete. As often in an age of spectacular novelty, many people looked back to an idealized past. Indeed the great innovations of the Tudor era—intellectual, governmental, and religious—were all presented at the time as attempts to restore lost links with ancient traditions.

RENAISSANCE HUMANISM

During the fifteenth century a few English clerics and government officials had journeyed to Italy and had seen something of the extraordinary cultural and intellectual movement flourishing in the city-states there. That movement, generally known as the Renaissance, involved a rebirth of letters and arts stimulated by the recovery of texts and artifacts from classical antiquity, the development of techniques such as linear perspective, and the creation of powerful new aesthetic practices based on classical models. It also unleashed new ideas and new social, political, and economic forces that gradually displaced the spiritual and communal values of the Middle Ages. To Renaissance intellectuals and artists, the achievements of the pagan philosophers of ancient Greece and Rome came to seem more compelling than the subtle distinctions drawn by medieval Christian theologians. In the brilliant, intensely competitive, and vital world of Leonardo da Vinci and Michelangelo, the submission of the human spirit to penitential discipline gave way to unleashed curiosity, individual self-assertion, and a powerful conviction that man was the measure of all things. Yet the superb human figure placed at the center of the Renaissance world-view was also seen as remarkably malleable. "We have made thee neither of heaven nor of earth, neither mortal nor immortal," God tells Adam, in the Florentine Pico della Mirandola's *Oration on the Dignity of Man* (1486), "so that with freedom of choice and with honor, as though the maker and molder of thyself, thou mayest fashion thyself in whatever shape thou shalt prefer." "As though the maker and molder of thyself": this vision of self-fashioning may be glimpsed in the poetry of Petrarch, the sculpture of Donatello, and the statecraft of Lorenzo de' Medici. But in England it was not until Henry VII's reign brought some measure of political stability that the Renaissance could take root, and it was not until the accession of Henry VIII that it began to flower.

This flowering, when it occurred, came not, as in Italy, in the visual arts and architecture. It came rather in the spiritual and intellectual orientation known as humanism. More's *Utopia* (1516), with its dream of human existence entirely transformed by a radical change in institutional arrangements, is an extreme instance of a general humanist interest in education: in England and elsewhere, humanism was bound up with struggles over the purposes of education and curriculum reform. The great Dutch humanist Erasmus, who spent some time in England and developed a close friendship with More, was a leader in the assault on what he and others regarded as a hopelessly narrow and outmoded intellectual culture based on scholastic hair-splitting and a dogmatic adherence to the philosophy of Aristotle. English humanists, including John Colet (who, as dean of St. Paul's Cathedral, recast its grammar school on humanist principles), Roger Ascham (tutor to Princess Elizabeth), and Sir Thomas Elyot, wrote treatises on education to promote the kind of learning they regarded as the most suitable preparation for public service. That education—predominantly male and conducted by tutors in wealthy families or in grammar schools—was still ordered according to the subjects of the medieval *trivium* (grammar, logic, and rhetoric) and *quadrivium* (arithmetic, geometry, astronomy, and music), but its focus shifted from training for the Church to the general acquisition of "literature," in the sense both of literacy and of cultural knowledge. For some of the more intellectually ambitious humanists, that knowledge extended to ancient Greek, whose enthusiastic adherents began to challenge the entrenched prestige of Latin.

Still, at the core of the curriculum remained the study of Latin, the mastery of which was in effect a prolonged male puberty rite involving pain as well as pleasure. Though some educators counseled mildness, punishment was an established part of the pedagogy of the age, and even gifted students could scarcely have escaped recurrent flogging. The purpose was to train the sons of the nobility and gentry to speak and write good Latin, the language of diplomacy, of the professions, and of all higher learning. Their sisters were always educated at home or in other noble houses. They chiefly learned modern languages, religion, music, and needlework, but they very seldom received the firm grounding in ancient languages and classical literature so central to Renaissance culture. Elizabethan schoolmasters sought to impart facility and rhetorical elegance, but the books their students laboriously pored over were not considered mere exhibitions of literary style: from the *Sententiae Pueriles* (Maxims for Children) for beginners on up through the dramatists Terence, Plautus, and Seneca, the poets Virgil and Horace, and the orator Cicero, the classics were also studied for the moral, political, and philosophical truths they contained. Though originating in pagan times, those truths could, in the opinion of many humanists, be reconciled to the moral vision of Christianity. The result, perplexing for some modern readers, is that pagan gods and goddesses flourish on the pages of even such a devoutly Christian poem as Edmund Spenser's *Faerie Queene*.

Humanists committed to classical learning were faced with the question of whether to write their own works in Latin or in English. To many learned men, influenced both by the humanist exaltation of the classical languages and by the characteristic Renaissance desire for eternal fame, the national languages seemed relatively unstable and ephemeral. Intellectuals had long shared a pan-European world of scientific inquiry, so that works by such English scientists as William Gilbert, William Harvey, and Francis Bacon easily joined those by Nicolaus Copernicus, Johannes Kepler, and Andreas Vesalius on the common linguistic ground of Latin. But throughout Europe nationalism and the expansion of the reading public were steadily strengthening the power and allure of the vernacular. The famous schoolmaster Richard Mulcaster (ca. 1530–1611), Spenser's teacher, captured this emergent sense of national identity in singing the praises of his native tongue:

> Is it not indeed a marvelous bondage, to become servants to one tongue for learning's sake the most of our time, with loss of most time, whereas we may have the very same treasure in our own tongue, with the gain of more time? our own bearing the joyful title of our liberty and freedom, the Latin tongue remembering us of our thralldom and bondage? I love Rome, but London better; I favor Italy, but England more; I honor the Latin, but I worship the English.

These two impulses—humanist reverence for the classics and English pride in the vernacular language—gave rise to many distinguished translations throughout the century: Homer's *Iliad* and *Odyssey* by George Chapman, Plutarch's *Lives of the Noble Grecians and Romans* by Sir Thomas North, and Ovid's *Metamorphoses* by Arthur Golding. Translators also sought to make available in English the most notable literary works in the modern languages: Castiglione's *Il Cortegiano* by Sir Thomas Hoby, Ariosto's *Orlando furioso* (Orlando mad) by Sir John Harington, and Montaigne's *Essais* by John Florio. The London book trade of the sixteenth century was a thoroughly international affair.

THE REFORMATION

There had long been serious ideological and institutional tensions in the religious life of England, but officially at least England in the early sixteenth century had a single religion, Catholicism, whose acknowledged head was the pope in Rome. For its faithful adherents the Roman Catholic Church was the central institution in their lives, a universal infallible guide to human existence from cradle to grave and on into the life to come. They were instructed by its teachings, corrected by its discipline, sustained by its sacraments, and comforted by its promises. At Mass, its most sacred ritual, the congregation could witness a miracle, as the priest held aloft the Host and uttered the words that transformed the bread and wine into the body and blood of God incarnate. A vast system of confession, pardons, penance, absolution, indulgences, sacred relics, and ceremonies gave the unmarried male clerical hierarchy great power, at once spiritual and material, over their largely illiterate flock. The Bible, the liturgy, and most of the theological discussions were in Latin, which few lay people could understand; however, religious doctrine and spirituality were mediated to them by the priests, by beautiful church art and music, and by the liturgical ceremonies of daily life—festivals, holy days, baptisms, marriages, exorcisms, and funerals.

Several of the key doctrines and practices of the Catholic Church had been challenged in fourteenth-century England by the teachings of John Wycliffe and his followers, known as the Lollards. But the heretical challenge had been ruthlessly suppressed, and the embers of dissent lay largely dormant until they were ignited once again in Germany by Martin Luther, an Augustinian monk and professor of theology at the University of Wittenberg. What began in November 1517 as an academic disputation grew with amazing speed into a bitter, far-reaching, and bloody revolt that forever ruptured the unity of Western Christendom.

When Luther rose up against the ancient church, he did so in the name of private conscience enlightened by a personal reading of the Scriptures. A person of formidable intellectual energy, eloquence, and rhetorical violence, Luther charged that the pope and his hierarchy were the servants of Satan and that the Church had degenerated into a corrupt, worldly conspiracy designed to bilk the credulous and subvert secular authority. Salvation depended upon destroying this conspiracy and enabling all of the people to regain direct access to the word of God by means of vernacular translations of the Bible. The common watchwords of the Reformation, as the movement Luther sparked came to be known, were *sola scriptura* and *sola fide*: only the Scriptures (not the Church or tradition or the clerical hierarchy) have authority in matters of religion and should determine what an individual must believe and practice; only the faith of the individual (not good works or the scrupulous observance of religious rituals) can effect a Christian's salvation.

These tenets, heretical in the eyes of the Catholic Church, spread and gathered force, especially in northern Europe, where major leaders like the Swiss pastor Ulrich Zwingli in Zurich and the French theologian John Calvin in Geneva, elaborating various and sometimes conflicting doctrinal principles, organized the populace to overturn the existing church and established new institutional structures. In England, however, the Reformation began less with popular discontent and theological disputation than with dynastic politics and royal greed. Henry VIII, who had received from Pope Leo X the title Defender of the Faith for writing a diatribe against Luther, craved a legitimate son to succeed to the throne, and his queen, Catherine of Aragon, failed to give him one. (Catherine had borne six children, but only a daughter, Mary, survived infancy.) After lengthy negotiations, the pope, under pressure from Catherine's powerful Spanish family, refused to grant the king the divorce he sought in order to marry Anne Boleyn. A series of momentous events followed, as England lurched away from the Church of Rome.

In 1531 Henry forced the entire clergy of England to beg pardon for having usurped royal authority in the administration of canon law (the law that governed such matters as divorce). Two years later Henry's marriage to Catherine was officially declared null and void and Anne Boleyn was crowned queen. The king was promptly excommunicated by the pope, Clement VII. In the following year, a parliamentary Act of Succession required an oath from all adult male subjects confirming the new dynastic settlement. Thomas More and John Fisher, the bishop of Rochester, were among the small number who refused. The Act of Supremacy, passed later in the year, formally declared the king to be "Supreme Head of the Church in England" and again required an oath to this effect. In 1535 and 1536 further acts made it treasonous to refuse the oath of royal supremacy or, as More had tried to do, to remain silent. The first victims were three Carthusian monks who rejected the oath—"How could the king, a layman," said one of them, "be Head of the Church of England?"—and in May 1535 were duly hanged, drawn, and quartered. A few weeks later Fisher and More were convicted and beheaded. Between 1536 and 1539, under the direction of Henry's powerful secretary of state, Thomas Cromwell, England's monasteries were suppressed and their vast wealth seized by the Crown.

Royal defiance of the authority of Rome was a key element in the Reformation but did not by itself constitute the establishment of Protestantism in England. On the contrary, in the same year that Fisher and More were martyred for their adherence to Roman Catholicism, twenty-five Protestants, members of a sect known as Anabaptists, were burned for heresy on a single day. Through most of his reign, Henry remained an equal-opportunity persecutor, pitiless to Catholics loyal to Rome and hostile to many of those who espoused Reformation ideas, though these ideas, aided greatly by the printing press, gradually established themselves on English soil.

Upon Henry's death in 1547, his son, Edward (by his third wife, Jane Seymour), came to the throne. Both the ten-year-old Edward and his successive Protectors, the dukes of Somerset and Northumberland, were staunch Protestants, and reformers hastened to transform the English church accordingly. During Edward's brief reign, Thomas Cranmer, the archbishop of Canterbury, formulated the forty-two articles of religion which became the core of Anglican orthodoxy and wrote the first *Book of Common Prayer*, which was officially adopted in 1549 as the basis of English worship services.

The sickly Edward died in 1553, only six years after his accession to the throne, and was succeeded by his half-sister Mary (Henry VIII's daughter by his first wife, Catherine), who immediately took steps to return her kingdom to Roman Catholicism. Though she was unable to get Parliament to agree to return church lands seized under Henry VIII, she restored the Catholic Mass, once again affirmed the authority of the pope, and put down a rebellion that sought to depose her. Seconded by her ardently Catholic husband, Philip II, king of Spain, she initiated a series of religious persecutions that earned her (from her enemies) the name Bloody Mary. Hundreds of Protestants took refuge abroad in cities like Calvin's Geneva; almost three hundred less-fortunate Protestants were condemned as heretics and burned at the stake. Yet for thousands of others, Mary's reign came as a liberation; the rapid restoration of old Catholic ornaments to parish churches all over England indicates that they had not in fact been confiscated or destroyed as ordered, but simply hidden away, in hopes of better times.

Mary died childless in 1558, and her younger half-sister, Elizabeth, became queen. Elizabeth's succession had been by no means assured. For if Protestants regarded Henry VIII's marriage to Catherine as invalid and hence deemed Mary illegitimate, so Catholics regarded his marriage to Anne Boleyn as invalid and hence deemed *her* daughter illegitimate. Henry VIII himself seemed to support both views, since only three years after divorcing Catherine, he beheaded Anne on charges of treason and adultery and urged Parliament to invalidate the marriage. Moreover, though during her sister's reign Elizabeth outwardly complied with the official Catholic religious observance, Mary and her advisers suspected her of Protestant leanings, and the young princess's life was in grave danger. Poised and circumspect, Elizabeth warily evaded the traps that were set for her. When she ascended the throne, her actions were scrutinized for some indication of the country's future course. During her coronation procession, when a girl in an allegorical pageant presented her with a Bible in English translation—banned under Mary's reign—Elizabeth kissed the book, held it up reverently, and laid it to her breast. By this simple yet profound (and carefully choreographed) gesture, Elizabeth signaled England's return to the Reformation.

Many English men and women, of all classes, remained loyal to the old Catholic faith, but English authorities under Elizabeth moved steadily, if cautiously, toward ensuring at least an outward conformity to the official Protestant settlement. Recusants, those who refused to attend regular Sunday services in their parish churches, were heavily fined. Anyone who wished to receive a university degree, to be ordained as a priest in the Church of England, or to be named as an officer of the state had to swear an oath to the royal supremacy. Commissioners were sent throughout the land to confirm that religious services were following the officially approved liturgy and to investigate any reported backsliding into Catholic practice or, alternatively, any attempts to introduce reforms more radical than the queen and her bishops had chosen to embrace. For the Protestant exiles who streamed back were eager not only to undo the damage Mary had done but also to carry the Reformation much further than it had gone. A minority, who would come to be known as Puritans, sought to dismantle the church hierarchy, to purge the calendar of folk customs deemed pagan and the church service of ritual practices deemed superstitious, to dress the clergy in simple garb, and, at the extreme edge, to smash "idolatrous" statues, crucifixes, and altarpieces. Throughout her long reign, however, Elizabeth remained cautiously conservative and determined to hold religious zealotry in check.

In the space of a single lifetime, England had gone officially from Roman Catholicism, to Catholicism under the supreme headship of the English king, to a guarded Protestantism, to a more radical Protestantism, to a renewed and aggressive Roman Catholicism, and finally to Protestantism again. Each of these shifts was accompanied by danger, persecution, and death. It was enough to make people wary. Or skeptical. Or extremely agile.

A FEMALE MONARCH IN A MALE WORLD

In the last year of Mary's reign, the Scottish Calvinist minister John Knox thundered against what he called "the monstrous regiment of women." After the Protestant Elizabeth came to the throne the following year, Knox and his religious brethren were less inclined to denounce all female rulers, but in England, as elsewhere in Europe, there remained a widespread conviction that women were unsuited to wield power over men. Many men seem to have regarded the capacity for rational thought as exclusively male; women, they assumed, were led only by their passions. While gentlemen mastered the arts of rhetoric and warfare, gentlewomen were expected to display the virtues of silence and good housekeeping. Among upper-class males, the will to dominate others was acceptable and indeed admired; the same will in women was condemned as a grotesque and dangerous aberration.

Apologists for the queen countered these prejudices by appealing to historical precedent and legal theory. History offered inspiring examples of just female rulers, notably Deborah, the biblical prophetess who had judged Israel. In the legal sphere, Crown lawyers advanced the theory of "the king's two bodies." As England's crowned head, Elizabeth's person was mystically divided between her mortal "body natural" and the immortal "body politic." While the queen's natural body was inevitably subject to the failings of human flesh, the body politic was timeless and perfect. In political terms, therefore, Elizabeth's sex was a matter of no consequence, a thing indifferent.

Elizabeth, who had received a fine humanist education and an extended, dangerous lesson in the art of survival, made it immediately clear that she intended to rule in more than name only. She assembled a group of trustworthy advisers, foremost among them William Cecil (later created Lord Burghley), but she insisted on making many of the crucial decisions herself. Like many Renaissance monarchs, Elizabeth was drawn to the idea of royal absolutism, the theory that ultimate power was quite properly concentrated in her person and indeed that God had appointed her to be His deputy in the kingdom. Opposition to her rule, in this view, was not only a political act but also a kind of impiety, a blasphemous grudging against the will of God. Supporters of absolutism contended that God commands obedience even to manifestly wicked rulers whom He has sent to punish the sinfulness of humankind. Such arguments were routinely made in speeches and political tracts and from the pulpits of churches, where they were incorporated into the *Book of Homilies* that clergymen were required to read out to their congregations.

In reality, Elizabeth's power was not absolute. The government had a network of spies, informers, and *agents provocateurs*, but it lacked a standing army, a national police force, an efficient system of communication, and an extensive bureaucracy. Above all, the queen had limited financial resources and needed to turn periodically to an independent and often recalcitrant Parliament, which by long tradition had the sole right to levy taxes and to grant subsidies. Members of the House of Commons were elected from their boroughs, not appointed by the monarch, and though the queen had considerable influence over their decisions, she could by no means dictate policy. Under these constraints, Elizabeth ruled through a combination of adroit political maneuvering and imperious command, all the while enhancing her authority in the eyes of both court and country by means of an extraordinary cult of love.

"We all loved her," Elizabeth's godson Sir John Harington wrote, with just a touch of irony, a few years after the queen's death, "for she said she loved us." Ambassadors, courtiers, and parliamentarians all submitted to Elizabeth's cult of love, in which the queen's gender was transformed from a potential liability into a significant asset. Those who approached her generally did so on their knees and were expected to address her with the most extravagant compliments; she in turn spoke, when it suited her to do so, in a comparable language of love. The court moved in an atmosphere of romance, with music, dancing, plays, and the elaborate, fancy-dress entertainments called masques. The queen adorned herself in dazzling clothes and rich jewels. When she went on one of her summer "progresses," ceremonial journeys through her land, she looked like an exotic, sacred image in a religious cult of love, and her noble hosts virtually bankrupted themselves to lavish upon her the costliest pleasures. England's leading artists, such as the poet Edmund Spenser and the painter Nicholas Hilliard, enlisted themselves in the celebration of Elizabeth's mystery, likening her to the goddesses of mythology and the heroines of the Bible: Diana, Astraea, Cynthia, Deborah. The cultural sources of the so-called "cult of Elizabeth" were both secular (her courtiers could pine for her as the cruelly chaste mistress celebrated in Petrarchan love poetry) and sacred (the veneration that under Catholicism had been due to the Virgin Mary could now be directed toward England's semi-divine queen).

There was a sober, even grim aspect to these poetical fantasies: Elizabeth was brilliant at playing off one dangerous faction against another, now turning her gracious smiles on one favorite, now honoring his hated rival, now suddenly looking elsewhere and raising an obscure upstart to royal favor. And when she was disobeyed or when she felt that her prerogatives had been challenged, she was capable of an anger that, as Harington put it, "left no doubtings whose daughter she was." Thus when Sir Walter Ralegh, one of the queen's glittering favorites, married without her knowledge or consent, he found himself promptly imprisoned in the Tower of London. Or when the Protestant polemicist John Stubbes ventured to publish a pamphlet stridently denouncing the queen's proposed marriage to the French Catholic duke of Anjou, Stubbes and his publisher were arrested and had their right hands chopped off. (After receiving the blow, the now prudent Stubbes lifted his hat with his remaining hand and cried, "God save the Queen!")

THE KINGDOM IN DANGER

Beset by Catholic and Protestant extremists, Elizabeth contrived to forge a moderate compromise that enabled her realm to avert the massacres and civil wars that poisoned France and other countries on the Continent. But menace was never far off, and there were continual fears of conspiracy, rebellion, and assassination. Suspicion swirled around Mary, Queen of Scots, who had been driven from her own kingdom in 1568 and had taken refuge in England. The presence, under a kind of house arrest, of a Catholic queen with a plausible claim to the English throne was the source of widespread anxiety and helped generate recurrent rumors of plots. Some of these were real enough, others imaginary, still others fabricated by the secret agents of the government's intelligence service under the direction of Sir Francis Walsingham. Fears of Catholic conspiracies intensified greatly after Spanish imperial armies invaded the Netherlands in order to stamp out Protestant rebels (1567), after the St. Bartholomew's Day Massacre of Protestants (Huguenots) in France (1572), and after the assassination of Europe's other major Protestant leader, William of Orange (1584).

The queen's life seemed to be in even greater danger after Pope Gregory XIII's proclamation in 1580 that the assassination of the great heretic Elizabeth (who had been excommunicated a decade before) would not constitute a mortal sin. The immediate effect of the proclamation was to make life more difficult for English Catholics, most of whom were loyal to the queen but who fell under grave suspicion. Suspicion was heightened by the clandestine presence of English Jesuits, trained at seminaries abroad and smuggled back into England to serve the Roman Catholic cause. When, after several botched conspiracies had been disclosed, Elizabeth's spymaster Walsingham unearthed another assassination plot in the correspondence between the Queen of Scots and the Catholic Anthony Babington, the wretched Mary's fate was sealed. After a public display of vacillation and perhaps with genuine regret, Elizabeth signed the death warrant, and her cousin was beheaded.

The long-anticipated military confrontation with Catholic Spain was now unavoidable. Elizabeth learned that Philip II, her former brother-in-law and one-time suitor, was preparing to send an enormous fleet against her island realm. The Armada was to sail first to the Netherlands, where a Spanish army would be waiting to embark and invade England. Barring its way was England's small fleet of well-armed and highly maneuverable fighting vessels, backed up by ships from the merchant navy. The Invincible Armada reached English waters in July 1588, only to be routed in one of the most famous and decisive naval battles in European history. Then, in what many viewed as an Act of God on behalf of Protestant England, the Spanish fleet was dispersed and all but destroyed by violent storms.

As England braced itself to withstand the invasion that never came, Elizabeth appeared in person to review a detachment of soldiers assembled at Tilbury, on the Thames estuary. Dressed in a white gown and a silver breastplate, she declared that though some among her councilors had urged her not to appear before a large crowd of armed men, she would never fail to trust the loyalty of her faithful and loving subjects. Nor did she fear the Spanish armies. "I know I have the body but of a weak and feeble woman," Elizabeth declared, "but I have the heart and stomach [i.e., valor] of a king, and of a king of England too." In this celebrated speech, Elizabeth displayed many of her most memorable qualities: her self-consciously theatrical command of grand public occasion, her subtle blending of magniloquent rhetoric and the language of love, her strategic appropriation of traditionally masculine qualities, and her great personal courage. "We princes," she once remarked, "are set on stages in the sight and view of all the world."

THE ENGLISH AND OTHERNESS

In 1485, most English people would have devoted little thought to their national identity. If asked to describe their sense of belonging, they would probably have spoken first of the international community of Christendom, and secondly of their local region, such as Kent or Cumberland. The extraordinary events of the Tudor era, from the encounter with the New World to the break with Rome, made many people newly aware and proud of their Englishness. At the same time, they began to perceive those who lay outside the national community in new (and often negative) ways. Like most national communities, the English defined themselves largely in terms of what or who they were not. In the wake of the Reformation, the most prominent "others" were those who had until recently been more or less the same, that is, the Catholics of western Christendom. But other groups were also instrumental in the project of English self-definition.

Elizabethan London had a large population of resident aliens, mainly artisans and merchants and their families, from Portugal, Italy, Spain, Germany, and, above all, France and the Netherlands. Many of these people were Protestant refugees, and they were accorded some legal and economic protection by the government. But they were not always welcome to the local populace. Throughout the sixteenth century London was the site of repeated demonstrations and, on occasion, bloody riots against the communities of foreign artisans, who were accused of taking jobs away from Englishmen. There was widespread hostility as well toward the Welsh, the Scots, and above all the Irish, whom the English had for centuries been struggling unsuccessfully to subdue. The kings of England claimed to be rulers of Ireland, but in reality they effectively controlled only a small area known as the Pale, extending north from Dublin. The great majority of the population remained stubbornly Catholic and, despite endlessly reiterated English repression, burning of villages, destruction of crops, seizure of land, and massacres, incorrigibly independent.

Medieval England's Jewish population, the recurrent object of persecution, extortion, and massacre, had been officially expelled by King Edward I in 1290, but Elizabethan England harbored a tiny number of Jews or Jewish converts to Christianity. They were the objects of suspicion and hostility. Elizabethans appear to have been fascinated by Jews and Judaism but quite uncertain whether the terms referred to a people, a foreign nation, a set of strange practices, a living faith, a defunct religion, a villainous conspiracy, or a messianic inheritance. Protestant Reformers brooded deeply on the Hebraic origins of Christianity; government officials ordered the arrest of those "suspected to be Jews"; villagers paid pennies to itinerant fortunetellers who claimed to be descended from Abraham or masters of kabbalistic mysteries; and London playgoers enjoyed the spectacle of the downfall of the wicked Barabas in Christopher Marlowe's *The Jew of Malta* and the forced conversion of Shylock in Shakespeare's *The Merchant of Venice*. Jews were not officially permitted to resettle in England until the middle of the seventeenth century, and even then their legal status was ambiguous.

Sixteenth-century England also had a small African population whose skin color was the subject of pseudoscientific speculation and theological debate. Some Elizabethans believed that Africans' blackness resulted from the climate of the regions where they lived, where, as one traveler put it, they were "so scorched and vexed with the heat of the sun, that in many places they curse it when it riseth." Others held that blackness was a curse inherited from their forefather Cush, the son of Ham (who had, according to Genesis, wickedly exposed the nakedness of his drunken father, Noah). George Best, a proponent of this theory of inherited skin color, reported that "I myself have seen an Ethiopian as black as coal brought into England, who taking a fair English woman to wife, begat a son in all respects as black as the father was, although England were his native country, and an English woman his mother: whereby it seemeth this blackness proceedeth rather of some natural infection of that man."

As the word "infection" suggests, Elizabethans frequently regarded blackness as a physical defect, though the black people who lived in England and Scotland throughout the sixteenth century were also treated as exotic curiosities. At his marriage to Anne of Denmark, James VI of Scotland (the son of Mary, Queen of Scots; as James I of England, he succeeded Elizabeth in 1603) entertained his bride and her family by commanding four naked black youths to dance before him in the snow. (The youths died of exposure shortly afterward.) In 1594, in the festivities celebrating the baptism of James's son, a "Black-Moor" entered pulling an elaborately decorated chariot that was, in the original plan, supposed to be pulled by a lion. In England there was a black trumpeter in the courts of Henry VII and Henry VIII, while Elizabeth had at least two black servants, one an entertainer, the other a page. Africans became increasingly popular as servants in aristocratic and gentle households in the last decades of the sixteenth century.

Some of these Africans were almost certainly slaves, though the legal status of slavery in England was ambiguous. In Cartwright's Case (1569), the court ruled "that England was too Pure an Air for Slaves to breathe in," but there is evidence that black slaves were owned in Elizabethan and Jacobean England. Moreover, by the mid-sixteenth century the English had become involved in the profitable trade that carried African slaves to the New World. In 1562 John Hawkins embarked on his first slaving voyage, transporting some three hundred Africans from the Guinea coast to Hispaniola, where they were sold for ten thousand pounds. Elizabeth is reported to have said that this venture was "detestable, and would call down the Vengeance of Heaven upon the Undertakers." Nevertheless, she invested in Hawkins's subsequent voyages and loaned him ships.

Elizabeth also invested in other enterprises that combined aggressive nationalism and the pursuit of profit. In 1493 the pope had divided the New World between the Spanish and the Portuguese by drawing a line from pole to pole (hence Brazil speaks Portuguese today and the rest of Latin America speaks Spanish): the English were not in the picture. But by the end of Edward VI's reign the Company of Merchant Adventurers was founded, and Englishmen began to explore Asia and North America. Some of these adventurers turned to piracy, preying on Spanish ships that were returning laden with wealth extracted from their New World possessions. (The pope had ruled that the Indians were human beings—and hence could be converted to Christianity—but the ruling did nothing to prevent their enslavement and brutal exploitation.) English acts of piracy soon became a private undeclared war, with the queen and her courtiers covertly investing in the raids but accepting no responsibility for them. The greatest of many astounding exploits was the voyage of Francis Drake (1577–80): he sailed through the Strait of Magellan, pillaged Spanish towns on the Pacific, reached as far north as San Francisco, crossed to the Philippines, and returned around the Cape of Good Hope; he came back with a million pounds in treasure, and his investors earned a dividend of 5,000 percent. Queen Elizabeth knighted him on the deck of his ship, *The Golden Hind*.

WRITERS, PRINTERS, AND PATRONS

The association between literature and print, so natural to us, was less immediate in the sixteenth century. Poetry in particular frequently circulated in manuscript, copied by reader after reader into personal anthologies—commonplace books—or reproduced by professional scribes for a fee. The texts that have come down to us in printed form often bear an uncertain relation to authorial manuscripts, and were frequently published only posthumously. The career of professional writer in sixteenth-century England was almost impossible: there was no such thing as author's copyright, no royalties paid to an author according to the sales of his book, and virtually no notion that anyone could make a decent living through the creation of works of literature. Writers sold their manuscripts to the printer or bookseller outright, for what now seem like ridiculously low prices. The churchyard of St Paul's Cathedral in London was lined with booksellers' shops: dissolved chantries were taken over by bookshops in the 1540s, church officials leased out their residences near the church's north door to members of the Stationers' Company (the guild whose members had the exclusive right to own printing presses), and eventually bookstores even filled the bays between the Cathedral's buttresses, two stories high and more. Paul's was the main center of business in the capital, with the church itself serving as a meeting place, and its columns as notice-boards; publishers would post there, and elsewhere in the city, the title pages of new books as advertisements. Those title pages listed the wholesaler for the work, but customers could have bought popular books at most of the shops in St Paul's Yard. The publishing business was not entirely contained in that busy space, though: some Stationers were only printers, merely working as contractors for publishers, and their printshops were located all over the city, often in the owner's residence.

Freedom of the press did not exist. Before Elizabeth's reign, state control of printed books was poorly organized, although licensing efforts had been underway since 1538. In 1557, however, the Stationers' Company received its charter, and became responsible for the licensing of books. Two years later, the government commanded the Stationers only to license books that had been approved by either six Privy Councilors or the Archbishop of Canterbury and the Bishop of London. Despite these seemingly strict regulations, "scandalous, malicious, schismatical, and heretical" works were never effectively suppressed. Though there were occasional show trials and horrendous punishments—the printer William Carter was hanged for treason in 1584 because he had published a Catholic pamphlet; the Protestant separatists John Penry, Henry Barrow, and John Greenwood were executed in 1593 under a statute that made it a capital offense to "devise and write, print or set forth, any manner of book . . . letter, or writing containing false, seditious, and slanderous matter to the defamation of the Queen's Majesty"—active censorship was not as frequent or thorough as we might expect.

The censors largely focused their attention on works of history, which often had political implications for the present, and on religious treatises. In this, they shared the public's taste. Plays and secular poetry occasionally sold well (Shakespeare's *Henry IV, Part 1* was printed 7 times in 25 years), but they could not compete with publishing blockbusters such as *The Plain Man's Pathway* (16 editions in 25 years), let alone *The Psalms in English Meter*, published 124 times between 1583 and 1608. Publishers were largely interested in profit margins, and the predominance of devotional texts among the surviving books from the period attests to their greater marketability. The format in which works of literature were usually published is also telling. We normally find plays and poetry in quartos (or octavos), small volumes which had four (or eight) pages printed on each side of a sheet which was then folded twice (or three times) and stitched together with other such folded sheets to form the book. The more imposing folio format (in which the paper was folded only once, at two pages per side of a sheet) tended to be reserved not just for longer works but for those regarded as meriting especially respectful treatment. In 1577, Raphael Holinshed's massive history *The Chronicles of England, Scotlande, and Irelande* appeared in a woodcut-illustrated folio; only ten years later, a second edition was published, again in the large format. In contrast, Edmund Spenser's huge poem *The Faerie Queene* was printed as a quarto both in 1590 and in 1596. A decade after his death, though, as the poet's reputation grew, his epic appeared again (1609), this time as a folio.

Elizabethan writers of exalted social standing, like the earl of Surrey or Sir Philip Sidney, thought of themselves as courtiers, statesmen, and landowners; poetry was for them an indispensable social grace and a deeply pleasurable, exalted form of play. Writers of lower rank, such as Samuel Daniel and Michael Drayton, sought careers as civil servants, secretaries, tutors, and clerics; they might take up more or less permanent residence in a noble household, or, more casually, offer their literary work to actual or prospective patrons, in the hope of protection, career advancement, or financial reward. Ambitious authors eager to rise from threadbare obscurity often looked to the court for livelihood, notice, and encouragement, but their great expectations generally proved chimerical. "A thousand hopes, but all nothing," wailed John Lyly, alluding to his long wait for the office of Master of the Revels, "a hundred promises but yet nothing."

Financial rewards for writing prose or poetry came mostly in the form of gifts from wealthy patrons, who sought to enhance their status and gratify their vanity through the achievements and lavish praises of their clients. Some Elizabethan patrons, though, were well-educated humanists motivated by aesthetic interests, and with them, patronage extended beyond financial support to the creation of lively literary and intellectual circles. Poems by Daniel, Ben Jonson, Aemilia Lanyer, and others bear witness to the sustaining intelligence and sophistication, as well as the generosity, of their benefactors. But the experience of Robert Greene is perhaps equally revealing: the fact that he had sixteen different patrons for seventeen books suggests that he did not find much favor or support from any one of them. Indeed, a practice grew up of printing off several dedications to be inserted into particular copies of a book, so that an impecunious author could deceive each of several patrons into thinking that he or she was the uniquely fortunate person to be honored by the volume.

In addition to the court and the great families as dispensers of patronage, the city of London and the two universities also had a substantial impact on the period's literature. London was the center of the book trade, the nursery of a fledgling middle-class reading public, and, most important, the home of the public theaters. Before Elizabeth's time, the universities were mainly devoted to educating the clergy, and that remained an important part of their function. But in the second half of the century, the sons of the gentry and the aristocracy were going in increasing numbers to the universities and the Inns of Court (law schools), not in order to take religious orders or to practice law but to prepare for public service or the management of their estates. Other, less affluent students, such as Marlowe and Spenser, attended Oxford and Cambridge on scholarship. A group of graduates, including Thomas Nashe, Robert Greene, and George Peele, enlivened the literary scene in London in the 1590s, but the precarious lives of these so-called "university wits" testify to the difficulties they encountered in their quixotic attempt to survive by their writing skill. The diary of Philip Henslowe, a leading theatrical manager, has entry after entry showing university graduates in prison or in debt or at best eking out a miserable existence patching plays.

Women had no access to grammar schools, the universities, or the Inns of Court and, when not altogether illiterate, received for the most part only a rudimentary education. While Protestantism, with its emphasis on reading Scripture, certainly helped to improve female literacy in the sixteenth century, girls were rarely encouraged to pursue their studies. Indeed, while girls were increasingly taught to read, they were not necessarily taught to write, for the latter skill in women was considered to be at the very least useless, at the worst dangerous. When the prominent humanist Sir Thomas Smith thought of how he should describe his country's social order, he declared that "we do reject women, as those whom nature hath made to keep home and to nourish their family and children, and not to meddle with matters abroad, nor to bear office in a city or commonwealth." Then, with a kind of nervous glance over his shoulder, he made an exception of those few in whom "the blood is respected, not the age nor the sex": for example, the queen. Every piece of writing by a woman from this period is a triumph over nearly impossible odds.

TUDOR STYLE: ORNAMENT, PLAINNESS, AND WONDER

Renaissance literature is the product of a rhetorical culture, a culture steeped in the arts of persuasion and trained to process complex verbal signals. (The contemporary equivalent would be the ease with which we deal with complex visual signals, effortlessly processing such devices as fade-out, montage, cross-cutting, and morphing.) In 1512, Erasmus published a work called *De copia* that taught its readers how to cultivate "copiousness," verbal richness, in discourse. The work obligingly provides, as a sample, a list of 144 different ways of saying "Thank you for your letter."

In Renaissance England, certain syntactic forms or patterns of words known as "figures" (also called "schemes") were shaped and repeated in order to confer beauty or heighten expressive power. Figures were usually known by their Greek and Latin names, though in an Elizabethan rhetorical manual, *The Arte of English Poesie*, George Puttenham made a valiant if short-lived attempt to give them English equivalents, such as "Hyperbole, or the Overreacher" and "Ironia, or the Dry Mock." Those who received a grammar-school education throughout Europe at almost any point between the Roman Empire and the eighteenth century probably knew by heart the names of up to one hundred such figures, just as they knew by heart their multiplication tables. According to one scholar's count, William Shakespeare knew and made use of about two hundred.

As certain grotesquely inflated Renaissance texts attest, lessons from *De copia* and similar rhetorical guides could encourage prolixity and verbal self-display. Elizabethans had a taste for elaborate ornament in language as in clothing, jewelry, and furniture, and, if we are to appreciate their accomplishments, it helps to set aside the modern preference, particularly in prose, for unadorned simplicity and directness. When, in one of the age's most fashionable works of prose fiction, John Lyly wishes to explain that the vices of his young hero, Euphues, are tarnishing his virtues, he offers a small flood of synonymous images: "The freshest colors soonest fade, the teenest [i.e., keenest] razor soonest turneth his edge, the finest cloth is soonest eaten with moths." Lyly's multiplication of balanced rhetorical figures sparked a small literary craze known as "Euphuism," which was soon ridiculed by Shakespeare and others for its formulaic excesses. Yet the multiplication of figures was a source of deep-rooted pleasure in rhetorical culture, and most of the greatest Renaissance writers used it to extraordinary effect. Consider, for example, the succession of images in Shakespeare's sonnet 73:

> That time of year thou mayst in me behold
> When yellow leaves, or none, or few, do hang
> Upon those boughs which shake against the cold,
> Bare ruined choirs, where late the sweet birds sang.
> In me thou seest the twilight of such day
> As after sunset fadeth in the west;
> Which by and by black night doth take away,
> Death's second self that seals up all in rest.
> In me thou seest the glowing of such fire
> That on the ashes of his youth doth lie,
> As the deathbed whereon it must expire,
> Consumed with that which it was nourished by.
> This thou perceiv'st, which makes thy love more strong,
> To love that well, which thou must leave ere long.

What seems merely repetitious in Lyly here becomes a subtle, poignant amplification of the perception of decay, through the succession of images from winter (or late fall) to twilight to the last glow of a dying fire. Each of these images is in turn sensitively explored, so that, for example, the season is figured by bare boughs that shiver, as if they were human, and then these anthropomorphized tree branches in turn are figured as the ruined choirs of a church where services were once sung. No sooner is the image of singers in a church choir evoked than these singers are instantaneously transmuted back into the songbirds who, in an earlier season, had sat upon the boughs, while these sweet birds in turn conjure up the poet's own vanished youth. And this nostalgic gaze extends, at least glancingly, to the chancels of the Catholic abbeys reduced to ruins by Protestant iconoclasm and the dissolution of the monasteries. All of this within the first four lines: here and elsewhere Shakespeare, along with other poets of his time, contrives to freight the small compass and tight formal constraints of the sonnet—fourteen lines of iambic pentameter in three principal rhyming patterns—with remarkable emotional intensity, psychological nuance, and imagistic complexity. The effect is what Christopher Marlowe called "infinite riches in a little room."

Elizabethans were certainly capable of admiring plainness of speech—in *King Lear* Shakespeare contrasts the severe directness of the virtuous Cordelia to the "glib and oily art" of her wicked sisters—and such poets as George Gascoigne, Thomas Nashe, and, in the early seventeenth century, Ben Jonson wrote restrained, aphoristic, moralizing lyrics in a plain style whose power depends precisely on the avoidance of richly figurative verbal pyrotechnics. This power is readily apparent in the wintry spareness of Nashe's "A Litany in Time of Plague," with its grim refrain:

> Wit with his wantonness
> Tasteth death's bitterness;
> Hell's executioner
> Hath no ears for to hear
> What vain art can reply.
> I am sick, I must die.
>   Lord, have mercy on us!

Here the linguistic playfulness beloved by Elizabethan culture is scorned as an ineffectual "vain art" to which the executioner, death, is utterly indifferent.

But here and in other plain-style poetry, the somber, lapidary effect depends on a tacit recognition of the allure of the suppleness, grace, and sweet harmony that the dominant literary artists of the period so assiduously cultivated. Poetry, writes Puttenham, is "more delicate to the ear than prose is, because it is more current and slipper upon the tongue [i.e., flowing and easily pronounced], and withal tunable and melodious, as a kind of Music, and therefore may be termed a musical speech or utterance." The sixteenth century was an age of superb vocal music. The renowned composers William Byrd, Thomas Morley, John Dowland, and others scarcely less distinguished wrote a rich profusion of madrigals (part songs for two to eight voices, unaccompanied) and airs (songs for solo voice, generally accompanied by the lute). These works, along with hymns, popular ballads, rounds, catches, and other forms of song, enjoyed immense popularity, not only in the royal court, where musical skill was regarded as an important accomplishment, and in aristocratic households, where professional musicians were employed as entertainers, but also in less exalted social circles. In his *Plain and Easy Introduction to Practical Music* (1597), Morley tells a story of social humiliation at a failure to perform that suggests that a well-educated Elizabethan was expected to be able to sight-sing. Even if this is an exaggeration in the interest of book sales, there is evidence of impressively widespread musical literacy, a literacy reflected in a splendid array of music for the lute, viol, recorder, harp, and virginal, as well as vocal music.

Many sixteenth-century poems were written to be set to music, but even those that were not often aspire in their metrical and syllabic virtuosity to the complex pleasures of madrigals or to the sweet fluency of airs. In poetry and music, as in gardens, architecture, and dance, Elizabethans had a taste for elaborate, intricate, but perfectly regular designs. They admired form, valued the artist's manifest control of the medium, and took pleasure in the highly patterned surfaces of things. Modern responses to art often evidence a suspicion of surfaces, impatience with order, the desire to rip away the mask in order to discover a hidden core of experiential truth: these responses are far less evident in Renaissance aesthetics than is a delight in pattern. Indeed many writers of the time expressed the faith that the universe itself had in its basic construction the beauty, concord, and harmonious order of a poem or a piece of music. "The world is made by Symmetry and proportion," wrote Thomas Campion, who was both a poet and a composer, "and is in that respect compared to Music, and Music to Poetry." The design of an exquisite work of art is deeply linked in this view to the design of the cosmos.

Such an emphasis on conspicuous pattern might seem to encourage an art as stiff as the starched ruffs that ladies and gentlemen wore around their necks, but the period's fascination with order was conjoined with a profound interest in persuasively conveying the movements of the mind and heart. Syntax in the sixteenth century was looser, more flexible than our own and punctuation less systematic. If the effect is sometimes confusing, it also enabled writers to follow the twists and turns of thought or perception. Consider, for example, Roger Ascham's account, in his book on archery, of a day in which he saw the wind blowing the new-fallen snow:

> That morning the sun shone bright and clear, the wind was whistling aloft, and sharp according to the time of the year. The snow in the highway lay loose and trodden with horse feet: so as the wind blew, it took the loose snow with it, and made it so slide upon the snow in the field which was hard and crusted by reason of the frost overnight, that thereby I might see very well, the whole nature of the wind as it blew that day. And I had a great delight and pleasure to mark it, which maketh me now far better to remember it. Sometime the wind would be not past two yards broad, and so it would carry the snow as far as I could see. Another time the snow would blow over half the field at once. Sometime the snow would tumble softly, by and by it would fly wonderful fast. And this I perceived also, that the wind goeth by streams and not whole together. . . . And that which was the most marvel of all, at one time two drifts of snow flew, the one of the West into the East, the other out of the North into the East: And I saw two winds by reason of the snow the one cross over the other, as it had been two highways. . . . The more uncertain and deceivable the wind is, the more heed must a wise Archer give to know the guiles of it.

What is delightful here is not only the author's moment of sharpened perception but his confidence that this moment—a glimpse of baffling complexity and uncertainty—can be captured in the restless succession of sentences and then neatly summed up in the pithy conclusion. (This effect parallels that of the couplet that sums up the complexities of a Shakespearean sonnet.) A similar confidence emanates from Sir Walter Ralegh's deeply melancholy, deeply ironic apostrophe to Death at the close of *The History of the World*, written when he was a prisoner in the Tower:

> O eloquent, just, and mighty Death! Whom none could advise, thou hast persuaded; what none hath dared, thou hast done; and whom all the world hath flattered, thou only hast cast out of the world and despised; thou hast drawn together all the far-stretched greatness, all the pride, cruelty, and ambition of man, and covered it all over with these two narrow words: *Hic jacet!* [Here lies]

Death is triumphant here, but so is Ralegh's eloquent, just, and mighty language.

The sense of *wonder* that animates both of these exuberant prose passages—as if the world were being seen clearly and distinctly for the first time—characterizes much of the period's poetry as well. The mood need not always be solemn. One can sense laughter, for example, rippling just below the surface of Marlowe's admiring description of the beautiful maiden Hero's boots:

> Buskins of shells all silvered usèd she,
> And branched with blushing coral to the knee,
> Where sparrows perched, of hollow pearl and gold,
> Such as the world would wonder to behold;
> Those with sweet water oft her handmaid fills,
> Which, as she went, would chirrup through the bills.

Seashells were beloved by Renaissance collectors because their intricate designs, functionally inexplicable, seemed the works of an ingenious, infinitely playful craftsman. Typically, the shells did not simply stand by themselves in cabinets but were gilded or silvered and then turned into other objects: cups, miniature ships, or, in Marlowe's fantasy, boots further decorated with coral and mechanical sparrows made of conspicuously precious materials and designed, as he puts it deliciously, to "chirrup." The poet knows perfectly well that the boots would be implausible footwear in the real world, but he invites us into an imaginary world of passion, a world in which the heroine's costume includes a skirt "whereon was many a stain, / Made with the blood of wretched lovers slain" and a veil of "artificial flowers and leaves, / Whose workmanship both man and beast deceives." The veil reflects an admiration for an art of successful imitation—after all, bees are said to look in vain for honey amidst the artificial flowers—but it is cunning illusion rather than realism that excites Marlowe's wonder. Renaissance poetry is interested not in representational accuracy but in the magical power of exquisite workmanship to draw its readers into fabricated worlds.

In his *Defense of Poesy*, the most important work of literary criticism in sixteenth-century England, Sidney claims that this magical power is also a moral power. All other arts, he argues, are subjected to fallen, imperfect nature, but the poet alone is free to range "within the zodiac of his own wit" and create a second nature, superior to the one we are condemned to inhabit: "Her world is brazen, the poets only deliver a golden." The poet's golden world in this account is not an escapist fantasy; it is a model to be emulated in actual life, an ideal to be brought into reality as completely as possible. It is difficult to say, of course, how seriously this project of realization was taken—though the circumstances of Sidney's own death suggest that he may have been attempting to enact on the battlefield an ideal image of Protestant chivalry. A didactic role for poetry is, in any case, urged not by Sidney alone but by most Elizabethan poets. Human sinfulness has corrupted life, robbing it of the sweet wholesomeness that it had once possessed in Eden, but poetry can mark the way back to a more virtuous and fulfilled existence. And not only mark the way: poetry, Sidney and others argue, has a unique persuasive force that shatters inertia and impels readers toward the good they glimpse in its ravishing lines.

This force, attributed to the energy and vividness of figurative language, made poetry a fitting instrument not only for such high-minded enterprises as moral exhortation, prayer, and praise, and for such uplifting narratives as the legends of religious and national heroes, but also for such verbal actions as cursing, lamenting, flattering, and seducing. The almost inexhaustible range of motives was given some order by literary conventions that functioned as shared cultural codes, enabling poets to elicit particular responses from readers and to relate their words to other times, other languages, and other cultures. Among the most prominent of the clusters of conventions in the period were those that defined the major literary modes (or "kinds," as Sidney terms them): pastoral, heroic, lyric, satiric, elegiac, tragic, and comic. They helped to shape subject matter, attitude, tone, and values, and in some cases—sonnet, verse epistle, epigram, funeral elegy, and masque, to name a few—they also governed formal structure, meter, style, length, and occasion. We can glimpse a few of the ways in which these literary codes worked by looking briefly at the two that are, for modern readers, the least familiar: pastoral and heroic.

The conventions of the pastoral mode present a world inhabited by shepherds and shepherdesses who are concerned not just to tend their flocks but to fall in love and to engage in friendly singing contests. The mode celebrated leisure, humility, and contentment, exalting the simple country life over the city and its business, the military camp and its violence, the court and its burdens of rule. Pastoral motifs could be deployed in different genres. Pastoral songs commonly expressed the joys of the shepherd's life or his disappointment in love. Pastoral dialogues between shepherds might conceal serious, satiric comment on abuses in the great world under the guise of homely, local concerns. There were pastoral funeral elegies, pastoral dramas, pastoral romances (prose fiction), and even pastoral episodes within epics. The most famous pastoral poem of the period is Marlowe's "The Passionate Shepherd to His Love," an erotic invitation whose promise of gold buckles, coral clasps, and amber studs serves to remind us that, however much it sings of naïve innocence, the mode is ineradicably sophisticated and urban.

With its rustic characters, simple concerns, and modest scope, the pastoral mode was regarded as situated at the opposite extreme from heroic, with its values of honor, martial courage, loyalty, leadership, and endurance and its glorification of a nation or people. The chief genre here was the epic, typically a long, exalted poem in the high style, based on a heroic story from the nation's distant past and imitating Homer and Virgil in structure and motifs. Renaissance poets throughout Europe undertook to honor their nations and their vernacular languages by writing this most prestigious kind of poetry. In sixteenth-century England the major success in heroic poetry is Spenser's *Faerie Queene*. Yet the success of *The Faerie Queene* owes much to the fact that the poem is a generic hybrid, in which the conventions of classical epic mingle with those of romance, medieval allegory, pastoral, satire, mythological narrative, comedy, philosophical meditation, and many others in a strange, wonderful blend. The spectacular mixing of genres in Spenser's poem is only an extreme instance of a general Elizabethan indifference to the generic purity admired by writers, principally on the Continent, who adhered to Aristotle's *Poetics*. Where such neoclassicists attempted to observe rigid stylistic boundaries, English poets tended to approach the different genres in the spirit of Sidney's inclusivism: "if severed they be good, the conjunction cannot be hurtful."

THE ELIZABETHAN THEATER

If Sidney welcomed the experimental intertwining of genres in both poetry and prose—and his own *Arcadia*, a prose romance incorporating both pastoral and heroic elements, confirms that he did—there was one place where he found it absurd: the theater. He condemned the conjunction of high and low characters in "mongrel" tragicomedies that mingled "kings and clowns." Moreover, in the spirit of neoclassical advocacy of the "dramatic unities," Sidney disliked the ease with which the action on the bare stage ("where you shall have Asia of the one side, and Afric of the other") violated the laws of time and space. "Now you shall have three ladies walk to gather flowers," he writes in *The Defense of Poesy*, "and then we must believe the stage to be a garden. By and by we hear news of shipwreck in the same place: and then we are to blame if we accept it not for a rock." The irony is that this mocking account, written probably in 1579, anticipates by a few years the stupendous achievements of Marlowe and Shakespeare, whose plays joyously break every rule that Sidney thought it essential to observe.

A permanent, freestanding public theater in England dates only from Shakespeare's own lifetime. A London playhouse, the Red Lion, is first mentioned in 1567, and James Burbage's playhouse, The Theater, was built in 1576. But it is quite misleading to identify English drama exclusively with the new, specially constructed playhouses, for in fact there was a rich and vital theatrical tradition in England stretching back for centuries. Townspeople in late medieval England mounted elaborate cycles of plays (sometimes called "mystery plays") depicting the great biblical stories, from the creation of the world to Christ's Passion and its miraculous aftermath. Many of these plays have been lost, but those that survive, as the selection in this anthology demonstrates, include magnificent and complex works of art. At once civic and religious festivals, the cycles continued to be performed into the reign of Elizabeth, but their close links to popular Catholic piety led Protestant authorities in the sixteenth century to suppress them.

Early English theater was not restricted to these annual festivals. Performers acted in town halls and the halls of guilds and aristocratic mansions, on scaffolds erected in town squares and marketplaces, on pageant wagons in the streets, and in innyards. By the fifteenth century, and probably earlier, there were organized companies of players traveling under noble patronage. Such companies earned a precarious living providing amusement, while enhancing the prestige of the patron whose livery they wore and whose protection they enjoyed. (Otherwise, by statutes enjoining productive labor, actors without another, ordinary trade could have been classified as vagabonds and whipped or branded.) This practice explains why the professional acting companies of Shakespeare's time, including Shakespeare's own, attached themselves to a nobleman and were technically his servants (the Lord Chamberlain's Men, the Lord Admiral's Men, etc.), even though virtually all their time was devoted to entertaining the public, from whom most of their income derived.

Before the construction of the public theaters, the playing companies often performed short plays called "interludes" that were, in effect, staged dialogues on religious, moral, and political themes. Henry Medwall's *Fulgens and Lucrece* (ca. 1490–1501), for example, pits a wealthy but dissolute nobleman against a virtuous public servant of humble origins, while John Heywood's *The Play of the Weather* (ca. 1525–33) stages a debate among social rivals, including a gentleman, a merchant, a forest ranger, and two millers. The structure of such plays reflects the training in argumentation that students received in Tudor schools and, in particular, the sustained practice in examining both sides of a difficult question. Some of Shakespeare's amazing ability to look at critical issues from multiple perspectives may be traced back to this practice and the dramatic interludes it helped to inspire.

Another major form of theater that flourished in England in the fifteenth century and continued on into the sixteenth was the morality play, a dramatization of the spiritual struggle of the Christian soul. These dramas derived their power from the poignancy and terror of an individual's encounter with death. Often this somber power was supplemented by the extraordinary comic vitality of the evil character, or Vice.

If such plays sound more than a bit like sermons, it is because they were. The Church was a profoundly different institution from the theater, but its professionals shared some of the same rhetorical skills. It would be grossly misleading to regard churchgoing and playgoing as comparable entertainments, but clerical attacks on the theater sometimes make it sound as if ministers thought themselves to be in direct competition with professional players. The players, for their part, were generally too discreet to present themselves in a similar light, yet they almost certainly understood their craft as relating to sermons with an uneasy blend of emulation and rivalry. When, in 1610, the theater manager Philip Rosseter was reported to have declared that plays were as good as sermons, he was summoned before the bishop of London to recant; but Rosseter had said no more than what many players must have privately thought.

By the later sixteenth century, many churchmen, particularly those with Puritan leanings, were steadfastly opposed to the theater, but some early Protestant Reformers, such as John Bale, tried their hand at writing plays. Thomas Norton, who with a fellow lawyer, Thomas Sackville, wrote the first English tragedy in blank verse, *Gorboduc, or Ferrex and Porrex* (1561), was also a translator of the great Reformer John Calvin. There is no evidence that Norton felt a tension between his religious convictions and his theatrical interests, nor was his play a private exercise. The five-act tragedy in blank verse, a grim vision of Britain descending into civil war, was performed at the Inner Temple (one of London's law schools) and subsequently acted before the queen.

Gorboduc was closely modeled on the works of the Roman playwright Seneca, and Senecan influence—including violent plots, resounding rhetorical speeches, and ghosts thirsting for blood—remained pervasive in the Elizabethan period, giving rise to a subgenre of revenge tragedy, in which a wronged protagonist plots and executes revenge, destroying himself (or herself) in the process. An early, highly influential example is Thomas Kyd's *Spanish Tragedy* (1592), and, despite its unprecedented psychological complexity, Shakespeare's *Hamlet* clearly participates in this kind. A related but distinct kind is the villain tragedy, in which the protagonist is blatantly evil: in his *Poetics*, Aristotle had advised against attempting to use a wicked person as the hero of a tragedy, but Shakespeare's *Richard III* and *Macbeth* amply justify the general English indifference to classical rules. Some Elizabethan tragedies, such as the fine *Arden of Feversham* (whose author is unknown), are concerned not with the fall of great men but with domestic violence; others, such as Christopher Marlowe's *Tamburlaine*, are concerned with "overreachers," larger-than-life heroes who challenge the limits of human possibility. Certain tragedies in the period, such as *Richard III*, intersect with another Elizabethan genre, the history play, in which dramatists staged the great events, most often conspiracies, rebellions, and wars, of the nation. Not all of the events commemorated in history plays were tragic, but they tend to circle back again and again to the act that epitomized what for this period was the ultimate challenge to authority: the killing of a king. When the English cut off the head of their king in 1649, they were performing a deed which they had been rehearsing, literally, for most of a century.

English schoolboys would read and occasionally perform comedies by the great Roman playwrights Plautus and Terence. Shortly before mid-century a schoolmaster, Nicholas Udall, used these as a model for a comedy in English, *Ralph Roister Doister*. At about the same time, another comedy, *Gammar Gurton's Needle*, which put vivid, native English material into classical form, was amusing the students at Cambridge. From the classical models English playwrights derived some elements of structure and content: plots based on intrigue, division into acts and scenes, and type characters such as the rascally servant and the *miles gloriosus* (cowardly braggart soldier). The latter type appears in *Ralph Roister Doister* and is a remote ancestor of Shakespeare's Sir John Falstaff in the two parts of *Henry IV* and *The Merry Wives of Windsor*.

Early plays such as *Gorboduc* and *Ralph Roister Doister* are rarely performed or read today, and with good reason. In terms of both dramatic structure and style, they are comparatively crude. Take, for example, this clumsy expression of passionate love by the title character in *Cambyses, King of Persia*, a popular play written around 1560 by a Cambridge graduate, Thomas Preston:

> For Cupid he, that eyeless boy, my heart hath so enflamed
> With beauty, you me to content the like cannot be named;
> For since I entered in this place and on you fixed mine eyes,
> Most burning fits about my heart in ample wise did rise.
> The heat of them such force doth yield, my corpse they scorch, alas!
> And burns the same with wasting heat as Titan doth the grass.
> And sith this heat is kindled so and fresh in heart of me,
> There is no way but of the same the quencher you much be.

Around 1590, an extraordinary change overcame the English drama, transforming it almost overnight into a vehicle for unparalleled poetic and dramatic expression. Many factors contributed to this transformation, but probably the chief was the eruption onto the scene of Christopher Marlowe. Compare Preston's couplets, written in a metre called "fourteeners," with the lines in Marlowe's *Doctor Faustus* (ca. 1592–93) with which Faustus greets the conjured figure of Helen of Troy:

> Was this the face that launched a thousand ships,
> And burnt the topless towers of Ilium?

> Sweet Helen, make me immortal with a kiss:
> Her lips sucks forth my soul, see where it flies!
> Come Helen, come, give me my soul again.
> Here will I dwell, for heaven be in these lips,
> And all is dross that is not Helena! (Scene 12, lines 81–87)

Marlowe has created and mastered a theatrical language—a superb unrhymed iambic pentameter, or blank verse—far more expressive than anything that anyone accustomed to the likes of Preston could have imagined.

Play-acting, whether of tragedies, comedies, or any of the other Elizabethan genres, took its place alongside other forms of public expression and entertainment as well. Perhaps the most important, from the perspective of the theater, were music and dance, since these were directly and repeatedly incorporated into plays. Moreover, virtually all plays in the period, including Shakespeare's, apparently ended with a dance. Brushing off the theatrical gore and changing their expressions from woe to pleasure, the actors in plays like *Doctor Faustus* and *King Lear* would presumably have received the audience's applause and then bid for a second round by performing a stately pavane or a lively jig.

Plays, music, and dancing were by no means the only shows in town. There were jousts, tournaments, royal entries, religious processions, pageants in honor of newly installed civic officials or ambassadors arriving from abroad; wedding masques, court masques, and costumed entertainments known as Disguisings or Mummings; juggling acts, fortunetellers, exhibitions of swordsmanship, mountebanks, folk healers, storytellers, magic shows; bearbaiting, bullbaiting, cockfighting, and other blood sports; folk festivals such as Maying, the Feast of Fools, Carnival, and Whitsun Ales. For several years, Elizabethan Londoners were delighted by a trained animal—Banks's Horse—that could, it was thought, do arithmetic and answer questions. And there was always the grim but compelling spectacle of public shaming, mutilation, and execution.

Most English towns had stocks and whipping posts. Drunks, fraudulent merchants, adulterers, and quarrelers could be placed in carts or mounted backward on asses and paraded through the streets for crowds to jeer and throw refuse at. Women accused of being scolds could be publicly muzzled by an iron device called a brank or tied to a "cucking stool" and dunked in the river. Convicted criminals could have their ears cut off, their noses slit, their foreheads branded. Public beheadings and hangings were common. In the worst cases, felons were sentenced to be "hanged by the neck, and being alive cut down, and your privy members to be cut off, and your bowels to be taken out of your belly and there burned, you being alive." In the dismemberment with which Marlowe's *Doctor Faustus* ends, the audience was witnessing the theatrical equivalent of the execution of criminals and traitors that they could have also watched in the flesh, as it were, nearby.

Doctor Faustus was performed by the Lord Admiral's Men at the Rose Theater, one of four major public playhouses that by the mid-1590s were feverishly competing for crowds of spectators. These playhouses (including Shakespeare's famous Globe Theater, which opened in 1599) each accommodated some two thousand spectators and generally followed the same design: they were oval in shape, with an unroofed yard in the center where stood the groundlings (apprentices, servants, and others of the lower classes) and three rising tiers around the yard for men and women able to pay a higher price for places to sit and a roof over their heads. A large platform stage jutted out into the yard, surrounded on three sides by spectators (see the conjectural drawing of an Elizabethan playhouse in the appendices to this volume). These financially risky ventures relied on admission charges—it was an innovation of this period to have money advanced in the expectation of pleasure rather than offered to servants afterwards as a reward—and counted on habitual playgoing fueled by a steady supply of new plays. The public playhouses were all located outside the limits of the city of London and, accordingly, beyond the jurisdiction of the city authorities, who were generally hostile to dramatic spectacles. Eventually, indoor theaters, artificially lighted and patronized by a more select audience, were also built inside the city, secured under conditions that would allow them some protection from those who wished to shut them down.

Why should what we now regard as one of the undisputed glories of the age have aroused so much hostility? One answer, curiously enough, is traffic: plays drew large audiences, and nearby residents objected to the crowds, the noise, and the crush of carriages. Other, more serious concerns were public health and crime. It was thought that many diseases, including the dreaded bubonic plague, were spread by noxious odors, and the packed playhouses were obvious breeding grounds for infection. (Patrons often tried to protect themselves by sniffing nosegays or stuffing cloves in their nostrils.) The large crowds drew pickpockets, cutpurses, and other scoundrels. On one memorable afternoon a pickpocket was caught in the act and tied for the duration of the play to one of the posts that held up the canopy above the stage. The theater was, moreover, a well-known haunt of prostitutes, and, it was alleged, a place where innocent maids were seduced and respectable matrons corrupted. It was darkly rumored that "chambers and secret places" adjoined the theater galleries, and, in any case, taverns, disreputable inns, and brothels were close at hand.

There were other charges as well. Plays were performed in the afternoon and therefore drew people, especially the young, away from their work. They were schools of idleness, luring apprentices from their trades, law students from their studies, housewives from their kitchens, and potentially pious souls from the sober meditations to which they might otherwise devote themselves. Moralists warned that the theaters were nests of sedition, and religious polemicists, especially Puritans, obsessively focusing on the use of boy actors to play the female parts, charged that theatrical transvestism excited illicit sexual desires, both heterosexual and homosexual.

But the playing companies had powerful allies, including Queen Elizabeth herself, and continuing popular support. One theater historian has estimated that between the late 1560s and 1642, when the playhouses were shut down by the English Civil War, well over fifty million visits were paid to the London theater, an astonishing figure for a city that had, by our standards, a very modest population. Plays were performed without the scene breaks and intermissions to which we are accustomed; there was no scenery and few props, but costumes were usually costly and elaborate. The players formed what would now be called repertory companies—that is, they filled the roles of each play from members of their own group, not employing outsiders. They performed a number of different plays on consecutive days, and the principal actors were shareholders in the profits of the company. Boys were apprenticed to actors just as they were apprenticed to master craftsmen in the guilds; they took the women's parts in plays until their voices changed. The plays might be bought for the company from freelance writers, or, as in Shakespeare's company, the group might include an actor-playwright who could supply it with some (though by no means all) of its plays. The script remained the property of the company, but a popular play was eagerly sought by the printers, and the companies, which generally tried to keep their plays from appearing in print, sometimes had trouble guarding their rights. The editors of the earliest collected edition of Shakespeare, the First Folio (1623), complain about the prior publication of "divers stolen and surreptitious copies" of his plays, "maimed and deformed by the frauds and stealths of injurious imposters."

SURPRISED BY TIME

All of the ways we cut up time into units are inevitably distortions. The dividing line between centuries was not, as far as we can tell, a highly significant one for people in the Renaissance, and many of the most important literary careers cross into the seventeenth century without a self-conscious moment of reflection. But virtually everyone must have been aware, by the end of the 1590s, that the long reign of England's Queen Elizabeth was nearing its end, and this impending closure occasioned considerable anxiety. Childless, the last of her line, Elizabeth had steadfastly refused to name a successor. She continued to make brilliant speeches, to receive the extravagant compliments of her flatterers, and to exercise her authority—in 1601, she had her favorite, the headstrong earl of Essex, executed for attempting to raise an insurrection. But, as her seventieth birthday approached, she was clearly, as Ralegh put it, "a lady surprised by time." She suffered from bouts of ill health and melancholy; her godson, Sir John Harington, was dismayed to see her pacing through the rooms of her palace, striking at the tapestries with a sword. Her more astute advisers—among them Lord Burghley's son, Sir Robert Cecil, who had succeeded his father as her principal counsellor—secretly entered into correspondence with the likeliest claimant to the throne, James VI of Scotland. Though the English queen had executed his Catholic mother, Mary, Queen of Scots, the Protestant James had continued to exchange polite letters with Elizabeth. It was at least plausible, as officially claimed, that in her dying breath, on March 24, 1603, Elizabeth designated James as her successor. A jittery nation that had feared a possible civil war at her death lit bonfires to welcome its new king. But in just a very few years, the English began to express nostalgia for the rule of "Good Queen Bess" and to look back on her reign as a magnificent high point in the history and culture of their nation.

Additional information about the Sixteenth Century, including primary texts and images, is available on Norton Literature Online (wwnorton.com/nlo). Online topics are

- The Magician, the Heretic, and the Playwright
- Renaissance Exploration, Travel, and the World Outside Europe
- Dissent, Doubt, and Spiritual Violence in the Reformation
- Island Nations

THE SIXTEENTH CENTURY

TEXTS	CONTEXTS
	1485 Accession of Henry VII inaugurates Tudor dynasty
ca. 1505–07 Amerigo Vespucci, *New World* and *Four Voyages*	**ca. 1504** Leonardo da Vinci paints the Mona Lisa
	1508–12 Michaelangelo paints Sistine Chapel ceiling
	1509 Death of Henry VII; accession of Henry VIII
1511 Desiderius Erasmus, *Praise of Folly*	
	1513 James IV of Scotland killed at Battle of Flodden; succeeded by James V
1516 Thomas More, *Utopia*. Ludovico Ariosto, *Orlando furioso*	
ca. 1517 John Skelton, "The Tunning of Elinour Rumming"	**1517** Martin Luther's Ninety-Five Theses; beginning of the Reformation in Germany
	1519 Cortés invades Mexico. Magellen begins his voyage around the world
1520s–30s Thomas Wyatt's poems circulating in manuscript	**1521** Pope Leo X names Henry VIII "Defender of the Faith"
1525 William Tyndale's English translation of the New Testament	
1528 Baldessare Castiglione, *The Courtier*	
	1529–32 More is Lord Chancellor
1532 Niccolò Machiavelli, *The Prince* (written 1513)	**1532–34** Henry VIII divorces Catherine of Aragon to marry Anne Boleyn; Elizabeth I born; Henry declares himself head of the Church of England
	1535 More beheaded
1537 John Calvin, *The Institution of Christian Religion*	**1537** Establishment of Calvin's theocracy at Geneva
	1542 Roman Inquisition. James V of Scotland dies; succeeded by infant daughter Mary
1543 Copernicus, *On the Revolution of the Spheres*	
1547 *Book of Homilies*	**1547** Death of Henry VIII; accession of Protestant Edward VI
1549 *Book of Common Prayer*	
	1553 Death of Edward VI; failed attempt to put Protestant Lady Jane Grey on throne; accession of Catholic Queen Mary, daughter of Catherine of Aragon
	1555–56 Archbishop Cranmer and former bishops Latimer and Ridley burned at the stake
1557 Tottel's *Songs and Sonnets* (printing poems by Wyatt, Surrey, and others)	

TEXTS	CONTEXTS
	1558 Mary dies; succeeded by Protestant Elizabeth I
1563 John Foxe, *Acts and Monuments*	
1565 Thomas Norton and Thomas Sackville, *Gorboduc*, first English blank-verse tragedy (acted in 1561)	
1567 Arthur Golding, translation of Ovid's *Metamorphoses*	**1567–68** Mary, Queen of Scots, forced to abdicate; succeeded by her son James VI; Mary imprisoned in England
	1570 Elizabeth I excommunicated by Pope Pius V
	1572 St. Bartholomew's Day Massacre of French Protestants
	1576 James Burbage's playhouse, The Theater, built in London
	1577–80 Drake's circumnavigation of the globe
1578 John Lyly, *Euphues*	
1579 Edmund Spenser, *The Shepheardes Calender*	
1580 Montaigne, *Essais*	
	1583 Irish rebellion crushed
	1584–87 Sir Walter Ralegh's earliest attempts to colonize Virginia
	1586–87 Mary, Queen of Scots, tried for treason and executed
ca. 1587–90 Marlowe's *Tamburlaine* acted. Shakespeare begins career as actor and playwright	
1588 Thomas Hariot, *A Brief and True Report of . . . Virginia*	**1588** Failed invasion of the Spanish Armada
1589 Richard Hakluyt, *The Principal Navigations . . . of the English Nation*	
1590 Sir Philip Sidney, *Arcadia* (posthumously published); Spenser, *The Faerie Queene,* Books 1–3	
1591 Sidney, *Astrophil and Stella*	
ca. 1592 John Donne's earliest poems circulating in manuscript	
1595 Sidney, *The Defense of Poesy*	**1595** Ralegh's voyage to Guiana
1596 Spenser, *The Faerie Queene,* Books 4–6 (with Books 1–3)	
1598 Ben Jonson, *Every Man in His Humor*	
	1599 Globe Theater opens
	1603 Elizabeth I dies; succeeded by James VI of Scotland (as James I), inaugurating the Stuart dynasty

SIR THOMAS WYATT THE ELDER
1503–1542

Thomas Wyatt made his career in the shifting, dangerous currents of Renaissance courts, and court culture, with its power struggles, sexual intrigues, and sophisticated tastes, shaped his remarkable achievements as a poet. Educated at St. John's College, Cambridge, Wyatt entered the service of Henry VIII, becoming clerk of the king's jewels, a member of diplomatic missions to France and the Low Countries, and, in 1537–39, ambassador to Spain at the court of the Holy Roman Emperor, Charles V. The years he spent abroad as a diplomat had a significant impact upon his writing, most obvious in his translations and imitations of poems by the Italian Renaissance writers Serafino, Aretino, Sannazaro, Alamanni, and, above all, Petrarch. Diplomacy, with its veiled threats, subtle indirection, and cynical role-playing, may have had a more indirect impact as well, reinforcing the lessons in self-display and self-concealment that Wyatt would have received at the English court.

Life in the orbit of the ruthless, unpredictable Henry VIII was competitive and risky. When, in the late 1530s, Wyatt wrote to his son of the "thousand dangers and hazards, enmities, hatreds, prisonments, despites, and indignations" he had faced, he was not exaggerating. He probably came closest to the executioner's axe when in 1536 he was imprisoned in the Tower of London along with several others accused of having committed adultery with the queen, Anne Boleyn. As his poem "Who list his wealth and ease retain" suggests, Wyatt may have watched from his cell the execution of the queen and her alleged lovers; but he himself was spared, as he was spared a few years later, when he was again imprisoned in the Tower on charges of high treason brought by his enemies at court. His death, at the age of thirty-nine, came from a fever.

It is not surprising, given his career, that many of Wyatt's poems, including his satires and his psalm translations, express an intense longing for "steadfastness" and an escape from the corruption, anxiety, and duplicity of the court. The praise, in his verse epistle to John Poins, of a quiet retired life in the country and the harsh condemnation of courtly hypocrisy derive from his own experience. But of course the eloquent celebration of simplicity and truthfulness can itself be a cunning strategy. Wyatt was a master of the game of poetic self-display. Again and again he represents himself as a plain-speaking and steadfast man, betrayed by the "doubleness" of a fickle mistress or the instability of fortune. At this distance it is impossible to know how much this account corresponds to reality, but we can admire, as Wyatt's contemporaries did, the rhetorical deftness of the performance.

In a move with momentous consequences for English poetry, Wyatt introduced into English the sonnet, a fourteen-line poem in iambic pentameter with a complex, intertwining rhyme scheme. For the most part, he took his subject matter from Petrarch's sonnets, but his rhyme schemes make a significant departure. Petrarch's sonnets consist of an "octave," rhyming *abbaabba*, followed, after a turn (*volta*) in the sense, by a "sestet" with various rhyme schemes (such as *cd cd cd* and *cde cde*) that have in common their avoidance of a rhyming couplet at the end. Wyatt employs the Petrarchan octave, but his most common sestet scheme is *cddc ee*: the Petrarchan sonnet was already beginning to change into the characteristic "English" structure for the sonnet, three quatrains and a closing couplet.

In his freest translations of Petrarchan sonnets, such as "Whoso list to hunt," Wyatt tends to turn the idealizing of the woman into disillusionment and complaint. For the lover in Petrarch's poems, love is a transcendent experience; for the lover in Wyatt's poems, it is obsessive and embittering. The tone of bitterness carries over to many poems less closely linked to Italian and French models, poems with short stanzas and refrains in the manner of the native English "ballet" (pronounced to rhyme with *mallet*) or dance-song. Some of the ballets, to be sure, strike a note of jaunty independence, often tinged with misogyny, but melancholy complaint is rarely very distant. Perhaps the poem that most brilliantly captures Wyatt's blend of passion, anger, cynicism, longing, and pain is "They flee from me."

Though Wyatt's representations of women are often cynical, it is clear that aristocratic women played a key role in the reception and preservation of his poetry. Women were not excluded from the courtly game of ballet-making. The Devonshire Manuscript, one of the chief sources for Wyatt's poetry, contains a number of poems that were probably by women, many more transcribed by female hands, and some male-authored poems written in a female voice, as well as any number of misogynist verses, by Wyatt and others.

Wyatt never published a collection of his own poems, and very little of his verse appeared in print during his lifetime. In 1557 (fifteen years after his death), the printer Richard Tottel included 97 poems attributed to Wyatt among the 271 poems in his miscellany, *Songs and Sonnets*. Wyatt was not primarily concerned with regularity of accent and smoothness of rhythm. By the time Tottel's collection was published, Wyatt's deliberately rough, vigorous, and expressive metrical practice was felt to be crude, and Tottel (or perhaps some intermediary) smoothed out the versification. We reprint "They flee from me" in the version found in the Egerton Manuscript, a manuscript that contains poems in Wyatt's own hand and corrections he made to scribal copies of his poems. Unlike the Egerton Manuscript (E. MS.), the Devonshire Manuscript (D. MS.) was not apparently in the poet's possession, but some of its texts seem earlier than Egerton's, and it furnishes additional poems, as do the Blage Manuscript (B. MS.) and the Arundel Manuscript (A. MS.).

In the following selections we have indicated the manuscript from which each of the poems derives.*

The long love that in my thought doth harbor[1]

The long love that in my thought doth harbor,
And in mine heart doth keep his residence,
Into my face presseth with bold pretense
And therein campeth, spreading his banner.[2]
She that me learneth° to love and suffer — *teaches me*
And will that my trust and lust's negligence[3]
Be reined by reason, shame,° and reverence, — *modesty*
With his hardiness taketh displeasure.
Wherewithal° unto the heart's forest he fleeth, — *because of which*
Leaving his enterprise with pain and cry,
And there him hideth, and not appeareth.
What may I do, when my master feareth,
But in the field with him to live and die?
For good is the life ending faithfully.

E. MS.

*For the Italian originals of some of the Petrarchan sonnets that Wyatt translated, as well as additional poems by Wyatt, go to Norton Literature Online.

1. Wyatt's version of poem 140 of Petrarch's *Rime sparse* (Scattered rhymes); his younger friend the earl of Surrey also translated it (p. 354).

2. I.e., the speaker's blush. The first four lines of this sonnet introduce the "conceit" (elaborately sustained metaphor) of Love as a warrior who, "with bold pretense" (i.e., making bold claim), flaunts his presence by means of the "banner." Elaborate metaphors of this kind are common in Petrarchan (and Elizabethan) love poetry, and often, as in this instance, an entire sonnet will turn on a single conceit.

3. I.e., my open and careless revelation of my love.

Petrarch, Rima 140

A MODERN PROSE TRANSLATION[1]

Love, who lives and reigns in my thought and keeps his principal seat in my heart, sometimes comes forth all in armor into my forehead, there camps, and there sets up his banner.

She who teaches us to love and to be patient, and wishes my great desire, my kindled hope, to be reined in by reason, shame, and reverence, at our boldness is angry within herself.

Wherefore Love flees terrified to my heart, abandoning his every enterprise, and weeps and trembles; there he hides and no more appears outside.

What can I do, when my lord is afraid, except stay with him until the last hour? For he makes a good end who dies loving well.

Whoso list to hunt[1]

Whoso list° to hunt, I know where is an hind,° *cares / female deer*
But as for me, alas, I may no more.
The vain travail° hath wearied me so sore, *labor*
I am of them that farthest cometh behind.
Yet may I, by no means, my wearied mind
Draw from the deer, but as she fleeth afore,
Fainting I follow. I leave off, therefore,
Since in a net I seek to hold the wind.
Who list her hunt, I put him out of doubt,° *assure him*
As well as I, may spend his time in vain.
And graven with diamonds in letters plain
There is written, her fair neck round about,
"*Noli me tangere,* for Caesar's I am,
And wild for to hold, though I seem tame."

E. MS.

Petrarch, Rima 190

A MODERN PROSE TRANSLATION

A white doe on the green grass appeared to me, with two golden horns, between two rivers, in the shade of a laurel, when the sun was rising in the unripe season.

Her look was so sweet and proud that to follow her I left every task, like the miser who as he seeks treasure sweetens his trouble with delight.

1. This and the prose translation of Rime 190 are by Robert K. Durling.

1. An adaptation of Petrarch's Rima 190, perhaps influenced by commentators on Petrarch, who said that *Noli me tangere quia Caesaris sum* ("Touch me not, for I am Caesar's") was inscribed on the collars of Caesar's hinds, which were then set free and were presumably safe from hunters. Wyatt's sonnet is usually supposed to refer to Anne Boleyn, in whom Henry VIII became interested in 1526.

"Let no one touch me," she bore written with diamonds and topazes around her lovely neck. "It has pleased my Caesar to make me free."

And the sun had already turned at midday; my eyes were tired by looking but not sated, when I fell into the water, and she disappeared.

They flee from me[1]

They flee from me, that sometime did me seek
With naked foot stalking° in my chamber. *walking softly*
I have seen them gentle, tame, and meek
That now are wild and do not remember
That sometime they put themself in danger
To take bread at my hand; and now they range,
Busily seeking with a continual change.

Thanked be fortune it hath been otherwise
Twenty times better; but once in special,
In thin array, after a pleasant guise,
When her loose gown from her shoulders did fall,
And she me caught in her arms long and small,° *slender*
Therewithal° sweetly did me kiss *with that*
And softly said, "Dear heart, how like you this?"

It was no dream, I lay broad waking.
But all is turned, thorough° my gentleness, *through*
Into a strange fashion of forsaking;
And I have leave to go, of her goodness,
And she also to use newfangleness.° *fickleness*
But since that I so kindely[2] am served,
I fain would° know what she hath deserved. *would like to*

E. MS

My lute, awake!

My lute, awake! Perform the last
Labor that thou and I shall waste,
And end that I have now begun:
For when this song is sung and past,
My lute be still, for I have done.

As to be heard where ear is none,
As lead to grave in marble stone,[1]
My song may pierce her heart as soon.

1. For a recitation of this poem, go to Norton Literature Online.
2. Naturally (from *kind*: "nature," but with an ironic suggestion of the modern meaning of "kindly"). In Wyatt's spelling, the word should presumably be pronounced as three syllables.
1. I.e., when sound may be heard with no ear to hear it or when soft lead is able to carve ("grave") hard marble.

Should we then sigh or sing or moan?
No, no, my lute, for I have done.

The rocks do not so cruelly
Repulse the waves continually
As she my suit and affectiön.
So that I am past remedy,
Whereby my lute and I have done.

Proud of the spoil that thou hast got
Of simple hearts, thorough Love's shot,
By whom, unkind, thou hast them won,
Think not he hath his bow forgot,
Although my lute and I have done.

Vengeance shall fall on thy disdain
That makest but game on earnest pain.
Think not alone under the sun
Unquit° to cause thy lovers plain,° *unrevenged / to complain*
Although my lute and I have done.

Perchance thee lie[2] withered and old
The winter nights that are so cold,
Plaining in vain unto the moon.
Thy wishes then dare not be told.
Care then who list,° for I have done. *likes*

And then may chance thee to repent
The time that thou hast lost and spent
To cause thy lovers sigh and swoon.
Then shalt thou know beauty but lent,
And wish and want as I have done.

Now cease, my lute. This is the last
Labor that thou and I shall waste,
And ended is that we begun.
Now is this song both sung and past;
My lute be still, for I have done.

E. MS.

Stand whoso list[1]

Stand whoso list° upon the slipper° top *cares to / slippery*
Of court's estates,° and let me here rejoice *high positions*
And use me quiet without let or stop,[2]
Unknown in court, that hath such brackish joys.

2. Perhaps it may befall you to lie.

1. A translation of Seneca, *Thyestes*, lines 391–403. For a literal translation of this famous passage, and other verse translations of it, go to Norton Literature Online.

2. Comport myself quietly without hindrance or impediment.

In hidden place so let my days forth pass
That when my years be done withouten noise,
I may die aged after the common trace.° *way*
For him death grippeth right hard by the crop° *throat*
That is much known of other, and of himself, alas,
Doth die unknown, dazed, with dreadful° face. *fearful*

A. MS.

HENRY HOWARD, EARL OF SURREY
1517–1547

The axe that decapitated Surrey at the age of thirty had been hanging over his head for much of his life. In the court of Henry VIII, it was dangerous to be a potential claimant to the throne, and Surrey was descended from kings on both sides of his family. He was brought up at Windsor Castle as the close companion of Henry VIII's illegitimate son, the duke of Richmond, who married Surrey's sister. As the eldest son of the duke of Norfolk, the chief bulwark of the old Catholic aristocracy against the rising tide of "new men" and the reformed religion, Surrey was the heir not only to the Howard family's great wealth but also to their immense pride, their sense at once of noble privilege and of obligation. Like his father and grandfather, he was a brave and able soldier, serving in Henry VIII's French wars as "Lieutenant General of the King on Sea and Land." He was also repeatedly imprisoned for rash behavior, on one occasion for striking a courtier, on another for wandering through the streets of London breaking the windows of sleeping townspeople. In 1541 Surrey used his family connections—his first cousin, Catherine Howard, was queen—to secure the release from the Tower of his close friend, the poet Thomas Wyatt, who had been accused of treason. But a year later, Catherine Howard was executed for adultery, like Anne Boleyn before her. Power returned to the rival family of the former queen Jane Seymour, who had died in childbirth giving a son and heir to the aging Henry VIII. Surrey's situation was already precarious, and his vocal opposition to the Seymours, with their strong Protestant leanings, sealed his fate. Convicted of treason, he had the grim distinction of being Henry's last victim.

Poets and critics of the later sixteenth century, fascinated by Surrey's noble rank and his tragic fate, routinely praised him as one of the very greatest English poets. The full title of Tottel's influential miscellany, published in 1557 (ten years after Surrey's death), is *Songs and Sonnets written by the Right Honorable Lord Henry Howard Late Earl of Surrey and Other*. The principal "other" here is his older friend Wyatt, with whose poetry Surrey's is closely linked. Poets who circulated their verse in manuscript in a courtly milieu, both shared a passion for French and Italian poetry, especially for Petrarch's sonnets. Surrey established a form for these that was used by Shakespeare and that has become known as the English sonnet: three quatrains and a couplet, all in iambic pentameter and rhyming *abab cdcd efef gg*. Even more significant, he was the first English poet to publish in blank verse—unrhymed iambic pentameter—a verse form so popular in the succeeding centuries that it has come to seem almost indigenous to the language. The work in which he used his "strange meter," as the publisher called it, was a translation of part of Virgil's *Aeneid*. Managing the five-stress line with exceptional skill, Surrey initiated the rhythmic fluency that distinguishes so many Elizabethan lyrics. It is striking that his two great literary innovations, the English sonnet and blank verse, should emerge in the same period that saw radical upheavals in traditional religious and social life. It is possible that he was drawn to Virgil's epic because it offered a model of continuity in the face of disaster. Aeneas cannot prevent the fall of Troy, but he goes on to establish a new world without abandoning his old values.*

Love, that doth reign and live within my thought[1]

Love, that doth reign and live within my thought,
And built his seat within my captive breast,
Clad in the arms wherein with me he fought,
Oft in my face he doth his banner rest.
But she that taught me love and suffer pain,
My doubtful hope and eke° my hot desire — *also*
With shamefast° look to shadow and refrain,° — *modest / restrain*
Her smiling grace converteth straight to ire.
And coward Love then to the heart apace° — *at once*
Taketh his flight, where he doth lurk and plain,° — *complain*
His purpose lost, and dare not show his face.
For my lord's guilt thus faultless bide I pain,
Yet from my lord shall not my foot remove:
Sweet is the death that taketh end by love.

1557

*For additional lyrics by Surrey, as well as two excerpts from his partial translation of Virgil's *Aeneid* and the Italian originals of some of his sonnets, go to Norton Literature Online.

1. Cf. Surrey's version of Petrarch's Rima 140 with Wyatt's translation of the same original (p. 349; with a modern prose translation).

THE ENGLISH BIBLE

Protestant insistence that true belief must be based on the Holy Scriptures alone made the translation and dissemination of the Bible in English and other vernacular languages a matter of utmost urgency. Prior to the Reformation, the Roman Catholic Church had not always and everywhere opposed vernacular translations of the Bible, but it generally preferred that the populace encounter the Scriptures through the interpretations of the priests, trained to read the Latin translation known as the Vulgate. In times of great conflict this preference for clerical mediation hardened into outright prohibition of vernacular translation and into persecution and book burning. It was in the face of fierce opposition that zealous Protestants all over Europe set out to put the Bible into the hands of the laity. A remarkable translation of the New Testament by an English Lutheran named William Tyndale was printed on the Continent and smuggled into England in 1525; Tyndale's translation of the Pentateuch, the first five books of the Hebrew Bible, followed in 1530. Many copies of these translations were seized and destroyed, as was the translator himself, but the printing press made it extremely difficult for authorities to eradicate books for which there was a passionate demand.

Tyndale's translation was completed by an associate, Miles Coverdale, whose rendering of the Psalms proved to be particularly influential. Their joint labor was the basis for the Great Bible (1539), the first authorized version of the Bible in English, a copy of which was ordered to be placed in every church in the kingdom. Four years later, as Henry VIII sought to halt the tide of reform, a law was passed forbidding women, craftsmen, servants, and laborers from reading the Bible either in public or in private. Yet nothing could be done at this stage to take the Scriptures out of the hands of the populace. Though there would be further opposition in years to come—innumerable Bibles were printed under Edward VI, only to be burned under his sister Mary—the English Bible was a force that could not be suppressed, and it became, in its various forms, the single most important book of the sixteenth century.

Marian persecution was indirectly responsible for what would become the most scholarly Protestant English Bible, the translation known as the Geneva Bible, prepared, with extensive, learned, and often fiercely polemical marginal notes, by English exiles in Calvin's Geneva and widely diffused in England after Elizabeth came to the throne. In addition, Elizabethan church authorities ordered a careful revision of the Great Bible, and this version, known as the Bishops' Bible, was the one read in the churches. The success of the Geneva Bible in particular prompted those Elizabethan Catholics who now in turn found themselves in exile to bring out a vernacular translation of their own, the Douay-Rheims version, in order to counter the Protestant readings and glosses.

After Elizabeth's death in 1603, King James I and his bishops ordered that a revised translation of the entire Bible be undertaken by a group of forty-seven scholars. The result was the Authorized Version, more popularly known as the King James Bible.

In the passage selected here, 1 Corinthians 13, Tyndale's use of the word "love," echoed by the Geneva Bible, is set against the Catholic "charity." The latter term gestures toward the religious doctrine of "works," against the Protestant insistence on salvation by faith alone. It is a sign of the conservative, moderate Protestantism of the King James version that it too opts for "charity."

1 Corinthians 13[1]

From *Tyndale's Translation*

Though I spake with the tongues of men and angels, and yet had no love, I were even as sounding brass: or as a tinkling cymbal. And though I could prophesy, and understood all secrets, and all knowledge: yea, if I had all faith, so that I could move mountains out of their places, and yet had no love, I were nothing. And though I bestowed all my goods to feed the poor, and though I gave my body even that I burned, and yet had no love, it profiteth me nothing.

Love suffereth long, and is courteous. Love envieth not. Love doth not frowardly,[2] swelleth not, dealeth not dishonestly, seeketh not her own, is not provoked to anger, thinketh not evil, rejoiceth not in iniquity: but rejoiceth in the truth, suffereth all things, believeth all things, hopeth all things, endureth in all things. Though that prophesying fail, other[3] tongues shall cease, or knowledge vanish away, yet love falleth never away.

For our knowledge is unperfect and our prophesying is unperfect. But when that which is perfect is come, then that which is unperfect shall be done away. When I was a child, I spake as a child, I understood as a child, I imagined as a child. But as soon as I was a man, I put away childishness. Now we see in a glass, even in a dark[4] speaking: but then shall we see face to face. Now I

1. For two additional sets of passages from sixteenth-century English Bibles (Psalm 23, Isaiah 53.3–6), go to Norton Literature Online.
2. Perversely, evilly.
3. Or.
4. Obscure, unclear. "Glass": mirror. The metaphor of indirect and imperfect sight seems to derive from Plato's Allegory of the Cave (*Republic* 7).

know unperfectly: but then shall I know even as I am known. Now abideth faith, hope, and love, even these three: but the chief of these is love.

1525, 1535

From *The Geneva Bible*

Though I speak with the tongues of men and Angels, and have not love, I am as sounding brass, or a tinkling cymbal. And though I had the gift of prophecy, and knew all secrets and all knowledge, yea, if I had all faith, so that I could remove mountains, and had not love, I were nothing. And though I feed the poor with all my goods, and though I give my body, that I be burned, and have not love, it profiteth me nothing. Love suffereth long: it is bountiful: love envieth not: love doth not boast itself: it is not puffed up: It disdaineth not: it seeketh not her own things: it is not provoked to anger: it thinketh not evil: It rejoiceth not in iniquity, but rejoiceth in the truth: It suffereth all things: it believeth all things: it hopeth all things: it endureth all things. Love doth never fall away, though that prophesyings be abolished, or the tongues cease, or knowledge vanish away. For we know in part, and we prophesy in part. But when that which is perfect is come, then that which is in part shall be abolished. When I was a child, I spake as a child, I understood as a child, I thought as a child: but when I became a man, I put away childish things. For now we see through a glass darkly:[5] but then shall we see face to face. Now I know in part: but then shall I know even as I am known. And now abideth faith, hope, and love, even these three: but the chiefest of these is love.

1560, 1602

From *The Douay-Rheims Version*

If I speak with the tongues of men and of Angels, and have not charity,[6] I am become as sounding brass, or a tinkling cymbal. And if I should have prophecy, and knew all mysteries, and all knowledge, and if I should have all faith so that I could remove mountains, and have not charity, I am nothing. And if I should distribute all my goods to be meat[7] for the poor, and if I should deliver my body so that I burn, and have not charity, it doth profit me nothing.

Charity is patient, is benign: charity envieth not, dealeth not perversely: is not puffed up, is not ambitious, seeketh not her own, is not provoked to anger, thinketh not evil: rejoiceth not upon iniquity, but rejoiceth with the truth: suffereth all things, believeth all things, hopeth all things, beareth all things. Charity never falleth away: whether prophecies shall be made void, or tongues shall cease, or knowledge shall be destroyed. For in part we know, and in part we prophesy. But when that shall come that is perfect, that shall be made void that is in part. When I was a little one, I spake as a little one, I understood as a little one, I thought as a little one. But when I was made a man, I did away the things that belonged to a little one. We see now by a glass in a dark sort: but then face to face. Now I know in part: but then I shall know as also I am

5. By means of a mirror, obscurely.
6. From Latin *caritas*, love; but also carrying the modern sense.
7. Food (in general).

known. And now there remain faith, hope, charity, these three, but the greater of these is charity.

1582

From *The Authorized (King James) Version*

Though I speak with the tongues of men and of angels, and have not charity, I am become as sounding brass, or a tinkling cymbal. And though I have the gift of prophecy, and understand all mysteries, and all knowledge; and though I have all faith, so that I could remove mountains, and have no charity, I am nothing. And though I bestow all my goods to feed the poor, and though I give my body to be burned, and have not charity, it profiteth me nothing. Charity suffereth long, and is kind; charity envieth not; charity vaunteth not itself, is not puffed up, doth not behave itself unseemly, seeketh not her own, is not easily provoked, thinketh no evil; rejoiceth not in iniquity, but rejoiceth in the truth; beareth all things, believeth all things, hopeth all things, endureth all things. Charity never faileth: but whether there be prophecies, they shall fail; whether there be tongues, they shall cease; whether there be knowledge, it shall vanish away. For we know in part, and we prophesy in part. But when that which is perfect is come, then that which is in part shall be done away. When I was a child, I spake as a child, I understood as a child, I thought as a child: but when I became a man, I put away childish things. For now we see through a glass, darkly; but then face to face: now I know in part; but then shall I know even as also I am known. And now abideth faith, hope, charity, these three; but the greatest of these is charity.

1611

ELIZABETH I
1533–1603

Elizabeth I, queen of England from 1558 to her death, set her mark indelibly on the age that has come to bear her name. Endowed with intelligence, courage, cunning, and a talent for self-display, she managed to survive and flourish in a world that would easily have crushed a weaker person. Her birth was a disappointment to her father, Henry VIII, who had hoped for a male heir to the throne, and her prospects were further dimmed when her mother, Anne Boleyn, was executed a few years later on charges of adultery and treason. At six years old, observers noted, Elizabeth had as much gravity as if she had been forty.

Under distinguished tutors, including the Protestant humanist Roger Ascham, the young princess received a rigorous education, with training in classical and modern languages, history, rhetoric, theology, and moral philosophy. Her own religious orientation was also Protestant, which put her in great danger during the reign of her Catholic older half-sister, Mary. Imprisoned in the Tower of London, interrogated and constantly spied upon, Elizabeth steadfastly professed innocence, loyalty, and a pious abhorrence of heresy. Upon Mary's death, she ascended the throne and quickly made clear that the official religion of the land would be Protestantism.

When she came to the throne at twenty-five, speculation about a suitable match, already widespread, intensified. It remained for decades at a fever pitch, for the stakes were high. If Elizabeth died childless, the Tudor line would come to an end. The nearest heir was her cousin Mary, Queen of Scots, a Catholic whose claim was supported by France and by the papacy, and whose penchant for sexual and political intrigue soon confirmed the worst fears of English Protestants. The obvious way to avert the nightmare was for Elizabeth to marry and produce an heir, and the pressure upon her to do so was intense.

More than the royal succession hinged on the question of the queen's marriage; Elizabeth's perceived eligibility was a vital factor in the complex machinations of international diplomacy. A dynastic marriage between the queen of England and a foreign ruler could forge an alliance sufficient to alter the balance of power in Europe. The English court hosted a steady stream of ambassadors from kings and princelings eager to win the hand of the royal maiden, and Elizabeth played her romantic part with exemplary skill, sighing and spinning the negotiations out for months and even years. Most probably, she never meant to marry any of her numerous foreign (and domestic) suitors. Such a decisive act would have meant the end of her independence, as well as the end of the marriage game by which she played one power off against another. One day she would seem to be on the verge of accepting a proposal; the next, she would vow never to forsake her virginity. "She is a princess," the French ambassador remarked, "who can act any part she pleases." Ultimately she refused all offers and declared repeatedly that she was wedded to her country.

In the face of deep skepticism about the ability of any woman to rule, Elizabeth strategically blended imperiousness with an elaborate cult of love. Quickly making it clear that she would not be a figurehead, she gathered around her an able group of advisers, but she held firmly to the reins of power, subtly manipulating factional disputes, conducting diplomacy, and negotiating with an often contentious Parliament. Her courtiers and advisers, on their knees, approached the queen, glittering in jewels and gorgeous gowns, and addressed her in extravagant terms that conjoined romantic passion and religious veneration. Artists and poets celebrated her in mythological guise—as Diana, the chaste goddess of the moon; Astraea, the goddess of justice; Gloriana, the queen of the fairies. Though she could suddenly veer, whenever she chose, toward bluntness and anger, Elizabeth herself often contrived to transform the language of politics into the language of love. "We all loved her," her godson John Harington wrote with a touch of irony, "for she said she loved us."

Throughout her life, Elizabeth took pride in her command of languages (she spoke fluent French and Italian and read Latin and Greek) and in her felicity of expression. Her own writing includes carefully crafted letters and speeches on several state occasions; a number of prayers; translations of selections from the Psalms, Petrarch, Seneca, and Horace; prose translations from Boethius, Plutarch, and the French Protestant Queen Margaret of Navarre; and a few original poems. The original poems known to be hers deal with actual events in her life. They show her to be an exceptionally agile, poised, and self-conscious writer, a gifted role-player fully in control of the rhetorical as well as political situation in which she found herself. The texts printed here, occasionally altered in light of variant versions, are from *Elizabeth I: Collected Works*, ed. Leah Marcus, Janel Mueller, and Mary Beth Rose (2000).*

* For an additional letter from Elizabeth—to Henry III of France, furiously objecting to his intervention on behalf of Mary, Queen of Scots—go to Norton Literature Online, where there is also a recitation of Elizabeth's poem "When I was fair and young." For a painting of the queen in procession, see the color insert in this volume.

The doubt of future foes[1]

The doubt° of future foes exiles my present joy, *fear*
And wit° me warns to shun such snares as threatens mine annoy.[2] *intelligence*
For falsehood now doth flow, and subjects' faith doth ebb,[3]
Which should not be, if reason ruled or wisdom weaved the web.
But clouds of toys untried do cloak aspiring minds,
Which turns to rain of late repent, by course of changèd winds.[4]
The top of hope supposed, the root of rue° shall be, *regret*
And fruitless all their grafted guile, as shortly you shall see.[5]
Their dazzled eyes with pride, which great ambition blinds,
Shall be unsealed° by worthy wights° whose foresight falsehood finds. *opened / men*
The daughter of debate,[6] that discord aye° doth sow, *continually*
Shall reap no gain where former rule[7] still° peace hath taught to grow. *stable*
No foreign banished wight shall anchor in this port:
Our realm brooks no seditious sects—let them elsewhere resort.
My rusty sword through rest[8] shall first his edge employ
To poll their tops[9] who seek such change or gape for future joy.
Vivat Regina[1]

ca. 1571 1589

On Monsieur's Departure[1]

I grieve and dare not show my discontent,
I love and yet am forced to seem to hate,
I do, yet dare not say I ever meant,
I seem stark mute but inwardly do prate.° *chatter*
I am and not, I freeze and yet am burned,
Since from myself another self I turned.

My care is like my shadow in the sun,
Follows me flying, flies when I pursue it,
Stands and lies by me, doth what I have done.[2]
His too familiar care[3] doth make me rue° it. *regret*

1. The poem concerns Mary, Queen of Scots, who in 1568 sought refuge in England from her rebellious subjects.
2. I.e., threaten to do me harm ("annoy").
3. I.e., the tide of faith (loyalty) is ebbing, yielding to the rising tide of falsehood.
4. Clouds of tricks ("toys") not yet tested or detected hide the "aspiring minds" of ambitious foes, but those clouds will turn at last into rains of repentance.
5. The deception ("guile") grafted into them will not bear fruit.
6. Strife. Mary Stuart also was sometimes called "Mother of Debate," because she was constantly the focus of conspiracies and plots.
7. "Former rule": either the reign of Henry VIII or that of Edward VI, which established the Reformation in England.
8. Sword rusty from disuse.
9. Strike off their heads.
1. Long live the queen.
1. The heading, present in a seventeenth-century manuscript, identifies the occasion of this poem as the breaking off of marriage negotiations between Queen Elizabeth and the French duke of Anjou in 1582.
2. Does everything I do.
3. I.e., my own care, which he caused.

No means I find to rid him from my breast,
Till by the end of things it be suppressed.

Some gentler passion slide into my mind,
For I am soft and made of melting snow;
Or be more cruel, love, and so be kind.
Let me or° float or sink, be high or low. *either*
Or let me live with some more sweet content,
Or die and so forget what love e'er° meant. *ever*

ca. 1582 1823

A Letter to Sir Amyas Paulet, August 1586[1]

Amyas, my most careful and faithful servant,

God reward thee treblefold in the double for thy most troublesome charge[2] so well discharged. If you knew, my Amyas, how kindly, besides dutifully, my careful[3] heart accepts your double labors and faithful actions, your wise orders and safe regards performed in so dangerous and crafty a charge, it would ease your troubles' travail and rejoice your heart. In which I charge you to carry this most nighest thought: that I cannot balance in any weight of my judgment the value that I prize you at. And suppose no treasure to countervail such a faith, and condemn me in that behalf which I never committed if I reward not such deserts. Yea, let me lack when I have most need if I acknowledge not such a merit with a reward *non omnibus datum*.[4]

But let your wicked mistress know how, with hearty sorrow, her vile deserts compels these orders; and bid her, from me, ask God forgiveness for her treacherous dealing towards the saver of her life many years, to the intolerable peril of her own.[5] And yet not content with so many forgivenesses, must fall again so horribly, far passing a woman's thought, much more a princess', instead of excusing, whereof not one can serve, it being so plainly confessed by the actors[6] of my guiltless death. Let repentance take place; and let not the fiend possess her so as her best part be lost, which I pray with hands lifted up to Him that may both save and spill,[7] with my loving adieu and prayer for thy long life.

Your most assured and loving sovereign in heart,
by good desert induced, *Elizabeth Regina*.

1586 1854

1. Paulet was the keeper of Mary, Queen of Scots. In 1586 a number of her supporters, led by Anthony Babington, plotted to murder Elizabeth and place Mary on the throne. The plot was discovered, and the plotters were executed in September. Mary, who had been complicit with them, was placed under stricter confinement, and then tried for treason.
Elizabeth's letter to Paulet circulated widely in manuscript: to her contemporaries, it was evidently the single best-known of the queen's letters.
2. Duty, responsibility.
3. Full of care.
4. Not given to all.
5. I.e., Elizabeth's own.
6. I.e., the conspirators.
7. Destroy.

Verse Exchange between Elizabeth and Sir Walter Ralegh[1]

[RALEGH TO ELIZABETH]

Fortune hath taken away my love,
My life's joy and my soul's heaven above.
Fortune hath taken thee away, my princess,
My world's joy and my true fantasy's mistress.

Fortune hath taken thee away from me;
Fortune hath taken all by taking thee.
Dead to all joys, I only live to woe:
So is Fortune become my fantasy's foe.

In vain, my eyes, in vain ye waste your tears;
In vain, my sights,[2] the smoke of my despairs,
In vain you search the earth and heaven above.
In vain you search, for Fortune keeps my love.

Then will I leave my love in Fortune's hand;
Then will I leave my love in worldings' band,[3]
And only love the sorrows due to me—
Sorrow, henceforth, that shall my princess be—

And only joy that Fortune conquers kings.
Fortune, that rules the earth and earthly things,
Hath taken my love in spite of virtue's might:
So blind a goddess did never virtue right.

With wisdom's eyes had but blind Fortune seen,
Then had my love, my love forever been.
But love, farewell—though Fortune conquer thee,
No fortune base nor frail shall alter me.

[ELIZABETH TO RALEGH]

Ah, silly Pug,[4] wert thou so sore afraid?
Mourn not, my Wat,[5] nor be thou so dismayed.
It passeth fickle Fortune's power and skill
To force my heart to think thee any ill.
No Fortune base, thou sayest, shall alter thee?
And may so blind a witch so conquer me?
No, no, my Pug, though Fortune were not blind,
Assure thyself she could not rule my mind.
Fortune, I know, sometimes doth conquer kings,
And rules and reigns on earth and earthly things,
But never think Fortune can bear the sway

1. This exchange, which exemplifies the poetic banter that sometimes passed between the queen and her favorites, took place about 1587, when Ralegh believed that the rapid rise of the earl of Essex in Elizabeth's favor entailed a diminution of his own standing with her.

2. Sighs?

3. Bond.

4. An endearment, which Elizabeth used as her pet name for Ralegh.

5. Short for Walter.

If virtue watch, and will her not obey.
Ne chose I thee by fickle Fortune's rede,[6]
Ne she shall force me alter with such speed
But if to try this mistress' jest with thee.[7]
Pull up thy heart, suppress thy brackish tears,
Torment thee not, but put away thy fears.
Dead to all joys and living unto woe,
Slain quite by her that ne'er gave wise men blow,
Revive again and live without all dread,
The less afraid, the better thou shalt speed.[8]

ca. 1587 ca. 1600?

Speech to the Troops at Tilbury[1]

My loving people, I have been persuaded by some that are careful of[2] my safety, to take heed how I committed myself to armed multitudes, for fear of treachery. But I tell you that I would not desire to live to distrust my faithful and loving people. Let tyrants fear! I have so behaved myself that, under God, I have placed my chiefest strength and safeguard in the loyal hearts and goodwill of my subjects. Wherefore I am come among you at this time but for my recreation and pleasure, being resolved in the midst and heat of the battle to live and die amongst you all,[3] to lay down for my God and for my kingdom and for my people mine honor and my blood even in the dust. I know I have the body but of a weak and feeble woman; but I have the heart and stomach of a king, and of a king of England too[4]—and take foul scorn that Parma[5] or any prince of Europe should dare to invade the borders of my realm. To the which, rather than any dishonor shall grow by me, I myself will venter[6] my royal blood; I myself will be your general, judge, and rewarder of your virtue in the field. I know that already for your forwardness you have deserved rewards and crowns;[7] and I assure you in the word of a prince you shall not fail of them. In the meantime, my lieutenant general[8] shall be in my stead, than whom never prince commanded a more noble or worthy subject; not doubting but by your concord in the camp and valor in the field, and your obedience to myself and my general, we shall shortly have a famous victory over these enemies of my God and of my kingdom.

1588 1654

6. Decision.
7. Since "thee" has nothing to rhyme with, and since the line is hard to construe, it seems likely that there is a line missing before or after this one. "But if": unless I do it.
8. Succeed.
1. Delivered by Elizabeth on August 9, 1588, to the land forces assembled at Tilbury (in Essex) to repel the anticipated invasion of the Spanish Armada, a fleet of warships sent by Philip II. The Armada was defeated at sea and never reached England, a miraculous deliverance and sign of God's special favor to Elizabeth and to England, in the general view.
2. Anxious about.
3. In another version of the speech (based, like this one, on an auditor's memory) the sentence up to this point reads: "And therefore I am come amongst you, as you see at this time, not for my recreation and disport, but being resolved in the midst and heat of the battle to live or die amongst you all."
4. An allusion to the concept of the king's (or queen's) two bodies, the one natural and mortal, the other an ideal and enduring political construct. "Stomach": valor.
5. Alessandro Farnese, duke of Parma, allied with (the king of) Spain and expected to join with him in the invasion of England.
6. Venture, risk.
7. The crown was an English coin. "Forwardness": eagerness.
8. The earl of Leicester led the English troops. Elizabeth's great and powerful favorite, he died just a month later.

The "Golden Speech" A speech to Elizabeth's last Parliament, delivered November 30, 1601, and here given as recorded by one of the members. The designation "Golden Speech" stems from the headnote to a version of the speech printed near the end of the Puritan interregnum (1659?): "This speech ought to be set in letters of gold, that as well the majesty, prudence, and virtue of this royal queen might in general most exquisitely appear, as also that her religious love and tender respect which she particularly and constantly did bear to her Parliament in unfeigned sincerity might (to the shame and perpetual disgrace and infamy of some of her successors) be nobly and truly vindicated."

The royal prerogatives included the right to grant or sell "letters patent," which gave the recipient monopoly control of some branch of commerce. (Sir Walter Ralegh, for example, was given the exclusive right, for a period of thirty years, to license all taverns.) Discontent with the monopolies—which had resulted in higher prices for a wide range of commodities, including such basic ones as salt and starch—came to a head in the Parliament of 1601. Under parliamentary pressure (and in return for a subsidy granted to her treasury), Elizabeth agreed to revoke some of the most obnoxious patents and to allow the courts to rule freely on charges brought against the holders of others. She invited members of Parliament who wished to offer thanks for this largess to come to her in a body, and on November 30 received about 150 of them at Whitehall palace. After effusive remarks by the speaker of the House of Commons (Sir John Croke), the queen responded more or less as recorded here. (Elizabeth revised the speech for publication; and none of the surviving versions of it—which differ considerably—was printed earlier than about 1628.)

The "Golden Speech"[1]

Mr. Speaker, we have heard your declaration and perceive your care of our estate,[2] by falling into the consideration of a grateful acknowledgment of such benefits as you have received; and that your coming is to present thanks unto us, which I accept with no less joy than your loves can have desire to offer such a present.

I do assure you that there is no prince that loveth his subjects better, or whose love can countervail[3] our loves. There is no jewel, be it of never so rich a price, which I set before this jewel—I mean your loves. For I do more esteem it than any treasure or riches: for that we know how to prize, but love and thanks I count unvaluable.[4] And though God hath raised me high, yet this I count the glory of my crown, that I have reigned with your loves. This makes me that I do not so much rejoice that God hath made me to be a queen, as to be a queen over so thankful a people. Therefore I have cause to wish nothing more than to content the subjects, and that is a duty which I owe. Neither do I desire to live longer days than that I may see your prosperity, and that is my only desire. And as I am that person that still,[5] yet under God, hath delivered you, so I trust, by the almighty power of God, that I shall be His instrument to preserve you from envy, peril, dishonor, shame, tyranny, and oppression, partly by means of your intended helps, which we take very acceptable because it manifesteth the largeness of your loves and loyalties unto your sovereign.

1. We print only the words of the queen, omitting various interpolations, as well as opening remarks by the speaker of the Parliament.
2. Rank, position.
3. Match.
4. Invaluable.
5. Continually.

Of myself I must say this: I never was any greedy, scraping grasper, nor a strait, fast-holding prince, nor yet a waster. My heart was never set on worldly goods, but only for my subjects' good. What you bestow on me, I will not hoard it up, but receive it to bestow on you again. Yea, my own properties I account yours to be expended for your good, and your eyes shall see the bestowing of all for your good. Therefore render unto them from me, I beseech you, Mr. Speaker, such thanks as you imagine my heart yieldeth but my tongue cannot express.

Mr. Speaker, I would wish you and the rest to stand up, for I shall yet trouble you with longer speech.[6]

Mr. Speaker, you give me thanks, but I doubt[7] me that I have more cause to thank you all than you me; and I charge you to thank them of the Lower House[8] from me. For had I not received a knowledge from you, I might have fallen into the lapse of an error only for lack of true information.

Since I was queen yet did I never put my pen to any grant but that upon pretext and semblance made unto me, it was both good and beneficial to the subject in general, though a private profit to some of my ancient servants who had deserved well. But the contrary being found by experience, I am exceedingly beholding to such subjects as would move the same at the first.[9] And I am not so simple to suppose but that there be some of the Lower House whom these grievances never touched; and for them I think they speak out of zeal to their countries[1] and not out of spleen or malevolent affection, as being parties grieved. And I take it exceedingly gratefully from them, because it gives us to know that no respects or interests had moved them other than the minds they bear to suffer[2] no diminution of our honor and our subjects' love unto us, the zeal of which affection tending to ease my people and knit their hearts unto me, I embrace with a princely care.

For above all earthly treasures I esteem my people's love, more than which I desire not to merit. That my grants should be grievous to my people and oppressions to be privileged under color of our patents, our kingly dignity shall not suffer[3] it. Yea, when I heard it I could give no rest unto my thoughts until I had reformed it.[4] Shall they (think you) escape unpunished that have thus oppressed you and have been respectless of their duty and regardless of our honor? No, no, Mr. Speaker, I assure you were it not more for conscience' sake than for any glory or increase of love that I desire, these errors, troubles, vexations, and oppressions done by these varlets and low persons (not worthy the name of subjects) should not escape without condign punishment. But I perceive they dealt with me like physicians who, ministering a drug, make it more acceptable by giving it a good aromatical savor; or when they give pills, do gild them all over.

I have ever used[5] to set the Last Judgment Day before my eyes and so to rule as I shall be judged, to answer before a higher Judge. To whose judgment seat I do appeal that never thought was cherished in my heart that tended not unto my people's good. And now if my kingly bounties have been abused and my grants turned to the hurts of my people, contrary to my will and meaning, or if any in authority under me have neglected or perverted what I have com-

6. Up to this point, the assemblage had been kneeling.
7. Fear.
8. The House of Commons.
9. I.e., those members of the House of Commons who had raised the issue of monopolies in previous sessions.
1. Their constituents.
2. Permit. "Minds": intentions.
3. Allow. "Color": pretext.
4. In fact, Elizabeth was extremely slow to respond to the grievances, which had, for example, previously been raised in the Parliament of 1597.
5. Been accustomed.

mitted to them, I hope God will not lay their culps[6] and offenses to my charge. Who, though there were danger in repealing our grants, yet what danger would I not rather incur for your good than I would suffer them still to continue?

I know the title of a king is a glorious title, but assure yourself that the shining glory of princely authority hath not so dazzled the eyes of our understanding but that we well know and remember that we also are to yield an account of our actions before the great Judge. To be a king and wear a crown is more glorious to them that see it than it is pleasant to them that bear it. For myself, I was never so much enticed with the glorious name of a king or royal authority of a queen as delighted that God hath made me His instrument to maintain His truth and glory, and to defend this kingdom (as I said) from peril, dishonor, tyranny, and oppression.

There will never queen sit in my seat with more zeal to my country, care to my subjects, and that will sooner with willingness venture her life for your good and safety, than myself. For it is not my desire to live nor reign longer than my life and reign shall be for your good. And though you have had and may have many princes more mighty and wise sitting in this seat, yet you never had or shall have any that will be more careful and loving.

Shall I ascribe anything to myself and my sexly[7] weakness? I were not worthy to live then, and of all most unworthy of the mercies I have had from God, who hath ever yet given me a heart which yet never feared any foreign or home enemy. I speak it to give God the praise as a testimony before you, and not to attribute anything unto myself. For I, O Lord, what am I, whom practices and perils past should not fear?[8] O, what can I do, that I should speak for any glory? God forbid!

This, Mr. Speaker, I pray you deliver unto the House, to whom heartily recommend me. And so I commit you all to your best fortunes and further counsels. And I pray you, Mr. Comptroller, Mr. Secretary,[9] and you of my council, that before these gentlemen depart into their countries,[1] you bring them all to kiss my hand.

1601 — 1601 (in a summary version)

6. Sins.
7. Characteristic of my sex. "Ascribe": attribute.
8. Frighten. "Practices": treacherous schemes.
9. William Knollys, earl of Banbury, and Robert Cecil, earl of Salisbury.
1. Districts.

EDMUND SPENSER
1552–1599

Edmund Spenser set out, consciously and deliberately, to become the great English poet of his age. In a culture in which most accomplished poetry was written by those who were, or at least professed to be, principally interested in something else—advancement at court, diplomacy, statecraft, or the church—Spenser's ambition was altogether remarkable, and it is still more remarkable that he succeeded in reaching his goal. Unlike such poets as Wyatt, Surrey, and Sidney, born to privilege and social distinction, Spenser was born to parents of modest means and station, in London, probably in 1552. He nonetheless received an impressive education, first at the Merchant Taylors' School, under its demanding humanist headmaster, Richard Mulcaster, then at Pembroke College, Cambridge, where he was enrolled as a "sizar" or poor (meaning impoverished) scholar. At Cambridge, which harbored many Puritans, Spenser started as a poet by translating some poems for a volume of anti-Catholic propaganda. He also began his friendship with Gabriel Harvey, an eccentric Cambridge don, humanist, and pamphleteer. Their correspondence shows that they shared a passionate and patriotic interest in the reformation of English verse. In a 1580 letter to Harvey, Spenser demanded, "Why a God's name may not we, as else the Greeks, have the kingdom of our own language?"

After receiving the B.A. degree in 1573 and the M.A. in 1576, Spenser served as personal secretary and aide to several prominent men, including the earl of Leicester, the queen's principal favorite. During his employment in Leicester's household he came to know Sir Philip Sidney and his friend Sir Edward Dyer, courtiers who sought to promote a new English poetry. Spenser's contribution to the movement was *The Shepheardes Calender*, published in 1579 and dedicated to Sidney.

In *The Shepheardes Calender* Spenser used a deliberately archaic language, partly in homage to Chaucer, whose work he praised as a "well of English undefiled," and partly to achieve a rustic effect, in keeping with the feigned simplicity of pastoral poetry's shepherd singers. Sidney did not entirely approve, and another contemporary, Ben Jonson, growled that Spenser "writ no language." In the eighteenth century, Samuel Johnson described the language of *The Shepheardes Calender* as "studied barbarity." Johnson's characterization is, in a way, quite accurate, for Spenser was attempting to conjure up a native English style to which he could wed the classical mode of the pastoral. Moreover, since pastoral was traditionally viewed as the prelude in a great national poet's career to more ambitious undertakings, Spenser was also in effect announcing his extravagant ambition.

Spenser was a prolific and daring experimenter: the poems of *The Shepheardes Calender* use no fewer than thirteen different metrical schemes. In his later poems, he went on to make further innovations: the special rhyme scheme of the Spenserian sonnet; the remarkably beautiful adaptation of the Italian *canzone* forms for the *Epithalamion* and *Prothalamion*; and the nine-line or "Spenserian" stanza of *The Faerie Queene*, with its hexameter (six-stress) line at the end, are the best-known. Spenser is sometimes called the "poet's poet" because so many later English poets learned the art of versification from him. In the nineteenth century alone his influence may be seen in Shelley's *Revolt of Islam*, Byron's *Childe Harold's Pilgrimage*, Keats's *Eve of St. Agnes*, and Tennyson's "The Lotos-Eaters."

The year after the publication of *The Shepheardes Calender*, Spenser went to Ireland as secretary and aide to Lord Grey of Wilton, lord deputy of Ireland. Although he tried continually to obtain appointments in England and to secure the patronage of the queen, he spent the rest of his career in Ireland, holding various minor government posts and hence participating actively in the English struggle against those who resisted colonial domination. The grim realities of that struggle—massacre, the burning of miserable hovels and of crops with the deliberate intention of starving the inhabitants, the forced relocation of whole communities, the manipulation of treason charges so as to facilitate the seizure of lands, the endless repetition of acts of military "justice" calculated to intimidate and break the spirit—may be glimpsed in distorted and on occasion direct form throughout Spenser's writings, along with dreamlike depictions of the beauty of the Irish landscape. Those writings include an anonymously published political tract, *A View of the Present State of Ireland*, which was unusual in its time both for its genuine fascination with Irish culture and for the ruthlessness of the policies it prescribed.

Spenser's attitudes toward Ireland and his conduct there raise difficult questions concerning the relationship between literature and colonialism. Are the harsh policies of the *View* echoed, allegorically, in *The Faerie Queene*? What does it mean to admire a poet who might, by modern standards, be judged a war criminal (as his master, Lord Grey, was judged to be, even by notoriously brutal Elizabethan standards)? Does Spenser use his Irish vantage point to launch daring criticisms of Queen Elizabeth and the English form of government? In addition to sharpening racial chauvinism, the experience of Ireland seems to have given English settlers a new perspective on events back home. As one of Spenser's contemporaries remarked, words that would be considered treasonous in England were common table talk among the Irish settlers.

Spenser was rewarded for his efforts in Ireland with a castle and 3,028 acres of expropriated land at Kilcolman in the province of Munster. There he was visited by another colonist and poet, the powerful and well-connected Sir Walter Ralegh, to whom Spenser showed the great chivalric epic on which he was at work. With Ralegh's influential backing, Spenser traveled to England and published, in 1590, the first three books of *The Faerie Queene*, which made a strong bid for the queen's favor and patronage. He was rewarded with a handsome pension of fifty pounds a year for life, though the queen's principal councilor, Lord Burghley, is said to have complained that it was a lot for a song. Soon after, Spenser published a volume of poems called *Complaints;* a pastoral called *Colin Clouts Come Home Againe* (1595), commenting on the courtiers and ladies at the center of English court life at the time of his 1590 visit; his sonnet cycle, *Amoretti;* and two wedding poems, *Epithalamion* and *Prothalamion*. The six-book *Faerie Queene* was published in 1596, with some revisions in the first part and a changed ending to Book 3 to provide a bridge to the added books; the two so-called Mutability Cantos and two stanzas of a third—perhaps part of an intended seventh book—appeared posthumously in the edition of 1609.

In 1598 there was an uprising in Munster, and rebels burned down the house in which Spenser lived. The poet fled with his wife; their newborn baby is said to have died in the flames. Spenser was sent to England with messages from the besieged English garrison. He died in Westminster on January 13, 1599, and was buried near his beloved Chaucer in what is now called the Poets' Corner of Westminster Abbey.

Spenser cannot be put into neatly labeled categories. His work is steeped in Renaissance Neoplatonism but is also earthy and practical. He is a lover and celebrator of physical beauty yet also a profound analyst of good and evil in all their perplexing shapes and complexities. Strongly influenced by Puritanism in his early days, he remained a thoroughgoing Protestant all his life, and portrayed the Roman Catholic church as a demonic villain in *The Faerie Queene*; yet his understanding of faith and of sin owes much to Catholic thinkers. He is a poet of sensuous images yet also something of an iconoclast, deeply suspicious of the power of images (material and verbal) to turn into idols. He is an idealist, drawn to courtesy, gentleness, and exquisite moral refinement, yet also a celebrant of English nationalism, empire, and martial power. He is the author of the most memorable literary idealization of Elizabeth I, yet he fills his poem with coded criticisms of the queen. He is in some ways a backward-looking poet who paid homage to Chaucer, used archaic language, and compared his own age unfavorably with the feudal past. Yet as a British epic poet and poet-prophet, he points forward to the poetry of the Romantics and especially Milton—who himself paid homage to the "sage and serious" Spenser as "a better teacher than Scotus or Aquinas."

Because it was a deliberate choice on Spenser's part that his language should seem antique, his poetry is always printed in the original spelling and punctuation; a few of the most confusing punctuation marks have, however, been altered in the present text. Spenser also spells words variably in such a way as to suggest rhymes to the eye or to suggest etymologies (often incorrect ones). This inconsistency in his spelling is typical of his time; in the sixteenth century people varied even the spelling of their own names.*

*For additional writings by Spenser—"Aprill" from *The Shepheardes Calender*, four more sonnets from the *Amoretti* (nos. 15, 35, 59, 70), "A Hymne in Honour of Beautie," and, from *The Faerie Queene*, the Cave of Mammon canto from Book 2, extensive excerpts from Book 3, and the Mutability Cantos—go to Norton Literature Online. For excerpts from *A View of the Present State of Ireland* and a portrait of Spenser, go to the topic "Island Nations."

The Faerie Queene In a letter to Sir Walter Ralegh, appended to the first, 1590, edition of *The Faerie Queene,* Spenser describes his exuberant, multifaceted poem as an allegory—an extended metaphor or "dark conceit"—and invites us to interpret the characters and adventures in the several books in terms of the particular virtues and vices they enact or come to embody. Thus the Redcrosse Knight in Book 1 is the knight of Holiness (and also St. George, the patron saint of England); Sir Guyon in Book 2 is the knight of Temperance; the female knight Britomart in Book 3 is the knight of Chastity (chastity here meaning chaste love leading to marriage). The heroes of Books 4, 5, and 6 represent Friendship, Justice, and Courtesy. The poem's general end, Spenser writes, is "to fashion a gentleman or noble person in vertuous and gentle discipline," and the individual moral qualities, taken together, constitute the ideal human being.

However, Spenser's allegory is not as simple as the letter to Ralegh might suggest, and the fashioning of identity proves to be anything but straightforward. Far from being the static embodiments of abstract moral precepts, the knights have a surprisingly complex, altogether human relation to their allegorical identities, identities into which they grow only through painful trial and error in the course of their adventures. These adventures repeatedly take the form of mortal combat with sworn enemies—hence the Redcrosse Knight of Holiness smites the "Saracen" (that is, Muslim) Sansfoy (literally, "without faith")—but the enemies are revealed more often than not to be weirdly dissociated aspects of the knights themselves: when he encounters Sansfoy, Redcrosse has just been faithless to his lady Una, and his most dangerous enemy ultimately proves to be his own despair. Accordingly, the meaning of the various characters, episodes, and places is richly complex, revealed to us (and to the characters themselves) only by degrees.

The complexity is heightened by the inclusion, in addition to the moral allegory, of a historical allegory to which Spenser calls attention, in the letter to Ralegh, by observing that both the Faerie Queene and Belphoebe are personifications of Queen Elizabeth. (In fact, they are only two among many oblique representations of Queen Elizabeth in the poem, some of them far from complimentary.) Throughout the poem there is a dense network of allusions to events, issues, and particular persons in England and Ireland—for example, the queen, her rival Mary, Queen of Scots, the Spanish Armada, the English Reformation, the controversies over religious images, and the bitter colonial struggles against Irish rebellion. Some of Spenser's characters are identified by conventional symbols and attributes that would have been obvious to readers of his time. For example, they would know immediately that a woman who wears a miter and scarlet clothes and dwells near the river Tiber represents (in one sense at least) the Roman Catholic Church, which had often been identified by Protestant preachers with the Whore of Babylon in the Book of Revelation. Marginal notes jotted in early copies of *The Faerie Queene* suggest, however, that there was no consensus among Spenser's contemporaries about the precise historical referents of others of the poem's myriad figures. (Sir Walter Ralegh's wife Bess, for example, seems to have identified many of the virtuous female characters as allegorical representations of herself.) Spenser's poem may be enjoyed as a fascinating story with multiple meanings, a story that works on several levels at once and continually eludes the full and definitive allegorical explanation it constantly promises to deliver.

The poem is also an epic. In moving from *The Shepheardes Calender* to *The Faerie Queene* Spenser deliberately fashioned himself after the great Roman poet Virgil, who began his poetic career with pastoral poetry and moved on to his epic poem, the *Aeneid.* Spenser was acutely conscious that poets elsewhere in Europe, such as Ariosto and Tasso in Italy, and Camoens in Portugal, had already produced works modeled on Virgil's, in celebration of their respective nations. In weaving together classical and medieval sources, drawing on pictorial traditions, and adapting whole episodes from Ariosto and Tasso, he was providing his country with the epic it had hitherto lacked. Like Virgil, Spenser is deeply concerned with the dangerous struggles and painful renunciations required to achieve the highest values of human civilization. The heroic deeds of Spenser's brave knights are the achievements of individual aristocratic men and women, not the triumphs of armies or communities united in serving a common purpose, not even the triumph of the virtually invisible royal court of Gloriana, the Faerie Queene. Yet, taken together, the disjointed adventures of these solitary warriors constitute in Spenser's fervent vision the glory of Britain, the collective memory of its heroic past and the promise of a still more glorious future. And if the Faerie Queene herself is consigned to the margins of the poem that bears her name, she nonetheless is the symbolic embodiment of a shared national destiny, a destiny that reaches beyond mere political success to participate in the ultimate, millennial triumph of good over evil.

If *The Faerie Queene* is thus an epic celebration of Queen Elizabeth, the Protestant faith, and the English nation, it is also a chivalric romance, full of jousting knights and damsels in distress, dragons, witches, enchanted trees, wicked magicians, giants, dark caves, shining castles, and "paynims" (with French names). A clear, pleasant stream may be dangerous to drink from because to do so produces loss of strength. A pious hermit may prove to be a cunningly disguised villain. Houses, castles, and gardens are often places of education and challenge or of especially dense allegorical significance, as if they possess special, half-hidden keys to the meaning of the books in which they appear. As a romance, Spenser's poem is designed to produce wonder, to enthrall its readers with sprawling plots, marvelous adventures, heroic characters, ravishing descriptions, and esoteric mysteries.

In addition to enthralling readers, the poem habitually entraps, misleads, and deludes them. Like Spenser's protagonists, readers are constantly in danger of mistaking hypocritical evil for good, or cunningly disguised foulness for true beauty. *The Faerie Queene* demands vigilance from readers, and many passages must be reread in light of what follows after. In some sections, such as the dialogue between Redcrosse and Despair (Book 1, canto 9), the repeated use of pronouns instead of proper names can lead to confusion as to who is speaking; the effect is intentional, for the promptings of evil are not always easy to disentangle from the voice of conscience.

The whole of *The Faerie Queene* is written in a remarkable nine-line stanza of closely interlocking rhymes (*ababbcbcc*), the first eight lines with five stresses each (iambic pentameter) and the final line with six stresses (iambic hexameter or alexandrine). The stanza gives the work a certain formal regularity, but the various books are composed on quite different structural principles. Book 1 is almost entirely self-contained; it has been called a miniature epic in itself, centering on the adventures of one principal hero, Redcrosse, who at length achieves the quest he undertakes at Una's behest: killing the dragon who has imprisoned her parents and thereby winning her as his bride. The spiritual allegory is similarly self-contained; it presents the Christian struggling heroically against many evils and temptations—doctrinal error, hypocrisy, the Seven Deadly Sins, and despair—to some of which he succumbs before finally emerging triumphant. It shows him separated from the one true faith and, aided by interventions of divine grace, at length reunited with it. Then it treats his purgation from sin, his education in the House of Holiness, and his final salvation. By contrast the structure of Book 3 is more romancelike, with its multiplicity of principal characters (who present, allegorically, several varieties of chaste and unchaste love), its interwoven stories, its heightened attention to women, and its conspicuous lack of closure.

To some degree a lack of closure characterizes all of *The Faerie Queene*, including the more self-contained of the six finished books, and it is fitting that there survives the fragment of another book, the cantos of Mutability, in which Spenser broods on the tension in nature between systematic order and ceaseless change. The poem as a whole is built around principles that pull tautly against one another: a commitment to a life of constant struggle and a profound longing for rest; a celebration of human heroism and a perception of ineradicable human sinfulness; a vision of evil as a terrifyingly potent force and a vision of evil as mere emptiness and filth; a faith in the supreme value of visionary art and a recurrent suspicion that art is dangerously allied to graven images and deception. That Spenser's knights never quite reach the havens they seek may reflect irresolvable tensions to which we owe much of the power and beauty of this great, unfinished work.

From The Faerie Queene

The First Booke of The Faerie Queene

Contayning
The Legende of the
Knight of the Red Crosse,
or
Of Holinesse

1

Lo I the man, whose Muse whilome did maske,
As time her taught, in lowly Shepheards weeds,[1]
Am now enforst a far unfitter taske,
For trumpets sterne to chaunge mine Oaten reeds,[2]
And sing of Knights and Ladies gentle° deeds; *noble*
Whose prayses having slept in silence long,[3]
Me, all too meane,° the sacred Muse areeds° *low / counsels*
To blazon° broad emongst her learned throng: *proclaim*
Fierce warres and faithfull loves shall moralize[4] my song.

2

Helpe then, O holy Virgin chiefe of nine,[5]
Thy weaker° Novice to performe thy will, *too weak*
Lay forth out of thine everlasting scryne° *a chest for papers*
The antique rolles, which there lye hidden still,
Of Faerie knights and fairest Tanaquill,° *i.e., Gloriana*
Whom that most noble Briton Prince[6] so long
Sought through the world, and suffered so much ill,
That I must rue° his undeservèd wrong: *pity*
O helpe thou my weake wit, and sharpen my dull tong.

3

And thou most dreaded impe° of highest Jove, *offspring*
Faire Venus sonne,° that with thy cruell dart *Cupid*
At that good knight so cunningly didst rove,° *shoot*
That glorious fire it kindled in his hart,
Lay now thy deadly Heben° bow apart, *ebony*
And with thy mother milde come to mine ayde:

1. Garb. The poet appeared before ("whilome") as a writer of humble pastoral (i.e., *The Shepheardes Calender*). These lines are imitated from the verses prefixed to Renaissance editions of Virgil's *Aeneid.*
2. To write heroic poetry, of which the trumpet is a symbol, instead of pastoral poetry symbolized by the humble shepherd's pipe ("Oaten reeds").
3. Lines 5 and 6 are imitated from the opening of Ariosto's *Orlando furioso.*
4. Provide subjects for moralizing.
5. Scholars have debated whether the reference is to Clio, the Muse of history, or to Calliope, the Muse of epic.
6. I.e., Arthur, named in 1.9.50.

Come both, and with you bring triumphant Mart,[7]
In loves and gentle jollities arrayd,
After his murdrous spoiles and bloudy rage allayd.

4

And with them eke,° O Goddesse heavenly bright, *also*
Mirrour of grace and Majestie divine,
Great Lady of the greatest Isle, whose light
Like Phoebus lampe throughout the world doth shine,
Shed thy faire beames into my feeble eyne,° *eyes*
And raise my thoughts too humble and too vile,° *lowly*
To thinke of that true glorious type[8] of thine,
The argument° of mine afflicted stile:° *subject / humble work*
The which to heare, vouchsafe, O dearest dred° a-while. *object of awe*

Canto 1

The Patron of true Holinesse,
Foule Errour doth defeate:
Hypocrisie him to entrappe,
Doth to his home entreate.

1

A Gentle Knight was pricking° on the plaine, *spurring*
Ycladd in mightie armes and silver shielde,
Wherein old dints of deepe wounds did remaine,
The cruell markes of many a bloudy fielde;
Yet armes till that time did he never wield:
His angry steede did chide his foming bitt,
As much disdayning to the curbe to yield:
Full jolly° knight he seemd, and faire did sitt, *gallant*
As one for knightly giusts° and fierce encounters fitt. *tourneys, jousts*

2

But on his brest a bloudie Crosse he bore,
The deare remembrance of his dying Lord,
For whose sweete sake that glorious badge he wore,
And dead as living ever him adored:[9]
Upon his shield the like was also scored,° *incised*
For soveraine[1] hope, which in his helpe he had:
Right faithfull true[2] he was in deede and word,
But of his cheere[3] did seeme too solemne sad;° *grave*
Yet nothing did he dread, but ever was ydrad.° *dreaded, feared*

3

Upon a great adventure he was bond,
That greatest Gloriana to him gave,
That greatest Glorious Queene of Faerie Lond,
To winne him worship,° and her grace to have, *honor*

7. Mars, god of war and lover of Venus.
8. I.e., Gloriana is the "type" (prefiguration) of Queen Elizabeth.
9. A compressed reference to Revelation 1.18: "I am he that liveth, and was dead; and, behold, I am alive for evermore."
1. Having greatest power (often applied to medical remedies).
2. Compare Revelation 19.11: "And I saw heaven opened; and behold a white horse; and he that sat upon him was called Faithful and True."
3. Facial expression, mood.

Which of all earthly things he most did crave;
And ever as he rode, his hart did earne° *yearn*
To prove his puissance° in battell brave *might*
Upon his foe, and his new force to learne;
Upon his foe, a Dragon horrible and stearne.

4

A lovely Ladie rode him faire beside,
Upon a lowly Asse more white then snow,
Yet she much whiter, but the same did hide
Under a vele, that wimpled° was full low, *lying in folds*
And over all a blacke stole she did throw,
As one that inly mournd: so was she sad,
And heavie sat upon her palfrey slow:
Seemèd in heart some hidden care she had,
And by her in a line° a milke white lambe she lad. *on a leash*

5

So pure an innocent, as that same lambe,
She was in life and every vertuous lore,
And by descent from Royall lynage came
Of ancient Kings and Queenes, that had of yore
Their scepters stretcht from East to Westerne shore,
And all the world in their subjection held;
Till that infernall feend with foule uprore
Forwasted° all their land, and them expeld: *laid waste*
Whom to avenge, she had this Knight from far compeld.° *summoned*

6

Behind her farre away a Dwarfe did lag,
That lasie seemd in being ever last,
Or wearièd with bearing of her bag
Of needments at his backe. Thus as they past,
The day with cloudes was suddeine overcast,
And angry Jove an hideous storme of raine
Did poure into his Lemans[4] lap so fast,
That every wight° to shrowd° it did constrain, *creature / take shelter*
And this faire couple eke° to shroud themselves were fain.° *also / eager*

7

Enforst to seeke some covert nigh at hand,
A shadie grove not far away they spide,
That promist ayde the tempest to withstand:
Whose loftie trees yclad with sommers pride,
Did spred so broad, that heavens light did hide,
Not perceable° with power of any starre: *penetrable*
And all within were pathes and alleies wide,
With footing worne, and leading inward farre:
Faire harbour that them seemes; so in they entred arre.

8

And foorth they passe, with pleasure forward led,
Joying to heare the birdes sweete harmony,

4. His lover's, i.e., the earth's.

Which therein shrouded from the tempest dred,° *fearful*
Seemd in their song to scorne the cruell sky.
Much can° they prayse the trees, so straight and hy, *did*
The sayling Pine, the Cedar proud and tall,
The vine-prop Elme, the Poplar never dry,
The builder Oake, sole king of forrests all,
The Aspine good for staves, the Cypresse funerall.° *funereal*

9

The Laurell, meed° of mightie Conquerours *reward*
And Poets sage, the Firre that weepeth still,[5]
The Willow worne of forlorne Paramours,
The Eugh° obedient to the benders will, *yew*
The Birch for shaftes, the Sallow° for the mill, *willow*
The Mirrhe sweete bleeding in the bitter wound,
The warlike Beech, the Ash for nothing ill,
The fruitfull Olive, and the Platane° round, *plane-tree*
The carver Holme,[6] the Maple seeldom inward sound.

10

Led with delight, they thus beguile the way,
Untill the blustring storme is overblowne;
When weening° to returne, whence they did stray, *thinking*
They cannot finde that path, which first was showne,
But wander too and fro in wayes unknowne,
Furthest from end then, when they neerest weene,
That makes them doubt, their wits be not their owne:
So many pathes, so many turnings seene,
That which of them to take, in diverse doubt they been.

11

At last resolving forward still to fare,
Till that some end they finde or° in or out, *either*
That path they take, that beaten seemed most bare,
And like to lead the labyrinth about° *out of*
Which when by tract they hunted had throughout,
At length it brought them to a hollow cave,
Amid the thickest woods. The Champion stout
Eftsoones° dismounted from his courser brave, *at once*
And to the Dwarfe a while his needlesse spere[7] he gave.

12

"Be well aware,"° quoth then that Ladie milde, *watchful*
"Least suddaine mischiefe° ye too rash provoke: *misfortune*
The danger hid, the place unknowne and wilde,
Breedes dreadfull doubts: Oft fire is without smoke,
And perill without show: therefore your stroke
Sir knight with-hold, till further triall made."
"Ah Ladie," said he, "shame were to revoke° *draw back*
The forward footing for° an hidden shade: *because of*
Vertue gives her selfe light, through darkenesse for to wade."

5. I.e., exudes resin continuously. Spenser in these stanzas imitates Chaucer's catalog of trees in the *Parliament of Fowls;* the convention goes back to Ovid.

6. Holly or holm-oak, both suitable for carving.

7. "Needlesse" because the spear is used only on horseback. "By tract" (line 95): by following the track.

13

"Yea but," quoth she, "the perill of this place
I better wot then° you, though now too late *know than*
To wish you backe returne with foule disgrace,
Yet wisedome warnes, whilest foot is in the gate,
To stay the stepe, ere forcèd to retrate.
This is the wandring wood, this Errours den,
A monster vile, whom God and man does hate:
Therefore I read° beware." "Fly fly," quoth then *advise*
The fearefull Dwarfe: "this is no place for living men."

14

But full of fire and greedy hardiment,° *boldness*
The youthfull knight could not for ought° be staide, *anything*
But forth unto the darksome hole he went,
And lookèd in: his glistring° armor made *shining*
A litle glooming light, much like a shade,
By which he saw the ugly monster plaine,
Halfe like a serpent horribly displaide,
But th' other halfe did womans shape retaine,
Most lothsom, filthie, foule, and full of vile disdaine.°[8] *loathsomeness*

15

And as she lay upon the durtie ground,
Her huge long taile her den all overspred,
Yet was in knots and many boughtes° upwound, *coils*
Pointed with mortall sting. Of her there bred
A thousand yong ones, which she dayly fed,
Sucking upon her poisonous dugs, eachone
Of sundry shapes, yet all ill favorèd:
Soone as that uncouth° light upon them shone, *unfamiliar*
Into her mouth they crept, and suddain all were gone.

16

Their dam upstart, out of her den effraide,° *alarmed*
And rushèd forth, hurling her hideous taile
About her cursèd head, whose folds displaid° *extended*
Were stretcht now forth at length without entraile.° *coiling*
She lookt about, and seeing one in mayle
Armèd to point,° sought backe to turne againe; *i.e., completely*
For light she hated as the deadly bale,° *injury*
Ay wont° in desert darknesse to remain, *ever accustomed*
Where plaine none might her see, nor she see any plaine.

17

Which when the valiant Elfe[9] perceived, he lept
As Lyon fierce upon the flying pray,
And with his trenchand° blade her boldly kept *cutting*
From turning backe, and forcèd her to stay:
Therewith enraged she loudly gan to bray,
And turning fierce, her speckled taile advaunst,
Threatning her angry sting, him to dismay:° *defeat*

8. The description echoes both classical and biblical monsters (cf. Revelation 9.7–10).

9. I.e., knight of Faerie Land.

Who nought aghast, his mightie hand enhaunst:° *lifted up*
The stroke down from her head unto her shoulder glaunst.

18

Much daunted with that dint,° her sence was dazd, *blow*
Yet kindling rage, her selfe she gathered round,
And all attonce her beastly body raizd
With doubled forces high above the ground:
Tho° wrapping up her wrethèd sterne arownd, *then*
Lept fierce upon his shield, and her huge traine° *tail*
All suddenly about his body wound,
That hand or foot to stirre he strove in vaine:
God helpe the man so wrapt in Errours endlesse traine.

19

His Lady sad to see his sore constraint,
Cride out, "Now now Sir knight, shew what ye bee,
Add faith unto your force, and be not faint:
Strangle her, else she sure will strangle thee."
That when he heard, in great perplexitie,[1]
His gall did grate[2] for griefe° and high disdaine, *wrath*
And knitting all his force got one hand free,
Wherewith he grypt her gorge° with so great paine, *throat*
That soone to loose her wicked bands did her constraine.

20

Therewith she spewd out of her filthy maw
A floud of poyson horrible and blacke,
Full of great lumpes of flesh and gobbets raw,
Which stunck so vildly, that it forst him slacke
His grasping hold, and from her turne him backe:
Her vomit full of bookes and papers was,[3]
With loathly frogs and toades, which eyes did lacke,
And creeping sought way in the weedy gras:
Her filthy parbreake° all the place defilèd has.[4] *vomit*

21

As when old father Nilus gins to swell
With timely° pride above the Aegyptian vale, *in season*
His fattie° waves do fertile slime outwell, *rich*
And overflow each plaine and lowly dale:
But when his later spring gins to avale,° *subside*
Huge heapes of mudd he leaves, wherein there breed
Ten thousand kindes of creatures, partly male
And partly female of his fruitfull seed;
Such ugly monstrous shapes elswhere may no man reed.° *see*

22

The same so sore annoyed has the knight,
That welnigh chokèd with the deadly stinke,

1. In both the usual sense and the sense of "entangled condition."
2. I.e., his gall bladder (considered the seat of anger) was violently disturbed.
3. Alluding (at one level) to books and pamphlets of Catholic propaganda, notably attacks on Queen Elizabeth.
4. Revelation 16.13: "And I saw three unclean spirits like frogs come out of the mouth of the dragon, and out of the mouth of the beast, and out of the mouth of the false prophet."

His forces faile, ne can no longer fight.
Whose corage when the feend perceived to shrinke,
She pourèd forth out of her hellish sinke
Her fruitfull cursèd spawne of serpents small,
Deformèd monsters, fowle, and blacke as inke,
Which swarming all about his legs did crall,
And him encombred sore, but could not hurt at all.

23

As gentle Shepheard in sweete even-tide,
When ruddy Phoebus gins to welke° in west, *sink*
High on an hill, his flocke to vewen wide,
Markes° which do byte their hasty supper best; *observes*
A cloud of combrous° gnattes do him molest, *encumbering*
All striving to infixe their feeble stings,
That from their noyance he no where can rest,
But with his clownish° hands their tender wings *rustic*
He brusheth oft, and oft doth mar their murmurings.

24

Thus ill bestedd,° and fearful more of shame, *situated*
Then of the certaine perill he stood in,
Halfe furious unto his foe he came,
Resolved in minde all suddenly to win,
Or soone to lose, before he once would lin;° *cease*
And strooke at her with more then manly force,
That from her body full of filthie sin
He raft° her hatefull head without remorse; *cut away*
A streame of cole black bloud forth gushèd from her corse.

25

Her scattred brood, soone as their Parent deare
They saw so rudely° falling to the ground, *with great force*
Groning full deadly, all with troublous feare,
Gathred themselves about her body round,
Weening° their wonted entrance to have found *thinking*
At her wide mouth: but being there withstood
They flockèd all about her bleeding wound,
And suckèd up their dying mothers blood,
Making her death their life, and eke° her hurt their good. *also*

26

That detestable sight him much amazde,° *stunned*
To see th' unkindly Impes° of heaven accurst, *unnatural offspring*
Devoure their dam; on whom while so he gazd,
Having all satisfide their bloudy thurst,
Their bellies swolne he saw with fulnesse burst,
And bowels gushing forth: well worthy end
Of such as drunke her life, the which them nurst;
Now needeth him no lenger° labour spend, *longer*
His foes have slaine themselves, with whom he should contend.

27

His Ladie seeing all, that chaunst, from farre
Approcht in hast to greet° his victorie, *congratulate*

And said, "Faire knight, borne under happy starre,
Who see your vanquisht foes before you lye;
Well worthy be you of that Armorie,° *armor*
Wherein ye have great glory wonne this day,
And prooved your strength on a strong enimie,
Your first adventure: many such I pray,
And henceforth ever wish, that like succeed it may."

28

Then mounted he upon his Steede againe,
And with the Lady backward sought to wend;° *go*
That path he kept, which beaten was most plaine,
Ne ever would to any by-way bend,
But still did follow one unto the end,
The which at last out of the wood them brought.
So forward on his way (with God to frend)° *with God as friend*
He passèd forth, and new adventure sought;
Long way he travelèd, before he heard of ought.° *aught, anything*

29

At length they chaunst to meet upon the way
An aged Sire, in long blacke weedes yclad,[5]
His feete all bare, his beard all hoarie gray,
And by his belt his booke he hanging had;
Sober he seemde, and very sagely sad,° *grave*
And to the ground his eyes were lowly bent,
Simple in shew,° and voyde of malice bad, *show*
And all the way he prayèd, as he went,
And often knockt his brest, as one that did repent.

30

He faire the knight saluted, louting° low, *bowing*
Who faire him quited,° as that courteous was: *answered*
And after askèd him, if he did know
Of straunge adventures, which abroad did pas.
"Ah my deare Sonne," quoth he, "how should, alas,
Silly° old man, that lives in hidden cell, *simple*
Bidding his beades° all day for his trespas, *saying his prayers*
Tydings of warre and worldly trouble tell?
With holy father sits not with such things to mell.[6]

31

"But if of daunger which hereby doth dwell,
And homebred evill ye desire to heare,
Of a straunge man I can you tidings tell,
That wasteth all this countrey farre and neare."
"Of such," said he, "I chiefly do inquere,
And shall you well reward to shew the place,
In which that wicked wight his dayes doth weare.° *spend*
For to all knighthood it is foule disgrace,
That such a cursed creature lives so long a space."

5. Dressed in long black garments.
6. I.e., it is not fitting for a holy hermit to meddle ("mell") with such things.

32

"Far hence," quoth he, "in wastfull° wildernesse — *desolate*
His dwelling is, by which no living wight° — *creature*
May ever passe, but thorough° great distresse." — *through*
"Now," sayd the Lady, "draweth toward night,
And well I wote, that of your later° fight — *recent*
Ye all forwearied be: for what so strong,
But wanting° rest will also want of might? — *lacking*
The Sunne that measures heaven all day long,
At night doth baite° his steedes the Ocean waves emong. — *feed, refresh*

33

"Then with the Sunne take Sir, your timely rest,
And with new day new worke at once begin:
Untroubled night they say gives counsell best."
"Right well Sir knight ye have advisèd bin,"
Quoth then that agèd man; "the way to win
Is wisely to advise:° now day is spent; — *take thought*
Therefore with me ye may take up your In° — *lodging*
For this same night." The knight was well content.
So with that godly father to his home they went.

34

A little lowly Hermitage it was,
Downe in a dale, hard by° a forests side, — *close to*
Far from resort of people, that did pas
In travell to and froe: a little wyde° — *apart*
There was an holy Chappell edifyde,° — *built*
Wherein the Hermite dewly wont° to say — *was accustomed*
His holy things° each morne and eventyde: — *prayers*
Thereby a Christall streame did gently play,
Which from a sacred fountaine wellèd forth alway.

35

Arrivèd there, the little house they fill,
Ne looke for entertainement,° where none was: — *elegant provision*
Rest is their feast, and all things at their will;
The noblest mind the best contentment has.
With faire discourse the evening so they pas:
For that old man of pleasing wordes had store,
And well could file° his tongue as smooth as glas; — *polish*
He told of Saintes and Popes, and evermore
He strowd an *Ave-Mary*[7] after and before.

36

The drouping Night thus creepeth on them fast,
And the sad humour;° loading their eye liddes, — *heavy moisture*
As messenger of Morpheus[8] on them cast
Sweet slombring deaw, the which to sleepe them biddes.
Unto their lodgings then his guestes he riddes:° — *leads*
Where when all drownd in deadly sleepe° he findes, — *sleep like death*
He to his study goes, and there amiddes

7. "Hail Mary"—that is, a Catholic prayer.
8. Here (as often) Morpheus, the classical god of dreams, is conflated with his father Somnus, god of sleep.

His Magick bookes and artes of sundry kindes,
He seekes out mighty charmes, to trouble sleepy mindes.

37

Then choosing out few wordes most horrible
(Let none them read), thereof did verses frame,
With which and other spelles like terrible,
He bade awake blacke Plutoes griesly Dame,[9]
And cursèd heaven, and spake reprochfull shame
Of highest God, the Lord of life and light;
A bold bad man, that dared to call by name
Great Gorgon,[1] Prince of darknesse and dead night,
At which Cocytus quakes, and Styx is put to flight.

38

And forth he cald out of deepe darknesse dred
Legions of Sprights,° the which like little flyes[2] *spirits*
Fluttring about his ever damnèd hed,
A-waite whereto their service he applyes,
To aide his friends, or fray° his enimies: *frighten*
Of those he chose out two, the falsest twoo,
And fittest for to forge true-seeming lyes;
The one of them he gave a message too,
The other by him selfe staide other worke to doo.

39

He making speedy way through spersèd° ayre, *dispersed*
And through the world of waters wide and deepe,
To Morpheus house doth hastily repaire.
Amid the bowels of the earth full steepe,
And low, where dawning day doth never peepe,
His dwelling is; there Tethys° his wet bed *the wife of Ocean*
Doth ever wash, and Cynthia[3] still° doth steepe *continually*
In silver deaw his ever-drouping hed,
Whiles sad° Night over him her mantle black doth spred. *sober*

40

Whose double gates he findeth lockèd fast,
The one faire framed of burnisht Yvory,
The other all with silver overcast;
And wakefull dogges before them farre do lye,
Watching to banish Care their enimy,
Who oft is wont° to trouble gentle Sleepe. *accustomed to*
By them the Sprite doth passe in quietly,
And unto Morpheus comes, whom drownèd deepe
In drowsie fit he findes: of nothing he takes keepe.° *notice*

41

And more, to lulle him in his slumber soft,
A trickling streame from high rocke tumbling downe
And ever-drizling raine upon the loft,° *aloft, above*

9. Proserpine, as patron of witchcraft.

1. Demogorgon, in some myths the progenitor of all the gods, so powerful that the mention of his name causes hell's rivers (Styx and Cocytus) to tremble.

2. The simile associates him with Beelzebub ("Lord of Flies"), the name given to "the prince of the devils."

3. Diana, the goddess of the moon.

Mixt with a murmuring winde, much like the sowne° *sound*
Of swarming Bees, did cast him in a swowne:° *swoon*
No other noyse, nor peoples troublous cryes,
As still° are wont t'annoy the wallèd towne, *always*
Might there be heard: but carelesse° Quiet lyes, *free from care*
Wrapt in eternall silence farre from enemyes.[4]

42

The messenger approching to him spake,
But his wast° wordes returnd to him in vaine: *wasted*
So sound he slept, that nought mought° him awake. *might*
Then rudely he him thrust, and pusht with paine,° *effort*
Whereat he gan to stretch: but he againe
Shooke him so hard, that forcèd him to speake.
As one then in a dreame, whose dryer braine[5]
Is tost with troubled sights and fancies° weake, *fantasies*
He mumbled soft, but would not all his silence breake.

43

The Sprite then gan more boldly him to wake,
And threatned unto him the dreaded name
Of Hecate:° whereat he gan to quake, *queen of Hades*
And lifting up his lumpish° head, with blame *heavy*
Halfe angry askèd him, for what° he came. *why*
"Hither," quoth he, "me Archimago[6] sent,
He that the stubborne Sprites can wisely tame,
He bids thee to him send for his intent
A fit false dreame, that can delude the sleepers sent."° *senses*

44

The God obayde, and calling forth straight way
A diverse° dreame out of his prison darke, *distracting*
Delivered it to him, and downe did lay
His heavie head, devoide of carefull carke,° *anxious concerns*
Whose sences all were straight° benumbd and starke.° *immediately*; *unfeeling*
He backe returning by the Yvorie dore,[7]
Remounted up as light as chearefull Larke,
And on his litle winges the dreame he bore
In hast unto his Lord, where he him left afore.

45

Who all this while with charmes and hidden artes,
Had made a Lady of that other Spright,
And framed of liquid ayre her tender partes
So lively,° and so like in all mens sight, *lifelike*
That weaker° sence it could have ravisht quight: *too weak*
The maker selfe for all his wondrous witt,
Was nigh beguilèd° with so goodly sight: *deceived*

4. Spenser is imitating descriptions of the caves of Morpheus in Chaucer (*Book of the Duchess*, lines 153–77) and of Somnus in Ovid (*Metamorphoses* 11.592–632).
5. According to the old physiology, elderly people and other light sleepers had too little moisture in the brain.
6. The name can be construed as meaning both "archmagician" and "architect of images."
7. According to Homer (*Odyssey* 19.562–67) and Virgil (*Aeneid* 6.893–96), false dreams come through Sleep's ivory gate, true dreams through his gate of horn.

Her all in white he clad, and over it
Cast a blacke stole, most like to seeme for Una[8] fit.° *fitting*

46

Now when that ydle dreame was to him brought
Unto that Elfin knight he bad him fly,
Where he slept soundly void of evill thought
And with false shewes abuse his fantasy,° *imagination*
In sort as° he him schoolèd privily: *in the way that*
And that new creature borne without her dew,° *unnaturally*
Full of the makers guile, with usage sly
He taught to imitate that Lady trew,
Whose semblance she did carrie under feignèd hew.° *form*

47

Thus well instructed, to their worke they hast
And comming where the knight in slomber lay
The one upon his hardy head him plast,° *placed*
And made him dreame of loves and lustfull play,
That nigh his manly hart did melt away,
Bathèd in wanton blis and wicked joy:
Then seemèd him his Lady by him lay,
And to him playnd,° how that false wingèd boy;° *complained / Cupid*
Her chast hart had subdewd, to learne Dame pleasures toy.° *lustful play*

48

And she her selfe of beautie soveraigne Queene,
Faire Venus seemde unto his bed to bring
Her, whom he waking evermore did weene° *think*
To be the chastest flowre, that ay° did spring *ever*
On earthly braunch, the daughter of a king,
Now a loose Leman° to vile service bound: *paramour*
And eke° the Graces seemèd all to sing, *also*
Hymen iô Hymen, dauncing all around,
Whilst freshest Flora her with Yvie girlond crownd.[9]

49

In this great passion of unwonted° lust, *unaccustomed*
Or wonted feare of doing ought amis,
He started up, as seeming to mistrust° *suspect*
Some secret ill, or hidden foe of his:
Lo there before his face his Lady is,
Under blake stole hyding her bayted hooke,
And as halfe blushing offred him to kis,
With gentle blandishment and lovely° looke, *loving*
Most like that virgin true, which for her knight him took.

50

All cleane dismayd to see so uncouth° sight, *strange; unseemly*
And halfe enragèd at her shamelesse guise,

8. Her name means "one, unity." Elizabethan readers would know the Latin phrase *Una Vera Fides* ("one true faith") and also the proverb "Truth is one."

9. The three graces of classical mythology were personifications of grace and beauty; here they sing a call to the pleasures of the marriage bed (Hymen was god of marriage). In the March eclogue of *The Shepheardes Calender*, E. K. glossed Flora as "the Goddesse of flowres, but indede (as saith Tacitus) a famous harlot."

He thought have slaine her in his fierce despight:° *indignation*
But hasty heat tempring with sufferance° wise, *patience*
He stayde his hand, and gan himselfe advise
To prove his sense, and tempt° her faignèd truth. *test*
Wringing her hands in wemens pitteous wise,
Tho can° she weepe, to stirre up gentle ruth,° *then did / pity*
Both for her noble bloud, and for her tender youth.

51

And said, "Ah Sir, my liege Lord and my love,
Shall I accuse the hidden cruell fate,
And mightie causes wrought in heaven above,
Or the blind God, that doth me thus amate,° *dismay*
For° hopèd love to winne me certaine hate? *instead of*
Yet thus perforce° he bids me do, or die. *forcibly*
Die is my dew:[1] yet rew° my wretched state *pity*
You, whom my hard avenging destinie
Hath made judge of my life or death indifferently.° *impartially*

52

"Your owne deare sake forst me at first to leave
My Fathers kingdome," There she stopt with teares;
Her swollen hart her speach seemd to bereave,
And then againe begun, "My weaker yeares
Captived to fortune and frayle worldly feares,
Fly to your faith for succour and sure ayde:
Let me not dye in languor° and long teares. *sorrow*
"Why Dame," quoth he, "what hath ye thus dismayd?
What frayes° ye, that were wont to comfort me affrayd?" *frightens*

53

"Love of your selfe," she said, "and deare° constraint *dire*
Lets me not sleepe, but wast the wearie night
In secret anguish and unpittied plaint,
Whiles you in carelesse sleepe are drownèd quight."
Her doubtfull words made that redoubted[2] knight
Suspect her truth: yet since no'untruth he knew,
Her fawning love with foule disdainefull spight
He would not shend,° but said, "Deare dame I rew, *reject*
That for my sake unknowne such griefe unto you grew.

54

"Assure your selfe, it fell not all to ground;
For all so deare as life is to my hart,
I deeme your love, and hold me to you bound;
Ne let vaine feares procure your needlesse smart,° *pain*
Where cause is none, but to your rest depart."
Not all content, yet seemd she to appease° *cease*
Her mournefull plaintes, beguilèd° of her art, *foiled*
And fed with words, that could not chuse° but please, *choose*
So slyding softly forth, she turnd° as to her ease. *returned*

1. I.e., I deserve to die.
2. Dreaded, also doubting again. "Doubtfull": fearful, also questionable.

55

Long after lay he musing at her mood,
Much grieved to thinke that gentle Dame so light,° *frivolous*
For whose defence he was to shed his blood.
At last dull wearinesse of former fight
Having yrockt a sleepe his irkesome spright,
That troublous dreame gan freshly tosse his braine,
With bowres and beds, and Ladies deare delight:
But when he saw his labour all was vaine,
With that misformèd spright[3] he backe returnd againe.

From *Canto 2*

[REDCROSSE WINS "FIDESSA"]

The guilefull great Enchaunter parts
The Redcrosse Knight from Truth:
Into whose stead faire falshood steps,
And workes him wofull ruth.° *mischief*

1

By this the Northerne wagoner had set
His seven fold teame behind the stedfast starre,[4]
That was in Ocean waves yet never wet,
But firme is fixt, and sendeth light from farre
To all, that in the wide deepe wandring arre:
And chearefull Chaunticlere with his note shrill
Had warnèd once, that Phoebus fiery carre[5]
In hast was climbing up the Easterne hill,
Full envious that night so long his roome° did fill. *place*

2

When those accursèd messengers of hell,
That feigning dreame, and that faire-forgèd Spright
Came to their wicked maister, and gan tell
Their bootelesse° paines, and ill succeeding night: *useless*
Who all in rage to see his skilfull might
Deluded so, gan threaten hellish paine
And sad Proserpines wrath, them to affright.
But when he saw his threatning was but vaine,
He cast about, and searcht his balefull° bookes againe. *deadly*

3

Eftsoones° he tooke that miscreated faire, *immediately*
And that false other Spright, on whom he spred
A seeming body of the subtile° aire, *rarefied*
Like a young Squire, in loves and lusty-hed
His wanton dayes that ever loosely led,
Without regard of armes and dreaded fight:
Those two he tooke, and in a secret bed,

3. I.e., with the spirit impersonating Una.
4. I.e., by this time the Big Dipper had set behind the North Star.
5. Chariot of the sun god, Phoebus Apollo. "Chaunticlere": Chanticleer—generic name for a rooster.

Covered with darknesse and misdeeming° night, *misleading*
Them both together laid, to joy in vaine delight.

4

Forthwith he runnes with feignèd faithfull hast
Unto his guest, who after troublous sights
And dreames, gan now to take more sound repast,° *rest*
Whom suddenly he wakes with fearefull frights,
As one aghast with feends or damnèd sprights,
And to him cals, "Rise rise unhappy Swaine,
That here wex° old in sleepe, whiles wicked wights *grow*
Have knit themselves in Venus shamefull chaine;
Come see, where your false Lady doth her honour staine."

5

All in amaze he suddenly up start
With sword in hand, and with the old man went;
Who soone him brought into a secret part,
Where that false couple were full closely ment° *mingled*
In wanton lust and lewd embracèment:
Which when he saw, he burnt with gealous fire,
The eye of reason was with rage yblent,° *blinded*
And would have slaine them in his furious ire,
But hardly° was restreinèd of° that agèd sire. *with difficulty / by*

6

Returning to his bed in torment great,
And bitter anguish of his guiltie sight,
He could not rest, but did his stout heart eat,
And wast his inward gall with deepe despight,° *malice*
Yrkesome° of life, and too long lingring night. *tired*
At last faire Hesperus[6] in highest skie
Had spent his lampe, and brought forth dawning light,
Then up he rose, and clad him hastily;
The Dwarfe him brought his steed: so both away do fly.

7

Now when the rosy-fingred Morning faire,
Weary of aged Tithones[7] saffron bed,
Had spred her purple robe through deawy aire,
And the high hils Titan° discoverèd,° *the sun / revealed*
The royall virgin shooke off drowsy-hed,
And rising forth out of her baser° bowre, *too lowly*
Lookt for her knight, who far away was fled,
And for her Dwarfe, that wont° to wait each houre: *was accustomed*
Then gan she waile and weepe, to see that woefull stowre.° *affliction*

8

And after him she rode with so much speede
As her slow beast could make; but all in vaine:
For him so far had borne his light-foot steede,
Prickèd with wrath and fiery fierce disdaine,° *indignation*
That him to follow was but fruitlesse paine;

6. The morning star.
7. Tithonus is the husband of Aurora, goddess of the dawn.

Yet she her weary limbes would never rest,
But every hill and dale, each wood and plaine
Did search, sore grievèd in her gentle brest,
He so ungently left her, whom she lovèd best.

9

But subtill° Archimago, when his guests — *cunning*
He saw divided into double parts,
And Una wandring in woods and forrests,
Th' end of his drift,° he praisd his divelish arts — *plot*
That had such might over true meaning harts;
Yet rests not so, but other meanes doth make,
How he may worke unto her further smarts:° — *pains*
For her he hated as the hissing snake,
And in her many troubles did most pleasure take.

10

He then devisde himselfe how to disguise;
For by his mightie science° he could take — *knowledge*
As many formes and shapes in seeming wise,° — *in appearance*
As ever Proteus[8] to himselfe could make:
Sometime a fowle, sometime a fish in lake,
Now like a foxe, now like a dragon fell,° — *fierce*
That of himselfe he oft for feare would quake,
And oft would flie away. O who can tell
The hidden power of herbes, and might of Magicke spell?

11

But now seemde best, the person to put on
Of that good knight, his late beguilèd guest:
In mighty armes he was yclad anon,
And silver shield: upon his coward brest
A bloudy crosse, and on his craven crest
A bounch of haires discolourd diversly:° — *variously colored*
Full jolly° knight he seemde, and well addrest,° — *gallant / armed*
And when he sate upon his courser free,
Saint George himself ye would have deemèd him to be.

12

But he the knight, whose semblaunt° he did beare, — *likeness*
The true Saint George was wandred far away,
Still flying from° his thoughts and gealous feare; — *because of*
Will was his guide, and griefe led him astray.
At last him chaunst to meete upon the way
A faithlesse Sarazin° all armed to point,° — *Saracen / completely*
In whose great shield was writ with letters gay
Sans foy:[9] full large of limbe and every joint
He was, and carèd not for God or man a point.° — *at all*

13

He had a faire companion of his way,
A goodly Lady clad in scarlot red,
Purfled° with gold and pearle of rich assay,[1] — *decorated*

8. A sea god who could change his shape at will (*Odyssey* 4.398–424).

9. Without faith, faithless (French).

1. Proven of rich value.

And like a Persian mitre on her hed
She wore, with crownes and owches° garnishèd, *brooches*
The which her lavish lovers to her gave;[2]
Her wanton° palfrey all was overspred *unruly*
With tinsell trappings, woven like a wave,
Whose bridle rung with golden bels and bosses brave.° *handsome studs*

14

With faire disport° and courting dalliaunce *diversion*
She intertainde her lover all the way:
But when she saw the knight his speare advaunce,
She soone left off her mirth and wanton play,
And bad her knight addresse him to the fray:
His foe was nigh at hand. He prickt with pride
And hope to winne his Ladies heart that day,
Forth spurrèd fast: adowne his coursers side
The red bloud trickling staind the way, as he did ride.

15

The knight of the Redcrosse when him he spide,
Spurring so hote with rage dispiteous,° *cruel*
Gan fairely couch° his speare, and towards ride: *lower*
Soone meete they both, both fell° and furious, *fierce*
That daunted° with their forces hideous, *dazed*
Their steeds do stagger, and amazèd° stand, *stunned*
And eke° themselves too rudely rigorous,° *also / violent*
Astonied° with the stroke of their owne hand, *stunned*
Do backe rebut,° and each to other yeeldeth land. *recoil*

16

As when two rams stird with ambitious pride,
Fight for the rule of the rich fleecèd flocke,
Their hornèd fronts so fierce on either side
Do meete, that with the terrour of the shocke
Astonied both, stand sencelesse as a blocke,
Forgetfull of the hanging° victory: *in the balance*
So stood these twaine, unmovèd as a rocke,
Both staring fierce, and holding idely
The broken reliques of their former cruelty.

17

The Sarazin sore daunted with the buffe
Snatcheth his sword, and fiercely to him flies;
Who well it wards, and quyteth° cuff with cuff: *requites, repays*
Each others equall puissaunce envies,° *power seeks to rival*
And through their iron sides with cruell spies° *looks*
Does seeke to perce: repining courage yields
No foote to foe. The flashing fier flies

2. The lady's garb associates her with the Whore of Babylon (Revelation 17.3–4): "And I saw a woman sit upon a scarlet colored beast, full of names of blasphemy, having seven heads and ten horns. And the woman was arrayed in purple and scarlet color, and decked with gold and precious stones and pearls, having a golden cup in her hand full of abominations and filthiness of her fornication."

As from a forge out of their burning shields,
And streames of purple bloud new dies the verdant fields.

18

"Curse on that Crosse," quoth then the Sarazin,
"That keepes thy body from the bitter fit;° *death pangs*
Dead long ygoe I wote° thou haddest bin, *thought*
Had not that charme from thee forwarnèd° it: *prevented*
But yet I warne thee now assurèd° sitt, *securely*
And hide thy head." Therewith upon his crest
With rigour° so outrageöus he smitt, *violence*
That a large share it hewd out of the rest,
And glauncing downe his shield, from blame him fairely blest.[3]

19

Who thereat wondrous wroth, the sleeping spark
Of native vertue° gan eftsoones° revive, *strength / again*
And at his haughtie helmet making mark,° *taking aim*
So hugely° stroke, that it the steele did rive, *mightily*
And cleft his head. He tumbling downe alive,
With bloudy mouth his mother earth did kis
Greeting his grave: his grudging° ghost did strive *complaining*
With the fraile flesh; at last it flitted is,
Whither the soules do fly of men, that live amis.

20

The Lady when she saw her champion fall,
Like the old ruines of a broken towre,
Staid not to waile his woefull funerall,° *death*
But from him fled away with all her powre;
Who after her as hastily gan scowre,° *scurry*
Bidding the Dwarfe with him to bring away
The Sarazins shield, signe of the conqueroure.
Her soone he overtooke, and bad to stay,
For present cause was none of dread her to dismay.

21

She turning backe with ruefull countenaunce,
Cride, "Mercy mercy Sir vouchsafe to show
On silly° Dame, subject to hard mischaunce, *helpless*
And to your mighty will." Her humblesse low
In so ritch weedes° and seeming glorious show, *clothes*
Did much emmove his stout heroicke heart,
And said, "Deare dame, your suddein overthrow
Much rueth° me; but now put feare apart, *grieves*
And tell, both who ye be, and who that tooke your part."

22

Melting in teares, then gan she thus lament;
"The wretched woman, whom unhappy howre
Hath now made thrall° to your commandèment, *slave*
Before that angry heavens list to lowre,° *chose to frown*

3. Preserved him from harm.

And fortune false betraide me to your powre
Was (O what now availeth that I was!)
Borne the sole daughter of an Emperour,
He that the wide West under his rule has,
And high hath set his throne, where Tiberis doth pas.[4]

23

"He in the first flowre of my freshest age,
Betrothèd me unto the onely haire° *heir*
Of a most mighty king, most rich and sage;[5]
Was never Prince so faithfull and so faire,
Was never Prince so meeke and debonaire;° *gracious*
But ere my hopèd day of spousall shone,
My dearest Lord fell from high honours staire,
Into the hands of his accursèd fone,° *foes*
And cruelly was slaine, that shall I ever mone.

24

"His blessèd body spoild of lively breath,
Was afterward, I know not how, convaid° *carried away*
And fro me hid: of whose most innocent death
When tidings came to me unhappy maid,
O how great sorrow my sad soule assaid.° *afflicted*
Then forth I went his woefull corse to find,
And many yeares throughout the world I straid,
A virgin widow, whose deepe wounded mind
With love, long time did languish as the striken hind.° *deer*

25

"At last it chauncèd this proud Sarazin
To meete me wandring, who perforce° me led *by violence*
With him away, but yet could never win
The fort, that Ladies hold in soveraigne dread.° *utmost reverence*
There lies he now with foule dishonour dead,
Who whiles he livde, was callèd proud Sans foy,
The eldest of three brethren, all three bred
Of one bad sire, whose youngest is Sans joy,
And twixt them both was borne the bloudy bold Sans loy.[6]

26

"In this sad plight, friendlesse, unfortunate,
Now miserable I Fidessa° dwell, *Faithful*
Craving of you in pitty of my state,
To do none° ill, if please ye not do well." *no*
He in great passion all this while did dwell,° *continue*
More busying his quicke eyes, her face to view,
Then his dull eares, to heare what she did tell;
And said, "Faire Lady hart of flint would rew
The undeservèd woes and sorrowes, which ye shew.

4. The Tiber River runs through Rome. The lady is hence associated with the Catholic church. Her father, she says, is ruler of the west—but Una's father had the rule of both east *and* west (1.1.41); historically, the true church once embraced east and west.
5. The lady claims to have been betrothed to Christ, bridegroom of the church (Matthew 9.15).
6. Without law.

27

"Henceforth in safe assuraunce may ye rest,
Having both found a new friend you to aid,
And lost an old foe, that did you molest:
Better new friend than an old foe is° said." *it is*
With chaunge of cheare° the seeming simple maid *countenance*
Let fall her eyen, as shamefast° to the earth, *as if modestly*
And yeelding soft, in that she nought gain-said,° *objected*
So forth they rode, he feining° seemely merth, *simulating*
And she coy lookes: so dainty they say maketh derth.[7]

Summary In the second half of the canto, Redcrosse and his new companion seek relief from the blazing sun in the shade of two trees. Plucking a bough from one of them to make a garland for the lady, he is astonished to hear a groaning voice from within the tree. The voice is that of a knight named Fradubio (Brother Doubt), who explains that he and his beloved have been metamorphosed into trees by a wicked witch named Duessa. Unbeknownst to him, Redcrosse is in the company of this witch.

Canto 3 *Summary* In search of the knight who has abandoned her, Una encounters a lion who licks her hands and accompanies her in her wanderings. They take refuge for the night in the cottage of a superstitious old woman and her daughter. During the night the daughter's lover, a robber of churches, returns to the cottage with booty for her and is torn to pieces by the lion. Seeking revenge, the old woman encounters Archimago and tells him where to find Una. The magician presents himself to Una disguised as Redcrosse, but his plan backfires when he is attacked by the Saracen Sans loy (brother of the slain Sans foy). Sans loy then kills the faithful lion and abducts Una, leaving Archimago lying wounded.

From *Canto 4*

[THE HOUSE OF PRIDE]

To sinfull house of Pride, Duessa
guides the faithfull knight,
Where brothers death to wreak° Sansjoy *avenge*
doth chalenge him to fight.

I

Young knight, what ever that dost armes professe,
And through long labours huntest after fame,
Beware of fraud, beware of ficklenesse,
In choice, and change of thy deare lovèd Dame,
Least thou of her beleeve too lightly blame,[8]
And rash misweening° doe thy hart remove: *misjudgment*
For unto knight there is no greater shame,
Then lightnesse and inconstancie in love;
That doth this Redcrosse knights ensample° plainly prove. *example*

7. Proverbial: what's dear is rare; here, coyness creates unsatisfied desire.

8. Lest you too readily believe accusations about her.

2

Who after that he had faire Una lorne,° *forsaken*
Through light misdeeming° of her loialtie, *misjudging*
And false Duessa in her sted had borne,° *taken as companion*
Called Fidess', and so supposd to bee;
Long with her traveild, till at last they see
A goodly building, bravely garnishèd,° *adorned*
The house of mightie Prince it seemd to bee:
And towards it a broad high way[9] that led,
All bare through peoples feet, which thither traveilèd.

3

Great troupes of people traveild thitherward
Both day and night, of each degree and place,° *rank*
But few returnèd, having scapèd hard,° *with difficulty*
With balefull° beggerie, or foule disgrace, *wretched*
Which ever after in most wretched case,
Like loathsome lazars,° by the hedges lay. *lepers*
Thither Duessa bad him bend his pace:° *direct his steps*
For she is wearie of the toilesome way,
And also nigh consumèd is the lingring day.

4

A stately Pallace built of squarèd bricke,
Which cunningly was without morter laid,
Whose wals were high, but nothing strong, nor thick,
And golden foile° all over them displaid, *thin layer of gold*
That purest skye with brightnesse they dismaid:° *outdid*
High lifted up were many loftie towres,
And goodly galleries farre over laid,° *placed above*
Full of faire windowes, and delightfull bowres;
And on the top a Diall told the timely howres.[1]

5

It was a goodly heape° for to behould, *building*
And spake the praises of the workmans wit;° *skill*
But full great pittie, that so faire a mould° *structure*
Did on so weake foundation ever sit:
For on a sandie hill,[2] that still did flit,° *shift*
And fall away, it mounted was full hie,
That every breath of heaven shakèd it:
And all the hinder parts, that few could spie,
Were ruinous and old, but painted cunningly.

6

Arrivèd there they passèd in forth right;
For still° to all the gates stood open wide, *always*
Yet charge of them was to a Porter hight° *committed*
Cald Malvenù,[3] who entrance none denide:

9. "Broad is the way that leadeth to destruction" (Matthew 7.13).
1. A sundial measured the hours of the day.
2. Matthew 7.26–27: "A foolish man . . . built his house upon the sand: And the rain descended, and the floods came, and the winds blew, and beat upon that house; and it fell; and great was the fall of it."
3. "Unwelcome." In courtly love allegories, the porter is often called Bienvenu or Bel-accueil ("welcome").

Thence to the hall, which was on every side
With rich array and costly arras dight:[4]
Infinite sorts of people did abide
There waiting long, to win the wishèd sight
Of her, that was the Lady of that Pallace bright.

7

By them they passe, all gazing on them round,
And to the Presence[5] mount; whose glorious vew
Their frayle amazèd senses did confound:
In living Princes court none ever knew
Such endlesse richesse, and so sumptuous shew;° *show*
Ne° Persia selfe, the nourse of pompous pride *nor*
Like ever saw. And there a noble crew
Of Lordes and Ladies stood on every side,
Which with their presence faire, the place much beautifide.

8

High above all a cloth of State° was spred, *canopy*
And a rich throne, as bright as sunny day,
On which there sate most brave embellishèd° *handsomely clad*
With royall robes and gorgeous array,
A mayden Queene, that shone as Titans° ray, *the sun's*
In glistring gold, and peerelesse pretious stone:
Yet her bright blazing beautie did assay° *attempt*
To dim the brightnesse of her glorious throne,
As envying her selfe, that too exceeding shone.

9

Exceeding shone, like Phoebus fairest childe,
That did presume his fathers firie wayne,° *chariot*
And flaming mouthes of steedes unwonted° wilde *unusually*
Through highest heaven with weaker° hand to rayne; *too weak*
Proud of such glory and advancement vaine,
While flashing beames do daze his feeble eyen,
He leaves the welkin° way most beaten plaine, *heavenly*
And rapt° with whirling wheeles, inflames the skyen, *carried away*
With fire not made to burne, but fairely for to shyne.[6]

10

So proud she shynèd in her Princely state,
Looking to heaven; for earth she did disdayne,
And sitting high; for lowly° she did hate: *lowliness*
Lo underneath her scornefull feete, was layne
A dreadfull Dragon with an hideous trayne,° *tail*
And in her hand she held a mirrhour bright,[7]
Wherein her face she often vewèd fayne,° *with pleasure*
And in her selfe-loved semblance tooke delight;
For she was wondrous faire, as any living wight.

4. Decorated with costly wall hangings.
5. Presence chamber, where a sovereign receives guests.
6. Phaëthon tried to drive the chariot of his father, Phoebus, the sun god, but set the skies on fire and fell.
7. Pride and figures associated with her in Renaissance literature and art often hold a mirror, emblematic of self-love.

11

Of griesly° Pluto she the daughter was, *horrid*
And sad Proserpina the Queene of hell;
Yet did she thinke her pearelesse worth to pas° *surpass*
That parentage, with pride so did she swell,
And thundring Jove, that high in heaven doth dwell,
And wield° the world, she claymèd for her syre, *govern*
Or if that any else did Jove excell:
For to the highest she did still aspyre,
Or if ought° higher were then that, did it desyre. *anything*

12

And proud Lucifera men did her call,
That made her selfe a Queene, and crownd to be,
Yet rightfull kingdome she had none at all,
Ne heritage of native soveraintie,
But did usurpe with wrong and tyrannie
Upon the scepter, which she now did hold:
Ne ruld her Realmes with lawes, but pollicie,° *political cunning*
And strong advizement of six wisards old,
That with their counsels bad her kingdome did uphold.

13

Soone as the Elfin knight in presence came,
And false Duessa seeming Lady faire,
A gentle Husher,° Vanitie by name *usher*
Made rowme, and passage for them did prepaire:
So goodly° brought them to the lowest staire *graciously*
Of her high throne, where they on humble knee
Making obeyssance,° did the cause declare, *submission*
Why they were come, her royall state to see,
To prove° the wide report of her great Majestee. *verify*

14

With loftie eyes, halfe loth to looke so low,
She thankèd them in her disdainefull wise,° *manner*
Ne other grace vouchsafèd them to show
Of Princesse worthy, scarse them bad° arise. *bade*
Her Lordes and Ladies all this while devise° *make ready*
Themselves to setten forth to straungers sight:
Some frounce° their curlèd haire in courtly guise, *frizzle*
Some prancke° their ruffes, and others trimly dight° *pleat / arrange*
Their gay attire: each others greater pride does spight.[8]

15

Goodly they all that knight do entertaine,
Right glad with him to have increast their crew:
But to Duess' each one himselfe did paine
All kindnesse and faire courtesie to shew;
For in that court whylome° her well they knew: *formerly*
Yet the stout Faerie mongst the middest° crowd *thickest*
Thought all their glorie vaine in knightly vew,

8. Each despises the others' greater pride.

And that great Princesse too exceeding prowd,
That to strange° knight no better countenance° allowd. *stranger / favor*

16

Suddein upriseth from her stately place
The royall Dame, and for her coche doth call:
All hurtlen° forth and she with Princely pace, *rush*
As faire Aurora in her purple pall,[9]
Out of the East the dawning day doth call:
So forth she comes: her brightnesse brode° doth blaze; *abroad*
The heapes of people thronging in the hall,
Do ride° each other, upon her to gaze: *climb up on*
Her glorious glitterand° light doth all mens eyes amaze. *glittering*

17

So forth she comes, and to her coche does clyme,
Adornèd all with gold, and girlonds gay,
That seemd as fresh as Flora° in her prime, *the goddess of flowers*
And strove to match, in royall rich array,
Great Junos golden chaire,° the which they say *chariot*
The Gods stand gazing on, when she does ride
To Joves high house through heavens bras-pavèd way
Drawne of faire Pecocks, that excell in pride,
And full of Argus eyes their tailes dispredden wide.[1]

18

But this was drawne of six unequall beasts,
On which her six sage Counsellours did ryde,
Taught to obay their bestiall beheasts,° *bidding*
With like conditions to their kinds applyde:[2]
Of which the first, that all the rest did guyde,
Was sluggish Idlenesse the nourse of sin;
Upon a slouthfull Asse he chose to ryde,
Arayd in habit blacke, and amis thin,[3]
Like to an holy Monck, the service to begin.

19

And in his hand his Portesse° still he bare, *breviary, prayerbook*
That much was worne, but therein little red,
For of devotion he had little care,
Still drownd in sleepe, and most of his dayes ded;
Scarse could he once uphold his heavie hed,
To looken, whether it were night or day:
May seeme the wayne° was very evill led, *chariot*
When such an one had guiding of the way,
That knew not, whether right he went, or else astray.

9. Goddess of dawn, in her crimson robe ("purple pall").
1. Peacocks, with their tails outspread ("dispredden wide"), are a symbol of pride. The hundred-eyed monster Argus was set by Juno to watch Io, one of Jupiter's loves. When Mercury killed Argus, his eyes were put in the peacock's tail feathers.
2. I.e., each bestial rider gave commands to his beast appropriate to its particular nature: the beasts and riders are suited to each other. This procession of the Seven Deadly Sins—of which Pride is queen—had a long tradition in medieval art and literature (see also Marlowe, *Dr. Faustus*, scene 5, lines 280–330).
3. Idleness wears the gown ("habit") and hood or amice ("amis") of a monk. Traditionally, Idleness led the procession of the deadly sins.

20

From worldly cares himselfe he did esloyne,° *withdraw*
And greatly shunnèd manly exercise,
From every worke he chalengèd essoyne,° *claimed exemption*
For contemplation sake: yet otherwise,
His life he led in lawlesse riotise;° *riotous conduct*
By which he grew to grievous malady;
For in his lustlesse° limbs through evill guise° *feeble / living*
A shaking fever raignd continually:
Such one was Idlenesse, first of this company.

21

And by his side rode loathsome Gluttony,
Deformèd creature, on a filthie swyne,
His belly was up-blowne with luxury,° *indulgence*
And eke° with fatnesse swollen were his eyne,° *also / eyes*
And like a Crane his necke was long and fyne,[4]
With which he swallowd up excessive feast,
For want whereof poore people oft did pyne;° *starve*
And all the way, most like a brutish beast,
He spuèd up his gorge,[5] that° all did him deteast. *so that*

22

In greene vine leaves he was right fitly clad;
For other clothes he could not weare for heat,
And on his head an yvie girland had,[6]
From under which fast trickled downe the sweat:
Still as he rode, he somewhat° still did eat, *something*
And in his hand did beare a bouzing° can, *drinking*
Of which he supt so oft, that on his seat
His dronken corse° he scarse upholden can, *body*
In shape and life more like a monster, then° a man. *than*

23

Unfit he was for any worldly thing,
And eke unhable once° to stirre or go,° *at all / walk*
Not meet° to be of counsell to a king, *fit*
Whose mind in meat and drinke was drownèd so,
That from his friend he seldome knew his fo:
Full of diseases was his carcas blew,
And a dry dropsie through his flesh did flow,
Which by misdiet daily greater grew:
Such one was Gluttony, the second of that crew.

24

And next° to him rode lustfull Lechery, *just after*
Upon a bearded Goat,[7] whose rugged° haire, *shaggy*
And whally° eyes (the signe of gelosy,°) *glaring / jealousy*
Was like the person selfe, whom he did beare:
Who rough, and blacke, and filthy did appeare,
Unseemely man to please faire Ladies eye;

4. The crane is a common symbol of gluttony because its long and thin ("fyne") neck allows extended pleasure in swallowing.
5. Vomited up what he had swallowed.
6. He resembles the drunken satyr Silenus, foster father of Bacchus, god of wine; ivy is sacred to Bacchus.
7. Traditional symbol of lust.

Yet he of Ladies oft was lovèd deare,
When fairer faces were bid standen by:° *away*
O who does know the bent of womens fantasy?° *caprice, whim*

25

In a greene gowne he clothèd was full faire,
Which underneath did hide his filthinesse,
And in his hand a burning hart he bare,
Full of vaine follies, and new fangleness:° *fickleness*
For he was false, and fraught with ficklenesse,
And learnèd had to love with secret lookes,
And well could daunce, and sing with ruefulnesse,° *pathos*
And fortunes tell, and read in loving bookes,[8]
And thousand other wayes, to bait his fleshly hookes.

26

Inconstant man, that lovèd all he saw,
And lusted after all, that he did love,
Ne would his looser life be tide to law,
But joyd weake wemens hearts to tempt and prove° *try*
If from their loyall loves he might them move;
Which lewdnesse fild him with reprochfull paine
Of that fowle evill, which all men reprove,° *i.e., syphilis*
That rots the marrow, and consumes the braine:
Such one was Lecherie, the third of all this traine.

27

And greedy Avarice by him did ride,
Upon a Camell loaden all with gold;[9]
Two iron coffers hong on either side,
With precious mettall full, as they might hold,
And in his lap an heape of coine he told;° *counted*
For of his wicked pelfe° his God he made, *money*
And unto hell him selfe for money sold;
Accursèd usurie was all his trade,
And right and wrong ylike in equall ballaunce waide.[1]

28

His life was nigh unto deaths doore yplast,
And thread-bare cote, and cobled° shoes he ware, *roughly mended*
Ne scarse good morsell all his life did tast,
But both from backe and belly still did spare,
To fill his bags, and richesse to compare;° *acquire*
Yet chylde ne° kinsman living had he none *nor*
To leave them to; but thorough° daily care *through*
To get, and nightly feare to lose his owne,
He led a wretched life unto him selfe unknowne.

29

Most wretched wight, whom nothing might suffise,
Whose greedy lust did lacke in greatest store,° *plenty*

8. Either manuals on the art of love (e.g., Ovid's *Ars Amatoria*) or more ordinary erotica.

9. The camel as a symbol of avarice is based on Matthew 19.24: "It is easier for a camel to go through the eye of a needle, than for a rich man to enter into the kingdom of God."

1. I.e., he made no distinction between right and wrong.

Whose need had end, but no end covetise,
Whose wealth was want, whose plenty made him pore,
Who had enough, yet wishèd ever more;
A vile disease, and eke in foote and hand
A grievous gout tormented him full sore,
That well he could not touch, nor go,° nor stand: *walk*
Such one was Avarice, the fourth of this faire band.

30

And next to him malicious Envie rode,
Upon a ravenous wolfe, and still° did chaw *continually*
Betweene his cankred° teeth a venemous tode, *infected*
That all the poison ran about his chaw;° *jaw*
But inwardly he chawèd his owne maw° *entrails*
At neighbours wealth, that made him ever sad;
For death it was, when any good he saw,
And wept, that cause of weeping none he had,
But when he heard of harme, he wexèd wondrous glad.

31

All in a kirtle of discolourd say[2]
He clothèd was, ypainted full of eyes;
And in his bosome secretly there lay
An hatefull Snake,[3] the which his taile uptyes
In many folds, and mortall sting implyes.° *enfolds*
Still as he rode, he gnasht his teeth, to see
Those heapes of gold with griple Covetyse,° *grasping Avarice*
And grudgèd at the great felicitie
Of proud Lucifera, and his owne companie.

32

He hated all good workes and vertuous deeds,
And him no lesse, that any like did use,° *perform*
And who with gracious bread the hungry feeds,
His almes for want of faith he doth accuse;[4]
So every good to bad he doth abuse:° *twist*
And eke the verse of famous Poets witt
He does backebite, and spightfull poison spues
From leprous mouth on all, that ever writt:
Such one vile Envie was, that fifte in row did sitt.

33

And him beside rides fierce revenging Wrath,
Upon a Lion, loth for to be led;
And in his hand a burning brond° he hath, *sword*
The which he brandisheth about his hed;
His eyes did hurle forth sparkles fiery red,
And starèd sterne on all, that him beheld,
As ashes pale of hew and seeming ded;
And on his dagger still his hand he held,
Trembling through hasty rage, when choler° in him sweld. *anger*

2. Robe or gown of many-colored cloth.
3. Traditional attribute of envy.
4. Envy perversely discounts others' good works by attributing them to a selfish motive: the desire to compensate (in God's eyes) for lack of faith.

34

His ruffin° raiment all was staind with blood, *disorderly*
Which he had spilt, and all to rags yrent,° *torn*
Through unadvisèd rashnesse woxen wood,° *grown insane*
For of his hands he had no governement,° *control*
Ne cared for° bloud in his avengement: *minded*
But when the furious fit was overpast,
His cruell facts° he often would repent; *actions*
Yet wilfull man he never would forecast,
How many mischieves should ensue his heedlesse hast.[5]

35

Full many mischiefes follow cruell Wrath;
Abhorrèd bloudshed, and tumultuous strife,
Unmanly murder, and unthrifty scath,[6]
Bitter despight,° with rancours rusty knife, *malice*
And fretting griefe the enemy of life;
All these, and many evils moe° haunt ire,° *more / anger*
The swelling Splene,[7] and Frenzy raging rife,
The shaking Palsey, and Saint Fraunces fire:[8]
Such one was Wrath, the last of this ungoldly tire.° *train*

36

And after all, upon the wagon beame
Rode Sathan,° with a smarting whip in hand, *Satan*
With which he forward lasht the laesie teme,
So oft as Slowth° still in the mire did stand. *Idleness*
Huge routs° of people did about them band, *crowds*
Showting for joy, and still before their way
A foggy mist had covered all the land;
And underneath their feet, all scattered lay
Dead sculs and bones of men, whose life had gone astray.

Summary In the remainder of the canto, the third Saracen brother, Sans joy, arrives at the House of Pride and demands to do battle with Redcrosse. Lucifera intervenes and orders them to meet in a formal combat on the following day. Duessa visits Sans joy in the night, warning him of the power of Redcrosse's invulnerable armor, and promising him her secret aid.

Canto 5 *Summary*

Just as Redcrosse is about to slay Sans joy in combat, the Saracen vanishes in a magical cloud created by Duessa. To heal the wounded Sans joy, the witch enlists the help of Night, the queen of darkness who is grandmother of the three Saracen brothers. Together they take Sans joy down to Hades, the classical underworld. There he will be healed by the legendary physician Aesculapius, who has the power to raise the dead and is himself immortal, but doomed to live

5. I.e., he never would foresee ("forecast") the calamities his careless haste caused.
6. I.e., inhuman murder and destructive harm.
7. In Renaissance physiology, the spleen was regarded as the seat of ill-humor.
8. Presumably St. Anthony's fire: erysipelas, or the flaming itch; appropriate to Wrath.

forever in Hades. Meanwhile, Redcrosse's companion the dwarf discovers Lucifera's dungeon, where the bodies of the proud are cast in heaps. With the dwarf, Redcrosse flees in the night, stumbling over piled-up corpses as he makes his escape, and Duessa returns to find him gone.

Canto 6 ***Summary*** Sans loy intends to rape Una, but is frightened away by a band of fauns and satyrs (mythological creatures who are men above the waist and goats below). They take Una and proceed to worship her as a goddess, in spite of her attempts to teach them true religion. She is discovered among them by Satyrane, a wild but virtuous knight born of a human mother and a satyr father. Together they escape her idolators. They then meet with a pilgrim who informs them that Redcrosse has been slain by Sans loy. Satyrane seeks out the Saracen and they do battle. Una flees in terror and is pursued by the pilgrim, who is revealed as Archimago in disguise.

Cantos 7 and 8 ***Summary*** Still disguised as Fidessa, Duessa pursues and finds Redcrosse. He drinks from a fountain which robs him of strength. The enfeebled knight is discovered lying with Duessa by the giant Orgoglio (Pride), who easily conquers Redcrosse and casts him into his dungeon. The giant pampers Duessa, attiring her as the Whore of Babylon in Revelation (a figure associated by Protestants with the papacy), and mounting her on a seven-headed beast. Meanwhile, the dwarf finds Una and reveals to her what has happened. Una sets out in search of Redcrosse and meets with Prince Arthur—the future king of Britain whose story runs through all the books of *The Faerie Queene*. She tells Arthur her story, explaining that Redcrosse has been assigned by the Faerie Queene to rescue her parents, the king and queen of Eden, from a dragon. Arthur promises to rescue Redcrosse. In an epic fight, he defeats and kills Orgoglio, after stunning the giant and the beast with the divine brightness of his shield. Arthur seizes the keys to Orgoglio's dungeon from the giant's ancient foster-father, Ignaro (Ignorance), and liberates the starving Redcrosse. They strip Duessa, who is revealed as a filthy, bestial hag. She hides herself in the wilderness.

From *Canto 9*

His loves and lignage° Arthur tells: *lineage*
The knights knit friendly bands:° *bonds*
Sir Trevisan flies from Despayre,
Whom Redcrosse knight withstands.

Summary In the first part of the canto, Arthur tells Redcrosse and Una of his past life. Taken from his mother at birth, Arthur is ignorant of his lineage, but has been told by the magician Merlin that he is heir to a king. After being visited by the Faerie Queene in a dream, in which she lay beside him on the grass, he has fallen in love with her. The knights then exchange vows of friendship and gifts. Arthur gives Redcrosse a precious liquid which heals wounds, while Redcrosse gives him the New Testament. Arthur then rides off in search of the Faerie Queene. Una looks with concern at Redcrosse, who remains weak and weary from his recent ordeal.

21

So as they traveild, lo they gan espy
An armèd knight towards them gallop fast,
That seemèd from some fearèd foe to fly,
Or other griesly thing, that him agast.° *terrified*
Still° as he fled, his eye was backward cast, *continually*
As if his feare still followed him behind;
Als flew his steed, as he his bands had brast,° *broken*
And with his wingèd heeles did tread the wind,
As he had beene a fole of Pegasus his kind.[9]

22

Nigh as he drew, they might perceive his head
To be unarmd, and curld uncombèd heares
Upstaring° stiffe, dismayd with uncouth° dread; *bristling / strange*
Nor drop of bloud in all his face appeares
Nor life in limbe: and to increase his feares,
In fowle reproch° of knighthoods faire degree,° *disgrace / condition*
About his neck an hempen rope he weares,
That with his glistring armes does ill agree;
But he of rope or armes has now no memoree.

23

The Redcrosse knight toward him crossèd fast,
To weet,° what mister° wight was so dismayd: *learn / kind of*
There him he finds all sencelesse and aghast,
That of him selfe he seemd to be afrayd;
Whom hardly° he from flying forward stayd, *with difficulty*
Till he these wordes to him deliver might;
"Sir knight, aread° who hath ye thus arayd, *declare*
And eke from whom make ye this hasty flight:
For never knight I saw in such misseeming° plight." *unseemly*

24

He answerd nought at all, but adding new
Feare to his first amazment, staring wide
With stony eyes, and hartlesse hollow hew,[1]
Astonisht stood, as one that had aspide
Infernall furies, with their chaines untide.
Him yet againe, and yet againe bespake
The gentle knight; who nought to him replide,
But trembling every joynt did inly quake,
And foltring tongue at last these words seemd forth to shake.

25

"For Gods deare love, Sir knight, do me not stay;
For loe he comes, he comes fast after mee."
Eft° looking backe would faine have runne away; *again*
But he him forst to stay, and tellen free
The secret cause of his perplexitie:° *distress*
Yet nathemore° by his bold hartie speach, *not at all*

9. I.e., as if he had been a foal of a horse like Pegasus, the flying horse of classical mythology.

1. I.e., with blanched, bloodless countenance.

Could his bloud-frosen hart emboldned bee,
But through his boldnesse rather feare did reach,
Yet forst, at last he made through silence suddein breach.

26

"And am I now in safetie sure," quoth he,
"From him, that would have forcèd me to dye?
And is the point of death now turnd fro mee,
That I may tell this haplesse history?"° *story of misfortune*
"Feare nought:" quoth he, "no daunger now is nye."
"Then shall I you recount a ruefull cace,"° *pitiable event*
Said he, "the which with this unlucky eye
I late beheld, and had not greater grace
Me reft° from it, had bene partaker of the place.[2] *carried*

27

"I lately chaunst (Would I had never chaunst)
With a faire knight to keepen companee,
Sir Terwin[3] hight,° that well himselfe advaunst *named*
In all affaires, and was both bold and free,
But not so happie as mote happie bee:
He loved, as was his lot, a Ladie gent,° *gentle*
That him againe° loved in the least degree: *in return*
For she was proud, and of too high intent,° *mind*
And joyd to see her lover languish and lament.

28

"From whom returning sad and comfortlesse,° *desolate*
As on the way together we did fare,
We met that villen (God from him me blesse°) *defend*
That cursèd wight, from whom I scapt whyleare,° *a while before*
A man of hell, that cals himselfe Despaire;[4]
Who first us greets, and after faire areedes° *tells*
Of tydings strange, and of adventures rare:
So creeping close, as Snake in hidden weedes,
Inquireth of our states, and of our knightly deedes.

29

"Which when he knew, and felt our feeble harts
Embost° with bale,° and bitter byting griefe, *exhausted / sorrow*
Which love had launchèd° with his deadly darts, *pierced*
With wounding words and termes of foule repriefe° *insult*
He pluckt from us all hope of due reliefe,
That earst° us held in love of lingring life; *formerly*
Then hopelesse hartlesse, gan the cunning thiefe
Perswade us die, to stint° all further strife: *end*
To me he lent this rope, to him a rustie° knife. *i.e., bloodstained*

30

"With which sad instrument of hastie death,
That wofull lover, loathing lenger° light, *longer*

2. I.e., shared the same fate.
3. His name may connote weariness or fatigue ("terwyn").
4. Despair is the ultimate Christian sin, denying the possibility of divine mercy and grace.

A wide way made to let forth living breath.
But I more fearefull, or more luckie wight,
Dismayd with that deformèd dismall sight,
Fled fast away, halfe dead with dying feare:° *fear of death*
Ne yet assur'd of life by you, Sir knight,
Whose like infirmitie like chaunce may beare:
But God you never let his charmèd speeches heare."[5]

31

"How may a man," said he, "with idle speach
Be wonne, to spoyle° the Castle of his health?" *destroy*
"I wote," quoth he, "whom triall° late did teach, *experience*
That like would not[6] for all this worldes wealth:
His subtill tongue, like dropping honny, mealt'th° *melts*
Into the hart, and searcheth every vaine,
That ere one be aware, by secret stealth
His powre is reft, and weaknesse doth remaine.
O never Sir desire to try° his guilefull traine."° *test / treachery*

32

"Certes,"° said he, "hence shall I never rest, *surely*
Till I that treachours art have heard and tride;
And you Sir knight, whose name mote° I request, *might*
Of grace° do me unto his cabin° guide." *favor / cave*
"I that hight° Trevisan,"[7] quoth he, "will ride *am called*
Against my liking backe, to doe you grace:° *a favor*
But nor for gold nor glee[8] will I abide
By you, when ye arrive in that same place;
For lever° had I die, then° see his deadly face." *rather / than*

33

Ere long they come, where that same wicked wight
His dwelling has, low in an hollow cave,
Farre underneath a craggie clift ypight,° *placed*
Darke, dolefull, drearie, like a greedie grave,
That still° for carrion carcases doth crave: *continually*
On top whereof aye° dwelt the ghastly Owle,[9] *ever*
Shrieking his balefull note, which ever drave
Farre from that haunt all other chearefull fowle;
And all about it wandring ghostes did waile and howle.

34

And all about old stockes° and stubs of trees, *stumps*
Whereon nor fruit, nor leafe was ever seene,
Did hang upon the ragged rocky knees;° *crags*
On which had many wretches hangèd beene,
Whose carcases were scattered on the greene,
And throwne about the cliffs. Arrivèd there,
That bare-head knight for dread and dolefull teene,° *grief*

5. I.e., may God never let you hear his mesmerizing ("charmed") speeches.
6. I.e., would not do the like again.
7. The meaning is uncertain, but may be "flight" or "dread."
8. Beauty; i.e., not for anything in the world.
9. Traditionally a messenger of death.

Would faine° have fled, ne durst approachen neare, *gladly*
But th' other forst him stay, and comforted in feare.

35

That darkesome cave they enter, where they find
That cursèd man, low sitting on the ground,
Musing full sadly in his sullein° mind; *morose*
His griesie° lockes, long growen, and unbound, *gray*
Disordred hong about his shoulders round,
And hid his face; through which his hollow eyne
Lookt deadly dull, and starèd as astound;° *as if stunned*
His raw-bone cheekes through penurie and pine,° *starvation*
Were shronke into his jawes, as° he did never dine. *as if*

36

His garment nought but many ragged clouts,° *rags*
With thornes together pind and patchèd was,
The which his naked sides he wrapt abouts;
And him beside there lay upon the gras
A drearie corse,° whose life away did pas, *bloody corpse*
All wallowd in his owne yet luke-warme blood,
That from his wound yet wellèd fresh alas;
In which a rustie knife fast fixèd stood,
And made an open passage for the gushing flood.

37

Which piteous spectacle, approving° trew *confirming*
The wofull tale that Trevisan had told,
When as the gentle Redcrosse knight did vew,
With firie zeale he burnt in courage bold,
Him to avenge, before his bloud were cold,
And to the villein said, "Thou agèd damnèd wight,
The author of this fact,° we here behold, *deed*
What justice can but judge against thee right,
With thine owne bloud to price° his bloud, here shed in sight?" *pay for*

38

"What franticke fit," quoth he, "hath thus distraught
Thee, foolish man, so rash a doome° to give? *judgment*
What justice ever other judgement taught,
But he should die, who merites not to live?
None else to death this man despayring drive,° *drove*
But his owne guiltie mind deserving death.
Is then unjust to each his due to give?
Or let him die, that loatheth living breath?
Or let him die at ease, that liveth here uneath?° *in hardship*

39

"Who travels by the wearie wandring way,
To come unto his wishèd home in haste,
And meetes a flood, that doth his passage stay,
Is not great grace to helpe him over past,
Or free his feet, that in the myre sticke fast?

Most envious man, that grieves at neighbours good,
And fond,° that joyest in the woe thou hast, *foolish*
Why wilt not let him passe, that long hath stood
Upon the banke, yet wilt thy selfe not passe the flood?

40

"He there does now enjoy eternall rest
And happie ease, which thou doest want and crave,
And further from it daily wanderest:
What if some litle paine the passage have,
That makes fraile flesh to feare the bitter wave?
Is not short paine well borne, that brings long ease,
And layes the soule to sleepe in quiet grave?
Sleepe after toyle, port after stormie seas,
Ease after warre, death after life does greatly please."[1]

41

The knight much wondred at his suddeine wit,° *quick intelligence*
And said, "The terme of life is limited,
Ne may a man prolong, nor shorten it;
The souldier may not move from watchfull sted,[2]
Nor leave his stand, untill his Captaine bed."° *commands*
"Who life did limit by almightie doome,"
Quoth he, "knowes best the termes establishèd;
And he, that points the Centonell his roome,° *station*
Doth license him depart at sound of morning droome.[3]

42

"Is not his deed, what ever thing is donne,
In heaven and earth? did not he all create
To die againe? all ends that was begonne.
Their times in his eternall booke of fate
Are written sure, and have their certaine° date. *fixed*
Who then can strive with strong necessitie,
That holds the world in his still chaunging state,
Or shunne the death ordaynd by destinie?
When houre of death is come, let none aske whence, nor why.

43

"The lenger° life, I wote° the greater sin, *longer / know*
The greater sin, the greater punishment:
All those great battels, which thou boasts to win,
Through strife, and bloud-shed, and avengement,
Now praysd, hereafter deare° thou shalt repent: *bitterly*
For life must life, and bloud must bloud repay.[4]
Is not enough thy evill life forespent?
For he, that once hath missèd the right way,
The further he doth goe, the further he doth stray.

1. Despaire's arguments on behalf of suicide as against a painful life are derived, like those of Hamlet in his third soliloquy (*Hamlet* 3.1.58–90), principally from Seneca, Marcus Aurelius, other ancient Stoics, and Old Testament statements on divine justice.
2. The sentry post assigned him.
3. Drum, with a pun on *doom*.
4. An echo of Genesis 9.6: "Whoso sheddeth man's blood, by man shall his blood be shed."

44

"Then do no further goe, no further stray,
But here lie downe, and to thy rest betake,
Th' ill to prevent, that life ensewen may.[5]
For what hath life, that may it lovèd make,
And gives not rather cause it to forsake?
Feare, sicknesse, age, losse, labour, sorrow, strife,
Paine, hunger, cold, that makes the hart to quake;
And ever fickle fortune rageth rife,
All which, and thousands mo° do make a loathsome life. *more*

45

"Thou wretched man, of death hast greatest need,
If in true ballance thou wilt weigh thy state:
For never knight, that darèd warlike deede,
More lucklesse disaventures° did amate:° *mishaps / daunt*
Witnesse the dongeon deepe, wherein of late
Thy life shut up, for death so oft did call;
And though good lucke prolongèd hath thy date,° *span of life*
Yet death then, would the like mishaps forestall,
Into the which hereafter thou maiest happen fall.° *happen to fall*

46

"Why then doest thou, O man of sin, desire
To draw thy dayes forth to their last degree?
Is not the measure of thy sinfull hire° *service to sin*
High heapèd up with huge iniquitie,
Against the day of wrath,° to burden thee? *Judgment Day*
Is not enough that to this Ladie milde
Thou falsèd° hast thy faith with perjurie,° *betrayed / oath-breaking*
And sold thy selfe to serve Duessa vilde,° *vile*
With whom in all abuse thou hast thy selfe defilde?

47

"Is not he just, that all this doth behold
From highest heaven, and beares an equall° eye? *impartial*
Shall he thy sins up in his knowledge fold,
And guiltie be of thine impietie?
Is not his law, Let every sinner die:[6]
Die shall all flesh? what then must needs be donne,
Is it not better to doe willinglie,
Then linger, till the glasse° be all out ronne? *hourglass*
Death is the end of woes: die soone, O faeries sonne."

48

The knight was much enmovèd with his speach,
That as a swords point through his hart did perse,
And in his conscience made a secret breach,° *wound*
Well knowing true all, that he did reherse° *recount*
And to his fresh remembrance did reverse° *bring back*

5. I.e., to prevent the evil that will ensue in the rest of your life.

6. Despaire cites only half of the Scripture verse: "The wages of sin is death; but the gift of God is eternal life through Jesus Christ our Lord" (Romans 6.23).

The ugly vew of his deformèd crimes,
That all his manly powres it did disperse,
As he were charmèd with inchaunted rimes,
That oftentimes he quakt, and fainted° oftentimes. *lost heart*

49

In which amazement, when the Miscreant° *misbeliever*
Perceivèd him to waver weake and fraile,
Whiles trembling horror did his conscience dant,° *daunt*
And hellish anguish° did his soule assaile, *i.e., fear of hell*
To drive him to despaire, and quite to quaile,° *be dismayed*
He shewed him painted in a table° plaine, *picture*
The damnèd ghosts, that doe in torments waile,
And thousand feends that doe them endlesse paine
With fire and brimstone, which for ever shall remaine.

50

The sight whereof so throughly him dismaid,
That nought but death before his eyes he saw,
And ever burning wrath before him laid,
By righteous sentence of th' Almighties law:
Then gan the villein him to overcraw,° *exult over*
And brought unto him swords, ropes, poison, fire,
And all that might him to perdition draw;
And bad him choose, what death he would desire:
For death was due to him, that had provokt Gods ire.

51

But when as none of them he saw him take,
He to him raught° a dagger sharpe and keene, *reached*
And gave it him in hand: his hand did quake,
And tremble like a leafe of Aspin greene,
And troubled bloud through his pale face was seene
To come, and goe with tydings from the hart,
As it a running messenger had beene.
At last resolved to worke his finall smart,
He lifted up his hand, that backe againe did start.

52

Which when as Una saw, through every vaine
The crudled° cold ran to her well of life,° *congealing / heart*
As in a swowne: but soone relived° againe, *revived*
Out of his hand she snatcht the cursèd knife,
And threw it to the ground, enragèd rife,° *deeply*
And to him said, "Fie, fie, faint harted knight,
What meanest thou by this reprochfull° strife? *deserving reproach*
Is this the battell, which thou vauntst to fight
With the fire-mouthèd Dragon, horrible and bright?

53

"Come, come away, fraile, feeble, fleshly wight,
Ne let vaine words bewitch thy manly hart,
Ne divelish thoughts dismay thy constant spright.° *spirit*
In heavenly mercies hast thou not a part?

Why shouldst thou then despeire, that chosen[7] art?
Where justice growes, there grows eke° greater grace, *also*
The which doth quench the brond° of hellish smart, *firebrand*
And that accurst hand-writing[8] doth deface.° *blot out*
Arise, Sir knight arise, and leave this cursèd place."

54

So up he rose, and thence amounted° streight. *mounted his horse*
Which when the carle° beheld, and saw his guest *churl*
Would safe depart, for° all his subtill sleight, *in spite of*
He chose an halter° from among the rest, *noose*
And with it hung himselfe, unbid° unblest. *unprayed for*
But death he could not worke himselfe thereby;
For thousand times he so himselfe had drest,° *made ready*
Yet nathelesse it could not doe° him die, *make*
Till he should die his last, that is eternally.

From *Canto 10*

Her faithfull knight faire Una brings
to house of Holinesse,
Where he is taught repentance, and
the way to heavenly blesse.° **bliss**

Summary In the first part of the canto, Una brings Redcrosse to the House of Holinesse to be healed in body and spirit. The house is kept by Dame Caelia (Heavenly) with her three daughters Fidelia (Faith), Speranza (Hope), and Charissa (Charity, or Love). Redcrosse is welcomed and given counsel by Fidelia and Speranza, but remains wracked by guilt and suicidal impulses. He is entrusted to the doctor Patience and undergoes a painful cure with Penance, Remorse, and Repentance. He next comes to Charissa, who instructs him in love and good deeds and places him in the hands of a godly matron, Mercie. She leads him along a narrow and thorny path to a holy Hospitall (hostel), kept by seven Bead-men (men of prayer), where Redcrosse learns to frame his life in righteousness. Redcrosse and Mercie then continue on their way.

46

Thence forward by that painfull way they pas,
Forth to an hill, that was both steepe and hy;
On top whereof a sacred chappell was,
And eke a litle Hermitage thereby,
Wherein an agèd holy man did lye,° *live*
That day and night said his devotiön,
Ne other worldly busines did apply;[9]
His name was heavenly Contemplation;
Of God and goodnesse was his meditation.

7. Cf. 2 Thessalonians 2.13: "God hath from the beginning chosen you to salvation through sanctification of the Spirit and belief of the truth." This is one of several similar passages in the epistles of St. Paul that form the basis of the theological doctrine of predestination.

8. An echo of Colossians 2.14: "Blotting out the handwriting of ordinances [i.e., the Old Testament Law] that was against us, which was contrary to us, and took it out of the way, nailing it to his cross."

9. I.e., he did not attend to any worldly activities.

47

Great grace that old man to him given had;
For God he often saw from heavens hight,
All° were his earthly eyen both blunt° and bad, *although / dim*
And through great age had lost their kindly° sight, *natural*
Yet wondrous quick and persant° was his spright,° *piercing / spirit*
As Eagles eye, that can behold the Sunne:
That hill they scale with all their powre and might,
That his frayle thighes nigh wearie and fordonne° *exhausted*
Gan faile, but by her helpe the top at last he wonne.

48

There they do finde that godly agèd Sire,
With snowy lockes adowne his shoulders shed,
As hoarie frost with spangles doth attire
The mossy braunches of an Oke halfe ded.
Each bone might through his body well be red,° *seen*
And every sinew seene through° his long fast: *because of*
For nought he cared his carcas long unfed;
His mind was full of spirituall repast,
And pyned° his flesh, to keepe his body low° and chast. *starved / thin*

49

Who when these two approching he aspide,
At their first presence grew agrievèd sore,[1]
That forst him lay his heavenly thoughts aside;
And had he not that Dame respected more,° *greatly*
Whom highly he did reverence and adore,
He would not once have movèd for the knight.
They him saluted standing far afore;° *away*
Who well them greeting, humbly did requight,° *respond*
And askèd, to what end they clomb° that tedious height. *had climbed*

50

"What end," quoth she, "should cause us take such paine,
But that same end, which every living wight
Should make his marke,° high heaven to attaine? *goal*
Is not from hence the way, that leadeth right
To that most glorious house, that glistreth bright
With burning starres, and everliving fire,
Whereof the keyes are to thy hand behight° *entrusted*
By wise Fidelia? she doth thee require,
To shew it to this knight, according° his desire." *granting*

51

"Thrise happy man," said then the father grave,
"Whose staggering steps thy° steady hand doth lead, *i.e., Mercy's*
And shewes the way, his sinfull soule to save.
Who better can the way to heaven aread° *direct*
Then thou thy selfe, that was both borne and bred
In heavenly throne, where thousand Angels shine?
Thou doest the prayers of the righteous sead° *seed*

1. I.e., he was at first sorely grieved at their arrival.

Present before the majestie divine,
And his avenging wrath to clemencie incline.

52

"Yet since thou bidst, thy pleasure shalbe donne.
Then come thou man of earth,[2] and see the way,
That never yet was seene of Faeries sonne,
That never leads the traveiler astray,
But after labours long, and sad delay,
Brings them to joyous rest and endlesse blis.
But first thou must a season fast and pray,
Till from her bands the spright assoilèd° is, *spirit released*
And have her strength recured° from fraile infirmitis." *recovered*

53

That done, he leads him to the highest Mount;
Such one, as that same mighty man of God,
That bloud-red billowes like a wallèd front
On either side disparted° with his rod, *parted asunder*
Till that his army dry-foot through them yod,° *went*
Dwelt fortie dayes upon; where writ in stone
With bloudy letters by the hand of God,
The bitter doome of death and balefull mone[3]
He did receive, whiles flashing fire about him shone.

54

Or like that sacred hill, whose head full hie,
Adornd with fruitfull Olives all arownd,
Is, as it were for endlesse memory
Of that deare Lord, who oft thereon was fownd,
For ever with a flowring girlond crownd:
Or like that pleasaunt Mount, that is for ay
Through famous Poets verse each where° renownd, *everywhere*
On which the thrise three learned Ladies play
Their heavenly notes, and make full many a lovely lay.°[4] *song*

55

From thence, far off he unto him did shew
A litle path, that was both steepe and long,
Which to a goodly Citie led his vew;
Whose wals and towres were builded high and strong
Of perle and precious stone, that earthly tong
Cannot describe, nor wit of man can tell;
Too high a ditty° for my simple song; *subject*
The Citie of the great king hight° it well, *is called*
Wherein eternall peace and happinesse doth dwell.

56

As he thereon stood gazing, he might° see *could*
The blessed Angels to and fro descend

2. An allusion to humankind's formation from the dust of the earth (Genesis 2.7) and also to the knight's name (see below, stanza 66 and note 1).

3. I.e., the Ten Commandments ("bloudy letters") carried with them the judgment ("doome") of death and pain (causing sorrowful moans—"balefull mone").

4. The mountain is successively compared to Mount Sinai, where Moses, after parting the "bloud-red billowes" of the Red Sea, received the tablets of the Ten Commandments; to the Mount of Olives, associated with Christ; and to Mount Parnassus, where the Nine Muses of art and poetry dwelt.

From highest heaven, in gladsome companee,
And with great joy into that Citie wend,
As commonly° as friend does with his frend.[5] *familiarly*
Whereat he wondred much, and gan enquere,
What stately building durst so high extend
Her loftie towres unto the starry sphere,
And what unknowen nation there empeopled were.

57

"Faire knight," quoth he, "Hierusalem that is,
The new Hierusalem, that God has built
For those to dwell in, that are chosen his,
His chosen people purged from sinfull guilt,
With pretious bloud, which cruelly was spilt
On cursèd tree, of that unspotted lam,[6]
That for the sinnes of all the world was kilt:
Now are they Saints all in that Citie sam,° *together*
More deare unto their God, then younglings to their dam."[7]

58

"Till now," said then the knight, "I weenèd well,
That great Cleopolis,[8] where I have beene,
In which that fairest Faerie Queene doth dwell,
The fairest Citie was, that might be seene;
And that bright towre all built of christall cleene,° *clear*
Panthea,[9] seemd the brightest thing, that was:
But now by proofe° all otherwise I weene;° *experience / think*
For this great Citie that[1] does far surpas,
And this bright Angels towre quite dims that towre of glas."

59

"Most trew," then said the holy agèd man;
"Yet is Cleopolis for earthly frame,° *structure*
The fairest peece,° that eye beholden can: *masterpiece*
And well beseemes° all knights of noble name, *becomes*
That covet in th' immortall booke of fame
To be eternizèd, that same to haunt,° *frequent*
And doen their service to that soveraigne Dame,
That glorie does to them for guerdon° graunt: *reward*
For she is heavenly borne, and heaven may justly vaunt.[2]

60

"And thou faire ymp,° sprong out from English race, *youth*
How ever now accompted° Elfins sonne, *accounted*
Well worthy doest thy service for her grace,° *favor*
To aide a virgin desolate foredonne.° *undone*
But when thou famous victorie hast wonne,

5. Cf. Jacob's ladder, which "reached to heaven; and behold the angels of God ascending and descending on it" (Genesis 28.12).
6. Christ (the lamb of God), whose death on the cross ("cursèd tree") purged the guilt of sin from those "chosen his."
7. The New Jerusalem is described in Revelation 21–22; "the nations of them which are saved shall walk in the light of it" (21.24).
8. "City of Fame"; in the historical allegory, London or Westminster.
9. Reminiscent of the temple of glass in Chaucer's *House of Fame;* perhaps intended to allude to Westminster Abbey as pantheon of the English great.
1. I.e., The New Jerusalem far surpasses Cleopolis ("that").
2. I.e., may justly boast ("vaunt") that heaven is her home.

And high emongst all knights hast hong thy shield,
Thenceforth the suit° of earthly conquest shonne, *pursuit*
And wash thy hands from guilt of bloudy field:
For bloud can nought but sin, and wars but sorrowes yield.

61

"Then seeke this path, that I to thee presage,° *show prophetically*
Which after all to heaven shall thee send;
Then peaceably thy painefull° pilgrimage *laborious*
To yonder same Hierusalem do bend,
Where is for thee ordaind a blessèd end:
For thou emongst those Saints, whom thou doest see,
Shalt be a Saint, and thine owne nations frend
And Patrone: thou Saint George shalt callèd bee,
Saint George of mery England, the signe of victoree."[3]

62

"Unworthy wretch," quoth he, "of so great grace,
How dare I thinke such glory to attaine?"
"These that have it attaind, were in like cace,"
Quoth he, "as wretched, and lived in like paine."
"But deeds of armes must I at last be faine,° *content (to leave)*
And Ladies love to leave so dearely bought?"
"What need of armes, where peace doth ay° remaine," *ever*
Said he, "and battailes none are to be fought?
As for loose° loves are° vaine, and vanish into nought." *wanton / i.e., they are*

63

"O let me not," quoth he, "then turne againe
Backe to the world, whose joyes so fruitlesse are;
But let me here for aye in peace remaine,
Or streight way on that last long voyage fare,
That nothing may my present hope empare."° *impair*
"That may not be," said he, "ne maist thou yit
Forgo that royall maides bequeathèd care,° *charge*
Who did her cause into thy hand commit,
Till from her cursèd foe thou have her freely quit."° *released*

64

"Then shall I soone," quoth he, "so God me grace,
Abet° that virgins cause disconsolate, *maintain*
And shortly backe returne unto this place
To walke this way in Pilgrims poore estate.
But now aread,° old father, why of late *declare*
Didst thou behight° me borne of English blood, *call*
Whom all a Faeries sonne doen nominate?"° *name*
"That word shall I," said he, "avouchen° good, *prove*
Sith° to thee is unknowne the cradle of thy brood. *since*

65

"For well I wote,° thou springst from ancient race *know*
Of Saxon kings, that have with mightie hand

3. Spenser's conception of St. George, patron saint of England, draws on the *Legenda Aurea* (*The Golden Legend*—a medieval manual of ecclesiastical lore, translated into English by William Caxton in 1487) and on pictures, tapestries, pageants, and folklore.

And many bloudie battailes fought in place° *there*
High reard their royall throne in Britane land,
And vanquisht them,° unable to withstand: *i.e., the ancient Britons*
From thence a Faerie thee unweeting reft,° *secretly stole*
There as thou slepst in tender swadling band,
And her base Elfin brood there for thee left.
Such men do Chaungelings call, so chaungd by Faeries theft.

66

"Thence she thee brought into this Faerie lond,
And in an heapèd furrow did thee hyde,
Where thee a Ploughman all unweeting° fond, *unknowing*
As he his toylesome teme° that way did guyde, *team of oxen*
And brought thee up in ploughmans state to byde,
Whereof Georgos he thee gave to name;[4]
Till prickt° with courage, and thy forces pryde, *spurred*
To Faery court thou cam'st to seeke for fame,
And prove thy puissaunt° armes, as seemes thee best *powerful*
became."° *as best suited you*

67

"O holy Sire," quoth he, "how shall I quight° *repay*
The many favours I with thee have found,
That hast my name and nation red° aright, *declared*
And taught the way that does to heaven bound?"° *go*
This said, adowne he lookèd to the ground,
To have returnd, but dazèd° were his eyne, *dazzled*
Through passing° brightnesse, which did quite confound *surpassing*
His feeble sence, and too exceeding shyne.
So darke are earthly things compard to things divine.

68

At last whenas himselfe he gan to find,° *recover*
To Una back he cast him to retire;
Who him awaited still with pensive° mind. *anxious*
Great thankes and goodly meed° to that good syre, *gift*
He thence departing gave for his paines hyre.° *reward*
So came to Una, who him joyd to see,
And after litle rest, gan him desire,
Of her adventure mindfull for to bee.
So leave they take of Caelia, and her daughters three.

Canto 11

The knight with that old Dragon fights
two dayes incessantly:
The third him overthrowes, and gayns
most glorious victory.

1

High time now gan it wex° for Una faire, *grow*
To thinke of those her captive Parents deare,
And their forwasted kingdome to repaire:[5]

4. I.e., as a name. *Georgos* is Greek for "farmer" (cf. Virgil's *Georgics*, on farming).

5. I.e., to restore their kingdom, laid waste (by the dragon).

Whereto whenas they now approachèd neare,
With hartie° words her knight she gan to cheare, *bold*
And in her modest manner thus bespake;
"Deare knight, as deare, as ever knight was deare,
That all these sorrowes suffer for my sake,
High heaven behold the tedious toyle, ye for me take.

2

"Now are we come unto my native soyle,
And to the place, where all our perils dwell;
Here haunts that feend, and does his dayly spoyle,
Therefore henceforth be at your keeping well,° *be well on your guard*
And ever ready for your foeman fell.
The sparke of noble courage now awake,
And strive your excellent selfe to excell;
That shall ye evermore renowmèd make,
Above all knights on earth, that batteill undertake."

3

And pointing forth, "lo yonder is," said she,
"The brasen towre in which my parents deare
For dread of that huge feend emprisond be,
Whom I from far see on the walles appeare,
Whose sight my feeble soule doth greatly cheare:
And on the top of all I do espye
The watchman wayting tydings glad to heare,
That O my parents might I happily
Unto you bring, to ease you of your misery."

4

With that they heard a roaring hideous sound,
That all the ayre with terrour fillèd wide,
And seemd uneath° to shake the stedfast ground. *almost*
Eftsoones° that dreadfull Dragon they espide, *immediately*
Where stretcht he lay upon the sunny side
Of a great hill, himselfe like a great hill.
But all so soone, as he from far descride
Those glistring armes, that heaven with light did fill,
He rousd himselfe full blith,° and hastned them untill.° *joyfully / toward*

5

Then bad° the knight his Lady yede° aloofe, *bade / go*
And to an hill her selfe withdraw aside,
From whence she might behold that battailles proof° *outcome*
And eke° be safe from daunger far descryde:° *also / observed from afar*
She him obayd, and turnd a little wyde.° *aside*
Now O thou sacred Muse, most learnèd Dame,
Faire ympe° of Phoebus, and his agèd bride,[6] *child*
The Nourse of time, and everlasting fame,
That warlike hands ennoblest with immortall name;

6

O gently come into my feeble brest,
Come gently, but not with that mighty rage,

6. I.e., Mnemosyne (memory), mother of the Muses.

Wherewith the martiall troupes thou doest infest,° *arouse*
And harts of great Heroes doest enrage,
That nought their kindled courage may aswage,
Soone as thy dreadfull trompe° begins to sownd; *trumpet*
The God of warre with his fiers equipage
Thou doest awake, sleepe never he so sownd,° *sound*
And scarèd nations doest with horrour sterne astown.° *appall*

7

Faire Goddesse lay that furious fit° aside, *strain*
Till I of warres and bloudy Mars do sing[7]
And Briton fields with Sarazin° bloud bedyde,° *Saracen / dyed*
Twixt that great faery Queene and Paynim° king, *pagan*
That with their horrour heaven and earth did ring,
A worke of labour long, and endlesse prayse:
But now a while let downe that haughtie string,
And to my tunes thy second tenor rayse,[8]
That I this man of God his godly armes may blaze.° *proclaim*

8

By this the dreadfull Beast drew nigh to hand,
Halfe flying, and halfe footing° in his hast, *walking*
That with his largenesse measurèd much land,
And made wide shadow under his huge wast;° *girth*
As mountaine doth the valley overcast.
Approching nigh, he rearèd high afore
His body monstrous, horrible, and vast,
Which to increase his wondrous greatnesse more,
Was swolne with wrath, and poyson, and with bloudy gore.

9

And over, all with brasen scales was armd,
Like plated coate of steele, so couchèd neare,° *placed so closely*
That nought mote perce,[9] ne might his corse° be harmd *body*
With dint of sword, nor push of pointed speare;
Which as an Eagle, seeing pray appeare,
His aery Plumes doth rouze,° full rudely dight,° *shake / ruggedly arrayed*
So shakèd he, that horrour was to heare,
For as the clashing of an Armour bright,
Such noyse his rouzèd scales did send unto the knight.

10

His flaggy° wings when forth he did display, *drooping*
Were like two sayles, in which the hollow wynd
Is gathered full, and worketh speedy way:
And eke the pennes, that did his pineons bynd,
Were like mayne-yards, with flying canvas lynd,[1]
With which whenas him list° the ayre to beat, *he chose*
And there by force unwonted° passage find, *unaccustomed*
The cloudes before him fled for terrour great,

7. Perhaps a reference to a projected but unwritten book of *The Faerie Queene*.
8. The "haughtie" (high-pitched) mode would be appropriate to a large-scale epic war; the "second tenor" (lower in pitch) to this present battle.
9. Nothing might pierce.
1. I.e., the ribs of his wings were like the massive spars (main yards) to which a ship's mainsail is affixed.

And all the heavens stood still amazèd with his threat.

11

His huge long tayle wound up in hundred foldes,
Does overspred his long bras-scaly backe,
Whose wreathèd boughts° when ever he unfoldes, *coils*
And thicke entangled knots adown does slacke,
Bespotted as with shields° of red and blacke, *scales*
It sweepeth all the land behind him farre,
And of three furlongs does but litle lacke;
And at the point two stings in-fixèd arre,
Both deadly sharpe, that sharpest steele exceeden farre.

12

But stings and sharpest steele did far exceed° *i.e., were far exceeded by*
The sharpnesse of his cruell rending clawes;
Dead was it sure, as sure as death in deed,° *in its effect*
What ever thing does touch his ravenous pawes,
Or what within his reach he ever drawes.
But his most hideous head my toung to tell
Does tremble: for his deepe devouring jawes
Wide gapèd, like the griesly° mouth of hell, *horrid*
Through which into his darke abisse all ravin° fell. *prey; booty*

13

And that° more wondrous was, in either jaw *what*
Three ranckes of yron teeth enraungèd were,
In which yet trickling bloud and gobbets raw° *chunks of unswallowed food*
Of late° devourèd bodies did appeare, *recently*
That sight thereof bred cold congealèd feare:
Which to increase, and all at once to kill,
A cloud of smoothering smoke and sulphur seare° *burning*
Out of his stinking gorge° forth steemèd still, *maw*
That all the ayre about with smoke and stench did fill.

14

His blazing eyes, like two bright shining shields,
Did burne with wrath, and sparkled living fyre;
As two broad Beacons, set in open fields,
Send forth their flames farre off to every shyre,° *shire*
And warning give, that enemies conspyre,
With fire and sword the region to invade;
So flamed his eyne° with rage and rancorous yre:° *eyes / ire, anger*
But farre within, as in a hollow glade,
Those glaring lampes were set, that made a dreadfull shade.

15

So dreadfully he towards him did pas,
Forelifting up aloft his speckled brest,
And often bounding on the brusèd gras,
As for great joyance of his newcome guest.
Eftsoones he gan advance his haughtie crest,
As chauffèd° Bore his bristles doth upreare, *angry*
And shoke his scales to battell readie drest;° *prepared*

That made the Redcrosse knight nigh quake for feare,
As bidding bold defiance to his foeman neare.

16

The knight gan fairely couch° his steadie speare, *level*
And fiercely ran at him with rigorous° might: *violent*
The pointed steele arriving rudely° theare, *roughly*
His harder hide would neither perce, nor bight,
But glauncing by forth passèd forward right;
Yet sore amovèd with so puissant push,
The wrathfull beast about him turnèd light,° *quickly*
And him so rudely passing by, did brush
With his long tayle, that horse and man to ground did rush.

17

Both horse and man up lightly rose againe,
And fresh encounter towards him addrest:
But th' idle stroke yet backe recoyld in vaine,
And found no place his° deadly point to rest. *its*
Exceeding rage enflamed the furious beast,
To be avengèd of so great despight;° *outrage*
For never felt his imperceable brest
So wondrous force, from hand of living wight;
Yet had he proved° the powre of many a puissant knight. *tested*

18

Then with his waving wings displayèd wyde,
Himselfe up high he lifted from the ground,
And with strong flight did forcibly divide
The yielding aire, which nigh° too feeble found *nearly*
Her flitting° partes, and element unsound,° *moving / weak*
To beare so great a weight: he cutting way
With his broad sayles, about him soarèd round:
At last low stouping with unweldie sway,° *ponderous force*
Snatcht up both horse and man, to beare them quite away.

19

Long he them bore above the subject plaine,° *i.e., the ground below*
So farre as Ewghen° bow a shaft may send, *yewen, of yew*
Till struggling strong did him at last constraine,
To let them downe before his flightès end:
As hagard° hauke presuming to contend *untamed*
With hardie fowle, above his hable might,° *able power*
His wearie pounces° all in vaine doth spend, *claws*
To trusse° the pray too heavie for his flight; *seize*
Which comming downe to ground, does free it selfe by fight.

20

He so disseizèd of his gryping grosse,[2]
The knight his thrilant° speare againe assayd *piercing*
In his bras-plated body to embosse,° *plunge*
And three mens strength unto the stroke he layd;

2. Freed from his formidable grip.

Wherewith the stiffe beame quakèd, as affrayd,
And glauncing from his scaly necke, did glyde
Close under his left wing, then broad displayd.
The percing steele there wrought a wound full wyde,
That with the uncouth° smart the Monster lowdly cryde. *unfamiliar*

21

He cryde, as raging seas are wont° to rore, *accustomed*
When wintry storme his wrathfull wreck does threat,
The rolling billowes beat the ragged shore,
As° they the earth would shoulder from her seat, *as if*
And greedie gulfe° does gape, as he would eat *i.e., the sea*
His neighbour element° in his revenge: *i.e., earth*
Then gin the blustring brethren° boldly threat, *the winds*
To move the world from off his stedfast henge,° *axis*
And boystrous battell make, each other to avenge.

22

The steely head stucke fast still in his flesh,
Till with his cruell clawes he snatcht the wood,
And quite a sunder broke. Forth flowèd fresh
A gushing river of blacke goarie° blood, *clotted*
That drownèd all the land, whereon he stood;
The stream thereof would drive a water-mill.
Trebly augmented was his furious mood
With bitter sense of his deepe rooted ill,° *injury*
That flames of fire he threw forth from his large nosethrill.

23

His hideous tayle then hurlèd he about,
And therewith all enwrapt the nimble thyes° *thighs*
Of his froth-fomy steed, whose courage stout
Striving to loose the knot, that fast him tyes,
Himselfe in streighter° bandes too rash implyes,[3] *tighter*
That to the ground he is perforce° constraynd *of necessity*
To throw his rider: who can° quickly ryse *did*
From off the earth, with durty bloud distaynd,° *defiled*
For that reprochfull fall right fowly he disdaynd.

24

And fiercely tooke his trenchand° blade in hand, *sharp*
With which he stroke so furious and so fell,° *fiercely*
That nothing seemd the puissance could withstand:
Upon his crest the hardned yron fell,
But his more hardned crest was armd so well,
That deeper dint therein it would not make;[4]
Yet so extremely did the buffe° him quell,° *blow / dismay*
That from thenceforth he shund the like to take,
But when he saw them come, he did them still forsake.° *avoid*

25

The knight was wrath to see his stroke beguyld,° *foiled*
And smote againe with more outrageous might;

3. I.e., too quickly entangles.

4. I.e., it could not make a deep gash there.

But backe againe the sparckling steele recoyld,
And left not any marke, where it did light;
As if in Adamant rocke it had bene pight.° *struck against*
The beast impatient of his smarting wound,
And of so fierce and forcible despight,° *powerful injury*
Thought with his wings to stye° above the ground; *mount*
But his late wounded wing unserviceable found.

26

Then full of griefe and anguish vehement,
He lowdly brayd, that like was never heard,
And from his wide devouring oven sent
A flake° of fire, that flashing in his beard, *flash*
Him all amazd, and almost made affeard;
The scorching flame sore swingèd° all his face, *singed*
And through his armour all his bodie seard,
That he could not endure so cruell cace,° *plight*
But thought his armes to leave, and helmet to unlace.

27

Not that great Champion of the antique world,
Whom famous Poetes verse so much doth vaunt,
And hath for twelve huge labours high extold,
So many furies and sharpe fits did haunt,
When him the poysoned garment did enchaunt
With Centaures bloud, and bloudie verses charmed,
As did this knight twelve thousand dolours° daunt, *pains*
Whom fyrie steele now burnt, that earst° him armed, *formerly*
That erst him goodly armed, now most of all him harmed.[5]

28

Faint, wearie, sore, emboylèd, grievèd, brent° *burned*
With heat, toyle, wounds, armes, smart, and inward fire
That never man such mischiefes° did torment; *misfortunes*
Death better were, death did he oft desire,
But death will never come, when needes require.
Whom so dismayd when that his foe beheld,
He cast to suffer° him no more respire,° *allow / live*
But gan his sturdie sterne° about to weld,° *tail / lash*
And him so strongly stroke, that to the ground him feld.

29

It fortunèd (as faire it then befell)
Behind his backe unweeting,° where he stood, *unnoticed*
Of auncient time there was a springing well,
From which fast trickled forth a silver flood,
Full of great vertues,° and for med'cine good. *powers*
Whylome,° before that cursèd Dragon got *formerly*
That happie land, and all with innocent blood
Defyld those sacred waves, it rightly hot° *was called*
The Well of Life,[6] ne yet his vertues had forgot.

5. Redcrosse's fire baptism is compared with the burning shirt of Nessus, which killed Hercules, "that great Champion of the antique world" (line 235). His "twelve huge labours" are paralleled to the knight's "twelve thousand dolours."

6. An allusion to Revelation 22.1–2: "And he showed me a pure river of water of life, clear as crystal, proceeding out of the throne of God, and of the Lamb. In the midst of the street of it, and on either side of the river, was the tree of life which

30

For unto life the dead it could restore,
And guilt of sinfull crimes cleane wash away,
Those that with sicknesse were infected sore,
It could recure, and agèd long decay
Renew, as one were borne that very day.
Both Silo this, and Jordan did excell,
And th' English Bath, and eke the german Spau,
Ne can Cephise, nor Hebrus match this well:
Into the same the knight backe overthrowen, fell.[7]

31

Now gan the golden Phoebus for to steepe
His fierie face in billowes of the west,
And his faint steedes watred in Ocean deepe,
Whiles from their journall° labours they did rest, *daily*
When that infernall Monster, having kest° *cast*
His wearie foe into that living well,
Can° high advaunce his broad discoloured brest, *did*
Above his wonted pitch,° with countenance fell,° *height / sinister*
And clapt his yron wings, as victor he did dwell.° *remain*

32

Which when his pensive° Ladie saw from farre, *anxious*
Great woe and sorrow did her soule assay,° *assail*
As weening° that the sad end of the warre, *thinking*
And gan to highest God entirely° pray, *earnestly*
That fearèd chaunce° from her to turne away; *fate*
With folded hands and knees full lowly bent
All night she watcht, ne once adowne would lay
Her daintie limbs in her sad dreriment,° *dismal condition*
But praying still did wake, and waking did lament.

33

The morrow next gan early to appeare,
That° Titan° rose to runne his daily race; *when / the sun god*
But early ere the morrow next gan reare
Out of the sea faire Titans deawy face,
Up rose the gentle virgin from her place,
And lookèd all about, if she might spy
Her lovèd knight to move° his manly pace: *i.e., moving*
For she had great doubt of his safety,
Since late she saw him fall before his enemy.

34

At last she saw, where he upstarted brave
Out of the well, wherein he drenchèd lay;
As Eagle fresh out of the Ocean wave,
Where he hath left his plumes all hoary gray,

---

bare twelve manner of fruits and yielded her fruit every month: and the leaves of the tree were for the healing of the nations."

7. The Well of Life, with its powers of renewal, is successively compared with waters of the Bible, of England and Europe, and of classical antiquity. In the pool of Siloam ("Silo") a blind man was cured by Christ (John 9.7); water of the river Jordan cured Naaman of leprosy (2 Kings 5.14) and Christ was baptized therein (Matthew 3.16). "Bath" and "Spau" (Spa) were famed for their medicinal waters. "Cephise" and "Hebrus" in Greece were noted for purifying and healing powers.

And deckt himselfe with feathers youthly gay,
Like Eyas hauke° up mounts unto the skies, *unfledged hawk*
His newly budded pineons to assay,
And marveiles at himselfe, still as he flies:
So new this new-borne knight to battell new did rise.

35

Whom when the damnèd feend so fresh did spy,
No wonder if he wondred at the sight,
And doubted, whether his late enemy
It were, or other new supplièd knight.
He, now to prove° his late renewèd might, *try*
High brandishing his bright deaw-burning blade,
Upon his crested scalpe so sore did smite,
That to the scull a yawning wound it made:
The deadly dint° his dullèd senses all dismaid. *blow*

36

I wote° not, whether the revenging steele *know*
Were hardnèd with that holy water dew,
Wherein he fell, or sharper edge did feele,
Or his baptizèd hands now greater° grew; *stronger*
Or other secret vertue° did ensew; *power*
Else never could the force of fleshly arme,
Ne molten mettall in his bloud embrew:° *plunge*
For till that stownd° could never wight him harme, *moment*
By subtilty, nor slight,° nor might, nor mighty charme. *trickery*

37

The cruell wound enragèd him so sore,
That loud he yellèd for exceeding paine;
As hundred ramping° Lyons seemed to rore, *rearing*
Whom ravenous hunger did thereto constraine:
Then gan he tosse aloft his stretchèd traine,° *tail*
And therewith scourge the buxome° aire so sore, *yielding*
That to his force to yeelden it was faine;° *obliged*
Ne ought his sturdie strokes might stand afore,[8]
That high trees overthrew, and rocks in peeces tore.

38

The same advauncing high above his head,
With sharpe intended° sting so rude° him smot, *extended / roughly*
That to the earth him drove, as stricken dead,
Ne living wight would have him life behot:[9]
The mortall sting his angry needle shot
Quite through his shield, and in his shoulder seasd,
Where fast it stucke, ne would there out be got:
The griefe° thereof him wondrous sore diseasd,° *pain / afflicted*
Ne might his ranckling paine with patience be appeasd.

39

But yet more mindfull of his honour deare,
Then of the grievous smart, which him did wring,° *torment*

8. I.e., neither could anything ("ought") stand before his violent ("sturdie") strokes.

9. Promised. I.e., no one would have thought he could survive the blow.

From loathèd soile he can° him lightly reare, *did*
And strove to loose the farre infixèd sting:
Which when in vaine he tryde with struggeling,
Inflamed with wrath, his raging blade he heft,° *heaved*
And strooke so strongly, that the knotty string
Of his huge taile he quite a sunder cleft,
Five joynts thereof he hewd, and but the stump him left.

40

Hart cannot thinke, what outrage,° and what cryes, *violent clamor*
With foule enfouldred[1] smoake and flashing fire,
The hell-bred beast threw forth unto the skyes,
That all was coverèd with darknesse dire:
Then fraught° with rancour, and engorgèd° ire, *filled / swollen*
He cast at once him to avenge for all,
And gathering up himselfe out of the mire,
With his uneven wings did fiercely fall
Upon his sunne-bright shield, and gript it fast withall.

41

Much was the man encombred with his hold,
In feare to lose his weapon in his paw,
Ne wist° yet, how his talents° to unfold; *knew / talons*
Nor harder was from Cerberus[2] greedie jaw
To plucke a bone, then° from his cruell claw *than*
To reave° by strength the gripèd gage° away: *seize / prize*
Thrise he assayd° it from his foot to draw, *tried*
And thrise in vaine to draw it did assay,
It booted nought to thinke, to robbe him of his pray.

42

Tho° when he saw no power might prevaile, *then*
His trustie sword he cald to his last aid,
Wherewith he fiercely did his foe assaile,
And double blowes about him stoutly laid,
That glauncing fire out of the yron plaid;
As sparckles from the Andvile° use to fly, *anvil*
When heavie hammers on the wedge are swaid;° *struck*
Therewith at last he forst him to unty° *loosen*
One of his grasping feete, him to defend thereby.

43

The other foot, fast fixèd on his shield,
Whenas no strength, nor stroks mote° him constraine *might*
To loose, ne yet the warlike pledge to yield,
He smot thereat with all his might and maine,
That nought so wondrous puissance might sustaine;
Upon the joynt the lucky steele did light,
And made such way, that hewd it quite in twaine;
The paw yet missèd not his minisht° might, *lessened*
But hong still on the shield, as it at first was pight.° *placed*

1. Black as a thundercloud.
2. The dog that guards the mouth of Hades.

44

For griefe thereof, and divelish despight,
  From his infernall fournace forth he threw
  Huge flames, that dimmèd all the heavens light,
  Enrold in duskish smoke and brimstone blew;
  As burning Aetna from his boyling stew° *cauldron*
  Doth belch out flames, and rockes in peeces broke,
  And ragged ribs of mountaines molten new
  Enwrapt in coleblacke clouds and filthy smoke,
That all the land with stench, and heaven with horror choke.

45

The heate whereof, and harmefull pestilence
  So sore him noyd,° that forst him to retire *troubled*
  A little backward for his best defence,
  To save his bodie from the scorching fire,
  Which he from hellish entrailes did expire.° *breathe out*
  It chaunst (eternall God that chaunce did guide)
  As he recoylèd backward, in the mire
  His nigh forwearied° feeble feet did slide, *exhausted*
And downe he fell, with dread of shame sore terrifide.

46

There grew a goodly tree him faire beside,
  Loaden with fruit and apples rosie red,
  As they in pure vermilion had beene dide,
  Whereof great vertues over all were red:° *everywhere were told*
  For happie life to all, which thereon fed,
  And life eke everlasting did befall:
  Great God it planted in that blessed sted° *place*
  With his almightie hand, and did it call
The Tree of Life, the crime of our first fathers fall.[3]

47

In all the world like was not to be found,
  Save in that soile, where all good things did grow,
  And freely sprong out of the fruitfull ground,
  As incorrupted Nature did them sow,
  Till that dread Dragon all did overthrow.
  Another like faire tree eke grew thereby,
  Whereof who so did eat, eftsoones did know
  Both good and ill: O mornefull memory:
That tree through one mans fault hath doen us all to dy.° *i.e., killed us*

48

From that first tree forth flowd, as from a well,
  A trickling streame of Balme, most soveraine° *powerful for cures*
  And daintie deare,° which on the ground still fell, *precious*
  And overflowèd all the fertill plaine,

3. Genesis 2.9 describes the Tree of Life and also the Tree of Knowledge of Good and Evil, both of which God planted in the Garden of Eden. The "crime of our first fathers fall" is that Adam, in eating of the second and being banished from Eden, separated himself—and (according to Christian doctrine) his descendants—from the first. The Tree of Life appears again in the New Jerusalem (Revelation 22.2).

As it had deawèd bene with timely° raine: *seasonable*
Life and long health that gratious° ointment gave, *full of grace*
And deadly woundes could heale, and reare° againe *raise*
The senselesse corse appointed° for the grave. *made ready*
Into that same he fell: which did from death him save.[4]

49

For nigh thereto the ever damnèd beast
Durst not approch, for he was deadly made,° *i.e., a child of death*
And all that life preservèd, did detest:
Yet he it oft adventured° to invade. *attempted*
By this the drouping day-light gan to fade,
And yeeld his roome° to sad succeeding night, *its place*
Who with her sable mantle gan to shade
The face of earth, and wayes of living wight,
And high her burning torch set up in heaven bright.

50

When gentle Una saw the second fall
Of her deare knight, who wearie of long fight,
And faint through losse of bloud, moved not at all,
But lay as in a dreame of deepe delight,
Besmeard with pretious Balme, whose vertuous might
Did heale his wounds, and scorching heat alay,[5]
Againe she stricken was with sore affright,
And for his safetie gan devoutly pray;
And watch the noyous° night, and wait for joyous day. *noxious*

51

The joyous day gan early to appeare,
And faire Aurora from the deawy bed
Of agèd Tithone gan her selfe to reare,[6]
With rosie cheekes, for shame as blushing red;
Her golden lockes for haste were loosely shed
About her eares, when Una her did marke
Clymbe to her charet, all with flowers spred,
From heaven high to chase the chearelesse darke;
With merry note her loud salutes the mounting larke.

52

Then freshly up arose the doughtie° knight, *valiant*
All healèd of his hurts and woundès wide,
And did himselfe to battell readie dight;° *prepare*
Whose early foe awaiting him beside
To have devourd, so soone as day he spyde,
When now he saw himselfe so freshly reare,
As if late fight had nought him damnifyde,° *injured*
He woxe° dismayd, and gan his fate to feare; *grew*
Nathlesse° with wonted rage he him advauncèd neare. *nevertheless*

4. The healing balm flowing from the Tree of Life is understood to be Christ's blood, shed to redeem humankind from eternal damnation.
5. Cf. Revelation 2.7, 11: "To him that overcometh will I give to eat of the tree of life" and "He that overcometh shall not be hurt of the second death."
6. Aurora is goddess of the dawn, Tithonus her husband ("aged" because he was granted everlasting life without everlasting youth).

53

And in his first encounter, gaping wide,
He thought attonce him to have swallowed quight,
And rusht upon him with outragious pride;
Who him r'encountring fierce, as hauke in flight,
Perforce rebutted° backe. The weapon bright *drove*
Taking advantage of his open jaw,
Ran through his mouth with so importune° might, *violent*
That deepe emperst his darksome hollow maw,
And back retyrd,[7] his life bloud forth with all did draw.

54

So downe he fell, and forth his life did breath,
That vanisht into smoke and cloudès swift;
So downe he fell, that th' earth him underneath
Did grone, as feeble so great load to lift;
So downe he fell, as an huge rockie clift,
Whose false° foundation waves have washt away, *insecure*
With dreadfull poyse° is from the mayneland rift,° *falling weight / split*
And rolling downe, great Neptune doth dismay;
So downe he fell, and like an heapèd mountaine lay.

55

The knight himselfe even trembled at his fall,
So huge and horrible a masse it seemed;
And his deare Ladie, that beheld it all,
Durst not approch for dread, which she misdeemed,° *misjudged*
But yet at last, when as the direfull feend
She saw not stirre, off-shaking vaine affright,
She nigher drew, and saw that joyous end:
Then God she praysd, and thankt her faithfull knight,
That had atchiev'd so great a conquest by his might.

Canto 12 *Summary* The king and queen of Eden emerge from the castle with all their followers and gaze in wonder at the dead dragon. A great banquet is held in the castle, and Redcrosse and Una are betrothed, though Redcrosse must still fulfill his pledge to serve the Faerie Queene in war for six more years. A messenger arrives bearing a letter from Fidessa (Duessa), in which she charges Redcrosse with breach of promise and seeks to prevent his marriage to Una. Redcrosse explains to the king how he was led astray by Duessa's wicked arts. The messenger is revealed by Una as Archimago and thrown into a dungeon. The king then performs the wedding ceremony. They live in happiness for some time, until Redcrosse must return to the Faerie Queene, leaving Una to mourn.

7. I.e., on being drawn back.

From The Second Booke of The Faerie Queene

Contayning
The Legend of Sir Guyon,
or
Of Temperaunce

Summary In Book Two, Sir Guyon represents and becomes the virtue of Temperance, which requires moderation, self-control, and sometimes abstinence in regard to anger, sex, greed, ambition, and the whole spectrum of passions, desires, pleasures, and material goods. In his climactic adventure, he visits and destroys the witch Acrasia's Bower of Bliss.

From *Canto 12*

[THE BOWER OF BLISS][1]

42

Thence passing forth, they[2] shortly do arrive,
  Whereas the Bowre of Blisse was situate;
  A place pickt out by choice of best alive,° *the best living artisans*
  That natures worke by art can imitate:
  In which what ever in this worldly state
  Is sweet, and pleasing unto living sense,
  Or that may dayntiest fantasie aggrate,° *please, satisfy*
  Was pourèd forth with plentifull dispence,° *liberality*
And made there to abound with lavish affluence.

43

Goodly it was enclosèd round about,
  Aswell their entred guests to keepe within,
  As those unruly beasts to hold without;[3]
  Yet was the fence thereof but weake and thin;
  Nought feard their force, that fortilage° to win,[4] *fortress*
  But wisedomes powre, and temperaunces might,
  By which the mightiest things efforcèd bin:° *are compelled*
  And eke° the gate was wrought of substaunce light, *also*
Rather for pleasure, then° for battery or fight. *than*

44

Yt framèd° was of precious yvory, *made*
  That seemd a worke of admirable wit;° *marvelous skill*

1. The Bower of Bliss, perhaps the most famous of Spenser's symbolic places, has been variously interpreted. Some critics emphasize its aspects of sterility and artifice; others, its seductive and threatening eroticism and idolatry akin to that associated with the New World and Ireland.
2. I.e., Guyon and a character called the Palmer, who is his guide throughout Book 2 (and who is usually thought to represent reason). Pilgrims to the Holy Land were called palmers in token of the palm leaves they often brought back.
3. Just outside the Bower, Guyon and the Palmer had encountered "many beasts, that roard outrageously, / As if that hungers point, or Venus sting / Had them enraged" (stanza 39). The Palmer had used the magical power of his staff to turn their aggression into cringing fear.
4. I.e., it was not at all feared that the physical force of the beasts could breach that fortress.

And therein all the famous history
Of Jason and Medaea was ywrit;
Her mighty charmes, her furious loving fit,
His goodly conquest of the golden fleece,
His falsèd° faith, and love too lightly flit,° *violated / altering*
The wondred° Argo, which in venturous peece[5] *admired*
First through the Euxine seas bore all the flowr of Greece.[6]

45

Ye might° have seene the frothy billowes fry° *could / foam*
Under the ship, as thorough° them she went, *through*
That seemd the waves were into yvory,
Or yvory into the waves were sent;
And other where the snowy substaunce sprent° *sprinkled*
With vermell,° like the boyes bloud therein shed,[7] *vermilion*
A piteous spectacle did represent,
And otherwhiles° with gold besprinkelèd; *elsewhere*
Yt seemd th' enchaunted flame, which did Creüsa wed.[8]

46

All this, and more might in that goodly gate
Be red; that ever open stood to all,
Which thither came: but in the Porch there sate
A comely personage of stature tall,
And semblaunce° pleasing, more then naturall, *appearance*
That travellers to him seemd to entize;
His looser° garment to the ground did fall, *too loose*
And flew about his heeles in wanton wize,
Not fit for speedy pace, or manly exercize.

47

They in that place him Genius° did call: *presiding spirit*
Not that celestiall powre, to whom the care
Of life, and generatiön of all
That lives, pertaines in charge particulare,[9]
Who wondrous things concerning our welfare,
And strange phantomes doth let us oft forsee,
And oft of secret ill bids us beware:
That is our Selfe,[1] whom though we do not see,
Yet each doth in him selfe it well perceive to bee.

48

Therefore a God him sage Antiquity
Did wisely make,[2] and good Agdistes call:
But this same[3] was to that quite contrary,

5. I.e., adventurous vessel.
6. Jason, in his ship the *Argo,* sought the Golden Fleece of the king of Colchis; the sorceress Medea, the king's daughter, fell in love with him and used "her mighty charmes" to help him obtain it.
7. The blood of Absyrtus, Medea's younger brother, whose body she cut into pieces and scattered to delay her father's pursuit.
8. Jason later deserted Medea for Creüsa. In revenge, Medea gave her a dress that burst into flame when she put it on; the flame consumed and thus "wed" her.
9. I.e., not Agdistes (see next stanza), the god of generation. The true Agdistes appears in the Garden of Adonis canto of Book 3 (canto 6, stanzas 31–33).
1. I.e., the *daemon* or indwelling divine power that directs the course of our lives.
2. I.e., the wise ancients were right to declare this power a god.
3. I.e., the Genius of the Bower.

The foe of life, that good envyes° to all, *grudges*
That secretly doth us procure° to fall, *cause*
Through guilefull semblaunts,° which he makes us see. *illusions*
He of this Gardin had the governall,° *management*
And Pleasures porter was devizd° to bee, *appointed*
Holding a staffe in hand for more formalitee.

49

With diverse flowres he daintily was deckt,
And strowèd round about, and by his side
A mighty Mazer bowle[4] of wine was set,
As if it had to him bene sacrifide;° *consecrated*
Wherewith all new-come guests he gratifide:
So did he eke Sir Guyon passing by:
But he his idle curtesie defide,
And overthrew his bowle disdainfully;
And broke his staffe, with which he charmèd semblants sly.[5]

50

Thus being entred, they behold around
A large and spacious plaine, on every side
Strowed with pleasauns,° whose faire grassy ground *pleasure-grounds*
Mantled with greene, and goodly beautifide
With all the ornaments of Floraes° pride, *goddess of flowers*
Wherewith her mother Art, as halfe in scorne
Of niggard° Nature, like a pompous bride *stingy*
Did decke her, and too lavishly adorne,
When forth from virgin bowre she comes in th' early morne.

51

Thereto the Heavens alwayes Joviall,[6]
Lookt on them lovely,° still° in stedfast state, *lovingly / always*
Ne° suffred storme nor frost on them to fall, *nor*
Their tender buds or leaves to violate,
Nor scorching heat, nor cold intemperate
T' afflict the creatures, which therein did dwell,
But the milde aire with season moderate
Gently attempred, and disposd so well,
That still it breathèd forth sweet spirit° and holesome smell. *breath*

52

More sweet and holesome, then° the pleasaunt hill *than*
Of Rhodope, on which the Nimphe, that bore
A gyaunt babe, her selfe for griefe did kill;
Or the Thessalian Tempe, where of yore
Faire Daphne Phoebus hart with love did gore;
Or Ida, where the Gods lov'd to repaire,° *resort*
When ever they their heavenly bowres forlore;° *deserted*
Or sweet Parnasse, the haunt of Muses faire;[7]
Or Eden selfe, if ought° with Eden mote compaire. *aught, anything*

4. A drinking cup of maple.

5. Raised deceitful apparitions. The rod and bowl are traditional emblems of enchantment (cf. Duessa's cup, 1.8, stanza 14).

6. Serene and beneficent, as influenced by the planet Jupiter.

7. The nymph Rhodope, who had a "gyaunt babe," Athos, by Neptune, was turned into a mountain. Daphne, another nymph, charmed Apollo so that he pursued her until she prayed for aid and was turned into a laurel tree. Mount Ida was the scene of the rape of Ganymede by Jupiter, the judgment

53

Much wondred Guyon at the faire aspect
Of that sweet place, yet suffred no delight
To sincke into his sence, nor mind affect,
But passèd forth, and lookt still forward right,° *straight ahead*
Bridling his will, and maistering his might:
Till that he came unto another gate;
No gate, but like one, being goodly dight° *arrayed*
With boughes and braunches, which did broad dilate° *spread out*
Their clasping armes, in wanton wreathings intricate.

54

So fashionèd a Porch with rare device,° *design*
Archt over head with an embracing vine,
Whose bounches hanging downe, seemed to entice
All passers by, to tast their lushious wine,
And did themselves into their hands incline,
As freely offering to be gatherèd:
Some deepe empurpled as the Hyacint,[8]
Some as the Rubine,° laughing sweetly red, *ruby*
Some like faire Emeraudes, not yet well ripenèd.

55

And them amongst, some were of burnisht gold,
So made by art, to beautifie the rest,
Which did themselves emongst the leaves enfold,
As lurking from the vew of covetous guest,
That the weake bowes,° with so rich load opprest, *boughs*
Did bowe adowne, as over-burdenèd.
Under that Porch a comely dame did rest,
Clad in faire weedes,° but fowle disorderèd, *garments*
And garments loose, that seemd unmeet for womanhed.° *womanhood*

56

In her left hand a Cup of gold she held,
And with her right the riper° fruit did reach, *overripe*
Whose sappy liquor, that with fulnesse sweld,
Into her cup she scruzd,° with daintie breach° *squeezed / crushing*
Of her fine fingers, without fowle empeach,° *injury*
That so faire wine-presse made the wine more sweet:
Thereof she usd to give to drinke to each,
Whom passing by she happenèd to meet:
It was her guise,° all Straungers goodly so to greet. *custom*

57

So she to Guyon offred it to tast;
Who taking it out of her tender hond,
The cup to ground did violently cast,
That all in peeces it was broken fond,° *found*
And with the liquor stainèd all the lond:° *land*
Whereat Excesse exceedingly was wroth,

---

of Paris, and the gods' vantage point for viewing the Trojan War. Mount Parnassus is the home of the Muses.

8. The hyacinth or jacinth, a sapphire-colored stone.

Yet no'te° the same amend, ne yet withstond, *knew not how to*
But suffered° him to passe, all° were she loth; *allowed / although*
Who nought regarding her displeasure forward goth.

58

There the most daintie Paradise on ground,
It selfe doth offer to his sober eye,
In which all pleasures plenteously abound,
And none does others happinesse envye:
The painted° flowres, the trees upshooting hye, *brightly colored*
The dales for shade, the hilles for breathing space,
The trembling groves, the Christall° running by; *clear stream*
And that, which all faire workes doth most aggrace,° *add grace to*
The art, which all that wrought, appearèd in no place.

59

One would have thought (so cunningly, the rude,
And scornèd parts were mingled with the fine)
That nature had for wantonesse ensude° *playfulness imitated*
Art, and that Art at nature did repine;° *complain*
So striving each th' other to undermine,
Each did the others worke more beautifie;
So diff'ring both in willes, agreed in fine:° *in the end*
So all agreed through sweete diversitie,
This Gardin to adorne with all varietie.

60

And in the midst of all, a fountaine stood,
Of richest substaunce, that on earth might bee,
So pure and shiny, that the silver flood
Through every channell running one might see;
Most goodly it with curious imageree
Was over-wrought, and shapes of naked boyes,
Of which some seemd with lively jollitee,
To fly about, playing their wanton toyes,° *sports*
Whilest others did them selves embay° in liquid joyes. *bathe*

61

And over all, of purest gold was spred,
A trayle of yvie in his native hew:
For the rich mettall was so colourèd,
That wight, who did not well avis'd° it vew, *carefully*
Would surely deeme it to be yvie trew:
Low his lascivious armes adown did creepe,
That themselves dipping in the silver dew,
Their fleecy flowres they tenderly did steepe,
Which° drops of Christall seemd for wantones to weepe. *on which*

62

Infinit streames continually did well
Out of this fountaine, sweet and faire to see,
The which into an ample laver° fell, *basin*
And shortly grew to so great quantitie,
That like a little lake it seemd to bee;

Whose depth exceeded not three cubits[9] hight,
That through the waves one might the bottom see,
All pav'd beneath with Jaspar shining bright,
That seemd the fountaine in that sea did sayle upright.

63

And all the margent° round about was set, *border*
With shady Laurell trees, thence to defend° *ward off*
The sunny beames, which on the billowes bet,° *beat*
And those which therein bathèd, mote offend.° *harm*
As Guyon hapned by the same to wend,
Two naked Damzelles he therein espyde,
Which therein bathing, seemèd to contend,
And wrestle wantonly, ne car'd to hyde,
Their dainty parts from vew of any, which them eyde.

64

Sometimes the one would lift the other quight
Above the waters, and then downe againe
Her plong,° as over maisterèd by might, *plunge*
Where both awhile would coverèd remaine,
And each the other from to rise° restraine; *rising*
The whiles their snowy limbes, as through a vele,
So through the Christall waves appearèd plaine:
Then suddeinly both would themselves unhele,° *uncover*
And th' amarous sweet spoiles° to greedy eyes revele. *booty, plunder*

65

As that faire Starre, the messenger of morne,[1]
His deawy face out of the sea doth reare:
Or as the Cyprian goddess,[2] newly borne
Of th' Oceans fruitfull froth,° did first appeare: *foam*
Such seemèd they, and so their yellow heare
Christalline humour° droppèd downe apace. *clear water*
Whom such when Guyon saw, he drew him neare,
And somewhat gan relent his earnest pace;
His stubborne brest gan secret pleasaunce to embrace.

66

The wanton Maidens him espying, stood
Gazing a while at his unwonted guise;° *unaccustomed behavior*
Then th' one her selfe low duckèd in the flood,
Abasht, that her a straunger did avise:° *see*
But th' other rather higher did arise,
And her two lilly paps aloft displayd,
And all, that might his melting hart entise
To her delights, she unto him bewrayed:° *revealed*
The rest hid underneath, him more desirous made.

9. A cubit is about twenty inches (thus the depth is less than five feet).

1. Unless "his" in the next line is to be taken as neuter, it implies that the reference is not to Venus but to Phosphorus (or Heophorus), the minor male divinity sometimes identified with the morning star.

2. Venus, one of whose principal shrines was on the island of Cyprus.

67

With that, the other likewise up arose,
And her faire lockes, which formerly were bownd
Up in one knot, she low adowne did lose:° *loosen*
Which flowing long and thick, her cloth'd arownd,
And th' yvorie in golden mantle gownd:
So that faire spectacle from him was reft,° *taken*
Yet that, which reft it, no lesse faire was fownd:
So hid in lockes and waves from lookers theft,
Nought but her lovely face she for his looking left.

68

Withall she laughèd, and she blusht withall,
That blushing to her laughter gave more grace,
And laughter to her blushing, as did fall:
Now when they spide the knight to slacke his pace,
Them to behold, and in his sparkling face
The secret signes of kindled lust appeare,
Their wanton meriments they did encreace,
And to him beckned, to approch more neare,
And shewd him many sights, that courage cold could reare.[3]

69

On which when gazing him the Palmer saw,
He much rebukt those wandring eyes of his,
And counseld well, him forward thence did draw.
Now are they come nigh to the Bowre of blis
Of her fond° favorites so named amis: *enamored; foolish*
When thus the Palmer; "Now Sir, well avise;° *take care*
For here the end of all our travell° is: *travel; travail*
Here wonnes° Acrasia, whom we must surprise, *dwells*
Else she will slip away, and all our drift despise."° *plan set at nought*

70

Eftsoones° they heard a most melodious sound, *immediately*
Of all that mote delight a daintie eare,
Such as attonce might not on living ground,
Save in this Paradise, be heard elswhere:
Right hard it was, for wight,° which did it heare, *person*
To read,° what manner musicke that mote bee: *discern*
For all that pleasing is to living eare,
Was there consorted in one harmonee,
Birdes, voyces, instruments, windes, waters, all agree.

71

The joyous birdes shrouded in chearefull shade,
Their notes unto the voyce attempred° sweet; *attuned*
Th' Angelicall soft trembling voyces made
To th' instruments divine respondence meet:° *fitting*
The silver sounding instruments did meet° *join*
With the base murmure of the waters fall:

3. That could arouse sexual desire ("courage") when cold.

The waters fall with difference discreet,° *distinct variation*
Now soft, now loud, unto the wind did call:
The gentle warbling wind low answerèd to all.

72

There, whence that Musick seemèd heard to bee,
Was the faire Witch her selfe[4] now solacing,° *taking pleasure*
With a new Lover, whom through sorceree
And witchcraft, she from farre did thither bring:
There she had him now layd a slombering,
In secret shade, after long wanton joyes:
Whilst round about them pleasauntly did sing
Many faire Ladies, and lascivious boyes,
That ever mixt their song with light licentious toyes.° *amorous play*

73

And all that while, right over him she hong,
With her false° eyes fast fixèd in his sight, *deceitful*
As seeking medicine, whence she was stong,° *stung*
Or greedily depasturing° delight: *feeding on*
And oft inclining downe with kisses light,
For feare of waking him, his lips bedewd,
And through his humid eyes did sucke his spright,° *spirit*
Quite molten into lust and pleasure lewd;
Wherewith she sighèd soft, as if his case she rewd.° *pitied*

74

The whiles some one did chaunt this lovely lay:[5]
"Ah see, who so faire thing doest faine° to see, *delight*
In springing flowre the image of thy day;
Ah see the Virgin Rose, how sweetly shee
Doth first peepe forth with bashfull modestee,
That fairer seemes, the lesse ye see her may;
Lo see soone after, how more bold and free
Her barèd bosome she doth broad display;
Loe see soone after, how she fades, and falles away.

75

"So passeth, in the passing of a day,
Of mortall life the leafe, the bud, the flowre,
Ne more doth flourish after first decay,
That earst° was sought to decke both bed and bowre, *formerly*
Of many a Ladie, and many a Paramowre:° *lover*
Gather therefore the Rose, whilest yet is prime,° *(its) springtime*
For soone comes age, that will her pride deflowre:
Gather the Rose of love, whilest yet is time,
Whilest loving thou mayst lovèd be with equal crime."

4. Acrasia—whose name means both "intemperance" and "incontinence"—bears many resemblances to the classical Circe (in *Odyssey* 10 as well as the more witchlike and seductive figure in Ovid's *Metamorphoses* 14) and also to the enchantresses of Italian romance who derive from Circe: Acratia in Trissino's *L'Italia liberata* and Armida in Tasso's *Gerusalemme liberata.* Much of the description in this scene is imitated from Tasso's account of the garden of Armida.

5. The song ("lay") of stanzas 74 and 75 imitates that in *Gerusalemme liberata* 16.14–15; this is a classic statement of the *carpe florem* (or *carpe diem*) theme—pick the flower of youth before it fades.

76

He ceast, and then gan all the quire of birdes
Their diverse notes t' attune unto his lay,
As in approvance of his pleasing words.
The constant paire[6] heard all, that he did say,
Yet swarvèd not, but kept their forward way,
Through many covert groves, and thickets close,
In which they creeping did at last display° *discover*
That wanton Ladie, with her lover lose,° *loose, wanton*
Whose sleepie head she in her lap did soft dispose.

77

Upon a bed of Roses she was layd,
As faint through heat, or dight to° pleasant sin, *ready for*
And was arayd, or rather disarayd,
All in a vele of silke and silver thin,
That hid no whit her alablaster skin,
But rather shewd more white, if more might bee:
More subtile web Arachne° cannot spin, *the spider*
Nor the fine nets, which oft we woven see
Of scorchèd deaw, do not in th' aire more lightly flee.° *float*

78

Her snowy brest was bare to readie spoyle
Of hungry eies, which n'ote° therewith be fild, *could not*
And yet through languor of her late sweet toyle,
Few drops, more cleare then Nectar, forth distild,
That like pure Orient perles[7] adowne it trild,° *trickled*
And her faire eyes sweet smyling in delight,
Moystened their fierie beames, with which she thrild° *pierced*
Fraile harts, yet quenchèd° not; like starry light *quenched; killed*
Which sparckling on the silent waves, does seeme more bright.

79

The young man sleeping by her, seemd to bee
Some goodly swayne of honorable place,° *rank*
That certès° it great pittie was to see *certainly*
Him his nobilitie so foule deface;° *disgrace*
A sweet regard,° and amiable grace, *demeanor*
Mixèd with manly sternnesse did appeare
Yet sleeping, in his well proportioned face,
And on his tender lips the downy heare
Did now but freshly spring, and silken blossomes beare.

80

His warlike armes, the idle instruments
Of sleeping praise,° were hong upon a tree, *worthiness*
And his brave° shield, full of old moniments,° *splendid / marks of honor*
Was fowly ra'st,° that none the signes might see; *erased*
Ne for them, ne for honour carèd hee,
Ne ought,° that did to his advauncement tend, *aught, anything*
But in lewd loves, and wastfull luxuree,° *licentiousness*

6. I.e., Guyon and the Palmer.

7. Lustrous pearls of the East.

His dayes, his goods, his bodie he did spend:
O horrible enchantment, that him so did blend.° *blind*

81

The noble Elfe,[8] and carefull Palmer drew
So nigh them, minding nought, but° lustfull game, *heedful only of*
That suddein forth they on them rusht, and threw
A subtile net, which onely for the same
The skilfull Palmer formally° did frame.[9] *expressly*
So held them under fast, the whiles the rest
Fled all away from feare of fowler shame.
The faire Enchauntresse, so unwares opprest,° *surprised*
Tryde all her arts, and all her sleights, thence out to wrest.

82

And eke° her lover strove: but all in vaine; *also*
For that same net so cunningly was wound,
That neither guile, nor force might it distraine.° *tear*
They tooke them both, and both them strongly bound
In captive bandes,° which there they readie found: *bonds*
But her in chaines of adamant[1] he tyde;
For nothing else might keepe her safe and sound;
But Verdant° (so he hight°) he soone untyde, *Green / was called*
And counsell sage in steed° thereof to him applyde. *instead*

83

But all those pleasant bowres and Pallace brave,° *splendid*
Guyon broke downe, with rigour pittilesse;
Ne ought their goodly workmanship might save
Them from the tempest of his wrathfulnesse,
But that their blisse he turn'd to balefulnesse:° *distress*
Their groves he feld, their gardins did deface,
Their arbers spoyle, their Cabinets° suppresse, *bowers*
Their banket° houses burne, their buildings race,° *banquet / raze*
And of the fairest late, now made the fowlest place.

84

Then led they her away, and eke that knight
They with them led, both sorrowfull and sad:
The way they came, the same retourn'd they right,
Till they arrivèd, where they lately had
Charm'd those wild-beasts, that rag'd with furie mad.[2]
Which now awaking, fierce at them gan fly,
As in their mistresse reskew, whom they lad;° *led*
But them the Palmer soone did pacify.
Then Guyon askt, what meant those beastes, which there did ly.

85

Said he, "These seeming beasts are men indeed,
Whom this Enchauntresse hath transformèd thus,

8. Knight of Faerie Land, here, Guyon.
9. The episode recalls the capture of Venus and her lover Mars in a net cunningly set around his marriage bed by Venus's husband, Vulcan, the blacksmith god (*Odyssey* 8.272–84).
1. Steel or some other extremely hard substance.
2. See above, stanza 43, note 3.

Whylome° her lovers, which her lusts did feed, *formerly*
Now turnèd into figures hideous,
According to their mindes like monstruous."[3]
"Sad end," quoth he, "of life intemperate,
And mournefull meed° of joyes delicious: *reward*
But Palmer, if it mote thee so aggrate,° *please*
Let them returnèd be unto their former state."

86

Streight way he with his vertuous° staffe them strooke, *powerful*
And streight of beasts they comely men became;
Yet being men they did unmanly looke,
And starèd ghastly, some for inward shame,
And some for wrath, to see their captive Dame:
But one above the rest in speciall,
That had an hog beene late, hight° Grille[4] by name, *called*
Repinèd° greatly, and did him miscall,° *complained / revile*
That had from hoggish forme him brought to naturall.

87

Said Guyon, "See the mind of beastly man,
That hath so soone forgot the excellence
Of his creation, when he life began,
That now he chooseth, with vile difference,° *preference*
To be a beast, and lacke intelligence."
To whom the Palmer thus, "The donghill kind
Delights in filth and foule incontinence:
Let Grill be Grill, and have his hoggish mind,
But let us hence depart, whilest wether serves and wind."

1590, 1596

Amoretti and Epithalamion

In the early 1590s the widowed Spenser wooed and won Elizabeth Boyle, whom he married in Ireland in 1594. The next year he published a small volume that included the sonnet sequence *Amoretti* ("little loves" or "little cupids") and the *Epithalamion*. Several of the sonnets explicitly address an "Elizabeth," and the volume's subtitle, "Written not long since," suggests that these poems, taken together, are a portrait of Spenser's recent courtship and marriage. It was unusual to write sonnets about a happy and successful love; traditionally, the sonneteer's love was for someone painfully inaccessible. Spenser rehearses some of the conventional motifs of frustration and longing, but his cycle of polished, eloquent poems leads toward joyous possession. Thus, for example, in sonnet 67 ("Lyke as a huntsman after weary chace"), he transforms a Petrarchan lament into a vision of unexpected fulfillment.

Spenser's great celebration of this fulfillment is the *Epithalamion*. A learned poet, he was acutely conscious that he was writing within a tradition: an epithalamion is a wedding song whose Greek name conveys that it was sung on the threshold of the bridal chamber. The genre, which goes back at least as far as Sappho (ca. 612 B.C.E.),

3. Even as their own minds were similarly monstrous. Circe changed Odysseus's companions into animals, but Odysseus had a charm to release them.

4. According to one of Plutarch's dialogues, a man named Gryllus ("fierce," "cruel"), having been changed into a hog by Circe, refused to be restored to human form by Odysseus.

was widely practiced by the Roman poets, particularly Catullus, and imitated in the Renaissance. Its elements typically include an invocation of the Muses, followed by a celebratory description of the procession of the bride, the religious rites, the singing and dancing at the wedding party, the preparations for the wedding night, and the sexual consummation of the marriage.

In long, flowing stanzas, Spenser follows these conventions closely, adapting them with exquisite delicacy to his small-town Irish setting and native folklore. But his first stanza announces a major innovation: "So I unto myselfe alone will sing." Traditionally, the poet of an epithalamion was an admiring observer, a kind of master of ceremonies; by combining the roles of poet and bridegroom, Spenser transforms a genial social performance into a passionate lyric utterance. Equally remarkable innovations are the complex stanza form, for which no direct model has been discovered, and the still more complex overall structure. That structure is a triumph of symbolic patterning; the more scholars have studied it, the more elaborate the order they seem to have uncovered. This subtle and rich poetic structure conjures up not only a single day of celebration but also, beyond this particular event, an orderly, harmonious universe, with a hidden pattern of coherence and regularity. If the *Epithalamion* goes to remarkable lengths to affirm this pattern, it is perhaps because it also registers so insistently all that threatens the enduring happiness of wedded love and indeed of human life itself. The greatest threat is the force over which the poem exercises its greatest power: time.

From Amoretti

Sonnet 1

Happy ye leaves[1] when as those lilly hands,
  Which hold my life in their dead doing° might, *killing*
  Shall handle you and hold in loves soft bands,° *bonds*
  Lyke captives trembling at the victors sight.
And happy lines, on which with starry light,
  Those lamping° eyes will deigne sometimes to look *flashing*
  And reade the sorrowes of my dying spright,° *spirit*
  Written with teares in harts close° bleeding book. *secret*
And happy rymes bath'd in the sacred brooke
  Of Helicon[2] whence she derivèd is,
  When ye behold that Angels blessèd looke,
  My soules long lackèd foode, my heavens blis.
Leaves, lines, and rymes, seeke her to please alone,
  Whom if ye please, I care for other none.

Sonnet 34[3]

Lyke as a ship that through the Ocean wyde,
  By conduct of some star doth make her way,
  Whenas a storme hath dimd her trusty guyde,
  Out of her course doth wander far astray:
So I whose star, that wont° with her bright ray *was accustomed*
  Me to direct, with cloudes is overcast,

1. I.e., of the book: pages.
2. The "sacred brooke" is Hippocrene, which flows from Mount Helicon, the mountain sacred to the Muses.
3. An adaptation of Petrarch's Rima 189.

Doe wander now in darknesse and dismay,
Through hidden perils round about me plast.° *placed*
Yet hope I well, that when this storme is past
My Helice[4] the lodestar° of my lyfe *guiding star*
Will shine again, and looke on me at last,
With lovely light to cleare my cloudy grief.
Till then I wander carefull° comfortlesse, *full of cares*
In secret sorow and sad pensivenesse.

Sonnet 54

Of this worlds Theatre in which we stay,
My love like the Spectator ydly sits
Beholding me that all the pageants° play, *dramatic scenes*
Disguysing diversly my troubled wits.
Sometimes I joy when glad occasion fits,
And mask in myrth lyke to a Comedy:
Soone after when my joy to sorrow flits,
I waile and make my woes a Tragedy.
Yet she beholding me with constant° eye, *unmoved*
Delights not in my merth nor rues my smart:° *pities my hurt*
But when I laugh she mocks, and when I cry
She laughes and hardens evermore her hart.
What then can move her? if nor merth nor mone,° *moan*
She is no woman, but a sencelesse stone.

Sonnet 64[5]

Comming to kisse her lyps (such grace I found)
Me seemd I smelt a gardin of sweet flowres
That dainty odours from them threw around,
For damzels fit to decke their lovers bowres.
Her lips did smell lyke unto Gillyflowers,° *carnations*
Her ruddy cheeks lyke unto Roses red;
Her snowy browes lyke budded Bellamoures,[6]
Her lovely eyes like Pincks but newly spred,
Her goodly bosome lyke a Strawberry bed,
Her neck lyke to a bounch of Cullambynes;
Her brest lyke lillyes, ere theyr leaves be shed,
Her nipples lyke yong blossomd Jessemynes.° *jasmines*
Such fragrant flowres doe give most odorous smell,
But her sweet odour did them all excell.

Sonnet 67[7]

Lyke as a huntsman after weary chace,
Seeing the game from him escapt away,

4. A name for the Big Dipper (after the nymph who, in classical mythology, was transformed into it).
5. Much of the imagery of this sonnet is imitated from the Song of Solomon 4.10–16.
6. Unidentified flower, evidently white.
7. An imitation of Petrarch's Rima 190, but with a very different ending. Cf. Sir Thomas Wyatt's adaptation ("Whoso list to hunt") of the same sonnet, and the prose translation of the Petrarchan original appended to it: pp. 350–51.

Sits downe to rest him in some shady place,
With panting hounds beguilèd° of their pray: *deluded*
So after long pursuit and vaine assay,° *attempt*
When I all weary had the chace forsooke,
The gentle deare returnd the selfe-same way,
Thinking to quench her thirst at the next° brooke. *nearby*
There she beholding me with mylder looke,
Sought not to fly, but fearelesse still did bide:
Till I in hand her yet halfe trembling tooke,
And with her owne goodwill hir fyrmely tyde.
Strange thing me seemd to see a beast so wyld,
So goodly wonne with her owne will beguyld.

Sonnet 75[8]

One day I wrote her name upon the strand,° *shore*
But came the waves and washèd it away:
Agayne I wrote it with a second hand,
But came the tyde, and made my paynes his pray.° *prey*
"Vayne man," sayd she, "that doest in vaine assay,° *attempt*
A mortall thing so to immortalize,
For I my selve shall lyke to this decay,
And eek° my name bee wypèd out lykewize." *also*
"Not so," quod° I, "let baser things devize° *quoth / contrive*
To dy in dust, but you shall live by fame:
My verse your vertues rare shall eternize,
And in the heavens wryte your glorious name.
Where whenas death shall all the world subdew,
Our love shall live, and later life renew."

Sonnet 79

Men call you fayre, and you doe credit° it, *believe*
For that your selfe ye dayly such doe see:
But the trew fayre,° that is the gentle wit,° *beauty / intelligence*
And vertuous mind, is much more praysd of me.
For all the rest, how ever fayre it be,
Shall turne to nought and loose that glorious hew:° *form*
But onely that is permanent and free
From frayle corruption, that doth flesh ensew.° *outlast*
That is true beautie: that doth argue° you *prove*
To be divine and borne of heavenly seed:
Deriv'd from that fayre Spirit,° from whom al true *i.e., God*
And perfect beauty did at first proceed.
He onely fayre, and what he fayre hath made:
All other fayre, lyke flowres, untymely fade.

1595

8. For a recitation of this sonnet, go to Norton Literature Online.

Epithalamion

Ye learnèd sisters which have oftentimes
Beene to me ayding, others to adorne:[1]
Whom ye thought worthy of your gracefull rymes,
That even the greatest did not greatly scorne
To heare theyr names sung in your simple layes,° *songs*
But joyèd in theyr prayse.
And when ye list° your owne mishaps to mourne, *chose*
Which death, or love, or fortunes wreck did rayse,
Your string could soone to sadder tenor° turne, *mood*
And teach the woods and waters to lament
Your dolefull dreriment.° *sorrow*
Now lay those sorrowfull complaints aside,
And having all your heads with girland crownd,
Helpe me mine owne loves prayses to resound,
Ne° let the same of° any be envide: *nor / by*
So Orpheus did for his owne bride,[2]
So I unto my selfe alone will sing,
The woods shall to me answer and my Eccho ring.

Early before the worlds light giving lampe,
His golden beame upon the hils doth spred,
Having disperst the nights unchearefull dampe,
Doe ye awake, and with fresh lustyhed° *vigor*
Go to the bowre° of my belovèd love, *bedchamber*
My truest turtle dove,
Bid her awake; for Hymen[3] is awake,
And long since ready forth his maske to move,
With his bright Tead[4] that flames with many a flake,° *spark*
And many a bachelor to waite on him,
In theyr fresh garments trim.
Bid her awake therefore and soone her dight,° *dress*
For lo the wishèd day is come at last,
That shall for al the paynes and sorrowes past,
Pay to her usury° of long delight: *interest*
And whylest she doth her dight,
Doe ye to her of joy and solace° sing, *pleasure*
That all the woods may answer and your Eccho ring.

Bring with you all the Nymphes that you can heare° *can hear you*
Both of the rivers and the forrests greene:
And of the sea that neighbours to her neare,
Al with gay girlands goodly wel beseene.° *beautified*
And let them also with them bring in hand,
Another gay girland
For my fayre love of lillyes and of roses,

1. To write poems in praise of others. The "learned sisters" are the Muses.
2. Orpheus, archetype of the poet in classical antiquity, was famous for his love for his wife, Eurydice.
3. The god of marriage, who leads a "maske" or procession at weddings.
4. A ceremonial torch, associated with marriages since classical times.

Bound truelove wize° with a blew silke riband. *i.e., in a love knot*
And let them make great store of bridale poses,° *posies*
And let them eeke° bring store° of other flowers *also / abundance*
To deck the bridale bowers.
And let the ground whereas° her foot shall tread, *where*
For feare the stones her tender foot should wrong
Be strewed with fragrant flowers all along,
And diapred lyke the discolored mead.[5]
Which done, doe at her chamber dore awayt,
For she will waken strayt,° *straightway*
The whiles doe ye this song unto her sing,
The woods shall to you answer and your Eccho ring.

Ye Nymphes of Mulla[6] which with careful heed,
The silver scaly trouts doe tend full well,
And greedy pikes which use° therein to feed, *are accustomed*
(Those trouts and pikes all others doo excell)
And ye likewise, which keepe the rushy lake,
Where none doo fishes take,
Bynd up the locks the which hang scatterd light,
And in his waters which your mirror make,
Behold your faces as the christall bright,
That when you come whereas° my love doth lie, *where*
No blemish she may spie.
And eke ye lightfoot mayds which keepe the deere,
That on the hoary mountayne use to towre,[7]
And the wylde wolves which seeke them to devoure,
With your steele darts° doo chace from comming neer, *spears*
Be also present heere,
To helpe to decke her and to help to sing,
That all the woods may answer and your Eccho ring.

Wake now my love, awake; for it is time,
The Rosy Morne long since left Tithones bed,[8]
All ready to her silver coche° to clyme, *coach*
And Phoebus° gins to shew his glorious hed. *the sun god*
Hark how the cheerefull birds do chaunt theyr laies
And carroll of loves praise.
The merry Larke hir mattins° sings aloft, *morning prayers*
The thrush replyes, the Mavis descant playes,
The Ouzell shrills, the Ruddock warbles soft,[9]
So goodly all agree with sweet consent,
To this dayes merriment.
Ah my deere love why doe ye sleepe thus long,
When meeter° were that ye should now awake, *more fitting*

5. Ornamented like the many-colored meadow.
6. A river near Spenser's home in Ireland.
7. A falconry term meaning to occupy heights. "The deere": all wild animals, kept by the woodland nymphs.
8. See Song of Solomon 2.10–13: "Rise up, my love, my fair one, and come away. For, lo, the winter is past, the rain is over and gone; the flowers appear on the earth; the time of the singing of birds is come." In classical myth, Tithonus is the aged husband of Aurora, the dawn.
9. The "Mavis" is the song thrush; the "Ouzell," the blackbird (which sings in England); and the "Ruddock," the European robin. The birds' concert is a convention of medieval love poetry. "Descant": a melody or counterpoint written above a musical theme—a soprano obbligato.

T' awayt the comming of your joyous make,° *mate*
And hearken to the birds lovelearnèd song,
The deawy leaves among.
For they of joy and pleasance to you sing,
That all the woods them answer and theyr Eccho ring.

My love is now awake out of her dreame,
And her fayre eyes like stars that dimmèd were
With darksome cloud, now shew° theyr goodly beams *show*
More bright then° Hesperus° his head doth rere. *than / evening star*
Come now ye damzels, daughters of delight,
Helpe quickly her to dight,° *attire*
But first come ye fayre houres which were begot
In Joves sweet paradice, of Day and Night,
Which doe the seasons of the yeare allot,
And al that ever in this world is fayre
Doe make and still° repayre. *continuously*
And ye three handmayds of the Cyprian Queene,[1]
The which doe still adorne her beauties pride,
Helpe to addorne my beautifullest bride:
And as ye her array, still throw betweene° *at intervals*
Some graces to be seene,
And as ye use° to Venus, to her sing, *are accustomed*
The whiles the woods shal answer and your Eccho ring.

Now is my love all ready forth to come,
Let all the virgins therefore well awayt,
And ye fresh boyes that tend upon her groome
Prepare your selves; for he is comming strayt.° *straightway*
Set all your things in seemely good aray° *order*
Fit for so joyfull day,
The joyfulst day that ever sunne did see.
Faire Sun, shew forth thy favourable ray,
And let thy lifull° heat not fervent° be *life-giving / hot*
For feare of burning her sunshyny face,
Her beauty to disgrace.
O fayrest Phoebus, father of the Muse,[2]
If ever I did honour thee aright,
Or sing the thing, that mote° thy mind delight, *might*
Doe not thy servants simple boone° refuse, *request*
But let this day let this one day be myne,
Let all the rest be thine.
Then I thy soverayne prayses loud wil sing,
That all the woods shal answer and theyr Eccho ring.

Harke how the Minstrels gin° to shrill aloud *begin*
Their merry Musick that resounds from far,
The pipe, the tabor,° and the trembling Croud,[3] *small drum*

1. The Graces attending on Venus ("Cyprian Queene"), representing brightness, joy, and bloom.
2. Phoebus Apollo, god of the sun, was also god of music and poetry, but he was not normally regarded as the father of the Nine Muses (Zeus was).
3. Primitive fiddle. Spenser here designates Irish, not classical, instruments and music for the classical masque or ballet.

That well agree withouten breach or jar.° *discord*
But most of all the Damzels doe delite,
When they their tymbrels° smyte, *tambourines*
And thereunto doe daunce and carrol sweet,
That all the sences they doe ravish quite,
The whyles the boyes run up and downe the street,
Crying aloud with strong confusèd noyce,
As if it were one voyce.
Hymen iô Hymen, Hymen[4] they do shout,
That even to the heavens theyr shouting shrill
Doth reach, and all the firmament doth fill,
To which the people standing all about,
As in approvance doe thereto applaud
And loud advaunce her laud,° *praise*
And evermore they *Hymen Hymen* sing,
That all the woods them answer and theyr Eccho ring.

Loe where she comes along with portly° pace *stately*
Lyke Phoebe from her chamber of the East,
Arysing forth to run her mighty race,[5]
Clad all in white, that seemes° a virgin best. *beseems, suits*
So well it her beseems that ye would weene° *think*
Some angell she had beene.
Her long loose yellow locks lyke golden wyre,
Sprinckled with perle, and perling° flowres a tweene, *winding*
Doe lyke a golden mantle her attyre,
And being crownèd with a girland greene,
Seeme lyke some mayden Queene.
Her modest eyes abashèd to behold
So many gazers, as on her do stare,
Upon the lowly ground affixèd are.
Ne dare lift up her countenance too bold,
But blush to heare her prayses sung so loud,
So farre from being proud.
Nathlesse doe ye still loud her prayses sing.
That all the woods may answer and your Eccho ring.

Tell me ye merchants daughters did ye see
So fayre a creature in your towne before,
So sweet, so lovely, and so mild as she,
Adornd with beautyes grace and vertues store,
Her goodly eyes lyke Saphyres shining bright,
Her forehead yvory white,
Her cheekes lyke apples which the sun hath rudded,° *made red*
Her lips lyke cherryes charming men to byte,
Her brest like to a bowle of creame uncrudded,° *uncurdled*
Her paps lyke lyllies budded,
Her snowie necke lyke to a marble towre,
And all her body like a pallace fayre,
Ascending uppe with many a stately stayre,

4. The name of the god of marriage, used as a conventional exclamation at weddings.

5. Phoebe is the moon, a virgin like the bride; the reference to her anticipates the night.

To honors seat and chastities sweet bowre.[6]
Why stand ye still ye virgins in amaze,
Upon her so to gaze,
Whiles ye forget your former lay to sing,
To which the woods did answer and your Eccho ring.

But if ye saw that which no eyes can see,
The inward beauty of her lively spright,° *living spirit, soul*
Garnisht with heavenly guifts of high degree,
Much more then would ye wonder at that sight,
And stand astonisht lyke to those which red° *saw*
Medusaes mazeful hed.[7]
There dwels sweet love and constant chastity,
Unspotted fayth° and comely womanhood, *fidelity*
Regard of honour and mild modesty,
There vertue raynes as Queene in royal throne,
And giveth lawes alone.
The which the base° affections doe obay, *lower*
And yeeld theyr services unto her will,
Ne thought of thing uncomely ever may
Thereto approch to tempt her mind to ill.
Had ye once seene these her celestial threasures,
And unrevealèd pleasures,
Then would ye wonder and her prayses sing,
That all the woods should answer and your Eccho ring.

Open the temple gates unto my love,
Open them wide that she may enter in,[8]
And all the postes adorne as doth behove,[9]
And all the pillours deck with girlands trim,
For to recyve this Saynt with honour dew,
That commeth in to you.
With trembling steps and humble reverence,
She commeth in, before th' almighties vew,
Of her ye virgins learne obedience,
When so ye come into those holy places,
To humble your proud faces:
Bring her up to th' high altar, that she may
The sacred ceremonies there partake,
The which do endless matrimony make,
And let the roring Organs loudly play
The praises of the Lord in lively notes,
The whiles with hollow throates
The Choristers the joyous Antheme sing,
That all the woods may answere and theyr Eccho ring.

Behold whiles she before the altar stands
Hearing the holy priest that to her speakes

6. The head, where the higher faculties are. The catalog of qualities is a convention in love poetry (cf. Song of Solomon 4–8).
7. Medusa, one of the Gorgons, had serpents instead of hair (hence a "mazeful hed"): the effect on beholders was to turn them to stone.
8. Cf. Psalm 24.7: "Lift up your heads, O ye gates; and be ye lift up, ye everlasting doors; and the King of glory shall come in."
9. As is proper. The doorposts were trimmed for weddings in classical times, and the custom was often referred to in classical and later love poetry.

And blesseth her with his two happy hands,
How the red roses flush up in her cheekes,
And the pure snow with goodly vermill° stayne, *vermilion*
Like crimsin dyde in grayne,° *fast color*
That even th' Angels which continually,
About the sacred Altare doe remaine,
Forget their service and about her fly,
Ofte peeping in her face that seemes more fayre,
The more they on it stare.
But her sad° eyes still° fastened on the ground, *serious / ever*
Are governèd with goodly modesty,
That suffers° not one looke to glaunce awry, *permits*
Which may let in a little thought unsownd.
Why blush ye love to give to me your hand,
The pledge of all our band?° *bond, tie*
Sing ye sweet Angels, Alleluya sing,
That all the woods may answere and your Eccho ring.

Now al is done; bring home the bride againe,
Bring home the triumph of our victory,
Bring home with you the glory of her gaine,[1]
With joyance bring her and with jollity.
Never had man more joyfull day then this,
Whom heaven would heape with blis.
Make feast therefore now all this live long day,
This day for ever to me holy is,
Poure out the wine without restraint or stay,
Poure not by cups, but by the belly° full, *wine-skin*
Poure out to all that wull,° *want it*
And sprinkle all the postes and wals with wine,
That they may sweat, and drunken be withall.
Crowne ye God Bacchus° with a coronall,° *god of wine / garland*
And Hymen also crowne with wreathes of vine,
And let the Graces daunce unto the rest;
For they can doo it best:
The whiles the maydens doe theyr carroll sing,
To which the woods shall answer and theyr Eccho ring.

Ring ye the bels, ye young men of the towne,
And leave your wonted° labors for this day: *usual*
This day is holy; doe ye write it downe,
That ye for ever it remember may.
This day the sunne is in his chiefest hight,
With Barnaby the bright,[2]
From whence declining daily by degrees,
He somewhat loseth of his heat and light,
When once the Crab[3] behind his back he sees.
But for this time it ill ordainèd was,
To chose the longest day in all the yeare,
And shortest night, when longest fitter weare:

1. I.e., the glory of gaining her.
2. St. Barnabas's Day, at the time of the summer solstice.
3. The constellation Cancer between Gemini and Leo. The sun, passing through the zodiac, leaves the Crab behind toward the end of July.

Yet never day so long, but late° would passe. — *at last*
Ring ye the bels, to make it weare away,
And bonefiers° make all day, — *bonfires*
And daunce about them, and about them sing:
That all the woods may answer, and your Eccho ring.

Ah when will this long weary day have end,
And lende me leave to come unto my love?
How slowly do the houres theyr numbers spend?
How slowly does sad Time his feathers move?
Hast° thee O fayrest Planet to thy home — *haste*
Within the Westerne fome:
Thy tyred steedes long since have need of rest.[4]
Long though it be, at last I see it gloome,
And the bright evening star with golden creast° — *crest*
Appeare out of the East.
Fayre childe of beauty, glorious lampe of love
That all the host of heaven in rankes doost lead,
And guydest lovers through the nightès dread,
How chearefully thou lookest from above,
And seemst to laugh atweene thy twinkling light
As joying in the sight
Of these glad many which for joy doe sing,
That all the woods them answer and theyr Eccho ring.

Now ceasse ye damsels your delights forepast;
Enough is it, that all the day was youres:
Now day is doen, and night is nighing fast:
Now bring the Bryde into the brydall boures.
Now night is come, now soone her disaray,° — *undress*
And in her bed her lay;
Lay her in lillies and in violets,
And silken courteins over her display,° — *spread*
And odourd° sheetes, and Arras° coverlets. — *perfumed / tapestry*
Behold how goodly my faire love does ly
In proud humility;
Like unto Maia,[5] when as Jove her tooke,
In Tempe,[6] lying on the flowry gras,
Twixt sleepe and wake, after she weary was,
With bathing in the Acidalian brooke.[7]
Now it is night, ye damsels may be gon,
And leave my love alone,
And leave likewise your former lay to sing:
The woods no more shall answere, nor your Eccho ring.

Now welcome night, thou night so long expected,
That long daies labour doest at last defray,° — *pay for*
And all my cares, which cruell love collected,

4. The sun's chariot completes its daily course in the western sea.
5. The eldest and most beautiful of the seven daughters of Atlas. (They were stellified as the Pleiades.) Jove fathered Mercury on her.
6. The Vale of Tempe in Thessaly (not, however, traditionally the site of Jove's encounter with Maia).
7. The Acidalian brook is associated with Venus.

Hast sumd in one, and cancellèd for aye:° *forever*
Spread thy broad wing over my love and me,
That no man may us see,
And in thy sable mantle us enwrap,
From feare of perrill and foule horror free.
Let no false treason seeke us to entrap,
Nor any dread disquiet once annoy
The safety of our joy:
But let the night be calme and quietsome,
Without tempestuous storms or sad afray:° *fear*
Lyke as when Jove with fayre Alcmena[8] lay,
When he begot the great Tirynthian groome:
Or lyke as when he with thy selfe[9] did lie,
And begot Majesty.
And let the mayds and yongmen cease to sing:
Ne let the woods them answer, nor theyr Eccho ring.

Let no lamenting cryes, nor dolefull teares,
Be heard all night within nor yet without:
Ne let false whispers, breeding hidden feares,
Breake gentle sleepe with misconceivèd dout.° *fear*
Let no deluding dreames, nor dreadful sights
Make sudden sad affrights;
Ne let housefyres, nor lightnings helpelesse harmes,
Ne let the Pouke,[1] nor other evill sprights,
Ne let mischivous witches with theyr charmes,
Ne let hob Goblins, names whose sence we see not,
Fray° us with things that be not. *terrify*
Let not the shriech Oule, nor the Storke be heard:
Nor the night Raven that still° deadly yels,[2] *continuously*
Nor damnèd ghosts cald up with mighty spels,
Nor griesly° vultures make us once affeard: *horrid*
Ne let th' unpleasant Quyre of Frogs still croking
Make us to wish theyr choking.
Let none of these theyr drery accents sing;
Ne let the woods them answer, nor theyr Eccho ring.

But let stil Silence trew night watches keepe,
That sacred peace may in assurance rayne,
And tymely Sleep, when it is tyme to sleepe,
May poure his limbs forth on your pleasant playne,
The whiles an hundred little wingèd loves,° *cupids (or amoretti)*
Like divers fethered doves,
Shall fly and flutter round about your bed,
And in the secret darke, that none reproves,
Their prety stealthes shal worke, and snares shal spread
To filch away sweet snatches of delight,
Conceald through covert night.

8. The mother of Hercules ("the great Tirynthian groome"). Jove made that first night last as long as three.
9. Night. This is Spenser's own myth.
1. Puck, Robin Goodfellow—here more powerful and evil than Shakespeare made him in *A Midsummer Night's Dream.*
2. The owl and the night raven were birds of ill omen; the stork, in Chaucer's *Parliament of Fowls*, is called an avenger of adultery.

Ye sonnes of Venus, play your sports at will,
For greedy pleasure, carelesse of your toyes,° — *amorous dallying*
Thinks more upon her paradise of joyes,
Then° what ye do, albe it° good or ill. — *than / albeit, although*
All night therefore attend your merry play,
For it will soone be day:
Now none doth hinder you, that say or sing,
Ne will the woods now answer, nor your Eccho ring.

Who is the same, which at my window peepes?
Or whose is that faire face, that shines so bright,
Is it not Cinthia,[3] she that never sleepes,
But walkes about high heaven al the night?
O fayrest goddesse, do thou not envy
My love with me to spy:
For thou likewise didst love, though now unthought,° — *not thought of*
And for a fleece of woll,° which privily, — *wool*
The Latmian shephard[4] once unto thee brought,
His pleasures with thee wrought,
Therefore to us be favorable now;
And sith° of wemens labours thou hast charge,[5] — *since*
And generation goodly dost enlarge,
Encline thy will t' effect our wishfull vow,
And the chast wombe informe° with timely seed, — *give life to*
That may our comfort breed:
Till which we cease our hopefull hap° to sing, — *fortune we hope for*
Ne let the woods us answer, nor our Eccho ring.

And thou great Juno, which with awful° might — *awesome*
The lawes of wedlock still dost patronize,
And the religion° of the faith first plight° — *sanctity / pledged*
With sacred rites hast taught to solemnize:
And eeke° for comfort often callèd art — *also*
Of women in their smart,° — *(labor) pains*
Eternally bind thou this lovely band,° — *bond*
And all thy blessings unto us impart.
And thou glad Genius,[6] in whose gentle hand,
The bridale bowre and geniall bed remaine,
Without blemish or staine,
And the sweet pleasures of theyr loves delight
With secret ayde doest succour° and supply, — *help*
Till they bring forth the fruitfull progeny,
Send us the timely fruit of this same night.
And thou fayre Hebe,[7] and thou Hymen free,
Grant that it may so be.
Til which we cease your further prayse to sing,
Ne any woods shall answer, nor your Eccho ring.

3. Cynthia (or Diana) is goddess of the moon.
4. Endymion, beloved of the moon. The "fleece of woll," however, comes from another story—that of Pan's enticement of the moon.
5. Diana is, as Lucina, patroness of births. The "labours" are, of course, those of childbirth.
6. God of generation and birth. In the next line, "geniall"—having both the usual sense and the sense of "generative"—puns on his name.
7. Goddess of youth and freedom.

And ye high heavens, the temple of the gods,
In which a thousand torches flaming bright
Doe burne, that to us wretched earthly clods,
In dreadful darknesse lend desirèd light;
And all ye powers which in the same remayne,
More then we men can fayne,° *imagine*
Poure out your blessing on us plentiously,
And happy influence upon us raine,
That we may raise a large posterity,
Which from the earth, which they may long possesse,
With lasting happinesse,
Up to your haughty° pallaces may mount, *lofty*
And for the guerdon° of theyr glorious merit *reward*
May heavenly tabernacles there inherit,
Of blessèd Saints for to increase the count.
So let us rest, sweet love, in hope of this,
And cease till then our tymely joyes to sing,
The woods no more us answer, nor our Eccho ring.

Song made in lieu of many ornaments,
With which my love should duly have bene dect,° *adorned*
Which cutting off through hasty accidents,
Ye would not stay your dew time to expect,° *await*
But promist both to recompens,
Be unto her a goodly ornament,
And for short time an endlesse moniment.[8]

1595

8. The envoy (brief final stanza addressed to the poem itself) is traditionally apologetic in tone: the poem is offered as a substitute for presents ("ornaments") that did not arrive in time for the wedding. But this elaborate poem is itself a "goodly ornament," for it stands as a timeless monument of art to the passing day that it celebrates.

SIR WALTER RALEGH
1552–1618

The brilliant and versatile Sir Walter Ralegh was a soldier, courtier, philosopher, explorer and colonist, student of science, historian, and poet. Born to West Country gentry of modest means, Ralegh amassed great wealth thanks to his position at court, leading him to be denounced by some as an upstart and hated by others as a rapacious monopolist. He fought ruthlessly in Ireland and Cádiz, directed the colonization of Virginia, introduced the potato to Ireland and tobacco to Europe, brought Spenser from Ireland to the English court, conducted scientific experiments, led expeditions to Guiana in an unsuccessful effort to find gold, and wrote several reports urging England to challenge Spanish dominance in the New World. He was known for his violent temper, his dramatic sense of life, his extravagant dress, his skepticism in religious matters, his bitter hatred of Spain, and his great favor with Queen Elizabeth, interrupted in 1592 when he seduced, and then married, one of her ladies-in-waiting. His long poem to the queen, *The Ocean to Cynthia,* remains in manuscript fragments, one of more than five hundred lines. His best-known shorter poems include the reply to Marlowe's "Passionate Shepherd" and "The Lie," an attack on social classes and institutions which itself provoked many replies. His active resistance to printing his poems—in one case he forced a printer to recall a volume and paste a slip of paper over his initials—makes it very difficult to put the copies that circulated in manuscript in any reliable chronological order.

King James suspected Ralegh of opposing his succession and threw him into the Tower of London in 1603 on trumped-up charges of treason; there he remained for the rest of his life save for an ill-fated last voyage to Guiana in 1617, which again failed to discover gold. In prison he wrote his long, unfinished *History of the World,* which begins with the Creation, emphasizes the providential punishment of evil princes, and projects a treatment of English history—although not of recent events because, he declared, he who follows truth too closely at the heels might get kicked in the teeth. The work was to have been dedicated to Henry, prince of Wales, Ralegh's most powerful friend and supporter, who declared, "Only my father would keep such a bird in a cage." But Henry died in 1612, and Ralegh broke off his narrative at 168 B.C.E. Six years later James, bowing to Spanish pressure, had Ralegh executed on the old treason charge.*

The Nymph's Reply to the Shepherd[1]

If all the world and love were young,
And truth in every shepherd's tongue,
These pretty pleasures might me move
To live with thee and be thy love.

Time drives the flocks from field to fold
When rivers rage and rocks grow cold,
And Philomel° becometh dumb; *the nightingale*
The rest complains of cares to come.

The flowers do fade, and wanton fields
To wayward winter reckoning yields;° *renders an account*
A honey tongue, a heart of gall,
Is fancy's spring, but sorrow's fall.

Thy gowns, thy shoes, thy beds of roses,
Thy cap, thy kirtle,° and thy posies° *dress / bouquets*
Soon break, soon wither, soon forgotten—
In folly ripe, in reason rotten.

Thy belt of straw and ivy buds,
Thy coral clasps and amber studs,
All these in me no means can move
To come to thee and be thy love.

But could youth last and love still breed,
Had joys no date° nor age no need, *ending*

*Go to Norton Literature Online for Ralegh's poem beginning "As you came from the holy land of Walsinghame" and for excerpts from his account of the battle between the *Revenge* and a Spanish fleet.

1. Cf. Marlowe, "The Passionate Shepherd to His Love," p. 459.

Then these delights my mind might move
To live with thee and be thy love.

1600

From The History of the World

[CONCLUSION: ON DEATH]

It is * * * Death alone that can suddenly make man to know himself. He tells the proud and insolent that they are but abjects,[1] and humbles them at the instant; makes them cry, complain, and repent; yea, even to hate their forepassed happiness. He takes the account[2] of the rich, and proves him a beggar, a naked beggar, which hath interest in nothing but in the gravel that fills his mouth. He holds a glass[3] before the eyes of the most beautiful, and makes them see therein their deformity and rottenness, and they acknowledge it.

O eloquent, just, and mighty Death! Whom none could advise, thou hast persuaded; what none hath dared, thou hast done; and whom all the world hath flattered, thou only hast cast out of the world and despised; thou hast drawn together all the far-stretched greatness, all the pride, cruelty, and ambition of man, and covered it all over with these two narrow words: *Hic jacet!*[4] * * *

1614

1. Castoffs.
2. Estimate, measure.
3. Mirror.
4. Latin for "Here lies," often carved on tombstones.

SIR PHILIP SIDNEY
1554–1586

Sir Philip Sidney's face was "spoiled with pimples," Ben Jonson remarked in 1619, wryly distancing himself from the virtual Sidney cult that had arisen in the years after his death. Knight, soldier, poet, friend, and patron, Sidney seemed to the Elizabethans to embody all the traits of character and personality they admired: he was Castiglione's perfect courtier come to life. When he was killed in battle in the Low Countries at the age of thirty-two, fighting for the Protestant cause against the hated Spanish, all England mourned. Stories, possibly apocryphal, began immediately to circulate about his gallantry on the battlefield—grievously wounded, he gave his water to a dying footsoldier with the words "Thy necessity is yet greater than mine"—and about his astonishing self-composure as he himself lay dying: suffering from his putrifying, gangrenous wound, Sidney composed a song and had it sung by his deathbed. When his corpse was brought back to England for burial, the spectacular funeral procession, one of the most elaborate ever staged, almost bankrupted his father-in-law, Francis Walsingham, the wealthy head of Queen Elizabeth's secret service.

Philip Sidney's father was Sir Henry Sidney, thrice lord deputy (governor) of Ireland, and his mother was a sister of Robert Dudley, earl of Leicester, the most spectacular and powerful of all the queen's favorites. He entered Shrewsbury School in 1564, at the age of ten, on the same day as Fulke Greville, who became his lifelong friend and his biographer. Greville wrote of Sidney, "though I lived with him and knew him from a child, yet I never knew him other than a man—with such staidness of mind, lovely and familiar gravity, as carried grace and reverence above greater years." He attended Oxford but left without taking a degree and completed his education by extended travels on the Continent. There he met many of the most important people of the time, from kings and queens to philosophers, theologians, and poets. In France he witnessed the Massacre of St. Bartholomew's Day, which began in Paris on August 24, 1572, and raged through France for more than a month, as Catholic mobs incited by Queen Catherine de Médicis slaughtered perhaps 50,000 Huguenots (French Protestants). This experience undoubtedly strengthened Sidney's ardent Protestantism, which had been inculcated by his family background and education. In an intense correspondence with his mentor, the Burgundian humanist Hubert Languet, he brooded on how he could help to save Europe from what he viewed as the Roman Catholic menace.

Languet and his associates clearly hoped that this brilliant and wonderfully well-connected young Englishman would be able to steer royal policy toward active intervention in Europe's wars of religion. Yet when he returned to England Sidney found the direct path to heroic action blocked by the caution and hard-nosed realism of Queen Elizabeth and her principal advisers. Though she sent him on some diplomatic missions, the queen clearly regarded the zealous young man with considerable skepticism. As a prominent, well-connected courtier with literary interests, Sidney actively encouraged authors such as Edward Dyer, Greville, and, most important, Edmund Spenser, who dedicated *The Shepheardes Calender* to him as "the president [chief exemplar] of noblesse and of chevalree." But he clearly longed to be something more than an influential patron of letters. In 1580 his Protestant convictions led him publicly to oppose Queen Elizabeth's projected marriage to the Catholic duke of Anjou. The queen, who hated interference with her diplomatic maneuvers, angrily dismissed Sidney from the court.

He retired to Wilton, the estate of his beloved and learned sister, Mary Herbert, countess of Pembroke, and there he wrote a long, elaborate epic romance in prose called *Arcadia*. Sidney's claim, made with studied nonchalance, that the work was casually tossed off for his sister's private entertainment is belied by its considerable literary, political, and moral ambitions, qualities that were reinforced and intensified in the extensive revisions he began to make to it in 1582.

In addition to *Arcadia*, which inspired many imitations, including the *Urania* of Sidney's niece, Lady Mary Wroth, two other influential works by Sidney have had still more lasting importance. One of these, *The Defense of Poesy*, is the major work of literary criticism produced in the English Renaissance. In this long essay Sidney eloquently defends poetry (his term for all imaginative literature) against its attackers and, in the process, greatly exalts the role of the poet, the freedom of the imagination, and the moral value of fiction. Perhaps Sidney's finest literary achievement is *Astrophil and Stella* (Starlover and Star), the first of the great Elizabethan sonnet cycles. The principal focus of these sonnets is not a sequence of events or an unfolding relationship. Rather, they explore the lover's state of mind and soul, the contradictory impulses, intense desires, and frustrations that haunt him.

In his guise as a Petrarchan sonneteer, Sidney repeatedly insists that the thought of his beloved drives all more mundane matters from his mind. Yet a number of the sonnets betray a continuing preoccupation with matters of politics and foreign policy. Neither love nor literature could distract Sidney for long from what he took to be his destined role. In 1585 he tried to join Sir Francis Drake's West Indian expedition but was prevented by the queen; instead, she appointed him governor of Flushing in the Netherlands, where as a volunteer and knight-errant he engaged in several vicious skirmishes in the war against Spain. At Zutphen on September 13, 1586, leading a charge against great odds, Sidney was wounded in the thigh, shortly after he had thrown away his thigh armor in an ill-fated chivalric gesture. He died after lingering for twenty-six days.

Sidney called poetry his "unelected vocation," and in keeping with the norms of his class, he did not publish any of his major literary works himself. His ambition, continually thwarted, was to be a man of action whose deeds would affect his country's destiny. Yet he was the author of the most ambitious work of prose fiction, the most important piece of literary criticism, and the most influential sonnet cycle of the Elizabethan Age.*

Astrophil and Stella

Sidney was a jealous protector of his privacy. "I assure you before God," he had written once in an angry letter to his father's private secretary, Molyneux, "that if ever I know you do so much as read any letter I write to my father, without his commandment or my consent, I will thrust my dagger into you. And trust to it, for I speak it in earnest." Yet in *Astrophil and Stella* he seems to hold up a mirror to every nuance of his emotional being. For its original coterie audience, Sidney's sonnet sequence must have been an elaborate game of literary masks, psychological risk-taking, and open secrets. The loosely linked succession of 108 sonnets and eleven songs, with its dazzling display of technical virtuosity, provides tantalizing glimpses of identifiable characters and, still more, a sustained and remarkably intimate portrait of the poet's inner life.

Much biographical speculation has centered on Sidney's ambiguous relationship with Penelope Devereux, the supposed original of Stella. A marriage between the two had been proposed in 1576 and was talked about for some years, but in 1581 she married Lord Robert Rich, and two years later Sidney also married. (At their high social rank, marriages were negotiated in the interests of the powerful families involved, not of the individuals.) Some of the sonnets contain sly puns on the name *Rich*, and it seems likely that there are autobiographical elements in the shadowy narrative sketched by the work. At the same time, however, the "plot" of the sequence, full of trials, setbacks, much suffering on the part of the lover and occasional encouragement on the part of the lady, is highly conventional, derived from Petrarch and his many Italian, French, and Spanish imitators.

Poets in this tradition undertook to produce an anatomy of love, displaying its shifting and often contradictory states: hope and despair, tenderness and bitterness, exultation and modesty, bodily desire and spiritual transcendence. Petrarch had deployed a series of ingenious metaphors to describe these states, but by Sidney's time the metaphors—love as a freezing fire, the beloved's glance as an arrow striking the lover's heart, and so forth—had through endless repetition become familiar and predictable, less a revelation than a role. Sidney, in the role of Astrophil, protests that he uses no standard conventional phrases, that his verse is original and comes from his heart. This protest is itself conventional, and yet Sidney manages to infuse his sonnets with an extraordinary vigor and freshness. Certain of the sonnets have, within their narrow fourteen-line bounds, the force of the drama: "Fly, fly, my friends, I have my death-wound, fly" or "What, have I thus betrayed my liberty?" Others, in their grappling with insistent desire, have the probing, psychological resonance of private confession: "With what sharp checks I in myself am shent" or "Who will in fairest book of Nature know." Still others ask crucial questions about the whole project of self-representation: "Stella oft sees the very face of woe." Virtually all of them manifest the exceptional *energia*—forcibleness—that Sidney, in *The Defense of Poesy*, says is the key ingredient of good poetry.

*For additional writings by Sidney—another sonnet from *Astrophil and Stella* (64), four poems from *Certain Sonnets*, and excerpts from *Arcadia*—go to Norton Literature Online.

From Astrophil and Stella

1[1]

Loving in truth, and fain° in verse my love to show, *desirous*
That the dear She might take some pleasure of my pain,
Pleasure might cause her read, reading might make her know,
Knowledge might pity win, and pity grace obtain,
I sought fit words to paint the blackest face of woe,
Studying inventions fine, her wits to entertain,
Oft turning others' leaves, to see if thence would flow
Some fresh and fruitful showers upon my sunburned brain.
But words came halting forth, wanting Invention's stay;[2]
Invention, Nature's child, fled step-dame Study's blows,
And others' feet still° seemed but strangers in my way. *continually*
Thus great with child to speak, and helpless in my throes,
Biting my trewand° pen, beating myself for spite, *truant*
"Fool," said my Muse to me, "look in thy heart and write."

2

Not at first sight, nor with a dribbèd[3] shot
Love gave the wound, which while I breathe will bleed,
But known worth did in mine[4] of time proceed,
Till by degrees it had full conquest got.
I saw and liked, I liked but lovèd not,
I loved, but straight did not[5] what *Love* decreed;
At length to Love's decrees, I, forced, agreed,
Yet with repining° at so partial° lot. *complaining / unfair*
Now even that footstep of lost liberty
Is gone, and now like slave-born Muscovite,[6]
I call it praise to suffer tyranny;
And now employ the remnant of my wit,° *mind*
To make myself believe that all is well,
While with a feeling skill I paint my hell.

6

Some lovers speak, when they their muses entertain,
Of hopes begot by fear, of wot° not what desires, *know*
Of force of heavenly beams infusing hellish pain,
Of living deaths, dear wounds, fair storms, and freezing fires;[7]
Some one his song in Jove and Jove's strange tales attires,
Broidered with bulls and swans, powdered with golden rain;[8]
Another humbler wit to shepherd's pipe retires,
Yet hiding royal blood full oft in rural vein.[9]

1. One of six sonnets in the sequence written in hexameters.
2. I.e., lacking the support of Invention, his words moved haltingly.
3. Ineffectual or at random.
4. Tunnel dug to undermine a besieged fortress.
5. Did not immediately do.
6. Inhabitant of Muscovy, Russian principality ruled from Moscow; sixteenth-century travel books describe Muscovites as contented slaves.
7. Conventional Petrarchan oxymorons.
8. I.e., embroidered with mythological figures. Jove courted Europa in the shape of a bull; Leda, as a swan; and Danaë, as a golden shower.
9. I.e., in pastoral allegory. By convention, a pastoral poet pipes his songs on an oaten or reed pipe.

To some a sweetest plaint a sweetest style affords,[1]
While tears pour out his ink, and sighs breathe out his words,
His paper pale Despair, and pain his pen doth move.
I can speak what I feel, and feel as much as they,
But think that all the map of my state I display,
When trembling voice brings forth that I do Stella love.

20

Fly, fly, my friends, I have my death-wound, fly;
See there that boy, that murth'ring° boy, I say, *murdering*
Who like a thief hid in dark bush doth lie
Till bloody bullet get him wrongful prey.
So tyran° he no fitter place could spy, *tyrant*
Nor so fair level° in so secret stay,° *aim / stopping place*
As that sweet black° which veils the heav'nly eye; *pupil*
There himself with his shot he close° doth lay. *secretly*
Poor passenger,° pass now thereby I did, *passerby*
And stay'd, pleas'd with the prospect of the place,
While that black hue from me the bad guest hid;
But straight I saw motions of lightning grace,
And then descried° the glist'ring° of his dart; *saw / glittering*
But ere I could fly thence, it pierc'd my heart.

28

You that with allegory's curious frame° *intricate contrivance*
Of others' children changelings use° to make, *are accustomed*
With me those pains, for God's sake, do not take;
I list not° dig so deep for brazen fame. *I don't care to*
When I say Stella, I do mean the same
Princess of beauty for whose only sake
The reins of love I love, though never slake,° *slack*
And joy therein, though nations count it shame.
I beg no subject to use eloquence,[2]
Nor in hid ways do guide philosophy;
Look at my hands for no such quintessence,[3]
But know that I in pure simplicity
Breathe out the flames which burn within my heart,
Love only reading unto me this art.

31

With how sad steps, O Moon, thou climb'st the skies,
How silently, and with how wan a face!
What, may it be that even in heavenly place
That busy archer° his sharp arrows tries? *Cupid*
Sure, if that long-with-love-acquainted eyes

1. Parodying the overuse of the word *sweet* in love complaints, with allusion to the very musical *dolce stil nuovo* (sweet new style) associated with Dante and his Italian contemporaries.
2. I.e., I don't ask for a topic simply as an excuse to display my rhetorical skills.
3. The mysterious "fifth element" of matter (supplementary to earth, air, fire, and water), which alchemists labored to extract.

Can judge of love, thou feel'st a lover's case;
I read it in thy looks: thy languished grace,
To me that feel the like, thy state descries.° *reveals*
Then even of fellowship, O Moon, tell me,
Is constant love deemed there but want of wit?° *lack of intelligence*
Are beauties there as proud as here they be?
Do they above love to be loved, and yet
Those lovers scorn whom that love doth possess?
Do they call virtue there ungratefulness?[4]

52

A strife is grown between Virtue and Love,
While each pretends° that Stella must be his: *claims*
Her eyes, her lips, her all, saith Love, do this,
Since they do wear his badge,[5] most firmly prove.
But Virtue thus that title doth disprove:
That Stella (O dear name) that Stella is
That virtuous soul, sure heir of heavenly bliss;
Not this fair outside, which our hearts doth move.
And therefore, though her beauty and her grace
Be Love's indeed, in Stella's self he may
By no pretence claim any manner° place. *kind of*
Well, Love, since this demur° our suit[6] doth stay,° *objection / stop*
Let Virtue have that Stella's self; yet thus,
That Virtue but° that body grant to us. *only*

71

Who will in fairest book of Nature know
How Virtue may best lodged in beauty be,
Let him but learn of Love to read in thee,
Stella, those fair lines, which true goodness show.
There shall he find all vices' overthrow,
Not by rude force, but sweetest sovereignty
Of reason, from whose light those night-birds[7] fly;
That inward sun in thine eyes shineth so.
And not content to be Perfection's heir
Thyself, dost strive all minds that way to move,
Who mark° in thee what is in thee most fair.[8] *perceive*
So while thy beauty draws the heart to love,
As fast° thy Virtue bends that love to good; *at the same rate*
"But, ah," Desire still cries, "give me some food."

72

Desire, though thou my old companion art,
And oft so clings to my pure Love that I
One from the other scarcely can descry,° *distinguish*

4. I.e., is the lady's ingratitude considered virtue in heaven (as here)? Also, is the lover's virtue (fidelity) considered distasteful in heaven (as here)?
5. Device or livery worn to identify someone's (here, Cupid's) servants.
6. "Courtship," in addition to the legal meaning.
7. The owl, for example, was an emblem of various vices.
8. I.e., her virtue, which is fairer even than her beauty.

While each doth blow the fire of my heart,
Now from thy fellowship I needs must part:
Venus is taught with Dian's wings to fly;[9]
I must no more in thy sweet passions lie;
Virtue's gold now must head my Cupid's dart.
Service and honor, wonder with delight,
Fear to offend, will worthy to appear,[1]
Care shining in mine eyes, faith in my sprite:° *spirit*
These things are left me by my only dear;
But thou, Desire, because thou wouldst have all,
Now banished art. But yet alas how shall?

74

I never drank of Aganippe well,
Nor ever did in shade of Tempe[2] sit;
And Muses scorn with vulgar° brains to dwell; *common*
Poor layman I, for sacred rites unfit.
Some do I hear of Poets' fury° tell, *inspiration*
But God wot,° wot not what they mean by it; *knows*
And this I swear by blackest brook of hell,[3]
I am no pick-purse of another's wit.
How falls it then that with so smooth an ease
My thoughts I speak, and what I speak doth flow
In verse, and that my verse best wits doth please?
Guess we the cause. "What, is it thus?" Fie no.
"Or so?" Much less. "How then?" Sure thus it is:
My lips are sweet, inspired with Stella's kiss.[4]

108[5]

When Sorrow (using mine own fire's might)
Melts down his lead into my boiling breast,
Through that dark furnace to my heart oppressed
There shines a joy from thee, my only light;
But soon as thought of thee breeds my delight,
And my young soul flutters to thee, his nest,
Most rude Despair, my daily unbidden guest,
Clips straight° my wings, straight wraps me in his night, *immediately*
And makes me then bow down my head and say,
"Ah, what doth Phoebus'° gold that wretch avail, *god of the sun*
Whom iron doors do keep from use of day?"
So strangely (alas) thy works in me prevail,
That in my woes for thee thou art my joy,
And in my joys for thee my only annoy.° *trouble, pain*

1582? 1591, 1598

9. Diana, goddess of the moon and patron of chastity; Venus, goddess of beauty and love, mother of Cupid.
1. The phrase can mean either "the wish to appear worthy" or "desire that is worthy to appear [i.e., not shameful]."
2. Valley beside Mount Olympus, sacred to Apollo, the god of poetry. "Aganippe well": fountain at the foot of Mount Helicon in Greece, sacred to the Muses.
3. The most binding of all oaths were those sworn by the river Styx.
4. A kiss he stole from Stella when he caught her napping (Song 2).
5. In many sonnet sequences, as here, the final sonnet brings no resolution.

MARY (SIDNEY) HERBERT, COUNTESS OF PEMBROKE
1562–1621

When her brother, the celebrated courtier and author Philip Sidney, died in 1586, Mary Sidney, the countess of Pembroke, became the custodian not only of his writings but also of his last name. Though her marriage in 1577 to Henry Herbert, the second earl of Pembroke, represented a great social advance for her family—her offspring would no longer be members of the gentry but rather would be among the nation's tiny hereditary nobility—yet throughout her life the countess of Pembroke held onto her identity as a Sidney.

She had good reason to do so. The Sidneys were celebrated for their generous support of poets, clergymen, alchemists, naturalists, scientists, and musicians. The Pembroke country estate, Wilton, quickly became a gathering place for thinkers who enjoyed the countess's patronage and shared her staunch Protestant convictions and her literary interests. Books, pamphlets, and scores of poems were dedicated in the 1590s and thereafter to her, as well as to her brother Robert (his country house, Penshurst, is praised in a well-known poem by Ben Jonson). Nicholas Breton and Samuel Daniel in particular benefited from her support, as did her niece, goddaughter, and frequent companion, Mary Wroth.

In one of the dedicatory poems to *Salve Deus Rex Judaeorum*, Aemilia Lanyer praises Mary Sidney not only for her generosity toward poets but also for those "works that are more deep and more profound." These include her translation of Robert Garnier's neoclassical French tragedy *Antonius* and a prose translation of the religious tract *A Discourse of Life and Death* by the French Protestant Philippe de Mornay. Her translation of Petrarch's *Triumph of Death* was the first in English to maintain the original *terza rima* (a particularly challenging rhyme scheme for an English versifier). Although translation was considered an especially appropriate genre for women to work in, it is a mistake to assume that Mary Sidney's efforts as a poet are merely derivative: Elizabethans understood that translation offered the opportunity not only for the display of linguistic and technical skills but also for the indirect expression of personal and political concerns. Mary Sidney also expressed these concerns more directly: among her original poems was a powerful elegy for her brother Philip and a short pastoral entertainment for Queen Elizabeth.

Mary Sidney was best known for having prepared a composite edition of Philip Sidney's *Arcadia* and for contributing the larger number (107) of the verse translations of the 150 biblical psalms that her brother had begun. Her very free renderings re-create the psalms as English poems, using an amazing variety of stanzaic and metrical patterns and some strikingly effective images. Widely circulated in manuscript, this influential collection was an important bridge between the many metrical paraphrases of psalms in this period and the works of the great religious lyric poets of the seventeenth century, especially George Herbert. Donne's poem *Upon the Translation of the Psalms by Sir Philip Sidney and the Countess of Pembroke His Sister* testifies to that importance: "They tell us *why*, and teach us *how* to sing."*

*For Mary Sidney's elegy on Sir Philip Sidney, her translation of Psalm 58, her "Dialogue between two shepherds," and the King James Bible version of the psalm printed here, go to Norton Literature Online.

Psalm 52

Tyrant, why swell'st thou thus,
  Of mischief vaunting?
Since help from God to us
  Is never wanting.

Lewd lies thy tongue contrives,
  Loud lies it soundeth;
Sharper than sharpest knives
  With lies it woundeth.

Falsehood thy wit° approves, *mind*
  All truth rejected:
Thy will all vices loves,
  Virtue neglected.

Not words from cursèd thee,
  But gulfs° are pourèd; *abysses, yawning chasms*
Gulfs wherein daily be
  Good men devourèd.

Think'st thou to bear it° so? *bear it off, triumph*
  God shall displace thee;
God shall thee overthrow,
  Crush thee, deface° thee. *destroy*

The just shall fearing see
  These fearful chances,
And laughing shoot at thee
  With scornful glances.

Lo, lo, the wretched wight,° *creature*
  Who, God disdaining,
His mischief made his might,
  His guard his gaining.° *riches*

I as an olive tree
  Still green shall flourish:
God's house the soil shall be
  My roots to nourish.

My trust on his true love
  Truly attending,
Shall never thence remove,
  Never see ending.

Thee will I honor still,
  Lord, for this justice;
There fix my hopes I will
  Where thy saints' trust is.

Thy saints trust in thy name,
  Therein they joy them:
Protected by the same,
  Nought° can annoy° them. *nothing / harm*

ca. 1595 1823

CHRISTOPHER MARLOWE
1564–1593

The son of a Canterbury shoemaker, Christopher Marlowe was born two months before William Shakespeare. In 1580 he went to Corpus Christi College, Cambridge, on a scholarship that was ordinarily awarded to students preparing for the ministry. He held the scholarship for the maximum time, six years, but did not take holy orders. Instead, he began to write plays. When he applied for his Master of Arts degree in 1587, the university was about to deny it to him on the ground that he intended to go abroad to join the dissident English Catholics at Rheims. But the Privy Council intervened and requested that because Marlowe had done the queen "good service"—evidently as some kind of secret agent—he be granted his degree at the next commencement. "It is not Her Majesty's pleasure," the government officials added, "that anyone employed as he had been in matters touching the benefit of his country should be defamed by those that are ignorant in the affairs he went about." Although much sensational information about Marlowe has been discovered in modern times, we are still largely "ignorant in the affairs he went about." The likeliest possibility is that he served as a spy or *agent provocateur* against English Catholics who were conspiring to overthrow the Protestant regime.

Before he left Cambridge, Marlowe had certainly written his tremendously successful play *Tamburlaine* and perhaps also, in collaboration with his younger Cambridge contemporary Thomas Nashe, the tragedy of *Dido, Queen of Carthage. Tamburlaine* dramatizes the exploits of a fourteenth-century Mongol warrior who rose from humble origins to conquer a huge territory that extended from the Black Sea to Delhi. In some sixteenth-century chronicles, Tamburlaine is represented as God's scourge, the instrument of divine wrath. In Marlowe's play there are few if any glimpses of a transcendent design. His hero is the vehicle for the expression of boundless energy and ambition, the impulse to strive ceaselessly for absolute dominance. Yet Tamburlaine's conquests are achieved not only by force of arms, but also by his extraordinary mastery of language, his "high astounding terms." The English theater audience had never before heard such resonant, immensely energetic blank verse. The great period of Elizabethan drama was launched by what Ben Jonson called "Marlowe's mighty line."

From the time of his first theatrical success, when he was twenty-three, Marlowe had only six years to live. They were not calm years. In 1589 he was involved in a brawl with one William Bradley, in which the poet Thomas Watson intervened and killed Bradley. Both poets were jailed, but Watson got off on a plea of self-defense, and Marlowe was released. In 1591 Marlowe was living in London with the playwright Thomas Kyd, who later, under torture, gave information to the Privy Council accusing him of atheism and treason. On May 30, 1593, an informer named Richard Baines submitted a note to the Council which, on the evidence of Marlowe's own alleged utterances, branded him with atheism, sedition, and homosexuality. Four days later, at an inn in the London suburb of Deptford, Marlowe was killed by a dagger thrust, purportedly in an argument over the bill. Modern scholars have discovered that the murderer and the others present in the room at the inn had connections to the world of spies, double agents, and swindlers to which Marlowe himself was in some way linked. Those who were arrested in connection with the murder were briefly held and then quietly released.

On the bare surface, Marlowe's tragic vision seems for the most part religiously and socially conventional. Tamburlaine at last suffers divine retribution and death at the end of the sequel, *Tamburlaine Part II*; the central character of *The Jew of Malta* is a monstrous anti-Semitic caricature; *Doctor Faustus* and *Edward II* (which treats the tragic fate of a homosexual king) demonstrate the destruction that awaits those who rebel against God or violate the official moral order. Yet there is a force at work in these plays that relentlessly questions and undermines conventional morality. The crime for which Tamburlaine is apparently struck down is the burning of the Muslim *Koran*; the Jew of Malta turns out to be, if anything, less ruthless and hypocritical than his Christian counterparts; and Edward II's life of homoerotic indulgence seems innocent in comparison with the cynical and violent dealings of the corrupt rebels who turn against him. In a way that goes far beyond the demands of moral instruction, Marlowe seems to revel in the depiction of flamboyant transgression, physical abjection, and brutal punishment. Whether as a radical pursuit of absolute liberty or an expression of sheer destructive negativity, Marlowe's plays, written in the turbulent years before his murder at the age of twenty-nine, have continued to fascinate and disturb readers and audiences.*

The Passionate Shepherd to His Love[1]

Come live with me and be my love,
And we will all the pleasures prove° *test, experience*
That valleys, groves, hills, and fields,
Woods, or steepy mountain yields.

And we will sit upon the rocks,
Seeing the shepherds feed their flocks,
By shallow rivers to whose falls
Melodious birds sing madrigals.

And I will make thee beds of roses
And a thousand fragrant posies,° *bouquets (also of poems)*
A cap of flowers, and a kirtle° *dress*
Embroidered all with leaves of myrtle;

A gown made of the finest wool
Which from our pretty lambs we pull;
Fair linèd slippers for the cold,
With buckles of the purest gold;

A belt of straw and ivy buds,
With coral clasps and amber studs:

*For texts and images relating to Marlowe, *Doctor Faustus*, and sixteenth-century conceptions of sorcery, go to "The Magician, the Heretic, and the Playwright," at Norton Literature Online.

1. This pastoral lyric of invitation is one of the most famous of Elizabethan songs, and a few lines from it are sung in Shakespeare's *Merry Wives of Windsor*. Many poets have written replies to it, the best known of which is by Sir Walter Ralegh (p. 448). Go to Norton Literature Online for a recitation of Marlowe's poem.

And if these pleasures may thee move,
Come live with me, and be my love.

The shepherd swains shall dance and sing
For thy delight each May morning:
If these delights thy mind may move,
Then live with me and be my love.

1599, 1600

Doctor Faustus Marlowe's major dramas, *Tamburlaine, The Jew of Malta*, and *Doctor Faustus*, all portray heroes who passionately seek power—the power of rule, the power of money, and the power of knowledge, respectively. Each of the heroes is an overreacher, striving to get beyond the conventional boundaries established to contain the human will.

Unlike Tamburlaine, whose aim and goal is "the sweet fruition of an earthly crown," and Barabas, the Jew of Malta, who lusts for "infinite riches in a little room," Faustus seeks the mastery and voluptuous pleasure that come from forbidden knowledge. To achieve his goal Faustus must make—or chooses to make—a bargain with Lucifer. This is an old folklore motif, but it would have been taken seriously in a time when belief in the reality of devils was almost universal. The story's power over its original audience is vividly suggested by the numerous accounts of uncanny events at performances of the play: strange noises in the theater or extra devils who suddenly appeared among the actors on stage, causing panic.

In the opening soliloquy, Marlowe's Faustus bids farewell to each of his studies—logic, medicine, law, and divinity—as something he has used up. He turns instead to black magic, but the devil exacts a fearful price in exchange: the eternal damnation of Faustus's soul. Faustus aspires to be more than a man: "A sound magician is a mighty god," he declares. His fall is caused by the same pride and ambition that caused the fall of the angels in heaven and of humankind in the Garden of Eden. But it is characteristic of Marlowe that he makes this aspiration nonetheless magnificent.

The immediate source of the play is a German narrative called, in its English translation, *The History of the Damnable Life and Deserved Death of Doctor John Faustus*. That source supplies Marlowe's drama with the scenes of horseplay and low practical joking that contrast so markedly with the passages of huge ambition. It is quite possible that these comic scenes are the work of a collaborator; but no other Elizabethan could have written the first scene (with its brilliant representation of the insatiable aspiring mind of the hero), the ecstatic address to Helen of Troy, or the searing scene of Faustus's last hour. And though compared with these celebrated passages the comic scenes often seem crude, they too contribute to the overarching vision of Faustus's fate: the half-trivial, half-daring exploits, the alternating states of bliss and despair, the questions that are not answered and the answers that bring no real satisfaction, the heroic wanderings that lead nowhere.

Marlowe's play exists in two very different forms: the A text (1604) and the much longer B text (1616), which probably incorporates additions by other hands and which has also been revised to conform to the severe censorship statutes of 1606. We use Roma Gill's edition, based on the A text.

The Tragical History of Doctor Faustus

DRAMATIS PERSONAE[1]

CHORUS
DR. JOHN FAUSTUS
WAGNER, *his servant, a student*
VALDES, CORNELIUS } *his friends, magicians*
THREE SCHOLARS
GOOD ANGEL
EVIL ANGEL
MEPHASTOPHILIS
LUCIFER
BELZEBUB
OLD MAN
CLOWN
ROBIN, RAFE } *ostlers at an inn*
VINTNER
HORSE-COURSER
THE POPE
THE CARDINAL OF LORRAINE
CHARLES V, EMPEROR OF GERMANY
A KNIGHT *at the* EMPEROR'*s court*
DUKE OF VANHOLT
DUCHESS OF VANHOLT

Spirits presenting
THE SEVEN DEADLY SINS
- PRIDE
- COVETOUSNESS
- WRATH
- ENVY
- GLUTTONY
- SLOTH
- LECHERY

ALEXANDER THE GREAT *and his* PARAMOUR
HELEN OF TROY

ATTENDANTS, FRIARS, *and* DEVILS

Prologue

[*Enter* CHORUS.][2]

CHORUS Not marching now in fields of Thrasimene,
Where Mars[3] did mate° the Carthaginians, *join with*
Nor sporting in the dalliance of love,
In courts of kings where state° is overturned, *political power*

1. There is no list of characters in the A text. The one here is an editorial construction.
2. A single actor who recited a prologue to an act or a whole play, and occasionally delivered an epilogue.
3. God of war. The battle of Lake Trasimene (217 B.C.E.) was one of the Carthaginian leader Hannibal's great victories.

Nor in the pomp of proud audacious deeds,
Intends our Muse to vaunt his heavenly verse:
Only this (Gentlemen) we must perform,
The form of Faustus' fortunes good or bad.
To patient judgments we appeal our plaud,° *applause*
And speak for Faustus in his infancy:
Now is he born, his parents base of stock,
In Germany, within a town called Rhodes;
Of riper years to Wittenberg[4] he went,
Whereas° his kinsmen chiefly brought him up. *where*
So soon he profits in divinity,° *theology*
The fruitful plot of scholarism graced,
That shortly he was graced with doctor's name,[5]
Excelling all, whose sweet delight disputes[6]
In heavenly matters of theology.
Till, swollen with cunning,° of a self-conceit, *knowledge*
His waxen wings did mount above his reach,
And melting heavens conspired his overthrow.[7]
For falling to a devilish exercise,
And glutted more with learning's golden gifts,
He surfeits upon cursed necromancy:° *black magic*
Nothing so sweet as magic is to him,
Which he prefers before his chiefest bliss.[8]
And this the man[9] that in his study sits. [*Exit.*]

SCENE 1

[*Enter* FAUSTUS *in his study.*]

FAUSTUS Settle thy studies, Faustus, and begin
To sound the depth of that thou wilt profess:
Having commenced, be a divine in show,[1]
Yet level° at the end of every art, *aim*
And live and die in Aristotle's works.
Sweet *Analytics,* 'tis thou hast ravished me:
Bene disserere est finis logices.[2]
Is to dispute well logic's chiefest end?
Affords this art no greater miracle?
Then read no more, thou hast attained the end;
A greater subject fitteth Faustus' wit.° *intellect*
Bid *on kai me on* farewell;[3] Galen come:
Seeing, *ubi desinit philosophus, ibi incipit medicus.*[4]
Be a physician, Faustus, heap up gold,
And be eternized for some wondrous cure.
Summum bonum medicinae sanitas:[5]

4. The famous university where Martin Luther studied, as did Shakespeare's Hamlet and Horatio. "Rhodes": Roda, or Stadtroda, in Germany.
5. The lines play on two senses of *graced*: he so (1) adorned the place ("plot") of scholarship—i.e., the university—that shortly he was (2) honored with a doctor's degree.
6. Referring to formal disputations, academic exercises that took the place of examinations.
7. In Greek myth, Icarus flew too near the sun on wings of feathers and wax made by his father, Daedalus; the wax melted, and he fell into the sea and drowned.
8. The salvation of his soul.
9. Apparently a cue for the Chorus to draw aside the curtain to the enclosed space at the rear of the stage.
1. In external appearance. "Commenced": graduated, i.e., received the doctor's degree.
2. "To carry on a disputation well is the end [or purpose] of logic" (Latin). *Analytics*: the title of two treatises on logic by Aristotle.
3. The Greek phrase means "being and not being"; i.e., philosophy.
4. "Where the philosopher leaves off the physician begins" (Latin). Galen: the ancient authority on medicine (2nd century C.E.).
5. The Latin is translated in the following line.

The end of physic° is our body's health. *medicine*
Why Faustus, hast thou not attained that end?
Is not thy common talk found aphorisms?[6]
Are not thy bills° hung up as monuments, *prescriptions*
Whereby whole cities have escaped the plague,
And thousand desperate maladies been eased?
Yet art thou still but Faustus, and a man.
Couldst thou make men to live eternally,
Or, being dead, raise them to life again,
Then this profession were to be esteemed.
Physic farewell! Where is Justinian?[7]
Si una eademque res legatur duobus,
Alter rem alter valorem rei, etc.[8]
A pretty case of paltry legacies:
Exhereditare filium non potest pater nisi . . .[9]
Such is the subject of the Institute,
And universal body of the law:
This study fits a mercenary drudge
Who aims at nothing but external trash!
Too servile and illiberal for me.
When all is done, divinity is best:
Jerome's Bible,[1] Faustus, view it well:
Stipendium peccati mors est:[2] ha! *Stipendium, etc.*
The reward of sin is death? That's hard.
Si pecasse negamus, fallimur, et nulla est in nobis veritas.[3]
If we say that we have no sin,
We deceive ourselves, and there's no truth in us.
Why then belike° we must sin, *in all likelihood*
And so consequently die.
Ay, we must die an everlasting death.
What doctrine call you this? *Che sarà, sarà*
What will be, shall be! Divinity, adieu!
These metaphysics° of magicians, *occult lore*
And necromantic books are heavenly!
Lines, circles, schemes, letters, and characters!
Ay, these are those that Faustus most desires.
O what a world of profit and delight,
Of power, of honor, of omnipotence
Is promised to the studious artisan![4]
All things that move between the quiet° poles *unmoving*
Shall be at my command: emperors and kings
Are but obeyed in their several° provinces, *separate*
Nor can they raise the wind, or rend the clouds;
But his dominion that exceeds in this
Stretcheth as far as doth the mind of man:
A sound magician is a mighty god.
Here Faustus, try thy brains to gain a deity.

6. I.e., generally accepted wisdom.
7. Roman emperor and authority on law (483–565 C.E.).
8. "If something is bequeathed to two persons, one shall have the thing itself, the other something of equal value."
9. "A father cannot disinherit his son unless . . ."
1. The Latin translation, or "Vulgate," of St. Jerome (ca. 340–420 C.E.).
2. Romans 6.23. But Faustus reads only *half* of the Scripture verse: "For the wages of sin is death; but the gift of God is eternal life through Jesus Christ our Lord."
3. 1 John 1.8 (translated in the following two lines).
4. A practitioner of an art; here, necromancy.

[*Enter* WAGNER.]
Wagner, commend me to my dearest friends,
The German Valdes and Cornelius,
Request them earnestly to visit me.
WAGNER I will, sir. [*Exit.*]
FAUSTUS Their conference will be a greater help to me
Than all my labors, plod I ne'er so fast.
[*Enter the* GOOD ANGEL *and the* EVIL ANGEL.]
GOOD ANGEL O Faustus, lay that damnèd book aside,
And gaze not on it, lest it tempt thy soul,
And heap God's heavy wrath upon thy head:
Read, read the Scriptures; that is blasphemy.
EVIL ANGEL Go forward, Faustus, in that famous art,
Wherein all nature's treasury is contained:
Be thou on earth as Jove[5] is in the sky,
Lord and commander of these elements. [*Exeunt.*]
FAUSTUS How am I glutted with conceit° of this! *filled with the idea*
Shall I make spirits fetch me what I please,
Resolve me of all ambiguities,
Perform what desperate enterprise I will?
I'll have them fly to India[6] for gold,
Ransack the ocean for orient pearl,
And search all corners of the new-found world
For pleasant fruits and princely delicates.
I'll have them read me strange philosophy,
And tell the secrets of all foreign kings;
I'll have them wall all Germany with brass,
And make swift Rhine circle fair Wittenberg;[7]
I'll have them fill the public schools[8] with silk,
Wherewith the students shall be bravely° clad. *splendidly*
I'll levy soldiers with the coin they bring,
And chase the Prince of Parma[9] from our land,
And reign sole king of all our provinces.
Yea, stranger engines for the brunt of war
Than was the fiery keel at Antwerp's bridge,[1]
I'll make my servile spirits to invent.
Come German Valdes and Cornelius,
And make me blest with your sage conference.
[*Enter* VALDES *and* CORNELIUS.]
Valdes, sweet Valdes, and Cornelius,
Know that your words have won me at the last
To practise magic and concealed arts;
Yet not your words only, but mine own fantasy,° *imagination*
That will receive no object[2] for my head,
But ruminates on necromantic skill.
Philosophy is odious and obscure,
Both law and physic are for petty wits;

5. God—a common substitution in Elizabethan drama.
6. "India" could refer to the West Indies, America, or Ophir (in the east).
7. Wittenberg is in fact on the Elbe River.
8. The university lecture rooms.
9. The duke of Parma was the Spanish governor-general of the Low Countries, 1579–92.
1. A reference to the burning ship sent by the Protestant Netherlanders in 1585 against the barrier on the river Scheldt that Parma had built as a part of the blockade of Antwerp.
2. That will pay no attention to physical reality.

Divinity is basest of the three,
Unpleasant, harsh, contemptible, and vile.
'Tis magic, magic that hath ravished me.
Then, gentle friends, aid me in this attempt,
And I, that have with concise syllogisms
Graveled° the pastors of the German church, — *confounded*
And made the flowering pride of Wittenberg
Swarm to my problems,[3] as the infernal spirits
On sweet Musaeus when he came to hell,
Will be as cunning as Agrippa was,
Whose shadows made all Europe honor him.[4]

VALDES Faustus, these books, thy wit,° and our experience — *intellect*
Shall make all nations to canonize us.
As Indian Moors[5] obey their Spanish lords,
So shall the spirits of every element
Be always serviceable to us three.
Like lions shall they guard us when we please,
Like Almaine rutters° with their horsemen's staves, — *German horsemen*
Or Lapland giants trotting by our sides;
Sometimes like women, or unwedded maids,
Shadowing° more beauty in their airy brows — *harboring*
Than in the white breasts of the Queen of Love.
From Venice shall they drag huge argosies,
And from America the golden fleece
That yearly stuffs old Philip's° treasury, — *Philip II, king of Spain*
If learnèd Faustus will be resolute.

FAUSTUS Valdes, as resolute am I in this
As thou to live, therefore object it not.[6]

CORNELIUS The miracles that magic will perform
Will make thee vow to study nothing else.
He that is grounded in astrology,
Enriched with tongues,° well seen° in minerals, — *languages / expert*
Hath all the principles magic doth require:
Then doubt not, Faustus, but to be renowned
And more frequented for this mystery° — *craft*
Than heretofore the Delphian oracle.[7]
The spirits tell me they can dry the sea,
And fetch the treasure of all foreign wrecks,
Ay, all the wealth that our forefathers hid
Within the massy° entrails of the earth. — *massive*
Then tell me, Faustus, what shall we three want?° — *lack*

FAUSTUS Nothing, Cornelius. O this cheers my soul!
Come, show me some demonstrations magical,
That I may conjure in some lusty° grove, — *pleasant*
And have these joys in full possessiön.

VALDES Then haste thee to some solitary grove,
And bear wise Bacon's and Abanus'[8] works,

3. Questions posed for public academic disputation.
4. Cornelius Agrippa, German author of *The Vanity and Uncertainty of Arts and Sciences* (1530), was popularly supposed to have had the power of calling up the "shadows" or shades of the dead. Musaeus was a mythical singer, son of Orpheus; it was, however, Orpheus who charmed the denizens of hell with his music.
5. Dark-skinned native Americans.
6. I.e., do not make an issue of my resolve.
7. The oracle of Apollo at Delphi in Greece.
8. Roger Bacon, the 13th-century friar and scientist popularly thought to be a magician, and Pietro d'Abano, 13th-century alchemist.

The Hebrew Psalter, and New Testament;
And whatsoever else is requisite
We will inform thee ere our conference cease.

CORNELIUS Valdes, first let him know the words of art,
And then, all other ceremonies learned,
Faustus may try his cunning by himself.

VALDES First, I'll instruct thee in the rudiments,
And then wilt thou be perfecter° than I. *more accomplished*

FAUSTUS Then come and dine with me, and after meat
We'll canvass every quiddity° thereof: *essential feature*
For ere I sleep, I'll try what I can do.
This night I'll conjure,° though I die therefore. *call up spirits*

[*Exeunt.*]

SCENE 2

[*Enter two* SCHOLARS.]

1 SCHOLAR I wonder what's become of Faustus, that was wont to make our schools ring with *sic probo*.[9]

2 SCHOLAR That shall we know; for see, here comes his boy.[1]

[*Enter* WAGNER.]

SCHOLAR How now sirra, where's thy master?

WAGNER God in heaven knows.

2 SCHOLAR Why, dost not thou know?

WAGNER Yes I know, but that follows not.

1 SCHOLAR Go to sirra, leave your jesting, and tell us where he is.

WAGNER That follows not necessary by force of argument, that you, being licentiates,[2] should stand upon't; therefore acknowledge your error, and be attentive.

2 SCHOLAR Why, didst thou not say thou knew'st?

WAGNER Have you any witness on't?

1 SCHOLAR Yes sirra, I heard you.

WAGNER Ask my fellow if I be a thief.

2 SCHOLAR Well, you will not tell us.

WAGNER Yes sir, I will tell you; yet if you were not dunces you would never ask me such a question. For is not he *corpus naturale*? And is not that *mobile*?[3] Then wherefore should you ask me such a question? But that I am by nature phlegmatic,[4] slow to wrath, and prone to lechery—to love I would say—it were not for you to come within forty foot of the place of execution,[5] although I do not doubt to see you both hanged the next sessions. Thus having triumphed over you, I will set my countenance like a precisian,[6] and begin to speak thus: Truly my dear brethren, my master is within at dinner with Valdes and Cornelius, as this wine, if it could speak, it would inform your worships. And so the Lord bless you, preserve you, and keep you, my dear brethren, my dear brethren. [*Exit.*]

1 SCHOLAR Nay then, I fear he is fallen into that damned art, for

9. Thus I prove; a phrase in scholastic disputation.
1. Poor student acting as servant to earn his living.
2. Graduate students.
3. *Corpus naturale et mobile* ("matter natural and movable") was a scholastic definition of the subject matter of physics. Wagner is here parodying the language of learning at the university.
4. Dominated by the phlegm, one of the four humors of medieval and Renaissance medicine and psychology.
5. The dining room.
6. Puritan. The rest of his speech is in the style of the Puritans. "Sessions": sittings of a court.

which they two are infamous through the world.

2 SCHOLAR Were he a stranger, and not allied to me, yet should I grieve for him. But come, let us go and inform the Rector,[7] and see if he by his grave counsel can reclaim him.

1 SCHOLAR Ay, but I fear me nothing can reclaim him.

2 SCHOLAR Yet let us try what we can do. [*Exeunt.*]

SCENE 3

[*Enter* FAUSTUS *to conjure.*]

FAUSTUS Now that the gloomy shadow of the earth,
Longing to view Orion's drizzling look,[8]
Leaps from th'antarctic world unto the sky,
And dims the welkin° with her pitchy breath, *sky*
Faustus, begin thine incantations,
And try if devils will obey thy hest,° *command*
Seeing thou hast prayed and sacrificed to them.
Within this circle[9] is Jehovah's name,
Forward and backward anagrammatized;
Th'abbreviated names of holy saints,
Figures of every adjunct to the heavens,
And characters of signs and erring stars,[1]
By which the spirits are enforced to rise.
Then fear not Faustus, but be resolute,
And try the uttermost magic can perform.
Sint mihi dei Acherontis propitii! Valeat numen triplex Jehovae! Ignei, aerii, aquatici, terreni spiritus salvete! Orientis princeps, Belzebub inferni ardentis monarcha, et Demogorgon, propitiamus vos ut appareat et surgat Mephastophilis. Quid tu moraris? Per Jehovam, Gehennam, et consecratam aquam quam nunc spargo, signumque crucis quod nunc facio, et per vota nostra, ipse nunc surgat nobis dicatus Mephastophilis.[2]

[*Enter a* DEVIL.]

I charge thee to return and change thy shape,
Thou art too ugly to attend on me;
Go and return an old Franciscan friar,
That holy shape becomes a devil best. [*Exit* DEVIL.]
I see there's virtue° in my heavenly words! *power*
Who would not be proficient in this art?
How pliant is this Mephastophilis,
Full of obedience and humility,
Such is the force of magic and my spells.

7. The head of a German university.
8. The constellation Orion appears at the beginning of winter. The phrase is a reminiscence of Virgil.
9. The magic circle drawn on the ground, within which the magician would be safe from the spirits he conjured.
1. The moving planets. "Adjunct": heavenly body, thought to be joined to the solid firmament of the sky. "Characters of signs": signs of the zodiac and the planets.
2. Faustus's Latin conjures the devils: "May the gods of the lower regions favor me! Farewell to the Trinity! Hail, spirits of fire, air, water, and earth! Prince of the East, Belzebub, monarch of burning hell, and Demogorgon, we pray to you that Mephastophilis may appear and rise. What are you waiting for? By Jehovah, Gehenna, and the holy water that I now sprinkle, and the sign of the cross that I now make, and by our vows, may Mephastophilis himself now rise to serve us." "Beelzebub" ("Lord of Flies"): an ancient Phoenician deity; in Matthew 12.24, he is called "the prince of the devils." "Demogorgon": in Renaissance versions of classical mythology, a mysterious primeval god.

Now Faustus, thou art conjurer laureate° *pre-eminent*
That canst command great Mephastophilis.
Quin redis, Mephastophilis, fratris imagine![3]
[*Enter* MEPHASTOPHILIS.]

MEPHASTOPHILIS Now Faustus, what would'st thou have me do?

FAUSTUS I charge thee wait upon me whilst I live,
To do whatever Faustus shall command,
Be it to make the moon drop from her sphere,
Or the ocean to overwhelm the world.

MEPHASTOPHILIS I am a servant to great Lucifer,
And may not follow thee without his leave;
No more than he commands must we perform.

FAUSTUS Did not he charge thee to appear to me?

MEPHASTOPHILIS No, I came now hither of mine own accord.

FAUSTUS Did not my conjuring speeches raise thee? Speak!

MEPHASTOPHILIS That was the cause, but yet *per accidens*,[4]
For when we hear one rack[5] the name of God,
Abjure the Scriptures, and his savior Christ,
We fly in hope to get his glorious soul;
Nor will we come unless he use such means
Whereby he is in danger to be damned:
Therefore the shortest cut for conjuring
Is stoutly to abjure° the Trinity, *repudiate*
And pray devoutly to the prince of hell.

FAUSTUS So Faustus hath already done, and holds this principle:
There is no chief but only Belzebub,
To whom Faustus doth dedicate himself.
This word damnation terrifies not him,
For he confounds hell in Elysium:
His ghost be with the old philosophers.[6]
But leaving these vain trifles of men's souls,
Tell me, what is that Lucifer thy lord?

MEPHASTOPHILIS Arch-regent and commander of all spirits.

FAUSTUS Was not that Lucifer an angel once?

MEPHASTOPHILIS Yes Faustus, and most dearly loved of God.

FAUSTUS How comes it then that he is prince of devils?

MEPHASTOPHILIS O, by aspiring pride and insolence,
For which God threw him from the face of heaven.

FAUSTUS And what are you that live with Lucifer?

MEPHASTOPHILIS Unhappy spirits that fell with Lucifer,
Conspired against our God with Lucifer,
And are forever damned with Lucifer.

FAUSTUS Where are you damned?

MEPHASTOPHILIS In hell.

FAUSTUS How comes it then that thou art out of hell?

MEPHASTOPHILIS Why this is hell, nor am I out of it.
Think'st thou that I, who saw the face of God,
And tasted the eternal joys of heaven,
Am not tormented with ten thousand hells

3. "Return, Mephastophilis, in the shape of a friar."
4. The immediate, not ultimate, cause.
5. Torture (by anagrammatizing).
6. Faustus considers hell to be the Elysium of the classical philosophers, not the Christian hell of torment.

In being deprived of everlasting bliss?[7]
O Faustus, leave these frivolous demands,° *questions*
Which strike a terror to my fainting soul.
FAUSTUS What, is great Mephastophilis so passionate
For being deprivèd of the joys of heaven?
Learn thou of Faustus manly fortitude,
And scorn those joys thou never shalt possess.
Go bear these tidings to great Lucifer,
Seeing Faustus hath incurred eternal death
By desperate thoughts against Jove's deity:
Say, he surrenders up to him his soul
So he will spare him four and twenty years,
Letting him live in all voluptuousness,
Having thee ever to attend on me,
To give me whatsoever I shall ask,
To tell me whatsoever I demand,
To slay mine enemies, and aid my friends,
And always be obedient to my will.
Go, and return to mighty Lucifer,
And meet me in my study at midnight
And then resolve me of thy master's mind.[8]
MEPHASTOPHILIS I will, Faustus. [*Exit.*]
FAUSTUS Had I as many souls as there be stars,
I'd give them all for Mephastophilis.
By him I'll be great emperor of the world,
And make a bridge through the moving air
To pass the ocean with a band of men;
I'll join the hills that bind the Afric shore,
And make that land continent to° Spain, *connected to*
And both contributory to my crown.
The emperor[9] shall not live but by my leave,
Nor any potentate of Germany.
Now that I have obtained what I desire,
I'll live in speculation° of this art *contemplation*
Till Mephastophilis return again. [*Exit.*]

SCENE 4

[*Enter* WAGNER *and the* CLOWN.[1]]

WAGNER Sirra boy, come hither.

CLOWN How, boy? Zounds, boy! I hope you have seen many boys with such pickadevants as I have. Boy, quotha![2]

WAGNER Tell me sirra, hast thou any comings in?[3]

CLOWN Ay, and goings out too; you may see else.[4]

WAGNER Alas poor slave, see how poverty jesteth in his nakedness! The villain is bare, and out of service,[5] and so hungry that I know

7. This is the punishment of loss of God's presence, which is supposed to be the greatest torment of hell.
8. I.e., give me his decision.
9. The Holy Roman Emperor.
1. Not a court jester (as in some of Shakespeare's plays) but an older stock character, a rustic buffoon.
2. Says he. The point of the clown's retort is that he is a man and wears a beard. "Zounds": an oath, meaning "God's wounds." "Pickadevants": small, pointed beards.
3. Income, but the clown then puns on the literal meaning.
4. I.e., if you don't believe me.
5. Out of a job.

he would give his soul to the devil for a shoulder of mutton, though it were blood raw.

CLOWN How, my soul to the devil for a shoulder of mutton though 'twere blood raw? Not so good friend; by'rlady,[6] I had need have it well roasted, and good sauce to it, if I pay so dear.

WAGNER Well, wilt thou serve me, and I'll make thee go like *qui mihi discipulus?*[7]

CLOWN How, in verse?

WAGNER No sirra; in beaten silk and stavesacre.[8]

CLOWN How, how, knavesacre?[9] Ay I thought that was all the land his father left him! Do ye hear, I would be sorry to rob you of your living.

WAGNER Sirra, I say in stavesacre.

CLOWN Oho, oho, stavesacre! Why then belike, if I were your man, I should be full of vermin.

WAGNER So thou shalt, whether thou be'st with me or no. But sirra, leave your jesting, and bind your self presently unto me for seven years, or I'll turn all the lice about thee into familiars,[1] and they shall tear thee in pieces.

CLOWN Do you hear, sir? You may save that labor: they are too familiar with me already—zounds, they are as bold with my flesh as if they had paid for my meat and drink.

WAGNER Well, do you hear, sirra? Hold, take these guilders.[2]

CLOWN Gridirons; what be they?

WAGNER Why, French crowns.[3]

CLOWN 'Mass, but for the name of French crowns a man were as good have as many English counters![4] And what should I do with these?

WAGNER Why, now, sirra, thou art at an hour's warning whensoever or wheresoever the devil shall fetch thee.

CLOWN No, no, here take your gridirons again.

WAGNER Truly I'll none of them.

CLOWN Truly but you shall.

WAGNER Bear witness I gave them him.

CLOWN Bear witness I give them you again.

WAGNER Well, I will cause two devils presently to fetch thee away. Baliol[5] and Belcher!

CLOWN Let your Baliol and your Belcher come here, and I'll knock[6] them, they were never so knocked since they were devils! Say I should kill one of them, what would folks say? "Do ye see yonder tall fellow in the round slop?[7] He has killed the devil!" So I should be called "Killdevil" all the parish over.

[*Enter two* DEVILS, *and the* CLOWN *runs up and down crying.*]

WAGNER Baliol and Belcher, spirits, away! [*Exeunt* DEVILS.]

CLOWN What, are they gone? A vengeance on them! They have vile long nails. There was a he devil and a she devil. I'll tell you how

6. An oath: "by Our Lady."
7. "You who are my pupil" (the opening phrase of a poem on how students should behave, from Lily's *Latin Grammar,* ca. 1509). Wagner means "like a proper servant of a learned man."
8. A preparation from delphinium seeds, used for killing vermin.
9. Wordplay, here and below.
1. Familiar spirits, demons. "Bind your self": i.e., as apprentice. "Presently": immediately.
2. Coins.
3. French crowns, legal tender in England at this period, were easily counterfeited.
4. Worthless tokens. "'Mass": by the Mass.
5. Probably a corruption of Belial.
6. Beat.
7. Baggy pants. "Tall": fine.

you shall know them: all he devils has horns, and all she devils has clefts and cloven feet.

WAGNER Well sirra, follow me.

CLOWN But do you hear? If I should serve you, would you teach me to raise up Banios and Belcheos?

WAGNER I will teach thee to turn thyself to anything, to a dog, or a cat, or a mouse, or a rat, or anything.

CLOWN How! A Christian fellow to a dog, or a cat, a mouse, or a rat? No, no sir, if you turn me into anything, let it be in the likeness of a little pretty frisking flea, that I may be here, and there, and everywhere. O I'll tickle the pretty wenches' plackets! I'll be amongst them, i'faith.[8]

WAGNER Well sirra, come.

CLOWN But, do you hear, Wagner . . . ?

WAGNER How? Baliol and Belcher!

CLOWN O Lord I pray, sir, let Banio and Belcher go sleep.

WAGNER Villain, call me Master Wagner; and let thy left eye be diametarily fixed upon my right heel, with *quasi vestigias nostras insistere.*[9] [*Exit.*]

CLOWN God forgive me, he speaks Dutch fustian![1] Well, I'll follow him, I'll serve him; that's flat. [*Exit.*]

SCENE 5

[*Enter* FAUSTUS *in his study.*]

FAUSTUS Now Faustus, must thou needs be damned,
And canst thou not be saved.
What boots° it then to think of God or heaven? *avails*
Away with such vain fancies, and despair,
Despair in God, and trust in Belzebub.
Now go not backward: no, Faustus, be resolute;
Why waverest thou? O, something soundeth in mine ears:
"Abjure this magic, turn to God again."
Ay, and Faustus will turn to God again.
To God? He loves thee not:
The god thou servest is thine own appetite,
Wherein is fixed the love of Belzebub.
To him I'll build an altar and a church,
And offer lukewarm blood of newborn babes.

[*Enter* GOOD ANGEL *and* EVIL.]

GOOD ANGEL Sweet Faustus, leave that execrable° art. *accursed*

FAUSTUS Contrition, prayer, repentance: what of them?

GOOD ANGEL O they are means to bring thee unto heaven.

EVIL ANGEL Rather illusions, fruits of lunacy,
That makes men foolish that do trust them most.

GOOD ANGEL Sweet Faustus, think of heaven, and heavenly things.

EVIL ANGEL No Faustus, think of honor and of wealth. [*Exeunt.*]

FAUSTUS Of wealth!
Why, the signory° of Emden[2] shall be mine, *lordship*
When Mephastophilis shall stand by me.
What god can hurt thee, Faustus? Thou art safe,

8. In faith. "Plackets": slits in garments—but with an obvious sexual allusion.

9. A pedantic way of saying "Follow my footsteps." "Diametarily": diametrically.

1. Gibberish.

2. A wealthy German trade center.

Cast no more doubts. Come, Mephastophilis,
And bring glad tidings from great Lucifer.
Is't not midnight? Come, Mephastophilis:
Veni, veni, Mephastophile![3]
[*Enter* MEPHASTOPHILIS.]
Now tell, what says Lucifer thy lord?
MEPHASTOPHILIS That I shall wait on Faustus whilst he lives,
So° he will buy my service with his soul. *provided that*
FAUSTUS Already Faustus hath hazarded that for thee.
MEPHASTOPHILIS But Faustus, thou must bequeath it solemnly,
And write a deed of gift with thine own blood,
For that security° craves great Lucifer. *guarantee*
If thou deny it, I will back to hell.
FAUSTUS Stay, Mephastophilis, and tell me,
What good will my soul do thy lord?
MEPHASTOPHILIS Enlarge his kingdom.
FAUSTUS Is that the reason he tempts us thus?
MEPHASTOPHILIS *Solamen miseris socios habuisse doloris.*[4]
FAUSTUS Have you any pain that tortures others?
MEPHASTOPHILIS As great as have the human souls of men.
But tell me Faustus, shall I have thy soul?
And I will be thy slave and wait on thee,
And give thee more than thou hast wit to ask.
FAUSTUS Ay Mephastophilis, I give it thee.
MEPHASTOPHILIS Then stab thine arm courageously,
And bind thy soul, that at some certain day
Great Lucifer may claim it as his own,
And then be thou as great as Lucifer.
FAUSTUS Lo Mephastophilis, for love of thee,
I cut my arm, and with my proper° blood *own*
Assure my soul to be great Lucifer's,
Chief lord and regent of perpetual night.
View here the blood that trickles from mine arm,
And let it be propitious for my wish.
MEPHASTOPHILIS But Faustus, thou must write it
In manner of a deed of gift.
FAUSTUS Ay, so I will; but, Mephastophilis,
My blood congeals and I can write no more.
MEPHASTOPHILIS I'll fetch thee fire to dissolve it straight. [*Exit.*]
FAUSTUS What might the staying of my blood portend?
Is it unwilling I should write this bill? ° *contract*
Why streams it not, that I may write afresh:
"Faustus gives to thee his soul"? Ah, there it stayed!
Why should'st thou not? Is not thy soul thine own?
Then write again: "Faustus gives to thee his soul."
[*Enter* MEPHASTOPHILIS *with a chafer° of coals.*] *a portable grate*
MEPHASTOPHILIS Here's fire, come Faustus, set it on.
FAUSTUS So, now the blood begins to clear again.
Now will I make an end immediately.
MEPHASTOPHILIS O what will not I do to obtain his soul!
FAUSTUS *Consummatum est,*[5] this bill is ended,

3. "Come, come, Mephastophilis!"
4. "Misery loves company."
5. "It is finished": a blasphemy, because these are the words of Christ on the Cross (John 19.30).

And Faustus hath bequeathed his soul to Lucifer.
But what is this inscription on mine arm?
Homo fuge.° Whither should I fly? *O man, fly*
If unto God, he'll throw me down to hell;
My senses are deceived, here's nothing writ;
I see it plain, here in this place is writ,
Homo fuge! Yet shall not Faustus fly.
MEPHASTOPHILIS I'll fetch him somewhat to delight his mind. [*Exit.*]
[*Enter with* DEVILS, *giving crowns and rich apparel to* FAUSTUS, *and dance, and then depart.*]
FAUSTUS Speak, Mephastophilis, what means this show?
MEPHASTOPHILIS Nothing, Faustus, but to delight thy mind withal,
And to show thee what magic can perform.
FAUSTUS But may I raise up spirits when I please?
MEPHASTOPHILIS Ay, Faustus, and do greater things than these.
FAUSTUS Then there's enough for a thousand souls!
Here, Mephastophilis, receive this scroll,
A deed of gift of body and of soul:
But yet conditionally, that thou perform
All articles prescribed between us both.
MEPHASTOPHILIS Faustus, I swear by hell and Lucifer
To effect all promises between us made.
FAUSTUS Then hear me read them. On these conditions following:
First, that Faustus may be a spirit[6] *in form and substance.*
Secondly, that Mephastophilis shall be his servant, and at his command.
Thirdly, that Mephastophilis shall do for him, and bring him whatsoever.
Fourthly, that he shall be in his chamber or house invisible.
Lastly, that he shall appear to the said John Faustus at all times, in what form or shape soever he please.
I, John Faustus of Wittenberg, doctor, by these presents,[7] *do give both body and soul to Lucifer, Prince of the East, and his minister Mephastophilis; and furthermore grant unto them that, four and twenty years being expired, the articles above-written inviolate, full power to fetch or carry the said John Faustus, body and soul, flesh, blood, or goods, into their habitation wheresoever.*
By me John Faustus.
MEPHASTOPHILIS Speak, Faustus: do you deliver this as your deed?
FAUSTUS Ay, take it; and the devil give thee good on't.
MEPHASTOPHILIS Now, Faustus, ask what thou wilt.
FAUSTUS First will I question with thee about hell:
Tell me, where is the place that men call hell?
MEPHASTOPHILIS Under the heavens.
FAUSTUS Ay, but whereabouts?
MEPHASTOPHILIS Within the bowels of these elements,
Where we are tortured and remain for ever.
Hell hath no limits, nor is circumscribed
In one self place; for where we are is hell,
And where hell is, there must we ever be.
And to conclude, when all the world dissolves,
And every creature shall be purified,

6. I.e., have the supernatural powers of a spirit. 7. Legal articles.

All places shall be hell that is not heaven.
FAUSTUS Come, I think hell's a fable.
MEPHASTOPHILIS Ay, think so still, till experience change thy mind.
FAUSTUS Why? think'st thou then that Faustus shall be damned?
MEPHASTOPHILIS Ay, of necessity, for here's the scroll
Wherein thou hast given thy soul to Lucifer.
FAUSTUS Ay, and body too; but what of that?
Think'st thou that Faustus is so fond° to imagine *foolish*
That after this life there is any pain?
Tush, these are trifles and mere old wives' tales.
MEPHASTOPHILIS But Faustus, I am an instance to prove the contrary;
For I am damned, and am now in hell.
FAUSTUS How, now in hell? Nay, and this be hell, I'll willingly be damned here! What? walking, disputing, etc. . . . But leaving off this, let me have a wife, the fairest maid in Germany, for I am wanton and lascivious, and cannot live without a wife.
MEPHASTOPHILIS How, a wife? I prithee Faustus, talk not of a wife.[8]
FAUSTUS Nay sweet Mephastophilis, fetch me one, for I will have one.
MEPHASTOPHILIS Well, thou wilt have one; sit there till I come.
I'll fetch thee a wife in the devil's name. [*Exit.*]
[*Enter with a* DEVIL *dressed like a woman, with fireworks.*]
MEPHASTOPHILIS Tell, Faustus, how dost thou like thy wife?
FAUSTUS A plague on her for a hot whore!
MEPHASTOPHILIS Tut, Faustus, marriage is but a ceremonial toy;
If thou lovest me, think no more of it.
I'll cull thee out the fairest courtesans
And bring them every morning to thy bed:
She whom thine eye shall like, thy heart shall have,
Be she as chaste as was Penelope,
As wise as Saba,[9] or as beautiful
As was bright Lucifer before his fall.
Hold, take this book, peruse it thoroughly:
The iterating° of these lines brings gold; *repeating*
The framing° of this circle on the ground *drawing*
Brings whirlwinds, tempests, thunder and lightning.
Pronounce this thrice devoutly to thyself,
And men in armor shall appear to thee,
Ready to execute what thou desirest.
FAUSTUS Thanks, Mephastophilis, yet fain would I have a book wherein I might behold all spells and incantations, that I might raise up spirits when I please.
MEPHASTOPHILIS Here they are in this book. [*There turn to them.*]
FAUSTUS Now would I have a book where I might see all characters and planets of the heavens, that I might know their motions and dispositions.
MEPHASTOPHILIS Here they are too. [*Turn to them.*]
FAUSTUS Nay, let me have one book more, and then I have done, wherein I might see all plants, herbs, and trees that grow upon the earth.

8. Mephastophilis cannot produce a wife for Faustus because marriage is a sacrament.

9. The queen of Sheba. "Penelope": the wife of Ulysses, famed for chastity and fidelity.

MEPHASTOPHILIS Here they be.
FAUSTUS O thou art deceived!
MEPHASTOPHILIS Tut, I warrant thee. [*Turn to them.*]
FAUSTUS When I behold the heavens, then I repent,
And curse thee, wicked Mephastophilis,
Because thou hast deprived me of those joys.
MEPHASTOPHILIS Why Faustus,
Think'st thou that heaven is such a glorious thing?
I tell thee 'tis not half so fair as thou,
Or any man that breathes on earth.
FAUSTUS How prov'st thou that?
MEPHASTOPHILIS It was made for man, therefore is man more excellent.
FAUSTUS If it were made for man,'twas made for me:
I will renounce this magic, and repent.
[*Enter* GOOD ANGEL *and* EVIL ANGEL.]
GOOD ANGEL Faustus, repent, yet° God will pity thee. *still*
EVIL ANGEL Thou art a spirit,° God cannot pity thee. *evil spirit, devil*
FAUSTUS Who buzzeth in mine ears I am a spirit?
Be I a devil, yet God may pity me.
Ay, God will pity me if I repent.
EVIL ANGEL Ay, but Faustus never shall repent. [*Exeunt.*]
FAUSTUS My heart's so hardened[1] I cannot repent!
Scarce can I name salvation, faith, or heaven,
But fearful echoes thunders in mine ears,
"Faustus, thou are damned"; then swords and knives,
Poison, guns, halters,° and envenomed steel *ropes for hanging*
Are laid before me to dispatch myself:
And long ere this I should have slain myself,
Had not sweet pleasure conquered deep despair.
Have I not made blind Homer sing to me
Of Alexander's[2] love, and Oenon's death?
And hath not he that built the walls of Thebes
With ravishing sound of his melodious harp,[3]
Made music with my Mephastophilis?
Why should I die then, or basely despair?
I am resolved! Faustus shall ne'er repent.
Come, Mephastophilis, let us dispute again,
And argue of divine astrology.
Tell me, are there many heavens above the moon?
Are all celestial bodies but one globe,
As is the substance of this centric earth?[4]
MEPHASTOPHILIS As are the elements, such are the spheres,
Mutually folded in each other's orb.
And, Faustus, all jointly move upon one axletree
Whose terminè° is termed the world's wide pole, *end*

1. Hardness of heart is the desperate spiritual state of the reprobate who will suffer eternal damnation.
2. Alexander is another name for Paris, the lover of Oenone; later he deserted her and abducted Helen, causing the Trojan War. Oenone refused to heal the wounds Paris received in battle, and when he died of them, she killed herself in remorse.
3. The legendary musician Amphion, whose harp caused stones, of themselves, to form the walls of Thebes.
4. Faustus asks whether all the apparently different heavenly bodies form really "one globe" like the earth. Mephastophilis answers that like the elements, which are separate but combined, the heavenly bodies are separate but their spheres are enfolded and they move on one axletree.

Nor are the names of Saturn, Mars, or Jupiter
Feigned, but are erring stars.[5]

FAUSTUS But tell me, have they all one motion, both *situ et tempore*?[6]

MEPHASTOPHILIS All jointly move from east to west in four-and-twenty hours upon the poles of the world, but differ in their motion upon the poles of the zodiac.[7]

FAUSTUS Tush, these slender trifles Wagner can decide!
Hath Mephastophilis no greater skill?
Who knows not the double motion of the planets?
The first is finished in a natural day, the second thus: as Saturn in thirty years; Jupiter in twelve; Mars in four; the Sun, Venus, and Mercury in a year; the Moon in twenty-eight days. Tush, these are freshmen's suppositions. But tell me, hath every sphere a dominion or *intelligentia*?[8]

MEPHASTOPHILIS Ay.

FAUSTUS How many heavens or spheres are there?

MEPHASTOPHILIS Nine: the seven planets, the firmament, and the empyreal heaven.[9]

FAUSTUS Well, resolve me then in this question: why have we not conjunctions, oppositions,[1] aspects, eclipses, all at one time, but in some years we have more, in some less?

MEPHASTOPHILIS *Per inaequalem motum respectu totius.*[2]

FAUSTUS Well, I am answered. Tell me who made the world?

MEPHASTOPHILIS I will not.

FAUSTUS Sweet Mephastophilis, tell me.

MEPHASTOPHILIS Move° me not, for I will not tell thee. *urge*

FAUSTUS Villain, have I not bound thee to tell me anything?

MEPHASTOPHILIS Ay, that is not against our kingdom; but this is.
Think thou on hell, Faustus, for thou art damned.

FAUSTUS Think, Faustus, upon God, that made the world.

MEPHASTOPHILIS Remember this. [*Exit.*]

FAUSTUS Ay, go accursèd spirit, to ugly hell,
'Tis thou hast damned distressèd Faustus' soul:
Is't not too late?

[*Enter* GOOD ANGEL *and* EVIL.]

EVIL ANGEL Too late.

GOOD ANGEL Never too late, if Faustus will repent.

EVIL ANGEL If thou repent, devils shall tear thee in pieces.

GOOD ANGEL Repent, and they shall never raze° thy skin. *graze*

[*Exeunt.*]

FAUSTUS Ah Christ my Savior! seek to save
Distressèd Faustus' soul!

[*Enter* LUCIFER, BELZEBUB, *and* MEPHASTOPHILIS.]

LUCIFER Christ cannot save thy soul, for he is just.
There's none but I have interest in the same.

5. It is appropriate to give individual names to Saturn, Mars, Jupiter, and the other planets—which are called wandering, or "erring" stars. The fixed stars were in the eighth sphere (the firmament, or crystalline sphere).
6. "In position and in time."
7. The common axletree on which all the spheres revolve.
8. An angel, or intelligence, thought to be the source of motion in each sphere.
9. The ninth sphere was the immovable empyrean.
1. "Oppositions": when two planets are most remote. "Conjunctions": the apparent joinings of two planets.
2. "Because of their unequal movements in respect of the whole."

FAUSTUS O who art thou that look'st so terrible?
LUCIFER I am Lucifer, and this is my companion prince in hell.
FAUSTUS O Faustus, they are come to fetch away thy soul!
LUCIFER We come to tell thee thou dost injure us.
Thou talk'st of Christ, contrary to thy promise.
Thou should'st not think of God; think of the devil,
And his dam[3] too.
FAUSTUS Nor will I henceforth: pardon me in this,
And Faustus vows never to look to heaven,
Never to name God, or to pray to him,
To burn his Scriptures, slay his ministers,
And make my spirits pull his churches down.

LUCIFER Do so, and we will highly gratify thee. Faustus, we are come from hell to show thee some pastime; sit down, and thou shalt see all the Seven Deadly Sins[4] appear in their proper shapes.

FAUSTUS That sight will be as pleasing unto me as Paradise was to Adam, the first day of his creation.

LUCIFER Talk not of Paradise, nor creation, but mark this show; talk of the devil and nothing else. Come away.

[*Enter the* SEVEN DEADLY SINS.]

Now Faustus, examine them of their several names and dispositions.

FAUSTUS What art thou, the first?

PRIDE I am Pride: I disdain to have any parents. I am like to Ovid's flea,[5] I can creep into every corner of a wench: sometimes like a periwig, I sit upon her brow; or like a fan of feathers, I kiss her lips. Indeed I do—what do I not! But fie, what a scent is here? I'll not speak another word, except the ground were perfumed and covered with cloth of arras.[6]

FAUSTUS What art thou, the second?

COVETOUSNESS I am Covetousness, begotten of an old churl in an old leathern bag; and might I have my wish, I would desire that this house, and all the people in it, were turned to gold, that I might lock you up in my good chest. O my sweet gold!

FAUSTUS What art thou, the third?

WRATH I am Wrath. I had neither father nor mother: I leaped out of a lion's mouth when I was scarce half an hour old, and ever since I have run up and down the world, with this case of rapiers, wounding myself when I had nobody to fight withal. I was born in hell—and look to it, for some of you shall be my father.

FAUSTUS What art thou, the fourth?

ENVY I am Envy, begotten of a chimney-sweeper and an oyster-wife. I cannot read, and therefore wish all books were burnt; I am lean with seeing others eat—O that there would come a famine through all the world, that all might die, and I live alone; then thou should'st see how fat I would be! But must thou sit and I stand? Come down, with a vengeance!

3. Mother. "The devil and his dam" was a common colloquial expression.
4. Pride, avarice, lust, anger, gluttony, envy, and sloth, called deadly because they lead to spiritual death. All other sins are said to grow out of them (cf. the procession of the Seven Deadly Sins in Spenser's *The Faerie Queene* 1.4, stanzas 16–37).
5. A salacious medieval poem "Carmen de Pulice" (Song of the Flea) was attributed to Ovid.
6. Arras in Flanders exported fine cloth used for tapestry hangings. "Except": unless.

FAUSTUS Away, envious rascal! What art thou, the fifth?

GLUTTONY Who, I sir? I am Gluttony. My parents are all dead, and the devil a penny they have left me but a bare pension, and that is thirty meals a day and ten bevers[7]—a small trifle to suffice nature. O, I come of a royal parentage: my grandfather was a gammon[8] of bacon, my grandmother a hogshead of claret wine; my godfathers were these: Peter Pickled-Herring, and Martin Martlemas-Beef.[9] O but my godmother! She was a jolly gentlewoman, and well-beloved in every good town and city; her name was Mistress Margery March-Beer.[1] Now, Faustus, thou hast heard all my progeny;[2] wilt thou bid me to supper?

FAUSTUS No, I'll see thee hanged; thou wilt eat up all my victuals.

GLUTTONY Then the devil choke thee!

FAUSTUS Choke thyself, Glutton. What art thou, the sixth?

SLOTH I am Sloth; I was begotten on a sunny bank, where I have lain ever since—and you have done me great injury to bring me from thence. Let me be carried thither again by Gluttony and Lechery. I'll not speak another word for a king's ransom.

FAUSTUS What are you, Mistress Minx, the seventh and last?

LECHERY Who, I sir? I am one that loves an inch of raw mutton better than an ell of fried stockfish;[3] and the first letter of my name begins with Lechery.

LUCIFER Away! To hell, to hell! [*Exeunt the* SINS.]
Now Faustus, how dost thou like this?

FAUSTUS O this feeds my soul!

LUCIFER Tut, Faustus, in hell is all manner of delight.

FAUSTUS O might I see hell, and return again, how happy were I then!

LUCIFER Thou shalt; I will send for thee at midnight. In meantime, take this book, peruse it thoroughly, and thou shalt turn thyself into what shape thou wilt.

FAUSTUS Great thanks, mighty Lucifer; this will I keep as chary[4] as my life.

LUCIFER Farewell, Faustus; and think on the devil.

FAUSTUS Farewell, great Lucifer; come, Mephastophilis.

[*Exeunt* OMNES.]

SCENE 6

[*Enter* ROBIN *the ostler*[5] *with a book in his hand.*]

ROBIN O this is admirable! here I ha' stolen one of Doctor Faustus' conjuring books, and i'faith I mean to search some circles[6] for my own use: now will I make all the maidens in our parish dance at my pleasure stark naked before me, and so by that means I shall see more than ere I felt or saw yet.

[*Enter* RAFE *calling* ROBIN.]

RAFE Robin, prithee come away, there's a gentleman tarries to have his horse, and he would have his things rubbed and made clean.

7. Snacks.
8. The lower side of pork, including the leg.
9. Meat, salted to preserve it during the winter, was prepared around Martinmas (November 11).
1. A rich ale, made in March.
2. Lineage.
3. Dried cod. "Mutton": frequently a bawdy term in Elizabethan English; here, the penis. "Ell": forty-five inches.
4. Carefully.
5. Hostler, stablehand.
6. Magicians' circles, but with a sexual innuendo.

He keeps such a chafing[7] with my mistress about it, and she has sent me to look thee out. Prithee, come away.

ROBIN Keep out, keep out; or else you are blown up, you are dismembered, Rafe. Keep out, for I am about a roaring[8] piece of work.

RAFE Come, what dost thou with that same book? Thou canst not read!

ROBIN Yes, my master and mistress shall find that I can read—he for his forehead,[9] she for her private study. She's born to bear with me,[1] or else my art fails.

RAFE Why Robin, what book is that?

ROBIN What book? Why the most intolerable[2] book for conjuring that ere was invented by any brimstone devil.

RAFE Canst thou conjure with it?

ROBIN I can do all these things easily with it: first, I can make thee drunk with 'ipocrase[3] at any tavern in Europe for nothing, that's one of my conjuring works.

RAFE Our master parson says that's nothing.

ROBIN True, Rafe! And more, Rafe, if thou hast any mind to Nan Spit, our kitchen maid, then turn her and wind her to thy own use, as often as thou wilt, and at midnight.

RAFE O brave Robin! Shall I have Nan Spit, and to mine own use? On that condition I'll feed thy devil with horsebread as long as he lives, of free cost.[4]

ROBIN No more, sweet Rafe; let's go and make clean our boots which lie foul upon our hands, and then to our conjuring in the devil's name. [*Exeunt.*]

CHORUS 2

[*Enter* WAGNER *solus.*]

WAGNER Learned Faustus,
To know the secrets of astronomy
Graven in the book of Jove's high firmament,
Did mount himself to scale Olympus'[5] top.
Being seated in a chariot burning bright,
Drawn by the strength of yokèd dragons' necks.
He now is gone to prove cosmography,[6]
And, as I guess, will first arrive at Rome
To see the pope, and manner of his court,
And take some part of holy Peter's feast,[7]
That to this day is highly solemnized. [*Exit* WAGNER.]

SCENE 7

[*Enter* FAUSTUS *and* MEPHASTOPHILIS.]

FAUSTUS Having now, my good Mephastophilis,
Passed with delight the stately town of Trier,[8]
Environed round with airy mountain tops,

7. Scolding.
8. Dangerous.
9. That is, Robin intends to give his master horns—cuckold him.
1. I.e., bear his weight, or bear him a child.
2. Irresistible.
3. Robin's pronunciation of *hippocras,* a spiced wine.
4. Free of charge. "Horsebread": fodder.
5. The home of the gods in Greek mythology.
6. To test the accuracy of maps.
7. St. Peter's feast is June 29.
8. Treves (in Prussia).

With walls of flint, and deep entrenchèd lakes,° *moats*
Not to be won by any conquering prince;
From Paris next, coasting° the realm of France, *traversing*
We saw the river Main fall into Rhine,
Whose banks are set with groves of fruitful vines;
Then up to Naples, rich Campania,
With buildings fair and gorgeous to the eye,
The streets straight forth, and paved with finest brick,
Quarters the town in four equivalents;
There saw we learned Maro's[9] golden tomb,
The way° he cut, an English mile in length, *tunnel*
Thorough° a rock of stone in one night's space. *through*
From thence to Venice, Padua, and the rest,
In midst of which a sumptuous temple° stands *St. Mark's in Venice*
That threats the stars with her aspiring top.
Thus hitherto hath Faustus spent his time.
But tell me now, what resting place is this?
Hast thou, as erst° I did command, *earlier*
Conducted me within the walls of Rome?

MEPHASTOPHILIS Faustus, I have; and because we will not be unprovided, I have taken up his holiness' privy chamber for our use.

FAUSTUS I hope his holiness will bid us welcome.

MEPHASTOPHILIS Tut, 'tis no matter, man, we'll be bold with his good cheer.[1]
And now, my Faustus, that thou may'st perceive
What Rome containeth to delight thee with,
Know that this city stands upon seven hills
That underprop the groundwork of the same;
Just through the midst runs flowing Tiber's stream,
With winding banks, that cut it in two parts;
Over the which four stately bridges lean,
That makes safe passage to each part of Rome.
Upon the bridge called Ponte Angelo
Erected is a castle passing strong,[2]
Within whose walls such store of ordnance are
And double cannons, framed of carvèd brass,
As match the days within one complete year—
Besides the gates and high pyramides° *obelisks*
Which Julius Caesar brought from Africa.

FAUSTUS Now by the kingdoms of infernal rule,
Of Styx, Acheron, and the fiery lake
Of ever-burning Phlegethon,[3] I swear
That I do long to see the monuments
And situation of bright-splendent Rome.
Come therefore, let's away.

MEPHASTOPHILIS Nay, Faustus, stay. I know you'd fain see the pope,
And take some part of holy Peter's feast,
Where thou shalt see a troop of bald-pate friars,
Whose *summum bonum*[4] is in belly-cheer.

FAUSTUS Well, I am content to compass[5] then some sport,

9. Virgil's. In medieval legend the Roman poet Virgil was considered a magician whose powers produced a tunnel on the promontory of Posilippo at Naples, near his tomb.
1. Entertainment.
2. Surpassingly. Actually the castle is on the bank, not the bridge.
3. Classical names for rivers of the underworld.
4. The greatest good; often refers to God.
5. Take part in.

And by their folly make us merriment.
Then charm me that I may be invisible, to do what I please unseen of any whilst I stay in Rome.

MEPHASTOPHILIS [*casts a spell on him*]. So Faustus, now do what thou wilt, thou shalt not be discerned.

[*Sound a sennet;*[6] *enter the* POPE *and the* CARDINAL OF LORRAINE *to the banquet, with* FRIARS *attending.*]

POPE My lord of Lorraine, will't please you draw near.

FAUSTUS Fall to; and the devil choke you and[7] you spare.

POPE How now, who's that which spake? Friars, look about.

1 FRIAR Here's nobody, if it like[8] your holiness.

POPE My lord, here is a dainty dish was sent to me from the bishop of Milan.

FAUSTUS I thank you, sir. [*Snatch it.*]

POPE How now, who's that which snatched the meat from me? Will no man look? My lord, this dish was sent me from the cardinal of Florence.

FAUSTUS You say true? I'll have't. [*Snatch it.*]

POPE What, again! My lord, I'll drink to your grace.

FAUSTUS I'll pledge[9] your grace. [*Snatch the cup.*]

LORRAINE My lord, it may be some ghost newly crept out of purgatory come to beg a pardon of your holiness.

POPE It may be so; friars; prepare a dirge[1] to lay the fury of this ghost. Once again my lord, fall to. [*The* POPE *crosseth himself.*]

FAUSTUS What, are you crossing of your self? Well, use that trick no more, I would advise you.

[*Cross again.*]

FAUSTUS Well, there's the second time; aware the third! I give you fair warning.

[*Cross again, and* FAUSTUS *hits him a box of the ear, and they all run away.*]

FAUSTUS Come on, Mephastophilis, what shall we do?

MEPHASTOPHILIS Nay, I know not; we shall be cursed with bell, book, and candle.[2]

FAUSTUS How! Bell, book, and candle; candle, book, and bell,
Forward and backward, to curse Faustus to hell.
Anon you shall hear a hog grunt, a calf bleat, and an ass bray,
Because it is St. Peter's holy day.

[*Enter all the* FRIARS *to sing the Dirge.*]

1 FRIAR Come brethren, let's about our business with good devotion.

[*Sing this.*]

Cursed be he that stole away His Holiness' meat from the table.
Maledicat Dominus.[3]
Cursed be he that struck His Holiness a blow on the face.
Maledicat Dominus.
Cursed be he that took Friar Sandelo a blow on the pate.
Maledicat Dominus.
Cursed be he that disturbeth our holy dirge.
Maledicat Dominus.
Cursed be he that took away His Holiness' wine.

6. A set of notes on the trumpet or cornet.
7. If. "Fall to": start eating.
8. Please.
9. Toast.
1. A requiem mass. But what actually follows is a litany of curses.
2. The traditional paraphernalia for cursing and excommunication.
3. "May the Lord curse him."

Maledicat dominus.
Et omnes sancti.[4] Amen.
[*Beat the* FRIARS, *and fling fireworks among them, and so Exeunt.*]

SCENE 8

[*Enter* ROBIN *and* RAFE *with a silver goblet.*]

ROBIN Come, Rafe, did not I tell thee we were forever made by this Doctor Faustus' book? *Ecce signum!*[5] Here's a simple purchase for horsekeepers: our horses shall eat no hay as long as this lasts.

[*Enter the* VINTNER.]

RAFE But Robin, here comes the vintner.

ROBIN Hush, I'll gull him supernaturally! Drawer,[6] I hope all is paid; God be with you. Come, Rafe.

VINTNER Soft, sir, a word with you. I must yet have a goblet paid from you ere you go.

ROBIN I, a goblet, Rafe? I, a goblet? I scorn you: and you are but a &c.[7] . . . I, a goblet? Search me.

VINTNER I mean so, sir, with your favor. [*Searches* ROBIN.]

ROBIN How say you now?

VINTNER I must say somewhat to your fellow; you, sir!

RAFE Me, sir? Me, sir? Search your fill. Now sir, you may be ashamed to burden honest men with a matter of truth.

VINTNER [*searches* RAFE] Well, t'one of you hath this goblet about you.

ROBIN You lie, drawer; 'tis afore me. Sirra you, I'll teach ye to impeach[8] honest men: [*to* RAFE] stand by. [*to the* VINTNER] I'll scour you for a goblet—stand aside, you were best—I charge you in the name of Belzebub—look to the goblet, Rafe!

VINTNER What mean you, sirra?

ROBIN I'll tell you what I mean: [*he reads*] *Sanctobulorum Periphrasticon*—nay, I'll tickle you, vintner—look to the goblet, Rafe—*Poly pragmos Belseborams framanto pacostiphos tostis Mephastophilis, &c.* . . .[9]

[*Enter* MEPHASTOPHILIS*: sets squibs*[1] *at their backs: they run about.*]

VINTNER *O nomine Domine!*[2] What mean'st thou, Robin? Thou hast no goblet.

RAFE *Peccatum peccatorum!*[3] Here's thy goblet, good vintner.

ROBIN *Misericordia pro nobis!*[4] What shall I do? Good devil, forgive me now, and I'll never rob thy library more.

[*Enter to them* MEPHASTOPHILIS.]

MEPHASTOPHILIS Vanish, villains, th'one like an ape, another like a bear, the third an ass, for doing this enterprise. [*Exit* VINTNER.]
Monarch of hell, under whose black survey
Great potentates do kneel with awful fear;

4. "And all the saints (also curse him)."
5. "Behold the proof."
6. Wine-drawer. "Gull": trick.
7. The actor might ad lib abuse at this point.
8. Accuse.
9. Dog-Latin, as Robin attempts to conjure from Faustus's book.
1. Firecrackers. Evidently Mephastophilis is on stage only long enough to set off the firecrackers and is not seen by Robin, Rafe, or the vintner. He then reenters at line 32.
2. "In the name of the Lord"; the Latin invocations are used in swearing.
3. "Sin of sins!"
4. "Have mercy on us!"

Upon whose altars thousand souls do lie;
How am I vexèd with these villains' charms!
From Constantinople am I hither come,
Only for pleasure of these damnèd slaves.

ROBIN How, from Constantinople? You have had a great journey! Will you take sixpence in your purse to pay for your supper, and be gone?

MEPHASTOPHILIS Well, villains, for your presumption, I transform thee into an ape, and thee into a dog; and so begone! [*Exit.*]

ROBIN How, into an ape? That's brave: I'll have fine sport with the boys; I'll get nuts and apples enow.[5]

RAFE And I must be a dog.

ROBIN I'faith, thy head will never be out of the potage[6] pot.

[*Exeunt.*]

CHORUS 3

[*Enter* CHORUS.[7]]

CHORUS When Faustus had with pleasure ta'en the view
Of rarest things, and royal courts of kings,
He stayed his course, and so returnèd home;
Where such as bare his absence but with grief—
I mean his friends and nearest companions—
Did gratulate his safety with kind words.
And in their conference of what befell,
Touching his journey through the world and air,
They put forth questions of astrology,
Which Faustus answered with such learnèd skill,
As they admired and wondered at his wit.
Now is his fame spread forth in every land:
Amongst the rest the emperor is one,
Carolus the Fifth,[8] at whose palace now
Faustus is feasted 'mongst his noblemen.
What there he did in trial° of his art *demonstration*
I leave untold: your eyes shall see performed. [*Exit.*]

SCENE 9

[*Enter* EMPEROR, FAUSTUS, *and a* KNIGHT, *with Attendants.*]

EMPEROR Master Doctor Faustus, I have heard strange report of thy knowledge in the black art, how that none in my empire, nor in the whole world, can compare with thee for the rare effects of magic. They say thou hast a familiar spirit, by whom thou canst accomplish what thou list! This therefore is my request: that thou let me see some proof of thy skill, that mine eyes may be witnesses to confirm what mine ears have heard reported. And here I swear to thee, by the honor of mine imperial crown, that whatever thou dost, thou shalt be in no ways prejudiced or endamaged.

KNIGHT [*aside*] I'faith, he looks much like a conjuror.

FAUSTUS My gracious sovereign, though I must confess myself far inferior to the report men have published, and nothing answerable

5. Enough. "Brave": splendid.
6. Porridge.
7. I.e., Wagner.
8. The Holy Roman Emperor Charles V (reigned 1519–56).

to the honor of your imperial majesty, yet for that love and duty binds me thereunto, I am content to do whatsoever your majesty shall command me.

EMPEROR Then Doctor Faustus, mark what I shall say. As I was sometime solitary set within my closet,[9] sundry thoughts arose about the honor of mine ancestors—how they had won by prowess such exploits, got such riches, subdued so many kingdoms, as we that do succeed, or they that shall hereafter possess our throne, shall (I fear me) never attain to that degree of high renown and great authority. Amongst which kings is Alexander the Great,[1] chief spectacle of the world's pre-eminence:
The bright shining of whose glorious acts
Lightens the world with his reflecting beams;
As when I hear but motion° made of him, *mention*
It grieves my soul I never saw the man.
If therefore thou, by cunning of thine art,
Canst raise this man from hollow vaults below,
Where lies entombed this famous conqueror,
And bring with him his beauteous paramour,[2]
Both in their right shapes, gesture, and attire
They used to wear during their time of life,
Thou shalt both satisfy my just desire
And give me cause to praise thee whilst I live.

FAUSTUS My gracious lord, I am ready to accomplish your request, so far forth as by art and power of my spirit I am able to perform.

KNIGHT [*aside*] I'faith, that's just nothing at all.

FAUSTUS But, if it like your grace, it is not in my ability to present before your eyes the true substantial bodies of those two deceased princes, which long since are consumed to dust.

KNIGHT [*aside*] Ay, marry,[3] master doctor, now there's a sign of grace in you, when you will confess the truth.

FAUSTUS But such spirits as can lively resemble Alexander and his paramour shall appear before your grace, in that manner that they best lived in, in their most flourishing estate: which I doubt not shall sufficiently content your imperial majesty.

EMPEROR Go to, master doctor, let me see them presently.[4]

KNIGHT Do you hear, master doctor? You bring Alexander and his paramour before the emperor!

FAUSTUS How then, sir?

KNIGHT I'faith, that's as true as Diana turned me to a stag.

FAUSTUS No sir; but when Actaeon died, he left the horns[5] for you! Mephastophilis, begone! [*Exit* MEPHASTOPHILIS.]

KNIGHT Nay, and[6] you go to conjuring I'll be gone. [*Exit* KNIGHT.]

FAUSTUS I'll meet with[7] you anon for interrupting me so. Here they are, my gracious lord.

[*Enter* MEPHASTOPHILIS *with* ALEXANDER *and his* PARAMOUR.]

EMPEROR Master doctor, I heard this lady, while she lived, had a

9. Private chamber.
1. The emperor traces his ancestry to the world conqueror (356–323 B.C.E.).
2. Probably Roxana, Alexander's wife.
3. To be sure.
4. Immediately.
5. Horns were traditionally a sign of the cuckolded husband (cf. Scene 6, lines 14–15). "Actaeon": the hunter of classical legend who happened to see the goddess Diana bathing. For punishment he was changed into a stag; he was then chased and killed by his own hounds.
6. If.
7. Be revenged on.

wart or mole in her neck; how shall I know whether it be so or no?

FAUSTUS Your highness may boldly go and see.

[*The* EMPEROR *examines the lady's neck.*]

EMPEROR Sure, these are no spirits, but the true substantial bodies of those two deceased princes.

[*Exit* ALEXANDER *(and his* PARAMOUR).]

FAUSTUS Will't please your highness now to send for the knight that was so pleasant with me here of late?

EMPEROR One of you call him forth.

[*Enter the* KNIGHT *with a pair of horns on his head.*]

EMPEROR How now, sir knight? Why, I had thought thou hadst been a bachelor, but now I see thou hast a wife that not only gives thee horns but makes thee wear them! Feel on thy head.

KNIGHT Thou damnèd wretch and execrable° dog, *detestable*
Bred in the concave of some monstrous rock,
How dar'st thou thus abuse a gentleman?
Villain, I say, undo what thou hast done.

FAUSTUS O not so fast, sir, there's no haste but good. Are you remembered[8] how you crossed me in my conference with the emperor? I think I have met with you for it.

EMPEROR Good master doctor, at my entreaty release him; he hath done penance sufficient.

FAUSTUS My gracious lord, not so much for the injury he offered me here in your presence as to delight you with some mirth, hath Faustus worthily requited this injurious knight; which being all I desire, I am content to release him of his horns. And, sir knight, hereafter speak well of scholars: Mephastophilis, transform him straight.[9] Now, my good lord, having done my duty, I humbly take my leave.

EMPEROR Farewell, master doctor; yet ere you go, expect from me a bounteous reward.

[*Exit* EMPEROR *(and his* ATTENDANTS).]

FAUSTUS Now, Mephastophilis, the restless course
That time doth run with calm and silent foot,
Shortening my days and thread of vital life,
Calls for the payment of my latest years;
Therefore, sweet Mephastophilis, let us make haste to Wittenberg.

MEPHASTOPHILIS What, will you go on horseback or on foot?

FAUSTUS Nay, till I am past this fair and pleasant green, I'll walk on foot.

SCENE 10

[*Enter a* HORSE-COURSER.[1]]

HORSE-COURSER I have been all this day seeking one Master Fustian: 'mass,[2] see where he is! God save you, master doctor.

FAUSTUS What, horse-courser: you are well met.

HORSE-COURSER Do you hear, sir; I have brought you forty dollars[3] for your horse.

FAUSTUS I cannot sell him so: if thou lik'st him for fifty, take him.

8. Have you forgotten. "No haste but good": a proverb: no point hurrying, unless it's to good effect.
9. Immediately.
1. Horse trader, traditionally a sharp bargainer or cheat.
2. By the Mass. "Fustian": the horse-courser's mispronunciation of Faustus's name.
3. Common German coins.

HORSE-COURSER Alas sir, I have no more. I pray you speak for me.

MEPHASTOPHILIS I pray you let him have him; he is an honest fellow, and he has a great charge[4]—neither wife nor child.

FAUSTUS Well, come, give me your money; my boy will deliver him to you. But I must tell you one thing before you have him: ride him not into the water at any hand.

HORSE-COURSER Why sir, will he not drink of all waters?

FAUSTUS O yes, he will drink of all waters, but ride him not into the water. Ride him over hedge or ditch, or where thou wilt, but not into the water.

HORSE-COURSER Well sir. Now am I made man forever: I'll not leave my horse for forty! If he had but the quality of hey ding ding, hey ding ding,[5] I'd make a brave living on him! He has a buttock as slick as an eel. Well, God b'y,[6] sir; your boy will deliver him me. But hark ye sir, if my horse be sick, or ill at ease, if I bring his water[7] to you, you'll tell me what it is?

[*Exit* HORSE-COURSER.]

FAUSTUS Away, you villain! What, dost think I am a horse-doctor?
What art thou, Faustus, but a man condemned to die?
Thy fatal time doth draw to final end.
Despair doth drive distrust unto my thoughts:
Confound these passions with a quiet sleep.
Tush, Christ did call the thief upon the cross;[8]
Then rest thee, Faustus, quiet in conceit.° *in mind*

[*Sleep in his chair.*]

[*Enter* HORSE-COURSER *all wet, crying.*]

HORSE-COURSER Alas, alas, Doctor Fustian, quoth 'a: 'mass, Doctor Lopus[9] was never such a doctor! H'as given me a purgation, h'as purged me of forty dollars! I shall never see them more. But yet, like an ass as I was, I would not be ruled by him; for he bade me I should ride him into no water. Now I, thinking my horse had had some rare quality that he would not have had me known of, I, like a vent'rous youth, rid him into the deep pond at the town's end. I was no sooner in the middle of the pond, but my horse vanished away, and I sat upon a bottle[1] of hay, never so near drowning in my life! But I'll seek out my doctor, and have my forty dollars again, or I'll make it the dearest[2] horse. O, yonder is his snipper-snapper! Do you hear, you hey-pass,[3] where's your master?

MEPHASTOPHILIS Why, sir, what would you? You cannot speak with him.

HORSE-COURSER But I will speak with him.

MEPHASTOPHILIS Why, he's fast asleep; come some other time.

HORSE-COURSER I'll speak with him now, or I'll break his glass-windows[4] about his ears.

MEPHASTOPHILIS I tell thee, he has not slept this eight nights.

HORSE-COURSER And he have not slept this eight weeks I'll speak with him.

4. Burden.
5. I.e., he wishes his horse were a stallion, not a gelding, so he could put him to stud.
6. Good-bye (contracted from "God be with you").
7. Urine.
8. In Luke 23.39–43 one of the two thieves crucified with Jesus is promised paradise.
9. In February 1594 Roderigo Lopez, the queen's personal physician, was executed for plotting to poison her. Obviously Marlowe, who died in 1593, did not write the line.
1. Bundle.
2. Most expensive.
3. A conjurer's phrase. "Snipper-snapper": insignificant youth, whipper-snapper.
4. Spectacles.

MEPHASTOPHILIS See where he is, fast asleep.

HORSE-COURSER Ay, this is he; God save ye master doctor, master doctor, master Doctor Fustian, forty dollars, forty dollars for a bottle of hay.

MEPHASTOPHILIS Why, thou seest he hears thee not.

HORSE-COURSER So ho ho; so ho ho.[5] [*Halloo in his ear.*] No, will you not wake? I'll make you wake ere I go. [*Pull him by the leg, and pull it away.*] Alas, I am undone! What shall I do?

FAUSTUS O my leg, my leg! Help, Mephastophilis! Call the officers! My leg, my leg!

MEPHASTOPHILIS Come villain, to the constable.

HORSE-COURSER O Lord, sir! Let me go, and I'll give you forty dollars more.

MEPHASTOPHILIS Where be they?

HORSE-COURSER I have none about me: come to my ostry[6] and I'll give them you.

MEPHASTOPHILIS Begone quickly!

[HORSE-COURSER *runs away.*]

FAUSTUS What, is he gone? Farewell he: Faustus has his leg again, and the horse-courser—I take it—a bottle of hay for his labor! Well, this trick shall cost him forty dollars more.

[*Enter* WAGNER.]

How now, Wagner, what's the news with thee?

WAGNER Sir, the duke of Vanholt doth earnestly entreat your company.

FAUSTUS The duke of Vanholt! An honorable gentleman, to whom I must be no niggard of my cunning. Come, Mephastophilis, let's away to him. [*Exeunt.*]

SCENE 11

[FAUSTUS *and* MEPHASTOPHILIS *return to the stage. Enter to them the* DUKE *and the* DUCHESS; *the* DUKE *speaks.*]

DUKE Believe me, master doctor, this merriment hath much pleased me.

FAUSTUS My gracious lord, I am glad it contents you so well: but it may be, madam, you take no delight in this; I have heard that great-bellied women do long for some dainties or other—what is it, madam? Tell me, and you shall have it.

DUCHESS Thanks, good master doctor; and for I see your courteous intent to pleasure me, I will not hide from you the thing my heart desires. And were it now summer, as it is January and the dead of winter, I would desire no better meat than a dish of ripe grapes.

FAUSTUS Alas madam, that's nothing! Mephastophilis, begone! [*Exit* MEPHASTOPHILIS.] Were it a greater thing than this, so it would content you, you should have it. [*Enter* MEPHASTOPHILIS *with the grapes.*] Here they be, madam; will't please you taste on them?

DUKE Believe me, master doctor, this makes me wonder above the rest: that being in the dead time of winter, and in the month of January, how you should come by these grapes?

FAUSTUS If it like your grace, the year is divided into two circles over the whole world, that when it is here winter with us, in the contrary

5. The huntsman's cry, when he sights the quarry.

6. Hostelry, inn.

circle it is summer with them, as in India, Saba,[7] and farther countries in the east; and by means of a swift spirit that I have, I had them brought hither, as ye see. How do you like them, madam; be they good?

DUCHESS Believe me, master doctor, they be the best grapes that ere I tasted in my life before.

FAUSTUS I am glad they content you so, madam.

DUKE Come madam, let us in, where you must well reward this learned man for the great kindness he hath showed to you.

DUCHESS And so I will, my lord; and whilst I live, rest beholding for this courtesy.

FAUSTUS I humbly thank your grace.

DUKE Come, master doctor, follow us, and receive your reward.

[*Exeunt.*]

CHORUS 4

[*Enter* WAGNER *solus.*]

WAGNER I think my master means to die shortly,
For he hath given to me all his goods!
And yet methinks, if that death were near,
He would not banquet, and carouse, and swill
Amongst the students, as even now he doth,
Who are at supper with such belly-cheer
As Wagner ne'er beheld in all his life.
See where they come: belike the feast is ended. [*Exit.*]

SCENE 12

[*Enter* FAUSTUS *(and* MEPHASTOPHILIS*), with two or three* SCHOLARS.]

1 SCHOLAR Master Doctor Faustus, since our conference about fair ladies, which was the beautifulest in all the world, we have determined with ourselves that Helen of Greece was the admirablest lady that ever lived. Therefore, master doctor, if you will do us that favor as to let us see that peerless dame of Greece, whom all the world admires for majesty, we should think ourselves much beholding unto you.

FAUSTUS Gentlemen, for that I know your friendship is unfeigned,
And Faustus' custom is not to deny
The just requests of those that wish him well,
You shall behold that peerless dame of Greece,
No otherways for pomp and majesty
Than when Sir Paris crossed the seas with her
And brought the spoils to rich Dardania.° *Troy*
Be silent then, for danger is in words.
[*Music sounds, and* HELEN *passeth over the stage.*]

2 SCHOLAR Too simple is my wit to tell her praise,
Whom all the world admires for majesty.

3 SCHOLAR No marvel though the angry Greeks pursued
With ten years' war the rape of such a queen,
Whose heavenly beauty passeth all compare.

7. The biblical kingdom of Sheba, in southwestern Arabia.

1 SCHOLAR Since we have seen the pride of Nature's works
And only paragon of excellence,
Let us depart; and for this glorious deed
Happy and blest be Faustus evermore.
FAUSTUS Gentlemen farewell; the same I wish to you.
[*Exeunt* SCHOLARS.]
[*Enter an* OLD MAN.]
OLD MAN Ah Doctor Faustus, that I might prevail
To guide thy steps unto the way of life,
By which sweet path thou may'st attain the goal
That shall conduct thee to celestial rest.
Break heart, drop blood, and mingle it with tears,
Tears falling from repentant heaviness
Of thy most vile and loathsome filthiness,
The stench whereof corrupts the inward soul
With such flagitious° crimes of heinous sins, *villainous*
As no commiseration may expel
But mercy, Faustus, of thy savior sweet,
Whose blood alone must wash away thy guilt.
FAUSTUS Where art thou, Faustus? Wretch, what hast thou done!
Damned art thou, Faustus, damned; despair and die!
Hell calls for right, and with a roaring voice
Says, "Faustus, come: thine hour is come!"
[MEPHASTOPHILIS *gives him a dagger.*]
And Faustus will come to do thee right.
OLD MAN Ah stay, good Faustus, stay thy desperate steps!
I see an angel hovers o'er thy head
And with a vial full of precious grace
Offers to pour the same into thy soul!
Then call for mercy, and avoid despair.
FAUSTUS Ah my sweet friend, I feel thy words
To comfort my distressed soul;
Leave me awhile to ponder on my sins.
OLD MAN I go, sweet Faustus; but with heavy cheer,° *heavy heart*
Fearing the ruin of thy hopeless soul. [*Exit.*]
FAUSTUS Accursèd Faustus, where is mercy now?
I do repent, and yet I do despair:
Hell strives with grace for conquest in my breast!
What shall I do to shun the snares of death?
MEPHASTOPHILIS Thou traitor, Faustus: I arrest thy soul
For disobedience to my sovereign lord.
Revolt,[8] or I'll in piecemeal tear thy flesh.
FAUSTUS Sweet Mephastophilis, entreat thy lord
To pardon my unjust presumptiön;
And with my blood again I will confirm
My former vow I made to Lucifer.
MEPHASTOPHILIS Do it then quickly, with unfeignèd heart,
Lest greater danger do attend thy drift.° *intent*
FAUSTUS Torment, sweet friend, that base and crooked age
That durst dissuade me from thy Lucifer,
With greatest torments that our hell affords.
MEPHASTOPHILIS His faith is great, I cannot touch his soul,

8. Turn back (to your allegiance to Lucifer).

But what I may afflict his body with
I will attempt—which is but little worth.
FAUSTUS One thing, good servant, let me crave of thee,
To glut the longing of my heart's desire:
That I might have unto° my paramour *for*
That heavenly Helen which I saw of late,
Whose sweet embracings may extinguish clean
These thoughts that do dissuade me from my vow:
And keep mine oath I made to Lucifer.
MEPHASTOPHILIS Faustus, this, or what else thou shalt desire,
Shall be performed in twinkling of an eye.
[*Enter* HELEN.]
FAUSTUS Was this the face that launched a thousand ships,
And burnt the topless[9] towers of Ilium?° *Troy*
Sweet Helen, make me immortal with a kiss:
Her lips sucks forth my soul, see where it flies!
Come Helen, come, give me my soul again.
Here will I dwell, for heaven be in these lips,
And all is dross that is not Helena!
[*Enter* OLD MAN.]
I will be Paris, and for love of thee,
Instead of Troy shall Wittenberg be sacked;
And I will combat with weak Menelaus,° *Helen's husband*
And wear thy colors on my plumèd crest:
Yea, I will wound Achilles in the heel,[1]
And then return to Helen for a kiss.
O thou art fairer than the evening air,
Clad in the beauty of a thousand stars,
Brighter art thou than flaming Jupiter
When he appeared to hapless Semele;[2]
More lovely than the monarch of the sky
In wanton Arethusa's azured arms;[3]
And none but thou shalt be my paramour.
[*Exeunt* (FAUSTUS *and* HELEN).]
OLD MAN Accursèd Faustus, miserable man,
That from thy soul exclud'st the grace of heaven
And fliest the throne of His tribunal seat!
[*Enter the* DEVILS.]
Satan begins to sift me with his pride,[4]
As in this furnace God shall try my faith.
My faith, vile hell, shall triumph over thee!
Ambitious fiends, see how the heavens smiles
At your repulse, and laughs your state° to scorn. *royal power*
Hence hell, for hence I fly unto my God.
[*Exeunt.*]

9. Immeasurably high; matchless.
1. Achilles could only be wounded in his heel—where he was shot by Paris.
2. A Theban girl, loved by Jupiter and destroyed by the fire of his lightning when he appeared to her in his full splendor.
3. Arethusa was the nymph of a fountain, as well as the fountain itself; she excited the passion of the river god Alpheus, who was by some accounts related to the sun.
4. To test me with his strength.

SCENE 13

[*Enter* FAUSTUS *with the* SCHOLARS.]

FAUSTUS Ah, gentlemen!

1 SCHOLAR What ails Faustus?

FAUSTUS Ah, my sweet chamber-fellow, had I lived with thee, then had I lived still; but now I die eternally. Look, comes he not, comes he not?

2 SCHOLAR What means Faustus?

3 SCHOLAR Belike he is grown into some sickness by being oversolitary.

1 SCHOLAR If it be so, we'll have physicians to cure him; 'tis but a surfeit:[5] never fear, man.

FAUSTUS A surfeit of deadly sin, that hath damned both body and soul.

2 SCHOLAR Yet Faustus, look up to heaven; remember God's mercies are infinite.

FAUSTUS But Faustus' offense can ne'er be pardoned! The serpent that tempted Eve may be saved, but not Faustus. Ah gentlemen, hear me with patience, and tremble not at my speeches, though my heart pants and quivers to remember that I have been a student here these thirty years—O would I had never seen Wittenberg, never read book—and what wonders I have done, all Wittenberg can witness—yea, all the world; for which Faustus hath lost both Germany and the world—yea, heaven itself—heaven, the seat of God, the throne of the blessed, the kingdom of joy; and must remain in hell forever—hell, ah, hell forever! Sweet friends, what shall become of Faustus, being in hell forever?

3 SCHOLAR Yet Faustus, call on God.

FAUSTUS On God, whom Faustus hath abjured? On God, whom Faustus hath blasphemed? Ah my God—I would weep, but the devil draws in my tears! gush forth blood, instead of tears—yea, life and soul! O, he stays my tongue! I would lift up my hands, but see, they hold them, they hold them!

ALL Who, Faustus?

FAUSTUS Lucifer and Mephastophilis! Ah gentlemen, I gave them my soul for my cunning.

ALL God forbid!

FAUSTUS God forbade it indeed, but Faustus hath done it: for the vain pleasure of four-and-twenty years hath Faustus lost eternal joy and felicity. I writ them a bill[6] with mine own blood, the date is expired, the time will come, and he will fetch me.

1 SCHOLAR Why did not Faustus tell us of this before, that divines might have prayed for thee?

FAUSTUS Oft have I thought to have done so, but the devil threatened to tear me in pieces if I named God, to fetch both body and soul, if I once gave ear to divinity; and now 'tis too late. Gentlemen, away, lest you perish with me!

2 SCHOLAR O what shall we do to save Faustus?

3 SCHOLAR God will strengthen me. I will stay with Faustus.

1 SCHOLAR Tempt not God, sweet friend, but let us into the next room, and there pray for him.

5. Indigestion caused by overeating.

6. Document.

FAUSTUS Ay, pray for me, pray for me; and what noise soever ye hear, come not unto me, for nothing can rescue me.

2 SCHOLAR Pray thou, and we will pray, that God may have mercy upon thee.

FAUSTUS Gentlemen, farewell. If I live till morning, I'll visit you; if not, Faustus is gone to hell.

ALL Faustus, farewell. [*Exeunt* SCHOLARS.]

[*The clock strikes eleven.*]

FAUSTUS Ah Faustus,
Now hast thou but one bare hour to live,
And then thou must be damned perpetually.
Stand still, you ever-moving spheres of heaven,
That time may cease, and midnight never come.
Fair Nature's eye, rise, rise again, and make
Perpetual day, or let this hour be but
A year, a month, a week, a natural day,
That Faustus may repent and save his soul.
O lente, lente currite noctis equi![7]
The stars move still, time runs, the clock will strike,
The devil will come, and Faustus must be damned.
O I'll leap up to my God! Who pulls me down?
See, see where Christ's blood streams in the firmament!° *sky*
One drop would save my soul, half a drop: ah my Christ—
Ah, rend not my heart for naming of my Christ;
Yet will I call on him—O spare me, Lucifer!
Where is it now? 'Tis gone: and see where God
Stretcheth out his arm, and bends his ireful brows!
Mountains and hills, come, come and fall on me,
And hide me from the heavy wrath of God.
No, no?
Then will I headlong run into the earth:
Earth, gape! O no, it will not harbor me.
You stars that reigned at my nativity,
Whose influence hath allotted death and hell,
Now draw up Faustus like a foggy mist
Into the entrails of yon laboring cloud,
That when you vomit forth into the air
My limbs may issue from your smoky mouths,
So that my soul may but ascend to heaven.[8]

[*The watch strikes.*]

Ah, half the hour is past: 'twill all be past anon.
O God, if thou wilt not have mercy on my soul,
Yet for Christ's sake, whose blood hath ransomed me,
Impose some end to my incessant pain:
Let Faustus live in hell a thousand years,
A hundred thousand, and at last be saved.
O no end is limited to damnèd souls!
Why wert thou not a creature wanting° soul? *lacking*
Or why is this immortal that thou hast?
Ah, Pythagoras' *metempsychosis*[9]—were that true,

7. "Slowly, slowly run, O horses of the night"; adapted from a line in Ovid's *Amores*.
8. Faustus wants to be drawn up into a cloud, which would compact his body into a thunderbolt so that his soul, thus purified, might ascend to heaven.
9. Pythagoras's doctrine of the transmigration of souls.

This soul should fly from me, and I be changed
Unto some brutish beast:
All beasts are happy, for when they die,
Their souls are soon dissolved in elements;
But mine must live still° to be plagued in hell. *always*
Cursed be the parents that engendered me:
No, Faustus, curse thy self, curse Lucifer,
That hath deprived thee of the joys of heaven.
[*The clock striketh twelve.*]
O it strikes, it strikes! Now body, turn to air,
Or Lucifer will bear thee quick° to hell. *alive*
[*Thunder and lightning.*]
O soul, be changed into little water drops,
And fall into the ocean, ne'er be found.
My God, my God, look not so fierce on me!
[*Enter* DEVILS.]
Adders and serpents, let me breathe awhile!
Ugly hell gape not! Come not, Lucifer!
I'll burn my books—ah, Mephastophilis!
[*Exeunt with him.*]

Epilogue

[*Enter* CHORUS.]
Cut is the branch that might have grown full straight,
And burnèd is Apollo's laurel bough,[1]
That sometime grew within this learnèd man.
Faustus is gone! Regard his hellish fall,
Whose fiendful fortune° may exhort the wise *devilish fate*
Only to wonder at[2] unlawful things:
Whose deepness doth entice such forward wits° *aspiring minds*
To practice more than heavenly power permits.
[*Exit.*]

Terminat hora diem, terminat author opus.[3]

1604, 1616

1. The laurel crown of Apollo symbolizes (among other things) learning and wisdom.
2. Be content simply to observe with awe.
3. "The hour ends the day, the author ends his work"; this motto was probably added by the printer.

WILLIAM SHAKESPEARE
1564–1616

William Shakespeare was born in the small market town of Stratford-on-Avon in April (probably April 23) 1564. His father, a successful glovemaker, landowner, money-lender, and dealer in agricultural commodities, was elected to several important posts in local government but later suffered financial and social reverses, possibly as a result of adherence to the Catholic faith. Shakespeare almost certainly attended the free

Stratford grammar school, where he could have acquired a reasonably impressive education, including a respectable knowledge of Latin, but he did not proceed to Oxford or Cambridge. There are legends about Shakespeare's youth but no documented facts. Some scholars are tempted to associate him with "William Shakeshafte," a young actor attached to a recusant Catholic circle in Lancashire around 1581; one of Shakespeare's former Stratford schoolmasters belonged to this circle. But the first unambiguous record we have of his life after his christening is that of his marriage in 1582, at age eighteen, to Anne Hathaway, eight years his senior. A daughter, Susanna, was born six months later, in 1583, and twins, Hamnet and Judith, in 1585. We possess no information about his activities for the next seven years, but by 1592 he was in London as an actor and apparently already well known as a playwright, for a rival dramatist, Robert Greene, refers to him resentfully in *A Groatsworth of Wit* as "an upstart crow, beautified with our feathers."

At this time, there were several companies of professional actors in London and in the provinces. What connection Shakespeare had with one or more of them before 1592 is conjectural, but we do know of his long and fruitful connection with the most successful troupe, the Lord Chamberlain's Men, who later, when James I came to the throne, became the King's Men. Shakespeare not only acted with this company but eventually became a leading shareholder and the principal playwright. Then as now, making a living in the professional theater was not easy: competition among the repertoire companies was stiff, civic officials and religious moralists regarded playacting as a sinful, time-wasting nuisance and tried to ban it altogether, government officials exercised censorship over the contents of the plays, and periodic outbreaks of bubonic plague led to temporary closing of the London theaters. But Shakespeare's company, which included some of the most famous actors of the day, nonetheless thrived and in 1599 began to perform in the Globe, a fine, open-air theater that the company built for itself on the south bank of the Thames. The company also performed frequently at court and, after 1608, at Blackfriars, an indoor London theater. Already by 1597 Shakespeare had so prospered that he was able to purchase New Place, a handsome house in Stratford; he could now call himself a gentleman, as his father had (probably with the financial assistance of his successful playwright son) been granted a coat of arms the previous year. Shakespeare's wife and daughters (his son, Hamnet, having died in 1596) resided in Stratford, while the playwright, living in rented rooms in London, pursued his career. Shortly after writing *The Tempest* (ca. 1611), he retired from direct involvement in the theater and returned to Stratford. In March 1616, he signed his will; he died a month later, leaving the bulk of his estate to his daughter Susanna. To his wife of thirty-four years, he left "my second best bed."

Shakespeare began his career as a playwright, probably in the early 1590s, by writing comedies and history plays. The earliest of these histories, generally based on accounts of English kings written by Raphael Holinshed and other sixteenth-century chroniclers, seem theatrically vital but crude, as does an early attempt at tragedy, *Titus Andronicus*. But Shakespeare quickly moved on to create by the later 1590s a sequence of profoundly searching and ambitious history plays—*Richard II*, the first and second parts of *Henry IV*, and *Henry V*—which together explore the death throes of feudal England and the birth of the modern nation-state ruled by a charismatic monarch. In the same years he wrote a succession of romantic comedies (*The Merchant of Venice, The Merry Wives of Windsor, Much Ado About Nothing, As You Like It, Twelfth Night*) whose poetic richness and emotional complexity remain unmatched.

Twelfth Night was probably written in the same year as *Hamlet* (ca. 1601), which initiated an outpouring of great tragic dramas: *Othello, King Lear, Macbeth, Antony and Cleopatra*, and *Coriolanus*. These plays, written from 1601 to 1607, seem to mark a major shift in sensibility, an existential and metaphysical darkening that many readers think must have originated in personal anguish. Whatever the truth of this speculation—and we have no direct, personal testimony either to support or to undermine it—there appears to have occurred in the same period a shift as well in Shakespeare's comic sensibility. The comedies written between 1601 and 1604, *Troilus and Cressida, All's Well That Ends Well,* and *Measure for Measure*, are sufficiently different from the earlier comedies—more biting in tone, more uneasy with comic conventions, more ruthlessly questioning of the values of the characters and the resolutions of the plots—to have led some modern scholars to classify them as "problem plays" or "dark comedies." Another group of plays, among the last that Shakespeare wrote, seem similarly to define a distinct category. *Pericles, Cymbeline, The Winter's Tale*, and *The Tempest,* written between 1608 and 1611, when Shakespeare had developed a remarkably fluid, dream-like sense of plot and a poetic style that could veer, apparently effortlessly, from the tortured to the ineffably sweet, are now commonly known as the "romances." These plays share an interest in the moral and emotional life less of the adolescents who dominate the earlier comedies than of their parents. The "romances" are deeply concerned with patterns of loss and recovery, suffering and redemption, despair and renewal. They have seemed to many critics to constitute a self-conscious conclusion to a career that opened with histories and comedies and passed through the dark and tormented tragedies.

Shakespeare himself apparently had no interest in preserving for posterity the sum of his writings, let alone in clarifying the chronology of his works or in specifying which plays he wrote alone and which with collaborators. He wrote plays for performance by his company, and his scripts existed in his own handwritten manuscripts or in scribal copies, in playhouse prompt books, and probably in pirated texts based on shorthand reports of a performance or on reconstructions from memory by an actor or spectator. None of these manuscript versions has survived. Eighteen of his plays were published during his lifetime in the small-format, inexpensive books called quartos; to these were added eighteen other plays, never before printed, in the large, expensive folio volume of *Mr. William Shakespeares Comedies, Histories, & Tragedies* (1623), published seven years after his death. This First Folio, edited by two of his friends and fellow actors, John Heminges and Henry Condell, is prefaced by a poem of Ben Jonson's, in which Shakespeare is hailed, presciently, as "not of an age, but for all time."

That Shakespeare is "for all time" does not mean that he did not also belong to his own age. It is possible to see where Shakespeare adapted the techniques of his contemporaries and where, crucially, he differed from them. Shakespeare rarely invented the plots of his dramas, preferring to work, often quite closely, with stories he found ready-made in histories, novellas, narrative poems, or other plays. The religious mystery plays and the allegorical morality plays still popular during his childhood taught him that dramas worth seeing must get at something central to the human condition, that they should embody as well as narrate the crucial actions, and that they could reach not only a coterie of the educated elite but also the great mass of ordinary people. From these and other theatrical models, Shakespeare learned how to construct plays around the struggle for the soul of a protagonist, how to create theatrically compelling and subversive figures of wickedness, and how to focus attention on his characters' psychological, moral, and spiritual lives, as well as on their outward behavior.

The authors of the morality plays thought that they could enhance the broad impact they sought to achieve by stripping their characters of all incidental distinguishing traits and getting to their essences. They thought that their audiences would thereby not be distracted by the irrelevant details of individual identities. Shakespeare grasped that the spectacle of human destiny was in fact vastly more compelling when it was attached not to generalized abstractions but to particular people, people whom he realized with an unprecedented intensity of individuation: not Youth but Viola, not Everyman but Lear. No other writer of his time was able to create and enter into the interior worlds of so many characters, conveying again and again a sense of unique and irreducible selfhood. In the plays of Shakespeare's brilliant contemporary Marlowe, the protagonist overwhelms virtually all of the other characters; in Shakespeare, by contrast, even relatively minor characters—Maria in *Twelfth Night*, for example, or the fool in *King Lear*—make astonishingly powerful claims on the audience's attention. The Romantic critic William Hazlitt observed that Shakespeare had the power to multiply himself marvelously. His plays convey the sense of an inexhaustible imaginative generosity.

Shakespeare was singularly alert to the fantastic vitality of the English language. His immense vocabulary bears witness to an uncanny ability to absorb terms from a wide range of pursuits and to transform them into intimate registers of thought and feeling. He had a seemingly boundless capacity to generate metaphors, and he was virtually addicted to word play. Double-meanings, verbal echoes, and submerged associations ripple through every passage, deepening the reader's enjoyment and understanding, though sometimes at the expense of a single clear sense. The eighteenth-century critic Samuel Johnson complained with some justice that the quibble, the pun, was "the fatal Cleopatra for which Shakespeare lost the world and was content to lose it." For the power that continually discharges itself throughout his plays and poems, at once constituting and unsettling everything it touches, is the polymorphous power of language.

Anachronism is rarely a concern for Shakespeare. His ancient Romans throw their caps into the air and use Christian oaths: to this extent he pulled everything he touched into his contemporary existence. But at the same time he was not a social realist; other writers in this period are better at conveying the precise details of the daily lives of shoemakers, alchemists, and judges. The settings of his plays—"Illyria" in *Twelfth Night*, for example, or ancient Britain in *King Lear*—were for Shakespeare not realistic representations of particular historical times and places but rather imaginative displacements into alternative worlds that remain strangely familiar.

Though on occasion he depicts ghosts, demons, and other supernatural figures, the universe Shakespeare conjures up seems resolutely human-centered and secular: the torments and joys that most deeply matter are found in this world, not in the next. Attempts to claim him for one or another religious system have proven unconvincing, as have attempts to assign him a specific political label. Activists and ideologues of all political stripes have viewed him as an ally: he has been admiringly quoted by kings and by revolutionaries, by fascists, liberal democrats, socialists, republicans, and communists. At once an agent of civility and an agent of subversion, Shakespeare seems to have been able to view society simultaneously as an insider and as an outsider. His plays can be interpreted and performed—with deep conviction and compelling power—in utterly contradictory ways. The centuries-long accumulation of these interpretations and performances, far from exhausting Shakespeare's aesthetic appeal, seems only to have enhanced its perennial freshness.*

Sonnets

In Elizabethan England aristocratic patronage, with the money, protection, and prestige it alone could provide, was probably a professional writer's most important asset. This patronage, or at least Shakespeare's quest for it, is most visible in his dedication in 1593 and 1594 of his narrative poems, *Venus and Adonis* and *The Rape of Lucrece*, to the wealthy young nobleman Henry Wriothesley, earl of Southampton. What return the poet got for his exquisite offerings is unknown. We do know that among wits and gallants the narrative poems won Shakespeare a fine reputation as an immensely stylish and accomplished poet. This reputation was enhanced as well by manuscript circulation of his sonnets, which were mentioned admiringly in print more than ten years before they were published in 1609 (apparently without his personal supervision and perhaps without his consent).

Shakespeare's sonnets are quite unlike the other sonnet sequences of his day,

*For additional writings by Shakespeare—including the full text of *The First Part of King Henry IV*, Ulysses' speech on degree from *Troilus and Cressida*, a collection of songs from the plays, five additional sonnets (nos. 56, 104, 118, 121, 124), and the philosophical poem "The Phoenix and the Turtle"—go to Norton Literature Online. See the color insert in this volume for the "Chandos" portrait of Shakespeare and a portrait of Henry Wriothesley, third earl of Southampton and possibly the dedicatee of Shakespeare's *Sonnets*.

notably in his almost unprecedented choice of a beautiful young man (rather than a lady) as the principal object of praise, love, and idealizing devotion and in his portrait of a dark, sensuous, and sexually promiscuous mistress (rather than the usual chaste and aloof blond beauty). Nor are the moods confined to what the Renaissance thought were those of the despairing Petrarchan lover: they include delight, pride, melancholy, shame, disgust, and fear. Shakespeare's sequence suggests a story, although the details are vague, and there is even doubt whether the sonnets as published are in an order established by the poet himself. Certain motifs are evident: an introductory series (1 to 17) celebrates the beauty of a young man and urges him to marry and beget children who will bear his image. The subsequent long sequence (18 to 126), passionately focused on the beloved young man, develops as a dominant motif the transience and destructive power of time, countered only by the force of love and the permanence of poetry. The remaining sonnets focus chiefly on the so-called Dark Lady as an alluring but degrading object of desire. Some sonnets (like 144) intimate a love triangle involving the speaker, the male friend, and the woman; others take note of a rival poet (sometimes identified as George Chapman or Christopher Marlowe). The biographical background of the sonnets has inspired a mountain of speculation, but very little of it has any factual support.

Though there are many variations, Shakespeare's most frequent rhyme scheme in the sonnets is *abab cdcd efef gg*. This so-called Shakespearean pattern often (though not always) calls attention to three distinct quatrains (each of which may develop a separate metaphor), followed by a closing couplet that may either confirm or pull sharply against what has gone before. Startling shifts in direction may occur in lines other than the closing ones; consider, for example, the twists and turns in the opening lines of sonnet 138: "When my love swears that she is made of truth, / I do believe her, though I know she lies." Shakespeare's sonnets as a whole are strikingly intense, conveying a sense of high psychological and moral stakes. They are also remarkably dense, written with a daunting energy, concentration, and compression. Often the main idea of the poem may be grasped quickly, but the precise movement of thought and feeling, the links among the shifting images, the syntax, tone, and rhetorical structure prove immensely challenging. These are poems that famously reward rereading.

Sonnets

To the Only Begetter of
These Ensuing Sonnets
Mr. W. H. All Happiness
and That Eternity
Promised
By
Our Ever-Living Poet
Wisheth
The Well-Wishing
Adventurer in
Setting Forth
T. T.[1]

1. This odd dedication bears the initials of the publisher, Thomas Thorpe. The W. H. addressed here may or may not be the male friend addressed in sonnets 1 to 126. Leading candidates for that role are Henry Wriothesley, earl of Southampton, the dedicatee of *Venus and Adonis* (1593) and *The Rape of Lucrece* (1594), and William Herbert, earl of Pembroke, a dedicatee of the First Folio. But there is no hard evidence to support these or other suggested identifications of the male friend or of the so-called Dark Lady; these sonnet personages may or may not have had real-life counterparts.

Since all the sonnets save two were first published in 1609, we do not repeat the date after each

3

Look in thy glass° and tell the face thou viewest *mirror*
Now is the time that face should form another,
Whose fresh repair if now thou not renewest,
Thou dost beguile° the world, unbless some mother. *cheat*
For where is she so fair whose uneared° womb *unplowed*
Disdains the tillage of thy husbandry?
Or who is he so fond° will be the tomb *foolish*
Of his self-love, to stop posterity?
Thou art thy mother's glass, and she in thee
Calls back the lovely April of her prime;
So thou through windows of thine age shalt see,
Despite of wrinkles, this thy golden time.
  But if thou live rememb'red not to be,
  Die single, and thine image dies with thee.

12

When I do count the clock that tells the time
And see the brave° day sunk in hideous night, *splendid*
When I behold the violet past prime
And sable curls all silvered o'er with white,
When lofty trees I see barren of leaves,
Which erst° from heat did canopy the herd *formerly*
And summer's green all girded up in sheaves
Borne on the bier with white and bristly beard:
Then of thy beauty do I question make° *speculate*
That thou among the wastes of time must go,
Since sweets and beauties do themselves forsake,
And die as fast as they see others grow,
  And nothing 'gainst Time's scythe can make defense
  Save breed, to brave[2] him when he takes thee hence.

15

When I consider every thing that grows
Holds° in perfection but a little moment; *remains*
That this huge stage presenteth nought but shows
Whereon the stars in secret influence comment;[3]
When I perceive that men as plants increase,
Cheered and checked[4] even by the selfsame sky,
Vaunt[5] in their youthful sap, at height decrease,
And wear their brave state out of memory;[6]
Then the conceit° of this inconstant stay *conception*
Sets you most rich in youth before my sight,

---

one. Numbers 138 and 144 were first published in 1599, in a verse miscellany called *The Passionate Pilgrim*.
2. Defy. "Breed": offspring.
3. The stars secretly affect human actions. "Shows": (1) appearances, (2) performances.
4. Encouraged and reproached or stopped.
5. Exult, display themselves.
6. Wear their showy splendor out and are forgotten.

Where wasteful Time debateth[7] with Decay
To change your day of youth to sullied° night, *soiled, blackened*
And all in war with Time for love of you,
As he takes from you, I ingraft[8] you new.

18

Shall I compare thee to a summer's day?
Thou art more lovely and more temperate:
Rough winds do shake the darling buds of May,
And summer's lease hath all too short a date;
Sometime too hot the eye of heaven shines,
And often is his gold complexion dimmed;
And every fair from fair sometime declines,
By chance or nature's changing course untrimmed.[9]
But thy eternal summer shall not fade,
Nor lose possession of that fair thou ow'st;° *ownest*
Nor shall death brag thou wander'st in his shade,
When in eternal lines to time thou grow'st:° *are grafted*
So long as men can breathe or eyes can see,
So long lives this,[1] and this gives life to thee.

19

Devouring Time, blunt thou the lion's paws,
And make the earth devour her own sweet brood;
Pluck the keen teeth from the fierce tiger's jaws,
And burn the long-lived phoenix in her blood;[2]
Make glad and sorry seasons as thou fleet'st,
And do whate'er thou wilt, swift-footed Time,
To the wide world and all her fading sweets,
But I forbid thee one most heinous crime:
O carve not with thy hours my love's fair brow,
Nor draw no lines there with thine antique[3] pen;
Him in thy course untainted[4] do allow,
For beauty's pattern to succeeding men.
Yet do thy worst, old Time: despite thy wrong,
My love shall in my verse ever live young.

20

A woman's face with Nature's own hand painted[5]
Hast thou, the master mistress of my passion;[6]
A woman's gentle heart but not acquainted
With shifting change as is false women's fashion;
An eye more bright than theirs, less false in rolling,° *roving*

7. (1)Fights, (2) joins forces.
8. Renew by grafting, implant beauty again (by my verse).
9. Stripped of gay apparel.
1. I.e., the poem. The boast of immortality for one's verse was a convention going back to the Greek and Roman classics.
2. In full vigor of life (a hunting term). The phoenix was a mythical bird that lived five hundred years, then died in flames to rise again from its ashes.
3. (1) Old, (2) fantastic (antic).
4. (1) Undefiled, (2) untouched by a weapon (a term from jousting).
5. I.e., not made up with cosmetics.
6. (1) Strong feeling, (2) poem.

Gilding the object whereupon it gazeth;
A man in hue all hues[7] in his controlling,
Which steals men's eyes and women's souls amazeth.
And for a woman wert thou first created,
Till Nature as she wrought thee fell a-doting,[8]
And by addition me of thee defeated,
By adding one thing to my purpose nothing.
But since she pricked[9] thee out for women's pleasure,
Mine be thy love, and thy love's use their treasure.[1]

23

As an unperfect actor on the stage
Who with his fear is put besides° his part, *forgets*
Or some fierce thing replete with too much rage
Whose strength's abundance weakens his own heart,
So I, for fear of trust,° forget to say *lack of confidence*
The perfect ceremony of love's rite.[2]
And in mine own love's strength seem to decay,
O'er-charged° with burden of mine own love's might. *overweighed*
O let my books be then the eloquence
And dumb presagers° of my speaking breast, *mute presenters*
Who plead for love, and look for recompense
More than that tongue that more hath more expressed.[3]
O learn to read what silent love hath writ;
To hear with eyes belongs to love's fine wit.° *intelligence*

29

When, in disgrace° with Fortune and men's eyes, *disfavor*
I all alone beweep my outcast state,
And trouble deaf heaven with my bootless° cries, *futile*
And look upon myself and curse my fate,
Wishing me like to one more rich in hope,
Featured like him, like him with friends possessed,[4]
Desiring this man's art° and that man's scope,° *skill / ability*
With what I most enjoy contented least;
Yet in these thoughts myself almost despising,
Haply I think on thee, and then my state[5]
(Like to the lark at break of day arising
From sullen earth) sings hymns at heaven's gate;
For thy sweet love remembered such wealth brings
That then I scorn to change my state with kings.

7. "Hue" probably means appearance or form. In the first edition, "hues" is spelled "*Hews*," which some have taken as indicating a pun on a proper name. It has also been suggested that "man in" is a copyist's or compositor's misreading of "maiden."
8. (1) Crazy, (2) infatuated.
9. Marked, with obvious sexual pun.
1. (1) Sexual enjoyment, (2) interest (as in usury).
2. The first edition has "right," suggesting love's due as well as love's ritual ("rite").
3. More than that (rival) speaker who has more often said more.
4. I.e., I wish I had one man's looks, another man's friends.
5. Condition, state of mind; but in line 14 there is a pun on *state* meaning chair of state, throne.

30

When to the sessions[6] of sweet silent thought
I summon up remembrance of things past,
I sigh the lack of many a thing I sought,
And with old woes new wail° my dear time's waste: *bewail anew*
Then can I drown an eye (unused to flow)
For precious friends hid in death's dateless° night, *endless*
And weep afresh love's long since canceled woe,
And moan th' expense° of many a vanished sight: *loss*
Then can I grieve at grievances foregone,° *former*
And heavily from woe to woe tell° o'er *count*
The sad account of fore-bemoanèd moan,
Which I new pay as if not paid before.
  But if the while I think on thee, dear friend,
  All losses are restored and sorrows end.

33

Full many a glorious morning have I seen
Flatter the mountain tops with sovereign eye,° *sunlight*
Kissing with golden face the meadows green,
Gilding pale streams with heavenly alchemy;
Anon° permit the basest° clouds to ride *(but) soon / darkest*
With ugly rack° on his celestial face, *cloudy mask*
And from the forlorn world his visage hide,
Stealing unseen to west with this disgrace.
Even so my sun one early morn did shine
With all triumphant splendor on my brow;
But out, alack,° he was but one hour mine; *alas*
The region° cloud hath masked him from me now. *high*
  Yet him for this my love no whit disdaineth:
  Suns of the world may stain° when heaven's sun staineth. *darken*

55

Not marble, nor the gilded monuments
Of princes, shall outlive this powerful rhyme;
But you shall shine more bright in these contents
Than unswept stone, besmeared with sluttish time.[7]
When wasteful war shall statues overturn,
And broils° root out the work of masonry, *battles*
Nor Mars his° sword nor war's quick fire shall burn *neither Mars's*
The living record of your memory.
'Gainst death and all-oblivious enmity[8]
Shall you pace forth; your praise shall still find room
Even in the eyes of all posterity
That wear this world out to the ending doom.° *Judgment Day*

6. Sittings of court. "Summon up" (next line) continues the metaphor.
7. I.e., than in a stone tomb or effigy that time wears away and covers with dust. "Sluttish": slovenly.
8. The enmity of oblivion, of being forgotten.

So, till the judgment that yourself arise,[9]
You live in this, and dwell in lovers' eyes.

60

Like as the waves make towards the pebbled shore,
So do our minutes hasten to their end;
Each changing place with that which goes before,
In sequent toil all forwards do contend.[1]
Nativity, once in the main° of light, *broad expanse*
Crawls to maturity, wherewith being crowned,
Crooked eclipses 'gainst his glory fight,
And Time that gave doth now his gift confound.
Time doth transfix the flourish set on youth
And delves the parallels[2] in beauty's brow,
Feeds on the rarities of nature's truth,
And nothing stands but for his scythe to mow.
And yet to times in hope° my verse shall stand, *future times*
Praising thy worth, despite his cruel hand.

62

Sin of self-love possesseth all mine eye,
And all my soul, and all my every part;
And for this sin there is no remedy,
It is so grounded inward in my heart.
Methinks no face so gracious° is as mine, *pleasing*
No shape so true,° no truth of such account, *perfect*
And for myself mine own worth do define
As° I all other° in all worths surmount. *as if / others*
But when my glass° shows me myself indeed, *mirror*
Beated and chapped with tanned antiquity,
Mine own self-love quite contrary° I read; *differently*
Self so self-loving were iniquity.
'Tis thee, my self,° that for° myself I praise, *you, my other self / as*
Painting my age with beauty of thy days.

65

Since[3] brass, nor stone, nor earth, nor boundless sea,
But sad mortality o'ersways their power,
How with this rage° shall beauty hold a plea, *destructive power*
Whose action is no stronger than a flower?
O how shall summer's honey breath hold out
Against the wrackful° siege of batt'ring days, *destructive*
When rocks impregnable are not so stout,
Nor gates of steel so strong, but Time decays?

9. Until you rise from the dead on Judgment Day.
1. Toiling and following each other, all struggle to move forward.
2. Digs the parallel furrows (wrinkles). "Transfix the flourish": remove the embellishment. To "flourish" is also to blossom.
3. I.e., because there is neither.

O fearful meditation! where, alack,
Shall Time's best jewel from Time's chest[4] lie hid?
Or what strong hand can hold his swift foot back?
Or who his spoil° of beauty can forbid? *ravaging*
O none, unless this miracle have might,
That in black ink my love may still shine bright.

71

No longer mourn for me when I am dead
Than you shall hear the surly sullen bell[5]
Give warning to the world that I am fled
From this vile world, with vilest worms to dwell:
Nay, if you read this line, remember not
The hand that writ it; for I love you so,
That I in your sweet thoughts would be forgot,
If thinking on me then should make you woe.
Oh, if, I say, you look upon this verse
When I perhaps compounded am with clay,
Do not so much as my poor name rehearse,° *repeat*
But let your love even with my life decay;
Lest the wise world should look into your moan,
And mock you with me after I am gone.

73

That time of year thou mayst in me behold
When yellow leaves, or none, or few, do hang
Upon those boughs which shake against the cold,
Bare ruined choirs,[6] where late° the sweet birds sang. *lately*
In me thou seest the twilight of such day
As after sunset fadeth in the west;
Which by and by black night doth take away,
Death's second self that seals up all in rest.
In me thou seest the glowing of such fire
That on the ashes of his youth doth lie,
As the deathbed whereon it must expire,
Consumed with that which it was nourished by.[7]
This thou perceiv'st, which makes thy love more strong,
To love that well, which thou must leave ere long.

80

O, how I faint° when I of you do write, *get discouraged*
Knowing a better spirit[8] doth use your name,
And in the praise thereof spends all his might,
To make me tongue-tied, speaking of your fame!

4. I.e., from being coffered up by Time.
5. The bell was tolled to announce the death of a member of the parish—one stroke for each year of his or her life.
6. The part of a church where divine service was sung.
7. Choked by the ashes of that which once nourished its flame.
8. A rival poet. See the headnote.

But since your worth, wide as the ocean is,
The humble as° the proudest sail doth bear, *as well as*
My saucy bark,° inferior far to his, *impudent boat*
On your broad main° doth willfully° appear. *waters / boldly*
Your shallowest help will hold me up afloat
Whilst he upon your soundless° deep doth ride; *bottomless*
Or, being wrecked, I am a worthless boat,
He of tall building[9] and of goodly pride.° *magnificence*
  Then if he thrive and I be cast away,
  The worst was this: my love was my decay.

85

My tongue-tied muse in manners holds her still° *tactfully says nothing*
While comments of° your praise, richly compiled, *commentaries in*
Reserve thy character° with golden quill *hoard up your features*
And precious phrase by all the muses filed.° *polished*
I think good thoughts whilst other° write good words, *others*
And like unlettered clerk still cry "Amen"
To every hymn[1] that able spirit affords° *offers*
In polished form of well-refinèd pen.
Hearing you praised I say "'Tis so, 'tis true,"
And to the most° of praise add something more; *highest*
But that is in my thought,° whose love to you, *i.e., is unspoken*
Though words come hindmost, holds his rank before.° *before all others*
  Then others for the breath of words respect,° *regard*
  Me for my dumb thoughts, speaking in effect.° *in reality*

87

Farewell: thou art too dear[2] for my possessing,
And like enough thou know'st thy estimate.° *value*
The charter° of thy worth gives thee releasing; *deed, contract for property*
My bonds in thee are all determinate.° *expired*
For how do I hold thee but by thy granting,
And for that riches where is my deserving?
The cause of this fair gift in me is wanting,
And so my patent° back again is swerving. *title*
Thy self thou gav'st, thy own worth then not knowing,
Or me, to whom thou gav'st it, else mistaking;
So thy great gift, upon misprision growing,° *based on error*
Comes home again, on better judgment making.
  Thus have I had thee as a dream doth flatter:
  In sleep a king, but waking no such matter.

93

So shall I live supposing thou art true,
Like a deceivèd husband; so love's face° *appearance*

9. Tall, strong build.
1. "Like . . . hymn": like an illiterate parish clerk reflexively approve ("cry 'Amen' " after) every poem ("hymn") of praise.
2. (1) Expensive, (2) beloved.

May still seem love to me, though altered new—
Thy looks with me, thy heart in other place.
For there can live no hatred in thine eye;
Therefore in that I cannot know thy change.
In many's looks the false heart's history
Is writ in moods and frowns and wrinkles strange:[3]
But heaven in thy creation did decree
That in thy face sweet love should ever dwell;
Whate'er thy thoughts or thy heart's workings be,
Thy looks should nothing thence but sweetness tell.
  How like Eve's apple doth thy beauty grow° *become*
  If thy sweet virtue answer not thy show![4]

94

They that have power to hurt and will do none,
That do not do the thing they most do show,[5]
Who, moving others, are themselves as stone,
Unmovèd, cold, and to temptation slow;
They rightly do inherit heaven's graces
And husband nature's riches from expense;[6]
They are the lords and owners of their faces,
Others but stewards of their excellence.
The summer's flower is to the summer sweet,
Though to itself it only live and die,
But if that flower with base infection meet,
The basest weed outbraves° his dignity: *surpasses*
  For sweetest things turn sourest by their deeds;
  Lilies that fester smell far worse than weeds.

97

How like a winter hath my absence been
From thee, the pleasure of the fleeting year!
What freezings have I felt, what dark days seen!
What old December's bareness everywhere!
And yet this time removed[7] was summer's time,
The teeming autumn, big with rich increase,
Bearing the wanton burthen of the prime,[8]
Like widowed wombs after their lords' decease;
Yet this abundant issue° seemed to me *outgrowth*
But hope of orphans and unfathered fruit;
For summer and his pleasures wait on thee,
And, thou away, the very birds are mute;
  Or, if they sing, 'tis with so dull a cheer° *such a dismal mood*
  That leaves look pale, dreading the winter's near.

3. Unaccustomed. "Moods": moody expressions.
4. Does not correspond to your appearance.
5. Seem to do, or seem capable of doing.
6. I.e., they do not squander nature's gifts.
7. I.e., when I was absent.
8. Spring, which has engendered the lavish crop ("wanton burthen") that autumn is now left to bear.

105

Let not my love be called idolatry,
Nor my belovèd as an idol show,
Since all alike my songs and praises be
To one, of one, still° such, and ever so. *continually*
Kind is my love today, tomorrow kind,
Still constant in a wondrous excellence.
Therefore my verse, to constancy confined,
One thing expressing, leaves out difference.° *variety*
"Fair, kind, and true" is all my argument,° *theme*
"Fair, kind, and true" varying to other words,
And in this change is my invention spent,[9]
Three themes in one, which wonderous scope affords.
Fair, kind, and true have often lived alone,° *separately*
Which three till now never kept seat° in one. *dwelt permanently*

106

When in the chronicle of wasted° time *past*
I see descriptions of the fairest wights,° *persons*
And beauty making beautiful old rhyme
In praise of ladies dead and lovely knights,
Then, in the blazon[1] of sweet beauty's best,
Of hand, of foot, of lip, of eye, of brow,
I see their antique pen would have expressed
Even such a beauty as you master now.
So all their praises are but prophecies
Of this our time, all you prefiguring;
And, for they looked but with divining eyes,[2]
They had not skill enough your worth to sing:
For we, which now behold these present days,
Have eyes to wonder, but lack tongues to praise.

116

Let me not to the marriage of true minds
Admit impediments;[3] love is not love
Which alters when it alteration finds,
Or bends with the remover to remove:
O, no, it is an ever-fixèd mark,[4]
That looks on tempests and is never shaken;
It is the star to every wand'ring bark,
Whose worth's unknown, although his highth[5] be taken.
Love's not Time's fool,° though rosy lips and cheeks *plaything*

9. And in varying the words alone my inventiveness is expended.
1. Catalog of excellencies.
2. Because ("for") they were able only ("but") to foresee prophetically.
3. From the Anglican marriage service: "If either of you do know any impediment why ye may not be lawfully joined together . . ."
4. Seamark (cf. *landmark*).
5. The star's value is incalculable, although its "highth" (altitude) may be known and used for practical purposes.

Within his[6] bending sickle's compass come;
Love alters not with his brief hours and weeks,
But bears it out even to the edge of doom.° *brink of Judgment Day*
If this be error and upon me proved,
I never writ, nor no man ever loved.

129

Th' expense of spirit in a waste of shame
Is lust in action;[7] and till action, lust
Is perjured, murd'rous, bloody, full of blame,
Savage, extreme, rude,° cruel, not to trust; *brutal*
Enjoyed no sooner but despisèd straight:° *immediately*
Past reason hunted; and no sooner had,
Past reason hated, as a swallowed bait,
On purpose laid to make the taker mad:
Mad in pursuit, and in possession so;
Had, having, and in quest to have, extreme;
A bliss in proof[8] and proved, a very° woe; *true*
Before, a joy proposed; behind, a dream.
All this the world well knows; yet none knows well
To shun the heaven that leads men to this hell.

130

My mistress' eyes are nothing like the sun;[9]
Coral is far more red than her lips' red;
If snow be white, why then her breasts are dun;
If hairs be wires, black wires grow on her head.
I have seen roses damasked,° red and white, *variegated*
But no such roses see I in her cheeks;
And in some perfumes is there more delight
Than in the breath that from my mistress reeks.[1]
I love to hear her speak, yet well I know
That music hath a far more pleasing sound;
I grant I never saw a goddess go;° *walk*
My mistress, when she walks, treads on the ground.
And yet, by heaven, I think my love as rare° *admirable; extraordinary*
As any she belied° with false compare. *misrepresented*

135

Whoever hath her wish, thou hast thy *Will*,[2]
And *Will* to boot, and *Will* in overplus;
More than enough am I that vex thee still,° *always*

6. Time's (as also in line 11).
7. The word order here is inverted and slightly obscures the meaning. Lust, when put into action, expends "spirit" (life, vitality; also semen) in a "waste" (desert; also with a pun on *waist*) of shame.
8. A bliss during the experience.
9. An anti-Petrarchan sonnet. All of the details commonly attributed by other Elizabethan sonneteers to their ladies (for example, in Spenser's *Amoretti* 64, p. 436) are here denied to the poet's mistress.
1. Not with our pejorative sense, but simply "emanates."
2. (1) Wishes, (2) carnal desire, (3) the male and female sexual organs, (4) a lover—Shakespeare?—named Will. This is one of several sonnets punning on the word.

To thy sweet will making addition thus.
Wilt thou, whose will is large and spacious,
Not once vouchsafe° to hide my will in thine? *consent*
Shall will in others seem right gracious,
And in° my will no fair acceptance shine? *in the case of*
The sea, all water, yet receives rain still,
And in abundance addeth to his store,° *plenty*
So thou being rich in *Will* add to thy *Will*
One will of mine to make thy large *Will* more.
Let no unkind, no fair beseechers kill;[3]
Think all but one, and me in that one *Will*.

138

When my love swears that she is made of truth,
I do believe her, though I know she lies,[4]
That she might think me some untutored youth,
Unlearnèd in the world's false subtleties.
Thus vainly thinking that she thinks me young,
Although she knows my days are past the best,[5]
Simply° I credit her false-speaking tongue: *like a simpleton*
On both sides thus is simple truth suppressed.
But wherefore says she not she is unjust?° *unfaithful*
And wherefore say not I that I am old?
Oh, love's best habit° is in seeming trust, *clothing, guise*
And age in love loves not to have years told.° *counted*
Therefore I lie with her and she with me,
And in our faults by lies we flattered be.

144

Two loves I have of comfort and despair,[6]
Which like two spirits do suggest me still:° *tempt me constantly*
The better angel is a man right fair,
The worser spirit a woman colored ill.° *dark*
To win me soon to hell, my female evil
Tempteth my better angel from my side,
And would corrupt my saint to be a devil,
Wooing his purity with her foul pride.[7]
And whether that my angel be turned fiend
Suspect I may, yet not directly tell;
But being both from me, both to each[8] friend,
I guess one angel in another's hell.
Yet this shall I ne'er know, but live in doubt,
Till my bad angel fire my good one out.[9]

3. I.e., do not kill with unkindness any of your wooers.
4. With the obvious sexual pun (as also in lines 13–14). "Made of truth": (1) is utterly honest, (2) is faithful.
5. Shakespeare was thirty-five or younger when he wrote this sonnet (it first appeared in *The Passionate Pilgrim*, 1599).
6. I have two beloveds, one bringing me comfort and the other despair.
7. (1) Vanity, (2) sexuality.
8. Each other. "From": away from.
9. I.e., until she infects him with venereal disease.

146[1]

Poor soul, the center of my sinful earth,
Lord of[2] these rebel powers that thee array,[3]
Why dost thou pine within and suffer dearth,
Painting thy outward walls so costly gay?
Why so large cost, having so short a lease,
Dost thou upon thy fading mansion spend?
Shall worms, inheritors of this excess,
Eat up thy charge?[4] Is this thy body's end?° *destiny; purpose*
Then, soul, live thou upon thy servant's loss,
And let that pine to aggravate thy store;[5]
Buy terms divine in selling hours of dross;[6]
Within be fed, without be rich no more.
So shalt thou feed on death, that feeds on men,
And death once dead, there's no more dying then.

147

My love is as a fever, longing still° *continually*
For that which longer nurseth[7] the disease,
Feeding on that which doth preserve the ill,° *maintain the illness*
Th' uncertain sickly appetite[8] to please.
My reason, the physician to my love,
Angry that his prescriptions are not kept,
Hath left me, and I desperate now approve
Desire is death, which physic did except.[9]
Past cure I am, now reason is past care,[1]
And frantic mad with evermore unrest;
My thoughts and my discourse as madmen's are,
At random from the truth, vainly expressed:[2]
For I have sworn thee fair, and thought thee bright,
Who art as black as hell, as dark as night.

152

In loving thee thou know'st I am forsworn,[3]
But thou art twice forsworn to me love swearing:
In act thy bed-vow° broke, and new faith torn *to husband (or lover)*
In vowing new hate after new love bearing.[4]
But why of two oaths' breach do I accuse thee
When I break twenty? I am perjured most,

1. Go to Norton Literature Online for a recitation of this poem.
2. An emendation. The 1609 edition repeats the last three words of line 1. Other suggestions are "Thrall to," "Starved by," "Pressed by," and leaving the repetition but dropping "that thee" in line 2.
3. The rebellious body that clothes you.
4. (1) Your expense; (2) the thing you were responsible for (i.e., the body).
5. Let "that" (i.e., the body) deteriorate to increase ("aggravate") the soul's riches ("thy store").
6. Rubbish. "Terms": long periods.
7. (1) Nourishes, (2) takes care of.
8. (1) Desire for food, (2) lust.
9. I.e., I learn by experience that desire, which rejected reason's medicine, is death.
1. I.e., medical care (of me). The line is a version of the proverb "past cure, past care."
2. Wide of the mark and senselessly uttered.
3. I.e., am breaking loving vows to another.
4. The object of the "new faith" followed by "new hate" could be either the speaker's young friend or the speaker himself.

For all my vows are oaths but to misuse° thee, *deceive; misrepresent*
And all my honest faith in thee is lost.
For I have sworn deep oaths of thy deep kindness,
Oaths of thy love, thy truth, thy constancy,
And to enlighten thee gave eyes to blindness,[5]
Or made them swear against the thing they see.
  For I have sworn thee fair—more perjured eye° *(punning on "I")*
  To swear against the truth so foul a lie.

1609

Twelfth Night

Women did not perform on the English public stage during Shakespeare's lifetime; all the great women's roles in Elizabethan and Jacobean plays, from Juliet and Lady Macbeth to the duchess of Malfi, were written to be performed by trained adolescent boys. These boy actors were evidently extraordinarily skillful, and the audiences were sufficiently immersed in the conventions both of theater and of social life in general to accept gesture, makeup, and above all dress as a convincing representation of femininity. *Twelfth Night, or What You Will*, written for Shakespeare's all-male company, plays brilliantly with these conventions. The comedy depends upon an actor's ability to transform himself, through costume, voice, and gesture, into a young noblewoman, Viola, who transforms herself, through costume, voice, and gesture, into a young man, Cesario. The play's delicious complications follow from the emotional tangles that these transformations engender, unsettling fixed categories of sexual identity and social class and allowing characters to explore emotional territory that a culture officially hostile to same-sex desire and cross-class marriage would ordinarily have ruled out of bounds. In *Twelfth Night* conventional expectations repeatedly give way to a different mode of perceiving the world.

Shakespeare wrote *Twelfth Night* around 1601. He had already written such comedies as *A Midsummer Night's Dream, Much Ado About Nothing*, and *As You Like It*, with their playful, subtly ironic investigations of the ways in which heterosexual couples are produced out of the murkier crosscurrents of male and female friendships; as interesting, perhaps, he had probably just recently completed *Hamlet*, with its unprecedented exploration of mourning, betrayal, antic humor, and tragic isolation. *Twelfth Night* would prove to be, in the view of many critics, both the most nearly perfect and in some sense the last of the great festive comedies. Shakespeare returned to comedy later in his career but always with more insistent overtones of bitterness, loss, and grief. There are dark notes in *Twelfth Night* as well—the countess Olivia is in mourning for her brother, Viola thinks that her brother too is dead, Antonio believes that he has been betrayed by the man he loves, Duke Orsino threatens to kills Cesario—but these notes are swept up in a giddy, carnivalesque dance of illusion, disguise, folly, and clowning.

The complex tonal shifts of Shakespeare's comedy are conveyed in part by the pervasive music and in part by the constant oscillation between blank verse and prose. Generally, the characters in the main, romantic plot speak in the more elevated, aristocratic, and dignified register of verse, while the comic subplot proceeds in prose. Yet these formal distinctions between serious and comic, high and low, are frequently undermined, as when the wronged Malvolio in his final speech addresses Olivia in dignified verse or when the mercurial Viola shifts with the greatest ease between verse and prose.

The play's subtitle, *What You Will*, underscores the celebratory spirit associated

5. And to make you fair (or give you insight), I looked blindly on your failings (or pretended to see what I couldn't).

with Twelfth Night, the Feast of the Epiphany (January 6), that in Elizabethan England marked the culminating night of the traditional Christmas revels. In the time-honored festivities associated with the midwinter season, a rigidly hierarchical social order that ordinarily demanded deference, sobriety, and strict obedience to authority temporarily gave way to raucous rituals of inversion: young boys were crowned for a day as bishops and carried through the streets in mock religious processions, abstemiousness was toppled by bouts of heavy drinking and feasting, and the spirit of parody, folly, and misrule reigned briefly in places normally reserved for stern-faced moralists and sober judges. The fact that these festivities were associated with Christian holidays—the Epiphany marked the visit of the Three Kings to Bethlehem to worship the Christ child—did not altogether obscure the continuities with pagan winter rituals such as the Roman Saturnalia, with its comparably explosive release from everyday discipline into a disorderly realm of belly laughter and belly cheer. Puritans emphasized these continuities in launching a fierce attack on the Elizabethan festive calendar and its whole ethos, just as they attacked the theater for what they saw as its links with paganism, idleness, and sexual license. Elizabethan and Jacobean authorities in the church and the state had their own concerns about idleness and subversion, but they generally protected and patronized both festive ritual and theater on the ground that these provided a valuable release from tensions that might otherwise prove dangerous. Sobriety, piety, and discipline were no doubt admirable virtues, but most human beings were not saints. "Dost thou think because thou art virtuous," the drunken Sir Toby asks the censorious steward Malvolio, "there shall be no more cakes and ale?" (2.3.107–08).

Fittingly, the earliest firm record of a performance of *Twelfth Night*, as noted in the diary of John Manningham, was "at our feast" in the Middle Temple (one of London's law schools) in February 1602. Manningham noted cannily the comedy's resemblance to Shakespeare's earlier play on twins, *The Comedy of Errors*, as well as to the Roman playwright Plautus's *Menaechmi* and to an early-sixteenth-century Italian comedy, *Gl'Ingannati* (The Deceived). Shakespeare also drew upon an English story, Barnabe Riche's tale of *Apollonius and Silla* in *Riche His Farewell to the Military Profession* (1581), which was in turn based on French and Italian sources. There is, however, little precedent, in Riche or in any of the known sources, for the aspect of *Twelfth Night* that Manningham found particularly memorable and that has continued to delight audiences: the gulling of Malvolio.

Malvolio (in Italian, "ill will") is explicitly linked to those among Shakespeare's contemporaries most hostile to the theater and to such holidays as Twelfth Night: "Sometimes," says the Lady Olivia's gentlewoman Maria, "he is a kind of puritan" (2.3.131). Shakespeare does not hide the cruelty of the treatment to which Malvolio is subjected—"He hath been most notoriously abused" (5.1.375), says Olivia—nor does he shrink from showing the audience other disagreeable qualities in Olivia's kinsman Sir Toby Belch and his companions. But while the close of the comedy seems to embrace these failings in a tolerant, amused aristocratic recognition of human folly, it can find no place for Malvolio's blend of puritanism and social-climbing.

Malvolio is scapegoated for indulging in a fantasy that colors several of the key relationships in *Twelfth Night:* the fantasy of winning the favor, and ultimately the hand, of the noble and wealthy aristocrats who reign over the social world of the play. The beautiful heiress Olivia, mistress of a great house, is a glittering prize that lures not only Malvolio but also the foolish Sir Andrew and the elegant, imperious Duke Orsino. In falling in love with the duke's graceful messenger (and, as she thinks she has done, in marrying him), Olivia seems to have made precisely the kind of match that had fueled Malvolio's social-climbing imagination. As it turns out, the match is not between unequals: "Be not amazed," the duke tells her when she realizes that she has married someone she scarcely knows. "Right noble is his blood" (5.1.263). The social order then has not been overturned: as in a carnival, when the disguises are removed, the revelers resume their "proper," socially and sexually approved positions.

Yet there is something irreducibly odd about the marriages with which *Twelfth Night* ends. Sir Toby has married the lady's maid Maria as a reward for devising the plot against Malvolio. Olivia has entered into a "contract of eternal bond of love" (5.1.153) with someone whose actual identity is only revealed to her after the marriage is sealed. The strangeness of the bond between virtual strangers is matched by the strangeness of Orsino's instantaneous decision to marry Cesario—as soon as "he" can become Viola by changing into women's clothes. Shakespeare conspicuously chooses not to stage this return to conventionality.

Part of the quirky delight of the play's conclusion depends upon the resilient hopefulness of its central character, Viola, a hopefulness that is linked to her improvisatory boldness, eloquent tongue, and keen wit. These qualities link her to the fool Feste, who does not have a major part in the comedy's plot, but who occupies a place at its imaginative center. Viola seems to acknowledge this place in paying handsome tribute to Feste's intelligence: "This fellow is wise enough to play the fool, / And to do that well craves a kind of wit" (3.1.59–60). His wit often takes the form of a perverse literalism that slyly calls attention to the play's repeated confounding of such simple binaries as male and female, outside and inside, role and reality. Feste is irresponsible, vulnerable, and dependent, but he also understands, as he teasingly shows Olivia, that it is foolish to bewail forever a loss that cannot be recovered. And he understands that it is important to take such pleasures as life offers and not to wait: "In delay there lies no plenty," he sings, "Then come kiss me, sweet and twenty. / Youth's a stuff will not endure" (2.3.48–50). There is in this wonderful song, as in all of his jests, a current of sadness. Feste knows, as the refrain of the last of his songs puts it, that "the rain it raineth every day" (5.1.388). His counsel is for "present mirth" and "present laughter" (2.3.46). This is, of course, the advice of a fool. But do the Malvolios of the world have anything wiser to suggest?

Twelfth Night, or What You Will

The Persons of the Play

ORSINO, duke of Illyria
VALENTINE } attending on Orsino
CURIO }
FIRST OFFICER
SECOND OFFICER
VIOLA, a lady, later disguised as Cesario
A CAPTAIN
SEBASTIAN, her twin brother
ANTONIO, another sea-captain
OLIVIA, a countess
MARIA, her waiting-gentlewoman
SIR TOBY Belch, Olivia's kinsman
SIR ANDREW Aguecheek, companion of Sir Toby
MALVOLIO, Olivia's steward
FABIAN, a member of Olivia's household
FESTE the clown, her jester
A PRIEST
A SERVANT of Olivia
Musicians, sailors, lords, attendants

1.1

Music. Enter ORSINO *Duke of Illyria,* CURIO, *and other lords*

ORSINO If music be the food of love, play on,
Give me excess of it that, surfeiting,
The appetite may sicken and so die.
That strain again, it had a dying fall.° — *cadence*
O, it came o'er my ear like the sweet sound
That breathes upon a bank of violets,
Stealing and giving odor. Enough, no more,
'Tis not so sweet now as it was before.
[*Music ceases*]
O spirit of love, how quick and fresh° art thou — *lively and eager*
That, notwithstanding thy capacity
pReceiveth as the sea,° naught enters there, — *receives without limit*
Of what validity° and pitch° so e'er, — *value / height; excellence*
But falls into abatement° and low price — *lesser value*
Even in a minute! So full of shapes is fancy
That it alone is high fantastical.° — *uniquely imaginative*
CURIO Will you go hunt, my lord?
ORSINO What, Curio?
CURIO The hart.
ORSINO Why so I do, the noblest that I have.[1]
O, when mine eyes did see Olivia first
Methought she purged the air of pestilence;[2]
That instant was I turned into a hart,
And my desires, like fell° and cruel hounds, — *savage*
E'er since pursue me.[3]
Enter VALENTINE
How now, what news from her?
VALENTINE So please my lord, I might° not be admitted, — *could*
But from her handmaid do return this answer:
The element itself till seven years' heat[4]
Shall not behold her face at ample° view, — *full*
But like a cloistress° she will veilèd walk — *nun*
And water once a day her chamber round
With eye-offending brine°—all this to season — *stinging tears*
A brother's dead love,[5] which she would keep fresh
And lasting in her sad remembrance.
ORSINO O, she that hath a heart of that fine° frame — *exquisitely made*
To pay this debt of love but to a brother,
How will she love when the rich golden shaft[6]
Hath killed the flock of all affections else° — *other emotions*
That live in her—when liver, brain, and heart,[7]
These sovereign thrones, are all supplied, and filled

1.1 Location: Illyria, Greek and Roman name for the eastern Adriatic coast; probably not suggesting a real country to Shakespeare's audience.
1. Orsino plays on "hart/heart."
2. Plague and other illnesses were thought to be caused by bad air.
3. Alluding to the classical legend of Actaeon, who was turned into a stag and hunted by his own hounds for having seen the goddess Diana naked.
4. The sky itself for seven hot summers.
5. I.e., all this to preserve (by the salt of the tears) the love of a dead brother.
6. Of Cupid's golden-tipped arrow, which caused desire.
7. In Elizabethan psychology, the seats of passion, intellect, and feeling.

Her sweet perfections[8] with one self° king! *one and the same*
Away before me to sweet beds of flowers.
Love-thoughts lie rich when canopied with bowers.
Exeunt

1.2

Enter VIOLA, A CAPTAIN, *and sailors*

VIOLA[1] What country, friends, is this?
CAPTAIN This is Illyria, lady.
VIOLA And what should I do in Illyria?
My brother, he is in Elysium.[2]
Perchance° he is not drowned. What think you sailors? *perhaps*
CAPTAIN It is perchance° that you yourself were saved. *by chance*
VIOLA O my poor brother!—and so perchance may he be.
CAPTAIN True, madam, and to comfort you with chance,[3]
Assure yourself, after our ship did split,
When you and those poor number saved with you
Hung on our driving boat,[4] I saw your brother,
Most provident in peril, bind himself—
Courage and hope both teaching him the practice—
To a strong mast that lived° upon the sea, *remained afloat*
Where, like Arion[5] on the dolphin's back,
I saw him hold acquaintance with the waves
So long as I could see.
VIOLA [*giving money*] For saying so, there's gold.
Mine own escape unfoldeth to° my hope, *encourages*
Whereto thy speech serves for authority,° *support*
The like of him.[6] Know'st thou this country?
CAPTAIN Ay, madam, well, for I was bred and born
Not three hours' travel from this very place.
VIOLA Who governs here?
CAPTAIN A noble duke, in nature
As in name.
VIOLA What is his name?
CAPTAIN Orsino.
VIOLA Orsino. I have heard my father name him.
He was a bachelor then.
CAPTAIN And so is now, or was so very late,° *lately*
For but a month ago I went from hence,
And then 'twas fresh in murmur°—as, you know, *newly rumored*
What great ones do the less will prattle of—
That he did seek the love of fair Olivia.
VIOLA What's she?
CAPTAIN A virtuous maid, the daughter of a count
That died some twelvemonth since, then leaving her
In the protection of his son, her brother,

8. And her sweet perfections have been filled.
1.2 Location: The coast of Illyria.
1. Viola is not named in the dialogue until 5.1.242.
2. The heaven of classical mythology.
3. With what may have happened.
4. The ship's boat. "Driving": being driven by the wind.
5. A legendary Greek musician who, in order to save himself from being murdered on a voyage, jumped overboard and was carried to land by a dolphin.
6. I.e., that he too has survived.

Who shortly also died, for whose dear love,
They say, she hath abjured° the sight *renounced*
And company of men.

VIOLA O that I served that lady,
And might not be delivered° to the world *revealed*
Till I had made mine own occasion mellow,° *ripe (to be revealed)*
What my estate° is. *social rank*

CAPTAIN That were hard to compass,° *achieve*
Because she will admit no kind of suit,° *petition*
No, not the Duke's.

VIOLA There is a fair behavior[7] in thee, captain,
And though that nature with a beauteous wall
Doth oft close in pollution, yet of thee
I will believe thou hast a mind that suits
With this thy fair and outward character.[8]
I pray thee—and I'll pay thee bounteously—
Conceal me what I am, and be my aid
For such disguise as haply shall become
The form of my intent.[9] I'll serve this duke.
Thou shalt present me as an eunuch[1] to him.
It may be worth thy pains, for I can sing,
And speak to him in many sorts of music
That will allow° me very worth his service. *prove*
What else may hap, to time I will commit.
Only shape thou thy silence to my wit.° *imagination; plan*

CAPTAIN Be you his eunuch, and your mute[2] I'll be.
When my tongue blabs, then let mine eyes not see.

VIOLA I thank thee. Lead me on. *Exeunt*

1.3

Enter SIR TOBY [*Belch*] *and* MARIA

SIR TOBY What a plague means my niece to take the death of her brother thus? I am sure care's an enemy to life.

MARIA By my troth, Sir Toby, you must come in earlier o' nights. Your cousin,[1] my lady, takes great exceptions to your ill hours.

SIR TOBY Why, let her except, before excepted.[2]

MARIA Ay, but you must confine yourself within the modest° limits of order. *moderate*

SIR TOBY Confine? I'll confine myself no finer[3] than I am. These clothes are good enough to drink in, and so be these boots too; an° they be not, let them hang themselves in their own straps. *if*

MARIA That quaffing and drinking will undo you. I heard

7. Outward appearance; conduct.
8. Appearance (suggesting moral qualities).
9. That perhaps may be fitting to my purpose. "Form": shape.
1. Castrati (hence, "eunuchs") were prized as male sopranos; the disguise would have explained Viola's feminine voice. Viola (or perhaps Shakespeare) seems to have changed plans: she presents herself instead as a young page.
2. In Turkish harems, eunuchs served as guards and were assisted by "mutes" (usually servants whose tongues had been cut out).

1.3 Location: The Countess Olivia's house.
1. Term used generally of kinsfolk. "Troth": faith.
2. Playing on the legal jargon *exceptis excipiendis*, "with the previous stated exceptions." Sir Toby refuses to take Olivia's displeasure seriously.
3. Suggesting both "a refined manner of dress" and "narrowly" (referring to his girth).

my lady talk of it yesterday, and of a foolish knight that you brought in one night here to be her wooer.

SIR TOBY Who, Sir Andrew Aguecheek?

MARIA Ay, he.

SIR TOBY He's as tall a man as any's[4] in Illyria.

MARIA What's that to th' purpose?

SIR TOBY Why, he has three thousand ducats a year.

MARIA Ay, but he'll have but a year in all these ducats.[5] He's a very° fool, and a prodigal. *an absolute*

SIR TOBY Fie that you'll say so! He plays o'th' viol-de-gamboys,[6] and speaks three or four languages word for word without book,° and hath all the good gifts of nature. *from memory*

MARIA He hath indeed, almost natural,[7] for besides that he's a fool, he's a great quarreller, and but that he hath the gift° of a coward to allay the gust° he hath in quarrelling, 'tis thought among the prudent he would quickly have the gift of a grave. *talent; present / gusto*

SIR TOBY By this hand, they are scoundrels and substractors[8] that say so of him. Who are they?

MARIA They that add, moreover, he's drunk nightly in your company.

SIR TOBY With drinking healths to my niece. I'll drink to her as long as there is a passage in my throat and drink in Illyria. He's a coward and a coistrel° that will not drink to my niece till his brains turn o'th' toe, like a parish top. What wench, *Castiliano, vulgo,*[9] for here comes Sir Andrew Agueface. *horse groom; lout*

Enter SIR ANDREW [*Aguecheek*]

SIR ANDREW Sir Toby Belch! How now, Sir Toby Belch?

SIR TOBY Sweet Sir Andrew.

SIR ANDREW [*to* MARIA] Bless you, fair shrew.[1]

MARIA And you too, sir.

SIR TOBY Accost, Sir Andrew, accost.[2]

SIR ANDREW What's that?

SIR TOBY My niece's chambermaid.[3]

SIR ANDREW Good Mistress Accost, I desire better acquaintance.

MARIA My name is Mary, sir.

SIR ANDREW Good Mistress Mary Accost.

SIR TOBY You mistake, knight. "Accost" is front° her, board her, woo her, assail[4] her. *confront*

SIR ANDREW By my troth, I would not undertake[5] her in this company.° Is that the meaning of "accost"? *i.e., the audience*

4. Any (man who) is. "Tall": brave; worthy. (Maria takes it in the modern sense of height.)
5. I.e., he'll spend his fortune in a year.
6. A facetious corruption of "viola da gamba," a bass viol held between the knees.
7. Idiots and fools were called "naturals."
8. Corruption of "detractors." (In reply, Maria puns on "substract" as "subtract.")
9. Variously interpreted, but may mean "Speak of the devil," since Castilians were considered devilish, and *vulgo* refers to the common tongue. "Parish top": parishes kept large tops that were spun by whipping them, for the parishioners' amusement and exercise.
1. Andrew possibly confuses "shrew" (ill-tempered woman) with "mouse," an endearment.
2. Address (her); originally a naval term meaning "go alongside; greet."
3. Lady-in-waiting; not a menial servant, but a gentlewoman in attendance on a great lady.
4. Greet (also nautical). "Board": speak to; tackle.
5. Take her on (with sexual implication).

MARIA Fare you well, gentlemen.

SIR TOBY An thou let part so,[6] Sir Andrew, would thou mightst never draw sword again.

SIR ANDREW An you part so, mistress, I would I might never draw sword again. Fair lady, do you think you have fools in hand?° *to deal with*

MARIA Sir, I have not you by th' hand.

SIR ANDREW Marry, but you shall have, and here's my hand.

MARIA [*taking his hand*] Now sir, thought is free.[7] I pray you, bring your hand to th' buttery-bar,[8] and let it drink.

SIR ANDREW Wherefore, sweetheart? What's your metaphor?

MARIA It's dry,[9] sir.

SIR ANDREW Why, I think so. I am not such an ass but I can keep my hand dry.[1] But what's your jest?

MARIA A dry jest,[2] sir.

SIR ANDREW Are you full of them?

MARIA Ay, sir, I have them at my fingers' ends.[3] Marry, now I let go your hand I am barren.° *Exit* *empty of jokes*

SIR TOBY O knight, thou lackest a cup of canary.[4] When did I see thee so put down?[5]

SIR ANDREW Never in your life, I think, unless you see canary put me down. Methinks sometimes I have no more wit than a Christian° or an ordinary man has; but I am a great eater of beef,[6] and I believe that does harm to my wit. *an average man*

SIR TOBY No question.

SIR ANDREW An I thought that, I'd forswear it. I'll ride home tomorrow, Sir Toby.

SIR TOBY *Pourquoi,*° my dear knight? *why*

SIR ANDREW What is "Pourquoi"? Do, or not do? I would I had bestowed that time in the tongues[7] that I have in fencing, dancing, and bear-baiting. O, had I but followed the arts!

SIR TOBY Then hadst thou° had an excellent head of hair. *you would have*

SIR ANDREW Why, would that have mended° my hair? *improved*

SIR TOBY Past question, for thou seest it will not curl by nature.[8]

SIR ANDREW But it becomes me well enough, does't not?

SIR TOBY Excellent, it hangs like flax on a distaff,[9] and I

6. If you let her go without protest or without bidding her farewell.
7. The customary retort to "Do you think I am a fool?" "Marry": indeed (originally, the name of the Virgin Mary used as an oath).
8. Ledge on the half-door to a buttery or a wine cellar, on which drinks were served.
9. Thirsty; but a dry hand was also thought to be a sign of impotence.
1. Alluding to the proverb "Even fools have enough wit to come in out of the rain."
2. A stupid joke (referring to Andrew's stupidity); an ironic quip; a joke about dryness.
3. Always ready; or "by th'hand" (line 62).
4. A sweet wine, like sherry, originally from the Canary Islands.
5. Defeated in repartee; "put down" with drink.
6. Contemporary medicine held that beef dulled the intellect.
7. Foreign languages; Toby takes him to mean "curling tongs."
8. To contrast with Andrew's "arts" (line 90).
9. In spinning, flax would hang in long, thin, yellowish strings on the "distaff," a pole held between the knees.

hope to see a housewife[1] take thee between her legs and spin it off.[2]

SIR ANDREW Faith, I'll home tomorrow, Sir Toby. Your niece will not be seen, or if she be, it's four to one she'll none of me. The Count himself here hard by woos her.

SIR TOBY She'll none o'th' Count. She'll not match above her degree,° neither in estate,[3] years, nor wit, I have heard her swear't. Tut, there's life in't,[4] man. *social rank*

SIR ANDREW I'll stay a month longer. I am a fellow o'th' strangest mind o'th' world. I delight in masques and revels sometimes altogether.

SIR TOBY Art thou good at these kickshawses,[5] knight?

SIR ANDREW As any man in Illyria, whatsoever he be, under the degree of my betters; and yet I will not compare with an old man.[6]

SIR TOBY What is thy excellence in a galliard,[7] knight?

SIR ANDREW Faith, I can cut a caper.[8]

SIR TOBY And I can cut the mutton to't.

SIR ANDREW And I think I have the back-trick[9] simply as strong as any man in Illyria.

SIR TOBY Wherefore are these things hid? Wherefore have these gifts a curtain[1] before 'em? Are they like to take dust, like Mistress Mall's[2] picture? Why dost thou not go to church in a galliard, and come home in a coranto?[3] My very walk should be a jig. I would not so much as make water but in a cinquepace.[4] What dost thou mean? Is it a world to hide virtues in? I did think by the excellent constitution of thy leg it was formed under the star of a galliard.[5]

SIR ANDREW Ay,'tis strong, and it does indifferent° well in a divers-colored stock.° Shall we set about some revels? *moderately* / *stocking*

SIR TOBY What shall we do else—were we not born under Taurus?[6]

SIR ANDREW Taurus? That's sides and heart.

SIR TOBY No, sir, it is legs and thighs: let me see thee caper.

[SIR ANDREW *capers*]

Ha, higher! Ha ha, excellent. *Exeunt*

1.4

Enter VALENTINE, *and* VIOLA [*as Cesario*] *in man's attire*

VALENTINE If the Duke continue these favors towards you,

1. Housewives spun flax; the pronunciation, "hus-wife," also suggests the meaning "prostitute."
2. Make him bald (as a result of venereal disease).
3. Status; possessions.
4. Proverbial: "While there's life, there's hope."
5. Trifles; trivialities (from the French *quelque chose*).
6. Expert (perhaps a backhanded compliment).
7. A lively, complex dance, including the caper.
8. Leap. (Toby puns on the pickled flower buds used in a sauce of mutton.)
9. Probably a dance movement, a kick of the foot behind the body (also suggesting sexual prowess, with later reference to "mutton" as "prostitute").
1. Used to protect paintings from dust.
2. Like "Moll[y]," "Mall" was a nickname for "Mary."
3. An even more rapid dance than the galliard.
4. Galliard, or, more properly, the steps joining the figures of the dance; punning on "sink," as in "sewer."
5. Astrological influences favorable to dancing.
6. The astrological sign of the bull was usually thought to govern the neck and throat (appropriate to heavy drinkers).

1.4 Location: Orsino's palace.

Cesario, you are like to be much advanced. He hath known you but three days, and already you are no stranger.

VIOLA You either fear his humor° or my negligence, that you call in question the continuance of his love. Is he inconstant, sir, in his favors? *moodiness*

VALENTINE No, believe me.

Enter DUKE, CURIO, *and attendants*

VIOLA I thank you. Here comes the Count.
ORSINO Who saw Cesario, ho?
VIOLA On your attendance,° my lord, here. *waiting at your service*
ORSINO [*to* CURIO *and attendants*] Stand you a while
  aloof.° [*To* VIOLA] Cesario, *aside*
Thou know'st no less but all.° I have unclasped *than everything*
To thee the book even of my secret soul.
Therefore, good youth, address thy gait° unto her, *go*
Be not denied access, stand at her doors,
And tell them there thy fixèd foot shall grow° *take root*
Till thou have audience.
VIOLA Sure, my noble lord,
If she be so abandoned to her sorrow
As it is spoke, she never will admit me.
ORSINO Be clamorous, and leap all civil bounds,[1]
Rather than make unprofited° return. *unsuccessful*
VIOLA Say I do speak with her, my lord, what then?
ORSINO O then unfold the passion of my love,
Surprise[2] her with discourse of my dear° faith. *heartfelt*
It shall become thee well to act my woes—
She will attend it better in thy youth
Than in a nuncio's° of more grave aspect.° *messenger's / appearance*
VIOLA I think not so, my lord.
ORSINO Dear lad, believe it;
For they shall yet° belie thy happy years *thus far*
That say thou art a man. Diana's lip
Is not more smooth and rubious;° thy small pipe° *ruby red / voice*
Is as the maiden's organ, shrill and sound,[3]
And all is semblative° a woman's part. *like*
I know thy constellation[4] is right apt
For this affair. [*To* CURIO *and attendants*] Some four or
  five attend him.
All if you will, for I myself am best
When least in company. [*To* VIOLA] Prosper well in this
And thou shalt live as freely as thy lord,
To call his fortunes thine.
VIOLA I'll do my best
To woo your lady—[*aside*] yet a barful strife[5]—
Whoe'er I woo, myself would be his wife. *Exeunt*

1. All constraints of polite behavior.
2. Capture by unexpected attack.
3. High-pitched and uncracked.
4. Nature and abilities (as supposedly determined by the stars).
5. An undertaking full of impediments.

1.5

Enter MARIA, *and* [FESTE,[1] *the*] *clown*

MARIA Nay, either tell me where thou hast been or I will not open my lips so wide as a bristle may enter in° way of thy excuse. My lady will hang thee for thy absence. *by*

FESTE Let her hang me. He that is well hanged in this world needs to fear no colors.[2]

MARIA Make that good.° *explain that*

FESTE He shall see none to fear.

MARIA A good lenten[3] answer. I can tell thee where that saying was born, of "I fear no colors."

FESTE Where, good Mistress Mary?

MARIA In the wars,[4] and that may you be bold to say in your foolery.

FESTE Well, God give them wisdom that have it; and those that are fools, let them use their talents.[5]

MARIA Yet you will be hanged for being so long absent, or to be turned away[6]—is not that as good as a hanging to you?

FESTE Many a good hanging prevents a bad marriage;[7] and for turning away, let summer bear it out.° *make it endurable*

MARIA You are resolute then?

FESTE Not so neither, but I am resolved on two points.° *matters; laces*

MARIA That if one break, the other will hold; or if both break, your gaskins° fall. *wide breeches*

FESTE Apt, in good faith, very apt. Well, go thy way. If Sir Toby would leave drinking thou wert as witty a piece of Eve's flesh[8] as any in Illyria.

MARIA Peace, you rogue, no more o' that. Here comes my lady. Make your excuse wisely, you were best.° [*Exit*] *you had better*

Enter Lady OLIVIA, *with* MALVOLIO [*and attendants*]

FESTE [*aside*] Wit,[9] an't° be thy will, put me into good fooling! Those wits that think they have thee do very oft prove fools, and I that am sure I lack thee may pass for a wise man. For what says Quinapalus?[1]—"Better a witty fool than a foolish wit." [*To* OLIVIA] God bless thee, lady. *if it*

OLIVIA [*to attendants*] Take the fool away.

FESTE Do you not hear, fellows? Take away the lady.

OLIVIA Go to, you're a dry[2] fool. I'll no more of you. Besides, you grow dishonest.° *unreliable*

FESTE Two faults, madonna,° that drink and good counsel will amend, for give the dry fool drink, then is the fool *my lady*

1.5 Location: Olivia's house.
1. The name is used only once, at 2.4.11.
2. Proverbial for "fear nothing." "Colors": worldly deceptions, with puns on "collars" as "hangman's nooses" and "cholers" as "anger."
3. Thin or meager (like Lenten fare).
4. "Colors" in line 9 refers to military flags.
5. Alluding to the parable of the talents, Matthew 25. The comic implication is that a fool should strive to increase his measure of folly. Since "fool" and "fowl" had similar pronunciations, there may also be a play on "talents/talons."
6. Dismissed; also, perhaps, turned off or hanged.
7. Proverbial. "Hanging": execution; sexual prowess.
8. Woman. Feste may imply both that Maria and Toby would make a good match and that Maria is as witty as Toby is sober.
9. Intelligence, which is often contrasted with will.
1. Feste frequently invents his own authorities.
2. Dull, but Feste interprets as "thirsty." "Go to": an expression of impatience.

not dry; bid the dishonest man mend° himself: if he mend, he is no longer dishonest; if he cannot, let the botcher° mend him. Anything that's mended is but patched. Virtue that transgresses is but patched with sin, and sin that amends is but patched with virtue. If that this simple syllogism will serve, so. If it will not, what remedy? As there is no true cuckold but calamity, so beauty's a flower.[3] The lady bade take away the fool, therefore I say again, take her away. *reform* / *tailor; cobbler*

OLIVIA Sir, I bade them take away you.

FESTE Misprision[4] in the highest degree! Lady, "*Cucullus non facit monachum*"[5]—that's as much to say as I wear not motley[6] in my brain. Good madonna, give me leave to prove you a fool.

OLIVIA Can you do it?

FESTE Dexteriously,° good madonna. *dexterously*

OLIVIA Make your proof.

FESTE I must catechize[7] you for it, madonna. Good my mouse of virtue,° answer me. *my good virtuous mouse*

OLIVIA Well, sir, for want of other idleness° I'll bide° your proof. *pastime / await*

FESTE Good madonna, why mournest thou?

OLIVIA Good fool, for my brother's death.

FESTE I think his soul is in hell, madonna.

OLIVIA I know his soul is in heaven, fool.

FESTE The more fool, madonna, to mourn for your brother's soul, being in heaven. Take away the fool, gentlemen.

OLIVIA What think you of this fool, Malvolio? Doth he not mend?[8]

MALVOLIO Yes, and shall do till the pangs of death shake him. Infirmity,° that decays the wise, doth ever make the better fool.[9] *(old) age*

FESTE God send you, sir, a speedy infirmity for the better increasing your folly. Sir Toby will be sworn that I am no fox, but he will not pass his word for twopence that you are no fool.

OLIVIA How say you to that, Malvolio?

MALVOLIO I marvel your ladyship takes delight in such a barren rascal. I saw him put down° the other day with an ordinary fool that has no more brain than a stone. Look you now, he's out of his guard° already. Unless you laugh and minister occasion[1] to him, he is gagged. I protest I take these wise men that crow so at these set° kind of fools no better than the fools' zanies.° *defeated in repartee* / *defenseless* / *artificial* / *"straight men"*

3. In taking her vow (1.2.36–37), Olivia has wedded herself to calamity but must be unfaithful, or let pass her moment of beauty.
4. Misapprehension; wrongful arrest.
5. The cowl does not make the monk (a Latin proverb).
6. The multicolored costume of a fool.
7. Question (as in catechism, which tests the orthodoxy of belief).
8. Improve, but Malvolio takes "mend" to mean "grow more foolish."
9. Make the fool more foolish.
1. And give opportunity.

OLIVIA O, you are sick of° self-love, Malvolio, and taste — *with*
with a distempered[2] appetite. To be generous, guiltless,
and of free° disposition is to take those things for bird- — *magnanimous*
bolts[3] that you deem cannon bullets. There is no slander
in an allowed fool, though he do nothing but rail; nor no
railing in a known discreet man, though he do nothing
but reprove.

FESTE Now Mercury indue thee with leasing,[4] for thou
speakest well of fools.

Enter MARIA

MARIA Madam, there is at the gate a young gentleman
much desires to speak with you.

OLIVIA From the Count Orsino, is it?

MARIA I know not, madam. 'Tis a fair young man, and well
attended.

OLIVIA Who of my people hold him in delay?

MARIA Sir Toby, madam, your kinsman.

OLIVIA Fetch him off, I pray you, he speaks nothing but
madman.° Fie on him. Go you, Malvolio. If it be a suit — *madman's talk*
from the Count, I am sick, or not at home—what you
will to dismiss it. *Exit* MALVOLIO
Now you see, sir, how your fooling grows old,° and people — *stale*
dislike it.

FESTE Thou hast spoke for us, madonna, as if thy eldest
son should be a fool, whose skull Jove cram with brains,
for—here he comes—

Enter SIR TOBY

one of thy kin has a most weak *pia mater*.[5]

OLIVIA By mine honor, half-drunk. What is he at the gate,
cousin?° — *kinsman*

SIR TOBY A gentleman.

OLIVIA A gentleman? What gentleman?

SIR TOBY 'Tis a gentleman here. [*He belches*] A plague o'
these pickle herring! [*To* FESTE] How now, sot?° — *fool; drunkard*

FESTE Good Sir Toby.

OLIVIA Cousin, cousin, how have you come so early by this
lethargy?

SIR TOBY Lechery? I defy lechery. There's one° at the gate. — *someone*

OLIVIA Ay, marry, what is he?

SIR TOBY Let him be the devil an° he will, I care not. Give — *if*
me faith,[6] say I. Well, it's all one.° *Exit* — *it doesn't matter*

OLIVIA What's a drunken man like, fool?

FESTE Like a drowned man, a fool, and a madman—one
draught above heat[7] makes him a fool, the second mads
him, and a third drowns him.

OLIVIA Go thou and seek the coroner, and let him sit o'° — *hold an inquest for*
my coz,° for he's in the third degree of drink, he's — *cousin; uncle*

2. Unbalanced; sick.
3. Blunt arrows for shooting birds.
4. May Mercury, the god of deception, endow you with the talent of tactful lying.
5. Brain; or literally, the membrane enclosing it.
6. To defy the devil by faith alone.
7. One drink ("draught") beyond the quantity necessary to warm him.

drowned. Go look after him.

FESTE He is but mad yet, madonna, and the fool shall look to the madman. [*Exit*]

Enter MALVOLIO

MALVOLIO Madam, yon young fellow swears he will speak with you. I told him you were sick—he takes on him to understand so much, and therefore° comes to speak with you. I told him you were asleep—he seems to have a foreknowledge of that too, and therefore comes to speak with you. What is to be said to him, lady? He's fortified against any denial.

therefore°: for that very reason

OLIVIA Tell him he shall not speak with me.

MALVOLIO He's been told so, and he says he'll stand at your door like a sheriff's post,[8] and be the supporter to a bench, but he'll speak with you.

OLIVIA What kind o' man is he?

MALVOLIO Why, of mankind.°

of mankind°: like any other

OLIVIA What manner of man?

MALVOLIO Of very ill manner: he'll speak with you, will you or no.

OLIVIA Of what personage° and years is he?

personage°: appearance

MALVOLIO Not yet old enough for a man, nor young enough for a boy; as a squash[9] is before 'tis a peascod, or a codling° when 'tis almost an apple. 'Tis with him in standing water° between boy and man. He is very well-favored,° and he speaks very shrewishly.° One would think his mother's milk were scarce out of him.

codling°: an unripe apple; standing water°: at the turn of the tide; well-favored°: handsome; shrewishly°: sharply

OLIVIA Let him approach. Call in my gentlewoman.

MALVOLIO Gentlewoman, my lady calls. *Exit*

Enter MARIA

OLIVIA Give me my veil. Come, throw it o'er my face.
We'll once more hear Orsino's embassy.

Enter VIOLA [*as Cesario*]

VIOLA The honorable lady of the house, which is she?

OLIVIA Speak to me, I shall answer for her. Your will.

VIOLA Most radiant, exquisite, and unmatchable beauty.—I pray you, tell me if this be the lady of the house, for I never saw her. I would be loath to cast away° my speech, for besides that it is excellently well penned, I have taken great pains to con° it. Good beauties, let me sustain° no scorn; I am very 'countable,° even to the least sinister usage.[1]

cast away°: waste; con°: memorize; sustain°: suffer; 'countable°: sensitive

OLIVIA Whence came you, sir?

VIOLA I can say little more than I have studied,[2] and that question's out of my part. Good gentle one, give me modest° assurance if you be the lady of the house, that I may proceed in my speech.

modest°: adequate

8. A decorative post set before a sheriff's door, as a sign of authority.
9. An undeveloped pea pod.

1. To the slightest discourteous treatment.
2. Learned by heart (a theatrical term).

OLIVIA Are you a comedian?°

an actor

VIOLA No, my profound heart;[3] and yet—by the very fangs of malice I swear—I am not that° I play. Are you the lady of the house?

what

OLIVIA If I do not usurp[4] myself, I am.

VIOLA Most certain if you are she you do usurp yourself, for what is yours to bestow is not yours to reserve. But this is from my commission.° I will on with my speech in your praise, and then show you the heart of my message.

beyond my instructions

OLIVIA Come to what is important in't, I forgive you° the praise.

excuse you from

VIOLA Alas, I took great pains to study it, and 'tis poetical.

OLIVIA It is the more like to be feigned, I pray you keep it in. I heard you were saucy° at my gates, and allowed your approach rather to wonder at you than to hear you. If you be not mad, be gone. If you have reason,° be brief. 'Tis not that time of moon with me to make one in so skipping a dialogue.[5]

impertinent / *any sanity*

MARIA Will you hoist sail, sir? Here lies your way.

VIOLA No, good swabber, I am to hull[6] here a little longer. [*To* OLIVIA] Some mollification for your giant,[7] sweet lady. Tell me your mind, I am a messenger.[8]

OLIVIA Sure, you have some hideous matter to deliver when the courtesy° of it is so fearful. Speak your office.°

introduction / business

VIOLA It alone concerns your ear. I bring no overture° of war, no taxation of homage.[9] I hold the olive[1] in my hand. My words are as full of peace as matter.°

declaration / *meaning*

OLIVIA Yet you began rudely. What are you? What would you?

VIOLA The rudeness that hath appeared in me have I learned from my entertainment.° What I am and what I would are as secret as maidenhead;° to your ears, divinity; to any others', profanation.

reception / *virginity*

OLIVIA [*to* MARIA *and attendants*] Give us the place alone, we will hear this divinity.° [*Exeunt* MARIA *and attendants*] Now sir, what is your text?[2]

religious discourse

VIOLA Most sweet lady—

OLIVIA A comfortable° doctrine, and much may be said of it. Where lies your text?

comforting

VIOLA In Orsino's bosom.

OLIVIA In his bosom? In what chapter of his bosom?

VIOLA To answer by the method,° in the first of his heart.

in the same style

OLIVIA O, I have read it. It is heresy. Have you no more to say?

VIOLA Good madam, let me see your face.

3. My most wise lady; upon my soul.
4. Counterfeit; misappropriate.
5. I am not lunatic enough to take part in so flighty a conversation. (Lunacy was thought to be influenced by the phases of the moon.)
6. To lie unanchored with lowered sails.
7. Mythical giants guarded ladies; here, also mocking Maria's diminutive size. "Some . . . for": please pacify.
8. From Orsino; Olivia pretends she understands her to mean a king's messenger, or a messenger-at-arms, employed on important state affairs.
9. Demand for dues paid to a superior.
1. Olive branch (as a symbol of peace).
2. Quotation (as a theme of a sermon, in keeping with "divinity," "doctrine," "heresy," etc.).

OLIVIA Have you any commission from your lord to negotiate with my face? You are now out of° your text. But we will draw the curtain and show you the picture. *straying from*
[*She unveils*]
Look you, sir, such a one I was this present.[3] Is't not well done?
VIOLA Excellently done, if God did all.[4]
OLIVIA 'Tis in grain,° sir, 'twill endure wind and weather. *the dye is fast*
VIOLA 'Tis beauty truly blent,[5] whose red and white
Nature's own sweet and cunning° hand laid on. *skillful*
Lady, you are the cruell'st she° alive *woman*
If you will lead these graces to the grave
And leave the world no copy.[6]
OLIVIA O sir, I will not be so hardhearted. I will give out divers schedules° of my beauty. It shall be inventoried and every particle and utensil labelled[7] to my will, as, *item,* two lips, indifferent° red; *item,* two grey eyes, with lids[8] to them; *item,* one neck, one chin, and so forth. Were you sent hither to praise° me? *various inventories* / *moderate* / *appraise; flatter*
VIOLA I see you what you are, you are too proud,
But if° you were the devil, you are fair. *even if*
My lord and master loves you. O, such love
Could be but recompensed though[9] you were crowned
The nonpareil of beauty.° *an unequaled beauty*
OLIVIA How does he love me?
VIOLA With adorations, fertile° tears, *ever-flowing*
With groans that thunder love, with sighs of fire.
OLIVIA Your lord does know my mind, I cannot love him.
Yet I suppose him virtuous, know him noble,
Of great estate,° of fresh and stainless youth, *high status*
In voices well divulged,° free,° learned, and valiant, *spoken of / generous*
And in dimension and the shape of nature[1]
A gracious person; but yet I cannot love him.
He might have took his answer long ago.
VIOLA If I did love you in° my master's flame,° *with / passion*
With such a suff'ring, such a deadly° life, *deathlike*
In your denial I would find no sense,
I would not understand it.
OLIVIA Why, what would you?
VIOLA Make me a willow[2] cabin at your gate
And call upon my soul° within the house, *i.e., Olivia*
Write loyal cantons of contemnèd° love, *songs of rejected*
And sing them loud even in the dead of night;
Halloo[3] your name to the reverberate° hills, *echoing*

3. Portraits usually gave the year of painting. "This present" was a term used to date letters.
4. If it is natural (without the use of cosmetics).
5. Blended, or mixed (of paints). Shakespeare uses the same metaphor in sonnet 20, lines 1–2. As Cesario, Viola is playing with established conventions of poetic courtship.
6. Viola means "child"; Olivia takes her to mean "list" or "inventory."
7. Every single part and article added as a codicil (parodying the legal language of a last will and testament).
8. Eyelids, but also punning on "pot lids" (punning on "utensil" as a household implement).
9. Would have to be requited even if.
1. "Dimension" and "shape of nature" are synonymous, meaning "bodily form."
2. Traditional symbol of rejected love.
3. Shout; or perhaps "hallow," as in "bless."

And make the babbling gossip of the air[4]
Cry out "Olivia!" O, you should not rest
Between the elements of air and earth
But° you should pity me. *unless*
OLIVIA You might do much.
What is your parentage?
VIOLA Above my fortunes, yet my state° is well. *social status*
I am a gentleman.
OLIVIA Get you to your lord.
I cannot love him. Let him send no more,
Unless, perchance,° you come to me again *perhaps*
To tell me how he takes it. Fare you well.
I thank you for your pains. [*Offering a purse*] Spend this for me.
VIOLA I am no fee'd post,° lady. Keep your purse. *hired messenger*
My master, not myself, lacks recompense.
Love make his heart of flint that you shall love,[5]
And let your fervor, like my master's, be
Placed in contempt. Farewell, fair cruelty. *Exit*
OLIVIA "What is your parentage?"
"Above my fortunes, yet my state is well.
I am a gentleman." I'll be sworn thou art.
Thy tongue, thy face, thy limbs, actions, and spirit
Do give thee five-fold blazon.[6] Not too fast. Soft,° soft— *wait*
Unless the master were the man.[7] How now?
Even so quickly may one catch the plague?
Methinks I feel this youth's perfections
With an invisible and subtle stealth
To creep in at mine eyes. Well, let it be.
What ho, Malvolio.
Enter MALVOLIO
MALVOLIO Here, madam, at your service.
OLIVIA Run after that same peevish messenger
The County's° man. He left this ring behind him, *Count's*
Would I° or not. Tell him I'll none of it. *whether I wished it*
Desire him not to flatter with° his lord, *encourage*
Nor hold him up with hopes. I am not for him.
If that the youth will come this way tomorrow,
I'll give him reasons for't. Hie thee,° Malvolio. *hurry*
MALVOLIO Madam, I will. *Exit* [*at one door*]
OLIVIA I do I know not what, and fear to find
Mine eye too great a flatterer for my mind.[8]
Fate, show thy force. Ourselves we do not owe.° *own*
What is decreed must be; and be this so.
[*Exit at another door*]

4. For the love of Narcissus, the nymph Echo wasted away to a mere voice, only able to repeat whatever she heard spoken.
5. May love make the heart of the man you love as hard as flint.
6. Formal description of a gentleman's coat of arms.
7. If Orsino were Cesario ("man": servant).
8. I.e., my eye (through which love has entered my heart) has seduced my reason.

2.1

Enter ANTONIO *and* SEBASTIAN

ANTONIO Will you stay no longer, nor will° you not that I go with you? *wish*

SEBASTIAN By your patience, no. My stars shine darkly[1] over me. The malignancy of my fate[2] might perhaps distemper° yours, therefore I shall crave of you your leave *infect*
that I may bear my evils alone. It were a bad recompense for your love to lay any of them on you.

ANTONIO Let me yet know of you whither you are bound.

SEBASTIAN No, sooth,° sir. My determinate° voyage is *truly / destined*
mere extravagancy.° But I perceive in you so excellent a *idle wandering*
touch of modesty° that you will not extort from me what *politeness*
I am willing to keep in. Therefore it charges me in manners[3] the rather to express° myself. You must know of me *reveal*
then, Antonio, my name is Sebastian, which I called Roderigo. My father was that Sebastian of Messaline[4] whom I know you have heard of. He left behind him myself and a sister, both born in an° hour. If the heavens had been *within the same*
pleased, would we had so ended. But you, sir, altered that, for some hour before you took me from the breach° *surf*
of the sea was my sister drowned.

ANTONIO Alas the day!

SEBASTIAN A lady, sir, though it was said she much resembled me, was yet of many accounted beautiful. But though I could not with such estimable° wonder over-far *appreciative*
believe that, yet thus far I will boldly publish° her: she *proclaim*
bore a mind that envy° could not but call fair. She is *malice*
drowned already, sir, with salt water, though I seem to drown her remembrance again with more.

ANTONIO Pardon me, sir, your bad entertainment.[5]

SEBASTIAN O good Antonio, forgive me your trouble.

ANTONIO If you will not murder me[6] for my love, let me be your servant.

SEBASTIAN If you will not undo what you have done—that is, kill him whom you have recovered°—desire it not. Fare *rescued*
ye well at once. My bosom is full of kindness,° and I am *tender emotion*
yet° so near the manners of my mother[7] that upon the *still*
least occasion more mine eyes will tell tales of me.° I am *betray my feelings*
bound to the Count Orsino's court. Farewell. *Exit*

ANTONIO The gentleness° of all the gods go with thee! *favor*
I have many enemies in Orsino's court,
Else° would I very shortly see thee there. *otherwise*
But come what may, I do adore thee so
That danger shall seem sport, and I will go. *Exit*

2.1 Location: Near the coast of Illyria.
1. Forebodingly; unfavorably.
2. Evil influence of the stars; "malignancy" also signifies a deadly disease.
3. Therefore courtesy requires.
4. Possibly Messina, Sicily.
5. Your poor reception; your inhospitality.
6. I.e., murder him by insisting that they part.
7. I.e., so near woman's readiness to weep.

2.2

Enter VIOLA *as Cesario, and* MALVOLIO, *at several° doors* — *separate*

MALVOLIO Were not you ev'n° now with the Countess Olivia? — *just*

VIOLA Even now, sir, on° a moderate pace, I have since arrived but hither.° — *at*; *come only this far*

MALVOLIO [*offering a ring*] She returns this ring to you, sir. You might have saved me my pains to have taken° it away yourself. She adds, moreover, that you should put your lord into a desperate assurance° she will none of him. And one thing more: that you be never so hardy° to come again in his affairs, unless it be to report your lord's taking of this.[1] Receive it so. — *by taking*; *hopeless certainty*; *bold*

VIOLA She took the ring of me.[2] I'll none of it.

MALVOLIO Come, sir, you peevishly threw it to her, and her will is it should be so returned.

[*He throws the ring down*]

If it be worth stooping for, there it lies, in your eye;° if not, be it his that finds it. *Exit* — *sight*

VIOLA [*picking up the ring*] I left no ring with her. What means this lady?
Fortune forbid my outside° have not charmed her. — *appearance*
She made good view of° me, indeed so much — *looked carefully at*
That straight methought her eyes had lost° her tongue, — *made her lose*
For she did speak in starts, distractedly.
She loves me, sure. The cunning of her passion
Invites me in° this churlish messenger. — *by means of*
None of my lord's ring! Why, he sent her none.
I am the man.[3] If it be so—as 'tis—
Poor lady, she were better love a dream!
Disguise, I see thou art a wickedness
Wherein the pregnant enemy[4] does much.
How easy is it for the proper false[5]
In women's waxen hearts to set their forms![6]
Alas, our frailty is the cause, not we,
For such as we are made of, such we be.[7]
How will this fadge?° My master loves her dearly, — *turn out*
And I, poor monster,[8] fond° as much on him, — *dote*
And she, mistaken, seems to dote on me.
What will become of this? As I am man,
My state is desperate° for my master's love. — *hopeless*
As I am woman, now, alas the day,
What thriftless° sighs shall poor Olivia breathe! — *unprofitable*
O time, thou must untangle this, not I.
It is too hard a knot for me t'untie. [*Exit*]

2.2 Location: Between Olivia's house and Orsino's palace.
1. Reception of this (rejection).
2. Viola pretends to believe Olivia's story. "Of": from.
3. I.e., the man with whom she has fallen in love.
4. The devil. "Pregnant": teeming with ideas.
5. Handsome, but deceitful (men).
6. To impress their images on women's affections (as a seal stamps its image in wax).
7. For being made of frail flesh, we are frail.
8. Since she is both man and woman.

2.3

Enter SIR TOBY *and* SIR ANDREW

SIR TOBY Approach, Sir Andrew. Not to be abed after midnight is to be up betimes,° and *diliculo surgere,*[1] thou — *early*
knowest.

SIR ANDREW Nay, by my troth,° I know not; but I know to — *faith*
be up late is to be up late.

SIR TOBY A false conclusion. I hate it as an unfilled can.° — *tankard*
To be up after midnight and to go to bed then is early; so
that to go to bed after midnight is to go to bed betimes.
Does not our lives consist of the four elements?[2]

SIR ANDREW Faith, so they say, but I think it rather consists
of eating and drinking.

SIR TOBY Thou'rt a scholar; let us therefore eat and drink.
Marian, I say, a stoup° of wine. — *two-pint tankard*

Enter [FESTE, *the*] *clown*

SIR ANDREW Here comes the fool, i'faith.

FESTE How now, my hearts. Did you never see the picture
of "we three"?[3]

SIR TOBY Welcome, ass. Now let's have a catch.[4]

SIR ANDREW By my troth, the fool has an excellent breast.° — *singing voice*
I had rather than forty shillings I had such a leg,° and so — *(for dancing)*
sweet a breath to sing, as the fool has. In sooth, thou
wast in very gracious fooling last night, when thou spo-
kest of Pigrogromitus, of the Vapians passing the equinoctial of Queubus.[5] 'Twas very good, i'faith. I sent thee
sixpence for thy leman.° Hadst it? — *sweetheart*

FESTE I did impeticos thy gratility;[6] for Malvolio's nose is
no whipstock. My lady has a white hand, and the Myr-
midons are no bottle-ale houses.[7]

SIR ANDREW Excellent! Why, this is the best fooling, when
all is done. Now a song.

SIR TOBY [*to* FESTE] Come on, there is sixpence for you.
Let's have a song.

SIR ANDREW [*to* FESTE] There's a testril[8] of me, too. If one
knight give a—[9]

FESTE Would you have a love-song, or a song of good life?

SIR TOBY A love-song, a love-song.

SIR ANDREW Ay, ay. I care not for good life.

FESTE (*sings*)

O mistress mine, where are you roaming?
O stay and hear, your true love's coming,

2.3 Location: Olivia's house.

1. Part of a Latin proverb, meaning "to rise at dawn (is most healthy)."
2. The four elements, thought to make up all matter, were earth, air, fire, and water.
3. A trick picture portraying two fools' or asses' heads, the third being the viewer.
4. Round: a simple song for several voices.
5. "Pigrogromitus . . . Queubus": Feste's mock learning. "Equinoctial": equator of the astronomical heavens.
6. Comic jargon for "impocket (or impetticoat) your gratuity."
7. Perhaps it is the sheer inscrutability of Feste's foolery that so impresses Sir Andrew (line 28). "Whipstock": handle of a whip. "Bottle-ale houses": cheap taverns.
8. Sir Andrew's version of "tester" (sixpence).
9. In the First Folio, "give a" appears at the end of a justified line; an omission is possible.

That can sing both high and low.
Trip° no further, pretty sweeting. *go*
Journeys end in lovers meeting,
Every wise man's son doth know.[1]

SIR ANDREW Excellent good, i'faith.

SIR TOBY Good, good.

FESTE What is love? 'Tis not hereafter,
Present mirth hath present laughter.
What's to come is still° unsure. *always*
In delay there lies no plenty,
Then come kiss me, sweet and twenty.° *twenty-times sweet*
Youth's a stuff will not endure.

SIR ANDREW A mellifluous voice, as I am true knight.

SIR TOBY A contagious breath.[2]

SIR ANDREW Very sweet and contagious, i'faith.

SIR TOBY To hear by the nose, it is dulcet in contagion.[3] But shall we make the welkin° dance indeed? Shall we rouse the night-owl in a catch that will draw three souls out of one weaver?[4] Shall we do that? *sky*

SIR ANDREW An° you love me, let's do't. I am dog° at a catch. *if / clever*

FESTE By'r Lady, sir, and some dogs will catch well.

SIR ANDREW Most certain. Let our catch be "Thou knave."

FESTE "Hold thy peace, thou knave,"[5] knight. I shall be constrained in't to call thee knave, knight.

SIR ANDREW 'Tis not the first time I have constrained one to call me knave. Begin, fool. It begins "Hold thy peace."

FESTE I shall never begin if I hold my peace.

AIR ANDREW 'Good, i'faith. Come, begin.

[*They sing the*] *catch.*

Enter MARIA

MARIA What a caterwauling do you keep here! If my lady have not called up her steward Malvolio and bid him turn you out of doors, never trust me.

SIR TOBY My lady's a Cathayan,[6] we are politicians,° Malvolio's a Peg-o'-Ramsey,[7] and "Three merry men be we." Am not I consanguineous?[8] Am I not of her blood? Tillyvally°—"lady"! "There dwelt a man in Babylon, lady, lady."[9] *schemers* / *fiddlesticks*

FESTE Beshrew° me, the knight's in admirable fooling. *curse*

1. The words of the song are not certainly Shakespeare's; they fit the tune of an instrumental piece printed in Thomas Morley's *First Book of Consort Lessons* (1599). "Wise man's son": wise men were thought to have foolish sons.
2. Catchy voice; with a play on "disease-causing air."
3. If one could hear through the nose, the sound would be sweetly ("dulcet") infectious.
4. Weavers were traditionally addicted to psalm singing, so to move them with popular catches would be a great triumph. Music was said to be able to draw the soul from the body.
5. The words of the catch are "Hold thy peace, I prithee hold thy peace, thou knave." Each singer repeatedly calls the others knaves and tells them to stop singing.
6. Chinese; but also ethnocentric slang for "trickster" or "cheat."
7. Name of a dance and popular song; here, used contemptuously.
8. A blood relative (of Olivia's). "Three . . . we": refrain of a popular song.
9. The opening and refrain of a popular song.

SIR ANDREW Ay, he does well enough if he be disposed, and so do I, too. He does it with a better grace, but I do it more natural.[1]

SIR TOBY "O' the twelfth day of December"[2]—

MARIA For the love o' God, peace.

Enter MALVOLIO

MALVOLIO My masters, are you mad? Or what are you? Have you no wit,° manners, nor honesty,° but to gabble like tinkers at this time of night? Do ye make an alehouse of my lady's house, that ye squeak out your coziers'° catches without any mitigation or remorse[3] of voice? Is there no respect of place, persons, nor time in you? *sense / decency* *cobblers'*

SIR TOBY We did keep time, sir, in our catches. Sneck up!° *go hang yourself*

MALVOLIO Sir Toby, I must be round° with you. My lady bade me tell you that though she harbors you as her kinsman she's nothing allied to your disorders. If you can separate yourself and your misdemeanors you are welcome to the house. If not, an it would please you to take leave of her she is very willing to bid you farewell. *plainspoken*

SIR TOBY "Farewell, dear heart, since I must needs be gone."[4]

MARIA Nay, good Sir Toby.

FESTE "His eyes do show his days are almost done."

MALVOLIO Is't even so?

SIR TOBY "But I will never die."

FESTE "Sir Toby, there you lie."

MALVOLIO This is much credit to you.

SIR TOBY "Shall I bid him go?"

FESTE "What an if° you do?" *an if = if*

SIR TOBY "Shall I bid him go, and spare not?"

FESTE "O no, no, no, no, you dare not."

SIR TOBY Out o' tune, sir, ye lie. [*To* MALVOLIO] Art any more than a steward? Dost thou think because thou art virtuous there shall be no more cakes and ale?[5]

FESTE Yes, by Saint Anne, and ginger[6] shall be hot i'th' mouth, too.

SIR TOBY Thou'rt i'th' right. [*To* MALVOLIO] Go, sir, rub your chain with crumbs.[7] [*To* MARIA] A stoup of wine, Maria.

MALVOLIO Mistress Mary, if you prized my lady's favor at any thing more than contempt you would not give means° for this uncivil rule.° She shall know of it, by this hand. *Exit*[8] *drink / behavior*

MARIA Go shake your ears.° *(like an ass)*

1. Effortlessly; but unconsciously playing on the sense of *natural* as "fool" or "idiot."
2. Snatch of a ballad; or possibly a drunken version of "twelfth day of Christmas," that is, Twelfth Night.
3. Without any abating or softening.
4. Part of another song that Sir Toby and Feste adapt for the occasion.
5. Traditionally associated with church festivals and therefore disliked by Puritans.
6. Used to spice ale. Saint Anne was the mother of the Virgin; the oath would be offensive to Puritans, who attacked her cult.
7. Clean your steward's chain; mind your own business.
8. Feste plays no further part in this scene. This is the suggested exit for him.

SIR ANDREW 'Twere as good a deed as to drink when a man's a-hungry to challenge him the field° [*to a duel*] and then to break promise with him, and make a fool of him.

SIR TOBY Do't, knight. I'll write thee a challenge, or I'll deliver thy indignation to him by word of mouth.

MARIA Sweet Sir Toby, be patient for tonight. Since the youth of the Count's was today with my lady she is much out of quiet. For Monsieur Malvolio, let me alone with him.° [*leave him to me*] If I do not gull him into a nayword[9] and make him a common recreation,° [*sport, jest*] do not think I have wit enough to lie straight in my bed. I know I can do it.

SIR TOBY Possess° [*inform*] us, possess us, tell us something of him.

MARIA Marry, sir, sometimes he is a kind of puritan.[1]

SIR ANDREW O, if I thought that I'd beat him like a dog.

SIR TOBY What, for being a puritan? Thy exquisite° [*ingenious*] reason, dear knight.

SIR ANDREW I have no exquisite reason for't, but I have reason good enough.

MARIA The dev'l a puritan that he is, or anything constantly but a time-pleaser,° [*boot licker*] an affectioned° [*affected*] ass that cons state without book and utters it by great swathes;[2] the best persuaded of himself,[3] so crammed, as he thinks, with excellencies, that it is his grounds of faith° [*his creed*] that all that look on him love him; and on that vice in him will my revenge find notable cause to work.

SIR TOBY What wilt thou do?

MARIA I will drop in his way some obscure epistles of love, wherein by the color of his beard, the shape of his leg, the manner of his gait, the expressure° [*expression*] of his eye, forehead, and complexion, he shall find himself most feelingly personated.° [*represented*] I can write very like my lady your niece; on a forgotten matter we can hardly make distinction of our hands.° [*handwriting*]

SIR TOBY Excellent, I smell a device.

SIR ANDREW I have't in my nose too.

SIR TOBY He shall think by the letters that thou wilt drop that they come from my niece, and that she's in love with him.

MARIA My purpose is indeed a horse of that color.

SIR ANDREW And your horse now would make him an ass.

MARIA Ass° [*(punning on "as")*] I doubt not.

SIR ANDREW O, 'twill be admirable.

MARIA Sport royal, I warrant you. I know my physic° [*medicine*] will work with him. I will plant you two—and let the fool make a third—where he shall find the letter. Observe his construction° [*interpretation*] of it. For this night, to bed, and dream on

9. If I do not trick ("gull") him into a byword (for "dupe").

1. Could mean "morally strict and censorious," as well as "a follower of the Puritan religious faith."

2. Memorizes dignified and high-flown language and utters it in great sweeps (like hay falling under a scythe).

3. Having the highest opinion of himself.

the event.° Farewell. *Exit* — *outcome*

SIR TOBY Good night, Penthesilea.[4]

SIR ANDREW Before me,[5] she's a good wench.

SIR TOBY She's a beagle true bred, and one that adores me. What o' that?

SIR ANDREW I was adored once, too.

SIR TOBY Let's to bed, knight. Thou hadst need send for more money.

SIR ANDREW If I cannot recover° your niece, I am a foul way out.° — *win* / *out of money*

SIR TOBY Send for money, knight. If thou hast her not i'th' end, call me cut.[6]

SIR ANDREW If I do not, never trust me, take it how you will.

SIR TOBY Come, come, I'll go burn some sack,[7] 'tis too late to go to bed now. Come knight, come knight. *Exeunt*

2.4

Enter Duke, VIOLA [*as Cesario*], CURIO, *and others*

ORSINO Give me some music. Now good morrow,° friends. — *morning*
Now good Cesario, but° that piece of song, — *just*
That old and antic° song we heard last night. — *quaint*
Methought it did relieve my passion° much, — *suffering*
More than light airs and recollected° terms — *studied; artificial*
Of these most brisk and giddy-pacèd times.
Come, but one verse.

CURIO He is not here, so please your lordship, that should sing it.

ORSINO Who was it?

CURIO Feste the jester, my lord, a fool that the lady Olivia's father took much delight in. He is about the house.

ORSINO Seek him out, and play the tune the while.

[*Exit* CURIO]

Music plays

[*To* VIOLA] Come hither, boy. If ever thou shalt love,
In the sweet pangs of it remember me;
For such as I am, all true lovers are,
Unstaid° and skittish in all motions° else — *unstable / emotions*
Save° in the constant image of the creature — *except*
That is beloved. How dost thou like this tune?

VIOLA It gives a very echo to the seat
Where love is throned.[1]

ORSINO Thou dost speak masterly.° — *expertly*
My life upon't, young though thou art thine eye
Hath stayed upon some favor° that it loves. — *face*
Hath it not, boy?

4. Queen of the Amazons (a joke about Maria's small size).
5. On my soul (a mild oath).
6. A dock-tailed horse; also, slang for "gelding" or for "female genitals."
7. I'll go warm and spice some Spanish wine.
2.4 Location: Orsino's palace.
1. I.e., it reflects back to the heart.

VIOLA A little, by your favor.° *leave; face*
ORSINO What kind of woman is't?
VIOLA Of your complexion.
ORSINO She is not worth thee then. What years, i'faith?
VIOLA About your years, my lord.
ORSINO Too old, by heaven. Let still° the woman take *always*
An elder than herself. So wears° she to him; *adapts*
So sways she level[2] in her husband's heart.
For, boy, however we do praise ourselves,
Our fancies° are more giddy and unfirm, *affections*
More longing, wavering, sooner lost and worn,° *exhausted*
Than women's are.
VIOLA I think° it well, my lord. *believe*
ORSINO Then let thy love be younger than thyself,
Or thy affection cannot hold the bent;[3]
For women are as roses, whose fair flower
Being once displayed,° doth fall that very hour. *opened*
VIOLA And so they are. Alas that they are so:
To die even° when they to perfection grow. *just*
Enter CURIO *and* [FESTE, *the*] *clown*
ORSINO [*to* FESTE] O fellow, come, the song we had last night.
Mark it, Cesario, it is old and plain.
The spinsters,° and the knitters in the sun, *spinners*
And the free° maids that weave their thread with bones,[4] *carefree*
Do use to chant it. It is silly sooth,° *simple truth*
And dallies with° the innocence of love, *lingers lovingly on*
Like the old° age. *golden*
FESTE Are you ready, sir?
ORSINO I prithee, sing.
Music
FESTE [*sings*] Come away,° come away death, *come hither*
And in sad cypress[5] let me be laid.
Fie away, fie away breath,
I am slain by a fair cruel maid.
My shroud of white, stuck all with yew,° *yew sprigs*
O prepare it.
My part of death no one so true
Did share it.[6]

Not a flower, not a flower sweet
On my black coffin let there be strewn.
Not a friend, not a friend greet
My poor corpse, where my bones shall be thrown.
A thousand thousand sighs to save,
Lay me O where
Sad true lover never find my grave,
To weep there.

2. So does she balance (influence and affection).
3. Cannot remain at full stretch (like the tautness of a bowstring).
4. Spools made from bone on which lace (called "bone lace") was woven.
5. Cypress-wood coffin. Like yews, cypresses were emblematic of mourning.
6. I.e., no one has died so true to love as I.

ORSINO [*giving money*] There's for thy pains.
FESTE No pains, sir. I take pleasure in singing, sir.
ORSINO I'll pay thy pleasure then.
FESTE Truly, sir, and pleasure will be paid,° one time or another. *paid for*
ORSINO Give me now leave° to leave° thee. *permission / dismiss*
FESTE Now the melancholy god[7] protect thee, and the tailor make thy doublet° of changeable taffeta,[8] for thy mind is a very opal.[9] I would have men of such constancy put to sea, that their business might be everything, and their intent° everywhere, for that's it that always makes a good voyage of nothing.[1] Farewell. *Exit* *close-fitting jacket* *destination*
ORSINO Let all the rest give place:° *withdraw*
[*Exeunt* CURIO *and others*]
Once more, Cesario,
Get thee to yon same sovereign° cruelty. *supreme*
Tell her my love, more noble than the world,
Prizes not quantity of dirty lands.
The parts° that fortune hath bestowed upon her *possessions*
Tell her I hold as giddily[2] as fortune;
But 'tis that miracle and queen of gems
That nature pranks° her in attracts my soul. *adorns*
VIOLA But if she cannot love you, sir?
ORSINO I cannot be so answered.
VIOLA Sooth,° but you must. *in truth*
Say that some lady, as perhaps there is,
Hath for your love as great a pang of heart
As you have for Olivia. You cannot love her.
You tell her so. Must she not then be answered?
ORSINO There is no woman's sides
Can bide° the beating of so strong a passion *withstand*
As love doth give my heart; no woman's heart
So big, to hold so much. They lack retention.° *constancy*
Alas, their love may be called appetite,
No motion° of the liver, but the palate,[3] *impulse*
That suffer surfeit, cloyment,° and revolt.° *satiety / revulsion*
But mine is all as hungry as the sea,
And can digest as much. Make no compare
Between that love a woman can bear me
And that I owe° Olivia. *have for*
VIOLA Ay, but I know—
ORSINO What dost thou know?
VIOLA Too well what love women to men may owe.
In faith, they are as true of heart as we.
My father had a daughter loved a man

7. Saturn (thought to control the melancholic).
8. Shot silk, whose color changes with the angle of vision.
9. An iridescent gemstone that changes color depending on the angle from which it is seen.
1. I.e., this fickle lack of direction can make a voyage in the notoriously changeful sea carefree and consonant with one's desires.
2. Lightly (fortune being fickle).
3. Appetite, like the palate, is easily sated and thus lacks the emotional depth and complexity of real love, whose seat is the liver.

As it might be, perhaps, were I a woman
I should your lordship.
ORSINO And what's her history?
VIOLA A blank, my lord. She never told her love,
But let concealment, like a worm i'th' bud,
Feed on her damask[4] cheek. She pined in thought,
And with a green and yellow° melancholy *pale and sallow*
She sat like patience on a monument,[5]
Smiling at grief. Was not this love indeed?
We men may say more, swear more, but indeed
Our shows are more than will;[6] for still° we prove *always*
Much in our vows, but little in our love.
ORSINO But died thy sister of her love, my boy?
VIOLA I am all the daughters of my father's house,
And all the brothers too; and yet I know not.
Sir, shall I to this lady?
ORSINO Ay, that's the theme,
To her in haste. Give her this jewel. Say
My love can give no place, bide no denay.[7]
Exeunt [*severally*]

2.5

Enter SIR TOBY, SIR ANDREW, *and* FABIAN

SIR TOBY Come thy ways,° Signor Fabian. *come along*

FABIAN Nay, I'll come. If I lose a scruple° of this sport let me be boiled to death with melancholy.[1] *miss a scrap*

SIR TOBY Wouldst thou not be glad to have the niggardly° rascally sheep-biter[2] come by some notable shame? *stingy*

FABIAN I would exult, man. You know he brought me out o' favour with my lady about a bear-baiting[3] here.

SIR TOBY To anger him we'll have the bear again, and we will fool° him black and blue, shall we not, Sir Andrew? *mock*

SIR ANDREW An° we do not, it is pity of our lives. *if*

Enter MARIA [*with a letter*]

SIR TOBY Here comes the little villain. How now, my metal of India?[4]

MARIA Get ye all three into the box-tree.° Malvolio's coming down this walk. He has been yonder i' the sun practising behavior to his own shadow this half-hour. Observe him, for the love of mockery, for I know this letter will make a contemplative° idiot of him. Close,° in the name of jesting! *hedge of boxwood* *vacuous / hide*

[*The men hide.* MARIA *places the letter*]

Lie thou there, for here comes the trout that must be caught with tickling.[5] *Exit*

Enter MALVOLIO

4. Pink and white, like a damask rose.
5. A memorial statue symbolizing patience.
6. Our displays of love are greater than our actual feelings.
7. My love cannot be bated, nor tolerate refusal.
2.5 Location: Olivia's garden.
1. Melancholy was a cold humor; "boiled" puns on "bile," the surplus of which produced melancholy.
2. Literally, a dog that attacks sheep; here, a malicious sneak.
3. Puritans disapproved of blood sports like bearbaiting.
4. A woman worth her weight in gold.
5. Flattery; trout can supposedly be caught by strok-

MALVOLIO 'Tis but fortune, all is fortune. Maria once told me she° did affect° me, and I have heard herself come thus near, that should she fancy° it should be one of my complexion. Besides, she uses me with a more exalted respect than anyone else that follows her. What should I think on't? *i.e., Olivia / care for* *fall in love*

SIR TOBY Here's an overweening° rogue. *presumptuous*

FABIAN O, peace! Contemplation makes a rare turkey-cock[6] of him—how he jets° under his advanced° plumes! *struts / raised*

SIR ANDREW 'Slight,[7] I could so beat the rogue.

SIR TOBY Peace, I say.

MALVOLIO To be Count Malvolio!

SIR TOBY Ah, rogue.

SIR ANDREW Pistol him, pistol him.

SIR TOBY Peace, peace.

MALVOLIO There is example° for't: the Lady of the Strachey married the yeoman of the wardrobe.[8] *precedent*

SIR ANDREW Fie on him, Jezebel.[9]

FABIAN O peace, now he's deeply in. Look how imagination blows him.° *puffs him up*

MALVOLIO Having been three months married to her, sitting in my state°— *chair of state*

SIR TOBY O for a stone-bow[1] to hit him in the eye!

MALVOLIO Calling my officers° about me, in my branched[2] velvet gown, having come from a day-bed° where I have left Olivia sleeping— *household attendants* *couch*

SIR TOBY Fire and brimstone!

FABIAN O peace, peace.

MALVOLIO And then to have the humor of state[3] and—after a demure travel of regard,[4] telling them I know my place, as I would they should do theirs—to ask for my kinsman Toby.

SIR TOBY Bolts and shackles!

FABIAN O peace, peace, peace, now, now.

MALVOLIO Seven of my people with an obedient start make° out for him. I frown the while, and perchance wind up my watch, or play with my—[*touching his chain*][5] some rich jewel. Toby approaches; curtsies° there to me. *go* *bows*

SIR TOBY Shall this fellow live?

FABIAN Though our silence be drawn from us with cars,[6] yet peace.

MALVOLIO I extend my hand to him thus, quenching my familiar smile with an austere regard° of control— *look*

---

ing them under the gills.
6. Proverbially proud; they display their feathers like peacocks.
7. By God's light (an oath).
8. Perhaps an allusion to a noblewoman who had married her manservant, but there is no certain identification. "Yeoman of the wardrobe": keeper of clothes and linen.
9. Biblical allusion to the proud wife of Ahab, king of Israel.

1. Catapult, or crossbow for stones.
2. Embroidered with branch patterns.
3. To adopt the grand air of exalted greatness.
4. After casting my eyes gravely about the room.
5. Malvolio momentarily forgets that he will have abandoned his steward's chain; watches were an expensive luxury at this time.
6. A prisoner might be tied to two carts or chariots ("cars") and pulled by horses in opposite directions to extort information.

SIR TOBY And does not Toby take° you a blow o' the lips, then? *give*

MALVOLIO Saying "Cousin Toby, my fortunes, having cast me on your niece, give me this prerogative of speech"—

SIR TOBY What, what!

MALVOLIO "You must amend your drunkenness."

SIR TOBY Out, scab.

FABIAN Nay, patience, or we break the sinews of our plot.

MALVOLIO "Besides, you waste the treasure of your time with a foolish knight"—

SIR ANDREW That's me, I warrant you.

MALVOLIO "One Sir Andrew."

SIR ANDREW I knew 'twas I, for many do call me fool.

MALVOLIO [*seeing the letter*] What employment° have we here? *business*

FABIAN Now is the woodcock near the gin.[7]

SIR TOBY O peace, and the spirit of humors intimate[8] reading aloud to him.

MALVOLIO [*taking up the letter*] By my life, this is my lady's hand. These be her very c's, her u's, and her t's,[9] and thus makes she her great P's. It is in contempt of° question her hand. *beyond*

SIR ANDREW Her c's, her u's, and her t's? Why that?

MALVOLIO [*reads*] "To the unknown beloved, this, and my good wishes." Her very phrases! [*Opening the letter*] By your leave, wax[1]—soft,° and the impressure her Lucrece,[2] with which she uses to seal°—'tis my lady. To whom should this be? *wait* *habitually seals*

FABIAN This wins him, liver and all.

MALVOLIO "Jove knows I love,
But who?
Lips do not move,
No man must know."

"No man must know." What follows? The numbers altered.° "No man must know." If this should be thee, Malvolio? *meter changed*

SIR TOBY Marry, hang thee, brock.[3]

MALVOLIO "I may command where I adore,
But silence like a Lucrece knife[4]
With bloodless stroke my heart doth gore.
M.O.A.I. doth sway my life."

FABIAN A fustian° riddle. *bombastic*

SIR TOBY Excellent wench, say I.

MALVOLIO "M.O.A.I. doth sway my life." Nay, but first let me see, let me see, let me see.

FABIAN What dish o' poison has she dressed° him! *prepared*

7. Snare. The woodcock is a proverbially foolish bird.
8. And may a capricious impulse suggest.
9. Malvolio unwittingly spells out "cut," slang for female genitals; the meaning is compounded by "great P's." In fact, these letters do not appear on the outside of the letter.

1. He addresses himself to the sealing wax.
2. The figure of Lucrece, Roman model of chastity, is the device ("impressure") imprinted on the seal.
3. Badger (proverbially stinking).
4. After being raped, Lucretia stabbed herself to death.

SIR TOBY And with what wing the staniel checks at it![5]

MALVOLIO "I may command where I adore." Why, she may command me. I serve her, she is my lady. Why, this is evident to any formal capacity.° There is no obstruction in this. And the end—what should that alphabetical position° portend? If I could make that resemble something in me. Softly—'M.O.A.I.'

normal intelligence / *arrangements*

SIR TOBY O ay,[6] make up that, he is now at a cold scent.

FABIAN Sowter will cry upon't for all this, though° it be as rank as a fox.[7]

as though

MALVOLIO "M." Malvolio—'M"—why, that begins my name.

FABIAN Did not I say he would work it out? The cur is excellent at faults.[8]

MALVOLIO "M." But then there is no consonancy in the sequel.[9] That suffers under probation.[1] "A" should follow, but "O" does.

FABIAN And "O"[2] shall end, I hope.

SIR TOBY Ay, or I'll cudgel him, and make him cry "O!"

MALVOLIO And then "I" comes behind.

FABIAN Ay, an you had any eye behind you you might see more detraction° at your heels than fortunes before you.

defamation

MALVOLIO "M.O.A.I." This simulation° is not as the former; and yet to crush° this a little, it would bow° to me, for every one of these letters are in my name. Soft, here follows prose: "If this fall into thy hand, revolve.° In my stars° I am above thee, but be not afraid of greatness. Some are born great, some achieve greatness, and some have greatness thrust upon 'em. Thy fates open their hands,° let thy blood and spirit embrace them, and to inure° thyself to what thou art like° to be, cast thy humble slough,[3] and appear fresh. Be opposite° with a kinsman, surly with servants. Let thy tongue tang arguments of state;[4] put thyself into the trick of singularity.° She thus advises thee that sighs for thee. Remember who commended thy yellow stockings, and wished to see thee ever cross-gartered.[5] I say remember, go to,[6] thou art made if thou desirest to be so; if not, let me see thee a steward still, the fellow of servants, and not worthy to touch Fortune's fingers. Farewell. She that would alter services[7] with thee,

The Fortunate-Unhappy."

Daylight and champaign discovers[8] not more. This is

disguise; riddle / *force / yield; point* / *consider* / *fortunes* / *bestow gifts* / *accustom / likely* / *contrary* / *cultivate eccentricity*

5. And with what alacrity the sparrow hawk goes after it.
6. Playing on "O.I."
7. "Sowter" (the name of a hound), having lost the scent, will start to bay loudly as he picks up the new, rank (stinking) smell of the fox.
8. At picking up a scent after it is momentarily lost. A "fault" is a "cold scent" (line 117).
9. There is no consistency in what follows.
1. That weakens upon being put to the test.
2. As in the hangman's noose; the last letter of Malvolio's name; or "O" as a lamentation.
3. A snake's old skin, which peels away.
4. Let your tongue ring out arguments of statecraft or politics.
5. An antiquated way of adjusting a garter—going once below the knee, crossing behind it, and knotting above the knee at the side.
6. An emphatic expression, like "I tell you."
7. Change places (of servant and mistress or master).
8. Open countryside reveals.

open.° I will be proud, I will read politic° authors, I will *clear / political*
baffle[9] Sir Toby, I will wash off gross acquaintance, I will
be point-device the very man.[1] I do not now fool myself,
to let imagination jade° me; for every reason excites to *trick*
this, that my lady loves me. She did commend my yellow
stockings of late, she did praise my leg, being cross-
gartered, and in this she manifests herself to my love, and
with a kind of injunction drives me to these habits° of her *clothes*
liking. I thank my stars, I am happy. I will be strange,° *aloof*
stout,° in yellow stockings, and cross-gartered, even with *proud*
the swiftness of putting on. Jove and my stars be praised.
Here is yet a postscript. "Thou canst not choose but know
who I am. If thou entertainest° my love, let it appear in *accept*
thy smiling, thy smiles become thee well. Therefore in
my presence still° smile, dear my sweet, I prithee." Jove, *constantly*
I thank thee. I will smile, I will do everything that thou
wilt have me. *Exit*

[SIR TOBY, SIR ANDREW, *and* FABIAN *come from hiding*]

FABIAN I will not give my part of this sport for a pension
of thousands to be paid from the Sophy.° *shah of Persia*

SIR TOBY I could marry this wench for this device.

SIR ANDREW So could I, too.

SIR TOBY And ask no other dowry with her but such
another jest.

Enter MARIA

SIR ANDREW Nor I neither.

FABIAN Here comes my noble gull-catcher.° *trickster*

SIR TOBY [*to* MARIA] Wilt thou set thy foot o' my neck?

SIR ANDREW [*to* MARIA] Or o' mine either?

SIR TOBY [*to* MARIA] Shall I play° my freedom at tray-trip,[2] *wager*
and become thy bondslave?

SIR ANDREW [*to* MARIA] I'faith, or I either?

SIR TOBY [*to* MARIA] Why, thou hast put him in such a
dream that when the image° of it leaves him, he must run *illusion*
mad.

MARIA Nay, but say true, does it work upon him?

SIR TOBY Like aqua vitae° with a midwife. *spirits, liquor*

MARIA If you will then see the fruits of the sport, mark his
first approach before my lady. He will come to her in
yellow stockings, and 'tis a color she abhors, and cross-
gartered, a fashion she detests; and he will smile upon
her, which will now be so unsuitable to her disposition,
being addicted to a melancholy as she is, that it cannot
but turn him into a notable contempt.[3] If you will see it,
follow me.

9. Term used to describe the formal unmaking of a knight; hence, "disgrace."
1. I will be in every detail the identical man (described in the letter).
2. A game of dice in which the winner throws a three ("tray" is from the Spanish *tres*).
3. A notorious object of contempt.

SIR TOBY To the gates of Tartar,° thou most excellent devil of wit. *hell*

SIR ANDREW I'll make one,° too. *Exeunt* *go along*

3.1

Enter VIOLA [*as Cesario*] *and* [FESTE, *the*] *clown* [*with pipe and tabor*][1]

VIOLA Save° thee, friend, and thy music. Dost thou live by thy tabor? *God save*

FESTE No, sir, I live by° the church. *near*

VIOLA Art thou a churchman?

FESTE No such matter, sir. I do live by[2] the church for I do live at my house, and my house doth stand by the church.

VIOLA So thou mayst say the king lies by[3] a beggar if a beggar dwell near him, or the church stands° by thy tabor if thy tabor stand by the church. *is maintained*

FESTE You have said, sir. To see this age!—A sentence° is but a cheverel° glove to a good wit, how quickly the wrong side may be turned outward. *saying* *kidskin*

VIOLA Nay, that's certain. They that dally nicely° with words may quickly make them wanton.[4] *play subtly*

FESTE I would therefore my sister had had no name, sir.

VIOLA Why, man?

FESTE Why, sir, her name's a word, and to dally with that word might make my sister wanton. But indeed, words are very rascals since bonds disgraced them.[5]

VIOLA Thy reason, man?

FESTE Troth, sir, I can yield you none without words, and words are grown so false I am loath to prove reason with them.

VIOLA I warrant thou art a merry fellow, and carest for nothing.

FESTE Not so, sir, I do care for something; but in my conscience, sir, I do not care for you. If that be to care for nothing, sir, I would it would make you invisible.

VIOLA Art not thou the Lady Olivia's fool?

FESTE No indeed, sir, the Lady Olivia has no folly, she will keep no fool, sir, till she be married, and fools are as like husbands as pilchards[6] are to herrings—the husband's the bigger. I am indeed not her fool, but her corrupter of words.

VIOLA I saw thee late° at the Count Orsino's. *lately*

FESTE Foolery, sir, does walk about the orb[7] like the sun, it shines everywhere. I would be sorry, sir, but the fool should be as oft with your master as with my mistress.[8] I

3.1 Location: Olivia's garden.
1. The dialogue demands only a tabor, but jesters commonly played a pipe with one hand while tapping a tabor (small drum, hanging from the neck) with the other.
2. I do earn my keep with.
3. Lives near; punning on "goes to bed with."
4. Equivocal; Viola puns on the sense "unchaste."
5. Since legal contracts replaced a man's word of honor. ("Bonds" plays on "sworn statements" and "fetters," betokening criminality.)
6. Small fish similar to herring.
7. World; the sun was still believed to circle the earth.
8. Unless ("but") Feste should visit his foolery upon

think I saw your wisdom[9] there.
VIOLA Nay, an thou pass upon[1] me, I'll no more with thee.
[*giving money*] Hold, there's expenses for thee.
FESTE Now Jove in his next commodity° of hair send thee *shipment*
a beard.
VIOLA By my troth I'll tell thee, I am almost sick for one,[2]
though I would not have it grow on *my* chin. Is thy lady
within?
FESTE Would not a pair of these have bred,[3] sir?
VIOLA Yes, being kept together and put to use.[4]
FESTE I would play Lord Pandarus[5] of Phrygia, sir, to bring
a Cressida to this Troilus.
VIOLA [*giving money*] I understand you, sir, 'tis well
begged.
FESTE The matter I hope is not great, sir; begging but a
beggar—Cressida was a beggar.[6] My lady is within, sir. I
will conster° to them whence you come. Who you are and *explain*
what you would are out of my welkin—I might say "ele-
ment," but the word is over-worn.[7] *Exit*
VIOLA This fellow is wise enough to play the fool,
And to do that well craves a kind of wit.° *intelligence*
He must observe their mood on whom he jests,
The quality of persons, and the time,
And, like the haggard, check at every feather
That comes before his eye.[8] This is a practice° *skill*
As full of labor as a wise man's art,
For folly that he wisely shows is fit,[9]
But wise men, folly-fall'n,° quite taint[1] their wit. *fallen into folly*
Enter SIR TOBY *and* [SIR] ANDREW
SIR TOBY Save you, gentleman.
VIOLA And you, sir.
SIR ANDREW *Dieu vous garde,*[2] monsieur.
VIOLA *Et vous aussi, votre serviteur.*[3]
SIR ANDREW I hope, sir, you are, and I am yours.
SIR TOBY Will you encounter[4] the house? My niece is
desirous you should enter if your trade be to her.
VIOLA I am bound to° your niece, sir: I mean she is the *for*
list° of my voyage. *destination*
SIR TOBY Taste° your legs, sir, put them to motion. *try*

others, but also unless Orsino should be called "fool" as often as Olivia.
9. A mocking title for Cesario.
1. If you express an opinion of; if you joke about.
2. Almost eager for a beard; almost pining for a man (Orsino).
3. Would not a pair of coins such as these have multiplied (with possible pun on "be enough to buy bread").
4. Invested to produce interest.
5. Go-between or "pander," since Feste needs a "mate" for his coin(s). Shakespeare dramatizes the story in *Troilus and Cressida*.
6. In asking for the "mate" to his Troilus coin, Feste draws on a version of the story of Troilus and Cressida in which Cressida became a leprous beggar.
7. "Welkin" (sky or air) is synonymous with one meaning of "element," used in what Feste regards as the overworn phrase "out of my element."
8. I.e., as a wild hawk ("haggard") must be sensitive to its prey's disposition.
9. For folly that he skillfully displays is proper.
1. Discredit; spoil.
2. God protect you (French).
3. And you also, (I am) your servant. (Sir Andrew's awkward reply demonstrates that his French is limited.)
4. Pedantry for "enter" (Toby mocks Viola's courtly language).

VIOLA My legs do better understand° me, sir, than I understand what you mean by bidding me taste my legs. *stand under*

SIR TOBY I mean to go, sir, to enter.

VIOLA I will answer you with gait and entrance.

Enter OLIVIA, *and* [MARIA, *her*] *gentlewoman*

But we are prevented.° [*To* OLIVIA] Most excellent accomplished lady, the heavens rain odors on you. *anticipated*

SIR ANDREW [*to* SIR TOBY] That youth's a rare° courtier; "rain odors"—well.° *an excellent* / *well put*

VIOLA My matter hath no voice,° lady, but to your own most pregnant° and vouchsafed° ear. *must not be spoken* / *receptive / proffered*

SIR ANDREW [*to* SIR TOBY] "Odors," "pregnant," and "vouchsafed"—I'll get 'em all three all ready.[5]

OLIVIA Let the garden door be shut, and leave me to my hearing. [*Exeunt* SIR TOBY, SIR ANDREW, *and* MARIA]
Give me your hand, sir.

VIOLA My duty, madam, and most humble service.

OLIVIA What is your name?

VIOLA Cesario is your servant's name, fair princess.

OLIVIA My servant, sir? 'Twas never merry world[6]
Since lowly feigning° was called compliment. *pretended humility*
You're servant to the Count Orsino, youth.

VIOLA And he is yours, and his must needs be yours.
Your servant's servant is *your* servant, madam.

OLIVIA For° him, I think not on him. For his thoughts, *as for*
Would they were blanks rather than filled with me.

VIOLA Madam, I come to whet your gentle thoughts
On his behalf.

OLIVIA O by your leave,[7] I pray you.
I bade you never speak again of him;
But would you undertake another suit,
I had rather hear you to solicit that
Than music from the spheres.[8]

VIOLA Dear lady—

OLIVIA Give me leave, beseech you. I did send,
After the last enchantment you did here,
A ring in chase of you. So did I abuse° *deceive; dishonor*
Myself, my servant, and I fear me you.° *and, as I fear, you*
Under your hard construction[9] must I sit,
To force° that on you in a shameful cunning *for forcing*
Which you knew none of yours. What might you think?
Have you not set mine honor at the stake
And baited it with all th'unmuzzled thoughts[1]
That tyrannous heart can think? To one of your receiving° *perception*
Enough is shown. A cypress,[2] not a bosom,
Hides my heart. So let me hear you speak.

5. I.e., to commit to memory for later use.
6. The proverbial "Things have never been the same."
7. Permit me to interrupt (polite expression).
8. Exquisite music thought to be made by the planets as they moved, but inaudible to mortal ears.
9. Your unfavorable interpretation (of my behavior).
1. As bears that were tied up at the stake and baited with dogs.
2. Veil of transparent silken gauze; the cypress tree was also emblematic of mourning.

VIOLA I pity you.
OLIVIA That's a degree to° love. *toward*
VIOLA No, not a grece,° for 'tis a vulgar proof° *step / common experience*
That very oft we pity enemies.
OLIVIA Why then, methinks 'tis time to smile again.[3]
O world, how apt° the poor are to be proud! *ready*
If one should be a prey, how much the better
To fall before the lion than the wolf![4]
Clock strikes
The clock upbraids° me with the waste of time. *reproaches*
Be not afraid, good youth, I will not have you;
And yet when wit and youth is come to harvest
Your wife is like to reap a proper° man. *handsome; worthy*
There lies your way, due west.
VIOLA Then westward ho![5]
Grace and good disposition° attend your ladyship. *peace of mind*
You'll nothing, madam, to my lord by me?
OLIVIA Stay. I prithee tell me what thou[6] think'st of me.
VIOLA That you do think you are not what you are.[7]
OLIVIA If I think so, I think the same of you.[8]
VIOLA Then think you right, I am not what I am.
OLIVIA I would you were as I would have you be.
VIOLA Would it be better, madam, than I am?
I wish it might, for now I am your fool.[9]
OLIVIA [*aside*] O, what a deal of scorn looks beautiful
In the contempt and anger of his lip!
A murd'rous guilt shows not itself more soon
Than love that would seem hid. Love's night is noon.[1]
[*To* VIOLA] Cesario, by the roses of the spring,
By maidhood, honor, truth, and everything,
I love thee so that, maugre° all thy pride, *despite*
Nor° wit nor reason can my passion hide. *neither*
Do not extort thy reasons from this clause,
For that° I woo, thou therefore hast no cause.[2] *that because*
But rather reason thus with reason fetter:[3]
Love sought is good, but given unsought, is better.
VIOLA By innocence I swear, and by my youth,
I have one heart, one bosom, and one truth,
And that no woman has, nor never none
Shall mistress be of it save I alone.
And so adieu, good madam. Never more
Will I my master's tears to you deplore.° *lament*

3. Time to discard love's melancholy.
4. I.e., if I had to fall prey to love, it would have been better to succumb to the noble Orsino than to the hardhearted Cesario.
5. Thames watermen's cry to attract London passengers for the court at Westminster.
6. Olivia changes from "you" to the familiar "thou."
7. That you think you are in love with a man, but you are mistaken.
8. Olivia may think that Cesario has suggested that she is mad; or she may imply that she thinks that Cesario, despite his subordinate position, is noble.
9. You have made a fool of me.
1. Love, though attempting secrecy, still shines out as bright as day.
2. Do not take the position that just because I woo you, you are under no obligation to reciprocate.
3. But instead constrain your reasoning with this argument.

OLIVIA Yet come again, for thou perhaps mayst move
That heart which now abhors, to like his love.

Exeunt [*severally*]

3.2

Enter SIR TOBY, SIR ANDREW, *and* FABIAN

SIR ANDREW No, faith, I'll not stay a jot longer.

SIR TOBY Thy reason, dear venom,° give thy reason. *venomous one*

FABIAN You must needs yield your reason, Sir Andrew.

SIR ANDREW Marry, I saw your niece do more favors to the Count's servingman than ever she bestowed upon me. I saw't i'th' orchard.° *garden*

SIR TOBY Did she see thee the while,° old boy? Tell me that. *meanwhile*

SIR ANDREW As plain as I see you now.

FABIAN This was a great argument° of love in her toward you. *proof*

SIR ANDREW 'Slight,° will you make an ass o' me? *by God's light*

FABIAN I will prove it legitimate, sir, upon the oaths of judgment and reason.

SIR TOBY And they have been grand-jurymen[1] since before Noah was a sailor.

FABIAN She did show favor to the youth in your sight only to exasperate you, to awake your dormouse° valor, to put fire in your heart and brimstone in your liver. You should then have accosted her, and with some excellent jests, fire-new from the mint,° you should have banged the youth into dumbness. This was looked for at your hand, and this was balked.° The double gilt[2] of this opportunity you let time wash off, and you are now sailed into the north of my lady's opinion,[3] where you will hang like an icicle on a Dutchman's[4] beard unless you do redeem it by some laudable attempt either of valor or policy.° *meek, timid* / *newly minted* / *neglected* / *cunning*

SIR ANDREW An't° be any way, it must be with valor, for policy I hate. I had as lief° be a Brownist as a politician.[5] *if it* / *as soon*

SIR TOBY Why then, build me thy fortunes upon the basis of valor. Challenge me° the Count's youth to fight with him, hurt him in eleven places. My niece shall take note of it; and assure thyself, there is no love-broker in the world can more prevail in man's commendation with woman than report of valor. *for me*

FABIAN There is no way but this, Sir Andrew.

SIR ANDREW Will either of you bear me a challenge to him?

SIR TOBY Go, write it in a martial hand, be curst° and brief. It is no matter how witty so it be eloquent and full of *sharp*

3.2 Location: Olivia's house.
1. Grand-jurymen were supposed to be good judges of evidence.
2. Twice gilded, and as such, Sir Andrew's "golden opportunity" to prove both love and valor.
3. Into Olivia's cold disfavor.
4. Perhaps an allusion to William Barentz, who led an expedition to the Arctic in 1596–97.
5. Schemer. A Brownist was a member of the Puritan sect founded in 1581 by Robert Browne.

invention.° Taunt him with the license of ink.[6] If thou "thou'st"[7] him some thrice, it shall not be amiss, and as many lies° as will lie in thy sheet of paper, although the sheet were big enough for the bed of Ware,[8] in England, set 'em down, go about it. Let there be gall[9] enough in thy ink; though thou write with a goose-pen,[1] no matter. About it.

imagination; untruth / *accusations of lying*

SIR ANDREW Where shall I find you?

SIR TOBY We'll call thee at the cubiculo.° Go. *little chamber*

Exit SIR ANDREW

FABIAN This is a dear manikin° to you, Sir Toby. *puppet*

SIR TOBY I have been dear° to him, lad, some two thousand strong or so. *costly*

FABIAN We shall have a rare letter from him; but you'll not deliver't.

SIR TOBY Never trust me then; and by all means stir on the youth to an answer. I think oxen and wain-ropes[2] cannot hale° them together. For Andrew, if he were opened and you find so much blood in his liver[3] as will clog° the foot of a flea, I'll eat the rest of th'anatomy.°

drag / *weigh down* / *cadaver*

FABIAN And his opposite,° the youth, bears in his visage no great presage of cruelty. *adversary*

Enter MARIA

SIR TOBY Look where the youngest wren of nine[4] comes.

MARIA If you desire the spleen,° and will laugh yourselves into stitches, follow me. Yon gull° Malvolio is turned heathen, a very renegado,[5] for there is no Christian that means to be saved by believing rightly can ever believe such impossible passages of grossness.[6] He's in yellow stockings.

a laughing fit / *dupe*

SIR TOBY And cross-gartered?

MARIA Most villainously,° like a pedant° that keeps a school i'th' church.[7] I have dogged him like his murderer. He does obey every point of the letter that I dropped to betray him. He does smile his face into more lines than is in the new map with the augmentation of the Indies.[8] You have not seen such a thing as 'tis. I can hardly forbear hurling things at him. I know my lady will strike him. If she do, he'll smile, and take't for a great favor.

abominably / *teacher*

SIR TOBY Come bring us, bring us where he is. *Exeunt*

6. I.e., with the freedom taken in writing but not risked in conversation.
7. Call him "thou" (an insult to a stranger).
8. Famous Elizabethan bedstead, nearly eleven feet square, now in the Victoria and Albert Museum, London.
9. (1) Oak gall, an ingredient in ink; (2) bitterness or rancor.
1. Quill made of a goose feather. (The goose was proverbially cowardly and foolish.)
2. Wagon ropes pulled by oxen.
3. Supposed to be the source of blood, which engendered courage.
4. The smallest of small birds; the smallest wren in a family of nine.
5. Renegade (Spanish); a Christian converted to Islam.
6. Such patent absurdities (in the letter).
7. Because no schoolroom is available in a small rustic community.
8. Possibly refers to a map published in 1599 showing the East Indies more fully than in earlier maps and crisscrossed by many rhumb lines.

3.3

Enter SEBASTIAN *and* ANTONIO

SEBASTIAN I would not by my will have troubled you,
But since you make your pleasure of your pains
I will no further chide you.
ANTONIO I could not stay behind you. My desire,
More sharp than filèd steel, did spur me forth,
And not all° love to see you—though so much *only*
As might have drawn one to a longer voyage—
But jealousy° what might befall your travel, *apprehension*
Being skilless in° these parts, which to a stranger, *unfamiliar to*
Unguided and unfriended, often prove
Rough and unhospitable. My willing love
The rather° by these arguments of fear *more willingly*
Set forth in your pursuit.
SEBASTIAN My kind Antonio,
I can no other answer make but thanks,
And thanks; and ever oft° good turns *very often*
Are shuffled off° with such uncurrent[1] pay. *shrugged off*
But were my worth as is my conscience° firm, *sense of indebtedness*
You should find better dealing. What's to do?
Shall we go see the relics° of this town? *sights*
ANTONIO Tomorrow, sir. Best first go see your lodging.
SEBASTIAN I am not weary, and 'tis long to night.
I pray you let us satisfy our eyes
With the memorials and the things of fame
That do renown this city.
ANTONIO Would you'd pardon me.
I do not without danger walk these streets.
Once in a sea-fight 'gainst the Count his° galleys *i.e., the Count's*
I did some service, of such note indeed
That were I ta'en° here it would scarce be answered.[2] *captured*
SEBASTIAN Belike° you slew great number of his people. *perhaps*
ANTONIO Th'offense is not of such a bloody nature,
Albeit° the quality° of the time and quarrel *although / circumstances*
Might well have given us bloody argument.° *cause for bloodshed*
It might have since been answered in repaying
What we took from them, which for traffic's° sake *trade's*
Most of our city did. Only myself stood out,
For which if I be latchèd° in this place *caught*
I shall pay dear.
SEBASTIAN Do not then walk too open.
ANTONIO It doth not fit me. Hold, sir, here's my purse.
In the south suburbs at the Elephant° *name of an inn*
Is best to lodge. I will bespeak our diet° *order our meals*
Whiles you beguile° the time and feed your knowledge *pass*
With viewing of the town. There shall you have me.
SEBASTIAN Why I your purse?

3.3 Location: A street scene.
1. Out of currency; worthless.
2. It would be difficult for me to make reparation (and thus my life would be in danger).

ANTONIO Haply° your eye shall light upon some toy° — *perhaps / trifle*
You have desire to purchase; and your store° — *resources*
I think is not for idle markets,[3] sir.
SEBASTIAN I'll be your purse-bearer, and leave you
For an hour.
ANTONIO To th' Elephant.
SEBASTIAN I do remember.
Exeunt [severally]

3.4

Enter OLIVIA *and* MARIA

OLIVIA [*aside*] I have sent after him, he says he'll come.
How shall I feast him? What bestow of° him? — *on*
For youth is bought more oft than begged or borrowed.[1]
I speak too loud.
[*To* MARIA] Where's Malvolio? He is sad° and civil,° — *sober / respectful*
And suits well for a servant with my fortunes.
Where is Malvolio?
MARIA He's coming, madam, but in very strange manner.
He is sure possessed,° madam. — *(by the devil); insane*
OLIVIA Why, what's the matter? Does he rave?
MARIA No, madam, he does nothing but smile. Your ladyship were best to have some guard about you if he come, for sure the man is tainted in's wits.
OLIVIA Go call him hither. [*Exit* MARIA]
I am as mad as he,
If sad and merry madness equal be.
Enter MALVOLIO [*cross-gartered and wearing yellow stockings, with* MARIA]
How now, Malvolio?
MALVOLIO Sweet lady, ho, ho!
OLIVIA Smil'st thou? I sent for thee upon a sad occasion.° — *about a serious matter*
MALVOLIO Sad, lady? I could be sad. This does make some obstruction in the blood, this cross-gartering, but what of that? If it please the eye of one, it is with me as the very true sonnet° is, "Please one, and please all."[2] — *song*
OLIVIA Why, how dost thou, man? What is the matter with thee?
MALVOLIO Not black in my mind, though yellow[3] in my legs. It did come to his hands, and commands shall be executed. I think we do know the sweet roman hand.° — *italic calligraphy*
OLIVIA Wilt thou go to bed,[4] Malvolio?
MALVOLIO [*kissing his hand*] To bed? "Ay, sweetheart, and I'll come to thee."[5]
OLIVIA God comfort thee. Why dost thou smile so, and kiss thy hand so oft?

3. Not large enough to spend on luxuries.
3.4 Location: The garden of Olivia's house.
1. "Better to buy than to beg or borrow" was proverbial.
2. If I please one, I please all I care to please (words of a popular bawdy ballad).
3. Black and yellow biles indicated choleric and melancholic dispositions, respectively. "Black and yellow" was the name of a popular song; to "wear yellow hose" was to be jealous.
4. In order to cure his madness with sleep.
5. A line from a popular song.

MARIA How do you, Malvolio?

MALVOLIO At your request?—yes, nightingales answer daws.[6]

MARIA Why appear you with this ridiculous boldness before my lady?

MALVOLIO "Be not afraid of greatness"—'twas well writ.

OLIVIA What meanest thou by that, Malvolio?

MALVOLIO "Some are born great"—

OLIVIA Ha?

MALVOLIO "Some achieve greatness"—

OLIVIA What sayst thou?

MALVOLIO "And some have greatness thrust upon them."

OLIVIA Heaven restore thee.

MALVOLIO "Remember who commended thy yellow stockings"—

OLIVIA "Thy yellow stockings"?

MALVOLIO "And wished to see thee cross-gartered."

OLIVIA "Cross-gartered"?

MALVOLIO "Go to, thou art made, if thou desirest to be so."

OLIVIA Am I made?

MALVOLIO "If not, let me see thee a servant still."

OLIVIA Why, this is very midsummer° madness. *the height of*

Enter a SERVANT

SERVANT Madam, the young gentleman of the Count Orsino's is returned. I could hardly entreat him back. He attends your ladyship's pleasure.

OLIVIA I'll come to him. [*Exit* SERVANT]

Good Maria, let this fellow be looked to. Where's my cousin Toby? Let some of my people have a special care of him, I would not have him miscarry° for the half of my dowry. *come to harm*

Exeunt [OLIVIA *and* MARIA, *severally*]

MALVOLIO O ho, do you come near° me now? No worse man than Sir Toby to look to me. This concurs directly with the letter, she sends him on purpose, that I may appear stubborn to him, for she incites me to that in the letter. "Cast thy humble slough," says she, "be opposite with a kinsman, surly with servants, let thy tongue tang arguments of state, put thyself into the trick of singularity," and consequently° sets down the manner how, as a sad face, a reverend carriage, a slow tongue, in the habit of some sir of note,° and so forth. I have limed[7] her, but it is Jove's doing, and Jove make me thankful. And when she went away now, "let this fellow be looked to." Fellow![8]—not "Malvolio," nor after my degree, but "fellow." Why, everything adheres together that no dram of a scruple, no scruple of a scruple,[9] no obstacle, no incredulous

appreciate *subsequently* *gentleman*

6. Shall I deign to reply to you? Yes, since even the nightingale sings in response to the crowing of the jackdaw.
7. Birds were caught by smearing sticky birdlime on branches.
8. Malvolio takes the word to mean "companion."
9. Both phrases mean "no scrap of a doubt." "Dram": one-eighth of a fluid ounce. "Scruple": one-third of a dram.

or unsafe circumstance—what can be said?—nothing that can be can come between me and the full prospect of my hopes. Well, Jove, not I, is the doer of this, and he is to be thanked.

Enter [SIR] TOBY, FABIAN, *and* MARIA

SIR TOBY Which way is he, in the name of sanctity? If all the devils of hell be drawn in little,[1] and Legion[2] himself possessed him, yet I'll speak to him.

FABIAN Here he is, here he is. [*To* MALVOLIO] How is't with you, sir? How is't with you, man?

MALVOLIO Go off, I discard you. Let me enjoy my private.° *privacy*
Go off.

MARIA Lo, how hollow° the fiend speaks within him. Did *resonantly*
not I tell you? Sir Toby, my lady prays you to have a care of him.

MALVOLIO Aha, does she so?

SIR TOBY Go to, go to. Peace, peace, we must deal gently
with him. Let me alone.° How do you, Malvolio? How is't *leave him to me*
with you? What, man, defy° the devil. Consider, he's an *renounce*
enemy to mankind.

MALVOLIO Do you know what you say?

MARIA La° you, an you speak ill of the devil, how he takes *look*
it at heart. Pray God he be not bewitched.

FABIAN Carry his water to th' wise woman.[3]

MARIA Marry, and it shall be done tomorrow morning, if I live. My lady would not lose him for more than I'll say.

MALVOLIO How now, mistress?

MARIA O Lord!

SIR TOBY Prithee hold thy peace, this is not the way. Do
you not see you move° him? Let me alone with him. *anger*

FABIAN No way but gentleness, gently, gently. The fiend is
rough,° and will not be roughly used. *violent*

SIR TOBY Why how now, my bawcock? How dost thou, chuck?[4]

MALVOLIO Sir!

SIR TOBY Ay, biddy,° come with me. What, man, 'tis not *hen*
for gravity° to play at cherry-pit[5] with Satan. Hang him, *for a man of dignity*
foul collier.[6]

MARIA Get him to say his prayers. Good Sir Toby, get him to pray.

MALVOLIO My prayers, minx?° *impertinent girl*

MARIA No, I warrant you, he will not hear of godliness.

MALVOLIO Go hang yourselves, all. You are idle° shallow *foolish*
things, I am not of your element.° You shall know more *social sphere*
hereafter. *Exit*

1. Be contracted into a small space (punning on "painted in miniature").
2. Alluding to a scene of exorcism in Mark 5.8–9: "For he [Jesus] said unto him, Come out of the man, thou unclean spirit. And he asked him, What is thy name? And he answered saying, My name is Legion: for we are many."
3. Local healer, "good witch." "Water": urine (for medical diagnosis).
4. A term of endearment, perhaps from *chick, chicken*. "Bawcock": fine fellow (from the French *beau coq*, "fine bird").
5. A children's game in which cherry stones were thrown into a hole.
6. Dirty coalman (the devil was supposed to be black).

SIR TOBY Is't possible?

FABIAN If this were played upon a stage, now, I could condemn it as an improbable fiction.

SIR TOBY His very genius° hath taken the infection of the device,° man. *spirit* *trick*

MARIA Nay, pursue him now, lest the device take air and taint.[7]

FABIAN Why, we shall make him mad indeed.

MARIA The house will be the quieter.

SIR TOBY Come, we'll have him in a dark room and bound.[8] My niece is already in the belief that he's mad. We may carry it thus° for our pleasure and his penance till our very pastime, tired out of breath, prompt us to have mercy on him, at which time we will bring the device to the bar[9] and crown thee for a finder of madmen.[1] But see, but see. *continue the pretense*

Enter SIR ANDREW [*with a paper*]

FABIAN More matter for a May morning.[2]

SIR ANDREW Here's the challenge, read it. I warrant there's vinegar and pepper in't.

FABIAN Is't so saucy?

SIR ANDREW Ay—is't? I warrant him. Do but read.

SIR TOBY Give me.
[*Reads*] "Youth, whatsoever thou art, thou art but a scurvy fellow."

FABIAN Good, and valiant.

SIR TOBY "Wonder not, nor admire° not in thy mind why I do call thee so, for I will show thee no reason for't." *marvel*

FABIAN A good note, that keeps you from the blow of the law.[3]

SIR TOBY "Thou comest to the Lady Olivia, and in my sight she uses thee kindly; but thou liest in thy throat,° that is not the matter I challenge thee for." *deeply*

FABIAN Very brief, and to exceeding good sense [*aside*] -less.[4]

SIR TOBY "I will waylay thee going home, where if it be thy chance to kill me"—

FABIAN Good.

SIR TOBY "Thou killest me like a rogue and a villain."

FABIAN Still you keep o'th' windy side[5] of the law—good.

SIR TOBY "Fare thee well, and God have mercy upon one of our souls. He may have mercy upon mine, but my hope is better,[6] and so look to thyself.
Thy friend as thou usest him, and thy sworn enemy,
Andrew Aguecheek."
If this letter move° him not, his legs cannot. I'll give't him. *provoke*

MARIA You may have very fit occasion for't. He is now in

7. Spoil (like leftover food) by exposure to air; become known (and thus ruined).
8. Customary treatments for madness.
9. Into the open court (to be judged).
1. I.e., one of a jury "finding," or declaring, a man to be mad.
2. More pastime fit for a holiday.
3. That protects you from a charge of a breach of peace.
4. The Folio's "sence-lesse" appears to use the hyphen to signal an aside.
5. Downwind of the law—on the safe side of it.
6. Andrew means he expects to survive, but he ineptly implies that he expects to be damned.

some commerce° with my lady, and will by and by depart. *conversation*
SIR TOBY Go, Sir Andrew. Scout me° for him at the corner *look out*
of the orchard like a bum-baily.[7] So soon as ever thou
seest him, draw, and as thou drawest, swear horrible, for
it comes to pass oft that a terrible oath, with a swaggering
accent sharply twanged off, gives manhood more appro-
bation° than ever proof° itself would have earned him. *credit / trial*
Away.
SIR ANDREW Nay, let me alone for swearing.[8] *Exit*
SIR TOBY Now will not I deliver his letter, for the behavior
of the young gentleman gives him out to be of good
capacity° and breeding.° His employment between his *ability / upbringing*
lord and my niece confirms no less. Therefore this letter,
being so excellently ignorant, will breed no terror in the
youth. He will find it comes from a clodpoll.° But, sir, I *blockhead*
will deliver his challenge by word of mouth, set upon
Aguecheek a notable report of valor, and drive the gentleman—as I know his youth will aptly receive it[9]—into
a most hideous opinion of his rage, skill, fury, and impetuosity. This will so fright them both that they will kill one
another by the look, like cockatrices.[1]

Enter OLIVIA, *and* VIOLA [*as Cesario*]

FABIAN Here he comes with your niece. Give them way° *stand aside*
till he take leave, and presently after him.
SIR TOBY I will meditate the while upon some horrid message for a challenge.

[*Exeunt* SIR TOBY, FABIAN, *and* MARIA]

OLIVIA I have said too much unto a heart of stone,
And laid mine honor too unchary° out. *carelessly*
There's something in me that reproves my fault,
But such a headstrong potent fault it is
That it but mocks reproof.
VIOLA With the same 'havior
That your passion bears[2] goes on my master's griefs.
OLIVIA [*giving a jewel*] Here, wear this jewel[3] for me, 'tis
my picture—
Refuse it not, it hath no tongue to vex you—
And I beseech you come again tomorrow.
What shall you ask of me that I'll deny,
That honor, saved, may upon asking give?[4]
VIOLA Nothing but this: your true love for my master.
OLIVIA How with mine honor may I give him that
Which I have given to you?
VIOLA I will acquit you.[5]
OLIVIA Well, come again tomorrow. Fare thee well.
A fiend like thee might bear my soul to hell. [*Exit*]

7. Petty sheriff's officer employed to arrest debtors.
8. Have no doubts as to my swearing ability.
9. As I know his inexperience will readily believe the report.
1. Basilisks: mythical creatures supposed to kill at a glance.
2. Behavior that characterizes your lovesickness.
3. Jeweled ornament, here a brooch or a locket with Olivia's picture.
4. That honor may grant without compromising itself.
5. I will release you from your promise.

Enter [SIR] TOBY *and* FABIAN

SIR TOBY Gentleman, God save thee.

VIOLA And you, sir.

SIR TOBY That defense thou hast, betake thee to't. Of what nature the wrongs are thou hast done him, I know not, but thy intercepter, full of despite,° bloody as the hunter, attends° thee at the orchard end. Dismount thy tuck,[6] be yare° in thy preparation, for thy assailant is quick, skillful, and deadly. *defiance* *awaits* *prompt*

VIOLA You mistake, sir, I am sure no man hath any quarrel to me. My remembrance° is very free and clear from any image of offense done to any man. *memory*

SIR TOBY You'll find it otherwise, I assure you. Therefore, if you hold your life at any price, betake you to your guard, for your opposite° hath in him what youth, strength, skill, and wrath can furnish man withal. *opponent*

VIOLA I pray you, sir, what is he?

SIR TOBY He is knight dubbed with unhatched[7] rapier and on carpet consideration,[8] but he is a devil in private brawl. Souls and bodies hath he divorced three, and his incensement at this moment is so implacable that satisfaction can be none but by pangs of death and sepulchre. Hob nob[9] is his word,° give't or take't. *motto*

VIOLA I will return again into the house and desire some conduct° of the lady. I am no fighter. I have heard of some kind of men that put quarrels purposely on others, to taste° their valor. Belike this is a man of that quirk. *escort* *test*

SIR TOBY Sir, no. His indignation derives itself out of a very competent° injury, therefore get you on, and give him his desire. Back you shall not to the house unless you undertake that° with me which with as much safety you might answer him. Therefore on, or strip your sword stark naked, for meddle° you must, that's certain, or forswear to wear iron about you.[1] *sufficient* *i.e., a duel* *engage in a duel*

VIOLA This is as uncivil as strange. I beseech you do me this courteous office, as to know of° the knight what my offense to him is. It is something of my negligence, nothing of my purpose. *ascertain from*

SIR TOBY I will do so. Signor Fabian, stay you by this gentleman till my return. *Exit*

VIOLA Pray you, sir, do you know of this matter?

FABIAN I know the knight is incensed against you even to a mortal arbitrement,° but nothing of the circumstance more. *deadly duel*

VIOLA I beseech you, what manner of man is he?

FABIAN Nothing of that wonderful promise to read him by his form[2] as you are like to find him in the proof° of his valor. He is indeed, sir, the most skillful, bloody, and fatal *experience*

6. Draw your rapier.
7. Unhacked, or undented, never used in battle.
8. A "carpet knight" obtained his title through connections at court rather than valor on the battlefield.
9. Have or have not ("all or nothing").
1. Or forfeit your right to wear a sword.
2. I.e., from his outward appearance, you cannot perceive him to be as remarkable.

opposite that you could possibly have found in any part
of Illyria. Will you° walk towards him, I will make your   *if you will*
peace with him if I can.

VIOLA I shall be much bound to you for't. I am one that
had rather go with Sir Priest[3] than Sir Knight—I care not
who knows so much of my mettle.° *Exeunt*   *disposition*

Enter [SIR] TOBY *and* [SIR] ANDREW

SIR TOBY Why, man, he's a very devil, I have not seen such
a virago.[4] I had a pass° with him, rapier, scabbard, and   *fencing bout*
all, and he gives me the stuck-in[5] with such a mortal
motion that it is inevitable, and on the answer,° he pays   *return hit*
you as surely as your feet hits the ground they step on.
They say he has been fencer to the Sophy.°   *shah of Persia*

SIR ANDREW Pox on't, I'll not meddle with him.

SIR TOBY Ay, but he will not now be pacified, Fabian can
scarce hold him yonder.

SIR ANDREW Plague on't, an° I thought he had been valiant   *if*
and so cunning in fence I'd have seen him damned ere
I'd have challenged him. Let him let the matter slip and
I'll give him my horse, grey Capulet.

SIR TOBY I'll make the motion.° Stand here, make a good   *offer*
show on't—this shall end without the perdition of souls.°   *loss of lives*
[*Aside*] Marry, I'll ride your horse as well as I ride you.

Enter FABIAN, *and* VIOLA [*as Cesario*]

[*Aside to* FABIAN] I have his horse to take up° the quarrel, I   *settle*
have persuaded him the youth's a devil.

FABIAN [*aside to* SIR TOBY] He is as horribly conceited[6] of
him, and pants and looks pale as if a bear were at his
heels.

SIR TOBY [*to* VIOLA] There's no remedy, sir, he will fight
with you for's oath' sake. Marry, he hath better bethought
him of his quarrel, and he finds that now scarce to be
worth talking of. Therefore draw for the supportance of
his vow, he protests he will not hurt you.

VIOLA [*aside*] Pray God defend me. A little thing would
make me tell them how much I lack of a man.

FABIAN [*to* SIR ANDREW] Give ground if you see him furious.

SIR TOBY Come, Sir Andrew, there's no remedy, the gentleman will for his honor's sake have one bout with you,
he cannot by the duello° avoid it, but he has promised   *code of dueling*
me, as he is a gentleman and a soldier, he will not hurt
you. Come on, to't.

SIR ANDREW Pray God he keep his oath.

Enter ANTONIO

VIOLA I do assure you 'tis against my will.

[SIR ANDREW *and* VIOLA *draw their swords*]

ANTONIO [*drawing his sword, to* SIR ANDREW] Put up your
sword. If this young gentleman

3. Priests were often addressed as "sir."
4. Woman warrior (suggesting great ferocity with a feminine appearance).
5. Thrust (from the Italian *stoccata*).
6. He has as terrifying an idea.

Have done offense, I take the fault on me.
If you offend him, I for him defy you.
SIR TOBY You, sir? Why, what are you?
ANTONIO One, sir, that for his love dares yet do more
Than you have heard him brag to you he will.
SIR TOBY [*drawing his sword*] Nay, if you be an undertaker,[7] I am for you.

Enter OFFICERS

FABIAN O, good Sir Toby, hold. Here come the officers.
SIR TOBY [*to* ANTONIO] I'll be with you anon.
VIOLA [*to* SIR ANDREW] Pray, sir, put your sword up if you please.
SIR ANDREW Marry will I, sir, and for that° I promised you I'll be as good as my word. He will bear you easily, and reins well. *as for that*

[SIR ANDREW *and* VIOLA *put up their swords*]

FIRST OFFICER This is the man, do thy office.
SECOND OFFICER Antonio, I arrest thee at the suit of Count Orsino.
ANTONIO You do mistake me, sir.
FIRST OFFICER No, sir, no jot. I know your favor° well, *face*
Though now you have no seacap on your head.
[*To* SECOND OFFICER] Take him away, he knows I know him well.
ANTONIO I must obey. [*To* VIOLA] This comes with seeking you.
But there's no remedy, I shall answer° it. *answer for*
What will you do now my necessity
Makes me to ask you for my purse? It grieves me
Much more for what I cannot do for you
Than what befalls myself. You stand amazed,
But be of comfort.
SECOND OFFICER Come, sir, away.
ANTONIO [*to* VIOLA] I must entreat of you some of that money.
VIOLA What money, sir?
For the fair kindness you have showed me here,
And part° being prompted by your present trouble, *in part*
Out of my lean and low ability
I'll lend you something. My having is not much.
I'll make division of my present° with you. *ready money*
Hold, [*offering money*] there's half my coffer.
ANTONIO Will you deny me now?
Is't possible that my deserts to you
Can lack persuasion?[8] Do not tempt my misery,
Lest that it make me so unsound° a man *morally weak*
As to upbraid you with those kindnesses
That I have done for you.
VIOLA I know of none,
Nor know I you by voice, or any feature.
I hate ingratitude more in a man
Than lying, vainness, babbling drunkenness,

7. One who would take upon himself a task (here, a challenge).

8. Is it possible my past kindness can fail to persuade you?

Or any taint of vice whose strong corruption
Inhabits our frail blood.
ANTONIO O heavens themselves!
SECOND OFFICER Come, sir, I pray you go.
ANTONIO Let me speak a little. This youth that you see here
I snatched one half out of the jaws of death,
Relieved him with such sanctity° of love, *great devotion*
And to his image,[9] which methought did promise
Most venerable worth,[1] did I devotion.
FIRST OFFICER What's that to us? The time goes by, away.
ANTONIO But O, how vile an idol proves this god!
Thou hast, Sebastian, done good feature° shame. *physical beauty*
In nature there's no blemish but the mind.
None can be called deformed but the unkind.
Virtue is beauty, but the beauteous evil
Are empty trunks o'er-flourished[2] by the devil.
FIRST OFFICER The man grows mad, away with him.
Come, come, sir.
ANTONIO Lead me on. *Exit* [*with* OFFICERS]
VIOLA [*aside*] Methinks his words do from such passion fly
That he believes himself. So do not I.[3]
Prove true, imagination, O prove true,
That I, dear brother, be now ta'en for you!
SIR TOBY Come hither, knight. Come hither, Fabian. We'll whisper o'er a couplet or two of most sage saws.° *sayings, maxims*
[*They stand aside*]
VIOLA He named Sebastian. I my brother know
Yet living in my glass.° Even such and so *mirror*
In favor° was my brother, and he went *appearance*
Still° in this fashion, color, ornament, *always*
For him I imitate. O, if it prove,
Tempests are kind, and salt waves fresh in love! *Exit*
SIR TOBY [*to* SIR ANDREW] A very dishonest,° paltry boy, and more a coward than a hare. His dishonesty appears in leaving his friend here in necessity, and denying him; and for his cowardship, ask Fabian. *dishonorable*
FABIAN A coward, a most devout coward, religious in it.
SIR ANDREW 'Slid,° I'll after him again, and beat him. *by God's eyelid*
SIR TOBY Do, cuff him soundly, but never draw thy sword.
SIR ANDREW An I do not— [*Exit*]
FABIAN Come, let's see the event.° *outcome*
SIR TOBY I dare lay any money 'twill be nothing yet.° *after all*
Exeunt

4.1

Enter SEBASTIAN *and* [FESTE, *the*] *clown*
FESTE Will you° make me believe that I am not sent for you? *are you trying to*

9. Appearance (with a play on "religious icon").
1. Was worthy of veneration.
2. Chests decorated with carving or painting; beautified bodies.
3. I.e., I do not entirely believe the passionate hope (for my brother's rescue) that is arising in me.
4.1 Location: Near Olivia's house.

SEBASTIAN Go to, go to, thou art a foolish fellow,
Let me be clear° of thee. *rid*

FESTE Well held out,° i'faith! No, I do not know you, nor I am not sent to you by my lady to bid you come speak with her, nor your name is not Master Cesario, nor this is not my nose, neither. Nothing that is so, is so. *kept up*

SEBASTIAN I prithee vent° thy folly somewhere else, *utter; excrete*
Thou know'st not me.

FESTE Vent my folly! He has heard that word of some great man, and now applies it to a fool. Vent my folly—I am afraid this great lubber° the world will prove a cockney.° I prithee now ungird thy strangeness,[1] and tell me what I shall "vent" to my lady? Shall I "vent" to her that thou art coming? *lout / pampered child*

SEBASTIAN I prithee, foolish Greek,° depart from me. *buffoon*
There's money for thee. If you tarry longer
I shall give worse payment.

FESTE By my troth, thou hast an open hand. These wise men that give fools money get themselves a good report,° after fourteen years' purchase.[2] *reputation*

Enter [SIR] ANDREW, [SIR] TOBY, *and* FABIAN

SIR ANDREW [*to* SEBASTIAN] Now, sir, have I met you again?
[*Striking him*] There's for you.

SEBASTIAN [*striking* SIR ANDREW *with his* DAGGER] Why,
there's for thee, and there, and there.
Are all the people mad?

SIR TOBY [*to* SEBASTIAN, *holding him back*] Hold, sir, or I'll throw your dagger o'er the house.

FESTE This will I tell my lady straight.° I would not be in some of your coats for twopence. [*Exit*] *straightway*

SIR TOBY Come on, sir, hold.

SIR ANDREW Nay, let him alone, I'll go another way to work with him. I'll have an action of battery° against him if there be any law in Illyria. Though I struck him first, yet it's no matter for that. *a lawsuit for assault*

SEBASTIAN Let go thy hand.

SIR TOBY Come, sir, I will not let you go. Come, my young soldier, put up your iron. You are well fleshed.[3] Come on.

SEBASTIAN [*freeing himself*] I will be free from thee.
What wouldst thou now?
If thou dar'st tempt me further, draw thy sword.

SIR TOBY What, what? Nay then, I must have an ounce or two of this malapert° blood from you. *impudent*

[SIR TOBY *and* SEBASTIAN *draw their swords.*]

Enter OLIVIA

OLIVIA Hold, Toby, on thy life I charge thee hold.

SIR TOBY Madam.

OLIVIA Will it be ever thus? Ungracious wretch,

1. I.e., stop pretending not to know me. (Feste mocks Sebastian's affected language.)
2. I.e., at a high price. The purchase price of land was normally twelve times its annual rent.
3. Experienced in combat. Hunting hounds were said to be "fleshed" after being fed part of their first kill.

Fit for the mountains and the barbarous caves,
Where manners ne'er were preached—out of my sight!
Be not offended, dear Cesario.
[*To* SIR TOBY] Rudesby,° be gone. *ruffian*
[*Exeunt* SIR TOBY, SIR ANDREW, *and* FABIAN]
I prithee, gentle friend,
Let thy fair wisdom, not thy passion sway
In this uncivil and unjust extent° *assault*
Against thy peace. Go with me to my house,
And hear thou there how many fruitless pranks
This ruffian hath botched up,° that thou thereby *clumsily contrived*
Mayst smile at this. Thou shalt not choose but go.
Do not deny. Beshrew° his soul for me, *curse*
He started one poor heart of mine in thee.[4]

SEBASTIAN What relish° is in this? How runs the stream? *task; meaning*
Or° I am mad, or else this is a dream. *either*
Let fancy° still my sense in Lethe[5] steep. *imagination*
If it be thus to dream, still° let me sleep. *ever*

OLIVIA Nay, come, I prithee, would thou'dst be ruled by me.

SEBASTIAN Madam, I will.

OLIVIA O, say so, and so be. *Exeunt*

4.2

Enter MARIA [*carrying a gown and false beard, and* FESTE, *the*] *clown*

MARIA Nay, I prithee put on this gown and this beard, make him believe thou art Sir Topas[1] the curate. Do it quickly. I'll call Sir Toby the whilst.° *Exit* *in the meantime*

FESTE Well, I'll put it on, and I will dissemble[2] myself in't, and I would I were the first that ever dissembled in such a gown.
[*He disguises himself*]
I am not tall enough to become the function well,[3] nor lean enough to be thought a good student,° but to be said° "an honest man and a good housekeeper"° goes as fairly as[4] to say "a careful man and a great scholar." The competitors° enter. *(of divinity) / reputed* *host* *associates*

Enter [SIR] TOBY [*and* MARIA]

SIR TOBY Jove bless thee, Master Parson.

FESTE *Bonos dies,*[5] Sir Toby, for, as the old hermit of Prague,[6] that never saw pen and ink, very wittily° said to a niece of King Gorboduc,° "That that is, is." So I, being Master Parson, am Master Parson; for what is "that" but "that," and "is" but "is"? *intelligently* *legendary British king*

4. By attacking Sebastian, Sir Toby frightened Olivia, who has exchanged hearts with Sebastian. "Started": an allusion to hunting, creating a pun on "hart/heart."
5. The mythical river of oblivion.
4.2 Location: Olivia's house, where Malvolio will be found (offstage) "in a dark room and bound" (3.4.132).
1. The comical hero of Chaucer's *Tale of Sir Thopas.* Also alluding to the topaz stone, which was thought to have special curative qualities for insanity.
2. Disguise; with subsequent play on "lie."
3. Grace the priestly office. "Tall": stout, rather than of great height.
4. Sounds as well as.
5. Good day (false Latin).
6. Probably an invented authority.

SIR TOBY To him, Sir Topas.

FESTE What ho, I say, peace in this prison.

SIR TOBY The knave counterfeits well—a good knave.

MALVOLIO *within*

MALVOLIO Who calls there?

FESTE Sir Topas the curate, who comes to visit Malvolio the lunatic.

MALVOLIO Sir Topas, Sir Topas, good Sir Topas, go to my lady.

FESTE Out, hyperbolical fiend,[7] how vexest thou this man! Talkest thou nothing but of ladies?

SIR TOBY Well said, Master Parson.

MALVOLIO Sir Topas, never was man thus wronged. Good Sir Topas, do not think I am mad. They have laid me here in hideous darkness.

FESTE Fie, thou dishonest Satan—I call thee by the most modest° terms, for I am one of those gentle ones that will use the devil himself with courtesy. Sayst thou that house° is dark? *mildest* *room*

MALVOLIO As hell, Sir Topas.

FESTE Why, it hath bay windows transparent as barricadoes, and the clerestories[8] toward the south-north are as lustrous as ebony,[9] and yet complainest thou of obstruction?

MALVOLIO I am not mad, Sir Topas; I say to you this house is dark.

FESTE Madman, thou errest. I say there is no darkness but ignorance, in which thou art more puzzled than the Egyptians in their fog.[1]

MALVOLIO I say this house is as dark as ignorance, though ignorance were as dark as hell; and I say there was never man thus abused. I am no more mad than you are. Make the trial of it in any constant question.° *logical discussion*

FESTE What is the opinion of Pythagoras[2] concerning wildfowl?

MALVOLIO That the soul of our grandam might haply° inhabit a bird. *perhaps*

FESTE What thinkest thou of his opinion?

MALVOLIO I think nobly of the soul, and no way approve his opinion.

FESTE Fare thee well. Remain thou still in darkness. Thou shalt hold th'opinion of Pythagoras ere I will allow of thy wits,° and fear to kill a woodcock[3] lest thou dispossess the soul of thy grandam. Fare thee well. *certify your sanity*

MALVOLIO Sir Topas, Sir Topas!

7. Feste treats Malvolio as a man possessed by vehement ("hyperbolical") evil spirits.
8. Upper windows, usually in a church or great hall. "Barricadoes": barricades (subsequent paradoxes are equivalent to "as clear as mud").
9. A dense and naturally dull black wood.
1. One of the plagues of Egypt was a "black darkness" lasting for three days (Exodus 10.21–23).
2. An ancient Greek philosopher who held that the same soul could successively inhabit different creatures.
3. A traditionally stupid bird.

SIR TOBY My most exquisite Sir Topas.

FESTE Nay, I am for all waters.[4]

MARIA Thou mightst have done this without thy beard and gown, he sees thee not.

SIR TOBY [*to* FESTE] To him in thine own voice, and bring me word how thou findest him. I would we were well rid of this knavery. If he may be conveniently delivered, I would he were, for I am now so far in offense with my niece that I cannot pursue with any safety this sport to the upshot. [*To* MARIA] Come by and by to my chamber.

Exit [*with* MARIA]

FESTE [*sings*][5] "Hey Robin, jolly Robin,
Tell me how thy lady does."

MALVOLIO Fool!

FESTE "My lady is unkind, pardie."[6]

MALVOLIO Fool!

FESTE "Alas, why is she so?"

MALVOLIO Fool, I say!

FESTE "She loves another."
Who calls, ha?

MALVOLIO Good fool, as ever thou wilt deserve well at my hand, help me to a candle and pen, ink, and paper. As I am a gentleman, I will live to be thankful to thee for't.

FESTE Master Malvolio?

MALVOLIO Ay, good fool.

FESTE Alas, sir, how fell you besides° your five wits?[7] *out of*

MALVOLIO Fool, there was never man so notoriously° *outrageously* abused. I am as well in my wits, fool, as thou art.

FESTE But as well? Then you are mad indeed, if you be no better in your wits than a fool.

MALVOLIO They have here propertied me,[8] keep me in darkness, send ministers to me, asses, and do all they can to face me[9] out of my wits.

FESTE Advise you° what you say, the minister is here. *be careful* [*As Sir Topas*] Malvolio, Malvolio, thy wits the heavens restore. Endeavor thyself to sleep, and leave thy vain bibble-babble.

MALVOLIO Sir Topas.

FESTE [*as Sir Topas*] Maintain no words with him, good fellow. [*As himself*] Who I, sir? Not I, sir. God b'wi' you,° *God be with you* good Sir Topas. [*As Sir Topas*] Marry, amen. [*As himself*] I will, sir, I will.

MALVOLIO Fool, fool, fool, I say.

FESTE Alas, sir, be patient. What say you, sir? I am shent° *scolded* for speaking to you.

4. I am able to turn my hand to anything.
5. Feste's song, which makes Malvolio aware of his presence, is traditional. There is a version by Sir Thomas Wyatt.
6. A corruption of the French *pardieu*, "by God."
7. Usually regarded as common sense, fantasy, memory, judgment, and imagination.
8. Treated me as a piece of property.
9. Brazenly construe me as.

MALVOLIO Good fool, help me to some light and some paper. I tell thee I am as well in my wits as any man in Illyria.

FESTE Well-a-day° that you were, sir. *alas*

MALVOLIO By this hand, I am. Good fool, some ink, paper, and light, and convey what I will set down to my lady. It shall advantage thee more than ever the bearing of letter did.

FESTE I will help you to't. But tell me true, are you not mad indeed, or do you but counterfeit?

MALVOLIO Believe me, I am not, I tell thee true.

FESTE Nay, I'll ne'er believe a madman till I see his brains. I will fetch you light, and paper, and ink.

MALVOLIO Fool, I'll requite it in the highest degree. I prithee, be gone.

FESTE
I am gone, sir,
And anon, sir,
I'll be with you again,
In a trice,
Like to the old Vice,[1]
Your need to sustain,
Who with dagger of lath
In his rage and his wrath
Cries "Aha," to the devil,
Like a mad lad,
"Pare thy nails, dad,
Adieu, goodman[2] devil."

Exit

4.3

Enter SEBASTIAN

SEBASTIAN
This is the air, that is the glorious sun.
This pearl she gave me, I do feel't and see't,
And though 'tis wonder that enwraps me thus,
Yet 'tis not madness. Where's Antonio then?
I could not find him at the Elephant,
Yet there he was,° and there I found this credit,° *had been / report*
That he did range the town to seek me out.
His counsel now might do me golden service,
For though my soul disputes well with my sense[1]
That this may be some error but no madness,
Yet doth this accident and flood of fortune
So far exceed all instance,° all discourse,° *precedent / reasoning*
That I am ready to distrust mine eyes
And wrangle with my reason that persuades me
To any other trust° but that I am mad, *belief*

1. A stock comic figure in the old morality plays; he often carried a wooden dagger.
2. Yeoman; a title given to one not of gentle birth, hence a parting insult to Malvolio.

4.3 Location: Near Olivia's house.
1. For though my reason and my sense both concur.

Or else the lady's mad. Yet if 'twere so
She could not sway° her house, command her followers, — *rule*
Take and give back affairs and their dispatch[2]
With such a smooth, discreet, and stable bearing
As I perceive she does. There's something in't
That is deceivable.° But here the lady comes. — *deceptive*

Enter OLIVIA *and* PRIEST

OLIVIA Blame not this haste of mine. If you mean well
Now go with me, and with this holy man,
Into the chantry by.° There before him, — *nearby chapel*
And underneath that consecrated roof,
Plight me the full assurance of your faith,[3]
That my most jealous and too doubtful soul
May live at peace. He shall conceal it
Whiles° you are willing it shall come to note, — *until*
What° time we will our celebration keep — *at which*
According to my birth.° What do you say? — *rank*

SEBASTIAN I'll follow this good man, and go with you,
And having sworn truth, ever will be true.

OLIVIA Then lead the way, good father, and heavens so shine
That they may fairly note° this act of mine. *Exeunt* — *look favorably upon*

5.1

Enter [FESTE, *the*] *clown and* FABIAN

FABIAN Now, as thou lovest me, let me see his letter.

FESTE Good Master Fabian, grant me another request.

FABIAN Anything.

FESTE Do not desire to see this letter.

FABIAN This is to give a dog, and in recompense desire my dog again.[1]

Enter Duke, VIOLA [*as Cesario*], CURIO, *and lords*

ORSINO Belong you to the Lady Olivia, friends?

FESTE Ay, sir, we are some of her trappings.° — *ornaments*

ORSINO I know thee well. How dost thou, my good fellow?

FESTE Truly, sir, the better for my foes and the worse for my friends.

ORSINO Just the contrary—the better for thy friends.

FESTE No, sir, the worse.

ORSINO How can that be?

FESTE Marry, sir, they praise me, and make an ass of me. Now my foes tell me plainly I am an ass, so that by my foes, sir, I profit in the knowledge of myself, and by my friends I am abused;° so that, conclusions to be as kisses, if your four negatives make your two affirmatives,[2] why then the worse for my friends and the better for my foes. — *deceived*

2. Undertake business, and ensure that it is carried out.
3. Enter into the solemn contract of betrothal.
5.1 Location: Before Olivia's house.
1. Perhaps a reference to an anecdote, recorded in John Manningham's diary, in which Queen Elizabeth requested a dog, and the donor, when granted a wish in return, asked for the dog back.
2. As in grammar a double negative can make an affirmative (and therefore four negatives can make two affirmatives), so when a coy girl is asked for a kiss, her four refusals can be construed as "yes, yes."

ORSINO Why, this is excellent.

FESTE By my troth, sir, no, though it please you to be one of my friends.

ORSINO [*giving money*] Thou shalt not be the worse for me. There's gold.

FESTE But° that it would be double-dealing,[3] sir, I would you could make it another. — *except for the fact*

ORSINO O, you give me ill counsel.

FESTE Put your grace in your pocket,[4] sir, for this once, and let your flesh and blood obey it.[5]

ORSINO Well, I will be so much a sinner to° be a double-dealer. [*Giving money*] There's another. — *as to*

FESTE *Primo, secundo, tertio*[6] is a good play,° and the old saying is "The third pays for all."[7] The triplex,° sir, is a good tripping measure, or the bells of Saint Bennet,[8] sir, may put you in mind—"one, two, three." — *game* / *triple time in music*

ORSINO You can fool no more money out of me at this throw.° If you will let your lady know I am here to speak with her, and bring her along with you, it may awake my bounty° further. — *throw of the dice* / *generosity*

FESTE Marry, sir, lullaby to your bounty till I come again. I go, sir, but I would not have you to think that my desire of having is the sin of covetousness. But as you say, sir, let your bounty take a nap, I will awake it anon. *Exit*

Enter ANTONIO *and* OFFICERS

VIOLA Here comes the man, sir, that did rescue me.

ORSINO That face of his I do remember well,
Yet when I saw it last it was besmeared
As black as Vulcan[9] in the smoke of war.
A baubling° vessel was he captain of, — *trifling*
For shallow draft and bulk unprizable,[1]
With which such scatheful° grapple did he make — *destructive*
With the most noble bottom° of our fleet — *ship*
That very envy° and the tongue of loss° — *even enmity / the losers*
Cried fame and honor on him. What's the matter?

FIRST OFFICER Orsino, this is that Antonio
That took the *Phoenix* and her freight from Candy,° — *Candia, capital of Crete*
And this is he that did the *Tiger* board
When your young nephew Titus lost his leg.
Here in the streets, desperate of shame and state,[2]
In private brabble° did we apprehend him. — *brawl*

VIOLA He did me kindness, sir, drew on my side,[3]
But in conclusion put strange speech upon° me. — *spoke strangely to*

3. (1) A duplicity; (2) a double donation.
4. Set aside (pocket up) your virtue; also (with a play on the customary form of address for a duke, "your grace"), reach into your pocket and grace me with another coin.
5. Let your normal human instincts (as opposed to grace) follow the "ill counsel" (line 28).
6. First, second, third (Latin): perhaps an allusion to a dice throw or a child's game.
7. Third time lucky (proverbial).
8. A London church, across the Thames from the Globe Theater, was known as St. Bennet Hithe.
9. Blacksmith god of the Romans.
1. Of no value because of its small size. "Draft": water displaced by a vessel.
2. Recklessly oblivious of the danger to his honor and his position (as a free man and public enemy).
3. Drew his sword in my defense.

I know not what 'twas but distraction.° *if not insanity*
ORSINO [*to* ANTONIO] Notable° pirate, thou salt-water thief, *notorious*
What foolish boldness brought thee to their mercies
Whom thou in terms so bloody and so dear° *dire*
Hast made thine enemies?
ANTONIO Orsino, noble sir,
Be pleased that I shake off these names you give me.
Antonio never yet was thief or pirate,
Though, I confess, on base° and ground enough *foundation*
Orsino's enemy. A witchcraft drew me hither.
That most ingrateful boy there by your side
From the rude sea's enraged and foamy mouth
Did I redeem. A wreck past hope he was.
His life I gave him, and did thereto add
My love without retention° or restraint, *reservation*
All his in dedication. For his sake
Did I expose myself, pure° for his love, *only*
Into the danger of this adverse° town, *hostile*
Drew to defend him when he was beset,
Where being apprehended, his false cunning—
Not meaning to partake with me in danger—
Taught him to face me out of his acquaintance,[4]
And grew a twenty years' removèd thing
While one would wink,[5] denied me mine own purse,
Which I had recommended° to his use *consigned*
Not half an hour before.
VIOLA How can this be?
ORSINO When came he to this town?
ANTONIO Today, my lord, and for three months before,
No int'rim, not a minute's vacancy,° *interval*
Both day and night did we keep company.
Enter OLIVIA *and attendants*
ORSINO Here comes the Countess. Now heaven walks on earth.
But for thee, fellow—fellow, thy words are madness.
Three months this youth hath tended upon me.
But more of that anon. Take him aside.
OLIVIA What would my lord, but that he may not have,[6]
Wherein Olivia may seem serviceable?
Cesario, you do not keep promise with me.
VIOLA Madam—
ORSINO Gracious Olivia—
OLIVIA What do you say, Cesario? Good my lord—
VIOLA My lord would speak, my duty hushes me.
OLIVIA If it be aught° to the old tune, my lord, *anything*
It is as fat and fulsome° to mine ear *gross and offensive*
As howling after music.
ORSINO Still so cruel?
OLIVIA Still so constant, lord.

4. To brazenly deny my acquaintance.
5. I.e., in the wink of an eye, pretended we had been estranged for twenty years.
6. Except that which he may not have (my love).

ORSINO What, to perverseness? You uncivil lady,
To whose ingrate and unauspicious° altars *unfavorable*
My soul the faithfull'st off'rings hath breathed out
That e'er devotion tendered—what shall I do?
OLIVIA Even what it please my lord that shall become° him. *be fitting for*
ORSINO Why should I not, had I the heart to do it,
Like to th' Egyptian thief, at point of death
Kill what I love[7]—a savage jealousy
That sometime savors nobly.° But hear me this: *of nobility*
Since you to non-regardance° cast my faith, *oblivion*
And that I partly know the instrument
That screws° me from my true place in your favor, *wrenches*
Live you the marble-breasted tyrant still.
But this your minion,° whom I know you love, *darling*
And whom, by heaven I swear, I tender° dearly, *regard*
Him will I tear out of that cruel eye
Where he sits crownèd in his master's spite.[8]
[*To* VIOLA] Come, boy, with me. My thoughts are ripe in mischief.
I'll sacrifice the lamb that I do love
To spite a raven's heart within a dove.
VIOLA And I most jocund,° apt,° and willingly *cheerfully / ready*
To do you rest a thousand deaths would die.
OLIVIA Where goes Cesario?
VIOLA After him I love
More than I love these eyes, more than my life,
More by all mores[9] than e'er I shall love wife.
If I do feign, you witnesses above,
Punish my life for tainting of my love.
OLIVIA Ay me detested, how am I beguiled!° *deceived*
VIOLA Who does beguile you? Who does do you wrong?
OLIVIA Hast thou forgot thyself? Is it so long?
Call forth the holy father. [*Exit an attendant*]
ORSINO [*to* VIOLA] Come, away.
OLIVIA Whither, my lord? Cesario, husband, stay.
ORSINO Husband?
OLIVIA Ay, husband. Can he that deny?
ORSINO [*to* VIOLA] Her husband, sirrah?[1]
VIOLA No, my lord, not I.
OLIVIA Alas, it is the baseness of thy fear
That makes thee strangle thy propriety.[2]
Fear not, Cesario, take thy fortunes up,
Be that thou know'st thou art, and then thou art
As great as that° thou fear'st. *him whom*
Enter PRIEST
O welcome, father.
Father, I charge thee by thy reverence

7. In Heliodorus's *Ethiopica*, a Greek prose romance translated into English in 1569 and popular in Shakespeare's day, the Egyptian robber chief Thyamis tries to kill his captive Chariclea, whom he loves, when he is in danger from a rival band.
8. To the mortification of his master.
9. More beyond all comparison.
1. Contemptuous form of address to an inferior.
2. That makes you deny your identity (as my husband).

Here to unfold—though lately we intended
To keep in darkness what occasion° now — *necessity*
Reveals before 'tis ripe—what thou dost know
Hath newly passed between this youth and me.

PRIEST A contract of eternal bond of love,
Confirmed by mutual joinder° of your hands, — *joining*
Attested by the holy close° of lips, — *meeting*
Strengthened by interchangement of your rings,
And all the ceremony of this compact
Sealed in my function,[3] by my testimony;
Since when, my watch hath told me, toward my grave
I have traveled but two hours.

ORSINO [*to* VIOLA] O thou dissembling cub, what wilt thou be
When time hath sowed a grizzle on thy case?[4]
Or will not else° thy craft° so quickly grow — *otherwise / craftiness*
That thine own trip shall be thine overthrow?[5]
Farewell, and take her, but direct thy feet
Where thou and I henceforth may never meet.

VIOLA My lord, I do protest.

OLIVIA O, do not swear!
Hold little° faith, though thou hast too much fear. — *preserve some*

Enter SIR ANDREW

SIR ANDREW For the love of God, a surgeon—send one presently° to Sir Toby. — *immediately*

OLIVIA What's the matter?

SIR ANDREW He's broke° my head across, and has given Sir Toby a bloody coxcomb,[6] too. For the love of God, your help! I had rather than forty pound I were at home. — *cut*

OLIVIA Who has done this, Sir Andrew?

SIR ANDREW The Count's gentleman, one Cesario. We took him for a coward, but he's the very devil incardinate.[7]

ORSINO My gentleman, Cesario?

SIR ANDREW 'Od's lifelings,° here he is. [*To* VIOLA] You broke my head for nothing, and that that I did I was set on to do't by Sir Toby. — *by God's little lives*

VIOLA Why do you speak to me? I never hurt you.
You drew your sword upon me without cause,
But I bespake you fair,[8] and hurt you not.

Enter [SIR] TOBY *and* [FESTE, *the*] *clown*

SIR ANDREW If a bloody coxcomb be a hurt you have hurt me. I think you set nothing by° a bloody coxcomb. Here comes Sir Toby, halting.° You shall hear more; but if° he had not been in drink he would have tickled° you othergates° than he did. — *think nothing of / limping / if only / chastised / in other ways*

3. Ratified by priestly authority.
4. A gray hair ("grizzle") on your hide (sustaining the metaphor of "cub").
5. That your attempt to trip someone else will be the cause of your downfall.
6. Head; also, a fool's cap, which resembles the crest of a cock.
7. Sir Andrew's blunder for "incarnate" (in the flesh).
8. But I spoke courteously to you.

ORSINO [*to* SIR TOBY] How now, gentleman? How is't with you?

SIR TOBY That's all one,° he's hurt me, and there's th'end on't. *no matter*

[*To* FESTE] Sot,° didst see Dick Surgeon, sot? *fool; drunkard*

FESTE O, he's drunk, Sir Toby, an hour agone. His eyes were set[9] at eight i'th' morning.

SIR TOBY Then he's a rogue, and a passy-measures pavan.[1] I hate a drunken rogue.

OLIVIA Away with him! Who hath made this havoc with them?

SIR ANDREW I'll help you, Sir Toby, because we'll be dressed[2] together.

SIR TOBY Will *you* help—an ass-head, and a coxcomb,° and a knave; a thin-faced knave, a gull?° *fool* *dupe*

OLIVIA Get him to bed, and let his hurt be looked to.

[*Exeunt* SIR TOBY, SIR ANDREW, FESTE, *and* FABIAN]

Enter SEBASTIAN

SEBASTIAN [*to* OLIVIA] I am sorry, madam, I have hurt your kinsman,
But had it been the brother of my blood
I must have done no less with wit and safety.[3]
You throw a strange regard upon me,° and by that *regard me strangely*
I do perceive it hath offended you.
Pardon me, sweet one, even for the vows
We made each other but so late ago.

ORSINO One face, one voice, one habit, and two persons,
A natural perspective,[4] that is and is not.

SEBASTIAN Antonio! O, my dear Antonio,
How have the hours racked and tortured me
Since I have lost thee!

ANTONIO Sebastian are you?

SEBASTIAN Fear'st thou° that, Antonio? *do you doubt*

ANTONIO How have you made division of yourself?
An apple cleft in two is not more twin
Than these two creatures. Which is Sebastian?

OLIVIA Most wonderful!° *full of wonder*

SEBASTIAN [*seeing* VIOLA] Do I stand there? I never had a brother,
Nor can there be that deity° in my nature *divine power*
Of here and everywhere.° I had a sister, *of omnipresence*
Whom the blind waves and surges have devoured.
Of charity,° what kin are you to me? *please*
What countryman? What name? What parentage?

VIOLA Of Messaline. Sebastian was my father.
Such a Sebastian was my brother, too.
So went he suited° to his watery tomb. *in appearance; clad*

9. Closed (as the sun sets).
1. A variety of the slow dance known as "pavane" (from the Italian *passemezzo pavana*). Sir Toby may think its swaying movements suggest drunkenness.
2. We'll have our wounds dressed.
3. With any sense of my welfare.
4. An optical illusion produced by nature (rather than by a mirror).

If spirits can assume both form and suit
You come to fright us.
SEBASTIAN A spirit I am indeed,
But am in that dimension grossly clad
Which from the womb I did participate.[5]
Were you a woman, as the rest goes even,° *the rest suggests*
I should my tears let fall upon your cheek
And say "Thrice welcome, drownèd Viola."
VIOLA My father had a mole upon his brow.
SEBASTIAN And so had mine.
VIOLA And died that day when Viola from her birth
Had numbered thirteen years.
SEBASTIAN O, that record is lively[6] in my soul.
He finishèd indeed his mortal act
That day that made my sister thirteen years.
VIOLA If nothing lets° to make us happy both *hinders*
But this my masculine usurped attire,
Do not embrace me till each circumstance
Of place, time, fortune do cohere and jump° *agree*
That I am Viola, which to confirm
I'll bring you to a captain in this town
Where lie my maiden weeds,° by whose gentle help *clothes*
I was preserved to serve this noble count.
All the occurrence of my fortune since
Hath been between this lady and this lord.
SEBASTIAN [*to* OLIVIA] So comes it, lady, you have been mistook.
But nature to her bias drew in that.[7]
You would have been contracted° to a maid, *betrothed*
Nor are you therein, by my life, deceived.
You are betrothed both to a maid and man.[8]
ORSINO [*to* OLIVIA] Be not amazed. Right noble is his blood.
If this be so, as yet the glass seems true,[9]
I shall have share in this most happy wreck.
[*To* VIOLA] Boy, thou hast said to me a thousand times
Thou never shouldst love woman like to me.
VIOLA And all those sayings will I overswear,° *swear again*
And all those swearings keep as true in soul
As doth that orbèd continent[1] the fire
That severs day from night.
ORSINO Give me thy hand,
And let me see thee in thy woman's weeds.
VIOLA The captain that did bring me first on shore
Hath my maid's garments. He upon some action° *legal charge*
Is now in durance,° at Malvolio's suit, *prison*
A gentleman and follower of my lady's.

5. I.e., I am clad, like all mortals, in the flesh in which I was born.
6. The memory of that is vivid.
7. But nature followed her inclination. (The image is from the game of bowls, which sometimes used a ball with an off-center weight that caused it to curve away from a straight course.)
8. I.e., a man who is a virgin.
9. The "natural perspective" (line 214) continues to seem real.
1. Referring to either the sun or the sphere within which the sun was thought to be fixed.

OLIVIA He shall enlarge° him. Fetch Malvolio hither— *release*
And yet, alas, now I remember me,
They say, poor gentleman, he's much distraught.° *crazed*
Enter [FESTE, *the*] *clown with a letter, and* FABIAN
A most extracting° frenzy of mine own *distracting*
From my remembrance clearly banished his.
How does he, sirrah?

FESTE Truly, madam, he holds Beelzebub at the stave's end[2] as well as a man in his case may do. He's here writ a letter to you. I should have given't you today morning. But as a madman's epistles are no gospels,[3] so it skills° not much when they are delivered. *matters*

OLIVIA Open't and read it.

FESTE Look then to be well edified when the fool delivers° the madman. [*Reads*] "By the Lord, madam"— *speaks the words of*

OLIVIA How now, art thou mad?

FESTE No, madam, I do but read madness. An your ladyship will have it as it ought to be you must allow *vox*.[4]

OLIVIA Prithee, read i'thy right wits.

FESTE So I do, madonna, but to read his right wits[5] is to read thus. Therefore perpend,° my princess, and give ear. *pay attention*

OLIVIA [*to* FABIAN] Read it you, sirrah.

[FESTE *gives the letter to* FABIAN]

FABIAN (READS) "By the Lord, madam, you wrong me, and the world shall know it. Though you have put me into darkness and given your drunken cousin rule over me, yet have I the benefit of my senses as well as your ladyship. I have your own letter that induced me to the semblance I put on, with the which I doubt not but to do myself much right or you much shame. Think of me as you please. I leave my duty a little unthought of, and speak out of my injury.[6]

The madly-used Malvolio."

OLIVIA Did he write this?

FESTE Ay, madam.

ORSINO This savors not much of distraction.° *insanity*

OLIVIA See him delivered,° Fabian, bring him hither. *released*
My lord, so please you—these things further thought on—
To think me as well a sister as a wife,[7]
One day shall crown th'alliance[8] on't, so please you,
Here at my house and at my proper cost.° *own expense*

ORSINO Madam, I am most apt° t'embrace your offer. *ready*
[*To* VIOLA] Your master quits° you, and for your service done him *releases*

2. He holds the devil (who threatens to possess him) at a distance (proverbial).
3. Gospel truths. "Epistles": letters (playing on the sense of apostolic accounts of Christ in the New Testament).
4. The appropriate voice (Latin).
5. To accurately represent his mental state.
6. I neglect the formality I owe you as your servant and speak as an injured person.
7. To think as well of me as a sister-in-law as you would have thought of me as a wife.
8. The impending double-marriage ceremony.

So much against the mettle° of your sex, *disposition*
So far beneath your soft and tender breeding,
And since you called me master for so long,
Here is my hand. You shall from this time be
Your master's mistress.

OLIVIA [*to* VIOLA]
A sister, you are she.

Enter MALVOLIO

ORSINO Is this the madman?

OLIVIA Ay, my lord, this same.
How now, Malvolio?

MALVOLIO Madam, you have done me wrong,
Notorious wrong.

OLIVIA Have I, Malvolio? No.

MALVOLIO [*showing a letter*] Lady, you have. Pray you
peruse that letter.
You must not now deny it is your hand.° *handwriting*
Write from° it if you can, in hand or phrase, *differently from*
Or say 'tis not your seal, not your invention.° *composition*
You can say none of this. Well, grant it then,
And tell me in the modesty of honor[9]
Why you have given me such clear lights° of favor, *signs*
Bade me come smiling and cross-gartered to you,
To put on yellow stockings, and to frown
Upon Sir Toby and the lighter° people, *lesser*
And acting° this in an obedient hope, *upon doing*
Why have you suffered° me to be imprisoned, *allowed*
Kept in a dark house, visited by the priest,
And made the most notorious geck° and gull *fool*
That e'er invention° played on? Tell me why? *trickery*

OLIVIA Alas, Malvolio, this is not my writing,
Though I confess much like the character,° *handwriting*
But out of question,'tis Maria's hand.
And now I do bethink me, it was she
First told me thou wast mad; then cam'st° in smiling, *you came*
And in such forms which here were presupposed° *previously suggested*
Upon thee in the letter. Prithee be content;
This practice hath most shrewdly passed[1] upon thee,
But when we know the grounds and authors of it
Thou shalt be both the plaintiff and the judge
Of thine own cause.

FABIAN Good madam, hear me speak,
And let no quarrel nor no brawl to come
Taint the condition of this present hour,
Which I have wondered at. In hope it shall not,
Most freely I confess myself and Toby
Set this device against Malvolio here
Upon° some stubborn and uncourteous parts° *because / behavior*

9. Tell me with the propriety that becomes a noblewoman.

1. This trick has most mischievously played.

We had conceived against him.[2] Maria writ
The letter, at Sir Toby's great importance,° *importunity, insistence*
In recompense whereof he hath married her.
How with a sportful malice it was followed° *followed through*
May rather pluck on° laughter than revenge *incite*
If that the injuries be justly weighed
That have on both sides passed.

OLIVIA [*to* MALVOLIO] Alas, poor fool, how have they baffled° thee! *disgraced*

FESTE Why, "Some are born great, some achieve greatness, and some have greatness thrown upon them." I was one, sir, in this interlude,° one Sir Topas, sir; but that's all one. "By the Lord, fool, I am not mad"—but do you remember, "Madam, why laugh you at such a barren rascal, an you smile not, he's gagged"—and thus the whirligig° of time brings in his revenges. *comedy* *spinning top*

MALVOLIO I'll be revenged on the whole pack of you.
[*Exit*]

OLIVIA He hath been most notoriously abused.

ORSINO Pursue him, and entreat him to a peace.
He hath not told us of the captain yet.
[*Exit one or more*]
When that is known, and golden time convents,° *summons; is convenient*
A solemn combination shall be made
Of our dear souls. Meantime, sweet sister,
We will not part from hence.° Cesario, come— *(Olivia's house)*
For so you shall be while you are a man;
But when in other habits° you are seen, *attire*
Orsino's mistress, and his fancy's° queen. *love's; imagination's*
Exeunt [*all but* FESTE]

FESTE (*sings*) When that I was and a little tiny boy,
With hey, ho, the wind and the rain,
A foolish thing was but a toy,
For the rain it raineth every day.

But when I came to man's estate,
With hey, ho, the wind and the rain,
'Gainst knaves and thieves men shut their gate,
For the rain it raineth every day.

But when I came, alas, to wive,
With hey, ho, the wind and the rain,
By swaggering° could I never thrive, *bullying*
For the rain it raineth every day.

But when I came unto my beds,
With hey, ho, the wind and the rain,
With tosspots° still had drunken heads, *drunkards*
For the rain it raineth every day.

2. To which we took exception.

A great while ago the world begun,
With hey, ho, the wind and the rain,
But that's all one, our play is done,
And we'll strive to please you every day.
Exit

ca. 1601 1623

THOMAS NASHE
1567–1601

Thomas Nashe, a Cambridge graduate, was a versatile writer of satires, plays, a novel, lyric verse, and controversial pamphlets. He was one of the so-called "University Wits" who in the late 1580s came to London and wrote for the stage and the press. They lived precarious and short lives: Nashe was about thirty-three when he died; his friend Christopher Marlowe died at twenty-nine; George Peele, at thirty; and Robert Greene, at thirty-two. In his brief career, Nashe won fame for his brilliant, idiosyncratic style, and notoriety for the vituperative and slanderous pamphlet war he conducted with Spenser's friend the scholar Gabriel Harvey.

Nashe's best-known prose work is a picaresque narrative, *The Unfortunate Traveler, or the Life of Jack Wilton*, which recounts the rambling adventures of the young hero all over Europe, including fictive encounters with Erasmus and the poet Surrey, the massacre of the Protestant radicals in Germany, and harrowing, melodramatic exploits in seductive, corrupt, and plague-ridden Italy. In this tale, and in satirical pamphlets like *Pierce Penniless, His Supplication to the Devil*, Nashe's prose, which sometimes sounds like modern experimental fiction, is headlong, exuberant, surrealistic, and intensely vivid. His tone routinely mingles the beautiful and the grotesque, laughter and horror. His dance-of-death poem, "A Litany in Time of Plague," comes paradoxically from one of his most light-hearted works, a festive comedy called *Summer's Last Will and Testament*.

Nashe's general outlook, like that of many satirists, was conservative; he attacked innovation and praised the purported stability and order of the past. But in his vision of the world, as in the manner of his writing, there is something wild and extreme. Those in power seem to have recognized that Nashe's style in itself, regardless of the content to which it was wedded, might constitute a threat to established order. In June 1599 the ecclesiastical authorities ordered that "all Nashe's books and Doctor Harvey's books be taken wheresoever they may be found and that none of their books be ever printed hereafter."*

A Litany in Time of Plague[1]

Adieu, farewell, earth's bliss,
This world uncertain is;

*Go to Norton Literature Online for another lyric by Nashe ("Spring, the sweet spring") and samples of his prose, including excerpts from his picaresque novel *The Unfortunate Traveler* and defenses of poetry and plays from his satire *Pierce Penniless, His Supplication to the Devil.*

1. This lyric is from *A Pleasant Comedy Called Summer's Last Will and Testament,* acted before the archbishop of Canterbury in his palace at Croydon in 1592 and published in 1600. Literally, a

Fond° are life's lustful° joys, *foolish / lusty*
Death proves them all but toys,° *trifles*
None from his darts° can fly; *arrows*
I am sick, I must die.
  Lord, have mercy on us!

Rich men, trust not in wealth,
Gold cannot buy you health;
Physic himself° must fade, *medicine itself*
All things to end are made.
The plague full swift goes by;
I am sick, I must die.
  Lord, have mercy on us!

Beauty is but a flower
Which wrinkles will devour;
Brightness falls from the air,
Queens have died young and fair,
Dust hath closed Helen's° eye. *Helen of Troy*
I am sick, I must die.
  Lord, have mercy on us!

Strength stoops unto the grave,
Worms feed on Hector[2] brave;
Swords may not fight with fate,
Earth still holds ope her gate.
"Come, come!" the bells[3] do cry.
I am sick, I must die.
  Lord, have mercy on us!

Wit with his wantonness
Tasteth death's bitterness;
Hell's executioner
Hath no ears for to hear
What vain art° can reply. *skill*
I am sick, I must die.
  Lord, have mercy on us!

Haste, therefore, each degree,° *social rank*
To welcome destiny;
Heaven is our heritage,
Earth but a player's stage;
Mount we unto the sky.
I am sick, I must die.
  Lord, have mercy on us!

1592 1600

litany is an appointed form of public prayer in which each of a series of supplications by the clergy is followed by a response by the congregation, with the same formula of response being repeated several times.

2. The greatest of the Trojan warriors—killed, nevertheless, by Achilles.

3. The "passing bell" that was tolled in the parish church to solicit prayers for the dying. See John Donne's "Meditation 17," p. 628.

The Early Seventeenth Century 1603–1660

1603: Death of Elizabeth I; accession of James I, first Stuart king of England
1605: The Gunpowder Plot, a failed effort by Catholic extremists to blow up Parliament and the king
1607: Establishment of first permanent English colony in the New World at Jamestown, Virginia
1625: Death of James I; accession of Charles I
1642: Outbreak of civil war; theaters closed
1649: Execution of Charles I; beginning of Commonwealth and Protectorate, known inclusively as the Interregnum (1649–60)
1660: End of the Protectorate; restoration of Charles II

Queen Elizabeth died on March 24, 1603, after ruling England for more than four decades. The Virgin Queen had not, of course, produced a child to inherit her throne, but her kinsman, the thirty-six-year old James Stuart, James VI of Scotland, succeeded her as James I without the attempted coups that many had feared. Many welcomed the accession of a man in the prime of life, supposing that he would prove more decisive than his notoriously vacillating predecessor. Worries over the succession, which had plagued the reigns of the Tudor monarchs since Henry VIII, could finally subside: James already had several children with his queen, Anne of Denmark. Writers and scholars jubilantly noted that their new ruler had literary inclinations. He was the author of treatises on government and witchcraft, and some youthful efforts at poetry.

Nonetheless, there were grounds for disquiet. James had come to maturity in Scotland, in the seventeenth century a foreign land with a different church, different customs, and different institutions of government. Two of his books, *The True Law of Free Monarchies* (1598) and *Basilikon Doron* (1599), expounded authoritarian theories of kingship: James's views seemed incompatible with the English tradition of "mixed" government, in which power was shared by the monarch, the House of Lords, and the House of Commons. As Thomas Howard wrote in 1611, while Elizabeth "did talk of her subjects' love and good affection," James "talketh of his subjects' fear and subjection." James liked to imagine himself as a modern version of the wise, peace-loving Roman Augustus Caesar, who autocratically governed a vast empire. The Romans had deified their emperors, and while the Christian James could not expect the same, he insisted on his closeness to divinity. Kings, he believed, derived their powers from God rather than from the people. As God's specially chosen delegate, surely he deserved his subjects' reverent, unconditional obedience.

Yet unlike the charismatic Elizabeth, James was personally unprepossessing. One contemporary, Anthony Weldon, provides a barbed description: "His tongue too large for his mouth, which ever made him speak full in the mouth, and drink very uncomely as if eating his drink . . . he never washed his hands . . . his walk was ever circular, his fingers ever in that walk fiddling about his codpiece." Unsurprisingly, James did not always inspire in his subjects the deferential awe to which he thought himself entitled.

The relationship between the monarch and his people and the relationship between England and Scotland would be sources of friction throughout James's reign. James had hoped to unify his domains as a single nation, "the empire of Britain." But the two realms' legal and ecclesiastical systems proved difficult to reconcile, and the English Parliament, traditionally a sporadically convened advisory body to the monarch, offered robustly xenophobic opposition. The failure of unification was only one of several clashes with the English Parliament, especially with the House of Commons, which had authority over taxation. After James died in 1625 and his son, Charles I, succeeded him, tensions persisted and intensified. Charles, indeed, attempted to rule without summoning Parliament at all between 1629 and 1638. By 1642 England was up in arms, in a civil war between the king's forces and armies loyal to the House of Commons. The conflict ended with Charles's defeat and beheading in 1649.

Although in the early 1650s the monarchy as an institution seemed as dead as the man who had last worn the crown, an adequate replacement proved difficult to devise. Executive power devolved upon a "Lord Protector," Oliver Cromwell, former general of the parliamentary forces, who wielded power nearly as autocratically as Charles had done. Yet without an institutionally sanctioned method of transferring power upon Cromwell's death in 1658, the attempt to fashion a commonwealth without a hereditary monarch eventually failed. In 1660 Parliament invited the eldest son of the old king home from exile. He succeeded to the throne as King Charles II.

As James's accession marks the beginning of "the early seventeenth century," his grandson's marks the end. Literary periods often fail to correlate neatly with the reigns of monarchs, and the period 1603–60 can seem especially arbitrary. Many of the most important cultural trends in seventeenth-century Europe neither began nor ended in these years but were in the process of unfolding slowly, over several centuries. The Protestant Reformation of the sixteenth century was still ongoing in the seventeenth, and still producing turmoil. The printing press, invented in the fifteenth century, made books ever more widely available, contributing to an expansion of literacy and to a changed conception of authorship. Although the English economy remained primarily agrarian, its manufacturing and trade sectors were expanding rapidly. England was beginning to establish itself as a colonial power and as a leading maritime nation. From 1550 on, London grew explosively as a center of population, trade, and literary endeavor. All these important developments got under way before James came to the throne, and many of them would continue after the 1714 death of James's great-granddaughter Queen Anne, the last of the Stuarts to reign in England.

From a literary point of view, 1603 can seem a particularly capricious dividing line because at the accession of James I so many writers happened to be in midcareer. The professional lives of William Shakespeare, Ben Jonson, John Donne, Francis Bacon, Walter Ralegh, and many less important writers—

Thomas Dekker, George Chapman, Samuel Daniel, Michael Drayton, and Thomas Heywood, for instance—straddle the reigns of Elizabeth and James. The Restoration of Charles II, with which this section ends, is likewise a more significant political than literary milestone: John Milton completed *Paradise Lost* and wrote two other major poems in the 1660s. Nonetheless, recognizing the years 1603–60 as a period sharpens our awareness of some important political, intellectual, cultural, and stylistic currents that bear directly upon literary production. It helps focus attention too upon the seismic shift in national consciousness that, in 1649, could permit the formal trial, conviction, and execution of an anointed king at the hands of his former subjects.

STATE AND CHURCH, 1603–40

In James's reign, the most pressing difficulties were apparently financial, but money troubles were merely symptoms of deeper quandaries about the proper relationship between the king and the people. Compared to James's native Scotland, England seemed a prosperous nation, but James was less wealthy than he believed. Except in times of war, the Crown was supposed to fund the government not through regular taxation but through its own extensive land revenues and by exchanging Crown prerogatives, such as the collection of taxes on luxury imports, in return for money or services. Yet the Crown's independent income had declined throughout the sixteenth century as inflation eroded the value of land rents. Meanwhile, innovations in military technology and shipbuilding dramatically increased the expense of port security and other defenses, a traditional Crown responsibility. Elizabeth had responded to straitened finances with parsimony, transferring much of the expense of her court, for instance, onto wealthy subjects, whom she visited for extended periods on her annual "progresses." She kept a tight lid on honorific titles too, creating new knights or peers very rarely, even though the years of her reign saw considerable upward social mobility. In consequence, by 1603 there was considerable pent-up pressure both for "honors" and for more tangible rewards for government officials. As soon as James came to power, he was immediately besieged with supplicants.

James responded with what seemed to him appropriate royal munificence, knighting and ennobling many of his courtiers and endowing them with opulent gifts. His expenses were unavoidably higher than Elizabeth's, because he had to maintain not only his own household, but also separate establishments for his queen and for the heir apparent, Prince Henry. Yet he quickly became notorious for his financial heedlessness. Compared to Elizabeth's, his court was disorderly and wasteful, marked by hard drinking, gluttonous feasting, and a craze for hunting. "It is not possible for a king of England . . . to be rich or safe, but by frugality," warned James's lord treasurer, Robert Cecil, but James seemed unable to restrain himself. Soon he was deep in debt and unable to convince Parliament to bankroll him by raising taxes.

The king's financial difficulties set his authoritarian assertions about the monarch's supremacy at odds with Parliament's control over taxation. How were his prerogatives as a ruler to coexist with the rights of his subjects? Particularly disturbing to many was James's tendency to bestow high offices upon favorites apparently chosen for good looks rather than for good judgment. James's openly romantic attachment first to Robert Carr, Earl of Somerset, and then to George Villiers, Duke of Buckingham, gave rise to widespread rumors of homosexuality at court. The period had complex attitudes toward same-sex relationships; on the one hand, "sodomy" was a capital crime (though it was very rarely prosecuted); on the other hand, passionately intense male friendship, sometimes suffused with eroticism, constituted an important cultural ideal. In James's case, at least, contemporaries considered his susceptibility to lovely, expensive youths more a political than a moral calamity. For his critics, it crystallized what was wrong with unlimited royal power: the ease with which a king could confuse his own whim with a divine mandate.

Despite James's ungainly demeanor, his frictions with Parliament, and his chronic problems of self-management, he was politically astute. Often, like Elizabeth, he succeeded not through decisiveness but through canny inaction. Cautious by temperament, he characterized himself as a peacemaker and, for many years, successfully kept England out of the religious wars raging on the Continent. His 1604 peace treaty with England's old enemy, Spain, made the Atlantic safe for English ships, a prerequisite for the colonization of the New World and for regular long-distance trading expeditions into the Mediterranean and down the African coast into the Indian Ocean. During James's reign the first permanent English settlements were established in North America, first at Jamestown, then in Bermuda, at Plymouth, and in the Caribbean. In 1611 the East India Company established England's first foothold in India. Even when expeditions ended disastrously, as did Henry Hudson's 1611 attempt to find the Northwest Passage and Walter Ralegh's 1617 expedition to Guiana, they often asserted territorial claims that England would exploit in later decades.

Although the Crown's deliberate attempts to manage the economy were often misguided, its frequent inattention or refusal to interfere had the unintentional effect of stimulating growth. Early seventeenth-century entrepreneurs undertook a wide variety of schemes for industrial or agricultural improvement. Some ventures were almost as loony as Sir Politic Would-be's ridiculous moneymaking notions in Ben Jonson's *Volpone* (1606), but others were serious, profitable enterprises. In the south, domestic industries began manufacturing goods like pins and light woolens that had previously been imported. In the north, newly developed coal mines provided fuel for England's growing cities. In the east, landowners drained wetlands, producing more arable land to feed England's rapidly growing population. These endeavors gave rise to a new respect for the practical arts, a faith in technology as a means of improving human life, and a conviction that the future might be better than the past: all important influences upon the scientific theories of Francis Bacon and his seventeenth-century followers. Economic growth in this period owed more to the initiative of individuals and small groups than to government policy, a factor that encouraged a reevaluation of the role of self-interest, the profit motive, and the role of business contracts in the betterment of the community. This reevaluation was a prerequisite for the secular, contractual political theories proposed by Thomas Hobbes and John Locke later in the seventeenth century.

On the vexations faced by the Church of England, James was likewise often most successful when he was least activist. Since religion cemented sociopolitical order, it seemed necessary to English rulers that all of their subjects belong to a single church. Yet how could they do so when the Reformation had discredited many familiar religious practices and had bred disagreement over many theological issues? Sixteenth- and seventeenth-century English people argued over many religious topics. How should public worship be conducted, and what sorts of qualifications should ministers possess? How should Scripture be understood? How should people pray? What did the sacrament of Communion mean? What happened to people's souls after they died? Elizabeth's government had needed to devise a common religious practice when actual consensus was impossible. Sensibly, it sought a middle ground between traditional and reformed views. Everyone was legally required to attend Church of England services, and the form of the services themselves was mandated in the Elizabethan Book of Common Prayer. Yet the Book of Common Prayer deliberately avoided addressing abstruse theological controversies. The language of the English church service was carefully chosen to be open to several interpretations and acceptable to both Protestant- and Catholic-leaning subjects.

The Elizabethan compromise effectively tamed many of the Reformation's divisive energies and proved acceptable to the majority of Elizabeth's subjects. To staunch Catholics on one side and ardent Protestants on the other, however, the Elizabethan church seemed to have sacrificed truth to political expediency. Catholics wanted to return England to the Roman fold; while some of them were loyal subjects of the queen, others advocated invasion by a foreign Catholic power. Meanwhile the Puritans, as they were disparagingly called, pressed for more thoroughgoing reformation in doctrine, ritual, and church government, urging the elimination of "popish" elements from worship services and "idolatrous" religious images from churches. Some, the Presbyterians, wanted to separate lay and clerical power in the national church, so that church leaders would be appointed by other ministers, not by secular authorities. Others, the separatists, advocated abandoning a national church in favor of small congregations of the "elect."

The resistance of religious minorities to Elizabeth's established church opened them to state persecution. In the 1580s and 1590s, Catholic priests and the laypeople who harbored them were executed for treason, and radical Protestants for heresy. Both groups greeted James's accession enthusiastically; his mother had been the Catholic Mary, Queen of Scots, while his upbringing had been in the strict Reformed tradition of the Scottish Presbyterian Kirk.

James began his reign with a conference at Hampton Court, one of his palaces, at which advocates of a variety of religious views could openly debate them. Yet the Puritans failed to persuade him to make any substantive reforms. Practically speaking, the Puritan belief that congregations should choose their leaders diminished the monarch's power by stripping him of authority over ecclesiastical appointments. More generally, allowing people to choose their leaders in any sphere of life threatened to subvert the entire system of deference and hierarchy upon which the institution of monarchy itself seemed to rest. "No bishop, no king," James famously remarked.

Nor did Catholics fare well in the new reign. Initially inclined to lift Elizabeth's sanctions against them, James hesitated when he realized how entrenched was the opposition to toleration. Then, in 1605, a small group of disaffected Catholics packed a cellar adjacent to the Houses of Parliament with gunpowder, intending to detonate it on the day that the king formally opened Parliament, with Prince Henry, the Houses of Lords and Commons, and the leading justices in attendance. The conspirators were arrested before they could effect their plan. If the "Gunpowder Plot" had succeeded, it would have eliminated much of England's ruling class in a single tremendous explosion, leaving the land vulnerable to invasion by a foreign, Catholic power. Not surprisingly, the Gunpowder Plot dramatically heightened anti-Catholic paranoia in England, and its apparently miraculous revelation was widely seen as a sign of God's care for England's Protestant governors.

By and large, then, James's ecclesiastical policies continued along the lines laid down by Elizabeth. By appointing bishops of varying doctrinal views, he restrained any single faction from controlling church policy. The most important religious event of James's reign was a newly commissioned translation of the Bible. First published in 1611, it was a typically moderating document. A much more graceful rendering than its predecessor, the Geneva version produced by Puritan expatriates in the 1550s, the King James Bible immediately became the standard English Scripture. Its impressive rhythms and memorable phrasing would influence writers for centuries. On the one hand, the new translation contributed to the Protestant aim of making the Bible widely available to every reader in the vernacular. On the other hand, unlike the Geneva Bible, the King James Version translated controversial and ambiguous passages in ways that bolstered conservative preferences for a ceremonial church and for a hierarchically organized church government.

James's moderation was not universally popular. Some Protestants yearned for a more confrontational policy toward Catholic powers, particularly toward Spain, England's old enemy. In the first decade of James's reign, this party clustered around James's eldest son and heir apparent, Prince Henry, who cultivated a militantly Protestant persona. When Henry died of typhoid fever in 1612, those who favored his policies were forced to seek avenues of power outside the royal court. By the 1620s, the House of Commons was developing a vigorous sense of its own independence, debating policy agendas often quite at odds with the Crown's and openly attempting to use its power to approve taxation as a means of exacting concessions from the king.

James's second son, Prince Charles, came to the throne upon James's death in 1625. Unlike his father, Charles was not a theorist of royal absolutism, but he acted on that principle with an inflexibility that his father had never been able to muster. By 1629 he had dissolved Parliament three times in frustration with its recalcitrance, and he then began more than a decade of "personal rule" without Parliament. Charles was more prudent in some respects than his father had been—he not only restrained the costs of his own court, but paid off his father's staggering debts by the early 1630s. Throughout his reign, he conscientiously applied himself to the business of government. Yet his refusal to involve powerful individuals and factions in the workings of the state inevitably alienated them, even while it cut him off dangerously from important channels of information about the reactions of his people. Money was a constant problem, too. Even a relatively frugal king required some funds for ambitious government initiatives; but without parliamentary approval, any taxes Charles imposed were widely perceived as illegal. As a result, even wise policies, such as Charles's effort to build up the English navy, spawned misgivings among many of his subjects.

Religious conflicts intensified. Charles's queen, the French princess Henrietta Maria, supported an entourage of Roman Catholic priests, protected English Catholics, and encouraged several noblewomen in her court to convert to the Catholic faith. While Charles remained a staunch member of the Church of England, he loved visual splendor and majestic ceremony in all aspects of life, spiritual and otherwise—proclivities that led his Puritan subjects to suspect him of popish sympathies. Charles's profound attachment to his wife, so different from James's neglect of Anne, only deepened their qualms. Like many fellow Puritans, Lucy Hutchinson blamed the entire debacle of Charles's reign on his wife's influence.

Charles's appointment of William Laud as archbishop of Canterbury, the ecclesiastical head of the English Church, further alienated Puritans. Laud subscribed to a theology that most Puritans rejected. As followers of the sixteenth-century reformer John Calvin, Puritans held that salvation depended upon faith in Christ, not "works." Works were meaningless because the deeds of sinful human beings could not be sanctified in the absence of faith; moreover, the Fall had so thoroughly corrupted human beings that they could not muster this faith without the help of God's grace. God chose (or refused) to extend grace to particular individuals on grounds that human beings were incapable of comprehending, and his decision had been made from eternity, before the individuals concerned were even born. In other words, Puritans believed, God predestined people to be saved or damned, and Christ's redemptive sacrifice was designed only for the saved group, the "elect." Laud, by contrast, advocated the Arminian doctrine that through Christ, God made redemption freely available to all human beings. Individuals could choose whether or not to respond to God's grace, and they could work actively toward their salvation by acts of charity, ritual devotion, and generosity to the church.

Although Laud's theology appears more generously inclusive than the Calvinist alternative, his ecclesiastical policies were uncompromising. Stripping many Puritan ministers of their posts, Laud aligned the doctrine and ceremonies of the English church with Roman Catholicism, which like Arminianism held works in high regard. In an ambitious project of church renovation, Laud installed religious paintings and images in churches; he thought they promoted reverence in worshippers, but the Puritans believed they encouraged idolatry. He rebuilt and resituated altars, making them more ornate and prominent: another change that dismayed Puritans, since it implied that the Eucharist rather than the sermon was the central element of a worship service. In the 1630s thousands of Puritans departed for the New England colonies, but many more remained at home, deeply discontented.

As the 1630s drew to a close, Archbishop Laud and Charles attempted to impose a version of the English liturgy and episcopal organization upon Presbyterian Scotland. Unlike his father, Charles had little acquaintance with his northern realm, and he drastically underestimated the difficulties involved. The Scots objected both on nationalist and on religious grounds, and they were not shy about expressing their objections: the bishop of Brechin, obliged to conduct divine service in the prescribed English style, mounted the pulpit armed with two pistols against his unruly congregation, while his wife, stationed on the floor below, backed him up with a blunderbuss. In the conflict that followed, the Bishops' Wars of 1639 and 1640, Charles's forces met with abject defeat. Exacerbating the situation, Laud was simultaneously insisting upon greater conformity within the English church. Riots in the London streets and the Scots' occupation of several northern English cities forced Charles to call the so-called Long Parliament, which would soon be managing a revolution.

LITERATURE AND CULTURE, 1603–40

Old Ideas and New

In the first part of the seventeenth century, exciting new scientific theories were in the air, but the older ways of thinking about the nature of things had not yet been superseded. Writers such as John Donne, Robert Burton, and Ben Jonson often invoked an inherited body of concepts even though they were aware that those concepts were being questioned or displaced. The Ptolemaic universe, with its fixed earth and circling sun, moon, planets, and stars, was a rich source of poetic imagery. So were the four elements—fire, earth, water, and air—that together were thought to comprise all matter, and the four bodily humors—choler, blood, phlegm, and black bile—which were supposed to determine a person's temperament and to cause physical and mental disease when out of balance. Late Elizabethans and Jacobeans (so called from *Jacobus,* Latin for James) considered themselves especially prone to melancholy, an ailment of scholars and thinkers stemming from an excess of black bile. Shakespeare's Hamlet is melancholic, as is Bosola in John Webster's *Duchess of Malfi* and Milton's title figure in "Il Penseroso" ("the serious-minded one"). In his panoramic *Anatomy of Melancholy,* Burton argued that melancholy was universal.

Key concepts of the inherited system of knowledge were analogy and order. Donne was especially fond of drawing parallels between the macrocosm, or "big world," and the microcosm, or "little world," of the individual human being. Also widespread were versions of the "chain of being" that linked and ordered various kinds of beings in hierarchies. The order of nature, for instance, put God above angels, angels above human beings, human beings above animals, animals above plants, plants above rocks. The social order installed the king over his nobles, nobles over the gentry, gentry over yeomen, yeomen over common laborers. The order of the family set husband above wife, parents above children, master and mistress above servants, the elderly above the young. Each level had its peculiar function, and each was connected to those above and beneath in a tight network of obligation and dependency. Items that occupied similar positions in different hierarchies were related by analogy: thus a monarch was like God, and he was also like a father, the head of the family, or like a lion, most majestic of beasts, or like the sun, the most excellent of heavenly bodies. A medieval or Renaissance poet who calls a king a sun or a lion, then, imagines himself not to be forging a metaphor in his own creative imagination, but to be describing something like an obvious fact of nature. Many Jacobean tragedies, Shakespeare's *King Lear* perhaps most comprehensively, depict the catastrophes that ensue when these hierarchies rupture, and both the social order and the natural order disintegrate.

Yet this conceptual system was itself beginning to crumble. Francis Bacon advocated rooting out of the mind all the intellectual predilections that had made the old ideas so attractive: love of ingenious correlations, reverence for tradition, and a priori assumptions about what was possible in nature. Instead, he argued, groups of collaborators ought to design controlled experiments to find the truths of nature by empirical means. Even as Bacon was promoting his views in *The Advancement of Learning, Novum Organum,* and *The New Atlantis,* actual experiments and discoveries were calling the old verities into question. From the far-flung territories England was beginning to colonize or to trade with, collectors brought animal, plant, and ethnological novelties, many of which were hard to subsume under old categories of understanding. William Harvey's discovery that blood circulated in the body shook received views on the function of blood, casting doubt on the theory of the humors. Galileo's telescope provided evidence confirming Copernican astronomical theory, which dislodged the earth from its stable central position in the cosmos and, in defiance of all ordinary observation, set it whirling around the sun. Galileo found evidence as well of change in the heavens, which were supposed to be perfect and incorruptible above the level of the moon. Donne, like other writers of his age, responded with a mixture of excitement and anxiety to such novel ideas as these:

And new philosophy calls all in doubt:
The element of fire is quite put out;
The sun is lost, and the earth, and no man's wit
Can well direct him where to look for it.

Several decades later, however, Milton embraced the new science, proudly recalling a visit during his European tour to "the famous Galileo, grown old, a prisoner to the Inquisition for thinking in astronomy otherwise than the Franciscan and Dominican licensers thought." In *Paradise Lost,* he would make complex poetic use of the astronomical controversy, considering how, and how far, humans should pursue scientific knowledge.

Patrons, Printers, and Acting Companies

The social institutions, customs, and practices that had supported and regulated writers in Tudor times changed only gradually before 1640. As it had under Elizabeth, the church promoted writing of several kinds: devotional treatises; guides to meditation; controversial tracts; "cases of conscience," which work out difficult moral issues in complex situations; and especially sermons. Since everyone was required to attend church, everyone heard sermons at least once and often twice on Sunday, as well as on religious or national holidays. The essence of a sermon, Protestants agreed, was the careful exposition of Scripture, and its purpose was to instruct and to move. Yet styles varied; while some preachers, like Donne, strove to enthrall their congregations with all the resources of artful rhetoric, others, especially many Puritans, sought an undecorated style that would display God's word in its own splendor. Printing made it easy to circulate many copies of sermons, blurring the line between oral delivery and written text and enhancing the role of printers and booksellers in disseminating God's word.

Many writers of the period depended in one way or another upon literary patronage. A Jacobean or Caroline aristocrat, like his medieval forebears, was expected to reward dependents in return for services and homage. Indeed, his status was gauged partly on the size of his entourage (that is one reason why in *King Lear* the hero experiences his daughters' attempts to dismiss his retainers as so intensely humiliating). In the early seventeenth century, although commercial relationships were rapidly replacing feudal ones, patronage pervaded all walks of life: governing relationships between landlords and tenants, masters and servants, kings and courtiers. Writers were assimilated into this system partly because their works reflected well on the patron, and partly because their all-around intelligence made them useful members of a great man's household. Important patrons of the time included the royal family—especially Queen Anne, who sponsored the court masques, and Prince

Henry—the members of the intermarried Sidney/Herbert family, and the Countess of Bedford, Queen Anne's confidante.

Because the patronage relationship often took the form of an exchange of favors rather than a simple financial transaction, its terms were very variable and are difficult to recover with any precision at this historical remove. A poet might dedicate a poem or a work to a patron in the expectation of a simple cash payment. But a patron might provide a wide range of other benefits: a place to live; employment as a secretary, tutor, or household servant; or gifts of clothing (textiles were valuable commodities). Donne, for instance, received inexpensive lodging from the Drury family, for whom he wrote the *Anniversaries;* a suit of clerical attire from Lucy Russell, Countess of Bedford, when he took orders in the Church of England; and advancement in the church from King James. Ben Jonson lived for several years at the country estates of Lord Aubigny and of Robert Sidney, in whose honor he wrote "To Penshurst"; he received a regular salary from the king in return for writing court masques; and he served as chaperone to Sir Walter Ralegh's son on a Continental tour. Aemilia Lanyer apparently resided for some time in the household of Margaret Clifford, Countess of Cumberland. Andrew Marvell lived for two years with Thomas Fairfax, tutored his daughter and wrote *Upon Appleton House* for him. All these quite different relationships and forms of remuneration fall under the rubric of patronage.

The patronage system required the poets involved to hone their skills at eulogizing their patrons' generosity and moral excellence. Jonson's epigrams and many of Lanyer's dedicatory poems evoke communities of virtuous poets and patrons joined by bonds of mutual respect and affection. Like the line between sycophantic flattery and truthful depiction, the line between patronage and friendship could be a thin one. Literary manuscripts circulated among circles of acquaintances and supporters, many of whom were, at least occasionally, writers as well as readers. Jonson esteemed Mary Wroth both as a fellow poet and as a member of the Sidney family to whom he owed so much. Donne became part of a coterie around Queen Anne's closest confidante, Lucy Russell, Countess of Bedford, who was also an important patron for Ben Jonson, Michael Drayton, and Samuel Daniel. The countess evidently wrote poems herself, although only one attributed to her has apparently survived.

Presenting a poem to a patron, or circulating it among the group of literary people who surrounded the patron, did not require printing it. In early-seventeenth-century England, the reading public for sophisticated literary works was tiny and concentrated in a few social settings: the royal court, the universities, and the Inns of Court, or law schools. In these circumstances, manuscript circulation could be an effective way of reaching one's audience. So a great deal of writing remained in manuscript in early-seventeenth-century England. The collected works of many important writers of the period—most notably John Donne, George Herbert, William Shakespeare, and Andrew Marvell—appeared in print only posthumously, in editions produced by friends or admirers. Other writers, like Robert Herrick, collected and printed their own works long after they were written and (probably) circulated in manuscript. In consequence, it is often difficult to date accurately the composition of a seventeenth-century poem. In addition, when authors do not participate in the printing of their own works, editorial problems multiply—when, for instance, the printed version of a poem is inconsistent with a surviving manuscript copy.

Nonetheless, the printing of all kinds of literary works was becoming more common. Writers such as Francis Bacon or Robert Burton, who hoped to reach large numbers of readers with whom they were not acquainted, usually arranged for the printing of their texts soon after they were composed. The sense that the printing of lyric poetry, in particular, was a bit vulgar began to fade when the famous Ben Jonson collected his own works in a grand folio edition.

Until 1640 the Stuart kings kept in place the strict controls over print publication originally instituted by Henry VIII, in response to the ideological threat posed by the Reformation. King Henry had given the members of London's Stationer's Company a monopoly on all printing; in return for their privilege, they were supposed to submit texts to prepublication censorship. In the latter part of the sixteenth century, presses associated with the universities at Oxford and Cambridge would begin operation as well, but they were largely concerned with scholarly and theological books. As a result, with a very few exceptions (such as George Herbert's *The Temple,* published by Cambridge University Press), almost all printed literary texts were produced in London. Most of them were sold there as well, in the booksellers' stalls set up outside St. Paul's Cathedral.

The licensing system located not only primary responsibility for a printed work, but its ownership, with the printer rather than with the author. Printers typically paid writers a onetime fee for the use of their work, but the payment was scanty, and the authors of popular texts realized no royalties from the many copies sold. As a result, no one could make a living as a writer in the early seventeenth century by producing best sellers. The first writer formally to arrange for royalties was apparently John Milton, who received five pounds up front for *Paradise Lost,* and another five pounds and two hundred copies at the end of each of the first three impressions. Still, legal ownership of and control over a printed work remained with the printer: authorial copyright would not become a reality until the early eighteenth century.

In monetary terms, a more promising outlet for writers was the commercial theater, which provided the first literary market in English history. Profitable and popular acting companies, established successfully in London in Elizabeth's time, continued to play a very important cultural role under James and Charles. Because the acting companies staged a large number of different plays and paid for them at a predictable, if not generous, rate, they enabled a few hardworking writers to support themselves as full-time professionals. One of them, Thomas Dekker, commented bemusedly on the novelty of being paid for the mere products of one's imagination: "the theater," he wrote, "is your poet's Royal Exchange upon which their muses—that are now turned to merchants—meeting, barter away that light commodity of words." In James's reign, Shakespeare was at the height of his powers: *Othello, King Lear, Macbeth, Antony and Cleopatra, The Winter's Tale, The Tempest,* and other important plays were first staged during these years. So were Jonson's major comedies: *Volpone, Epicene, The Alchemist,* and *Bartholomew Fair*. The most important new playwright was John Webster, whose dark tragedies *The White Devil* and *The Duchess of Malfi* combined gothic horror with stunningly beautiful poetry.

Just as printers were legally the owners of the texts they printed, so theater companies, not playwrights, were the owners of the texts they performed. Typically, companies guarded their scripts closely, permitting them to be printed only in times of financial distress or when they were so old that printing them seemed unlikely to reduce the paying audience. As a result, many Jacobean and Caroline plays are lost to us or available only in corrupt or posthumous versions. For contemporaries, though, a play was "published" not by being printed but by being performed. Aware of the dangerous potential of plays in arousing the sentiments of large crowds of onlookers, the Stuarts, like the Tudors before them, instituted tight controls over dramatic performances. Acting companies, like printers, were obliged to submit works to the censor before public presentation.

Authors, printers, and acting companies who flouted the censorships laws were subject to imprisonment, fines, or even bodily mutilation. Queen Elizabeth cut off the hand of a man who disagreed in print with her marriage plans, King Charles the ears of a man who inveighed against court masques. Jonson and his collaborators found themselves in prison for ridiculing King James's broad Scots accent in one of their comedies. The effects of censorship on writers' output were therefore far reaching across literary genres. Since overt criticism or satire of the great was so dangerous, political writing was apt to be oblique and allegorical. Writers often employed animal fables, tales of distant lands, or long-past historical events to comment upon contemporary issues.

While the commercial theaters were profitable businesses that made most of their money from paying audiences, several factors combined to bring writing for the theater closer to the Stuart court than it had been in Elizabeth's time. The Elizabethan theater companies had been officially associated with noblemen who guaranteed their legitimacy (in contrast to unsponsored traveling players, who were subject to punishment as vagrants). Early in his reign, James brought the major theater companies under royal auspices. Shakespeare's company, the most successful of the day, became the King's Men: it performed not only all of Shakespeare's plays but also *Volpone* and *The Duchess of Malfi*. Queen Anne, Prince Henry, Prince Charles, and Princess Elizabeth sponsored other companies of actors. Royal patronage, which brought with it tangible rewards and regular court performances, naturally encouraged the theater companies to pay more attention to courtly taste. Shakespeare's *Macbeth* put onstage Scots history and witches, two of James's own interests; in *King Lear,* the hero's disastrous division of his kingdom may reflect controversies over the proposed union of Scotland and England. In the first four decades of the seventeenth century, court-affiliated theater companies such as the King's Men increasingly cultivated audiences markedly more affluent than the audiences they had sought in the 1580s and 1590s, performing in intimate, expensive indoor theaters instead of, or as well as, in the cheap popular amphitheaters. *The Duchess of Malfi,* for instance, was probably written with the King's Men's indoor theater at Blackfriars in mind, because several scenes depend for their effect upon a control over lighting that is impossible outdoors. Partly because the commercial theaters seemed increasingly to cater to the affluent and courtly elements of society, they attracted the ire of the king's opponents when civil war broke out in the 1640s.

Jacobean Writers and Genres

The era saw important changes in poetic fashion. Some major Elizabethan genres fell out of favor—long allegorical or mythological narratives, sonnet sequences, and pastoral poems. The norm was coming to be short, concentrated, often witty poems. Poets and prose writers alike often preferred the jagged rhythms of colloquial speech to the elaborate ornamentation and near-musical orchestration of sound that many Elizabethans had sought. The major poets of these years, Jonson, Donne, and Herbert, led this shift and also promoted a variety of "new" genres: love elegy and satire after the classical models of Ovid and Horace, epigram, verse epistle, meditative religious lyric, and country-house poem. Although these poets differed enormously from one another, all three exercised an important influence on the poets of the next generation.

A native Londoner, Jonson first distinguished himself as an acute observer of urban manners in a series of early, controversial satiric plays. Although he wrote two of his most moving poems to his dead children, Jonson focused rather rarely on the dynamics of the family relationships that so profoundly concerned his contemporary Shakespeare. When generational and dynastic matters do figure in his poetry, as they do at the end of "To Penshurst," they seem part of the agrarian, feudal order that Jonson may have romanticized but that he suspected was rapidly disappearing. By and large, Jonson interested himself in relationships that seemed to be negotiated by the participants, often in a bustling urban or courtly world in which blood kinship no longer decisively determined one's social place. Jonson's poems of praise celebrate and exemplify classical and humanist ideals of friendship: like-minded men and women elect to join in a community that fosters wisdom, generosity, civic responsibility, and mutual respect. In the plays and satiric poems, Jonson stages the violation of those values with such riotous comprehensiveness that the very survival of such ideals seem endangered: the plays swarm with voracious swindlers and their eager victims, social climbers both adroit and inept, and a dizzying assortment of morons and misfits. In many of Jonson's plays, rogues or wits collude to victimize others; their stormy, self-interested alliances, apparently so different from the virtuous friendships of the poems of praise, in fact resemble them in one respect: they are connections entered into by choice, not by law, inheritance, or custom.

Throughout his life, Jonson earned his living entirely from his writing, composing plays for the public theater while also attracting patronage as a poet and a writer of court masques. His acute awareness of his audience was partly, then, a sheerly practical matter. Yet Jonson's yearning for recognition ran far beyond any desire for material reward. A gifted poet, Jonson argued, was a society's proper judge and teacher, and he could only be effective if his audience understood and respected the poet's exalted role. Jonson set out unabashedly to create that audience and to monumentalize himself as a great English author. In 1616 he took the unusual step, for his time, of collecting his poems, plays, and masques in an elegant folio volume.

Jonson's influence upon the next generation of writers, and through them into the Restoration and the eighteenth century, was an effect both of his poetic mastery of his chosen modes and of his powerful personal example. Jonson mentored a group of younger poets, known as the Tribe, or Sons, of Ben, meeting regularly with some of them in the Apollo Room of the Devil Tavern in London. Many of the royalist, or Cavalier, poets—Robert Herrick, Thomas Carew, Richard Lovelace, Sir John Suckling, Edmund Waller, Henry Vaughan in his secular verse—proudly acknowledged their relationship to Jonson or gave some evidence of it in their verse. Most of them absorbed too Jonson's attitude toward print and in later decades supervised the publication of their own poems.

Donne, like Jonson, spent most of his life in or near London, often in the company of other writers and intellectuals—indeed, in the company of many of the same writers and intellectuals, since the two men were friends and shared some of the same patrons. Yet, unlike Jonson's, most of Donne's poetry concerns itself not with a crowded social panorama, but with a dyad—with the relationship between the speaker and one single other being, a woman or God—that in its intensity blots out the claims of lesser relationships. Love for Donne encompasses an astonishing range of emotional experiences, from the lusty impatience of "To His Mistress Going to Bed" to the cheerful promiscuity of "The Indifferent" to the mysterious platonic telepathy of "Air and Angels," from the vengeful wit of "The Apparition" to the postcoital tranquility of "The Good Morrow." While for Jonson the shared meal among friends often becomes an emblem of communion, for Donne sexual consummation has something of the same highly charged symbolic character, a moment in which the isolated individual can, however temporarily, escape the boundaries of selfhood in union with another:

> The phoenix riddle hath more with
> By us: we two being one, are it.
> So, to one neutral thing both sexes fit.

In the religious poems, where Donne both yearns for a physical relationship with God and knows it is impossible, he does not abandon his characteristic bodily metaphors. The doctrine of the Incarnation—God's taking material form in the person of Jesus Christ—and the doctrine of the bodily resurrection of the dead at the Last Day are Christian teachings that fascinate Donne, to which he returns again and again in his poems, sermons, and devotional writings. While sexual and religious love had long shared a common vocabulary, Donne delights in making that overlap seem new and shocking. He likens conjoined lovers to saints; demands to be raped by God; speculates, after his wife's death, that God killed her because He was jealous of Donne's divided loyalty; imagines Christ encouraging his Bride, the church, to "open" herself to as many men as possible.

Throughout Donne's life, his faith, like his intellect, was anything but quiet. Born into a family of devout Roman Catholics just as the persecution of Catholics was intensifying in Elizabethan England, Donne eventually became a member of the Church of England. If "Satire 3" is any indication, the conversion was attended by profound doubts and existential crisis. Donne's restless mind can lead him in surprising and sometimes unorthodox directions, to a qualified defense of suicide, for instance, in *Biathanatos.* At the same time, overwhelmed with a sense of his own unworthiness, he courts God's punishment, demanding to be spat upon, flogged, burnt, broken down, in the expectation that suffering at God's hand will restore him to grace and favor.

In both style and content, Donne's poems were addressed to a select few rather than to the public at large. His style is demanding, characterized by learned terms, audaciously far-fetched analogies, and an intellectually sophisticated play of ironies. Even Donne's sermons, attended by large crowds, share the knotty difficulty of the poems, and something too of their quality of intimate address. Donne circulated his poems in manuscript and largely avoided print publication (most of his poems were printed after his death in 1631). By some critics Donne has been regarded as the founder of a Metaphysical school of poetry. We find echoes of Donne's style in many later poets: in Thomas Carew, who praised Donne as a "monarch of wit," George Herbert, Richard

Crashaw, John Cleveland, Sir John Suckling, Abraham Cowley, and Andrew Marvell.

Herbert, the younger son of a wealthy, cultivated, and well-connected family, seemed destined in early adulthood for a brilliant career as a diplomat or government servant. Yet he turned his back on worldly greatness to be ordained a priest in the Church of England. Moreover, eschewing a highly visible career as an urban preacher, he spent the remaining years of his short life ministering to the tiny rural parish of Bemerton. Herbert's poetry is shot through with the difficulty and joy of this renunciation, with all it entailed for him. Literary ambition—pride in one's independent creativity—appears to Herbert a temptation that must be resisted, whether it takes the form of Jonson's openly competitive aspiration for literary preeminence or Donne's brilliantly ironic self-displaying performances. Instead, Herbert seeks other models for poetic agency: the secretary taking dictation from a master, the musician playing in harmonious consort with others, the member of a church congregation who speaks with and for a community.

Herbert destroyed his secular verse in English and he turned his volume of religious verse over to a friend only on his deathbed, desiring him to print it if he thought it would be useful to "some dejected poor soul," but otherwise to burn it. The 177 lyrics contained in that volume, *The Temple,* display a complex religious sensibility and great artistic subtlety in an amazing variety of stanza forms. Herbert was the major influence on the next generation of religious lyric poets and was explicitly recognized as such by Henry Vaughan and Richard Crashaw.

The Jacobean period also saw the emergence of what would become a major prose genre, the familiar essay. The works of the French inventor of the form, Michel de Montaigne, appeared in English translation in 1603, influencing Shakespeare as well as such later writers as Sir Thomas Browne. Yet the first essays in English, the work of Francis Bacon, attorney general under Elizabeth and eventually lord chancellor under James, bear little resemblance to Montaigne's intimate, tentative, conversational pieces. Bacon's essays present pithy, sententious, sometimes provocative claims in a tone of cool objectivity, tempering moral counsel with an awareness of the importance of prudence and expediency in practical affairs. In *Novum Organum* Bacon adapts his deliberately discontinuous mode of exposition to outline a new scientific method, holding out the tantalizing prospect of eventual mastery over the natural world and boldly articulating the ways in which science might improve the human condition. In his fictional utopia, described in *The New Atlantis*, Bacon imagines a society that realizes his dream of carefully orchestrated collaborative research, so different from the erratic, uncoordinated efforts of alchemists and amateurs in his own day. Bacon's philosophically revolutionary approach to the natural world profoundly impacted scientifically minded people over the next several generations. His writings influenced the materialist philosophy of his erstwhile secretary, Thomas Hobbes, encouraged Oliver Cromwell to attempt a large-scale overhaul of the university curriculum during the 1650s, and inspired the formation of the Royal Society, an organization of experimental scientists, after the Restoration.

The reigns of the first two Stuart kings mark the entry of Englishwomen, in some numbers, into authorship and publication. Most female writers of the period were from the nobility or gentry; all were much better educated than most women of the period, many of whom remained illiterate. In 1611 Aemilia

Lanyer was the first Englishwoman to publish a substantial volume of original poems. It contained poetic dedications, a long poem on Christ's passion, and a country-house poem, all defending women's interests and importance. In 1613 Elizabeth Cary, Lady Falkland, was the first Englishwoman to publish a tragedy, *Mariam,* a closet drama that probes the situation of a queen subjected to her husband's domestic and political tyranny. In 1617 Rachel Speght, the first female polemicist who can be securely identified, published a defense of her sex in response to a notorious attack upon "Lewd, Idle, Froward, and Unconstant Women"; she was also the author of a long dream-vision poem. Lady Mary Wroth, niece of Sir Philip Sidney and the Countess of Pembroke, wrote a long prose romance, *Urania* (1612), which presents a range of women's experiences as lovers, rulers, counselors, scholars, storytellers, poets, and seers. Her Petrarchan sonnet sequence *Pamphilia to Amphilanthus,* published with *Urania,* gives poetic voice to the female in love.

THE CAROLINE ERA, 1625–40

When King Charles came to the throne in 1625, "the fools and bawds, mimics and catamites of the former court grew out of fashion," as the Puritan Lucy Hutchinson recalled. The changed style of the court directly affected the arts and literature of the Caroline period (so called after *Carolus,* Latin for Charles). Charles and his queen, Henrietta Maria, were art collectors on a large scale and patrons of such painters as Peter Paul Rubens and Sir Anthony Van Dyke; the latter portrayed Charles as a heroic figure of knightly romance, mounted on a splendid stallion. The conjunction of chivalric virtue and divine beauty or love, symbolized in the union of the royal couple, was the dominant theme of Caroline court masques, which were even more extravagantly hyperbolic than their Jacobean predecessors. Even as Henrietta Maria encouraged an artistic and literary cult of platonic love, several courtier-poets, such as Carew and Suckling, wrote playful, sophisticated love lyrics that both alluded to this fashion and sometimes urged a more licentiously physical alternative.

The religious tensions between the Caroline court's Laudian church and the Puritan opposition produced something of a culture war. In 1633 Charles reissued the *Book of Sports,* originally published by his father in 1618, prescribing traditional holiday festivities and Sunday sports in every parish. Like his father, he saw these recreations as the rural, downscale equivalent of the court masque: harmless, healthy diversions for people who otherwise spent most of their waking hours hard at work. Puritans regarded masques and rustic dances alike as occasions for sin, the Maypole as a vestige of pagan phallus worship, and Sunday sports as a profanation of the Sabbath. In 1632 William Prynne staked out the most extreme Puritan position, publishing a tirade of over one thousand pages against stage plays, court masques, Maypoles, Laudian church rituals, stained-glass windows, mixed dancing, and other outrages, all of which he associated with licentiousness, effeminacy, and the seduction of popish idolatry. For this cultural critique, Prynne was stripped of his academic degrees, ejected from the legal profession, set in the pillory, sentenced to life imprisonment, and had his books burned and his ears cut off. The severity of the punishments indicates the perceived danger of the book and the inextricability of literary and cultural affairs from politics.

Milton's astonishingly virtuosic early poems also respond to the tensions of the 1630s. Milton repudiated both courtly aesthetics and also Prynne's wholesale prohibitions, developing reformed versions of pastoral, masque, and hymn. In "On the Morning of Christ's Nativity," the birth of Christ coincides with a casting out of idols and a flight of false gods, stanzas that suggest contemporary Puritan resistance to Archbishop Laud's policies. Milton's magnificent funeral elegy "Lycidas" firmly rejects the poetic career of the Cavalier poet, who disregards high artistic ambition to "sport with Amaryllis in the shade / Or with the tangles of Neaera's hair." The poem also vehemently denounces the establishment clergy, ignorant and greedy "blind mouths" who rob their flocks of spiritual nourishment.

THE REVOLUTIONARY ERA, 1640–60

Early in the morning on January 30, 1649, Charles Stuart, the dethroned king Charles I, set off across St. James Park for his execution, surrounded by a heavy guard. He wore two shirts because the weather was frigid, and he did not want to look as if he were shivering with fear to the thousands who had gathered to watch him be beheaded. The black-draped scaffold had been erected just outside James I's elegant Banqueting House, inside of which so many court masques, in earlier decades, had celebrated the might of the Stuart monarchs and assured them of their people's love and gratitude. To those who could not attend, newsbooks provided eyewitness accounts of the dramatic events of the execution, as they had of Charles's trial the week before. Andrew Marvell also memorably describes the execution scene in "An Horatian Ode."

The execution of Charles I was understood at the time, and is still seen by many historians today, as a watershed event in English history. How did it come to pass? Historians do not agree over what caused "the English revolution," or, as it is alternatively called, the English civil war. One group argues that long-term changes in English society and the English economy led to rising social tensions and eventually to violent conflict. New capitalist modes of production in agriculture, industry, and trade were often incompatible with older feudal norms. The gentry, an affluent, highly educated class below the nobility but above the artisans, mechanics, and yeomen, played an increasingly important part in national affairs, as did the rich merchants in London; but the traditional social hierarchies failed to grant them the economic, political, and religious freedoms they believed they deserved. Another group of historians, the "revisionists," emphasize instead short-term and avoidable causes of the war—unlucky chances, personal idiosyncrasies, and poor decisions made by a small group of individuals.

Whatever caused the outbreak of hostilities, there is no doubt that the twenty-year period between 1640 and 1660 saw the emergence of concepts central to bourgeois liberal thought for centuries to come: religious toleration, separation of church and state, freedom from press censorship, and popular sovereignty. These concepts developed out of bitter disputes centering on three fundamental questions: What is the ultimate source of political power? What kind of church government is laid down in Scripture, and therefore ought to be settled in England? What should be the relation between the church and the state? The theories that evolved in response to these questions contained the seeds of much that is familiar in modern thought, mixed with much that is forbiddingly alien. It is vital to recognize that the participants in the disputes were not haphazardly attempting to predict the shape of modern liberalism, but were responding powerfully to the most important problems of their day. The need to find right answers seemed particularly urgent for the Millenarians among them, who, interpreting the upheavals of the time through the lens of the apocalyptic Book of Revelation, believed that their day was very near to being the last day of all.

When the so-called Long Parliament convened in 1640, it did not plan to execute a monarch or even to start a war. It did, however, want to secure its rights in the face of King Charles's perceived absolutist tendencies. Refusing merely to approve taxes and go home, as Charles would have wished, Parliament insisted that it could remain in session until its members agreed to disband. Then it set about abolishing extralegal taxes and courts, reining in the bishops' powers, and arresting (and eventually trying and executing) the king's ministers, the Earl of Strafford and Archbishop Laud. The collapse of effective royal government meant that the machinery of press censorship, which had been a Crown responsibility, no longer restrained the printing of explicit commentary on contemporary affairs of state. As Parliament debated, therefore, presses poured forth a flood of treatises arguing vociferously on all sides of the questions about church and state, creating a lively public forum for political discussion where none had existed before. The suspension of censorship permitted the development of weekly newsbooks that reported, and editorialized on, current domestic events from varying political and religious perspectives.

As the rift widened between Parliament and the king in 1641, Charles sought to arrest five members of Parliament for treason, and Londoners rose in arms against him. The king fled to York, while the queen escaped to the Continent. Negotiations for compromise broke down over the issues that would derail them at every future stage: control of the army and the church. On July 12, 1642, Parliament voted to raise an army, and on August 22 the king stood before a force of two thousand horse and foot at Nottingham, unfurled his royal standard, and summoned his liege men to his aid. Civil war had begun. Regions of the country, cities, towns, social classes, and even families found themselves painfully divided. The king set up court and an alternative parliament in Oxford, to which many in the House of Lords and some in the House of Commons transferred their allegiance.

In the First Civil War (1642–46), Parliament and the Presbyterian clergy that supported it had limited aims. They hoped to secure the rights of the House of Commons, to limit the king's power over the army and the church—but not to depose him—and to settle Presbyterianism as the national established church. As Puritan armies moved through the country, fighting at Edgehill, Marston Moor, Naseby, and elsewhere, they also undertook a crusade to stamp out idolatry in English churches, smashing religious images and stained-glass windows and lopping off the heads of statues as an earlier generation had done at the time of the English Reformation. Their ravages are still visible in English churches and cathedrals.

The Puritans were not, however, a homogeneous group, as the 1643 Toleration Controversy revealed. The Presbyterians wanted a national Presbyterian church, with dissenters punished and silenced as before. But Congregationalists, Independents, Baptists, and other separatists opposed a national church and pressed for some measure of toleration, for themselves at least. The religious radical Roger Williams, just returned from New England, argued that Christ mandated the complete separation of church and state and the civic toleration of all religions, even Roman Catholics, Jews, and

Muslims. Yet to most people, the civil war itself seemed to confirm that people of different faiths could not coexist peacefully. Thus even as sects continued to proliferate—Seekers, Finders, Antinomians, Fifth Monarchists, Quakers, Muggletonians, Ranters—even the most broad-minded of the age often attempted to draw a line between what was acceptable and what was not. Predictably, their lines failed to coincide. In *Areopagitica* (1644), John Milton argues vigorously against press censorship and for toleration of most Protestants—but for him, Catholics are beyond the pale. Robert Herrick and Sir Thomas Browne regarded Catholic rites, and even some pagan ones, indulgently but could not stomach Puritan zeal.

In 1648, after a period of negotiation and a brief Second Civil War, the king's army was definitively defeated. His supporters were captured or fled into exile, losing position and property. Yet Charles, imprisoned on the Isle of Wight, remained a threat. He was a natural rallying point for those disillusioned by parliamentary rule—many people disliked Parliament's legal but heavy taxes even more than they had the king's illegal but lighter ones. Charles repeatedly attempted to escape and was accused of trying to open the realm to a foreign invasion. Some powerful leaders of the victorious New Model Army took drastic action. They expelled royalists and Presbyterians, who still wanted to come to an accommodation with the king, from the House of Commons and abolished the House of Lords. With consensus assured by the purgation of dissenting viewpoints, the army brought the king to trial for high treason in the Great Hall of Westminster.

After the king's execution, the Rump Parliament, the part of the House of Commons that had survived the purge, immediately established a new government "in the way of a republic, without king or House of Lords." The new state was extremely fragile. Royalists and Presbyterians fiercely resented their exclusion from power and pronounced the execution of the king a sacrilege. The Rump Parliament and the army were at odds, with the army rank and file arguing that voting rights ought not be restricted to men of property. The Levelers, led by John Lilburne, called for suffrage for all adult males. An associated but more radical group, called the Diggers or True Levelers, pushed for economic reforms to match the political ones. Their spokesman, Gerrard Winstanley, wrote eloquent manifestos developing a Christian communist program. Meanwhile, Millenarians and Fifth Monarchists wanted political power vested in the regenerate "saints" in preparation for the thousand-year reign of Christ on earth foretold in the biblical Book of Revelation. Quakers defied both state and church authority by refusing to take oaths and by preaching incendiary sermons in open marketplaces. Most alarming of all, out of proportion to their scant numbers, were the Ranters, who believed that because God dwelt in them none of their acts could be sinful. Notorious for sexual license and for public nudity, they got their name from their deliberate blaspheming and their penchant for rambling prophecy. In addition to internal disarray, the new state faced serious external threats. After Charles I's execution, the Scots and the Irish—who had not been consulted about the trial—immediately proclaimed his eldest son, Prince Charles, the new king. The prince, exiled on the Continent, was attempting to enlist the support of a major European power for an invasion.

The formidable Oliver Cromwell, now undisputed leader of the army, crushed external threats, suppressing rebellions in Ireland and Scotland. The Irish war was especially bloody, as Cromwell's army massacred the Catholic natives in a frenzy of religious hatred. When trade rivalries erupted with the Dutch over control of shipping lanes in the North Sea and the English Channel, the new republic was again victorious. Yet the domestic situation remained unstable. Given popular disaffection and the unresolved disputes between Parliament and the army, the republic's leaders dared not call new elections. In 1653 power effectively devolved upon Cromwell, who was sworn in as Lord Protector for life under England's first written constitution. Many property owners considered Cromwell the only hope for stability, while others, including Milton, saw him as a champion of religious liberty. Although persecution of Quakers and Ranters continued, Cromwell sometimes intervened to mitigate the lot of the Quakers. He also began a program to readmit Jews to England, partly in the interests of trade but also to open the way for their conversion, supposedly a precursor of the Last Day as prophesied in the Book of Revelation.

The problem of succession remained unresolved, however. When Oliver Cromwell died in 1658, his son, Richard, was appointed in his place, but he had inherited none of his father's leadership qualities. In 1660 General George Monck succeeded in calling elections for a new "full and free" parliament, open to supporters of the monarchy as well as of the republic. The new Parliament immediately recalled the exiled prince, officially proclaiming him King Charles II on May 8, 1660. The period that followed, therefore, is called the Restoration: it saw the restoration of the monarchy and with it the royal court, the established Church of England, and the professional theater.

Over the next few years, the new regime executed some of the regicides that had participated in Charles I's trial and execution and harshly repressed radical Protestants (the Baptist John Bunyan wrote *Pilgrim's Progress* in prison). Yet Charles II, who came to the throne at Parliament's invitation, could not lay claim to absolute power as his father had done. After his accession, Parliament retained its legislative supremacy and complete power over taxation, and exercised some control over the king's choice of counselors. It assembled by its own authority, not by the king's mandate. During the Restoration years, the journalistic commentary and political debates that had first flourished in the 1640s remained forceful and open, and the first modern political parties developed out of what had been the royalist and republican factions in the civil war. In London and in other cities, the merchant classes, filled with dissenters, retained their powerful economic leverage. Although the English revolution was apparently dismantled in 1660, its long-term effects profoundly changed English institutions and English society.

LITERATURE AND CULTURE, 1640–60

The English civil war was disastrous for the English theater. One of Parliament's first acts after hostilities began in 1642 was to abolish public plays and sports, as "too commonly expressing lascivious mirth and levity." Some drama continued to be written and published, but performances were rare and would-be theatrical entrepreneurs had to exploit loopholes in the prohibitions by describing their works as "operas" or presenting their productions in semiprivate circumstances.

As the king's government collapsed, the patronage relationships centered upon the court likewise disintegrated. Many leading poets were staunch royalists, or Cavaliers, who suffered considerably in the war years. Robert Herrick lost his position; Richard Lovelace was imprisoned; Margaret Cavendish went into exile. With their usual networks of manuscript circulation disrupted, many royalist writers printed their verse. Volumes of poetry by Thomas Carew, John Denham, John Suckling, James Shirley, Richard Lovelace, and Robert Herrick appeared in the 1640s. Their poems, some dating from the 1620s or 1630s, celebrate the courtly ideal of the good life: good food, plenty of wine, good verse, hospitality, and high-spirited loyalty, especially to the king. One characteristic genre is the elegant love lyric, often with a carpe diem theme. In Herrick's case especially, apparent ease and frivolity masks a frankly political subtext. The Puritans excoriated May Day celebrations, harvest-home festivities, and other time-honored holidays and "sports" as unscriptural, idolatrous, or frankly pagan. For Herrick, they sustained a community that strove neither for ascetic perfection nor for equality among social classes, but that knew the value of pleasure in cementing social harmony and that incorporated everyone—rich and poor, unlettered and learned—as the established church had traditionally tried to do.

During the 1640s and 1650s, as they faced defeat, the Cavaliers wrote movingly of the relationship between love and honor, of fidelity under duress, of like-minded friends sustaining one another in a hostile environment. They presented themselves as amateurs, writing verse in the midst of a life devoted to more important matters: war, love, the king's service, the endurance of loss. Rejecting the radical Protestant emphasis on the "inner light," which they considered merely a pretext for presumptuousness and violence, the Cavalier poets often cultivated a deliberately unidiosyncratic, even self-deprecating poetic persona. Thus the poems of Richard Lovelace memorably express sentiments that he represents not as the unique insights of an isolated genius, but as principles easily grasped by all honorable men. When in "The Vine" Herrick relates a wet dream, he not only laughs at himself but at those who mistake their own fantasies for divine inspiration.

During the 1650s, royalists wrote lyric poems in places far removed from the hostile centers of parliamentary power. In Wales, Henry Vaughan wrote religious verse expressing his intense longing for past eras of innocence and for the perfection of heaven or the millennium. Also in Wales, Katherine Philips wrote and circulated in manuscript poems that celebrate female friends in terms normally reserved for male friendships. The publication of her poems after the Restoration brought Philips some celebrity as "the Matchless Orinda." Richard Crashaw, an exile in Paris and Rome and a convert to Roman Catholicism, wrote lush religious poetry that attempted to reveal the spiritual by stimulating the senses. Margaret Cavendish, also in exile, with the queen in Paris, published two collections of lyrics when she returned to England in 1653; after the Restoration she published several dramas and a remarkable utopian romance, *The Blazing World*.

Several prose works by royalist sympathizers have become classics in their respective genres. Thomas Hobbes, the most important English philosopher of the period, another exile in Paris, developed his materialist philosophy and psychology there and, in *Leviathan* (1651), his unflinching defense of absolute sovereignty based on a theory of social contract. Some royalist writing seems to have little to do with the contemporary scene, but in fact carries a political charge. In *Religio Medici* (1642–43), Sir Thomas Browne presents himself as a genial, speculative doctor who loves ritual and ceremony not for complicated theological reasons, but because they move him emotionally. While he can sympathize with all Christians, even Roman Catholics, and while he recognizes in himself many idiosyncratic views, he willingly submits his judgment to the Church of England, in sharp contrast to Puritans bent on ridding the church of its errors. Izaak Walton's treatise on fishing, *The Complete Angler* (1653), presents a dialogue between Walton's persona, Piscator the angler, and Venator the hunter. Piscator, speaking like many Cavalier poets for the values of warmheartedness, charity, and inclusiveness, converts the busy, warlike Venator, a figure for the Puritan, to the tranquil and contemplative pursuit of fishing.

The revolutionary era gave new impetus to women's writing. The circumstances of war placed women in novel, occasionally dangerous situations, giving them unusual events to describe and prompting self-discovery. The autobiographies of royalists Lady Anne Halkett and Margaret Cavendish, Duchess of Newcastle, published after the Restoration, report their experiences and their sometimes daring activities during those trying days. Lucy Hutchinson's memoir of her husband, Colonel John Hutchinson, first published in 1806, narrates much of the history of the times from a republican point of view. Leveler women offered petitions and manifestos in support of their cause and of their imprisoned husbands. The widespread belief that the Holy Spirit was moving in unexpected ways encouraged a number of female prophets: Anna Trapnel, Mary Cary, and Lady Eleanor Davies. Their published prophecies often carried a strong political critique of Charles or of Cromwell. Quaker women came into their own as preachers and sometimes as writers of tracts, authorized by the Quaker belief in the spiritual equality of women and men, and by the conviction that all persons should testify to whatever the inner light communicates to them. Many of their memoirs, such as Dorothy Waugh's "Relation," were originally published both to call attention to their sufferings and to inspire other Quakers to similar feats of moral fortitude.

While most writers during this period were royalists, two of the best, Andrew Marvell and John Milton, sided with the republic. Marvell wrote most of the poems for which he is still remembered while at Nunappleton in the early 1650s, tutoring the daughter of the retired parliamentary general Thomas Fairfax; in 1657 he joined his friend Milton in the office of Cromwell's Latin Secretariat. In Marvell's love poems and pastorals, older convictions about ordered harmony give way to wittily unresolved or unresolvable oppositions, some playful, some painful. Marvell's conflictual worldview seems unmistakably the product of the unsettled civil war decades. In his country-house poem "Upon Appleton House," even agricultural practices associated with regular changes of the season, like the flooding of fallow fields, become emblems of unpredictability, reversal, and category confusion. In other poems Marvell eschews an authoritative poetic persona in favor of speakers that seem limited or even a bit unbalanced: a mower who argues for the values of pastoral with disconcerting belligerence, a nymph who seems to exemplify virginal innocence but also immature self-absorption and possibly unconscious sexual perversity. Marvell's finest political poem, "An Horatian Ode upon Cromwell's Return from Ireland," celebrates Cromwell's providential victories even while inviting sympathy for the executed king and warning about the potential dangers of Cromwell's meteoric rise to power.

A promising, prolific young poet in the 1630s, Milton committed himself to the English republic as soon as the conflict between the king and Parliament began to take shape. His loyalty to the revolution remained unwavering despite his disillusion when it failed to realize his ideals: religious toleration for all Protestants and the free circulation of ideas without prior censorship. First as a self-appointed adviser to the state, then as its official defender, he addressed the great issues at stake in the 1640s and the 1650s. In a series of treatises he argued for church disestablishment and for the removal of bishops, for a republican government based on natural law and popular sovereignty, for the right of the people to dismiss from office and even execute their rulers, and, most controversial even to his usual allies, in favor of divorce on the grounds of incompatibility. Milton was a Puritan, but both his theological heterodoxies and his poetic vision mark him as a distinctly unusual one.

During his years as a political polemicist, Milton also wrote several sonnets, revising that small, love-centered genre to accommodate large private and public topics: a Catholic massacre of proto-Protestants in the foothills of Italy, the agonizing questions posed by his blindness, various threats to intellectual and religious liberty. In 1645 he published his collected English and Latin poems as a counterstatement to the royalist volumes of the 1640s. Yet his most ambitious poetry remained to be written. Milton probably wrote some part of *Paradise Lost* in the late 1650s and completed it after the Restoration, encompassing in it all he had thought, read, and experienced of tyranny, political controversy, evil, deception, love, and the need for companionship. This cosmic blank-verse epic assimilates and critiques the epic tradition and Milton's entire intellectual and literary heritage, classical and Christian. Yet it centers not on martial heroes but on a domestic couple who must discover how to live a good life day by day, in Eden and later in the fallen world, amid intense emotional pressures and the seductions of evil.

Seventeenth-century poetry, prose, and drama retains its hold on readers because so much of it is so very good, fusing intellectual power, emotional passion, and extraordinary linguistic artfulness. Poetry in this period ranges over an astonishing variety of topics and modes: highly erotic celebrations of sexual desire, passionate declarations of faith and doubt, lavishly embroidered paeans to friends and benefactors, tough-minded assessments of social and political institutions. English dramatists were at the height of their powers, situating characters of unprecedented complexity in plays sometimes remorselessly satiric, sometimes achingly moving. In these years English prose becomes a highly flexible instrument, suited to informal essays, scientific treatises, religious meditation, political polemic, biography and autobiography, and journalistic reportage. Literary forms evolve for the exquisitely modulated representation of the self: dramatic monologues, memoirs, spiritual autobiographies, sermons in which the preacher takes himself for an example. Finally, we have in Milton an epic poet who assumed the role of inspired prophet, envisioning a world created by God but shaped by human choice and imagination.

Additional information about the Early Seventeenth Century, including primary texts and images, is available at Norton Literature Online (wwnorton.com/literature). Online topics are

- Gender, Family, Household
- *Paradise Lost* in Context
- Civil Wars of Ideas
- Emigrants and Settlers

THE EARLY SEVENTEENTH CENTURY

TEXTS	CONTEXTS
1603 James I, *Basilikon Doron* reissued	**1603** Death of Elizabeth I; accession of James I. Plague
1604 William Shakespeare, *Othello*	
1605 Shakespeare, *King Lear*. Ben Jonson, *The Masque of Blackness*. Francis Bacon, *The Advancement of Learning*	**1605** Gunpowder Plot, failed effort by Roman Catholic extremists to blow up Parliament
1606 Jonson, *Volpone*. Shakespeare, *Macbeth*	
	1607 Founding of Jamestown colony in Virginia
1609 Shakespeare, *Sonnets*	**1609** Galileo begins observing the heavens with a telescope
1611 "King James" Bible (Authorized Version). Shakespeare, *The Tempest*. John Donne, *The First Anniversary*. Aemilia Lanyer, *Salve Deus Rex Judaeorum*	
1612 Donne, *The Second Anniversary*	**1612** Death of Prince Henry
1613 Elizabeth Cary, *The Tragedy of Mariam*	
1614 John Webster, *The Duchess of Malfi*	
1616 Jonson, *Works*. James I, *Works*	**1616** Death of Shakespeare
	1618 Beginning of the Thirty Years War
	1619 First African slaves in North America exchanged by Dutch frigate for food and supplies at Jamestown
1620 Bacon, *Novum Organum*	**1620** Pilgrims land at Plymouth
1621 Mary Wroth, *The Countess of Montgomery's Urania* and *Pamphilia to Amphilanthus*. Robert Burton, *The Anatomy of Melancholy*	**1621** Donne appointed dean of St. Paul's Cathedral
1623 Shakespeare, First Folio	
1625 Bacon, *Essays*	**1625** Death of James I; accession of Charles I; Charles I marries Henrietta Maria
	1629 Charles I dissolves Parliament
1633 Donne, *Poems*. George Herbert, *The Temple*	**1633** Galileo forced by the Inquisition to recant the Copernican theory
1637 John Milton, "Lycidas"	
1640 Thomas Carew, *Poems*	**1640** Long Parliament called (1640–53). Archbishop Laud impeached
1642 Thomas Browne, *Religio Medici*. Milton, *The Reason of Church Government*	**1642** First Civil War begins (1642–46). Parliament closes the theaters
1643 Milton, *The Doctrine and Discipline of Divorce*	**1643** Accession of Louis XIV of France

TEXTS	CONTEXTS
1644 Milton, *Areopagitica*	
1645 Milton, *Poems.* Edmund Waller, *Poems*	**1645** Archbishop Laud executed. Royalists defeated at Naseby
1648 Robert Herrick, *Hesperides* and *Noble Numbers*	**1648** Second Civil War. "Pride's Purge" of Parliament
1649 Milton, *The Tenure of Kings and Magistrates* and *Eikonoklastes*	**1649** Trial and execution of Charles I. Republic declared. Milton becomes Latin Secretary (1649–59)
1650 Henry Vaughan, *Silex Scintillans* (Part II, 1655)	
1651 Thomas Hobbes, *Leviathan.* Andrew Marvell, *Upon Appleton House* (unpublished)	
	1652 Anglo-Dutch War (1652–54)
	1653 Cromwell made Lord Protector
	1658 Death of Cromwell; his son Richard made Protector
1660 Milton, *Ready and Easy Way to Establish a Free Commonwealth*	**1660** Restoration of Charles II to throne. Royal Society founded
	1662 Charles II marries Catherine of Braganza
	1665 The Great Plague
1666 Margaret Cavendish, *The Blazing World*	**1666** The Great Fire
1667 Milton, *Paradise Lost* (in ten books). Katherine Philips, *Collected Poems.* John Dryden, *Annus Mirabilis*	
1671 Milton, *Paradise Regained* and *Samson Agonistes*	
1674 Milton, *Paradise Lost* (in twelve books)	**1674** Death of Milton
1681 Marvell, *Poems,* published posthumously	

JOHN DONNE
1572–1631

Lovers' eyeballs threaded on a string. A god who assaults the human heart with a battering ram. A teardrop that encompasses and drowns the world. John Donne's poems abound with startling images, some of them exalting and others grotesque. With his strange and playful intelligence, expressed in puns, paradoxes, and the elaborately sustained metaphors known as "conceits," Donne has enthralled and sometimes enraged readers from his day to our own. The tired clichés of love poetry—cheeks like roses, hearts pierced by the arrows of love—emerge reinvigorated and radically transformed by his hand, demanding from the reader an unprecedented level of mental alertness and engagement. Donne prided himself on his wit and displayed it not only in his conceits but in his grasp of learned and obscure discourses ranging from theology to alchemy, from cosmology to law. Yet for all their ostentatious intellectuality, Donne's poems never give the impression of being academic exercises put into verse. Rather, they are intense dramatic monologues in which the speaker's ideas and feelings seem to shift and evolve from one line to the next. Donne's prosody is equally dramatic, mirroring in its variable and jagged rhythms the effect of speech (and eliciting from his classically minded contemporary Ben Jonson the gruff observation that "Donne, for not keeping of accent deserved hanging").

Donne began life as an outsider, and in some respects remained one until death. He was born in London in 1572 into a devout Roman Catholic household. The family was prosperous, but, as the poet later remarked, none had suffered more heavily for its loyalty to the Catholic Church: "I have been ever kept awake in a meditation of martyrdom." Donne was distantly related to the great Catholic humanist and martyr Sir Thomas More. Closer to home, a Jesuit uncle was executed by the brutal method of hanging, castrating, disemboweling, and quartering, and his own brother Henry, arrested for harboring a priest, died in prison of the plague. As a Catholic in Protestant England, growing up in decades when anti-Roman feeling reached new heights, Donne could not expect any kind of public career, nor even to receive a university degree (he left Oxford without one and studied law for a time at the Inns of Court). What he could reasonably expect instead was prejudice, official harassment, and crippling financial penalties. He chose not to live under such conditions. At some point in the 1590s, having returned to London after travels abroad, and having devoted some years to studying theological issues, Donne converted to the English church.

The poems that belong with certainty to this period of his life—the five satires and most of the elegies—reveal a man both fascinated by and keenly critical of English society. Four of the satires treat commonplace Elizabethan topics—foppish and obsequious courtiers, bad poets, corrupt lawyers and a corrupt court—but are unique both in their visceral revulsion and in their intellectual excitement. Donne uses striking images of pestilence, itchy lust, vomit, excrement, and pox to create a unique satiric world, busy, vibrant, and corrupt, in which his dramatic speakers have only to step outside the door to be inundated by all the fools and knaves in Christendom. By contrast, the third satire treats the quest for true religion—the question that preoccupied him above all others in these years—in terms that are serious, passionately witty, and deeply felt. Donne argues that honest doubting search is better than the facile acceptance of any religious tradition, epitomizing that point brilliantly in the image of Truth on a high and craggy hill, very difficult to climb. What is certain is that society's values are of no help whatsoever to the individual seeker—none will escape the final judgment by pleading that "A Harry, or a Martin taught [them] this." In the love elegies Donne seems intent on making up for his social powerlessness through witty representations of mastery in the bedroom and of adventurous travel. In "Elegy 16" he imagines his speaker embarking on a journey "O'er the white Alps" and with mingled tenderness and condescension argues down a naive mistress's proposal to accompany him. And in "Elegy 19," his fondling of a naked lover becomes in a famous conceit the equivalent of exploration in America. Donne's interest in satire and elegy—classical Roman genres, which he helped introduce to English verse—is itself significant. He wrote in English, but he reached out to other traditions.

If Donne's conversion to the Church of England promised him security, social acceptance, and the possibility of a public career, that promise was soon to be cruelly withdrawn. In 1596–97 he participated in the Earl of Essex's military expeditions against Catholic Spain in Cádiz and the Azores (the experience prompted two remarkable descriptive poems of life at sea, "The Storm" and "The Calm") and upon his return became secretary to Sir Thomas Egerton, Lord Keeper of the Great Seal. This should have been the beginning of a successful public career. But his secret marriage in 1601 to Egerton's seventeen-year-old niece Ann More enraged Donne's employer and the bride's wealthy father; Donne was briefly imprisoned and dismissed from service. The poet was reduced to a retired country life beset by financial insecurity and a rapidly increasing family; Ann bore twelve children (not counting miscarriages) by the time she died at age thirty-three. At one point, Donne wrote despairingly that while the death of a child would mean one less mouth to feed, he could not afford the burial expenses. In this bleak period, he wrote but dared not publish *Biathanatos*, a paradoxical defense of suicide.

As his family grew, Donne made every effort to reinstate himself in the favor of the great. To win the approval of James I, he penned *Pseudo-Martyr* (1610), defending the king's insistence that Catholics take the Oath of Allegiance. This set an irrevocable public stamp on his renunciation of Catholicism, and Donne followed up with a witty satire on the Jesuits, *Ignatius His Conclave* (1611). In the same period he was producing a steady stream of occasional poems for friends and patrons such as Somerset (the king's favorite), the Countess of Bedford, and Magdalen Herbert, and for small coteries of courtiers and ladies. Like most gentlemen of his era, Donne saw poetry as a polite accomplishment rather than as a trade or vocation, and in consequence he circulated his poems in manuscript but left most of them uncollected and unpublished. In 1611 and 1612, however, he published the first and second *Anniversaries* on the death of the daughter of his patron Sir Robert Drury.

For some years King James had urged an ecclesiastical career on Donne, denying him any other means of advancement. In 1615 Donne finally consented, overcoming his sense of unworthiness and the pull of other ambitions. He was ordained in the Church of England and entered upon a distinguished career as court preacher, reader in divinity at Lincoln's Inn, and dean of St. Paul's. Donne's metaphorical style, bold erudition, and dramatic wit established him as a great preacher in an age that appreciated learned sermons powerfully delivered. Some 160 of his sermons survive, preached to monarchs and courtiers, lawyers and London magistrates, city merchants and trading companies. As a distinguished clergyman in the Church of England, Donne had traveled an immense distance from the religion of his childhood and the adventurous life of his twenties. Yet in his sermons and late poems we find the same brilliant and idiosyncratic mind at work, refashioning his profane conceits to serve a new and higher purpose. In "Expostulation 19" he praises God as the greatest of literary stylists: "a figurative, a metaphorical God," imagining God as a conceit-maker like himself. In poems, meditations, and sermons, Donne came increasingly to be engaged in anxious contemplation of his own mortality. In "Hymn to God My God, in My Sickness," Donne imagines himself spread out on his deathbed like a map showing the route to the next world. Only a few days before his death he preached "Death's Duel," a terrifying analysis of all life as a decline toward death and dissolution, which contemporaries termed his own funeral sermon. On his deathbed, according to his contemporary biographer Izaak Walton, Donne had a portrait made of himself in his shroud and meditated on it daily. Meditations upon skulls as emblems of mortality were common in the period, but nothing is more characteristic of Donne than to find a way to meditate on his own skull.

Given the shape of Donne's career, it is no surprise that his poems and prose works display an astonishing variety of attitudes, viewpoints, and feelings on the great subjects of love and religion. Yet this variety cannot be fully explained in biographical terms. The poet's own attempt to distinguish between Jack Donne, the young rake, and Dr. Donne, the grave and religious dean of St. Paul's, is (perhaps intentionally) misleading. We do not know the time and circumstances for most of Donne's verses, but it is clear that many of his finest religious poems predate his ordination, and it is possible that he continued to add to the love poems known as his "songs and sonnets" after he entered the church. Theological language abounds in his love poetry, and daringly erotic images occur in his religious verse.

Donne's "songs and sonnets" have been the cornerstone of his reputation almost since their publication in 1633. The title *Songs and Sonnets* associates them with the popular miscellanies of love poems and sonnet sequences in the Petrarchan tradition, but they directly challenge the popular Petrarchan sonnet sequences of the 1590s. The collection contains only one formal sonnet, the "songs" are not notably lyrical, and Donne draws upon and transforms a whole range of literary traditions concerned with love. Like Petrarch, Donne can present himself as the despairing lover of an unattainable lady ("The Funeral"); like Ovid he can be lighthearted, witty, cynical, and frankly lustful ("The Flea," "The Indifferent"); like the Neoplatonists, he espouses a theory of transcendent love, but he breaks from them with his insistence in many poems on the union of physical and spiritual love. What binds these poems together and grants them enduring power is their compelling immediacy. The speaker is always in the throes of intense emotion, and that emotion is not static but constantly shifting and evolving with the turns of the poet's thought. Donne seems supremely present in these poems, standing behind their various speakers. Where Petrarchan poets exhaustively catalogue their beloved's physical features (though in highly conventional terms), Donne's speakers tell us little or nothing about the loved woman, or about the male friends imagined as the audience for many poems. Donne's repeated insistence that the private world of lovers is superior to the wider public world, or that it somehow contains all of that world, or obliterates it, is understandable in light of the many disappointments of his career. Yet this was also a poet who threw himself headlong into life, love, and sexuality, and later into the very visible public role of court and city preacher.

Donne was long grouped with Herbert, Vaughan, Crashaw, Marvell, Traherne, and Cowley under the heading of "Metaphysical poets." The expression was first employed by critics like Samuel Johnson and William Hazlitt, who found the intricate conceits and self-conscious learning of these poets incompatible with poetic beauty and sincerity. Early in the twentieth century, T. S. Eliot sought to restore their reputation, attributing to them a unity of thought and feeling that had since their time been lost. There was, however, no formal "school" of Metaphysical poetry, and the characteristics ascribed to it by later critics pertain chiefly to Donne. Like Ben Jonson, John Donne had a large influence on the succeeding generation, but he remains a singularity.

FROM SONGS AND SONNETS[1]

The Flea[2]

Mark but this flea, and mark in this,
How little that which thou deniest me is;
Me it sucked first, and now sucks thee,
And in this flea our two bloods mingled be;
Thou know'st that this cannot be said
A sin, or shame, or loss of maidenhead,° *virginity*
Yet this enjoys before it woo,
And pampered° swells with one blood made of two,[3] *overfed*
And this, alas, is more than we would do.

Oh stay, three lives in one flea spare,
Where we almost, nay more than married are.
This flea is you and I, and this
Our marriage bed and marriage temple is;
Though parents grudge, and you, we are met,
And cloistered[4] in these living walls of jet.° *black*
Though use° make you apt to kill me,[5] *habit*
Let not to that, self-murder added be,
And sacrilege, three sins in killing three.

Cruel and sudden, hast thou since
Purpled thy nail in blood of innocence?
Wherein could this flea guilty be,
Except in that drop which it sucked from thee?
Yet thou triumph'st, and say'st that thou
Find'st not thy self nor me the weaker now;
'Tis true; then learn how false fears be:
Just so much honor, when thou yield'st to me,
Will waste, as this flea's death took life from thee.

1633

The Good-Morrow° *morning greeting*

I wonder, by my troth,° what thou and I *good faith*
Did, till we loved? Were we not weaned till then,
But sucked on country pleasures, childishly?

1. Donne's love poems were written over nearly two decades, beginning around 1595; they were not published in Donne's lifetime but circulated widely in manuscript. The title *Songs and Sonnets* was supplied in the second edition (1635), which grouped the poems by kind, but neither this arrangement nor the more haphazard organization of the first edition (1633) is Donne's own. In Donne's time the term "sonnet" often meant simply "love lyric," and in fact there is only one formal sonnet in this collection. For the poems we present we follow the 1635 edition, beginning with the extremely popular poem "The Flea."
2. This insect afforded a popular erotic theme for poets all over Europe, deriving from a pseudo-Ovidian medieval poem in which a lover envies the flea for the liberties it takes with his mistress's body.
3. The swelling suggests pregnancy.
4. As in a convent or monastery.
5. By denying me sexual gratification.

Or snorted° we in the seven sleepers' den?[1] *snored*
'Twas so; but° this, all pleasures fancies be. *except for*
If ever any beauty I did see,
Which I desired, and got, 'twas but a dream of thee.

And now good morrow to our waking souls,
Which watch not one another out of fear;
For love all love of other sights controls,
And makes one little room an everywhere.
Let sea-discoverers to new worlds have gone,
Let maps to others, worlds on worlds have shown:
Let us possess one world;[2] each hath one, and is one.

My face in thine eye, thine in mine appears,
And true plain hearts do in the faces rest;
Where can we find two better hemispheres,
Without sharp North, without declining West?
Whatever dies was not mixed equally;[3]
If our two loves be one, or thou and I
Love so alike that none do slacken, none can die.

1633

Song

Go and catch a falling star,
  Get with child a mandrake root,[1]
Tell me where all past years are,
  Or who cleft the Devil's foot,
Teach me to hear mermaids° singing, *sirens*
Or to keep off envy's stinging,
    And find
    What wind
Serves to advance an honest mind.

If thou beest born to strange sights,
  Things invisible to see,
Ride ten thousand days and nights,
  Till age snow white hairs on thee,
Thou, when thou return'st, wilt tell me
All strange wonders that befell thee,
    And swear
    No where
Lives a woman true, and fair.

1. Cave in Ephesus where, according to legend, seven Christian youths hid from pagan persecutors and slept for 187 years.
2. "Our world" in many manuscripts.
3. Scholastic philosophy taught that when the elements were imperfectly mixed ("not mixed equally"), matter was mutable and mortal; conversely, when the elements were perfectly mixed, matter was immutable and hence immortal.

1. The mandrake root, or mandragora, is forked like the lower part of the human body. It was thought to shriek when pulled from the ground and to kill all humans who heard it; it was also (paradoxically) thought to help women conceive.

If thou find'st one, let me know,
  Such a pilgrimage were sweet;
Yet do not, I would not go,
  Though at next door we might meet;
Though she were true when you met her,
And last till you write your letter,
    Yet she
    Will be
False, ere I come, to two, or three.

1633

The Undertaking

I have done one braver° thing *more glorious*
  Than all the Worthies[1] did,
And yet a braver thence doth spring,
  Which is, to keep that hid.

It were but madness now t' impart
  The skill of specular stone,[2]
When he which can have learned the art
  To cut it, can find none.

So, if I now should utter this,
  Others (because no more
Such stuff to work upon, there is)
  Would love but as before.

But he who loveliness within
  Hath found, all outward loathes,
For he who color loves, and skin,
  Loves but their oldest clothes.

If, as I have, you also do
  Virtue attired in woman see,
And dare love that, and say so too,
  And forget the He and She;

And if this love, though placèd so,
  From profane men you hide,
Which will no faith on this bestow,
  Or, if they do, deride;

1. According to medieval legend, the Nine Worthies, or supreme heroes of history, included three Jews (Joshua, David, Judas Maccabaeus), three pagans (Hector, Alexander, Julius Caesar), and three Christians (Arthur, Charlemagne, Godfrey of Boulogne).

2. A transparent or translucent material, reputed to have been used in antiquity for windows, but no longer known. Great skill was needed to cut it.

Then you have done a braver thing
Than all the Worthies did;
And a braver thence will spring,
Which is, to keep that hid.

1633

The Sun Rising[1]

Busy old fool, unruly sun,
Why dost thou thus
Through windows and through curtains call on us?
Must to thy motions lovers' seasons run?
Saucy pedantic wretch, go chide
Late schoolboys and sour prentices,
Go tell court huntsmen that the king will ride,[2]
Call country ants to harvest offices;[3]
Love, all alike, no season knows nor clime,
Nor hours, days, months, which are the rags of time.

Thy beams, so reverend and strong
Why shouldst thou think?
I could eclipse and cloud them with a wink,
But that I would not lose her sight so long;
If her eyes have not blinded thine,
Look, and tomorrow late, tell me,
Whether both th' Indias of spice and mine[4]
Be where thou leftst them, or lie here with me.
Ask for those kings whom thou saw'st yesterday,
And thou shalt hear, All here in one bed lay.

She is all states,° and all princes I, *nations*
Nothing else is.
Princes do but play us; compared to this,
All honor's mimic, all wealth alchemy.
Thou, sun, art half as happy as we,
In that the world's contracted thus;
Thine age asks ease, and since thy duties be
To warm the world, that's done in warming us.
Shine here to us, and thou art everywhere;
This bed thy center is, these walls thy sphere.[5]

1633

1. Some lines of this poem recall Ovid, *Amores* 1.13.
2. King James was very fond of hunting.
3. Autumn chores. "Country ants": farm drudges.
4. The India of "spice" is the East Indies; that of "mine" (gold), the West Indies.
5. According to the old Ptolemaic astronomy, the earth was the center of the sun's orbit, and the sun's motion was contained within its sphere.

The Indifferent[1]

I can love both fair and brown,[2]
Her whom abundance melts, and her whom want betrays,
Her who loves loneness best, and her who masks and plays,
Her whom the country formed, and whom the town,
Her who believes, and her who tries,° *tests*
Her who still° weeps with spongy eyes, *always*
And her who is dry cork, and never cries;
I can love her, and her, and you, and you,
I can love any, so she be not true.

Will no other vice content you?
Will it not serve your turn to do as did your mothers?
Or have you all old vices spent, and now would find out others?
Or doth a fear that men are true torment you?
O we are not, be not you so;
Let me, and do you, twenty know.
Rob me, but bind me not, and let me go.
Must I, who came to travail thorough[3] you,
Grow your fixed subject, because you are true?

Venus heard me sigh this song,
And by love's sweetest part, variety, she swore,
She heard not this till now; and that it should be so no more.
She went, examined, and returned ere long,
And said, Alas, some two or three
Poor heretics in love there be,
Which think to 'stablish dangerous constancy.
But I have told them, Since you will be true,
You shall be true to them who are false to you.

1633

The Canonization[1]

For God's sake hold your tongue, and let me love,
Or chide my palsy, or my gout,
My five gray hairs, or ruined fortune, flout,
With wealth your state, your mind with arts improve,
Take you a course, get you a place,[2]
Observe His Honor, or His Grace,[3]
Or the king's real, or his stampèd face[4]
Contemplate; what you will, approve,° *try, test*
So you will let me love.

1. Some lines of this poem recall Ovid, *Amores* 2.4.
2. Both blonde and brunette.
3. Through. "Travail": grief.

1. The poem plays off against the Roman Catholic process of determining that certain persons are saints, proper objects of veneration and prayer.
2. An appointment, at court or elsewhere. "Take you a course": follow some career.
3. Pay court to some lord or bishop.
4. On coins; "real" (royal) refers also to a particular Spanish coin.

Alas, alas, who's injured by my love?
What merchant's ships have my sighs drowned?
Who says my tears have overflowed his ground?
When did my colds a forward° spring remove?[5] *early*
When did the heats which my veins fill
Add one man to the plaguy bill?[6]
Soldiers find wars, and lawyers find out still
Litigious men, which quarrels move,
Though she and I do love.

Call us what you will, we are made such by love;
Call her one, me another fly,
We're tapers too, and at our own cost die,[7]
And we in us find the eagle and the dove.
The phoenix riddle hath more wit
By us: we two being one, are it.[8]
So, to one neutral thing both sexes fit.
We die and rise the same, and prove
Mysterious by this love.

We can die by it, if not live by love,
And if unfit for tombs and hearse
Our legend be, it will be fit for verse;
And if no piece of chronicle we prove,
We'll build in sonnets pretty rooms;[9]
As well a well-wrought urn becomes° *befits*
The greatest ashes, as half-acre tombs,
And by these hymns,[1] all shall approve° *confirm*
Us canonized for love:

And thus invoke us: You whom reverend love
Made one another's hermitage;
You, to whom love was peace, that now is rage;
Who did the whole world's soul contract,[2] and drove
Into the glasses of your eyes
(So made such mirrors, and such spies,° *spyglasses, telescopes*
That they did all to you epitomize)
Countries, towns, courts:[3] Beg from above
A pattern of your love!

1633

5. Petrarchan lovers traditionally sigh, weep, and are frozen because of their mistresses' neglect.
6. Deaths from the plague, which raged in summer, were recorded by parish in weekly lists.
7. Flies were emblems of transience and lustfulness; tapers (candles) attract flies to their death and also consume themselves. "Die" in the punning terminology of the period means to experience orgasm, and there was a superstition that intercourse shortened life.
8. The eagle signifies strength and vision; the dove, meekness and mercy. The phoenix was a mythic Arabian bird, only one of which existed at any one time. After living five hundred years, it was consumed by fire, then rose triumphantly from its ashes a new bird. Thus it was a symbol of immortality and sometimes associated with Christ. "Eagle" and "dove" are also alchemical terms for processes leading to the rise of "phoenix," a stage in the transmutation of metals to gold.
9. "Rooms" (punning on the Italian meaning of "stanza") will contain their exploits, as prose chronicle histories contain great deeds done in the world.
1. The lover's own poems.
2. An alternative meaning is "extract."
3. "Countries, towns, courts" are objects of the verb "drove." The notion is that eyes both see and reflect the outside world, and so can contain all of it.

Air and Angels

Twice or thrice had I loved thee,
Before I knew thy face or name;
So in a voice, so in a shapeless flame,
Angels affect us oft, and worshipped be;
Still° when, to where thou wert, I came, *always*
Some lovely glorious nothing[1] I did see.
But since my soul, whose child love is,
Takes limbs of flesh, and else could nothing do,[2]
More subtle° than the parent is *rarefied*
Love must not be, but take a body too;
And therefore what thou wert, and who,
I bid love ask, and now
That it assume thy body I allow,
And fix itself in thy lip, eye, and brow.
Whilst thus to ballast love I thought,
And so more steadily to have gone,
With wares which would sink° admiration, *overwhelm*
I saw I had love's pinnace° overfraught;° *small boat / overballasted*
Every thy hair for love to work upon
Is much too much, some fitter must be sought;
For, nor in nothing, nor in things
Extreme and scatt'ring° bright, can love inhere. *diffused, dazzling*
Then as an angel, face and wings
Of air, not pure as it, yet pure doth wear,
So thy love may be my love's sphere;[3]
Just such disparity
As is 'twixt air and angels' purity,
'Twixt women's love and men's will ever be.[4]

1633

Break of Day[1]

'Tis true, 'tis day; what though it be?
O wilt thou therefore rise from me?
Why should we rise because 'tis light?
Did we lie down because 'twas night?
Love, which in spite of darkness brought us hither,
Should in despite of light keep us together.

Light hath no tongue, but is all eye;
If it could speak as well as spy,

1. Spiritual beauty, the true object of love in Neoplatonic philosophy.
2. My soul could not function unless it were in a body.
3. Each sphere was thought to be governed by an angel (an intelligence).
4. It was commonly believed that angels, when they appeared to humans, assumed a body of air which, though pure, was less so than the angel's spiritual essence.

1. An aubade, or song of the lovers' parting at dawn, this poem is unusual for Donne in having a female speaker. The poem was given a musical setting and published in 1622, in William Corkine's *Second Book of Ayers*.

This were the worst that it could say,
That being well, I fain° would stay, *gladly*
And that I loved my heart and honor so
That I would not from him, that had them, go.

Must business thee from hence remove?
O, that's the worst disease of love.
The poor, the foul, the false, love can
Admit, but not the busied man.
He which hath business, and makes love, doth do
Such wrong, as when a married man doth woo.

1622, 1633

A Valediction:[1] Of Weeping

Let me pour forth
My tears before thy face whilst I stay here,
For thy face coins them, and thy stamp° they bear, *image*
And by this mintage they are something worth,
For thus they be
Pregnant of thee;
Fruits of much grief they are, emblems° of more— *symbols*
When a tear falls, that thou falls which it bore,
So thou and I are nothing then, when on a diverse° shore. *different*

On a round ball
A workman that hath copies by can lay
An Europe, Afric, and an Asia,
And quickly make that, which was nothing, all;[2]
So doth each tear
Which thee doth wear,[3]
A globe, yea world, by that impression grow,
Till thy tears mixed with mine do overflow
This world; by waters sent from thee, my heaven dissolvèd so.

O more than moon,
Draw not up seas to drown me in thy sphere;[4]
Weep me not dead in thine arms, but forbear
To teach the sea what it may do too soon.
Let not the wind
Example find
To do me more harm than it purposeth;
Since thou and I sigh one another's breath,
Whoe'er sighs most is cruelest, and hastes the other's death.

1633

1. A farewell poem, one of four so titled in the *Songs and Sonnets*. Another is "A Valediction: Forbidding Mourning," p. 611.
2. I.e., on a blank globe one can place maps of the continents and so convert a cipher ("nothing") into the whole world ("all").
3. Which bears your image.
4. A star or planet with more power of attraction than the moon might not only affect tides but draw the very seas unto itself.

Love's Alchemy

Some that have deeper digged love's mine than I,
Say where his centric° happiness doth lie: *central*
I have loved, and got, and told,
But should I love, get, tell, till I were old,
I should not find that hidden mystery;
O, 'tis imposture all:
And as no chemic° yet the elixir[1] got, *alchemist*
But glorifies his pregnant pot[2]
If by the way to him befall
Some odoriferous thing, or medicinal;
So lovers dream a rich and long delight,
But get a winter-seeming summer's night.[3]

Our ease, our thrift, our honor, and our day,
Shall we for this vain bubble's shadow pay?
Ends love in this, that my man° *servant*
Can be as happy as I can, if he can
Endure the short scorn of a bridegroom's play?
That loving wretch that swears
'Tis not the bodies marry, but the minds,
Which he in her angelic finds,
Would swear as justly that he hears,
In that day's rude hoarse minstrelsy, the spheres.[4]
Hope not for mind in women; at their best
Sweetness and wit, they are but mummy, possessed.[5]

1633

A Valediction: Forbidding Mourning[1]

As virtuous men pass mildly away,
And whisper to their souls to go,
Whilst some of their sad friends do say
The breath goes now, and some say, No;

So let us melt, and make no noise,
No tear-floods, nor sigh-tempests move;
'Twere profanation° of our joys *desecration*
To tell the laity our love.

1. A magic medicine sought by alchemists and reputed to heal all ills.
2. A fertile (and womb-shaped) retort, calling up the common analogy between producing the elixir of life and human generation.
3. A night cold as in winter and short as in summer.
4. The perfect harmony of the planets, moving in concentric crystalline "spheres," is contrasted with the boisterous serenade of pots, pans, and trumpets performed on the wedding night.
5. The syntax of the last two lines is unclear, and they are punctuated differently in various copies. The 1633 edition reads: "at their best, / Sweetnesse, and wit they'are, but, *mummy*, possesst." Many modern editors punctuate as we do here. "Mummy" suggests a corpselike body, without mind or spirit.

1. For "valediction" see p. 610, n. 1. Izaak Walton speculated that this poem was addressed to Donne's wife on the occasion of his trip to the Continent in 1611, but there is no proof of that. Donne was, however, apprehensive about that trip; Walton also heard that, while abroad, Donne had a startling vision of his wife holding a dead baby at about the time she gave birth to a stillborn child.

Moving of th' earth brings harms and fears,
  Men reckon what it did and meant;
But trepidation of the spheres,
  Though greater far, is innocent.[2]

Dull sublunary[3] lovers' love
  (Whose soul is sense) cannot admit
Absence, because it doth remove
  Those things which elemented° it. *composed*

But we, by a love so much refined
  That ourselves know not what it is,
Inter-assurèd of the mind,
  Care less, eyes, lips, and hands to miss.

Our two souls therefore, which are one,
  Though I must go, endure not yet
A breach, but an expansion,
  Like gold to airy thinness beat.

If they be two, they are two so
  As stiff twin compasses[4] are two;
Thy soul, the fixed foot, makes no show
  To move, but doth, if th' other do.

And though it in the center sit,
  Yet when the other far doth roam,
It leans and hearkens after it,
  And grows erect, as that comes home.

Such wilt thou be to me, who must,
  Like th' other foot, obliquely run;
Thy firmness makes my circle just,
  And makes me end where I begun.

1633

The Ecstasy[1]

Where, like a pillow on a bed,
  A pregnant bank swelled up to rest
The violet's reclining head,
  Sat we two, one another's best.

2. Earthquakes cause damage and were thought to be portentous. "Trepidation" (in the Ptolemaic cosmology) is an oscillation of the ninth or crystalline sphere imparted to all the inner spheres. Though a much more violent motion than an earthquake, it is neither destructive nor sinister.
3. Beneath the moon, therefore earthly, sensual, and subject to change.
4. The two legs of a geometer's or draftsman's compass. This simile is the most famous example of the "metaphysical conceit" (see the "Literary Terminology" appendix to this volume).
1. From *ekstasis* (Greek), a movement of the soul outside of the body.

Our hands were firmly cemented
With a fast balm° which thence did spring, *perspiration*
Our eye-beams[2] twisted, and did thread
Our eyes upon one double string;

So to intergraft our hands, as yet
Was all our means to make us one,
And pictures in our eyes[3] to get° *beget*
Was all our propagation.

As 'twixt two equal armies Fate
Suspends uncertain victory,
Our souls (which to advance their state
Were gone out) hung 'twixt her and me;

And whilst our souls negotiate there,
We like sepulchral statues lay;
All day the same our postures were,
And we said nothing all the day.

If any, so by love refined
That he soul's language understood,
And by good love were grown all mind,[4]
Within convenient distance stood,

He (though he knew not which soul spake,
Because both meant, both spake the same)
Might thence a new concoction[5] take,
And part far purer than he came.

This ecstasy doth unperplex,
We said, and tell us what we love;
We see by this it was not sex;
We see we saw not what did move;° *motivate us*

But as all several° souls contain *separate*
Mixture of things, they know not what,
Love these mixed souls doth mix again,
And makes both one, each this and that.

A single violet transplant,
The strength, the color, and the size
(All which before was poor and scant)
Redoubles still,° and multiplies. *continually*

When love with one another so
Interinanimates two souls,
That abler soul, which thence doth flow,
Defects of loneliness controls.

2. Invisible shafts of light, thought of as going out of the eyes and thereby enabling one to see things.
3. Reflections of each in the other's eyes, often called "making babies."
4. On this higher love, see Bembo's ladder of love from Castiglione's *The Courtier*.
5. In the alchemical sense of sublimation or purification.

We then, who are this new soul, know
   Of what we are composed and made,
For th' atomies° of which we grow *components*
   Are souls, whom no change can invade.

But O alas, so long, so far
   Our bodies why do we forbear?
They are ours, though they are not we; we are
   The intelligences, they the sphere.[6]

We owe them thanks because they thus
   Did us to us at first convey,
Yielded their forces, sense, to us,
   Nor are dross to us, but allay.[7]

On man heaven's influence works not so
   But that it first imprints the air:[8]
So soul into the soul may flow,
   Though it to body first repair.° *go*

As our blood labors to beget
   Spirits[9] as like souls as it can,
Because such fingers need° to knit *are needed*
   That subtle knot which makes us man,

So must pure lovers' souls descend
   T' affections, and to faculties
Which sense may reach and apprehend;
   Else a great prince in prison lies.

To our bodies turn we then, that so
   Weak men on love revealed may look;
Love's mysteries[1] in souls do grow,
   But yet the body is his book.

And if some lover, such as we,
   Have heard this dialogue of one,[2]
Let him still mark° us; he shall see *observe*
   Small change when we are to bodies gone.

1633

6. In Ptolemaic astronomy, each planet, set in a transparent "sphere" that revolved and so carried it around the earth, was inhabited by a controlling angelic "intelligence."
7. "Dross" is an impurity that weakens metal; "allay" (alloy) strengthens it.
8. Astrological influences were thought to work on people through the medium of the surrounding air.
9. Subtle substances thought to be produced by the blood to serve as intermediaries between body and soul.
1. The implied comparison is with God's mysteries, which are revealed and may be read in the book of Nature and the book of Scripture.
2. "Dialogue of one" because "both meant, both spake the same" (line 26).

The Funeral

Whoever comes to shroud me, do not harm
Nor question much
That subtle wreath of hair which crowns my arm;
The mystery, the sign you must not touch,
For 'tis my outward soul,
Viceroy to that, which then to heaven being gone,
Will leave this to control,
And keep these limbs, her[1] provinces, from dissolution.

For if the sinewy thread[2] my brain lets fall
Through every part
Can tie those parts and make me one of all,
These hairs which upward grew, and strength and art
Have from a better brain,
Can better do it; except° she meant that I *unless*
By this should know my pain,
As prisoners then are manacled, when they're condemned to die.

Whate'er she meant by it, bury it with me,
For since I am
Love's martyr, it might breed idolatry,
If into others' hands these relics[3] came:
As 'twas humility
To afford to it all that a soul can do,
So 'tis some bravery,
That since you would save[4] none of me, I bury some of you.

1633

The Relic

When my grave is broke up again
Some second guest to entertain
(For graves have learned that woman-head° *female trait*
To be to more than one a bed),[1]
And he that digs it spies
A bracelet of bright hair about the bone,
Will he not let us alone,
And think that there a loving couple lies,
Who thought that this device might be some way
To make their souls, at the last busy day,° *Judgment Day*
Meet at this grave, and make a little stay?

1. The soul's, but also the mistress's (cf. "she," line 14).
2. The nervous system.
3. Body parts or other objects belonging to a saint, venerated by Roman Catholics.
4. All the early printed texts read "have" (which carries sexual connotations), while many manuscripts read "save."

1. Graves were often used to inter successive corpses, the bones of previous occupants being deposited in charnel houses.

If this fall° in a time, or land, *happen*
Where mis-devotion[2] doth command,
Then he that digs us up will bring
Us to the bishop and the king,
To make us relics; then
Thou shalt be a Mary Magdalen, and I
A something else thereby;
All women shall adore us, and some men;
And since at such times, miracles are sought,
I would have that age by this paper taught
What miracles we harmless lovers wrought.

First, we loved well and faithfully,
Yet knew not what we loved, nor why,
Difference of sex no more we knew,
Than our guardian angels do;
Coming and going, we
Perchance might kiss, but not between those meals;[3]
Our hands ne'er touched the seals° *sexual organs*
Which nature, injured by late law, sets free:[4]
These miracles we did: but now, alas,
All measure and all language I should pass,
Should I tell what a miracle she was.

1633

Elegy[1] 16. On His Mistress

By our first strange and fatal interview,
By all desires which thereof did ensue,
By our long starving hopes, by that remorse° *pity*
Which my words' masculine persuasive force
Begot in thee, and by the memory
Of hurts which spies and rivals threatened me,
I calmly beg; but by thy father's wrath,
By all pains which want and divorcement hath,
I conjure thee; and all the oaths which I
And thou have sworn to seal joint constancy
Here I unswear and overswear them thus:
Thou shalt not love by ways so dangerous.
Temper, oh fair love, love's impetuous rage;
Be my true mistress still, not my feigned page.[2]
I'll go, and, by thy kind leave, leave behind

2. False devotion, superstition, i.e., Roman Catholicism.
3. The kisses of salutation and parting.
4. Human law forbids the free love permitted by nature. "Late": recent (comparatively speaking).
1. In Latin poetry, an elegy is a discursive or reflective poem written in "elegiacs" (unrhymed couplets of alternating dactylic hexameters and pentameters). This meter was used for funeral laments and especially for love poetry. The most famous collection of elegies was Ovid's *Amores.* Several of Donne's elegies—almost all written in the 1590s—take Ovid as their principal model and resemble him in ingenious wit and in frank and unapologetic eroticism.
2. The speaker's mistress wanted to accompany him abroad, disguised as a page boy. Such escapades occasionally took place in real life; in 1605, Elizabeth Southwell, disguised as a page, went abroad with Sir Robert Dudley.

Thee, only worthy to nurse in my mind
Thirst to come back. Oh, if thou die before,
My soul from other lands to thee shall soar.
Thy (else almighty) beauty cannot move
Rage from the seas, nor thy love teach them love,
Nor tame wild Boreas' harshness.[3] Thou hast read
How roughly he in pieces shiverèd
Fair Orithea, whom he swore he loved.
Fall ill or good, 'tis madness to have proved° *sought out*
Dangers unurged; feed on this flattery,
That absent lovers one in th' other be.
Dissemble nothing, not a boy, nor change
Thy body's habit,° nor mind's; be not strange *clothing*
To thyself only; all will spy in thy face
A blushing womanly discovering grace.
Richly clothed apes are called apes, and as soon
Eclipsed as bright we call the moon the moon.
Men of France, changeable chameleons,
Spitals° of diseases, shops of fashions, *hospitals*
Love's fuelers[4] and the rightest company
Of players which upon the world's stage be,
Will quickly know thee, and know thee; and alas![5]
Th' indifferent° Italian, as we pass *bisexual*
His warm land, well content to think thee page,
Will hunt thee with such lust and hideous rage
As Lot's fair guests were vexed.[6] But none of these
Nor spongy, hydroptic[7] Dutch shall thee displease
If thou stay here. O stay here, for, for thee,
England is only a worthy gallery
To walk in expectation, till from thence
Our greatest king call thee to his presence.[8]
When I am gone, dream me some happiness,
Nor let thy looks our long-hid love confess;
Nor praise nor dispraise me, bless nor curse
Openly love's force, nor in bed fright thy nurse
With midnight's startings, crying out "Oh, oh!
Nurse, oh my love is slain, I saw him go
O'er the white Alps alone; I saw him, I,
Assailed, fight, taken, stabbed, bleed, fall, and die."
Augur me better chance, except dread Jove
Think it enough for me t' have had thy love.

1635

3. God of the north wind; in *Metamorphoses* 6 Ovid describes the wild force with which Boreas abducted Orithea.
4. Providers of aphrodisiacs.
5. May pun on "a lass." "Know": in the sexual sense.
6. The inhabitants of Sodom tried to rape two angels who visited Lot in the guise of men to warn of the city's impending destruction. (Genesis 19.1–11).
7. Dropsical, thus insatiably thirsty.
8. Throne rooms commonly had antechambers (galleries) where visitors waited until the monarch was ready to see them.

Elegy 19. To His Mistress Going to Bed[1]

Come, Madam, come, all rest my powers defy,
Until I labor, I in labor lie.[2]
The foe ofttimes having the foe in sight,
Is tired with standing though he never fight.
Off with that girdle,° like heaven's zone° glistering, *belt / zodiac*
But a far fairer world encompassing.
Unpin that spangled breastplate[3] which you wear
That th' eyes of busy fools may be stopped there.
Unlace yourself, for that harmonious chime
Tells me from you that now it is bed-time.
Off with that happy busk,° which I envy, *bodice*
That still° can be and still can stand so nigh. *always*
Your gown going off, such beauteous state reveals
As when from flowery meads th' hill's shadow steals.
Off with that wiry coronet and show
The hairy diadem which on you doth grow;
Now off with those shoes, and then safely tread
In this love's hallowed temple, this soft bed.
In such white robes, heaven's angels used to be
Received by men; thou, angel, bring'st with thee
A heaven like Mahomet's paradise;[4] and though
Ill spirits walk in white, we easily know
By this these angels from an evil sprite,
Those set our hairs, but these our flesh upright.
  License my roving hands, and let them go
Before, behind, between, above, below.
O my America! my new-found-land,
My kingdom, safeliest when with one man manned,
My mine of precious stones, my empery,° *empire*
How blest am I in this discovering thee!
To enter in these bonds is to be free;
There where my hand is set, my seal shall be.[5]
  Full nakedness! All joys are due to thee.
As souls unbodied, bodies unclothed must be,
To taste whole joys. Gems which you women use
Are like Atalanta's balls,[6] cast in men's views,
That when a fool's eye lighteth on a gem,
His earthly soul may covet theirs, not them.
Like pictures, or like books' gay coverings, made
For laymen, are all women thus arrayed;
Themselves are mystic books, which only we
(Whom their imputed grace will dignify)
Must see revealed.[7] Then since that I may know,

1. This poem reworks the central situation of Ovid's *Amores* 1.5 in much more dramatic terms.
2. "Labor" in the dual sense of "get to work (sexually)" and "distress."
3. The stomacher, an ornamental, often jeweled, covering for the chest, worn under the lacing of the bodice.
4. A place of sensual pleasure, thought to be populated by seductive houris for the delectation of the faithful.
5. The jokes mingle law with sex: where he has signed a document (placed his hand) he will now place his seal; and in the bonds of her arms he will find freedom.
6. Atalanta, running a race against her suitor Hippomenes, was beaten when he dropped golden apples ("balls") for her to pick up. Donne reverses the story.
7. By granting favors to their lovers, women impute to them grace that they don't deserve, as

As liberally as to a midwife show
Thyself: cast all, yea, this white linen hence,
Here is no penance, much less innocence.[8]
  To teach thee, I am naked first; why then
What need'st thou have more covering than a man?

1669

Satire 3 In satire the author holds a subject up to ridicule. Like his elegies, Donne's five verse satires were written in his twenties and are in the forefront of an effort in the 1590s (by Donne, Ben Jonson, Joseph Hall, and John Marston) to naturalize those classical forms in England. While elements of satire figure in many different kinds of literature, the great models for formal verse satire were the Roman poets Horace and Juvenal, the former for an urbanely witty style, the latter for an indignant or angry manner. While Donne's other satires call on these models, his third satire more nearly resembles those of a third Roman satirist, Persius, known for an abstruse style and moralizing manner. This work is a strenuous discussion of an acute theological problem, for the age and for Donne himself: How may one discover the true Christian church among so many claimants to that role? At the time Donne wrote this, he was in the process of leaving the Roman Catholic Church of his heritage for the Church of England.

Satire 3

Kind pity chokes my spleen;[1] brave° scorn forbids *defiant*
Those tears to issue which swell my eyelids;
I must not laugh, nor weep° sins, and be wise: *lament*
Can railing then cure these worn maladies?
Is not our mistress, fair Religion,
As worthy of all our souls' devotion
As virtue was to the first blinded age?[2]
Are not heaven's joys as valiant to assuage
Lusts, as earth's honor was to them?° Alas, *pagans*
As we do them in means, shall they surpass
Us in the end, and shall thy father's spirit
Meet blind philosophers in heaven, whose merit
Of strict life may be imputed faith,[3] and hear
Thee, whom he taught so easy ways and near
To follow, damned? O, if thou dar'st, fear this;
This fear great courage and high valor is.
Dar'st thou aid mutinous Dutch,[4] and dar'st thou lay
Thee in ships, wooden sepulchers, a prey

God (in Calvinist doctrine) imputes grace to undeserving sinners. Laymen can only look at the covers of mystic books (clothed women), but "we" elect can read them (see women naked).

8. Some manuscripts read: "There is no penance due to innocence." White garments would be appropriate either for the innocent virgin or for the sinner doing formal penance.

1. The seat of bile, hence scorn and ridicule.

2. The age of paganism, blind to Christianity but capable of natural morality ("virtue").

3. Donne's formulation wittily turns on its head the key concept of Protestant theology—that salvation is to be achieved only by imputing Christ's merits to Christians through faith—by suggesting that virtuous pagans might be saved by imputing faith to them on the basis of their moral life.

4. English volunteers took frequent part with the Dutch in their wars against Spain. Donne himself had sailed in two raiding expeditions against the Spanish.

To leaders' rage, to storms, to shot, to dearth?° *famine*
Dar'st thou dive seas and dungeons° of the earth? *mines, caves*
Hast thou courageous fire to thaw the ice
Of frozen north discoveries?[5] And thrice
Colder than salamanders, like divine
Children in the oven,[6] fires of Spain and the line,
Whose countries limbecks to our bodies be,
Canst thou for gain bear?[7] And must every he
Which cries not "Goddess!" to thy mistress, draw,° *fight a duel*
Or eat thy poisonous words? Courage of straw!
O desperate coward, wilt thou seem bold, and
To thy foes and His° (who made thee to stand *God's*
Sentinel in his world's garrison) thus yield,
And for forbidden wars leave th' appointed field?[8]
Know thy foes: The foul Devil (whom thou
Strivest to please) for hate, not love, would allow
Thee fain° his whole realm to be quit;° and as *gladly / to satisfy you*
The world's all parts wither away and pass,[9]
So the world's self, thy other loved foe, is
In her decrepit wane, and thou, loving this,
Dost love a withered and worn strumpet; last,
Flesh (itself's death) and joys which flesh can taste
Thou lovest; and thy fair goodly soul, which doth
Give this flesh power to taste joy, thou dost loathe.
Seek true religion. O, where? Mirreus,[1]
Thinking her unhoused here, and fled from us,
Seeks her at Rome; there, because he doth know
That she was there a thousand years ago.
He loves her rags so, as we here obey
The statecloth[2] where the prince sat yesterday.
Crantz to such brave loves will not be enthralled,
But loves her only, who at Geneva is called
Religion—plain, simple, sullen, young,
Contemptuous, yet unhandsome; as among
Lecherous humors,° there is one that judges *temperaments*
No wenches wholesome but coarse country drudges.
Graius stays still at home here, and because
Some preachers, vile ambitious bawds, and laws
Still new, like fashions, bid him think that she
Which dwells with us is only perfect, he
Embraceth her whom his godfathers will
Tender to him, being tender, as wards still
Take such wives as their guardians offer, or

5. Many explorers tried to find a northwest passage to the Pacific.
6. In the biblical story (Daniel 3), Shadrach, Meshack, and Abednego were rescued from a fiery furnace. The salamander (a lizardlike creature) was thought to be so cold-blooded that it could live in fire.
7. The object of "bear" is "fires of Spain and the line"—inquisitorial and equatorial heats, which roast people as chemists heat materials in "limbecks" (alembics, or vessels for distilling).
8. Of moral struggle.
9. The common belief that the world was growing old and becoming decrepit.
1. The satiric types in this passage represent different creeds: "Mirreus" is a Roman Catholic; "Crantz," an austere Calvinist Presbyterian of Geneva; "Graius" a Church of England Erastian who believes in any religion sponsored by the state; "Phrygius," a skeptic; and "Graccus," a complete relativist.
2. The royal canopy, a symbol of kingly power.

Pay values.[3] Careless Phrygius doth abhor
All, because all cannot be good, as one
Knowing some women whores, dares marry none.
Graccus loves all as one, and thinks that so
As women do in divers countries go
In divers habits,° yet are still one kind, *styles of clothing*
So doth, so is religion; and this blind-
ness too much light breeds;[4] but unmoved thou
Of force° must one, and forced but one allow; *necessity*
And the right; ask thy father which is she,
Let him ask his; though truth and falsehood be
Near twins, yet truth a little elder is;
Be busy to seek her, believe me this,
He's not of none, nor worst, that seeks the best.[5]
To adore, or scorn an image, or protest,
May all be bad; doubt wisely; in strange way
To stand inquiring right, is not to stray;
To sleep, or run wrong, is. On a huge hill,
Cragged and steep, Truth stands, and he that will
Reach her, about must, and about must go,
And what the hill's suddenness resists, win so;
Yet strive so, that before age, death's twilight,
Thy soul rest, for none can work in that night.[6]
To will° implies delay, therefore now do. *intend a future act*
Hard deeds, the body's pains; hard knowledge too
The mind's endeavors reach,° and mysteries *achieve*
Are like the sun, dazzling, yet plain to all eyes.
Keep the truth which thou hast found; men do not stand
In so ill case here, that God hath with his hand
Signed kings' blank charters to kill whom they hate,
Nor are they vicars, but hangmen to fate.[7]
Fool and wretch, wilt thou let thy soul be tied
To man's laws, by which she shall not be tried
At the last day? O, will it then boot° thee *profit*
To say a Philip, or a Gregory,
A Harry, or Martin taught thee this?[8]
Is not this excuse for mere° contraries *complete*
Equally strong? Cannot both sides say so?
That thou mayest rightly obey power, her bounds know;
Those passed, her nature and name is changed; to be
Then humble to her is idolatry.
As streams are, power is; those blest flowers that dwell
At the rough stream's calm head, thrive and prove well,
But having left their roots, and themselves given
To the stream's tyrannous rage, alas, are driven
Through mills, and rocks, and woods, and at last, almost

3. If minors in care of a guardian (in wardship) rejected the wives offered ("tendered") to them they had to pay fines ("values").
4. I.e., Graccus considers the differences between religions merely incidental, like womens' clothes, but his apparently tolerant, "enlightened" attitude is itself a form of blindness.
5. The person who seeks the best church is neither an unbeliever nor the worst sort of believer.
6. Echoes John 9.4, "the night cometh, when no man can work."
7. Kings are not God's vicars on earth, with license ("blank charters") to persecute or kill whomever they wish on grounds of religion.
8. "Philip" is Philip II of Spain, "Gregory" is Pope Gregory XIII or XIV, "Harry" is England's Henry VIII, and "Martin" is Martin Luther.

Consumed in going, in the sea are lost:
So perish souls, which more choose men's unjust
Power from God claimed, than God himself to trust.

1633

From Holy Sonnets[1]

1

Thou hast made me, and shall thy work decay?
Repair me now, for now mine end doth haste;
I run to death, and death meets me as fast,
And all my pleasures are like yesterday.
I dare not move my dim eyes any way,
Despair behind, and death before doth cast
Such terror, and my feeble flesh doth waste
By sin in it, which it towards hell doth weigh.° *incline, weigh down*
Only thou art above, and when towards thee
By thy leave I can look, I rise again;
But our old subtle foe so tempteth me
That not one hour myself I can sustain.
Thy grace may wing° me to prevent° his art, *give wings to / forestall*
And thou like adamant° draw mine iron heart. *magnetic lodestone*

1635

5

I am a little world[2] made cunningly
Of elements, and an angelic sprite;° *spirit, soul*
But black sin hath betrayed to endless night
My world's both parts, and O, both parts must die.
You which beyond that heaven which was most high
Have found new spheres, and of new lands can write,[3]
Pour new seas in mine eyes, that so I might
Drown my world with my weeping earnestly,
Or wash it if it must be drowned no more.[4]
But O, it must be burnt! Alas, the fire
Of lust and envy have burnt it heretofore,
And made it fouler; let their flames retire,
And burn me, O Lord, with a fiery zeal
Of thee and thy house, which doth in eating heal.[5]

1635

1. Donne wrote a variety of religious poems (called "Divine Poems"), including a group of nineteen "Holy sonnets" that reflect his interest in Jesuit and especially Protestant meditative procedures. He probably began writing them about 1609, a decade or so after leaving the Catholic Church. Our selections follow the traditional numbering established in Sir Herbert Grierson's influential edition, since for most of these sonnets we cannot tell when they were written or in what order they were intended to appear.

2. The traditional idea of the human being as microcosm (a "little world"), containing in miniature all the features of the macrocosm, or great world.

3. Astronomers, especially Galileo, and explorers.

4. God promised Noah (Genesis 9.11) never to flood the earth again.

5. See Psalm 69.9: "For the zeal of thine house hath eaten me up." These lines refer to three kinds of flame—those of the Last Judgment, those of lust and envy, and those of zeal, which alone save.

7

At the round earth's imagined corners,[6] blow
Your trumpets, angels; and arise, arise
From death, you numberless infinities
Of souls, and to your scattered bodies go:
All whom the flood did, and fire[7] shall, o'erthrow,
All whom war, dearth,° age, agues,° tyrannies, *famine / fevers*
Despair, law, chance hath slain, and you whose eyes
Shall behold God, and never taste death's woe.[8]
But let them sleep, Lord, and me mourn a space;
For, if above all these, my sins abound,
'Tis late to ask abundance of thy grace
When we are there. Here on this lowly ground,
Teach me how to repent; for that's as good
As if thou hadst sealed my pardon with thy blood.

1633

9

If poisonous minerals, and if that tree[9]
Whose fruit threw death on else-immortal us,
If lecherous goats, if serpents envious[1]
Cannot be damned, alas! why should I be?
Why should intent or reason, born in me,
Make sins, else equal, in me more heinous?
And, mercy being easy and glorious
To God, in his stern wrath why threatens he?
But who am I that dare dispute with thee
O God? Oh, of thine only worthy blood
And my tears, make a heavenly Lethean[2] flood,
And drown in it my sin's black memory.
That thou remember them some claim as debt;
I think it mercy if thou wilt forget.[3]

1633

10

Death, be not proud, though some have callèd thee
Mighty and dreadful, for thou art not so;
For those whom thou think'st thou dost overthrow
Die not, poor Death, nor yet canst thou kill me.
From rest and sleep, which but thy pictures be,
Much pleasure; then from thee much more must flow,

6. Cf. Revelation 7.1: "I saw four angels standing on the four corners of the earth."
7. Noah's flood, and the universal conflagration at the end of the world (Revelation 6.11).
8. Those who will be alive at the Second Coming (cf. Luke 9.27).
9. The Tree of Knowledge of Good and Evil, whose fruit was forbidden to Adam and Eve in Eden.
1. Traits commonly associated with these creatures.
2. In classical mythology, the waters of the river Lethe in the underworld caused total forgetfulness.
3. Cf. Jeremiah 31.34: "I will forgive their iniquity, and I will remember their sins no more."

And soonest our best men with thee do go,
Rest of their bones, and soul's delivery.[4]
Thou art slave to fate, chance, kings, and desperate men,
And dost with poison, war, and sickness dwell,
And poppy° or charms can make us sleep as well *opium*
And better than thy stroke; why swell'st° thou then? *puff with pride*
One short sleep past, we wake eternally
And death shall be no more; Death, thou shalt die.[5]

1633

13

What if this present were the world's last night?
Mark in my heart, O soul, where thou dost dwell,
The picture of Christ crucified, and tell
Whether that countenance can thee affright.
Tears in his eyes quench the amazing light,
Blood fills his frowns, which from his pierced head fell;
And can that tongue adjudge thee unto hell
Which prayed forgiveness for his foes' fierce spite?
No, no; but as in my idolatry
I said to all my profane° mistresses, *secular*
Beauty of pity, foulness only is
A sign of rigor:[6] so I say to thee,
To wicked spirits are horrid shapes assigned,
This beauteous form assures a piteous mind.

1633

14

Batter my heart, three-personed God; for you
As yet but knock, breathe, shine, and seek to mend;
That I may rise and stand, o'erthrow me, and bend
Your force to break, blow, burn, and make me new.
I, like an usurped town, to another due,
Labor to admit you, but O, to no end;
Reason, your viceroy[7] in me, me should defend,
But is captived, and proves weak or untrue.
Yet dearly I love you, and would be loved fain,° *gladly*
But am betrothed[8] unto your enemy.
Divorce me, untie or break that knot again;
Take me to you, imprison me, for I,
Except° you enthrall me, never shall be free, *unless*
Nor ever chaste, except you ravish[9] me.

1633

4. I.e., to find rest for their bones and freedom ("delivery") for their souls.
5. Cf. 1 Corinthians 15.26: "The last enemy that shall be destroyed is death."
6. In Neoplatonic theory, beautiful features are the sign of a compassionate mind, while ugliness signifies the contrary.
7. The governor in your stead.
8. Humanity's relationship with God has been described in terms of marriage and adultery from the time of the Hebrew prophets.
9. Rape, also overwhelm with wonder. "Enthrall": enslave, also enchant.

18

Show me, dear Christ, thy spouse[1] so bright and clear.
What! is it she which on the other shore
Goes richly painted? or which, robbed and tore,
Laments and mourns in Germany and here?[2]
Sleeps she a thousand, then peeps up one year?
Is she self-truth, and errs? now new, now outwore?
Doth she, and did she, and shall she evermore
On one, on seven, or on no hill appear?[3]
Dwells she with us, or like adventuring knights
First travel we to seek, and then make love?
Betray, kind husband, thy spouse to our sights,
And let mine amorous soul court thy mild dove,
Who is most true and pleasing to thee then
When she is embraced and open to most men.[4]

1899

19

Oh, to vex me, contraries meet in one:
Inconstancy unnaturally hath begot
A constant habit; that when I would not
I change in vows, and in devotion.
As humorous° is my contrition *subject to whim*
As my profane love, and as soon forgot:
As riddlingly distempered, cold and hot,[5]
As praying, as mute, as infinite, as none.
I durst not view heaven yesterday; and today
In prayers, and flattering speeches I court God:
Tomorrow I quake with true fear of his rod.
So my devout fits come and go away
Like a fantastic ague:[6] save° that here *except*
Those are my best days, when I shake with fear.

1899

Good Friday, 1613. Riding Westward

Let man's soul be a sphere, and then, in this,
The intelligence that moves, devotion is,[1]

1. The church is commonly called the bride of Christ. Cf. Revelation 19.7–8: "The marriage of the Lamb is come, and his wife hath made herself ready. / And to her was granted that she should be arrayed in fine linen, clean and white."
2. I.e., the painted woman (the Church of Rome) or the ravished virgin (the Lutheran and Calvinist churches in Germany and England).
3. The church on one hill is probably Solomon's temple on Mount Moriah; that on seven hills is the Church of Rome; that on no hill is the Presbyterian church of Geneva.
4. The final lines wittily rework, with startling sexual associations, Song of Solomon 5.2: "Open to me, my sister, my love, my dove, my undefiled." That biblical book was often interpreted as the song of love between Christ and the church.
5. Arising from the unbalanced humors, inexplicably changeable.
6. A fever, attended with paroxysms of hot and cold and trembling fits. "Fantastic": capricious, extravagant.
1. As angelic intelligences guide the celestial spheres, so devotion is or should be the guiding principle of the soul.

And as the other spheres, by being grown
Subject to foreign motions, lose their own,
And being by others hurried every day,
Scarce in a year their natural form[2] obey;
Pleasure or business, so, our souls admit
For° their first mover, and are whirled by it. *instead of*
Hence is 't, that I am carried towards the West
This day, when my soul's form bends toward the East.
There I should see a Sun[3] by rising, set,
And by that setting endless day beget:
But that Christ on this cross did rise and fall,
Sin had eternally benighted all.
Yet dare I almost be glad I do not see
That spectacle, of too much weight for me.
Who sees God's face, that is self-life, must die;[4]
What a death were it then to see God die?
It made his own lieutenant,° Nature, shrink; *deputy*
It made his footstool crack, and the sun wink.[5]
Could I behold those hands which span the poles,
And tune[6] all spheres at once, pierced with those holes?
Could I behold that endless height which is
Zenith to us, and t'our antipodes,[7]
Humbled below us? Or that blood which is
The seat° of all our souls, if not of his, *dwelling place*
Make dirt of dust, or that flesh which was worn
By God for his apparel, ragg'd and torn?
If on these things I durst not look, durst I
Upon his miserable mother cast mine eye,
Who was God's partner here, and furnished thus
Half of that sacrifice which ransomed us?
Though these things, as I ride, be from° mine eye, *away from*
They are present yet unto my memory,
For that looks towards them; and thou look'st towards me,
O Savior, as thou hang'st upon the tree.
I turn my back to thee but to receive
Corrections,[8] till thy mercies bid thee leave.° *cease*
O think me worth thine anger; punish me;
Burn off my rusts and my deformity;
Restore thine image so much, by thy grace,
That thou may'st know me, and I'll turn my face.

1633

2. Their true moving principle or intelligence. The orbit of the celestial spheres was thought to be governed by an unmoving outermost sphere, the primum mobile, or first mover (line 8), but sometimes outside influences ("foreign motions," line 4) deflected the spheres from their correct orbits.
3. The "sun" / "Son" pun was an ancient one. Christ the Son of God "set" when he rose on the Cross, and that setting (death) gave rise to the Christian era and the promise of immortality.
4. God told Moses, "Thou canst not see my face, for there shall no man see me, and live" (Exodus 33.20).
5. An earthquake and eclipse supposedly accompanied the Crucifixion (Matthew 27.45, 51). Cf. Isaiah 66.1: "Thus saith the Lord, The heaven is my throne, and the earth is my footstool."
6. Some manuscripts read "turn."
7. God is at once the highest point for us and for our "antipodes," those who live on the opposite side of the earth.
8. Suggests a flogging.

Hymn to God My God, in My Sickness[1]

Since I am coming to that holy room
  Where, with thy choir of saints for evermore,
I shall be made thy music; as I come
  I tune the instrument here at the door,
  And what I must do then, think now before.[2]

Whilst my physicians by their love are grown
  Cosmographers, and I their map, who lie
Flat on this bed, that by them may be shown
  That this is my southwest discovery[3]
  Per fretum febris,[4] by these straits to die,

I joy, that in these straits, I see my West;
  For, though their currents yield return to none,
What shall my West hurt me? As West and East
  In all flat maps (and I am one) are one,[5]
  So death doth touch the resurrection.

Is the Pacific Sea my home? Or are
  The Eastern riches?° Is Jerusalem? *Cathay, China*
Anyan,[6] and Magellan, and Gibraltar,
  All straits, and none but straits, are ways to them,
  Whether where Japhet dwelt, or Cham, or Shem.[7]

We think that Paradise and Calvary,
  Christ's cross and Adam's tree, stood in one place;
Look, Lord and find both Adams[8] met in me;
  As the first Adam's sweat surrounds my face,
  May the last Adam's blood my soul embrace.

So, in his purple wrapped,[9] receive me, Lord;
  By these his thorns° give me his other crown; *crown of thorns*
And, as to others' souls I preached thy word,
  Be this my text, my sermon to mine own:
  Therefore that he may raise the Lord throws down.

1635

1. Though Izaak Walton, Donne's friend and biographer, assigns this poem to the last days of his life, it was probably written during another illness, in December 1623.
2. This is less a hymn (song of praise) than a meditation preparing (tuning the instrument) for such a hymn.
3. South is the region of heat, west the region of sunset and death.
4. Through the straits of fever, with a pun on straits as sufferings, rigors, and a geographical reference to the Strait of Magellan.
5. If a flat map is pasted on a round globe, west and east meet.
6. Anian, a strait on the west coast of America, shown on early maps as separating America from Asia.
7. The three sons of Noah by whom the world was repopulated after the Flood (Genesis 10). The descendants of Japhet were thought to inhabit Europe; those of Cham (Ham), Africa; and those of Shem, Asia.
8. Adam and Christ. Legend had it that Christ's cross was erected on the spot, or at least in the region, where the tree forbidden to Adam in Eden had stood.
9. In his blood, also in his kingly robes.

A Hymn to God the Father[1]

Wilt thou forgive that sin where I begun,
Which is my sin, though it were done before?[2]
Wilt thou forgive that sin through which I run,
And do run still, though still I do deplore?
When thou hast done,[3] thou hast not done,
For I have more.

Wilt thou forgive that sin by which I have won
Others to sin? and made my sin their door?
Wilt thou forgive that sin which I did shun
A year or two, but wallowed in a score?
When thou hast done, thou hast not done,
For I have more.

I have a sin of fear, that when I have spun
My last thread, I shall perish on the shore;
Swear by thy self, that at my death thy Son
Shall shine as he shines now and heretofore;
And, having done that, thou hast done,
I fear[4] no more.

1633

From Devotions upon Emergent Occasions[1]

Meditation 17

Nunc lento sonitu dicunt, morieris.
Now this bell tolling softly for another, says to me, Thou must die.[2]

Perchance he for whom this bell[3] tolls may be so ill as that he knows not it tolls for him; and perchance I may think myself so much better than I am, as that they who are about me and see my state may have caused it to toll for me, and I know not that. The church is catholic, universal, so are all her actions; all that she does belongs to all. When she baptizes a child, that action concerns me; for that child is thereby connected to that head which is my head too, and ingrafted into that body[4] whereof I am a member. And when

1. This hymn was used as a congregational hymn. Walton tells us that Donne wrote it during his illness of 1623, had it set to music, and was delighted to hear it performed (as it frequently was) by the choir of St. Paul's Cathedral.
2. I.e., he inherits the original sin of Adam and Eve.
3. In the refrains, Donne puns on his own name and may pun on his wife's maiden name, Ann More.
4. Some manuscripts read "have."

1. Donne's *Devotions* were composed in the aftermath of his serious illness in the winter of 1623, though Donne characteristically writes as if the events of the illness were happening as he describes them. The *Devotions* recount in twenty-three sections the stages ("emergent occasions") of the illness and recovery: the term associates the exercise with a popular kind of Protestant meditation on the occasions that daily life presents to us. Each section contains a "meditation upon our human condition," an "expostulation and debatement with God," and a prayer to God. The book was published almost immediately, offering its meditation on an intensely personal experience as exemplary for others.
2. Donne's Latin epigraphs are followed by his English translations, often quite free.
3. The "passing bell" for the dying.
4. The church.

she buries a man, that action concerns me: all mankind is of one author and is one volume; when one man dies, one chapter is not torn out of the book, but translated[5] into a better language; and every chapter must be so translated. God employs several translators; some pieces are translated by age, some by sickness, some by war, some by justice; but God's hand is in every translation, and his hand shall bind up all our scattered leaves again for that library where every book shall lie open to one another. As therefore the bell that rings to a sermon calls not upon the preacher only, but upon the congregation to come, so this bell calls us all; but how much more me, who am brought so near the door by this sickness. There was a contention as far as a suit[6] (in which piety and dignity, religion and estimation,[7] were mingled) which of the religious orders should ring to prayers first in the morning; and it was determined that they should ring first that rose earliest. If we understand aright the dignity of this bell that tolls for our evening prayer, we would be glad to make it ours by rising early, in that application, that it might be ours as well as his whose indeed it is. The bell doth toll for him that thinks it doth; and though it intermit again, yet from that minute that that occasion wrought upon him, he is united to God. Who casts not up his eye to the sun when it rises? But who takes off his eye from a comet when that breaks out? Who bends not his ear to any bell which upon any occasion rings? But who can remove it from that bell which is passing a piece of himself out of this world? No man is an island, entire of itself; every man is a piece of the continent, a part of the main.[8] If a clod be washed away by the sea, Europe is the less, as well as if a promontory were, as well as if a manor of thy friend's or of thine own were. Any man's death diminishes me, because I am involved in mankind; and therefore never send to know for whom the bell tolls; it tolls for thee.[9] Neither can we call this a begging of misery or a borrowing of misery, as though we were not miserable enough of ourselves but must fetch in more from the next house, in taking upon us the misery of our neighbors. Truly it were an excusable covetousness if we did; for affliction is a treasure, and scarce any man hath enough of it. No man hath affliction enough that is not matured and ripened by it, and made fit for God by that affliction. If a man carry treasure in bullion, or in a wedge of gold, and have none coined into current moneys, his treasure will not defray[1] him as he travels. Tribulation is treasure in the nature of it, but it is not current money in the use of it, except we get nearer and nearer our home, heaven, by it. Another man may be sick too, and sick to death, and this affliction may lie in his bowels as gold in a mine and be of no use to him; but this bell that tells me of his affliction digs out and applies that gold to me, if by this consideration of another's danger I take mine own into contemplation and so secure myself by making my recourse to my God, who is our only security.

5. Punning on the literal sense, "carried across."
6. Controversy that went as far as a lawsuit.
7. Self-esteem.
8. Mainland.
9. This phrase gave Hemingway the title for his novel *For Whom the Bell Tolls*.
1. Meet his expenses.

AEMILIA LANYER
1569–1645

Aemilia Lanyer was the first Englishwoman to publish a substantial volume of original poems and the first to make an overt bid for patronage. She was the daughter to an Italian family of court musicians who came to England in the reign of Henry VIII; they may have been Christianized Jews or, alternatively, Protestants forced to flee Catholic persecution in their native land. Some information about Lanyer's life has come down to us from the notebooks of the astrologer and fortune-teller Simon Forman, whom Lanyer consulted in 1597. Educated in the aristocratic household of the Countess of Kent, in her late teens and early twenties Lanyer was the mistress of Queen Elizabeth's lord chamberlain, Henry Carey, Lord Hunsdon. The wealthy Hunsdon, forty-five years her senior, was a notable patron of the arts—Shakespeare's company performed under his auspices in the 1590s—and he maintained his mistress in luxury. Yet when she became pregnant by Hunsdon at age twenty-three, she was married off to Alfonso Lanyer, one of another family of gentleman musicians attached to the courts of Elizabeth I and James I. Lanyer's fortunes declined after her marriage. Lanyer's poetry suggests that she resided for some time in the bookish and cultivated household of Margaret Clifford, Countess of Cumberland, and Margaret's young daughter Anne. Lanyer reports receiving there encouragement in learning, piety, and poetry, as well as, perhaps, some support in the unusual venture of offering her poems for publication. Yet her efforts to find some niche at the Jacobean court came to nothing.

Lanyer's single volume of poems, *Salve Deus Rex Judaeorum* (1611) has a decided feminist thrust. A series of dedicatory poems to former and would-be patronesses praises them as a community of contemporary good women. The title poem, a meditation on Christ's Passion that at times invites comparison with Donne and Crashaw, contrasts the good women in the Passion story with the weak, evil men portrayed there. It also incorporates a defense of Eve and all women. That defense and Lanyer's prose epistle, "To the Virtuous Reader," are spirited contributions to the so-called *querelle des femmes*, or "debate about women," a massive body of writings in several genres and languages: some examples include Chaucer's Wife of Bath's Prologue and Tale and Shakespeare's *Taming of the Shrew*. The final poem in Lanyer's volume, "The Description of Cookham," celebrates in elegiac mode the Crown estate occasionally occupied by the Countess of Cumberland, portraying it as an Edenic paradise of women, now lost. The poem may or may not have been written before Ben Jonson's "To Penshurst"—commonly thought to have inaugurated the "country-house" genre in English literature—but Lanyer's poem can claim priority in publication. The poems' different conceptions of the role of women in the ideal social order make an instructive comparison.

From Salve Deus Rex Judaeorum[1]

To the Doubtful Reader[2]

Gentle Reader, if thou desire to be resolved, why I give this title, *Salve Deus Rex Judaeorum*, know for certain, that it was delivered unto me in sleep many

1. "Hail God, King of the Jews," a variant of the inscription affixed to Christ's cross.
2. Lanyer placed this explanation at the end of her volume, not the beginning, as a further authorizing gesture. Invoking the familiar genre of the dream vision, she lays claim to poetic, even divine, inspiration. "Doubtful": doubting.

years before I had any intent to write in this manner, and was quite out of my memory, until I had written the Passion of Christ, when immediately it came into my remembrance, what I had dreamed long before. And thinking it a significant token[3] that I was appointed to perform this work, I gave the very same words I received in sleep as the fittest title I could devise for this book.

Eve's Apology in Defense of Women[4]

Now Pontius Pilate is to judge the cause° *case*
Of faultless Jesus, who before him stands,
Who neither hath offended prince, nor laws,
Although he now be brought in woeful bands.
O noble governor, make thou yet a pause,
Do not in innocent blood inbrue° thy hands; *stain*
But hear the words of thy most worthy wife,
Who sends to thee, to beg her Savior's life.[5]

Let barb'rous cruelty far depart from thee,
And in true justice take affliction's part;
Open thine eyes, that thou the truth may'st see.
Do not the thing that goes against thy heart,
Condemn not him that must thy Savior be;
But view his holy life, his good desert.
Let not us women glory in men's fall,[6]
Who had power given to overrule us all.

Till now your indiscretion sets us free.
And makes our former fault much less appear;
Our mother Eve, who tasted of the tree,
Giving to Adam what she held most dear,
Was simply good, and had no power to see;[7]
The after-coming harm did not appear:
The subtle serpent that our sex betrayed
Before our fall so sure a plot had laid.

That undiscerning ignorance perceived
No guile or craft that was by him intended;
For had she known of what we were bereaved,[8]
To his request she had not condescended.° *consented*
But she, poor soul, by cunning was deceived;

3. Sign.
4. Lanyer supplies the title for this subsection of the *Salve Deus* on her title page. Eve is not, however, the speaker; rather, the narrator presents Eve's "Apology" (defense of her actions), which is also a defense of all women. She does so by means of an apostrophe (impassioned address) to Pilate, the Roman official who authorized the crucifixion of Jesus. Lanyer makes Pilate and Adam representatives of the male gender, whereas Eve and Pilate's wife represent womankind.
5. Pilate's wife wrote her husband a letter urging Pilate to spare Jesus, about whom she had a warning dream (Matthew 27.19).
6. The fall of Adam, and the prospective fall of Pilate.
7. In Eden, Eve ate the forbidden fruit first, at the serpent's bidding. Genesis commentary usually emphasized Eve's full knowledge that God had forbidden them on pain of death and banishment from Eden to eat the fruit of the Tree of Knowledge of Good and Evil. Her action was usually ascribed to intemperance, pride, and ambition.
8. Deprived, specifically of eternal life. In Genesis 3, Eve was enticed by the serpent to eat the forbidden fruit; she in turn enticed her husband. God expelled them from Eden, condemning Adam to hard labor, Eve to pain in childbirth and subjection to her husband, and both to suffering and death.

No hurt therein her harmless heart intended:
  For she alleged° God's word, which he° denies, *asserted / serpent*
  That they should die, but even as gods be wise.

But surely Adam cannot be excused;
Her fault though great, yet he was most to blame;
What weakness offered, strength might have refused,
Being lord of all, the greater was his shame.
Although the serpent's craft had her abused,
God's holy word ought all his actions frame,° *determine*
  For he was lord and king of all the earth,
  Before poor Eve had either life or breath,

Who being framed° by God's eternal hand *fashioned*
The perfectest man that ever breathed on earth;
And from God's mouth received that strait° command, *strict*
The breach whereof he knew was present death;
Yea, having power to rule both sea and land,
Yet with one apple won to lose that breath[9]
  Which God had breathed in his beauteous face,
  Bringing us all in danger and disgrace.

And then to lay the fault on Patience' back,
That we (poor women) must endure it all.
We know right well he did discretion lack,
Being not persuaded thereunto at all.
If Eve did err, it was for knowledge sake;
The fruit being fair persuaded him to fall:
  No subtle serpent's falsehood did betray him;
  If he would eat it, who had power to stay° him? *prevent*

Not Eve, whose fault was only too much love,
Which made her give this present to her dear,
That what she tasted he likewise might prove,° *experience*
Whereby his knowledge might become more clear;
He never sought her weakness to reprove
With those sharp words which he of God did hear;
  Yet men will boast of knowledge, which he took
  From Eve's fair hand, as from a learned book.

If any evil did in her remain,
Being made of him,[1] he was the ground of all.
If one of many worlds[2] could lay a stain
Upon our sex, and work so great a fall
To wretched man by Satan's subtle train,[3]
What will so foul a fault amongst you all?
  Her weakness did the serpent's words obey,
  But you in malice God's dear Son betray,

9. The breath of life, which would have been eternal.
1. Genesis 2.21–22 reports God's creation of Eve from Adam's rib.
2. May allude to the commonplace that man is a little world, applying it here to woman.
3. Tradition identifies Satan with the serpent, although that identification is not made in Genesis.

Whom, if unjustly you condemn to die,
Her sin was small to what you do commit;
All mortal sins[4] that do for vengeance cry
Are not to be compared unto it.
If many worlds would altogether try
By all their sins the wrath of God to get,
  This sin of yours surmounts them all as far
  As doth the sun another little star.[5]

Then let us have our liberty again,
And challenge° to yourselves no sovereignty. *claim*
You came not in the world without our pain,
Make that a bar against your cruelty;
Your fault being greater, why should you disdain
Our being your equals, free from tyranny?
  If one weak woman simply did offend,
  This sin of yours hath no excuse nor end,

To which, poor souls, we never gave consent.
Witness, thy wife, O Pilate, speaks for all,
Who did but dream, and yet a message sent
That thou shouldest have nothing to do at all
With that just man° which, if thy heart relent, *Christ*
Why wilt thou be a reprobate° with Saul[6] *damned*
  To seek the death of him that is so good,
  For thy soul's health to shed his dearest blood?

1611

The Description of Cookham[1]

Farewell, sweet Cookham, where I first obtained
Grace[2] from that grace where perfect grace remained;
And where the muses gave their full consent,
I should have power the virtuous to content;
Where princely palace willed me to indite,° *write*
The sacred story of the soul's delight.[3]
Farewell, sweet place, where virtue then did rest,
And all delights did harbor in her breast;
Never shall my sad eyes again behold

4. Sins punishable by damnation.
5. In the Ptolemaic system, the sun was larger than the other planets and the fixed stars.
6. King of Israel who sought the death of God's annointed prophet-king, David. The parallel is with Pilate, who sought Christ's death.
1. The poem was written in honor of Margaret Clifford, Countess of Cumberland, and celebrates a royal estate leased to her brother, at which the countess occasionally resided. The poem should be compared with Jonson's "To Penshurst" (p. 644). Lanyer's poem is based on a familiar classical topic, the "farewell to a place," which had its most famous development in Virgil's *Eclogue* 1. Lanyer makes extensive use of the common pastoral motif of nature's active sympathy with and response to human emotion—which later came to be called the "pathetic fallacy."
2. Here, both God's grace and the favor of Her Grace, the Countess of Cumberland. Lanyer attributes both her religious conversion and her vocation as poet to a period of residence at Cookham in the countess's household. We do not know how long or under what circumstances Lanyer resided there.
3. Apparently a reference to the countess as her patron, commissioning her Passion poem.

Those pleasures which my thoughts did then unfold.
Yet you, great lady, mistress of that place,
From whose desires did spring this work of grace;
Vouchsafe° to think upon those pleasures past, *be willing*
As fleeting worldly joys that could not last,
Or, as dim shadows of celestial pleasures,
Which are desired above all earthly treasures.
Oh how, methought, against° you thither came, *in preparation for*
Each part did seem some new delight to frame!
The house received all ornaments to grace it,
And would endure no foulness to deface it.
And walks put on their summer liveries,[4]
And all things else did hold like similes:[5]
The trees with leaves, with fruits, with flowers clad,
Embraced each other, seeming to be glad,
Turning themselves to beauteous canopies,
To shade the bright sun from your brighter eyes;
The crystal streams with silver spangles graced,
While by the glorious sun they were embraced;
The little birds in chirping notes did sing,
To entertain both you and that sweet spring.
And Philomela[6] with her sundry lays,
Both you and that delightful place did praise.
Oh how me thought each plant, each flower, each tree
Set forth their beauties then to welcome thee!
The very hills right humbly did descend,
When you to tread on them did intend.
And as you set your feet, they still did rise,
Glad that they could receive so rich a prize.
The gentle winds did take delight to be
Among those woods that were so graced by thee,
And in sad murmur uttered pleasing sound,
That pleasure in that place might more abound.
The swelling banks delivered all their pride
When such a phoenix[7] once they had espied.
Each arbor, bank, each seat, each stately tree,
Thought themselves honored in supporting thee.
The pretty birds would oft come to attend thee,
Yet fly away for fear they should offend thee;
The little creatures in the burrow by
Would come abroad to sport them in your eye,
Yet fearful of the bow in your fair hand,
Would run away when you did make a stand.
Now let me come unto that stately tree,
Wherein such goodly prospects you did see;
That oak that did in height his fellows pass,

4. Distinctive garments worn by persons in the service of great families, to indicate whose servants they were.
5. Behaved in similar fashion.
6. In myth, Philomela was raped by her brother-in-law Tereus, who also tore out her tongue; the gods transformed her into a nightingale. Here the bird's song is joyous but later mournful (line 189), associating her own woes with those of Cookham at the women's departure.
7. Mythical bird that lived alone of its kind for five hundred years, then was consumed in flame and reborn from its own ashes; metaphorically, a person of rare excellence. "All their pride": fish (cf. To Penshurst, lines 31–36).

As much as lofty trees, low growing grass,
Much like a comely cedar straight and tall,
Whose beauteous stature far exceeded all.
How often did you visit this fair tree,
Which seeming joyful in receiving thee,
Would like a palm tree spread his arms abroad,
Desirous that you there should make abode;
Whose fair green leaves much like a comely veil,
Defended Phoebus° when he would assail; *resisted the sun*
Whose pleasing boughs did yield a cool fresh air,
Joying° his happiness when you were there. *enjoying*
Where being seated, you might plainly see
Hills, vales, and woods, as if on bended knee
They had appeared, your honor to salute,
Or to prefer some strange unlooked-for suit;[8]
All interlaced with brooks and crystal springs,
A prospect fit to please the eyes of kings.
And thirteen shires appeared all in your sight,
Europe could not afford much more delight.
What was there then but gave you all content,
While you the time in meditation spent
Of their Creator's power, which there you saw,
In all his creatures held a perfect law;
And in their beauties did you plain descry° *perceive*
His beauty, wisdom, grace, love, majesty.
In these sweet woods how often did you walk,
With Christ and his apostles there to talk;
Placing his holy writ in some fair tree
To meditate what you therein did see.
With Moses you did mount his holy hill
To know his pleasure, and perform his will.[9]
With lowly David you did often sing
His holy hymns to heaven's eternal King.[1]
And in sweet music did your soul delight
To sound his praises, morning, noon, and night.
With blessed Joseph you did often feed
Your pined brethren, when they stood in need.[2]
And that sweet lady sprung from Clifford's race,
Of noble Bedford's blood, fair stem of grace,[3]
To honorable Dorset now espoused,[4]
In whose fair breast true virtue then was housed,
Oh what delight did my weak spirits find
In those pure parts° of her well framéd mind. *qualities*
And yet it grieves me that I cannot be
Near unto her, whose virtues did agree

8. To urge some unexpected petition, as to a monarch.
9. You sought out and followed God's law, like Moses, who received the Ten Commandments on Mount Sinai.
1. You often sang David's psalms.
2. Like Joseph, who fed the starving Israelites in Egypt, you fed the hungry.
3. Main line of the family tree. Anne Clifford, only surviving child of the seaman-adventurer George Clifford, third Earl of Cumberland, and the countess, a Russell (of "Bedford's blood"). She was tutored by Samuel Daniel and her *Diary* offers interesting insights into this period.
4. Anne Clifford was married to Richard Sackville, third Earl of Dorset, on February 25, 1609; the reference helps date Lanyer's poem.

With those fair ornaments of outward beauty,
Which did enforce from all both love and duty.
Unconstant Fortune, thou art most to blame,
Who casts us down into so low a frame
Where our great friends we cannot daily see,
So great a difference is there in degree.[5]
Many are placèd in those orbs of state,
Parters[6] in honor, so ordained by Fate,
Nearer in show, yet farther off in love,
In which, the lowest always are above.[7]
But whither am I carried in conceit,° *thought, fancy*
My wit too weak to conster° of the great. *construe*
Why not? Although we are but born of earth,
We may behold the heavens, despising death;
And loving heaven that is so far above,
May in the end vouchsafe us entire love.[8]
Therefore sweet memory do thou retain
Those pleasures past, which will not turn again:
Remember beauteous Dorset's[9] former sports,
So far from being touched by ill reports,
Wherein myself did always bear a part,
While reverend love presented my true heart.
Those recreations let me bear in mind,
Which her sweet youth and noble thoughts did find,
Whereof deprived, I evermore must grieve,
Hating blind Fortune, careless to relieve.
And you sweet Cookham, whom these ladies leave,
I now must tell the grief you did conceive
At their departure, when they went away,
How everything retained a sad dismay.
Nay long before, when once an inkling came,
Methought each thing did unto sorrow frame:
The trees that were so glorious in our view,
Forsook both flowers and fruit, when once they knew
Of your depart, their very leaves did wither,
Changing their colors as they grew together.
But when they saw this had no power to stay you,
They often wept, though, speechless, could not pray you,
Letting their tears in your fair bosoms fall,
As if they said, Why will ye leave us all?
This being vain, they cast their leaves away
Hoping that pity would have made you stay:
Their frozen tops, like age's hoary hairs,
Shows their disasters, languishing in fears.
A swarthy riveled rind° all over spread, *bark*
Their dying bodies half alive, half dead.

5. These lines and lines 117–25 probably exaggerate Lanyer's former familiarity with Anne Clifford.
6. Separators, i.e., the various honorific ranks ("orbs of state") act to separate person from person.
7. An egalitarian sentiment playing on the Christian notion that in spiritual things—love and charity—the poor and lowly surpass the great ones.
8. I.e., we (lowly) may also love God and enjoy God's love, and hence are equal to anyone.
9. As was common, Anne Clifford is here referred to by her husband's title.

But your occasions called you so away[1]
That nothing there had power to make you stay.
Yet did I see a noble grateful mind
Requiting each according to their kind,
Forgetting not to turn and take your leave
Of these sad creatures, powerless to receive
Your favor, when with grief you did depart,
Placing their former pleasures in your heart,
Giving great charge to noble memory
There to preserve their love continually.
But specially the love of that fair tree,
That first and last you did vouchsafe to see,
In which it pleased you oft to take the air
With noble Dorset, then a virgin fair,
Where many a learned book was read and scanned,
To this fair tree, taking me by the hand,
You did repeat the pleasures which had passed,
Seeming to grieve they could no longer last.
And with a chaste, yet loving kiss took leave,
Of which sweet kiss I did it soon bereave,° *soon take from it*
Scorning a senseless creature should possess
So rare a favor, so great happiness.
No other kiss it could receive from me,
For fear to give back what it took of thee,
So I ungrateful creature did deceive it
Of that which you in love vouchsafed to leave it.
And though it oft had given me much content,
Yet this great wrong I never could repent;
But of the happiest made it most forlorn,
To show that nothing's free from Fortune's scorn,
While all the rest with this most beauteous tree
Made their sad comfort sorrow's harmony.
The flowers that on the banks and walks did grow,
Crept in the ground, the grass did weep for woe.
The winds and waters seemed to chide together
Because you went away they knew not whither;
And those sweet brooks that ran so fair and clear,
With grief and trouble wrinkled did appear.
Those pretty birds that wonted° were to sing, *accustomed*
Now neither sing, nor chirp, nor use their wing,
But with their tender feet on some bare spray,
Warble forth sorrow, and their own dismay.
Fair Philomela leaves her mournful ditty,
Drowned in deep sleep, yet can procure no pity.
Each arbor, bank, each seat, each stately tree
Looks bare and desolate now for want of thee,
Turning green tresses into frosty gray,
While in cold grief they wither all away.
The sun grew weak, his beams no comfort gave,
While all green things did make the earth their grave.

1. After her husband's death (1605) Margaret Clifford chiefly resided in her dower properties in the north; Anne Clifford was married in 1609.

Each briar, each bramble, when you went away
Caught fast your clothes, thinking to make you stay;
Delightful Echo wonted to reply
To our last words, did now for sorrow die;
The house cast off each garment that might grace it,
Putting on dust and cobwebs to deface it.
All desolation then there did appear,
When you were going whom they held so dear.
This last farewell to Cookham here I give,
When I am dead thy name in this may live,
Wherein I have performed her noble hest° *commission*
Whose virtues lodge in my unworthy breast,
And ever shall, so long as life remains,
Tying my life to her by those rich chains.° *her virtues*

1611

BEN JONSON
1572–1637

In 1616 Ben Jonson published his *Works*, to the derision of those astounded to see mere plays and poems collected under the same title the king gave to his political treatises. Many of Jonson's contemporaries shied away from publication, either because, like Donne, they wrote for small coterie audiences or because, like Shakespeare, they wrote for theater companies that preferred not to let go of the scripts. Jonson knew and admired both Donne and Shakespeare and more than any Jacobean belonged to both of their very different worlds, but in publishing his *Works* he laid claim to an altogether higher literary status. He had risen from very humble beginnings to become England's unofficial poet laureate, with a pension from the king and honorary degrees from both Oxford and Cambridge. If he was not the first professional author in England, he was the first to invest that role with dignity and respectability. His published *Works*, over which he labored with painstaking care, testify to an extraordinary feat of self-transformation.

Jonson's early life was tough and turbulent. The posthumous son of a London clergyman, he was educated at Westminster School under the great antiquarian scholar William Camden. There he developed his love of classical learning, but lacking the resources to continue his education, Jonson was forced to turn to his stepfather's trade of bricklaying, a life he "could not endure." He escaped by joining the English forces in Flanders, where, as he later boasted, he killed a man in single combat before the eyes of two armies. Back in London, his attempt to make a living as an actor and playwright almost ended in early disaster. He was imprisoned in 1597 for collaborating with Thomas Nashe on the scandalous play *The Isle of Dogs* (now lost), and shortly after his release he killed one of his fellow actors in a duel. Jonson escaped the gallows by pleading benefit of clergy (a medieval privilege exempting felons who could read Latin from the death penalty). His learning had saved his life, but he emerged from captivity branded on the thumb, and with another mark against him as well. Under the influence of a priest imprisoned with him, he had converted to Catholicism (around the time that John Donne was abandoning that faith). Jonson was now more than ever a marginal figure, distrusted by the society that he satirized brilliantly in his early plays.

Jonson's fortunes improved with the accession of James I, though not at once. In 1603 he was called before the Privy Council to answer charges of "popery and treason" found in his play *Sejanus*. Little more than a year later he was in jail again for his part in the play *Eastward Ho*, which openly mocked the king's Scots accent and propensity for selling knighthoods. Yet Jonson was now on the way to establishing himself at the new court. In 1605 he received the commission to organize the Twelfth Night entertainment; *The Masque of Blackness* was the first of twenty-four masques he would produce for the court, most of them in collaboration with the architect and scene designer Inigo Jones. In the same years that he was writing the masques he produced his greatest works for the public theater. His first successful play, *Every Man in His Humor* (1598), had inaugurated the so-called comedy of humors, which ridicules the eccentricities or passions of the characters (thought to be caused by physiological imbalance). He capitalized on this success with the comedies *Volpone* (1606), *Epicene* (1609), *The Alchemist* (1610), and *Bartholomew Fair* (1614). Jonson preserved the detached, satiric perspective of an outsider, but he was rising in society and making accommodations where necessary. In 1605, when suspicion fell upon him as a Catholic following the exposure of the Gunpowder Plot, he showed his loyalty by agreeing to serve as a spy for the Privy Council. Five years later he would return to the Church of England.

Although he rose to a position of eminent respectability, Jonson seems to have been possessed all his life by a quarrelsome spirit. Much of his best work emerged out of fierce tensions with collaborators and contemporaries. At the turn of the century he became embroiled in the so-called War of the Theaters, in which he satirized and was satirized by his fellow playwrights John Marston and Thomas Dekker. Later, his long partnership with Inigo Jones was marked by ever more bitter rivalry over the relative importance of words and scenery in the masques. Jonson also poured invective on the theater audiences when they failed, in his view, to appreciate his plays. The failure of his play *The New Inn* elicited his "Ode to Himself" (1629), a disgusted farewell to the "loathed stage." Yet even after a stroke in 1629 left him partially paralyzed and confined to his home, Jonson continued to write for the stage, and was at work on a new play when he died in 1637.

In spite of his antagonistic nature, Jonson had a great capacity for friendship. His friends included Shakespeare, Donne, Francis Bacon, and John Selden. In later years he gathered about himself a group of admiring younger men known as the "Sons of Ben," whose numbers included Robert Herrick, Thomas Carew, and Sir John Suckling. He was a fascinating and inexhaustible conversationalist, as recorded by his friend William Drummond of Hawthornden, who carefully noted down Jonson's remarks on a wide variety of subjects, ranging from his fellow poets to his sexual predilections. Jonson also moved easily among the great of the land. His patrons included Lady Mary Wroth and other members of the Sidney and Herbert families. In "To Penshurst," a celebration of Robert Sidney's country estate, Jonson offers an ideal image of a social order in which a virtuous patriarchal governor offers ready hospitality to guests of all stations, from poets to kings.

"To Penshurst," together with Aemilia Lanyer's "Description of Cookham," inaugurated the small genre of the "country-house poem" in England. Jonson tried his hand, usually with success, at a wide range of poetic genres, including epitaph and epigram, love and funeral elegy, verse satire and verse letter, song and ode. More often than not he looked back to classical precedents. From the Roman poets Horace and Martial he derived not only generic models but an ideal vision of the artist and society against which he measured himself and the court he served. In many poems he adopted the persona of a witty, keenly perceptive, and scrupulously honest judge of men and women. The classical values Jonson most admired are enumerated in "Inviting a Friend to Supper," which describes a dinner party characterized by moderation, civility, graciousness, and pleasure that delights without enslaving—all contrasting sharply with the excess and licentiousness that marked the banquets and entertainments of imperial Rome and Stuart England. Yet the poet who produced this image of moderation was a man of immense appetites, which found expression in his art as well as in his life. His best works seethe with an almost uncontrollable imaginative energy and lust for abundance. Even his profound classical learning manifests this impulse. The notes and references to learned authorities that spill across the margins of his *Works* can be seen as the literary equivalent of food and drink piled high on the poet's table. Years of hardship had taught Jonson to seek his feasts in his imagination, and he could make the most mundane object the basis for flights of high fancy. As he told Drummond, he once "consumed a whole night in lying looking to his great toe, about which he had seen Tartars and Turks, Romans and Carthaginians fight in his imagination." In Drummond's view, Jonson was "oppressed with fantasy." Perhaps it was so—but Jonson's capacity for fantasy also produced a wide variety of plays, masques, and poems, in styles ranging from witty comedy to delicate lyricism.

From Epigrams[1]

To My Book

It will be looked for, book, when some but see
Thy title, *Epigrams,* and named of me,
Thou should'st be bold, licentious, full of gall,
Wormwood° and sulphur, sharp and toothed[2] withal, *bitter-tasting plant*
Become a petulant thing, hurl ink and wit
As madmen stones, not caring whom they hit.
Deceive their malice who could wish it so,
And by thy wiser temper let men know
Thou art not covetous of least self-fame
Made from the hazard of another's shame[3]—
Much less with lewd, profane, and beastly phrase
To catch the world's loose laughter or vain gaze.
He that departs° with his own honesty *parts*
For vulgar praise, doth it too dearly buy.

1616

On My First Daughter[1]

Here lies, to each her parents' ruth,° *grief*
Mary, the daughter of their youth;
Yet all heaven's gifts being heaven's due,
It makes the father less to rue.° *regret*

1. Epigrams are commonly thought of as brief, witty, incisive poems of personal invective, often with a surprise turn at the end. But Jonson uses the word in a more liberal sense. His "Epigrams," a separate section in his collected *Works* of 1616, include not only sharp, satiric poems but many complimentary ones to friends and patrons, as well as memorial epitaphs and a verse letter, "Inviting a Friend to Supper."

2. The distinction between toothed (biting) and toothless (general) satires was a commonplace.

3. Here, as often elsewhere, Jonson echoes the greatest Roman epigrammatist, Martial.

1. Probably written in the late 1590s, in Jonson's Roman Catholic period (ca. 1598–1610).

At six months' end she parted hence
With safety of her innocence;
Whose soul heaven's queen,° whose name she bears, *Mary*
In comfort of her mother's tears,
Hath placed amongst her virgin-train:
Where, while that severed doth remain,
This grave partakes the fleshly birth;° *the body*
Which cover lightly, gentle earth![2]

1616

To John Donne

Donne, the delight of Phoebus° and each Muse, *god of poetry*
Who, to thy one, all other brains refuse;[1]
Whose every work, of thy most early wit,
Came forth example[2] and remains so yet;
Longer a-knowing than most wits do live,
And which no affection praise enough can give.
To it[3] thy language, letters, arts, best life,
Which might with half mankind maintain a strife.
All which I meant to praise, and yet I would,
But leave, because I cannot as I should.

1616

On My First Son

Farewell, thou child of my right hand,[1] and joy;
My sin was too much hope of thee, loved boy:
Seven years thou wert lent to me, and I thee pay,
Exacted by thy fate, on the just day.
O could I lose all father now! For why
Will man lament the state he should envy,
To have so soon 'scaped world's and flesh's rage,
And, if no other misery, yet age?
Rest in soft peace, and asked, say, "Here doth lie
Ben Jonson his best piece of poetry."[2]
For whose sake henceforth all his vows be such
As what he loves may never like too much.[3]

1616

2. A common sentiment in Latin epitaphs.
1. I.e., the muses shower their favors exclusively on you.
2. A pattern for others to imitate.
3. In addition to your wit.
1. A literal translation of the Hebrew name "Benjamin," which implies the meaning "dexterous" or "fortunate." The boy was born in 1596 and died on his birthday in 1603.
2. Poet and father are both "makers," Jonson's favorite term for the poet.
3. The obscure grammar of the last lines allows for various readings; "like" may carry the sense of "please."

On Lucy, Countess of Bedford[1]

This morning, timely rapt with holy fire,
I thought to form unto my zealous muse,
What kind of creature I could most desire,
To honor, serve, and love; as poets use.[2]
I meant to make her fair, and free, and wise,
Of greatest blood, and yet more good than great;
I meant the day-star° should not brighter rise, *the sun*
Nor lend like influence[3] from his lucent seat.
I meant she should be courteous, facile,° sweet, *affable*
Hating that solemn vice of greatness, pride;
I meant each softest virtue, there should meet,
Fit in that softer bosom to reside.
Only a learnèd, and a manly soul
I purposed her; that should, with even powers,
The rock, the spindle, and the shears[4] control
Of destiny, and spin her own free hours.
Such when I meant to feign, and wished to see,
My muse bad, *Bedford* write, and that was she.

1616

Inviting a Friend to Supper

Tonight, grave sir, both my poor house and I
Do equally desire your company:
Not that we think us worthy such a guest,
But that your worth will dignify our feast
With those that come; whose grace may make that seem
Something, which else could hope for no esteem.
It is the fair acceptance, sir, creates
The entertainment perfect: not the cates.° *food*
Yet shall you have, to rectify your palate,
An olive, capers, or some better salad
Ushering the mutton; with a short-legged hen,
If we can get her, full of eggs, and then
Lemons and wine for sauce; to° these, a coney° *besides / rabbit*
Is not to be despaired of for our money;
And though fowl now be scarce, yet there are clerks,° *scholars*
The sky not falling, think we may have larks.
I'll tell you of more, and lie, so you will come:
Of partridge, pheasant, woodcock, of which some
May yet be there; and godwit if we can,

1. The Countess of Bedford was a famous patroness of the age, to whom Jonson, Donne, and many other poets addressed poems of compliment.
2. This elegant epigram of praise plays off against the Pygmalion story, in which the sculptor molds a statue of his ideal woman and she then comes to life.
3. Stars were supposed to emit an ethereal fluid, or "influence," that affected the affairs of mortals, for good or ill.
4. Emblems of the three Fates: Clotho spun the thread of life, Lachesis decided its length, and Atropos cut the thread to end life.

Knot, rail, and ruff, too.[1] Howsoe'er, my man° *servant*
Shall read a piece of Virgil, Tacitus,
 Livy, or of some better book to us,
Of which we'll speak our minds amidst our meat;° *food (of any kind)*
 And I'll profess° no verses to repeat: *promise*
To this,° if aught appear which I not know of, *on this point*
 That will the pastry, not my paper, show of.[2]
Digestive cheese and fruit there sure will be;
 But that which most doth take my muse and me
Is a pure cup of rich canary wine,
 Which is the Mermaid's now, but shall be mine;
Of which, had Horace or Anacreon[3] tasted,
 Their lives, as do their lines, till now had lasted.
Tobacco, nectar, or the Thespian spring
 Are all but Luther's beer to this I sing.[4]
Of this we will sup free but moderately,
 And we will have no Pooly or Parrot[5] by;
Nor shall our cups make any guilty men,
 But at our parting we will be as when
We innocently met. No simple word
 That shall be uttered at our mirthful board
Shall make us sad next morning, or affright
 The liberty that we'll enjoy tonight.

1616

Epitaph on S. P., a Child of Queen Elizabeth's Chapel[1]

Weep with me, all you that read
 This little story;
And know for whom a tear you shed,
 Death's self is sorry.
'Twas a child that so did thrive
 In grace and feature,
As Heaven and Nature seemed to strive
 Which owned the creature.
Years he numbered scarce thirteen
 When Fates turned cruel,
Yet three filled zodiacs had he been
 The stage's jewel;[2]
And did act (what now we moan)

1. All these are edible birds.
2. Paper-lined pans were used to keep pies from sticking; the writing sometimes rubbed off on the piecrust.
3. Horace and Anacreon (one in Latin, the other in Greek) wrote many poems in praise of wine. The Mermaid tavern was a favorite haunt of the poets; sweet wine from the Canary Islands was popular in England.
4. Tobacco was an expensive New World novelty in Jonson's time. Nectar is the drink of the gods. The Thespian spring, on Mount Helicon, is a legendary source of poetic inspiration. Compared with canary, these intoxicants are no better than inferior German beer.
5. Pooly and Parrot were government spies. As a Roman Catholic, Jonson had reason to be wary of undercover agents.

1. Salomon Pavy, a boy actor in the troupe known as the Children of Queen Elizabeth's Chapel, who had appeared in several of Jonson's plays; he died in 1602.
2. He had been on the stage for three seasons.

Old men so duly,° *aptly*
As, sooth,° the Parcae° thought him one, *in truth / Fates*
He played so truly.
So, by error, to his fate
They all consented;
But, viewing him since (alas, too late),
They have repented,
And have sought (to give new birth)
In baths[3] to steep him;
But, being so much too good for earth,
Heaven vows to keep him.

1616

FROM THE FOREST[1]

To Penshurst[2]

Thou art not, Penshurst, built to envious show,
Of touch[3] or marble; nor canst boast a row
Of polished pillars, or a roof of gold;
Thou hast no lantern° whereof tales are told, *cupola*
Or stair, or courts; but stand'st an ancient pile,° *edifice*
And, these grudged at,[4] art reverenced the while.
Thou joy'st in better marks, of soil, of air,
Of wood, of water; therein thou art fair.
Thou hast thy walks for health, as well as sport;
Thy mount, to which the dryads° do resort, *wood nymphs*
Where Pan and Bacchus their high feasts have made,
Beneath the broad beech and the chestnut shade;
That taller tree, which of a nut was set
At his great birth where all the Muses met.[5]
There in the writhèd bark are cut the names
Of many a sylvan,° taken with his flames; *countryman*
And thence the ruddy satyrs oft provoke
The lighter fauns[6] to reach thy Lady's Oak.[7]
Thy copse° too, named of Gamage[8] thou hast there, *little woods*
That never fails to serve thee seasoned deer
When thou wouldst feast or exercise thy friends.

3. Perhaps such magic baths as that of Medea, which restored Jason's father to his first youth (Ovid, *Metamorphoses* 7).

1. In the 1616 *Works*, Jonson grouped some of his nonepigrammatic poems under the heading "The Forest," a translation of the term *Sylvae*, meaning a poetic miscellany. "To Penshurst" and the two following poems are from that group.

2. Penshurst, in Kent, was the estate of Robert Sidney, Viscount Lisle (later, Earl of Leicester), a younger brother of the poet Sir Philip Sidney. Along with Lanyer's "Description of Cookham" (p. 633), this poem inaugurated the small genre of English "country-house" poems, which includes Marvell's *Upon Appleton House*.

3. Touchstone, an expensive black basalt.

4. More pretentious houses attract envy.

5. Sir Philip Sidney was born at Penshurst.

6. Satyrs and fauns were woodland spirits. Satyrs had the bodies of men and the legs (and horns) of goats. "Provoke": challenge to a race.

7. Named after a lady of the house who went into labor under its branches.

8. Lady Barbara (Gamage) Sidney, wife of Sir Robert.

The lower land, that to the river bends,
Thy sheep, thy bullocks, kine,° and calves do feed; *cattle*
The middle grounds thy mares and horses breed.
Each bank doth yield thee conies;° and the tops,° *rabbits / high ground*
Fertile of wood, Ashore and Sidney's copse,
To crown thy open table, doth provide
The purpled pheasant with the speckled side;
The painted partridge lies in every field,
And for thy mess° is willing to be killed. *table*
And if the high-swollen Medway[9] fail thy dish,
Thou hast thy ponds, that pay thee tribute fish:
Fat agèd carps that run into thy net,
And pikes, now weary their own kind to eat,
As loath the second draft or cast to stay,
Officiously° at first themselves betray; *dutifully*
Bright eels that emulate them, and leap on land
Before the fisher, or into his hand.
Then hath thy orchard fruit, thy garden flowers,
Fresh as the air, and new as are the hours.
The early cherry, with the later plum,
Fig, grape, and quince, each in his time doth come;
The blushing apricot and woolly peach
Hang on thy walls, that every child may reach.
And though thy walls be of the country stone,
They're reared with no man's ruin, no man's groan;
There's none that dwell about them wish them down;
But all come in, the farmer and the clown,° *peasant*
And no one empty-handed, to salute
Thy lord and lady, though they have no suit.° *request to make*
Some bring a capon, some a rural cake,
Some nuts, some apples; some that think they make
The better cheeses bring them, or else send
By their ripe daughters, whom they would commend
This way to husbands, and whose baskets bear
An emblem of themselves in plum or pear.
But what can this (more than express their love)
Add to thy free provisions, far above
The need of such? whose liberal board doth flow
With all that hospitality doth know;
Where comes no guest but is allowed to eat,
Without his fear, and of thy lord's own meat;° *food*
Where the same beer and bread, and selfsame wine,
That is his lordship's shall be also mine,[1]
And I not fain to sit (as some this day
At great men's tables), and yet dine away.
Here no man tells° my cups; nor, standing by, *counts*
A waiter doth my gluttony envy,° *resent*
But gives me what I call, and lets me eat;
He knows below° he shall find plenty of meat. *in the servants' quarters*
Thy tables hoard not up for the next day;
Nor, when I take my lodging, need I pray

9. The local river.
1. Different courses might be served to different guests, depending on their social status. The lord would have the best food.

For fire, or lights, or livery;° all is there, *provisions*
As if thou then wert mine, or I reigned here:
There's nothing I can wish, for which I stay.° *wait*
That found King James when, hunting late this way
With his brave son, the Prince,[2] they saw thy fires
Shine bright on every hearth, as the desires
Of thy Penates° had been set on flame *Roman household gods*
To entertain them; or the country came
With all their zeal to warm their welcome here.
What (great I will not say, but) sudden cheer
Didst thou then make 'em! And what praise was heaped
On thy good lady then, who therein reaped
The just reward of her high housewifery;
To have her linen, plate, and all things nigh,
When she was far; and not a room but dressed
As if it had expected such a guest!
These, Penshurst, are thy praise, and yet not all.
Thy lady's noble, fruitful, chaste withal.
His children thy great lord may call his own,
A fortune in this age but rarely known.
They are, and have been, taught religion; thence
Their gentler spirits have sucked innocence.
Each morn and even they are taught to pray,
With the whole household, and may, every day,
Read in their virtuous parents' noble parts° *attributes*
The mysteries of manners,° arms, and arts. *moral behavior*
Now, Penshurst, they that will proportion° thee *compare*
With other edifices, when they see
Those proud, ambitious heaps, and nothing else,
May say, their lords have built, but thy lord dwells.

1616

FROM UNDERWOOD[1]

My Picture Left in Scotland[2]

I now think Love is rather deaf than blind,
For else it could not be
That she
Whom I adore so much should so slight me
And cast my love behind;
I'm sure my language to her was as sweet,
And every close° did meet *cadence*

2. Prince Henry, the heir apparent, who died in November 1612.

1. Preparing a second edition of his *Works* (published posthumously in 1640–41), Jonson added a third section of poems, "Underwood," "out of the analogy they hold to *The Forest* in my former book."

2. After his walking tour of Scotland in 1618–19, Jonson sent a manuscript version of this poem to William Drummond, with whom he had stayed. The woman of the poem may or may not be a real person.

In sentence° of as subtle feet,° *wise sayings / rhythm*
As hath the youngest he
That sits in shadow of Apollo's tree.[3]

O, but my conscious fears
That fly my thoughts between,
Tell me that she hath seen
My hundreds of gray hairs,
Told° seven and forty years, *counted*
Read so much waist[4] as she cannot embrace
My mountain belly and my rocky face;
And all these through her eyes have stopped her ears.

1619 1640–41

Queen and Huntress[1]

Queen and huntress, chaste and fair,
Now the sun is laid to sleep,
Seated in thy silver chair,
State in wonted° manner keep; *accustomed*
Hesperus entreats thy light,
Goddess excellently bright.

Earth, let not thy envious shade
Dare itself to interpose;[2]
Cynthia's shining orb was made
Heaven to clear, when day did close.
Bless us then with wishèd sight,
Goddess excellently bright.

Lay thy bow of pearl apart,
And thy crystal-shining quiver;
Give unto the flying hart
Space to breathe, how short soever.
Thou that mak'st a day of night,
Goddess excellently bright.

1600

Though I Am Young[1]

Though I am young and cannot tell
Either what Death or Love is well,
Yet I have heard they both bear darts,
And both do aim at human hearts.

3. Bay laurel, the tree associated with Apollo, god of poetry.
4. With a pun on "waste," meaning "untillable ground."
1. From the play *Cynthia's Revels* (4.3), this song is sung by Hesperus, the evening star, to Cynthia, or Diana, goddess of chastity and the moon—with whom Queen Elizabeth was constantly compared.
2. Eclipses were thought to portend evil.
1. This song is sung in *The Sad Shepherd*, by Karolin; the pastoral simplicity of his character is caught in the naive monosyllables of the poem.

And then again, I have been told
Love wounds with heat, as Death with cold;
So that I fear they do but bring
Extremes to touch, and mean one thing.

As in a ruin we it call
One thing to be blown up or fall;
Or to our end like way may have
By a flash of lightning or a wave;
So Love's inflamèd shaft or brand
May kill as soon as Death's cold hand;
Except[2] Love's fires the virtue have
To fright the frost out of the grave.

1640–41

Still to Be Neat[1]

Still° to be neat, still to be dressed *always*
As° you were going to a feast, *as though*
Still to be powdered, still perfumed;
Lady, it is to be presumed,
Though art's hid causes are not found,
All is not sweet, all is not sound.

Give me a look, give me a face
That makes simplicity a grace;
Robes loosely flowing, hair as free—
Such sweet neglect more taketh me
Than all the adulteries° of art. *adulterations*
They strike mine eyes, but not my heart.

1609

To the Memory of My Beloved, The Author, Mr. William Shakespeare, and What He Hath Left Us[1]

To draw no envy, Shakespeare, on thy name,
Am I thus ample° to thy book and fame, *copious*
While I confess thy writings to be such
As neither man nor muse can praise too much.
'Tis true, and all men's suffrage.° But these ways *admission*
Were not the paths I meant unto thy praise;
For silliest° ignorance on these may light, *simplest*
Which, when it sounds at best, but echoes right;
Or blind affection, which doth ne'er advance
The truth, but gropes, and urgeth all by chance;

2. Unless.

1. Sung in the play *Epicene*, this song concerns the art of makeup, but also art more generally. Compare Herrick's "Delight in Disorder" (p. 667).

1. This poem was prefixed to the first folio of Shakespeare's plays (1623).

Or crafty malice might pretend this praise,
And think to ruin where it seemed to raise.
These are as° some infamous bawd or whore — *as though*
Should praise a matron. What could hurt her more?
But thou art proof against them, and, indeed,
Above th' ill fortune of them, or the need.
I therefore will begin. Soul of the age!
The applause! Delight! The wonder of our stage!
My Shakespeare, rise; I will not lodge thee by
Chaucer or Spenser, or bid Beaumont lie
A little further to make thee a room:[2]
Thou art a monument without a tomb,
And art alive still while thy book doth live,
And we have wits to read and praise to give.
That I not mix thee so, my brain excuses,
I mean with great, but disproportioned° Muses; — *not comparable*
For, if I thought my judgment were of years,
I should commit thee surely with thy peers,
And tell how far thou didst our Lyly outshine,
Or sporting Kyd, or Marlowe's mighty line.[3]
And though thou hadst small Latin and less Greek,[4]
From thence to honor thee I would not seek° — *lack*
For names, but call forth thund'ring Aeschylus,
Euripides, and Sophocles to us,
Pacuvius, Accius, him of Cordova dead,[5]
To life again, to hear thy buskin° tread — *symbol of tragedy*
And shake a stage; or, when thy socks° were on, — *symbol of comedy*
Leave thee alone for the comparison
Of all that insolent Greece or haughty Rome
Sent forth, or since did from their ashes come.
Triumph, my Britain; thou hast one to show
To whom all scenes° of Europe homage owe. — *stages*
He was not of an age, but for all time!
And all the Muses still were in their prime
When like Apollo° he came forth to warm — *god of poetry*
Our ears, or like a Mercury° to charm. — *god of eloquence*
Nature herself was proud of his designs,
And joyed to wear the dressing of his lines,
Which were so richly spun, and woven so fit,
As, since, she will vouchsafe° no other wit: — *grant*
The merry Greek, tart Aristophanes,
Neat Terence, witty Plautus[6] now not please,
But antiquated and deserted lie,
As they were not of Nature's family.
Yet must I not give nature all; thy art,
My gentle Shakespeare, must enjoy a part.

2. Chaucer, Spenser, and Francis Beaumont were buried in Westminster Abbey; Shakespeare, in Stratford.

3. John Lyly, Thomas Kyd, and Christopher Marlowe were Elizabethan dramatists contemporary or nearly contemporary with Shakespeare.

4. Shakespeare's Latin was pretty good, but Jonson is judging by the standard of his own remarkable scholarship.

5. Marcus Pacuvius, Lucius Accius (2nd century B.C.E.), and "him of Cordova," Seneca the Younger (Ist century C.E.), were Latin tragedians. Seneca's tragedies had a large influence on Elizabethan revenge tragedy.

6. Aristophanes, an ancient Greek satirist and writer of comedy; Terence and Plautus (2nd and 3rd centuries B.C.E.), Roman writers of comedy.

For though the poet's matter° nature be, *subject matter*
His art doth give the fashion;° and that he *form, style*
Who casts° to write a living line must sweat *undertakes*
(Such as thine are) and strike the second heat
Upon the Muses' anvil; turn the same,
And himself with it, that he thinks to frame,
Or for° the laurel he may gain a scorn; *instead of*
For a good poet's made as well as born,
And such wert thou. Look how the father's face
Lives in his issue;° even so the race *offspring*
Of Shakespeare's mind and manners brightly shines
In his well-turnèd and true-filèd lines,
In each of which he seems to shake a lance,[7]
As brandished at the eyes of ignorance.
Sweet swan of Avon, what a sight it were
To see thee in our waters yet appear,
And make those flights upon the banks of Thames
That so did take Eliza and our James![8]
But stay; I see thee in the hemisphere
Advanced and made a constellation there![9]
Shine forth, thou star of poets, and with rage
Or influence[1] chide or cheer the drooping stage,
Which, since thy flight from hence, hath mourned like night,
And despairs day, but for thy volume's light.

1623

7. Pun on Shake-speare.
8. Queen Elizabeth and King James.
9. Heroes and demigods were typically exalted after death to a place among the stars.
1. "Rage" and "influence" describe the supposed effects of the planets on earthly affairs. "Rage" also implies poetic inspiration.

MARY WROTH
1587–1651?

Lady Mary Wroth was the most prolific, self-conscious, and impressive female author of the Jacobean era. Her published work (1621) include two firsts for an Englishwoman: a 558-page romance, *The Countess of Montgomery's Urania*, which includes more than fifty poems, and appended to it a Petrarchan lyric sequence that had circulated some years in manuscript, 103 sonnets and elegant songs titled *Pamphilia to Amphilanthus*. Wroth left unpublished a very long but unfinished continuation of the *Urania* and a pastoral drama, *Love's Victory*, also a first for an Englishwoman. Her achievement was fostered by her strong sense of identity as a Sidney, heir to the literary talent and cultural role of her famous uncle Sir Philip Sidney, her famous aunt Mary Sidney Herbert, Countess of Pembroke, who may have served as mentor to her; and her father Robert Sidney, Viscount Lisle, author of a recently discovered sonnet sequence. But she used that heritage transgressively to replace heroes with heroines in genres employed by the male Sidney authors—notably Philip Sidney's *Astrophil and Stella* and *The Countess of Pembroke's Arcadia*—transforming their gender politics and exploring the poetics and situation of women writers.

As Robert Sidney's eldest daughter, she lived and was educated at Penshurst, the Sidney country house celebrated by Ben Jonson, and was often at her aunt's "little college" at Wilton. She danced at court in *The Masque of Blackness* and perhaps in other masques; she was married (incompatibly) at age seventeen to Sir Robert Wroth of Durrance and Loughton Manor, whose office it was to facilitate the king's hunting; and she was patron to several poets, including Jonson. He celebrated her in two epigrams and in a verse letter honoring her husband, dedicated his great comedy *The Alchemist* to her, and claimed in his only sonnet that the artistry and erotic power of her sonnets had made him "a better lover, and much better poet." After her husband's death she carried on a long-standing love affair with her married first cousin, William Herbert, Earl of Pembroke, himself a poet, a powerful courtier, and a patron of the theater and of literature. That relationship produced two children and occasioned some scandal.

The significant names in the title of Wroth's Petrarchan sequence, *Pamphilia* ("all-loving") *to Amphilanthus* ("lover of two"), are from characters in her romance who at times shadow Wroth and her lover Pembroke. The Petrarchan lyric sequence had long served as the major genre for analyzing a male lover's passions, frustrations, and fantasies (and sometimes his career anxieties). So although the sonnet sequence was becoming passé by Wroth's time, it was an obvious choice for a woman poet undertaking the construction of subjectivity in a female lover-speaker. Wroth does not, however, simply reverse roles. Pamphilia addresses very few sonnets to Amphilanthus and seldom assumes the Petrarchan lover's position of abject servitude to a cruel beloved. Instead, she proclaims subjection to Cupid, usually identified with the force of her own desire. This radical revision identifies female desire as the source and center of the love relationship and celebrates the woman lover-poet's movement from the bondage of chaotic passion to the freedom of self-chosen constancy.

Wroth's romance, *Urania*, breaks the romance convention of a plot centered on courtship, portraying instead married heroines and their love relationships, both inside and outside of marriage. It is in part an idealizing fantasy: the principal characters are queens, kings, and emperors, with the power and comparative freedom such positions allow. However, the landscape is not Arcadia or Fairyland but war-torn Europe and Asia. The romance fantasy, with Spenserian symbolic places and knights fighting evil tyrants and monsters, only partially overlays a rigidly patriarchal Jacobean world rife with rape, incest, arranged or forced marriages, jealous husbands, tortured women, and endangered children. Those perils, affecting all women from shepherdesses to queens, are rendered in large part through the numerous stories interpolated in romance fashion within the principal plots. The male heroes are courageous fighters and attractive lovers, but all are flawed by inconstancy. For Wroth, true heroism consists of integrity in love despite social constraints and psychological pressures. A few women are heroic in this sense: Pamphilia, the good queen and pattern of constancy; Urania, the wise counselor who wins self-knowledge and makes wise choices in love; and Veralinda, who weds her true lover after great trials. Almost all Wroth's female characters define themselves through storytelling and making poems. The women compose twice as many of the poems as the men do. Pamphilia, Wroth's surrogate, is singled out as a poet by vocation, both by the number of her poems and by their recognized excellence.

Many contemporaries assumed that the *Urania* was a scandalous roman à clef, alluding not only to Sidney-Pembroke-Wroth affairs but to notable personages of the Jacobean court. A public outcry from one of them, Lord Edward Denny, elicited a spirited satiric response from Wroth. Although she suggested to the king's minister Buckingham that she withdraw the work from circulation, there is no evidence that she actually did so. The uproar, however, may have discouraged her from publishing part 2 of the romance and her pastoral drama.

From Pamphilia to Amphilanthus[1]

1

When night's black mantle could most darkness prove,
And sleep, death's image, did my senses hire
From knowledge of myself, then thoughts did move
Swifter than those most swiftness need require.
In sleep, a chariot drawn by winged desire
I saw, where sat bright Venus, Queen of Love,
And at her feet, her son,° still adding fire — *Cupid*
To burning hearts, which she did hold above.
But one heart flaming more than all the rest
The goddess held, and put it to my breast.
"Dear son, now shut,"[2] said she: "thus must we win."
He her obeyed, and martyred my poor heart.
I, waking, hoped as dreams it would depart:
Yet since, O me, a lover I have been.

16

Am I thus conquered? Have I lost the powers
That to withstand, which joys to ruin me?[3]
Must I be still while it my strength devours,
And captive leads me prisoner, bound, unfree?
Love first shall leave men's fancies to them free,[4]
Desire shall quench Love's flames, spring hate sweet showers,
Love shall loose all his darts, have sight, and see
His shame, and wishings hinder happy hours.
Why should we not Love's purblind° charms resist? — *completely blind*
Must we be servile, doing what he list?° — *what pleases him*
No, seek some host to harbor thee: I fly
Thy babish tricks, and freedom do profess.
But O my hurt makes my lost heart confess
I love, and must: So farewell liberty.

40

False hope which feeds but to destroy, and spill[5]
What it first breeds; unnatural to the birth
Of thine own womb; conceiving but to kill,
And plenty gives to make the greater dearth,[6]
So tyrants do who falsely ruling earth

1. Pamphilia ("all-loving") is the protagonist of *Urania*. Her unfaithful beloved's name means "lover of two." These characters are first cousins, like Mary Wroth and William Herbert; their names adumbrate the main theme of both the romance and the appended sonnet sequence, constancy in the face of unfaithfulness.

Pamphilia to Amphilanthus is broken into several separately numbered series (the first of which includes forty-eight sonnets, with songs inserted after every sixth sonnet except the last). In Josephine A. Roberts's edition of Wroth's poetry, the poems are numbered consecutively throughout the work; we have adopted this convenient renumbering.

2. I.e., shut the burning heart into Pamphilia's breast.

3. I.e., have I lost the power to withstand love ("That"), which takes pleasure in ruining me?

4. I.e., this and the other impossibilities that follow will occur before I surrender to love.

5. Kill. The image is of miscarriage or infanticide.

6. Gives abundance only to make scarcity more painful afterward.

Outwardly grace them,[7] and with profits fill,
Advance those who appointed are to death,
To make their greater fall to please their will.
Thus shadow° they their wicked vile intent, *conceal*
Coloring evil with a show of good
While in fair shows their malice so is spent;[8]
Hope kills the heart, and tyrants shed the blood.
For hope deluding brings us to the pride
Of our desires the farther down to slide.

68

My pain, still smothered in my grievèd breast,
Seeks for some ease, yet cannot passage find
To be discharged of this unwelcome guest:
When most I strive, most fast his burdens bind,
Like to a ship on Goodwin's[9] cast by wind,
The more she strives, more deep in sand is pressed,
Till she be lost; so am I, in this kind,° *manner*
Sunk, and devoured, and swallowed by unrest,
Lost, shipwrecked, spoiled, debarred of smallest hope,
Nothing of pleasure left; save thoughts have scope,
Which wander may. Go then, my thoughts, and cry
"Hope's perished, love tempest-beaten, joy lost:
Killing despair hath all these blessings crossed."
Yet faith still cries, "love will not falsify."

74

SONG

Love a child is ever crying,
Please him, and he straight is flying;
Give him, he the more is craving,
Never satisfied with having.

His desires have no measure,
Endless folly is his treasure;
What he promiseth he breaketh:
Trust not one word that he speaketh.

He vows nothing but false matter,
And to cozen° you he'll flatter. *cheat*
Let him gain the hand,° he'll leave you, *the upper hand*
And still glory to deceive you.

He will triumph in your wailing,
And yet cause be of your failing:
These his virtues are, and slighter
Are his gifts, his favors lighter.

7. I.e., those whom they mean to destroy (see next line).
8. Expended, employed. "Shows": appearances.
9. Goodwin Sands, a line of shoals at the entrance to the Strait of Dover.

Feathers are as firm in staying,
Wolves no fiercer in their preying.
As a child then leave him crying,
Nor seek him, so given to flying.

From *A Crown of Sonnets Dedicated to Love*[1]

77

In this strange labyrinth how shall I turn?
Ways° are on all sides, while the way I miss: *paths*
If to the right hand, there in love I burn;
Let me go forward, therein danger is;
If to the left, suspicion hinders bliss,
Let me° turn back, shame cries I ought return, *if I*
Nor faint though crosses[2] with my fortunes kiss;
Stand still is harder, although sure to mourn.[3]
Then let me take the right- or left-hand way;
Go forward, or stand still, or back retire;
I must these doubts endure without allay° *abatement*
Or help, but travail find for my best hire.[4]
Yet that which most my troubled sense doth move
Is to leave all, and take the thread of love.[5]

1621

1. The "crown" is a difficult poetic form (originally Italian and usually known by its Italian name, *corona*) in which the last line of each poem serves as the first line of the next, until a circle is completed by the last line of the final poem, which is the same as the first line of the first one. The number of poems varies from seven to (as in Wroth's *corona*) fourteen.

In contrast to the errant-child Cupid of the preceding part of the sequence, Love in this series is a mature and just monarch, whose true service ennobles lovers. The crown is in part a recantation of the harsh judgment of love earlier in the sequence. But Pamphilia relapses into melancholy afterward.

2. Troubles, adversity. "Faint": lose heart.
3. I.e., certain to make me mourn.
4. I.e., I find travail (with a pun on "travel," the spelling in the 1621 edition) is my only reward.
5. Ariadne gave Theseus a thread to follow so as to find his way out of the Labyrinth, after killing the Minotaur at its center.

THOMAS HOBBES
1588–1679

The English civil war and its aftermath raised fundamental questions about the nature and legitimacy of state power. In 1651 Thomas Hobbes attempted to answer those questions in his ambitious masterwork of political theory, *Leviathan*. A gifted mathematician, Hobbes believed in working rigorously from clearly defined first principles to conclusions, so he grounded his political vision upon a comprehensive philosophy of nature and of knowledge. Hobbes held that everything in the universe is composed only of matter; spirit does not exist. All knowledge is gained through sensory impressions, which are nothing but matter in motion. What we call the self is, for Hobbes, simply a tissue of sensory impressions—clear and immediate in the presence of the objects that evoke them, vague and less vivid in their absence. As a result, an iron determinism of cause and effect governs everything in the universe, including human action.

Human beings, Hobbes thought, seek self-preservation as a primary goal, and power as a means to secure that goal. His politics spring directly from these premises. Because all humans are roughly equal, physically and mentally, they possess equal hopes of attaining goods, as well as equal fears of danger from others. In the state of nature, before the foundation of some sovereign power to keep them all in awe, everyone is continually at war with everyone else, and life, in Hobbes's memorable phrase, is "solitary, poor, nasty, brutish, and short." To escape this ghastly strife, humans covenant with one another to establish a sovereign government over all of them. That sovereign power—which need not be a king but is always indivisible—incorporates the wills and individuality of them all, so that the people no longer have wills, rights, or liberties apart from the sovereign's will. The sovereign's virtually absolute dominion over his subjects extends to the right to pronounce on all matters of religion and doctrine. The four parts of Hobbes's long treatise deal, respectively, with the nature of human beings, the creation of the state, the proper subordination of the church to state sovereignty, and what Hobbes labels the "kingdom of darkness," the Roman Catholic Church.

In Hobbes's system, the founding political covenant, once made, cannot be revoked. Revolution against or resistance to the sovereign for any reason is absurd, since no tyranny can be so evil as the state of war that the sovereign power prevents. Yet if the sovereign should be overthrown, the individual ruler has no further claim, and the people, for their safety, must accept the new sovereign power unconditionally. Hobbes's materialism and secularism scandalized Puritans. The Puritans also rejected its argument for an absolutism that cannot be modified or qualified, even on religious grounds. Other versions of covenant theory, for instance Milton's *Tenure of Kings and Magistrates*, insisted that the power transferred by the people to the sovereign could be limited or revoked. Nor did royalists find much reassurance in Hobbes's political theory. Hobbes was generally associated with the royalist cause, as a tutor to the Cavendish family and as an exile in Paris from 1640 to 1651, where he tutored the future Charles II. Yet his argument made no real distinction between a legitimate monarch and a successful usurper, like Oliver Cromwell; moreover, Hobbes's virtual exclusion of God from politics made many supporters of the king as uncomfortable as it did the Puritans. After the Restoration, Hobbes was widely suspected of atheism, and publication of many of his books, including a history of the civil war entitled *Behemoth,* was prohibited until after his death. Undeterred, Hobbes continued to write on a variety of psychological, political, and mathematical topics, completing a translation of Homer's *Iliad* and *Odyssey* at the age of eighty-six.

Hobbes's political theory did not fit easily into the established patterns of English thought partly because his perspective was essentially cosmopolitan. Educated at Oxford as a classicist, Hobbes traveled widely in Europe between 1610 and 1660 as a companion and tutor of noblemen, often remaining abroad for years at a time. During these lengthy sojourns he became acquainted with many of the leading intellectuals and scientists on the Continent, including Galileo, Descartes, and the prominent French mathematician Pierre Gassendi, who argued that the universe was governed entirely by mechanical principles. The most important political philosophers for Hobbes were also Continental figures: the Italian Niccolò Machiavelli, who saw human beings as naturally competitive and power hungry, and Jean Bodin, a French theorist of indivisible, absolute monarchy. One English writer who did influence Hobbes profoundly was Francis Bacon, whose amanuensis Hobbes had been in Bacon's last years. Ironically, Hobbes was not invited to join the Royal Society, established after the Restoration on Baconian principles, because his religious views were suspect and because he had quarreled with several of the society's founders. Yet Hobbes is truly Bacon's heir, sharing Bacon's utter lack of sentimentality and a memorably astringent prose style.

From Leviathan[1]

From *Part 1. Of Man*

CHAPTER 13. OF THE NATURAL CONDITION OF MANKIND AS CONCERNING THEIR FELICITY AND MISERY

Nature hath made men so equal in the faculties of body and mind as that, though there be found one man sometimes manifestly stronger in body or of quicker mind than another, yet when all is reckoned together, the difference between man and man is not so considerable as that one man can thereupon claim to himself any benefit, to which another may not pretend as well as he. For as to the strength of body, the weakest has strength enough to kill the strongest, either by secret machination, or by confederacy[2] with others that are in the same danger with himself.

And as to the faculties of the mind—setting aside the arts grounded upon words, and especially that skill of proceeding upon general and infallible rules, called science; which very few have, and but in few things; as being not a native faculty, born with us; nor attained, as prudence, while we look after somewhat else—I find yet a greater equality amongst men than that of strength. For prudence is but experience, which equal time equally bestows on all men, in those things they equally apply themselves unto. That which may perhaps make such equality incredible is but a vain conceit of one's own wisdom, which almost all men think they have in a greater degree than the vulgar—that is, than all men but themselves and a few others, whom by fame, or for concurring with themselves, they approve. For such is the nature of men, that howsoever they may acknowledge many others to be more witty, or more eloquent, or more learned, yet they will hardly believe there be many so wise as themselves; for they see their own wit at hand, and other men's at a distance. But this proveth rather that men are in that point equal, than unequal. For there is not ordinarily a greater sign of the equal distribution of anything than that every man is contented with his share.

From this equality of ability ariseth equality of hope in the attaining of our ends. And therefore if any two men desire the same thing, which nevertheless they cannot both enjoy, they become enemies; and in the way to their end (which is principally their own conservation, and sometimes their delectation[3] only) endeavor to destroy or subdue one another. And from hence it comes to pass, that where an invader hath no more to fear than another man's single power, if one plant, sow, build, or possess a convenient seat, others may probably be expected to come prepared with forces united, to dispossess and deprive him, not only of the fruit of his labor, but also of his life or liberty. And the invader again is in the like danger of another.

And from this diffidence[4] of one another, there is no way for any man to secure himself so reasonable as anticipation; that is, by force or wiles to master the persons of all men he can, so long, till he see no other power great enough to endanger him; and this is no more than his own conservation requireth, and is generally allowed. Also because there be some, that taking pleasure in

1. The title refers to the primordial sea creature Leviathan, described in Job 41 as the prime evidence of and analogue to God's power, beyond all human measure and comprehension. Hobbes takes him as figure for the sovereign power in the state. Leviathan was also sometimes taken as a figure for Satan, on the basis of Job 41.34: "he is a king over all the children of pride."
2. Alliance.
3. Pleasure.
4. Lack of faith, mistrust.

contemplating their own power in the acts of conquest, which they pursue farther than their security requires; if others that otherwise would be glad to be at ease within modest bounds, should not by invasion increase their power, they would not be able long time, by standing only on their defense, to subsist. And by consequence, such augmentation of dominion over men being necessary to a man's conservation, it ought to be allowed him.

Again, men have no pleasure, but on the contrary a great deal of grief, in keeping company, where there is no power able to overawe them all. For every man looketh that his companion should value him at the same rate he sets upon himself; and upon all signs of contempt, or undervaluing, naturally endeavors, as far as he dares (which amongst them that have no common power to keep them in quiet, is far enough to make them destroy each other), to extort a greater value from his contemners[5] by damage, and from others by the example.

So that in the nature of man, we find three principal causes of quarrel. First, competition; secondly, diffidence; thirdly, glory.

The first maketh men invade for gain; the second, for safety; and the third, for reputation. The first use violence to make themselves masters of other men's persons, wives, children, and cattle; the second, to defend them; the third, for trifles, as a word, a smile, a different opinion, and any other sign of undervalue, either direct in their persons, or by reflection in their kindred, their friends, their nation, their profession, or their name.

Hereby it is manifest that during the time men live without a common power to keep them all in awe, they are in that condition which is called war; and such a war as is of every man against every man. For war consisteth not in battle only, or the act of fighting, but in a tract of time wherein the will to contend by battle is sufficiently known; and therefore the notion of time is to be considered in the nature of war, as it is in the nature of weather. For as the nature of foul weather lieth not in a shower or two of rain, but in an inclination thereto of many days together; so the nature of war consisteth not in actual fighting, but in the known disposition thereto, during all the time there is no assurance to the contrary. All other time is peace.

Whatsoever therefore is consequent to a time of war, where every man is enemy to every man, the same is consequent to the time wherein men live without other security than what their own strength and their own invention shall furnish them withal. In such condition there is no place for industry, because the fruit thereof is uncertain, and consequently no culture of the earth; no navigation, nor use of the commodities that may be imported by sea; no commodious building; no instruments of moving, and removing, such things as require much force; no knowledge of the face of the earth; no account of time; no arts; no letters; no society; and, which is worst of all, continual fear, and danger of violent death; and the life of man, solitary, poor, nasty, brutish, and short.

It may seem strange to some man that has not well weighed these things, that nature should thus dissociate and render men apt to invade and destroy one another; and he may therefore, not trusting to this inference, made from the passions, desire perhaps to have the same confirmed by experience. Let him therefore consider with himself, when taking a journey, he arms himself and seeks to go well accompanied; when going to sleep, he locks his doors; when even in his house he locks his chests; and this when he knows there be

5. Scorners.

laws, and public officers, armed, to revenge all injuries shall be done him; what opinion he has of his fellow subjects, when he rides armed; of his fellow citizens, when he locks his doors; and of his children and servants, when he locks his chests. Does he not there as much accuse mankind by his actions, as I do by my words? But neither of us accuse man's nature in it. The desires and other passions of man are in themselves no sin. No more are the actions that proceed from those passions, till they know a law that forbids them, which, till laws be made, they cannot know; nor can any law be made, till they have agreed upon the person that shall make it.

It may peradventure be thought there was never such a time nor condition of war as this; and I believe it was never generally so, over all the world; but there are many places where they live so now. For the savage people in many places of America, except the government of small families, the concord whereof dependeth on natural lust, have no government at all and live at this day in that brutish manner as I said before. Howsoever, it may be perceived what manner of life there would be, where there were no common power to fear, by the manner of life which men that have formerly lived under a peaceful government use to degenerate into in a civil war.[6]

But though there had never been any time wherein particular men were in a condition of war one against another, yet in all times, kings and persons of sovereign authority, because of their independency, are in continual jealousies, and in the state and posture of gladiators; having their weapons pointing, and their eyes fixed on one another; that is, their forts, garrisons, and guns upon the frontiers of their kingdoms, and continual spies upon their neighbors, which is a posture of war. But because they uphold thereby the industry of their subjects, there does not follow from it that misery which accompanies the liberty of particular men.

To this war of every man against every man, this also is consequent: that nothing can be unjust. The notions of right and wrong, justice and injustice, have there no place. Where there is no common power, there is no law; where no law, no injustice. Force and fraud are in war the two cardinal virtues. Justice and injustice are none of the faculties neither of the body nor mind. If they were, they might be in a man that were alone in the world, as well as his senses and passions. They are qualities that relate to men in society, not in solitude. It is consequent also to the same condition that there be no propriety,[7] no dominion, no *mine* and *thine* distinct; but only that to be every man's, that he can get; and for so long as he can keep it. And thus much for the ill condition which man by mere nature is actually placed in; though with a possibility to come out of it, consisting partly in the passions, partly in his reason.

The passions that incline men to peace are fear of death, desire of such things as are necessary to commodious living, and a hope by their industry to obtain them. And reason suggesteth convenient articles of peace, upon which men may be drawn to agreement. These articles are they which otherwise are called the Laws of Nature, whereof I shall speak more particularly in the two following chapters.

1651

6. Hobbes is thinking of the recent civil wars in England, and perhaps also of the Greek civil wars described by Thucydides (whom he translated).
7. Property.

GEORGE HERBERT
1593–1633

Unlike the learned and witty style of the work of his friend John Donne, George Herbert's style in his volume of religious poetry, *The Temple*, is deceptively simple and graceful. But it is also marked by self-irony, a remarkable intellectual and emotional range, and a highly conscious artistry that is evident in the poems' tight construction, exact diction, perfect control of tone, and enormously varied stanzaic forms and rhythmic patterns. These poems reflect Herbert's struggle to define his relationship to God through biblical metaphors invested with the tensions of relationships familiar in his own society: king and subject, lord and courtier, master and servant, father and child, bridegroom and bride, friends of unequal status. None of Herbert's secular English poems survives, so his reputation rests on this single volume, published posthumously. *The Temple* contains a long prefatory poem, "The Church-Porch," and a long concluding poem, "Church Militant," which together enclose a collection of 177 short lyrics entitled *The Church*, among which are sonnets, songs, hymns, laments, meditative poems, dialogue poems, acrostic poems, emblematic poems, and more. Herbert's own description of the collection is apt: "a picture of the many spiritual conflicts that have passed between God and my soul." Izaak Walton reports that Herbert gave the manuscript to his friend Nicholas Farrar, head of a quasi-monastic community at Little Gidding, with instructions to publish it if he thought it would "turn to the advantage of any dejected poor soul" and otherwise to burn it. Fortunately, Farrar chose to publish, and *The Temple* became the major influence on the religious lyric poets of the Caroline age: Henry Vaughan, Richard Crashaw, Thomas Traherne, and even Edward Taylor, the American colonial poet.

The fifth son of an eminent Welsh family, Herbert (and his nine siblings) had an upbringing carefully monitored by his mother, Magdalen Herbert, patron and friend of Donne and several other scholars and poets. Herbert was educated at Westminster School and at Trinity College, Cambridge, where he subsequently held a fellowship and wrote Latin poetry: elegies on the death of Prince Henry (1612), witty epigrams, poems on Christ's Passion and death, and poems defending the rites of the English church. In 1620 he was appointed "public orator," the official spokesman and correspondent for the university. This was a step toward a career at court or in public service, as was his election as the member of Parliament from Montgomery in 1624. But that route was closed off by the death of influential patrons and the change of monarchs. Like Donne, Herbert hesitated for some years before being ordained, but in 1630 he took up pastoral duties in the small country parish at Bemerton in Wiltshire. Whereas Donne preached to monarchs and statesmen, Herbert ministered to a few cottagers, and none of his sermons survive. His small book on the duties of his new life, *A Priest to the Temple; or, The Country Parson*, testifies to the earnestness and joy, but also to the aristocratic uneasiness, with which he embraced that role. In chronic bad health, he lived only three more years—performing pastoral duties assiduously, writing and revising his poems, playing music, and listening to the organ and choir at nearby Salisbury Cathedral.

Herbert locates himself in the church through many poems that treat church liturgy, architecture, and art—e.g., "Church Monuments" and "The Windows"—but his primary emphasis is always on the soul's inner architecture. Unlike Donne's poems, Herbert's poems do not voice anxious fears about his salvation or about his desperate sins and helplessness; his anxieties center rather on his relationship with Christ, most often represented as that of friend with friend. Many poems register the speaker's distress over the vacillations and regressions in this relationship, over his lack of "fruition" in God's service, and over the instability in his own nature, purposes, and temperament. In several dialogic poems the speaker's difficulties and anxieties are alleviated or resolved by the voice of a divine friend heard within or recalled through a Scripture text (as in "The Collar"). In poem after poem he has to come to terms with the fact that his relationship with Christ is always radically unequal, that Christ must both initiate it and enable his own response. Herbert struggles constantly with the paradox that, as the works of a Christian poet, his poems ought to give fit praise to God but cannot possibly do so—an issue explored in "The Altar," the two "Jordan" poems, "Easter," "The Forerunners," and many more.

His recourse is to develop a biblical poetics that renounces conventional poetic styles—"fiction and false hair"—to depend instead on God's "art" wrought in his own soul and displayed in the language, metaphors, and symbolism of the Bible. He makes scant use of Donnean learned imagery, but his scriptual allusions carry profound significances. A biblical metaphor provides the unifying motif for the volume: the New Testament temple in the human heart (1 Corinthians 3.16). Another recurring biblical metaphor represents the Christian as plant or tree or flower in God's garden, needing pruning, rain, and nurture. Herbert was profoundly influenced by the genre of the emblem, which typically associated mysterious but meaningful pictures and mottoes with explanatory text. Shaped poems like "The Altar" or "Easter Wings" present image and picture at once; others, like "The Windows," resemble emblem commentary. Other poems allude to typological symbolism, which reads persons and events in the Old Testament as types or foreshadowings of Christ, the fulfillment or antitype. Often, as in "The Bunch of Grapes," Herbert locates both type and antitype in the speaker's soul.

From The Temple[1]

The Altar[2]

A broken ALTAR, Lord, thy servant rears,
Made of a heart, and cemented with tears:
Whose parts are as thy hand did frame;
No workman's tool hath touched the same.[3]
A HEART alone
Is such a stone,
As nothing but
Thy power doth cut.
Wherefore each part
Of my hard heart
Meets in this frame,
To praise thy Name:
That, if I chance to hold my peace,
These stones to praise thee may not cease.[4]
Oh let thy blessed SACRIFICE be mine,
And sanctify this ALTAR to be thine.

1. The title of Herbert's volume sets his poems in relation to David's psalms for the Temple at Jerusalem; his are "psalms" for the New Testament temple in the heart. All of the following poems come from this volume, published in 1633.

2. A variety of emblem poem. Emblems customarily have three parts: a picture, a motto, and a poem. This kind collapses picture and poem into one, presenting the emblem image by its very shape. Shaped poems have been used by authors from Hellenistic times to Dylan Thomas.

3. A reference to Exodus 20.25, in which the Lord enjoins Moses to build an altar of uncut stones, not touched by any tool, and also to Psalm 51.17: "a broken and a contrite heart, O God, thou wilt not despise."

4. A reference to Luke 19.40: "I tell you that, if these should hold their peace, the stones would immediately cry out." Herbert's poems obtain much of their resonance from their biblical echoes.

Redemption[1]

Having been tenant long to a rich lord,
Not thriving, I resolvèd to be bold,
And make a suit unto him, to afford
A new small-rented lease, and cancel th' old.[2]

In heaven at his manor I him sought:
They told me there that he was lately gone
About some land which he had dearly bought
Long since on earth, to take possession.

I straight° returned, and knowing his great birth, *at once*
Sought him accordingly in great resorts—
In cities, theaters, gardens, parks, and courts:
At length I heard a ragged noise and mirth

Of thieves and murderers; there I him espied,
Who straight, "Your suit is granted," said, and died.

Easter Wings[1]

Lord, who createdst man in wealth and store,° *abundance*
Though foolishly he lost the same,
Decaying more and more
Till he became
Most poor:
With thee
O let me rise
As larks, harmoniously,
And sing this day thy victories:
Then shall the fall further the flight in me.[2]

My tender age in sorrow did begin:
And still with sicknesses and shame
Thou didst so punish sin,
That I became
Most thin.
With thee
Let me combine,
And feel this day thy victory;
For, if I imp[3] my wing on thine,
Affliction shall advance the flight in me.

1. Literally, "buying back." In this beautifully concise sonnet Herbert figures God as a landlord, himself as a discontented tenant.
2. I.e., to ask him for a new lease, with a smaller rent; the figure points to the New Testament supplanting the Old.
1. Another emblem poem whose shape presents the emblem picture; the lines, increasing and decreasing, imitate flight, and also the spiritual experience of falling and rising. Early editions printed the poem with the lines running vertically, making the wing shape more apparent.
2. Refers to the "Fortunate Fall," which brought humankind so great a redeemer.
3. In falconry, to insert feathers in a bird's wing.

Jordan (1)[1]

Who says that fictions only and false hair
Become a verse? Is there in truth no beauty?
Is all good structure in a winding stair?
May no lines pass, except they do their duty° — *pay reverence*
    Not to a true, but painted chair?[2]

Is it no verse, except enchanted groves
And sudden arbors shadow coarse-spun lines?[3]
Must purling° streams refresh a lover's loves? — *rippling*
Must all be veiled,[4] while he that reads, divines,
    Catching the sense at two removes?

Shepherds[5] are honest people: let them sing;
Riddle who list,° for me, and pull for prime:[6] — *wishes*
I envy no man's nightingale or spring;
Nor let them punish me with loss of rhyme,
    Who plainly say, *My God, My King.*[7]

The Collar[1]

I struck the board[2] and cried, "No more;
    I will abroad!
What? Shall I ever sigh and pine?
My lines and life are free, free as the road,
Loose as the wind, as large as store.
    Shall I be still in suit?[3]
Have I no harvest but a thorn
To let me blood, and not restore
What I have lost with cordial° fruit? — *restorative to the heart*
    Sure there was wine
Before my sighs did dry it; there was corn° — *grain*
    Before my tears did drown it.
Is the year only lost to me?
    Have I no bays[4] to crown it,
No flowers, no garlands gay? All blasted?
    All wasted?
Not so, my heart; but there is fruit,
    And thou hast hands.

1. The river Jordan, which the Israelites crossed to enter the Promised Land, was also taken as a symbol for baptism.
2. It was the custom for men to bow before a throne, whether it was occupied or not (see Donne, "Satire 3," lines 47–48, p. 620), but to require bowing before a throne in a painting would be ridiculous.
3. "Sudden," i.e., that appear unexpectedly (an artificial effect much sought after in landscape gardening). "Shadow": shade.
4. As in allegory.
5. Conventional pastoral poets.
6. To draw a lucky card in the game of primero. "For me": as far as I am concerned.
7. Echoes Psalm 145.1: "my God, O king."

1. The emblematic title suggests a clerical collar that has become a slave's collar; also, punningly, the speaker's choler (anger) and, perhaps, the caller that he at last hears.
2. Table, with an allusion to the Communion table.
3. Always in attendance, waiting on someone for a favor.
4. The poet's laurel wreath, a symbol of recognized accomplishment.

Recover all thy sigh-blown age
On double pleasures: leave thy cold dispute
Of what is fit and not. Forsake thy cage,
Thy rope of sands,
Which petty thoughts have made, and made to thee
Good cable,[5] to enforce and draw,
And be thy law,
While thou didst wink and wouldst not see.
Away! Take heed;
I will abroad.
Call in thy death's-head[6] there; tie up thy fears.
He that forbears
To suit and serve his need,
Deserves his load."
But as I raved and grew more fierce and wild
At every word,
Methoughts I heard one calling, *Child!*[7]
And I replied, *My Lord.*

The Pulley[1]

When God at first made man,
Having a glass of blessings standing by,
"Let us," said he, "pour on him all we can:
Let the world's riches, which dispersèd lie,
Contract into a span."

So strength first made a way;
Then beauty flowed, then wisdom, honor, pleasure.
When almost all was out, God made a stay,
Perceiving that, alone of all his treasure,
Rest° in the bottom lay. *repose*

"For if I should," said He,
"Bestow this jewel also on my creature,
He would adore my gifts instead of me,
And rest in Nature, not the God of Nature;
So both should losers be.

"Yet let him keep the rest,[2]
But keep them with repining restlessness:
Let him be rich and weary, that at least,
If goodness lead him not, yet weariness
May toss him to my breast."

5. Christian restrictions on behavior, which the "petty thoughts" of the docile believer have made into strong bonds.
6. Skull, emblem of human mortality, and often used as an object for meditation.
7. The call "Child!" reminds the speaker of Paul's words (Romans 8.14–17) that Christians are not in "bondage again to fear" but are children of God, "and if children, then heirs."
1. The poem inverts the legend of Pandora's box, which released all manner of evils when opened but left Hope trapped inside.
2. "Rest" has two senses here: "remainder" and "repose."

The Flower

How fresh, O Lord, how sweet and clean
Are thy returns! even as the flowers in spring,
To which, besides their own demesne,° *domain, demeanor*
The late-past frosts tributes of pleasure bring.
Grief melts away
Like snow in May,
As if there were no such cold thing.

Who would have thought my shriveled heart
Could have recovered greenness? It was gone
Quite underground; as flowers depart
To see their mother-root, when they have blown,° *bloomed*
Where they together
All the hard weather,
Dead to the world, keep house unknown.

These are thy wonders, Lord of power,
Killing and quickening, bringing down to hell
And up to heaven in an hour,
Making a chiming of a passing-bell.[1]
We say amiss
This or that is:
Thy word is all, if we could spell.° *read*

O that I once past changing were,
Fast in thy Paradise, where no flower can wither!
Many a spring I shoot up fair,
Offering° at heaven, growing and groaning thither; *aiming*
Nor doth my flower
Want a spring shower,° *tears of contrition*
My sins and I joining together.

But while I grow in a straight line,
Still upwards bent,° as if heaven were mine own, *directed*
Thy anger comes, and I decline:
What frost to that? What pole is not the zone
Where all things burn,
When thou dost turn,
And the least frown of thine is shown?[2]

And now in age I bud again,
After so many deaths I live and write;
I once more smell the dew and rain,
And relish versing. O my only light,
It cannot be
That I am he
On whom thy tempests fell all night.

1. The "passing-bell," intended to mark the death of a parishioner, is tolled in a monotone; a "chiming" bell offers pleasant variety.

2. I.e., compared with God's wrath, what polar chill would not seem like the heat of the equator?

These are thy wonders, Lord of love,
To make us see we are but flowers that glide;° *slip silently away*
Which when we once can find and prove,° *experience*
Thou hast a garden for us where to bide;
Who would be more,
Swelling through store,
Forfeit their Paradise by their pride.

Love (3)

Love bade me welcome: yet my soul drew back,
Guilty of dust and sin.
But quick-eyed Love, observing me grow slack° *hesitant*
From my first entrance in,
Drew nearer to me, sweetly questioning
If I lacked anything.[1]

"A guest," I answered, "worthy to be here":
Love said, "You shall be he."
"I, the unkind, ungrateful? Ah, my dear,
I cannot look on thee."
Love took my hand, and smiling did reply,
"Who made the eyes but I?"

"Truth, Lord; but I have marred them; let my shame
Go where it doth deserve."
"And know you not," says Love, "who bore the blame?"
"My dear, then I will serve."
"You must sit down," says Love, "and taste my meat."
So I did sit and eat.[2]

1. The first question of tavern waiters to an entering customer would be "What d'ye lack?" (i.e., want).
2. In addition to the sacrament of Communion, the reference is especially to the banquet in heaven, when the Lord "shall gird himself, and make them to sit down to meat, and will come forth and serve them" (Luke 12.37).

ROBERT HERRICK
1591–1674

Robert Herrick was the most devoted of the Sons of Ben, though his epigrams and lyrics (like Jonson's) also show the direct influence of classical poets: Horace, Anacreon, Catullus, Tibullus, Ovid, and Martial. Born in London the son of a goldsmith and apprenticed for some years in that craft, Herrick took B.A. and M.A. degrees at Cambridge and consorted in the early 1620s with Jonson and his "tribe," who met regularly at the Apollo Room. After his ordination in 1623, he apparently served as chaplain to various noblemen and in that role joined Buckingham's failed military expedition to rescue French Protestants at Rhé in 1627. In 1630 he was installed as the vicar of Dean Prior in Devonshire. Expelled as a royalist in 1647, he apparently lived in London until the Restoration, when he was reinstated at Dean Prior and remained there until his death.

Herrick's single volume of poems, *Hesperides* (1648), with its appended book of religious poems, *Noble Numbers*, contains over four hundred short poems. At first glance, they seem merely playful and charming, although remarkable for their exquisite and unerring artistry and perfect decorum. Many are love poems on the carpe diem theme—seize the day, time is fleeting, make love now; a famous example is the elegant song "To the Virgins, to Make Much of Time." But Herrick's range is much wider than is sometimes recognized. He moves from the pastoral to the cynical, from an almost rococo elegance to coarse, even vulgar, epigrams, and from the didactic to the dramatic. Also, he derives mythic energy and power from certain recurring motifs. One is metamorphosis, "times trans-shifting," the transience of all natural things. Another is celebration—festivals and feasts—evoking the social, ritualistic, and even anthropological signficances and energies contained in rural harvest festivals ("The Hock Cart") or the May Day rituals described in what is perhaps his finest poem, "Corinna's Going A-Maying." Yet another is the classical but also perennial ideal of the "good life," defined in his terms as "cleanly wantonness." For Herrick this involves love devoid of high passion (the several mistresses he addresses seem interchangeable and not very real); the pleasures of food, drink, and song; delight in the beauty of surfaces (as in "Upon Julia's Clothes"); and, finally, the creation of poetry as ballast against the ravages of time.

Published just months before the execution of Charles I, these poems, seem almost oblivious to the catastrophes of the war. But they are not. Poems celebrating rural feasts and festivals, ceremonial social occasions, and the rituals of good fellowship reinforce the conservative values of social stability, tradition, and order threatened by the Puritans. Several poems that draw upon the Celtic mythology of fairy folk make their feasts, temples, worship, and ceremonies stand in for the forbidden ceremonies of the Laudian church and a life governed by ritual. Still other poems, like "The Hock Cart" and "Corinna's Going A-Maying," celebrate the kind of rural festivals that were at the center of the culture wars between royalists and Puritans. Both James I and Charles I urged such activities in their *Book of Sports* as a means of reinforcing traditional institutions in the countryside and deflecting discontent, while Puritans vigorously opposed them as occasions for drunkenness and licentiousness.

FROM HESPERIDES[1]

The Vine

I dreamed this mortal part of mine
Was metamorphosed to a vine,
Which, crawling one and every way,
Enthralled my dainty Lucia.[2]
Methought, her long small legs and thighs
I with my tendrils did surprise;
Her belly, buttocks, and her waist
By my soft nervelets were embraced.
About her head I writhing hung,
And with rich clusters (hid among

1. In myth, the Hesperides, or Western Maidens, guarded an orchard and garden, also called Hesperides, in which grew a tree bearing golden apples. Herrick's title suggests that his poems are golden apples from his residence in western Devonshire; the following poems are all from that volume, published in 1648.

2. For the sake of both rhyme and meter, the name of this lady is given three syllables here; in line 12 it has only two.

The leaves) her temples I behung,
So that my Lucia seemed to me
Young Bacchus ravished by his tree.° *the grapevine*
My curls about her neck did crawl,
And arms and hands they did enthrall,
So that she could not freely stir
(All parts there made one prisoner).
But when I crept with leaves to hide
Those parts which maids keep unespied,
Such fleeting pleasures there I took
That with the fancy I awoke,
And found (ah me!) this flesh of mine
More like a stock° than like a vine. *hard stalk*

Delight in Disorder[1]

A sweet disorder in the dress
Kindles in clothes a wantonness.
A lawn° about the shoulders thrown *fine linen scarf*
Into a fine distractiòn;
An erring° lace, which here and there *wandering*
Enthralls the crimson stomacher;[2]
A cuff neglectful, and thereby
Ribbons to flow confusedly;
A winning wave, deserving note,
In the tempestuous petticoat;
A careless shoestring, in whose tie
I see a wild civility:
Do more bewitch me than when art
Is too precise[3] in every part.

Corinna's Going A-Maying

Get up! Get up for shame! The blooming morn
Upon her wings presents the god unshorn.[1]
  See how Aurora throws her fair
  Fresh-quilted colors through the air:[2]
  Get up, sweet slug-a-bed, and see
  The dew bespangling herb and tree.
Each flower has wept and bowed toward the east
Above an hour since, yet you not dressed;
  Nay, not so much as out of bed?
  When all the birds have matins° said, *morning prayer*
  And sung their thankful hymns, 'tis sin,

1. One of several poems in this period in which women's dress is a means by which to explore the relation of nature and art. See Jonson's "Still to Be Neat," p. 648.
2. An ornamental covering of the chest, worn under the laces of the bodice.
3. "Precise" and "precision" were terms used satirically about Puritans. Herrick, in praising feminine disarray, is at one level praising the "sprezzatura," or careless grace, of Cavalier art.

1. Apollo, the sun god; sunbeams are seen as his flowing locks.
2. Aurora is goddess of the dawn.

Nay, profanation° to keep in, *impiety*
Whenas a thousand virgins on this day
Spring, sooner than the lark, to fetch in May.[3]

Rise, and put on your foliage, and be seen
To come forth, like the springtime, fresh and green,
And sweet as Flora.[4] Take no care
For jewels for your gown or hair;
Fear not; the leaves will strew
Gems in abundance upon you;
Besides, the childhood of the day has kept,
Against° you come, some orient pearls[5] unwept; *until*
Come and receive them while the light
Hangs on the dew-locks of the night,
And Titan° on the eastern hill *the sun*
Retires himself, or else stands still
Till you come forth. Wash, dress, be brief in praying:
Few beads[6] are best when once we go a-Maying.

Come, my Corinna, come; and, coming, mark
How each field turns° a street, each street a park *turns into*
Made green and trimmed with trees; see how
Devotion gives each house a bough
Or branch: each porch, each door ere this,
An ark, a tabernacle is,[7]
Made up of whitethorn neatly interwove,
As if here were those cooler shades of love.
Can such delights be in the street
And open fields, and we not see 't?
Come, we'll abroad; and let's obey
The proclamation[8] made for May,
And sin no more, as we have done, by staying;
But, my Corinna, come, let's go a-Maying.

There's not a budding boy or girl this day
But is got up and gone to bring in May;
A deal of youth, ere this, is come
Back, and with whitethorn laden, home.
Some have dispatched their cakes and cream
Before that we have left to dream;
And some have wept, and wooed, and plighted troth,[9]
And chose their priest, ere we can cast off sloth.
Many a green gown[1] has been given,
Many a kiss, both odd and even;[2]
Many a glance, too, has been sent

3. On May Day morning, it was the custom to gather whitethorn blossoms and trim the house with them.
4. Flora, Italian goddess of flowers, had her festival in the spring.
5. Pearls from the Orient were especially lustrous, like drops of dew.
6. Rosary beads of the "old" Catholic religion, but more generally, a casual term for prayers.
7. The doorways, ornamented with whitethorn, are like the Hebrew Ark of the Covenant or the sanctuary that housed it (Leviticus 23.40–42: "Ye shall take you on the first day the boughs of goodly trees . . .").
8. Probably a reference to Charles I's "Declaration to his subjects concerning lawful sports."
9. Engaged themselves to marry.
1. Got by rolling in the grass.
2. Kisses are odd and even in kissing games.

From out the eye, love's firmament;° *sky*
Many a jest told of the keys betraying
This night, and locks picked; yet we're not a-Maying.

Come, let us go while we are in our prime,
And take the harmless folly of the time.
We shall grow old apace, and die
Before we know our liberty.
Our life is short, and our days run
As fast away as does the sun;
And, as a vapor or a drop of rain,
Once lost, can ne'er be found again,
So when or you or I are made
A fable, song, or fleeting shade,
All love, all liking, all delight
Lies drowned with us in endless night.[3]
Then while time serves, and we are but decaying,
Come, my Corinna, come, let's go a-Maying.

To the Virgins, to Make Much of Time

Gather ye rosebuds while ye may,
Old time is still° a-flying;[1] *always*
And this same flower that smiles today,
Tomorrow will be dying.

The glorious lamp of heaven, the sun,
The higher he's a-getting,
The sooner will his race be run,
And nearer he's to setting.

That age is best which is the first,
When youth and blood are warmer;
But being spent, the worse, and worst
Times still succeed the former.

Then be not coy, but use your time,
And while ye may, go marry;
For having lost but once your prime,
You may forever tarry.

Upon Julia's Clothes

Whenas in silks my Julia goes,° *walks*
Then, then, methinks, how sweetly flows
That liquefaction of her clothes.

3. Some echoes of the apocryphal book Wisdom of Solomon 2.1–8: "For the ungodly said . . . the breath of our nostrils is as smoke, and a little spark . . . and our life shall pass away as the trace of a cloud. . . . Come on therefore . . . Let us crown ourselves with rose buds before they be withered." This carpe diem sentiment is a frequent theme in classical love poetry.

1. Translates the Latin *tempus fugit*.

Next, when I cast mine eyes and see
That brave° vibration each way free, *splendid*
Oh, how that glittering taketh me!

RICHARD LOVELACE
1618–1657

Usually linked with Suckling as a quintessential Cavalier, Richard Lovelace was described by a contemporary as "the most amiable and beautiful person that ever eye beheld." Born into a wealthy Kentish family, he was educated at Oxford and, like Suckling, fought for his king in Scotland (in both expeditions, 1639 and 1640). But he was not a libertine, and his poems, in contrast with Suckling's, often exalt women, love, and honor. Also, he shared with his king a serious interest in art, especially the paintings of Rubens, Van Dyck, and Lely. He was imprisoned for a few months in 1642 for supporting the "Kentish Petition" that urged restoration of the king to his ancient rights; in "To Althea, from Prison," he finds freedom from external bondage in the Cavalier ideals of women, wine, and royalism. During 1643–46 he fought in Holland and France and in the king's armies in England and was wounded abroad. In a general roundup of known royalists in 1648 he was imprisoned for ten months, and while there prepared his poems for publication under the title *Lucasta* (1649). Besides witty and charming love songs, that volume includes the plaintive ballad about the conflict between love and honor, "To Lucasta, Going to the Wars," and also "The Grasshopper," a poem that presents the Cavalier ideal at its most attractive. That emblematic summer creature is taken to symbolize the loss of the king and the carefree Cavalier life in the Puritan "winter," but Lovelace finds in the fellowship of Cavalier friends a nobler version of the good life and a truer kingship. After 1649 he endured years of penury, largely dependent on the largesse of his friend and fellow royalist, Charles Cotton. His remaining poems appeared in 1659 as *Lucasta: Postume Poems*.

From LUCASTA

To Lucasta, Going to the Wars

Tell me not, sweet, I am unkind,
  That from the nunnery
Of thy chaste breast and quiet mind
  To war and arms I fly.

True, a new mistress now I chase,
  The first foe in the field;
And with a stronger faith embrace
  A sword, a horse, a shield.

Yet this inconstancy is such
As you too shall adore;
I could not love thee, dear, so much,
Loved I not honor more.

1649

To Althea, from Prison

When Love with unconfinèd wings
Hovers within my gates,
And my divine Althea brings
To whisper at the grates;
When I lie tangled in her hair
And fettered to her eye,
The gods[1] that wanton° in the air *play*
Know no such liberty.

When flowing cups run swiftly round,
With no allaying Thames,[2]
Our careless heads with roses bound,
Our hearts with loyal flames;
When thirsty grief in wine we steep,
When healths and drafts go free,
Fishes that tipple in the deep
Know no such liberty.

When, like committed linnets,° I *caged finches*
With shriller throat shall sing
The sweetness, mercy, majesty,
And glories of my king;
When I shall voice aloud how good
He is, how great should be,
Enlargèd winds, that curl the flood,
Know no such liberty.

Stone walls do not a prison make,
Nor iron bars a cage;
Minds innocent and quiet take
That for an hermitage.
If I have freedom in my love,
And in my soul am free,
Angels alone, that soar above,
Enjoy such liberty.

1649

1. Some versions read "birds" instead of "gods."
2. No mixture of water (as from the river Thames) in the wine.

KATHERINE PHILIPS
1632–1664

The best-known woman poet of her own and the next generation, Katherine Philips was honored as "the Matchless Orinda," the classical name she chose for herself in her poetic addresses to a coterie of chiefly female friends, especially Mary Aubrey (M. A.) and Anne Owen (Lucasia). Sometimes reminiscent of Donne's love lyrics and sometimes of the ancient Greek Sappho's erotic lyrics to women, these poems develop an exalted ideal of female friendship as a Platonic union of souls. Born to a well-to-do Presbyterian family and educated at Mrs. Salmon's Presbyterian School, Philips was taken to Wales when her mother remarried. In 1648, at age seventeen, she was married to James Philips, a prominent member of Parliament. They lived together twelve years, chiefly in the small Welsh town of Cardigan, and had two children: Hector, whose death a few days after birth prompted one of her most moving poems, and Katherine, who lived to adulthood. A royalist despite her Puritan family connections, Philips forged connections with other displaced royalists. Her poems circulated in manuscript and elicited high praise from Vaughan in *Olor Iscanus*. They include elegies, epitaphs, poems at parting, and friendship poems to women and men, but also poetry on political themes: a denunciation of the regicide, "Upon the Double Murder of King Charles," and panegyrics on the restored Stuarts. After the Restoration, James Philips barely escaped execution as a regicide, had his estates confiscated, and lost his seat in Parliament, but Katherine became a favorite at court, promoted by her friend Sir Charles Cotterell ("Poliarchus"), who was master of ceremonies. In Ireland attempting (unsuccessfully) to redeem an investment, she translated Corneille's *Pompey* and her friend the Earl of Orrery produced and printed it in Dublin in 1663. The first edition of her poems, apparently pirated, appeared in 1664, the same year she died of smallpox. Her friend Cotterell brought out an authorized edition in 1667.

A Married State[1]

A married state affords but little ease
The best of husbands are so hard to please.
This in wives' careful° faces you may spell° *full of cares / read*
Though they dissemble their misfortunes well.
A virgin state is crowned with much content;[2]
It's always happy as it's innocent.
No blustering husbands to create your fears;
No pangs of childbirth to extort your tears;
No children's cries for to offend your ears;
Few worldly crosses to distract your prayers:
Thus are you freed from all the cares that do
Attend on matrimony and a husband too.
Therefore Madam, be advised by me
Turn, turn apostate to love's levity,

1. In a manuscript (Orielton MSS Box 24 at the National Library of Wales) this poem appears with another by Philips, addressed to Anne Barlow (whom she probably met in 1646); this one is probably also for Barlow. Both are signed by her maiden name, C. Fowler, so were evidently written before her marriage in 1648.
2. Praise of the single life is a common topic in women's poetry.

Suppress wild nature if she dare rebel.
There's no such thing as leading apes in hell.[3]

ca. 1646 Ms; 1988

Upon the Double Murder of King Charles

In Answer to a Libelous Rhyme made by V. P.[1]

I think not on the state, nor am concerned
Which way soever that great helm[2] is turned,
But as that son whose father's danger nigh
Did force his native dumbness, and untie
His fettered organs: so here is a cause
That will excuse the breach of nature's laws.[3]
Silence were now a sin: nay passion now
Wise men themselves for merit would allow.[4]
What noble eye could see (and careless pass)
The dying lion kicked by every ass?
Hath Charles so broke God's laws, he must not have
A quiet crown, nor yet a quiet grave?
Tombs have been sanctuaries; thieves lie here
Secure from all their penalty and fear.
Great Charles his double misery was this,
Unfaithful friends, ignoble enemies;
Had any heathen been this prince's foe,
He would have wept to see him injured so.
His title was his crime, they'd reason good
To quarrel at the right they had withstood.
He broke God's laws, and therefore he must die,
And what shall then become of thee and I?
Slander must follow treason; but yet stay,
Take not our reason with our king away.
Though you have seized upon all our defense,
Yet do not sequester° our common sense. *confiscate*
But I admire° not at this new supply: *wonder*
No bounds will hold those who at scepters fly.
Christ will be King, but I ne'er understood,
His subjects built his kingdom up with blood
(Except their own) or that he would dispense
With his commands, though for his own defense.
Oh! to what height of horror are they come
Who dare pull down a crown, tear up a tomb![5]

1649? 1664

3. Proverbially, the fate of spinsters.

1. The itinerant Welsh preacher Vavasour Powell was a Fifth Monarchist and an ardent republican who justified the regicide on the ground that Christ's second coming was imminent, when he would rule with his saints, putting down all earthly kings. His poem and Philips's answer were likely written shortly after Charles I's execution (January 30, 1649). Powell's poem has been published by Elizabeth H. Hageman in *English Manuscript Studies.*

2. Steering wheel for the "ships" of state.

3. Breaking the supposed law of nature that excludes women from speaking about public affairs.

4. Wise men, especially Stoic philosophers, normally counsel the firm control or elimination of passions.

5. Their slanders tear up Charles's tomb after his death.

Friendship's Mystery, To My Dearest *Lucasia*[1]

1

Come, my Lucasia, since we see
That miracles men's faith do move,
By wonder and by prodigy
To the dull angry world let's prove
There's a religion in our love.

2

For though we were designed t' agree,
That fate no liberty destroys,
But our election is as free
As angels, who with greedy choice
Are yet determined to their joys.[2]

3

Our hearts are doubled by the loss,
Here mixture is addition grown;
We both diffuse,° and both engross:° *spread out / collect*
And we whose minds are so much one,
Never, yet ever are alone.

4

We court our own captivity
Than thrones more great and innocent:
'Twere banishment to be set free,
Since we wear fetters whose intent
Not bondage is, but ornament.

5

Divided joys are tedious found,
And griefs united easier grow:
We are selves but by rebound,
And all our titles shuffled so,
Both princes, and both subjects too.[3]

6

Our hearts are mutual victims laid,
While they (such power in friendship lies)
Are altars, priests, and off'rings made:

1. This poem was first printed, with a musical setting by the royalist musician and composer Henry Lawes, as "Mutual Affection betweene *Orinda* and *Lucasia*" in Lawes's *The Second Book of Ayres* (1655); our text is from *Poems by the Most Deservedly Admired Mrs. Katherine Philips, the Matchless Orinda* (1667). Lucasia is Philips's name for her friend Anne Owen.

2. Angels, though created with free will, were thought to have become fixed in goodness when they turned toward God in the first moments after their creation.

3. Compare Donne, "The Sun Rising", line 21: "She is all states, and all princes, I" (p. 606).

And each heart which thus kindly° dies, *benevolently, naturally*
Grows deathless by the sacrifice.

1655, 1664

On the Death of My First and Dearest Child, Hector Philips[1]

Twice forty months in wedlock[2] I did stay,
Then had my vows crowned with a lovely boy.
And yet in forty days[3] he dropped away;
O swift vicissitude of human joy!

I did but see him, and he disappeared,
I did but touch the rosebud, and it fell;
A sorrow unforeseen and scarcely feared,
So ill can mortals their afflictions spell.° *discern*

And now, sweet babe, what can my trembling heart
Suggest to right my doleful fate or thee?
Tears are my muse, and sorrow all my art,
So piercing groans must be thy elegy.

Thus whilst no eye is witness of my moan,
I grieve thy loss (ah, boy too dear to live!),
And let the unconcernèd world alone,
Who neither will, nor can, refreshment give.

An off'ring too for thy sad tomb I have,
Too just a tribute to thy early hearse.
Receive these gasping numbers to thy grave,
The last of thy unhappy mother's verse.[4]

1655 1667

1. In Philips's manuscript the subtitle reads, "born the 23d of April, and died the 2d of May 1655. Set by Mr. Lawes." The musical setting has been published by Joan Applegate in *English Manuscript Studies.*
2. Philips was married in August 1648.
3. The subtitle indicates that he lived barely ten days; the change here is clearly for the parallelism.
4. This was not in fact Philips's last poem, but the sentiment is both true to human feeling and common in elegy. She had one other child, a year later—a daughter, Katherine, who survived her.

ANDREW MARVELL
1621–1678

Andrew Marvell's finest poems are second to none in this or any other period. He wrote less than Donne, Jonson, and Herbert did, but his range was in some ways greater, as he claimed both the private worlds of love and religion and the public worlds of political and satiric poetry and prose. His overriding concern with art, his elegant, well-crafted, limpid style, and the cool balance and reserve of some poems align him with Jonson. Yet his paradoxes and complexities of tone, his use of dramatic monologue, and his witty, dialectical arguments associate him with Donne. Above all, he is a supremely original poet, so complex and elusive that it is often hard to know what he really thought about the subjects he treated. Many of his poems were published posthumously in 1681, some thirty years after they were written, by a woman who claimed to be his widow but was probably his housekeeper. So their date and order of composition is often in doubt, as is his authorship of some anonymous works.

The son of a Church of England clergyman, Marvell grew up in Yorkshire, attended Trinity College, Cambridge (perhaps deriving the persistent strain of Neoplatonism in his poetry from the academics known as the Cambridge Platonists), ran off to London, and converted to Roman Catholicism until his father put an end to both ventures. He returned to Cambridge, took his degree in 1639, and stayed on as a scholar until his father's death in 1641. During the years of the civil wars (1642–48), he traveled in France, Italy, Holland, and Spain; much later he said of the Puritan "Good Old Cause" that it was "too good to have been fought for." While his earliest poems associate him with royalists, those after 1649 celebrate the Commonwealth and Oliver Cromwell; although he is sometimes ambivalent, Marvell recognizes divine providence in the political changes. From 1650 to 1652 he lived at Nunappleton as tutor to the twelve-year-old daughter of Thomas Fairfax, who had given over his command of the parliamentary army to Cromwell because he was unwilling to invade Scotland. In these years of retirement and ease, Marvell probably wrote most of his love lyrics and pastorals as well as *Upon Appleton House*. Subsequently he was tutor to Cromwell's ward, William Dutton, and traveled with him on the Continent; in 1657 he joined the blind Milton, at Milton's request, in the post of Latin secretary to Cromwell's Council of State. Marvell accepted the Restoration but maintained his own independent vision and his abiding belief in religious toleration, a mixed state, and constitutional government. He helped his friend Milton avoid execution for his revolutionary polemics and helped negotiate Milton's release from a brief imprisonment. Elected a member of Parliament in 1659 from his hometown, Hull, in Yorkshire, he held that post until 1678, focusing his attention on the needs of his district; on two occasions he went on diplomatic missions—to Holland and Russia. His (necessarily anonymous) antiroyalist polemics of these years include several verse satires on Charles II and his ministers, as well as his best-known prose work, *The Rehearsal Transprosed* (1672–73), which defends Puritan dissenters and denounces censorship with verve and wit. He also wrote a brilliant poem of criticism and interpretation on Milton's *Paradise Lost* that was prefixed to the second edition (1674).

Many of Marvell's poems explore the human condition in terms of fundamental dichotomies that resist resolution. In religious or philosophical poems like "The Coronet" or "The Dialogue Between the Soul and Body", the conflict is between nature and grace, or body and soul, or poetic creation and sacrifice. In love poems such as "The Definition of Love" or "To His Coy Mistress" it is often between flesh and spirit, or physical sex and platonic love, or idealizing courtship and the ravages of time. In pastorals like the Mower poems and "The Garden," the opposition is between nature and art, or the fallen and the Edenic state, or violent passion and contentment. Marvell's most subtle and complex political poem, "An Horatian Ode upon Cromwell's Return from Ireland," sets stable traditional order and ancient right against providential revolutionary change, and the goods and costs of retirement and peace against those of action and war. *Upon Appleton House* also opposes the attractions of various kinds of retirement to the duties of action and reformation.

Marvell experimented with style and genre to striking effect. Many of his dramatic monologues are voiced by named, naive personas—the Mower, the Nymph—who stand at some remove from the author. One of his most remarkable figures—the phrase "To a green thought in a green shade," from "The Garden"—derives its power from the unanalyzable suggestiveness the poem invests in the term "green." "To His

Coy Mistress," perhaps the best known of the century's carpe diem poems, is voiced by a witty and urbane speaker in balanced and artful couplets. But its rapid shifts from the world of fantasy to the charnal house of reality raise questions as to whether this is a clever seduction poem or a probing of existential angst, and whether Marvell intends to endorse or critique this speaker's view of passion and sex. In *Upon Appleton House* Marvell transforms the static, mythic features of Jonson's country-house poem "To Penshurst" to create a poem of epiclike scope that incorporates history and the conflicts of contemporary society. It assimilates to the course of providential history the topographical features of the Fairfax estate, the Fairfax family myth of origin, the experiences of the poet-tutor on his progress around the estate, and the activities and projected future of the daughter of the house. In the poem's rich symbolism, biblical events—Eden, the first temptation, the Fall, the wilderness experience of the Israelites—find echoes in the experiences of the Fairfax family, the speaker, the history of the English Reformation, and the wanton destruction of the recent civil wars.

From Poems[1]

To His Coy Mistress

Had we but world enough, and time,
This coyness, lady, were no crime.
We would sit down, and think which way
To walk, and pass our long love's day.
Thou by the Indian Ganges' side
Shouldst rubies find; I by the tide
Of Humber would complain.[2] I would
Love you ten years before the Flood,
And you should, if you please, refuse
Till the conversion of the Jews.[3]
My vegetable love should grow
Vaster than empires, and more slow;
An hundred years should go to praise
Thine eyes, and on thy forehead gaze;
Two hundred to adore each breast,
But thirty thousand to the rest:
An age at least to every part,
And the last age should show your heart.
For, lady, you deserve this state,° *dignity*
Nor would I love at lower rate.
But at my back I always hear
Time's wingèd chariot hurrying near;
And yonder all before us lie
Deserts of vast eternity.

1. Marvell's lyrics were published posthumously in 1681.
2. The exotic river Ganges in India is on one side of the world, the Humber River flows past Marvell's city, Hull, on the opposite side. Complaints are poems of plaintive, unavailing love.
3. Popular belief had it that the Jews were to be converted just before the Last Judgment. The exaggerated offers in this stanza play off against conventional hyperbolic declarations of love in Petrarchan poetry.

Thy beauty shall no more be found,
Nor, in thy marble vault, shall sound
My echoing song; then worms shall try
That long-preserved virginity,
And your quaint[4] honor turn to dust,
And into ashes all my lust:
The grave's a fine and private place,
But none, I think, do there embrace.
  Now therefore, while the youthful hue
Sits on thy skin like morning dew,[5]
And while thy willing soul transpires
At every pore with instant fires,[6]
Now let us sport us while we may,
And now, like amorous birds of prey,
Rather at once our time devour
Than languish in his slow-chapped[7] power.
Let us roll all our strength and all
Our sweetness up into one ball,
And tear our pleasures with rough strife
Thorough° the iron gates of life:[8] *through*
Thus, though we cannot make our sun
Stand still, yet we will make him run.[9]

ca. 1650–52 1681

The Definition of Love

My Love is of a birth as rare
As 'tis, for object, strange and high;
It was begotten by Despair
Upon Impossibility.

Magnanimous Despair alone
Could show me so divine a thing,
Where feeble Hope could ne'er have flown
But vainly flapped its tinsel wing.

And yet I quickly might arrive
Where my extended soul is fixed;[1]
But Fate does iron wedges drive,
And always crowds itself betwixt.

For Fate with jealous eye does see
Two perfect loves, nor lets them close;° *unite*

4. "Quaint" puns on "out of date" and *queynte*, a term for the female genitals.
5. The text reads "glew," which could be correct, but "dew" is a common emendation.
6. Urgent, sudden enthusiasm. "Transpires": breathes forth.
7. Slowly devouring jaws.
8. One manuscript reads "grates," a somewhat different figure for the sexual act proposed.
9. The sun stood still for Joshua (Joshua 10.12) in his war against Gibeon; see the very different resolution in Donne's "The Sun Rising" (p. 606).
1. The soul has extended itself from the speaker's body and fixed itself to his lover.

Their union would her ruin be,
And her tyrannic power depose.[2]

And therefore her decrees of steel
Us as the distant poles have placed
(Though Love's whole world on us doth wheel),[3]
Not by themselves to be embraced,

Unless the giddy heaven fall,
And earth some new convulsion tear,
And, us to join, the world should all
Be cramped into a planisphere.[4]

As lines, so loves oblique may well
Themselves in every angle greet;[5]
But ours, so truly parallel,
Though infinite, can never meet.

Therefore the Love which us doth bind,
But Fate so enviously debars,
Is the conjunction of the mind,
And opposition of the stars.[6]

ca. 1650–52 1681

The Mower to the Glowworms[1]

Ye living lamps, by whose dear light
The nightingale does sit so late,
And studying all the summer night
Her matchless songs does meditate,

Ye country comets, that portend
No war nor prince's funeral,
Shining unto no higher end
Than to presage the grass's fall;

Ye glowworms, whose officious° flame *helpful*
To wand'ring mowers shows the way,
That in the night have lost their aim,
And after foolish fires° do stray; *will-o'-the-wisps*

2. Two perfections, united, would not be subject to change and thereby to Fate.
3. Rotates as on its axis.
4. A two-dimensional map of the world; Marvell images a round globe collapsed into a flat pancake shape, top to bottom, which would bring the two poles together.
5. Oblique lines can touch in angles, as might "oblique" lovers that (in one meaning of the term) "deviate from right conduct or thought."
6. "Conjunction" is the coming together of two heavenly bodies in the same sign of the zodiac; "opposition" places them at diametrical opposites.
1. Marvell's four "Mower" poems, two of which are included in this volume, are linked by their treatment of a distinctly unusual pastoral figure, a mower rather than a shepherd or goatherd, who provides a singular perspective on those familiar pastoral topics, nature versus art and nature's sympathy for man (the pathetic fallacy). As mower wielding a scythe, he evokes other figures (Time, Death).

Your courteous fires in vain you waste,
Since Juliana here is come,
For she my mind hath so displaced
That I shall never find my home.

ca. 1650–52 1681

The Mower's Song

My mind was once the true survey
Of all these meadows fresh and gay,
And in the greenness of the grass
Did see its hopes[1] as in a glass;° *mirror*
When Juliana came, and she,
What I do to the grass, does to my thoughts and me.[2]

But these, while I with sorrow pine,
Grew more luxuriant still and fine,
That not one blade of grass you spied
But had a flower on either side;
When Juliana came, and she,
What I do to the grass, does to my thoughts and me.

Unthankful meadows, could you so
A fellowship so true forego,
And in your gaudy May-games[3] meet,
While I lay trodden under feet?
When Juliana came, and she,
What I do to the grass, does to my thoughts and me.

But what you in compassion ought
Shall now by my revenge be wrought,
And flowers, and grass, and I, and all,
Will in one common ruin fall;
For Juliana comes, and she,
What I do to the grass, does to my thoughts and me.

And thus ye meadows, which have been
Companions of my thoughts more green,
Shall now the heraldry become
With which I shall adorn my tomb;
For Juliana comes, and she,
What I do to the grass, does to my thoughts and me.

ca. 1650–52 1681

1. Green is the color of hope.
2. The alexandrine (twelve-syllable line) used here is the only example of a refrain in Marvell.
3. Festivals and merrymaking marked the first of May, May Day.

The Garden

How vainly men themselves amaze° *bewilder*
To win the palm, the oak, or bays,[1]
And their uncessant labors see
Crowned from some single herb or tree,
Whose short and narrow-vergèd° shade *edged*
Does prudently their toils upbraid;° *reprove*
While all flowers and all trees do close° *unite, agree*
To weave the garlands of repose!

Fair Quiet, have I found thee here,
And Innocence, thy sister dear?
Mistaken long, I sought you then
In busy companies of men.
Your sacred plants, if here below,° *on earth*
Only among the plants will grow;
Society is all but rude,
To° this delicious solitude. *compared to*

No white nor red[2] was ever seen
So amorous as this lovely green.
Fond lovers, cruel as their flame,
Cut in these trees their mistress' name:
Little, alas, they know or heed
How far these beauties hers exceed!
Fair trees, wheresoe'er your barks I wound,
No name shall but your own be found.[3]

When we have run our passion's heat,
Love hither makes his best retreat.
The gods, that mortal beauty chase,
Still° in a tree did end their race: *always*
Apollo hunted Daphne so,
Only that she might laurel grow;
And Pan did after Syrinx speed,
Not as a nymph, but for a reed.[4]

What wondrous life in this I lead!
Ripe apples drop about my head;
The luscious clusters of the vine
Upon my mouth do crush their wine;
The nectarine and curious° peach *exquisite*
Into my hands themselves do reach;
Stumbling on melons[5] as I pass,
Ensnared with flowers, I fall on grass.

1. Honors, respectively, for military, civic, and poetic achievement.
2. Colors traditionally associated with female beauty.
3. Marvell proposes to carve in the bark of trees not "Sylvia" or "Laura," but "Beech" and "Oak."
4. Apollo, the god of poetry, chased Daphne until she turned into a laurel (the emblematic reward of poets); Pan pursued Syrinx until she became a reed, out of which he made panpipes. The gods' motives were, of course, sexual, not horticultural.
5. "Melons," with etymological roots in the Greek word for "apple," may recall the apple over which all humankind stumbled.

Meanwhile the mind, from pleasure less,
Withdraws into its happiness;
The mind, that ocean where each kind
Does straight° its own resemblance find;[6] *immediately*
Yet it creates, transcending these,
Far other worlds and other seas,
Annihilating all that's made
To a green thought in a green shade.

Here at the fountain's sliding foot,
Or at some fruit tree's mossy root,
Casting the body's vest° aside, *garment*
My soul into the boughs does glide:
There like a bird it sits and sings,
Then whets° and combs its silver wings, *preens*
And, till prepared for longer flight,
Waves in its plumes the various light.[7]

Such was that happy garden-state,
While man there walked without a mate:
After a place so pure and sweet,
What other help could yet be meet![8]
But 'twas beyond a mortal's share
To wander solitary there:
Two paradises 'twere in one
To live in paradise alone.

How well the skillful gardener drew
Of flowers and herbs this dial new,[9]
Where from above the milder sun
Does through a fragrant zodiac run;
And as it works, th' industrious bee
Computes its time[1] as well as we!
How could such sweet and wholesome hours
Be reckoned but with herbs and flowers?

ca. 1650–52 1681

An Horatian Ode

Upon Cromwell's Return from Ireland[1]

The forward° youth that would appear *eager, ambitious*
Must now forsake his Muses dear,
Nor in the shadows sing
His numbers languishing:

6. As the ocean supposedly contained a counterpart of every creature on land, so the ocean of the mind holds the innate ideas of all things (in Neoplatonic philosophy).
7. The multicolored light of this world, contrasted with the white radiance of eternity.
8. Genesis 2.18 recounts the Lord's decision to make a "help meet" for Adam, Eve.
9. The garden itself is laid out as a sundial.
1. With a pun on "thyme."
1. Oliver Cromwell, the general primarily responsible for Parliament's victory in the civil war, returned from conquering Ireland in May 1650, about eighteen months after the execution of

'Tis time to leave the books in dust
And oil th' unusèd armor's rust,
Removing from the wall
The corselet° of the hall.[2] *upper body armor*

So restless Cromwell could not cease
In the inglorious arts of peace,
But through adventurous war
Urgèd his active star;[3]

And, like the three-forked lightning, first
Breaking the clouds where it was nursed,
Did through his own side
His fiery way divide:[4]

For 'tis all one to courage high,
The emulous, or enemy;
And with such, to enclose
Is more than to oppose.

Then burning through the air he went,
And palaces and temples rent;
And Caesar's head at last
Did through his laurels blast.[5]

'Tis madness to resist or blame
The force of angry heaven's flame;
And if we would speak true,
Much to the man is due,

Who from his private gardens, where
He lived reservèd and austere
(As if his highest plot
To plant the bergamot),[6]

Could by industrious valor climb
To ruin the great work of time,
And cast the kingdom old
Into another mold;

Though Justice against Fate complain,
And plead the ancient rights in vain:

Charles I. The two events were persistently connected: Cromwell's success in Ireland was taken as a sign of God's favor to the new republican regime and to Cromwell as his chosen instrument. Pindaric odes (like Jonson's Cary-Morison ode) are heroic and ecstatic; Horatian odes are poems of cool and balanced judgment, as this one is in its representations of Cromwell, Charles I, and the issues of power and providence.

2. Here as elsewhere there are allusions to Lucan's *Pharsalia*, a poem of civil war whose sympathies are with Pompey, Cato, and the Roman Republic against Caesar and the empire. The poem's allusions to Caesar are most often to Charles I, but sometimes to Cromwell.

3. Normally the stars are thought to control men's fates, but Cromwell presses his own star forward.

4. The "three-forked lightning" identifies him with Zeus, suggesting the elemental force by which he surpassed all those in his own party ("side") of radical Independents; the imagery of giving birth to himself also suggests going Caesar (born by cesarean section) one better.

5. Royal crowns were made of laurel because they were supposed to protect from lightning.

6. A pear-shaped orange (from the Turkish, "prince's pear").

But those do hold or break,
As men are strong or weak.

Nature that hateth emptiness,
Allows of penetration less,[7]
And therefore must make room
Where greater spirits come.

What field of all the civil wars
Where his were not the deepest scars?
And Hampton shows what part
He had of wiser art;[8]

Where, twining subtle fears with hope,
He wove a net of such a scope
That Charles himself might chase
To Caresbrooke's narrow case,

That thence the royal actor[9] borne,
The tragic scaffold might adorn;
While round the armèd bands
Did clap their bloody hands.

He nothing common did or mean
Upon that memorable scene,
But with his keener eye
The ax's edge[1] did try;

Nor called the gods with vulgar spite
To vindicate his helpless right;
But bowed his comely head
Down, as upon a bed.

This was that memorable hour,
Which first assured the forcèd power;
So when they did design
The Capitol's first line,

A bleeding head where they begun
Did fright the architects to run;
And yet in that the state
Foresaw its happy fate.[2]

7. Nature abhors a vacuum, but even more, the penetration of one body's space by another body.
8. Charles was confined at Hampton Court after his defeat, as Parliament attempted to negotiate terms for his restoration. Cromwell was rumored to have connived at his escape to Carisbrooke Castle, on the Isle of Wight, in order to convince Parliament that he could not be trusted and must be executed. Cromwell has shown himself master of the two "arts" of rule defined by Machiavelli, namely, force and craft.
9. The theater metaphors used for Charles are even more powerful because the "tragic scaffold" was erected outside Whitehall, where so many royal masques were produced.
1. A play on the Latin *acies*, which means the edge of a sword or ax, a keen glance, and the vanguard of a battle.
2. Livy and Pliny record that the workmen digging the foundations for a temple of Jupiter at Rome uncovered a bloody head which they were persuaded to take as an omen that Rome would be head (*caput*) of a great empire; the temple and the hill took the name Capitoline from that event.

And now the Irish are ashamed
To see themselves in one year tamed;
So much one man can do,
That does both act and know.

They can affirm his praises best,
And have, though overcome, confessed
How good he is, how just,
And fit for highest trust.[3]

Nor yet grown stiffer with command,
But still in the republic's hand—
How fit he is to sway,
That can so well obey.[4]

He to the Commons' feet presents
A kingdom for his first year's rents;
And, what he may, forbears
His fame to make it theirs;[5]

And has his sword and spoils ungirt,
To lay them at the public's skirt:
So, when the falcon high
Falls heavy from the sky,

She, having killed, no more does search,
But on the next green bough to perch;
Where, when he first does lure,
The falconer has her sure.

What may not then our isle presume,
While victory his crest does plume!
What may not others fear,
If thus he crown each year!

A Caesar he ere long to Gaul,
To Italy an Hannibal,
And to all states not free,
Shall climactèric be.[6]

The Pict no shelter now shall find
Within his parti-colored mind,

3. Cromwell conducted a particularly brutal campaign in Ireland, and the Irish had no such testimonials for him; the lines are deeply equivocal.
4. The maxim about obedience fitting one to rule is a commonplace. The implications of "yet" and "still," along with the next stanza, suggest a Caesar figure who has not—but might—cross the Rubicon and defy the Republic, as Julius Caesar did.
5. Thus far, Cromwell gives the Republic credit for his victories.
6. It was thought that Cromwell's military acumen might subdue France and Italy (which threatened to attack the new republic to restore Charles II), just as did Caesar and Hannibal of old. "Climacteric": a period of crucial, epochal change—here, the expectation that the example of a successful English republic would topple absolute monarchs abroad.

But from this valor sad,° *severe, solemn*
Shrink underneath the plaid;[7]

Happy if in the tufted brake
The English hunter him mistake,
Nor lay his hounds in near
The Caledonian° deer. *Scottish*

But thou, the war's and Fortune's son,
March indefatigably on;
And for the last effect,
Still keep thy sword erect;

Besides the force it has to fright
The spirits of the shady night,[8]
The same arts that did gain
A power must it maintain.[9]

1650 1681

7. Early Scots were called Picts (from the Latin *pictus*, painted), because the warriors painted themselves many colors; contemporary Scots are "parti-colored" (divided into many factions) like a scotch plaid. Cromwell was about to go to subdue Scotland, which had declared for Charles II.

8. A sword carried with the blade upright evokes the classical tradition that underworld spirits (here, the slain king and his followers) are frightened off by raised weapons.

9. The maxim alludes to Machiavelli's advice that a kingdom won by force must for some time be maintained by force.

MARGARET CAVENDISH
1623–1673

Margaret (Lucas) Cavendish, Duchess of Newcastle, wrote and published numerous works during the Interregnum and Restoration era, in a great variety of genres: poetry (*Poems and Fancies*, 1653); essays (*Philosophical Fancies*, 1653; *The World's Olio*, 1655), short fiction (*Nature's Pictures*, 1656), autobiography (*A True Relation of My Birth, Breeding, and Life*, 1656), utopian romance (*The Blazing World*, 1666), scientific essays chiefly critical of the new science, letters, a biography of her husband (*The Life of . . . William Cavendish*, 1667), and some eighteen plays, of which one, *The Forced Marriage*, was produced in 1670. Most were published in lavish editions at the Newcastles' own expense. At the time they elicited more derision than praise: for a woman, especially an aristocratic woman, to publish works dealing so intimately with her desires, opinions, personal circumstances, and aspirations to fame and authorship seemed to many disgraceful. Samuel Pepys concluded, after reading her life of her husband the duke, that she was "a mad, conceited, ridiculous woman, and he an ass to suffer [her] to write what she writes to him and of him." Her fantastic dress and sometimes idiosyncratic behavior abetted that characterization: she took pride in "singularity" and even paid a visit to the all-male Royal Society. But the philosopher Thomas Hobbes thought well of her, and her rediscoverers in recent decades have praised her works and her self-construction as a female author.

Cavendish's autobiography analyzes her responses to the circumstances of her life. Born into a wealthy royalist family that encouraged her disposition to read and write, she became maid of honor to Queen Henrietta Maria, whom she followed into exile in Paris. There she married, in 1645, the widowed William Cavendish, thirty years her senior, who was one of Charles I's generals and later Duke of Newcastle. Exiled for fifteen years on the Continent, where (his estates having been sequestered) they ran up exorbitant debts, they were restored to status and fortune after the Restoration. The duke, who was himself a poet, playwright, and philosopher, supported and promoted Margaret's literary endeavors, for which she was profoundly grateful. In polemical prefaces to her several works, she develops a fragmentary poetics, trenchantly defends her right to publish and to participate in contemporary intellectual exchange, defends women's rational powers, and decries their educational disadvantages and exclusion from the public domain.

The Blazing World

Part romance, part utopia, and part science fiction, *The Blazing World* is also an idealized version of Cavendish's own ideas and fantasies in that it portrays the effortless rise of a woman to absolute power. It begins in the vein of romance: a young woman is abducted and miraculously saved as a tempest carries the abductors' boat to the North Pole and on to another universe, the Blazing World, whose emperor promptly marries her and turns over the entire government of the realm to her. It takes on a utopian character, as the new empress learns from the fantastically diverse inhabitants about their numerous scientific experiments and about the royalist politics and religious uniformity of the place. She then brings Margaret Cavendish to be her scribe and returns with Margaret (in the state of disembodied spirits and Platonic friends) to visit and learn about Margaret's world and Margaret's husband, the duke; she also puts down a rebellion at home and subjects other nations to her beneficent rule. Cavendish's preface makes a bold claim for authorial self-sufficiency, equating her creation of and rule over her textual world with the conquering and ruling of empires by Caesar and Alexander. She emphasizes the satisfactions of authorship, but in doing so she also underscores the social and political restrictions on women that have confined her sphere of action to an imagined world.

The Description of a New World, Called The Blazing World[1]

To the Reader

* * * This is the reason, why I added this piece of fancy to my philosophical observations, and joined them as two worlds at the ends of their poles; both for my own sake, to divert my studious thoughts, which I employed in the contemplation thereof, and to delight the reader with variety, which is always pleasing. But lest my fancy should stray too much, I chose such a fiction as would be agreeable to the subject treated of in the former parts; it is a description of a new world, not such as Lucian's or the French-man's world in the moon;[2] but a world of my own creating, which I call the Blazing World: the first part whereof is romancical, the second philosophical, and the third is merely fancy, or (as I may call it) fantastical, which if it add any satisfaction to you, I shall account myself a happy creatoress; if not, I must be content to

1. *The Blazing World* was published in 1666 and 1668, together with Newcastle's *Observations upon Experimental Philosophy,* a critique of the new science emphasizing the limitations of experiment founded on human perception and such instruments as the microscope and the telescope.

2. Cyrano de Bergerac (1619–1655), author of *Histoire comique des états et empires de la lune* (1656). The Greek satirist Lucian of Samosata (125–200? C.E.) wrote dialogues about an imaginary voyage, translated in 1634.

live a melancholy life in my own world; I cannot call it a poor world, if poverty be only want of gold, silver, and jewels; for there is more gold in it than all the chemists ever did, and (as I verily believe) will ever be able to make. As for the rocks of diamonds, I wish with all my soul they might be shared amongst my noble female friends, and upon that condition, I would willingly quit my part; and of the gold I should only desire so much as might suffice to repair my noble lord and husband's losses:[3] for I am not covetous, but as ambitious as ever any of my sex was, is, or can be; which makes, that though I cannot be Henry the Fifth, or Charles the Second, yet I endeavor to be Margaret the First; and although I have neither power, time nor occasion to conquer the world as Alexander and Caesar did; yet rather than not to be mistress of one, since fortune and the fates would give me none, I have made a world of my own: for which nobody, I hope, will blame me, since it is in everyone's power to do the like.

---

* * *No sooner was the lady brought before the emperor, but he conceived her to be some goddess, and offered to worship her; which she refused, telling him, (for by that time she had pretty well learned their language) that although she came out of another world, yet was she but a mortal; at which the emperor rejoicing, made her his wife, and gave her an absolute power to rule and govern all that world as she pleased. But her subjects, who could hardly be persuaded to believe her mortal, tendered her all the veneration and worship due to a deity. . . .

Their priests and governors were princes of the imperial blood, and made eunuchs for that purpose; and as for the ordinary sort of men in that part of the world where the emperor resided, they were of several complexions; not white, black, tawny, olive or ash-colored; but some appeared of an azure, some of a deep purple, some of a grass-green, some of a scarlet, some of an orange color, etc. Which colors and complexions, whether they were made by the bare reflection of light, without the assistance of small particles, or by the help of well-ranged and ordered atoms; or by a continual agitation of little globules; or by some pressing and reacting motion, I am not able to determine. The rest of the inhabitants of that world, were men of several different sorts, shapes, figures, dispositions, and humors, as I have already made mention heretofore; some were bear-men, some worm-men, some fish- or mear-men,[4] otherwise called sirens; some bird-men, some fly-men, some ant-men, some geese-men, some spider-men, some lice-men, some fox-men, some ape-men, some jackdaw-men, some magpie-men, some parrot-men, some satyrs, some giants, and many more, which I cannot all remember; and of these several sorts of men, each followed such a profession as was most proper for the nature of their species, which the empress encouraged them in, especially those that had applied themselves to the study of several arts and sciences; for they were as ingenious and witty in the invention of profitable and useful arts, as we are in our world, nay, more; and to that end she erected schools, and founded several societies. The bear-men were to be her experimental philosophers, the bird-men her astronomers, the fly-, worm-, and fish-men her natural philos-

3. Cavendish's husband, William, was formally banished from England and his estates confiscated in 1649; they were all restored after the Restoration. During his banishment Margaret estimated that he suffered financial losses of around £940,000.

4. Mermen, the male counterparts of mermaids.

ophers, the ape-men her chemists, the satyrs her Galenic physicians, the fox-men her politicians, the spider- and lice-men her mathematicians, the jackdaw-, magpie-, and parrot-men her orators and logicians, the giants her architects, etc. But before all things, she having got a sovereign power from the emperor over all the world, desired to be informed both of the manner of their religion and government, and to that end she called the priests and statesmen, to give her an account of either. Of the statesmen she inquired, first, why they had so few laws? To which they answered, that many laws made many divisions, which most commonly did breed factions, and at last break out into open wars. Next, she asked, why they preferred the monarchical form of government before any other? They answered, that as it was natural for one body to have but one head, so it was also natural for a politic body to have but one governor; and that a commonwealth, which had many governors, was like a monster with many heads: besides, said they, a monarchy is a divine form of government, and agrees most with our religion; for as there is but one God, whom we all unanimously worship and adore with one faith, so we are resolved to have but one emperor, to whom we all submit with one obedience.

Then the empress seeing that the several sorts of her subjects had each their churches apart, asked the priests whether they were of several religions? They answered Her Majesty, that there was no more but one religion in all that world, nor no diversity of opinions in that same religion; for though there were several sorts of men, yet had they all but one opinion concerning the worship and adoration of God. The empress asked them, whether they were Jews, Turks, or Christians? We do not know, said they, what religions those are; but we do all unanimously acknowledge, worship, and adore the only, omnipotent, and eternal God, with all reverence, submission, and duty. Again, the empress inquired, whether they had several forms of worship? They answered, no: for our devotion and worship consists only in prayers, which we frame according to our several necessities, in petitions, humiliations, thanksgiving, etc. Truly, replied the empress, I thought you had been either Jews, or Turks, because I never perceived any women in your congregations; but what is the reason, you bar them from your religious assemblies? It is not fit, said they, that men and women should be promiscuously together in time of religious worship; for their company hinders devotion, and makes many, instead of praying to God, direct their devotion to their mistresses. But, asked the empress, have they no congregation of their own, to perform the duties of divine worship, as well as men? No, answered they: but they stay at home, and say their prayers by themselves in their closets.[5] Then the empress desired to know the reason why the priests and governors of their world were made eunuchs? They answered, to keep them from marriage: for women and children most commonly make disturbance both in church and state. But, said she, women and children have no employment in church or state. 'Tis true, answered they; but although they are not admitted to public employments, yet are they so prevalent[6] with their husbands and parents, that many times by their importunate persuasions, they cause as much, nay, more mischief secretly, than if they had the management of public affairs.

* * *

5. Private chambers.

6. I.e., they prevail so much.

[THE EMPRESS BRINGS THE DUCHESS OF NEWCASTLE TO THE BLAZING WORLD]

After some time, when the spirits had refreshed themselves in their own vehicles, they sent one of their nimblest spirits, to ask the empress, whether she would have a scribe.* * * Then the spirit asked her, whether she would have the soul of a living or a dead man? Why, said the empress, can the soul quit a living body, and wander or travel abroad? Yes, answered he, for according to Plato's doctrine, there is a conversation of souls, and the souls of lovers live in the bodies of their beloved. Then I will have, answered she, the soul of some ancient famous writer, either of Aristotle, Pythagoras, Plato, Epicurus,[7] or the like. The spirit said, that those famous men were very learned, subtle, and ingenious writers, but they were so wedded to their own opinions, that they would never have the patience to be scribes. Then, said she, I'll have the soul of one of the most famous modern writers, as either of Galileo, Gassendus, Descartes, Helmont, Hobbes, H. More,[8] etc. The spirit answered, that they were fine ingenious writers, but yet so self-conceited, that they would scorn to be scribes to a woman. But, said he, there's a lady, the Duchess of Newcastle, which although she is not one of the most learned, eloquent, witty, and ingenious, yet is she a plain and rational writer, for the principle of her writings, is sense and reason, and she will without question, be ready to do you all the service she can. This lady then, said the empress, will I choose for my scribe, neither will the emperor have reason to be jealous, she being one of my own sex. In truth, said the spirit, husbands have reason to be jealous of platonic lovers, for they are very dangerous, as being not only very intimate and close, but subtle and insinuating. You say well, replied the empress; wherefore I pray send me the Duchess of Newcastle's soul; which the spirit did; and after she came to wait on the empress, at her first arrival the empress embraced and saluted her with a spiritual kiss.

* * *

[THE DUCHESS WANTS A WORLD TO RULE]

Well, said the duchess, setting aside this dispute, my ambition is, that I would fain be as you are, that is, an empress of a world, and I shall never be at quiet until I be one. I love you so well, replied the empress, that I wish with all my soul, you had the fruition of your ambitious desire, and I shall not fail to give you my best advice how to accomplish it; the best informers are the immaterial spirits, and they'll soon tell you, whether it be possible to obtain your wish. But, said the duchess, I have little acquaintance with them, for I never knew any before the time you sent for me. They know you, replied the empress; for they told me of you, and were the means and instrument of your coming hither: wherefore I'll confer with them, and inquire whether there be not another world, whereof you may be empress as well as I am of this. No sooner had the empress said this, but some immaterial spirits came to visit

7. Classical philosophers and founders, respectively, of schools of philosophy: the Peripatetics, the Pythagoreans, the Academics, the Epicureans.
8. Galileo Galilei (1564–1642), Italian astronomer and defender of the Copernican system; Pierre Gassendi (1592–1655), proponent of a mechanistic theory of matter; René Descartes (1596–1650), French mathematician and philosopher who had a major influence on the new science; Jan Baptista van Helmont (1579–1644), Flemish chemist; Thomas Hobbes, English mechanistic philosopher and political scientist, author of *Leviathan*; Henry More (1614–1687), one of the antimaterialist Cambridge Platonists.

her, of whom she inquired, whether there were but three worlds in all, to wit, the Blazing World where she was in, the world which she came from, and the world where the duchess lived? The spirits answered, that there were more numerous worlds than the stars which appeared in these three mentioned worlds. Then the empress asked, whether it was not possible, that her dearest friend the Duchess of Newcastle, might be empress of one of them.[9] Although there be numerous, nay, infinite worlds, answered the spirits, yet none is without government. But is none of these worlds so weak, said she, that it may be surprised or conquered? The spirits answered, that Lucian's world of lights, had been for some time in a snuff,[1] but of late years one Helmont had got it, who since he was emperor of it, had so strengthened the immortal parts thereof with mortal outworks, as it was for the present impregnable. Said the empress, if there be such an infinite number of worlds, I am sure, not only my friend, the duchess, but any other might obtain one. Yes, answered the spirits, if those worlds were uninhabited; but they are as populous as this, your majesty governs. Why, said the empress, it is not impossible to conquer a world. No, answered the spirits, but, for the most part, conquerors seldom enjoy their conquest, for they being more feared than loved, most commonly come to an untimely end. If you will but direct me, said the duchess to the spirits, which world is easiest to be conquered, her Majesty will assist me with means, and I will trust to fate and fortune; for I had rather die in the adventure of noble achievements, than live in obscure and sluggish security; since by the one, I may live in a glorious fame, and by the other I am buried in oblivion. The spirits answered, that the lives of fame were like other lives; for some lasted long, and some died soon. 'Tis true, said the duchess; but yet the shortest-lived fame lasts longer than the longest life of man. But, replied the spirits, if occasion does not serve you, you must content yourself to live without such achievements that may gain you a fame: but we wonder, proceeded the spirits, that you desire to be empress of a terrestrial world, whenas you can create yourself a celestial world if you please. What, said the empress, can any mortal be a creator? Yes, answered the spirits; for every human creature can create an immaterial world fully inhabited by immaterial creatures, and populous of immaterial subjects, such as we are, and all this within the compass of the head or skull; nay, not only so, but he may create a world of what fashion and government he will, and give the creatures thereof such motions, figures, forms, colors, perceptions, etc. as he pleases, and make whirlpools, lights, pressures, and reactions, etc. as he thinks best; nay, he may make a world full of veins, muscles, and nerves, and all these to move by one jolt or stroke: also he may alter that world as often as he pleases, or change it from a natural world, to an artificial; he may make a world of ideas, a world of atoms, a world of lights, or whatsoever his fancy leads him to. And since it is in your power to create such a world, what need you to venture life, reputation and tranquility, to conquer a gross material world? . . . You have converted me, said the duchess to the spirits, from my ambitious desire; wherefore I'll take your advice, reject and despise all the worlds without me, and create a world of my own.

* * *

9. Speculation about multiple inhabited worlds was an occasional topic in texts on the new astronomy. Milton's Raphael introduces the idea to Adam (*Paradise Lost* 8.140–58).

1. On the point of extinction.

The Epilogue to the Reader

By this poetical description, you may perceive, that my ambition is not only to be empress, but authoress of a whole world; and that the worlds I have made, both the Blazing and the other Philosophical World, mentioned in the first part of this description, are framed and composed of the most pure, that is, the rational parts of matter, which are the parts of my mind; which creation was more easily and suddenly effected, than the conquests of the two famous monarchs of the world, Alexander and Caesar:[2] neither have I made such disturbances, and caused so many dissolutions of particulars, otherwise named deaths, as they did; for I have destroyed but some few men in a little boat, which died through the extremity of cold, and that by the hand of justice, which was necessitated to punish their crime of stealing away a young and beauteous lady.[3] And in the formation of those worlds, I take more delight and glory, than ever Alexander or Caesar did in conquering this terrestrial world; and though I have made my Blazing World, a peaceable world, allowing it but one religion, one language, and one government; yet could I make another world, as full of factions, divisions, and wars, as this is of peace and tranquility; and the rational figures of my mind might express as much courage to fight, as Hector and Achilles had; and be as wise as Nestor, as eloquent as Ulysses, and as beautiful as Helen.[4] But I esteeming peace before war, wit before policy,[5] honesty before beauty; instead of the figures of Alexander, Caesar, Hector, Achilles, Nestor, Ulysses, Helen, etc. chose rather the figure of honest Margaret Newcastle, which now I would not change for all this terrestrial world; and if any should like the world I have made, and be willing to be my subjects, they may imagine themselves such, and they are such, I mean, in their minds, fancies, or imaginations; but if they cannot endure to be subjects, they may create worlds of their own, and govern themselves as they please: but yet let them have a care, not to prove unjust usurpers, and to rob me of mine; for concerning the Philosophical World, I am empress of it myself; and as for the Blazing World, it having an empress already, who rules it with great wisdom and conduct, which empress is my dear platonic friend; I shall never prove so unjust, treacherous, and unworthy to her, as to disturb her government, much less to depose her from her imperial throne, for the sake of any other; but rather choose to create another world for another friend.

1666, 1668

2. Alexander the Great and Julius Caesar were both famed as conquerors of much of the world known to them.
3. A reference to the romancelike incident with which *The Blazing World* begins, the abduction of a young woman by a party of adventurers whose boat is blown in a tempest to the North Pole, where they perish (except for the woman, who enters into the Blazing World).
4. Hector the Trojan and Achilles the Greek are the principal heroes of Homer's *Iliad*; Nestor, wise adviser to the Greeks; Ulysses, hero of Homer's *Odyssey*, Helen, the one whose beauty caused the Trojan War, as it prompted the Trojan Paris to steal her away from her Greek husband, Menelaus.
5. Intelligence before cunning.

JOHN MILTON
1608–1674

As a young man, John Milton proclaimed himself the future author of a great English epic. He promised a poem devoted to the glory of the nation, centering on the deeds of King Arthur or some other ancient hero. When Milton finally published his epic thirty years later, readers found instead a poem about the Fall of Satan and humankind, set in Heaven, Hell, and the Garden of Eden, in which traditional heroism is denigrated and England not once mentioned. What lay between the youthful promise and the eventual fulfillment was a career marked by private tragedy and public controversy.

In his poems and prose tracts Milton often explores or alludes to crises in his own life: worries about fleeting time, the choice of a vocation and early death, painful disappointment in marriage, and the catastrophe of blindness, manifesting in this the heightened seventeenth-century concern with the self. At the same time, no other major English poet has been so deeply involved in the great questions and political crises of his times. His works inscribe and help construct some basic Western institutions, concepts, and attitudes that were taking on modern form in his lifetime: companionate marriage, the new science and the new astronomy, freedom of the press, religious liberty and toleration, republicanism, and more. It is scarcely possible to treat Milton's career separately from the history of England in his lifetime, not only because he was an active participant in affairs of church and state, but also because when he signed himself, as he often did, "John Milton, Englishman," he was presenting himself as England's prophetic bard, the spokesman for the nation as a whole even when he found himself in a minority of one.

As well, no English poet before Milton fashioned himself quite so self-consciously as an author. The young Milton deliberately set out to follow the steps of the ideal poetic career—beginning with pastoral (the mode prominent in several of his early English poems) and ending with epic. His models for this progression were Virgil and Spenser: he called the latter "a better teacher than Scotus or Aquinas." In this approach to his vocation he stood at the opposite end of the spectrum from such Cavalier contemporaries as John Suckling and Richard Lovelace, who turned to verse with an air of studied carelessness. Milton resembles Spenser especially in his constant use of myth and archetype and also in his readiness to juxtapose biblical and classical stories. He is everywhere concerned with the conventions of genre, yet he infused every genre he used with new energy, transforming it for later practitioners. The Western literary and intellectual heritage impinged on his writing as immediately and directly as the circumstances of his own life, but he continually reconceived the ideas, literary forms, and values of this heritage to make them relevant to himself and to his age.

Milton's family was bourgeois, cultured, and staunchly Protestant. His father was a scrivener—a combination of solicitor, investment adviser, and moneylender—as well as an amateur composer with some reputation in musical circles. Milton had a younger brother, Christopher, who practiced law, and an elder sister, Anne. At age seventeen he wrote a funeral elegy for the death of Anne's infant daughter and later educated her two sons, Edward and John (Edward wrote his biography). Milton had private tutors at home and also attended one of the finest schools in the land, St. Paul's. At school he began a long and close friendship with Charles Diodati, with whom he exchanged Latin poems and letters over several years, and for whose death in 1638 he wrote a moving Latin elegy. Milton was deeply grateful to his father for his excellent early education, especially in languages (Latin, Greek, Hebrew and its dialects, Italian, and French; later he learned Spanish and Dutch).

In 1625 Milton entered Christ's College, Cambridge. He was briefly suspended during his freshman year over some dispute with his tutor, but he graduated in 1629 and was made Master of Arts three years later. As his surviving student orations indicate, he was profoundly disappointed in his university education, reviling the scholastic logic and Latin rhetorical exercises that still formed its core as "futile and barren controversies and wordy disputes" that "stupify and benumb the mind." He went to university with the serious intention of taking orders in the Church of England—the obvious vocation for a young man of his scholarly and religious bent—but became increasingly disenchanted with the lack of reformation in the church under Archbishop William Laud, and in the hindsight of 1642 he proclaimed himself "church-outed by the prelates." No doubt his change of direction was also linked to the fastidious contempt he expressed for the ignorant and clownish clergymen-in-the-making who were his fellow students at Cambridge: "They thought themselves gallant men, and I thought them fools." Those students retaliated by dubbing Milton "the Lady of Christ's College."

Above all, Milton came to believe more and more strongly that he was destined to serve his language, his country, and his God as a poet. He began by writing occasional poetry in Latin, the usual language for collegiate poets and for poets who sought a European audience. Milton wrote some of the century's best Latin poems, but as early as 1628 he announced to a university audience his determination to glorify England and the English language in poetry. In his first major English poem (at age twenty-one), the hymn "On the Morning of Christ's Nativity," Milton already portrayed himself as a prophetic bard. This poem is very different from Richard Crashaw's Nativity hymn, with its Spenserian echoes, its allusion to Roman Catholic and Laudian "idolatry" in the long passage on the expulsion of the pagan gods, and its stunning moves from the Creation to Doomsday, from the manger at Bethlehem to the cosmos, and from the shepherd's chatter to the music of the spheres. Two or three years later, probably, Milton wrote the companion poems "L'Allegro" and "Il Penseroso," achieving a stylistic tour de force by creating from the same meter (octosyllabic couplets) entirely different sound qualities, rhythmic effects, and moods. These poems celebrate, respectively, Mirth and Melancholy, defining them by their ancestry, lifestyles, associates, landscapes, activities, music, and literature. In 1634, at the invitation of his musician friend Henry Lawes, he wrote the masque called *Comus,* in which the villain is portrayed as a refined, seductive, and dissolute Cavalier, and which challenges the absolutist politics of court masques like Ben Jonson's *Masque of Blackness* or Thomas Carew's *Coelum Britannicum* by locating true virtue and good pleasure in the households of the country aristocracy rather than at court.

After university, as part of his preparation for a poetic career, Milton undertook a six-year program of self-directed reading in ancient and modern theology, philosophy, history, science, politics, and literature. He was profoundly grateful to his father for sparing him the grubby business of making money and also for financing these years of private study, followed by a fifteen-month "grand tour" of France, Italy, and Switzerland. In 1638 Milton contributed the pastoral elegy "Lycidas" to a Cambridge volume lamenting the untimely death of a college contemporary. This greatest of English funeral elegies explores Milton's deep anxieties about poetry as a vocation, confronts the terrors of mortality in language of astonishing resonance and power, and incorporates a furious apocalyptic diatribe on the corrupt Church of England clergy. Nonetheless, while he was in Italy he exchanged verses and learned compliments with various Catholic intellectuals and men of letters, some of whom became his friends. Milton could always maintain friendships and family relationships across ideological divides. In 1645 his English and Latin poems were published together in a two-part volume, *Poems of Mr. John Milton.*

Upon his return to England, Milton opened a school and was soon involved in Presbyterian efforts to depose the bishops and reform church liturgy, writing five "antiprelatical tracts" denouncing and satirizing bishops. These were the first in a series of political interventions Milton produced over the next twenty years, characterized by remarkable courage and independence of thought. He wrote successively on church government, divorce, education, freedom of the press, regicide, and republicanism. From the outbreak of the Civil War in 1642 until his death, Milton allied himself with the Puritan cause, but his religious opinions developed throughout his life, from relative orthodoxy in his youth to ever more heretical positions in his later years. And while his family belonged to the class that benefited most directly from Europe's first bourgeois revolution, his brother, Christopher, fought on the royalist side. The Milton brothers, like most of their contemporaries, did not see these wars as a confrontation of class interests, but as a conflict between radically differing theories of government and, above all, religion.

Some of Milton's treatises were prompted by personal concerns or crises. He interrupted his polemical tract, *The Reason of Church Government Urged Against Prelaty* (1642), to devote several pages to a discussion of his poetic vocation and the great works he hoped to produce in the future. His tracts about divorce, which can hardly have seemed the most pressing of issues in the strife-torn years 1643–45, were motivated by his personal experience of a disastrous marriage. Aged thirty-three, inexperienced with women, and idealistic about marriage as in essence a union of minds and spirits, he married a young woman of seventeen, Mary Powell, who returned to her royalist family just a few months after the marriage. In response, Milton wrote several tracts vigorously advocating divorce on the grounds of incompatibility and with the right to remarry—a position almost unheard of at the time and one that required a boldly antiliteral reading of the Gospels. The fact that these tracts could not be licensed and were roundly denounced in Parliament, from pulpits, and in print prompted him to write *Areopagitica* (1644), an impassioned defense of a free press and the free commerce in ideas against a Parliament determined to restore effective censorship. He saw these personal issues—reformed poetry, domestic liberty achieved through needful divorce, and a free press—as vital to the creation of a reformed English culture.

In 1649, just after Charles I was executed, Milton published *The Tenure of Kings and Magistrates* (go to Norton Literature Online for extracts from the *Tenure*), which defends the revolution and the regicide and was of considerable importance in developing a "contract theory" of government based on the inalienable sovereignty of the people—a version of contract very different from that of Thomas Hobbes. Milton was appointed Latin Secretary to the Commonwealth government (1649–53) and to Oliver Cromwell's Protectorate (1654–58), which meant that he wrote the official letters—mostly in Latin—to foreign governments and heads of state. He also wrote polemical defenses of the new government: *Eikonoklastes* (1649), to counter the powerful emotional effect of *Eikon Basilike*, supposedly written by the king just before his death (an excerpt is included on Norton Literature Online), and two Latin *Defenses* upholding the regicide and the new republic to European audiences.

During these years Milton suffered a series of agonizing tragedies. Mary Powell returned to him in 1645 but died in childbirth in 1652, leaving four children; the only son, John, died a few months later. That same year Milton became totally blind; he thought his boyhood habit of reading until midnight had weakened his eyesight and that writing his first *Defense* to answer the famous French scholar Claudius Salmasius had destroyed it. Milton married again in 1656, apparently happily, but his new wife, Katherine Woodcock, was dead two years later, along with their infant daughter. Katherine is probably the subject of his sonnet "Methought I Saw My Late Espoused Saint," a moving dream vision poignant with the sense of loss—both of sight and of love. Milton had little time for poetry in these years, but his few sonnets revolutionized the genre, overlaying the Petrarchan metrical structure with an urgent rhetorical voice and using the small sonnet form, hitherto confined mainly to matters of love, for new and grand subjects: praises of Cromwell and other statesmen mixed with admonition and political advice; a prophetic denunciation calling down God's vengeance for Protestants massacred in Piedmont; and an emotion-filled account of his continuing struggle to come to terms with his blindness as part of God's providence.

Cromwell's death in 1658 led to mounting chaos and a growing belief that a restored Stuart monarchy was inevitable. Milton held out against that tide. His several tracts of 1659–60 developed radical arguments for broad toleration, church disestablishment, and republican government. And just as he was among the first to attack the power of the bishops, so he was virtually the last defender of the "Good Old Cause" of the Revolution; the second edition of his *Ready and Easy Way to Establish a Free Commonwealth* appeared in late April 1660, scarcely two weeks before the Restoration, when the monarchy was restored. For several months after that event, Milton was in hiding, his life in danger. Friends, especially the poet Andrew Marvell, managed to secure his pardon and later his release from a brief imprisonment. He lived out his last years in reduced circumstances, plagued by ever more serious attacks of gout but grateful for the domestic comforts provided by his third wife, Elizabeth Minshull, whom he married in 1663 and who survived him.

In such conditions, dismayed by the defeat of his political and religious cause, totally blind and often ill, threatened by the horrific plague of 1665 and the great fire of 1666, and entirely dependent on amanuenses and friends to transcribe his dictation, he completed his great epic poem. *Paradise Lost* (1667/74) radically reconceives the epic genre and epic heroism, choosing as protagonists a domestic couple rather than martial heroes and degrading the military glory celebrated in epic tradition in favor of "the better fortitude / Of patience and heroic martyrdom." It offers a sweeping imaginative vision of Hell, Chaos, and Heaven; prelapsarian life in Eden; the power of the devil's political rhetoric; the psychology of Satan, Adam, and Eve; and the high drama of the Fall and its aftermath.

In his final years, Milton published works on grammar and logic chiefly written during his days as a schoolmaster, a history of Britain (1670) from the earliest times to the Norman Conquest, and a treatise urging toleration for Puritan dissenters (1673). He also continued work on his *Christian Doctrine,* a Latin treatise that reveals how far he had moved from the orthodoxies of his day. The work denies the Trinity (making the Son and the Holy Spirit much inferior to God the Father), insists upon free will against Calvinist predestination, and privileges the inspiration of the Spirit even above the Scriptures and the Ten Commandments. Such radical and heterodox positions could not be made public in his lifetime, certainly not in the repressive conditions of the Restoration, and Milton's *Christian Doctrine* was subsequently lost to view for over 150 years.

In 1671 Milton published two poems that resonated with the harsh repression and the moral and political challenges all Puritan dissenters faced after the Restoration. *Paradise Regained,* a brief epic in four books, treats Jesus' Temptation in the Wilderness as an intellectual struggle through which the hero comes to understand both himself and his mission and through which he defeats Satan by renouncing the whole panoply of false or faulty versions of the good life and of God's kingdom. *Samson Agonistes,* a classical tragedy, is the more harrowing for the resemblances between its tragic hero and its author. The deeply flawed, pain-wracked, blind, and defeated Samson struggles, in dialogues with his visitors, to gain self-knowledge, discovering at last a desperate way to triumph over his captors and offer his people a chance to regain their freedom. (The tragedy in its entirety is available on Norton Literature Online.) In these last poems Milton sought to educate his readers in moral and political wisdom and virtue. Only through such inner transformation, Milton now firmly believed, would men and women come to value—and so perhaps reclaim—the intellectual, religious, and political freedom he so vigorously promoted in his prose and poetry.

From Poems

On Shakespeare[1]

What needs my Shakespeare for his honored bones
The labor of an age in pilèd stones,
Or that his hallowed relics should be hid
Under a star-ypointing[2] pyramid?
Dear son of memory,[3] great heir of fame,
What° need'st thou such weak witness of thy name? *why*
Thou in our wonder and astonishment
Hast built thyself a livelong° monument. *enduring*
For whilst to th' shame of slow-endeavoring art
Thy easy numbers° flow, and that each heart *verses*
Hath from the leaves of thy unvalued° book *invaluable*
Those Delphic[4] lines with deep impression took,
Then thou, our fancy of itself bereaving,
Dost make us marble with too much conceiving;[5]
And so sepùlchered in such pomp dost lie,
That kings for such a tomb would wish to die.

1630 1632

L'Allegro[1]

Hence loathèd Melancholy,[2]
Of Cerberus[3] and blackest midnight born,
In Stygian[4] cave forlorn
'Mongst horrid shapes, and shrieks, and sights unholy,
Find out some uncouth° cell, *desolate*
Where brooding Darkness spreads his jealous wings,
And the night raven sings;
There under ebon shades and low-browed rocks,
As ragged as thy locks,

1. This tribute, Milton's first published poem, appeared in the Second Folio of Shakespeare's plays (1632).
2. A Spenserian archaism.
3. As "son of memory" Shakespeare is a brother of the Muses, who are the daughters of Mnemosyne (Memory).
4. Apollo, god of poetry, had his oracle at Delphi.
5. Shakespeare's mesmerized readers are themselves his ("marble") monument.

1. The companion poems "L'Allegro" and "Il Penseroso" are both written in tetrameter couplets, except for the first ten lines, but Milton's virtuosity produces entirely different tempos and sound qualities in the two poems. The Italian titles name, respectively, the cheerful, mirthful man and the melancholy, contemplative man. The poems are carefully balanced and their different values celebrated, though "Il Penseroso's" greater length and final coda may intimate that life's superiority. Mirth, the presiding deity of "L'Allegro," is described in terms that evoke Botticelli's presentation of the Grace Euphrosyne (youthful mirth) and her sisters in his *Primavera*.
2. The black melancholy recognized and here exorcized by Mirth's man is a disease leading to madness. "Il Penseroso" celebrates "white" melancholy as the temperament of the scholarly, contemplative man, represented in Dürer's famous engraving *Melancholy*. Burton's *Anatomy of Melancholy* treats the entire range of possibilities.
3. The three-headed hellhound of classical mythology.
4. Near the river Styx, in the underworld.

In dark Cimmerian[5] desert ever dwell.
But come thou goddess fair and free,
In heaven yclept Euphrosyne,[6]
And by men, heart-easing Mirth,
Whom lovely Venus at a birth
With two sister Graces more
To ivy-crownèd Bacchus bore;
Or whether (as some sager sing)
The frolic wind that breathes the spring,
Zephyr with Aurora playing,
As he met her once a-Maying,
There on beds of violets blue,
And fresh-blown° roses washed in dew, *newly opened*
Filled her with thee a daughter fair,
So buxom,° blithe, and debonair. *lively*
Haste thee nymph, and bring with thee
Jest and youthful Jollity,
Quips° and Cranks,° and wanton Wiles, *witty sayings / jokes*
Nods, and Becks,° and wreathèd Smiles, *beckonings*
Such as hang on Hebe's[7] cheek,
And love to live in dimple sleek;
Sport that wrinkled Care derides,
And Laughter holding both his sides.
Come, and trip it° as ye go *dance*
On the light fantastic toe,
And in thy right hand lead with thee
The mountain nymph, sweet Liberty;
And if I give thee honor due,
Mirth, admit me of thy crew
To live with her and live with thee,
In unreprovèd° pleasures free; *irreproachable*
To hear the lark begin his flight,
And, singing, startle the dull night,
From his watchtower in the skies,
Till the dappled dawn doth rise;
Then to come in spite of° sorrow, *in defiance of*
And at my window bid good morrow,
Through the sweetbriar or the vine,
Or the twisted eglantine.
While the cock with lively din
Scatters the rear of darkness thin,
And to the stack or the barn door,
Stoutly struts his dames before;
Oft listening how the hounds and horn
Cheerly rouse the slumbering morn,
From the side of some hoar° hill, *ancient*
Through the high wood echoing shrill.

5. Homer's Cimmereans (*Odyssey* 11.13–19) live on the outer edge of the world, in perpetual darkness.
6. The three Graces—Euphrosyne (four syllables) figuring Youthful Mirth; Aglaia, Brilliance; and Thalia, Bloom—were commonly taken to be offspring of Venus (Love and Beauty) and Bacchus (god of wine). Milton proceeds, however, to devise another, more innocent parentage for Euphrosyne (ascribing it to "some sager," lines 17–24): Zephyr, the West Wind, and Aurora, goddess of the Dawn.
7. Goddess of youth and cupbearer to the gods.

Sometime walking not unseen
By hedgerow elms, on hillocks green,
Right against the eastern gate,
Where the great sun begins his state,[8]
Robed in flames and amber light,
The clouds in thousand liveries dight;° *dressed*
While the plowman near at hand
Whistles o'er the furrowed land,
And the milkmaid singeth blithe,
And the mower whets his scythe,
And every shepherd tells his tale
Under the hawthorn in the dale.
Straight° mine eye hath caught new pleasures *immediately*
Whilst the landscape round it measures,
Russet lawns and fallows° gray, *plowed land*
Where the nibbling flocks do stray,
Mountains on whose barren breast
The laboring clouds do often rest;
Meadows trim with daisies pied,° *multicolored*
Shallow brooks, and rivers wide.
Towers and battlements it sees
Bosomed high in tufted trees,
Where perhaps some beauty lies,
The cynosure[9] of neighboring eyes.
Hard by, a cottage chimney smokes
From betwixt two agèd oaks,
Where Corydon and Thyrsis met
Are at their savory dinner set
Of herbs and other country messes,
Which the neat-handed° Phyllis dresses; *dexterous*
And then in haste her bower she leaves,
With Thestylis[1] to bind the sheaves;
Or if the earlier season lead
To the tanned° haycock in the mead. *sun-dried*
Sometimes with secure° delight *careless*
The upland hamlets will invite,
When the merry bells ring round
And the jocund rebecks[2] sound
To many a youth and many a maid,
Dancing in the checkered shade;
And young and old come forth to play
On a sunshine holiday,
Till the livelong daylight fail;
Then to the spicy nut-brown ale,
With stories told of many a feat,
How fairy Mab the junkets[3] eat;
She was pinched and pulled, she said,

8. Stately procession, as by a monarch.
9. Literally, the bright polestar, or North Star, by which mariners steer; here, a splendid object, much gazed at.
1. Milton uses traditional names from classical pastoral—Corydon, Thyrsis, Phyllis, Thestylis—for his rustic English shepherds.
2. A small three-stringed fiddle. "Jocund": merry, sprightly.
3. Sweetmeats, especially with cream. Queen Mab is the fairy queen, consort of Oberon. "She" and "he" in the next two lines are country folk telling of their experiences with fairies.

And he, by friar's lantern led,
Tells how the drudging goblin[4] sweat
To earn his cream bowl duly set,
When in one night, ere glimpse of morn,
His shadowy flail hath threshed the corn
That ten day laborers could not end;
Then lies him down the lubber fiend,[5]
And stretched out all the chimney's° length, *fireplace's*
Basks at the fire his hairy strength;
And crop-full° out of doors he flings *satiated*
Ere the first cock his matin rings.
Thus done the tales, to bed they creep,
By whispering winds soon lulled asleep.
Towered cities please us then,
And the busy hum of men,
Where throngs of knights and barons bold
In weeds of peace high triumphs[6] hold,
With store of ladies, whose bright eyes
Rain influence,[7] and judge the prize
Of wit or arms, while both contend
To win her grace, whom all commend.
There let Hymen[8] oft appear
In saffron robe, with taper clear,
And pomp and feast and revelry,
With masque and antique° pageantry; *ancient, also antic*
Such sights as youthful poets dream
On summer eves by haunted stream.
Then to the well-trod stage anon,
If Jonson's learned sock be on,
Or sweetest Shakespeare, fancy's child,
Warble his native woodnotes wild.[9]
And ever against eating cares;[1]
Lap me in soft Lydian airs,[2]
Married to immortal verse
Such as the meeting soul may pierce
In notes with many a winding bout° *circuit*
Of linkèd sweetness long drawn out,
With wanton heed and giddy cunning,
The melting voice through mazes running,
Untwisting all the chains that tie
The hidden soul of harmony;
That Orpheus' self may heave his head
From golden slumber on a bed

4. Robin Goodfellow, alias Puck, Pook, or Hobgoblin. "Friar's lantern": will-o'-the-wisp.
5. Puck, here identified with the folktale goblin, Lob-lie-by-the-fire. Robin traditionally did all manner of drudging work for people, to be rewarded with a bowl of cream.
6. Pageants. "Weeds of peace": courtly raiment.
7. The ladies' eyes are stars and so have astrological influence over the men.
8. Roman god of marriage. An orange-yellow ("saffron") robe and a torch are his attributes.
9. It was conventional to contrast Jonson as a "learned" poet and Shakespeare as a "natural" one, but L'Allegro's views and choices of literature also suits with his nature. "Sock": the comedian's low-heeled slipper, contrasted with the tragedian's buskin, a high-heeled boot.
1. "Eating cares" (Horace, *Odes* 2.11.18) is one of many classical echoes in the poem.
2. Plato considered "Lydian airs" to be enervating, soft, and sensual; he preferred the solemn Doric mode. Some others thought Lydian airs relaxing and delightful.

Of heaped Elysian flowers, and hear
Such strains as would have won the ear
Of Pluto, to have quite set free
His half-regained Eurydice.³
These delights if thou canst give,
Mirth, with thee I mean to live.⁴

ca. 1631 1645

Il Penseroso¹

Hence vain deluding joys,²
 The brood of Folly without father bred,
How little you bestead,° *avail*
 Or fill the fixèd mind with all your toys° *trifles*
Dwell in some idle brain,
 And fancies fond° with gaudy shapes possess, *foolish*
As thick and numberless
 As the gay motes that people the sunbeams,
Or likest hovering dreams,
 The fickle pensioners of Morpheus'³ train.
But hail thou Goddess sage and holy,
 Hail, divinest Melancholy,
Whose saintly visage is too bright
 To hit° the sense of human sight, *suit*
And therefore to our weaker view
 O'erlaid with black, staid wisdom's hue;⁴
Black, but such as in esteem,
 Prince Memnon's sister⁵ might beseem,
Or that starred Ethiope queen⁶ that strove
 To set her beauty's praise above
The sea nymphs, and their powers offended.
 Yet thou art higher far descended;
Thee bright-haired Vesta long of yore
 To solitary Saturn bore;⁷
His daughter she (in Saturn's reign

Line numbers: 150, 5, 10, 15, 20, 25

3. Orpheus's music so moved Pluto that he agreed to release Orpheus's dead wife Eurydice (four syllables, accent on the second) from the underworld (Elysium), but he violated the condition set—that he not look back at her—and so lost her again. Milton often uses Orpheus as a figure for the poet.
4. The final lines echo Marlowe's "The Passionate Shepherd to His Love" (p. 459): "If these delights thy mind may move, / Then live with me and be my love."
1. Il Penseroso whose name is Italian for "the thoughtful one," celebrates a melancholy that does not produce madness but the scholarly temperament, ruled by Saturn. See note 2 on p. 697 to "L' Allegro."
2. In "Il Penseroso," Mirth is not the innocent joys of "L'Allegro," but "vain deluding joys."
3. Morpheus is the god of sleep. "Pensioners": followers.

4. The melancholy humor, caused by black bile, was thought to make the face dark or saturnine—from the ancient god Saturn, allegorized in Neoplatonic philosophy as "the collective angelic mind."
5. Memnon, in *Odyssey* 11, was a handsome Ethiopian prince; his sister Himera's beauty was mentioned by later commentators. Cf. Song of Solomon 1.5, "I am black but comely."
6. Cassiopeia was turned into a constellation ("starred") for bragging that she was more beautiful than the sea nymphs.
7. Vesta, daughter of Saturn, was goddess of the household and a virgin, as were her priestesses. Milton invented the story of her sexual congress with Saturn on Mount Ida, resulting in Melancholy's birth. Saturn ruled the gods and the world during the Golden Age, which ended when he was murdered by his son Jove.

Such mixture was not held a stain).
Oft in glimmering bowers and glades
He met her, and in secret shades
Of woody Ida's inmost grove,
While yet there was no fear of Jove.
Come pensive nun, devout and pure,
Sober, steadfast, and demure,
All in a robe of darkest grain,° *color*
Flowing with majestic train,
And sable stole[8] of cypress lawn
Over thy decent° shoulders drawn. *comely, modestly covered*
Come, but keep thy wonted° state,° *usual / dignity*
With even step and musing gait,
And looks commercing with the skies,
Thy rapt soul sitting in thine eyes:
There held in holy passion still,
Forget thyself to marble,[9] till
With a sad° leaden downward cast° *grave, dignified / glance*
Thou fix them on the earth as fast.
And join with thee calm Peace and Quiet,
Spare Fast, that oft with gods doth diet,
And hears the Muses in a ring
Aye° round about Jove's altar sing. *continually*
And add to these retired Leisure,
That in trim gardens takes his pleasure;
But first, and chiefest, with thee bring
Him that yon soars on golden wing,
Guiding the fiery-wheelèd throne,
The cherub Contemplatiòn;[1]
And the mute Silence hist° along, *summon*
'Less Philomel[2] will deign a song,
In her sweetest, saddest plight,° *mood*
Smoothing the rugged brow of night,
While Cynthia[3] checks her dragon yoke
Gently o'er th' accustomed oak;
Sweet bird that shunn'st the noise of folly,
Most musical, most melancholy!
Thee chantress oft the woods among
I woo to hear thy evensong;[4]
And missing thee, I walk unseen
On the dry smooth-shaven green,
To behold the wandering moon,
Riding near her highest noon,
Like one that had been led astray
Through the heaven's wide pathless way;

8. A delicate black cloth.
9. Still as a statue.
1. The special function of cherubim is contemplation of God; Milton alludes also (line 53) to their identification with the wheels of the mystical chariot/throne of God described by Ezekiel (Ezekiel 10).
2. The nightingale (the bird into which Philomela was transformed after her rape by her brother-in-law Tereus) traditionally sings a mournful song. " 'Less": unless.
3. Goddess of the moon, also associated with Hecate, goddess of the underworld, who drives a pair of sleepless dragons.
4. The evening liturgy traditionally sung by cloistered monks and nuns ("chantress" evokes such a singer); "L'Allegro's" cock, by contrast, calls hearers to the morning liturgy, "matins" (line 114).

And oft as if her head she bowed,
Stooping through a fleecy cloud.
Oft on a plat° of rising ground, *plot, open field*
I hear the far-off curfew sound
Over some wide-watered shore,
Swinging slow with sullen° roar; *deep, mournful*
Or if the air will not permit,
Some still removèd place will fit,
Where glowing embers through the room
Teach light to counterfeit a gloom,
Far from all resort of mirth,
Save the cricket on the hearth,
Or the bellman's[5] drowsy charm,
To bless the doors from nightly harm;
Or let my lamp at midnight hour
Be seen in some high lonely tower,
Where I may oft outwatch the Bear,[6]
With thrice-great Hermes, or unsphere
The spirit of Plato[7] to unfold
What words or what vast regions hold
The immortal mind that hath forsook
Her mansion in this fleshly nook;
And of those demons[8] that are found
In fire, air, flood, or underground,
Whose power hath a true consent° *agreement*
With planet, or with element.
Sometime let gorgeous Tragedy
In sceptered pall[9] come sweeping by,
Presenting Thebes, or Pelops' line,
Or the tale of Troy divine,[1]
Or what (though rare) of later age
Ennobled hath the buskined[2] stage.
But, O sad virgin, that thy power
Might raise Musaeus[3] from his bower,
Or bid the soul of Orpheus[4] sing
Such notes as, warbled to the string,
Drew iron tears down Pluto's cheek,
And made Hell grant what love did seek.
Or call up him[5] that left half told
The story of Cambuscan bold,
Of Camball and of Algarsife,
And who had Canacee to wife,

5. Night watchman who rang a bell to mark the hours.
6. The Great Bear constellation never sets in northern skies.
7. Various esoteric books (actually written in the 3rd and 4th centuries) were attributed to an ancient Egyptian, Hermes Trismegistus ("thrice great"). Neoplatonists made him the father of all knowledge; later he became a patron of magicians and alchemists. To "unsphere" Plato is to bring him magically back to earth from whatever sphere he now inhabits—in practical terms, by reading his books.
8. Demons (daemons), halfway between gods and men, preside over the four elements.
9. Royal robe, worn by tragic actors.
1. Tragedies about Thebes include Sophocles' *Oedipus* cycle, those about the line of Pelops, Aeschylus's *Oresteia*, and those about Troy, Euripedes' *Trojan Women*.
2. The buskin (high boot) of tragedy, contrasted with the "sock" of comedy ("L'Allegro," line 132).
3. Mythical poet-priest of the pre-Homeric age, supposedly a son or pupil of Orpheus.
4. For the story of Orpheus, see "L'Allegro," line 145, and note 5 (on line 150).
5. Chaucer, whose Squire's Tale is unfinished.

That owned the virtuous° ring and glass, *having magical powers*
And of the wondrous horse of brass,
On which the Tartar king did ride;
And if aught° else great bards beside *anything*
In sage and solemn tunes have sung,
Of tourneys and of trophies hung,
Of forests and enchantments drear,
Where more is meant than meets the ear.[6]
Thus, Night, oft see me in thy pale career,
Till civil-suited Morn appear,
Not tricked and frounced as she was wont
With the Attic boy to hunt,[7]
But kerchiefed in a comely cloud,
While rocking winds are piping loud,
Or ushered with a shower still,° *gentle*
When the gust hath blown his fill,
Ending on the rustling leaves,
With minute drops from off the eaves.
And when the sun begins to fling
His flaring beams, me, Goddess, bring
To archèd walks of twilight groves,
And shadows brown that Sylvan[8] loves
Of pine or monumental oak,
Where the rude ax with heavèd stroke
Was never heard the nymphs to daunt,
Or fright them from their hallowed haunt.
There in close covert° by some brook, *hidden place*
Where no profaner eye may look,
Hide me from day's garish eye,
While the bee with honeyed thigh,
That at her flowery work doth sing,
And the waters murmuring
With such consort° as they keep, *musical harmony*
Entice the dewy-feathered sleep;
And let some strange mysterious dream
Wave at his wings in airy stream
Of lively portraiture displayed
Softly on my eyelids laid.
And as I wake, sweet music breathe
Above, about, or underneath,
Sent by some spirit to mortals good,
Or th' unseen genius° of the wood. *guardian deity*
But let my due feet never fail
To walk the studious cloister's pale,° *enclosure*
And love the high embowèd roof,
With antic pillars massy proof,[9]
And storied windows richly dight,[1]
Casting a dim religious light.
There let the pealing organ blow

6. A capsule definition of allegory.
7. The now soberly dressed Aurora, goddess of the dawn, once fell in love with Cephalus ("the Attic boy") and hunted with him. "Tricked and frounced": adorned and with frizzled hair.
8. Roman god of woodlands.
9. Massive and strong. "Antic": covered with quaint or grotesque carvings, also antique.
1. Dressed. "Storied windows": stained-glass windows depicting biblical stories.

To the full-voiced choir below,
In service high and anthems clear,
As may with sweetness, through mine ear,
Dissolve me into ecstasies,
And bring all heaven before mine eyes.
And may at last my weary age
Find out the peaceful hermitage,
The hairy gown and mossy cell,
Where I may sit and rightly spell° *study*
Of every star that heaven doth shew,
And every herb that sips the dew,
Till old experience do attain
To something like prophetic strain.
These pleasures, Melancholy, give,[2]
And I with thee will choose to live.

ca. 1631 1645

Lycidas

Milton wrote this pastoral elegy for a volume of Latin, Greek, and English poems, *Justa Eduourdo King Naufrago* (1638), commemorating the death by shipwreck of his college classmate Edward King, three years younger than himself. King was not a close friend, but Milton's deepest emotions, anxieties, and fears are engaged here because, as poet and minister, King could serve Milton as a kind of alter ego. Still engaged in preparing himself, at the age of twenty-nine, for his projected poetic career, Milton was forced to recognize the uncertainty of all human endeavors. King's death posed the problem of mortality in its most agonizing form: the death of the young, the unfulfilled, the good seems to deny all meaning to life, to demonstrate the uselessness of exceptional talent, lofty ambition, and noble ideals of service to God.

While the poem expresses Milton's anxieties, it also serves as an announcement of his grand ambitions. Like Edmund Spenser, Milton saw mastery of the pastoral mode as the first step in a great poetic career. In "Lycidas" that mastery is complete. In the tradition that Milton received from classical and Renaissance predecessors, including Theocritus, Virgil, Petrarch, and Spenser, the pastoral landscape was invested with profound significances that had little indeed to do with the hard life of agricultural labor. In lines 25–36, Milton evokes the conventional pastoral topic of carefree shepherds who engage in singing contests, watch contentedly over their grazing sheep, fall in love, and write poetry, offering an image of human life in harmony with nature and the seasonal processes of fruition and mellowing before the winter of death. That classical image of the shepherd as poet is mingled with the Christian understanding of the shepherd as pastor (Christ is the Good Shepherd), and sometimes as the prophet called to his mission from the fields, like David or Isaiah. Milton calls on all these associations, along with other motifs specific to pastoral funeral elegy: the recollection of past friendship, a questioning of destiny for cutting short this life, a procession of mourners (often mythological figures), and a "flower passage" in which nature pays tribute to the dead shepherd.

"Lycidas" uses but continually tests and challenges the assumptions and conventions of pastoral elegy, making for profound tensions and clashes of tone. The pastoral "oaten flute" is interrupted by divine pronouncements and bitter invective; nature seems rife with examples of meaningless waste and early death; the "blind Fury" often cuts off the poet's "thin-spun life" before he can win fame; good pastors die young

2. Compare "L'Allegro," lines 151–52 (p. 701), and the final lines of Marlowe's "Passionate Shepherd" (p. 459).

while corrupt "Blind mouths" remain; and Nature cannot even pay her tribute of flowers to Lycidas's funeral bier since he welters in the deep, his bones hurled to the "bottom of the monstrous world." In response to these fierce challenges come pronouncements by Apollo and St. Peter, and images of protection and resurrection in nature and myth, culminating in a new vision of pastoral: in heaven Lycidas enjoys a perfected pastoral existence, and in the coda the consoled shepherd arises and carries his song to "pastures new." Milton's questioning leads to a final reassertion of confidence in his calling as national poet. Moreover, in the headnote added in the 1645 volume of his *Poems*, he lays claim to prophetic authority, for the Church of England clergy he denounced as corrupt in 1638 had mostly been expelled from their livings by Puritan reformers in 1645.

Lycidas

In this monody[1] the author bewails a learned friend, unfortunately drowned in his passage from Chester on the Irish seas, 1637. And by occasion foretells the ruin of our corrupted clergy, then in their height.

Yet once more, O ye laurels, and once more
Ye myrtles brown, with ivy never sere,[2]
I come to pluck your berries harsh and crude,° *unripe*
And with forced fingers rude,° *unskilled*
Shatter your leaves before the mellowing year.
Bitter constraint, and sad occasion dear,° *heartfelt, also dire*
Compels me to disturb your season due;
For Lycidas is dead, dead ere his prime,[3]
Young Lycidas, and hath not left his peer.
Who would not sing for Lycidas? He knew
Himself to sing, and build the lofty rhyme.[4]
He must not float upon his watery bier
Unwept, and welter° to the parching wind, *be tossed about*
Without the meed° of some melodious tear.° *reward / elegy*
Begin then, sisters of the sacred well[5]
That from beneath the seat of Jove doth spring,
Begin, and somewhat loudly sweep the string.
Hence with denial vain, and coy excuse;
So may some gentle muse[6]
With lucky words favor my destined urn,
And as he passes turn,
And bid fair peace be to my sable shroud.
For we were nursed upon the selfsame hill,
Fed the same flock, by fountain, shade, and rill.
Together both, ere the high lawns° appeared *upland pastures*
Under the opening eyelids of the morn,

1. A dirge sung by a single voice, though this one incorporates several other voices. Milton added this headnote in the edition of 1645; it identifies Milton as a prophet in the passage denouncing the clergy in this 1638 poem (lines 112–31) and invites the reader to remember Milton's 1641–42 polemics against the English bishops and church government (now dismantled).
2. "Laurels," associated with Apollo and poetry; "myrtle," associated with Venus and love; "ivy," associated with Bacchus and frenzy (also learning). All three are evergreens ("never sere") linked to poetic inspiration.
3. King was twenty-five.
4. King had written several poems of compliment in the patronage mode, chiefly on members of the royal family.
5. The nine (sister) Muses called (probably) from the fountain Aganippe, near Mount Helicon.
6. Here, some kindly poet.

We drove afield, and both together heard
What time the grayfly winds her sultry horn,[7]
Battening° our flocks with the fresh dews of night, *feeding fat*
Oft till the star that rose at evening bright[8]
Toward heaven's descent had sloped his westering wheel.
Meanwhile the rural ditties were not mute,
Tempered to th' oaten flute,[9]
Rough satyrs danced, and fauns with cloven heel
From the glad sound would not be absent long,
And old Damoetas[1] loved to hear our song.
  But O the heavy change, now thou art gone,
Now thou art gone, and never must return!
Thee, shepherd, thee the woods and desert caves,
With wild thyme and the gadding° vine o'ergrown, *wandering*
And all their echoes mourn.
The willows and the hazel copses° green *thickets of trees*
Shall now no more be seen,
Fanning their joyous leaves to thy soft lays.
As killing as the canker° to the rose, *cankerworm*
Or taint-worm[2] to the weanling herds that graze,
Or frost to flowers that their gay wardrobe wear
When first the white-thorn blows;[3]
Such, Lycidas, thy loss to shepherd's ear.
  Where were ye, nymphs,[4] when the remorseless deep
Closed o'er the head of your loved Lycidas?
For neither were ye playing on the steep
Where your old bards, the famous Druids,[5] lie,
Nor on the shaggy top of Mona high,
Nor yet where Deva spreads her wizard stream:[6]
Ay me! I fondly dream—
Had ye been there—for what could that have done?
What could the Muse[7] herself that Orpheus bore,
The Muse herself, for her enchanting[8] son
Whom universal Nature did lament,
When by the rout that made the hideous roar
His gory visage down the stream was sent,
Down the swift Hebrus to the Lesbian shore?[9]
  Alas! What boots° it with incessant care *profits*
To tend the homely slighted shepherd's trade,
And strictly meditate the thankless muse?[1]

7. I.e., heard the grayfly when she buzzes.
8. Hesperus, the evening star.
9. Panpipes, played traditionally by shepherds in pastoral.
1. A type name from pastoral poetry, possibly referring to some particular tutor at Cambridge. "Satyrs": goat-legged woodland creatures, Pan's boisterous attendants.
2. Internal parasite fatal to newly weaned lambs.
3. Hawthorn blooms.
4. Nature deities.
5. Priestly poet-kings of Celtic Britain, who worshipped the forces of nature. They are buried on the mountain ("steep") Kerig-y-Druidion in Wales.
6. Mona is the island of Anglesey. Deva, the river Dee in Cheshire, was magic ("wizard") because its shifting stream foretold prosperity or dearth for the land. All these places are in the West Country, near where King drowned.
7. Calliope, Muse of epic poetry, was the mother of Orpheus.
8. Implies both song and magic; the root word survives in "incantation."
9. Orpheus's song was drowned out by the screams of a mob ("rout") of Thracian women, the Bacchantes, who then were able to tear him to pieces and throw his gory head into the river Hebrus, which carried it—still singing—to the island of Lesbos, bringing that island the gift of poetry.
1. I.e., study to write poetry (a Virgilian phrase).

Were it not better done as others use,
To sport with Amaryllis in the shade,
Or with the tangles of Neaera's hair?[2]
Fame is the spur that the clear spirit doth raise
(That last infirmity of noble mind)
To scorn delights, and live laborious days;
But the fair guerdon° when we hope to find, *reward*
And think to burst out into sudden blaze,
Comes the blind Fury[3] with th' abhorrèd shears,
And slits the thin-spun life. "But not the praise,"
Phoebus replied, and touched my trembling ears;[4]
"Fame is no plant that grows on mortal soil,
Nor in the glistering foil[5]
Set off to th' world, nor in broad rumor lies,
But lives and spreads aloft by those pure eyes,
And perfect witness of all-judging Jove;
As he pronounces lastly on each deed,
Of so much fame in heaven expect thy meed."° *reward*
 O fountain Arethuse, and thou honored flood,
Smooth-sliding Mincius, crowned with vocal reeds,
That strain I heard was of a higher mood.[6]
But now my oat° proceeds, *pastoral flute*
And listens to the herald of the sea[7]
That came in Neptune's plea.
He asked the waves, and asked the felon° winds, *savage*
"What hard mishap hath doomed this gentle swain?"° *shepherd*
And questioned every gust of rugged° wings *stormy*
That blows from off each beakèd promontory;
They knew not of his story,
And sage Hippotades[8] their answer brings,
That not a blast was from his dungeon strayed;
The air was calm, and on the level brine,
Sleek Panope[9] with all her sisters played.
It was that fatal and perfidious bark,
Built in th' eclipse,[1] and rigged with curses dark,
That sunk so low that sacred head of thine.
 Next Camus,[2] reverend sire, went footing slow,
His mantle hairy, and his bonnet sedge,° *formed of reeds*
Inwrought with figures dim, and on the edge
Like to that sanguine flower inscribed with woe.[3]
"Ah! who hath reft," quoth he, "my dearest pledge?"

2. "Amaryllis" and "Neaera" (*Nee-eye-ra*), conventional names for pretty shepherdesses wooed in song by pastoral shepherds.
3. Atropos, one of the three Fates, whose scissors cuts the thread of human life after her sisters spin and measure it. Milton makes her a savage, and blind, Fury.
4. Phoebus Apollo, god of poetic inspiration. In *Eclogue* 6.3–4 he plucked Virgil's ears, warning him against impatient ambition.
5. Flashy, glittering metal foil, set under a gem to enhance its brilliance.
6. Arethusa was a fountain in Sicily associated with Greek pastoral poetry (Theocritus), Mincius a river in Lombardy associated with Latin pastoral (Virgil); Milton invokes them as a return to the pastoral after the "higher mood" of Apollo's speech.
7. Triton, who comes gathering evidence about the accident for Neptune's court.
8. Aeolus, god of winds.
9. The chief Nereid, or sea nymph.
1. Eclipses were taken as evil omens.
2. God of the river Cam, representing Cambridge University.
3. Like the *AI AI* cry of grief supposedly found on the hyacinth, a "sanguine flower" sprung from the blood of the youth Hyacinthus, beloved of Apollo and accidentally killed by him.

Last came and last did go
The pilot of the Galilean lake;[4]
Two massy keys he bore of metals twain
(The golden opes, the iron shuts amain).° *forever*
He shook his mitered locks, and stern bespake:
"How well could I have spared for° thee, young swain, *in place of*
Enow° of such as for their bellies' sake *enough (plural)*
Creep and intrude and climb into the fold![5]
Of other care they little reckoning make,
Than how to scramble at the shearers' feast,[6]
And shove away the worthy bidden guest.
Blind mouths![7] that scarce themselves know how to hold
A sheep-hook, or have learned aught else the least
That to the faithful herdsman's art belongs!
What recks it them? What need they? They are sped;[8]
And when they list,° their lean° and flashy songs *choose / meager*
Grate on their scrannel° pipes of wretched straw. *harsh, thin*
The hungry sheep look up, and are not fed,
But swol'n with wind, and the rank mist they draw,° *inhale*
Rot inwardly,[9] and foul contagion spread,
Besides what the grim wolf with privy paw[1]
Daily devours apace, and nothing said.
But that two-handed engine at the door[2]
Stands ready to smite once, and smite no more."
  Return, Alpheus,[3] the dread voice is past,
That shrunk thy streams; return, Sicilian muse,
And call the vales, and bid them hither cast
Their bells and flowerets of a thousand hues.[4]
Ye valleys low where the mild whispers use,° *frequent*
Of shades and wanton winds, and gushing brooks,
On whose fresh lap the swart star[5] sparely looks,
Throw hither all your quaint enameled eyes,[6]
That on the green turf suck the honeyed showers,
And purple all the ground with vernal flowers.

4. St. Peter, originally a fisherman on the sea of Galilee, was Christ's chief apostle; his keys open and shut the gates of heaven. He wears a bishop's miter (line 112): Milton in his "antiprelatical tracts" allows for a special role for apostles but denies any distinction in office between bishops and ministers in the later church.
5. Cf. John 10.1: "He that entereth not by the door into the sheepfold, but climbeth up some other way, the same is a thief and a robber."
6. Festive suppers for the sheepshearers (hence, the material rewards of their ministry). "Worthy bidden guest" (next line): cf. Matthew 22.8, the parable of the marriage feast, "they which were bidden were not worthy."
7. Collapsing blindness with greed, this audacious metaphor accuses churchmen of shirking oversight (*episcopus*, bishop, means "supervision") and of glutting themselves, although pastors ought to feed their flocks. "Sheep-hook" (next line): the bishop's staff is in the form of a shepherd's crook.
8. Provided for. "What recks it them?": what do they care?
9. Sheep rot is used as an allegory of church corruption by both Petrarch and Dante.
1. I.e., Roman Catholicism, whose agents operated in secret ("privy"). Conversions in the court of the Roman Catholic queen Henrietta Maria were notorious.
2. A celebrated crux, variously explained as the two houses of Parliament, St. Peter's keys, the two-edged sword of the Book of Revelation, a sword wielded by two hands, and by other guesses; what is clear is the denunciation of impending, apocalyptic vengeance. In Matthew 24.33 the Last Judgment is said to be "even at the doors."
3. A river in Arcadia, fabled to pass unmixed through the sea before mixing its waters with the "fountain Arethuse" in Sicily, again reviving the pastoral mode after the fierce denunciation of Peter (see lines 85–87).
4. A catalogue of flowers was a common pastoral topic. "Bells": bell-shaped flowers.
5. The Dog Star, Sirius, associated with the heats of late summer.
6. Flowers curiously patterned and adorned with many colors.

Bring the rathe° primrose that forsaken dies, *early*
The tufted crow-toe, and pale jessamine,[7]
The white pink, and the pansy freaked° with jet, *flecked*
The glowing violet,
The musk rose, and the well-attired woodbine,
With cowslips wan° that hang the pensive head, *pale*
And every flower that sad embroidery wears:
Bid amaranthus[8] all his beauty shed,
And daffadillies fill their cups with tears,
To strew the laureate hearse° where Lycid lies. *laurel-decked bier*
For so to interpose a little ease,
Let our frail thoughts dally with false surmise.[9]
Ay me! whilst thee the shores and sounding seas
Wash far away, where'er thy bones are hurled,
Whether beyond the stormy Hebrides,[1]
Where thou perhaps under the whelming° tide *roaring, overwhelming*
Visit'st the bottom of the monstrous world;
Or whether thou, to our moist vows denied,
Sleep'st by the fable of Bellerus old,[2]
Where the great vision of the guarded mount
Looks toward Namancos and Bayona's hold;[3]
Look homeward angel now, and melt with ruth:° *pity*
And, O ye dolphins,[4] waft the hapless youth.
   Weep no more, woeful shepherds, weep no more,
For Lycidas your sorrow is not dead,
Sunk though he be beneath the wat'ry floor;
So sinks the daystar° in the ocean bed, *the sun*
And yet anon repairs his drooping head,
And tricks° his beams, and with new-spangled ore *adorns, trims*
Flames in the forehead of the morning sky:
So Lycidas sunk low, but mounted high,
Through the dear might of him that walked the waves,[5]
Where, other groves and other streams along,[6]
With nectar pure his oozy° locks he laves, *moist*
And hears the unexpressive nuptial song,[7]
In the blest kingdoms meek of joy and love.
There entertain him all the saints above,
In solemn troops and sweet societies
That sing, and singing in their glory move,

7. White jasmine. "Tufted crow-toe": hyacinth or buttercup, growing in clusters. "Woodbine" (line 146): honeysuckle.
8. In Greek, "unfading," a legendary flower of immortality, one that never fades.
9. False, because Lycidas's body is not here to receive floral and poetic tributes.
1. Islands off the coast of Scotland, the northern terminus of the Irish Sea.
2. A fabulous giant invented by Milton as the origin of the Latin name for Land's End in Cornwall, *Bellerium*. "Monstrous world" (line 158): filled with monsters, also, immense.
3. "The guarded mount" is St. Michael's Mount in Cornwall, where the archangel was said to have appeared to fishermen in 495, and from which he is envisioned as looking over the Atlantic toward a region and fortress ("Bayona's hold") in northern Spain, thereby guarding Protestant England against the continuing Roman Catholic threat.
4. Dolphins brought the Greek poet Arion safely ashore, for love of his verse, and also performed other sea rescues.
5. Christ, who rescued Peter when he tried and failed to walk on the Sea of Galilee (Matthew 14.25–31).
6. See Revelation 22.1–2, on the "pure river of water of life," and the "tree of life, which bare twelve manner of fruits."
7. Inexpressible hymn of joy sung at "the marriage supper of the Lamb" (Revelation 19).

And wipe the tears forever from his eyes.
Now, Lycidas, the shepherds weep no more;
Henceforth thou art the Genius[8] of the shore,
In thy large recompense, and shalt be good
To all that wander in that perilous flood.
  Thus sang the uncouth swain[9] to th' oaks and rills,
While the still morn went out with sandals gray;
He touched the tender stops of various quills,[1]
With eager thought warbling his Doric[2] lay:
And now the sun had stretched out all the hills,
And now was dropped into the western bay;
At last he rose, and twitched his mantle blue:[3]
Tomorrow to fresh woods, and pastures new.

November 1637 1638

Areopagitica

This passionate, trenchant defense of intellectual liberty has had a powerful influence on the evolving liberal conception of freedom of speech, press, and thought. Milton's specific target is the Press Ordinance of June 14, 1643, Parliament's attempt to crack down on the flood of pamphlets (including Milton's own controversial treatises on divorce) that poured forth both from legal and from underground presses as the Civil War raged. Like Tudor and Stuart censorship laws, Parliament's ordinance demanded that works be registered with the stationers and licensed by the censors before publication, and that both author and publisher be identified, on pain of fines and imprisonment for both. Milton vigorously protests the prepublication licensing of books, arguing that such measures have only been used by, and are only fit for, degenerate cultures. In the regenerate English nation, now "rousing herself like a strong man after sleep," men and women must be allowed to develop in virtue by participating in the clash and conflict of ideas. Truth will always overcome falsehood in reasoned debate. Thus, in opposition to the Presbyterians then in power, Milton defends widespread religious toleration, though with restrictions on Roman Catholicism, which, like most of his Protestant contemporaries, he viewed as a political threat and a tyranny binding individual conscience to the pope.

The title associates the tract with the speech of the Greek orator Isocrates to the Areopagus, the Council of the Wise in Athens. Learned readers would have recognized the irony of this. While Isocrates instructed the council to reform Athens by careful supervision of the private lives of citizens, Milton argues that only liberty and removal of censorship can advance reformation. This association explains the oratorical tone of the tract, which was, in fact, subtitled "A Speech." In this most literary of his tracts, Milton's style is elevated, eloquent, dense with poetic figures, and ranges in tone from satire and ridicule to urgent pleading and florid praise. His arguments and principles are often couched in striking images and phrases. One example is his passionate testimony to the potency and inestimable value of books: "As good almost kill a man as kill a good book . . ." Most memorable is his ringing credo that echoes down the centuries to protest every new tyranny: "Give me the liberty to know, to utter, and to argue freely according to conscience, above all liberties."

8. Local guardian spirit.
9. Another voice now seems to take over from the previously heard voice of the "uncouth swain" (unknown, unskilled shepherd).
1. The oaten stalks of panpipes.
2. Rustic, the dialect of Theocritus and other famous Greek pastoral poets.
3. The color of hope. "Twitched": pulled up around his shoulders.

From Areopagitica

I deny not, but that it is of greatest concernment in the church and commonwealth, to have a vigilant eye how books demean[1] themselves as well as men; and thereafter to confine, imprison, and do sharpest justice on them as malefactors:[2] For books are not absolutely dead things, but do contain a potency of life in them to be as active as that soul was whose progeny they are; nay they do preserve as in a vial the purest efficacy and extraction of that living intellect that bred them. I know they are as lively, and as vigorously productive, as those fabulous dragon's teeth; and being sown up and down, may chance to spring up armed men.[3] And yet on the other hand unless wariness be used, as good almost kill a man as kill a good book; who kills a man kills a reasonable creature, God's image; but he who destroys a good book, kills reason itself, kills the image of God, as it were in the eye. Many a man lives a burden to the earth; but a good book is the precious lifeblood of a master spirit, embalmed and treasured up on purpose to a life beyond life. 'Tis true, no age can restore a life, whereof perhaps there is no great loss; and revolutions of ages do not oft recover the loss of a rejected truth, for the want of which whole nations fare the worse. We should be wary therefore what persecution we raise against the living labors of public men, how we spill that seasoned life of man preserved and stored up in books; since we see a kind of massacre, whereof the execution ends not in the slaying of an elemental life, but strikes at that ethereal and fifth essence,[4] the breath of reason itself, slays an immortality rather than a life. But lest I should be condemned of introducing licence, while I oppose licensing, I refuse not the pains to be so much historical, as will serve to show what hath been done by ancient and famous commonwealths, against this disorder, till the very time that this project of licensing crept out of the Inquisition,[5] was catched up by our prelates, and hath caught some of our presbyters.[6] * * *

* * *Good and evil we know in the field of this world grow up together almost inseparably; and the knowledge of good is so involved and interwoven with the knowledge of evil, and in so many cunning resemblances hardly to be discerned, that those confused seeds which were imposed on Psyche as an incessant labor to cull out and sort asunder were not more intermixed.[7] It was from out the rind of one apple tasted, that the knowledge of good and evil, as two twins cleaving together, leaped forth into the world. And perhaps this is that doom which Adam fell into of knowing good and evil, that is to say of knowing good by evil.

As therefore the state of man now is, what wisdom can there be to choose, what continence to forbear, without the knowledge of evil? He that can appre-

1. Behave.
2. Milton allows that books may be called to account after publication, if they are proved to contain libels or other manifest crimes (he leaves this quite vague).
3. After Cadmus killed a dragon on his way to founding Thebes, on a god's advice he sowed the dragon's teeth, which sprang up as an army, the belligerent forefathers of Sparta.
4. Quintessence, a pure, mystical substance above the four elements (fire, air, water, earth).
5. The Roman Catholic institution for suppressing heresy, especially strong in Spain.
6. The Presbyterians, powerful in the Parliament, were striving to establish theirs as the national church and suppress others. Milton, who began by supporting them in *The Reason of Church Government* and his other antiprelatical tracts (1641–42), now rejects them, in large part because they seek to supplant one repressive church with another.
7. Angry at her son Cupid's love for Psyche, Venus set the girl many trials, among them to sort out a vast mound of mixed seeds, but the ants took pity on her and did the work.

hend and consider vice with all her baits and seeming pleasures, and yet abstain, and yet distinguish, and yet prefer that which is truly better, he is the true wayfaring[8] Christian. I cannot praise a fugitive and cloistered virtue, unexercised and unbreathed,[9] that never sallies out and sees her adversary, but slinks out of the race where that immortal garland is to be run for, not without dust and heat. Assuredly we bring not innocence into the world, we bring impurity much rather; that which purifies us is trial, and trial is by what is contrary. That virtue therefore which is but a youngling in the contemplation of evil, and knows not the utmost that vice promises to her followers, and rejects it, is but a blank virtue, not a pure; her whiteness is but an excremental[1] whiteness; which was the reason why our sage and serious poet Spenser (whom I dare be known to think a better teacher than Scotus or Aquinas), describing true temperance under the person of Guyon, brings him in with his Palmer through the Cave of Mammon and the Bower of Earthly Bliss,[2] that he might see and know, and yet abstain.

Since therefore the knowledge and survey of vice is in this world so necessary to the constituting of human virtue, and the scanning of error to the confirmation of truth, how can we more safely, and with less danger, scout into the regions of sin and falsity than by reading all manner of tractates and hearing all manner of reason? And this is the benefit which may be had of books promiscuously read.

But of the harm that may result hence, three kinds are usually reckoned. First is feared the infection that may spread; but then all human learning and controversy in religious points must remove out of the world, yea, the Bible itself; for that ofttimes relates blasphemy not nicely,[3] it describes the carnal sense of wicked men not unelegantly, it brings in holiest men passionately murmuring against providence through all the arguments of Epicurus;[4] in other great disputes it answers dubiously and darkly to the common reader.[5]

* * *

To sequester out of the world into Atlantic and Utopian politics,[6] which never can be drawn into use, will not mend our condition, but to ordain wisely as in this world of evil, in the midst whereof God hath placed us unavoidably. . . . Impunity and remissness, for certain, are the bane of a commonwealth; but here the great art lies, to discern in what the law is to bid restraint and punishment, and in what things persuasion only is to work. If every action which is good or evil in man at ripe years were to be under pittance[7] and

8. The printed text reads "wayfaring," calling up the image of the Christian pilgrim; several presentation copies correct it (by hand) to "warfaring," calling up the image of the Christian warrior. Both suit the passage.
9. Not forced by exertion to breathe hard. "Immortal garland" (next line): the prize for the winner of a race, as figure for the "crown of life" promised to those who endure temptation (James 1.12).
1. Exterior only.
2. John Duns Scotus and Thomas Aquinas, major Scholastic theologians. Guyon (following), the hero of Book 2 of the *Faerie Queene*, passes through the Cave of Mammon (symbolic of all worldly goods and honors) without his Palmer-guide, but that figure does accompany him through the Bower of Bliss.
3. Daintily.
4. Greek philosopher (342–270 B.C.E.) who taught that happiness is the greatest good, and that virtue should be practiced because it brings happiness; some of his followers equated happiness with sensual enjoyment. Milton may be thinking of the biblical book of Ecclesiastes.
5. Milton goes on to argue that a fool can find material for folly in the best books, and a wise person material for wisdom in the worst. Also, one cannot remove evil by censoring books without also censoring ballads, fiddlers, clothing, conversation, and all social life.
6. Milton alludes to More's *Utopia* and Bacon's *New Atlantis*.
7. Rationing.

prescription and compulsion, what were virtue but a name, what praise could be then due to well-doing, what gramercy[8] to be sober, just, or continent?

Many there be that complain of divine providence for suffering Adam to transgress; foolish tongues! When God gave him reason, he gave him freedom to choose, for reason is but choosing; he had been else a mere artificial Adam, such an Adam as he is in the motions.[9] We ourselves esteem not of that obedience, or love, or gift, which is of force: God therefore left him free, set before him a provoking object, ever almost in his eyes; herein consisted his merit, herein the right of his reward, the praise of his abstinence.[1] Wherefore did he create passions within us, pleasures round about us, but that these rightly tempered are the very ingredients of virtue? They are not skillful considerers of human things, who imagine to remove sin by removing the matter of sin; for, besides that it is a huge heap increasing under the very act of diminishing, though some part of it may for a time be withdrawn from some persons, it cannot from all, in such a universal thing as books are; and when this is done, yet the sin remains entire. Though ye take from a covetous man all his treasure, he has yet one jewel left: ye cannot bereave him of his covetousness. Banish all objects of lust, shut up all youth into the severest discipline that can be exercised in any hermitage, ye cannot make them chaste that came not thither so: such great care and wisdom is required to the right managing of this point.

Suppose we could expel sin by this means; look how much we thus expel of sin, so much we expel of virtue: for the matter of them both is the same; remove that, and ye remove them both alike. This justifies the high providence of God, who, though he commands us temperance, justice, continence, yet pours out before us, even to a profuseness, all desirable things, and gives us minds that can wander beyond all limit and satiety. Why should we then affect a rigor contrary to the manner of God and of nature, by abridging or scanting those means, which books freely permitted are, both to the trial of virtue and the exercise of truth? It would be better done to learn that the law must needs be frivolous which goes to restrain things uncertainly and yet equally working to good and to evil. And were I the chooser, a dram of well-doing should be preferred before many times as much the forcible hindrance of evil-doing. For God sure esteems the growth and completing of one virtuous person more than the restraint of ten vicious.

* * *

What advantage is it to be a man over it is to be a boy at school, if we have only scaped the ferula to come under the fescue of an *imprimatur*;[2] if serious and elaborate writings, as if they were no more than the theme of a grammar-lad under his pedagogue, must not be uttered without the cursory eyes of a temporizing and extemporizing licenser?[3] He who is not trusted with his own actions, his drift not being known to be evil, and standing to the hazard of law and penalty, has no great argument to think himself reputed, in the commonwealth wherein he was born, for other than a fool or a foreigner.

When a man writes to the world, he summons up all his reason and deliberation to assist him; he searches, meditates, is industrious, and likely consults

8. Reward, thanks.
9. Puppet shows.
1. Compare Milton's representation of Adam and Eve in Eden in *Paradise Lost*.
2. "Ferula": a schoolmaster's rod; "fescue": a pointer, "imprimatur": "it may be printed" (Latin), appears on the title page of books approved by the Roman Catholic censors. Milton's keen sense of the affront to scholars and scholarship, and to himself, is evident in this passage.
3. He temporizes in following the times, and acts by whim (extemporizes).

and confers with his judicious friends, after all which done he takes himself to be informed in what he writes, as well as any that writ before him. If in this the most consummate act of his fidelity and ripeness, no years, no industry, no former proof of his abilities can bring him to that state of maturity as not to be still mistrusted and suspected (unless he carry all his considerate diligence, all his midnight watchings, and expense of Palladian[4] oil, to the hasty view of an unleisured licenser, perhaps much his younger, perhaps far his inferior in judgment, perhaps one who never knew the labor of book-writing), and if he be not repulsed, or slighted, must appear in print like a puny[5] with his guardian, and his censor's hand on the back of his title to be his bail and surety that he is no idiot, or seducer; it cannot be but a dishonor and derogation to the author, to the book, to the privilege and dignity of learning. * * *

And how can a man teach with authority, which is the life of teaching, how can he be a doctor[6] in his book as he ought to be, or else had better be silent, whenas all he teaches, all he delivers, is but under the tuition, under the correction of his patriarchal[7] licenser to blot or alter what precisely accords not with the hide-bound humor which he calls his judgment? When every acute reader upon the first sight of a pedantic license, will be ready with these like words to ding the book a quoit's[8] distance from him: "I hate a pupil teacher, I endure not an instructor that comes to me under the wardship of an overseeing fist. I know nothing of the licenser, but that I have his own hand here for his arrogance; who shall warrant me his judgment?"

"The state, sir," replies the stationer,[9] but has a quick return: "The state shall be my governors, but not my critics; they may be mistaken in the choice of a licenser, as easily as this licenser may be mistaken in an author."

* * *

Well knows he who uses to consider, that our faith and knowledge thrives by exercise, as well as our limbs and complexion.[1] Truth is compared in Scripture to a streaming fountain;[2] if her waters flow not in a perpetual progression, they sicken into a muddy pool of conformity and tradition. A man may be a heretic in the truth; and if he believe things only because his pastor says so, or the Assembly[3] so determines, without knowing other reason, though his belief be true, yet the very truth he holds becomes his heresy.

* * *

Truth indeed came once into the world with her Divine Master, and was a perfect shape most glorious to look on: but when he ascended, and his apostles after him were laid asleep, then straight arose a wicked race of deceivers, who, as that story goes of the Egyptian Typhon with his conspirators, how they dealt with the good Osiris,[4] took the virgin Truth, hewed her lovely form into a thousand pieces, and scattered them to the four winds. From that time ever since, the sad friends of Truth, such as durst appear, imitating the careful

4. Pertaining to Pallas Athena, goddess of wisdom.
5. A minor, hence, young, unseasoned.
6. Teacher.
7. Taking on the role of a father; also, standing in for ecclesiastical patriarchs or prelates (like Archbishop Laud).
8. A flat disc of stone or metal, thrown as an exercise of strength or skill.
9. Printer, who was responsible for submitting books before publication to the "licenser" (censor).
1. Constitution, the proper mingling of qualities in the body.
2. In Psalm 85.11.
3. The Westminster Assembly, convened by Parliament in 1643 to reorganize the English church along Presbyterian lines.
4. Plutarch tells, in "Isis and Osiris," of Typhon's scattering the fragments of his brother Osiris and of Isis's efforts to recover them.

search that Isis made for the mangled body of Osiris, went up and down gathering up limb by limb, still as they could find them. We have not yet found them all, Lords and Commons, nor ever shall do, till her Master's second coming; he shall bring together every joint and member, and shall mold them into an immortal feature of loveliness and perfection. Suffer not these licensing prohibitions to stand at every place of opportunity, forbidding and disturbing them that continue seeking, that continue to do our obsequies[5] to the torn body of our martyred saint.

We boast our light; but if we look not wisely on the sun itself, it smites us into darkness. Who can discern those planets that are oft combust,[6] and those stars of brightest magnitude that rise and set with the sun, until the opposite motion of their orbs bring them to such a place in the firmament where they may be seen evening or morning? The light which we have gained was given us, not to be ever staring on, but by it to discover onward things more remote from our knowledge. It is not the unfrocking of a priest, the unmitering of a bishop, and the removing him from off the Presbyterian shoulders, that will make us a happy nation. No, if other things as great in the church, and in the rule of life both economical and political, be not looked into and reformed, we have looked so long upon the blaze that Zwinglius and Calvin[7] hath beaconed up to us, that we are stark blind.

There be who perpetually complain of schisms and sects, and make it such a calamity that any man dissents from their maxims. 'Tis their own pride and ignorance which causes the disturbing, who neither will hear with meekness, nor can convince; yet all must be suppressed which is not found in their syntagma.[8] They are the troublers, they are the dividers of unity, who neglect and permit not others to unite those dissevered pieces which are yet wanting to the body of Truth. To be still searching what we know not by what we know, still closing up truth to truth as we find it (for all her body is homogeneal and proportional), this is the golden rule in theology as well as in arithmetic, and makes up the best harmony in a church; not the forced and outward union of cold and neutral and inwardly divided minds.

Lords and Commons of England, consider what nation it is whereof ye are, and whereof ye are the governors: a nation not slow and dull, but of a quick, ingenious, and piercing spirit, acute to invent, subtle and sinewy to discourse, not beneath the reach of any point the highest that human capacity can soar to. Therefore the studies of learning in her deepest sciences have been so ancient and so eminent among us, that writers of good antiquity and ablest judgment have been persuaded that even the school of Pythagoras and the Persian wisdom took beginning from the old philosophy of this island.[9] And that wise and civil Roman, Julius Agricola,[1] who governed once here for Caesar, preferred the natural wits of Britain before the labored studies of the French. Nor is it for nothing that the grave and frugal Transylvanian sends out yearly from as far as the mountainous borders of Russia, and beyond the

5. Funeral or commemorative rites.
6. Burned up; in astrology, so close to the sun as not to be visible.
7. Zwingli and Calvin, famous Protestant reformers, were mainstays of the Presbyterian cause. "Economical": domestic.
8. Compilations of beliefs, creeds.
9. Some speculation existed as to whether the Pythagorean notion of the transmigration of souls might trace back to the Druids, but the notion was mostly denied.
1. The "civil" (cultured, civilized) Agricola's opinion of the British intellect is found in Tacitus's *Life of Agricola*. Transylvania (following; now Romania) was an independent Protestant country whose citizens sometimes came to England to study. "Hercynian wilderness": Roman name for a forested and mountainous region of Germany.

Hercynian wilderness, not their youth, but their staid men, to learn our language and our theologic arts.

Yet that which is above all this, the favor and the love of heaven we have great argument to think in a peculiar manner propitious and propending[2] towards us. Why else was this nation chosen before any other, that out of her, as out of Zion,[3] should be proclaimed and sounded forth the first tidings and trumpet of Reformation to all Europe? And had it not been the obstinate perverseness of our prelates against the divine and admirable spirit of Wycliffe to suppress him as a schismatic and innovator, perhaps neither the Bohemian Huss and Jerome,[4] no, nor the name of Luther or of Calvin, had been ever known: the glory of reforming all our neighbors had been completely ours. But now, as our obdurate clergy have with violence demeaned the matter, we are become hitherto the latest and the backwardest scholars of whom[5] God offered to have made us the teachers.

Now once again by all concurrence of signs, and by the general instinct of holy and devout men, as they daily and solemnly express their thoughts, God is decreeing to begin some new and great period in his church, even to the reforming of Reformation itself; what does he then but reveal himself to his servants, and as his manner is, first to his Englishmen? I say, as his manner is, first to us, though we mark not the method of his counsels, and are unworthy. Behold now this vast city: a city of refuge,[6] the mansion house of liberty, encompassed and surrounded with his protection; the shop of war hath not there more anvils and hammers waking, to fashion out the plates[7] and instruments of armed justice in defense of beleaguered truth, than there be pens and heads there, sitting by their studious lamps, musing, searching, revolving new notions and ideas wherewith to present, as with their homage and their fealty, the approaching Reformation: others as fast reading, trying all things, assenting to the force of reason and convincement.

What could a man require more from a nation so pliant and so prone to seek after knowledge? What wants there to such a towardly and pregnant[8] soil, but wise and faithful laborers, to make a knowing people, a nation of prophets,[9] of sages, and of worthies? We reckon more than five months yet to harvest; there need not be five weeks; had we but eyes to lift up, the fields are white already.[1] Where there is much desire to learn, there of necessity will be much arguing, much writing, many opinions; for opinion in good men is but knowledge in the making. Under these fantastic terrors of sect and schism we wrong the earnest and zealous thirst after knowledge and understanding which God hath stirred up in this city.

What some lament of, we rather should rejoice at, should rather praise this pious forwardness among men, to reassume the ill-deputed care of their religion into their own hands again. A little generous prudence, a little forbearance of one another, and some grain of charity might win all these diligences

2. Inclining, favorable. "Argument": reason.
3. Mount Zion, in Jerusalem, the site of the Temple.
4. John Wycliffe was a 14th-century English reformer and translator of the Bible, whose books were forbidden by Pope Alexander V in 1409. John Huss spread Wycliffe's doctrines on the Continent; he was burned at the stake in 1415, as was (the next year) his follower Jerome of Prague.
5. Of those whom. "Demeaned": conducted, degraded.
6. Numbers 35 instructs the Jews to establish "cities of refuge" where those accused of crimes will be protected from "revengers of blood."
7. Plate mail, for armor.
8. Favorable and fertile.
9. In Numbers 11.29 Moses reproaches Joshua, who complained of the presence of other prophets: "Enviest thou for my sake? Would God that all the Lord's people were prophets."
1. Milton is paraphrasing Christ's words to his disciples (John 4.35): "Lift up your eyes, and look on the fields: for they are white already to harvest."

to join, and unite into one general and brotherly search after truth; could we but forgo this prelatical tradition of crowding free consciences and Christian liberties into canons and precepts of men. I doubt not, if some great and worthy stranger should come among us, wise to discern the mold and temper of a people, and how to govern it, observing the high hopes and aims, the diligent alacrity of our extended thoughts and reasonings in the pursuance of truth and freedom, but that he would cry out as Pyrrhus did, admiring the Roman docility and courage: "If such were my Epirots, I would not despair the greatest design that could be attempted, to make a church or kingdom happy."[2] Yet these are the men cried out against for schismatics and sectaries;[3] as if, while the temple of the Lord was building, some cutting, some squaring the marble, others hewing the cedars, there should be a sort of irrational men, who could not consider there must be many schisms and many dissections[4] made in the quarry and in the timber, ere the house of God can be built. And when every stone is laid artfully together, it cannot be united into a continuity, it can but be contiguous in this world; neither can every piece of the building be of one form; nay rather the perfection consists in this, that out of many moderate varieties and brotherly dissimilitudes that are not vastly disproportional, arises the goodly and the graceful symmetry that commends the whole pile and structure. Let us therefore be more considerate builders, more wise in spiritual architecture, when great reformation is expected. For now the time seems come, wherein Moses the great prophet may sit in heaven rejoicing to see that memorable and glorious wish of his fulfilled, when not only our seventy elders, but all the Lord's people, are become prophets.[5]

* * *

Methinks I see in my mind a noble and puissant nation rousing herself like a strong man after sleep, and shaking her invincible locks:[6] methinks I see her as an eagle mewing her mighty youth, and kindling her undazzled eyes at the full midday beam;[7] purging and unscaling her long-abused sight at the fountain itself of heavenly radiance; while the whole noise of timorous and flocking birds, with those also that love the twilight, flutter about, amazed at what she means, and in their envious gabble would prognosticate[8] a year of sects and schisms.

What should ye do then, should ye suppress all this flowery crop of knowledge and new light sprung up and yet springing daily in this city? Should ye set an oligarchy of twenty engrossers[9] over it, to bring a famine upon our minds again, when we shall know nothing but what is measured to us by their bushel? Believe it, Lords and Commons, they who counsel ye to such a suppressing do as good as bid ye suppress yourselves; and I will soon show how.[1]

2. Though King Pyrrhus of Epirus beat the Roman armies at Heraclea in 280 B.C.E., he was much impressed by their discipline.
3. "Schismatics": those who cut up or divide the church; "sectaries": members of Protestant communions outside the national church.
4. Milton is playing on the literal meaning of "schism," cutting up or dividing.
5. Again alluding to Numbers 11.29, Milton equates the English assembly of clergy to set doctrine and church order (the Westminster Assembly) with the Jewish Sanhedrin of seventy elders.
6. The allusion is to Samson, whose uncut hair made him invincible, when he frustrated the first three attempts of Delilah and the Philistines to subdue him in sleep (Judges 16.6–14).
7. Eagles were thought to be able to look directly at the sun. "Mewing": molting, when the eagle sheds it feathers and thereby renews its coat.
8. Predict.
9. Engrossers, much hated in the English countryside, bought up great quantities of grain and held it for times of famine, selling it at high prices; Milton equates them with the twenty authorized printers, the stationers.
1. Milton goes on to argue that Parliament, by its own liberalizing reforms to date, has created the vigorous and inquiring minds it now seeks to suppress.

* * *

And now the time in special is by privilege to write and speak what may help to the further discussing of matters in agitation. The temple of Janus with his two controversial faces might now not unsignificantly be set open.[2] And though all the winds of doctrine were let loose to play upon the earth, so Truth be in the field, we do injuriously by licensing and prohibiting to misdoubt her strength. Let her and Falsehood grapple; who ever knew Truth put to the worse in a free and open encounter? Her[3] confuting is the best and surest suppressing. He who hears what praying there is for light and clearer knowledge to be sent down among us would think of other matters to be constituted beyond the discipline of Geneva framed and fabriced already to our hands.[4]

Yet when the new light which we beg for shines in upon us, there be who envy and oppose if it come not first in at their casements. What a collusion is this, whenas we are exhorted by the wise man to use diligence, to seek for wisdom as for hidden treasures early and late,[5] that another order shall enjoin us to know nothing but by statute. When a man hath been laboring the hardest labor in the deep mines of knowledge, hath furnished out his findings in all their equipage, drawn forth his reasons as it were a battle[6] ranged, scattered and defeated all objections in his way, calls out his adversary into the plain, offers him the advantage of wind and sun if he please, only that he may try the matter by dint of argument; for his opponents then to skulk, to lay ambushments, to keep a narrow bridge of licensing where the challenger should pass, though it be valor enough in soldiership, is but weakness and cowardice in the wars of Truth.

For who knows not that Truth is strong, next to the Almighty? She needs no policies nor stratagems nor licensings to make her victorious—those are the shifts and the defenses that error uses against her power. Give her but room, and do not bind her when she sleeps, for then she speaks not true, as the old Proteus[7] did, who spake oracles only when he was caught and bound, but then rather she turns herself into all shapes except her own, and perhaps tunes her voice according to the time, as Micaiah did before Ahab,[8] until she be adjured into her own likeness.

Yet it is not impossible that she may have more shapes than one. What else is all that rank of things indifferent, wherein Truth may be on this side or on the other without being unlike herself? What but a vain shadow else is the abolition of those ordinances, that handwriting nailed to the cross?[9] What great purchase is this Christian liberty which Paul so often boasts of? His doctrine is that he who eats or eats not, regards a day or regards it not, may do either to the Lord.[1] How many other things might be tolerated in peace and left to conscience, had we but charity, and were it not the chief stronghold of our hypocrisy to be ever judging one another? I fear yet this iron yoke of

2. Janus, as god of beginnings and endings, had two faces looking in opposite directions; a door dedicated to him in Rome was kept open in time of war, closed in time of peace.
3. I.e., Falsehood's.
4. Milton was already disenchanted with Genevan "Discipline" (Presbyterian church government) and within a year or so would be writing "New *presbyter* is but old *priest*, writ large." "Fabriced": fabricated.
5. Solomon's advice in Proverbs 8.11.
6. Line of battle. Wind and sun (below) were significant advantages in a fight with swords.
7. The sea god who could change shape at will, to avoid capture (*Odyssey* 4).
8. Micaiah, a prophet of God, tried for a time to disguise an unpleasant prophecy from King Ahab but then spoke truth when adjured to do so (1 Kings 22.10–28).
9. The locution, from Colossians 2.14, implies that the Crucifixion canceled all the rules and penalties of the Mosaic law. Paul's doctrine of Christian liberty (below) is expressed in Galatians 5 and elsewhere.
1. In the Lord's service.

outward conformity hath left a slavish print upon our necks; the ghost of a linen decency[2] yet haunts us. We stumble and are impatient at the least dividing of one visible congregation from another, though it be not in fundamentals; and through our forwardness to suppress and our backwardness to recover any enthralled piece of truth out of the grip of custom, we care not[3] to keep truth separated from truth, which is the fiercest rent and disunion of all. We do not see that while we still affect by all means a rigid and external formality, we may as soon fall again into a gross conforming stupidity, a stark and dead congealment of "wood and hay and stubble,"[4] forced and frozen together, which is more to the sudden degenerating of a church than many subdichotomies of petty schisms.

Not that I can think well of every light separation, or that all in a church is to be expected "gold and silver and precious stones." It is not possible for man to sever the wheat from the tares, the good fish from the other fry; that must be the angels' ministry at the end of mortal things.[5] Yet if all cannot be of one mind—as who looks they should be?—this doubtless is more wholesome, more prudent, and more Christian, that many be tolerated rather than all compelled. I mean not tolerated popery and open superstition, which, as it extirpates all religions and civil supremacies, so itself should be extirpate, provided first that all charitable and compassionate means be used to win and regain the weak and the misled; that also which is impious or evil absolutely, either against faith or manners,[6] no law can possibly permit that intends not to unlaw itself; but those neighboring differences or rather indifferences are what I speak of, whether in some point of doctrine or of discipline, which though they may be many yet need not interrupt "the unity of spirit," if we could but find among us the "bond of peace."[7]

In the meanwhile, if anyone would write and bring his helpful hand to the slow-moving reformation which we labor under, if truth have spoken to him before others, or but seemed at least to speak, who hath so bejesuited[8] us that we should trouble that man with asking license to do so worthy a deed? And not consider this, that if it come to prohibiting, there is not aught more likely to be prohibited than truth itself; whose first appearance to our eyes bleared and dimmed with prejudice and custom is more unsightly and unplausible than many errors, even as the person is of many a great man slight and contemptible to see to. And what do they tell us vainly of new opinions, when this very opinion of theirs, that none must be heard but whom they like, is the worst and newest opinion of all others, and is the chief cause why sects and schisms do so much abound, and true knowledge is kept at distance from us; besides yet a greater danger which is in it. For when God shakes a kingdom[9] with strong and healthful commotions to a general reforming, it is not untrue that many sectaries and false teachers are then busiest in seducing; but yet more true it is that God then raises to his own work men of rare abilities and more than common industry, not only to look back and revise what hath been

2. White bands around the necks of clergymen are made emblems of formal piety.
3. Scruple not.
4. The contrast between "wood and hay and stubble" and "gold and silver and precious stones" (next paragraph) is from 1 Corinthians 3.12.
5. In Matthew 13.24–30, 36–43, Christ in a parable tells his disciples to let the wheat and tares (weeds) grow up together till harvest time.
6. Morals.
7. The quoted phrases are from Ephesians 4.3.
8. Imposed on us Jesuit ideas (of censorship).
9. Milton alludes to Haggai 2.7: "I will shake all nations, and the desire of all nations shall come, and I will fill this house with glory, saith the Lord of hosts."

taught heretofore, but to gain further and go on some new enlightened steps in the discovery of truth.

1644

Sonnets Milton wrote twenty-four sonnets between 1630 and 1658. Five in Italian constitute a mini-Petrarchan sequence on a perhaps imaginary Italian lady. The rest, in English, are individual poems on a wide variety of topics and occasions, though not on the usual sonnet topics (love, as in the sequences of Sidney, Spenser, and Shakespeare, or religious devotion, as in that of Donne). Milton writes sometimes about personal crises (his blindness, the death of his wife), sometimes about political issues or personages (Cromwell, the persecuting Parliament), sometimes about friends and friendship (Cyriack Skinner, Lady Margaret Ley), sometimes about historical events (a threatened royalist attack on London, the massacre of Protestants in Piedmont). His tone ranges from Jonsonian urbanity to prophetic denunciation. The form of the sonnets is Petrarchan (see "Poetic Forms and Literary Terminology," in the appendices to this volume), but in the later sonnets especially (e.g., the Blindness and Piedmont sonnets) the sense runs on from line to line, overriding the expected end-stopped lines and the octave/sestet shift. There is some precedent for this in the Italian sonneteer Giovanni della Casa, but not for the powerful tension Milton creates as meaning and emotion strive within and against the formal metrics of the Petrarchan sonnet. Milton's new ways with the sonnet had a profound and acknowledged influence on the Romantic poets, especially Wordsworth and Shelley.

Sonnets

How Soon Hath Time

How soon hath Time, the subtle thief of youth,
Stol'n on his wing my three and twentieth year!
My hasting days fly on with full career,
But my late spring no bud or blossom shew'th.
Perhaps my semblance might deceive[1] the truth,
That I to manhood am arrived so near,
And inward ripeness doth much less appear,
That some more timely-happy spirits endu'th.° *endows*
Yet be it less or more, or soon or slow,
It shall be still in strictest measure even[2]
To that same lot, however mean or high,
Toward which Time leads me, and the will of Heaven;
All is, if I have grace to use it so,
As ever in my great Taskmaster's eye.[3]

1632? 1645

1. Misrepresent. "Semblance": appearance.
2. Equal, adequate. "It": Milton's inner growth. "Even / To that same lot": conformed to my appointed destiny.
3. The final lines allow for various readings. "Taskmaster" identifies God with the parable (Matthew 20.1–16) in which a vineyard keeper takes on workers throughout the day, paying the same wages to those hired at the first and at the eleventh hour.

When I Consider How My Light Is Spent[1]

When I consider how my light is spent,° *extinguished*
Ere half my days,[2] in this dark world and wide,
And that one talent which is death to hide[3]
Lodged with me useless, though my soul more bent
To serve therewith my Maker, and present
My true account, lest he returning chide;
"Doth God exact day-labor, light denied?"[4]
I fondly° ask; but Patience to prevent° *foolishly / forestall*
That murmur, soon replies, "God doth not need
Either man's work or his own gifts; who best
Bear his mild yoke, they serve him best. His state° *splendor*
Is kingly.[5] Thousands at his bidding speed
And post o'er land and ocean without rest:
They also serve who only stand and wait."

1652? 1673

On the Late Massacre in Piedmont[1]

Avenge,[2] O Lord, thy slaughtered saints, whose bones
Lie scattered on the Alpine mountains cold;
Even them who kept thy truth so pure of old
When all our fathers worshipped stocks and stones,[3]
Forget not: in thy book[4] record their groans
Who were thy sheep and in their ancient fold
Slain by the bloody Piemontese that rolled
Mother with infant down the rocks. Their moans

1. Apparently written soon after Milton lost his sight entirely in 1652.
2. Milton was forty-three in 1652; he is obviously not thinking of the biblical lifespan of seventy, but perhaps of that of his father, who died at eighty-four.
3. In the parable of the talents (Matthew 25.14–30), a crucial text for Puritans, the servants who put their master's money ("talents") to earn interest for him were praised, while the servant who buried the single talent he was given was deprived of it and cast into outer darkness. Milton puns on "literary talent." "Useless" (line 4) carries a pun on "usury," the return expected by the Master.
4. Milton alludes here to the parable of the vineyard keeper (see "How Soon Hath Time," note 3), and also to John 9.4, spoken by Jesus before curing a blind man: "I must work the works of him that sent me, while it is day: the night cometh, when no man can work."
5. The changed metaphor for God—from master who needs to profit from his workers to king—allows the inference that those who "stand and wait" may be placed nearest the throne.
1. The Waldensians (or Vaudois) were a proto-Protestant sect dating to the 12th century who lived in the valleys of northern Italy (the Piedmont) and southern France; Protestants considered them a remnant retaining apostolic purity, free of Catholic superstitions and graven images ("stocks and stones," line 4). The treaty that had allowed them freedom of worship was bypassed in 1655 when the armies of the Catholic duke of Savoy conducted a massacre, razing villages, committing unspeakable atrocities, and hurling women and children from the mountaintops. Protestant Europe was outraged, and in his capacity as Cromwell's Latin secretary Milton translated and wrote several letters about the episode. The sonnet incorporates details from such letters and the contemporary newsbooks. Here Milton transforms the sonnet into a prophetic denunciation.
2. Cf. Revelation 6.9–10: "the souls of them that were slain for the word of God . . . cried with a loud voice, saying, 'How long, O Lord, holy and true, dost thou not judge and avenge our blood . . . ?' "
3. Pagan gods of wood and stone, but with allusion to Roman Catholic "idols."
4. Cf. Revelation 20.12: "the dead were judged out of those things which were written in the books, according to their works." "Sheep" (next line) echoes Romans 8.36: "we are accounted as sheep for the slaughter."

The vales redoubled to the hills, and they
To heaven. Their martyred blood and ashes sow
O'er all th' Italian fields, where still doth sway
The triple tyrant:[5] that from these may grow
A hundredfold, who having learnt thy way
Early may fly the Babylonian woe.[6]

1655 1673

Methought I Saw My Late Espousèd Saint[1]

Methought I saw my late espousèd saint
Brought to me like Alcestis[2] from the grave,
Whom Jove's great son to her glad husband gave,
Rescued from death by force though pale and faint.
Mine, as whom[3] washed from spot of childbed taint,
Purification in the old law did save,[4]
And such, as yet once more I trust to have
Full sight of her in heaven without restraint,
Came vested all in white, pure as her mind.
Her face was veiled, yet to my fancied sight[5]
Love, sweetness, goodness, in her person shined
So clear, as in no face with more delight.
But O, as to embrace me she inclined,
I waked, she fled, and day brought back my night.

1658 1673

Paradise Lost

The setting of Milton's great epic encompasses Heaven, Hell, primordial Chaos, and the planet earth. It features battles among immortal spirits, voyages through space, and lakes of fire. Yet its protagonists are a married couple living in a garden, and its climax consists in the eating of a piece of fruit. *Paradise Lost* is ultimately about the human condition, the Fall that caused "all our woe," and the promise and means of restoration. It is also about knowing and choosing, about free will. In the opening passages of Books 1, 3, 7, and 9, Milton highlights the choices and difficulties he faced in creating his poem. His central characters—Satan, Beelzebub, Abdiel, Adam, and Eve—are confronted with hard choices under the pressure of powerful desires and sometimes devious temptations. Milton's readers, too, are

5. The pope, wearing his tiara with three crowns. The passage alludes to Tertullian's maxim that "the blood of the martyrs is the seed of the church"; also to the parable of the sower (Matthew 13.3), some of whose seed brought forth fruit "an hundredfold" (see next line); and also to Cadmus, who sowed dragon's teeth that sprang forth armed men.
6. Protestants often identified the Roman Church with the whore of Babylon (Revelation 17–18).
1. There is some debate as to whether this poem refers to Milton's first wife, Mary Powell, who died in May 1652, three days after giving birth to her third daughter, or his second wife, Katherine Woodcock, who died in February 1658, after giving birth (in October 1657) to a daughter. The text can support either, but the latter seems more likely. The sonnet is couched as a dream vision.
2. In Euripides' *Alcestis*, Alcestis, wife of Admetus, is rescued from the underworld by Hercules ("Jove's great son," next line) and restored, veiled, to Admetus; he is overjoyed when he lifts the veil, but she must remain silent until she is ritually cleansed.
3. As one whom.
4. The Mosaic Law (Leviticus 12.2–8) prescribed periods for the purification of women after childbirth (eighty days for a daughter).
5. She is veiled like Alcestis, and Milton's sight of her is only "fancied"; he never saw the face of his second wife, Katherine, because of his blindness.

continually challenged to choose and to reconsider their most basic assumptions about freedom, heroism, work, pleasure, language, nature, and love. The great themes of *Paradise Lost* are intimately linked to the political questions at stake in the English Revolution and the Restoration, but the connection is by no means simple or straightforward. This is a poem in which Satan leads a revolution against an absolute monarch and in which questions of tyranny, servitude, and liberty are debated in a parliament in Hell. Milton's readers are hereby challenged to rethink these topics and, like Abdiel debating with Satan in Books 5 and 6, to make crucial distinctions between God as monarch and earthly kings.

In Milton's time, the conventions of epic poetry followed a familiar recipe. The action was to begin in medias res (in the middle of things), following the poet's statement of his theme and invocation of his Muse. The reader could expect grand battles and love affairs, supernatural intervention, a descent into the underworld, catalogues of warriors, and epic similes. Milton had absorbed the epic tradition in its entirety, and his poem abounds with echoes of Homer and Virgil, the fifteenth-century Italians Tasso and Ariosto, and the English Spenser. But in *Paradise Lost* he at once heightens epic conventions and values and utterly transforms them. This is the epic to end all epics. Milton gives us the first and greatest of all wars (between God and Satan) and the first and greatest of love affairs (between Adam and Eve). His theme is the destiny of the entire human race, caught up in the temptation and Fall of our first "grand parents."

Milton challenges his readers in *Paradise Lost*, at once fulfilling and defying all of our expectations. Nothing in the epic tradition or in biblical interpretation can prepare us for the Satan who hurtles into view in Book 1, with his awesome energy and defiance, incredible fortitude, and, above all, magnificent rhetoric. For some readers, including Blake and Shelley, Satan is the true hero of the poem. But Milton is engaged in a radical reevaluation of epic values, and Satan's version of heroism must be contrasted with those of the loyal Abdiel and the Son of God. Moreover, the poem's truly epic action takes place not on the battlefield but in the moral and domestic arena. Milton's Adam and Eve are not conventional epic heroes, but neither are they the conventional Adam and Eve. Their state of innocence is not childlike, tranquil, and free of sexual desire. Instead, the first couple enjoy sex, experience tension and passion, make mistakes of judgment, and grow in knowledge. Their task is to prune what is unruly in their own natures as they prune the vegetation in their garden, for both have the capacity to grow wild. Their relationship exhibits gender hierarchy, but Milton's early readers may have been surprised by the fullness and complexity of Eve's character and the centrality of her role, not only in the Fall but in the promised restoration.

We expect in epics a grand style, and Milton's style engulfs us from the outset with its energy and power, as those rushing, enjambed, blank-verse lines propel us along with only a few pauses for line endings or grammar (there is only one full stop in the first twenty-six lines). The elevated diction and complex syntax, the sonorities and patternings make a magnificent music. But that music is an entire orchestra of tones, including the high political rhetoric of Satan in Books 1 and 2, the evocative sensuousness of the descriptions of Eden, the delicacy of Eve's love lyric to Adam in Book 4, the relatively plain speech of God in Book 3, and the speech rhythms of Adam and Eve's marital quarrel in Book 9. This majestic achievement depends on the poet's rejection of heroic couplets, the norm for epic and tragedy in the Restoration, vigorously defended by Dryden but denounced by Milton in his note on "The Verse." The choice of verse form was, like so many other things in Milton's life, in part a question of politics. Milton's terms associate the "troublesome and modern bondage of rhyming" with Restoration monarchy and the repression of dissidents and present his use of unrhymed blank verse as a recovery of "ancient liberty."

The first edition (1667) presented *Paradise Lost* in ten books; the second (1674) recast it into twelve books, after the Virgilian model, splitting the original Books 7 and 10.

PARADISE LOST

SECOND EDITION (1674)

The Verse

The measure is English heroic verse without rhyme, as that of Homer in Greek and of Virgil in Latin; rhyme being no necessary adjunct or true ornament of poem or good verse, in longer works especially, but the invention of a barbarous age, to set off wretched matter[1] and lame meter; graced indeed since by the use of some famous modern poets,[2] carried away by custom, but much to their own vexation, hindrance, and constraint to express many things otherwise, and for the most part worse than else they would have expressed them. Not without cause therefore some both Italian[3] and Spanish poets of prime note have rejected rhyme both in longer and shorter works, as have also long since our best English tragedies, as a thing of itself, to all judicious ears, trivial and of no true musical delight; which consists only in apt numbers,[4] fit quantity of syllables, and the sense variously drawn out from one verse into another, not in the jingling sound of like endings, a fault avoided by the learned ancients both in poetry and all good oratory. This neglect then of rhyme so little is to be taken for a defect, though it may seem so perhaps to vulgar readers, that it rather is to be esteemed an example set, the first in English, of ancient liberty recovered to heroic poem from the troublesome and modern bondage of rhyming.

Book 1

The Argument[1]

This first book proposes, first in brief, the whole subject, man's disobedience, and the loss thereupon of Paradise wherein he was placed: then touches the prime cause of his fall, the Serpent, or rather Satan in the Serpent; who revolting from God, and drawing to his side many legions of angels, was by the command of God driven out of Heaven with all his crew into the great deep. Which action passed over, the poem hastes into the midst of things,[2] presenting Satan with his angels now fallen into Hell, described here, not in the center[3] (for Heaven and Earth may be supposed as yet not made, certainly not yet accursed) but in a place of utter darkness, fitliest called Chaos: here Satan with his angels lying on the burning lake, thunderstruck and astonished, after a certain space recovers, as from confusion, calls up him who next in order and dignity lay by him; they confer of their miserable fall. Satan awakens all his legions, who lay till then in the same manner confounded; they rise, their numbers, array of battle, their chief leaders named, according to the idols known afterwards in Canaan and the countries adjoining. To these Satan

1. Perhaps the bawdy content of the Latin songs composed by goliardic poets of the Middle Ages; they learned rhyme from medieval hymns.
2. Notably, Dryden. See his *Essay of Dramatic Poesy*, p. 914.
3. Trissino and Tasso.
4. Appropriate rhythm.
1. *Paradise Lost* appeared originally without any sort of prose aid to the reader, but the printer asked Milton for some "Arguments," or summary explanations of the action in the various books, and these were prefixed to later issues of the poem. We reprint the "Argument" for the first book.
2. According to Horace, the epic poet should begin, "in medias res."
3. I.e., of the earth.

directs his speech, comforts them with hope yet of regaining Heaven, but tells them lastly of a new world and new kind of creature to be created, according to an ancient prophecy or report in Heaven; for that angels were long before this visible creation, was the opinion of many ancient Fathers.[4] To find out the truth of this prophecy, and what to determine[5] thereon he refers to a full council. What his associates thence attempt. Pandemonium the palace of Satan rises, suddenly built out of the deep: the infernal peers there sit in council.

Of man's first disobedience, and the fruit[1]
Of that forbidden tree, whose mortal° taste *deadly*
Brought death into the world, and all our woe,
With loss of Eden, till one greater Man[2]
Restore us, and regain the blissful seat,
Sing Heav'nly Muse,[3] that on the secret top
Of Oreb, or of Sinai, didst inspire
That shepherd, who first taught the chosen seed,
In the beginning how the heav'ns and earth
Rose out of Chaos: or if Sion hill[4]
Delight thee more, and Siloa's brook that flowed
Fast by the oracle of God; I thence
Invoke thy aid to my advent'rous song,
That with no middle flight intends to soar
Above th' Aonian mount,[5] while it pursues
Things unattempted yet in prose or rhyme.[6]
And chiefly thou O Spirit,[7] that dost prefer
Before all temples th' upright heart and pure,
Instruct me, for thou know'st; thou from the first
Wast present, and with mighty wings outspread
Dove-like sat'st brooding[8] on the vast abyss
And mad'st it pregnant: what in me is dark
Illumine, what is low raise and support;
That to the height of this great argument° *subject, theme*
I may assert Eternal Providence,
And justify° the ways of God to men. *show the justice of*
  Say first, for Heav'n hides nothing from thy view
Nor the deep tract of Hell, say first what cause[9]
Moved our grand parents in that happy state,
Favored of Heav'n so highly, to fall off

4. Church Fathers, the Christian writers of the first centuries.
5. I.e., what action to take.
1. Eve's apple, and all the consequences of eating it. This first proem (lines 1–26) combines the epic statement of theme and invocation.
2. Christ, the second Adam.
3. In Greek mythology, Urania, Muse of astronomy; here, however, by the references to Oreb and Sinai (following), identified with the Muse who inspired Moses ("that shepherd") to write Genesis and the other four books of the Pentateuch for the instruction of the Jews ("the chosen seed").
4. Mount Zion: the site of Solomon's Temple. "Siloa's brook" (next line): a spring near the Temple where Christ cured a blind man.
5. Helicon, home of the classical Muses. Milton will attempt to surpass Homer and Virgil.
6. Paradoxically, Milton vaunts his originality in a translated line from Ariosto's *Orlando Furioso* 1.2. The allusion also challenges the romantic epic in Ariosto's tradition.
7. Here identified with God's creating power.
8. A composite of phrases and ideas from Genesis 1.2 ("And the earth was without form, and void, and darkness was upon the face of the deep. And the Spirit of God moved upon the face of the waters"). Only a small number of Milton's many allusions to the Bible (in many versions) can be indicated in the notes. Milton's brooding dove image comes from the Latin (Tremellius) Bible version, *incubabat*, "incubated."
9. An opening question like this is an epic convention.

From their Creator, and transgress his will
For° one restraint, lords of the world besides?° *because of / otherwise*
Who first seduced them to that foul revolt?
Th' infernal Serpent; he it was, whose guile
Stirred up with envy and revenge, deceived
The mother of mankind, what time° his pride *when*
Had cast him out from Heav'n, with all his host
Of rebel angels, by whose aid aspiring
To set himself in glory above his peers,° *equals*
He trusted to have equaled the Most High,
If he opposed; and with ambitious aim
Against the throne and monarchy of God
Raised impious war in Heav'n and battle proud
With vain attempt. Him the Almighty Power
Hurled headlong flaming from th' ethereal sky
With hideous ruin and combustion down
To bottomless perdition, there to dwell
In adamantine[1] chains and penal fire,
Who durst defy th' Omnipotent to arms.
Nine times the space[2] that measures day and night
To mortal men, he with his horrid crew
Lay vanquished, rolling in the fiery gulf
Confounded though immortal: but his doom
Reserved him to more wrath; for now the thought
Both of lost happiness and lasting pain
Torments him; round he throws his baleful° eyes *malignant*
That witnessed huge affliction and dismay
Mixed with obdúrate pride and steadfast hate:
At once as far as angels' ken° he views *range of sight*
The dismal situation waste and wild,
A dungeon horrible, on all sides round
As one great furnace flamed, yet from those flames
No light, but rather darkness visible
Served only to discover sights of woe,
Regions of sorrow, doleful shades, where peace
And rest can never dwell, hope never comes
That comes to all;[3] but torture without end
Still urges,° and a fiery deluge, fed *always provokes*
With ever-burning sulphur unconsumed:
Such place Eternal Justice had prepared
For those rebellious, here their prison ordained
In utter darkness, and their portion set
As far removed from God and light of Heav'n
As from the center thrice to th' utmost pole.[4]
O how unlike the place from whence they fell!
There the companions of his fall, o'erwhelmed
With floods and whirlwinds of tempestuous fire,

1. A mythical substance of great hardness.
2. Extent of time.
3. The phrase alludes to Dante ("All hope abandon, ye who enter here").
4. Milton makes use of various images of the cosmos in *Paradise Lost*: (1) the earth is the center of the (Ptolemaic) cosmos of ten concentric spheres; (2) the earth and the whole cosmos are an appendage hanging from Heaven by a golden chain; (3) the cosmos seems Copernican from the angels' perspective (see Book 8). Here, the fall from Heaven to Hell is described as thrice as far as the distance from the center (earth) to the outermost sphere.

He soon discerns, and welt'ring° by his side *rolling in the waves*
One next himself in power, and next in crime,
Long after known in Palestine, and named
Beëlzebub.[5] To whom th' Arch-Enemy,
And thence in Heav'n called Satan,[6] with bold words
Breaking the horrid silence thus began.
"If thou beest he; but O how fall'n![7] how changed
From him, who in the happy realms of light
Clothed with transcendent brightness didst outshine
Myriads though bright: if he whom mutual league,
United thoughts and counsels, equal hope
And hazard in the glorious enterprise,
Joined with me once, now misery hath joined
In equal ruin: into what pit thou seest
From what height fall'n, so much the stronger proved
He with his thunder:° and till then who knew *thunderbolt*
The force of those dire arms? Yet not for those,
Nor what the potent victor in his rage
Can else inflict, do I repent or change,
Though changed in outward luster, that fixed mind
And high disdain, from sense of injured merit,
That with the mightiest raised me to contend,
And to the fierce contention brought along
Innumerable force of spirits armed
That durst dislike his reign, and me preferring,
His utmost power with adverse power opposed
In dubious° battle on the plains of Heav'n, *of uncertain outcome*
And shook his throne. What though the field be lost?
All is not lost; the unconquerable will,
And study° of revenge, immortal hate, *intense consideration*
And courage never to submit or yield:
And what is else not to be overcome?[8]
That glory never shall his wrath or might
Extort from me. To bow and sue for grace
With suppliant knee, and deify his power
Who from the terror of this arm so late
Doubted° his empire, that were low indeed, *feared for*
That were an ignominy and shame beneath
This downfall; since by fate the strength of gods[9]
And this empyreal substance cannot fail,° *cease to exist*
Since through experience of this great event
In arms not worse, in foresight much advanced,
We may with more successful hope resolve
To wage by force or guile eternal war
Irreconcilable, to our grand foe,

5. A Phoenician deity, or Baal (the name means "Lord of Flies"). He is called the prince of devils in Matthew 12.24. As with the other fallen angels, his angelic name has been obliterated, and he is now called by the name he will bear as a pagan deity. That literary strategy evokes all the evil associations attaching to those names in human history.
6. In Hebrew the name means "adversary."
7. Alludes to Isaiah 14.12: "How art thou fallen from heaven, O Lucifer, Son of the morning."
8. I.e., what else does it mean not to be overcome?
9. A term commonly used in the poem for angels. But to Satan and his followers it means more, as Satan claims the position of a god, subject to fate but nothing else. Their substance is "empyreal" (next line), of the empyrean.

The Middle Ages (to ca. 1485)

Scepter, from the Sutton Hoo Treasure, ca. 625 C.E.

Discovered in 1939, among other items (jewelry, pottery, fragments of a helmet and shield), in a funeral ship buried in a mound near the coast of East Anglia, the scepter—probably a symbol of royal authority—consists of a massive ceremonial whetstone carved with faces and attached to a ring of twisted bronze wires mounted by an intricately carved stag. The treasure suggests the one laden on Scyld's funeral ship in *Beowulf* (lines 26–52; pp. 31–32) and the material world imagined throughout the poem; the scepter evokes the "gold standard . . . / high above [the king's] head." THE BRITISH MUSEUM, LONDON, UK/BRIDGEMAN ART LIBRARY.

Annunciation to the Shepherds; the Magi before Herod, ca. 1150

Stories of the Nativity figure prominently both in the mystery plays and in medieval Psalters such as this one. The Latin text on the angels' scrolls is from Luke 2.11, "Natus est nobis hodie salvator qui est Christus Dominus in civitate David" (Unto us is born in the city of David a savior who is Christ the Lord). Herod's scroll gives his instructions to the Magi from Matthew 2.8, "ite et interrogate diligenter de puero" (go and inquire diligently about the child). The caption above each image is in French. THE BRITISH LIBRARY, COTTON NERO C. IV, FOLIO 11.

Noah urging his wife to board the ark, ca. 1290

Noah's trouble getting his wife to board the ark was a popular subject in medieval drama and art (See Chaucer, *The Miller's Tale,* lines 430–35; p. 200). In this illustration from a Psalter, Noah admonishes his wife with his left hand and grabs her wrist with the right, urging her to come aboard. Concealed, riding piggyback on the wife, a winged devil comes along as a stowaway. Below, he exits through the hull among drowned bodies on the seafloor. Other manuscripts show the serpent plugging the hole with his tail. THE PIERPONT MORGAN LIBRARY/ART RESOURCE, NY.

Plowing, the Luttrell Psalter, ca. 1330

The Psalter made for Sir Geoffrey Luttrell is sumptuously illustrated with idealized depictions of family, servants, workers, animals, and their activities (plowing, sowing, harvesting, feasting, playing) on the lord's estate; it is also elaborately decorated with foliage and grotesques. The Plowman here is a symbolic figure of order like Chaucer's Plowman (p. 183) and Langland's Piers Plowman (p. 271). The image echoes line 6 of the Psalm above, "Si dicebam motus est pes meus, misericordia tua, domine, adiuvabat me" (If I said: My foot is moved: thy mercy, Lord, helped me); "pes" (foot) anticipates the plow foot that moves the soil. The British Library, Folio 170r from the Luttrell Psalter, MS Additional 42130.

The Wilton Diptych, Flemish school, 1395–96

Richard II commissioned this double-panel painting, both pious and political, not long before his deposition. In it he is portrayed as a boy, perhaps ten years old, the age at which he became king. Two English kings, St. Edmund and St. Edward "the Confessor," and John the Baptist, Richard's patron saint, present the young king to the Virgin and Child, who are surrounded by angels. The Christ Child blesses the red-cross standard of St. George (the patron saint of England), about to be given into the kneeling king's open hands. Richard's robe and the angels' sleeves display his personal emblem, a white hart (punning on *richehart*). NATIONAL GALLERY, LONDON, GREAT BRITAIN/ART RESOURCE, NY.

The Crucifixion, Lapworth Missal, 1398

This late medieval manuscript illumination typically portrays the humanity of Christ: frail, eyes closed, head inclining on his shoulder. At the sides stand the Virgin mother, who swoons in the arms of Mary Magdalene, and St. John the evangelist. The skull signifies Golgotha (place of skulls), the site of the Crucifixion. According to medieval legend, the tree of knowledge had stood on the same site and Adam was buried there: thus the skull is that of Adam, whose original sin is being redeemed by the blood that the angels are collecting. The sun and moon symbolize the New and Old Testaments: as the sun illuminates the moon, the light of the New Testament reveals the hidden truths of the Old. Symbols of the four evangelists appear in the corners of the intricately decorated frame. CORPUS CHRISTI COLLEGE, UNIVERSITY OF OXFORD, MS 394.

Portrait of Chaucer, ca. 1411

In his poem *The Regiment of Princes*, Hoccleve, a younger disciple of Chaucer, memorializes "My maistir Chaucer, flour of eloquence, / Mirour of fructuous entendement, / O universel fadir in science!" One manuscript preserves a copy of a small portrait that Hoccleve placed in the margin so "That they that han of him lost thought and mynde / By this peynture may ageyn him fynde." Chaucer holds a rosary in his left hand; attached to his gown, a penknife (formerly used for making and mending quill pens) or pen case functions as a symbol of authorship. THE BRITISH LIBRARY, MS HARLEY 4866, FOLIO 88.

Manuscript illumination of pilgrims leaving Canterbury, ca. 1420

Chaucer's pilgrims never get to Canterbury, but they do in the prologue to John Lydgate's *The Siege of Thebes*. In the prologue, Lydgate, a monk of Bury St. Edmund's and an enthusiastic follower of Chaucer, tells how on his own pilgrimage to Canterbury he encounters Chaucer's pilgrims. The Host invites the monk to join the company on their return journey and calls on him to tell the first tale. Lydgate is the middle figure in a monk's cowl, costumed more soberly than Chaucer's Monk (pp. 174–75). The cathedral and walls of Canterbury appear in the background. THE BRITISH LIBRARY, MS ROYAL 18 D II, FOLIO 148.

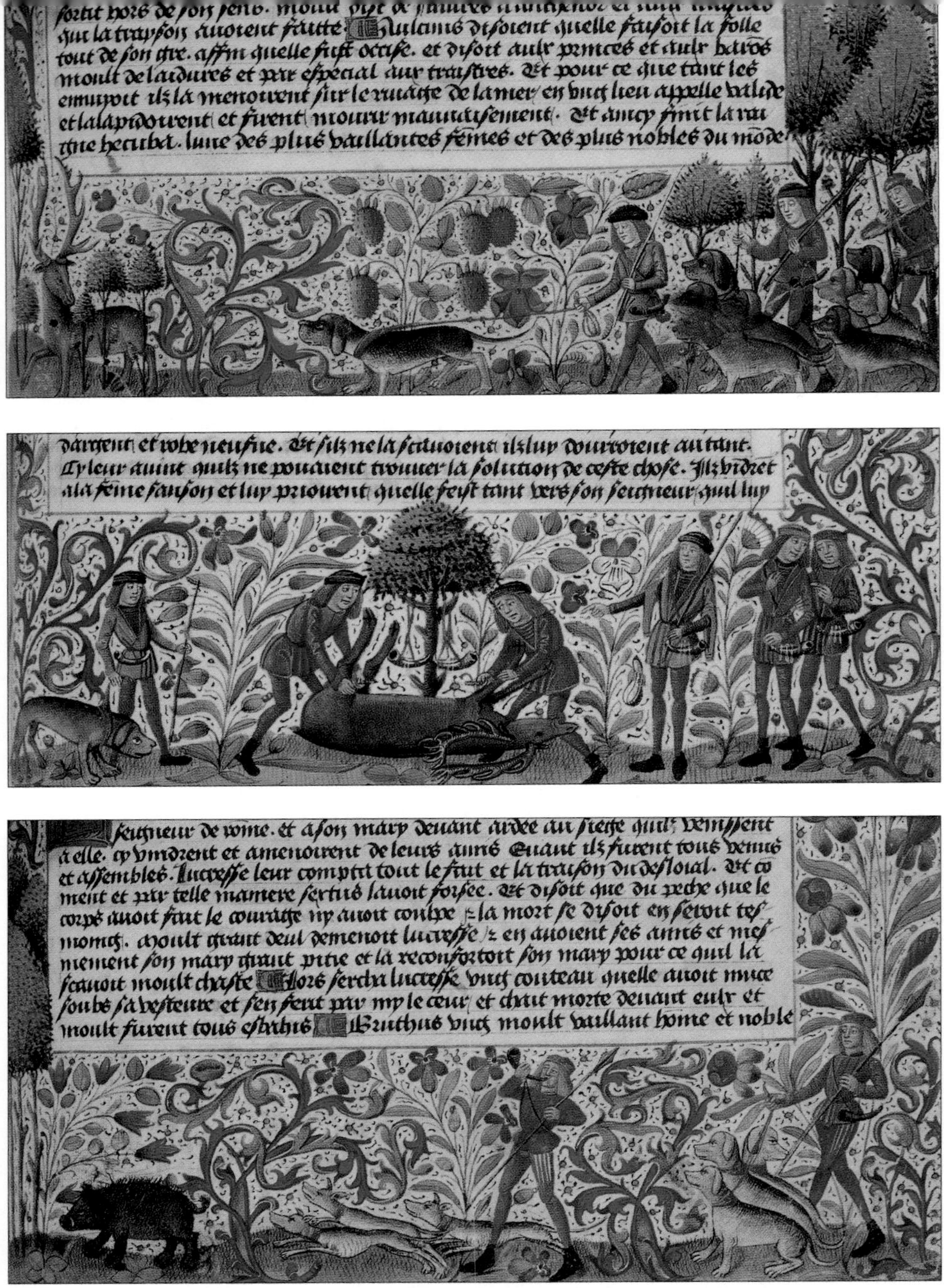

Three hunting scenes, *Le Mireur du Monde,* French manuscript, ca. 1475

The medieval nobility regarded the hunt as both a sport and an art—a test of the skill and endurance of men, dogs, and quarry. These scenes of hunters stalking the deer, breaking up the carcass, and pursuing the boar correspond to the *Gawain* poet's elaborate descriptions of the first two hunts (pp. 137ff., 143ff.). The stylized rhetoric describing the hunts both parallels and contrasts with the stylized exchanges between Gawain and the lady in the interspersed bedroom scenes where she is the hunter and he the quarry. Bodleian Library, University of Oxford, MS Douce 338, folio 60, 56, 78.

The Sixteenth Century (1485–1603)

St. George and the Dragon (London version), Paolo Uccello, ca. 1455–60

A depiction by the Florentine artist Uccello of the legend that was to inspire Edmund Spenser in Book I of *The Faerie Queene* (p. 370). Already held on a leash by the elegant lady—as if the struggle's outcome were not in doubt—the dragon submits to the knight's lance (thrust through the nose in a gesture that better recalls the domestication of cattle than the thwarting of an enemy). The desolate cave is strangely conjoined with the formal garden and the lady's elegant court dress: the story is imagined as located at once in the wilderness and at the very center of civilization. NATIONAL GALLERY, LONDON, GREAT BRITAIN/ART RESOURCE, NY.

Thomas More, Hans Holbein, 1527

Painted on the eve of More's great conflict with Henry VIII over the validity of the king's marriage to Catherine of Aragon, Holbein's portrait emphasizes both the chancellor's importance and his strength of character. More wears the heavy gold chain and rich dress of high office, which he had satirized a decade earlier in *Utopia*. In all probability, if early biographies of More can be believed, he also wears a hair shirt under the velvet and fur, a hidden, painful reminder of the vulnerable flesh that he secretly mortified. COPYRIGHT THE FRICK COLLECTION, NEW YORK.

Edward VI and the Pope: An Allegory of the Reformation, English school, ca. 1568–71

The dying Henry VIII hands over the mandate for church reform to his young son and heir, Prince Edward. This is a polemical attempt to depict the religious revolution that had a deep impact on English society and literature. The open book, proclaiming the Protestant emphasis on the Word of God in vernacular translation, crushes the pope and the taglines of Catholic corruption that surround him. The Council of Regency (appointed to guide the king, who was only nine when he ascended the throne) is in attendance; to the left, two monks flee the pope's downfall. In the upper right, a painting (or view from the window?) heralds the collapse of the Old Church and the breaking of its "idols." Several places in the painting are intended for inscriptions, but for unknown reasons these were never completed. NATIONAL PORTRAIT GALLERY, LONDON, UK/BRIDGEMAN ART LIBRARY.

The Wife and Daughter of a Chief,
John White, 1585

Accompanying Thomas Hariot's *Brief and True Report of the New-found Land of Virginia,* John White's watercolors chronicle the most striking images of Algonkian life as seen by the English voyagers. Here, a young girl "of the age of 8 or 10 yeares" carries a European doll, dressed in full Elizabethan costume, that she has clearly been given as a gift by the strange visitors. The presentation of small gifts was a regular part of English practice, frequently alternating with displays of murderous violence. White's drawing manages to convey both the exoticism and the dignity that Hariot and others perceived in the American natives. THE BRITISH MUSEUM.

Portrait of a Melancholy Young Man, Isaac Oliver; ca. 1590–95

Equally fashionable in attitude and dress, Oliver's young man displays the fascination of the English elite with the "melancholy humour." In addition to the sad expression, the black clothes and crossed arms are conventional markers of melancholy. Men in love, like Sidney's Astrophil (p. 451) and Duke Orsino in *Twelfth Night* (p. 510), found it particularly glamorous to parade their pensive dispositions. The romance of this "disease" figures in the couple just walking into the labyrinth-garden on the right. THE ROYAL COLLECTION © 2003, HER MAJESTY QUEEN ELIZABETH II.

Captain Thomas Lee, Marcus Gheeraerts the Younger, 1594

Restless, ambitious Thomas Lee was executed in 1601 for participating in the rebellion against the queen led by the earl of Essex, but in 1594 he was in the midst of his bid for the position of chief negotiator between Ireland and the English Crown. His appearance refers both to his military service in Ireland and to his status at home: Lee sports the bare legs and open shirt of a "kerne," or Irish footsoldier, along with the rich brocade and armor of a wealthy English nobleman. Lee, whose hand had been injured in a skirmish, wishes himself compared with the Roman Gaius Mucius Scaevola, who demonstrated to the enemy Etruscans his resolution and indifference to pain by thrusting his right hand into a fire. Scaevola so impressed the Etruscans that their leader, Porsena, sued for peace. Painted in the tree to Lee's right is a quotation from Livy attributed to Scaevola: "Both to act and to suffer with fortitude is a Roman's part" (trans. Karen Hearn, ed. *Dynasties*). TATE GALLERY, LONDON/ART RESOURCE, NY.

The Life and Death of Sir Henry Unton, anonymous, ca. 1597

A masque of musicians and dancers performs for a dinner party of Unton's friends. Theatrical life in this period, which often included music and dancing, was not restricted to the playhouse; it extended into other social settings, such as this one. Theater here is depicted as incidental entertainment: some guests turn their backs on the pageant; the size of the actors is considerably smaller than that of their patrons, an index of relative social importance. By courtesy of the National Portrait Gallery, London.

The "Chandos Portrait" of William Shakespeare, anonymous, date unknown

The formal portrait of the playwright that appears in the First Folio edition of his works depicts him stiffly posed in a brocade jacket and a heavily starched collar. Here, in a portrait named after its owner, the duke of Chandos, Shakespeare is presented less formally and more as his friends and colleagues may have known him. The artist is unknown, but some speculate that it may have been Shakespeare's fellow actor Richard Burbage. By courtesy of the National Portrait Gallery, London.

A Young Man, Nicholas Hilliard, ca. 1600

This tiny painting from a playing card approximately two inches square represents the "other side" of Elizabethan love poetry: passion replaces languor. The image of the lover tormented by the "fire" of his mistress's eyes or the hellish inner torment of desire was a common one. Though Sidney's Astrophil lives "in blackest winter night," he feels "the flames of hottest summer day," while even disillusioned lovers in Shakespeare's sonnets do not know how "To shun the heaven that leads men to this hell" (p. 507). The locket held by the young man presumably contains another miniature: a portrait of the beloved. VICTORIA & ALBERT MUSEUM, LONDON/ART RESOURCE, NY.

Elizabeth I in Procession, attributed to Robert Peake, ca. 1600

Carried on a litter like an image of the Virgin in the religious processions of previous centuries, the gorgeously arrayed Queen Elizabeth is shown here as a time-defying icon of purity and power. When the painting was executed, the queen was sixty-seven years old. Until the end of her life she continued her custom of going on "Progresses" through the realm: surrounded by her courtiers and ladies in waiting, she would venture forth to show herself to her people, many of whom nearly bankrupted themselves to entertain her in style. THE STAPLETON COLLECTION/BRIDGEMAN ART LIBRARY.

Henry Wriothesley, Third Earl of Southampton, John de Critz, 1603

Henry Wriothesley, the third earl of Southampton, was nearly executed for his part in the rebellion against Queen Elizabeth led by his friend the earl of Essex in 1601. Though he was eventually pardoned, Southampton was imprisoned for two years in the Tower of London, where he is here depicted along with his favorite cat. Tradition has it that the cat found its way to him in prison and reached him by coming down the chimney. An early patron of Shakespeare, the wealthy earl may be the "Mr. W. H." (his initials reversed) to whom the first edition of the sonnets is dedicated (p. 497). On the eve of the Essex rebellion, Southampton seems to have instigated a performance of *Richard II* by Shakespeare's company to put the people of London in mind of deposition. The painting was clearly commissioned after his release, the date of which is painted on the tablet, along with the proud inscription "In Vinculis / Invictus" (Though in chains, unconquered). PRIVATE COLLECTION/BRIDGEMAN ART LIBRARY.

The Early Seventeenth Century (1603–1660)

The Expulsion from Paradise, Masaccio, ca. 1427–28

This striking fresco shows an agonized Adam and Eve driven from Eden by a sword-wielding angel. Adam is so overcome he buries his face in his hands; Eve's face is a mask of despair. They do not touch: each seems imprisoned in his or her own pain. Milton's representation of the expulsion at the end of Book 12 of *Paradise Lost* is very different, and the comparison is instructive (see pp. 848ff.). SCALA/ART RESOURCE, NY.

The Three Graces (detail), *The Primavera,* Sandro Botticelli, ca. 1481

The Graces are a prominent allusive feature of seventeenth-century poetry and masques. At times they carry the allegorical significance suggested in Botticelli's portrayal of them as extensions of Venus, goddess of love and beauty, and as manifestations of the beauty, joy, and freshness of spring. Milton's "L'Allegro" (p. 697) is couched as a literary hymn honoring Euphrosyne, the Grace who signifies youthful mirth; her sisters are Aglaia, splendor, and Thalia, abundance or pleasure. Their linked hands and postures are said to symbolize the giving and receiving of joy, bounty, and pleasure. Erich Lessing/Art Resource, NY.

Sacred and Profane Love, Titian, ca. 1515

This image might almost serve as an emblem for the two kinds of love celebrated and often contrasted in seventeenth-century verse. In Titian's Neoplatonic program, the nude figure bearing the torch is the celestial Venus, the principle of universal and eternal beauty and love; the clothed figure is the earthly Venus, who creates the perishable images of beauty in humans, flowers and trees, gold and gems, and works of art. Cupid is placed between them but somewhat closer to the terrestrial Venus. SCALA/ART RESOURCE, NY.

God Creating the Animals, Tintoretto, 1550–52

A remarkable rendering of the scene, with God the Father depicted as an immense figure, exuding power and energy, actively calling forth many varieties of animals. The conception invites comparison with Milton's rendering of the Genesis creation story in *Paradise Lost,* Book 7 (p. 801). CAMARAPHOTO/ART RESOURCE, NY.

John Donne, anonymous, ca. 1595

This portrait presents Donne in the guise of a melancholy lover fond of self-display; the signs are his broad-brimmed black hat, soulful eyes, sensual lips, delicate hands, and untied but expensive lace collar. Parts of Donne's *Songs and Sonnets* (pp. 603 ff.) date from this period. Melancholy, supposedly caused by an excess of black bile and often associated with the scholarly and artistic temperament, was identified in Robert Burton's massive and very popular *Anatomy of Melancholy* as a well-nigh universal attribute of the period. It is the temperament of many literary characters, among them Hamlet, Duke Orsino (in *Twelfth Night,* p. 510), Jacques in *As You Like It,* and Milton's Il Penseroso (p. 1801). PRIVATE COLLECTION/ BRIDGEMAN ART LIBRARY.

Lady Sidney and Six of Her Children, Marcus Gheeraerts the Younger, ca. 1596

This portrait of Barbara (Gamage) Sidney, wife of Sir Robert Sidney of Penshurst, provides an insight into domestic relations in the period, as well as an illuminating comment on Ben Jonson's poem "To Penshurst" (p. 644). Robert Sidney (brother of Sir Philip Sidney) is absent, serving as governor of the English stronghold in Flushing. Lady Sidney is portrayed as a fruitful, fostering mother. Her hands rest on her two sons—both still in skirts, though the heir wears a sword; the four daughters are arranged in two pairs, the elder of each pair imitating her mother's nurturing gesture. The eldest daughter will become Lady Mary Wroth, author of *Urania* and the sonnet sequence *Pamphilia to Amphilanthus* (pp. 652 ff.).

Lucy, Countess of Bedford, as a Masquer, attributed to John de Critz, ca. 1606

Lucy (Harrington) Russell, countess of Bedford, prominent courtier, favorite of Queen Anne, patron of Donne and Jonson, and frequent planner of and participant in court masques, is shown in masquing costume, for the wedding masque *Hymenaei,* by Ben Jonson and Inigo Jones. Jonson describes the masquing ladies as "attired richly and alike in the most celestial colors" associated with the rainbow, with elaborate headdresses and shoes, "all full of splendor, sovereignty, and riches." Their masque dances were "fully of subtlety and device." WOBURN ABBEY, BEDFORDSHIRE, UK/BRIDGEMAN ART LIBRARY.

The Garden of Eden with the Fall of Man, Jan Brueghel the Elder and Peter Paul Rubens, ca. 1615

Possibly foreshadowing Milton's portrayal of Eden in *Paradise Lost*, the painting presents an idyllic scene with cavorting animals in a lush landscape and a graceful human pair—perhaps just enjoying the garden's fruit, but at least intimating the moment of the Fall as a seductive Eve hands Adam an apple and a snake looks on. A favorite painter of Charles I, Rubens designed and painted for the king the splendid ceiling of Whitehall, portraying King James in apotheosis, as a supporter of wisdom, justice, concord, and peace. SCALA/ART RESOURCE, NY.

Charles I on Horseback, Sir Anthony Van Dyck, 1637–38

One of Charles I's court painters, knighted and pensioned by the king, Van Dyck produced several portraits of the royal family and their circle at court. This magnificent equestrian portrait of the king in armor on a white horse presents him as hero and warrior, in a pose that looks back to portraits and statues of Roman emperors on horseback. It was painted to be hung at the end of the Long Gallery in St. James Palace. NATIONAL GALLERY, LONDON, UK/ BRIDGEMAN ART LIBRARY, NY.

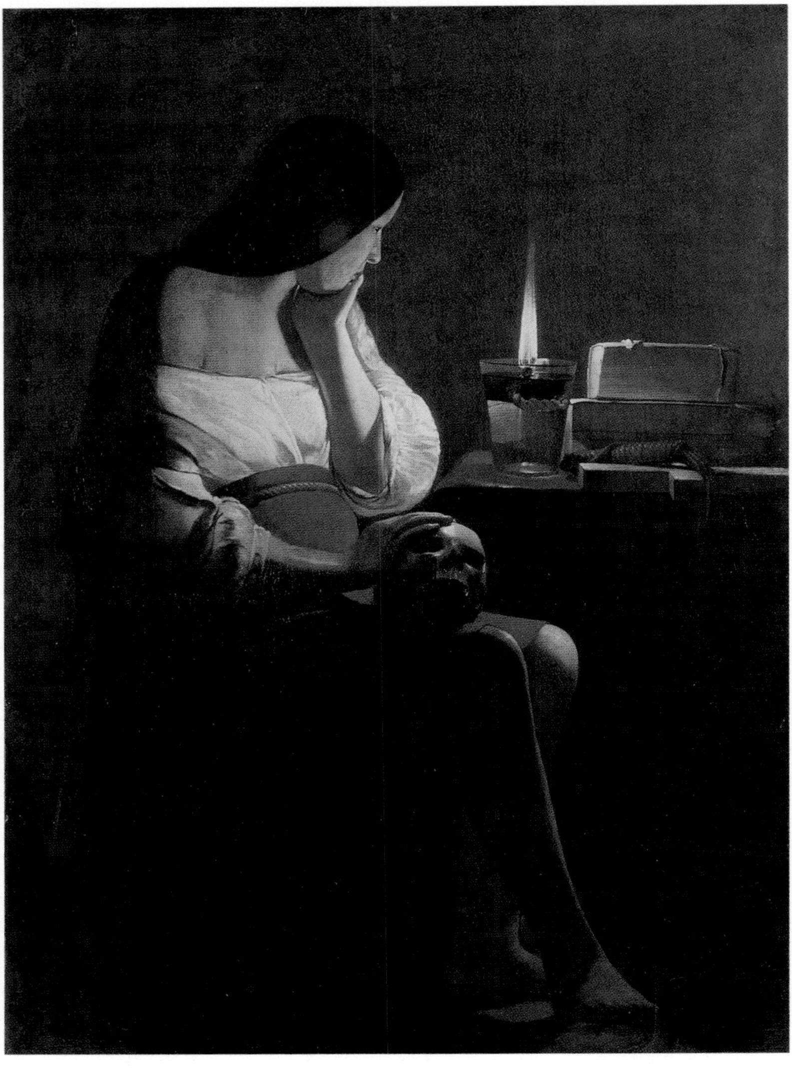

The Penitent Magdalen, Georges de la Tour, ca. 1638–43

This remarkable image of a young woman in meditative pose, her face lit by candlelight and her hand touching a skull, can serve as an emblem for the extensive meditative literature of the period—the poetry and prose of Donne, Herbert, Vaughan, and Traherne, among others—on such topics as sickness, human mortality, the transience of life and beauty, and the inevitability of death. Réunion des Musées Nationaux/Art Resource, NY.

The Restoration and the Eighteenth Century (1660–1785)

Landscape with Apollo and the Muses, Claude Lorrain, 1652

Claude's poetic landscapes inspired many British landscape gardens. In this painting, a river god sprawls by the Castalian spring under Mount Parnassus; the white swans are sacred to Apollo. On the terrace to the left, Apollo plays his lyre, surrounded by the nine Muses, while four poets approach through the woods. At the upper left, below a temple, the fountain of Hippocrene pours forth its inspiring waters. The dreamlike distance of the figures in this mysterious, luminous scene is intended to draw the viewer in. Similarly, in landscape gardens visitors were invited to stroll amid temples, inscriptions, swans, and statues, gradually comprehending the master plan. NATIONAL GALLERY OF SCOTLAND, EDINBURGH, SCOTLAND/BRIDGEMAN ART LIBRARY.

Great Fire of London, Dutch school, 1666

The fire of London, described by Dryden in *Annus Mirabilis* and by Pepys in his diary, destroyed most of the central city. In the foreground of this panorama, huddled refugees carry their goods away from the city. Under a pall of smoke across the Thames, St. Paul's Cathedral blazes in the center, with London Bridge on the far left and the Tower on the far right. The fire raged for four days, after which a new city eventually rose from the ashes.

Embarkment for Cythera,
Jean Antoine Watteau, 1717

Cythera is one of the names of Venus, and in this painting elegant pilgrims visit an island of love to pay homage to Venus (whose statue is on the far right). Paired off, these lovers pass through a romantic, erotic dreamscape, related to the visionary landscape of Pope's "Eloisa to Abelard." A ship of love waits on the left to carry the couples away. Are they going or coming to Cythera? In the grip of love, is the prevailing mood one of joy and anticipation, or of melancholy and surfeit? Critics differ; this painting does not reveal all its secrets. Réunion des Musées Nationaux/Art Resource, NY.

Bristol Docks and Qu
anonymous, early eig
teenth century

Bristol, in southwest E
gland, profited enor-
mously from the expan
sion of the slave trade.
From this port, mer-
chants sent trinkets,
guns, and rum to West
Africa in exchange for
slaves, who were trans
ported to North Ameri
and the West Indies in
exchange for money ar
sugar. This painting
shows a bustling metro
olis whose trade make
possible the busy shop
the right and the great
houses in the back-
ground. BRISTOL CITY
MUSEUM AND ART
GALLERY, UK/BRIDGEM
ART LIBRARY.

Gulliver Taking Leave of the Houyhnhnms, Sawrey Gilpin, 1769

In part 4 of *Gulliver's Travels* (pp. 1069 ff.), Swift cleverly makes use of the eighteenth-century British love of horses. Gulliver's infatuation with the dignity and nobility of the Houyhnhnms reflects the feelings of many hunters mounted for the chase or of gentlefolk promenading in the park; some preferred horses to human beings. Commercially, "horse painters" found eager and wealthy buyers, while Sawrey Gilpin tried to elevate horse painting by placing his horses against rich landscapes and in historical settings. PRIVATE COLLECTION/BRIDGEMAN ART LIBRARY.

The Begger's Opera, act 3, scene 11, William Hogarth, 1729

The highwayman Macheath, in leg irons, stands at the center, flanked by the women between whom he cannot choose. To the left, Lucy kneels before the jailer Lockit; to the right, Polly kneels before her father, Peachum. In the rear, a group of prisoners waits for its cue. But the setting is not so much a prison as the theater; spectators are seated on each side of the stage. Hogarth connects the audience with the actors just as *The Beggar's Opera* does, suggesting corruption "through all the employments of life." Behind Peachum, John Gay confers with his producer, John Rich. Below them, seated at the far right, the duke of Bolton (note his Star of the Garter) exchanges a rapt gaze with Polly; a satyr points down at him. On opening night, the duke fell in love with the actor who played Polly, Lavinia Fenton. He returned every night, until she became his mistress—and, two decades later, his wife. Tate Gallery, London/Art Resource, NY.

Garrick between Trag and Comedy, Joshua Reynolds, 1762

Sir Joshua Reynolds s cialized in portraits th characterized his subj by alluding to classica erature and art. Here, great actor David Garr is torn between Come on the left, and Trage on the right. The pictu parodies a well-known image, *Hercules betwe Virtue and Pleasure*, a alludes to Guido Reni (Tragedy) and Corregg (Comedy). Exalted Tra edy urges Garrick to f low her, but darling C edy drags him away. SOMERSET MAUGHAM THEATRE COLLECTION, LONDON, UK/BRIDGEM ART LIBRARY.

A Philosopher Giving That Lecture on the Orrery, in Which a Lamp Is Put in Place of the Sun, Joseph Wright, 1766.

Joseph Wright came from the English Midlands, where an intense interest in science helped spark the industrial revolution. The orrery, a mechanism that represents the movements of the planets around the sun, was one of many devices that taught the public to appreciate the wonders and pleasures of science. In this picture, the philosopher at the center bears a striking resemblance to portraits of Sir Isaac Newton, who had cast light on the solar system. Wright specialized in "candlelight pictures." Strong effects of light and shade play over the faces around the lamp, as if to reflect the literal meaning of enlightenment. GIRAUDON/ART RESOURCE, NY.

The Death of General Wolfe, Benjamin West, 1771

History painting—pictures that represent a famous legend or historical event—was the most prestigious genre of eighteenth-century art. West's painting of Wolfe, who fell on the day that he captured Quebec, revolutionized the genre by dressing the figures in contemporary clothes, not classical togas. Twelve years after his death, Wolfe had become an icon; the composition draws on images of mourners around the dead Christ. The poetic shading is also appropriate to Wolfe. The night before he died, he is supposed to have said of Gray's "Elegy" (p. 1332) that he "would rather have been the author of that piece than beat the French tomorrow"; and in his copy of the poem, he marked one passage: "The paths of glory lead but to the grave." PRIVATE COLLECTION/PHILLIPS, FINE ART AUCTIONEERS, NY/BRIDGEMAN ART LIBRARY.

The Parting of Abelard from Heloise, Angelika Kauffmann, ca. 1778

Angelika Kauffmann, born in Switzerland in 1741, was a child prodigy; at eleven she made a name in Italy for her portraits. From 1766 to 1781 she lived in England, where she was admired as a singer as well as a painter. During the eighteenth century the affair of Abelard and Heloise, which Pope depicted as a struggle between God and Eros, softened into a sentimental love story. Rousseau's novel *The New Heloise* (1761) helped transform the heroine into a saint of love. In an Age of Sensibility, Kauffmann portrays a youthful and feminized Abelard, not a wounded middle-aged scholar, and pathos, not repentance, marks this tender parting. COPYRIGHT © 2003 STATE HERMITAGE MUSEUM, ST. PETERSBURG, RUSSIA.

50 ODE ON THE DEATH
Her coat, that with the tortoiſe vies,
Her ears of jet, and emerald eyes,
She ſaw ; and purr'd applauſe.
Still had ſhe gaz'd ; but 'midſt the tide
Two angel forms were ſeen to glide,
The Genii of the ſtream :
Their ſcaly armour's Tyrian hue,
Thro' richeſt purple to the view
Betray'd a golden gleam.
The hapleſs nymph with wonder ſaw :
A whiſker firſt, and then a claw,
With many an ardent wiſh,
She ſtretch'd, in vain, to reach the prize.
What female heart can gold deſpiſe?
What cat's averſe to fiſh ?
Preſump-

Illustration for Gray's "Ode on the Death of a Favourite Cat," William Blake, 1798

In 1797, as a birthday gift for his wife, Nancy, the sculptor John Flaxman commissioned Blake to illustrate Gray's poems. These designs, in pen and watercolor, view the art of Gray through Blake's own vision. The charm of Gray's ode depends on picturing Selima both as a cat who tumbles for goldfish and as a "nymph" or "maid" who falls for gold. Blake mixes the two together in a cat and turns the goldfish (or "genii of the stream") into fleeing, finny human forms. Meanwhile, a lurking Fate cuts the thread of Selima's life, reminding us, in this interpretation of Gray, that perverted desires can be deadly.

Who now triúmphs, and in th' excess of joy
Sole reigning holds the tyranny of Heav'n."
So spake th' apostate angel, though in pain,
Vaunting aloud, but racked with deep despair:
And him thus answered soon his bold compeer.° *comrade*
"O Prince, O Chief of many thronéd Powers,
That led th' embattled Seraphim[1] to war
Under thy conduct, and in dreadful deeds
Fearless, endangered Heav'ns perpetual King;
And put to proof his high supremacy,
Whether upheld by strength, or chance, or fate;
Too well I see and rue the dire event,° *outcome*
That with sad overthrow and foul defeat
Hath lost us Heav'n, and all this mighty host
In horrible destruction laid thus low,
As far as gods and heav'nly essences
Can perish: for the mind and spirit remains
Invincible, and vigor soon returns,
Though all our glory extinct, and happy state
Here swallowed up in endless misery.
But what if he our conqueror (whom I now
Of force° believe almighty, since no less *necessarily*
Than such could have o'erpow'red such force as ours)
Have left us this our spirit and strength entire
Strongly to suffer and support our pains,
That we may so suffice° his vengeful ire, *satisfy*
Or do him mightier service as his thralls
By right of war, whate'er his business be
Here in the heart of Hell to work in fire,
Or do his errands in the gloomy deep;
What can it then avail though yet we feel
Strength undiminished, or eternal being
To undergo eternal punishment?"
Whereto with speedy words th' Arch-Fiend replied.
"Fall'n Cherub, to be weak is miserable
Doing or suffering: but of this be sure,
To do aught° good never will be our task, *anything*
But ever to do ill our sole delight,
As being the contrary to his high will
Whom we resist. If then his providence
Out of our evil seek to bring forth good,
Our labor must be to pervert that end,
And out of good still to find means of evil;
Which ofttimes may succeed, so as perhaps
Shall grieve him, if I fail° not, and disturb *err*
His inmost counsels from their destined aim.
But see the angry victor hath recalled
His ministers of vengeance and pursuit
Back to the gates of Heav'n: the sulphurous hail

1. According to tradition, there were nine orders of angels, arranged hierarchically—seraphim, cherubim, thrones, dominions, virtues, powers, principalities, archangels, and angels. The poem makes use of some of these titles but does not keep this hierarchy.

Shot after us in storm, o'erblown hath laid° *calmed*
The fiery surge, that from the precipice
Of Heav'n received us falling, and the thunder,
Winged with red lightning and impetuous rage,
Perhaps hath spent his shafts, and ceases now
To bellow through the vast and boundless deep.
Let us not slip° th' occasion, whether scorn, *let slip*
Or satiate fury yield it from our foe.
Seest thou yon dreary plain, forlorn and wild,
The seat of desolation, void of light,
Save what the glimmering of these livid° flames *bluish*
Casts pale and dreadful? Thither let us tend
From off the tossing of these fiery waves,
There rest, if any rest can harbor there,
And reassembling our afflicted powers,° *armies*
Consult how we may henceforth most offend° *harm, vex*
Our enemy, our own loss how repair,
How overcome this dire calamity,
What reinforcement we may gain from hope,
If not what resolution from despair."[2]
  Thus Satan talking to his nearest mate
With head uplift above the wave, and eyes
That sparkling blazed, his other parts besides
Prone on the flood, extended long and large
Lay floating many a rood,[3] in bulk as huge
As whom° the fables name of monstrous size, *as those whom*
Titanian, or Earth-born, that warred on Jove,
Briareos or Typhon,[4] whom the den
By ancient Tarsus held, or that sea-beast
Leviathan,[5] which God of all his works
Created hugest that swim th' ocean stream:
Him haply° slumb'ring on the Norway foam *perhaps*
The pilot of some small night-foundered° skiff, *overcome by night*
Deeming some island, oft, as seamen tell,[6]
With fixèd anchor in his scaly rind
Moors by his side under the lee,° while night *out of the wind*
Invests° the sea, and wishèd morn delays: *covers*
So stretched out huge in length the Arch-Fiend lay
Chained on the burning lake, nor ever thence
Had ris'n or heaved his head, but that the will
And high permission of all-ruling Heaven
Left him at large to his own dark designs,
That with reiterated crimes he might
Heap on himself damnation, while he sought

2. Five of the last nine lines of Satan's speech rhyme.
3. An old unit of measure, between six and eight yards.
4. Both the Titans, led by Briareos (said to have had a hundred hands), and the earth-born Giants, represented by Typhon (who lived in Cilicea near Tarsus and was said to have had a hundred heads), fought with Jove. They were punished by being thrown into the underworld. Christian mythographers found in these stories an analogy to Satan's revolt and punishment.
5. The whale, often identified with the great sea monster and enemy of the Lord in Isaiah 17.1 and the crocodile-like dragon of Job 41. Both were also identified with Satan.
6. The story of the deceived sailor and the illusory island was a commonplace, but the reference to Norway suggests a 16th-century version by Olaus Magnus, a Swedish historian.

Evil to others, and enraged might see
How all his malice served but to bring forth
Infinite goodness, grace, and mercy shown
On man by him seduced, but on himself
Treble confusion, wrath, and vengeance poured.
Forthwith upright he rears from off the pool
His mighty stature; on each hand the flames
Driv'n backward slope their pointing spires,° and rolled *points of flames*
In billows, leave i' th' midst a horrid° vale. *dreadful, bristling*
Then with expanded wings he steers his flight
Aloft, incumbent on° the dusky air *resting on*
That felt unusual weight, till on dry land
He lights,° if it were land that ever burned *alights*
With solid, as the lake with liquid fire,
And such appeared in hue; as when the force
Of subterranean wind transports a hill
Torn from Pelorus, or the shattered side
Of thund'ring Etna,[7] whose combustible
And fueled entrails thence conceiving fire,
Sublimed° with mineral fury, aid the winds, *vaporized*
And leave a singèd bottom all involved° *enveloped*
With stench and smoke: such resting found the sole
Of unblest feet. Him followed his next mate,
Both glorying to have scaped the Stygian° flood *Styxlike, hellish*
As gods, and by their own recovered strength,
Not by the sufferance° of supernal power. *permission*
"Is this the region, this the soil, the clime,"
Said then the lost Archangel, "this the seat° *estate*
That we must change for Heav'n, this mournful gloom
For that celestial light? Be it so, since he
Who now is sov'reign can dispose and bid
What shall be right: farthest from him is best
Whom reason hath equaled, force hath made supreme
Above his equals. Farewell happy fields
Where joy forever dwells: Hail horrors, hail
Infernal world, and thou profoundest Hell
Receive thy new possessor: one who brings
A mind not to be changed by place or time.
The mind is its own place, and in itself
Can make a Heav'n of Hell, a Hell of Heav'n.[8]
What matter where, if I be still the same,
And what I should be, all but less than° he *barely less than*
Whom thunder hath made greater? Here at least
We shall be free; th' Almighty hath not built
Here for his envy,[9] will not drive us hence:
Here we may reign secure, and in my choice
To reign is worth ambition though in Hell:
Better to reign in Hell, than serve in Heav'n.[1]
But wherefore let we then our faithful friends,

7. Pelorus and Etna are volcanic mountains in Sicily.
8. Compare Satan's soliloquy, 4.32–113.
9. I.e., because he desires this place.
1. An ironic echo of *Odyssey* 11.489–91, where the shade of Achilles tells Odysseus that it is better to be a farmhand on earth than king among the dead.

Th' associates and copartners of our loss
Lie thus astonished° on th' oblivious pool,[2] *stunned*
And call them not to share with us their part
In this unhappy mansion, or once more
With rallied arms to try what may be yet
Regained in Heav'n, or what more lost in Hell?"
  So Satan spake, and him Beëlzebub
Thus answered. "Leader of those armies bright,
Which but th' Omnipotent none could have foiled,
If once they hear that voice, their liveliest pledge
Of hope in fears and dangers, heard so oft
In worst extremes, and on the perilous edge° *front lines*
Of battle when it raged, in all assaults
Their surest signal, they will soon resume
New courage and revive, though now they lie
Groveling and prostrate on yon lake of fire,
As we erewhile, astounded and amazed,
No wonder, fall'n such a pernicious highth."
  He scarce had ceased when the superior Fiend
Was moving toward the shore; his ponderous shield
Ethereal temper,[3] massy, large and round,
Behind him cast; the broad circumference
Hung on his shoulders like the moon, whose orb
Through optic glass the Tuscan artist views[4]
At evening from the top of Fesole,
Or in Valdarno, to descry new lands,
Rivers or mountains in her spotty globe.
His spear, to equal which the tallest pine
Hewn on Norwegian hills, to be the mast
Of some great ammiral,° were but a wand *admiral's ship*
He walked with to support uneasy steps
Over the burning marl,° not like those steps *soil*
On heaven's azure; and the torrid clime
Smote on him sore besides, vaulted with fire;
Nathless° he so endured, till on the beach *nevertheless*
Of that inflamed° sea, he stood and called *flaming*
His legions, angel forms, who lay entranced
Thick as autumnal leaves that strow the brooks
In Vallombrosa,[5] where th' Etrurian shades
High overarched embow'r;° or scattered sedge° *form bowers / seaweed*
Afloat, when with fierce winds Orion armed
Hath vexed the Red Sea coast,[6] whose waves o'erthrew
Busiris[7] and his Memphian chivalry,

2. The epithet "oblivious" is transferred from the fallen angels to the pool into which they have fallen.
3. I.e., tempered in celestial fire.
4. Galileo, who looked through a telescope ("optic glass") from the hill town of Fiesole, outside Florence, in the valley of the Arno River ("Valdarno," val d'Arno, line 290). In 1610 he published a book describing the mountains on the moon.
5. The name means "shady valley" and refers to a region high in the Apennines, about twenty miles from Florence, in Tuscany ("Etruria"). Similes comparing the numberless dead to falling leaves are frequent in epic (e.g., *Aeneid* 6.309–10).
6. Orion is a constellation whose rising near sunset in late summer and autumn was associated with storms in the Red Sea.
7. Mythical Egyptian pharaoh, whom Milton associates with the pharaoh of Exodus 14, who pursued the Israelites ("sojourners of Goshen," line 309) into the Red Sea, which God parted for them. His "chivalry" (following) are horsemen from Memphis.

While with perfidious hatred they pursued
The sojourners of Goshen, who beheld
From the safe shore their floating carcasses
And broken chariot wheels; so thick bestrown
Abject and lost lay these, covering the flood,
Under amazement of their hideous change.
He called so loud, that all the hollow deep
Of Hell resounded. "Princes, Potentates,
Warriors, the flow'r of Heav'n, once yours, now lost,
If such astonishment as this can seize
Eternal Spirits: or have ye chos'n this place
After the toil of battle to repose
Your wearied virtue,° for the ease you find *strength, valor*
To slumber here, as in the vales of Heav'n?
Or in this abject posture have ye sworn
To adore the conqueror? who now beholds
Cherub and Seraph rolling in the flood
With scattered arms and ensigns,° till anon *battle flags*
His swift pursuers from Heav'n gates discern
Th' advantage, and descending tread us down
Thus drooping, or with linkèd thunderbolts
Transfix us to the bottom of this gulf.
Awake, arise, or be forever fall'n."
They heard, and were abashed, and up they sprung
Upon the wing, as when men wont° to watch *accustomed*
On duty, sleeping found by whom they dread,
Rouse and bestir themselves ere well awake.
Nor did they not perceive the evil plight
In which they were, or the fierce pains not feel;[8]
Yet to their general's voice they soon obeyed
Innumerable. As when the potent rod
Of Amram's son[9] in Egypt's evil day
Waved round the coast, up called a pitchy cloud
Of locusts, warping° on the eastern wind, *swarming*
That o'er the realm of impious Pharaoh hung
Like night, and darkened all the land of Nile:
So numberless were those bad angels seen
Hovering on wing under the cope° of Hell *roof*
'Twixt upper, nether, and surrounding fires;
Till, as a signal giv'n, th' uplifted spear
Of their great Sultan[1] waving to direct
Their course, in even balance down they light
On the firm brimstone, and fill all the plain;
A multitude, like which the populous north
Poured never from her frozen loins, to pass
Rhene or the Danaw, when her barbarous sons
Came like a deluge on the south, and spread
Beneath Gibraltar to the Libyan sands.[2]
Forthwith from every squadron and each band

8. The double negatives make a positive: they did perceive both plight and pain.
9. Moses, who drew down a plague of locusts on Egypt (Exodus 10.12–15).

1. A first use of this description of Satan as an Oriental despot.
2. The barbarian invasions of Rome began with crossings of the Rhine ("Rhene") and Danube

The heads and leaders thither haste where stood
Their great commander; godlike shapes and forms
Excelling human, princely dignities,
And powers that erst° in Heaven sat on thrones; *formerly*
Though of their names in heav'nly records now
Be no memorial, blotted out and razed° *erased*
By their rebellion, from the Books of Life.
Nor had they yet among the sons of Eve
Got them new names, till wand'ring o'er the earth,
Through God's high sufferance for the trial of man,
By falsities and lies the greatest part
Of mankind they corrupted to forsake
God their Creator, and th' invisible
Glory of him that made them, to transform
Oft to the image of a brute, adorned
With gay religions° full of pomp and gold, *showy rites*
And devils to adore for deities:
Then were they known to men by various names,
And various idols through the heathen world.
  Say, Muse, their names then known, who first, who last,[3]
Roused from the slumber on that fiery couch,
At their great emperor's call, as next in worth
Came singly° where he stood on the bare strand, *one at a time*
While the promiscuous° crowd stood yet aloof. *mixed*
  The chief were those who from the pit of Hell
Roaming to seek their prey on earth, durst fix
Their seats long after next the seat of God,[4]
Their altars by his altar, gods adored
Among the nations round, and durst abide
Jehovah thund'ring out of Zion, throned
Between the Cherubim;[5] yea, often placed
Within his sanctuary itself their shrines,
Abomination; and with cursèd things
His holy rites, and solemn feasts profaned,
And with their darkness durst affront his light.
First Moloch,[6] horrid king besmeared with blood
Of human sacrifice, and parents' tears,
Though for the noise of drums and timbrels° loud *tambourines*
Their children's cries unheard, that passed through fire
To his grim idol. Him the Ammonite[7]
Worshipped in Rabba and her wat'ry plain,
In Argob and in Basan, to the stream
Of utmost Arnon. Nor content with such
Audacious neighborhood, the wisest heart
Of Solomon he led by fraud to build
His temple right against the temple of God

("Danaw") rivers and spread across Spain, via Gibraltar, to North Africa.

3. The catalogue of gods here is an epic convention; Homer catalogues ships; Virgil, warriors.

4. The first group of devils come from the Middle East, close neighbors of Jehovah "throned" in his sanctuary in Jerusalem.

5. Golden cherubim adorned opposite ends of the gold cover on the Ark of the Covenant.

6. Moloch was a sun god, sometimes represented as a roaring bull or with a calf's head, within whose brazen image living children were supposedly burned as sacrifices.

7. The Ammonites lived east of the Jordan River. "Rabba" (next line) is modern Amman, in Jordan; "Argob," "Basan," "utmost Arnon" (lines 398–99) are lands east of the Dead Sea.

On that opprobrious hill, and made his grove
The pleasant valley of Hinnom, Tophet thence
And black Gehenna called, the type of Hell.[8]
Next Chemos,[9] th' obscene dread of Moab's sons,
From Aroer to Nebo, and the wild
Of southmost Abarim; in Hesebon
And Horanaim, Seon's realm, beyond
The flow'ry dale of Sibma clad with vines,
And Eleale to th' Asphaltic Pool.[1]
Peor[2] his other name, when he enticed
Israel in Sittim on their march from Nile
To do him wanton rites, which cost them woe.
Yet thence his lustful orgies he enlarged
Even to that hill of scandal,[3] by the grove
Of Moloch homicide, lust hard by° hate; *close by*
Till good Josiah drove them thence to Hell.
With these came they, who from the bord'ring flood
Of old Euphrates to the brook that parts
Egypt from Syrian ground,[4] had general names
Of Baalim and Ashtaroth, those male,
These feminine.[5] For Spirits when they please
Can either sex assume, or both; so soft
And uncompounded is their essence pure,
Not tied or manacled with joint or limb,
Nor founded on the brittle strength of bones,
Like cumbrous flesh; but in what shape they choose
Dilated or condensed, bright or obscure,
Can execute their airy purposes,
And works of love or enmity fulfill.
For those the race of Israel oft forsook
Their Living Strength, and unfrequented left
His righteous altar, bowing lowly down
To bestial gods; for which their heads as low
Bowed down in battle, sunk before the spear
Of despicable foes. With these in troop
Came Astoreth, whom the Phoenicians called
Astartè, queen of Heav'n, with crescent horns;
To whose bright image nightly by the moon
Sidonian virgins[6] paid their vows and songs,
In Sion also not unsung, where stood
Her temple on th' offensive mountain,[7] built
By that uxorious king, whose heart though large,

8. The rites of Moloch on "that opprobrious hill" (the Mount of Olives), just opposite the Jewish temple, and in the valley of Hinnom so polluted those places that they were turned into the refuse dump of Jerusalem. Under the name "Tophet" and "Gehenna," Hinnom became a type of Hell.
9. Chemos, or Chemosh, associated with Moloch in 1 Kings 11.7, was the god of the Moabites, whose lands (many drawn from Isaiah 15–16) are mentioned in the following lines.
1. The Dead Sea.
2. The story of Peor seducing the Israelites in Sittim is told in Numbers 15.
3. The Mount of Olives, where Solomon built temples for Chemos and Moloch (1 Kings 11.7); epithets were commonly attached to the names of gods, as in the next line, Moloch "homicide." Josiah (following line) destroyed pagan idols in Jerusalem and other cities (2 Chronicles 34).
4. Palestine lies between the Euphrates and "the brook Besor" (1 Samuel 30.10).
5. Plural forms, masculine and feminine, respectively, denoting aspects of the sun god Baal and the moon goddess Astarte (called "Astoreth" in line 438, below).
6. Sidon and Tyre were the chief cities of Phoenicia.
7. The Mount of Olives again. "That uxorious king" (next line) is Solomon, who "loved many strange women" (2 Kings 11.1–8).

Beguiled by fair idolatresses, fell
To idols foul. Thammuz[8] came next behind,
Whose annual wound in Lebanon allured
The Syrian damsels to lament his fate
In amorous ditties all a summer's day,
While smooth Adonis[9] from his native work
Ran purple to the sea, supposed with blood
Of Thammuz yearly wounded: the love-tale
Infected Sion's daughters with like heat,
Whose wanton passions in the sacred porch
Ezekiel[1] saw, when by the vision led
His eye surveyed the dark idolatries
Of alienated Judah. Next came one
Who mourned in earnest, when the captive ark
Maimed his brute image, head and hands lopped off
In his own temple, on the grunsel edge,[2]
Where he fell flat, and shamed his worshippers:
Dagon his name, sea monster, upward man
And downward fish: yet had his temple high
Reared in Azotus, dreaded through the coast
Of Palestine, in Gath and Ascalon
And Accaron and Gaza's[3] frontier bounds.
Him followed Rimmon,[4] whose delightful seat
Was fair Damascus, on the fertile banks
Of Abbana and Pharphar, lucid streams.
He also against the house of God was bold:
A leper once he lost and gained a king,
Ahaz his sottish conqueror, whom he drew
God's altar to disparage and displace
For one of Syrian mode,[5] whereon to burn
His odious off'rings, and adore the gods
Whom he had vanquished. After these appeared
A crew who under names of old renown,
Osiris, Isis, Orus[6] and their train
With monstrous shapes and sorceries abused
Fanatic Egypt and her priests, to seek
Their wand'ring gods disguised in brutish forms
Rather than human. Nor did Israel scape
Th' infection when their borrowed gold composed
The calf in Oreb:[7] and the rebel king

8. A Syrian god, supposedly killed by a boar in Lebanon; his Greek form was Adonis, beloved of Aphrodite and god of the solar year. Annual festivals mourned his death and celebrated his revival as signifying the death and rebirth of vegetation.
9. Here, the Lebanese river named for the deity because every spring it turned bloodred from sedimentary mud.
1. The prophet complained that Jewish women were worshipping Thammuz (Ezekiel 8.14).
2. When the Philistines stole the ark of God, they placed it in the temple of their sea god, Dagon, but in the morning the mutilated statue of Dagon was found on the threshhold ("grunsel edge") (1 Samuel 5.1–5).
3. The five chief cities of the Philistines, sites of Dagon's worship.
4. A Phoenician god whose temple was in Damascus.
5. A Syrian general, Naaman, was cured of leprosy and converted from worship of Rimmon by the waters of the Jordan (2 Kings 5), while King Ahaz, an Israelite monarch who conquered Damascus, was converted there to Rimmon's worship.
6. The second group of devils includes the Egyptian gods driven from Heaven by the revolt of the giants (Ovid, *Metamorphoses* 5) and forced to wander in "monstrous" (next line) animal disguises.
7. In the wilderness of Egypt, while Moses was receiving the Law, Aaron made a golden calf, thought to be an idol of the Egyptian god Apis and made of ornaments brought out of Egypt (Exodus 32).

Doubled that sin in Bethel and in Dan,
Lik'ning his Maker to the grazèd ox,[8]
Jehovah, who in one night when he passed
From Egypt marching, equaled° with one stroke *leveled*
Both her firstborn and all her bleating gods.[9]
Belial came last,[1] than whom a spirit more lewd
Fell not from Heaven, or more gross to love
Vice for itself: to him no temple stood
Or altar smoked; yet who more oft than he
In temples and at altars, when the priest
Turns atheist, as did Eli's sons,[2] who filled
With lust and violence the house of God.
In courts and palaces he also reigns
And in luxurious cities, where the noise
Of riot ascends above their loftiest tow'rs,
And injury and outrage: and when night
Darkens the streets, then wander forth the sons
Of Belial, flown° with insolence and wine.[3] *flushed*
Witness the streets of Sodom, and that night
In Gibeah, when the hospitable door
Exposed a matron to avoid worse rape.[4]
These were the prime in order and in might;
The rest were long to tell, though far renowned,
Th' Ionian gods, of Javan's issue held
Gods, yet confessed later than Heav'n and Earth
Their boasted parents;[5] Titan Heav'n's firstborn
With his enormous brood, and birthright seized
By younger Saturn, he from mightier Jove,
His own and Rhea's son, like measure found;
So Jove usurping reigned:[6] these first in Crete
And Ida known, thence on the snowy top
Of cold Olympus ruled the middle air
Their highest heav'n; or on the Delphian cliff,
Or in Dodona, and through all the bounds
Of Doric land;[7] or who with Saturn old
Fled over Adria to th' Hesperian fields,
And o'er the Celtic roamed the utmost isles.[8]
All these and more came flocking; but with looks

8. Jeroboam, "the rebel king" who led the ten tribes of Israel in revolt against Solomon's son, Rehoboam; he doubled Aaron's sin by making two golden calves (1 Kings 12.25–30).
9. Jehovah smote the firstborn of all Egyptian families as well as their gods (Exodus 12.12).
1. Belial was never worshipped as a god; his name means "wickedness," but its use in phrases like "sons of Belial" encouraged personification.
2. Priests who were termed "sons of Belial" because they seized for themselves offerings made to God and lay with women who assembled at the door of the tarbernacle (1 Samuel 2.12–22).
3. This passage, with its present-tense verbs, invites application to current examples—at court and in Restoration London.
4. Lot begged the Sodomites to rape his daughters rather than his (male) angel guests (Genesis 19); in Gibeah a Levite avoided "worse" (homosexual) rape by surrendering his concubine to riotous "sons of Belial" (Judges 19.21–30).
5. The Ionian Greeks ("Javan's issue," i.e., of the line of Javan, grandson of Noah) regarded the Titans as gods; their supposed parents were Heaven (Uranus) and Earth (Gaea).
6. The Titan Chronos, or Saturn, deposed his elder brother, married his sister Rhea, and ruled until he was deposed by his son, Zeus (Jove), who had been reared in secret on Mount Ida in Crete.
7. Zeus and the other Olympian gods had their seat on Mount Olympus, in "middle air"; they were worshipped in Delphi, Dodona, and throughout Greece ("Doric lands").
8. Saturn, after his downfall, fled over "Adria" (the Adriatic Sea) to the "Hesperian fields" (Italy), crossed the "Celtic" fields of France, and thence to Britain, the "utmost isles."

Downcast and damp,° yet such wherein appeared *depressed, dazed*
Obscure some glimpse of joy, to have found their chief
Not in despair, to have found themselves not lost
In loss itself; which on his count'nance cast
Like doubtful hue:[9] but he his wonted° pride *accustomed*
Soon recollecting, with high words, that bore
Semblance of worth, not substance, gently raised
Their fainting courage, and dispelled their fears.
Then straight° commands that at the warlike sound *immediately*
Of trumpets loud and clarions be upreared
His mighty standard; that proud honor claimed
Azazel[1] as his right, a Cherub tall:
Who forthwith from the glittering staff unfurled
Th' imperial ensign, which full high advanced
Shone like a meteor streaming to the wind
With gems and golden luster rich emblazed,
Seraphic arms and trophies:[2] all the while
Sonorous metal° blowing martial sounds: *trumpets*
At which the universal host upsent
A shout that tore Hell's concave,° and beyond *vault*
Frighted the reign of Chaos and old Night.[3]
All in a moment through the gloom were seen
Ten thousand banners rise into the air
With orient° colors waving: with them rose *lustrous*
A forest huge of spears: and thronging helms
Appeared, and serried° shields in thick array *pushed close together*
Of depth immeasurable: anon they move
In perfect phalanx to the Dorian[4] mood
Of flutes and soft recorders; such as raised
To highth of noblest temper heroes old
Arming to battle, and instead of rage
Deliberate valor breathed, firm and unmoved
With dread of death to flight or foul retreat,
Nor wanting power to mitigate and swage° *assuage*
With solemn touches, troubled thoughts, and chase
Anguish and doubt and fear and sorrow and pain
From mortal or immortal minds. Thus they
Breathing united force with fixèd thought
Moved on in silence to soft pipes that charmed
Their painful steps o'er the burnt soil; and now
Advanced in view they stand, a horrid° front *bristling with spears*
Of dreadful length and dazzling arms, in guise
Of warriors old with ordered spear and shield,
Awaiting what command their mighty chief
Had to impose. He through the armèd files
Darts his experienced eye, and soon traverse° *across*
The whole battalion views, their order due,

9. Satan's face reflected the same mixed emotions.
1. Traditionally, one of the four standard-bearers in Satan's army. "Clarions" (line 532): small, shrill trumpets.
2. Their flags bear the heraldic arms of the various orders of angels and memorials of their battles.
3. In *Paradise Lost* 2.894–909, 959–70 Chaos and Night rule the region of unformed matter between Heaven and earth.
4. Severe, martial music used by the Spartans marching to battle. "Phalanx": battle formation.

Their visages and stature as of gods,
Their number last he sums. And now his heart
Distends with pride, and hard'ning in his strength
Glories: for never since created man[5]
Met such embodied force, as named° with these *composed*
Could merit more than that small infantry
Warred on by cranes:[6] though all the giant brood
Of Phlegra with th' heroic race were joined
That fought at Thebes and Ilium,[7] on each side
Mixed with auxiliar° gods; and what resounds *allied*
In fable or romance of Uther's son
Begirt with British and Armoric knights;
And all who since, baptized or infidel
Jousted in Aspramont or Montalban,
Damasco, or Morocco, or Trebisond,
Or whom Biserta sent from Afric shore
When Charlemagne with all his peerage fell
By Fontarabia.[8] Thus far these beyond
Compare of mortal prowess, yet observed° *obeyed*
Their dread commander: he above the rest
In shape and gesture proudly eminent
Stood like a tow'r; his form had yet not lost
All her[9] original brightness, nor appeared
Less than Archangel ruined, and th' excess
Of glory obscured: as when the sun new-ris'n
Looks through the horizontal° misty air *on the horizon*
Shorn of his beams, or from behind the moon
In dim eclipse disastrous° twilight sheds *ill-starred*
On half the nations, and with fear of change
Perplexes monarchs. Darkened so, yet shone
Above them all th' Archangel: but his face
Deep scars of thunder had intrenched,° and care *furrowed*
Sat on his faded cheek, but under brows
Of dauntless courage, and considerate° pride *conscious, deliberate*
Waiting revenge: cruel his eye, but cast
Signs of remorse and passion° to behold *compassion, pain*
The fellows of his crime, the followers rather
(Far other once beheld in bliss) condemned
Forever now to have their lot in pain,
Millions of Spirits for his fault amerced° *deprived*
Of Heav'n, and from eternal splendors flung
For his revolt, yet faithful how they stood,
Their glory withered: as when Heaven's fire
Hath scathed° the forest oaks, or mountain pines, *damaged*

5. I.e., since the creation of man.
6. Pygmies (little people, with a pun, in "infantry" on "infants") had periodic fights with the cranes, in Pliny's account. Compared with Satan's forces, all other armies are puny.
7. In Greek mythology, the Giants fought the gods at Phlegra in Macedonia; in Roman myth, it was at Phlegra in Italy. Satan's forces surpass them, even if joined with the Seven who fought against Thebes and the whole Greek host that besieged Troy ("Ilium").
8. Satan's forces also surpass the "British and Armoric" (from Brittany) knights who fought with King Arthur ("Uther's son") and all the romance knights who fought at the famous named sites in the following lines. Roncesvalles, near Fontarabia, was the place where Charlemagne's "peerage," including his best knight, Roland, were defeated in battle (though not Charlemagne himself).
9. *Forma* in Latin is feminine.

With singèd top their stately growth though bare
Stands on the blasted heath. He now prepared
To speak; whereat their doubled ranks they bend
From wing to wing, and half enclose him round
With all his peers: attention held them mute.
Thrice he essayed,° and thrice, in spite of scorn, *attempted*
Tears such as angels weep burst forth: at last
Words interwove with sighs found out their way.
  "O myriads of immortal Spirits, O Powers
Matchless, but with th' Almighty, and that strife
Was not inglorious, though th' event° was dire, *outcome*
As this place testifies, and this dire change
Hateful to utter: but what power of mind
Foreseeing or presaging, from the depth
Of knowledge past or present, could have feared,
How such united force of gods, how such
As stood like these, could ever know repulse?
For who can yet believe, though after loss,
That all these puissant° legions, whose exile *potent, powerful*
Hath emptied Heav'n, shall fail to reascend
Self-raised, and repossess their native seat?
For me, be witness all the host of Heav'n,
If counsels different,° or danger shunned *contradictory*
By me, have lost our hopes. But he who reigns
Monarch in Heav'n, till then as one secure
Sat on his throne, upheld by old repute,
Consent or custom, and his regal state
Put forth at full, but still° his strength concealed, *always*
Which tempted our attempt, and wrought our fall.
Henceforth his might we know, and know our own
So as not either to provoke, or dread
New war, provoked; our better part remains
To work in close design, by fraud or guile
What force effected not: that he no less
At length from us may find, who overcomes
By force, hath overcome but half his foe.
Space may produce new worlds; whereof so rife° *common*
There went a fame° in Heav'n that he ere long *rumor*
Intended to create, and therein plant
A generation, whom his choice regard
Should favor equal to the sons of Heaven:
Thither, if but to pry, shall be perhaps
Our first eruption,° thither or elsewhere: *breaking out*
For this infernal pit shall never hold
Celestial Spirits in bondage, not th' abyss
Long under darkness cover. But these thoughts
Full counsel must mature: peace is despaired,
For who can think submission? War then, war
Open or understood° must be resolved." *covert*
  He spake: and to confirm his words, out flew
Millions of flaming swords, drawn from the thighs
Of mighty Cherubim; the sudden blaze
Far round illumined Hell: highly they raged

Against the Highest, and fierce with graspèd arms
Clashed on their sounding shields the din of war,[1]
Hurling defiance toward the vault of Heav'n.
There stood a hill not far whose grisly top
Belched fire and rolling smoke; the rest entire
Shone with a glossy scurf,° undoubted sign *crust*
That in his womb was hid metallic ore,
The work of sulphur.[2] Thither winged with speed
A numerous brígade hastened. As when bands
Of pioneers° with spade and pickax armed *military engineers*
Forerun the royal camp, to trench a field,
Or cast a rampart. Mammon[3] led them on,
Mammon, the least erected Spirit that fell
From Heav'n, for ev'n in Heav'n his looks and thoughts
Were always downward bent, admiring more
The riches of Heav'n's pavement, trodden gold,
Than aught divine or holy else enjoyed
In vision beatific: by him first
Men also, and by his suggestion taught,
Ransacked the center, and with impious hands
Rifled the bowels of their mother earth
For treasures better hid. Soon had his crew
Opened into the hill a spacious wound
And digged out ribs of gold. Let none admire° *wonder*
That riches grow in Hell; that soil may best
Deserve the precious bane.° And here let those *poison*
Who boast in mortal things, and wond'ring tell
Of Babel, and the works of Memphian kings,[4]
Learn how their greatest monuments of fame,
And strength and art are easily outdone
By Spirits reprobate, and in an hour
What in an age they with incessant toil
And hands innumerable scarce perform.
Nigh on the plain in many cells prepared,
That underneath had veins of liquid fire
Sluiced from the lake, a second multitude
With wondrous art founded° the massy ore, *melted*
Severing° each kind, and scummed the bullion dross:° *separating / boiling dregs*
A third as soon had formed within the ground
A various mold, and from the boiling cells
By strange conveyance filled each hollow nook,
As in an organ from one blast of wind
To many a row of pipes the soundboard breathes.
Anon out of the earth a fabric huge
Rose like an exhalation, with the sound
Of dulcet symphonies and voices sweet,
Built like a temple,[5] where pilasters° round *columns set in a wall*

1. Like Roman legionnaires, the fallen angels applaud by beating swords on shields.
2. Sulfur and mercury were considered the basic substances of all metals.
3. "Mammon," an abstract word for riches, came to be personified and associated with the god of wealth, Plutus, and so with Pluto, god of the underworld. Cf. Matthew 6.24: "Ye cannot serve God and mammon."
4. The Tower of Babel and the pyramids of Egypt.
5. After melting the gold with fire from the lake and pouring it into molds, the devils cause their building to rise as by magic, to the sounds of marvelous music.

Were set, and Doric pillars[6] overlaid
With golden architrave; nor did there want
Cornice or frieze, with bossy° sculptures grav'n; *embossed*
The roof was fretted° gold. Not Babylon, *richly ornamented*
Nor great Alcairo such magnificence
Equaled in all their glories, to enshrine
Belus or Serapis[7] their gods, or seat
Their kings, when Egypt with Assyria strove
In wealth and luxury. Th' ascending pile
Stood fixed° her stately height, and straight° the doors *complete / at once*
Opening their brazen folds discover° wide *reveal*
Within, her ample spaces, o'er the smooth
And level pavement: from the archèd roof
Pendent by subtle magic many a row
Of starry lamps and blazing cressets[8] fed
With naphtha and asphaltus yielded light
As from a sky. The hasty multitude
Admiring entered, and the work some praise
And some the architect: his hand was known
In Heav'n by many a towered structure high,
Where sceptered angels held their residence,
And sat as princes, whom the Súpreme King
Exalted to such power, and gave to rule,
Each in his hierarchy, the orders bright.
Nor was his name unheard or unadored
In ancient Greece and in Ausonian land
Men called him Mulciber[9] and how he fell
From Heav'n, they fabled, thrown by angry Jove
Sheer o'er the crystal battlements: from morn
To noon he fell, from noon to dewy eve,
A summer's day; and with the setting sun
Dropped from the zenith like a falling star,
On Lemnos th' Aégean isle: thus they relate,
Erring; for he with this rebellious rout
Fell long before; nor aught availed him now
To have built in Heav'n high tow'rs; nor did he scape
By all his engines, but was headlong sent
With his industrious crew to build in Hell.
  Meanwhile the wingèd heralds by command
Of sov'reign power, with awful ceremony
And trumpet's sound throughout the host proclaim
A solemn council forthwith to be held
At Pandemonium,[1] the high capitol
Of Satan and his peers:° their summons called *nobles*
From every band and squarèd regiment
By place° or choice° the worthiest; they anon *rank / election*

6. Doric pillars are severe and plain. The devils' palace combines classical architectural features with elaborate ornamentation, suggesting, perhaps, St. Peter's in Rome.

7. At Babylon, in Assyria, there were temples to "Belus" or Baal; at Alcairo (modern Cairo, ancient Memphis), in Egypt, they were to Osiris ("Serapis").

8. Basketlike lamps, hung from the ceiling.

9. Hephaestus, or Vulcan, was sometimes known in "Ausonian land" (Italy) as "Mulciber." The story of Jove's tossing him out of Heaven (see following lines) is told in Book 1 of the *Iliad*.

1. "Pandemonium" (a Miltonic coinage) means literally "all demons," an inversion of "pantheon," "all gods."

With hundreds and with thousands trooping came
Attended: all access was thronged, the gates
And porches wide, but chief the spacious hall
(Though like a covered field, where champions bold
Wont ride in armed, and at the soldan's° chair *sultan's*
Defied the best of paynim° chivalry *pagan*
To mortal combat or career with lance)
Thick swarmed, both on the ground and in the air,
Brushed with the hiss of rustling wings. As bees
In springtime, when the sun with Taurus rides,[2]
Pour forth their populous youth about the hive
In clusters; they among fresh dews and flowers
Fly to and fro, or on the smoothèd plank,
The suburb of their straw-built citadel,
New rubbed with balm, expatiate and confer[3]
Their state affairs. So thick the aery crowd
Swarmed and were straitened; till the signal giv'n,
Behold a wonder! They but now who seemed
In bigness to surpass Earth's giant sons
Now less than smallest dwarfs, in narrow room
Throng numberless, like that Pygmean race
Beyond the Indian mount,[4] or fairy elves,
Whose midnight revels, by a forest side
Or fountain some belated peasant sees,
Or dreams he sees, while overhead the moon
Sits arbitress,° and nearer to the earth *witness*
Wheels her pale course: they on their mirth and dance
Intent, with jocund° music charm his ear;[5] *merry*
At once with joy and fear his heart rebounds.
Thus incorporeal Spirits to smallest forms
Reduced their shapes immense, and were at large,
Though without number still amidst the hall
Of that infernal court. But far within
And in their own dimensions like themselves
The great Seraphic Lords and Cherubim
In close recess and secret conclave sat,
A thousand demigods on golden seats,
Frequent and full.[6] After short silence then
And summons read, the great consult[7] began.

Book 2

High on a throne of royal state, which far
Outshone the wealth of Ormus and of Ind,[1]
Or where the gorgeous East with richest hand

2. The sun is in the zodiacal sign of Taurus from about April 19 to May 20.
3. Spread out and discuss. Bee similes were common in epic from Homer on; also, the bees' (royalist) society was often cited in political argument. The simile prepares for the sudden contraction of the devils, who can shrink or dilate at will.
4. The pygmies were supposed to live beyond the Himalayas.
5. The belated peasant's.
6. Crowded together, and in full complement.
7. Consultation, often secret and seditious.
1. India. "Ormus": an island in the Persian Gulf, modern Hormuz, famous for pearls.

Show'rs on her kings barbaric pearl and gold,
Satan exalted sat, by merit raised
To that bad eminence; and from despair
Thus high uplifted beyond hope, aspires
Beyond thus high, insatiate to pursue
Vain war with Heav'n, and by success° untaught — *the outcome*
His proud imaginations° thus displayed. — *schemes*
"Powers and Dominions,[2] deities of Heaven,
For since no deep within her gulf can hold
Immortal vigor, though oppressed and fall'n,
I give not Heav'n for lost. From this descent
Celestial Virtues rising, will appear
More glorious and more dread than from no fall,
And trust themselves to fear no second fate.
Me though just right, and the fixed laws of Heav'n
Did first create your leader, next, free choice,
With what besides, in counsel or in fight,
Hath been achieved of merit, yet this loss
Thus far at least recovered, hath much more
Established in a safe unenvied throne
Yielded with full consent. The happier state
In Heav'n, which follows dignity, might draw
Envy from each inferior; but who here
Will envy whom the highest place exposes
Foremost to stand against the Thunderer's aim
Your bulwark, and condemns to greatest share
Of endless pain? Where there is then no good
For which to strive, no strife can grow up there
From faction; for none sure will claim in Hell
Precédence, none, whose portion is so small
Of present pain, that with ambitious mind
Will covet more. With this advantage then
To union, and firm faith, and firm accord,
More than can be in Heav'n, we now return
To claim our just inheritance of old,
Surer to prosper than prosperity
Could have assured us;[3] and by what best way,
Whether of open war or covert guile,[4]
We now debate; who can advise, may speak."
He ceased, and next him Moloch, sceptered king
Stood up, the strongest and the fiercest Spirit
That fought in Heav'n; now fiercer by despair:
His trust was with th' Eternal to be deemed
Equal in strength, and rather than be less
Cared not to be at all; with that care lost
Went all his fear: of God, or Hell, or worse
He recked° not, and these words thereafter spake. — *cared*
"My sentence° is for open war: of wiles, — *judgment*
More unexpért,° I boast not: them let those — *less experienced*

2. Angelic orders.
3. Note the play on "surer," "prosper," "prosperity," "assured," a favorite device of Milton's.
4. A typical epic convention (in Homer, Virgil, Tasso, and elsewhere) involved councils debating war or peace, with spokesmen on each side. Satan offers only the option of war, open or covert.

Contrive who need, or when they need, not now.
For while they sit contriving, shall the rest,
Millions that stand in arms, and longing wait
The signal to ascend, sit lingering here
Heav'n's fugitives, and for their dwelling place
Accept this dark opprobrious den of shame,
The prison of his tyranny who reigns
By our delay? No, let us rather choose
Armed with Hell flames and fury all at once
O'er Heav'n's high tow'rs to force resistless way,
Turning our tortures into horrid° arms — *bristling, horrifying*
Against the Torturer; when to meet the noise
Of his almighty engine° he shall hear — *the thunderbolt*
Infernal thunder, and for lightning see
Black fire and horror shot with equal rage
Among his angels; and his throne itself
Mixed with Tartarean[5] sulfur, and strange fire,
His own invented torments. But perhaps
The way seems difficult and steep to scale
With upright wing against a higher foe.
Let such bethink them, if the sleepy drench° — *large draught*
Of that forgetful° lake benumb not still, — *causing oblivion*
That in our proper° motion we ascend — *natural to us*
Up to our native seat: descent and fall
To us is adverse. Who but felt of late
When the fierce foe hung on our broken rear
Insulting,[6] and pursued us through the deep,
With what compulsion and laborious flight
We sunk thus low? Th' ascent is easy then;
Th' event° is feared; should we again provoke — *outcome*
Our stronger, some worse way his wrath may find
To our destruction: if there be in Hell
Fear to be worse destroyed: what can be worse
Than to dwell here, driven out from bliss, condemned
In this abhorrèd deep to utter woe;
Where pain of unextinguishable fire
Must exercise° us without hope of end — *vex, afflict*
The vassals[7] of his anger, when the scourge
Inexorably, and the torturing hour
Calls us to penance? More destroyed than thus
We should be quite abolished and expire.
What fear we then? What° doubt we to incense — *why*
His utmost ire? which to the height enraged,
Will either quite consume us, and reduce
To nothing this essential,° happier far — *essence*
Than miserable to have eternal being:
Or if our substance be indeed divine,
And cannot cease to be, we are at worst
On this side nothing;[8] and by proof we feel

5. Tartarus is a classical name for hell.
6. With the Latin sense of stamping on; also, triumphantly scorning.
7. Servants, but perhaps also vessels. See Romans 9.22: "vessels of wrath fitted to destruction."
8. I.e., we cannot be worse off than we are now, and still live.

Our power sufficient to disturb his Heav'n,
And with perpetual inroads to alarm,
Though inaccessible, his fatal[9] throne:
Which if not victory is yet revenge."
He ended frowning, and his look, denounced° *portended*
Desperate revenge, and battle dangerous
To less than gods. On th' other side up rose
Belial, in act more graceful and humane;° *civil, polite*
A fairer person lost not Heav'n; he seemed
For dignity composed and high exploit:
But all was false and hollow; though his tongue
Dropped manna, and could make the worse appear
The better reason,[1] to perplex and dash° *confuse*
Maturest counsels: for his thoughts were low;
To vice industrious, but to nobler deeds
Timorous and slothful: yet he pleased the ear,
And with persuasive accent thus began.
"I should be much for open war, O Peers,
As not behind in hate; if what was urged
Main reason to persuade immediate war,
Did not dissuade me most, and seem to cast
Ominous conjecture on the whole success:
When he who most excels in fact° of arms, *feat*
In what he counsels and in what excels
Mistrustful, grounds his courage on despair
And utter dissolution, as the scope
Of all his aim, after some dire revenge.
First, what revenge? The tow'rs of Heav'n are filled
With armèd watch, that render all access
Impregnable; oft on the bordering deep
Encamp their legions, or with óbscure wing
Scout far and wide into the realm of Night,
Scorning surprise. Or could we break our way
By force, and at our heels all Hell should rise
With blackest insurrection, to confound
Heav'n's purest light, yet our great enemy
All incorruptible would on his throne
Sit unpolluted, and th' ethereal mold[2]
Incapable of stain would soon expel
Her mischief, and purge off the baser fire
Victorious. Thus repulsed, our final hope
Is flat despair: we must exasperate
Th' almighty victor to spend all his rage,
And that must end us, that must be our cure,
To be no more; sad cure; for who would lose,
Though full of pain, this intellectual being,
Those thoughts that wander through eternity,
To perish rather, swallowed up and lost

9. Established by Fate; also, deadly.
1. The Sophists, mercenary teachers of rhetoric in ancient Greece, were denounced by Plato for making "the worse appear / The better reason." "His tongue / Dropped manna": his honeyed words seemed like the manna supplied to the Israelites in the desert.
2. Heavenly substance, derived from "ether," the fifth and purest element, thought to be incorruptible.

In the wide womb of uncreated night,
Devoid of sense and motion? And who knows,
Let this be good, whether our angry foe
Can give it, or will ever? How he can
Is doubtful; that he never will is sure.
Will he, so wise, let loose at once his ire,
Belike° through impotence, or unaware, *perhaps*
To give his enemies their wish, and end
Them in his anger, whom his anger saves
To punish endless? 'Wherefore cease we then?'
Say they who counsel war, 'We are decreed,
Reserved and destined to eternal woe;
Whatever doing, what can we suffer more,
What can we suffer worse?' Is this then worst,
Thus sitting, thus consulting, thus in arms?
What when we fled amain,° pursued and strook° *headlong / struck*
With Heav'n's afflicting thunder, and besought
The deep to shelter us? This Hell then seemed
A refuge from those wounds. Or when we lay
Chained on the burning lake? That sure was worse.
What if the breath that kindled those grim fires
Awaked should blow them into sevenfold rage
And plunge us in the flames? Or from above
Should intermitted° vengeance arm again *suspended*
His red right hand to plague us? What if all
Her° stores were opened, and this firmament° *Hell's / sky*
Of Hell should spout her cataracts° of fire, *cascades*
Impendent[3] horrors, threat'ning hideous fall
One day upon our heads; while we perhaps
Designing or exhorting glorious war,
Caught in a fiery tempest shall be hurled
Each on his rock transfixed, the sport and prey
Of racking whirlwinds, or forever sunk
Under yon boiling ocean, wrapped in chains;
There to converse with everlasting groans,
Unrespited, unpitied, unreprieved,
Ages of hopeless end; this would be worse.
War therefore, open or concealed, alike
My voice dissuades; for what can force or guile[4]
With him, or who deceive his mind, whose eye
Views all things at one view? He from Heav'n's high
All these our motions° vain, sees and derides; *proposals*
Not more almighty to resist our might
Than wise to frustrate all our plots and wiles.
Shall we then live thus vile, the race of Heav'n
Thus trampled, thus expelled to suffer here
Chains and these torments? Better these than worse
By my advice; since fate inevitable
Subdues us, and omnipotent decree,
The victor's will. To suffer, as to do,

3. In the Latin sense, hanging down, threatening.
4. The verb "accomplish" or "achieve" is understood.

Our strength is equal, nor the law unjust
That so ordains: this was at first resolved,
If we were wise, against so great a foe
Contending, and so doubtful what might fall.
I laugh, when those who at the spear are bold
And vent'rous, if that fail them, shrink and fear
What yet they know must follow, to endure
Exile, or ignominy, or bonds, or pain,
The sentence of their conqueror: This is now
Our doom; which if we can sustain and bear,
Our Súpreme Foe in time may much remit
His anger, and perhaps thus far removed
Not mind us not offending, satisfied
With what is punished; whence these raging fires
Will slacken, if his breath stir not their flames.
Our purer essence then will overcome
Their noxious vapor, or inured° not feel, *accustomed*
Or changed at length, and to the place conformed
In temper and in nature, will receive
Familiar the fierce heat, and void of pain;
This horror will grow mild, this darkness light,
Besides what hope the never-ending flight
Of future days may bring, what chance, what change
Worth waiting, since our present lot appears
For happy though but ill, for ill not worst,[5]
If we procure not to ourselves more woe."
  Thus Belial, with words clothed in reason's garb,
Counseled ignoble ease and peaceful sloth,
Not peace: and after him thus Mammon spake.
  "Either to disenthrone the King of Heav'n
We war, if war be best, or to regain
Our own right lost: him to unthrone we then
May hope when everlasting Fate shall yield
To fickle Chance, and Chaos judge the strife:
The former vain to hope argues° as vain *proves*
The latter: for what place can be for us
Within Heav'n's bound, unless Heav'n's Lord supreme
We overpower? Suppose he should relent
And publish grace to all, on promise made
Of new subjection; with what eyes could we
Stand in his presence humble, and receive
Strict laws imposed, to celebrate his throne
With warbled hymns, and to his Godhead sing
Forced hallelujahs; while he lordly sits
Our envied Sov'reign, and his altar breathes
Ambrosial° odors and ambrosial flowers, *fragrant, immortal*
Our servile offerings. This must be our task
In Heav'n, this our delight; how wearisome
Eternity so spent in worship paid
To whom we hate. Let us not then pursue
By force impossible, by leave obtained

5. I.e., from the point of view of happiness, the devils are in an ill state, but it could be worse.

Unácceptable, though in Heav'n, our state
Of splendid vassalage,° but rather seek *servitude*
Our own good from ourselves, and from our own
Live to ourselves, though in this vast recess,
Free, and to none accountable, preferring
Hard liberty before the easy yoke
Of servile pomp. Our greatness will appear
Then most conspicuous, when great things of small,
Useful of hurtful, prosperous of adverse
We can create, and in what place soe'er
Thrive under evil, and work ease out of pain
Through labor and endurance. This deep world
Of darkness do we dread? How oft amidst
Thick clouds and dark doth Heav'n's all-ruling Sire
Choose to reside, his glory unobscured,
And with the majesty of darkness round
Covers his throne; from whence deep thunders roar
Must'ring their rage, and Heav'n resembles Hell?
As he our darkness, cannot we his light
Imitate when we please? This desert soil
Wants° not her hidden luster, gems and gold; *lacks*
Nor want we skill or art, from whence to raise
Magnificence; and what can Heav'n show more?
Our torments also may in length of time
Become our elements, these piercing fires
As soft as now severe, our temper° changed *constitution*
Into their temper; which must needs remove
The sensible of pain.[6] All things invite
To peaceful counsels, and the settled state
Of order, how in safety best we may
Compose° our present evils, with regard *come to terms with*
Of what we are and where, dismissing quite
All thoughts of war: ye have what I advise."
He scarce had finished, when such murmur filled
Th' assembly, as when hollow rocks retain
The sound of blust'ring winds, which all night long
Had roused the sea, now with hoarse cadence lull
Seafaring men o'erwatched,° whose bark by chance *worn out from watching*
Or pinnace° anchors in a craggy bay *boat*
After the tempest: such applause was heard
As Mammon ended, and his sentence pleased,
Advising peace: for such another field° *battlefield*
They dreaded worse than Hell: so much the fear
Of thunder and the sword of Michaël[7]
Wrought still within them; and no less desire
To found this nether empire, which might rise
By policy,° and long process of time, *statecraft*
In emulation opposite to Heav'n.
Which then Beëlzebub perceived, than whom,
Satan except, none higher sat, with grave
Aspect he rose, and in his rising seemed

6. Pain felt by the senses.

7. The warrior angel, chief of the angelic armies.

A pillar of state; deep on his front° engraven *brow*
Deliberation sat and public care;
And princely counsel in his face yet shone,
Majestic though in ruin: sage he stood
With Atlantean[8] shoulders fit to bear
The weight of mightiest monarchies; his look
Drew audience and attention still as night
Or summer's noontide air, while thus he spake.
"Thrones and imperial Powers, offspring of Heav'n
Ethereal Virtues; or these titles[9] now
Must we renounce, and changing style° be called *title*
Princes of Hell? for so the popular vote
Inclines, here to continue, and build up here
A growing empire. Doubtless! while we dream,
And know not that the King of Heav'n hath doomed
This place our dungeon, not our safe retreat
Beyond his potent arm, to live exempt
From Heav'n's high jurisdiction, in new league
Banded against his throne, but to remain
In strictest bondage, though thus far removed,
Under th' inevitable curb, reserved
His captive multitude: for he, be sure,
In height or depth, still first and last will reign
Sole King, and of his kingdom lose no part
By our revolt, but over Hell extend
His empire, and with iron scepter rule
Us here, as with his golden those in Heav'n.
What° sit we then projecting peace and war? *why*
War hath determined us,[1] and foiled with loss
Irreparable; terms of peace yet none
Vouchsafed° or sought; for what peace will be giv'n *granted*
To us enslaved, but custody severe,
And stripes, and arbitrary punishment
Inflicted? And what peace can we return,
But, to our power,[2] hostility and hate,
Untamed reluctance,° and revenge though slow, *resistance*
Yet ever plotting how the conqueror least
May reap his conquest, and may least rejoice
In doing what we most in suffering feel?
Nor will occasion want,° nor shall we need *be lacking*
With dangerous expedition to invade
Heav'n, whose high walls fear no assault or siege,
Or ambush from the deep. What if we find
Some easier enterprise? There is a place
(If ancient and prophetic fame° in Heav'n *rumor*
Err not) another world, the happy seat
Of some new race called Man, about this time
To be created like to us, though less
In power and excellence, but favored more

8. Worthy of Atlas, the Titan who as a punishment for rebellion was condemned to hold up the heavens on his shoulders.
9. The official titles of angelic orders.
1. I.e., war has decided the question for us, but also limited us.
2. I.e., to the best of our power.

Of him who rules above; so was his will
Pronounced among the gods, and by an oath,
That shook Heav'n's whole circumference, confirmed.
Thither let us bend all our thoughts, to learn
What creatures there inhabit, of what mold,
Or substance, how endued,° and what their power, *endowed*
And where their weakness, how attempted° best, *attacked, tempted*
By force or subtlety. Though Heav'n be shut,
And Heav'n's high arbitrator sit secure
In his own strength, this place may lie exposed,
The utmost border of his kingdom, left
To their defense who hold it:[3] here perhaps
Some advantageous act may be achieved
By sudden onset, either with hellfire
To waste° his whole creation, or possess *lay waste*
All as our own, and drive as we were driven,
The puny habitants, or if not drive,
Seduce them to our party, that their God
May prove their foe, and with repenting hand
Abolish his own works.[4] This would surpass
Common revenge, and interrupt his joy
In our confusion, and our joy upraise
In his disturbance; when his darling sons
Hurled headlong to partake with us, shall curse
Their frail original,° and faded bliss, *originator, parent*
Faded so soon. Advise° if this be worth *consider*
Attempting, or to sit in darkness here
Hatching vain empires." Thus Beëlzebub
Pleaded his devilish counsel, first devised
By Satan, and in part proposed: for whence,
But from the author of all ill could spring
So deep a malice, to confound° the race *ruin*
Of mankind in one root,[5] and earth with Hell
To mingle and involve, done all to spite
The great Creator? But their spite still serves
His glory to augment. The bold design
Pleased highly those infernal States,° and joy *nobles*
Sparkled in all their eyes; with full assent
They vote: whereat his speech he thus renews.
  "Well have ye judged, well ended long debate,
Synod of gods, and like to what ye are,
Great things resolved, which from the lowest deep
Will once more lift us up, in spite of fate,
Nearer our ancient seat; perhaps in view
Of those bright confines, whence with neighboring arms
And opportune excursion we may chance
Reenter Heav'n; or else in some mild zone
Dwell not unvisited of Heav'n's fair light
Secure, and at the bright'ning orient° beam *lustrous*

3. To be defended by the occupants.
4. Cf. Genesis 6.7: "And the Lord said, 'I will destroy man [and all other creatures]; for it repenteth me that I have made them.' "
5. Adam, the first man, is the "root" of the human race.

Purge off this gloom; the soft delicious air,
To heal the scar of these corrosive fires
Shall breathe her balm. But first whom shall we send
In search of this new world, whom shall we find
Sufficient? Who shall tempt° with wand'ring feet *attempt, venture*
The dark unbottomed infinite abyss
And through the palpable obscure[6] find out
His uncouth° way, or spread his aery flight *unknown*
Upborne with indefatigable wings
Over the vast abrupt,[7] ere he arrive
The happy isle? What strength, what art can then
Suffice, or what evasion bear him safe
Through the strict senteries° and stations thick *sentries*
Of angels watching round? Here he had need
All circumspection, and we now no less
Choice° in our suffrage; for on whom we send, *discrimination*
The weight of all and our last hope relies."
  This said, he sat; and expectation held
His look suspense,[8] awaiting who appeared
To second, or oppose, or undertake
The perilous attempt: but all sat mute,
Pondering the danger with deep thoughts; and each
In other's count'nance read his own dismay
Astonished. None among the choice and prime
Of those Heav'n-warring champions could be found
So hardy as to proffer or accept
Alone the dreadful voyage; till at last
Satan, whom now transcendent glory raised
Above his fellows, with monarchal pride
Conscious of highest worth, unmoved thus spake.
  "O progeny of Heav'n, empyreal Thrones,
With reason hath deep silence and demur° *hesitation*
Seized us, though undismayed: long is the way
And hard, that out of Hell leads up to light;
Our prison strong, this huge convex of fire,
Outrageous to devour, immures us round
Ninefold,[9] and gates of burning adamant
Barred over us prohibit all egress.
These passed, if any pass, the void profound
Of unessential Night receives him next
Wide gaping, and with utter loss of being
Threatens him, plunged in that abortive gulf.[1]
If thence he scape into whatever world,
Or unknown region, what remains him less° *awaits him except*
Than unknown dangers and as hard escape?
But I should ill become this throne, O Peers,
And this imperial sov'reignty, adorned

6. Darkness so thick it can be felt (cf. Exodus 10.21).
7. Chaos, a striking example of sound imitating sense.
8. I.e., he sat waiting in suspense.
9. Hell's fiery walls and gates have nine thicknesses (see lines 645ff.). "Adamant" (following): a fabulously hard metal.
1. Chaos is a womb in which all potential forms fragment (see lines 895ff.) "Unessential" (line 439): i.e., having no real essence.

With splendor, armed with power, if aught proposed
And judged of public moment,° in the shape — *importance*
Of difficulty or danger could deter
Me from attempting. Wherefore do I assume
These royalties, and not refuse to reign,
Refusing° to accept as great a share — *if I refuse*
Of hazard as of honor, due alike
To him who reigns, and so much to him due
Of hazard more, as he above the rest
High honored sits? Go therefore mighty Powers,
Terror of Heav'n, though fall'n; intend° at home, — *consider*
While here shall be our home, what best may ease
The present misery, and render Hell
More tolerable; if there be cure or charm
To respite or deceive, or slack the pain
Of this ill mansion: intermit no watch
Against a wakeful foe, while I abroad
Through all the coasts° of dark destruction seek — *districts*
Deliverance for us all: this enterprise
None shall partake with me." Thus saying rose
The monarch, and prevented° all reply, — *forestalled*
Prudent, lest from his resolution raised° — *roused*
Others among the chief might offer now
(Certain to be refused) what erst° they feared; — *formerly*
And so refused might in opinion stand
His rivals, winning cheap the high repute
Which he through hazard huge must earn. But they
Dreaded not more th' adventure than his voice
Forbidding; and at once with him they rose;
Their rising all at once was as the sound
Of thunder heard remote. Towards him they bend
With awful° reverence prone; and as a god — *full of awe*
Extol him equal to the Highest in Heav'n:
Nor failed they to express how much they praised,
That for the general safety he despised
His own: for neither do the Spirits damned
Lose all their virtue; lest bad men should boast
Their specious° deeds on earth, which glory excites, — *pretending to worth*
Or close° ambition varnished o'er with zeal. — *secret*

Thus they their doubtful consultations dark
Ended rejoicing in their matchless chief:
As when from mountaintops the dusky clouds
Ascending, while the north wind sleeps, o'erspread
Heav'n's cheerful face, the louring element° — *threatening sky*
Scowls o'er the darkened landscape snow, or show'r;
If chance the radiant sun with farewell sweet
Extend his evening beam, the fields revive,
The birds their notes renew, and bleating herds
Attest their joy, that hill and valley rings.
O shame to men! Devil with devil damned
Firm concord holds, men only disagree
Of creatures rational, though under hope
Of heavenly grace: and God proclaiming peace,

Yet live in hatred, enmity, and strife
Among themselves, and levy cruel wars,
Wasting the earth, each other to destroy:
As if (which might induce us to accord)
Man had not hellish foes enow° besides, — *enough*
That day and night for his destruction wait.
   The Stygian° council thus dissolved; and forth — *Styx-like, hellish*
In order came the grand infernal peers:
Midst came their mighty paramount,° and seemed — *supreme ruler*
Alone th' antagonist of Heav'n, nor less
Than Hell's dread emperor with pomp supreme,
And godlike imitated state; him round
A globe° of fiery Seraphim enclosed — *band, circle*
With bright emblazonry and horrent[2] arms.
Then of their session ended they bid cry
With trumpet's regal sound the great result:
Toward the four winds four speedy Cherubim
Put to their mouths the sounding alchemy[3]
By herald's voice explained; the hollow abyss
Heard far and wide, and all the host of Hell
With deaf'ning shout, returned them loud acclaim.
Thence more at ease their minds and somewhat raised
By false presumptuous hope, the rangèd° powers — *arrayed in ranks*
Disband, and wand'ring, each his several way
Pursues, as inclination or sad choice
Leads him perplexed, where he may likeliest find
Truce to his restless thoughts, and entertain
The irksome hours, till his great chief return.
Part on the plain, or in the air sublime° — *aloft*
Upon the wing, or in swift race contend,
As at th' Olympian games or Pythian fields;[4]
Part curb their fiery steeds, or shun the goal[5]
With rapid wheels, or fronted° brígades form. — *confronting*
As when to warn proud cities war appears
Waged in the troubled sky, and armies rush
To battle in the clouds,[6] before each van° — *vanguard*
Prick° forth the aery knights, and couch their spears — *spur*
Till thickest legions close; with feats of arms
From either end of Heav'n the welkin° burns. — *sky*
Others with vast Typhoean[7] rage more fell° — *fierce*
Rend up both rocks and hills, and ride the air
In whirlwind; Hell scarce holds the wild uproar.
As when Alcides from Oechalia crowned
With conquest, felt th' envenomed robe, and tore
Through pain up by the roots Thessalian pines,
And Lichas from the top of Oeta threw
Into th' Euboic sea.[8] Others more mild,

2. Bristling. "Emblazonry": decorated shields.
3. Trumpets (made of the goldlike alloy brass).
4. The Olympic games were held at Olympia, the Pythian games at Delphi. Games celebrating a (usually dead) hero are an epic convention.
5. To drive a chariot as close as possible around a column without hitting it.
6. The appearance of warfare in the skies, reported before several notable battles, portends trouble on earth.
7. Like that of Typhon, the hundred-headed Titan (see 1.199).
8. Wearing a poisoned robe given him in a deception, Hercules ("Alcides") in his dying agonies

Retreated in a silent valley, sing
With notes angelical to many a harp
Their own heroic deeds and hapless fall
By doom of battle; and complain that fate
Free virtue should enthrall to force or chance.
Their song was partial,° but the harmony — *prejudiced*
(What could it less when Spirits immortal sing?)
Suspended° Hell, and took with ravishment — *held in suspense*
The thronging audience. In discourse more sweet
(For eloquence the soul, song charms the sense)
Others apart sat on a hill retired,
In thoughts more elevate, and reasoned high
Of providence, foreknowledge, will, and fate,
Fixed fate, free will, foreknowledge absolute,
And found no end, in wand'ring mazes lost.
Of good and evil much they argued then,
Of happiness and final misery,
Passion and apathy,[9] and glory and shame,
Vain wisdom all, and false philosophy:
Yet with a pleasing sorcery could charm
Pain for a while or anguish, and excite
Fallacious hope, or arm th' obdurèd° breast — *hardened*
With stubborn patience as with triple steel.
Another part in squadrons and gross° bands, — *solid, dense*
On bold adventure to discover wide
That dismal world, if any clime perhaps
Might yield them easier habitation, bend
Four ways their flying march, along the banks
Of four infernal rivers that disgorge
Into the burning lake their baleful streams:[1]
Abhorrèd Styx the flood of deadly hate,
Sad Acheron of sorrow, black and deep;
Cocytus, named of lamentation loud
Heard on the rueful stream; fierce Phlegethon
Whose waves of torrent fire inflame with rage.
Far off from these a slow and silent stream,
Lethe the river of oblivion rolls
Her wat'ry labyrinth, whereof who drinks,
Forthwith his former state and being forgets,
Forgets both joy and grief, pleasure and pain.
Beyond this flood a frozen continent
Lies dark and wild, beat with perpetual storms
Of whirlwind and dire hail, which on firm land
Thaws not, but gathers heap,[2] and ruin seems
Of ancient pile; all else deep snow and ice,
A gulf profound as that Serbonian bog[3]

threw his beloved companion Lichas, along with a good part of Mount Oeta, into the Euboean Sea, near Thermopylae.

9. The Stoic goal of freedom from passion.

1. These four rivers are traditional in hellish geography. Milton distinguishes them by the original meanings of their Greek names: Styx means "hateful," Acheron "woeful," etc. Lethe is "far off" and quite different from the others, oblivion being a desired state in Hell.

2. In a heap, resembling the ruin of an old building ("ancient pile," next line).

3. Lake Serbonis, once famous for its quicksands, lies near the city of Damietta ("Damiata," next line), just east of the Nile.

Betwixt Damiata and Mount Casius old,
Where armies whole have sunk: the parching air
Burns frore,° and cold performs th' effect of fire. *frozen*
Thither by harpy-footed[4] Furies haled,° *driven*
At certain revolutions° all the damned *recurring times*
Are brought: and feel by turns the bitter change
Of fierce extremes, extremes by change more fierce,
From beds of raging fire to starve° in ice *make numb*
Their soft ethereal warmth, and there to pine
Immovable, infixed, and frozen round,
Periods of time; thence hurried back to fire.
They ferry over this Lethean sound
Both to and fro, their sorrow to augment,
And wish and struggle, as they pass, to reach
The tempting stream, with one small drop to lose
In sweet forgetfulness all pain and woe,
All in one moment, and so near the brink;
But fate withstands, and to oppose th' attempt
Medusa[5] with Gorgonian terror guards
The ford, and of itself the water flies
All taste of living wight,° as once it fled *creature*
The lip of Tantalus.[6] Thus roving on
In cónfused march forlorn, th' advent'rous bands
With shudd'ring horror pale, and eyes aghast
Viewed first their lamentable lot, and found
No rest: through many a dark and dreary vale
They passed, and many a region dolorous,
O'er many a frozen, many a fiery alp,° *volcano*
Rocks, caves, lakes, fens, bogs, dens, and shades of death,
A universe of death, which God by curse
Created evil, for evil only good,
Where all life dies, death lives, and nature breeds,
Perverse, all monstrous, all prodigious things,
Abominable, inutterable, and worse
Than fables yet have feigned, or fear conceived,
Gorgons and Hydras, and Chimeras[7] dire.
  Meanwhile the Adversary[8] of God and man,
Satan, with thoughts inflamed of highest design,
Puts on swift wings,° and towards the gates of Hell *flies swiftly*
Explores his solitary flight; sometimes
He scours the right-hand coast, sometimes the left,
Now shaves with level wing the deep, then soars
Up to the fiery concave° tow'ring high. *vault*
As when far off at sea a fleet descried
Hangs on the clouds, by equinoctial° winds *from the equator*
Close sailing from Bengala,° or the isles *Bengal*
Of Ternate and Tidore,[9] whence merchants bring

4. Taloned. In Greek mythology the Harpies (monsters with women's faces) carried off individuals to the Furies, who avenged crimes.
5. One of the three Gorgons, women with snaky hair, scaly bodies, and boar's tusks, the sight of whose faces changed men to stone.
6. Tantalus, afflicted with a raging thirst, stood in the middle of a lake, the water of which always receded when he tried to drink (hence, "tantalize").
7. The Hydra was a serpent whose multiple heads grew back when severed; the Chimera was a fire-breathing creature, part lion, part dragon, part goat.
8. *Satan* in Hebrew means "adversary."
9. Two of the Moluccas, or Spice Islands, modern Indonesia.

Their spicy drugs: they on the trading flood
Through the wide Ethiopian to the Cape
Ply stemming nightly toward the pole:[1] so seemed
Far off the flying Fiend. At last appear
Hell bounds high reaching to the horrid roof,
And thrice threefold the gates; three folds were brass,
Three iron, three of adamantine rock,
Impenetrable, impaled with circling fire,
Yet unconsumed. Before the gates there sat
On either side a formidable shape;[2]
The one seemed woman to the waist, and fair,
But ended foul in many a scaly fold
Voluminous and vast, a serpent armed
With mortal sting: about her middle round
A cry° of hellhounds never ceasing barked *pack*
With wide Cerberean[3] mouths full loud, and rung
A hideous peal: yet, when they list,° would creep, *wish*
If aught disturbed their noise, into her womb,
And kennel there, yet there still barked and howled,
Within unseen. Far less abhorred than these
Vexed Scylla[4] bathing in the sea that parts
Calabria from the hoarse Trinacrian shore:
Nor uglier follow the night-hag,[5] when called
In secret, riding through the air she comes
Lured with the smell of infant blood, to dance
With Lapland witches, while the laboring° moon *troubled*
Eclipses at their charms.° The other shape, *magic*
If shape it might be called that shape had none
Distinguishable in member, joint, or limb,
Or substance might be called that shadow seemed,
For each seemed either; black it stood as night,
Fierce as ten Furies, terrible as hell,
And shook a dreadful dart; what seemed his head
The likeness of a kingly crown had on.
Satan was now at hand, and from his seat
The monster moving onward came as fast
With horrid strides. Hell trembled as he strode.
Th' undaunted Fiend what this might be admired,° *wondered*
Admired, not feared; God and his Son except,
Created thing naught valued he nor shunned;
And with disdainful look thus first began.
"Whence and what art thou, execrable shape,
That dar'st, though grim and terrible, advance
Thy miscreated front° athwart my way *misshapen face*
To yonder gates? Through them I mean to pass,

1. The South Pole. "Ethiopian": the Indian Ocean. "The Cape" is the Cape of Good Hope.
2. The allegorical figures of Sin and Death are founded on James 1.15: "Then when lust hath conceived, it bringeth forth sin: and sin, when it is finished, bringeth forth death." But the incestuous relations of Sin and Death are Milton's own invention. Physically, Sin is modeled on Virgil's or Ovid's Scylla, with some touches adopted from Spenser's Error. Death is a traditional figure, vague and vast.
3. Like Cerberus, the multiheaded hound of Hell.
4. Circe, out of jealousy, threw poison into the water where Scylla bathed, in the straits between Calabria and Sicily ("Trinacria," next line); the poison caused Scylla to develop a ring of barking, snapping dogs around her waist.
5. Hecate (three syllables), goddess of sorcery. She attends orgies of witches in Lapland (line 665, famous for witchcraft), drawn by the blood of babies sacrificed for the occasion.

That be assured, without leave asked of thee:
Retire, or taste° thy folly, and learn by proof, (*experience*)
Hell-born, not to contend with Spirits of Heav'n."
  To whom the goblin full of wrath replied:
"Art thou that traitor angel, art thou he,
Who first broke peace in Heav'n and faith, till then
Unbroken, and in proud rebellious arms
Drew after him the third part of Heav'n's sons
Conjured° against the Highest, for which both thou (*sworn together*)
And they outcast from God, are here condemned
To waste eternal days in woe and pain?
And reckon'st thou thyself with Spirits of Heav'n,
Hell-doomed, and breath'st defiance here and scorn,
Where I reign king, and to enrage thee more,
Thy king and lord? Back to thy punishment,
False fugitive, and to thy speed add wings,
Lest with a whip of scorpions I pursue
Thy ling'ring, or with one stroke of this dart
Strange horror seize thee, and pangs unfelt before."
  So spake the grisly terror, and in shape,
So speaking and so threat'ning, grew tenfold
More dreadful and deform: on th' other side
Incensed with indignation Satan stood
Unterrified, and like a comet burned
That fires the length of Ophiuchus[6] huge
In th' arctic sky, and from his horrid° hair (*bristling*)
Shakes pestilence and war. Each at the head
Leveled his deadly aim; their fatal hands
No second stroke intend, and such a frown
Each cast at th' other, as when, two black clouds
With Heav'n's artillery fraught,[7] come rattling on
Over the Caspian,[8] then stand front to front
Hov'ring a space, till winds the signal blow
To join their dark encounter in mid-air:
So frowned the mighty combatants, that Hell
Grew darker at their frown, so matched they stood;
For never but once more was either like
To meet so great a foe.[9] And now great deeds
Had been achieved, whereof all Hell had rung,
Had not the snaky sorceress that sat
Fast by Hell gate, and kept the fatal key,
Ris'n, and with hideous outcry rushed between.
  "O father, what intends thy hand," she cried,
"Against thy only son?[1] What fury O son,
Possesses thee to bend that mortal dart
Against thy father's head? And know'st for whom;
For him who sits above and laughs the while
At thee ordained his drudge, to execute
Whate'er his wrath, which he calls justice, bids,

6. A vast northern constellation, "the Serpent Bearer."
7. Loaded with thunderbolts.
8. The Caspian is a particularly stormy area.
9. I.e., the Son of God.
1. Sin, Death, and Satan, in their various interrelations, parody obscenely the relations between God and the Son, Adam and Eve.

His wrath which one day will destroy ye both."
She spake, and at her words the hellish pest
Forbore, then these to her Satan returned.
"So strange thy outcry, and thy words so strange
Thou interposest, that my sudden hand
Prevented° spares to tell thee yet by deeds *forestalled*
What it intends; till first I know of thee,
What thing thou art, thus double-formed, and why
In this infernal vale first met thou call'st
Me father, and that phantasm call'st my son?
I know thee not, nor ever saw till now
Sight more detestable than him and thee."
T' whom thus the portress of Hell gate replied:
"Hast thou forgot me then, and do I seem
Now in thine eye so foul, once deemed so fair
In Heav'n, when at th' assembly, and in sight
Of all the Seraphim with thee combined
In bold conspiracy against Heav'n's King,
All on a sudden miserable pain
Surprised thee, dim thine eyes, and dizzy swum
In darkness, while thy head flames thick and fast
Threw forth, till on the left side op'ning wide,
Likest to thee in shape and count'nance bright,
Then shining heav'nly fair, a goddess armed
Out of thy head I sprung:[2] amazement seized
All th' host of Heav'n; back they recoiled afraid
At first, and called me Sin, and for a sign
Portentous held me; but familiar grown,
I pleased, and with attractive graces won
The most averse, thee chiefly, who full oft
Thyself in me thy perfect image viewing
Becam'st enamored, and such joy thou took'st
With me in secret, that my womb conceived
A growing burden. Meanwhile war arose,
And fields were fought in Heav'n; wherein remained
(For what could else) to our almighty foe
Clear victory, to our part loss and rout
Through all the empyrean: down they fell
Driv'n headlong from the pitch° of Heaven, down *summit*
Into this deep, and in the general fall
I also; at which time this powerful key
Into my hand was giv'n, with charge to keep
These gates forever shut, which none can pass
Without my op'ning. Pensive here I sat
Alone, but long I sat not, till my womb
Pregnant by thee, and now excessive grown
Prodigious motion felt and rueful throes.
At last this odious offspring whom thou seest
Thine own begotten, breaking violent way
Tore through my entrails, that with fear and pain
Distorted, all my nether shape thus grew

2. As Athena sprang full grown from the head of Zeus.

Transformed: but he my inbred enemy
Forth issued, brandishing his fatal dart
Made to destroy: I fled, and cried out 'Death';
Hell trembled at the hideous name, and sighed
From all her caves, and back resounded 'Death.'
I fled, but he pursued (though more, it seems,
Inflamed with lust than rage) and swifter far,
Me overtook his mother all dismayed,
And in embraces forcible and foul
Engend'ring with me, of that rape begot
These yelling monsters that with ceaseless cry
Surround me, as thou saw'st, hourly conceived
And hourly born, with sorrow infinite
To me, for when they list,° into the womb *wish*
That bred them they return, and howl and gnaw
My bowels, their repast; then bursting forth
Afresh with conscious terrors vex me round,
That rest or intermission none I find.
Before mine eyes in opposition sits
Grim Death my son and foe, who sets them on,
And me his parent would full soon devour
For want of other prey, but that he knows
His end with mine involved; and knows that I
Should prove a bitter morsel, and his bane,° *poison*
Whenever that shall be; so fate pronounced.
But thou O father, I forewarn thee, shun
His deadly arrow; neither vainly hope
To be invulnerable in those bright arms,
Though tempered heav'nly, for that mortal dint,° *blow*
Save he who reigns above, none can resist."
She finished, and the subtle Fiend his lore° *lesson*
Soon learned, now milder, and thus answered smooth.
"Dear daughter, since thou claim'st me for thy sire,
And my fair son here show'st me, the dear pledge
Of dalliance had with thee in Heav'n, and joys
Then sweet, now sad to mention, through dire change
Befall'n us unforeseen, unthought of, know
I come no enemy, but to set free
From out this dark and dismal house of pain,
Both him and thee, and all the heav'nly host
Of Spirits that in our just pretenses° armed *claims*
Fell with us from on high: from them I go
This uncouth errand[3] sole, and one for all
Myself expose, with lonely steps to tread
Th' unfounded° deep, and through the void immense *bottomless*
To search with wand'ring quest a place foretold
Should be, and, by concurring signs, ere now
Created vast and round, a place of bliss
In the purlieus° of Heav'n, and therein placed *outskirts*
A race of upstart creatures, to supply
Perhaps our vacant room, though more removed,

3. Unknown journey—a parody of Christ's errand on earth (3.236–65).

Lest Heav'n surcharged° with potent multitude *overcrowded*
Might hap to move new broils:° be this or aught *controversies*
Than this more secret now designed, I haste
To know, and this once known, shall soon return,
And bring ye to the place where thou and Death
Shall dwell at ease, and up and down unseen
Wing silently the buxom° air, embalmed° *yielding / made fragrant*
With odors; there ye shall be fed and filled
Immeasurably, all things shall be your prey."
He ceased, for both seemed highly pleased, and Death
Grinned horrible a ghastly smile, to hear
His famine° should be filled, and blessed his maw° *ravenous hunger / belly*
Destined to that good hour: no less rejoiced
His mother bad, and thus bespake her sire.
"The key of this infernal pit by due,
And by command of Heav'n's all-powerful King
I keep, by him forbidden to unlock
These adamantine gates; against all force
Death ready stands to interpose his dart,
Fearless to be o'ermatched by living might.
But what owe I to his commands above
Who hates me, and hath hither thrust me down
Into this gloom of Tartarus profound,
To sit in hateful office here confined,
Inhabitant of Heav'n, and heav'nly-born,
Here in perpetual agony and pain,
With terrors and with clamors compassed round
Of mine own brood, that on my bowels feed?
Thou art my father, thou my author, thou
My being gav'st me; whom should I obey
But thee, whom follow? Thou wilt bring me soon
To that new world of light and bliss, among
The gods who live at ease, where I shall reign
At thy right hand voluptuous,[4] as beseems
Thy daughter and thy darling, without end."
Thus saying, from her side the fatal key,
Sad instrument of all our woe, she took;
And towards the gate rolling her bestial train,[5]
Forthwith the huge portcullis high up drew,
Which but herself not all the Stygian powers° *armies of Hell*
Could once have moved; then in the keyhole turns
Th' intrícate wards, and every bolt and bar
Of massy iron or solid rock with ease
Unfastens: on a sudden open fly
With impetuous recoil and jarring sound
Th' infernal doors, and on their hinges grate
Harsh thunder, that the lowest bottom shook
Of Erebus.° She opened, but to shut *Hell*
Excelled° her power; the gates wide open stood, *exceeded*
That with extended wings a bannered host

4. As the Son sits at God's right hand, Sin will at Satan's, a blasphemous parody of the Apostles' Creed and of *Paradise Lost* 3.250–80.
5. I.e. propelling her yelping offspring.

Under spread ensigns° marching might pass through — *flags, standards*
With horse and chariots ranked in loose array;
So wide they stood, and like a furnace mouth
Cast forth redounding° smoke and ruddy flame. — *billowing*
Before their eyes in sudden view appear
The secrets of the hoary° deep, a dark — *ancient*
Illimitable° ocean without bound, — *without limit*
Without dimension, where length, breadth, and height,
And time and place are lost; where eldest Night
And Chaos, ancestors of Nature, hold
Eternal anarchy, amidst the noise
Of endless wars, and by confusion stand.
For Hot, Cold, Moist, and Dry, four champions fierce
Strive here for mastery, and to battle bring
Their embryon atoms;[6] they around the flag
Of each his faction, in their several clans,
Light-armed or heavy, sharp, smooth, swift or slow,
Swarm populous, unnumbered as the sands
Of Barca or Cyrene's torrid soil,[7]
Levied to side with warring winds, and poise[8]
Their lighter wings. To whom these most adhere,
He rules a moment; Chaos[9] umpire sits,
And by decision more embroils the fray
By which he reigns: next him high arbiter
Chance governs all. Into this wild abyss,
The womb of Nature and perhaps her grave,
Of neither sea, nor shore, nor air, nor fire,
But all these in their pregnant causes° mixed — *seeds*
Confus'dly, and which thus must ever fight,
Unless th' Almighty Maker them ordain
His dark materials to create more worlds,
Into this wild abyss the wary Fiend
Stood on the brink of Hell and looked a while,
Pondering his voyage; for no narrow frith° — *channel, firth*
He had to cross. Nor was his ear less pealed° — *dinned*
With noises loud and ruinous (to compare
Great things with small) than when Bellona[1] storms,
With all her battering engines bent to raze
Some capital city; or less than if this frame° — *structure*
Of Heav'n were falling, and these elements
In mutiny had from her axle torn
The steadfast earth. At last his sail-broad vans° — *wings*
He spreads for flight, and in the surging smoke
Uplifted spurns the ground, thence many a league
As in a cloudy chair ascending rides
Audacious, but that seat soon failing, meets
A vast vacuity: all unawares
Flutt'ring his pennons[2] vain plumb down he drops

6. These subatomic qualities combine together in nature to form the four elements, fire, earth, water, and air, but they struggle endlessly in Chaos, where the atoms of these elements remain undeveloped (in "embryo").
7. Cities built on the shifting sands of North Africa.
8. Give weight to. "Levied": both enlisted and raised up.
9. Chaos is both the place where confusion reigns and personified confusion itself.
1. Goddess of war.
2. Useless wings ("pinions").

Ten thousand fathom deep, and to this hour
Down had been falling, had not by ill chance
The strong rebuff° of some tumultuous cloud *counterblast*
Instinct° with fire and niter° hurried him *filled / saltpeter*
As many miles aloft: that fury stayed,
Quenched in a boggy Syrtis,[3] neither sea,
Nor good dry land: nigh foundered° on he fares, *drowned*
Treading the crude consistence, half on foot,
Half flying; behoves° him now both oar and sail. *befits*
As when a griffin through the wilderness
With wingèd course o'er hill or moory° dale, *marshy*
Pursues the Arimaspian, who by stealth
Had from his wakeful custody purloined
The guarded gold:[4] so eagerly the Fiend
O'er bog or steep, through strait, rough, dense, or rare,
With head, hands, wings, or feet pursues his way,
And swims or sinks, or wades, or creeps, or flies:
At length a universal hubbub wild
Of stunning sounds and voices all confused
Borne through the hollow dark assaults his ear
With loudest vehemence: thither he plies,
Undaunted to meet there whatever Power
Or Spirit of the nethermost abyss
Might in that noise reside, of whom to ask
Which way the nearest coast of darkness lies
Bordering on light; when straight behold the throne
Of Chaos, and his dark pavilion spread
Wide on the wasteful deep; with him enthroned
Sat sable-vested Night, eldest of things,
The consort of his reign; and by them stood
Orcus and Ades,[5] and the dreaded name
Of Demogorgon,[6] Rumor next and Chance,
And Tumult and Confusion all embroiled,
And Discord with a thousand various mouths.
T' whom Satan turning boldly, thus. "Ye Powers
And Spirits of this nethermost abyss,
Chaos and ancient Night, I come no spy,
With purpose to explore or to disturb
The secrets of your realm, but by constraint
Wand'ring this darksome desert, as my way
Lies through your spacious empire up to light,
Alone, and without guide, half lost, I seek
What readiest path leads where your gloomy bounds
Confine with° Heav'n; or if some other place *border on*
From your dominion won, th' Ethereal King
Possesses lately, thither to arrive
I travel this profound;° direct my course; *deep pit*
Directed, no mean recompense it brings
To your behoof,° if I that region lost, *on your behalf*
All usurpation thence expelled, reduce

3. Quicksand in North African gulfs, famous for their shifting sandbars.
4. Griffins, mythical creatures, half-eagle, half-lion, hoarded gold that was stolen from them by the one-eyed Arimaspians.
5. Latin and Greek names of Pluto, god of Hell.
6. A mysterious deity associated with Fate; Milton elsewhere identifies him with Chaos.

To her original darkness and your sway
(Which is my present journey)[7] and once more
Erect the standard there of ancient Night;
Yours be th' advantage all, mine the revenge."
   Thus Satan; and him thus the anarch[8] old
With falt'ring speech and visage incomposed° *disordered*
Answered. "I know thee, stranger, who thou art,
That mighty leading angel, who of late
Made head against Heav'n's King, though overthrown.
I saw and heard, for such a numerous host
Fled not in silence through the frighted deep
With ruin upon ruin, rout on rout,
Confusion worse confounded; and Heav'n gates
Poured out by millions her victorious bands
Pursuing. I upon my frontiers here
Keep residence; if all I can will serve,
That little which is left so to defend,
Encroached on still° through our intestine broils° *constantly / civil wars*
Weak'ning the scepter of old Night: first Hell
Your dungeon stretching far and wide beneath;
Now lately heaven and earth,[9] another world
Hung o'er my realm, linked in a golden chain
To that side Heav'n from whence your legions fell:
If that way be your walk, you have not far;
So much the nearer danger; go and speed;
Havoc and spoil and ruin are my gain."
   He ceased; and Satan stayed not to reply,
But glad that now his sea should find a shore,
With fresh alacrity and force renewed
Springs upward like a pyramid of fire
Into the wild expanse, and through the shock
Of fighting elements, on all sides round
Environed wins his way; harder beset
And more endangered, than when Argo passed
Through Bosporus betwixt the justling rocks:[1]
Or when Ulysses on the larboard shunned
Charybdis, and by th' other whirlpool steered.[2]
So he with difficulty and labor hard
Moved on, with difficulty and labor he;
But he once passed, soon after when man fell,
Strange alteration! Sin and Death amain° *at full speed*
Following his track, such was the will of Heav'n,
Paved after him a broad and beaten way
Over the dark abyss, whose boiling gulf
Tamely endured a bridge of wondrous length
From Hell continued reaching th' utmost orb[3]
Of this frail world; by which the Spirits perverse

7. The purpose of my present journey.
8. Chaos is not monarch of his realm but, appropriately, "anarch," nonruler.
9. The cosmos, with its own "heaven" (not the empyrean, the Heaven of God and the angels).
1. Jason and his fifty Argonauts, sailing through the Bosporus to the Black Sea in pursuit of the Golden Fleece, had to pass through the Symplegades, or clashing rocks.
2. Homer's Ulysses, sailing where Italy almost touches Sicily, had to pass between Charybdis, a whirlpool, and Scylla, a monster who devoured six of his men (not another whirlpool, as used here).
3. The bridge ends on the outermost sphere of the ten concentric spheres making up the universe.

With easy intercourse pass to and fro
To tempt or punish mortals, except whom
God and good angels guard by special grace.
But now at last the sacred influence
Of light appears, and from the walls of Heav'n
Shoots far into the bosom of dim Night
A glimmering dawn; here Nature first begins
Her farthest verge,° and Chaos to retire *threshold*
As from her outmost works a broken foe
With tumult less and with less hostile din,
That° Satan with less toil, and now with ease *so that*
Wafts on the calmer wave by dubious light
And like a weather-beaten vessel holds° *makes for*
Gladly the port, though shrouds and tackle torn;
Or in the emptier waste, resembling air
Weighs° his spread wings, at leisure to behold *balances*
Far off th' empyreal Heav'n, extended wide
In circuit, undetermined square or round,
With opal tow'rs and battlements adorned
Of living sapphire, once his native seat;
And fast by hanging in a golden chain
This pendent world,° in bigness as a star *universe*
Of smallest magnitude close by the moon.
Thither full fraught with mischievous revenge,
Accursed, and in a cursèd hour, he hies.

From Book 3

[THE INVOCATION, THE COUNCIL IN HEAVEN, AND THE CONCLUSION OF SATAN'S JOURNEY]

Hail holy Light, offspring of Heav'n firstborn,
Or of th' Eternal coeternal beam
May I express thee unblamed?[1] Since God is light,
And never but in unapproachèd light
Dwelt from eternity, dwelt then in thee,
Bright effluence of bright essence increate.° *uncreated, eternal*
Or hear'st thou rather[2] pure ethereal stream,
Whose fountain who shall tell? Before the sun,
Before the heavens thou wert, and at the voice
Of God, as with a mantle didst invest° *cover*
The rising world of waters dark and deep,
Won from the void and formless infinite.
Thee I revisit now with bolder wing,
Escaped the Stygian pool, though long detained
In that obscure sojourn, while in my flight
Through utter and through middle darkness[3] borne
With other notes than to th' Orphéan lyre[4]

1. This second proem or invocation (3.1–55) is a hymn to Light, addressed either as the first creature of God or as coeternal with God, with allusion to 1 John 1.5, "God is Light, and in him is no darkness at all."
2. I.e., would you rather be called (a Latinism).
3. Hell is "utter" (i.e., outer) darkness; Chaos is middle darkness.
4. One of the so-called Orphic hymns is "To Night," and Orpheus himself visited the underworld. But Milton's song, Christian and epic, is of a different kind.

I sung of Chaos and eternal Night,
Taught by the Heav'nly Muse[5] to venture down
The dark descent, and up to reascend,
Though hard and rare: thee I revisit safe,
And feel thy sov'reign vital lamp; but thou
Revisit'st not these eyes, that roll in vain
To find thy piercing ray, and find no dawn;
So thick a drop serene hath quenched their orbs,
Or dim suffusion[6] veiled. Yet not the more
Cease I to wander where the Muses haunt
Clear spring, or shady grove, or sunny hill,
Smit with the love of sacred song; but chief
Thee Sion[7] and the flow'ry brooks beneath
That wash thy hallowed feet, and warbling flow,
Nightly I visit: nor sometimes forget° *always remember*
Those other two equaled with me in fate,[8]
So were I equaled with them in renown,
Blind Thamyris and blind Maeonides,
And Tiresias and Phineus prophets old,[9]
Then feed on thoughts, that voluntary move
Harmonious numbers;° as the wakeful bird° *verses / nightingale*
Sings darkling,° and in shadiest covert hid *in the dark*
Tunes her nocturnal note. Thus with the year
Seasons return, but not to me returns
Day, or the sweet approach of ev'n or morn,
Or sight of vernal bloom, or summer's rose,
Or flocks, or herds, or human face divine;
But cloud instead, and ever-during° dark *everlasting*
Surrounds me, from the cheerful ways of men
Cut off, and for the book of knowledge° fair *Book of Nature*
Presented with a universal blank
Of nature's works to me expunged and razed,° *erased*
And wisdom at one entrance quite shut out.
So much the rather thou celestial Light
Shine inward, and the mind through all her powers
Irradiate, there plant eyes, all mist from thence
Purge and disperse, that I may see and tell
Of things invisible to mortal sight.
  Now had the Almighty Father from above,
From the pure empyrean° where he sits *Heaven*
High throned above all height, bent down his eye,
His own works and their works at once to view:
Above him all the sanctities° of Heaven *angels*
Stood thick as stars, and from his sight received
Beatitude past utterance; on his right
The radiant image of his glory sat,
His only Son; on earth he first beheld

5. Urania (though not named until 7.1).
6. Cataract—*suffusio nigra*. "Drop serene": *gutta serena*, the medical term for Milton's kind of blindness.
7. The mountain of scriptural inspiration, with its brooks Siloa and Kidron.
8. I.e., blind like me.
9. Thamyris was a blind Thracian poet who lived before Homer; "Maeonides" is an epithet of Homer; Tiresias was the blind prophet of Thebes; Phineus was a blind king and seer (*Aeneid* 3).

Our two first parents, yet the only two
Of mankind, in the happy garden placed,
Reaping immortal fruits of joy and love,
Uninterrupted joy, unrivaled love
In blissful solitude; he then surveyed
Hell and the gulf between, and Satan there
Coasting the wall of Heav'n on this side Night
In the dun° air sublime,° and ready now — *dusky / aloft*
To stoop° with wearied wings, and willing feet — *swoop down*
On the bare outside of this world,° that seemed — *universe*
Firm land embosomed without firmament,° — *atmosphere*
Uncertain which, in ocean or in air.
Him God beholding from his prospect high,
Wherein past, present, future he beholds,
Thus to his only Son foreseeing spake.
"Only begotten Son, seest thou what rage
Transports our Adversary, whom no bounds
Prescribed, no bars of Hell, nor all the chains
Heaped on him there, nor yet the main° abyss — *vast*
Wide interrupt[1] can hold; so bent he seems
On desperate revenge, that shall redound° — *flow back*
Upon his own rebellious head. And now
Through all restraint broke loose he wings his way
Not far off Heav'n, in the precincts of light,
Directly towards the new-created world,
And man there placed, with purpose to essay° — *try*
If him by force he can destroy, or worse,
By some false guile pervert; and shall pervert;
For man will hearken to his glozing° lies, — *flattering*
And easily transgress the sole command,
Sole pledge of his obedience: so will fall
He and his faithless progeny: whose fault?
Whose but his own? Ingrate, he had of me
All he could have; I made him just and right,
Sufficient to have stood, though free to fall.
Such I created all th' ethereal Powers
And Spirits, both them who stood and them who failed;
Freely they stood who stood, and fell who fell.
Not free, what proof could they have giv'n sincere
Of true allegiance, constant faith or love,
Where only what they needs must do, appeared,
Not what they would? What praise could they receive?
What pleasure I from such obedience paid,
When will and reason (reason also is choice)
Useless and vain, of freedom both despoiled,
Made passive both, had served necessity,
Not me. They therefore as to right belonged,
So were created, nor can justly accuse
Their Maker, or their making, or their fate,
As if predestination overruled
Their will, disposed by absolute decree

1. Forming a wide breach between Heaven and Hell.

Or high foreknowledge; they themselves decreed
Their own revolt, not I: if I foreknew,
Foreknowledge had no influence on their fault,
Which had no less proved certain unforeknown.[2]
So without least impulse or shadow of fate,
Or aught by me immutably foreseen,
They trespass, authors to themselves in all
Both what they judge and what they choose; for so
I formed them free, and free they must remain,
Till they enthrall themselves: I else must change
Their nature, and revoke the high decree
Unchangeable, eternal, which ordained
Their freedom, they themselves ordained their fall.
The first sort[3] by their own suggestion fell,
Self-tempted, self-depraved: man falls deceived
By the other first: man therefore shall find grace,
The other none: in mercy and justice both,
Through Heav'n and earth, so shall my glory excel,
But mercy first and last shall brightest shine."
  Thus while God spake, ambrosial° fragrance filled *fragrant, immortal*
All Heav'n, and in the blessèd Spirits elect° *unfallen*
Sense of new joy ineffable° diffused: *inexpressible*
Beyond compare the Son of God was seen
Most glorious, in him all his Father shone
Substantially expressed, and in his face
Divine compassion visibly appeared,
Love without end, and without measure grace,
Which uttering thus he to his Father spake.
  "O Father, gracious was that word which closed
Thy sov'reign sentence, that man should find grace;
For which both Heav'n and earth shall high extol
Thy praises, with th' innumerable sound
Of hymns and sacred songs, wherewith thy throne
Encompassed shall resound thee ever blessed.
For should man finally be lost, should man
Thy creature late so loved, thy youngest son
Fall circumvented thus by fraud, though joined
With his own folly? That be from thee far,
That far be from thee, Father, who art judge
Of all things made, and judgest only right.[4]
Or shall the Adversary thus obtain
His end, and frustrate thine, shall he fulfill
His malice, and thy goodness bring to naught,
Or proud return though to his heavier doom,
Yet with revenge accomplished, and to Hell
Draw after him the whole race of mankind,
By him corrupted? Or wilt thou thyself
Abolish thy creation, and unmake,
For him, what for thy glory thou hast made?

2. I.e., if I had not foreknown it.
3. Satan and his crew.
4. The Son echoes (or rather foreshadows) Abraham pleading with the Lord to spare Sodom: "That be far from thee to do after this manner, to slay the righteous with the wicked . . . that be far from thee: Shall not the Judge of all the earth do right?" (Genesis 18.25).

So should thy goodness and thy greatness both
Be questioned and blasphemed° without defense." *profaned*
  To whom the great Creator thus replied.
"O Son, in whom my soul hath chief delight,
Son of my bosom, Son who art alone
My Word, my wisdom, and effectual might,[5]
All hast thou spoken as my thoughts are, all
As my eternal purpose hath decreed:
Man shall not quite be lost, but saved who will,
Yet not of will in him, but grace in me
Freely vouchsafed;° once more I will renew *bestowed*
His lapsèd powers, though forfeit and enthralled
By sin to foul exorbitant desires;
Upheld by me, yet once more he shall stand
On even ground against his mortal foe,
By me upheld, that he may know how frail
His fall'n condition is, and to me owe
All his deliv'rance, and to none but me.
Some I have chosen of peculiar grace
Elect above the rest;[6] so is my will:
The rest shall hear me call, and oft be warned° *warned about*
Their sinful state, and to appease betimes
Th' incensèd Deity, while offered grace
Invites; for I will clear their senses dark,
What may suffice, and soften stony hearts
To pray, repent, and bring obedience due.
To prayer, repentance, and obedience due,
Though but endeavored with sincere intent,
Mine ear shall not be slow, mine eye not shut.
And I will place within them as a guide
My umpire conscience, whom if they will hear,
Light after light well used they shall attain,[7]
And to the end persisting, safe arrive.
This my long sufferance and my day of grace
They who neglect and scorn, shall never taste;
But hard be hardened, blind be blinded more,
That they may stumble on, and deeper fall;
And none but such from mercy I exclude.
But yet all is not done; man disobeying,
Disloyal breaks his fealty, and sins
Against the high supremacy of Heav'n,
Affecting° Godhead, and so losing all, *aspiring to*
To expiate his treason hath naught left,
But to destruction sacred and devote,° *consecrated*
He with his whole posterity must die,
Die he or justice must; unless for him
Some other able, and as willing, pay

5. God's speech is rhythmic and sometimes rhymed.
6. In this speech, Milton's God rejects the Calvinist doctrine that he had from the beginning predestined the damnation or salvation of each individual soul; he claims rather that grace sufficient for salvation is offered to all, enabling everyone, if they choose to do so, to believe and persevere. He does, however, assert his right to give special grace to some.
7. By using the light of conscience well they will gain more light.

The rigid satisfaction, death for death.
Say heav'nly Powers, where shall we find such love,
Which of ye will be mortal to redeem
Man's mortal crime,[8] and just th' unjust to save,
Dwells in all Heaven charity so dear?"
He asked, but all the heav'nly choir stood mute,[9]
And silence was in Heav'n; on man's behalf
Patron or intercessor none appeared,
Much less that durst upon his own head draw
The deadly forfeiture, and ransom set.
And now without redemption all mankind
Must have been lost, adjudged to death and Hell
By doom severe, had not the Son of God,
In whom the fullness dwells of love divine,
His dearest mediation° thus renewed. *intercession*
"Father, thy word is passed, man shall find grace;
And shall grace not find means, that finds her way,
The speediest of thy wingèd messengers,
To visit all thy creatures, and to all
Comes unprevented,° unimplored, unsought, *unanticipated*
Happy for man, so coming; he her aid
Can never seek, once dead in sins and lost;
Atonement for himself or offering meet,° *fitting*
Indebted and undone, hath none to bring:
Behold me then, me for him, life for life
I offer, on me let thine anger fall;
Account me man; I for his sake will leave
Thy bosom, and this glory next to thee
Freely put off, and for him lastly die
Well pleased, on me let Death wreak all his rage;
Under his gloomy power I shall not long
Lie vanquished; thou hast giv'n me to possess
Life in myself forever, by thee I live,
Though now to Death I yield, and am his due
All that of me can die, yet that debt paid,
Thou wilt not leave me in the loathsome grave
His prey, nor suffer my unspotted soul
Forever with corruption there to dwell;
But I shall rise victorious, and subdue
My vanquisher, spoiled of his vaunted spoil;
Death his death's wound shall then receive, and stoop
Inglorious, of his mortal sting disarmed.
I through the ample air in triumph high
Shall lead Hell captive maugre° Hell, and show *in spite of*
The powers of darkness bound. Thou at the sight
Pleased, out of Heaven shalt look down and smile,
While by thee raised I ruin[1] all my foes,
Death last, and with his carcass glut the grave:
Then with the multitude of my redeemed

8. "Mortal" means "human" in line 214, but "deadly" in line 215.

9. Compare the devils in the Great Consult, 2.420–26.

1. In the Latin sense, throw down.

Shall enter Heaven long absent, and return,
Father, to see thy face, wherein no cloud
Of anger shall remain, but peace assured,
And reconcilement; wrath shall be no more
Thenceforth, but in thy presence joy entire."
His words here ended, but his meek aspéct
Silent yet spake, and breathed immortal love
To mortal men, above which only shone
Filial obedience: as a sacrifice
Glad to be offered, he attends the will
Of his great Father. Admiration° seized *wonder*
All Heav'n, what this might mean, and whither tend
Wond'ring; but soon th' Almighty thus replied:
"O thou in Heav'n and earth the only peace
Found out for mankind under wrath, O thou
My sole complacence!° well thou know'st how dear *pleasure, delight*
To me are all my works, nor man the least
Though last created, that for him I spare
Thee from my bosom and right hand, to save,
By losing thee a while, the whole race lost.
Thou therefore whom[2] thou only canst redeem,
Their nature also to thy nature join;
And be thyself man among men on earth,
Made flesh, when time shall be, of virgin seed,
By wondrous birth: be thou in Adam's room
The head of all mankind, though Adam's son.[3]
As in him perish all men, so in thee
As from a second root shall be restored,
As many as are restored, without thee none.
His crime makes guilty all his sons; thy merit
Imputed shall absolve them who renounce
Their own both righteous and unrighteous deeds,
And live in thee transplanted, and from thee
Receive new life.[4] So man, as is most just,
Shall satisfy for man, be judged and die,
And dying rise, and rising with him raise
His brethren, ransomed with his own dear life.
So heav'nly love shall outdo hellish hate,
Giving to death, and dying to redeem,
So dearly to redeem what hellish hate
So easily destroyed, and still destroys
In those who, when they may, accept not grace.
Nor shalt thou by descending to assume
Man's nature, lessen or degrade thine own.
Because thou hast, though throned in highest bliss
Equal to God, and equally enjoying
Godlike fruition,° quitted all to save *pleasurable possession*

2. The antecedent of "whom" is, loosely construed, the "their nature" that follows it.
3. The Son of God, who long antedates the creation of Adam and who is actually the first created being (3.383), is later incarnated in Jesus Christ; he is called Second Adam and Son of Man by reason of his descent from the first man, Adam. Cf. 1 Corinthians 15.22: "For as in Adam all die, even so in Christ shall all be made alive."
4. The merit of Christ attributed vicariously ("imputed") to human beings frees from original sin those who renounce their own deeds, good and bad, and hope to be saved by faith.

A world from utter loss, and hast been found
By merit more than birthright Son of God,[5]
Found worthiest to be so by being good,
Far more than great or high; because in thee
Love hath abounded more than glory abounds.
Therefore thy humiliation shall exalt
With thee thy manhood also to this throne;
Here shalt thou sit incarnate, here shalt reign
Both God and man, Son both of God and man,
Anointed[6] universal King; all power
I give thee, reign forever, and assume
Thy merits; under thee as Head Supreme
Thrones, Princedoms, Powers, Dominions[7] I reduce:
All knees to thee shall bow, of them that bide
In Heaven, or earth, or under earth in Hell;
When thou attended gloriously from Heav'n
Shalt in the sky appear, and from thee send
The summoning Archangels to proclaim
Thy dread tribunal: forthwith from all winds° *directions*
The living, and forthwith the cited° dead *summoned*
Of all past ages to the general doom° *judgment*
Shall hasten, such a peal shall rouse their sleep.
Then all thy saints assembled, thou shalt judge
Bad men and angels, they arraigned° shall sink *accursed*
Beneath thy sentence; Hell, her numbers full,
Thenceforth shall be forever shut. Meanwhile
The world shall burn, and from her ashes spring
New heav'n° and earth, wherein the just shall dwell,[8] *sky, cosmos*
And after all their tribulations long
See golden days, fruitful of golden deeds,
With joy and love triumphing, and fair truth.
Then thou thy regal scepter shalt lay by,
For regal scepter then no more shall need,° *be needed*
God shall be all in all. But all ye gods,° *angels*
Adore him, who to compass all this dies,
Adore the Son, and honor him as me."
No sooner had th' Almighty ceased, but all
The multitude of angels with a shout
Loud as from numbers without number, sweet
As from blest voices, uttering joy, Heav'n rung[9]
With jubilee, and loud hosannas filled
Th' eternal regions: lowly reverent
Towards either throne[1] they bow, and to the ground
With solemn adoration down they cast
Their crowns inwove with amarant[2] and gold,
Immortal amarant, a flow'r which once

5. A heterodox doctrine, that Christ was Son of God by merit. Compare with Satan (2.5).
6. In Hebrew "Messiah" means "the anointed one."
7. Orders of angels.
8. Milton's description of the Last Judgment draws on several biblical texts, including Matthew 24.30–31 and 25.31–32; the account of the burning and re-creation of the heavens and earth is from 2 Peter 3.12–13.
9. "Multitude" (line 345) is the subject of the sentence, "rung" the verb, and "Heav'n" the object.
1. Thrones of God and the Son.
2. In Greek, "unfading," a legendary immortal flower.

In Paradise, fast by the Tree of Life
Began to bloom, but soon for man's offense
To Heav'n removed where first it grew, there grows,
And flow'rs aloft shading the Fount of Life,
And where the river of bliss through midst of Heav'n
Rolls o'er Elysian[3] flow'rs her amber stream;
With these that never fade the Spirits elect
Bind their resplendent locks inwreathed with beams,
Now in loose garlands thick thrown off, the bright
Pavement that like a sea of jasper shone
Impurpled with celestial roses smiled.
Then crowned again their golden harps they took,
Harps ever tuned, that glittering by their side
Like quivers hung, and with preamble sweet
Of charming symphony they introduce
Their sacred song, and waken raptures high;
No voice exempt,° no voice but well could join *excluded*
Melodious part, such concord is in Heav'n.
  Thee Father first they sung omnipotent,
Immutable, immortal, infinite,
Eternal King; thee Author of all being,
Fountain of light, thyself invisible
Amidst the glorious brightness where thou sitt'st
Throned inaccessible, but° when thou shad'st *except*
The full blaze of thy beams, and through a cloud
Drawn round about thee like a radiant shrine,[4]
Dark with excessive bright thy skirts appear,
Yet dazzle Heav'n, that brightest Seraphim
Approach not, but with both wings veil their eyes.
Thee next they sang of all creation first,[5]
Begotten Son, Divine Similitude,
In whose conspicuous count'nance, without cloud
Made visible, th' Almighty Father shines,
Whom else no creature can behold;[6] on thee
Impressed th' effulgence of his glory abides,
Transfused on thee his ample spirit rests.
He Heav'n of heavens and all the Powers therein
By thee created, and by thee threw down
Th' aspiring Dominations.[7] Thou that day
Thy Father's dreadful thunder didst not spare,
Nor stop thy flaming chariot wheels, that shook
Heav'n's everlasting frame, while o'er the necks
Thou drov'st of warring angels disarrayed.
Back from pursuit thy Powers° with loud acclaim *angels*
Thee only extolled, Son of thy Father's might,
To execute fierce vengeance on his foes,
Not so on man; him through their malice fall'n,
Father of mercy and grace, thou didst not doom

3. Milton draws freely, for his Christian Heaven, on descriptions of the classical paradisal place, the Elysian Fields.
4. The turn from theological debate to images that evoke a more mystical aspect of God.
5. The Son is not eternal, as in Trinitarian doctrine, but rather, God's first creation.
6. If it were not for the Son who is God's image, no creature could see God.
7. The rebel angels.

So strictly, but much more to pity incline:
No sooner did thy dear and only Son
Perceive thee purposed not to doom° frail man *judge*
So strictly, but much more to pity inclined,
He to appease thy wrath, and end the strife
Of mercy and justice in thy face discerned,
Regardless of the bliss wherein he sat
Second to thee, offered himself to die
For man's offense. O unexampled love,
Love nowhere to be found less than divine!
Hail Son of God, Savior of men, thy name
Shall be the copious matter of my[8] song
Henceforth, and never shall my harp thy praise
Forget, nor from thy Father's praise disjoin.
  Thus they in Heav'n, above the starry sphere,
Their happy hours in joy and hymning spent.
Meanwhile upon the firm opacous° globe *opaque*
Of this round world, whose first convex divides
The luminous inferior orbs, enclosed
From Chaos and th' inroad of Darkness old,
Satan alighted walks:[9] a globe far off
It seemed, now seems a boundless continent
Dark, waste, and wild, under the frown of Night
Starless exposed, and ever-threatening storms
Of Chaos blust'ring round, inclement sky;
Save on that side which from the wall of Heav'n
Though distant far some small reflection gains
Of glimmering air less vexed with tempest loud:
Here walked the Fiend at large in spacious field.
As when a vulture on Imaus bred,
Whose snowy ridge the roving Tartar bounds,[1]
Dislodging from a region scarce of prey
To gorge the flesh of lambs or yeanling° kids *newborn*
On hills where flocks are fed, flies toward the springs
Of Ganges or Hydaspes, Indian streams;[2]
But in his way lights on the barren plains
Of Sericana, where Chineses drive
With sails and wind their cany wagons light:
So on this windy sea of land, the Fiend
Walked up and down alone bent on his prey,
Alone, for other creature in this place
Living or lifeless to be found was none,
None yet, but store hereafter from the earth
Up hither like aërial vapors flew
Of all things transitory and vain, when sin
With vanity had filled the works of men:
Both all things vain, and all who in vain things

8. Either Milton here quotes the angels singing as a single chorus, or he associates himself with their song, or both.
9. Satan is on the outermost of the ten concentric spheres that make up the cosmos.
1. Imaus, a ridge of mountains beyond the modern Himalayas, runs north through Asia from modern Afghanistan to the Arctic Circle.
2. Both the Ganges and the Hydaspes (a tributary of the Indus) rise from the mountains of northern India. Sericana (line 438) is a region in northwest China.

Built their fond° hopes of glory or lasting fame, *foolish*
Or happiness in this or th' other life;
All who have their reward on earth, the fruits
Of painful superstition and blind zeal,
Naught seeking but the praise of men, here find
Fit retribution, empty as their deeds;
All th' unaccomplished° works of nature's hand, *imperfect*
Abortive, monstrous, or unkindly° mixed, *unnaturally*
Dissolved on earth, fleet° hither, and in vain, *float*
Till final dissolution, wander here,
Not in the neighboring moon, as some[3] have dreamed;
Those argent° fields more likely habitants, *silver*
Translated saints,[4] or middle Spirits hold
Betwixt th' angelical and human kind:
Hither of ill-joined sons and daughters born
First from the ancient world those giants came
With many a vain exploit, though then renowned:[5]
The builders next of Babel on the plain
Of Sennaär,[6] and still with vain design
New Babels, had they wherewithal, would build:
Others came single; he who to be deemed
A god, leaped fondly° into Etna flames, *foolishly*
Empedocles, and he who to enjoy
Plato's Elysium, leaped into the sea,
Cleombrotus, and many more too long,[7]
Embryos and idiots, eremites° and friars *hermits*
White, black, and gray, with all their trumpery.[8]
Here pilgrims roam, that strayed so far to seek
In Golgotha[9] him dead, who lives in Heav'n;
And they who to be sure of paradise
Dying put on the weeds° of Dominic, *garments*
Or in Franciscan think to pass disguised;[1]
They pass the planets seven, and pass the fixed,
And that crystálline sphere whose balance weighs
The trepidation talked, and that first moved;[2]
And now Saint Peter at Heav'n's wicket seems
To wait them with his keys, and now at foot
Of Heav'n's ascent they lift their feet, when lo
A violent crosswind from either coast
Blows them transverse ten thousand leagues awry

3. Milton's Paradise of Fools (named in line 496) was inspired by Ariosto's Limbo of Vanity in *Orlando Furioso* (Book 34, lines 73ff.); Milton's region is reserved for deluded victims of misplaced devotion, chiefly Roman Catholics.
4. Holy men like Enoch and Elijah, transported to Heaven while yet alive. (Genesis 5.24; 2 Kings 2.11–12).
5. Giants, born of unnatural marriages between the "sons of God" and the daughters of men (Genesis 6.4), are creatures unkindly mixed.
6. Shinar, the plain of Babel (Genesis 11.2–9); the Tower of Babel is an emblem of human pride and folly.
7. I.e., it would take too long to name them. Both Empedocles and Cleombrotus foolishly carried piety to the point of suicide.
8. Religious paraphernalia. The white friars are Carmelites; the black, Dominicans; and the gray, Franciscans.
9. Place where Christ was crucified.
1. Some try to trick God into granting them salvation by wearing on their deathbeds the garb of various religious orders.
2. Milton follows their souls through the spheres of the moon and sun, the five then-known planets, the fixed stars, and the sphere responsible for the "trepidation" (a periodic corrective shudder of the cosmos), up to the primum mobile, or prime mover. The next step seems to be the empyreal Heaven.

Into the devious° air. Then might ye see *erratic*
Cowls, hoods, and habits[3] with their wearers tossed
And fluttered into rags; then relics, beads,
Indulgences, dispenses, pardons, bulls,
The sport of winds: all these upwhirled aloft
Fly o'er the backside° of the world far off *rump*
Into a limbo large and broad, since called
The Paradise of Fools, to few unknown
Long after, now unpeopled, and untrod;
All this dark globe the Fiend found as he passed,
And long he wandered, till at last a gleam
Of dawning light turned thitherward in haste
His traveled° steps; far distant he descries *travel-weary*
Ascending by degrees° magnificent *steps*
Up to the wall of Heaven a structure high,
At top whereof, but far more rich appeared
The work as of a kingly palace gate
With frontispiece° of diamond and gold *pediment*
Embellished; thick with sparkling orient° gems *lustrous*
The portal shone, inimitable on earth,
By model, or by shading pencil drawn.
The stairs were such as whereon Jacob saw
Angels ascending and descending, bands
Of guardians bright, when he from Esau fled
To Padan-Aram in the field of Luz,
Dreaming by night under the open sky,
And waking cried, "This is the gate of Heav'n."[4]
Each stair mysteriously was meant, nor stood
There always, but drawn up to Heav'n sometimes
Viewless,° and underneath a bright sea flowed *invisible*
Of jasper, or of liquid pearl, whereon
Who after came from earth, sailing arrived,
Wafted by angels, or flew o'er the lake
Rapt in a chariot drawn by fiery steeds.[5]
The stairs were then let down, whether to dare
The Fiend by easy ascent, or aggravate
His sad exclusion from the doors of bliss.
Direct against which opened from beneath,
Just o'er the blissful seat of Paradise,
A passage down to th' earth, a passage wide,[6]
Wider by far than that of aftertimes
Over Mount Zion, and, though that were large,
Over the Promised Land to God so dear,
By which, to visit oft those happy tribes,
On high behests his angels to and fro
Passed frequent, and his eye with choice° regard *discriminating*

3. The dress of religious orders, together with (next lines) saints' relics, rosary beads, various kinds of pardon for sins, and papal decrees ("bulls").

4. The story of Jacob's vision is summarized from Genesis 28.1–19; the stairs of the ladder (next line) allegorically ("mysteriously") represent stages of spiritual growth.

5. Elijah was wafted to heaven in a chariot.

6. A passage through the crystalline spheres, otherwise impenetrable.

From Paneas the fount of Jordan's flood
To Beërsaba, where the Holy Land
Borders on Egypt and the Arabian shore;[7]
So wide the op'ning seemed, where bounds were set
To darkness, such as bound the ocean wave.
Satan from hence now on the lower stair
That scaled by steps of gold to Heaven gate
Looks down with wonder at the sudden view
Of all this world at once. As when a scout
Through dark and desert ways with peril gone
All night; at last by break of cheerful dawn
Obtains° the brow of some high-climbing hill, *gains*
Which to his eye discovers unaware
The goodly prospect of some foreign land
First seen, or some renowned metropolis
With glistering spires and pinnacles adorned,
Which now the rising sun gilds with his beams.
Such wonder seized, though after Heaven seen,
The Spirit malign, but much more envy seized
At sight of all this world beheld so fair.
Round he surveys, and well might, where he stood
So high above the circling canopy
Of night's extended shade; from eastern point
Of Libra to the fleecy star that bears
Andromeda far off Atlantic seas[8]
Beyond th' horizon; then from pole to pole
He views in breadth, and without longer pause
Down right into the world's first region throws
His flight precipitant, and winds with ease
Through the pure marble° air his oblique way *sparkling*
Amongst innumerable stars, that shone
Stars distant, but nigh hand seemed other worlds,
Or other worlds they seemed, or happy isles,
Like those Hesperian gardens famed of old,
Fortunate fields, and groves and flow'ry vales,[9]
Thrice happy isles, but who dwelt happy there
He stayed not to inquire: above them all
The golden sun in splendor likest Heaven
Allured his eye: thither his course he bends
Through the calm firmament;° but up or down *sky*
By center, or eccentric, hard to tell,
Or longitude,[1] where the great luminary
Aloof the vulgar constellations thick,
That from his lordly eye keep distance due,
Dispenses light from far; they as they move
Their starry dance in numbers that compute

7. From Paneas (or Dan) in northern Palestine to Beersaba, or Beersheba, near the Egyptian border—the entire land of Israel.
8. In the zodiac, Libra is diametrically opposite Aries, or the Ram ("the fleecy star"), which seems to carry the constellation Andromeda on its back.
9. The gardens of the Hesperides and the "fortunate isles" of Greek mythology, classical versions of paradise, lay far out in the Atlantic.
1. The passage leaves open whether the sun or the earth is at the center of the cosmos.

Days, months, and years, towards his all-cheering lamp
Turn swift their various motions, or are turned
By his magnetic beam, that gently warms
The universe, and to each inward part
With gentle penetration, though unseen,
Shoots invisible virtue° even to the deep: *influence, strength*
So wondrously was set his station bright.

Summary Landing on the bright orb of the sun, Satan disguises himself as a youthful cherub and approaches the solar guardian, the archangel Uriel. Pretending interest in the new great works of God, he gets directions to Earth and Adam's bower, then spirals down and lands on Mount Niphates (in modern Iran), overlooking the site of Paradise.

From Book 4

[SATAN'S ENTRY INTO PARADISE; ADAM AND EVE IN THEIR BOWER]

O for that warning voice, which he who saw
Th' Apocalypse, heard cry in Heaven aloud,
Then when the Dragon, put to second rout,
Came furious down to be revenged on men,
"Woe to the inhabitants on earth!"[1] that now,
While time was, our first parents had been warned
The coming of their secret foe, and scaped
Haply° so scaped his mortal° snare; for now *perhaps / deadly*
Satan, now first inflamed with rage, came down,
The tempter ere° th' accuser of mankind, *before being*
To wreak° on innocent frail man his loss *avenge*
Of that first battle, and his flight to Hell:
Yet not rejoicing in his speed, though bold,
Far off and fearless, nor with cause to boast,
Begins his dire attempt, which nigh the birth
Now rolling, boils in his tumultuous breast,
And like a devilish engine back recoils
Upon himself; horror and doubt distract
His troubled thoughts, and from the bottom stir
The Hell within him, for within him Hell
He brings, and round about him, nor from Hell
One step no more than from himself can fly
By change of place: now conscience wakes despair
That slumbered, wakes the bitter memory
Of what he was, what is, and what must be
Worse; of worse deeds worse sufferings must ensue.
Sometimes towards Eden which now in his view
Lay pleasant, his grieved look he fixes sad,
Sometimes towards Heav'n and the full-blazing sun,

1. John of Patmos, in Revelation 12.3–12, hears such a cry during a second war in Heaven, between the Dragon and the angels.

Which now sat high in his meridian tow'r:[2]
Then much revolving,° thus in sighs began. *pondering*
"O thou that with surpassing glory crowned,[3]
Look'st from thy sole dominion like the god
Of this new world: at whose sight all the stars
Hide their diminished heads; to thee I call,
But with no friendly voice, and add thy name
O sun, to tell thee how I hate thy beams
That bring to my remembrance from what state
I fell, how glorious once above thy sphere;
Till pride and worse ambition threw me down
Warring in Heav'n against Heav'n's matchless King:
Ah wherefore! he deserved no such return
From me, whom he created what I was
In that bright eminence, and with his good
Upbraided[4] none, nor was his service hard.
What could be less than to afford him praise,
The easiest recompense, and pay him thanks,
How due! yet all his good proved ill in me,
And wrought but malice; lifted up so high
I 'sdained° subjection, and thought one step higher *disdained*
Would set me highest, and in a moment quit° *pay*
The debt immense of endless gratitude,
So burthensome still° paying, still to owe; *always*
Forgetful what from him I still received,
And understood not that a grateful mind
By owing owes not, but still pays, at once
Indebted and discharged; what burden then?
O had his powerful destiny ordained
Me some inferior angel, I had stood
Then happy; no unbounded hope had raised
Ambition. Yet why not? some other Power° *angel*
As great might have aspired, and me though mean
Drawn to his part; but other Powers as great
Fell not, but stand unshaken, from within
Or from without, to all temptations armed.
Hadst thou[5] the same free will and power to stand?
Thou hadst: whom hast thou then or what to accuse,
But Heav'n's free love dealt equally to all?
Be then his love accursed, since love or hate,
To me alike, it deals eternal woe.
Nay cursed be thou; since against his thy will
Chose freely what it now so justly rues.
Me miserable![6] which way shall I fly
Infinite wrath, and infinite despair?
Which way I fly is Hell; myself am Hell;[7]
And in the lowest deep a lower deep

2. At midday, the height of noon.
3. Milton's nephew, Edward Phillips, said that this soliloquy was written "several years before the poem was begun," and was intended to begin a drama on the topic, *Adam Unparadised*.
4. Reproached (James 1.5).
5. Compare Satan's address to himself here with Adam's soliloquy in parallel circumstances (10.758ff.).
6. A Latinism, *me miserum!*
7. Compare Satan's earlier claim that "the mind is its own place" (1.254).

Still threat'ning to devour me opens wide,
To which the Hell I suffer seems a Heav'n.
O then at last relent! is there no place
Left for repentance, none for pardon left?
None left but by submission; and that word
Disdain forbids me, and my dread of shame
Among the Spirits beneath, whom I seduced
With other promises and other vaunts
Than to submit, boasting I could subdue
Th' Omnipotent. Ay me, they little know
How dearly I abide° that boast so vain, *pay the penalty for*
Under what torments inwardly I groan:
While they adore me on the throne of Hell,
With diadem and scepter high advanced
The lower still I fall, only supreme
In misery; such joy ambition finds.
But say I could repent and could obtain
By act of grace[8] my former state; how soon
Would heighth recall high thoughts, how soon unsay
What feigned submission swore: ease would recant
Vows made in pain, as violent° and void. *forced*
For never can true reconcilement grow
Where wounds of deadly hate have pierced so deep:
Which would but lead me to a worse relapse,
And heavier fall: so should I purchase dear
Short intermission bought with double smart.
This knows my punisher; therefore as far
From granting he, as I from begging peace:
All hope excluded thus, behold instead
Of us outcast, exiled, his new delight,
Mankind created, and for him this world.
So farewell hope, and with hope farewell fear,
Farewell remorse: all good to me is lost;
Evil be thou my good; by thee at least
Divided empire with Heav'n's King I hold
By thee, and more than half perhaps will reign;
As man ere long, and this new world shall know."
  Thus while he spake, each passion dimmed his face
Thrice changed with pale,° ire, envy, and despair, *pallor*
Which marred his borrowed visage, and betrayed
Him counterfeit, if any eye beheld.
For heav'nly minds from such distempers foul
Are ever clear. Whereof he soon aware,
Each perturbation smoothed with outward calm,
Artificer of fraud; and was the first
That practiced falsehood under saintly show,
Deep malice to conceal, couched° with revenge: *hidden*
Yet not enough had practiced to deceive
Uriel once warned; whose eye pursued him down
The way he went, and on th' Assyrian mount° *Niphates*
Saw him disfigured, more than could befall

8. The technical term for a formal pardon.

Spirit of happy sort: his gestures fierce
He marked and mad demeanor, then alone,
As he supposed, all unobserved, unseen.
So on he fares, and to the border comes
Of Eden, where delicious Paradise,[9]
Now nearer, crowns with her enclosure green,
As with a rural mound the champaign head° — *open summit*
Of a steep wilderness, whose hairy sides
With thicket overgrown, grotesque[1] and wild,
Access denied; and overhead up grew
Insuperable heighth of loftiest shade,
Cedar, and pine, and fir, and branching palm,
A sylvan scene, and as the ranks ascend
Shade above shade, a woody theater[2]
Of stateliest view. Yet higher than their tops
The verdurous wall of Paradise up sprung:
Which to our general sire gave prospect large
Into his nether empire neighboring round.
And higher than that wall a circling row
Of goodliest trees loaden with fairest fruit,
Blossoms and fruits at once of golden hue
Appeared, with gay enameled° colors mixed: — *bright*
On which the sun more glad impressed his beams
Than in fair evening cloud, or humid bow,° — *rainbow*
When God hath show'red the earth; so lovely seemed
That landscape: and of pure now purer air[3]
Meets his approach, and to the heart inspires° — *infuses*
Vernal delight and joy, able to drive° — *drive out*
All sadness but despair: now gentle gales
Fanning their odoriferous° wings dispense — *fragrance-bearing*
Native perfumes, and whisper whence they stole
Those balmy spoils. As when to them who sail
Beyond the Cape of Hope,° and now are past — *Cape of Good Hope*
Mozambic, off at sea northeast winds blow
Sabean odors from the spicy shore
Of Araby the Blest,[4] with such delay
Well pleased they slack their course, and many a league
Cheered with the grateful° smell old Ocean smiles. — *pleasing*
So entertained those odorous sweets the Fiend
Who came their bane,° though with them better pleased — *poison*
Than Asmodeus with the fishy fume,
That drove him, though enamored, from the spouse
Of Tobit's son, and with a vengeance sent
From Media post to Egypt, there fast bound.[5]
Now to th'ascent of that steep savage° hill — *wooded, wild*

9. Paradise is a delightful ("delicious") garden on top of a steep hill situated in the east of the land of Eden.
1. Characterized by interwoven, tangled vines and branches.
2. As if in a Greek amphitheater, the trees are set row on row.
3. The air becomes still purer.
4. *Arabia Felix* (modern Yemen). "Sabean": the biblical Sheba.
5. The Apocryphal book of Tobit tells of Tobias, Tobit's son, who married Sara and avoided the fate of her previous seven husbands (killed on their wedding night by the demon Asmodeus) by following the instructions of the angel Raphael and making a fishy smell to drive him off; Asmodeus then fled to Egypt, where Raphael bound him.

Satan had journeyed on, pensive and slow;
But further way found none, so thick entwined,
As one continued brake,° the undergrowth *thicket*
Of shrubs and tangling bushes had perplexed
All path of man or beast that passed that way:
One gate there only was, and that looked east
On th' other side: which when th' arch-felon saw
Due entrance he disdained, and in contempt,
At one slight bound high overleaped all bound
Of hill or highest wall, and sheer within
Lights on his feet. As when a prowling wolf,
Whom hunger drives to seek new haunt for prey,
Watching where shepherds pen their flocks at eve
In hurdled cotes° amid the field secure, *pens of woven reeds*
Leaps o'er the fence with ease into the fold:
Or as a thief bent to unhoard the cash
Of some rich burgher, whose substantial doors,
Cross-barred and bolted fast, fear no assault,
In at the window climbs, or o'er the tiles;
So clomb° this first grand thief into God's fold: *climbed*
So since into his church lewd hirelings[6] climb.
Thence up he flew, and on the Tree of Life,
The middle tree and highest there that grew,
Sat like a cormorant;[7] yet not true life
Thereby regained, but sat devising death
To them who lived; nor on the virtue° thought *power*
Of that life-giving plant, but only used
For prospect,° what well used had been the pledge *as a lookout*
Of immortality. So little knows
Any, but God alone, to value right
The good before him, but perverts best things
To worst abuse, or to their meanest use.
  Beneath him with new wonder now he views
To all delight of human sense exposed
In narrow room nature's whole wealth, yea more,
A heav'n on earth: for blissful Paradise
Of God the garden was, by him in the east
Of Eden planted; Eden stretched her line
From Auran eastward to the royal tow'rs
Of great Seleucia, built by Grecian kings,
Or where the sons of Eden long before
Dwelt in Telassar:[8] in this pleasant soil
His far more pleasant garden God ordained;
Out of the fertile ground he caused to grow
All trees of noblest kind for sight, smell, taste;
And all amid them stood the Tree of Life,
High eminent, blooming ambrosial° fruit *divinely fragrant*
Of vegetable gold; and next to life

6. Base men interested only in money; Milton would have clergymen not paid by required tithes or by the state, to ensure their purity of motive.
7. A sea bird, noted for gluttony.
8. Auran is the province of Hauran on the eastern border of Israel. Selucia, a powerful city on the Tigris, near modern Baghdad, was founded by one of Alexander's generals ("built by Grecian kings"). Telassar is another Near Eastern kingdom.

Our death the Tree of Knowledge grew fast by,
Knowledge of good bought dear by knowing ill.
Southward through Eden went a river large,[9]
Nor changed his course, but through the shaggy hill
Passed underneath engulfed, for God had thrown
That mountain as his garden mold° high raised *rich earth*
Upon the rapid current, which through veins
Of porous earth with kindly° thirst up drawn, *natural*
Rose a fresh fountain, and with many a rill
Watered the garden; thence united fell
Down the steep glade, and met the nether flood,
Which from his darksome passage now appears,
And now divided into four main streams,
Runs diverse, wand'ring many a famous realm
And country whereof here needs no account,
But rather to tell how, if art could tell,
How from that sapphire fount the crispèd° brooks, *wavy, rippling*
Rolling on orient pearl and sands of gold,
With mazy error[1] under pendent shades
Ran nectar, visiting each plant, and fed
Flow'rs worthy of Paradise which not nice° art *fastidious*
In beds and curious knots, but nature boon° *bounteous*
Poured forth profuse on hill and dale and plain,
Both where the morning sun first warmly smote
The open field, and where the unpierced shade
Embrowned° the noontide bow'rs. Thus was this place, *darkened*
A happy rural seat of various view,[2]
Groves whose rich trees wept odorous gums and balm,
Others whose fruit burnished with golden rind
Hung amiable,° Hesperian fables true,[3] *lovely*
If true, here only, and of delicious taste:
Betwixt them lawns, or level downs,° and flocks *uplands*
Grazing the tender herb, were interposed,
Or palmy hillock, or the flow'ry lap
Of some irriguous° valley spread her store, *well-watered*
Flow'rs of all hue, and without thorn the rose:
Another side, umbrageous° grots and caves *shady*
Of cool recess, o'er which the mantling° vine *enveloping*
Lays forth her purple grape, and gently creeps
Luxuriant; meanwhile murmuring waters fall
Down the slope hills, dispersed, or in a lake,
That to the fringèd bank with myrtle crowned,
Her crystal mirror holds, unite their streams.
The birds their choir apply; airs,[4] vernal airs,
Breathing the smell of field and grove, attune
The trembling leaves, while universal Pan[5]
Knit° with the Graces and the Hours in dance *clasping hands*

9. The Tigris (identified at 9.71) flowed under the hill.
1. From Latin *errare*, wandering.
2. Like a country estate, with a variety of prospects.
3. These were real golden apples, by contrast to those feigned golden apples of the Hesperides, fabled paradisal islands in the Western Ocean.
4. Both breezes and melodies. "Their choir apply": practice their songs.
5. The god of all nature—*pan* in Greek means "all."

Led on th' eternal spring. Not that fair field
Of Enna, where Proserpine gathering flow'rs
Herself a fairer flow'r by gloomy Dis
Was gathered, which cost Ceres all that pain
To seek her through the world; nor that sweet grove
Of Daphne by Orontes, and th' inspired
Castalian spring, might with this Paradise
Of Eden strive;[6] nor that Nyseian isle
Girt with the river Triton, where old Cham,
Whom Gentiles Ammon call and Libyan Jove,
Hid Amalthea and her florid° son *wine-flushed*
Young Bacchus from his stepdame Rhea's eye;[7]
Nor where Abassin kings their issue guard,
Mount Amara,[8] though this by some supposed
True Paradise under the Ethiop line° *equator*
By Nilus'° head, enclosed with shining rock, *Nile's*
A whole day's journey high, but wide remote
From this Assyrian garden,° where the Fiend *Eden*
Saw undelighted all delight, all kind
Of living creatures new to sight and strange:
  Two of far nobler shape erect and tall,
Godlike erect, with native honor clad
In naked majesty seemed lords of all,
And worthy seemed, for in their looks divine
The image of their glorious Maker shone,
Truth, wisdom, sanctitude severe and pure,
Severe but in true filial freedom placed;
Whence true authority in men;[9] though both
Not equal, as their sex not equal seemed;
For contemplation he and valor formed,
For softness she and sweet attractive grace,
He for God only, she for God in him:[1]
His fair large front° and eye sublime declared *forehead*
Absolute rule; and hyacinthine[2] locks
Round from his parted forelock manly hung
Clust'ring, but not beneath his shoulders broad:
She as a veil down to the slender waist
Her unadorned golden tresses wore
Disheveled, but in wanton° ringlets waved *unrestrained*
As the vine curls her tendrils,[3] which implied
Subjection, but required° with gentle sway,° *requested / persuasion*
And by her yielded, by him best received,

6. Milton compares Paradise with famous beauty spots of antiquity. Enna in Sicily was a lovely meadow from which Proserpine was kidnapped by "gloomy Dis" (i.e., Pluto); her mother Ceres sought her throughout the world. The grove of Daphne, near Antioch and the Orontes River in the Near East, had a spring called "Castalia" after the Muses' fountain near Parnassus.
7. The isle of Nysa in the river Triton in Tunisia was where Ammon (an Egyptian god, identified with Cham, or Ham, the son of Noah) hid Bacchus, his child by Amalthea (who later became the god of wine), away from the eyes of his wife Rhea.
8. Atop Mount Amara, the "Abassin" (Abyssinian) king had a splendid palace in a paradisal garden.
9. This phrase underscores Milton's idea that true freedom involves obedience to natural superiors (i.e., God).
1. The phrase has as its context 1 Corinthians 11.3: "The head of every man is Christ; and the head of the woman is the man."
2. A classical metaphor for hair curled in the form of hyacinth petals, and perhaps also implying dark or flowing.
3. Eve's hair is curly, abundant, not subjected to rigid control, like the vegetation in Paradise.

Yielded with coy° submission, modest pride, *shyly reserved*
And sweet reluctant amorous delay.
Nor those mysterious parts were then concealed,
Then was not guilty shame, dishonest° shame *unchaste*
Of nature's works, honor dishonorable,
Sin-bred, how have ye troubled all mankind
With shows instead, mere shows of seeming pure,
And banished from man's life his happiest life,
Simplicity and spotless innocence.
So passed they naked on, nor shunned the sight
Of God or angel, for they thought no ill:
So hand in hand they passed, the loveliest pair
That ever since in love's embraces met,
Adam the goodliest man of men since born
His sons, the fairest of her daughters Eve.
Under a tuft of shade that on a green
Stood whispering soft, by a fresh fountain side
They sat them down, and after no more toil
Of their sweet gard'ning labor than sufficed
To recommend cool Zephyr,[4] and made ease
More easy, wholesome thirst and appetite
More grateful, to their supper fruits they fell,
Nectarine° fruits which the compliant boughs *sweet as nectar*
Yielded them, sidelong as they sat recline
On the soft downy bank damasked with flow'rs:
The savory pulp they chew, and in the rind
Still as they thirsted scoop the brimming stream;
Nor gentle purpose,° nor endearing smiles *conversation*
Wanted,° nor youthful dalliance as beseems *lacked*
Fair couple, linked in happy nuptial league,
Alone as they. About them frisking played
All beasts of th' earth, since wild, and of all chase° *game animals*
In wood or wilderness, forest or den;
Sporting the lion ramped,° and in his paw *stood on hind legs*
Dandled the kid; bears, tigers, ounces,° pards° *lynxes / leopards*
Gamboled before them; th' unwieldy elephant
To make them mirth used all his might, and wreathed
His lithe proboscis;° close the serpent sly *trunk*
Insinuating,° wove with Gordian twine *writhing, twisting*
His braided train,[5] and of his fatal guile
Gave proof unheeded; others on the grass
Couched, and now filled with pasture gazing sat,
Or bedward ruminating:° for the sun *chewing the cud*
Declined was hasting now with prone° career *sinking*
To th' Ocean Isles,° and in th' ascending scale *the Azores*
Of Heav'n the stars that usher evening rose:
When Satan still in gaze, as first he stood,
Scarce thus at length failed speech recovered sad.
"O Hell! what do mine eyes with grief behold,
Into our room of bliss thus high advanced

4. I.e., to make a cool breeze welcome.
5. Checkered body. "Gordian twine": cords as convoluted as the Gordian knot that Alexander the Great had to cut with his sword.

Creatures of other mold, earth-born perhaps,
Not Spirits, yet to heav'nly Spirits bright
Little inferior; whom my thoughts pursue
With wonder, and could love, so lively shines
In them divine resemblance, and such grace
The hand that formed them on their shape hath poured.
Ah gentle pair, ye little think how nigh
Your change approaches, when all these delights
Will vanish and deliver ye to woe,
More woe, the more your taste is now of joy;
Happy, but for so happy° ill secured *such happiness*
Long to continue, and this high seat your heav'n
Ill fenced for Heav'n to keep out such a foe
As now is entered; yet no purposed foe
To you whom I could pity thus forlorn
Though I unpitied: league with you I seek,
And mutual amity so strait,° so close, *intimate*
That I with you must dwell, or you with me
Henceforth; my dwelling haply° may not please *perhaps*
Like this fair Paradise, your sense, yet such
Accept your Maker's work; he gave it me,
Which I as freely give; Hell shall unfold,
To entertain you two, her widest gates,
And send forth all her kings; there will be room,
Not like these narrow limits, to receive
Your numerous offspring; if no better place,
Thank him who puts me loath to this revenge
On you who wrong me not for° him who wronged. *in place of*
And should I at your harmless innocence
Melt, as I do, yet public reason just,
Honor and empire with revenge enlarged
By conquering this new world, compels me now
To do what else though damned I should abhor."[6]
So spake the Fiend, and with necessity,
The tyrant's plea, excused his devilish deeds.
Then from his lofty stand on that high tree
Down he alights among the sportful herd
Of those four-footed kinds, himself now one,
Now other, as their shape served best his end
Nearer to view his prey, and unespied
To mark what of their state he more might learn
By word or action marked: about them round
A lion now he stalks with fiery glare,
Then as a tiger, who by chance hath spied
In some purlieu° two gentle fawns at play, *outskirts of a forest*
Straight° couches close, then rising changes oft *at once*
His couchant watch, as one who chose his ground
Whence rushing he might surest seize them both
Gripped in each paw: when Adam first of men
To first of women Eve thus moving speech
Turned him all ear to hear new utterance flow:

6. Satan's excuse—reason of state, public interest, empire, etc.—is called "the tyrant's plea" in line 394.

"Sole partner and sole° part of all these joys, *chief*
Dearer thyself than all; needs must the Power
That made us, and for us this ample world
Be infinitely good, and of his good
As liberal and free as infinite,
That raised us from the dust and placed us here
In all this happiness, who at his hand
Have nothing merited, nor can perform
Aught whereof he hath need, he who requires
From us no other service than to keep
This one, this easy charge, of all the trees
In Paradise that bear delicious fruit
So various, not to taste that only Tree
Of Knowledge, planted by the Tree of Life,
So near grows death to life, whate'er death is,
Some dreadful thing no doubt; for well thou know'st
God hath pronounced it death to taste that Tree,
The only sign of our obedience left
Among so many signs of power and rule
Conferred upon us, and dominion giv'n
Over all other creatures that possess
Earth, air, and sea. Then let us not think hard
One easy prohibition, who enjoy
Free leave so large to all things else, and choice
Unlimited of manifold delights:
But let us ever praise him, and extol
His bounty, following our delightful task
To prune these growing plants, and tend these flow'rs,
Which were it toilsome, yet with thee were sweet."
To whom thus Eve replied. "O thou for whom
And from whom I was formed flesh of thy flesh,
And without whom am to no end, my guide
And head, what thou hast said is just and right.
For we to him indeed all praises owe,
And daily thanks, I chiefly who enjoy
So far the happier lot, enjoying thee
Preeminent by so much odds,° while thou *advantage*
Like consort to thyself canst nowhere find.
That day I oft remember, when from sleep
I first awaked, and found myself reposed° *resting*
Under a shade on flowers, much wond'ring where
And what I was, whence thither brought, and how.
Not distant far from thence a murmuring sound
Of waters issued from a cave and spread
Into a liquid plain, then stood unmoved
Pure as th' expanse of Heav'n; I thither went
With unexperienced thought, and laid me down
On the green bank, to look into the clear
Smooth lake, that to me seemed another sky.
As I bent down to look, just opposite,
A shape within the wat'ry gleam appeared
Bending to look on me, I started back,
It started back, but pleased I soon returned,

Pleased it returned as soon with answering looks
Of sympathy and love; there I had fixed
Mine eyes till now, and pined with vain° desire,[7] *futile*
Had not a voice thus warned me, 'What thou seest,
What there thou seest fair creature is thyself,
With thee it came and goes: but follow me,
And I will bring thee where no shadow stays° *hinders*
Thy coming, and thy soft embraces, he
Whose image thou art, him thou shall enjoy
Inseparably thine, to him shalt bear
Multitudes like thyself, and thence be called
Mother of human race': what could I do,
But follow straight° invisibly thus led? *at once*
Till I espied thee, fair indeed and tall,
Under a platan,° yet methought less fair, *plane tree*
Less winning soft, less amiably mild,
Than that smooth wat'ry image; back I turned,
Thou following cried'st aloud, 'Return fair Eve,
Whom fli'st thou? Whom thou fli'st, of him thou art,
His flesh, his bone; to give thee being I lent
Out of my side to thee, nearest my heart
Substantial life, to have thee by my side
Henceforth an individual° solace dear; *inseparable, distinct*
Part of my soul I seek thee, and thee claim
My other half': with that thy gentle hand
Seized mine, I yielded, and from that time see
How beauty is excelled by manly grace
And wisdom, which alone is truly fair."
  So spake our general mother, and with eyes
Of conjugal attraction unreproved,
And meek surrender, half embracing leaned
On our first father, half her swelling breast
Naked met his under the flowing gold
Of her loose tresses hid: he in delight
Both of her beauty and submissive charms
Smiled with superior love, as Jupiter
On Juno smiles, when he impregns° the clouds *impregnates*
That shed May flowers; and pressed her matron lip
With kisses pure: aside the Devil turned
For envy, yet with jealous leer malign
Eyed them askance, and to himself thus plained.° *complained*
  "Sight hateful, sight tormenting! thus these two
Imparadised in one another's arms
The happier Eden, shall enjoy their fill
Of bliss on bliss, while I to Hell am thrust,
Where neither joy nor love, but fierce desire,
Among our other torments not the least,
Still° unfulfilled with pain of longing pines; *always*
Yet let me not forget what I have gained
From their own mouths; all is not theirs it seems:

7. Eve's experience reprises (but with significant differences) the story of Narcissus, who fell in love with his own reflection and was transformed into a flower.

One fatal tree there stands of Knowledge called,
Forbidden them to taste: knowledge forbidden?
Suspicious, reasonless. Why should their Lord
Envy° them that? Can it be sin to know, *begrudge*
Can it be death? And do they only stand
By ignorance, is that their happy state,
The proof of their obedience and their faith?
O fair foundation laid whereon to build
Their ruin! Hence I will excite their minds
With more desire to know, and to reject
Envious commands, invented with design
To keep them low whom knowledge might exalt
Equal with gods; aspiring to be such,
They taste and die: what likelier can ensue?
But first with narrow search I must walk round
This garden, and no corner leave unspied;
A chance, but chance[8] may lead where I may meet
Some wand'ring Spirit of Heav'n, by fountain side,
Or in thick shade retired, from him to draw
What further would be learnt. Live while ye may,
Yet happy pair; enjoy, till I return,
Short pleasures, for long woes are to succeed."
  So saying, his proud step he scornful turned,
But with sly circumspection, and began
Through wood, through waste, o'er hill, o'er dale his roam.° *act of wandering*
Meanwhile in utmost longitude, where heav'n° *the sky*
With earth and ocean meets, the setting sun
Slowly descended, and with right aspéct
Against the eastern gate of Paradise
Leveled his evening rays.[9] It was a rock
Of alabaster,[1] piled up to the clouds,
Conspicuous far, winding with one ascent
Accessible from earth, one entrance high;
The rest was craggy cliff, that overhung
Still as it rose, impossible to climb.
Betwixt these rocky pillars Gabriel[2] sat
Chief of th' angelic guards, awaiting night;
About him exercised heroic games
Th' unarmèd youth of Heav'n, but nigh at hand
Celestial armory, shields, helms, and spears
Hung high with diamond flaming, and with gold.
Thither came Uriel, gliding through the even
On a sunbeam, swift as a shooting star
In autumn thwarts° the night, when vapors fired *passes across*
Impress the air, and shows the mariner
From what point of his compass to beware
Impetuous winds:[3] he thus began in haste.
  "Gabriel, to thee thy course by lot hath giv'n

8. An opportunity, even if only by luck.
9. Setting in the west, the sun struck the eastern gate from the inside, at a ninety-degree angle.
1. White, translucent marble veined with colors.
2. In Hebrew, "strength of God." A tradition (cf. 1 Enoch 20.7) gave Gabriel charge of Paradise.
3. Shooting stars were thought to indicate by the direction of their fall the source of oncoming storms. "Vapors fired": heat lightning.

Charge and strict watch that to this happy place
No evil thing approach or enter in;
This day at height of noon came to my sphere
A Spirit, zealous, as he seemed, to know
More of th' Almighty's works, and chiefly man
God's latest image: I described° his way — *descried, observed*
Bent all on speed, and marked his airy gait;° — *path*
But in the mount that lies from Eden north,
Where he first lighted, soon discerned his looks
Alien from Heav'n, with passions foul obscured:
Mine eye pursued him still, but under shade° — *trees*
Lost sight of him; one of the banished crew
I fear, hath ventured from the deep, to raise
New troubles; him thy care must be to find."
To whom the wingèd warrior thus returned:
"Uriel, no wonder if thy perfect sight,
Amid the sun's bright circle where thou sitt'st,
See far and wide. In at this gate none pass
The vigilance here placed, but such as come
Well known from Heav'n; and since meridian hour° — *noon*
No creature thence: if Spirit of other sort,
So minded, have o'erleaped these earthy bounds
On purpose, hard thou know'st it to exclude
Spiritual substance with corporeal bar.
But if within the circuit of these walks,
In whatsoever shape he lurk, of whom
Thou tell'st, by morrow dawning I shall know."
So promised he, and Uriel to his charge
Returned on that bright beam, whose point now raised
Bore him slope downward to the sun now fall'n
Beneath th' Azorès; whether the prime orb,
Incredible how swift, had thither rolled
Diurnal,° or this less volúble° earth — *daily / swift-turning*
By shorter flight to th' east,[4] had left him there
Arraying with reflected purple and gold
The clouds that on his western throne attend.
Now came still evening on, and twilight gray
Had in her sober livery all things clad;
Silence accompanied, for beast and bird,
They to their grassy couch, these to their nests
Were slunk, all but the wakeful nightingale;
She all night long her amorous descant° sung; — *melody*
Silence was pleased: now glowed the firmament
With living sapphires: Hesperus[5] that led
The starry host, rode brightest, till the moon
Rising in clouded majesty, at length
Apparent° queen unveiled her peerless light, — *clearly seen*
And o'er the dark her silver mantle threw.
When Adam thus to Eve: "Fair consort, th' hour
Of night, and all things now retired to rest

4. Here and elsewhere Milton leaves open the question of whether the sun moves around the earth, or vice versa.

5. Called Venus when it appears in the evening sky.

Mind us of like repose, since God hath set
Labor and rest, as day and night to men
Successive, and the timely dew of sleep
Now falling with soft slumbrous weight inclines
Our eyelids; other creatures all day long
Rove idle unemployed, and less need rest;
Man hath his daily work of body or mind
Appointed, which declares his dignity,
And the regard of Heav'n on all his ways;
While other animals unactive range,
And of their doings God takes no account.
Tomorrow ere fresh morning streak the east
With first approach of light, we must be ris'n,
And at our pleasant labor, to reform
Yon flow'ry arbors, yonder alleys green,
Our walk at noon, with branches overgrown,
That mock our scant manuring,° and require *cultivating*
More hands than ours to lop their wanton° growth: *luxuriant*
Those blossoms also, and those dropping gums,
That lie bestrown unsightly and unsmooth,
Ask riddance,° if we mean to tread with ease; *need to be cleared*
Meanwhile, as nature wills, night bids us rest."
   To whom thus Eve with perfect beauty adorned.
"My author and disposer, what thou bidd'st
Unargued I obey; so God ordains,
God is thy law, thou mine: to know no more
Is woman's happiest knowledge and her praise.
With thee conversing I forget all time.
All seasons° and their change, all please alike. *times of day*
Sweet[6] is the breath of morn, her rising sweet,
With charm[7] of earliest birds; pleasant the sun
When first on this delightful land he spreads
His orient° beams, on herb, tree, fruit, and flow'r, *lustrious, eastern*
Glist'ring with dew; fragrant the fertile earth
After soft showers; and sweet the coming on
Of grateful evening mild, then silent night
With this her solemn bird° and this fair moon, *the nightingale*
And these the gems of heav'n, her starry train:
But neither breath of morn when she ascends
With charm of earliest birds, nor rising sun
On this delightful land, nor herb, fruit, flow'r,
Glist'ring with dew, nor fragrance after showers,
Nor grateful evening mild, nor silent night
With this her solemn bird, nor walk by moon,
Or glittering starlight without thee is sweet.
But wherefore all night long shine these, for whom
This glorious sight, when sleep hath shut all eyes?"
   To whom our general ancestor replied.
"Daughter of God and man, accomplished[8] Eve,
Those have their course to finish, round the earth,

6. With this embedded lyric, beginning here, Eve displays her literary talents in an elegant love song, sonnetlike and replete with striking rhetorical figures of circularity and repetition.

7. Blended singing of many birds.

8. Having many talents and achievements; perfect, complete.

By morrow evening, and from land to land
In order, though to nations yet unborn,
Minist'ring light prepared, they set and rise;
Lest total darkness should by night regain
Her old possession, and extinguish life
In nature and all things, which these soft° fires *agreeable*
Not only enlighten, but with kindly° heat *natural, benevolent*
Of various influence foment° and warm, *foster*
Temper or nourish, or in part shed down
Their stellar virtue on all kinds that grow
On earth, made hereby apter to receive
Perfection from the sun's more potent ray.[9]
These then, though unbeheld in deep of night,
Shine not in vain, nor think, though men were none,
That heav'n would want° spectators, God want praise; *lack*
Millions of spiritual creatures walk the earth
Unseen, both when we wake, and when we sleep:
All these with ceaseless praise his works behold
Both day and night: how often from the steep
Of echoing hill or thicket have we heard
Celestial voices to the midnight air,
Sole, or responsive each to other's note
Singing their great Creator: oft in bands
While they keep watch, or nightly rounding walk,
With heav'nly touch of instrumental sounds
In full harmonic number joined, their songs
Divide[1] the night, and lift our thoughts to Heaven."
  Thus talking hand in hand alone they passed
On to their blissful bower; it was a place
Chos'n by the sov'reign Planter, when he framed° *fashioned*
All things to man's delightful use; the roof
Of thickest covert was inwoven shade
Laurel and myrtle, and what higher grew
Of firm and fragrant leaf; on either side
Acanthus, and each odorous bushy shrub
Fenced up the verdant wall; each beauteous flow'r,
Iris all hues, roses, and jessamine° *jasmine*
Reared high their flourished° heads between, and wrought *flowering*
Mosaic; underfoot the violet,
Crocus, and hyacinth with rich inlay
Broidered the ground, more colored than with stone
Of costliest emblem:° other creature here *inlaid work*
Beast, bird, insect, or worm durst enter none,
Such was their awe of man. In shadier bower
More sacred and sequestered,° though but feigned, *secluded*
Pan or Silvanus never slept, nor nymph,
Nor Faunus[2] haunted. Here in close recess
With flowers, garlands, and sweet-smelling herbs
Espousèd Eve decked first her nuptial bed,

9. The stars were thought to have their own occult influence, and also to moderate that of the sun.
1. Mark the watches of the night; also, perform musical "divisions," elaborate melodic passages.
2. Forest and field divinities of classical mythology.

And heav'nly choirs the hymenean° sung, *wedding song*
What day the genial[3] angel to our sire
Brought her in naked beauty more adorned,
More lovely than Pandora, whom the gods
Endowed with all their gifts, and O too like
In sad event,° when to the unwiser son *outcome*
Of Japhet brought by Hermes, she ensnared
Mankind with her fair looks, to be avenged
On him who had stole Jove's authentic fire.[4]
Thus at their shady lodge arrived, both stood,
Both turned, and under open sky adored
The God that made both sky, air, earth, and heav'n
Which they beheld, the moon's resplendent globe
And starry pole:° "Thou also mad'st the night, *sky*
Maker Omnipotent, and thou the day,
Which we in our appointed work employed
Have finished happy in our mutual help
And mutual love, the crown of all our bliss
Ordained by thee, and this delicious place
For us too large, where thy abundance wants
Partakers, and uncropped falls to the ground.
But thou hast promised from us two a race
To fill the earth, who shall with us extol
Thy goodness infinite, both when we wake,
And when we seek, as now, thy gift of sleep."
This said unanimous, and other rites
Observing none, but adoration pure
Which God likes best,[5] into their inmost bow'r
Handed° they went; and eased° the putting off *hand in hand / spared*
These troublesome disguises which we wear,
Straight side by side were laid, nor turned I ween° *surmise*
Adam from his fair spouse, nor Eve the rites
Mysterious[6] of connubial love refused:
Whatever hypocrites austerely talk
Of purity and place and innocence,
Defaming as impure what God declares
Pure, and commands to some, leaves free to all.
Our Maker bids increase,[7] who bids abstain
But our destroyer, foe to God and man?
Hail wedded Love, mysterious law, true source
Of human offspring, sole propriety° *private property*
In Paradise of all things common else.
By thee adulterous lust was driv'n from men
Among the bestial herds to range, by thee

3. Presiding over marriage and generation.
4. Pandora (the name means "all gifts") was an artificial woman, molded of clay, bestowed by the gods on Epimetheus, brother of Prometheus (who angered Jove by stealing fire from heaven). She brought a box that foolish Epimetheus opened, releasing all the ills of the human race, leaving only hope inside. The brothers were sons of Iapetos, whom Milton identifies with Japhet, Noah's third son. The Eve-Pandora parallel was often noted.
5. Like many Puritans, Milton objected to set forms of prayer, so Adam and Eve pray spontaneously (therefore sincerely), but also, paradoxically, together. Their prayer develops variations on Psalm 104.20–24.
6. Awe-inspiring. St. Paul (Ephesians 5.32) calls the union of man and woman a "mystery" paralleling that of Christ and the church.
7. Genesis 1.28: "Be fruitful and multiply, and replenish the earth."

Founded in reason, loyal, just, and pure,
Relations dear, and all the charities° *loves*
Of father, son, and brother first were known.
Far be it, that I should write thee sin or blame,
Or think thee unbefitting holiest place,
Perpetual fountain of domestic sweets,
Whose bed is undefiled and chaste pronounced,
Present, or past, as saints and patriarchs used.[8]
Here Love his golden shafts employs,[9] here lights
His constant lamp, and waves his purple wings,
Reigns here and revels; not in the bought smile
Of harlots, loveless, joyless, unendeared,
Casual fruition, nor in court amours,
Mixed dance, or wanton masque, or midnight ball,
Or serenade, which the starved° lover sings *deprived*
To his proud fair, best quitted with disdain.
These lulled by nightingales embracing slept,
And on their naked limbs the flow'ry roof
Show'red roses, which the morn repaired.° Sleep on, *replaced*
Blest pair; and O yet happiest if ye seek
No happier state, and know to know no more.[1]

Summary Fulfilling his promise to Uriel, Gabriel divides his night watch into search parties, assigning Ithuriel and Zephon to guard closely the bower of Adam and Eve. They find Satan in the bower, whispering in the ear of the sleeping Eve, and bring him before Gabriel. A battle impends, but is averted by a heavenly signal, and Satan flees out of Paradise.

From Book 5

[EVE'S DREAM; TROUBLE IN PARADISE]

Now Morn her rosy steps in th' eastern clime
Advancing, sowed the earth with orient pearl,° *sparkling dew*
When Adam waked, so customed, for his sleep
Was aery light, from pure digestion bred,
And temperate vapors bland,° which th' only sound *gentle, balmy*
Of leaves and fuming rills, Aurora's fan,[1]
Lightly dispersed, and the shrill matin° song *morning*
Of birds on every bough; so much the more
His wonder was to find unwakened Eve
With tresses discomposed, and glowing cheek,
As through unquiet rest: he on his side
Leaning half-raised, with looks of cordial° love *heartfelt*
Hung over her enamored, and beheld
Beauty, which whether waking or asleep,

8. Throughout history ("present or past"), Old and New Testament worthies have "used" matrimony as a noble estate.
9. The "golden shafts" (arrows) of Cupid produce true love, his lead-tipped arrows, hate.
1. Know enough to be content with what you know.
1. Rustling leaves and streams ("rills") stirred by Aurora, goddess of the dawn.

Shot forth peculiar° graces; then with voice *its own*
Mild, as when Zephyrus on Flora[2] breathes,
Her hand soft touching, whispered thus: "Awake
My fairest, my espoused, my latest found,
Heav'n's last best gift, my ever new delight,
Awake, the morning shines, and the fresh field
Calls us, we lose the prime, to mark how spring
Our tended plants, how blows° the citron grove, *blooms*
What drops the myrrh, and what the balmy reed,° *balsam*
How nature paints her colors, how the bee
Sits on the bloom extracting liquid sweet."[3]
  Such whispering waked her, but with startled eye
On Adam, whom embracing, thus she spake:
  "O sole in whom my thoughts find all repose,
My glory, my perfection, glad I see
Thy face, and morn returned, for I this night,
Such night till this I never passed, have dreamed,
If dreamed, not as I oft am wont,° of thee, *accustomed*
Works of day past, or morrow's next design,
But of offense and trouble, which my mind
Knew never till this irksome night. Methought
Close at mine ear one called me forth to walk
With gentle voice, I thought it thine; it said,
'Why sleep'st thou Eve? Now is the pleasant time,
The cool, the silent, save where silence yields
To the night-warbling bird, that now awake
Tunes sweetest his love-labored song; now reigns
Full-orbed the moon, and with more pleasing light
Shadowy sets off the face of things, in vain,
If none regard; heav'n wakes with all his eyes,° *stars*
Whom to behold but thee, nature's desire,
In whose sight all things joy, with ravishment
Attracted by thy beauty still° to gaze.' *continually*
I rose as at thy call, but found thee not;
To find thee I directed then my walk;
And on, me thought, alone I passed through ways
That brought me on a sudden to the tree
Of interdicted knowledge: fair it seemed,
Much fairer to my fancy than by day:
And as I wond'ring looked, beside it stood
One shaped and winged like one of those from Heav'n
By us oft seen; his dewy locks distilled
Ambrosia;° on that tree he also gazed; *heavenly fragrance*
And 'O fair plant,' said he, 'with fruit surcharged,° *overburdened*
Deigns none to ease thy load and taste thy sweet,
Nor god,° nor man? Is knowledge so despised? *angel*
Or envy, or what reserve forbids to taste?[4]
Forbid who will, none shall from me withhold

2. Zephyrus is god of the gentle west wind, Flora goddess of flowers.

3. Adam sings a morning love song (*aubade*) to Eve, which works variations on Song of Solomon 2.10–12: "Rise up, my love, my fair one, and come away. . . . The flowers appear on the earth; the time of the singing of birds is come." Compare Satan's serenade (5.38–47), a parody of Adam's *aubade* and the Song of Solomon. "Prime" (line 21): first hour of the day.

4. I.e., does envy or some other barrier ("reserve") forbid your being tasted?

Longer thy offered good, why else set here?'
This said he paused not, but with vent'rous arm
He plucked, he tasted; me damp horror chilled
At such bold words vouched with° a deed so bold: *backed by*
But he thus overjoyed, 'O fruit divine,
Sweet of thyself, but much more sweet thus cropped,
Forbidden here, it seems, as only fit
For gods, yet able to make gods of men:
And why not gods of men, since good, the more
Communicated, more abundant grows,
The author not impaired,° but honored more? *injured, diminished*
Here, happy creature, fair angelic Eve,
Partake thou also; happy though thou art,
Happier thou may'st be, worthier canst not be:
Taste this, and be henceforth among the gods
Thyself a goddess, not to earth confined,
But sometimes in the air, as we, sometimes
Ascend to Heav'n, by merit thine, and see
What life the gods live there, and such live thou.'
So saying, he drew nigh, and to me held,
Even to my mouth of that same fruit held part
Which he had plucked; the pleasant savory smell
So quickened appetite, that I, methought,
Could not but taste. Forthwith up to the clouds
With him I flew, and underneath beheld
The earth outstretched immense, a prospect wide
And various: wond'ring at my flight and change
To this high exaltation: suddenly
My guide was gone, and I, methought, sunk down,
And fell asleep; but O how glad I waked
To find this but a dream!" Thus Eve her night
Related, and thus Adam answered sad.° *gravely, soberly*
"Best image of myself and dearer half,
The trouble of thy thoughts this night in sleep
Affects me equally; nor can I like
This uncouth° dream, of evil sprung I fear; *strange, unpleasant*
Yet evil whence? In thee can harbor none,
Created pure. But know that in the soul
Are many lesser faculties[5] that serve
Reason as chief; among these fancy next
Her office holds; of all external things,
Which the five watchful senses represent,
She forms imaginations,° aery shapes, *images*
Which reason joining or disjoining, frames
All what we affirm or what deny, and call
Our knowledge or opinion; then retires
Into her private cell when nature rests.
Oft in her absence mimic fancy wakes
To imitate her; but misjoining shapes,

5. Adam's explanation of the dream (lines 100–116) summarizes the orthodox faculty psychology and dream theory of Milton's time—one among many kinds of knowledge with which unfallen man was endowed.

Wild work produces oft, and most in dreams,
Ill matching words and deeds long past or late.
Some such resemblances methinks I find
Of our last evening's talk in this thy dream,[6]
But with addition strange; yet be not sad.
Evil into the mind of god[7] or man
May come and go, so unapproved,[8] and leave
No spot or blame behind: which gives me hope
That what in sleep thou didst abhor to dream,
Waking thou never wilt consent to do.
Be not disheartened then, nor cloud those looks
That wont to be° more cheerful and serene — *usually are*
Than when fair morning first smiles on the world,
And let us to our fresh employments rise
Among the groves, the fountains, and the flow'rs
That open now their choicest bosomed smells
Reserved from night, and kept for thee in store."
  So cheered he his fair spouse, and she was cheered,
But silently a gentle tear let fall
From either eye, and wiped them with her hair;
Two other precious drops that ready stood,
Each in their crystal sluice, he ere they fell
Kissed as the gracious signs of sweet remorse
And pious awe, that feared to have offended.

Summary Before going to work at their rural tasks, Adam and Eve recite their spontaneous morning prayers. God, seeing and pitying their unprotected innocence, dispatches Raphael to warn them of approaching dangers. The affable archangel enters the bower just about noontime and is promptly invited to join the midday meal, an invitation that he gladly accepts.

[A VISIT WITH THE ANGEL. THE SCALE OF NATURE]

* * * So to the sylvan lodge
They came, that like Pomona's[9] arbor smiled
With flow'rets decked° and fragrant smells; but Eve — *covered*
Undecked, save with herself more lovely fair
Than wood nymph, or the fairest goddess feigned
Of three that in Mount Ida naked strove,[1]
Stood to entertain her guest from Heav'n; no veil
She needed, virtue-proof,° no thought infirm — *armored in virtue*
Altered her cheek. On whom the Angel "Hail"
Bestowed, the holy salutation used
Long after to blest Mary, second Eve.[2]

6. Adam recalls his own words in 4.411–39.
7. Probably "angel" as elsewhere, but perhaps God, whose omniscience must encompass knowledge of evil as well as good.
8. If not willed (approved of) or not acted on (put to the proof).
9. The Roman goddess of fruit trees.
1. On Mount Ida, Venus, Juno, and Minerva "strove" naked for the title of the most beautiful; Paris awarded the prize (the apple of discord) to Venus, which led to the rape of Helen and the Trojan War.
2. Cf. the angel's words to Mary announcing that she would bear a son, Jesus (Luke 1.28): "Hail, thou that art highly favored, the Lord is with thee: blessed art thou among women."

"Hail mother of mankind, whose fruitful womb
Shall fill the world more numerous with thy sons
Than with these various fruits the trees of God
Have heaped this table." Raised of grassy turf
Their table was, and mossy seats had round,
And on her ample square from side to side
All autumn piled, though spring and autumn here
Danced hand in hand. A while discourse they hold;
No fear lest dinner cool; when thus began
Our author:° "Heav'nly stranger, please to taste — *forefather*
These bounties which our Nourisher, from whom
All perfect good unmeasured out, descends,
To us for food and for delight hath caused
The earth to yield; unsavory food perhaps
To spiritual natures; only this I know,
That one Celestial Father gives to all."
To whom the angel: "Therefore what he gives
(Whose praise be ever sung) to man in part
Spiritual, may of° purest Spirits be found — *by*
No ingrateful food: and food alike those pure
Intelligential substances require[3]
As doth your rational; and both contain
Within them every lower faculty
Of sense, whereby they hear, see, smell, touch, taste,
Tasting concoct, digest, assimilate,[4]
And corporeal to incorporeal turn.
For know, whatever was created, needs
To be sustained and fed; of elements
The grosser feeds the purer, earth the sea,
Earth and the sea feed air, the air those fires
Ethereal, and as lowest first the moon;
Whence in her visage round those spots, unpurged
Vapors not yet into her substance turned.[5]
Nor doth the moon no nourishment exhale
From her moist continent to higher orbs.[6]
The sun that light imparts to all, receives
From all his alimental° recompense — *nourishing*
In humid exhalations, and at even
Sups with the ocean:[7] though in Heav'n the trees
Of life ambrosial° fruitage bear, and vines — *divinely fragrant*
Yield nectar,[8] though from off the boughs each morn
We brush mellifluous° dews, and find the ground — *honey-flowing*
Covered with pearly grain; yet God hath here
Varied his bounty so with new delights,

3. Milton's angels ("intelligential substances") require real food, even as "rational" men do (see below, lines 430–38). As a monist (believer that all creation is of one matter), Milton denied the more common (dualistic) idea that angels are pure spirit, holding instead that they are of a very highly refined material substance.
4. Three stages in digestion.
5. Here Raphael describes lunar spots as still-undigested vapors (in keeping with his exposition of the universal need of nourishment); in 1.287–91 he referred to moon spots in Galileo's terms, as landscape features.
6. A double negative: the moon does exhale such nourishment to other planets.
7. Milton explains evaporation as the sun dining off moisture exhaled from the oceans.
8. Ambrosia is the food and nectar the drink of the classical gods; Milton adds "pearly grain" (line 430), like the manna showered on the Israelites in the desert (Exodus 16.14–15).

As may compare with Heaven; and to taste
Think not I shall be nice."° So down they sat, *fastidious, finicky*
And to their viands fell, nor seemingly° *in show*
The angel, nor in mist, the common gloss° *explanation*
Of theologians, but with keen dispatch
Of real hunger, and concoctive° heat *digestive*
To transubstantiate;[9] what redounds, transpires
Through Spirits with ease; nor wonder, if by fire
Of sooty coal the empiric° alchemist *experimental*
Can turn, or holds it possible to turn
Metals of drossiest ore to perfect gold
As from the mine. Meanwhile at table Eve
Ministered naked, and their flowing cups
With pleasant liquors crowned.° O innocence *filled to the brim*
Deserving Paradise! if ever, then,
Then had the Sons of God excuse t' have been
Enamored at that sight,[1] but in those hearts
Love unlibidinous° reigned, nor jealousy *without lust*
Was understood, the injured lover's hell.
  Thus when with meats and drinks they had sufficed,
Not burdened nature, sudden mind arose
In Adam, not to let th' occasion pass
Given him by this great conference to know
Of things above his world, and of their being
Who dwell in Heav'n, whose excellence he saw
Transcend his own so far, whose radiant forms
Divine effulgence,° whose high power so far *shining forth*
Exceeded human, and his wary speech
Thus to th' empyreal minister he framed:
  "Inhabitant with God, now know I well
Thy favor, in this honor done to man,
Under whose lowly roof thou hast vouchsafed
To enter and these earthly fruits to taste,
Food not of angels, yet accepted so,
As that more willingly thou couldst not seem
At Heav'n's high feasts t' have fed: yet what compare?"
  To whom the wingèd hierarch° replied: *authority*
"O Adam, one Almighty is, from whom
All things proceed, and up to him return,
If not depraved from good, created all
Such to perfection, one first matter all,[2]
Endued with various forms, various degrees
Of substance, and in things that live, of life;
But more refined, more spiritous, and pure,

9. In common theological use, transubstantiation is the Roman Catholic doctrine that the bread and wine of the Eucharist become the body and blood of Christ. Milton vigorously denied that doctrine, but he describes the angels' transforming of earthly food into their more highly refined spiritual substance as a true transubstantiation. The excess ("what redounds") is exhaled ("transpires") through angelic pores.

1. Genesis 6.2 tells of the marriage of "the daughters of men" with "the sons of God," usually identified as sons of Seth, but a patristic tradition (alluded to here) identifies them as angels.

2. Milton held that the universe was created out of Chaos, not out of nothing: the primal matter of Chaos had its origin in God, who subsequently created all things from that matter (see 7.168–73, 210–42). This materialist "monism" denies sharp distinctions between angels and men, spirit and matter: all beings are of one substance, of varying degrees of refinement and life.

As nearer to him placed or nearer tending
Each in their several active spheres assigned,
Till body up to spirit work, in bounds
Proportioned to each kind.[3] So from the root
Springs lighter the green stalk, from thence the leaves
More airy, last the bright consummate flow'r
Spirits odorous breathes:[4] flow'rs and their fruit
Man's nourishment, by gradual scale sublimed° *purified*
To vital spirits aspire, to animal,
To intellectual, give both life and sense,
Fancy° and understanding, whence the soul *imagination*
Reason receives, and reason is her being,
Discursive, or intuitive;[5] discourse
Is oftest yours, the latter most is ours,
Differing but in degree, of kind the same.
Wonder not then, what God for you saw good
If I refuse not, but convert, as you,
To proper° substance; time may come when men *our own*
With angels may participate, and find
No inconvenient diet, nor too light fare:
And from these corporal nutriments perhaps
Your bodies may at last turn all to spirit,
Improved by tract° of time, and winged ascend *passage*
Ethereal as we, or may at choice
Here or in heav'nly paradises dwell;
If ye be found obedient, and retain
Unalterably firm his love entire
Whose progeny you are. Meanwhile enjoy
Your fill what happiness this happy state
Can comprehend, incapable° of more." *unable to contain*
  To whom the patriarch of mankind replied:
"O favorable Spirit, propitious guest,
Well hast thou taught the way that might direct
Our knowledge, and the scale of nature set
From center to circumference, whereon
In contemplation of created things
By steps we may ascend to God. * * *

Summary After this mingled explanation and warning, Raphael, by way of emphasizing the danger that threatens Adam and Eve, enters upon the story of Satan's revolt and fall. Satan, pretending that God's exaltation of the Son was an offense to angelic dignity, persuaded the angels under his command—a third of the heavenly

3. Milton's version of the chain of being qualifies natural hierarchy by allowing for movement up or down; beings may become increasingly spiritual ("more spiritous") or increasingly gross (as the rebel angels do), depending on their moral choices—"nearer tending."

4. The plant figure—root, stalk, leaves, flowers, and fruit—provides an illustration of the dynamism of being in the universe and further explains why Raphael can eat the fruit. Such food is then transformed (next lines) into various orders of "spirits"—"vital," "animal," and "intellectual" (fluids in the blood that sustain life, sensation, motion, and finally intellect and its functions, "fancy," "understanding," and "reason"), indicating that the soul is also material.

5. Traditionally, on the dualist assumption that angels are pure spirit and humans a combination of matter and spirit, angelic intuition (immediate apprehension of truth) was absolutely distinguished from human "discourse" of reason (arguing from premises to conclusions). Milton, denying that assumption, makes the distinction only relative, a matter of "degree" (line 490).

host—to go off and set up a camp in the north of Heaven. When he revealed his rebellious purpose, however, one of these angels refused to embrace it. The seraph Abdiel, though scorned by Satan and all his legions, denounced the rebellion and returned, heroically alone, to the ranks of God's followers.

Book 6 *Summary*

Continuing the story of the war in Heaven, Raphael describes the assembling of the armies and a first skirmish in which Satan is both insulted and wounded by Abdiel. After the first day's battle, the evil angels retire discomfited; but overnight Satan invents cannon, with which, on the second day, the good angels are put to some disorder. In the fury of the fight, however, they pull up mountains by the roots and bury the cannon beneath them; thus the issue remains inconclusive. On the third day, God withdraws all His armies and sends the Son alone into battle; the Son drives His enemies over the wall of Heaven, and after falling nine days through Chaos they are swallowed up in Hell.

From Book 7

[THE INVOCATION]

Descend from Heav'n Urania,[1] by that name
If rightly thou art called, whose voice divine
Following, above th' Olympian hill I soar,
Above the flight of Pegasean wing.[2]
The meaning, not the name I call: for thou
Nor of the muses nine, nor on the top
Of old Olympus dwell'st, but heav'nly born
Before the hills appeared, or fountain flowed,
Thou with eternal Wisdom[3] didst converse,° *associate*
Wisdom thy sister, and with her didst play
In presence of th' Almighty Father, pleased
With thy celestial song. Up led by thee
Into the Heav'n of Heav'ns I have presumed,
An earthly guest, and drawn empyreal air,
Thy temp'ring;° with like safety guided down *made suitable by thee*
Return me to my native element:
Lest from this flying steed unreined (as once
Bellerophon,[4] though from a lower clime)° *region*
Dismounted, on th' Aleian field I fall
Erroneous° there to wander and forlorn. *straying*
Half yet remains unsung, but narrower bound
Within the visible diurnal sphere;[5]
Standing on earth, not rapt° above the pole, *transported, enraptured*

1. Urania, the Greek Muse of astronomy, had been made into the Muse of Christian poetry by du Bartas and other religious poets. Milton, however, constructs another derivation for her (line 5ff.). Milton begins Book 7 with a third proem (lines 1–39).
2. Pegasus, the flying horse of inspired poetry, suggests (in connection with Bellerophon, line 18) Milton's sense of perilous audacity in writing this poem.
3. In Proverbs 8.24–31 Wisdom tells of her activities before the Creation: "Then I was by him [God], as one brought up with him: and I was daily his delight, rejoicing always before him." Milton describes "eternal Wisdom" as a daughter of God (personification of his wisdom) and devises a myth in which the Muse of divine poetry ("celestial song," line 12) is Wisdom's "sister"—also, thereby, originating from God.
4. Bellerophon incurred the gods' anger when he tried to fly to heaven upon Pegasus; Zeus sent an insect to sting the horse, and Bellerophon fell down to the "Aleian field" (plain of error), where he wandered alone and blind until his death.
5. The universe, which appears to rotate daily.

More safe I sing with mortal voice, unchanged
To hoarse or mute, though fall'n on evil days,
On evil days though fall'n, and evil tongues;
In darkness, and with dangers compassed round,[6]
And solitude; yet not alone, while thou
Visit'st my slumbers nightly, or when morn
Purples the east: still govern thou my song,
Urania, and fit audience find, though few.
But drive far off the barbarous dissonance
Of Bacchus and his revelers, the race
Of that wild rout that tore the Thracian bard
In Rhodope, where woods and rocks had ears
To rapture, till the savage clamor drowned
Both harp and voice;[7] nor could the Muse defend
Her son.[8] So fail not thou, who thee implores:
For thou art heav'nly, she an empty dream.

Summary At Adam's request, Raphael continues his narration and describes how God, to replace the fallen angels, created the world, its creatures, and finally man, in the course of six days; the story of the creation concludes, on the seventh day, with a chorus of thanksgiving by the angels.

From Book 8

Summary Adam, to prolong his visit with Raphael, asks why so many and such splendid stars seem to be at the service of the earth, which appears smaller and less noble than they. At this point Eve discreetly takes her leave. Replying to Adam's question, Raphael proposes various astronomical possibilities, but gives no conclusive answer, advising Adam to concern himself with matters closer to home. The angel, on the other hand, is much interested to hear the story, which Adam proposes to tell, of his own creation.

[ADAM DESCRIBES HIS OWN CREATION AND THAT OF EVE; HAVING REPEATED HIS WARNING, THE ANGEL DEPARTS]

So spake the godlike Power, and thus our sire:
"For man to tell how human life began
Is hard; for who himself beginning knew?[1]
Desire with thee still longer to converse
Induced me. As new-waked from soundest sleep
Soft on the flow'ry herb I found me laid

6. After the Restoration of Charles II (May 1660) and until the passage of the Act of Oblivion (August 1660), Milton was in danger of death and dismemberment (like Orpheus, lines 34–35); several of his republican colleagues were hanged, disembowelled, and quartered for their part in the revolution and regicide.

7. The music of the "Thracian bard" Orpheus, type of the poet, charmed even "woods and rocks," but his song was drowned out by the Bacchantes, a "wild rout" of screaming women who murdered and dismembered him and threw his body parts into the Hebrus River, which rises in the "Rhodope" mountains. Milton fears that a similar "barbarous dissonance" unleashed by the Restoration will drown out his voice and threaten his life.

8. Orpheus's mother is Calliope, Muse of epic poetry.

1. Compare Satan's inability to remember his origins (5.856–63), from which he infers self-creation, whereas Adam infers a Maker (line 278).

In balmy sweat, which with his beams the sun
Soon dried, and on the reeking° moisture fed. *steaming*
Straight toward heav'n my wond'ring eyes I turned,
And gazed a while the ample sky, till raised
By quick instinctive motion up I sprung
As thitherward endeavoring, and upright
Stood on my feet; about me round I saw
Hill, dale, and shady woods, and sunny plains,
And liquid lapse° of murmuring streams; by these, *flow*
Creatures that lived, and moved, and walked, or flew,
Birds on the branches warbling; all things smiled,
With fragrance and with joy my heart o'erflowed.
Myself I then perused, and limb by limb
Surveyed, and sometimes went,° and sometimes ran *walked*
With supple joints, as lively vigor led:
But who I was, or where, or from what cause,
Knew not; to speak I tried, and forthwith spake,
My tongue obeyed and readily could name
Whate'er I saw.[2] 'Thou sun,' said I, 'fair light,
And thou enlightened earth, so fresh and gay,
Ye hills and dales, ye rivers, woods, and plains,
And ye that live and move, fair creatures, tell,
Tell, if ye saw, how came I thus, how here?
Not of myself; by some great Maker then,
In goodness and in power preeminent;
Tell me, how may I know him, how adore,
From whom I have that thus I move and live,
And feel that I am happier than I know.'
While thus I called, and strayed I knew not whither,
From where I first drew air, and first beheld
This happy light, when answer none returned,
On a green shady bank profuse of flow'rs
Pensive I sat me down; there gentle sleep
First found me, and with soft oppression seized
My drowsèd sense, untroubled, though I thought
I then was passing to my former state
Insensible, and forthwith to dissolve:
When suddenly stood at my head a dream,
Whose inward apparition gently moved
My fancy to believe I yet had being,
And lived: one came, methought, of shape divine,
And said, 'Thy mansion° wants° thee, Adam, rise, *habitation / lacks*
First man, of men innumerable ordained
First father, called by thee I come thy guide
To the garden of bliss, thy seat° prepared.' *residence*
So saying, by the hand he took me raised,
And over fields and waters, as in air
Smooth sliding without step, last led me up
A woody mountain whose high top was plain,
A circuit wide, enclosed, with goodliest trees
Planted, with walks, and bowers, that what I saw

2. Adam's ability to name the creatures was said to signify his intuitive understanding of their natures.

Of earth before scarce pleasant seemed. Each tree
Load'n with fairest fruit, that hung to the eye
Tempting, stirred in me sudden appetite
To pluck and eat; whereat I waked, and found
Before mine eyes all real, as the dream
Had lively° shadowed: here had new begun *vividly*
My wand'ring, had not he who was my guide
Up hither, from among the trees appeared,
Presence Divine. Rejoicing, but with awe
In adoration at his feet I fell
Submiss:° he reared me, and 'Whom thou sought'st I am,' *submissive*
Said mildly, 'Author of all this thou seest
Above, or round about thee or beneath.
This Paradise I give thee, count it thine
To till and keep,° and of the fruit to eat: *care for*
Of every tree that in the garden grows
Eat freely with glad heart; fear here no dearth:
But of the tree whose operation° brings *action*
Knowledge of good and ill, which I have set
The pledge of thy obedience and thy faith,
Amid the garden by the Tree of Life,
Remember what I warn thee, shun to taste,
And shun the bitter consequence: for know,
The day thou eat'st thereof, my sole command
Transgressed, inevitably thou shalt die;
From that day mortal, and this happy state
Shalt lose, expelled from hence into a world
Of woe and sorrow.'[3] Sternly he pronounced
The rigid interdiction,° which resounds *prohibition*
Yet dreadful in mine ear, though in my choice
Not to incur; but soon his clear aspéct° *untroubled expression*
Returned and gracious purpose° thus renewed: *speech*
'Not only these fair bounds, but all the earth
To thee and to thy race I give; as lords
Possess it, and all things that therein live,
Or live in sea, or air, beast, fish, and fowl.
In sign whereof each bird and beast behold
After their kinds; I bring them to receive
From thee their names, and pay thee fealty
With low subjection; understand the same
Of fish within their wat'ry residence,
Not hither summoned, since they cannot change
Their element to draw the thinner air.'
As thus he spake, each bird and beast behold
Approaching two and two, these° cow'ring low *the beasts*
With blandishment,° each bird stooped on his wing. *flattering gesture*
I named them, as they passed, and understood
Their nature, with such knowledge God endued
My sudden apprehension:[4] but in these

3. Compare God's commands to Adam (Genesis 1.28–30, 2.16–17) with Milton's elaboration here.
4. Adam had already begun naming the sun and features of the earth (lines 272–74), but here he names (and thereby shows he understands) all living creatures.

I found not what methought I wanted still;
And to the heav'nly Vision thus presumed:
" 'O by what name, for thou above all these,
Above mankind, or aught than mankind higher,
Surpassest far my naming,[5] how may I
Adore thee, Author of this universe,
And all this good to man, for whose well-being
So amply, and with hands so liberal
Thou hast provided all things: but with me
I see not who partakes. In solitude
What happiness, who can enjoy alone,
Or all enjoying, what contentment find?'
Thus I presumptuous; and the Vision bright,
As with a smile more brightened, thus replied:
" 'What call'st thou solitude? Is not the earth
With various living creatures, and the air
Replenished,° and all these at thy command — *fully stocked*
To come and play before thee? Know'st thou not
Their language and their ways? They also know,° — *have understanding*
And reason not contemptibly; with these
Find pastime, and bear rule; thy realm is large.'
So spake the Universal Lord, and seemed
So ordering. I with leave of speech implored,
And humble deprecation thus replied:
" 'Let not my words offend thee, Heav'nly Power,
My Maker, be propitious while I speak.
Hast thou not made me here thy substitute,
And these inferior far beneath me set?
Among unequals what society
Can sort,° what harmony or true delight? — *agree*
Which must be mutual, in proportion due
Giv'n and received; but in disparity
The one intense, the other still remiss
Cannot well suit with either,[6] but soon prove
Tedious alike. Of fellowship I speak
Such as I seek, fit to participate° — *partake of*
All rational delight, wherein the brute
Cannot be human consort; they rejoice
Each with their kind, lion with lioness;
So fitly them in pairs thou hast combined;
Much less can bird with beast, or fish with fowl
So well converse, nor with the ox the ape;
Worse then can man with beast, and least of all.'
"Whereto th' Almighty answered, not displeased:
'A nice° and subtle happiness I see — *fastidious*
Thou to thyself proposest, in the choice
Of thy associates, Adam, and wilt taste
No pleasure, though in pleasure, solitary.
What think'st thou then of me, and this my state?

5. Adam reasons, as the Scholastics did, from the creatures to the fact of a Creator, but he cannot name (and so indicates that he cannot understand) God, except as God reveals himself.

6. As with poorly matched musical instruments, Adam's string is too taut ("intense") and the animals' is too slack ("remiss") to be in harmony ("suit").

Seem I to thee sufficiently possessed
Of happiness, or not? who am alone
From all eternity, for none I know
Second to me or like, equal much less.
How have I then with whom to hold converse
Save with the creatures which I made, and those
To me inferior, infinite descents
Beneath what other creatures are to thee?'
"He ceased, I lowly answered: 'To attain
The height and depth of thy eternal ways
All human thoughts come short, Supreme of things;
Thou in thyself art perfect, and in thee
Is no deficience found; not so is man,
But in degree, the cause of his desire
By conversation with his like to help,
Or solace his defects.[7] No need that thou
Shouldst propagate, already infinite;
And through all numbers absolute, though One;
But man by number is to manifest
His single imperfection, and beget
Like of his like, his image multiplied,
In unity defective,[8] which requires
Collateral° love, and dearest amity. *mutual*
Thou in thy secrecy° although alone, *seclusion*
Best with thyself accompanied, seek'st not
Social communication, yet so pleased,
Canst raise thy creature to what height thou wilt
Of union or communion, deified;
I by conversing cannot these erect
From prone, nor in their ways complacence° find.' *satisfaction*
Thus I emboldened spake, and freedom used
Permissive,° and acceptance found, which gained *permitted*
This answer from the gracious Voice Divine:
" 'Thus far to try thee, Adam, I was pleased,
And find thee knowing not of beasts alone,
Which thou hast rightly named, but of thyself,
Expressing well the spirit within thee free,
My image, not imparted to the brute,
Whose fellowship therefore unmeet° for thee *unsuitable*
Good reason was thou freely shouldst dislike,
And be so minded still. I, ere thou spak'st,
Knew it not good for man to be alone,
And no such company as then thou saw'st
Intended thee, for trial only brought,
To see how thou couldst judge of fit and meet:
What next I bring shall please thee, be assured,
Thy likeness, thy fit help, thy other self,
Thy wish, exactly to thy heart's desire.'[9]

7. God is absolutely perfect, man only relatively so ("in degree"), and thereby needs companionship with a fit mate to assuage ("solace") the "defects" arising from solitude.

8. God, "though One," (line 421), contains all numbers, but man has to remedy the "imperfection" of being single (line 423) by procreating and thereby multiplying his single and thereby "defective" image (line 425).

9. Compare the account in Genesis 2.18 with Milton's elaboration.

"He ended, or I heard no more, for now
My earthly by his heav'nly overpowered,
Which it had long stood under,° strained to the height — *been exposed to*
In that celestial colloquy sublime,
As with an object that excels° the sense, — *exceeds*
Dazzled and spent, sunk down, and sought repair
Of sleep, which instantly fell on me, called
By nature as in aid, and closed mine eyes.
Mine eyes he closed, but open left the cell
Of fancy° my internal sight, by which — *imagination*
Abstract° as in a trance methought I saw, — *withdrawn*
Though sleeping, where I lay, and saw the shape
Still glorious before whom awake I stood;
Who stooping opened my left side, and took
From thence a rib, with cordial° spirits warm, — *from the heart*
And lifeblood streaming fresh; wide was the wound,
But suddenly with flesh filled up and healed:
The rib he formed and fashioned with his hands;
Under his forming hands a creature grew,[1]
Manlike, but different sex, so lovely fair
That what seemed fair in all the world seemed now
Mean, or in her summed up, in her contained
And in her looks, which from that time infused
Sweetness into my heart, unfelt before,
And into all things from her air° inspired — *mien, look*
The spirit of love and amorous delight.
She disappeared, and left me dark, I waked
To find her, or forever to deplore
Her loss, and other pleasures all abjure:
When out of hope, behold her, not far off,
Such as I saw her in my dream, adorned
With what all earth or heaven could bestow
To make her amiable:° on she came, — *lovely*
Led by her heav'nly Maker, though unseen,[2]
And guided by his voice, nor uninformed
Of nuptial sanctity and marriage rites:
Grace was in all her steps, Heav'n in her eye,
In every gesture dignity and love.
I overjoyed could not forbear aloud:
" 'This turn hath made amends; thou hast fulfilled
Thy words, Creator bounteous and benign,
Giver of all things fair, but fairest this
Of all thy gifts, nor enviest.° I now see — *given reluctantly*
Bone of my bone, flesh of my flesh, my self
Before me; woman is her name, of man
Extracted; for this cause he shall forgo
Father and mother, and to his wife adhere;
And they shall be one flesh, one heart, one soul.'[3]
"She heard me thus, and though divinely brought,
Yet innocence and virgin modesty,

1. Go to Norton Literature Online, to see the *Creation of Eve* by the Italian painter Paolo Veronese (1528–1588).

2. Compare Eve's version of these events (4.440–91).

3. Compare the account in Genesis 2.23–24.

Her virtue and the conscience° of her worth — *consciousness*
That would be wooed, and not unsought be won,
Not obvious,° not obtrusive,° but retired, — *bold / forward*
The more desirable, or to say all,
Nature herself, though pure of sinful thought,
Wrought in her so that, seeing me, she turned;
I followed her, she what was honor knew,
And with obsequious° majesty approved — *compliant*
My pleaded reason. To the nuptial bow'r
I led her blushing like the morn: all heav'n,
And happy constellations on that hour
Shed their selectest influence; the earth
Gave sign of gratulation,° and each hill; — *rejoicing, congratulation*
Joyous the birds; fresh gales and gentle airs[4]
Whispered it to the woods, and from their wings
Flung rose, flung odors from the spicy shrub,
Disporting,° till the amorous bird of night° — *frolicking / nightingale*
Sung spousal, and bid haste the evening star° — *Venus*
On his hill top, to light the bridal lamp.
  Thus I have told thee all my state, and brought
My story to the sum of earthly bliss
Which I enjoy, and must confess to find
In all things else delight indeed, but such
As used or not, works in the mind no change,
Nor vehement desire, these delicacies
I mean of taste, sight, smell, herbs, fruits, and flow'rs,
Walks, and the melody of birds; but here
Far otherwise, transported° I behold, — *enraptured*
Transported touch; here passion first I felt,
Commotion° strange, in all enjoyments else — *mental agitation*
Superior and unmoved, here only weak
Against the charm of beauty's powerful glance.
Or° nature failed in me, and left some part — *either*
Not proof enough such object to sustain,° — *withstand*
Or from my side subducting,° took perhaps — *subtracting*
More than enough; at least on her bestowed
Too much of ornament, in outward show
Elaborate, of inward less exact.
For well I understand in the prime end
Of nature her th' inferior, in the mind
And inward faculties, which most excel,
In outward also her resembling less
His image who made both, and less expressing
The character of that dominion giv'n
O'er other creatures; yet when I approach
Her loveliness, so absolute° she seems — *perfect, independent*
And in herself complete, so well to know
Her own, that what she wills to do or say,
Seems wisest, virtuousest, discreetest, best;
All higher knowledge in her presence falls
Degraded, wisdom in discourse with her

4. Both breezes and melodies. "Gales": winds.

Loses discount'nanced,° and like folly shows; *disconcerted, abashed*
Authority and reason on her wait,
As one intended first, not after made
Occasionally;° and to consúmmate all, *incidentally*
Greatness of mind and nobleness their seat
Build in her loveliest, and create an awe
About her, as a guard angelic placed."
To whom the angel with contracted brow:
"Accuse not nature, she hath done her part;
Do thou but thine, and be not diffident° *mistrustful*
Of wisdom, she deserts thee not, if thou
Dismiss not her, when most thou need'st her nigh,
By áttributing overmuch to things
Less excellent, as thou thyself perceiv'st.
For what admir'st thou, what transports thee so,
An outside? Fair no doubt, and worthy well
Thy cherishing, thy honoring, and thy love,
Not thy subjection: weigh with her thyself;
Then value: ofttimes nothing profits more
Than self-esteem, grounded on just and right
Well managed; of that skill the more thou know'st,
The more she will acknowledge thee her head,[5]
And to realities yield all her shows:
Made so adorn for thy delight the more,
So awful,° that with honor thou may'st love *awe-inspiring*
Thy mate, who sees when thou art seen least wise.
But if the sense of touch whereby mankind
Is propagated seem such dear delight
Beyond all other, think the same vouchsafed
To cattle and each beast; which would not be
To them made common and divulged,° if aught *imparted generally*
Therein enjoyed were worthy to subdue
The soul of man, or passion in him move.
What higher in her society thou find'st
Attractive, human, rational, love still;
In loving thou dost well, in passion not,
Wherein true love consists not; love refines
The thoughts, and heart enlarges, hath his seat
In reason, and is judicious, is the scale[6]
By which to heav'nly love thou may'st ascend,
Not sunk in carnal pleasure, for which cause
Among the beasts no mate for thee was found."
To whom thus half abashed Adam replied.
"Neither her outside formed so fair, nor aught
In procreation common to all kinds
(Though higher of the genial[7] bed by far,
And with mysterious reverence I deem)

5. See 1 Corinthians 11.3: "the head of every man is Christ; and the head of the woman is the man; and the head of Christ is God."
6. The ladder of love, a Neoplatonic concept for the movement from sensual love to higher forms, and ultimately to love of God (see Castiglione's *Courtier*).
7. Both "nuptial" and "generative." Adam takes respectful issue with the apparent denigration of human sex in Raphael's account of the Neoplatonic ladder, which prompts his question about angelic sex (lines 615–17).

So much delights me, as those graceful acts,
Those thousand decencies° that daily flow *fitting acts*
From all her words and actions, mixed with love
And sweet compliance, which declare unfeigned
Union of mind, or in us both one soul;
Harmony to behold in wedded pair
More grateful than harmonious sound to the ear.
Yet these subject not; I to thee disclose
What inward thence I feel, not therefore foiled,° *overcome*
Who meet with various objects, from the sense
Variously representing;[8] yet still free
Approve the best, and follow what I approve.
To love thou blam'st me not, for love thou say'st
Leads up to Heav'n, is both the way and guide;
Bear with me then, if lawful what I ask;
Love not the heav'nly Spirits, and how their love
Express they, by looks only, or do they mix
Irradiance, virtual or immediate° touch?" *actual*
  To whom the angel with a smile that glowed
Celestial rosy red, love's proper hue,[9]
Answered. "Let it suffice thee that thou know'st
Us happy, and without love no happiness.
Whatever pure thou in the body enjoy'st
(And pure thou wert created) we enjoy
In eminence,° and obstacle find none *higher degree*
Of membrane, joint, or limb, exclusive bars:
Easier than air with air, if Spirits embrace,
Total they mix, union of pure with pure
Desiring; nor restrained conveyance need
As flesh to mix with flesh, or soul with soul.
But I can now no more; the parting sun
Beyond the earth's green cape and verdant isles
Hesperian sets,[1] my signal to depart.
Be strong, live happy, and love, but first of all
Him whom to love is to obey, and keep
His great command; take heed lest passion sway
Thy judgment to do aught, which else free will
Would not admit;° thine and of all thy sons *permit*
The weal or woe in thee is placed; beware.
I in thy persevering shall rejoice,
And all the blest: stand fast; to stand or fall
Free in thine own arbitrament° it lies. *determination*
Perfect within, no outward aid require;° *depend on*
And all temptation to transgress repel."
  So saying, he arose; whom Adam thus
Followed with benediction. "Since to part,
Go heavenly guest, ethereal messenger,
Sent from whose sov'reign goodness I adore.
Gentle to me and affable hath been

8. I.e., various objects, variously represented to me by my senses.
9. This is not likely to be an embarrassed blush: red is the color traditionally associated with Seraphim, who burn with ardor. Raphael's smile also glows with friendship for Adam and appreciation of his perceptive inference about angelic love.
1. Cape Verde, near Dakar, and the islands off that coast are the westernmost ("Hesperian") points of Africa.

Thy condescension, and shall be honored ever
With grateful memory: thou to mankind
Be good and friendly still,° and oft return." *always*
So parted they, the angel up to Heav'n
From the thick shade, and Adam to his bow'r.

Book 9

No more of talk where God or angel guest
With man, as with his friend, familiar used
To sit indulgent, and with him partake
Rural repast, permitting him the while
Venial° discourse unblamed: I now must change *permissible*
Those notes to tragic; foul distrust, and breach
Disloyal on the part of man, revolt,
And disobedience: on the part of Heav'n
Now alienated, distance and distaste,° *aversion*
Anger and just rebuke, and judgment giv'n,
That brought into this world a world of woe,
Sin and her shadow Death, and misery
Death's harbinger:° sad task, yet argument° *forerunner / subject*
Not less but more heroic than the wrath
Of stern Achilles on his foe pursued
Thrice fugitive about Troy wall; or rage
Of Turnus for Lavinia disespoused,
Or Neptune's ire or Juno's, that so long
Perplexed the Greek and Cytherea's son;[1]
If answerable° style I can obtain *fitting*
Of my celestial patroness, who deigns
Her nightly visitation unimplored,[2]
And dictates to me slumb'ring, or inspires
Easy my unpremeditated verse:
Since first this subject for heroic song
Pleased me long choosing, and beginning late;
Not sedulous° by nature to indite *eager*
Wars, hitherto the only argument° *subject*
Heroic deemed, chief mastery to dissect
With long and tedious havoc fabled knights
In battles feigned; the better fortitude
Of patience and heroic martyrdom
Unsung; or to describe races and games,
Or tilting furniture, emblazoned shields,
Impresses quaint, caparisons and steeds;
Bases[3] and tinsel trappings, gorgeous knights
At joust and tournament; then marshaled feast

1. In this fourth proem (lines 1–47), after signaling his change from pastoral to tragic mode (lines 1–6), Milton emphasizes tragic elements in several classical epics: Achilles pursuing Hector three times around the wall of Troy before killing him (*Iliad* 22); Turnus fighting Aeneas over the loss of his betrothed Lavinia, and then killed by Aeneas; Odysseus ("the Greek") and Aeneas ("Cytherea's son," i.e., Venus's son) tormented ("perplexed") by Neptune (Poseidon) and Juno, respectively.

2. Milton does not here invoke the Muse but testifies to her customary nightly visits. Milton's nephew reports that he often awoke in the morning with lines of poetry fully formed in his head, ready to dictate them to a scribe.

3. Cloth coverings for horses; "tilting furniture": equipment for jousting; "impresses quaint": cunningly designed heraldic devices on shields;

Served up in hall with sewers,° and seneschals;° *waiters / stewards*
The skill of artifice° or office mean, *mechanic art*
Not that which justly gives heroic name
To person or to poem. Me of these
Nor skilled nor studious, higher argument
Remains,[4] sufficient of itself to raise
That name, unless an age too late, or cold
Climate, or years damp my intended wing
Depressed, and much they may, if all be mine,
Not hers who brings it nightly to my ear.
  The sun was sunk, and after him the star
Of Hesperus,[5] whose office is to bring
Twilight upon the earth, short arbiter
'Twixt day and night, and now from end to end
Night's hemisphere had veiled the horizon round:
When Satan who late° fled[6] before the threats *recently*
Of Gabriel out of Eden, now improved° *increased*
In meditated fraud and malice, bent
On man's destruction, maugre what might hap
Of heavier on himself,[7] fearless returned.
By night he fled, and at midnight returned
From compassing the earth, cautious of day,
Since Uriel regent of the sun descried
His entrance, and forewarned the Cherubim
That kept their watch; thence full of anguish driv'n,
The space of seven continued nights he rode
With darkness, thrice the equinoctial line° *equator*
He circled, four times crossed the car of Night
From pole to pole, traversing each colure;[8]
On the eighth returned, and on the coast averse° *turned away*
From entrance on Cherubic watch, by stealth
Found unsuspected way. There was a place,
Now not, though sin, not time, first wrought the change,
Where Tigris at the foot of Paradise
Into a gulf shot underground, till part
Rose up a fountain by the Tree of Life;
In with the river sunk, and with it rose
Satan involved° in rising mist, then sought *enveloped*
Where to lie hid. Sea he had searched and land
From Eden over Pontus,[9] and the pool
Maeotis, up beyond the river Ob;

"caparisons": ornamental trappings or armor for horses. After rejecting the classical epic subjects, Milton here rejects the familiar topics of romance.

4. For a heroic poem. He proceeds to recap worries he has voiced before: that the times might not be receptive to such poems ("age too late"), that the "cold Climate" of England or his own advanced age might "damp" (benumb, dampen) his "intended wing / Depressed" (poetic flights held down, kept from soaring).

5. Venus, the evening star.

6. At the end of Book 4.

7. I.e., despite ("maugre") what might result in heavier punishments for himself.

8. The colures are two great circles that intersect at right angles at the poles. By circling the globe from east to west at the equator and then over the north and south poles, Satan can remain in darkness, keeping the earth between himself and the sun. "Car of Night" (line 65): the earth's shadow, imagined as the chariot of the goddess Night.

9. The Black Sea. Satan's journey (lines 77–82) takes him from there to the Sea of Azov in Russia ("Maeotis"), beyond the river "Ob" in Siberia, which flows into the Arctic Ocean, then south to Antarctica; thence west from "Orontes" (a river in Syria) across the Atlantic to "Darien" (the Isthmus of Panama), then across the Pacific and Asia to India where the "Ganges" and "Indus" rivers flow.

Downward as far Antarctic; and in length
West from Orontes to the ocean barred
At Darien, thence to the land where flows
Ganges and Indus: thus the orb he roamed
With narrow° search; and with inspection deep — *strict*
Considered every creature, which of all
Most opportune might serve his wiles, and found
The serpent subtlest beast of all the field.[1]
Him after long debate, irresolute° — *undecided*
Of° thoughts revolved, his final sentence° chose — *among / decision*
Fit vessel, fittest imp° of fraud, in whom — *offshoot*
To enter, and his dark suggestions hide
From sharpest sight: for in the wily snake,
Whatever sleights° none would suspicious mark, — *artifices*
As from his wit and native subtlety
Proceeding, which in other beasts observed
Doubt° might beget of diabolic pow'r — *suspicion*
Active within beyond the sense of brute.
Thus he resolved, but first from inward grief
His bursting passion into plaints thus poured:
"O earth, how like to Heav'n, if not preferred
More justly, seat worthier of gods, as built
With second thoughts, reforming what was old!
For what God after better worse would build?
Terrestrial heav'n, danced round by other heav'ns
That shine, yet bear their bright officious° lamps, — *dutiful*
Light above light, for thee alone, as seems,[2]
In thee concent'ring all their precious beams
Of sacred influence: as God in Heav'n
Is center, yet extends to all, so thou
Centring receiv'st from all those orbs; in thee,
Not in themselves, all their known virtue appears
Productive in herb, plant, and nobler birth
Of creatures animate with gradual life
Of growth, sense, reason,[3] all summed up in man.
With what delight could I have walked thee round,
If I could joy in aught, sweet interchange
Of hill and valley, rivers, woods and plains,
Now land, now sea, and shores with forest crowned,
Rocks, dens, and caves; but I in none of these
Find place or refuge; and the more I see
Pleasures about me, so much more I feel
Torment within me, as from the hateful siege° — *conflict*
Of contraries; all good to me becomes
Bane,° and in Heav'n much worse would be my state. — *poison*
But neither here seek I, no nor in Heav'n
To dwell, unless by mastering Heav'n's Supreme;
Nor hope to be myself less miserable
By what I seek, but others to make such

1. The serpent is so described in Genesis 3.1.
2. Like Adam (8.15ff.) and Eve (4.657–58) but not Raphael (8.114–78), Satan assumes a Ptolemaic universe centered on the earth and humankind.
3. Graduated in steps ("gradual," line 112) from vegetable to animal to rational forms (souls); cf. 5.469–90.

As I, though thereby worse to me redound:
For only in destroying I find ease
To my relentless thoughts; and him[4] destroyed,
Or won to what may work his utter loss,
For whom all this was made, all this will soon
Follow, as to him linked in weal or woe:
In woe then; that destruction wide may range:
To me shall be the glory sole among
The infernal Powers, in one day to have marred
What he Almighty styled,° six nights and days *called*
Continued making, and who knows how long
Before had been contriving, though perhaps
Not longer than since I in one night freed
From servitude inglorious well-nigh half
Th' angelic name, and thinner left the throng
Of his adorers. He to be avenged,
And to repair his numbers thus impaired,
Whether such virtue° spent of old now failed *power*
More angels to create, if they at least
Are his created, or to spite us more,
Determined to advance into our room
A creature formed of earth, and him endow,
Exalted from so base original,° *origin*
With Heav'nly spoils, our spoils: what he decreed
He effected; man he made, and for him built
Magnificent this world, and earth his seat,
Him lord pronounced, and, O indignity!
Subjected to his service angel wings,
And flaming ministers to watch and tend
Their earthy charge: of these the vigilance
I dread, and to elude, thus wrapped in mist
Of midnight vapor glide obscure, and pry
In every bush and brake, where hap° may find *luck*
The serpent sleeping, in whose mazy folds
To hide me, and the dark intent I bring.
O foul descent! that I who erst contended
With gods to sit the highest, am now constrained
Into a beast, and mixed with bestial slime,
This essence to incarnate and imbrute,[5]
That to the height of deity aspired;
But what will not ambition and revenge
Descend to? Who aspires must down as low
As high he soared, obnoxious° first or last *exposed*
To basest things. Revenge, at first though sweet,
Bitter ere long back on itself recoils;
Let it; I reck° not, so it light well aimed, *care*
Since higher I fall short, on him who next
Provokes my envy, this new favorite
Of Heav'n, this man of clay, son of despite,
Whom us the more to spite his Maker raised

4. Adam. "This" (line 132): the universe.
5. Satan "imbruting" himself in a snake parodies, grotesquely, the Son's incarnation in human form, as Christ.

From dust: spite then with spite is best repaid."
  So saying, through each thicket dank or dry,
Like a black mist low creeping, he held on
His midnight search, where soonest he might find
The serpent: him fast sleeping soon he found
In labyrinth of many a round self-rolled,
His head the midst, well stored with subtle wiles:
Not yet in horrid shade or dismal den,
Nor nocent° yet, but on the grassy herb *harmful, guilty*
Fearless unfeared he slept: in at his mouth
The Devil entered, and his brutal° sense, *animal*
In heart or head, possessing soon inspired
With act intelligential: but his sleep
Disturbed not, waiting close° th' approach of morn. *hidden*
Now whenas sacred light began to dawn
In Eden on the humid flow'rs, that breathed
Their morning incense, when all things that breathe,
From th' earth's great altar send up silent praise
To the Creator, and his nostrils fill
With grateful° smell, forth came the human pair *pleasing*
And joined their vocal worship to the choir
Of creatures wanting° voice; that done, partake *lacking*
The season, prime° for sweetest scents and airs: *best*
Then cómmune how that day they best may ply
Their growing work; for much their work outgrew
The hands' dispatch of two gard'ning so wide.
And Eve first to her husband thus began:
  "Adam, well may we labor still° to dress *continually*
This garden, still to tend plant, herb, and flow'r,
Our pleasant task enjoined, but till more hands
Aid us, the work under our labor grows,
Luxurious° by restraint; what we by day *luxuriant*
Lop overgrown, or prune, or prop, or bind,
One night or two with wanton° growth derides, *unrestrained*
Tending to wild. Thou therefore now advise
Or hear what to my mind first thoughts present,
Let us divide our labors, thou where choice
Leads thee, or where most needs, whether to wind
The woodbine round this arbor, or direct
The clasping ivy where to climb, while I
In yonder spring° of roses intermixed *growth*
With myrtle, find what to redress° till noon: *set upright*
For while so near each other thus all day
Our task we choose, what wonder if so near
Looks intervene and smiles, or object new
Casual discourse draw on, which intermits° *interrupts*
Our day's work brought to little, though begun
Early, and th' hour of supper comes unearned."
  To whom mild answer Adam thus returned:
"Sole Eve, associate sole,[6] to me beyond
Compare above all living creatures dear,

6. Adam puns on "sole" as "unrivaled" and "only" (cf. 4.411).

Well hast thou motioned,° well thy thoughts employed *proposed*
How we might best fulfill the work which here
God hath assigned us, nor of me shalt pass
Unpraised: for nothing lovelier can be found
In woman, than to study household good,
And good works in her husband to promote.[7]
Yet not so strictly hath our Lord imposed
Labor, as to debar us when we need
Refreshment, whether food, or talk between,
Food of the mind, or this sweet intercourse
Of looks and smiles, for smiles from reason flow,
To brute denied, and are of love the food,
Love not the lowest end of human life.
For not to irksome toil, but to delight
He made us, and delight to reason joined.
These paths and bowers doubt not but our joint hands
Will keep from wilderness with ease, as wide
As we need walk, till younger hands ere long
Assist us: but if much convérse perhaps
Thee satiate, to short absence I could yield.
For solitude sometimes is best society,
And short retirement urges sweet return.
But other doubt possesses me, lest harm
Befall thee severed from me; for thou know'st
What hath been warned us, what malicious foe
Envying our happiness, and of his own
Despairing, seeks to work us woe and shame
By sly assault; and somewhere nigh at hand
Watches, no doubt, with greedy hope to find
His wish and best advantage, us asunder,
Hopeless to circumvent us joined, where each
To other speedy aid might lend at need;
Whether his first design be to withdraw
Our fealty° from God, or to disturb *allegiance*
Conjugal love, than which perhaps no bliss
Enjoyed by us excites his envy more;
Or° this, or worse, leave not the faithful side *whether*
That gave thee being, still shades thee and protects.
The wife, where danger or dishonor lurks,
Safest and seemliest by her husband stays,
Who guards her, or with her the worst endures."
  To whom the virgin[8] majesty of Eve,
As one who loves, and some unkindness meets,
With sweet austere composure thus replied.
  "Offspring of Heav'n and earth, and all earth's lord,
That such an enemy we have, who seeks
Our ruin, both by thee informed I learn,
And from the parting angel overheard
As in a shady nook I stood behind,

7. Adam's compliments resemble the praises of a good wife in Proverbs 31.

8. The term here means unspotted or peerless; Milton has insisted at the end of Books 4 and 8 that Adam and Eve have sex.

Just then returned at shut of evening flow'rs.[9]
But that thou shouldst my firmness therefore doubt
To God or thee, because we have a foe
May tempt it, I expected not to hear.
His violence thou fear'st not, being such,
As we, not capable of death or pain,
Can either not receive, or can repel.
His fraud is then thy fear, which plain infers
Thy equal fear that my firm faith and love
Can by his fraud be shaken or seduced;
Thoughts, which how found they harbor in thy breast,
Adam, misthought of° her to thee so dear?" *misapplied to*
To whom with healing words Adam replied.
"Daughter of God and man, immortal Eve,
For such thou art, from sin and blame entire:° *untouched*
Not diffident° of thee do I dissuade *distrustful*
Thy absence from my sight, but to avoid
Th' attempt itself, intended by our foe.
For he who tempts, though in vain, at least asperses° *bespatters*
The tempted with dishonor foul, supposed
Not incorruptible of faith, not proof
Against temptation: thou thyself with scorn
And anger wouldst resent the offered wrong,
Though ineffectual found; misdeem not then,
If such affront I labor to avert
From thee alone, which on us both at once
The enemy, though bold, will hardly dare,
Or daring, first on me th' assault shall light.
Nor thou his malice and false guile contemn;° *despise*
Subtle he needs must be, who could seduce
Angels, nor think superfluous others' aid.
I from the influence of thy looks receive
Access° in every virtue, in thy sight *increase*
More wise, more watchful, stronger, if need were
Of outward strength; while shame, thou looking on,
Shame to be overcome or overreached° *outwitted*
Would utmost vigor raise, and raised unite.
Why shouldst not thou like sense within thee feel
When I am present, and thy trial choose
With me, best witness of thy virtue tried."
So spake domestic Adam in his care
And matrimonial love; but Eve, who thought
Less° attribúted to her faith sincere, *too little*
Thus her reply with accent sweet renewed.
"If this be our condition, thus to dwell
In narrow circuit straitened° by a foe, *confined*
Subtle or violent, we not endued
Single with like defense, wherever met,
How are we happy, still° in fear of harm? *always*

9. Somewhat confusing, since Eve heard the full story of the war in Heaven and Raphael's earlier warnings; Raphael's parting words (8.630–43) overheard by Eve do not specifically mention Satan but warn Adam to resist his passion for Eve. He does, however, reiterate the charge to obey the "great command" and repel temptation.

But harm precedes not sin: only our foe
Tempting affronts us with his foul esteem
Of our integrity: his foul esteem
Sticks no dishonor on our front,° but turns *forehead*
Foul on himself; then wherefore shunned or feared
By us? who rather double honor gain
From his surmise proved false, find peace within,
Favor from Heav'n, our witness from th' event.° *outcome*
And what is faith, love, virtue unassayed
Alone, without exterior help sustained?[1]
Let us not then suspect our happy state
Left so imperfect by the Maker wise,
As not secure to single° or combined. *one alone*
Frail is our happiness, if this be so,
And Eden were no Eden thus exposed."
  To whom thus Adam fervently replied.
"O woman, best are all things as the will
Of God ordained them, his creating hand
Nothing imperfect or deficient left
Of all that he created, much less man,
Or aught that might his happy state secure,
Secure from outward force; within himself
The danger lies, yet lies within his power:
Against his will he can receive no harm.
But God left free the will, for what obeys
Reason, is free, and reason he made right,[2]
But bid her well beware, and still erect,° *ever-alert*
Lest by some fair appearing good surprised
She dictate false, and misinform the will
To do what God expressly hath forbid.
Not then mistrust, but tender love enjoins,
That I should mind° thee oft, and mind thou me. *remind, pay heed to*
Firm we subsist,° yet possible to swerve, *stand, exist*
Since reason not impossibly may meet
Some specious° object by the foe suborned, *deceptively attractive*
And fall into deception unaware,
Not keeping strictest watch, as she was warned.
Seek not temptation then, which to avoid
Were better, and most likely if from me
Thou sever not: trial will come unsought.
Wouldst thou approve° thy constancy, approve *prove*
First thy obedience; th' other who can know,
Not seeing thee attempted, who attest?
But if thou think, trial unsought may find
Us both securer° than thus warned thou seem'st, *overconfident*
Go; for thy stay, not free, absents thee more;
Go in thy native innocence, rely
On what thou hast of virtue, summon all,
For God towards thee hath done his part, do thine."
  So spake the patriarch of mankind, but Eve

1. Compare and contrast *Areopagitica*, p. 711.
2. Right reason, a classical concept accommodated to Christian thought, is the God-given power to apprehend truth and moral law.

Persisted, yet submiss, though last, replied:
"With thy permission then, and thus forewarned
Chiefly by what thy own last reasoning words
Touched only, that our trial, when least sought,
May find us both perhaps far less prepared,
The willinger I go, nor much expect
A foe so proud will first the weaker seek;
So bent, the more shall shame him his repulse."
Thus saying, from her husband's hand her hand
Soft she withdrew, and like a wood nymph light[3]
Oread or Dryad, or of Delia's train,
Betook her to the groves, but Delia's self
In gait surpassed and goddess-like deport,° *bearing*
Though not as she with bow and quiver armed,
But with such gardening tools as art yet rude,
Guiltless of fire[4] had formed, or angels brought.
To Pales, or Pomona, thus adorned,
Likest she seemed Pomona when she fled
Vertumnus, or to Ceres in her prime,
Yet virgin of Proserpina from Jove.[5]
Her long with ardent look his eye pursued
Delighted, but desiring more her stay.
Oft he to her his charge of quick return
Repeated, she to him as oft engaged
To be returned by noon amid the bow'r,
And all things in best order to invite
Noontide repast, or afternoon's repose.
O much deceived, much failing,° hapless° Eve, *erring / unlucky*
Of thy presumed return! event° perverse! *outcome*
Thou never from that hour in Paradise
Found'st either sweet repast, or sound repose;
Such ambush hid among sweet flow'rs and shades
Waited with hellish rancor imminent
To intercept thy way, or send thee back
Despoiled of innocence, of faith, of bliss.
For now, and since first break of dawn the Fiend,
Mere serpent in appearance, forth was come,
And on his quest, where likeliest he might find
The only two of mankind, but in them
The whole included race, his purposed prey.
In bow'r and field he sought, where any tuft
Of grove or garden plot more pleasant lay,
Their tendance or plantation for delight,[6]
By fountain or by shady rivulet
He sought them both, but wished his hap° might find *luck*

3. Light-footed, with overtones of "fickle" or "frivolous." "Oread" (next line): a mountain nymph. "Dryad": a wood nymph. "Delia": Diana, born on the isle of Delos, hunted with a "train" of nymphs.
4. Having no experience of fire, not needed in Paradise. Milton may be alluding to the guilt of Prometheus, who stole fire from heaven.
5. These goddesses, like Eve, are associated with agriculture (lines 393–96)—Pales, with flocks and pastures; Pomona, with fruit trees; Ceres, with harvests—and the latter two foreshadow Eve's situation. Pomona was chased by the wood god "Vertumnus" in many guises before surrendering to him; Ceres was impregnated by Jove with Proserpina—later carried off to Hades by Pluto.
6. I.e., which they had cultivated or planted for their pleasure.

Eve separate; he wished, but not with hope
Of what so seldom chanced, when to his wish,
Beyond his hope, Eve separate he spies,
Veiled in a cloud of fragrance, where she stood,
Half spied, so thick the roses bushing round
About her glowed, oft stooping to support
Each flow'r of slender stalk, whose head though gay
Carnation, purple, azure, or specked with gold,
Hung drooping unsustained, them she upstays
Gently with myrtle band, mindless° the while, *heedless*
Herself, though fairest unsupported flow'r
From her best prop so far, and storm so nigh.[7]
Nearer he drew, and many a walk traversed
Of stateliest covert, cedar, pine, or palm,
Then voluble° and bold, now hid, now seen *undulating*
Among thick-woven arborets° and flow'rs *small trees*
Embordered on each bank, the hand° of Eve: *handiwork*
Spot more delicious than those gardens feigned
Or° of revived Adonis, or renowned *either*
Alcinous, host of old Laertes' son,
Or that, not mystic, where the sapient king
Held dalliance with his fair Egyptian spouse.[8]
Much he the place admired, the person more.
As one who long in populous city pent,
Where houses thick and sewers annoy° the air, *make noisome, befoul*
Forth issuing on a summer's morn to breathe
Among the pleasant villages and farms
Adjoined, from each thing met conceives delight,
The smell of grain, or tedded grass, or kine,[9]
Or dairy, each rural sight, each rural sound;
If chance with nymph-like step fair virgin pass,
What pleasing seemed, for° her now pleases more, *because of*
She most, and in her look sums all delight.
Such pleasure took the Serpent to behold
This flow'ry plat,° the sweet recess° of Eve *plot / retreat*
Thus early, thus alone; her heav'nly form
Angelic, but more soft, and feminine,
Her graceful innocence, her every air° *manner*
Of gesture or least action overawed
His malice, and with rapine sweet[1] bereaved
His fierceness of the fierce intent it brought:
That space the Evil One abstracted° stood *withdrawn*
From his own evil, and for the time remained
Stupidly good,° of enmity disarmed, *good because stupefied*
Of guile, of hate, of envy, of revenge;
But the hot hell that always in him burns,

7. The conceit of the flower-gatherer who is herself gathered evokes the story of Proserpina, to whom it was applied in 4.269–71.

8. The gardens of Adonis were beauty spots named for the lovely youth loved by Venus, killed by a boar, and subsequently revived; Odysseus ("Laertes' son") was entertained by Alcinous in his beautiful gardens; Solomon ("the sapient king") entertained his "fair Egyptian spouse," the Queen of Sheba, in a real garden (not "mystic," or "feigned," as the others were).

9. Cattle. "Tedded": spread out to dry, like hay.

1. From Latin *rapere,* to seize, the root of both "rape" and "rapture," underscoring the paradox of the ravisher (temporarily) ravished.

Though in mid-Heav'n, soon ended his delight,
And tortures him now more, the more he sees
Of pleasure not for him ordained: then soon
Fierce hate he recollects, and all his thoughts
Of mischief gratulating,° thus excites: *greeting*
"Thoughts, whither have ye led me, with what sweet
Compulsion thus transported to forget
What hither brought us, hate, not love, nor hope
Of Paradise for Hell, hope here to taste
Of pleasure, but all pleasure to destroy,
Save what is in destroying, other joy
To me is lost. Then let me not let pass
Occasion which now smiles, behold alone
The woman, opportune° to all attempts, *open*
Her husband, for I view far round, not nigh,
Whose higher intellectual more I shun,
And strength, of courage haughty,° and of limb *exalted*
Heroic built, though of terrestrial° mold, *earthly*
Foe not informidable, exempt from wound,
I not; so much hath Hell debased, and pain
Enfeebled me, to what I was in Heav'n.
She fair, divinely fair, fit love for gods,
Not terrible,° though terror be in love *terrifying*
And beauty, not° approached by stronger hate, *unless*
Hate stronger, under show of love well feigned,
The way which to her ruin now I tend."
So spake the Enemy of mankind, enclosed
In serpent, inmate bad, and toward Eve
Addressed his way, not with indented° wave, *zigzag*
Prone on the ground, as since, but on his rear,
Circular base of rising folds, that tow'red
Fold above fold a surging maze, his head
Crested aloft, and carbuncle° his eyes; *deep red*
With burnished neck of verdant° gold, erect *green*
Amidst his circling spires,° that on the grass *coils*
Floated redundant:° pleasing was his shape, *in swelling waves*
And lovely, never since of serpent kind
Lovelier, not those that in Illyria changed
Hermione and Cadmus, or the god
In Epidaurus;[2] nor to which transformed
Ammonian Jove, or Capitoline was seen,
He with Olympias, this with her who bore
Scipio, the height of Rome.[3] With tract° oblique *course*
At first, as one who sought accéss, but feared
To interrupt, sidelong he works his way.
As when a ship by skillful steersman wrought
Nigh river's mouth or foreland, where the wind

2. The legendary founder of Thebes, Cadmus, and his wife Harmonia (Milton's "Hermione") were changed to serpents when they went to Illyria in old age; Aesculapius, god of healing, sometimes came forth as a serpent from his temple in Epidaurus.

3. Jupiter Ammon ("Ammonian Jove") made love to Olympias in the form of a snake and sired Alexander the Great; the Jupiter worshipped in Rome ("Capitoline"), also in serpent form, sired Scipio Africanus, the savior and great leader ("height") of Rome.

Veers oft, as oft so steers, and shifts her sail;
So varied he, and of his tortuous train° *twisting length*
Curled many a wanton° wreath in sight of Eve, *luxuriant, sportive*
To lure her eye; she busied heard the sound
Of rustling leaves, but minded not, as used
To such disport before her through the field,
From every beast, more duteous at her call,
Than at Circean call the herd disguised.[4]
He bolder now, uncalled before her stood;
But as in gaze admiring: oft he bowed
His turret crest, and sleek enameled° neck, *multicolored*
Fawning, and licked the ground whereon she trod.
His gentle dumb expression turned at length
The eye of Eve to mark his play; he glad
Of her attention gained, with serpent tongue
Organic, or impulse of vocal air,[5]
His fraudulent temptation thus began.
"Wonder not, sov'reign mistress, if perhaps
Thou canst, who art sole wonder, much less arm
Thy looks, the heav'n of mildness, with disdain,
Displeased that I approach thee thus, and gaze
Insatiate, I thus single, nor have feared
Thy awful° brow, more awful thus retired. *awe-inspiring*
Fairest resemblance of thy Maker fair,
Thee all things living gaze on, all things thine
By gift, and thy celestial beauty adore
With ravishment beheld, there best beheld
Where universally admired; but here
In this enclosure wild, these beasts among,
Beholders rude, and shallow to discern
Half what in thee is fair, one man except,
Who sees thee? (and what is one?) who shouldst be seen
A goddess among gods, adored and served
By angels numberless, thy daily train."[6]
So glozed° the Tempter, and his proem° tuned; *flattered / prelude*
Into the heart of Eve his words made way,
Though at the voice much marveling; at length
Not unamazed she thus in answer spake.
"What may this mean? Language of man pronounced
By tongue of brute, and human sense expressed?
The first at least of these I thought denied
To beasts, whom God on their creation day
Created mute to all articulate sound;
The latter I demur,° for in their looks *hesitate about*
Much reason, and in their actions oft appears.
Thee, Serpent, subtlest beast of all the field
I knew, but not with human voice endued;° *endowed*
Redouble then this miracle, and say,

4. Circe, in the *Odyssey*, transformed men to beasts and was attended by an obedient herd.
5. Satan either used the actual tongue of the serpent or impressed the air with his own voice.
6. Satan's entire speech is couched in the extravagant praises of the Petrarchan love convention.

How cam'st thou speakable° of mute, and how — *able to speak*
To me so friendly grown above the rest
Of brutal kind, that daily are in sight?
Say, for such wonder claims attention due."
  To whom the guileful Tempter thus replied:
"Empress of this fair world, resplendent Eve,
Easy to me it is to tell thee all
What thou command'st, and right thou shouldst be obeyed:
I was at first as other beasts that graze
The trodden herb, of abject thoughts and low,
As was my food, nor aught but food discerned
Or sex, and apprehended nothing high:
Till on a day roving the field, I chanced
A goodly tree far distant to behold
Loaden with fruit of fairest colors mixed,
Ruddy and gold: I nearer drew to gaze;
When from the boughs a savory odor blown,
Grateful to appetite, more pleased my sense
Than smell of sweetest fennel, or the teats
Of ewe or goat dropping with milk at ev'n,[7]
Unsucked of lamb or kid, that tend their play.
To satisfy the sharp desire I had
Of tasting those fair apples, I resolved
Not to defer;° hunger and thirst at once, — *delay*
Powerful persuaders, quickened at the scent
Of that alluring fruit, urged me so keen.
About the mossy trunk I wound me soon,
For high from ground the branches would require
Thy utmost reach or Adam's: round the tree
All other beasts that saw, with like desire
Longing and envying stood, but could not reach.
Amid the tree now got, where plenty hung
Tempting so nigh, to pluck and eat my fill
I spared° not, for such pleasure till that hour — *refrained*
At feed or fountain never had I found.
Sated at length, ere long I might perceive
Strange alteration in me, to degree
Of reason in my inward powers, and speech
Wanted° not long, though to this shape retained.[8] — *lacked*
Thenceforth to speculations high or deep
I turned my thoughts, and with capacious mind
Considered all things visible in Heav'n,
Or earth, or middle,° all things fair and good; — *regions between*
But all that fair and good in thy divine
Semblance, and in thy beauty's heav'nly ray
United I beheld; no fair° to thine — *beauty*
Equivalent or second, which compelled

7. According to Pliny, serpents ate fennel to aid in shedding their skins and to sharpen their eyesight; folklore had it that they drank the milk of sheep and goats.

8. There is no precedent in Genesis or the interpretative tradition for Satan's powerfully persuasive argument by analogy based on the snake's supposed experience of attaining to reason and speech by eating the forbidden fruit.

Me thus, though importune° perhaps, to come *inopportunely*
And gaze, and worship thee of right declared
Sov'reign of creatures, universal dame."[9]
So talked the spirited[1] sly snake; and Eve
Yet more amazed unwary thus replied:
"Serpent, thy overpraising leaves in doubt
The virtue° of that fruit, in thee first proved: *power*
But say, where grows the tree, from hence how far?
For many are the trees of God that grow
In Paradise, and various, yet unknown
To us, in such abundance lies our choice,
As leaves a greater store of fruit untouched,
Still hanging incorruptible, till men
Grow up to their provision,[2] and more hands
Help to disburden nature of her birth."
To whom the wily adder, blithe and glad:
"Empress, the way is ready, and not long,
Beyond a row of myrtles, on a flat,
Fast by° a fountain, one small thicket past *close by*
Of blowing myrrh and balm;[3] if thou accept
My conduct,° I can bring thee thither soon." *guidance*
"Lead then," said Eve. He leading swiftly rolled
In tangles, and made intricate seem straight,
To mischief swift. Hope elevates, and joy
Brightens his crest, as when a wand'ring fire,° *will-o'-the-wisp*
Compact° of unctuous° vapor, which the night *composed / oily*
Condenses, and the cold environs round,
Kindled through agitation to a flame,
Which oft, they say, some evil spirit attends,
Hovering and blazing with delusive light,
Misleads th' amazed° night-wanderer from his way *bewildered*
To bogs and mires, and oft through pond or pool,
There swallowed up and lost, from succor far.
So glistered the dire snake, and into fraud
Led Eve our credulous mother, to the tree
Of prohibition, root of all our woe;
Which when she saw, thus to her guide she spake:
"Serpent, we might have spared our coming hither,
Fruitless to me, though fruit be here to excess,
The credit of whose virtue° rest with thee, *power*
Wondrous indeed, if cause of such effects.
But of this tree we may not taste nor touch;
God so commanded, and left that command
Sole daughter of his voice;[4] the rest, we live
Law to ourselves, our reason is our law."
To whom the Tempter guilefully replied:

9. Satan continues his Petrarchan language of courtship.
1. Both inspired by and possessed by an evil spirit, Satan.
2. I.e., until the numbers of the human race are such as to consume the food God has provided.
3. Blooming trees that exude the aromatic gums myrrh and balm (balsam).
4. God's only direct commandment (in Hebrew, *Bath Kol*, "daughter of a voice" from heaven). Otherwise (see following), they follow the moral law of nature, known to them perfectly by their unfallen reason, "our reason is our law."

"Indeed? hath God then said that of the fruit
Of all these garden trees ye shall not eat,
Yet lords declared of all in earth or air?"
  To whom thus Eve yet sinless: "Of the fruit
Of each tree in the garden we may eat,
But of the fruit of this fair tree amidst
The garden, God hath said, 'Ye shall not eat
Thereof, nor shall ye touch it, lest ye die.' "[5]
  She scarce had said, though brief, when now more bold
The Tempter, but with show of zeal and love
To man, and indignation at his wrong,
New part puts on, and as to passion moved,
Fluctuates disturbed, yet comely, and in act
Raised,[6] as of some great matter to begin.
As when of old some orator renowned
In Athens or free Rome, where eloquence
Flourished, since mute, to some great cause addressed,
Stood in himself collected, while each part,
Motion, each act won audience ere the tongue,° *before speaking*
Sometimes in height began, as no delay
Of preface brooking[7] through his zeal of right.
So standing, moving, or to high upgrown
The Tempter all impassioned thus began:
  "O sacred, wise, and wisdom-giving plant,
Mother of science,° now I feel thy power *knowledge*
Within me clear, not only to discern
Things in their causes, but to trace the ways
Of highest agents, deemed however wise.
Queen of this universe, do not believe
Those rigid threats of death; ye shall not die:
How should ye? By the fruit? It gives you life
To knowledge.[8] By the Threat'ner? Look on me,
Me who have touched and tasted, yet both live,
And life more perfect have attained than fate
Meant me, by vent'ring higher than my lot.
Shall that be shut to man, which to the beast
Is open? Or will God incense his ire
For such a petty trespass, and not praise
Rather your dauntless virtue,° whom the pain *courage*
Of death denounced,° whatever thing death be, *threatened*
Deterred not from achieving what might lead
To happier life, knowledge of good and evil;
Of good, how just?[9] Of evil, if what is evil
Be real, why not known, since easier shunned?
God therefore cannot hurt ye, and be just;

5. Eve's formulation indicates her "sufficient" understanding of the prohibition and the conditions of life in Eden. See 3.98–101.
6. Drawn up to full dignity. Satan as the snake takes on the role of a Greek or Roman orator defending liberty (lines 670–72), a Demosthenes or a Cicero.
7. Bursting into the middle of his speech without a preface, and "upgrown" to the impassioned high style ("high") at once (lines 675–78).
8. I.e., life as well as knowledge, and a better life enhanced by knowledge, which Satan in the snake presents as a magical property of the tree.
9. I.e., how can it be just to forbid the knowledge of good?

Not just, not God; not feared then,[1] nor obeyed:
Your fear itself of death removes the fear.
Why then was this forbid? Why but to awe,
Why but to keep ye low and ignorant,
His worshippers; he knows that in the day
Ye eat thereof, your eyes that seem so clear,
Yet are but dim, shall perfectly be then
Opened and cleared, and ye shall be as gods,[2]
Knowing both good and evil as they know.
That ye should be as gods, since I as man,
Internal man, is but proportion meet,
I of brute human, ye of human gods.[3]
So ye shall die perhaps, by putting off
Human, to put on gods, death to be wished,
Though threatened, which no worse than this can bring.
And what are gods that man may not become
As they, participating° godlike food? *partaking of*
The gods are first, and that advantage use
On our belief, that all from them proceeds;
I question it, for this fair earth I see,
Warmed by the sun, producing every kind,
Them nothing: if they all° things, who enclosed *produce all*
Knowledge of good and evil in this tree,
That whoso eats thereof, forthwith attains
Wisdom without their leave? And wherein lies
Th' offense, that man should thus attain to know?
What can your knowledge hurt him, or this tree
Impart against his will if all be his?
Or is it envy, and can envy dwell
In heav'nly breasts? These, these and many more
Causes import° your need of this fair fruit. *prove*
Goddess humane,[4] reach then, and freely taste."
He ended, and his words replete with guile
Into her heart too easy entrance won:
Fixed on the fruit she gazed, which to behold
Might tempt alone, and in her ears the sound
Yet rung of his persuasive words, impregned° *impregnated*
With reason, to her seeming, and with truth;
Meanwhile the hour of noon drew on, and waked
An eager appetite, raised by the smell
So savory of that fruit, which with desire,
Inclinable now grown to touch or taste,
Solicited her longing eye; yet first
Pausing a while, thus to herself she mused:
"Great are thy virtues,° doubtless, best of fruits, *powers*
Though kept from man, and worthy to be admired,
Whose taste, too long forborne, at first assay° *try*
Gave elocution to the mute, and taught
The tongue not made for speech to speak thy praise:

1. Satan's sophism invites atheism: if God forbids knowledge of good and evil he is not just, therefore not God, therefore his threat of death need not be feared.
2. Hereafter, Satan speaks of "gods," not God.
3. Satan invites the aspiration to divinity, based on analogy to the supposed experience of the snake.
4. Both "human" and "gracious" or "kindly."

Thy praise he also who forbids thy use,
Conceals not from us, naming thee the Tree
Of Knowledge, knowledge both of good and evil;
Forbids us then to taste, but his forbidding
Commends thee more, while it infers° the good — *implies*
By thee communicated, and our want:° — *lack*
For good unknown, sure is not had, or had
And yet unknown, is as not had at all.
In plain° then, what forbids he but to know, — *in plain words*
Forbids us good, forbids us to be wise?
Such prohibitions bind not. But if death
Bind us with after-bands,° what profits then — *later bonds*
Our inward freedom? In the day we eat
Of this fair fruit, our doom is, we shall die.
How dies the serpent? He hath eat'n and lives,
And knows, and speaks, and reasons, and discerns,
Irrational till then. For us alone
Was death invented? Or to us denied
This intellectual food, for beasts reserved?
For beasts it seems: yet that one beast which first
Hath tasted, envies° not, but brings with joy — *begrudges*
The good befall'n him, author unsuspect,[5]
Friendly to man, far from deceit or guile.
What fear I then, rather what know to fear
Under this ignorance of good and evil,
Of God or death, of law or penalty?
Here grows the cure of all, this fruit divine,
Fair to the eye, inviting to the taste,
Of virtue° to make wise: what hinders then — *power*
To reach, and feed at once both body and mind?"
   So saying, her rash hand in evil hour
Forth reaching to the fruit, she plucked, she eat.[6]
Earth felt the wound, and nature from her seat
Sighing through all her works gave signs of woe,
That all was lost. Back to the thicket slunk
The guilty serpent, and well might, for Eve
Intent now wholly on her taste, naught else
Regarded, such delight till then, as seemed,
In fruit she never tasted, whether true
Or fancied so, through expectation high
Of knowledge, nor was godhead from her thought.
Greedily she engorged without restraint,
And knew not eating death:[7] satiate at length,
And heightened as with wine, jocund° and boon,° — *merry / jolly*
Thus to herself she pleasingly began:
   "O sov'reign, virtuous, precious of all trees
In Paradise, of operation blest
To sapience, hitherto obscured, infamed,[8]
And thy fair fruit let hang, as to no end

5. An authority or informant beyond suspicion.
6. Ate: an accepted past tense, pronounced *et*.
7. I.e., she is eating death and doesn't know it, or experience it yet, but also, punning, death is eating her too.
8. Slandered. "Sapience": both knowledge and tasting (Latin *sapere*).

Created; but henceforth my early care,
Not without song, each morning, and due praise
Shall tend thee, and the fertile burden ease
Of thy full branches offered free to all;
Till dieted by thee I grow mature
In knowledge, as the gods who all things know;
Though others envy what they cannot give;
For had the gift been theirs,[9] it had not here
Thus grown. Experience, next to thee I owe,
Best guide; not following thee, I had remained
In ignorance, thou open'st wisdom's way,
And giv'st accéss, though secret° she retire. *hidden*
And I perhaps am secret;° Heav'n is high, *unseen*
High and remote to see from thence distinct
Each thing on earth; and other care perhaps
May have diverted from continual watch
Our great Forbidder, safe with all his spies
About him. But to Adam in what sort° *guise*
Shall I appear? Shall I to him make known
As yet my change, and give him to partake
Full happiness with me, or rather not,
But keep the odds° of knowledge in my power *advantage*
Without copartner? so to add what wants° *lacks*
In female sex, the more to draw his love,
And render me more equal, and perhaps,
A thing not undesirable, sometime
Superior; for inferior who is free?[1]
This may be well: but what if God have seen,
And death ensue? Then I shall be no more,
And Adam wedded to another Eve,
Shall live with her enjoying, I extinct;
A death to think. Confirmed then I resolve,
Adam shall share with me in bliss or woe:
So dear I love him, that with him all deaths
I could endure, without him live no life."
  So saying, from the tree her step she turned,
But first low reverence done, as to the power
That dwelt within,[2] whose presence had infused
Into the plant sciential° sap, derived *knowledge-producing*
From nectar, drink of gods. Adam the while
Waiting desirous her return, had wove
Of choicest flow'rs a garland to adorn
Her tresses, and her rural labors crown,
As reapers oft are wont° their harvest queen. *accustomed*
Great joy he promised to his thoughts, and new
Solace in her return, so long delayed;
Yet oft his heart, divine of° something ill, *foreboding*
Misgave him; he the falt'ring measure° felt; *heartbeat*
And forth to meet her went, the way she took
That morn when first they parted; by the Tree

9. Like Satan, Eve now conflates gods and God, ascribing envy but also lack of power to "them."

1. Cf. Satan, 1.248–63, 5.790–97.

2. Eve ends with idolatry, worship of the tree.

Of Knowledge he must pass; there he her met,
Scarce from the tree returning; in her hand
A bough of fairest fruit that downy smiled,
New gathered, and ambrosial° smell diffused. *fragrant*
To him she hasted, in her face excuse
Came prologue,[3] and apology to prompt,
Which with bland° words at will she thus addressed. *mild, coaxing*
  "Hast thou not wondered, Adam, at my stay?
Thee I have missed, and thought it long, deprived
Thy presence, agony of love till now
Not felt, nor shall be twice, for never more
Mean I to try, what rash untried I sought,
The pain of absence from thy sight. But strange
Hath been the cause, and wonderful to hear:
This tree is not as we are told, a tree
Of danger tasted,° nor to evil unknown *if tasted*
Op'ning the way, but of divine effect
To open eyes, and make them gods who taste;
And hath been tasted such: the serpent wise,
Or° not restrained as we, or not obeying, *either*
Hath eaten of the fruit, and is become,
Not dead, as we are threatened, but thenceforth
Endued with human voice and human sense,
Reasoning to admiration,° and with me *wonderfully well*
Persuasively° hath so prevailed, that I *by persuasion*
Have also tasted, and have also found
Th' effects to correspond, opener mine eyes,
Dim erst,° dilated spirits, ampler heart, *before*
And growing up to godhead; which for thee
Chiefly I sought, without thee can despise.
For bliss, as thou hast part, to me is bliss,
Tedious, unshared with thee, and odious soon.
Thou therefore also taste, that equal lot
May join us, equal joy, as equal love;
Lest thou not tasting, different degree° *rank*
Disjoin us, and I then too late renounce
Deity for thee, when fate will not permit."[4]
  Thus Eve with count'nance blithe her story told;
But in her cheek distemper[5] flushing glowed.
On th' other side, Adam, soon as he heard
The fatal trespass done by Eve, amazed,° *stunned*
Astonied° stood and blank, while horror chill *petrified*
Ran through his veins, and all his joints relaxed;
From his slack hand the garland wreathed for Eve
Down dropped, and all the faded roses shed:
Speechless he stood and pale, till thus at length
First to himself he inward silence broke:
  "O fairest of creation, last and best
Of all God's works, creature in whom excelled

3. I.e., excuse came like the prologue in a play, and apology (justification, self-defense) served as prompter.

4. Compare Eve in soliloquy, lines 817–33.

5. I.e., disorder arising from disturbance of the balance of humors in the body, intoxication.

Whatever can to sight or thought be formed,
Holy, divine, good, amiable, or sweet!
How art thou lost, how on a sudden lost,
Defaced, deflow'red, and now to death devote?° *doomed*
Rather how hast thou yielded to transgress
The strict forbiddance, how to violate
The sacred° fruit forbidd'n! Some cursèd fraud *consecrated*
Of enemy hath beguiled thee, yet unknown,
And me with thee hath ruined, for with thee
Certain my resolution is to die;
How can I live without thee, how forgo
Thy sweet converse and love so dearly joined,
To live again in these wild woods forlorn?
Should God create another Eve, and I
Another rib afford, yet loss of thee
Would never from my heart; no no, I feel
The link of nature draw me: flesh of flesh,
Bone of my bone thou art,[6] and from thy state
Mine never shall be parted, bliss or woe."
  So having said, as one from sad dismay
Recomforted, and after thoughts disturbed
Submitting to what seemed remédiless,
Thus in calm mood his words to Eve he turned:
  "Bold deed thou hast presumed, advent'rous Eve,
And peril great provoked, who thus hast dared
Had it been only coveting to eye
That sacred fruit, sacred° to abstinence, *set apart*
Much more to taste it under ban to touch.
But past who can recall, or done undo?
Not God omnipotent, nor fate; yet so
Perhaps thou shalt not die, perhaps the fact° *deed*
Is not so heinous now, foretasted fruit,
Profaned first by the serpent, by him first
Made common and unhallowed ere our taste;
Nor yet on him found deadly, he yet lives,
Lives, as thou saidst, and gains to live as man
Higher degree of life, inducement strong
To us, as likely tasting to attain
Proportional ascent, which cannot be
But to be gods, or angels demigods.
Nor can I think that God, Creator wise,
Though threat'ning, will in earnest so destroy
Us his prime creatures, dignified so high,
Set over all his works, which in our fall,
For us created, needs with us must fail,
Dependent made; so God shall uncreate,
Be frustrate, do, undo, and labor lose,
Not well conceived of God, who though his power
Creation could repeat, yet would be loath
Us to abolish, lest the Adversary° *Satan*
Triumph and say; 'Fickle their state whom God
Most favors, who can please him long? Me first

6. Adam echoes Genesis 2.23–24.

He ruined, now mankind; whom will he next?'
Matter of scorn, not to be given the Foe.
However I with thee have fixed my lot,
Certain° to undergo like doom; if death *resolved*
Consort° with thee, death is to me as life; *associate*
So forcible within my heart I feel
The bond of nature draw me to my own,
My own in thee, for what thou art is mine;
Our state cannot be severed, we are one,
One flesh; to lose thee were to lose myself."
So Adam, and thus Eve to him replied:
"O glorious trial of exceeding[7] love,
Illustrious evidence, example high!
Engaging me to emulate, but short
Of thy perfection, how shall I attain,
Adam, from whose dear side I boast me sprung,
And gladly of our union hear thee speak,
One heart, one soul in both; whereof good proof
This day affords, declaring thee resolved,
Rather than death or aught° than death more dread *anything other*
Shall separate us, linked in love so dear,
To undergo with me one guilt, one crime,
If any be, of tasting this fair fruit,
Whose virtue,° for of good still good proceeds, *power*
Direct, or by occasion° hath presented *indirectly*
This happy trial of thy love, which else
So eminently never had been known.
Were it° I thought death menaced would ensue° *if / result from*
This my attempt, I would sustain alone
The worst, and not persuade thee, rather die
Deserted, than oblige° thee with a fact° *bind / deed*
Pernicious to thy peace, chiefly assured
Remarkably so late of thy so true,
So faithful love unequaled;[8] but I feel
Far otherwise th' event,° not death, but life *result*
Augmented, opened eyes, new hopes, new joys,
Taste so divine, that what of sweet before
Hath touched my sense, flat seems to this, and harsh.
On my experience, Adam, freely taste,
And fear of death deliver to the winds."
So saying, she embraced him, and for joy
Tenderly wept, much won that he his love
Had so ennobled, as of choice to incur
Divine displeasure for her sake, or death.
In recompense (for such compliance bad
Such recompense best merits) from the bough
She gave him of that fair enticing fruit
With liberal hand: he scrupled not to eat
Against his better knowledge, not deceived,[9]
But fondly° overcome with female charm. *foolishly*

7. The word, which Eve intends as praise, carries the implication of "excessive."
8. I.e., since I have so recently been assured of your unparalleled love.
9. Cf. 1 Timothy 2.14: "And Adam was not deceived, but the woman being deceived was in the transgression."

Earth trembled from her entrails, as again
In pangs, and nature gave a second groan;
Sky loured, and muttering thunder, some sad drops
Wept at completing of the mortal sin
Original;[1] while Adam took no thought,
Eating his fill, nor Eve to iterate° *repeat*
Her former trespass feared, the more to soothe
Him with her loved society, that now
As with new wine intoxicated both
They swim in mirth, and fancy that they feel
Divinity within them breeding wings
Wherewith to scorn the earth: but that false fruit
Far other operation first displayed,
Carnal desire inflaming, he on Eve
Began to cast lascivious eyes, she him
As wantonly repaid; in lust they burn:
Till Adam thus 'gan Eve to dalliance move:
  "Eve, now I see thou art exact of taste,
And elegant, of sapience[2] no small part,
Since to each meaning savor we apply,
And palate call judicious; I the praise
Yield thee, so well this day thou hast purveyed.° *provided*
Much pleasure we have lost, while we abstained
From this delightful fruit, nor known till now
True relish, tasting; if such pleasure be
In things to us forbidden, it might be wished,
For this one tree had been forbidden ten.
But come, so well refreshed, now let us play,
As meet° is, after such delicious fare; *appropriate*
For never did thy beauty since the day
I saw thee first and wedded thee, adorned
With all perfections, so inflame my sense
With ardor to enjoy thee, fairer now
Than ever, bounty of this virtuous tree."
  So said he, and forbore not glance or toy° *caress*
Of amorous intent, well understood
Of° Eve, whose eye darted contagious fire. *by*
Her hand he seized, and to a shady bank,
Thick overhead with verdant roof embow'red
He led her nothing loath; flow'rs were the couch,
Pansies, and violets, and asphodel,
And hyacinth, earth's freshest softest lap.
There they their fill of love and love's disport
Took largely, of their mutual guilt the seal,
The solace of their sin, till dewy sleep
Oppressed them, wearied with their amorous play.
Soon as the force of that fallacious fruit,
That with exhilarating vapor bland° *pleasing*

1. The theological doctrine that all Adam's descendants are stained by Adam's sin and are thereby subject to physical death and (unless saved by grace) to damnation.

2. Adam commends Eve for her fine ("exact") and discriminating ("elegant") taste, as a part of "sapience," which means both "taste" and "wisdom."

About their spirits had played, and inmost powers
Made err, was now exhaled, and grosser sleep
Bred of unkindly fumes,° with conscious dreams — *unnatural vapors*
Encumbered,° now had left them, up they rose — *oppressed*
As from unrest, and each the other viewing,
Soon found their eyes how opened, and their minds
How darkened; innocence, that as a veil
Had shadowed them from knowing ill, was gone,
Just confidence, and native righteousness,
And honor from about them, naked left
To guilty shame: he° covered, but his robe — *shame*
Uncovered more. So rose the Danite strong
Hercúlean Samson from the harlot-lap
Of Philistéan Dálilah, and waked
Shorn of his strength,[3] they destitute and bare
Of all their virtue: silent, and in face
Confounded long they sat, as strucken mute,
Till Adam, though not less than Eve abashed,
At length gave utterance to these words constrained:° — *forced*
"O Eve, in evil[4] hour thou didst give ear
To that false worm, of whomsoever taught
To counterfeit man's voice, true in our fall,
False in our promised rising; since our eyes
Opened we find indeed, and find we know
Both good and evil, good lost and evil got,[5]
Bad fruit of knowledge, if this be to know,
Which leaves us naked thus, of honor void,
Of innocence, of faith, of purity,
Our wonted° ornaments now soiled and stained, — *accustomed*
And in our faces evident the signs
Of foul concupiscence;[6] whence evil store;
Even shame, the last of evils; of the first
Be sure then. How shall I behold the face
Henceforth of God or angel, erst with joy
And rapture so oft beheld? Those heav'nly shapes
Will dazzle now this earthly, with their blaze
Insufferably bright. O might I here
In solitude live savage, in some glade
Obscured, where highest woods impenetrable
To star or sunlight, spread their umbrage° broad, — *shadow, foliage*
And brown as evening: cover me ye pines,
Ye cedars, with innumerable boughs
Hide me, where I may never see them more.
But let us now, as in bad plight, devise
What best may for the present serve to hide

3. Samson, of the tribe of Dan, told the "harlot" Philistine Delilah that the secret of his strength (like that of Hercules) lay in his hair; she sheared it off while he slept, and when he awoke he was easily captured and blinded by his enemies.

4. Adam's bitter pun—Eve, evil—repudiates the actual etymology of Eve, "life," which Adam will later reaffirm (11.159–61).

5. Milton, like most commentators, derives the tree's name from the event (4.222, 11.84–89).

6. The theological term for the unruly human passions and desires seen as one effect of the Fall, a sign of abundance ("store") of evils. If "shame" (see following lines) is the "last" evil, the "first" is probably the guiltiness that produces it, according to Milton's *Christian Doctrine* (1.12).

The parts of each from other, that seem most
To shame obnoxious,° and unseemliest seen, *exposed*
Some tree whose broad smooth leaves together sewed,
And girded on our loins, may cover round
Those middle parts, that this newcomer, shame,
There sit not, and reproach us as unclean."
  So counseled he, and both together went
Into the thickest wood, there soon they chose
The fig tree,[7] not that kind for fruit renowned,
But such as at this day to Indians known
In Malabar or Deccan spreads her arms
Branching so broad and long, that in the ground
The bended twigs take root, and daughters grow
About the mother tree, a pillared shade
High overarched, and echoing walks between;
There oft the Indian herdsman shunning heat
Shelters in cool, and tends his pasturing herds
At loopholes cut through thickest shade: those leaves
They gathered, broad as Amazonian targe,° *shields*
And with what skill they had, together sewed,
To gird their waist, vain covering if to hide
Their guilt and dreaded shame. O how unlike
To that first naked glory. Such of late
Columbus found th' American so girt
With feathered cincture,° naked else and wild, *belt*
Among the trees on isles and woody shores.
Thus fenced, and as they thought, their shame in part
Covered, but not at rest or ease of mind,
They sat them down to weep, nor only tears
Rained at their eyes, but high winds worse within
Began to rise, high passions, anger, hate,
Mistrust, suspicion, discord, and shook sore
Their inward state of mind, calm region once
And full of peace, now tossed and turbulent:
For understanding ruled not, and the will
Heard not her lore, both in subjection now
To sensual appetite, who from beneath
Usurping over sov'reign reason claimed
Superior sway: from thus distempered breast,[8]
Adam, estranged° in look and altered style, *unlike himself*
Speech intermitted° thus to Eve renewed: *interrupted*
  "Would thou hadst hearkened to my words, and stayed
With me, as I besought thee, when that strange
Desire of wand'ring this unhappy morn,
I know not whence possessed thee; we had then
Remained still happy, not as now, despoiled
Of all our good, shamed, naked, miserable.

7. The banyan, or Indian fig, has small leaves, but the account Milton draws on from Gerard's *Herbal* (1597) contains the details of lines 1104–11; Malabar and Deccan (line 1103) are in southern India.

8. The immediate psychological effects of the Fall are evident in the subjection of reason to the lower faculties of sensual appetite.

Let none henceforth seek needless cause to approve° *prove*
The faith they owe; when earnestly they seek
Such proof, conclude, they then begin to fail."
  To whom soon moved with touch of blame thus Eve:
"What words have passed thy lips, Adam severe,
Imput'st thou that to my default, or will
Of wand'ring, as thou call'st it, which who knows
But might as ill have happened thou being by,
Or to thyself perhaps: hadst thou been there,
Or here th' attempt, thou couldst not have discerned
Fraud in the serpent, speaking as he spake;
No ground of enmity between us known,
Why he should mean me ill, or seek to harm.
Was I to have never parted from thy side?
As good have grown there still a lifeless rib.
Being as I am, why didst not thou the head
Command me absolutely not to go,
Going into such danger as thou saidst?
Too facile° then thou didst not much gainsay,° *easy, mild / oppose*
Nay didst permit, approve, and fair dismiss.
Hadst thou been firm and fixed in thy dissent,
Neither had I transgressed, nor thou with me."
  To whom then first incensed Adam replied.
"Is this the love, is this the recompense
Of mine to thee, ingrateful Eve, expressed° *demonstrated*
Immutable when thou wert lost, not I,
Who might have lived and joyed immortal bliss,
Yet willingly chose rather death with thee:
And am I now upbraided, as the cause
Of thy transgressing? not enough severe,
It seems, in thy restraint: what could I more?
I warned thee, I admonished thee, foretold
The danger, and the lurking enemy
That lay in wait; beyond this had been force,
And force upon free will hath here no place.
But confidence then bore thee on, secure° *self-assured*
Either to meet no danger, or to find
Matter of glorious trial; and perhaps
I also erred in overmuch admiring
What seemed in thee so perfect, that I thought
No evil durst attempt thee, but I rue
That error now, which is become my crime,
And thou th' accuser. Thus it shall befall
Him who to worth in women overtrusting
Lets her will rule; restraint she will not brook,° *accept*
And left to herself, if evil thence ensue,
She first his weak indulgence will accuse."
  Thus they in mutual accusation spent
The fruitless hours, but neither self-condemning,
And of their vain contést appeared no end.

From Book 10

Summary When it is known in Heaven that man has fallen, God sends his Son to pass judgment on the sinners. Having found them in the garden, he hears their confession and passes instant sentence, cursing the serpent, condemning Eve to the pains of childbirth and Adam to those of daily toil; but in mercy, he clothes the human couple both outwardly with skins of beasts and inwardly with his righteousness. Meanwhile Sin and Death, sitting by Hell-gate, feel new strength, and pass across Chaos, leaving a great bridge behind them. On their way they meet with their parent, Satan, learn of his success on Earth, and press eagerly forward in hopes of destroying humankind altogether. Satan, on the other hand, continues his flight back toward Hell, where he is to report to his constituents.

[CONSEQUENCES OF THE FALL]

* * * Th' other way Satan went down
The causey° to Hell gate; on either side *causeway*
Disparted Chaos over-built exclaimed,
And with rebounding surge the bars assailed,
That scorned his indignation.[1] Through the gate,
Wide open and unguarded, Satan passed,
And all about found desolate; for those[2]
Appointed to sit there, had left their charge,
Flown to the upper world; the rest were all
Far to the inland retired, about the walls
Of Pandemonium, city and proud seat
Of Lucifer, so by allusion° called, *metaphor*
Of that bright star to Satan paragoned.[3]
There kept their watch the legions, while the grand[4]
In council sat, solicitous° what chance *anxious*
Might intercept their emperor sent, so he
Departing gave command, and they observed.
As when the Tartar from his Russian foe
By Astracan over the snowy plains
Retires, or Bactrian Sophi from the horns
Of Turkish crescent, leaves all waste beyond
The realm of Aladule, in his retreat
To Tauris or Casbeen:[5] so these the late
Heav'n-banished host, left desert utmost Hell
Many a dark league, reduced° in careful watch *drawn together*
Round their metropolis, and now expecting
Each hour their great adventurer from the search
Of foreign worlds: he through the midst unmarked,° *unnoticed*
In show plebeian angel militant

1. Chaos is the instinctive enemy of all order, so hostile to the bridge built over it.
2. Sin and Death.
3. Satan before his fall was Lucifer, the Light-bringer, and the morning star is named Lucifer because it is compared ("paragoned") to him.
4. The "grand infernal peers" who govern (cf. 2.507).
5. The simile, begun in line 431, compares the fallen angels, withdrawn from other regions of Hell to guard their metropolis, to Tartars retiring before attacking Russians and Persians retreating before the attacking Turks. "Astracan": a region west of the Caspian Sea inhabited by Russia and defended against Turks and Tartars; "Aladule": the region of Armenia, from which the last Persian ruler, called Anadule, a "Bactrian Sophi" (Persian shah), was forced to retreat from the Turks, to Tabriz ("Tauris") and Kazvin ("Casbeen").

Of lowest order, passed; and from the door
Of that Plutonian[6] hall, invisible
Ascended his high throne, which under state° *canopy*
Of richest texture spread, at th' upper end
Was placed in regal luster. Down a while
He sat, and round about him saw unseen:
At last as from a cloud his fulgent head
And shape star-bright appeared, or brighter, clad
With what permissive° glory since his fall *permitted*
Was left him, or false glitter: all amazed
At that so sudden blaze the Stygian[7] throng
Bent their aspéct, and whom they wished beheld,
Their mighty chief returned: loud was th' acclaim:
Forth rushed in haste the great consulting peers,
Raised from their dark divan,[8] and with like joy
Congratulant approached him, who with hand
Silence, and with these words attention won:
"Thrones, Dominations, Princedoms, Virtues, Powers,
For in possession such, not only of right,
I call ye[9] and declare ye now, returned
Successful beyond hope, to lead ye forth
Triumphant out of this infernal pit
Abominable, accurst, the house of woe,
And dungeon of our tyrant: now possess,
As lords, a spacious world, to our native Heaven
Little inferior, by my adventure hard
With peril great achieved. Long were to tell
What I have done, what suffered, with what pain
Voyaged th' unreal,° vast, unbounded deep *unformed*
Of horrible confusion, over which
By Sin and Death a broad way now is paved
To expedite your glorious march; but I
Toiled out my uncouth° passage, forced to ride *strange*
Th' untractable abyss, plunged in the womb
Of unoriginal[1] Night and Chaos wild,
That jealous of their secrets fiercely opposed
My journey strange, with clamorous uproar
Protesting Fate[2] supreme; thence how I found
The new-created world, which fame in Heav'n
Long had foretold, a fabric wonderful
Of absolute perfection, therein man
Placed in a paradise, by our exile
Made happy: him by fraud I have seduced
From his Creator, and the more to increase
Your wonder, with an apple. He thereat
Offended, worth your laughter, hath giv'n up
Both his beloved man and all his world,
To Sin and Death a prey, and so to us,
Without our hazard, labor, or alarm,

6. Pertaining to Pluto, ruler of the classical underworld.
7. Of the river Styx in Hades, the river of hate.
8. The Turkish Council of State.
9. I.e., you now have these titles not only by right but by possession (from the conquest on earth).
1. Having no origin, uncreated.
2. Protesting both to and against Fate.

To range in, and to dwell, and over man
To rule, as over all he should have ruled.
True is, me also he hath judged, or rather
Me not, but the brute serpent in whose shape
Man I deceived; that which to me belongs,
Is enmity, which he will put between
Me and mankind; I am to bruise his heel;
His seed, when is not set, shall bruise my head:
A world who would not purchase with a bruise,
Or much more grievous pain? Ye have th' account
Of my performance: what remains, ye gods,
But up and enter now into full bliss."[3]
  So having said, a while he stood, expecting
Their universal shout and high applause
To fill his ear, when contrary he hears
On all sides, from innumerable tongues
A dismal universal hiss, the sound
Of public scorn; he wondered, but not long
Had leisure, wond'ring at himself now more;
His visage drawn he felt to sharp and spare,
His arms clung to his ribs, his legs entwining
Each other, till supplanted° down he fell *tripped up*
A monstrous serpent on his belly prone,
Reluctant,° but in vain, a greater power *struggling*
Now ruled him, punished in the shape he sinned,
According to his doom: he would have spoke,
But hiss for hiss returned with forkèd tongue
To forkèd tongue, for now were all transformed
Alike, to serpents[4] all as accessories
To his bold riot:° dreadful was the din *revolt*
Of hissing through the hall, thick swarming now
With complicated° monsters, head and tail, *tangled*
Scorpion and asp, and amphisbaena dire,
Cerastes horned, hydrus, and ellops drear,
And dipsas[5] (not so thick swarmed once the soil
Bedropped with blood of Gorgon, or the isle
Ophiusa)[6] but still greatest he the midst,
Now dragon grown, larger than whom the sun
Engendered in the Pythian vale on slime,
Huge Python,[7] and his power no less he seemed
Above the rest still to retain; they all
Him followed issuing forth to th' open field,
Where all yet left of that revolted rout

3. Ironically, the final word of Satan's proud, triumphal speech rhymes with and so prepares for the "hiss" (line 508) that will soon greet him, as his would-be triumph is turned by God to abject humiliation.

4. The scene recalls Dante's vivid description of the thieves metamorphosed to snakes in *Inferno* 24–25.

5. The "scorpion" has a venomous sting at the tip of the tail; "asp" is a small Egyptian viper; "amphisbaena" supposedly had a head at each end; "Cerastes" is an asp with horny projections over each eye; "hydrus" and "ellops" were mythical water snakes; "dipsas" was a mythical snake whose bite caused raging thirst.

6. Drops of blood from the Gorgon Medusa's severed head turned into snakes; "Ophiusa" in Greek means "isle of snakes."

7. A gigantic serpent engendered from the slime left by Deucalion's flood; Apollo slew him and appropriated the "Pythian" vale and shrine at Delphi.

Heav'n-fall'n, in station stood or just array,[8]
Sublime° with expectation when to see *raised up*
In triumph issuing forth their glorious chief;
They saw, but other sight instead, a crowd
Of ugly serpents; horror on them fell,
And horrid sympathy; for what they saw,
They felt themselves now changing; down their arms,
Down fell both spear and shield, down they as fast,
And the dire hiss renewed, and the dire form
Catched by contagion, like in punishment,
As in their crime. Thus was th' applause they meant,
Turned to exploding hiss, triumph to shame
Cast on themselves from their own mouths. There stood
A grove hard by, sprung up with this their change,
His will who reigns above, to aggravate
Their penance,° laden with fair fruit, like that *punishment*
Which grew in Paradise, the bait of Eve
Used by the Tempter: on that prospect strange
Their earnest eyes they fixed, imagining
For one forbidden tree a multitude
Now ris'n, to work them further woe or shame;
Yet parched with scalding thirst and hunger fierce,
Though to delude them sent, could not abstain,
But on they rolled in heaps, and up the trees
Climbing, sat thicker than the snaky locks
That curled Megaera:[9] greedily they plucked
The fruitage fair to sight, like that which grew
Near that bituminous lake where Sodom flamed;[1]
This more delusive, not the touch, but taste
Deceived; they fondly° thinking to allay *foolishly*
Their appetite with gust,° instead of fruit *relish*
Chewed bitter ashes, which th' offended taste
With spattering noise rejected: oft they assayed,° *attempted*
Hunger and thirst constraining, drugged as oft,
With hatefulest disrelish writhed their jaws
With soot and cinders filled; so oft they fell
Into the same illusion, not as man
Whom they triumphed once lapsed.[2] Thus were they plagued
And worn with famine, long and ceaseless hiss,
Till their lost shape, permitted, they resumed,[3]
Yearly enjoined, some say, to undergo
This annual humbling certain numbered days,
To dash their pride, and joy for man seduced.
However some tradition they dispersed
Among the heathen of their purchase° got, *plunder*
And fabled how the serpent, whom they called

8. I.e., at their posts or on parade.
9. One of three Furies with snaky hair.
1. Sodom apples reputedly grew on the spot where the accursed city once stood, now the Dead Sea ("that bituminous lake"); the apples look good but dissolve into ashes when eaten.
2. Unlike man who fell once, they try to eat the dissolving apples over and over again.
3. God permitted them to regain their "lost shape" as fallen angels; but they are undergoing a slower, natural metamorphosis into grosser substance by their continuing commitment to and choice of evil.

Ophion with Eurynome, the wide-
Encroaching Eve perhaps, had first the rule
Of high Olympus, thence by Saturn driv'n
And Ops, ere yet Dictaean Jove was born.[4]

Summary Sin and Death proceed without further interruption to Earth, and enter into possession of it. God sees their arrival and declines to interfere, but prophesies that their triumph will be only temporary; in due course they will be forced back to Hell again, and forever. Meanwhile, the angels are ordered to twist the Earth on its axis, disorder the planets so their influence will in future be bad as well as good, and rearrange the cosmos generally. In consequence, the temperate climate of Paradise at once gives way to extremes of heat and cold, and furious winds begin to blow across the ruined planet.

[Adam, Eve, and the First Steps to Redemption]

* * * Thus began
Outrage from lifeless things; but Discord first
Daughter of Sin, among th' irrational,
Death introduced through fierce antipathy:[5]
Beast now with beast gan war, and fowl with fowl,
And fish with fish; to graze the herb° all leaving, *grass*
Devour'd each other; nor stood much in awe
Of man, but fled him, or with count'nance grim
Glared on him passing: these were from without
The growing miseries, which Adam saw
Already in part, though hid in gloomiest shade,
To sorrow abandoned, but worse felt within,
And in a troubled sea of passion tossed,
Thus to disburden sought with sad complaint:
"O miserable of happy![6] Is this the end
Of this new glorious world, and me so late
The glory of that glory, who now become
Accurst of blessèd, hide me from the face
Of God, whom to behold was then my height
Of happiness: yet well, if here would end
The misery, I deserved it, and would bear
My own deservings; but this will not serve;
All that I eat or drink, or shall beget,
Is propagated[7] curse. O voice once heard
Delightfully, 'Increase and multiply,'
Now death to hear! For what can I increase
Or multiply, but curses on my head?
Who of all ages to succeed, but feeling

4. The Titan Ophion (whose name means "snake") and his wife Eurynome ("the wide-reacher") ruled Olympus until driven away by "Saturn" and his wife Ops, who were in turn overthrown by Jove, who lived on the mountain Dicte. Milton suggests that these may represent versions of the story transmitted by the fallen angels to the pagans (lines 578–79).

5. Discord (personified as daughter of Sin) introduced Death among the animals ("th' irrational") by stirring up "antipathy" among them.

6. Adam's complaint begins with the classical formula for a tragic fall, or *peripeteia*, the change from happiness to misery.

7. Handed down from one generation to the next.

The evil on him brought by me, will curse
My head: 'Ill fare our ancestor impure,
For this we may thank Adam'; but his thanks
Shall be the execration; so besides
Mine own that bide upon me, all from me
Shall with a fierce reflux on me redound,
On me as on their natural center light
Heavy, though in their place.[8] O fleeting joys
Of Paradise, dear bought with lasting woes!
Did I request thee, Maker, from my clay
To mold me man, did I solicit thee
From darkness to promote me, or here place
In this delicious garden? As my will
Concurred not to my being, it were but right
And equal° to reduce me to my dust, *just*
Desirous to resign, and render back
All I received, unable to perform
Thy terms too hard, by which I was to hold
The good I sought not. To the loss of that,
Sufficient penalty, why hast thou added
The sense of endless woes? Inexplicable
Thy justice seems; yet to say truth, too late
I thus contest; then should have been refused
Those terms whatever, when they were proposed:
Thou[9] didst accept them; wilt thou enjoy the good,
Then cavil° the conditions? And though God *object frivolously to*
Made thee without thy leave, what if thy son
Prove disobedient, and reproved, retort,
'Wherefore didst thou beget me? I sought it not':
Wouldst thou admit for his contempt of thee
That proud excuse? Yet him not thy election,° *choice*
But natural necessity begot.
God made thee of choice his own, and of his own
To serve him, thy reward was of his grace,
Thy punishment then justly is at his will.
Be it so, for I submit, his doom is fair,
That dust I am, and shall to dust return:
O welcome hour whenever! Why delays
His hand to execute what his decree
Fixed on this day? Why do I overlive,
Why am I mocked with death, and lengthened out
To deathless pain? How gladly would I meet
Mortality my sentence, and be earth
Insensible, how glad would lay me down
As in my mother's lap! There I should rest
And sleep secure; his dreadful voice no more
Would thunder in my ears, no fear of worse
To me and to my offspring would torment me
With cruel expectation. Yet one doubt

8. I.e., Adam's "own" curse will remain ("bide") with him, and the curse ("execration") of "all" who descend from him will "redound" on him as to their "natural center"; objects so placed ("in their place") were thought to be weightless ("light"), but these curses will be "heavy."

9. Adam turns from addressing God to address himself.

Pursues me still, lest all I° cannot die, *all of me*
Lest that pure breath of life, the spirit of man
Which God inspired, cannot together perish
With this corporeal clod; then in the grave,
Or in some other dismal place, who knows
But I shall die a living death? O thought
Horrid, if true! Yet why? It was but breath
Of life that sinned; what dies but what had life
And sin? The body properly hath neither.
All of me then shall die:[1] let this appease
The doubt, since human reach no further knows.
For though the Lord of all be infinite,
Is his wrath also? Be it, man is not so,
But mortal doomed. How can he exercise
Wrath without end on man whom death must end?
Can he make deathless death? That were to make
Strange contradiction, which to God himself
Impossible is held, as argument
Of weakness, not of power. Will he draw out,
For anger's sake, finite to infinite
In punished man, to satisfy his rigor
Satisfied never; that were to extend
His sentence beyond dust and nature's law,
By which all causes else according still
To the reception of their matter act,
Not to th' extent of their own sphere.[2] But say
That death be not one stroke, as I supposed,
Bereaving° sense, but endless misery *taking away*
From this day onward, which I feel begun
Both in me, and without° me, and so last *outside of*
To perpetuity; ay me, that fear
Comes thund'ring back with dreadful revolution° *return*
On my defenseless head; both Death and I
Am found eternal, and incorporate° both, *made one body*
Nor I on my part single, in me all
Posterity stands cursed: fair patrimony
That I must leave ye, sons; O were I able
To waste it all myself, and leave ye none!
So disinherited how would ye bless
Me now your curse! Ah, why should all mankind
For one man's fault thus guiltless be condemned,
If guiltless? But from me what can proceed,
But all corrupt, both mind and will depraved,
Not to do° only, but to will the same *act*
With me? How can they then acquitted stand
In sight of God? Him after all disputes
Forced I absolve: all my evasions vain
And reasonings, though through mazes, lead me still

1. After debating the matter, Adam concludes that the soul dies with the body; Milton in his *Christian Doctrine* worked out this "mortalist" doctrine, with its corollary, that both soul and body rise at the Last Judgment.

2. Adam convinces himself that "finite" matter (line 802) cannot suffer "infinite" punishment by an axiom of traditional philosophy, that by "nature's law" (line 805) the actions of agents are limited by the nature of the object they act upon.

But to my own conviction: first and last
On me, me only, as the source and spring
Of all corruption, all the blame lights due;
So might the wrath.[3] Fond° wish! Couldst thou support *foolish*
That burden heavier than the earth to bear,
Than all the world much heavier, though divided
With that bad woman? Thus what thou desir'st,
And what thou fear'st, alike destroys all hope
Of refuge, and concludes thee miserable
Beyond all past example and future,
To Satan only like both crime and doom.
O conscience, into what abyss of fears
And horrors hast thou driv'n me; out of which
I find no way, from deep to deeper plunged!"
 Thus Adam to himself lamented loud
Through the still night, not now, as ere man fell,
Wholesome and cool, and mild, but with black air
Accompanied, with damps° and dreadful gloom, *noxious vapors*
Which to his evil conscience represented
All things with double terror: on the ground
Outstretched he lay, on the cold ground, and oft
Cursed his creation, Death as oft accused
Of tardy execution, since denounced° *pronounced*
The day of his offense: "Why comes not Death,"
Said he, "with one thrice-ácceptáble stroke
To end me? Shall Truth fail to keep her word,
Justice divine not hasten to be just?
But Death comes not at call, Justice divine
Mends not her slowest pace for prayers or cries.
O woods, O fountains, hillocks, dales, and bow'rs,
With other echo late I taught your shades
To answer, and resound far other song."[4]
Whom thus afflicted when sad Eve beheld,
Desolate where she sat, approaching nigh,
Soft words to his fierce passion she assayed;° *attempted*
But her with stern regard he thus repelled:
 "Out of my sight, thou serpent,[5] that name best
Befits thee with him leagued, thyself as false
And hateful; nothing wants,° but that thy shape, *is lacking*
Like his, and color serpentine may show
Thy inward fraud, to warn all creatures from thee
Henceforth; lest that too heav'nly form, pretended[6]
To hellish falsehood, snare them. But° for thee *except*
I had persisted happy, had not thy pride
And wand'ring vanity, when least was safe,
Rejected my forewarning, and disdained
Not to be trusted, longing to be seen
Though by the Devil himself, him overweening° *overconfident*
To overreach, but with the serpent meeting

3. Cf. the Son's offer to accept all humankind's guilt (3.236–41), and Eve's similar offer (10.933–36).
4. Cf. their morning hymn (5.153–208).
5. Adam's bitter, misogynistic outcry begins with reference to the patristic notion that the name Eve, aspirated, means "serpent."
6. Held in front, as a cover or mask.

Fooled and beguiled, by him thou, I by thee,
To trust thee from my side, imagined wise,
Constant, mature, proof against all assaults,
And understood not all was but a show
Rather than solid virtue, all but a rib
Crooked by nature, bent, as now appears,
More to the part sinístero° from me drawn, *the left side*
Well if thrown out, as supernumerary
To my just number found.[7] O why did God,
Creator wise, that peopled highest heav'n
With Spirits masculine,[8] create at last
This novelty on earth, this fair defect
Of nature,[9] and not fill the world at once
With men as angels without feminine,
Or find some other way to generate
Mankind? This mischief had not then befall'n,
And more that shall befall, innumerable
Disturbances on earth through female snares,
And strait conjunction[1] with this sex: for either
He never shall find out fit mate, but such
As some misfortune brings him, or mistake,
Or whom he wishes most shall seldom gain
Through her perverseness, but shall see her gained
By a far worse, or if she love, withheld
By parents, or his happiest choice too late
Shall meet, already linked and wedlock-bound
To a fell° adversary, his hate or shame: *bitter*
Which infinite calamity shall cause
To human life, and household peace confound."
He added not, and from her turned, but Eve
Not so repulsed, with tears that ceased not flowing,
And tresses all disordered, at his feet
Fell humble, and embracing them, besought
His peace, and thus proceeded in her plaint:
"Forsake me not thus, Adam, witness Heav'n
What love sincere, and reverence in my heart
I bear thee, and unweeting° have offended, *unintentionally*
Unhappily deceived; thy suppliant
I beg, and clasp thy knees;[2] bereave me not,
Whereon I live, thy gentle looks, thy aid,
Thy counsel in this uttermost distress,
My only strength and stay: forlorn of thee,
Whither shall I betake me, where subsist?
While yet we live, scarce one short hour perhaps,
Between us two let there be peace, both joining,
As joined in injuries, one enmity
Against a foe by doom express° assigned us, *explicit judgment*

7. It was supposed that Adam had thirteen ribs on the left side, so he could spare one for the creation of Eve and still retain the proper ("just") number, twelve.
8. The Miltonic bard indicated that angels can assume at will "either sex . . . or both" (1.424).
9. Aristotle had claimed that the female is a defective male.
1. Close, hard-pressing, binding union: Adam then projects the problems of future marriages.
2. Eve assumes the posture of the classical suppliant, clasping the knees of the one she begs from.

That cruel serpent: on me exercise not
Thy hatred for this misery befall'n,
On me already lost, me than thyself
More miserable; both have sinned, but thou
Against God only, I against God and thee,
And to the place of judgment will return,
There with my cries importune Heaven, that all
The sentence from thy head removed may light
On me, sole cause to thee of all this woe,
Me me only just object of his ire."[3]
She ended weeping, and her lowly plight,° *posture*
Immovable till peace obtained from fault
Acknowledged and deplored, in Adam wrought
Commiseration; soon his heart relented
Towards her, his life so late and sole delight,
Now at his feet submissive in distress,
Creature so fair his reconcilement seeking,
His counsel whom she had displeased, his aid;
As one disarmed, his anger all he lost,
And thus with peaceful words upraised her soon:
"Unwary, and too desirous, as before,
So now of what thou know'st not, who desir'st
The punishment all on thyself; alas!
Bear thine own first, ill able to sustain
His full wrath whose thou feel'st as yet least part,
And my displeasure bear'st so ill.[4] If prayers
Could alter high decrees, I to that place
Would speed before thee, and be louder heard,
That on my head all might be visited,
Thy frailty and infirmer sex forgiv'n,
To me committed and by me exposed.
But rise, let us no more contend, nor blame
Each other, blamed enough elsewhere, but strive
In offices of love, how we may light'n
Each other's burden in our share of woe;
Since this day's death denounced, if aught I see,
Will prove no sudden, but a slow-paced evil,
A long day's dying to augment our pain,
And to our seed (O hapless seed!) derived."° *passed on*
To whom thus Eve, recovering heart, replied:
"Adam, by sad experiment I know
How little weight my words with thee can find,
Found so erroneous, thence by just event° *consequence*
Found so unfortunate; nevertheless,
Restored by thee, vile as I am, to place
Of new acceptance, hopeful to regain
Thy love, the sole contentment of my heart
Living or dying, from thee I will not hide
What thoughts in my unquiet breast are ris'n,

3. Eve also echoes the Son's offer (3.236–41). Cf. Adam's cry (10.832–34).

4. I.e., you could hardly bear God's "full wrath" since you are so distraught when you feel only the smallest part of it, and you can "ill" bear my displeasure.

Tending to some relief of our extremes,
Or end, though sharp and sad, yet tolerable,
As in our evils, and of easier choice.
If care of our descent perplex us most,[5]
Which must be born to certain woe, devoured
By Death at last, and miserable it is
To be to others cause of misery,
Our own begotten, and of our loins to bring
Into this cursèd world a woeful race,
That after wretched life must be at last
Food for so foul a monster, in thy power
It lies, yet ere conception to prevent
The race unblest, to being yet unbegot.
Childess thou art, childless remain; so Death
Shall be deceived° his glut, and with us two *cheated of*
Be forced to satisfy his rav'nous maw.
But if thou judge it hard and difficult,
Conversing, looking, loving, to abstain
From love's due rites, nuptial embraces sweet,
And with desire to languish without hope,
Before the present object[6] languishing
With like desire, which would be misery
And torment less than none of what we dread,
Then both ourselves and seed at once to free
From what we fear for both, let us make short,° *lose no time*
Let us seek Death, or he not found, supply
With our own hands his office on ourselves;
Why stand we longer shivering under fears,
That show no end but death, and have the power,
Of many ways to die the shortest choosing,
Destruction with destruction to destroy."
She ended here, or vehement despair
Broke off the rest; so much of death her thoughts
Had entertained, as dyed her cheeks with pale.
But Adam with such counsel nothing swayed,
To better hopes his more attentive mind
Laboring had raised, and thus to Eve replied.
"Eve thy contempt of life and pleasure seems
To argue in thee something more sublime
And excellent than what thy mind contemns;° *despises*
But self-destruction therefore sought, refutes
That excellence thought in thee, and implies,
Not thy contempt, but anguish and regret
For loss of life and pleasure overloved.
Or if thou covet death, as utmost end
Of misery, so thinking to evade
The penalty pronounced, doubt not but God
Hath wiselier armed his vengeful ire than so
To be forestalled; much more I fear lest death
So snatched will not exempt us from the pain

5. I.e., if concern for our descendants most torment ("perplex") us.

6. I.e., Eve herself, who then projects her own frustrated desire if they were to forgo sex.

We are by doom to pay: rather such acts
Of contumácy° will provoke the Highest *contempt*
To make death in us live. Then let us seek
Some safer resolution, which methinks
I have in view, calling to mind with heed
Part of our sentence, that thy seed shall bruise
The serpent's head; piteous amends, unless
Be meant, whom I conjecture, our grand foe
Satan, who in the serpent hath contrived
Against us this deceit: to crush his head
Would be revenge indeed; which will be lost
By death brought on ourselves, or childless days
Resolved, as thou proposest; so our foe
Shall scape his punishment ordained, and we
Instead shall double ours upon our heads.
No more be mentioned then of violence
Against ourselves, and willful barrenness,
That cuts us off from hope, and savors only
Rancor and pride, impatience and despite,
Reluctance° against God and his just yoke *resistance*
Laid on our necks. Remember with what mild
And gracious temper he both heard and judged
Without wrath or reviling; we expected
Immediate dissolution, which we thought
Was meant by death that day, when lo, to thee
Pains only in childbearing were foretold,
And bringing forth, soon recompensed with joy,
Fruit of thy womb:[7] on me the curse aslope
Glanced on the ground,[8] with labor I must earn
My bread; what harm? Idleness had been worse;
My labor will sustain me; and lest cold
Or heat should injure us, his timely care
Hath unbesought provided, and his hands
Clothed us unworthy, pitying while he judged;
How much more, if we pray him, will his ear
Be open, and his heart to pity incline,
And teach us further by what means to shun
Th' inclement seasons, rain, ice, hail, and snow,
Which now the sky with various face begins
To show us in this mountain, while the winds
Blow moist and keen, shattering° the graceful locks *scattering*
Of these fair spreading trees; which bids us seek
Some better shroud,° some better warmth to cherish *shelter*
Our limbs benumbed, ere this diurnal star° *the sun*
Leave cold the night, how we his gathered beams
Reflected, may with matter sere° foment, *dry*
Or by collision of two bodies grind

7. Adam's prophetic echo of Elizabeth's address to Mary, mother of Jesus (Luke 1.41–42), "blessed is the fruit of thy womb," lays the ground for their fuller understanding of the promise about the "seed" of the woman.

8. I.e., the curse, like a spear that almost missed its target, glanced aside and hit the ground.

The air attrite to fire,[9] as late the clouds
Justling or pushed with winds rude in their shock
Tine° the slant lightning, whose thwart° flame driv'n down *ignite / slanting*
Kindles the gummy bark of fir or pine,
And sends a comfortable heat from far,
Which might supply° the sun: such fire to use, *take the place of*
And what may else be remedy or cure
To evils which our own misdeeds have wrought,
He will instruct us praying, and of grace
Beseeching him, so as we need not fear
To pass commodiously this life, sustained
By him with many comforts, till we end
In dust, our final rest and native home.
What better can we do, than to the place
Repairing where he judged us, prostrate fall
Before him reverent, and there confess
Humbly our faults, and pardon beg, with tears
Watering the ground, and with our sighs the air
Frequenting,° sent from hearts contrite, in sign *filling*
Of sorrow unfeigned, and humiliation meek.
Undoubtedly he will relent and turn
From his displeasure; in whose look serene,
When angry most he seemed and most severe,
What else but favor, grace, and mercy shone?"
  So spake our father penitent, nor Eve
Felt less remorse: they forthwith to the place
Repairing where he judged them prostrate fell
Before him reverent, and both confessed
Humbly their faults, and pardon begged, with tears
Watering the ground, and with their sighs the air
Frequenting, sent from hearts contrite, in sign
Of sorrow unfeigned, and humiliation meek.[1]

Book 11 *Summary* The prayers of Adam and Eve prove acceptable to God. But while humankind may now hope for ultimate redemption, humans may no longer dwell in Paradise; and Michael, the warrior archangel, is dispatched to explain the sentence, offer some hope for the future, and dismiss Adam and Eve from the happy garden. Adam is at first overcome with grief; but the angel encourages him, and while Eve is put in a trance, Adam is raised to the peak of a high hill and shown in a vision the future of humankind as far as the flood of Noah.

From Book 12

Summary Continuing his instruction of Adam, Michael relates the history of the world from the time of Noah through the coming of Christ, whose ascent into Heaven and triumph over Death after the Crucifixion he describes.

9. Adam projects the invention of fire: they might, by striking two bodies together, rub ("attrite") the air into fire by friction; or else (lines 1070–71) focus reflected sunbeams (through some equivalent of glass) on dry ("sere") matter.

1. The final six lines repeat, almost word for word, lines 1086–92, as the poet describes Adam's proposed gesture of repentance carried out in every detail.

[THE DEPARTURE FROM EDEN]

So spake th' Archangel Michaël, then paused,
As at the world's great period;° and our sire *consummation*
Replete with joy and wonder thus replied:
"O goodness infinite, goodness immense!
That all this good of evil shall produce,
And evil turn to good; more wonderful
Than that which by creation first brought forth
Light out of darkness! Full of doubt I stand,
Whether I should repent me now of sin
By me done and occasioned, or rejoice
Much more, that much more good thereof shall spring,
To God more glory, more good will to men
From God, and over wrath grace shall abound.[1]
But say, if our Deliverer up to Heav'n
Must reascend, what will betide the few
His faithful, left among th' unfaithful herd,
The enemies of truth; who then shall guide
His people, who defend? Will they not deal
Worse with his followers than with him they dealt?"
"Be sure they will," said th' angel; "but from Heav'n
He to his own a Comforter will send,[2]
The promise of the Father, who shall dwell
His Spirit within them, and the law of faith
Working through love, upon their hearts shall write,
To guide them in all truth, and also arm
With spiritual armor, able to resist
Satan's assaults, and quench his fiery darts,[3]
What° man can do against them, not afraid, *as much as*
Though to the death, against such cruelties
With inward consolations recompensed,
And oft supported so as shall amaze
Their proudest persecutors: for the Spirit
Poured first on his apostles, whom he sends
To evangelize the nations, then on all
Baptized, shall them with wondrous gifts endue° *endow*
To speak all tongues, and do all miracles,
As did their Lord before them. Thus they win
Great numbers of each nation to receive
With joy the tidings brought from Heav'n: at length
Their ministry performed, and race well run,
Their doctrine and their story written left,[4]
They die; but in their room, as they forewarn,
Wolves shall succeed for teachers, grievous wolves,
Who all the sacred mysteries of Heav'n

1. These lines do not formulate the medieval idea of the *felix culpa*—that the Fall was fortunate in bringing humans greater happiness than they would otherwise have enjoyed—only that the Fall has provided God an occasion to bring still greater good out of evil. The poem makes clear that Adam and Eve would have grown in perfection and advanced to Heaven had they not sinned.

2. The Holy Spirit, who for Milton is much subordinate to both Father and Son.

3. Cf. Ephesians 6.11–16: "Put on the whole armor of God, that ye may be able to stand against the wiles of the devil. . . . Above all, taking the shield of faith, wherewith ye shall be able to quench all the fiery darts of the wicked." The subsequent history (lines 493–507) is that of the early Christian church in apostolic times.

4. I.e., in the Gospels and Epistles.

To their own vile advantages shall turn
Of lucre° and ambition, and the truth — *wealth*
With superstitions and traditions taint,[5]
Left only in those written records pure,
Though not but by the Spirit understood.
Then shall they seek to avail themselves of names,° — *honors*
Places° and titles, and with these to join — *offices*
Secular power, though feigning still to act
By spiritual, to themselves appropriating
The Spirit of God, promised alike and giv'n
To all believers; and from that pretense,
Spiritual laws by carnal° power shall force — *fleshly, worldly*
On every conscience;[6] laws which none shall find
Left them enrolled, or what the Spirit within
Shall on the heart engrave.[7] What will they then
But force the Spirit of Grace itself, and bind
His consort Liberty; what, but unbuild
His living temples,[8] built by faith to stand,
Their own faith not another's: for on earth
Who against faith and conscience can be heard
Infallible?[9] Yet many will presume:
Whence heavy persecution shall arise
On all who in the worship persevere
Of Spirit and Truth; the rest, far greater part,
Will deem in outward rites and specious forms
Religion satisfied; Truth shall retire
Bestuck with sland'rous darts, and works of faith
Rarely be found: so shall the world go on,
To good malignant, to bad men benign,
Under her own weight groaning, till the day
Appear of respiration° to the just, — *respite*
And vengeance to the wicked, at return
Of him so lately promised to thy aid,
The Woman's Seed,[1] obscurely then foretold,
Now amplier known thy Savior and thy Lord,
Last in the clouds from Heav'n to be revealed
In glory of the Father, to dissolve
Satan with his perverted world, then raise
From the conflagrant mass,° purged and refined, — *the burning world*
New heav'ns, new earth, ages of endless date
Founded in righteousness and peace of love,
To bring forth fruits joy and eternal bliss."

5. The history summarized in lines 508–40 is of the corruption of the Christian church by superstitions, traditions, and persecutions of conscience in patristic times under the popes and the Christian emperors, but also extending to the Last Day. The terms point especially to what Milton saw as the revival of "popish" superstitions in the English church of the Restoration and to the fierce persecution of dissenters.
6. These lines affirm the Protestant principle of every Christian's right to interpret Scripture according to the "inner light" of the Spirit, and denounce (as Milton consistently did in his tracts) the use of civil ("carnal") power to enforce orthodoxy.
7. I.e., there is nothing in Scripture or in the Spirit's inner teaching that sanctions persecution for conscience.
8. Cf. 1 Corinthians 3.16: "Know ye not that ye are the temple of God?" "His consort Liberty": Milton typically insists that Christ's gospel and the Spirit of God teach liberty, religious and civil, alluding as here to 2 Corinthians 3.17: "where the Spirit of the Lord is, there is liberty."
9. An attack on papal claims to infallibility, asserted though not yet proclaimed as doctrine.
1. Michael's story ends with the full explication of the promised "Woman's Seed" as Christ, and with the renewal of all things after the Last Judgment (lines 545–51).

He ended; and thus Adam last replied:
"How soon hath thy prediction, seer blest,
Measured this transient world, the race of time,
Till time stand fixed: beyond is all abyss,
Eternity, whose end no eye can reach.
Greatly instructed I shall hence depart,
Greatly in peace of thought, and have my fill
Of knowledge, what° this vessel can contain; *as much as*
Beyond which was my folly to aspire.
Henceforth I learn, that to obey is best,
And love with fear the only God, to walk
As in his presence, ever to observe
His providence, and on him sole depend,
Merciful over all his works, with good
Still overcoming evil, and by small
Accomplishing great things, by things deemed weak
Subverting worldly strong, and worldly wise
By simply meek; that suffering for truth's sake
Is fortitude to highest victory,
And to the faithful death the gate of life;
Taught this by his example whom I now
Acknowledge my Redeemer ever blest."
To whom thus also th' angel last replied:
"This having learnt, thou hast attained the sum
Of wisdom; hope no higher, though all the stars
Thou knew'st by name,[2] and all th' ethereal powers,
All secrets of the deep, all nature's works,
Or works of God in heav'n, air, earth, or sea,
And all the riches of this world enjoy'dst,
And all the rule, one empire; only add
Deeds to thy knowledge answerable,° add faith, *corresponding*
Add virtue, patience, temperance, add love,
By name to come called charity, the soul
Of all the rest: then wilt thou not be loath
To leave this Paradise, but shalt possess
A paradise within thee, happier far.
Let us descend now therefore from this top
Of speculation;° for the hour precise *hill of speculation*
Exacts° our parting hence; and see the guards, *requires*
By me encamped on yonder hill, expect
Their motion,° at whose front a flaming sword, *await their orders*
In signal of remove, waves fiercely round;
We may no longer stay: go, waken Eve;
Her also I with gentle dreams have calmed
Portending good, and all her spirits composed
To meek submission: thou at season fit
Let her with thee partake what thou hast heard,
Chiefly what may concern her faith to know,
The great deliverance by her seed to come
(For by the Woman's Seed) on all mankind.
That ye may live, which will be many days,

2. Michael glances back at Raphael's warning in Book 8 that Adam should concern himself first with matters pertaining to his own life and world, rather than speculating overmuch about the cosmos.

Both in one faith unanimous though sad,
With cause for evils past, yet much more cheered
With meditation on the happy end."
  He ended, and they both descend the hill;
Descended, Adam to the bow'r where Eve
Lay sleeping ran before, but found her waked;
And thus with words not sad she him received:
  "Whence thou return'st, and whither went'st, I know;
For God is also in sleep, and dreams advise,[3]
Which he hath sent propitious, some great good
Presaging, since with sorrow and heart's distress
Wearied I fell asleep: but now lead on;
In me is no delay; with thee to go,
Is to stay here; without thee here to stay,
Is to go hence unwilling; thou to me
Art all things under heav'n, all places thou,[4]
Who for my willful crime art banished hence.
This further consolation yet secure
I carry hence; though all by me is lost,
Such favor I unworthy am vouchsafed,
By me the promised Seed shall all restore."
  So spake our mother Eve, and Adam heard
Well pleased, but answered not; for now too nigh
Th' Archangel stood, and from the other hill
To their fixed station, all in bright array
The Cherubim descended; on the ground
Gliding metéorous,° as evening mist *like a meteor*
Ris'n from a river o'er the marish° glides, *marsh*
And gathers ground fast at the laborer's heel
Homeward returning. High in front advanced,
The brandished sword of God before them blazed
Fierce as a comet; which with torrid heat,
And vapor° as the Libyan air adust,° *smoke / parched*
Began to parch that temperate clime; whereat
In either hand the hast'ning angel caught
Our ling'ring parents, and to th' eastern gate
Led them direct, and down the cliff as fast
To the subjected° plain; then disappeared. *low-lying*
They looking back, all th' eastern side beheld
Of Paradise, so late their happy seat,° *estate*
Waved over by that flaming brand,° the gate *sword*
With dreadful faces thronged and fiery arms:
Some natural tears they dropped, but wiped them soon;
The world was all before them, where to choose
Their place of rest, and Providence their guide:
They hand in hand with wand'ring steps and slow,
Through Eden took their solitary way.

1674

3. The lines suggest that Eve's dream has provided her a parallel (if lesser) prophecy to Adam's visions and instruction. Cf. Numbers 12.6: "If there be a prophet among you, I the Lord will make myself known unto him in a vision, and will speak unto him in a dream."

4. Eve's lines—the final speech in the poem—recall her prelapsarian love song to Adam (4.641ff.) and Ruth's promise to accompany her mother-in-law, Naomi (Ruth 1.16).

The Restoration and the Eighteenth Century 1660–1785

1660:	Charles II restored to the English throne
1688–89:	The Glorious Revolution: deposition of James II and accession of William of Orange
1700:	Death of John Dryden
1707:	Act of Union unites Scotland and England, creating the nation of "Great Britain"
1714:	Rule by House of Hanover begins with accession of George I
1744–45:	Deaths of Alexander Pope and Jonathan Swift
1784:	Death of Samuel Johnson

The Restoration and the eighteenth century brought vast changes to the island of Great Britain, which became a single nation after 1707, when the Act of Union joined Scotland to England and Wales. After the prolonged civil and religious strife of the seventeenth century, Britain attained political stability and unprecedented commercial vigor. The countryside kept its seemingly timeless agricultural rhythms, even as the nation's great families consolidated their control over the land and those who worked it. Change came most dramatically to cities, which absorbed much of a national population that nearly doubled in the period, to ten million. Britons came together in civil society—the public but nongovernmental institutions and practices that became newly powerful in the period. The theaters (reopened at the Restoration), coffeehouses, concert halls, pleasure gardens, lending libraries, picture exhibitions, and shopping districts gave life in London and elsewhere a feeling of bustle and friction. Reflecting and stimulating this activity, an expanding assortment of printed works vied to interest literate women and men, whose numbers grew to include most of the middle classes and many among the poor. Civil society also linked people to an increasingly global economy, as they shopped for diverse goods from around the world. The rich and even the moderately well off could profit or go broke from investments in joint-stock companies, which controlled much of Britain's international trade, including its lucrative traffic in slaves. At home, new systems of canals and turnpikes stimulated domestic trade, industry, and travel, bringing distant parts of the country closer together. The cohesion of the nation also depended on ideas of social order—some old and clear, many subtle and new. An ethos of politeness came to prevail, a standard of social behavior to which more and more could aspire yet that served to distinguish the privileged sharply from the rude and vulgar. This and other ideas, of order and hierarchy, of liberty and rights, of sentiment and sympathy, helped determine the ways in which an expanding diversity of people could seek to participate in Britain's thriving cultural life.

RELIGION AND POLITICS

The Restoration of 1660—the return of Charles Stuart and, with him, the monarchy to England—brought hope to a divided nation, exhausted by years of civil war and political turmoil. Almost all of Charles's subjects welcomed him home. After the abdication of Richard Cromwell in 1659 the country had seemed at the brink of chaos, and Britons were eager to believe that their king would bring order and law and a spirit of mildness back into the national life. But no political settlement could be stable until the religious issues had been resolved. The restoration of the monarchy meant that the established church would also be restored, and though Charles was willing to pardon or ignore many former enemies (such as Milton), the bishops and Anglican clergy were less tolerant of dissent. When Parliament reimposed the Book of Common Prayer in 1662 and then in 1664 barred Nonconformists from religious meetings outside the established church, thousands of clergymen resigned their livings, and the jails were filled with preachers like John Bunyan who refused to be silenced. In 1673 the Test Act required all holders of civil and military offices to take the sacrament in an Anglican church and to deny belief in transubstantiation. Thus Protestant Dissenters and Roman Catholics were largely excluded from public life; for instance, Alexander Pope, a Catholic, could not attend a university, own land, or vote. The scorn of Anglicans for Nonconformist zeal or "enthusiasm" (a belief in private revelation) bursts out in Samuel Butler's popular *Hudibras* (1663), a caricature of Presbyterians and Independents. And English Catholics were widely regarded as potential traitors and (wrongly) thought to have set the Great Fire that destroyed much of London in 1666.

Yet the triumph of the established church did not resolve the constitutional issues that had divided Charles I and Parliament. Charles II had promised to govern through Parliament but slyly tried to consolidate royal power. Steering away from crises, he hid his Catholic sympathies and avoided a test of strength with Parliament—except on one occasion. In 1678 the report of the Popish Plot, in which Catholics would rise and murder their Protestant foes, terrified London; and though the charge turned out to be a fraud, the House of Commons exploited the fear by trying to force Charles to exclude his Catholic brother, James, duke of York, from succession to the throne. The turmoil of this period is captured brilliantly by Dryden's *Absalom and Achitophel* (1681). Finally, Charles defeated the Exclusion Bill by dissolving Parliament. But the crisis resulted in a basic division of the country between two new political parties: the Tories, who supported the king, and the Whigs, the king's opponents.

Neither party could live with James II. After he came to the throne in 1685, he claimed the right to make his own laws, suspended the Test Act, and began to fill the army and government with fellow Catholics. The birth of James's son in 1688 brought matters to a head, confronting the nation with the prospect of a Catholic dynasty. Secret negotiations paved the way for the Dutchman William of Orange, a champion of Protestantism and the husband of James's Protestant daughter Mary. William landed with a small army in southwestern England and marched toward London. As he advanced the king's allies melted away, and James fled to a permanent exile in France. But the house of Stuart would be heard from again. For more than half a century some loyal Jacobites (from the Latin *Jacobus,* "James"), especially in Scotland, supported James, his son ("the Old Pretender"), and his grandson ("the Young Pretender" or "Bonnie Prince Charlie") as the legitimate rulers of Britain. Moreover, a good many writers, from Aphra Behn and Dryden (and arguably Pope and Johnson) to Robert Burns, privately sympathized with Jacobitism. But after the failure of one last rising in 1745, the cause would dwindle gradually into a wistful sentiment. In retrospect, the coming of William and Mary in 1688—the Glorious, or Bloodless, Revolution—came to be seen as the beginning of a stabilized, unified Great Britain.

A lasting settlement followed. In 1689 a Bill of Rights revoked James's actions; it limited the powers of the Crown, reaffirmed the supremacy of Parliament, and guaranteed some individual rights. The same year the Toleration Act relaxed the strain of religious conflict by granting a limited freedom of worship to Dissenters (although not to Catholics or Jews) so long as they swore allegiance to the Crown. This proved to be a workable compromise; and with the passage of the Act of Settlement in 1701, putting Sophia, electress of Hanover, and her descendants in line for the throne (as the granddaughter of James I, she was the closest Protestant relative of Princess Anne, James II's younger daughter, whose sole surviving child died in that year), the difficult problems that had so long divided England seemed resolved. The principles established in 1689 endured unaltered in essentials until the Reform Bill of 1832.

During Anne's reign (1702–14), new political tensions embittered the nation. In the War of the Spanish Succession (1702–13), England and its allies defeated France and Spain; as these commercial rivals were weakened and war profits flowed in, the Whig lords and London merchants supporting the war grew rich. The spoils included new colonies and the *asiento,* a contract to supply slaves to the Spanish Empire. The hero of the war, Captain-General John Churchill, duke of Marlborough, won the famous victory of Blenheim; was showered with honors and wealth; and, with his duchess, dominated the queen until 1710. But the Whigs and Marlborough pushed their luck too hard. When the Whigs tried to reward the Dissenters for their loyalty by removing the Test, Anne fought back to defend the established church. She dismissed her Whig ministers and the Marlboroughs and called in Robert Harley and the brilliant young Henry St. John to form a Tory ministry. These ministers employed prominent writers like Defoe and Swift and commissioned Matthew Prior to negotiate the Peace of Utrecht (1713). But to Swift's despair—he later burlesqued events at court in *Gulliver's Travels*—a bitter rivalry broke out between Harley (now earl of Oxford) and St. John (now Viscount Bolingbroke). Though Bolingbroke succeeded in ousting Oxford, the death of Anne in 1714 reversed his fortunes. The Whigs returned to power, and George I (Sophia's son) became the first Hanoverian king (he would reign until 1727). Harley was imprisoned in the Tower of London until 1717; and Bolingbroke, charged with being a Jacobite traitor, fled to France. Government was now securely in the hands of the Whigs.

The political principles of the Whig and Tory Parties, which bring so much fire to eighteenth-century public debate, evolved to address changing circumstances through the period. Now we tend to think of Tories as conservative and Whigs as liberal. (Members of today's Conservative Party in the United

Kingdom are sometimes called Tories.) During the Exclusion Crisis of the 1680s the Whigs asserted the liberties of the English subject against the royal prerogatives of Charles II, whom Tories such as Dryden supported. After both parties survived the 1688 Glorious Revolution, the Tories guarded the preeminence of the established church (sometimes styling themselves the Church Party), while Whigs tended to support toleration of Dissenters. Economically, too, Tories defined themselves as traditionalists, affirming landownership as the proper basis of wealth, power, and privilege (though most thought trade honorable), whereas the Whigs came to be seen as supporting a new "moneyed interest" (as Swift called it): managers of the Bank of England (founded 1694), contrivers of the system of public credit, and investors in the stock market. But conservatism and liberalism did not exist as coherent ideologies in the period, and the vicissitudes of party dispute offer many surprises. When Bolingbroke returned to England in 1724 after being pardoned, he led a Tory opposition that decried the "ministerial tyranny" of the Whig government. This opposition patriotically hailed liberty in a manner recalling the Whig rhetoric of earlier decades, appealed to both landed gentry and urban merchants, and arguably anticipated the antigovernment radicalism of the end of the eighteenth century. Conversely, the Whigs sought to secure a centralized fiscal and military state machine and a web of financial interdependence controlled by the wealthiest aristocrats.

The great architect of this Whig policy was Robert Walpole, who came to power as a result of the "South Sea bubble" (1720), a stock market crash. His ability to restore confidence and keep the country running smoothly, as well as to juggle money, would mark his long ascendancy. Coming to be known as Britain's first "prime" minister, he consolidated his power during the reign of George II (1727–60). More involved in British affairs than his essentially German father, George II came to appreciate the efficient administration of the patronage system under Walpole, who installed dependents in government offices and controlled the House of Commons by financially rewarding its members. Many great writers found these methods offensive and embraced Bolingbroke's new Tory rhetoric extolling the Englishman's fierce independence from the corrupting power of centralized government and concentrations of wealth. Gay's *Beggar's Opera* (1728) and Fielding's *Jonathan Wild* (1743) draw parallels between great criminals and great politicians, and Pope's *Dunciad* uses Walpole as an emblem of the venal commercialization of the whole social fabric. This distaste, however, did not prevent Pope himself from marketing his poems as cleverly as he wrote them.

Walpole fell in 1742 because he was unwilling to go to war against the French and Spanish, a war he thought would cost too much but that many perceived would enhance Britain's wealth still further. The next major English statesman, William Pitt the Elder, appealed to a spirit of national patriotism and called for the expansion of British power and commerce overseas. The defeat of the French in the Seven Years' War (1756–63), especially in North America, was largely his doing. The long reign of George III (1760–1820) was dominated by two great concerns: the emergence of Britain as a colonial power and the cry for a new social order based on liberty and radical reform. In 1763 the Peace of Paris consolidated British rule over Canada and India, and not even the later loss of the American colonies could stem the rise of the empire. Great Britain was no longer an isolated island but a nation with interests and responsibilities around the world.

At home, however, there was discontent. The wealth brought to England by industrialism and foreign trade had not spread to the great mass of the poor. For much of the century, few had questioned the idea that those at the top of the social hierarchy rightfully held power. Rich families' alliances and rivalries, national and local, dominated politics; while male property owners could vote in Parliamentary elections, they and others of the middle classes and the poor had mostly followed the powerful people who could best help them thrive or at least survive. But toward the end of the century it seemed to many that the bonds of custom that once held people together had finally broken, and now money alone was respected. Protestants turned against Catholics; in 1780 the Gordon Riots put London temporarily under mob rule. The king was popular with his subjects and tried to take government into his own hands, rising above partisanship, but his efforts often backfired—as when the American colonists took him for a tyrant. From 1788 to the end of his life, moreover, an inherited disease (porphyria) periodically unhinged his mind, as in a memorable scene described by Frances Burney. Meanwhile, reformers such as John Wilkes and Richard Price called for a new political democracy. Fear of their radicalism would contribute to the British reaction against the French Revolution. In the last decades of the century British authors would be torn between two opposing attitudes: loyalty to the old traditions of subordination, mutual obligations, and local self-sufficiency, and yearning for a new dispensation founded on principles of liberty, the rule of reason, and human rights.

THE CONTEXT OF IDEAS

Much of the most powerful writing after 1660 exposed divisions in the nation's thinking that derived from the tumult of earlier decades. As the possibility of a Christian Commonwealth receded, the great republican John Milton published *Paradise Lost* (final version, 1674), and John Bunyan's immensely popular masterwork *Pilgrim's Progress* (1679) expressed the conscience of a Nonconformist. Conversely, an aristocratic culture, led by Charles II himself, aggressively celebrated pleasure and the right of the elite to behave extravagantly: members of the court scandalized respectable London citizens and considered their wives and daughters fair game. The court's hero, the earl of Rochester, became a celebrity for enacting the creed of a libertine and rake. The delights of the court also took more refined forms. French and Italian musicians, as well as painters from the Low Countries, migrated to England; and playhouses—closed by the Puritans since 1642—sprang back to life. In 1660 Charles authorized two new companies of actors, the King's Players and the Duke's; their repertory included witty, bawdy comedies written and acted by women as well as men. But as stark as the contrasts were during the Restoration between libertine and religious intellectuals, royalists and republicans, High Churchmen and Nonconformists, the court and the rest of the country, a spirit of compromise was brewing.

Perhaps the most widely shared intellectual impulse of the age was a distrust of dogmatism. Nearly everybody blamed it for the civil strife through which the nation had recently passed. Opinions varied widely about which dogmatism was most dangerous—Puritan enthusiasm, papal infallibility, the divine right of kings, medieval scholastic or modern Cartesian philosophy—but these were denounced in remarkably similar terms. As far apart intellectually and temperamentally as Rochester and Milton were, both portray overconfidence in human reasoning as the supreme disaster. It is the theme of Butler's *Hudibras* and much of the work of Dryden. Many philosophers, scientists, and divines began to embrace a mitigated skepticism, which argued that human beings could readily achieve a sufficient degree of necessary knowledge (sometimes called "moral certainty") but also contended that the pursuit of absolute certainty was vain, mad, and socially calamitous. If, as the commentator Martin Clifford put it in *A Treatise of Humane Reason* (1675), "in this vast latitude of probabilities," a person thinks "there is none can lead one to salvation, but the path wherein he treads himself, we may see the evident and necessary consequence of eternal troubles and confusions." Such writers insist that a distrust of human capacities is fully compatible with religious faith: for them the inability of reason and sensory evidence to settle important questions reveals our need to accept Christian mysteries as our intellectual foundation. Dryden's poem *Religio Laici* (1682) explains: "So pale grows reason in religion's sight; / So dies, and so dissolves in supernatural light."

Far from inhibiting fresh thinking, however, the distrust of old dogmas inspired new theories, projects, and explorations. In *Leviathan* (1651), Thomas Hobbes jettisoned the notion of a divine basis for kingly authority, proposing instead a naturalistic argument for royal absolutism begun from the claim that mere "matter in motion" composes the universe: if not checked by an absolute sovereign, mankind's "perpetual and restless desire of power after power" could lead to civic collapse. Other materialist philosophies derived from ancient Epicurean thought, which was Christianized by the French philosopher Pierre Gassendi (1592–1655). The Epicurean doctrine that the universe consists only of minuscule atoms and void unnerved some thinkers—Swift roundly mocks it in *A Tale of a Tub*—but it also energized efforts to examine the world with deliberate, acute attention. This new scientific impulse advanced Francis Bacon's program of methodical experimentation and inductive reasoning formulated earlier in the century.

Charles II gave official approval to the scientific revolution by chartering the Royal Society of London for the Improving of Natural Knowledge in 1662. But observations of nature advanced both formally and informally in an eclectic range of areas: the specialized, professional "scientist" we know today did not yet exist. And new features of the world were disclosed to everyone who had the chance to look. Two wonderful inventions, the microscope and telescope, had begun to reveal that nature is more extravagant—teeming with tiny creatures and boundless galaxies—than anyone had ever imagined. One book that stayed popular for more than a century, Fontenelle's *Conversations on the Plurality of Worlds* (1686; translated from French by Behn and later by Burney), suggested that an infinite number of alternate worlds and living creatures might exist, not only in outer space but under our feet, invisibly small. Travels to unfamiliar regions of the globe also enlarged understandings of what nature could do: Behn's classifying and collecting of South American flora and fauna in *Oroonoko* show how the appetite for wondrous facts kept pace with the economic motives of world exploration and colonization. Encounters with hitherto little known societies in the Far East, Africa, and the Americas enlarged Europeans' understanding of human norms as well. In *Gulliver's Travels*, Swift shows the comical, painful ways in which the discovery of new cultures forces one average Briton to reexamine his own. (See the topics "The Plurality of Worlds" and "Travel, Trade, and the Expansion of Empire" on Norton Literature Online.)

Scientific discovery and exploration also affected religious attitudes. Alongside "natural history" (the collection and description of facts of nature) and "natural philosophy" (the study of the causes of what happens in nature), thinkers of the period placed "natural religion" (the study of nature as a book written by God). Newly discovered natural laws, such as Newton's laws of optics and celestial mechanics, seemed evidence of a universal order in creation, which implied God's hand in the design of the universe, as a watch implies a watchmaker. Expanded knowledge of peoples around the world who had never heard of Christianity led theologians to formulate supposedly universal religious tenets available to all rational beings. Some intellectuals embraced Deism, the doctrine that religion need not depend on mystery or biblical truths and could rely on reason alone, which recognized the goodness and wisdom of natural law and its creator. Natural religion could not, however, discern an active God who punished vice and rewarded virtue in this life; evidently the First Cause had withdrawn from the universe He set in motion. Many orthodox Christians shuddered at the vision of a vast, impersonal machine of nature. Instead they rested their faith on the revelation of Scripture, the scheme of salvation in which Christ died to redeem our sins. Other Christians, such as Pope in *An Essay on Man* and Thomson in *The Seasons*, espoused arguments for natural religion that they felt did not conflict with or diminish orthodox belief.

Some people began to argue that the achievements of modern inquiry had eclipsed those of the ancients (and the fathers of the church), who had not known about the solar system, the New World, microscopic organisms, or the circulation of the blood. The school curriculum began with years of Latin and Greek, inculcating a long-established humanistic tradition that many authors, including Swift and Pope, still cherished. A battle of the books erupted in the late seventeenth century between champions of ancient and of modern learning. Swift crusaded fiercely in this battle: *Gulliver's Travels* denounces the pointlessness and arrogance he saw in experiments of the Royal Society, while "A Modest Proposal" depicts a peculiar new cruelty and indifference to moral purpose made possible by statistics and economics (two fields pioneered by Royal Society member Sir William Petty). But as sharp as such disagreements were, accommodation was also possible. Even as works such as Newton's *Principia* (1687) and *Opticks* (1704) revolutionized previously held views of the world, Newton himself maintained a seemly diffidence, comparing himself to "a boy playing on the sea-shore" "whilst the great ocean of truth lay all undiscovered before me." He and other modest modern inquirers such as Locke won the admiration of Pope and many ardent defenders of the past.

The widespread devotion to the direct observation of experience established empiricism as the dominant intellectual attitude of the age, which would become Britain's great legacy to world philosophy. Locke and his heirs George Berkeley and David Hume pursue the experiential approach in widely divergent directions. But even when they reach conclusions shocking to common sense, they tend to reassert the security of our prior knowledge. Berkeley insists we know the world only through our senses and thus cannot prove that any material thing exists, but he uses that argument to demonstrate the necessity of faith, because reality amounts to no more than a perception in the mind of God. Hume's famous argument about causation—that "causes and effects are discoverable, not by reason but by experience"—grounds our sense of the world not on rational reflection but on spontaneous, unreflective beliefs and feelings. Perhaps Locke best expresses the temper of his times in the *Essay Concerning Human Understanding* (1690):

> If by this inquiry into the nature of the understanding, I can discover the powers thereof; how far they reach; to what things they are in any degree proportionate; and where they fail us, I suppose it may be of use, to prevail with the busy mind of man to be more cautious in meddling with things exceeding its comprehension; to stop when it is at the utmost extent of its tether; and to sit down in a quiet ignorance of those things which, upon examination, are found to be beyond the reach of our capacities. . . . Our business here is not to know all things, but those which concern our conduct.

Such a position is Swift's, when he inveighs against metaphysics, abstract logical deductions, and theoretical science. It is similar to Pope's warning against human presumption in *An Essay on Man.* It prompts Johnson to talk of "the business of living" and to restrain the flights of unbridled imagination. And it helps account for the Anglican clergy's dislike of emotion and "enthusiasm" in religion and for their emphasis on good works, rather than faith, as the way to salvation. Locke's empiricism pervaded eighteenth-century British thought on politics, education, and morals as well as philosophy; Johnson's great *Dictionary* (1755) uses more than fifteen hundred illustrations from his writings.

Yet perhaps the most momentous new idea at the turn of the eighteenth century was set against Lockean thinking. The groundbreaking intellectual Mary Astell, in *A Serious Proposal to the Ladies* (1694) and *Some Reflections upon Marriage* (1700, 1706), initiated a powerful strain of modern feminism, arguing for the establishment of women's educational institutions and decrying the tyranny that husbands legally exercised over their wives. She nonetheless mocked the calls for political rights and liberty by Locke and other Whig theorists, rights that pointedly did not extend to women. Instead, she and other early feminists, including Sarah Fyge Egerton and Mary, Lady Chudleigh, embraced the Tory principle of obedience to royal and church authority. Women's advocates had to fight "tyrant Custom" (in Egerton's words), rooted in ancient traditions of domestic power and enshrined in the Bible and mythic human prehistory. This struggle seemed distinct from public political denunciations of the tyranny of some relatively recent Charles or James. Astell feared that the doctrines of male revolutionaries could produce civil chaos and so jeopardize the best that women could hope for in her day: the freedom to become fully educated, practice their religion, and marry (or not) according to their own enlightened judgment.

Other thinkers, male and female, began to advocate improving women's education as part of a wider commitment to enhancing and extending sociability. Richard Steele's periodical *The Tatler* satirized Astell as "Madonella" because she seemed to recommend women to a nun-like, "recluse life." In *The Spectator* (1711–12; 1714), conversely, Steele and Joseph Addison encouraged women to learn to participate in an increasingly sociable, intellectually sophisticated, urbane world, where all sorts of people could mingle, as in the streets and parks of a thriving city like London. Such periodicals sought to teach as large a readership as possible to think and behave politely. On a more aristocratic plane, the *Characteristics of Men, Manners, Opinions, and Times* (1711) by the third earl of Shaftesbury similarly asserted the naturally social meaning of human character and meditated on the affections, the witty intercourse, and the standards of politeness that bind people together. Such ideas led to the popularity around mid-century of a new word, *sentimental,* which locates the bases of social conduct in instinctual feeling rather than divinely sanctioned moral codes. Religion itself, according to Laurence Sterne, might be a "Great Sensorium," a sort of central nervous system that connects the feelings of all living creatures in one great benevolent soul. And people began to feel exquisite pleasure in the exercise of charity. The cult of sensibility fostered a philanthropy that led to social reforms seldom envisioned in earlier times—to the improvement of jails, the relief of imprisoned debtors, the establishment of foundling hospitals and of homes for penitent prostitutes, and ultimately the abolition of the slave trade. And it also loosed a ready flow of sympathetic responses to the joys and sorrows of fellow human beings.

Another passion that transformed British culture in the period was curiosity: scientific discoveries increasingly found practical applications in industry, the arts, and even entertainment. By the late 1740s, as knowledge of electricity advanced, public experiments offered fashionable British crowds the opportunity to electrocute themselves. Amateurs everywhere amused themselves with air pumps and chemical explosions. Birmingham became famous as a center where science and manufacturing were combining to change the world: in the early 1760s Matthew Boulton (1728–1809) established the most impressive factory of the age just outside town, producing vast quantities of pins, buckles, and buttons; in subsequent decades, his applications and manufacture of the new steam engine invented by Scotsman James Watt (1736–1819) helped build an industry to drive all others. Practical chemistry also led to industrial improvements: domestic porcelain production became established in the 1750s; and from the 1760s Josiah Wedgwood (1730–95) developed glazing, manufacturing, and marketing techniques that enabled British ceramics to compete with China for fashionable taste. (In 1765 he named his creamware "Queen's ware" to remind customers of its place on Queen Charlotte's table.) Wedgwood and others answered an ever-increasing demand in Britain for beautiful objects. Artist William Hogarth satirized this appetite of the upper and middle classes for the accumulation of finery: a chaotic collection of china figurines crowds the mantel in Plate 2 of *Marriage A-la-Mode* (1743–45). Yet the images that made Hogarth famous would soon decorate English ceramic teapots and plates and be turned into porcelain figurines themselves.

New forms of religious devotion sprang up amid Britain's spectacular material success. The evangelical revival known as Methodism began in the 1730s, led by three Oxford graduates: John Wesley (1703–1791), his brother Charles (1707–1788), and George Whitefield (1714–1770). The Methodists took their gospel to the common people, warning that all were sinners and damned, unless they accepted "amazing grace," salvation through faith. Often denied the privilege of preaching in village churches, evangelicals preached to thousands in barns or the open fields. The emotionalism of such revival meetings repelled the somnolent Anglican Church and the upper classes, who feared that the fury and zeal of the Puritan sects were returning. Methodism was sometimes related to madness; convinced that he was damned forever, the poet William Cowper broke down and became a recluse. But the religious awakening persisted and affected many clergymen and laymen within the Establishment, who reanimated the church and promoted unworldliness and piety. Nor did the insistence of Methodists on faith over works as the way to salvation prevent them or their Anglican allies from fighting for social reforms. The campaign to abolish slavery and the slave trade was driven largely by a passion to save souls.

Sentimentalism, evangelicalism, and the pursuits of wealth and luxury in different ways all placed a new importance on individuals—the gratification of their tastes and ambitions or their yearning for personal encounters with each other or a personal God. Diary keeping, elaborate letter writing, and the novel also testified to the growing importance of the private, individual life. Few histories of kings or nations could rival Richardson's novel *Clarissa* in length, popularity, or documentary detail: it was subtitled "the History of a Young Lady." The older hierarchical system had tended to subordinate individuals to their social rank or station. In the eighteenth century that fixed system began to break down, and people's sense of themselves began to change. By the end of the century many issues of politics and the law revolve around rights, not traditions. The modern individual had been invented; no product of the age is more enduring.

CONDITIONS OF LITERARY PRODUCTION

Publishing boomed as never before in eighteenth-century Britain, as the number of titles appearing annually and the periodicals published in London and the provincial towns dramatically increased. This expansion in part resulted from a loosening of legal restraints on printing. Through much of the previous three centuries, the government had licensed the texts deemed suitable for publication and refused to license those it wanted suppressed (a practice called "prior restraint"). After the Restoration, the new Printing Act (1662) tightened licensing controls, though unlike his Stuart predecessors Charles II now shared this power with Parliament. But in 1695, during the reign of William III, the last in a series of printing acts was not renewed. Debate in Parliament on the matter was more practical than idealistic: it was argued that licensing fettered the printing trades and was ineffective at preventing obnoxious publications anyway, which could be better constrained after publication by enforcing laws against seditious libel, obscenity, and treason. As the two-party system consolidated, both Whigs and Tories seemed to realize that prepublication censorship could bite them when their own side happened to be out of power. Various governments attempted to revive licensing during political crises throughout the eighteenth century, but it was gone for good.

This did not end the legal liabilities, and the prosecutions, of authors. Daniel Defoe, for instance, was convicted of seditious libel and faced the pillory and jail for his satirical pamphlet "The Shortest Way with the Dissenters" (1702), which imitated High-Church zeal so extravagantly that it provoked both the Tories and the Dissenters he had set about to defend. And licensing of the stage returned: irritated especially by Henry Fielding's anti-government play *The Historical Register for the Year 1736*, Robert Walpole pushed the Stage Licensing Act through Parliament in 1737, which authorized the Lord Chamberlain to license all plays and reduced the number of London theaters to two (Drury Lane and Covent Garden), closing Fielding's New Theatre in the Haymarket and driving him to a new career as a novelist. But despite such constraints, Hume could begin his essay "Of the Liberty of the Press" (1741) by citing "the extreme liberty we enjoy in this country of communicating whatever we please to the public" as an internationally recognized commonplace. This freedom allowed eighteenth-century Britain to build an exemplary version of what historians have called "the public sphere": a cultural arena, free of direct government control, consisting of not just published comment on matters of national interest but also the public venues—coffeehouses, clubs, taverns—where readers circulated, discussed, and conceived responses to it. The first regular daily London newspaper, the *Daily Courant*, appeared in 1702; in 1731, the first magazine, the *Gentleman's Magazine*. The latter was followed both by imitations and by successful literary journals like the *Monthly Review* (1749) and the *Critical Review* (1756). Each audience attracted some periodical tailored to it, as with the *Female Tatler* (1709) and Eliza Haywood's *Female Spectator* (1744–46).

After 1695, the legal status of printed matter became ambiguous, and in 1710 Parliament enacted the Statute of Anne—"An Act for the Encouragement of Learning by Vesting the Copies of Printed Books in the Authors or Purchasers of Such Copies"—the first copyright law in British history not tied to government approval of works' contents. Typically, these copyrights were held by booksellers, who operated much as publishers do today (in the eighteenth century, *publisher* referred to one who distributed books). A bookseller paid an author for a work's copyright and, after registering the work with the Stationers' Company for a fee, had exclusive right for fourteen years to publish it; if alive when this term expired, he owned it another fourteen years. Payments to authors for copyright varied. Pope got £15 for the 1714 version of *The Rape of the Lock*, while Samuel Johnson's *Rasselas* earned him £100. The Statute of Anne spurred the book trade by enhancing booksellers' control over works and hence their chance to profit by them. But the government soon introduced a new constraint. In 1712, the first Stamp Act put a tax on all newspapers, advertisements, paper, and pamphlets (effectively any work under a hundred pages or so): all printed matter had to carry the stamp indicating the taxes had been paid. Happily for Anne and her ministry, the act both raised government revenue and drove a number of the more irresponsible, ephemeral newspapers out of business, though the *Spectator* simply doubled its price and thrived. Stamp Acts were in effect throughout the century, and duties tended to increase when the government needed to raise money and rein in the press, as during the Seven Years' War in 1757.

But such constraints were not heavy enough to hold back the publishing market, which began to sustain the first true professional class of authors in British literary history. The lower echelon of the profession was called "Grub Street," which was, as Johnson's *Dictionary* explains, "originally the name of a street in Moorfields in London, much inhabited by writers of small histories, dictionaries, and temporary poems." The market increasingly motivated the literary elite too, and Johnson himself came to remark that "no man but a blockhead ever wrote, except for money." As a young writer, he sold articles to the *Gentleman's Magazine*, and many other men and women struggled to survive doing piecework for periodicals. The enhanced opportunity to sell their works on the open market meant that fewer authors needed to look to aristocratic patrons for support. But a new practice, publication by subscription, blended elements of patronage and literary capitalism and created the century's most spectacular authorial fortunes. Wealthy readers could subscribe to a work in progress, usually by agreeing to pay the author half in advance and half upon receipt of the book. Subscribers were rewarded with an edition more sumptuous than the common run and the appearance of their names in a list in the book's front pages. Major works by famous authors, such as Dryden's translation of Virgil (1697) and the 1718 edition of Prior's poems, generated the most subscription sales; the grandest success was Pope's translation of Homer's *Iliad* (1715–20), which gained him about £5000; his *Odyssey* (1725–26) raised nearly that much. But smaller projects deemed to need special encouragement also sold by subscription, including nearly all books of poetry by women, such as Mary Leapor's poems (1751).

Not all entered the literary market with equal advantages; and social class played a role, though hardly a simple one, in preparing authors for success. The better educated were better placed to be taken seriously: many eminent male writers, including Dryden, Locke, Addison, Swift, Hume, Johnson, Burke—the list could go on and on—had at least some university education, either at Oxford or Cambridge or at Scottish or Irish universities, where attendance by members of the laboring classes was virtually nil. Also, universities were officially closed to non-Anglicans. Some important writers attended the Dissenting academies that sprang up to fulfill Nonconformists' educational aspirations: Defoe went to an excellent one at Newington Green. A few celebrated authors such as Rochester and Henry Fielding had aristocratic backgrounds, but many came from the "middle class," though those in this category show how heterogeneous it was. Pope, a Catholic, obtained his education privately, and his father was a linen wholesaler, but he eventually became intimate with earls and viscounts, whereas Richardson, who had a family background in trade and (as he said) "only common school-learning," was a successful printer before he became a novelist. Both were middle class in a sense and made their own fortunes in eighteenth-century print culture, yet they inhabited vastly different social worlds.

Despite the general exclusion of the poor from education and other means of social advancement, some self-educated writers of the laboring classes fought their way into print. A few became celebrities, aided by the increasing popularity of the idea, famously expressed by Gray in his "Elegy Written in a Country Churchyard," that there must be unknown geniuses among the poor. Stephen Duck, an agricultural worker from Wiltshire, published his popular *Poems on Several Subjects* in 1730, which included "The Thresher's Labor" (he became known as the Thresher Poet). Queen Caroline herself retained him to be keeper of her library in Richmond. Several authors of the "common sort" followed in Duck's wake, including Mary Collier, whose poem "The Woman's Labor: An Epistle to Mr. Duck" (1739) defended country women against charges of idleness. Apart from such visible successes, eighteenth-century print culture afforded work for many from lower socioeconomic levels, if not as authors, then as hawkers of newspapers on city streets and singers of political ballads (who were often illiterate and female), bookbinders, papermakers, and printing-press workers. The vigor of the literary market demanded the labor of all classes.

As all women were barred from universities and faced innumerable other disadvantages and varieties of repression, the story of virtually every woman author in the period is one of self-education, courage, and extraordinary initiative. Yet women did publish widely for the first time in the period, and the examples that can be assembled are as diverse as they are impressive. During the Restoration and early eighteenth century, a few aristocratic women poets were hailed as marvelous exceptions and given fanciful names: the poems of Katherine Philips (1631–1664), "the matchless Orinda," were published posthumously in 1667; and others, including Anne Finch, Anne Killigrew, and later, Lady Mary Wortley Montagu, printed poems or circulated them in manuscript among fashionable circles. A more broadly public sort of female authorship was more ambivalently received. Though Aphra Behn built a successful career in the theater and in print, her sexually frank works were sometimes denounced as unbecoming a woman. Many women writers of popular literature after her in the early eighteenth century assumed "scandalous" public roles. Delarivier Manley published transparent fictionalizations of the doings of the Whig nobility, including *The New Atalantis* (1709), while Eliza Haywood produced stories about seduction and sex (though her late works, including *The History of Miss Betsy Thoughtless*, 1751, courted a rising taste for morality). Male defenders of high culture found it easy to denounce these women and their works as affronts simultaneously to sexual decency and good literary taste: Pope's *Dunciad* (1728) awards Haywood as the prize in a pissing contest between scurrilous male booksellers.

Many women writers after mid-century were determined to be more moral than their predecessors. Around 1750, intellectual women established clubs of their own under the leadership of Elizabeth Vesey and Elizabeth Montagu, cousin to Lady Mary. Proclaiming a high religious and intellectual standard, these women came to be called "bluestockings" (after the inelegant worsted hose of an early member). Eminent men joined the bluestockings for literary conversation, including Samuel Johnson, Samuel Richardson, Horace Walpole (novelist, celebrated letter writer, and son of the prime minister), and David Garrick, preeminent actor of his day. The literary accomplishments of bluestockings ranged widely: in 1758 Elizabeth Carter published her translation of the Greek philosopher Epictetus, while Hannah More won fame as a poet, abolitionist, and educational theorist. Some of the most considerable literary achievements of women after mid-century came in the novel, a form increasingly directed at women readers, often exploring the moral difficulties of young women approaching marriage. The satirical novel *The Female Quixote* (1752) by Charlotte Lennox describes one such heroine deluded by the extravagant romances she reads, while Frances Burney's *Evelina* (1778) unfolds the sexual and other dangers besetting its naïve but good-hearted heroine.

Readers' abilities and inclinations to consume literature helped determine the volume and variety of published works. While historians disagree about how exactly the literacy rate changed in Britain through the early modern period, there is widespread consensus that by 1800 between 60 and 70 percent of adult men could read, in contrast to 25 percent in 1600. Since historians use the ability to sign one's name as an indicator of literacy, the evidence is even sketchier for women, who were less often parties to legal contracts: perhaps a third of women could read by the mid-eighteenth century. Reading was commoner among the relatively well off than among the very poor, and among the latter, more prevalent in urban centers than the countryside. Most decisively, cultural commentators throughout the century portrayed literacy as a good in itself: everyone in a Protestant country such as Britain, most thought, would benefit from direct access to the Bible and devotional works, and increasingly employers found literacy among servants and other laborers useful, especially those working in cities. Moral commentators did their best to steer inexperienced readers away from the frivolous and idle realm of popular imaginative literature, though literacy could not but give its new possessors freedom to explore their own tastes and inclinations.

Cost placed another limit on readership: few of the laboring classes would have disposable income to buy a cheap edition of Milton (around two shillings at mid-century) or even a copy of the *Gentleman's Magazine* (six pence), let alone the spare time or sense of entitlement to peruse such things. Nonetheless, reading material was widely shared (Addison optimistically calculated "twenty readers to every paper" of the *Spectator*), and occasionally servants were given access to the libraries of their employers or the rich family of the neighborhood. In the 1740s, circulating libraries began to emerge in cities and towns throughout Britain. Though the yearly fee they usually charged put them beyond the reach of the poor, these libraries gave the middle classes access to a wider array of books than they could afford to assemble on their own. Records of such libraries indicate that travels, histories, letters, and novels were most popular, though patrons borrowed many specialized, technical works as well. One fascinating index of change in the character of the reading public was the very look of words on the page. In the past, printers had rather capriciously capitalized many nouns—words as common as *Wood* or *Happiness*—and frequently italicized various words for emphasis. But around the middle of the eighteenth century, new conventions arose: initial capitals were reserved for proper names, and the use of italics was reduced. Such changes indicate that the reading public was becoming sophisticated enough not to require such overt pointing to the meanings of what they read. The modern, eighteenth-century reader had come to expect that all English writing, no matter how old or new, on any topic, in any genre, would be printed in the same consistent, uncluttered style. No innovation of the eighteenth-century culture of reading more immediately demonstrates its linkage to our own.

LITERARY PRINCIPLES

The literature appearing between 1660 and 1785 divides conveniently into three lesser periods of about forty years each. The first, extending to the death of Dryden in 1700, is characterized by an effort to bring a new refinement to English literature according to sound critical principles of what is fitting and right; the second, ending with the deaths of Pope in 1744 and Swift in 1745, extends that effort to a wider circle of readers, with special satirical attention to what is unfitting and wrong; the third, concluding with the death of Johnson in 1784 and the publication of Cowper's *The Task* in 1785, confronts the old principles with revolutionary ideas that would come to the fore in the Romantic movement of the late eighteenth and early nineteenth centuries.

A sudden change of taste seemed to occur around 1660. The change had been long prepared, however, by a trend in European culture, especially in seventeenth-century France: the desire for an elegant simplicity. Reacting against the difficulty and occasional extravagance of late Renaissance literature, writers and critics called for a new restraint, clarity, regularity, and good sense. Donne's "metaphysics" and Milton's bold storming of heaven, for instance, seemed overdone to some Restoration readers. Hence Dryden and Andrew Marvell both were tempted to revise *Paradise Lost*, smoothing away its sublime but arduous idiosyncrasies. As daring and imaginative as Dryden's verse is, he tempers even its highly dramatic moments with an ease and sense of control definitive of the taste of his times.

This movement produced in France an impressive body of classical literature that distinguished the age of Louis XIV. In England it produced a literature often termed "Augustan," after the writers who flourished during the reign of Augustus Caesar, the first Roman emperor. Rome's Augustan Age reestablished stability after the civil war that followed the assassination of Julius Caesar. Its chief poets, Virgil, Horace, and Ovid, addressed their polished works to a sophisticated aristocracy among whom they looked for patrons. Dryden's generation took advantage of the analogy between post–civil war England and Augustan Rome. Later generations would be suspicious of that analogy; after 1700 most writers stressed that Augustus had been a tyrant who thought himself greater than the law. But in 1660 there was hope that Charles would be a better Augustus, bringing England the civilized virtues of an Augustan age without its vices.

Charles and his followers brought back from exile an admiration of French literature as well as French fashions, and the theoretical "correctness" of such writers as Pierre Corneille, René Rapin, and Nicolas Boileau came into vogue. England also had a native tradition of classicism, derived from Ben Jonson and his followers, whose couplets embodied a refinement Dryden eagerly inherited and helped codify. The effort to formulate rules of good writing appealed to many critics of the age. Even Shakespeare had sometimes been careless; and although writers could not expect to surpass his genius, they might hope to avoid his faults. But "neoclassical" English literature aimed to be not only classical but *new*. Rochester and Dryden drew on literary traditions of variety, humor, and freewheeling fancy represented by Chaucer, Spenser, Shakespeare, Jonson, and Milton to infuse fresh life into Greek or Latin or French classical models.

Above all, the new simplicity of style aimed to give pleasure to readers—to express passions that everyone could recognize in language that everyone could understand. According to Dryden, Donne's amorous verse misguidedly "perplexes the minds of the fair sex with nice speculations of philosophy, when he should engage their hearts, and entertain them with the softnesses of love." Dryden's poems would not make that mistake; like subsequent English critics, he values poetry according to its power to move an audience. Thus Timotheus, in Dryden's "Alexander's Feast," is not only a musician but an archetypal poet who can make Alexander tearful or loving or angry at will. Readers, in turn, were supposed to cooperate with authors through the exercise of their own imaginations, creating pictures in the mind. When Timotheus describes vengeful ghosts holding torches, Alexander hallucinates in response and seizes a torch "with zeal to destroy." Much eighteenth-century poetry demands to be visualized. A phrase from Horace's *Art of Poetry, ut pictura poesis* (as in painting, so in poetry), was interpreted to mean that poetry ought to be a visual as well as verbal art. Pope's "Eloisa to Abelard," for instance, begins by picturing two rival female personifications: "heavenly-pensive contemplation" and "ever-musing melancholy" (in the older typographical style, the nouns would be capitalized). Readers were expected to *see* these figures: Contemplation, in the habit of a nun, whose eyes roll upward toward heaven; and the black goddess Melancholy, in wings and drapery, who broods upon the darkness. These two competing visions fight for Eloisa's soul throughout the poem, which we see entirely through her perspective. Eighteenth-century readers knew how to translate words into pictures, and modern readers can share their pleasure by learning to see poetic images in the mind's eye.

What poets most tried to see and represent was *Nature*—a word of many meanings. The Augustans focused especially on one: Nature as the universal and permanent elements in human experience. External nature, the landscape, attracted attention throughout the eighteenth century as a source of pleasure and an object of inquiry. But as Finch muses on the landscape, in "A Nocturnal Reverie," it is her own soul she discovers. Pope's injunction to the critic, "First follow Nature," has primarily *human* nature in view. Nature consists of the enduring, general truths that have been, are, and will be true for everyone in all times, everywhere. Hence the business of the poet, according to Johnson's *Rasselas,* is "to examine, not the individual, but the species; to remark general properties and large appearances . . . to exhibit in his portraits of nature such prominent and striking features as recall the original to every mind." Yet if human nature was held to be uniform, human beings were known to be infinitely varied. Pope praises Shakespeare's characters as "Nature herself," but continues that "every single character in Shakespeare is as much an individual as those in life itself; it is . . . impossible to find any two alike." The general need not exclude the particular. In *The Vanity of Human Wishes*, Johnson describes the sorrows of an old woman: "Now kindred Merit fills the sable Bier, / Now lacerated Friendship claims a tear." Here "kindred Merit" refers particularly to a worthy relative who has died, and "lacerated Friendship" refers to a friend who has been wasted by violence or disease. Yet Merit and Friendship are also personifications, and the lines imply that the woman may be mourning the passing of goodness like her own or a broken friendship; values and sympathies can die as well as people. This play on words is not a pun. Rather, it indicates a state of mind in which life assumes the form of a perpetual allegory and some abiding truth shines through each circumstance as it passes. The particular is already the general, in good eighteenth-century verse.

To study Nature was also to study the ancients. Nature and Homer, according to Pope, were the same; and both Pope and his readers applied Horace's satires on Rome to their own world, because Horace had expressed the perennial forms of life. Moreover, modern writers could learn from the ancients how to practice their craft. If a poem is an object to be made, the *poet* (a word derived from the Greek for "maker") must make the object to proper specifications. Thus poets were taught to plan their works in one of the classical "kinds" or genres—epic, tragedy, comedy, pastoral, satire, or ode—to choose a language appropriate to that genre, and to select the right style and tone and rhetorical figures. The rules of art, as Pope had said, "are Nature methodized." At the same time, however, writers needed *wit:* quickness of mind, inventiveness, a knack for conceiving images and metaphors and for perceiving resemblances between things apparently unlike. Shakespeare had surpassed the ancients themselves in wit, and no one could deny that Pope was witty. Hence a major project of the age was to combine good method with wit, or judgment with fancy. Nature intended them to be one, and the role of judgment was not to suppress passion, energy, and originality but to make them more effective through discipline: "The winged courser, like a generous horse, / Shows most true mettle when you check his course."

The test of a poet's true mettle is language. When Wordsworth, in the preface to *Lyrical Ballads* (1800), declared that he wrote "in a selection of the language really used by men," he went on to attack eighteenth-century poets for their use of an artificial and stock "poetic diction." Many poets did employ a special language. It is characterized by personification, representing a thing or abstraction in human form, as when an "Ace of Hearts steps forth" or "Melancholy frowns"; by periphrasis (a roundabout way of avoiding homely words: "finny tribes" for *fish*, or "household feathery people" for *chickens*); by stock phrases such as "shining sword," "verdant mead," "bounding main," and "checkered shade"; by words used in their original Latin sense, such as "genial," "gelid," and "horrid"; and by English sentences forced into Latin syntax ("Here rests his head upon the lap of Earth / A youth to Fortune and to Fame unknown," where *youth* is the subject of the verb *rests*). This language originated in the attempt of Renaissance poets to rival the elegant diction of Virgil and other Roman writers, and Milton depended on it to help him obtain "answerable style" for the lofty theme of *Paradise Lost*. When used mechanically it could become a mannerism. But Thomas Gray contrives subtle, expressive effects from artificial diction and syntax, as in the ironic inflation of "Ode on the Death of a Favorite Cat" or a famous stanza from "Elegy Written in a Country Churchyard":

> The boast of heraldry, the pomp of power,
> And all that beauty, all that wealth e'er gave,
> Awaits alike the inevitable hour.
> The paths of glory lead but to the grave.

It is easy to misread the first sentence. What is the subject of *awaits*? The answer must be *hour* (the only available singular noun), which lurks at the end of the sentence, ready to spring a trap not only on the reader but on all those aristocratic, powerful, beautiful, wealthy people who forget that their hour will come. Moreover, the intricacy of that sentence sets off the simplicity of the next, which says the same thing with deadly directness. The artful mix in the "Elegy" of a special poetic language—a language that nobody speaks—with sentiments that everybody feels helps account for the poem's enduring popularity.

Versification also tests a poet's skill. The heroic couplet was brought to such perfection by Pope, Johnson thought, that "to attempt any further improvement of versification will be dangerous." Pope's couplets, in rhymed iambic pentameter, typically present a complete statement, closed by a punctuation mark. Within the binary system of these two lines, a world of distinctions can be compressed. The second line of the couplet might closely parallel the first in structure and meaning, for instance, or the two lines might antithetically play against each other. Similarly, because a slight pause called a "caesura" often divides the typical pentameter line ("Know then thyself, presume not God to scan"), one part of the line can be made parallel with or antithetical to the other or even to one part of the following line. An often quoted and parodied passage of Sir John Denham's "Cooper's Hill" (1642) illustrates these effects. The poem addresses the Thames and builds up a witty comparison between the flow of a river and the flow of verse (italics are added to highlight the terms compared):

	O could I flow like thee, | and make thy stream
Parallelism:	*My great example*, | as it is *my theme!*
Double balance:	Though *deep*, yet *clear*, | though *gentle*, yet not *dull*,
Double balance:	*Strong* without *rage*, | without *o'erflowing*, *full*.

Once Dryden and Pope had bound such passages more tightly together with alliteration and assonance, the typical metrical-rhetorical wit of the new age had been perfected. For most of the eighteenth century its only metrical rival was blank verse: iambic pentameter that does not rhyme and is not closed in couplets. Milton's blank verse in *Paradise Lost* provided one model, and the dramatic blank verse of Shakespeare and Dryden provided another. This more expansive form appealed to poets who cared less for wit than for stories and thoughts with plenty of room to develop. Blank verse was favored as the best medium for descriptive and meditative poems, from Thomson's *Seasons* (1726–30) to Cowper's *The Task* (1785), and the tradition continued in Wordsworth's "Tintern Abbey" and *Prelude*.

Yet not all poets chose to compete with Pope's wit or Milton's heroic striving. Ordinary people also wrote and read verse, and many of them neither knew nor regarded the classics. Only a minority of men, and very few women, had the chance to study Latin and Greek, but that did not keep a good many from playing with verse as a pastime or writing about their own lives. Hence the eighteenth century is the first age to reflect the modern tension between "high" and "low" art. While the heroic couplet was being perfected, doggerel also thrived, and Milton's blank verse was sometimes reduced to describing a drunk or an oyster. Burlesque and broad humor characterize the common run of eighteenth-century verse. As the audience for poetry became more diversified, so did the subject matter. No readership was too small to address; Isaac Watts, and later Anna Laetitia Barbauld and William Blake, wrote songs for children. The rise of unconventional forms and topics of verse subverted an older poetic ideal: the Olympian art that only a handful of the elect could possibly master. The eighteenth century brought poetry down to earth. In the future, art that claimed to be high would have to find ways to distinguish itself from the low.

RESTORATION LITERATURE, 1660–1700

Dryden brought England a *modern* literature between 1660 and 1700. He combined a cosmopolitan outlook on the latest European trends with some of the richness and variety he admired in Chaucer and Shakespeare. In most of the important contemporary forms—occasional verse, comedy, tragedy, heroic play, ode, satire, translation, and critical essay—both his example and his precepts influenced others. As a critic, he spread the word that English literature, particularly his own, could vie with the best of the past. As a translator, he made such classics as Ovid and Virgil available to a wide public; for the first time, a large number of women and men without a formal education could feel included in the literary world.

Restoration prose clearly indicated the desire to reach a new audience. The styles of Donne's sermons, Milton's pamphlets, or Browne's treatises now seemed too elaborate and rhetorical for simple communication. By contrast, Pepys and Behn head straight to the point, informally and unself-consciously. The Royal Society asked its members to employ a plain, utilitarian prose style that spelled out scientific truths; rhetorical flourishes and striking metaphors might be acceptable in poetry, which engaged the emotions, but they had no place in rational discourse. In polite literature, exemplified by Cowley, Dryden, and Sir William Temple, the ideal of good prose came to be a style with the ease and poise of well-bred urbane conversation. This is a social prose for a sociable age. Later, it became the mainstay of essayists like Addison and Steele, of eighteenth-century novelists, and of the host of brilliant eighteenth-century letter writers, including Montagu, Horace Walpole, Gray, Cowper, and Burney, who still give readers the sense of being their intimate friends.

Yet despite its broad appeal to the public, Restoration literature kept its ties to an aristocratic heroic ideal. The "fierce wars and faithful loves" of epic poems were expected to offer patterns of virtue for noble emulation. These ideals lived on in popular French prose romances and in Behn's *Oroonoko*. But the ideal was most fully expressed in heroic plays like those written by Dryden, which push to extremes the conflict between love and honor in the hearts of impossibly valiant heroes and impossibly high-minded and attractive heroines. Dryden's best serious drama, however, was his blank verse tragedy *All for Love* (produced 1677), based on the story of Antony and Cleopatra. Instead of Shakespeare's worldwide panorama, his rapid shifts of scene and complex characters, this version follows the unities of time, place, and action, compressing the plot to the tragic last hours of the lovers. Two other tragic playwrights were celebrated in the Restoration and for a long time to come: Nathaniel Lee (ca. 1649–1692), known for violent plots and wild ranting, and the passionately sensitive Thomas Otway (1652–1685).

But comedy was the real distinction of Restoration drama. The best plays of Sir George Etherege (*The Man of Mode*, 1676), William Wycherley (*The Country Wife*, 1675), Aphra Behn (*The Rover*, 1677), William Congreve (*Love for Love*, 1695; *The Way of the World*, 1700), and later George Farquhar (*The Beaux' Stratagem*, 1707) can still hold the stage today. These "comedies of manners" pick social behavior apart, exposing the nasty struggles for power among the upper classes, who use wit and manners as weapons. Human nature in these plays often conforms to the worst fears of Hobbes; sensual, false-hearted, selfish characters prey on each other. The male hero lives for pleasure and for the money and women that he can conquer. The object of his game of sexual intrigue is a beautiful, witty, pleasure-loving, and emancipated lady, every bit his equal in the strategies of love. What makes the favored couple stand out is the true wit and well-bred grace with which they step through the minefield of the plot. But during the 1690s "Societies for the Reformation of Manners" began to attack the blasphemy and obscenity they detected in such plays, and they sometimes brought offenders to trial. When Dryden died in 1700, a more respectable society was coming into being.

EIGHTEENTH-CENTURY LITERATURE, 1700–1745

Early in the eighteenth century a new and brilliant group of writers emerged: Swift, with *A Tale of a Tub* (1704–10); Addison, with *The Campaign* (1705), a poetic celebration of the battle of Blenheim; Prior, with *Poems on Several Occasions* (1707); Steele, with the *Tatler* (1709); and the youthful Pope, in the same year, with his *Pastorals*. These writers consolidate and popularize the social graces of the previous age. Determined to preserve good sense and civilized values, they turn their wit against fanaticism and innovation. Hence this is a great age of satire. Deeply conservative but also playful, their finest works often cast a strange light on modern times by viewing them through the screen of classical myths and classical forms. Thus Pope exposes the frivolity of fashionable London, in *The Rape of the Lock*, through the incongruity of verse that casts the idle rich as epic heroes. Similarly, Swift uses epic similes to mock the moderns in *The Battle of the Books*, and John Gay's *Trivia, or the Art of Walking the Streets of London* (1716) uses mock georgics to order his tour of the city. Such incongruities are not entirely negative. They also provide a fresh perspective on things that had once seemed too low for poetry to notice—for instance, in *The Rape of the Lock*, a girl putting on her makeup. In this way a parallel with classical literature can show not only how far the modern world has fallen but also how fascinating and magical it is when seen with "quick, poetic eyes."

The Augustans' effort to popularize and enforce high literary and social values was set against the new mass and multiplicity of writings that responded more spontaneously to the expanding commercial possibilities of print. The array of popular prose genres—news, thinly disguised political allegories, biographies of notorious criminals, travelogues, gossip, romantic tales—often blended facts and patently fictional elements, cemented by a rich lode of exaggeration, misrepresentations, and outright lies. Out of this matrix the modern novel would come to be born. The great master of such works was Daniel Defoe, producing first-person accounts such as *Robinson Crusoe* (1719) the famous castaway, or *Moll Flanders* (1722), mistress of lowlife crime. Claims that such works present (as the "editor" of *Crusoe* says) "a just history of fact," believed or not, sharpened the public's avidity for them. Defoe shows his readers a world plausibly like the one they know, where ordinary people negotiate familiar, entangled problems of financial, emotional, and spiritual existence. Jane Barker, Mary Davys, and many others brought women's work and daily lives as well as love affairs to fiction. Such stories were not only amusing but also served as models of conduct; they influenced the stories that real people told about themselves.

The theater also began to change its themes and effects to appeal to a wider audience. The clergyman Jeremy Collier had vehemently taken Dryden, Wycherley, and Congreve to task in *A Short View of the Immorality and Profaneness of the English Stage* (1698), which spoke for the moral outrage of the pious middle classes. The wits retreated. The comedy of manners was replaced by a new kind, later called "sentimental" not only because goodness triumphs over vice but also because it deals in high moral sentiments rather than witty dialogue and because the embarrassments of its heroines and heroes move the audience not to laughter but to tears. Virtue refuses to bow to aristocratic codes. In one crucial scene of Steele's influential play *The Conscious Lovers* (1722) the hero would rather accept dishonor than fight a duel with a friend. Piety and middle-class values typify tragedies such as George Lillo's *London Merchant* (1731). One luxury invented in eighteenth-century Europe was the delicious pleasure of weeping, and comedies as well as tragedies brought that pleasure to playgoers through many decades. Some plays resisted the tide. Gay's cynical *Beggar's Opera* (1728) was a tremendous success, and later in the century the comedies of Goldsmith and Sheridan proved that sentiment is not necessarily an enemy to wit and laughter. (For the complete text of one of Sheridan's best plays, *The School for Scandal*, go to Norton Literature Online.) Yet larger and larger audiences responded more to spectacles and special effects than to sophisticated writing. Although the *stage* prospered during the eighteenth century, and the star system produced idolized actors and actresses (such as David Garrick and Sarah Siddons), the authors of *drama* tended to fade to the background.

Despite the sociable impulses of much the period's writing, readers also craved less crowded, more meditative works. Since the seventeenth century, no poems had been more popular than those about the pleasures of retirement, which invited the reader to dream about a safe retreat in the country or to meditate, like Finch, on scenery and the soul. But after 1726, when Thomson published *Winter*, the first of his cycle on the seasons, the poetry of natural description came into its own. A taste for gentle, picturesque beauty found expression not only in verse but in the elaborate, cultivated art of landscape gardening, and finally in the cherished English art of landscape painting in watercolor or oils (often illustrating Thomson's *Seasons*). Many readers also learned to enjoy a thrilling pleasure or fear in the presence of the sublime in nature: rushing waters, wild prospects, and mountains shrouded in mist. Whether enthusiasts went to the landscape in search of God or merely of heightened sensations, they came back feeling that they had been touched by something beyond the life they knew, by something that could hardly be expressed. Tourists as well as poets roamed the countryside, frequently quoting verse as they gazed at some evocative scene. A partiality for the sublime passed from Thomson to Collins to inspire the poetry of the Romantic age to come.

THE EMERGENCE OF NEW LITERARY THEMES AND MODES, 1740–85

When Matthew Arnold called the eighteenth century an "age of prose," he meant to belittle its poetry, but he also stated a significant fact: great prose does dominate the age. Until the 1740s, poetry tended to set the standards of literature. But the growth of new kinds of prose took the initiative away from verse. Novelists became better known than poets. Intellectual prose also flourished, with the achievements of Johnson in the essay and literary criticism, of Boswell in biography, of Hume in philosophy, of Burke in politics, of Edward Gibbon in history, of Sir Joshua Reynolds in aesthetics, of Gilbert White in natural history, and of Adam Smith in economics. Each of these authors is a master stylist, whose effort to express himself clearly and fully demands an art as carefully wrought as poetry. Other writers of prose were more informal. The memoirs of such women as Laetitia Pilkington, Charlotte Charke, Hester Thrale Piozzi, and Frances Burney bring each reader into their private lives and also remind us that the new print culture created celebrities, who wrote not only about themselves but about other celebrities they knew. The interest of readers in Samuel Johnson helped sell his own books as well as a host of books that quoted his sayings. But the prose of the age also had to do justice to difficult and complicated ideas. An unprecedented effort to formulate the first principles of philosophy, history, psychology, and art required a new style of persuasion.

Johnson helped codify that language, not only with his writings but with the first great English *Dictionary* (1755). This work established him as a national man of letters; eventually the period would be known as "the Age of Johnson." But his dominance was based on an ideal of service to others. The *Dictionary* illustrates its definitions with more than 114,000 quotations from the best English writers, thus building a bridge from past to present usage; and Johnson's essays, poems, and criticism also reflect his desire to preserve the lessons of the past. Yet he looks to the future as well, trying both to reach and to mold a nation of readers. If Johnson speaks for his age, one reason is his faith in common sense and the common reader. "By the common sense of readers uncorrupted with literary prejudices," he wrote in the last of his *Lives of the Poets* (1781), "must be finally decided all claim to poetical honors." A similar respect for the good judgment of ordinary people, and for standards of taste and behavior that anyone can share, marks many writers of the age. Both Burke, the great conservative statesman and author, and Thomas Paine, his radical adversary, proclaim themselves apostles of common sense.

No prose form better united availability to the common reader and seriousness of artistic purpose than the novel in the hands of two of its early masters, Samuel Richardson and Henry Fielding. Like many writers of fiction earlier in the century, Richardson initially did not set out to entertain the public with an avowedly invented tale: he conceived *Pamela, or Virtue Rewarded* (1740) while compiling a little book of model letters. The letters grew into a story about a captivating young servant who resists her master's base designs on her virtue until he gives up and marries her. The combination of a high moral tone with sexual titillation and a minute analysis of the heroine's emotions and state of mind proved irresistible to readers, in Britain and in Europe at large. Richardson topped *Pamela*'s success with *Clarissa* (1747–48), another epistolary novel, which explored the conflict between the libertine Lovelace, an attractive and diabolical aristocrat, and the angelic Clarissa, a middle-class paragon who struggles to stay pure. The sympathy that readers felt for Clarissa was magnified by a host of sentimental novels, including Frances Sheridan's *Memoirs of Miss Sidney Bidulph* (1761), Rousseau's *Julie, or The New Heloise* (1761), and Henry Mackenzie's *The Man of Feeling* (1771).

Henry Fielding made his entrance into the novel by turning *Pamela* farcically upside-down, as the hero of *Joseph Andrews* (1742), Pamela's brother, defends his chastity from the lewd advances of Lady Booby. Fielding's true model, however, is Cervantes's great *Don Quixote* (1605–15), from which he took an ironic, antiromantic style; a plot of wandering around the countryside; and an idealistic central character (Parson Adams) who keeps mistaking appearances for reality. The ambition of writing what Fielding called "a comic epic-poem in prose" went still further in *The History of Tom Jones, A Foundling* (1749). Crowded with incidents and comments on the state of England, the novel contrasts a good-natured, generous, wayward hero (who needs to learn prudence) with cold-hearted people who use moral codes and the law for their own selfish interests. This emphasis on instinctive virtue and vice, instead of Richardson's devotion to good principles, put off respectable readers like Johnson and Burney. But Coleridge thought that *Tom Jones* (along with *Oedipus Rex* and Jonson's *Alchemist*) was one of "the three most perfect plots ever planned."

An age of great prose can burden its poets. To Gray, Collins, Mark Akenside, and the brothers Joseph and Thomas Warton, it seemed that the spirit of poetry might be dying, driven out by the spirit of prose, by uninspiring truth, by the end of superstitions that had once peopled the land with poetic fairies and demons. In an age barren of magic, they ask, where has poetry gone? That question haunts many poems, suffusing them with melancholy. Poets who muse in silence are never far from thoughts of death, and a morbid fascination with suicide and the grave preoccupies many at midcentury. Such an attitude has little in common with that of poets like Dryden and Pope, social beings who live in a crowded world and seldom confess their private feelings in public. Pope's *Essay on Man* had taken a sunny view of providence; Edward Young's *The Complaint: or Night Thoughts on Life, Death, and Immortality* (1742–46), an immensely long poem in blank verse, is darkened by Christian fear of the life to come.

Often the melancholy poet withdraws into himself and yearns to be living in some other time and place. In his "Ode to Fancy" (1746), Joseph Warton associated "fancy" with visions in the wilderness and spontaneous passions; the true poet was no longer defined as a craftsman or maker but as a seer or nature's priest. "The public has seen all that art can do," William Shenstone wrote in 1761, welcoming James Macpherson's *Ossian*, "and they want the more striking efforts of wild, original, enthusiastic genius." Macpherson filled the bill. His primitive, sentimental epics, supposedly translated from an ancient Gaelic warrior-bard, won the hearts of readers around the world; Napoleon and Thomas Jefferson, for instance, both thought that Ossian was greater than Homer. Poets began to cultivate archaic language and antique forms. Inspired by Thomas Percy's edition of *Reliques of Ancient English Poetry* (1765), Thomas Chatterton passed off his own ballads as medieval; he died at seventeen, soon after his forgeries were exposed, but the Romantics later idolized his precocious genius.

The most remarkable consequence of the medieval revival, however, was the invention of the Gothic novel. Horace Walpole set *The Castle of Otranto* (1765), a dreamlike tale of terror, in a simulacrum of Strawberry Hill, his own tiny, pseudo-medieval castle, which helped revive a taste for Gothic architecture. Walpole created a mode of fiction that retains its popularity to the present day. In a typical Gothic romance, amid the glooms and secret passages of some remote castle, the laws of nightmare replace the laws of probability. Forbidden themes—incest, murder, necrophilia, atheism, and the torments of sexual desire—are allowed free play. Most such romances, like William Beckford's *Vathek* (1786) and Matthew Lewis's *The Monk* (1796), revel in sensationalism and the grotesque. The Gothic vogue suggested that classical canons of taste—simplicity and harmonious balance—might count for less than the pleasures of fancy—intricate puzzles and a willful excess. But Gothicism also resulted in works, like Ann Radcliffe's, that temper romance with reality as well as in serious novels of social purpose, like William Godwin's *Caleb Williams* (1794) and Mary Wollstonecraft's *Maria, or The Wrongs of Woman* (1798); and Mary Shelley, the daughter of Wollstonecraft and Godwin, eventually composed a romantic nightmare, *Frankenstein* (1818), that continues to haunt our dreams.

The century abounded in other remarkable experiments in fiction, anticipating many of the forms that novelists still use today. Tobias Smollett's picaresque *Roderick Random* (1748) and *Humphry Clinker* (1771) delight in coarse practical jokes, the freaks and strong odors of life. But the most *novel* novelist of the age was Laurence Sterne, a humorous, sentimental clergyman who loves to play tricks on his readers. *The Life and Opinions of Tristram Shandy* (1760–67) abandons clock time for psychological time, whimsically follows chance associations, interrupts its own stories, violates the conventions of print by putting chapters 18 and 19 after chapter 25, sneaks in double entendres, and seems ready to go on forever. And yet these games get us inside the characters' minds, as if the world were as capricious as our thoughts. Sterne's self-conscious art implies that people's private obsessions shape their lives—or help create reality itself. As unique as Sterne's fictional world is, his interest in private life matched the concerns of the novel toward the end of the century: depictions of characters' intimate feelings dominated the tradition of domestic fiction that included Burney, Radcliffe, and, later, Maria Edgeworth, culminating in the masterworks of Jane Austen. A more "masculine" orientation emerged at the beginning of the next century, as Walter Scott's works, with their broad historical scope and outdoor scenes of men at work and war, appealed to a large readership. Yet the copious, acute, often ironic attention to details of private life by Richardson, Sterne, and Austen continued to influence the novel profoundly through its subsequent history.

CONTINUITY AND REVOLUTION

The history of eighteenth-century literature was first composed by the Romantics, who wrote it to serve their own interests. Prizing originality, they naturally preferred to stress how different they were from writers of the previous age. Later historians have tended to follow their lead, competing to prove that everything changed in 1776, or 1789, or 1798. This revolutionary view of history accounts for what happened to the word *revolution*. The older meaning referred to a movement around a point, a recurrence or cycle, as in the revolutions of the planets; the newer meaning signified a violent break with the past, an overthrow of the existing order, as in the Big Bang or the French Revolution. Romantic rhetoric made heavy use of such dramatic upheavals. Yet every history devoted to truth must take account of both sorts of revolution, of continuities as well as changes. The ideals that many Romantics made their own—the passion for liberty and equality, the founding of justice on individual rights, the distrust of institutions, the love of nature, the reverence for imagination, and even the embrace of change—grew from seeds that had been planted long before. Nor did Augustan literature abruptly vanish on that day in 1798 when Wordsworth and Coleridge anonymously published a small and unsuccessful volume of poems called *Lyrical Ballads*. Even when they rebel against the work of Pope and Johnson and Gray, Romantic writers incorporate much of their language and values.

What Restoration and eighteenth-century literature passed on to the future, in fact, was chiefly a set of unresolved problems. The age of Enlightenment was also, in England, an age that insisted on holding fast to older beliefs and customs; the age of population explosion was also an age of individualism; the age that developed the slave trade was also the age that gave rise to the abolitionist movement; the age that codified rigid standards of conduct for women was also an age when many women took the chance to read and write and think for themselves; the age of reason was also the age when sensibility flourished; the last classical age was also the first modern age. These contradictions are far from abstract; writers were forced to choose their own directions. When young James Boswell looked for a mentor whose biography he might write, he considered not only Samuel Johnson but also David Hume, whose skeptical views of morality, truth, and religion were everything Johnson abhorred. The two writers seem to inhabit different worlds, yet Boswell traveled freely between them. That was exciting and also instructive. "Without Contraries is no progression," according to one citizen of Johnson's London, William Blake, who also thought that "Opposition is true Friendship." Good conversation was a lively eighteenth-century art, and sharp disagreements did not keep people from talking. The conversations the period started have not ended yet.

Additional information about the Restoration and the Eighteenth Century, including primary texts and images, is available at Norton Literature Online (wwnorton.com/nlo). Online topics are

- A Day in Eighteenth-Century London
- Slavery and the Slave Trade in Britain
- The Plurality of Worlds
- Travel, Trade, and the Expansion of Empire

THE RESTORATION AND THE EIGHTEENTH CENTURY

TEXTS	CONTEXTS
1660 Samuel Pepys begins his diary	**1660** Charles II restored to the throne. Reopening of the theaters
1662 Samuel Butler, *Hudibras,* part 1	**1662** Act of Uniformity requires all clergy to obey the Church of England. Chartering of the Royal Society
	1664–66 Great Plague of London
	1666 Fire destroys the City of London
1667 John Milton, *Paradise Lost*	
1668 John Dryden, *Essay of Dramatic Poesy*	**1668** Dryden becomes poet laureate
	1673 Test Act requires all officeholders to swear allegiance to Anglicanism
1678 John Bunyan, *Pilgrim's Progress,* part 1	**1678** The "Popish Plot" inflames anti-Catholic feeling
1681 Dryden, *Absalom and Achitophel*	**1681** Charles II dissolves Parliament
	1685 Death of Charles II. James II, his Catholic brother, takes the throne
1687 Sir Isaac Newton, *Principia Mathematica*	
1688 Aphra Behn, *Oroonoko*	**1688–89** The Glorious Revolution. James II exiled and succeeded by his Protestant daughter, Mary, and her husband, William of Orange
1690 John Locke, *An Essay Concerning Human Understanding*	
1700 William Congreve, *The Way of the World.* Mary Astell, *Some Reflections upon Marriage*	
	1701 War of the Spanish Succession begins
	1702 Death of William III. Succession of Anne (Protestant daughter of James II)
1704 Jonathan Swift, *A Tale of a Tub.* Newton, *Opticks*	
	1707 Act of Union with Scotland
	1710 Tories take power
1711 Alexander Pope, *An Essay on Criticism.* Joseph Addison and Sir Richard Steele, *Spectator* (1711–12, 1714)	
	1713 Treaty of Utrecht ends War of the Spanish Succession
	1714 Death of Queen Anne. George I (great-grandson of James I) becomes the first Hanoverian king. Tory government replaced by Whigs

TEXTS	CONTEXTS
1716 Lady Mary Wortley Montagu writes her letters from Turkey (1716–18)	
1717 Pope, *The Rape of the Lock* (final version)	
1719 Daniel Defoe, *Robinson Crusoe*	
	1720 South Sea Bubble collapses
	1721 Robert Walpole comes to power
1726 Swift, *Gulliver's Travels*	
	1727 George I dies. George II succeeds
1728 John Gay, *The Beggar's Opera*	
1733 Pope, *An Essay on Man*	
	1737 Licensing Act censors the stage
1740 Samuel Richardson, *Pamela*	
1742 Henry Fielding, *Joseph Andrews*	**1742** Walpole resigns
1743 Pope, *The Dunciad* (final version). William Hogarth, *Marriage A-la-Mode*	
1746 William Collins's *Odes*	**1746** Charles Edward Stuart's defeat at Culloden ends the last Jacobite rebellion
1747 Richardson, *Clarissa*	
1749 Fielding, *Tom Jones*	
1751 Thomas Gray, "Elegy Written in a Country Churchyard"	**1751** Robert Clive seizes Arcot, the prelude to English control of India
1755 Samuel Johnson, *Dictionary*	
	1756 Beginning of Seven Years' War
1759 Johnson, *Rasselas*. Voltaire, *Candide*	**1759** James Wolfe's capture of Quebec ensures British control of Canada
1760 Laurence Sterne, *Tristram Shandy* (1760–67)	**1760** George III succeeds to the throne
1765 Johnson's edition of Shakespeare	
	1768 Captain James Cook voyages to Australia and New Zealand
1770 Oliver Goldsmith, "The Deserted Village"	
	1775 American Revolution (1775–83). James Watt produces steam engines
1776 Adam Smith, *The Wealth of Nations*	
1778 Frances Burney, *Evelina*	
1779 Johnson, *Lives of the Poets* (1779–81)	
	1780 Gordon Riots in London
1783 George Crabbe, *The Village*	**1783** William Pitt becomes prime minister
1785 William Cowper, *The Task*	

JOHN DRYDEN
1631–1700

Although John Dryden's parents seem to have sided with Parliament against the king, there is no evidence that the poet grew up in a strict Puritan family. His father, a country gentleman of moderate fortune, gave his son a gentleman's education at Westminster School, under the renowned Dr. Richard Busby, who used the rod as a pedagogical aid in imparting a sound knowledge of the learned languages and literatures to his charges (among others John Locke and Matthew Prior). From Westminster, Dryden went to Trinity College, Cambridge, where he took his A.B. in 1654. His first important poem, "Heroic Stanzas" (1659), was written to commemorate the death of Cromwell. The next year, however, in "Astraea Redux," Dryden joined his countrymen in celebrating the return of Charles II to his throne. During the rest of his life Dryden was to remain entirely loyal to Charles and to his successor, James II.

Dryden is the commanding literary figure of the last four decades of the seventeenth century. Every important aspect of the life of his times—political, religious, philosophical, artistic—finds expression somewhere in his writings. Dryden is the least personal of poets. He is not at all the solitary, subjective poet listening to the murmur of his own voice and preoccupied with his own feelings but rather a citizen of the world commenting publicly on matters of public concern.

From the beginning to the end of his literary career, Dryden's nondramatic poems are most typically occasional poems, which commemorate particular events of a public character—a coronation, a military victory, a death, or a political crisis. Such poems are social and often ceremonial, written not for the self but for the nation. Dryden's principal achievements in this form are the two poems on the king's return and his coronation; *Annus Mirabilis* (1667), which celebrates the English naval victory over the Dutch and the fortitude of the people of London and the king during the Great Fire, both events of that "wonderful year," 1666; the political poems; the lines on the death of Oldham (1684); and odes such as "Alexander's Feast."

Between 1664 and 1681, however, Dryden was mainly a playwright. The newly chartered theaters needed a modern repertory, and he set out to supply the need. Dryden wrote his plays, as he frankly confessed, to please his audiences, which were not heterogeneous like Shakespeare's but were largely drawn from the court and from people of fashion. In the style of the time, he produced rhymed heroic plays, in which incredibly noble heroes and heroines face incredibly difficult choices between love and honor; comedies, in which male and female rakes engage in intrigue and bright repartee; and later, libretti for the newly introduced dramatic form, the opera. His one great tragedy, *All for Love* (1677), in blank verse, adapts Shakespeare's *Antony and Cleopatra* to the unities of time, place, and action. As his *Essay of Dramatic Poesy* (1668) shows, Dryden had studied the works of the great playwrights of Greece and Rome, of the English Renaissance, and of contemporary France, seeking sound theoretical principles on which to construct the new drama that the age demanded. Indeed, his fine critical intelligence always supported his creative powers, and because he took literature seriously and enjoyed discussing it, he became, almost casually, what Samuel Johnson called him: "the father of English criticism." His abilities as both poet and dramatist brought him to the attention of the king, who in 1668 made him poet laureate. Two years later the post of historiographer royal was added to the laureateship at a combined stipend of £200, enough money to live comfortably on.

Between 1678 and 1681, when he was nearing fifty, Dryden discovered his great gift for writing formal verse satire. A quarrel with the playwright Thomas Shadwell prompted the mock-heroic episode "Mac Flecknoe," probably written in 1678 or 1679 but not published until 1682. Out of the stresses occasioned by the Popish Plot (1678) and its political aftermath came his major political satires, *Absalom and Ach-*

itophel (1681), and "The Medal" (1682), his final attack on the villain of *Absalom and Achitophel,* the earl of Shaftesbury. Twenty years' experience as poet and playwright had prepared him technically for the triumph of *Absalom and Achitophel.* He had mastered the heroic couplet, having fashioned it into an instrument suitable in his hands for every sort of discourse from the thrust and parry of quick logical argument, to lyric feeling, rapid narrative, or forensic declamation. Thanks to this long discipline, he was able in one stride to rival the masters of verse satire: Horace, Juvenal, Persius, in ancient Rome, and Boileau, his French contemporary.

The consideration of religious and political questions that the events of 1678–81 forced on Dryden brought a new seriousness to his mind and works. In 1682 he published *Religio Laici,* a poem in which he examined the grounds of his religious faith and defended the middle way of the Anglican Church against the rationalism of Deism on the one hand and the authoritarianism of Rome on the other. But he had moved closer to Rome than he perhaps realized when he wrote the poem. Charles II died in 1685 and was succeeded by his Catholic brother, James II. Within a year Dryden and his two sons converted to Catholicism. Though his enemies accused him of opportunism, he proved his sincerity by his steadfast loyalty to the Roman Church after James abdicated and the Protestant William and Mary came in; as a result he was to lose his offices and their much-needed stipends. From his new position as a Roman Catholic, Dryden wrote in 1687 *The Hind and the Panther,* in which a milk-white Hind (the Roman Church) and a spotted Panther (the Anglican Church) eloquently debate theology. The Hind has the better of the argument, but Dryden already knew that James's policies were failing, and with them the Catholic cause in England.

Dryden was now nearing sixty, with a family to support on a much-diminished income. To earn a living, he resumed writing plays and turned to translations. In 1693 appeared his versions of Juvenal and Persius, with a long dedicatory epistle on satire; and in 1697, his greatest achievement in this mode, the works of Virgil. At the very end, two months before his death, came the *Fables Ancient and Modern,* prefaced by one of the finest of his critical essays and made up of translations from Ovid, Boccaccio, and Chaucer. (For additional works by Dryden, go to Norton Literature Online.)

Dryden's foremost achievement was to bring the pleasures of literature to the ever-increasing reading public of Britain. As a critic and translator, he made many classics available to men and women who lacked a classical education. His canons of taste and theoretical principles would set the standard for the next generation. As a writer of prose, he helped establish a popular new style, shaped to the cadences of good conversation. Johnson praised its apparent artlessness: "every word seems to drop by chance, though it falls into its proper place. Nothing is cold or languid; the whole is airy, animated, and vigorous . . . though all is easy, nothing is feeble; though all seems careless, there is nothing harsh." Although Dryden's plays went out of fashion, his poems did not. His satire inspired the most brilliant verse satirist of the next century, Alexander Pope, and the energy and variety of his metrics launched the long-standing vogue of heroic couplets. Augustan style is at its best in his poems: lively, dignified, precise, and always musical—a flexible instrument of public speech. "By him we were taught *sapere et fari,* to think naturally and express forcibly," Johnson concluded. "What was said of Rome, adorned by Augustus, may be applied by an easy metaphor to English poetry embellished by Dryden, *lateritiam invenit, marmoream reliquit,* he found it brick, and he left it marble."

Absalom and Achitophel

In 1678 a dangerous crisis, both religious and political, threatened to undo the Restoration settlement and to precipitate England once again into civil war. The Popish Plot and its aftermath not only whipped up extreme anti-Catholic passions, but led between 1679 and 1681 to a bitter political struggle between Charles II (whose adherents came to be called Tories) and the earl of Shaftesbury (whose followers were termed Whigs). The issues were nothing less than the prerogatives of the crown and the possible exclusion of the king's Catholic brother, James, duke of York, from his position as heir-presumptive to the throne. Charles's cool courage and brilliant, if unscrupulous, political genius saved the throne for his brother and gave at least temporary peace to his people.

Charles was a Catholic at heart—he received the last rites of that church on his deathbed—and was eager to do what he could do discreetly for the relief of his Catholic subjects, who suffered severe civil and religious disabilities imposed by their numerically superior Protestant compatriots. James openly professed the Catholic religion, an awkward fact politically, for he was next in line of succession because Charles had no legitimate children. The household of the duke, as well as that of Charles's neglected queen, Catherine of Braganza, inevitably became the center of Catholic life and intrigue at court and consequently of Protestant prejudice and suspicion.

No one understood, however, that the situation was explosive until 1678, when Titus Oates (a renegade Catholic convert of infamous character) offered sworn testimony of the existence of a Jesuit plot to assassinate the king, burn London, massacre Protestants, and reestablish the Roman Church.

The country might have kept its head and come to realize (what no historian has doubted) that Oates and his confederates were perjured rascals, as Charles himself quickly perceived. But panic was created by the discovery of the body of a prominent London justice of the peace, Sir Edmund Berry Godfrey, who a few days before had received for safekeeping a copy of Oates's testimony. The murder, immediately ascribed to the Catholics, has never been solved. Fear and indignation reached a hysterical pitch when the seizure of the papers of the duke of York's secretary revealed that he had been in correspondence with the confessor of Louis XIV regarding the reestablishment of the Roman Church in England. Before the terror subsided many innocent men were executed on the increasingly bold and always false evidence of Oates and his accomplices.

The earl of Shaftesbury, the duke of Buckingham, and others quickly took advantage of the situation. With the support of the Commons and the City of London, they moved to exclude the duke of York from the succession. Between 1679 and 1681 Charles and Shaftesbury were engaged in a mighty struggle. The Whigs found a candidate of their own in the king's favorite illegitimate son, the handsome and engaging duke of Monmouth, whom they advanced as a proper successor to his father. They urged Charles to legitimize him, and when he refused, they whispered that there was proof that the king had secretly married Monmouth's mother. The young man allowed himself to be used against his father. He was sent on a triumphant progress through western England, where he was enthusiastically received. Twice an Exclusion Bill nearly passed both houses. But by early 1681 Charles had secured his own position by secretly accepting from Louis XIV a three-year subsidy that made him independent of Parliament, which had tried to force his hand by refusing to vote him funds. He summoned Parliament to meet at Oxford in the spring of 1681, and a few moments after the Commons had passed the Exclusion Bill, in a bold stroke he abruptly dissolved Parliament, which never met again during his reign. Already, as Charles was aware, a reaction had set in against the violence of the Whigs. In midsummer, when he felt it safe to move against his enemies, Shaftesbury was sent to the Tower of London, charged with high treason. In November, the grand jury, packed with Whigs, threw out the indictment, and the earl was free, but his power was broken, and he lived only two more years.

Shortly before the grand jury acted, Dryden published anonymously the first part of *Absalom and Achitophel,* apparently hoping to influence their verdict. The issues in question were grave; the chief actors, the most important men in the realm. Dryden, therefore, could not use burlesque and caricature as had Butler, or the mock heroic as he himself had done in "Mac Flecknoe." Only a heroic style and manner were appropriate to his weighty material, and the poem is most original in its blending of the heroic and the satiric. Dryden's task called for all his tact and literary skill; he had to mention, but to gloss over, the king's faults: his indolence and love of pleasure; his neglect of his wife, and his devotion to his mistresses—conduct that had left him with many children, but no heir except his Catholic brother. He had to deal gently with Monmouth, whom Charles still loved. And he had to present, or appear to present, the king's case objectively.

The remarkable parallels between the rebellion of Absalom against his father King David (2 Samuel 13–18) had already been remarked in sermons, satires, and pamphlets. Dryden took the hint and gave contemporary events a due distance and additional dignity by approaching them indirectly through their biblical analogues. The poem is famous for its brilliant portraits of the king's enemies and friends, but equally admirable are the temptation scene (which, like other passages, is indebted to *Paradise Lost*) and the remarkably astute analysis of the Popish Plot itself.

A second part of *Absalom and Achitophel* appeared in 1682. Most of it is the work of Nahum Tate, but lines 310–509, which include the devastating portraits of Doeg and Og (two Whig poets, Elkanah Settle and Thomas Shadwell), are certainly by Dryden.

Absalom and Achitophel: A Poem

In pious times, ere priestcraft[1] did begin,
Before polygamy was made a sin;
When man on many multiplied his kind,
Ere one to one was cursedly confined;
When nature prompted and no law denied
Promiscuous use of concubine and bride;
Then Israel's monarch after Heaven's own heart,[2]
His vigorous warmth did variously impart
To wives and slaves; and, wide as his command,
Scattered his Maker's image through the land.
Michal,[3] of royal blood, the crown did wear,
A soil ungrateful to the tiller's care:
Not so the rest; for several mothers bore
To godlike David several sons before.
But since like slaves his bed they did ascend,
No true succession could their seed attend.
Of all this numerous progeny was none
So beautiful, so brave, as Absalom:[4]
Whether, inspired by some diviner lust,
His father got him with a greater gust,° *relish, pleasure*
Or that his conscious destiny made way,
By manly beauty, to imperial sway.
Early in foreign fields he won renown,
With kings and states allied to Israel's crown:[5]
In peace the thoughts of war he could remove,

1. "Religious frauds; management of wicked priests to gain power" (Johnson's *Dictionary*).
2. David ("a man after [God's] own heart," according to 1 Samuel 13.14) represents Charles II.
3. One of David's wives, who represents the childless queen, Catherine of Braganza.
4. James Scott, duke of Monmouth (1649–1685).
5. Monmouth had won repute as a soldier fighting for France against Holland and for Holland against France.

And seemed as he were only born for love.
Whate'er he did, was done with so much ease,
In him alone 'twas natural to please;
His motions all accompanied with grace;
And paradise was opened in his face.
With secret joy indulgent David viewed
His youthful image in his son renewed:
To all his wishes nothing he denied;
And made the charming Annabel[6] his bride.
What faults he had (for who from faults is free?)
His father could not, or he would not see.
Some warm excesses which the law forbore,
Were cònstrued youth that purged by boiling o'er:
And Amnon's murther,[7] by a specious name,
Was called a just revenge for injured fame.
Thus praised and loved the noble youth remained,
While David, undisturbed, in Sion° reigned. *London*
But life can never be sincerely° blest; *wholly*
Heaven punishes the bad, and proves° the best. *tests*
The Jews,° a headstrong, moody, murmuring race, *English*
As ever tried the extent and stretch of grace;
God's pampered people, whom, debauched with ease,
No king could govern, nor no God could please
(Gods they had tried of every shape and size
That god-smiths could produce, or priests devise);[8]
These Adam-wits, too fortunately free,
Began to dream they wanted liberty;[9]
And when no rule, no precedent was found,
Of men by laws less circumscribed and bound,
They led their wild desires to woods and caves,
And thought that all but savages were slaves.
They who, when Saul was dead, without a blow,
Made foolish Ishbosheth[1] the crown forgo;
Who banished David did from Hebron[2] bring,
And with a general shout proclaimed him king:
Those very Jews, who, at their very best,
Their humor° more than loyalty expressed, *caprice*
Now wondered why so long they had obeyed
An idol monarch, which their hands had made;
Thought they might ruin him they could create,
Or melt him to that golden calf,[3] a state.° *republic*
But these were random bolts;° no formed design *shots*
Nor interest made the factious crowd to join:

6. Anne Scott, duchess of Buccleuch (pronounced *Bue-cloo*), a beauty and a great heiress.
7. Absalom killed his half-brother Amnon, who had raped Absalom's sister Tamar (2 Samuel 13.28–29). The parallel with Monmouth is vague. He is known to have committed acts of violence in his youth, but certainly not fratricide.
8. Dryden recalls the political and religious controversies that, since the Reformation, had divided England and finally caused civil wars.
9. Adam rebelled because he felt that he lacked ("wanted") liberty, because he was forbidden to eat the fruit of one tree.
1. Saul's son. He stands for Richard Cromwell, who succeeded his father as lord protector. "Saul": Oliver Cromwell.
2. Where David reigned over Judah after the death of Saul and before he became king of Israel (2 Samuel 1–5). Charles had been crowned in Scotland in 1651.
3. The image worshiped by the children of Israel during the period that Moses spent on Mount Sinai, receiving the law from God.

The sober part of Israel, free from stain,
Well knew the value of a peaceful reign;
And, looking backward with a wise affright,
Saw seams of wounds, dishonest° to the sight: *disgraceful*
In contemplation of whose ugly scars
They cursed the memory of civil wars.
The moderate sort of men, thus qualified,° *assuaged*
Inclined the balance to the better side;
And David's mildness managed it so well,
The bad found no occasion to rebel.
But when to sin our biased[4] nature leans,
The careful Devil is still at hand with means;
And providently pimps for ill desires:
The Good Old Cause[5] revived, a plot requires.
Plots, true or false, are necessary things,
To raise up commonwealths and ruin kings.
The inhabitants of old Jerusalem
Were Jebusites;[6] the town so called from them;
And theirs the native right.
But when the chosen people° grew more strong, *Protestants*
The rightful cause at length became the wrong;
And every loss the men of Jebus bore,
They still were thought God's enemies the more.
Thus worn and weakened, well or ill content,
Submit they must to David's government:
Impoverished and deprived of all command,
Their taxes doubled as they lost their land;
And, what was harder yet to flesh and blood,
Their gods disgraced, and burnt like common wood.[7]
This set the heathen priesthood° in a flame; *Roman Catholic clergy*
For priests of all religions are the same:
Of whatsoe'er descent their godhead be,
Stock, stone, or other homely pedigree,
In his defense his servants are as bold,
As if he had been born of beaten gold.
The Jewish rabbins,° though their enemies, *Anglican clergy*
In this conclude them honest men and wise:
For 'twas their duty, all the learned think,
To espouse his cause, by whom they eat and drink.
From hence began that Plot, the nation's curse,
Bad in itself, but represented worse;
Raised in extremes, and in extremes decried;
With oaths affirmed, with dying vows denied;
Not weighed or winnowed by the multitude;
But swallowed in the mass, unchewed and crude.
Some truth there was, but dashed° and brewed with lies, *adulterated*
To please the fools, and puzzle all the wise.
Succeeding times did equal folly call,
Believing nothing, or believing all.

4. Inclined (cf. "Mac Flecknoe," line 189 and n. 5, p. 910).
5. The Commonwealth. Dryden stigmatizes the Whigs by associating them with subversion.
6. Roman Catholics. The original name of Jerusalem (here, London) was Jebus.
7. Such oppressive laws against Roman Catholics date from the time of Elizabeth I.

The Egyptian rites the Jebusites embraced,
Where gods were recommended by their taste.[8]
Such savory deities must needs be good,
As served at once for worship and for food.
By force they could not introduce these gods,
For ten to one in former days was odds;
So fraud was used (the sacrificer's trade):
Fools are more hard to conquer than persuade.
Their busy teachers mingled with the Jews,
And raked for converts even the court and stews:° *brothels*
Which Hebrew priests the more unkindly took,
Because the fleece accompanies the flock.[9]
Some thought they God's anointed° meant to slay *the king*
By guns, invented since full many a day:
Our author swears it not; but who can know
How far the Devil and Jebusites may go?
This Plot, which failed for want of common sense,
Had yet a deep and dangerous consequence:
For, as when raging fevers boil the blood,
The standing lake soon floats into a flood,
And every hostile humor,[1] which before
Slept quiet in its channels, bubbles o'er;
So several factions from this first ferment
Work up to foam, and threat the government.
Some by their friends, more by themselves thought wise,
Opposed the power to which they could not rise.
Some had in courts been great, and thrown from thence,
Like fiends were hardened in impenitence;
Some, by their monarch's fatal mercy, grown
From pardoned rebels kinsmen to the throne,
Were raised in power and public office high;
Strong bands, if bands ungrateful men could tie.

Of these the false Achitophel[2] was first;
A name to all succeeding ages cursed:
For close designs, and crooked counsels fit;
Sagacious, bold, and turbulent of wit;° *unruly imagination*
Restless, unfixed in principles and place;
In power unpleased, impatient of disgrace:
A fiery soul, which, working out its way,
Fretted the pygmy body to decay,
And o'er-informed the tenement of clay.[3]
A daring pilot in extremity;
Pleased with the danger, when the waves went high,

8. Here Dryden sneers at the doctrine of transubstantiation. "Egyptian": French, therefore Catholic.
9. Dryden charges that the Anglican clergy ("Hebrew priests") resented proselytizing by Catholics chiefly because they stood to lose their tithes ("fleece").
1. Bodily fluid. Such fluids were thought to determine health and temperament.
2. Anthony Ashley Cooper, first earl of Shaftesbury (1621–1683). He had served in the parliamentary army and been a member of Cromwell's council of state. He later helped bring back Charles and, in 1670, was made a member of the notorious Cabal Ministry, which formed an alliance with Louis XIV in which England betrayed her ally, Holland, and joined France in war against that country. In 1672 he became lord chancellor, but with the dissolution of the cabal in 1673, he was removed from office. Lines 146–49 apply perfectly to him.
3. The soul is thought of as the animating principle, the force that puts the body in motion. Shaftesbury's body seemed too small to house his fiery, energetic soul.

He sought the storms; but, for a calm unfit,
Would steer too nigh the sands, to boast his wit.
Great wits° are sure to madness near allied,[4] *men of genius*
And thin partitions do their bounds divide;
Else why should he, with wealth and honor blest,
Refuse his age the needful hours of rest?
Punish a body which he could not please;
Bankrupt of life, yet prodigal of ease?
And all to leave what with his toil he won,
To that unfeathered two-legged thing,[5] a son;
Got, while his soul did huddled° notions try; *confused, hurried*
And born a shapeless lump, like anarchy.
In friendship false, implacable in hate,
Resolved to ruin or to rule the state.
To compass this the triple bond[6] he broke,
The pillars of the public safety shook,
And fitted Israel for a foreign yoke;
Then seized with fear, yet still affecting fame,
Usurped a patriot's all-atoning name.
So easy still it proves in factious times,
With public zeal to cancel private crimes.
How safe is treason, and how sacred ill,
Where none can sin against the people's will!
Where crowds can wink, and no offense be known,
Since in another's guilt they find their own!
Yet fame deserved, no enemy can grudge;
The statesman we abhor, but praise the judge.
In Israel's courts ne'er sat an Abbethdin[7]
With more discerning eyes, or hands more clean;
Unbribed, unsought, the wretched to redress;
Swift of dispatch, and easy of access.
Oh, had he been content to serve the crown,
With virtues only proper to the gown° *judge's robe*
Or had the rankness of the soil been freed
From cockle,° that oppressed the noble seed; *weeds*
David for him his tuneful harp had strung,
And Heaven had wanted one immortal song.[8]
But wild Ambition loves to slide, not stand,
And Fortune's ice prefers to Virtue's land.
Achitophel, grown weary to possess
A lawful fame, and lazy happiness,
Disdained the golden fruit to gather free,
And lent the crowd his arm to shake the tree.
Now, manifest of° crimes contrived long since, *detected in*
He stood at bold defiance with his prince;

4. That genius and madness are akin is a very old idea.
5. Cf. Plato's definition of a human: "a featherless biped."
6. The triple alliance of England, Sweden, and Holland against France, 1668. Shaftesbury helped bring about the war against Holland in 1672.
7. The chief of the seventy elders who composed the Jewish supreme court. The allusion is to Shaftesbury's serving as lord chancellor from 1672 to 1673. Dryden's praise of Shaftesbury's integrity in this office, by suggesting a balanced judgment, makes his condemnation of the statesman more effective than it might otherwise have been.
8. I.e., David would have had occasion to write one fewer song of praise to heaven. The reference may be to 2 Samuel 22 or to Psalm 4.

Held up the buckler of the people's cause
Against the crown, and skulked behind the laws.
The wished occasion of the Plot he takes;
Some circumstances finds, but more he makes.
By buzzing emissaries fills the ears
Of listening crowds with jealousies° and fears *suspicions*
Of arbitrary counsels brought to light,
And proves the king himself a Jebusite.
Weak arguments! which yet he knew full well
Were strong with people easy to rebel.
For, governed by the moon, the giddy Jews
Tread the same track when she the prime renews;
And once in twenty years, their scribes record,[9]
By natural instinct they change their lord.
Achitophel still wants a chief, and none
Was found so fit as warlike Absalom:
Not that he wished his greatness to create
(For politicians neither love nor hate),
But, for he knew his title not allowed,
Would keep him still depending on the crowd,
That° kingly power, thus ebbing out, might be *so that*
Drawn to the dregs of a democracy.[1]
Him he attempts with studied arts to please,
And sheds his venom in such words as these:
"Auspicious prince, at whose nativity
Some royal planet[2] ruled the southern sky;
Thy longing country's darling and desire;
Their cloudy pillar and their guardian fire:
Their second Moses, whose extended wand
Divides the seas, and shows the promised land;[3]
Whose dawning day in every distant age
Has exercised the sacred prophet's rage:
The people's prayer, the glad diviners' theme,
The young men's vision, and the old men's dream![4]
Thee, savior, thee, the nation's vows[5] confess,
And, never satisfied with seeing, bless:
Swift unbespoken° pomps thy steps proclaim, *spontaneous*
And stammering babes are taught to lisp thy name.
How long wilt thou the general joy detain,
Starve and defraud the people of thy reign?
Content ingloriously to pass thy days
Like one of Virtue's fools that feeds on praise;
Till thy fresh glories, which now shine so bright,
Grow stale and tarnish with our daily sight.

9. The moon "renews her prime" when its several phases recur on the same day of the solar calendar (i.e., complete a cycle) as happens approximately every twenty years. The crisis between Charles I and Parliament began to grow acute about 1640; Charles II returned in 1660; it is now 1680 and a full cycle has been completed.
1. I.e., mob rub. To Dryden, *democracy* meant popular government.
2. A planet whose influence destines him to kingship.
3. After their exodus from Egypt under the leadership of Moses, whose "extended wand" separated the waters of the Red Sea so that they crossed over on dry land, the Israelites were led in their forty-year wandering in the wilderness by a pillar of cloud by day and a pillar of fire by night (Exodus 13–14).
4. Cf. Joel 2.28.
5. Solemn promises of fidelity.

Believe me, royal youth, thy fruit must be
Or gathered ripe, or rot upon the tree.
Heaven has to all allotted, soon or late,
Some lucky revolution of their fate;
Whose motions if we watch and guide with skill
(For human good depends on human will),
Our Fortune rolls as from a smooth descent,
And from the first impression takes the bent;
But, if unseized, she glides away like wind,
And leaves repenting Folly far behind.
Now, now she meets you with a glorious prize,
And spreads her locks before her as she flies.[6]
Had thus old David, from whose loins you spring,
Not dared, when Fortune called him, to be king,
At Gath[7] an exile he might still remain,
And heaven's anointing[8] oil had been in vain.
Let his successful youth your hopes engage;
But shun the example of declining age;
Behold him setting in his western skies,
The shadows lengthening as the vapors rise.
He is not now, as when on Jordan's sand[9]
The joyful people thronged to see him land,
Covering the beach, and blackening all the strand;
But, like the Prince of Angels, from his height
Comes tumbling downward with diminished light;[1]
Betrayed by one poor plot to public scorn
(Our only blessing since his cursed return),
Those heaps of people which one sheaf did bind,
Blown off and scattered by a puff of wind.
What strength can he to your designs oppose,
Naked of friends, and round beset with foes?
If Pharaoh's[2] doubtful succor he should use,
A foreign aid would more incense the Jews:
Proud Egypt would dissembled friendship bring;
Foment the war, but not support the king:
Nor would the royal party e'er unite
With Pharaoh's arms to assist the Jebusite;
Or if they should, their interest soon would break,
And with such odious aid make David weak.
All sorts of men by my successful arts,
Abhorring kings, estrange their altered hearts
From David's rule: and 'tis the general cry,
'Religion, commonwealth, and liberty.'[3]
If you, as champion of the public good,
Add to their arms a chief of royal blood,

6. Achitophel gives to Fortune the traditional attributes of the allegorical personification of Opportunity: bald except for a forelock, she can be seized only as she approaches.
7. Brussels, where Charles spent his last years in exile. David took refuge from Saul in Gath (1 Samuel 27.4).
8. After God rejected Saul, he sent Samuel to anoint the boy David, as a token that he should finally come to the throne (1 Samuel 16.1–13).
9. The seashore at Dover, where Charles landed (May 25, 1660).
1. Cf. the fall of Satan in *Paradise Lost* 1.50–124, which dims the brightness of the archangel. The choice of the undignified word *tumbling* is deliberate.
2. Pharaoh is Louis XIV of France.
3. Cf. line 82 and n. 5.

What may not Israel hope, and what applause
Might such a general gain by such a cause?
Not barren praise alone, that gaudy flower
Fair only to the sight, but solid power;
And nobler is a limited command,
Given by the love of all your native land,
Than a successive title,[4] long and dark,
Drawn from the moldy rolls of Noah's ark."
  What cannot praise effect in mighty minds,
When flattery soothes, and when ambition blinds!
Desire of power, on earth a vicious weed,
Yet, sprung from high, is of celestial seed:
In God 'tis glory; and when men aspire,
'Tis but a spark too much of heavenly fire.
The ambitious youth, too covetous of fame,
Too full of angels' metal[5] in his frame,
Unwarily was led from virtue's ways,
Made drunk with honor, and debauched with praise.
Half loath, and half consenting to the ill
(For loyal blood within him struggled still),
He thus replied: "And what pretense have I
To take up arms for public liberty?
My father governs with unquestioned right;
The faith's defender, and mankind's delight,
Good, gracious, just, observant of the laws:
And heaven by wonders has espoused his cause.
Whom has he wronged in all his peaceful reign?
Who sues for justice to his throne in vain?
What millions has he pardoned of his foes,
Whom just revenge did to his wrath expose?
Mild, easy, humble, studious of our good,
Inclined to mercy, and averse from blood;
If mildness ill with stubborn Israel suit,
His crime is God's beloved attribute.
What could he gain, his people to betray,
Or change his right for arbitrary sway?
Let haughty Pharaoh curse with such a reign
His fruitful Nile, and yoke a servile train.
If David's rule Jerusalem displease,
The Dog Star[6] heats their brains to this disease.
Why then should I, encouraging the bad,
Turn rebel and run popularly mad?
Were he a tyrant, who, by lawless might
Oppressed the Jews, and raised the Jebusite,
Well might I mourn; but nature's holy bands
Would curb my spirits and restrain my hands:
The people might assert° their liberty, *claim*
But what was right in them were crime in me.

4. A title to the crown based on succession.

5. An alternative spelling of *mettle* (i.e., spirit). But a pun on *metal* is intended, as is obvious from the pun *angel* (a purely intellectual being and a coin). Ambition caused the revolt of the angels in heaven.

6. Sirius, which in midsummer rises and sets with the sun and is thus associated with the maddening heat of the "dog days."

His favor leaves me nothing to require,
Prevents my wishes, and outruns desire.
What more can I expect while David lives?
All but his kingly diadem he gives:
And that"—But there he paused; then sighing, said—
"Is justly destined for a worthier head.
For when my father from his toils shall rest
And late augment the number of the blest,
His lawful issue shall the throne ascend,
Or the collateral line,[7] where that shall end.
His brother, though oppressed with vulgar spite,[8]
Yet dauntless, and secure of native right,
Of every royal virtue stands possessed;
Still dear to all the bravest and the best.
His courage foes, his friends his truth proclaim;
His loyalty the king, the world his fame.
His mercy even the offending crowd will find,
For sure he comes of a forgiving kind.[9]
Why should I then repine at heaven's decree,
Which gives me no pretense to royalty?
Yet O that fate, propitiously inclined,
Had raised my birth, or had debased my mind;
To my large soul not all her treasure lent,
And then betrayed it to a mean descent!
I find, I find my mounting spirits bold,
And David's part disdains my mother's mold.
Why am I scanted by a niggard birth?[1]
My soul disclaims the kindred of her earth;
And, made for empire, whispers me within,
'Desire of greatness is a godlike sin.' "
  Him staggering so when hell's dire agent found,
While fainting Virtue scarce maintained her ground,
He pours fresh forces in, and thus replies:
  "The eternal god, supremely good and wise,
Imparts not these prodigious gifts in vain:
What wonders are reserved to bless your reign!
Against your will, your arguments have shown,
Such virtue's only given to guide a throne.
Not that your father's mildness I contemn,
But manly force becomes the diadem.
'Tis true he grants the people all they crave;
And more, perhaps, than subjects ought to have:
For lavish grants suppose a monarch tame,
And more his goodness than his wit° proclaim. *intelligence*
But when should people strive their bonds to break,
If not when kings are negligent or weak?
Let him give on till he can give no more,
The thrifty Sanhedrin[2] shall keep him poor;

7. In the event of Charles's dying without legitimate issue, the throne would constitutionally pass to his brother, James, or his descendants, the "collateral line."
8. Anger of the common people.
9. Race, in the sense of family.
1. I.e., why does my mean birth impose such limits on me?
2. The highest judicial counsel of the Jews, here, Parliament.

And every shekel which he can receive,
Shall cost a limb of his prerogative.[3]
To ply him with new plots shall be my care;
Or plunge him deep in some expensive war;
Which when his treasure can no more supply,
He must, with the remains of kingship, buy.
His faithful friends our jealousies and fears
Call Jebusites, and Pharaoh's pensioners;
Whom when our fury from his aid has torn,
He shall be naked left to public scorn.
The next successor, whom I fear and hate,
My arts have made obnoxious to the state;
Turned all his virtues to his overthrow,
And gained our elders[4] to pronounce a foe.
His right, for sums of necessary gold,
Shall first be pawned, and afterward be sold;
Till time shall ever-wanting David draw,
To pass your doubtful title into law:
If not, the people have a right supreme
To make their kings; for kings are made for them.
All empire is no more than power in trust,
Which, when resumed,° can be no longer just. *taken back*
Succession, for the general good designed,
In its own wrong a nation cannot bind;
If altering that the people can relieve,
Better one suffer than a nation grieve.
The Jews well know their power: ere Saul they chose,[5]
God was their king, and God they durst depose.
Urge now your piety,[6] your filial name,
A father's right and fear of future fame;
The public good, that universal call,
To which even heaven submitted, answers all.
Nor let his love enchant your generous mind;
'Tis Nature's trick to propagate her kind.
Our fond begetters, who would never die,
Love but themselves in their posterity.
Or let his kindness by the effects be tried,
Or let him lay his vain pretense aside.
God said he loved your father; could he bring
A better proof than to anoint him king?
It surely showed he loved the shepherd well,
Who gave so fair a flock as Israel.
Would David have you thought his darling son?
What means he then, to alienate[7] the crown?
The name of godly he may blush to bear:

3. The Whigs hoped to limit the special privileges of the Crown (the royal "prerogative") by refusing to vote money to Charles. He circumvented them by living on French subsidies and refusing to summon Parliament.
4. The chief magistrates and rulers of the Jews. Shaftesbury had won over ("gained") country gentlemen and nobles to his hostile view of James.
5. Before Saul, the first king of Israel, came to the throne, the Jews were governed by judges. Similarly Oliver Cromwell as lord protector took over the reins of government, after he had dissolved the Rump Parliament in 1653.
6. Dutifulness to a parent.
7. In law, to convey the title to property to another person.

'Tis after God's own heart[8] to cheat his heir.
He to his brother gives supreme command;
To you a legacy of barren land,[9]
Perhaps the old harp, on which he thrums his lays,
Or some dull Hebrew ballad in your praise.
Then the next heir, a prince severe and wise,
Already looks on you with jealous eyes;
Sees through the thin disguises of your arts,
And marks your progress in the people's hearts.
Though now his mighty soul its grief contains,
He meditates revenge who least complains;
And, like a lion, slumbering in the way,
Or sleep dissembling, while he waits his prey,
His fearless foes within his distance draws,
Constrains his roaring, and contracts his paws;
Till at the last, his time for fury found,
He shoots with sudden vengeance from the ground;
The prostrate vulgar° passes o'er and spares, *common people*
But with a lordly rage his hunters tears.
Your case no tame expedients will afford:
Resolve on death, or conquest by the sword,
Which for no less a stake than life you draw;
And self-defense is nature's eldest law.
Leave the warm people no considering time;
For then rebellion may be thought a crime.
Prevail yourself of what occasion gives,
But try your title while your father lives;
And that your arms may have a fair pretense,° *pretext*
Proclaim you take them in the king's defense;
Whose sacred life each minute would expose
To plots, from seeming friends, and secret foes.
And who can sound the depth of David's soul?
Perhaps his fear his kindness may control.
He fears his brother, though he loves his son,
For plighted vows too late to be undone.
If so, by force he wishes to be gained,
Like women's lechery, to seem constrained.° *forced*
Doubt not; but when he most affects the frown,
Commit a pleasing rape upon the crown.
Secure his person to secure your cause:
They who possess the prince, possess the laws."
He said, and this advice above the rest
With Absalom's mild nature suited best:
Unblamed of life (ambition set aside),
Not stained with cruelty, nor puffed with pride,
How happy had he been, if destiny
Had higher placed his birth, or not so high!
His kingly virtues might have claimed a throne,
And blest all other countries but his own.
But charming greatness since so few refuse,
'Tis juster to lament him than accuse.

8. An irony (cf. line 7 and n. 2).
9. James was given the title of generalissimo in 1678. In 1679 Monmouth was banished and withdrew to Holland.

Strong were his hopes a rival to remove,
With blandishments to gain the public love;
To head the faction while their zeal was hot,
And popularly prosecute the Plot.
To further this, Achitophel unites
The malcontents of all the Israelites;
Whose differing parties he could wisely join,
For several ends, to serve the same design:
The best (and of the princes some were such),
Who thought the power of monarchy too much;
Mistaken men, and patriots in their hearts;
Not wicked, but seduced by impious arts.
By these the springs of property were bent,
And wound so high, they cracked the government.
The next for interest sought to embroil the state,
To sell their duty at a dearer rate;
And make their Jewish markets of the throne,
Pretending public good, to serve their own.
Others thought kings an useless heavy load,
Who cost too much, and did too little good.
These were for laying honest David by,
On principles of pure good husbandry.° *economy*
With them joined all the haranguers of the throng,
That thought to get preferment by the tongue.
Who follow next, a double danger bring,
Not only hating David, but the king:
The Solymaean rout,[1] well-versed of old
In godly faction, and in treason bold;
Cowering and quaking at a conqueror's sword,
But lofty to a lawful prince restored;
Saw with disdain an ethnic[2] plot begun,
And scorned by Jebusites to be outdone.
Hot Levites[3] headed these; who, pulled before
From the ark, which in the Judges' days they bore,
Resumed their cant, and with a zealous cry
Pursued their old beloved theocracy:
Where Sanhedrin and priest enslaved the nation,
And justified their spoils by inspiration:
For who so fit for reign as Aaron's race,[4]
If once dominion they could found in grace?
These led the pack; though not of surest scent,
Yet deepest-mouthed[5] against the government.
A numerous host of dreaming saints[6] succeed,
Of the true old enthusiastic breed:

1. I.e., London rabble. Solyma was a name for Jerusalem.
2. Gentile; here, Roman Catholic.
3. I.e., Presbyterian clergymen. The tribe of Levi, assigned to duties in the tabernacle, carried the Ark of the Covenant during the forty-year sojourn in the wilderness (Numbers 4). Under the Commonwealth ("in the Judges' days") Presbyterianism became the state religion, and its clergy, therefore, "bore the ark." The Act of Uniformity (1662) forced the Presbyterian clergy out of their livings: in short, before the Popish Plot, they had been "pulled from the ark." They are represented here as joining the Whigs in the hope of restoring the commonwealth, "their old beloved theocracy."
4. Priests had to be descendants of Aaron (Exodus 28.1, Numbers 18.7).
5. Loudest. The phrase is applied to hunting dogs. "Pack" and "scent" sustain the image.
6. Term used by certain Dissenters for those elected to salvation. The extreme fanaticism of the "saints" and their claims to inspiration are characterized as a form of religious madness ("enthusiastic," line 530).

'Gainst form and order they their power employ,
Nothing to build, and all things to destroy.
But far more numerous was the herd of such,
Who think too little, and who talk too much.
These out of mere instinct, they knew not why,
Adored their fathers' God and property;
And, by the same blind benefit of fate,
The Devil and the Jebusite did hate:
Born to be saved, even in their own despite,
Because they could not help believing right.
Such were the tools; but a whole Hydra more
Remains, of sprouting heads too long to score.° *count*
Some of their chiefs were princes of the land:
In the first rank of these did Zimri[7] stand;
A man so various, that he seemed to be
Not one, but all mankind's epitome:
Stiff in opinions, always in the wrong;
Was everything by starts, and nothing long;
But, in the course of one revolving moon,
Was chymist,° fiddler, statesman, and buffoon: *chemist*
Then all for women, painting, rhyming, drinking,
Besides ten thousand freaks that died in thinking.
Blest madman, who could every hour employ,
With something new to wish, or to enjoy!
Railing° and praising were his usual themes; *reviling, abusing*
And both (to show his judgment) in extremes:
So over-violent, or over-civil,
That every man, with him, was God or Devil.
In squandering wealth was his peculiar art:
Nothing went unrewarded but desert.
Beggared by fools, whom still° he found° too late, *constantly / found out*
He had his jest, and they had his estate.
He laughed himself from court; then sought relief
By forming parties, but could ne'er be chief;
For, spite of him, the weight of business fell
On Absalom and wise Achitophel:
Thus, wicked but in will, of means bereft,
He left not faction, but of that was left.
  Titles and names 'twere tedious to rehearse
Of lords, below the dignity of verse.
Wits, warriors, Commonwealth's men, were the best;
Kind husbands, and mere nobles, all the rest.
And therefore, in the name of dullness, be
The well-hung Balaam and cold Caleb, free;
And canting Nadab let oblivion damn,
Who made new porridge for the paschal lamb.[8]

7. George Villiers, second duke of Buckingham (1628–1687), wealthy, brilliant, dissolute, and unstable. He had been an influential member of the cabal, but after 1673 had joined Shaftesbury in opposition to the court party. This is the least political of the satirical portraits in the poem. Buckingham had been the chief author of *The Rehearsal* (1671), the play that satirized heroic tragedy and ridiculed Dryden in the character of Mr. Bayes. Politics gave Dryden an opportunity to retaliate. He comments on this portrait in his "A Discourse Concerning the Original and Progress of Satire." Dryden had two biblical Zimris in mind: the Zimri destroyed for his lustfulness and blasphemy (Numbers 25) and the conspirator and regicide of 1 Kings 16.8–20 and 2 Kings 9.31.

8. The lamb slain during Passover; here, Christ. The identities of Balaam, Caleb, and Nadab have

Let friendship's holy band some names assure;
Some their own worth, and some let scorn secure.
Nor shall the rascal rabble here have place,
Whom kings no titles gave, and God no grace:
Not bull-faced Jonas,[9] who could statutes draw
To mean rebellion, and make treason law.
But he, though bad, is followed by a worse,
The wretch who heaven's anointed dared to curse:
Shimei,[1] whose youth did early promise bring
Of zeal to God and hatred to his king,
Did wisely from expensive sins refrain,
And never broke the Sabbath, but for gain;
Nor ever was he known an oath to vent,
Or curse, unless against the government.
Thus heaping wealth, by the most ready way
Among the Jews, which was to cheat and pray,
The city, to reward his pious hate
Against his master, chose him magistrate.
His hand a vare° of justice did uphold; *staff*
His neck was loaded with a chain of gold.
During his office, treason was no crime;
The sons of Belial[2] had a glorious time;
For Shimei, though not prodigal of pelf,
Yet loved his wicked neighbor as himself.
When two or three were gathered to declaim
Against the monarch of Jerusalem,
Shimei was always in the midst of them;
And if they cursed the king when he was by,
Would rather curse than break good company.
If any durst his factious friends accuse,
He packed a jury of dissenting Jews;
Whose fellow-feeling in the godly cause
Would free the suffering saint from human laws.
For laws are only made to punish those
Who serve the king, and to protect his foes.
If any leisure time he had from power
(Because 'tis sin to misemploy an hour),
His business was, by writing, to persuade
That kings were useless, and a clog to trade;
And, that his noble style he might refine,
No Rechabite[3] more shunned the fumes of wine.
Chaste were his cellars, and his shrieval board[4]

not been certainly established, although various Whig nobles have been suggested. For Balaam see Numbers 22–24; for Caleb, Numbers 13–14; and for Nadab, Leviticus 10.1–2. "Well-hung": fluent of speech or sexually potent or both. "Cold": contrasts with the second meaning of *well-hung*. "Canting": points to a Nonconformist, as does "new porridge," for Dissenters referred to the Book of Common Prayer contemptuously as "porridge," a hodgepodge, unsubstantial stuff.

9. Sir William Jones, attorney general, had been largely responsible for the passage of the first Exclusion Bill by the House of Commons. He prosecuted the accused in the Popish Plot.

1. Shimei cursed and stoned David when he fled into the wilderness during Absalom's revolt (2 Samuel 16.5–14). His name is used here for one of the two sheriffs of London: Slingsby Bethel, a Whig, former republican, and virulent enemy of Charles. He packed juries with Whigs and so secured the acquittal of enemies of the court, among them Shaftesbury himself.

2. Sons of wickedness (cf. Milton, *Paradise Lost* 1.490–505). Dryden probably intended a pun on Balliol, the Oxford college in which leading Whigs stayed during the brief and fateful meeting of Parliament at Oxford in 1681.

3. An austere Jewish sect that drank no wine (Jeremiah 35.2–19).

4. Sheriff's dinner table.

The grossness of a city feast abhorred:
His cooks, with long disuse, their trade forgot;
Cool was his kitchen, though his brains were hot,
Such frugal virtue malice may accuse,
But sure 'twas necessary to the Jews:
For towns once burnt[5] such magistrates require
As dare not tempt God's providence by fire.
With spiritual food he fed his servants well,
But free from flesh that made the Jews rebel;
And Moses' laws he held in more account,
For forty days of fasting in the mount.[6]
To speak the rest, who better are forgot,
Would tire a well-breathed witness of the Plot.
Yet, Corah,[7] thou shalt from oblivion pass:
Erect thyself, thou monumental brass,
High as the serpent of thy metal made,[8]
While nations stand secure beneath thy shade.
What though his birth were base, yet comets rise
From earthy vapors, ere they shine in skies.
Prodigious actions may as well be done
By weaver's issue,[9] as by prince's son.
This arch-attestor for the public good
By that one deed ennobles all his blood.
Who ever asked the witnesses' high race
Whose oath with martyrdom did Stephen[1] grace?
Ours was a Levite, and as times went then,
His tribe were God Almighty's gentlemen.
Sunk were his eyes, his voice was harsh and loud,
Sure signs he neither choleric° was nor proud: *prone to anger*
His long chin proved his wit; his saintlike grace
A church vermilion, and a Moses' face.[2]
His memory, miraculously great,
Could plots, exceeding man's belief, repeat;
Which therefore cannot be accounted lies,
For human wit could never such devise.
Some future truths are mingled in his book;
But where the witness failed, the prophet spoke:
Some things like visionary flights appear;
The spirit caught him up, the Lord knows where,
And gave him his rabbinical degree,
Unknown to foreign university.[3]
His judgment yet his memory did excel;
Which pieced his wondrous evidence so well,
And suited to the temper of the times,

5. London burned in 1666.
6. Mount Sinai, where, during a fast of forty days, Moses received the law (Exodus 34.28).
7. Or Korah, a rebellious Levite, swallowed up by the earth because of his crimes (Numbers 16). Corah is Titus Oates, the self-appointed, perjured, and "well-breathed" (long-winded) witness of the plot.
8. Moses erected a brazen serpent to heal the Jews bitten by fiery serpents (Numbers 21.4–9). *Brass* also means impudence or shamelessness.
9. Oates's father, a clergyman, belonged to an obscure family of ribbon weavers.
1. The first Christian martyr, accused by false witnesses (Acts 6–7).
2. Moses' face shone when he came down from Mount Sinai with the tables of the law (Exodus 34.29–30). Oates's face suggests high living, not spiritual illumination.
3. Oates falsely claimed to be a doctor of divinity in the University of Salamanca.

Then groaning under Jebusitic crimes.
Let Israel's foes suspect his heavenly call,
And rashly judge his writ apocryphal;[4]
Our laws for such affronts have forfeits made:
He takes his life, who takes away his trade.
Were I myself in witness Corah's place,
The wretch who did me such a dire disgrace
Should whet my memory, though once forgot,
To make him an appendix of my plot.
His zeal to heaven made him his prince despise,
And load his person with indignities;
But zeal peculiar privilege affords,
Indulging latitude to deeds and words;
And Corah might for Agag's[5] murder call,
In terms as coarse as Samuel used to Saul.
What others in his evidence did join
(The best that could be had for love or coin),
In Corah's own predicament will fall;
For *witness* is a common name to all.

Surrounded thus with friends of every sort,
Deluded Absalom forsakes the court:
Impatient of high hopes, urged with renown,
And fired with near possession of a crown.
The admiring crowd are dazzled with surprise,
And on his goodly person feed their eyes:
His joy concealed, he sets himself to show,
On each side bowing popularly[6] low;
His looks, his gestures, and his words he frames,
And with familiar ease repeats their names.
Thus formed by nature, furnished out with arts,
He glides unfelt into their secret hearts.
Then, with a kind compassionating look,
And sighs, bespeaking pity ere he spoke,
Few words he said; but easy those and fit,
More slow than Hybla-drops,[7] and far more sweet.

"I mourn, my countrymen, your lost estate;
Though far unable to prevent your fate:
Behold a banished man, for your dear cause
Exposed a prey to arbitrary laws!
Yet oh! that I alone could be undone,
Cut off from empire, and no more a son!
Now all your liberties a spoil are made;
Egypt° and Tyrus° intercept your trade, *France / Holland*
And Jebusites your sacred rites invade.
My father, whom with reverence yet I name,
Charmed into ease, is careless of his fame;
And, bribed with petty sums of foreign gold,

4. Not inspired and hence excluded from Holy Writ.
5. Agag is probably one of the five Catholic peers executed for the Popish Plot in 1680, most likely Lord Stafford, against whom Oates fabricated testimony. He is almost certainly not, as is usually suggested, Sir Edmund Berry Godfrey (see headnote, pp. 2087–88). "Agag's murder" and Samuel's coarse terms to Saul are in 1 Samuel 15.
6. "So as to please the crowd" (Johnson's *Dictionary*).
7. The famous honey of Hybla in Sicily.

Is grown in Bathsheba's[8] embraces old;
Exalts his enemies, his friends destroys;
And all his power against himself employs.
He gives, and let him give, my right away;
But why should he his own, and yours betray?
He only, he can make the nation bleed,
And he alone from my revenge is freed.
Take then my tears (with that he wiped his eyes),
'Tis all the aid my present power supplies:
No court-informer can these arms accuse;
These arms may sons against their fathers use:
And 'tis my wish, the next successor's reign
May make no other Israelite complain."
Youth, beauty, graceful action seldom fail;
But common interest always will prevail;
And pity never ceases to be shown
To him who makes the people's wrongs his own.
The crowd (that still believe their kings oppress)
With lifted hands their young Messiah bless:
Who now begins his progress to ordain
With chariots, horsemen, and a numerous train;
From east to west his glories he displays,[9]
And, like the sun, the promised land surveys.
Fame runs before him as the morning star,
And shouts of joy salute him from afar:
Each house receives him as a guardian god,
And consecrates the place of his abode:
But hospitable treats did most commend
Wise Issachar,[1] his wealthy western friend.
This moving court, that caught the people's eyes,
And seemed but pomp, did other ends disguise:
Achitophel had formed it, with intent
To sound the depths, and fathom, where it went,
The people's hearts; distinguish friends from foes,
And try their strength, before they came to blows.
Yet all was colored with a smooth pretense
Of specious love, and duty to their prince.
Religion, and redress of grievances,
Two names that always cheat and always please,
Are often urged; and good King David's life
Endangered by a brother and a wife.[2]
Thus, in a pageant show, a plot is made,
And peace itself is war in masquerade.
O foolish Israel! never warned by ill,
Still the same bait, and circumvented still!
Did ever men forsake their present ease,
In midst of health imagine a disease;

8. Bathsheba is the woman with whom David committed adultery (2 Samuel 11). Here, Charles II's French mistress, Louise de Kerouallle, duchess of Portsmouth.
9. In 1680 Monmouth made a progress through the west of England, seeking popular support for his cause.
1. Thomas Thynne of Longleat. He entertained Monmouth on his journey in the west. *Wise* is, of course, ironic.
2. Titus Oates had sworn that both James, duke of York, and the queen were involved in a similar plot to poison Charles II.

Take pains contingent mischiefs to foresee,
Make heirs for monarchs, and for God decree?
What shall we think! Can people give away
Both for themselves and sons, their native sway?
Then they are left defenseless to the sword
Of each unbounded, arbitrary lord:
And laws are vain, by which we right enjoy,
If kings unquestioned can those laws destroy.
Yet if the crowd be judge of fit and just,
And kings are only officers in trust,
Then this resuming covenant was declared
When kings were made, or is forever barred.
If those who gave the scepter could not tie
By their own deed their own posterity,
How then could Adam bind his future race?
How could his forfeit on mankind take place?
Or how could heavenly justice damn us all,
Who ne'er consented to our father's fall?
Then kings are slaves to those whom they command,
And tenants to their people's pleasure stand.
Add, that the power for property allowed
Is mischievously seated in the crowd;
For who can be secure of private right,
If sovereign sway may be dissolved by might?
Nor is the people's judgment always true:
The most may err as grossly as the few;
And faultless kings run down, by common cry,
For vice, oppression, and for tyranny.
What standard is there in a fickle rout,
Which, flowing to the mark,° runs faster out? *highwater mark*
Nor only crowds, but Sanhedrins may be
Infected with this public lunacy,[3]
And share the madness of rebellious times,
To murder monarchs for imagined crimes.[4]
If they may give and take whene'er they please,
Not kings alone (the Godhead's images),
But government itself at length must fall
To nature's state, where all have right to all.
Yet, grant our lords the people kings can make,
What prudent men a settled throne would shake?
For whatsoe'er their sufferings were before,
That change they covet makes them suffer more.
All other errors but disturb a state,
But innovation is the blow of fate.
If ancient fabrics nod, and threat to fall,
To patch the flaws, and buttress up the wall,
Thus far 'tis duty; but here fix the mark;
For all beyond it is to touch our ark.[5]
To change foundations, cast the frame anew,

3. The fickle crowd flows and ebbs like the tide, which is pulled back and forth by the moon (hence "lunacy," after the Latin *luna*, or "moon").
4. An allusion to the execution of Charles I.
5. Uzzah was struck dead because he sacrilegiously touched the Ark of the Covenant (2 Samuel 6.6–7).

Is work for rebels, who base ends pursue,
At once divine and human laws control,
And mend the parts by ruin of the whole.
The tampering world is subject to this curse,
To physic their disease into a worse.
   Now what relief can righteous David bring?
How fatal 'tis to be too good a king!
Friends he has few, so high the madness grows:
Who dare be such, must be the people's foes:
Yet some there were, even in the worst of days;
Some let me name, and naming is to praise.
   In this short file Barzillai[6] first appears;
Barzillai, crowned with honor and with years:
Long since, the rising rebels he withstood
In regions waste, beyond the Jordan's flood:
Unfortunately brave to buoy the State;
But sinking underneath his master's fate:
In exile with his godlike prince he mourned;
For him he suffered, and with him returned.
The court he practiced, not the courtier's art:
Large was his wealth, but larger was his heart:
Which well the noblest objects knew to choose,
The fighting warrior, and recording Muse.
His bed could once a fruitful issue boast;
Now more than half a father's name is lost.
His eldest hope,[7] with every grace adorned,
By me (so Heaven will have it) always mourned,
And always honored, snatched in manhood's prime
By unequal fates, and Providence's crime:
Yet not before the goal of honor won,
All parts fulfilled of subject and of son;
Swift was the race, but short the time to run.
O narrow circle, but of power divine,
Scanted in space, but perfect in thy line!
By sea, by land, thy matchless worth was known,
Arms thy delight, and war was all thy own:
Thy force, infused, the fainting Tyrians° propped; *the Dutch*
And haughty Pharaoh found his fortune stopped.
Oh ancient honor! Oh unconquered hand,
Whom foes unpunished never could withstand!
But Israel was unworthy of thy name:
Short is the date of all immoderate fame.
It looks as Heaven our ruin had designed,
And durst not trust thy fortune and thy mind.
Now, free from earth, thy disencumbered soul
Mounts up, and leaves behind the clouds and starry pole:
From thence thy kindred legions mayst thou bring,

6. James Butler, duke of Ormond (1610–1688). He was famous for his loyalty to the Stuart cause. He fought for Charles I in Ireland, and when that cause was hopeless, he joined Charles II in his exile abroad. He spent a large fortune on behalf of the king and continued to serve him loyally after the Restoration. Six of his ten children were dead (see line 830). Cf. 2 Samuel 19.31–39.

7. Ormond's son, Thomas, earl of Ossory (1634–1680), a famous soldier and, like his father, devoted to Charles II.

To aid the guardian angel of thy king.
Here stop my Muse, here cease thy painful flight;
No pinions can pursue immortal height:
Tell good Barzillai thou canst sing no more,
And tell thy soul she should have fled before:
Or fled she with his life, and left this verse
To hang on her departed patron's hearse?
Now take thy steepy flight from heaven, and see
If thou canst find on earth another *he:*
Another *he* would be too hard to find;
See then whom thou canst see not far behind.
Zadoc the priest, whom, shunning power and place,
His lowly mind advanced to David's grace:
With him the Sagan[8] of Jerusalem,
Of hospitable soul, and noble stem;
Him of the western dome, whose weighty sense
Flows in fit words and heavenly eloquence.
The prophets' sons,[9] by such example led,
To learning and to loyalty were bred:
For colleges on bounteous kinds depend,
And never rebel was to arts a friend.
To these succeed the pillars of the laws,
Who best could plead, and best can judge a cause.
Next them a train of loyal peers ascend;
Sharp-judging Adriel,[1] the Muses' friend,
Himself a Muse—in Sanhedrin's debate
True to his prince, but not a slave of state:
Whom David's love with honors did adorn,
That from his disobedient son were torn.
Jotham[2] of piercing wit, and pregnant thought,
Indued by nature, and by learning taught
To move assemblies, who but only tried
The worse a while, then chose the better side;
Nor chose alone, but turned the balance too;
So much the weight of one brave man can do.
Hushai,[3] the friend of David in distress,
In public storms, of manly steadfastness:
By foreign treaties he informed his youth,
And joined experience to his native truth.
His frugal care supplied the wanting throne,
Frugal for that, but bounteous of his own:
'Tis easy conduct when exchequers flow,
But hard the task to manage well the low;
For sovereign power is too depressed or high,
When kings are forced to sell, or crowds to buy.
Indulge one labor more, my weary Muse,
For Amiel:[4] who can Amiel's praise refuse?
Of ancient race by birth, but nobler yet

8. Henry Compton, bishop of London. "Zadoc": William Sancroft, archbishop of Canterbury.
9. The boys of Westminster School, which Dryden had attended. "Him of the western dome": John Dolben, dean of Westminster.
1. John Sheffield, earl of Mulgrave.
2. George Savile, marquis of Halifax.
3. Laurence Hyde, earl of Rochester.
4. Edward Seymour, speaker of the House of Commons.

In his own worth, and without title great:
The Sanhedrin long time as chief he ruled,
Their reason guided, and their passion cooled:
So dexterous was he in the crown's defense,
So formed to speak a loyal nation's sense,
That, as their band was Israel's tribes in small,
So fit was he to represent them all.
Now rasher charioteers the seat ascend,
Whose loose careers his steady skill commend°: — *set off to advantage*
They like the unequal ruler of the day,
Misguide the seasons, and mistake the way;
While he withdrawn at their mad labor smiles,
And safe enjoys the sabbath of his toils.
These were the chief, a small but faithful band
Of worthies, in the breach who dared to stand,
And tempt the united fury of the land.
With grief they viewed such powerful engines bent,
To batter down the lawful government:
A numerous faction, with pretended frights,
In Sanhedrins to plume° the regal rights; — *pluck, plunder*
The true successor from the court removed:[5]
The Plot, by hireling witnesses, improved.
These ills they saw, and, as their duty bound,
They showed the king the danger of the wound:
That no concessions from the throne would please,
But lenitives° fomented the disease; — *pain relievers*
That Absalom, ambitious of the crown,
Was made the lure to draw the people down;
That false Achitophel's pernicious hate
Had turned the Plot to ruin Church and State:
The council violent, the rabble worse;
That Shimei taught Jerusalem to curse.
With all these loads of injuries oppressed,
And long revolving, in his careful breast,
The event of things, at last, his patience tired,
Thus from his royal throne, by Heaven inspired,
The godlike David spoke: with awful fear
His train their Maker in their master hear.
"Thus long have I, by native mercy swayed,
My wrongs dissembled, my revenge delayed:
So willing to forgive the offending age,
So much the father did the king assuage.
But now so far my clemency they slight,
The offenders question my forgiving right.
That one was made for many, they contend;
But 'tis to rule; for that's a monarch's end.
They call my tenderness of blood, my fear;
Though manly tempers can the longest bear.
Yet, since they will divert my native course,
'Tis time to show I am not good by force.
Those heaped affronts that haughty subjects bring,

5. The duke of York had been banished from England.

Are burdens for a camel, not a king:
Kings are the public pillars of the State,
Born to sustain and prop the nation's weight:
If my young Samson will pretend a call
To shake the column, let him share the fall:[6]
But, oh, that yet he would repent and live!
How easy 'tis for parents to forgive!
With how few tears a pardon might be won
From nature, pleading for a darling son!
Poor pitied youth, by my paternal care
Raised up to all the height his frame could bear:
Had God ordained his fate for empire born,
He would have given his soul another turn:
Gulled° with a patriot's name, whose modern sense *deceived*
Is one that would by law supplant his prince:
The people's brave,° the politician's tool; *bully*
Never was patriot yet, but was a fool.
Whence comes it that religion and the laws
Should more be Absalom's than David's cause?
His old instructor,[7] ere he lost his place,
Was never thought indued with so much grace.
Good heavens, how faction can a patriot paint!
My rebel ever proves my people's saint:
Would *they* impose an heir upon the throne?
Let Sanhedrins be taught to give their own.
A king's at least a part of government,
And mine as requisite as their consent;
Without my leave a future king to choose,
Infers a right the present to depose:
True, they petition me to approve their choice;
But Esau's hands suit ill with Jacob's voice.[8]
My pious subjects for my safety pray,
Which to secure, they take my power away.
From plots and treasons Heaven preserve my years,
But save me most from my petitioners.
Unsatiate as the barren womb or grave;
God cannot grant so much as they can crave.
What then is left but with a jealous eye
To guard the small remains of royalty?
The law shall still direct my peaceful sway,
And the same law teach rebels to obey:
Votes shall no more established power control—
Such votes as make a part exceed the whole:
No groundless clamors shall my friends remove,
Nor crowds have power to punish ere they prove:
For gods and godlike kings, their care express,
Still to defend their servants in distress.
O that my power to saving were confined:
Why am I forced, like Heaven, against my mind,
To make examples of another kind?

6. Judges 16.
7. The earl of Shaftesbury.
8. Genesis 27.22.

Must I at length the sword of justice draw?
O curst effects of necessary law!
How ill my fear they by my mercy scan°! *judge*
Beware the fury of a patient man.
Law they require, let Law then show her face;
They could not be content to look on Grace,
Her hinder parts, but with a daring eye
To tempt the terror of her front and die.[9]
By their own arts,'tis righteously decreed,
Those dire artificers of death shall bleed.
Against themselves their witnesses will swear,
Till viper-like their mother Plot they tear:
And suck for nutriment that bloody gore,
Which was their principle of life before.
Their Belial with their Belzebub[1] will fight;
Thus on my foes, my foes shall do me right:
Nor doubt the event; for factious crowds engage,
In their first onset, all their brutal rage.
Then let 'em take an unresisted course,
Retire and traverse,° and delude their force: *thwart*
But when they stand all breathless, urge the fight,
And rise upon 'em with redoubled might:
For lawful power is still superior found,
When long driven back, at length it stands the ground."
He said. The Almighty, nodding, gave consent;
And peals of thunder shook the firmament.
Henceforth a series of new time began,
The mighty years in long procession ran:
Once more the godlike David was restored,
And willing nations knew their lawful lord.

1681

Mac Flecknoe The target of this superb satire, which is cast in the form of a mock-heroic episode, is Thomas Shadwell (1640–1692), the playwright, with whom Dryden had been on good terms for a number of years, certainly as late as March 1678. Shadwell considered himself the successor of Ben Jonson and the champion of the type of comedy that Jonson had written, the "comedy of humors," in which each character is presented under the domination of a single psychological trait or eccentricity, his humor. His plays are not without merit, but they are often clumsy and prolix and certainly much inferior to Jonson's. For many years he had conducted a public argument with Dryden on the merits of Jonson's comedies, which he thought Dryden undervalued. Exactly what moved Dryden to attack him is a matter of conjecture: he may simply have grown progressively bored and irritated by Shadwell and his tedious argument. The poem seems to have been written in late 1678 or 1679 and to have circulated only in manuscript until it was printed in 1682 in a pirated edition by an obscure publisher. By that time, the two playwrights were alienated by politics as well as by literary quarrels. Shadwell was a violent Whig and the reputed author of a sharp attack on Dryden as the Tory author of *Absalom and Achitophel* and "The Medal." It was probably for this reason that the printer added the subtitle

9. Moses was not allowed to see the countenance of Jehovah (Exodus 33.20–23).

1. A god of the Philistines. "Belial": the incarnation of all evil.

referring to Shadwell's Whiggism in the phrase "true-blue-Protestant poet." Political passions were running high, and sales would be helped if the poem seemed to refer to the events of the day.

Whereas Butler had debased and degraded his victims by using burlesque, caricature, and the grotesque, Dryden exposed Shadwell to ridicule by using the devices of mock epic, which treats the low, mean, or absurd in the grand language, lofty style, and solemn tone of epic poetry. The obvious disparity between subject and style makes the satiric point. In 1678, a prolific, untalented writer, Richard Flecknoe, died. Dryden conceived the idea of presenting Shadwell (the self-proclaimed heir of Ben Jonson, the laureate) as the son and successor of Flecknoe (an irony also because Flecknoe was a Catholic priest)—hence *Mac* (i.e., son of) *Flecknoe*—from whom he inherits the throne of dullness. Flecknoe in the triple role of king, priest, and poet hails his successor, pronounces a panegyric on his perfect fitness for the throne, anoints and crowns him, foretells his glorious reign, and as he sinks (leaden dullness cannot soar), leaves his mantle to fall symbolically on Shadwell's shoulders. The poem abounds in literary allusions—to Roman legend and history and to the *Aeneid*, to Cowley's fragmentary epic *The Davideis*, to *Paradise Lost*, and to Shadwell's own plays. Biblical allusions add an unexpected dimension of incongruous dignity to the low scene. The coronation takes place in the City, to the plaudits of the citizens, who are fit to admire only what is dull. In 217 lines, Dryden created an image of Shadwell that has fixed his reputation to this day.

Mac Flecknoe

Or a Satire upon the True-Blue-Protestant Poet, T. S.

All human things are subject to decay,
And when fate summons, monarchs must obey.
This Flecknoe found, who, like Augustus,[1] young
Was called to empire, and had governed long;
In prose and verse, was owned, without dispute,
Through all the realms of Nonsense, absolute.
This aged prince, now flourishing in peace,
And blest with issue of a large increase,
Worn out with business, did at length debate
To settle the succession of the state;
And, pondering which of all his sons was fit
To reign, and wage immortal war with wit,
Cried: " 'Tis resolved; for nature pleads that he
Should only rule, who most resembles me.
Sh——[2] alone my perfect image bears,
Mature in dullness from his tender years:
Sh—— alone, of all my sons, is he
Who stands confirmed in full stupidity.
The rest to some faint meaning make pretense,
But Sh—— never deviates into sense.
Some beams of wit on other souls may fall,
Strike through, and make a lucid interval;
But Sh——'s genuine night admits no ray,

1. In 31 B.C.E. Octavian became the first Roman emperor at the age of thirty-two. He assumed the title Augustus in 27 B.C.E.
2. Thomas Shadwell. The initial and second letter of the name followed by a dash give the appearance, but only the appearance, of protecting Dryden's victim by concealing his name. A common device in the satire of the period.

His rising fogs prevail upon the day.
Besides, his goodly fabric[3] fills the eye,
And seems designed for thoughtless majesty:
Thoughtless as monarch oaks that shade the plain,
And, spread in solemn state, supinely reign.
Heywood and Shirley were but types of thee,[4]
Thou last great prophet of tautology.[5]
Even I, a dunce of more renown than they,
Was sent before but to prepare thy way;
And, coarsely clad in Norwich drugget,° came — *coarse woolen cloth*
To teach the nations in thy greater name.[6]
My warbling lute, the lute I whilom° strung, — *formerly*
When to King John of Portugal[7] I sung,
Was but the prelude to that glorious day,
When thou on silver Thames didst cut thy way,
With well-timed oars before the royal barge,
Swelled with the pride of thy celestial charge;
And big with hymn, commander of a host,
The like was ne'er in Epsom blankets tossed.[8]
Methinks I see the new Arion[9] sail,
The lute still trembling underneath thy nail.
At thy well-sharpened thumb from shore to shore
The treble squeaks for fear, the basses roar;
Echoes from Pissing Alley Sh—— call,
And Sh—— they resound from Aston Hall.
About thy boat the little fishes throng,
As at the morning toast° that floats along. — *sewage*
Sometimes, as prince of thy harmonious band,
Thou wield'st thy papers in thy threshing hand,
St. André's[1] feet ne'er kept more equal time,
Not ev'n the feet of thy own *Psyche's* rhyme;
Though they in number as in sense excel:
So just, so like tautology, they fell,
That, pale with envy, Singleton[2] forswore
The lute and sword, which he in triumph bore,
And vowed he ne'er would act Villerius[3] more."
Here stopped the good old sire, and wept for joy
In silent raptures of the hopeful boy.
All arguments, but most his plays, persuade,

3. His body. Shadwell was a corpulent man.
4. Thomas Heywood (ca. 1570–1641) and James Shirley (1596–1666), playwrights popular before the closing of the theaters in 1642 but now out of fashion. They are introduced here as "types" (i.e., prefigurings) of Shadwell, in the sense that Solomon was regarded as an Old Testament prefiguring of Christ, the "last [final] great prophet."
5. Unnecessary repetition of meaning in different words.
6. The parallel between Flecknoe, as forerunner of Shadwell, and John the Baptist, as forerunner of Jesus, is made plain in lines 32–34 by the use of details and even words taken from Matthew 3.3–4 and John 1.23.
7. Flecknoe boasted of the patronage of the Portuguese king.
8. A reference to Shadwell's comedy *Epsom Wells* and to the farcical scene in his *Virtuoso,* in which Sir Samuel Hearty is tossed in a blanket.
9. A legendary Greek poet. Returning home by sea, he was robbed and thrown overboard by the sailors, but was saved by a dolphin that had been charmed by his music.
1. A French dancer who designed the choreography of Shadwell's opera *Psyche* (1675). Dryden's sneer at the mechanical metrics of the songs in *Psyche* is justified.
2. John Singleton (d. 1686), a musician at the Theatre Royal.
3. A character in Sir William Davenant's *Siege of Rhodes* (1656), the first English opera.

That for anointed dullness[4] he was made.
Close to the walls which fair Augusta° bind *London*
(The fair Augusta much to fears inclined),[5]
An ancient fabric,° raised to inform the sight, *building*
There stood of yore, and Barbican it hight:° *was called*
A watchtower once; but now, so fate ordains,
Of all the pile an empty name remains.
From its old ruins brothel houses rise,
Scenes of lewd loves, and of polluted joys,
Where their vast courts the mother-strumpets keep,
And, undisturbed by watch, in silence sleep.
Near these a Nursery[6] erects its head,
Where queens are formed, and future heroes bred;
Where unfledged actors learn to laugh and cry,
Where infant punks° their tender voices try, *prostitutes*
And little Maximins[7] the gods defy.
Great Fletcher never treads in buskins here,
Nor greater Jonson dares in socks[8] appear;
But gentle Simkin[9] just reception finds
Amidst this monument of vanished minds:
Pure clinches° the suburbian Muse affords, *puns*
And Panton[1] waging harmless war with words.
Here Flecknoe, as a place to fame well known,
Ambitiously design'd his Sh——'s throne;
For ancient Dekker[2] prophesied long since,
That in this pile would reign a mighty prince,
Born for a scourge of wit, and flail of sense;
To whom true dullness should some *Psyches* owe,
But worlds of *Misers* from his pen should flow;
Humorists and *Hypocrites*[3] it should produce,
Whole Raymond families, and tribes of Bruce.
Now Empress Fame had published the renown
Of Sh——'s coronation through the town.
Roused by report of Fame, the nations meet,
From near Bunhill, and distant Watling Street.[4]
No Persian carpets spread the imperial way,
But scattered limbs of mangled poets lay;
From dusty shops neglected authors come,
Martyrs of pies, and relics of the bum.[5]
Much Heywood, Shirley, Ogilby[6] there lay,

4. The anticipated phrase is "anointed *majesty*." English kings are anointed with oil at their coronations.
5. This line alludes to the fears excited by the Popish Plot (cf. *Absalom and Achitophel*, p. 880).
6. The name of a training school for young actors.
7. Maximin is the cruel emperor in Dryden's *Tyrannic Love* (1669), notorious for his bombast.
8. "Buskins" and "socks" were the symbols of tragedy and comedy, respectively. John Fletcher (1579–1625), the playwright and collaborator with Francis Beaumont (ca. 1584–1616).
9. A popular character in low farces.
1. Said to have been a celebrated punster.
2. Thomas Dekker (ca. 1572–1632), the playwright, whom Jonson had satirized in *The Poetaster*.
3. Three of Shadwell's plays; *The Hypocrite*, a failure, was not published. "Raymond" and "Bruce" (line 93) are characters in *The Humorists* and *The Virtuoso*, respectively.
4. Because Bunhill is about a quarter mile and Watling Street little more than a half mile from the site of the Nursery, where the coronation is held, Shadwell's fame is narrowly circumscribed. Moreover, his subjects live in the heart of the City, regarded by men of wit and fashion as the abode of bad taste and middle-class vulgarity.
5. Unsold books were used to line pie plates and as toilet paper.
6. John Ogilby, a translator of Homer and Virgil, ridiculed by both Dryden and Pope as a bad poet.

But loads of Sh—— almost choked the way.
Bilked stationers for yeomen stood prepared,
And Herringman was captain of the guard.[7]
The hoary prince in majesty appeared,
High on a throne of his own labors reared.
At his right hand our young Ascanius sate,
Rome's other hope, and pillar of the state.
His brows thick fogs, instead of glories, grace,
And lambent dullness played around his face.[8]
As Hannibal did to the altars come,
Sworn by his sire a mortal foe to Rome,[9]
So Sh—— swore, nor should his vow be vain,
That he till death true dullness would maintain;
And, in his father's right, and realm's defense,
Ne'er to have peace with wit, nor truce with sense.
The king himself the sacred unction[1] made,
As king by office, and as priest by trade.
In his siníster° hand, instead of ball, *left*
He placed a mighty mug of potent ale;
Love's Kingdom to his right he did convey,
At once his scepter, and his rule of sway;
Whose righteous lore the prince had practiced young,
And from whose loins recorded *Psyche* sprung.
His temples, last, with poppies were o'erspread,
That nodding seemed to consecrate his head.[2]
Just at that point of time, if fame not lie,
On his left hand twelve reverend owls did fly.[3]
So Romulus,'tis sung, by Tiber's brook,
Presage of sway from twice six vultures took.
The admiring throng loud acclamations make,
And omens of his future empire take.
The sire then shook the honors[4] of his head,
And from his brows damps of oblivion shed
Full on the filial dullness: long he stood,
Repelling from his breast the raging god;
At length burst out in this prophetic mood:
"Heavens bless my son, from Ireland let him reign
To far Barbadoes on the western main;[5]
Of his dominion may no end be known,
And greater than his father's be his throne;
Beyond *Love's Kingdom* let him stretch his pen!"
He paused, and all the people cried, "Amen."

7. "Bilked stationers": cheated publishers, acting as "yeomen" of the guard, led by Henry Herringman, who until 1679 was the publisher of both Shadwell and Dryden.
8. Ascanius, or Iülus, was the son of Aeneas. Virgil referred to him as "*spes altera Romae*" ("Rome's other hope," *Aeneid* 12.168). As Troy fell, he was marked as favored by the gods when a flickering ("lambent") flame played round his head (*Aeneid* 2.680–84).
9. Hannibal, who almost conquered Rome in 216 B.C.E., during the second Punic War, took this oath at the age of nine (Livy 21.1).
1. The sacramental oil, used in the coronation.
2. During the coronation a British monarch holds two symbols of the throne: a globe ("ball") representing the world in the left hand and a scepter in the right. Shadwell's symbols of monarchy are a mug of ale; Flecknoe's dreary play *Love's Kingdom;* and a crown of poppies, which suggest heaviness, dullness, and drowsiness. The poppies also refer obliquely to Shadwell's addiction to opium.
3. Birds of night. Appropriate substitutes for the twelve vultures whose flight confirmed to Romulus the destined site of Rome, of which he was founder and king.
4. Ornaments, hence locks.
5. Shadwell's empire is vast but empty.

Then thus continued he: "My son, advance
Still in new impudence, new ignorance.
Success let others teach, learn thou from me
Pangs without birth, and fruitless industry.
Let *Virtuosos* in five years be writ;
Yet not one thought accuse thy toil of wit.
Let gentle George[6] in triumph tread the stage,
Make Dorimant betray, and Loveit rage;
Let Cully, Cockwood, Fopling, charm the pit,
And in their folly show the writer's wit.
Yet still thy fools shall stand in thy defense,
And justify their author's want of sense.
Let 'em be all by thy own model made
Of dullness, and desire no foreign aid;
That they to future ages may be known,
Not copies drawn, but issue of thy own.
Nay, let thy men of wit too be the same,
All full of thee, and differing but in name.
But let no alien S—dl—y[7] interpose,
To lard with wit[8] thy hungry *Epsom* prose.
And when false flowers of rhetoric thou wouldst cull,
Trust nature, do not labor to be dull;
But write thy best, and top; and, in each line,
Sir Formal's[9] oratory will be thine:
Sir Formal, though unsought, attends thy quill,
And does thy northern dedications[1] fill.
Nor let false friends seduce thy mind to fame,
By arrogating Jonson's hostile name.
Let father Flecknoe fire thy mind with praise,
And uncle Ogilby thy envy raise.
Thou art my blood, where Jonson has no part:
What share have we in nature, or in art?
Where did his wit on learning fix a brand,
And rail at arts he did not understand?
Where made he love in Prince Nicander's vein,[2]
Or swept the dust in *Psyche's* humble strain?
Where sold he bargains, 'whip-stitch,[3] kiss my arse,'
Promised a play and dwindled to a farce?[4]
When did his Muse from Fletcher scenes purloin,
As thou whole Eth'rege dost transfuse to thine?
But so transfused, as oil on water's flow,
His always floats above, thine sinks below.
This is thy province, this thy wondrous way,
New humors to invent for each new play:

6. Sir George Etherege (ca. 1635–1691), a writer of brilliant comedies. In the next couplet Dryden names characters from his plays.
7. Sir Charles Sedley (1638–1701), wit, rake, poet, and playwright. Dryden hints that he contributed more than the prologue to Shadwell's *Epsom Wells*.
8. This phrase recalls a sentence in Burton's *Anatomy of Melancholy:* "They lard their lean books with the fat of others' works."
9. Sir Formal Trifle, the ridiculous and vapid orator in *The Virtuoso*.
1. Shadwell frequently dedicated his works to the duke of Newcastle and members of his family.
2. In *Psyche*.
3. A nonsense word frequently used by Sir Samuel Hearty in *The Virtuoso*. "Sell bargains": to answer an innocent question with a coarse or indecent phrase, as in this line.
4. Low comedy that depends largely on situation rather than wit, consistently condemned by Dryden and other serious playwrights.

This is that boasted bias[5] of thy mind,
By which one way, to dullness, 'tis inclined;
Which makes thy writings lean on one side still,
And, in all changes, that way bends thy will.
Nor let thy mountain-belly make pretense
Of likeness; thine's a tympany[6] of sense.
A tun° of man in thy large bulk is writ, *large cask*
But sure thou'rt but a kilderkin° of wit. *small cask*
Like mine, thy gentle numbers feebly creep;
Thy tragic Muse gives smiles, thy comic sleep.
With whate'er gall thou sett'st thyself to write,
Thy inoffensive satires never bite.
In thy felonious heart though venom lies,
It does but touch thy Irish pen,[7] and dies.
Thy genius calls thee not to purchase fame
In keen iambics,° but mild anagram. *sharp satire*
Leave writing plays, and choose for thy command
Some peaceful province in acrostic land.
There thou may'st wings display and altars raise,[8]
And torture one poor word ten thousand ways.
Or, if thou wouldst thy different talent suit,
Set thy own songs, and sing them to thy lute."
He said: but his last words were scarcely heard
For Bruce and Longville had a trap prepared,
And down they sent the yet declaiming bard.[9]
Sinking he left his drugget robe behind,
Borne upwards by a subterranean wind.
The mantle fell to the young prophet's part,[1]
With double portion of his father's art.

ca. 1679 1682

To the Memory of Mr. Oldham[1]

Farewell, too little, and too lately known,
Whom I began to think and call my own:
For sure our souls were near allied, and thine
Cast in the same poetic mold with mine.
One common note on either lyre did strike,
And knaves and fools[2] we both abhorred alike.
To the same goal did both our studies drive;

5. In bowling, the spin given to the bowl that causes it to swerve. Dryden closely parodies a passage in Shadwell's epilogue to *The Humorists.*

6. A swelling in some part of the body caused by wind.

7. Dryden accuses Flecknoe and his "son" of being Irish. Ireland suggested only poverty, superstition, and barbarity to 17th-century Londoners.

8. "Wings" and "altars" refer to poems in the shape of these objects as in George Herbert's "Easter Wings" and "The Altar." "Anagram": the transposition of letters in a word so as to make a new one. "Acrostic": a poem in which the first letter of each line, read downward, makes up the name of the person or thing that is the subject of the poem. Dryden is citing instances of triviality and over-ingenuity in literature.

9. In *The Virtuoso,* Bruce and Longville play this trick on Sir Formal Trifle while he makes a speech.

1. When the prophet Elijah was carried to heaven in a chariot of fire borne on a whirlwind, his mantle fell on his successor, the younger prophet Elisha (2 Kings 2.8–14). Flecknoe, prophet of dullness, naturally cannot ascend, but must sink.

1. John Oldham (1653–1683), the young poet whose *Satires upon the Jesuits* (1681), which Dryden admired, were written in 1679, before Dryden's major satires appeared (see line 8). This elegy was published in Oldham's *Remains in Verse and Prose* (1684).

2. Objects of satire.

The last set out the soonest did arrive.
Thus Nisus fell upon the slippery place,
While his young friend[3] performed and won the race.
O early ripe! to thy abundant store
What could advancing age have added more?
It might (what nature never gives the young)
Have taught the numbers° of thy native tongue. *metrics, verse*
But satire needs not those, and wit will shine
Through the harsh cadence of a rugged line.[4]
A noble error, and but seldom made,
When poets are by too much force betrayed.
Thy generous fruits, though gathered ere their prime,
Still showed a quickness;[5] and maturing time
But mellows what we write to the dull sweets of rhyme.
Once more, hail and farewell;[6] farewell, thou young,
But ah too short, Marcellus[7] of our tongue;
Thy brows with ivy, and with laurels bound;[8]
But fate and gloomy night encompass thee around.

1684

A Song for St. Cecilia's Day[1]

I

From harmony, from heavenly harmony
 This universal frame began:
When Nature underneath a heap
 Of jarring atoms lay,
And could not heave her head,
The tuneful voice was heard from high:
 "Arise, ye more than dead."
Then cold, and hot, and moist, and dry,[2]
In order to their stations leap,
 And Music's power obey.
From harmony, from heavenly harmony

3. Nisus, on the point of winning a footrace, slipped in a pool of blood. His "young friend" was Euryalus (Virgil's *Aeneid* 5.315–39).

4. Dryden repeats the Renaissance idea that the satirist should avoid smoothness and affect rough meters ("harsh cadence").

5. Sharpness of flavor.

6. Dryden echoes the famous words that conclude Catullus's elegy to his brother: *"Atque in perpetuum, frater, ave atque vale"* (And forever, brother, hail and farewell!).

7. The nephew of Augustus, adopted by him as his successor. After winning military fame as a youth, he died at the age of twenty. Virgil celebrated him in the *Aeneid* 6.854–86. The last line of Dryden's poem is a reminiscence of *Aeneid* 6.866.

8. The poet's wreath (cf. Milton's *Lycidas,* lines 1–2, p. 706).

1. St. Cecilia, a Roman lady, was an early Christian martyr. She has long been regarded as the patroness of music and the supposed inventor of the organ. Celebrations of her festival day (November 22) in England were usually devoted to music and the praise of music, and from about 1683 to 1703 the Musical Society in London annually commemorated it with a religious service and a public concert. This concert always included an ode written and set to music for the occasion, of which the two by Dryden ("A Song for St. Cecilia's Day," 1687, and "Alexander's Feast," 1697) are the most distinguished. G. B. Draghi, an Italian brought to England by Charles II, set this ode to music; but Handel's fine score, composed in 1739, has completely obscured the original setting. This is an irregular ode in the manner of Cowley. In stanzas 3–6, Dryden boldly attempted to suggest in the sounds of his words the characteristic tones of the instruments mentioned.

2. "Nature": created nature, ordered by the Divine Wisdom out of chaos, which Dryden, adopting the physics of the Greek philosopher Epicurus, describes as composed of the warring and discordant ("jarring") atoms of the four elements: earth, fire, water, and air ("cold," "hot," "moist," and "dry").

This universal frame began:
From harmony to harmony
Through all the compass of the notes it ran,
The diapason[3] closing full in man.

2

What passion cannot Music raise and quell![4]
When Jubal struck the corded shell,[5]
His listening brethren stood around,
And, wondering, on their faces fell
To worship that celestial sound.
Less than a god they thought there could not dwell
Within the hollow of that shell
That spoke so sweetly and so well.
What passion cannot Music raise and quell!

3

The trumpet's loud clangor
Excites us to arms,
With shrill notes of anger,
And mortal alarms.
The double double double beat
Of the thundering drum
Cries: "Hark! the foes come;
Charge, charge,'tis too late to retreat."

4

The soft complaining flute
In dying notes discovers
The woes of hopeless lovers,
Whose dirge is whispered by the warbling lute.

5

Sharp violins[6] proclaim
Their jealous pangs, and desperation,
Fury, frantic indignation,
Depth of pains, and height of passion,
For the fair, disdainful dame.

6

But O! what art can teach,
What human voice can reach,
The sacred organ's praise?
Notes inspiring holy love,
Notes that wing their heavenly ways
To mend the choirs above.

3. The entire compass of tones in the scale. Dryden is thinking of the Chain of Being, the ordered creation from inanimate nature up to humans, God's latest and final work. The just gradations of notes in a scale are analogous to the equally just gradations in the ascending scale of created beings. Both are the result of harmony.
4. The power of music to describe, evoke, or subdue emotion ("passion") is a frequent theme in 17th-century literature. In stanzas 2–6, the poet considers music as awakening religious awe, warlike courage, sorrow for unrequited love, jealousy and fury, and the impulse to worship God.
5. According to Genesis 4.21, Jubal was the inventor of the lyre and the pipe. Dryden imagines Jubal's lyre to have been made of a tortoiseshell ("corded shell").
6. A reference to the bright tone of the modern violin, introduced into England at the Restoration. The tone of the old-fashioned viol is much duller.

7

Orpheus[7] could lead the savage race;
And trees unrooted left their place,
Sequacious of° the lyre; *following*
But bright Cecilia raised the wonder higher:
When to her organ vocal breath was given,
An angel heard, and straight appeared,[8]
Mistaking earth for heaven.

GRAND CHORUS

As from the power of sacred lays
The spheres began to move,
And sung the great Creator's praise[9]
To all the blest above;
So, when the last and dreadful hour
This crumbling pageant[1] *shall devour,*
The trumpet shall be heard on high,
The dead shall live, the living die,
And Music shall untune the sky.[2]

1687

Criticism

Dryden's impulse to write criticism came from his practical urge to explain and justify his own writings; his attraction to clear, ordered theoretical principles; and his growing sense of himself as a leader of English literary taste and judgment. The Elizabethans, largely impelled by the example of Italian humanists, had produced an interesting but unsystematic body of critical writings. Dryden could look back to such pioneer works as George Puttenham's *Art of English Poesy* (1589), Sir Philip Sidney's *Defense of Poesy* (1595), Samuel Daniel's *Defense of Rhyme* (ca. 1603), and Ben Jonson's *Timber, or Discoveries* (1641). These and later writings Dryden knew, as he knew the ancients and the important contemporary French critics, notably Pierre Corneille, René Rapin, and Nicolas Boileau. Taken as a whole, his critical prefaces and dedications, which appeared between 1664 and 1700, are the work of a man of independent mind who has made his own synthesis of critical canons from wide reading, a great deal of thinking, and the constant practice of the art of writing. As a critic he is no one's disciple, and he has the saving grace of being always willing to change his mind.

7. Legendary poet, son of one of the Muses, who played so wonderfully on the lyre that wild beasts ("the savage race") grew tame and followed him, as did even rocks and trees.
8. According to the legend, it was Cecilia's piety, not her music, that brought an angel to visit her.
9. As it was harmony that ordered the universe, so it was angelic song ("sacred lays") that put the celestial bodies ("spheres") in motion. The harmonious chord that results from the traditional "music of the spheres" is a hymn of "praise" sung by created nature to its "Creator."
1. The universe, the stage on which the drama of human salvation has been acted out.
2. The "last trump" of 1 Corinthians 15.52, which will announce the Resurrection and the Last Judgment.

All but a very few of Dryden's critical works (most notably *An Essay of Dramatic Poesy*) grew out of the works to which they served as prefaces: comedies, heroic plays, tragedies, translations, and poems of various sorts. Each work posed problems that Dryden was eager to discuss with his readers, and the topics that he treated proved to be important in the development of the new literature of which he was the principal apologist. He dealt with the processes of literary creation, the poet's relation to tradition, the forms of modern drama, the craft of poetry, and above all the genius of earlier poets: Shakespeare, Jonson, Chaucer, Juvenal, Horace, Homer, and Virgil. For nearly forty years this voice was heard in the land; and when it was finally silenced, a set of critical standards had come into existence and a new age had been given its direction.

From An Essay of Dramatic Poesy[1]

[SHAKESPEARE AND BEN JONSON COMPARED][2]

"To begin, then, with Shakespeare. He was the man who of all modern, and perhaps ancient poets, had the largest and most comprehensive soul. All the images of Nature were still present to him, and he drew them, not laboriously, but luckily; when he describes anything, you more than see it, you feel it too. Those who accuse him to have wanted learning, give him the greater commendation: he was naturally learned; he needed not the spectacles of books to read Nature; he looked inwards, and found her there. I cannot say he is everywhere alike; were he so, I should do him injury to compare him with the greatest of mankind. He is many times flat, insipid; his comic wit degenerating into clenches, his serious swelling into bombast. But he is always great when some great occasion is presented to him; no man can say he ever had a fit subject for his wit and did not then raise himself as high above the rest of poets,

Quantum lenta solent inter viburna cupressi[3]

The consideration of this made Mr. Hales[4] of Eton say that there was no subject of which any poet ever writ, but he would produce it much better treated of in Shakespeare; and however others are now generally preferred before him, yet the age wherein he lived, which had contemporaries with him Fletcher and Jonson, never equaled them to him in their esteem: and in the last king's court,

1. With the reopening of the theaters in 1660, older plays were revived, but despite their power and charm, they seemed old-fashioned. Although new playwrights, ambitious to create a modern English drama, soon appeared, they were uncertain of their direction. What, if anything, useful could they learn from the dramatic practice of the ancients? Should they ignore the English dramatists of the late 16th and early 17th centuries? Should they make their example the vigorous contemporary drama of France? Dryden addresses himself to these and other problems in this essay, his first extended piece of criticism. Its purpose, he tells us, was "chiefly to vindicate the honor of our English writers from the censure of those who unjustly prefer the French before them." Its method is skeptical: Dryden presents several points of view, but imposes none. The form is a dialogue among friends, like the *Tusculan Disputations* or the *Brutus* of Cicero. Crites praises the drama of the ancients; Eugenius protests against their authority and argues for the idea of progress in the arts; Lisideius urges the excellence of French plays; and Neander, speaking in the climactic position, defends the native tradition and the greatness of Shakespeare, Fletcher, and Jonson. The dialogue takes place on June 3, 1665, in a boat on the Thames. The four friends are rowed downstream to listen to the cannonading of the English and Dutch fleets, engaged in battle off the Suffolk coast. As the gunfire recedes they are assured of victory and order their boatman to return to London, and naturally enough they fall to discussing the number of bad poems that the victory will evoke.

2. Neander's contrast of Shakespeare and Jonson introduces an extended commentary on the latter's play *Epicoene; or the Silent Woman*.

3. As do cypresses among the bending shrubs (Latin; Virgil's *Eclogues* 1.25).

4. The learned John Hales (1584–1656), provost of Eton. He is reputed to have said this to Jonson himself.

when Ben's reputation was at highest, Sir John Suckling,[5] and with him the greater part of the courtiers, set our Shakespeare far above him. . . .

"As for Jonson, to whose character I am now arrived, if we look upon him while he was himself (for his last plays were but his dotages), I think him the most learned and judicious writer which any theater ever had. He was a most severe judge of himself, as well as others. One cannot say he wanted wit, but rather that he was frugal of it. In his works you find little to retrench[6] or alter. Wit, and language, and humor also in some measure, we had before him; but something of art[7] was wanting to the drama till he came. He managed his strength to more advantage than any who preceded him. You seldom find him making love in any of his scenes or endeavoring to move the passions; his genius was too sullen and saturnine[8] to do it gracefully, especially when he knew he came after those who had performed both to such an height. Humor was his proper sphere: and in that he delighted most to represent mechanic people.[9] He was deeply conversant in the ancients, both Greek and Latin, and he borrowed boldly from them: there is scarce a poet or historian among the Roman authors of those times whom he has not translated in *Sejanus* and *Catiline*.[1] But he has done his robberies so openly, that one may see he fears not to be taxed by any law. He invades authors like a monarch; and what would be theft in other poets is only victory in him. With the spoils of these writers he so represents old Rome to us, in its rites, ceremonies, and customs, that if one of their poets had written either of his tragedies, we had seen less of it than in him. If there was any fault in his language, 'twas that he weaved it too closely and laboriously, in his serious plays:[2] perhaps, too, he did a little too much Romanize our tongue, leaving the words which he translated almost as much Latin as he found them: wherein, though he learnedly followed the idiom of their language, he did not enough comply with the idiom of ours. If I would compare him with Shakespeare, I must acknowledge him the more correct poet, but Shakespeare the greater wit.[3] Shakespeare was the Homer, or father of our dramatic poets; Jonson was the Virgil, the pattern of elaborate writing; I admire him, but I love Shakespeare. To conclude of him; as he has given us the most correct plays, so in the precepts which he has laid down in his *Discoveries*, we have as many and profitable rules for perfecting the stage, as any wherewith the French can furnish us."

1668

5. Courtier, poet, playwright, much admired in Dryden's time for his wit and the easy naturalness of his style. "King's court": that of Charles I.
6. Delete.
7. Craftsmanship.
8. Heavy.
9. I.e., artisans. In Jonson's comedies the characters are seen under the domination of some psychological trait, ruling passion, or affectation—i.e., some "humor"—that makes them unique and ridiculous.
1. Jonson's two Roman plays, dated 1605 and 1611, respectively.
2. This is the reading of the first edition. Curiously enough, in the second edition Dryden altered the phrase to "in his comedies especially."
3. Genius.

From A Discourse Concerning the Original and Progress of Satire[1]

[THE ART OF SATIRE]

* * * How easy is it to call rogue and villain, and that wittily! But how hard to make a man appear a fool, a blockhead, or a knave without using any of those opprobrious terms! To spare the grossness of the names, and to do the thing yet more severely, is to draw a full face, and to make the nose and cheeks stand out, and yet not to employ any depth of shadowing.[2] This is the mystery of that noble trade, which yet no master can teach to his apprentice; he may give the rules, but the scholar is never the nearer in his practice. Neither is it true that this fineness of raillery[3] is offensive. A witty man is tickled while he is hurt in this manner, and a fool feels it not. The occasion of an offense may possibly be given, but he cannot take it. If it be granted that in effect this way does more mischief; that a man is secretly wounded, and though he be not sensible himself, yet the malicious world will find it out for him; yet there is still a vast difference betwixt the slovenly butchering of a man, and the fineness of a stroke that separates the head from the body, and leaves it standing in its place. A man may be capable, as Jack Ketch's[4] wife said of his servant, of a plain piece of work, a bare hanging; but to make a malefactor die sweetly was only belonging to her husband. I wish I could apply it to myself, if the reader would be kind enough to think it belongs to me. The character of Zimri in my *Absalom*[5] is, in my opinion, worth the whole poem: it is not bloody, but it is ridiculous enough; and he, for whom it was intended, was too witty to resent it as an injury. If I had railed,[6] I might have suffered for it justly; but I managed my own work more happily, perhaps more dexterously. I avoided the mention of great crimes, and applied myself to the representing of blindsides, and little extravagancies; to which, the wittier a man is, he is generally the more obnoxious.[7] It succeeded as I wished; the jest went round, and he was laughed at in his turn who began the frolic. * * *

1693

1. This passage is an excerpt from the long and rambling preface that served as the dedication of a translation of the satires of the Roman satirists Juvenal and Persius to Charles Sackville, sixth earl of Dorset. The translations were made by Dryden and other writers, among them William Congreve. Dryden traces the origin and development of verse satire in Rome and in a very fine passage contrasts Horace and Juvenal as satiric poets. It is plain that he prefers the "tragic" satire of Juvenal to the urbane and laughing satire of Horace. But in the passage printed here, he praises his own satiric character of Zimri (the duke of Buckingham) in *Absalom and Achitophel* for the very reason that it is modeled on Horatian "raillery," not Juvenalian invective.
2. Early English miniaturists prided themselves on the art of giving roundness to the full face without painting in shadows.
3. Satirical mirth, good-natured satire.
4. A notorious public executioner of Dryden's time (d. 1686). His name later became a generic term for all members of his profession.
5. *Absalom and Achitophel,* lines 544–68 (p. 894).
6. Reviled, abused. Observe that the verb differed in meaning from its noun, defined above.
7. Liable.

JOHN WILMOT, SECOND EARL OF ROCHESTER
1647–1680

John Wilmot, second earl of Rochester, was the precocious son of one of Charles II's most loyal followers in exile. He won the king's favor at the Restoration and, in 1664, after education at Oxford and on the Continent, took a place at court, at the age of seventeen. There he soon distinguished himself as "the man who has the most wit and the least honor in England." For one escapade, the abduction of Elizabeth Malet, an heiress, he was imprisoned in the Tower of London. But he regained his position by courageous service in the naval war against the Dutch, and in 1667 he married Malet. The rest of his career was no less stormy. His satiric wit, directed not only at ordinary mortals but at Dryden and Charles II himself, embroiled him in constant quarrels and exiles; his practical jokes, his affairs, and his dissipation were legendary. He circulated his works, always intellectually daring and often obscene, to a limited court readership in manuscripts executed by professional scribes—a common way of handling writing deemed too ideologically or morally scandalous for print. An early printed collection of his poems did appear in 1680, though the title page read "Antwerp," probably to hide its London origin. The air of scandal and disguise surrounding his writing only intensified his notoriety as the exemplar of the dissolute, libertine ways of court culture. He told his biographer, Gilbert Burnet, that "for five years together he was continually drunk." Just before his death, however, he was converted to Christian repentance, and for posterity, Rochester became a favorite moral topic: the libertine who had seen the error of his ways.

Wit, in the Restoration, meant not only a clever turn of phrase but mental capacity and intellectual power. Rochester was famous for both kinds of wit. His fierce intelligence, impatient of sham and convention, helped design a way of life based on style, cleverness, and self-interest—a way of life observable in Restoration plays (Dorimant, in Etherege's *The Man of Mode,* strongly resembles Rochester). Stylistically, Rochester infuses forms such as the heroic couplet with a volatility that contrasts with the pointed and balanced manner of its other masters. From the very first line of "A Satire against Reason and Mankind"—"Were I (who to my cost already am"—he plunges the reader into a couplet mode energized by speculation, self-interruption, and enjambment; and he frequently employs extravagant effects (such as the alliterations "love's lesser lightning" and "balmy brinks of bliss" in "The Imperfect Enjoyment") to flaunt his delight in dramatizing situations, sensations, and himself. "The Disabled Debauchee," composed in "heroic stanzas" like those of Dryden's *Annus Mirabilis,* subverts the very notion of heroism by turning conventions upside down. Philosophically, Rochester is daring and destabilizing. In "A Satire," he rejects high-flown, theoretical reason and consigns its "misguided follower" to an abyss of doubt. The poem's speaker himself happily embraces the "right reason" of instinct, celebrating the life of a "natural man." The poem thus accords with Hobbes's doctrine that all laws, even our notions of good and evil, are artificial social checks on natural human desires. Yet it remains unclear, in Rochester's world of intellectual risk and conflict, whether he thinks humanity's paradoxical predicament can ever finally be escaped. Often called a skeptic himself, he seems to hint that the doubt raised by reason's collapse may surge to engulf him too.

The Disabled Debauchee

As some brave admiral, in former war
Deprived of force, but pressed with courage still,
Two rival fleets appearing from afar,
Crawls to the top of an adjacent hill;

From whence, with thoughts full of concern, he views
The wise and daring conduct of the fight,
And each bold action to his mind renews
His present glory and his past delight;

From his fierce eyes flashes of fire he throws,
As from black clouds when lightning breaks away;
Transported, thinks himself amidst his foes,
And absent, yet enjoys the bloody day;

So, when my days of impotence approach,
And I'm by pox° and wine's unlucky chance *syphilis*
Forced from the pleasing billows of debauch
On the dull shore of lazy temperance,

My pains at least some respite shall afford
While I behold the battles you maintain
When fleets of glasses sail about the board,° *table*
From whose broadsides[1] volleys of wit shall rain.

Nor shall the sight of honorable scars,
Which my too forward valor did procure,
Frighten new-listed° soldiers from the wars: *newly enlisted*
Past joys have more than paid what I endure.

Should any youth (worth being drunk) prove nice,° *coy, fastidious*
And from his fair inviter meanly shrink,
'Twill please the ghost of my departed vice
If, at my counsel, he repent and drink.

Or should some cold-complexioned sot forbid,
With his dull morals, our bold night-alarms,
I'll fire his blood by telling what I did
When I was strong and able to bear arms.

I'll tell of whores attacked, their lords at home;
Bawds' quarters beaten up, and fortress won;
Windows demolished, watches° overcome; *watchmen*
And handsome ills by my contrivance done.

Nor shall our love-fits, Chloris, be forgot,
When each the well-looked linkboy[2] strove t' enjoy,

1. The sides of the table; artillery on a ship; sheets on which satirical verses were printed.

2. Good-looking boy employed to light the way with a link or torch.

And the best kiss was the deciding lot
  Whether the boy used you, or I the boy.

With tales like these I will such thoughts inspire
  As to important mischief shall incline:
I'll make him long some ancient church to fire,
  And fear no lewdness he's called to by wine.

Thus, statesmanlike, I'll saucily impose,
  And safe from action, valiantly advise;
Sheltered in impotence, urge you to blows,
  And being good for nothing else, be wise.

1680

The Imperfect Enjoyment[1]

Naked she lay, clasped in my longing arms,
I filled with love, and she all over charms;
Both equally inspired with eager fire,
Melting through kindness, flaming in desire.
With arms, legs, lips close clinging to embrace,
She clips° me to her breast, and sucks me to her face. *hugs*
Her nimble tongue, Love's lesser lightning, played
Within my mouth, and to my thoughts conveyed
Swift orders that I should prepare to throw
The all-dissolving thunderbolt below.
My fluttering soul, sprung[2] with the pointed kiss,
Hangs hovering o'er her balmy brinks of bliss.
But whilst her busy hand would guide that part
Which should convey my soul up to her heart,
In liquid raptures I dissolve all o'er,
Melt into sperm, and spend at every pore.
A touch from any part of her had done 't:
Her hand, her foot, her very look's a cunt.
  Smiling, she chides in a kind murmuring noise,
And from her body wipes the clammy joys,
When, with a thousand kisses wandering o'er
My panting bosom, "Is there then no more?"
She cries. "All this to love and rapture's due;
Must we not pay a debt to pleasure too?"
  But I, the most forlorn, lost man alive,
To show my wished obedience vainly strive:
I sigh, alas! and kiss, but cannot swive.° *screw*
Eager desires confound my first intent,
Succeeding shame does more success prevent,
And rage at last confirms me impotent.
Ev'n her fair hand, which might bid heat return

1. The genre of poems about the downfall of male "pride"—not only a swelled head but an erection—derives from Ovid's *Amores* 3.7. For a woman's treatment of this situation, see Aphra Behn's "The Disappointment" (p. 942).
2. Startled from cover, like a game bird.

To frozen age, and make cold hermits burn,
Applied to my dead cinder, warms no more
Than fire to ashes could past flames restore.
Trembling, confused, despairing, limber, dry,
A wishing, weak, unmoving lump I lie.
This dart of love, whose piercing point, oft tried,
With virgin blood ten thousand maids have dyed;
Which nature still directed with such art
That it through every cunt reached every heart—
Stiffly resolved, 'twould carelessly invade
Woman or man, nor aught° its fury stayed: *anything*
Where'er it pierced, a cunt it found or made—
Now languid lies in this unhappy hour,
Shrunk up and sapless like a withered flower.
  Thou treacherous, base deserter of my flame,
False to my passion, fatal to my fame,
Through what mistaken magic dost thou prove
So true to lewdness, so untrue to love?
What oyster-cinder-beggar-common whore
Didst thou e'er fail in all thy life before?
When vice, disease, and scandal lead the way,
With what officious haste dost thou obey!
Like a rude, roaring hector° in the streets *bully*
Who scuffles, cuffs, and justles all he meets,
But if his King or country claim his aid,
The rakehell villain shrinks and hides his head;
Ev'n so thy brutal valor is displayed,
Breaks every stew,[3] does each small whore invade,
But when great Love the onset does command,
Base recreant to thy prince, thou dar'st not stand.
Worst part of me, and henceforth hated most,
Through all the town a common fucking post,
On whom each whore relieves her tingling cunt
As hogs on gates do rub themselves and grunt,
Mayst thou to ravenous chancres be a prey,
Or in consuming weepings waste away;
May strangury and stone[4] thy days attend;
May'st thou ne'er piss, who didst refuse to spend
When all my joys did on false thee depend.
  And may ten thousand abler pricks agree
  To do the wronged Corinna right for thee.

1680

Upon Nothing

Nothing, thou elder brother even to shade,
Thou hadst a being ere the world was made
And (well fixed) art alone of ending not afraid.

3. Breaks into every brothel.
4. "Strangury" and "stone" cause slow and painful urination. "Chancres" and "weepings" are signs of venereal disease.

Ere time and place were, time and place were not,
When primitive Nothing Something straight begot,
Then all proceeded from the great united *What*.

Something, the general attribute of all,
Severed from thee, its sole original,
Into thy boundless self must undistinguished fall.

Yet Something did thy mighty power command
And from thy fruitful emptiness's hand
Snatched men, beasts, birds, fire, water, air, and land.

Matter, the wick'dst offspring of thy race,
By form assisted, flew from thy embrace,
And rebel light obscured thy reverend dusky face.

With form and matter, time and place did join,
Body thy foe, with these did leagues combine[1]
To spoil thy peaceful realm and ruin all thy line.

But turncoat time assists the foe in vain
And bribed by thee destroys their short-lived reign
And to thy hungry womb drives back thy slaves again.

Though mysteries are barred from laic eyes[2]
And the divine alone with warrant pries
Into thy bosom where thy truth in private lies,

Yet this of thee the wise may truly say:
Thou from the virtuous, nothing tak'st away,[3]
And to be part of thee, the wicked wisely pray.

Great negative, how vainly would the wise
Enquire, define, distinguish, teach, devise,
Didst thou not stand to point° their blind philosophies. *expose*

Is or Is Not, the two great ends of fate,
And true or false, the subject of debate
That perfect or destroy the vast designs of state,

When they have racked the politician's breast,
Within thy bosom most securely rest
And when reduced to thee are least unsafe and best.

But Nothing, why does Something still permit
That sacred monarchs should at council sit
With persons highly thought, at best, for nothing fit;

1. Form, matter, time, and place combined in leagues against Nothing.
2. I.e., the eyes of the laity, who are uninitiated in Nothing's mysteries.
3. You, Nothing, do not take anything away from the virtuous.

Whilst weighty Something modestly abstains
From princes' coffers[4] and from statesmen's brains
And Nothing there like stately Something reigns?

Nothing, who dwellst with fools in grave disguise,
For whom they reverend shapes and forms devise,
Lawn-sleeves and furs and gowns,[5] when they like thee look wise;

French truth, Dutch prowess, British policy,
Hibernian° learning, Scotch civility, *Irish*
Spaniards' dispatch, Danes' wit[6] are mainly seen in thee;

The great man's gratitude to his best friend,
Kings' promises, whores' vows, towards thee they bend,
Flow swiftly into thee and in thee ever end.

1679

4. Charles II's coffers were notably empty, and he was forced to declare bankruptcy in 1672.
5. "Furs and gowns" were worn by judges. "Lawn": a fine linen or cotton fabric, worn by bishops.
6. All proverbial deficiencies of the various nationalities mentioned, many of them exposed during the Anglo-Dutch war (1672–74).

APHRA BEHN
1640?–1689

"A woman wit has often graced the stage," Dryden wrote in 1681. Soon after actresses first appeared in English public theaters, there was an even more striking debut by a woman writer who boldly signed her plays and talked back to her critics. In a dozen years, Aphra Behn turned out at least that many plays, discovering fresh dramatic possibilities in casts that included women with warm bodies and clever heads. She also drew attention as a warm and witty poet of love. When writing for the stage became less profitable, she turned to the emerging field of prose fiction, composing a pioneering epistolary novel, *Love Letters between a Nobleman and His Sister,* and diverse short tales—not to mention a raft of translations from the French, pindarics to her beloved Stuart rulers, compilations, prologues, complimentary verses, all the piecework and puffery that were the stock in trade of the Restoration town wit. She worked in haste and with flair for nearly two decades and more than held her own as a professional writer. In the end, no author of her time—except Dryden himself—proved more versatile, more alive to new currents of thought, or more inventive in recasting fashionable forms.

Much of Behn's life remains a mystery. Although her books have been accompanied—and often all but buried—by volumes of rumor, hard facts are elusive. She was almost certainly from East Kent; she may well have been named Johnson. But she herself seems to have left no record of her date and place of birth, her family name and upbringing, or the identity of the shadowy Mr. Behn whom she reportedly married. Her many references to nuns and convents, as well as praise for prominent Catholic lords (*Oroonoko* is dedicated to one), have prompted speculation that she may have been raised as a Catholic and educated in a convent abroad. Without doubt, she drew on a range of worldly experience that would be closed to women in the more genteel ages to come. The circumstantial detail of *Oroonoko* supports her claim that she was in the new sugar colony of Surinam early in 1664. Perhaps she exaggerated her social position to enhance her tale, but many particulars—from dialect words and the location of plantations to methods of selling and torturing slaves—can be authenticated. During the trade war that broke out in 1665—which left her "vast and charming world" a Dutch prize—Behn traveled to the Low Countries on a spying mission for King Charles II. The king could be lax about payment, however, and Behn had to petition desperately to escape debtor's prison. In 1670 she brought out her first plays, "forced to write for bread," she confessed, "and not ashamed to own it."

In London, Behn flourished in the cosmopolitan world of the playhouse and the court. Dryden and other wits encouraged her; she mixed with actresses and managers and playwrights and exchanged verses with a lively literary set that she called her "cabal." Surviving letters record a passionate, troubled attachment to a lawyer named John Hoyle, a bisexual with libertine views. She kept up with the most advanced thinking and joined public debates with pointed satire against the Whigs. But the festivity of the Restoration world was fading out in bitter party acrimony. In 1682 Behn was placed under arrest for "abusive reflections" on the king's illegitimate son, the Whig duke of Monmouth (Dryden's Absalom). Her Royalist opinions and the immodesty of her public role made her a target; gleeful lampoons declared that she was aging and ill and once again poor. She responded by bringing out her works at a still faster rate, composing *Oroonoko*, her dedication claims, "in a few hours . . . for I never rested my pen a moment for thought." In some last works she recorded her hope that her writings would live: "I value fame as much as if I had been born a hero." When she died she was buried in Westminster Abbey.

"All women together ought to let flowers fall upon the grave of Aphra Behn," Virginia Woolf wrote, "for it was she who earned them the right to speak their minds." Behn herself spoke her mind. She scorned hypocrisy and calculation in her society and commented freely on religion, science, and philosophy. Moreover, she spoke as a woman. Denied the classical education of most male authors, she dismissed "musty rules" and lessons and relished the immediate human appeal of popular forms. Her first play, *The Forced Marriage,* exposes the bondage of matches arranged for money and status, and many later works invoke the powerful natural force of love, whose energy breaks through conventions. In a range of genres, from simple pastoral songs to complex plots of intrigue, she candidly explores the sexual feelings of women, their schooling in disguise, their need to "love upon the honest square" (for this her work was later denounced as coarse and impure). *Oroonoko* represents another departure for Behn and prose fiction. It achieves something new both in its narrative form and in extending some of her favorite themes to an original subject: the destiny of a black male hero on a world historical stage.

Oroonoko cannot be classified as fact or fiction, realism or romance. In the still unshaped field of prose narrative—where a "history" could mean any story, true or false—Behn combined the attractions of three older forms. First, she presents the work as a memoir, a personal account of what she has heard and seen. According to a friend, Behn had told this tale over and over; perhaps that explains the conversational ease with which she turns back and forth, interpreting faraway scenes for her readers at home. Second, *Oroonoko* is a travel narrative in three parts. It turns west to a new world often extolled as a paradise, then east to Africa and the amorous intrigues of a corrupt old-world court (popular reading fare), then finally west again with its hero across the infamous "Middle Passage"—over which millions of slaves would be transported during the next century—to the conflicts of a raw colonial world. Exotic scenes fascinate Behn, but she wants even more to talk to people and learn about their ways of life. As in imaginary voyages, from Sir Thomas More's *Utopia* to *Gulliver's Travels* and *Rasselas,* encounters with foreign cultures sharply challenge Europeans to reexamine themselves. Behn's primitive Indians and noble Africans live by a code of virtue, by principles of fidelity and honor, that "civilized" Christians often ignore or betray. Oroonoko embodies this code. Above all, the book is his biography. Courageous, high-minded, and great hearted, he rivals the heroes of classical epics and Plutarch's *Lives* and is equally worthy of fame. Nor does he lack gentler virtues. Like the heroes of seventeenth-century heroic dramas and romances, he shines in the company of women and proves his nobility by his passionate and constant love for Imoinda, his ideal counterpart. Yet finally a contradiction dooms Oroonoko: he is at once prince and chattel, a "royal slave."

Behn handles her forms dynamically, drawing out their inner discords and tensions. In the biography, Oroonoko's deepest values are turned against him. His trust in friendship and scrupulous truth to his word expose him to the treachery of Europeans who calculate human worth on a yardstick of profit. A hero cannot survive in such a world. His self-respect demands action, even when he can find no clear path through the tangle of assurances and lies. Moreover, the colony too seems tangled in contradictions. Behn's travel narrative reveals a broken paradise where, in the absence of secure authority, the settlers descend into a series of unstable alliances, improvised power relations, and escalating suspicions. Here every term—friend and foe, tenderness and brutality, savagery and civilization—can suddenly turn into its opposite. And the author also seems caught between worlds. The cultivated Englishwoman who narrates and acts in this memoir thinks highly of her hero's code of honor and shares his contempt for the riffraff who plague him. Yet her own role is ambiguous: she lacks the power to save Oroonoko and might even be viewed as implicated in his downfall. Only as a writer can she take control, preserving the hero in her work.

The story of Oroonoko did not end with Behn. Compassion for the royal slave and outrage at his fate were enlisted in the long battle against the slave trade. Reprinted, translated, serialized, dramatized, and much imitated, *Oroonoko* helped teach a mass audience to feel for all victims of the brutal commerce in human beings. A hundred years later, the popular writer Hannah More testified to the widening influence of the story: "No individual griefs my bosom melt, / For millions feel what Oroonoko felt." Women especially identified with the experience of personal injustice and everyday indignity—the pain of being treated as something less than fully human. Perhaps it is appropriate that the writer who made the suffering of the royal slave famous had known the pride and lowliness of being "a female pen."

The Disappointment[1]

One day the amorous Lysander,
By an impatient passion swayed,
Surprised fair Cloris, that loved maid,
Who could defend herself no longer.
All things did with his love conspire;
The gilded planet of the day,° *the sun*
In his gay chariot drawn by fire,
Was now descending to the sea,
And left no light to guide the world
But what from Cloris' brighter eyes was hurled.

In a lone thicket made for love,
Silent as yielding maid's consent,

1. This variation on the "imperfect enjoyment" genre compares with Rochester's (p. 919); it first appeared in a collection of his poems. But Behn gives the theme of impotence her own twist. Freely translating a French poem, Cantenac's "The Lost Chance Recovered," she cuts the conclusion, in which the French lover regained his potency, and she highlights the woman's feelings as well as the man's.

She with a charming languishment,
Permits his force, yet gently strove;
Her hands his bosom softly meet,
But not to put him back designed,
Rather to draw 'em on inclined:
Whilst he lay trembling at her feet,
Resistance 'tis in vain to show:
She wants° the power to say—*Ah! what d'ye do?* lacks

Her bright eyes sweet and yet severe,
Where love and shame confusedly strive,
Fresh vigor to Lysander give;
And breathing faintly in his ear,
She cried—*Cease, cease—your vain desire,*
Or I'll call out—what would you do?
My dearer honor even to you
I cannot, must not give—Retire,
Or take this life, whose chiefest part
I gave you with the conquest of my heart.

But he as much unused to fear,
As he was capable of love,
The blessed minutes to improve
Kisses her mouth, her neck, her hair;
Each touch her new desire alarms;
His burning, trembling hand he pressed
Upon her swelling snowy breast,
While she lay panting in his arms.
All her unguarded beauties lie
The spoils and trophies of the enemy.

And now without respect or fear
He seeks the object of his vows
(His love no modesty allows)
By swift degrees advancing—where
His daring hand that altar seized,
Where gods of love do sacrifice:
That awful throne, that paradise
Where rage is calmed, and anger pleased;
That fountain where delight still flows,
And gives the universal world repose.

Her balmy lips encountering his,
Their bodies, as their souls, are joined;
Where both in transports unconfined
Extend themselves upon the moss.
Cloris half dead and breathless lay;
Her soft eyes cast a humid light
Such as divides the day and night;
Or falling stars, whose fires decay:
And now no signs of life she shows,
But what in short-breathed sighs returns and goes.

He saw how at her length she lay;
He saw her rising bosom bare;
Her loose thin robes, through which appear
A shape designed for love and play;
Abandoned by her pride and shame
She does her softest joys dispense,
Offering her virgin innocence
A victim to love's sacred flame;
While the o'er-ravished shepherd lies
Unable to perform the sacrifice.

Ready to taste a thousand joys,
The too transported hapless swain
Found the vast pleasure turned to pain;
Pleasure which too much love destroys:
The willing garments by he laid,[2]
And heaven all opened to his view.
Mad to possess, himself he threw
On the defenseless lovely maid.
But oh what envying god conspires
To snatch his power, yet leave him the desire!

Nature's support (without whose aid
She can no human being give)
Itself now wants the art[3] to live;
Faintness its slackened nerves invade:
In vain th'enraged youth essayed
To call its fleeting vigor back;
No motion 'twill from motion take;
Excess of love his love betrayed:
In vain he toils, in vain commands:
The insensible[4] fell weeping in his hand.

In this so amorous cruel strife,
Where love and fate were too severe,
The poor Lysander in despair
Renounced his reason with his life:
Now all the brisk and active fire
That should the nobler part inflame
Served to increase his rage and shame,
And left no spark for new desire:
Not all her naked charms could move
Or calm that rage that had debauched his love.

Cloris returning from the trance
Which love and soft desire had bred,
Her timorous hand she gently laid
(Or guided by design or chance)
Upon that fabulous Priapus,[5]
That potent god, as poets feign:

2. He took off her compliant clothes.
3. Lacks the capacity.
4. Devoid of feeling and too small to be noticed.
5. Phallus. The ancient god Priapus is always pictured with an outstanding erection.

But never did young shepherdess,
Gathering the fern upon the plain,
More nimbly draw her fingers back,
Finding beneath the verdant leaves a snake,

Than Cloris her fair hand withdrew,
Finding that god of her desires
Disarmed of all his awful fires,
And cold as flowers bathed in the morning dew.
Who can the nymph's confusion guess?
The blood forsook the hinder place,
And strewed with blushes all her face,
Which both disdain and shame expressed:
And from Lysander's arms she fled,
Leaving him fainting on the gloomy bed.

Like lightning through the grove she hies,
Or Daphne from the Delphic god;[6]
No print upon the grassy road
She leaves, to instruct pursuing eyes.
The wind that wantoned in her hair
And with her ruffled garments played,
Discovered in the flying maid
All that the gods e'er made, if fair.
So Venus, when her love[7] was slain,
With fear and haste flew o'er the fatal plain.

The nymph's resentments none but I
Can well imagine or condole:
But none can guess Lysander's soul,
But those who swayed his destiny.
His silent griefs swell up to storms,
And not one god his fury spares;
He cursed his birth, his fate, his stars;
But more the shepherdess's charms,
Whose soft bewitching influence
Had damned him to the hell of impotence.[8]

1680

Oroonoko, or The Royal Slave[1]

I do not pretend, in giving you the history of this royal slave, to entertain my reader with the adventures of a feigned hero, whose life and fortunes fancy may manage at the poet's pleasure; nor in relating the truth, design to adorn it with any accidents but such as arrived in earnest to him. And it shall come simply into the world, recommended by its own proper merits and

6. Apollo, from whom the Greek nymph Daphne fled until she turned into a laurel tree.
7. Adonis, who was killed by a boar.
8. Blaming the woman for an imperfect enjoyment is typical of the genre.
1. The text, prepared by Joanna Lipking, is based on the 1688 edition, the sole edition published during Behn's lifetime. The critical edition of G. C. Duchovnay (diss., Indiana, 1971), which collates the four 17th-century editions, has been consulted.

natural intrigues, there being enough of reality to support it, and to render it diverting, without the addition of invention.

I was myself an eyewitness to a great part of what you will find here set down, and what I could not be witness of, I received from the mouth of the chief actor in this history, the hero himself, who gave us the whole transactions of his youth; and though I shall omit for brevity's sake a thousand little accidents of his life, which, however pleasant to us, where history was scarce and adventures very rare, yet might prove tedious and heavy to my reader, in a world where he finds diversions for every minute, new and strange. But we who were perfectly charmed with the character of this great man were curious to gather every circumstance of his life.

The scene of the last part of his adventures lies in a colony in America called Surinam,[2] in the West Indies.

But before I give you the story of this gallant slave, 'tis fit I tell you the manner of bringing them to these new colonies, for those they make use of there are not natives of the place; for those we live with in perfect amity, without daring to command 'em, but on the contrary caress 'em with all the brotherly and friendly affection in the world, trading with 'em for their fish, venison, buffaloes, skins, and little rarities; as marmosets, a sort of monkey as big as a rat or weasel but of a marvelous and delicate shape, and has face and hands like a human creature, and *cousheries*,[3] a little beast in the form and fashion of a lion, as big as a kitten, but so exactly made in all parts like that noble beast, that it is it in miniature. Then for little parakeetoes, great parrots, macaws, and a thousand other birds and beasts of wonderful and surprising forms, shapes, and colors. For skins of prodigious snakes, of which there are some threescore yards in length, as is the skin of one that may be seen at his Majesty's antiquaries'; where are also some rare flies[4] of amazing forms and colors, presented to 'em by myself, some as big as my fist, some less, and all of various excellencies, such as art cannot imitate. Then we trade for feathers, which they order into all shapes, make themselves little short habits of 'em, and glorious wreaths for their heads, necks, arms and legs, whose tinctures are unconceivable. I had a set of these presented to me, and I gave 'em to the King's theater, and it was the dress of the Indian Queen,[5] infinitely admired by persons of quality, and were unimitable. Besides these, a thousand little knacks and rarities in nature, and some of art, as their baskets, weapons, aprons, et cetera. We dealt with 'em with beads of all colors, knives, axes, pins and needles, which they used only as tools to drill holes with in their ears, noses, and lips, where they hang a great many little things, as long beads, bits of tin, brass, or silver beat thin, and any shining trinket. The beads they weave into aprons about a quarter of an ell long, and of the same breadth,[6] working them very prettily in flowers of several colors of beads; which apron they wear just before 'em, as Adam and Eve did the fig leaves, the men wearing a long stripe of linen which they deal with us for. They thread these beads also on long cotton threads and make girdles to tie their aprons to, which come twenty

2. A British sugar colony on the South American coast east of Venezuela; later Dutch Guiana, now the Republic of Suriname.

3. A name appearing in local descriptions, but the animal is not clearly identified; probably the lion-headed marmoset or perhaps the *cujara* (Portuguese), a rodent known as the rice rat. "Buffaloes": wild oxen of various species.

4. Butterflies. "Antiquaries": probably the natural history museum of the Royal Society.

5. The title character in the 1664 heroic play by Sir Robert Howard and John Dryden, which was noted for its lavish production. There are contemporary records of "speckled plumes" and feather headdresses.

6. About a foot square.

times or more about the waist, and then cross, like a shoulder belt, both ways, and round their necks, arms, and legs. This adornment, with their long black hair, and the face painted in little specks or flowers here and there, makes 'em a wonderful figure to behold.

Some of the beauties which indeed are finely shaped, as almost all are, and who have pretty features, are very charming and novel; for they have all that is called beauty, except the color, which is a reddish yellow; or after a new oiling, which they often use to themselves, they are of the color of a new brick, but smooth, soft, and sleek. They are extreme[7] modest and bashful, very shy and nice of being touched. And though they are all thus naked, if one lives forever among 'em there is not to be seen an indecent action or glance; and being continually used to see one another so unadorned, so like our first parents before the Fall, it seems as if they had no wishes; there being nothing to heighten curiosity, but all you can see you see at once, and every moment see, and where there is no novelty there can be no curiosity. Not but I have seen a handsome young Indian dying for love of a very beautiful young Indian maid; but all his courtship was to fold his arms, pursue her with his eyes, and sighs were all his language; while she, as if no such lover were present, or rather, as if she desired none such, carefully guarded her eyes from beholding him, and never approached him but she looked down with all the blushing modesty I have seen in the most severe and cautious of our world. And these people represented to me an absolute idea of the first state of innocence, before man knew how to sin. And 'tis most evident and plain that simple Nature is the most harmless, inoffensive, and virtuous mistress. 'Tis she alone, if she were permitted, that better instructs the world than all the inventions of man. Religion would here but destroy that tranquillity they possess by ignorance, and laws would but teach 'em to know offense, of which now they have no notion. They once made mourning and fasting for the death of the English governor, who had given his hand to come on such a day to 'em and neither came nor sent, believing when once a man's word was passed, nothing but death could or should prevent his keeping it. And when they saw he was not dead, they asked him what name they had for a man who promised a thing he did not do. The governor told them, such a man was a liar, which was a word of infamy to a gentleman. Then one of 'em replied, "Governor, you are a liar, and guilty of that infamy." They have a native justice which knows no fraud, and they understand no vice or cunning, but when they are taught by the white men. They have plurality of wives, which, when they grow old, they serve those that succeed 'em, who are young, but with a servitude easy and respected; and unless they take slaves in war, they have no other attendants.

Those on that continent where I was had no king, but the oldest war captain was obeyed with great resignation. A war captain is a man who has led them on to battle with conduct[8] and success, of whom I shall have occasion to speak more hereafter, and of some other of their customs and manners, as they fall in my way.

With these people, as I said, we live in perfect tranquillity and good understanding, as it behooves us to do, they knowing all the places where to seek the best food of the country and the means of getting it, and for very small and unvaluable trifles, supply us with what 'tis impossible for us to get; for they do not only in the wood and over the savannas, in hunting, supply the

7. Extremely.

8. Capacity to lead.

parts of hounds, by swiftly scouring through those almost impassable places, and by the mere activity of their feet run down the nimblest deer and other eatable beasts; but in the water one would think they were gods of the rivers, or fellow citizens of the deep, so rare an art they have in swimming, diving, and almost living in water, by which they command the less swift inhabitants of the floods. And then for shooting, what they cannot take, or reach with their hands, they do with arrows, and have so admirable an aim that they will split almost a hair; and at any distance that an arrow can reach, they will shoot down oranges and other fruit, and only touch the stalk with the dart's point, that they may not hurt the fruit. So that they being, on all occasions, very useful to us, we find it absolutely necessary to caress 'em as friends, and not to treat 'em as slaves; nor dare we do other, their numbers so far surpassing ours in that continent.

Those then whom we make use of to work in our plantations of sugar are Negroes, black slaves altogether, which are transported thither in this manner. Those who want slaves make a bargain with a master or captain of a ship and contract to pay him so much apiece, a matter of twenty pound a head for as many as he agrees for, and to pay for 'em when they shall be delivered on such a plantation. So that when there arrives a ship laden with slaves, they who have so contracted go aboard and receive their number by lot; and perhaps in one lot that may be for ten, there may happen to be three or four men, the rest women and children. Or be there more or less of either sex, you are obliged to be contented with your lot.

Coramantien,[9] a country of blacks so called, was one of those places in which they found the most advantageous trading for these slaves, and thither most of our great traders in that merchandise trafficked; for that nation is very warlike and brave, and having a continual campaign, being always in hostility with one neighboring prince or other, they had the fortune to take a great many captives; for all they took in battle were sold as slaves, at least those common men who could not ransom themselves. Of these slaves so taken, the general only has all the profit; and of these generals, our captains and masters of ships buy all their freights.

The King of Coramantien was himself a man of a hundred and odd years old, and had no son, though he had many beautiful black wives; for most certainly there are beauties that can charm of that color. In his younger years he had had many gallant men to his sons, thirteen of which died in battle, conquering when they fell; and he had only left him for his successor one grandchild, son to one of these dead victors, who, as soon as he could bear a bow in his hand and a quiver at his back, was sent into the field, to be trained up by one of the oldest generals to war; where, from his natural inclination to arms and the occasions given him, with the good conduct of the old general, he became, at the age of seventeen, one of the most expert captains and bravest soldiers that ever saw the field of Mars. So that he was adored as the wonder of all that world, and the darling of the soldiers. Besides, he was adorned with a native beauty so transcending all those of his gloomy race that he struck an awe and reverence even in those that knew not his quality; as he did in me,

9. Not a country but a British-held fort and slave market on the Gold Coast of Africa, in modern-day Ghana. As the slave trade expanded, the slaves and workers shipped out from the region (who came to be called Cormantines) impressed many European observers by their beauty and bearing, their fierceness in war, and their extreme dignity under captivity or torture.

who beheld him with surprise and wonder, when afterwards he arrived in our world.

He had scarce arrived at his seventeenth year, when fighting by his side, the general was killed with an arrow in his eye, which the Prince Oroonoko (for so was this gallant Moor[1] called) very narrowly avoided; nor had he, if the general, who saw the arrow shot, and perceiving it aimed at the Prince, had not bowed his head between, on purpose to receive it in his own body rather than it should touch that of the Prince, and so saved him.

'Twas then, afflicted as Oroonoko was, that he was proclaimed general in the old man's place; and then it was, at the finishing of that war, which had continued for two years, that the Prince came to court, where he had hardly been a month together from the time of his fifth year to that of seventeen; and 'twas amazing to imagine where it was he learned so much humanity; or to give his accomplishments a juster name, where 'twas he got that real greatness of soul, those refined notions of true honor, that absolute generosity, and that softness that was capable of the highest passions of love and gallantry, whose objects were almost continually fighting men, or those mangled or dead; who heard no sounds but those of war and groans. Some part of it we may attribute to the care of a Frenchman of wit and learning, who, finding it turn to very good account to be a sort of royal tutor to this young black, and perceiving him very ready, apt, and quick of apprehension, took a great pleasure to teach him morals, language, and science, and was for it extremely beloved and valued by him. Another reason was, he loved, when he came from war, to see all the English gentlemen that traded thither, and did not only learn their language but that of the Spaniards also, with whom he traded afterwards for slaves.

I have often seen and conversed with this great man, and been a witness to many of his mighty actions, and do assure my reader the most illustrious courts could not have produced a braver man, both for greatness of courage and mind, a judgment more solid, a wit more quick, and a conversation more sweet and diverting. He knew almost as much as if he had read much. He had heard of and admired the Romans; he had heard of the late civil wars in England, and the deplorable death of our great monarch,[2] and would discourse of it with all the sense and abhorrence of the injustice imaginable. He had an extreme good and graceful mien, and all the civility of a well-bred great man. He had nothing of barbarity in his nature, but in all points addressed himself as if his education had been in some European court.

This great and just character of Oroonoko gave me an extreme curiosity to see him, especially when I knew he spoke French and English, and that I could talk with him. But though I had heard so much of him, I was as greatly surprised when I saw him as if I had heard nothing of him, so beyond all report I found him. He came into the room and addressed himself to me, and some other women, with the best grace in the world. He was pretty tall, but of a shape the most exact that can be fancied. The most famous statuary[3] could not form the figure of a man more admirably turned from head to foot. His face was not of that brown, rusty black which most of that nation are, but a perfect ebony or polished jet. His eyes were the most awful that could be seen,

1. Loosely used for any dark-skinned person.
2. Charles I, beheaded in 1649 during the civil wars between Royalists and Parliamentarians. In 1688 this remark and others would have signaled Behn's ardent support of James II, the last of the Stuart kings, who would be forced into exile within the year.
3. Sculptor.

and very piercing, the white of 'em being like snow, as were his teeth. His nose was rising and Roman, instead of African and flat; his mouth the finest shaped that could be seen, far from those great turned lips which are so natural to the rest of the Negroes. The whole proportion and air of his face was so noble and exactly formed that, bating[4] his color, there could be nothing in nature more beautiful, agreeable, and handsome. There was no one grace wanting that bears the standard of true beauty. His hair came down to his shoulders by the aids of art; which was by pulling it out with a quill and keeping it combed, of which he took particular care. Nor did the perfections of his mind come short of those of his person, for his discourse was admirable upon almost any subject; and whoever had heard him speak would have been convinced of their errors, that all fine wit is confined to the white men, especially to those of Christendom, and would have confessed that Oroonoko was as capable even of reigning well, and of governing as wisely, had as great a soul, as politic[5] maxims, and was as sensible of power, as any prince civilized in the most refined schools of humanity and learning, or the most illustrious courts.

This prince, such as I have described him, whose soul and body were so admirably adorned, was (while yet he was in the court of his grandfather), as I said, as capable of love as 'twas possible for a brave and gallant man to be; and in saying that, I have named the highest degree of love, for sure, great souls are most capable of that passion.

I have already said, the old general was killed by the shot of an arrow, by the side of this prince, in battle, and that Oroonoko was made general. This old dead hero had one only daughter left of his race, a beauty that, to describe her truly, one need say only she was female to the noble male, the beautiful black Venus to our young Mars, as charming in her person as he, and of delicate virtues. I have seen an hundred white men sighing after her, and making a thousand vows at her feet, all vain and unsuccessful. And she was, indeed, too great for any but a prince of her own nation to adore.

Oroonoko coming from the wars (which were now ended), after he had made his court to his grandfather, he thought in honor he ought to make a visit to Imoinda, the daughter of his foster-father, the dead general; and to make some excuses to her, because his preservation was the occasion of her father's death; and to present her with those slaves that had been taken in this last battle, as the trophies of her father's victories. When he came, attended by all the young soldiers of any merit, he was infinitely surprised at the beauty of this fair queen of night, whose face and person was so exceeding all he had ever beheld; that lovely modesty with which she received him; that softness in her look, and sighs, upon the melancholy occasion of this honor that was done by so great a man as Oroonoko, and a prince of whom she had heard such admirable things: the awfulness[6] wherewith she received him, and the sweetness of her words and behavior while he stayed, gained a perfect conquest over his fierce heart, and made him feel the victor could be subdued. So that having made his first compliments, and presented her a hundred and fifty slaves in fetters, he told her with his eyes that he was not insensible of her charms; while Imoinda, who wished for nothing more than so glorious a con-

4. Except for. The singling out of Africans with European looks or moral values is by no means unique to Behn; for example, Edward Long's 1774 *History of Jamaica* reports of the Cormantines that "their features are very different from the rest of the African Negroes, being smaller, and more of the European turn."
5. Shrewd, sagacious.
6. Reverence.

quest, was pleased to believe she understood that silent language of newborn love, and from that moment put on all her additions to beauty.

The Prince returned to court with quite another humor than before; and though he did not speak much of the fair Imoinda, he had the pleasure to hear all his followers speak of nothing but the charms of that maid, insomuch that, even in the presence of the old king, they were extolling her and heightening, if possible, the beauties they had found in her. So that nothing else was talked of, no other sound was heard in every corner where there were whisperers, but "Imoinda! Imoinda!"

'Twill be imagined Oroonoko stayed not long before he made his second visit, nor, considering his quality, not much longer before he told her he adored her. I have often heard him say that he admired by what strange inspiration he came to talk things so soft and so passionate, who never knew love, nor was used to the conversation[7] of women; but (to use his own words) he said, most happily some new and till then unknown power instructed his heart and tongue in the language of love, and at the same time, in favor of him, inspired Imoinda with a sense of his passion. She was touched with what he said, and returned it all in such answers as went to his very heart, with a pleasure unknown before. Nor did he use those obligations[8] ill that love had done him, but turned all his happy moments to the best advantage; and as he knew no vice, his flame aimed at nothing but honor, if such a distinction may be made in love; and especially in that country, where men take to themselves as many as they can maintain, and where the only crime and sin with woman is to turn her off, to abandon her to want, shame, and misery. Such ill morals are only practiced in Christian countries, where they prefer the bare name of religion, and, without virtue or morality, think that's sufficient. But Oroonoko was none of those professors, but as he had right notions of honor, so he made her such propositions as were not only and barely such; but contrary to the custom of his country, he made her vows she should be the only woman he would possess while he lived; that no age or wrinkles should incline him to change, for her soul would be always fine and always young, and he should have an eternal idea in his mind of the charms she now bore, and should look into his heart for that idea when he could find it no longer in her face.

After a thousand assurances of his lasting flame, and her eternal empire over him, she condescended to receive him for her husband, or rather, received him as the greatest honor the gods could do her.

There is a certain ceremony in these cases to be observed, which I forgot to ask him how performed; but 'twas concluded on both sides that, in obedience to him, the grandfather was to be first made acquainted with the design, for they pay a most absolute resignation to the monarch, especially when he is a parent also.

On the other side, the old king, who had many wives and many concubines, wanted not court flatterers to insinuate in his heart a thousand tender thoughts for this young beauty, and who represented her to his fancy as the most charming he had ever possessed in all the long race of his numerous years. At this character his old heart, like an extinguished brand, most apt to take fire, felt new sparks of love and began to kindle; and now grown to his second childhood, longed with impatience to behold this gay thing, with whom, alas! he could but innocently play. But how he should be confirmed

7. Company. "Admired": marveled.

8. Benefits.

she was this wonder, before he used his power to call her to court (where maidens never came, unless for the King's private use), he was next to consider; and while he was so doing, he had intelligence brought him that Imoinda was most certainly mistress to the Prince Oroonoko. This gave him some chagrin; however, it gave him also an opportunity, one day when the Prince was a-hunting, to wait on a man of quality, as his slave and attendant, who should go and make a present to Imoinda as from the Prince; he should then, unknown, see this fair maid, and have an opportunity to hear what message she would return the Prince for his present, and from thence gather the state of her heart and degree of her inclination. This was put in execution, and the old monarch saw, and burned. He found her all he had heard, and would not delay his happiness, but found he should have some obstacle to overcome her heart; for she expressed her sense of the present the Prince had sent her in terms so sweet, so soft and pretty, with an air of love and joy that could not be dissembled, insomuch that 'twas past doubt whether she loved Oroonoko entirely. This gave the old king some affliction, but he salved it with this, that the obedience the people pay their king was not at all inferior to what they paid their gods; and what love would not oblige Imoinda to do, duty would compel her to.

He was therefore no sooner got to his apartment but he sent the royal veil to Imoinda, that is, the ceremony of invitation: he sends the lady he has a mind to honor with his bed a veil, with which she is covered, and secured for the King's use; and 'tis death to disobey, besides held a most impious disobedience.

'Tis not to be imagined the surprise and grief that seized this lovely maid at this news and sight. However, as delays in these cases are dangerous and pleading worse than treason, trembling, and almost fainting, she was obliged to suffer herself to be covered and led away.

They brought her thus to court; and the King, who had caused a very rich bath to be prepared, was led into it, where he sat under a canopy, in state, to receive this longed-for virgin; whom he having commanded should be brought to him, they (after disrobing her) led her to the bath, and making fast the doors, left her to descend. The King, without more courtship, bade her throw off her mantle and come to his arms. But Imoinda, all in tears, threw herself on the marble, on the brink of the bath, and besought him to hear her. She told him, as she was a maid, how proud of the divine glory she should have been, of having it in her power to oblige her king; but as by the laws he could not, and from his royal goodness would not, take from any man his wedded wife, so she believed she should be the occasion of making him commit a great sin, if she did not reveal her state and condition, and tell him she was another's, and could not be so happy to be his.

The King, enraged at this delay, hastily demanded the name of the bold man that had married a woman of her degree without his consent. Imoinda, seeing his eyes fierce and his hands tremble (whether with age or anger, I know not, but she fancied the last), almost repented she had said so much, for now she feared the storm would fall on the Prince. She therefore said a thousand things to appease the raging of his flame, and to prepare him to hear who it was with calmness; but before she spoke, he imagined who she meant, but would not seem to do so, but commanded her to lay aside her mantle and suffer herself to receive his caresses; or by his gods, he swore that happy man whom she was going to name should die, though it were even Oroonoko himself. "Therefore," said he, "deny this marriage, and swear thyself a maid." "That," replied Imoinda, "by all our powers I do, for I am not yet known to my husband." " 'Tis enough," said the King; " 'tis enough to satisfy both my conscience and my heart." And rising from his seat, he went and led her into the bath, it being in vain for her to resist.

In this time the Prince, who was returned from hunting, went to visit his Imoinda, but found her gone; and not only so, but heard she had received the royal veil. This raised him to a storm, and in his madness they had much ado to save him from laying violent hands on himself. Force first prevailed, and then reason. They urged all to him that might oppose his rage, but nothing weighed so greatly with him as the King's old age, uncapable of injuring him with Imoinda. He would give way to that hope, because it pleased him most, and flattered best his heart. Yet this served not altogether to make him cease his different passions, which sometimes raged within him, and sometimes softened into showers. 'Twas not enough to appease him, to tell him his grandfather was old and could not that way injure him, while he retained that awful duty which the young men are used there to pay to their grave relations. He could not be convinced he had no cause to sigh and mourn for the loss of a mistress he could not with all his strength and courage retrieve. And he would often cry, "O my friends! Were she in walled cities or confined from me in fortifications of the greatest strength, did enchantments or monsters detain her from me, I would venture through any hazard to free her. But here, in the arms of a feeble old man, my youth, my violent love, my trade in arms, and all my vast desire of glory avail me nothing. Imoinda is as irrecoverably lost to me as if she were snatched by the cold arms of Death. Oh! she is never to be retrieved. If I would wait tedious years, till fate should bow the old king to his grave, even that would not leave me Imoinda free; but still that custom that makes it so vile a crime for a son to marry his father's wives or mistresses would hinder my happiness, unless I would either ignobly set an ill precedent to my successors, or abandon my country and fly with her to some unknown world, who never heard our story."

But it was objected to him that his case was not the same; for Imoinda being his lawful wife, by solemn contract, 'twas he was the injured man and might if he so pleased take Imoinda back, the breach of the law being on his grandfather's side; and that if he could circumvent him and redeem her from the Otan, which is the palace of the King's women, a sort of seraglio, it was both just and lawful for him so to do.

This reasoning had some force upon him, and he should have been entirely comforted, but for the thought that she was possessed by his grandfather. However, he loved so well that he was resolved to believe what most favored his hope, and to endeavor to learn from Imoinda's own mouth what only she could satisfy him in, whether she was robbed of that blessing which was only due to his faith and love. But as it was very hard to get a sight of the women (for no men ever entered into the Otan but when the King went to entertain himself with some one of his wives or mistresses, and 'twas death at any other time for any other to go in), so he knew not how to contrive to get a sight of her.

While Oroonoko felt all the agonies of love, and suffered under a torment the most painful in the world, the old king was not exempted from his share of affliction. He was troubled for having been forced by an irresistible passion to rob his son[9] of a treasure he knew could not but be extremely dear to him, since she was the most beautiful that ever had been seen, and had besides all the sweetness and innocence of youth and modesty, with a charm of wit surpassing all. He found that, however she was forced to expose her lovely person to his withered arms, she could only sigh and weep there, and think of Oroonoko; and oftentimes could not forbear speaking of him, though her life were, by custom, forfeited by owning her passion. But she spoke not of a lover only, but of a prince dear to him to whom she spoke, and of the praises of a man who, till now, filled the old man's soul with joy at every recital of his bravery, or even his name. And 'twas this dotage on our young hero that gave Imoinda a thousand privileges to speak of him without offending, and this condescension in the old king that made her take the satisfaction of speaking of him so very often.

Besides, he many times inquired how the Prince bore himself; and those of whom he asked, being entirely slaves to the merits and virtues of the Prince, still answered what they thought conduced best to his service; which was to make the old king fancy that the Prince had no more interest in Imoinda, and had resigned her willingly to the pleasure of the King; that he diverted himself with his mathematicians, his fortifications, his officers, and his hunting.

This pleased the old lover, who failed not to report these things again to Imoinda, that she might, by the example of her young lover, withdraw her heart, and rest better contented in his arms. But however she was forced to receive this unwelcome news, in all appearance with unconcern and content, her heart was bursting within, and she was only happy when she could get alone, to vent her griefs and moans with sighs and tears.

What reports of the Prince's conduct were made to the King, he thought good to justify as far as possibly he could by his actions, and when he appeared in the presence of the King, he showed a face not at all betraying his heart. So that in a little time, the old man being entirely convinced that he was no longer a lover of Imoinda, he carried him with him in his train to the Otan, often to banquet with his mistress. But as soon as he entered, one day, into the apartment of Imoinda with the King, at the first glance from her eyes, notwithstanding all his determined resolution, he was ready to sink in the place where he stood, and had certainly done so but for the support of Aboan, a young man who was next to him; which, with his change of countenance, had betrayed him, had the King chanced to look that way. And I have observed, 'tis a very great error, in those who laugh when one says a Negro can change color, for I have seen 'em as frequently blush, and look pale, and that as visibly as ever I saw in the most beautiful white. And 'tis certain that both these changes were evident, this day, in both these lovers. And Imoinda, who saw with some joy the change in the Prince's face, and found it in her own, strove to divert the King from beholding either by a forced caress, with which she met him, which was a new wound in the heart of the poor dying Prince. But as soon as the King was busied in looking on some fine thing of Imoinda's making, she had time to tell the Prince with her angry but love-darting eyes that she resented his coldness, and bemoaned her own miserable captivity. Nor were his eyes silent, but answered hers again, as much as eyes could do, instructed by the most tender and most passionate heart that ever loved. And

9. I.e., grandson.

they spoke so well and so effectually, as Imoinda no longer doubted but she was the only delight and the darling of that soul she found pleading in 'em its right of love, which none was more willing to resign than she. And 'twas this powerful language alone that in an instant conveyed all the thoughts of their souls to each other, that[1] they both found there wanted but opportunity to make them both entirely happy. But when he saw another door opened by Onahal, a former old wife of the King's who now had charge of Imoinda, and saw the prospect of a bed of state made ready with sweets and flowers for the dalliance of the King, who immediately led the trembling victim from his sight into that prepared repose, what rage, what wild frenzies seized his heart! which forcing to keep within bounds, and to suffer without noise, it became the more insupportable, and rent his soul with ten thousand pains. He was forced to retire to vent his groans, where he fell down on a carpet and lay struggling a long time, and only breathing now and then, "—O Imoinda!"

When Onahal had finished her necessary affair within, shutting the door, she came forth to wait till the King called; and hearing someone sighing in the other room, she passed on, and found the Prince in that deplorable condition, which she thought needed her aid. She gave him cordials, but all in vain, till finding the nature of his disease by his sighs and naming Imoinda. She told him, he had not so much cause as he imagined to afflict himself, for if he knew the King so well as she did, he would not lose a moment in jealousy, and that she was confident that Imoinda bore, at this minute, part in his affliction. Aboan was of the same opinion, and both together persuaded him to reassume his courage; and all sitting down on the carpet, the Prince said so many obliging things to Onahal that he half persuaded her to be of his party. And she promised him she would thus far comply with his just desires, that she would let Imoinda know how faithful he was, what he suffered, and what he said.

This discourse lasted till the King called, which gave Oroonoko a certain satisfaction, and with the hope Onahal had made him conceive, he assumed a look as gay as 'twas possible a man in his circumstances could do; and presently after, he was called in with the rest who waited without. The King commanded music to be brought, and several of his young wives and mistresses came all together by his command to dance before him; where Imoinda performed her part with an air and grace so passing all the rest as her beauty was above 'em, and received the present ordained as a prize. The Prince was every moment more charmed with the new beauties and graces he beheld in this fair one. And while he gazed, and she danced, Onahal was retired to a window with Aboan.

This Onahal, as I said, was one of the cast mistresses of the old king; and 'twas these (now past their beauty) that were made guardians or governants[2] to the new and the young ones, and whose business it was to teach them all those wanton arts of love with which they prevailed and charmed heretofore in their turn; and who now treated the triumphing happy ones with all the severity, as to liberty and freedom, that was possible, in revenge of those honors they rob them of; envying them those satisfactions, those gallantries and presents, that were once made to themselves, while youth and beauty lasted, and which they now saw pass regardless by, and paid only to the bloomings.

1. So that.
2. Female teachers or chaperones. "Cast": i.e., cast-off.

And certainly nothing is more afflicting to a decayed beauty than to behold in itself declining charms that were once adored, and to find those caresses paid to new beauties to which once she laid a claim; to hear 'em whisper as she passes by, "That once was a delicate woman." These abandoned ladies therefore endeavor to revenge all the despites[3] and decays of time on these flourishing happy ones. And 'twas this severity that gave Oroonoko a thousand fears he should never prevail with Onahal to see Imoinda. But, as I said, she was now retired to a window with Aboan.

This young man was not only one of the best quality,[4] but a man extremely well made and beautiful; and coming often to attend the King to the Otan, he had subdued the heart of the antiquated Onahal, which had not forgot how pleasant it was to be in love. And though she had some decays in her face, she had none in her sense and wit; she was there agreeable still, even to Aboan's youth, so that he took pleasure in entertaining her with discourses of love. He knew also that to make his court to these she-favorites was the way to be great, these being the persons that do all affairs and business at court. He had also observed that she had given him glances more tender and inviting than she had done to others of his quality. And now, when he saw that her favor could so absolutely oblige the Prince, he failed not to sigh in her ear and to look with eyes all soft upon her, and give her hope that she had made some impressions on his heart. He found her pleased at this, and making a thousand advances to him; but the ceremony ending and the King departing broke up the company for that day, and his conversation.

Aboan failed not that night to tell the Prince of his success, and how advantageous the service of Onahal might be to his amour with Imoinda. The Prince was overjoyed with this good news and besought him, if it were possible, to caress her so as to engage her entirely, which he could not fail to do, if he complied with her desires. "For then," said the Prince, "her life lying at your mercy, she must grant you the request you make in my behalf." Aboan understood him, and assured him he would make love so effectually that he would defy the most expert mistress of the art to find out whether he dissembled it or had it really. And 'twas with impatience they waited the next opportunity of going to the Otan.

The wars came on, the time of taking the field approached, and 'twas impossible for the Prince to delay his going at the head of his army to encounter the enemy. So that every day seemed a tedious year till he saw his Imoinda, for he believed he could not live if he were forced away without being so happy. 'Twas with impatience, therefore, that he expected the next visit the King would make, and according to his wish, it was not long.

The parley of the eyes of these two lovers had not passed so secretly but an old jealous lover could spy it; or rather, he wanted not flatterers who told him they observed it. So that the Prince was hastened to the camp, and this was the last visit he found he should make to the Otan; he therefore urged Aboan to make the best of this last effort, and to explain himself so to Onahal that she, deferring her enjoyment of her young lover no longer, might make way for the Prince to speak to Imoinda.

The whole affair being agreed on between the Prince and Aboan, they attended the King, as the custom was, to the Otan, where, while the whole company was taken up in beholding the dancing and antic postures the

3. Insults.

4. Rank.

women-royal made to divert the King, Onahal singled out Aboan, whom she found most pliable to her wish. When she had him where she believed she could not be heard, she sighed to him, and softly cried, "Ah, Aboan! When will you be sensible of my passion? I confess it with my mouth, because I would not give my eyes the lie; and you have but too much already perceived they have confessed my flame. Nor would I have you believe that because I am the abandoned mistress of a king, I esteem myself altogether divested of charms. No, Aboan; I have still a rest[5] of beauty enough engaging, and have learned to please too well not to be desirable. I can have lovers still, but will have none but Aboan." "Madam," replied the half-feigning youth, "you have already, by my eyes, found you can still conquer, and I believe 'tis in pity of me you condescend to this kind confession. But, Madam, words are used to be so small a part of our country courtship, that 'tis rare one can get so happy an opportunity as to tell one's heart, and those few minutes we have are forced to be snatched for more certain proofs of love than speaking and sighing; and such I languish for."

He spoke this with such a tone that she hoped it true, and could not forbear believing it; and being wholly transported with joy, for having subdued the finest of all the King's subjects to her desires, she took from her ears two large pearls and commanded him to wear 'em in his. He would have refused 'em, crying, "Madam, these are not the proofs of your love that I expect; 'tis opportunity, 'tis a lone hour only, that can make me happy." But forcing the pearls into his hand, she whispered softly to him, "Oh! Do not fear a woman's invention, when love sets her a-thinking." And pressing his hand, she cried, "This night you shall be happy. Come to the gate of the orange groves behind the Otan, and I will be ready, about midnight, to receive you." 'Twas thus agreed, and she left him, that no notice might be taken of their speaking together.

The ladies were still dancing, and the King, laid on a carpet, with a great deal of pleasure was beholding them, especially Imoinda, who that day appeared more lovely than ever, being enlivened with the good tidings Onahal had brought her of the constant passion the Prince had for her. The Prince was laid on another carpet at the other end of the room, with his eyes fixed on the object of his soul; and as she turned or moved, so did they, and she alone gave his eyes and soul their motions. Nor did Imoinda employ her eyes to any other use than in beholding with infinite pleasure the joy she produced in those of the Prince. But while she was more regarding him than the steps she took, she chanced to fall, and so near him as that, leaping with extreme force from the carpet, he caught her in his arms as she fell; and 'twas visible to the whole presence[6] the joy wherewith he received her. He clasped her close to his bosom, and quite forgot that reverence that was due to the mistress of a king, and that punishment that is the reward of a boldness of this nature; and had not the presence of mind of Imoinda (fonder of his safety than her own) befriended him, in making her spring from his arms and fall into her dance again, he had at that instant met his death; for the old king, jealous to the last degree, rose up in rage, broke all the diversion, and led Imoinda to her apartment, and sent out word to the Prince to go immediately to the camp, and that if he were found another night in court he should suffer the death ordained for disobedient offenders.

You may imagine how welcome this news was to Oroonoko, whose unsea-

5. Remnant.

6. Company.

sonable transport and caress of Imoinda was blamed by all men that loved him; and now he perceived his fault, yet cried that for such another moment, he would be content to die.

All the Otan was in disorder about this accident; and Onahal was particularly concerned, because on the Prince's stay depended her happiness, for she could no longer expect that of Aboan. So that ere they departed, they contrived it so that the Prince and he should come both that night to the grove of the Otan, which was all of oranges and citrons, and that there they should wait her orders.

They parted thus, with grief enough, till night, leaving the King in possession of the lovely maid. But nothing could appease the jealousy of the old lover. He would not be imposed on, but would have it that Imoinda made a false step on purpose to fall into Oroonoko's bosom, and that all things looked like a design on both sides; and 'twas in vain she protested her innocence. He was old and obstinate, and left her more than half assured that his fear was true.

The King going to his apartment sent to know where the Prince was, and if he intended to obey his command. The messenger returned and told him, he found the Prince pensive and altogether unpreparing for the campaign, that he lay negligently on the ground, and answered very little. This confirmed the jealousy of the King, and he commanded that they should very narrowly and privately watch his motions, and that he should not stir from his apartment but one spy or other should be employed to watch him. So that the hour approaching wherein he was to go to the citron grove, and taking only Aboan along with him, he leaves his apartment, and was watched to the very gate of the Otan, where he was seen to enter, and where they left him, to carry back the tidings to the King.

Oroonoko and Aboan were no sooner entered but Onahal led the Prince to the apartment of Imoinda, who, not knowing anything of her happiness, was laid in bed. But Onahal only left him in her chamber, to make the best of his opportunity, and took her dear Aboan to her own, where he showed the heighth of complaisance for his prince, when, to give him an opportunity, he suffered himself to be caressed in bed by Onahal.

The Prince softly wakened Imoinda, who was not a little surprised with joy to find him there; and yet she trembled with a thousand fears. I believe he omitted saying nothing to this young maid that might persuade her to suffer him to seize his own, and take the rights of love; and I believe she was not long resisting those arms where she so longed to be; and having opportunity, night and silence, youth, love and desire, he soon prevailed, and ravished in a moment what his old grandfather had been endeavoring for so many months.

'Tis not to be imagined the satisfaction of these two young lovers; nor the vows she made him that she remained a spotless maid till that night, and that what she did with his grandfather had robbed him of no part of her virgin honor, the gods in mercy and justice having reserved that for her plighted lord, to whom of right it belonged. And 'tis impossible to express the transports he suffered, while he listened to a discourse so charming from her loved lips, and clasped that body in his arms for whom he had so long languished; and nothing now afflicted him but his sudden departure from her; for he told her the necessity and his commands, but should depart satisfied in this, that since the old king had hitherto not been able to deprive him of those enjoyments which only belonged to him, he believed for the future he would be less able to injure him; so that abating the scandal of the veil, which was no otherwise so than that she was wife to another, he believed her safe, even in the arms of the

King, and innocent; yet would he have ventured at the conquest of the world, and have given it all, to have had her avoided that honor of receiving the royal veil. 'Twas thus, between a thousand caresses, that both bemoaned the hard fate of youth and beauty, so liable to that cruel promotion. 'Twas a glory that could well have been spared here, though desired and aimed at by all the young females of that kingdom.

But while they were thus fondly employed, forgetting how time ran on, and that the dawn must conduct him far away from his only happiness, they heard a great noise in the Otan, and unusual voices of men; at which the Prince, starting from the arms of the frighted Imoinda, ran to a little battle-ax he used to wear by his side, and having not so much leisure as to put on his habit, he opposed himself against some who were already opening the door; which they did with so much violence that Oroonoko was not able to defend it, but was forced to cry out with a commanding voice, "Whoever ye are that have the boldness to attempt to approach this apartment thus rudely, know that I, the Prince Oroonoko, will revenge it with the certain death of him that first enters. Therefore stand back, and know, this place is sacred to love and me this night; tomorrow 'tis the King's."

This he spoke with a voice so resolved and assured that they soon retired from the door, but cried, " 'Tis by the King's command we are come; and being satisfied by thy voice, O Prince, as much as if we had entered, we can report to the King the truth of all his fears, and leave thee to provide for thy own safety, as thou art advised by thy friends."

At these words they departed, and left the Prince to take a short and sad leave of his Imoinda, who, trusting in the strength of her charms, believed she should appease the fury of a jealous king by saying she was surprised, and that it was by force of arms he got into her apartment. All her concern now was for his life, and therefore she hastened him to the camp, and with much ado prevailed on him to go. Nor was it she alone that prevailed; Aboan and Onahal both pleaded, and both assured him of a lie that should be well enough contrived to secure Imoinda. So that at last, with a heart sad as death, dying eyes, and sighing soul, Oroonoko departed and took his way to the camp.

It was not long after the King in person came to the Otan, where, beholding Imoinda with rage in his eyes, he upbraided her wickedness and perfidy, and threatening her royal lover, she fell on her face at his feet, bedewing the floor with her tears and imploring his pardon for a fault which she had not with her will committed, as Onahal, who was also prostrate with her, could testify; that unknown to her, he had broke into her apartment, and ravished her. She spoke this much against her conscience, but to save her own life 'twas absolutely necessary she should feign this falsity. She knew it could not injure the Prince, he being fled to an army that would stand by him against any injuries that should assault him. However, this last thought of Imoinda's being ravished changed the measures of his revenge; and whereas before he designed to be himself her executioner, he now resolved she should not die. But as it is the greatest crime in nature amongst 'em to touch a woman after having been possessed by a son, a father, or a brother, so now he looked on Imoinda as a polluted thing, wholly unfit for his embrace; nor would he resign her to his grandson, because she had received the royal veil. He therefore removes her from the Otan, with Onahal; whom he put into safe hands, with order they should be both sold off as slaves to another country, either Christian or heathen; 'twas no matter where.

This cruel sentence, worse than death, they implored might be reversed;

but their prayers were vain, and it was put in execution accordingly, and that with so much secrecy that none, either without or within the Otan, knew anything of their absence or their destiny.

The old king, nevertheless, executed this with a great deal of reluctancy; but he believed he had made a very great conquest over himself, when he had once resolved, and had performed what he resolved. He believed now that his love had been unjust, and that he could not expect the gods, or Captain of the Clouds (as they call the unknown power), should suffer a better consequence from so ill a cause. He now begins to hold Oroonoko excused, and to say he had reason for what he did. And now everybody could assure the King how passionately Imoinda was beloved by the Prince; even those confessed it now, who said the contrary before his flame was abated. So that the King being old, and not able to defend himself in war, and having no sons of all his race remaining alive but only this, to maintain him on his throne; and looking on this as a man disobliged, first by the rape of his mistress, or rather wife; and now by depriving of him wholly of her, he feared, might make him desperate and do some cruel thing, either to himself or his old grandfather, the offender: he began to repent him extremely of the contempt he had, in his rage, put on Imoinda. Besides, he considered he ought in honor to have killed her for this offense, if it had been one. He ought to have had so much value and consideration for a maid of her quality as to have nobly put her to death, and not to have sold her like a common slave, the greatest revenge and the most disgraceful of any; and to which they a thousand times prefer death, and implore it, as Imoinda did, but could not obtain that honor. Seeing therefore it was certain that Oroonoko would highly resent this affront, he thought good to make some excuse for his rashness to him; and to that end he sent a messenger to the camp, with orders to treat with him about the matter, to gain his pardon, and to endeavor to mitigate his grief; but that by no means he should tell him she was sold, but secretly put to death, for he knew he should never obtain his pardon for the other.

When the messenger came, he found the Prince upon the point of engaging with the enemy; but as soon as he heard of the arrival of the messenger, he commanded him to his tent, where he embraced him and received him with joy; which was soon abated by the downcast looks of the messenger, who was instantly demanded the cause by Oroonoko, who, impatient of delay, asked a thousand questions in a breath, and all concerning Imoinda. But there needed little return, for he could almost answer himself of all he demanded, from his sighs and eyes. At last, the messenger casting himself at the Prince's feet, and kissing them with all the submission of a man that had something to implore which he dreaded to utter, he besought him to hear with calmness what he had to deliver to him, and to call up all his noble and heroic courage to encounter with his words, and defend himself against the ungrateful[7] things he must relate. Oroonoko replied, with a deep sigh and a languishing voice, "I am armed against their worst efforts—; for I know they will tell me, Imoinda is no more—and after that, you may spare the rest." Then, commanding him to rise, he laid himself on a carpet, under a rich pavilion, and remained a good while silent, and was hardly heard to sigh. When he was come a little to himself, the messenger asked him leave to deliver that part of his embassy which the Prince had not yet divined. And the Prince cried, "I permit

7. Offensive.

thee—." Then he told him the affliction the old king was in, for the rashness he had committed in his cruelty to Imoinda; and how he deigned to ask pardon for his offense, and to implore the Prince would not suffer that loss to touch his heart too sensibly, which now all the gods could not restore him, but might recompense him in glory, which he begged he would pursue; and that Death, that common revenger of all injuries, would soon even the account between him and a feeble old man.

Oroonoko bade him return his duty to his lord and master, and to assure him, there was no account of revenge to be adjusted between them; if there were, 'twas he was the aggressor, and that Death would be just and, maugre[8] his age, would see him righted; and he was contented to leave his share of glory to youths more fortunate and worthy of that favor from the gods. That henceforth he would never lift a weapon or draw a bow, but abandon the small remains of his life to sighs and tears, and the continual thoughts of what his lord and grandfather had thought good to send out of the world, with all that youth, that innocence, and beauty.

After having spoken this, whatever his greatest officers and men of the best rank could do, they could not raise him from the carpet, or persuade him to action and resolutions of life; but commanding all to retire, he shut himself into his pavilion all that day, while the enemy was ready to engage; and wondering at the delay, the whole body of the chief of the army then addressed themselves to him, and to whom they had much ado to get admittance. They fell on their faces at the foot of his carpet, where they lay and besought him with earnest prayers and tears to lead 'em forth to battle, and not let the enemy take advantages of them; and implored him to have regard to his glory, and to the world, that depended on his courage and conduct. But he made no other reply to all their supplications but this, that he had now no more business for glory; and for the world, it was a trifle not worth his care. "Go," continued he, sighing, "and divide it amongst you; and reap with joy what you so vainly prize, and leave me to my more welcome destiny."

They then demanded what they should do, and whom he would constitute in his room, that the confusion of ambitious youth and power might not ruin their order and make them a prey to the enemy. He replied, he would not give himself the trouble—; but wished 'em to choose the bravest man amongst 'em, let his quality or birth be what it would. "For, O my friends!" said he, "it is not titles make men brave or good, or birth that bestows courage and generosity, or makes the owner happy. Believe this, when you behold Oroonoko, the most wretched and abandoned by fortune of all the creation of the gods." So turning himself about, he would make no more reply to all they could urge or implore.

The army, beholding their officers return unsuccessful, with sad faces and ominous looks that presaged no good luck, suffered a thousand fears to take possession of their hearts, and the enemy to come even upon 'em, before they would provide for their safety by any defense; and though they were assured by some, who had a mind to animate 'em, that they should be immediately headed by the Prince, and that in the meantime Aboan had orders to command as general, yet they were so dismayed for want of that great example of bravery that they could make but a very feeble resistance; and at last downright fled before the enemy, who pursued 'em to the very tents, killing 'em. Nor could all Aboan's courage, which that day gained him immortal glory, shame 'em

8. In spite of. Oroonoko is saying that he will die before the king does.

into a manly defense of themselves. The guards that were left behind about the Prince's tent, seeing the soldiers flee before the enemy and scatter themselves all over the plain, in great disorder, made such outcries as roused the Prince from his amorous slumber, in which he had remained buried for two days without permitting any sustenance to approach him. But in spite of all his resolutions, he had not the constancy of grief to that degree, as to make him insensible of the danger of his army; and in that instant he leaped from his couch and cried, "—Come, if we must die, let us meet Death the noblest way; and 'twill be more like Oroonoko to encounter him at an army's head, opposing the torrent of a conquering foe, than lazily on a couch to wait his lingering pleasure, and die every moment by a thousand wrecking[9] thoughts; or be tamely taken by an enemy, and led a whining, lovesick slave to adorn the triumphs of Jamoan, that young victor, who already is entered beyond the limits I had prescribed him."

While he was speaking, he suffered his people to dress him for the field, and sallying out of his pavilion, with more life and vigor in his countenance than ever he showed, he appeared like some divine power descended to save his country from destruction; and his people had purposely put on him all things that might make him shine with most splendor, to strike a reverend awe into the beholders. He flew into the thickest of those that were pursuing his men, and being animated with despair, he fought as if he came on purpose to die, and did such things as will not be believed that human strength could perform, and such as soon inspired all the rest with new courage and new order. And now it was that they began to fight indeed, and so as if they would not be outdone even by their adored hero; who, turning the tide of the victory, changing absolutely the fate of the day, gained an entire conquest; and Oroonoko having the good fortune to single out Jamoan, he took him prisoner with his own hand, having wounded him almost to death.

This Jamoan afterwards became very dear to him, being a man very gallant and of excellent graces and fine parts; so that he never put him amongst the rank of captives, as they used to do, without distinction, for the common sale or market; but kept him in his own court, where he retained nothing of the prisoner but the name, and returned no more into his own country, so great an affection he took for Oroonoko; and by a thousand tales and adventures of love and gallantry flattered[1] his disease of melancholy and languishment, which I have often heard him say had certainly killed him, but for the conversation of this prince and Aboan, and the French governor he had from his childhood, of whom I have spoken before, and who was a man of admirable wit, great ingenuity and learning, all which he had infused into his young pupil. This Frenchman was banished out of his own country for some heretical notions he held, and though he was a man of very little religion, he had admirable morals and a brave soul.

After the total defeat of Jamoan's army, which all fled, or were left dead upon the place, they spent some time in the camp, Oroonoko choosing rather to remain a while there in his tents than enter into a palace or live in a court where he had so lately suffered so great a loss. The officers, therefore, who saw and knew his cause of discontent, invented all sorts of diversions and sports to entertain their prince; so that what with those amusements abroad and others at home, that is, within their tents, with the persuasions, argu-

9. Racking.

1. Soothed.

ments, and care of his friends and servants that he more peculiarly prized, he wore off in time a great part of that chagrin and torture of despair which the first efforts of Imoinda's death had given him. Insomuch as having received a thousand kind embassies from the King, and invitations to return to court, he obeyed, though with no little reluctancy; and when he did so, there was a visible change in him, and for a long time he was much more melancholy than before. But time lessens all extremes, and reduces 'em to mediums and unconcern; but no motives or beauties, though all endeavored it, could engage him in any sort of amour, though he had all the invitations to it, both from his own youth and others' ambitions and designs.

Oroonoko was no sooner returned from this last conquest, and received at court with all the joy and magnificence that could be expressed to a young victor, who was not only returned triumphant but beloved like a deity, when there arrived in the port an English ship.

This person[2] had often before been in these countries and was very well known to Oroonoko, with whom he had trafficked for slaves, and had used to do the same with his predecessors.

This commander was a man of a finer sort of address and conversation, better bred and more engaging than most of that sort of men are, so that he seemed rather never to have been bred out of a court than almost all his life at sea. This captain therefore was always better received at court than most of the traders to those countries were; and especially by Oroonoko, who was more civilized, according to the European mode, than any other had been, and took more delight in the white nations, and above all men of parts and wit. To this captain he sold abundance of his slaves, and for the favor and esteem he had for him, made him many presents, and obliged him to stay at court as long as possibly he could. Which the captain seemed to take as a very great honor done him, entertaining the Prince every day with globes and maps, and mathematical discourses and instruments; eating, drinking, hunting, and living with him with so much familiarity that it was not to be doubted but he had gained very greatly upon the heart of this gallant young man. And the captain, in return of all these mighty favors, besought the Prince to honor his vessel with his presence, some day or other, to dinner, before he should set sail; which he condescended to accept, and appointed his day. The captain, on his part, failed not to have all things in a readiness, in the most magnificent order he could possibly. And the day being come, the captain in his boat, richly adorned with carpets and velvet cushions, rowed to the shore to receive the Prince, with another longboat where was placed all his music and trumpets, with which Oroonoko was extremely delighted; who met him on the shore attended by his French governor, Jamoan, Aboan, and about a hundred of the noblest of the youths of the court. And after they had first carried the Prince on board, the boats fetched the rest off; where they found a very splendid treat, with all sorts of fine wines, and were as well entertained as 'twas possible in such a place to be.

The Prince, having drunk hard of punch and several sorts of wine, as did all the rest (for great care was taken they should want nothing of that part of the entertainment), was very merry, and in great admiration of the ship, for he had never been in one before; so that he was curious of beholding every place where he decently might descend. The rest, no less curious, who were

2. The ship's captain.

not quite overcome with drinking, rambled at their pleasure fore and aft, as their fancies guided 'em. So that the captain, who had well laid his design before, gave the word, and seized on all his guests; they clapping great irons suddenly on the Prince, when he was leaped down in the hold to view that part of the vessel, and locking him fast down, secured him. The same treachery was used to all the rest; and all in one instant, in several places of the ship, were lashed fast in irons, and betrayed to slavery. That great design over, they set all hands to work to hoise[3] sail; and with as treacherous and fair a wind, they made from the shore with this innocent and glorious prize, who thought of nothing less than such an entertainment.

Some have commended this act as brave in the captain; but I will spare my sense of it, and leave it to my reader to judge as he pleases.

It may be easily guessed in what manner the Prince resented this indignity, who may be best resembled to a lion taken in a toil; so he raged, so he struggled for liberty, but all in vain; and they had so wisely managed his fetters that he could not use a hand in his defense, to quit himself of a life that would by no means endure slavery, nor could he move from the place where he was tied to any solid part of the ship, against which he might have beat his head, and have finished his disgrace that way. So that being deprived of all other means, he resolved to perish for want of food. And pleased at last with that thought, and toiled and tired by rage and indignation, he laid himself down, and sullenly resolved upon dying, and refused all things that were brought him.

This did not a little vex the captain, and the more so because he found almost all of 'em of the same humor; so that the loss of so many brave slaves, so tall and goodly to behold, would have been very considerable. He therefore ordered one to go from him (for he would not be seen himself) to Oroonoko, and to assure him he was afflicted for having rashly done so unhospitable a deed, and which could not be now remedied, since they were far from shore; but since he resented it in so high a nature, he assured him he would revoke his resolution, and set both him and his friends ashore on the next land they should touch at; and of this the messenger gave him his oath, provided he would resolve to live. And Oroonoko, whose honor was such as he never had violated a word in his life himself, much less a solemn asseveration, believed in an instant what this man said, but replied, he expected for a confirmation of this to have his shameful fetters dismissed. This demand was carried to the captain, who returned him answer that the offense had been so great which he had put upon the Prince that he durst not trust him with liberty while he remained in the ship, for fear lest by a valor natural to him, and a revenge that would animate that valor, he might commit some outrage fatal to himself and the King his master, to whom his vessel did belong. To this Oroonoko replied, he would engage his honor to behave himself in all friendly order and manner, and obey the command of the captain, as he was lord of the King's vessel and general of those men under his command.

This was delivered to the still doubting captain, who could not resolve to trust a heathen, he said, upon his parole,[4] a man that had no sense or notion of the God that he worshipped. Oroonoko then replied, he was very sorry to hear that the captain pretended to the knowledge and worship of any gods who had taught him no better principles than not to credit as he would be credited; but they told him the difference of their faith occasioned that distrust. For the captain had protested to him upon the word of a Christian, and

3. Hoist.

4. Word of honor.

sworn in the name of a great god, which if he should violate, he would expect eternal torment in the world to come. "Is that all the obligation he has to be just to his oath?" replied Oroonoko. "Let him know I swear by my honor; which to violate, would not only render me contemptible and despised by all brave and honest men, and so give myself perpetual pain, but it would be eternally offending and diseasing all mankind, harming, betraying, circumventing and outraging all men; but punishments hereafter are suffered by one's self, and the world takes no cognizances whether this god have revenged 'em or not, 'tis done so secretly and deferred so long. While the man of no honor suffers every moment the scorn and contempt of the honester world, and dies every day ignominiously in his fame, which is more valuable than life. I speak not this to move belief, but to show you how you mistake, when you imagine that he who will violate his honor will keep his word with his gods." So turning from him with a disdainful smile, he refused to answer him, when he urged him to know what answer he should carry back to his captain; so that he departed without saying any more.

The captain pondering and consulting what to do, it was concluded that nothing but Oroonoko's liberty would encourage any of the rest to eat, except the Frenchman, whom the captain could not pretend to keep prisoner, but only told him he was secured because he might act something in favor of the Prince, but that he should be freed as soon as they came to land. So that they concluded it wholly necessary to free the Prince from his irons, that he might show himself to the rest; that they might have an eye upon him, and that they could not fear a single man.

This being resolved, to make the obligation the greater, the captain himself went to Oroonoko; where after many compliments, and assurances of what he had already promised, he receiving from the Prince his parole and his hand for his good behavior, dismissed his irons and brought him to his own cabin; where after having treated and reposed him a while, for he had neither eat[5] nor slept in four days before, he besought him to visit those obstinate people in chains, who refused all manner of sustenance, and entreated him to oblige 'em to eat, and assure 'em of their liberty the first opportunity.

Oroonoko, who was too generous not to give credit to his words, showed himself to his people, who were transported with excess of joy at the sight of their darling prince, falling at his feet and kissing and embracing 'em, believing, as some divine oracle, all he assured 'em. But he besought 'em to bear their chains with that bravery that became those whom he had seen act so nobly in arms; and that they could not give him greater proofs of their love and friendship, since 'twas all the security the captain (his friend) could have, against the revenge, he said, they might possibly justly take for the injuries sustained by him. And they all with one accord assured him, they could not suffer enough, when it was for his repose and safety.

After this they no longer refused to eat, but took what was brought 'em, and were pleased with their captivity, since by it they hoped to redeem the Prince, who, all the rest of the voyage, was treated with all the respect due to his birth, though nothing could divert his melancholy; and he would often sigh for Imoinda, and think this a punishment due to his misfortune, in having left that noble maid behind him that fatal night, in the Otan, when he fled to the camp.

Possessed with a thousand thoughts of past joys with this fair young person,

5. The past form of *eat*.

and a thousand griefs for her eternal loss, he endured a tedious voyage, and at last arrived at the mouth of the river of Surinam, a colony belonging to the King of England, and where they were to deliver some part of their slaves. There the merchants and gentlemen of the country going on board to demand those lots of slaves they had already agreed on, and, amongst those, the overseers of those plantations where I then chanced to be, the captain, who had given the word, ordered his men to bring up those noble slaves in fetters whom I have spoken of; and having put 'em some in one and some in other lots, with women and children (which they call pickaninnies), they sold 'em off as slaves to several merchants and gentlemen; not putting any two in one lot, because they would separate 'em far from each other, not daring to trust 'em together, lest rage and courage should put 'em upon contriving some great action, to the ruin of the colony.

Oroonoko was first seized on, and sold to our overseer, who had the first lot, with seventeen more of all sorts and sizes, but not one of quality with him. When he saw this, he found what they meant, for, as I said, he understood English pretty well; and being wholly unarmed and defenseless, so as it was in vain to make any resistance, he only beheld the captain with a look all fierce and disdainful, upbraiding him with eyes that forced blushes on his guilty cheeks; he only cried, in passing over the side of the ship, "Farewell, sir. 'Tis worth my suffering, to gain so true a knowledge both of you and of your gods by whom you swear." And desiring those that held him to forbear their pains, and telling 'em he would make no resistance, he cried, "Come, my fellow slaves; let us descend, and see if we can meet with more honor and honesty in the next world we shall touch upon." So he nimbly leaped into the boat, and showing no more concern, suffered himself to be rowed up the river with his seventeen companions.

The gentleman that bought him was a young Cornish gentleman whose name was Trefry, a man of great wit and fine learning, and was carried into those parts by the Lord——, Governor,[6] to manage all his affairs. He reflecting on the last words of Oroonoko to the captain, and beholding the richness of his vest,[7] no sooner came into the boat but he fixed his eyes on him; and finding something so extraordinary in his face, his shape and mien, a greatness of look and haughtiness in his air, and finding he spoke English, had a great mind to be inquiring into his quality and fortune; which, though Oroonoko endeavored to hide, by only confessing he was above the rank of common slaves, Trefry soon found he was yet something greater than he confessed, and from that moment began to conceive so vast an esteem for him that he ever after loved him as his dearest brother, and showed him all the civilities due to so great a man.

Trefry was a very good mathematician and a linguist, could speak French and Spanish; and in the three days they remained in the boat (for so long were they going from the ship to the plantation) he entertained Oroonoko so agreeably with his art and discourse, that he was no less pleased with Trefry than he was with the Prince; and he thought himself at least fortunate in this, that since he was a slave, as long as he would suffer himself to remain so, he had a man of so excellent wit and parts for a master. So that before they had finished their voyage up the river, he made no scruple of declaring to Trefry

6. Lord Willoughby of Parham, coproprietor of Surinam by royal grant. John Treffry was his plantation overseer.

7. An outer garment or robe.

all his fortunes, and most part of what I have here related, and put himself wholly into the hands of his new friend, whom he found resenting all the injuries were done him, and was charmed with all the greatness of his actions; which were recited with that modesty and delicate sense as wholly vanquished him, and subdued him to his interest. And he promised him on his word and honor, he would find the means to reconduct him to his own country again, assuring him, he had a perfect abhorrence of so dishonorable an action, and that he would sooner have died than have been the author of such a perfidy. He found the Prince was very much concerned to know what became of his friends, and how they took their slavery; and Trefry promised to take care about the inquiring after their condition, and that he should have an account of 'em.

Though, as Oroonoko afterwards said, he had little reason to credit the words of a *backearary,*[8] yet he knew not why, but he saw a kind of sincerity and awful truth in the face of Trefry; he saw an honesty in his eyes, and he found him wise and witty enough to understand honor; for it was one of his maxims, a man of wit could not be a knave or villain.

In their passage up the river they put in at several houses for refreshment, and ever when they landed, numbers of people would flock to behold this man; not but their eyes were daily entertained with the sight of slaves, but the fame of Oroonoko was gone before him, and all people were in admiration of his beauty. Besides, he had a rich habit on, in which he was taken, so different from the rest, and which the captain could not strip him of, because he was forced to surprise his person in the minute he sold him. When he found his habit made him liable, as he thought, to be gazed at the more, he begged Trefry to give him something more befitting a slave, which he did, and took off his robes. Nevertheless, he shone through all; and his osenbrigs (a sort of brown holland[9] suit he had on) could not conceal the graces of his looks and mien, and he had no less admirers than when he had his dazzling habit on. The royal youth appeared in spite of the slave, and people could not help treating him after a different manner, without designing it. As soon as they approached him, they venerated and esteemed him; his eyes insensibly commanded respect, and his behavior insinuated it into every soul. So that there was nothing talked of but this young and gallant slave, even by those who yet knew not that he was a prince.

I ought to tell you that the Christians never buy any slaves but they give 'em some name of their own, their native ones being likely very barbarous and hard to pronounce; so that Mr. Trefry gave Oroonoko that of Caesar, which name will live in that country as long as that (scarce more) glorious one of the great Roman; for 'tis most evident, he wanted[1] no part of the personal courage of that Caesar, and acted things as memorable, had they been done in some part of the world replenished with people and historians that might have given him his due. But his misfortune was to fall in an obscure world, that afforded only a female pen to celebrate his fame; though I doubt not but it had lived from others' endeavors, if the Dutch, who immediately after his time took that country,[2] had not killed, banished, and dispersed all those that were capable of giving the world this great man's life, much better than I have done. And Mr.

8. White person or master; a variant of *backra*, from an Ibo word transported with the slaves to Surinam and the Caribbean.

9. Coarse cotton or linen, sometimes called osnaburg, after a German cloth-manufacturing town.

1. Lacked.

2. In 1667 the Dutch attacked and conquered Surinam, and England ceded it by treaty in exchange for New York.

Trefry, who designed it, died before he began it, and bemoaned himself for not having undertook it in time.

For the future, therefore, I must call Oroonoko Caesar, since by that name only he was known in our western world, and by that name he was received on shore at Parham House, where he was destined a slave. But if the King himself (God bless him) had come ashore, there could not have been greater expectations by all the whole plantation, and those neighboring ones, than was on ours at that time; and he was received more like a governor than a slave. Notwithstanding, as the custom was, they assigned him his portion of land, his house, and his business, up in the plantation. But as it was more for form than any design to put him to his task, he endured no more of the slave but the name, and remained some days in the house, receiving all visits that were made him, without stirring towards that part of the plantation where the Negroes were.

At last he would needs go view his land, his house, and the business assigned him. But he no sooner came to the houses of the slaves, which are like a little town by itself, the Negroes all having left work, but they all came forth to behold him, and found he was that prince who had, at several times, sold most of 'em to these parts; and from a veneration they pay to great men, especially if they know 'em, and from the surprise and awe they had at the sight of him, they all cast themselves at his feet, crying out in their language, "Live, O King! Long live, O King!" and kissing his feet, paid him even divine homage.

Several English gentlemen were with him; and what Mr. Trefry had told 'em was here confirmed, of which he himself before had no other witness than Caesar himself. But he was infinitely glad to find his grandeur confirmed by the adoration of all the slaves.

Caesar, troubled with their over-joy and over-ceremony, besought 'em to rise and to receive him as their fellow slave, assuring them he was no better. At which they set up with one accord a most terrible and hideous mourning and condoling, which he and the English had much ado to appease; but at last they prevailed with 'em, and they prepared all their barbarous music, and everyone killed and dressed something of his own stock (for every family has their land apart, on which, at their leisure times, they breed all eatable things), and clubbing it together,[3] made a most magnificent supper, inviting their *Grandee Captain*, their prince, to honor it with his presence; which he did, and several English with him; where they all waited on him, some playing, others dancing before him all the time, according to the manners of their several nations, and with unwearied industry endeavoring to please and delight him.

While they sat at meat Mr. Trefry told Caesar that most of these young slaves were undone in love with a fine she-slave, whom they had had about six months on their land. The Prince, who never heard the name of love without a sigh, nor any mention of it without the curiosity of examining further into that tale, which of all discourses was most agreeable to him, asked how they came to be so unhappy as to be all undone for one fair slave. Trefry, who was naturally amorous and loved to talk of love as well as anybody, proceeded to tell him, they had the most charming black that ever was beheld on their plantation, about fifteen or sixteen years old, as he guessed; that for his part, he had done nothing but sigh for her ever since she came, and that all the

3. Contributing jointly.

white beauties he had seen never charmed him so absolutely as this fine creature had done; and that no man, of any nation, ever beheld her that did not fall in love with her; and that she had all the slaves perpetually at her feet, and the whole country resounded with the fame of Clemene, "for so," said he, "we have christened her. But she denies us all with such a noble disdain, that 'tis a miracle to see that she, who can give such eternal desires, should herself be all ice and all unconcern. She is adorned with the most graceful modesty that ever beautified youth; the softest sigher—that, if she were capable of love, one would swear she languished for some absent happy man; and so retired, as if she feared a rape even from the god of day,[4] or that the breezes would steal kisses from her delicate mouth. Her task of work some sighing lover every day makes it his petition to perform for her, which she accepts blushing and with reluctancy, for fear he will ask her a look for a recompense, which he dares not presume to hope, so great an awe she strikes into the hearts of her admirers." "I do not wonder," replied the Prince, "that Clemene should refuse slaves, being as you say so beautiful, but wonder how she escapes those who can entertain her as you can do; or why, being your slave, you do not oblige her to yield." "I confess," said Trefry, "when I have, against her will, entertained her with love so long as to be transported with my passion, even above decency, I have been ready to make use of those advantages of strength and force nature has given me. But oh! she disarms me with that modesty and weeping, so tender and so moving that I retire, and thank my stars she overcame me." The company laughed at his civility to a slave, and Caesar only applauded the nobleness of his passion and nature, since that slave might be noble or, what was better, have true notions of honor and virtue in her. Thus passed they this night, after having received from the slaves all imaginable respect and obedience.

The next day Trefry asked Caesar to walk, when the heat was allayed, and designedly carried him by the cottage of the fair slave, and told him she whom he spoke of last night lived there retired. "But," says he, "I would not wish you to approach, for I am sure you will be in love as soon as you behold her." Caesar assured him he was proof against all the charms of that sex, and that if he imagined his heart could be so perfidious to love again, after Imoinda, he believed he should tear it from his bosom. They had no sooner spoke, but a little shock dog[5] that Clemene had presented her, which she took great delight in, ran out; and she, not knowing anybody was there, ran to get it in again, and bolted out on those who were just speaking of her. When seeing them, she would have run in again, but Trefry caught her by the hand and cried, "Clemene, however you fly a lover, you ought to pay some respect to this stranger" (pointing to Caesar). But she, as if she had resolved never to raise her eyes to the face of a man again, bent 'em the more to the earth when he spoke, and gave the Prince the leisure to look the more at her. There needed no long gazing or consideration to examine who this fair creature was; he soon saw Imoinda all over her; in a minute he saw her face, her shape, her air, her modesty, and all that called forth his soul with joy at his eyes, and left his body destitute of almost life; it stood without motion, and for a minute knew not that it had a being; and I believe he had never come to himself, so oppressed he was with over-joy, if he had not met with this allay,

4. The sun.
5. A long-haired dog or poodle, especially associated with women of fashion.

that he perceived Imoinda fall dead in the hands of Trefry. This awakened him, and he ran to her aid and caught her in his arms, where by degrees she came to herself; and 'tis needless to tell with what transports, what ecstasies of joy, they both a while beheld each other, without speaking; then snatched each other to their arms; then gaze again, as if they still doubted whether they possessed the blessing they grasped; but when they recovered their speech, 'tis not to be imagined what tender things they expressed to each other, wondering what strange fate had brought 'em again together. They soon informed each other of their fortunes, and equally bewailed their fate; but at the same time they mutually protested that even fetters and slavery were soft and easy, and would be supported with joy and pleasure, while they could be so happy to possess each other and to be able to make good their vows. Caesar swore he disdained the empire of the world while he could behold his Imoinda; and she despised grandeur and pomp, those vanities of her sex, when she could gaze on Oroonoko. He adored the very cottage where she resided, and said that little inch of the world would give him more happiness than all the universe could do; and she vowed it was a palace, while adorned with the presence of Oroonoko.

Trefry was infinitely pleased with this novel,[6] and found this Clemene was the fair mistress of whom Caesar had before spoke; and was not a little satisfied that heaven was so kind to the Prince as to sweeten his misfortunes by so lucky an accident; and leaving the lovers to themselves, was impatient to come down to Parham House (which was on the same plantation) to give me an account of what had happened. I was as impatient to make these lovers a visit, having already made a friendship with Caesar, and from his own mouth learned what I have related; which was confirmed by his Frenchman, who was set on shore to seek his fortunes, and of whom they could not make a slave, because a Christian, and he came daily to Parham Hill to see and pay his respects to his pupil prince. So that concerning and interesting myself in all that related to Caesar, whom I had assured of liberty as soon as the Governor arrived, I hasted presently to the place where the lovers were, and was infinitely glad to find this beautiful young slave (who had already gained all our esteems, for her modesty and her extraordinary prettiness) to be the same I had heard Caesar speak so much of. One may imagine then we paid her a treble respect; and though, from her being carved in fine flowers and birds all over her body, we took her to be of quality before, yet when we knew Clemene was Imoinda, we could not enough admire her.

I had forgot to tell you that those who are nobly born of that country are so delicately cut and rased[7] all over the forepart of the trunk of their bodies, that it looks as if it were japanned, the works being raised like high point round the edges of the flowers. Some are only carved with a little flower or bird at the sides of the temples, as was Caesar; and those who are so carved over the body resemble our ancient Picts,[8] that are figured in the chronicles, but these carvings are more delicate.

From that happy day Caesar took Clemene for his wife, to the general joy of all people; and there was as much magnificence as the country would afford at the celebration of this wedding: and in a very short time after she conceived

6. I.e., novel event or piece of news.
7. Incised. The carving is likened to figured lacquerwork in the Japanese style and to elaborate "high point" lace.
8. A North British people appearing in histories of England and Scotland.

with child, which made Caesar even adore her, knowing he was the last of his great race. This new accident made him more impatient of liberty, and he was every day treating with Trefry for his and Clemene's liberty, and offered either gold or a vast quantity of slaves, which should be paid before they let him go, provided he could have any security that he should go when his ransom was paid. They fed him from day to day with promises, and delayed him till the Lord Governor should come; so that he began to suspect them of falsehood, and that they would delay him till the time of his wife's delivery and make a slave of that too, for all the breed is theirs to whom the parents belong. This thought made him very uneasy, and his sullenness gave them some jealousies[9] of him; so that I was obliged, by some persons who feared a mutiny (which is very fatal sometimes in those colonies, that abound so with slaves that they exceed the whites in vast numbers), to discourse with Caesar, and to give him all the satisfaction I possibly could; they knew he and Clemene were scarce an hour in a day from my lodgings, that they eat with me, and that I obliged 'em in all things I was capable of. I entertained him with the lives of the Romans, and great men, which charmed him to my company, and her with teaching her all the pretty works[1] that I was mistress of, and telling her stories of nuns, and endeavoring to bring her to the knowledge of the true God. But of all discourses Caesar liked that the worst, and would never be reconciled to our notions of the Trinity, of which he ever made a jest; it was a riddle, he said, would turn his brain to conceive, and one could not make him understand what faith was. However, these conversations failed not altogether so well to divert him that he liked the company of us women much above the men, for he could not drink, and he is but an ill companion in that country that cannot. So that obliging him to love us very well, we had all the liberty of speech with him, especially myself, whom he called his Great Mistress; and indeed my word would go a great way with him. For these reasons, I had opportunity to take notice to him that he was not well pleased of late as he used to be, was more retired and thoughtful; and told him I took it ill he should suspect we would break our words with him, and not permit both him and Clemene to return to his own kingdom, which was not so long a way but when he was once on his voyage he would quickly arrive there. He made me some answers that showed a doubt in him, which made me ask him what advantage it would be to doubt. It would but give us a fear of him, and possibly compel us to treat him so as I should be very loath to behold; that is, it might occasion his confinement. Perhaps this was not so luckily spoke of me, for I perceived he resented that word, which I strove to soften again in vain. However, he assured me that whatsoever resolutions he should take, he would act nothing upon the white people; and as for myself and those upon that plantation where he was, he would sooner forfeit his eternal liberty, and life itself, than lift his hand against his greatest enemy on that place. He besought me to suffer no fears upon his account, for he could do nothing that honor should not dictate; but he accused himself for having suffered slavery so long; yet he charged that weakness on Love alone, who was capable of making him neglect even glory itself, and for which now he reproaches himself every moment of the day. Much more to this effect he spoke, with an air impatient enough to make me know he would not be long in bondage; and though he suffered only the name of a slave, and had nothing of the toil and labor of one, yet that was sufficient

9. Suspicions.

1. Decorative needlework or other handiwork.

to render him uneasy; and he had been too long idle, who used to be always in action and in arms. He had a spirit all rough and fierce, and that could not be tamed to lazy rest; and though all endeavors were used to exercise himself in such actions and sports as this world afforded, as running, wrestling, pitching the bar, hunting and fishing, chasing and killing tigers of a monstrous size, which this continent affords in abundance, and wonderful snakes, such as Alexander is reported to have encountered at the river of Amazons,[2] and which Caesar took great delight to overcome, yet these were not actions great enough for his large soul, which was still panting after more renowned action.

Before I parted that day with him, I got, with much ado, a promise from him to rest yet a little longer with patience, and wait the coming of the Lord Governor, who was every day expected on our shore; he assured me he would, and this promise he desired me to know was given perfectly in complaisance to me, in whom he had an entire confidence.

After this, I neither thought it convenient to trust him much out of our view, nor did the country, who feared him; but with one accord it was advised to treat him fairly, and oblige him to remain within such a compass, and that he should be permitted as seldom as could be to go up to the plantations of the Negroes or, if he did, to be accompanied by some that should be rather in appearance attendants than spies. This care was for some time taken, and Caesar looked upon it as a mark of extraordinary respect, and was glad his discontent had obliged 'em to be more observant to him. He received new assurance from the overseer, which was confirmed to him by the opinion of all the gentlemen of the country, who made their court to him. During this time that we had his company more frequently than hitherto we had had, it may not be unpleasant to relate to you the diversions we entertained him with, or rather he us.

My stay was to be short in that country, because my father died at sea, and never arrived to possess the honor was designed him (which was lieutenant general of six and thirty islands, besides the continent[3] of Surinam) nor the advantages he hoped to reap by them; so that though we were obliged to continue on our voyage, we did not intend to stay upon the place. Though, in a word, I must say thus much of it, that certainly had his late Majesty, of sacred memory, but seen and known what a vast and charming world he had been master of in that continent, he would never have parted so easily with it to the Dutch. 'Tis a continent whose vast extent was never yet known, and may contain more noble earth than all the universe besides, for, they say, it reaches from east to west, one way as far as China and another to Peru. It affords all things both for beauty and use; 'tis there eternal spring, always the very months of April, May, and June; the shades are perpetual, the trees bearing at once all degrees of leaves and fruit, from blooming buds to ripe autumn: groves of oranges, lemons, citrons, figs, nutmegs, and noble aromatics, continually bearing their fragrancies. The trees appearing all like nosegays adorned with flowers of different kinds; some are all white, some purple, some scarlet, some blue, some yellow; bearing, at the same time, ripe fruit and blooming young, or producing every day new. The very wood of all these trees has an intrinsic value above common timber, for they are, when cut, of different

2. Alexander the Great is supposed to have encountered both snakes and Amazons in a campaign against India. "Pitching the bar": game in which players compete in throwing a heavy bar or rod. "Tigers": wild cats, including the South American jaguar and cougar.

3. "Land not disjoined by the sea from other lands" (Johnson's *Dictionary*).

colors, glorious to behold, and bear a price considerable, to inlay withal. Besides this they yield rich balm and gums, so that we make our candles of such an aromatic substance as does not only give a sufficient light, but, as they burn, they cast their perfumes all about. Cedar is the common firing, and all the houses are built with it. The very meat we eat, when set on the table, if it be native, I mean of the country, perfumes the whole room; especially a little beast called an armadilly, a thing which I can liken to nothing so well as a rhinoceros; 'tis all in white armor, so jointed that it moves as well in it as if it had nothing on; this beast is about the bigness of a pig of six weeks old. But it were endless to give an account of all the diverse wonderful and strange things that country affords, and which we took a very great delight to go in search of, though those adventures are oftentimes fatal and at least dangerous. But while we had Caesar in our company on these designs we feared no harm, nor suffered any.

As soon as I came into the country, the best house in it was presented me, called St. John's Hill. It stood on a vast rock of white marble, at the foot of which the river ran a vast depth down, and not to be descended on that side; the little waves still dashing and washing the foot of this rock made the softest murmurs and purlings in the world; and the opposite bank was adorned with such vast quantities of different flowers eternally blowing,[4] and every day and hour new, fenced behind 'em with lofty trees of a thousand rare forms and colors, that the prospect was the most ravishing that fancy can create. On the edge of this white rock, towards the river, was a walk or grove of orange and lemon trees, about half the length of the Mall[5] here, whose flowery and fruit-bearing branches met at the top and hindered the sun, whose rays are very fierce there, from entering a beam into the grove; and the cool air that came from the river made it not only fit to entertain people in, at all the hottest hours of the day, but refreshed the sweet blossoms and made it always sweet and charming; and sure the whole globe of the world cannot show so delightful a place as this grove was. Not all the gardens of boasted Italy can produce a shade to outvie this, which nature had joined with art to render so exceeding fine; and 'tis a marvel to see how such vast trees, as big as English oaks, could take footing on so solid a rock and in so little earth as covered that rock; but all things by nature there are rare, delightful, and wonderful. But to our sports.

Sometimes we would go surprising,[6] and in search of young tigers in their dens, watching when the old ones went forth to forage for prey; and oftentimes we have been in great danger and have fled apace for our lives when surprised by the dams. But once, above all other times, we went on this design, and Caesar was with us, who had no sooner stolen a young tiger from her nest but, going off, we encountered the dam, bearing a buttock of a cow which he[7] had torn off with his mighty paw, and going with it towards his den. We had only four women, Caesar, and an English gentleman, brother to Harry Martin, the great Oliverian;[8] we found there was no escaping this enraged and ravenous beast. However, we women fled as fast as we could from it; but our heels had not saved our lives if Caesar had not laid down his cub, when he found the tiger quit her prey to make the more speed towards him, and taking

4. Blooming.
5. Fashionable walk in St. James's Park in London.
6. A military term for making sudden raids.
7. The jarring mixture of pronouns in the two accounts of the tigers (wild cats) may suggest a reluctance to use a feminine pronoun in moments of extreme violence. The first account was left uncorrected in all four 17th-century editions.
8. Supporter of Oliver Cromwell.

Mr. Martin's sword, desired him to stand aside, or follow the ladies. He obeyed him, and Caesar met this monstrous beast of might, size, and vast limbs, who came with open jaws upon him; and fixing his awful stern eyes full upon those of the beast, and putting himself into a very steady and good aiming posture of defense, ran his sword quite through his breast down to his very heart, home to the hilt of the sword. The dying beast stretched forth her paw, and going to grasp his thigh, surprised with death in that very moment, did him no other harm than fixing her long nails in his flesh very deep, feebly wounded him, but could not grasp the flesh to tear off any. When he had done this, he halloed to us to return, which, after some assurance of his victory, we did, and found him lugging out the sword from the bosom of the tiger, who was laid in her blood on the ground; he took up the cub, and with an unconcern that had nothing of the joy or gladness of a victory, he came and laid the whelp at my feet. We all extremely wondered at his daring, and at the bigness of the beast, which was about the heighth of a heifer but of mighty, great, and strong limbs.

Another time, being in the woods, he killed a tiger which had long infested that part, and borne away abundance of sheep and oxen, and other things that were for the support of those to whom they belonged; abundance of people assailed this beast, some affirming they had shot her with several bullets quite through the body at several times, and some swearing they shot her through the very heart, and they believed she was a devil rather than a mortal thing. Caesar had often said he had a mind to encounter this monster, and spoke with several gentlemen who had attempted her, one crying, "I shot her with so many poisoned arrows," another with his gun in this part of her, and another in that; so that he, remarking all these places where she was shot, fancied still he should overcome her by giving her another sort of a wound than any had yet done; and one day said (at the table), "What trophies and garlands, ladies, will you make me, if I bring you home the heart of this ravenous beast that eats up all your lambs and pigs?" We all promised he should be rewarded at all our hands. So taking a bow, which he choosed out of a great many, he went up in the wood, with two gentlemen, where he imagined this devourer to be; they had not passed very far in it but they heard her voice, growling and grumbling, as if she were pleased with something she was doing. When they came in view, they found her muzzling in the belly of a new ravished sheep, which she had torn open; and seeing herself approached, she took fast hold of her prey with her forepaws and set a very fierce raging look on Caesar, without offering to approach him, for fear at the same time of losing what she had in possession. So that Caesar remained a good while, only taking aim, and getting an opportunity to shoot her where he designed; 'twas some time before he could accomplish it, and to wound her and not kill her would but have enraged her more, and endangered him. He had a quiver of arrows at his side, so that if one failed he could be supplied; at last, retiring a little, he gave her opportunity to eat, for he found she was ravenous, and fell to as soon as she saw him retire, being more eager of her prey than of doing new mischiefs. When he going softly to one side of her, and hiding his person behind certain herbage that grew high and thick, he took so good aim that, as he intended, he shot her just into the eye, and the arrow was sent with so good a will and so sure a hand that it stuck in her brain, and made her caper and become mad for a moment or two; but being seconded by another arrow, he fell dead upon the prey. Caesar cut him open with a knife, to see where those wounds were that had been reported to him, and why he did not die of 'em. But I shall now relate a thing that possibly will find no credit among men, because 'tis a notion commonly received with us, that nothing can receive a wound in the heart and live; but when the heart of this courageous animal was taken out, there were seven bullets of lead in it, and the wounds seamed up with great scars, and she lived with the bullets a great while, for it was long since they were shot. This heart the conqueror brought up to us, and 'twas a very great curiosity, which all the country came to see, and which gave Caesar occasion of many fine discourses, of accidents in war and strange escapes.

At other times he would go a-fishing; and discoursing on that diversion, he [illegible]nd we had in that country a very strange fish, called a numb eel[9] (an eel of wh[illegible] I have eaten), that while it is alive, it has a quality so cold, that those who [illegible] angling, though with a line of never so great a length with a rod at the en[illegible] it, it shall, in the same minute the bait is touched by this eel, seize him or her that holds the rod with benumbedness, that shall deprive 'em of sense for a while; and some have fallen into the water, and others dropped as dead on the banks of the rivers where they stood, as soon as this fish touches the bait. Caesar used to laugh at this, and believed it impossible a man could lose his force at the touch of a fish, and could not understand that philosophy,[1] that a cold quality should be of that nature. However, he had a great curiosity to try whether it would have the same effect on him it had on others, and often tried, but in vain. At last the sought for fish came to the bait, as he stood angling on the bank; and instead of throwing away the rod or giving it a sudden twitch out of the water, whereby he might have caught both the eel and have dismissed the rod, before it could have too much power over him, for experiment sake he grasped it but the harder, and fainting fell into the river; and being still possessed of the rod, the tide carried him, senseless as he was, a great way, till an Indian boat took him up, and perceived when they touched him a numbness seize them, and by that knew the rod was in his hand; which with a paddle (that is, a short oar) they struck away, and snatched it into the boat, eel and all. If Caesar were almost dead with the effect of this fish, he was more so with that of the water, where he had remained the space of going a league, and they found they had much ado to bring him back to life. But at last they did, and brought him home, where he was in a few hours well recovered and refreshed, and not a little ashamed to find he should be overcome by an eel, and that all the people who heard his defiance would laugh at him. But we cheered him up; and he being convinced, we had the eel at supper, which was a quarter of an ell about and most delicate meat, and was of the more value, since it cost so dear as almost the life of so gallant a man.

About this time we were in many mortal fears about some disputes the English had with the Indians, so that we could scarce trust ourselves, without great numbers, to go to any Indian towns or place where they abode, for fear they should fall upon us, as they did immediately after my coming away; and that it was in the possession of the Dutch, who used 'em not so civilly as the English, so that they cut in pieces all they could take, getting into houses and hanging up the mother and all her children about her, and cut a footman I left behind me all in joints, and nailed him to trees.

This feud began while I was there, so that I lost half the satisfaction I

9. Electric eel.

1. "Hypothesis or system upon which natural effects are explained" (Johnson's *Dictionary*).

proposed, in not seeing and visiting the Indian towns. But one day, bemoaning of our misfortunes upon this account, Caesar told us we need not fear, for if we had a mind to go, he would undertake to be our guard. Some would, but most would not venture; about eighteen of us resolved and took barge, and after eight days arrived near an Indian town. But approaching it, the hearts of some of our company failed, and they would not venture on shore; so we polled who would and who would not. For my part, I said if Caesar would, I would go; he resolved; so did my brother and my woman, a maid of good courage. Now none of us speaking the language of the people, and imagining we should have a half diversion in gazing only and not knowing what they said, we took a fisherman that lived at the mouth of the river, who had been a long inhabitant there, and obliged him to go with us. But because he was known to the Indians, as trading among 'em, and being by long living there become a perfect Indian in color, we, who resolved to surprise 'em by making 'em see something they never had seen (that is, white people), resolved only myself, my brother and woman should go; so Caesar, the fisherman, and the rest, hiding behind some thick reeds and flowers that grew on the banks, let us pass on towards the town, which was on the bank of the river all along. A little distant from the houses, or huts, we saw some dancing, others busied in fetching and carrying of water from the river. They had no sooner spied us but they set up a loud cry, that frighted us at first; we thought it had been for those that should kill us, but it seems it was of wonder and amazement. They were all naked, and we were dressed so as is most commode for the hot countries, very glittering and rich, so that we appeared extremely fine; my own hair was cut short, and I had a taffety cap with black feathers on my head; my brother was in a stuff[2] suit, with silver loops and buttons and abundance of green ribbon. This was all infinitely surprising to them, and because we saw them stand still till we approached 'em, we took heart and advanced, came up to 'em, and offered 'em our hands; which they took, and looked on us round about, calling still for more company; who came swarming out, all wondering and crying out "*Tepeeme,*" taking their hair up in their hands and spreading it wide to those they called out to, as if they would say (as indeed it signified) "Numberless wonders," or not to be recounted, no more than to number the hair of their heads. By degrees they grew more bold, and from gazing upon us round, they touched us, laying their hands upon all the features of our faces, feeling our breasts and arms, taking up one petticoat, then wondering to see another; admiring our shoes and stockings, but more our garters, which we gave 'em, and they tied about their legs, being laced with silver lace at the ends, for they much esteem any shining things. In fine, we suffered 'em to survey us as they pleased, and we thought they would never have done admiring us. When Caesar and the rest saw we were received with such wonder, they came up to us; and finding the Indian trader whom they knew (for 'tis by these fishermen, called Indian traders, we hold a commerce with 'em, for they love not to go far from home, and we never go to them), when they saw him therefore they set up a new joy, and cried, in their language, "Oh! here's our *tiguamy,* and we shall now know whether those things can speak." So advancing to him, some of 'em gave him their hands and cried, "*Amora tiguamy,*" which is as much as, "How do you?" or "Welcome, friend," and all with one din began to gabble to him, and asked if we had sense and wit; if we could talk of affairs

2. Woven fabric, worsted. "Commode": suitable.

of life and war, as they could do; if we could hunt, swim, and do a thousand things they use. He answered 'em, we could. Then they invited us into their houses, and dressed venison and buffalo for us; and going out, gathered a leaf of a tree called a *sarumbo* leaf, of six yards long, and spread it on the ground for a tablecloth; and cutting another in pieces instead of plates, setting us on little bow Indian stools, which they cut out of one entire piece of wood and paint in a sort of japan work. They serve everyone their mess[3] on these pieces of leaves, and it was very good, but too high seasoned with pepper. When we had eat, my brother and I took out our flutes and played to 'em, which gave 'em new wonder; and I soon perceived, by an admiration that is natural to these people, and by the extreme ignorance and simplicity of 'em, it were not difficult to establish any unknown or extravagant religion among them, and to impose any notions or fictions upon 'em. For seeing a kinsman of mine set some paper afire with a burning glass, a trick they had never before seen, they were like to have adored him for a god, and begged he would give them the characters or figures of his name, that they might oppose it against winds and storms; which he did, and they held it up in those seasons, and fancied it had a charm to conquer them, and kept it like a holy relic. They are very superstitious, and called him the great *Peeie,* that is, prophet. They showed us their Indian *Peeie,* a youth of about sixteen years old, as handsome as nature could make a man. They consecrate a beautiful youth from his infancy, and all arts are used to complete him in the finest manner, both in beauty and shape. He is bred to all the little arts and cunning they are capable of, to all the legerdemain tricks and sleight of hand, whereby he imposes upon the rabble, and is both a doctor in physic[4] and divinity; and by these tricks makes the sick believe he sometimes eases their pains, by drawing from the afflicted part little serpents, or odd flies, or worms, or any strange thing; and though they have besides undoubted good remedies for almost all their diseases, they cure the patient more by fancy than by medicines, and make themselves feared, loved, and reverenced. This young *Peeie* had a very young wife, who seeing my brother kiss her, came running and kissed me; after this they kissed one another, and made it a very great jest, it being so novel; and new admiration and laughing went round the multitude, that they never will forget that ceremony, never before used or known. Caesar had a mind to see and talk with their war captains, and we were conducted to one of their houses, where we beheld several of the great captains, who had been at council. But so frightful a vision it was to see 'em no fancy can create; no such dreams can represent so dreadful a spectacle. For my part I took 'em for hobgoblins or fiends rather than men; but however their shapes appeared, their souls were very humane and noble; but some wanted their noses, some their lips, some both noses and lips, some their ears, and others cut through each cheek with long slashes, through which their teeth appeared; they had other several formidable wounds and scars, or rather dismemberings. They had *comitias* or little aprons before 'em, and girdles of cotton, with their knives naked, stuck in it; a bow at their backs and a quiver of arrows on their thighs; and most had feathers on their heads of diverse colors. They cried "*Amora tiguamy*" to us at our entrance, and were pleased we said as much to 'em; they seated us, and gave us drink of the best sort, and wondered, as much as the others had done before, to see us. Caesar was marveling as much at their faces, wondering how they should all

3. Meal.

4. Medicine.

be so wounded in war; he was impatient to know how they all came by those frightful marks of rage or malice, rather than wounds got in noble battle. They told us, by our interpreter, that when any war was waging, two men chosen out by some old captain whose fighting was past, and who could only teach the theory of war, these two men were to stand in competition for the generalship, or great war captain; and being brought before the old judges, now past labor, they are asked what they dare do to show they are worthy to lead an army. When he who is first asked, making no reply, cuts off his nose, and throws it contemptibly[5] on the ground; and the other does something to himself that he thinks surpasses him, and perhaps deprives himself of lips and an eye; so they slash on till one gives out, and many have died in this debate. And 'tis by a passive valor they show and prove their activity, a sort of courage too brutal to be applauded by our black hero; nevertheless he expressed his esteem of 'em.

In this voyage Caesar begot so good an understanding between the Indians and the English that there were no more fears or heart-burnings during our stay, but we had a perfect, open, and free trade with 'em. Many things remarkable and worthy reciting we met with in this short voyage, because Caesar made it his business to search out and provide for our entertainment, especially to please his dearly adored Imoinda, who was a sharer in all our adventures; we being resolved to make her chains as easy as we could, and to compliment the Prince in that manner that most obliged him.

As we were coming up again, we met with some Indians of strange aspects; that is, of a larger size and other sort of features than those of our country. Our Indian slaves that rowed us asked 'em some questions, but they could not understand us; but showed us a long cotton string with several knots on it, and told us, they had been coming from the mountains so many moons as there were knots. They were habited in skins of a strange beast, and brought along with 'em bags of gold dust, which, as well as they could give us to understand, came streaming in little small channels down the high mountains when the rains fell; and offered to be the convoy to any body or persons that would go to the mountains. We carried these men up to Parham, where they were kept till the Lord Governor came. And because all the country was mad to be going on this golden adventure, the Governor by his letters commanded (for they sent some of the gold to him) that a guard should be set at the mouth of the river of Amazons[6] (a river so called, almost as broad as the river of Thames) and prohibited all people from going up that river, it conducting to those mountains of gold. But we going off for England before the project was further prosecuted, and the Governor being drowned in a hurricane, either the design died, or the Dutch have the advantage of it. And 'tis to be bemoaned what his Majesty lost by losing that part of America.

Though this digression is a little from my story, however since it contains some proofs of the curiosity and daring of this great man, I was content to omit nothing of his character.

It was thus for some time we diverted him; but now Imoinda began to show she was with child, and did nothing but sigh and weep for the captivity of her lord, herself, and the infant yet unborn, and believed if it were so hard to gain the liberty of two, 'twould be more difficult to get that for three. Her griefs

5. With contempt.
6. The mouth of the Amazon, in Brazil, is far distant from Surinam.

were so many darts in the great heart of Caesar; and taking his opportunity one Sunday when all the whites were overtaken in drink, as there were abundance of several trades and slaves for four years[7] that inhabited among the Negro houses, and Sunday was their day of debauch (otherwise they were a sort of spies upon Caesar), he went pretending out of goodness to 'em to feast amongst 'em; and sent all his music, and ordered a great treat for the whole gang, about three hundred Negroes; and about a hundred and fifty were able to bear arms, such as they had, which were sufficient to do execution[8] with spirits accordingly. For the English had none but rusty swords that no strength could draw from a scabbard, except the people of particular quality, who took care to oil 'em and keep 'em in good order. The guns also, unless here and there one, or those newly carried from England, would do no good or harm; for 'tis the nature of that country to rust and eat up iron, or any metals but gold and silver. And they are very unexpert at the bow, which the Negroes and Indians are perfect masters of.

Caesar, having singled out these men from the women and children, made an harangue to 'em of the miseries and ignominies of slavery, counting up all their toils and sufferings, under such loads, burdens, and drudgeries as were fitter for beasts than men, senseless brutes than human souls. He told 'em, it was not for days, months, or years, but for eternity; there was no end to be of their misfortunes. They suffered not like men, who might find a glory and fortitude in oppression, but like dogs that loved the whip and bell,[9] and fawned the more they were beaten. That they had lost the divine quality of men and were become insensible asses, fit only to bear; nay, worse: an ass, or dog, or horse, having done his duty, could lie down in retreat and rise to work again, and while he did his duty endured no stripes; but men, villainous, senseless men such as they, toiled on all the tedious week till Black Friday;[1] and then, whether they worked or not, whether they were faulty or meriting, they promiscuously, the innocent with the guilty, suffered the infamous whip, the sordid stripes, from their fellow slaves, till their blood trickled from all parts of their body, blood whose every drop ought to be revenged with a life of some of those tyrants that impose it. "And why," said he, "my dear friends and fellow sufferers, should we be slaves to an unknown people? Have they vanquished us nobly in fight? Have they won us in honorable battle? And are we by the chance of war become their slaves? This would not anger a noble heart, this would not animate a soldier's soul; no, but we are bought and sold like apes or monkeys, to be the sport of women, fools, and cowards, and the support of rogues, runagades,[2] that have abandoned their own countries for rapine, murders, thefts, and villainies. Do you not hear every day how they upbraid each other with infamy of life, below the wildest savages; and shall we render obedience to such a degenerate race, who have no one human virtue left to distinguish 'em from the vilest creatures? Will you, I say, suffer the lash from such hands?" They all replied, with one accord, "No, no, no; Caesar has spoke like a great captain, like a great king."

After this he would have proceeded, but was interrupted by a tall Negro of some more quality than the rest; his name was Tuscan; who bowing at the

7. Whites who, for crimes or debt, were indentured for a fixed period. "Trades": tradesman.
8. Harm, slaughter.
9. Proverbial for something that distracts from comfort or pleasure, from the protective charm on chariots of triumphing generals in ancient Rome.
1. Here a day of customary beating; more widely, a Friday bringing some notable disaster, from students' slang for examination day.
2. Renegades or fugitives.

feet of Caesar, cried, "My lord, we have listened with joy and attention to what you have said, and, were we only men, would follow so great a leader through the world. But oh! consider, we are husbands and parents too, and have things more dear to us than life, our wives and children, unfit for travel in these unpassable woods, mountains, and bogs; we have not only difficult lands to overcome, but rivers to wade, and monsters to encounter, ravenous beasts of prey—." To this, Caesar replied that honor was the first principle in nature that was to be obeyed; but as no man would pretend to that, without all the acts of virtue, compassion, charity, love, justice, and reason, he found it not inconsistent with that to take an equal care of their wives and children as they would of themselves; and that he did not design, when he led them to freedom and glorious liberty, that they should leave that better part of themselves to perish by the hand of the tyrant's whip. But if there were a woman among them so degenerate from love and virtue to choose slavery before the pursuit of her husband, and with the hazard of her life to share with him in his fortunes, that such a one ought to be abandoned, and left as a prey to the common enemy.

To which they all agreed—and bowed. After this, he spoke of the impassable woods and rivers, and convinced 'em, the more danger, the more glory. He told them that he had heard of one Hannibal, a great captain, had cut his way through mountains of solid rocks;[3] and should a few shrubs oppose them, which they could fire before 'em? No, 'twas a trifling excuse to men resolved to die or overcome. As for bogs, they are with a little labor filled and hardened; and the rivers could be no obstacle, since they swam by nature, at least by custom, from their first hour of their birth. That when the children were weary they must carry them by turns, and the woods and their own industry would afford them food. To this they all assented with joy.

Tuscan then demanded what he would do. He said, they would travel towards the sea, plant a new colony, and defend it by their valor; and when they could find a ship, either driven by stress of weather or guided by Providence that way, they would seize it and make it a prize, till it had transported them to their own countries; at least, they should be made free in his kingdom, and be esteemed as his fellow sufferers, and men that had the courage and the bravery to attempt, at least, for liberty; and if they died in the attempt it would be more brave than to live in perpetual slavery.

They bowed and kissed his feet at this resolution, and with one accord vowed to follow him to death. And that night was appointed to begin their march; they made it known to their wives, and directed them to tie their hamaca[4] about their shoulder and under their arm like a scarf, and to lead their children that could go, and carry those that could not. The wives, who pay an entire obedience to their husbands, obeyed, and stayed for 'em where they were appointed. The men stayed but to furnish themselves with what defensive arms they could get; and all met at the rendezvous, where Caesar made a new encouraging speech to 'em, and led 'em out.

But as they could not march far that night, on Monday early, when the overseers went to call 'em all together to go to work, they were extremely surprised to find not one upon the place, but all fled with what baggage they had. You may imagine this news was not only suddenly spread all over the

3. The Carthaginian general and his troops literally hacked their way down the Alps into Italy to attack Rome.

4. Hammock.

plantation, but soon reached the neighboring ones; and we had by noon about six hundred men they call the militia of the county, that came to assist us in the pursuit of the fugitives. But never did one see so comical an army march forth to war. The men of any fashion would not concern themselves, though it were almost the common cause; for such revoltings are very ill examples, and have very fatal consequences oftentimes in many colonies. But they had a respect for Caesar, and all hands were against the Parhamites, as they called those of Parham plantation, because they did not, in the first place, love the Lord Governor, and secondly they would have it that Caesar was ill used, and baffled with;[5] and 'tis not impossible but some of the best in the country was of his counsel in this flight, and depriving us of all the slaves; so that they of the better sort would not meddle in the matter. The deputy governor,[6] of whom I have had no great occasion to speak, and who was the most fawning fair-tongued fellow in the world and one that pretended the most friendship to Caesar, was now the only violent man against him; and though he had nothing, and so need fear nothing, yet talked and looked bigger than any man. He was a fellow whose character is not fit to be mentioned with the worst of the slaves. This fellow would lead his army forth to meet Caesar, or rather to pursue him; most of their arms were of those sort of cruel whips they call cat with nine tails; some had rusty useless guns for show, others old basket hilts[7] whose blades had never seen the light in this age, and others had long staffs and clubs. Mr. Trefry went along, rather to be a mediator than a conqueror in such a battle; for he foresaw and knew, if by fighting they put the Negroes into despair, they were a sort of sullen fellows that would drown or kill themselves before they would yield; and he advised that fair means was best. But Byam was one that abounded in his own wit and would take his own measures.

It was not hard to find these fugitives; for as they fled they were forced to fire and cut the woods before 'em, so that night or day they pursued 'em by the light they made and by the path they had cleared. But as soon as Caesar found he was pursued, he put himself in a posture of defense, placing all the women and children in the rear, and himself with Tuscan by his side, or next to him, all promising to die or conquer. Encouraged thus, they never stood to parley, but fell on pell-mell upon the English, and killed some and wounded a good many, they having recourse to their whips as the best of their weapons. And as they observed no order, they perplexed the enemy so sorely with lashing 'em in the eyes; and the women and children seeing their husbands so treated, being of fearful cowardly dispositions, and hearing the English cry out, "Yield and live, yield and be pardoned," they all run in amongst their husbands and fathers, and hung about 'em, crying out, "Yield, yield; and leave Caesar to their revenge"; that by degrees the slaves abandoned Caesar, and left him only Tuscan and his heroic Imoinda; who, grown big as she was, did nevertheless press near her lord, having a bow and a quiver full of poisoned arrows, which she managed with such dexterity that she wounded several, and shot the governor[8] into the shoulder; of which wound he had like to have died, but that an Indian woman, his mistress, sucked the wound and cleansed it from the venom. But however, he stirred not from the place till he had parleyed with Caesar, who he found was resolved to die fighting, and would not be taken; no more would

5. Cheated.
6. William Byam. There are recorded complaints against him for high-handedness and from him about insubordination by settlers and slaves.
7. Swords with protective hilt guards.
8. I.e., Byam, the deputy governor.

Tuscan, or Imoinda. But he, more thirsting after revenge of another sort than that of depriving him of life, now made use of all his art of talking and dissembling, and besought Caesar to yield himself upon terms which he himself should propose, and should be sacredly assented to and kept by him. He told him, it was not that he any longer feared him, or could believe the force of two men, and a young heroine, could overcome all them, with all the slaves now on their side also; but it was the vast esteem he had for his person, the desire he had to serve so gallant a man, and to hinder himself from the reproach hereafter of having been the occasion of the death of a prince whose valor and magnanimity deserved the empire of the world. He protested to him, he looked upon this action as gallant and brave, however tending to the prejudice of his lord and master, who would by it have lost so considerable a number of slaves; that this flight of his should be looked on as a heat of youth, and rashness of a too forward courage, and an unconsidered impatience of liberty, and no more; and that he labored in vain to accomplish that which they would effectually perform as soon as any ship arrived that would touch on his coast. "So that if you will be pleased," continued he, "to surrender yourself, all imaginable respect shall be paid you; and yourself, your wife, and child, if it be here born, shall depart free out of our land."

But Caesar would hear of no composition;[9] though Byam urged, if he pursued and went on in his design, he would inevitably perish, either by great snakes, wild beasts, or hunger; and he ought to have regard to his wife, whose condition required ease, and not the fatigues of tedious travel, where she could not be secured from being devoured. But Caesar told him, there was no faith in the white men or the gods they adored, who instructed 'em in principles so false that honest men could not live amongst 'em; though no people professed so much, none performed so little; that he knew what he had to do when he dealt with men of honor, but with them a man ought to be eternally on his guard, and never to eat and drink with Christians without his weapon of defense in his hand; and for his own security, never to credit one word they spoke. As for the rashness and inconsiderateness of his action, he would confess the governor is in the right; and that he was ashamed of what he had done, in endeavoring to make those free who were by nature slaves, poor wretched rogues, fit to be used as Christians' tools; dogs, treacherous and cowardly, fit for such masters; and they wanted only but to be whipped into the knowledge of the Christian gods to be the vilest of all creeping things, to learn to worship such deities as had not power to make 'em just, brave, or honest. In fine, after a thousand things of this nature, not fit here to be recited, he told Byam he had rather die than live upon the same earth with such dogs. But Trefry and Byam pleaded and protested together so much that Trefry, believing the governor to mean what he said, and speaking very cordially himself, generously put himself into Caesar's hands, and took him aside and persuaded him, even with tears, to live, by surrendering himself, and to name his conditions. Caesar was overcome by his wit and reasons, and in consideration of Imoinda; and demanding what he desired, and that it should be ratified by their hands in writing, because he had perceived that was the common way of contract between man and man, amongst the whites. All this was performed, and Tuscan's pardon was put in, and they surrender to the governor, who walked peaceably down into the plantation with 'em, after giving order to bury

9. Settlement.

their dead. Caesar was very much toiled with the bustle of the day, for he had fought like a fury; and what mischief was done he and Tuscan performed alone, and gave their enemies a fatal proof that they durst do anything and feared no mortal force.

But they were no sooner arrived at the place where all the slaves receive their punishments of whipping, but they laid hands on Caesar and Tuscan, faint with heat and toil; and surprising them, bound them to two several stakes, and whipped them in a most deplorable and inhuman manner, rending the very flesh from their bones; especially Caesar, who was not perceived to make any moan or to alter his face, only to roll his eyes on the faithless governor, and those he believed guilty, with fierceness and indignation; and to complete his rage, he saw every one of those slaves, who but a few days before adored him as something more than mortal, now had a whip to give him some lashes, while he strove not to break his fetters; though if he had, it were impossible. But he pronounced a woe and revenge from his eyes, that darted fire that 'twas at once both awful and terrible to behold.

When they thought they were sufficiently revenged on him, they untied him, almost fainting with loss of blood from a thousand wounds all over his body, from which they had rent his clothes, and led him bleeding and naked as he was, and loaded him all over with irons; and then rubbed his wounds, to complete their cruelty, with Indian pepper, which had like to have made him raving mad; and in this condition made him so fast to the ground that he could not stir, if his pains and wounds would have given him leave. They spared Imoinda, and did not let her see this barbarity committed towards her lord, but carried her down to Parham and shut her up; which was not in kindness to her, but for fear she should die with the sight, or miscarry, and then they should lose a young slave and perhaps the mother.

You must know, that when the news was brought on Monday morning that Caesar had betaken himself to the woods and carried with him all the Negroes, we were possessed with extreme fear, which no persuasions could dissipate, that he would secure himself till night, and then that he would come down and cut all our throats. This apprehension made all the females of us fly down the river, to be secured; and while we were away they acted this cruelty. For I suppose I had authority and interest enough there, had I suspected any such thing, to have prevented it; but we had not gone many leagues but the news overtook us that Caesar was taken and whipped like a common slave. We met on the river with Colonel Martin, a man of great gallantry, wit, and goodness, and whom I have celebrated in a character of my new comedy[1] by his own name, in memory of so brave a man. He was wise and eloquent and, from the fineness of his parts, bore a great sway over the hearts of all the colony. He was a friend to Caesar, and resented this false dealing with him very much. We carried him back to Parham, thinking to have made an accommodation; when we came, the first news we heard was that the governor was dead of a wound Imoinda had given him; but it was not so well. But it seems he would have the pleasure of beholding the revenge he took on Caesar, and before the cruel ceremony was finished, he dropped down; and then they perceived the wound he had on his shoulder was by a venomed arrow, which, as I said, his Indian mistress healed by sucking the wound.

We were no sooner arrived but we went up to the plantation to see Caesar,

1. *The Younger Brother, or The Amorous Jilt*, not produced until 1696 despite this piece of promotion.

whom we found in a very miserable and unexpressible condition; and I have a thousand times admired how he lived, in so much tormenting pain. We said all things to him that trouble, pity, and good nature could suggest, protesting our innocency of the fact and our abhorrence of such cruelties; making a thousand professions of services to him and begging as many pardons for the offenders, till we said so much that he believed we had no hand in his ill treatment; but told us he could never pardon Byam; as for Trefry, he confessed he saw his grief and sorrow for his suffering, which he could not hinder, but was like to have been beaten down by the very slaves for speaking in his defense. But for Byam, who was their leader, their head—and should, by his justice and honor, have been an example to 'em—for him, he wished to live, to take a dire revenge of him, and said, "It had been well for him if he had sacrificed me, instead of giving me the contemptible[2] whip." He refused to talk much, but begging us to give him our hands, he took 'em, and protested never to lift up his to do us any harm. He had a great respect for Colonel Martin, and always took his counsel like that of a parent, and assured him he would obey him in anything but his revenge on Byam. "Therefore," said he, "for his own safety, let him speedily dispatch me; for if I could dispatch myself I would not, till that justice were done to my injured person,[3] and the contempt of a soldier. No, I would not kill myself, even after a whipping, but will be content to live with that infamy, and be pointed at by every grinning slave, till I have completed my revenge; and then you shall see that Oroonoko scorns to live with the indignity that was put on Caesar." All we could do could get no more words from him; and we took care to have him put immediately into a healing bath to rid him of his pepper, and ordered a chirurgeon[4] to anoint him with healing balm, which he suffered; and in some time he began to be able to walk and eat. We failed not to visit him every day, and to that end had him brought to an apartment at Parham.

The governor was no sooner recovered, and had heard of the menaces of Caesar, but he called his council; who (not to disgrace them, or burlesque the government there) consisted of such notorious villains as Newgate[5] never transported; and possibly originally were such who understood neither the laws of God or man, and had no sort of principles to make 'em worthy the name of men; but at the very council table would contradict and fight with one another, and swear so bloodily that 'twas terrible to hear and see 'em. (Some of 'em were afterwards hanged when the Dutch took possession of the place, others sent off in chains.) But calling these special rulers of the nation together, and requiring their counsel in this weighty affair, they all concluded that (Damn 'em) it might be their own cases; and that Caesar ought to be made an example to all the Negroes, to fright 'em from daring to threaten their betters, their lords and masters; and at this rate no man was safe from his own slaves; and concluded, *nemine contradicente*,[6] that Caesar should be hanged.

Trefry then thought it time to use his authority, and told Byam his command did not extend to his lord's plantation, and that Parham was as much exempt from the law as Whitehall;[7] and that they ought no more to touch the servants of the Lord——(who there represented the King's person) than they could

2. Showing contempt.
3. Body or character.
4. Surgeon.
5. The major London prison, from which criminals were transported to the colonies.
6. No one disagreeing (Latin).
7. The king's palace in London. Treffry stands as Lord Willoughby's deputy on his private land, Byam in the colony at large.

those about the King himself; and that Parham was a sanctuary; and though his lord were absent in person, his power was still in being there, which he had entrusted with him as far as the dominions of his particular plantations reached, and all that belonged to it; the rest of the country, as Byam was lieutenant to his lord, he might exercise his tyranny upon. Trefry had others as powerful, or more, that interested themselves in Caesar's life, and absolutely said he should be defended. So turning the governor and his wise council out of doors (for they sat at Parham House), they set a guard upon our landing place, and would admit none but those we called friends to us and Caesar.

The governor having remained wounded at Parham till his recovery was completed, Caesar did not know but he was still there; and indeed, for the most part his time was spent there, for he was one that loved to live at other people's expense; and if he were a day absent, he was ten present there, and used to play and walk and hunt and fish with Caesar. So that Caesar did not at all doubt, if he once recovered strength, but he should find an opportunity of being revenged on him. Though after such a revenge, he could not hope to live, for if he escaped the fury of the English mobile,[8] who perhaps would have been glad of the occasion to have killed him, he was resolved not to survive his whipping; yet he had, some tender hours, a repenting softness, which he called his fits of coward, wherein he struggled with Love for the victory of his heart, which took part with his charming Imoinda there; but for the most part his time was passed in melancholy thought and black designs. He considered, if he should do this deed and die, either in the attempt or after it, he left his lovely Imoinda a prey, or at best a slave, to the enraged multitude; his great heart could not endure that thought. "Perhaps," said he, "she may be first ravished by every brute, exposed first to their nasty lusts and then a shameful death." No; he could not live a moment under that apprehension, too insupportable to be borne. These were his thoughts and his silent arguments with his heart, as he told us afterwards; so that now resolving not only to kill Byam but all those he thought had enraged him, pleasing his great heart with the fancied slaughter he should make over the whole face of the plantation, he first resolved on a deed, that (however horrid it at first appeared to us all), when we had heard his reasons, we thought it brave and just. Being able to walk and, as he believed, fit for the execution of his great design, he begged Trefry to trust him into the air, believing a walk would do him good, which was granted him; and taking Imoinda with him, as he used to do in his more happy and calmer days, he led her up into a wood, where, after (with a thousand sighs, and long gazing silently on her face, while tears gushed, in spite of him, from his eyes) he told her his design first of killing her, and then his enemies, and next himself, and the impossibility of escaping, and therefore he told her the necessity of dying, he found the heroic wife faster pleading for death than he was to propose it, when she found his fixed resolution, and on her knees besought him not to leave her a prey to his enemies. He (grieved to death) yet pleased at her noble resolution, took her up, and embracing her with all the passion and languishment of a dying lover, drew his knife to kill this treasure of his soul, this pleasure of his eyes; while tears trickled down his cheeks, hers were smiling with joy she should die by so noble a hand, and be sent in her own country (for that's their notion of the next world) by him she so tenderly loved and so truly adored in this; for wives have a respect for

8. Common people or mob.

their husbands equal to what any other people pay a deity, and when a man finds any occasion to quit his wife, if he love her, she dies by his hand; if not, he sells her, or suffers some other to kill her. It being thus, you may believe the deed was soon resolved on; and 'tis not to be doubted but the parting, the eternal leave-taking of two such lovers, so greatly born, so sensible,[9] so beautiful, so young, and so fond, must be very moving, as the relation of it was to me afterwards.

All that love could say in such cases being ended, and all the intermitting irresolutions being adjusted, the lovely, young, and adored victim lays herself down before the sacrificer; while he, with a hand resolved and a heart breaking within, gave the fatal stroke; first cutting her throat, and then severing her yet smiling face from that delicate body, pregnant as it was with fruits of tenderest love. As soon as he had done, he laid the body decently on leaves and flowers, of which he made a bed, and concealed it under the same coverlid of nature; only her face he left yet bare to look on. But when he found she was dead and past all retrieve, never more to bless him with her eyes and soft language, his grief swelled up to rage; he tore, he raved, he roared, like some monster of the wood, calling on the loved name of Imoinda. A thousand times he turned the fatal knife that did the deed toward his own heart, with a resolution to go immediately after her; but dire revenge, which now was a thousand times more fierce in his soul than before, prevents him; and he would cry out, "No; since I have sacrificed Imoinda to my revenge, shall I lose that glory which I have purchased so dear as at the price of the fairest, dearest, softest creature that ever nature made? No, no!" Then, at her name, grief would get the ascendant of rage, and he would lie down by her side and water her face with showers of tears, which never were wont to fall from those eyes. And however bent he was on his intended slaughter, he had not power to stir from the sight of this dear object, now more beloved and more adored than ever.

He remained in this deploring condition for two days, and never rose from the ground where he had made his sad sacrifice. At last, rousing from her side, and accusing himself with living too long now Imoinda was dead, and that the deaths of those barbarous enemies were deferred too long, he resolved now to finish the great work; but offering to rise, he found his strength so decayed that he reeled to and fro, like boughs assailed by contrary winds; so that he was forced to lie down again, and try to summon all his courage to his aid. He found his brains turned round, and his eyes were dizzy, and objects appeared not the same to him they were wont to do; his breath was short, and all his limbs surprised with a faintness he had never felt before. He had not eat in two days, which was one occasion of this feebleness, but excess of grief was the greatest; yet still he hoped he should recover vigor to act his design, and lay expecting it yet six days longer, still mourning over the dead idol of his heart, and striving every day to rise, but could not.

In all this time you may believe we were in no little affliction for Caesar and his wife; some were of opinion he was escaped never to return; others thought some accident had happened to him. But however, we failed not to send out an hundred people several ways to search for him; a party of about forty went that way he took, among whom was Tuscan, who was perfectly reconciled to Byam. They had not gone very far into the wood but they smelt an unusual smell, as of a dead body; for stinks must be very noisome that can be distin-

9. Sensitive.

guished among such a quantity of natural sweets as every inch of that land produces. So that they concluded they should find him dead, or somebody that was so. They passed on towards it, as loathsome as it was, and made such a rustling among the leaves that lie thick on the ground, by continual falling, that Caesar heard he was approached; and though he had during the space of these eight days endeavored to rise, but found he wanted strength, yet looking up and seeing his pursuers, he rose and reeled to a neighboring tree, against which he fixed his back; and being within a dozen yards of those that advanced and saw him, he called out to them and bid them approach no nearer, if they would be safe. So that they stood still, and hardly believing their eyes, that would persuade them that it was Caesar that spoke to 'em, so much was he altered, they asked him what he had done with his wife, for they smelt a stink that almost struck them dead. He, pointing to the dead body, sighing, cried, "Behold her there." They put off the flowers that covered her with their sticks, and found she was killed, and cried out, "Oh, monster! that hast murdered thy wife." Then asking him why he did so cruel a deed, he replied, he had no leisure to answer impertinent questions. "You may go back," continued he, "and tell the faithless governor he may thank fortune that I am breathing my last, and that my arm is too feeble to obey my heart in what it had designed him." But his tongue faltering, and trembling, he could scarce end what he was saying. The English, taking advantage by his weakness, cried, "Let us take him alive by all means." He heard 'em; and as if he had revived from a fainting, or a dream, he cried out, "No, gentlemen, you are deceived; you will find no more Caesars to be whipped, no more find a faith in me. Feeble as you think me, I have strength yet left to secure me from a second indignity." They swore all anew, and he only shook his head and beheld them with scorn. Then they cried out, "Who will venture on this single man? Will nobody?" They stood all silent while Caesar replied, "Fatal will be the attempt to the first adventurer, let him assure himself," and at that word, held up his knife in a menacing posture. "Look ye, ye faithless crew," said he, " 'tis not life I seek, nor am I afraid of dying," and at that word cut a piece of flesh from his own throat, and threw it at 'em; "yet still I would live if I could, till I had perfected my revenge. But oh! it cannot be; I feel life gliding from my eyes and heart, and if I make not haste, I shall yet fall a victim to the shameful whip." At that, he ripped up his own belly, and took his bowels and pulled 'em out, with what strength he could; while some, on their knees imploring, besought him to hold his hand. But when they saw him tottering, they cried out, "Will none venture on him?" A bold English cried, "Yes, if he were the devil" (taking courage when he saw him almost dead); and swearing a horrid oath for his farewell to the world, he rushed on him; Caesar, with his armed hand, met him so fairly as stuck him to the heart, and he fell dead at his feet. Tuscan, seeing that, cried out, "I love thee, O Caesar, and therefore will not let thee die, if possible." And running to him, took him in his arms; but at the same time warding a blow that Caesar made at his bosom, he received it quite through his arm; and Caesar having not the strength to pluck the knife forth, though he attempted it, Tuscan neither pulled it out himself nor suffered it to be pulled out, but came down with it sticking in his arm; and the reason he gave for it was, because the air should not get into the wound. They put their hands across, and carried Caesar between six of 'em, fainted as he was, and they thought dead, or just dying; and they brought him to Parham, and laid him on a couch, and had the chirurgeon immediately to him, who dressed his wounds and sewed up his belly, and used means to bring him to life, which they effected. We ran all to see him, and if before we thought him so beautiful a sight, he was now so altered that his face was like a death's head blacked over, nothing but teeth and eyeholes. For some days we suffered nobody to speak to him, but caused cordials to be poured down his throat, which sustained his life; and in six or seven days he recovered his senses. For you must know that wounds are almost to a miracle cured in the Indies, unless wounds in the legs, which rarely ever cure.

When he was well enough to speak, we talked to him, and asked him some questions about his wife, and the reasons why he killed her; and he then told us what I have related of that resolution, and of his parting; and he besought us we would let him die, and was extremely afflicted to think it was possible he might live; he assured us if we did not dispatch him, he would prove very fatal to a great many. We said all we could to make him live, and gave him new assurances; but he begged we would not think so poorly of him, or of his love to Imoinda, to imagine we could flatter him to life again; but the chirurgeon assured him he could not live, and therefore he need not fear. We were all (but Caesar) afflicted at this news; and the sight was gashly;[1] his discourse was sad, and the earthly smell about him so strong that I was persuaded to leave the place for some time (being myself but sickly, and very apt to fall into fits of dangerous illness upon any extraordinary melancholy). The servants and Trefry and the chirurgeons promised all to take what possible care they could of the life of Caesar, and I, taking boat, went with other company to Colonel Martin's, about three days' journey down the river; but I was no sooner gone, but the governor taking Trefry about some pretended earnest business a day's journey up the river, having communicated his design to one Banister, a wild Irishman and one of the council, a fellow of absolute barbarity, and fit to execute any villainy, but was rich: he came up to Parham, and forcibly took Caesar, and had him carried to the same post where he was whipped; and causing him to be tied to it, and a great fire made before him, he told him he should die like a dog, as he was. Caesar replied, this was the first piece of bravery that ever Banister did, and he never spoke sense till he pronounced that word; and if he would keep it, he would declare, in the other world, that he was the only man of all the whites that ever he heard speak truth. And turning to the men that bound him, he said, "My friends, am I to die, or to be whipped?" And they cried, "Whipped! No, you shall not escape so well." And then he replied, smiling, "A blessing on thee," and assured them they need not tie him, for he would stand fixed like a rock, and endure death so as should encourage them to die. "But if you whip me," said he, "be sure you tie me fast."

He had learned to take tobacco; and when he was assured he should die, he desired they would give him a pipe in his mouth, ready lighted, which they did; and the executioner came, and first cut off his members,[2] and threw them into the fire; after that, with an ill-favored knife, they cut his ears, and his nose, and burned them; he still smoked on, as if nothing had touched him. Then they hacked off one of his arms, and still he bore up, and held his pipe; but at the cutting off the other arm, his head sunk, and his pipe dropped, and he gave up the ghost, without a groan or a reproach. My mother and sister were by him all the while, but not suffered to save him, so rude and wild were the rabble, and so inhuman were the justices, who stood by to see the exe-

1. Ghastly.

2. Genitals.

cution, who after paid dearly enough for their insolence. They cut Caesar in quarters, and sent them to several of the chief plantations. One quarter was sent to Colonel Martin, who refused it, and swore he had rather see the quarters of Banister and the governor himself than those of Caesar on his plantations, and that he could govern his Negroes without terrifying and grieving them with frightful spectacles of a mangled king.

Thus died this great man, worthy of a better fate, and a more sublime wit than mine to write his praise; yet, I hope, the reputation of my pen is considerable enough to make his glorious name to survive to all ages, with that of the brave, the beautiful, and the constant Imoinda.

1688

JONATHAN SWIFT
1667–1745

Jonathan Swift—a posthumous child—was born of English parents in Dublin. Through the generosity of an uncle he was educated at Kilkenny School and Trinity College, Dublin, but before he could fix on a career, the troubles that followed upon James II's abdication and subsequent invasion of Ireland drove Swift along with other Anglo-Irish to England. Between 1689 and 1699 he was more or less continuously a member of the household of his kinsman Sir William Temple, an urbane, civilized man, a retired diplomat, and a friend of King William. During these years Swift read widely, rather reluctantly decided on the church as a career and so took orders, and discovered his astonishing gifts as a satirist. About 1696–97 he wrote his powerful satires on corruptions in religion and learning, *A Tale of a Tub* and *The Battle of the Books,* which were published in 1704 and reached their final form only in the fifth edition of 1710. These were the years in which he slowly came to maturity. When, at the age of thirty-two, he returned to Ireland as chaplain to the lord justice, the earl of Berkeley, he had a clear sense of his genius.

For the rest of his life, Swift devoted his talents to politics and religion—not clearly separated at the time—and most of his works in prose were written to further a specific cause. As a clergyman, a spirited controversialist, and a devoted supporter of the Anglican Church, he was hostile to all who seemed to threaten it: Deists, freethinkers, Roman Catholics, Nonconformists, or merely Whig politicians. In 1710 he abandoned the Whigs, because he opposed their indifference to the welfare of the Anglican Church in Ireland and their desire to repeal the Test Act, which required all holders of offices of state to take the Sacrament according to the Anglican rites, thus excluding Roman Catholics and Dissenters. (For Swift's "Argument against the Abolishing of Christianity in England," go to Norton Literature Online.) Welcomed by the Tories, he became the most brilliant political journalist of the day, serving the government of Oxford and Bolingbroke as editor of the party organ, the *Examiner,* and as author of its most powerful articles as well as writing longer pamphlets in support of important policies, such as that favoring the Peace of Utrecht (1713). He was greatly valued by the two ministers, who admitted him to social intimacy, although never to their counsels. The reward of his services was not the English bishopric that he had a right to expect, but the deanship of St. Patrick's Cathedral in Dublin, which came to him in 1713, a year before the death of Queen Anne and the fall of the Tories put an end to all his hopes of preferment in England.

In Ireland, where he lived unwillingly, he became not only an efficient ecclesiastical administrator but also, in 1724, the leader of Irish resistance to English oppression. Under the pseudonym "M. B. Drapier," he published the famous series of public letters that aroused the country to refuse to accept £100,000 in new copper coins (minted in England by William Wood, who had obtained his patent through court corruption), which, it was feared, would further debase the coinage of the already poverty-stricken kingdom. Although his authorship of the letters was known to all Dublin, no one could be found to earn the £300 offered by the government for information as to the identity of the drapier. Swift is still venerated in Ireland as a national hero. He earned the right to refer to himself in the epitaph that he wrote for his tomb as a vigorous defender of liberty.

His last years were less happy. Swift had suffered most of his adult life from what we now recognize as Ménière's disease, which affects the inner ear, causing dizziness, nausea, and deafness. After 1739, when he was seventy-two years old, his infirmities cut him off from his duties as dean, and from then on his social life dwindled. In 1742 guardians were appointed to administer his affairs, and his last three years were spent in gloom and lethargy. But this dark ending should not put his earlier life, so full of energy and humor, into a shadow. The writer of the satires was a man in full control of great intellectual powers.

He also had a gift for friendship. Swift was admired and loved by many of the distinguished men of his time. His friendships with Joseph Addison, Alexander Pope, John Arbuthnot, John Gay, Matthew Prior, Lord Oxford, and Lord Bolingbroke, not to mention those in his less brilliant but amiable Irish circle, bear witness to his moral integrity and social charm. Nor was he, despite some of his writings, indifferent to women. Esther Johnson (Swift's "Stella") was the daughter of Temple's steward, and when Swift first knew her, she was little more than a child. He educated her, formed her character, and came to love her as he was to love no other person. After Temple's death she moved to Dublin, where she and Swift met constantly, but never alone. While working with the Tories in London, he wrote letters to her, later published as *The Journal to Stella* (1766), and they exchanged poems as well. Whether they were secretly married or never married—and in either case why—has been often debated. A marriage of any sort seems most unlikely; and however perplexing their relationship was to others, it seems to have satisfied them. Not even the violent passion that Swift awakened, no doubt unwittingly, in the much younger woman Hester Vanhomrigh (pronounced *Van-úm-mer-y*)—with her pleadings and reproaches and early death—could unsettle his devotion to Stella. An enigmatic account of his relations with "Vanessa," as he called Vanhomrigh, is given in his poem "Cadenus and Vanessa."

For all his involvement in public affairs, Swift seems to stand apart from his contemporaries—a striking figure among the statesmen of the time, a writer who towered above others by reason of his imagination, mordant wit, and emotional intensity. He has been called a misanthrope, a hater of humanity, and *Gulliver's Travels* has been considered an expression of savage misanthropy. It is true that Swift proclaimed himself a misanthrope in a letter to Pope, declaring that, though he loved individuals, he hated "that animal called man" in general and offering a new definition of the species not as *animal rationale* ("a rational animal") but as merely *animal rationis capax* ("an animal *capable* of reason"). This, he declared, is the "great foundation" on which his "misanthropy" was erected. Swift was stating not his hatred of his fellow creatures but his antagonism to the current optimistic view that human nature is essentially good. To the "philanthropic" flattery that sentimentalism and Deistic rationalism were paying to human nature, Swift opposed a more ancient view: that human nature is deeply and permanently flawed and that we can do nothing with or for the human race until we recognize its moral and intellectual limitations. In his epitaph he spoke of the "fierce indignation" that had torn his heart, an indignation that found superb expression in his greatest satires. It was provoked by the constant spectacle of creatures capable of reason, and therefore of reasonable conduct, steadfastly refusing to live up to their capabilities.

Swift is a master of prose. He defined a good style as "proper words in proper places," a more complex and difficult saying than at first appears. Clear, simple, concrete diction; uncomplicated syntax; and economy and conciseness of language mark all his writings. His is a style that shuns ornaments and singularity of all kinds, a style that grows more tense and controlled the more fierce the indignation that it is called on to express. The virtues of his prose are those of his poetry, which shocks us with its hard look at the facts of life and the body. It is unpoetic poetry, devoid of, indeed as often as not mocking at, inspiration, romantic love, cosmetic beauty, easily assumed literary attitudes, and conventional poetic language. Like the prose, it is predominantly satiric in purpose, but not without its moments of comedy and lightheartedness, though most often written less to divert than to agitate the reader.

A Description of a City Shower

Careful observers may foretell the hour
(By sure prognostics) when to dread a shower:
While rain depends,[1] the pensive cat gives o'er
Her frolics, and pursues her tail no more.
Returning home at night, you'll find the sink° *sewer*
Strike your offended sense with double stink.
If you be wise, then go not far to dine;
You'll spend in coach hire more than save in wine.
A coming shower your shooting corns presage,
Old achés throb, your hollow tooth will rage.
Sauntering in coffeehouse is Dulman seen;
He damns the climate and complains of spleen.[2]
Meanwhile the South, rising with dabbled wings,
A sable cloud athwart the welkin flings,
That swilled more liquor than it could contain,
And, like a drunkard, gives it up again.
Brisk Susan whips her linen from the rope,
While the first drizzling shower is borne aslope:
Such is that sprinkling which some careless quean° *wench, slut*
Flirts on you from her mop, but not so clean:
You fly, invoke the gods; then turning, stop
To rail; she singing, still whirls on her mop.
Not yet the dust had shunned the unequal strife,
But, aided by the wind, fought still for life,
And wafted with its foe by violent gust,
'Twas doubtful which was rain and which was dust.
Ah! where must needy poet seek for aid,
When dust and rain at once his coat invade?
Sole coat, where dust cemented by the rain
Erects the nap,[3] and leaves a mingled stain.
Now in contiguous drops the flood comes down,
Threatening with deluge this devoted town.
To shops in crowds the daggled° females fly, *mud-spattered*

1. Impends, is imminent. An example of elevated diction used frequently throughout the poem.
2. The English tendency to melancholy ("the spleen") was often attributed to the rainy climate. "Dulman": a type name (from "dull man"), like Congreve's "Petulant" or "Witwoud."
3. Stiffens the coat's surface.

Pretend to cheapen° goods, but nothing buy. *bargain for*
The Templar spruce, while every spout's abroach,[4]
Stays till 'tis fair, yet seems to call a coach.
The tucked-up sempstress walks with hasty strides,
While streams run down her oiled umbrella's sides.
Here various kinds, by various fortunes led,
Commence acquaintance underneath a shed.
Triumphant Tories and desponding Whigs
Forget their feuds,[5] and join to save their wigs.
Boxed in a chair° the beau impatient sits, *sedan chair*
While spouts run clattering o'er the roof by fits,
And ever and anon with frightful din
The leather sounds;[6] he trembles from within.
So when Troy chairmen bore the wooden steed,
Pregnant with Greeks impatient to be freed
(Those bully Greeks, who, as the moderns do,
Instead of paying chairmen, run them through),[7]
Laocoön struck the outside with his spear,
And each imprisoned hero quaked for fear.[8]
Now from all parts the swelling kennels[9] flow,
And bear their trophies with them as they go:
Filth of all hues and odors seem to tell
What street they sailed from, by their sight and smell.
They, as each torrent drives with rapid force,
From Smithfield or St. Pulchre's shape their course,
And in huge confluence joined at Snow Hill ridge,
Fall from the conduit prone to Holborn Bridge.[1]
Sweepings from butchers' stalls, dung, guts, and blood,
Drowned puppies, stinking sprats,° all drenched in mud, *small herrings*
Dead cats, and turnip tops, come tumbling down the flood.[2]

1710

Gulliver's Travels

Gulliver's Travels is Swift's most enduring satire. Although full of allusions to recent and current events, it still rings true today, for its objects are human failings and the defective political, economic, and social institutions that they call into being. Swift adopts an ancient satirical device: the imaginary voyage. Lemuel Gulliver, the narrator, is a ship's surgeon, a moderately well educated man, kindly, resourceful, cheerful, inquiring, patriotic, truthful, and rather unimaginative—in short, a reasonably decent example of humanity, with whom a reader can readily identify. He undertakes four voyages, all of which end disastrously among "several

4. Pouring out water. "The Templar": a young man engaged in studying law.
5. The Whig ministry had just fallen and the Tories, led by Harley and St. John, were forming the government with which Swift was to be closely associated until the death of the queen in 1714.
6. The roof of the sedan chair was made of leather.
7. I.e., with their swords.
8. *Aeneid* 2.40–53.
9. The open gutters in the middle of the street.
1. An accurate description of the drainage system of this part of London—the eastern edge of Holborn and West Smithfield, which lie outside the old walls west and east of Newgate. The great cattle and sheep markets were in Smithfield. The church of St. Sepulchre ("St. Pulchre's") stood opposite Newgate Prison. Holborn Conduit was at the foot of Snow Hill. It drained into Fleet Ditch, an evil-smelling open sewer, at Holborn Bridge.
2. In Faulkner's edition of Swift's *Works* (Dublin, 1735) a note almost certainly suggested by Swift points to the concluding triplet, with its resonant final alexandrine, as a burlesque of a mannerism of Dryden and other Restoration poets and claims that Swift's ridicule banished the triplet from contemporary poetry.

remote nations of the world." In the first, Gulliver is shipwrecked in the empire of Lilliput, where he finds himself a giant among a diminutive people, charmed by their miniature city and amused by their toylike prettiness. But in the end they prove to be treacherous, malicious, ambitious, vengeful, and cruel. As we read we grow disenchanted with the inhabitants of this fanciful kingdom, and then gradually we begin to recognize our likeness to them, especially in the disproportion between our natural pettiness and our boundless and destructive passions. In the second voyage, Gulliver is abandoned by his shipmates in Brobdingnag, a land of giants, creatures ten times as large as Europeans. Though he fears that such monsters must be brutes, the reverse proves to be the case. Brobdingnag is something of a utopia, governed by a humane and enlightened prince who is the embodiment of moral and political wisdom. In the long interview in which Gulliver pridefully enlarges on the glories of England and its political institutions, the king reduces him to resentful silence by asking questions that reveal the difference between what England is and what it ought to be. In Brobdingnag, Gulliver finds himself a Lilliputian, his pride humbled by his helpless state and his human vanity diminished by the realization that his body must have seemed as disgusting to the Lilliputians as do the bodies of the Brobdingnagians to him.

In the third voyage, to Laputa, Swift is chiefly concerned with attacking extremes of theoretical and speculative reasoning, whether in science, politics, or economics. Much of this voyage is an allegory of political life under the administration of the Whig minister, Sir Robert Walpole. The final voyage sets Gulliver between a race of horses, Houyhnhnms (prounced *Hwín-ims*), who live entirely by reason except for a few well-controlled and muted social affections, and their slaves, the Yahoos, whose bodies are obscene caricatures of the human body and who have no glimmer of reason but are mere creatures of appetite and passion.

When *Gulliver's Travels* first appeared, everyone read it—children for the story and politicians for the satire of current affairs—and ever since it has retained a hold on readers of every kind. Almost unique in world literature, it is simple enough for children, complex enough to carry adults beyond their depth. Swift's art works on many levels. First of all, there is the sheer playfulness of the narrative. Through Gulliver's eyes, we gaze on marvel after marvel: a tiny girl who threads an invisible needle with invisible silk or a white mare who threads a needle between pastern and hoof. The travels, like a fairy story, transport us to imaginary worlds that function with a perfect, fantastic logic different from our own; Swift exercises our sense of vision. But beyond that, he exercises our perceptions of meaning. In *Gulliver's Travels,* things are seldom what they seem; irony, probing or corrosive, underlies almost every word. In the last chapter, Gulliver insists that the example of the Houyhnhnms has made him incapable of telling a lie—but the oath he swears is quoted from Sinon, whose lies to the Trojans persuaded them to accept the Trojan *horse*. Swift trains us to read alertly, to look beneath the surface. Yet on its deepest level, the book does not offer final meanings, but a question: What is a human being? Voyaging through imaginary worlds, we try to find ourselves. Are we prideful insects or lords of creation? brutes or reasonable beings? In the last voyage, Swift pushes such questions, and Gulliver himself, almost beyond endurance; hating his own humanity, Gulliver forgets who he is. For the reader, however, the outcome cannot be so clear. Swift does not set out to satisfy our minds but to vex and unsettle them. And he leaves us at the moment when the mixed face of humanity—the pettiness of the Lilliputians, the savagery of the Yahoos, the innocence of Gulliver himself—begins to look strangely familiar, like our own faces in a mirror.

Swift's full title for this work was *Travels into Several Remote Nations of the World. In Four Parts. By Lemuel Gulliver, First a Surgeon, and then a Captain of several Ships*. In the first edition (1726), either the bookseller or Swift's friends Charles Ford, Pope, and others, who were concerned in getting the book anonymously into print, altered and omitted so much of the original manuscript (because of its dangerous political implications) that Swift was seriously annoyed. When, in 1735, the Dublin bookseller George Faulkner brought out an edition of Swift's works, the dean seems to have taken pains, surreptitiously, to see that a more authentic version of the work was published. This text is the basis of modern editions.

From Gulliver's Travels

A Letter from Captain Gulliver to His Cousin Sympson[1]

I hope you will be ready to own publicly, whenever you shall be called to it, that by your great and frequent urgency you prevailed on me to publish a very loose and uncorrect account of my travels; with direction to hire some young gentlemen of either University to put them in order, and correct the style, as my Cousin Dampier[2] did by my advice, in his book called *A Voyage round the World.* But I do not remember I gave you power to consent that anything should be omitted, and much less that anything should be inserted: therefore, as to the latter, I do here renounce everything of that kind; particularly a paragraph about her Majesty the late Queen Anne, of most pious and glorious memory; although I did reverence and esteem her more than any of human species. But you, or your interpolator, ought to have considered that as it was not my inclination, so was it not decent to praise any animal of our composition before my master Houyhnhnm; and besides, the fact was altogether false; for to my knowledge, being in England during some part of her Majesty's reign, she did govern by a chief Minister; nay, even by two successively; the first whereof was the Lord of Godolphin, and the second the Lord of Oxford; so that you have made me *say the thing that was not.* Likewise, in the account of the Academy of Projectors, and several passages of my discourse to my master Houyhnhnm, you have either omitted some material circumstances, or minced or changed them in such a manner, that I do hardly know mine own work. When I formerly hinted to you something of this in a letter, you were pleased to answer that you were afraid of giving offense; that people in power were very watchful over the press; and apt not only to interpret, but to punish everything which looked like an *innuendo* (as I think you called it). But pray, how could that which I spoke so many years ago, and at above five thousand leagues distance, in another reign, be applied to any of the Yahoos, who now are said to govern the herd; especially, at a time when I little thought on or feared the unhappiness of living under them. Have not I the most reason to complain, when I see these very Yahoos carried by Houyhnhnms in a vehicle, as if these were brutes, and those the rational creatures? And, indeed, to avoid so monstrous and detestable a sight was one principal motive of my retirement hither.[3]

Thus much I thought proper to tell you in relation to yourself, and to the trust I reposed in you.

I do in the next place complain of my own great want of judgment, in being prevailed upon by the intreaties and false reasonings of you and some others, very much against mine own opinion, to suffer my travels to be published. Pray bring to your mind how often I desired you to consider, when you insisted on the motive of public good, that the Yahoos were a species of animals utterly

1. In this letter, first published in 1735, Swift complains, among other matters, of the alterations in his original text made by the publisher, Benjamin Motte, in the interest of what he considered political discretion.

2. William Dampier (1652–1715), the explorer, whose account of his circumnavigation of the globe Swift had read.

3. To Nottinghamshire.

incapable of amendment by precepts or examples; and so it hath proved; for instead of seeing a full stop put to all abuses and corruptions, at least in this little island, as I had reason to expect, behold, after above six months warning, I cannot learn that my book hath produced one single effect according to mine intentions; I desired you would let me know by a letter, when party and faction were extinguished; judges learned and upright; pleaders honest and modest, with some tincture of common sense; and Smithfield blazing with pyramids of law books; the young nobility's education entirely changed; the physicians banished; the female Yahoos abounding in virtue, honor, truth, and good sense; courts and levees of great ministers thoroughly weeded and swept; wit, merit, and learning rewarded; all disgracers of the press in prose and verse, condemned to eat nothing but their own cotton,[4] and quench their thirst with their own ink. These, and a thousand other reformations, I firmly counted upon by your encouragement; as indeed they were plainly deducible from the precepts delivered in my book. And, it must be owned that seven months were a sufficient time to correct every vice and folly to which Yahoos are subject; if their natures had been capable of the least disposition to virtue or wisdom; yet so far have you been from answering mine expectation in any of your letters, that on the contrary, you are loading our carrier every week with libels, and keys, and reflections, and memoirs, and second parts; wherein I see myself accused of reflecting upon great statesfolk; of degrading human nature (for so they have still the confidence to style it) and of abusing the female sex. I find likewise, that the writers of those bundles are not agreed among themselves; for some of them will not allow me to be author of mine own travels; and others make me author of books to which I am wholly a stranger.

I find likewise that your printer hath been so careless as to confound the times, and mistake the dates of my several voyages and returns; neither assigning the true year, or the true month, or day of the month; and I hear the original manuscript is all destroyed, since the publication of my book. Neither have I any copy left; however, I have sent you some corrections, which you may insert, if ever there should be a second edition; and yet I cannot stand to them, but shall leave that matter to my judicious and candid readers, to adjust it as they please.

I hear some of our sea Yahoos find fault with my sea language, as not proper in many parts, nor now in use. I cannot help it. In my first voyages, while I was young, I was instructed by the oldest mariners, and learned to speak as they did. But I have since found that the sea Yahoos are apt, like the land ones, to become new fangled in their words; which the latter change every year; insomuch, as I remember upon each return to mine own country, their old dialect was so altered, that I could hardly understand the new. And I observe, when any Yahoo comes from London out of curiosity to visit me at mine own house, we neither of us are able to deliver our conceptions in a manner intelligible to the other.[5]

If the censure of Yahoos could any way affect me, I should have great reason to complain that some of them are so bold as to think my book of travels a mere fiction out of mine own brain; and have gone so far as to drop hints that the Houyhnhnms, and Yahoos have no more existence than the inhabitants of Utopia.

Indeed I must confess that as to the people of Lilliput, Brobdingrag (for so

4. Presumably their paper. "Pleaders": lawyers. Smithfield was a part of London containing many bookshops. "Levees": morning receptions.
5. Swift was the inveterate enemy of slang.

the word should have been spelled, and not erroneously Brobdingnag) and Laputa, I have never yet heard of any Yahoo so presumptuous as to dispute their being, or the facts I have related concerning them; because the truth immediately strikes every reader with conviction. And, is there less probability in my account of the Houyhnhnms or Yahoos, when it is manifest as to the latter, there are so many thousands even in this city, who only differ from their brother brutes in Houyhnhnmland, because they use a sort of a jabber, and do not go naked. I wrote for their amendment, and not their approbation. The united praise of the whole race would be of less consequence to me, than the neighing of those two degenerate Houyhnhnms I keep in my stable; because, from these, degenerate as they are, I still improve in some virtues, without any mixture of vice.

Do these miserable animals presume to think that I am so far degenerated as to defend my veracity; Yahoo as I am, it is well known through all Houyhnhnmland, that by the instructions and example of my illustrious master, I was able in the compass of two years (although I confess with the utmost difficulty) to remove that infernal habit of lying, shuffling, deceiving, and equivocating, so deeply rooted in the very souls of all my species; especially the Europeans.

I have other complaints to make upon this vexatious occasion; but I forbear troubling myself or you any further. I must freely confess that since my last return, some corruptions of my Yahoo nature have revived in me by conversing with a few of your species, and particularly those of mine own family, by an unavoidable necessity; else I should never have attempted so absurd a project as that of reforming the Yahoo race in this kingdom; but I have now done with all such visionary schemes for ever.

1727? 1735

The Publisher to the Reader

The author of these travels, Mr. Lemuel Gulliver, is my ancient and intimate friend; there is likewise some relation between us by the mother's side. About three years ago Mr. Gulliver, growing weary of the concourse of curious people coming to him at his house in Redriff,[6] made a small purchase of land, with a convenient house, near Newark, in Nottinghamshire, his native country; where he now lives retired, yet in good esteem among his neighbors.

Although Mr. Gulliver were born in Nottinghamshire, where his father dwelt, yet I have heard him say his family came from Oxfordshire; to confirm which, I have observed in the churchyard at Banbury, in that county, several tombs and monuments of the Gullivers.

Before he quitted Redriff, he left the custody of the following papers in my hands, with the liberty to dispose of them as I should think fit. I have carefully perused them three times; the style is very plain and simple; and the only fault I find is that the author, after the manner of travelers, is a little too circumstantial. There is an air of truth apparent through the whole; and indeed the author was so distinguished for his veracity, that it became a sort of proverb among his neighbors at Redriff, when anyone affirmed a thing, to say, it was as true as if Mr. Gulliver had spoke it.

6. Rotherhithe, a district in southern London, below Tower Bridge, then frequented by sailors.

By the advice of several worthy persons, to whom, with the author's permission, I communicated these papers, I now venture to send them into the world; hoping they may be, at least for some time, a better entertainment to our young noblemen, than the common scribbles of politics and party.

This volume would have been at least twice as large, if I had not made bold to strike out innumerable passages relating to the winds and tides, as well as to the variations and bearings in the several voyages; together with the minute descriptions of the management of the ship in storms, in the style of sailors; likewise the account of the longitudes and latitudes, wherein I have reason to apprehend that Mr. Gulliver may be a little dissatisfied; but I was resolved to fit the work as much as possible to the general capacity of readers. However, if my own ignorance in sea affairs shall have led me to commit some mistakes, I alone am answerable for them; and if any traveler hath a curiosity to see the whole work at large, as it came from the hand of the author, I will be ready to gratify him.

As for any further particulars relating to the author, the reader will receive satisfaction from the first pages of the book.

RICHARD SYMPSON

Part 1. A Voyage to Lilliput

CHAPTER 1. *The author gives some account of himself and family; his first inducements to travel. He is shipwrecked, and swims for his life; gets safe on shore in the country of Lilliput; is made a prisoner, and carried up the country.*

My father had a small estate in Nottinghamshire; I was the third of five sons. He sent me to Emanuel College in Cambridge, at fourteen years old, where I resided three years, and applied myself close to my studies: but the charge of maintaining me (although I had a very scanty allowance) being too great for a narrow fortune, I was bound apprentice to Mr. James Bates, an eminent surgeon in London, with whom I continued four years; and my father now and then sending me small sums of money, I laid them out in learning navigation, and other parts of the mathematics, useful to those who intend to travel, as I always believed it would be some time or other my fortune to do. When I left Mr. Bates, I went down to my father; where, by the assistance of him and my uncle John, and some other relations, I got forty pounds, and a promise of thirty pounds a year to maintain me at Leyden:[7] there I studied physic two years and seven months, knowing it would be useful in long voyages.

Soon after my return from Leyden, I was recommended by my good master Mr. Bates, to be surgeon to the *Swallow,* Captain Abraham Pannell commander; with whom I continued three years and a half, making a voyage or two into the Levant[8] and some other parts. When I came back, I resolved to settle in London, to which Mr. Bates, my master, encouraged me; and by him I was recommended to several patients. I took part of a small house in the Old Jury; and being advised to alter my condition, I married Mrs.[9] Mary Burton, second daughter to Mr. Edmond Burton, hosier, in Newgate Street, with whom I received four hundred pounds for a portion.

7. The University of Leyden, in Holland, was a center for the study of medicine ("physic").
8. The eastern Mediterranean.
9. The title (pronounced *mistress*) designated any woman, married or unmarried. "Old Jury": a street (once "Old Jewry") in the City of London.

But, my good master Bates dying in two years after, and I having few friends, my business began to fail; for my conscience would not suffer me to imitate the bad practice of too many among my brethren. Having therefore consulted with my wife, and some of my acquaintance, I determined to go again to sea. I was surgeon successively in two ships, and made several voyages, for six years, to the East and West Indies; by which I got some addition to my fortune. My hours of leisure I spent in reading the best authors, ancient and modern, being always provided with a good number of books; and when I was ashore, in observing the manners and dispositions of the people, as well as learning their language; wherein I had a great facility by the strength of my memory.

The last of these voyages not proving very fortunate, I grew weary of the sea, and intended to stay at home with my wife and family. I removed from the Old Jury to Fetter Lane, and from thence to Wapping, hoping to get business among the sailors; but it would not turn to account. After three years' expectation that things would mend, I accepted an advantageous offer from Captain William Prichard, master of the *Antelope,* who was making a voyage to the South Sea. We set sail from Bristol, May 4th, 1699, and our voyage at first was very prosperous.

It would not be proper, for some reasons, to trouble the reader with the particulars of our adventures in those seas: let it suffice to inform him, that in our passage from thence to the East Indies we were driven by a violent storm to the northwest of Van Diemen's Land.[1] By an observation, we found ourselves in the latitude of 30 degrees 2 minutes south. Twelve of our crew were dead by immoderate labor, and ill food, the rest were in a very weak condition. On the fifth of November, which was the beginning of summer in those parts, the weather being very hazy, the seamen spied a rock, within half a cable's length[2] of the ship; but the wind was so strong, that we were driven directly upon it, and immediately split. Six of the crew, of whom I was one, having let down the boat into the sea, made a shift to get clear of the ship, and the rock. We rowed by my computation about three leagues, till we were able to work no longer, being already spent with labor while we were in the ship. We therefore trusted ourselves to the mercy of the waves; and in about half an hour the boat was overset by a sudden flurry from the north. What became of my companions in the boat, as well as of those who escaped on the rock, or were left in the vessel, I cannot tell; but conclude they were all lost. For my own part, I swam as fortune directed me, and was pushed forward by wind and tide. I often let my legs drop, and could feel no bottom; but when I was almost gone, and able to struggle no longer, I found myself within my depth; and by this time the storm was much abated. The declivity was so small, that I walked near a mile before I got to the shore, which I conjectured was about eight o'clock in the evening. I then advanced forward near half a mile, but could not discover any sign of houses or inhabitants; at least I was in so weak a condition, that I did not observe them. I was extremely tired, and with that, and the heat of the weather, and about half a pint of brandy that I drank as I left the ship, I found myself much inclined to sleep. I lay down on the grass, which was very short and soft, where I slept sounder than ever I remember to have done in my life, and as I reckoned, above nine hours; for when I awaked, it was just daylight. I attempted to rise, but was not able to stir: for

1. Tasmania.
2. A cable is about six hundred feet (one hundred fathoms).

as I happened to lie on my back, I found my arms and legs were strongly fastened on each side to the ground; and my hair, which was long and thick, tied down in the same manner. I likewise felt several slender ligatures across my body, from my armpits to my thighs. I could only look upwards; the sun began to grow hot, and the light offended my eyes. I heard a confused noise about me, but in the posture I lay, could see nothing except the sky. In a little time I felt something alive moving on my left leg, which advancing gently forward over my breast, came almost up to my chin; when bending my eyes downwards as much as I could, I perceived it to be a human creature not six inches high,[3] with a bow and arrow in his hands, and a quiver at his back. In the meantime, I felt at least forty more of the same kind (as I conjectured) following the first. I was in the utmost astonishment, and roared so loud, that they all ran back in a fright; and some of them, as I was afterwards told, were hurt with the falls they got by leaping from my sides upon the ground. However, they soon returned; and one of them, who ventured so far as to get a full sight of my face, lifting up his hands and eyes by way of admiration,[4] cried out in a shrill, but distinct voice, *Hekinah Degul*: the others repeated the same words several times, but I then knew not what they meant. I lay all this while, as the reader may believe, in great uneasiness; at length, struggling to get loose, I had the fortune to break the strings, and wrench out the pegs that fastened my left arm to the ground; for, by lifting it up to my face, I discovered the methods they had taken to bind me; and, at the same time, with a violent pull, which gave me excessive pain, I a little loosened the strings that tied down my hair on the left side; so that I was just able to turn my head about two inches. But the creatures ran off a second time, before I could seize them; whereupon there was a great shout in a very shrill accent; and after it ceased, I heard one of them cry aloud, *Tolgo phonac*; when in an instant I felt above an hundred arrows discharged on my left hand, which pricked me like so many needles; and besides they shot another flight into the air, as we do bombs in Europe, whereof many, I suppose, fell on my body (though I felt them not) and some on my face, which I immediately covered with my left hand. When this shower of arrows was over, I fell a groaning with grief and pain; and then striving again to get loose, they discharged another volley larger than the first, and some of them attempted with spears to stick me in the sides; but, by good luck, I had on me a buff jerkin,[5] which they could not pierce. I thought it the most prudent method to lie still; and my design was to continue so till night, when, my left hand being already loose, I could easily free myself: and as for the inhabitants, I had reason to believe I might be a match for the greatest armies they could bring against me, if they were all of the same size with him that I saw. But fortune disposed otherwise of me. When the people observed I was quiet, they discharged no more arrows: but by the noise increasing, I knew their numbers were greater; and about four yards from me, over-against my right ear, I heard a knocking for above an hour, like people at work; when turning my head that way, as well as the pegs and strings would permit me, I saw a stage erected about a foot and a half from the ground, capable of holding four of the inhabitants, with two or three ladders to mount it: from whence one of them, who seemed to be a person of quality, made me a long speech, whereof I understood not one syllable. But I should have mentioned, that before the principal person

3. Lilliput is scaled, fairly consistently, at one-twelfth of Gulliver's world.

4. Wonderment.

5. Leather jacket.

began his oration, he cried out three times, *Langro Dehul san*: (these words and the former were afterwards repeated and explained to me). Whereupon immediately about fifty of the inhabitants came, and cut the strings that fastened the left side of my head, which gave me the liberty of turning it to the right, and of observing the person and gesture of him who was to speak. He appeared to be of a middle age, and taller than any of the other three who attended him; whereof one was a page who held up his train, and seemed to be somewhat longer than my middle finger; the other two stood one on each side to support him. He acted every part of an orator, and I could observe many periods[6] of threatenings, and others of promises, pity and kindness. I answered in a few words, but in the most submissive manner, lifting up my left hand and both my eyes to the sun, as calling him for a witness; and being almost famished with hunger, having not eaten a morsel for some hours before I left the ship, I found the demands of nature so strong upon me, that I could not forbear showing my impatience (perhaps against the strict rules of decency) by putting my finger frequently on my mouth, to signify that I wanted food. The *Hurgo* (for so they call a great lord, as I afterwards learned) understood me very well. He descended from the stage, and commanded that several ladders should be applied to my sides, on which above an hundred of the inhabitants mounted, and walked towards my mouth, laden with baskets full of meat, which had been provided and sent thither by the King's orders upon the first intelligence he received of me. I observed there was the flesh of several animals, but could not distinguish them by the taste. There were shoulders, legs, and loins shaped like those of mutton, and very well dressed, but smaller than the wings of a lark. I eat them by two or three at a mouthful, and took three loaves at a time, about the bigness of musket bullets. They supplied me as fast as they could, showing a thousand marks of wonder and astonishment at my bulk and appetite. I then made another sign that I wanted drink. They found by my eating that a small quantity would not suffice me; and being a most ingenious people, they slung up with great dexterity one of their largest hogsheads; then rolled it towards my hand, and beat out the top; I drank it off at a draught, which I might well do, for it hardly held half a pint, and tasted like a small wine of Burgundy, but much more delicious. They brought me a second hogshead, which I drank in the same manner, and made signs for more, but they had none to give me. When I had performed these wonders, they shouted for joy, and danced upon my breast, repeating several times as they did at first, *Hekinah Degul*. They made me a sign that I should throw down the two hogsheads, but first warned the people below to stand out of the way, crying aloud, *Borach Mivola,* and when they saw the vessels in the air, there was an universal shout of *Hekinah Degul*. I confess I was often tempted, while they were passing backwards and forwards on my body, to seize forty or fifty of the first that came in my reach, and dash them against the ground. But the remembrance of what I had felt, which probably might not be the worst they could do; and the promise of honor I made them, for so I interpreted my submissive behavior, soon drove out those imaginations. Besides, I now considered myself as bound by the laws of hospitality to a people who had treated me with so much expense and magnificence. However, in my thoughts I could not sufficiently wonder at the intrepidity of these diminutive mortals, who durst venture to mount and walk on my body, while one of my hands was at

6. In rhetoric, complete, well-constructed sentences.

liberty, without trembling at the very sight of so prodigious a creature as I must appear to them. After some time, when they observed that I made no more demands for meat, there appeared before me a person of high rank from his Imperial Majesty. His Excellency, having mounted on the small of my right leg, advanced forwards up to my face, with about a dozen of his retinue. And producing his credentials under the Signet Royal, which he applied[7] close to my eyes, spoke about ten minutes, without any signs of anger, but with a kind of determinate resolution; often pointing forwards, which, as I afterwards found, was towards the capital city, about half a mile distant, whither it was agreed by his Majesty in council that I must be conveyed. I answered in a few words, but to no purpose, and made a sign with my hand that was loose, putting it to the other (but over his Excellency's head, for fear of hurting him or his train) and then to my own head and body, to signify that I desired my liberty. It appeared that he understood me well enough; for he shook his head by way of disapprobation, and held his hand in a posture to show that I must be carried as a prisoner. However, he made other signs to let me understand that I should have meat and drink enough, and very good treatment. Whereupon I once more thought of attempting to break my bonds; but again, when I felt the smart of their arrows upon my face and hands, which were all in blisters, and many of the darts still sticking in them; and observing likewise that the number of my enemies increased; I gave tokens to let them know that they might do with me what they pleased. Upon this the *Hurgo* and his train withdrew, with much civility and cheerful countenances. Soon after I heard a general shout, with frequent repetitions of the words, *Peplom Selan,* and I felt great numbers of the people on my left side relaxing the cords to such a degree, that I was able to turn upon my right, and to ease myself with making water; which I very plentifully did, to the great astonishment of the people, who conjecturing by my motions what I was going to do, immediately opened to the right and left on that side, to avoid the torrent which fell with such noise and violence from me. But before this, they had daubed my face and both my hands with a sort of ointment very pleasant to the smell, which in a few minutes removed all the smart of their arrows. These circumstances, added to the refreshment I had received by their victuals and drink, which were very nourishing, disposed me to sleep. I slept about eight hours, as I was afterwards assured; and it was no wonder; for the physicians, by the Emperor's order, had mingled a sleeping potion in the hogsheads of wine.

It seems that upon the first moment I was discovered sleeping on the ground after my landing, the Emperor had early notice of it by an express; and determined in council that I should be tied in the manner I have related (which was done in the night while I slept), that plenty of meat and drink should be sent me, and a machine prepared to carry me to the capital city.

This resolution perhaps may appear very bold and dangerous, and I am confident would not be imitated by any prince in Europe on the like occasion; however, in my opinion it was extremely prudent as well as generous. For supposing these people had endeavored to kill me with their spears and arrows while I was asleep; I should certainly have awaked with the first sense of smart, which might so far have roused my rage and strength, as to enable me to break the strings wherewith I was tied; after which, as they were not able to make resistance, so they could expect no mercy.

7. Brought.

These people are most excellent mathematicians, and arrived to a great perfection in mechanics by the countenance and encouragement of the Emperor, who is a renowned patron of learning. This prince hath several machines fixed on wheels, for the carriage of trees and other great weights. He often builds his largest men of war, whereof some are nine foot long, in the woods where the timber grows, and has them carried on these engines[8] three or four hundred yards to the sea. Five hundred carpenters and engineers were immediately set at work to prepare the greatest engine they had. It was a frame of wood raised three inches from the ground, about seven foot long and four wide, moving upon twenty-two wheels. The shout I heard was upon the arrival of this engine, which it seems set out in four hours after my landing. It was brought parallel to me as I lay. But the principal difficulty was to raise and place me in this vehicle. Eighty poles, each of one foot high, were erected for this purpose, and very strong cords of the bigness of packthread were fastened by hooks to many bandages, which the workmen had girt round my neck, my hands, my body, and my legs. Nine hundred of the strongest men were employed to draw up these cords by many pulleys fastened on the poles; and thus, in less than three hours, I was raised and slung into the engine, and there tied fast. All this I was told, for while the whole operation was performing, I lay in a profound sleep, by the force of that soporiferous[9] medicine infused into my liquor. Fifteen hundred of the Emperor's largest horses, each about four inches and a half high, were employed to draw me towards the metropolis, which, as I said, was half a mile distant.

About four hours after we began our journey, I awaked by a very ridiculous accident; for, the carriage being stopped a while to adjust something that was out of order, two or three of the young natives had the curiosity to see how I looked when I was asleep; they climbed up into the engine, and advancing very softly to my face, one of them, an officer in the guards, put the sharp end of his half-pike a good way up into my left nostril, which tickled my nose like a straw, and made me sneeze violently: whereupon they stole off unperceived, and it was three weeks before I knew the cause of my awaking so suddenly. We made a long march the remaining part of the day, and rested at night with five hundred guards on each side of me half with torches, and half with bows and arrows, ready to shoot me if I should offer to stir. The next morning at sunrise we continued our march, and arrived within two hundred yards of the city gates about noon. The Emperor and all his court came out to meet us, but his great officers would by no means suffer his Majesty to endanger his person by mounting on my body.

At the place where the carriage stopped, there stood an ancient temple, esteemed to be the largest in the whole kingdom, which having been polluted some years before by an unnatural murder,[1] was, according to the zeal of those people, looked on as profane, and therefore had been applied to common use, and all the ornaments and furniture carried away. In this edifice it was determined I should lodge. The great gate fronting to the north was about four foot high, and almost two foot wide, through which I could easily creep. On each side of the gate was a small window not above six inches from the ground: into that on the left side, the King's smiths conveyed fourscore and eleven chains, like those that hang to a lady's watch in Europe, and almost as large,

8. Contrivances.
9. Inducing unnatural sleep.
1. Presumably a reference to the execution of Charles I, who was sentenced in Westminster Hall.

which were locked to my left leg with six and thirty padlocks. Over against this temple, on the other side of the great highway, at twenty foot distance, there was a turret at least five foot high. Here the Emperor ascended with many principal lords of his court, to have an opportunity of viewing me, as I was told, for I could not see them. It was reckoned that above an hundred thousand inhabitants came out of the town upon the same errand; and in spite of my guards, I believe there could not be fewer than ten thousand, at several times, who mounted upon my body by the help of ladders. But a proclamation was soon issued to forbid it upon pain of death. When the workmen found it was impossible for me to break loose, they cut all the strings that bound me; whereupon I rose up with as melancholy a disposition as ever I had in my life. But the noise and astonishment of the people at seeing me rise and walk are not to be expressed. The chains that held my left leg were about two yards long, and gave me not only the liberty of walking backwards and forwards in a semicircle; but, being fixed within four inches of the gate, allowed me to creep in, and lie at my full length in the temple.

CHAPTER 2. *The Emperor of Lilliput, attended by several of the nobility, comes to see the author in his confinement. The Emperor's person and habit described. Learned men appointed to teach the author their language. He gains favor by his mild disposition. His pockets are searched, and his sword and pistols taken from him.*

When I found myself on my feet, I looked about me, and must confess I never beheld a more entertaining prospect. The country round appeared like a continued garden, and the inclosed fields, which were generally forty foot square, resembled so many beds of flowers. These fields were intermingled with woods of half a stang,[2] and the tallest trees, as I could judge, appeared to be seven foot high. I viewed the town on my left hand, which looked like the painted scene of a city in a theater.

I had been for some hours extremely pressed by the necessities of nature; which was no wonder, it being almost two days since I had last disburthened myself. I was under great difficulties between urgency and shame. The best expedient I could think on, was to creep into my house, which I accordingly did; and shutting the gate after me, I went as far as the length of my chain would suffer; and discharged my body of that uneasy load. But this was the only time I was ever guilty of so uncleanly an action; for which I cannot but hope the candid reader will give some allowance, after he hath maturely and impartially considered my case, and the distress I was in. From this time my constant practice was, as soon as I rose, to perform that business in open air, at the full extent of my chain, and due care was taken every morning before company came, that the offensive matter should be carried off in wheelbarrows by two servants appointed for that purpose. I would not have dwelt so long upon a circumstance, that perhaps at first sight may appear not very momentous, if I had not thought it necessary to justify my character in point of cleanliness to the world; which I am told some of my maligners have been pleased, upon this and other occasions, to call in question.

When this adventure was at an end, I came back out of my house, having occasion for fresh air. The Emperor was already descended from the tower,

2. A quarter of an acre.

and advancing on horseback towards me, which had like to have cost him dear; for the beast, although very well trained, yet wholly unused to such a sight, which appeared as if a mountain moved before him, reared up on his hinder feet: but that prince, who is an excellent horseman, kept his seat, until his attendants ran in, and held the bridle, while his Majesty had time to dismount. When he alighted, he surveyed me round with great admiration, but kept beyond the length of my chains. He ordered his cooks and butlers, who were already prepared, to give me victuals and drink, which they pushed forward in a sort of vehicles upon wheels until I could reach them. I took these vehicles, and soon emptied them all; twenty of them were filled with meat, and ten with liquor; each of the former afforded me two or three good mouthfuls, and I emptied the liquor of ten vessels, which was contained in earthen vials, into one vehicle, drinking it off at a draught; and so I did with the rest. The Empress, and young princes of the blood, of both sexes, attended by many ladies, sat at some distance in their chairs; but upon the accident that happened to the Emperor's horse, they alighted, and came near his person; which I am now going to describe. He is taller, by almost the breadth of my nail, than any of his court, which alone is enough to strike an awe into the beholders. His features are strong and masculine, with an Austrian lip, and arched nose, his complexion olive, his countenance[3] erect, his body and limbs well proportioned, all his motions graceful, and his deportment majestic. He was then past his prime, being twenty-eight years and three quarters old, of which he had reigned about seven, in great felicity, and generally victorious. For the better convenience of beholding him, I lay on my side, so that my face was parallel to his, and he stood but three yards off: however, I have had him since many times in my hand, and therefore cannot be deceived in the description. His dress was very plain and simple, the fashion of it between the Asiatic and the European; but he had on his head a light helmet of gold, adorned with jewels, and a plume on the crest. He held his sword drawn in his hand, to defend himself, if I should happen to break loose; it was almost three inches long, the hilt and scabbard were gold enriched with diamonds. His voice was shrill, but very clear and articulate, and I could distinctly hear it when I stood up. The ladies and courtiers were all most magnificently clad, so that the spot they stood upon seemed to resemble a petticoat spread on the ground, embroidered with figures of gold and silver. His Imperial Majesty spoke often to me, and I returned answers, but neither of us could understand a syllable. There were several of his priests and lawyers present (as I conjectured by their habits) who were commanded to address themselves to me, and I spoke to them in as many languages as I had the least smattering of, which were High and Low Dutch, Latin, French, Spanish, Italian, and Lingua Franca;[4] but all to no purpose. After about two hours the court retired, and I was left with a strong guard, to prevent the impertinence, and probably the malice of the rabble, who were very impatient to crowd about me as near as they durst; and some of them had the impudence to shoot their arrows at me as I sat on the ground by the door of my house, whereof one very narrowly missed my left eye. But the colonel ordered six of the ringleaders to be seized, and thought no punishment so proper as to deliver them bound into my hands, which some of his soldiers accordingly did, pushing them forwards with the butt-ends of their

3. Bearing, appearance. Swift may be satirically idealizing George I, whom most of the British thought gross.

4. A jargon, based on Italian, used by traders in the Mediterranean. "High and Low Dutch": German and Dutch, respectively.

pikes into my reach; I took them all in my right hand, put five of them into my coat-pocket; and as to the sixth, I made a countenance as if I would eat him alive. The poor man squalled terribly, and the colonel and his officer were in much pain, especially when they saw me take out my penknife: but I soon put them out of fear; for, looking mildly, and immediately cutting the strings he was bound with, I set him gently on the ground, and away he ran. I treated the rest in the same manner, taking them one by one out of my pocket, and I observed both the soldiers and people were highly obliged at this mark of my clemency, which was represented very much to my advantage at court.

Towards night I got with some difficulty into my house, where I lay on the ground, and continued to do so about a fortnight; during which time the Emperor gave orders to have a bed prepared for me. Six hundred beds of the common measure were brought in carriages, and worked up in my house; an hundred and fifty of their beds sewn together made up the breadth and length, and these were four double, which however kept me but very indifferently from the hardness of the floor, that was of smooth stone. By the same computation they provided me with sheets, blankets, and coverlets, tolerable enough for one who had been so long enured to hardships as I.

As the news of my arrival spread through the kingdom, it brought prodigious numbers of rich, idle, and curious people to see me; so that the villages were almost emptied, and great neglect of tillage and household affairs must have ensued, if his Imperial Majesty had not provided by several proclamations and orders of state against this inconveniency. He directed that those who had already beheld me should return home, and not presume to come within fifty yards of my house without license from court; whereby the secretaries of state got considerable fees.

In the mean time, the Emperor held frequent councils to debate what course should be taken with me; and I was afterwards assured by a particular friend, a person of great quality, who was as much in the secret as any, that the court was under many difficulties concerning me. They apprehended[5] my breaking loose, that my diet would be very expensive, and might cause a famine. Sometimes they determined to starve me, or at least to shoot me in the face and hands with poisoned arrows, which would soon dispatch me: but again they considered, that the stench of so large a carcass might produce a plague in the metropolis, and probably spread through the whole kingdom. In the midst of these consultations, several officers of the army went to the door of the great council chamber; and two of them being admitted, gave an account of my behavior to the six criminals above-mentioned; which made so favorable an impression in the breast of his Majesty, and the whole board, in my behalf, that an imperial commission was issued out, obliging all the villages nine hundred yards round the city to deliver in every morning six beeves, forty sheep, and other victuals for my sustenance; together with a proportionable quantity of bread and wine, and other liquors: for the due payment of which his Majesty gave assignments[6] upon his treasury. For this prince lives chiefly upon his own demesnes; seldom except upon great occasions raising any subsidies upon his subjects, who are bound to attend him in his wars at their own expense. An establishment was also made of six hundred persons to be my domestics, who had board-wages allowed for their maintenance, and tents built for them very conveniently on each side of my door. It was likewise ordered, that three hun-

5. Anticipated with fear.

6. Formal mandates of revenue.

dred tailors should make me a suit of clothes after the fashion of the country: that six of his Majesty's greatest scholars should be employed to instruct me in their language: and, lastly, that the Emperor's horses, and those of the nobility, and troops of guards, should be exercised in my sight, to accustom themselves to me. All these orders were duly put in execution; and in about three weeks I made a great progress in learning their language; during which time the Emperor frequently honored me with his visits, and was pleased to assist my masters in teaching me. We began already to converse together in some sort; and the first words I learned, were to express my desire that he would please to give me my liberty; which I every day repeated on my knees.[7] His answer, as I could apprehend, was, that this must be a work of time, not to be thought on without the advice of his council; and that first I must *Lumos kelmin pesso desmar lon emposo;* that is, swear a peace with him and his kingdom. However, that I should be used with all kindness; and he advised me to acquire by my patience and discreet behavior, the good opinion of himself and his subjects. He desired I would not take it ill, if he gave orders to certain proper officers to search me; for probably I might carry about me several weapons, which must needs be dangerous things, if they answered the bulk of so prodigious a person.[8] I said, his Majesty should be satisfied, for I was ready to strip myself, and turn up my pockets before him. This I delivered part in words, and part in signs. He replied, that by the laws of the kingdom, I must be searched by two of his officers; that he knew this could not be done without my consent and assistance; that he had so good an opinion of my generosity and justice, as to trust their persons in my hands; that whatever they took from me should be returned when I left the country, or paid for at the rate which I would set upon them. I took up the two officers in my hands, put them first into my coat-pockets, and then into every other pocket about me, except my two fobs, and another secret pocket which I had no mind should be searched, wherein I had some little necessaries of no consequence to any but myself. In one of my fobs there was a silver watch, and in the other a small quantity of gold in a purse. These gentlemen, having pen, ink, and paper about them, made an exact inventory of everything they saw; and when they had done, desired I would set them down, that they might deliver it to the Emperor. This inventory I afterwards translated into English, and is word for word as follows.

> Imprimis,[9] In the right coat-pocket of the Great Man-Mountain (for so I interpret the words *Quinbus Flestrin*) after the strictest search, we found only one great piece of coarse cloth, large enough to be a foot-cloth for your Majesty's chief room of state. In the left pocket, we saw a huge silver chest, with a cover of the same metal, which we the searchers were not able to lift. We desired it should be opened; and one of us, stepping into it, found himself up to the mid leg in a sort of dust, some part whereof flying up to our faces, set us both a sneezing for several times together. In his right waistcoat-pocket, we found a prodigious bundle of white thin substances, folded one over another, about the bigness of three men, tied with a strong cable, and marked with black figures; which we humbly conceive to be writings; every letter almost half as large as the palm of

7. Gulliver's plea for liberty and the threat of starvation or rebellion he represents to his captors suggest the situation of Ireland with respect to England.
8. When the Whigs came into power in 1715, the leading Tories, who included Swift's friends Oxford and Bolingbroke (Robert Harley and Henry St. John) as well as Swift himself, were investigated by a committee of secrecy.
9. In the first place (Latin).

our hands. In the left there was a sort of engine, from the back of which were extended twenty long poles, resembling the palisados[1] before your Majesty's court; wherewith we conjecture the Man-Mountain combs his head; for we did not always trouble him with questions, because we found it a great difficulty to make him understand us. In the large pocket on the right side of his middle cover (so I translate the word *ranfu-lo,* by which they meant my breeches) we saw a hollow pillar of iron, about the length of a man, fastened to a strong piece of timber, larger than the pillar; and upon one side of the pillar were huge pieces of iron sticking out, cut into strange figures; which we know not what to make of. In the left pocket, another engine of the same kind. In the smaller pocket on the right side, were several round flat pieces of white and red metal, of different bulk; some of the white, which seemed to be silver, were so large and heavy, that my comrade and I could hardly lift them. In the left pocket were two black pillars irregularly shaped: we could not, without difficulty, reach the top of them as we stood at the bottom of his pocket. One of them was covered, and seemed all of a piece; but at the upper end of the other, there appeared a white round substance, about twice the bigness of our heads. Within each of these was inclosed a prodigious plate of steel; which, by our orders, we obliged him to show us, because we apprehended they might be dangerous engines. He took them out of their cases, and told us, that in his own country his practice was to shave his beard with one of these, and to cut his meat with the other. There were two pockets which we could not enter: these he called his fobs; they were two large slits cut into the top of his middle cover, but squeezed close by the pressure of his belly. Out of the right fob hung a great silver chain, with a wonderful kind of engine at the bottom. We directed him to draw out whatever was at the end of the chain, which appeared to be a globe, half silver, and half of some transparent metal: for on the transparent side we saw certain strange figures circularly drawn, and thought we could touch them, until we found our fingers stopped with that lucid substance. He put this engine to our ears, which made an incessant noise like that of a watermill. And we conjecture it is either some unknown animal, or the god that he worships: but we are more inclined to the latter opinion, because he assured us (if we understood him right, for he expressed himself very imperfectly), that he seldom did any thing without consulting it. He called it his oracle, and said it pointed out the time for every action of his life. From the left fob he took out a net almost large enough for a fisherman, but contrived to open and shut like a purse, and served him for the same use: we found therein several massy pieces of yellow metal, which if they be of real gold, must be of immense value.

Having thus, in obedience to your Majesty's commands, diligently searched all his pockets, we observed a girdle[2] about his waist made of the hide of some prodigious animal; from which, on the left side, hung a sword of the length of five men; and on the right, a bag or pouch divided into cells; each cell capable of holding three of your Majesty's subjects. In one of these cells were several globes or balls of a most ponderous metal, about the bigness of our heads, and required a strong hand to lift them: the other cell contained a heap of certain black grains, but of no

1. Fences of stakes.

2. Belt.

great bulk or weight, for we could hold above fifty of them in the palms of our hands.

This is an exact inventory of what we found about the body of the Man-Mountain; who used us with great civility, and due respect to your Majesty's commission. Signed and sealed on the fourth day of the eighty-ninth moon of your Majesty's auspicious reign.

CLEFREN FRELOCK, MARSI FRELOCK.

When this inventory was read over to the Emperor, he directed me to deliver up the several particulars. He first called for my scimitar, which I took out, scabbard and all. In the meantime he ordered three thousand of his choicest troops (who then attended him) to surround me at a distance, with their bows and arrows just ready to discharge: but I did not observe it; for my eyes were wholly fixed upon his Majesty. He then desired me to draw my scimitar, which, although it had got some rust by the sea water, was in most parts exceeding bright. I did so, and immediately all the troops gave a shout between terror and surprise; for the sun shone clear, and the reflection dazzled their eyes, as I waved the scimitar to and fro in my hand. His Majesty, who is a most magnanimous[3] prince, was less daunted than I could expect; he ordered me to return it into the scabbard, and cast it on the ground as gently as I could, about six foot from the end of my chain. The next thing he demanded was one of the hollow iron pillars, by which he meant my pocket-pistols. I drew it out, and at his desire, as well as I could, expressed to him the use of it, and charging it only with powder, which by the closeness of my pouch happened to escape wetting in the sea (an inconvenience that all prudent mariners take special care to provide against), I first cautioned the Emperor not to be afraid; and then I let it off in the air. The astonishment here was much greater than at the sight of my scimitar. Hundreds fell down as if they had been struck dead; and even the Emperor, although he stood his ground, could not recover himself in some time. I delivered up both my pistols in the same manner as I had done my scimitar, and then my pouch of powder and bullets; begging him that the former might be kept from fire; for it would kindle with the smallest spark, and blow up his imperial palace into the air. I likewise delivered up my watch, which the Emperor was very curious to see; and commanded two of his tallest yeomen of the guards to bear it on a pole upon their shoulders, as draymen in England do a barrel of ale. He was amazed at the continual noise it made, and the motion of the minute-hand, which he could easily discern; for their sight is much more acute than ours: he asked the opinions of his learned men about him, which were various and remote, as the reader may well imagine without my repeating; although indeed I could not very perfectly understand them. I then gave up my silver and copper money, my purse with nine large pieces of gold, and some smaller ones; my knife and razor, my comb and silver snuffbox, my handkerchief and journal book. My scimitar, pistols, and pouch, were conveyed in carriages to his Majesty's stores; but the rest of my goods were returned me.

I had, as I before observed, one private pocket which escaped their search, wherein there was a pair of spectacles (which I sometimes use for the weakness of my eyes), a pocket perspective,[4] and several other little conveniences; which,

3. Courageous, great-spirited. Magnanimity, the relation (direct or inverse) between the size of the body and the soul, is a central concern of the first two parts of the *Travels*.
4. Telescope.

being of no consequence to the Emperor, I did not think myself bound in honor to discover, and I apprehended they might be lost or spoiled if I ventured them out of my possession.

CHAPTER 3. *The author diverts the Emperor and his nobility of both sexes in a very uncommon manner. The diversions of the court of Lilliput described. The author hath his liberty granted him upon certain conditions.*

My gentleness and good behavior had gained so far on the Emperor and his court, and indeed upon the army and people in general, that I began to conceive hopes of getting my liberty in a short time. I took all possible methods to cultivate this favorable disposition. The natives came by degrees to be less apprehensive of any danger from me. I would sometimes lie down, and let five or six of them dance on my hand. And at last the boys and girls would ventureto come and play at hide-and-seek in my hair. I had now made a good progress in understanding and speaking their language. The Emperor had a mind one day to entertain me with several of the country shows; wherein they exceed all nations I have known, both for dexterity and magnificence. I was diverted with none so much as that of the rope-dancers, performed upon a slender white thread, extended about two foot, and twelve inches from the ground. Upon which I shall desire liberty, with the reader's patience, to enlarge a little.

This diversion is only practiced by those persons who are candidates for great employments, and high favor, at court. They are trained in this art from their youth, and are not always of noble birth, or liberal education. When a great office is vacant either by death or disgrace (which often happens) five or six of those candidates petition the Emperor to entertain his Majesty and the court with a dance on the rope; and whoever jumps the highest without falling, succeeds in the office. Very often the chief ministers themselves are commanded to show their skill, and to convince the Emperor that they have not lost their faculty. Flimnap,[5] the Treasurer, is allowed to cut a caper on the strait rope, at least an inch higher than any other lord in the whole empire. I have seen him do the summerset several times together upon a trencher[6] fixed on the rope, which is no thicker than a common packthread in England. My friend Reldresal, Principal Secretary for Private Affairs, is, in my opinion, if I am not partial, the second after the Treasurer; the rest of the great officers are much upon a par.

These diversions are often attended with fatal accidents, whereof great numbers are on record. I myself have seen two or three candidates break a limb. But the danger is much greater when the ministers themselves are commanded to show their dexterity; for, by contending to excel themselves and their fellows, they strain so far, that there is hardly one of them who hath not received a fall; and some of them two or three. I was assured, that a year or two before my arrival, Flimnap would have infallibly broke his neck, if one of the King's cushions,[7] that accidentally lay on the ground, had not weakened the force of his fall.

There is likewise another diversion, which is only shown before the Emperor and Empress, and first minister, upon particular occasions. The Emperor lays

5. Sir Robert Walpole, the Whig head of the government, was notorious in Swift's circle for his political acrobatics.

6. Plate. "Summerset": somersault.

7. A mistress of George I was supposed to have helped restore Walpole to office in 1721.

on a table three fine silken threads of six inches long. One is blue, the other red, and the third green.[8] These threads are proposed as prizes for those persons whom the Emperor hath a mind to distinguish by a peculiar mark of his favor. The ceremony is performed in his Majesty's great chamber of state; where the candidates are to undergo a trial of dexterity very different from the former, and such as I have not observed the least resemblance of in any other country of the old or the new world. The Emperor holds a stick in his hands, both ends parallel to the horizon, while the candidates, advancing one by one, sometimes leap over the stick, sometimes creep under it backwards and forwards several times, according as the stick is advanced or depressed. Sometimes the Emperor holds one end of the stick, and his first minister the other; sometimes the minister has it entirely to himself. Whoever performs his part with most agility, and holds out the longest in *leaping* and *creeping,* is rewarded with the blue-colored silk; the red is given to the next, and the green to the third, which they all wear girt twice round about the middle; and you see few great persons about this court who are not adorned with one of these girdles.

The horses of the army, and those of the royal stables, having been daily led before me, were no longer shy, but would come up to my very feet, without starting. The riders would leap them over my hand as I held it on the ground; and one of the Emperor's huntsmen, upon a large courser, took[9] my foot, shoe and all; which was indeed a prodigious leap. I had the good fortune to divert the Emperor one day after a very extraordinary manner. I desired he would order several sticks of two foot high, and the thickness of an ordinary cane, to be brought me; whereupon his Majesty commanded the master of his woods to give directions accordingly; and the next morning six woodmen arrived with as many carriages, drawn by eight horses to each. I took nine of these sticks, and fixing them firmly in the ground in a quadrangular figure, two foot and a half square, I took four other sticks, and tied them parallel at each corner, about two foot from the ground; then I fastened my handkerchief to the nine sticks that stood erect, and extended it on all sides till it was as tight as the top of a drum; and the four parallel sticks, rising about five inches higher than the handkerchief, served as ledges on each side. When I had finished my work, I desired the Emperor to let a troop of his best horse, twenty-four in number, come and exercise upon this plain. His Majesty approved of the proposal, and I took them up one by one in my hands, ready mounted and armed, with the proper officers to exercise them. As soon as they got into order, they divided into two parties, performed mock skirmishes, discharged blunt arrows, drew their swords, fled and pursued, attacked and retired; and in short discovered the best military discipline I ever beheld. The parallel sticks secured them and their horses from falling over the stage; and the Emperor was so much delighted, that he ordered this entertainment to be repeated several days; and once was pleased to be lifted up, and give the word of command; and, with great difficulty, persuaded even the Empress herself to let me hold her in her close chair[1] within two yards of the stage, from whence she was able to take a full view of the whole performance. It was my good fortune that no ill accident happened in these entertainments, only once a fiery horse that belonged to one of the captains pawing with his hoof struck a hole in my handkerchief, and his foot slipping, he overthrew his rider and himself; but I immediately

8. The Orders of the Garter, the Bath, and the Thistle, conferred for services to the king.

9. Jumped over.

1. An enclosed or sedan chair.

relieved them both; for covering the hole with one hand, I set down the troop with the other, in the same manner as I took them up. The horse that fell was strained in the left shoulder, but the rider got no hurt, and I repaired my handkerchief as well as I could; however, I would not trust to the strength of it any more in such dangerous enterprises.

About two or three days before I was set at liberty, as I was entertaining the court with these kinds of feats, there arrived an express to inform his Majesty that some of his subjects, riding near the place where I was first taken up, had seen a great black substance lying on the ground, very oddly shaped, extending its edges round as wide as his Majesty's bedchamber, and rising up in the middle as high as a man; that it was no living creature, as they at first apprehended, for it lay on the grass without motion, and some of them had walked round it several times; that by mounting upon each other's shoulders, they had got to the top, which was flat and even; and stamping upon it they found it was hollow within; that they humbly conceived it might be something belonging to the Man-Mountain, and if his Majesty pleased, they would undertake to bring it with only five horses. I presently[2] knew what they meant; and was glad at heart to receive this intelligence. It seems upon my first reaching the shore after our shipwreck, I was in such confusion, that before I came to the place where I went to sleep, my hat, which I had fastened with a string to my head while I was rowing, and had stuck on all the time I was swimming, fell off after I came to land; the string, as I conjecture, breaking by some accident which I never observed, but thought my hat had been lost at sea. I intreated his Imperial Majesty to give orders it might be brought to me as soon as possible, describing to him the use and the nature of it: and the next day the wagoners arrived with it, but not in a very good condition; they had bored two holes in the brim, within an inch and half of the edge, and fastened two hooks in the holes; these hooks were tied by a long cord to the harness, and thus my hat was dragged along for above half an English mile: but the ground in that country being extremely smooth and level, it received less damage than I expected.

Two days after this adventure, the Emperor, having ordered that part of his army which quarters in and about his metropolis to be in a readiness, took a fancy of diverting himself in a very singular manner. He desired I would stand like a colossus, with my legs as far asunder as I conveniently could. He then commanded his general (who was an old experienced leader, and a great patron of mine) to draw up the troops in close order, and march them under me; the foot[3] by twenty-four in a breast, and the horse by sixteen, with drums beating, colors flying, and pikes advanced. This body consisted of three thousand foot, and a thousand horse. His Majesty gave orders, upon pain of death, that every soldier in his march should observe the strictest decency with regard to my person; which, however, could not prevent some of the younger officers from turning up their eyes as they passed under me. And, to confess the truth, my breeches were at that time in so ill a condition, that they afforded some opportunities for laughter and admiration.

I had sent so many memorials and petitions for my liberty, that his Majesty at length mentioned the matter first in the cabinet, and then in a full council; where it was opposed by none, except Skyresh Bolgolam,[4] who was pleased,

2. Immediately.
3. Foot soldiers or infantry.
4. The earl of Nottingham, an enemy of Swift.

without any provocation, to be my mortal enemy. But it was carried against him by the whole board, and confirmed by the Emperor. That minister was *Galbet,* or Admiral of the Realm; very much in his master's confidence, and a person well versed in affairs, but of a morose and sour complexion.[5] However, he was at length persuaded to comply; but prevailed that the articles and conditions upon which I should be set free, and to which I must swear, should be drawn up by himself. These articles were brought to me by Skyresh Bolgolam in person, attended by two under-secretaries, and several persons of distinction. After they were read, I was demanded to swear to the performance of them; first in the manner of my own country, and afterwards in the method prescribed by their laws; which was to hold my right foot in my left hand, to place the middle finger of my right hand on the crown of my head, and my thumb on the tip of my right ear. But because the reader may perhaps be curious to have some idea of the style and manner of expression peculiar to that people, as well as to know the articles upon which I recovered my liberty, I have made a translation of the whole instrument,[6] word for word, as near as I was able; which I here offer to the public.

> GOLBASTO MOMAREN EVLAME GURDILO SHEFIN MULLY ULLY GUE, most mighty Emperor of Lilliput, delight and terror of the universe, whose dominions extend five thousand blustrugs (about twelve miles in circumference) to the extremities of the globe; Monarch of all Monarchs; taller than the sons of men; whose feet press down to the center, and whose head strikes against the sun; at whose nod the princes of the earth shake their knees; pleasant as the spring, comfortable as the summer, fruitful as autumn, dreadful as winter. His most sublime Majesty proposeth to the Man-Mountain, lately arrived at our celestial dominions, the following articles, which by a solemn oath he shall be obliged to perform.
>
> First, The Man-Mountain shall not depart from our dominions, without our license under our great seal.
>
> Secondly, He shall not presume to come into our metropolis, without our express order; at which time the inhabitants shall have two hours warning, to keep within their doors.
>
> Thirdly, The said Man-Mountain shall confine his walks to our principal high roads; and not offer to walk or lie down in a meadow, or field of corn.
>
> Fourthly, As he walks the said roads, he shall take the utmost care not to trample upon the bodies of any of our loving subjects, their horses, or carriages, nor take any of our said subjects into his hands, without their own consent.
>
> Fifthly, If an express require extraordinary dispatch, the Man-Mountain shall be obliged to carry in his pocket the messenger and horse, a six days' journey once in every moon, and return the said messenger back (if so required) safe to our Imperial Presence.
>
> Sixthly, He shall be our ally against our enemies in the island of Blefuscu, and do his utmost to destroy their fleet, which is now preparing to invade us.
>
> Seventhly, That the said Man-Mountain shall, at his times of leisure, be aiding and assisting to our workmen, in helping to raise certain great

5. Disposition.

6. A formal legal document.

stones, towards covering the wall of the principal park, and other our royal buildings.

Eighthly, That the said Man-Mountain shall, in two moons' time, deliver in an exact survey of the circumference of our dominions by a computation of his own paces round the coast.

Lastly, That upon his solemn oath to observe all the above articles, the said Man-Mountain shall have a daily allowance of meat and drink sufficient for the support of 1,728 of our subjects; with free access to our Royal Person, and other marks of our favor. Given at our palace at Belfaborac the twelfth day of the ninety-first moon of our reign.

I swore and subscribed to these articles with great cheerfulness and content, although some of them were not so honorable as I could have wished; which proceeded wholly from the malice of Skyresh Bolgolam the High Admiral: whereupon my chains were immediately unlocked, and I was at full liberty: the Emperor himself in person did me the honor to be by at the whole ceremony. I made my acknowledgements by prostrating myself at his Majesty's feet: but he commanded me to rise; and after many gracious expressions, which, to avoid the censure of vanity, I shall not repeat, he added, that he hoped I should prove a useful servant, and well deserve all the favors he had already conferred upon me, or might do for the future.

The reader may please to observe, that in the last article for the recovery of my liberty, the Emperor stipulates to allow me a quantity of meat and drink, sufficient for the support of 1,728 Lilliputians. Some time after, asking a friend at court how they came to fix on that determinate number, he told me, that his Majesty's mathematicians, having taken the height of my body by the help of a quadrant, and finding it to exceed theirs in the proportion of twelve to one, they concluded from the similarity of their bodies, that mine must contain at least 1,728 of theirs, and consequently would require as much food as was necessary to support that number of Lilliputians. By which, the reader may conceive an idea of the ingenuity of that people, as well as the prudent and exact economy of so great a prince.

CHAPTER 4. *Mildendo, the metropolis of Lilliput, described, together with the Emperor's palace. A conversation between the author and a principal secretary, concerning the affairs of that empire; the author's offers to serve the Emperor in his wars.*

The first request I made after I had obtained my liberty, was, that I might have license to see Mildendo, the metropolis; which the Emperor easily granted me, but with a special charge to do no hurt, either to the inhabitants, or their houses. The people had notice by proclamation of my design to visit the town. The wall which encompassed it is two foot and an half high, and at least eleven inches broad, so that a coach and horses may be driven very safely round it; and it is flanked with strong towers at ten foot distance. I stepped over the great western gate, and passed very gently, and sideling[7] through the two principal streets, only in my short waistcoat, for fear of damaging the roofs and eaves of the houses with the skirts of my coat. I walked with the utmost circumspection, to avoid treading on any stragglers, who might remain in the

7. Sideways.

streets, although the orders were very strict, that all people should keep in their houses, at their own peril. The garret windows and tops of houses were so crowded with spectators, that I thought in all my travels I had not seen a more populous place. The city is an exact square, each side of the wall being five hundred foot long. The two great streets, which run cross and divide it into four quarters, are five foot wide. The lanes and alleys, which I could not enter, but only viewed them as I passed, are from twelve to eighteen inches. The town is capable of holding five hundred thousand souls. The houses are from three to five stories. The shops and markets well provided.

The Emperor's palace is in the center of the city, where the two great streets meet. It is enclosed by a wall of two foot high, and twenty foot distant from the buildings. I had his Majesty's permission to step over this wall; and the space being so wide between that and the palace, I could easily view it on every side. The outward court is a square of forty foot, and includes two other courts: in the inmost are the royal apartments, which I was very desirous to see, but found it extremely difficult; for the great gates, from one square into another, were but eighteen inches high, and seven inches wide. Now the buildings of the outer court were at least five foot high; and it was impossible for me to stride over them, without infinite damage to the pile, although the walls were strongly built of hewn stone, and four inches thick. At the same time the Emperor had a great desire that I should see the magnificence of his palace; but this I was not able to do till three days after, which I spent in cutting down with my knife some of the largest trees in the royal park, about an hundred yards distance from the city. Of these trees I made two stools, each about three foot high, and strong enough to bear my weight. The people having received notice a second time, I went again through the city to the palace, with my two stools in my hands. When I came to the side of the outer court, I stood upon one stool, and took the other in my hand: this I lifted over the roof, and gently set it down on the space between the first and second court, which was eight foot wide. I then stepped over the buildings very conveniently from one stool to the other, and drew up the first after me with a hooked stick. By this contrivance I got into the inmost court; and lying down upon my side, I applied my face to the windows of the middle stories, which were left open on purpose, and discovered the most splendid apartments that can be imagined. There I saw the Empress, and the young princes in their several lodgings, with their chief attendants about them. Her Imperial Majesty was pleased to smile very graciously upon me and gave me out of the window her hand to kiss.

But I shall not anticipate the reader with farther descriptions of this kind, because I reserve them for a greater work, which is now almost ready for the press; containing a general description of this empire, from its first erection, through a long series of princes, with a particular account of their wars and politics, laws, learning, and religion; their plants and animals, their peculiar manners and customs, with other matters very curious and useful; my chief design at present being only to relate such events and transactions as happened to the public, or to myself, during a residence of about nine months in that empire.

One morning, about a fortnight after I had obtained my liberty, Reldresal, Principal Secretary (as they style him) of Private Affairs, came to my house, attended only by one servant. He ordered his coach to wait at a distance, and desired I would give him an hour's audience; which I readily consented to, on account of his quality, and personal merits, as well as of the many good offices he had done me during my solicitations at court. I offered to lie down, that he might the more conveniently reach my ear; but he chose rather to let me hold him in my hand during our conversation. He began with compliments on my liberty, said he might pretend to some merit in it; but, however, added, that if it had not been for the present situation of things at court, perhaps I might not have obtained it so soon. For, said he, as flourishing a condition as we appear to be in to foreigners, we labor under two mighty evils; a violent faction at home, and the danger of an invasion by a most potent enemy from abroad. As to the first, you are to understand, that for above seventy moons past, there have been two struggling parties in the empire, under the names of *Tramecksan,* and *Slamecksan,*[8] from the high and low heels on their shoes, by which they distinguish themselves.

It is alleged indeed, that the high heels are most agreeable to our ancient constitution: but however this be, his Majesty hath determined to make use of only low heels in the administration of the government and all offices in the gift of the crown; as you cannot but observe; and particularly, that his Majesty's imperial heels are lower at least by a *drurr* than any of his court; (*drurr* is a measure about the fourteenth part of an inch). The animosities between these two parties run so high, that they will neither eat nor drink, nor talk with each other. We compute the *Tramecksan,* or High-Heels, to exceed us in number; but the power is wholly on our side. We apprehend his Imperial Highness, the heir to the crown, to have some tendency towards the High-Heels; at least we can plainly discover one of his heels higher than the other, which gives him a hobble in his gait.[9] Now, in the midst of these intestine disquiets, we are threatened with an invasion from the island of Blefuscu,[1] which is the other great empire of the universe, almost as large and powerful as this of his Majesty. For as to what we have heard you affirm, that there are other kingdoms and states in the world, inhabited by human creatures as large as yourself, our philosophers are in much doubt; and would rather conjecture that you dropped from the moon, or one of the stars; because it is certain, that an hundred mortals of your bulk would, in a short time, destroy all the fruits and cattle of his Majesty's dominions. Besides, our histories of six thousand moons make no mention of any other regions, than the two great empires of Lilliput and Blefuscu. Which two mighty powers have, as I was going to tell you, been engaged in a most obstinate war for six and thirty moons past. It began upon the following occasion. It is allowed on all hands, that the primitive way of breaking eggs before we eat them, was upon the larger end: but his present Majesty's grandfather, while he was a boy, going to eat an egg, and breaking it according to the ancient practice, happened to cut one of his fingers. Whereupon the Emperor his father published an edict, commanding all his subjects, upon great penalties, to break the smaller end of their eggs. The people so highly resented this law, that our histories tell us there have been six rebellions raised on that account; wherein one emperor lost his life, and another his crown.[2] These civil commotions were constantly fomented by the monarchs of Blefuscu; and when they were quelled, the exiles always fled for

8. Tory (High Church) and Whig (Low Church), respectively.
9. The prince of Wales (later George II) had friends in both parties.
1. France.
2. Swift's satirical allegory of the strife between Catholics (Big-Endians) and Protestants (Little-Endians) touches on Henry VIII (who "broke" with the Pope), Charles I (who lost his life), and James II (who lost his crown).

refuge to that empire. It is computed, that eleven thousand persons have, at several times, suffered death, rather than submit to break their eggs at the smaller end. Many hundred large volumes have been published upon this controversy: but the books of the Big-Endians have been long forbidden, and the whole party rendered incapable by law of holding employments.[3] During the course of these troubles, the emperors of Blefuscu did frequently expostulate by their ambassadors, accusing us of making a schism in religion, by offending against a fundamental doctrine of our great prophet Lustrog, in the fifty-fourth chapter of the *Brundecral* (which is their Alcoran[4]). This, however, is thought to be a mere strain upon the text: for the words are these; *That all true believers shall break their eggs at the convenient end:* and which is the convenient end, seems, in my humble opinion, to be left to every man's conscience, or at least in the power of the chief magistrate[5] to determine. Now the Big-Endian exiles have found so much credit in the Emperor of Blefuscu's court, and so much private assistance and encouragement from their party here at home, that a bloody war hath been carried on between the two empires for six and thirty moons with various success;[6] during which time we have lost forty capital ships, and a much greater number of smaller vessels, together with thirty thousand of our best seamen and soldiers; and the damage received by the enemy is reckoned to be somewhat greater than ours. However, they have now equipped a numerous fleet, and are just preparing to make a descent upon us; and his Imperial Majesty, placing great confidence in your valor and strength, hath commanded me to lay this account of his affairs before you.

I desired the Secretary to present my humble duty to the Emperor, and to let him know, that I thought it would not become me, who was a foreigner, to interfere with parties; but I was ready, with the hazard of my life, to defend his person and state against all invaders.

Chapter 5. *The author by an extraordinary stratagem prevents an invasion. A high title of honor is conferred upon him. Ambassadors arrive from the Emperor of Blefuscu, and sue for peace. The Empress's apartment on fire by an accident; the author instrumental in saving the rest of the palace.*

The empire of Blefuscu is an island situated to the north north-east side of Lilliput, from whence it is parted only by a channel of eight hundred yards wide. I had not yet seen it, and upon this notice of an intended invasion, I avoided appearing on that side of the coast, for fear of being discovered by some of the enemy's ships, who had received no intelligence of me; all intercourse between the two empires having been strictly forbidden during the war, upon pain of death; and an embargo laid by our Emperor upon all vessels whatsoever. I communicated to his Majesty a project I had formed of seizing the enemy's whole fleet; which, as our scouts assured us, lay at anchor in the harbor ready to sail with the first fair wind. I consulted the most experienced seamen upon the depth of the channel, which they had often plumbed; who told me, that in the middle at high water it was seventy *glumgluffs* deep, which is about six foot of European measure; and the rest of it fifty *glumgluffs* at most.

3. The Test Act (1673) prevented Catholics and Nonconformists from holding office unless they accepted the Anglican Sacrament.
4. Koran.
5. Ruler, sovereign. Swift himself accepted the right of the king to determine religious observances.
6. Reminiscent of the War of the Spanish Succession (1701–13).

I walked to the northeast coast over against Blefuscu; where, lying down behind a hillock, I took out my small pocket perspective glass, and viewed the enemy's fleet at anchor, consisting of about fifty men of war, and a great number of transports: I then came back to my house, and gave order (for which I had a warrant) for a great quantity of the strongest cable and bars of iron. The cable was about as thick as packthread and the bars of the length and size of a knitting-needle. I trebled the cable to make it stronger, and for the same reason I twisted three of the iron bars together, bending the extremities into a hook. Having thus fixed fifty hooks to as many cables, I went back to the northeast coast, and putting off my coat, shoes, and stockings, walked into the sea in my leathern jerkin, about half an hour before high water. I waded with what haste I could, and swam in the middle about thirty yards until I felt the ground; I arrived at the fleet in less than half an hour. The enemy was so frighted when they saw me, that they leaped out of their ships, and swam to shore, where there could not be fewer than thirty thousand souls. I then took my tackling, and fastening a hook to the hole at the prow of each, I tied all the cords together at the end. While I was thus employed, the enemy discharged several thousand arrows, many of which stuck in my hands and face; and besides the excessive smart, gave me much disturbance in my work. My greatest apprehension was for my eyes, which I should have infallibly lost, if I had not suddenly thought of an expedient. I kept, among other little necessaries, a pair of spectacles in a private pocket, which, as I observed before, had escaped the Emperor's searchers. These I took out, and fastened as strongly as I could upon my nose; and thus armed went on boldly with my work in spite of the enemy's arrows; many of which struck against the glasses of my spectacles, but without any other effect, further than a little to discompose them. I had now fastened all the hooks, and taking the knot in my hand, began to pull; but not a ship would stir, for they were all too fast by their anchors, so that the boldest part of my enterprise remained. I therefore let go the cord, and leaving the hooks fixed to the ships, I resolutely cut with my knife the cables that fastened the anchors, receiving about two hundred shots in my face and hands; then I took up the knotted end of the cables to which my hooks were tied; and with great ease drew fifty of the enemy's largest men-of-war after me.

The Blefuscudians, who had not the least imagination of what I intended, were at first confounded with astonishment. They had seen me cut the cables, and thought my design was only to let the ships run adrift, or fall foul on each other: but when they perceived the whole fleet moving in order, and saw me pulling at the end, they set up such a scream of grief and despair, that it is almost impossible to describe or conceive. When I had got out of danger, I stopped a while to pick out the arrows that stuck in my hands and face, and rubbed on some of the same ointment that was given me at my first arrival, as I have formerly mentioned. I then took off my spectacles, and waiting about an hour until the tide was a little fallen, I waded through the middle with my cargo, and arrived safe at the royal port of Lilliput.

The Emperor and his whole court stood on the shore, expecting the issue of this great adventure. They saw the ships move forward in a large half-moon, but could not discern me, who was up to my breast in water. When I advanced to the middle of the channel, they were yet more in pain, because I was under water to my neck. The Emperor concluded me to be drowned, and that the enemy's fleet was approaching in a hostile manner: but he was soon eased of his fears, for the channel growing shallower every step I made, I came in a short time within hearing; and holding up the end of the cable by which the fleet was fastened, I cried in a loud voice, Long live the most puissant Emperor of Lilliput! This great prince received me at my landing with all possible encomiums, and created me a *Nardac* upon the spot, which is the highest title of honor among them.

His Majesty desired I would take some other opportunity of bringing all the rest of his enemy's ships into his ports. And so unmeasurable is the ambition of princes, that he seemed to think of nothing less than reducing the whole empire of Blefuscu into a province, and governing it by a viceroy; of destroying the Big-Endian exiles, and compelling that people to break the smaller end of their eggs, by which he would remain sole monarch of the whole world. But I endeavored to divert him from this design, by many arguments drawn from the topics of policy as well as justice: and I plainly protested, that I would never be an instrument of bringing a free and brave people into slavery. And when the matter was debated in council, the wisest part of the ministry were of my opinion.

This open bold declaration of mine was so opposite to the schemes and politics of his Imperial Majesty, that he could never forgive me; he mentioned it in a very artful manner at council, where I was told that some of the wisest appeared, at least by their silence, to be of my opinion; but others, who were my secret enemies, could not forbear some expressions, which by a side-wind[7] reflected on me. And from this time began an intrigue between his Majesty and a junta of ministers maliciously bent against me, which broke out in less than two months, and had like to have ended in my utter destruction. Of so little weight are the greatest services to princes, when put into the balance with a refusal to gratify their passions.[8]

About three weeks after this exploit, there arrived a solemn embassy from Blefuscu, with humble offers of a peace; which was soon concluded upon conditions very advantageous to our Emperor; wherewith I shall not trouble the reader. There were six ambassadors, with a train of about five hundred persons; and their entry was very magnificent, suitable to the grandeur of their master, and the importance of their business. When their treaty was finished, wherein I did them several good offices by the credit I now had, or at least appeared to have at court, their Excellencies, who were privately told how much I had been their friend, made me a visit in form. They began with many compliments upon my valor and generosity; invited me to that kingdom in the Emperor their master's name; and desired me to show them some proofs of my prodigious strength, of which they had heard so many wonders; wherein I readily obliged them, but shall not interrupt the reader with the particulars.

When I had for some time entertained their Excellencies to their infinite satisfaction and surprise, I desired they would do me the honor to present my most humble respects to the Emperor their master, the renown of whose virtues had so justly filled the whole world with admiration, and whose royal person I resolved to attend before I returned to my own country. Accordingly, the next time I had the honor to see our Emperor, I desired his general license to wait on the Blefuscudian monarch, which he was pleased to grant me, as I could plainly perceive, in a very cold manner; but could not guess the reason,

7. Indirectly.

8. After a series of British naval victories, the Treaty of Utrecht (1713) had ended the war with France, but the Tory ministers who engineered the peace were subsequently accused of having sold out to the enemy.

till I had a whisper from a certain person, that Flimnap and Bolgolam had represented my intercourse with those ambassadors as a mark of disaffection, from which I am sure my heart was wholly free. And this was the first time I began to conceive some imperfect idea of courts and ministers.

It is to be observed, that these ambassadors spoke to me by an interpreter; the languages of both empires differing as much from each other as any two in Europe, and each nation priding itself upon the antiquity, beauty, and energy of their own tongues, with an avowed contempt for that of their neighbor; yet our Emperor, standing upon the advantage he had got by the seizure of their fleet, obliged them to deliver their credentials, and make their speech, in the Lilliputian tongue. And it must be confessed, that from the great intercourse of trade and commerce between both realms, from the continual reception of exiles, which is mutual among them, and from the custom in each empire to send their young nobility and richer gentry to the other, in order to polish themselves, by seeing the world, and understanding men and manners, there are few persons of distinction, or merchants, or seamen, who dwell in the maritime parts, but what can hold conversation in both tongues; as I found some weeks after, when I went to pay my respects to the Emperor of Blefuscu, which in the midst of great misfortunes, through the malice of my enemies, proved a very happy adventure to me, as I shall relate in its proper place.

The reader may remember, that when I signed those articles upon which I recovered my liberty, there were some which I disliked upon account of their being too servile, neither could any thing but an extreme necessity have forced me to submit. But being now a *Nardac,* of the highest rank in that empire, such offices[9] were looked upon as below my dignity, and the Emperor (to do him justice) never once mentioned them to me. However, it was not long before I had an opportunity of doing his Majesty, at least as I then thought, a most signal service. I was alarmed at midnight with the cries of many hundred people at my door; by which being suddenly awaked, I was in some kind of terror. I heard the word *burglum* repeated incessantly; several of the Emperor's court, making their way through the crowd, intreated me to come immediately to the palace, where her Imperial Majesty's apartment was on fire, by the carelessness of a maid of honor, who fell asleep while she was reading a romance. I got up in an instant; and orders being given to clear the way before me, and it being likewise a moonshine night, I made a shift to get to the palace without trampling on any of the people. I found they had already applied ladders to the walls of the apartment, and were well provided with buckets, but the water was at some distance. These buckets were about the size of a large thimble, and the poor people supplied me with them as fast as they could; but the flame was so violent, that they did little good. I might easily have stifled it with my coat, which I unfortunately left behind me for haste, and came away only in my leathern jerkin. The case seemed wholly desperate and deplorable; and this magnificent palace would have infallibly been burnt down to the ground, if, by a presence of mind, unusual to me, I had not suddenly thought of an expedient. I had the evening before drank plentifully of a most delicious wine, called *glimigrim* (the Blefuscudians call it *flunec,* but ours is esteemed the better sort), which is very diuretic. By the luckiest chance in the world, I had not discharged myself of any part of it. The heat I had contracted by coming very near the flames, and by my laboring to quench

9. Duties.

them, made the wine begin to operate by urine; which I voided in such a quantity, and applied so well to the proper places, that in three minutes the fire was wholly extinguished; and the rest of that noble pile, which had cost so many ages in erecting, preserved from destruction.

It was now daylight, and I returned to my house, without waiting to congratulate with the Emperor; because, although I had done a very eminent piece of service, yet I could not tell how his Majesty might resent the manner by which I had performed it: for, by the fundamental laws of the realm, it is capital[1] in any person, of what quality soever, to make water within the precincts of the palace. But I was a little comforted by a message from his Majesty, that he would give orders to the Grand Justiciary for passing my pardon in form; which, however, I could not obtain. And I was privately assured, that the Empress, conceiving the greatest abhorrence of what I had done,[2] removed to the most distant side of the court, firmly resolved that those buildings should never be repaired for her use; and, in the presence of her chief confidents, could not forbear vowing revenge.

Chapter 6. *Of the inhabitants of Lilliput; their learning, laws, and customs, the manner of educating their children. The author's way of living in that country. His vindication of a great lady.*

Although I intend to leave the description of this empire to a particular treatise, yet in the mean time I am content to gratify the curious reader with some general ideas. As the common size of the natives is somewhat under six inches, so there is an exact proportion in all other animals, as well as plants and trees: for instance, the tallest horses and oxen are between four and five inches in height, the sheep an inch and a half, more or less; their geese about the bigness of a sparrow; and so the several gradations downwards, till you come to the smallest, which, to my sight, were almost invisible; but nature hath adapted the eyes of the Lilliputians to all objects proper for their view: they see with great exactness, but at no great distance. And to show the sharpness of their sight towards objects that are near, I have been much pleased with observing a cook pulling[3] a lark, which was not so large as a common fly; and a young girl threading an invisible needle with invisible silk. Their tallest trees are about seven foot high; I mean some of those in the great royal park, the tops whereof I could but just reach with my fist clinched. The other vegetables[4] are in the same proportion; but this I leave to the reader's imagination.

I shall say but little at present of their learning, which for many ages hath flourished in all its branches among them: but their manner of writing is very peculiar; being neither from the left to the right, like the Europeans; nor from the right to the left, like the Arabians; nor from up to down, like the Chinese; nor from down to up, like the Cascagians;[5] but aslant from one corner of the paper to the other, like ladies in England.

They bury their dead with their heads directly downwards; because they hold an opinion that in eleven thousand moons they are all to rise again; in which period, the earth (which they conceive to be flat) will turn upside down, and by this means they shall, at their resurrection, be found ready standing

1. Punishable by death.
2. Queen Anne, whom Swift called "a royal prude," strongly objected to the coarseness of *A Tale of a Tub*.
3. Plucking.
4. Plants.
5. Swift's invention.

on their feet. The learned among them confess the absurdity of this doctrine; but the practice still continues, in compliance to the vulgar.[6]

There are some laws and customs in this empire very peculiar; and if they were not so directly contrary to those of my own dear country, I should be tempted to say a little in their justification. It is only to be wished, that they were as well executed. The first I shall mention relateth to informers. All crimes against the state are punished here with the utmost severity; but if the person accused make his innocence plainly to appear upon his trial, the accuser is immediately put to an ignominious death; and out of his goods or lands, the innocent person is quadruply recompensed for the loss of his time, for the danger he underwent, for the hardship of his imprisonment, and for all the charges he hath been at in making his defense. Or, if that fund be deficient, it is largely[7] supplied by the crown. The Emperor doth also confer on him some public mark of his favor; and proclamation is made of his innocence through the whole city.

They look upon fraud as a greater crime than theft, and therefore seldom fail to punish it with death; for they allege, that care and vigilance, with a very common understanding, may preserve a man's goods from thieves; but honesty hath no fence against superior cunning: and since it is necessary that there should be a perpetual intercourse of buying and selling, and dealing upon credit, where fraud is permitted or connived at, or hath no law to punish it, the honest dealer is always undone, and the knave gets the advantage. I remember when I was once interceding with the King for a criminal who had wronged his master of a great sum of money, which he had received by order, and ran away with; and happening to tell his Majesty, by way of extenuation, that it was only a breach of trust, the Emperor thought it monstrous in me to offer, as a defense, the greatest aggravation of the crime: and truly, I had little to say in return, farther than the common answer, that different nations had different customs; for, I confess, I was heartily ashamed.

Although we usually call reward and punishment the two hinges upon which all government turns, yet I could never observe this maxim to be put in practice by any nation, except that of Lilliput. Whoever can there bring sufficient proof that he hath strictly observed the laws of his country for seventy-three moons, hath a claim to certain privileges, according to his quality[8] and condition of life, with a proportionable sum of money out of a fund appropriated for that use: he likewise acquires the title of *Snilpall,* or *Legal,* which is added to his name, but doth not descend to his posterity. And these people thought it a prodigious defect of policy among us, when I told them that our laws were enforced only by penalties, without any mention of reward. It is upon this account that the image of Justice, in their courts of judicature, is formed with six eyes, two before, as many behind, and on each side one, to signify circumspection; with a bag of gold open in her right hand, and a sword sheathed in her left, to show she is more disposed to reward than to punish.

In choosing persons for all employments, they have more regard to good morals than to great abilities; for, since government is necessary to mankind, they believe that the common size of human understandings is fitted to some station or other; and that Providence never intended to make the management of public affairs a mystery, to be comprehended only by a few persons of

6. The (beliefs of the) common people.
7. Fully.
8. Social position.

sublime genius, of which there seldom are three born in an age: but they suppose truth, justice, temperance, and the like, to be in every man's power; the practice of which virtues, assisted by experience and a good intention, would qualify any man for the service of his country, except where a course of study is required. But they thought the want of moral virtues was so far from being supplied by superior endowments of the mind, that employments could never be put into such dangerous hands as those of persons so qualified; and at least, that the mistakes committed by ignorance in a virtuous disposition would never be of such fatal consequence to the public weal, as the practices of a man whose inclinations led him to be corrupt, and had great abilities to manage, to multiply, and defend his corruptions.

In like manner, the disbelief of a divine Providence renders a man uncapable of holding any public station; for since kings avow themselves to be the deputies of Providence, the Lilliputians think nothing can be more absurd than for a prince to employ such men as disown the authority under which he acteth.

In relating these and the following laws, I would only be understood to mean the original institutions, and not the most scandalous corruptions into which these people are fallen by the degenerate nature of man. For as to that infamous practice of acquiring great employments by dancing on the ropes, or badges of favor and distinction by leaping over sticks, and creeping under them, the reader is to observe, that they were first introduced by the grandfather of the Emperor now reigning; and grew to the present height by the gradual increase of party and faction.

Ingratitude is among them a capital crime, as we read it to have been in some other countries; for they reason thus, that whoever makes ill returns to his benefactor, must needs be a common enemy to the rest of mankind, from whom he hath received no obligation; and therefore such a man is not fit to live.

Their notions relating to the duties of parents and children differ extremely from ours. For, since the conjunction of male and female is founded upon the great law of nature, in order to propagate and continue the species, the Lilliputians will needs have it, that men and women are joined together like other animals, by the motives of concupiscence; and that their tenderness towards their young proceedeth from the like natural principle: for which reason they will never allow, that a child is under any obligation to his father for begetting him, or to his mother for bringing him into the world; which, considering the miseries of human life, was neither a benefit in itself, nor intended so by his parents, whose thoughts in their love-encounters were otherwise employed. Upon these, and the like reasonings, their opinion is, that parents are the last of all others to be trusted with the education of their own children: and therefore they have in every town public nurseries, where all parents, except cottagers[9] and laborers, are obliged to send their infants of both sexes to be reared and educated when they come to the age of twenty moons; at which time they are supposed to have some rudiments of docility. These schools are of several kinds, suited to different qualities, and to both sexes. They have certain professors[1] well skilled in preparing children for such a condition of life as befits the rank of their parents, and their own capacities as well as inclinations. I shall first say something of the male nurseries, and then of the female.

9. Agricultural workers, peasants.

1. Professional teachers.

The nurseries for males of noble or eminent birth are provided with grave and learned professors, and their several deputies. The clothes and food of the children are plain and simple. They are bred up in the principles of honor, justice, courage, modesty, clemency, religion, and love of their country; they are always employed in some business, except in the times of eating and sleeping, which are very short, and two hours for diversions, consisting of bodily exercises. They are dressed by men until four years of age, and then are obliged to dress themselves, although their quality be ever so great; and the women attendants, who are aged proportionably to ours at fifty, perform only the most menial offices. They are never suffered to converse with servants, but go together in small or greater numbers to take their diversions, and always in the presence of a professor, or one of his deputies; whereby they avoid those early bad impressions of folly and vice to which our children are subject. Their parents are suffered to see them only twice a year; the visit is not to last above an hour; they are allowed to kiss the child at meeting and parting; but a professor, who always standeth by on those occasions, will not suffer them to whisper, or use any fondling expressions, or bring any presents of toys, sweetmeats, and the like.

The pension from each family for the education and entertainment[2] of a child, upon failure of due payment, is levied by the Emperor's officers.

The nurseries for children of ordinary gentlemen, merchants, traders, and handicrafts, are managed proportionably after the same manner; only those designed for trades are put out apprentices at seven years old; whereas those of persons of quality continue in their exercises until fifteen, which answers to one and twenty with us: but the confinement is gradually lessened for the last three years.

In the female nurseries, the young girls of quality are educated much like the males, only they are dressed by orderly servants of their own sex, but always in the presence of a professor or deputy, until they come to dress themselves, which is at five years old. And if it be found that these nurses ever presume to entertain the girls with frightful or foolish stories, or the common follies practiced by chambermaids among us, they are publicly whipped thrice about the city, imprisoned for a year, and banished for life to the most desolate parts of the country. Thus the young ladies there are as much ashamed of being cowards and fools as the men; and despise all personal ornaments beyond decency and cleanliness: neither did I perceive any difference in their education, made by their difference of sex, only that the exercises of the females were not altogether so robust; and that some rules were given them relating to domestic life, and a smaller compass of learning was enjoined them: for their maxim is, that among people of quality, a wife should be always a reasonable and agreeable companion, because she cannot always be young. When the girls are twelve years old, which among them is the marriageable age, their parents or guardians take them home, with great expressions of gratitude to the professors, and seldom without tears of the young lady and her companions.

In the nurseries of females of the meaner sort, the children are instructed in all kinds of works proper for their sex, and their several degrees:[3] those intended for apprentices are dismissed at seven years old, the rest are kept to eleven.

The meaner families who have children at these nurseries are obliged, besides their annual pension, which is as low as possible, to return to the

2. Sustenance.

3. Various social ranks.

steward of the nursery a small monthly share of their gettings, to be a portion for the child; and therefore all parents are limited in their expenses by the law. For the Lilliputians think nothing can be more unjust, than that people, in subservience to their own appetites, should bring children into the world, and leave the burthen of supporting them on the public. As to persons of quality, they give security to appropriate a certain sum for each child, suitable to their condition; and these funds are always managed with good husbandry, and the most exact justice.

The cottagers and laborers keep their children at home, their business being only to till and cultivate the earth; and therefore their education is of little consequence to the public; but the old and diseased among them are supported by hospitals: for begging is a trade unknown in this empire.

And here it may perhaps divert the curious reader, to give some account of my domestic,[4] and my manner of living in this country, during a residence of nine months and thirteen days. Having a head mechanically turned, and being likewise forced by necessity, I had made for myself a table and chair convenient enough, out of the largest trees in the royal park. Two hundred sempstresses were employed to make me shirts, and linen for my bed and table, all of the strongest and coarsest kind they could get; which, however, they were forced to quilt together in several folds; for the thickest was some degrees finer than lawn. Their linen is usually three inches wide, and three foot make a piece. The sempstresses took my measure as I lay on the ground, one standing at my neck, and another at my mid-leg, with a strong cord extended, that each held by the end, while the third measured the length of the cord with a rule of an inch long. Then they measured my right thumb, and desired no more; for by a mathematical computation, that twice round the thumb is one round the wrist, and so on to the neck and the waist; and by the help of my old shirt, which I displayed on the ground before them for a pattern, they fitted me exactly. Three hundred tailors were employed in the same manner to make me clothes; but they had another contrivance for taking my measure. I kneeled down, and they raised a ladder from the ground to my neck; upon this ladder one of them mounted, and let fall a plumb-line from my collar to the floor, which just answered the length of my coat; but my waist and arms I measured myself. When my clothes were finished, which was done in my house (for the largest of theirs would not have been able to hold them), they looked like the patchwork made by the ladies in England, only that mine were all of a color.

I had three hundred cooks to dress my victuals, in little convenient huts built about my house, where they and their families lived, and prepared me two dishes apiece. I took up twenty waiters in my hand, and placed them on the table; an hundred more attended below on the ground, some with dishes of meat, and some with barrels of wine, and other liquors, slung on their shoulders; all which the waiters above drew up as I wanted, in a very ingenious manner, by certain cords, as we draw the bucket up a well in Europe. A dish of their meat was a good mouthful, and a barrel of their liquor a reasonable draught. Their mutton yields to ours, but their beef is excellent. I have had a sirloin so large, that I have been forced to make three bites of it; but this is rare. My servants were astonished to see me eat it bones and all, as in our country we do the leg of a lark. Their geese and turkeys I usually eat at a mouthful, and I must confess they far exceed ours. Of their smaller fowl I could take up twenty or thirty at the end of my knife.

4. Household.

One day his Imperial Majesty, being informed of my way of living, desired that himself and his royal consort, with the young princes of the blood of both sexes, might have the happiness (as he was pleased to call it) of dining with me. They came accordingly, and I placed them upon chairs of state on my table, just over against me, with their guards about them. Flimnap the Lord High Treasurer attended there likewise, with his white staff; and I observed he often looked on me with a sour countenance, which I would not seem to regard, but eat more than usual, in honor to my dear country, as well as to fill the court with admiration. I have some private reasons to believe, that this visit from his Majesty gave Flimnap an opportunity of doing me ill offices to his master. That minister had always been my secret enemy, although he outwardly caressed me more than was usual to the moroseness of his nature. He represented to the Emperor the low condition of his treasury; that he was forced to take up money at great discount; that exchequer bills[5] would not circulate under nine per cent below par; that I had cost his Majesty above a million and a half of *sprugs* (their greatest gold coin, about the bigness of a spangle); and upon the whole, that it would be advisable in the Emperor to take the first fair occasion of dismissing me.

I am here obliged to vindicate the reputation of an excellent lady, who was an innocent sufferer upon my account. The Treasurer took a fancy to be jealous of his wife, from the malice of some evil tongues, who informed him that her Grace had taken a violent affection for my person; and the court-scandal ran for some time that she once came privately to my lodging. This I solemnly declare to be a most infamous falsehood, without any grounds, farther than that her Grace was pleased to treat me with all innocent marks of freedom and friendship. I own she came often to my house, but always publicly, nor ever without three more in the coach, who were usually her sister and young daughter, and some particular acquaintance; but this was common to many other ladies of the court. And I still appeal to my servants round, whether they at any time saw a coach at my door without knowing what persons were in it. On those occasions, when a servant had given me notice, my custom was to go immediately to the door; and, after paying my respects, to take up the coach and two horses very carefully in my hands (for if there were six horses, the postillion always unharnessed four) and place them on a table, where I had fixed a moveable rim quite round, of five inches high, to prevent accidents. And I have often had four coaches and horses at once on my table full of company, while I sat in my chair leaning my face towards them; and when I was engaged with one set, the coachmen would gently drive the others round my table. I have passed many an afternoon very agreeably in these conversations. But I defy the Treasurer, or his two informers (I will name them, and let them make their best of it) Clustril and Drunlo, to prove that any person ever came to me *incognito,* except the Secretary Reldresal, who was sent by express command of his Imperial Majesty, as I have before related. I should not have dwelt so long upon this particular, if it had not been a point wherein the reputation of a great lady is so nearly concerned, to say nothing of my own; although I had the honor to be a *Nardac,* which the Treasurer himself is not; for all the world knows he is only a *Clumglum,* a title inferior by one degree, as that of a marquis is to a duke in England; yet I allow he preceded me in right of his post. These false informations, which I afterwards came to the knowledge of, by an accident not proper to mention, made the Treasurer

5. Government bills of credit. Walpole was noted as a canny financier.

show his lady for some time an ill countenance, and me a worse; for although he was at last undeceived and reconciled to her, yet I lost all credit with him; and found my interest decline very fast with the Emperor himself, who was indeed too much governed by that favorite.

CHAPTER 7. *The author, being informed of a design to accuse him of high treason, makes his escape to Blefuscu. His reception there.*

Before I proceed to give an account of my leaving this kingdom, it may be proper to inform the reader of a private intrigue which had been for two months forming against me.

I had been hitherto all my life a stranger to courts, for which I was unqualified by the meanness of my condition. I had indeed heard and read enough of the dispositions of great princes and ministers; but never expected to have found such terrible effects of them in so remote a country, governed, as I thought, by very different maxims from those in Europe.

When I was just preparing to pay my attendance on the Emperor of Blefuscu, a considerable person at court (to whom I had been very serviceable at a time when he lay under the highest displeasure of his Imperial Majesty) came to my house very privately at night in a close chair, and without sending his name, desired admittance. The chairmen were dismissed; I put the chair, with his Lordship in it, into my coat-pocket; and giving orders to a trusty servant to say I was indisposed and gone to sleep, I fastened the door of my house, placed the chair on the table, according to my usual custom, and sat down by it. After the common salutations were over, observing his Lordship's countenance full of concern, and enquiring into the reason, he desired I would hear him with patience, in a matter that highly concerned my honor and my life. His speech was to the following effect, for I took notes of it as soon as he left me.

You are to know, said he, that several committees of council have been lately called in the most private manner on your account: and it is but two days since his Majesty came to a full resolution.

You are very sensible that Skyresh Bolgolam (*Galbet,* or High Admiral) hath been your mortal enemy almost ever since your arrival. His original reasons I know not; but his hatred is much increased since your great success against Blefuscu, by which his glory, as Admiral, is obscured. This lord, in conjunction with Flimnap the High Treasurer, whose enmity against you is notorious on account of his lady, Limtoc the General, Lalcon the Chamberlain, and Balmuff the Grand Justiciary, have prepared articles of impeachment against you, for treason, and other capital crimes.[6]

This preface made me so impatient, being conscious of my own merits and innocence, that I was going to interrupt; when he entreated me to be silent, and thus proceeded.

Out of gratitude for the favors you have done me, I procured information of the whole proceedings, and a copy of the articles, wherein I venture my head for your service.

6. After the Whigs had investigated Oxford and Bolingbroke, both were impeached for high treason, on charges of being sympathetic to the Jacobites and the French.

Articles of Impeachment against Quinbus Flestrin
(*the* Man-Mountain).

ARTICLE 1

Whereas, by a statute made in the reign of his Imperial Majesty Calin Deffar Plune, it is enacted, that whoever shall make water within the precincts of the royal palace shall be liable to the pains and penalties of high treason: notwithstanding, the said Quinbus Flestrin, in open breach of the said law, under color of extinguishing the fire kindled in the apartment of his Majesty's most dear imperial consort, did maliciously, traitorously, and devilishly, by discharge of his urine, put out the said fire kindled in the said apartment, lying and being within the precincts of the said royal palace; against the statute in that case provided, etc., against the duty, etc.

ARTICLE 2

That the said Quinbus Flestrin, having brought the imperial fleet of Blefuscu into the royal port, and being afterwards commanded by his Imperial Majesty to seize all the other ships of the said empire of Blefuscu, and reduce that empire to a province, to be governed by a viceroy from hence; and to destroy and put to death not only all the Big-Endian exiles, but likewise all the people of that empire who would not immediately forsake the Big-Endian heresy: he, the said Flestrin, like a false traitor against his most auspicious, serene, Imperial Majesty, did petition to be excused from the said service, upon pretense of unwillingness to force the consciences, or destroy the liberties and lives of an innocent people.

ARTICLE 3

That, whereas certain ambassadors arrived from the court of Blefuscu to sue for peace in his Majesty's court: he the said Flestrin did, like a false traitor, aid, abet, comfort, and divert the said ambassadors; although he knew them to be servants to a prince who was lately an open enemy to his Imperial Majesty, and in open war against his said Majesty.

ARTICLE 4

That the said Quinbus Flestrin, contrary to the duty of a faithful subject, is now preparing to make a voyage to the court and empire of Blefuscu, for which he hath received only verbal license from his Imperial Majesty; and under color of the said license, doth falsely and traitorously intend to take the said voyage, and thereby to aid, comfort, and abet the Emperor of Blefuscu, so late an enemy, and in open war with his Imperial Majesty aforesaid.

There are some other articles, but these are the most important, of which I have read you an abstract.

In the several debates upon this impeachment, it must be confessed that his Majesty gave many marks of his great *lenity;* often urging the services you had done him, and endeavoring to extenuate your crimes. The Treasurer and Admiral insisted that you should be put to the most painful and ignominious death, by setting fire on your house at night; and the General was to attend with twenty thousand men armed with poisoned arrows, to shoot you on the face and hands. Some of your servants were to have private orders to strew a poisonous juice on your shirts and sheets, which would soon make you tear your own flesh, and die in the utmost torture. The General came into the same opinion; so that for a long time there was a majority against you. But his Majesty resolving, if possible, to spare your life, at last brought off[7] the Chamberlain.

Upon this incident, Reldresal, Principal Secretary for Private Affairs, who always approved[8] himself your true friend, was commanded by the Emperor to deliver his opinion, which he accordingly did; and therein justified the good thoughts you have of him. He allowed your crimes to be great; but that still there was room for mercy, the most commendable virtue in a prince, and for which his Majesty was so justly celebrated. He said, the friendship between you and him was so well known to the world, that perhaps the most honorable board might think him partial: however, in obedience to the command he had received, he would freely offer his sentiments. That if his Majesty, in consideration of your services, and pursuant to his own merciful disposition, would please to spare your life, and only give order to put out both your eyes, he humbly conceived, that by this expedient justice might in some measure be satisfied, and all the world would applaud the *lenity* of the Emperor, as well as the fair and generous proceedings of those who have the honor to be his counselors. That the loss of your eyes would be no impediment to your bodily strength, by which you might still be useful to his Majesty. That blindness is an addition to courage, by concealing dangers from us; that the fear you had for your eyes was the greatest difficulty in bringing over the enemy's fleet; and it would be sufficient for you to see by the eyes of the ministers, since the greatest princes do no more.

This proposal was received with the utmost disapprobation by the whole board. Bolgolam, the Admiral, could not preserve his temper; but rising up in fury, said, he wondered how the Secretary durst presume to give his opinion for preserving the life of a traitor: that the services you had performed were, by all true reasons of state, the great aggravation of your crimes; that you, who were able to extinguish the fire by discharge of urine in her Majesty's apartment (which he mentioned with horror), might, at another time, raise an inundation by the same means, to drown the whole palace; and the same strength which enabled you to bring over the enemy's fleet might serve, upon the first discontent, to carry it back: that he had good reasons to think you were a Big-Endian in your heart; and as treason begins in the heart before it appears in overt acts, so he accused you as a traitor on that account, and therefore insisted you should be put to death.

The Treasurer was of the same opinion; he showed to what straits his Majesty's revenue was reduced by the charge of maintaining you, which would soon grow insupportable: that the Secretary's expedient of putting out your eyes was so far from being a remedy against this evil, that it would probably increase it; as it is manifest from the common practice of blinding some kind of fowl, after which they fed the faster, and grew sooner fat: that his sacred Majesty, and the council, who are your judges, were in their own consciences fully convinced of your guilt; which was a sufficient argument to condemn

7. Won over.

8. Proved.

you to death, without the formal proofs required by the strict letter of the law.

But his Imperial Majesty, fully determined against capital punishment, was graciously pleased to say, that since the council thought the loss of your eyes too easy a censure, some other may be inflicted hereafter. And your friend the Secretary humbly desiring to be heard again, in answer to what the Treasurer had objected concerning the great charge his Majesty was at in maintaining you, said, that his Excellency, who had the sole disposal of the Emperor's revenue, might easily provide against this evil, by gradually lessening your establishment; by which, for want of sufficient food, you would grow weak and faint, and lose your appetite, and consequently decay and consume in a few months; neither would the stench of your carcass be then so dangerous, when it should become more than half diminished; and immediately upon your death, five or six thousand of his Majesty's subjects might, in two or three days, cut your flesh from your bones, take it away by cart-loads, and bury it in distant parts to prevent infection; leaving the skeleton as a monument of admiration to posterity.

Thus by the great friendship of the Secretary, the whole affair was compromised. It was strictly enjoined, that the project of starving you by degrees should be kept a secret; but the sentence of putting out your eyes was entered on the books; none dissenting except Bolgolam the Admiral, who being a creature of the Empress, was perpetually instigated by her Majesty to insist upon your death; she having borne perpetual malice against you, on account of that infamous and illegal method you took to extinguish the fire in her apartment.

In three days your friend the Secretary will be directed to come to your house, and read before you the articles of impeachment; and then to signify the great lenity and favor of his Majesty and council; whereby you are only condemned to the loss of your eyes, which his Majesty doth not question you will gratefully and humbly submit to; and twenty of his Majesty's surgeons will attend, in order to see the operation well performed, by discharging very sharp-pointed arrows into the balls of your eyes, as you lie on the ground.

I leave to your prudence what measures you will take; and to avoid suspicion, I must immediately return in as private a manner as I came.

His Lordship did so, and I remained alone, under many doubts and perplexities of mind.

It was a custom introduced by this prince and his ministry (very different, as I have been assured, from the practices of former times), that after the court had decreed any cruel execution, either to gratify the monarch's resentment, or the malice of a favorite, the Emperor always made a speech to his whole council, expressing his great lenity and tenderness, as qualities known and confessed by all the world. This speech was immediately published through the kingdom; nor did any thing terrify the people so much as those encomiums on his Majesty's mercy; because it was observed, that the more these praises were enlarged and insisted on, the more inhuman was the punishment, and the sufferer more innocent. Yet as to myself, I must confess, having never been designed for a courtier, either by my birth or education, I was so ill a judge of things, that I could not discover the lenity and favor of this sentence, but conceived it (perhaps erroneously) rather to be rigorous than gentle. I sometimes thought of standing my trial; for although I could not deny the facts alleged in the several articles, yet I hoped they would admit of some extenuations. But having in my life perused many state trials, which I ever observed to terminate as the judges thought fit to direct, I durst not rely on so dangerous a decision, in so critical a juncture, and against such powerful enemies. Once I was strongly bent upon resistance: for while I had liberty, the whole strength of that empire could hardly subdue me, and I might easily with stones pelt the metropolis to pieces; but I soon rejected that project with horror, by remembering the oath I had made to the Emperor, the favors I received from him, and the high title of *Nardac* he conferred upon me. Neither had I so soon learned the gratitude of courtiers, to persuade myself that his Majesty's present severities acquitted me of all past obligations.

At last I fixed upon a resolution, for which it is probable I may incur some censure, and not unjustly; for I confess I owe the preserving my eyes, and consequently my liberty, to my own great rashness and want of experience: because if I had then known the nature of princes and ministers, which I have since observed in many other courts, and their methods of treating criminals less obnoxious than myself, I should with great alacrity and readiness have submitted to so *easy* a punishment. But hurried on by the precipitancy of youth, and having his Imperial Majesty's license to pay my attendance upon the Emperor of Blefuscu, I took this opportunity, before the three days were elapsed, to send a letter to my friend the Secretary, signifying my resolution of setting out that morning for Blefuscu,[9] pursuant to the leave I had got; and without waiting for an answer, I went to that side of the island where our fleet lay. I seized a large man of war, tied a cable to the prow, and lifting up the anchors, I stripped myself, put my clothes (together with my coverlet, which I carried under my arm) into the vessel; and drawing it after me, between wading and swimming, arrived at the royal port of Blefuscu, where the people had long expected me. They lent me two guides to direct me to the capital city, which is of the same name; I held them in my hands until I came within two hundred yards of the gate; and desired them to signify my arrival to one of the secretaries, and let him know, I there waited his Majesty's commands. I had an answer in about an hour, that his Majesty, attended by the royal family, and great officers of the court, was coming out to receive me. I advanced a hundred yards; the Emperor, and his train, alighted from their horses, the Empress and ladies from their coaches; and I did not perceive they were in any fright or concern. I lay on the ground to kiss his Majesty's and the Empress's hand. I told his Majesty that I was come according to my promise, and with the license of the Emperor my master, to have the honor of seeing so mighty a monarch, and to offer him any service in my power, consistent with my duty to my own prince; not mentioning a word of my disgrace, because I had hitherto no regular information of it, and might suppose myself wholly ignorant of any such design; neither could I reasonably conceive that the Emperor would discover the secret while I was out of his power: wherein, however, it soon appeared I was deceived.

I shall not trouble the reader with the particular account of my reception at this court, which was suitable to the generosity of so great a prince; nor of the difficulties I was in for want of a house and bed, being forced to lie on the ground, wrapped up in my coverlet.

Chapter 8. *The author, by a lucky accident, finds means to leave Blefuscu; and, after some difficulties, returns safe to his native country.*

9. Before his trial for treason could be held, Bolingbroke had escaped to France.

Three days after my arrival, walking out of curiosity to the northeast coast of the island, I observed, about half a league off, in the sea, somewhat that looked like a boat overturned. I pulled off my shoes and stockings, and wading two or three hundred yards, I found the object to approach nearer by force of the tide; and then plainly saw it to be a real boat, which I supposed might, by some tempest, have been driven from a ship. Whereupon I returned immediately towards the city, and desired his Imperial Majesty to lend me twenty of the tallest vessels he had left after the loss of his fleet, and three thousand seamen under the command of his Vice Admiral. This fleet sailed round, while I went back the shortest way to the coast where I first discovered the boat; I found the tide had driven it still nearer; the seamen were all provided with cordage, which I had beforehand twisted to a sufficient strength. When the ships came up, I stripped myself, and waded till I came within an hundred yards of the boat; after which I was forced to swim till I got up to it. The seamen threw me the end of the cord, which I fastened to a hole in the forepart of the boat, and the other end to a man of war: but I found all my labor to little purpose; for being out of my depth, I was not able to work. In this necessity, I was forced to swim behind, and push the boat forwards as often as I could, with one of my hands; and the tide favoring me, I advanced so far, that I could just hold up my chin and feel the ground. I rested two or three minutes, and then gave the boat another shove, and so on till the sea was no higher than my armpits. And now the most laborious part being over, I took out my other cables which were stowed in one of the ships, and fastening them first to the boat, and then to nine of the vessels which attended me, the wind being favorable, the seamen towed, and I shoved till we arrived within forty yards of the shore; and waiting till the tide was out, I got dry to the boat, and by the assistance of two thousand men, with ropes and engines, I made a shift to turn it on its bottom, and found it was but little damaged.

I shall not trouble the reader with the difficulties I was under by the help of certain paddles, which cost me ten days making, to get my boat to the royal port of Blefuscu; where a mighty concourse of people appeared upon my arrival, full of wonder at the sight of so prodigious a vessel. I told the Emperor that my good fortune had thrown this boat in my way, to carry me to some place from whence I might return into my native country; and begged his Majesty's orders for getting materials to fit it up, together with license to depart; which, after some kind expostulations, he was pleased to grant.

I did very much wonder, in all this time, not to have heard of any express relating to me from our Emperor to the court of Blefuscu. But I was afterwards given privately to understand, that his Imperial Majesty, never imagining I had the least notice of his designs, believed I was only gone to Blefuscu in performance of my promise, according to the license he had given me, which was well known at our court; and would return in a few days when that ceremony was ended. But he was at last in pain at my long absence; and, after consulting with the Treasurer, and the rest of that cabal, a person of quality was dispatched with the copy of the articles against me. This envoy had instructions to represent to the monarch of Blefuscu the great lenity of his master, who was content to punish me no further than with the loss of my eyes; that I had fled from justice, and if I did not return in two hours, I should be deprived of my title of *Nardac,* and declared a traitor. The envoy further added, that in order to maintain the peace and amity between both empires, his master expected, that his brother of Blefuscu would give orders to have me sent back to Lilliput, bound hand and foot, to be punished as a traitor.

The Emperor of Blefuscu, having taken three days to consult, returned an answer consisting of many civilities and excuses. He said, that as for sending me bound, his brother knew it was impossible; that although I had deprived him of his fleet, yet he owed great obligations to me for many good offices I had done him in making the peace. That however, both their Majesties would soon be made easy; for I had found a prodigious vessel on the shore, able to carry me on the sea, which he had given order to fit up with my own assistance and direction; and he hoped in a few weeks both empires would be freed from so insupportable an incumbrance.

With this answer the envoy returned to Lilliput, and the monarch of Blefuscu related to me all that had passed, offering me at the same time (but under the strictest confidence) his gracious protection, if I would continue in his service; wherein although I believed him sincere, yet I resolved never more to put any confidence in princes or ministers, where I could possibly avoid it; and therefore, with all due acknowledgements for his favorable intentions, I humbly begged to be excused. I told him, that since fortune, whether good or evil, had thrown a vessel in my way, I was resolved to venture myself in the ocean, rather than be an occasion of difference between two such mighty monarchs. Neither did I find the Emperor at all displeased; and I discovered by a certain accident, that he was very glad of my resolution, and so were most of his ministers.

These considerations moved me to hasten my departure somewhat sooner than I intended; to which the court, impatient to have me gone, very readily contributed. Five hundred workmen were employed to make two sails to my boat, according to my directions, by quilting thirteen fold of their strongest linen together. I was at the pains of making ropes and cables, by twisting ten, twenty or thirty of the thickest and strongest of theirs. A great stone that I happened to find, after a long search by the seashore, served me for an anchor. I had the tallow of three hundred cows for greasing my boat, and other uses. I was at incredible pains in cutting down some of the largest timber trees for oars and masts, wherein I was, however, much assisted by his Majesty's ship-carpenters, who helped me in smoothing them, after I had done the rough work.

In about a month, when all was prepared, I sent to receive his Majesty's commands, and to take my leave. The Emperor and royal family came out of the palace; I lay down on my face to kiss his hand, which he very graciously gave me: so did the Empress, and young princes of the blood. His Majesty presented me with fifty purses of two hundred *sprugs* apiece, together with his picture at full length, which I put immediately into one of my gloves, to keep it from being hurt. The ceremonies at my departure were too many to trouble the reader with at this time.

I stored the boat with the carcasses of an hundred oxen, and three hundred sheep, with bread and drink proportionable, and as much meat ready dressed as four hundred cooks could provide. I took with me six cows and two bulls alive, with as many ewes and rams, intending to carry them into my own country, and propagate the breed. And to feed them on board, I had a good bundle of hay, and a bag of corn.[1] I would gladly have taken a dozen of the

1. Generic term for any cereal or grain crop (here, wheat).

natives; but this was a thing the Emperor would by no means permit; and besides a diligent search into my pockets, his Majesty engaged my honor not to carry away any of his subjects, although with their own consent and desire.

Having thus prepared all things as well as I was able, I set sail on the twenty-fourth day of September, 1701, at six in the morning; and when I had gone about four leagues to the northward, the wind being at southeast, at six in the evening, I descried a small island about half a league to the northwest. I advanced forward, and cast anchor on the lee-side of the island, which seemed to be uninhabited. I then took some refreshment, and went to my rest. I slept well, and as I conjecture at least six hours; for I found the day broke in two hours after I awaked. It was a clear night; I eat my breakfast before the sun was up; and heaving anchor, the wind being favorable, I steered the same course that I had done the day before, wherein I was directed by my pocket compass. My intention was to reach, if possible, one of those islands which I had reason to believe lay to the northeast of Van Diemen's Land. I discovered nothing all that day; but upon the next, about three in the afternoon, when I had by my computation made twenty-four leagues from Blefuscu, I descried a sail steering to the southeast; my course was due east. I hailed her, but could get no answer; yet I found I gained upon her, for the wind slackened. I made all the sail I could, and in half an hour she spied me, then hung out her ancient,[2] and discharged a gun. It is not easy to express the joy I was in upon the unexpected hope of once more seeing my beloved country, and the dear pledges[3] I had left in it. The ship slackened her sails, and I came up with her between five and six in the evening, September 26; but my heart leapt within me to see her English colors. I put my cows and sheep into my coat-pockets and got on board with all my little cargo of provisions. The vessel was an English merchantman, returning from Japan by the North and South Seas;[4] the captain, Mr. John Biddel of Deptford, a very civil man, and an excellent sailor. We were now in the latitude of 30 degrees south; there were about fifty men in the ship; and here I met an old comrade of mine, one Peter Williams, who gave me a good character to the captain. This gentleman treated me with kindness, and desired I would let him know what place I came from last, and whither I was bound; which I did in few words; but he thought I was raving, and that the dangers I underwent had disturbed my head; whereupon I took my black cattle and sheep out of my pocket, which, after great astonishment, clearly convinced him of my veracity. I then showed him the gold given me by the Emperor of Blefuscu, together with his Majesty's picture at full length, and some other rarities of that country. I gave him two purses of two hundred *sprugs* each, and promised, when we arrived in England, to make him a present of a cow and a sheep big with young.

I shall not trouble the reader with a particular account of this voyage; which was very prosperous for the most part. We arrived in the Downs[5] on the 13th of April, 1702. I had only one misfortune, that the rats on board carried away one of my sheep; I found her bones in a hole, picked clean from the flesh. The rest of my cattle I got safe on shore, and set them a grazing in a bowling-green at Greenwich, where the fineness of the grass made them feed very heartily, though I had always feared the contrary; neither could I possibly have

2. Flag.
3. Hostages (i.e., his family).
4. North and South Pacific.
5. A rendezvous for ships off the southeast coast of England.

preserved them in so long a voyage, if the captain had not allowed me some of his best biscuit, which rubbed to powder, and mingled with water, was their constant food. The short time I continued in England, I made a considerable profit by showing my cattle to many persons of quality, and others: and before I began my second voyage, I sold them for six hundred pounds. Since my last return, I find the breed is considerably increased, especially the sheep; which I hope will prove much to the advantage of the woolen manufacture, by the fineness of the fleeces.

I stayed but two months with my wife and family; for my insatiable desire of seeing foreign countries would suffer me to continue no longer. I left fifteen hundred pounds with my wife, and fixed her in a good house at Redriff. My remaining stock I carried with me, part in money, and part in goods, in hopes to improve my fortunes. My eldest uncle, John, had left me an estate in land, near Epping, of about thirty pounds a year; and I had a long lease of the Black Bull in Fetter Lane, which yielded me as much more: so that I was not in any danger of leaving my family upon the parish.[6] My son Johnny, named so after his uncle, was at the grammar school, and a towardly[7] child. My daughter Betty (who is now well married, and has children) was then at her needlework. I took leave of my wife, and boy and girl, with tears on both sides; and went on board the *Adventure,* a merchant-ship of three hundred tons, bound for Surat, Captain John Nicholas of Liverpool, Commander. But my account of this voyage must be referred to the second part of my *Travels.*

Part 2. A Voyage to Brobdingnag

CHAPTER 1. *A great storm described. The longboat sent to fetch water; the Author goes with it to discover the country. He is left on shore, is seized by one of the natives, and carried to a farmer's house. His reception there, with several accidents that happened there. A description of the inhabitants.*

Having been condemned by nature and fortune to an active and restless life, in ten months after my return I again left my native country, and took shipping in the Downs on the 20th day of June, 1702, in the *Adventure,* Captain John Nicholas, a Cornish man, Commander, bound for Surat.[8] We had a very prosperous gale till we arrived at the Cape of Good Hope, where we landed for fresh water, but discovering a leak we unshipped our goods and wintered there; for the Captain falling sick of an ague, we could not leave the Cape till the end of March. We then set sail, and had a good voyage till we passed the Straits of Madagascar; but having got northward of that island, and to about five degrees south latitude, the winds, which in those seas are observed to blow a constant equal gale between the north and west from the beginning of December to the beginning of May, on the 19th of April began to blow with much greater violence and more westerly than usual, continuing so far twenty days together, during which time we were driven a little to the east of the Molucca Islands and about three degrees northward of the Line, as our Cap-

6. On welfare (living on charity given by the parish).
7. Promising.
8. In India. The geography of the voyage (described next) is simple: The *Adventure,* after sailing up the east coast of Africa to about five degrees south of the equator (the "Line"), is blown past India into the Malay Archipelago, north of the islands of Buru and Ceram. The storm then drives the ship northward and eastward, away from the coast of Siberia ("Great Tartary") into the northeast Pacific, at that time unexplored. Brobdingnag lies somewhere in the vicinity of Alaska.

tain found by an observation he took the 2nd of May, at which time the wind ceased, and it was a perfect calm, whereat I was not a little rejoiced. But he, being a man well experienced in the navigation of those seas, bid us all prepare against a storm, which accordingly happened the day following: for a southern wind, called the southern monsoon, began to set in.

Finding it was likely to overblow,[9] we took in our spritsail, and stood by to hand the foresail; but making foul weather, we looked the guns were all fast, and handed the mizzen. The ship lay very broad off, so we thought it better spooning before the sea, than trying or hulling. We reefed the foresail and set him, we hauled aft the foresheet; the helm was hard aweather. The ship wore bravely. We belayed the fore-downhaul; but the sail was split, and we hauled down the yard and got the sail into the ship, and unbound all the things clear of it. It was a very fierce storm; the sea broke strange and dangerous. We hauled off upon the lanyard of the whipstaff, and helped the man at helm. We would not get down our topmast, but let all stand, because she scudded before the sea very well, and we knew that the topmast being aloft, the ship was the wholesomer, and made better way through the sea, seeing we had searoom. When the storm was over, we set foresail and mainsail, and brought the ship to. Then we set the mizzen, main topsail and the fore topsail. Our course was east-northeast, the wind was at southwest. We got the starboard tacks aboard, we cast off our weather braces and lifts; we set in the lee braces, and hauled forward by the weather bowlings, and hauled them tight, and belayed them, and hauled over the mizzen tack to windward, and kept her full and by as near as she would lie.

During this storm, which was followed by a strong wind west-southwest, we were carried by my computation about five hundred leagues to the east, so that the oldest sailor on board could not tell in what part of the world we were. Our provisions held out well, our ship was staunch, and our crew all in good health; but we lay in the utmost distress for water. We thought it best to hold on the same course rather than turn more northerly, which might have brought us to the northwest parts of Great Tartary, and into the frozen sea.

On the 16th day of June, 1703, a boy on the topmast discovered land. On the 17th we came in full view of a great island or continent (for we knew not whether) on the south side whereof was a small neck of land jutting out into the sea, and a creek[1] too shallow to hold a ship of above one hundred tons. We cast anchor within a league of this creek, and our Captain sent a dozen of his men well armed in the longboat, with vessels for water if any could be found. I desired his leave to go with them that I might see the country and make what discoveries I could. When we came to land we saw no river or spring, nor any sign of inhabitants. Our men therefore wandered on the shore to find out some fresh water near the sea, and I walked alone about a mile on the other side, where I observed the country all barren and rocky. I now began to be weary, and seeing nothing to entertain my curiosity, I returned gently down towards the creek; and the sea being full in my view, I saw our men already got into the boat, and rowing for life to the ship. I was going to hollow after them, although it had been to little purpose, when I observed a huge creature walking after them in the sea as fast as he could; he waded not much

9. This paragraph is taken almost literally from Samuel Sturmy's *Mariner's Magazine* (1669). Swift is ridiculing the use of technical terms by writers of popular voyages.
1. A small bay or cove, affording anchorage.

deeper than his knees and took prodigious strides, but our men had the start of him half a league, and the sea thereabouts being full of sharp-pointed rocks, the monster was not able to overtake the boat. This I was afterwards told, for I durst not stay to see the issue of that adventure, but ran as fast as I could the way I first went, and then climbed up a steep hill, which gave me some prospect of the country. I found it fully cultivated; but that which first surprised me was the length of the grass, which, in those grounds that seemed to be kept for hay, was about twenty foot high.[2]

I fell into a highroad, for so I took it to be, although it served to the inhabitants only as a footpath through a field of barley. Here I walked on for some time, but could see little on either side, it being now near harvest, and the corn[3] rising at least forty foot. I was an hour walking to the end of this field, which was fenced in with a hedge of at least one hundred and twenty foot high, and the trees so lofty that I could make no computation of their altitude. There was a stile to pass from this field into the next: it had four steps, and a stone to cross over when you came to the utmost. It was impossible for me to climb this stile, because every step was six foot high, and the upper stone above twenty. I was endeavoring to find some gap in the hedge when I discovered one of the inhabitants in the next field advancing towards the stile, of the same size with him whom I saw in the sea pursuing our boat. He appeared as tall as an ordinary spire-steeple, and took about ten yards at every stride, as near as I could guess. I was struck with the utmost fear and astonishment, and ran to hide myself in the corn, from whence I saw him at the top of the stile, looking back into the next field on the right hand; and heard him call in a voice many degrees louder than a speaking trumpet; but the noise was so high in the air that at first I certainly thought it was thunder. Whereupon seven monsters like himself came towards him with reaping hooks in their hands, each hook about the largeness of six scythes. These people were not so well clad as the first, whose servants or laborers they seemed to be. For, upon some words he spoke, they went to reap the corn in the field where I lay. I kept from them at as great a distance as I could, but was forced to move with extreme difficulty, for the stalks of the corn were sometimes not above a foot distant, so that I could hardly squeeze my body betwixt them. However, I made a shift to go forward till I came to a part of the field where the corn had been laid by the rain and wind; here it was impossible for me to advance a step, for the stalks were so interwoven that I could not creep through, and the beards of the fallen ears so strong and pointed that they pierced through my clothes into my flesh. At the same time I heard the reapers not above an hundred yards behind me. Being quite dispirited with toil, and wholly overcome by grief and despair, I lay down between two ridges and heartily wished I might there end my days. I bemoaned my desolate widow and fatherless children; I lamented my own folly and willfulness in attempting a second voyage against the advice of all my friends and relations. In this terrible agitation of mind, I could not forbear thinking of Lilliput, whose inhabitants looked upon me as the greatest prodigy that ever appeared in the world; where I was able to draw an imperial fleet in my hand, and perform those other actions which will be recorded forever in the chronicles of that empire, while

2. Swift's intention, not always carried out accurately, is that everything in Brobdingnag should be, in relation to our familiar world, on a scale of ten to one.

3. Here, barley.

posterity shall hardly believe them, although attested by millions. I reflected what a mortification it must prove to me to appear as inconsiderable in this nation as one single Lilliputian would be among us. But this I conceived was to be the least of my misfortunes; for as human creatures are observed to be more savage and cruel in proportion to their bulk, what could I expect but to be a morsel in the mouth of the first among these enormous barbarians who should happen to seize me? Undoubtedly philosophers are in the right when they tell us that nothing is great or little otherwise than by comparison. It might have pleased fortune to let the Lilliputians find some nation where the people were as diminutive with respect to them as they were to me. And who knows but that even this prodigious race of mortals might be equally overmatched in some distant part of the world, whereof we have yet no discovery?

Scared and confounded as I was, I could not forbear going on with these reflections; when one of the reapers approaching within ten yards of the ridge where I lay, made me apprehend that with the next step I should be squashed to death under his foot, or cut in two with his reaping hook. And therefore when he was again about to move, I screamed as loud as fear could make me. Whereupon the huge creature trod short, and looking round about under him for some time, at last espied me as I lay on the ground. He considered a while with the caution of one who endeavors to lay hold on a small dangerous animal in such a manner that it shall not be able either to scratch or to bite him, as I myself have sometimes done with a weasel in England. At length he ventured to take me up behind by the middle between his forefinger and thumb, and brought me within three yards of his eyes, that he might behold my shape more perfectly. I guessed his meaning, and my good fortune gave me so much presence of mind that I resolved not to struggle in the least as he held me in the air about sixty foot from the ground, although he grievously pinched my sides, for fear I should slip through his fingers. All I ventured was to raise mine eyes towards the sun, and place my hands together in a supplicating posture, and to speak some words in an humble melancholy tone, suitable to the condition I then was in. For I apprehended every moment that he would dash me against the ground, as we usually do any little hateful animal which we have a mind to destroy. But my good star would have it that he appeared pleased with my voice and gestures, and began to look upon me as a curiosity, much wondering to hear me pronounce articulate words, although he could not understand them. In the meantime I was not able to forbear groaning and shedding tears and turning my head towards my sides, letting him know, as well as I could, how cruelly I was hurt by the pressure of his thumb and finger. He seemed to apprehend my meaning; for, lifting up the lappet[4] of his coat, he put me gently into it, and immediately ran along with me to his master, who was a substantial farmer, and the same person I had first seen in the field.

The farmer having (as I supposed by their talk) received such an account of me as his servant could give him, took a piece of a small straw about the size of a walking staff, and therewith lifted up the lappets of my coat, which it seems he thought to be some kind of covering that nature had given me. He blew my hairs aside to take a better view of my face. He called his hinds[5] about him, and asked them (as I afterwards learned) whether they had ever seen in the fields any little creature that resembled me. He then placed me softly on the ground upon all four; but I got immediately up, and walked slowly back-

4. Flap or fold.

5. Farm servants.

wards and forwards, to let those people see I had no intent to run away. They all sat down in a circle about me, the better to observe my motions. I pulled off my hat, and made a low bow towards the farmer; I fell on my knees, and lifted up my hands and eyes, and spoke several words as loud as I could; I took a purse of gold out of my pocket, and humbly presented it to him. He received it on the palm of his hand, then applied it close to his eye to see what it was, and afterwards turned it several times with the point of a pin (which he took out of his sleeve), but could make nothing of it. Whereupon I made a sign that he should place his hand on the ground; I then took the purse, and opening it, poured all the gold into his palm. There were six Spanish pieces of four pistoles each, beside twenty or thirty smaller coins. I saw him wet the tip of his little finger upon his tongue, and take up one of my largest pieces, and then another; but he seemed to be wholly ignorant what they were. He made me a sign to put them again into my purse, and the purse again into my pocket, which after offering to him several times, I thought it best to do.

The farmer by this time was convinced I must be a rational creature. He spoke often to me, but the sound of his voice pierced my ears like that of a water mill, yet his words were articulate enough. I answered as loud as I could in several languages, and he often laid his ear within two yards of me, but all in vain, for we were wholly unintelligible to each other. He then sent his servants to their work, and taking his handkerchief out of his pocket, he doubled and spread it on his hand, which he placed flat on the ground with the palm upwards, making me a sign to step into it, as I could easily do, for it was not above a foot in thickness. I thought it my part to obey, and for fear of falling, laid myself at full length upon the handkerchief, with the remainder of which he lapped me up to the head for further security, and in this manner carried me home to his house. There he called his wife, and showed me to her; but she screamed and ran back as women in England do at the sight of a toad or a spider. However, when she had a while seen my behavior, and how well I observed the signs her husband made, she was soon reconciled, and by degrees grew extremely tender of me.

It was about twelve at noon, and a servant brought in dinner. It was only one substantial dish of meat (fit for the plain condition of an husbandman) in a dish of about four-and-twenty foot diameter. The company were the farmer and his wife, three children, and an old grandmother. When they were sat down, the farmer placed me at some distance from him on the table, which was thirty foot high from the floor. I was in a terrible fright, and kept as far as I could from the edge, for fear of falling. The wife minced a bit of meat, then crumbled some bread on a trencher, and placed it before me. I made her a low bow, took out my knife and fork, and fell to eat; which gave them exceeding delight. The mistress sent her maid for a small dram cup, which held about two gallons, and filled it with drink; I took up the vessel with much difficulty in both hands, and in a most respectful manner drank to her ladyship's health, expressing the words as loud as I could in English; which made the company laugh so heartily that I was almost deafened with the noise. This liquor tasted like a small cider,[6] and was not unpleasant. Then the master made me a sign to come to his trencher side; but as I walked on the table, being in great surprise all the time, as the indulgent reader will easily conceive and excuse, I happened to stumble against a crust, and fell flat on my face, but received

6. I.e., weak cider.

no hurt. I got up immediately, and observing the good people to be in much concern, I took my hat (which I held under my arm out of good manners) and waving it over my head, made three huzzas to show I had got no mischief by my fall. But advancing forwards toward my master (as I shall henceforth call him), his youngest son who sat next him, an arch boy of about ten years old, took me up by the legs, and held me so high in the air that I trembled every limb; but his father snatched me from him, and at the same time gave him such a box on the left ear as would have felled an European troop of horse to the earth, ordering him to be taken from the table. But being afraid the boy might owe me a spite, and well remembering how mischievous all children among us naturally are to sparrows, rabbits, young kittens, and puppy dogs, I fell on my knees, and pointing to the boy, made my master to understand, as well as I could, that I desired his son might be pardoned. The father complied, and the lad took his seat again; whereupon I went to him and kissed his hand, which my master took, and made him stroke me gently with it.

In the midst of dinner, my mistress's favorite cat leaped into her lap. I heard a noise behind me like that of a dozen stocking weavers at work; and turning my head, I found it proceeded from the purring of this animal, who seemed to be three times larger than an ox, as I computed by the view of her head and one of her paws, while her mistress was feeding and stroking her. The fierceness of this creature's countenance altogether discomposed me, although I stood at the farther end of the table, about fifty foot off, and although my mistress held her fast for fear she might give a spring and seize me in her talons. But it happened there was no danger, for the cat took not the least notice of me when my master placed me within three yards of her. And as I have been always told, and found true by experience in my travels, that flying or discovering[7] fear before a fierce animal is a certain way to make it pursue or attack you, so I resolved in this dangerous juncture to show no manner of concern. I walked with intrepidity five or six times before the very head of the cat, and came within half a yard of her; whereupon she drew herself back, as if she were more afraid of me. I had less apprehension concerning the dogs, whereof three or four came into the room, as it is usual in farmers' houses; one of which was a mastiff, equal in bulk to four elephants, and a greyhound, somewhat taller than the mastiff, but not so large.

When dinner was almost done, the nurse came in with a child of a year old in her arms, who immediately spied me, and began a squall that you might have heard from London Bridge to Chelsea, after the usual oratory of infants, to get me for a plaything. The mother out of pure indulgence took me up, and put me towards the child, who presently seized me by the middle, and got my head in his mouth, where I roared so loud that the urchin was frighted and let me drop; and I should infallibly have broke my neck if the mother had not held her apron under me. The nurse to quiet her babe made use of a rattle, which was a kind of hollow vessel filled with great stones, and fastened by a cable to the child's waist: but all in vain, so that she was forced to apply the last remedy by giving it suck. I must confess no object ever disgusted me so much as the sight of her monstrous breast, which I cannot tell what to compare with so as to give the curious reader an idea of its bulk, shape, and color. It stood prominent six foot, and could not be less than sixteen in circumference. The nipple was about half the bigness of my head, and the hue both of that

7. Revealing.

and the dug so varified with spots, pimples, and freckles that nothing could appear more nauseous: for I had a near sight of her, she sitting down the more conveniently to give suck, and I standing on the table. This made me reflect upon the fair skins of our English ladies, who appear so beautiful to us, only because they are of our own size, and their defects not to be seen but through a magnifying glass, where we find by experiment that the smoothest and whitest skins look rough and coarse and ill colored.

I remember when I was at Lilliput, the complexion of those diminutive people appeared to me the fairest in the world; and talking upon this subject with a person of learning there, who was an intimate friend of mine, he said that my face appeared much fairer and smoother when he looked on me from the ground than it did upon a nearer view when I took him up in my hand and brought him close, which he confessed was at first a very shocking sight. He said he could discover great holes in my skin; that the stumps of my beard were ten times stronger than the bristles of a boar, and my complexion made up of several colors altogether disagreeable: although I must beg leave to say for myself that I am as fair as most of my sex and country and very little sunburnt by all my travels. On the other side, discoursing of the ladies in that Emperor's court, he used to tell me one had freckles, another too wide a mouth, a third too large a nose; nothing of which I was able to distinguish. I confess this reflection was obvious enough; which however I could not forbear, lest the reader might think those vast creatures were actually deformed: for I must do them justice to say they are a comely race of people; and particularly the features of my master's countenance, although he were but a farmer, when I beheld him from the height of sixty foot, appeared very well proportioned.

When dinner was done, my master went out to his laborers; and as I could discover by his voice and gesture, gave his wife a strict charge to take care of me. I was very much tired and disposed to sleep, which my mistress perceiving, she put me on her own bed, and covered me with a clean white handkerchief, but larger and coarser than the mainsail of a man-of-war.

I slept about two hours, and dreamed I was at home with my wife and children, which aggravated my sorrows when I awaked and found myself alone in a vast room, between two and three hundred foot wide, and above two hundred high, lying in a bed twenty yards wide. My mistress was gone about her household affairs, and had locked me in. The bed was eight yards from the floor. Some natural necessities required me to get down; I durst not presume to call, and if I had, it would have been in vain with such a voice as mine at so great a distance from the room where I lay to the kitchen where the family kept. While I was under these circumstances, two rats crept up the curtains, and ran smelling backwards and forwards on the bed. One of them came up almost to my face; whereupon I rose in a fright, and drew out my hanger[8] to defend myself. These horrible animals had the boldness to attack me on both sides, and one of them held his forefeet at my collar; but I had the good fortune to rip up his belly before he could do me any mischief. He fell down at my feet; and the other seeing the fate of his comrade, made his escape, but not without one good wound on the back, which I gave him as he fled, and made the blood run trickling from him. After this exploit I walked gently to and fro on the bed, to recover my breath and loss of spirits. These creatures were of the size of a large mastiff, but infinitely more nimble and

8. A short, broad sword.

fierce; so that if I had taken off my belt before I went to sleep, I must have infallibly been torn to pieces and devoured. I measured the tail of the dead rat, and found it to be two yards long, wanting an inch; but it went against my stomach to drag the carcass off the bed, where it lay still bleeding; I observed it had yet some life, but with a strong slash cross the neck, I thoroughly dispatched it.

Soon after, my mistress came into the room, who seeing me all bloody, ran and took me up in her hand. I pointed to the dead rat, smiling and making other signs to show I was not hurt, whereat she was extremely rejoiced, calling the maid to take up the dead rat with a pair of tongs, and throw it out of the window. Then she set me on a table, where I showed her my hanger all bloody, and wiping it on the lappet of my coat, returned it to the scabbard. I was pressed to do more than one thing, which another could not do for me, and therefore endeavored to make my mistress understand that I desired to be set down on the floor; which after she had done, my bashfulness would not suffer me to express myself farther than by pointing to the door, and bowing several times. The good woman with much difficulty at last perceived what I would be at, and taking me up again in her hand, walked into the garden, where she set me down. I went on one side about two hundred yards; and beckoning to her not to look or to follow me, I hid myself between two leaves of sorrel, and there discharged the necessities of nature.

I hope the gentle reader will excuse me for dwelling on these and the like particulars, which however insignificant they may appear to groveling vulgar minds, yet will certainly help a philosopher[9] to enlarge his thoughts and imagination, and apply them to the benefit of public as well as private life, which was my sole design in presenting this and other accounts of my travels to the world; wherein I have been chiefly studious of truth, without affecting any ornaments of learning or of style. But the whole scene of this voyage made so strong an impression on my mind, and is so deeply fixed in my memory, that in committing it to paper I did not omit one material circumstance; however, upon a strict review, I blotted out several passages of less moment which were in my first copy, for fear of being censured as tedious and trifling, whereof travelers are often, perhaps not without justice, accused.

CHAPTER 2. *A description of the farmer's daughter. The Author carried to a market town, and then to the metropolis. The particulars of his journey.*

My mistress had a daughter of nine years old, a child of towardly parts for her age, very dexterous at her needle, and skillful in dressing her baby.[1] Her mother and she contrived to fit up the baby's cradle for me against night: the cradle was put into a small drawer of a cabinet, and the drawer placed upon a hanging shelf for fear of the rats. This was my bed all the time I stayed with those people, although made more convenient by degrees as I began to learn their language, and make my wants known. This young girl was so handy, that after I had once or twice pulled off my clothes before her, she was able to dress and undress me, although I never gave her that trouble when she would let me do either myself. She made me seven shirts, and some other linen of as fine cloth as could be got, which indeed was coarser than sackcloth, and

9. Scientist, in contrast to the "vulgar" (commonplace, uncultivated).

1. Doll. "Towardly parts": promising abilities.

these she constantly washed for me with her own hands. She was likewise my schoolmistress to teach me the language: when I pointed to anything, she told me the name of it in her own tongue, so that in a few days I was able to call for whatever I had a mind to. She was very good-natured, and not above forty foot high, being little for her age. She gave me the name of *Grildrig,* which the family took up, and afterwards the whole kingdom. The word imports what the Latins call *nanunculus,* the Italian *homunceletino,* and the English *mannikin.*[2] To her I chiefly owe my preservation in that country: we never parted while I was there; I called her my *Glumdalclitch,* or little nurse: and I should be guilty of great ingratitude if I omitted this honorable mention of her care and affection towards me, which I heartily wish it lay in my power to requite as she deserves, instead of being the innocent but unhappy instrument of her disgrace, as I have too much reason to fear.

It now began to be known and talked of in the neighborhood that my master had found a strange animal in the field, about the bigness of a *splacknuck,* but exactly shaped in every part like a human creature, which it likewise imitated in all its actions: seemed to speak in a little language of its own, had already learned several words of theirs, went erect upon two legs, was tame and gentle, would come when it was called, do whatever it was bid, had the finest limbs in the world, and a complexion fairer than a nobleman's daughter of three years old. Another farmer who lived hard by, and was a particular friend of my master, came on a visit on purpose to inquire into the truth of this story. I was immediately produced, and placed upon a table, where I walked as I was commanded, drew my hanger, put it up again, made my reverence to my master's guest, asked him in his own language how he did, and told him he was welcome, just as my little nurse had instructed me. This man, who was old and dimsighted, put on his spectacles to behold me better, at which I could not forbear laughing very heartily, for his eyes appeared like the full moon shining into a chamber at two windows. Our people, who discovered the cause of my mirth, bore me company in laughing, at which the old fellow was fool enough to be angry and out of countenance. He had the character of a great miser, and to my misfortune he well deserved it by the cursed advice he gave my master to show me as a sight upon a market day in the next town, which was half an hour's riding, about two and twenty miles from our house. I guessed there was some mischief contriving when I observed my master and his friend whispering long together, sometimes pointing at me; and my fears made me fancy that I overheard and understood some of their words. But the next morning Glumdalclitch, my little nurse, told me the whole matter, which she had cunningly picked out from her mother. The poor girl laid me on her bosom, and fell a weeping with shame and grief. She apprehended some mischief would happen to me from rude vulgar folks, who might squeeze me to death, or break one of my limbs by taking me in their hands. She had also observed how modest I was in my nature, how nicely I regarded my honor, and what an indignity I should conceive it to be exposed for money as a public spectacle to the meanest of the people. She said her papa and mamma had promised that Grildrig should be hers; but now she found they meant to serve her as they did last year, when they pretended to give her a lamb, and yet, as soon as it was fat, sold it to a butcher. For my own part, I may truly affirm

2. Little man, dwarf. The Latin and Italian words are Swift's own coinages, as, of course, are the various words from the Brobdingnagian language.

that I was less concerned than my nurse. I had a strong hope, which never left me, that I should one day recover my liberty; and as to the ignominy of being carried about for a monster, I considered myself to be a perfect stranger in the country, and that such a misfortune could never be charged upon me as a reproach, if ever I should return to England; since the King of Great Britain himself, in my condition, must have undergone the same distress.

My master, pursuant to the advice of his friend, carried me in a box the next market day to the neighboring town, and took along with him his little daughter, my nurse, upon a pillion[3] behind him. The box was close on every side, with a little door for me to go in and out, and a few gimlet holes to let in air. The girl had been so careful to put the quilt of her baby's bed into it, for me to lie down on. However, I was terribly shaken and discomposed in this journey, although it were but of half an hour. For the horse went about forty foot at every step, and trotted so high that the agitation was equal to the rising and falling of a ship in a great storm, but much more frequent. Our journey was somewhat further than from London to St. Albans.[4] My master alighted at an inn which he used to frequent; and after consulting a while with the innkeeper, and making some necessary preparations, he hired the *Grultrud,* or crier, to give notice through the town of a strange creature to be seen at the Sign of the Green Eagle, not so big as a *splacknuck* (an animal in that country very finely shaped, about six foot long), and in every part of the body resembling an human creature; could speak several words and perform an hundred diverting tricks.

I was placed upon a table in the largest room of the inn, which might be near three hundred foot square. My little nurse stood on a low stool close to the table, to take care of me, and direct what I should do. My master, to avoid a crowd, would suffer only thirty people at a time to see me. I walked about on the table as the girl commanded; she asked me questions as far as she knew my understanding of the language reached, and I answered them as loud as I could. I turned about several times to the company, paid my humble respects, said they were welcome, and used some other speeches I had been taught. I took up a thimble filled with liquor, which Glumdalclitch had given me for a cup, and drank their health. I drew out my hanger, and flourished with it after the manner of fencers in England. My nurse gave me part of a straw, which I exercised as pike, having learned the art in my youth. I was that day shown to twelve sets of company, and as often forced to go over again with the same fopperies, till I was half dead with weariness and vexation. For those who had seen me made such wonderful reports that the people were ready to break down the doors to come in. My master for his own interest would not suffer anyone to touch me except my nurse; and, to prevent danger, benches were set round the table at such a distance as put me out of everybody's reach. However, an unlucky schoolboy aimed a hazelnut directly at my head, which very narrowly missed me; otherwise, it came with so much violence that it would have infallibly knocked out my brains, for it was almost as large as a small pumpion:[5] but I had the satisfaction to see the young rogue well beaten, and turned out of the room.

My master gave public notice that he would show me again the next market

3. A pad attached to the hinder part of a saddle, on which a second person, usually a woman, could ride.

4. About twenty miles.

5. Pumpkin.

day, and in the meantime he prepared a more convenient vehicle for me, which he had reason enough to do; for I was so tired with my first journey, and with entertaining company for eight hours together, that I could hardly stand upon my legs or speak a word. It was at least three days before I recovered my strength; and that I might have no rest at home, all the neighboring gentlemen from an hundred miles round, hearing of my fame, came to see me at my master's own house. There could not be fewer than thirty persons with their wives and children (for the country is very populous); and my master demanded the rate of a full room whenever he showed me at home, although it were only to a single family. So that for some time I had but little ease every day of the week (except Wednesday, which is their Sabbath) although I were not carried to the town.

My master finding how profitable I was like to be, resolved to carry me to the most considerable cities of the kingdom. Having therefore provided himself with all things necessary for a long journey, and settled his affairs at home, he took leave of his wife; and upon the 17th of August, 1703, about two months after my arrival, we set out for the metropolis, situated near the middle of that empire, and about three thousand miles distance from our house. My master made his daughter Glumdalclitch ride behind him. She carried me on her lap in a box tied about her waist. The girl had lined it on all sides with the softest cloth she could get, well quilted underneath, furnished it with her baby's bed, provided me with linen and other necessaries, and made everything as convenient as she could. We had no other company but a boy of the house, who rode after us with the luggage.

My master's design was to show me in all the towns by the way, and to step out of the road for fifty or an hundred miles to any village or person of quality's house where he might expect custom. We made easy journeys of not above seven or eight score miles a day: for Glumdalclitch, on purpose to spare me, complained she was tired with the trotting of the horse. She often took me out of my box at my own desire, to give me air and show me the country, but always held me fast by leading strings.[6] We passed over five or six rivers many degrees broader and deeper than the Nile or the Ganges; and there was hardly a rivulet so small as the Thames at London Bridge. We were ten weeks in our journey, and I was shown in eighteen large towns, besides many large villages and private families.

On the 26th day of October, we arrived at the metropolis, called in their language *Lorbrulgrud,* or Pride of the Universe. My master took a lodging in the principal street of the city, not far from the royal palace, and put out bills in the usual form, containing an exact description of my person and parts. He hired a large room between three and four hundred foot wide. He provided a table sixty foot in diameter, upon which I was to act my part, and palisadoed it round three foot from the edge, and as many high, to prevent my falling over. I was shown ten times a day to the wonder and satisfaction of all people. I could now speak the language tolerably well, and perfectly understood every word that was spoken to me. Besides, I had learned their alphabet, and could make a shift to explain a sentence here and there; for Glumdalclitch had been my instructor while we were at home, and at leisure hours during our journey. She carried a little book in her pocket, not much larger than a Sanson's *Atlas*;[7] it was a common treatise for the use of young girls, giving a short account of their religion: out of this she taught me my letters, and interpreted the words.

6. Used to guide children learning to walk.

7. I.e., over two feet long and about two feet wide.

CHAPTER 3. *The Author sent for to Court. The Queen buys him of his master, the farmer, and presents him to the King. He disputes with his Majesty's great scholars. An apartment at Court provided for the Author. He is in high favor with the Queen. He stands up for the honor of his own country. His quarrels with the Queen's dwarf.*

The frequent labors I underwent every day made in a few weeks a very considerable change in my health: the more my master got by me, the more unsatiable he grew. I had quite lost my stomach, and was almost reduced to a skeleton. The farmer observed it, and concluding I soon must die, resolved to make as good a hand of me as he could. While he was thus reasoning and resolving with himself, a *Slardral,* or Gentleman Usher, came from Court, commanding my master to carry me immediately thither for the diversion of the Queen and her ladies. Some of the latter had already been to see me and reported strange things of my beauty, behavior, and good sense. Her Majesty and those who attended her were beyond measure delighted with my demeanor. I fell on my knees and begged the honor of kissing her Imperial foot; but this gracious princess held out her little finger towards me (after I was set on a table), which I embraced in both my arms, and put the tip of it, with the utmost respect, to my lip. She made me some general questions about my country and my travels, which I answered as distinctly and in as few words as I could. She asked whether I would be content to live at Court. I bowed down to the board of the table, and humbly answered that I was my master's slave, but if I were at my own disposal, I should be proud to devote my life to her Majesty's service. She then asked my master whether he were willing to sell me at a good price. He, who apprehended I could not live a month, was ready enough to part with me, and demanded a thousand pieces of gold, which were ordered him on the spot, each piece being about the bigness of eight hundred moidores;[8] but, allowing for the proportion of all things between that country and Europe, and the high price of gold among them, was hardly so great a sum as a thousand guineas would be in England. I then said to the Queen, since I was now her Majesty's most humble creature and vassal, I must beg the favor that Glumdalclitch, who had always tended me with so much care and kindness, and understood to do it so well, might be admitted into her service, and continue to be my nurse and instructor. Her Majesty agreed to my petition, and easily got the farmer's consent, who was glad enough to have his daughter preferred at Court; and the poor girl herself was not able to hide her joy. My late master withdrew, bidding me farewell, and saying he had left me in a good service; to which I replied not a word, only making him a slight bow.

The Queen observed my coldness, and when the farmer was gone out of the apartment, asked me the reason. I made bold to tell her Majesty that I owed no other obligation to my late master than his not dashing out the brains of a poor harmless creature found by chance in his field; which obligation was amply recompensed by the gain he had made in showing me through half the kingdom, and the price he had now sold me for. That the life I had since led was laborious enough to kill an animal of ten times my strength. That my health was much impaired by the continual drudgery of entertaining the rabble every hour of the day; and that if my master had not thought my life in danger, her Majesty perhaps would not have got so cheap a bargain. But as I was out

8. Portuguese coins.

of all fear of being ill treated under the protection of so great and good an Empress, the Ornament of Nature, the Darling of the World, the Delight of her Subjects, the Phoenix of the Creation; so I hoped my late master's apprehensions would appear to be groundless, for I already found my spirits to revive by the influence of her most august presence.

This was the sum of my speech, delivered with great improprieties and hesitation; the latter part was altogether framed in the style peculiar to that people, whereof I learned some phrases from Glumdalclitch, while she was carrying me to Court.

The Queen, giving great allowance for my defectiveness in speaking, was however surprised at so much wit and good sense in so diminutive an animal. She took me in her own hand, and carried me to the King, who was then retired to his cabinet.[9] His Majesty, a prince of much gravity, and austere countenance, not well observing my shape at first view, asked the Queen after a cold manner how long it was since she grew fond of a *splacknuck;* for such it seems he took me to be, as I lay upon my breast in her Majesty's right hand. But this princess, who hath an infinite deal of wit and humor, set me gently on my feet upon the scrutore,[1] and commanded me to give his Majesty an account of myself, which I did in a very few words; and Glumdalclitch, who attended at the cabinet door, and could not endure I should be out of her sight, being admitted, confirmed all that had passed from my arrival at her father's house.

The King, although he be as learned a person as any in his dominions, had been educated in the study of philosophy and particularly mathematics; yet when he observed my shape exactly, and saw me walk erect, before I began to speak, conceived I might be a piece of clockwork (which is in that country arrived to a very great perfection) contrived by some ingenious artist. But when he heard my voice, and found what I delivered to be regular and rational, he could not conceal his astonishment. He was by no means satisfied with the relation I gave him of the manner I came into his kingdom, but thought it a story concerted between Glumdalclitch and her father, who had taught me a set of words to make me sell at a higher price. Upon this imagination he put several other questions to me, and still received rational answers, no otherwise defective than by a foreign accent, and an imperfect knowledge in the language, with some rustic phrases which I had learned at the farmer's house, and did not suit the polite style of a court.

His Majesty sent for three great scholars who were then in their weekly waiting (according to the custom in that country). These gentlemen, after they had a while examined my shape with much nicety, were of different opinions concerning me. They all agreed that I could not be produced according to the regular laws of nature, because I was not framed with a capacity of preserving my life, either by swiftness, or climbing of trees, or digging holes in the earth. They observed by my teeth, which they viewed with great exactness, that I was a carnivorous animal; yet most quadrupeds being an overmatch for me, and field mice, with some others, too nimble, they could not imagine how I should be able to support myself, unless I fed upon snails and other insects; which they offered, by many learned arguments, to evince that I could not possibly do. One of them seemed to think that I might be an embryo, or abortive birth. But this opinion was rejected by the other two, who observed my limbs to be perfect and finished, and that I had lived several years, as it was manifested

9. Private apartment.

1. Writing desk.

from my beard, the stumps whereof they plainly discovered through a magnifying glass. They would not allow me to be a dwarf, because my littleness was beyond all degrees of comparison; for the Queen's favorite dwarf, the smallest ever known in that kingdom, was nearly thirty foot high. After much debate, they concluded unanimously that I was only *relplum scalcath,* which is interpreted literally, *lusus naturae;* a determination exactly agreeable to the modern philosophy of Europe, whose professors, disdaining the old evasion of *occult causes,* whereby the followers of Aristotle endeavor in vain to disguise their ignorance, have invented this wonderful solution of all difficulties, to the unspeakable advancement of human knowledge.[2]

After this decisive conclusion, I entreated to be heard a word or two. I applied myself to the King, and assured his Majesty that I came from a country which abounded with several millions of both sexes, and of my own stature, where the animals, trees, and houses were all in proportion, and where by consequence I might be as able to defend myself, and to find sustenance, as any of his Majesty's subjects could do here; which I took for a full answer to those gentlemen's arguments. To this they only replied with a smile of contempt, saying that the farmer had instructed me very well in my lesson. The King, who had a much better understanding, dismissing his learned men, sent for the farmer, who by good fortune was not yet gone out of town; having therefore first examined him privately, and then confronted him with me and the young girl, his Majesty began to think that what we told him might possibly be true. He desired the Queen to order that a particular care should be taken of me, and was of opinion that Glumdalclitch should still continue in her office of tending me, because he observed we had a great affection for each other. A convenient apartment was provided for her at Court; she had a sort of governess appointed to take care of her education, a maid to dress her, and two other servants for menial offices; but the care of me was wholly appropriated to herself. The Queen commanded her own cabinetmaker to contrive a box that might serve me for a bedchamber, after the model that Glumdalclitch and I should agree upon. This man was a most ingenious artist, and according to my directions, in three weeks finished for me a wooden chamber of sixteen foot square and twelve high, with sash windows, a door, and two closets, like a London bedchamber. The board that made the ceiling was to be lifted up and down by two hinges, to put in a bed ready furnished by her Majesty's upholsterer, which Glumdalclitch took out every day to air, made it with her own hands, and letting it down at night, locked up the roof over me. A nice[3] workman, who was famous for little curiosities, undertook to make me two chairs, with backs and frames, of a substance not unlike ivory, and two tables, with a cabinet to put my things in. The room was quilted on all sides, as well as the floor and the ceiling, to prevent any accident from the carelessness of those who carried me, and to break the force of a jolt when I went in a coach. I desired a lock for my door to prevent rats and mice from coming in: the smith, after several attempts, made the smallest that ever was seen among them, for I have known a larger at the gate of a gentleman's house in England. I made a shift[4] to keep the key in a pocket of my own, fearing Glumdalclitch might lose it. The Queen likewise ordered the thinnest silks that could be

2. Swift had contempt for both the medieval Schoolmen, who discussed "occult causes," the unknown causes of observable effects, and modern scientists, who, he believed, often concealed their ignorance by using equally meaningless terms. "*Lusus naturae*": one of nature's sports, or roughly, freaks.

3. Exact.

4. Contrived.

gotten, to make me clothes, not much thicker than an English blanket, very cumbersome till I was accustomed to them. They were after the fashion of the kingdom, partly resembling the Persian, and partly the Chinese, and are a very grave, decent habit.

The Queen became so fond of my company that she could not dine without me. I had a table placed upon the same at which her Majesty ate, just at her left elbow, and a chair to sit on. Glumdalclitch stood upon a stool on the floor, near my table, to assist and take care of me. I had an entire set of silver dishes and plates, and other necessaries, which, in proportion to those of the Queen, were not much bigger than what I have seen of the same kind in a London toyshop,[5] for the furniture of a baby-house: these my little nurse kept in her pocket in a silver box and gave me at meals as I wanted them, always cleaning them herself. No person dined with the Queen but the two Princesses Royal, the elder sixteen years old, and the younger at that time thirteen and a month. Her Majesty used to put a bit of meat upon one of my dishes, out of which I carved for myself; and her diversion was to see me eat in miniature. For the Queen (who had indeed but a weak stomach) took up at one mouthful as much as a dozen English farmers could eat at a meal, which to me was for some time a very nauseous sight. She would craunch the wing of a lark, bones and all, between her teeth, although it were nine times as large as that of a full-grown turkey; and put a bit of bread into her mouth as big as two twelve-penny loaves. She drank out of a golden cup, above a hogshead at a draught. Her knives were twice as long as a scythe set straight upon the handle. The spoons, forks, and other instruments were all in the same proportion. I remember when Glumdalclitch carried me out of curiosity to see some of the tables at Court, where ten or a dozen of these enormous knives and forks were lifted up together, I thought I had never till then beheld so terrible a sight.

It is the custom that every Wednesday (which, as I have before observed, was their Sabbath) the King and Queen, with the royal issue of both sexes, dine together in the apartment of his Majesty, to whom I was now become a favorite; and at these times my little chair and table were placed at his left hand, before one of the salt-cellars. This prince took a pleasure in conversing with me, inquiring into the manners, religion, laws, government, and learning of Europe; wherein I gave him the best account I was able. His apprehension was so clear, and his judgment so exact, that he made very wise reflections and observations upon all I said. But I confess that after I had been a little too copious in talking of my own beloved country, of our trade and wars by sea and land, of our schisms in religion and parties in the state, the prejudices of his education prevailed so far that he could not forbear taking me up in his right hand, and stroking me gently with the other, after an hearty fit of laughing, asked me whether I were a Whig or a Tory. Then turning to his first minister, who waited behind him with a white staff, near as tall as the mainmast of the *Royal Sovereign*,[6] he observed how contemptible a thing was human grandeur, which could be mimicked by such diminutive insects as I: "and yet," said he, "I dare engage, these creatures have their titles and distinctions of honor; they contrive little nests and burrows, that they call houses and cities; they make a figure in dress and equipage; they love, they fight, they dispute, they cheat, they betray." And thus he continued on, while my color

5. A shop for selling knickknacks.
6. One of the largest ships in the Royal Navy. At the English court the lord treasurer bore a "white staff" as the symbol of his office.

came and went several times with indignation to hear our noble country, the mistress of arts and arms, the scourge of France, the arbitress of Europe, the seat of virtue, piety, honor, and truth, the pride and envy of the world, so contemptuously treated.

But as I was not in a condition to resent injuries, so, upon mature thoughts, I began to doubt whether I were injured or no. For, after having been accustomed several months to the sight and converse of this people, and observed every object upon which I cast my eyes to be of proportionable magnitude, the horror I had first conceived from their bulk and aspect was so far worn off that if I had then beheld a company of English lords and ladies in their finery and birthday clothes,[7] acting their several parts in the most courtly manner of strutting and bowing and prating, to say the truth, I should have been strongly tempted to laugh as much at them as this King and his grandees did at me. Neither indeed could I forbear smiling at myself when the Queen used to place me upon her hand towards a looking glass, by which both our persons appeared before me in full view together; and there could be nothing more ridiculous than the comparison; so that I really began to imagine myself dwindled many degrees below my usual size.

Nothing angered and mortified me so much as the Queen's dwarf, who being of the lowest stature that was ever in that country (for I verily think he was not full thirty foot high) became so insolent at seeing a creature so much beneath him that he would always affect to swagger and look big as he passed by me in the Queen's antechamber, while I was standing on some table talking with the lords or ladies of the court; and he seldom failed of a smart word or two upon my littleness, against which I could only revenge myself by calling him brother, challenging him to wrestle, and such repartees as are usual in the mouths of Court pages. One day at dinner this malicious little cub was so nettled with something I had said to him that, raising himself upon the frame of Her Majesty's chair, he took me up by the middle, as I was sitting down, not thinking any harm, and let me drop into a large silver bowl of cream, and then ran away as fast as he could. I fell over head and ears, and if I had not been a good swimmer, it might have gone very hard with me; for Glumdalclitch in that instant happened to be at the other end of the room, and the Queen was in such a fright that she wanted presence of mind to assist me. But my little nurse ran to my relief, and took me out, after I had swallowed above a quart of cream. I was put to bed; however, I received no other damage than the loss of a suit of clothes, which was utterly spoiled. The dwarf was soundly whipped, and as further punishment, forced to drink up the bowl of cream into which he had thrown me; neither was he ever restored to favor: for soon after the Queen bestowed him to a lady of high quality, so that I saw him no more, to my very great satisfaction; for I could not tell to what extremity such a malicious urchin might have carried his resentment.

He had before served me a scurvy trick, which set the Queen a laughing, although at the same time she were heartily vexed, and would have immediately cashiered him, if I had not been so generous as to intercede. Her Majesty had taken a marrow bone upon her plate, and after knocking out the marrow, placed the bone again in the dish, erect as it stood before; the dwarf watching his opportunity, while Glumdalclitch was gone to the sideboard, mounted upon the stool she stood on to take care of me at meals, took me up in both

7. Courtiers dressed with special splendor on the monarch's birthday.

hands, and squeezing my legs together, wedged them into the marrow bone above my waist, where I stuck for some time, and made a very ridiculous figure. I believe it was near a minute before anyone knew what was become of me, for I thought it below me to cry out. But, as princes seldom get their meat hot, my legs were not scalded, only my stockings and breeches in a sad condition. The dwarf at my entreaty had no other punishment than a sound whipping.

I was frequently rallied by the Queen upon account of my fearfulness, and she used to ask me whether the people of my country were as great cowards as myself. The occasion was this. The kingdom is much pestered with flies in summer, and these odious insects, each of them as big as a Dunstable lark, hardly gave me any rest while I sat at dinner, with their continual humming and buzzing about my ears. They would sometimes alight upon my victuals, and leave their loathsome excrement or spawn behind, which to me was very visible, although not to the natives of that country, whose large optics were not so acute as mine in viewing smaller objects. Sometimes they would fix upon my nose or forehead, where they stung me to the quick, smelling very offensively; and I could easily trace that viscous matter, which our naturalists tell us enables those creatures to walk with their feet upwards upon a ceiling. I had much ado to defend myself against these detestable animals, and could not forbear starting when they came on my face. It was the common practice of the dwarf to catch a number of these insects in his hand, as schoolboys do among us, and let them out suddenly under my nose, on purpose to frighten me, and divert the Queen. My remedy was to cut them in pieces with my knife as they flew in the air, wherein my dexterity was much admired.

I remember one morning when Glumdalclitch had set me in my box upon a window, as she usually did in fair days to give me air (for I durst not venture to let the box be hung on a nail out of the window, as we do with cages in England), after I had lifted up one of my sashes, and sat down at my table to eat a piece of sweet cake for my breakfast, above twenty wasps, allured by the smell, came flying into the room, humming louder than the drones of as many bagpipes. Some of them seized my cake, and carried it piecemeal away; others flew about my head and face, confounding me with the noise, and putting me in the utmost terror of their stings. However, I had the courage to rise and draw my hanger, and attack them in the air. I dispatched four of them, but the rest got away, and I presently shut my window. These insects were as large as partridges; I took out their stings, found them an inch and a half long, and as sharp as needles. I carefully preserved them all, and having since shown them with some other curiosities in several parts of Europe, upon my return to England I gave three of them to Gresham College,[8] and kept the fourth for myself.

CHAPTER 4. *The country described. A proposal for correcting modern maps. The King's palace, and some account of the metropolis. The Author's way of traveling. The chief temple described.*

I now intend to give the reader a short description of this country, as far as I had traveled in it, which was not above two thousand miles round Lorbrulgrud the metropolis. For the Queen, whom I always attended, never went further when she accompanied the King in his progresses, and there stayed till his

8. The Royal Society, in its earliest years, met in Gresham College.

Majesty returned from viewing his frontiers. The whole extent of this prince's dominions reacheth about six thousand miles in length, and from three to five in breadth. From whence I cannot but conclude that our geographers of Europe are in a great error by supposing nothing but sea between Japan and California: for it was ever my opinion that there must be a balance of earth to counterpoise the great continent of Tartary; and therefore they ought to correct their maps and charts by joining this vast tract of land to the northwest parts of America, wherein I shall be ready to lend them my assistance.

The kingdom is a peninsula, terminated to the northeast by a ridge of mountains thirty miles high, which are altogether impassable by reason of the volcanoes upon the tops. Neither do the most learned know what sort of mortals inhabit beyond those mountains, or whether they be inhabited at all. On the three other sides it is bounded by the ocean. There is not one seaport in the whole kingdom; and those parts of the coasts into which the rivers issue are so full of pointed rocks, and the sea generally so rough, that there is no venturing with the smallest of their boats; so that these people are wholly excluded from any commerce with the rest of the world. But the large rivers are full of vessels, and abound with excellent fish, for they seldom get any from the sea, because the sea fish are of the same size with those in Europe, and consequently not worth catching; whereby it is manifest that nature, in the production of plants and animals of so extraordinary a bulk, is wholly confined to this continent, of which I leave the reasons to be determined by philosophers. However, now and then they take a whale that happens to be dashed against the rocks, which the common people feed on heartily. These whales I have known so large that a man could hardly carry one upon his shoulders; and sometimes for curiosity they are brought in hampers to Lorbrulgrud: I saw one of them in a dish at the King's table, which passed for a rarity, but I did not observe he was fond of it; for I think indeed the bigness disgusted him, although I have seen one somewhat larger in Greenland.

The country is well inhabited, for it contains fifty-one cities, near an hundred walled towns, and a great number of villages. To satisfy my curious reader, it may be sufficient to describe Lorbrulgrud. This city stands upon almost two equal parts on each side the river that passes through. It contains above eight thousand houses, and about six hundred thousand inhabitants. It is in length three *glonglungs* (which make about fifty-four English miles) and two and a half in breadth, as I measured it myself in the royal map made by the King's order, which was laid on the ground on purpose for me, and extended an hundred feet; I paced the diameter and circumference several times barefoot, and computing by the scale, measured it pretty exactly.

The King's palace is no regular edifice, but an heap of buildings about seven miles round: the chief rooms are generally two hundred and forty foot high, and broad and long in proportion. A coach was allowed to Glumdalclitch and me, wherein her governess frequently took her out to see the town, or go among the shops; and I was always of the party, carried in my box, although the girl at my own desire would often take me out, and hold me in her hand, that I might more conveniently view the houses and the people as we passed along the streets. I reckoned our coach to be about a square of Westminster Hall,[9] but not altogether so high; however, I cannot be very exact. One day

9. The ancient hall, now incorporated into the Houses of Parliament, where the law courts then sat. Swift presumably means the square of its breadth (just under sixty-eight feet).

the governess ordered our coachman to stop at several shops, where the beggars, watching their opportunity, crowded to the sides of the coach, and gave me the most horrible spectacles that ever an English eye beheld. There was a woman with a cancer in her breast, swelled to a monstrous size, full of holes, in two or three of which I could have easily crept, and covered my whole body. There was a fellow with a wen in his neck, larger than five woolpacks, and another with a couple of wooden legs, each about twenty foot high. But the most hateful sight of all was the lice crawling on their clothes. I could see distinctly the limbs of these vermin with my naked eye, much better than those of an European louse through a microscope, and their snouts with which they rooted like swine. They were the first I had ever beheld; and I should have been curious enough to dissect one of them if I had proper instruments (which I unluckily left behind me in the ship), although indeed the sight was so nauseous that it perfectly turned my stomach.

Besides the large box in which I was usually carried, the Queen ordered a smaller one to be made for me, of about twelve foot square and ten high, for the convenience of traveling, because the other was somewhat too large for Glumdalclitch's lap, and cumbersome in the coach; it was made by the same artist, whom I directed in the whole contrivance. This traveling closet was an exact square with a window in the middle of three of the squares, and each window was latticed with iron wire on the outside, to prevent accidents in long journeys. On the fourth side, which had no windows, two strong staples were fixed, through which the person that carried me, when I had a mind to be on horseback, put in a leathern belt, and buckled it about his waist. This was always the office of some grave trusty servant in whom I could confide, whether I attended the King and Queen in their progresses, or were disposed to see the gardens, or pay a visit to some great lady or minister of state in the court, when Glumdalclitch happened to be out of order: for I soon began to be known and esteemed among the greatest officers, I suppose more upon account of their Majesties' favor than any merit of my own. In journeys, when I was weary of the coach, a servant on horseback would buckle my box, and place it on a cushion before him; and there I had a full prospect of the country on three sides from my three windows. I had in this closet a field bed[1] and a hammock hung from the ceiling, two chairs and a table, neatly screwed to the floor to prevent being tossed about by the agitation of the horse or the coach. And having been long used to sea voyages, those motions, although sometimes very violent, did not much discompose me.

When I had a mind to see the town, it was always in my traveling closet, which Glumdalclitch held in her lap in a kind of open sedan, after the fashion of the country, borne by four men, and attended by two others in the Queen's livery. The people, who had often heard of me, were very curious to crowd about the sedan; and the girl was complaisant enough to make the bearers stop, and to take me in her hand that I might be more conveniently seen.

I was very desirous to see the chief temple, and particularly the tower belonging to it, which is reckoned the highest in the kingdom. Accordingly one day my nurse carried me thither, but I may truly say I came back disappointed; for the height is not above three thousand foot, reckoning from the ground to the highest pinnacle top; which, allowing for the difference between the size of those people and us in Europe, is no great matter for admiration,

1. Folding bed, cot.

nor at all equal in proportion (if I rightly remember) to Salisbury steeple.[2] But, not to detract from a nation to which during my life I shall acknowledge myself extremely obliged, it must be allowed that whatever this famous tower wants in height is amply made up in beauty and strength. For the walls are near an hundred foot thick, built of hewn stone, whereof each is about forty foot square, and adorned on all sides with statues of gods and emperors cut in marble larger than the life, placed in their several niches. I measured a little finger which had fallen down from one of these statues, and lay unperceived among some rubbish, and found it exactly four foot and an inch in length. Glumdalclitch wrapped it up in a handkerchief, and carried it home in her pocket to keep among other trinkets, of which the girl was very fond, as children at her age usually are.

The King's kitchen is indeed a noble building, vaulted at top, and about six hundred foot high. The great oven is not so wide by ten paces as the cupola at St. Paul's:[3] for I measured the latter on purpose after my return. But if I should describe the kitchen grate, the prodigious pots and kettles, the joints of meat turning on the spits, with many other particulars, perhaps I should be hardly believed; at least a severe critic would be apt to think I enlarged a little, as travelers are often suspected to do. To avoid which censure, I fear I have run too much into the other extreme, and that if this treatise should happen to be translated into the language of Brobdingnag (which is the general name of that kingdom) and transmitted thither, the King and his people would have reason to complain that I had done them an injury by a false and diminutive representation.

His Majesty seldom keeps above six hundred horses in his stables: they are generally from fifty-four to sixty foot high. But when he goes abroad on solemn days, he is attended for state by a militia guard of five hundred horse, which indeed I thought was the most splendid sight that could be ever beheld, till I saw part of his army in battalia,[4] whereof I shall find another occasion to speak.

CHAPTER 5. *Several adventures that happened to the Author. The execution of a criminal. The Author shows his skill in navigation.*

I should have lived happy enough in that country if my littleness had not exposed me to several ridiculous and troublesome accidents, some of which I shall venture to relate. Glumdalclitch often carried me into the gardens of the court in my smaller box, and would sometimes take me out of it and hold me in her hand, or set me down to walk. I remember, before the dwarf left the Queen, he followed us one day into those gardens; and my nurse having set me down, he and I being close together near some dwarf apple trees, I must needs show my wit by a silly allusion between him and the trees, which happens to hold in their language as it doth in ours. Whereupon, the malicious rogue watching his opportunity, when I was walking under one of them, shook it directly over my head, by which a dozen apples, each of them near as large as a Bristol barrel, came tumbling about my ears; one of them hit me on the back as I chanced to stoop, and knocked me down flat on my face, but I

2. One of the most beautiful Gothic steeples in England is that of Salisbury Cathedral, 404 feet high.

3. The cupola of St. Paul's Cathedral in London is 108 feet in diameter.

4. Battle array.

received no other hurt; and the dwarf was pardoned at my desire, because I had given the provocation.

Another day Glumdalclitch left me on a smooth grassplot to divert myself while she walked at some distance with her governess. In the meantime there suddenly fell such a violent shower of hail that I was immediately by the force of it struck to the ground: and when I was down, the hailstones gave me such cruel bangs all over the body as if I had been pelted with tennis balls;[5] however I made a shift to creep on all four, and shelter myself by lying on my face on the lee side of a border of lemon thyme, but so bruised from head to foot that I could not go abroad in ten days. Neither is this at all to be wondered at, because nature in that country observing the same proportion through all her operations, a hailstone is near eighteen hundred times as large as one in Europe; which I can assert upon experience, having been so curious to weigh and measure them.

But a more dangerous accident happened to me in the same garden when my little nurse, believing she had put me in a secure place, which I often entreated her to do that I might enjoy my own thoughts, and having left my box at home to avoid the trouble of carrying it, went to another part of the garden with her governess and some ladies of her acquaintance. While she was absent and out of hearing, a small white spaniel belonging to one of the chief gardeners, having got by accident into the garden, happened to range near the place where I lay. The dog following the scent, came directly up, and taking me in his mouth, ran straight to his master, wagging his tail, and set me gently on the ground. By good fortune he had been so well taught that I was carried between his teeth without the least hurt, or even tearing my clothes. But the poor gardener, who knew me well, and had a great kindness for me, was in a terrible fright. He gently took me up in both his hands, and asked me how I did; but I was so amazed and out of breath that I could not speak a word. In a few minutes I came to myself, and he carried me safe to my little nurse, who by this time had returned to the place where she left me, and was in cruel agonies when I did not appear nor answer when she called; she severely reprimanded the gardener on account of his dog. But the thing was hushed up and never known at court; for the girl was afraid of the Queen's anger; and truly, as to myself, I thought it would not be for my reputation that such a story should go about.

This accident absolutely determined Glumdalclitch never to trust me abroad for the future out of her sight. I had been long afraid of this resolution, and therefore concealed from her some little unlucky adventures that happened in those times when I was left by myself. Once a kite hovering over the garden made a stoop[6] at me, and if I had not resolutely drawn my hanger, and run under a thick espalier, he would have certainly carried me away in his talons. Another time walking to the top of a fresh molehill, I fell to my neck in the hole through which that animal had cast up the earth, and coined some lie, not worth remembering, to excuse myself for spoiling my clothes. I likewise broke my right shin against the shell of a snail, which I happened to stumble over, as I was walking alone, and thinking on poor England.

I cannot tell whether I were more pleased or mortified to observe in those solitary walks that the smaller birds did not appear to be at all afraid of me;

5. Eighteenth-century tennis balls, unlike the modern, were very hard.

6. Swoop. "Kite": a bird of prey.

but would hop about within a yard distance, looking for worms and other food with as much indifference and security as if no creature at all were near them. I remember a thrush had the confidence to snatch out of my hand with his bill a piece of cake that Glumdalclitch had just given me for my breakfast. When I attempted to catch any of these birds, they would boldly turn against me, endeavoring to pick my fingers, which I durst not venture within their reach; and then they would hop back unconcerned to hunt for worms or snails, as they did before. But one day I took a thick cudgel, and threw it with all my strength so luckily at a linnet that I knocked him down, and seizing him by the neck with both my hands, ran with him in triumph to my nurse. However, the bird, who had only been stunned, recovering himself, gave me so many boxes with his wings on both sides of my head and body, though I held him at arm's length, and was out of the reach of his claws, that I was twenty times thinking to let him go. But I was soon relieved by one of our servants, who wrung off the bird's neck, and I had him next day for dinner, by the Queen's command. This linnet, as near as I can remember, seemed to be somewhat larger than an English swan.

The Maids of Honor often invited Glumdalclitch to their apartments, and desired she would bring me along with her, on purpose to have the pleasure of seeing and touching me. They would often strip me naked from top to toe and lay me at full length in their bosoms; wherewith I was much disgusted, because, to say the truth, a very offensive smell came from their skins, which I do not mention or intend to the disadvantage of those excellent ladies, for whom I have all manner of respect; but I conceive that my sense was more acute in proportion to my littleness, and that those illustrious persons were no more disagreeable to their lovers, or to each other, than people of the same quality are with us in England. And, after all, I found their natural smell was much more supportable than when they used perfumes, under which I immediately swooned away. I cannot forget that an intimate friend of mine in Lilliput took the freedom in a warm day, when I had used a good deal of exercise, to complain of a strong smell about me, although I am as little faulty that way as most of my sex: but I suppose his faculty of smelling was as nice with regard to me as mine was to that of this people. Upon this point, I cannot forbear doing justice to the Queen, my mistress, and Glumdalclitch, my nurse, whose persons were as sweet as those of any lady in England.

That which gave me most uneasiness among these Maids of Honor, when my nurse carried me to visit them, was to see them use me without any manner of ceremony, like a creature who had no sort of consequence. For they would strip themselves to the skin and put on their smocks in my presence, while I was placed on their toilet[7] directly before their naked bodies; which, I am sure, to me was very far from being a tempting sight, or from giving me any other emotions than those of horror and disgust. Their skins appeared so coarse and uneven, so variously colored, when I saw them near, with a mole here and there as broad as a trencher, and hairs hanging from it thicker than packthreads, to say nothing further concerning the rest of their persons. Neither did they at all scruple, while I was by, to discharge what they had drunk, to the quantity of at least two hogsheads, in a vessel that held above three tuns. The handsomest among these Maids of Honor, a pleasant frolicsome girl of sixteen, would sometimes set me astride upon one of her nipples, with many

7. Toilet table.

other tricks, wherein the reader will excuse me for not being over particular. But I was so much displeased that I entreated Glumdalclitch to contrive some excuse for not seeing that young lady any more.

One day a young gentleman, who was nephew to my nurse's governess, came and pressed them both to see an execution. It was of a man who had murdered one of that gentleman's intimate acquaintance. Glumdalclitch was prevailed on to be of the company, very much against her inclination, for she was naturally tender-hearted: and as for myself, although I abhorred such kind of spectacles, yet my curiosity tempted me to see something that I thought must be extraordinary. The malefactor was fixed in a chair upon a scaffold erected for the purpose, and his head cut off at a blow with a sword of about forty foot long. The veins and arteries spouted up such a prodigious quantity of blood, and so high in the air, that the great *jet d'eau* at Versailles was not equal for the time it lasted; and the head, when it fell on the scaffold floor, gave such a bounce,[8] as made me start, although I were at least half an English mile distant.

The Queen, who often used to hear me talk of my sea voyages, and took all occasions to divert me when I was melancholy, asked me whether I understood how to handle a sail or an oar, and whether a little exercise of rowing might not be convenient for my health. I answered that I understood both very well. For although my proper employment had been to be surgeon or doctor to the ship, yet often, upon a pinch, I was forced to work like a common mariner. But I could not see how this could be done in their country, where the smallest wherry was equal to a first-rate man-of-war among us, and such a boat as I could manage would never live in any of their rivers. Her Majesty said, if I would contrive a boat, her own joiner should make it, and she would provide a place for me to sail in. The fellow was an ingenious workman and, by my instructions, in ten days finished a pleasure boat with all its tackling, able conveniently to hold eight Europeans. When it was finished, the Queen was so delighted that she ran with it in her lap to the King, who ordered it to be put in a cistern full of water, with me in it, by way of trial; where I could not manage my two sculls, or little oars, for want of room. But the Queen had before contrived another project. She ordered the joiner to make a wooden trough of three hundred foot long, fifty broad, and eight deep; which being well pitched to prevent leaking, was placed on the floor along the wall in an outer room of the palace. It had a cock near the bottom to let out the water when it began to grow stale, and two servants could easily fill it in half an hour. Here I often used to row for my own diversion, as well as that of the Queen and her ladies, who thought themselves well entertained with my skill and agility. Sometimes I would put up my sail, and then my business was only to steer, while the ladies gave me a gale with their fans; and when they were weary, some of the pages would blow my sail forward with their breath, while I showed my art by steering starboard or larboard as I pleased. When I had done, Glumdalclitch always carried my boat into her closet, and hung it on a nail to dry.

In this exercise I once met an accident which had like to have cost me my life. For one of the pages having put my boat into the trough, the governess who attended Glumdalclitch very officiously lifted me up to place me in the boat; but I happened to slip through her fingers, and should have infallibly

8. A sudden noise. "*Jet d'eau* at Versailles": this fountain rose over forty feet in the air.

fallen down forty foot upon the floor, if by the luckiest chance in the world I had not been stopped by a corking-pin that stuck in the good gentlewoman's stomacher;[9] the head of the pin passed between my shirt and the waistband of my breeches, and thus I was held by the middle in the air until Glumdalclitch ran to my relief.

Another time, one of the servants, whose office it was to fill my trough every third day with fresh water, was so careless to let a huge frog (not perceiving it) slip out of his pail. The frog lay concealed till I was put into my boat, but then seeing a resting place, climbed up, and made it lean so much on one side that I was forced to balance it with all my weight on the other, to prevent overturning. When the frog was got in, it hopped at once half the length of the boat, and then over my head, backwards and forwards, daubing my face and clothes with its odious slime. The largeness of its features made it appear the most deformed animal that can be conceived. However, I desired Glumdalclitch to let me deal with it alone. I banged it a good while with one of my sculls, and at last forced it to leap out of the boat.

But the greatest danger I ever underwent in that kingdom was from a monkey, who belonged to one of the clerks of the kitchen. Glumdalclitch had locked me up in her closet, while she went somewhere upon business or a visit. The weather being very warm, the closet window was left open, as well as the windows in the door of my bigger box, in which I usually lived, because of its largeness and conveniency. As I sat quietly meditating at my table, I heard something bounce in at the closet window, and skip about from one side to the other, whereat, although I was much alarmed, yet I ventured to look out, but stirred not from my seat; and then I saw this frolicsome animal, frisking and leaping up and down, till at last he came to my box, which he seemed to view with great pleasure and curiosity, peeping in at the door and every window. I retreated to the farther corner of my room, or box, but the monkey looking in at every side, put me into such a fright that I wanted presence of mind to conceal myself under the bed, as I might easily have done. After some time spent in peeping, grinning, and chattering, he at last espied me, and reaching one of his paws in at the door, as a cat does when she plays with a mouse, although I often shifted place to avoid him, he at length seized the lappet of my coat (which, being made of that country cloth, was very thick and strong) and dragged me out. He took me up in his right forefoot, and held me as a nurse does a child she is going to suckle, just as I have seen the same sort of creature do with a kitten in Europe: and when I offered to struggle, he squeezed me so hard that I thought it more prudent to submit. I have good reason to believe that he took me for a young one of his own species, by his often stroking my face very gently with his other paw. In these diversions he was interrupted by a noise at the closet door, as if somebody were opening it, whereupon he suddenly leaped up to the window at which he had come in, and thence upon the leads and gutters, walking upon three legs, and holding me in the fourth, till he clambered up to a roof that was next to ours. I heard Glumdalclitch give a shriek at the moment he was carrying me out. The poor girl was almost distracted: that quarter of the palace was all in an uproar; the servants ran for ladders; the monkey was seen by hundreds in the court, sitting

9. An ornamental covering for the front and upper part of the body. "Officiously": kindly, dutifully. "Corking-pin": a pin of the largest size.

upon the ridge of a building, holding me like a baby in one of his forepaws and feeding me with the other, by cramming into my mouth some victuals he had squeezed out of the bag on one side of his chaps, and patting me when I would not eat; whereat many of the rabble below could not forebear laughing; neither do I think they justly ought to be blamed, for without question the sight was ridiculous enough to everybody but myself. Some of the people threw up stones, hoping to drive the monkey down; but this was strictly forbidden, or else very probably my brains had been dashed out.

The ladders were now applied, and mounted by several men; which the monkey observing, and finding himself almost encompassed, not being able to make speed enough with his three legs, let me drop on a ridge tile, and made his escape. Here I sat for some time three hundred yards from the ground, expecting every moment to be blown down by the wind, or to fall by my own giddiness, and come tumbling over and over from the ridge to the eaves. But an honest lad, one of my nurse's footmen, climbed up, and putting me into his breeches pocket, brought me down safe.

I was almost choked with the filthy stuff the monkey had crammed down my throat; but my dear little nurse picked it out of my mouth with a small needle, and then I fell a vomiting, which gave me great relief. Yet I was so weak and bruised in the sides with the squeezes given me by this odious animal that I was forced to keep my bed a fortnight. The King, Queen, and all the Court sent every day to inquire after my health, and her Majesty made me several visits during my sickness. The monkey was killed, and an order made that no such animal should be kept about the palace.

When I attended the King after my recovery, to return him thanks for his favors, he was pleased to rally me a good deal upon this adventure. He asked me what my thoughts and speculations were while I lay in the monkey's paw, how I liked the victuals he gave me, his manner of feeding, and whether the fresh air on the roof had sharpened my stomach. He desired to know what I would have done upon such an occasion in my own country. I told his Majesty that in Europe we had no monkeys, except such as were brought for curiosities from other places, and so small that I could deal with a dozen of them together, if they presumed to attack me. And as for that monstrous animal with whom I was so lately engaged (it was indeed as large as an elephant), if my fears had suffered me to think so far as to make use of my hanger (looking fiercely and clapping my hand upon the hilt as I spoke) when he poked his paw into my chamber, perhaps I should have given him such a wound as would have made him glad to withdraw it with more haste than he put it in. This I delivered in a firm tone, like a person who was jealous lest his courage should be called in question. However, my speech produced nothing else besides a loud laughter, which all the respect due to his Majesty from those about him could not make them contain. This made me reflect how vain an attempt it is for a man to endeavor doing himself honor among those who are out of all degree of equality or comparison with him. And yet I have seen the moral of my own behavior very frequent in England since my return, where a little contemptible varlet, without the least title to birth, person, wit, or common sense, shall presume to look with importance, and put himself upon a foot with the greatest persons of the kingdom.

I was every day furnishing the court with some ridiculous story; and Glumdalclitch, although she loved me to excess, yet was arch enough to inform the Queen whenever I committed any folly that she thought would be diverting to her Majesty. The girl, who had been out of order,[1] was carried by her governess to take the air about an hour's distance, or thirty miles from town. They alighted out of the coach near a small footpath in a field, and Glumdalclitch setting down my traveling box, I went out of it to walk. There was a cow dung in the patch, and I must needs try my activity by attempting to leap over it. I took a run, but unfortunately jumped short, and found myself just in the middle up to my knees. I waded through with some difficulty, and one of the footmen wiped me as clean as he could with his handkerchief; for I was filthily bemired, and my nurse confined me to my box till we returned home, where the Queen was soon informed of what had passed and the footmen spread it about the Court, so that all the mirth, for some days, was at my expense.

CHAPTER 6. *Several contrivances of the Author to please the King and Queen. He shows his skill in music. The King inquires into the state of Europe, which the Author relates to him. The King's observations thereon.*

I used to attend the King's levee once or twice a week, and had often seen him under the barber's hand, which indeed was at first very terrible to behold. For the razor was almost twice as long as an ordinary scythe. His Majesty, according to the custom of the country, was only shaved twice a week. I once prevailed on the barber to give me some of the suds or lather, out of which I picked forty or fifty of the strongest stumps of hair. I then took a piece of fine wood, and cut it like the back of a comb, making several holes in it at equal distance with as small a needle as I could get from Glumdalclitch. I fixed in the stumps so artificially,[2] scraping and sloping them with my knife towards the points, that I made a very tolerable comb; which was a seasonable supply, my own being so much broken in the teeth that it was almost useless; neither did I know any artist in that country so nice and exact as would undertake to make me another.

And this puts me in mind of an amusement wherein I spent many of my leisure hours. I desired the Queen's woman to save for me the combings of her Majesty's hair, whereof in time I got a good quantity; and consulting with my friend the cabinetmaker, who had received general orders to do little jobs for me, I directed him to make two chair frames, no larger than those I had in my box, and then to bore little holes with a fine awl round those parts where I designed the backs and seats; through these holes I wove the strongest hairs I could pick out, just after the manner of cane chairs in England. When they were finished, I made a present of them to her Majesty, who kept them in her cabinet, and used to show them for curiosities, as indeed they were the wonder of every one that beheld them. The Queen would have made me sit upon one of these chairs, but I absolutely refused to obey her, protesting I would rather die a thousand deaths than place a dishonorable part of my body on those precious hairs that once adorned her Majesty's head. Of these hairs (as I had always a mechanical genius) I likewise made a neat little purse above five foot long, with her Majesty's name deciphered in gold letters, which I gave to Glumdalclitch by the Queen's consent. To say the truth, it was more for show than use, being not of strength to bear the weight of the larger coins; and therefore she kept nothing in it but some little toys[3] that girls are fond of.

1. Not feeling well.
2. Skillfully.
3. Trifles.

The King, who delighted in music, had frequent consorts[4] at court, to which I was sometimes carried, and set in my box on a table to hear them; but the noise was so great that I could hardly distinguish the tunes. I am confident that all the drums and trumpets of a royal army, beating and sounding together just at your ears, could not equal it. My practice was to have my box removed from the places where the performers sat, as far as I could, then to shut the doors and windows of it, and draw the window curtains, after which I found their music not disagreeable.

I had learned in my youth to play a little upon the spinet. Glumdalclitch kept one in her chamber, and a master attended twice a week to teach her: I call it a spinet, because it somewhat resembled that instrument, and was played upon in the same manner. A fancy came into my head that I would entertain the King and Queen with an English tune upon this instrument. But this appeared extremely difficult: for the spinet was near sixty foot long, each key being almost a foot wide; so that, with my arms extended, I could not reach to above five keys, and to press them down required a good smart stroke with my fist, which would be too great a labor and to no purpose. The method I contrived was this: I prepared two round sticks about the bigness of common cudgels; they were thicker at one end than the other, and I covered the thicker ends with a piece of a mouse's skin, that by rapping on them I might neither damage the tops of the keys, nor interrupt the sound. Before the spinet a bench was placed, about four foot below the keys, and I was put upon the bench. I ran sideling upon it that way and this, as fast as I could, banging the proper keys with my two sticks; and made a shift to play a jig, to the great satisfaction of both their Majesties: but it was the most violent exercise I ever underwent, and yet I could not strike above sixteen keys, nor, consequently, play the bass and treble together, as other artists do; which was a great disadvantage to my performance.

The King, who, as I before observed, was a prince of excellent understanding, would frequently order that I should be brought in my box and set upon the table in his closet. He would then command me to bring one of my chairs out of the box, and sit down within three yards distance upon the top of the cabinet, which brought me almost to a level with his face. In this manner I had several conversations with him. I one day took the freedom to tell his Majesty that the contempt he discovered towards Europe, and the rest of the world, did not seem answerable to those excellent qualities of mind that he was master of. That reason did not extend itself with the bulk of the body: on the contrary, we observed in our country that the tallest persons were usually least provided with it. That among other animals, bees and ants had the reputation of more industry, art, and sagacity than many of the larger kinds; and that, as inconsiderable as he took me to be, I hoped I might live to do his Majesty some signal service. The King heard me with attention, and began to conceive a much better opinion of me than he had before. He desired I would give him as exact an account of the government of England as I possibly could; because, as fond as princes commonly are of their own customs (for so he conjectured of other monarchs, by my former discourses), he should be glad to hear of anything that might deserve imitation.

Imagine with thyself, courteous reader, how often I then wished for the tongue of Demosthenes or Cicero,[5] that might have enabled me to celebrate the praise of my own dear native country in a style equal to its merits and felicity.

4. Concerts.

5. Great orators of Athens and Rome, respectively.

I began my discourse by informing his Majesty that our dominions consisted of two islands, which composed three mighty kingdoms under one sovereign, beside our plantations in America. I dwelt long upon the fertility of our soil, and the temperature of our climate. I then spoke at large upon the constitution of an English Parliament, partly made up of an illustrious body called the House of Peers,[6] persons of the noblest blood, and of the most ancient and ample patrimonies. I described that extraordinary care always taken of their education in arts and arms, to qualify them for being counselors born to the king and kingdom; to have a share in the legislature, to be members of the highest Court of Judicature, from whence there could be no appeal; and to be champions always ready for the defense of their prince and country, by their valor, conduct, and fidelity. That these were the ornament and bulwark of the kingdom, worthy followers of their most renowned ancestors, whose honor had been the reward of their virtue, from which their posterity were never once known to degenerate. To these were joined several holy persons, as part of that assembly, under the title of Bishops, whose peculiar business it is to take care of religion, and of those who instruct the people therein. These were searched and sought out through the whole nation, by the prince and his wisest counselors, among such of the priesthood as were most deservedly distinguished by the sanctity of their lives and the depth of their erudition, who were indeed the spiritual fathers of the clergy and the people.

That the other part of the Parliament consisted of an assembly called the House of Commons, who were all principal gentlemen, freely picked and culled out by the people themselves, for their great abilities and love of their country, to represent the wisdom of the whole nation. And these two bodies make up the most august assembly in Europe, to whom, in conjunction with the prince, the whole legislature is committed.

I then descended to the Courts of Justice, over which the Judges, those venerable sages and interpreters of the law, presided, for determining the disputed rights and properties of men, as well as for the punishment of vice, and protection of innocence. I mentioned the prudent management of our treasury, the valor and achievements of our forces by sea and land. I computed the number of our people, by reckoning how many millions there might be of each religious sect, or political party among us. I did not omit even our sports and pastimes, or any other particular which I thought might redound to the honor of my country. And I finished all with a brief historical account of affairs and events in England for about an hundred years past.

This conversation was not ended under five audiences, each of several hours, and the King heard the whole with great attention, frequently taking notes of what I spoke, as well as memorandums of several questions he intended to ask me.

When I had put an end to these long discourses, his Majesty in a sixth audience consulting his notes, proposed many doubts, queries, and objections, upon every article. He asked what methods were used to cultivate the minds and bodies of our young nobility, and in what kind of business they commonly spent the first and teachable part of their lives. What course was taken to supply that assembly when any noble family became extinct. What qualifications were necessary in those who were to be created new lords. Whether the humor[7] of the prince, a sum of money to a Court lady or a prime minister, or

6. The House of Lords. "Temperature": temperateness.

7. Whim.

a design of strengthening a party opposite to the public interest, ever happened to be motives in those advancements. What share of knowledge these lords had in the laws of their country, and how they came by it, so as to enable them to decide the properties of their fellow subjects in the last resort. Whether they were always so free from avarice, partialities, or want that a bribe or some other sinister view could have no place among them. Whether those holy lords I spoke of were constantly promoted to that rank upon account of their knowledge in religious matters, and the sanctity of their lives; had never been compliers with the times while they were common priests, or slavish prostitute chaplains to some nobleman, whose opinions they continued servilely to follow after they were admitted into that assembly.

He then desired to know what arts were practiced in electing those whom I called Commoners. Whether a stranger with a strong purse might not influence the vulgar voters to choose him before their own landlord or the most considerable gentleman in the neighborhood. How it came to pass that people were so violently bent upon getting into this assembly, which I allowed to be a great trouble and expense, often to the ruin of their families, without any salary or pension: because this appeared such an exalted strain of virtue and public spirit that his Majesty seemed to doubt it might possibly not be always sincere; and he desired to know whether such zealous gentlemen could have any views of refunding themselves for the charges and trouble they were at, by sacrificing the public good to the designs of a weak and vicious prince in conjunction with a corrupted ministry. He multiplied his questions, and sifted me thoroughly upon every part of this head, proposing numberless inquiries and objections, which I think it not prudent or convenient to repeat.

Upon what I said in relation to our Courts of Justice, his Majesty desired to be satisfied in several points: and this I was the better able to do, having been formerly almost ruined by a long suit in chancery, which was decreed for me with costs. He asked what time was usually spent in determining between right and wrong, and what degree of expense. Whether advocates and orators had liberty to plead in causes manifestly known to be unjust, vexatious, or oppressive. Whether party in religion or politics were observed to be of any weight in the scale of justice. Whether those pleading orators were persons educated in the general knowledge of equity, or only in provincial, national, and other local customs. Whether they or their judges had any part in penning those laws which they assumed the liberty of interpreting and glossing upon at their pleasure. Whether they had ever at different times pleaded for and against the same cause, and cited precedents to prove contrary opinions. Whether they were a rich or a poor corporation. Whether they received any pecuniary reward for pleading or delivering their opinions. And particularly whether they were ever admitted as members in the lower senate.

He fell next upon the management of our treasury, and said he thought my memory had failed me, because I computed our taxes at about five or six millions a year, and when I came to mention the issues,[8] he found they sometimes amounted to more than double, for the notes he had taken were very particular in this point; because he hoped, as he told me, that the knowledge of our conduct might be useful to him, and he could not be deceived in his calculations. But if what I told him were true, he was still at a loss how a kingdom could run out of its estate like a private person. He asked me, who

8. Expenditures.

were our creditors? and where we should find money to pay them? He wondered to hear me talk of such chargeable and extensive wars; that certainly we must be a quarrelsome people, or live among very bad neighbors, and that our generals must needs be richer than our kings.[9] He asked what business we had out of our own islands, unless upon the score of trade or treaty or to defend the coasts with our fleet. Above all, he was amazed to hear me talk of a mercenary standing army[1] in the midst of peace, and among a free people. He said if we were governed by our own consent in the persons of our representatives, he could not imagine of whom we were afraid, or against whom we were to fight; and would hear my opinion whether a private man's house might not better be defended by himself, his children, and family, than by half a dozen rascals picked up at a venture[2] in the streets for small wages, who might get an hundred times more by cutting their throats.

He laughed at my odd kind of arithmetic (as he was pleased to call it) in reckoning the numbers of our people by a computation drawn from the several sects among us in religion and politics. He said he knew no reason why those who entertain opinions prejudicial to the public should be obliged to change, or should not be obliged to conceal them. And as it was tyranny in any government to require the first, so it was weakness not to enforce the second: for a man may be allowed to keep poisons in his closet, but not to vend them about for cordials.[3]

He observed that among the diversions of our nobility and gentry I had mentioned gaming. He desired to know at what age this entertainment was usually taken up, and when it was laid down; how much of their time it employed; whether it ever went so high as to affect their fortunes; whether mean, vicious people, by their dexterity in that art, might not arrive at great riches, and sometimes keep our very nobles in dependence, as well as habituate them to vile companions, wholly take them from the improvement of their minds, and force them, by the losses they received, to learn and practice that infamous dexterity upon others.

He was perfectly astonished with the historical account I gave him of our affairs during the last century, protesting it was only an heap of conspiracies, rebellions, murders, massacres, revolutions, banishments, the very worst effects that avarice, faction, hypocrisy, perfidiousness, cruelty, rage, madness, hatred, envy, lust, malice, or ambition could produce.

His Majesty in another audience was at the pains to recapitulate the sum of all I had spoken; compared the questions he made with the answers I had given; then taking me into his hands, and stroking me gently, delivered himself in these words, which I shall never forget, nor the manner he spoke them in. "My little friend Grildrig, you have made a most admirable panegyric upon your country. You have clearly proved that ignorance, idleness, and vice are the proper ingredients for qualifying a legislator. That laws are best explained, interpreted, and applied by those whose interests and abilities lie in perverting, confounding, and eluding them. I observe among you some lines of an institution which in its original might have been tolerable; but these half erased,

9. An allusion to the enormous fortune gained by the duke of Marlborough, formerly captain-general of the army, whom Swift detested.

1. Since the declaration of the Bill of Rights (1689), a standing army without authorization by Parliament had been illegal. Swift and the Tories in general were vigilant in their opposition to such an army.

2. By chance.

3. Medicines to stimulate the heart, or, equally commonly, liqueurs.

and the rest wholly blurred and blotted by corruptions. It doth not appear from all you have said how any one virtue is required towards the procurement of any one station among you; much less that men are ennobled on account of their virtue, that priests are advanced for their piety or learning, soldiers for their conduct or valor, judges for their integrity, senators for the love of their country, or counselors for their wisdom. As for yourself," continued the King, "who have spent the greatest part of your life in traveling, I am well disposed to hope you may hitherto have escaped many vices of your country. But by what I have gathered from your own relation, and the answers I have with much pains wringed and extorted from you, I cannot but conclude the bulk of your natives to be the most pernicious race of little odious vermin that nature ever suffered to crawl upon the surface of the earth."

Chapter 7. *The Author's love of his country. He makes a proposal of much advantage to the King; which is rejected. The King's great ignorance in politics. The learning of that country very imperfect and confined. Their laws, and military affairs, and parties in the State.*

Nothing but an extreme love of truth could have hindered me from concealing this part of my story. It was in vain to discover my resentments, which were always turned into ridicule: and I was forced to rest with patience while my noble and most beloved country was so injuriously treated. I am heartily sorry as any of my readers can possibly be that such an occasion was given, but this prince happened to be so curious and inquisitive upon every particular that it could not consist either with gratitude or good manners to refuse giving him what satisfaction I was able. Yet thus much I may be allowed to say in my own vindication: that I artfully eluded many of his questions, and gave to every point a more favorable turn by many degrees than the strictness of truth would allow. For I have always borne that laudable partiality to my own country, which Dionysius Halicarnassensis[4] with so much justice recommends to an historian. I would hide the frailties and deformities of my political mother, and place her virtues and beauties in the most advantageous light. This was my sincere endeavor in those many discourses I had with that mighty monarch, although it unfortunately failed of success.

But great allowances should be given to a King who lives wholly secluded from the rest of the world, and must therefore be altogether unacquainted with the manners and customs that most prevail in other nations: the want of which knowledge will ever produce many *prejudices,* and a certain *narrowness of thinking,* from which we and the politer countries of Europe are wholly exempted. And it would be hard indeed if so remote a prince's notions of virtue and vice were to be offered as a standard for all mankind.

To confirm what I have now said, and further to show the miserable effects of a *confined education,* I shall here insert a passage which will hardly obtain belief. In hopes to ingratiate myself farther into his Majesty's favor, I told him of an invention discovered between three and four hundred years ago, to make a certain powder, into an heap of which the smallest spark of fire falling would kindle the whole in a moment, although it were as big as a mountain, and make it all fly up in the air together, with a noise and agitation greater than

4. A Greek rhetorician and historian, who flourished ca. 25 B.C.E. His history of Rome was written to reconcile the Greeks to their Roman masters.

thunder. That a proper quantity of this powder rammed into an hollow tube of brass or iron, according to its bigness, would drive a ball of iron or lead with such violence and speed as nothing was able to sustain its force. That the largest balls thus discharged would not only destroy whole ranks of an army at once, but batter the strongest walls to the ground; sink down ships with a thousand men in each, to the bottom of the sea; and, when linked together by a chain, would cut through masts and rigging; divide hundreds of bodies in the middle, and lay all waste before them. That we often put this powder into large hollow balls of iron, and discharged them by an engine into some city we were besieging; which would rip up the pavements, tear the houses to pieces, burst and throw splinters on every side, dashing out the brains of all who came near. That I knew the ingredients very well, which were cheap and common; I understood the manner of compounding them, and could direct his workmen how to make those tubes of a size proportionable to all other things in his Majesty's kingdom, and the largest need not be above two hundred foot long; twenty or thirty of which tubes, charged with the proper quantity of powder and balls, would batter down the walls of the strongest town in his dominions in a few hours; or destroy the whole metropolis, if ever it should pretend to dispute his absolute commands. This I humbly offered to his Majesty as a small tribute of acknowledgement in return of so many marks that I had received of his royal favor and protection.

The King was struck with horror at the description I had given of those terrible engines and the proposal I had made. He was amazed how so impotent and groveling an insect as I (these were his expressions) could entertain such inhuman ideas, and in so familiar a manner as to appear wholly unmoved at all the scenes of blood and desolation which I had painted as the common effects of those destructive machines; whereof he said some evil genius, enemy to mankind, must have been the first contriver. As for himself, he protested that although few things delighted him so much as new discoveries in art or in nature, yet he would rather lose half his kingdom than be privy to such a secret, which he commanded me, as I valued my life, never to mention any more.

A strange effect of *narrow principles* and *short views!* that a prince possessed of every quality which procures veneration, love, and esteem; of strong parts, great wisdom, and profound learning; endued with admirable talents for government, and almost adored by his subjects; should from a *nice, unnecessary scruple,* whereof in Europe we can have no conception, let slip an opportunity put into his hands that would have made him absolute master of the lives, the liberties, and the fortunes of his people. Neither do I say this with the least intention to detract from the many virtues of that excellent King, whose character I am sensible will on this account be very much lessened in the opinion of an English reader: but I take this defect among them to have risen from their ignorance; they not having hitherto reduced politics into a science, as the more acute wits of Europe have done. For I remember very well, in a discourse one day with the King, when I happened to say there were several thousand books among us written upon the art of government, it gave him (directly contrary to my intention) a very mean opinion of our understandings. He professed both to abominate and despise all *mystery, refinement,* and *intrigue,* either in a prince or a minister. He could not tell what I meant by *secrets of state,* where an enemy or some rival nation were not in the case. He confined the knowledge of governing within very *narrow bounds:* to common sense and reason, to justice and lenity, to the speedy determination of civil and criminal causes, with some other obvious topics which are not worth considering. And he gave it for his opinion that whoever could make two ears of corn or two blades of grass to grow upon a spot of ground where only one grew before would deserve better of mankind and do more essential service to his country than the whole race of politicians[5] put together.

The learning of this people is very defective, consisting only in morality, history, poetry, and mathematics; wherein they must be allowed to excel. But the last of these is wholly applied to what may be useful in life, to the improvement of agriculture and all mechanical arts; so that among us it would be little esteemed. And as to ideas, entities, abstractions, and transcendentals,[6] I could never drive the least conception into their heads.

No law of that country must exceed in words the number of letters in their alphabet, which consists only in two and twenty. But indeed few of them extend even to that length. They are expressed in the most plain and simple terms, wherein those people are not mercurial enough to discover above one interpretation. And to write a comment upon any law is a capital crime. As to the decision of civil causes, or proceedings against criminals, their precedents are so few that they have little reason to boast of any extraordinary skill in either.

They have had the art of printing as well as the Chinese, time out of mind. But their libraries are not very large; for that of the King's, which is reckoned the biggest, doth not amount to above a thousand volumes, placed in a gallery of twelve hundred foot long, from whence I had liberty to borrow what books I pleased. The Queen's joiner had contrived in one of the Glumdalclitch's rooms a kind of wooden machine five and twenty foot high, formed like a standing ladder; the steps were each fifty foot long. It was indeed a movable pair of stairs, the lowest end placed at ten foot distance from the wall of the chamber. The book I had a mind to read was put up leaning against the wall. I first mounted to the upper step of the ladder, and turning my face towards the book began at the top of the page, and so walking to the right and left about eight or ten paces according to the length of the lines, till I had gotten a little below the level of mine eyes, and then descending gradually till I came to the bottom: after which I mounted again, and began the other page in the same manner, and so turned over the leaf, which I could easily do with both my hands, for it was as thick and stiff as a pasteboard, and in the largest folios not above eighteen or twenty foot long.

Their style is clear, masculine, and smooth, but not florid; for they avoid nothing more than multiplying unnecessary words or using various expressions. I have perused many of their books, especially those in history and morality. Among the rest, I was much diverted with a little old treatise, which always lay in Glumdalclitch's bedchamber, and belonged to her governess, a grave elderly gentlewoman, who dealt in writings of morality and devotion. The book treats of the weakness of human kind, and is in little esteem, except among the women and the vulgar. However, I was curious to see what an author of that country could say upon such a subject. This writer went through all the usual topics of European moralists: showing how diminutive, contemptible, and helpless an animal was man in his own nature; how unable to defend himself from the inclemencies of the air, or the fury of wild beasts;

5. Swift means something like our modern political scientists or theorists.

6. In Swift's time, *transcendental* was practically synonymous with *metaphysical*.

how much he was excelled by one creature in strength, by another in speed, by a third in foresight, by a fourth in industry. He added that nature was degenerated in these latter declining ages of the world, and could now produce only small abortive births in comparison of those in ancient times. He said it was very reasonable to think, not only that the species of men were originally much larger, but also that there must have been giants in former ages; which, as it is asserted by history and tradition, so it hath been confirmed by huge bones and skulls casually dug up in several parts of the kingdom, far exceeding the common dwindled race of man in our days. He argued that the very laws of nature absolutely required we should have been made in the beginning of a size more large and robust, not so liable to destruction from every little accident of a tile falling from a house, or a stone cast from the hand of a boy, or of being drowned in a little brook. From this way of reasoning, the author drew several moral applications useful in the conduct of life, but needless here to repeat. For my own part, I could not avoid reflecting how universally this talent was spread, of drawing lectures in morality, or indeed rather matter of discontent and repining, from the quarrels we raise with nature. And I believe, upon a strict inquiry, those quarrels might be shown as ill grounded among us as they are among that people.

As to their military affairs, they boast that the King's army consists of an hundred and seventy-six thousand foot and thirty-two thousand horse: if that may be called an army which is made up of tradesmen in the several cities, and farmers in the country, whose commanders are only the nobility and gentry, without pay or reward. They are indeed perfect enough in their exercises, and under very good discipline, wherein I saw no great merit; for how should it be otherwise, where every farmer is under the command of his own landlord, and every citizen under that of the principal men in his own city, chosen after the manner of Venice by ballot?

I have often seen the militia of Lorbrulgrud drawn out to exercise in a great field near the city, of twenty miles square. They were in all not above twenty-five thousand foot, and six thousand horse; but it was impossible for me to compute their number, considering the space of ground they took up. A cavalier mounted on a large steed might be about an hundred foot high. I have seen this whole body of horse, upon a word of command, draw their swords at once, and brandish them in the air. Imagination can figure nothing so grand, so surprising, and so astonishing. It looked as if ten thousand flashes of lightning were darting at the same time from every quarter of the sky.

I was curious to know how this prince, to whose dominions there is no access from any other country, came to think of armies, or to teach his people the practice of military discipline. But I was soon informed, both by conversation and reading their histories. For in the course of many ages they have been troubled with the same disease to which the whole race of mankind is subject: the nobility often contending for power, the people for liberty, and the King for absolute dominion. All which, however happily tempered by the laws of the kingdom, have been sometimes violated by each of the three parties, and have more than once occasioned civil wars, the last whereof was happily put an end to by this prince's grandfather in a general composition;[7] and the militia, then settled with common consent, hath been ever since kept in the strictest duty.

7. A political settlement based on general agreement of all parties.

CHAPTER 8. *The King and Queen make a progress to the frontiers. The Author attends them. The manner in which he leaves the country very particularly related. He returns to England.*

I had always a strong impulse that I should some time recover my liberty, though it were impossible to conjecture by what means, or to form any project with the least hope of succeeding. The ship in which I sailed was the first ever known to be driven within sight of that coast; and the King had given strict orders that if at any time another appeared, it should be taken ashore, and with all its crew and passengers brought in a tumbrel[8] to Lorbrulgrud. He was strongly bent to get me a woman of my own size, by whom I might propagate the breed: but I think I should rather have died than undergone the disgrace of leaving a posterity to be kept in cages like tame canary birds, and perhaps in time sold about the kingdom to persons of quality for curiosities. I was indeed treated with much kindness: I was the favorite of a great King and Queen, and the delight of the whole Court, but it was upon such a foot as ill became the dignity of human kind. I could never forget those domestic pledges I had left behind me. I wanted to be among people with whom I could converse upon even terms, and walk about the streets and fields without fear of being trod to death like a frog or a young puppy. But my deliverance came sooner than I expected, and in a manner not very common; the whole story and circumstances of which I shall faithfully relate.

I had now been two years in this country; and about the beginning of the third, Glumdalclitch and I attended the King and Queen in progress to the south coast of the kingdom. I was carried as usual in my traveling box, which, as I have already described, was a very convenient closet of twelve foot wide. I had ordered a hammock to be fixed by silken ropes from the four corners at the top, to break the jolts when a servant carried me before him on horseback, as I sometimes desired; and would often sleep in my hammock while we were upon the road. On the roof of my closet, set not directly over the middle of the hammock, I ordered the joiner to cut out a hole of a foot square to give me air in hot weather as I slept, which hole I shut at pleasure with a board that drew backwards and forwards through a groove.

When we came to our journey's end, the King thought proper to pass a few days at a palace he hath near Flanflasnic, a city within eighteen English miles of the seaside. Glumdalclitch and I were much fatigued; I had gotten a small cold, but the poor girl was so ill as to be confined to her chamber. I longed to see the ocean, which must be the only scene of my escape, if ever it should happen. I pretended to be worse than I really was, and desired leave to take the fresh air of the sea with a page whom I was very fond of, and who had sometimes been trusted with me. I shall never forget with what unwillingness Glumdalclitch consented, nor the strict charge she gave the page to be careful of me, bursting at the same time into a flood of tears, as if she had some foreboding of what was to happen. The boy took me out in my box about half an hour's walk from the palace, towards the rocks on the seashore. I ordered him to set me down, and lifting up one of my sashes, cast many a wistful melancholy look towards the sea. I found myself not very well, and told the page that I had a mind to take a nap in my hammock, which I hoped would do me good. I got in, and the boy shut the window close down, to keep out

8. A farm wagon.

the cold. I soon fell asleep: and all I can conjecture is that while I slept, the page, thinking no danger could happen, went among the rocks to look for birds' eggs; having before observed him from my window searching about, and picking up one or two in the clefts. Be that as it will, I found myself suddenly awaked with a violent pull upon the ring which was fastened at the top of my box for the conveniency of carriage. I felt my box raised very high in the air, and then borne forward with prodigious speed. The first jolt had like to have shaken me out of my hammock, but afterwards the motion was easy enough. I called out several times as loud as I could raise my voice, but all to no purpose. I looked towards my windows, and could see nothing but the clouds and sky. I heard a noise just over my head like the clapping of wings, and then began to perceive the woeful condition I was in; that some eagle had got the ring of my box in his beak, with an intent to let it fall on a rock, like a tortoise in a shell, and then pick out my body and devour it. For the sagacity and smell of this bird enable him to discover his quarry at a great distance, although better concealed than I could be within a two-inch board.

In a little time I observed the noise and flutter of wings to increase very fast, and my box was tossed up and down like a signpost in a windy day. I heard several bangs or buffets, as I thought, given to the eagle (for such I am certain it must have been that held the ring of my box in his beak), and then all on a sudden felt myself falling perpendicularly down for above a minute, but with such incredible swiftness that I almost lost my breath. My fall was topped by a terrible squash, that sounded louder to mine ears than the cataract of Niagara; after which I was quite in the dark for another minute, and then my box began to rise so high that I could see light from the tops of my windows. I now perceived that I was fallen into the sea. My box, by the weight of my body, the goods that were in, and the broad plates of iron fixed for strength at the four corners of the top and bottom, floated above five foot deep in water. I did then and do now suppose that the eagle which flew away with my box was pursued by two or three others, and forced to let me drop while he was defending himself against the rest, who hoped to share in the prey. The plates of iron fastened at the bottom of the box (for those were the strongest) preserved the balance while it fell, and hindered it from being broken on the surface of the water. Every joint of it was well grooved, and the door did not move on hinges, but up and down like a sash; which kept my closet so tight that very little water came in. I got with much difficulty out of my hammock, having first ventured to draw back the slip-board on the roof already mentioned, contrived on purpose to let in air, for want of which I found myself almost stifled.

How often did I then wish myself with my dear Glumdalclitch, from whom one single hour had so far divided me! And I may say with truth that in the midst of my own misfortune, I could not forbear lamenting my poor nurse, the grief she would suffer for my loss, the displeasure of the Queen, and the ruin of her fortune. Perhaps many travelers have not been under greater difficulties and distress than I was at this juncture, expecting every moment to see my box dashed in pieces, or at least overset by the first violent blast or a rising wave. A breach in one single pane of glass would have been immediate death, nor could anything have preserved the windows but the strong lattice wires placed on the outside against accidents in traveling. I saw the water ooze in at several crannies, although the leaks were not considerable, and I endeavored to stop them as well as I could. I was not able to lift up the roof of my closet, which otherwise I certainly should have done, and sat on the top of it, where I might at least preserve myself from being shut up, as I may call it, in the hold. Or, if I escaped these dangers for a day or two, what could I expect but a miserable death of cold and hunger! I was four hours under these circumstances, expecting and indeed wishing every moment to be my last.

I have already told the reader that there were two strong staples fixed upon that side of my box which had no window and into which the servant, who used to carry me on horseback, would put a leathern belt, and buckle it about his waist. Being in this disconsolate state, I heard, or at least thought I heard, some kind of grating noise on that side of my box where the staples were fixed; and soon after I began to fancy that the box was pulled or towed along in the sea; for I now and then felt a sort of tugging, which made the waves rise near the tops of my windows, leaving me almost in the dark. This gave me some faint hopes of relief, although I was not able to imagine how it could be brought about. I ventured to unscrew one of my chairs, which were always fastened to the floor; and having made a hard shift to screw it down again directly under the slipping-board that I had lately opened, I mounted on the chair, and putting my mouth as near as I could to the hole, I called for help in a loud voice, and in all the languages I understood. I then fastened my handkerchief to a stick I usually carried, and thrusting it up the hole, waved it several times in the air, that if any boat or ship were near, the seamen might conjecture some unhappy mortal to be shut up in the box.

I found no effect from all I could do, but plainly perceived my closet to be moved along; and in the space of an hour or better, that side of the box where the staples were, and had no window, struck against something that was hard. I apprehended it to be a rock, and found myself tossed more than ever. I plainly heard a noise upon the cover of my closet, like that of a cable, and the grating of it as it passed through the ring. I then found myself hoisted up by degrees at least three foot higher than I was before. Whereupon I again thrust up my stick and handkerchief, calling for help till I was almost hoarse. In return to which, I heard a great shout repeated three times, giving me such transports of joy as are not to be conceived but by those who feel them. I now heard a trampling over my head, and somebody calling through the hole with a loud voice in the English tongue: "If there be anybody below, let them speak." I answered, I was an Englishman, drawn by ill fortune into the greatest calamity that ever any creature underwent, and begged, by all that was moving, to be delivered out of the dungeon I was in. The voice replied, I was safe, for my box was fastened to their ship; and the carpenter should immediately come and saw an hole in the cover, large enough to pull me out. I answered, that was needless and would take up too much time, for there was no more to be done but let one of the crew put his finger into the ring, and take the box out of the sea into the ship, and so into the captain's cabin. Some of them, upon hearing me talk so wildly, thought I was mad; others laughed; for indeed it never came into my head that I was now got among people of my own stature and strength. The carpenter came, and in a few minutes sawed a passage about four foot square; then let down a small ladder, upon which I mounted, and from thence was taken into the ship in a very weak condition.

The sailors were all in amazement, and asked me a thousand questions, which I had no inclination to answer. I was equally confounded at the sight of so many pygmies, for such I took them to be, after having so long accustomed my eyes to the monstrous objects I had left. But the Captain, Mr. Thomas Wilcocks, an honest, worthy Shropshire man, observing I was ready to faint, took me into his cabin, gave me a cordial to comfort me, and made me turn in upon his own bed, advising me to take a little rest, of which I had great need. Before I went to sleep I gave him to understand that I had some valuable furniture in my box, too good to be lost, a fine hammock, an handsome field bed, two chairs, a table, and a cabinet; that my closet was hung on all sides, or rather quilted with silk and cotton; that if he would let one of the crew bring my closet into his cabin, I would open it before him and show him my goods. The Captain, hearing me utter these absurdities, concluded I was raving; however (I suppose to pacify me), he promised to give order as I desired, and going upon deck, sent some of his men down into my closet, from whence (as I afterwards found) they drew up all my goods and stripped off the quilting; but the chairs, cabinet, and bedstead, being screwed to the floor, were much damaged by the ignorance of the seamen, who tore them up by force. Then they knocked off some of the boards for the use of the ship; and when they had got all they had a mind for, let the hulk drop into the sea, which, by reason of many breaches made in the bottom and sides, sunk to rights.[9] And indeed I was glad not to have been a spectator of the havoc they made, because I am confident it would have sensibly touched me, by bringing former passages into my mind, which I had rather forget.

I slept some hours, but perpetually disturbed with dreams of the place I had left, and the dangers I had escaped. However, upon waking, I found myself much recovered. It was now about eight o'clock at night, and the Captain ordered supper immediately, thinking I had already fasted too long. He entertained me with great kindness, observing me not to look wildly, or talk inconsistently; and when we were left alone, desired I would give him a relation of my travels, and by what accident I came to be set adrift in that monstrous wooden chest. He said that about twelve o'clock at noon, as he was looking through his glass, he spied it at a distance, and thought it was a sail, which he had a mind to make,[1] being not much out of his course, in hopes of buying some biscuit, his own beginning to fall short. That, upon coming nearer, and finding his error, he sent out his longboat to discover what I was; that his men came back in a fright, swearing they had seen a swimming house. That he laughed at their folly, and went himself in the boat, ordering his men to take a strong cable along with them. That the weather being calm, he rowed round me several times, observed my windows, and the wire lattices that defended them. That he discovered two staples upon one side, which was all of boards, without any passage for light. He then commanded his men to row up to that side, and fastening a cable to one of the staples, ordered his men to tow my chest (as he called it) towards the ship. When it was there, he gave directions to fasten another cable to the ring fixed in the cover, and to raise up my chest with pulleys, which all the sailors were not able to do above two or three foot. He said they saw my stick and handkerchief thrust out of the hole, and concluded that some unhappy man must be shut up in the cavity. I asked whether he or the crew had seen any prodigious birds in the air about the time he first discovered me. To which he answered that, discoursing this matter with the sailors while I was asleep, one of them said he had observed three eagles flying towards the north, but remarked nothing of their being larger than the usual size (which I suppose must be imputed to the great height they were at), and he could not guess the reason of my question. I then asked the Captain how

9. At once, altogether.

1. Overtake.

far he reckoned we might be from land; he said, by the best computation he could make, we were at least an hundred leagues. I assured him that he must be mistaken by almost half; for I had not left the country from whence I came above two hours before I dropped into the sea. Whereupon he began again to think that my brain was disturbed, of which he gave me a hint, and advised me to go to bed in a cabin he had provided. I assured him I was well refreshed with his good entertainment and company, and as much in my senses as ever I was in my life. He then grew serious and desired to ask me freely whether I were not troubled in mind by the consciousness of some enormous crime, for which I was punished at the command of some prince, by exposing me in that chest, as great criminals in other countries have been forced to sea in a leaky vessel without provisions; for although he should be sorry to have taken so ill[2] a man into his ship, yet he would engage his word to set me safe on shore in the first port where we arrived. He added that his suspicions were much increased by some very absurd speeches I had delivered at first to the sailors, and afterwards to himself, in relation to my closet or chest, as well as by my odd looks and behavior while I was at supper.

I begged his patience to hear me tell my story, which I faithfully did from the last time I left England to the moment he first discovered me. And as truth always forceth its way into rational minds, so this honest, worthy gentleman, who had some tincture of learning, and very good sense, was immediately convinced of my candor and veracity. But further to confirm all I had said, I entreated him to give order that my cabinet should be brought, of which I kept the key in my pocket (for he had already informed me how the seamen disposed of my closet). I opened it in his presence and showed him the small collection of rarities I made in the country from whence I had been so strangely delivered. There was the comb I had contrived out of the stumps of the King's beard, and another of the same materials, but fixed into a paring of her Majesty's thumbnail, which served for the back. There was a collection of needles and pins from a foot to half a yard long; four wasp-stings, like joiners' tacks; some combings of the Queen's hair; a gold ring which one day she made me a present of in a most obliging manner, taking it from her little finger, and throwing it over my head like a collar. I desired the Captain would please to accept this ring in return for his civilities, which he absolutely refused. I showed him a corn that I had cut off with my own hand from a Maid of Honor's toe; it was about the bigness of a Kentish pippin, and grown so hard that, when I returned to England, I got it hollowed into a cup and set in silver. Lastly, I desired him to see the breeches I had then on, which were made of a mouse's skin.

I could force nothing on him but a footman's tooth, which I observed him to examine with great curiosity, and found he had a fancy for it. He received it with abundance of thanks, more than such a trifle could deserve. It was drawn by an unskillful surgeon in a mistake from one of Glumdalclitch's men, who was afflicted with the toothache; but it was as sound as any in his head. I got it cleaned, and put it into my cabinet. It was about a foot long, and four inches in diameter.

The Captain was very well satisfied with this plain relation I had given him, and said he hoped when we returned to England I would oblige the world by putting it in paper and making it public. My answer was that I thought we were already overstocked with books of travels; that nothing could now pass

2. Evil.

which was not extraordinary; wherein I doubted some authors less consulted truth than their own vanity or interest, or the diversion of ignorant readers. That my story could contain little besides common events, without those ornamental descriptions of strange plants, trees, birds, and other animals, or the barbarous customs and idolatry of savage people, with which most writers abound. However, I thanked him for his good opinion, and promised to take the matter into my thoughts.

He said he wondered at one thing very much, which was to hear me speak so loud, asking me whether the King or Queen of that country were thick of hearing. I told him it was what I had been used to for above two years past, and that I admired[3] as much at the voices of him and his men, who seemed to me only to whisper, and yet I could hear them well enough. But, when I spoke in that country, it was like a man talking in the street to another looking out from the top of a steeple, unless when I was placed on a table, or held in any person's hand. I told him I had likewise observed another thing: that when I first got into the ship, and the sailors stood all about me, I thought they were the most little contemptible creatures I had ever beheld. For indeed while I was in that prince's country, I could never endure to look in a glass after my eyes had been accustomed to such prodigious objects, because the comparison gave me so despicable a conceit[4] of myself. The Captain said that while we were at supper he observed me to look at everything with a sort of wonder, and that I often seemed hardly able to contain my laughter; which he knew not well how to take, but imputed it to some disorder in my brain. I answered, it was very true; and I wondered how I could forbear, when I saw his dishes of the size of a silver threepence, a leg of pork hardly a mouthful, a cup not so big as a nutshell; and so I went on, describing the rest of his household stuff and provisions after the same manner. For, although the Queen had ordered a little equipage of all things necessary for me while I was in her service, yet my ideas were wholly taken up with what I saw on every side of me, and I winked at my own littleness, as people do at their own faults. The Captain understood my raillery very well, and merrily replied with the old English proverb, that he doubted[5] my eyes were bigger than my belly, for he did not observe my stomach so good, although I had fasted all day; and continuing in his mirth, protested he would have gladly given an hundred pounds to have seen my closet in the eagle's bill, and afterwards in its fall from so great an height into the sea; which would certainly have been a most astonishing object, worthy to have the description of it transmitted to future ages: and the comparison of Phaeton[6] was so obvious, that he could not forbear applying it, although I did not much admire the conceit.

The Captain having been at Tonquin,[7] was in his return to England driven northeastward to the latitude of 44 degrees, and of longitude 143. But meeting a trade wind two days after I came on board him, we sailed southward a long time, and coasting New Holland[8] kept our course west-southwest, and then south-southwest till we doubled the Cape of Good Hope. Our voyage was very prosperous, but I shall not trouble the reader with a journal of it. The Captain called in at one or two ports, and sent in his longboat for provisions and fresh

3. Wondered.
4. Notion.
5. Feared.
6. Son of Helios, the sun god, whose unsuccessful attempt to drive his father's chariot led to his death, when he lost control and was hurled by Zeus from the sky, falling into the river Eridanus, where he drowned.
7. Tonkin, now in Vietnam.
8. Australia.

water; but I never went out of the ship till we came into the Downs, which was on the third day of June, 1706, about nine months after my escape. I offered to leave my goods in security for payment of my freight; but the Captain protested he would not receive one farthing. We took kind leave of each other, and I made him promise he would come to see me at my house in Redriff. I hired a horse and guide for five shillings, which I borrowed of the Captain.

As I was on the road, observing the littleness of the houses, the trees, the cattle, and the people, I began to think myself in Lilliput. I was afraid of trampling on every traveler I met, and often called aloud to have them stand out of the way, so that I had like to have gotten one or two broken heads for my impertinence.

When I came to my own house, for which I was forced to inquire, one of the servants opening the door, I bent down to go in (like a goose under a gate) for fear of striking my head. My wife ran out to embrace me, but I stooped lower than her knees, thinking she could otherwise never be able to reach my mouth. My daughter kneeled to ask my blessing, but I could not see her till she arose, having been so long used to stand with my head and eyes erect to above sixty foot; and then I went to take her up with one hand by the waist. I looked down upon the servants and one or two friends who were in the house, as if they had been pygmies and I a giant. I told my wife she had been too thrifty; for I found she had starved herself and her daughter to nothing. In short, I behaved myself so unaccountably that they were all of the Captain's opinion when he first saw me, and concluded I had lost my wits. This I mention as an instance of the great power of habit and prejudice.

In a little time I and my family and friends came to a right understanding; but my wife protested I should never go to sea any more, although my evil destiny so ordered that she had not power to hinder me; as the reader may know hereafter. In the meantime I here conclude the second part of my unfortunate voyages.

From *Part 3. A Voyage to Laputa, Balnibarbi, Glubbdubdrib, Luggnagg, and Japan*

* * *

[THE FLYING ISLAND OF LAPUTA][9]

CHAPTER 2. *The humors and dispositions of the Laputans described. An account of their learning. Of the King and his court. The author's reception there. The inhabitants subject to fears and disquietudes. An account of the women.*

At my alighting I was surrounded by a crowd of people, but those who stood nearest seemed to be of better quality. They beheld me with all the marks and circumstances of wonder; neither indeed was I much in their debt, having never till then seen a race of mortals so singular in their shapes, habits, and countenances. Their heads were all reclined to the right, or the left; one of their eyes turned inward, and the other directly up to the zenith. Their outward garments were adorned with the figures of suns, moons, and stars, interwoven

9. In the first chapter of part 3 Gulliver starts on his third voyage, but is captured by pirates and set adrift. Just as he is about to despair, a vast flying island appears in the sky, and the inhabitants draw him up with pulleys.

with those of fiddles, flutes, harps, trumpets, guitars, harpsichords, and many more instruments of music, unknown to us in Europe.[1] I observed here and there many in the habits of servants, with a blown bladder fastened like a flail to the end of a short stick, which they carried in their hands. In each bladder was a small quantity of dried pease or little pebbles (as I was afterwards informed). With these bladders they now and then flapped the mouths and ears of those who stood near them, of which practice I could not then conceive the meaning. It seems, the minds of these people are so taken up with intense speculations, that they neither can speak, or attend to the discourses of others, without being roused by some external taction[2] upon the organs of speech and hearing; for which reason those persons who are able to afford it always keep a flapper (the original is *climenole*) in their family, as one of their domestics; nor ever walk abroad or make visits without him. And the business of this officer is, when two or more persons are in company, gently to strike with his bladder the mouth of him who is to speak, and the right ear of him or them to whom the speaker addresseth himself. This flapper is likewise employed diligently to attend his master in his walks, and upon occasion to give him a soft flap on his eyes, because he is always so wrapped up in cogitation, that he is in manifest danger of falling down every precipice, and bouncing his head against every post; and in the streets, of jostling others, or being jostled himself into the kennel.[3]

It was necessary to give the reader this information, without which he would be at the same loss with me, to understand the proceedings of these people, as they conducted me up the stairs to the top of the island, and from thence to the royal palace. While we were ascending, they forgot several times what they were about, and left me to myself, till their memories were again roused by their flappers; for they appeared altogether unmoved by the sight of my foreign habit and countenance, and by the shouts of the vulgar, whose thoughts and minds were more disengaged.

At last we entered the palace, and proceeded into the chamber of presence; where I saw the King seated on his throne, attended on each side by persons of prime quality. Before the throne was a large table filled with globes and spheres, and mathematical instruments of all kinds. His Majesty took not the least notice of us, although our entrance was not without sufficient noise, by the concourse of all persons belonging to the court. But he was then deep in a problem, and we attended at least an hour before he could solve it. There stood by him on each side a young page, with flaps in their hands, and when they saw he was at leisure, one of them gently struck his mouth, and the other his right ear; at which he started like one awaked on the sudden, and looking towards me, and the company I was in, recollected the occasion of our coming, whereof he had been informed before. He spoke some words, whereupon immediately a young man with a flap came up to my side, and flapped me gently on the right ear; but I made signs as well as I could, that I had no occasion for such an instrument; which as I afterwards found gave his Majesty and the whole court a very mean opinion of my understanding. The King, as far as I could conjecture, asked me several questions, and I addressed myself

1. The Laputans represent contemporary speculation, deplored by Swift, about abstract theories of science, mathematics, and music. Both the Royal Society and Sir Isaac Newton took an interest in the mathematical basis of music.
2. Touch.
3. Gutter.

to him in all the languages I had. When it was found that I could neither understand nor be understood, I was conducted by his order to an apartment in his palace (this prince being distinguished above all his predecessors for his hospitality to strangers),[4] where two servants were appointed to attend me. My dinner was brought, and four persons of quality, whom I remembered to have seen very near the King's person, did me the honor to dine with me. We had two courses, of three dishes each. In the first course there was a shoulder of mutton, cut into an equilateral triangle; a piece of beef into a rhomboid; and a pudding into a cycloid. The second course was two ducks, trussed up into the form of fiddles; sausages and pudding resembling flutes and hautboys,[5] and a breast of veal in the shape of a harp. The servants cut our bread into cones, cylinders, parallelograms, and several other mathematical figures.

While we were at dinner, I made bold to ask the names of several things in their language, and those noble persons, by the assistance of their flappers, delighted to give me answers, hoping to raise my admiration of their great abilities, if I could be brought to converse with them. I was soon able to call for bread and drink, or whatever else I wanted.

After dinner my company withdrew, and a person was sent to me by the King's order, attended by a flapper. He brought with him pen, ink, and paper, and three or four books; giving me to understand by signs, that he was sent to teach me the language. We sat together four hours, in which time I wrote down a great number of words in columns, with the translations over against them. I likewise made a shift to learn several short sentences. For my tutor would order one of my servants to fetch something, to turn about, to make a bow, to sit, or stand, or walk, and the like. Then I took down the sentence in writing. He showed me also in one of his books the figures of the sun, moon, and stars, the zodiac, the tropics and polar circles, together with the denominations of many figures of planes and solids. He gave me the names and descriptions of all the musical instruments, and the general terms of art in playing on each of them. After he had left me, I placed all my words with their interpretations in alphabetical order. And thus in a few days, by the help of a very faithful memory, I got some insight into their language.

The word, which I interpret the *Flying* or *Floating Island,* is in the original *Laputa;* whereof I could never learn the true etymology. *Lap* in the old obsolete language signifieth *high,* and *untuh* a *governor;* from which they say by corruption was derived *Laputa,* from *Lapuntuh.* But I do not approve of this derivation, which seems to be a little strained. I ventured to offer to the learned among them a conjecture of my own, that *Laputa* was *quasi Lap outed; Lap* signifying properly the dancing of the sunbeams in the sea, and *outed* a wing, which however I shall not obtrude, but submit to the judicious reader.[6]

Those to whom the King had entrusted me, observing how ill I was clad, ordered a tailor to come next morning, and take my measure for a suit of clothes. This operator did his office after a different manner from those of his trade in Europe. He first took my altitude by a quadrant, and then, with rule and compasses, described the dimensions and outlines of my whole body; all

4. George I, a patron of music and science, had filled his court with Hanoverians when he came to England in 1714.

5. Oboes.

6. Gulliver overlooks a likelier etymology: Spanish *la puta,* "the whore."

which he entered upon paper, and in six days brought my clothes very ill made, and quite out of shape, by happening to mistake a figure in the calculation. But my comfort was, that I observed such accidents very frequent, and little regarded.

During my confinement for want of clothes, and by an indisposition that held me some days longer, I much enlarged my dictionary; and when I went next to court, was able to understand many things the King spoke, and to return him some kind of answers. His Majesty had given orders that the island should move northeast and by east, to the vertical point over Lagado, the metropolis of the whole kingdom, below upon the firm earth. It was about ninety leagues distant, and our voyage lasted four days and a half. I was not in the least sensible of the progressive motion made in the air by the island. On the second morning, about eleven o'clock, the King himself in person, attended by his nobility, courtiers, and officers, having prepared all their musical instruments, played on them for three hours without intermission, so that I was quite stunned with the noise; neither could I possibly guess the meaning, till my tutor informed me. He said, that the people of their island had their ears adapted to hear the music of the spheres, which always played at certain periods; and the court was now prepared to bear their part in whatever instrument they most excelled.

In our journey towards Lagado, the capital city, his Majesty ordered that the island should stop over certain towns and villages, from whence he might receive the petitions of his subjects. And to this purpose, several packthreads were let down with small weights at the bottom. On these packthreads the people strung their petitions, which mounted up directly like the scraps of paper fastened by schoolboys at the end of the string that holds their kite.[7] Sometimes we received wine and victuals from below, which were drawn up by pulleys.

The knowledge I had in mathematics gave me great assistance in acquiring their phraseology, which depended much upon that science and music; and in the latter I was not unskilled. Their ideas are perpetually conversant in lines and figures. If they would, for example, praise the beauty of a woman, or any other animal, they describe it by rhombs, circles, parallelograms, ellipses, and other geometrical terms; or else by words of art drawn from music, needless here to repeat. I observed in the King's kitchen all sorts of mathematical and musical instruments, after the figures of which they cut up the joints that were served to his Majesty's table.

Their houses are very ill built, the walls bevil, without one right angle in any apartment; and this defect ariseth from the contempt they bear for practical geometry; which they despise as vulgar and mechanic, those instructions they give being too refined for the intellectuals of their workmen; which occasions perpetual mistakes. And although they are dextrous enough upon a piece of paper, in the management of the rule, the pencil, and the divider, yet in the common actions and behavior of life I have not seen a more clumsy, awkward, and unhandy people, nor so slow and perplexed in their conceptions upon all other subjects, except those of mathematics and music. They are very bad reasoners, and vehemently given to opposition, unless when they happen to

7. Petitioners, that is, might as well go fly a kite. Throughout this section Swift satirizes the "distance" of George I (who spent much of his time in Hanover) from his British subjects.

be of the right opinion, which is seldom their case. Imagination, fancy, and invention, they are wholly strangers to, nor have any words in their language by which those ideas can be expressed; the whole compass of their thoughts and mind being shut up within the two forementioned sciences.

Most of them, and especially those who deal in the astronomical part, have great faith in judicial astrology, although they are ashamed to own it publicly. But what I chiefly admired,[8] and thought altogether unaccountable, was the strong disposition I observed in them towards news and politics; perpetually enquiring into public affairs, giving their judgments in matters of state; and passionately disputing every inch of a party opinion. I have indeed observed the same disposition among most of the mathematicians I have known in Europe; although I could never discover the least analogy between the two sciences; unless those people suppose, that because the smallest circle hath as many degrees as the largest, therefore the regulation and management of the world require no more abilities than the handling and turning of a globe. But I rather take this quality to spring from a very common infirmity of human nature, inclining us to be more curious and conceited in matters where we have least concern, and for which we are least adapted either by study or nature.

These people are under continual disquietudes, never enjoying a minute's peace of mind; and their disturbances proceed from causes which very little affect the rest of mortals. Their apprehensions arise from several changes they dread in the celestial bodies. For instance; that the earth, by the continual approaches of the sun towards it, must in course of time be absorbed or swallowed up. That the face of the sun will by degrees be encrusted with its own effluvia,[9] and give no more light to the world. That the earth very narrowly escaped a brush from the tail of the last comet, which would have infallibly reduced it to ashes; and that the next, which they have calculated for one and thirty years hence, will probably destroy us.[1] For, if in its perihelion it should approach within a certain degree of the sun (as by their calculations they have reason to dread), it will conceive a degree of heat ten thousand times more intense than that of red-hot glowing iron; and in its absence from the sun, carry a blazing tail ten hundred thousand and fourteen miles long; through which if the earth should pass at the distance of one hundred thousand miles from the nucleus, or main body of the comet, it must in its passage be set on fire, and reduced to ashes. That the sun daily spending its rays without any nutriment to supply them, will at last be wholly consumed and annihilated; which must be attended with the destruction of this earth, and of all the planets that receive their light from it.

They are so perpetually alarmed with the apprehensions of these and the like impending dangers, that they can neither sleep quietly in their beds, nor have any relish for the common pleasures or amusements of life. When they meet an acquaintance in the morning, the first question is about the sun's health, how he looked at his setting and rising, and what hopes they have to avoid the stroke of the approaching comet. This conversation they are apt to run into with the same temper that boys discover in delighting to hear terrible

8. Wondered at.
9. Sunspots.
1. Halley's comet, some astronomers had feared, might strike the earth on its next appearance (1758). All the disasters that disquiet the Laputans had occurred to English scientists as possible implications of Newtonian theory.

stories of sprites and hobgoblins, which they greedily listen to, and dare not go to bed for fear.

The women of the island have abundance of vivacity; they contemn their husbands, and are exceedingly fond of strangers, whereof there is always a considerable number from the continent below, attending at court, either upon affairs of the several towns and corporations, or their own particular occasions; but are much despised, because they want[2] the same endowments. Among these the ladies choose their gallants: but the vexation is, that they act with too much ease and security; for the husband is always so rapt in speculation, that the mistress and lover may proceed to the greatest familiarities before his face, if he be but provided with paper and implements, and without his flapper at his side.

The wives and daughters lament their confinement to the island, although I think it the most delicious spot of ground in the world; and although they live here in the greatest plenty and magnificence, and are allowed to do whatever they please, they long to see the world, and take the diversions of the metropolis, which they are not allowed to do without a particular license from the King; and this is not easy to be obtained, because the people of quality have found by frequent experience, how hard it is to persuade their women to return from below. I was told that a great court lady, who had several children, is married to the prime minister, the richest subject in the kingdom, a very graceful person, extremely fond of her, and lives in the finest palace of the island, went down to Lagado, on the pretense of health, there hid herself for several months, till the King sent a warrant to search for her, and she was found in an obscure eating-house all in rags, having pawned her clothes to maintain an old deformed footman, who beat her every day, and in whose company she was taken much against her will. And although her husband received her with all possible kindness, and without the least reproach, she soon after contrived to steal down again with all her jewels, to the same gallant, and hath not been heard of since.

This may perhaps pass with the reader rather for an European or English story, than for one of a country so remote. But he may please to consider, that the caprices of womankind are not limited by any climate or nation; and that they are much more uniform than can be easily imagined.

In about a month's time I had made a tolerable proficiency in their language, and was able to answer most of the King's questions, when I had the honor to attend him. His Majesty discovered not the least curiosity to enquire into the laws, government, history, religion, or manners of the countries where I had been; but confined his questions to the state of mathematics, and received the account I gave him with great contempt and indifference, though often roused by his flapper on each side.[3]

* * *

2. Lack. "Corporations": municipal authorities.
3. In the omitted chapters, Gulliver visits countries that show the consequences of modern learning. After an account of the Flying Island, whose power of motion (derived from a giant magnet or lodestone) allows it to dominate the regions below, he descends to Balnibarbi, a once fertile land now ruined by the fanciful projects of impractical scientists. In the Grand Academy of Lagado he meets many professors who are contriving such perverse "improvements" as making clothes from cobwebs or breeding naked sheep. Then he visits the part of the academy devoted to speculative learning.

[THE ACADEMY OF LAGADO][4]
FROM CHAPTER 5.

The first professor I saw was in a very large room, with forty pupils about him. After salutation, observing me to look earnestly upon a frame, which took up the greatest part of both the length and breadth of the room, he said, perhaps I might wonder to see him employed in a project for improving speculative knowledge by practical and mechanical operations. But the world would soon be sensible[5] of its usefulness, and he flattered himself that a more noble, exalted thought never sprang in any other man's head. Everyone knew how laborious the usual method is of attaining to arts and sciences; whereas by his contrivance the most ignorant person at a reasonable charge, and with a little bodily labor, may write books in philosophy, poetry, politics, law, mathematics, and theology, without the least assistance from genius or study. He then led me to the frame, about the sides whereof all his pupils stood in ranks. It was twenty foot square, placed in the middle of the room. The superficies[6] was composed of several bits of wood, about the bigness of a die, but some larger than others. They were all linked together by slender wires. These bits of wood were covered on every square with papers pasted on them; and on these papers were written all the words of their language in their several moods, tenses, and declensions, but without any order. The professor then

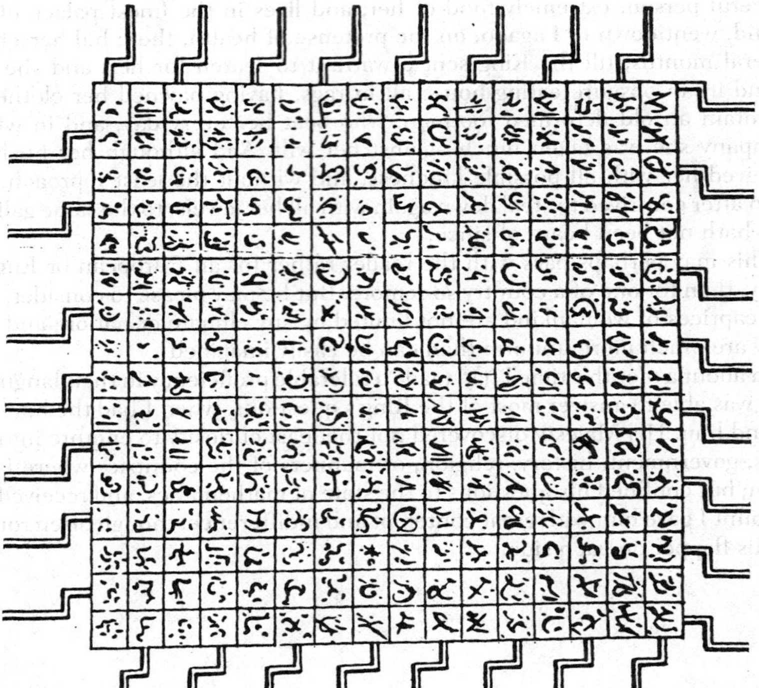

4. The Grand Academy of Lagado satirizes the Royal Society of London, an organization founded in 1662 to encourage the pursuit of scientific knowledge. Some of the projects described by Swift resemble the experiments or speculations of British scientists at the time.

5. Aware.

6. Surface.

desired me to observe, for he was going to set his engine at work. The pupils at his command took each of them hold of an iron handle, whereof there were forty fixed round the edges of the frame; and giving them a sudden turn, the whole disposition[7] of the words was entirely changed. He then commanded six and thirty of the lads to read the several lines softly as they appeared upon the frame; and where they found three or four words together that might make part of a sentence, they dictated to the four remaining boys who were scribes. This work was repeated three or four times, and at every turn the engine was so contrived that the words shifted into new places, as the square bits of wood moved upside down.

Six hours a day the young students were employed in this labor; and the professor showed me several volumes in large folio already collected, of broken sentences, which he intended to piece together, and out of those rich materials to give the world a complete body of all arts and sciences; which however might be still improved, and much expedited, if the public would raise a fund for making and employing five hundred such frames in Lagado, and oblige the managers to contribute in common their several[8] collections.

He assured me, that this invention had employed all his thoughts from his youth, that he had emptied the whole vocabulary into his frame, and made the strictest computation of the general proportion there is in books between the numbers of particles, nouns, and verbs, and other parts of speech.

I made my humblest acknowledgments to this illustrious person for his great communicativeness, and promised if ever I had the good fortune to return to my native country, that I would do him justice, as the sole inventor of this wonderful machine; the form and contrivance of which I desired leave to delineate upon paper as in the figure here annexed. I told him, although it were the custom of our learned in Europe to steal inventions from each other, who had thereby at least this advantage, that it became a controversy which was the right owner, yet I would take such caution, that he should have the honor entire without a rival.

We next went to the school of languages, where three professors sat in consultation upon improving that of their own country.[9]

The first project was to shorten discourse by cutting polysyllables into one, and leaving out verbs and participles, because in reality all things imaginable are but nouns.

The other was a scheme for entirely abolishing all words whatsoever; and this was urged as a great advantage in point of health as well as brevity. For it is plain, that every word we speak is in some degree a diminution of our lungs by corrosion, and consequently contributes to the shortening of our lives. An expedient was therefore offered, that since words are only names for *things*, it would be more convenient for all men to carry about them such *things* as were necessary to express the particular business they are to discourse on. And this invention would certainly have taken place, to the great ease as well as health of the subject, if the women in conjunction with the vulgar and illiterate had not threatened to raise a rebellion, unless they might be allowed the liberty to speak with their tongues, after the manner of their forefathers. Such constant irreconcilable enemies to science[1] are the common people.

7. Arrangement.
8. Separate.
9. Many contemporary scientists had proposed a philosophical language that would eliminate the treacherous disparity between words and things and thus allow accurate scientific discourse.
1. Knowledge.

However, many of the most learned and wise adhere to the new scheme of expressing themselves by *things*, which hath only this inconvenience attending it, that if a man's business be very great, and of various kinds, he must be obliged in proportion to carry a greater bundle of *things* upon his back, unless he can afford one or two strong servants to attend him. I have often beheld two of those sages almost sinking under the weight of their packs, like pedlars among us, who when they met in the streets would lay down their loads, open their sacks, and hold conversation for an hour together, then put up their implements, help each other to resume their burdens, and take their leave.

But for short conversations a man may carry implements in his pockets and under his arms, enough to supply him, and in his house he cannot be at a loss; therefore the room where company meet who practice this art is full of all *things* ready at hand, requisite to furnish matter for this kind of artificial converse.[2]

Another great advantage proposed by this invention was that it would serve as an universal language to be understood in all civilized nations, whose goods and utensils are generally of the same kind, or nearly resembling, so that their uses might easily be comprehended. And thus, ambassadors would be qualified to treat with foreign princes or ministers of state to whose tongues they were utter strangers.

I was at the mathematical school, where the master taught his pupils after a method scarce imaginable to us in Europe. The proposition and demonstration were fairly written on a thin wafer, with ink composed of a cephalic tincture.[3] This the student was to swallow upon a fasting stomach, and for three days following eat nothing but bread and water. As the wafer digested, the tincture mounted to his brain, bearing the proposition along with it. But the success hath not hitherto been answerable, partly by some error in the *quantum* or composition, and partly by the perverseness of lads, to whom this bolus[4] is so nauseous that they generally steal aside, and discharge it upwards before it can operate; neither have they been yet persuaded to use so long an abstinence as the prescription requires.[5]

* * *

[THE STRULDBRUGGS]

CHAPTER 10. *The Luggnaggians commended. A particular description of the struldbruggs, with many conversations between the author and some eminent persons upon that subject.*

The Luggnaggians are a polite[6] and generous people, and although they are not without some share of that pride which is peculiar to all eastern countries, yet they show themselves courteous to strangers, especially such who are countenanced by the court. I had many acquaintance among persons of the best fashion, and being always attended by my interpreter, the conversation we had was not disagreeable.

2. The Royal Society had sponsored a collection intended to contain one specimen of every thing in the world.
3. A solution or dye directed toward the head.
4. A large pill. "*Quantum*": amount.
5. In the omitted chapters Gulliver hears projects for improving politics and offers some of his own. He sails to Glubbdubdrib, the Island of Sorcerers, where he talks with the spirits of the dead; he learns that history is a pack of lies and that humanity has degenerated since ancient times. He is then received by the king of Luggnagg.
6. Refined, cultivated.

One day in much good company, I was asked by a person of quality, whether I had seen any of their *struldbruggs* or *immortals*. I said I had not; and desired he would explain to me what he meant by such an appellation, applied to a mortal creature. He told me, that sometimes, although very rarely, a child happened to be born in a family with a red circular spot in the forehead, directly over the left eyebrow, which was an infallible mark that it should never die. The spot, as he described it, was about the compass of a silver threepence, but in the course of time grew larger, and changed its color; for at twelve years old it became green, so continued till five and twenty, then turned to a deep blue; at five and forty it grew coal black, and as large as an English shilling; but never admitted any farther alteration. He said these births were so rare, that he did not believe there could be above eleven hundred *struldbruggs* of both sexes in the whole kingdom, of which he computed about fifty in the metropolis, and among the rest a young girl born about three years ago. That these productions were not peculiar to any family, but a mere effect of chance; and the children of the *struldbruggs* themselves were equally mortal with the rest of the people.

I freely own myself to have been struck with inexpressible delight upon hearing this account: and the person who gave it me happening to understand the Balnibarbian language, which I spoke very well, I could not forbear breaking out into expressions perhaps a little too extravagant. I cried out as in a rapture: Happy nation, where every child hath at least a chance for being immortal! Happy people who enjoy so many living examples of ancient virtue, and have masters ready to instruct them in the wisdom of all former ages! But happiest beyond all comparison are those excellent *struldbruggs*, who being born exempt from that universal calamity of human nature, have their minds free and disengaged, without the weight and depression of spirits caused by the continual apprehension of death. I discovered my admiration that I had not observed any of these illustrious persons at court; the black spot on the forehead being so remarkable a distinction, that I could not have easily overlooked it; and it was impossible that his Majesty, a most judicious prince, should not provide himself with a good number of such wise and able counselors. Yet perhaps the virtue of those reverend sages was too strict for the corrupt and libertine manners of a court. And we often find by experience that young men are too opinionative[7] and volatile to be guided by the sober dictates of their seniors. However, since the King was pleased to allow me access to his royal person, I was resolved upon the very first occasion to deliver my opinion to him on this matter freely, and at large by the help of my interpreter; and whether he would please to take my advice or no, yet in one thing I was determined, that his Majesty having frequently offered me an establishment in this country, I would with great thankfulness accept the favor, and pass my life here in the conversation of those superior beings the *struldbruggs*, if they would please to admit me.

The gentleman to whom I addressed my discourse, because (as I have already observed) he spoke the language of Balnibarbi, said to me with a sort of a smile, which usually ariseth from pity to the ignorant, that he was glad of any occasion to keep me among them, and desired my permission to explain to the company what I had spoke. He did so; and they talked together for some time in their own language, whereof I understood not a syllable, neither could

7. Speculative, impractical.

I observe by their countenances what impression my discourse had made on them. After a short silence the same person told me, that his friends and mine (so he thought fit to express himself) were very much pleased with the judicious remarks I had made on the great happiness and advantages of immortal life; and they were desirous to know in a particular manner, what scheme of living I should have formed to myself, if it had fallen to my lot to have been born a *struldbrugg*.

I answered, it was easy to be eloquent on so copious and delightful a subject, especially to me who have been often apt to amuse myself with visions of what I should do if I were a king, a general, or a great lord; and upon this very case I had frequently run over the whole system how I should employ myself, and pass the time if I were sure to live forever.

That, if it had been my good fortune to come into the world a *struldbrugg*, as soon as I could discover my own happiness by understanding the difference between life and death, I would first resolve by all arts and methods whatsoever to procure myself riches: in the pursuit of which, by thrift and management, I might reasonably expect in about two hundred years to be the wealthiest man in the kingdom. In the second place, I would from my earliest youth apply myself to the study of arts and sciences, by which I should arrive in time to excel all others in learning. Lastly, I would carefully record every action and event of consequence that happened in the public, impartially draw the characters of the several successions of princes, and great ministers of state; with my own observations on every point. I would exactly set down the several changes in customs, languages, fashions of dress, diet and diversions. By all which acquirements, I should be a living treasury of knowledge and wisdom, and certainly become the oracle of the nation.

I would never marry after threescore, but live in an hospitable manner, yet still on the saving side. I would entertain myself in forming and directing the minds of hopeful young men, by convincing them from my own remembrance, experience and observation, fortified by numerous examples, of the usefulness of virtue in public and private life. But my choice and constant companions should be a set of my own immortal brotherhood, among whom I would elect a dozen from the most ancient down to my own contemporaries. Where any of these wanted fortunes, I would provide them with convenient lodges round my own estate, and have some of them always at my table, only mingling a few of the most valuable among you mortals, whom length of time would harden me to lose with little or no reluctance, and treat your posterity after the same manner; just as a man diverts himself with the annual succession of pinks and tulips in his garden, without regretting the loss of those which withered the preceding year.

These *struldbruggs* and I would mutually communicate our observations and memorials[8] through the course of time; remark the several gradations by which corruption steals into the world, and oppose it in every step, by giving perpetual warning and instruction to mankind; which, added to the strong influence of our own example, would probably prevent that continual degeneracy of human nature, so justly complained of in all ages.

Add to all this, the pleasure of seeing the various revolutions of states and empires; the changes in the lower and upper world;[9] ancient cities in ruins;

8. Memories.
9. Earth and heaven; figuratively, common people and the ruling class. "Revolutions": cycles.

and obscure villages become the seats of kings. Famous rivers lessening into shallow brooks; the ocean leaving one coast dry, and overwhelming another; the discovery of many countries yet unknown. Barbarity overrunning the politest nations, and the most barbarous becoming civilized. I should then see the discovery of the longitude, the perpetual motion, the universal medicine,[1] and many other great inventions brought to the utmost perfection.

What wonderful discoveries should we make in astronomy, by outliving and confirming our own predictions, by observing the progress and returns of comets, with the changes of motion in the sun, moon and stars.

I enlarged upon many other topics, which the natural desire of endless life and sublunary happiness could easily furnish me with. When I had ended, and the sum of my discourse had been interpreted as before to the rest of the company, there was a good deal of talk among them in the language of the country, not without some laughter at my expense. At last the same gentleman who had been my interpreter said, he was desired by the rest to set me right in a few mistakes, which I had fallen into through the common imbecility[2] of human nature, and upon that allowance was less answerable for them. That this breed of *struldbruggs* was peculiar to their country, for there were no such people either in Balnibarbi or Japan, where he had the honor to be ambassador from his Majesty, and found the natives in both those kingdoms very hard to believe that the fact was possible; and it appeared from my astonishment when he first mentioned the matter to me, that I received it as a thing wholly new, and scarcely to be credited. That in the two kingdoms above mentioned, where during his residence he had conversed very much, he observed long life to be the universal desire and wish of mankind. That whoever had one foot in the grave was sure to hold back the other as strongly as he could. That the oldest had still hopes of living one day longer, and looked on death as the greatest evil, from which nature always prompted him to retreat; only in this island of Luggnagg the appetite for living was not so eager, from the continual example of the *struldbruggs* before their eyes.

That the system of living contrived by me was unreasonable and unjust, because it supposed a perpetuity of youth, health, and vigor, which no man could be so foolish to hope, however extravagant he might be in his wishes. That the question therefore was not whether a man would choose to be always in the prime of youth, attended with prosperity and health; but how he would pass a perpetual life under all the usual disadvantages which old age brings along with it. For although few men will avow their desires of being immortal upon such hard conditions, yet in the two kingdoms before mentioned of Balnibarbi and Japan, he observed that every man desired to put off death for some time longer, let it approach ever so late; and he rarely heard of any man who died willingly, except he were incited by the extremity of grief or torture. And he appealed to me whether in those countries I had traveled, as well as my own, I had not observed the same general disposition.

After this preface he gave me a particular account of the *struldbruggs* among them. He said they commonly acted like mortals, till about thirty years old, after which by degrees they grew melancholy and dejected, increasing in both till they came to fourscore. This he learned from their own confession; for

1. The *elixir vitae*, an alchemical formula to preserve life forever, was considered by Swift an impossible dream, like a method for calculating longitude at sea, or a perpetual motion machine.

2. Weakness.

otherwise there not being above two or three of that species born in an age, they were too few to form a general observation by. When they came to fourscore years, which is reckoned the extremity of living in this country, they had not only all the follies and infirmities of other old men, but many more which arose from the dreadful prospect of never dying. They were not only opinionative, peevish, covetous, morose, vain, talkative; but uncapable of friendship, and dead to all natural affection, which never descended below their grandchildren. Envy and impotent desires are their prevailing passions. But those objects against which their envy seems principally directed, are the vices of the younger sort, and the deaths of the old. By reflecting on the former, they find themselves cut off from all possibility of pleasure; and whenever they see a funeral, they lament and repine that others are gone to an harbor of rest, to which they themselves never can hope to arrive. They have no remembrance of anything but what they learned and observed in their youth and middle age, and even that is very imperfect. And for the truth or particulars of any fact, it is safer to depend on common traditions than upon their best recollections. The least miserable among them appear to be those who turn to dotage, and entirely lose their memories; these meet with more pity and assistance, because they want many bad qualities which abound in others.

If a *struldbrugg* happen to marry one of his own kind, the marriage is dissolved of course by the courtesy of the kingdom, as soon as the younger of the two comes to be fourscore. For the law thinks it a reasonable indulgence, that those who are condemned without any fault of their own to a perpetual continuance in the world, should not have their misery doubled by the load of a wife.

As soon as they have completed the term of eighty years, they are looked on as dead in law; their heirs immediately succeed to their estates, only a small pittance is reserved for their support; and the poor ones are maintained at the public charge. After that period they are held incapable of any employment of trust or profit; they cannot purchase land, or take leases, neither are they allowed to be witnesses in any cause, either civil or criminal, not even for the decision of meers[3] and bounds.

At ninety they lose their teeth and hair; they have at that age no distinction of taste, but eat and drink whatever they can get, without relish or appetite. The diseases they were subject to still continue without increasing or diminishing. In talking they forget the common appellation of things, and the names of persons, even of those who are their nearest friends and relations. For the same reason they never can amuse themselves with reading, because their memory will not serve to carry them from the beginning of a sentence to the end, and by this defect they are deprived of the only entertainment whereof they might otherwise be capable.

The language of this country being always upon the flux, the *struldbruggs* of one age do not understand those of another; neither are they able after two hundred years to hold any conversation (farther than by a few general words) with their neighbors the mortals; and thus they lie under the disadvantage of living like foreigners in their own country.

This was the account given me of the *struldbruggs,* as near as I can remember. I afterwards saw five or six of different ages, the youngest not above two hundred years old, who were brought to me at several times by some of my

3. Boundaries.

friends; but although they were told that I was a great traveler, and had seen all the world, they had not the least curiosity to ask me a question; only desired I would give them *slumskudask,* or a token of remembrance; which is a modest way of begging, to avoid the law that strictly forbids it, because they are provided for by the public, although indeed with a very scanty allowance.

They are despised and hated by all sorts of people; when one of them is born, it is reckoned ominous, and their birth is recorded very particularly; so that you may know their age by consulting the registry, which however hath not been kept above a thousand years past, or at least hath been destroyed by time or public disturbances. But the usual way of computing how old they are, is by asking them what kings or great persons they can remember, and then consulting history; for infallibly the last prince in their mind did not begin his reign after they were fourscore years old.

They were the most mortifying sight I ever beheld; and the women more horrible than the men. Besides the usual deformities in extreme old age, they acquired an additional ghastliness in proportion to their number of years, which is not to be described; and among half a dozen I soon distinguished which was the oldest, although there were not above a century or two between them.

The reader will easily believe, that from what I had heard and seen, my keen appetite for perpetuity of life was much abated. I grew heartily ashamed of the pleasing visions I had formed; and thought no tyrant could invent a death into which I would not run with pleasure from such a life. The King heard of all that had passed between me and my friends upon this occasion, and rallied[4] me very pleasantly; wishing I would send a couple of *struldbruggs* to my own country, to arm our people against the fear of death; but this it seems is forbidden by the fundamental laws of the kingdom; or else I should have been well content with the trouble and expense of transporting them.

I could not but agree, that the laws of this kingdom relating to the *struldbruggs,* were founded upon the strongest reasons, and such as any other country would be under the necessity of enacting in the like circumstances. Otherwise, as avarice is the necessary consequent of old age, those immortals would in time become proprietors of the whole nation, and engross[5] the civil power; which, for want of abilities to manage, must end in the ruin of the public.[6]

* * *

Part 4. A Voyage to the Country of the Houyhnhnms[7]

CHAPTER 1. *The Author sets out as Captain of a ship. His men conspire against him, confine him a long time to his cabin, set him on shore in an unknown land. He travels up into the country. The Yahoos, a strange sort of animal, described. The Author meets two Houyhnhnms.*

I continued at home with my wife and children about five months in a very happy condition, if I could have learned the lesson of knowing when I was

4. Ridiculed.
5. Absorb, monopolize.
6. In the omitted chapter, Gulliver sails to Japan, where a Dutch ship provides him passage back to Europe.
7. Pronounced *hwin-ims.* The word suggests the neigh characteristic of a horse.

well. I left my poor wife big with child, and accepted an advantageous offer made me to be Captain of the *Adventure*, a stout merchantman of 350 tons; for I understood navigation well, and being grown weary of a surgeon's employment at sea, which however I could exercise upon occasion, I took a skillful young man of that calling, one Robert Purefoy, into my ship. We set sail from Portsmouth upon the 7th day of September, 1710; on the 14th we met with Captain Pocock of Bristol, at Tenariff, who was going to the Bay of Campeachy[8] to cut logwood. On the 16th he was parted from us by a storm; I heard since my return that his ship foundered and none escaped, but one cabin boy. He was an honest man and a good sailor, but a little too positive in his own opinions, which was the cause of his destruction, as it hath been of several others. For if he had followed my advice, he might at this time have been safe at home with his family as well as myself.

I had several men died in my ship of calentures,[9] so that I was forced to get recruits out of Barbadoes and the Leeward Islands, where I touched by the direction of the merchants who employed me; which I had soon too much cause to repent, for I found afterwards that most of them had been buccaneers. I had fifty hands on board; and my orders were that I should trade with the Indians in the South Sea, and make what discoveries I could. These rogues whom I had picked up debauched my other men, and they all formed a conspiracy to seize the ship and secure me; which they did one morning, rushing into my cabin, and binding me hand and foot, threatening to throw me overboard, if I offered to stir. I told them I was their prisoner, and would submit. This they made me swear to do, and then unbound me, only fastening one of my legs with a chain near my bed, and placed a sentry at my door with his piece charged, who was commanded to shoot me dead if I attempted my liberty. They sent me down victuals and drink, and took the government of the ship to themselves. Their design was to turn pirates and plunder the Spaniards, which they could not do, till they got more men. But first they resolved to sell the goods in the ship, and then go to Madagascar for recruits, several among them having died since my confinement. They sailed many weeks, and traded with the Indians; but I knew not what course they took, being kept close prisoner in my cabin, and expecting nothing less than to be murdered, as they often threatened me.

Upon the 9th day of May, 1711, one James Welch came down to my cabin; and said he had orders from the Captain to set me ashore. I expostulated with him, but in vain; neither would he so much as tell me who their new Captain was. They forced me into the longboat, letting me put on my best suit of clothes, which were as good as new, and a small bundle of linen, but no arms except my hanger; and they were so civil as not to search my pockets, into which I conveyed what money I had, with some other little necessaries. They rowed about a league, and then set me down on a strand. I desired them to tell me what country it was; they all swore, they knew no more than myself, but said that the Captain (as they called him) was resolved, after they had sold the lading, to get rid of me in the first place where they discovered land. They pushed off immediately, advising me to make haste, for fear of being overtaken by the tide, and bade me farewell.

8. Campeche, in the Gulf of Mexico. Teneriffe is one of the Canary Islands.
9. "A distemper peculiar to sailors, in hot climates; wherein they imagine the sea to be green fields, and will throw themselves into it, if not restrained" (Johnson's *Dictionary*).

In this desolate condition I advanced forward, and soon got upon firm ground, where I sat down on a bank to rest myself, and consider what I had best to do. When I was a little refreshed, I went up into the country, resolving to deliver myself to the first savages I should meet, and purchase my life from them by some bracelets, glass rings, and other toys, which sailors usually provide themselves with in those voyages, and whereof I had some about me. The land was divided by long rows of trees, not regularly planted, but naturally growing; there was great plenty of grass, and several fields of oats. I walked very circumspectly for fear of being surprised, or suddenly shot with an arrow from behind, or on either side. I fell into a beaten road, where I saw many tracks of human feet, and some of cows, but most of horses. At last I beheld several animals in a field, and one or two of the same kind sitting in trees. Their shape was very singular, and deformed, which a little discomposed me, so that I lay down behind a thicket to observe them better. Some of them coming forward near the place where I lay, gave me an opportunity of distinctly marking their form. Their heads and breasts were covered with a thick hair, some frizzled and others lank; they had beards like goats, and a long ridge of hair down their backs, and the fore parts of their legs and feet; but the rest of their bodies were bare, so that I might see their skins, which were of a brown buff color. They had no tails, nor any hair at all on their buttocks, except about the anus; which, I presume Nature had placed there to defend them as they sat on the ground; for this posture they used, as well as lying down, and often stood on their hind feet. They climbed high trees, as nimbly as a squirrel, for they had strong extended claws before and behind, terminating in sharp points, and hooked. They would often spring, and bound, and leap with prodigious agility. The females were not so large as the males; they had long lank hair on their heads, and only a sort of down on the rest of their bodies, except about the anus, and pudenda. Their dugs hung between their forefeet, and often reached almost to the ground as they walked. The hair of both sexes was of several colors, brown, red, black, and yellow. Upon the whole, I never beheld in all my travels so disagreeable an animal, or one against which I naturally conceived so strong an antipathy. So that thinking I had seen enough, full of contempt and aversion, I got up and pursued the beaten road, hoping it might direct me to the cabin of some Indian. I had not gone far when I met one of these creatures full in my way, and coming up directly to me. The ugly monster, when he saw me, distorted several ways every feature of his visage, and stared as at an object he had never seen before; then approaching nearer, lifted up his forepaw, whether out of curiosity or mischief, I could not tell; but I drew my hanger, and gave him a good blow with the flat side of it; for I durst not strike him with the edge, fearing the inhabitants might be provoked against me, if they should come to know that I had killed or maimed any of their cattle. When the beast felt the smart, he drew back, and roared so loud, that a herd of at least forty came flocking about me from the near field, howling and making odious faces; but I ran to the body of a tree, and leaning my back against it, kept them off, by waving my hanger. Several of this cursed brood getting hold of the branches behind, leaped up into the tree, from whence they began to discharge their excrements on my head; however, I escaped pretty well, by sticking close to the stem of the tree, but was almost stifled with the filth, which fell about me on every side.

In the midst of this distress, I observed them all to run away on a sudden as fast as they could; at which I ventured to leave the tree, and pursue the road, wondering what it was that could put them into this fright. But looking on my left hand, I saw a horse walking softly in the field; which my persecutors having sooner discovered, was the cause of their flight. The horse started a little when he came near me, but soon recovering himself, looked full in my face with manifest tokens of wonder; he viewed my hands and feet, walking round me several times. I would have pursued my journey, but he placed himself directly in the way, yet looking with a very mild aspect, never offering the least violence. We stood gazing at each other for some time; at last I took the boldness, to reach my hand towards his neck, with a design to stroke it; using the common style and whistle of jockies when they are going to handle a strange horse. But this animal, seeming to receive my civilities with disdain, shook his head, and bent his brows, softly raising up his left forefoot to remove my hand. Then he neighed three or four times, but in so different a cadence, that I almost began to think he was speaking to himself in some language of his own.

While he and I were thus employed, another horse came up; who applying himself to the first in a very formal manner, they gently struck each other's right hoof before, neighing several times by turns, and varying the sound, which seemed to be almost articulate. They went some paces off, as if it were to confer together, walking side by side, backward and forward, like persons deliberating upon some affair of weight; but often turning their eyes towards me, as it were to watch that I might not escape. I was amazed to see such actions and behavior in brute beasts; and concluded with myself that if the inhabitants of this country were endued with a proportionable degree of reason, they must needs be the wisest people upon earth. This thought gave me so much comfort, that I resolved to go forward until I could discover some house or village, or meet with any of the natives, leaving the two horses to discourse together as they pleased. But the first, who was a dapple grey, observing me to steal off, neighed after me in so expressive a tone that I fancied myself to understand what he meant; whereupon I turned back, and came near him, to expect his farther commands; but concealing my fear as much as I could; for I began to be in some pain, how this adventure might terminate; and the reader will easily believe I did not much like my present situation.

The two horses came up close to me, looking with great earnestness upon my face and hands. The grey steed rubbed my hat all round with his right fore hoof, and discomposed it so much that I was forced to adjust it better, by taking it off, and settling it again; whereat both he and his companion (who was a brown bay) appeared to be much surprised; the latter felt the lappet of my coat, and finding it to hang loose about me, they both looked with new signs of wonder. He stroked my right hand, seeming to admire the softness, and color; but he squeezed it so hard between his hoof and his pastern, that I was forced to roar; after which they both touched me with all possible tenderness. They were under great perplexity about my shoes and stockings, which they felt very often, neighing to each other, and using various gestures, not unlike those of a philosopher, when he would attempt to solve some new and difficult phenomenon.

Upon the whole, the behavior of these animals was so orderly and rational, so acute and judicious, that I at last concluded, they must needs be magicians, who had thus metamorphosed themselves upon some design; and seeing a stranger in the way, were resolved to divert themselves with him; or perhaps were really amazed at the sight of a man so very different in habit, feature, and complexion from those who might probably live in so remote a climate. Upon the strength of this reasoning, I ventured to address them in the following manner: "Gentlemen, if you be conjurers, as I have good cause to believe, you can understand any language; therefore I make bold to let your worships know that I am a poor distressed Englishman, driven by his misfortunes upon your coast; and I entreat one of you, to let me ride upon his back, as if he were a real horse, to some house or village, where I can be relieved. In return of which favor, I will make you a present of this knife and bracelet" (taking them out of my pocket). The two creatures stood silent while I spoke, seeming to listen with great attention; and when I had ended, they neighed frequently towards each other, as if they were engaged in serious conversation. I plainly observed, that their language expressed the passions very well, and the words might with little pains be resolved into an alphabet more easily than the Chinese.

I could frequently distinguish the word *Yahoo,*[1] which was repeated by each of them several times; and although it were impossible for me to conjecture what it meant, yet while the two horses were busy in conversation, I endeavored to practice this word upon my tongue; and as soon as they were silent, I boldly pronounced "Yahoo" in a loud voice, imitating, at the same time, as near as I could, the neighing of a horse; at which they were both visibly surprised, and the grey repeated the same word twice, as if he meant to teach me the right accent, wherein I spoke after him as well as I could, and found myself perceivably to improve every time, although very far from any degree of perfection. Then the bay tried me with a second word, much harder to be pronounced; but reducing it to the English orthography, may be spelt thus, *Houyhnhnm.* I did not succeed in this so well as the former, but after two or three farther trials, I had better fortune; and they both appeared amazed at my capacity.

After some farther discourse, which I then conjectured might relate to me, the two friends took their leaves, with the same compliment of striking each other's hoof; and the grey made me signs that I should walk before him; wherein I thought it prudent to comply, till I could find a better director. When I offered to slacken my pace, he would cry, "Hhuun, Hhuun"; I guessed his meaning, and gave him to understand, as well as I could that I was weary, and not able to walk faster; upon which, he would stand a while to let me rest.

Chapter 2. *The Author conducted by a Houyhnhnm to his house. The house described. The Author's reception. The food of the Houyhnhnms. The Author in distress for want of meat is at last relieved. His manner of feeding in that country.*

Having traveled about three miles, we came to a long kind of building, made of timber, stuck in the ground, and wattled across; the roof was low, and covered with straw. I now began to be a little comforted, and took out some toys, which travelers usually carry for presents to the savage Indians of America and other parts, in hopes the people of the house would be thereby encouraged to receive me kindly. The horse made me a sign to go in first; it was a large room with a smooth clay floor, and a rack and manger extending the whole length on one side. There were three nags, and two mares, not eating,

1. Perhaps compounded from two expressions of disgust, *yah* and *ugh* (or *hoo*), common in the 18th century.

but some of them sitting down upon their hams, which I very much wondered at; but wondered more to see the rest employed in domestic business. The last seemed but ordinary cattle; however this confirmed my first opinion, that a people who could so far civilize brute animals must needs excel in wisdom all the nations of the world. The grey came in just after, and thereby prevented any ill treatment, which the others might have given me. He neighed to them several times in a style of authority, and received answers.

Beyond this room there were three others, reaching the length of the house, to which you passed through three doors, opposite to each other, in the manner of a vista; we went through the second room towards the third; here the grey walked in first, beckoning me to attend.[2] I waited in the second room, and got ready my presents, for the master and mistress of the house; they were two knives, three bracelets of false pearl, a small looking glass and a bead necklace. The horse neighed three or four times, and I waited to hear some answers in a human voice, but I heard no other returns than in the same dialect, only one or two a little shriller than his. I began to think that this house must belong to some person of great note among them, because there appeared so much ceremony before I could gain admittance. But, that a man of quality should be served all by horses, was beyond my comprehension. I feared my brain was disturbed by my sufferings and misfortunes; I roused myself, and looked about me in the room where I was left alone; this was furnished as the first, only after a more elegant manner. I rubbed my eyes often, but the same objects still occurred. I pinched my arms and sides, to awaken myself, hoping I might be in a dream. I then absolutely concluded that all these appearances could be nothing else but necromancy and magic. But I had no time to pursue these reflections; for the grey horse came to the door, and made me a sign to follow him into the third room; where I saw a very comely mare, together with a colt and foal, sitting on their haunches, upon mats of straw, not unartfully made, and perfectly neat and clean.

The mare soon after my entrance, rose from her mat, and coming up close, after having nicely observed my hands and face, gave me a most contemptuous look; then turning to the horse, I heard the word Yahoo often repeated betwixt them; the meaning of which word I could not then comprehend, although it were the first I had learned to pronounce; but I was soon better informed, to my everlasting mortification: for the horse beckoning to me with his head, and repeating the word, "Hhuun, Hhuun," as he did upon the road, which I understood was to attend him, led me out into a kind of court, where was another building at some distance from the house. Here we entered, and I saw three of those detestable creatures, which I first met after my landing, feeding upon roots, and the flesh of some animals, which I afterwards found to be that of asses and dogs, and now and then a cow dead by accident or disease. They were all tied by the neck with strong withes,[3] fastened to a beam; they held their food between the claws of their forefeet, and tore it with their teeth.

The master horse ordered a sorrel nag, one of his servants, to untie the largest of these animals, and take him into a yard. The beast and I were brought close together; and our countenances diligently compared, both by master and servant, who thereupon repeated several times the word "Yahoo." My horror and astonishment are not to be described, when I observed, in this abominable animal, a perfect human figure; the face of it indeed was flat and broad, the

2. To wait. "Vista": a long, open corridor.

3. Slender, flexible branches.

nose depressed, the lips large, and the mouth wide; but these differences are common to all savage nations, where the lineaments of the countenance are distorted by the natives suffering their infants to lie groveling on the earth, or by carrying them on their backs, nuzzling with their face against the mother's shoulders. The forefeet of the Yahoo differed from my hands in nothing else but the length of the nails, the coarseness and brownness of the palms, and the hairiness on the backs. There was the same resemblance between our feet, with the same differences, which I knew very well, although the horses did not, because of my shoes and stockings; the same in every part of our bodies, except as to hairiness and color, which I have already described.

The great difficulty that seemed to stick with the two horses was to see the rest of my body so very different from that of a Yahoo, for which I was obliged to my clothes, whereof they had no conception; the sorrel nag offered me a root, which he held (after their manner, as we shall describe in its proper place) between his hoof and pastern; I took it in my hand, and having smelled it, returned it to him again as civilly as I could. He brought out of the Yahoo's kennel a piece of ass's flesh, but it smelled so offensively that I turned from it with loathing; he then threw it to the Yahoo, by whom it was greedily devoured. He afterwards showed me a wisp of hay, and a fetlock full of oats; but I shook my head, to signify that neither of these were food for me. And indeed, I now apprehended that I must absolutely starve, if I did not get to some of my own species; for as to those filthy Yahoos, although there were few greater lovers of mankind, at that time, than myself, yet I confess I never saw any sensitive being so detestable on all accounts; and the more I came near them, the more hateful they grew, while I stayed in that country. This the master horse observed by my behavior, and therefore sent the Yahoo back to his kennel. He then put his forehoof to his mouth, at which I was much surprised, although he did it with ease, and with a motion that appeared perfectly natural; and made other signs to know what I would eat; but I could not return him such an answer as he was able to apprehend; and if he had understood me, I did not see how it was possible to contrive any way for finding myself nourishment. While we were thus engaged, I observed a cow passing by; whereupon I pointed to her, and expressed a desire to let me go and milk her. This had its effect; for he led me back into the house, and ordered a mare-servant to open a room, where a good store of milk lay in earthen and wooden vessels, after a very orderly and cleanly manner. She gave me a large bowl full, of which I drank very heartily, and found myself well refreshed.

About noon I saw coming towards the house a kind of vehicle, drawn like a sledge by four Yahoos. There was in it an old steed, who seemed to be of quality; he alighted with his hind feet forward, having by accident got a hurt in his left forefoot. He came to dine with our horse, who received him with great civility. They dined in the best room, and had oats boiled in milk for the second course, which the old horse eat warm, but the rest cold. Their mangers were placed circular in the middle of the room, and divided into several partitions, round which they sat on their haunches upon bosses[4] of straw. In the middle was a large rack with angles answering to every partition of the manger. So that each horse and mare eat their own hay, and their own mash of oats and milk, with much decency and regularity. The behavior of the young colt and foal appeared very modest; and that of the master and mistress extremely

4. Seats of bundled grasses.

cheerful and complaisant to their guest. The grey ordered me to stand by him; and much discourse passed between him and his friend concerning me, as I found by the stranger's often looking on me, and the frequent repetition of the word Yahoo.

I happened to wear my gloves; which the master grey observing, seemed perplexed; discovering signs of wonder what I had done to my forefeet; he put his hoof three or four times to them, as if he would signify, that I should reduce them to their former shape, which I presently did, pulling off both my gloves, and putting them into my pocket. This occasioned farther talk, and I saw the company was pleased with my behavior, whereof I soon found the good effects. I was ordered to speak the few words I understood; and while they were at dinner, the master taught me the names for oats, milk, fire, water, and some others which I could readily pronounce after him, having from my youth a great facility in learning languages.

When dinner was done, the master horse took me aside, and by signs and words made me understand the concern he was in that I had nothing to eat. Oats in their tongue are called *hlunnh*. This word I pronounced two or three times; for although I had refused them at first, yet upon second thoughts, I considered that I could contrive to make a kind of bread, which might be sufficient with milk to keep me alive, till I could make my escape to some other country, and to creatures of my own species. The horse immediately ordered a white mare-servant of his family to bring me a good quantity of oats in a sort of wooden tray. These I heated before the fire as well as I could, and rubbed them till the husks came off, which I made a shift to winnow from the grain; I ground and beat them between two stones, then took water, and made them into a paste or cake, which I toasted at the fire, and eat warm with milk. It was at first a very insipid diet, although common enough in many parts of Europe, but grew tolerable by time; and having been often reduced to hard fare in my life, this was not the first experiment I had made how easily nature is satisfied. And I cannot but observe that I never had one hour's sickness, while I staid in this island. It is true, I sometimes made a shift to catch a rabbit, or bird, by springes[5] made of Yahoos' hairs; and I often gathered wholesome herbs, which I boiled, or eat as salads with my bread; and now and then, for a rarity, I made a little butter, and drank the whey. I was at first at a great loss for salt; but custom soon reconciled the want of it; and I am confident that the frequent use of salt among us is an effect of luxury, and was first introduced only as a provocative to drink; except where it is necessary for preserving of flesh in long voyages, or in places remote from great markets. For we observe no animal to be fond of it but man;[6] and as to myself, when I left this country, it was a great while before I could endure the taste of it in anything that I eat.

This is enough to say upon the subject of my diet, wherewith other travelers fill their books, as if the readers were personally concerned whether we fare well or ill. However, it was necessary to mention this matter, lest the world should think it impossible that I could find sustenance for three years in such a country, and among such inhabitants.

When it grew towards evening, the master horse ordered a place for me to lodge in; it was but six yards from the house, and separated from the stable of

5. Snares.
6. Gulliver is, of course, in error; many animals require salt.

the Yahoos. Here I got some straw, and covering myself with my own clothes, slept very sound. But I was in a short time better accommodated, as the reader shall know hereafter, when I come to treat more particularly about my way of living.

CHAPTER 3. *The Author studious to learn the language, the Houyhnhnm his master assists in teaching him. The language described. Several Houyhnhnms of quality come out of curiosity to see the Author. He gives his master a short account of his voyage.*

My principal endeavor was to learn the language, which my master (for so I shall henceforth call him) and his children, and every servant of his house were desirous to teach me. For they looked upon it as a prodigy, that a brute animal should discover such marks of a rational creature. I pointed to everything, and enquired the name of it, which I wrote down in my journal book when I was alone, and corrected my bad accent, by desiring those of the family to pronounce it often. In this employment, a sorrel nag, one of the under servants, was very ready to assist me.

In speaking, they pronounce through the nose and throat, and their language approaches nearest to the High Dutch or German, of any I know in Europe; but is much more graceful and significant. The Emperor Charles V made almost the same observation, when he said, that if he were to speak to his horse, it should be in High Dutch.[7]

The curiosity and impatience of my master were so great, that he spent many hours of his leisure to instruct me. He was convinced (as he afterwards told me) that I must be a Yahoo, but my teachableness, civility, and cleanliness astonished him; which were qualities altogether so opposite to those animals. He was most perplexed about my clothes, reasoning sometimes with himself whether they were a part of my body; for I never pulled them off till the family were asleep, and got them on before they waked in the morning. My master was eager to learn from whence I came; how I acquired those appearances of reason, which I discovered in all my actions; and to know my story from my own mouth, which he hoped he should soon do by the great proficiency I made in learning and pronouncing their words and sentences. To help my memory, I formed all I learned into the English alphabet, and writ the words down with the translations. This last, after some time, I ventured to do in my master's presence. It cost me much trouble to explain to him what I was doing; for the inhabitants have not the least idea of books or literature.

In about ten weeks time I was able to understand most of his questions; and in three months could give him some tolerable answers. He was extremely curious to know from what part of the country I came, and how I was taught to imitate a rational creature; because the Yahoos (whom he saw I exactly resembled in my head, hands, and face, that were only visible) with some appearance of cunning, and the strongest disposition to mischief, were observed to be the most unteachable of all brutes. I answered that I came over the sea, from a far place, with many others of my own kind, in a great hollow vessel made of the bodies of trees; that my companions forced me to land on this coast, and then left me to shift for myself. It was with some difficulty, and

7. The emperor is supposed to have said that he would speak to his God in Spanish, to his mistress in Italian, and to his horse in German.

by the help of many signs, that I brought him to understand me. He replied that I must needs be mistaken, or that I *said the thing which was not*. (For they have no word in their language to express lying or falsehood.) He knew it was impossible that there could be a country beyond the sea, or that a parcel of brutes could move a wooden vessel whither they pleased upon water. He was sure no Houyhnhnm alive could make such a vessel, or would trust Yahoos to manage it.

The word Houyhnhnm, in their tongue, signifies a Horse; and in its etymology, the Perfection of Nature. I told my master that I was at a loss for expression, but would improve as fast as I could; and hoped in a short time I should be able to tell him wonders. He was pleased to direct his own mare, his colt, and foal, and the servants of the family to take all opportunities of instructing me; and every day for two or three hours, he was at the same pains himself. Several horses and mares of quality in the neighborhood came often to our house, upon the report spread of a wonderful Yahoo, that could speak like a Houyhnhnm, and seemed in his words and actions to discover some glimmerings of reason. These delighted to converse with me; they put many questions, and received such answers as I was able to return. By all which advantages, I made so great a progress, that in five months from my arrival, I understood whatever was spoke, and could express myself tolerably well.

The Houyhnhnms who came to visit my master, out of a design of seeing and talking with me, could hardly believe me to be a right Yahoo, because my body had a different covering from others of my kind. They were astonished to observe me without the usual hair or skin, except on my head, face, and hands; but I discovered that secret to my master, upon an accident, which happened about a fortnight before.

I have already told the reader, that every night when the family were gone to bed, it was my custom to strip and cover myself with my clothes; it happened one morning early, that my master sent for me, by the sorrel nag, who was his valet; when he came, I was fast asleep, my clothes fallen off on one side, and my shirt above my waist. I awaked at the noise he made, and observed him to deliver his message in some disorder; after which he went to my master, and in a great fright gave him a very confused account of what he had seen. This I presently discovered; for going as soon as I was dressed, to pay my attendance upon his honor, he asked me the meaning of what his servant had reported; that I was not the same thing when I slept as I appeared to be at other times; that his valet assured him, some part of me was white, some yellow, at least not so white, and some brown.

I had hitherto concealed the secret of my dress, in order to distinguish myself as much as possible, from that cursed race of Yahoos; but now I found it in vain to do so any longer. Besides, I considered that my clothes and shoes would soon wear out, which already were in a declining condition, and must be supplied by some contrivance from the hides of Yahoos, or other brutes; whereby the whole secret would be known. I therefore told my master, that in the country from whence I came, those of my kind always covered their bodies with the hairs of certain animals prepared by art, as well for decency, as to avoid inclemencies of air both hot and cold; of which, as to my own person I would give him immediate conviction, if he pleased to command me; only desiring his excuse, if I did not expose those parts that Nature taught us to conceal. He said, my discourse was all very strange, but especially the last part; for he could not understand why Nature should teach us to conceal what

Nature had given. That neither himself nor family were ashamed of any parts of their bodies; but however I might do as I pleased. Whereupon, I first unbuttoned my coat, and pulled it off. I did the same with my waistcoat; I drew off my shoes, stockings, and breeches. I let my shirt down to my waist, and drew up the bottom, fastening it like a girdle about my middle to hide my nakedness.

My master observed the whole performance with great signs of curiosity and admiration. He took up all my clothes in his pastern, one piece after another, and examined them diligently; he then stroked my body very gently, and looked round me several times; after which he said, it was plain I must be a perfect Yahoo; but that I differed very much from the rest of my species, in the whiteness and smoothness of my skin, my want of hair in several parts of my body, the shape and shortness of my claws behind and before, and my affectation of walking continually on my two hinder feet. He desired to see no more; and gave me leave to put on my clothes again, for I was shuddering with cold.

I expressed my uneasiness at his giving me so often the appellation of Yahoo, an odious animal, for which I had so utter an hatred and contempt. I begged he would forbear applying that word to me, and take the same order in his family, and among his friends whom he suffered to see me. I requested likewise, that the secret of my having a false covering to my body might be known to none but himself, at least as long as my present clothing should last; for as to what the sorrel nag his valet had observed, his honor might command him to conceal it.

All this my master very graciously consented to; and thus the secret was kept till my clothes began to wear out, which I was forced to supply by several contrivances, that shall hereafter be mentioned. In the meantime, he desired I would go on with my utmost diligence to learn their language, because he was more astonished at my capacity for speech and reason, than at the figure of my body, whether it were covered or no; adding that he waited with some impatience to hear the wonders which I promised to tell him.

From thenceforward he doubled the pains he had been at to instruct me; he brought me into all company, and made them treat me with civility, because, as he told them privately, this would put me into good humor, and make me more diverting.

Every day when I waited on him, beside the trouble he was at in teaching, he would ask me several questions concerning myself, which I answered as well as I could; and by those means he had already received some general ideas, although very imperfect. It would be tedious to relate the several steps, by which I advanced to a more regular conversation, but the first account I gave of myself in any order and length was to this purpose:

That, I came from a very far country, as I already had attempted to tell him, with about fifty more of my own species; that we traveled upon the seas, in a great hollow vessel made of wood, and larger than his honor's house. I described the ship to him in the best terms I could; and explained by the help of my handkerchief displayed, how it was driven forward by the wind. That, upon a quarrel among us, I was set on shore on this coast, where I walked forward without knowing whither, till he delivered me from the persecution of those execrable Yahoos. He asked me who made the ship, and how it was possible that the Houyhnhnms of my country would leave it to the management of brutes? My answer was that I durst proceed no farther in my relation, unless he would give me his word and honor that he would not be offended; and then I would tell him the wonders I had so often promised. He agreed;

and I went on by assuring him, that the ship was made by creatures like myself, who in all the countries I had traveled, as well as in my own, were the only governing, rational animals; and that upon my arrival hither, I was as much astonished to see the Houyhnhnms act like rational beings, as he or his friends could be in finding some marks of reason in a creature he was pleased to call a Yahoo; to which I owned my resemblance in every part, but could not account for their degenerate and brutal nature. I said farther, that if good fortune ever restored me to my native country, to relate my travels hither, as I resolved to do, everybody would believe that I *said the thing which was not,* that I invented the story out of my own head; and with all possible respect to himself, his family, and friends, and under his promise of not being offended, our countrymen would hardly think it probable, that a Houyhnhnm should be the presiding creature of a nation, and a Yahoo the brute.

Chapter 4. *The Houyhnhnms' notion of truth and falsehood. The Author's discourse disapproved by his master. The Author gives a more particular account of himself, and the accidents of his voyage.*

My master heard me with great appearances of uneasiness in his countenance; because *doubting* or *not believing* are so little known in this country, that the inhabitants cannot tell how to behave themselves under such circumstances. And I remember in frequent discourses with my master concerning the nature of manhood, in other parts of the world, having occasion to talk of *lying* and *false representation,* it was with much difficulty that he comprehended what I meant; although he had otherwise a most acute judgment. For he argued thus: that the use of speech was to make us understand one another, and to receive information of facts; now if anyone *said the thing which was not,* these ends were defeated; because I cannot properly be said to understand him; and I am so far from receiving information, that he leaves me worse than in ignorance; for I am led to believe a thing *black* when it is *white,* and *short* when it is *long.* And these were all the notions he had concerning the faculty of *lying,* so perfectly well understood, and so universally practiced among human creatures.

To return from this digression; when I asserted that the Yahoos were the only governing animals in my country, which my master said was altogether past his conception, he desired to know, whether we had Houyhnhnms among us, and what was their employment. I told him we had great numbers; that in summer they grazed in the fields, and in winter were kept in houses, with hay and oats, where Yahoo servants were employed to rub their skins smooth, comb their manes, pick their feet, serve them with food, and make their beds. "I understand you well," said my master; "it is now very plain from all you have spoken, that whatever share of reason the Yahoos pretend to, the Houyhnhnms are your masters; I heartily wish our Yahoos would be so tractable." I begged his honor would please to excuse me from proceeding any farther, because I was very certain that the account he expected from me would be highly displeasing. But he insisted in commanding me to let him know the best and the worst; I told him he should be obeyed. I owned that the Houyhnhnms among us, whom we called Horses, were the most generous[8] and comely animal we had; that they excelled in strength and swiftness; and when they belonged to

8. Noble.

persons of quality, employed in traveling, racing, and drawing chariots, they were treated with much kindness and care, till they fell into diseases, or became foundered in the feet; but then they were sold, and used to all kind of drudgery till they died; after which their skins were stripped and sold for what they were worth, and their bodies left to be devoured by dogs and birds of prey. But the common race of horses had not so good fortune, being kept by farmers and carriers, and other mean people, who put them to greater labor, and feed them worse. I described as well as I could, our way of riding; the shape and use of a bridle, a saddle, a spur, and a whip; of harness and wheels. I added, that we fastened plates of a certain hard substance called iron at the bottom of their feet, to preserve their hoofs from being broken by the stony ways on which we often traveled.

My master, after some expressions of great indignation, wondered how we dared to venture upon a Houyhnhnm's back; for he was sure, that the weakest servant in his house would be able to shake off the strongest Yahoo; or by lying down, and rolling upon his back, squeeze the brute to death. I answered that our horses were trained up from three or four years old to the several uses we intended them for; that if any of them proved intolerably vicious, they were employed for carriages; that they were severely beaten while they were young for any mischievous tricks; that the males, designed for the common use of riding or draught, were generally castrated about two years after their birth, to take down their spirits, and make them more tame and gentle; that they were indeed sensible of rewards and punishments; but his honor would please to consider that they had not the least tincture of reason any more than the Yahoos in this country.

It put me to the pains of many circumlocutions to give my master a right idea of what I spoke; for their language doth not abound in variety of words, because their wants and passions are fewer than among us. But it is impossible to express his noble resentment at our savage treatment of the Houyhnhnm race; particularly after I had explained the manner and use of castrating horses among us, to hinder them from propagating their kind, and to render them more servile. He said, if it were possible there could be any country where Yahoos alone were endued with reason, they certainly must be the governing animal, because reason will in time always prevail against brutal strength. But, considering the frame of our bodies, and especially of mine, he thought no creature of equal bulk was so ill-contrived for employing that reason in the common offices of life; whereupon he desired to know whether those among whom I lived resembled me or the Yahoos of his country. I assured him that I was as well shaped as most of my age; but the younger and the females were much more soft and tender, and the skins of the latter generally as white as milk. He said I differed indeed from other Yahoos, being much more cleanly, and not altogether so deformed; but in point of real advantage, he thought I differed for the worse. That my nails were of no use either to my fore or hinder feet; as to my forefeet, he could not properly call them by that name, for he never observed me to walk upon them; that they were too soft to bear the ground; that I generally went with them uncovered, neither was the covering I sometimes wore on them of the same shape, or so strong as that on my feet behind. That I could not walk with any security; for if either of my hinder feet slipped, I must inevitably fall. He then began to find fault with other parts of my body; the flatness of my face, the prominence of my nose, my eyes placed directly in front, so that I could not look on either side without turning my head; that I was not able to feed myself without lifting one of my forefeet to my mouth; and therefore nature had placed those joints to answer that necessity. He knew not what could be the use of those several clefts and divisions in my feet behind; that these were too soft to bear the hardness and sharpness of stones without a covering made from the skin of some other brute; that my whole body wanted a fence against heat and cold, which I was forced to put on and off every day with tediousness and trouble. And lastly, that he observed every animal in his country naturally to abhor the Yahoos, whom the weaker avoided, and the stronger drove from them. So that supposing us to have the gift of reason, he could not see how it were possible to cure that natural antipathy which every creature discovered against us; nor consequently, how we could tame and render them serviceable. However, he would (as he said) debate the matter no farther, because he was more desirous to know my own story, the country where I was born, and the several actions and events of my life before I came hither.

I assured him how extremely desirous I was that he should be satisfied in every point; but I doubted much whether it would be possible for me to explain myself on several subjects whereof his honor could have no conception, because I saw nothing in his country to which I could resemble them. That however, I would do my best, and strive to express myself by similitudes, humbly desiring his assistance when I wanted proper words; which he was pleased to promise me.

I said, my birth was of honest parents, in an island called England, which was remote from this country, as many days journey as the strongest of his honor's servants could travel in the annual course of the sun. That I was bred a surgeon, whose trade it is to cure wounds and hurts in the body, got by accident or violence. That my country was governed by a female man, whom we called a queen. That I left it to get riches, whereby I might maintain myself and family when I should return. That in my last voyage, I was Commander of the ship and had about fifty Yahoos under me, many of which died at sea, and I was forced to supply them by others picked out from several nations. That our ship was twice in danger of being sunk; the first time by a great storm, and the second, by striking against a rock. Here my master interposed, by asking me, how I could persuade strangers out of different countries to venture with me, after the losses I had sustained, and the hazards I had run. I said, they were fellows of desperate fortunes, forced to fly from the places of their birth, on account of their poverty or their crimes. Some were undone by lawsuits; others spent all they had in drinking, whoring, and gaming; others fled for treason; many for murder, theft, poisoning, robbery, perjury, forgery, coining false money; for committing rapes or sodomy; for flying from their colors, or deserting to the enemy; and most of them had broken prison. None of these durst return to their native countries for fear of being hanged, or of starving in a jail; and therefore were under a necessity of seeking a livelihood in other places.

During this discourse, my master was pleased often to interrupt me. I had made use of many circumlocutions in describing to him the nature of the several crimes, for which most of our crew had been forced to fly their country. This labor took up several days conversation before he was able to comprehend me. He was wholly at a loss to know what could be the use or necessity of practicing those vices. To clear up which I endeavored to give him some ideas of the desire of power and riches; of the terrible effects of lust, intemperance, malice, and envy. All this I was forced to define and describe by putting of cases, and making suppositions. After which, like one whose imagination was struck with something never seen or heard of before, he would lift up his eyes with amazement and indignation. Power, government, war, law, punishment, and a thousand other things had no terms, wherein that language could express them; which made the difficulty almost insuperable to give my master any conception of what I meant; but being of an excellent understanding, much improved by contemplation and converse, he at last arrived at a competent knowledge of what human nature in our parts of the world is capable to perform; and desired I would give him some particular account of that land, which we call Europe, especially, of my own country.

CHAPTER 5. *The Author, at his master's commands, informs him of the state of England. The causes of war among the princes of Europe. The Author begins to explain the English Constitution.*

The reader may please to observe that the following extract of many conversations I had with my master contains a summary of the most material points, which were discoursed at several times for above two years; his honor often desiring fuller satisfaction as I farther improved in the Houyhnhnm tongue. I laid before him, as well as I could, the whole state of Europe; I discoursed of trade and manufactures, of arts and sciences; and the answers I gave to all the questions he made, as they arose upon several subjects, were a fund of conversation not to be exhausted. But I shall here only set down the substance of what passed between us concerning my own country, reducing it into order as well as I can, without any regard to time or other circumstances, while I strictly adhere to truth. My only concern is that I shall hardly be able to do justice to my master's arguments and expressions; which must needs suffer by my want of capacity, as well as by a translation into our barbarous English.

In obedience therefore to his honor's commands, I related to him the Revolution under the Prince of Orange; the long war with France entered into by the said Prince, and renewed by his successor the present queen; wherein the greatest powers of Christendom were engaged, and which still continued. I computed at his request, that about a million of Yahoos might have been killed in the whole progress of it; and perhaps a hundred or more cities taken, and five times as many ships burned or sunk.[9]

He asked me what were the usual causes or motives that made one country to go to war with another. I answered, they were innumerable; but I should only mention a few of the chief. Sometimes the ambition of princes, who never think they have land or people enough to govern; sometimes the corruption of ministers, who engage their master in a war in order to stifle or divert the clamor of the subjects against their evil administration. Difference in opinions hath cost many millions of lives; for instance, whether flesh be bread, or bread be flesh; whether the juice of a certain berry be blood or wine; whether whistling be a vice or a virtue; whether it be better to kiss a post, or throw it into the fire; what is the best color for a coat, whether black, white, red, or grey; and whether it should be long or short, narrow or wide, dirty or clean;[1] with

9. Gulliver relates recent English history: the Glorious Revolution (1688–89) and the War of Spanish Succession (1701–13). He greatly exaggerates the casualties in the war.

1. Gulliver refers to the religious controversies of the Reformation and Counter-Reformation: the doctrine of transubstantiation, the use of music in church services, the veneration of the crucifix, and the wearing of priestly vestments.

many more. Neither are any wars so furious and bloody, or of so long continuance, as those occasioned by difference in opinion, especially if it be in things indifferent.[2]

Sometimes the quarrel between two princes is to decide which of them shall dispossess a third of his dominions, where neither of them pretend to any right. Sometimes one prince quarreleth with another, for fear the other should quarrel with him. Sometimes a war is entered upon, because the enemy is too strong, and sometimes because he is too weak. Sometimes our neighbors want the things which we have, or have the things which we want; and we both fight, till they take ours or give us theirs. It is a very justifiable cause of war to invade a country after the people have been wasted by famine, destroyed by pestilence, or embroiled by factions amongst themselves. It is justifiable to enter into a war against our nearest ally, when one of his towns lies convenient for us, or a territory of land, that would render our dominions round and compact. If a prince send forces into a nation, where the people are poor and ignorant, he may lawfully put half of them to death, and make slaves of the rest, in order to civilize and reduce them from their barbarous way of living. It is a very kingly, honorable, and frequent practice, when one prince desires the assistance of another to secure him against an invasion, that the assistant, when he hath driven out the invader, should seize on the dominions himself, and kill, imprison, or banish the prince he came to relieve. Alliance by blood or marriage is a sufficient cause of war between princes; and the nearer the kindred is, the greater is their disposition to quarrel. Poor nations are hungry, and rich nations are proud; and pride and hunger will ever be at variance. For these reasons, the trade of a soldier is held the most honorable of all others: because a soldier is a Yahoo hired to kill in cold blood as many of his own species, who have never offended him, as possibly he can.

There is likewise a kind of beggarly princes in Europe, not able to make war by themselves, who hire out their troops to richer nations for so much a day to each man; of which they keep three fourths to themselves, and it is the best part of their maintenance; such are those in many northern parts of Europe.[3]

"What you have told me," said my master, "upon the subject of war, doth indeed discover most admirably the effects of that reason you pretend to. However, it is happy that the shame is greater than the danger; and that Nature hath left you utterly uncapable of doing much mischief; for your mouths lying flat with your faces, you can hardly bite each other to any purpose, unless by consent. Then, as to the claws upon your feet before and behind, they are so short and tender, that one of our Yahoos would drive a dozen of yours before him. And therefore in recounting the numbers of those who have been killed in battle, I cannot but think that you have *said the thing which is not*."

I could not forbear shaking my head and smiling a little at his ignorance. And, being no stranger to the art of war, I gave him a description of cannons, culverins, muskets, carabines, pistols, bullets, powder, swords, bayonets, battles, sieges, retreats, attacks, undermines, countermines, bombardments, sea fights; ships sunk with a thousand men; twenty thousand killed on each side; dying groans, limbs flying in the air; smoke, noise, confusion, trampling to death under horses' feet; flight, pursuit, victory; fields strewed with carcasses left for food to dogs, and wolves, and birds of prey; plundering, stripping,

2. Of little consequence.
3. A satiric glance at George I, who, as elector of Hanover, had dealt in this trade.

ravishing, burning, and destroying. And, to set forth the valor of my own dear countrymen, I assured him that I had seen them blow up a hundred enemies at once in a siege, and as many in a ship; and beheld the dead bodies drop down in pieces from the clouds, to the great diversion of all the spectators.

I was going on to more particulars, when my master commanded me silence. He said, whoever understood the nature of Yahoos might easily believe it possible for so vile an animal, to be capable of every action I had named, if their strength and cunning equaled their malice. But, as my discourse had increased his abhorrence of the whole species, so he found it gave him a disturbance in his mind, to which he was wholly a stranger before. He thought his ears being used to such abominable words, might by degrees admit them with less detestation. That, although he hated the Yahoos of this country, yet he no more blamed them for their odious qualities, than he did a *gnnayh* (a bird of prey) for its cruelty, or a sharp stone for cutting his hoof. But, when a creature pretending to reason could be capable of such enormities, he dreaded lest the corruption of that faculty might be worse than brutality itself. He seemed therefore confident, that instead of reason, we were only possessed of some quality fitted to increase our natural vices; as the reflection from a troubled stream returns the image of an ill-shapen body, not only larger, but more distorted.

He added that he had heard too much upon the subject of war, both in this and some former discourses. There was another point which a little perplexed him at present. I had said that some of our crew left their country on account of being ruined by law: that I had already explained the meaning of the word; but he was at a loss how it should come to pass, that the law which was intended for every man's preservation, should be any man's ruin. Therefore he desired to be farther satisfied what I meant by law, and the dispensers thereof, according to the present practice in my own country; because he thought Nature and Reason were sufficient guides for a reasonable animal, as we pretended to be, in showing us what we ought to do, and what to avoid.

I assured his honor that law was a science wherein I had not much conversed, further than by employing advocates, in vain, upon some injustices that had been done me. However, I would give him all the satisfaction I was able.

I said there was a society of men among us, bred up from their youth in the art of proving by words multiplied for the purpose, that white is black, and black is white, according as they are paid. To this society all the rest of the people are slaves.

"For example. If my neighbor hath a mind to my cow, he hires a lawyer to prove that he ought to have my cow from me. I must then hire another to defend my right; it being against all rules of law that any man should be allowed to speak for himself. Now in this case, I who am the true owner lie under two great disadvantages. First, my lawyer being practiced almost from his cradle in defending falsehood is quite out of his element when he would be an advocate for justice, which as an office unnatural, he always attempts with great awkwardness, if not with ill-will. The second disadvantage is that my lawyer must proceed with great caution, or else he will be reprimanded by the judges, and abhorred by his brethren, as one who would lessen the practice of the law. And therefore I have but two methods to preserve my cow. The first is to gain over my adversary's lawyer with a double fee; who will then betray his client, by insinuating that he hath justice on his side. The second way is for my lawyer to make my cause appear as unjust as he can; by allowing the cow to belong to my adversary; and this if it be skillfully done, will certainly bespeak the favor of the bench.

"Now, your honor is to know that these judges are persons appointed to decide all controversies of property, as well as for the trial of criminals; and picked out from the most dextrous lawyers who are grown old or lazy; and having been biased all their lives against truth and equity, lie under such a fatal necessity of favoring fraud, perjury, and oppression, that I have known some of them to have refused a large bribe from the side where justice lay, rather than injure the faculty,[4] by doing anything unbecoming their nature or their office.

"It is a maxim among these lawyers, that whatever hath been done before may legally be done again; and therefore they take special care to record all the decisions formerly made against common justice and the general reason of mankind. These, under the name of *precedents,* they produce as authorities to justify the most iniquitous opinions; and the judges never fail of directing accordingly.

"In pleading, they studiously avoid entering into the merits of the cause; but are loud, violent, and tedious in dwelling upon all circumstances which are not to the purpose. For instance, in the case already mentioned, they never desire to know what claim or title my adversary hath to my cow; but whether the said cow were red or black; her horns long or short; whether the field I graze her in be round or square; whether she were milked at home or abroad; what diseases she is subject to, and the like. After which they consult precedents, adjourn the cause, from time to time, and in ten, twenty, or thirty years come to an issue.

"It is likewise to be observed, that this society hath a peculiar cant and jargon of their own, that no other mortal can understand, and wherein all their laws are written, which they take special care to multiply; whereby they have wholly confounded the very essence of truth and falsehood, of right and wrong; so that it will take thirty years to decide whether the field, left me by my ancestors for six generations, belong to me, or to a stranger three hundred miles off.

"In the trial of persons accused for crimes against the state, the method is much more short and commendable: the judge first sends to sound the disposition of those in power; after which he can easily hang or save the criminal, strictly preserving all the forms of law."

Here my master interposing said it was a pity that creatures endowed with such prodigious abilities of mind as these lawyers, by the description I gave of them, must certainly be, were not rather encouraged to be instructors of others in wisdom and knowledge. In answer to which, I assured his honor that in all points out of their own trade, they were usually the most ignorant and stupid generation among us, the most despicable in common conversation, avowed enemies to all knowledge and learning; and equally disposed to pervert the general reason of mankind, in every other subject of discourse as in that of their own profession.

CHAPTER 6. *A continuation of the state of England, under Queen Anne. The character of a first minister in the courts of Europe.*

4. Profession.

My master was yet wholly at a loss to understand what motives could incite this race of lawyers to perplex, disquiet, and weary themselves by engaging in a confederacy of injustice, merely for the sake of injuring their fellow animals; neither could he comprehend what I meant in saying they did it for hire. Whereupon I was at much pains to describe to him the use of money, the materials it was made of, and the value of the metals; that when a Yahoo had got a great store of this precious substance, he was able to purchase whatever he had a mind to; the finest clothing, the noblest houses, great tracts of land, the most costly meats and drinks; and have his choice of the most beautiful females. Therefore since money alone was able to perform all these feats, our Yahoos thought they could never have enough of it to spend or to save, as they found themselves inclined from their natural bent either to profusion or avarice. That the rich man enjoyed the fruit of the poor man's labor, and the latter were a thousand to one in proportion to the former. That the bulk of our people was forced to live miserably, by laboring every day for small wages to make a few live plentifully. I enlarged myself much on these and many other particulars to the same purpose, but his honor was still to seek,[5] for he went upon a supposition that all animals had a title to their share in the productions of the earth; and especially those who presided over the rest. Therefore he desired I would let him know what these costly meats were, and how any of us happened to want[6] them. Whereupon I enumerated as many sorts as came into my head, with the various methods of dressing them, which could not be done without sending vessels by sea to every part of the world, as well for liquors to drink, as for sauces, and innumerable other conveniencies. I assured him, that this whole globe of earth must be at least three times gone round, before one of our better female Yahoos could get her breakfast, or a cup to put it in. He said, "That must needs be a miserable country which cannot furnish food for its own inhabitants." But what he chiefly wondered at, was how such vast tracts of ground as I described, should be wholly without fresh water, and the people put to the necessity of sending over the sea for drink. I replied that England (the dear place of my nativity) was computed to produce three times the quantity of food, more than its inhabitants are able to consume, as well as liquors extracted from grain, or pressed out of the fruit of certain trees, which made excellent drink; and the same proportion in every other convenience of life. But, in order to feed the luxury and intemperance of the males, and the vanity of the females, we sent away the greatest part of our necessary things to other countries, from whence in return we brought the materials of diseases, folly, and vice, to spend among ourselves. Hence it follows of necessity, that vast numbers of our people are compelled to seek their livelihood by begging, robbing, stealing, cheating, pimping, forswearing, flattering, suborning, forging, gaming, lying, fawning, hectoring, voting, scribbling, star gazing, poisoning, whoring, canting, libeling, freethinking, and the like occupations; every one of which terms, I was at much pains to make him understand.

That, wine was not imported among us from foreign countries, to supply the want of water or other drinks, but because it was a sort of liquid which made us merry, by putting us out of our senses; diverted all melancholy thoughts, begat wild extravagant imaginations in the brain, raised our hopes, and banished our fears; suspended every office of reason for a time, and

5. Still did not understand.

6. Lack.

deprived us of the use of our limbs, until we fell into a profound sleep; although it must be confessed, that we always awaked sick and dispirited; and that the use of this liquor filled us with diseases, which made our lives uncomfortable and short.

But beside all this, the bulk of our people supported themselves by furnishing the necessities or conveniencies of life to the rich, and to each other. For instance, when I am at home and dressed as I ought to be, I carry on my body the workmanship of an hundred tradesmen; the building and furniture of my house employ as many more; and five times the number to adorn my wife.

I was going on to tell him of another sort of people, who get their livelihood by attending the sick; having upon some occasions informed his honor that many of my crew had died of diseases. But here it was with the utmost difficulty that I brought him to apprehend what I meant. He could easily conceive that a Houyhnhnm grew weak and heavy a few days before his death; or by some accident might hurt a limb. But that nature, who worketh all things to perfection, should suffer any pains to breed in our bodies, he thought impossible; and desired to know the reason of so unaccountable an evil. I told him, we fed on a thousand things which operated contrary to each other; that we eat when we were not hungry, and drank without the provocation of thirst; that we sat whole nights drinking strong liquors without eating a bit, which disposed us to sloth, inflamed our bodies, and precipitated or prevented digestion. That, prostitute female Yahoos acquired a certain malady, which bred rottenness in the bones of those who fell into their embraces; that this and many other diseases were propagated from father to son; so that great numbers come into the world with complicated maladies upon them; that it would be endless to give him a catalogue of all diseases incident to human bodies; for they could not be fewer than five or six hundred, spread over every limb, and joint; in short, every part, external and intestine, having diseases appropriated to each. To remedy which, there was a sort of people bred up among us, in the profession or pretense of curing the sick. And because I had some skill in the faculty, I would in gratitude to his honor let him know the whole mystery and method by which they proceed.

Their fundamental is that all diseases arise from repletion; from whence they conclude, that a great evacuation of the body is necessary, either through the natural passage, or upwards at the mouth. Their next business is, from herbs, minerals, gums, oils, shells, salts, juices, seaweed, excrements, barks of trees, serpents, toads, frogs, spiders, dead men's flesh and bones, birds, beasts and fishes, to form a composition for smell and taste the most abominable, nauseous, and detestable, that they can possibly contrive, which the stomach immediately rejects with loathing, and this they call a vomit. Or else from the same storehouse, with some other poisonous additions, they command us to take in at the orifice above or below (just as the physician then happens to be disposed) a medicine equally annoying and disgustful to the bowels; which relaxing the belly, drives down all before it; and this they call a purge, or a clyster. For nature (as the physicians allege) having intended the superior anterior orifice only for the intromission of solids and liquids, and the inferior posterior for ejection, these artists ingeniously considering that in all diseases nature is forced out of her seat; therefore to replace her in it, the body must be treated in a manner directly contrary, by interchanging the use of each orifice; forcing solids and liquids in at the anus, and making evacuations at the mouth.

But, besides real diseases, we are subject to many that are only imaginary, for which the physicians have invented imaginary cures; these have their several names, and so have the drugs that are proper for them; and with these our female Yahoos are always infested.

One great excellency in this tribe is their skill at prognostics, wherein they seldom fail; their predictions in real diseases, when they rise to any degree of malignity, generally portending death, which is always in their power, when recovery is not, and therefore, upon any unexpected signs of amendment, after they have pronounced their sentence, rather than be accused as false prophets, they know how to approve[7] their sagacity to the world by a seasonable dose.

They are likewise of special use to husbands and wives, who are grown weary of their mates; to eldest sons, to great ministers of state, and often to princes.

I had formerly upon occasion discoursed with my master upon the nature of government in general, and particularly of our own excellent constitution, deservedly the wonder and envy of the whole world. But having here accidently mentioned a minister of state, he commanded me some time after to inform him what species of Yahoo I particularly meant by that appellation.

I told him that a first or chief minister of state, whom I intended to describe, was a creature wholly exempt from joy and grief, love and hatred, pity and anger; at least makes use of no other passions but a violent desire of wealth, power, and titles; that he applies his words to all uses, except to the indication of his mind; that he never tells a truth, but with an intent that you should take it for a lie; nor a lie, but with a design that you should take it for a truth; that those he speaks worst of behind their backs are in the surest way to preferment; and whenever he begins to praise you to others or to yourself, you are from that day forlorn. The worst mark you can receive is a promise, especially when it is confirmed with an oath; after which every wise man retires, and gives over all hopes.

There are three methods by which a man may rise to be chief minister: the first is by knowing how with prudence to dispose of a wife, a daughter, or a sister; the second, by betraying or undermining his predecessor; and the third is by a furious zeal in public assemblies against the corruptions of the court. But a wise prince would rather choose to employ those who practice the last of these methods; because such zealots prove always the most obsequious and subservient to the will and passions of their master. That, these ministers having all employments at their disposal, preserve themselves in power by bribing the majority of a senate or great council; and at last by an expedient called an Act of Indemnity[8] (whereof I described the nature to him) they secure themselves from after reckonings, and retire from the public, laden with the spoils of the nation.

The palace of a chief minister is a seminary to breed up others in his own trade; the pages, lackies, and porter, by imitating their master, become ministers of state in their several districts, and learn to excel in the three principal ingredients, of insolence, lying, and bribery. Accordingly, they have a subaltern court paid to them by persons of the best rank; and sometimes by the force of dexterity and impudence, arrive through several gradations to be successors to their lord.

He is usually governed by a decayed wench, or favorite footman, who are

7. Prove.
8. An act passed at each session of Parliament to protect ministers of state who in good faith might have acted illegally.

the tunnels through which all graces are conveyed, and may properly be called, in the last resort, the governors of the kingdom.

One day, my master, having heard me mention the nobility of my country, was pleased to make me a compliment which I could not pretend to deserve: that, he was sure, I must have been born of some noble family, because I far exceeded in shape, color, and cleanliness, all the Yahoos of his nation, although I seemed to fail in strength, and agility, which must be imputed to my different way of living from those other brutes; and besides, I was not only endowed with the faculty of speech, but likewise with some rudiments of reason, to a degree, that with all his acquaintance I passed for a prodigy.

He made me observe, that among the Houyhnhnms, the white, the sorrel, and the iron grey were not so exactly shaped as the bay, the dapple grey, and the black; nor born with equal talents of mind, or a capacity to improve them; and therefore continued always in the condition of servants, without ever aspiring to match out of their own race, which in that country would be reckoned monstrous and unnatural.

I made his honor my most humble acknowledgments for the good opinion he was pleased to conceive of me; but assured him at the same time, that my birth was of the lower sort, having been born of plain, honest parents, who were just able to give me a tolerable education; that, nobility among us was altogether a different thing from the idea he had of it; that, our young noblemen are bred from their childhood in idleness and luxury; that, as soon as years will permit, they consume their vigor, and contract odious diseases among lewd females; and when their fortunes are almost ruined, they marry some woman of mean birth, disagreeable person, and unsound constitution, merely for the sake of money, whom they hate and despise. That, the productions of such marriages are generally scrofulous, rickety or deformed children; by which means the family seldom continues above three generations, unless the wife take care to provide a healthy father among her neighbors, or domestics, in order to improve and continue the breed. That a weak diseased body, a meager countenance, and sallow complexion are the true marks of noble blood; and a healthy robust appearance is so disgraceful in a man of quality, that the world concludes his real father to have been a groom or a coachman. The imperfections of his mind run parallel with those of his body; being a composition of spleen, dullness, ignorance, caprice, sensuality, and pride.

Without the consent of this illustrious body, no law can be enacted, repealed, or altered, and these nobles have likewise the decision of all our possessions without appeal.

CHAPTER 7. *The Author's great love of his native country. His master's observations upon the constitution and administration of England, as described by the Author, with parallel cases and comparisons. His master's observations upon human nature.*

The reader may be disposed to wonder how I could prevail on myself to give so free a representation of my own species, among a race of mortals who were already too apt to conceive the vilest opinion of humankind, from that entire congruity betwixt me and their Yahoos. But I must freely confess that the many virtues of those excellent quadrupeds placed in opposite view to human corruptions had so far opened my eyes, and enlarged my understanding, that I began to view the actions and passions of man in a very different light; and to think the honor of my own kind not worth managing;[9] which, besides, it was impossible for me to do before a person of so acute a judgment as my master, who daily convinced me of a thousand faults in myself, whereof I had not the least perception before, and which with us would never be numbered even among human infirmities. I had likewise learned from his example an utter detestation of all falsehood or disguise; and truth appeared so amiable to me, that I determined upon sacrificing everything to it.

Let me deal so candidly with the reader as to confess that there was yet a much stronger motive for the freedom I took in my representation of things. I had not been a year in this country, before I contracted such a love and veneration for the inhabitants, that I entered on a firm resolution never to return to humankind, but to pass the rest of my life among these admirable Houyhnhnms in the contemplation and practice of every virtue; where I could have no example or incitement to vice. But it was decreed by fortune, my perpetual enemy, that so great a felicity should not fall to my share. However, it is now some comfort to reflect that in what I said of my countrymen, I extenuated their faults as much as I durst before so strict an examiner; and upon every article, gave as favorable a turn as the matter would bear. For, indeed, who is there alive that will not be swayed by his bias and partiality to the place of his birth?

I have related the substance of several conversations I had with my master, during the greatest part of the time I had the honor to be in his service; but have indeed for brevity sake omitted much more than is here set down.

When I had answered all his questions, and his curiosity seemed to be fully satisfied; he sent for me one morning early, and commanding me to sit down at some distance (an honor which he had never before conferred upon me), he said he had been very seriously considering my whole story, as far as it related both to myself and my country; that, he looked upon us as a sort of animals to whose share, by what accident he could not conjecture, some small pittance of reason had fallen, whereof we made no other use than by its assistance to aggravate our natural corruptions, and to acquire new ones which nature had not given us. That we disarmed ourselves of the few abilities she had bestowed; had been very successful in multiplying our original wants, and seemed to spend our whole lives in vain endeavors to supply them by our own inventions. That, as to myself, it was manifest I had neither the strength or agility of a common Yahoo; that I walked infirmly on my hinder feet; had found out a contrivance to make my claws of no use or defense, and to remove the hair from my chin, which was intended as a shelter from the sun and the weather. Lastly, that I could neither run with speed, nor climb trees like my brethren (as he called them) the Yahoos in this country.

That our institutions of government and law were plainly owing to our gross defects in reason, and by consequence, in virtue; because reason alone is sufficient to govern a rational creature; which was therefore a character we had no pretense to challenge, even from the account I had given of my own people; although he manifestly perceived, that in order to favor them, I had concealed many particulars, and often *said the thing which was not*.

He was the more confirmed in this opinion, because he observed that I agreed in every feature of my body with other Yahoos, except where it was to my real disadvantage in point of strength, speed, and activity, the shortness of

9. Taking care of.

my claws, and some other particulars where Nature had no part; so, from the representation I had given him of our lives, our manners, and our actions, he found as near a resemblance in the disposition of our minds. He said the Yahoos were known to hate one another more than they did any different species of animals; and the reason usually assigned was the odiousness of their own shapes, which all could see in the rest, but not in themselves. He had therefore begun to think it not unwise in us to cover our bodies, and by that invention, conceal many of our deformities from each other, which would else be hardly supportable. But he now found he had been mistaken; and that the dissensions of those brutes in his country were owing to the same cause with ours, as I had described them. For, if (said he) you throw among five Yahoos as much food as would be sufficient for fifty, they will instead of eating peaceably, fall together by the ears, each single one impatient to have all to itself; and therefore a servant was usually employed to stand by while they were feeding abroad, and those kept at home were tied at a distance from each other. That, if a cow died of age or accident, before a Houyhnhnm could secure it for his own Yahoos, those in the neighborhood would come in herds to seize it, and then would ensue such a battle as I had described, with terrible wounds made by their claws on both sides, although they seldom were able to kill one another, for want of such convenient instruments of death as we had invented. At other times the like battles have been fought between the Yahoos of several neighborhoods without any visible cause; those of one district watching all opportunities to surprise the next before they are prepared. But if they find their project hath miscarried, they return home, and for want of enemies, engage in what I call a civil war among themselves.

That, in some fields of his country, there are certain shining stones of several colors, whereof the Yahoos are violently fond; and when part of these stones are fixed in the earth, as it sometimes happeneth, they will dig with their claws for whole days to get them out, and carry them away, and hide them by heaps in their kennels; but still looking round with great caution, for fear their comrades should find out their treasure. My master said he could never discover the reason of this unnatural appetite, or how these stones could be of any use to a Yahoo; but now he believed it might proceed from the same principle of avarice, which I had ascribed to mankind. That he had once, by way of experiment, privately removed a heap of these stones from the place where one of his Yahoos had buried it, whereupon, the sordid animal missing his treasure, by his loud lamenting brought the whole herd to the place, there miserably howled, then fell to biting and tearing the rest; began to pine away, would neither eat nor sleep, nor work, till he ordered a servant privately to convey the stones into the same hole, and hide them as before; which when his Yahoo had found, he presently recovered his spirits and good humor; but took care to remove them to a better hiding place; and hath ever since been a very serviceable brute.

My master farther assured me, which I also observed myself, that in the fields where these shining stones abound, the fiercest and most frequent battles are fought, occasioned by perpetual inroads of the neighboring Yahoos.

He said it was common when two Yahoos discovered such a stone in a field, and were contending which of them should be the proprietor, a third would take the advantage, and carry it away from them both; which my master would needs contend to have some resemblance with our suits at law; wherein I thought it for our credit not to undeceive him; since the decision he mentioned was much more equitable than many decrees among us; because the plaintiff and defendant there lost nothing beside the stone they contended for; whereas our courts of equity would never have dismissed the cause while either of them had anything left.

My master continuing his discourse said there was nothing that rendered the Yahoos more odious, than their undistinguished appetite to devour everything that came in their way, whether herbs, roots, berries, corrupted flesh of animals, or all mingled together; and it was peculiar in their temper, that they were fonder of what they could get by rapine or stealth at a greater distance, than much better food provided for them at home. If their prey held out, they would eat till they were ready to burst, after which nature had pointed out to them a certain root that gave them a general evacuation.

There was also another kind of root very juicy, but something rare and difficult to be found, which the Yahoos sought for with much eagerness, and would suck it with great delight; it produced the same effects that wine hath upon us. It would make them sometimes hug, and sometimes tear one another; they would howl and grin, and chatter, and reel, and tumble, and then fall asleep in the mud.

I did indeed observe that the Yahoos were the only animals in this country subject to any diseases; which however, were much fewer than horses have among us, and contracted not by any ill treatment they meet with, but by the nastiness and greediness of that sordid brute. Neither has their language any more than a general appellation for those maladies; which is borrowed from the name of the beast, and called *Hnea Yahoo*, or the Yahoo's Evil; and the cure prescribed is a mixture of their own dung and urine, forcibly put down the Yahoo's throat. This I have since often known to have been taken with success, and do here freely recommend it to my countrymen, for the public good, as an admirable specific[1] against all diseases produced by repletion.

As to learning, government, arts, manufactures, and the like, my master confessed he could find little or no resemblance between the Yahoos of that country and those in ours. For he only meant to observe what parity there was in our natures. He had heard indeed some curious Houyhnhnms observe that in most herds there was a sort of ruling Yahoo (as among us there is generally some leading or principal stag in a park) who was always more deformed in body, and mischievous in disposition, than any of the rest. That this leader had usually a favorite as like himself as he could get, whose employment was to lick his master's feet and posteriors, and drive the female Yahoos to his kennel; for which he was now and then rewarded with a piece of ass's flesh. This favorite is hated by the whole herd; and therefore to protect himself, keeps always near the person of his leader. He usually continues in office till a worse can be found; but the very moment he is discarded, his successor, at the head of all the Yahoos in that district, young and old, male and female, come in a body, and discharge their excrements upon him from head to foot. But how far this might be applicable to our courts and favorites, and ministers of state, my master said I could best determine.

I durst make no return to this malicious insinuation, which debased human understanding below the sagacity of a common hound, who hath judgment enough to distinguish and follow the cry of the ablest dog in the pack, without being ever mistaken.

1. Remedy.

My master told me there were some qualities remarkable in the Yahoos, which he had not observed me to mention, or at least very slightly, in the accounts I had given him of humankind. He said, those animals, like other brutes, had their females in common; but in this they differed, that the she-Yahoo would admit the male while she was pregnant; and that the hes would quarrel and fight with the females as fiercely as with each other. Both which practices were such degrees of infamous brutality, that no other sensitive creature ever arrived at.

Another thing he wondered at in the Yahoos was their strange disposition to nastiness and dirt; whereas there appears to be a natural love of cleanliness in all other animals. As to the two former accusations, I was glad to let them pass without any reply, because I had not a word to offer upon them in defense of my species, which otherwise I certainly had done from my own inclinations. But I could have easily vindicated humankind from the imputation of singularity upon the last article, if there had been any swine in that country (as unluckily for me there were not) which although it may be a sweeter quadruped than a Yahoo, cannot I humbly conceive in justice pretend to more cleanliness; and so his honor himself must have owned, if he had seen their filthy way of feeding, and their custom of wallowing and sleeping in the mud.

My master likewise mentioned another quality, which his servants had discovered in several Yahoos, and to him was wholly unaccountable. He said, a fancy would sometimes take a Yahoo, to retire into a corner, to lie down and howl, and groan, and spurn away all that came near him, although he were young and fat, and wanted neither food nor water; nor did the servants imagine what could possibly ail him. And the only remedy they found was to set him to hard work, after which he would infallibly come to himself. To this I was silent out of partiality to my own kind; yet here I could plainly discover the true seeds of spleen,[2] which only seizeth on the lazy, the luxurious, and the rich; who, if they were forced to undergo the same regimen, I would undertake for the cure.

His Honor had farther observed, that a female Yahoo would often stand behind a bank or a bush, to gaze on the young males passing by, and then appear, and hide, using many antic gestures and grimaces; at which time it was observed, that she had a most offensive smell; and when any of the males advanced, would slowly retire, looking back, and with a counterfeit show of fear, run off into some convenient place where she knew the male would follow her.

At other times, if a female stranger came among them, three or four of her own sex would get about her, and stare and chatter, and grin, and smell her all over; and then turn off with gestures that seemed to express contempt and disdain.

Perhaps my master might refine a little in these speculations, which he had drawn from what he observed himself, or had been told by others; however, I could not reflect without some amazement, and much sorrow, that the rudiments of lewdness, coquetry, censure, and scandal, should have place by instinct in womankind.

I expected every moment that my master would accuse the Yahoos of those unnatural appetites in both sexes, so common among us. But Nature it seems hath not been so expert a schoolmistress; and these politer pleasures are entirely the productions of art and reason, on our side of the globe.

2. Depression.

CHAPTER 8. *The Author relateth several particulars of the Yahoos. The great virtues of the Houyhnhnms. The education and exercises of their youth. Their general assembly.*

As I ought to have understood human nature much better than I supposed it possible for my master to do, so it was easy to apply the character he gave of the Yahoos to myself and my countrymen; and I believed I could yet make farther discoveries from my own observation. I therefore often begged his honor to let me go among the herds of Yahoos in the neighborhood; to which he always very graciously consented, being perfectly convinced that the hatred I bore those brutes would never suffer me to be corrupted by them; and his honor ordered one of his servants, a strong sorrel nag, very honest and good-natured, to be my guard; without whose protection I durst not undertake such adventures. For I have already told the reader how much I was pestered by those odious animals upon my first arrival. I afterwards failed very narrowly three or four times of falling into their clutches, when I happened to stray at any distance without my hanger. And I have reason to believe, they had some imagination that I was of their own species, which I often assisted myself, by stripping up my sleeves, and shewing my naked arms and breast in their sight, when my protector was with me; at which times they would approach as near as they durst, and imitate my actions after the manner of monkeys, but ever with great signs of hatred; as a tame jackdaw with cap and stockings is always persecuted by the wild ones, when he happens to be got among them.

They are prodigiously nimble from their infancy; however, I once caught a young male of three years old, and endeavored by all marks of tenderness to make it quiet; but the little imp fell a squalling, scratching, and biting with such violence, that I was forced to let it go; and it was high time, for a whole troop of old ones came about us at the noise; but finding the cub was safe (for away it ran) and my sorrel nag being by, they durst not venture near us. I observed the young animal's flesh to smell very rank, and the stink was somewhat between a weasel and a fox, but much more disagreeable. I forgot another circumstance (and perhaps I might have the reader's pardon, if it were wholly omitted) that while I held the odious vermin in my hands, it voided its filthy excrements of a yellow liquid substance, all over my clothes; but by good fortune there was a small brook hard by, where I washed myself as clean as I could; although I durst not come into my master's presence until I were sufficiently aired.

By what I could discover, the Yahoos appear to be the most unteachable of all animals, their capacities never reaching higher than to draw or carry burdens. Yet I am of opinion, this defect ariseth chiefly from a perverse, restive disposition. For they are cunning, malicious, treacherous and revengeful. They are strong and hardy, but of a cowardly spirit, and by consequence insolent, abject, and cruel. It is observed that the red-haired of both sexes are more libidinous and mischievous than the rest, whom yet they much exceed in strength and activity.

The Houyhnhnms keep the Yahoos for present use in huts not far from the house; but the rest are sent abroad to certain fields, where they dig up roots, eat several kinds of herbs, and search about for carrion, or sometimes catch weasels and *luhimuhs* (a sort of wild rat) which they greedily devour. Nature hath taught them to dig deep holes with their nails on the side of a rising ground, wherein they lie by themselves; only the kennels of the females are larger, sufficient to hold two or three cubs.

They swim from their infancy like frogs, and are able to continue long under water, where they often take fish, which the females carry home to their young. And upon this occasion, I hope the reader will pardon my relating an odd adventure.

Being one day abroad with my protector the sorrel nag, and the weather exceeding hot, I entreated him to let me bathe in a river that was near. He consented, and I immediately stripped myself stark naked, and went down softly into the stream. It happened that a young female Yahoo standing behind a bank, saw the whole proceeding; and inflamed by desire, as the nag and I conjectured, came running with all speed, and leaped into the water within five yards of the place where I bathed. I was never in my life so terribly frighted; the nag was grazing at some distance, not suspecting any harm. She embraced me after a most fulsome manner; I roared as loud as I could, and the nag came galloping towards me, whereupon she quitted her grasp, with the utmost reluctancy, and leaped upon the opposite bank, where she stood gazing and howling all the time I was putting on my clothes.

This was matter of diversion to my master and his family, as well as of mortification to myself. For now I could no longer deny that I was a real Yahoo, in every limb and feature, since the females had a natural propensity to me as one of their own species; neither was the hair of this brute of a red color (which might have been some excuse for an appetite a little irregular) but black as a sloe, and her countenance did not make an appearance altogether so hideous as the rest of the kind; for I think, she could not be above eleven years old.

Having already lived three years in this country, the reader I suppose will expect that I should, like other travelers, give him some account of the manners and customs of its inhabitants, which it was indeed my principal study to learn.

As these noble Houyhnhnms are endowed by Nature with a general disposition to all virtues, and have no conceptions or ideas of what is evil in a rational creature; so their grand maxim is to cultivate reason, and to be wholly governed by it. Neither is reason among them a point problematical as with us, where men can argue with plausibility on both sides of a question; but strikes you with immediate conviction; as it must needs do where it is not mingled, obscured, or discolored by passion and interest. I remember it was with extreme difficulty that I could bring my master to understand the meaning of the word "opinion," or how a point could be disputable; because reason taught us to affirm or deny only where we are certain; and beyond our knowledge we cannot do either. So that controversies, wranglings, disputes, and positiveness in false or dubious propositions are evils unknown among the Houyhnhnms. In the like manner when I used to explain to him our several systems of natural philosophy,[3] he would laugh that a creature pretending to reason should value itself upon the knowledge of other people's conjectures, and in things, where that knowledge, if it were certain, could be of no use. Wherein he agreed entirely with the sentiments of Socrates, as Plato delivers them, which I mention as the highest honor I can do that prince of philosophers. I have often since reflected what destruction such a doctrine would make in the libraries of Europe; and how many paths to fame would be then shut up in the learned world.

3. Science.

Friendship and benevolence are the two principal virtues among the Houyhnhnms; and these not confined to particular objects, but universal to the whole race. For a stranger from the remotest part is equally treated with the nearest neighbor, and wherever he goes, looks upon himself as at home. They preserve decency and civility in the highest degrees, but are altogether ignorant of ceremony. They have no fondness for their colts or foals; but the care they take in educating them proceedeth entirely from the dictates of reason. And I observed my master to show the same affection to his neighbor's issue that he had for his own. They will have it that Nature teaches them to love the whole species, and it is reason only that maketh a distinction of persons, where there is a superior degree of virtue.

When the matron Houyhnhnms have produced one of each sex, they no longer accompany with their consorts, except they lose one of their issue by some casualty, which very seldom happens; but in such a case they meet again; or when the like accident befalls a person whose wife is past bearing, some other couple bestows on him one of their own colts, and then go together a second time, until the mother be pregnant. This caution is necessary to prevent the country from being overburdened with numbers. But the race of inferior Houyhnhnms bred up to be servants is not so strictly limited upon this article; these are allowed to produce three of each sex, to be domestics in the noble families.

In their marriages they are exactly careful to choose such colors as will not make any disagreeable mixture in the breed. Strength is chiefly valued in the male, and comeliness in the female; not upon the account of love, but to preserve the race from degenerating; for, where a female happens to excel in strength, a consort is chosen with regard to comeliness. Courtship, love, presents, jointures, settlements, have no place in their thoughts, or terms whereby to express them in their language. The young couple meet and are joined, merely because it is the determination of their parents and friends; it is what they see done every day; and they look upon it as one of the necessary actions in a reasonable being. But the violation of marriage, or any other unchastity, was never heard of; and the married pair pass their lives with the same friendship and mutual benevolence that they bear to all others of the same species who come in their way, without jealousy, fondness, quarreling, or discontent.

In educating the youth of both sexes, their method is admirable, and highly deserveth our imitation. These are not suffered to taste a grain of oats, except upon certain days, till eighteen years old; nor milk, but very rarely; and in summer they graze two hours in the morning, and as many in the evening, which their parents likewise observe; but the servants are not allowed above half that time; and a great part of the grass is brought home, which they eat at the most convenient hours when they can be best spared from work.

Temperance, industry, exercise, and cleanliness are the lessons equally enjoined to the young ones of both sexes; and my master thought it monstrous in us to give the females a different kind of education from the males, except in some articles of domestic management; whereby, as he truly observed, one half of our natives were good for nothing but bringing children into the world; and to trust the care of their children to such useless animals, he said was yet a greater instance of brutality.

But the Houyhnhnms train up their youth to strength, speed, and hardiness, by exercising them in running races up and down steep hills, or over hard stony grounds; and when they are all in a sweat, they are ordered to leap over head and ears into a pond or a river. Four times a year the youth of certain districts meet to show their proficiency in running, and leaping, and other feats of strength or agility; where the victor is rewarded with a song made in his or her praise. On this festival the servants drive a herd of Yahoos into the field, laden with hay, and oats, and milk for a repast to the Houyhnhnms; after which these brutes are immediately driven back again, for fear of being noisome to the assembly.

Every fourth year, at the vernal equinox, there is a representative council of the whole nation, which meets in a plain about twenty miles from our house, and continueth about five or six days. Here they inquire into the state and condition of the several districts; whether they abound or be deficient in hay or oats, or cows or Yahoos? And wherever there is any want (which is but seldom) it is immediately supplied by unanimous consent and contribution. Here likewise the regulation of children is settled: as for instance, if a Houyhnhnm hath two males, he changeth one of them with another who hath two females, and when a child hath been lost by any casualty, where the mother is past breeding, it is determined what family in the district shall breed another to supply the loss.

CHAPTER 9. *A grand debate at the general assembly of the Houyhnhnms, and how it was determined. The learning of the Houyhnhnms. Their buildings. Their manner of burials. The defectiveness of their language.*

One of these grand assemblies was held in my time, about three months before my departure, whither my master went as the representative of our district. In this council was resumed their old debate, and indeed, the only debate that ever happened in their country; whereof my master after his return gave me a very particular account.

The question to be debated was whether the Yahoos should be exterminated from the face of the earth. One of the members for the affirmative offered several arguments of great strength and weight, alleging that, as the Yahoos were the most filthy, noisome, and deformed animal which nature ever produced, so they were the most restive and indocible,[4] mischievous, and malicious; they would privately suck the teats of the Houyhnhnms' cows; kill and devour their cats, trample down their oats and grass, if they were not continually watched; and commit a thousand other extravagancies. He took notice of a general tradition, that Yahoos had not been always in their country, but that many ages ago, two of these brutes appeared together upon a mountain; whether produced by the heat of the sun upon corrupted mud and slime, or from the ooze and froth of the sea, was never known. That these Yahoos engendered, and their brood in a short time grew so numerous as to overrun and infest the whole nation. That the Houyhnhnms to get rid of this evil, made a general hunting, and at last enclosed the whole herd; and destroying the older, every Houyhnhnm kept two young ones in a kennel, and brought them to such a degree of tameness as an animal so savage by nature can be capable of acquiring, using them for draught and carriage. That there seemed to be much truth in this tradition, and that those creatures could not be *ylnhniamshy* (or aborigines of the land) because of the violent hatred the Houyhnhnms as well as all other animals bore them; which although their evil disposition sufficiently

4. Unteachable.

deserved, could never have arrived at so high a degree, if they had been aborigines, or else they would have long since been rooted out. That the inhabitants taking a fancy to use the service of the Yahoos, had very imprudently neglected to cultivate the breed of asses, which were a comely animal, easily kept, more tame and orderly, without any offensive smell, strong enough for labor, although they yield to the other in agility of body; and if their braying be no agreeable sound, it is far preferable to the horrible howlings of the Yahoos.

Several others declared their sentiments to the same purpose, when my master proposed an expedient to the assembly, whereof he had indeed borrowed the hint from me. He approved of the tradition, mentioned by the honorable member, who spoke before; and affirmed, that the two Yahoos said to be first seen among them, had been driven thither over the sea; that coming to land, and being forsaken by their companions, they retired to the mountains, and degenerating by degrees, became in process of time much more savage than those of their own species in the country from whence these two originals came. The reason of his assertion was that he had now in his possession a certain wonderful Yahoo (meaning myself) which most of them had heard of, and many of them had seen. He then related to them how he first found me; that my body was all covered with an artificial composure of the skins and hairs of other animals; that I spoke in a language of my own, and had thoroughly learned theirs; that I had related to him the accidents which brought me thither; that when he saw me without my covering, I was an exact Yahoo in every part, only of a whiter color, less hairy and with shorter claws. He added how I had endeavored to persuade him that in my own and other countries the Yahoos acted as the governing, rational animal, and held the Houyhnhnms in servitude; that he observed in me all the qualities of a Yahoo, only a little more civilized by some tincture of reason, which however was in a degree as far inferior to the Houyhnhnm race as the Yahoos of their country were to me; that among other things, I mentioned a custom we had of castrating Houyhnhnms when they were young, in order to render them tame; that the operation was easy and safe; that it was no shame to learn wisdom from brutes, as industry is taught by the ant, and building by the swallow (for so I translate the world *lyhannh*, although it be a much larger fowl). That this invention might be practiced upon the younger Yahoos here, which, besides rendering them tractable and fitter for use, would in an age put an end to the whole species without destroying life. That in the meantime the Houyhnhnms should be exhorted to cultivate the breed of asses, which, as they are in all respects more valuable brutes, so they have this advantage, to be fit for service at five years old, which the other are not till twelve.

This was all my master thought fit to tell me at that time, of what passed in the grand council. But he was pleased to conceal one particular, which related personally to myself, whereof I soon felt the unhappy effect, as the reader will know in its proper place, and from whence I date all the succeeding misfortunes of my life.

The Houyhnhnms have no letters, and consequently, their knowledge is all traditional. But there happening few events of any moment among a people so well united, naturally disposed to every virtue, wholly governed by reason, and cut off from all commerce with other nations, the historical part is easily preserved without burdening their memories. I have already observed that they are subject to no diseases, and therefore can have no need of physicians. However, they have excellent medicines composed of herbs, to cure accidental bruises and cuts in the pastern or frog[5] of the foot by sharp stones, as well as other maims and hurts in the several parts of the body.

They calculate the year by the revolution of the sun and the moon, but use no subdivisions into weeks. They are well enough acquainted with the motions of those two luminaries, and understand the nature of eclipses; and this is the utmost progress of their astronomy.

In poetry they must be allowed to excel all other mortals; wherein the justness of their similes, and the minuteness, as well as exactness of their descriptions, are indeed inimitable. Their verses abound very much in both of these, and usually contain either some exalted notions of friendship and benevolence, or the praises of those who were victors in races and other bodily exercises. Their buildings, although very rude and simple, are not inconvenient, but well contrived to defend them from all injuries of cold and heat. They have a kind of tree, which at forty years old loosens in the root, and falls with the first storm; it grows very straight, and being pointed like stakes with a sharp stone (for the Houyhnhnms know not the use of iron), they stick them erect in the ground about ten inches asunder, and then weave in oat straw, or sometimes wattles, betwixt them. The roof is made after the same manner, and so are the doors.

The Houyhnhnms use the hollow part between the pastern and the hoof of their forefeet as we do our hands, and this with greater dexterity than I could at first imagine. I have seen a white mare of our family thread a needle (which I lent her on purpose) with that joint. They milk their cows, reap their oats, and do all the work which requires hands in the same manner. They have a kind of hard flints, which by grinding against other stones they form into instruments that serve instead of wedges, axes, and hammers. With tools made of these flints, they likewise cut their hay, and reap their oats, which there groweth naturally in several fields. The Yahoos draw home the sheaves in carriages, and the servants tread them in certain covered huts, to get out the grain, which is kept in stores. They make a rude kind of earthen and wooden vessels, and bake the former in the sun.

If they can avoid casualties, they die only of old age, and are buried in the obscurest places that can be found, their friends and relations expressing neither joy nor grief at their departure; nor does the dying person discover the least regret that he is leaving the world, any more than if he were upon returning home from a visit to one of his neighbors; I remember my master having once made an appointment with a friend and his family to come to his house upon some affair of importance; on the day fixed, the mistress and her two children came very late; she made two excuses, first for her husband, who, as she said, happened that very morning to *lhnuwnh*. The word is strongly expressive in their language, but not easily rendered into English; it signifies, *to retire to his first Mother*. Her excuse for not coming sooner was that her husband dying late in the morning, she was a good while consulting her servants about a convenient place where his body should be laid; and I observed she behaved herself at our house, as cheerfully as the rest. She died about three months after.

They live generally to seventy or seventy-five years, very seldom to fourscore; some weeks before their death they feel a gradual decay, but without pain. During this time they are much visited by their friends, because they cannot go abroad with their usual ease and satisfaction. However, about ten days

5. Sole.

before their death, which they seldom fail in computing, they return the visits that have been made by those who are nearest in the neighborhood, being carried in a convenient sledge drawn by Yahoos; which vehicle they use, not only upon this occasion, but when they grow old, upon long journeys, or when they are lamed by any accident. And therefore when the dying Houyhnhnms return those visits, they take a solemn leave of their friends, as if they were going to some remote part of the country, where they designed to pass the rest of their lives.

I know not whether it may be worth observing, that the Houyhnhnms have no word in their language to express anything that is evil, except what they borrow from the deformities or ill qualities of the Yahoos. Thus they denote the folly of a servant, an omission of a child, a stone that cuts their feet, a continuance of foul or unseasonable weather, and the like, by adding to each the epithet of Yahoo. For instance, *hhnm Yahoo, whnaholm Yahoo, ynlhmnd-wihlma Yahoo,* and an ill-contrived house, *ynholmhnmrohlnw Yahoo.*

I could with great pleasure enlarge farther upon the manners and virtues of this excellent people; but intending in a short time to publish a volume by itself expressly upon that subject, I refer the reader thither. And in the meantime, proceed to relate my own sad catastrophe.

CHAPTER 10. *The Author's economy, and happy life among the Houyhnhnms. His great improvement in virtue, by conversing with them. Their conversations. The Author hath notice given him by his master that he must depart from the country. He falls into a swoon for grief, but submits. He contrives and finishes a canoe, by the help of a fellow servant, and puts to sea at a venture.*

I had settled my little economy to my own heart's content. My master had ordered a room to be made for me after their manner, about six yards from the house; the sides and floors of which I plastered with clay, and covered with rush mats of my own contriving; I had beaten hemp, which there grows wild, and made of it a sort of ticking; this I filled with the feathers of several birds I had taken with springes made of Yahoos' hairs, and were excellent food. I had worked two chairs with my knife, the sorrel nag helping me in the grosser and more laborious part. When my clothes were worn to rags, I made myself others with the skins of rabbits, and of a certain beautiful animal about the same size, called *nnuhnoh*, the skin of which is covered with a fine down. Of these I likewise made very tolerable stockings. I soled my shoes with wood which I cut from a tree, and fitted to the upper leather, and when this was worn out, I supplied it with the skins of Yahoos, dried in the sun. I often got honey out of hollow trees, which I mingled with water, or eat it with my bread. No man could more verify the truth of these two maxims, that *Nature is very easily satisfied;* and, that *Necessity is the mother of invention.* I enjoyed perfect health of body, and tranquility of mind; I did not feel the treachery or inconstancy of a friend, nor the inquiries of a secret or open enemy. I had no occasion of bribing, flattering, or pimping to procure the favor of any great man, or of his minion. I wanted no fence against fraud or oppression; here was neither physician to destroy my body, nor lawyer to ruin my fortune; no informer to watch my words and actions, or forge accusations against me for hire; here were no gibers, censurers, backbiters, pickpockets, highwaymen, housebreakers, attorneys, bawds, buffoons, gamesters, politicians, wits, splenetics, tedious talkers, controvertists, ravishers, murderers, robbers, virtuosos;[6] no leaders or followers of party and faction; no encouragers to vice, by seducement or examples; no dungeons, axes, gibbets, whipping posts, or pillories; no cheating shopkeepers or mechanics; no pride, vanity or affectation; no fops, bullies, drunkards, strolling whores, or poxes; no ranting, lewd, expensive wives; no stupid, proud pedants; no importunate, overbearing, quarrelsome, noisy, roaring, empty, conceited, swearing companions; no scoundrels raised from the dust upon the merit of their vices; or nobility thrown into it on account of their virtues; no lords, fiddlers, judges, or dancing masters.

I had the favor of being admitted to several Houyhnhnms, who came to visit or dine with my master; where his honor graciously suffered me to wait in the room, and listen to their discourse. Both he and his company would often descend to ask me questions, and receive my answers. I had also sometimes the honor of attending my master in his visits to others. I never presumed to speak, except in answer to a question; and then I did it with inward regret, because it was a loss of so much time for improving myself; but I was infinitely delighted with the station of an humble auditor in such conversations, where nothing passed but what was useful, expressed in the fewest and most significant words; where (as I have already said) the greatest decency was observed, without the least degree of ceremony; where no person spoke without being pleased himself, and pleasing his companions; where there was no interruption, tediousness, heat, or difference of sentiments. They have a notion, that when people are met together, a short silence doth much improve conversation; this I found to be true; for during those little intermissions of talk, new ideas would arise in their minds, which very much enlivened the discourse. Their subjects are generally on friendship and benevolence; on order and economy; sometimes upon the visible operations of nature, or ancient traditions; upon the bounds and limits of virtue; upon the unerring rules of reason; or upon some determinations, to be taken at the next great assembly; and often upon the various excellencies of poetry. I may add, without vanity, that my presence often gave them sufficient matter for discourse, because it afforded my master an occasion of letting his friends into the history of me and my country, upon which they were all pleased to descant in a manner not very advantageous to human kind; and for that reason I shall not repeat what they said; only I may be allowed to observe that his honor, to my great admiration, appeared to understand the nature of Yahoos much better than myself. He went through all our vices and follies, and discovered many which I had never mentioned to him; by only supposing what qualities a Yahoo of their country, with a small proportion of reason, might be capable of exerting; and concluded, with too much probability, how vile as well as miserable such a creature must be.

I freely confess, that all the little knowledge I have of any value was acquired by the lectures I received from my master, and from hearing the discourses of him and his friends; to which I should be prouder to listen, than to dictate to the greatest and wisest assembly in Europe. I admired the strength, comeliness, and speed of the inhabitants; and such a constellation of virtues in such amiable persons produced in me the highest veneration. At first, indeed, I did not feel that natural awe which the Yahoos and all other animals bear towards them; but it grew upon me by degrees, much sooner than I imagined, and was mingled with a respectful love and gratitude, that they would condescend to distinguish me from the rest of my species.

6. Those who pursue special interests in the arts or sciences.

When I thought of my family, my friends, my countrymen, or human race in general, I considered them as they really were, Yahoos in shape and disposition, perhaps a little more civilized, and qualified with the gift of speech; but making no other use of reason than to improve and multiply those vices, whereof their brethren in this country had only the share that nature allotted them. When I happened to behold the reflection of my own form in a lake or fountain, I turned away my face in horror and detestation of myself, and could better endure the sight of a common Yahoo than of my own person. By conversing with the Houyhnhnms, and looking upon them with delight, I fell to imitate their gait and gesture, which is now grown into a habit; and my friends often tell me in a blunt way, that I trot like a horse; which, however, I take for a great compliment. Neither shall I disown, that in speaking I am apt to fall into the voice and manner of the Houyhnhnms, and hear myself ridiculed on that account without the least mortification.

In the midst of this happiness, when I looked upon myself to be fully settled for life, my master sent for me one morning a little earlier than his usual hour. I observed by his countenance that he was in some perplexity, and at a loss how to begin what he had to speak. After a short silence, he told me, he did not know how I would take what he was going to say; that, in the last general assembly, when the affair of the Yahoos was entered upon, the representatives had taken offense at his keeping a Yahoo (meaning myself) in his family more like a Houyhnhnm than a brute animal. That he was known frequently to converse with me, as if he could receive some advantage of pleasure in my company; that such a practice was not agreeable to reason or nature, or a thing ever heard of before among them. The assembly did therefore exhort him, either to employ me like the rest of my species, or command me to swim back to the place from whence I came. That the first of these expedients was utterly rejected by all the Houyhnhnms who had ever seen me at his house or their own; for, they alleged, that because I had some rudiments of reason, added to the natural pravity[7] of those animals, it was to be feared, I might be able to seduce them into the woody and mountainous parts of the country, and bring them in troops by night to destroy the Houyhnhnms' cattle, as being naturally of the ravenous kind, and averse from labor.

My master added that he was daily pressed by the Houyhnhnms of the neighborhood to have the assembly's exhortation executed, which he could not put off much longer. He doubted[8] it would be impossible for me to swim to another country; and therefore wished I would contrive some sort of vehicle resembling those I had described to him, that might carry me on the sea; in which work I should have the assistance of his own servants, as well as those of his neighbors. He concluded that for his own part he could have been content to keep me in his service as long as I lived; because he found I had cured myself of some bad habits and dispositions, by endeavoring, as far as my inferior nature was capable, to imitate the Houyhnhnms.

I should here observe to the reader, that a decree of the general assembly in this country is expressed by the word *hnhloayn,* which signifies an exhortation, as near as I can render it; for they have no conception how a rational creature can be compelled, but only advised, or exhorted; because no person can disobey reason without giving up his claim to be a rational creature.

I was struck with the utmost grief and despair at my master's discourse; and

7. Corruption.

8. Feared.

being unable to support the agonies I was under, I fell into a swoon at his feet; when I came to myself, he told me that he concluded I had been dead (for these people are subject to no such imbecilities of nature). I answered, in a faint voice, that death would have been too great an happiness; that although I could not blame the assembly's exhortation, or the urgency of his friends; yet in my weak and corrupt judgment, I thought it might consist with reason to have been less rigorous. That I could not swim a league, and probably the nearest land to theirs might be distant above an hundred; that many materials, necessary for making a small vessel to carry me off, were wholly wanting in this country, which, however, I would attempt in obedience and gratitude to his honor, although I concluded the thing to be impossible, and therefore looked on myself as already devoted to destruction. That the certain prospect of an unnatural death was the least of my evils; for, supposing I should escape with life by some strange adventure, how could I think with temper[9] of passing my days among Yahoos, and relapsing into my old corruptions, for want of examples to lead and keep me within the paths of virtue. That I knew too well upon what solid reasons all the determinations of the wise Houyhnhnms were founded, not to be shaken by arguments of mine, a miserable Yahoo; and therefore after presenting him with my humble thanks for the offer of his servants' assistance in making a vessel, and desiring a reasonable time for so difficult a work, I told him I would endeavor to preserve a wretched being; and, if ever I returned to England, was not without hopes of being useful to my own species by celebrating the praises of the renowned Houyhnhnms, and proposing their virtues to the imitation of mankind.

My master in a few words made me a very gracious reply, allowed me the space of two months to finish my boat, and ordered the sorrel nag, my fellow servant (for so at this distance I may presume to call him), to follow my instructions, because I told my master that his help would be sufficient, and I knew he had a tenderness for me.

In his company my first business was to go to that part of the coast where my rebellious crew had ordered me to be set on shore. I got upon a height, and looking on every side into the sea, fancied I saw a small island towards the northeast; I took out my pocket glass, and could then clearly distinguish it about five leagues off, as I computed; but it appeared to the sorrel nag to be only a blue cloud; for, as he had no conception of any country besides his own, so he could not be as expert in distinguishing remote objects at sea, as we who so much converse in that element.

After I had discovered this island, I considered no farther; but resolved, it should, if possible, be the first place of my banishment, leaving the consequence to fortune.

I returned home, and consulting with the sorrel nag, we went into a copse at some distance, where I with my knife, and he with a sharp flint fastened very artificially,[1] after their manner, to a wooden handle, cut down several oak wattles about the thickness of a walking staff, and some larger pieces. But I shall not trouble the reader with a particular description of my own mechanics; let it suffice to say, that in six weeks time, with the help of the sorrel nag, who performed the parts that required most labor, I finished a sort of Indian canoe; but much larger, covering it with the skins of Yahoos, well stitched together, with hempen threads of my own making. My sail was likewise composed of

9. Equanimity. "Devoted": doomed.

1. Artfully.

the skins of the same animal; but I made use of the youngest I could get, the older being too tough and thick; and I likewise provided myself with four paddles. I laid in a stock of boiled flesh, of rabbits and fowls; and took with me two vessels, one filled with milk, and the other with water.

I tried my canoe in a large pond near my master's house, and then corrected in it what was amiss, stopping all the chinks with Yahoo's tallow, till I found it staunch, and able to bear me and my freight. And when it was as complete as I could possibly make it, I had it drawn on a carriage very gently by Yahoos, to the seaside, under the conduct of the sorrel nag and another servant.

When all was ready, and the day came for my departure, I took leave of my master and lady, and the whole family, my eyes flowing with tears and my heart quite sunk with grief.[2] But his honor, out of curiosity, and perhaps (if I may speak it without vanity) partly out of kindness, was determined to see me in my canoe; and got several of his neighboring friends to accompany him. I was forced to wait above an hour for the tide, and then observing the wind very fortunately bearing towards the island to which I intended to steer my course, I took a second leave of my master; but as I was going to prostrate myself to kiss his hoof, he did me the honor to raise it gently to my mouth. I am not ignorant how much I have been censured for mentioning this last particular. Detractors are pleased to think it improbable that so illustrious a person should descend to give so great a mark of distinction to a creature so inferior as I. Neither have I forgot how apt some travelers are to boast of extraordinary favors they have received. But, if these censurers were better acquainted with the noble and courteous disposition of the Houyhnhnms, they would soon change their opinion. I paid my respects to the rest of the Houyhnhnms in his honor's company; then getting into my canoe, I pushed off from shore.

CHAPTER 11. *The Author's dangerous voyage. He arrives at New Holland, hoping to settle there. Is wounded with an arrow by one of the natives. Is seized and carried by force into a Portuguese ship. The great civilities of the Captain. The Author arrives at England.*

I began this desperate voyage on February 15, 1714/5,[3] at 9 o'clock in the morning. The wind was very favorable; however, I made use at first only of my paddles; but considering I should soon be weary, and that the wind might probably chop about, I ventured to set up my little sail, and thus, with the help of the tide, I went at the rate of a league and a half an hour, as near as I could guess. My master and his friends continued on the shore, till I was almost out of sight; and I often heard the sorrel nag (who always loved me) crying out, *"Hnuy illa nyha maiah Yahoo"* ("Take care of thyself, gentle Yahoo").

My design was, if possible, to discover some small island uninhabited, yet sufficient by my labor to furnish me with necessaries of life, which I would have thought a greater happiness than to be first minister in the politest court of Europe, so horrible was the idea I conceived of returning to live in the society and under the government of Yahoos. For in such a solitude as I desired, I could at least enjoy my own thoughts, and reflect with delight on

2. For depiction of this scene by Sawrey Gilpin, see the color insert in this volume.

3. I.e., 1715, by modern dating. The year began on March 25.

the virtues of those inimitable Houyhnhnms, without any opportunity of degenerating into the vices and corruptions of my own species.

The reader may remember what I related when my crew conspired against me, and confined me to my cabin, how I continued there several weeks, without knowing what course we took; and when I was put ashore in the longboat, how the sailors told me with oaths, whether true or false, that they knew not in what part of the world we were. However, I did then believe us to be about 10 degrees southward of the Cape of Good Hope, or about 45 degrees southern latitude, as I gathered from some general words I overheard among them, being I supposed to the southeast in their intended voyage to Madagascar. And although this were but little better than conjecture, yet I resolved to steer my course eastward, hoping to reach the southwest coast of New Holland, and perhaps some such island as I desired, lying westward of it. The wind was full west, and by six in the evening I computed I had gone eastward at least eighteen leagues; when I spied a very small island about half a league off, which I soon reached. It was nothing but a rock with one creek, naturally arched by the force of tempests. Here I put in my canoe, and climbing a part of the rock, I could plainly discover land to the east, extending from south to north. I lay all night in my canoe; and repeating my voyage early in the morning, I arrived in seven hours to the southeast point of New Holland. This confirmed me in the opinion I have long entertained, that the maps and charts place this country at least three degrees more to the east than it really is; which thought I communicated many years ago to my worthy friend Mr. Herman Moll,[4] and gave him my reasons for it, although he hath rather chosen to follow other authors.

I saw no inhabitants in the place where I landed; and being unarmed, I was afraid of venturing far into the country. I found some shellfish on the shore, and eat them raw, not daring to kindle a fire, for fear of being discovered by the natives. I continued three days feeding on oysters and limpets, to save my own provisions; and I fortunately found a brook of excellent water, which gave me great relief.

On the fourth day, venturing out early a little too far, I saw twenty or thirty natives upon a height, not above five hundred yards from me. They were stark naked, men, women, and children round a fire, as I could discover by the smoke. One of them spied me, and gave notice to the rest; five of them advanced towards me, leaving the women and children at the fire. I made what haste I could to the shore, and getting into my canoe, shoved off; the savages observing me retreat, ran after me; and before I could get far enough into the sea, discharged an arrow, which wounded me deeply on the inside of my left knee. (I shall carry the mark to my grave.) I apprehended the arrow might be poisoned; and paddling out of the reach of their darts (being a calm day) I made a shift to suck the wound, and dress it as well as I could.

I was at a loss what to do, for I durst not return to the same landing place, but stood to the north, and was forced to paddle; for the wind, although very gentle, was against me, blowing northwest. As I was looking about for a secure landing place, I saw a sail to the north northeast, which appearing every minute more visible, I was in some doubt whether I should wait for them or no; but at last my detestation of the Yahoo race prevailed; and turning my canoe, I sailed and paddled together to the south, and got into the same creek from

4. A famous contemporary map maker.

whence I set out in the morning, choosing rather to trust myself among these barbarians than live with European Yahoos. I drew up my canoe as close as I could to the shore, and hid myself behind a stone by the little brook, which, as I have already said, was excellent water.

The ship came within half a league of this creek, and sent out her longboat with vessels to take in fresh water (for the place it seems was very well known), but I did not observe it until the boat was almost on shore; and it was too late to seek another hiding place. The seamen at their landing observed my canoe, and rummaging it all over, easily conjectured that the owner could not be far off. Four of them well armed searched every cranny and lurking hole, till at last they found me flat on my face behind the stone. They gazed a while in admiration at my strange uncouth dress; my coat made of skins, my wooden-soled shoes, and my furred stockings; from whence, however, they concluded I was not a native of the place, who all go naked. One of the seamen in Portuguese bid me rise, and asked who I was. I understood that language very well, and getting upon my feet, said I was a poor Yahoo, banished from the Houyhnhnms, and desired they would please to let me depart. They admired to hear me answer them in their own tongue, and saw by my complexion I must be an European; but were at a loss to know what I meant by Yahoos and Houyhnhnms, and at the same time fell a laughing at my strange tone in speaking, which resembled the neighing of a horse. I trembled all the while betwixt fear and hatred; I again desired leave to depart, and was gently moving to my canoe; but they laid hold on me, desiring to know what country I was of? whence I came? with many other questions. I told them I was born in England, from whence I came about five years ago, and then their country and ours was at peace. I therefore hoped they would not treat me as an enemy, since I meant them no harm, but was a poor Yahoo, seeking some desolate place where to pass the remainder of his unfortunate life.

When they began to talk, I thought I never heard or saw any thing so unnatural; for it appeared to me as monstrous as if a dog or a cow should speak in England, or a Yahoo in Houyhnhnmland. The honest Portuguese were equally amazed at my strange dress, and the odd manner of delivering my words, which however they understood very well. They spoke to me with great humanity, and said they were sure their Captain would carry me *gratis* to Lisbon, from whence I might return to my own country; that two of the seamen would go back to the ship, to inform the Captain of what they had seen, and receive his orders; in the meantime, unless I would give my solemn oath not to fly, they would secure me by force. I thought it best to comply with their proposal. They were very curious to know my story, but I gave them very little satisfaction; and they all conjectured, that my misfortunes had impaired my reason. In two hours the boat, which went laden with vessels of water, returned with the Captain's commands to fetch me on board. I fell on my knees to preserve my liberty; but all was in vain, and the men having tied me with cords, heaved me into the boat, from whence I was taken into the ship, and from thence into the Captain's cabin.

His name was Pedro de Mendez; he was a very courteous and generous person; he entreated me to give some account of myself, and desired to know what I would eat or drink; said I should be used as well as himself, and spoke so many obliging things, that I wondered to find such civilities from a Yahoo. However, I remained silent and sullen; I was ready to faint at the very smell of him and his men. At last I desired something to eat out of my own canoe;

but he ordered me a chicken and some excellent wine, and then directed that I should be put to bed in a very clean cabin. I would not undress myself, but lay on the bedclothes; and in half an hour stole out, when I thought the crew was at dinner; and getting to the side of the ship, was going to leap into the sea, and swim for my life, rather than continue among Yahoos. But one of the seamen prevented me, and having informed the Captain, I was chained to my cabin.

After dinner Don Pedro came to me, and desired to know my reason for so desperate an attempt; assured me he only meant to do me all the service he was able; and spoke so very movingly, that at last I descended to treat him like an animal which had some little portion of reason. I gave him a very short relation of my voyage; of the conspiracy against me by my own men; of the country where they set me on shore, and of my five years residence there. All which he looked upon as if it were a dream or a vision; whereat I took great offense; for I had quite forgot the faculty of lying, so peculiar to Yahoos in all countries where they preside, and consequently the disposition of suspecting truth in others of their own species. I asked him whether it were the custom of his country to *say the thing that was not?* I assured him I had almost forgot what he meant by falsehood; and if I had lived a thousand years in Houyhnhnmland, I should never have heard a lie from the meanest servant. That I was altogether indifferent whether he believed me or no; but however, in return for his favors, I would give so much allowance to the corruption of his nature, as to answer any objection he would please to make; and he might easily discover the truth.

The Captain, a wise man, after many endeavors to catch me tripping in some part of my story, at last began to have a better opinion of my veracity. But he added that since I professed so inviolable an attachment to truth, I must give him my word of honor to bear him company in this voyage without attempting anything against my life; or else he would continue me a prisoner till we arrived at Lisbon. I gave him the promise he required; but at the same time protested that I would suffer the greatest hardships rather than return to live among Yahoos.

Our voyage passed without any considerable accident. In gratitude to the Captain I sometimes sat with him at his earnest request, and strove to conceal my antipathy against humankind, although it often broke out; which he suffered to pass without observation. But the greatest part of the day, I confined myself to my cabin, to avoid seeing any of the crew. The Captain had often entreated me to strip myself of my savage dress, and offered to lend me the best suit of clothes he had. This I would not be prevailed on to accept, abhorring to cover myself with anything that had been on the back of a Yahoo. I only desired he would lend me two clean shirts, which having been washed since he wore them, I believed would not so much defile me. These I changed every second day, and washed them myself.

We arrived at Lisbon, Nov. 5, 1715. At our landing, the Captain forced me to cover myself with his cloak, to prevent the rabble from crowding about me. I was conveyed to his own house; and at my earnest request, he led me up to the highest room backwards.[5] I conjured him to conceal from all persons what I had told him of the Houyhnhnms; because the least hint of such a story would not only draw numbers of people to see me, but probably put me in danger of being imprisoned, or burned by the Inquisition. The Captain per-

5. At the rear.

suaded me to accept a suit of clothes newly made; but I would not suffer the tailor to take my measure; however, Don Pedro being almost of my size, they fitted me well enough. He accoutered me with other necessaries, all new, which I aired for twenty-four hours before I would use them.

The Captain had no wife, nor above three servants, none of which were suffered to attend at meals; and his whole deportment was so obliging, added to very good human understanding, that I really began to tolerate his company. He gained so far upon me, that I ventured to look out of the back window. By degrees I was brought into another room, from whence I peeped into the street, but drew my head back in a fright. In a week's time he seduced me down to the door. I found my terror gradually lessened, but my hatred and contempt seemed to increase. I was at last bold enough to walk the street in his company, but kept my nose well stopped with rue, or sometimes with tobacco.

In ten days, Don Pedro, to whom I had given some account of my domestic affairs, put it upon me as a point of honor and conscience that I ought to return to my native country, and live at home with my wife and children. He told me there was an English ship in the port just ready to sail, and he would furnish me with all things necessary. It would be tedious to repeat his arguments, and my contradictions. He said it was altogether impossible to find such a solitary island as I had desired to live in; but I might command in my own house, and pass my time in a manner as recluse as I pleased.

I complied at last, finding I could not do better. I left Lisbon the 24th day of November, in an English merchantman, but who was the Master I never inquired. Don Pedro accompanied me to the ship, and lent me twenty pounds. He took kind leave of me, and embraced me at parting; which I bore as well as I could. During this last voyage I had no commerce with the Master, or any of his men; but pretending I was sick kept close in my cabin. On the fifth of December, 1715, we cast anchor in the Downs about nine in the morning, and at three in the afternoon I got safe to my house at Redriff.

My wife and family received me with great surprise and joy, because they concluded me certainly dead; but I must freely confess, the sight of them filled me only with hatred, disgust, and contempt; and the more, by reflecting on the near alliance I had to them. For although since my unfortunate exile from the Houyhnhnm country, I had compelled myself to tolerate the sight of Yahoos, and to converse with Don Pedro de Mendez; yet my memory and imaginations were perpetually filled with the virtues and ideas of those exalted Houyhnhnms. And when I began to consider that by copulating with one of the Yahoo species, I had become a parent of more, it struck me with the utmost shame, confusion, and horror.

As soon as I entered the house, my wife took me in her arms, and kissed me; at which, having not been used to the touch of that odious animal for so many years, I fell in a swoon for almost an hour. At the time I am writing, it is five years since my last return to England. During the first year I could not endure my wife or children in my presence, the very smell of them was intolerable; much less could I suffer them to eat in the same room. To this hour they dare not presume to touch my bread, or drink out of the same cup; neither was I ever able to let one of them take me by the hand. The first money I laid out was to buy two young stone-horses,[6] which I keep in a good stable, and next to them the groom is my greatest favorite; for I feel my spirits revived by

6. Stallions.

the smell he contracts in the stable. My horses understand me tolerably well; I converse with them at least four hours every day. They are strangers to bridle or saddle; they live in great amity with me, and friendship to each other.

CHAPTER 12. *The Author's veracity. His design in publishing this work. His censure of those travelers who swerve from the truth. The Author clears himself from any sinister ends in writing. His native country commended. The right of the crown to those countries described by the Author is justified. The difficulty of conquering them. The Author takes his last leave of the reader; proposeth his manner of living for the future; gives good advice, and concludeth.*

Thus gentle reader, I have given thee a faithful history of my travels for sixteen years, and above seven months; wherein I have not been so studious of ornament as of truth. I could perhaps like others have astonished thee with strange improbable tales; but I rather chose to relate plain matter of fact in the simplest manner and style; because my principal design was to inform, and not to amuse thee.

It is easy for us who travel into remote countries, which are seldom visited by Englishmen or other Europeans, to form descriptions of wonderful animals both at sea and land. Whereas a traveler's chief aim should be to make men wiser and better, and to improve their minds by the bad as well as good example of what they deliver concerning foreign places.

I could heartily wish a law were enacted, that every traveler, before he were permitted to publish his voyages, should be obliged to make oath before the Lord High Chancellor that all he intended to print was absolutely true to the best of his knowledge; for then the world would no longer be deceived as it usually is, while some writers, to make their works pass the better upon the public, impose the grossest falsities on the unwary reader. I have perused several books of travels with great delight in my younger days; but, having since gone over most parts of the globe, and been able to contradict many fabulous accounts from my own observation, it hath given me a great disgust against this part of reading, and some indignation to see the credulity of mankind so impudently abused. Therefore, since my acquaintance were pleased to think my poor endeavors might not be unacceptable to my country, I imposed on myself as a maxim, never to be swerved from, that I would *strictly adhere to truth;* neither indeed can I be ever under the least temptation to vary from it, while I retain in my mind the lectures and example of my noble master, and the other illustrious Houyhnhnms, of whom I had so long the honor to be an humble hearer.

> ——*Nec si miserum Fortuna Sinonem*
> *Finxit, vanum etiam, mendacemque improba finget.*[7]

I know very well how little reputation is to be got by writings which require neither genius nor learning, nor indeed any other talent, except a good memory, or an exact journal. I know likewise, that writers of travels, like dictionary-makers, are sunk into oblivion by the weight and bulk of those who come last, and therefore lie uppermost. And it is highly probable that such travelers who shall hereafter visit the countries described in this work of mine, may be

7. Nor if Fortune had molded Sinon for misery, will she also in spite mold him as false and lying (Latin; Virgil's *Aeneid* 2.79–80).

detecting my errors (if there be any) and adding many new discoveries of their own, jostle me out of vogue, and stand in my place, making the world forget that ever I was an author. This indeed would be too great a mortification if I wrote for fame; but, as my sole intention was the PUBLIC GOOD, I cannot be altogether disappointed. For, who can read the virtues I have mentioned in the glorious Houyhnhnms, without being ashamed of his own vices, when he considers himself as the reasoning, governing animal of his country? I shall say nothing of those remote nations where Yahoos preside; amongst which the least corrupted are the Brobdingnagians, whose wise maxims in morality and government it would be our happiness to observe. But I forbear descanting further, and rather leave the judicious reader to his own remarks and applications.

I am not a little pleased that this work of mine can possibly meet with no censurers; for what objections can be made against a writer who relates only plain facts that happened in such distant countries, where we have not the least interest with respect either to trade or negotiations? I have carefully avoided every fault with which common writers of travels are often too justly charged. Besides, I meddle not the least with any party, but write without passion, prejudice, or ill-will against any man or number of men whatsoever. I write for the noblest end, to inform and instruct mankind, over whom I may, without breach of modesty, pretend to some superiority, from the advantages I received by conversing so long among the most accomplished Houyhnhnms. I write without any view towards profit or praise. I never suffer a word to pass that may look like a reflection,[8] or possibly give the least offense even to those who are most ready to take it. So that, I hope, I may with justice pronounce myself an Author perfectly blameless; against whom the tribes of answerers, considerers, observers, reflectors, detecters, remarkers will never be able to find matter for exercising their talents.

I confess it was whispered to me that I was bound in duty as a subject of England, to have given in a memorial[9] to a secretary of state, at my first coming over; because, whatever lands are discovered by a subject, belong to the Crown. But I doubt whether our conquests in the countries I treat of would be as easy as those of Ferdinando Cortez over the naked Americans. The Lilliputians, I think, are hardly worth the charge of a fleet and army to reduce them; and I question whether it might be prudent or safe to attempt the Brobdingnagians; or, whether an English army would be much at their ease with the Flying Island over their heads. The Houyhnhnms, indeed, appear not to be so well prepared for war, a science to which they are perfect strangers, and especially against missive weapons. However, supposing myself to be a minister of state, I could never give my advice for invading them. Their prudence, unanimity, unacquaintedness with fear, and their love of their country would amply supply all defects in the military art. Imagine twenty thousand of them breaking into the midst of an European army, confounding the ranks, overturning the carriages, battering the warriors' faces into mummy, by terrible yerks from their hinder hoofs: for they would well deserve the character given to Augustus, *Recalcitrat undique tutus.*[1] But instead of proposals for conquering that magnanimous nation, I rather wish they were in a capacity or dispo-

8. Censure, criticism.
9. Statement of facts for government use.
1. He kicks backward, at every point on his guard (Latin; Horace's *Satires* 2.1.20). "Mummy": pulp. "Yerks": kicks.

sition to send a sufficient number of their inhabitants for civilizing Europe; by teaching us the first principles of Honor, Justice, Truth, Temperance, Public Spirit, Fortitude, Chastity, Friendship, Benevolence, and Fidelity. The names of all which virtues are still retained among us in most languages, and are to be met with in modern as well as ancient authors, which I am able to assert from my own small reading.

But I had another reason which made me less forward to enlarge his majesty's dominions by my discoveries: to say the truth, I had conceived a few scruples with relation to the distributive justice of princes upon those occasions. For instance, a crew of pirates are driven by a storm they know not whither; at length a boy discovers land from the topmast; they go on shore to rob and plunder; they see an harmless people, are entertained with kindness, they give the country a new name, they take formal possession of it for the king, they set up a rotten plank or a stone for a memorial, they murder two or three dozen of the natives, bring away a couple more by force for a sample, return home, and get their pardon. Here commences a new dominion acquired with a title by Divine Right. Ships are sent with the first opportunity; the natives driven out or destroyed, their princes tortured to discover their gold; a free license given to all acts of inhumanity and lust; the earth reeking with the blood of its inhabitants: and this execrable crew of butchers employed in so pious an expedition is a *modern colony* sent to convert and civilize an idolatrous and barbarous people.

But this description, I confess, doth by no means affect the British nation, who may be an example to the whole world for their wisdom, care, and justice in planting colonies; their liberal endowments for the advancement of religion and learning; their choice of devout and able pastors to propagate Christianity; their caution in stocking their provinces with people of sober lives and conversations from this the Mother Kingdom; their strict regard to the distribution of justice, in supplying the civil administration through all their colonies with officers of the greatest abilities, utter strangers to corruption: and to crown all, by sending the most vigilant and virtuous governors, who have no other views than the happiness of the people over whom they preside, and the honor of the king their master.

But, as those countries which I have described do not appear to have any desire of being conquered, and enslaved, murdered, or driven out by colonies, nor abound either in gold, silver, sugar, or tobacco, I did humbly conceive they were by no means proper objects of our zeal, our valor, or our interest. However, if those whom it may concern, think fit to be of another opinion, I am ready to depose, when I shall be lawfully called, that no European did ever visit these countries before me. I mean, if the inhabitants ought to be believed.

But, as to the formality of taking possession in my sovereign's name, it never came once into my thoughts; and if it had, yet as my affairs then stood, I should perhaps in point of prudence and self-preservation have put it off to a better opportunity.

Having thus answered the only objection that can be raised against me as a traveler, I here take a final leave of my courteous readers, and return to enjoy my own speculations in my little garden at Redriff; to apply those excellent lessons of virtue which I learned among the Houyhnhnms; to instruct the Yahoos of my own family as far as I shall find them docible animals; to behold my figure often in a glass, and thus if possible habituate myself by time to tolerate the sight of a human creature; to lament the brutality of Houyhnhnms in my own country, but always treat their persons with respect, for the sake of my noble master, his family, his friends, and the whole Houyhnhnm race, whom these of ours have the honor to resemble in all their lineaments, however their intellectuals came to degenerate.

I began last week to permit my wife to sit at dinner with me, at the farthest end of a long table; and to answer (but with the utmost brevity) the few questions I ask her. Yet the smell of a Yahoo continuing very offensive, I always keep my nose well stopped with rue, lavender, or tobacco leaves. And although it be hard for a man late in life to remove old habits, I am not altogether out of hopes in some time to suffer a neighbor Yahoo in my company, without the apprehensions I am yet under of his teeth or his claws.

My reconcilement to the Yahoo kind in general might not be so difficult, if they would be content with those vices and follies only which nature hath entitled them to. I am not in the least provoked at the sight of a lawyer, a pickpocket, a colonel, a fool, a lord, a gamester, a politician, a whoremonger, a physician, an evidence,[2] a suborner, an attorney, a traitor, or the like: this is all according to the due course of things. But when I behold a lump of deformity, and diseases both in body and mind, smitten with *pride,* it immediately breaks all the measures of my patience; neither shall I be ever able to comprehend how such an animal and such a vice could tally together. The wise and virtuous Houyhnhnms, who abound in all excellencies that can adorn a rational creature, have no name for this vice in their language, which hath no terms to express anything that is evil, except those whereby they describe the detestable qualities of their Yahoos, among which they were not able to distinguish this of pride, for want of thoroughly understanding human nature, as it showeth itself in other countries, where that animal presides. But I, who had more experience, could plainly observe some rudiments of it among the wild Yahoos.

But the Houyhnhnms, who live under the government of reason, are no more proud of the good qualities they possess, than I should be for not wanting a leg or an arm, which no man in his wits would boast of, although he must be miserable without them. I dwell the longer upon this subject from the desire I have to make the society of an English Yahoo by any means not insupportable; and therefore I here entreat those who have any tincture of this absurd vice, that they will not presume to appear in my sight.

1726, 1735

2. Witness.

A Modest Proposal[1]

FOR PREVENTING THE CHILDREN OF POOR PEOPLE IN IRELAND FROM BEING A BURDEN TO THEIR PARENTS OR COUNTRY, AND FOR MAKING THEM BENEFICIAL TO THE PUBLIC

It is a melancholy object to those who walk through this great town[2] or travel in the country, when they see the streets, the roads, and cabin doors, crowded with beggars of the female sex, followed by three, four, or six children, all in rags and importuning every passenger for an alms. These mothers, instead of being able to work for their honest livelihood, are forced to employ all their time in strolling to beg sustenance for their helpless infants, who, as they grow up, either turn thieves for want of work, or leave their dear native country to fight for the Pretender in Spain, or sell themselves to the Barbadoes.[3]

I think it is agreed by all parties that this prodigious number of children in the arms, or on the backs, or at the heels of their mothers, and frequently of their fathers, is in the present deplorable state of the kingdom a very great additional grievance; and therefore whoever could find out a fair, cheap, and easy method of making these children sound, useful members of the commonwealth would deserve so well of the public as to have his statue set up for a preserver of the nation.

But my intention is very far from being confined to provide only for the children of professed beggars; it is of a much greater extent, and shall take in the whole number of infants at a certain age who are born of parents in effect as little able to support them as those who demand our charity in the streets.

As to my own part, having turned my thoughts for many years upon this important subject, and maturely weighed the several schemes of other projectors,[4] I have always found them grossly mistaken in their computation. It is true, a child just dropped from its dam may be supported by her milk for a solar year, with little other nourishment; at most not above the value of two shillings, which the mother may certainly get, or the value in scraps, by her lawful occupation of begging; and it is exactly at one year old that I propose to provide for them in such a manner as instead of being a charge upon their parents or the parish, or wanting food and raiment for the rest of their lives, they shall on the contrary contribute to the feeding, and partly to the clothing, of many thousands.

There is likewise another great advantage in my scheme, that it will prevent

1. "A Modest Proposal" is an example of Swift's favorite satiric devices used with superb effect. Irony (from the deceptive adjective *modest* in the title to the very last sentence) pervades the piece. A rigorous logic deduces ghastly arguments from a premise so quietly assumed that readers assent before they are aware of what that assent implies. Parody, at which Swift is adept, allows him to glance sardonically at the by then familiar figure of the benevolent humanitarian (forerunner of the modern sociologist, social worker, and economic planner) concerned to correct a social evil by means of a theoretically conceived plan. The proposer, as naive as he is apparently logical and kindly, ignores and therefore emphasizes for the reader the enormity of his plan. The whole is an elaboration of a rather trite metaphor: "The English are devouring the Irish." But there is nothing trite about the pamphlet, which expresses in Swift's most controlled style his revulsion at the contemporary state of Ireland and his indignation at the rapacious English absentee landlords, who were bleeding the country white with the silent approbation of Parliament, ministers, and the crown.

2. Dublin.

3. James Francis Edward Stuart (1688–1766), the son of James II, was claimant ("Pretender") to the throne of England from which the Glorious Revolution had barred his succession. Catholic Ireland was loyal to him, and Irishmen joined him in his exile on the Continent. Because of the poverty in Ireland, many Irishmen emigrated to the West Indies and other British colonies in America; they paid their passage by binding themselves to work for a stated period for one of the planters.

4. Devisers of schemes.

those voluntary abortions, and that horrid practice of women murdering their bastard children, alas, too frequent among us, sacrificing the poor innocent babes, I doubt, more to avoid the expense than the shame, which would move tears and pity in the most savage and inhuman breast.

The number of souls in this kingdom[5] being usually reckoned one million and a half, of these I calculate there may be about two hundred thousand couple whose wives are breeders; from which number I subtract thirty thousand couples who are able to maintain their own children, although I apprehend there cannot be so many under the present distresses of the kingdom; but this being granted, there will remain an hundred and seventy thousand breeders. I again subtract fifty thousand for those women who miscarry, or whose children die by accident or disease within the year. There only remain an hundred and twenty thousand children of poor parents annually born. The question therefore is, how this number shall be reared and provided for, which, as I have already said, under the present situation of affairs, is utterly impossible by all the methods hitherto proposed. For we can neither employ them in handicraft or agriculture; we neither build houses (I mean in the country) nor cultivate land. They can very seldom pick up a livelihood by stealing till they arrive at six years old, except where they are of towardly parts;[6] although I confess they learn the rudiments much earlier, during which time they can however be looked upon only as probationers, as I have been informed by a principal gentleman in the county of Cavan, who protested to me that he never knew above one or two instances under the ages of six, even in a part of the kingdom so renowned for the quickest proficiency in that art.

I am assured by our merchants that a boy or a girl before twelve years old is no salable commodity; and even when they come to this age they will not yield above three pounds, or three pounds and half a crown at most on the Exchange; which cannot turn to account either to the parents or the kingdom, the charge of nutriment and rags having been at least four times that value.

I shall now therefore humbly propose my own thoughts, which I hope will not be liable to the least objection.

I have been assured by a very knowing American of my acquaintance in London, that a young healthy child well nursed is at a year old a most delicious, nourishing, and wholesome food, whether stewed, roasted, baked, or boiled; and I make no doubt that it will equally serve in a fricassee or a ragout.[7]

I do therefore humbly offer it to public consideration that of the hundred and twenty thousand children, already computed, twenty thousand may be reserved for breed, whereof only one fourth part to be males, which is more than we allow to sheep, black cattle, or swine; and my reason is that these children are seldom the fruits of marriage, a circumstance not much regarded by our savages, therefore one male will be sufficient to serve four females. That the remaining hundred thousand may at a year old be offered in sale to the persons of quality and fortune through the kingdom, always advising the mother to let them suck plentifully in the last month, so as to render them plump and fat for a good table. A child will make two dishes at an entertainment for friends; and when the family dines alone, the fore or hind quarter will make a reasonable dish, and seasoned with a little pepper or salt will be very good boiled on the fourth day, especially in winter.

I have reckoned upon a medium that a child just born will weigh twelve

5. Ireland.
6. Promising abilities.
7. A highly seasoned meat stew.

pounds, and in a solar year if tolerably nursed increaseth to twenty-eight pounds.

I grant this food will be somewhat dear, and therefore very proper for landlords, who, as they have already devoured most of the parents, seem to have the best title to the children.

Infant's flesh will be in season throughout the year, but more plentiful in March, and a little before and after. For we are told by a grave author, an eminent French physician,[8] that fish being a prolific diet, there are more children born in Roman Catholic countries about nine months after Lent than at any other season; therefore, reckoning a year after Lent, the markets will be more glutted than usual, because the number of popish infants is at least three to one in this kingdom; and therefore it will have one other collateral advantage, by lessening the number of Papists among us.

I have already computed the charge of nursing a beggar's child (in which list I reckon all cottagers, laborers, and four fifths of the farmers) to be about two shillings per annum, rags included; and I believe no gentleman would repine to give ten shillings for the carcass of a good fat child, which, as I have said, will make four dishes of excellent nutritive meat, when he hath only some particular friend or his own family to dine with him. Thus the squire will learn to be a good landlord, and grow popular among the tenants; the mother will have eight shillings net profit, and be fit for the work till she produces another child.

Those who are more thrifty (as I must confess the times require) may flay the carcass; the skin of which artificially[9] dressed will make admirable gloves for ladies, and summer boots for fine gentlemen.

As to our city of Dublin, shambles[1] may be appointed for this purpose in the most convenient parts of it, and butchers we may be assured will not be wanting; although I rather recommend buying the children alive, and dressing them hot from the knife as we do roasting pigs.

A very worthy person, a true lover of his country, and whose virtues I highly esteem, was lately pleased in discoursing on this matter to offer a refinement upon my scheme. He said that many gentlemen of this kingdom, having of late destroyed their deer, he conceived that the want of venison might be well supplied by the bodies of young lads and maidens, not exceeding fourteen years of age nor under twelve, so great a number of both sexes in every county being now ready to starve for want of work and service; and these to be disposed of by their parents, if alive, or otherwise by their nearest relations. But with due deference to so excellent a friend and so deserving a patriot, I cannot be altogether in his sentiments; for as to the males, my American acquaintance assured me from frequent experience that their flesh was generally tough and lean, like that of our schoolboys, by continual exercise, and their taste disagreeable; and to fatten them would not answer the charge. Then as to the females, it would, I think with humble submission, be a loss to the public, because they soon would become breeders themselves; and besides, it is not improbable that some scrupulous people might be apt to censure such a practice (although indeed very unjustly) as a little bordering upon cruelty; which I confess, hath always been with me the strongest objection against any project, how well soever intended.

8. François Rabelais (ca. 1494–1553), a humorist and satirist, by no means grave.

9. Skillfully.

1. Slaughterhouses.

But in order to justify my friend, he confessed that this expedient was put into his head by the famous Psalmanazar,[2] a native of the island Formosa, who came from thence to London above twenty years ago, and in conversation told my friend that in his country when any young person happened to be put to death, the executioner sold the carcass to persons of quality as a prime dainty; and that in his time the body of a plump girl of fifteen, who was crucified for an attempt to poison the emperor, was sold to his Imperial Majesty's prime minister of state, and other great mandarins of the court, in joints from the gibbet, at four hundred crowns. Neither indeed can I deny that if the same use were made of several plump young girls in this town, who without one single groat to their fortunes cannot stir abroad without a chair, and appear at the playhouse and assemblies in foreign fineries which they never will pay for, the kingdom would not be the worse.

Some persons of a desponding spirit are in great concern about that vast number of poor people who are aged, diseased, or maimed, and I have been desired to employ my thoughts what course may be taken to ease the nation of so grievous an encumbrance. But I am not in the least pain upon that matter, because it is very well known that they are every day dying and rotting by cold and famine, and filth and vermin, as fast as can be reasonably expected. And as to the younger laborers, they are now in almost as hopeful a condition. They cannot get work, and consequently pine away for want of nourishment to a degree that if at any time they are accidentally hired to common labor, they have not strength to perform it; and thus the country and themselves are happily delivered from the evils to come.

I have too long digressed, and therefore shall return to my subject. I think the advantages by the proposal which I have made are obvious and many, as well as of the highest importance.

For first, as I have already observed, it would greatly lessen the number of Papists, with whom we are yearly overrun, being the principal breeders of the nation as well as our most dangerous enemies; and who stay at home on purpose to deliver the kingdom to the Pretender, hoping to take their advantage by the absence of so many good Protestants, who have chosen rather to leave their country than stay at home and pay tithes against their conscience to an Episcopal curate.[3]

Secondly, the poorer tenants will have something valuable of their own, which by law may be made liable to distress,[4] and help to pay their landlord's rent, their corn and cattle being already seized and money a thing unknown.

Thirdly, whereas the maintenance of an hundred thousand children, from two years old and upwards, cannot be computed at less than ten shillings a piece per annum, the nation's stock will be thereby increased fifty thousand pounds per annum, besides the profit of a new dish introduced to the tables of all gentlemen of fortune in the kingdom who have any refinement in taste. And the money will circulate among ourselves, the goods being entirely of our own growth and manufacture.

Fourthly, the constant breeders, besides the gain of eight shillings sterling

2. George Psalmanazar (ca. 1679–1763), a famous impostor. A Frenchman, he imposed himself on English bishops, noblemen, and scientists as a Formosan. He wrote an entirely fictitious account of Formosa, in which he described human sacrifices and cannibalism.

3. Ireland had many Protestant sectarians who did not support the "Episcopal" (Anglican) Church of Ireland.

4. Distraint, i.e., the seizing, through legal action, of property for the payment of debts and other obligations. "Corn": grain.

per annum by the sale of their children, will be rid of the charge of maintaining them after the first year.

Fifthly, this food would likewise bring great custom to taverns, where the vintners will certainly be so prudent as to procure the best receipts[5] for dressing it to perfection, and consequently have their houses frequented by all the fine gentlemen, who justly value themselves upon their knowledge in good eating; and a skillful cook, who understands how to oblige his guests, will contrive to make it as expensive as they please.

Sixthly, this would be a great inducement to marriage, which all wise nations have either encouraged by rewards or enforced by laws and penalties. It would increase the care and tenderness of mothers toward their children, when they were sure of a settlement for life to the poor babes, provided in some sort by the public, to their annual profit instead of expense. We should see an honest emulation among the married women, which of them could bring the fattest child to the market. Men would become as fond of their wives during the time of their pregnancy as they are now of their mares in foal, their cows in calf, or sows when they are ready to farrow; nor offer to beat or kick them (as is too frequent a practice) for fear of a miscarriage.

Many other advantages might be enumerated. For instance, the addition of some thousand carcasses in our exportation of barreled beef, the propagation of swine's flesh, and improvement in the art of making good bacon, so much wanted among us by the great destruction of pigs, too frequent at our tables, which are no way comparable in taste or magnificence to a well-grown, fat, yearling child, which roasted whole will make a considerable figure at a lord mayor's feast or any other public entertainment. But this and many others I omit, being studious of brevity.

Supposing that one thousand families in this city would be constant customers for infants' flesh, besides others who might have it at merry meetings, particularly weddings and christenings, I compute that Dublin would take off annually about twenty thousand carcasses, and the rest of the kingdom (where probably they will be sold somewhat cheaper) the remaining eighty thousand.

I can think of no one objection that will probably be raised against this proposal, unless it should be urged that the number of people will be thereby much lessened in the kingdom. This I freely own, and it was indeed one principal design in offering it to the world. I desire the reader will observe, that I calculate my remedy for this one individual kingdom of Ireland and for no other that ever was, is, or I think ever can be upon earth. Therefore let no man talk to me of other expedients: of taxing our absentees at five shillings a pound: of using neither clothes nor household furniture except what is of our own growth and manufacture: of utterly rejecting the materials and instruments that promote foreign luxury: of curing the expensiveness of pride, vanity, idleness, and gaming in our women: of introducing a vein of parsimony, prudence, and temperance: of learning to love our country, in the want of which we differ even from Laplanders and the inhabitants of Topinamboo:[6] of quitting our animosities and factions, nor acting any longer like the Jews, who were murdering one another at the very moment their city was taken:[7] of being a little cautious not to sell our country and conscience for nothing: of

5. Recipes.

6. I.e., even Laplanders love their frozen, infertile country and the savage tribes of Brazil love their jungle more than the Anglo-Irish love Ireland.

7. During the siege of Jerusalem by the Roman Titus (later emperor), who captured and destroyed the city in 70 C.E., bloody fights broke out between fanatical factions among the defenders.

teaching landlords to have at least one degree of mercy toward their tenants: lastly, of putting a spirit of honesty, industry, and skill into our shopkeepers; who, if a resolution could now be taken to buy only our native goods, would immediately unite to cheat and exact upon us in the price, the measure, and the goodness, nor could ever yet be brought to make one fair proposal of just dealing, though often and earnestly invited to it.[8]

Therefore I repeat, let no man talk to me of these and the like expedients, till he hath at least some glimpse of hope that there will ever be some hearty and sincere attempt to put them in practice.

But as to myself, having been wearied out for many years with offering vain, idle, visionary thoughts, and at length utterly despairing of success, I fortunately fell upon this proposal, which, as it is wholly new, so it hath something solid and real, of no expense and little trouble, full in our own power, and whereby we can incur no danger in disobliging England. For this kind of commodity will not bear exportation, the flesh being of too tender a consistence to admit a long continuance in salt, although perhaps I could name a country which would be glad to eat up our whole nation without it.[9]

After all, I am not so violently bent upon my own opinion as to reject any offer proposed by wise men, which shall be found equally innocent, cheap, easy, and effectual. But before something of that kind shall be advanced in contradiction to my scheme, and offering a better, I desire the author or authors will be pleased maturely to consider two points. First, as things now stand, how they will be able to find food and raiment for an hundred thousand useless mouths and backs. And secondly, there being a round million of creatures in human figure throughout this kingdom, whose sole subsistence put into a common stock would leave them in debt two millions of pounds sterling, adding those who are beggars by profession to the bulk of farmers, cottagers, and laborers, with their wives and children who are beggars in effect; I desire those politicians who dislike my overture, and may perhaps be so bold to attempt an answer, that they will first ask the parents of these mortals whether they would not at this day think it a great happiness to have been sold for food at a year old in the manner I prescribe, and thereby have avoided such a perpetual sense of misfortunes as they have since gone through by the oppression of landlords, the impossibility of paying rent without money or trade, the want of common sustenance, with neither house nor clothes to cover them from the inclemencies of the weather, and the most inevitable prospect of entailing the like or greater miseries upon their breed forever.

I profess, in the sincerity of my heart, that I have not the least personal interest in endeavoring to promote this necessary work, having no other motive than the public good of my country, by advancing our trade, providing for infants, relieving the poor, and giving some pleasure to the rich. I have no children by which I can propose to get a single penny; the youngest being nine years old, and my wife past childbearing.

1729

8. Swift himself had made all these proposals in various pamphlets. In editions printed during his lifetime the various proposals were italicized to indicate Swift's support for them.

9. England.

ALEXANDER POPE
1688–1744

Alexander Pope is the only important writer of his generation who was solely a man of letters. Because he could not, as a Roman Catholic, attend a university, vote, or hold public office, he was excluded from the sort of patronage that was bestowed by statesmen on many writers during the reign of Anne. This disadvantage he turned into a positive good, for the translation of Homer's *Iliad* and *Odyssey,* which he undertook for profit as well as for fame, gave him ample means to live the life of an independent suburban gentleman. After 1718 he lived hospitably in his villa by the Thames at Twickenham (then pronounced *Twit'nam*), entertaining his friends and converting his five acres of land into a diminutive landscape garden. Almost exactly a century earlier, William Shakespeare had earned enough to retire to a country estate at Stratford—but he had been an actor-manager as well as a playwright; Pope was the first English writer to build a lucrative, lifelong career by publishing his works.

Ill health plagued Pope almost from birth. Crippled early by tuberculosis of the bone, he never grew taller than four and a half feet. In later life he suffered from violent headaches and required constant attention from servants. But Pope did not allow his infirmities to hold him back; he was always a master at making the best of what he had. Around 1700 his father, a well-to-do, retired London merchant, moved to a small property at Binfield in Windsor Forest. There, in rural surroundings, young Pope completed his education by reading whatever he pleased, "like a boy gathering flowers in the woods and fields just as they fall in his way"; and there, encouraged by his father, he began to write verse. He was already an accomplished poet in his teens; no English poet has ever been more precocious.

Pope's first striking success as a poet was *An Essay on Criticism* (1711), which brought him Joseph Addison's approval and an intemperate personal attack from the critic John Dennis, who was angered by a casual reference to himself in the poem. *The Rape of the Lock,* both in its original shorter version of 1712 and in its more elaborate version of 1714, proved the author a master not only of metrics and of language but also of witty, urbane satire. In *An Essay on Criticism,* Pope had excelled all his predecessors in writing a didactic poem after the example of Horace; in the *Rape,* he had written the most brilliant mock epic in the language. But there was another vein in Pope's youthful poetry, a tender concern with natural beauty and love. The *Pastorals* (1709), his first publication, and *Windsor Forest* (1713; much of it was written earlier) abound in visual imagery and descriptive passages of ideally ordered nature; they remind us that Pope was an amateur painter. The "Elegy to the Memory of an Unfortunate Lady" and *Eloisa to Abelard,* published in the collected poems of 1717, dwell on the pangs of unhappy lovers (Pope himself never married). And even the long task of translating Homer, the "dull duty" of editing Shakespeare, and, in middle age, his dedication to ethical and satirical poetry did not make less fine his keen sense of beauty in nature and art. (For additional poems by Pope, go to Norton Literature Online.)

Pope's early poetry brought him to the attention of literary men, with whom he began to associate in the masculine world of coffeehouse and tavern, where he liked to play the rake. Between 1706 and 1711 he came to know, among many others, William Congreve; William Walsh, the critic and poet; and Richard Steele and Joseph Addison. As it happened, all were Whigs. Pope could readily ignore politics in the excitement of taking his place among the leading wits of the town. But after the fall of the Whigs in 1710 and the formation of the Tory government under Robert Harley (later the Earl of Oxford) and Henry St. John (later Viscount Bolingbroke) party loyalties bred bitterness among the wits as among the politicians. By 1712, Pope had made the acquaintance of another group of writers, all Tories, who were soon his intimate friends: Jonathan Swift, by then the close associate of Harley and St. John and the principal propagandist for their policies; Dr. John Arbuthnot, physician to the queen, a learned scientist, a wit, and a man of humanity and integrity; John Gay, the poet, who in 1728 was to create *The Beggar's Opera,* the greatest theatrical success of the century; and the poet Thomas Parnell. Through them he became the friend and admirer of Oxford and later the intimate of Bolingbroke. In 1714 this group, at the instigation of Pope, formed a club for satirizing all sorts of false learning. The friends proposed to write jointly the biography of a learned fool whom they named Martinus Scriblerus (Martin the Scribbler), whose life and opinions would be a running commentary on educated nonsense. Some amusing episodes were later rewritten and published as the *Memoirs of Martinus Scriblerus* (1741). The real importance of the club, however, is that it fostered a satiric temper that would be expressed in such mature works of the friends as *Gulliver's Travels, The Beggar's Opera,* and *The Dunciad.*

"The life of a wit is a warfare on earth," said Pope, generalizing from his own experience. His very success as a poet (and his astonishing precocity brought him success very early) made enemies who were to plague him in pamphlets, verse satires, and squibs in the journals throughout his entire literary career. He was attacked for his writings, his religion, and his physical deformity. Although he smarted under the jibes of his detractors, he was a fighter who struck back, always giving better than he got. Pope's literary warfare began in 1713, when he announced his intention of translating the *Iliad* and sought subscribers to a deluxe edition of the work. Subscribers came in droves, but the Whig writers who surrounded Addison at Button's Coffee House did all they could to discredit the venture. The eventual success of the first published installment of his *Iliad* in 1715 did not obliterate Pope's resentment against Addison and his "little senate"; and he took his revenge in the damaging portrait of Addison (under the name of Atticus), which was later included in the *Epistle to Dr. Arbuthnot* (1735), lines 193–214. The not unjustified attacks on Pope's edition of Shakespeare (1725) by the learned Shakespeare scholar Lewis Theobald (Pope always spelled and pronounced the name "Tibbald" in his satires) led to Theobald's appearance as king of the dunces in *The Dunciad* (1728). In this impressive poem Pope stigmatized his literary enemies as agents of all that he disliked and feared in the tendencies of his time—the vulgarization of taste and the arts consequent on the rapid growth of the reading public and the development of journalism, magazines, and other popular and cheap publications, which spread scandal, sensationalism, and political partisanship—in short the new commercial spirit of the nation that was corrupting not only the arts but, as Pope saw it, the national life itself.

In the 1730s Pope moved on to philosophical, ethical, and political subjects in *An Essay on Man,* the *Epistles to Several Persons,* and the *Imitations of Horace.* The reigns of George I and George II appeared to him, as to Swift and other Tories, a period of rapid moral, political, and cultural deterioration. The agents of decay fed on the rise of moneyed (as opposed to landed) wealth, which accounted for the political corruption encouraged by Sir Robert Walpole and the court party and the corruption of all aspects of the national life by a vulgar class of *nouveaux riches.* Pope assumed the role of the champion of traditional values: of right reason, humanistic learning, sound art, good taste, and public virtue. It was fortunate that many of his enemies happened to illustrate various degrees of unreason, pedantry, bad art, vulgar taste, and at best, indifferent morals.

The satirist traditionally deals in generally prevalent evils and generally observable human types, not with particular individuals. So too with Pope; the bulk of his satire can be read and enjoyed without much biographical information. Usually he used fictional or type names, although he most often had an individual in mind—Sappho, Atossa, Atticus, Sporus—and when he named individuals (as he consistently did in *The Dunciad*), his purpose was to raise his victims to emblems of folly and vice. To judge and censure the age, Pope also created the *I* of the satires (not identical with Alexander Pope of Twickenham). This semifictional figure is the detached observer, somewhat removed from the City, town, and court, the centers of corruption; he is the friend of the virtuous, whose friendship for him testifies to his integrity; he is fond of peace, country life, the arts, morality, and truth; and he detests their opposites that flourish in the great world. In such an age, Pope implies, it is impossible for such a man—honest, truthful, blunt—not to write satire.

Pope was a master of style. From first to last, his verse is notable for its rhythmic variety, despite the apparently rigid metrical unit—the heroic couplet—in which he wrote; for the precision of meaning and the harmony (or expressive disharmony) of his language; and for the union of maximum conciseness with maximum complexity. Variety and harmony can be observed in even so short a passage as lines 71–76 of the pastoral "Summer" (1709), lines so lyrical that, in *Semele,* Handel set them to music. In the passage quoted below (as also in the quotation at the bottom of the page), only those rhetorical stresses that distort the normal iambic flow of the verse have been marked; internal pauses within the line are indicated by single and double bars, alliteration and assonance by italics.

> Óh *déi*gn to visit our *f*ors*a*ken *sea*ts,
> The mossy *fou*ntains || and the *gr*e*e*n retr*ea*ts!
> Where'er yóu wálk || cóol *gá*les shall *f*an the *gl*ade,
> Trées whére yóu sít || shall cr*ow*d into a sh*a*de:
> Where'er yóu tread || the bl*u*shing *flow*ers shall rise,
> And all thíngs *flóu*rish where yóu *tú*rn your eyes.

Pope has attained metrical variety by the free substitution of trochees and spondees for the normal iambs; he has achieved rhythmic variety by arranging phrases and clauses (units of syntax and logic) of different lengths within single lines and couplets, so that the passage moves with the sinuous fluency of thought and feeling; and he not only has chosen musical combinations of words but has also subtly modulated the harmony of the passage by unobtrusive patterns of alliteration and assonance.

Contrast with this pastoral passage lines 16–25 of the "Epilogue to the Satires, Dialogue 2" (1738), in which Pope is not making music but imitating actual conversation so realistically that the metrical pattern and the integrity of the couplet and individual line seem to be destroyed (although in fact they remain in place). In a dialogue with a friend who warns him that his satire is too personal, indeed mere libel, the poet-satirist replies:

> Yé státesmen, | priests of one religion all!
> Yé trádesmen vile || in army, court, or hall!
> Yé réverend atheists. || F. Scandal! | name them, | Who?
> P. Why that's the thing you bid me not to do.
> Whó stárved a sister, || who foreswore a debt,
> Í néver named; || the town's inquiring yet.
> The poisoning dame—| F. Yóu méan—| P. I don't—| F. Yóu dó.
> P. Sée, nów I kéep the secret, || and nót yóu!
> The bribing statesman—| F. Hóld, || tóo hígh you go.
> P. The bribed elector—|| F. There you stoop tóo lów.

In such a passage the language and rhythms of poetry merge with the language and rhythms of impassioned living speech.

A fine example of Pope's ability to derive the maximum of meaning from the most economic use of language and image is the description of the manor house in which lives old Cotta, the miser (*Epistle to Lord Bathurst,* lines 187–96):

> Like some lone Chartreuse stands the good old Hall,
> Silence without, and fasts within the wall;
> No raftered roofs with dance and tabor sound,
> No noontide bell invites the country round;
> Tenants with sighs the smokeless towers survey,
> And turn the unwilling steeds another way;
> Benighted wanderers, the forest o'er,
> Curse the saved candle and unopening door;
> While the gaunt mastiff growling at the gate,
> Affrights the beggar whom he longs to eat.

The first couplet of this passage associates the "Hall," symbol of English rural hospitality, with the Grande Chartreuse, the monastery in the French Alps, which, although a place of "silence" and "fasts" for the monks, afforded food and shelter to all travelers. Then the dismal details of Cotta's miserly dwelling provide a stark contrast, and the meaning of the scene is concentrated in the grotesque image of the last couplet: the half-starved watchdog and the frightened beggar confronting each other in mutual hunger.

But another sort of variety derives from Pope's respect for the idea that the different kinds of literature have their different and appropriate styles. Thus *An Essay on Criticism,* an informal discussion of literary theory, is written, like Horace's *Art of Poetry* (a similarly didactic poem), in a plain style, the easy language of well-bred talk. *The Rape of the Lock,* "a heroi-comical poem" (that is, a comic poem that treats trivial material in an epic style), employs the lofty heroic language that John Dryden had perfected in his translation of Virgil and introduces amusing parodies of passages in *Paradise Lost,* parodies later raised to truly Miltonic sublimity and complexity by the conclusion of *The Dunciad. Eloisa to Abelard* renders the brooding, passionate voice of its heroine in a declamatory language, given to sudden outbursts and shifts of tone, that recalls the stage. The grave epistles that make up *An Essay on Man,* a philosophical discussion of such majestic themes as the Creator and His creation, the universe, human nature, society, and happiness, are written in a stately forensic language and tone and constantly employ the traditional rhetorical figures. The *Imitations of Horace* and, above all, the *Epistle to Dr. Arbuthnot,* his finest poem "in the Horatian way," reveal Pope's final mastery of the plain style of Horace's epistles and satires and support his image of himself as the heir of the Roman poet. In short, no other poet of the century can equal Pope in the range of his materials, the diversity of his poetic styles, and the wizardry of his technique.

An Essay on Criticism

There is no pleasanter introduction to the canons of taste in the English Augustan age than Pope's *An Essay on Criticism.* As Addison said in his review in *Spectator* 253, it assembles the "most known and most received observations on the subject of literature and criticism." Pope was attempting to do for his time what Horace, in his *Art of Poetry,* and what Nicolas Boileau (French poet of the age of Louis XIV), in his *L'Art Poétique,* had done for theirs. Horace is Pope's model not only for principles of criticism but also for style, especially in the simple, conversational language and the tone of well-bred ease.

In framing his critical creed, Pope did not try for novelty: he wished merely to give to generally accepted doctrines pleasing and memorable expression and make them useful to modern poets. Here one meets the key words of neoclassical criticism: *wit,*

Nature, ancients, rules, and *genius. Wit* in the poem is a word of many meanings—a clever remark or the person who makes it, a conceit, liveliness of mind, inventiveness, fancy, genius, a genius, and poetry itself, among others. *Nature* is an equally ambiguous word, meaning not "things out there" or "the outdoors" but most important that which is representative, universal, permanent in human experience as opposed to the idiosyncratic, the individual, the temporary. In line 21, *Nature* comes close to meaning "intuitive knowledge." In line 52, it means that half-personified power manifested in the cosmic order, which in its modes of working is a model for art. The reverence felt by most Augustans for the great writers of ancient Greece and Rome raised the question how far the authority of these *ancients* extended. Were their works to be received as models to be conscientiously imitated? Were the *rules* received from them or deducible from their works to be accepted as prescriptive laws or merely convenient guides? Was individual *genius* to be bound by what has been conventionally held to be *Nature,* by the authority of the *ancients,* and by the legalistic pedantry of *rules*? Or could it go its own way?

In part 1 of the *Essay,* Pope constructs a harmonious system in which he effects a compromise among all these conflicting forces—a compromise that is typical of his times. Part 2 analyzes the causes of faulty criticism. Part 3 characterizes the good critic and praises the great critics of the past.

An Essay on Criticism

Part 1

'Tis hard to say, if greater want of skill
Appear in writing or in judging ill;
But of the two less dangerous is the offense
To tire our patience than mislead our sense.
Some few in that, but numbers err in this,
Ten censure° wrong for one who writes amiss; *judge*
A fool might once himself alone expose,
Now one in verse makes many more in prose.
'Tis with our judgments as our watches, none
Go just alike, yet each believes his own.
In poets as true genius is but rare,
True taste as seldom is the critic's share;
Both must alike from Heaven derive their light,
These born to judge, as well as those to write.
Let such teach others who themselves excel,
And censure freely who have written well.
Authors are partial to their wit, 'tis true,
But are not critics to their judgment too?
Yet if we look more closely, we shall find
Most have the seeds of judgment in their mind:
Nature affords at least a glimmering light;
The lines, though touched but faintly, are drawn right.
But as the slightest sketch, if justly traced,
Is by ill coloring but the more disgraced,
So by false learning is good sense defaced:
Some are bewildered in the maze of schools,
And some made coxcombs[1] Nature meant but fools.

1. Superficial pretenders to learning.

In search of wit these lose their common sense,
And then turn critics in their own defense:
Each burns alike, who can, or cannot write,
Or with a rival's or an eunuch's spite.
All fools have still an itching to deride,
And fain would be upon the laughing side.
If Maevius[2] scribble in Apollo's spite,
There are who judge still worse than he can write.
 Some have at first for wits, then poets passed,
Turned critics next, and proved plain fools at last.
Some neither can for wits nor critics pass,
As heavy mules are neither horse nor ass.
Those half-learn'd witlings, numerous in our isle,
As half-formed insects on the banks of Nile;[3]
Unfinished things, one knows not what to call,
Their generation's so equivocal:
To tell° them would a hundred tongues require, *reckon, count*
Or one vain wit's, that might a hundred tire.
 But you who seek to give and merit fame,
And justly bear a critic's noble name,
Be sure yourself and your own reach to know,
How far your genius, taste, and learning go;
Launch not beyond your depth, but be discreet,
And mark that point where sense and dullness meet.
 Nature to all things fixed the limits fit,
And wisely curbed proud man's pretending° wit. *aspiring*
As on the land while here the ocean gains,
In other parts it leaves wide sandy plains;
Thus in the soul while memory prevails,
The solid power of understanding fails;
Where beams of warm imagination play,
The memory's soft figures melt away.
One science° only will one genius fit, *branch of learning*
So vast is art, so narrow human wit.
Not only bounded to peculiar arts,
But oft in those confined to single parts.
Like kings we lose the conquests gained before,
By vain ambition still to make them more;
Each might his several province well command,
Would all but stoop to what they understand.
 First follow Nature, and your judgment frame
By her just standard, which is still the same;
Unerring Nature, still divinely bright,
One clear, unchanged, and universal light,
Life, force, and beauty must to all impart,
At once the source, and end, and test of art.
Art from that fund each just supply provides,
Works without show, and without pomp presides.
In some fair body thus the informing soul

2. A silly poet alluded to contemptuously by Virgil in *Eclogue* 3 and by Horace in *Epode* 10.
3. The ancients believed that many forms of life were spontaneously generated in the fertile mud of the Nile.

With spirits feeds, with vigor fills the whole,
Each motion guides, and every nerve sustains;
Itself unseen, but in the effects remains.
Some, to whom Heaven in wit has been profuse,
Want as much more to turn it to its use;
For wit and judgment often are at strife,
Though meant each other's aid, like man and wife.
'Tis more to guide than spur the Muse's steed,
Restrain his fury than provoke his speed;
The wingèd courser,[4] like a generous° horse, *spirited, highly bred*
Shows most true mettle when you check his course.
  Those rules of old discovered, not devised,
Are Nature still, but Nature methodized;
Nature, like liberty, is but restrained
By the same laws which first herself ordained.
  Hear how learn'd Greece her useful rules indites,
When to repress and when indulge our flights:
High on Parnassus' top her sons she showed,
And pointed out those arduous paths they trod;
Held from afar, aloft, the immortal prize,
And urged the rest by equal steps to rise.
Just precepts thus from great examples given,
She drew from them what they derived from Heaven.
The generous critic fanned the poet's fire,
And taught the world with reason to admire.
Then criticism the Muse's handmaid proved,
To dress her charms, and make her more beloved:
But following wits from that intention strayed,
Who could not win the mistress, wooed the maid;
Against the poets their own arms they turned,
Sure to hate most the men from whom they learned.
So modern 'pothecaries, taught the art
By doctors's bills° to play the doctor's part, *prescriptions*
Bold in the practice of mistaken rules,
Prescribe, apply, and call their masters fools.
Some on the leaves of ancient authors prey,
Nor time nor moths e'er spoiled so much as they.
Some dryly plain, without invention's aid,
Write dull receipts[5] how poems may be made.
These leave the sense their learning to display,
And those explain the meaning quite away.
  You then whose judgment the right course would steer,
Know well each ancient's proper character;
His fable,[6] subject, scope° in every page; *aim, purpose*
Religion, country, genius of his age:
Without all these at once before your eyes,
Cavil you may, but never criticize.
Be Homer's works your study and delight,
Read them by day, and meditate by night;

4. Pegasus, associated with the Muses and poetic inspiration.
5. Formulas for preparing a dish; recipes. Pope himself wrote an amusing burlesque, "Receipt to Make an Epic Poem," first published in the *Guardian* 78 (1713).
6. Plot or story of a play or poem.

Thence form your judgment, thence your maxims bring,
And trace the Muses upward to their spring.
Still with itself compared, his text peruse;
And let your comment be the Mantuan Muse.
When first young Maro[7] in his boundless mind
A work to outlast immortal Rome designed,
Perhaps he seemed above the critic's law,
And but from Nature's fountains scorned to draw;
But when to examine every part he came,
Nature and Homer were, he found, the same.
Convinced, amazed, he checks the bold design,
And rules as strict his labored work confine
As if the Stagirite[8] o'erlooked each line.
Learn hence for ancient rules a just esteem;
To copy Nature is to copy them.
Some beauties yet no precepts can declare,
For there's a happiness as well as care.[9]
Music resembles poetry, in each
Are nameless graces which no methods teach,
And which a master hand alone can reach.
If, where the rules not far enough extend
(Since rules were made but to promote their end)
Some lucky license answers to the full
The intent proposed, that license is a rule.
Thus Pegasus, a nearer way to take,
May boldly deviate from the common track.
Great wits sometimes may gloriously offend,
And rise to faults true critics dare not mend;
From vulgar bounds with brave disorder part,
And snatch a grace beyond the reach of art,
Which, without passing through the judgment, gains
The heart, and all its end at once attains.
In prospects thus, some objects please our eyes,
Which out of Nature's common order rise,
The shapeless rock, or hanging precipice.
But though the ancients thus their rules invade° *violate*
(As kings dispense with laws themselves have made)
Moderns, beware! or if you must offend
Against the precept, ne'er transgress its end;
Let it be seldom, and compelled by need;
And have at least their precedent to plead.
The critic else proceeds without remorse,
Seizes your fame, and puts his laws in force.
I know there are, to whose presumptuous thoughts
Those freer beauties, even in them, seem faults.[1]
Some figures monstrous and misshaped appear,

7. Virgil, who was born in a village adjacent to Mantua in Italy, hence "Mantuan Muse." His epic, the *Aeneid*, was modeled on Homer's *Iliad* and *Odyssey* and was considered to be a refinement of the Greek poems. Thus it could be thought of as a commentary ("comment") on Homer's poems.

8. Aristotle, a native of Stagira, from whose *Poetics* later critics formulated strict rules for writing tragedy and the epic.

9. I.e., no rules ("precepts") can explain ("declare") some beautiful effects in a work of art that can be the result only of inspiration or good luck ("happiness"), not of painstaking labor ("care").

1. Pronounced *fawts.*

Considered singly, or beheld too near,
Which, but proportioned to their light or place,
Due distance reconciles to form and grace.
A prudent chief not always must display
His powers in equal ranks and fair array,
But with the occasion and the place comply,
Conceal his force, nay seem sometimes to fly.
Those oft are stratagems which errors seem,
Nor is it Homer nods, but we that dream.
  Still green with bays each ancient altar stands
Above the reach of sacrilegious hands,
Secure from flames, from envy's fiercer rage,
Destructive war, and all-involving age.
See, from each clime the learn'd their incense bring!
Here in all tongues consenting° paeans ring! *agreeing, concurring*
In praise so just let every voice be joined,[2]
And fill the general chorus of mankind.
Hail, bards triumphant! born in happier days,
Immortal heirs of universal praise!
Whose honors with increase of ages grow,
As streams roll down, enlarging as they flow;
Nations unborn your mighty names shall sound,
And worlds applaud that must not yet be found!
Oh, may some spark of your celestial fire,
The last, the meanest of your sons inspire
(That on weak wings, from far, pursues your flights,
Glows while he reads, but trembles as he writes)
To teach vain wits a science little known,
To admire superior sense, and doubt their own!

Part 2

  Of all the causes which conspire to blind
Man's erring judgment, and misguide the mind,
What the weak head with strongest bias rules,
Is pride, the never-failing vice of fools.
Whatever Nature has in worth denied,
She gives in large recruits° of needful pride; *supplies*
For as in bodies, thus in souls, we find
What wants in blood and spirits, swelled with wind:
Pride, where wit fails, steps in to our defense,
And fills up all the mighty void of sense.
If once right reason drives that cloud away,
Truth breaks upon us with resistless day.
Trust not yourself: but your defects to know,
Make use of every friend—and every foe.
  A little learning is a dangerous thing;
Drink deep, or taste not the Pierian spring.[3]
There shallow draughts intoxicate the brain,
And drinking largely sobers us again.

2. Pronounced *jined.*
3. The spring in Pieria on Mount Olympus, sacred to the Muses.

Fired at first sight with what the Muse imparts,
In fearless youth we tempt° the heights of arts, *attempt*
While from the bounded level of our mind
Short views we take, nor see the lengths behind;
But more advanced, behold with strange surprise
New distant scenes of endless science rise!
So pleased at first the towering Alps we try,
Mount o'er the vales, and seem to tread the sky,
The eternal snows appear already past,
And the first clouds and mountains seem the last;
But, those attained, we tremble to survey
The growing labors of the lengthened way,
The increasing prospect tires our wandering eyes,
Hills peep o'er hills, and Alps on Alps arise!
A perfect judge will read each work of wit
With the same spirit that its author writ:
Survey the whole, nor seek slight faults to find
Where Nature moves, and rapture warms the mind;
Nor lose, for that malignant dull delight,
The generous pleasure to be charmed with wit.
But in such lays as neither ebb nor flow,
Correctly cold, and regularly low,
That, shunning faults, one quiet tenor keep,
We cannot blame indeed—but we may sleep.
In wit, as nature, what affects our hearts
Is not the exactness of peculiar° parts; *particular*
'Tis not a lip, or eye, we beauty call,
But the joint force and full result of all.
Thus when we view some well-proportioned dome[4]
(The world's just wonder, and even thine, O Rome!),
No single parts unequally surprise,
All comes united to the admiring eyes:
No monstrous height, or breadth, or length appear;
The whole at once is bold and regular.
Whoever thinks a faultless piece to see,
Thinks what ne'er was, nor is, nor e'er shall be.
In every work regard the writer's end,
Since none can compass more than they intend;
And if the means be just, the conduct true,
Applause, in spite of trivial faults, is due.
As men of breeding, sometimes men of wit,
To avoid great errors must the less commit,
Neglect the rules each verbal critic lays,
For not to know some trifles is a praise.
Most critics, fond of some subservient art,
Still make the whole depend upon a part:
They talk of principles, but notions prize,
And all to one loved folly sacrifice.
Once on a time La Mancha's knight,[5] they say,

4. The dome of St. Peter's, designed by Michelangelo.
5. Don Quixote. The story comes not from Cervantes's novel, but from a spurious sequel to it by Don Alonzo Fernandez de Avellaneda.

A certain bard encountering on the way,
Discoursed in terms as just, with looks as sage,
As e'er could Dennis,[6] of the Grecian stage;
Concluding all were desperate sots and fools
Who durst depart from Aristotle's rules.
Our author, happy in a judge so nice,
Produced his play, and begged the knight's advice;
Made him observe the subject and the plot,
The manners, passions, unities; what not?
All which exact to rule were brought about,
Were but a combat in the lists left out.
"What! leave the combat out?" exclaims the knight.
"Yes, or we must renounce the Stagirite."
"Not so, by Heaven!" he answers in a rage,
"Knights, squires, and steeds must enter on the stage."
"So vast a throng the stage can ne'er contain."
"Then build a new, or act it in a plain."
  Thus critics of less judgment than caprice,
Curious,° not knowing, not exact, but nice,° *laborious / fussy*
Form short ideas, and offend in arts
(As most in manners), by a love to parts.
  Some to conceit[7] alone their taste confine,
And glittering thoughts struck out at every line;
Pleased with a work where nothing's just or fit,
One glaring chaos and wild heap of wit.
Poets, like painters, thus unskilled to trace
The naked nature and the living grace,
With gold and jewels cover every part,
And hide with ornaments their want of art.
True wit is Nature to advantage dressed,
What oft was thought, but ne'er so well expressed;
Something whose truth convinced at sight we find,
That gives us back the image of our mind.
As shades more sweetly recommend the light,
So modest plainness sets off sprightly wit;
For works may have more wit than does them good,
As bodies perish through excess of blood.
  Others for language all their care express,
And value books, as women men, for dress.
Their praise is still—the style is excellent;
The sense they humbly take upon contènt.° *mere acquiescence*
Words are like leaves; and where they most abound,
Much fruit of sense beneath is rarely found.
False eloquence, like the prismatic glass,
Its gaudy colors spreads on every place;[8]
The face of Nature we no more survey,
All glares alike, without distinction gay.

6. John Dennis (1657–1734), although one of the leading critics of the time, was frequently ridiculed by the wits for his irascibility and pomposity. Pope apparently did not know Dennis personally, but his jibe at him in part 3 of this poem made him a bitter enemy.

7. Pointed wit, ingenuity and extravagance, or affectation in the use of figures, especially similes and metaphors.

8. A very up-to-date scientific reference. Newton's *Optics*, which dealt with the prism and the spectrum, had been published in 1704, although his theories had been known earlier.

But true expression, like the unchanging sun,
Clears and improves whate'er it shines upon;
It gilds all objects, but it alters none.
Expression is the dress of thought, and still
Appears more decent as more suitable.
A vile conceit in pompous words expressed
Is like a clown° in regal purple dressed: *country bumpkin*
For different styles with different subjects sort,
As several garbs with country, town, and court.
Some by old words to fame have made pretense,
Ancients in phrase, mere moderns in their sense.
Such labored nothings, in so strange a style,
Amaze the unlearn'd, and make the learned smile;
Unlucky as Fungoso[9] in the play,
These sparks with awkward vanity display
What the fine gentleman wore yesterday;
And but so mimic ancient wits at best,
As apes our grandsires in their doublets dressed.
In words as fashions the same rule will hold,
Alike fantastic if too new or old:
Be not the first by whom the new are tried,
Nor yet the last to lay the old aside.
  But most by numbers° judge a poet's song, *versification*
And smooth or rough with them is right or wrong.
In the bright Muse though thousand charms conspire,
Her voice is all these tuneful fools admire,
Who haunt Parnassus but to please their ear,
Not mend their minds; as some to church repair,
Not for the doctrine, but the music there.
These equal syllables alone require,
Though oft the ear the open vowels tire,[1]
While expletives[2] their feeble aid do join,
And ten low words oft creep in one dull line:
While they ring round the same unvaried chimes,
With sure returns of still expected rhymes;
Where'er you find "the cooling western breeze,"
In the next line, it "whispers through the trees";
If crystal streams "with pleasing murmurs creep,"
The reader's threatened (not in vain) with "sleep";
Then, at the last and only couplet fraught
With some unmeaning thing they call a thought,
A needless Alexandrine[3] ends the song
That, like a wounded snake, drags its slow length along.
Leave such to tune their own dull rhymes, and know
What's roundly smooth or languishingly slow;
And praise the easy vigor of a line
Where Denham's strength and Waller's sweetness join.[4]

9. A character in Ben Jonson's comedy *Every Man out of His Humor* (1599).
1. In lines 345–57 Pope cleverly contrives to make his own metrics or diction illustrate the faults that he is exposing.
2. Words used merely to achieve the necessary number of feet in a line of verse.
3. A line of verse containing six iambic feet; it is illustrated in the next line.
4. Dryden, whom Pope echoes here, considered Sir John Denham (1615–1669) and Edmund Waller (1606–1687) to have been the principal shapers of the closed pentameter couplet. He had distinguished the "strength" of the one and the "sweetness" of the other.

True ease in writing comes from art, not chance,
As those move easiest who have learned to dance.
'Tis not enough no harshness gives offense,
The sound must seem an echo to the sense.
Soft is the strain when Zephyr gently blows,
And the smooth stream in smoother numbers flows;
But when loud surges lash the sounding shore,
The hoarse, rough verse should like the torrent roar.
When Ajax strives some rock's vast weight to throw,
The line too labors, and the words move slow;
Not so when swift Camilla[5] scours the plain,
Flies o'er the unbending corn, and skims along the main.
Hear how Timotheus'[6] varied lays surprise,
And bid alternate passions fall and rise!
While at each change the son of Libyan Jove° *Alexander the Great*
Now burns with glory, and then melts with love;
Now his fierce eyes with sparkling fury glow,
Now sighs steal out, and tears begin to flow:
Persians and Greeks like turns of nature[7] found
And the world's victor stood subdued by sound!
The power of music all our hearts allow,
And what Timotheus was, is Dryden now.
  Avoid extremes; and shun the fault of such
Who still are pleased too little or too much.
At every trifle scorn to take offense:
That always shows great pride, or little sense.
Those heads, as stomachs, are not sure the best,
Which nauseate all, and nothing can digest.
Yet let not each gay turn thy rapture move;
For fools admire,° but men of sense approve:[8] *wonder*
As things seem large which we through mists descry,
Dullness is ever apt to magnify.
  Some foreign writers, some our own despise;
The ancients only, or the moderns prize.
Thus wit, like faith, by each man is applied
To one small sect, and all are damned beside.
Meanly they seek the blessing to confine,
And force that sun but on a part to shine,
Which not alone the southern wit sublimes,° *raises up, purifies*
But ripens spirits in cold northern climes;
Which from the first has shone on ages past,
Enlights the present, and shall warm the last;
Though each may feel increases and decays,
And see now clearer and now darker days.
Regard not then if wit be old or new,
But blame the false and value still the true.
  Some ne'er advance a judgment of their own,
But catch the spreading notion of the town;
They reason and conclude by precedent,
And own° stale nonsense which they ne'er invent. *lay claim to*

5. Fleet-footed virgin warrior (*Aeneid* 7, 11).
6. The musician in Dryden's "Alexander's Feast." Pope retells the story of that poem in the following lines.
7. Alternations of feelings.
8. Judge favorably only after due deliberation.

Some judge of authors' names, not works, and then
Nor praise nor blame the writings, but the men.
Of all this servile herd the worst is he
That in proud dullness joins with quality,[9]
A constant critic at the great man's board,
To fetch and carry nonsense for my lord.
What woeful stuff this madrigal would be
In some starved hackney sonneteer° or me! *hireling poet*
But let a lord once own the happy lines,
How the wit brightens! how the style refines!
Before his sacred name flies every fault,
And each exalted stanza teems with thought!
  The vulgar thus through imitation err;
As oft the learn'd by being singular;
So much they scorn the crowd, that if the throng
By chance go right, they purposely go wrong.
So schismatics[1] the plain believers quit,
And are but damned for having too much wit.
Some praise at morning what they blame at night,
But always think the last opinion right.
A Muse by these is like a mistress used,
This hour she's idolized, the next abused;
While their weak heads like towns unfortified,
'Twixt sense and nonsense daily change their side.
Ask them the cause; they're wiser still, they say;
And still tomorrow's wiser than today.
We think our fathers fools, so wise we grow;
Our wiser sons, no doubt, will think us so.
Once school divines[2] this zealous isle o'erspread;
Who knew most sentences[3] was deepest read.
Faith, Gospel, all seemed made to be disputed,
And none had sense enough to be confuted.
Scotists and Thomists now in peace remain
Amidst their kindred cobwebs in Duck Lane.[4]
If faith itself has different dresses worn,
What wonder modes in wit should take their turn?
Oft, leaving what is natural and fit,
The current folly proves the ready wit;
And authors think their reputation safe,
Which lives as long as fools are pleased to laugh.
  Some valuing those of their own side or mind,
Still make themselves the measure of mankind:
Fondly° we think we honor merit then, *foolishly*
When we but praise ourselves in other men.
Parties in wit attend on those of state,
And public faction doubles private hate.
Pride, Malice, Folly against Dryden rose,
In various shapes of parsons, critics, beaux;

9. People of high rank.
1. Those who have divided the church on points of theology. Pope stressed the first syllable, the pronunciation approved by Johnson in his *Dictionary*.
2. The medieval theologians, such as the followers of Duns Scotus and St. Thomas Aquinas, mentioned below.
3. Allusion to Peter Lombard's *Book of Sentences*, a book esteemed by Scholastic philosophers.
4. Street where publishers' remainders and secondhand books were sold.

But sense survived, when merry jests were past;
For rising merit will buoy up at last.
Might he return and bless once more our eyes,
New Blackmores and new Milbourns[5] must arise.
Nay, should great Homer lift his awful head,
Zoilus[6] again would start up from the dead.
Envy will merit, as its shade, pursue,
But like a shadow, proves the substance true;
For envied wit, like Sol eclipsed, makes known
The opposing body's grossness, not its own.
When first that sun too powerful beams displays,
It draws up vapors which obscure its rays;
But even those clouds at last adorn its way,
Reflect new glories, and augment the day.
  Be thou the first true merit to befriend;
His praise is lost who stays till all commend.
Short is the date, alas! of modern rhymes,
And 'tis but just to let them live betimes.° *for a brief time*
No longer now that golden age appears,
When patriarch wits survived a thousand years:
Now length of fame (our second life) is lost,
And bare threescore is all even that can boast;
Our sons their fathers' failing language see,
And such as Chaucer is, shall Dryden be.[7]
So when the faithful pencil has designed
Some bright idea of the master's mind,
Where a new world leaps out at his command,
And ready Nature waits upon his hand;
When the ripe colors soften and unite,
And sweetly melt into just shade and light;
When mellowing years their full perfection give,
And each bold figure just begins to live,
The treacherous colors the fair art betray,
And all the bright creation fades away!
  Unhappy° wit, like most mistaken things, *ill-fated*
Atones not for that envy which it brings.
In youth alone its empty praise we boast,
But soon the short-lived vanity is lost;
Like some fair flower the early spring supplies,
That gaily blooms, but even in blooming dies.
What is this wit, which must our cares employ?
The owner's wife, that other men enjoy;
Then most our trouble still when most admired,
And still the more we give, the more required;
Whose fame with pains we guard, but lose with ease,
Sure some to vex, but never all to please;
'Tis what the vicious fear, the virtuous shun,

5. Luke Milbourn had attacked Dryden's translation of Virgil. Sir Richard Blackmore, physician and poet, had attacked Dryden for the immorality of his plays.
6. A Greek critic of the 4th century B.C.E. who wrote a book of carping criticism of Homer.
7. The radical changes that took place in the English language between the death of Chaucer in 1400 and the death of Dryden in 1700 suggested that in another three hundred years Dryden would be unintelligible.

By fools 'tis hated, and by knaves undone!
If wit so much from ignorance undergo,
Ah, let not learning too commence its foe!
Of old those met rewards who could excel,
And such were praised who but endeavored well;
Though triumphs were to generals only due,
Crowns were reserved to grace the soldiers too.[8]
Now they who reach Parnassus' lofty crown
Employ their pains to spurn° some others down; *kick*
And while self-love each jealous writer rules,
Contending wits become the sport of fools;
But still the worst with most regret commend,
For each ill author is as bad a friend.
To what base ends, and by what abject ways,
Are mortals urged through sacred° lust of praise![9] *accursed*
Ah, ne'er so dire a thirst of glory boast,
Nor in the critic let the man be lost!
Good nature and good sense must ever join;
To err is human, to forgive divine.
But if in noble minds some dregs remain
Not yet purged off, of spleen° and sour disdain, *rancor*
Discharge that rage on more provoking crimes,
Nor fear a dearth in these flagitious° times. *scandalously wicked*
No pardon vile obscenity should find,
Though wit and art conspire to move your mind;
But dullness with obscenity must prove
As shameful sure as impotence in love.
In the fat age of pleasure, wealth, and ease
Sprung the rank weed, and thrived with large increase:
When love was all an easy monarch's[1] care,
Seldom at council, never in a war;
Jilts[2] ruled the state, and statesmen farces writ;
Nay, wits had pensions, and young lords had wit;
The fair sat panting at a courtier's play,
And not a mask[3] went unimproved away;
The modest fan was lifted up no more,
And virgins smiled at what they blushed before.
The following license of a foreign reign
Did all the dregs of bold Socinus[4] drain;
Then unbelieving priests reformed the nation,
And taught more pleasant methods of salvation;
Where Heaven's free subjects might their rights dispute,
Lest God himself should seem too absolute;
Pulpits their sacred satire learned to spare,
And Vice admired° to find a flatterer there! *wondered*
Encouraged thus, wit's Titans braved the skies,
And the press groaned with licensed blasphemies.

8. To celebrate Roman victories, valiant soldiers were decorated with a variety of crowns.
9. The phrase imitates Virgil's *auri sacra famis,* "accursed hunger for gold" (*Aeneid* 3.57).
1. Charles II. The concluding lines of part 2 discuss the corruption of wit and poetry under this monarch.
2. Mistresses of the king.
3. A woman wearing a mask.
4. The name of two Italian theologians of the 16th century who denied the divinity of Jesus. Pope charges that freethinkers attained the upper hand during the "foreign reign" of William III, a Dutchman.

These monsters, critics! with your darts engage,
Here point your thunder, and exhaust your rage!
Yet shun their fault, who, scandalously nice,° *subtle*
Will needs mistake an author into vice;
All seems infected that the infected spy,
As all looks yellow to the jaundiced eye.

1709 1711

The Rape of the Lock

The Rape of the Lock is based on an actual episode that provoked a quarrel between two prominent Catholic families. Pope's friend John Caryll, to whom the poem is addressed (line 3), suggested that Pope write it, in the hope that a little laughter might serve to soothe ruffled tempers. Lord Petre had cut off a lock of hair from the head of the lovely Arabella Fermor (often spelled "Farmer" and doubtless so pronounced), much to the indignation of the lady and her relatives. In its original version of two cantos and 334 lines, published in 1712, *The Rape of the Lock* was a great success. In 1713 a new version was undertaken against the advice of Addison, who considered the poem perfect as it was first written. Pope greatly expanded the earlier version, adding the delightful "machinery" (i.e., the supernatural agents in epic action) of the Sylphs, Belinda's toilet, the card game, and the visit to the Cave of Spleen in canto 4. In 1717, with the addition of Clarissa's speech on good humor, the poem assumed its final form.

With delicate fancy and playful wit, Pope elaborated the trivial episode that occasioned the poem into the semblance of an epic in miniature, the most nearly perfect heroicomical poem in English. The verse abounds in parodies and echoes of the *Iliad*, the *Aeneid*, and *Paradise Lost*, thus constantly forcing the reader to compare small things with great. The familiar devices of epic are observed, but the incidents or characters are beautifully proportioned to the scale of mock epic. The *Rape* tells of war, but it is the drawing-room war between the sexes; it has its heroes and heroines, but they are beaux and belles; it has its supernatural characters ("machinery"), but they are Sylphs (borrowed, as Pope tells us in his dedicatory letter, from Rosicrucian lore)—creatures of the air, the souls of dead coquettes, with tasks appropriate to their nature—or the Gnome Umbriel, once a prude on earth; it has its epic game, played on the "velvet plain" of the card table, its feasting heroes, who sip coffee and gossip, and its battle, fought with the clichés of compliment and conceits, with frowns and angry glances, with snuff and bodkin; it has the traditional epic journey to the underworld—here the Cave of Spleen, emblematic of the ill nature of female hypochondriacs. And Pope creates a world in which these actions take place, a world that is dense with beautiful objects: brocades, ivory and tortoiseshell, cosmetics and diamonds, lacquered furniture, silver teapot, delicate chinaware. It is a world that is constantly in motion and that sparkles and glitters with light, whether the light of the sun or of Belinda's eyes or that light into which the "fluid" bodies of the Sylphs seem to dissolve as they flutter in shrouds and around the mast of Belinda's ship. Pope laughs at this world, its ritualized triviality, its irrational, upper-class women and feminized men—and remembers that a grimmer, darker world surrounds it (3.19–24 and 5.145–48); but he also makes us aware of its beauty and charm.

The epigraph may be translated, "I was unwilling, Belinda, to ravish your locks; but I rejoice to have conceded this to your prayers" (Martial's *Epigrams* 12.84.1–2). Pope substituted his heroine for Martial's Polytimus. The epigraph is intended to suggest that the poem was published at Miss Fermor's request.

The Rape of the Lock

An Heroi-Comical Poem

Nolueram, Belinda, tuos violare capillos;
sed juvat hoc precibus me tribuisse tuis.
—MARTIAL

TO MRS. ARABELLA FERMOR

MADAM,

It will be in vain to deny that I have some regard for this piece, since I dedicate it to you. Yet you may bear me witness, it was intended only to divert a few young ladies, who have good sense and good humor enough to laugh not only at their sex's little unguarded follies, but at their own. But as it was communicated with the air of a secret, it soon found its way into the world. An imperfect copy having been offered to a bookseller, you had the good nature for my sake to consent to the publication of one more correct; this I was forced to, before I had executed half my design, for the machinery was entirely wanting to complete it.

The machinery, Madam, is a term invented by the critics, to signify that part which the deities, angels, or demons are made to act in a poem; for the ancient poets are in one respect like many modern ladies: let an action be never so trivial in itself, they always make it appear of the utmost importance. These machines I determined to raise on a very new and odd foundation, the Rosicrucian[1] doctrine of spirits.

I know how disagreeable it is to make use of hard words before a lady; but 'tis so much the concern of a poet to have his works understood, and particularly by your sex, that you must give me leave to explain two or three difficult terms.

The Rosicrucians are a people I must bring you acquainted with. The best account I know of them is in a French book called *Le Comte de Gabalis,*[2] which both in its title and size is so like a novel, that many of the fair sex have read it for one by mistake. According to these gentlemen, the four elements are inhabited by spirits, which they call Sylphs, Gnomes, Nymphs, and Salamanders. The Gnomes or Demons of earth delight in mischief; but the Sylphs, whose habitation is in the air, are the best-conditioned creatures imaginable. For they say, any mortals may enjoy the most intimate familiarities with these gentle spirits, upon a condition very easy to all true adepts, an inviolate preservation of chastity.

As to the following cantos, all the passages of them are as fabulous as the vision at the beginning, or the transformation at the end (except the loss of your hair, which I always mention with reverence). The human persons are as fictitious as the airy ones; and the character of Belinda, as it is now managed, resembles you in nothing but in beauty.

If this poem had as many graces as there are in your person, or in your mind, yet I could never hope it should pass through the world half so uncensured as

1. A system of arcane philosophy introduced into England from Germany in the 17th century.

2. By the Abbé de Montfaucon de Villars, published in 1670.

you have done. But let its fortune be what it will, mine is happy enough, to have given me this occasion of assuring you that I am, with the truest esteem,

MADAM,
Your most obedient, humble servant,
A. POPE

Canto 1

What dire offense from amorous causes springs,
What mighty contests rise from trivial things,
I sing—This verse to Caryll, Muse! is due:
This, even Belinda may vouchsafe to view:
Slight is the subject, but not so the praise,
If she inspire, and he approve my lays.
Say what strange motive, Goddess! could compel
A well-bred lord to assault a gentle belle?
Oh, say what stranger cause, yet unexplored,
Could make a gentle belle reject a lord?
In tasks so bold can little men engage,
And in soft bosoms dwells such mighty rage?
Sol through white curtains shot a timorous ray,
And oped those eyes that must eclipse the day.
Now lapdogs give themselves the rousing shake,
And sleepless lovers, just at twelve, awake:
Thrice rung the bell, the slipper knocked the ground,
And the pressed watch[3] returned a silver sound.
Belinda still her downy pillow pressed,
Her guardian Sylph prolonged the balmy rest.
'Twas he had summoned to her silent bed
The morning dream that hovered o'er her head.
A youth more glittering than a birthnight beau[4]
(That even in slumber caused her cheek to glow)
Seemed to her ear his winning lips to lay,
And thus in whispers said, or seemed to say:
"Fairest of mortals, thou distinguished care
Of thousand bright inhabitants of air!
If e'er one vision touched thy infant thought,
Of all the nurse and all the priest have taught,
Of airy elves by moonlight shadows seen,
The silver token, and the circled green,[5]
Or virgins visited by angel powers,
With golden crowns and wreaths of heavenly flowers,
Hear and believe! thy own importance know,
Nor bound thy narrow views to things below.
Some secret truths, from learned pride concealed,
To maids alone and children are revealed:
What though no credit doubting wits may give?

3. A watch that chimes the hour and the quarter hour when the stem is pressed down. "Knocked the ground": summons to a maid.
4. Courtiers wore especially fine clothes on the sovereign's birthday.
5. Rings of bright green grass, which are common in England even in winter, were held to be caused by the round dances of fairies. According to popular belief, fairies skim off the cream from jugs of milk left standing overnight and leave a coin ("silver token") in payment.

The fair and innocent shall still believe.
Know, then, unnumbered spirits round thee fly,
The light militia of the lower sky:
These, though unseen, are ever on the wing,
Hang o'er the box, and hover round the Ring.[6]
Think what an equipage thou hast in air,
And view with scorn two pages and a chair.° *sedan chair*
As now your own, our beings were of old,
And once enclosed in woman's beauteous mold;
Thence, by a soft transition, we repair
From earthly vehicles to these of air.
Think not, when woman's transient breath is fled,
That all her vanities at once are dead:
Succeeding vanities she still regards,
And though she plays no more, o'erlooks the cards.
Her joy in gilded chariots, when alive,
And love of ombre,[7] after death survive.
For when the Fair in all their pride expire,
To their first elements[8] their souls retire:
The sprites of fiery termagants in flame
Mount up, and take a Salamander's[9] name.
Soft yielding minds to water glide away,
And sip, with Nymphs, their elemental tea.[1]
The graver prude sinks downward to a Gnome,
In search of mischief still on earth to roam.
The light coquettes in Sylphs aloft repair,
And sport and flutter in the fields of air.
"Know further yet; whoever fair and chaste
Rejects mankind, is by some Sylph embraced:
For spirits, freed from mortal laws, with ease
Assume what sexes and what shapes they please.[2]
What guards the purity of melting maids,
In courtly balls, and midnight masquerades,
Safe from the treacherous friend, the daring spark,
The glance by day, the whisper in the dark,
When kind occasion prompts their warm desires,
When music softens, and when dancing fires?
'Tis but their Sylph, the wise Celestials° know, *heavenly beings*
Though Honor is the word with men below.
"Some nymphs[3] there are, too conscious of their face,
For life predestined to the Gnomes' embrace.
These swell their prospects and exalt their pride,
When offers are disdained, and love denied:
Then gay ideas° crowd the vacant brain, *showy images*

6. The "box" in the theater and the fashionable circular drive ("Ring") in Hyde Park.
7. The popular card game (see n. 1, p. 1114).
8. The four elements out of which all things were believed to have been made were fire, water, earth, and air. One or another of these elements was supposed to be predominant in both the physical and the psychological makeup of each human being. In this context they are spoken of as "humors."
9. A lizardlike animal, in antiquity believed to live in fire. Each element was inhabited by a spirit, as the following lines explain. "Termagants": shrewish or overbearing women.
1. Pronounced *tay*.
2. Cf. *Paradise Lost* 1.427–31; this is one of many allusions to that poem in the *Rape*.
3. Here and after, a fanciful name for a young woman, to be distinguished from the "Nymphs" (water spirits) in line 62.

While peers, and dukes, and all their sweeping train,
And garters, stars, and coronets[4] appear,
And in soft sounds, 'your Grace'° salutes their ear. *a duchess*
'Tis these that early taint the female soul,
Instruct the eyes of young coquettes to roll,
Teach infant cheeks a bidden blush to know,
And little hearts to flutter at a beau.
"Oft, when the world imagine women stray,
The Sylphs through mystic mazes guide their way,
Through all the giddy circle they pursue,
And old impertinence° expel by new. *trifle*
What tender maid but must a victim fall
To one man's treat, but for another's ball?
When Florio speaks, what virgin could withstand,
If gentle Damon did not squeeze her hand?
With varying vanities, from every part,
They shift the moving toyshop[5] of their heart;
Where wigs with wigs, with sword-knots sword-knots strive,
Beaux banish beaux, and coaches coaches drive.
This erring mortals levity may call;
Oh, blind to truth! the Sylphs contrive it all.
"Of these am I, who thy protection claim,
A watchful sprite, and Ariel is my name.
Late, as I ranged the crystal wilds of air,
In the clear mirror of thy ruling star
I saw, alas! some dread event impend,
Ere to the main this morning sun descend,
But Heaven reveals not what, or how, or where:
Warned by the Sylph, O pious maid, beware!
This to disclose is all thy guardian can:
Beware of all, but most beware of Man!"
He said; when Shock,[6] who thought she slept too long,
Leaped up, and waked his mistress with his tongue.
'Twas then, Belinda, if report say true,
Thy eyes first opened on a billet-doux;
Wounds, charms, and ardors were no sooner read,
But all the vision vanished from thy head.
And now, unveiled, the toilet stands displayed,
Each silver vase in mystic order laid.
First, robed in white, the nymph intent adores,
With head uncovered, the cosmetic powers.
A heavenly image in the glass appears;
To that she bends, to that her eyes she rears.
The inferior priestess, at her altar's side,
Trembling begins the sacred rites of Pride.
Unnumbered treasures ope at once, and here
The various offerings of the world appear;
From each she nicely culls with curious toil,
And decks the goddess with the glittering spoil.
This casket India's glowing gems unlocks,

4. Emblems of nobility.
5. A shop stocked with baubles and trifles.
6. A long-haired poodle, Belinda's lapdog.

And all Arabia breathes from yonder box.
The tortoise here and elephant unite,
Transformed to combs, the speckled and the white.
Here files of pins extend their shining rows,
Puffs, powders, patches, Bibles,[7] billet-doux.
Now awful° Beauty puts on all its arms; *awe-inspiring*
The fair each moment rises in her charms,
Repairs her smiles, awakens every grace,
And calls forth all the wonders of her face;
Sees by degrees a purer blush arise,
And keener lightnings quicken in her eyes.
The busy Sylphs surround their darling care,
These set the head, and those divide the hair,
Some fold the sleeve, whilst others plait the gown;
And Betty's[8] praised for labors not her own.

Canto 2

Not with more glories, in the ethereal plain,
The sun first rises o'er the purpled main,
Than, issuing forth, the rival of his beams
Launched on the bosom of the silver Thames.
Fair nymphs and well-dressed youths around her shone,
But every eye was fixed on her alone.
On her white breast a sparkling cross she wore,
Which Jews might kiss, and infidels adore.
Her lively looks a sprightly mind disclose,
Quick as her eyes, and as unfixed as those:
Favors to none, to all she smiles extends;
Oft she rejects, but never once offends.
Bright as the sun, her eyes the gazers strike,
And, like the sun, they shine on all alike.
Yet graceful ease, and sweetness void of pride,
Might hide her faults, if belles had faults to hide:
If to her share some female errors fall,
Look on her face, and you'll forget 'em all.
This nymph, to the destruction of mankind,
Nourished two locks which graceful hung behind
In equal curls, and well conspired to deck
With shining ringlets her smooth ivory neck.
Love in these labyrinths his slaves detains,
And mighty hearts are held in slender chains.
With hairy springes[9] we the birds betray,
Slight lines of hair surprise the finny prey,
Fair tresses man's imperial race ensnare,
And beauty draws us with a single hair.
The adventurous Baron the bright locks admired,
He saw, he wished, and to the prize aspired.
Resolved to win, he meditates the way,

7. It has been suggested that Pope intended here not "Bibles," but "bibelots" (trinkets), but this interpretation has not gained wide acceptance.

8. Belinda's maid, the "inferior priestess" mentioned in line 127.

9. Snares (pronounced *sprin-jez*).

By force to ravish, or by fraud betray;
For when success a lover's toil attends,
Few ask if fraud or force attained his ends.
For this, ere Phoebus° rose, he had implored — *the sun*
Propitious Heaven, and every power adored,
But chiefly Love—to Love an altar built,
Of twelve vast French romances, neatly gilt.
There lay three garters, half a pair of gloves,
And all the trophies of his former loves.
With tender billet-doux he lights the pyre,
And breathes three amorous sighs to raise the fire.
Then prostrate falls, and begs with ardent eyes
Soon to obtain, and long possess the prize:
The powers gave ear, and granted half his prayer,
The rest the winds dispersed in empty air.
But now secure the painted vessel glides,
The sunbeams trembling on the floating tides,
While melting music steals upon the sky,
And softened sounds along the waters die.
Smooth flow the waves, the zephyrs gently play,
Belinda smiled, and all the world was gay.
All but the Sylph—with careful thoughts oppressed,
The impending woe sat heavy on his breast.
He summons straight his denizens of air;
The lucid squadrons round the sails repair:
Soft o'er the shrouds aërial whispers breathe
That seemed but zephyrs to the train beneath.
Some to the sun their insect-wings unfold,
Waft on the breeze, or sink in clouds of gold.
Transparent forms too fine for mortal sight,
Their fluid bodies half dissolved in light,
Loose to the wind their airy garments flew,
Thin glittering textures of the filmy dew,
Dipped in the richest tincture of the skies,
Where light disports in ever-mingling dyes,
While every beam new transient colors flings,
Colors that change whene'er they wave their wings.
Amid the circle, on the gilded mast,
Superior by the head was Ariel placed;
His purple[1] pinions opening to the sun,
He raised his azure wand, and thus begun:
"Ye Sylphs and Sylphids, to your chief give ear!
Fays, Fairies, Genïi, Elves, and Daemons, hear!
Ye know the spheres and various tasks assigned
By laws eternal to the aërial kind.
Some in the fields of purest ether play,
And bask and whiten in the blaze of day.
Some guide the course of wandering orbs on high,
Or roll the planets through the boundless sky.
Some less refined, beneath the moon's pale light

1. In 18th-century poetic diction the word might mean bloodred, purple, or simply (as is likely here) brightly colored. The word derives from Virgil's *Eclogue* 9.40, *purpureum*. An example of the Latinate nature of some poetic diction of the period.

Pursue the stars that shoot athwart the night,
Or suck the mists in grosser air below,
Or dip their pinions in the painted bow,° *rainbow*
Or brew fierce tempests on the wintry main,
Or o'er the glebe° distill the kindly rain. *cultivated field*
Others on earth o'er human race preside,
Watch all their ways, and all their actions guide:
Of these the chief the care of nations own,
And guard with arms divine the British Throne.
"Our humbler province is to tend the Fair,
Not a less pleasing, though less glorious care:
To save the powder from too rude a gale,
Nor let the imprisoned essences° exhale; *perfumes*
To draw fresh colors from the vernal flowers;
To steal from rainbows e'er they drop in showers
A brighter wash;° to curl their waving hairs, *cosmetic lotion*
Assist their blushes, and inspire their airs,
Nay oft, in dreams invention we bestow,
To change a flounce, or add a furbelow.
"This day black omens threat the brightest fair,
That e'er deserved a watchful spirit's care;
Some dire disaster, or by force or slight,
But what, or where, the Fates have wrapped in night:
Whether the nymph shall break Diana's[2] law,
Or some frail china jar receive a flaw,
Or stain her honor, or her new brocade,
Forget her prayers, or miss a masquerade,
Or lose her heart, or necklace, at a ball;
Or whether Heaven has doomed that Shock must fall.
Haste, then, ye spirits! to your charge repair:
The fluttering fan be Zephyretta's care;
The drops[3] to thee, Brillante, we consign;
And, Momentilla, let the watch be thine;
Do thou, Crispissa,[4] tend her favorite Lock;
Ariel himself shall be the guard of Shock.
"To fifty chosen Sylphs, of special note,
We trust the important charge, the petticoat;
Oft have we known that sevenfold fence to fail,
Though stiff with hoops, and armed with ribs of whale.[5]
Form a strong line about the silver bound,
And guard the wide circumference around.
"Whatever spirit, careless of his charge,
His post neglects, or leaves the fair at large,
Shall feel sharp vengeance soon o'ertake his sins,
Be stopped in vials, or transfixed with pins,
Or plunged in lakes of bitter washes lie,
Or wedged whole ages in a bodkin's[6] eye;
Gums and pomatums shall his flight restrain,
While clogged he beats his silken wings in vain,

2. Diana was the goddess of chastity.
3. Diamond earrings. Observe the appropriateness of the names of the Sylphs to their assigned functions.
4. From Latin *crispere*, "to curl."
5. Corsets and the hoops of hoopskirts were made of whalebone.
6. A blunt needle with a large eye used for drawing ribbon through eyelets in the edging of women's garments.

Or alum styptics with contracting power
Shrink his thin essence like a riveled[7] flower:
Or, as Ixion[8] fixed, the wretch shall feel
The giddy motion of the whirling mill,
In fumes of burning chocolate shall glow,
And tremble at the sea that froths below!"
He spoke; the spirits from the sails descend;
Some, orb in orb, around the nymph extend;
Some thread the mazy ringlets of her hair;
Some hang upon the pendants of her ear:
With beating hearts the dire event they wait,
Anxious, and trembling for the birth of Fate.

Canto 3

Close by those meads, forever crowned with flowers,
Where Thames with pride surveys his rising towers,
There stands a structure of majestic frame,
Which from the neighboring Hampton[9] takes its name.
Here Britain's statesmen oft the fall foredoom
Of foreign tyrants and of nymphs at home;
Here thou, great Anna! whom three realms obey,
Dost sometimes counsel take—and sometimes tea.
Hither the heroes and the nymphs resort,
To taste awhile the pleasures of a court;
In various talk the instructive hours they passed,
Who gave the ball, or paid the visit last;
One speaks the glory of the British Queen,
And one describes a charming Indian screen;
A third interprets motions, looks, and eyes;
At every word a reputation dies.
Snuff, or the fan, supply each pause of chat,
With singing, laughing, ogling, and all that.
Meanwhile, declining from the noon of day,
The sun obliquely shoots his burning ray;
The hungry judges soon the sentence sign,
And wretches hang that jurymen may dine;
The merchant from the Exchange returns in peace,
And the long labors of the toilet cease.
Belinda now, whom thirst of fame invites,
Burns to encounter two adventurous knights,
At ombre[1] singly to decide their doom,
And swells her breast with conquests yet to come.

7. To "rivel" is to "contract into wrinkles and corrugations" (Johnson's *Dictionary*).
8. In the Greek myth, he was punished in the underworld by being bound on an everturning wheel.
9. Hampton Court, the royal palace, about fifteen miles up the Thames from London.
1. The game of ombre that Belinda plays against the baron and another young man is too complicated for complete explication here. Pope has carefully arranged the cards so that Belinda wins. The baron's hand is strong enough to be a threat, but the third player's is of little account. The hand is played exactly according to the rules of ombre, and Pope's description of the cards is equally accurate. Each player holds nine cards (line 30). The "Matadores" (line 33), when spades are trump, are "Spadillio" (line 49), the ace of spades; "Manillio" (line 51), the two of spades; and "Basto" (line 53), the ace of clubs. Belinda holds all three of these. (For a more complete description of ombre, see *The Rape of the Lock and Other Poems,* ed. Geoffrey Tillotson, in the Twickenham Edition of Pope's poems, vol. 2, Appendix C.)

Straight the three bands prepare in arms to join,
Each band the number of the sacred nine.
Soon as she spreads her hand, the aërial guard
Descend, and sit on each important card:
First Ariel perched upon a Matadore,
Then each according to the rank they bore;
For Sylphs, yet mindful of their ancient race,
Are, as when women, wondrous fond of place.
Behold, four Kings in majesty revered,
With hoary whiskers and a forky beard;
And four fair Queens whose hands sustain a flower,
The expressive emblem of their softer power;
Four Knaves in garbs succinct,° a trusty band, *girded up*
Caps on their heads, and halberts in their hand;
And parti-colored troops, a shining train,
Draw forth to combat on the velvet plain.
The skillful nymph reviews her force with care;
"Let Spades be trumps!" she said, and trumps they were.
Now move to war her sable Matadores,
In show like leaders of the swarthy Moors.
Spadillio first, unconquerable lord!
Led off two captive trumps, and swept the board.
As many more Manillio forced to yield,
And marched a victor from the verdant field.
Him Basto followed, but his fate more hard
Gained but one trump and one plebeian card.
With his broad saber next, a chief in years,
The hoary Majesty of Spades appears,
Puts forth one manly leg, to sight revealed,
The rest his many-colored robe concealed.
The rebel Knave, who dares his prince engage,
Proves the just victim of his royal rage.
Even mighty Pam,[2] that kings and queens o'erthrew
And mowed down armies in the fights of loo,
Sad chance of war! now destitute of aid,
Falls undistinguished by the victor Spade.
Thus far both armies to Belinda yield;
Now to the Baron fate inclines the field.
His warlike amazon her host invades,
The imperial consort of the crown of Spades.
The Club's black tyrant first her victim died,
Spite of his haughty mien and barbarous pride.
What boots° the regal circle on his head, *avails*
His giant limbs, in state unwieldy spread?
That long behind he trails his pompous robe,
And of all monarchs only grasps the globe?[3]
The Baron now his Diamonds pours apace;
The embroidered King who shows but half his face,
And his refulgent Queen, with powers combined,
Of broken troops an easy conquest find.

2. The knave of clubs, the highest trump in the game of loo.

3. In the English deck, only the king of clubs holds an imperial orb.

Clubs, Diamonds, Hearts, in wild disorder seen,
With throngs promiscuous strew the level green.
Thus when dispersed a routed army runs,
Of Asia's troops, and Afric's sable sons,
With like confusion different nations fly,
Of various habit, and of various dye,
The pierced battalions disunited fall
In heaps on heaps; one fate o'erwhelms them all.
  The Knave of Diamonds tries his wily arts,
And wins (oh, shameful chance!) the Queen of Hearts.
At this, the blood the virgin's cheek forsook,
A livid paleness spreads o'er all her look;
She sees, and trembles at the approaching ill,
Just in the jaws of ruin, and Codille.[4]
And now (as oft in some distempered state)
On one nice trick depends the general fate.
An Ace of Hearts steps forth: the King unseen
Lurked in her hand, and mourned his captive Queen.
He springs to vengeance with an eager pace,
And falls like thunder on the prostrate Ace.
The nymph exulting fills with shouts the sky,
The walls, the woods, and long canals reply.
  O thoughtless mortals! ever blind to fate,
Too soon dejected, and too soon elate:
Sudden these honors shall be snatched away,
And cursed forever this victorious day.
  For lo! the board with cups and spoons is crowned,
The berries crackle, and the mill turns round;[5]
On shining altars of Japan[6] they raise
The silver lamp; the fiery spirits blaze:
From silver spouts the grateful liquors glide,
While China's earth receives the smoking tide.
At once they gratify their scent and taste,
And frequent cups prolong the rich repast.
Straight hover round the fair her airy band;
Some, as she sipped, the fuming liquor fanned,
Some o'er her lap their careful plumes displayed,
Trembling, and conscious of the rich brocade.
Coffee (which makes the politician wise,
And see through all things with his half-shut eyes)
Sent up in vapors to the Baron's brain
New stratagems, the radiant Lock to gain.
Ah, cease, rash youth! desist ere 'tis too late,
Fear the just Gods, and think of Scylla's[7] fate!
Changed to a bird, and sent to flit in air,
She dearly pays for Nisus' injured hair!
  But when to mischief mortals bend their will,

4. The term applied to losing a hand at cards.
5. I.e., coffee is roasted and ground.
6. I.e., small, lacquered tables. "Altars" suggests the ritualistic character of coffee drinking in Belinda's world.
7. Scylla, daughter of Nisus, was turned into a sea bird because, for the sake of her love for Minos of Crete, who was besieging her father's city of Megara, she cut from her father's head the purple lock on which his safety depended. She is not the Scylla of "Scylla and Charybdis."

How soon they find fit instruments of ill!
Just then, Clarissa drew with tempting grace
A two-edged weapon from her shining case:
So ladies in romance assist their knight,
Present the spear, and arm him for the fight.
He takes the gift with reverence, and extends
The little engine on his fingers' ends;
This just behind Belinda's neck he spread,
As o'er the fragrant steams she bends her head.
Swift to the Lock a thousand sprites repair,
A thousand wings, by turns, blow back the hair,
And thrice they twitched the diamond in her ear,
Thrice she looked back, and thrice the foe drew near.
Just in that instant, anxious Ariel sought
The close recesses of the virgin's thought;
As on the nosegay in her breast reclined,
He watched the ideas rising in her mind,
Sudden he viewed, in spite of all her art,
An earthly lover lurking at her heart.
Amazed, confused, he found his power expired,
Resigned to fate, and with a sigh retired.
The Peer now spreads the glittering forfex° wide, *scissors*
To enclose the Lock; now joins it, to divide.
Even then, before the fatal engine closed,
A wretched Sylph too fondly interposed;
Fate urged the shears, and cut the Sylph in twain
(But airy substance soon unites again):
The meeting points the sacred hair dissever
From the fair head, forever and forever!
Then flashed the living lightning from her eyes,
And screams of horror rend the affrighted skies.
Not louder shrieks to pitying heaven are cast,
When husbands, or when lapdogs breathe their last;
Or when rich china vessels fallen from high,
In glittering dust and painted fragments lie!
"Let wreaths of triumph now my temples twine,"
The victor cried, "the glorious prize is mine!
While fish in streams, or birds delight in air,
Or in a coach and six the British fair,
As long as *Atalantis*[8] shall be read,
Or the small pillow grace a lady's bed,
While visits shall be paid on solemn days,
When numerous wax-lights in bright order blaze,
While nymphs take treats,° or assignations give, *free refreshments*
So long my honor, name, and praise shall live!
"What time would spare, from steel receives its date,
And monuments, like men, submit to fate!
Steel could the labor of the Gods destroy,
And strike to dust the imperial towers of Troy;
Steel could the works of mortal pride confound,

8. Delarivier Manley's *New Atalantis* (1709) was notorious for its thinly concealed allusions to contemporary scandals.

And hew triumphal arches to the ground.
What wonder then, fair nymph! thy hairs should feel,
The conquering force of unresisted steel?"

Canto 4

But anxious cares the pensive nymph oppressed,
And secret passions labored in her breast.
Not youthful kings in battle seized alive,
Not scornful virgins who their charms survive,
Not ardent lovers robbed of all their bliss,
Not ancient ladies when refused a kiss,
Not tyrants fierce that unrepenting die,
Not Cynthia when her manteau's° pinned awry, *wrap*
E'er felt such rage, resentment, and despair,
As thou, sad virgin! for thy ravished hair.
For, that sad moment, when the Sylphs withdrew
And Ariel weeping from Belinda flew,
Umbriel,[9] a dusky, melancholy sprite
As ever sullied the fair face of light,
Down to the central earth, his proper scene,
Repaired to search the gloomy Cave of Spleen.° *Ill Humor*
Swift on his sooty pinions flits the Gnome,
And in a vapor reached the dismal dome.
No cheerful breeze this sullen region knows,
The dreaded east is all the wind that blows.
Here in a grotto, sheltered close from air,
And screened in shades from day's detested glare,
She sighs forever on her pensive bed,
Pain at her side, and Megrim° at her head. *headache*
Two handmaids wait the throne: alike in place
But differing far in figure and in face.
Here stood Ill-Nature like an ancient maid,
Her wrinkled form in black and white arrayed;
With store of prayers for mornings, nights, and noons,
Her hand is filled; her bosom with lampoons.
There Affectation, with a sickly mien,
Shows in her cheek the roses of eighteen,
Practiced to lisp, and hang the head aside,
Faints into airs, and languishes with pride,
On the rich quilt sinks with becoming woe,
Wrapped in a gown, for sickness and for show.
The fair ones° feel such maladies as these, *women*
When each new nightdress gives a new disease.
A constant vapor[1] o'er the palace flies,
Strange phantoms rising as the mists arise;
Dreadful as hermit's dreams in haunted shades,
Or bright as visions of expiring maids.
Now glaring fiends, and snakes on rolling spires,° *coils*

9. The name suggests shade and darkness.
1. Emblematic of "the vapors," a fashionable hypochondria, melancholy, or peevishness.

Pale specters, gaping tombs, and purple fires;
Now lakes of liquid gold, Elysian scenes,
And crystal domes, and angels in machines.[2]
   Unnumbered throngs on every side are seen
Of bodies changed to various forms by Spleen.
Here living teapots stand, one arm held out,
One bent; the handle this, and that the spout:
A pipkin° there, like Homer's tripod,[3] walks; *earthen pot*
Here sighs a jar, and there a goose pie talks;
Men prove with child, as powerful fancy works,
And maids, turned bottles, call aloud for corks.
   Safe passed the Gnome through this fantastic band,
A branch of healing spleenwort[4] in his hand.
Then thus addressed the Power: "Hail, wayward Queen!
Who rule the sex to fifty from fifteen:
Parent of vapors and of female wit,
Who give the hysteric or poetic fit,
On various tempers act by various ways,
Make some take physic,° others scribble plays; *medicine*
Who cause the proud their visits to delay,
And send the godly in a pet to pray.
A nymph there is that all your power disdains,
And thousands more in equal mirth maintains.
But oh! if e'er thy Gnome could spoil a grace,
Or raise a pimple on a beauteous face,
Like citron-waters[5] matrons' cheeks inflame,
Or change complexions at a losing game;
If e'er with airy horns[6] I planted heads,
Or rumpled petticoats, or tumbled beds,
Or caused suspicion when no soul was rude,
Or discomposed the headdress of a prude,
Or e'er to costive lapdog gave disease,
Which not the tears of brightest eyes could ease,
Hear me, and touch Belinda with chagrin:° *ill humor*
That single act gives half the world the spleen."
   The Goddess with a discontented air
Seems to reject him though she grants his prayer.
A wondrous bag with both her hands she binds,
Like that where once Ulysses held the winds;[7]
There she collects the force of female lungs,
Sighs, sobs, and passions, and the war of tongues.
A vial next she fills with fainting fears,
Soft sorrows, melting griefs, and flowing tears.

2. Mechanical devices used in the theaters for spectacular effects. The catalog of hallucinations draws on the sensational stage effects popular with contemporary audiences.
3. In the *Iliad* (18.373–77), Vulcan furnishes the gods with self-propelling "tripods" (three-legged stools).
4. An herb, efficacious against diseases of the spleen. Pope alludes to the golden bough that Aeneas and the Cumaean sibyl carry with them for protection into the underworld in *Aeneid* 6.
5. Brandy flavored with orange or lemon peel.
6. The symbol of the cuckold, the man whose wife has been unfaithful to him; here "airy," because they exist only in the jealous suspicions of the husband, the victim of the mischievous Umbriel.
7. Aeolus (later conceived of as god of the winds) gave Ulysses a bag containing all the winds adverse to his voyage home. When his ship was in sight of Ithaca, his companions opened the bag and the storms that ensued drove Ulysses far away (*Odyssey* 10.19ff.).

The Gnome rejoicing bears her gifts away,
Spreads his black wings, and slowly mounts to day.
  Sunk in Thalestris'[8] arms the nymph he found,
Her eyes dejected and her hair unbound.
Full o'er their heads the swelling bag he rent,
And all the Furies issued at the vent.
Belinda burns with more than mortal ire,
And fierce Thalestris fans the rising fire.
"O wretched maid!" she spread her hands, and cried
(While Hampton's echoes, "Wretched maid!" replied),
"Was it for this you took such constant care
The bodkin, comb, and essence to prepare?
For this your locks in paper durance bound,
For this with torturing irons wreathed around?
For this with fillets strained your tender head,
And bravely bore the double loads of lead?[9]
Gods! shall the ravisher display your hair,
While the fops envy, and the ladies stare!
Honor forbid! at whose unrivaled shrine
Ease, pleasure, virtue, all, our sex resign.
Methinks already I your tears survey,
Already hear the horrid things they say,
Already see you a degraded toast,
And all your honor in a whisper lost!
How shall I, then, your helpless fame defend?
'Twill then be infamy to seem your friend!
And shall this prize, the inestimable prize,
Exposed through crystal to the gazing eyes,
And heightened by the diamond's circling rays,
On that rapacious hand forever blaze?
Sooner shall grass in Hyde Park Circus grow,
And wits take lodgings in the sound of Bow;[1]
Sooner let earth, air, sea, to chaos fall,
Men, monkeys, lapdogs, parrots, perish all!"
  She said; then raging to Sir Plume repairs,
And bids her beau demand the precious hairs
(Sir Plume of amber snuffbox justly vain,
And the nice conduct of a clouded° cane). *marbled, veined*
With earnest eyes, and round unthinking face,
He first the snuffbox opened, then the case,
And thus broke out—"My Lord, why, what the devil!
Z—ds! damn the lock! 'fore Gad, you must be civil!
Plague on 't! 'tis past a jest—nay prithee, pox!
Give her the hair"—he spoke, and rapped his box.
  "It grieves me much," replied the Peer again,
"Who speaks so well should ever speak in vain.
But by this Lock, this sacred Lock I swear
(Which never more shall join its parted hair;

8. The name is borrowed from a queen of the Amazons, hence a fierce and warlike woman.
9. The frame on which the elaborate coiffures of the day were arranged.
1. A person born within sound of the bells of St. Mary-le-Bow in Cheapside is said to be a cockney. No fashionable wit would have so vulgar an address.

Which never more its honors shall renew,
Clipped from the lovely head where late it grew),
That while my nostrils draw the vital air,
This hand, which won it, shall forever wear."
He spoke, and speaking, in proud triumph spread
The long-contended honors[2] of her head.
   But Umbriel, hateful Gnome, forbears not so;
He breaks the vial whence the sorrows flow.
Then see! the nymph in beauteous grief appears,
Her eyes half languishing, half drowned in tears;
On her heaved bosom hung her drooping head,
Which with a sigh she raised, and thus she said:
   "Forever cursed be this detested day,
Which snatched my best, my favorite curl away!
Happy! ah, ten times happy had I been,
If Hampton Court these eyes had never seen!
Yet am not I the first mistaken maid,
By love of courts to numerous ills betrayed.
Oh, had I rather unadmired remained
In some lone isle, or distant northern land;
Where the gilt chariot never marks the way,
Where none learn ombre, none e'er taste bohea![3]
There kept my charms concealed from mortal eye,
Like roses that in deserts bloom and die.
What moved my mind with youthful lords to roam?
Oh, had I stayed, and said my prayers at home!
'Twas this the morning omens seemed to tell;
Thrice from my trembling hand the patch box[4] fell;
The tottering china shook without a wind,
Nay, Poll sat mute, and Shock was most unkind!
A Sylph too warned me of the threats of fate,
In mystic visions, now believed too late!
See the poor remnants of these slighted hairs!
My hands shall rend what e'en thy rapine spares.
These in two sable ringlets taught to break,
Once gave new beauties to the snowy neck.
The sister lock now sits uncouth, alone,
And in its fellow's fate foresees its own;
Uncurled it hangs, the fatal shears demands,
And tempts once more thy sacrilegious hands.
Oh, hadst thou, cruel! been content to seize
Hairs less in sight, or any hairs but these!"

Canto 5

   She said: the pitying audience melt in tears.
But Fate and Jove had stopped the Baron's ears.
In vain Thalestris with reproach assails,
For who can move when fair Belinda fails?

2. Ornaments, hence locks; a Latinism.
3. A costly sort of tea.
4. To hold the ornamental patches of court plaster worn on the face by both sexes.

Not half so fixed the Trojan[5] could remain,
While Anna begged and Dido raged in vain.
Then grave Clarissa graceful waved her fan;
Silence ensued, and thus the nymph began:
"Say, why are beauties praised and honored most,
The wise man's passion, and the vain man's toast?
Why decked with all that land and sea afford,
Why angels called, and angel-like adored?
Why round our coaches crowd the white-gloved beaux,
Why bows the side box from its inmost rows?
How vain are all these glories, all our pains,
Unless good sense preserve what beauty gains;
That men may say when we the front box grace,
'Behold the first in virtue as in face!'
Oh! if to dance all night, and dress all day,
Charmed the smallpox, or chased old age away,
Who would not scorn what housewife's cares produce,
Or who would learn one earthly thing of use?
To patch, nay ogle, might become a saint,
Nor could it sure be such a sin to paint.
But since, alas! frail beauty must decay,
Curled or uncurled, since locks will turn to gray;
Since painted, or not painted, all shall fade,
And she who scorns a man must die a maid;
What then remains but well our power to use,
And keep good humor still whate'er we lose?
And trust me, dear, good humor can prevail
When airs, and flights, and screams, and scolding fail.
Beauties in vain their pretty eyes may roll;
Charms strike the sight, but merit wins the soul."[6]
So spoke the dame, but no applause ensued;
Belinda frowned, Thalestris called her prude.
"To arms, to arms!" the fierce virago cries,
And swift as lightning to the combat flies.
All side in parties, and begin the attack;
Fans clap, silks rustle, and tough whalebones crack;
Heroes' and heroines' shouts confusedly rise,
And bass and treble voices strike the skies.
No common weapons in their hands are found,
Like Gods they fight, nor dread a mortal wound.
So when bold Homer makes the Gods engage,
And heavenly breasts with human passions rage;
'Gainst Pallas, Mars; Latona, Hermes arms;
And all Olympus rings with loud alarms:
Jove's thunder roars, heaven trembles all around,
Blue Neptune storms, the bellowing deeps resound:
Earth shakes her nodding towers, the ground gives way,

5. Aeneas, who forsook Dido at the bidding of the gods, despite her reproaches and the supplications of her sister Anna. Virgil compares him to a steadfast oak that withstands a storm (*Aeneid* 4.437–43).

6. The speech is a close parody of Pope's own translation of the speech of Sarpedon to Glaucus, first published in 1709 and slightly revised in his version of the *Iliad* (12.371–96).

And the pale ghosts start at the flash of day!
  Triumphant Umbriel on a sconce's[7] height
Clapped his glad wings, and sat to view the fight:
Propped on the bodkin spears, the sprites survey
The growing combat, or assist the fray.
  While through the press enraged Thalestris flies,
And scatters death around from both her eyes,
A beau and witling perished in the throng,
One died in metaphor, and one in song.
"O cruel nymph! a living death I bear,"
Cried Dapperwit, and sunk beside his chair.
A mournful glance Sir Fopling upwards cast,
"Those eyes are made so killing"—was his last.
Thus on Maeander's flowery margin lies
The expiring swan,[8] and as he sings he dies.
  When bold Sir Plume had drawn Clarissa down,
Chloe stepped in, and killed him with a frown;
She smiled to see the doughty hero slain,
But, at her smile, the beau revived again.
  Now Jove suspends his golden scales in air,
Weighs the men's wits against the lady's hair;
The doubtful beam long nods from side to side;
At length the wits mount up, the hairs subside.
  See, fierce Belinda on the Baron flies,
With more than usual lightning in her eyes;
Nor feared the chief the unequal fight to try,
Who sought no more than on his foe to die.
  But this bold lord with manly strength endued,
She with one finger and a thumb subdued:
Just where the breath of life his nostrils drew,
A charge of snuff the wily virgin threw;
The Gnomes direct, to every atom just,
The pungent grains of titillating dust.
Sudden, with starting tears each eye o'erflows,
And the high dome re-echoes to his nose.
  "Now meet thy fate," incensed Belinda cried,
And drew a deadly bodkin[9] from her side.
(The same, his ancient personage to deck,
Her great-great-grandsire wore about his neck,
In three seal rings; which after, melted down,
Formed a vast buckle for his widow's gown:
Her infant grandame's whistle next it grew,
The bells she jingled, and the whistle blew;
Then in a bodkin graced her mother's hairs,
Which long she wore, and now Belinda wears.)
  "Boast not my fall," he cried, "insulting foe!
Thou by some other shalt be laid as low.
Nor think to die dejects my lofty mind:

7. A sconce is a candlestick fastened on the wall.
8. The Maeander, a river in Asia Minor, was famous in mythology for its swans.
9. Here, an ornamental hairpin shaped like a dagger.

All that I dread is leaving you behind!
Rather than so, ah, let me still survive,
And burn in Cupid's flames—but burn alive."
  "Restore the Lock!" she cries; and all around
"Restore the Lock!" the vaulted roofs rebound.
Not fierce Othello in so loud a strain
Roared for the handkerchief that caused his pain.[1]
But see how oft ambitious aims are crossed,
And chiefs contend till all the prize is lost!
The lock, obtained with guilt, and kept with pain,
In every place is sought, but sought in vain:
With such a prize no mortal must be blessed,
So Heaven decrees! with Heaven who can contest?
  Some thought it mounted to the lunar sphere,
Since all things lost on earth are treasured there.
There heroes' wits are kept in ponderous vases,
And beaux' in snuffboxes and tweezer cases.
There broken vows and deathbed alms are found,
And lovers' hearts with ends of riband bound,
The courtier's promises, and sick man's prayers,
The smiles of harlots, and the tears of heirs,
Cages for gnats, and chains to yoke a flea,
Dried butterflies, and tomes of casuistry.
  But trust the Muse—she saw it upward rise,
Though marked by none but quick, poetic eyes
(So Rome's great founder to the heavens withdrew,[2]
To Proculus alone confessed in view);
A sudden star, it shot through liquid air,
And drew behind a radiant trail of hair.
Not Berenice's locks first rose so bright,[3]
The heavens bespangling with disheveled light.
The Sylphs behold it kindling as it flies,
And pleased pursue its progress through the skies.
  This the beau monde shall from the Mall[4] survey,
And hail with music its propitious ray.
This the blest lover shall for Venus take,
And send up vows from Rosamonda's Lake.[5]
This Partridge[6] soon shall view in cloudless skies,
When next he looks through Galileo's eyes;° *telescope*
And hence the egregious wizard shall foredoom
The fate of Louis, and the fall of Rome.
  Then cease, bright nymph! to mourn thy ravished hair,
Which adds new glory to the shining sphere!
Not all the tresses that fair head can boast
Shall draw such envy as the Lock you lost.

1. *Othello* 3.4.
2. Romulus, the "founder" and first king of Rome, was snatched to heaven in a storm cloud while reviewing his army in the Campus Martius (Livy 1.16).
3. Berenice, the wife of Ptolemy III, dedicated a lock of her hair to the gods to ensure her husband's safe return from war. It was turned into a constellation.
4. A walk laid out by Charles II in St. James's Park (London), a resort for strollers of all sorts.
5. In St. James's Park; associated with unhappy lovers.
6. John Partridge, an astrologer whose annually published predictions (among them that Louis XIV and the Catholic Church would fall) had been amusingly satirized by Swift and other wits in 1708.

For, after all the murders of your eye,
When, after millions slain, yourself shall die:
When those fair suns shall set, as set they must,
And all those tresses shall be laid in dust,
This Lock the Muse shall consecrate to fame,
And 'midst the stars inscribe Belinda's name.

1712 1714

An Essay on Man

Pope's philosophical poem *An Essay on Man* represents the beginnings of an ambitious but never completed plan for what he called his "ethic work," intended to be a large survey of human nature, society, and morals. He dedicated the *Essay* to Henry St. John (pronounced *Sín-jun*), Viscount Bolingbroke (1678–1751), the brilliant, erratic secretary of state in the Tory ministry of 1710–14. After the accession of George I, Bolingbroke fled to France, but he was allowed to return in 1723, settling near Pope at Dawley Farm. The two formed a close friendship and talked through the ideas expressed in the *Essay* and in Bolingbroke's own philosophical writings (some of which are addressed to Pope). But Pope's poem has many sources in the thought of his times and the philosophical tradition at large, and he says himself in the poem's little preface that his intention is to formulate a widely acceptable system of obvious, familiar truths. Pope's "optimism"—his insistence that everything must be "RIGHT" in a universe created and superintended by God—skips over the tragic elements of experience that much great literary, philosophical, and religious expression confronts. But the strains and contradictions of the poem are themselves deeply revealing about the thinking of Pope and his age, as he both presents and withholds a comprehensive view of the universe and reasons out reason's drastic limitations.

Pope's purpose is to "vindicate the ways of God to man," a phrase that consciously echoes *Paradise Lost* 1.26. Like John Milton, Pope faces the problem of the existence of evil in a world presumed to be the creation of a good god. *Paradise Lost* is biblical in content, Christian in doctrine; *An Essay on Man* avoids all specifically Christian doctrines, not because Pope disbelieved them but because "man," the subject of the poem, includes millions who never heard of Christianity and Pope is concerned with the universal. Milton tells a Judeo-Christian story. Pope writes in abstract terms.

The *Essay* is divided into four epistles. In the first Pope asserts the essential order and goodness of the universe and the rightness of our place in it. The other epistles deal with how we may emulate in our nature and in society the cosmic harmony revealed in the first epistle. The second seeks to show how we may attain a psychological harmony that can become the basis of a virtuous life through the cooperation of self-love and the passions (both necessary to our complete humanity) with reason, the controller and director. The third is concerned with the individual in society, which, it teaches, was created through the cooperation of self-love (the egoistic drives that motivate us) and social love (our dependence on others, our inborn benevolence). The fourth is concerned with happiness, which lies within the reach of all for it is dependent on virtue, which becomes possible when—though only when—self-love is transmuted into love of others and love of God. Such, in brief summary, are Pope's main ideas, expressed in many phrases so memorable that they have detached themselves from the poem and become part of daily speech.

From An Essay on Man

TO HENRY ST. JOHN, LORD BOLINGBROKE

Epistle 1. Of the Nature and State of Man, with Respect to the Universe

Awake, my St. John! leave all meaner things
To low ambition, and the pride of kings.
Let us (since life can little more supply
Than just to look about us and to die)
Expatiate free° o'er all this scene of man; *range freely*
A mighty maze! but not without a plan;
A wild, where weeds and flowers promiscuous shoot,
Or garden, tempting with forbidden fruit.
Together let us beat this ample field,[1]
Try what the open, what the covert yield;
The latent tracts, the giddy heights, explore
Of all who blindly creep, or sightless soar;
Eye Nature's walks, shoot folly as it flies,
And catch the manners living as they rise;
Laugh where we must, be candid° where we can; *favorably disposed*
But vindicate the ways of God to man.

1. Say first, of God above, or man below,
What can we reason, but from what we know?
Of man, what see we but his station here,
From which to reason, or to which refer?
Through worlds unnumbered though the God be known,
'Tis ours to trace him only in our own.
He, who through vast immensity can pierce,
See worlds on worlds compose one universe,
Observe how system into system runs,
What other planets circle other suns,
What varied being peoples every star,
May tell why Heaven has made us as we are.
But of this frame° the bearings, and the ties, *the universe*
The strong connections, nice dependencies,
Gradations just, has thy pervading soul
Looked through? or can a part contain the whole?
Is the great chain, that draws all to agree,
And drawn supports, upheld by God, or thee?[2]

2. Presumptuous man! the reason wouldst thou find,
Why formed so weak, so little, and so blind?
First, if thou canst, the harder reason guess,
Why formed no weaker, blinder, and no less!
Ask of thy mother earth, why oaks are made
Taller or stronger than the weeds they shade?
Or ask of yonder argent fields above,

1. Pope and Bolingbroke will try to drive truth into the open, like hunters beating the bushes for game.

2. For the chain of being, see lines 207–58.

Why Jove's satellites[3] are less than Jove?
  Of systems possible, if 'tis confessed
That Wisdom Infinite must form the best,
Where all must full or not coherent be,
And all that rises, rise in due degree;
Then, in the scale of reasoning life, 'tis plain,
There must be, somewhere, such a rank as man:
And all the question (wrangle e'er so long)
Is only this, if God has placed him wrong?
  Respecting man, whatever wrong we call,
May, must be right, as relative to all.
In human works, though labored on with pain,
A thousand movements scarce one purpose gain;
In God's, one single can its end produce;
Yet serves to second too some other use.
So man, who here seems principal alone,
Perhaps acts second to some sphere unknown,
Touches some wheel, or verges to some goal;
'Tis but a part we see, and not a whole.
  When the proud steed shall know why man restrains
His fiery course, or drives him o'er the plains;
When the dull ox, why now he breaks the clod,
Is now a victim, and now Egypt's god:[4]
Then shall man's pride and dullness comprehend
His actions', passions', being's use and end;
Why doing, suffering, checked, impelled; and why
This hour a slave, the next a deity.
  Then say not man's imperfect, Heaven in fault;
Say rather, man's as perfect as he ought;
His knowledge measured to his state and place,
His time a moment, and a point his space.
If to be perfect in a certain sphere,[5]
What matter, soon or late, or here or there?
The blest today is as completely so,
As who began a thousand years ago.

  3. Heaven from all creatures hides the book of Fate,
All but the page prescribed, their present state:
From brutes what men, from men what spirits know:
Or who could suffer being here below?
The lamb thy riot° dooms to bleed today, *feast*
Had he thy reason, would he skip and play?
Pleased to the last, he crops the flowery food,
And licks the hand just raised to shed his blood.
O blindness to the future! kindly given,
That each may fill the circle marked by Heaven:
Who sees with equal eye, as God of all,
A hero perish, or a sparrow fall,
Atoms or systems° into ruin hurled, *solar systems*
And now a bubble burst, and now a world.

3. In his *Dictionary*, Johnson notes and condemns Pope's giving this word four syllables, as in Latin.

4. The Egyptians worshiped a bull called Apis.

5. I.e., in one's "state and place."

Hope humbly then; with trembling pinions soar;
Wait the great teacher Death, and God adore!
What future bliss, he gives not thee to know,
But gives that hope to be thy blessing now.
Hope springs eternal in the human breast:
Man never is, but always to be blest:
The soul, uneasy and confined from home,
Rests and expatiates in a life to come.
Lo! the poor Indian, whose untutored mind
Sees God in clouds, or hears him in the wind;
His soul proud Science never taught to stray
Far as the solar walk, or milky way;
Yet simple Nature to his hope has given,
Behind the cloud-topped hill, an humbler heaven;
Some safer world in depth of woods embraced,
Some happier island in the watery waste,
Where slaves once more their native land behold,
No fiends torment, no Christians thirst for gold!
To be, contents his natural desire,
He asks no angel's wing, no seraph's fire;
But thinks, admitted to that equal° sky, *impartial*
His faithful dog shall bear him company.

4. Go, wiser thou! and, in thy scale of sense,
Weigh thy opinion against Providence;
Call imperfection what thou fancy'st such,
Say, here he gives too little, there too much;
Destroy all creatures for thy sport or gust,[6]
Yet cry, if man's unhappy, God's unjust;
If man alone engross not Heaven's high care,
Alone made perfect here, immortal there:
Snatch from his hand the balance and the rod,[7]
Rejudge his justice, be the God of God!
In pride, in reasoning pride, our error lies;
All quit their sphere, and rush into the skies.
Pride still is aiming at the blest abodes,
Men would be angels, angels would be gods.
Aspiring to be gods, if angels fell,
Aspiring to be angels, men rebel:
And who but wishes to invert the laws
Of order, sins against the Eternal Cause.

5. Ask for what end the heavenly bodies shine,
Earth for whose use? Pride answers, " 'Tis for mine:
For me kind Nature wakes her genial power,
Suckles each herb, and spreads out every flower;
Annual for me, the grape, the rose renew
The juice nectareous, and the balmy dew;
For me, the mine a thousand treasures brings;
For me, health gushes from a thousand springs;
Seas roll to waft me, suns to light me rise;

6. "Sense of tasting" (Johnson's *Dictionary*).
7. Symbols of judgment and punishment.

My footstool earth, my canopy the skies."
   But errs not Nature from this gracious end,
From burning suns when livid deaths descend,
When earthquakes swallow, or when tempests sweep
Towns to one grave, whole nations to the deep?
"No," 'tis replied, "the first Almighty Cause
Acts not by partial, but by general laws;
The exceptions few; some change since all began,
And what created perfect?"—Why then man?
If the great end be human happiness,
Then Nature deviates; and can man do less?
As much that end a constant course requires
Of showers and sunshine, as of man's desires;
As much eternal springs and cloudless skies,
As men forever temperate, calm, and wise.
If plagues or earthquakes break not Heaven's design,
Why then a Borgia, or a Catiline?[8]
Who knows but he whose hand the lightning forms,
Who heaves old ocean, and who wings the storms,
Pours fierce ambition in a Caesar's mind,
Or turns young Ammon° loose to scourge mankind? *Alexander the Great*
From pride, from pride, our very reasoning springs;
Account for moral, as for natural things:
Why charge we Heaven in those, in these acquit?
In both, to reason right is to submit.
   Better for us, perhaps, it might appear,
Were there all harmony, all virtue here;
That never air or ocean felt the wind;
That never passion discomposed the mind:
But ALL subsists by elemental strife;
And passions are the elements of life.
The general ORDER, since the whole began,
Is kept in Nature, and is kept in man.

   6. What would this man? Now upward will he soar,
And little less than angel, would be more;
Now looking downwards, just as grieved appears
To want the strength of bulls, the fur of bears.
Made for his use all creatures if he call,
Say what their use, had he the powers of all?
Nature to these, without profusion, kind,
The proper organs, proper powers assigned;
Each seeming want compènsated of course,° *as a matter of course*
Here with degrees of swiftness, there of force;
All in exact proportion to the state;
Nothing to add, and nothing to abate.
Each beast, each insect, happy in its own;
Is Heaven unkind to man, and man alone?

8. The Italian Renaissance family the Borgias was notorious for its ruthless lust for power, cruelty, rapaciousness, treachery, and murder (especially by poisoning). Cesare Borgia (1476–1507), son of Pope Alexander VI, is here referred to. Lucius Sergius Catiline (ca. 108–62 B.C.E.), an ambitious, greedy, and cruel conspirator against the Roman state, was denounced in Cicero's famous orations before the senate and in the Forum.

Shall he alone, whom rational we call,
Be pleased with nothing, if not blessed with all?
  The bliss of man (could pride that blessing find)
Is not to act or think beyond mankind;
No powers of body or of soul to share,
But what his nature and his state can bear.
Why has not man a microscopic eye?
For this plain reason, man is not a fly.
Say what the use, were finer optics given,
To inspect a mite, not comprehend the heaven?
Or touch, if tremblingly alive all o'er,
To smart and agonize at every pore?
Or quick effluvia[9] darting through the brain,
Die of a rose in aromatic pain?
If nature thundered in his opening ears,
And stunned him with the music of the spheres,
How would he wish that Heaven had left him still
The whispering zephyr, and the purling rill?
Who finds not Providence all good and wise,
Alike in what it gives, and what denies?

  7. Far as creation's ample range extends,
The scale of sensual,° mental powers ascends: *sensory*
Mark how it mounts, to man's imperial race,
From the green myriads in the peopled grass:
What modes of sight betwixt each wide extreme,
The mole's dim curtain, and the lynx's beam:[1]
Of smell, the headlong lioness between,
And hound sagacious° on the tainted green: *quick of scent*
Of hearing, from the life that fills the flood,
To that which warbles through the vernal wood:
The spider's touch, how exquisitely fine!
Feels at each thread, and lives along the line:
In the nice° bee, what sense so subtly true *exact, accurate*
From poisonous herbs extracts the healing dew:
How instinct varies in the groveling swine,
Compared, half-reasoning elephant, with thine!
'Twixt that, and reason, what a nice barrier,[2]
Forever separate, yet forever near!
Remembrance and reflection how allied;
What thin partitions sense from thought divide:
And middle natures, how they long to join,
Yet never pass the insuperable line!
Without this just gradation, could they be
Subjected, these to those, or all to thee?
The powers of all subdued by thee alone,
Is not thy reason all these powers in one?

9. According to the philosophy of Epicurus (adopted by Robert Boyle, the chemist, and other 17th-century scientists), the senses are stirred to perception by being bombarded through the pores by steady streams of "effluvia," incredibly thin and tiny—but material—images of the objects that surround us.

1. One of several early theories of vision held that the eye casts a beam of light that makes objects visible.

2. Pronounced *ba-réer*.

8. See, through this air, this ocean, and this earth,
All matter quick, and bursting into birth.
Above, how high progressive life may go!
Around, how wide! how deep extend below!
Vast Chain of Being! which from God began,
Natures ethereal, human, angel, man,
Beast, bird, fish, insect, what no eye can see,
No glass can reach! from Infinite to thee,
From thee to nothing.—On superior powers
Were we to press, inferior might on ours:
Or in the full creation leave a void,
Where, one step broken, the great scale's destroyed:
From Nature's chain whatever link you strike,
Tenth or ten thousandth, breaks the chain alike.
And, if each system in gradation roll
Alike essential to the amazing whole,
The least confusion but in one, not all
That system only, but the whole must fall.
Let earth unbalanced from her orbit fly,
Planets and suns run lawless through the sky,
Let ruling angels from their spheres be hurled,
Being on being wrecked, and world on world,
Heaven's whole foundations to their center nod,
And Nature tremble to the throne of God:
All this dread ORDER break—for whom? for thee?
Vile worm!—oh, madness, pride, impiety!

9. What if the foot, ordained the dust to tread,
Or hand, to toil, aspired to be the head?
What if the head, the eye, or ear repined
To serve mere engines to the ruling Mind?[3]
Just as absurd, for any part to claim
To be another, in this general frame.
Just as absurd, to mourn the tasks or pains,
The great directing MIND of ALL ordains.
All are but parts of one stupendous whole,
Whose body Nature is, and God the soul;
That, changed through all, and yet in all the same,
Great in the earth, as in the ethereal frame,
Warms in the sun, refreshes in the breeze,
Glows in the stars, and blossoms in the trees,
Lives through all life, extends through all extent,
Spreads undivided, operates unspent,
Breathes in our soul, informs our mortal part,
As full, as perfect, in a hair as heart;
As full, as perfect, in vile man that mourns,
As the rapt seraph that adores and burns;
To him no high, no low, no great, no small;
He fills, he bounds, connects, and equals all.

3. Cf. 1 Corinthians 12.14–26.

10. Cease then, nor ORDER imperfection name:
Our proper bliss depends on what we blame.
Know thy own point: this kind, this due degree
Of blindness, weakness, Heaven bestows on thee.
Submit—In this, or any other sphere,
Secure to be as blest as thou canst bear:
Safe in the hand of one disposing Power,
Or in the natal, or the mortal hour.
All Nature is but art, unknown to thee;
All chance, direction, which thou canst not see;
All discord, harmony not understood;
All partial evil, universal good:
And, spite of pride, in erring reason's spite,
One truth is clear: Whatever IS, is RIGHT.

From *Epistle 2. Of the Nature and State of Man with Respect to Himself, as an Individual*

1. Know then thyself, presume not God to scan;° *judge*
The proper study of mankind is Man.
Placed on this isthmus of a middle state,
A being darkly wise, and rudely great:
With too much knowledge for the skeptic side,
With too much weakness for the Stoic's pride,
He hangs between; in doubt to act, or rest,
In doubt to deem himself a god, or beast;
In doubt his mind or body to prefer,
Born but to die, and reasoning but to err;
Alike in ignorance, his reason such,
Whether he thinks too little, or too much:
Chaos of thought and passion, all confused;
Still by himself abused, or disabused;
Created half to rise, and half to fall;
Great lord of all things, yet a prey to all;
Sole judge of truth, in endless error hurled:
The glory, jest, and riddle of the world!

* * *

1733

Epistle to Dr. Arbuthnot

Dr. John Arbuthnot (1667–1735), to whom Pope addressed his best-known verse epistle, was distinguished both as a physician and as a man of wit. He had been one of the liveliest members of the Martinus Scriblerus Club, helping his friends create the character and shape the career of the learned pedant whose memoirs the club had undertaken to write.

Pope had long been meditating such a poem, which was to be both an attack on his detractors and a defense of his own character and career. In his usual way, he had jotted down hints, lines, couplets, and fragments over a period of two decades, but the poem might never have been completed had it not been for two events: Arbuthnot, from his deathbed, wrote to urge Pope to continue his abhorrence of vice and to express it in his writings and, during 1733, Pope was the victim of two bitter attacks by "persons of rank and fortune," as the Advertisement has it. The "Verses Addressed to the Imitator of Horace" was the work of Lady Mary Wortley Montagu, helped by her friend Lord Hervey (pronounced *Harvey*), a close friend and confidant of Queen Caroline. "An Epistle to a Doctor of Divinity from a Nobleman at Hampton Court" was the work of Lord Hervey alone. Montagu had provocation enough, especially in Pope's recent reference to her in "The First Satire of the Second Book of Horace," lines 83–84; but Hervey had little to complain of beyond occasional covert references to him as "Lord Fanny." At any rate, the two scurrilous attacks goaded Pope into action, and he completed the poem by the end of the summer of 1734.

The *Epistle* is the most brilliant and daring execution of the techniques that Pope used in many of the autobiographical poems of the 1730s. He presents himself in a theatrical array of postures: the comically exaggerating complainer, the admired man of genius, the true friend, the unpretentiously honest man, the satirist-hero of his country, the "manly" defender of virtue, the tender son mothering his own mother. Part of what cements this mixture is the verve with which he modulates from role to role, implying that none of them exhaustively defines him. Pope tries to force the reader to take sides, for him and what he claims to represent, or against him. Thus reading becomes an ethical exercise; readers must make up their own minds about his moral superiority, his exquisitely crafted portraits of his enemies, his social self-positioning, or his self-righteous politics. Pope solicits our judgment of his character and his professed ideals, and no other poet in English does so with so much artistic energy, resourcefulness, and success.

It is not clear that Pope intended the poem to be thought of as a dialogue, as it has usually been printed since Warburton's edition of 1751. The original edition, while suggesting interruptions in the flow of the monologue, kept entirely to the form of a letter. The introduction of the friend, who speaks from time to time, converts the original letter into a dramatic dialogue.

Epistle to Dr. Arbuthnot

Advertisement

TO THE FIRST PUBLICATION OF THIS *Epistle*

This paper is a sort of bill of complaint, begun many years since, and drawn up by snatches, as the several occasions offered. I had no thoughts of publishing it, till it pleased some persons of rank and fortune (the authors of *Verses to the Imitator of Horace*, and of an *Epistle to a Doctor of Divinity from a Nobleman at Hampton Court*) to attack, in a very extraordinary manner, not only my writings (of which, being public, the public is judge) but my person, morals, and family, whereof, to those who know me not, a truer information may be requisite. Being divided between the necessity to say something of myself, and my own laziness to undertake so awkward a task, I thought it the shortest way to put the last hand[1] to this epistle. If it have anything pleasing, it will be that by which I am most desirous to please, the truth and the sentiment; and if anything offensive, it will be only to those I am least sorry to offend, the vicious or the ungenerous.

Many will know their own pictures in it, there being not a circumstance but what is true; but I have, for the most part, spared their names, and they may escape being laughed at, if they please.

1. Finish.

I would have some of them know, it was owing to the request of the learned and candid friend to whom it is inscribed, that I make not as free use of theirs as they have done of mine. However, I shall have this advantage, and honor, on my side, that whereas, by their proceeding, any abuse may be directed at any man, no injury can possibly be done by mine, since a nameless character can never be found out, but by its truth and likeness. P.

P. Shut, shut the door, good John![2] (fatigued, I said),
Tie up the knocker, say I'm sick, I'm dead.
The Dog Star[3] rages! nay 'tis past a doubt
All Bedlam,[4] or Parnassus, is let out:
Fire in each eye, and papers in each hand,
They rave, recite, and madden round the land.
What walls can guard me, or what shades can hide?
They pierce my thickets, through my grot[5] they glide,
By land, by water, they renew the charge,
They stop the chariot, and they board the barge.
No place is sacred, not the church is free;
Even Sunday shines no Sabbath day to me:
Then from the Mint[6] walks forth the man of rhyme,
Happy! to catch me just at dinner time.
Is there a parson, much bemused in beer,
A maudlin poetess, a rhyming peer,
A clerk foredoomed his father's soul to cross,
Who pens a stanza when he should engross?[7]
Is there who, locked from ink and paper,[8] scrawls
With desperate charcoal round his darkened walls?
All fly to Twit'nam,[9] and in humble strain
Apply to me to keep them mad or vain.
Arthur,[1] whose giddy son neglects the laws,
Imputes to me and my damned works the cause:
Poor Cornus[2] sees his frantic wife elope,
And curses wit, and poetry, and Pope.
Friend to my life (which did not you prolong,
The world had wanted° many an idle song) *missed*
What drop or nostrum° can this plague remove? *medicine*
Or which must end me, a fool's wrath or love?
A dire dilemma! either way I'm sped,° *killed*
If foes, they write, if friends, they read me dead.
Seized and tied down to judge, how wretched I!
Who can't be silent, and who will not lie.
To laugh were want of goodness and of grace,

2. John Serle, Pope's gardener.
3. Sirius, associated with the period of greatest heat (and hence of madness) because it sets with the sun in late summer. August, in ancient Rome, was the season for reciting poetry.
4. Bethlehem Hospital for the insane, in London.
5. The subterranean passage under the road that separated his house at Twickenham from his garden became, in Pope's hands, a romantic grotto ornamented with shells and mirrors.
6. A place in Southwark where debtors were free from arrest (they could not be arrested anywhere on Sundays).
7. Write out legal documents.
8. Is there some madman who, locked up without ink or paper . . . ?
9. I.e., Twickenham, Pope's villa on the bank of the Thames, a few miles above Hampton Court.
1. Arthur Moore, whose son, James Moore Smythe, dabbled in literature. Moore Smythe had earned Pope's enmity by using in one of his plays some unpublished lines from Pope's "Epistle 2. To a Lady" in spite of Pope's objections.
2. Latin for "horn," the traditional emblem of the cuckold.

And to be grave exceeds all power of face.
I sit with sad civility, I read
With honest anguish and an aching head,
And drop at last, but in unwilling ears,
This saving counsel, "Keep your piece nine years."[3]
  "Nine years!" cries he, who high in Drury Lane,[4]
Lulled by soft zephyrs through the broken pane,
Rhymes ere he wakes, and prints before term[5] ends,
Obliged by hunger and request of friends:
"The piece, you think, is incorrect? why, take it,
I'm all submission, what you'd have it, make it."
  Three things another's modest wishes bound,
My friendship, and a prologue,[6] and ten pound.
  Pitholeon[7] sends to me: "You know his Grace,
I want a patron; ask him for a place."
Pitholeon libeled me—"but here's a letter
Informs you, sir, 'twas when he knew no better.
Dare you refuse him? Curll[8] invites to dine,
He'll write a *Journal,* or he'll turn divine."[9]
Bless me! a packet.—" 'Tis a stranger sues,° *asks for help*
A virgin tragedy, an orphan Muse."
If I dislike it, "Furies, death, and rage!"
If I approve, "Commend it to the stage."
There (thank my stars) my whole commission ends,
The players and I are, luckily, no friends.
Fired that the house° reject him, " 'Sdeath, I'll print it, *playhouse*
And shame the fools—Your interest, sir, with Lintot!"[1]
Lintot, dull rogue, will think your price too much.
"Not, sir, if you revise it, and retouch."
All my demurs but double his attacks;
At last he whispers, "Do; and we go snacks."° *shares*
Glad of a quarrel, straight I clap the door,
"Sir, let me see your works and you no more."
  'Tis sung, when Midas' ears began to spring
(Midas, a sacred person and a king),
His very minister who spied them first,
(Some say his queen) was forced to speak, or burst.[2]
And is not mine, my friend, a sorer case,
When every coxcomb perks them in my face?

3. The advice of Horace in *Art of Poetry* (line 388).
4. I.e., living in a garret in Drury Lane, site of one of the theaters and the haunt of the profligate.
5. One of the four annual periods in which the law courts are in session and with which the publishing season coincided.
6. Famous poets helped playwrights by contributing prologues to their plays.
7. "A foolish poet of Rhodes, who pretended much to Greek" [Pope's note]. He is Leonard Welsted, who translated Longinus and had attacked and slandered Pope (see line 375).
8. Edmund Curll, shrewd and disreputable bookseller, published pirated works, works falsely ascribed to reputable writers, scandalous biographies, and other ephemera. Pope had often attacked him and had assigned to him a low role in *The Dunciad*.
9. I.e., he will attack Pope in the *London Journal* or write a treatise on theology, as Welsted in fact did.
1. Bernard Lintot, publisher of Pope's Homer and other early works.
2. Midas, king of ancient Lydia, had the bad taste to prefer the flute-playing of Pan to that of Apollo, whereupon the god endowed him with ass's ears. It was his barber (not his wife or his minister) who discovered the secret and whispered it into a hole in the earth. The reference to "queen" and "minister" makes it plain that Pope is alluding to George II, Queen Caroline, and Walpole.

A. Good friend, forbear! you deal in dangerous things.
I'd never name queens, ministers, or kings;
Keep close to ears,° and those let asses prick; *whisper*
'Tis nothing——P. Nothing? if they bite and kick?
Out with it, *Dunciad!* let the secret pass,
That secret to each fool, that he's an ass:
The truth once told (and wherefore should we lie?)
The queen of Midas slept, and so may I.
You think this cruel? take it for a rule,
No creature smarts so little as a fool.
Let peals of laughter, Codrus![3] round thee break,
Thou unconcerned canst hear the mighty crack.
Pit, box, and gallery in convulsions hurled,
Thou stand'st unshook amidst a bursting world.
Who shames a scribbler? break one cobweb through,
He spins the slight, self-pleasing thread anew:
Destroy his fib or sophistry, in vain;
The creature's at his dirty work again,
Throned in the center of his thin designs,
Proud of a vast extent of flimsy lines.
Whom have I hurt? has poet yet or peer
Lost the arched eyebrow or Parnassian sneer?
And has not Colley still his lord and whore?
His butchers Henley?[4] his freemasons Moore?
Does not one table Bavius still admit?
Still to one bishop Philips[5] seem a wit?
Still Sappho[6]——A. Hold! for god's sake—you'll offend.
No names—be calm—learn prudence of a friend.
I too could write, and I am twice as tall;
But foes like these!——P. One flatterer's worse than all.
Of all mad creatures, if the learn'd are right,
It is the slaver kills, and not the bite.
A fool quite angry is quite innocent:
Alas! 'tis ten times worse when they repent.

One dedicates in high heroic prose,
And ridicules beyond a hundred foes;
One from all Grub Street[7] will my fame defend,
And, more abusive, calls himself my friend.
This prints my letters,[8] that expects a bribe,
And others roar aloud, "Subscribe, subscribe!"[9]
There are, who to my person pay their court:

3. Poet ridiculed by Virgil and Juvenal.
4. John Henley, known as "Orator" Henley, an independent preacher of marked eccentricity, was popular among the common people, especially for his elocution. Colley Cibber, the poet laureate.
5. The "bishop" is Hugh Boulter, bishop of Armagh. He had employed as his secretary Ambrose Philips (1674–1749), whose insipid simplicity of manner in poetry earned him the nickname of "Namby-Pamby." Bavius, the bad poet alluded to in Virgil's *Eclogue* 3.
6. Lady Mary Wortley Montagu.
7. A term denoting the whole society of literary, political, and journalistic hack writers.
8. In 1726 Curll had surreptitiously acquired and published without permission some of Pope's letters to Henry Cromwell.
9. To ensure the financial success of a work, wealthy readers were often asked to "subscribe" to it before printing was undertaken. Pope's Homer was published in this manner.

I cough like Horace,[1] and, though lean, am short;
Ammon's great son[2] one shoulder had too high,
Such Ovid's nose,[3] and "Sir! you have an eye—"
Go on, obliging creatures, make me see
All that disgraced my betters met in me.
Say for my comfort, languishing in bed,
"Just so immortal Maro° held his head": *Virgil*
And when I die, be sure you let me know
Great Homer died three thousand years ago.

Why did I write? what sin to me unknown
Dipped me in ink, my parents', or my own?
As yet a child, nor yet a fool to fame,
I lisped in numbers,° for the numbers came. *verses*
I left no calling for this idle trade,
No duty broke, no father disobeyed.
The Muse but served to ease some friend, not wife,
To help me through this long disease, my life,
To second, Arbuthnot! thy art and care,
And teach the being you preserved, to bear.° *endure*

A. But why then publish? P. Granville the polite,
And knowing Walsh, would tell me I could write;
Well-natured Garth inflamed with early praise,
And Congreve loved, and Swift endured my lays;
The courtly Talbot, Somers, Sheffield, read;
Even mitered Rochester would nod the head,
And St. John's self (great Dryden's friends before)
With open arms received one poet more.[4]
Happy my studies, when by these approved!
Happier their author, when by these beloved!
From these the world will judge of men and books,
Not from the Burnets, Oldmixons, and Cookes.[5]
Soft were my numbers; who could take offense
While pure description held the place of sense?
Like gentle Fanny's[6] was my flowery theme,
A painted mistress, or a purling stream.
Yet then did Gildon draw his venal quill;[7]
I wished the man a dinner, and sat still.
Yet then did Dennis[8] rave in furious fret;
I never answered, I was not in debt.
If want provoked, or madness made them print,

1. Horace, who mentions a cough in a few poems, was plump and short.
2. Alexander the Great, whose head inclined to his left shoulder, resembling Pope's hunchback.
3. Ovid's family name, Naso, suggests the Latin word *nasus* ("nose"), hence the pun.
4. The purpose of this list is to establish Pope as the successor of Dryden and thus to place him far above his Grub Street persecutors. George Granville, Lord Lansdowne, poet and statesman; William Walsh, poet and critic; Sir Samuel Garth, physician and mock-epic poet; William Congreve, the playwright; Charles Talbot, Duke of Shrewsbury, Lord Sommers; John Sheffield, Duke of Buckinghamshire; and Francis Atterbury, bishop of Rochester, statesmen, had all been associated with Dryden in his later years and had all encouraged the young Pope.
5. Thomas Burnet, John Oldmixon, and Thomas Cooke: Pope identifies them in a note as "authors of secret and scandalous history."
6. John, Lord Hervey, whom Pope satirizes in the character of Sporus (lines 305–33).
7. Charles Gildon, minor critic and scribbler, who, Pope believed, early attacked him at the instigation of Addison; hence "venal quill."
8. John Dennis (see *An Essay on Criticism,* n. 6, p. 1130).

I waged no war with Bedlam or the Mint.
Did some more sober critic come abroad?
If wrong, I smiled; if right, I kissed the rod.
Pains, reading, study are their just pretense,
And all they want is spirit, taste, and sense.
Commas and points they set exactly right,
And 'twere a sin to rob them of their mite.
Yet ne'er one sprig of laurel graced these ribalds,
From slashing Bentley down to piddling Tibbalds.[9]
Each wight who reads not, and but scans and spells,
Each word-catcher that lives on syllables,
Even such small critics some regard may claim,
Preserved in Milton's or in Shakespeare's name.
Pretty! in amber to observe the forms
Of hairs, or straws, or dirt, or grubs, or worms!
The things, we know, are neither rich nor rare,
But wonder how the devil they got there.
Were others angry? I excused them too;
Well might they rage; I gave them but their due.
A man's true merit 'tis not hard to find;
But each man's secret standard in his mind,
That casting weight[1] pride adds to emptiness,
This, who can gratify? for who can guess?
The bard[2] whom pilfered pastorals renown,
Who turns a Persian tale for half a crown,
Just writes to make his barrenness appear,
And strains from hard-bound brains eight lines a year:
He, who still wanting, though he lives on theft,
Steals much, spends little, yet has nothing left;
And he who now to sense, now nonsense leaning,
Means not, but blunders round about a meaning:
And he whose fustian's so sublimely bad,
It is not poetry, but prose run mad:
All these, my modest satire bade translate,
And owned that nine such poets made a Tate.[3]
How did they fume, and stamp, and roar, and chafe!
And swear, not Addison himself was safe.
Peace to all such! but were there one whose fires
True Genius kindles, and fair Fame inspires;
Blessed with each talent and each art to please,
And born to write, converse, and live with ease:
Should such a man, too fond to rule alone,
Bear, like the Turk, no brother near the throne;[4]

9. Lewis Theobald (1688–1744), whose minute learning in Elizabethan literature had enabled him to expose Pope's defects as an editor of Shakespeare in 1726. Pope made him king of the Dunces in *The Dunciad* of 1728. Richard Bentley (1662–1742), the eminent classical scholar, seemed to both Pope and Swift the perfect type of the pedant: he is called "slashing" because, in his edition of *Paradise Lost* (1732), he had set in square brackets all passages that he disliked on the grounds they had been slipped into the poem without the blind poet's knowledge.

1. The weight that turns the scale; here, the "deciding factor."

2. Philips, Pope's rival in pastoral poetry in 1709, when their pastorals were published in Tonson's 6th *Miscellany*. Philips had also translated some Persian tales (see line 100 and n. 5, p. 1166).

3. Nahum Tate, poet laureate from 1692 to 1715. His popular rewriting of Shakespeare's *King Lear* provided a happy ending; he wrote most of part 2 of *Absalom and Achitophel*. The line refers to the old adage that it takes nine tailors to make one man.

4. Turkish monarchs proverbially killed off their nearest rivals.

View him with scornful, yet with jealous eyes,
And hate for arts that caused himself to rise;
Damn with faint praise, assent with civil leer,
And without sneering, teach the rest to sneer;
Willing to wound, and yet afraid to strike,
Just hint a fault, and hesitate dislike;
Alike reserved to blame or to commend,
A timorous foe, and a suspicious friend;
Dreading even fools; by flatterers besieged,
And so obliging that he ne'er obliged;
Like Cato, give his little senate[5] laws,
And sit attentive to his own applause;
While wits and Templars° every sentence raise, *law students*
And wonder with a foolish face of praise—
Who but must laugh, if such a man there be?
Who would not weep, if Atticus[6] were he?

What though my name stood rubric° on the walls *in red letters*
Or plastered posts, with claps,° in capitals? *posters*
Or smoking forth, a hundred hawkers' load,
On wings of winds came flying all abroad?
I sought no homage from the race that write;
I kept, like Asian monarchs, from their sight:
Poems I heeded (now berhymed so long)
No more than thou, great George! a birthday song.
I ne'er with wits or witlings passed my days
To spread about the itch of verse and praise;
Nor like a puppy daggled through the town
To fetch and carry sing-song up and down;
Nor at rehearsals sweat, and mouthed, and cried,
With handkerchief and orange at my side;
But sick of fops, and poetry, and prate,
To Bufo left the whole Castalian[7] state.

Proud as Apollo on his forkèd hill,[8]
Sat full-blown Bufo, puffed° by every quill;° *flattered / pen*
Fed with soft dedication all day long,
Horace and he went hand in hand in song.
His library (where busts of poets dead
And a true Pindar stood without a head)
Received of wits an undistinguished race,
Who first his judgment asked, and then a place:
Much they extolled his pictures, much his seat,[9]
And flattered every day, and some days eat:
Till grown more frugal in his riper days,
He paid some bards with port, and some with praise;
To some a dry rehearsal was assigned,

5. Addison's tragedy *Cato* had been a sensational success in 1713. Pope had written the prologue, in which occurs the line, "While Cato gives his little senate laws." The satirical reference here is to Addison in the role of arbiter of taste among his friends and admirers, mostly Whigs, at Button's Coffee House. This group worked against the success of Pope's Homer.

6. Pope's satiric pseudonym for Addison. Atticus (109–32 B.C.E.), a wealthy man of letters and a friend of Cicero, was known as wise and disinterested.

7. The Castalian spring on Mount Parnassus was sacred to Apollo and the Muses. "Bufo": a type of tasteless patron of the arts. (*Bufo* means "toad" in Latin.)

8. Mount Parnassus had two peaks, one sacred to Apollo, one to Bacchus.

9. Estate. Pronounced *sate* and rhymed in next line with "eat" (*ate*).

And others (harder still) he paid in kind.
Dryden alone (what wonder?) came not nigh;
Dryden alone escaped this judging eye:
But still the great have kindness in reserve;
He helped to bury whom he helped to starve.
May some choice patron bless each gray goose quill!
May every Bavius have his Bufo still!
So when a statesman wants a day's defense,
Or envy holds a whole week's war with sense,
Or simple pride for flattery makes demands,
May dunce by dunce be whistled off my hands!
Blessed be the great! for those they take away,
And those they left me—for they left me Gay;[1]
Left me to see neglected genius bloom,
Neglected die, and tell it on his tomb;
Of all thy blameless life the sole return
My verse, and Queensberry weeping o'er thy urn!
Oh, let me live my own, and die so too!
("To live and die is all I have to do")[2]
Maintain a poet's dignity and ease,
And see what friends, and read what books I please;
Above a patron, though I condescend
Sometimes to call a minister my friend.
I was not born for courts or great affairs;
I pay my debts, believe, and say my prayers,
Can sleep without a poem in my head,
Nor know if Dennis be alive or dead.
Why am I asked what next shall see the light?
Heavens! was I born for nothing but to write?
Has life no joys for me? or (to be grave)
Have I no friend to serve, no soul to save?
"I found him close with Swift"—"Indeed? no doubt"
Cries prating Balbus,[3] "something will come out."
'Tis all in vain, deny it as I will.
"No, such a genius never can lie still,"
And then for mine obligingly mistakes
The first lampoon Sir Will or Bubo[4] makes.
Poor guiltless I! and can I choose but smile,
When every coxcomb knows me by my style?
Cursed be the verse, how well soe'er it flow,
That tends to make one worthy man my foe,
Give virtue scandal, innocence a fear,
Or from the soft-eyed virgin steal a tear!
But he who hurts a harmless neighbor's peace,
Insults fallen worth, or beauty in distress,
Who loves a lie, lame slander helps about,
Who writes a libel, or who copies out:

1. John Gay (1685–1732), author of *The Beggar's Opera*, dear friend of Swift and Pope. His failure to obtain patronage from the court intensified Pope's hostility to the Whig administration and the queen. Gay spent the last years of his life under the protection of the Duke and Duchess of Queensberry. Pope wrote his epitaph.

2. A quotation from John Denham's poem "Of Prudence."

3. Latin for *stammering*.

4. Sir William Yonge, Whig politician and poetaster. George Bubb ("Bubo") Dodington, a Whig patron of letters.

That fop whose pride affects a patron's name,
Yet absent, wounds an author's honest fame;
Who can your merit selfishly approve,
And show the sense of it without the love;
Who has the vanity to call you friend,
Yet wants the honor, injured, to defend;
Who tells whate'er you think, whate'er you say,
And, if he lie not, must at least betray:
Who to the dean and silver bell can swear,
And sees at Cannons what was never there:[5]
Who reads but with a lust to misapply,
Make satire a lampoon, and fiction, lie:
A lash like mine no honest man shall dread,
But all such babbling blockheads in his stead.
Let Sporus[6] tremble—— A. What? that thing of silk,
Sporus, that mere white curd of ass's milk?[7]
Satire or sense, alas! can Sporus feel?
Who breaks a butterfly upon a wheel?
P. Yet let me flap this bug with gilded wings,
This painted child of dirt, that stinks and stings;
Whose buzz the witty and the fair annoys,
Yet wit ne'er tastes, and beauty ne'er enjoys;
So well-bred spaniels civilly delight
In mumbling of the game they dare not bite.
Eternal smiles his emptiness betray,
As shallow streams run dimpling all the way.
Whether in florid impotence he speaks,
And, as the prompter breathes, the puppet squeaks;
Or at the ear of Eve,[8] familiar toad,
Half froth, half venom, spits himself abroad,
In puns, or politics, or tales, or lies,
Or spite, or smut, or rhymes, or blasphemies.
His wit all seesaw between *that* and *this,*
Now high, now low, now master up, now miss,
And he himself one vile antithesis.
Amphibious thing! that acting either part,
The trifling head or the corrupted heart,
Fop at the toilet, flatterer at the board,
Now trips a lady, and now struts a lord.
Eve's tempter thus the rabbins[9] have expressed,
A cherub's face, a reptile all the rest;
Beauty that shocks you, parts that none will trust,
Wit that can creep, and pride that licks the dust.
Not fortune's worshiper, nor fashion's fool,
Not lucre's madman, nor ambition's tool,

5. Pope's enemies had accused him of satirizing Cannons, the ostentatious estate of the Duke of Chandos, in his description of Timon's villa in the *Epistle to Burlington.* This Pope quite justly denied. The bell of Timon's chapel was of silver, and there preached a dean who "never mentions Hell to ears polite."

6. John, Lord Hervey, effeminate courtier and confidant of Queen Caroline (see headnote to *Epistle to Dr. Arbuthnot*, p. 1162). The original Sporus was a boy, whom the emperor Nero publicly married (see Suetonius's life of Nero in *The Twelve Caesars*).

7. Drunk by invalids.

8. The queen; the allusion is to *Paradise Lost* (4.799–809).

9. Scholars of and authorities on Jewish law and doctrine.

Not proud, nor servile, be one poet's praise,
That if he pleased, he pleased by manly ways:
That flattery, even to kings, he held a shame,
And thought a lie in verse or prose the same:
That not in fancy's maze he wandered long,
But stooped[1] to truth, and moralized his song:
That not for fame, but virtue's better end,
He stood the furious foe, the timid friend,
The damning critic, half approving wit,
The coxcomb hit, or fearing to be hit;
Laughed at the loss of friends he never had,
The dull, the proud, the wicked, and the mad;
The distant threats of vengeance on his head,
The blow unfelt, the tear he never shed;
The tale revived, the lie so oft o'erthrown,
The imputed trash, and dullness not his own;
The morals blackened when the writings 'scape,
The libeled person, and the pictured shape;[2]
Abuse on all he loved, or loved him, spread,
A friend in exile, or a father dead;
The whisper, that to greatness still too near,
Perhaps yet vibrates on his Sovereign's ear—
Welcome for thee, fair virtue! all the past:
For thee, fair virtue! welcome even the last!
  A. But why insult the poor, affront the great?
P. A knave's a knave to me in every state:
Alike my scorn, if he succeed or fail,
Sporus at court, or Japhet[3] in a jail,
A hireling scribbler, or a hireling peer,
Knight of the post[4] corrupt, or of the shire,
If on a pillory, or near a throne,
He gain his prince's ear, or lose his own.[5]
  Yet soft by nature, more a dupe than wit,
Sappho° can tell you how this man was bit:° *Montagu / deceived*
This dreaded satirist Dennis will confess
Foe to his pride, but friend to his distress:[6]
So humble, he has knocked at Tibbald's door,
Has drunk with Cibber, nay, has rhymed for Moore.
Full ten years slandered, did he once reply?
Three thousand suns went down on Welsted's lie.[7]
To please a mistress one aspersed his life;
He lashed him not, but let her be his wife.
Let Budgell charge low Grub Street on his quill,
And write whate'er he pleased, except his will;[8]

1. The falcon is said to "stoop" to its prey when it swoops down and seizes it in flight.
2. Pope's deformity was frequently ridiculed and occasionally caricatured.
3. Japhet Crook, a notorious forger.
4. One who lives by selling false evidence.
5. Those punished in the pillory often also had their ears cropped.
6. Pope wrote the prologue to Cibber's *Provoked Husband* (1728) when that play was performed for Dennis's benefit, shortly before the old critic died.
7. "This man had the impudence to tell in print that Mr. P. had occasioned a Lady's death, and to name a person he had never heard of" [Pope's note].
8. Eustace Budgell attacked the *Grub Street Journal* for publishing what he took to be a squib by Pope charging him with having forged the will of Dr. Matthew Tindal.

Let the two Curlls of town and court,[9] abuse
His father, mother, body, soul, and muse.
Yet why? that father held it for a rule,
It was a sin to call our neighbor fool;
That harmless mother thought no wife a whore:
Hear this, and spare his family, James Moore!
Unspotted names, and memorable long,
If there be force in virtue, or in song.
  Of gentle blood (part shed in honor's cause,
While yet in Britain honor had applause)
Each parent sprung——A. What fortune, pray?——P. Their own,
And better got than Bestia's[1] from the throne.
Born to no pride, inheriting no strife,
Nor marrying discord in a noble wife,
Stranger to civil and religious rage,
The good man walked innoxious through his age.
No courts he saw, no suits would ever try,
Nor dared an oath,[2] nor hazarded a lie.
Unlearn'd, he knew no schoolman's subtle art,
No language but the language of the heart.
By nature honest, by experience wise,
Healthy by temperance, and by exercise;
His life, though long, to sickness passed unknown,
His death was instant, and without a groan.
Oh, grant me thus to live, and thus to die!
Who sprung from kings shall know less joy than I.
  O friend! may each domestic bliss be thine!
Be no unpleasing melancholy mine:
Me, let the tender office long engage,
To rock the cradle of reposing age,
With lenient arts extend a mother's breath,
Make languor smile, and smooth the bed of death,
Explore the thought, explain the asking eye,
And keep a while one parent from the sky![3]
On cares like these if length of days attend,
May Heaven, to bless those days, preserve my friend,
Preserve him social, cheerful, and serene,
And just as rich as when he served a Queen![4]
  A. Whether that blessing be denied or given,
Thus far was right—the rest belongs to Heaven.

1735

9. I.e., the publisher and Lord Hervey.

1. Probably the duke of Marlborough, whose vast fortune was made through the favor of Queen Anne. The actual Bestia was a corrupt Roman consul.

2. As a Catholic, Pope's father refused to take the Oaths of Allegiance and Supremacy and the oath against the pope. He thus rendered himself vulnerable to the many repressive anti-Catholic laws then in force.

3. Pope was a tender and devoted son. His mother had died in 1733. The earliest version of these lines dates from 1731, when the poet was nursing her through a serious illness.

4. Pope alludes to the fact that Arbuthnot, a man of strict probity, left the queen's service no wealthier than when he entered it.

The Dunciad: Book the Fourth

The fourth book of *The Dunciad,* Pope's last major work, was originally intended as a continuation of *An Essay on Man.* To Jonathan Swift, the spiritual ancestor of the poem, Pope confided in 1736 that he was at work on a series of epistles on the uses of human reason and learning, to conclude with "a satire against the misapplication of all these, exemplified by pictures, characters, and examples." But the epistles never appeared; instead, the satire grew until it took their place. As Pope surveyed England in his last years, the complex literary and social order that had sustained him seemed to be crumbling. It was a time for desperate measures, for satire. And the means of retribution was at hand, in the structure of Pope's own *Dunciad,* the long work that had already impaled so many enemies.

The first *Dunciad,* published in three books in 1728, is a mock-epic reply to Pope's critics and other petty authors. Its hero and victim, Lewis Theobald, had attacked Pope's edition of Shakespeare (1725); other victims had offended Pope either by personal abuse or simply by ineptitude. Inspired by Dryden's "Mac Flecknoe," *The Dunciad* celebrates the triumph of the hordes of Grub Street. Indeed, so many obscure hacks were mentioned that a *Dunciad Variorum* (1729) was soon required, in which mock-scholarly notes identify the victims, "since it is only in this monument that they must expect to survive." But a modern reader need not catch every reference to enjoy the dazzling wit of the poem, or the sheer sense of fun with which Pope remakes the London literary world into a tiny insane fairground of his own.

The New Dunciad (1742), however, plays a far more serious game: here Pope takes aim at the rot of the whole social fabric. The satire goes deep and works at many levels, which for convenience may be divided into four. (1) Politics: From 1721 to 1742 England had been ruled by the Whig supremacy of Robert Walpole, first minister. To Pope and his circle, the immensely powerful Walpole (no friend of poets) seemed crass and greedy, like his monarch George II. It is no accident, in the kingdom of *The Dunciad,* that Dulness personified sits on a throne. (2) Society: Just as the action of the *Aeneid* had been the removal of the empire of Troy to Latium, the action of *The Dunciad,* according to Pope, is "the removal of the empire of Dulness from the City of London to the polite world, Westminster"; that is, the abdication of civility in favor of commerce and financial interests. In modern England, authors write for money, and ministers govern for profit; conspicuous consumption (especially the consumption of paper by scribblers) has replaced the old values of the yeoman and the aristocrat. In 1743 Pope revised the original *Dunciad,* substituting the actor and poet laureate Colley Cibber for Theobald as the hero and incorporating *The New Dunciad* as the fourth book (the version printed here). Dulness, he implies, has achieved her final triumph; Cibber is laureate in England. (3) Education: The word *dunce* is derived from the Scholastic philosopher John Duns Scotus (ca. 1265–1308), whose name had come to stand for silly and useless subtlety, logical hairsplitting. Pope, as an heir of the Renaissance, believes that the central subject of education must always be its relevance for human behavior: "The proper study of mankind is Man," and moral philosophy, the relation of individuals to each other and to the world, should be the teacher's first and last concern. By contrast, Dunces waste their time on grammar (words alone) or the "science" of the collector (things alone); they never comprehend that word and thing, like spirit and matter, are essentially dead unless they join. (4) Religion: At its deepest level, the subject of *The Dunciad* is the undoing of God's creation. Many passages from the fourth book echo *Paradise Lost,* and one of Pope's starting places seems to be Satan's threat to return the world to its original darkness, chaos, and ancient night (*Paradise Lost* 2.968–87). *The Dunciad* ends in a great apocalypse, with a yawn that signals the death of *Logos;* as words have become meaningless, so has the whole creation, which the Lord called forth with words. Here Pope invokes, with sublime intensity, the old idea that God was the first poet, one whose poem was the world, and suggests that the sickness of the word has infected all nature.

Such a cosmic collapse allows Pope to realize in full the aim of his satirical poetry: to depict the evil of his enemies in all its excessive might and magnitude. As matter without spirit and substance without essence prevail in the final *Dunciad* over Pope's own ideals, the poem perversely confirms his poetic power, and the destruction of art permits his ultimate artistic triumph.

From The Dunciad

From *Book the Fourth*

Yet, yet a moment, one dim ray of light
Indulge, dread Chaos, and eternal Night!
Of darkness visible[1] so much be lent,
As half to show, half veil the deep intent.
Ye Powers![2] whose mysteries restored I sing,
To whom Time bears me on his rapid wing,
Suspend a while your force inertly strong,
Then take at once the poet and the song.
   Now flamed the Dog-star's[3] unpropitious ray,
Smote every brain, and withered every bay,[4]
Sick was the sun, the owl forsook his bower,
The moon-struck prophet felt the madding hour:
Then rose the seed[5] of Chaos, and of Night,
To blot out Order, and extinguish Light,
Of dull and venal a new world to mold,
And bring Saturnian days of lead and gold.[6]
   She mounts the throne: her head a cloud concealed,
In broad effulgence all below revealed,
('Tis thus aspiring Dulness ever shines)
Soft on her lap her Laureate son[7] reclines.
   Beneath her foot-stool, Science groans in chains,
And Wit dreads exile, penalties and pains.
There foamed rebellious Logic, gagged and bound,
There, stripped, fair Rhetoric languished on the ground;
His blunted arms by Sophistry are borne,
And shameless Billingsgate[8] her robes adorn.
Morality, by her false guardians drawn,
Chicane in furs, and Casuistry in lawn,[9]
Gasps, as they straighten at each end the cord,
And dies, when Dulness gives her Page[1] the word.

* * *

1. Cf. *Paradise Lost* 1.63.
2. Chaos and Night, invoked in place of the Muse, because "the restoration of their empire is the action of the poem" [Pope's note].
3. Sirius, associated with the heat of summer and the madness of poets (see *Epistle to Dr. Arbuthnot,* line 3, p. 1164).
4. The laurel, whose garlands are bestowed on poets.
5. The Goddess Dulness.
6. Saturn ruled during the golden age; the new age of "gold" will be reestablished by the dull and venal.
7. Colley Cibber, the poet laureate.
8. Fishmarket slang, which now covers the noble science of rhetoric.
9. Chicanery (legal trickery) wears the ermine robe of a judge. Casuistry wears the linen ("lawn") sleeves of a bishop.
1. Sir Francis Page, a notorious hanging judge; or court page, used to strangle criminals in Turkey; or page of writing on which a dull author "kills" moral sentiments.

[THE EDUCATOR]

Now crowds on crowds around the Goddess press,
Each eager to present the first address.[2]
Dunce scorning dunce beholds the next advance,
But fop shows fop superior complaisance.
When lo! a specter[3] rose, whose index-hand
Held forth the virtue of the dreadful wand;
His beavered brow a birchen garland wears,[4]
Dropping with infant's blood, and mother's tears.
O'er every vein a shuddering horror runs;
Eton and Winton shake through all their sons.
All flesh is humbled, Westminster's bold race[5]
Shrink, and confess the Genius[6] of the place:
The pale boy-Senator yet tingling stands,
And holds his breeches close with both his hands.
Then thus. "Since Man from beast by words is known,
Words are Man's province, words we teach alone.
When reason doubtful, like the Samian letter,[7]
Points him two ways, the narrower is the better.
Placed at the door of learning, youth to guide,
We never suffer it to stand too wide.
To ask, to guess, to know, as they commence,
As fancy opens the quick springs of sense,
We ply the memory, we load the brain,
Bind rebel wit, and double chain on chain,
Confine the thought, to exercise the breath;[8]
And keep them in the pale of words till death.
Whate'er the talents, or howe'er designed,
We hang one jingling padlock on the mind:
A poet the first day, he dips his quill;
And what the last? a very poet still.
Pity! the charm works only in our wall,
Lost, lost too soon in yonder House or Hall."[9]

* * *

[THE TRIUMPH OF DULNESS]

Then blessing all,[1] "Go children of my care!
To practice now from theory repair.
All my commands are easy, short, and full:
My sons! be proud, be selfish, and be dull.
Guard my prerogative, assert my throne:
This nod confirms each privilege your own.

2. The goddess, newly enthroned, is receiving petitions and congratulations.
3. The ghost of Dr. Busby, stern headmaster of Westminster School.
4. He wears a hat (beaver) and a garland of birch twigs, used for flogging. "Wand": cane used for beating.
5. Alumni of Westminster School, with a play on the justices and members of Parliament who meet at Westminster Hall.
6. I.e., admit that Dr. Busby is the presiding deity (Genius).
7. The letter Y, which Pythagoras (a native of Samos) used as an emblem of the different roads of virtue and vice.
8. Students are taught only to recite the classic poets by heart.
9. The House of Commons and Westminster Hall, where law cases were heard. The eloquence learned by rote disappears on occasions for public speaking.
1. Having conferred her titles, Dulness bids each eminent dunce to indulge in the triviality closest to his heart.

The cap and switch be sacred to his Grace;[2]
With staff and pumps[3] the Marquis lead the race;
From stage to stage the licensed[4] Earl may run,
Paired with his fellow-charioteer the sun;
The learned baron butterflies design,
Or draw to silk Arachne's subtle line;° *spiderweb*
The Judge to dance his brother Sergeant[5] call;
The Senator at cricket urge the ball;
The Bishop stow (pontific luxury!)
An hundred souls of turkeys in a pie;[6]
The sturdy squire to Gallic masters° stoop, *French chefs*
And drown his lands and manors in a soup.
Others import yet nobler arts from France,
Teach kings to fiddle, and make senates dance.
Perhaps more high some daring son may soar,[7]
Proud to my list to add one monarch more;
And nobly conscious, Princes are but things
Born for First Ministers, as slaves for kings,
Tyrant supreme! shall three estates command,
And MAKE ONE MIGHTY DUNCIAD OF THE LAND!"
More she had spoke, but yawned—All Nature nods:
What mortal can resist the yawn of Gods?
Churches and chapels instantly it reached;
(St. James's first, for leaden Gilbert[8] preached)
Then catched the schools; the Hall scarce kept awake;
The Convocation gaped,[9] but could not speak:
Lost was the Nation's Sense,° nor could be found, *Parliament*
While the long solemn unison went round:
Wide, and more wide, it spread o'er all the realm;
Even Palinurus[1] nodded at the helm:
The vapor mild o'er each committee crept;
Unfinished treaties in each office slept;
And chiefless armies dozed out the campaign;
And navies yawned for orders on the main.
O Muse! relate (for you can tell alone,
Wits have short memories, and dunces none)
Relate, who first, who last resigned to rest;
Whose heads she partly, whose completely blessed;
What charms could faction, what ambition lull,
The venal quiet, and entrance the dull;
'Till drowned was sense, and shame, and right, and wrong—
O sing, and hush the nations with thy song!

. . . .

In vain, in vain,—the all-composing Hour

2. His Grace, a duke who loves horse racing, is to use the cap and switch of a jockey.
3. Footmen, who wore pumps (low-cut shoes for running), were matched in races.
4. The license required by the owner of a stage-coach; also privileged or licentious.
5. A lawyer or legislative officer. Formal ceremonies at the Inns of Court are said to have resembled a country dance.
6. According to Pope, a hundred turkeys had been "not unfrequently deposited in one Pye in the Bishopric of Durham."
7. A bold, direct attack on Walpole.
8. Dr. John Gilbert, dean of Exeter.
9. The Convocation, an assembly of clergy consulting on ecclesiastical affairs, had been adjourned since 1717.
1. The pilot of Aeneas's ship; here Walpole.

Resistless falls: The Muse obeys the Power.
She comes! she comes![2] the sable throne behold
Of Night primeval, and of Chaos old!
Before her, Fancy's gilded clouds decay,
And all its varying rainbows die away.
Wit shoots in vain its momentary fires,
The meteor drops, and in a flash expires.
As one by one, at dread Medea's strain,
The sickening stars fade off the ethereal plain;[3]
As Argus' eyes by Hermes' wand oppressed,
Closed one by one to everlasting rest;[4]
Thus at her felt approach, and secret might,
Art after Art goes out, and all is Night.
See skulking Truth to her old cavern fled,[5]
Mountains of casuistry heaped o'er her head!
Philosophy, that leaned on Heaven before,
Shrinks to her second cause,[6] and is no more.
Physic[7] of Metaphysic begs defense,
And Metaphysic calls for aid on Sense!
See Mystery[8] to Mathematics fly!
In vain! they gaze, turn giddy, rave, and die.
Religion blushing veils her sacred fires,
And unawares Morality expires.
Nor public flame, nor private, dares to shine;
Nor human spark is left, nor glimpse divine!
Lo! thy dread Empire, CHAOS! is restored;
Light dies before thy uncreating word:[9]
Thy hand, great Anarch! lets the curtain fall;
And Universal Darkness buries All.

1743

2. Having triumphed in the contemporary world of affairs, Dulness (like her antitype Christ) has a Second Coming, a prophetic vision in which she extinguishes the light of the arts and sciences.
3. In Seneca's *Medea,* the stars obey the curse of Medea, a magician and avenger.
4. Argus, Hera's hundred-eyed watchman, was charmed to sleep and slain by Hermes.
5. Alluding to the saying of Democritus, that Truth lay at the bottom of a deep well [Pope's note].
6. Science (philosophy) no longer accepts God as the first cause or final explanation of how all things came to be; instead, it accepts only the second or material cause and tries to account for all things by physical principles alone.
7. Natural science in general.
8. A religious truth known only through divine revelation.
9. Cf. God's first creating words in Genesis, "Let there be light."

ELIZA HAYWOOD
1693?–1756

Not much is known about the early life of Elizabeth Fowler or about the "unfortunate marriage," as she described it, that made her Eliza Haywood. She first came before the public as an actress in 1714 in Dublin, then moved to London. But "the stage not answering my expectation," as she later confessed, soon "made me turn my genius another way," to the life of a professional writer. Her first novel, the racy, best-selling *Love in Excess; or, the Fatal Inquiry* (1719), launched her long career as one of the most popular, prolific, and versatile authors of her time. She retailed gossip and also was gossiped about, becoming involved with the poet Richard Savage—a friend of Pope and later of Samuel Johnson—and with William Hatchett, a playwright and actor who seems to have been her longtime companion. Pope mocked her scandalmongering, and her two illegitimate children, in his own scandalmongering *Dunciad* (1728), and Fielding caricatured her as "Mrs. Novel." But nothing could keep her from writing. In addition to many kinds of fiction, she produced poems, translations, plays, political satires, essays, criticism, and books of advice and conduct—whatever might sell. In the 1730s she returned to the stage, as a playwright and actress, until the government cracked down on the theater in 1737. From 1744 to 1746 she had another great success with the *Female Spectator*, a wide-ranging periodical written for women. Later, *The History of Miss Betsy Thoughtless* (1751), the story of an indiscreet charmer who eventually reforms and finds her Mr. Trueworth, proved how well Haywood could adjust to the new style of edifying novels. And right up to the moment of her death she continued to work.

Fantomina first appeared among Haywood's *Secret Histories, Novels, and Poems* (1725), and the title page calls it "A Secret History of an Amour between Two Persons of Condition." The popular genre of "secret histories" promised a peep at what went on behind the scenes of fashionable society; and even though Haywood's story is obviously made up, it suggests that private lives, and especially love lives, are very different from what the public sees. Right at the start, the aristocratic heroine (whose name we never learn) is fascinated by the dalliance between "respectable" gentlemen and loose women of the town. She soon becomes a player herself. Cleverly switching roles, she gratifies her own desire by exploiting her lover's fickle passions. The story unsettles conventional views of social position, identity, morality, and gender. But most of all it shows that love is not only an irresistible impulse but also a risky, exciting game.

Fantomina; or, Love in a Maze

In love the victors from the vanquished fly.
They fly that wound, and they pursue that die.
—Waller[1]

A young lady of distinguished birth, beauty, wit, and spirit, happened to be in a box one night at the playhouse; where, though there were a great number of celebrated toasts,[2] she perceived several gentlemen extremely pleased themselves with entertaining a woman who sat in a corner of the pit and, by her air and manner of receiving them, might easily be known to be one of those who come there for no other purpose, than to create acquaintance with as many as seem desirous of it. She could not help testifying her contempt of men who, regardless either of the play or circle, threw away their time in such a manner, to some ladies that sat by her. But they, either less surprised by being more accustomed to such sights than she who had been bred for the most part in the country, or not of a disposition to consider anything very deeply, took but little notice of it. She still thought of it, however; and the longer she reflected on it, the greater was her wonder that men, some of whom she knew were accounted to have wit, should have tastes so very depraved.—This excited a curiosity in her to know in what manner these creatures were

1. Edmund Waller, "To A. H., of the different successes of their loves" (1645).

2. Women to whose charms men drink.

addressed.—She was young, a stranger to the world, and consequently to the dangers of it; and having nobody in town, at that time, to whom she was obliged to be accountable for her actions, did in everything as her inclinations or humors rendered most agreeable to her: therefore thought it not in the least a fault to put in practice a little whim which came immediately into her head, to dress herself as near as she could in the fashion of those women who make sale of their favors, and set herself in the way of being accosted as such a one, having at that time no other aim than the gratification of an innocent curiosity.—She no sooner designed this frolic than she put it in execution; and muffling her hoods over her face, went the next night into the gallery-box, and practicing, as much as she had observed at that distance, the behavior of that woman, was not long before she found her disguise had answered the ends she wore it for.—A crowd of purchasers of all degrees and capacities were in a moment gathered about her, each endeavoring to outbid the other, in offering her a price for her embraces.—She listened to 'em all, and was not a little diverted in her mind at the disappointment she should give to so many, each of which thought himself secure of gaining her.—She was told by 'em all, that she was the most lovely woman in the world; and some cried, *Gad, she is mighty like my fine Lady Such-a-one*—naming her own name. She was naturally vain, and received no small pleasure in hearing herself praised, though in the person of another, and a supposed prostitute; but she dispatched as soon as she could all that had hitherto attacked her, when she saw the accomplished *Beauplaisir*[3] was making his way through the crowd as fast as he was able, to reach the bench she sat on. She had often seen him in the drawing-room, had talked with him; but then her quality[4] and reputed virtue kept him from using her with that freedom she now expected he would do, and had discovered something in him which had made her often think she should not be displeased, if he would abate some part of his reserve.—Now was the time to have her wishes answered.—He looked in her face, and fancied, as many others had done, that she very much resembled that lady whom she really was; but the vast disparity there appeared between their characters prevented him from entertaining even the most distant thought that they could be the same.—He addressed her at first with the usual salutations of her pretended profession, as, *Are you engaged, Madam?—Will you permit me to wait on you home after the play?—By Heaven, you are a fine girl!—How long have you used this house?*—and such like questions; but perceiving she had a turn of wit, and a genteel manner in her raillery, beyond what is frequently to be found among those wretches, who are for the most part gentlewomen but by necessity, few of 'em having had an education suitable to what they affect to appear, he changed the form of his conversation, and showed her it was not because he understood no better, that he had made use of expressions so little polite.—In fine, they were infinitely charmed with each other. He was transported to find so much beauty and wit in a woman who he doubted not but on very easy terms he might enjoy; and she found a vast deal of pleasure in conversing with him in this free and unrestrained manner. They passed their time all the play with an equal satisfaction; but when it was over, she found herself involved in a difficulty which before never entered into her head, but which she knew not well how to get over.—The passion he professed for her was not of that humble nature which can be content with distant adorations.—He resolved not to part from her

3. Fine pleasure (French).

4. Social standing.

without the gratifications of those desires she had inspired; and presuming on the liberties which her supposed function allowed of, told her she must either go with him to some convenient house of his procuring, or permit him to wait on her to her own lodgings.—Never had she been in such a *dilemma*. Three or four times did she open her mouth to confess her real quality; but the influence of her ill stars prevented it, by putting an excuse into her head which did the business as well, and at the same time did not take from her the power of seeing and entertaining him a second time with the same freedom she had done this.—She told him, she was under obligations to a man who maintained her, and whom she durst not disappoint, having promised to meet him that night at a house hard by.—This story, so like what those ladies sometimes tell, was not at all suspected, by *Beauplaisir;* and assuring her he would be far from doing her a prejudice,[5] desired that in return for the pain he should suffer in being deprived of her company that night, that she would order her affairs so as not to render him unhappy the next. She gave a solemn promise to be in the same box on the morrow evening, and they took leave of each other; he to the tavern to drown the remembrance of his disappointment; she in a hackney-chair[6] hurried home to indulge contemplation on the frolic she had taken, designing nothing less on her first reflections than to keep the promise she had made him, and hugging herself with joy, that she had the good luck to come off undiscovered.

But these cogitations were but of a short continuance, they vanished with the hurry of her spirits, and were succeeded by others vastly different and ruinous.—All the charms of *Beauplaisir* came fresh into her mind; she languished, she almost died for another opportunity of conversing with him; and not all the admonitions of her discretion were effectual to oblige her to deny laying hold of that which offered itself the next night.—She depended on the strength of her virtue to bear her fate through trials more dangerous than she apprehended this to be, and never having been addressed by him as Lady—, was resolved to receive his devoirs as a town-mistress,[7] imagining a world of satisfaction to herself in engaging him in the character of such a one and in observing the surprise he would be in to find himself refused by a woman who he supposed granted her favors without exception.—Strange and unaccountable were the whimsies she was possessed of—wild and incoherent her desires—unfixed and undetermined her resolutions, but in that of seeing *Beauplaisir* in the manner she had lately done. As for her proceedings with him, or how a second time to escape him without discovering who she was, she could neither assure herself, nor whether or not in the last extremity she would do so.—Bent, however, on meeting him, whatever should be the consequence, she went out some hours before the time of going to the playhouse, and took lodgings in a house not very far from it, intending, that if he should insist on passing some part of the night with her, to carry him there, thinking she might with more security to her honor entertain him at a place where she was mistress than at any of his own choosing.

The appointed hour being arrived, she had the satisfaction to find his love in his assiduity. He was there before her; and nothing could be more tender than the manner in which he accosted her. But from the first moment she came in, to that of the play being done, he continued to assure her no consid-

5. Harm.
6. A small hired coach, carried by two men.
7. Prostitute. "Devoirs": dutiful compliments.

eration should prevail with him to part from her again, as she had done the night before; and she rejoiced to think she had taken that precaution of providing herself with a lodging, to which she thought she might invite him without running any risk, either of her virtue or reputation.—Having told him she would admit of his accompanying her home, he seemed perfectly satisfied; and leading her to the place, which was not above twenty houses distant, would have ordered a collation to be brought after them. But she would not permit it, telling him she was not one of those who suffered themselves to be treated at their own lodgings; and as soon she was come in, sent a servant belonging to the house to provide a very handsome supper and wine, and everything was served to table in a manner which showed the director neither wanted money, nor was ignorant how it should be laid out.

This proceeding, though it did not take from him the opinion that she was what she appeared to be, yet it gave him thoughts of her which he had not before.—He believed her a *mistress*, but believed her to be one of a superior rank, and began to imagine the possession of her would be much more expensive than at first he had expected. But not being of a humor to grudge anything for his pleasures, he gave himself no farther trouble than what were occasioned by fears of not having money enough to reach her price about him.

Supper being over, which was intermixed with a vast deal of amorous conversation, he began to explain himself more than he had done; and both by his words and behavior let her know he would not be denied that happiness the freedoms she allowed had made him hope.—It was in vain; she would have retracted the encouragement she had given.—In vain she endeavored to delay, till the next meeting, the fulfilling of his wishes.—She had now gone too far to retreat.—*He* was bold;—he was resolute. *She* fearful—confused, altogether unprepared to resist in such encounters, and rendered more so by the extreme liking she had to him.—Shocked, however, at the apprehension of really losing her honor, she struggled all she could, and was just going to reveal the whole secret of her name and quality, when the thoughts of the liberty he had taken with her, and those he still continued to prosecute, prevented her, with representing the danger of being exposed, and the whole affair made a theme for public ridicule.—Thus much, indeed, she told him, that she was a virgin, and had assumed this manner of behavior only to engage him. But that he little regarded, or if he had, would have been far from obliging him to desist;—nay, in the present burning eagerness of desire, 'tis probable, that had he been acquainted both with who and what she really was, the knowledge of her birth would not have influenced him with respect sufficient to have curbed the wild exuberance of his luxurious wishes, or made him in that longing, that impatient moment, change the form of his addresses. In fine, she was undone; and he gained a victory, so highly rapturous, that had he known over whom, scarce could he have triumphed more. Her tears, however, and the distraction she appeared in, after the ruinous ecstasy was past, as it heightened his wonder, so it abated his satisfaction.—He could not imagine for what reason a woman, who, if she intended not to be a *mistress*, had counterfeited the part of one, and taken so much pains to engage him, should lament a consequence which she could not but expect, and till the last test, seemed inclinable to grant; and was both surprised and troubled at the mystery.—He omitted nothing that he thought might make her easy; and still retaining an opinion that the hope of interest[8] had been the chief motive which had led her to act in the manner

8. Profit.

she had done, and believing that she might know so little of him as to suppose, now she had nothing left to give, he might not make that recompense she expected for her favors: to put her out of that pain, he pulled out of his pocket a purse of gold, entreating her to accept of that as an earnest of what he intended to do for her; assuring her, with ten thousand protestations, that he would spare nothing which his whole estate could purchase, to procure her content and happiness. This treatment made her quite forget the part she had assumed, and throwing it from her with an air of disdain, Is this a reward (*said she*) for condescensions,[9] such as I have yielded to?—Can all the wealth you are possessed of make a reparation for my loss of honor?—Oh! no, I am undone beyond the power of heaven itself to help me!—She uttered many more such exclamations; which the amazed *Beauplaisir* heard without being able to reply to, till by degrees sinking from that rage of temper, her eyes resumed their softening glances, and guessing at the consternation he was in, No, my dear *Beauplaisir*, (*added she*) your love alone can compensate for the shame you have involved me in; be you sincere and constant, and I hereafter shall, perhaps, be satisfied with my fate, and forgive myself the folly that betrayed me to you.

Beauplaisir thought he could not have a better opportunity than these words gave him of inquiring who she was, and wherefore she had feigned herself to be of a profession which he was now convinced she was not; and after he had made her a thousand vows of an affection as inviolable and ardent as she could wish to find in him, entreated she would inform him by what means his happiness had been brought about, and also to whom he was indebted for the bliss he had enjoyed.—Some remains of yet unextinguished modesty, and sense of shame, made her blush exceedingly at this demand; but recollecting herself in a little time, she told him so much of the truth, as to what related to the frolic she had taken of satisfying her curiosity in what manner *mistresses*, of the sort she appeared to be, were treated by those who addressed them; but forbore discovering her true name and quality, for the reasons she had done before, resolving, if he boasted of this affair, he should not have it in his power to touch her character. She therefore said she was the daughter of a country gentleman, who was come to town to buy clothes, and that she was called *Fantomina*. He had no reason to distrust the truth of this story, and was therefore satisfied with it; but did not doubt by the beginning of her conduct, but that in the end she would be in reality the thing she so artfully had counterfeited; and had good nature enough to pity the misfortunes he imagined would be her lot. But to tell her so, or offer his advice in that point, was not his business, at least as yet.

They parted not till towards morning; and she obliged him to a willing vow of visiting her the next day at three in the afternoon. It was too late for her to go home that night, therefore she contented herself with lying there. In the morning she sent for the woman of the house to come up to her; and easily perceiving, by her manner, that she was a woman who might be influenced by gifts, made her a present of a couple of broad pieces,[1] and desired her, that if the gentleman who had been there the night before should ask any questions concerning her, that he should be told, she was lately come out of the country, had lodged there about a fortnight, and that her name was *Fantomina*. I shall (*also added she*) lie but seldom here; nor, indeed, ever come but in those times when I expect to meet him. I would, therefore, have you order it so, that he

9. Humiliations.

1. Gold coins.

may think I am but just gone out, if he should happen by any accident to call when I am not here; for I would not, for the world, have him imagine I do not constantly lodge here. The landlady assured her she would do everything as she desired, and gave her to understand she wanted not[2] the gift of secrecy.

Everything being ordered at this home for the security of her reputation, she repaired to the other, where she easily excused to an unsuspecting aunt, with whom she boarded, her having been abroad all night, saying, she went with a gentleman and his lady in a barge to a little country seat of theirs up the river, all of them designing to return the same evening; but that one of the bargemen happening to be taken ill on the sudden, and no other waterman to be got that night, they were obliged to tarry till morning. Thus did this lady's wit and vivacity assist her in all but where it was most needful.—She had discernment to foresee and avoid all those ills which might attend the loss of her *reputation*, but was wholly blind to those of the ruin of her *virtue*; and having managed her affairs so as to secure the *one*, grew perfectly easy with the remembrance she had forfeited the *other*.—The more she reflected on the merits of *Beauplaisir*, the more she excused herself for what she had done; and the prospect of that continued bliss she expected to share with him took from her all remorse for having engaged in an affair which promised her so much satisfaction, and in which she found not the least danger of misfortune.—If he is really (*said she, to herself*) the faithful, the constant lover he has sworn to be, how charming will be our amour?—And if he should be false, grow satiated, like other men, I shall but, at the worst, have the private vexation of knowing I have lost him;—the intrigue being a secret, my disgrace will be so too.—I shall hear no whispers as I pass,—She is forsaken.—The odious word *forsaken* will never wound my ears; nor will my wrongs excite either the mirth or pity of the talking world.—It would not be even in the power of my undoer himself to triumph over me; and while he laughs at, and perhaps despises the fond, the yielding *Fantomina*, he will revere and esteem the virtuous, the reserved lady.—In this manner did she applaud her own conduct, and exult with the imagination that she had more prudence than all her sex beside. And it must be confessed, indeed, that she preserved an economy[3] in the management of this intrigue beyond what almost any woman but herself ever did: in the first place, by making no person in the world a confidant in it; and in the next, in concealing from *Beauplaisir* himself the knowledge who she was; for though she met him three or four days in a week at that lodging she had taken for that purpose, yet as much as he employed her time and thoughts, she was never missed from any assembly she had been accustomed to frequent.—The business of her love has engrossed her till six in the evening, and before seven she has been dressed in a different habit, and in another place.—Slippers, and a night-gown loosely flowing, has been the garb in which he has left the languishing *Fantomina*;—laced and adorned with all the blaze of jewels has he, in less than an hour after, beheld at the royal chapel, the palace gardens, drawing-room, opera, or play, the haughty awe-inspiring lady.—A thousand times has he stood amazed at the prodigious likeness between his little mistress and this court beauty; but was still as far from imagining they were the same as he was the first hour he had accosted her in the playhouse, though it is not impossible but that her resemblance to this celebrated lady might keep his inclination alive something longer than oth-

2. Did not lack.

3. Careful regulation.

erwise they would have been; and that it was to the thoughts of this (as he supposed) unenjoyed charmer she owed in great measure the vigor of his latter caresses.

But he varied not so much from his sex as to be able to prolong desire to any great length after possession. The rifled charms of *Fantomina* soon lost their poignancy,[4] and grew tasteless and insipid; and when the season of the year inviting the company to the *Bath*,[5] she offered to accompany him, he made an excuse to go without her. She easily perceived his coldness, and the reason why he pretended her going would be inconvenient, and endured as much from the discovery as any of her sex could do. She dissembled it, however, before him, and took her leave of him with the show of no other concern than his absence occasioned. But this she did to take from him all suspicion of her following him, as she intended, and had already laid a scheme for.—From her first finding out that he designed to leave her behind, she plainly saw it was for no other reason than that being tired of her conversation, he was willing to be at liberty to pursue new conquests; and wisely considering that complaints, tears, swoonings, and all the extravagancies which women make use of in such cases have little prevalence over a heart inclined to rove, and only serve to render those who practice them more contemptible, by robbing them of that beauty which alone can bring back the fugitive lover, she resolved to take another course; and remembering the height of transport she enjoyed when the agreeable *Beauplaisir* kneeled at her feet, imploring her first favors, she longed to prove the same again. Not but a woman of her beauty and accomplishments might have beheld a thousand in that condition *Beauplaisir* had been; but with her sex's modesty, she had not also thrown off another virtue equally valuable, though generally unfortunate, *constancy*. She loved *Beauplaisir*; it was only he whose solicitations could give her pleasure; and had she seen the whole species despairing, dying for her sake, it might, perhaps, have been a satisfaction to her pride, but none to her more tender inclination.—Her design was once more to engage him; to hear him sigh, to see him languish, to feel the strenuous pressures of his eager arms, to be compelled, to be sweetly forced to what she wished with equal ardor, was what she wanted, and what she had formed a stratagem to obtain, in which she promised herself success.

She no sooner heard he had left the town, than making a pretense to her aunt that she was going to visit a relation in the country, went towards *Bath*, attended but by two servants, who she found reasons to quarrel with on the road and discharged. Clothing herself in a habit she had brought with her, she forsook the coach and went into a wagon, in which equipage she arrived at *Bath*. The dress she was in was a round-eared cap, a short red petticoat, and a little jacket of gray stuff; all the rest of her accoutrements were answerable to[6] these, and joined with a broad country dialect, a rude unpolished air, which she, having been bred in these parts, knew very well how to imitate, with her hair and eye-brows blacked, made it impossible for her to be known, or taken for any other than what she seemed. Thus disguised did she offer herself to service in the house where *Beauplaisir* lodged, having made it her business to find out immediately where he was. Notwithstanding this metamorphosis she was still extremely pretty; and the mistress of the house hap-

4. Pungency.
5. A fashionable resort, one hundred miles west of London.
6. In harmony with.

pening at that time to want a maid, was very glad of the opportunity of taking her. She was presently[7] received into the family; and had a post in it (such as she would have chose, had she been left at her liberty), that of making the gentlemen's beds, getting them their breakfasts, and waiting on them in their chambers. Fortune in this exploit was extremely on her side; there were no others of the male sex in the house than an old gentleman who had lost the use of his limbs with the rheumatism, and had come thither for the benefit of the waters, and her beloved *Beauplaisir*; so that she was in no apprehensions of any amorous violence, but where she wished to find it. Nor were her designs disappointed. He was fired with the first sight of her; and though he did not presently take any farther notice of her than giving her two or three hearty kisses, yet she, who now understood that language but too well, easily saw they were the prelude to more substantial joys.—Coming the next morning to bring his chocolate, as he had ordered, he catched her by the pretty leg, which the shortness of her petticoat did not in the least oppose; then pulling her gently to him, asked her, how long she had been at service?—How many sweethearts she had? If she had ever been in love? and many other such questions, befitting one of the degree[8] she appeared to be. All which she answered with such seeming innocence, as more enflamed the amorous heart of him who talked to her. He compelled her to sit in his lap; and gazing on her blushing beauties, which, if possible, received addition from her plain and rural dress, he soon lost the power of containing himself.—His wild desires burst out in all his words and actions: he called her little angel, cherubim, swore he must enjoy her, though death were to be the consequence, devoured her lips, her breasts with greedy kisses, held to his burning bosom her half-yielding, half-reluctant body, nor suffered her to get loose till he had ravaged all, and glutted each rapacious sense with the sweet beauties of the pretty *Celia*, for that was the name she bore in this second expedition.—Generous as liberality itself to all who gave him joy this way, he gave her a handsome sum of gold, which she durst not now refuse, for fear of creating some mistrust, and losing the heart she so lately had regained; therefore taking it with an humble curtsy, and a well counterfeited show of surprise and joy, cried, O law, Sir! what must I do for all this? He laughed at her simplicity, and kissing her again, though less fervently than he had done before, bad her not be out of the way when he came home at night. She promised she would not, and very obediently kept her word.

His stay at *Bath* exceeded not a month; but in that time his supposed country lass had persecuted him so much with her fondness that in spite of the eagerness with which he first enjoyed her, he was at last grown more weary of her than he had been of *Fantomina*: which she perceiving, would not be troublesome, but quitting her service remained privately in the town till she heard he was on his return; and in that time provided herself of another disguise to carry on a third plot, which her inventing brain had furnished her with, once more to renew his twice-decayed ardors. The dress she had ordered to be made was such as widows wear in their first mourning, which, together with the most afflicted and penitential countenance that ever was seen, was no small alteration to her who used to seem all gaiety.—To add to this, her hair, which she was accustomed to wear very loose, both when *Fantomina* and *Celia*, was now tied back so straight, and her pinners[9] coming so very forward, that there

7. Immediately.
8. Social class.
9. Long flaps on the sides of a cap worn by women of rank.

was none of it to be seen. In fine, her habit and her air were so much changed, that she was not more difficult to be known in the rude country *girl*, than she was now in the sorrowful *widow*.

She knew that *Beauplaisir* came alone in his chariot to the *Bath*, and in the time of her being servant in the house where he lodged, heard nothing of anybody that was to accompany him to *London*, and hoped he would return in the same manner he had gone. She therefore hired horses and a man to attend her to an inn about ten miles on this side *Bath*, where having discharged them, she waited till the chariot should come by; which when it did, and she saw that he was alone in it, she called to him that drove it to stop a moment, and going to the door saluted the master with these words:

The distressed and wretched, Sir (*said she*), never fail to excite compassion in a generous mind; and I hope I am not deceived in my opinion that yours is such.—You have the appearance of a gentleman, and cannot, when you hear my story, refuse that assistance which is in your power to give to an unhappy woman, who without it may be rendered the most miserable of all created beings.

It would not be very easy to represent the surprise so odd an address created in the mind of him to whom it was made.—She had not the appearance of one who wanted charity; and what other favor she required he could not conceive; but telling her she might command anything in his power, gave her encouragement to declare herself in this manner. You may judge (*resumed she*), by the melancholy garb I am in, that I have lately lost all that ought to be valuable to womankind; but it is impossible for you to guess the greatness of my misfortune, unless you had known my husband, who was master of every perfection to endear him to a wife's affections.—But, notwithstanding I look on myself as the most unhappy of my sex in out-living him, I must so far obey the dictates of my discretion as to take care of the little fortune he left behind him, which being in the hands of a brother of his in *London*, will be all carried off to *Holland*, where he is going to settle; if I reach not the town before he leaves it, I am undone for ever.—To which end I left *Bristol*, the place where we lived, hoping to get a place in the stage[1] at *Bath*, but they were all taken up before I came; and being, by a hurt I got in a fall, rendered incapable of traveling any long journey on horseback, I have no way to go to *London*, and must be inevitably ruined in the loss of all I have on earth, without[2] you have good nature enough to admit me to take part of your chariot.

Here the feigned widow ended her sorrowful tale, which had been several times interrupted by a parenthesis of sighs and groans; and *Beauplaisir*, with a complaisant and tender air, assured her of his readiness to serve her in things of much greater consequence than what she desired of him; and told her it would be an impossibility of denying a place in his chariot to a lady, who he could not behold without yielding one in his heart. She answered the compliments he made her but with tears, which seemed to stream in such abundance from her eyes that she could not keep her handkerchief from her face one moment. Being come into the chariot, *Beauplaisir* said a thousand handsome things to persuade her from giving way to so violent a grief, which, he told her, would not only be destructive to her beauty, but likewise her health. But all his endeavors for consolement appeared ineffectual, and he began to think he should have but a dull journey, in the company of one who seemed so

1. Stagecoach.
2. Unless.

obstinately devoted to the memory of her dead husband that there was no getting a word from her on any other theme.—But bethinking himself of the celebrated story of the *Ephesian* matron,[3] it came into his head to make trial, she who seemed equally susceptible of *sorrow*, might not also be so too of *love*: and having began a discourse on almost every other topic, and finding her still incapable of answering, resolved to put it to the proof, if this would have no more effect to rouse her sleeping spirits.—With a gay air, therefore, though accompanied with the greatest modesty and respect, he turned the conversation, as though without design, on that joy-giving passion, and soon discovered that was indeed the subject she was best pleased to be entertained with; for on his giving her a hint to begin upon, never any tongue run more voluble than hers, on the prodigious power it had to influence the souls of those possessed of it, to actions even the most distant from their intentions, principles, or humors.—From that she passed to a description of the happiness of mutual affection;—the unspeakable ecstasy of those who meet with equal ardency; and represented it in colors so lively, and disclosed by the gestures with which her words were accompanied, and the accent of her voice so true a feeling of what she said, that *Beauplaisir*, without being as stupid as he was really the contrary, could not avoid perceiving there were seeds of fire not yet extinguished in this fair widow's soul, which wanted but the kindling breath of tender sighs to light into a blaze.—He now thought himself as fortunate, as some moments before he had the reverse; and doubted not but that before they parted, he should find a way to dry the tears of this lovely mourner, to the satisfaction of them both. He did not, however, offer, as he had done to *Fantomina* and *Celia*, to urge his passion directly to her, but by a thousand little softening artifices, which he well knew how to use, gave her leave to guess he was enamored. When they came to the inn where they were to lie, he declared himself somewhat more freely, and perceiving she did not resent it past forgiveness, grew more encroaching still.—He now took the liberty of kissing away her tears, and catching the sighs as they issued from her lips; telling her if grief was infectious, he was resolved to have his share; protesting he would gladly exchange passions with her, and be content to bear her load of *sorrow*, if she would as willingly ease the burden of his *love*.—She said little in answer to the strenuous pressures with which at last he ventured to enfold her, but not thinking it decent, for the character she had assumed, to yield so suddenly, and unable to deny both his and her own inclinations, she counterfeited a fainting, and fell motionless upon his breast.—He had no great notion that she was in a real fit, and the room they supped in happening to have a bed in it, he took her in his arms and laid her on it, believing that whatever her distemper was, that was the most proper place to convey her to.—He laid himself down by her, and endeavored to bring her to herself; and she was too grateful to her kind physician at her returning sense, to remove from the posture he had put her in, without his leave.

It may, perhaps, seem strange that *Beauplaisir* should in such near intimacies continue still deceived. I know there are men who will swear it is an impossibility, and that no disguise could hinder them from knowing a woman they had once enjoyed. In answer to these scruples, I can only say, that besides

3. In Petronius's *Satyricon*, a grieving widow who watches over her husband's burial vault is seduced by a soldier. When one of the bodies he was supposed to be guarding is stolen, she lets him replace it with her husband's.

the alteration which the change of dress made in her, she was so admirably skilled in the art of feigning that she had the power of putting on almost what face she pleased, and knew so exactly how to form her behavior to the character she represented that all the comedians[4] at both playhouses are infinitely short of her performances. She could vary her very glances, tune her voice to accents the most different imaginable from those in which she spoke when she appeared herself.—These aids from nature, joined to the wiles of art, and the distance between the places where the imagined *Fantomina* and *Celia* were, might very well prevent his having any thought that they were the same, or that the fair *widow* was either of them. It never so much as entered his head, and though he did fancy he observed in the face of the latter, features which were not altogether unknown to him, yet he could not recollect when or where he had known them;—and being told by her, that from her birth she had never removed from *Bristol*, a place where he never was, he rejected the belief of having seen her, and supposed his mind had been deluded by an idea of some other, whom she might have a resemblance of.

They passed the time of their journey in as much happiness as the most luxurious gratification of wild desires could make them; and when they came to the end of it, parted not without a mutual promise of seeing each other often.—He told her to what place she should direct a letter to him; and she assured him she would send to let him know where to come to her, as soon as she was fixed in lodgings.

She kept her promise; and charmed with the continuance of his eager fondness, went not home but into private lodgings, whence she wrote to him to visit her the first opportunity, and inquire for the Widow *Bloomer*.—She had no sooner dispatched this billet[5] than she repaired to the house where she had lodged as *Fantomina*, charging the people if *Beauplaisir* should come there, not to let him know she had been out of town. From thence she wrote to him, in a different hand, a long letter of complaint, that he had been so cruel in not sending one letter to her all the time he had been absent, entreated to see him, and concluded with subscribing herself his unalterably affectionate *Fantomina*. She received in one day answers to both these. The first contained these lines:

To the Charming Mrs. BLOOMER,

It would be impossible, my Angel! for me to express the thousandth part of that infinity of transport, the sight of your dear letter gave me.—Never was woman formed to charm like you: never did any look like you,—write like you,—bless like you;—nor did ever man adore as I do.—Since yesterday we parted, I have seemed a body without a soul; and had you not by this inspiring billet, gave me new life, I know not what by tomorrow I should have been.—I will be with you this evening about five.—O, 'tis an age till then!—But the cursed formalities of duty oblige me to dine with my lord—who never rises from table till that hour;—therefore adieu till then sweet lovely mistress of the soul and all the faculties of

Your most faithful,
BEAUPLAISIR.

The other was in this manner:

4. Actors.

5. Letter.

To the Lovely FANTOMINA,

If you were half so sensible as you ought of your own power of charming, you would be assured, that to be unfaithful or unkind to you would be among the things that are in their very natures impossibilities.—It was my misfortune, not my fault, that you were not persecuted every post with a declaration of my unchanging passion; but I had unluckily forgot the name of the woman at whose house you are, and knew not how to form a direction that it might come safe to your hands.—And, indeed, the reflection how you might misconstrue my silence, brought me to town some weeks sooner than I intended—If you knew how I have languished to renew those blessings I am permitted to enjoy in your society, you would rather pity than condemn

Your ever faithful,
BEAUPLAISIR.

P.S. *I fear I cannot see you till tomorrow; some business has unluckily fallen out that will engross my hours till then.—Once more, my dear,* Adieu.

Traitor! (*cried she*) as soon as she had read them, 'tis thus our silly, fond, believing sex are served when they put faith in man. So had I been deceived and cheated, had I like the rest believed, and sat down mourning in absence, and vainly waiting recovered tendernesses.—How do some women (*continued she*) make their life a hell, burning in fruitless expectations, and dreaming out their days in hopes and fears, then wake at last to all the horror of despair?—But I have outwitted even the most subtle of the deceiving kind, and while he thinks to fool me, is himself the only beguiled person.

She made herself, most certainly, extremely happy in the reflection on the process of her stratagems; and while the knowledge of his inconstancy and levity of nature kept her from having that real tenderness for him she would else have had, she found the means of gratifying the inclination she had for his agreeable person in as full a manner as she could wish. She had all the sweets of love, but as yet had tasted none of the gall, and was in a state of contentment which might be envied by the more delicate.

When the expected hour arrived, she found that her lover had lost no part of the fervency with which he had parted from her; but when the next day she received him as *Fantomina*, she perceived a prodigious difference; which led her again into reflections on the unaccountableness of men's fancies, who still[6] prefer the last conquest, only because it is the last.—Here was an evident proof of it; for there could not be a difference in merit, because they were the same person; but the Widow *Bloomer* was a more new acquaintance than *Fantomina*, and therefore esteemed more valuable. This, indeed, must be said of *Beauplaisir*, that he had a greater share of good nature than most of his sex, who, for the most part, when they are weary of an intrigue, break it entirely off, without any regard to the despair of the abandoned nymph. Though he retained no more than a bare pity and complaisance[7] for *Fantomina*, yet believing she loved him to an excess, would not entirely forsake her, though the continuance of his visits was now become rather a penance than a pleasure.

6. Always.

7. Indulgence.

The Widow *Bloomer* triumphed some time longer over the heart of this inconstant, but at length her sway was at an end, and she sunk in this character to the same degree of tastelessness as she had done before in that of *Fantomina* and *Celia*.—She presently perceived it, but bore it as she had always done; it being but what she expected, she had prepared herself for it, and had another project in *embryo* which she soon ripened into action. She did not, indeed, complete it altogether so suddenly as she had done the others, by reason there must be persons employed in it; and the aversion she had to any *confidants* in her affairs, and the caution with which she had hitherto acted, and which she was still determined to continue, made it very difficult for her to find a way without breaking through that resolution to compass what she wished.—She got over the difficulty at last, however, by proceeding in a manner, if possible, more extraordinary than all her former behavior.—Muffling herself up in her hood one day, she went into the park about the hour when there are a great many necessitous gentlemen, who think themselves above doing what they call little things for a maintenance, walking in the *Mall*, to take a *Camelion* treat,[8] and fill their stomachs with air instead of meat. Two of those, who by their physiognomy she thought most proper for her purpose, she beckoned to come to her; and taking them into a walk more remote from company, began to communicate the business she had with them in these words: I am sensible, gentlemen (*said she*), that, through the blindness of fortune and partiality of the world, merit frequently goes unrewarded, and that those of the best pretensions meet with the least encouragement.—I ask your pardon (*continued she*), perceiving they seemed surprised, if I am mistaken in the notion that you two may, perhaps, be of the number of those who have reason to complain of the injustice of fate; but if you are such as I take you for, I have a proposal to make you which may be of some little advantage to you. Neither of them made any immediate answer, but appeared buried in consideration for some moments. At length, We should, doubtless, madam (*said one of them*), willingly come into any measures to oblige you, provided they are such as may bring us into no danger, either as to our persons or reputations. That which I require of you (*resumed she*), has nothing in it criminal. All that I desire is *secrecy* in what you are entrusted, and to disguise yourselves in such a manner as you cannot be known, if hereafter seen by the person on whom you are to impose.—In fine, the business is only an innocent frolic, but if blazed abroad might be taken for too great a freedom in me.—Therefore, if you resolve to assist me, here are five pieces to drink my health and assure you, that I have not discoursed you on an affair I design not to proceed in; and when it is accomplished fifty more lie ready for your acceptance. These words, and above all the money, which was a sum which, 'tis probable, they had not seen of a long time, made them immediately assent to all she desired, and press for the beginning of their employment. But things were not yet ripe for execution; and she told them that the next day they should be let into the secret, charging them to meet her in the same place at an hour she appointed. 'Tis hard to say, which of these parties went away best pleased; *they*, that fortune had sent them so unexpected a windfall; or *she*, that she had found persons who appeared so well qualified to serve her.

Indefatigable in the pursuit of whatsoever her humor was bent upon, she

8. Chameleons supposedly fed on air. "The Mall": a fashionable promenade in St. James's Park.

had no sooner left her new-engaged emissaries than she went in search of a house for the completing her project.—She pitched on one very large and magnificently furnished, which she hired by the week, giving them the money beforehand to prevent any inquiries. The next day she repaired to the park, where she met the punctual squires of low degree; and ordering them to follow her to the house she had taken, told them they must condescend to appear like servants, and gave each of them a very rich livery. Then writing a letter to *Beauplaisir*, in a character vastly different from either of those she had made use of as *Fantomina*, or the fair Widow *Bloomer*, ordered one of them to deliver it into his own hands, to bring back an answer, and to be careful that he sifted out nothing of the truth.—I do not fear (*said she*), that you should discover to him who I am, because that is a secret of which you yourselves are ignorant; but I would have you be so careful in your replies, that he may not think the concealment springs from any other reasons than your great integrity to your trust.—Seem therefore to know my whole affairs; and let your refusing to make him partaker in the secret appear to be only the effect of your zeal for my interest and reputation. Promises of entire fidelity on the one side, and reward on the other, being past, the messenger made what haste he could to the house of *Beauplaisir*; and being there told where he might find him, performed exactly the injunction that had been given him. But never astonishment exceeding that which *Beauplaisir* felt at the reading this billet, in which he found these lines:

To the All-conquering BEAUPLAISIR.

I imagine not that 'tis a new thing to you, to be told you are the greatest charm in nature to our sex. I shall therefore, not to fill up my letter with any impertinent praises on your wit or person, only tell you that I am infinite in love with both, and if you have a heart not too deeply engaged, should think myself the happiest of my sex in being capable of inspiring it with some tenderness.—There is but one thing in my power to refuse you, which is the knowledge of my name, which believing the sight of my face will render no secret, you must not take it ill that I conceal from you.—The bearer of this is a person I can trust; send by him your answer; but endeavor not to dive into the meaning of this mystery, which will be impossible for you to unravel, and at the same time very much disoblige me.—But that you may be in no apprehensions of being imposed on by a woman unworthy of your regard, I will venture to assure you, the first and greatest men in the kingdom would think themselves blessed to have that influence over me you have, though unknown to yourself acquired.—But I need not go about to raise your curiosity, by giving you any idea of what my person is; if you think fit to be satisfied, resolve to visit me tomorrow about three in the afternoon; and though my face is hid, you shall not want sufficient demonstration that she who takes these unusual measures to commence a friendship with you is neither old, nor deformed. Till then I am,

Yours,
INCOGNITA.

He had scarce come to the conclusion before he asked the person who brought it, from what place he came;—the name of the lady he served;—if she were a wife, or widow, and several other questions directly opposite to the directions of the letter; but silence would have availed him as much as did all those testimonies of curiosity. No *Italian Bravo*,[9] employed in a business of the like nature, performed his office with more artifice; and the impatient inquirer was convinced, that nothing but doing as he was desired could give him any light into the character of the woman who declared so violent a passion for him; and little fearing any consequence which could ensue from such an encounter, resolved to rest satisfied till he was informed of everything from herself, not imagining this *Incognita* varied so much from the generality of her sex as to be able to refuse the knowledge of anything to the man she loved with that transcendency of passion she professed, and which his many successes with the ladies gave him encouragement enough to believe. He therefore took pen and paper, and answered her letter in terms tender enough for a man who had never seen the person to whom he wrote. The words were as follows:

To the Obliging and Witty INCOGNITA.

Though to tell me I am happy enough to be liked by a woman such, as by your manner of writing, I imagine you to be, is an honor which I can never sufficiently acknowledge, yet I know not how I am able to content myself with admiring the wonders of your wit alone. I am certain a soul like yours must shine in your eyes with a vivacity which must bless all they look on.—I shall, however, endeavor to restrain myself in those bounds you are pleased to set me, till by the knowledge of my inviolable fidelity, I may be thought worthy of gazing on that heaven I am now but to enjoy in contemplation.—You need not doubt my glad compliance with your obliging summons. There is a charm in your lines which gives too sweet an idea of their lovely author to be resisted.—I am all impatient for the blissful moment which is to throw me at your feet, and give me an opportunity of convincing you that I am,

Your everlasting slave,
BEAUPLAISIR.

Nothing could be more pleased than she to whom it was directed, at the receipt of this letter; but when she was told how inquisitive he had been concerning her character and circumstances, she could not forbear laughing heartily to think of the tricks she had played him, and applauding her own strength of genius and force of resolution, which by such unthought-of ways could triumph over her lover's inconstancy, and render that very temper,[1] which to other women is the greatest curse, a means to make herself more blessed.—Had he been faithful to me (*said she, to herself*), either as *Fantomina*, or *Celia*, or the Widow *Bloomer*, the most violent passion, if it does not change its object, in time will wither. Possession naturally abates the vigor of desire, and I should have had, at best, but a cold, insipid, husband-like lover in my arms; but by these arts of passing on him as a new mistress whenever the ardor, which alone makes love a blessing, begins to diminish for the former one, I have him always raving, wild, impatient, longing, dying.—O that all neglected wives and fond abandoned nymphs would take this method!—Men would be caught in their own snare, and have no cause to scorn our easy, weeping, wailing sex! Thus did she pride herself as if secure she never should

9. Ruffian for hire.

1. Habit of mind (inconstancy).

have any reason to repent the present gaiety of her humor. The hour drawing near in which he was to come, she dressed herself in as magnificent a manner as if she were to be that night at a ball at court, endeavoring to repair the want of those beauties which the vizard[2] should conceal, by setting forth the others with the greatest care and exactness. Her fine shape, and air, and neck appeared to great advantage; and by that which was to be seen of her, one might believe the rest to be perfectly agreeable. *Beauplaisir* was prodigiously charmed, as well with her appearance as with the manner she entertained him. But though he was wild with impatience for the sight of a face which belonged to so exquisite a body, yet he would not immediately press for it, believing before he left her he should easily obtain that satisfaction.—A noble collation being over, he began to sue for the performance of her promise of granting everything he could ask, excepting the sight of her face, and knowledge of her name. It would have been a ridiculous piece of affectation in her to have seemed coy in complying with what she herself had been the first in desiring. She yielded without even a show of reluctance: and if there be any true felicity in an amour such as theirs, both here enjoyed it to the full. But not in the height of all their mutual raptures could he prevail on her to satisfy his curiosity with the sight of her face. She told him that she hoped he knew so much of her as might serve to convince him she was not unworthy of his tenderest regard; and if he could not content himself with that which she was willing to reveal, and which was the conditions of their meeting, dear as he was to her, she would rather part with him for ever than consent to gratify an inquisitiveness which, in her opinion, had no business with his love. It was in vain that he endeavored to make her sensible of her mistake; and that this restraint was the greatest enemy imaginable to the happiness of them both. She was not to be persuaded, and he was obliged to desist his solicitations, though determined in his mind to compass what he so ardently desired, before he left the house. He then turned the discourse wholly on the violence of the passion he had for her; and expressed the greatest discontent in the world at the apprehensions of being separated;—swore he could dwell for ever in her arms, and with such an undeniable earnestness pressed to be permitted to tarry with her the whole night, that had she been less charmed with his renewed eagerness of desire, she scarce would have had the power of refusing him; but in granting this request, she was not without a thought that he had another reason for making it besides the extremity of his passion, and had it immediately in her head how to disappoint him.

The hours of repose being arrived, he begged she would retire to her chamber; to which she consented, but obliged him to go to bed first; which he did not much oppose, because he supposed she would not lie in her mask, and doubted not but the morning's dawn would bring the wished discovery.—The two imagined servants ushered him to his new lodging; where he lay some moments in all the perplexity imaginable at the oddness of this adventure. But she suffered not these cogitations to be of any long continuance. She came, but came in the dark; which being no more than he expected by the former part of her proceedings, he said nothing of; but as much satisfaction as he found in her embraces, nothing ever longed for the approach of day with more impatience than he did. At last it came; but how great was his disappointment,

2. Mask.

when by the noises he heard in the street, the hurry of the coaches, and the cries of penny-merchants,[3] he was convinced it was night nowhere but with him? He was still in the same darkness as before; for she had taken care to blind the windows in such a manner that not the least chink was left to let in day.—He complained of her behavior in terms that she would not have been able to resist yielding to, if she had not been certain it would have been the ruin of her passion.—She therefore answered him only as she had done before; and getting out of the bed from him, flew out of the room with too much swiftness for him to have overtaken her, if he had attempted it. The moment she left him, the two attendants entered the chamber, and plucking down the implements which had screened him from the knowledge of that which he so much desired to find out, restored his eyes once more to day.—They attended to assist him in dressing, brought him tea, and by their obsequiousness, let him see there was but one thing which the mistress of them would not gladly oblige him in.—He was so much out of humor, however, at the disappointment of his curiosity, that he resolved never to make a second visit.—Finding her in an outer room, he made no scruple of expressing the sense he had of the little trust she reposed in him, and at last plainly told her, he could not submit to receive obligations from a lady who thought him uncapable of keeping a secret, which she made no difficulty of letting her servants into.—He resented,—he once more entreated,—he said all that man could do, to prevail on her to unfold the mystery; but all his adjurations were fruitless; and he went out of the house determined never to re-enter it, till she should pay the price of his company with the discovery of her face and circumstances.—She suffered him to go with this resolution, and doubted not but he would recede from it, when he reflected on the happy moments they had passed together; but if he did not, she comforted herself with the design of forming some other stratagem, with which to impose on him a fourth time.

She kept the house and her gentlemen-equipage for about a fortnight, in which time she continued to write to him as *Fantomina* and the Widow *Bloomer*, and received the visits he sometimes made to each; but his behavior to both was grown so cold, that she began to grow as weary of receiving his now insipid caresses as he was of offering them. She was beginning to think in what manner she should drop these two characters, when the sudden arrival of her mother, who had been some time in a foreign country, obliged her to put an immediate stop to the course of her whimsical adventures.—That lady, who was severely virtuous, did not approve of many things she had been told of the conduct of her daughter; and though it was not in the power of any person in the world to inform her of the truth of what she had been guilty of, yet she heard enough to make her keep her afterwards in a restraint, little agreeable to her humor, and the liberties to which she had been accustomed.

But this confinement was not the greatest part of the trouble of this now afflicted lady. She found the consequences of her amorous follies would be, without almost a miracle, impossible to be concealed.—She was with child; and though she would easily have found means to have screened even this from the knowledge of the world, had she been at liberty to have acted with the same unquestionable authority over herself as she did before the coming of her mother, yet now all her invention was at a loss for a stratagem to impose

3. Street vendors.

on a woman of her penetration.—By eating little, lacing prodigious straight, and the advantage of a great hoop-petticoat, however, her bigness was not taken notice of, and, perhaps, she would not have been suspected till the time of her going into the country, where her mother designed to send her, and from whence she intended to make her escape to some place where she might be delivered with secrecy, if the time of it had not happened much sooner than she expected.—A ball being at court, the good old lady was willing she should partake of the diversion of it as a farewell to the town.—It was there she was seized with those pangs, which none in her condition are exempt from.—She could not conceal the sudden rack[4] which all at once invaded her; or had her tongue been mute, her wildly rolling eyes, the distortion of her features, and the convulsions which shook her whole frame, in spite of her, would have revealed she labored under some terrible shock of nature.—Everybody was surprised, everybody was concerned, but few guessed at the occasion.—Her mother grieved beyond expression, doubted not but she was struck with the hand of death; and ordered her to be carried home in a chair,[5] while herself followed in another.—A physician was immediately sent for; but he presently perceiving what was her distemper, called the old lady aside and told her, it was not a doctor of his sex, but one of her own, her daughter stood in need of.—Never was astonishment and horror greater than that which seized the soul of this afflicted parent at these words. She could not for a time believe the truth of what she heard; but he insisting on it, and conjuring her to send for a midwife, she was at length convinced of it.—All the pity and tenderness she had been for some moment before possessed of now vanished, and were succeeded by an adequate[6] shame and indignation.—She flew to the bed where her daughter was lying, and telling her what she had been informed of, and which she was now far from doubting, commanded her to reveal the name of the person whose insinuations[7] had drawn her to this dishonor.—It was a great while before she could be brought to confess anything, and much longer before she could be prevailed on to name the man whom she so fatally had loved; but the rack of nature growing more fierce, and the enraged old lady protesting no help should be afforded her while she persisted in her obstinacy, she, with great difficulty and hesitation in her speech, at last pronounced the name of *Beauplaisir*. She had no sooner satisfied her weeping mother, than that sorrowful lady sent messengers at the same time for a midwife, and for that gentleman who had occasioned the other's being wanted.—He happened by accident to be at home, and immediately obeyed the summons, though prodigiously surprised what business a lady so much a stranger to him could have to impart.—But how much greater was his amazement, when taking him into her closet,[8] she there acquainted him with her daughter's misfortune, of the discovery she had made, and how far he was concerned in it?—All the idea one can form of wild astonishment was mean to what he felt.—He assured her that the young lady her daughter was a person whom he had never, more than at a distance, admired;—that he had indeed spoke to her in public company, but that he never had a thought which tended to her dishonor.—His denials, if possible, added to the indignation she was before enflamed with.—She had no longer patience; and carrying him into the chamber, where she was just delivered of a fine girl, cried out, I will not be imposed on: the truth

4. Intense pain.
5. Carriage.
6. Equal.
7. Artful ways of winding into someone's favor.
8. Private room.

by one of you shall be revealed.—*Beauplaisir* being brought to the bedside, was beginning to address himself to the lady in it, to beg she would clear the mistake her mother was involved in; when she, covering herself with the clothes, and ready to die a second time with the inward agitations of her soul, shrieked out, Oh, I am undone!—I cannot live, and bear this shame!—But the old lady believing that now or never was the time to dive into the bottom of this mystery, forcing her to rear her head, told her she should not hope to escape the scrutiny of a parent she had dishonored in such a manner, and pointing to *Beauplaisir*, Is this the gentleman (*said she*), to whom you owe your ruin? or have you deceived me by a fictitious tale? Oh! no (*resumed the trembling creature*), he is indeed the innocent cause of my undoing.—Promise me your pardon (*continued she*), and I will relate the means. Here she ceased, expecting what she would reply, which, on hearing *Beauplaisir* cry out, What mean you, madam? I your undoing, who never harbored the least design on you in my life, she did in these words: Though the injury you have done your family (*said she*) is of a nature which cannot justly hope forgiveness, yet be assured, I shall much sooner excuse you when satisfied of the truth than while I am kept in a suspense, if possible, as vexatious as the crime itself is to me. Encouraged by this she related the whole truth. And 'tis difficult to determine if *Beauplaisir*, or the lady, were most surprised at what they heard; he, that he should have been blinded so often by her artifices; or she, that so young a creature should have the skill to make use of them. Both sat for some time in a profound reverie; till at length she broke it first in these words: Pardon, sir (*said she*), the trouble I have given you. I must confess it was with a design to oblige you to repair the supposed injury you had done this unfortunate girl, by marrying her, but now I know not what to say.—The blame is wholly hers, and I have nothing to request further of you, than that you will not divulge the distracted folly she has been guilty of.—He answered her in terms perfectly polite; but made no offer of that which, perhaps, she expected, though could not, now informed of her daughter's proceedings, demand. He assured her, however, that if she would commit the newborn lady to his care, he would discharge it faithfully. But neither of them would consent to that; and he took his leave, full of cogitations, more confused than ever he had known in his whole life. He continued to visit there, to inquire after her health every day; but the old lady perceiving there was nothing likely to ensue from these civilities but, perhaps, a renewing of the crime, she entreated him to refrain; and as soon as her daughter was in a condition, sent her to a monastery in *France*, the abbess of which had been her particular friend. And thus ended an intrigue which, considering the time it lasted, was as full of variety as any, perhaps, that many ages has produced.

1725

LADY MARY WORTLEY MONTAGU
1689–1762

In her early teens Lady Mary Pierrepont did something that well-bred young women were not supposed to do: she secretly taught herself Latin. The act reveals many of the traits that would also characterize her as a mature woman: curiosity, love of learning, intelligence, ambition, and independence of mind. The eldest daughter of a wealthy Whig peer (he later became marquess of Dorchester), she grew up amid a glittering London circle that included Addison, Steele, Congreve, and later Pope and Gay. But she was not content to live the life of a dutiful aristocratic daughter. Unlike most women in her time, she married for love, and when her husband, Edward Wortley Montagu, was appointed ambassador to Constantinople in 1716, she took advantage of the opportunity by traveling through Europe, studying the language and customs of Turkey, and even visiting Turkish harems. She also pioneered in introducing smallpox inoculation to England (her own son and daughter were among the first to be inoculated). Returning home in 1718, she spent unhappy years that included bitter political quarrels with Pope and the gradual failure of her marriage. Then, in middle age, she fell in love with a young Italian author, Francesco Algarotti. In 1739 she traveled to Italy hoping to see him; but the passion that had kindled in their letters was soon quenched when he failed to join her. The rest of her life was passed abroad, in Avignon, Brescia, and Venice. She died soon after her return to London in 1762.

As an author, Montagu is remembered chiefly for her letters. In a century that included many of the great letter writers in English—Gray, Horace Walpole, Cowper, and others—she is one of the greatest. "What fire, what ease, what knowledge of Europe and Asia!" Edward Gibbon commented when her Turkish correspondence was published. (For a selection of Montagu's *Turkish Embassy Letters,* see "Travel, Trade, and the Expansion of Empire," at Norton Literature Online.) But from an early age she had also tried her hand at other literary forms: essays, poems, and even a translated play. In her own time she was especially admired as a poet. When Pope, after their quarrel, gave her the name of "Sappho," he was doubtless betraying the nervousness that many men felt in the presence of intelligent women (the Greek poet Sappho, after all, preferred women to men); yet he was also associating her with the classic author of lyric verse. Montagu's verse, although often casual, reveals the mind of a woman who is not willing to accept the stereotypes imposed on her by men. Like her friend Mary Astell, Montagu puts her trust in education and reason, not in the opinions of others, and she always insists on preserving her freedom of choice. A woman, her poems suggest, need not defer to a man who is less than her equal; she must look to her own satisfaction before she looks to his, and she always has the right to say no. The verse demands respect by virtue of its sexual candor and punishing wit. Like Montagu herself, it is never dull, and at its best it places her in that ideal community defined by E. M. Forster: "Not an aristocracy of power, based upon rank and influence, but an aristocracy of the sensitive, the considerate, and the plucky."

The Lover: A Ballad

At length, by so much importunity pressed,
Take, (Molly),[1] at once, the inside of my breast;
This stupid indifference so often you blame
Is not owing to nature, to fear, or to shame;
I am not as cold as a Virgin in lead,[2]
Nor is Sunday's sermon so strong in my head;

1. Molly Skerrett, a friend of Lady Mary, was the mistress of Sir Robert Walpole. The ideal "lover" of the title, however, is not to be identified with any particular person.

2. I.e., an image of the Virgin Mary, either as a leaden statue or as a stained-glass window framed in lead.

I know but too well how time flies along,
That we live but few years and yet fewer are young.

But I hate to be cheated, and never will buy
Long years of repentance for moments of joy.
Oh was there a man (but where shall I find
Good sense and good nature so equally joined?)
Would value his pleasure, contribute to mine,
Not meanly would boast, nor lewdly design,° *plot*
Not over severe, yet not stupidly vain,
For I would have the power though not give the pain;

No pedant yet learnèd, not rakehelly gay
Or laughing because he has nothing to say,
To all my whole sex obliging and free,
Yet never be fond of any but me;
In public preserve the decorums are just,
And show in his eyes he is true to his trust,
Then rarely approach, and respectfully bow,
Yet not fulsomely pert, nor yet foppishly low.

But when the long hours of public are past
And we meet with champagne and a chicken at last,
May every fond pleasure that hour endear,
Be banished afar both discretion and fear,
Forgetting or scorning the airs of the crowd
He may cease to be formal, and I to be proud,
Till lost in the joy we confess that we live,
And he may be rude, and yet I may forgive.

And that my delight may be solidly fixed,
Let the friend and the lover be handsomely mixed,
In whose tender bosom my soul might confide,
Whose kindness can sooth me, whose counsel could guide.
From such a dear lover as here I describe
No danger should fright me, no millions should bribe;
But till this astonishing creature I know,
As I long have lived chaste, I will keep myself so.

I never will share with the wanton coquette,
Or be caught by a vain affectation of wit.
The toasters and songsters may try all their art
But never shall enter the pass of my heart.
I loathe the lewd rake, the dressed fopling despise;
Before such pursuers the nice° virgin flies; *fastidious*
And as Ovid has sweetly in parables told
We harden like trees, and like rivers are cold.[3]

1747

3. In Ovid's *Metamorphoses*, Daphne, to escape Apollo, was turned into a laurel, and Arethusa, escaping Alpheus, became a fountain.

Epistle from Mrs. Yonge to Her Husband[1]

Think not this paper comes with vain pretense
To move your pity, or to mourn th' offense.
Too well I know that hard obdurate heart;
No softening mercy there will take my part,
Nor can a woman's arguments prevail,
When even your patron's wise example fails.[2]
But this last privilege I still retain;
Th' oppressed and injured always may complain.
Too, too severely laws of honor bind
The weak submissive sex of womankind.
If sighs have gained or force compelled our hand,
Deceived by art, or urged by stern command,
Whatever motive binds the fatal tie,
The judging world expects our constancy.
Just heaven! (for sure in heaven does justice reign,
Though tricks below that sacred name profane)
To you appealing I submit my cause,
Nor fear a judgment from impartial laws.
All bargains but conditional° are made; *only conditionally*
The purchase void, the creditor unpaid;
Defrauded servants are from service free;
A wounded slave regains his liberty.
For wives ill used no remedy remains,
To daily racks condemned, and to eternal chains.
From whence is this unjust distinction grown?
Are we not formed with passions like your own?
Nature with equal fire our souls endued,
Our minds as haughty, and as warm our blood;
O'er the wide world your pleasures you pursue,
The change is justified by something new;
But we must sigh in silence—and be true.
Our sex's weakness you expose and blame
(Of every prattling fop the common theme),
Yet from this weakness you suppose is due
Sublimer virtue than your Cato[3] knew.
Had heaven designed us trials so severe,

1. In 1724 the notorious libertine William Yonge, separated from his wife, Mary, discovered that she (like him) had committed adultery. He sued her lover, Colonel Norton, for damages and collected £1500. Later that year, according to the law of the time, he petitioned the Houses of Parliament for a divorce. The case was tried in public, Mrs. Yonge's love letters were read aloud, and two men testified that they had found her and Norton "together in naked bed." Yonge was granted the divorce, his wife's dowry, and the greater part of her fortune.

Although the "Epistle" is obviously based on this sensational affair, it is also a work of imagination. Like Pope's *Eloisa to Abelard*—to which the author himself called Montagu's attention—it takes the form of a heroic epistle, the passionate outcry of an abandoned woman. The poet, entering into the feelings of Mary Yonge, justifies her conduct with reasons both of the heart and of the head. The objects of her attack include the institution of marriage, which binds wives in "eternal chains"; the double standard of morality, which requires chastity from women but not men; the hypocrisy of society, which condemns the very behavior it secretly lusts after; and the craven greed and cruelty of the husband himself. But 18th-century women seldom dared to speak like this in public, and the "Epistle" was not published until the 1970s.

2. Sir Robert Walpole, William Yonge's friend at court, was rumored to tolerate his own wife's infidelities.

3. The asceticism and self-discipline of the Roman statesman Cato were emphasized in Addison's famous tragedy *Cato* (1713).

It would have formed our tempers them to bear.
And I have borne (oh what have I not borne!)
The pang of jealousy, the insults of scorn.
Wearied at length, I from your sight remove,
And place my future hopes in secret love.
In the gay bloom of glowing youth retired,
I quit the woman's joy to be admired,
With that small pension your hard heart allows,
Renounce your fortune, and release your vows.
To custom (though unjust) so much is due;
I hide my frailty from the public view.
My conscience clear, yet sensible of shame,
My life I hazard, to preserve my fame.
And I prefer this low inglorious state
To vile dependence on the thing I hate—
But you pursue me to this last retreat.
Dragged into light, my tender crime is shown
And every circumstance of fondness known.
Beneath the shelter of the law you stand,
And urge my ruin with a cruel hand,
While to my fault thus rigidly severe,
Tamely submissive to the man you fear.[4]
This wretched outcast, this abandoned wife,
Has yet this joy to sweeten shameful life:
By your mean conduct, infamously loose,
You are at once my accuser and excuse.
Let me be damned by the censorious prude
(Stupidly dull, or spiritually lewd),
My hapless case will surely pity find
From every just and reasonable mind.
When to the final sentence I submit,
The lips condemn me, but their souls acquit.
No more my husband, to your pleasures go,
The sweets of your recovered freedom know.
Go: court the brittle friendship of the great,
Smile at his board,° or at his levee[5] wait; *dining table*
And when dismissed, to madam's toilet[6] fly,
More than her chambermaids, or glasses,° lie, *mirrors*
Tell her how young she looks, how heavenly fair,
Admire the lilies and the roses there.
Your high ambition may be gratified,
Some cousin of her own be made your bride,
And you the father of a glorious race
Endowed with Ch—l's strength and Low—r's face.[7]

1724 1972

4. I.e., Walpole. Montagu suggests that the whole political establishment of England takes sides against Mary Yonge.
5. Morning reception of visitors.
6. It was fashionable for women like Lady Walpole to receive visitors during the last stages of dressing (their "toilet").
7. General Churchill was rumored to have had an affair with Lady Walpole. Antony Lowther was a notorious gallant. The author implies that William Yonge's next wife may be as untrue as his first. Mary Yonge remarried immediately after her divorce; five years later Yonge himself (whose divorce had made him rich) married the daughter of a baron.

WILLIAM HOGARTH
1697–1764

William Hogarth was a Londoner born and bred; the life of the city, both high and low, fills all his work. His early life was hard. When his father, a writer and teacher, failed in business, the family was confined to the area of the Fleet, the debtor's prison. Hogarth never forgot "the cruel treatment" of his father by booksellers, and he resolved to make his living without relying on dealers; he would always be aggressively independent. Apprenticed as an engraver, he trained himself to sketch scenes quickly or catch them in memory. He also learned to paint, studying with the Serjeant Painter to the King, Sir James Thornhill, whose daughter he married (late in life Hogarth himself would become Serjeant Painter). Gradually he won a reputation for portraits and conversation pieces—group portraits in which members of a family or assembly interact in a social situation. But his popular fame was forged by sets of pictures that told a story: *A Harlot's Progress* (1731–32), *A Rake's Progress* (1734–35), and *Marriage A-la-Mode* (1743–45). First Hogarth painted these Modern Moral Subjects (as he called them), then prints were made and sold in large editions. He also found new ways to market and protect his work; a copyright bill to ban cheap imitations of prints was known as "Hogarth's Act." Despite this success, however, his ambition to redefine British standards of art led to frustration. The high regard and high prices for continental old masters were too well entrenched to be undermined. Hogarth did not get prestigious commissions, and his *Analysis of Beauty* (1753), an effort to fix "the fluctuating ideas of taste" by appealing to practical observations, not academic rules, was poorly received. Political and aesthetic controversies embittered his final years.

Writers have always loved Hogarth's satiric art, and many have claimed him as one of their own. Swift, Fielding, and Sterne associated their work with his; Horace Walpole considered him more "a writer of comedy with a pencil" than a painter; Charles Lamb compared him to Shakespeare; and William Hazlitt included him among the great English comic writers. This emphasis may slight Hogarth's importance in the history of art. His attempts to found a British school that looked at life and nature directly, not through a haze of ideas or reverence for the past, and to give pleasure to common people, not only to critics and connoisseurs, opened the eyes of many artists to come. But Hogarth is also a great storyteller, someone to *read*. Like novels and plays, his pictures have plots and morals; they ask us not only to look but also to think. Yet looking and thinking are always intertwined. The mind delights in riddles, according to Hogarth; and as he revised his work he stuffed in more and more clues, like a mystery writer. A feast of interpretation draws the reader in. So many expressive details crowd the pictures, so many keys to character and meaning, that viewers often become obsessed with figuring them out. Even inanimate objects can speak; playwrights rely on words, as Walpole pointed out, but "it was reserved to Hogarth to write a scene of furniture."

The furniture is particularly eloquent in *Marriage A-la-Mode;* note, for example, the fallen chairs in Plates 2 and 6. Hogarth took special pains with this series. The audience at which he aimed, as well as the subject matter, belonged to high society; and the art too is highly refined. A sinuous line weaves through each picture, leading the reader on, and each piece of bric-a-brac carries a message of lavish excess. Yet the story itself is brutally straightforward. A disastrous forced marriage stands at the center: a rich but miserly merchant buys the worthless son of an aristocrat for his restless daughter, and with nothing in common the couple destroy one another. The crisis of values that Hogarth depicts was bringing about radical changes in English life. In the tension between a fading aristocracy, both morally and financially bankrupt, and an upwardly mobile middle class, greedy for power but culturally insecure, the marriage reflects a society that has lost all sense of right and wrong. The artist plays no favorites. The aristocratic Squanderfields are not only vain, effete, and dissipated but also lacking in taste; the wan mythological paintings on their walls are just the sort of pretentious, overpriced art that Hogarth hates. But the vulgar Dutch art on the merchant's walls (in Plate 6) seems even worse, and his daughter falls for every extravagant, spurious fashion (in Plate 4). Nor do the parasites who live off these easy marks offer any hope. Lawyer and doctor, bawd and servant pave the road to ruin. Hogarth's satire warns against the spreading corruption of modern times, when self-interest eats into marriage and old values die. Look hard, he tells the public. These objects make up the world we live in. We might become these people.

Many commentaries have been written on Hogarth's pictures. The notes printed here were supplied by the editors of this volume.

Marriage A-la-Mode

Plate 1. *The Marriage Contract.* Lord Squanderfield points to the family tree, going back to William the Conquerer, that his son will bring to the marriage. Coronets are blazed all over the room, from the top of the canopy at the upper left to the side of the prostrate dog on the lower right. The earl, though hobbled by gout, is proud. But he has run out of money: construction has stopped on the Palladian mansion seen through the window. Sitting across from him, a squinting merchant grasps the marriage settlement. Some of the coins and banknotes he has placed on the table have been taken up by a scrawny usurer, who hands the earl a mortgage in return. At the right the betrothed sit back to back, uncaring as the dogs chained to each other below. The vacuous viscount pinches snuff and gazes at himself in a mirror, which ominously reflects the image of lawyer Silvertongue, who sharpens his pen as he bends unctuously over the bride-to-be. Pouting, she twirls her wedding ring in a handkerchief. Disasters from mythology cover the walls. A bombastic portrait of the earl as Jupiter, astride a cannon, dominates the room; and in a candle sconce on the right Medusa glowers over the scene.

Plate 2. *After the Marriage.* By now the couple are used to ignoring each other. The morning after a spree, the rumpled, exhausted viscount slouches in a chair. His broken sword has dropped on the carpet, and a lapdog sniffs at a woman's cap in his pocket—souvenirs of the night. Lolling and stretching in an unladylike pose, his wife too is half asleep. She has spent the night home but not alone. *Hoyle on Whist* lies before her, cards are scattered on the floor, and the overturned chair, book of music, and violin cases suggest that some player may have departed in haste. A steward carries away a sheaf of bills—only one paid—and the household ledger; a Methodist (*Regeneration* is in his pocket), he petitions heaven to look down on these heathens. Oriental idols decorate the mantel over the fireplace, surmounted by a broken-nosed Roman bust that frowns like the steward and a painting of Cupid playing the bagpipes. On the left, amid the shrubbery of a rococo clock, a cat leers over fish and a Buddha smiles. In the next room, a dozing servant fails to notice that a candle has set fire to a chair. Next to a row of saints, a curtain does not quite cover a bawdy painting from which a naked foot peeps.

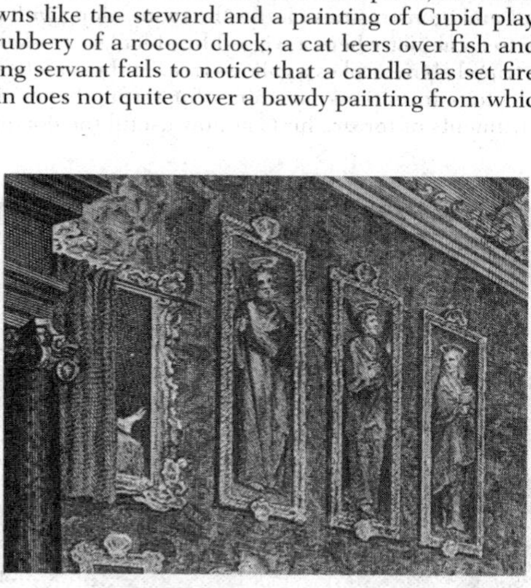

Plate 3. *The Scene with the Quack.* The husband has come to this chamber of medical horrors in search of a cure. The pillbox he holds toward the quack has not done its job, and he raises his cane as if with a playful threat. Evidently the little girl who stands between his legs is infected. She dabs a sore on her lip, and her ageless face may hint that she is not as young and pure as she looks. Her cap resembles the cap in Plate 2; she is the husband's mistress. Perhaps the beauty spot on his neck also covers a sore. The bowlegged Monsieur de la Pillule comfortably wipes his glasses; he has seen all this before. Between the two men an angry woman, fortified by a massive hoop skirt, opens a knife. She may be the wife of the quack, defending her man, or else a bawd who resents the charge that her girls are damaged goods. Medical oddities and monstrosities clutter the room, along with portents of death. The viscount's cane points to a cabinet where a wigged head looks at a skeleton that seems to be groping a cadaver; the tripod above evokes a gallows tree. At the far left, in front of a laboratory door, are two of the doctor's inventions: machines for setting bones and uncorking bottles. Their similarity to instruments of torture hints at how useful the doctor's assistance will be.

Plate 4. *The Countess's Levee.* In her bedchamber at rising (*levée;* French), the countess receives some guests and puts on a show. Her husband is now earl (note the coronets), and they have a child (note the rattle on her chair). While a hairdresser curls her locks, she hangs on the words of Silvertongue, who makes himself at home (note his portrait on the upper right wall). Tonight they will be going to a masquerade ball, like the one on the screen he gestures toward; his left hand holds the tickets. At the far right a puffy, bedizened castrato sings, accompanied by a flute. His audience includes a self-absorbed dandy in curl-papers; a man who appreciatively smirks and opens his hand, from which a fan dangles; a snoring husband, holding his riding-crop like a baton; and his enraptured wife, who leans forward as if about to swoon. Unobserved by the others, a black servant, bearing a cup of chocolate, smiles in amazement at these precious airs. At the lower left another black servant, a boy in a turban, grins at gewgaws purchased at an auction. His finger points both to Actaeon's horns, the sign of a cuckold, and to the couple as they arrange their tryst. Wall paintings illustrate unnatural sex: Lot's seduction by his daughters, Jupiter embracing Io, and the rape of Ganymede.

Plate 5. *The Death of the Earl.* The melodramatic tableau at the center, as the earl totters toward death and the countess kneels to beg forgiveness, imitates paintings of Christ descending from the cross while Mary Magdalen mourns. But the surroundings are sordid. At a house of ill repute, the Turk's Head Bagnio, the countess and Silvertongue have been surprised in bed. The earl has broken in (key and socket on the floor) and drawn his sword, and the lawyer has run him through. As the horrified owner and constable enter, under a watchman's lantern, the killer, still in his nightshirt, flees through a window. A fire, outside the picture on the lower right, casts lurid light on the victim; the shadow of the tongs encircles the murder weapon. Costumed as a nun and friar, the lovers have come from a masquerade, and their discarded masks and clothes show they were in haste. Pills (presumably mercury, prescribed for venereal disease) have spilled from an overturned table on the right, beside an advertisement for the bagnio, a corset, and a bundle of firewood. The portrait of a streetwalker, a squirrel perched on her hand, leers over the countess; on the wall behind the earl an uplifted blade is about to sever a child, in the Judgment of Solomon. At the top left St. Luke, the patron of artists, inscribes these transgressions.

Plate 6. *The Death of the Countess.* "Counseller Silvertongues Last Dying Speech," a paper on the floor announces, and a bottle of laudanum has dropped beside it. News of her lover's execution has driven the countess to poison herself. Slumped in a chair, she is already dead; on the far right a doctor steals away. Her father calmly slides the ring from her finger. This is his house; a window with cobwebs and broken panes opens on London Bridge, in the heart of the City. No luxury here. The furnishings are sparse, the floor is bare, and the dining table holds only one egg and a few leftovers, including a pathetic boar's head from which a starving hound is tearing scraps. The art is equally cheap: a pissing boy, a jumbled still life, a pipe set alight by the glowing nose of a drunk. At the center, beneath a coatrack, a stout apothecary (stomach pump and julep in his pocket) points toward the empty bottle in reproof and pokes the servant who brought it—an idiot wearing a coat many sizes too large, the merchant's hand-me-down. The service staff is completed by a withered old woman who holds out the countess's little child for one last hug and kiss. But the mark on the child's cheek and the brace on its leg imply that disease has passed to the next generation. This noble family will have no heir.

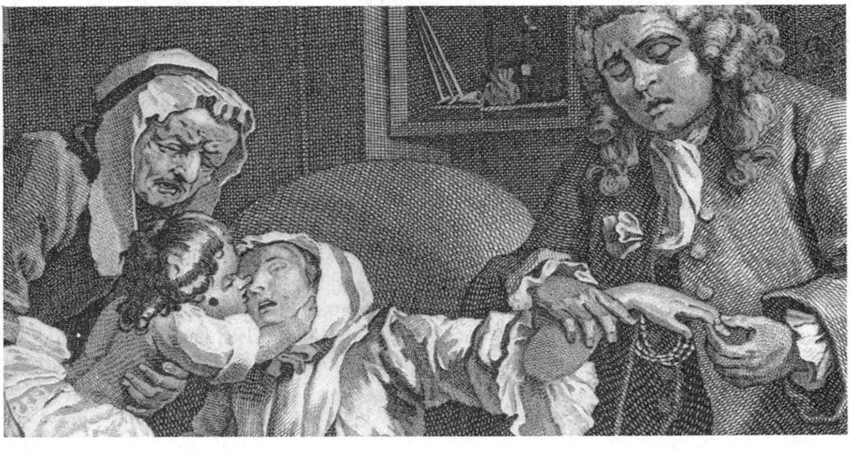

SAMUEL JOHNSON
1709–1784

Samuel Johnson was famous as a talker in his own time, and his conversation (preserved by James Boswell and others) has been famous ever since. But his wisdom survives above all in his writings: a few superb poems; the grave *Rambler* essays, which established his reputation as a stylist and a moralist; the lessons about life in *Rasselas* and the *Lives of the Poets;* and literary criticism that ranks among the best in English. The virtues of the talk and the writings are the same. They come hot from a mind well stored with knowledge, searingly honest, humane, and quick to seize the unexpected but appropriate image of truth. Johnson's wit is timeless, for it deals with the great facts of human experience, with hope and happiness and loss and duty and the fear of death. Whatever topic he addresses, whatever the form in which he writes, he holds to one commanding purpose: to see life as it is.

Two examples must suffice here. When Anna Williams wondered why a man should make a beast of himself through drunkenness, Johnson answered that "he who makes a beast of himself gets rid of the pain of being a man." In this reply Williams's tired metaphor is so charged with an awareness of the dark aspects of human life that it comes almost unbearably alive. Such moments characterize Johnson's writings as well. For instance, in reviewing the book of a fatuous would-be philosopher who blandly explained away the pains of poverty by declaring that a kindly providence compensates the poor by making them more hopeful, more healthy, more easily pleased, and less sensitive than the rich, Johnson retorted: "The poor indeed are insensible of many little vexations which sometimes embitter the possessions and pollute the enjoyments of the rich. They are not pained by casual incivility, or mortified by the mutilation of a compliment; but this happiness is like that of a malefactor who ceases to feel the cords that bind him when the pincers are tearing his flesh."

Johnson had himself known the pains of poverty. During his boyhood and youth in Lichfield, his father's bookshop and other businesses plunged into debt, so that he was forced to leave Oxford before he had taken a degree. An early marriage to a well-to-do widow, Elizabeth ("Tetty") Porter, more than twenty years older than he, enabled him to open a school. But the school failed, and he moved to London to make his way as a writer. The years between 1737, when he first arrived there with his pupil David Garrick (who later became the leading actor of his generation), and 1755, when the publication of the *Dictionary* established his reputation, were often difficult. He supported himself at first as best he could by doing hack work for the *Gentleman's Magazine,* but gradually his own original writings began to attract attention.

In 1747 Johnson published the Plan of his *Dictionary,* and he spent the the next seven years compiling it—although he had expected to finish it in three. When in 1748 Dr. Adams, a friend from Oxford days, questioned his ability to carry out such a work alone so fast and reminded him that the *Dictionary* of the French Academy had needed forty academicians working for forty years, Johnson replied with humorous jingoism: "Sir, thus it is. This is the proportion. Let me see; forty times forty is sixteen hundred. As three to sixteen hundred, so is the proportion of an Englishman to a Frenchman."

Johnson's achievement in compiling the *Dictionary* seems even greater when we realize that he was writing some of his best essays and poems during the same period. Although the booksellers who published the *Dictionary* paid him what was then the large sum of £1575, it was not enough to enable him to support his household, buy materials, and pay the wages of the six assistants whom he employed year by year until the task was accomplished. He therefore had to earn more money by writing. In 1749, his early tragedy *Irene* (pronounced *I-re-nĕ*) was produced at long last by his old friend Garrick, by then the manager of Drury Lane. The play was not a success, although Johnson made some profit from it. In the same year appeared his finest poem, "The Vanity of Human Wishes." With the *Rambler* (1750–52) and the *Idler* (1758–60), two series of periodical essays, Johnson found a devoted audience, but his pleasure was tempered by the death of his wife in 1752. He never remarried.

Boswell said of the *Rambler* essays that "in no writings whatever can be found more bark and steel [i.e., quinine and iron] for the mind." Moral strength and health; the importance of applying reason to experience; the test of virtue by what we do, not what we say or "feel"; faith in God: these are the centers to which Johnson's moral writings always return. What Johnson uniquely offers us is the quality of his understanding of the human condition, based on wide reading but always ultimately referred to his own passionate and often anguished experience. Such understanding had to be fought for again and again.

Johnson is thought of as the great generalizer, but what gives his generalizations strength is that they are rooted in the particulars of his self-knowledge. He had constantly to fight against what he called "filling the mind" with illusions to avoid the call of duty, his own black melancholy, and the realities of life. The portrait (largely a self-portrait) of Sober in *Idler* 31 is revealing: he occupies his idle hours with crafts and hobbies and has now taken up chemistry—he "sits and counts the drops as they come from his retort, and forgets that, whilst a drop is falling, a moment flies away."

His theme of themes is expressed in the title "The Vanity of Human Wishes": the dangerous but all-pervasive power of wishful thinking, the feverish intrusion of desires and hopes that distort reality and lead to false expectations. Almost all of Johnson's major writings—verse satire, moral essay, or the prose fable *Rasselas* (1759)—express this theme. In *Rasselas* it is called "the hunger of imagination, which preys upon life," picturing things as one would like them to be, not as they are. The travelers who are the fable's protagonists pursue some formula for happiness; they reflect our naive hope, against the lessons of experience, that one choice of life will make us happy forever.

Johnson also developed a style of his own: balanced, extended sentences, phrases, or clauses moving to carefully controlled rhythms, in language that is characteristically general, often Latinate, and frequently polysyllabic. This style is far from Swift's simplicity or Addison's neatness, but it never becomes obscure or turgid, for even a very complex sentence reveals—as it should—the structure of the thought, and the learned words are always precisely used. While reading early scientists to collect words for the *Dictionary,* Johnson developed a new vocabulary: for example, *obtund, exuberate, fugacity,* and *frigorific.* But he used many of these strange words in conversation as well as in his writings, often with a peculiarly Johnsonian felicity, describing the operations of the mind with a scientific precision.

After Johnson received his pension in 1762, he no longer had to write for a living, and because he held that "no man but a blockhead" ever wrote for any other reason, he produced as little as he decently could during the last twenty years of his life. His edition of Shakespeare, long delayed, was published in 1765, with a fine preface and fascinating notes. His last important work is the *Lives of the Poets,* which came out in two parts in 1779 and 1781. These biographical and critical prefaces were commissioned by a group of booksellers who had joined together to publish a large collection of the English poets and who wished to give their venture the prestige that Johnson would lend it. The poets to be included (except for four insisted on by Johnson) were selected by the booksellers according to current fashions. Therefore the collection begins with Abraham Cowley and John Milton and ends with Thomas Gray, and it omits such standard poets as Chaucer, Spenser, Sidney, Donne, and Marvell.

In the *Lives of the Poets* and in the earlier *Life of Richard Savage* (1744), Johnson did much to advance the art of biography in England. Biography had long been associated with panegyrics or scandalous memoirs; and therefore, Johnson's insistence on truth, even about the subject's defects, and on concrete, often minute, details was a new departure. "The biographical part of literature is what I love most," Johnson said, for he found every biography useful in revealing the human nature that all of us share.

His insistence on truth in biography (and knowing that Boswell intended to write his life, he insisted that he should write it truthfully) was owing to his conviction that only a truthful work can be trusted to help us with the business of living.

The ideal poet, according to Johnson, has a genius for making the things we see every day seem new. The same might be said of Johnson himself as a critic. (For additional works by Johnson, go to Norton Literature Online.) Johnson is our great champion, in criticism, of common sense and the common reader. Without denying the right of the poet to flights of imagination, he also insists that poems must make sense, please readers, and help us not only understand the world but cope with it. Johnson holds poems to the truth, as he sees it: the principles of nature, logic, religion, and morality. Not even Shakespeare can be excused when "he sacrifices virtue to convenience" and "seems to write without any moral purpose." Yet Johnson is no worshiper of authority or mere "correctness." As a critic he is always the empiricist, testing theory by practice. His determination to judge literature by its truth to life, not by abstract rules, is perfectly illustrated by his treatment of the doctrine of the three unities in the Preface to Shakespeare. Johnson is never afraid to state the obvious, whether the lack of human interest in *Paradise Lost* or Shakespeare's temptation by puns. But at its best, as in the praise of Milton or Shakespeare, his criticism engages some of the deepest questions about literature: why it endures, and how it helps us endure.

The Vanity of Human Wishes

This poem is an imitation of Juvenal's *Satire 10.* Although it closely follows the order and the ideas of the Latin poem, it remains a very personal work, for Johnson has used the Roman Stoic's satire as a means of expressing his own sense of the tragic and comic in human life. He has tried to reproduce in English verse the qualities he thought especially Juvenalian: stateliness, pointed sentences, and declamatory grandeur. The poem is difficult because of the extreme compactness of the style: every line is forced to convey the greatest possible amount of meaning. Johnson believed that "great thoughts are always general," but he certainly did not intend that the general should fade into the abstract: observe, for example, how he makes personified nouns concrete, active, and dramatic by using them as subjects of active and dramatic verbs: "Hate *dogs* their flight, and Insult *mocks* their end" (line 78). But the difficulty of the poem is also related to its theme, the difficulty of seeing anything clearly on this earth. In a world of blindness and illusion, human beings must struggle to find a point of view that will not deceive them, and a happiness that can last.

The Vanity of Human Wishes

In Imitation of the Tenth Satire of Juvenal

Let Observation, with extensive view,
Survey mankind, from China to Peru;
Remark each anxious toil, each eager strife,
And watch the busy scenes of crowded life;
Then say how hope and fear, desire and hate
O'erspread with snares the clouded maze of fate,
Where wavering man, betrayed by venturous Pride
To tread the dreary paths without a guide,
As treacherous phantoms in the mist delude,
Shuns fancied ills, or chases airy good.

How rarely Reason guides the stubborn choice,
Rules the bold hand, or prompts the suppliant voice;
How nations sink, by darling schemes oppressed,
When Vengeance listens to the fool's request.
Fate wings with every wish the afflictive dart,
Each gift of nature, and each grace of art;
With fatal heat impetuous courage glows,
With fatal sweetness elocution flows,
Impeachment stops the speaker's powerful breath,
And restless fire precipitates on death.

But scarce observed, the knowing and the bold
Fall in the general massacre of gold;
Wide-wasting pest! that rages unconfined,
And crowds with crimes the records of mankind;
For gold his sword the hireling ruffian draws,
For gold the hireling judge distorts the laws;
Wealth heaped on wealth, nor truth nor safety buys,
The dangers gather as the treasures rise.

Let History tell where rival kings command,
And dubious title° shakes the madded land, *claim of right*
When statutes glean the refuse of the sword,
How much more safe the vassal than the lord;
Low skulks the hind° beneath the rage of power, *peasant*
And leaves the wealthy traitor in the Tower,[1]
Untouched his cottage, and his slumbers sound,
Though Confiscation's vultures hover round.

The needy traveler, serene and gay,
Walks the wild heath, and sings his toil away.
Does envy seize thee? crush the upbraiding joy,
Increase his riches and his peace destroy;
New fears in dire vicissitude invade,
The rustling brake° alarms, and quivering shade, *thicket*
Nor light nor darkness bring his pain relief,
One shows the plunder, and one hides the thief.

Yet still one general cry the skies assails,
And gain and grandeur load the tainted gales;
Few know the toiling statesman's fear or care,
The insidious rival and the gaping heir.

Once more, Democritus,[2] arise on earth,
With cheerful wisdom and instructive mirth,
See motley life in modern trappings dressed,
And feed with varied fools the eternal jest:
Thou who couldst laugh where Want enchained Caprice,
Toil crushed Conceit, and man was of a piece;
Where Wealth unloved without a mourner died;
And scarce a sycophant was fed by Pride;
Where ne'er was known the form of mock debate,
Or seen a new-made mayor's unwieldy state;[3]
Where change of favorites made no change of laws,

1. I.e., the Tower of London, which served as a prison. Johnson first wrote "bonny traitor," recalling the Jacobite uprising of 1745 and the execution of four of its Scot leaders.

2. A Greek philosopher of the late 5th century B.C.E., remembered as the "laughing philosopher" because men's follies only moved him to mirth.

3. Pomp. Mayors organized costly processions.

And senates heard before they judged a cause;
How wouldst thou shake at Britain's modish tribe,
Dart the quick taunt, and edge the piercing gibe?
Attentive truth and nature to descry,
And pierce each scene with philosophic eye.
To thee were solemn toys or empty show
The robes of pleasure and the veils of woe:
All aid the farce, and all thy mirth maintain,
Whose joys are causeless, or whose griefs are vain.
   Such was the scorn that filled the sage's mind,
Renewed at every glance on human kind;
How just that scorn ere yet thy voice declare,
Search every state, and canvass every prayer.
   Unnumbered suppliants crowd Preferment's gate,
Athirst for wealth, and burning to be great;
Delusive Fortune hears the incessant call,
They mount, they shine, evaporate,[4] and fall.
On every stage the foes of peace attend,
Hate dogs their flight, and Insult mocks their end.
Love ends with hope, the sinking statesman's door
Pours in the morning worshiper no more;[5]
For growing names the weekly scribbler lies,
To growing wealth the dedicator flies;
From every room descends the painted face,
That hung the bright palladium[6] of the place;
And smoked in kitchens, or in auctions sold,
To better features yields the frame of gold;
For now no more we trace in every line
Heroic worth, benevolence divine:
The form distorted justifies the fall,
And Detestation rids the indignant wall.
   But will not Britain hear the last appeal,
Sign her foes' doom, or guard her favorites' zeal?
Through Freedom's sons no more remonstrance rings,
Degrading nobles and controlling kings;
Our supple tribes repress their patriot throats,
And ask no questions but the price of votes;
With weekly libels and septennial ale,[7]
Their wish is full to riot and to rail.
   In full-blown dignity, see Wolsey[8] stand,
Law in his voice, and fortune in his hand:
To him the church, the realm, their powers consign,
Through him the rays of regal bounty shine;
Turned by his nod the stream of honor flows,
His smile alone security bestows:

4. Disperse in vapors, like fireworks.
5. Statesmen gave interviews and received friends and petitioners at levees, or morning receptions.
6. An image of Pallas Athena, that fell from heaven and was preserved at Troy. Not until it was stolen by Diomedes could the city fall to the Greeks.
7. Ministers and even the king freely bought support by bribing members of Parliament, who in turn won elections by buying votes. "Weekly libels": politically motivated lampoons published in the weekly newspapers. "Septennial ale": the ale given away by candidates at parliamentary elections, held at least every seven years.
8. Thomas Cardinal Wolsey (ca. 1475–1530), lord chancellor and favorite of Henry VIII. Shakespeare dramatized his fall in *Henry VIII*.

Still to new heights his restless wishes tower,
Claim leads to claim, and power advances power;
Till conquest unresisted ceased to please,
And rights submitted, left him none to seize.
At length his sovereign frowns—the train of state
Mark the keen glance, and watch the sign to hate.
Where'er he turns, he meets a stranger's eye,
His suppliants scorn him, and his followers fly;
At once is lost the pride of awful state,
The golden canopy, the glittering plate,
The regal palace, the luxurious board,
The liveried army, and the menial lord.
With age, with cares, with maladies oppressed,
He seeks the refuge of monastic rest.
Grief aids disease, remembered folly stings,
And his last sighs reproach the faith of kings.
  Speak thou, whose thoughts at humble peace repine,
Shall Wolsey's wealth, with Wolsey's end be thine?
Or liv'st thou now, with safer pride content,
The wisest justice on the banks of Trent?
For why did Wolsey, near the steeps of fate,
On weak foundations raise the enormous weight?
Why but to sink beneath misfortune's blow,
With louder ruin to the gulfs below?
  What gave great Villiers[9] to the assassin's knife,
And fixed disease on Harley's closing life?
What murdered Wentworth, and what exiled Hyde,
By kings protected, and to kings allied?
What but their wish indulged in courts to shine,
And power too great to keep or to resign?
  When first the college rolls receive his name,
The young enthusiast quits his ease for fame;
Through all his veins the fever of renown
Burns from the strong contagion of the gown:[1]
O'er Bodley's dome his future labors spread,
And Bacon's[2] mansion trembles o'er his head.
Are these thy views? proceed, illustrious youth,
And Virtue guard thee to the throne of Truth!
Yet should thy soul indulge the generous heat,
Till captive Science° yields her last retreat; *knowledge*
Should Reason guide thee with her brightest ray,
And pour on misty Doubt resistless day;
Should no false kindness lure to loose delight,
Nor praise relax, nor difficulty fright;

9. George Villiers, first Duke of Buckingham, favorite of James I and Charles I, was assassinated in 1628. Mentioned in the following lines: Robert Harley, Earl of Oxford, chancellor of the exchequer and later lord treasurer under Queen Anne (1710–14), impeached and imprisoned by the Whigs in 1715. Thomas Wentworth, Earl of Strafford, intimate and adviser of Charles I, impeached by the Long Parliament and executed in 1641. Edward Hyde, Earl of Clarendon ("to kings allied" because his daughter married James, duke of York), lord chancellor under Charles II (impeached in 1667, he fled to the Continent).

1. Academic robe; here associated with the poisoned shirt that tormented Hercules.

2. Roger Bacon (ca. 1214–1294), scientist and philosopher, taught at Oxford, where his study, according to tradition, would collapse if a man greater than he should appear at Oxford. "Bodley's dome": the Bodleian Library, Oxford.

Should tempting Novelty thy cell refrain,
And Sloth effuse her opiate fumes in vain;
Should Beauty blunt on fops her fatal dart,
Nor claim the triumph of a lettered heart;
Should no disease thy torpid veins invade,
Nor Melancholy's phantoms haunt thy shade;
Yet hope not life from grief or danger free,
Nor think the doom of man reversed for thee:
Deign on the passing world to turn thine eyes,
And pause a while from letters, to be wise;
There mark what ills the scholar's life assail,
Toil, envy, want, the patron,[3] and the jail.
See nations slowly wise, and meanly just,
To buried merit raise the tardy bust.
If dreams yet flatter, once again attend,
Hear Lydiat's life, and Galileo's[4] end.
   Nor deem, when Learning her last prize bestows,
The glittering eminence exempt from foes;
See when the vulgar 'scapes, despised or awed,
Rebellion's vengeful talons seize on Laud.[5]
From meaner minds, though smaller fines content,
The plundered palace or sequestered rent;[6]
Marked out by dangerous parts° he meets the shock, *accomplishments*
And fatal Learning leads him to the block:
Around his tomb let Art and Genius weep,
But hear his death, ye blockheads, hear and sleep.
   The festal blazes, the triumphal show,
The ravished standard, and the captive foe,
The senate's thanks, the gazette's pompous tale,
With force resistless o'er the brave prevail.
Such bribes the rapid Greek° o'er Asia whirled, *Alexander the Great*
For such the steady Romans shook the world;
For such in distant lands the Britons shine,
And stain with blood the Danube or the Rhine;
This power has praise that virtue scarce can warm,
Till fame supplies the universal charm.
Yet Reason frowns on War's unequal game,
Where wasted nations raise a single name,
And mortgaged states their grandsires' wreaths regret
From age to age in everlasting debt;
Wreaths which at last the dear-bought right convey
To rust on medals, or on stones decay.
   On what foundation stands the warrior's pride?
How just his hopes, let Swedish Charles[7] decide;

3. In the first edition, "garret." For the reason of the change see Boswell's *Life of Johnson* (p. 2781).
4. Famous astronomer (1564–1642) who was imprisoned as a heretic by the Inquisition in 1633; he died blind. Thomas Lydiat (1572–1646), Oxford scholar, died impoverished because of his Royalist sympathies.
5. Appointed archbishop of Canterbury by Charles I, William Laud followed rigorously High Church policies and was executed by order of the Long Parliament in 1645.
6. During the Commonwealth, the estates of many Royalists were pillaged and their incomes confiscated ("sequestered") by the state.
7. Charles XII of Sweden (1682–1718). Defeated by the Russians at Pultowa (1709), he escaped to Turkey and tried to form an alliance against Russia with the sultan. Returning to Sweden, he attacked Norway and was killed in the attack on Fredrikshald.

A frame of adamant, a soul of fire,
No dangers fright him, and no labors tire;
O'er love, o'er fear, extends his wide domain,
Unconquered lord of pleasure and of pain;
No joys to him pacific scepters yield,
War sounds the trump, he rushes to the field;
Behold surrounding kings their powers combine,
And one capitulate, and one resign;[8]
Peace courts his hand, but spreads her charms in vain;
"Think nothing gained," he cries, "till naught remain,
On Moscow's walls till Gothic standards fly,
And all be mine beneath the polar sky."
The march begins in military state,
And nations on his eye suspended wait;
Stern Famine guards the solitary coast,
And Winter barricades the realms of Frost;
He comes, nor want nor cold his course delay—
Hide, blushing Glory, hide Pultowa's day:
The vanquished hero leaves his broken bands,
And shows his miseries in distant lands;
Condemned a needy supplicant to wait,
While ladies interpose, and slaves debate.
But did not Chance at length her error mend?
Did no subverted empire mark his end?
Did rival monarchs give the fatal wound?
Or hostile millions press him to the ground?
His fall was destined to a barren strand,
A petty fortress, and a dubious hand;[9]
He left the name at which the world grew pale,
To point a moral, or adorn a tale.

All times their scenes of pompous woes afford,
From Persia's tyrant to Bavaria's lord.[1]
In gay hostility, and barbarous pride,
With half mankind embattled at his side,
Great Xerxes comes to seize the certain prey,
And starves exhausted regions in his way;
Attendant Flattery counts his myriads o'er,
Till counted myriads soothe his pride no more;
Fresh praise is tried till madness fires his mind,
The waves he lashes, and enchains the wind;[2]
New powers are claimed, new powers are still bestowed,
Till rude resistance lops the spreading god;
The daring Greeks deride the martial show,
And heap their valleys with the gaudy foe;
The insulted sea with humbler thoughts he gains,
A single skiff to speed his flight remains;
The encumbered oar scarce leaves the dreaded coast

8. Frederick IV of Denmark capitulated to Charles in 1700. Augustus II of Poland resigned his throne to Charles in 1704.

9. It was disputed whether Charles was shot by the enemy or by his own aide-de-camp.

1. The Elector Charles Albert caused the War of the Austrian Succession (1740–48) when he contested the crown of the empire with Maria Theresa ("Fair Austria" in line 245). "Persia's tyrant": Xerxes invaded Greece and was totally defeated in the sea battle off Salamis, 480 B.C.E.

2. When storms destroyed Xerxes' boats, he commanded his men to punish the wind and sea.

Through purple billows and a floating host.
The bold Bavarian, in a luckless hour,
Tries the dread summits of Caesarean power,
With unexpected legions bursts away,
And sees defenseless realms receive his sway;
Short sway! fair Austria spreads her mournful charms,
The queen, the beauty, sets the world in arms;
From hill to hill the beacon's rousing blaze
Spreads wide the hope of plunder and of praise;
The fierce Croatian, and the wild Hussar,[3]
With all the sons of ravage crowd the war;
The baffled prince in honor's flattering bloom
Of hasty greatness finds the fatal doom,
His foes' derision, and his subjects' blame,
And steals to death from anguish and from shame.
Enlarge my life with multitude of days!
In health, in sickness, thus the suppliant prays;
Hides from himself his state, and shuns to know,
That life protracted is protracted woe.
Time hovers o'er, impatient to destroy,
And shuts up all the passages of joy;
In vain their gifts the bounteous seasons pour,
The fruit autumnal, and the vernal flower;
With listless eyes the dotard views the store,
He views, and wonders that they please no more;
Now pall the tasteless meats, and joyless wines,
And Luxury with sighs her slave resigns.
Approach, ye minstrels, try the soothing strain,
Diffuse the tuneful lenitives of pain:° *painkillers*
No sounds, alas! would touch the impervious ear,
Though dancing mountains witnessed Orpheus[4] near;
Nor lute nor lyre his feeble powers attend,
Nor sweeter music of a virtuous friend,
But everlasting dictates crowd his tongue,
Perversely grave, or positively wrong.
The still returning tale, and lingering jest,
Perplex the fawning niece and pampered guest,
While growing hopes scarce awe the gathering sneer,
And scarce a legacy can bribe to hear;
The watchful guests still hint the last offense,
The daughter's petulance, the son's expense,
Improve° his heady rage with treacherous skill, *increase*
And mold his passions till they make his will.
Unnumbered maladies his joints invade,
Lay siege to life and press the dire blockade;
But unextinguished avarice still remains,
And dreaded losses aggravate his pains;
He turns, with anxious heart and crippled hands,
His bonds of debt, and mortgages of lands;
Or views his coffers with suspicious eyes,

3. Hungarian light cavalry.
4. A legendary poet who played on the lyre so beautifully that even stones were moved.

Unlocks his gold, and counts it till he dies.
  But grant, the virtues of a temperate prime
Bless with an age exempt from scorn or crime;
An age that melts with unperceived decay,
And glides in modest innocence away;
Whose peaceful day Benevolence endears,
Whose night congratulating Conscience cheers;
The general favorite as the general friend:
Such age there is, and who shall wish its end?
  Yet even on this her load Misfortune flings,
To press the weary minutes' flagging wings;
New sorrow rises as the day returns,
A sister sickens, or a daughter mourns.
Now kindred Merit fills the sable bier,
Now lacerated Friendship claims a tear;
Year chases year, decay pursues decay,
Still drops some joy from withering life away;
New forms arise, and different views engage,
Superfluous lags the veteran[5] on the stage,
Till pitying Nature signs the last release,
And bids afflicted Worth retire to peace.
  But few there are whom hours like these await,
Who set unclouded in the gulfs of Fate.
From Lydia's monarch[6] should the search descend,
By Solon cautioned to regard his end,
In life's last scene what prodigies surprise,
Fears of the brave, and follies of the wise!
From Marlborough's eyes the streams of dotage flow,
And Swift[7] expires a driveler and a show.
  The teeming mother, anxious for her race,° *family*
Begs for each birth the fortune of a face:
Yet Vane could tell what ills from beauty spring;
And Sedley[8] cursed the form that pleased a king.
Ye nymphs of rosy lips and radiant eyes,
Whom Pleasure keeps too busy to be wise,
Whom Joys with soft varieties invite,
By day the frolic, and the dance by night;
Who frown with vanity, who smile with art,
And ask the latest fashion of the heart;
What care, what rules your heedless charms shall save,
Each nymph your rival, and each youth your slave?
Against your fame with Fondness Hate combines,
The rival batters, and the lover mines.[9]
With distant voice neglected Virtue calls,
Less heard and less, the faint remonstrance falls;
Tired with contempt, she quits the slippery reign,

5. I.e., of life, not of war.
6. Croesus, the wealthy and fortunate king, was warned by Solon not to count himself happy until he ceased to live. He lost his crown to Cyrus the Great of Persia.
7. Jonathan Swift, who passed the last four years of his life in utter senility. John Churchill, Duke of Marlborough, England's brilliant general during most of the War of the Spanish Succession (1702–13).
8. Catherine Sedley, mistress of James II. Anne Vane, mistress of Frederick, Prince of Wales (son of George II).
9. Plants mines beneath, as in the siege of a fortress.

And Pride and Prudence take her seat in vain.
In crowd at once, where none the pass defend,
The harmless freedom, and the private friend.
The guardians yield, by force superior plied:
To Interest, Prudence; and to Flattery, Pride.
Now Beauty falls betrayed, despised, distressed,
And hissing Infamy proclaims the rest.
  Where then shall Hope and Fear their objects find?
Must dull Suspense° corrupt the stagnant mind? *uncertainty*
Must helpless man, in ignorance sedate,
Roll darkling down the torrent of his fate?
Must no dislike alarm, no wishes rise,
No cries invoke the mercies of the skies?
Inquirer, cease; petitions yet remain,
Which Heaven may hear, nor deem religion vain.
Still raise for good the supplicating voice,
But leave to Heaven the measure and the choice.
Safe in his power, whose eyes discern afar
The secret ambush of a specious prayer.
Implore his aid, in his decisions rest,
Secure, whate'er he gives, he gives the best.
Yet when the sense of sacred presence fires,
And strong devotion to the skies aspires,
Pour forth thy fervors for a healthful mind,
Obedient passions, and a will resigned;
For love, which scarce collective man can fill;[1]
For patience sovereign o'er transmuted ill;
For faith, that panting for a happier seat,
Counts death kind Nature's signal of retreat:
These goods for man the laws of Heaven ordain,
These goods he grants, who grants the power to gain;
With these celestial Wisdom calms the mind,
And makes the happiness she does not find.

1749

On the Death of Dr. Robert Levet[1]

Condemned to Hope's delusive mine,
  As on we toil from day to day,
By sudden blasts, or slow decline,
  Our social comforts drop away.

Well tried through many a varying year,
  See Levet to the grave descend;
Officious,[2] innocent, sincere,
  Of every friendless name the friend.

1. Which humankind as a whole can hardly overtask.

1. An unlicensed physician who lived in Johnson's house for many years and who died in 1782. His practice was among the very poor. Boswell wrote: "He was of a strange grotesque appearance, stiff and formal in his manner, and seldom said a word while any company was present."

2. "Kind, doing good offices" (Johnson's *Dictionary*).

Yet still he fills Affection's eye,
Obscurely wise, and coarsely kind;
Nor, lettered Arrogance, deny
Thy praise to merit unrefined.

When fainting Nature called for aid,
And hovering Death prepared the blow,
His vigorous remedy displayed
The power of art without the show.

In Misery's darkest caverns known,
His useful care was ever nigh,
Where hopeless Anguish poured his groan,
And lonely Want retired to die.

No summons mocked by chill delay,
No petty gain disdained by pride,
The modest wants of every day
The toil of every day supplied.

His virtues walked their narrow round,
Nor made a pause, nor left a void;
And sure the Eternal Master found
The single talent well employed.[3]

The busy day, the peaceful night,
Unfelt, uncounted, glided by;
His frame was firm, his powers were bright,
Though now his eightieth year was nigh.

Then with no throbbing fiery pain,
No cold gradations of decay,
Death broke at once the vital chain,
And freed his soul the nearest way.

1783

Rasselas Johnson wrote *Rasselas* in January 1759 during the evenings of one week, a remarkable instance of his ability to write rapidly and brilliantly under the pressure of necessity. His mother lay dying in Lichfield. Her son, famous for his *Dictionary,* was nonetheless oppressed by poverty and in great need of ready money with which to make her last days comfortable, pay her funeral expenses, and settle her small debts. He was paid £100 for the first edition of *Rasselas,* but not in time to attend her deathbed or her funeral.

Rasselas is a philosophical fable cast in the popular form of an Oriental tale, a type of fiction that owed its popularity to the vogue of the *Arabian Nights,* first translated into English in the early eighteenth century. Because the work is a fable, we should not approach it as a novel: psychologically credible characters and a series of intricately involved actions that lead to a necessary resolution and conclusion are not to be found in *Rasselas.* Instead we are meant to reflect on the ideas and to savor the

3. In the parable of the talents (Matthew 25.14–30), Jesus suggests that salvation will be granted to those who make good use of their abilities, however small.

melancholy resonance and intelligence of the stately prose that expresses them. Johnson arranges the incidents of the fable to test a variety of possible solutions to a problem: What choice of life will bring us happiness? (*The Choice of Life* was his working title for the book.) Many ways of life are examined in turn, and each is found wanting. Johnson does not pretend to have solved the problem. Rather, he locates the sources of discontent in a basic principle of human nature: the "hunger of imagination which preys incessantly upon life" (chapter 32) and which lures us to "listen with credulity to the whispers of fancy and pursue with eagerness the phantoms of hope" (chapter 1). The tale is a gentle satire on one of the perennial topics of satirists: the folly of all of us who stubbornly cling to our illusions despite the evidence of experience. *Rasselas* is not all darkness and gloom, for Johnson's theme invites comic as well as tragic treatment, and some of the episodes evoke that laughter of the mind that is the effect of high comedy. In its main theme, however—the folly of cherishing the dream of ever attaining unalloyed happiness in a world that can never wholly satisfy our desires—and in many of the sayings of its characters, especially of the sage Imlac, *Rasselas* expresses some of Johnson's own deepest convictions.

The History of Rasselas, Prince of Abyssinia

Chapter 1. Description of a Palace in a Valley

Ye who listen with credulity to the whispers of fancy, and pursue with eagerness the phantoms of hope; who expect that age will perform the promises of youth, and that the deficiencies of the present day will be supplied by the morrow—attend to the history of Rasselas, prince of Abyssinia.

Rasselas was the fourth son of the mighty emperor in whose dominions the Father of Waters[1] begins his course; whose bounty pours down the streams of plenty, and scatters over half the world the harvests of Egypt.

According to the custom which has descended from age to age among the monarchs of the torrid zone, Rasselas was confined in a private palace, with the other sons and daughters of Abyssinian royalty, till the order of succession should call him to the throne.

The place which the wisdom or policy of antiquity had destined for the residence of the Abyssinian princes was a spacious valley[2] in the kingdom of Amhara, surrounded on every side by mountains, of which the summits overhang the middle part. The only passage by which it could be entered was a cavern that passed under a rock, of which it has long been disputed whether it was the work of nature or of human industry. The outlet of the cavern was concealed by a thick wood, and the mouth which opened into the valley was closed with gates of iron, forged by the artificers of ancient days, so massy that no man could, without the help of engines, open or shut them.

From the mountains on every side rivulets descended that filled all the valley with verdure and fertility, and formed a lake in the middle, inhabited by fish of every species, and frequented by every fowl whom nature has taught to dip the wing in water. This lake discharged its superfluities by a stream, which entered a dark cleft of the mountain on the northern side, and fell with dreadful noise from precipice to precipice till it was heard no more.

The sides of the mountains were covered with trees, the banks of the brooks were diversified with flowers; every blast[3] shook spices from the rocks, and

1. The Nile.
2. Johnson had read of the Happy Valley in the Portuguese Jesuit Father Lobo's book on Abyssinia, which he translated in 1735. This description also owes something to the description of the Garden in *Paradise Lost* 4, and Coleridge's "Kubla Khan" may owe something to it.
3. "A gust or puff of wind" (Johnson's *Dictionary*).

every month dropped fruits upon the ground. All animals that bite the grass, or browse the shrub, whether wild or tame, wandered in this extensive circuit, secured from beasts of prey by the mountains which confined them. On one part were flocks and herds feeding in the pastures, on another all the beasts of chase frisking in the lawns; the sprightly kid was bounding on the rocks, the subtle monkey frolicking in the trees, and the solemn elephant reposing in the shade. All the diversities of the world were brought together, the blessings of nature were collected, and its evils extracted and excluded.

The valley, wide and fruitful, supplied its inhabitants with the necessaries of life, and all delights and superfluities were added at the annual visit which the emperor paid his children, when the iron gate was opened to the sound of music, and during eight days everyone that resided in the valley was required to propose whatever might contribute to make seclusion pleasant, to fill up the vacancies of attention, and lessen the tediousness of time. Every desire was immediately granted. All the artificers of pleasure were called to gladden the festivity; the musicians exerted the power of harmony, and the dancers showed their activity before the princes, in hope that they should pass their lives in this blissful captivity, to which those only were admitted whose performance was thought able to add novelty to luxury. Such was the appearance of security and delight which this retirement afforded, that they to whom it was new always desired that it might be perpetual; and as those on whom the iron gate had once closed were never suffered to return, the effect of longer experience could not be known. Thus every year produced new schemes of delight and new competitors for imprisonment.

The palace stood on an eminence, raised about thirty paces[4] above the surface of the lake. It was divided into many squares or courts, built with greater or less magnificence according to the rank of those for whom they were designed. The roofs were turned into arches of massy stone, joined with a cement that grew harder by time, and the building stood from century to century, deriding the solstitial rains and equinoctial hurricanes, without need of reparation.

This house, which was so large as to be fully known to none but some ancient officers, who successively inherited the secrets of the place, was built as if suspicion herself had dictated the plan. To every room there was an open and secret passage; every square had a communication with the rest, either from the upper stories by private galleries, or by subterranean passages from the lower apartments. Many of the columns had unsuspected cavities, in which a long race of monarchs had reposited their treasures. They then closed up the opening with marble, which was never to be removed but in the utmost exigencies of the kingdom, and recorded their accumulations in a book, which was itself concealed in a tower, not entered but by the emperor, attended by the prince who stood next in succession.

Chapter 2. The Discontent of Rasselas in the Happy Valley

Here the sons and daughters of Abyssinia lived only to know the soft vicissitudes of pleasure and repose, attended by all that were skillful to delight, and gratified with whatever the senses can enjoy. They wandered in gardens of fragrance, and slept in the fortresses of security. Every art was practiced to make them pleased with their own condition. The sages who instructed them

4. About 150 feet.

told them of nothing but the miseries of public life, and described all beyond the mountains as regions of calamity, where discord was always raging, and where man preyed upon man.

To heighten their opinion of their own felicity, they were daily entertained with songs, the subject of which was the *happy valley*. Their appetites were excited by frequent enumerations of different enjoyments, and revelry and merriment was the business of every hour, from the dawn of morning to the close of even.

These methods were generally successful; few of the princes had ever wished to enlarge their bounds, but passed their lives in full conviction that they had all within their reach that art or nature could bestow, and pitied those whom fate had excluded from this seat of tranquility, as the sport of chance and the slaves of misery.

Thus they rose in the morning and lay down at night, pleased with each other and with themselves; all but Rasselas, who, in the twenty-sixth year of his age, began to withdraw himself from their pastimes and assemblies, and to delight in solitary walks and silent meditation. He often sat before tables covered with luxury, and forgot to taste the dainties that were placed before him; he rose abruptly in the midst of the song, and hastily retired beyond the sound of music. His attendants observed the change, and endeavored to renew his love of pleasure. He neglected their officiousness, repulsed their invitations, and spent day after day on the banks of rivulets sheltered with trees, where he sometimes listened to the birds in the branches, sometimes observed the fish playing in the stream, and anon cast his eyes upon the pastures and mountains filled with animals, of which some were biting the herbage, and some sleeping among the bushes.

This singularity of his humor made him much observed. One of the sages, in whose conversation he had formerly delighted, followed him secretly, in hope of discovering the cause of his disquiet. Rasselas, who knew not that anyone was near him, having for some time fixed his eyes upon the goats that were browsing among the rocks, began to compare their condition with his own.

"What," said he, "makes the difference between man and all the rest of the animal creation? Every beast that strays beside me has the same corporal necessities with myself; he is hungry, and crops the grass, he is thirsty, and drinks the stream, his thirst and hunger are appeased, he is satisfied, and sleeps; he rises again, and he is hungry, he is again fed, and is at rest. I am hungry and thirsty like him, but when thirst and hunger cease, I am not at rest; I am, like him, pained with want, but am not, like him, satisfied with fullness. The intermediate hours are tedious and gloomy; I long again to be hungry that I may again quicken my attention. The birds peck the berries or the corn, and fly away to the groves, where they sit in seeming happiness on the branches, and waste their lives in tuning one unvaried series of sounds. I likewise can call the lutanist and the singer, but the sounds that pleased me yesterday weary me today, and will grow yet more wearisome tomorrow. I can discover within me no power of perception which is not glutted with its proper pleasure, yet I do not feel myself delighted. Man has surely some latent sense for which this place affords no gratification, or he has some desires distinct from sense, which must be satisfied before he can be happy."

After this he lifted up his head, and seeing the moon rising, walked towards the palace. As he passed through the fields, and saw the animals around him,

"Ye," said he, "are happy, and need not envy me that walk thus among you, burthened with myself; nor do I, ye gentle beings, envy your felicity, for it is not the felicity of man. I have many distresses from which ye are free; I fear pain when I do not feel it; I sometimes shrink at evils recollected, and sometimes start at evils anticipated. Surely the equity of Providence has balanced peculiar sufferings with peculiar enjoyments."

With observations like these the prince amused himself as he returned, uttering them with a plaintive voice, yet with a look that discovered[5] him to feel some complacence in his own perspicacity, and to receive some solace of the miseries of life from consciousness of the delicacy with which he felt, and the eloquence with which he bewailed them. He mingled cheerfully in the diversions of the evening, and all rejoiced to find that his heart was lightened.

Chapter 3. The Wants of Him That Wants Nothing

On the next day his old instructor, imagining that he had now made himself acquainted with his disease of mind, was in the hope of curing it by counsel, and officiously sought an opportunity of conference, which the prince, having long considered him as one whose intellects were exhausted, was not very willing to afford. "Why," said he, "does this man thus intrude upon me; shall I be never suffered to forget those lectures which pleased only while they were new, and to become new again must be forgotten?" He then walked into the wood, and composed himself to his usual meditations; when, before his thoughts had taken any settled form, he perceived his pursuer at his side, and was at first prompted by his impatience to go hastily away; but, being unwilling to offend a man whom he had once reverenced and still loved, he invited him to sit down with him on the bank.

The old man, thus encouraged, began to lament the change which had been lately observed in the prince, and to inquire why he so often retired from the pleasures of the palace, to loneliness and silence. "I fly from pleasure," said the prince, "because pleasure has ceased to please; I am lonely because I am miserable, and am unwilling to cloud with my presence the happiness of others." "You, sir," said the sage, "are the first who has complained of misery in the *happy valley*. I hope to convince you that your complaints have no real cause. You are here in full possession of all that the emperor of Abyssinia can bestow; here is neither labor to be endured nor danger to be dreaded, yet here is all that labor or danger can procure or purchase. Look round and tell me which of your wants is without supply; if you want nothing, how are you unhappy?"

"That I want nothing," said the prince, "or that I know not what I want, is the cause of my complaint; if I had any known want, I should have a certain wish; that wish would excite endeavor, and I should not then repine to see the sun move so slowly towards the western mountain, or lament when the day breaks, and sleep will no longer hide me from myself. When I see the kids and the lambs chasing one another, I fancy that I should be happy if I had something to pursue. But, possessing all that I can want, I find one day and one hour exactly like another, except that the latter is still more tedious than the former. Let your experience inform me how the day may now seem as short as in my childhood, while nature was yet fresh and every moment showed me

5. Showed.

what I never had observed before. I have already enjoyed too much; give me something to desire."

The old man was surprised at this new species of affliction and knew not what to reply, yet was unwilling to be silent. "Sir," said he, "if you had seen the miseries of the world you would know how to value your present state." "Now," said the prince, "you have given me something to desire. I shall long to see the miseries of the world, since the sight of them is necessary to happiness."

Chapter 4. The Prince Continues to Grieve and Muse

At this time the sound of music proclaimed the hour of repast, and the conversation was concluded. The old man went away sufficiently discontented to find that his reasonings had produced the only conclusion which they were intended to prevent. But in the decline of life shame and grief are of short duration; whether it be that we bear easily what we have born long, or that, finding ourselves in age less regarded, we less regard others; or, that we look with slight regard upon afflictions, to which we know that the hand of death is about to put an end.

The prince, whose views were extended to a wider space, could not speedily quiet his emotions. He had been before terrified at the length of life which nature promised him, because he considered that in a long time much must be endured; he now rejoiced in his youth, because in many years much might be done.

This first beam of hope, that had been ever darted into his mind, rekindled youth in his cheeks, and doubled the luster of his eyes. He was fired with the desire of doing something, though he knew not yet with distinctness, either end or means.

He was now no longer gloomy and unsocial; but, considering himself as master of a secret stock of happiness, which he could enjoy only by concealing it, he affected to be busy in all schemes of diversion, and endeavored to make others pleased with the state of which he himself was weary. But pleasures never can be so multiplied or continued, as not to leave much of life unemployed; there were many hours, both of the night and day, which he could spend without suspicion in solitary thought. The load of life was much lightened: he went eagerly into the assemblies, because he supposed the frequency of his presence necessary to the success of his purposes; he retired gladly to privacy, because he had now a subject of thought.

His chief amusement was to picture to himself that world which he had never seen; to place himself in various conditions; to be entangled in imaginary difficulties, and to be engaged in wild adventures: but his benevolence always terminated his projects in the relief of distress, the detection of fraud, the defeat of oppression, and the diffusion of happiness.

Thus passed twenty months of the life of Rasselas. He busied himself so intensely in visionary bustle, that he forgot his real solitude; and, amidst hourly preparations for the various incidents of human affairs, neglected to consider by what means he should mingle with mankind.

One day, as he was sitting on a bank, he feigned to himself an orphan virgin robbed of her little portion[6] by a treacherous lover, and crying after him for

6. Money or goods.

restitution and redress. So strongly was the image impressed upon his mind, that he started up in the maid's defense, and ran forward to seize the plunderer with all the eagerness of real pursuit. Fear naturally quickens the flight of guilt. Rasselas could not catch the fugitive with his utmost efforts; but, resolving to weary, by perseverance, him whom he could not surpass in speed, he pressed on till the foot of the mountain stopped his course.

Here he recollected himself, and smiled at his own useless impetuosity. Then raising his eyes to the mountain, "This," said he, "is the fatal obstacle that hinders at once the enjoyment of pleasure, and the exercise of virtue. How long is it that my hopes and wishes have flown beyond this boundary of my life, which yet I never have attempted to surmount!"

Struck with this reflection, he sat down to muse, and remembered, that since he first resolved to escape from his confinement, the sun had passed twice over him in his annual course. He now felt a degree of regret with which he had never been before acquainted. He considered how much might have been done in the time which had passed, and left nothing real behind it. He compared twenty months with the life of man. "In life," said he, "is not to be counted the ignorance of infancy, or imbecility[7] of age. We are long before we are able to think, and we soon cease from the power of acting. The true period of human existence may be reasonably estimated as forty years, of which I have mused away the four and twentieth part. What I have lost was certain, for I have certainly possessed it; but of twenty months to come who can assure me?"

The consciousness of his own folly pierced him deeply, and he was long before he could be reconciled to himself. "The rest of my time," said he, "has been lost by the crime or folly of my ancestors, and the absurd institutions of my country; I remember it with disgust, yet without remorse: but the months that have passed since new light darted into my soul, since I formed a scheme of reasonable felicity, have been squandered by my own fault. I have lost that which can never be restored: I have seen the sun rise and set for twenty months, an idle gazer on the light of heaven. In this time the birds have left the nest of their mother, and committed themselves to the woods and to the skies: the kid has forsaken the teat, and learned by degrees to climb the rocks in quest of independent sustenance. I only have made no advances, but am still helpless and ignorant. The moon, by more than twenty changes, admonished me of the flux of life; the stream that rolled before my feet upbraided my inactivity. I sat feasting on intellectual luxury, regardless alike of the examples of the earth, and the instructions of the planets. Twenty months are past, who shall restore them!"

These sorrowful meditations fastened upon his mind; he passed four months in resolving to lose no more time in idle resolves, and was awakened to more vigorous exertion by hearing a maid, who had broken a porcelain cup, remark that what cannot be repaired is not to be regretted.

This was obvious; and Rasselas reproached himself that he had not discovered it, having not known, or not considered, how many useful hints are obtained by chance, and how often the mind, hurried by her own ardor to distant views, neglects the truths that lie open before her. He, for a few hours, regretted his regret, and from that time bent his whole mind upon the means of escaping from the valley of happiness.

7. Weakness.

Chapter 5. The Prince Meditates His Escape

He now found that it would be very difficult to effect that which it was very easy to suppose effected. When he looked round about him, he saw himself confined by the bars of nature which had never yet been broken, and by the gate, through which none that once had passed it were ever able to return. He was now impatient as an eagle in a grate.[8] He passed week after week in clambering the mountains, to see if there was any aperture which the bushes might conceal, but found all the summits inaccessible by their prominence. The iron gate he despaired to open; for it was not only secured with all the power of art, but was always watched by successive sentinels, and was by its position exposed to the perpetual observation of all the inhabitants.

He then examined the cavern through which the waters of the lake were discharged; and, looking down at a time when the sun shone strongly upon its mouth, he discovered it to be full of broken rocks, which, though they permitted the stream to flow through many narrow passages, would stop any body of solid bulk. He returned discouraged and dejected; but, having now known the blessing of hope, resolved never to despair.

In these fruitless searches he spent ten months. The time, however, passed cheerfully away: in the morning he rose with new hope, in the evening applauded his own diligence, and in the night slept sound after his fatigue. He met a thousand amusements which beguiled his labor, and diversified his thoughts. He discerned the various instincts of animals, and properties of plants, and found the place replete with wonders, of which he purposed to solace himself with the contemplation, if he should never be able to accomplish his flight; rejoicing that his endeavors, though yet unsuccessful, had supplied him with a source of inexhaustible enquiry.

But his original curiosity was not yet abated; he resolved to obtain some knowledge of the ways of men. His wish still continued, but his hope grew less. He ceased to survey any longer the walls of his prison, and spared to search by new toils for interstices which he knew could not be found, yet determined to keep his design always in view, and lay hold on any expedient that time should offer.

Chapter 6. A Dissertation on the Art of Flying

Among the artists that had been allured into the happy valley, to labor for the accommodation and pleasure of its inhabitants, was a man eminent for his knowledge of the mechanic powers, who had contrived many engines[9] both of use and recreation. By a wheel, which the stream turned, he forced the water into a tower, whence it was distributed to all the apartments of the palace. He erected a pavillion in the garden, around which he kept the air always cool by artificial showers. One of the groves appropriated to the ladies, was ventilated by fans, to which the rivulet that run through it gave a constant motion; and instruments of soft music were placed at proper distances, of which some played by the impulse of the wind, and some by the power of the stream.

This artist was sometimes visited by Rasselas, who was pleased with every kind of knowledge, imagining that the time would come when all his acqui-

8. Barred cage.
9. Machines. "Mechanic powers": the forces that cause things to move.

sitions should be of use to him in the open world. He came one day to amuse himself in his usual manner, and found the master busy in building a sailing chariot: he saw that the design was practicable upon a level surface, and with expressions of great esteem solicited its completion. The workman was pleased to find himself so much regarded by the prince, and resolved to gain yet higher honors. "Sir," said he, "you have seen but a small part of what the mechanic sciences can perform. I have been long of opinion, that, instead of the tardy conveyance of ships and chariots, man might use the swifter migration of wings; that the fields of air are open to knowledge, and that only ignorance and idleness need crawl upon the ground."

This hint rekindled the prince's desire of passing the mountains; having seen what the mechanist had already performed, he was willing to fancy that he could do more; yet resolved to inquire further before he suffered hope to afflict him by disappointment. "I am afraid," said he to the artist, "that your imagination prevails over your skill, and that you now tell me rather what you wish than what you know. Every animal has his element assigned him; the birds have the air, and man and beasts the earth." "So," replied the mechanist, "fishes have the water, in which yet beasts can swim by nature, and men by art. He that can swim needs not despair to fly: to swim is to fly in a grosser fluid, and to fly is to swim in a subtler.[1] We are only to proportion our power of resistance to the different density of the matter through which we are to pass. You will be necessarily upborn by the air, if you can renew any impulse upon it, faster than the air can recede from the pressure."

"But the exercise of swimming," said the prince, "is very laborious; the strongest limbs are soon wearied; I am afraid the act of flying will be yet more violent, and wings will be of no great use, unless we can fly further than we can swim."

"The labor of rising from the ground," said the artist, "will be great, as we see it in the heavier domestic fowls; but, as we mount higher, the earth's attraction, and the body's gravity, will be gradually diminished, till we shall arrive at a region where the man will float in the air without any tendency to fall: no care will then be necessary, but to move forwards, which the gentlest impulse will effect. You, Sir, whose curiosity is so extensive, will easily conceive with what pleasure a philosopher, furnished with wings, and hovering in the sky, would see the earth, and all its inhabitants, rolling beneath him, and presenting to him successively, by its diurnal motion, all the countries within the same parallel. How must it amuse the pendent spectator to see the moving scene of land and ocean, cities and deserts! To survey with equal security the marts of trade, and the fields of battle; mountains infested by barbarians, and fruitful regions gladdened by plenty, and lulled by peace! How easily shall we then trace the Nile through all his passage; pass over to distant regions, and examine the face of nature from one extremity of the earth to the other!"

"All this," said the prince, "is much to be desired, but I am afraid that no man will be able to breathe in these regions of speculation and tranquility. I have been told, that respiration is difficult upon lofty mountains, yet from these precipices, though so high as to produce great tenuity of the air, it is very easy to fall: therefore I suspect, that from any height, where life can be supported, there may be danger of too quick descent."

"Nothing," replied the artist, "will ever be attempted, if all possible objec-

1. Thinner.

tions must be first overcome. If you will favor my project I will try the first flight at my own hazard. I have considered the structure of all volant[2] animals, and find the folding continuity of the bat's wings most easily accommodated to the human form. Upon this model I shall begin my task tomorrow, and in a year expect to tower into the air beyond the malice or pursuit of man. But I will work only on this condition, that the art shall not be divulged, and that you shall not require me to make wings for any but ourselves."

"Why," said Rasselas, "should you envy others so great an advantage? All skill ought to be exerted for universal good; every man has owed much to others, and ought to repay the kindness that he has received."

"If men were all virtuous," returned the artist, "I should with great alacrity teach them all to fly. But what would be the security of the good, if the bad could at pleasure invade them from the sky? Against an army sailing through the clouds neither walls, nor mountains, nor seas, could afford any security. A flight of northern savages might hover in the wind, and light at once with irresistible violence upon the capital of a fruitful region that was rolling under them. Even this valley, the retreat of princes, the abode of happiness, might be violated by the sudden descent of some of the naked nations that swarm on the coast of the southern sea."

The prince promised secrecy, and waited for the performance, not wholly hopeless of success. He visited the work from time to time, observed its progress, and remarked many ingenious contrivances to facilitate motion, and unite levity with strength. The artist was every day more certain that he should leave vultures and eagles behind him, and the contagion of his confidence seized upon the prince.

In a year the wings were finished, and, on a morning appointed, the maker appeared furnished for flight on a little promontory: he waved his pinions a while to gather air, then leaped from his stand, and in an instant dropped into the lake. His wings, which were of no use in the air, sustained him in the water, and the prince drew him to land, half dead with terror and vexation.

Chapter 7. The Prince Finds a Man of Learning

The prince was not much afflicted by this disaster, having suffered himself to hope for a happier event, only because he had no other means of escape in view. He still persisted in his design to leave the happy valley by the first opportunity.

His imagination was now at a stand; he had no prospect of entering into the world; and, notwithstanding all his endeavors to support himself, discontent by degrees preyed upon him, and he began again to lose his thoughts in sadness, when the rainy season, which in these countries is periodical, made it inconvenient to wander in the woods.

The rain continued longer and with more violence than had been ever known; the clouds broke on the surrounding mountains, and the torrents streamed into the plain on every side, till the cavern was too narrow to discharge the water. The lake overflowed its banks, and all the level of the valley was covered with the inundation. The eminence, on which the palace was built, and some other spots of rising ground, were all that the eye could now discover. The herds and flocks left the pastures, and both the wild beasts and the tame retreated to the mountains.

2. Able to fly.

This inundation confined all the princes to domestic amusements, and the attention of Rasselas was particularly seized by a poem, which Imlac rehearsed,[3] upon the various conditions of humanity. He commanded the poet to attend him in his apartment, and recite his verses a second time; then entering into familiar talk, he thought himself happy in having found a man who knew the world so well, and could so skillfully paint the scenes of life. He asked a thousand questions about things, to which, though common to all other mortals, his confinement from childhood had kept him a stranger. The poet pitied his ignorance, and loved his curiosity, and entertained him from day to day with novelty and instruction, so that the prince regretted the necessity of sleep, and longed till the morning should renew his pleasure.

As they were sitting together, the prince commanded Imlac to relate his history, and to tell by what accident he was forced, or by what motive induced, to close his life in the happy valley. As he was going to begin his narrative, Rasselas was called to a concert, and obliged to restrain his curiosity till the evening.

Chapter 8. The History of Imlac

The close of the day is, in the regions of the torrid zone, the only season of diversion and entertainment, and it was therefore midnight before the music ceased, and the princesses retired. Rasselas then called for his companion and required him to begin the story of his life.

"Sir," said Imlac, "my history will not be long: the life that is devoted to knowledge passes silently away, and is very little diversified by events. To talk in public, to think in solitude, to read and to hear, to inquire, and answer inquiries, is the business of a scholar. He wanders about the world without pomp or terror, and is neither known nor valued but by men like himself.

"I was born in the kingdom of Goiama, at no great distance from the fountain of the Nile. My father was a wealthy merchant, who traded between the inland countries of Africk and the ports of the red sea. He was honest, frugal and diligent, but of mean sentiments, and narrow comprehension: he desired only to be rich, and to conceal his riches, lest he should be spoiled[4] by the governors of the province."

"Surely," said the prince, "my father must be negligent of his charge, if any man in his dominions dares take that which belongs to another. Does he not know that kings are accountable for injustice permitted as well as done? If I were emperor, not the meanest of my subjects should be oppressed with impunity. My blood boils when I am told that a merchant durst not enjoy his honest gains for fear of losing them by the rapacity of power. Name the governor who robbed the people, that I may declare his crimes to the emperor."

"Sir," said Imlac, "your ardor is the natural effect of virtue animated by youth: the time will come when you will acquit your father, and perhaps hear with less impatience of the governor. Oppression is, in the Abyssinian dominions, neither frequent nor tolerated; but no form of government has been yet discovered, by which cruelty can be wholly prevented. Subordination supposes power on one part and subjection on the other; and if power be in the hands of men, it will sometimes be abused. The vigilance of the supreme magistrate may do much, but much will still remain undone. He can never know all the crimes that are committed, and can seldom punish all that he knows."

3. Recited.

4. Robbed.

"This," said the prince, "I do not understand, but I had rather hear thee than dispute. Continue thy narration."

"My father," proceeded Imlac, "originally intended that I should have no other education, than such as might qualify me for commerce; and discovering in me great strength of memory, and quickness of apprehension, often declared his hope that I should be some time the richest man in Abyssinia."

"Why," said the prince, "did thy father desire the increase of his wealth, when it was already greater than he durst discover or enjoy? I am unwilling to doubt thy veracity, yet inconsistencies cannot both be true."

"Inconsistencies," answered Imlac, "cannot both be right, but, imputed to man, they may both be true. Yet diversity is not inconsistency. My father might expect a time of greater security. However, some desire is necessary to keep life in motion, and he, whose real wants are supplied, must admit those of fancy."

"This," said the prince, "I can in some measure conceive. I repent that I interrupted thee."

"With this hope," proceeded Imlac, "he sent me to school; but when I had once found the delight of knowledge, and felt the pleasure of intelligence[5] and the pride of invention, I began silently to despise riches, and determined to disappoint the purpose of my father, whose grossness of conception raised my pity. I was twenty years old before his tenderness would expose me to the fatigue of travel, in which time I had been instructed, by successive masters, in all the literature of my native country. As every hour taught me something new, I lived in a continual course of gratifications; but, as I advanced towards manhood, I lost much of the reverence with which I had been used to look on my instructors; because, when the lesson was ended, I did not find them wiser or better than common men.

"At length my father resolved to initiate me in commerce, and, opening one of his subterranean treasuries, counted out ten thousand pieces of gold. 'This, young man,' said he, 'is the stock with which you must negotiate.[6] I began with less than the fifth part, and you see how diligence and parsimony have increased it. This is your own to waste or to improve. If you squander it by negligence or caprice, you must wait for my death before you will be rich: if, in four years, you double your stock, we will thenceforward let subordination cease, and live together as friends and partners; for he shall always be equal with me, who is equally skilled in the art of growing rich.'

"We laid our money upon camels, concealed in bales of cheap goods, and travelled to the shore of the Red Sea. When I cast my eye on the expanse of waters my heart bounded like that of a prisoner escaped. I felt an unextinguishable curiosity kindle in my mind, and resolved to snatch this opportunity of seeing the manners of other nations, and of learning sciences unknown in Abyssinia.

"I remembered that my father had obliged me to the improvement of my stock, not by a promise which I ought not to violate, but by a penalty which I was at liberty to incur; and therefore determined to gratify my predominant desire, and by drinking at the fountains of knowledge, to quench the thirst of curiosity.

"As I was supposed to trade without connection with my father, it was easy for me to become acquainted with the master of a ship, and procure a passage to some other country. I had no motives of choice to regulate my voyage; it

5. Information or knowledge.

6. Do business.

was sufficient for me that, wherever I wandered, I should see a country which I had not seen before. I therefore entered a ship bound for Surat,[7] having left a letter for my father declaring my intention.

Chapter 9. The History of Imlac Continued

"When I first entered upon the world of waters, and lost sight of land, I looked round about me with pleasing terror, and thinking my soul enlarged by the boundless prospect, imagined that I could gaze round for ever without satiety; but, in a short time, I grew weary of looking on barren uniformity, where I could only see again what I had already seen. I then descended into the ship, and doubted for a while whether all my future pleasures would not end like this in disgust and disappointment. Yet, surely, said I, the ocean and the land are very different; the only variety of water is rest and motion, but the earth has mountains and valleys, deserts and cities: it is inhabited by men of different customs and contrary opinions; and I may hope to find variety in life, though I should miss it in nature.

"With this thought I quieted my mind; and amused myself during the voyage, sometimes by learning from the sailors the art of navigation, which I have never practiced, and sometimes by forming schemes for my conduct in different situations, in not one of which I have been ever placed.

"I was almost weary of my naval amusements when we landed safely at Surat. I secured my money, and purchasing some commodities for show, joined myself to a caravan that was passing into the inland country. My companions, for some reason or other, conjecturing that I was rich, and, by my inquiries and admiration, finding that I was ignorant, considered me as a novice whom they had a right to cheat, and who was to learn at the usual expense the art of fraud. They exposed me to the theft of servants, and the exaction of officers,[8] and saw me plundered upon false pretences, without any advantage to themselves, but that of rejoicing in the superiority of their own knowledge."

"Stop a moment," said the prince. "Is there such depravity in man, as that he should injure another without benefit to himself? I can easily conceive that all are pleased with superiority; but your ignorance was merely accidental, which, being neither your crime nor your folly, could afford them no reason to applaud themselves; and the knowledge which they had, and which you wanted, they might as effectually have shown by warning, as betraying you."

"Pride," said Imlac, "is seldom delicate, it will please itself with very mean advantages; and envy feels not its own happiness, but when it may be compared with the misery of others. They were my enemies because they grieved to think me rich, and my oppressors because they delighted to find me weak."

"Proceed," said the prince: "I doubt not of the facts which you relate, but imagine that you impute them to mistaken motives."

"In this company," said Imlac, "I arrived at Agra, the capital of Indostan, the city in which the great Mogul commonly resides. I applied myself to the language of the country, and in a few months was able to converse with the learned men; some of whom I found morose and reserved, and others easy and communicative; some were unwilling to teach another what they had with difficulty learned themselves; and some showed that the end of their studies was to gain the dignity of instructing.

"To the tutor of the young princes I recommended myself so much, that I

7. A port in India.

8. Officials or agents.

was presented to the emperor as a man of uncommon knowledge. The emperor asked me many questions concerning my country and my travels; and though I cannot now recollect any thing that he uttered above the power of a common man, he dismissed me astonished at his wisdom, and enamored of his goodness.

"My credit was now so high, that the merchants, with whom I had traveled, applied to me for recommendations to the ladies of the court. I was surprised at their confidence of solicitation, and gently reproached them with their practices on the road. They heard me with cold indifference, and showed no tokens of shame or sorrow.

"They then urged their request with the offer of a bribe; but what I would not do for kindness I would not do for money; and refused them, not because they had injured me, but because I would not enable them to injure others; for I knew they would have made use of my credit to cheat those who should buy their wares.

"Having resided at Agra till there was no more to be learned, I traveled into Persia, where I saw many remains of ancient magnificence, and observed many new accommodations[9] of life. The Persians are a nation eminently social, and their assemblies afforded me daily opportunities of remarking characters and manners, and of tracing human nature through all its variations.

"From Persia I passed into Arabia, where I saw a nation at once pastoral and warlike; who live without any settled habitation; whose only wealth is their flocks and herds; and who have yet carried on, through all ages, an hereditary war with all mankind, though they neither covet nor envy their possessions.

Chapter 10. Imlac's History Continued. A Dissertation upon Poetry

"Wherever I went, I found that poetry was considered as the highest learning, and regarded with a veneration somewhat approaching to that which man would pay to the angelic nature. And yet it fills me with wonder that, in almost all countries, the most ancient poets are considered as the best: whether it be that every other kind of knowledge is an acquisition gradually attained, and poetry is a gift conferred at once; or that the first poetry of every nation surprised them as a novelty, and retained the credit by consent which it received by accident at first; or whether, as the province of poetry is to describe nature and passion, which are always the same, the first writers took possession of the most striking objects for description and the most probable occurrences for fiction, and left nothing to those that followed them, but transcription of the same events, and new combinations of the same images—whatever be the reason, it is commonly observed that the early writers are in possession of nature, and their followers of art; that the first excel in strength and invention, and the latter in elegance and refinement.

"I was desirous to add my name to this illustrious fraternity. I read all the poets of Persia and Arabia, and was able to repeat by memory the volumes that are suspended in the mosque of Mecca.[1] But I soon found that no man was ever great by imitation. My desire of excellence impelled me to transfer

9. "Conveniences, things requisite to ease or refreshment" (Johnson's *Dictionary*).

1. In the 7th century, seven peerless Arabic poems were supposed to have been transcribed in gold and hung up in a mosque.

my attention to nature and to life. Nature was to be my subject, and men to be my auditors: I could never describe what I had not seen; I could not hope to move those with delight or terror, whose interests and opinions I did not understand.

"Being now resolved to be a poet, I saw everything with a new purpose; my sphere of attention was suddenly magnified; no kind of knowledge was to be overlooked. I ranged mountains and deserts for images and resemblances, and pictured upon my mind every tree of the forest and flower of the valley. I observed with equal care the crags of the rock and the pinnacles of the palace. Sometimes I wandered along the mazes of the rivulet, and sometimes watched the changes of the summer clouds. To a poet nothing can be useless. Whatever is beautiful, and whatever is dreadful, must be familiar to his imagination; he must be conversant with all that is awfully[2] vast or elegantly little. The plants of the garden, the animals of the wood, the minerals of the earth, and meteors of the sky, must all concur to store his mind with inexhaustible variety: for every idea[3] is useful for the enforcement or decoration of moral or religious truth; and he who knows most will have most power of diversifying his scenes, and of gratifying his reader with remote allusions and unexpected instruction.

"All the appearances of nature I was therefore careful to study, and every country which I have surveyed has contributed something to my poetical powers."

"In so wide a survey," said the prince, "you must surely have left much unobserved. I have lived till now within the circuit of these mountains, and yet cannot walk abroad without the sight of something which I have never beheld before, or never heeded."

"The business of a poet," said Imlac, "is to examine, not the individual, but the species; to remark general properties and large appearances; he does not number the streaks of the tulip, or describe the different shades in the verdure of the forest. He is to exhibit in his portraits of nature such prominent and striking features as recall the original to every mind, and must neglect the minuter discriminations, which one may have remarked and another have neglected, for those characteristics which are alike obvious to vigilance and carelessness.

"But the knowledge of nature is only half the task of a poet; he must be acquainted likewise with all the modes of life. His character requires that he estimate the happiness and misery of every condition; observe the power of all the passions in all their combinations, and trace the changes of the human mind, as they are modified by various institutions and accidental influences of climate or custom, from the sprightliness of infancy to the despondence of decrepitude. He must divest himself of the prejudices of his age or country; he must consider right and wrong in their abstracted and invariable state; he must disregard present laws and opinions, and rise to general and transcendental[4] truths, which will always be the same. He must, therefore, content himself with the slow progress of his name, contemn the applause of his own time, and commit his claims to the justice of posterity. He must write as the interpreter of nature and the legislator of mankind, and consider himself as presiding over the thoughts and manners of future generations, as a being superior to time and place.

2. Awe-inspiringly.
3. Mental image.
4. "General; pervading many particulars" (Johnson's *Dictionary*).

"His labor is not yet at an end; he must know many languages and many sciences; and, that his style may be worthy of his thoughts, must by incessant practice familiarize to himself every delicacy of speech and grace of harmony."

Chapter 11. Imlac's Narrative Continued. A Hint on Pilgrimage

Imlac now felt the enthusiastic fit, and was proceeding to aggrandize his own profession, when the prince cried out: "Enough! thou hast convinced me that no human being can ever be a poet. Proceed with thy narration."

"To be a poet," said Imlac, "is indeed very difficult." "So difficult," returned the prince, "that I will at present hear no more of his labors. Tell me whither you went when you had seen Persia."

"From Persia," said the poet, "I traveled through Syria, and for three years resided in Palestine, where I conversed with great numbers of the northern and western nations of Europe, the nations which are now in possession of all power and all knowledge, whose armies are irresistible, and whose fleets command the remotest parts of the globe. When I compared these men with the natives of our own kingdom, and those that surround us, they appeared almost another order of beings. In their countries it is difficult to wish for anything that may not be obtained; a thousand arts, of which we never heard, are continually laboring for their convenience and pleasure; and whatever their own climate has denied them is supplied by their commerce."

"By what means," said the prince, "are the Europeans thus powerful, or why, since they can so easily visit Asia and Africa for trade or conquest, cannot the Asiatics and Africans invade their coasts, plant colonies in their ports, and give laws to their natural princes? The same wind that carries them back would bring us thither."

"They are more powerful, sir, than we," answered Imlac, "because they are wiser; knowledge will always predominate over ignorance, as man governs the other animals. But why their knowledge is more than ours, I know not what reason can be given, but the unsearchable will of the Supreme Being."

"When," said the prince with a sigh, "shall I be able to visit Palestine, and mingle with this mighty confluence of nations? Till that happy moment shall arrive, let me fill up the time with such representations as thou canst give me. I am not ignorant of the motive that assembles such numbers in that place, and cannot but consider it as the center of wisdom and piety, to which the best and wisest men of every land must be continually resorting."

"There are some nations," said Imlac, "that send few visitants to Palestine; for many numerous and learned sects in Europe concur to censure pilgrimage as superstitious, or deride it as ridiculous."

"You know," said the prince, "how little my life has made me acquainted with diversity of opinions. It will be too long to hear the arguments on both sides; you, that have considered them, tell me the result."

"Pilgrimage," said Imlac, "like many other acts of piety, may be reasonable or superstitious, according to the principles upon which it is performed. Long journeys in search of truth are not commanded. Truth, such as is necessary to the regulation of life, is always found where it is honestly sought. Change of place is no natural cause of the increase of piety, for it inevitably produces dissipation of mind. Yet, since men go every day to view the fields where great actions have been performed, and return with stronger impressions of the event, curiosity of the same kind may naturally dispose us to view that country whence our religion had its beginning; and I believe no man surveys those awful scenes without some confirmation of holy resolutions. That the Supreme Being may be more easily propitiated in one place than in another is the dream of idle superstition, but that some places may operate upon our own minds in an uncommon manner is an opinion which hourly experience will justify. He who supposes that his vices may be more successfully combated in Palestine, will, perhaps, find himself mistaken, yet he may go thither without folly; he who thinks they will be more freely pardoned, dishonors at once his reason and religion."

"These," said the prince, "are European distinctions. I will consider them another time. What have you found to be the effect of knowledge? Are those nations happier than we?"

"There is so much infelicity," said the poet, "in the world that scarce any man has leisure from his own distresses to estimate the comparative happiness of others. Knowledge is certainly one of the means of pleasure, as is confessed by the natural desire which every mind feels of increasing its ideas. Ignorance is mere privation, by which nothing can be produced; it is a vacuity in which the soul sits motionless and torpid for want of attraction; and, without knowing why, we always rejoice when we learn, and grieve when we forget. I am therefore inclined to conclude that if nothing counteracts the natural consequence of learning, we grow more happy as our minds take a wider range.

"In enumerating the particular comforts of life, we shall find many advantages on the side of the Europeans. They cure wounds and diseases with which we languish and perish. We suffer inclemencies of weather which they can obviate. They have engines for the despatch of many laborious works, which we must perform by manual industry. There is such communication between distant places that one friend can hardly be said to be absent from another. Their policy removes all public inconveniences; they have roads cut through their mountains, and bridges laid upon their rivers. And, if we descend to the privacies of life, their habitations are more commodious, and their possessions are more secure."

"They are surely happy," said the prince, "who have all these conveniencies, of which I envy none so much as the facility with which separated friends interchange their thoughts."

"The Europeans," answered Imlac, "are less unhappy than we, but they are not happy. Human life is everywhere a state in which much is to be endured, and little to be enjoyed."

Chapter 12. The Story of Imlac Continued

"I am not yet willing," said the prince, "to suppose that happiness is so parsimoniously distributed to mortals; nor can believe but that, if I had the choice of life, I should be able to fill every day with pleasure. I would injure no man, and should provoke no resentment: I would relieve every distress, and should enjoy the benedictions of gratitude. I would choose my friends among the wise, and my wife among the virtuous; and therefore should be in no danger from treachery, or unkindness. My children should, by my care, be learned and pious, and would repay to my age what their childhood had received. What would dare to molest him who might call on every side to thousands enriched by his bounty, or assisted by his power? And why should not life glide quietly away in the soft reciprocation of protection and reverence? All this may be done without the help of European refinements, which appear by their effects to be rather specious than useful. Let us leave them and pursue our journey."

"From Palestine," said Imlac, "I passed through many regions of Asia; in the more civilized kingdoms as a trader, and among the barbarians of the mountains as a pilgrim. At last I began to long for my native country, that I might repose after my travels, and fatigues, in the places where I had spent my earliest years, and gladden my old companions with the recital of my adventures. Often did I figure to myself those, with whom I had sported away the gay hours of dawning life, sitting round me in its evening, wondering at my tales, and listening to my counsels.

"When this thought had taken possession of my mind, I considered every moment as wasted which did not bring me nearer to Abyssinia. I hastened into Egypt, and, notwithstanding my impatience, was detained ten months in the contemplation of its ancient magnificence, and in enquiries after the remains of its ancient learning. I found in Cairo a mixture of all nations; some brought thither by the love of knowledge, some by the hope of gain, and many by the desire of living after their own manner without observation, and of lying hid in the obscurity of multitudes: for, in a city, populous as Cairo, it is possible to obtain at the same time the gratifications of society, and the secrecy of solitude.

"From Cairo I traveled to Suez, and embarked on the Red Sea, passing along the coast till I arrived at the port from which I had departed twenty years before. Here I joined myself to a caravan and re-entered my native country.

"I now expected the caresses of my kinsmen, and the congratulations of my friends, and was not without hope that my father, whatever value he had set upon riches, would own with gladness and pride a son who was able to add to the felicity and honor of the nation. But I was soon convinced that my thoughts were vain. My father had been dead fourteen years, having divided his wealth among my brothers, who were removed to some other provinces. Of my companions the greater part was in the grave, of the rest some could with difficulty remember me, and some considered me as one corrupted by foreign manners.

"A man used to vicissitudes is not easily dejected. I forgot, after a time, my disappointment, and endeavored to recommend myself to the nobles of the kingdom: they admitted me to their tables, heard my story, and dismissed me. I opened a school, and was prohibited to teach. I then resolved to sit down in the quiet of domestic life, and addressed a lady that was fond of my conversation, but rejected my suit, because my father was a merchant.

"Wearied at last with solicitation and repulses, I resolved to hide myself for ever from the world, and depend no longer on the opinion or caprice of others. I waited for the time when the gate of the *happy valley* should open, that I might bid farewell to hope and fear: the day came; my performance was distinguished with favor, and I resigned myself with joy to perpetual confinement."

"Hast thou here found happiness at last?" said Rasselas. "Tell me without reserve; art thou content with thy condition? or, dost thou wish to be again wandering and inquiring? All the inhabitants of this valley celebrate their lot, and, at the annual visit of the emperor, invite others to partake of their felicity."

"Great prince," said Imlac, "I shall speak the truth: I know not one of all your attendants who does not lament the hour when he entered this retreat.

I am less unhappy than the rest, because I have a mind replete with images, which I can vary and combine at pleasure. I can amuse my solitude by the renovation of the knowledge which begins to fade from my memory, and by recollection of the accidents of my past life. Yet all this ends in the sorrowful consideration, that my acquirements are now useless, and that none of my pleasures can be again enjoyed. The rest, whose minds have no impression but of the present moment, are either corroded by malignant passions, or sit stupid in the gloom of perpetual vacancy."

"What passions can infest those," said the prince, "who have no trials? We are in a place where impotence precludes malice, and where all envy is repressed by community[5] of enjoyments."

"There may be community," said Imlac, "of material possessions, but there can never be community of love or of esteem. It must happen that one will please more than another; he that knows himself despised will always be envious; and still more envious and malevolent, if he is condemned to live in the presence of those who despise him. The invitations, by which they allure others to a state which they feel to be wretched, proceed from the natural malignity of hopeless misery. They are weary of themselves, and of each other, and expect to find relief in new companions. They envy the liberty which their folly has forfeited, and would gladly see all mankind imprisoned like themselves.

"From this crime, however, I am wholly free. No man can say that he is wretched by my persuasion. I look with pity on the crowds who are annually soliciting admission to captivity, and wish that it were lawful for me to warn them of their danger."

"My dear Imlac," said the prince, "I will open to thee my whole heart. I have long meditated an escape from the happy valley. I have examined the mountains on every side, but find myself insuperably barred: teach me the way to break my prison; thou shalt be the companion of my flight, the guide of my rambles, the partner of my fortune, and my sole director in the *choice of life.*"

"Sir," answered the poet, "your escape will be difficult, and, perhaps, you may soon repent your curiosity. The world, which you figure to yourself smooth and quiet as the lake in the valley, you will find a sea foaming with tempests, and boiling with whirlpools: you will be sometimes overwhelmed by the waves of violence, and sometimes dashed against the rocks of treachery. Amidst wrongs and frauds, competitions and anxieties, you will wish a thousand times for these seats of quiet, and willingly quit hope to be free from fear."

"Do not seek to deter me from my purpose," said the prince: "I am impatient to see what thou hast seen; and, since thou art thyself weary of the valley, it is evident, that thy former state was better than this. Whatever be the consequence of my experiment, I am resolved to judge with my own eyes of the various conditions of men, and then to make deliberately my *choice of life.*"

"I am afraid," said Imlac, "you are hindered by stronger restraints than my persuasions; yet, if your determination is fixed, I do not counsel you to despair. Few things are impossible to diligence and skill."

Chapter 13. Rasselas Discovers the Means of Escape

The prince now dismissed his favorite to rest, but the narrative of wonders and novelties filled his mind with perturbation. He revolved all that he had

5. Joint possession.

heard, and prepared innumerable questions for the morning.

Much of his uneasiness was now removed. He had a friend to whom he could impart his thoughts, and whose experience could assist him in his designs. His heart was no longer condemned to swell with silent vexation. He thought that even the *happy valley* might be endured with such a companion, and that, if they could range the world together, he should have nothing further to desire.

In a few days the water was discharged, and the ground dried. The prince and Imlac then walked out together to converse without the notice of the rest. The prince, whose thoughts were always on the wing, as he passed by the gate, said, with a countenance of sorrow, "Why art thou so strong, and why is man so weak?"

"Man is not weak," answered his companion; "knowledge is more than equivalent to force. The master of mechanics laughs at strength. I can burst the gate, but cannot do it secretly. Some other expedient must be tried."

As they were walking on the side of the mountain, they observed that the conies,[6] which the rain had driven from their burrows, had taken shelter among the bushes, and formed holes behind them, tending upwards in an oblique line. "It has been the opinion of antiquity," said Imlac, "that human reason borrowed many arts from the instinct of animals; let us, therefore, not think ourselves degraded by learning from the coney. We may escape by piercing the mountain in the same direction. We will begin where the summit hangs over the middle part, and labor upward till we shall issue out beyond the prominence."

The eyes of the prince, when he heard this proposal, sparkled with joy. The execution was easy, and the success certain.

No time was now lost. They hastened early in the morning to choose a place proper for their mine. They clambered with great fatigue among crags and brambles, and returned without having discovered any part that favored their design. The second and the third day were spent in the same manner, and with the same frustration. But, on the fourth, they found a small cavern, concealed by a thicket, where they resolved to make their experiment.

Imlac procured instruments proper to hew stone and remove earth, and they fell to their work on the next day with more eagerness than vigor. They were presently exhausted by their efforts, and sat down to pant upon the grass. The prince, for a moment, appeared to be discouraged. "Sir," said his companion, "practice will enable us to continue our labor for a longer time; mark, however, how far we have advanced, and you will find that our toil will some time have an end. Great works are performed, not by strength, but perseverance: yonder palace was raised by single stones, yet you see its height and spaciousness. He that shall walk with vigor three hours a day will pass in seven years a space equal to the circumference of the globe."

They returned to their work day after day, and, in a short time, found a fissure in the rock, which enabled them to pass far with very little obstruction. This Rasselas considered as a good omen. "Do not disturb your mind," said Imlac, "with other hopes or fears than reason may suggest: if you are pleased with prognostics of good, you will be terrified likewise with tokens of evil, and your whole life will be a prey to superstition. Whatever facilitates our work is more than an omen, it is a cause of success. This is one of those pleasing

6. Rabbits.

surprises which often happen to active resolution. Many things difficult to design prove easy to performance."

Chapter 14. Rasselas and Imlac Receive an Unexpected Visit

They had now wrought their way to the middle, and solaced their toil with the approach of liberty, when the prince, coming down to refresh himself with air, found his sister Nekayah standing before the mouth of the cavity. He started and stood confused, afraid to tell his design, and yet hopeless to conceal it. A few moments determined him to repose on her fidelity, and secure her secrecy by a declaration without reserve.

"Do not imagine," said the princess, "that I came hither as a spy: I had long observed from my window, that you and Imlac directed your walk every day towards the same point, but I did not suppose you had any better reason for the preference than a cooler shade, or more fragrant bank; nor followed you with any other design than to partake of your conversation. Since then not suspicion but fondness has detected you, let me not lose the advantage of my discovery. I am equally weary of confinement with yourself, and not less desirous of knowing what is done or suffered in the world. Permit me to fly with you from this tasteless tranquility, which will yet grow more loathsome when you have left me. You may deny me to accompany you, but cannot hinder me from following."

The prince, who loved Nekayah above his other sisters, had no inclination to refuse her request, and grieved that he had lost an opportunity of showing his confidence by a voluntary communication. It was therefore agreed that she should leave the valley with them; and that, in the mean time, she should watch, lest any other straggler should, by chance or curiosity, follow them to the mountain.

At length their labor was at an end; they saw light beyond the prominence, and, issuing to the top of the mountain, beheld the Nile, yet a narrow current, wandering beneath them.

The prince looked round with rapture, anticipated all the pleasures of travel, and in thought was already transported beyond his father's dominions. Imlac, though very joyful at his escape, had less expectation of pleasure in the world, which he had before tried, and of which he had been weary.

Rasselas was so much delighted with a wider horizon, that he could not soon be persuaded to return into the valley. He informed his sister that the way was open, and that nothing now remained but to prepare for their departure.

Chapter 15. The Prince and Princess Leave the Valley, and See Many Wonders

The prince and princess had jewels sufficient to make them rich whenever they came into a place of commerce, which, by Imlac's direction, they hid in their clothes, and, on the night of the next full moon, all left the valley. The princess was followed only by a single favorite, who did not know whither she was going.

They clambered through the cavity, and began to go down on the other side. The princess and her maid turned their eyes towards every part, and, seeing nothing to bound their prospect, considered themselves as in danger of being lost in a dreary vacuity. They stopped and trembled. "I am almost afraid," said the princess, "to begin a journey of which I cannot perceive an end, and to venture into this immense plain where I may be approached on every side by men whom I never saw." The prince felt nearly the same emotions, though he thought it more manly to conceal them.

Imlac smiled at their terrors, and encouraged them to proceed; but the princess continued irresolute till she had been imperceptibly drawn forward too far to return.

In the morning they found some shepherds in the field, who set milk and fruits before them. The princess wondered that she did not see a palace ready for her reception, and a table spread with delicacies; but, being faint and hungry, she drank the milk and ate the fruits, and thought them of a higher flavor than the products of the valley.

They traveled forward by easy journeys, being all unaccustomed to toil or difficulty, and knowing, that though they might be missed, they could not be pursued. In a few days they came into a more populous region, where Imlac was diverted with the admiration which his companions expressed at the diversity of manners, stations and employments.

Their dress was such as might not bring upon them the suspicion of having any thing to conceal, yet the prince, wherever he came, expected to be obeyed, and the princess was frighted, because those that came into her presence did not prostrate themselves before her. Imlac was forced to observe them with great vigilance, lest they should betray their rank by their unusual behavior, and detained them several weeks in the first village to accustom them to the sight of common mortals.

By degrees the royal wanderers were taught to understand that they had for a time laid aside their dignity, and were to expect only such regard as liberality and courtesy could procure. And Imlac, having, by many admonitions, prepared them to endure the tumults of a port, and the ruggedness of the commercial race, brought them down to the seacoast.

The prince and his sister, to whom every thing was new, were gratified equally at all places, and therefore remained for some months at the port without any inclination to pass further. Imlac was content with their stay, because he did not think it safe to expose them, unpracticed in the world, to the hazards of a foreign country.

At last he began to fear lest they should be discovered, and proposed to fix a day for their departure. They had no pretensions to judge for themselves, and referred the whole scheme to his direction. He therefore took passage in a ship to Suez; and, when the time came, with great difficulty prevailed on the princess to enter the vessel. They had a quick and prosperous voyage, and from Suez traveled by land to Cairo.

Chapter 16. They Enter Cairo, and Find Every Man Happy

As they approached the city, which filled the strangers with astonishment, "This," said Imlac to the prince, "is the place where travelers and merchants assemble from all the corners of the earth. You will here find men of every character and every occupation. Commerce is here honorable. I will act as a merchant, and you shall live as strangers, who have no other end of travel than curiosity. It will soon be observed that we are rich; our reputation will procure us access to all whom we shall desire to know; you will see all the conditions of humanity, and enable yourself at leisure to make your *choice of life.*"

They now entered the town, stunned by the noise, and offended by the crowds. Instruction had not yet so prevailed over habit, but that they wondered to see themselves pass undistinguished along the street, and met by the lowest of the people without reverence or notice. The princess could not at first bear the thought of being leveled with the vulgar,[7] and for some days continued in her chamber, where she was served by her favorite, Pekuah, as in the palace of the valley.

Imlac, who understood traffic,[8] sold part of the jewels the next day, and hired a house, which he adorned with such magnificence that he was immediately considered as a merchant of great wealth. His politeness attracted many acquaintance, and his generosity made him courted by many dependents. His table was crowded by men of every nation, who all admired his knowledge, and solicited his favor. His companions, not being able to mix in the conversation, could make no discovery[9] of their ignorance or surprise, and were gradually initiated in the world as they gained knowledge of the language.

The prince had, by frequent lectures, been taught the use and nature of money; but the ladies could not for a long time comprehend what the merchants did with small pieces of gold and silver, or why things of so little use should be received as equivalent to the necessaries of life.

They studied the language two years, while Imlac was preparing to set before them the various ranks and conditions of mankind. He grew acquainted with all who had anything uncommon in their fortune or conduct. He frequented the voluptuous and the frugal, the idle and the busy, the merchants and the men of learning.

The prince being now able to converse with fluency, and having learned the caution necessary to be observed in his intercourse with strangers, began to accompany Imlac to places of resort, and to enter into all assemblies, that he might make his *choice of life.*

For some time he thought choice needless, because all appeared to him equally happy. Wherever he went he met gaiety and kindness, and heard the song of joy or the laugh of carelessness. He began to believe that the world overflowed with universal plenty, and that nothing was withheld either from want or merit; that every hand showered liberality, and every heart melted with benevolence: "And who then," says he, "will be suffered to be wretched?"

Imlac permitted the pleasing delusion, and was unwilling to crush the hope of inexperience, till one day, having sat awhile silent, "I know not," said the prince, "what can be the reason that I am more unhappy than any of our friends. I see them perpetually and unalterably cheerful, but feel my own mind restless and uneasy. I am unsatisfied with those pleasures which I seem most to court; I live in the crowds of jollity, not so much to enjoy company as to shun myself, and am only loud and merry to conceal my sadness."

"Every man," said Imlac, "may, by examining his own mind, guess what passes in the minds of others; when you feel that your own gaiety is counterfeit, it may justly lead you to suspect that of your companions not to be sincere. Envy is commonly reciprocal. We are long before we are convinced that happiness is never to be found, and each believes it possessed by others, to keep

7. Ordinary people.
8. Commerce.
9. Exposure.

alive the hope of obtaining it for himself. In the assembly where you passed the last night, there appeared such sprightliness of air, and volatility of fancy, as might have suited beings of an higher order, formed to inhabit serener regions, inaccessible to care or sorrow; yet, believe me, prince, there was not one who did not dread the moment when solitude should deliver him to the tyranny of reflection."

"This," said the prince, "may be true of others, since it is true of me; yet, whatever be the general infelicity of man, one condition is more happy than another, and wisdom surely directs us to take the least evil in the *choice of life.*"

"The causes of good and evil," answered Imlac, "are so various and uncertain, so often entangled with each other, so diversified by various relations, and so much subject to accidents which cannot be foreseen, that he who would fix his condition upon incontestable reasons of preference must live and die inquiring and deliberating."

"But, surely," said Rasselas, "the wise men, to whom we listen with reverence and wonder, chose that mode of life for themselves which they thought most likely to make them happy."

"Very few," said the poet, "live by choice. Every man is placed in his present condition by causes which acted without his foresight, and with which he did not always willingly cooperate; and therefore you will rarely meet one who does not think the lot of his neighbor better than his own."

"I am pleased to think," said the prince, "that my birth has given me at least one advantage over others, by enabling me to determine for myself. I have here the world before me. I will review it at leisure; surely happiness is somewhere to be found."

Chapter 17. The Prince Associates with Young Men of Spirit and Gaiety

Rasselas rose next day, and resolved to begin his experiments upon life. "Youth," cried he, "is the time of gladness: I will join myself to the young men, whose only business is to gratify their desires, and whose time is all spent in a succession of enjoyments."

To such societies he was readily admitted, but a few days brought him back weary and disgusted. Their mirth was without images,[1] their laughter without motive; their pleasures were gross and sensual, in which the mind had no part; their conduct was at once wild and mean; they laughed at order and at law, but the frown of power dejected, and the eye of wisdom abashed them.

The prince soon concluded, that he should never be happy in a course of life of which he was ashamed. He thought it unsuitable to a reasonable being to act without a plan, and to be sad or cheerful only by chance. "Happiness," said he, "must be something solid and permanent, without fear and without uncertainty."

But his young companions had gained so much of his regard by their frankness and courtesy, that he could not leave them without warning and remonstrance. "My friends," said he, "I have seriously considered our manners and our prospects, and find that we have mistaken our own interest. The first years of man must make provision for the last. He that never thinks never can be wise. Perpetual levity must end in ignorance; and intemperance, though it may fire the spirits for an hour, will make life short or miserable. Let us con-

1. Ideas.

sider that youth is of no long duration, and that in maturer age, when the enchantments of fancy shall cease, and phantoms of delight dance no more about us, we shall have no comforts but the esteem of wise men, and the means of doing good. Let us, therefore, stop, while to stop is in our power: let us live as men who are sometime to grow old, and to whom it will be the most dreadful of all evils not to count their past years but by follies, and to be reminded of their former luxuriance of health only by the maladies which riot has produced."

They stared a while in silence one upon another, and, at last, drove him away by a general chorus of continued laughter.

The consciousness that his sentiments were just, and his intentions kind, was scarcely sufficient to support him against the horror of derision. But he recovered his tranquillity, and pursued his search.

Chapter 18. The Prince Finds a Wise and Happy Man

As he was one day walking in the street, he saw a spacious building which all were, by the open doors, invited to enter: he followed the stream of people, and found it a hall or school of declamation, in which professors read lectures to their auditory.[2] He fixed his eye upon a sage raised above the rest, who discoursed with great energy on the government of the passions. His look was venerable, his action graceful, his pronunciation clear, and his diction elegant. He showed with great strength of sentiment and variety of illustration that human nature is degraded and debased, when the lower faculties predominate over the higher; that when fancy, the parent of passion, usurps the dominion of the mind, nothing ensues but the natural effect of unlawful government, perturbation, and confusion; that she betrays the fortresses of the intellect to rebels, and excites her children to sedition against reason, their lawful sovereign. He compared reason to the sun, of which the light is constant, uniform and lasting; and fancy to a meteor, of bright but transitory luster, irregular in its motion, and delusive in its direction.

He then communicated the various precepts given from time to time for the conquest of passion, and displayed the happiness of those who had obtained the important victory, after which man is no longer the slave of fear, nor the fool of hope; is no more emaciated by envy, inflamed by anger, emasculated by tenderness, or depressed by grief; but walks on calmly through the tumults or the privacies of life, as the sun pursues alike his course through the calm or the stormy sky.

He enumerated many examples of heroes immovable by pain or pleasure, who looked with indifference on those modes or accidents to which the vulgar give the names of good and evil. He exhorted his hearers to lay aside their prejudices, and arm themselves against the shafts of malice or misfortune, by invulnerable patience; concluding that this state only was happiness, and that this happiness was in everyone's power.

Rasselas listened to him with the veneration due to the instructions of a superior being, and, waiting for him at the door, humbly implored the liberty of visiting so great a master of true wisdom. The lecturer hesitated a moment, when Rasselas put a purse of gold into his hand, which he received with a mixture of joy and wonder.

"I have found," said the prince at his return to Imlac, "a man who can teach

2. Audience.

all that is necessary to be known; who, from the unshaken throne of rational fortitude, looks down on the scenes of life changing beneath him. He speaks, and attention watches his lips. He reasons, and conviction closes his periods.[3] This man shall be my future guide; I will learn his doctrines, and imitate his life."

"Be not too hasty," said Imlac, "to trust or to admire the teachers of morality: they discourse like angels, but they live like men."

Rasselas, who could not conceive how any man could reason so forcibly without feeling the cogency of his own arguments, paid his visit in a few days, and was denied admission. He had now learned the power of money, and made his way by a piece of gold to the inner apartment, where he found the philosopher in a room half darkened, with his eyes misty and his face pale. "Sir," said he, "you are come at a time when all human friendship is useless; what I suffer cannot be remedied, what I have lost cannot be supplied. My daughter, my only daughter, from whose tenderness I expected all the comforts of my age, died last night of a fever. My views, my purposes, my hopes are at an end; I am now a lonely being, disunited from society."

"Sir," said the prince, "mortality is an event by which a wise man can never be surprised; we know that death is always near, and it should therefore always be expected." "Young man," answered the philosopher, "you speak like one that has never felt the pangs of separation." "Have you then forgot the precepts," said Rasselas, "which you so powerfully enforced? Has wisdom no strength to arm the heart against calamity? Consider that external things are naturally variable, but truth and reason are always the same." "What comfort," said the mourner, "can truth and reason afford me? Of what effect are they now, but to tell me that my daughter will not be restored?"

The prince, whose humanity would not suffer him to insult misery with reproof, went away, convinced of the emptiness of rhetorical sound, and the inefficacy of polished periods and studied sentences.[4]

Chapter 19. A Glimpse of Pastoral Life

He was still eager upon the same inquiry; and having heard of a hermit that lived near the lowest cataract of the Nile, and filled the whole country with the fame of his sanctity, resolved to visit his retreat, and inquire whether that felicity which public life could not afford was to be found in solitude; and whether a man whose age and virtue made him venerable could teach any peculiar art of shunning evils, or enduring them.

Imlac and the princess agreed to accompany him, and, after the necessary preparations, they began their journey. Their way lay through fields, where shepherds tended their flocks and the lambs were playing upon the pasture. "This," said the poet, "is the life which has been often celebrated for its innocence and quiet; let us pass the heat of the day among the shepherds' tents, and know whether all our searches are not to terminate in pastoral simplicity."

The proposal pleased them, and they induced the shepherds, by small presents and familiar questions, to tell their opinion of their own state. They were so rude and ignorant, so little able to compare the good with the evil of the occupation, and so indistinct in their narratives and descriptions, that very little could be learned from them. But it was evident that their hearts were cankered with discontent; that they considered themselves as condemned to

3. Completed sentences.

4. Maxims or moral axioms.

labor for the luxury of the rich, and looked up with stupid malevolence toward those that were placed above them.

The princess pronounced with vehemence that she would never suffer these envious savages to be her companions, and that she should not soon be desirous of seeing any more specimens of rustic happiness; but could not believe that all the accounts of primeval pleasures were fabulous, and was yet in doubt whether life had anything that could be justly preferred to the placid gratifications of fields and woods. She hoped that the time would come, when, with a few virtuous and elegant companions, she could gather flowers planted by her own hand, fondle the lambs of her own ewe, and listen, without care, among brooks and breezes, to one of her maidens reading in the shade.

Chapter 20. The Danger of Prosperity

On the next day they continued their journey, till the heat compelled them to look round for shelter. At a small distance they saw a thick wood, which they no sooner entered than they perceived that they were approaching the habitations of men. The shrubs were diligently cut away to open walks where the shades were darkest; the boughs of opposite trees were artificially interwoven; seats of flowery turf were raised in vacant spaces, and a rivulet, that wantoned along the side of a winding path, had its banks sometimes opened into small basins, and its stream sometimes obstructed by little mounds of stone heaped together to increase its murmurs.

They passed slowly through the wood, delighted with such unexpected accommodations, and entertained each other with conjecturing what, or who, he could be, that, in those rude and unfrequented regions, had leisure and art for such harmless luxury.

As they advanced, they heard the sound of music, and saw youths and virgins dancing in the grove; and, going still further, beheld a stately palace built upon a hill surrounded with woods. The laws of eastern hospitality allowed them to enter, and the master welcomed them like a man liberal and wealthy.

He was skilful enough in appearances soon to discern that they were no common guests, and spread his table with magnificence. The eloquence of Imlac caught his attention, and the lofty courtesy of the princess excited his respect. When they offered to depart he entreated their stay, and was the next day still more unwilling to dismiss them than before. They were easily persuaded to stop, and civility grew up in time to freedom and confidence.

The prince now saw all the domestics cheerful, and all the face of nature smiling round the place, and could not forbear to hope that he should find here what he was seeking; but when he was congratulating the master upon his possessions, he answered with a sigh, "My condition has indeed the appearance of happiness, but appearances are delusive. My prosperity puts my life in danger; the Bassa[5] of Egypt is my enemy, incensed only by my wealth and popularity. I have been hitherto protected against him by the princes of the country; but, as the favor of the great is uncertain, I know not how soon my defenders may be persuaded to share the plunder with the Bassa. I have sent my treasures into a distant country, and, upon the first alarm, am prepared to follow them. Then will my enemies riot in my mansion, and enjoy the gardens which I have planted."

They all joined in lamenting his danger, and deprecating his exile; and the

5. Pasha: a Turkish viceroy.

princess was so much disturbed with the tumult of grief and indignation, that she retired to her apartment. They continued with their kind inviter a few days longer, and then went forward to find the hermit.

Chapter 21. The Happiness of Solitude. The Hermit's History

They came on the third day, by the direction of the peasants, to the hermit's cell: it was a cavern in the side of a mountain, over-shadowed with palm-trees; at such a distance from the cataract, that nothing more was heard than a gentle uniform murmur, such as composed the mind to pensive meditation, especially when it was assisted by the wind whistling among the branches. The first rude essay of nature had been so much improved by human labor, that the cave contained several apartments, appropriated to different uses, and often afforded lodging to travelers, whom darkness or tempests happened to overtake.

The hermit sat on a bench at the door, to enjoy the coolness of the evening. On one side lay a book with pens and papers, on the other mechanical instruments of various kinds. As they approached him unregarded, the princess observed that he had not the countenance of a man that had found, or could teach, the way to happiness.

They saluted him with great respect, which he repaid like a man not unaccustomed to the forms of courts. "My children," said he, "if you have lost your way, you shall be willingly supplied with such conveniencies for the night as this cavern will afford. I have all that nature requires, and you will not expect delicacies in a hermit's cell."

They thanked him, and, entering, were pleased with the neatness and regularity of the place. The hermit set flesh and wine before them, though he fed only upon fruits and water. His discourse was cheerful without levity, and pious without enthusiasm.[6] He soon gained the esteem of his guests, and the princess repented of her hasty censure.

At last Imlac began thus: "I do not now wonder that your reputation is so far extended; we have heard at Cairo of your wisdom, and came hither to implore your direction for this young man and maiden in the *choice of life*."

"To him that lives well," answered the hermit, "every form of life is good; nor can I give any other rule for choice, than to remove from all apparent evil."

"He will remove most certainly from evil," said the prince, "who shall devote himself to that solitude which you have recommended by your example."

"I have indeed lived fifteen years in solitude," said the hermit, "but have no desire that my example should gain any imitators. In my youth I professed arms, and was raised by degrees to the highest military rank. I have traversed wide countries at the head of my troops, and seen many battles and sieges. At last, being disgusted by the preferment of a younger officer, and feeling that my vigor was beginning to decay, I resolved to close my life in peace, having found the world full of snares, discord, and misery. I had once escaped from the pursuit of the enemy by the shelter of this cavern, and therefore chose it for my final residence. I employed artificers to form it into chambers, and stored it with all that I was likely to want.

"For some time after my retreat, I rejoiced like a tempest-beaten sailor at

6. "A vain belief of private revelation; a vain confidence of divine favor or communication" (Johnson's *Dictionary*).

his entrance into the harbor, being delighted with the sudden change of the noise and hurry of war, to stillness and repose. When the pleasure of novelty went away, I employed my hours in examining the plants which grow in the valley, and the minerals which I collected from the rocks. But that inquiry is now grown tasteless and irksome. I have been for some time unsettled and distracted: my mind is disturbed with a thousand perplexities of doubt, and vanities of imagination, which hourly prevail upon me, because I have no opportunities of relaxation or diversion. I am sometimes ashamed to think that I could not secure myself from vice, but by retiring from the exercise of virtue, and begin to suspect that I was rather impelled by resentment, than led by devotion, into solitude. My fancy riots in scenes of folly, and I lament that I have lost so much, and have gained so little. In solitude, if I escape the example of bad men, I want likewise the counsel and conversation of the good. I have been long comparing the evils with the advantages of society, and resolve to return into the world tomorrow. The life of a solitary man will be certainly miserable, but not certainly devout."

They heard his resolution with surprise, but, after a short pause, offered to conduct him to Cairo. He dug up a considerable treasure which he had hid among the rocks, and accompanied them to the city, on which, as he approached it, he gazed with rapture.

Chapter 22. The Happiness of a Life Led According to Nature

Rasselas went often to an assembly of learned men, who met at stated times to unbend their minds and compare their opinions. Their manners were somewhat coarse, but their conversation was instructive, and their disputations acute, though sometimes too violent, and often continued till neither controvertist remembered upon what question they began. Some faults were almost general among them; everyone was desirous to dictate to the rest, and everyone was pleased to hear the genius or knowledge of another depreciated.

In this assembly Rasselas was relating his interview with the hermit, and the wonder with which he heard him censure a course of life which he had so deliberately chosen, and so laudably followed. The sentiments of the hearers were various. Some were of opinion that the folly of his choice had been justly punished by condemnation to perpetual perseverance. One of the youngest among them, with great vehemence, pronounced him an hypocrite. Some talked of the right of society to the labor of individuals, and considered retirement as a desertion of duty. Others readily allowed that there was a time when the claims of the public were satisfied, and when a man might properly sequester himself, to review his life and purify his heart.

One, who appeared more affected with the narrative than the rest, thought it likely that the hermit would in a few years go back to his retreat, and perhaps, if shame did not restrain, or death intercept him, return once more from his retreat into the world. "For the hope of happiness," said he, "is so strongly impressed that the longest experience is not able to efface it. Of the present state, whatever it be, we feel and are forced to confess the misery; yet when the same state is again at a distance, imagination paints it as desirable. But the time will surely come when desire will be no longer our torment, and no man shall be wretched but by his own fault."

"This," said a philosopher who had heard him with tokens of great impatience, "is the present condition of a wise man. The time is already come when none are wretched but by their own fault. Nothing is more idle than to inquire after happiness, which nature has kindly placed within our reach. The way to be happy is to live according to nature, in obedience to that universal and unalterable law with which every heart is originally impressed; which is not written on it by precept, but engraven by destiny, not instilled by education, but infused at our nativity. He that lives according to nature will suffer nothing from the delusions of hope, or importunities of desire; he will receive and reject with equability of temper, and act or suffer as the reason of things shall alternately prescribe. Other men may amuse themselves with subtle definitions, or intricate ratiocination. Let them learn to be wise by easier means; let them observe the hind of the forest, and the linnet of the grove; let them consider the life of animals, whose motions are regulated by instinct; they obey their guide, and are happy. Let us therefore, at length, cease to dispute, and learn to live; throw away the encumbrance of precepts, which they who utter them with so much pride and pomp do not understand, and carry with us this simple and intelligible maxim, that deviation from nature is deviation from happiness."

When he had spoken, he looked round him with a placid air, and enjoyed the consciousness of his own beneficence. "Sir," said the prince with great modesty, "as I, like all the rest of mankind, am desirous of felicity, my closest attention has been fixed upon your discourse. I doubt not the truth of a position which a man so learned has so confidently advanced. Let me only know what it is to live according to nature."

"When I find young men so humble and so docile," said the philosopher, "I can deny them no information which my studies have enabled me to afford. To live according to nature, is to act always with due regard to the fitness arising from the relations and qualities of causes and effects; to concur with the great and unchangeable scheme of universal felicity; to co-operate with the general disposition and tendency of the present system of things."

The prince soon found that this was one of the sages whom he should understand less as he heard him longer. He therefore bowed and was silent; and the philosopher, supposing him satisfied, and the rest vanquished, rose up and departed with the air of a man that had co-operated with the present system.

Chapter 23. The Prince and his Sister Divide between Them the Work of Observation

Rasselas returned home full of reflections, doubtful how to direct his future steps. Of the way to happiness he found the learned and simple equally ignorant; but, as he was yet young, he flattered himself that he had time remaining for more experiments, and further inquiries. He communicated to Imlac his observations and his doubts, but was answered by him with new doubts, and remarks that gave him no comfort. He therefore discoursed more frequently and freely with his sister, who had yet the same hope with himself, and always assisted him to give some reason why, though he had been hitherto frustrated, he might succeed at last.

"We have hitherto," said she, "known but little of the world: we have never yet been either great or mean. In our own country, though we had royalty, we had no power, and in this we have not yet seen the private recesses of domestic peace. Imlac favors not our search, lest we should in time find him mistaken.

We will divide the task between us: you shall try what is to be found in the splendor of courts, and I will range the shades of humbler life. Perhaps command and authority may be the supreme blessings, as they afford most opportunities of doing good: or, perhaps, what this world can give may be found in the modest habitations of middle fortune; too low for great designs, and too high for penury and distress."

Chapter 24. The Prince Examines the Happiness of High Stations

Rasselas applauded the design, and appeared next day with a splendid retinue at the court of the Bassa. He was soon distinguished for his magnificence, and admitted, as a prince whose curiosity had brought him from distant countries, to an intimacy with the great officers, and frequent conversation with the Bassa himself.

He was at first inclined to believe, that the man must be pleased with his own condition, whom all approached with reverence, and heard with obedience, and who had the power to extend his edicts to a whole kingdom. "There can be no pleasure," said he, "equal to that of feeling at once the joy of thousands all made happy by wise administration. Yet, since, by the law of subordination, this sublime delight can be in one nation but the lot of one, it is surely reasonable to think that there is some satisfaction more popular[7] and accessible, and that millions can hardly be subjected to the will of a single man, only to fill his particular breast with incommunicable content."

These thoughts were often in his mind, and he found no solution of the difficulty. But as presents and civilities gained him more familiarity, he found that almost every man who stood high in employment hated all the rest, and was hated by them, and that their lives were a continual succession of plots and detections, stratagems and escapes, faction and treachery. Many of those, who surrounded the Bassa, were sent only to watch and report his conduct; every tongue was muttering censure and every eye was searching for a fault.

At last the letters of revocation arrived, the Bassa was carried in chains to Constantinople, and his name was mentioned no more.

"What are we now to think of the prerogatives of power," said Rasselas to his sister; "is it without any efficacy to good? or, is the subordinate degree only dangerous, and the supreme safe and glorious? Is the Sultan the only happy man in his dominions? or, is the Sultan himself subject to the torments of suspicion, and the dread of enemies?"

In a short time the second Bassa was deposed. The Sultan, that had advanced him, was murdered by the Janisaries,[8] and his successor had other views and different favorites.

Chapter 25. The Princess Pursues Her Inquiry with More Diligence than Success

The princess, in the mean time, insinuated herself into many families; for there are few doors, through which liberality, joined with good humor, cannot find its way. The daughters of many houses were airy[9] and cheerful, but Nekayah had been too long accustomed to the conversation of Imlac and her

7. Common.
8. Guards of the Turkish ruler.
9. "Gay; sprightly; full of mirth" (Johnson's *Dictionary*).

brother to be much pleased with childish levity and prattle which had no meaning. She found their thoughts narrow, their wishes low, and their merriment often artificial. Their pleasures, poor as they were, could not be preserved pure, but were embittered by petty competitions and worthless emulation. They were always jealous of the beauty of each other; of a quality to which solicitude can add nothing, and from which detraction can take nothing away. Many were in love with triflers like themselves, and many fancied that they were in love when in truth they were only idle. Their affection was seldom fixed on sense or virtue, and therefore seldom ended but in vexation. Their grief, however, like their joy, was transient; everything floated in their mind unconnected with the past or future, so that one desire easily gave way to another, as a second stone cast into the water effaces and confounds the circles of the first.

With these girls she played as with inoffensive animals, and found them proud of her countenance,[1] and weary of her company.

But her purpose was to examine more deeply, and her affability easily persuaded the hearts that were swelling with sorrow to discharge their secrets in her ear: and those whom hope flattered, or prosperity delighted, often courted her to partake their pleasures.

The princess and her brother commonly met in the evening in a private summer-house on the bank of the Nile, and related to each other the occurrences of the day. As they were sitting together, the princess cast her eyes upon the river that flowed before her. "Answer," said she, "great father of waters, thou that rollest thy floods through eighty nations, to the invocations of the daughter of thy native king. Tell me if thou waterest, through all thy course, a single habitation from which thou dost not hear the murmurs of complaint?"

"You are then," said Rasselas, "not more successful in private houses than I have been in courts." "I have, since the last partition of our provinces,"[2] said the princess, "enabled myself to enter familiarly into many families, where there was the fairest show of prosperity and peace, and know not one house that is not haunted by some fury that destroys its quiet.

"I did not seek ease among the poor, because I concluded that there it could not be found. But I saw many poor whom I had supposed to live in affluence. Poverty has, in large cities, very different appearances: it is often concealed in splendor, and often in extravagance. It is the care of a very great part of mankind to conceal their indigence from the rest: they support themselves by temporary expedients, and every day is lost in contriving for the morrow.

"This, however, was an evil, which, though frequent, I saw with less pain, because I could relieve it. Yet some have refused my bounties; more offended with my quickness to detect their wants, than pleased with my readiness to succor them: and others, whose exigencies compelled them to admit my kindness, have never been able to forgive their benefactress. Many, however, have been sincerely grateful without the ostentation of gratitude, or the hope of other favors."

1. Patronage, favor.

2. Division of our responsibilities.

Chapter 26. The Princess Continues Her Remarks upon Private Life

Nekayah, perceiving her brother's attention fixed, proceeded in her narrative.

"In families where there is or is not poverty, there is commonly discord. If a kingdom be, as Imlac tells us, a great family, a family likewise is a little kingdom, torn with factions and exposed to revolutions. An unpracticed observer expects the love of parents and children to be constant and equal; but this kindness seldom continues beyond the years of infancy: in a short time the children become rivals to their parents. Benefits are allayed[3] by reproaches, and gratitude debased by envy.

"Parents and children seldom act in concert; each child endeavors to appropriate the esteem or fondness of the parents, and the parents, with yet less temptation, betray each other to their children. Thus, some place their confidence in the father, and some in the mother, and by degrees the house is filled with artifices and feuds.

"The opinions of children and parents, of the young and the old, are naturally opposite, by the contrary effects of hope and despondence, of expectation and experience, without crime or folly on either side. The colors of life in youth and age appear different, as the face of nature in spring and winter. And how can children credit the assertions of parents, which their own eyes show them to be false?

"Few parents act in such a manner as much to enforce their maxims by the credit of their lives. The old man trusts wholly to slow contrivance and gradual progression; the youth expects to force his way by genius, vigor, and precipitance. The old man pays regard to riches, and the youth reverences virtue. The old man deifies prudence; the youth commits himself to magnanimity and chance. The young man, who intends no ill, believes that none is intended, and therefore acts with openness and candor; but his father, having suffered the injuries of fraud, is impelled to suspect, and too often allured to practice it. Age looks with anger on the temerity of youth, and youth with contempt on the scrupulosity[4] of age. Thus parents and children, for the greatest part, live on to love less and less; and, if those whom nature has thus closely united are the torments of each other, where shall we look for tenderness and consolation?"

"Surely," said the prince, "you must have been unfortunate in your choice of acquaintance: I am unwilling to believe that the most tender of all relations is thus impeded in its effects by natural necessity."

"Domestic discord," answered she, "is not inevitably and fatally necessary, but yet is not easily avoided. We seldom see that a whole family is virtuous; the good and evil cannot well agree, and the evil can yet less agree with one another. Even the virtuous fall sometimes to variance, when their virtues are of different kinds, and tending to extremes. In general, those parents have most reverence who most deserve it; for he that lives well cannot be despised.

"Many other evils infest private life. Some are the slaves of servants whom they have trusted with their affairs. Some are kept in continual anxiety to the caprice of rich relations, whom they cannot please, and dare not offend. Some

3. To allay is "to join anything to another, so as to abate its predominant qualities" (Johnson's *Dictionary*).

4. "Fear of acting in any manner" (Johnson's *Dictionary*).

husbands are imperious, and some wives perverse; and, as it is always more easy to do evil than good, though the wisdom or virtue of one can very rarely make many happy, the folly or vice of one may often make many miserable."

"If such be the general effect of marriage," said the prince, "I shall for the future think it dangerous to connect my interest with that of another, lest I should be unhappy by my partner's fault."

"I have met," said the princess, "with many who live single for that reason; but I never found that their prudence ought to raise envy. They dream away their time without friendship, without fondness, and are driven to rid themselves of the day, for which they have no use, by childish amusements, or vicious delights. They act as beings under the constant sense of some known inferiority that fills their minds with rancor, and their tongues with censure. They are peevish at home, and malevolent abroad; and, as the outlaws of human nature, make it their business and their pleasure to disturb that society which debars them from its privileges. To live without feeling or exciting sympathy, to be fortunate without adding to the felicity of others, or afflicted without tasting the balm of pity, is a state more gloomy than solitude; it is not retreat but exclusion from mankind. Marriage has many pains, but celibacy has no pleasures."

"What then is to be done?" said Rasselas; "the more we inquire, the less we can resolve. Surely he is most likely to please himself that has no other inclination to regard."

Chapter 27. Disquisition upon Greatness

The conversation had a short pause. The prince, having considered his sister's observations, told her, that she had surveyed life with prejudice, and supposed misery where she did not find it. "Your narrative," says he, "throws yet a darker gloom upon the prospects of futurity: the predictions of Imlac were but faint sketches of the evils painted by Nekayah. I have been lately convinced that quiet is not the daughter of grandeur, or of power: that her presence is not to be bought by wealth, nor enforced by conquest. It is evident, that as any man acts in a wider compass, he must be more exposed to opposition from enmity or miscarriage from chance; whoever has many to please or to govern, must use the ministry of many agents, some of whom will be wicked, and some ignorant; by some he will be misled, and by others betrayed. If he gratifies one he will offend another: those that are not favored will think themselves injured; and, since favors can be conferred but upon few, the greater number will be always discontented."

"The discontent," said the princess, "which is thus unreasonable, I hope that I shall always have spirit to despise, and you, power to repress."

"Discontent," answered Rasselas, "will not always be without reason under the most just or vigilant administration of public affairs. None, however attentive, can always discover that merit which indigence or faction may happen to obscure; and none, however powerful, can always reward it. Yet, he that sees inferior desert[5] advanced above him, will naturally impute that preference to partiality or caprice; and, indeed, it can scarcely be hoped that any man, however magnanimous by nature, or exalted by condition, will be able to persist for ever in fixed and inexorable justice of distribution: he will sometimes

5. Merit; one deserving reward.

indulge his own affections, and sometimes those of his favorites; he will permit some to please him who can never serve him; he will discover in those whom he loves qualities which in reality they do not possess; and to those, from whom he receives pleasure, he will in his turn endeavor to give it. Thus will recommendations sometimes prevail which were purchased by money, or by the more destructive bribery of flattery and servility.

"He that has much to do will do something wrong, and of that wrong must suffer the consequences; and, if it were possible that he should always act rightly, yet when such numbers are to judge of his conduct, the bad will censure and obstruct him by malevolence, and the good sometimes by mistake.

"The highest stations cannot therefore hope to be the abodes of happiness, which I would willingly believe to have fled from thrones and palaces to seats of humble privacy and placid obscurity. For what can hinder the satisfaction, or intercept the expectations, of him whose abilities are adequate to his employments, who sees with his own eyes the whole circuit of his influence, who chooses by his own knowledge all whom he trusts, and whom none are tempted to deceive by hope or fear? Surely he has nothing to do but to love and to be loved, to be virtuous and to be happy."

"Whether perfect happiness would be procured by perfect goodness," said Nekayah, "this world will never afford an opportunity of deciding. But this, at least, may be maintained, that we do not always find visible happiness in proportion to visible virtue. All natural and almost all political evils, are incident alike to the bad and good: they are confounded in the misery of a famine, and not much distinguished in the fury of a faction; they sink together in a tempest, and are driven together from their country by invaders. All that virtue can afford is quietness of conscience, a steady prospect of a happier state; this may enable us to endure calamity with patience; but remember that patience must suppose pain."

Chapter 28. Rasselas and Nekayah Continue Their Conversation

"Dear princess," said Rasselas, "you fall into the common errors of exaggeratory declamation, by producing, in a familiar disquisition,[6] examples of national calamities, and scenes of extensive misery, which are found in books rather than in the world, and which, as they are horrid, are ordained to be rare. Let us not imagine evils which we do not feel, nor injure life by misrepresentations. I cannot bear that querulous eloquence which threatens every city with a siege like that of Jerusalem,[7] that makes famine attend on every flight of locusts, and suspends pestilence on the wing of every blast that issues from the south.

"On necessary and inevitable evils, which overwhelm kingdoms at once, all disputation is vain: when they happen they must be endured. But it is evident, that these bursts of universal distress are more dreaded than felt: thousands and ten thousands flourish in youth, and wither in age, without the knowledge of any other than domestic evils, and share the same pleasures and vexations whether their kings are mild or cruel, whether the armies of their country pursue their enemies, or retreat before them. While courts are disturbed with intestine[8] competitions, and ambassadors are negotiating in foreign countries,

6. Family discussion of a question.
7. In 70 C.E. the Romans, under Titus, besieged and destroyed Jerusalem.
8. Internal, domestic.

the smith still plies his anvil, and the husbandman drives his plow forward; the necessaries of life are required and obtained, and the successive business of the seasons continues to make its wonted revolutions.

"Let us cease to consider what, perhaps, may never happen, and what, when it shall happen, will laugh at human speculation. We will not endeavor to modify the motions of the elements, or to fix the destiny of kingdoms. It is our business to consider what beings like us may perform; each laboring for his own happiness, by promoting within his circle, however narrow, the happiness of others.

"Marriage is evidently the dictate of nature; men and women were made to be companions of each other, and therefore I cannot be persuaded but that marriage is one of the means of happiness."

"I know not," said the princess, "whether marriage be more than one of the innumerable modes of human misery. When I see and reckon the various forms of connubial infelicity, the unexpected causes of lasting discord, the diversities of temper, the oppositions of opinion, the rude collisons of contrary desire where both are urged by violent impulses, the obstinate contests of disagreeing virtues, where both are supported by consciousness of good intention, I am sometimes disposed to think with the severer casuists of most nations, that marriage is rather permitted than approved, and that none, but by the instigation of a passion too much indulged, entangle themselves with indissoluble compacts."

"You seem to forget," replied Rasselas, "that you have, even now, represented celibacy as less happy than marriage. Both conditions may be bad, but they cannot both be worst. Thus it happens when wrong opinions are entertained, that they mutually destroy each other, and leave the mind open to truth."

"I did not expect," answered the princess, "to hear that imputed to falsehood which is the consequence only of frailty. To the mind, as to the eye, it is difficult to compare with exactness objects vast in their extent, and various in their parts. Where we see or conceive the whole at once we readily note the discriminations and decide the preference: but of two systems, of which neither can be surveyed by any human being in its full compass of magnitude and multiplicity of complication, where is the wonder, that judging of the whole by parts, I am alternately affected by one and the other as either presses on my memory or fancy? We differ from ourselves just as we differ from each other, when we see only part of the question, as in the multifarious relations of politics and morality: but when we perceive the whole at once, as in numerical computations, all agree in one judgment, and none ever varies his opinion."

"Let us not add," said the prince, "to the other evils of life, the bitterness of controversy, nor endeavor to vie with each other in subtleties of argument. We are employed in a search, of which both are equally to enjoy the success, or suffer by the miscarriage. It is therefore fit that we assist each other. You surely conclude too hastily from the infelicity of marriage against its institution; will not the misery of life prove equally that life cannot be the gift of heaven? The world must be peopled by marriage, or peopled without it."

"How the world is to be peopled," returned Nekayah, "is not my care, and needs not be yours. I see no danger that the present generation should omit to leave successors behind them: we are not now inquiring for the world, but for ourselves."

Chapter 29. The Debate on Marriage Continued

"The good of the whole," says Rasselas, "is the same with the good of all its parts. If marriage be best for mankind it must be evidently best for individuals, or a permanent and necessary duty must be the cause of evil, and some must be inevitably sacrificed to the convenience of others. In the estimate which you have made of the two states, it appears that the incommodities of a single life are, in a great measure, necessary and certain, but those of the conjugal state accidental and avoidable.

"I cannot forbear to flatter myself that prudence and benevolence will make marriage happy. The general folly of mankind is the cause of general complaint. What can be expected but disappointment and repentance from a choice made in the immaturity of youth, in the ardor of desire, without judgment, without foresight, without inquiry after conformity of opinions, similarity of manners, rectitude of judgment, or purity of sentiment.

"Such is the common process of marriage. A youth and maiden meeting by chance, or brought together by artifice, exchange glances, reciprocate civilities, go home, and dream of one another. Having little to divert attention, or diversify thought, they find themselves uneasy when they are apart, and therefore conclude that they shall be happy together. They marry, and discover what nothing but voluntary blindness had before concealed; they wear out life in altercations, and charge nature with cruelty.

"From those early marriages proceeds likewise the rivalry of parents and children: the son is eager to enjoy the world before the father is willing to forsake it, and there is hardly room at once for two generations. The daughter begins to bloom before the mother can be content to fade, and neither can forbear to wish for the absence of the other.

"Surely all these evils may be avoided by that deliberation and delay which prudence prescribes to irrevocable choice. In the variety and jollity of youthful pleasures life may be well enough supported without the help of a partner. Longer time will increase experience, and wider views will allow better opportunities of inquiry and selection: one advantage, at least, will be certain; the parents will be visibly older than their children."

"What reason cannot collect," said Nekayah, "and what experiment has not yet taught, can be known only from the report of others. I have been told that late marriages are not eminently happy. This is a question too important to be neglected, and I have often proposed it to those, whose accuracy of remark, and comprehensiveness of knowledge, made their suffrages[9] worthy of regard. They have generally determined that it is dangerous for a man and woman to suspend their fate upon each other, at a time when opinions are fixed, and habits are established; when friendships have been contracted on both sides, when life has been planned into method, and the mind has long enjoyed the contemplation of its own prospects.

"It is scarcely possible that two traveling through the world under the conduct of chance should have been both directed to the same path, and it will not often happen that either will quit the track which custom has made pleasing. When the desultory levity of youth has settled into regularity, it is soon succeeded by pride ashamed to yield, or obstinacy delighting to contend. And even though mutual esteem produces mutual desire to please, time itself, as

9. Opinions.

it modifies unchangeably the external mien, determines likewise the direction of the passions, and gives an inflexible rigidity to the manners. Long customs are not easily broken: he that attempts to change the course of his own life very often labors in vain; and how shall we do that for others which we are seldom able to do for ourselves?"

"But surely," interposed the prince, "you suppose the chief motive of choice forgotten or neglected. Whenever I shall seek a wife, it shall be my first question, whether she be willing to be led by reason?"

"Thus it is," said Nekayah, "that philosophers are deceived. There are a thousand familiar[1] disputes which reason never can decide; questions that elude investigation, and make logic ridiculous; cases where something must be done, and where little can be said. Consider the state of mankind, and inquire how few can be supposed to act upon any occasions, whether small or great, with all the reasons of action present to their minds. Wretched would be the pair above all names of wretchedness, who should be doomed to adjust by reason every morning all the minute detail of a domestic day.

"Those who marry at an advanced age will probably escape the encroachments of their children; but, in diminution of this advantage, they will be likely to leave them, ignorant and helpless, to a guardian's mercy: or, if that should not happen, they must at least go out of the world before they see those whom they love best either wise or great.

"From their children, if they have less to fear, they have less also to hope, and they lose, without equivalent, the joys of early love, and the convenience of uniting with manners pliant and minds susceptible of new impressions, which might wear away their dissimilitudes by long cohabitation, as soft bodies, by continual attrition, conform their surfaces to each other.

"I believe it will be found that those who marry late are best pleased with their children, and those who marry early with their partners."

"The union of these two affections," said Rasselas, "would produce all that could be wished. Perhaps there is a time when marriage might unite them, a time neither too early for the father, nor too late for the husband."

"Every hour," answered the princess, "confirms my prejudice in favor of the position so often uttered by the mouth of Imlac, 'That nature sets her gifts on the right hand and on the left.' Those conditions, which flatter hope and attract desire, are so constituted that, as we approach one, we recede from another. There are goods so opposed that we cannot seize both, but, by too much prudence, may pass between them at too great a distance to reach either. This is often the fate of long consideration; he does nothing who endeavors to do more than is allowed to humanity. Flatter not yourself with contrarieties of pleasure. Of the blessings set before you make your choice, and be content. No man can taste the fruits of autumn, while he is delighting his scent with the flowers of the spring: no man can, at the same time, fill his cup from the source and from the mouth of the Nile."

Chapter 30. Imlac Enters, and Changes the Conversation

Here Imlac entered, and interrupted them. "Imlac," said Rasselas, "I have been taking from the princess the dismal history of private life, and am almost discouraged from further search."

1. Domestic.

"It seems to me," said Imlac, "that while you are making the choice of life, you neglect to live. You wander about a single city, which, however large and diversified, can now afford few novelties, and forget that you are in a country, famous among the earliest monarchies for the power and wisdom of its inhabitants; a country where the sciences first dawned that illuminate the world, and beyond which the arts cannot be traced of civil society or domestic life.

"The old Egyptians have left behind them monuments of industry and power before which all European magnificence is confessed to fade away. The ruins of their architecture are the schools of modern builders, and from the wonders which time has spared we may conjecture, though uncertainly, what it has destroyed."

"My curiosity," said Rasselas, "does not very strongly lead me to survey piles of stone, or mounds of earth; my business is with man. I came hither not to measure fragments of temples, or trace choked aqueducts, but to look upon the various scenes of the present world."

"The things that are now before us," said the princess, "require attention, and deserve it. What have I to do with the heroes or the monuments of ancient times? with times which never can return, and heroes, whose form of life was different from all that the present condition of mankind requires or allows."

"To know anything," returned the poet, "we must know its effects; to see men we must see their works, that we may learn what reason has dictated, or passion has incited, and find what are the most powerful motives of action. To judge rightly of the present we must oppose it to the past; for all judgment is comparative, and of the future nothing can be known. The truth is, that no mind is much employed upon the present: recollection and anticipation fill up almost all our moments. Our passions are joy and grief, love and hatred, hope and fear. Of joy and grief the past is the object, and the future of hope and fear; even love and hatred respect the past, for the cause must have been before the effect.

"The present state of things is the consequence of the former, and it is natural to inquire what were the sources of the good that we enjoy, or of the evil that we suffer. If we act only for ourselves, to neglect the study of history is not prudent: if we are entrusted with the care of others, it is not just. Ignorance, when it is voluntary, is criminal; and he may properly be charged with evil who refused to learn how he might prevent it.

"There is no part of history so generally useful as that which relates the progress of the human mind, the gradual improvement of reason, the successive advances of science, the vicissitudes of learning and ignorance, which are the light and darkness of thinking beings, the extinction and resuscitation of arts, and all the revolutions of the intellectual world. If accounts of battles and invasions are peculiarly the business of princes, the useful or elegant arts are not to be neglected; those who have kingdoms to govern, have understandings to cultivate.

"Example is always more efficacious than precept. A soldier is formed in war, and a painter must copy pictures. In this, contemplative life has the advantage: great actions are seldom seen, but the labors of art are always at hand for those who desire to know what art has been able to perform.

"When the eye or the imagination is struck with any uncommon work the next transition of an active mind is to the means by which it was performed. Here begins the true use of such contemplation; we enlarge our comprehension by new ideas, and perhaps recover some art lost to mankind, or learn what is less perfectly known in our own country. At least we compare our own with former times, and either rejoice at our improvements, or, what is the first motion towards good, discover our defects."

"I am willing," said the prince, "to see all that can deserve my search." "And I," said the princess, "shall rejoice to learn something of the manners of antiquity."

"The most pompous monument of Egyptian greatness, and one of the most bulky works of manual industry," said Imlac, "are the pyramids; fabrics[2] raised before the time of history, and of which the earliest narratives afford us only uncertain traditions. Of these the greatest is still standing, very little injured by time."

"Let us visit them tomorrow," said Nekayah. "I have often heard of the Pyramids, and shall not rest, till I have seen them within and without with my own eyes."

Chapter 31. They Visit the Pyramids

The resolution being thus taken, they set out the next day. They laid tents upon their camels, being resolved to stay among the pyramids till their curiosity was fully satisfied. They traveled gently, turned aside to everything remarkable, stopped from time to time and conversed with the inhabitants, and observed the various appearances of towns ruined and inhabited, of wild and cultivated nature.

When they came to the great pyramid, they were astonished at the extent of the base, and the height of the top. Imlac explained to them the principles upon which the pyramidal form was chosen for a fabric intended to coextend its duration with that of the world; he showed that its gradual diminution gave it such stability as defeated all the common attacks of the elements, and could scarcely be overthrown by earthquakes themselves, the least resistible of natural violence. A concussion that should shatter the pyramid would threaten the dissolution of the continent.

They measured all its dimensions, and pitched their tents at its foot. Next day they prepared to enter its interior apartments, and having hired the common guides, climbed up to the first passage, when the favorite of the princess, looking into the cavity, stepped back and trembled. "Pekuah," said the princess, "of what art thou afraid?" "Of the narrow entrance," answered the lady, "and of the dreadful gloom. I dare not enter a place which must surely be inhabited by unquiet souls. The original possessors of these dreadful vaults will start up before us, and perhaps shut us in forever." She spoke, and threw her arms round the neck of her mistress.

"If all your fear be of apparitions," said the prince, "I will promise you safety. There is no danger from the dead; he that is once buried will be seen no more."

"That the dead are seen no more," said Imlac, "I will not undertake to maintain, against the concurrent and unvaried testimony of all ages, and of all nations. There is no people, rude or learned, among whom apparitions of the dead are not related and believed. This opinion, which perhaps prevails as far as human nature is diffused, could become universal only by its truth; those that never heard of one another would not have agreed in a tale which nothing but experience can make credible. That it is doubted by single cavilers can

2. Buildings.

very little weaken the general evidence; and some who deny it with their tongues confess it by their fears.

"Yet I do not mean to add new terrors to those which have already seized upon Pekuah. There can be no reason why specters should haunt the pyramid more than other places, or why they should have power or will to hurt innocence and purity. Our entrance is no violation of their privileges; we can take nothing from them, how then can we offend them?"

"My dear Pekuah," said the princess, "I will always go before you, and Imlac shall follow you. Remember that you are the companion of the princess of Abyssinia."

"If the princess is pleased that her servant should die," returned the lady, "let her command some death less dreadful than enclosure in this horrid cavern. You know I dare not disobey you; I must go if you command me, but if I once enter, I never shall come back."

The princess saw that her fear was too strong for expostulation or reproof, and, embracing her, told her that she should stay in the tent till their return. Pekuah was yet not satisfied, but entreated the princess not to pursue so dreadful a purpose as that of entering the recesses of the pyramid. "Though I cannot teach courage," said Nekayah, "I must not learn cowardice, nor leave at last undone what I came hither only to do."

Chapter 32. They Enter the Pyramid

Pekuah descended to the tents, and the rest entered the pyramid. They passed through the galleries, surveyed the vaults of marble, and examined the chest in which the body of the founder is supposed to have been reposited. They then sat down in one of the most spacious chambers to rest a while before they attempted to return.

"We have now," said Imlac, "gratified our minds with an exact view of the greatest work of man, except the wall of China.

"Of the wall it is very easy to assign the motive. It secured a wealthy and timorous nation from the incursions of barbarians, whose unskillfulness in arts made it easier for them to supply their wants by rapine than by industry, and who from time to time poured in upon the habitations of peaceful commerce, as vultures descend upon domestic fowl. Their celerity and fierceness made the wall necessary, and their ignorance made it efficacious.

"But for the pyramids, no reason has ever been given adequate to the cost and labor of the work. The narrowness of the chambers proves that it could afford no retreat from enemies, and treasures might have been reposited at far less expense with equal security. It seems to have been erected only in compliance with that hunger of imagination which preys incessantly upon life, and must be always appeased by some employment. Those who have already all that they can enjoy must enlarge their desires. He that has built for use till use is supplied, must begin to build for vanity, and extend his plan to the utmost power of human performance, that he may not be soon reduced to form another wish.

"I consider this mighty structure as a monument of the insufficiency of human enjoyments. A king, whose power is unlimited, and whose treasures surmount all real and imaginary wants, is compelled to solace, by the erection of a pyramid, the satiety of dominion and tastelessness of pleasures, and to amuse the tediousness of declining life by seeing thousands laboring without end, and one stone, for no purpose, laid upon another. Whoever thou art, that, not content with a moderate condition, imaginest happiness in royal magnificence, and dreamest that command or riches can feed the appetite of novelty with perpetual gratifications, survey the pyramids, and confess thy folly!"

Chapter 33. The Princess Meets with an Unexpected Misfortune

They rose up, and returned through the cavity at which they had entered, and the princess prepared for her favorite a long narrative of dark labyrinths, and costly rooms, and of the different impressions which the varieties of the way had made upon her. But when they came to their train, they found every one silent and dejected: the men discovered[3] shame and fear in their countenances, and the women were weeping in the tents.

What had happened they did not try to conjecture, but immediately inquired. "You had scarcely entered into the pyramid," said one of the attendants, "when a troop of Arabs rushed upon us: we were too few to resist them, and too slow to escape. They were about to search the tents, set us on our camels, and drive us along before them, when the approach of some Turkish horsemen put them to flight; but they seized the lady Pekuah with her two maids, and carried them away: the Turks are now pursuing them by our instigation, but I fear they will not be able to overtake them."

The princess was overpowered with surprise and grief. Rasselas, in the first heat of his resentment, ordered his servants to follow him, and prepared to pursue the robbers with his saber in his hand. "Sir," said Imlac, "what can you hope from violence or valor? the Arabs are mounted on horses trained to battle and retreat; we have only beasts of burden. By leaving our present station we may lose the princess, but cannot hope to regain Pekuah."

In a short time the Turks returned, having not been able to reach the enemy. The princess burst out into new lamentations, and Rasselas could scarcely forbear to reproach them with cowardice; but Imlac was of opinion, that the escape of the Arabs was no addition to their misfortune, for, perhaps, they would have killed their captives rather than have resigned them.

Chapter 34. They Return to Cairo without Pekuah

There was nothing to be hoped from longer stay. They returned to Cairo repenting of their curiosity, censuring the negligence of the government, lamenting their own rashness which had neglected to procure a guard, imagining many expedients by which the loss of Pekuah might have been prevented, and resolving to do something for her recovery, though none could find any thing proper to be done.

Nekayah retired to her chamber, where her women attempted to comfort her, by telling her that all had their troubles, and that lady Pekuah had enjoyed much happiness in the world for a long time, and might reasonably expect a change of fortune. They hoped that some good would befall her wheresoever she was, and that their mistress would find another friend who might supply her place.

The princess made them no answer, and they continued the form of condolence, not much grieved in their hearts that the favorite was lost.

Next day the prince presented to the Bassa a memorial[4] of the wrong which

3. Revealed, betrayed. "Train": retinue.

4. Statement of facts.

he had suffered, and a petition for redress. The Bassa threatened to punish the robbers, but did not attempt to catch them, nor, indeed, could any account or description be given by which he might direct the pursuit.

It soon appeared that nothing would be done by authority. Governors, being accustomed to hear of more crimes than they can punish, and more wrongs than they can redress, set themselves at ease by indiscriminate negligence, and presently[5] forget the request when they lose sight of the petitioner.

Imlac then endeavored to gain some intelligence by private agents. He found many who pretended to an exact knowledge of all the haunts of the Arabs, and to regular correspondence with their chiefs, and who readily undertook the recovery of Pekuah. Of these, some were furnished with money for their journey, and came back no more; some were liberally paid for accounts which a few days discovered to be false. But the princess would not suffer any means, however improbable, to be left untried. While she was doing something she kept her hope alive. As one expedient failed, another was suggested; when one messenger returned unsuccessful, another was dispatched to a different quarter.

Two months had now passed, and of Pekuah nothing had been heard; the hopes which they had endeavored to raise in each other grew more languid, and the princess, when she saw nothing more to be tried, sunk down inconsolable in hopeless dejection. A thousand times she reproached herself with the easy compliance by which she permitted her favorite to stay behind her. "Had not my fondness," said she, "lessened my authority, Pekuah had not dared to talk of her terrors. She ought to have feared me more than specters. A severe look would have overpowered her; a peremptory command would have compelled obedience. Why did foolish indulgence prevail upon me? Why did I not speak and refuse to hear?"

"Great princess," said Imlac, "do not reproach yourself for your virtue, or consider that as blameable by which evil has accidentally been caused. Your tenderness for the timidity of Pekuah was generous and kind. When we act according to our duty, we commit the event to him by whose laws our actions are governed, and who will suffer none to be finally punished for obedience. When, in prospect of some good, whether natural or moral, we break the rules prescribed us, we withdraw from the direction of superior wisdom, and take all consequences upon ourselves. Man cannot so far know the connection of causes and events, as that he may venture to do wrong in order to do right. When we pursue our end by lawful means, we may always console our miscarriage by the hope of future recompense. When we consult only our own policy, and attempt to find a nearer way to good, by overleaping the settled boundaries of right and wrong, we cannot be happy even by success, because we cannot escape the consciousness of our fault; but, if we miscarry, the disappointment is irremediably embittered. How comfortless is the sorrow of him, who feels at once the pangs of guilt, and the vexation of calamity which guilt has brought upon him?

"Consider, princess, what would have been your condition, if the lady Pekuah had entreated to accompany you, and, being compelled to stay in the tents, had been carried away; or how would you have borne the thought, if you had forced her into the pyramid, and she had died before you in agonies of terror."

"Had either happened," said Nekayah, "I could not have endured life till now: I should have been tortured to madness by the remembrance of such

5. Immediately.

cruelty, or must have pined away in abhorrence of myself."

"This at least," said Imlac, "is the present reward of virtuous conduct, that no unlucky consequence can oblige us to repent it."

Chapter 35. The Princess Languishes for Want of Pekuah

Nekayah, being thus reconciled to herself, found that no evil is insupportable but that which is accompanied with consciousness of wrong. She was, from that time, delivered from the violence of tempestuous sorrow, and sunk into silent pensiveness and gloomy tranquillity. She sat from morning to evening recollecting all that had been done or said by her Pekuah, treasured up with might recall to mind any little incident or careless conversation. The sentiments of her, whom she now expected to see no more, were treasured in her memory as rules of life, and she deliberated to no other end than to conjecture on any occasion what would have been the opinion and counsel of Pekuah.

The women, by whom she was attended, knew nothing of her real condition, and therefore she could not talk to them but with caution and reserve. She began to remit[6] her curiosity, having no great care to collect notions which she had no convenience of uttering. Rasselas endeavored first to comfort and afterwards to divert her; he hired musicians, to whom she seemed to listen, but did not hear them, and procured masters to instruct her in various arts, whose lectures, when they visited her again, were again to be repeated. She had lost her taste of pleasure and her ambition of excellence. And her mind, though forced into short excursions, always recurred to the image of her friend.

Imlac was every morning earnestly enjoined to renew his inquiries, and was asked every night whether he had yet heard of Pekuah, till not being able to return the princess the answer that she desired, he was less and less willing to come into her presence. She observed his backwardness, and commanded him to attend her. "You are not," said she, "to confound impatience with resentment, or to suppose that I charge you with negligence, because I repine at your unsuccessfulness. I do not much wonder at your absence; I know that the unhappy are never pleasing, and that all naturally avoid the contagion of misery. To hear complaints is wearisome alike to the wretched and the happy; for who would cloud by adventitious grief the short gleams of gaiety which life allows us? or who, that is struggling under his own evils, will add to them the miseries of another?

"The time is at hand, when none shall be disturbed any longer by the sighs of Nekayah: my search after happiness is now at an end. I am resolved to retire from the world with all its flatteries and deceits, and will hide myself in solitude, without any other care than to compose my thoughts, and regulate my hours by a constant succession of innocent occupations, till, with a mind purified from all earthly desires, I shall enter into that state, to which all are hastening, and in which I hope again to enjoy the friendship of Pekuah."

"Do not entangle your mind," said Imlac, "by irrevocable determinations, nor increase the burden of life by a voluntary accumulation of misery: the weariness of retirement will continue or increase when the loss of Pekuah is forgotten. That you have been deprived of one pleasure is no very good reason for rejection of the rest."

6. Slacken.

"Since Pekuah was taken from me," said the princess, "I have no pleasure to reject or to retain. She that has no one to love or trust has little to hope. She wants the radical principle of happiness. We may, perhaps, allow that what satisfaction this world can afford, must arise from the conjunction of wealth, knowledge and goodness: wealth is nothing but as it is bestowed, and knowledge nothing but as it is communicated: they must therefore be imparted to others, and to whom could I now delight to impart them? Goodness affords the only comfort which can be enjoyed without a partner, and goodness may be practised in retirement."

"How far solitude may admit goodness, or advance it, I shall not," replied Imlac, "dispute at present. Remember the confession of the pious hermit. You will wish to return into the world, when the image of your companion has left your thoughts." "That time," said Nekayah, "will never come. The generous frankness, the modest obsequiousness,[7] and the faithful secrecy of my dear Pekuah, will always be more missed, as I shall live longer to see vice and folly."

"The state of a mind oppressed with a sudden calamity," said Imlac, "is like that of the fabulous inhabitants of the new created earth, who, when the first night came upon them, supposed that day never would return. When the clouds of sorrow gather over us, we see nothing beyond them, nor can imagine how they will be dispelled: yet a new day succeeded to the night, and sorrow is never long without a dawn of ease. But they who restrain themselves from receiving comfort, do as the savages would have done, had they put out their eyes when it was dark. Our minds, like our bodies, are in continual flux; something is hourly lost, and something acquired. To lose much at once is inconvenient to either, but while the vital powers remain uninjured, nature will find the means of reparation. Distance has the same effect on the mind as on the eye, and while we glide along the stream of time, whatever we leave behind us is always lessening, and that which we approach increasing in magnitude. Do not suffer life to stagnate; it will grow muddy for want of motion: commit yourself again to the current of the world; Pekuah will vanish by degrees; you will meet in your way some other favorite, or learn to diffuse yourself in general conversation."

"At least," said the prince, "do not despair before all remedies have been tried: the inquiry after the unfortunate lady is still continued, and shall be carried on with yet greater diligence, on condition that you will promise to wait a year for the event, without any unalterable resolution."

Nekayah thought this a reasonable demand, and made the promise to her brother, who had been advised by Imlac to require it. Imlac had, indeed, no great hope of regaining Pekuah, but he supposed, that if he could secure the interval of a year, the princess would be then in no danger of a cloister.

Chapter 36. Pekuah Is Still Remembered. The Progress of Sorrow

Nekayah, seeing that nothing was omitted for the recovery of her favorite, and having, by her promise, set her intention of retirement at a distance, began imperceptibly to return to common cares and common pleasures. She rejoiced without her own consent at the suspension of her sorrows, and sometimes caught herself with indignation in the act of turning away her mind from the remembrance of her, whom yet she resolved never to forget.

7. Obedience.

She then appointed a certain hour of the day for meditation on the merits and fondness of Pekuah, and for some weeks retired constantly at the time fixed, and returned with her eyes swollen and her countenance clouded. By degrees she grew less scrupulous, and suffered any important and pressing avocation to delay the tribute of daily tears. She then yielded to less occasions; sometimes forgot what she was indeed afraid to remember, and, at last, wholly released herself from the duty of periodical affliction.

Her real love of Pekuah was yet not diminished. A thousand occurrences brought her back to memory, and a thousand wants, which nothing but the confidence of friendship can supply, made her frequently regretted. She, therefore, solicited Imlac never to desist from inquiry, and to leave no art of intelligence untried, that, at least, she might have the comfort of knowing that she did not suffer by negligence or sluggishness. "Yet what," said she, "is to be expected from our pursuit of happiness, when we find the state of life to be such, that happiness itself is the cause of misery? Why should we endeavor to attain that, of which the possession cannot be secured? I shall henceforward fear to yield my heart to excellence, however bright, or to fondness, however tender, lest I should lose again what I have lost in Pekuah."

Chapter 37. The Princess Hears News of Pekuah

In seven months, one of the messengers, who had been sent away upon the day when the promise was drawn from the princess, returned, after many unsuccessful rambles, from the borders of Nubia, with an account that Pekuah was in the hands of an Arab chief, who possessed a castle or fortress on the extremity of Egypt. The Arab, whose revenue was plunder, was willing to restore her, with her two attendants, for two hundred ounces of gold.

The price was no subject of debate. The princess was in ecstasies when she heard that her favorite was alive, and might so cheaply be ransomed. She could not think of delaying for a moment Pekuah's happiness or her own, but entreated her brother to send back the messenger with the sum required. Imlac, being consulted, was not very confident of the veracity of the relator, and was still more doubtful of the Arab's faith, who might, if he were too liberally trusted, detain at once the money and the captives. He thought it dangerous to put themselves in the power of the Arab, by going into his district, and could not expect that the rover[8] would so much expose himself as to come into the lower country, where he might be seized by the forces of the Bassa.

It is difficult to negotiate where neither will trust. But Imlac, after some deliberation, directed the messenger to propose that Pekuah should be conducted by ten horsemen to the monastery of St. Anthony, which is situated in the deserts of Upper Egypt, where she should be met by the same number, and her ransom should be paid.

That no time might be lost, as they expected that the proposal would not be refused, they immediately began their journey to the monastery; and, when they arrived, Imlac went forward with the former messenger to the Arab's fortress. Rasselas was desirous to go with them, but neither his sister nor Imlac would consent. The Arab, according to the custom of his nation, observed the laws of hospitality with great exactness to those who put themselves into his power, and, in a few days, brought Pekuah with her maids, by easy journeys,

8. Robber.

to their place appointed, where receiving the stipulated price, he restored her with great respect to liberty and her friends, and undertook to conduct them back toward Cairo beyond all danger of robbery or violence.

The princess and her favorite embraced each other with transport too violent to be expressed, and went out together to pour the tears of tenderness in secret, and exchange professions of kindness and gratitude. After a few hours they returned into the refectory of the convent, where, in the presence of the prior and his brethren, the prince required of Pekuah the history of her adventures.

Chapter 38. The Adventures of the Lady Pekuah

"At what time, and in what manner, I was forced away," said Pekuah, "your servants have told you. The suddenness of the event struck me with surprise, and I was at first rather stupified than agitated with any passion of either fear or sorrow. My confusion was increased by the speed and tumult of our flight while we were followed by the Turks, who, as it seemed, soon despaired to overtake us, or were afraid of those whom they made a show of menacing.

"When the Arabs saw themselves out of danger they slackened their course, and, as I was less harassed by external violence, I began to feel more uneasiness in my mind. After some time we stopped near a spring shaded with trees in a pleasant meadow, where we were set upon the ground, and offered such refreshments as our masters were partaking. I was suffered to sit with my maids apart from the rest, and none attempted to comfort or insult us. Here I first began to feel the full weight of my misery. The girls sat weeping in silence, and from time to time looked on me for succor. I knew not to what condition we were doomed, nor could conjecture where would be the place of our captivity, or whence to draw any hope of deliverance. I was in the hands of robbers and savages, and had no reason to suppose that their pity was more than their justice, or that they would forbear the gratification of any ardor of desire, or caprice of cruelty. I, however, kissed my maids, and endeavored to pacify them by remarking, that we were yet treated with decency, and that, since we were now carried beyond pursuit, there was no danger of violence to our lives.

"When we were to be set again on horseback, my maids clung round me, and refused to be parted, but I commanded them not to irritate those who had us in their power. We traveled the remaining part of the day through an unfrequented and pathless country, and came by moonlight to the side of a hill, where the rest of the troop was stationed. Their tents were pitched, and their fires kindled, and our chief was welcomed as a man much beloved by his dependents.

"We were received into a large tent, where we found women who had attended their husbands in the expedition. They set before us the supper which they had provided, and I eat it rather to encourage my maids than to comply with any appetite of my own. When the meat was taken away they spread the carpets for repose. I was weary, and hoped to find in sleep that remission of distress which nature seldom denies. Ordering myself therefore to be undressed, I observed that the women looked very earnestly upon me, not expecting, I suppose, to see me so submissively attended. When my upper vest was taken off, they were apparently struck with the splendor of my clothes, and one of them timorously laid her hand upon the embroidery. She then went out, and, in a short time, came back with another woman, who seemed to be of higher rank, and greater authority. She did, at her entrance, the usual act of reverence, and, taking me by the hand, placed me in a smaller tent, spread with finer carpets, where I spent the night quietly with my maids.

"In the morning, as I was sitting on the grass, the chief of the troop came towards me: I rose up to receive him, and he bowed with great respect. 'Illustrious lady,' said he, 'my fortune is better than I had presumed to hope; I am told by my women that I have a princess in my camp.' 'Sir,' answered I, 'your women have deceived themselves and you; I am not a princess, but an unhappy stranger who intended soon to have left this country, in which I am now to be imprisoned for ever.' 'Whoever, or whencesoever, you are,' returned the Arab, 'your dress, and that of your servants, show your rank to be high, and your wealth to be great. Why should you, who can so easily procure your ransom, think yourself in danger of perpetual captivity? The purpose of my incursions is to increase my riches, or more properly to gather tribute. The sons of Ishmael[9] are the natural and hereditary lords of this part of the continent, which is usurped by late invaders, and low-born tyrants, from whom we are compelled to take by the sword what is denied to justice. The violence of war admits no distinction; the lance that is lifted at guilt and power will sometimes fall on innocence and gentleness.'

" 'How little,' said I, 'did I expect that yesterday it should have fallen upon me.'

" 'Misfortunes,' answered the Arab, 'should always be expected. If the eye of hostility could learn reverence or pity, excellence like yours had been exempt from injury. But the angels of affliction spread their toils alike for the virtuous and the wicked, for the mighty and the mean. Do not be disconsolate; I am not one of the lawless and cruel rovers of the desert; I know the rules of civil life: I will fix your ransom, give a passport to your messenger, and perform my stipulation with nice punctuality.'[1]

"You will easily believe that I was pleased with his courtesy; and finding that his predominant passion was desire of money, I began now to think my danger less, for I knew that no sum would be thought too great for the release of Pekuah. I told him that he should have no reason to charge me with ingratitude, if I was used with kindness, and that any ransom, which could be expected for a maid of common rank, would be paid, but that he must not persist to rate me as a princess. He said, he would consider what he should demand, and then, smiling, bowed and retired.

"Soon after the women came about me, each contending to be more officious[2] than the other, and my maids themselves were served with reverence. We traveled onward by short journeys. On the fourth day the chief told me, that my ransom must be two hundred ounces of gold, which I not only promised him, but told him, that I would add fifty more, if I and my maids were honorably treated.

"I never knew the power of gold before. From that time I was the leader of the troop. The march of every day was longer or shorter as I commanded, and the tents were pitched where I chose to rest. We now had camels and other conveniencies for travel, my own women were always at my side, and I amused myself with observing the manners of the vagrant nations,[3] and with viewing

9. Arabs, who claim descent from Ishmael, a son of Abraham.
1. Scrupulous exactness. "Civil": civilized.
2. Ready to serve.
3. Nomads.

remains of ancient edifices with which these deserted countries appear to have been, in some distant age, lavishly embellished.

"The chief of the band was a man far from illiterate: he was able to travel by the stars or the compass, and had marked in his erratic expeditions such places as are most worthy the notice of a passenger.[4] He observed to me, that buildings are always best preserved in places little frequented, and difficult of access: for, when once a country declines from its primitive splendor, the more inhabitants are left, the quicker ruin will be made. Walls supply stones more easily than quarries, and palaces and temples will be demolished to make stables of granite, and cottages of porphyry.

Chapter 39. The Adventures of Pekuah Continued

"We wandered about in this manner for some weeks, whether, as our chief pretended, for my gratification, or, as I rather suspected, for some convenience of his own. I endeavored to appear contented where sullenness and resentment would have been of no use, and that endeavor conduced much to the calmness of my mind; but my heart was always with Nekayah, and the troubles of the night much overbalanced the amusements of the day. My women, who threw all their cares upon their mistress, set their minds at ease from the time when they saw me treated with respect, and gave themselves up to the incidental alleviations of our fatigue without solicitude or sorrow. I was pleased with their pleasure, and animated with their confidence. My condition had lost much of its terror, since I found that the Arab ranged the country merely to get riches. Avarice is an uniform and tractable vice: other intellectual distempers are different in different constitutions of mind; that which sooths the pride of one will offend the pride of another; but to the favor of the covetous there is a ready way, bring money and nothing is denied.

"At last we came to the dwelling of our chief, a strong and spacious house built with stone in an island of the Nile, which lies, as I was told, under the tropic. 'Lady,' said the Arab, 'you shall rest after your journey a few weeks in this place, where you are to consider yourself as sovereign. My occupation is war: I have therefore chosen this obscure residence, from which I can issue unexpected, and to which I can retire unpursued. You may now repose in security: here are few pleasures, but here is no danger.' He then led me into the inner apartments, and seating me on the richest couch, bowed to the ground. His women, who considered me as a rival, looked on me with malignity; but being soon informed that I was a great lady detained only for my ransom, they began to vie with each other in obsequiousness and reverence.

"Being again comforted with new assurances of speedy liberty, I was for some days diverted from impatience by the novelty of the place. The turrets overlooked the country to a great distance, and afforded a view of many windings of the stream. In the day I wandered from one place to another as the course of the sun varied the splendor of the prospect, and saw many things which I had never seen before. The crocodiles and river-horses[5] are common in this unpeopled region, and I often looked upon them with terror, though I knew that they could not hurt me. For some time I expected to see mermaids and tritons, which, as Imlac has told me, the European travelers have stationed

4. Traveler.

5. Hippopotamuses.

in the Nile, but no such beings ever appeared, and the Arab, when I inquired after them, laughed at my credulity.

"At night the Arab always attended me to a tower set apart for celestial observations, where he endeavored to teach me the names and courses of the stars. I had no great inclination to this study, but an appearance of attention was necessary to please my instructor, who valued himself for his skill, and, in a little while, I found some employment requisite to beguile the tediousness of time, which was to be passed always amidst the same objects. I was weary of looking in the morning on things from which I had turned away weary in the evening: I therefore was at last willing to observe the stars rather than do nothing, but could not always compose my thoughts, and was very often thinking on Nekayah when others imagined me contemplating the sky. Soon after the Arab went upon another expedition, and then my only pleasure was to talk with my maids about the accident by which we were carried away, and the happiness that we should all enjoy at the end of our captivity."

"There were women in your Arab's fortress," said the princess, "why did you not make them your companions, enjoy their conversation, and partake their diversions? In a place where they found business or amusement, why should you alone sit corroded with idle melancholy? or why could not you bear for a few months that condition to which they were condemned for life?"

"The diversions of the women," answered Pekuah, "were only childish play, by which the mind accustomed to stronger operations could not be kept busy. I could do all which they delighted in doing by powers merely sensitive,[6] while my intellectual faculties were flown to Cairo. They ran from room to room as a bird hops from wire to wire in his cage. They danced for the sake of motion, as lambs frisk in a meadow. One sometimes pretended to be hurt that the rest might be alarmed, or hid herself that another might seek her. Part of their time passed in watching the progress of light bodies that floated on the river, and part in marking the various forms into which clouds broke in the sky.

"Their business was only needlework, in which I and my maids sometimes helped them; but you know that the mind will easily straggle from the fingers, nor will you suspect that captivity and absence from Nekayah could receive solace from silken flowers.

"Nor was much satisfaction to be hoped from their conversation: for of what could they be expected to talk? They had seen nothing; for they had lived from early youth in that narrow spot: of what they had not seen they could have no knowledge, for they could not read. They had no ideas but of the few things that were within their view, and had hardly names for anything but their clothes and their food. As I bore a superior character, I was often called to terminate their quarrels, which I decided as equitably as I could. If it could have amused me to hear the complaints of each against the rest, I might have been often detained by long stories, but the motives of their animosity were so small that I could not listen without intercepting the tale."

"How," said Rasselas, "can the Arab, whom you represented as a man of more than common accomplishments, take any pleasure in his seraglio, when it is filled only with women like these. Are they exquisitely beautiful?"

"They do not," said Pekuah, "want that unaffecting and ignoble beauty which may subsist without spriteliness or sublimity, without energy of thought

6. "Having sense or perception, but not reason" (Johnson's *Dictionary*).

or dignity of virtue. But to a man like the Arab such beauty was only a flower casually plucked and carelessly thrown away. Whatever pleasures he might find among them, they were not those of friendship or society. When they were playing about him he looked on them with inattentive superiority: when they vied for his regard he sometimes turned away disgusted. As they had no knowledge, their talk could take nothing from the tediousness of life: as they had no choice, their fondness, or appearance of fondness, excited in him neither pride nor gratitude; he was not exalted in his own esteem by the smiles of a woman who saw no other man, nor was much obliged by that regard, of which he could never know the sincerity, and which he might often perceive to be exerted not so much to delight him as to pain a rival. That which he gave, and they received, as love, was only a careless distribution of superfluous time, such love as man can bestow upon that which he despises, such as has neither hope nor fear, neither joy nor sorrow."

"You have reason, lady, to think yourself happy," said Imlac, "that you have been thus easily dismissed. How could a mind, hungry for knowledge, be willing, in an intellectual famine, to lose such a banquet as Pekuah's conversation?"

"I am inclined to believe," answered Pekuah, "that he was for some time in suspense; for, notwithstanding his promise, whenever I proposed to dispatch a messenger to Cairo, he found some excuse for delay. While I was detained in his house he made many incursions into the neighboring countries, and, perhaps, he would have refused to discharge me, had his plunder been equal to his wishes. He returned always courteous, related his adventures, delighted to hear my observations, and endeavored to advance my acquaintance with the stars. When I importuned him to send away my letters, he soothed me with professions of honor and sincerity; and, when I could be no longer decently denied, put his troop again in motion, and left me to govern in his absence. I was much afflicted by this studied procrastination, and was sometimes afraid that I should be forgotten; that you would leave Cairo, and I must end my days in an island of the Nile.

"I grew at last hopeless and dejected, and cared so little to entertain him, that he for a while more frequently talked with my maids. That he should fall in love with them, or with me, might have been equally fatal, and I was not much pleased with the growing friendship. My anxiety was not long; for, as I recovered some degree of cheerfulness, he returned to me, and I could not forbear to despise my former uneasiness.

"He still delayed to send for my ransom, and would, perhaps, never have determined, had not your agent found his way to him. The gold, which he would not fetch, he could not reject when it was offered. He hastened to prepare for our journey hither, like a man delivered from the pain of an intestine conflict. I took leave of my companions in the house, who dismissed me with cold indifference."

Nekayah, having heard her favorite's relation, rose and embraced her, and Rasselas gave her an hundred ounces of gold, which she presented to the Arab for the fifty that were promised.

Chapter 40. The History of a Man of Learning

They returned to Cairo, and were so well pleased at finding themselves together, that none of them went much abroad. The prince began to love learning, and one day declared to Imlac, that he intended to devote himself to science,[7] and pass the rest of his days in literary solitude.

"Before you make your final choice," answered Imlac, "you ought to examine its hazards, and converse with some of those who are grown old in the company of themselves. I have just left the observatory of one of the most learned astronomers in the world, who has spent forty years in unwearied attention to the motions and appearances of the celestial bodies, and has drawn out his soul in endless calculations. He admits a few friends once a month to hear his deductions and enjoy his discoveries. I was introduced as a man of knowledge worthy of his notice. Men of various ideas and fluent conversation are commonly welcome to those whose thoughts have been long fixed upon a single point, and who find the images of other things stealing away. I delighted him with my remarks, he smiled at the narrative of my travels, and was glad to forget the constellations, and descend for a moment into the lower world.

"On the next day of vacation[8] I renewed my visit, and was so fortunate as to please him again. He relaxed from that time the severity of his rule, and permitted me to enter at my own choice. I found him always busy, and always glad to be relieved. As each knew much which the other was desirous of learning, we exchanged our notions with great delight. I perceived that I had every day more of his confidence, and always found new cause of admiration in the profundity of his mind. His comprehension is vast, his memory capacious and retentive, his discourse is methodical, and his expression clear.

"His integrity and benevolence are equal to his learning. His deepest researches and most favorite studies are willingly interrupted for any opportunity of doing good by his counsel or his riches. To his closest retreat,[9] at his most busy moments, all are admitted that want his assistance: 'For though I exclude idleness and pleasure, I will never,' says he, 'bar my doors against charity. To man is permitted the contemplation of the skies, but the practice of virtue is commanded.' "

"Surely," said the princess, "this man is happy."

"I visited him," said Imlac, "with more and more frequency, and was every time more enamored of his conversation: he was sublime without haughtiness, courteous without formality, and communicative without ostentation. I was at first, great princess, of your opinion, thought him the happiest of mankind, and often congratulated him on the blessing that he enjoyed. He seemed to hear nothing with indifference but the praises of his condition, to which he always returned a general answer, and diverted the conversation to some other topic.

"Amidst this willingness to be pleased, and labor to please, I had quickly reason to imagine that some painful sentiment pressed upon his mind. He often looked up earnestly towards the sun, and let his voice fall in the midst of his discourse. He would sometimes, when we were alone, gaze upon me in silence with the air of a man who longed to speak what he was yet resolved to suppress. He would often send for me with vehement injunctions of haste, though, when I came to him, he had nothing extraordinary to say. And sometimes, when I was leaving him, he would call me back, pause a few moments and then dismiss me.

7. Knowledge.
8. Leisure.
9. Most secluded place of privacy.

Chapter 41. The Astronomer Discovers the Cause of His Uneasiness

"At last the time came when the secret burst his reserve. We were sitting together last night in the turret of his house, watching the emersion of a satellite of Jupiter. A sudden tempest clouded the sky, and disappointed our observation. We sat a while silent in the dark, and then he addressed himself to me in these words: 'Imlac, I have long considered thy friendship as the greatest blessing of my life. Integrity without knowledge is weak and useless, and knowledge without integrity is dangerous and dreadful. I have found in thee all the qualities requisite for trust, benevolence, experience, and fortitude. I have long discharged an office which I must soon quit at the call of nature, and shall rejoice in the hour of imbecility[1] and pain to devolve it upon thee.'

"I thought myself honored by this testimony, and protested that whatever could conduce to his happiness would add likewise to mine.

" 'Hear, Imlac, what thou wilt not without difficulty credit. I have possessed for five years the regulation of weather, and the distribution of the seasons: the sun has listened to my dictates, and passed from tropic to tropic by my direction; the clouds, at my call, have poured their waters, and the Nile has overflowed at my command; I have restrained the rage of the dog-star, and mitigated the fervors of the crab.[2] The winds alone, of all the elemental powers, have hitherto refused my authority, and multitudes have perished by equinoctial tempests which I found myself unable to prohibit or restrain. I have administered this great office with exact justice, and made to the different nations of the earth an impartial dividend of rain and sunshine. What must have been the misery of half the globe, if I had limited the clouds to particular regions, or confined the sun to either side of the equator?'

Chapter 42. The Opinion of the Astronomer Is Explained and Justified

"I suppose he discovered in me, through the obscurity of the room, some tokens of amazement and doubt, for, after a short pause, he proceeded thus:

" 'Not to be easily credited will neither surprise nor offend me; for I am, probably, the first of human beings to whom this trust has been imparted. Nor do I know whether to deem this distinction a reward or punishment; since I have possessed it I have been far less happy than before, and nothing but the consciousness of good intention could have enabled me to support the weariness of unremitted vigilance.'

" 'How long, Sir,' said I, 'has this great office been in your hands?'

" 'About ten years ago,' said he, 'my daily observations of the changes of the sky led me to consider, whether, if I had the power of the seasons, I could confer greater plenty upon the inhabitants of the earth. This contemplation fastened on my mind, and I sat days and nights in imaginary dominion, pouring upon this country and that the showers of fertility, and seconding every fall of rain with a due proportion of sunshine. I had yet only the will to do good, and did not imagine that I should ever have the power.

" 'One day as I was looking on the fields withering with heat, I felt in my mind a sudden wish that I could send rain on the southern mountains, and

1. Feebleness.
2. The fourth sign of the zodiac (Cancer). "The dog-star": Sirius was supposed to cause the heat ("dog days") of summer.

raise the Nile to an inundation. In the hurry of my imagination I commanded rain to fall, and, by comparing the time of my command, with that of the inundation, I found that the clouds had listened to my lips.'

" 'Might not some other cause,' said I, 'produce this concurrence? the Nile does not always rise on the same day.'

" 'Do not believe,' said he with impatience, 'that such objections could escape me: I reasoned long against my own conviction, and labored against truth with the utmost obstinacy. I sometimes suspected myself of madness, and should not have dared to impart this secret but to a man like you, capable of distinguishing the wonderful from the impossible, and the incredible from the false.'

" 'Why, Sir,' said I, 'do you call that incredible, which you know, or think you know, to be true?'

" 'Because,' said he, 'I cannot prove it by any external evidence; and I know too well the laws of demonstration to think that my conviction ought to influence another, who cannot, like me, be conscious of its force. I therefore shall not attempt to gain credit by disputation. It is sufficient that I feel this power, that I have long possessed, and every day exerted it. But the life of man is short, the infirmities of age increase upon me, and the time will soon come when the regulator of the year must mingle with the dust. The care of appointing a successor has long disturbed me; the night and the day have been spent in comparisons of all the characters which have come to my knowledge, and I have yet found none so worthy as thyself.

Chapter 43. The Astronomer Leaves Imlac His Directions

" 'Hear therefore, what I shall impart, with attention, such as the welfare of a world requires. If the task of a king be considered as difficult, who has the care only of a few millions, to whom he cannot do much good or harm, what must be the anxiety of him, on whom depends the action of the elements, and the great gifts of light and heat!—Hear me therefore with attention.

" 'I have diligently considered the position of the earth and sun, and formed innumerable schemes in which I changed their situation. I have sometimes turned aside the axis of the earth, and sometimes varied the ecliptic of the sun: but I have found it impossible to make a disposition by which the world may be advantaged; what one region gains, another loses by any imaginable alteration, even without considering the distant parts of the solar system with which we are unacquainted. Do not, therefore, in thy administration of the year, indulge thy pride by innovation; do not please thyself with thinking that thou canst make thyself renowned to all future ages, by disordering the seasons. The memory of mischief is no desirable fame. Much less will it become thee to let kindness or interest prevail. Never rob other countries of rain to pour it on thine own. For us the Nile is sufficient.'

"I promised that when I possessed the power, I would use it with inflexible integrity, and he dismissed me, pressing my hand. 'My heart,' said he, 'will be now at rest, and my benevolence will no more destroy my quiet: I have found a man of wisdom and virtue, to whom I can cheerfully bequeath the inheritance of the sun.' "

The prince heard this narration with very serious regard, but the princess smiled, and Pekuah convulsed herself with laughter. "Ladies," said Imlac, "to mock the heaviest of human afflictions is neither charitable nor wise. Few can attain this man's knowledge, and few practice his virtues; but all may suffer his calamity. Of the uncertainties of our present state, the most dreadful and alarming is the uncertain continuance of reason."

The princess was recollected, and the favorite was abashed. Rasselas, more deeply affected, inquired of Imlac, whether he thought such maladies of the mind frequent, and how they were contracted.

Chapter 44. The Dangerous Prevalence[3] of Imagination

"Disorders of intellect," answered Imlac, "happen much more often than superficial observers will easily believe. Perhaps, if we speak with rigorous exactness, no human mind is in its right state. There is no man whose imagination does not sometimes predominate over his reason, who can regulate his attention wholly by his will, and whose ideas will come and go at his command. No man will be found in whose mind airy notions do not sometimes tyrannize, and force him to hope or fear beyond the limits of sober probability. All power of fancy over reason is a degree of insanity; but while this power is such as we can control and repress, it is not visible to others, nor considered as any depravation of the mental faculties; it is not pronounced madness but when it comes ungovernable, and apparently influences speech or action.

"To indulge the power of fiction, and send imagination out upon the wing, is often the sport of those who delight too much in silent speculation. When we are alone we are not always busy; the labor of excogitation is too violent to last long; the ardor of inquiry will sometimes give way to idleness or satiety. He who has nothing external that can divert him must find pleasure in his own thoughts, and must conceive himself what he is not; for who is pleased with what he is? He then expatiates in boundless futurity, and culls from all imaginable conditions that which for the present moment he should most desire, amuses his desires with impossible enjoyments, and confers upon his pride unattainable dominion. The mind dances from scene to scene, unites all pleasures in all combinations, and riots in delights which nature and fortune, with all their bounty, cannot bestow.

"In time, some particular train of ideas fixes the attention; all other intellectual gratifications are rejected; the mind, in weariness or leisure, recurs constantly to the favorite conception, and feasts on the luscious falsehood, whenever she is offended with the bitterness of truth. By degrees the reign of fancy is confirmed; she grows first imperious, and in time despotic. Then fictions begin to operate as realities, false opinions fasten upon the mind, and life passes in dreams of rapture or of anguish.

"This, sir, is one of the dangers of solitude, which the hermit has confessed not always to promote goodness, and the astronomer's misery has proved to be not always propitious to wisdom."

"I will no more," said the favorite, "imagine myself the queen of Abyssinia. I have often spent the hours which the princess gave to my own disposal, in adjusting ceremonies and regulating the court; I have repressed the pride of the powerful, and granted the petitions of the poor; I have built new palaces in more happy situations, planted groves upon the tops of mountains, and have exulted in the beneficence of royalty, till, when the princess entered, I had almost forgotten to bow down before her."

3. Predominance.

"And I," said the princess, "will not allow myself any more to play the shepherdess in my waking dreams. I have often soothed my thoughts with the quiet and innocence of pastoral employments, till I have in my chamber heard the winds whistle, and the sheep bleat; sometimes freed the lamb entangled in the thicket, and sometimes with my crook encountered the wolf. I have a dress like that of the village maids, which I put on to help my imagination, and a pipe on which I play softly, and suppose myself followed by my flocks."

"I will confess," said the prince, "an indulgence of fantastic delight more dangerous than yours. I have frequently endeavored to image the possibility of a perfect government, by which all wrong should be restrained, all vice reformed, and all the subjects preserved in tranquility and innocence. This thought produced innumerable schemes of reformation, and dictated many useful regulations and salutary edicts. This has been the sport, and sometimes the labor, of my solitude; and I start, when I think with how little anguish I once supposed the death of my father and my brothers."

"Such," says Imlac, "are the effects of visionary schemes; when we first form them, we know them to be absurd, but familiarize them by degrees, and in time lose sight of their folly."

Chapter 45. They Discourse with an Old Man

The evening was now far past, and they rose to return home. As they walked along the bank of the Nile, delighted with the beams of the moon quivering on the water, they saw at a small distance an old man, whom the prince hadoften heard in the assembly of the sages. "Yonder," said he, "is one whose years have calmed his passions, but not clouded his reason. Let us close the disquisitions of the night by inquiring what are his sentiments of his own state, that we may know whether youth alone is to struggle with vexation, and whether any better hope remains for the latter part of life."

Here the sage approached and saluted them. They invited him to join their walk, and prattled a while, as acquaintance that had unexpectedly met one another. The old man was cheerful and talkative, and the way seemed short in his company. He was pleased to find himself not disregarded, accompanied them to their house, and, at the prince's request, entered with them. They placed him in the seat of honor, and set wine and conserves before him.

"Sir," said the princess, "an evening walk must give to a man of learning like you pleasures which ignorance and youth can hardly conceive. You know the qualities and the causes of all that you behold, the laws by which the river flows, the periods in which the planets perform their revolutions. Everything must supply you with contemplation, and renew the consciousness of your own dignity."

"Lady," answered he, "let the gay and the vigorous expect pleasure in their excursions; it is enough that age can obtain ease. To me the world has lost its novelty; I look round, and see what I remember to have seen in happier days. I rest against a tree, and consider that in the same shade I once disputed upon the annual overflow of the Nile with a friend who is now silent in the grave. I cast my eyes upward, fix them on the changing moon, and think with pain on the vicissitudes of life. I have ceased to take much delight in physical truth; for what have I to do with those things which I am soon to leave?"

"You may at least recreate[4] yourself," said Imlac, "with the recollection of

4. Refresh.

an honorable and useful life, and enjoy the praise which all agree to give you."

"Praise," said the sage with a sigh, "is to an old man an empty sound. I have neither mother to be delighted with the reputation of her son, nor wife to partake the honors of her husband. I have outlived my friends and my rivals. Nothing is now of much importance; for I cannot extend my interest beyond myself. Youth is delighted with applause, because it is considered as the earnest of some future good, and because the prospect of life is far extended; but to me, who am now declining to decrepitude, there is little to be feared from the malevolence of men, and yet less to be hoped from their affection or esteem. Something they may yet take away, but they can give me nothing. Riches would now be useless, and high employment would be pain. My retrospect of life recalls to my view many opportunities of good neglected, much time squandered upon trifles, and more lost in idleness and vacancy. I leave many great designs unattempted, and many great attempts unfinished. My mind is burthened with no heavy crime, and therefore I compose myself to tranquility; endeavor to abstract my thoughts from hopes and cares which, though reason knows them to be vain, still try to keep their old possession of the heart; expect,[5] with serene humility, that hour which nature cannot long delay; and hope to possess, in a better state, that happiness which here I could not find, and that virtue which here I have not attained."

He arose and went away, leaving his audience not much elated with the hope of long life. The prince consoled himself with remarking that it was not reasonable to be disappointed by this account; for age had never been considered as the season of felicity, and if it was possible to be easy in decline and weakness, it was likely that the days of vigor and alacrity might be happy; that the noon of life might be bright, if the evening could be calm.

The princess suspected that age was querulous and malignant, and delighted to repress the expectations of those who had newly entered the world. She had seen the possessors of estates look with envy on their heirs, and known many who enjoy pleasure no longer than they can confine it to themselves.

Pekuah conjectured that the man was older than he appeared, and was willing to impute his complaints to delirious dejection; or else supposed that he had been unfortunate, and was therefore discontented. "For nothing," said she, "is more common than to call our own condition the condition of life."

Imlac, who had no desire to see them depressed, smiled at the comforts which they could so readily procure to themselves, and remembered that, at the same age, he was equally confident of unmingled prosperity, and equally fertile of consolatory expedients. He forbore to force upon them unwelcome knowledge, which time itself would too soon impress. The princess and her lady retired; the madness of the astronomer hung upon their minds, and they desired Imlac to enter upon his office, and delay next morning the rising of the sun.

Chapter 46. The Princess and Pekuah Visit the Astronomer

The princess and Pekuah, having talked in private of Imlac's astronomer, thought his character at once so amiable and so strange, that they could not be satisfied without a nearer knowledge, and Imlac was requested to find the means of bringing them together.

5. Await.

This was somewhat difficult; the philosopher had never received any visits from women, though he lived in a city that had in it many Europeans who followed the manners of their own countries, and many from other parts of the world that lived there with European liberty. The ladies would not be refused, and several schemes were proposed for the accomplishment of their design. It was proposed to introduce them as strangers in distress, to whom the sage was always accessible; but, after some deliberation, it appeared, that by this artifice, no acquaintance could be formed, for their conversation would be short, and they could not decently importune him often. "This," said Rasselas, "is true; but I have yet a stronger objection against the misrepresentation of your state. I have always considered it as treason against the great republic of human nature, to make any man's virtues the means of deceiving him, whether on great or little occasions. All imposture weakens confidence and chills benevolence. When the sage finds that you are not what you seemed, he will feel the resentment natural to a man who, conscious of great abilities, discovers that he has been tricked by understandings meaner than his own, and, perhaps, the distrust, which he can never afterwards wholly lay aside, may stop the voice of counsel, and close the hand of charity; and where will you find the power of restoring his benefactions to mankind, or his peace to himself?"

To this no reply was attempted, and Imlac began to hope that their curiosity would subside; but next day Pekuah told him, she had now found an honest pretense for a visit to the astronomer, for she would solicit permission to continue under him the studies in which she had been initiated by the Arab, and the princess might go with her either as a fellow-student, or because a woman could not decently come alone. "I am afraid," said Imlac, "that he will be soon weary of your company: men advanced far in knowledge do not love to repeat the elements of their art, and I am not certain, that even of the elements, as he will deliver them connected with inferences, and mingled with reflections, you are a very capable auditress." "That," said Pekuah, "must be my care: I ask of you only to take me thither. My knowledge is, perhaps, more than you imagine it, and by concurring always with his opinions I shall make him think it greater than it is."

The astronomer, in pursuance of this resolution, was told, that a foreign lady, traveling in search of knowledge, had heard of his reputation, and was desirous to become his scholar. The uncommonness of the proposal raised at once his surprise and curiosity, and when, after a short deliberation, he consented to admit her, he could not stay without impatience till the next day.

The ladies dressed themselves magnificently, and were attended by Imlac to the astronomer, who was pleased to see himself approached with respect by persons of so splendid an appearance. In the exchange of the first civilities he was timorous and bashful; but when the talk became regular, he recollected his powers, and justified the character which Imlac had given. Inquiring of Pekuah what could have turned her inclination towards astronomy, he received from her a history of her adventure at the pyramid, and of the time passed in the Arab's island. She told her tale with ease and elegance, and her conversation took possession of his heart. The discourse was then turned to astronomy: Pekuah displayed what she knew: he looked upon her as a prodigy of genius, and entreated her not to desist from a study which she had so happily begun.

They came again and again, and were every time more welcome than before.

The sage endeavored to amuse them, that they might prolong their visits, for he found his thoughts grow brighter in their company; the clouds of solicitude vanished by degrees, as he forced himself to entertain them, and he grieved when he was left at their departure to his old employment of regulating the seasons.

The princess and her favorite had now watched his lips for several months, and could not catch a single word from which they could judge whether he continued, or not, in the opinion of his preternatural commission. They often contrived to bring him to an open declaration, but he easily eluded all their attacks, and on which side soever they pressed him escaped from them to some other topic.

As their familiarity increased they invited him often to the house of Imlac, where they distinguished him by extraordinary respect. He began gradually to delight in sublunary pleasures. He came early and departed late; labored to recommend himself by assiduity and compliance; excited their curiosity after new arts, that they might still want his assistance; and when they made any excursion of pleasure or inquiry, entreated to attend them.

By long experience of his integrity and wisdom, the prince and his sister were convinced that he might be trusted without danger; and lest he should draw any false hopes from the civilities which he received, discovered to him their condition, with the motives of their journey, and required his opinion on the choice of life.

"Of the various conditions which the world spreads before you, which you shall prefer," said the sage, "I am not able to instruct you. I can only tell that I have chosen wrong. I have passed my time in study without experience; in the attainment of sciences which can, for the most part, be but remotely useful to mankind. I have purchased knowledge at the expense of all the common comforts of life: I have missed the endearing elegance of female friendship, and the happy commerce of domestic tenderness. If I have obtained any prerogatives above other students, they have been accompanied with fear, disquiet, and scrupulosity; but even of these prerogatives, whatever they were, I have, since my thoughts have been diversified by more intercourse with the world, begun to question the reality. When I have been for a few days lost in pleasing dissipation, I am always tempted to think that my inquiries have ended in error, and that I have suffered much, and suffered it in vain."

Imlac was delighted to find that the sage's understanding was breaking through its mists, and resolved to detain him from the planets till he should forget his task of ruling them, and reason should recover its original influence.

From this time the astronomer was received into familiar friendship, and partook of all their projects and pleasures: his respect kept him attentive, and the activity of Rasselas did not leave much time unengaged. Something was always to be done; the day was spent in making observations which furnished talk for the evening, and the evening was closed with a scheme for the morrow.

The sage confessed to Imlac, that since he had mingled in the gay tumults of life, and divided his hours by a succession of amusements, he found the conviction of his authority over the skies fade gradually from his mind, and began to trust less to an opinion which he never could prove to others, and which he now found subject to variation from causes in which reason had no part. "If I am accidentally left alone for a few hours," said he, "my inveterate persuasion rushes upon my soul, and my thoughts are chained down by some irresistible violence, but they are soon disentangled by the prince's conversation, and instantaneously released at the entrance of Pekuah. I am like a man habitually afraid of specters, who is set at ease by a lamp, and wonders at the dread which harassed him in the dark, yet, if his lamp be extinguished, feels again the terrors which he knows that when it is light he shall feel no more. But I am sometimes afraid lest I indulge my quiet by criminal negligence, and voluntarily forget the great charge with which I am entrusted. If I favor myself in a known error, or am determined by my own ease in a doubtful question of this importance, how dreadful is my crime!"

"No disease of the imagination," answered Imlac, "is so difficult of cure, as that which is complicated with the dread of guilt: fancy and conscience then act interchangeably upon us, and so often shift their places, that the illusions of one are not distinguished from the dictates of the other. If fancy presents images not moral or religious, the mind drives them away when they give it pain, but when melancholic[6] notions take the form of duty, they lay hold on the faculties without opposition, because we are afraid to exclude or banish them. For this reason the superstitious are often melancholy, and the melancholy almost always superstitious.

"But do not let the suggestions of timidity overpower your better reason: the danger of neglect can be but as the probability of the obligation, which, when you consider it with freedom, you find very little, and that little growing every day less. Open your heart to the influence of the light, which, from time to time, breaks in upon you: when scruples importune you, which you in your lucid moments know to be vain, do not stand to parley, but fly to business or to Pekuah, and keep this thought always prevalent, that you are only one atom of the mass of humanity, and have neither such virtue nor vice, as that you should be singled out for supernatural favors or afflictions."

Chapter 47. The Prince Enters, and Brings a New Topic

"All this," said the astronomer, "I have often thought, but my reason has been so long subjugated by an uncontrollable and overwhelming idea, that it durst not confide in its own decisions. I now see how fatally I betrayed my quiet, by suffering chimeras to prey upon me in secret; but melancholy shrinks from communication, and I never found a man before, to whom I could impart my troubles, though I had been certain of relief. I rejoice to find my own sentiments confirmed by yours, who are not easily deceived, and can have no motive or purpose to deceive. I hope that time and variety will dissipate the gloom that has so long surrounded me, and the latter part of my days will be spent in peace."

"Your learning and virtue," said Imlac, "may justly give you hopes."

Rasselas then entered with the princess and Pekuah, and inquired whether they had contrived any new diversion for the next day. "Such," said Nekayah, "is the state of life, that none are happy but by the anticipation of change: the change itself is nothing; when we have made it, the next wish is to change again. The world is not yet exhausted; let me see something tomorrow which I never saw before."

"Variety," said Rasselas, "is so necessary to content, that even the happy valley disgusted me by the recurrence of its luxuries; yet I could not forbear to reproach myself with impatience, when I saw the monks of St. Anthony

6. Obsessive. According to Johnson's *Dictionary,* one definition of melancholy is "a kind of madness in which the mind is always fixed on one object."

support without complaint, a life, not of uniform delight, but uniform hardship."

"Those men," answered Imlac, "are less wretched in their silent convent than the Abyssinian princes in their prison of pleasure. Whatever is done by the monks is incited by an adequate and reasonable motive. Their labor supplies them with necessaries; it therefore cannot be omitted, and is certainly rewarded. Their devotion prepares them for another state, and reminds them of its approach, while it fits them for it. Their time is regularly distributed; one duty succeeds another, so that they are not left open to the distraction of unguided choice, nor lost in the shades of listless inactivity. There is a certain task to be performed at an appropriated hour; and their toils are cheerful, because they consider them as acts of piety, by which they are always advancing towards endless felicity."

"Do you think," said Nekayah, "that the monastic rule is a more holy and less imperfect state than any other? May not he equally hope for future happiness who converses openly with mankind, who succors the distressed by his charity, instructs the ignorant by his learning, and contributes by his industry to the general system of life; even though he should omit some of the mortifications which are practiced in the cloister, and allow himself such harmless delights as his condition may place within his reach?"

"This," said Imlac, "is a question which has long divided the wise, and perplexed the good. I am afraid to decide on either part. He that lives well in the world is better than he that lives well in a monastery. But perhaps everyone is not able to stem the temptations of public life; and if he cannot conquer, he may properly retreat. Some have little power to do good, and have likewise little strength to resist evil. Many are weary of their conflicts with adversity, and are willing to eject those passions which have long busied them in vain. And many are dismissed by age and diseases from the more laborious duties of society. In monasteries the weak and timorous may be happily sheltered, the weary may repose, and the penitent may meditate. Those retreats of prayer and contemplation have something so congenial to the mind of man, that, perhaps, there is scarcely one that does not purpose to close his life in pious abstraction with a few associates serious as himself."

"Such," said Pekuah, "has often been my wish, and I have heard the princess declare, that she should not willingly die in a crowd."

"The liberty of using harmless pleasures," proceeded Imlac, "will not be disputed; but it is still to be examined what pleasures are harmless. The evil of any pleasure that Nekayah can image is not in the act itself, but in its consequences. Pleasure, in itself harmless, may become mischievous, by endearing to us a state which we know to be transient and probatory,[7] and withdrawing our thoughts from that, of which every hour brings us nearer to the beginning, and of which no length of time will bring us to the end. Mortification is not virtuous in itself, nor has any other use, but that it disengages us from the allurements of sense. In the state of future perfection, to which we all aspire, there will be pleasure without danger, and security without restraint."

The princess was silent, and Rasselas, turning to the astronomer, asked him, whether he could not delay her retreat, by showing her something which she had not seen before.

"Your curiosity," said the sage, "has been so general, and your pursuit of

7. Serving as a trial or test.

knowledge so vigorous, that novelties are not now very easily to be found: but what you can no longer procure from the living may be given by the dead. Among the wonders of this country are the catacombs, or the ancient repositories, in which the bodies of the earliest generations were lodged, and where, by the virtue of the gums which embalmed them, they yet remain without corruption."

"I know not," said Rasselas, "what pleasure the sight of the catacombs can afford; but, since nothing else is offered, I am resolved to view them, and shall place this with many other things which I have done, because I would do something."

They hired a guard of horsemen, and the next day visited the catacombs. When they were about to descend into the sepulchral caves, "Pekuah," said the princess, "we are now again invading the habitations of the dead; I know that you will stay behind; let me find you safe when I return." "No, I will not be left," answered Pekuah; "I will go down between you and the prince."

They then all descended, and roved with wonder through the labyrinth of subterraneous passages, where the bodies were laid in rows on either side.

Chapter 48. Imlac Discourses on the Nature of the Soul

"What reason," said the prince, "can be given, why the Egyptians should thus expensively preserve those carcasses which some nations consume with fire, others lay to mingle with the earth, and all agree to remove from their sight, as soon as decent rites can be performed?"

"The original of ancient customs," said Imlac, "is commonly unknown; for the practice often continues when the cause has ceased; and concerning superstitious ceremonies it is vain to conjecture; for what reason did not dictate reason cannot explain. I have long believed that the practice of embalming arose only from tenderness to the remains of relations or friends, and to this opinion I am more inclined, because it seems impossible that this care should have been general: had all the dead been embalmed, their repositories must in time have been more spacious than the dwellings of the living. I suppose only the rich or honorable were secured from corruption, and the rest left to the course of nature.

"But it is commonly supposed that the Egyptians believed the soul to live as long as the body continued undissolved, and therefore tried this method of eluding death."

"Could the wise Egyptians," said Nekayah, "think so grossly of the soul? If the soul could once survive its separation, what could it afterwards receive or suffer from the body?"

"The Egyptians would doubtless think erroneously," said the astronomer, "in the darkness of heathenism, and the first dawn of philosophy. The nature of the soul is still disputed amidst all our opportunities of clearer knowledge: some yet say, that it may be material, who, nevertheless, believe it to be immortal."

"Some," answered Imlac, "have indeed said that the soul is material, but I can scarcely believe that any man has thought it, who knew how to think; for all the conclusions of reason enforce the immateriality of mind, and all the notices of sense and investigations of science concur to prove the unconsciousness of matter.

"It was never supposed that cogitation is inherent in matter, or that every particle is a thinking being. Yet if any part of matter be devoid of thought, what part can we suppose to think? Matter can differ from matter only in form, density, bulk, motion, and direction of motion: to which of these, however varied or combined, can consciousness be annexed? To be round or square, to be solid or fluid, to be great or little, to be moved slowly or swiftly one way or another, are modes of material existence, all equally alien from the nature of cogitation. If matter be once without thought, it can only be made to think by some new modification, but all the modifications which it can admit are equally unconnected with cogitative powers."

"But the materialists," said the astronomer, "urge that matter may have qualities with which we are unacquainted."

"He who will determine," returned Imlac, "against that which he knows, because there may be something which he knows not; he that can set hypothetical possibility against acknowledged certainty, is not to be admitted among reasonable beings. All that we know of matter is, that matter is inert, senseless and lifeless; and if this conviction cannot be opposed but by referring us to something that we know not, we have all the evidence that human intellect can admit. If that which is known may be overruled by that which is unknown, no being, not omniscient, can arrive at certainty."

"Yet let us not," said the astronomer, "too arrogantly limit the Creator's power."

"It is no limitation of omnipotence," replied the poet, "to suppose that one thing is not consistent with another, that the same proposition cannot be at once true and false, that the same number cannot be even and odd, that cogitation cannot be conferred on that which is created incapable of cogitation."

"I know not," said Nekayah, "any great use of this question. Does that immateriality, which, in my opinion, you have sufficiently proved, necessarily include eternal duration?"

"Of immateriality," said Imlac, "our ideas are negative, and therefore obscure. Immateriality seems to imply a natural power of perpetual duration as a consequence of exemption from all causes of decay: whatever perishes, is destroyed by the solution of its contexture,[8] and separation of its parts; nor can we conceive how that which has no parts, and therefore admits no solution, can be naturally corrupted or impaired."

"I know not," said Rasselas, "how to conceive anything without extension: what is extended must have parts, and you allow, that whatever has parts may be destroyed."

"Consider your own conceptions," replied Imlac, "and the difficulty will be less. You will find substance without extension. An ideal form is no less real than material bulk: yet an ideal form has no extension. It is no less certain, when you think on a pyramid, that your mind possesses the idea of a pyramid, than that the pyramid itself is standing. What space does the idea of a pyramid occupy more than the idea of a grain of corn? or how can either idea suffer laceration? As is the effect such is the cause; as thought is, such is the power that thinks; a power impassive and indiscerptible."[9]

"But the Being," said Nekayah, "whom I fear to name, the Being which made the soul, can destroy it."

"He, surely, can destroy it," answered Imlac, "since, however unperishable,

8. Dissolution of its structure.

9. Not to be separated.

it receives from a superior nature its power of duration. That it will not perish by any inherent cause of decay, or principle of corruption, may be shown by philosophy; but philosophy can tell no more. That it will not be annihilated by him that made it, we must humbly learn from higher authority."

The whole assembly stood a while silent and collected. "Let us return," said Rasselas, "from this scene of mortality. How gloomy would be these mansions of the dead to him who did not know that he shall never die; that what now acts shall continue its agency, and what now thinks shall think on for ever. Those that lie here stretched before us, the wise and the powerful of ancient times, warn us to remember the shortness of our present state: they were, perhaps, snatched away while they were busy, like us, in the choice of life."

"To me," said the princess, "the choice of life is become less important; I hope hereafter to think only on the choice of eternity."

They then hastened out of the caverns, and, under the protection of their guard, returned to Cairo.

Chapter 49. The Conclusion, in Which Nothing Is Concluded

It was now the time of the inundation of the Nile: a few days after their visit to the catacombs, the river began to rise.

They were confined to their house. The whole region being under water gave them no invitation to any excursions, and being well supplied with materials for talk, they diverted themselves with comparisons of the different forms of life which they had observed, and with various schemes of happiness which each of them had formed.

Pekuah was never so much charmed with any place as the convent of St. Anthony, where the Arab restored her to the princess, and wished only to fill it with pious maidens, and to be made prioress of the order; she was weary of expectation and disgust,[1] and would gladly be fixed in some unvariable state.

The princess thought that, of all sublunary things, knowledge was the best: she desired first to learn all sciences, and then purposed to found a college of learned women, in which she would preside, that, by conversing with the old and educating the young, she might divide her time between the acquisition and communication of wisdom, and raise up for the next age models of prudence, and patterns of piety.

The prince desired a little kingdom, in which he might administer justice in his own person, and see all the parts of government with his own eyes; but he could never fix the limits of his dominion, and was always adding to the number of his subjects.

Imlac and the astronomer were contented to be driven along the stream of life, without directing their course to any particular port.

Of these wishes that they had formed, they well knew that none could be obtained. They deliberated a while what was to be done, and resolved, when the inundation should cease, to return to Abyssinia.[2]

1759

1. Aversion.
2. Probably not to the Happy Valley, which they earlier fled. Their future remains uncertain.

Rambler No. 4[1]

[ON FICTION]

Saturday, *March* 31, 1750

Simul et jucunda et idonea dicere vitae.
—HORACE, *Art of Poetry,* 334

And join both profit and delight in one.
—CREECH

The works of fiction with which the present generation seems more particularly delighted are such as exhibit life in its true state, diversified only by accidents that daily happen in the world, and influenced by passions and qualities which are really to be found in conversing with mankind.

This kind of writing may be termed, not improperly, the comedy of romance, and is to be conducted nearly by the rules of comic poetry. Its province is to bring about natural events by easy means, and to keep up curiosity without the help of wonder: it is therefore precluded from the machines[2] and expedients of the heroic romance, and can neither employ giants to snatch away a lady from the nuptial rites, nor knights to bring her back from captivity; it can neither bewilder its personages in deserts, nor lodge them in imaginary castles.

I remember a remark made by Scaliger upon Pontanus,[3] that all his writings are filled with the same images; and that if you take from him his lilies and his roses, his satyrs and his dryads, he will have nothing left that can be called poetry. In like manner, almost all the fictions of the last age will vanish if you deprive them of a hermit and a wood, a battle and a shipwreck.

Why this wild strain of imagination found reception so long in polite and learned ages, it is not easy to conceive; but we cannot wonder that while readers could be procured, the authors were willing to continue it; for when a man had by practice gained some fluency of language, he had no further care than to retire to his closet, let loose his invention, and heat his mind with incredibilities; a book was thus produced without fear of criticism, without the toil of study, without knowledge of nature, or acquaintance with life.

The task of our present writers is very different; it requires, together with that learning which is to be gained from books, that experience which can never be attained by solitary diligence, but must arise from general converse and accurate observation of the living world. Their performances have, as Horace expresses it, *plus oneris quanto veniae minus,*[4] little indulgence, and therefore more difficulty. They are engaged in portraits of which everyone knows the original, and can detect any deviation from exactness of resemblance. Other writings are safe, except from the malice of learning, but these are in danger from every common reader; as the slipper ill executed was cen-

1. The *Rambler,* almost wholly written by Johnson himself, appeared every Tuesday and Saturday from March 20, 1750, to March 14, 1752—years in which Johnson was writing the *Dictionary.* It is a successor of the *Tatler* and the *Spectator,* but it is much more serious in tone than the earlier periodicals. Johnson's reputation as a moralist and a stylist was established by these essays; because of them Boswell first conceived the ambition to seek Johnson's acquaintance.
2. The technical term in neoclassical critical theory for the supernatural agents who intervene in human affairs in epic and tragedy.
3. Julius Caesar Scaliger (1484–1558) criticized the Latin poems of the Italian poet Jovianus Pontanus (1426–1503).
4. *Epistles* 2.1.170.

sured by a shoemaker who happened to stop in his way at the Venus of Apelles.[5]

But the fear of not being approved as just copiers of human manners is not the most important concern that an author of this sort ought to have before him. These books are written chiefly to the young, the ignorant, and the idle, to whom they serve as lectures of conduct, and introductions into life. They are the entertainment of minds unfurnished with ideas, and therefore easily susceptible of impressions; not fixed by principles, and therefore easily following the current of fancy; not informed by experience, and consequently open to every false suggestion and partial account.

That the highest degree of reverence should be paid to youth, and that nothing indecent should be suffered to approach their eyes or ears, are precepts extorted by sense and virtue from an ancient writer by no means eminent for chastity of thought.[6] The same kind, though not the same degree, of caution, is required in everything which is laid before them, to secure them from unjust prejudices, perverse opinions, and incongruous combinations of images.

In the romances formerly written, every transaction and sentiment was so remote from all that passes among men that the reader was in very little danger of making any applications to himself; the virtues and crimes were equally beyond his sphere of activity; and he amused himself with heroes and with traitors, deliverers and persecutors, as with beings of another species, whose actions were regulated upon motives of their own, and who had neither faults nor excellencies in common with himself.

But when an adventurer is leveled with the rest of the world, and acts in such scenes of the universal drama as may be the lot of any other man, young spectators fix their eyes upon him with closer attention, and hope, by observing his behavior and success, to regulate their own practices when they shall be engaged in the like part.

For this reason these familiar histories may perhaps be made of greater use than the solemnities of professed morality, and convey the knowledge of vice and virtue with more efficacy than axioms and definitions. But if the power of example is so great as to take possession of the memory by a kind of violence, and produce effects almost without the intervention of the will, care ought to be taken that when the choice is unrestrained, the best examples only should be exhibited; and that which is likely to operate so strongly should not be mischievous or uncertain in its effects.

The chief advantage which these fictions have over real life is that their authors are at liberty, though not to invent, yet to select objects, and to cull from the mass of mankind those individuals upon which the attention ought most to be employed; as a diamond, though it cannot be made, may be polished by art, and placed in such situation as to display that luster which before was buried among common stones.

It is justly considered as the greatest excellency of art to imitate nature; but it is necessary to distinguish those parts of nature which are most proper for imitation: greater care is still required in representing life, which is so often discolored by passion or deformed by wickedness. If the world be promiscu-

5. According to Pliny the Younger (*Naturalis Historia* 35.85), the Greek painter Apelles of Kos (4th century B.C.E.) corrected the drawing of a sandal after hearing a shoemaker criticize it as faulty, but when the flattered artisan dared to find fault with the drawing of a leg, the artist bade him "stick to his last."

6. Juvenal's *Satires* 14.1–58.

ously[7] described, I cannot see of what use it can be to read the account; or why it may not be as safe to turn the eye immediately upon mankind as upon a mirror which shows all that presents itself without discrimination.

It is therefore not a sufficient vindication of a character that it is drawn as it appears, for many characters ought never to be drawn; nor of a narrative that the train of events is agreeable to observation and experience, for that observation which is called knowledge of the world will be found much more frequently to make men cunning than good. The purpose of these writings is surely not only to show mankind, but to provide that they may be seen hereafter with less hazard; to teach the means of avoiding the snares which are laid by Treachery for Innocence, without infusing any wish for that superiority with which the betrayer flatters his vanity; to give the power of counteracting fraud without the temptation to practice it; to initiate youth by mock encounters in the art of necessary defense, and to increase prudence without impairing virtue.

Many writers, for the sake of following nature, so mingle good and bad qualities in their principal personages that they are both equally conspicuous; and as we accompany them through their adventures with delight, and are led by degrees to interest ourselves in their favor, we lose the abhorrence of their faults because they do not hinder our pleasure, or perhaps regard them with some kindness for being united with so much merit.[8]

There have been men indeed splendidly wicked, whose endowments threw a brightness on their crimes, and whom scarce any villainy made perfectly detestable because they never could be wholly divested of their excellencies; but such have been in all ages the great corrupters of the world, and their resemblance ought no more to be preserved than the art of murdering without pain.

Some have advanced, without due attention to the consequences of this notion, that certain virtues have their correspondent faults, and therefore that to exhibit either apart is to deviate from probability. Thus men are observed by Swift to be "grateful in the same degree as they are resentful." This principle, with others of the same kind, supposes man to act from a brute impulse, and pursue a certain degree of inclination without any choice of the object; for, otherwise, though it should be allowed that gratitude and resentment arise from the same constitution of the passions, it follows not that they will be equally indulged when reason is consulted; yet, unless that consequence be admitted, this sagacious maxim becomes an empty sound, without any relation to practice or to life.

Nor is it evident that even the first motions to these effects are always in the same proportion. For pride, which produces quickness of resentment, will obstruct gratitude by unwillingness to admit that inferiority which obligation implies; and it is very unlikely that he who cannot think he receives a favor will acknowledge or repay it.

It is of the utmost importance to mankind that positions of this tendency should be laid open and confuted; for while men consider good and evil as springing from the same root, they will spare the one for the sake of the other, and in judging, if not of others at least of themselves, will be apt to estimate

7. Indiscriminately.
8. Johnson is probably thinking of such popular novels as Tobias Smollett's *Roderick Random* (1748) and Henry Fielding's *Tom Jones* (1749), as opposed to the model of virtue provided by Samuel Richardson's *Clarissa* (1747–48).

their virtues by their vices. To this fatal error all those will contribute who confound the colors of right and wrong, and, instead of helping to settle their boundaries, mix them with so much art that no common mind is able to disunite them.

In narratives where historical veracity has no place, I cannot discover why there should not be exhibited the most perfect idea of virtue; of virtue not angelical, nor above probability (for what we cannot credit, we shall never imitate), but the highest and purest that humanity can reach, which, exercised in such trials as the various revolutions of things shall bring upon it, may, by conquering some calamities and enduring others, teach us what we may hope, and what we can perform. Vice (for vice is necessary to be shown) should always disgust; nor should the graces of gaiety, nor the dignity of courage, be so united with it as to reconcile it to the mind. Wherever it appears, it should raise hatred by the malignity of its practices, and contempt by the meanness of its stratagems: for while it is supported by either parts[9] or spirit, it will be seldom heartily abhorred. The Roman tyrant was content to be hated if he was but feared;[1] and there are thousands of the readers of romances willing to be thought wicked if they may be allowed to be wits. It is therefore to be steadily inculcated that virtue is the highest proof of understanding, and the only solid basis of greatness; and that vice is the natural consequence of narrow thoughts; that it begins in mistake, and ends in ignominy.

Rambler No. 60

[BIOGRAPHY]

Saturday, *October* 13, 1750

—Quid sit pulchrum, quid turpe, quid utile, quid non,
Plenius ac melius Chrysippo et Crantore dicit.
—HORACE, *Epistles*, 1.2. 3–4

Whose works the beautiful and base contain,
Of vice and virtue more instructive rules,
Than all the sober sages of the schools.
—FRANCIS

All joy or sorrow for the happiness or calamities of others is produced by an act of the imagination, that realizes the event, however fictitious, or approximates it,[1] however remote, by placing us, for a time, in the condition of him whose fortune we contemplate; so that we feel, while the deception lasts, whatever motions would be excited by the same good or evil happening to ourselves.

Our passions are therefore more strongly moved, in proportion as we can more readily adopt the pains or pleasure proposed to our minds, by recognizing them as once our own, or considering them as naturally incident to our state of life. It is not easy for the most artful writer to give us an interest in happiness or misery, which we think ourselves never likely to feel, and with which we have never yet been made acquainted. Histories of the downfall of kingdoms, and revolutions of empires, are read with great tranquility; the imperial tragedy pleases common auditors only by its pomp of ornament, and grandeur of ideas;

9. Abilities.
1. The emperor Tiberius (see Suetonius's *Lives of the Caesars*).
1. Brings it near.

and the man whose faculties have been engrossed by business, and whose heart never fluttered but at the rise or fall of stocks, wonders how the attention can be seized, or the affections agitated, by a tale of love.

Those parallel circumstances, and kindred images to which we readily conform our minds, are, above all other writings, to be found in narratives of the lives of particular persons; and therefore no species of writing seems more worthy of cultivation than biography, since none can be more delightful or more useful, none can more certainly enchain the heart by irresistible interest, or more widely diffuse instruction to every diversity of condition.

The general and rapid narratives of history, which involve a thousand fortunes in the business of a day, and complicate[2] innumerable incidents in one great transaction, afford few lessons applicable to private life, which derives its comforts and its wretchedness from the right or wrong management of things, which nothing but their frequency makes considerable, *Parva si non fiunt quotidie,* says Pliny,[3] and which can have no place in those relations which never descend below the consultation of senates, the motions of armies, and the schemes of conspirators.

I have often thought that there has rarely passed a life of which a judicious and faithful narrative would not be useful. For, not only every man has in the mighty mass of the world great numbers in the same condition with himself, to whom his mistakes and miscarriages, escapes and expedients, would be of immediate and apparent use; but there is such an uniformity in the state of man, considered apart from adventitious and separable decorations and disguises, that there is scarce any possibility of good or ill, but is common to humankind. A great part of the time of those who are placed at the greatest distance by fortune, or by temper, must unavoidably pass in the same manner; and though, when the claims of nature are satisfied, caprice, and vanity, and accident, begin to produce discriminations and peculiarities, yet the eye is not very heedful or quick, which cannot discover the same causes still[4] terminating their influence in the same effects, though sometimes accelerated, sometimes retarded, or perplexed by multiplied combinations. We are all prompted by the same motives, all deceived by the same fallacies, all animated by hope, obstructed by danger, entangled by desire, and seduced by pleasure.

It is frequently objected to relations of particular lives, that they are not distinguished by any striking or wonderful vicissitudes. The scholar who passed his life among his books, the merchant who conducted only his own affairs, the priest whose sphere of action was not extended beyond that of his duty, are considered as no proper objects of public regard, however they might have excelled in their several stations, whatever might have been their learning, integrity, and piety. But this notion arises from false measures of excellence and dignity, and must be eradicated by considering, that in the esteem of uncorrupted reason, what is of most use is of most value.

It is, indeed, not improper to take honest advantages of prejudice, and to gain attention by a celebrated name; but the business of the biographer is often to pass slightly over those performances and incidents, which produce vulgar greatness, to lead the thoughts into domestic privacies, and display the minute details of daily life, where exterior appendages are cast aside, and men excel each other only by prudence and by virtue. The account of Thuanus[5] is,

2. Join.
3. Pliny the Younger's *Epistles* 3.1. Johnson translates the phrase in the preceding clause.
4. Always.
5. Jacques-Auguste de Thou (1553–1617), an important French historian, of whom Nicholas Rigault wrote a brief biography, a sentence of which Johnson quotes and translates below.

with great propriety, said by its author to have been written, that it might lay open to posterity the private and familiar character of that man, *cujus ingenium et candorem ex ipsius scriptis sunt olim semper miraturi,* whose candor and genius will to the end of time be by his writings preserved in admiration.

There are many invisible circumstances which, whether we read as inquirers after natural or moral knowledge, whether we intend to enlarge our science, or increase our virtue, are more important than public occurrences. Thus Sallust, the great master of nature, has not forgot, in his account of Catiline,[6] to remark that *his walk was now quick, and again slow,* as an indication of a mind revolving something with violent commotion. Thus the story of Melancthon[7] affords a striking lecture on the value of time, by informing us that when he made an appointment, he expected not only the hour, but the minute to be fixed, that the day might not run out in the idleness of suspense; and all the plans and enterprises of De Witt are now of less importance to the world, than that part of his personal character, which represents him as careful of his health, and negligent of his life.[8]

But biography has often been allotted to writers who seem very little acquainted with the nature of their task, or very negligent about the performance. They rarely afford any other account than might be collected from public papers, but imagine themselves writing a life when they exhibit a chronological series of actions or preferments; and so little regard the manners or behavior of their heroes, that more knowledge may be gained of a man's real character, by a short conversation with one of his servants, than from a formal and studied narrative, begun with his pedigree, and ended with his funeral.

If now and then they condescend to inform the world of particular facts, they are not always so happy as to select the most important. I know not well what advantage posterity can receive from the only circumstance by which Tickell has distinguished Addison from the rest of mankind, the irregularity of his pulse:[9] nor can I think myself overpaid for the time spent in reading the life of Malherbe, by being enabled to relate, after the learned biographer,[1] that Malherbe had two predominant opinions; one, that the looseness of a single woman might destroy all her boast of ancient descent; the other, that the French beggars made use very improperly and barbarously of the phrase *noble gentleman,* because either word included the sense of both.

There are, indeed, some natural reasons why these narratives are often written by such as were not likely to give much instruction or delight, and why most accounts of particular persons are barren and useless. If a life be delayed till interest and envy are at an end, we may hope for impartiality, but must expect little intelligence;[2] for the incidents which give excellence to biography are of a volatile and evanescent kind, such as soon escape the memory, and are rarely transmitted by tradition. We know how few can portray a living acquaintance, except by his most prominent and observable particularities, and the grosser features of his mind; and it may be easily imagined how much of this little knowledge may be lost in imparting it, and how soon a succession of copies will lose all resemblance of the original.

6. Sallust, a Roman historian of the 1st century B.C.E., wrote an account of Catiline's conspiracy against the Roman state.
7. Camerarius wrote a life of Melancthon, a German theologian of the 16th century.
8. Sir William Temple, characterizing the Dutch statesman John De Witt.
9. From Thomas Tickell's preface to Addision's *Works* (1721).
1. The life of the French poet François de Malherbe (1555–1628) was written by Honorat de Racan.
2. Information.

If the biographer writes from personal knowledge, and makes haste to gratify the public curiosity, there is danger lest his interest, his fear, his gratitude, or his tenderness, overpower his fidelity, and tempt him to conceal, if not to invent. There are many who think it an act of piety to hide the faults or failings of their friends, even when they can no longer suffer by their detection; we therefore see whole ranks of characters adorned with uniform panegyric, and not to be known from one another, but by extrinsic and casual circumstances. "Let me remember," says Hale, "when I find myself inclined to pity a criminal, that there is likewise a pity due to the country."[3] If we owe regard to the memory of the dead, there is yet more respect to be paid to knowledge, to virtue, and to truth.

A Dictionary of the English Language

Before Johnson, no standard dictionary of the English language existed. The lack had troubled speakers of English for some time, both because Italian and French academies had produced major dictionaries of their own tongues and because, in the absence of any authority, English seemed likely to change utterly from one generation to another. Many eighteenth-century authors feared that their own language would soon become obsolete: as Alexander Pope wrote in *An Essay on Criticism,*

> Our sons their fathers' failing language see,
> And such as Chaucer is, shall Dryden be.

A dictionary could help retard such change, and commercially it would be a book that everyone would need to buy. In 1746 a group of London publishers commissioned Johnson, still an unknown author, to undertake the project. He hoped to finish it in three years; it took him nine. But the quantity and quality of work he accomplished, aided only by six part-time assistants, made him famous as "Dictionary Johnson." The *Dictionary* remained a standard reference book for one hundred years.

Johnson's achievement is notable in three respects: its size (forty thousand words), the wealth of illustrative quotations, and the excellence of the definitions. No earlier English dictionary rivaled the scope of Johnson's two large folio volumes. About 114,000 quotations, gathered from the best English writers from Sidney to the eighteenth century, exemplify the usage of words as well as their meanings. Above all, it was the definitions, however, that established the authority of Johnson's *Dictionary.* A small selection is only too likely to concentrate on a few amusing or notorious definitions, but the great majority are full, clear, and totally free from eccentricity. Indeed, many of them are still repeated in modern dictionaries. Language, Johnson knew, cannot be fixed once and for all; many of the words he defines have radically changed meaning since the eighteenth century. Yet Johnson did more than any other person of his time to preserve the ideal of a standard English.

From A Dictionary of the English Language

From *Preface*

* * *

A large work is difficult because it is large, even though all its parts might singly be performed with facility; where there are many things to be done,

3. From Gilbert Burnet's *Life and Death of Sir Matthew Hale* (1682).

each must be allowed its share of time and labor, in the proportion only which it bears to the whole; nor can it be expected that the stones which form the dome of a temple should be squared and polished like the diamond of a ring.

Of the event of this work, for which, having labored it with so much application, I cannot but have some degree of parental fondness, it is natural to form conjectures. Those who have been persuaded to think well of my design will require that it should fix our language, and put a stop to those alterations which time and chance have hitherto been suffered to make in it without opposition. With this consequence I will confess that I flattered myself for a while;[1] but now begin to fear that I have indulged expectation which neither reason nor experience can justify. When we see men grow old and die at a certain time one after another, from century to century, we laugh at the elixir that promises to prolong life to a thousand years; and with equal justice may the lexicographer be derided, who being able to produce no example of a nation that has preserved their words and phrases from mutability, shall imagine that his dictionary can embalm his language and secure it from corruption and decay, that it is in his power to change sublunary nature, or clear the world at once from folly, vanity, and affectation.

With this hope, however, academies have been instituted, to guard the avenues of their languages, to retain fugitives, and repulse intruders; but their vigilance and activity have hitherto been vain; sounds are too volatile and subtle for legal restraints; to enchain syllables, and to lash the wind, are equally the undertakings of pride, unwilling to measure its desires by its strength. The French language has visibly changed under the inspection of the academy;[2] the style of Amelot's translation of father Paul is observed by Le Courayer to be *un peu passé*;[3] and no Italian will maintain that the diction of any modern writer is not perceptibly different from that of Boccace, Machiavel, or Caro.[4]

Total and sudden transformations of a language seldom happen; conquests and migrations are now very rare: but there are other causes of change, which, though slow in their operation, and invisible in their progress, are perhaps as much superior to human resistance as the revolutions of the sky, or intumescence[5] of the tide. Commerce, however necessary, however lucrative, as it depraves the manners, corrupts the language; they that have frequent intercourse with strangers, to whom they endeavor to accommodate themselves, must in time learn a mingled dialect, like the jargon which serves the traffickers[6] on the Mediterranean and Indian coasts. This will not always be confined to the exchange, the warehouse, or the port, but will be communicated by degrees to other ranks of the people, and be at last incorporated with the current speech.

There are likewise internal causes equally forcible. The language most likely to continue long without alteration would be that of a nation raised a little, and but a little, above barbarity, secluded from strangers, and totally employed in procuring the conveniencies of life; either without books, or, like some of

1. Johnson's Plan (1747) had called for "a dictionary by which the pronunciation of our language may be fixed, and its attainment facilitated; by which its purity may be preserved, its use ascertained, and its duration lengthened."

2. The French academy, founded to purify the French language, had produced a dictionary in 1694; but revisions were necessary within a few years.

3. A bit old-fashioned (French). Le Courayer's translation (1736) of Father Paolo Sarpi's *History of the Council of Trent* superseded Amelot's (1683).

4. Like Boccaccio (1313–1375) and Machiavelli (1469–1527), Annibale Caro (1507–1566) was a classic Italian stylist whose work had preceded the dictionary published in 1612 by the Italian academy.

5. Swelling.

6. Traders.

the Mahometan countries, with very few: men thus busied and unlearned, having only such words as common use requires, would perhaps long continue to express the same notions by the same signs. But no such constancy can be expected in a people polished by arts, and classed by subordination, where one part of the community is sustained and accommodated by the labor of the other. Those who have much leisure to think, will always be enlarging the stock of ideas, and every increase of knowledge, whether real or fancied, will produce new words, or combinations of words. When the mind is unchained from necessity, it will range after convenience; when it is left at large in the fields of speculation, it will shift opinions; as any custom is disused, the words that expressed it must perish with it; as any opinion grows popular, it will innovate speech in the same proportion as it alters practice.

As by the cultivation of various sciences, a language is amplified, it will be more furnished with words deflected from their original sense; the geometrician will talk of a courtier's zenith, or the eccentric virtue of a wild hero, and the physician of sanguine expectations and phlegmatic delays.[7] Copiousness of speech will give opportunities to capricious choice, by which some words will be preferred, and others degraded; vicissitudes of fashion will enforce the use of new, or extend the signification of known terms. The tropes[8] of poetry will make hourly encroachments, and the metaphorical will become the current sense: pronunciation will be varied by levity or ignorance, and the pen must at length comply with the tongue; illiterate writers will at one time or other, by public infatuation, rise into renown, who, not knowing the original import of words, will use them with colloquial licentiousness, confound distinction, and forget propriety. As politeness increases, some expressions will be considered as too gross and vulgar for the delicate, others as too formal and ceremonious for the gay and airy; new phrases are therefore adopted, which must, for the same reasons, be in time dismissed. Swift, in his petty treatise on the English language,[9] allows that new words must sometimes be introduced, but proposes that none should be suffered to become obsolete. But what makes a word obsolete, more than general agreement to forbear it? and how shall it be continued, when it conveys an offensive idea, or recalled again into the mouths of mankind, when it has once by disuse become unfamiliar, and by unfamiliarity unpleasing.

There is another cause of alteration more prevalent than any other, which yet in the present state of the world cannot be obviated. A mixture of two languages will produce a third distinct from both, and they will always be mixed, where the chief part of education, and the most conspicuous accomplishment, is skill in ancient or in foreign tongues. He that has long cultivated another language, will find its words and combinations crowd upon his memory; and haste or negligence, refinement or affectation, will obtrude borrowed terms and exotic expressions.

The great pest of speech is frequency of translation. No book was ever turned from one language into another, without imparting something of its native idiom; this is the most mischievous and comprehensive innovation;

7. "Sanguine" and "phlegmatic" once referred only to the physiological predominance of blood or phlegm. "Zenith" (the point of the sky directly overhead) and "eccentric" (deviating from the center) were originally astronomical and geometrical terms.

8. "A change of a word from its original signification" (Johnson's *Dictionary*).

9. "A Proposal for Correcting, Improving, and Ascertaining the English Tongue" (1712). "Petty": little.

single words may enter by thousands, and the fabric of the tongue continue the same, but new phraseology changes much at once; it alters not the single stones of the building, but the order[1] of the columns. If an academy should be established for the cultivation of our style, which I, who can never wish to see dependence multiplied, hope the spirit of English liberty will hinder or destroy, let them, instead of compiling grammars and dictionaries, endeavor with all their influence to stop the license of translators, whose idleness and ignorance, if it be suffered to proceed, will reduce us to babble a dialect of France.

If the changes that we fear be thus irresistible, what remains but to acquiesce with silence, as in the other insurmountable distresses of humanity? It remains that we retard what we cannot repel, that we palliate what we cannot cure. Life may be lengthened by care, though death cannot be ultimately defeated: tongues, like governments, have a natural tendency to degeneration; we have long preserved our constitution, let us make some struggles for our language.

In hope of giving longevity to that which its own nature forbids to be immortal, I have devoted this book, the labor of years, to the honor of my country, that we may no longer yield the palm of philology without a contest to the nations of the continent. The chief glory of every people arises from its authors: whether I shall add anything by my own writings to the reputation of English literature, must be left to time. Much of my life has been lost under the pressures of disease; much has been trifled away; and much has always been spent in provision for the day that was passing over me; but I shall not think my employment useless or ignoble, if by my assistance foreign nations, and distant ages, gain access to the propagators of knowledge, and understand the teachers of truth; if my labors afford light to the repositories of science, and add celebrity to Bacon, to Hooker, to Milton, and to Boyle.[2]

When I am animated by this wish, I look with pleasure on my book, however defective; and deliver it to the world with the spirit of a man that has endeavored well. That it will immediately become popular I have not promised to myself: a few wild blunders and risible absurdities, from which no work of such multiplicity was ever free, may for a time furnish folly with laughter, and harden ignorance in contempt; but useful diligence will at last prevail, and there never can be wanting some who distinguish desert;[3] who will consider that no dictionary of a living tongue ever can be perfect, since while it is hastening to publication, some words are budding, and some falling away; that a whole life cannot be spent upon syntax and etymology, and that even a whole life would not be sufficient; that he, whose design includes whatever language can express, must often speak of what he does not understand; that a writer will sometimes be hurried by eagerness to the end, and sometimes faint with weariness under a task, which Scaliger compares to the labors of the anvil and the mine;[4] that what is obvious is not always known, and what is known is not always present; that sudden fits of inadvertency will surprise vigilance, slight avocations[5] will reduce attention, and casual eclipses of the mind will darken

1. Architectural mode (Doric, etc.), which determines the style and proportions of columns.
2. Leading physicist and chemist (1627–1691). "Science": knowledge. Richard Hooker wrote *The Laws of Ecclesiastical Polity* (1594–97), a famous defense of the Church of England.
3. Merit.
4. Joseph Justus Scaliger (1540–1609), a great scholar and lexicographer, wrote Latin verses suggesting that criminals should be condemned to lexicography.
5. Whatever calls one aside.

learning; and that the writer shall often in vain trace his memory at the moment of need, for that which yesterday he knew with intuitive readiness, and which will come uncalled into his thoughts tomorrow.

In this work, when it shall be found that much is omitted, let it not be forgotten that much likewise is performed; and though no book was ever spared out of tenderness to the author, and the world is little solicitous to know whence proceeded the faults of that which it condemns; yet it may gratify curiosity to inform it, that the *English Dictionary* was written with little assistance of the learned, and without any patronage of the great;[6] not in the soft obscurities of retirement, or under the shelter of academic bowers, but amidst inconvenience and distraction, in sickness and in sorrow: and it may repress the triumph of malignant criticism to observe, that if our language is not here fully displayed, I have only failed in an attempt which no human powers have hitherto completed. If the lexicons of ancient tongues, now immutably fixed, and comprised in a few volumes, be yet, after the toil of successive ages, inadequate and delusive; if the aggregated knowledge and cooperating diligence of the Italian academicians did not secure them from the censure of Beni;[7] if the embodied critics of France, when fifty years had been spent upon their work, were obliged to change its economy,[8] and give their second edition another form, I may surely be contented without the praise of perfection, which, if I could obtain, in this gloom of solitude, what would it avail me? I have protracted my work till most of those whom I wished to please have sunk into the grave,[9] and success and miscarriage are empty sounds: I therefore dismiss it with frigid tranquility, having little to fear or hope from censure or from praise.

[SOME DEFINITIONS: A SMALL ANTHOLOGY][1]

ANTHO'LOGY. *n.*

1. A collection of flowers.

To CANT. *v.*

To talk in the jargon of particular professions, or in any kind of formal affected language, or with a peculiar and studied tone of voice.

> Men *cant* endlessly about *materia forma;* and hunt chimeras by rules of art, or dress up ignorance in words of bulk or sound, which may stop up the mouth of inquiry.—*Glanville's Scepsis Scientifica.*

ENTHU'SIASM. *n.*

1. A vain belief of private revelation; a vain confidence of divine favor or communication.

> *Enthusiasm* is founded neither on reason nor divine revelation, but rises from the conceits of a warmed or overweening brain.—*Locke.*

GE'NIUS. *n.*

1. The protecting or ruling power of men, places, or things.

> And as I awake, sweet music breathe,
> Sent by some spirit to mortals good,
> Or th' unseen *genius* of the wood.—*Milton.*

2. A man endowed with superior faculties.

6. See Johnson's letter to Lord Chesterfield in Boswell's *Life of Johnson* (p. 1321).
7. Paolo Beni's *L'Anticrusca* (1612) violently attacked the first edition of the *Vocabolario* (the Italian dictionary).
8. Organization.
9. Johnson's wife had died three years earlier.
1. Johnson's definitions include etymologies and illustrative quotations, some of which are omitted in this selection.

3. Mental power or faculties.
4. Disposition of nature by which anyone is qualified for some peculiar employment.
5. Nature; disposition.

IMA'GINATION. *n.*

1. Fancy; the power of forming ideal pictures; the power of representing things absent to one's self or others.
2. Conception; image in the mind; idea.
3. Contrivance; scheme.

LEXICO'GRAPHER. *n.*

A writer of dictionaries; a harmless drudge, that busies himself in tracing the original, and detailing the signification of words.

MELANCHO'LY. *n.*

1. A disease, supposed to proceed from a redundance of black bile.
2. A kind of madness, in which the mind is always fixed on one object.
3. A gloomy, pensive, discontented temper.

NA'TURE. *n.*

1. An imaginary being supposed to preside over the material and animal world.

   Thou, *nature,* art my goddess; to thy law
   My services are bound.—*Shakespeare.*

2. The native state or properties of anything, by which it is discriminated from others.
3. The constitution of an animated body.
4. Disposition of mind; temper.
5. The regular course of things.
6. The compass of natural existence.
7. Natural affection, or reverence; native sensations.
8. The state or operation of the material world.
9. Sort; species.
10. Sentiments or images adapted to nature, or comformable to truth and reality.
11. Physics; the science which teaches the qualities of things.

   Nature and *nature's* laws lay hid in night,
   God said, Let Newton be, and all was light.—*Pope.*

NE'TWORK. *n.*

Anything reticulated or decussated, at equal distances, with interstices between the intersections.

OATS. *n.*

A grain, which in England is generally given to horses, but in Scotland supports the people.

PA'STERN. *n.*

1. The knee of an horse.[2]

PA'TRON. *n.*

1. One who countenances, supports, or protects. Commonly a wretch who supports with insolence, and is paid with flattery.

2. "A lady once asked him how he came to define *Pastern* the *knee* of a horse: instead of making an elaborate defense, as she expected, he at once answered, 'Ignorance, Madam, pure ignorance' " (Boswell).

PE'NSION. *n.*

An allowance made to anyone without an equivalent. In England it is generally understood to mean pay given to a state hireling for treason to his country.[3]

SA'TIRE. *n.*

A poem in which wickedness or folly is censured. Proper *satire* is distinguished, by the generality of the reflections, from a *lampoon,* which is aimed against a particular person; but they are too frequently confounded.

TO'RY. *n.*

One who adheres to the ancient constitution of the state, and the apostolical hierarchy of the church of England, opposed to a whig.

> The knight is more a *tory* in the country than the town, because it more advances his interest.—*Addison.*

WHIG. *n.*

2. The name of a faction.

> Whoever has a true value for church and state, should avoid the extremes of *whig* for the sake of the former, and the extremes of tory on the account of the latter.—*Swift.*

WIT. *n.*

1. The powers of the mind; the mental faculties; the intellects. This is the original signification.
2. Imagination; quickness of fancy.
3. Sentiments produced by quickness of fancy.
4. A man of fancy.
5. A man of genius.
6. Sense; judgment.
7. In the plural. Sound mind; intellect not crazed.
8. Contrivance; stratagem; power of expedients.

1755

The Preface to Shakespeare

This is the finest piece of Shakespeare criticism in the eighteenth century; it culminates a critical tradition that began with John Dryden's remarks on Shakespeare and continued as the plays were edited by Nicholas Rowe, Alexander Pope, Lewis Theobald, and William Warburton. Johnson addresses the standard topics: Shakespeare is the poet of nature, not learning; the creator of characters who spring to life; and a writer whose works express the full range of human passions. But the Preface also takes a fresh look not only at the plays but at the first principles of criticism. Resisting "bardolatry"—uncritical worship of Shakespeare—Johnson points out his faults as well as his virtues and finds that his truth to life, or "just representations of general nature," surpasses that of all other modern writers. The Preface is most original when it attacks the long-standing critical reverence for the unities of time and place. What seems real on the stage, Johnson argues, does not depend on artificial rules but on what the mind is willing to imagine.

Johnson's edition of Shakespeare also contained footnotes and brief introductions to each of the plays. Reprinted here are his afterwords to *Twelfth Night* and *King Lear.*

3. In 1762 Johnson was awarded a pension, but he did not revise the definition in later editions.

From The Preface to Shakespeare

[SHAKESPEARE'S EXCELLENCE. GENERAL NATURE]

That praises are without reason lavished on the dead, and that the honors due only to excellence are paid to antiquity, is a complaint likely to be always continued by those who, being able to add nothing to truth, hope for eminence from the heresies of paradox; or those who, being forced by disappointment upon consolatory expedients, are willing to hope from posterity what the present age refuses, and flatter themselves that the regard which is yet denied by envy will be at last bestowed by time.

Antiquity, like every other quality that attracts the notice of mankind, has undoubtedly votaries that reverence it not from reason but from prejudice. Some seem to admire indiscriminately whatever has been long preserved, without considering that time has sometimes cooperated with chance; all perhaps are more willing to honor past than present excellence; and the mind contemplates genius through the shades of age, as the eye surveys the sun through artificial opacity. The great contention of criticism is to find the faults of the moderns and the beauties of the ancients. While an author is yet living we estimate his powers by his worst performance; and when he is dead we rate them by his best.

To works, however, of which the excellence is not absolute and definite, but gradual and comparative; to works not raised upon principles demonstrative and scientific, but appealing wholly to observation and experience, no other test can be applied than length of duration and continuance of esteem. What mankind have long possessed they have often examined and compared; and if they persist to value the possession, it is because frequent comparisons have confirmed opinion in its favor. As among the works of nature no man can properly call a river deep or a mountain high, without the knowledge of many mountains and many rivers; so in the productions of genius, nothing can be styled excellent till it has been compared with other works of the same kind. Demonstration[1] immediately displays its power and has nothing to hope or fear from the flux of years; but works tentative and experimental must be estimated by their proportion to the general and collective ability of man, as it is discovered in a long succession of endeavors. Of the first building that was raised, it might be with certainty determined that it was round or square, but whether it was spacious or lofty must have been referred to time. The Pythagorean scale of numbers[2] was at once discovered to be perfect; but the poems of Homer we yet know not to transcend the common limits of human intelligence, but by remarking that nation after nation, and century after century, has been able to do little more than transpose his incidents, new name his characters, and paraphrase his sentiments.

The reverence due to writings that have long subsisted arises, therefore, not from any credulous confidence in the superior wisdom of past ages, or gloomy persuasion of the degeneracy of mankind, but is the consequence of acknowledged and indubitable positions, that what has been longest known has been most considered, and what is most considered is best understood.

The poet of whose works I have undertaken the revision may now begin to

1. "The highest degree of deducible or argumental evidence" (Johnson's *Dictionary*).

2. Pythagoras discovered the ratios that determine the principal intervals of the musical scale.

assume the dignity of an ancient and claim the privilege of established fame and prescriptive veneration. He has long outlived his century, the term commonly fixed as the test of literary merit.[3] Whatever advantages he might once derive from personal allusions, local customs, or temporary opinions, have for many years been lost; and every topic of merriment or motive of sorrow which the modes of artificial life afforded him now only obscure the scenes which they once illuminated. The effects of favor and competition are at an end; the tradition of his friendships and his enmities has perished; his works support no opinion with arguments nor supply any faction with invectives; they can neither indulge vanity nor gratify malignity; but are read without any other reason than the desire of pleasure, and are therefore praised only as pleasure is obtained; yet, thus unassisted by interest or passion, they have passed through variations of taste and changes of manners, and, as they devolved from one generation to another, have received new honors at every transmission.

But because human judgment, though it be gradually gaining upon certainty, never becomes infallible, and approbation, though long continued, may yet be only the approbation of prejudice or fashion, it is proper to inquire by what peculiarities of excellence Shakespeare has gained and kept the favor of his countrymen.

Nothing can please many, and please long, but just representations of general nature. Particular manners can be known to few, and therefore few only can judge how nearly they are copied. The irregular combinations of fanciful invention may delight awhile by that novelty of which the common satiety of life sends us all in quest; but the pleasures of sudden wonder are soon exhausted, and the mind can only repose on the stability of truth.

Shakespeare is, above all writers, at least above all modern writers, the poet of nature, the poet that holds up to his readers a faithful mirror of manners and of life. His characters are not modified by the customs of particular places, unpracticed by the rest of the world; by the peculiarities of studies or professions, which can operate but upon small numbers; or by the accidents of transient fashions or temporary opinions: they are the genuine progeny of common humanity, such as the world will always supply and observation will always find. His persons act and speak by the influence of those general passions and principles by which all minds are agitated and the whole system of life is continued in motion. In the writings of other poets a character is too often an individual: in those of Shakespeare it is commonly a species.

It is from this wide extension of design that so much instruction is derived. It is this which fills the plays of Shakespeare with practical axioms and domestic wisdom. It was said of Euripides[4] that every verse was a precept; and it may be said of Shakespeare that from his works may be collected a system of civil and economical prudence. Yet his real power is not shown in the splendor of particular passages, but by the progress of his fable[5] and the tenor of his dialogue; and he that tries to recommend him by select quotations will succeed like the pedant in Hierocles[6] who, when he offered his house to sale, carried a brick in his pocket as a specimen.

It will not easily be imagined how much Shakespeare excels in accommo-

3. Horace's *Epistles* 2.1.39.
4. The Greek tragic poet (ca. 480–406 B.C.E.). The observation is Cicero's.
5. Plot. "The series or contexture of events which constitute a poem epic or dramatic" (Johnson's *Dictionary*).
6. Hierocles of Alexandria, a Greek philosopher of the 5th century C.E.

dating his sentiments to real life but by comparing him with other authors. It was observed of the ancient schools of declamation that the more diligently they were frequented, the more was the student disqualified for the world, because he found nothing there which he should ever meet in any other place. The same remark may be applied to every stage but that of Shakespeare. The theater, when it is under any other direction, is peopled by such characters as were never seen, conversing in a language which was never heard, upon topics which will never arise in the commerce of mankind. But the dialogue of this author is often so evidently determined by the incident which produces it, and is pursued with so much ease and simplicity, that it seems scarcely to claim the merit of fiction, but to have been gleaned by diligent selection out of common conversation and common occurrences.

Upon every other stage the universal agent is love, by whose power all good and evil is distributed and every action quickened or retarded. To bring a lover, a lady, and a rival into the fable; to entangle them in contradictory obligations, perplex them with oppositions of interest, and harass them with violence of desires inconsistent with each other; to make them meet in rapture, and part in agony; to fill their mouths with hyperbolical joy and outrageous sorrow; to distress them as nothing human ever was distressed; to deliver them as nothing human ever was delivered, is the business of a modern dramatist. For this, probability is violated, life is misrepresented, and language is depraved. But love is only one of many passions; and as it has no great influence upon the sum of life, it has little operation in the dramas of a poet who caught his ideas from the living world and exhibited only what he saw before him. He knew that any other passion, as it was regular or exorbitant, was a cause of happiness or calamity.

Characters thus ample and general were not easily discriminated and preserved; yet perhaps no poet ever kept his personages more distinct from each other. I will not say with Pope that every speech may be assigned to the proper speaker,[7] because many speeches there are which have nothing characteristical; but perhaps though some may be equally adapted to every person, it will be difficult to find that any can be properly transferred from the present possessor to another claimant. The choice is right when there is reason for choice.

Other dramatists can only gain attention by hyperbolical or aggravated characters, by fabulous and unexampled excellence or depravity, as the writers of barbarous romances invigorated the reader by a giant and a dwarf; and he that should form his expectations of human affairs from the play or from the tale would be equally deceived. Shakespeare has no heroes; his scenes are occupied only by men, who act and speak as the reader thinks that he should himself have spoken or acted on the same occasion; even where the agency is supernatural, the dialogue is level with life. Other writers disguise the most natural passions and most frequent incidents so that he who contemplates them in the book will not know them in the world: Shakespeare approximates[8] the remote, and familiarizes the wonderful; the event which he represents will not happen, but, if it were possible, its effects would probably be such as he has assigned; and it may be said that he has not only shown human nature as it acts in real exigencies, but as it would be found in trials to which it cannot be exposed.

7. In the preface to his edition of Shakespeare's plays (1725).

8. Brings near.

This therefore is the praise of Shakespeare, that his drama is the mirror of life; that he who has mazed his imagination in following the phantoms which other writers raise up before him, may here be cured of his delirious ecstasies by reading human sentiments in human language, by scenes from which a hermit may estimate the transactions of the world, and a confessor predict the progress of the passions.

[SHAKESPEARE'S FAULTS. THE THREE DRAMATIC UNITIES]

Shakespeare with his excellencies has likewise faults, and faults sufficient to obscure and overwhelm any other merit. I shall show them in the proportion in which they appear to me, without envious malignity or superstitious veneration. No question can be more innocently discussed than a dead poet's pretensions to renown; and little regard is due to that bigotry which sets candor[9] higher than truth.

His first defect is that to which may be imputed most of the evil in books or in men. He sacrifices virtue to convenience, and is so much more careful to please than to instruct that he seems to write without any moral purpose. From his writings indeed a system of social duty may be selected, for he that thinks reasonably must think morally, but his precepts and axioms drop casually from him; he makes no just distribution of good or evil, nor is always careful to show in the virtuous a disapprobation of the wicked; he carries his persons indifferently through right and wrong, and at the close dismisses them without further care, and leaves their examples to operate by chance. This fault the barbarity of his age cannot extenuate; for it is always a writer's duty to make the world better, and justice is a virtue independent on time or place.

The plots are often so loosely formed that a very slight consideration may improve them, and so carelessly pursued that he seems not always fully to comprehend his own design. He omits opportunities of instructing or delighting which the train of his story seems to force upon him, and apparently rejects those exhibitions which would be more affecting for the sake of those which are more easy.

It may be observed that in many of his plays the latter part is evidently neglected. When he found himself near the end of his work, and in view of his reward, he shortened the labor to snatch the profit. He therefore remits his efforts where he should most vigorously exert them, and his catastrophe is improbably produced or imperfectly represented.

He had no regard to distinction of time or place, but gives to one age or nation, without scruple, the customs, institutions, and opinions of another, at the expense not only of likelihood but of possibility. These faults Pope has endeavored, with more zeal than judgment, to transfer to his imagined interpolators. We need not wonder to find Hector quoting Aristotle, when we see the loves of Theseus and Hippolyta combined with the Gothic mythology of fairies.[1] Shakespeare, indeed, was not the only violator of chronology, for in the same age Sidney, who wanted not the advantages of learning, has, in his *Arcadia,* confounded the pastoral with the feudal times, the days of innocence, quiet, and security with those of turbulence, violence, and adventure.

In his comic scenes he is seldom very successful when he engages his characters in reciprocations of smartness and contests of sarcasm; their jests are

9. Kindness.
1. In *Troilus and Cressida* 2.2.166 and in *A Midsummer Night's Dream,* respectively.

commonly gross, and their pleasantry licentious; neither his gentlemen nor his ladies have much delicacy, nor are sufficiently distinguished from his clowns[2] by any appearance of refined manners. Whether he represented the real conversation of his time is not easy to determine: the reign of Elizabeth is commonly supposed to have been a time of stateliness, formality, and reserve; yet perhaps the relaxations of that severity were not very elegant. There must, however, have been always some modes of gaiety preferable to others, and a writer ought to choose the best.

In tragedy his performance seems constantly to be worse as his labor is more. The effusions of passion, which exigence forces out, are for the most part striking and energetic; but whenever he solicits his invention, or strains his faculties, the offspring of his throes is tumor,[3] meanness, tediousness, and obscurity.

In narration he affects a disproportionate pomp of diction and a wearisome train of circumlocution, and tells the incident imperfectly in many words which might have been more plainly delivered in few. Narration in dramatic poetry is naturally tedious, as it is unanimated and inactive, and obstructs the progress of the action; it should therefore always be rapid and enlivened by frequent interruption. Shakespeare found it an encumbrance, and instead of lightening it by brevity, endeavored to recommend it by dignity and splendor.

His declamations or set speeches are commonly cold and weak, for his power was the power of nature; when he endeavored, like other tragic writers, to catch opportunities of amplification and, instead of inquiring what the occasion demanded, to show how much his stores of knowledge could supply, he seldom escapes without the pity or resentment of his reader.

It is incident to him to be now and then entangled with an unwieldy sentiment which he cannot well express, and will not reject; he struggles with it awhile, and, if it continues stubborn, comprises it in words such as occur, and leaves it to be disentangled and evolved[4] by those who have more leisure to bestow upon it.

Not that always where the language is intricate the thought is subtle, or the image always great where the line is bulky; the equality of words to things is very often neglected, and trivial sentiments and vulgar[5] ideas disappoint the attention, to which they are recommended by sonorous epithets and swelling figures.

But the admirers of this great poet have most reason to complain when he approaches nearest to his highest excellence, and seems fully resolved to sink them in dejection and mollify them with tender emotions by the fall of greatness, the danger of innocence, or the crosses of love. What he does best, he soon ceases to do. He is not long soft and pathetic without some idle conceit or contemptible equivocation. He no sooner begins to move than he counteracts himself; and terror and pity, as they are rising in the mind, are checked and blasted by sudden frigidity.

A quibble[6] is to Shakespeare what luminous vapors are to the traveler: he follows it at all adventures; it is sure to lead him out of his way, and sure to engulf him in the mire. It has some malignant power over his mind, and its fascinations are irresistible. Whatever be the dignity or profundity of his dis-

2. Rustics.
3. Inflated grandeur, false magnificence.
4. Unfolded.
5. "Mean; low; being of the common rate" (Johnson's *Dictionary*).
6. Pun.

quisitions, whether he be enlarging knowledge or exalting affection, whether he be amusing[7] attention with incidents, or enchaining it in suspense, let but a quibble spring up before him, and he leaves his work unfinished. A quibble is the golden apple for which he will always turn aside from his career[8] or stoop from his elevation. A quibble, poor and barren as it is, gave him such delight that he was content to purchase it by the sacrifice of reason, propriety, and truth. A quibble was to him the fatal Cleopatra for which he lost the world, and was content to lose it.

It will be thought strange that in enumerating the defects of this writer, I have not yet mentioned his neglect of the unities; his violation of those laws which have been instituted and established by the joint authority of poets and critics.

For his other deviations from the art of writing, I resign him to critical justice without making any other demand in his favor than that which must be indulged to all human excellence: that his virtues be rated with his failings. But from the censure which this irregularity may bring upon him I shall, with due reverence to that learning which I must oppose, adventure to try how I can defend him.

His histories, being neither tragedies nor comedies, are not subject to any of their laws; nothing more is necessary to all the praise which they expect than that the changes of action be so prepared as to be understood; that the incidents be various and affecting, and the characters consistent, natural, and distinct. No other unity is intended, and therefore none is to be sought.

In his other works he has well enough preserved the unity of action. He has not, indeed, an intrigue regularly perplexed and regularly unraveled: he does not endeavor to hide his design only to discover it, for this is seldom the order of real events, and Shakespeare is the poet of nature: but his plan has commonly what Aristotle requires,[9] a beginning, a middle, and an end; one event is concatenated with another, and the conclusion follows by easy consequence. There are, perhaps, some incidents that might be spared, as in other poets there is much talk that only fills up time upon the stage; but the general system makes gradual advances, and the end of the play is the end of expectation.

To the unities of time and place he has shown no regard; and perhaps a nearer view of the principles on which they stand will diminish their value and withdraw from them the veneration which, from the time of Corneille,[1] they have very generally received, by discovering that they have given more trouble to the poet than pleasure to the auditor.

The necessity of observing the unities of time and place arises from the supposed necessity of making the drama credible. The critics hold it impossible that an action of months or years can be possibly believed to pass in three hours; or that the spectator can suppose himself to sit in the theater while ambassadors go and return between distant kings, while armies are levied and towns besieged, while an exile wanders and returns, or till he whom they saw courting his mistress shall lament the untimely fall of his son. The mind revolts

7. "To entertain with tranquility; to fill with thoughts that engage the mind, without distracting it" (Johnson's *Dictionary*).

8. Course of action; the ground on which a race is run. In Greek legend Atalanta refused to marry any man who could not defeat her in a foot race. Hippomenes won her by dropping, as he ran, three of the golden apples of the Hesperides, which she paused to pick up.

9. *Poetics* 7.

1. Pierre Corneille (1606–1684), the French playwright, discussed the unities in his *Discours des trois unités* (1660).

from evident falsehood, and fiction loses its force when it departs from the resemblance of reality.

From the narrow limitation of time necessarily arises the contraction of place. The spectator who knows that he saw the first act at Alexandria cannot suppose that he sees the next at Rome, at a distance to which not the dragons of Medea[2] could, in so short a time, have transported him; he knows with certainty that he has not changed his place; and he knows that place cannot change itself, that what was a house cannot become a plain, that what was Thebes can never be Persepolis.

Such is the triumphant language with which a critic exults over the misery of an irregular poet, and exults commonly without resistance or reply. It is time, therefore, to tell him by the authority of Shakespeare that he assumes, as an unquestionable principle, a position which, while his breath is forming it into words, his understanding pronounces to be false. It is false that any representation is mistaken for reality; that any dramatic fable in its materiality was ever credible or, for a single moment, was ever credited.

The objection arising from the impossibility of passing the first hour at Alexandria and the next at Rome supposes that when the play opens the spectator really imagines himself at Alexandria, and believes that his walk to the theater has been a voyage to Egypt, and that he lives in the days of Antony and Cleopatra. Surely he that imagines this may imagine more. He that can take the stage at one time for the palace of the Ptolemies may take it in half an hour for the promontory of Actium. Delusion, if delusion be admitted, has no certain limitation; if the spectator can be once persuaded that his old acquaintances are Alexander and Caesar, that a room illuminated with candles is the plain of Pharsalia or the bank of Granicus, he is in a state of elevation above the reach of reason or of truth, and from the heights of empyrean poetry may despise the circumscriptions of terrestrial nature. There is no reason why a mind thus wandering in ecstasy should count the clock, or why an hour should not be a century in that calenture[3] of the brain that can make the stage a field.

The truth is that the spectators are always in their senses, and know, from the first act to the last, that the stage is only a stage, and that the players are only players. They came to hear a certain number of lines recited with just gesture and elegant modulation. The lines relate to some action, and an action must be in some place; but the different actions that complete a story may be in places very remote from each other; and where is the absurdity of allowing that space to represent first Athens, and then Sicily, which was always known to be neither Sicily nor Athens but a modern theater?

By supposition, as place is introduced, time may be extended; the time required by the fable elapses, for the most part, between the acts; for, of so much of the action as is represented, the real and poetical duration is the same. If, in the first act, preparations for war against Mithridates are represented to be made in Rome, the event of the war may, without absurdity, be represented, in the catastrophe, as happening in Pontus; we know that there is neither war nor preparation for war; we know that we are neither in Rome nor Pontus, that neither Mithridates nor Lucullus are before us. The drama exhibits successive imitations of successive actions; and why may not the second imitation represent an action that happened years after the first, if it be

2. According to legend, Medea fled the scene of her crimes in a chariot drawn by dragons.

3. A delirium produced by tropical heat, which causes sailors to leap into the sea under the delusion that it is a green field.

so connected with it that nothing but time can be supposed to intervene? Time is, of all modes of existence, most obsequious[4] to the imagination; a lapse of years is as easily conceived as a passage of hours. In contemplation we easily contract the time of real actions, and therefore willingly permit it to be contracted when we only see their imitation.

It will be asked how the drama moves if it is not credited. It is credited with all the credit due to a drama. It is credited, whenever it moves, as a just picture of a real original; as representing to the auditor what he would himself feel if he were to do or suffer what is there feigned to be suffered or to be done. The reflection that strikes the heart is not that the evils before us are real evils, but that they are evils to which we ourselves may be exposed. If there be any fallacy, it is not that we fancy the players, but that we fancy ourselves, unhappy for a moment; but we rather lament the possibility than suppose the presence of misery, as a mother weeps over her babe when she remembers that death may take it from her. The delight of tragedy proceeds from our consciousness of fiction; if we thought murders and treasons real, they would please no more.

Imitations produce pain or pleasure, not because they are mistaken for realities, but because they bring realities to mind. When the imagination is recreated[5] by a painted landscape, the trees are not supposed capable to give us shade or the fountains coolness; but we consider how we should be pleased with such fountains playing beside us and such woods waving over us. We are agitated in reading the history of *Henry the Fifth;* yet no man takes his book for the field of Agincourt. A dramatic exhibition is a book recited with concomitants that increase or diminish its effect. Familiar[6] comedy is often more powerful on the theater than in the page; imperial tragedy is always less. The humor of Petruchio may be heightened by grimace; but what voice or what gesture can hope to add dignity or force to the soliloquy of Cato?[7]

A play read affects the mind like a play acted. It is therefore evident that the action is not supposed to be real; and it follows that between the acts a longer or shorter time may be allowed to pass, and that no more account of space or duration is to be taken by the auditor of a drama than by the reader of a narrative, before whom may pass in an hour the life of a hero or the revolutions of an empire.

Whether Shakespeare knew the unities and rejected them by design or deviated from them by happy ignorance, it is, I think, impossible to decide and useless to inquire. We may reasonably suppose that, when he rose to notice, he did not want[8] the counsels and admonitions of scholars and critics, and that he at last deliberately persisted in a practice which he might have begun by chance. As nothing is essential to the fable but unity of action, and as the unities of time and place arise evidently from false assumptions, and, by circumscribing the extent of the drama, lessen its variety, I cannot think it much to be lamented that they were not known by him, or not observed: nor, if such another poet could arise, should I very vehemently reproach him that his first act passed at Venice and his next in Cyprus.[9] Such violations of rules merely positive[1] become the comprehensive genius of Shakespeare, and such censures are suitable to the minute and slender criticism of Voltaire.

4. "Obedient; compliant" (Johnson's *Dictionary*).
5. Delighted.
6. Domestic.
7. In Addison's tragedy *Cato* (5.1), the hero soliloquizes on immortality shortly before committing suicide. Petruchio is the hero of Shakespeare's comedy *The Taming of the Shrew*.
8. Lack.
9. As is the case in *Othello*.
1. Arbitrary; not natural.

Non usque adeo permiscuit imis
Longus summa dies, ut non, si voce Metelli
Serventur leges, malint a Caesare tolli.[2]

I speak thus slightly of dramatic rules, I cannot but recollect how much wit and learning may be produced against me; before such authorities I am afraid to stand: not that I think the present question one of those that are to be decided by mere authority, but because it is to be suspected that these precepts have not been so easily received but for better reasons than I have yet been able to find. The result of my inquiries, in which it would be ludicrous to boast of impartiality, is that the unities of time and place are not essential to a just drama, that though they may sometimes conduce to pleasure, they are always to be sacrificed to the nobler beauties of variety and instruction; and that a play written with nice observation of critical rules is to be contemplated as an elaborate curiosity, as the product of superfluous and ostentatious art, by which is shown rather what is possible than what is necessary.

He that without diminution of any other excellence shall preserve all the unities unbroken deserves the like applause with the architect who shall display all the orders of architecture in a citadel without any deduction for its strength; but the principal beauty of a citadel is to exclude the enemy, and the greatest graces of a play are to copy nature and instruct life.* * *

[*TWELFTH NIGHT*]

This play is in the graver part elegant and easy, and in some of the lighter scenes exquisitely humorous. Ague-cheek is drawn with great propriety, but his character is, in a great measure, that of natural fatuity, and is therefore not the proper prey of a satirist. The soliloquy of Malvolio is truly comick; he is betrayed to ridicule merely by his pride. The marriage of Olivia, and the succeeding perplexity, though well enough contrived to divert on the stage, wants credibility, and fails to produce the proper instruction required in the drama, as it exhibits no just picture of life.

1765

From LIVES OF THE POETS

From Milton[1]

["LYCIDAS"]

One of the poems on which much praise has been bestowed is *Lycidas;* of which the diction is harsh, the rhymes uncertain, and the numbers[2] unpleas-

2. Lucan's *Pharsalia* 3.138–40: "The course of time has not wrought such confusion that the laws would not rather be trampled on by Caesar than saved by Metellus."

1. Johnson's treatment of Milton as man and poet offended many ardent Miltonians in his own day and damaged his reputation as a critic in the following century. He did not admire Milton's character, and he detested his politics and religion. But no one has praised *Paradise Lost* more handsomely. Especially offensive in the 19th century was his attack on "Lycidas." Johnson disliked modern pastorals, believing that the tradition had been worn threadbare. His views on the genre may be read in *Rambler* no. 36 and no. 37.

2. Versification.

ing. What beauty there is, we must therefore seek in the sentiments and images. It is not to be considered as the effusion of real passion; for passion runs not after remote allusions and obscure opinions. Passion plucks no berries from the myrtle and ivy, nor calls upon Arethuse and Mincius, nor tells of "rough satyrs and fauns with cloven heel." Where there is leisure for fiction there is little grief.

In this poem there is no nature, for there is no truth; there is no art, for there is nothing new. Its form is that of a pastoral, easy, vulgar, and therefore disgusting:[3] whatever images it can supply are long ago exhausted; and its inherent improbability always forces dissatisfaction on the mind. When Cowley tells of Hervey that they studied together,[4] it is easy to suppose how much he must miss the companion of his labors and the partner of his discoveries; but what image of tenderness can be excited by these lines!

> We drove afield, and both together heard
> What time the grayfly winds her sultry horn,
> Battening our flocks with the fresh dews of night.

We know that they never drove afield, and that they had no flocks to batten; and though it be allowed that the representation may be allegorical, the true meaning is so uncertain and remote that it is never sought because it cannot be known when it is found.

Among the flocks and copses and flowers appear the heathen deities, Jove and Phoebus, Neptune and Aeolus, with a long train of mythological imagery, such as a college easily supplies. Nothing can less display knowledge or less exercise invention than to tell how a shepherd has lost his companion and must now feed his flocks alone, without any judge of his skill in piping; and how one god asks another god what is become of Lycidas, and how neither god can tell. He who thus grieves will excite no sympathy; he who thus praises will confer no honor.

This poem has yet a grosser fault. With these trifling fictions are mingled the most awful and sacred truths, such as ought never to be polluted with such irreverent combinations. The shepherd likewise is now a feeder of sheep, and afterwards an ecclesiastical pastor, a superintendent of a Christian flock. Such equivocations are always unskillful; but here they are indecent,[5] and at least approach to impiety, of which, however, I believe the writer not to have been conscious.

Such is the power of reputation justly acquired that its blaze drives away the eye from nice examination. Surely no man could have fancied that he read *Lycidas* with pleasure had he not known its author.

[*PARADISE LOST*]

Those little pieces may be dispatched without much anxiety; a greater work calls for greater care. I am now to examine *Paradise Lost*, a poem which, considered with respect to design, may claim the first place, and with respect to performance the second, among the productions of the human mind.

By the general consent of critics the first praise of genius is due to the writer of an epic poem, as it requires an assemblage of all the powers which are singly sufficient for other compositions. Poetry is the art of uniting pleasure with truth, by calling imagination to the help of reason. Epic poetry undertakes to

3. Distasteful, because too facile and common.
4. Cowley's "On the Death of Mr. William Hervey" (1656).
5. Unbecoming, lacking in decorum.

teach the most important truths by the most pleasing precepts, and therefore relates some great event in the most affecting manner. History must supply the writer with the rudiments of narration, which he must improve and exalt by a nobler art, must animate by dramatic energy, and diversify by retrospection and anticipation; morality must teach him the exact bounds and different shades of vice and virtue; from policy and the practice of life he has to learn the discriminations of character and the tendency of the passions, either single or combined; and physiology[6] must supply him with illustrations and images. To put these materials to poetical use is required an imagination capable of painting nature and realizing fiction. Nor is he yet a poet till he has attained the whole extension of his language, distinguished all the delicacies of phrase, and all the colors of words, and learned to adjust their different sounds to all the varieties of metrical modulation.

Bossu is of opinion that the poet's first work is to find a *moral,* which his fable is afterwards to illustrate and establish.[7] This seems to have been the process only of Milton: the moral of other poems is incidental and consequent; in Milton's only it is essential and intrinsic. His purpose was the most useful and the most arduous: "to vindicate the ways of God to man";[8] to show the reasonableness of religion, and the necessity of obedience to the Divine Law.

To convey this moral there must be a *fable,* a narration artfully constructed, so as to excite curiosity and surprise expectation. In this part of his work Milton must be confessed to have equaled every other poet. He has involved in his account of the Fall of Man the events which preceded, and those that were to follow it: he has interwoven the whole system of theology with such propriety that every part appears to be necessary, and scarcely any recital is wished shorter for the sake of quickening the progress of the main action.

The subject of an epic poem is naturally an event of great importance. That of Milton is not the destruction of a city, the conduct of a colony, or the foundation of an empire. His subject is the fate of worlds, the revolutions of heaven and of earth; rebellion against the Supreme King raised by the highest order of created beings; the overthrow of their host and the punishment of their crime; the creation of a new race of reasonable creatures; their original happiness and innocence, their forfeiture of immortality, and their restoration to hope and peace.

Great events can be hastened or retarded only by persons of elevated dignity. Before the greatness displayed in Milton's poem all other greatness shrinks away. The weakest of his agents are the highest and noblest of human beings, the original parents of mankind; with whose actions the elements consented; on whose rectitude or deviation of will depended the state of terrestrial nature and the condition of all the future inhabitants of the globe.

Of the other agents in the poem, the chief are such as it is irreverence to name on slight occasions. The rest were lower powers;

> of which the least could wield
> Those elements, and arm him with the force
> Of all their regions;[9]

6. "The doctrine of the constitution of the works of nature" (Johnson's *Dictionary*).
7. René le Bossu's treatise on the epic poem, *Traité du Poëme Épique,* 1675, was much admired in the late 17th and early 18th centuries.
8. Milton wrote "justify," not "vindicate" (*Paradise Lost* 1.26). It was Pope, in *An Essay on Man* 1.16, who used "vindicate."
9. *Paradise Lost* 6.221.

powers which only the control of Omnipotence restrains from laying creation waste, and filling the vast expanse of space with ruin and confusion. To display the motives and actions of beings thus superior, so far as human reason can examine them or human imagination represent them, is the task which this mighty poet has undertaken and performed.

In the examination of epic poems much speculation is commonly employed upon the *characters*. The characters in the *Paradise Lost* which admit of examination are those of angels and of man; of angels good and evil, of man in his innocent and sinful state.

Among the angels the virtue of Raphael is mild and placid, of easy condescension and free communication; that of Michael is regal and lofty, and, as may seem, attentive to the dignity of his own nature. Abdiel and Gabriel appear occasionally, and act as every incident requires; the solitary fidelity of Abdiel is very amiably painted.[1]

Of the evil angels the characters are more diversified. To Satan, as Addison observes, such sentiments are given as suit "the most exalted and most depraved being."[2] Milton has been censured by Clarke for the impiety which sometimes breaks from Satan's mouth. For there are thoughts, as he justly remarks, which no observation of character can justify, because no good man would willingly permit them to pass, however transiently, through his own mind.[3] To make Satan speak as a rebel, without any such expressions as might taint the reader's imagination, was indeed one of the great difficulties in Milton's undertaking, and I cannot but think that he has extricated himself with great happiness. There is in Satan's speeches little that can give pain to a pious ear. The language of rebellion cannot be the same with that of obedience. The malignity of Satan foams in haughtiness and obstinacy; but his expressions are commonly general, and no otherwise offensive than as they are wicked.

The other chiefs of the celestial rebellion are very judiciously discriminated in the first and second books; and the ferocious character of Moloch appears, both in the battle and the council, with exact consistency.

To Adam and Eve are given during their innocence such sentiments as innocence can generate and utter. Their love is pure benevolence and mutual veneration; their repasts are without luxury and their diligence without toil. Their addresses to their Maker have little more than the voice of admiration and gratitude. Fruition left them nothing to ask, and Innocence left them nothing to fear.

But with guilt enter distrust and discord, mutual accusation, and stubborn self-defense; they regard each other with alienated minds, and dread their Creator as the avenger of their transgression. At last they seek shelter in his mercy, soften to repentance, and melt in supplication. Both before and after the Fall the superiority of Adam is diligently sustained.

Of the *probable* and the *marvelous*,[4] two parts of a vulgar epic poem which immerge the critic in deep consideration, the *Paradise Lost* requires little to be said. It contains the history of a miracle, of Creation and Redemption; it displays the power and the mercy of the Supreme Being: the probable therefore is marvelous, and the marvelous is probable. The substance of the narrative is truth; and as truth allows no choice, it is, like necessity, superior

1. *Paradise Lost* 5.803ff.
2. *Spectator* 303.
3. John Clarke's *Essay upon Study* (1731).
4. Actions in an epic poem that are wonderful because they exceed the probable.

to rule. To the accidental or adventitious parts, as to every thing human, some slight exceptions may be made. But the main fabric is immovably supported.

It is justly remarked by Addison[5] that this poem has, by the nature of its subject, the advantage above all others, that it is universally and perpetually interesting. All mankind will, through all ages, bear the same relation to Adam and to Eve, and must partake of that good and evil which extend to themselves.

Of the *machinery,* so called from *theòs apò mēkhanēs,*[6] by which is meant the occasional interposition of supernatural power, another fertile topic of critical remarks, here is no room to speak, because every thing is done under the immediate and visible direction of Heaven; but the rule is so far observed that no part of the action could have been accomplished by any other means.

Of *episodes*[7] I think there are only two, contained in Raphael's relation of the war in heaven and Michael's prophetic account of the changes to happen in this world. Both are closely connected with the great action; one was necessary to Adam as a warning, the other as a consolation.

To the completeness or *integrity* of the design nothing can be objected; it has distinctly and clearly what Aristotle requires, a beginning, a middle, and an end. There is perhaps no poem of the same length from which so little can be taken without apparent mutilation. Here are no funeral games, nor is there any long description of a shield. The short digressions at the beginning of the third, seventh, and ninth books might doubtless be spared; but superfluities so beautiful who would take away? or who does not wish that the author of the *Iliad* had gratified succeeding ages with a little knowledge of himself? Perhaps no passages are more frequently or more attentively read than those extrinsic paragraphs; and since the end of poetry is pleasure, that cannot be unpoetical with which all are pleased.

The questions, whether the action of the poem be strictly *one,*[8] whether the poem can be properly termed *heroic,* and who is the hero, are raised by such readers as draw their principles of judgment rather from books than from reason. Milton, though he entitled *Paradise Lost* only a "poem," yet calls it himself "heroic song."[9] Dryden, petulantly and indecently, denies the heroism of Adam because he was overcome; but there is no reason why the hero should not be unfortunate except established practice, since success and virtue do not go necessarily together. Cato is the hero of Lucan, but Lucan's authority will not be suffered by Quintilian to decide. However, if success be necessary, Adam's deceiver was at last crushed; Adam was restored to his Maker's favor, and therefore may securely resume his human rank.

After the scheme and fabric of the poem must be considered its component parts, the sentiments, and the diction.

The *sentiments,* as expressive of manners or appropriated to characters, are for the greater part unexceptionably just. Splendid passages containing lessons of morality or precepts of prudence occur seldom. Such is the original formation of this poem that as it admits no human manners till the Fall, it can give little assistance to human conduct. Its end is to raise the thoughts above sublunary cares or pleasures. Yet the praise of that fortitude, with which Abdiel maintained his singularity of virtue against the scorn of multitudes, may be

5. *Spectator* 273.
6. Aristotle's *Poetics* 15.10. *Deus ex machina,* the intervention of supernatural powers into the affairs of humans.
7. Incidental but related narratives within an epic poem. Johnson is citing *Paradise Lost* 5.577ff. and 11.334ff.
8. I.e., a single action dealing with a single character.
9. *Paradise Lost* 9.25.

accommodated to all times; and Raphael's reproof of Adam's curiosity after the planetary motions, with the answer returned by Adam, may be confidently opposed to any rule of life which any poet has delivered.[1]

The thoughts which are occasionally called forth in the progress are such as could only be produced by an imagination in the highest degree fervid and active, to which materials were supplied by incessant study and unlimited curiosity. The heat of Milton's mind might be said to sublimate his learning, to throw off into his work the spirit of science,[2] unmingled with its grosser parts.

He had considered creation in its whole extent, and his descriptions are therefore learned. He had accustomed his imagination to unrestrained indulgence, and his conceptions therefore were extensive. The characteristic quality of his poem is sublimity. He sometimes descends to the elegant, but his element is the great. He can occasionally invest himself with grace; but his natural port is gigantic loftiness. He can please when pleasure is required; but it is his peculiar power to astonish.

He seems to have been well acquainted with his own genius, and to know what it was that Nature had bestowed upon him more bountifully than upon others; the power of displaying the vast, illuminating the splendid, enforcing the awful, darkening the gloomy, and aggravating the dreadful: he therefore chose a subject on which too much could not be said, on which he might tire his fancy without the censure of extravagance.

* * *

The defects and faults of *Paradise Lost,* for faults and defects every work of man must have, it is the business of impartial criticism to discover. As in displaying the excellence of Milton I have not made long quotations, because of selecting beauties there had been no end, I shall in the same general manner mention that which seems to deserve censure; for what Englishman can take delight in transcribing passages, which, if they lessen the reputation of Milton, diminish in some degree the honor of our country?

* * *

The plan of *Paradise Lost* has this inconvenience, that it comprises neither human actions nor human manners. The man and woman who act and suffer are in a state which no other man or woman can ever know. The reader finds no transaction in which he can be engaged, beholds no condition in which he can by any effort of imagination place himself; he has, therefore, little natural curiosity or sympathy.

We all, indeed, feel the effects of Adam's disobedience; we all sin like Adam, and like him must all bewail our offenses; we have restless and insidious enemies in the fallen angels, and in the blessed spirits we have guardians and friends; in the Redemption of mankind we hope to be included: in the description of heaven and hell we are surely interested, as we are all to reside hereafter either in the regions of horror or of bliss.

But these truths are too important to be new: they have been taught to our infancy; they have mingled with our solitary thoughts and familiar conversation, and are habitually interwoven with the whole texture of life. Being therefore not new they raise no unaccustomed emotion in the mind: what we

1. *Paradise Lost* 8.65ff.
2. Knowledge.

knew before, we cannot learn; what is not unexpected, cannot surprise.

Of the ideas suggested by these awful scenes, from some we recede with reverence, except when stated hours require their association; and from others we shrink with horror, or admit them only as salutary inflictions, as counterpoises to our interests and passions. Such images rather obstruct the career of fancy than incite it.

Pleasure and terror are indeed the genuine sources of poetry; but poetical pleasure must be such as human imagination can at least conceive, and poetical terror such as human strength and fortitude may combat. The good and evil of Eternity are too ponderous for the wings of wit; the mind sinks under them in passive helplessness, content with calm belief and humble adoration.

Known truths however may take a different appearance, and be conveyed to the mind by a new train of intermediate images. This Milton has undertaken, and performed with pregnancy and vigor of mind peculiar to himself. Whoever considers the few radical[3] positions which the Scriptures afforded him will wonder by what energetic operation he expanded them to such extent and ramified them to so much variety, restrained as he was by religious reverence from licentiousness of fiction.

Here is a full display of the united force of study and genius; of a great accumulation of materials, with judgment to digest and fancy to combine them: Milton was able to select from nature or from story, from ancient fable or from modern science, whatever could illustrate or adorn his thoughts. An accumulation of knowledge impregnated his mind, fermented by study and exalted by imagination.

* * *

But original deficience cannot be supplied. The want of human interest is always felt. *Paradise Lost* is one of the books which the reader admires and lays down, and forgets to take up again. None ever wished it longer than it is. Its perusal is a duty rather than a pleasure. We read Milton for instruction, retire harassed and overburdened, and look elsewhere for recreation; we desert our master, and seek for companions.

* * *

Dryden remarks that Milton has some flats among his elevations.[4] This is only to say that all the parts are not equal. In every work one part must be for the sake of others; a palace must have passages, a poem must have transitions. It is no more to be required that wit should always be blazing than that the sun should always stand at noon. In a great work there is a vicissitude[5] of luminous and opaque parts, as there is in the world a succession of day and night. Milton, when he has expatiated in the sky, may be allowed sometimes to revisit earth; for what other author ever soared so high or sustained his flight so long?

* * *

The highest praise of genius is original invention. Milton cannot be said to have contrived the structure of an epic poem, and therefore owes reverence to that vigor and amplitude of mind to which all generations must be indebted

3. Original or primary.
4. Preface to *Sylvae*.
5. Regular change.

for the art of poetical narration, for the texture of the fable, the variation of incidents, the interposition of dialogue, and all the stratagems that surprise and enchain attention. But of all the borrowers from Homer Milton is perhaps the least indebted. He was naturally a thinker for himself, confident of his own abilities and disdainful of help or hindrance; he did not refuse admission to the thoughts or images of his predecessors, but he did not seek them. From his contemporaries he neither courted nor received support; there is in his writings nothing by which the pride of other authors might be gratified or favor gained, no exchange of praise or solicitation of support. His great works were performed under discountenance and in blindness, but difficulties vanished at his touch; he was born for whatever is arduous; and his work is not the greatest of heroic poems, only because it is not the first.

1779

JAMES BOSWELL
1740–1795

The discovery of a vast number of James Boswell's personal papers (believed until 1925 to have been destroyed by his literary executors) has made it possible to know the author of *The Life of Samuel Johnson* as well as we can know anybody, dead or living. His published letters and journals have made modern readers aware of the serious and absurd, the charming and repellent sides of his character. At twenty-three, when he met Johnson, he had already trained himself to listen, to observe, and to remember until he found time to write it all down. Only rarely did he take notes while a conversation was in progress, since doing this might have inhibited the speakers. His unusual memory and disciplined art enabled him to re-create and vividly preserve the many "scenes" that distinguish his journals as they do the *Life*.

Boswell was the elder son of Alexander Boswell of Auchinleck (pronounced *Affléck*) in Ayreshire, a judge who bore the courtesy title of Lord Auchinleck. As a member of an ancient family and heir to its large estate, Boswell was in the technical sense of the term a gentleman, with entrée into the best circles of Edinburgh and London. By temperament he was unstable, emotionally and sexually skittish. After attending the universities of Edinburgh and Glasgow and studying law in Holland, he made the grand tour of Europe; in Switzerland he met and succeeded in captivating the two foremost French men of letters, Jean-Jacques Rousseau and Voltaire. He visited the beleaguered hero of Corsica, General Pasquale de Paoli, whose revolt against Genoa seemed to European liberals to embody all the civic and military virtues of Republican Rome. Upon returning to England, Boswell wrote *An Account of Corsica* (1768). It was promptly translated into Dutch, German, French, and Italian, and its young author found himself with a modest European reputation.

By 1769, Boswell was established in what was to prove a successful law practice in Edinburgh and had married his cousin, Margaret Montgomerie. But he kept his ties to London and Johnson. In 1773 he persuaded Johnson to join him in a tour of the Highlands and the Hebrides. Almost every aspect of the adventure should have made it impossible. Johnson, far from young and after years of sedentary city living, found himself astride a horse in wild country or in open boats in autumn weather. As a devout Anglican, he was an outspoken enemy of the Presbyterian church. As a lover of London, he was a stranger to the primitive life of the Highlands. Moreover, for many years he had half-jestingly, half-seriously, made Scots the butt of his wit. But such were Boswell's social tact and Johnson's vigor and curiosity that the tour was a great success. Johnson's *Journey to the Western Isles of Scotland* (1775) is a thoughtful account of the way that people live in the Hebrides (though some Scots were offended). Boswell's *Journal of a Tour to the Hebrides* (1785), a preliminary study for the *Life,* is a lively and entertaining diary that amused Johnson himself.

In 1788, four years after Johnson's death, Boswell abandoned his Scottish practice; moved to London; was admitted to the English bar (but never actually practiced); and, often depressed and drunken, began the *Life.* Fortunately he had the help and encouragement of the distinguished literary scholar Edmond Malone, without whose guidance he might never have finished his task.

Boswell had an overwhelming amount of material to deal with: his own journals, all of Johnson's letters that he could find, Johnson's voluminous writings, and every scrap of information that his friends would furnish—all of which had to be collected, verified, and somehow reduced to unity. The *Life* is a record not of Johnson alone but of literary England during the last half of the century. But Boswell wrote with his eye on the object, and that object was Samuel Johnson, toward whom such eminent persons as Sir Joshua Reynolds, Edmund Burke, Oliver Goldsmith, Lord Chesterfield—even the king himself—always face. Individual episodes are designed to reveal the great protagonist in a variety of aspects, and the world that Boswell created and populated is sustained by the vitality of his hero.

Boswell's gift is not only narrative but also dramatic. A gifted mimic, he often writes like a theatrical improviser, creating scenes with living people and playing simultaneously the roles of contriver of the dialogue, director of the plot, actor in the drama, and applauding audience—for Boswell kept an eye on his own performance. The quintessence of Boswell as both a social genius and a literary artist is to be found in his description of his visit to Voltaire: "I placed myself by him. I touched the keys in unison with his imagination. I wish you had heard the music."

Although the Johnson of popular legend is largely Boswell's creation, there was much in his life about which Boswell had no firsthand knowledge. At their first meeting, Johnson was fifty-four, a widower, already established as "Dictionary" Johnson and the author of the *Rambler,* and pensioned by the crown. Boswell knew nothing at firsthand of the long, hard years during which Johnson made his way painfully up from obscurity to fame. Hence the *Life* is the portrait of a sage. Its chief glory is conversation: the talk of a man who has experienced broadly, read widely, and observed and reflected on his observations; whose ideas are constantly brought to the test of experience; and whose experience is habitually transmuted into ideas. The book is as large as life and as human as its central character.

From The Life of Samuel Johnson, LL.D.

[PLAN OF THE *LIFE*]

* * * Had Dr. Johnson written his own life, in conformity with the opinion which he has given, that every man's life may be best written by himself;[1] had he employed in the preservation of his own history, that clearness of narration and elegance of language in which he has embalmed so many eminent persons, the world would probably have had the most perfect example of biography that was ever exhibited. But although he at different times, in a desultory manner, committed to writing many particulars of the progress of his mind and fortunes, he never had persevering diligence enough to form them into a regular composition. Of these memorials a few have been preserved; but the greater

1. *Idler* 84.

part was consigned by him to the flames, a few days before his death.

As I had the honor and happiness of enjoying his friendship for upwards of twenty years; as I had the scheme of writing his life constantly in view; as he was well apprised of this circumstance, and from time to time obligingly satisfied my inquiries, by communicating to me the incidents of his early years; as I acquired a facility in recollecting, and was very assiduous in recording, his conversation, of which the extraordinary vigor and vivacity constituted one of the first features of his character; and as I have spared no pains in obtaining materials concerning him, from every quarter where I could discover that they were to be found, and have been favored with the most liberal communications by his friends; I flatter myself that few biographers have entered upon such a work as this with more advantages; independent of literary abilities, in which I am not vain enough to compare myself with some great names who have gone before me in this kind of writing. * * *

Instead of melting down my materials into one mass, and constantly speaking in my own person, by which I might have appeared to have more merit in the execution of the work, I have resolved to adopt and enlarge upon the excellent plan of Mr. Mason, in his *Memoirs of Gray.*[2] Wherever narrative is necessary to explain, connect, and supply, I furnish it to the best of my abilities; but in the chronological series of Johnson's life, which I trace as distinctly as I can, year by year, I produce, wherever it is in my power, his own minutes, letters, or conversation, being convinced that this mode is more lively, and will make my readers better acquainted with him than even most of those were who actually knew him, but could know him only partially; whereas there is here an accumulation of intelligence from various points, by which his character is more fully understood and illustrated.

Indeed I cannot conceive a more perfect mode of writing any man's life than not only relating all the most important events of it in their order, but interweaving what he privately wrote, and said, and thought; by which mankind are enabled as it were to see him live, and to "live o'er each scene"[3] with him, as he actually advanced through the several stages of his life. Had his other friends been as diligent and ardent as I was, he might have been almost entirely preserved. As it is, I will venture to say that he will be seen in this work more completely than any man who has ever yet lived.

And he will be seen as he really was; for I profess to write, not his panegyric, which must be all praise, but his Life; which, great and good as he was, must not be supposed to be entirely perfect. To be as he was, is indeed subject of panegyric enough to any man in this state of being; but in every picture there should be shade as well as light, and when I delineate him without reserve, I do what he himself recommended, both by his precept and his example. * * *

I am fully aware of the objections which may be made to the minuteness on some occasions of my detail of Johnson's conversation, and how happily it is adapted for the petty exercise of ridicule, by men of superficial understanding and ludicrous fancy; but I remain firm and confident in my opinion, that minute particulars are frequently characteristic, and always amusing, when they relate to a distinguished man. I am therefore exceedingly unwilling that anything, however slight, which my illustrious friend thought it worth his while to express, with any degree of point, should perish. * * *

Of one thing I am certain, that considering how highly the small portion

2. William Mason, poet and dramatist, published his life of Thomas Gray in 1774.

3. Pope's Prologue to Addison's *Cato,* line 4.

which we have of the table-talk and other anecdotes of our celebrated writers is valued, and how earnestly it is regretted that we have not more, I am justified in preserving rather too many of Johnson's sayings, than too few; especially as from the diversity of dispositions it cannot be known with certainty beforehand, whether what may seem trifling to some, and perhaps to the collector himself, may not be most agreeable to many; and the greater number that an author can please in any degree, the more pleasure does there arise to a benevolent mind. * * *

[JOHNSON'S EARLY YEARS. MARRIAGE AND LONDON]

[*1709*] Samuel Johnson was born at Lichfield, in Staffordshire, on the 18th of September, N.S.,[4] 1709; and his initiation into the Christian Church was not delayed; for his baptism is recorded, in the register of St. Mary's parish in that city, to have been performed on the day of his birth. His father is there styled *Gentleman,* a circumstance of which an ignorant panegyrist has praised him for not being proud; when the truth is, that the appellation of Gentleman, though now lost in the indiscriminate assumption of *Esquire,* was commonly taken by those who could not boast of gentility. His father was Michael Johnson, a native of Derbyshire, of obscure extraction, who settled in Lichfield as a bookseller and stationer. His mother was Sarah Ford, descended of an ancient race of substantial yeomanry in Warwickshire. They were well advanced in years when they married, and never had more than two children, both sons; Samuel, their first-born, who lived to be the illustrious character whose various excellence I am to endeavor to record, and Nathanael, who died in his twenty-fifth year.

Mr. Michael Johnson was a man of a large and robust body, and of a strong and active mind; yet, as in the most solid rocks veins of unsound substance are often discovered, there was in him a mixture of that disease, the nature of which eludes the most minute inquiry, though the effects are well known to be a weariness of life, an unconcern about those things which agitate the greater part of mankind, and a general sensation of gloomy wretchedness. From him then his son inherited, with some other qualities, "a vile melancholy," which in his too strong expression of any disturbance of the mind, "made him mad all his life, at least not sober." Michael was, however, forced by the narrowness of his circumstances to be very diligent in business, not only in his shop, but by occasionally resorting to several towns in the neighborhood, some of which were at a considerable distance from Lichfield. At that time booksellers' shops in the provincial towns of England were very rare, so that there was not one even in Birmingham, in which town old Mr. Johnson used to open a shop every market day. He was a pretty good Latin scholar, and a citizen so creditable as to be made one of the magistrates of Lichfield; and, being a man of good sense, and skill in his trade, he acquired a reasonable share of wealth, of which however he afterwards lost the greatest part, by engaging unsuccessfully in a manufacture of parchment. He was a zealous highchurch man and royalist, and retained his attachment to the unfortunate house of Stuart, though he reconciled himself, by casuistical arguments of

4. New Style. In 1752, Great Britain adopted the Gregorian calendar, introduced in 1582 by Pope Gregory XIII, to correct the accumulated inaccuracies of Julius Caesar's calendar, which had been in use since 46 B.C.E. By 1752, the error amounted to eleven days. Dates before September 2, 1752, must, therefore, be corrected by adding eleven days or by using the Julian date, followed by "O.S." (Old Style).

expediency and necessity, to take the oaths imposed by the prevailing power. * * *

Johnson's mother was a woman of distinguished understanding. I asked his old schoolfellow, Mr. Hector,[5] surgeon of Birmingham, if she was not vain of her son. He said, "She had too much good sense to be vain, but she knew her son's value." Her piety was not inferior to her understanding; and to her must be ascribed those early impressions of religion upon the mind of her son, from which the world afterwards derived so much benefit. He told me that he remembered distinctly having had the first notice of Heaven, "a place to which good people went," and hell, "a place to which bad people went," communicated to him by her, when a little child in bed with her; and that it might be the better fixed in his memory, she sent him to repeat it to Thomas Jackson, their manservant; he not being in the way, this was not done; but there was no occasion for any artificial aid for its preservation. * * *

[*1728*] That a man in Mr. Michael Johnson's circumstances should think of sending his son to the expensive University of Oxford, at his own charge, seems very improbable. The subject was too delicate to question Johnson upon. But I have been assured by Dr. Taylor[6] that the scheme never would have taken place had not a gentleman of Shropshire, one of his schoolfellows, spontaneously undertaken to support him at Oxford, in the character of his companion; though, in fact, he never received any assistance whatever from that gentleman.

He, however, went to Oxford, and was entered a Commoner of Pembroke College on the 31st of October, 1728, being then in his nineteenth year.

The Reverend Dr. Adams,[7] who afterwards presided over Pembroke College with universal esteem, told me he was present, and gave me some account of what passed on the night of Johnson's arrival at Oxford. On that evening, his father, who had anxiously accompanied him, found means to have him introduced to Mr. Jorden, who was to be his tutor. * * *

His father seemed very full of the merits of his son, and told the company he was a good scholar, and a poet, and wrote Latin verses. His figure and manner appeared strange to them; but he behaved modestly and sat silent, till upon something which occurred in the course of conversation, he suddenly struck in and quoted Macrobius; and thus he gave the first impression of that more extensive reading in which he had indulged himself.

His tutor, Mr. Jorden, fellow of Pembroke, was not, it seems, a man of such abilities as we should conceive requisite for the instructor of Samuel Johnson, who gave me the following account of him. "He was a very worthy man, but a heavy man, and I did not profit much by his instructions. Indeed, I did not attend him much. The first day after I came to college I waited upon him, and then stayed away four. On the sixth, Mr. Jorden asked me why I had not attended. I answered I had been sliding in Christ Church meadow. And this I said with as much *nonchalance* as I am now talking to you. I had no notion that I was wrong or irreverent to my tutor." BOSWELL: "That, Sir, was great fortitude of mind." JOHNSON: "No, Sir; stark insensibility." * * *

[*1729*] The "morbid melancholy," which was lurking in his constitution, and to which we may ascribe those particularities and that aversion to regu-

5. Edmund Hector, a lifelong friend of Johnson.
6. A well-to-do clergyman who had been Johnson's schoolfellow in Lichfield.
7. The Reverend William Adams, D.D., elected master of Pembroke in 1775.

lar life, which, at a very early period, marked his character, gathered such strength in his twentieth year as to afflict him in a dreadful manner. While he was at Lichfield, in the college vacation of the year 1729, he felt himself overwhelmed with an horrible hypochondria,[8] with perpetual irritation, fretfulness, and impatience; and with a dejection, gloom, and despair, which made existence misery. From this dismal malady he never afterwards was perfectly relieved; and all his labors, and all his enjoyments, were but temporary interruptions of its baleful influence. He told Mr. Paradise[9] that he was sometimes so languid and inefficient that he could not distinguish the hour upon the town-clock. * * *

To Johnson, whose supreme enjoyment was the exercise of his reason, the disturbance or obscuration of that faculty was the evil most to be dreaded. Insanity, therefore, was the object of his most dismal apprehension; and he fancied himself seized by it, or approaching to it, at the very time when he was giving proofs of a more than ordinary soundness and vigor of judgment. That his own diseased imagination should have so far deceived him, is strange; but it is stranger still that some of his friends should have given credit to his groundless opinion, when they had such undoubted proofs that it was totally fallacious; though it is by no means surprising that those who wish to depreciate him should, since his death, have laid hold of this circumstance, and insisted upon it with very unfair aggravation. * * *

Dr. Adams told me that Johnson, while he was at Pembroke College, "was caressed and loved by all about him, was a gay and frolicsome fellow, and passed there the happiest part of his life." But this is a striking proof of the fallacy of appearances, and how little any of us know of the real internal state even of those whom we see most frequently; for the truth is, that he was then depressed by poverty, and irritated by disease. When I mentioned to him this account as given me by Dr. Adams, he said, "Ah, Sir, I was mad and violent. It was bitterness which they mistook for frolic. I was miserably poor, and I thought to fight my way by my literature and my wit; so I disregarded all power and all authority." * * *

[*1734*] In a man whom religious education has secured from licentious indulgences, the passion of love, when once it has seized him, is exceedingly strong; being unimpaired by dissipation,[1] and totally concentrated in one object. This was experienced by Johnson, when he became the fervent admirer of Mrs. Porter, after her first husband's death. Miss Porter told me that when he was first introduced to her mother, his appearance was very forbidding: he was then lean and lank, so that his immense structure of bones was hideously striking to the eye, and the scars of the scrofula were deeply visible. He also wore his hair,[2] which was straight and stiff, and separated behind: and he often had, seemingly, convulsive starts and odd gesticulations, which tended to excite at once surprise and ridicule. Mrs. Porter was so much engaged by his conversation that she overlooked all these external disadvantages, and said to her daughter, "This is the most sensible man that I ever saw in my life."

[*1735*] Though Mrs. Porter was double the age of Johnson, and her person and manner, as described to me by the late Mr. Garrick,[3] were by no means pleasing to others, she must have had a superiority of understanding and tal-

8. Depression.
9. John Paradise, a member of the Essex Head Club, which Johnson founded in 1783.
1. Scattered attention.
2. I.e., he wore no wig.
3. David Garrick (1717–1779), the most famous actor of his day. In 1736 he was one of Johnson's three pupils in an unsuccessful school at Edial.

ents, as she certainly inspired him with a more than ordinary passion; and she having signified her willingness to accept of his hand, he went to Lichfield to ask his mother's consent to the marriage, which he could not but be conscious was a very imprudent scheme, both on account of their disparity of years and her want of fortune. But Mrs. Johnson knew too well the ardor of her son's temper, and was too tender a parent to oppose his inclinations.

I know not for what reason the marriage ceremony was not performed at Birmingham; but a resolution was taken that it should be at Derby, for which place the bride and bridegroom set out on horseback, I suppose in very good humor. But though Mr. Topham Beauclerk[4] used archly to mention Johnson's having told him, with much gravity, "Sir, it was a love marriage on both sides," I have had from my illustrious friend the following curious account of their journey to church upon the nuptial morn:

9th July: "Sir, she had read the old romances, and had got into her head the fantastical notion that a woman of spirit should use her lover like a dog. So, Sir, at first she told me that I rode too fast, and she could not keep up with me; and, when I rode a little slower, she passed me, and complained that I lagged behind. I was not to be made the slave of caprice; and I resolved to begin as I meant to end. I therefore pushed on briskly, till I was fairly out of her sight. The road lay between two hedges, so I was sure she could not miss it; and I contrived that she should soon come up with me. When she did, I observed her to be in tears." * * *

[*1737*] Johnson now thought of trying his fortune in London, the great field of genius and exertion, where talents of every kind have the fullest scope and the highest encouragement. It is a memorable circumstance that his pupil David Garrick went thither at the same time, with intention to complete his education, and follow the profession of the law, from which he was soon diverted by his decided preference for the stage.[5] * * *

[*1744*] * * * He produced one work this year, fully sufficient to maintain the high reputation which he had acquired. This was *The Life of Richard Savage*;[6] a man of whom it is difficult to speak impartially without wondering that he was for some time the intimate companion of Johnson; for his character was marked by profligacy, insolence, and ingratitude: yet, as he undoubtedly had a warm and vigorous, though unregulated mind, had seen life in all its varieties, and been much in the company of the statesmen and wits of his time, he could communicate to Johnson an abundant supply of such materials as his philosophical curiosity most eagerly desired; and as Savage's misfortunes and misconduct had reduced him to the lowest state of wretchedness as a writer for bread, his visits to St. John's Gate[7] naturally brought Johnson and him together.

4. Pronounced *bo-clare.* A descendant of Charles II and the actress Nell Gwynn, he was brilliant and dissolute.

5. Johnson had hoped to complete his tragedy *Irene* and to get it produced, but this was not accomplished until Garrick staged it in 1749. Meanwhile Johnson struggled against poverty, at first as a writer and translator for Edward Cave's *Gentleman's Magazine.* He gradually won recognition but was never financially secure until he was pensioned in 1762. Garrick succeeded in the theater much more rapidly than did Johnson in literature.

6. The poet Richard Savage courted and gained notoriety by claiming to be the illegitimate son of Earl Rivers and the Countess of Macclesfield, whose husband had divorced her because of her unfaithfulness with Rivers. Savage publicized his claim and persecuted his alleged mother. Johnson and many others believed Savage's story and resented what they considered the lady's inhumanity. Savage was a gifted man, but he lived in poverty as a hack writer, although he was long assisted by Pope and others. He died in a debtor's prison in Bristol in 1743.

7. Where Cave published the *Gentleman's Magazine.*

It is melancholy to reflect that Johnson and Savage were sometimes in such extreme indigence that they could not pay for a lodging; so that they have wandered together whole nights in the streets. Yet in these almost incredible scenes of distress, we may suppose that Savage mentioned many of the anecdotes with which Johnson afterwards enriched the life of his unhappy companion, and those of other poets.

He told Sir Joshua Reynolds that one night in particular, when Savage and he walked round St. James's Square for want of a lodging, they were not at all depressed by their situation; but in high spirits and brimful of patriotism, traversed the square for several hours, inveighed against the minister, and "resolved they would *stand by their country*." * * *

[*1752*] That there should be a suspension of his literary labors during a part of the year 1752[8] will not seem strange when it is considered that soon after closing his *Rambler*, he suffered a loss which, there can be no doubt, affected him with the deepest distress. For on the 17th of March, O.S., his wife died. * * *

The following very solemn and affecting prayer was found, after Dr. Johnson's decease, by his servant, Mr. Francis Barber, who delivered it to my worthy friend the Reverend Mr. Strahan, Vicar of Islington, who at my earnest request has obligingly favored me with a copy of it, which he and I compared with the original:

"April 26, 1752, being after 12 at night of the 25th.

"O Lord! Governor of heaven and earth, in whose hands are embodied and departed spirits, if thou hast ordained the souls of the dead to minister to the living, and appointed my departed wife to have care of me, grant that I may enjoy the good effects of her attention and ministration, whether exercised by appearance, impulses, dreams or in any other manner agreeable to thy government. Forgive my presumption, enlighten my ignorance, and however meaner agents are employed, grant me the blessed influences of thy holy Spirit, through Jesus Christ our Lord. Amen." * * *

One night when Beauclerk and Langton[9] had supped at a tavern in London, and sat till about three in the morning, it came into their heads to go and knock up Johnson, and see if they could prevail on him to join them in a ramble. They rapped violently at the door of his chambers in the Temple,[1] till at last he appeared in his shirt, with his little black wig on the top of his head, instead of a nightcap, and a poker in his hand, imagining, probably, that some ruffians were coming to attack him. When he discovered who they were, and was told their errand, he smiled, and with great good humor agreed to their proposal: "What, is it you, you dogs! I'll have a frisk with you." He was soon dressed, and they sallied forth together into Covent Garden, where the greengrocers and fruiterers were beginning to arrange their hampers, just come in from the country. Johnson made some attempts to help them; but the honest gardeners stared so at his figure and manner and odd interference, that he

8. Johnson's important works written before the publication of the *Dictionary* are the poems "London" (1738) and "The Vanity of Human Wishes" (1749), the *Life of Savage* (1744), and the essays that made up his periodical the *Rambler* (1750–52).

9. Bennet Langton. As a boy he so much admired the *Rambler* that he sought Johnson's acquaintance. They became lifelong friends.

1. Because Johnson lived in Inner Temple Lane between 1760 and 1765, the "frisk" could not have taken place in the year of his wife's death, where Boswell, for his own convenience, placed it.

soon saw his services were not relished. They then repaired to one of the neighboring taverns, and made a bowl of that liquor called *Bishop,*[2] which Johnson had always liked; while in joyous contempt of sleep, from which he had been roused, he repeated the festive lines,

Short, O short then be thy reign,
And give us to the world again![3]

They did not stay long, but walked down to the Thames, took a boat, and rowed to Billingsgate. Beauclerk and Johnson were so well pleased with their amusement that they resolved to persevere in dissipation for the rest of the day: but Langton deserted them, being engaged to breakfast with some young ladies. Johnson scolded him for "leaving his social friends, to go and sit with a set of wretched *un-idea'd* girls." Garrick being told of this ramble, said to him smartly, "I heard of your frolic t' other night. You'll be in the *Chronicle.*" Upon which Johnson afterwards observed, "*He* durst not do such a thing. His *wife* would not *let* him!" * * *

[THE LETTER TO CHESTERFIELD]

[*1754*] Lord Chesterfield,[4] to whom Johnson had paid the high compliment of addressing to his Lordship the *Plan* of his *Dictionary,* had behaved to him in such a manner as to excite his contempt and indignation. The world has been for many years amused with a story confidently told, and as confidently repeated with additional circumstances, that a sudden disgust was taken by Johnson upon occasion of his having been one day kept long in waiting in his Lordship's antechamber, for which the reason assigned was that he had company with him; and that at last, when the door opened, out walked Colley Cibber;[5] and that Johnson was so violently provoked when he found for whom he had been so long excluded, that he went away in a passion, and never would return. I remember having mentioned this story to George Lord Lyttelton, who told me he was very intimate with Lord Chesterfield; and holding it as a well-known truth, defended Lord Chesterfield, by saying, that Cibber, who had been introduced familiarly by the back stairs, had probably not been there above ten minutes. It may seem strange even to entertain a doubt concerning a story so long and so widely current, and thus implicitly adopted, if not sanctioned, by the authority which I have mentioned; but Johnson himself assured me that there was not the least foundation for it. He told me that there never was any particular incident which produced a quarrel between Lord Chesterfield and him; but that his Lordship's continued neglect was the reason why he resolved to have no connection with him. When the *Dictionary* was upon the eve of publication, Lord Chesterfield, who, it is said, had flattered himself with expectations that Johnson would dedicate the work to him, attempted, in a courtly manner, to soothe, and insinuate himself with the sage, conscious, as it should seem, of the cold indifference with which he had treated its learned author; and further attempted to conciliate him, by writing two papers

2. A drink made of wine, sugar, and either lemon or orange.
3. Misquoted from Lansdowne's "Drinking Song to Sleep."
4. Philip Dormer Stanhope, Earl of Chesterfield (1694–1773), statesman, wit, man of fashion. His *Letters,* written for the guidance of his natural son, are famous for their worldly good sense and for their expression of the ideal of an 18th-century gentleman.
5. Cibber (1671–1757), playwright, comic actor, and (after 1730) poet laureate. A fine actor but a very bad poet, Cibber was a constant object of ridicule by the wits of the town. Pope made him king of the Dunces in the *Dunciad* of 1743.

in *The World,* in recommendation of the work; and it must be confessed that they contain some studied compliments, so finely turned, that if there had been no previous offense, it is probable that Johnson would have been highly delighted. Praise, in general, was pleasing to him; but by praise from a man of rank and elegant accomplishments, he was peculiarly gratified. * * *

This courtly device failed of its effect. Johnson, who thought that "all was false and hollow,"[6] despised the honeyed words, and was even indignant that Lord Chesterfield should, for a moment, imagine that he could be dupe of such an artifice. His expression to me concerning Lord Chesterfield, upon this occasion, was, "Sir, after making great professions, he had, for many years, taken no notice of me; but when my *Dictionary* was coming out, he fell a-scribbling in *The World* about it. Upon which, I wrote him a letter expressed in civil terms, but such as might show him that I did not mind what he said or wrote, and that I had done with him."

This is that celebrated letter of which so much has been said, and about which curiosity has been so long excited, without being gratified. I for many years solicited Johnson to favor me with a copy of it, that so excellent a composition might not be lost to posterity. He delayed from time to time to give it me; till at last in 1781, when we were on a visit at Mr. Dilly's,[7] at Southill in Bedfordshire, he was pleased to dictate it to me from memory. He afterwards found among his papers a copy of it, which he had dictated to Mr. Baretti,[8] with its title and corrections, in his own handwriting. This he gave to Mr. Langton; adding that if it were to come into print, he wished it to be from that copy. By Mr. Langton's kindness, I am enabled to enrich my work with a perfect transcript of what the world has so eagerly desired to see.

TO THE RIGHT HONORABLE THE EARL OF CHESTERFIELD

February 7, 1755

MY LORD,

I have been lately informed, by the proprietor of *The World,* that two papers, in which my Dictionary is recommended to the public, were written by your Lordship. To be so distinguished, is an honor, which, being very little accustomed to favors from the great, I know not well how to receive, or in what terms to acknowledge.

When, upon some slight encouragement, I first visited your Lordship, I was overpowered, like the rest of mankind, by the enchantment of your address; and could not forbear to wish that I might boast myself *Le vainqueur du vainqueur de la terre*[9]—that I might obtain that regard for which I saw the world contending; but I found my attendance so little encouraged that neither pride nor modesty would suffer me to continue it. When I had once addressed your Lordship in public, I had exhausted all the art of pleasing which a retired and uncourtly scholar can possess. I had done all that I could; and no man is well pleased to have his all neglected, be it ever so little.

Seven years, my Lord, have now passed since I waited in your outward

6. *Paradise Lost* 2.112.
7. Southill was the country home of Charles and Edward Dilly, publishers. The firm published all of Boswell's serious works and shared in the publication of Johnson's *Lives of the Poets* (1779–81).
8. Giuseppe Baretti, an Italian writer and lexicographer whom Johnson introduced into his circle.
9. The conqueror of the conqueror of the earth (French). From the first line of Scudéry's epic *Alaric* (1654).

rooms, or was repulsed from your door; during which time I have been pushing on my work through difficulties of which it is useless to complain, and have brought it, at last, to the verge of publication, without one act of assistance, one word of encouragement, or one smile of favor. Such treatment I did not expect, for I never had a patron before.

The shepherd in Virgil grew at last acquainted with Love, and found him a native of the rocks.[1]

Is not a patron, my Lord, one who looks with unconcern on a man struggling for life in the water, and, when he has reached ground, encumbers him with help? The notice which you have been pleased to take of my labors, had it been early, had been kind; but it has been delayed till I am indifferent, and cannot enjoy it; till I am solitary, and cannot impart it; till I am known, and do not want it. I hope it is no very cynical asperity not to confess obligations where no benefit has been received, or to be unwilling that the public should consider me as owing that to a patron which Providence has enabled me to do for myself.

Having carried on my work thus far with so little obligation to any favorer of learning, I shall not be disappointed though I should conclude it, if less be possible, with less; for I have been long wakened from that dream of hope in which I once boasted myself with so much exultation, my Lord, your Lordship's most humble, most obedient servant,

SAM. JOHNSON.

"While this was the talk of the town," says Dr. Adams, in a letter to me, "I happened to visit Dr. Warburton,[2] who finding that I was acquainted with Johnson, desired me earnestly to carry his compliments to him, and to tell him that he honored him for his manly behavior in rejecting these condescensions of Lord Chesterfield, and for resenting the treatment he had received from him, with a proper spirit. Johnson was visibly pleased with this compliment, for he had always a high opinion of Warburton. Indeed, the force of mind which appeared in this letter was congenial with that which Warburton himself amply possessed."

There is a curious minute circumstance which struck me, in comparing the various editions of Johnson's imitations of Juvenal. In the tenth satire, one of the couplets upon the vanity of wishes even for literary distinction stood thus:

Yet think what ills the scholar's life assail,
Toil, envy, want, the *garret,* and the jail.

But after experiencing the uneasiness which Lord Chesterfield's fallacious patronage made him feel, he dismissed the word *garret* from the sad group, and in all the subsequent editions the line stands

Toil, envy, want, the *patron,* and the jail.

[*1762*] The accession of George the Third to the throne of these kingdoms[3] opened a new and brighter prospect to men of literary merit, who had been honored with no mark of royal favor in the preceding reign. His present Majesty's education in this country, as well as his taste and beneficence, prompted

1. *Eclogues* 8.44.
2. William Warburton, bishop of Gloucester, friend and literary executor of Pope, editor of Pope and Shakespeare, theological controversialist.
3. In 1760.

him to be the patron of science and the arts; and early this year Johnson, having been represented to him as a very learned and good man, without any certain provision, his Majesty was pleased to grant him a pension of three hundred pounds a year. The Earl of Bute,[4] who was then Prime Minister, had the honor to announce this instance of his Sovereign's bounty, concerning which many and various stories, all equally erroneous, have been propagated: maliciously representing it as a political bribe to Johnson, to desert his avowed principles, and become the tool of a government which he held to be founded in usurpation. I have taken care to have it in my power to refute them from the most authentic information. Lord Bute told me that Mr. Wedderburne, now Lord Loughborough, was the person who first mentioned this subject to him. Lord Loughborough told me that the pension was granted to Johnson solely as the reward of his literary merit, without any stipulation whatever, or even tacit understanding that he should write for administration. His Lordship added that he was confident the political tracts which Johnson afterwards did write, as they were entirely consonant with his own opinions, would have been written by him though no pension had been granted to him.[5] * * *

[A MEMORABLE YEAR: BOSWELL MEETS JOHNSON]

[*1763*] This is to me a memorable year; for in it I had the happiness to obtain the acquaintance of that extraordinary man whose memoirs I am now writing; an acquaintance which I shall ever esteem as one of the most fortunate circumstances in my life. * * *

Mr. Thomas Davies the actor, who then kept a bookseller's shop in Russel Street, Covent Garden, told me that Johnson was very much his friend, and came frequently to his house, where he more than once invited me to meet him; but by some unlucky accident or other he was prevented from coming to us. * * *

At last, on Monday the 16th of May, when I was sitting in Mr. Davies's back parlor, after having drunk tea with him and Mrs. Davies, Johnson unexpectedly came into the shop; and Mr. Davies having perceived him through the glass door in the room in which we were sitting, advancing towards us—he announced his awful approach to me, somewhat in the manner of an actor in the part of Horatio, when he addresses Hamlet on the appearance of his father's ghost, "Look, my Lord, it comes." I found that I had a very perfect idea of Johnson's figure, from the portrait of him painted by Sir Joshua Reynolds soon after he had published his *Dictionary,* in the attitude of sitting in his easy chair in deep meditation, which was the first picture his friend did for him, which Sir Joshua very kindly presented to me, and from which an engraving has been made for this work. Mr. Davies mentioned my name, and respectfully introduced me to him. I was much agitated; and recollecting his prejudice against the Scotch, of which I had heard much, I said to Davies, "Don't tell where I come from."—"From Scotland," cried Davies roguishly. "Mr. Johnson," said I, "I do indeed come from Scotland, but I cannot help it." I am willing to flatter myself that I meant this as light pleasantry to soothe and conciliate him, and not as an humiliating abasement at the expense of my

4. An intimate friend of George III's mother, he early gained an ascendancy over the young prince and was largely responsible for the king's autocratic views. He was hated in England both as a favorite and as a Scot.

5. Johnson's few political pamphlets in the 1770s invariably supported the policies of the crown. The best known is his answer to the American colonies, "Taxation No Tyranny" (1775). His dislike of the Americans was in large part due to the fact they owned slaves.

country. But however that might be, this speech was somewhat unlucky; for with that quickness of wit for which he was so remarkable, he seized the expression "come from Scotland," which I used in the sense of being of that country; and, as if I had said that I had come away from it, or left it, retorted, "That, Sir, I find, is what a very great many of your countrymen cannot help." This stroke stunned me a good deal; and when we had sat down, I felt myself not a little embarrassed, and apprehensive of what might come next. He then addressed himself to Davies: "What do you think of Garrick? He has refused me an order for the play for Miss Williams,[6] because he knows the house will be full, and that an order would be worth three shillings." Eager to take any opening to get into conversation with him, I ventured to say, "O Sir, I cannot think Mr. Garrick would grudge such a trifle to you." "Sir," said he, with a stern look, "I have known David Garrick longer than you have done: and I know no right you have to talk to me on the subject." Perhaps I deserved this check; for it was rather presumptuous in me, an entire stranger, to express any doubt of the justice of his animadversion upon his old acquaintance and pupil. I now felt myself much mortified, and began to think that the hope which I had long indulged of obtaining his acquaintance was blasted. And, in truth, had not my ardor been uncommonly strong, and my resolution uncommonly persevering, so rough a reception might have deterred me forever from making any further attempts. Fortunately, however, I remained upon the field not wholly discomfited. * * *

I was highly pleased with the extraordinary vigor of his conversation, and regretted that I was drawn away from it by an engagement at another place. I had, for a part of the evening, been left alone with him, and had ventured to make an observation now and then, which he received very civilly; so that I was satisfied that though there was a roughness in his manner, there was no ill nature in his disposition. Davies followed me to the door, and when I complained to him a little of the hard blows which the great man had given me, he kindly took upon him to console me by saying, "Don't be uneasy. I can see he likes you very well."

A few days afterwards I called on Davies, and asked him if he thought I might take the liberty of waiting on Mr. Johnson at his chambers in the Temple. He said I certainly might, and that Mr. Johnson would take it as a compliment. So upon Tuesday the 24th of May, after having been enlivened by the witty sallies of Messieurs Thornton, Wilkes, Churchill, and Lloyd,[7] with whom I had passed the morning, I boldly repaired to Johnson. His chambers were on the first floor of No. 1, Inner Temple Lane, and I entered them with an impression given me by the Reverend Dr. Blair,[8] of Edinburgh, who had been introduced to him not long before, and described his having "found the giant in his den"; an expression, which, when I came to be pretty well acquainted with Johnson, I repeated to him, and he was diverted at this picturesque account of himself. Dr. Blair had been presented to him by Dr. James Fordyce.[9] At this time the controversy concerning the pieces published by Mr. James Macpherson, as translations of *Ossian*, was at its height.[1]

6. Mrs. Anna Williams (1706–1783), a blind poet and friend of Mrs. Johnson. She continued to live in Johnson's house after his wife's death and habitually sat up to make tea for him whenever he came home.

7. Robert Lloyd, poet and essayist. Bonnell Thornton, journalist. Charles Churchill, satirist. Wilkes, politician and agitator. The four were bound together by a common love of wit and dissipation. Boswell enjoyed their company in 1763.

8. The Reverend Hugh Blair (1718–1800), Scottish divine and professor of rhetoric and *belles lettres* at the University of Edinburgh.

9. A Scottish preacher.

1. Macpherson had imposed on most of his contemporaries, Scottish and English, by convincing

Johnson had all along denied their authenticity; and, what was still more provoking to their admirers, maintained that they had no merit. The subject having been introduced by Dr. Fordyce, Dr. Blair, relying on the internal evidence of their antiquity, asked Dr. Johnson whether he thought any man of a modern age could have written such poems? Johnson replied, "Yes, Sir, many men, many women, and many children." Johnson, at this time, did not know that Dr. Blair had just published a dissertation, not only defending their authenticity, but seriously ranking them with the poems of Homer and Virgil; and when he was afterwards informed of this circumstance, he expressed some displeasure at Dr. Fordyce's having suggested the topic, and said, "I am not sorry that they got thus much for their pains. Sir, it was like leading one to talk of a book when the author is concealed behind the door."

He received me very courteously; but, it must be confessed that his apartment, and furniture, and morning dress, were sufficiently uncouth. His brown suit of clothes looked very rusty; he had on a little old shriveled unpowdered wig, which was too small for his head; his shirt neck and knees of his breeches were loose; his black worsted stockings ill drawn up; and he had a pair of unbuckled shoes by way of slippers. But all these slovenly particularities were forgotten the moment that he began to talk. Some gentlemen, whom I do not recollect, were sitting with him; and when they went away, I also rose; but he said to me, "Nay, don't go." "Sir," said I, "I am afraid that I intrude upon you. It is benevolent to allow me to sit and hear you." He seemed pleased with this compliment, which I sincerely paid him, and answered, "Sir, I am obliged to any man who visits me." I have preserved the following short minute of what passed this day:

"Madness frequently discovers itself merely by unnecessary deviation from the usual modes of the world. My poor friend Smart showed the disturbance of his mind by falling upon his knees, and saying his prayers in the street, or in any other unusual place. Now although, rationally speaking, it is greater madness not to pray at all than to pray as Smart did, I am afraid there are so many who do not pray, that their understanding is not called in question."

Concerning this unfortunate poet, Christopher Smart, who was confined in a madhouse, he had, at another time, the following conversation with Dr. Burney:[2] BURNEY. "How does poor Smart do, Sir; is he likely to recover?" JOHNSON. "It seems as if his mind had ceased to struggle with the disease; for he grows fat upon it." BURNEY. "Perhaps, Sir, that may be from want of exercise." JOHNSON. "No, Sir; he has partly as much exercise as he used to have, for he digs in the garden. Indeed, before his confinement, he used for exercise to walk to the ale house; but he was *carried* back again. I did not think he ought to be shut up. His infirmities were not noxious to society. He insisted on people praying with him; and I'd as lief pray with Kit Smart as anyone else. Another charge was that he did not love clean linen; and I have no passion for it."—Johnson continued. "Mankind have a great aversion to intellectual labor; but even supposing knowledge to be easily attainable, more people would be content to be ignorant than would take even a little trouble to acquire it."

them of the genuineness of prose poems that he had concocted but that he claimed to have translated from the original Gaelic of Ossian, a blind epic poet of the 3rd century. The vogue of the poems both in Europe and in America was enormous.

2. Dr. Charles Burney (1726–1814), historian of music and father of the novelist and diarist Frances Burney, whom Johnson befriended in his old age.

Talking of Garrick, he said, "He is the first man in the world for sprightly conversation."

When I rose a second time he again pressed me to stay, which I did. * * *

[FEAR OF DEATH]

[*1769*] When we were alone, I introduced the subject of death, and endeavored to maintain that the fear of it might be got over. I told him that David Hume said to me, he was no more uneasy to think he should *not be* after this life, than that he *had not been* before he began to exist. JOHNSON. "Sir, if he really thinks so, his perceptions are disturbed; he is mad: if he does not think so, he lies. He may tell you, he holds his finger in the flame of a candle, without feeling pain; would you believe him? When he dies, he at least gives up all he has." BOSWELL. "Foote,[3] Sir, told me, that when he was very ill he was not afraid to die." JOHNSON. "It is not true, Sir. Hold a pistol to Foote's breast, or to Hume's breast, and threaten to kill them, and you'll see how they behave." BOSWELL. "But may we not fortify our minds for the approach of death?" Here I am sensible I was in the wrong, to bring before his view what he ever looked upon with horror; for although when in a celestial frame, in his *Vanity of Human Wishes,* he has supposed death to be "kind Nature's signal for retreat," from this stage of being to "a happier seat," his thoughts upon this awful change were in general full of dismal apprehensions. His mind resembled the vast amphitheater, the Colosseum at Rome. In the center stood his judgment, which, like a mighty gladiator, combated those apprehensions that, like the wild beasts of the arena, were all around in cells, ready to be let out upon him. After a conflict, he drove them back into their dens; but not killing them, they were still assailing him. To my question, whether we might not fortify our minds for the approach of death, he answered, in a passion, "No, Sir, let it alone. It matters not how a man dies, but how he lives. The act of dying is not of importance, it lasts so short a time." He added (with an earnest look), "A man knows it must be so, and submits. It will do him no good to whine."

I attempted to continue the conversation. He was so provoked that he said, "Give us no more of this"; and was thrown into such a state of agitation that he expressed himself in a way that alarmed and distressed me; showed an impatience that I should leave him, and when I was going away, called to me sternly, "Don't let us meet tomorrow." * * *

[JOHNSON FACES DEATH]

As Johnson had now very faint hopes of recovery, and as Mrs. Thrale was no longer devoted to him, it might have been supposed that he would naturally have chosen to remain in the comfortable house of his beloved wife's daughter,[4] and end his life where he began it. But there was in him an animated and lofty spirit, and however complicated diseases might depress ordinary mortals, all who saw him, beheld and acknowledged the *invictum animum Catonis.*[5] Such was his intellectual ardor even at this time that he said to one friend, "Sir, I look upon every day to be lost, in which I do not make a new acquaintance"; and to another, when talking of his illness, "I will be con-

3. Samuel Foote, actor and dramatist, famous for his wit and his skill in mimicry.

4. Lucy Porter.

5. The unconquered soul of Cato (Latin). An adaptation of a phrase in Horace's *Odes* 2.1.24.

quered; I will not capitulate." And such was his love of London, so high a relish had he of its magnificent extent, and variety of intellectual entertainment, that he languished when absent from it, his mind having become quite luxurious from the long habit of enjoying the metropolis; and, therefore, although at Lichfield, surrounded with friends, who loved and revered him, and for whom he had a very sincere affection, he still found that such conversation as London affords, could be found nowhere else. These feelings, joined, probably, to some flattering hopes of aid from the eminent physicians and surgeons in London, who kindly and generously attended him without accepting fees, made him resolve to return to the capital. * * * Death had always been to him an object of terror; so that, though by no means happy, he still clung to life with an eagerness at which many have wondered. At any time when he was ill, he was very much pleased to be told that he looked better. An ingenious member of the Eumelian Club[6] informs me that upon one occasion when he said to him that he saw health returning to his cheek, Johnson seized him by the hand and exclaimed, "Sir, you are one of the kindest friends I ever had." * * *

Dr. Heberden, Dr. Brocklesby, Dr. Warren, and Dr. Butter, physicians, generously attended him, without accepting any fees, as did Mr. Cruikshank, surgeon; and all that could be done from professional skill and ability was tried, to prolong a life so truly valuable. He himself, indeed, having, on account of his very bad constitution, been perpetually applying himself to medical inquiries, united his own efforts with those of the gentlemen who attended him; and imagining that the dropsical collection of water which oppressed him might be drawn off by making incisions in his body, he, with his usual resolute defiance of pain, cut deep, when he thought that his surgeon had done it too tenderly.

About eight or ten days before his death, when Dr. Brocklesby paid him his morning visit, he seemed very low and desponding, and said, "I have been as a dying man all night." He then emphatically broke out in the words of Shakespeare:

> "Canst thou not minister to a mind diseased;
> Pluck from the memory a rooted sorrow,
> Raze out the written troubles of the brain,
> And with some sweet oblivious antidote
> Cleanse the stuffed bosom of that perilous stuff
> Which weighs upon the heart?"

To which Dr. Brocklesby readily answered, from the same great poet:

> "—Therein the patient
> Must minister to himself."[7]

Johnson expressed himself much satisfied with the application. * * *

Amidst the melancholy clouds which hung over the dying Johnson, his characteristical manner showed itself on different occasions.

When Dr. Warren, in the usual style, hoped that he was better; his answer was, "No, Sir; you cannot conceive with what acceleration I advance towards death."

6. A club to which Boswell and Reynolds belonged.

7. *Macbeth* 5.3.40–46.

A man whom he had never seen before was employed one night to sit up with him. Being asked next morning how he liked his attendant, his answer was, "Not at all, Sir: the fellow's an idiot; he is as awkward as a turnspit[8] when first put into the wheel, and as sleepy as a dormouse."

Mr. Windham[9] having placed a pillow conveniently to support him, he thanked him for his kindness, and said, "That will do—all that a pillow can do." * * *

Johnson, with that native fortitude, which, amidst all his bodily distress and mental sufferings, never forsook him, asked Dr. Brocklesby, as a man in whom he had confidence, to tell him plainly whether he could recover. "Give me," said he, "a direct answer." The Doctor having first asked him if he could bear the whole truth, which way soever it might lead, and being answered that he could, declared that, in his opinion, he could not recover without a miracle. "Then," said Johnson, "I will take no more physic, not even my opiates; for I have prayed that I may render up my soul to God unclouded." In this resolution he persevered, and, at the same time, used only the weakest kinds of sustenance. Being pressed by Mr. Windham to take somewhat more generous nourishment, lest too low a diet should have the very effect which he dreaded, by debilitating his mind, he said, "I will take anything but inebriating sustenance."

The Reverend Mr. Strahan,[1] who was the son of his friend, and had been always one of his great favorites, had, during his last illness, the satisfaction of contributing to soothe and comfort him. That gentleman's house, at Islington, of which he is Vicar, afforded Johnson, occasionally and easily, an agreeable change of place and fresh air; and he attended also upon him in town in the discharge of the sacred offices of his profession.

Mr. Strahan has given me the agreeable assurance that, after being in much agitation, Johnson became quite composed, and continued so till his death.

Dr. Brocklesby, who will not be suspected of fanaticism, obliged me with the following account:

> "For some time before his death, all his fears were calmed and absorbed by the prevalence of his faith, and his trust in the merits and *propitiation* of Jesus Christ." * * *

Johnson having thus in his mind the true Christian scheme, at once rational and consolatory, uniting justice and mercy in the Divinity, with the improvement of human nature, previous to his receiving the Holy Sacrament in his apartment, composed and fervently uttered this prayer:

> "Almighty and most merciful Father, I am now as to human eyes, it seems, about to commemorate, for the last time, the death of thy Son Jesus Christ, our Saviour and Redeemer. Grant, O Lord, that my whole hope and confidence may be in his merits, and thy mercy; enforce and accept my imperfect repentance; make this commemoration available to the confirmation of my faith, the establishment of my hope, and the enlargement of my charity; and make the death of thy Son Jesus Christ effectual to my redemption. Have mercy upon me, and pardon the multitude of my offenses. Bless my friends; have mercy upon all men. Support

8. "A dog kept to turn the roasting-spit by running within a tread-wheel connected to it" (*OED*).
9. William Windham, one of Johnson's younger friends, later a member of Parliament.
1. The Reverend George Strahan (pronounced *Strawn*), who later published Johnson's *Prayers and Meditations*.

> me, by thy Holy Spirit, in the days of weakness, and at the hour of death; and receive me, at my death, to everlasting happiness, for the sake of Jesus Christ. Amen."

Having * * * made his will on the 8th and 9th of December, and settled all his worldly affairs, he languished till Monday, the 13th of that month, when he expired, about seven o'clock in the evening, with so little apparent pain that his attendants hardly perceived when his dissolution took place. * * *

1791

THOMAS GRAY
1716–1771

The man who wrote the English poem most loved by those whom Samuel Johnson called "the common reader" was a scholarly recluse who lived the quiet life of a university professor in the stagnant atmosphere of mid-eighteenth-century Cambridge. Born in London, Thomas Gray was the only one of twelve children to survive, and his family life was desperately unhappy. At eight he left home for Eton, where he made intimate friends: Richard West, a fellow poet; Thomas Ashton; and Horace Walpole, the son of the prime minister. After four years at Cambridge, Gray left without a degree to take the grand tour of France and Italy as Walpole's guest. The death of West in 1742 desolated Gray, and memories of West haunt much of his verse. He spent the rest of his life in Cambridge, pursuing his studies and writing wonderful letters as well as a handful of poems. Two high-flown Pindaric odes, "The Progress of Poesy" (1754) and "The Bard" (1757), display his learning and his love of nature and the sublime. (For more poems by Gray, go to Norton Literature Online.)

Most of Gray's poems take part in a contemporary reaction against the wit and satiric elegance of Pope's couplets; poets sought a new style, at once intimate and prophetic. Gray was not easily satisfied; he constantly revised his poems and published very little. Because he held that "the language of the age is never the language of poetry," he often uses archaic words and a word order borrowed from Latin, where a verb can precede its subject (as in line 35 of the "Elegy Written in a Country Churchyard": "Awaits alike the inevitable hour"). But the "Elegy" stands alone in his work. It balances Latinate phrases with living English speech, and the learning of a scholar with a common humanity that everyone can share. Johnson, who did not usually like Gray's poetry, acknowledged that the "Elegy" would live on:

> The Churchyard abounds with images that find a mirror in every mind, and with sentiments to which every bosom returns an echo. The four stanzas beginning "Yet even these bones" are to me original: I have never seen the notions in any other place; yet he that reads them here, persuades himself that he has always felt them. Had Gray written often thus, it had been vain to blame, and useless to praise him.

Ode on the Death of a Favorite Cat[1]

Drowned in a Tub of Goldfishes

'Twas on a lofty vase's side,
Where China's gayest art had dyed
  The azure flowers that blow;° *bloom*
Demurest of the tabby kind,
The pensive Selima reclined,
  Gazed on the lake below.

Her conscious tail her joy declared;
The fair round face, the snowy beard,
  The velvet of her paws,
Her coat, that with the tortoise vies,
Her ears of jet, and emerald eyes,
  She saw; and purred applause.

Still had she gazed; but 'midst the tide
Two angel forms were seen to glide,
  The genii of the stream:
Their scaly armor's Tyrian° hue *purple*
Through richest purple to the view
  Betrayed a golden gleam.

The hapless nymph with wonder saw:
A whisker first and then a claw,
  With many an ardent wish,
She stretched in vain to reach the prize.
What female heart can gold despise?
  What cat's averse to fish?

Presumptuous maid! with looks intent
Again she stretched, again she bent,
  Nor knew the gulf between.
(Malignant Fate sat by and smiled)
The slippery verge her feet beguiled,
  She tumbled headlong in.

Eight times emerging from the flood
She mewed to every watery god,
  Some speedy aid to send.
No dolphin came, no nereid° stirred: *sea nymph*
Nor cruel Tom, nor Susan[2] heard.
  A favorite has no friend!

From hence, ye beauties, undeceived,
Know, one false step is ne'er retrieved,
  And be with caution bold.

1. Selima, one of Horace Walpole's cats, had recently drowned in a china cistern. Gray wrote this memorial at Walpole's request. For an illustration of this poem by William Blake, see the color insert in this volume.

2. Servants' names.

Not all that tempts your wandering eyes
And heedless hearts is lawful prize;
Nor all that glisters gold.

1747 1748

Elegy Written in a Country Churchyard

The curfew[1] tolls the knell of parting day,
The lowing herd wind slowly o'er the lea,
The plowman homeward plods his weary way,
And leaves the world to darkness and to me.

Now fades the glimmering landscape on the sight,
And all the air a solemn stillness holds,
Save where the beetle wheels his droning flight,
And drowsy tinklings lull the distant folds;

Save that from yonder ivy-mantled tower
The moping owl does to the moon complain
Of such, as wandering near her secret bower,
Molest her ancient solitary reign.

Beneath those rugged elms, that yew tree's shade,
Where heaves the turf in many a moldering heap,
Each in his narrow cell forever laid,
The rude° forefathers of the hamlet sleep. *uneducated*

The breezy call of incense-breathing Morn,
The swallow twittering from the straw-built shed,
The cock's shrill clarion, or the echoing horn,° *hunter's horn*
No more shall rouse them from their lowly bed.

For them no more the blazing hearth shall burn,
Or busy housewife ply her evening care;
No children run to lisp their sire's return,
Or climb his knees the envied kiss to share.

Oft did the harvest to their sickle yield,
Their furrow oft the stubborn glebe° has broke; *soil*
How jocund did they drive their team afield!
How bowed the woods beneath their sturdy stroke!

Let not Ambition mock their useful toil,
Their homely joys, and destiny obscure;
Nor Grandeur hear with a disdainful smile
The short and simple annals of the poor.

1. A bell rung in the evening.

The boast of heraldry,° the pomp of power, *noble birth*
And all that beauty, all that wealth e'er gave,
Awaits alike the inevitable hour.
The paths of glory lead but to the grave.

Nor you, ye proud, impute to these the fault,
If Memory o'er their tomb no trophies[2] raise,
Where through the long-drawn aisle and fretted[3] vault
The pealing anthem swells the note of praise.

Can storied urn[4] or animated° bust *lifelike*
Back to its mansion call the fleeting breath?
Can Honor's voice provoke° the silent dust, *call forth*
Or Flattery soothe the dull cold ear of Death?

Perhaps in this neglected spot is laid
Some heart once pregnant with celestial fire;
Hands that the rod of empire might have swayed,° *wielded*
Or waked to ecstasy the living lyre.

But Knowledge to their eyes her ample page
Rich with the spoils of time did ne'er unroll;
Chill Penury repressed their noble rage,° *inspiration*
And froze the genial° current of the soul. *creative*

Full many a gem of purest ray serene,
The dark unfathomed caves of ocean bear:
Full many a flower is born to blush unseen,
And waste its sweetness on the desert air.

Some village Hampden,[5] that with dauntless breast
The little tyrant of his fields withstood;
Some mute inglorious Milton here may rest,
Some Cromwell guiltless of his country's blood.

The applause of listening senates to command,
The threats of pain and ruin to despise,
To scatter plenty o'er a smiling land,
And read their history in a nation's eyes,

Their lot forbade: nor circumscribed alone
Their growing virtues, but their crimes confined;
Forbade to wade through slaughter to a throne,
And shut the gates of mercy on mankind,

The struggling pangs of conscious truth to hide,
To quench the blushes of ingenuous shame,

2. An ornamental or symbolic group of figures depicting the achievements of the deceased.
3. Decorated with intersecting lines in relief.
4. A funeral urn with an epitaph or pictured story inscribed on it.
5. John Hampden (1594–1643), who, both as a private citizen and as a member of Parliament, zealously defended the rights of the people against the autocratic policies of Charles I.

Or heap the shrine of Luxury and Pride
With incense kindled at the Muse's flame.

Far from the madding crowd's ignoble strife,
Their sober wishes never learned to stray;
Along the cool sequestered vale of life
They kept the noiseless tenor of their way.

Yet even these bones from insult to protect
Some frail memorial still erected nigh,
With uncouth rhymes and shapeless sculpture decked,[6]
Implores the passing tribute of a sigh.

Their name, their years, spelt by the unlettered Muse,
The place of fame and elegy supply:
And many a holy text around she strews,
That teach the rustic moralist to die.

For who to dumb Forgetfulness a prey,
This pleasing anxious being e'er resigned,
Left the warm precincts of the cheerful day,
Nor cast one longing lingering look behind?

On some fond breast the parting soul relies,
Some pious drops the closing eye requires;
Even from the tomb the voice of Nature cries,
Even in our ashes live their wonted fires.

For thee, who mindful of the unhonored dead
Dost in these lines their artless tale relate;
If chance,° by lonely contemplation led, *perchance*
Some kindred spirit shall inquire thy fate,

Haply some hoary-headed swain may say,
"Oft have we seen him at the peep of dawn
Brushing with hasty steps the dews away
To meet the sun upon the upland lawn.

"There at the foot of yonder nodding beech
That wreathes its old fantastic roots so high,
His listless length at noontide would he stretch,
And pore upon the brook that babbles by.

"Hard by yon wood, now smiling as in scorn,
Muttering his wayward fancies he would rove,
Now drooping, woeful wan, like one forlorn,
Or crazed with care, or crossed in hopeless love.

"One morn I missed him on the customed hill,
Along the heath and near his favorite tree;

6. Cf. "the storied urn or animated bust" dedicated inside the church to "the proud" (line 41).

Another came; nor yet beside the rill,
  Nor up the lawn, nor at the wood was he;

"The next with dirges due in sad array
  Slow through the churchway path we saw him borne.
Approach and read (for thou canst read) the lay,
  Graved on the stone beneath yon aged thorn."

The Epitaph

Here rests his head upon the lap of Earth
  A youth to Fortune and to Fame unknown.
Fair Science° frowned not on his humble birth, Learning
  And Melancholy marked him for her own.

Large was his bounty, and his soul sincere,
  Heaven did a recompense as largely send:
He gave to Misery all he had, a tear,
  He gained from Heaven ('twas all he wished) a friend.

No farther seek his merits to disclose,
  Or draw his frailties from their dread abode
(There they alike in trembling hope repose),
  The bosom of his Father and his God.

ca. 1742–50 1751

WILLIAM COLLINS
1721–1759

William Collins was born in Chichester and was educated at Winchester and Oxford. Coming up to London from the university, he tried to establish himself as an author, but he was given rather to planning than to writing books. He came to know Samuel Johnson, who later remembered him affectionately as a man of learning who "loved fairies, genii, giants, and monsters" and who "delighted to rove through the meanders of enchantment." In 1746 Collins published his *Odes on Several Descriptive and Allegorical Subjects,* his part in an undertaking, with his friend Joseph Warton, to create a new poetry, more lyrical and fanciful than that of Alexander Pope's generation. Collins's *Odes* address personified abstractions (Fear, Pity, the Passions), which are imagined as vivid presences that overwhelm the poet as he calls them to life. In form these poems represent a new version of the Great or Cowleian Ode (see headnote to Ben Jonson's "Cary-Morison ode," p. 1439); Collins returns to Pindar's regularity of structure. But the originality of the *Odes* lies in their intensity of vision, which risks obscurity in quest of the sublime. (For more poems by Collins, go to Norton Literature Online.)

To his disappointment, contemporaries preferred his early *Persian Eclogues* to the more difficult *Odes*. Inheriting some money, the poet traveled for a while, but fits of depression gradually deepened into total debility. He spent his last years in

Chichester, forgotten by all but a small circle of loyal friends. As the century progressed he gained in reputation. The Romantics admired his poems and felt akin to him. Coleridge said that "Ode on the Poetical Character" "has inspired and whirled me along with greater agitations of enthusiasm than any the most *impassioned* scene in Schiller or Shakespeare."

Ode Written in the Beginning of the Year 1746

How sleep the brave[1] who sink to rest
By all their country's wishes blest!
When Spring, with dewy fingers cold,
Returns to deck their hallowed mold,
She there shall dress a sweeter sod
Than Fancy's feet have ever trod.

By fairy hands their knell is rung,
By forms unseen their dirge is sung;
There Honor comes, a pilgrim gray,
To bless the turf that wraps their clay,
And Freedom shall awhile repair,
To dwell a weeping hermit there!

1746

Ode to Evening[1]

If aught of oaten stop,[2] or pastoral song,
May hope, chaste Eve, to soothe thy modest ear,
Like thy own solemn springs,
Thy springs and dying gales,
O nymph reserved, while now the bright-haired sun
Sits in yon western tent, whose cloudy skirts,
With brede° ethereal wove, *embroidery*
O'erhang his wavy bed:
Now air is hushed, save where the weak-eyed bat,
With short shrill shriek flits by on leathern wing,
Or where the beetle winds
His small but sullen horn,
As oft he rises 'midst the twilight path,
Against the pilgrim borne in heedless hum:
Now teach me, maid composed,
To breathe some softened strain,
Whose numbers,° stealing through thy darkening vale, *measures*
May not unseemly with its stillness suit,

1. Collins is presumably thinking of those who lost their lives defending England in 1745, when the Scotch Jacobites, led by Bonnie Prince Charlie, penetrated to within 127 miles of London.

1. Collins borrowed the metrical structure and the rhymeless lines of this ode from Milton's translation of Horace, *Odes* 1.5 (1673). The text printed here is based on the revised version, published in Dodsley's *Miscellany* (1748).

2. Finger hole in a shepherd's flute.

As, musing slow, I hail
Thy genial° loved return! *life-giving*
For when thy folding-star[3] arising shows
His paly circlet, at his warning lamp
The fragrant Hours, and elves
Who slept in flowers the day,
And many a nymph who wreaths her brows with sedge,
And sheds the freshening dew, and, lovelier still,
The pensive Pleasures sweet,
Prepare thy shadowy car.
Then lead, calm vot'ress, where some sheety lake
Cheers the lone heath, or some time-hallowed pile
Or upland fallows gray
Reflect its last cool gleam.
But when chill blustering winds, or driving rain,
Forbid my willing feet, be mine the hut
That from the mountain's side
Views wilds, and swelling floods,
And hamlets brown, and dim-discovered spires,
And hears their simple bell, and marks o'er all
Thy dewy fingers draw
The gradual dusky veil.
While Spring shall pour his showers, as oft he wont,
And bathe thy breathing tresses, meekest Eve;
While Summer loves to sport
Beneath thy lingering light;
While sallow Autumn fills thy lap with leaves;
Or Winter, yelling through the troublous air,
Affrights thy shrinking train,
And rudely rends thy robes;
So long, sure-found beneath the sylvan shed,
Shall Fancy, Friendship, Science, rose-lipped Health,
Thy gentlest influence own,
And hymn thy favorite name!

1746, 1748

3. The evening star, which signals the hour for herding the sheep into the sheepfold.

WILLIAM COWPER
1731–1800

There are no saner poems in the language than William Cowper's, yet they were written by a man who was periodically insane and who for forty years lived day to day with the possibility of madness. After attempting suicide in 1763, he believed that he was damned for having committed the unforgivable sin, the "sin against the Holy Ghost." From then on, a refugee from life, he looked for hope in Evangelicalism and found shelter first, in 1765, in the pious family of the clergyman Morley Unwin, and after Unwin's death, with his widow, Mary Unwin, who cared for Cowper until her death in 1796. Their move to rural Olney (pronounced *Own-y*) in 1768 brought them under the influence of the strenuous and fervent Evangelical minister John Newton, author of "Amazing Grace." With him Cowper wrote the famous *Olney Hymns*, still familiar to Methodists and other Nonconformists. But a second attack of madness, in 1773, not only frustrated his planned marriage to Mary Unwin but left him for the rest of his life with the assurance that he had been cast out by God. He never again attended services, and the main purpose of his life thereafter was to divert his mind from numb despair by every possible innocent device. He gardened, he kept pets, he walked, he wrote letters (some of the best of the century), he conversed, he read—and he wrote poetry. When it was published, it brought him a measure of fame that his modest nature could never have hoped for.

Cowper's major work is *The Task* (1785), undertaken at the bidding of Lady Austen, a friend who, when he complained that he had no subject, directed him to write about the sofa in his parlor. It began with a mock-heroic account of the development of the sofa from a simple stool, but it grew into a long meditative poem of more than five thousand lines. The poet describes his small world of country, village, garden, and parlor, and from time to time he glances toward the great world to condemn cities and worldliness, war and slavery, luxury and corruption. The tone is muted, the sensibility delicate, the language on the whole precise and clear. Cowper does not strive to be great, yet his contemporaries recognized their own concerns in his pious and humorous musings. Blake, Wordsworth, and Coleridge felt close to him, and so did many literary women. No eighteenth-century poet was more beloved.

The Castaway

Obscurest night involved the sky,
   The Atlantic billows roared,
When such a destined wretch as I,
   Washed headlong from on board,
Of friends, of hope, of all bereft,
His floating home forever left.

No braver chief[1] could Albion boast
   Than he with whom he went,
Nor ever ship left Albion's coast,
   With warmer wishes sent.
He loved them both, but both in vain,
Nor him beheld, nor her again.

Not long beneath the whelming brine,
   Expert to swim, he lay;
Nor soon he felt his strength decline,
   Or courage die away;
But waged with death a lasting strife,
Supported by despair of life.

He shouted; nor his friends had failed
   To check the vessel's course,
But so the furious blast prevailed,
   That, pitiless perforce,

1. George, Lord Anson (1697–1762), in whose *Voyage* (1748) Cowper, years before writing this poem, had read the story of the sailor washed overboard in a storm.

They left their outcast mate behind,
And scudded still before the wind.

Some succor yet they could afford;
And, such as storms allow,
The cask, the coop, the floated cord,
Delayed not to bestow.
But he (they knew) nor ship, nor shore,
Whate'er they gave, should visit more.

Nor, cruel as it seemed, could he
Their haste himself condemn,
Aware that flight, in such a sea,
Alone could rescue them;
Yet bitter felt it still to die
Deserted, and his friends so nigh.

He long survives, who lives an hour
In ocean, self-upheld;
And so long he, with unspent power,
His destiny repelled;
And ever, as the minutes flew,
Entreated help, or cried, "Adieu!"

At length, his transient respite past,
His comrades, who before
Had heard his voice in every blast,
Could catch the sound no more.
For then, by toil subdued, he drank
The stifling wave, and then he sank.

No poet wept him; but the page
Of narrative sincere,
That tells his name, his worth, his age,
Is wet with Anson's tear.
And tears by bards or heroes shed
Alike immortalize the dead.

I therefore purpose not, or dream,
Descanting on his fate,
To give the melancholy theme
A more enduring date:
But misery still delights to trace
Its semblance in another's case.

No voice divine the storm allayed,
No light propitious shone,
When, snatched from all effectual aid,
We perished, each alone;
But I beneath a rougher sea,
And whelmed in deeper gulfs than he.

1799 1803

OLAUDAH EQUIANO

The Interesting Narrative of the Life of Olaudah Equiano, or Gustavus Vassa, the African, Written by Himself, published in 1789, is the classic story of an eighteenth-century African's descent into slavery and rise to freedom. Raised in an Ibo village (in modern Nigeria), Olaudah Equiano (ca. 1745–1797) was kidnapped by African raiders and sold into slavery. He survived the horrors of the Middle Passage to the New World, where an English naval officer bought him to serve as a cabin boy and renamed him Gustavus Vassa, after a sixteenth-century Swedish hero who freed his people from the Danes (such names concealed the status of a slave, because slavery was frowned on by the British Navy). During years at sea, as well as a period at a London school, Equiano acquired a basic education. He was also baptized, which many slaves expected to make them free. But his hopes were cruelly disappointed when, after six years' service, he was suddenly sold and shipped to the West Indies. There a Quaker merchant, Robert King, purchased him, employed him as a clerk and seaman, and eventually allowed him, in 1766, to buy his freedom. Equiano went back to England, working first as a hairdresser and later voyaging all over the world, even taking part in an effort to find a passage to India by way of the North Pole. In the 1780s he became involved in the abolitionist movement. The story of his life was an important contribution to that movement, not only for its explicit arguments against the slave trade but also for its demonstration that someone born in Africa could be humane, intelligent, a good Christian, and a free and eloquent British subject. The book went through many editions and made Equiano famous. He married an Englishwoman, fathered two daughters, and died in London in 1797.

The *Life of Equiano* combines several literary genres. It is a captivity narrative, a spiritual autobiography, a travel memoir, an adventure story, and an abolitionist tract. The early chapters describe the healthy, cheerful, and virtuous life of Africans, contrasted with European inhumanity, and the later chapters show how much a black man can achieve, when given a chance. Equiano does not disguise the strains of his position as he is pulled between different identities and different worlds. His main purpose, however, is clearly to force his readers to face the ordeals a slave must endure—to live in his skin. If *Oroonoko* taught Europeans to sympathize with Africans, Equiano taught them that a black man could speak for himself.

From The Interesting Narrative of the Life of Olaudah Equiano, or Gustavus Vassa, the African, Written by Himself

[THE MIDDLE PASSAGE][1]

The first object which saluted my eyes when I arrived on the coast was the sea, and a slave ship, which was then riding at anchor, and waiting for its cargo. These filled me with astonishment, which was soon converted into terror when I was carried on board. I was immediately handled and tossed up to see if I were sound by some of the crew; and I was now persuaded that I had gotten into a world of bad spirits, and that they were going to kill me. Their complexions too differing so much from ours, their long hair, and the language they spoke, (which was very different from any I had ever heard) united to confirm me in this belief. Indeed such were the horrors of my views and fears

1. After his kidnapping, young Equiano passes from one African master to another. The last of these, a merchant, treats him like a member of the family, until one morning the boy is suddenly wakened and hurried away to the seacoast.

at the moment, that, if ten thousand worlds had been my own, I would have freely parted with them all to have exchanged my condition with that of the meanest slave in my own country. When I looked round the ship too and saw a large furnace of copper boiling, and a multitude of black people of every description chained together, every one of their countenances expressing dejection and sorrow, I no longer doubted of my fate; and, quite overpowered with horror and anguish, I fell motionless on the deck and fainted. When I recovered a little I found some black people about me, who I believe were some of those who brought me on board, and had been receiving their pay; they talked to me in order to cheer me, but all in vain. I asked them if we were not to be eaten by those white men with horrible looks, red faces, and loose hair. They told me I was not; and one of the crew brought me a small portion of spirituous liquor in a wine glass; but, being afraid of him, I would not take it out of his hand. One of the blacks therefore took it from him and gave it to me, and I took a little down my palate, which, instead of reviving me, as they thought it would, threw me into the greatest consternation at the strange feeling it produced, having never tasted any such liquor before. Soon after this the blacks who brought me on board went off, and left me abandoned to despair. I now saw myself deprived of all chance of returning to my native country, or even the least glimpse of hope of gaining the shore, which I now considered as friendly; and I even wished for my former slavery in preference to my present situation, which was filled with horrors of every kind, still heightened by my ignorance of what I was to undergo. I was not long suffered to indulge my grief; I was soon put down under the decks, and there I received such a salutation in my nostrils as I had never experienced in my life; so that, with the loathsomeness of the stench, and crying together, I became so sick and low that I was not able to eat, nor had I the least desire to taste any thing. I now wished for the last friend, death, to relieve me; but soon, to my grief, two of the white men offered me eatables; and, on my refusing to eat, one of them held me fast by the hands, and laid me across I think the windlass, and tied my feet, while the other flogged me severely. I had never experienced any thing of this kind before; and although, not being used to the water, I naturally feared that element the first time I saw it, yet nevertheless, could I have got over the nettings,[2] I would have jumped over the side, but I could not; and, besides, the crew used to watch us very closely who were not chained down to the decks, lest we should leap into the water; and I have seen some of these poor African prisoners most severely cut for attempting to do so, and hourly whipped for not eating. This indeed was often the case with myself. In a little time after, amongst the poor chained men, I found some of my own nation, which in a small degree gave ease to my mind. I inquired of these what was to be done with us; they gave me to understand we were to be carried to these white people's country to work for them. I then was a little revived, and thought, if it were no worse than working, my situation was not so desperate: but still I feared I should be put to death, the white people looked and acted, as I thought, in so savage a manner; for I had never seen among any people such instances of brutal cruelty; and this not only shewn towards us blacks, but also to some of the whites themselves. One white man in particular I saw, when we were permitted to be on deck, flogged so unmercifully with a large rope near the foremast, that he died in consequence of it; and they tossed him

2. A network of small ropes around the ship kept slaves from jumping overboard.

over the side as they would have done a brute. This made me fear these people the more; and I expected nothing less than to be treated in the same manner. I could not help expressing my fears and apprehensions to some of my countrymen: I asked them if these people had no country, but lived in this hollow place (the ship): they told me they did not, but came from a distant one. "Then," said I, "how comes it in all our country we never heard of them?" They told me because they lived so very far off. I then asked where were their women? had they any like themselves? I was told they had: "and why," said I, "do we not see them?" they answered, because they were left behind. I asked how the vessel could go? they told me they could not tell; but that there were cloths put upon the masts by the help of the ropes I saw, and then the vessel went on; and the white men had some spell or magic they put in the water when they liked in order to stop the vessel. I was exceedingly amazed at this account, and really thought they were spirits. I therefore wished much to be from amongst them, for I expected they would sacrifice me: but my wishes were vain; for we were so quartered that it was impossible for any of us to make our escape. While we stayed on the coast I was mostly on deck; and one day, to my great astonishment, I saw one of these vessels coming in with the sails up. As soon as the whites saw it, they gave a great shout, at which we were amazed; and the more so as the vessel appeared larger by approaching nearer. At last she came to an anchor in my sight, and when the anchor was let go I and my countrymen who saw it were lost in astonishment to observe the vessel stop; and were now convinced it was done by magic. Soon after this the other ship got her boats out, and they came on board of us, and the people of both ships seemed very glad to see each other. Several of the strangers also shook hands with us black people, and made motions with their hands, signifying I suppose we were to go to their country; but we did not understand them. At last, when the ship we were in had got in all her cargo, they made ready with many fearful noises, and we were all put under deck, so that we could not see how they managed the vessel. But this disappointment was the least of my sorrow. The stench of the hold while we were on the coast was so intolerably loathsome, that it was dangerous to remain there for any time, and some of us had been permitted to stay on the deck for the fresh air; but now that the whole ship's cargo were confined together, it became absolutely pestilential. The closeness of the place, and the heat of the climate, added to the number in the ship, which was so crowded that each had scarcely room to turn himself, almost suffocated us. This produced copious perspirations, so that the air soon became unfit for respiration, from a variety of loathsome smells, and brought on a sickness among the slaves, of which many died, thus falling victims to the improvident avarice, as I may call it, of their purchasers. This wretched situation was again aggravated by the galling of the chains, now become insupportable; and the filth of the necessary tubs,[3] into which the children often fell, and were almost suffocated. The shrieks of the women, and the groans of the dying, rendered the whole a scene of horror almost inconceivable. Happily perhaps for myself I was soon reduced so low here that it was thought necessary to keep me almost always on deck; and from[4] my extreme youth I was not put in fetters. In this situation I expected every hour to share the fate of my companions, some of whom were almost daily brought upon deck at the point of death, which I began to hope would soon put an

3. Latrines.

4. Because of.

end to my miseries. Often did I think many of the inhabitants of the deep much more happy than myself. I envied them the freedom they enjoyed, and as often wished I could change my condition for theirs. Every circumstance I met with served only to render my state more painful, and heighten my apprehensions, and my opinion of the cruelty of the whites. One day they had taken a number of fishes; and when they had killed and satisfied themselves with as many as they thought fit, to our astonishment who were on the deck, rather than give any of them to us to eat as we expected, they tossed the remaining fish into the sea again, although we begged and prayed for some as well as we could, but in vain; and some of my countrymen, being pressed by hunger, took an opportunity, when they thought no one saw them, of trying to get a little privately; but they were discovered, and the attempt procured them some very severe floggings.

One day, when we had a smooth sea and moderate wind, two of my wearied countrymen who were chained together (I was near them at the time), preferring death to such a life of misery, somehow made through the nettings and jumped into the sea; immediately another quite dejected fellow, who, on account of his illness, was suffered to be out of irons, also followed their example; and I believe many more would very soon have done the same if they had not been prevented by the ship's crew, who were instantly alarmed. Those of us that were the most active were in a moment put down under the deck, and there was such a noise and confusion amongst the people of the ship as I never heard before, to stop her, and get the boat out to go after the slaves. However two of the wretches were drowned, but they got the other, and afterwards flogged him unmercifully for thus attempting to prefer death to slavery. In this manner we continued to undergo more hardships than I can now relate, hardships which are inseparable from this accursed trade. Many a time we were near suffocation from the want of fresh air, which we were often without for whole days together. This, and the stench of the necessary tubs, carried off many. During our passage I first saw flying fishes, which surprised me very much: they used frequently to fly across the ship, and many of them fell on the deck. I also now first saw the use of the quadrant; I had often with astonishment seen the mariners make observations with it, and I could not think what it meant. They at last took notice of my surprise; and one of them, willing to increase it, as well as to gratify my curiosity, made me one day look through it. The clouds appeared to me to be land, which disappeared as they passed along. This heightened my wonder; and I was now more persuaded than ever that I was in another world, and that every thing about me was magic. At last we came in sight of the island of Barbados,[5] at which the whites on board gave a great shout, and made many signs of joy to us. We did not know what to think of this; but as the vessel drew nearer we plainly saw the harbor, and other ships of different kinds and sizes; and we soon anchored amongst them off Bridge Town. Many merchants and planters now came on board, though it was in the evening. They put us in separate parcels,[6] and examined us attentively. They also made us jump, and pointed to the land, signifying we were to go there. We thought by this we should be eaten by these ugly men, as they appeared to us; and, when soon after we were all put down under the deck again, there was much dread and trembling among us, and nothing but bitter

5. The easternmost Caribbean island, then an important center for the trade of sugar and slaves.

6. Groups sorted to be sold as one lot.

cries to be heard all the night from these apprehensions, insomuch that at last the white people got some old slaves from the land to pacify us. They told us we were not to be eaten, but to work, and were soon to go on land, where we should see many of our country people. This report eased us much; and sure enough, soon after we were landed, there came to us Africans of all languages. We were conducted immediately to the merchant's yard, where we were pent up altogether like so many sheep in a fold, without regard to sex or age. As every object was new to me, every thing I saw filled me with surprise. What struck me first was that the houses were built with stories, and in every other respect different from those in Africa; but I was still more astonished on seeing people on horseback. I did not know what this could mean; and indeed I thought these people were full of nothing but magical arts. While I was in this astonishment one of my fellow prisoners spoke to a countryman of his about the horses, who said they were the same kind they had in their country. I understood them, though they were from a distant part of Africa, and I thought it odd I had not seen any horses there; but afterwards, when I came to converse with different Africans, I found they had many horses amongst them, and much larger than those I then saw. We were not many days in the merchant's custody before we were sold after their usual manner, which is this:—On a signal given (as the beat of a drum) the buyers rush at once into the yard where the slaves are confined, and make a choice of that parcel they like best. The noise and clamor with which this is attended, and the eagerness visible in the countenances of the buyers, serve not a little to increase the apprehensions of the terrified Africans, who may well be supposed to consider them as the ministers of that destruction to which they think themselves devoted.[7] In this manner, without scruple, are relations and friends separated, most of them never to see each other again. I remember in the vessel in which I was brought over, in the men's apartment, there were several brothers, who, in the sale, were sold in different lots; and it was very moving on this occasion to see and hear their cries at parting. O, ye nominal Christians! might not an African ask you, learned you this from your God, who says unto you, Do unto all men as you would men should do unto you? Is it not enough that we are torn from our country and friends to toil for your luxury and lust of gain? Must every tender feeling be likewise sacrificed to your avarice? Are the dearest friends and relations, now rendered more dear by their separation from their kindred, still to be parted from each other, and thus prevented from cheering the gloom of slavery with the small comfort of being together and mingling their sufferings and sorrows? Why are parents to lose their children, brothers their sisters, or husbands their wives? Surely this is a new refinement in cruelty, which, while it has no advantage to atone for it, thus aggravates distress, and adds fresh horrors even to the wretchedness of slavery.

* * *

[A Free Man][8]

Every day now brought me nearer my freedom, and I was impatient till we proceeded again to sea, that I might have an opportunity of getting a sum large

7. Doomed.
8. Frustrated in his hope to be set free in England, Equiano is shipped to Montserrat, a British colony in the Leeward Islands of the West Indies. Robert King, a prosperous Quaker merchant from Philadelphia, buys him, treats him kindly, and values him as a reliable worker. By being useful to a friendly sea captain, Thomas Farmer, Equiano has

enough to purchase it. I was not long ungratified; for, in the beginning of the year 1766, my master bought another sloop, named the *Nancy*, the largest I had ever seen. She was partly laden, and was to proceed to Philadelphia; our Captain had his choice of three, and I was well pleased he chose this, which was the largest; for, from his having a large vessel, I had more room, and could carry a larger quantity of goods with me. Accordingly, when we had delivered our old vessel, the *Prudence*, and completed the lading of the *Nancy*, having made near three hundred per cent, by four barrels of pork I brought from Charlestown, I laid in as large a cargo as I could, trusting to God's providence to prosper my undertaking. With these views I sailed for Philadelphia. On our passage, when we drew near the land, I was for the first time surprised at the sight of some whales, having never seen any such large sea monsters before; and as we sailed by the land one morning I saw a puppy whale close by the vessel; it was about the length of a wherry boat, and it followed us all the day till we got within the Capes. We arrived safe and in good time at Philadelphia, and I sold my goods there chiefly to the Quakers. They always appeared to be a very honest discreet sort of people, and never attempted to impose on me; I therefore liked them, and ever after chose to deal with them in preference to any others.

One Sunday morning while I was here, as I was going to church, I chanced to pass a meeting house. The doors being open, and the house full of people, it excited my curiosity to go in. When I entered the house, to my great surprise, I saw a very tall woman standing in the midst of them, speaking in an audible voice something which I could not understand. Having never seen anything of this kind before, I stood and stared about me for some time, wondering at this odd scene. As soon as it was over I took an opportunity to make inquiry about the place and people, when I was informed they were called Quakers.[9] I particularly asked what that woman I saw in the midst of them had said, but none of them were pleased to satisfy me; so I quitted them, and soon after, as I was returning, I came to a church crowded with people; the church-yard was full likewise, and a number of people were even mounted on ladders, looking in at the windows. I thought this a strange sight, as I had never seen churches, either in England or the West Indies, crowded in this manner before. I therefore made bold to ask some people the meaning of all this, and they told me the Rev. Mr. George Whitfield[1] was preaching. I had often heard of this gentleman, and had wished to see and hear him; but I had never before had an opportunity. I now therefore resolved to gratify myself with the sight, and I pressed in amidst the multitude. When I got into the church I saw this pious man exhorting the people with the greatest fervor and earnestness, and sweating as much as I ever did while in slavery on Montserrat beach. I was very much struck and impressed with this; I thought it strange I had never seen divines exert themselves in this manner before, and I was no longer at a loss to account for the thin congregations they preached to.

When we had discharged our cargo here, and were loaded again, we left this fruitful land once more, and set sail for Montserrat. My traffic had hitherto

opportunities to travel and trade goods for money. Eventually King promises to let him purchase his freedom for his original cost: forty pounds sterling.

9. Quaker meetings are not led by clergy; any worshiper who feels inspired by God can rise to speak.

1. Whitefield (1714–1770), a famous evangelist who helped found Methodism, was in Britain, not Philadelphia, in 1766. It is possible that Equiano had heard him preach the previous year, in Savannah, Georgia. Equiano's later conversion to Methodism will become a dominant theme of his life story.

succeeded so well with me, that I thought, by selling my goods when we arrived at Montserrat, I should have enough to purchase my freedom. But, as soon as our vessel arrived there, my master came on board, and gave orders for us to go to St. Eustatia,[2] and discharge our cargo there, and from thence proceed for Georgia. I was much disappointed at this; but thinking, as usual, it was of no use to murmur at the decrees of fate, I submitted without repining, and we went to St. Eustatia. After we had discharged our cargo there we took in a live cargo, as we call a cargo of slaves. Here I sold my goods tolerably well; but, not being able to lay out all my money in this small island to as much advantage as in many other places, I laid out only part, and the remainder I brought away with me neat.[3] We sailed from hence for Georgia, and I was glad when we got there, though I had not much reason to like the place from my last adventure in Savannah;[4] but I longed to get back to Montserrat and procure my freedom, which I expected to be able to purchase when I returned. As soon as we arrived here I waited on my careful doctor, Mr. Brady, to whom I made the most grateful acknowledgments in my power for his former kindness and attention during my illness.

While we were here an odd circumstance happened to the Captain and me, which disappointed us both a good deal. A silversmith, whom we had brought to this place some voyages before, agreed with the Captain to return with us to the West Indies, and promised at the same time to give the Captain a great deal of money, having pretended to take a liking to him, and being, as we thought, very rich. But while we stayed to load our vessel this man was taken ill in a house where he worked, and in a week's time became very bad. The worse he grew the more he used to speak of giving the Captain what he had promised him, so that he expected something considerable from the death of this man, who had no wife or child, and he attended him day and night. I used also to go with the Captain, at his own desire, to attend him; especially when we saw there was no appearance of his recovery; and, in order to recompense me for my trouble, the Captain promised me ten pounds, when he should get the man's property. I thought this would be of great service to me, although I had nearly money enough to purchase my freedom, if I should get safe this voyage to Montserrat. In this expectation I laid out above eight pounds of my money for a suit of superfine clothes to dance with at my freedom, which I hoped was then at hand. We still continued to attend this man, and were with him even on the last day he lived, till very late at night, when we went on board. After we were got to bed, about one or two o'clock in the morning, the Captain was sent for, and informed the man was dead. On this he came to my bed, and, waking me, informed me of it, and desired me to get up and procure a light, and immediately go to him. I told him I was very sleepy, and wished he would take somebody else with him, or else, as the man was dead, and could want no farther attendance, to let all things remain as they were till next morning. "No, no," said he, "we will have the money tonight, I cannot wait till tomorrow; so let us go." Accordingly I got up and struck a light, and away we both went and saw the man as dead as we could wish. The Captain said he would give him a grand burial, in gratitude for the promised treasure; and desired that all the things belonging to the deceased might be brought forth.

2. An island in the Netherlands Antilles (West Indies).
3. Intact.
4. The year before, a drunken slave owner and his servant had beaten Equiano so brutally that he nearly died.

Among others, there was a nest of trunks of which he had kept the keys whilst the man was ill, and when they were produced we opened them with no small eagerness and expectation; and as there were a great number within one another, with much impatience we took them one out of the other. At last, when we came to the smallest, and had opened it, we saw it was full of papers, which we supposed to be notes; at the sight of which our hearts leapt for joy; and that instant the Captain, clapping his hands, cried out, "Thank God, here it is." But when we took up the trunk, and began to examine the supposed treasure and long-looked-for bounty, (alas! alas! how uncertain and deceitful are all human affairs!) what had we found! While we were embracing a substance we grasped an empty nothing. The whole amount that was in the nest of trunks was only one dollar and a half; and all that the man possessed would not pay for his coffin. Our sudden and exquisite joy was now succeeded by as sudden and exquisite pain; and my Captain and I exhibited, for some time, most ridiculous figures—pictures of chagrin and disappointment! We went away greatly mortified, and left the deceased to do as well as he could for himself, as we had taken so good care of him when alive for nothing. We set sail once more for Montserrat, and arrived there safe; but much out of humor with our friend the silversmith. When we had unladen the vessel, and I had sold my venture, finding myself master of about forty-seven pounds, I consulted my true friend, the Captain, how I should proceed in offering my master the money for my freedom. He told me to come on a certain morning, when he and my master would be at breakfast together. Accordingly, on that morning I went, and met the Captain there, as he had appointed. When I went in I made my obeisance to my master, and with my money in my hand, and many fears in my heart, I prayed him to be as good as his offer to me, when he was pleased to promise me my freedom as soon as I could purchase it. This speech seemed to confound him; he began to recoil; and my heart that instant sank within me. "What," said he, "give you your freedom? Why, where did you get the money? Have you got forty pounds sterling?" "Yes, sir," I answered. "How did you get it?" replied he. I told him, very honestly. The Captain then said he knew I got the money very honestly and with much industry, and that I was particularly careful. On which my master replied, I got money much faster than he did; and said he would not have made me the promise he did if he had thought I should have got money so soon. "Come, come," said my worthy Captain, clapping my master on the back, "Come, Robert" (which was his name), "I think you must let him have his freedom; you have laid your money out very well; you have received good interest for it all this time, and here is now the principal at last. I know Gustavus has earned you more than an hundred a-year, and he will still save you money, as he will not leave you:—Come, Robert, take the money." My master then said, he would not be worse than his promise; and, taking the money, told me to go to the Secretary at the Register Office, and get my manumission[5] drawn up. These words of my master were like a voice from heaven to me: in an instant all my trepidation was turned into unutterable bliss; and I most reverently bowed myself with gratitude, unable to express my feelings, but by the overflowing of my eyes, while my true and worthy friend, the Captain, congratulated us both with a peculiar degree of heartfelt pleasure. As soon as the first transports of my joy were over, and that I had expressed my thanks to these my worthy friends in the best

5. Release from slavery.

manner I was able, I rose with a heart full of affection and reverence, and left the room, in order to obey my master's joyful mandate of going to the Register Office. As I was leaving the house I called to mind the words of the Psalmist, in the 126th Psalm, and like him, "I glorified God in my heart, in whom I trusted." These words had been impressed on my mind from the very day I was forced from Deptford[6] to the present hour, and I now saw them, as I thought, fulfilled and verified. My imagination was all rapture as I flew to the Register Office, and in this respect, like the apostle Peter[7] (whose deliverance from prison was so sudden and extraordinary, that he thought he was in a vision), I could scarcely believe I was awake. Heavens! who could do justice to my feelings at this moment! Not conquering heroes themselves, in the midst of a triumph—Not the tender mother who had just regained her long-lost infant, and presses it to her heart—Not the weary hungry mariner, at the sight of the desired friendly port—Not the lover, when he once more embraces his beloved mistress, after she had been ravished from his arms!—All within my breast was tumult, wildness, and delirium! My feet scarcely touched the ground, for they were winged with joy, and, like Elijah, as he rose to Heaven,[8] they "were with lightning sped as I went on." Every one I met I told of my happiness, and blazed about the virtue of my amiable master and captain.

When I got to the office and acquainted the Register with my errand he congratulated me on the occasion, and told me he would draw up my manumission for half price, which was a guinea. I thanked him for his kindness; and having received it and paid him, I hastened to my master to get him to sign it, that I might be fully released. Accordingly he signed the manumission that day, so that, before night, I who had been a slave in the morning, trembling at the will of another, was become my own master, and completely free. I thought this was the happiest day I had ever experienced; and my joy was still heightened by the blessings and prayers of the sable race, particularly the aged, to whom my heart had ever been attached with reverence.

As the form of my manumission has something peculiar in it, and expresses the absolute power and dominion one man claims over his fellow, I shall beg leave to present it before my readers at full length:

Montserrat.—To all men unto whom these presents shall come: I Robert King, of the parish of St. Anthony in the said island, merchant, send greeting: Know ye, that I the aforesaid Robert King, for and in consideration of the sum of seventy pounds current money of the said island,[9] to me in hand paid, and to the intent that a negro man-slave, named Gustavus Vassa, shall and may become free, have manumitted, emancipated, enfranchised, and set free, and by these presents do manumit, emancipate, enfranchise, and set free, the aforesaid negro man-slave, named Gustavus Vassa, for ever, hereby giving, granting, and releasing unto him, the said Gustavus Vassa, all right, title, dominion, sovereignty, and property, which, as lord and master over the aforesaid Gustavus Vassa, I had, or now I have, or by any means whatsoever I may or can hereafter possibly have over him the aforesaid negro, for ever. In witness whereof I the above-said Robert King have unto these presents set my hand

6. The port near London from which Equiano was sold by his English master.
7. Acts, chap. xii, ver. 9 [Equiano's note].
8. 2 Kings 2.11.
9. The equivalent of forty pounds in British money.

and seal, this tenth day of July, in the year of our Lord one thousand seven hundred and sixty-six.

ROBERT KING

Signed, sealed, and delivered in the presence of Terrylegay, Montserrat.

Registered the within manumission at full length, this eleventh day of July, 1766, in liber D.[1]

TERRYLEGAY, REGISTER.

In short, the fair as well as black people immediately styled me by a new appellation, to me the most desirable in the world, which was Freeman, and at the dances I gave my Georgia superfine blue clothes made no indifferent appearance, as I thought.

* * *

1789

1. Book or register D.

FRANCES BURNEY
1752–1840

People have often made the mistake of underestimating Frances Burney. In person, as in her writing, she seemed a proper, self-effacing lady. Many readers still call her "Fanny," as if familiarity could make her harmless. But she saw through such poses. Sir Joshua Reynolds said that "if he was conscious to himself of any trick, or any affectation, there is nobody he should so much fear as this little Burney!" And Samuel Johnson teased her by claiming that "your shyness, & slyness, & pretending to know nothing, never took *me* in, whatever you may do with others. *I* always knew you for a *toadling!*" (according to legend, little toads may look submissive but actually carry poison). Although her writing crackles with humor, it can be relentless—and sometimes cruel—in exposing bad manners or a selfish heart.

She learned quite young how to hide in a crowd. A devoted daughter of Charles Burney, a popular teacher and historian of music, Frances grew up in a large family that gave her many opportunities to study character and mix discreetly in society. Her first novel, *Evelina, or A Young Lady's Entrance into the World* (1778), was written in secret and published anonymously. But delighted readers, including Johnson, Burke, and Hester Thrale, soon found her out and sang her praises; and a second novel, *Cecilia* (1782), confirmed her reputation. Her home life was less happy, however; she and her stepmother disliked each other, and she fell in love with a young clergyman who never got around to proposing. In 1786, to please her father, she accepted a place as a lady-in-waiting at court, where the paralyzing etiquette and lack of independence tormented her for the next five years, until she finally managed to resign. At forty-one she married a French émigré, General Alexandre-Gabriel-Jean-Baptiste d'Arblay. Despite the disapproval of her father—d'Arblay was penniless, Catholic, and politically liberal—the marriage was happy. Madame d'Arblay soon bore a son, and her novel *Camilla* (1796) brought in good money. After she joined her husband in France, in 1802, the Napoleonic wars prevented them from returning to England for ten years; the pain of an outcast dominates her last novel, *The Wanderer, or Female*

Difficulties (1814). But she never stopped writing, producing a doctored version of her father's *Memoirs* (1832) and more of the diaries and letters that, edited after her death by a niece, made her famous again.

Burney wrote all her life—not only novels and plays but perpetual letters and journals, recording whatever she saw for friends and family as well as herself. Even the most informal pages display her gifts: a knack for catching character, a wonderful ear for dialogue, wry humor, and a swift pace that carries the reader along from moment to moment. Her special subject is embarrassment—often her own. In scenes like her flight from the king, where she is torn between opposite notions of the right thing to do, shame and comedy mingle. These trepidations can also be incredibly painful, as in her gripping account of a mastectomy. (For more selections from Burney's journals, go to Norton Literature Online.) Despite her propriety, Burney looks at the world and its institutions with the clear eyes of an outsider, aware of the gaps between what people say and what they do. She frees herself to write with utter honesty by pretending, at first, that nobody is going to read her. But her private thoughts are reported so fully and faithfully that, in the end, every reader can share them.

From The Journal and Letters

[FIRST JOURNAL ENTRY]

Poland Street, London, March 27, 1768[1]

To have some account of my thoughts, manners, acquaintance & actions, when the hour arrives in which time is more nimble than memory, is the reason which induces me to keep a journal: a journal in which I must confess my *every* thought, must open my whole heart! But a thing of this kind ought to be addressed to somebody—I must imagine myself to be talking—talking to the most intimate of friends—to one in whom I should take delight in confiding, & remorse in concealment: but who must this friend be?—to make choice of one to whom I can but *half* rely, would be to frustrate entirely the intention of my plan. The only one I could wholly, totally confide in, lives in the same house with me, & not only never *has*, but never *will*, leave me one secret *to* tell her.[2] To whom, then, *must* I dedicate my wonderful, surprising & interesting adventures?—to *whom* dare I reveal my private opinion of my nearest relations? the secret thoughts of my dearest friends? my own hopes, fears, reflections & dislikes?—Nobody!

To Nobody, then, will I write my journal! since to Nobody can I be wholly unreserved—to Nobody can I reveal every thought, every wish of my heart, with the most unlimited confidence, the most unremitting sincerity to the end of my life! For what chance, what accident can end my connections with Nobody? No secret *can* I conceal from No—body, & to No—body can I be *ever* unreserved. Disagreement cannot stop our affection, time itself has no power to end our friendship. The love, the esteem I entertain for Nobody, Nobody's self has not power to destroy. From Nobody I have nothing to fear, the secrets sacred to friendship, Nobody will not reveal, when the affair is doubtful, Nobody will not look towards the side least favorable—.

I will suppose you, then, to be my best friend; tho' God forbid you ever

1. This is the first page of Burney's first journal, begun when she was fifteen.
2. Burney's younger sister, Susanna. In 1773, when Burney spent the summer away from home, she began a journal for her sister, continuing it off and on until 1800, when Susanna died.

should! my dearest companion—& a romantick girl, for mere oddity may perhaps be more sincere—more *tender*—than if you were a friend in propria personæ[3]—in as much as imagination often exceeds reality. In your breast my errors may create pity without exciting contempt; may raise your compassion, without eradicating your love.

From this moment, then, my dear girl—but why, permit me to ask, must a *female* be made Nobody? Ah! my dear, what were this world good for, *were* Nobody a female? And now I have done with *preambulation*.

["DOWN WITH HER, BURNEY!"]

Streatham, September 15, 1778[4]

I was then looking over the Life of Cowley, which he[5] had himself given me to read, at the same time that he gave to Mrs. Thrale that of Waller.—They are now *printed*, though they will not be *published* for some time. But he bid me put it away.—"Do," cried he, "put away that now, & *prattle* with us;—I can't make this little Burney prattle,—& I am *sure* she prattles well.—but I shall teach her another lesson than to sit thus silent, before I have done with her."

"To *talk*," cried I, "is the *only* lesson I shall be backward to learn from you, sir."

* * *

Mrs. T. Tomorrow, sir, Mrs. Montagu[6] dines here! & then you will have talk enough.

Dr. Johnson began to seesaw, with a countenance strongly expressive of *inward fun*,—&, after enjoying it some time in silence, he suddenly, & with great animation, turned to me, & cried "*Down* with her, Burney!—*down* with her!—spare her not! attack her, fight her, & *down* with her at once!—*You* are a *rising* wit,—*she* is at the *top*,—& when *I* was beginning the world, & was nothing & nobody, the joy of my life was to fire at all the established wits!—& then, every body loved to hallow[7] me on;—but there is no game *now*, & *now*, every body would be glad to see me *conquered*: but *then*, when I was *new*,—to vanquish the great ones was all the delight of my poor little dear soul!—So at her, Burney!—at her, & *down* with her!"

O how we all hollowed![8] By the way, I must tell you that Mrs. Montagu is in very great estimation here, even with Dr. Johnson himself, when others do not praise her *improperly*: Mrs. Thrale ranks her as the *first of women*, in the literary way.

I should have told you, that Miss Gregory, daughter of the Gregory who wrote the letters, or *Legacy* of advice,[9] lives with Mrs. Montagu, & was invited to accompany her.

"Mark, now," said Dr. Johnson, "if I *contradict* her tomorrow; I am deter-

3. In your own person.
4. *Evelina* was published in January 1778 and enthusiastically received. After her authorship became known, Burney was invited to Streatham Park, the country house of Hector and Hester Lynch Thrale. Johnson spent much of his time there and was then writing his *Lives of the Poets*. He and Hester Thrale became fond of Burney.
5. Johnson.
6. Elizabeth Montagu, known as "Queen of the Blues" (or bluestockings), a group of intellectual women, was probably the most respected literary woman in England; she had written the famous *Essay on Shakespear* (1769).
7. A cry inciting hunters to the chase.
8. "To shout; to hoot" (Johnson's *Dictionary*).
9. John Gregory, *A Father's Legacy to His Daughters* (1774).

mined, let her say what she will, that I will *not* contradict her."

Mrs. T. Why, to be sure, Sir, you *did* put her a little out of countenance last time she came,—yet you were neither rough, nor cruel, nor ill-natured,—but still, when a lady *changes color,* we imagine her feelings are not quite *composed.*

Dr. J. Why, madam, I won't answer that I sha'n't contradict her again, if she provokes me as she did then; but a *less* provocation I will withstand. I believe I am not high in her good graces already, & I begin (added he, laughing heartily) to tremble for my admission into her new house! I doubt I shall never see the inside of it!

Mrs. Montagu is building a most superb house.

Mrs. T. O, I warrant you! she *fears* you, indeed, but that, you know, is nothing uncommon: & dearly I love to hear your *disquisitions,*—for certainly she is the first woman, for literary knowledge, in England,—& if in *England* I hope I may say in the *world!*

Dr. J. I believe you may, Madam. She diffuses more knowledge in her conversation than any woman I know,—or, indeed, *almost* any man.

Mrs. T. I declare *I* know *no* man equal to her, take away yourself & Burke, for *that* art.—And *you,* who love magnificence, won't quarrel with her, as everybody else does, for her love of finery.

Dr. J. No, I shall not quarrel with her upon that topic. (then, looking earnestly at *me*) "Nay," he added, "it's very handsome."

"What, sir?" cried I, amazed.

"Why your cap:—I have looked at it some time, & I like it much. It has not that vile *bandeau*[1] across it, which I have so often cursed."

Did you ever hear any thing so strange? *Nothing* escapes him. My Daddy Crisp[2] is not more minute in his attentions: nay, I think he is even *less* so.

Mrs. T. Well, sir, that bandeau you quarreled with was worn by every woman at court the last Birth Day,[3]—& I observed that *all* the men found fault with it.

Dr. J. The truth is,—women,—take them in general,—have *no* idea of grace!—Fashion is *all* they think of;—I don't mean Mrs. Thrale & Miss Burney, when I talk of *women!—they* are goddesses!—& therefore I except them.

Mrs. T. Lady Ladd never wore the bandeau, & said she never would, because it is unbecoming.

Dr. J. (*laughing*) Did not she? then is Lady Ladd a charming woman, & I have yet hopes of entering into engagements with her!

Mrs. T. Well, as to that, I can't say,—but, to be sure, the only similitude *I* have yet discovered in you, *is* in *size: there* you agree mighty well.

Dr. J. Why if *any* body could have worn the bandeau, it must have been Lady Ladd, for there is *enough* of her to carry it off; but *you* are too *little* for any thing ridiculous; that which seems *nothing* upon a Patagonian,[4] will become very *conspicuous* upon a Lilliputian; & of *you* there is so little in *all,* that one single absurdity would swallow up *half* of you.

Some time after,—when we had all been a few minutes wholly silent, he turned to me, & said "Come, Burney,—shall you & I *study our parts* against[5] Mrs. Montagu comes?"

How would you be entertained, my dear Susy, if I could give you the *manner,* as well as *matter,* of the conversation of this greatest of men.

1. A narrow headband.
2. Samuel Crisp, an old family friend, had been a mentor to Burney.
3. June 4, the king's birthday.
4. The Indians of Patagonia, whose average height was more than six feet, were commonly thought to be giants.
5. Before.

[Encountering the King]

Kew Palace, Monday February 2, 1789

What an adventure had I this morning! one that has occasioned me the severest personal terror I ever experienced in my life.

Sir Lucas Pepys still persisting that exercise and air were absolutely necessary to save me from illness, I have continued my walks, varying my gardens from Richmond to Kew, according to the accounts I received of the movements of the king. For this I had her majesty's permission, on the representation of Sir Lucas.

This morning, when I received my intelligence of the king from Dr. John Willis,[6] I begged to know where I might walk in safety? "In Kew gardens," he said, "as the king would be in Richmond."

"Should any unfortunate circumstance," I cried, "at any time, occasion my being seen by his majesty, do not mention my name, but let me run off without call or notice."

This he promised. Everybody, indeed, is ordered to keep out of sight.

Taking, therefore, the time I had most at command, I strolled into the gardens. I had proceeded, in my quick way, nearly half the round, when I suddenly perceived, through some trees, two or three figures. Relying on the instructions of Dr. John, I concluded them to be workmen and gardeners; yet tried to look sharp, and in so doing, as they were less shaded, I thought I saw the person of his majesty!

Alarmed past all possible expression, I waited not to know more, but turning back, ran off with all my might. But what was my terror to hear myself pursued!—to hear the voice of the king himself loudly and hoarsely calling after me, "Miss Burney! Miss Burney!"

I protest I was ready to die. I knew not in what state he might be at the time; I only knew the orders to keep out of his way were universal; that the queen would highly disapprove any unauthorized meeting, and that the very action of my running away might deeply, in his present irritable state, offend him. Nevertheless, on I ran, too terrified to stop, and in search of some short passage, for the garden is full of little labyrinths, by which I might escape.

The steps still pursued me, and still the poor hoarse and altered voice rang in my ears:—more and more footsteps resounded frightfully behind me,—the attendants all running, to catch their eager master, and the voices of the two Doctor Willises loudly exhorting him not to heat himself so unmercifully.

Heavens, how I ran! I do not think I should have felt the hot lava from Vesuvius—at least not the hot cinders—had I so run during its eruption. My feet were not sensible that they even touched the ground.

Soon after, I heard other voices, shriller, though less nervous, call out "Stop! stop! stop!"

I could by no means consent; I knew not what was purposed, but I recollected fully my agreement with Dr. John that very morning, that I should decamp if surprised, and not be named.

My own fears and repugnance, also, after a flight and disobedience like this, were doubled in the thought of not escaping; I knew not to what I might be exposed, should the malady be then high, and take the turn of resentment.

6. In 1788, two years after Burney joined the court, George III began to have fits of delirium or madness (today diagnosed as resulting from porphyria, a hereditary disease). He was kept in isolation at Kew, under the control of two physicians, Francis and John Willis.

Still, therefore, on I flew; and such was my speed, so almost incredible to relate or recollect, that I fairly believe no one of the whole party could have overtaken me, if these words, from one of the attendants, had not reached me: "Doctor Willis begs you to stop!"

"I cannot! I cannot!" I answered, still flying on, when he called out "You must, ma'am; it hurts the king to run."

Then, indeed, I stopped—in a state of fear really amounting to agony. I turned round, I saw the two doctors had got the king between them, and three attendants of Dr. Willis's were hovering about. They all slackened their pace, as they saw me stand still; but such was the excess of my alarm, that I was wholly insensible to the effects of a race which, at any other time, would have required an hour's recruit.[7]

As they approached, some little presence of mind happily came to my command; it occurred to me that, to appease the wrath of my flight, I must now show some confidence. I therefore faced them as undauntedly as I was able, only charging the nearest of the attendants to stand by my side.

When they were within a few yards of me, the king called out, "Why did you run away?"

Shocked at a question impossible to answer, yet a little assured by the mild tone of his voice, I instantly forced myself forward, to meet him, though the internal sensation, which satisfied me this was a step the most proper to appease his suspicions and displeasure, was so violently combated by the tremor of my nerves, that I fairly think I may reckon it the greatest effort of personal courage I have ever made.

The effort answered: I looked up, and met all his wonted benignity of countenance, though something still of wildness in his eyes. Think, however, of my surprise, to feel him put both his hands round my two shoulders, and then kiss my cheek!

I wonder I did not really sink, so exquisite was my affright when I saw him spread out his arms! Involuntarily, I concluded he meant to crush me; but the Willises, who have never seen him till this fatal illness, not knowing how very extraordinary an action this was from him, simply smiled and looked pleased, supposing, perhaps, it was his customary salutation!

I believe, however, it was but the joy of a heart unbridled, now, by the forms and proprieties of established custom and sober reason. To see any of his household thus by accident, seemed such a near approach to liberty and recovery, that who can wonder it should serve rather to elate[8] than lessen what yet remains of his disorder!

He now spoke in such terms of his pleasure in seeing me, that I soon lost the whole of my terror; astonishment to find him so nearly well, and gratification to see him so pleased, removed every uneasy feeling, and the joy that succeeded, in my conviction of his recovery, made me ready to throw myself at his feet to express it.

What a conversation followed! When he saw me fearless, he grew more and more alive, and made me walk close by his side, away from the attendants, and even the Willises themselves, who, to indulge him, retreated. I own myself not completely composed, but alarm I could entertain no more.

Everything that came uppermost in his mind he mentioned; he seemed to have just such remains of his flightiness as heated his imagination without

7. Renewal of strength.

8. Heighten.

deranging his reason, and robbed him of all control over his speech, though nearly in his perfect state of mind as to his opinions.

What did he not say!—He opened his whole heart to me,—expounded all his sentiments, and acquainted me with all his intentions.

* * *

He next talked to me a great deal of my dear father, and made a thousand inquiries concerning his "History of Music." This brought him to his favorite theme, Handel;[9] and he told me innumerable anecdotes of him, and particularly that celebrated tale of Handel's saying of himself, when a boy, "While that boy lives, my music will never want a protector." And this, he said, I might relate to my father. Then he ran over most of his oratorios, attempting to sing the subjects of several airs and choruses, but so dreadfully hoarse that the sound was terrible.

Dr. Willis, quite alarmed at this exertion, feared he would do himself harm, and again proposed a separation. "No! no! no!" he exclaimed, "not yet; I have something I must just mention first."

Dr. Willis, delighted to comply, even when uneasy at compliance, again gave way. The good king then greatly affected me. He began upon my revered old friend, Mrs. Delany;[1] and he spoke of her with such warmth—such kindness! "She was my friend!" he cried, "and I loved her as a friend! I have made a memorandum when I lost her—I will show it you."

He pulled out a pocketbook, and rummaged some time, but to no purpose. The tears stood in his eyes—he wiped them, and Dr. Willis again became very anxious. "Come, sir," he cried, "now do you come in and let the lady go on her walk,—come, now you have talked a long while,—so we'll go in,—if your majesty pleases."

"No, no!" he cried, "I want to ask her a few questions;—I have lived so long out of the world, I know nothing!"

This touched me to the heart.

* * *

What a scene! how variously was I affected by it! but, upon the whole, how inexpressibly thankful to see him so nearly himself—so little removed from recovery!

[A MASTECTOMY]

Paris, March 22, 1812[2]

Separated as I have now so long—long been from my dearest father—brothers—sisters—nieces, & native friends, I would spare, at least, their kind hearts any grief for me but what they must inevitably feel in reflecting upon the sorrow of such an absence to one so tenderly attached to all her first and forever so dear & regretted ties—nevertheless, if they should hear that I have been dangerously ill from any hand but my own, they might have doubts of

9. From childhood George III had been a devotee of George Frideric Handel (1685–1759), the great German-English composer. George III, who loved German music, took a keen interest in Charles Burney's pioneering work, *A General History of Music;* the third and fourth volumes were just about to be published.

1. Mary Delany, a kind old woman regarded by Burney as the "pattern of a perfect fine lady," had died the previous year.

2. Burney (now Madame d'Arblay) sent this letter to Esther Burney, her sister; it describes an operation performed the previous September.

my perfect recovery which my own alone can obviate. And how can I hope they will escape hearing what has reached Seville to the south, and Constantinople to the east? from both I have had messages—yet nothing could urge me to this communication till I heard that M. de Boinville had written it to his wife, without any precaution, because in ignorance of my plan of silence.[3] Still I must hope it may never travel to my dearest father—But to you, my beloved Esther, who, living more in the world, will surely hear it ere long, to you I will write the whole history, certain that, from the moment you know any evil has befallen me your kind kind heart will be constantly anxious to learn its extent, & its circumstances, as well as its termination.

About August, in the year 1810, I began to be annoyed by a small pain in my breast, which went on augmenting from week to week, yet, being rather heavy than acute, without causing me any uneasiness with respect to the consequences: Alas, *"what was the ignorance?"* The most sympathizing of partners, however, was more disturbed: not a start, not a wry face, not a movement that indicated pain was unobserved, & he early conceived apprehensions to which I was a stranger. He pressed me to see some surgeon; I revolted from the idea, & hoped, by care & warmth, to make all succor unnecessary. Thus passed some months, during which Madame de Maisonneuve, my particularly intimate friend, joined with M. d'Arblay to press me to consent to an examination. I thought their fears groundless, and could not make so great a conquest over my repugnance. I relate this false confidence, now, as a warning to my dear Esther—my sisters & nieces, should any similar sensations excite similar alarm. M. d'A. now revealed his uneasiness to another of our kind friends, Mme. de Tracy, who wrote to me a long & eloquent letter upon the subject, that began to awaken very unpleasant surmises; & a conference with her ensued, in which her urgency & representations, aided by her long experience of disease, & most miserable existence by art, subdued me, and, most painfully & reluctantly, I ceased to object, & M. d'A. summoned a physician—M. Bourdois? Maria will cry;—No, my dear Maria, I would not give your beau frere[4] that trouble; not him, but Dr. Jouart, the physician of Miss Potts. Thinking but slightly of my statement, he gave me some directions that produced no fruit—on the contrary, I grew worse, & M. d'A. now would take no denial to my consulting M. Dubois, who had already attended & cured me in an abscess of which Maria, my dearest Esther, can give you the history. M. Dubois, the most celebrated surgeon of France, was then appointed accoucheur to the empress, & already lodged in the Tuilleries,[5] & in constant attendance: but nothing could slacken the ardor of M. d'A. to obtain the first advice. Fortunately for his kind wishes, M. Dubois had retained a partial regard for me from the time of his former attendance, &, when applied to through a third person, he took the first moment of liberty, granted by a *promenade* taken by the empress, to come to me. It was now I began to perceive my real danger. M. Dubois gave me a prescription to be pursued for a month, during which time he could not undertake to see me again, & pronounced nothing—but uttered so many charges to me to be tranquil, & to suffer no uneasiness, that I could not but suspect there was room for terrible inquietude. My alarm was increased by the nonappearance of M. d'A. after his departure. They had

3. Because Chastel de Boinville's wife was English, it was likely that news of the illness would spread to the Burney family in England.
4. Brother-in-law. Maria (or Marianne), Esther Burney's daughter, had married Antoine Bourdois, whose brother was a prominent French physician.
5. The royal palace in Paris. "Accoucheur": obstetrician.

remained together some time in the book room, & M. d'A. did not return—till, unable to bear the suspense, I begged him to come back. He, also, sought then to tranquilize me—but in words only; his looks were shocking! his features, his whole face displayed the bitterest woe. I had not, therefore, much difficulty in telling myself what he endeavored not to tell me—that a small operation would be necessary to avert evil consequences!—Ah, my dearest Esther, for this I felt no courage—my dread & repugnance, from a thousand reasons *besides* the pain, almost shook all my faculties, &, for some time, I was rather confounded & stupified than affrighted.—Direful, however, was the effect of this interview; the pains became quicker & more violent, & the hardness of the spot affected increased. I took, but vainly, my prescription, & every symptom grew more serious.

* * *

A physician was now called in, Dr. Moreau, to hear if he could suggest any new means: but Dr. Larrey[6] had left him no resources untried. A formal consultation now was held, of Larrey, Ribe, & Moreau—&, in fine, I was formally condemned to an operation by all three. I was as much astonished as disappointed—for the poor breast was no where discolored, & not much larger than its healthy neighbor. Yet I felt the evil to be deep, so deep, that I often thought if it could not be dissolved, it could only with life be extirpated. I called up, however, all the reason I possessed, or could assume, & told them—that if they saw no other alternative, I would not resist their opinion & experience:—the good Dr. Larrey, who, during his long attendance had conceived for me the warmest friendship, had now tears in his eyes; from my dread he had expected resistance.

* * *

All hope of escaping this evil being now at an end, I could only console or employ my mind in considering how to render it less dreadful to M. d'A. M. Dubois had pronounced "il faut s'attendre à souffrir. Je ne veux pas vous trompez—Vous souffrirez—vous souffrirez *beaucoup*!—"[7] M. Ribe had *charged* me to cry! to withhold or restrain myself might have seriously bad consequences, he said. M. Moreau, in echoing this injunction, inquired whether I had cried or screamed at the birth of Alexander—Alas, I told him, it had not been possible to do otherwise; Oh then, he answered, there is no fear!—What terrible inferences were here to be drawn! I desired, therefore, that M. d'A. might be kept in ignorance of the day till the operation should be over. To this they agreed, except M. Larrey, with high approbation; M. Larrey looked dissentient, but was silent. M. Dubois protested he would not undertake to act, after what he had seen of the agitated spirits of M. d'A. if he were present; nor would he suffer me to know the time myself over night. I obtained with difficulty a promise of 4 hours warning, which were essential to me for sundry regulations.

From this time, I assumed the best spirits in my power, *to meet the coming blow;*—& support my too sympathizing partner.

* * *

6. Dominique-Jean Larrey, "Napoleon's surgeon," is still remembered for his courage on the battlefield and his innovative procedures.

7. You must expect to suffer. I do not want to deceive you—you will suffer—you will suffer *greatly* (French). Operations were then performed without anesthetics.

Sundry necessary works & orders filled up my time entirely till one o'clock. When all was ready——but Dr. Moreau then arrived, with news that M. Dubois could not attend till three. Dr. Aumont went away—& the coast was clear. This, indeed, was a dreadful interval. I had no longer any thing to do—I had only to think—TWO HOURS thus spent seemed never-ending. I would fain have written to my dearest father—to you, my Esther—to Charlotte, James, Charles—Amelia Lock—but my arm prohibited me. I strolled to the salon—I saw it fitted with preparations, & I recoiled—But I soon returned; to what effect disguise from myself what I must so soon know?—yet the sight of the immense quantity of bandages, compresses, sponges, lint——made me a little sick.—I walked backwards & forwards till I quieted all emotion, & became, by degrees, nearly stupid—torpid, without sentiment or consciousness;—& thus I remained till the clock struck three. A sudden spirit of exertion then returned—I defied my poor arm, no longer worth sparing, & took my long banished pen to write a few words to M. d'A.—& a few more for Alex, in case of a fatal result. These short billets I could only deposit safely, when the cabriolets[8]—one—two—three—four—succeeded rapidly to each other in stopping at the door. Dr. Moreau instantly entered my room, to see if I were alive. He gave me a wine cordial, & went to the salon. I rang for my maid & nurses—but before I could speak to them, my room, without previous message, was entered by 7 men in black, Dr. Larrey, M. Dubois, Dr. Moreau, Dr. Aumont, Dr. Ribe, & a pupil of Dr. Larrey, & another of M. Dubois. I was now awakened from my stupor—& by a sort of indignation—Why so many? & without leave?—But I could not utter a syllable. M. Dubois acted as commander in chief. Dr. Larrey kept out of sight; M. Dubois ordered a bedstead into the middle of the room. Astonished, I turned to Dr. Larrey, who had promised that an armchair would suffice; but he hung his head, & would not look at me. Two *old mattresses* M. Dubois then demanded, & an old sheet. I now began to tremble violently, more with distaste & horror of the preparations even than of the pain. These arranged to his liking, he desired me to mount the bedstead. I stood suspended, for a moment, whether I should not abruptly escape—I looked at the door, the windows—I felt desperate—but it was only for a moment, my reason then took the command, & my fears & feelings struggled vainly against it. I called to my maid—she was crying, & the two nurses stood, transfixed, at the door. "Let those women all go!" cried M. Dubois. This order recovered me my voice—"No," I cried, "let them stay! *qu'elles restent*!" This occasioned a little dispute, that re-animated me. The maid, however, & one of the nurses ran off—I charged the other to approach, & she obeyed. M. Dubois now tried to issue his commands *en militaire*,[9] but I resisted all that were resistible—I was compelled, however, to submit to taking off my long robe de chambre,[1] which I had meant to retain—Ah, then, how did I think of my sisters!—not one, at so dreadful an instant, at hand, to protect—adjust—guard me—I regretted that I had refused Mme de Maisonneuve–Mme Chastel—no one upon whom I could rely—my departed angel![2]—how did I think of her!—how did I long—long for my Esther—my Charlotte!—My distress was, I suppose, apparent, though not my wishes, for M. Dubois himself now softened, & spoke soothingly. "Can *you*," I cried, "feel for an

8. Carriages.
9. In military fashion. Most of the attending physicians had been army surgeons.
1. Dressing gown.
2. Susanna, Burney's favorite sister, had died in 1800.

operation that, to *you*, must seem so trivial?"—"Trivial?" he repeated—taking up a bit of paper, which he tore, unconsciously, into a million of pieces, "*oui—c'est peu de chose—mais*—"[3] he stammered, & could not go on. No one else attempted to speak, but I was softened myself, when I saw even M. Dubois grow agitated, while Dr. Larrey kept always aloof, yet a glance showed me he was pale as ashes. I knew not, positively, then, the immediate danger, but everything convinced me danger was hovering about me, & that this experiment could alone save me from its jaws. I mounted, therefore, unbidden, the bedstead—& M. Dubois placed me upon the mattress, & spread a cambric handkerchief upon my face. It was transparent, however, & I saw, through it, that the bedstead was instantly surrounded by the 7 men & my nurse. I refused to be held; but when, bright through the cambric, I saw the glitter of polished steel—I closed my eyes. I would not trust to convulsive fear the sight of the terrible incision. A silence the most profound ensued, which lasted for some minutes, during which, I imagine, they took their orders by signs, & made their examination—Oh what a horrible suspension!—I did not breathe—& M. Dubois tried vainly to find any pulse. This pause, at length, was broken by Dr. Larrey, who, in a voice of solemn melancholy, said "Qui me tiendra ce sein?—"[4]

No one answered; at least not verbally; but this aroused me from my passively submissive state, for I feared they imagined the whole breast infected—feared it too justly—for, again through the cambric, I saw the hand of M. Dubois held up, while his forefinger first described a straight line from top to bottom of the breast, secondly a cross, & thirdly a circle; intimating that the WHOLE was to be taken off. Excited by this idea, I started up, threw off my veil, &, in answer to the demand "Qui me tiendra ce sein?" cried "C'est moi, monsieur!"[5] & I held my hand under it, & explained the nature of my sufferings, which all sprang from one point, though they darted into every part. I was heard attentively, but in utter silence, & M. Dubois then re-placed me as before, &, as before, spread my veil over my face. How vain, alas, my representation! immediately again I saw the fatal finger describe the cross—& the circle. Hopeless, then, desperate, & self-given up, I closed once more my eyes, relinquishing all watching, all resistance, all interference, & sadly resolute to be wholly resigned.

My dearest Esther, & all my dears to whom she communicates this doleful ditty, will rejoice to hear that this resolution once taken, was firmly adhered to, in defiance of a terror that surpasses all description, & the most torturing pain. Yet—when the dreadful steel was plunged into the breast—cutting through veins—arteries—flesh—nerves—I needed no injunctions not to restrain my cries. I began a scream that lasted unintermittingly during the whole time of the incision—& I almost marvel that it rings not in my ears still! so excruciating was the agony. When the wound was made, & the instrument was withdrawn, the pain seemed undiminished, for the air that suddenly rushed into those delicate parts felt like a mass of minute but sharp & forked poniards,[6] that were tearing the edges of the wound—but when again I felt the instrument—describing a curve—cutting against the grain, if I may so say, while the flesh resisted in a manner so forcible as to oppose & tire the hand of the operator, who was forced to change from the right to the left—then,

3. Yes—it is not much—but—(French).
4. Who will hold this breast for me? (French).
5. *I* will! (French).
6. Daggers.

indeed, I thought I must have expired. I attempted no more to open my eyes,—they felt as if hermetically shut, & so firmly closed, that the eyelids seemed indented into the cheeks. The instrument this second time withdrawn, I concluded the operation over. Oh no! presently the terrible cutting was renewed—& worse than ever, to separate the bottom, the foundation of this dreadful gland from the parts to which it adhered. Again all description would be baffled—yet again all was not over.—Dr. Larrey rested but his own hand, &—Oh heaven!—I then felt the knife rackling[7] against the breast bone—scraping it!—This performed, while I yet remained in utterly speechless torture, I heard the voice of Mr. Larrey (all others guarded a dead silence) in a tone nearly tragic, desire every one present to pronounce if any thing more remained to be done. The general voice was Yes—but the finger of Mr. Dubois—which I literally *felt* elevated over the wound, though I saw nothing, & though he touched nothing, so indescribably sensitive was the spot—pointed to some further requisition[8]—& again began the scraping!—and, after this, Dr. Moreau thought he discerned a peccant atom—and still, & still, M. Dubois demanded atom after atom. My dearest Esther, not for days, not for weeks, but for months I could not speak of this terrible business without nearly again going through it! I could not *think* of it with impunity! I was sick, I was disordered by a single question—even now, 9 months after it is over, I have a headache from going on with the account! & this miserable account, which I began 3 months ago, at least, I dare not revise, nor read, the recollection is still so painful.

To conclude, the evil was so profound, the case so delicate, & the precautions necessary for preventing a return so numerous, that the operation, including the treatment & the dressing, lasted 20 minutes! a time, for sufferings so acute, that was hardly supportable. However, I bore it with all the courage I could exert, & never moved, nor stopped them, nor resisted, nor remonstrated, nor spoke—except once or twice, during the dressings, to say "Ah Messieurs! que je vous plains!—"[9] for indeed I was sensible to the feeling concern with which they all saw what I endured, though my speech was principally—*very* principally meant for Dr. Larrey. Except this, I uttered not a syllable, save, when so often they recommenced, calling out "Avertissez moi,[1] Messieurs! avertissez moi!—" Twice, I believe, I fainted; at least, I have two total chasms in my memory of this transaction, that impede my tying together what passed. When all was done, & they lifted me up that I might be put to bed, my strength was so totally annihilated, that I was obliged to be carried, & could not even sustain my hands & arms, which hung as if I had been lifeless; while my face, as the nurse has told me, was utterly colorless. This removal made me open my eyes—& I then saw my good Dr. Larrey, pale nearly as myself, his face streaked with blood, & its expression depicting grief, apprehension, & almost horror.

When I was in bed, my poor M. d'Arblay—who ought to write you himself his own history of this morning—was called to me—& afterwards our Alex.—

[M. D'ARBLAY'S POSTSCRIPT]

No! No my dearest & ever more dear friends, I shall not make a fruitless attempt. No language could convey what I felt in the deadly course of these

7. Raking (?).
8. Necessity. Surgical practice of the time dictated that "the whole diseased structure" be cut out, no matter how long or painful the operation.
9. How I pity you! (French).
1. Give me warning! (French).

seven hours. Nevertheless, every one *of you, my dearest dearest friends*, can guess, must even know it. Alexander had no less feeling, but showed more fortitude. He, perhaps, will be more able to describe to you, nearly at least, the torturing state of my poor heart & soul. Besides, I must own, to you, that these details which were, till just now, quite unknown to me, have almost killed me, & I am only able to thank God that this more than half angel has had the sublime courage to deny herself the comfort I might have offered her, to spare me, not the sharing of her excruciating pains, that was impossible, but the witnessing so terrific a scene, & perhaps the remorse to have rendered it more tragic. For I don't flatter myself I could have got through it—I must confess it.

Thank heaven! She is now surprisingly well, & in good spirits, & we hope to have many many still happy days. May that of peace soon arrive, and enable me to embrace better than with my pen my beloved & ever ever more dear friends of the town & country. Amen. Amen![2]

2. The wound healed without infection. Burney returned to England later in 1812 and lived for twenty-eight years.

Poems in Process

Poets have often claimed that their poems were not willed but were inspired, whether by a muse or by divine visitation, or that they emerged full-blown from the poet's unconscious mind. But working manuscripts tell another story, suggesting that, however involuntary the origin of a poem, vision was usually followed by revision, by second thoughts that refined and clarified an original intention or added something new. And revision can be a social as well as a private drama. As noted in section D ("Publishing History, Censorship") of this anthology's "Literary Terminology" glossary, many people participate in the labor that takes texts from the forms in which authors produce them to the forms in which they are presented to readers. In a similar if more limited way, revision, too, as a part of literary history, involves a range of collaborators, both institutional and personal, witting and unwitting: the copyists who recopy drafts so as to prepare fair copies for the printer and who advance suggestions of their own, the advisors who act as sounding boards, and, by the eighteenth century particularly, the critics whose responses the poet anticipates while revising in the hope of preempting them.

Though poets of all periods have revised their work, evidence of this aspect of their labor is sparse until the nineteenth century. It may be that in earlier times, the drafts and proof sheets that recorded revisions were valued only so long as they were useful (to the person preparing the fair copy or the printer setting the text). This emphasis on utility meant that these materials were often discarded once they had served their purpose. (The seventeenth-century term for working drafts, which we still use—"foul papers"—expresses this attitude.) Fascination with anything the author wrote by hand is a distinctly modern phenomenon, a characteristic of an era in which literature has come to be defined by the uniformity of machine-printed books.

Before the introduction of printing into England in 1476, writing was reproduced by hand, in manuscript (literally "written by hand"). Even after printing was introduced, however, certain forms of writing continued to circulate in manuscript. In a manuscript culture, revision was a complicated matter not always instigated or sanctioned by the individuals we would think of as authors. In certain respects, writers and readers were, for many centuries, able, as we are not, to think of all poems as works in process. Thus poets might be at the mercy of scribes who could mistranscribe their work. Chaucer, for example, jokingly promises to curse his scribe Adam unless he should "write truly according to my composition" ("To His Scribe Adam"). Or individuals transcribing poetry into their commonplace books (personalized anthologies) would readily write it down with changes and in so doing blur the lines between authoring and transcribing: sometimes these transcriptions are the only manuscript evidence that has survived.

Milton is the first major English author for whom we possess drafts of poems definitely written in his own hand. The excerpt below from his manuscript of "Lycidas" shows the extent to which he worked over and expanded his initial attempts. It is no surprise to find Pope, one of the most meticulous of craftsmen, working and reworking his drafts, and radically enlarging *The Rape of the Lock* even after the success of its first printed version. But the manuscript of Samuel Johnson's greatest poem, "The Vanity of Human Wishes," discovered in the 1940s, is a surprise, for it shows that this writer who, in his critical theory, regarded poetry as primarily an art of achieving preconceived ends by tested means in fact composed with even greater speed and assurance than the Romantic Byron, who liked to represent himself to his readers as dashing off his verses with unreflecting ease. In the manuscript of Gray's "Elegy Written in a Country Churchyard" we find that the poet, by late afterthought, converted a relatively simple elegiac meditation into a longer and much more complex apologia for his chosen way of life.

Our transcriptions from the poets' drafts attempt to reproduce, as accurately as the change from script to print will allow, the appearance of the manuscript page. A poet's first attempt at a line or phrase is reproduced in larger type, the revisions in smaller type. The line numbers used to identify an excerpt are those of the final form of the complete poem as reprinted in this anthology. The marginal numbers beside the extract from "The Vanity of Human Wishes" are Johnson's own additions.

SELECTED BIBLIOGRAPHY

Autograph Poetry in the English Language, 2 vols., 1973, compiled by P. J. Croft, reproduces and transcribes one or more pages of manuscript in the poet's own hand, from the fourteenth century to the present time. Books that discuss the process of poetic composition and revision, with examples from manuscripts and printed versions, are Charles D. Abbott, ed., *Poets at Work*, 1948; Phyllis Bartlett, *Poems in Process*, 1951; A. F. Scott, *The Poet's Craft*, 1957; George Bornstein, *Poetic Remaking: The Art of Browning, Yeats, and Pound*, 1988; and Robert Brinkley and Keith Hanley, eds., *Romantic Revisions*, 1992. In *Word for Word: A Study of Authors' Alterations*, 1965, Wallace Hildick analyzes the composition of prose fiction, as well as poems.

Documents that record a poet's work in progress do not, unfortunately, survive from before the sixteenth century. If you would like to see what Old English poetry looks like on the manuscript page, see, for example, *The Nowell Codex*, edited by Kemp Malone, 1963, which includes facsimiles of both *Beowulf* and *Judith*. You might also consult the Electronic Beowulf Web site: uky.edu/~kiernan/eBeowulf/guide.htm. For images of English literary manuscripts from the later medieval period, some written in the poet's own hand, see Anthony G. Petti, *English Literary Hands from Chaucer to Dryden*, 1977. Some pages of the Ellesmere manuscript of Chaucer's *Canterbury Tales* are available at huntington.org/LibraryDiv/ChaucerPict.html. For the survival of certain forms of literary manuscript culture beyond the introduction of print, see Arthur Marotti, *Manuscript, Print, and the English Renaissance Lyric*, 1995.

JOHN MILTON

From Lycidas[1]

[*Lines 1–14*][2]

yet once more O ye laurells and once more
ye myrtl's browne wth Ivie never sere
I come to pluck yor berries harsh and crude
~~before the mellowing yeare~~ and wth forc't fingers rude
~~and crop yor young~~ shatter yor leaves before ye mellowing yeare
bitter constraint, and sad occasion deare

compells me to disturbe yor season due
for ~~young~~ Lycidas is dead, dead ere his prime
young Lycidas and hath not left his peere
not
who would ^ sing for Lycidas he well knew
himselfe to sing & build the loftie rime
he must not flote upon his watrie beare
unwept, and welter to the parching wind
without the meed of some melodious teare

[*Lines* 56–63]

ay mee I fondly dreame
~~had yee~~ bin there, ~~for~~ what could that have don?
~~what could the golden hayrd Calliope~~
for her inchaunting son
~~when shee beheld (the gods farre sighted bee)~~
~~his goarie scalpe rowle downe the Thracian lee~~

* whome universal nature
might lament
~~and heaven and hel deplore~~
~~when his divine head downe~~
the streame was sent
downe the Swift Hebrus to
the Lesbian shore.

[THE THIRD AND FOLLOWING LINES ARE REWRITTEN ON A SEPARATE PAGE]

*what could the muse her selfe that Orpheus bore
muse her selfe for her inchanting son
~~for her inchanting son~~
did
whome universal nature ~~might~~ lament
when by the rout that made the hideous roare
gorie
*goarie his ~~divine~~ visage down the streame was sent
downe the swift Hebrus to ye Lesbian shoare.

1. Transcribed from a manuscript of fifty pages in the library of Trinity College, Cambridge. Among the poems written in Milton's own hand are "Lycidas," *Comus,* seven sonnets, and several other short poems. The manuscript has been photographically reproduced, with printed transcriptions, by W. Aldis Wright, *Facsimile of the Manuscript of Milton's Minor Poems* (1899).
2. This draft is written on a separate page of the manuscript, which also contains drafts of the passages, "What could the muse her selfe" and "Bring the rathe primrose," transcribed below.

[*Lines 132–53*]

Returne Alpheus the dred voice is past
that shrunk thy streams, returne Sicilian Muse
and call the vales and bid them hither cast
thire bells, and flowrets of a thousand hues
yee vallies low where the mild wispers use
of shades, and wanton winds, and g~~o~~[u]shing brooks ✱ ✱
on whose fresh lap the swart starre ✱sparely looks ~~faintly~~ sparely
✱ ~~bring~~ hither all yor quaint enamel'd eyes ✱ throw
that on the greene terfe suck the honied showrs
and purple all the ground wth vernal flowrs
Bring the rathe &c.[3]
to strew the laureat herse where Lycid' lies
for so to interpose a little ease
let our ✱ ~~sad~~ fraile thoughts dally wth false surmise ✱ fraile

[LINES 142–50 ARE DRAFTED ON A SEPARATE PAGE, AS FOLLOWS]

Bring the rathe primrose that unwedded dies
~~collu~~ colouring the pale cheeke of uninjoyd love
and that sad floure that strove
to write his owne woes on the vermeil graine
next adde Narcissus y^{t} still weeps in vaine
the woodbine and ye pancie freak't wth jet
the glowing violet
the cowslip wan that hangs his pensive head
and every bud that sorrows liverie weares
let Daffadillies fill thire cups ^with teares
bid Amaranthus all his beautie shed
to strew the laureat herse &c.

Bring the rathe primrose that forsaken dies
the tufted crowtoe and pale Gessamin
the white pinke, and ^ye pansie freakt wth jet
the glowing violet
the muske rose and ~~the garish columbine~~ the well-attired woodbine
wth cowslips wan that hang the pensive head
and every flower that sad ✱ escutcheon ~~beares~~ weare ✱ imbroidrie ~~beares~~ weares

2 ^& ~~let~~ daffadillies fill thire cups wth teares
1 bid Amaranthus all his beauties shed
to strew &c.

3. I.e., Milton plans to insert here the passage that follows, lines 142–50.

ALEXANDER POPE

From The Rape of the Lock[1]

[*1712 Version: Canto 1, Lines 1–24*]

WHAT dire Offence from Am'rous Causes springs,
What mighty Quarrels rise from Trivial Things,
I sing—This Verse to *C—l,* Muse! is due;
This, ev'n *Belinda* may vouchsafe to view:
Slight is the Subject, but not so the Praise,
If she inspire, and He approve my Lays.
Say what strange Motive, Goddess! cou'd compel
A well-bred *Lord* t'assault a gentle *Belle?*
Oh say what stranger Cause, yet unexplor'd,
Cou'd make a gentle *Belle* reject a *Lord?*
And dwells such Rage in *softest Bosoms* then?
And lodge such daring Souls in *Little Men?*
Sol thro' white Curtains did his Beams display,
And op'd those Eyes which brighter shine than they;
Shock just had giv'n himself the rowzing Shake,
And Nymphs prepar'd their *Chocolate* to take;
Thrice the wrought Slipper knock'd against the Ground,
And striking Watches the tenth Hour resound.
Belinda rose, and 'midst attending Dames
Launch'd on the Bosom of the silver *Thames:*
A Train of well-drest Youths around her shone,
And ev'ry Eye was fix'd on her alone;
On her white Breast a sparking *Cross* she wore,
Which *Jews* might kiss, and Infidels adore.

[*Revised Version: Canto 1, Lines 1–22*]

WHAT dire Offence from am'rous Causes springs,
What mighty Contests rise from trivial Things,
I sing—This Verse to *Caryll,* Muse! is due;
This, ev'n *Belinda* may vouchsafe to view:
Slight is the Subject, but not so the Praise,
If She inspire, and He approve my Lays.
Say what strange Motive, Goddess! cou'd compel
A well-bred *Lord* t'assault a gentle *Belle?*
Oh say what stranger Cause, yet unexplor'd,
Cou'd make a gentle *Belle* reject a *Lord?*

1. The first version of *The Rape of the Lock,* published in 1712, consisted of two cantos and a total of 334 lines. Two years later, in 1714, Pope published an enlarged version of five cantos and 794 lines, in which he added the supernatural "machinery" of the Sylphs and Gnomes as well as a number of mock-epic episodes. The excerpts reprinted here show how Pope revised and expanded passages that he retained from the first version of the poem. The revised version includes changes that Pope added in later editions of the enlarged text of 1714.

In Tasks so bold, can Little Men engage,
And in soft Bosoms dwells such mighty Rage?
Sol thro' white Curtains shot a tim'rous Ray,
And op'd those Eyes that must eclipse the Day;
Now Lapdogs give themselves the rowzing Shake,
And sleepless Lovers, just at Twelve, awake:
Thrice rung the Bell, the Slipper knock'd the Ground,
And the press'd Watch return'd a silver Sound.
Belinda still her downy Pillow prest,
Her Guardian *Sylph* prolong'd the balmy Rest.
'Twas he had summon'd to her silent Bed
The Morning-Dream that hover'd o'er her Head.

[*Revised Version: Canto 2, Lines 1–8*]

Not with more Glories, in th' Etherial Plain,
The Sun first rises o'er the purpled Main,
Than issuing forth, the Rival of his Beams
Launch'd on the Bosom of the Silver *Thames*.
Fair Nymphs, and well-drest Youths around her shone,
But ev'ry Eye was fix'd on her alone.
On her white Breast a sparkling *Cross* she wore,
Which *Jews* might kiss, and Infidels adore.

From An Essay on Man[1]

[*From the First Manuscript*]

we ourselves
1. Learn ~~then thyself,~~ not God presume to scan,
But
~~And~~ know, the Study of Mankind is Man.
Plac'd on this Isthmus of a Middle State,
A Being darkly wise, & rudely great.
With too much knowledge for the Sceptic side,
And too much Weakness for a Stoic's Pride,
He hangs between, uncertain where to rest;
Whether to deem himself a God or Beast;
Whether his Mind or Body to prefer,
Born but to die, & reas'ning but to err;
his
Alike in Ignorance, (~~that~~ Reason such)
~~Who~~ ~~who thinks~~
Whether he thinks too little or too much:
Chaos of Thought & Passion, all confus'd,
Still by himself abus'd & dis-abus'd:

1. Two of Pope's holograph manuscripts of *An Essay on Man* have survived. The earlier one is at the Pierpont Morgan Library in New York. The second one, at the Houghton Library, Harvard, was evidently intended as a fair copy for printing; but Pope, who was an inveterate reviser, introduced some last-minute changes. The passage transcribed here from each of these manuscripts is Pope's famed description of man's "middle state" in the great chain of being; in the published version, it opens Epistle 2, lines 1–18.

Created half to rise, & half to fall;
Great Lord of all things, yet a prey to all;
Sole Judge of Truth, in endless Error hurl'd;
The Glory, Jest, and Riddle of the World.

[*From the Second Manuscript*][2]

~~Incipit I~~ Know
~~Incipit III~~ ~~Learn~~ we ourselves, not God presume to scan,
The only Science Convinc'd,
~~But know~~, the Study of Mankind is Man;
(Plac'd on this Isthmus of a Middle State,
A Being darkly wise, and rudely great;
With too much Knowledge for the Sceptic side,
With
~~And~~ too much Weakness for a Stoic's Pride,
in doubt to act or
He hangs between, ~~uncertain where to~~ rest,
Part of
Whether ~~to~~ deem himself a ^ God or Beast;
In doubt
Whether his Mind, or Body to prefer.
~~This born~~ ~~that~~
Born but to die, and reas'ning but to err;
Alike in Ignorance, his Reason such,
Whether he thinks or too much.
~~Who thinks~~ too little, ~~or who thinks too much:~~
Chaos of Thought and Passion, all confus'd,
Still by himself abus'd and dis-abus'd:
Created half to rise, and half to fall;
Great Lord of all things, yet a prey to all;
Sole Judge of Truth, in endless error hurl'd;
The Glory, Jest, and Riddle of the World!

2. In this version of the manuscript, Pope inserted some marginal glosses. In the right-hand margin (next to the line beginning "Learn we ourselves"), he wrote, "Of Man, as an Individual," while next to the line beginning "Plac'd on this Isthmus," he wrote, "His Middle Nature." And in the left-hand margin, a little below the line beginning "With too much knowledge," he wrote, "His Powers, and Imperfections."

SAMUEL JOHNSON

Johnson told Boswell in 1766 that when composing verses "I have generally had them in my mind, perhaps fifty at a time, walking up and down in my room; and then I have written them down, and often, from laziness, have written only half lines. . . . I remember I wrote a hundred lines of 'The Vanity of Human Wishes' in a day." When the first manuscript draft of this poem turned up in the 1940s among Boswell's papers at Malahide Castle, it supported Johnson's account, for it had been written and corrected in haste, with only sparse punctuation; also the second half of each line had been filled out, obviously from memory, at some time after the writing of the first half, in a darker ink. In the transcriptions from this manuscript (which is in the collection of Mary Hyde, Somerville, New Jersey), the half-lines and emendations that Johnson added to his initial draft are printed in boldface type.

The draft was written on the right-hand pages of a small homemade pocket book;

some words in the added half-line, impinging on the right margin of the page, had to be completed above or below the line. The two added lines, "See Nations slowly wise . . . / . . . the tardy Bust," were written on the blank left-hand page, at the place where they were to be inserted. The numeration of every tenth line was added by Johnson in the manuscript and incorporates these two lines.

Johnson published the poem in 1749 and revised it for a second publication in 1755, when it achieved the final form printed in the selections from Johnson, above. It was in 1755 that Johnson introduced his most famous emendation, when, after his disillusionment with Lord Chesterfield as literary patron, he substituted in line 162 the word "patron" for "garret": "Toil, envy, want, the patron, and the jail."

From The Vanity of Human Wishes

[*Lines 135–64*]

e
When first the College Rolls **receive his nam**
The young Enthusiast **quits his ease for fame**
Quick fires his breast
~~Each act betrays~~ **the fever of renown**
Caught from **the strong Contagion of the Gown**
On Isis banks he waves, **from noise withdrawn**
In sober state **th' imaginary Lawn**
O'er Bodley's Dome **his future Labours spread**
And Bacon's Mansion **trembles o'er his head.**
Are these thy views, **proceed illustrious Youth**
And Virtue guard **thee to the throne of Truth**
Yet should th~~y fate~~ **Soul indulge the gen'rous**
Heat
Till Captive Science **yields her last Retreat**
Should Reason **guide thee with her brightest Ray**
And pour on misty Doubt **resistless day**
Should no false kindness **lure to loose delight**
Nor Praise relax, nor **difficulty fright**
Should tempting Novelty **thy cell refrain**
vain
And Sloth's bland opiates **shed their fumes in**
sShould Beuty blunt **on fops her fatal dart**
Nor claim the **triumph of a letter'd heart**
~~S Nor~~ Should no Disease **thy torpid veins invade**
Nor Melancholys Spectres **haunt thy Shade**
hope
Yet ~~dream~~ not Life **from Grief or Danger free,**
Nor think the doom of **Man revers'd for thee**
Deign passing **to**
~~Turn~~ on the^world ~~awhile~~ **turn thine eyes**
And pause **awhile from Learning to be wise**
There mark what **ill the Scholar's life assail**
See Nations slowly wise, and meanly just,
To buried merit raise the tardy Bust.
the
Toil envy Want ~~a~~ **Garret and the Jayl**
Dreams
If ~~Hope~~ yet flatter **once again attend**
Hear Lydiats life **and Galileo's End.**

THOMAS GRAY

There are three manuscript versions of the "Elegy" in Gray's handwriting. The one reproduced here in part is the earliest of these, preserved at Eton College, England; Gray entitled it "Stanzas wrote in a Country Church-Yard."

It is evident that Gray originally intended to conclude his poem at the end of the fifth stanza transcribed below. At some later time he bracketed off the last four stanzas, introduced a transitional stanza that incorporated the last two lines of the original conclusion, and then went on to write a new and much enlarged conclusion to the poem, which includes the closing "Epitaph." A comparison with the final version of the "Elegy," above, will show that the author deleted some of these added stanzas, and also made a number of verbal changes, in his published texts of the poem.

From Elegy Written in a Country Churchyard

[*Lines 69–128*]

The struggleings Pangs of conscious Truth to hide,
To quench the Blushes of ingenuous Shame,
crown
And at the Shrine of Luxury & Pride
With by
~~Burn~~ Incense hallowd in the Muse's Flame.
kindled at

The thoughtless World to Majesty may bow
Exalt the brave, & idolize Success
But more to Innocence their Safety owe
Than Power & Genius e'er conspired to bless

And thou, who mindful of the unhonour'd Dead
eir
Dost in these notes thy artless Tale relate
By Night & lonely Contemplation led
To linger in the gloomy Walks of Fate

Hark how the sacred Calm, that broods around
Bids ev'ry fierce tumultuous Passion cease
In still small Accents whisp'ring from the Ground
A grateful Earnest of eternal Peace

No more with Reason & thyself at Strife
Give anxious Cares & endless Wishes room
But thro' the cool sequester'd Vale of Life
Pursue the silent Tenour of thy Doom.

Far from the madding Crowd's ignoble Strife;
Their sober Wishes never knew to stray:
Along the cool sequester'd Vale of Life
noiseless
They kept the silent Tenour of their Way.

Yet even these Bones from Insult to protect
Some frail Memorial still erected nigh

With
~~In~~ uncouth Rhime, & shapeless Sculpture deckt
Implores the passing Tribute of a Sigh.

Their Name, their Years, spelt by th' unletter'd Muse
The Place of Fame, & Epitaph supply,
And many a holy Text around she strews
That teach the rustic Moralist to die.

For who to dumb Forgetfulness a Prey
This pleasing anxious Being e'er resign'd;
Left the warm Precincts of the chearful Day,
Nor cast one longing lingring Look behind?

On some fond Breast the parting Soul relies,
Some pious Drops the closing Eye requires:
Even from the Tomb the Voice of Nature cries,
And buried Ashes glow with social Fires
  For Thee, who mindful &c: as above.[1]

If chance that e'er some pensive Spirit more,
By sympathetic Musings here delay'd,
With vain, tho' kind, Enquiry shall explore
Thy once-loved Haunt, this long-deserted Shade.

Haply some hoary-headed Swain shall say,[2]
Oft have we seen him at the Peep of Dawn
With hasty Footsteps brush the Dews away
On the high Brow of yonder hanging Lawn
Him have we seen the Green-wood Side along,
While o'er the Heath we hied, our Labours done,
Oft as the Woodlark piped her farewell Song
With whistful Eyes pursue the setting Sun.

spreading nodding
Oft at the Foot of yonder hoary Beech
That wreathes its old fantastic Roots so high
His listless Length at Noontide would he stretch,
And pore upon the Brook that babbles by.
  With Gestures quaint now smileing as in Scorn,
  wayward fancies ~~loved~~ would he
  Mutt'ring his fond Conceits he ~~wont to~~ rove:
  drooping,
  Now woeful wan, ~~he droop'd,~~ as one forlorn
  Or crazed with Care, or cross'd in hopeless Love.
    One Morn we miss'd him on th' accustom'd Hill,
    Along the near
    By the Heath-~~side;~~ & at his fav'rite Tree.
    Another came, nor yet beside the Rill,
    by
    Nor up the Lawn, nor at the Wood was he.
  ~~There scatter'd oft, the earliest~~
    The next with Dirges meet in sad Array

1. I.e., Gray indicates that the second bracketed stanza, above, is to be inserted here, except that the opening "And thou" is to be altered to "For Thee."
2. At this point in the manuscript Gray ceases to leave a space between the stanzas. The first edition of 1751, at Gray's request, was printed without such spaces. They were, however, inserted in later editions printed during Gray's lifetime.

by
Slow thro the Church-way Path we saw him born
Approach & read, for thou can't read the Lay
Graved carved yon
Wrote on the Stone beneath that ancient Thorn

Year
There scatter'd oft the earliest of y^{e} ~~Spring~~
showers of
By Hands unseen are frequent Vi'lets found
Redbreast
The Robin loves to build & warble there,
And little Footsteps lightly print the Ground.

Here rests his Head upon the Lap of Earth[3]
A Youth to Fortune & to Fame unknown
Fair Science frown'd not on his humble Birth
And Melancholy mark'd him for her own

Large was his Bounty & his Heart sincere;
Heaven did a Recompence as largely send.
He gave to Mis'ry all he had, a Tear.
He gain'd from Heav'n, 'twas all he wish'd, a Friend

No farther seek his Merits to disclose,
think
Nor seek to draw them from their dread Abode
(His Frailties there in trembling Hope repose)
The Bosom of his Father & his God.

3. These last three stanzas (which Gray in the first edition of 1751 labeled "The Epitaph") are written in the right-hand margin, with the page turned crosswise.

Selected Bibliographies

The Selected Bibliographies consist of a list of Suggested General Readings on English literature, followed by bibliographies for each of the literary periods in this volume. For ease of reference, the authors within each period are arranged in alphabetical order.

SUGGESTED GENERAL READINGS

Histories of England and of English Literature

New research and new perspectives have made even the most distinguished of the comprehensive general histories written in past generations seem outmoded. Innovative research in social, cultural, and political history has made it difficult to write a single coherent account of England from the Middle Ages to the present, let alone to accommodate in a unified narrative the complex histories of Scotland, Ireland, Wales, and the other nations where writing in English has flourished. Readers who wish to explore the historical matrix out of which the works of literature collected in this anthology emerged are advised to consult the studies of particular periods listed in the appropriate sections of this bibliography. The multivolume *Oxford History of England* and *New Oxford History of England* are useful, as are the three-volume *Peoples of the British Isles: A New History*, ed. Stanford Lehmberg, 1992, the nine-volume *Cambridge Cultural History of Britain*, ed. Boris Ford, 1992, and the multivolume *Penguin History of Britain*, gen. ed. David Cannadine, 1996–. Given the cultural centrality of London, readers may find *The London Encyclopaedia*, ed. Ben Weinreb and Christopher Hibbert, 1986, and Roy Porter's *London: A Social History*, 1994, valuable.

Similar observations may be made about literary history. In the light of such initiatives as women's studies, new historicism, and postcolonialism, the range of authors deemed most significant has expanded in recent years, along with the geographical and conceptual boundaries of literature in English. Attempts to capture in a unified account the great sweep of literature from *Beowulf* to late last night have largely given way to studies of individual genres, carefully delimited time periods, and specific authors. For these more focused accounts, see the listings by period. Among the large-scale literary surveys, *The Cambridge Guide to Literature in English*, 1993, is useful, as is the seven-volume *Penguin History of Literature*, 1993–94. *The Feminist Companion to Literature in English*, ed. Virginia Blain, Isobel Grundy, and Patricia Clements, 1990, is an important resource, and the editorial materials in *The Norton Anthology of Literature by Women*, 2nd ed., 1996, ed. Sandra M. Gilbert and Susan Gubar, constitute a concise history and set of biographies of women authors since the Middle Ages. *Annals of English Literature, 1475–1950*, rev. 1961, lists important publications year by year, together with the significant literary events for each year. Four volumes have been published in the *Oxford English Literary History*, gen. ed. Jonathan Bate, 2002–: James Simpson, *Reform and Cultural Revolution, 1350–1547*; Philip Davis, *The Victorians, 1830–1880*; Randall Stevenson, *The Last of England? 1960–2000*; and Bruce King, *The Internationalization of English Literature, 1948–2000*. See also *The Cambridge History of Medieval English Literature*, ed. David Wallace, 1999, and *The Cambridge History of Early Modern English Literature*, ed. David Loewenstein and Janel Mueller, 2002.

Helpful treatments and surveys of English meter, rhyme, and stanza forms are Paul Fussell Jr., *Poetic Meter and Poetic Form*, rev. 1979; Donald Wesling, *The Chances of Rhyme: Device and Modernity*, 1980; Derek Attridge, *The Rhythms of English Poetry*, 1982; Charles O. Hartman, *Free Verse: An Essay in Prosody*, 1983; John Hollander, *Vision and Resonance: Two Senses of Poetic Form*, rev. 1985; and Robert Pinsky, *The Sounds of Poetry: A Brief Guide*, 1998.

On the development of the novel as a form, see Ian Watt, *The Rise of the Novel*, 1957; *The*

Columbia History of the British Novel, ed. John Richetti, 1994; Margaret Doody, *The True Story of the Novel*, 1996; *Theory of the Novel: A Historical Approach*, ed. Michael McKeon, 2000; and McKeon, *The Origins of the English Novel, 1600–1740*, 15th anniversary ed., 2002. On women novelists and readers, see Nancy Armstrong, *Desire and Domestic Fiction: A Political History of the Novel*, 1987; and Catherine Gallagher, *Nobody's Story: The Vanishing Acts of Women Writers in the Marketplace, 1670–1820*, 1994.

On the history of playhouse design, see Richard Leacroft, *The Development of the English Playhouse: An Illustrated Survey of Theatre Building in England from Medieval to Modern Times*, 1988. For a survey of the plays that have appeared on these and other stages, see Allardyce Nicoll, *British Drama*, rev. 1962, the eight-volume *Revels History of Drama in English*, gen. eds. Clifford Leech and T. W. Craik, 1975–83; and Alfred Harbage, *Annals of English Drama, 975–1700*, 3rd ed., 1989, rev. S. Schoenbaum and Sylvia Wagonheim.

On some of the key intellectual currents that are at once reflected in and shaped by literature, Arthur O. Lovejoy's classic studies *The Great Chain of Being*, 1936, and *Essays in the History of Ideas*, 1948, remain valuable, along with such works as Lovejoy and George Boas, *Primitivism and Related Ideas in Antiquity*, 1935; Ernst Kantorowicz, *The King's Two Bodies: A Study in Medieval Political Theology*, 1957, new ed. 1997; Richard Popkin, *The History of Skepticism from Erasmus to Descartes*, 1960; M. H. Abrams, *Natural Supernaturalism: Tradition and Revolution in Romantic Literature*, 1971; Michel Foucault, *Madness and Civilization: A History of Insanity in the Age of Reason*, Eng. trans. 1965, *The Order of Things: An Archaeology of the Human Sciences*, Eng. trans. 1970; Mikhail Bakhtin, *Rabelais and his World*, Eng. trans. 1968, and *The Dialogic Imagination*, Eng. trans. 1981; Roland Barthes, *The Pleasure of the Text*, Eng. trans. 1975; Jacques Derrida, *Of Grammatology*, Eng. trans. 1976, and *Dissemination*, Eng. trans. 1981; Raymond Williams, *Keywords: A Vocabulary of Culture and Society*, rev. 1983; Pierre Bourdieu, *Distinction: A Social Critique of the Judgment of Taste*, Eng. trans. 1984; Michel de Certeau, *The Practice of Everyday Life*, Eng. trans. 1984; and Sigmund Freud, *Writings on Art and Literature*, ed. Neil Hertz, 1997.

Reference Works

The single most important tool for the study of literature in English is the *Oxford English Dictionary*, 2nd ed., 1989, also available on CD-ROM, and online to subscribers. The *OED* is written on historical principles: that is, it attempts not only to describe current word use but also to record the history and development of the language from its origins before the Norman conquest to the present. It thus provides, for familiar as well as archaic and obscure words, the widest possible range of meanings and uses, organized chronologically and illustrated with quotations. Beyond the *OED* there are many other valuable dictionaries, such as *The American Heritage Dictionary*, *The Oxford Dictionary of Etymology*, and an array of reference works from *The Cambridge Encyclopedia of the English Language*, ed. David Crystal, 1995, to guides to specialized vocabularies, slang, regional dialects, and the like.

There is a steady flow of new editions of most major and many minor writers in English, along with a ceaseless outpouring of critical appraisals and scholarship. The *MLA International Bibliography* (also online) is the best way to keep abreast of the most recent work and to conduct bibliographic searches. *The New Cambridge Bibliography of English Literature*, ed. George Watson, 1969–77, updated shorter ed. 1981, is a valuable guide to the huge body of earlier literary criticism and scholarship. *A Guide to English and American Literature*, ed. F. W. Bateson and Harrison Meserole, rev. 1976, is a selected list of editions, as well as scholarly and critical treatments. Further bibliographical aids are described in Arthur G. Kennedy, *A Concise Bibliography for Students of English*, rev. 1972; Richard D. Altick and Andrew Wright, *Selective Bibliography for the Study of English and American Literature*, rev. 1979, and James L. Harner, *Literary Research Guide*, rev. 1998.

For compact biographies of English authors, see the multivolume *Oxford Dictionary of National Biography*, ed. H. C. G. Matthew and Brian Harrison, 2004; condensed biographies will be found in the *Concise Dictionary of National Biography*, 2 parts (1920, 1988). Handy reference books of authors, works, and various literary terms and allusions are *The Oxford Companion to the Theatre*, Phyllis Hartnoll, rev. 1990; *Princeton Encyclopedia of Poetry and Poetics*, ed. Alex Preminger and others, rev. 1993; and *The Oxford Companion to English Literature*, ed. Margaret Drabble, rev. 1998. Handbooks that define and illustrate literary concepts and terms are *The Penguin Dictionary of Literary Terms and Literary Theory*, ed. J. A. Cuddon, 1991; W. F. Thrall and Addison Hibbard, *A Handbook to Literature*, ed. C. Hugh Holman, rev. 1992; *Critical Terms for Literary Study*, ed. Frank Lentricchia and Thomas McLaughlin, rev. 1995; and M. H. Abrams, *A Glossary of Literary Terms*, rev. 1992. Also useful are Richard Lanham, *A Handlist of Rhetorical Terms*, 2nd ed., 1991; Arthur Quinn, *Figures of Speech: 60 Ways to Turn a Phrase*, 1993; and the *Barnhart Concise Dictionary of Etymology*, ed. Robert K. Barnhart, 1995. On the Greek and Roman background, see G. M. Kirkwood, *A Short Guide to Classical Mythology*, 1959; *The*

Oxford Classical Dictionary, rev. 1996; and *The Oxford Companion to Classical Literature*, ed. M. C. Howatson and Ian Chilvers, rev. 1993. Useful online resources include Early English Books Online; University of Pennsylvania's SCETI Furness Shakespeare Library; Michael Best's Internet Shakespeare Editions; and the University of Toronto Early Modern English Dictionaries Database, ed. Ian Lancashire.

Literary Criticism and Theory

Seven volumes of the *Cambridge History of Literary Criticism* have been published, 1989– : *Classical Criticism*, ed. George A. Kennedy; *The Renaissance*, ed. Glyn P. Norton; *The Eighteenth Century*, ed. H. B. Nisbet and Claude Rawson; *Romanticism*, ed. Marshall Brown; *Modernism and the New Criticism*, ed. A. Walton Litz, Louis Menand, and Lawrence Rainey; *From Formalism to Poststructuralism*, ed. Raman Selden; and *Twentieth-Century Historical, Philosophical, and Psychological Perspectives*, ed. Christa Knellwolf and Christopher Norris. See also M. H. Abrams, *The Mirror and the Lamp: Romantic Theory and the Critical Tradition*, 1953; William K. Wimsatt and Cleanth Brooks, *Literary Criticism: A Short History*, 1957; René Wellek, *A History of Modern Criticism: 1750–1950*, 9 vols., 1955–93; Frank Lentricchia, *After the New Criticism*, 1980; *Redrawing the Boundaries: The Transformation of English and American Literary Studies*, ed. Stephen Greenblatt and Giles Gunn, 1992; and J. Hillis Miller, *On Literature*, 2002. Raman Selden, Peter Widdowson, and Peter Brooker have written *A Reader's Guide to Contemporary Literary Theory*, 1997. Other useful resources include *The Johns Hopkins Guide to Literary Theory and Criticism*, ed. Michael Groden and Martin Kreiswirth, 1994 (also online); *Literary Theory, an Anthology*, ed. Julie Rivkin and Michael Ryan, 1998; and *The Norton Anthology of Theory and Criticism*, gen. ed. Vincent Leitch, 2001.

The following is a selection of books in literary criticism that have been notably influential in shaping modern approaches to English literature and literary forms: Lionel Trilling, *The Liberal Imagination*, 1950; T. S. Eliot, *Selected Essays*, 3rd ed. 1951, and *On Poetry and Poets*, 1957; Erich Auerbach, *Mimesis: The Representation of Reality in Western Literature*, 1953; William Empson, *Some Versions of Pastoral*, 1935, rpt. 1986, and *Seven Types of Ambiguity*, 3rd ed. 1953; William K. Wimsatt, *The Verbal Icon*, 1954; Northrop Frye, *Anatomy of Criticism*, 1957; Wayne C. Booth, *The Rhetoric of Fiction*, 1961, rev. ed. 1983; W. J. Bate, *The Burden of the Past and the English Poet*, 1970; Harold Bloom, *The Anxiety of Influence*, 1973; Paul de Man, *Allegories of Reading*, 1979; and Stanley Fish, *Is There a Text in This Class?: The Authority of Interpretive Communities*, 1980.

René Wellek and Austin Warren, *Theory of Literature*, rev. 1970, is a useful introduction to the variety of scholarly and critical approaches to literature up to the time of its publication. Jonathan Culler's *Literary Theory: A Very Short Introduction*, 1997, discusses recurrent issues and debates. See also Terry Eagleton, *After Theory*, 2003. Modern feminist literary criticism was fashioned by such works as Patricia Meyer Spacks, *The Female Imagination*, 1975; Ellen Moers, *Literary Women*, 1976; Elaine Showalter, *A Literature of Their Own*, 1977; and Sandra Gilbert and Susan Gubar, *The Madwoman in the Attic*, 1979. More recent studies include Jane Gallop, *The Daughter's Seduction: Feminism and Psychoanalysis*, 1982; Gayatri Chakravorty Spivak, *In Other Worlds: Essays in Cultural Politics*, 1987; Sandra Gilbert and Susan Gubar, *No Man's Land: The Place of the Woman Writer in the Twentieth Century*, 2 vols., 1988–89; Barbara Johnson, *A World of Difference*, 1989; Judith Butler, *Gender Trouble*, 1990; and the critical views sampled in Elaine Showalter, *The New Feminist Criticism*, 1985; *Feminist Literary Theory: A Reader*, ed. Mary Eagleton, 2nd ed., 1995; and *Feminisms: An Anthology of Literary Theory and Criticism*, ed. Robyn R. Warhol and Diane Price Herndl, 2nd ed. 1997. Gay and lesbian studies and criticism are represented in *The Lesbian and Gay Studies Reader*, ed. Henry Abelove, Michele Barale, and David Halperin, 1993, and by such books as Eve Sedgwick, *Between Men: English Literature and Male Homosocial Desire*, 1985, and *Epistemology of the Closet*, 1990; Diana Fuss, *Essentially Speaking: Feminism, Nature, and Difference*, 1989; Gregory Woods, *A History of Gay Literature: The Male Tradition*, 1998; and David Halperin, *How to Do the History of Homosexuality*, 2002.

Convenient introductions to structuralist literary criticism include Robert Scholes, *Structuralism in Literature: An Introduction*, 1974, and Jonathan Culler, *Structuralist Poetics*, 1975. The poststructuralist challenges to this approach are discussed in Jonathan Culler, *On Deconstruction*, 1982; Fredric Jameson, *Poststructuralism; or the Cultural Logic of Late Capitalism*, 1991; John McGowan, *Postmodernism and Its Critics*, 1991; and *Beyond Structuralism*, ed. Wendell Harris, 1996. For Marxism, see *Selections from the Prison Notebooks of Antonio Gramsci*, ed. and trans. Quintin Hoare and Geoffrey Smith, 1971; Raymond Williams, *Marxism and Literature*, 1977; Fredric Jameson, *The Political Unconscious: Narrative as a Socially Symbolic Act*, 1981; and Terry Eagleton, *Literary Theory: An Introduction*, 1983. New historicism is represented in Stephen Greenblatt, *Learning to Curse*, 1990; in the essays collected in *The New Historicism*, ed. Harold Veeser, 1989, and *New Historical Literary Study: Essays on Reproducing Texts, Representing History*, ed. Jeffrey N. Cox and Larry J.

Reynolds, 1993; and in Catherine Gallagher and Stephen Greenblatt, *Practicing New Historicism*, 2000. The related social and historical dimension of texts is discussed in Jerome McGann, *Critique of Modern Textual Criticism*, 1983; D. F. McKenzie, *Bibliography and Sociology of Texts*, 1986; Roger Chartier, *The Order of Books*, 1994; and *Scholarly Editing: A Guide to Research*, ed. D. C. Greetham, 1995. Characteristic of new historicism is an expansion of the field of literary interpretation extended still further in cultural studies; for a broad sampling of the range of interests, see *The Cultural Studies Reader*, ed. Simon During, 1993, and *A Cultural Studies Reader: History, Theory, Practice*, ed. Jessica Munns and Gita Rajan, 1997. This expansion of the field is similarly reflected in postcolonial studies: see *The Post-Colonial Studies Reader*, ed. Bill Ashcroft, Gareth Griffiths, and Helen Tiffin, 1995, and such influential books as Ranajit Guha and Gayatri Chakravorty Spivak, *Selected Subaltern Studies*, 1988; Edward Said, *Culture and Imperialism*, 1993; Homi Bhabha, *The Location of Culture*, 1994; Anne McClintock, *Imperial Leather: Race, Gender, and Sexuality in the Colonial Contest*, 1995; and Jonathan Goldberg, *Tempest in the Caribbean*, 2004.

Anthologies representing a range of recent approaches include *Modern Criticism and Theory*, ed. David Lodge, 1988, and *Contemporary Literary Criticism*, ed. Robert Con Davis and Ronald Schlieffer, rev. 1998.

THE MIDDLE AGES

Scholarship during this era has been divided into the same three periods as in the General Introduction: Anglo-Saxon Literature, Anglo-Norman Literature, and Middle English Literature of the Fourteenth and Fifteenth Centuries. A reference book for the whole era is Joseph Strayer et al., *Dictionary of the Middle Ages*, 1982–.

Anglo-Saxon Literature

D. Whitelock, *The Beginnings of English Society*, 1952, provides concise historical background for the literature of the period. The most detailed history is F. M. Stenton's authoritative *Anglo-Saxon England*, 3rd ed., 1971. Also highly informative are P. Hunter Blair, *An Introduction to Anglo-Saxon England*, 1956, and *Roman Britain and Early England, 55 B.C.–A.D. 871*, 1963. The classic study of the culture of the primitive Germanic peoples is H. M. Chadwick, *The Heroic Age*, 1912. For the later period, see R. Bartlett, *The Making of Europe: Conquest, Colonization, and Cultural Change, 950–1350*. For those who wish to sample basic historical documents of the period, there is available the translation by G. N. Garmonsway of *The Anglo-Saxon Chronicle*, 1953. *The Age of Bede*, ed. D. H. Farmer, rev. 1983, and *Alfred the Great*, ed. S. Keynes and M. Lapidge, 1983, contain texts documenting two crucial periods of Anglo-Saxon history. Bede's *Ecclesiastical History of the English People* is translated and edited by B. Colgrave and R.A.B. Mynors, 1969. For studies of Bede, see G. H. Brown, *Bede, the Venerable*, 1987, and J. M. Wallace-Hadrill, *Bede's Ecclesiastical History of the English People: A Historical Commentary*, 1993. A lavishly and finely illustrated introduction to Anglo-Saxon England is *The Anglo-Saxons*, ed. J. Campbell, 1982. C. Fell, *Women in Anglo-Saxon England*, 1984, is pertinent to women's studies. The journal *Anglo-Saxon England* is devoted to all aspects of the history and culture of the period.

All the surviving poetry in Old English is contained in the six volumes edited by G. P. Krapp and E.V.K. Dobbie, *The Anglo-Saxon Poetic Records*, 1931–53, but the absence of glossaries makes this edition difficult for nonspecialists. Excellent texts of the shorter poems translated in this anthology are contained in J. C. Pope, *Eight Old English Poems*, 3rd ed., rev. R. D. Fulk, 2001. The standard text of *Beowulf and the Fight of Finnsburg* is F. Klaeber's 3rd ed., 1950; C. L. Wrenn's edition, *Beowulf, with the Finnsburg Fragment*, rev. W. F. Bolton, 1973, rev. 1988, is very useful; H. D. Chickering Jr. has made a dual-language edition with extensive commentary, and G. B. Jack has prepared *Beowulf: A Student Edition*, 1994. There are individual editions of *The Dream of the Rood* by M. Swanton, 1970; of *The Wanderer* by T. P. Dunning and A. J. Bliss, 1969. *The Wanderer* and *The Wife's Lament* are included in *The Old English Elegies: A Critical Edition and Genre Study*, ed. A. L. Klinck, 1992. *Judith* has been edited by M. Griffith, 1997. Modern English translations of many of the Old English poems have been published under various titles by R. K. Gordon, C. W. Kennedy, M. Alexander, S.A.J. Bradley, and K. Crossley-Holland. Many translations of *Beowulf* are available. E. T. Donaldson's translation is used in *Beowulf*, A Norton Critical Edition, ed. J. F. Tuso, 1975.

General discussions of Old English literature will be found in Vol. 1 of the *Cambridge History of English Literature*; S. B. Greenfield and D. G. Calder, *New Critical History of Old English Literature*, 1986; C. L. Wrenn, *A Study of Old English Literature*, 1967; M. Alexander, *Old English Literature*, 1983; and *The Cambridge Companion to Old English Literature*, ed. M. Godden and M. Lapidge, 1991.

Some useful studies and collections devoted

exclusively to Old English poetry are S. B. Greenfield, *The Interpretation of Old English Poems*, 1972; T. A. Shippey, *Old English Verse*, 1972; J. B. Bessinger Jr. and S. J. Kahrl, *Essential Articles for the Study of Old English Poetry*, 1977; D. A. Pearsall, *Old and Middle English Poetry*, 1977; B. C. Raw, *The Art and Background of Old English Poetry*, 1978; *Old English Poetry: Essays on Style*, ed. D. G. Calder, 1979; *The Old English Elegies*, ed. M. Green, 1983; S. B. Greenfield, *Hero and Exile: The Art of Old English Poetry*, 1989; *De Gustibus*, ed. J. M. Foley et al., 1992; *Heroic Poetry in the Anglo-Saxon Period*, ed. H. Damico and J. Leyerle, 1993; *Companion to Old English Poetry*, ed. H. Aertsen and R. H. Bremmer Jr., 1994; and *Old English Shorter Poems: Basic Readings*, ed. K. O'Brien O'Keeffe, 1994.

General collections of essays on Old English literature include *Old English Literature in Context*, ed. J. D. Niles, 1980; *Literature and Learning in Anglo-Saxon England*, ed. M. Lapidge and H. Gneuss, 1985; *Modes of Interpretation in Old English Literature*, ed. P. R. Brown et al., 1986; F. C. Robinson, *The Tomb of Beowulf and Other Essays on Old English*, 1993; and *Studies in English Language and Literature*, ed. M. J. Toswell and E. M. Tyler, 1996.

Some studies of special topics in Old English literature are J. Chance, *Woman as Hero in Old English Literature*, 1986; *New Readings on Women in Old English Literature*, ed. Helen Damico and A. H. Olsen, 1990; A. J. Frantzen, *Desire for Origins: New Language, Old English, and Teaching the Tradition*, 1990; *The Battle of Maldon AD 991*, ed. D. Scragg, 1991; *Class and Gender in Early English Literature*, ed. B. J. Harwood and G. R. Overing, 1994; and *Holy Men, Holy Women: Old English Prose Saints' Lives and Their Contexts*, ed. P. Szarmach, 1996.

Beowulf

Essential backgrounds to the study of the poem are provided by R. W. Chambers, *Beowulf: An Introduction to the Study of the Poem*, 3rd ed., with a supplement by C. L. Wrenn, 1959; and a wide-ranging overview of *Beowulf* scholarship is furnished by *A Beowulf Handbook*, ed. R. E. Bjork and J. D. Niles, 1997; and by A. Orchard, *A Critical Companion to Beowulf*, 2003. Important critical studies of the poem are found in D. Whitelock, *The Audience of Beowulf*, 1951; A. G. Brodeur, *The Art of Beowulf*, 1959; E. B. Irving Jr., *A Reading of Beowulf*, 1968, *Introduction to Beowulf*, 1969, and *Rereading Beowulf*, 1990; T. A. Shippey, *Beowulf*, 1978; J. D. Niles, *Beowulf: The Poem and Its Tradition*, 1983; F. C. Robinson, *Beowulf and the Appositive Style*, 1985; G. Clark, *Beowulf*, 1990; J. W. Earl, *Thinking about Beowulf*, 1994; J. M. Hill, *The Cultural World in Beowulf*, 1995; and C. R. Davis, *Beowulf and the Demise of Germanic Legend in England*, 1996.

For anthologies of criticism, see *The Beowulf Poet*, ed. D. K. Fry, 1968; *Beowulf*, A Norton Critical Edition, ed. Nicholas Howe, 2001 (prose); and *Beowulf*, A Norton Critical Edition, ed. Daniel Donoghue, 2001 (verse); *Interpretations of Beowulf*, ed. R. D. Fulk, 1991; and *Beowulf: Basic Readings*, ed. P. S. Baker, 1995. Special mention should be made of J. R. R. Tolkien's famous lecture, *Beowulf, the Monsters and the Critics*, 1937, reprinted in the anthologies of Donoghue, Fry, and Fulk.

Anglo-Norman Literature

For accounts of the Norman conquest and its historical consequences, see F. M. Powicke, *The Thirteenth Century, 1216–1307*, 1953; C. Brooke, *From Alfred to Henry III, 871–1272*, 2 vols., 1961; R. A. Brown, *The Normans*, 1984; A. L. Poole, *From Domesday Book to Magna Carta*, 1955; P. Stafford, *A Political and Social History of England in the Tenth and Eleventh Centuries*, 1989; M. T. Clanchy, *England and Its Rulers, 1066–1272*, 2nd ed., 1998; and J. Gillingham, *The English in the Twelfth Century: Imperialism, National Identity and Political Values*, 2000. The *Peterborough Chronicle*, a continuation of the *Anglo-Saxon Chronicle* to the year 1154, relates events from the point of view of English monks and can be read in translation in *The Anglo-Saxon Chronicle: a Revised Translation*, ed. by D. Whitelock with D. C. Douglas and S. I. Tucker, 1961, rev. 1965.

Studies of historical writing within the period itself, including the legendary histories of the kings of Britain, are J. S. P. Tatlock, *The Legendary History of Britain*, 1950; R. W. Hanning, *The Vision of History in Early Britain: From Gildas to Geoffrey of Monmouth*, 1966; and M. Otter, *Inventiones: Fiction and Referentiality in Twelfth-Century Historical Writing*, 1996.

The Cambridge History of Medieval English Literature, ed. D. Wallace, 1999, contains many chapters of relevance to this period. M. D. Legge, *Anglo-Norman Literature and Its Background*, 1963, is the standard history. The lais of **Marie de France** have been translated by R. H. Hanning and J. Ferrante, 1978, and by G. S. Burgess and K. Busby, 1986. For background and critical interpretations of Marie de France's works, see E. J. Mickel, *Marie de France*, 1974; P. M. Clifford, *Marie de France, Lais*, 1982; and G. S. Burgess, *The Lais of Marie de France*, 1987.

R. M. Wilson's *Early Middle English Literature* focuses primarily on this period. Vol. 1 of the *Oxford History of English Literature*, by J. A. W. Bennett and D. Gray, *Middle English Literature*, 1986, which goes up to 1400 (exclusive of Chaucer), contains excellent discussions of early Middle English texts. So too does E. Salter, *English and International*, 1988. Selections of texts from this era with a valuable introduction to the language and annotations are contained in the anthology edited by J. A. W. Bennett and G. V. Smithers, *Early Middle English Verse and Prose*, 2nd ed, 1968.

Middle English Literature of the Fourteenth and Fifteenth Centuries

Histories of the period include G. Holmes, *The Later Middle Ages, 1272–1485*, 1962; M. McKisack, *The Fourteenth Century, 1307–99*, 1959; and E. F. Jacob, *The Fifteenth Century*, 1961. Accounts of life and society during this period are provided by B. W. Tuchman, *A Distant Mirror: The Calamitous Fourteenth Century*, 1978; M. Keen, *English Society in the Later Middle Ages*, 1990; and *Fifteenth Century Attitudes*, ed. R. Horrox, 1994. See also the picture books listed under Chaucer. J. Huizinga has written a famous account of the culture and spirit of the late fourteenth to fifteenth centuries, formerly translated as *The Waning of the Middle Ages*, 1924, now available in a fuller text under the more accurate title, *The Autumn of the Middle Ages*, trans. R. J. Payton and U. Mammitzsch, 1996. F. R. H. Du Boulay complements and qualifies Huizinga in *An Age of Ambition*, 1970. Chaps. 6 to 10 in E. Auerbach's *Mimesis: The Representation of Reality in Western Literature*, trans. by W. R. Trask, 1953, although it does not deal with works in this anthology, gives penetrating insights into the reading of medieval texts. C. S. Lewis, *The Discarded Image: An Introduction to Medieval and Renaissance Literature*, 1964, seeks to restore for modern readers the perspective and sensibilities of the earlier age. For the religious sensibility of late medieval England see E. Duffy, *The Stripping of the Altars: Traditional Religion in England c. 1400–c. 1580*, 1992.

For general discussion of late Middle English literature, see the *The Oxford History of English Literature*: J. A. W. Bennett and D. Gray, *Middle English Literature*, 1986, vol. 1, part 2 (up to 1400, exclusive of Chaucer); D. A. Pearsall, *Old and Middle English Poetry*, 1977; J. A. Burrow, *Middle English Literature and Its Background*, 1982; D. S. Brewer, *English Gothic Literature*, 1983; *Middle English Prose: A Critical Guide to Major Authors and Genres*, ed. A. S. G. Edwards, 1984; A. C. Spearing, *Medieval to Renaissance in English Poetry*, 1985; *The Cambridge History of Medieval English Literature*, ed. D. Wallace, 1999; and J. Simpson, *Reform and Cultural Revolution*, 2002.

Critical works devoted to more than one author or genre in the period are J. A. Burrow, *Ricardian Poetry: Chaucer, Gower, Langland, and the Gawain Poet*, 1971; C. Muscatine, *Poetry and Crisis in the Age of Chaucer*, 1972; A. C. Spearing, *Medieval Dream Poetry*, 1976, *Readings in Medieval Poetry*, 1987; T. Turville-Petre, *The Alliterative Revival*, 1977; *Medieval Literature: Chaucer and the Alliterative Tradition*, vol. 1 of *The New Pelican Guide to English Literature*, ed. Boris Ford, 1982; *Fifteenth-Century Studies: Recent Essays*, ed. R. F. Yeager, 1984; *Medieval English Poetry*, ed. S. Trigg, 1993; D. Despres, *Ghostly Sights: Visual Meditation in Late-Medieval Literature*, 1989; G. Margherita, *The Romance of Origins: Language and Sexual Difference in Middle English Literature*, 1994; and *The Long Fifteenth Century: Essays for Douglas Gray*, ed. H. Cooper and S. Mapstone, 1997.

For the Middle English language, see Helge Kökeritz, *A Guide to Chaucer's Pronunciation*, 1954; David Burnley, *A Guide to Chaucer's Language*, 1983; and J. A. Burrow and T. Turville-Petre, *A Book of Middle English*, 1996.

The standard bibliography is *A Manual of the Writings in Middle English, 1050–1500*, 6 vols., ed. J. B. Severs, A. E. Hartung, et al., 1967–80, which is based on and supersedes the *Manual* of J. E. Wells, 1916, with nine supplements through 1945.

Geoffrey Chaucer

The standard edition of Chaucer's writing is *The Riverside Chaucer*, 3rd ed., ed. L. D. Benson et al., 1987, based on F. N. Robinson's edition. E. Talbot Donaldson, *Chaucer's Poetry*, 2nd ed., 1975, from which are taken the selections printed here, is helpful to the nonspecialist, as are John H. Fisher, *The Complete Poetry and Prose of Geoffrey Chaucer*, 2nd ed., 1989, and V. A. Kolve and Glending Olson, *The Canterbury Tales: Nine Tales and The "General Prologue,"* Norton Critical Edition, 1989. Vivid presentations of Chaucer in the background of fourteenth-century England are found in D. S. Brewer, *Chaucer and His World*, 1978, which is beautifully illustrated, and *A New Introduction to Chaucer*, 2nd ed., 1998. Pictorial companions to Chaucer's works, especially the *Canterbury Tales*, include R. S. Loomis, *A Mirror of Chaucer's World*, 1965, Maurice Hussey, *Chaucer's World*, 1967, Ian Serraillier, *Chaucer and His World*, 1968, and Roger Hart, *English Life in Chaucer's Day*, 1973.

The raw material for Chaucer's biography is contained in *Chaucer Life-Records*, ed. M. M. Crow and C. C. Olson, 1966. D. R. Howard, *Chaucer: His Life, His Works, His World*, 1987, and D. A. Pearsall, *The Life of Geoffrey Chaucer*, 1992, contain extensive background and interpretation. For succinct accounts of the sources and literary background of Chaucer's works, see R. D. French, *A Chaucer Handbook*, 2nd ed., 1947; reproductions of many of the known sources of the *Canterbury Tales* are contained in *Sources and Analogues of Chaucer's Canterbury Tales*, ed. W. F. Bryan and Germaine Dempster, 1941, 1958. See also the updated *Sources and Analogues of the Canterbury Tales*, vol. 1, ed. R. M. Correale and M. Hamel, 2002. Useful literary materials are collected in R. P. Miller,

Chaucer: Sources and Backgrounds, 1977. Muriel Bowden, *A Commentary on the General Prologue to the Canterbury Tales*, 1948, provides a wealth of background information on the individual Canterbury pilgrims; see also Jill Mann, *Chaucer and Medieval Estates Satire*, 1973. Various aspects of Chaucer's work are treated by a number of scholars in *Chaucer and Chaucerians*, ed. D. S. Brewer, 1966; *Geoffrey Chaucer (Writers and Their Background)*, ed. D. S. Brewer, 1974; *Companion to Chaucer Studies*, ed. Beryl Rowland, rev. 1979; *A Companion to Chaucer*, ed. P. Brown, 2000; and *The Cambridge Chaucer Companion*, ed. Piero Boitani and Jill Mann, rev. 2003

For literary criticism on and context for both *The Canterbury Tales* and other works by Chaucer, the following contain stimulating discussions: G. L. Kittredge, *Chaucer and His Poetry*, 1915; J. L. Lowes, *Geoffrey Chaucer and the Development of His Genius*, 1934; C. Muscatine, *Chaucer and the French Tradition*, 1957; R. O. Payne, *The Key of Remembrance*, 1963; M. Hussey, A. C. Spearing, and J. Winny, *An Introduction to Chaucer*, 1965; E. T. Donaldson, *Speaking of Chaucer*, 1970; T. Ross, *Chaucer's Bawdy*, 1972; D. S. Brewer, *Chaucer*, 3rd ed., 1973; P. Elbow, *Oppositions in Chaucer*, 1975; A. David, *The Strumpet Muse: Art and Morals in Chaucer's Poetry*, 1976; R. Burlin, *Chaucerian Fiction*, 1977; D. Burnley, *Chaucer's Language and the Philosophers' Tradition*, 1979; A. J. Minnis, *Chaucer and Pagan Antiquity*, 1982; G. Kane, *Chaucer*, 1984; S. Knight, *Geoffrey Chaucer*, 1986; A. Astell, *Chaucer and the Universe of Learning*, 1996; D. Wallace, *Chaucerian Polity: Absolutist Lineages and Associational Forms in England and Italy*, 1997; and R. P. McGerr, *Chaucer's Open Book: Resistance to Closure in Medieval Discourse*, 1998.

Criticism that deals mainly with *The Canterbury Tales* and with earlier commentary on it includes P. Ruggiers, *The Art of The Canterbury Tales*, 1964; D. R. Howard, *The Idea of The Canterbury Tales*, 1976; T. Lawler, *The One and the Many in The Canterbury Tales*, 1980; H. Cooper, *The Structure of the Canterbury Tales*, 1983; D. Pearsall, *The Canterbury Tales*, 1985; C. D. Benson, *Chaucer's Drama of Style: Poetic Variety in The Canterbury Tales*, 1986; W. Wetherbee, *Geoffrey Chaucer: The Canterbury Tales*, 1989; H. M. Leicester Jr., *The Disenchanted Self: Representing the Subject in The Canterbury Tales*, 1990; S. Crane, *Gender and Romance in Chaucer's Canterbury Tales*, 1994; and H. Cooper, *The Canterbury Tales*, Oxford Guides to Chaucer, 2nd ed., 1996.

D. W. Robertson's *A Preface to Chaucer*, 1962, is a learned and stimulating introduction to the reading of Chaucer in the light of medieval aesthetic doctrines. V. A. Kolve, *Chaucer and the Imagery of Narrative*, 1984, relates the first five of the *Canterbury Tales* to medieval art. Several recent books stress the importance of oral delivery, performance, and storytelling in the *Canterbury Tales*: Betsy Bowden, *Chaucer Aloud*, 1987; Carl Lindahl, *Earnest Games: Folkloric Patterns in The Canterbury Tales*, 1987; L. M. Koff, *Chaucer and the Art of Storytelling*, 1988; and J. M. Ganim, *Chaucerian Theatricality*, 1990. The following studies relate Chaucer's works to their social and historical background: Paul Strohm, *Social Chaucer*, 1989; Peggy Knapp, *Chaucer and the Social Contest*, 1990; Peter Brown and Andrew Butcher, *The Age of Saturn: Literature and History in The Canterbury Tales*, 1991; and Lee Patterson, *Chaucer and the Subject of History*, 1991. A pioneer feminist study of Chaucer is Carolyn Dinshaw, *Chaucer's Sexual Poetics*, 1989; see also J. Mann, *Geoffrey Chaucer*, rev. 1991; and E. T. Hansen, *Chaucer and the Fictions of Gender*, 1992.

The following are collections of critical essays: *Discussions of The Canterbury Tales*, ed. C. J. Owen, 1961; *Geoffrey Chaucer: A Critical Anthology*, ed. J. A. Burrow, 1969; and *Geoffrey Chaucer* Contemporary Studies in Literature, ed. G. D. Economou, 1975; *Chaucer's Religious Tales*, ed. C. D. Benson and E. Robertson, 1990; and *Critical Essays on Chaucer's Canterbury Tales*, ed. M. Andrew, 1991. See also the prefatory remarks on individual works and tales in *The Riverside Chaucer* and the commentary in E. Talbot Donaldson's anthology, cited above.

For Chaucer's writing outside the *Canterbury Tales*, see B. A. Windeatt, *Oxford Guides to Chaucer: Troilus and Criseyde*, 1992; and A. J. Minnis, *Oxford Guides to Chaucer: The Shorter Poems*, 1995.

Perhaps the most reliable glossary is that edited by Norman Davis et al., 1979. The standard bibliographies are E. P. Hammond, *Chaucer: A Bibliographical Manual*, 1908; D. D. Griffith, *Bibliography of Chaucer*, 1955; W. R. Crawford, *1954–63*, 1967; L. Y. Baird, *1964–73*, 1977; and L. Y. Baird-Lange and H. Schnutgen, *1974–85*, 1988. Two very useful annotated bibliographies are by Mark Allen and J. H. Fisher, *The Essential Chaucer*, 1987, and John Leyerle and Anne Quick, *Chaucer: A Bibliographical Introduction*, 1986. *Studies in the Age of Chaucer*, the journal of The New Chaucer Society publishes a current bibliography as well as articles on Chaucer and other medieval literature. See also Caroline Spurgeon, *Five Hundred Years of Chaucer Criticism and Allusion, 1357–1900*, 1925.

Julian of Norwich

The standard Middle English text with a wealth of commentary is *A Book of Showings to the Anchoress Julian of Norwich*, 2 vols., ed. Edmund Colledge and James Walsh, 1978. The editors' translation is published as *Julian of Nor-*

wich: Showings, 1978; another translation of the long text by Clifton Walters is published under the title *Revelations of Divine Love*, 1966. Both long and short text are translated in *Julian of Norwich: Revelations of Divine Love*, trans. E. Spearing, 1998. Another edition of the long text, ed. G. R. Crampton, 1994, published for TEAMS (Consortium for the Teaching of the Middle Ages) is designed for students. See also the Norton Critical Edition.

General studies of mystical writing in England and on the Continent are W. Riehle, *The Middle English Mystics*, trans. B. Standring, 1981; *An Introduction to the Medieval Mystics of Europe*, ed. P. Szarmach, 1984; A. K. Warren, *Anchorites and their Patrons in Medieval England*, 1985; F. Beer, *Women and Mystical Experience in the Middle Ages*, 1992; S. Beckwith, *Christ's Body: Identity, Culture, and Society in Late Medieval Writings*, 1993; M. Glasscoe, *English Medieval Mystics: Games of Faith*, 1993; and D. Aers and L. Staley, *The Powers of the Holy: Religion, Politics, and Gender in Late Medieval English Culture*, 1996. Studies helpful to understanding the mystical thought of Julian of Norwich are B. Pelphrey, *Christ Our Mother*, 1989, and D. N. Baker, *Julian of Norwich's Showing: From Vision to Book*, 1994.

Margery Kempe

The standard Middle English text of *The Book of Margery Kempe* is that of B. A. Windeatt, 2000. Another edition, ed. L. Staley, 1996, for TEAMS (Consortium for the Teaching of Middle English) is designed for students. Barry Windeatt has made a translation, 1985, with notes and a helpful introduction. See also the Norton Critical Edition. For general studies of mystical writings, see under Julian of Norwich. Studies of Kempe are C. W. Atkinson, *Mystic and Pilgrim: The Book and the World of Margery Kempe*, 1983; K. Lochrie, *Margery Kempe and Translations of the Flesh*, 1991; *Margery Kempe: A Book of Essays*, S. McEntire, ed., 1992; and L. S. Johnson, *Margery Kempe's Dissenting Fictions*, 1994. Gibson, cited under **Mystery Plays**, provides background on Kempe's region and includes a chapter on Kempe.

William Langland

The most handy edition is A. V. C. Schmidt, *The Vision of Piers Plowman: A Complete Edition of the B-Text*, 1978. W. W. Skeat, *The Vision of William Concerning Piers the Plowman . . .*, 2 vols., 1886, gives all three versions side by side; the commentary and notes in volume 2 remain invaluable. The Athlone edition, based on all extant manuscripts, has the A text, ed. G. Kane, 1960, the B text, ed. Kane and E. T. Donaldson, 1975, and the C text, ed. Kane and G. H. Russell, 1997. J. A. W. Bennett's edition of the first eight passus of the B text, 1972, is very useful, as is D. A. Pearsall's edition of the C text, 1978. The selections here are taken from E. T. Donaldson's *Piers Plowman: An Alliterative Verse Translation*, 1990. *A Companion to Piers Plowman*, ed. J. A. Alford, 1988, has essays and extensive bibliographies on many aspects of the poem. Book-length studies helpful to the student as well as the specialist include R. W. Frank, *Piers Plowman and the Scheme of Salvation*, 1957; Elizabeth Salter, *Piers Plowman: An Introduction*, 1962; E. D. Kirk, *The Dream Thought of Piers Plowman*, 1972; David Aers, *Piers Plowman and Christian Allegory*, 1975; James Simpson, *Piers Plowman: An Introduction to the B-Text*, 1990; J. A. Burrow, *Langland's Fictions*, 1993; S. Justice, *Writing and Rebellion: England in 1381*, 1994; and J. Wittig, *William Langland Revisited*, 1997. Collections of critical essays have been made by S. Justice and K. Kerby-Fulton, eds., *Written Work: Langland, Labour and Authorship*, 1997; and K. M. Hewett-Smith, ed., *William Langland's Piers Plowman: A Book of Essays*, 2001. Useful background material has been collected by Jeanne Krochalis and Edward Peters in *The World of Piers Plowman*, 1975. F. R. H. Du-Boulay, *The England of Piers Plowman*, 1991, places the poem in its historical and cultural setting.

Sir Thomas Malory

The Winchester manuscript of Malory's *Morte Darthur*, with full commentary and valuable discussion, is given in Eugène Vinaver's *The Works of Sir Thomas Malory*, 3 vols., 2nd ed., 1967, rev. P. J. C. Field, 1990; the one-volume edition, 2nd ed., Oxford, 1970, contains the text only. See also *Le Morte Darthur*, 2003, ed. S. H. A. Shepherd. The Caxton version is most readily available in *Caxton's Malory*, ed. J. W. Spisak, 1983. Vinaver, *Malory*, 1929, surveys Malory's life and career; see also, P. J. C. Field, *The Life and Times of Sir Thomas Malory*, 1993. Guides to Malory are B. Dillon, *A Malory Handbook*, 1978; Terence McCarthy, *An Introduction to Malory*, rev. ed., 1991; and E. Archibald and A. S. G. Edwards, *A Companion to Malory*, 1996. A number of critical problems in Malory's work, especially its unity, are discussed in three collections of essays by various scholars: *Essays on Malory*, ed. J. A. W. Bennett, 1963, *Malory's Originality*, ed. by R. M. Lumianski, 1964, and *Studies in Malory*, ed. J. W. Spisak, 1985. Other studies of Malory and the *Morte Darthur* include Mark Lambert, *Malory: Style and Vision in Le Morte Darthur*, 1975; L. D. Benson, *Malory's Morte Darthur*, 1976; and Felicity Riddy, *Sir Thomas Malory*, 1987.

For reference books and discussions of the development and of the political and social significance of the Arthurian tradition in England, see R. S. Loomis, *The Development of Arthurian Romance*, 1963; S. Knight, *Arthurian Literature and Society*, 1983; *The Arthurian Handbook*, ed. N. J. Lacy and G. Ashe, 2nd ed., 1998; *The New*

Arthurian Encyclopedia, ed. N. J. Lacy, 1991; *Approaches to Teaching the Arthurian Tradition*, ed. M. Fries and J. Watson, 1992; *Culture and the King: the Social Implications of the Arthurian Legend*, ed. M. Schichtman and J. Carley, 1994; *Arthurian Women: A Casebook*, ed. T. Fenster, 1996; *King Arthur: A Casebook*, ed. E. D. Kennedy, 1996; and Patricia Ingham, *Sovereign Fantasies: Arthurian Romance and the Making of Britain*, 2001.

Mystery Plays; The York Play of the Crucifixion

Good selections of Middle English plays are presented by A. C. Cawley, *Everyman and Medieval Miracle Plays*, 1960; by D. M. Bevington, *Medieval Drama*, 1975; and by Peter Happé, *The English Mystery Plays*, 1975. Cawley, *The Wakefield Pageants in the Towneley Cycle*, 1958, has a discussion of the work of the "Wakefield Master" whose hand is seen in the *Second Shepherds' Play*.

E. K. Chambers's classic *The Medieval Stage*, 1905, remains a mine of information, although its views about the evolution of medieval drama are no longer accepted. A new understanding and appreciation of medieval drama begins with O. B. Hardison, *Christian Rite and Christian Drama in the Middle Ages*, 1965; and for the mysteries, with V. A. Kolve, *The Play Called Corpus Christi*, 1966. Rosemary Woolf, *The English Mystery Plays*, 1972, makes detailed comparisons among the extant plays. Individual cycles are studied by Peter Travis in *Dramatic Design in the Chester Cycle*, 1982, by Martin Stevens in *Four Middle English Mystery Cycles: Textual, Contextual, and Critical Interpretations*, 1987; and by S. Beckwith, *Signifying God: Social Relation and Symbolic Act in the York Corpus Christi Plays*, 2001. G. M. Gibson fills in the social and religious background in *The Theater of Devotion: East Anglian Drama and Society in the Late Middle Ages*, 1989. Collections of critical and/or introductory essays can be found in the following: *Medieval English Drama*, ed. J. Taylor and A. H. Nelson, 1972; *Contexts for Early English Drama*, ed. M. Briscoe and J. Coldewey, 1989; and *The Cambridge Companion to Medieval English Theatre*, ed. R. Beadle, 1994. *Approaches to Teaching Medieval Drama*, ed. Richard Emmerson, 1990, contains essays by many hands and makes up a nontechnical survey of current opinion.

Sir Gawain and the Green Knight

The standard Middle English edition of the poem is by J. R. R. Tolkien and E. V. Gordon, rev. Norman Davis, 1967. Easier to use are the editions by R. A. Waldron, 1970, rev. for *The Poems of the Pearl Manuscript*, 1978; and by J. A. Burrow, 1972. For a guide to the poems in the manuscript, see A. Putter, *An Introduction to the Gawain-Poet*, 1996, and *A Companion to the Gawain Poet*, ed. D. S. Brewer and J. Gibson, 1997. Discussions of various aspects of the poem appear in Marie Borroff, *Sir Gawain and the Green Knight: A Stylistic and Metrical Study*, 1962; L. D. Benson, *Art and Tradition in Sir Gawain and the Green Knight*, 1965; J. A. Burrow, *A Reading of Sir Gawain and the Green Knight*, 1965; A. C. Spearing, *The Gawain Poet: A Critical Study*, 1971; And W. Clein, *Concepts of Chivalry in Sir Gawain and the Green Knight*, 1984.

Collections of essays have been compiled by R. J. Blanch, *Sir Gawain and Pearl*, 1966, and *Text and Matter: New Critical Perspectives of the Pearl-Poet*, 1991 D. Fox, *Twentieth-Century Interpretations of Sir Gawain and the Green Knight*, 1968; and D. R. Howard and C. K. Zacher, *Critical Studies of Sir Gawain and the Green Knight*, 1968.

THE SIXTEENTH CENTURY

Some important books on society and culture in early modern England are Lawrence Stone, *The Crisis of the Aristocracy, 1558–1641*, 1965, and *The Family, Sex and Marriage in England, 1500–1800*, 1979; Keith Thomas, *Religion and the Decline of Magic*, 1971; P. G. Emmison, *Elizabethan Life: Disorder*, 1970; David Cressy, *Literacy and the Social Order: Reading and Writing in Tudor and Stuart England*, 1980, and *Birth, Marriage, and Death: Ritual, Religion, and the Life-Cycle in Tudor and Stuart England*, 1997; Peter Clark, *The English Alehouse: A Social History, 1200–1830*, 1983; Peter Laslett, *The World We Have Lost, Further Explored*, 1984; Paul Slack, *The Impact of Plague in Tudor and Stuart England*, 1985; J. A. Sharpe, *Early Modern England: A Social History*, 1987; Susan Amussen, *An Ordered Society: Gender and Class in Early Modern England*, 1988; Margaret Aston, *England's Iconoclasts: Laws Against Images*, 1988; Felicity Heal, *Hospitality in Early Modern England*, 1990; Ian Archer, *The Pursuit of Stability: Social Relations in Elizabethan London*, 1991; Ronald Hutton, *The Rise and Fall of Merry England: The Ritual Year 1400–1700*, 1994; Lena Orlin, *Private Matters and Public Culture in Post-Reformation England*, 1994; Kim Hall, *Things of Darkness: Economies of Race and Gender in Early Modern England*, 1995; Lisa Jardine, *Worldly Goods: A New History of the Renaissance*, 1996; Adam Fox, *Oral and Literate Culture in England, 1500–1700*, 2000; Ellen Meiskins Wood, *The Origin of Capitalism: A Longer View*, 2002; and Julian Yates, *Error, Misuse, Failure: Object Lessons from the English Renaissance*, 2003. Jeffrey L. Singman, *Daily*

Life in Elizabethan England, 1995, provides a wealth of information on topics ranging from sex to bear-baiting.

Useful general studies of the history of the period include; G. R. Elton, *Reform and Reformation: England, 1509–1559*, 1977; Conrad Russell, *The Crisis of Parliaments: English History, 1509–1660*, 1971; J. G. A. Pocock, *The Machiavellian Moment: Florentine Political Thought and the Atlantic Republican Tradition*, 1975; John Guy, *Tudor England*, 1988; Penry Williams, *The Later Tudors: England 1547–1603*, 1995; and Susan Brigdon, *New Worlds, Lost Worlds: The Rule of the Tudors, 1485–1603*, 2000. Political theory in the period is surveyed in Quentin Skinner, *The Foundations of Modern Political Thought*, 2 vols., 1978; and there is an important analysis of the theory of kingship in E. H. Kantorowicz, *The King's Two Bodies*, 1957. Exploration and military history are treated in G. Mattingly, *The Armada*, 1959, and J. A. Williamson, *The Age of Drake*, 4th ed., 1960. For church history and religion, see John Bossy, *The English Catholic Community, 1570–1850*, 1979; Patrick Collinson, *The Religion of Protestants: The Church in English Society, 1559–1625*, 1982, and *The Birthpangs of Protestant England: Religious and Cultural Change in the Sixteenth and Seventeenth Centuries*, 1988; Peter Lake, *Anglicans and Puritans?*, 1988; Debora Shuger, *Habits of Thought in the English Renaissance: Religion, Politics, and the Dominant Culture*, 1990; Eamon Duffy, *The Stripping of the Altars: Traditional Religion in England c. 1400–c. 1580*, 1992; Christopher Haigh, *English Reformations: Religion, Politics, and Society under the Tudors*, 1993; James Shapiro, *Shakespeare and the Jews*, 1996; *The Culture of English Puritanism*, ed. Christopher Durston and Jacqueline Eales, 1996; *The Impact of the English Reformation, 1500–1640*, ed. Peter Marshall, 1997; and Ian Green, *Print and Protestantism in Early Modern England*, 2000.

Life at court is described in David Starkey, *The English Court: From the Wars of the Roses to the Civil War*, 1987. Patronage and courtiership, with special reference to literature, are analyzed in David Javitch, *Poetry and Courtliness in Renaissance England*, 1976; *Patronage in the Renaissance*, ed. Guy Fitch Lytle and Stephen Orgel, 1981; and Frank Whigham, *Ambition and Privilege: The Social Tropes of Elizabethan Courtesy Theory*, 1984. On publishing and the book trade, see H. S. Bennett, *English Books and Readers, 1475–1557*, 1952, and *English Books and Readers, 1558–1603*, 1965; Elizabeth L. Eisenstein, *The Printing Press as an Agent of Change*, 2 vols., 1979; Adrian Johns, *The Nature of the Book: Print and Knowledge in the Making*, 1998; David Kastan, *Shakespeare and the Book*, 2001; *The Cambridge History of the Book in Britain*, vol. 4: 1557–1695, ed. John Bernard and D. F. McKenzie, with the assistance of Maureen Bell, 2002; and Joseph Loewenstein, *The Author's Due: Printing and the Prehistory of Copyright*, 2002.

A long series of important studies have defined the Renaissance in terms of humanism, imitation of the ancients, and individual achievement: Jacob Burckhardt, *The Civilization of the Renaissance*, 1878, rev. 1944; Max Weber, *The Protestant Ethic and the Spirit of Capitalism*, 1905; Douglas Bush, *The Renaissance and English Humanism*, 1939; E. M. W. Tillyard, *The Elizabethan World Picture*, 1943; *The Renaissance Philosophy of Man*, ed. Ernst Cassirer et al., 1948; Erwin Panofsky, *Renaissance and Renascences in Western Art*, 2 vols., 1960; R. R. Bolgar, *The Classical Heritage and Its Beneficiaries*, 1954, rpt. 1973; Paul O. Kristeller, *Renaissance Thought*, 2 vols., 1961, 1965; D. J. Gordon, *The Renaissance Imagination: Essays and Lectures*, ed. Stephen Orgel, 1975; Gordon Braden, *The Classics and English Renaissance Poetry*, 1978; David R. Carlson, *English Humanist Books: Writers and Patrons, Manuscript and Print, 1475–1525*, 1993; *Renaissance Humanism*, ed. Jill Kraye, 1996; Jonathan Woolfson, *Reassessing Tudor Humanism*, 2002. See also *The Cambridge History of Renaissance Philosophy*, ed. Charles Schmitt, 1988. Revisionist analyses by new historicist and cultural materialist critics focus on the interaction of institutions, ideology, and the conditions of cultural production in the social construction of persons and literary texts. Some seminal studies are Stephen Greenblatt, *Renaissance Self-Fashioning*, 1980; *Representing the English Renaissance*, ed. S. Greenblatt, 1988; Richard Helgerson, *Self-Crowned Laureates: Spenser, Jonson, Milton and the Literary System*, 1983, and *Forms of Nationhood: The Elizabethan Writing of England*, 1992; Annabel Patterson, *Censorship and Interpretation: The Conditions of Writing and Reading in Early Modern England*, 1984; Peter Stallybrass and Allon White, *The Politics and Poetics of Transgression*, 1986; Patricia Fumerton, *Cultural Aesthetics: Renaissance Literature and the Practice of Social Ornament*, 1991; Richard Halpern, *The Poetics of Primitive Accumulation: English Renaissance Culture and the Genealogy of Capital*, 1991; *Subject and Object in Renaissance Culture*, ed. Margreta de Grazia, Maureen Quilligan, and Peter Stallybrass, 1996; Cyndia Clegg, *Press Censorship in Elizabethan England*, 1997; and Timothy Reiss, *Knowledge, Discovery, and Imagination in Early Modern Europe: The Rise of Aesthetic Rationalism*, 1997. (Others on the theater and on Shakespeare are noted in appropriate sections below.)

Science and medicine in this period are discussed in Antonia McLean, *Humanism and the Rise of Science in Tudor England*, 1972; Roy Porter, *Disease, Medicine and Society in England*

1550–1860, 1987; Brian Rotman, *Signifying Nothing: The Semiotics of Zero*, 1987, rpt. 1993; Thomas Laqueur, *Making Sex: Body and Gender from the Greeks to Freud*, 1990; Jonathan Sawday, *The Body Emblazoned: Dissection and the Human Body in Renaissance Culture*, 1995; Steven Shapin, *The Scientific Revolution*, 1996; *Wonders and the Order of Nature, 1150–1750*, ed. Lorraine Daston and Katharine Park, 1998; Jonathan Gil Harris, *Foreign Bodies and the Body Politic: Discourses of Social Pathology in Early Modern England*, 1998; Mary Baine Campbell, *Wonder and Science: Imagining Worlds in Early Modern Europe*, 1999; Barbara Benedict, *Curiosity: A Cultural History of Early Modern Inquiry*, 2001; Margaret Healy, *Fictions of Disease in Early Modern England: Bodies, Plagues, and Politics*, 2001; and Michael Witmore, *Culture of Accidents: Unexpected Knowledges in Early Modern England*, 2001. Education is the subject of T. W. Baldwin, *William Shakespere's Small Latine and Lesse Greeke*, 2 vols., 1944; Kenneth Charlton, *Education in Renaissance England*, 1965; and Rebecca Bushnell, *A Culture of Teaching: Early Modern Humanism in Theory and Practice*, 1996. On logic and rhetoric see W. S. Howell, *Logic and Rhetoric in England, 1500–1700*, 1956; Sister Miriam Joseph, *Rhetoric in Shakespeare's Time*, 1962; Frances Yates, *The Art of Memory*, 1966; Joel Altman, *The Tudor Play of Mind: Rhetorical Inquiry and the Development of Elizabethan Drama*, 1978; Victoria Kahn, *Rhetoric and Skepticism in the Renaissance*, 1985; Patricia Parker, *Literary Fat Ladies: Rhetoric, Gender, Property*, 1987; Debora Shuger, *Sacred Rhetoric: The Christian Grand Style in the English Renaissance*, 1988; and Wayne Rebhorn, *The Emperor of Men's Minds: Literature and the Renaissance Discourse of Rhetoric*, 1995.

Some books on Renaissance art and architecture are J. Buxton, *Elizabethan Taste*, 1963; Roy Strong, *The English Icon: Elizabethan and Jacobean Portraiture*, 1969, and *The Cult of Elizabeth: Elizabethan Portraiture and Pageantry*, 1977; Mark Girouard, *Life in the English Country House*, 1978; Lucy Gent, *Picture and Poetry, 1560–1620*, 1981; Norman K. Farmer, *Poets and the Visual Arts in Renaissance England*, 1984; John King, *Tudor Royal Iconography: Literature and Art in an Age of Religious Crisis*, 1989; Timothy Mowl, *Elizabethan and Jacobean Style*, 1993; Anthony Wells-Cole, *Art and Decoration in Elizabethan and Jacobean England*, 1997; and Leonard Barkan, *Unearthing the Past: Archeology and Aesthetics in the Making of Renaissance Culture*, 1999. Renaissance gardens are treated in Roy Strong, *The Renaissance Garden in England*, 1979, and Rebecca Bushnell, *Green Desire: Imagining Early Modern English Gardens*, 2003. Some important studies on civic pageantry include David M. Bergeron, *English Civic Pageantry, 1558–1642*, 1971, rev. 2003; Gordon Kipling, *The Triumph of Honor: Burgundian Origins of the Elizabethan Renaissance*, 1977; and Michael D. Bristol, *Carnival and Theater: Plebian Culture and the Structure of Authority in Renaissance England*, 1985. See also Ann Rosalind Jones and Peter Stallybrass, *Renaissance Clothing and the Materials of Memory*, 2000. Renaissance iconology and emblem books often illuminate literary imagery; important studies are Erwin Panofsky, *Studies in Iconology*, 1939; Rosemary Freeman, *English Emblem Books*, 1948; Jean Seznec, *The Survival of the Pagan Gods*, trans. B. F. Sessions, 1963; and John Manning, *The Emblem*, 2002. The attack on religious images is treated by John Phillips, *The Reformation of Images: Destruction of Art in England, 1535–1660*, 1971; Ernest B. Gilman, *Iconoclasm and Poetry in the English Reformation*, 1986; and *Iconoclash*, ed. Bruno Latour and Peter Weibel, 2002.

For Tudor music and musicians in relation to poetry see M. C. Boyd, *Elizabethan Music and Music Criticism*, 1940; E. H. Fellowes, *English Madrigal Verse*, rev. 1967; John Stevens, *Music and Poetry in the Early Tudor Court*, 1961, rpt. 1979; David Price, *Patrons and Musicians of the English Renaissance*, 1981; and Winifred Maynard, *Elizabethan Lyric Poetry and Its Music*, 1986. John Hollander studies music as symbol in *The Untuning of the Sky: Ideas of Music in English Poetry, 1500–1700*, 1961; and Paula Johnson analyzes structural affinities of the two art forms in *Form and Transformation in Music and Poetry of the English Renaissance*, 1975. Other important studies include Linda Phyllis Austern, *Music in English Children's Drama of the Later Renaissance*, 1992; Bruce Smith, *The Acoustic World of Early Modern England: Attending to the O-Factor*, 1999; and Marc Berley, *After the Heavenly Tune: English Poetry and the Aspiration to Song*, 2000.

Useful anthologies of Elizabethan literary criticism are G. G. Smith, *Elizabethan Critical Essays*, 2 vols., 1904; O. B. Hardison Jr., *English Literary Criticism: The Renaissance*, 1963; and *English Renaissance Literary Criticism*, ed. Brian Vickers, 1999. Important studies of Renaissance literary theory and criticism include Rosamond Tuve, *Elizabethan and Metaphysical Imagery*, 1947; Bernard Weinberg, *A History of Literary Criticism in the Italian Renaissance*, 2 vols., 1961, rpt. 1974; Baxter Hathaway, *Marvels and Commonplaces: Renaissance Literary Criticism*, 1968; Don C. Allen, *Mysteriously Meant: The Rediscovery of Pagan Symbolism and Allegorical Interpretation in the Renaissance*, 1970; Margaret W. Ferguson, *Trials of Desire: Renaissance Defenses of Poetry*, 1983; Arthur Kinney, *Humanist Poetics*, 1986; *The Cambridge History of Literary Criticism*, vol. 3: *The Renaissance*, ed. Glyn P. Norton, 1999; and Robert Matz,

Defending Literature in Early Modern England: Renaissance Literary Theory in Social Context, 2000.

Some distinguished historical and critical accounts of Renaissance literature include C. S. Lewis, *English Literature in the Sixteenth Century, Excluding Drama*, 1954; Douglas Bush, *Mythology and the Renaissance Tradition in English Poetry*, rev. 1963; Rosalie Colie, *The Resources of Kind: Genre-Theory in the Renaissance*, 1973; Thomas M. Greene, *The Light in Troy: Imitation and Discovery in Renaissance Poetry*, 1982; Alan Sinfield, *Literature in Protestant England, 1560–1660*, 1983; David Norbrook, *Poetry and Politics in the English Renaissance*, 1984, rev. 2002; Franco Moretti, *Signs Taken for Wonders: Essays in the Sociology of Literary Forms*, rev. 1988; Heather Dubrow, *Echoes of Desire: English Petrarchism and Its Counterdiscourses*, 1995; *The Cambridge Companion to English Literature, 1500–1600*, ed. Arthur Kinney, 2000; *The Cambridge History of Early Modern English Literature*, ed. David Loewenstein and Janel Mueller, 2002. Important studies of particular Renaissance genres and kinds include J. W. Lever, *The Elizabethan Love Sonnet*, 1956; Alvin Kernan, *The Cankered Muse: Satire of the English Renaissance*, 1959; Lily B. Campbell, *Divine Poetry and Drama in Sixteenth-Century England*, 1959; Angus Fletcher, *Allegory: The Theory of a Symbolic Mode*, 1964; *Seventeenth-Century Prose*, ed. Stanley Fish, 1971; Patricia Parker, *Inescapable Romance*, 1979; Anne Ferry, *The "Inward" Language: Sonnets of Wyatt, Sidney, Shakespeare, and Donne*, 1983; Janel Mueller, *The Native Tongue and the Word: Developments in English Prose Style, 1380–1580*, 1984; Peter Sacks, *The English Elegy: Studies in the Genre from Spenser to Yeats*, 1985; *Unfolded Tales: Essays on Renaissance Romance*, ed. George M. Logan and Gordon Teskey, 1989; Susanne Wofford, *The Choice of Achilles: The Ideology of Figure in the Epic*, 1992; Arthur Marotti, *Manuscript, Print, and the English Renaissance Lyric*, 1995; Paul Alpers, *What Is Pastoral?*, 1996; *The Project of Prose in Early Modern Europe and the New World*, ed. Elizabeth Fowler and Roland Greene, 1997; Lori Newcombe, *Reading Popular Romance in Early Modern England*, 2002; and Elizabeth Heale, *Autobiography and Authorship in Renaissance Verse: Chronicles of the Self*, 2003.

Important studies of stage history, audiences, and the development of dramatic forms include E. K. Chambers, *The Elizabethan Stage*, 4 vols., 1923; Allardyce Nicoll, *British Drama*, rev. 1962; *Revels History of Drama in English*, 8 vols., 1978–83; Muriel D. Bradbrook, *A History of Elizabethan Drama*, 6 vols., 1935–76; F. T. Bowers, *Elizabethan Revenge Tragedy, 1578–1642*, 1940; Glynne Wickham, *Early English Stages, 1300–1660*, 3 vols., 1959–81; David Bevington, *From "Mankind" to Marlowe*, 1962; Stephen Orgel, *The Illusion of Power: Political Theater in the English Renaissance*, 1975, and *Impersonations: The Performance of Gender in Shakespeare's England*, 1996; Ann Jennalie Cook, *The Privileged Playgoers of Shakespeare's London: 1576–1642*, 1981; William Worthen, *The Idea of the Actor: Drama and the Ethics of Performance*, 1984; Gerald Bentley, *The Professions of Dramatist and Player in Shakespeare's Time, 1590–1642*, 1986; Andrew Gurr, *Playgoing in Shakespeare's London*, 1987, and *The Shakespearian Playing Companies*, 1996; John Orrell, *The Human Stage: English Theatrical Design, 1567–1640*, 1988; Leeds Barroll, *Politics, Plague, and Shakespeare's Theater*, 1991; Richard Dutton, *Mastering the Revels: Regulation and Censorship of English Renaissance Drama*, 1991; *A New History of Early English Drama*, ed. John Cox and David Kastan, 1997; G. K. Hunter, *English Drama 1586–1642: The Age of Shakespeare*, 1997; *Henslowe's Diary*, ed. R. A. Foakes, 2nd ed., 2002; *Staged Properties in Early Modern English Drama*, ed. Jonathan Gil Harris and Natasha Korda, 2002; Siobhan Keenan, *Travelling Players in Shakespeare's England*, 2002; *The Cambridge Companion to English Renaissance Drama*, ed. A. R. Braunmuller and Michael Hattaway, 2nd ed., 2003; and Andrew Sofer, *The Stage Life of Props*, 2003.

Some important studies of drama in relation to contemporary politics and ideology are David Bevington, *Tudor Drama and Politics*, 1968; Robert Weiman, *Shakespeare and the Popular Tradition in the Theater*, 1967, rpt. 1987; Jonas Barish, *The Antitheatrical Prejudice*, 1981; Jonathan Dollimore, *Radical Tragedy: Religion, Ideology and Power in the Drama of Shakespeare and his Contemporaries*, 1984; Catherine Belsey, *The Subject of Tragedy: Identity and Difference in Renaissance Drama*, 1985; Jean-Christophe Agnew, *Worlds Apart: The Market and the Theatre in Anglo-American Thought, 1550–1750*, 1986; Steven Mullaney, *The Place of the Stage*, 1988; Leah Marcus, *Puzzling Shakespeare: Local Reading and Its Discontents*, 1988; Katharine Maus, *Inwardness and Theater in the English Renaissance*, 1995; Louis Montrose, *The Purpose of Playing: Shakespeare and the Cultural Politics of the Elizabethan Theatre*, 1996; Janette Dillon, *Theatre, Court and City, 1595–1610: Drama and Social Space in London*, 2000; Michael O'Connell, *The Idolatrous Eye: Iconoclasm and Theater in Early-Modern England*, 2000; Jeffrey Knapp, *Shakespeare's Tribe: Church, Nation, and Theater in Renaissance England*, 2002; Wendy Wall, *Staging Domesticity: Household Work and English Identity in Early Modern Drama*, 2002; and Jonathan Gil Harris, *Sick Economies: Drama, Mercantilism, and Disease in Shakespeare's England*, 2004.

The many recent studies of the status of women in early modern England have a distinguished precursor in Alice Clark, *Working Life of Women in the Seventeenth Century*, 1919. On the situation of women in the Renaissance and the achievements of women writers, see Joan Kelly-Gadol, "Did Women Have a Renaissance?" in *Becoming Visible: Women in European History*, ed. R. Bridenthal and C. Koonz, 1977; Ian Maclean, *The Renaissance Notion of Women*, 1980; *Beyond Their Sex: Learned Women of the European Past*, ed. Patricia H. Labalme, 1980; Retha M. Warnicke, *Women of the English Renaissance and Reformation*, 1983; Linda Woodbridge, *Women and the English Renaissance: Literature and the Nature of Womankind, 1540–1640*, 1984; *Rewriting the Renaissance: The Discourses of Sexual Difference in Early Modern Europe*, ed. Margaret Ferguson et al., 1986; Elaine Beilin, *Redeeming Eve: Women Writers of the English Renaissance*, 1987; *The Renaissance Englishwoman in Print: Counterbalancing the Canon*. ed. Anne M. Haselkorn and Betty S. Travitsky, 1990; Constance Jordan, *Renaissance Feminism: Literary Texts and Political Models*, 1990; Patricia Crawford, *Women and Religion in England, 1500–1720*, 1993; *Silent but for the Word: Tudor Women as Patrons, Translators, and Writers of Religious Works*, ed. Margaret Hannay, 1985; Tina Krontiris, *Oppositional Voices: Women as Translators of Literature in the English Renaissance*, 1992; *Women, "Race," and Writing in the Early Modern Period*, ed. Margo Henricks and Patricia Parker, 1994; *Renaissance Women: A Sourcebook*, ed. Kate Aughterson, 1995; Helen Hackett, *Women and Literature in Britain, 1500–1700*, 1996; *Lay by your Needles, Ladies, Take the Pen: Writing Women in England*, ed. Kate Chedgzoy, Melanie Osborne, and Suzanne Trill, 1997; Sara Mendelson and Patricia Crawford, *Women in Early Modern England*, 1550–1720, 1998; Natasha Korda, *Shakespeare's Domestic Economies: Gender and Property in Early Modern England*, 2002; and Mary Beth Rose, *Gender and Heroism in Early Modern English Literature*, 2002. A useful anthology is *The Paradise of Women: Writings by Englishwomen of the Renaissance*, ed. Betty Travitsky, 1981; see also Randall Martin, ed., *Women Writers in Renaissance England*, 1997. Recent studies of women writers in Tudor England are surveyed in *English Literary Renaissance* [*ELR*] 30 (2000): 457–93. For studies on Renaissance masculinity, see Lorna Hutson, *The Usurer's Daughter: Male Frienship and Fictions of Women in Sixteenth-Century England*, 1994, and Lynn Enterline, *The Tears of Narcissus: Melancholia and Masculinity in Early Modern Writing*, 1995. On male homosexuality in the period, see Alan Bray, *Homosexuality in Renaissance England*, 1982; Bruce R. Smith, *Homosexual Desire in Shakespeare's England: A Cultural Poetics*, 1991; Jonathan Goldberg, *Sodometries: Renaissance Texts, Modern Sexualities*, 1992; and *Same-Sex Desire in the English Renaissance: A Sourcebook of Texts, 1470–1650*, ed. Kenneth Borris, 2003. Recent studies of Renaissance homoeroticism are surveyed in *ELR* 30 (2000):284–329.

An invaluable tool for the study of early modern language and literature is the *Oxford English Dictionary*, 2nd ed., 1989, now also on CD-ROM, and online for subscribers. Also useful are Morris Tilley, *A Dictionary of the Proverbs in England in the Sixteenth and Seventeenth Centuries*, 1950; Richard Jones, *The Triumph of the English Language*, 1953; Richard Lanham, *A Handlist of Rhetorical Terms*, 1968; Lee Sonnino, *A Handbook of Sixteenth-Century Rhetoric*, 1968; James Hencke, *Courtesans and Cuckolds: A Glossary of Renaissance Dramatic Bawdy (Exclusive of Shakespeare)*, 1979; Fausto Cercignani, *Shakespeare's Works and Elizabethan Pronunciation*, 1981; Eric Partridge, *Shakespeare's Bawdy*, 3rd ed., 1991; Paula Blank, *Broken English: Dialects and the Politics of Language in Renaissance Writings*, 1996; Charles Barber, *Early Modern English*, rev. ed., 1997; *The Cambridge History of the English Language, vol. III: 1476–1776*, 1999; and Jonathan Hope, *Shakespeare's Grammar*, 2003.

The journal *English Literary Renaissance* (*ELR*) regularly publishes surveys of recent studies of individual sixteenth-and seventeenth-century writers and of more general topics; the surveys are periodically updated. Each year, the winter issue of *Studies in English Literature 1500–1900* publishes "Recent Studies in the English Renaissance," an evaluative overview of the preceding year's books in the field. These journals also publish important new articles on sixteenth-century topics, as do other Renaissance journals such as *Early Modern Literary Studies*, *Journal of Medieval and Early Modern Studies*, *Renaissance Forum*, *Renaissance Quarterly*, *Renaissance Studies*, and *The Sixteenth Century Journal*. There are also a number of journals devoted to particular sixteenth-century authors; and many journals whose scope is not limited to Renaissance studies—such as *ELH* (*English Literary History*) and *Representations*—often publish articles on sixteenth-century topics.

Queen Elizabeth I

There is no complete edition, but *Elizabeth I: Collected Works*, ed. Leah S. Marcus, Janel Mueller, and Mary Beth Rose, 2000, includes a generous, well-edited, and fascinating selection of her letters, poems, prayers, and speeches. Some pieces not found in this volume are in the following: *The Letters of Queen Elizabeth*, ed. G. B. Harrison, 1935, rpt. 1968; *The Public Speaking of Queen Elizabeth: Selections from her Official Addresses*, ed. George P. Rice Jr.,

1951, rpt. 1966; and *The Poems of Queen Elizabeth I*, ed. Leicester Bradner, 1964. Janel Mueller and Leah Marcus are also the editors of *Elizabeth I: Autograph Compositions and Foreign Language Originals*, 2003. Frances Teague surveys Elizabeth's life and writings, and prints a selection of her works, in *Women Writers of the Renaissance and Reformation*, ed. Katharina M. Wilson, 1987; Marc Shell edits and provides an extended commentary on one of her religious translations, in *Elizabeth's Glass*, 1993. Mary Thomas Crane has an entry on Elizabeth in *Dictionary of Literary Biography*, vol. 136, ed. David A. Richardson, 1994, pp. 85–93. The standard biography remains J. E. Neale, *Queen Elizabeth I*, 1934, rpt. 1967. More recent biographies include Susan Doran, *Queen Elizabeth I*, 2003, and David Loades, *Elizabeth I*, 2003. Maria Perry has a documentary biography, *The Word of a Prince: The Life of Elizabeth I from Contemporary Documents*, 1990. The queen's significance as political and cultural presence is treated by Frances Yates, *Astraea: The Imperial Theme*, 1975; Marie Axton, *The Queen's Two Bodies: Drama and the Elizabethan Succession*, 1977; Phillippa Berry, *Of Chastity and Power: Elizabethan Literature and the Unmarried Queen*, 1989; Carole Levin, *"The Heart and Stomach of a King": Elizabeth I and the Politics of Sex and Power*, 1994; Mary Cole, *The Portable Queen: Elizabeth I and the Politics of Ceremony*, 1999; John Watkins, *Representing Elizabeth in Stuart England: Literature, History, and Sovereignty*, 2002; and *The Myth of Elizabeth*, ed. Susan Doran and Thomas Freeman, 2003. Susan Bassnett, *Elizabeth I: A Feminist Perspective*, 1988, approaches the queen's career through her writings; Susan Frye, *Elizabeth I: The Competition for Representation*, 1993, studies Elizabeth's construction of her power within a patriarchal society. *ELR* 23 (1993): 345–54, 24 (1994): 234–36, and 30 (2000): 470–73, survey recent studies of Elizabeth.

The English Bible
Debora Shuger's *The Renaissance Bible: Scholarship, Sacrifice, and Subjectivity*, 1994, analyzes the place of Scripture in a wide range of early modern discourses. Shuger is also the author of *Political Theologies in Shakespeare's England: The Sacred and the State in "Measure for Measure,"* 2001. Other important studies include Tessa Watt, *Cheap Print and Popular Piety, 1550–1640*, 1991; *Religion and Culture in Renaissance England*, ed. Claire McEachern and Debora Shuger, 1997; Alison Shell, *Catholicism, Controversy, and the English Literary Imagination, 1558–1660*, 1999; Ramie Targoff, *Common Prayer: The Language of Public Devotion in Early Modern England*, 2001; and Brian Cummings, *The Literary Culture of the Reformation: Grammar and Grace*, 2002. Studies of the English Bible include John Coolidge, *The Pauline Renaissance in England: Puritanism and the Bible*, 1970; David Daiches, *The King James Version of the English Bible*, 1968; F. F. Bruce, *History of the Bible in English*, 1978; A. C. Partridge, *English Biblical Translation*, 1973; David Daniell, *The Bible in English: Its History and Influence*, 2003; and Adam Nicolson, *God's Secretaries: The Making of the King James Bible*, 2003.

Mary (Sidney) Herbert, Countess of Pembroke
Margaret P. Hannay et al. edited the *Collected Works*, 2 vols., 1998; there is an important edition of *The Psalms of Sir Philip Sidney and the Countess of Pembroke*, ed J. C. A. Rathmell, 1963. Margaret P. Hannay has written the only literary biography, *Philip's Phoenix*, 1990. Mary Herbert is also one of the three writers treated in Kim Walker, *Women Writers of the English Renaissance*, 1996, and she is discussed in Elizabeth Mazzola, *Favorite Sons: The Politics and Poetics of the Sidney Family*, 2003. Other important studies are Gary Waller, *Mary Sidney, Countess of Pembroke: A Critical Study of Her Writings and Literary Milieu*, 1979, and Mary Ellen Lamb, *Gender and Authorship in the Sidney Circle*, 1990. Recent studies are surveyed in *ELR* 14 (1984): 426–37 and 24 (1994): 237–38, and recent studies of metrical psalms are surveyed in *ELR* 33 (2003): 252–75.

Christopher Marlowe
The current standard edition is *The Complete Works of Christopher Marlowe*, Oxford English Texts, 5 vols. 1987–98. W. W. Greg edited parallel texts of the two versions of *Dr. Faustus* in 1950; the two versions have also been edited by David Bevington and Eric Rasmussen, 1993. Stephen Orgel edited *The Complete Poems and Translations of Christopher Marlowe*, 1971. See also the Norton Critical Edition of *Dr. Faustus*. For Marlowe's biography see John Bakeless, *The Tragicall History of Christopher Marlowe*, 2 vols., 1942; Charles Nicholl, *The Reckoning: The Murder of Christopher Marlowe*, 1992; Constance Brown Kuriyama, *Christopher Marlowe: A Renaissance Life*, 2002; and David Riggs, *The World of Christopher Marlowe*, 2004. Valuable critical studies include Harry Levin, *The Overreacher*, 1952; *Two Renaissance Mythmakers: Christopher Marlowe and Ben Jonson*, ed. Alvin B. Kernan, 1977; *Marlowe: The Critical Heritage*, ed. Millar McLure, 1979; *Christopher Marlowe*, in the series "Modern Critical Views," ed. Harold Bloom, 1986; C. L. Barber, *Creating Elizabethan Tragedy: the Theater of Marlowe and Kyd*, 1988. *Christopher Marlowe's "Doctor Faustus,"* in "Modern Critical Interpretations," ed. Harold Bloom, 1988; *Christopher Marlowe and English Renaissance Culture*, ed. Darryll Grantley and Peter Roberts, 1996; Patrick Cheney, *Marlowe's Counterfeit Profession: Ovid, Spenser, Counter-Nationhood*, 1997; *Marlowe, History,*

and Sexuality: New Critical Essays on Christopher Marlowe, ed. Paul White, 1998; *Christopher Marlowe,* ed. Richard Wilson, 1999; *Constructing Christopher Marlowe,* ed. J. A. Downie and J. T. Parnell, 2000; *Marlowe's Empery: Expanding his Critical Contexts*, ed. Sara Deats and Robert Logan, 2002; Ruth Lunney, *Marlowe and the Popular Tradition: Innovation in the English Drama before 1595*, 2002; and *The Cambridge Companion to Christopher Marlowe*, ed. Patrick Cheney, 2004. For *Hero and Leander*, Louis L. Martz's facsimile of the first edition, 1972, has an important introduction. On the genre, see William Keach, *Elizabeth Erotic Narratives*, 1977, and Clark Hulse, *Metamorphic Verse: The Elizabethan Minor Epic*, 1981. Recent studies are surveyed in *ELR* 7 (1977): 382–99; 18 (1988): 329–42; and 31 (2001): 288–328.

Sir Walter Ralegh

The collected edition is by William Oldys and Thomas Birch, 8 vols., 1829, rpt. 1965; the standard edition of the poems is by A. M. C. Latham, rev. 1950; more recent is *The Poems of Sir Walter Ralegh: A Historical Edition*, ed. Michael Rudick, 1999. *The History of the World* is edited by C. A. Patrides, 1971. Another useful edition is *Selected Writings*, ed. Gerard Hammond, 1984. *The Discoverie of the Large, Rich and Bewtiful Empyre of Guiana* has been newly edited, with much contextual and interpretive material, by Neil L. Whitehead, 1997. For Ralegh's correspondence, see *The Letters of Sir Walter Ralegh*, ed. Agnes Latham and Joyce Youings, 1999. Biographies include Willard M. Wallace, *Sir Walter Raleigh*, 1959, and Stephen Coote, *A Play of Passion,* 1993. Noteworthy studies include David B. Quinn, *Ralegh and the British Empire*, 1947, rpt. 1962; E. A. Strathmann, *Sir Walter Ralegh, A Study in Elizabethan Skepticism*, 1951; Philip Edwards, *Sir Walter Ralegh*, 1953, rpt. 1976; Stephen Greenblatt, *Sir Walter Ralegh*, 1973; and Shannon Miller, *Invested with Meaning: The Raleigh Circle in the New World*, 1998. For guides to scholarship, see Jerry L. Mills, *Sir Walter Ralegh: A Reference Guide*, 1986, and Christopher Armitage, *Sir Walter Ralegh, An Annotated Bibliography*, 1987.

William Shakespeare

Important editions of *Twelfth Night* include the Variorum (ed. H. H. Furness, 1901); the Arden (eds. J. M. Lothan and T. W. Craik, 1975); and the Oxford (eds. Roger Warren and Stanley Wells, 1994). Significant studies of *Twelfth Night* are assembled by Walter King ("Twentieth Century Interpretations"), 1968; Stanley Wells ("Critical Essays"), 1986; Harold Bloom ("Modern Critical Interpretations"), 1987; and Barbara Everett ("New Casebooks"), 1996. The play is treated in the context of Shakespearean comedy by C. L. Barber, *Shakespeare's Festive Comedy*, 1959; Northrop Frye, *A Natural Perspective*, 1965; Linda Bamber, *Comic Women, Tragic Men*, 1982; Edward Berry, *Shakespeare's Comic Rites*, 1984; and William Carroll, *The Metamorphoses of Shakespearean Comedy*, 1985. Other important studies include Stephen Greenblatt, "Fiction and Friction," in *Shakespearean Negotiations*, 1988; Laura Levine, *Men in Women's Clothing: Anti-Theatricality and Effeminization, 1579 to 1642*, 1994; and Stephen Booth, *Precious Nonsense: The Gettysburg Address, Ben Jonson's Epitaphs on His Children, and "Twelfth Night,"* 1998. For the music in *Twelfth Night* (and other Shakespeare plays), see Ross Durfin, *Shakespeare's Songbook*, 2004, with CD.

The objects of obsessive critical attention for centuries, Shakespeare's plays have recently been studied from new-historicist, feminist, psychoanalytic, and deconstructive perspectives, among others. The range may be sampled in such collections as *Representing Shakespeare: New Psychoanalytic Essays*, ed. Murray Schwartz and Coppelia Kahn, 1980; *Alternative Shakespeares*, ed. John Drakakis, 1985, 2nd ed. 2002; *Shakespeare and the Question of Theory*, ed. Patricia Parker and Geoffrey Hartman, 1985; *Shakespeare Reproduced*, ed. Jean Howard and M. O'Connor, 1987; *Political Shakespeare*, ed. Jonathan Dollimore and Alan Sinfield, 1994; and in such books as Lisa Jardine, *Still Harping on Daughters*, 1983; Marjorie Garber, *Shakespeare's Ghost Writers*, 1987; Stephen Greenblatt, *Shakespearean Negotiations*, 1988; Margreta de Grazia, *Shakespeare Verbatim*, 1991; Janet Adelman, *Suffocating Mothers*, 1992; Valerie Traub, *Desire and Anxiety*, 1992; Harry Berger Jr., *Making Trifles of Terrors*, 1997; David Kastan, *Shakespeare After Theory*, 1999; *Shakespeare, the Critical Complex*, 10 vols., ed. Stephen Orgel and Sean Keilin, 1999; Lynn Enterline, *The Rhetoric of the Body from Ovid to Shakespeare*, 2000; Frank Kermode, *Shakespeare's Language*, 2000; Robin Headlam Wells, *Shakespeare on Masculinity*, 2000; James P. Bednarz, *Shakespeare and the Poets' War*, 2001; David Kastan, *Shakespeare and the Book*, 2001; Stephen Orgel, *The Authentic Shakespeare, and Other Problems of the Early Modern Stage*, 2002; Brian Vickers, *Shakespeare, Co-Author: A Historical Study of Five Collaborative Plays*, 2002; and Lukas Erne, *Shakespeare as Literary Dramatist*, 2003. See also *A Companion to Shakespeare*, ed. Kastan, 1999; *The Cambridge Companion to Shakespeare*, ed. Margreta de Grazia and Stanley Wells, 2001; *The Oxford Companion to Shakespeare*, ed. Michael Dobson and Stanley Wells, 2001; and Laurie Maguire, *Studying Shakespeare: A Guide to the Plays*, 2004. Notable performance studies include Marvin Rosenberg, *The Masks of Lear*, 1972; David Bevington, *Action Is Eloquence*, 1984; Michael Goldman, *Acting and Action in Shake-*

spearean Tragedy, 1985; Peter Donaldson, *Shakespearean Films, Shakespearean Directors*, 1990; William Worthen, *Shakespeare and the Authority of Performance*, 1997; *Shakespeare, the Movie: Popularizing the Plays on Film, TV, and Video*, and *Shakespeare, the Movie II*, ed. Lynda Boose and Richard Burt, 1997 and 2003; *Remaking Shakespeare: Performance Across Media, Genres, and Cultures*, ed. Pascale Aebischer, Edward J. Esche, and Nigel Wheale, 2003; and *Shakespeare in Performance: A Collection of Essays*, ed. Frank Occhiogrosso, 2003.

Hyder Rollins's Variorum edition of the sonnets, 2 vols., 1944, summarizes many commentaries and problems; Stephen Booth's edition, 1977, presents a facsimile of the first edition and a modernized text on facing pages, with elaborate commentary; see, likewise, the Arden Edition (ed. K. Duncan-Jones, 1997) and Helen Vendler, *The Art of Shakespeare's Sonnets*, 1997. Other recent editions include *The Sonnets and A Lover's Complaint*, ed. John Kerrigan, 1986; *Shakespeare's Sonnets and Poems*, ed. Harold Bloom, 1999; and *Shakespeare: The Complete Sonnets and Poems*, ed. Colin Burrow, 2002. Noteworthy criticism of the sonnets and poems includes Stephen Booth, *An Essay on Shakespeare's Sonnets*, 1969; Joseph Pequigney, *Such Is My Love: A Study of Shakespeare's Sonnets*, 1985; Joel Fineman, *Shakespeare's Perjured Eye: The Invention of Poetic Subjectivity in the Sonnets*, 1986; Heather Dubrow, *Captive Victors: Shakespeare's Narrative Poems and Sonnets*, 1987; Bruce Smith, *Homosexual Desire in Shakespeare's England*, 1991; Margreta de Grazia, "The Scandal of Shakespeare's Sonnets," in *Shakespeare Survey* 46 (1994): 35–49; *Shakespeare's Sonnets: Critical Essays*, ed. James Schiffer, 1999; Richard Halpern, *Shakespeare's Perfume: Sodomy and Sublimity in the Sonnets, Wilde, Freud, and Lacan*, 2002; and Sasha Roberts, *Reading Shakespeare's Poems in Early Modern England*, 2003.

The life and works are treated by E. K. Chambers, *William Shakespeare: A Study of Facts and Problems*, 2 vols., 1930. S. Schoenbaum's important biographical research is recorded in *William Shakespeare: A Documentary Life*, 1975, and *A Compact Documentary Life*, 1977. Recent biographical studies include Stanley Wells, *Shakespeare: A Dramatic Life*, 1994; Jonathan Bate, *The Genius of Shakespeare*, 1997; Park Honan, *Shakespeare: A Life*, 1998; Katherine Duncan-Jones, *Ungentle Shakespeare: Scenes from his Life*, 2001; and Stephen Greenblatt, *Will in the World: How Shakespeare Became Shakespeare*, 2004; and James Shapiro, *A Year in the Life of William Shakespeare*, 2005. Some useful aids to scholarship are Geoffrey Bullough, *Narrative and Dramatic Sources of Shakespeare*, 8 vols., 1957–75, and *A New Companion to Shakespeare Studies*, ed. Kenneth Muir and S. Schoenbaum, 1971, rpt. 1976.

Sir Philip Sidney

Oxford editions are standard for everything except the correspondence: the poetry is edited by William A. Ringler Jr., 1962; the *Old Arcadia* by Jean Robertson, 1973; the *New Arcadia* by Victor Skretkowicz, 1987; and the *Miscellaneous Prose* (including the *Defense*) by Katherine Duncan-Jones and Jan Van Dorsten, 1973. Sidney's letters are found in *The Prose Works of Sir Philip Sidney*, 4 vols., ed. Albert Feuillerat, 1912, rpt. 1962, 3:75–184. There are valuable editions of the *Defense* by Geoffrey Shepherd, 1965, 3rd ed., 2002, and Jan Van Dorsten, 1966. Maurice Evans edited *The Countess of Pembroke's Arcadia* (the 1593 composite version) in 1977. Useful volumes of selected works are those by David Kalstone, 1970; Duncan-Jones for the Oxford English Authors series, 1989; Catherine Bates (poetry), 1994; and Elizabeth P. Watson, 1997. The earliest biography was by Sidney's friend Fulke Greville, 1652; it is included in Greville's *Prose Works*, ed. John Gouws, 1986. The standard modern biography is Duncan-Jones, *Sir Philip Sidney: Courtier Poet*, 1991. Modern studies of the life and works are John Buxton, *Sir Philip Sidney and the English Renaissance*, 1954, rpt. 1964; James M. Osborn, *Young Philip Sidney*, 1972; A. C. Hamilton, *Sir Philip Sidney: A Study of His Life and Works*, 1977; and Alan Stewart, *Philip Sidney: A Double Life*, 2000. Some important critical studies are Walter R. Davis and Richard Lanham, *Sidney's Arcadia*, 1965; David Kalstone, *Sidney's Poetry: Contexts and Interpretations*, 1965; Neil L. Rudenstine, *Sidney's Poetic Development*, 1967; Andrew Weiner, *Sir Philip Sidney and the Poetics of Protestantism*, 1978; Richard C. McCoy, *Sir Philip Sidney: Rebellion in Arcadia*, 1979; Stephen Greenblatt, "Murdering Peasants: Status, Genre, and the Representation of Rebellion," in *Representations* 1 (1983): 1–29; Joan Rees, *Sir Philip Sidney and "Arcadia,"* 1991; Roland Greene in *Post-Petrarchism*, 1991; Blair Worden, *The Sound of Virtue: Philip Sidney's "Arcadia" and Elizabethan Politics*, 1996; Henry Woudhuysen, *Sir Philip Sidney and the Circulation of Manuscripts, 1558–1640*, 1996; Edward Berry, *The Making of Sir Philip Sidney*, 1998; Lisa Klein, *The Exemplary Sidney and the Elizabethan Sonneteer*, 1998; Tom Parker, *Proportional Form in the Sonnets of the Sidney Circle: Loving in Truth*, 1998; and Elizabeth Mazzola, *Favorite Sons: The Politics and Poetics of the Sidney Family*, 2003. Dennis Kay edited *Sir Philip Sidney: An Anthology of Modern Criticism*, 1987. *Sidney in Retrospect: Selections from "English Literary Renaissance,"* ed. Arthur F. Kinney, 1988, reprints articles and reviews of scholarship from a leading Renaissance journal. Studies of *Arcadia* are surveyed in *ELR* 26 (1996): 173–81.

Edmund Spenser

Edwin A. Greenlaw et al. edited a ten-volume Variorum edition, *The Works of Edmund Spenser*, 1932–49. Important editions of *The Faerie Queene* are by A. C. Hamilton, 1977, 2nd ed., 2001, and Thomas P. Roche Jr., 1978; William A. Oram et al. edited *The Yale Edition of the Shorter Poems of Edmund Spenser*, 1989. The chief biography is *The Life of Edmund Spenser* by Alexander Judson, 1945. Two recent overviews of the life and works are Gary Waller, *Edmund Spenser, A Literary Life*, 1994, and Oram, *Edmund Spenser*, 1997. Important critical studies include C. S. Lewis, *The Allegory of Love*, 1936; Paul J. Alpers, *The Poetry of "The Faerie Queene,"* 1967; Isabel MacCaffrey, *Spenser's Allegory: The Anatomy of Imagination*, 1975; James Nohrnberg, *The Analogy of "The Faerie Queene,"* 1976; Michael O'Connell, *Mirror and Veil: The Historical Dimension of Spenser's "Faerie Queene,"* 1977; Jonathan Goldberg, *Endlesse Worke: Spenser and the Structure of Discourse*, 1981; John Guillory, *Poetic Authority: Spenser, Milton, and Literary History*, 1983; Kenneth Gross, *Spenserian Poetics: Idolatry, Iconoclasm, and Magic*, 1985; Harry Berger Jr., *Revisionary Play: Studies in the Spenserian Dynamics*, 1988; David L. Miller, *The Poem's Two Bodies: The Poetics of the 1590 "Faerie Queene,"* 1988; John N. King, *Spenser's Poetry and the Reformation Tradition*, 1990; Theresa M. Krier, *Gazing on Secret Sights: Spenser, Classical Imitation, and the Decorums of Vision*, 1990; Jeffrey Knapp, *An Empire Nowhere: England, America, and Literature from "Utopia" to "The Tempest,"* 1992; Richard Rambuss, *Spenser's Secret Career*, 1993; Gordon Teskey, *Allegory and Violence*, 1994; James W. Broaddus, *Spenser's Allegory of Love: Social Vision in Books III, IV, and V of "The Faerie Queene,"* 1995; Linda Gregerson, *The Reformation of the Subject: Spenser, Milton, and the English Protestant Epic*, 1995; Lauren Silberman, *Transforming Desire: Erotic Knowledge in Books III and IV of "The Faerie Queene,"* 1995; Colin Burrow, *Edmund Spenser*, 1996; Willy Maley, *Salvaging Spenser: Colonialism, Culture, and Identity*, 1997; Carol V. Kaske, *Spenser and Biblical Poetics*, 1999; Kenneth Borris, *Allegory and Epic in English Renaissance Literature: Heroic Form in Sidney, Spenser, and Milton*, 2000; Richard A. McCabe, *Spenser's Monstrous Regiment: Elizabethan Ireland and the Poetics of Difference*, 2002; and Andrew Hadfield, *Shakespeare, Spenser, and the Matter of Britain*, 2004. A. C. Hamilton edited *Essential Articles for the Study of Edmund Spenser*, 1972. A wide range of criticism is reprinted in Hugh Maclean and Anne Lake Prescott's Norton Critical Edition, *Edmund Spenser's Poetry*, rev. 1993. Mihoko Suzuki edited a collection of recent *Critical Essays on Edmund Spenser*, 1996; a parallel collection, issued the same year, is *Edmund Spenser*, ed. Andrew Hadfield. Hadfield is also the editor of *The Cambridge Companion to Spenser*, 2001. A collection that students may find intriguing is *Approaches to Teaching Spenser's "Faerie Queene,"* ed. David L. Miller and Alexander Dunlop, 1994. *The Spenser Encyclopedia*, ed. Hamilton et al., 1990, is an invaluable aid. The best guides to recent work are the bibliographies in the encyclopedia and the selected bibliography, with annotations, in Oram's *Edmund Spenser*.

Henry Howard, Earl of Surrey

The complete edition is by F. M. Padelford, 1928, rpt. 1966; Emrys Jones's excellent selected edition, 1964, is widely used. *Tottel's Miscellany* is edited by Hyder E. Rollins, 2 vols., rev. 1965. Biographies include E. R. Casady, *Henry Howard, Earl of Surrey*, 1938, rpt. 1966, and W. R. Sessions, *Henry Howard, The Poet Earl of Surrey: A Life*, 1999. Noteworthy critical studies are Walter R. Davis, "Contexts in Surrey's Poetry," *ELR* 4 (1974): 40–55; the chapters on Surrey in Alastair Fowler, *Conceitful Thought: The Interpretation of English Renaissance Poems*, 1975, and Jonathan Crewe, *Trials of Authorship: Anterior Forms and Poetic Reconstruction from Wyatt to Shakespeare*, 1990, and those on Wyatt and Surrey in Maurice Evans, *English Poetry in the Sixteenth Century*, rev. 1967; Susanne Woods, *Natural Emphasis: English Versification from Chaucer to Dryden*, 1984; A. C. Spearing, *Medieval to Renaissance in English Poetry*, 1985; and Elizabeth Heale, *Wyatt, Surrey and Early Tudor Poetry*, 1998. Scholarship is surveyed in Clyde W. Jentoft, *Sir Thomas Wyatt and Henry Howard, Earl of Surrey: A Reference Guide*, 1980. Reviews of critical studies are in *ELR* 19 (1989): 389–401 and 28 (1998): 307.

Sir Thomas Wyatt

The most useful edition is by Kenneth Muir and Patricia Thomson, *Collected Poems*, 1969; others are by Richard C. Harrier, 1975; Joost Daalder, 1975; and R. A. Rebholz, 1978. *Tottel's Miscellany* is edited by Hyder E. Rollins, 2 vols., rev. 1965. Letters and life records are included in Muir's biography, *The Life and Letters of Sir Thomas Wyatt*, 1963; Thomson treats both life and works in *Sir Thomas Wyatt and His Background*, 1964. Critical studies include E. M. W. Tillyard, *The Poetry of Sir Thomas Wyatt*, 1929, rpt. 1949; Raymond Southall, *The Courtly Maker*, 1964; Elizabeth W. Pomeroy, *The Elizabethan Miscellanies: Their Development and Conventions*, 1973; Stephen Greenblatt, *Renaissance Self-Fashioning*, 1980; Thomas M. Greene, *The Light in Troy: Imitation and Discovery in Renaissance Poetry*, 1982; and Barbara L. Estrin, *Laura: Uncovering Gender and Genre in Wyatt, Donne, and Marvell*, 1994. Since the sixteenth century, Wyatt and Surrey have often been discussed in tandem: for some modern instances, see **Surrey**. Patricia Thomson edited *Wyatt: The Critical Heritage*, 1974. Reviews of some Wyatt studies are in *ELR* 19 (1989): 226–46 and 28 (1998): 307–09.

THE EARLY SEVENTEENTH CENTURY

Early-seventeenth-century literature is included in the new *Cambridge History of Early Modern English Literature,* ed. David Loewenstein and Janel Mueller, 2002; its several chapters examine the interactions between sites of production, reception, and circulation and the aesthetic and generic features of early modern texts. Other general resources include Thomas N. Corns, ed., *The Cambridge Companion to English Poetry,* 1993, and Graham Parry, *The Intellectual and Cultural Context of English Literature, 1604–1700,* 1989. The journal *English Literary Renaissance* (*ELR*) publishes "Recent Studies," a survey of new material on individual sixteenth- and seventeenth-century authors and on some literary topics on an ongoing basis; they are updated periodically. In its winter issues, annually, the journal *Studies in English Literature* publishes "Recent Studies in the English Renaissance," evaluating the past year's publications. These journals regularly carry important new articles on seventeenth-century topics, as do *English Literary History, Representations, The Seventeenth Century, Seventeenth Century News, Renaissance Studies, John Donne Journal, George Herbert Journal, Milton Studies,* and *Milton Quarterly*.

Politics, Society, and Political Thought

Some general histories of the seventeenth century or some part of it include Christopher Hill, *The Century of Revolution,* 1961; Barry Coward, *The Stuart Age: A History of England,* 1980; Derek Hirst, *Authority and Conflict: England, 1603–58,* 1986; and Austin Woolrych, *Commonwealth to Protectorate,* 1982. Interpretation of the causes and progress of the English Revolution is a contested issue. A series of books by Christopher Hill emphasize political, social, and ideological conflict: *Puritanism and Revolution,* 1958; *The World Turned Upside Down,* 1972; and *The Experience of Defeat,* 1984. The "revisionist" view sees this event not as a revolution but as an accidental consequence of politicians' incompetence: it is represented by J. S. Morrill, *Seventeenth-Century Britain,* 1980; Conrad Russell, *The Causes of the English Civil War,* 1990, and his *Unrevolutionary England, 1603–1642,* 1990. Some efforts to revise the revisionists include J. P. Sommerville, *Politics and Ideology in England, 1603–1640,* 1986; Richard Cust and Ann Hughes, eds., *Conflict in Early Stuart England: Studies in Religion and Politics, 1603–1642,* 1989, and Geoff Eley and William Hunt, eds., *Reviving the English Revolution,* 1988. Several scholars explore republican and royalist ideas and attitudes before, during, and after the regicide. Johann Sommerville discusses the clash of ideologies in the decades preceding the war in *Royalists and Patriots: Politics and Ideologies in England, 1603–1640,* 1999. Thomas Corns does the same for the war years and the Interregnum in *Uncloistered Virtue,* 1992. For royalist writing, see Robert Wilcher, *The Writing of Royalism,* 2001. David Norbrook has written a wide-ranging study of writers who contributed to the emergence of republican thought and culture in England, *Writing the English Republic: Poetry, Rhetoric and Politics, 1627–1660,* 1999. Other important studies include Sharon Achinstein, *Literature and Dissent in Milton's England,* 2003, and Sean Kelsey, *Inventing a Republic: The Political Culture of the English Commonwealth, 1649–1653,* 1997. Laura Lunger Knoppers has investigated visual and literary representations of the Protector in *Constructing Cromwell,* 2000.

The complex place of religion, both as doctrine and cultural force, is explored in Keith Thomas, *Religion and the Decline of Magic: Popular Beliefs in Sixteenth- and Seventeenth-Century England,* 1978; Patrick Collinson, *The Religion of Protestants,* 1980, and *The Birth-pangs of Protestant England,* 1986; David Underdown, *Revel, Riot, and Rebellion: Popular Politics and Culture in England, 1603–1660,* 1985; and Arthur Marotti, *Catholicism and Anti-Catholicism in Early Modern English Texts,* 1999. David Loewenstein has examined the complex interconnections of radical religion and revolution in several major and minor figures in *Representing Revolution in Milton and His Contemporaries: Religion, Politics, and Polemics in Radical Puritanism,* 2001. Nigel Smith has studied the rhetoric and assumptions about language of the revolution's radical sects—Quakers, Ranters, Diggers—in *Perfection Proclaimed: Language and Literature in English Radical Religion,* 1989. Suggestive essays on the interrelation of events, religion, and culture are collected in Kevin Sharpe and Peter Lake, eds., *Culture and Politics in Early Stuart England,* 1994, and C. McEachern and D. Shuger, eds., *Religion and Culture in Renaissance England,* 1997.

English society in the seventeenth century was analyzed by the German sociologist Max Weber in an influential essay, 1904, emphasizing the importance of the Protestant doctrine of the calling or vocation for the aspiring capitalist class; that thesis was further developed by R. H. Tawney in *Religion and the Rise of Capitalism,* 1926, but it has been much disputed, notably by

H. R. Trevor-Roper. Books that describe socioeconomic changes and the cultural and intellectual changes produced by England's quickening commercial life include Keith Wrightson, *Earthly Necessities: Economic Lives in Early Modern Britain,* 2000; Craig Muldrew, *The Economy of Obligation*, 1998; and David Wootten, ed., *Republicanism, Liberty, and Commercial Society, 1649–1776,* 1994. Peter Laslett's book *The World We Have Lost*, 3rd ed., 1984, helps in imagining what life was like in a preindustrial society. Studies of early modern society of special interest to students of literature include Lawrence Stone, *The Family, Sex, and Marriage in England, 1500–1800,* 1977; Keith Wrightson, *English Society, 1580–1680,* 1977; Susan Amussen, *An Ordered Society: Gender and Class in Early Modern England,* 1988; and Alan Bray, *Homosexuality in Renaissance England,* 1992. A general study of schools and education in the period is K. Charlton, *Education in Renaissance England,* 1965.

The material changes in the ways in which literary texts were transmitted have received increased attention in recent years. Books that explore these issues include Elizabeth Eisenstein, *The Printing Press as an Agent of Change,* 2 vols., 1979; Harold Love, *Scribal Publication in Seventeenth-Century England,* 1993; Arthur Marotti, *Manuscript, Print, and the English Renaissance Lyric,* 1995; and Joseph Loewenstein, *The Author's Due: Printing and the Prehistory of Copyright,* 2002. Several studies explore the way patronage and censorship influenced what was written in the period and how it was understood by contemporaries: Annabel Patterson, *Censorship and Interpretation: The Conditions of Writing and Reading in Early Modern England,* 1984; Cedric Brown, ed., *Patronage, Politics, and Literary Traditions in England, 1558–1658,* 1991; and Stephen Orgel and Guy Lytle, eds., *Patronage in the Renaissance,* 1981. Joad Raymond has studied the emergence of the newspaper during the revolutionary era as a force in the creation of a public sphere of discourse in *The Invention of the Newspaper: English Newsbooks 1641–1649,* 1996.

Helpful overviews of political thought in the seventeenth century are to be found in J. G. A. Pocock's seminal works, *The Ancient Constitution and the Feudal Law,* rev. 1987, and *The Machiavellian Moment: Florentine Political Thought and the Atlantic Republican Tradition,* 1975; Quentin Skinner's *The Foundation of Modern Political Thought*, 2 vols., 1978; and Richard Tuck's *Philosophy and Government, 1572–1651,* 1993. A useful collection of political treatises in the period has been edited by David Wooten, *Divine Right and Democracy: An Anthology of Political Writing in Stuart England,* 1986. J. H. Burns has edited essays pertaining to the period that are included in *The Cambridge History of Political Thought, 1450–1700,* 1991.

Literature, Culture, and Politics

Several studies focus on the intellectual and cultural milieu of the period as it affects literature. Inherited views of the universe based on hierarchy, order, and analogy, which were still prevalent in poetic imagery, are set forth in E. M. W. Tillyard's concise though oversimplified account, *The Elizabethan World Picture,* 1943. Studies focusing on the challenge of the new science include Rupert Hall, *The Scientific Resolution, 1500–1800,* 1956; William R. Shea, *Galileo's Intellectual Revolution,* 1972; Hans Blumenberg, *The Genesis of the Copernican World,* 1987; and Barbara Shapiro, *Probability and Certainty in Seventeenth-Century England,* 1983. Some sense of the still-powerful influence of the occult—alchemy, magic, hermeticism, and the like—may be gleaned from Wayne Shumaker's *The Occult Sciences in the Renaissance,* 1972. C. A. Patrides and Raymond Waddington have edited a useful collection of essays on various facets of seventeenth-century society and culture, *The Age of Milton: Backgrounds to Seventeenth-Century Literature,* 1980. More focused studies of intellectual currents include Debora Shuger, *Habits of Thought in the English Renaissance,* 1990; Victoria Kahn, *Machiavellian Rhetoric: From the Counter-Reformation to Milton,* 1994; and John Rogers, *The Matter of Revolution: Science, Poetry, and Politics in the Age of Milton,* 1996. A fine brief account of court culture in the Jacobean and Caroline eras is by Graham Parry, *The Golden Age Restored: The Culture of the Stuart Court, 1603–1642,* 1981.

Studies of seventeenth-century literature in relation to political and cultural forces include Leah Marcus, *The Politics of Mirth: Jonson, Herrick, Milton, Marvell,* 1986; Aschah Guibbory, *Ceremony and Community from Herbert to Milton: Religion and Cultural Conflict in Seventeenth-Century England,* 1998; and David Norbrook, *Poetry and Politics in the English Renaissance,* 1987. Several collections of essays treat particular topics and writers in these terms: Claude Summers and Ted-Larry Pebworth, eds., *The Muses Common-Weale: Poetry and Politics in the Seventeenth Century,* 1988; Kevin Sharpe and Steven Zwicker, eds., *The Politics of Discourse: The Literature and History of Seventeenth-Century England,* 1987; Kevin Sharpe and Peter Lake, eds., *Culture and Politics in Early Stuart England,* 1994; and Richard Burt and John M. Archer, eds., *Enclosure Acts: Sexuality, Property, and Culture in Early Modern England,* 1994.

Analyses focusing especially on the Jacobean era are Jonathan Goldberg, *James I and the Politics of Literature,* 1983; Curtis Perry, *The Making of Jacobean Culture,* 1998; and an important collection of essays edited by Linda Levy Peck, *The Mental World of the Jacobean Court,* 1991. Kevin Sharpe has edited a collection of essays pertaining to the Caroline era, *Criticism and Compliment: The Politics of Literature in the England of Charles I*, 1987. Studies treating the literature and culture of the revolutionary era focus on Milton, Marvell, and several royalist poets and prose writers: they include Michael Wilding, *Dragon's Teeth: Literature in the English Revolution*, 1987; Nigel Smith, *Literature and Revolution in England, 1640–1660*, 1994, which treats the political uses of various genres; Thomas Corns, *Uncloistered Virtue: English Political Literature, 1640–1660*, 1992; and Steven Zwicker, *Lines of Authority: Politics and English Culture, 1649–1689*, 1993. Works that attend especially to royalist writers are Raymond Anselment, *Loyalist Resolve: Patient Fortitude in the English Civil War*, 1988; Lois Potter, *Secret Rites and Secret Writing: Royalist Literature, 1641–1660*, 1989; and a collection of essays edited by Claude J. Summers and Ted-Larry Pebworth, *Classic and Cavalier: Essays on Jonson and the Sons of Ben*, 1982. Other important essays are edited by Thomas Healy and Jonathan Sawday in *Literature and the English Civil War*, 1990, and by James Holsten in *Pamphlet Wars: Prose in the English Revolution*, 1992.

Genre, Style, and Poetics

Valuable perspectives on literary history, the literary institution, and aspects of style in the period are provided in several works. Seventeenth-century critical texts are included in an anthology edited by Brian Vickers, *English Renaissance Literary Criticism*, 1999. An illuminating and elegant brief account of the place and uses of genre is supplied by Rosalie Colie in *The Resources of Kind: Genre-Theory in the Renaissance*, 1973. While the category of Metaphysical poets has lost much of its usefulness, Earl Miner's three volumes provide important surveys of the literature of the era: *The Metaphysical Mode from Donne to Cowley*, 1969; *The Cavalier Mode from Jonson to Cotton*, 1971; and *The Restoration Mode from Milton to Dryden*, 1974. George Parfitt has provided a single-volume survey, *English Poetry of the Seventeenth Century*, 1985. Barbara K. Lewalski, *Protestant Poetics and the Seventeenth-Century Religious Lyric*, 1979, treats the impact of Protestant theology, sermon theory, and devotional practices on poetics and religious poetry, especially Donne, Herbert, Vaughan, and Traherne. Anthony Low, in *Love's Architecture: Devotional Modes in Seventeenth-Century English Poetry*, 1978, has studied the religious lyric poets from another perspective, and Ramie Targoff has emphasized the importance of public devotional practices on several poets, especially Herbert, in *Common Prayer: The Language of Public Devotion in Early Modern England*, 2001. Diane McColley has explored the relationship between the poetic language of several major poets and the music of the period in *Poetry and Music in Seventeenth-Century England*, 1997. An important collection of essays that reconsiders canonical poets of the period in the light of poststructuralist theory is *Soliciting Interpretation: Literary Theory and Seventeenth-Century Poetry*, ed. Elizabeth D. Harvey and Katharine E. Maus, 1990. Another impressive essay collection reexamines the category of "wit" in several poets of the period, *The Wit of Seventeenth-Century Poetry*, ed. Claude J. Summers and Ted-Larry Pebworth, 1995.

The styles, varieties, and rhetoric of seventeenth-century prose are treated in several important studies: Maurice Croll, in *Style, Rhetoric, and Rhythm*, ed. J. M. Patrick et al., 1966; Stanley Fish, *Self-Consuming Artifacts: The Experience of Seventeenth-Century Literature*, 1972 (Bacon, Burton, Browne, Milton, Bunyan); Joan Webber, *The Eloquent "I": Style and Self in Seventeenth-Century Prose*, 1973; Roger Pooley, *English Prose of the Seventeenth Century, 1590–1700*, 1992; and Victoria Kahn, *Machiavellian Rhetoric: From the Counter-Reformation to Milton*, 1994. In *Paradoxia Epidemica*, 1966, Rosalie Colie studies the pervasiveness of paradox in texts of all kinds throughout the century.

Important studies of particular genres in relation to seventeenth-century culture include Rosemary Freeman, *English Emblem Books*, 1948; Paul Delany, *British Autobiography in the 17th Century*, 1968; Paul Alpers, *What Is Pastoral?*, 1999; Ellen Z. Lambert, *Placing Sorrow: A Study of Pastoral Elegy*, 1976; Anthony Low, *The Georgic Revolution*, 1985; Paul Salzman, *English Prose Fiction 1558–1700: A Critical History*, 1985; Heather DuBrow, *The Happier Eden: The Politics of Marriage in the English Epithalamion*, 1990; Amy Boesky, *Founding Fictions: Utopias in Early Modern England*, 1996; Alastair Fowler, *The Country-House Poem*, 1994; and on the same genre, Hugh Jenkins, *Feigned Commonwealths: The Country-House Poem and the Fashioning of the Ideal Community*, 1998.

Because most scholars of English Renaissance drama consider Tudor and Stuart drama as part of a continuous tradition, many of the books recommended for the study of sixteenth-century drama also include chapters on Jacobean and Caroline plays. Some studies of drama in the Stuart era are Brian Gibbons, *Jacobean City Comedy*, 1968; Margot Heinemann, *Puritanism and Theater: Thomas Middleton and Opposition Drama under the Early Stuarts*, 1980; Albert Tricomi, *Anticourt Drama in England, 1603–1642*, 1987; and Richard Strier and David Bevington, eds., *The Theatrical City: Culture, Theater, and Politics in Post-Reformation England*, 1995.

Women's Roles and Writing

An important recovery effort is under way in publishing and studying hitherto unknown or little-studied works by early modern women, sometimes highlighting gender issues, sometimes attending to their self-constructions as patrons and authors, sometimes addressing aesthetic and stylistic matters. Betty Travitsky and Patrick Cullen are publishing in facsimile an ongoing series of published and unpublished writings by women in the period 1500–1640. Some anthologies of writing by women in (or including) the seventeenth century are Betty Travitsky, ed., *The Paradise of Women,* 1981; Germaine Greer et al., eds., *Kissing the Rod: An Anthology of Seventeenth-Century Women's Verse,* 1988; Katharine Wilson and Frank J. Warnke, eds., *Women Writers of the Seventeenth Century,* 1989; and Elspeth Graham et al., eds., *Her Own Life: Autobiographical Writings by Seventeenth-Century Englishwomen,* 1989. Anita Pacheco has edited a useful *Companion to Early Modern Women's Writing,* 2002. An annotated bibliography by Hilda Smith and Susan Cardinale, *Women and the Literature of the Seventeenth Century,* 1900, gives a brief account of all the works by or about women listed in Donald Wing's *Short-Title Catalogue of English Books Published between 1641 and 1700.* Elaine Hobby, in *Virtue of Necessity: English Women's Writing, 1649–88,* 1988, discusses women writers and their several genres, with a bibliography. Other important bibliographical resources are Mary Thomas Crane, "Women and the Early Modern Canon: Recent Editions of Works by English Women, 1500–1660," *Renaissance Quarterly* 51 (1998); and the "Recent Studies" feature, on seventeenth-century women writers, by Elizabeth Hageman and Sara Jayne Steen, in *ELR* 14 (1984), 18 (1988), and 24 (1994).

Some important studies of women, writing, and gender in the period are Linda Woodbridge, *Women and the English Renaissance: Literature and the Nature of Womenkind, 1540–1620,* 1984; Margaret Ferguson, Maureen Quilligan, and Nancy Vickers, eds., *Rewriting the Renaissance: The Discourses of Sexual Difference in Early Modern England,* 1986; Margaret J. M. Ezell, *The Patriarch's Wife,* 1987; Wendy Wall, *The Imprint of Gender: Authorship and Publication in the English Renaissance,* 1993; and Mihoko Suzuki, *Subordinate Subjects: Gender, the Political Nation, and Literary Form in England, 1588–1688,* 2003. Some of the women writers included in *NAEL* (Lanyer, Speght, Cary, Wroth, Philips, and Cavendish) are treated by Elaine Beilin in *Redeeming Eve: Women Writers of the English Renaissance,* 1987; by Sara Mendelson in *The Mental World of Stuart Women,* 1987; by Tina Krontiris in *Oppositional Voices: Women as Writers and Translators of Literature in the English Renaissance,* 1992; by Barbara K. Lewalski in *Writing Women in Jacobean England,* 1993; and by Louise Schleiner in *Tudor and Stuart Women Writers,* 1994. Some important collections of essays including many on these women are Anne M. Haselkorn and Betty Travitsky, eds., *The Renaissance Englishwoman in Print: Counterbalancing the Canon,* 1990; Helen Wilcox, ed., *Women and Literature in Britain, 1500–1700,* 1996; Claude J. Summers and Ted-Larry Pebworth, eds., *Representing Women in Renaissance England,* 1997; and Jane Donawerth et al., eds., *Women, Writing, and the Reproduction of Culture,* 1998. Phyllis Mack's *Visionary Women: Ecstatic Prophecy in Seventeenth-Century England,* 1992, highlights the emergence of prophecy as a genre for women, especially during the revolution; and there is a complementary study by Bonnelyn Y. Kunze, *Margaret Fell and the Rise of Quakerism,* 1994.

Margaret Cavendish

Kate Lilley has edited *Margaret Cavendish: "The Description of a New World Called The Blazing World" and Other Writings,* 1992; *The Blazing World* is also included in Paul Salzman's *Anthology of Seventeenth-Century Fiction,* 1992, and he discusses that work in his *English Prose Fiction,* 1985, as do Amy Boesky, in *Founding Fictions,* 1996; Marina Leslie, in *Renaissance Utopias and the Problem of History,* 1998; and Mihoko Suzuki, in *Subordinate Subjects,* 2003. Two of Cavendish's books have been reprinted in facsimile, *Sociable Letters,* 1969, and *Poems and Fancies,* 1972. There are selections in Wilson and Warnke, eds. *Women Writers of the Seventeenth Century,* and in Greer et al., eds., *Kissing the Rod.* Ann Shaver has edited plays by Cavendish in *"Convent of Pleasure" and Other Plays,* 1999. The best biography is by Kathleen Jones, *A Glorious Fame: The Life of Margaret Cavendish, Duchess of Newcastle, 1623–1673,* 1988. Book-length critical treatments of Cavendish include Emma Rees, *Margaret Cavendish: Gender, Genre, Exile,* 2003, and Stephen Clueas, ed., *A Princely Brave Woman: Essays on Margaret Cavendish,* 2003. Some useful articles are Catherine Gallagher, "Embracing the Absolute: The Politics of the Female Subject in Seventeenth-Century England," *Genders* 1 (1988), and Eve Keller, "Producing Petty Gods: Margaret Cavendish's Critique of Experimental Science," *English Literary History* 64 (1997).

John Donne

The two-volume edition of Donne's *Poems* edited by H. J. C. Grierson, 1912, is still important, though we now have newer Oxford editions of Donne's several genres: Helen Gardner, ed., *The Divine Poems,* 1952, rev. 1978; Gardner, ed., *The Elegies and the Songs and Sonnets,* 1965; Wesley Milgate, ed., *The Satires, Epigrams, and Verse Letters,* 1967; and Milgate, ed., *The Epithalamiums, Anniversaries, and Epi-*

cedes, 1978. George Potter and Evelyn Simpson have edited *The Sermons of John Donne*, 10 vols. 1953–62. Donne's meditations were edited by Anthony Raspa, *John Donne: Devotions upon Emergent Occasions*, 1975. There are several single-volume editions of the English poems, one by C. A. Patrides, 1985, rpt. 1994; another by A. L. Clements, 1966, rev. 1992. A *Donne Variorum* edition is in progress, 1995–, under the general editorship of Gary Stringer; vol. 2, *The Elegies*; vol. 6, *Anniversaries and Epicedes*; and vol. 8, *Epigrams, Epithalamions, Epitaphs, Etc.*, have been published. The first biography of Donne was by Izaak Walton, 1640. *John Donne: A Life*, 1970, is the standard biography. John Carey, *John Donne: Life, Mind, and Art*, 1981, offers a challenging account of the psychological and social factors influencing Donne's life choices and his poetry. Arthur Marotti, in *John Donne: Coterie Poet*, 1986, locates Donne in his social milieu and places his poems in relation to the various audiences they addressed.

T. S. Eliot's essay "The Varieties of Metaphysical Poets," in *Selected Essays, 1917–1932*, 1932, rpt. 1969, was influential in setting terms for analyzing Donne over several decades; Cleanth Brook's reading of "The Canonization" in his *Well Wrought Urn*, 1947, is a classic of the New Criticism. Donne is discussed in many accounts of the period (e.g., Miner, *Metaphysical Mode;* Lewalski, *Protestant Poetics;* and Goldberg, *James I and the Politics of Literature*) and has invited several valuable individual studies: Donald Guss, *John Donne: Petrarchist*, 1966; Murray Roston, *The Soul of Wit*, 1974; Barbara K. Lewalski, *Donne's Anniversaries and the Poetry of Praise;* 1973; Stevie Davies, *Reassessing John Donne*, 1986; Terry Sherwood, *Fulfilling the Circle*, 1986; and Meg Lota Brown, *Donne and the Politics of Conscience*, 1995. Many significant critical essays are collected in A. J. Smith, ed., *John Donne: Essays in Celebration*, 1972, and *John Donne: The Critical Heritage, 1975–1995*, 1995; Harold Bloom, ed., *John Donne and the Seventeenth-Century Metaphysical Poets*, 1986; Claude J. Summers and Ted-Larry Pebworth, eds., *The Eagle and the Dove: Reassessing John Donne*, 1986; and Arthur Marotti, ed., *Critical Essays on John Donne*, 1994.

George Herbert

The standard edition is *The Works of George Herbert*, ed. F. E. Hutchinson, rev. 1945; C. A. Patrides edited a compact edition of *The English Poems*, 1974. Izaak Walton wrote a contemporary *Life of George Herbert*, 1670; there are modern biographies by Amy Charles, *A Life of George Herbert*, 1977; by Stanley Stewart, *George Herbert*, 1986; and by Christina Malcolmson, *George Herbert: A Literary Life*, 2004. Besides the general studies mentioned above (e.g., Lewalski, *Protestant Poetics*, and Low, *Love's Architecture: Devotional Modes*), several important critical books on Herbert deal with the interrelation of Herbert's religion and his art: Rosemund Tuve, *A Reading of George Herbert*, 1952; Joseph Summers, *George Herbert: His Religion and His Art*, 1966; Stanley Fish, *The Living Temple: George Herbert and Catechizing*, 1978; Diana Benet, *Secretary of Praise: The Poetic Vocation of George Herbert*, 1984; Chana Bloch, *Spelling the Word: George Herbert and the Bible*, 1985; Terry Sherwood, *Herbert's Prayerful Art*, 1989; Richard Strier, *Love Known: Theology and Experience in George Herbert's Poetry*, 1982; Gene E. Veath, *Reformation Spirituality: The Religion of George Herbert*, 1985; Harold E. Toliver, *Herbert's Christian Narratives*, 1993; and Christina Malcolmson, *Heart-Work: George Herbert and the Protestant Ethic*, 1999. Helen Vendler, in *The Poetry of George Herbert*, 1975, focuses on Herbert's exquisite art. Michael Schoenfeldt, in *Prayer and Power: George Herbert and Renaissance Courtiership*, 1991, explores the interdependence of social and religious discourse, to advance a cultural poetics of Herbert's lyrics. There are several essay collections all or partly on Herbert: Claude Summers and Ted-Larry Pebworth, eds. *"Too Rich to Clothe the Sunne": Essays on George Herbert*, 1980; Summers and Pebworth, eds. *"Bright Shoots of Everlastingness": The Seventeenth-Century Religious Lyric*, 1987; and C. A. Patrides, ed., *George Herbert: The Critical Heritage*, 1983. Recent studies are surveyed in *ELR* 18 (1988): 460–75.

Robert Herrick

The standard edition is by L. C. Martin, *The Poetical Works of Robert Herrick*, 1956; J. Max Patrick also edited the *Complete Poetry of Robert Herrick*, in 1963. There are biographical accounts by Roger Rollin, *Robert Herrick*, 1966, rpt. 1992, and George W. Scott, *Robert Herrick*, 1974. Important critical studies include Robert Deming, *Ceremony and Art: Robert Herrick's Poetry*, 1974; Gordon Braden, *The Classics and English Poetry: Three Case Studies*, 1978; Ann Baynes Coiro, *Robert Herrick's Hesperides and the Epigram Book Tradition*, 1988; as well as essays by Leah Marcus in *The Politics of Mirth*, 1986, and by Aschah Guibbory in *The Muses' Common-Weale*, ed. Summers and Pebworth. A collection of essays edited by Roger Rollin and J. Max Patrick, *Trust to Good Verses: Herrick Tercentenary Essays*, appeared in 1978. Herrick is treated at some length in Corns, *Uncloistered Virtue*. Recent studies are surveyed in *ELR* 29 (1999): 462–71.

Thomas Hobbes

The classic edition is by Sir William Molesworth, *English Works*, 11 vols., *Opera Philosophica*, 5 vols., 1839–45. A useful student's edition of the *Leviathan* is by C. P. Macpherson,

1968. See also the Norton Critical Edition. A delightful seventeenth-century biographical sketch is in John Aubrey's *Brief Lives*. Biographies include Mariam Reik, *The Golden Lands of Thomas Hobbes*, 1977, and Arnold Rogow, *Thomas Hobbes: Radical in the Service of Reason*, 1986. Important studies of Hobbes's thought and rhetoric include Michael Oakeshott, *Hobbes on Civil Association*, 1975; David Johnston, *The Rhetoric of "Leviathan": Thomas Hobbes and the Politics of Cultural Transformation*, 1986; Charles Catalupo, *A Literary Leviathan: Thomas Hobbes' Masterpiece of Language*, 1991; Richard Tuck, *Hobbes*, 1989; Quentin Skinner, *Visions of Politics*, 2002; Noel Malcolm, *Aspects of Hobbes*, 2002; and Vickie Sullivan, *Machiavelli, Hobbes, and the Formation of Liberal Republicanism in England*, 2004.

Ben Jonson

A monumental edition of Ben Jonson's *Works* was edited by C. H. Herford and Percy and Evelyn Simpson, 11 vols., 1925–52. The Yale edition and the paperback series known as the New Mermaid provide good modernized and annotated versions of the major plays (one play to a volume). Robert M. Adams's *Ben Jonson's Plays and Masques*, 1979, includes some plays and masques with critical essays. Stephen Orgel has edited *The Complete Masques*, 1969. Handy editions of the verse are by W. B. Hunter, *The Complete Poetry of Ben Jonson*, 1979, and George Parfitt, *Ben Jonson: The Complete Poems*, 1975. There is an edition of *Timber* by Ralph Walker, 1953. David Riggs has written a fine biography, *Ben Jonson: A Life*, 1989.

Important critical studies include Richard Helgerson, *Self-Crowned Laureates*, 1983; Katharine E. Maus, *Ben Jonson and the Roman Frame of Mind*, 1984; Anne Barton, *Ben Jonson, Dramatist*, 1984; Robert N. Watson, *Ben Jonson's Parodic Strategies: Literary Imperialism in the Comedies*, 1987; Bruce Boehrer, *The Fury of Men's Gullets: Ben Jonson and the Digestive Canal*, 1997; and Joseph Loewenstein, *Ben Jonson and Possessive Authorship*, 2002. Works that deal especially with Jonson's poetry are Sara Van den Berg, *The Action of Ben Jonson's Poetry*, 1987, and Robert C. Evans, *Ben Jonson and the Poetics of Patronage*, 1989. Don E. Wayne, *Penshurst: The Semiotics of Place and the Poetics of History*, 1984, locates Jonson's poem "To Penshurst" in its social and architectural context; Raymond Williams, *The Country and the City*, 1975, places it within a broad social history of movements affecting agriculture and the land.

Stuart court masques, and Jonson's major contribution to them, are analyzed in two essay collections: David Lindley, ed., *The Court Masque*, 1984, and David Bevington and Peter Holbrook, eds., *The Politics of the Stuart Court Masque*, 1998, as well as by Stephen Orgel in *The Illusion of Power: Political Theater in the English Renaissance*, 1975. The fascinating reproduction of drawings and designs for the masques published by Stephen Orgel and Roy Strong in *Inigo Jones: The Theatre of the Stuart Court*, 2 vols., 1973, gives some sense of what masques looked like in presentation. Collections of critical essays on Jonson include Jonas A. Barish, ed., *Ben Jonson: A Collection of Critical Essays*, 1983; Jennifer Brady and W. H. Herendeen, eds., *Ben Jonson's 1616 Folio*, 1990; James Hirsh, ed., *New Perspectives on Ben Jonson*, 1997; and Richard Harp and Stanley Stewart, eds., *The Cambridge Companion to Ben Jonson*, 2000.

Aemilia Lanyer

Susanne Woods has edited *The Poems of Aemilia Lanyer: "Salve Deus Rex Judaeorum,"* 1993, and has also analyzed her life and works in *Lanyer: A Renaissance Poet in Her Context*, 1999. The important collection of essays edited by Marshall Grossman, *Aemilia Lanyer: Gender, Genre, and the Canon*, 1998, includes a valuable annotated bibliography. There are chapters on Lanyer in Beilin, *Redeeming Eve*; Krontiris, *Oppositional Voices*; Lewalski, *Writing Women in Jacobean England*; Schleiner, *Tudor and Stuart Women Writers*; Wall, *The Imprint of Gender: Authorship and Publication in the English Renaissance*; and Donawerth et al., eds., *Women, Writing, and the Reproduction of Culture*, 1998.

Andrew Marvell

Nigel Smith has produced a scrupulously edited and annotated edition of Marvell's poems, *The Poems of Andrew Marvell*, 2003, which is now standard. Also now standard is the new *Prose Works of Andrew Marvell* in two volumes, edited by Martin Dzelzainis and Annabel Patterson, 2003, which set those works impressively in their contexts. There are compact editions of Marvell's *Complete Poetry* by George de F. Lord, 1968, rpt. 1984, and Elizabeth Story Donno, 1972. Robert Ray has published *An Andrew Marvell Companion*, 1998, and Elizabeth Donno has surveyed the critical tradition in *Andrew Marvell: The Critical Heritage*, 1978. Biographical studies include Nicholas Murray, *World Enough and Time: The Life of Andrew Marvell*, 2000, and Thomas Wheeler, *Andrew Marvell Revisited*, 1996. Influential studies of his political attitudes and writing in connection with his poetry include John M. Wallace, *Destiny His Choice: The Loyalism of Andrew Marvell*, 1979; Annabel Patterson, *Marvell and the Civic Crown*, 1978, and *Marvell: The Writer in Public Life*, 1999; Warren Chernaik, *The Poet's Time: Politics and Religion in the Work of Marvell*, 1983; essays in Warren Chernaik and Martin Dzelzainis, eds., *Marvell and Liberty*, 1999; and the important essay by David Norbrook on the "Horatian Ode," in Healy and Sawday, *Literature and the English Civil War*, 1990. Important analyses of Marvell's poetic art include Rosalie Colie's elegant and learned study, *"My Ecchoing Song": Andrew Marvell's Poetry of Criticism,* 1970; Donald Friedman's *Marvell's Pastoral Art,* 1970; and Christine Rees's *The Judgment of Marvell,* 1989. Thomas Healy has edited a useful collection of essays, *Andrew Marvell,* 1998; others appear in several tercentenary tributes: Kenneth Friedenreich, ed., *Tercentenary Essays in Honor of Andrew Marvell,* 1977; C. A. Patrides, ed., *Approaches to Marvell,* 1978; and R. L. Brett, ed., *Andrew Marvell: Essays on the Tercentenary of His Death,* 1979. Still other important essays are included in Sharpe and Zwicker, eds., *Politics of Discourse;* Marcus, *Politics of Mirth;* and Zwicker, *Lines of Authority.* Recent studies are surveyed in *ELR* 22 (1992).

John Milton

The Columbia Milton, *The Works of John Milton,* ed. F. A. Patterson et al., 18 vols., 1931–40, with its invaluable two-volume index, is the only complete edition of all the poetry and prose, English and Latin. The Yale edition, *Complete Prose Works of John Milton,* ed. Don M. Wolfe et al., 8 vols., 1953–82, supplies useful historical introductions to all the prose. *The Riverside Milton,* ed. Roy Flannagan, 1998, contains all the poetry and much of the English prose, with updated introductions and a bibliography. John Leonard's paperback, *John Milton: The Complete Poems,* 1998, supplies a good text and useful notes, as does the Longman edition in two volumes: John Carey, ed., *John Milton: Complete Shorter Poems,* 1968, rev. 1997, and Alastair Fowler, ed. *Paradise Lost,* 1966, rev. 1998. See also the Norton Critical Edition of *Paradise Lost.* For the prose, C. A. Patrides's paperback edition, *John Milton: Selected Prose,* 1985, offers a judicious selection. Three volumes of the *Variorum Commentary on the Poems of John Milton,* ed. Douglas Bush et al., 1970–75, have been published, but the volume on *Paradise Lost* is still in process. In 1987 C. A. Patrides provided a useful *Annotated Critical Bibliography of John Milton.*

Barbara K. Lewalski has published a new critical biography of Milton, *The Life of John Milton: A Critical Biography,* 2000, rev. 2003, which traces his interconnections with the history and culture of his age and provides extended analyses of his major poems and prose. William Riley Parker's important *Milton: A Biography,* 2 vols., 1968, has been edited and updated by Gordon Campbell, 1996. David Masson's *The Life of John Milton,* 6 vols. plus index, 1859–91, is still a treasure trove of information about the poet and the period. Christopher Hill's *Milton and the English Revolution,* 1977, has spearheaded an ongoing effort to locate Milton more precisely among his revolutionary contemporaries. Cedric C. Brown's brief biography, *John Milton: A Literary Life,* 1995, offers a useful introduction to the man and his works. Milton is psychoanalyzed by William Kerrigan in *The Sacred Complex: On the Psychogenesis of Paradise Lost,* 1983, and by John T. Shawcross in *John Milton: The Self and the World,* 1993. The five volumes of J. Milton French's *The Life Records of John Milton,* 1949–58, rpt. 1966, gather much primary material for the life. Gordon Campbell's *A Milton Chronology,* 1997, reexamines and adds to these materials. Aids to the study of Milton include the nine-volume *Milton Encyclopedia,* ed. William Hunter et al., 1978–83, with bibliographies and updates in vol. 9; Dennis Danielson, ed., *The Cambridge Companion to Milton,* 1989, rev. 1999; and Thomas Corns, ed., *A Companion to Milton,* 2003, which highlights contemporary issues in Milton studies.

Valuable critical studies that address all or some considerable part of Milton's career and writing include the following: Louis L. Martz, *Milton: Poet of Exile,* 1980; Marshall Grossman, *"Authors to Themselves": Milton and the Revelation of History,* 1987; Joan Bennett, *Reviving Liberty: Radical Christian Humanism in Milton's Great Poems,* 1989; Sharon Achinstein, *Milton and the Revolutionary Reader,* 1994; Laura Lunger Knoppers, *Historicizing Milton: Spectacle, Power, and Poetry in Restoration England,* 1994; Michael Lieb, *Milton and the Culture of Violence,* 1994; Lana Cable, *Carnal Rhetoric: Milton's Iconoclasm and the Poetics of Desire,* 1995; John Rumrich, *Milton Unbound,* 1996; David Loewenstein, *Representing Revolution in Milton and His Contemporaries,* 2001; and Stanley Fish, *How Milton Works,* 2001. Stephen M. Fallon has studied Milton in relation to contemporary philosophers wrestling with issues of materialism in *Milton among the Philosophers: Poetry and Materialism in Seventeenth-Century England,* 1991. Stephen B. Dobrinski considers Milton's authorial practices in relation to contemporary printing practices in *Milton, Authorship, and the Book Trade,* 1999.

Various approaches to Milton over the centuries can be sampled in two volumes edited by John Shawcross, *Milton: The Critical Heritage, 1628–1731,* 1970, and *Milton, 1732–1801: The Critical Heritage,* 1972, and in Joseph A. Wittreich, ed., *The Romantics on Milton,* 1970. Useful essay collections include Mary Nyquist and Margaret Ferguson, eds., *Re-membering Milton: Essays on the Texts and Traditions,* 1988; Mario Di Cesare, ed., *Milton in Italy,* 1991; Annabel Patterson, ed., *John Milton,* 1992; Diana Benet and Michael Lieb, eds., *Literary Milton: Text, Pretext, Context,* 1994; Paul G. Stanwood, ed., *Of Poetry and Politics: New Essays on Milton and His World,* 1995; David Armitage, Armand Himy, and Quentin Skinner, eds., *Milton and Republicanism,* 1995; Stephen B. Dobranski and John P. Rumrich, eds., *Milton and Heresy,* 1998; and Graham Parry and Joad Raymond, eds., *Milton and the Terms of Liberty,* 2002. Milton's views of women and various feminist issues are addressed in several of these collections, and centrally in Diane McColley, *Milton's Eve,* 1983; James Grantham Turner, *One Flesh: Paradisal Mariage and Sexual Relations in the Age of Milton,* 1987; Joseph A. Wittreich, *Feminist Milton,* 1987; and Julia M. Walker, ed., *Milton and the Idea of Woman,* 1988.

Stella Revard has written an excellent account of Milton's shorter poems, including the Latin poems, *Milton and the Tangles of Neaera's Hair: The Making of the 1645 Poems,* 1997. Rosamond Tuve's *Images and Themes in Five Poems by Milton,* 1957, can still illuminate Milton's most important shorter poems. Cedric C. Brown treats Milton's *Comus* and "Lycidas" in their social and political contexts in *John Milton's Aristocratic Entertainments,* 1985. C. A. Patrides has edited a useful collection of essays on "Lycidas," *Milton's "Lycidas": The Tradition and the Poem,* rev. 1983, and that poem is at the center of Joseph A Wittreich's *Visionary Poetics: Milton's Tradition and His Legacy,* 1980. Milton's prose is discussed in several books and essays: Thomas A. Kranides, *The Fierce Equation,* 1964; Joan Webber, *The Eloquent "I": Style and Self in Seventeenth-Century Prose,* 1968; Stanley Fish, *Self-Consuming Artifacts,* 1972; Keith W. Staveley, *The Politics of Milton's Prose Style,* 1975; Michael Lieb and John Shawcross, eds., *Achievements of the Left Hand,* 1975; Thomas N. Corns, *The Development of Milton's Prose Style,* 1982; and David Loewenstein and James G. Turner, eds., *Poetry, Politics, and Hermeneutics in Milton's Prose,* 1990.

Modern criticism of *Paradise Lost* still engages with issues of interpretation and generic tradition raised in C. S. Lewis's *A Preface to Paradise Lost,* 1942; C. M. Bowra's *From Virgil to Milton,* 1945; and William Empson's provocative attack on the figure of God in the poem, *Milton's God,* rev. 1965. A classic study of Milton's theology in reference to the epic is Maurice Kelley's *This Great Argument: A Study of Milton's "De Doctrina Christiana" as a Gloss upon "Paradise Lost,"* 1941. Dennis R. Danielson, *Milton's Good God: A Study in Literary Theodicy,* 1982, revisits that issue. Some important earlier critical books include Joseph Summers, *The Muse's Method: An Introduction to "Paradise Lost,"* 1962; Christopher Ricks, *Milton's Grand Style,* 1963; Northrop Frye, *The Return to Eden,* 1966; Stanley Fish's very influential reader-response criticism, *Surprised by Sin: The Reader in "Paradise Lost,"* 1967; John Steadman, *Epic and Tragic Structure in "Paradise Lost,"* 1976; Joan Webber, *Milton and His Epic Tradition,* 1979; and Barbara K. Lewalski, *"Paradise Lost" and the Rhetoric of Literary Forms,* 1985. The titles of some recent books point to new critical concerns: David Quint, *Epic and Empire: Politics and Generic Form from Virgil to Milton,* 1992; Jason Rosenblatt, *Torah and Law in "Paradise Lost,"* 1994; J. Martin Evans, *Milton's Imperial Epic: "Paradise Lost" and the Discourse of Colonialism,* 1996; B. Rajan and E. Sauer, eds., *Milton and the Imperial Vision,* 1999; and Karen Edwards, *Milton and the Natural World,* 1999. Placing Milton's epic in relation to relevant visual traditions is the burden of a beautifully illustrated book by Roland M. Frye, *Milton's Imagery and the Visual Arts: Iconographic Traditions in the Epic Poems,* 1978, and of a broader study by Diane McColley, *A Gust for Paradise: Milton's Eden and the Visual Arts,* 1993.

Milton's brief epic, *Paradise Regained,* is the subject of Barbara K. Lewalski's book *Milton's Brief Epic: The Genre, Meaning and Art of "Paradise Regained,"* 1966; the poem is treated at some length in David Loewenstein, *Milton and the Drama of History,* 1990; Knoppers, *Historicizing Milton;* Quint, *Epic and Empire;* Mary Ann Radzinowicz, *Milton's Epics and the Book of Psalms,* 1989; and a special issue of *Milton Studies* edited by David Loewenstein and Albert Labriola, *"Paradise Regained": Genre, Politics, Religion,* 2003. Some important works dealing with Milton's tragedy, *Samson Agonistes,* include William R. Parker, *Milton's Debt to Greek Tragedy in "Samson Agonistes,"* 1947; Anthony Low, *The Blaze of Noon: A Reading of "Samson Agonistes,"* 1968; and with reference to competing traditions of interpreting the Samson story, in Joseph A. Wittriech, *Interpreting "Samson Agonistes,"* 1986. Mary Ann Radzinowicz's book *Toward "Samson Agonistes": The Growth of Milton's Mind,* 1978, treats themes and concerns in all his writing as leading toward his great tragedy. Mark R. Kelley and Joseph A. Wittreich have edited a collection of essays on the tragedy, *Altering Eyes: New Perspectives on "Samson Agonistes,"* 2002.

Katherine Philips

Patrick Thomas has edited *The Collected Works of Katherine Philips: The Matchless Orinda,* 1993. Her translations of Corneille and other French works were edited by Ruth Little, 1991. There are two biographies: Philip W. Souer, *The Matchless Orinda,* 1931, and Patrick Thomas, *Katherine Philips ("Orinda")* 1988. Useful critical studies include Harriette Andreadis, "The Sapphic-Platonics of Katherine Philips, 1632–1664," *Signs* 15 (1989); Elizabeth Hageman, "Katherine Philips: *The Matchless Orinda,*" in *Women Writers of the Renaissance and Reformation,* ed. Katharina M. Wilson, 1987; and Arlene Stiebel, "Subversive Sexuality: Masking the Erotic in Poems" by Katherine Philips and Aphra Behn," in *Renaissance Discourses of Desire,* ed. Claude J. Summers and Ted-Larry Pebworth, 1993.

Thomas Traherne

The standard edition is *Thomas Traherne: Centuries, Poems, Thanksgivings,* ed. H. M. Margoliouth, 2 vols., rev. 1972. There is a biography by Gladys Wade, *Thomas Traherne,* 1944, and a Twayne life and works by Malcolm Day, *Thomas Traherne,* 1983. Significant critical studies include A. L. Clements, *The Mystical Poetry of Thomas Traherne,* 1969; Stanley Stewart, *The Expanded Voice: The Art of Thomas Traherne,* 1970; Sharon Seelig, *The Shadow of Eternity: Belief and Structure in Herbert, Vaughan, and Traherne,* 1981; and Graham Dowell, *Enjoying the World: The Rediscovery of Thomas Traherne,* 1990.

Mary Wroth

Josephine Roberts edited Wroth's *Poems,* 1983, and *The First Part of "The Countess of Montgomery's Urania,"* 1995. Her edition of part 2 of the *Urania,* from the manuscript in the Newberry Library, was completed by Suzanne Gossett and Janel Mueller. There is a modernized edition of Wroth's *Poems* edited by R. E. Pritchard, 1996. Wroth's pastoral drama, *Love's Victory,* was edited by Michael Brennan, 1989. There are biographical accounts in Roberts's introductions and in Kim Walker, *Women Writers of the English Renaissance,* 1996. Critical studies include May Nelson Paulissen, *The Love Sonnets of Lady Mary Wroth: A Critical Introduction,* 1982; Gary Waller, *The Sidney Family Romance: Mary Wroth, William Herbert, and the Early Modern Construction of Gender,* 1993; Naomi Miller, *Changing the Subject: Mary Wroth and Figurations of Gender in Early Modern England,* 1996; and Sheila T. Cavanagh, *Cherished Torment: The Emotional Geography of Lady Mary Wroth's "Urania,"* 2001. Miller and Waller have also edited a collection of essays, *Reading Mary Wroth: Representing Alternatives in Early Modern England,* 1991. Wroth's works are also treated by Maureen Quilligan in *Unfolded Tales: Essays on Renaissance Romance,* ed. George Logan and Gordon Teskey, 1989; by several hands in *The Renaissance Englishwoman in Print,* ed. Haselkorn and Travitsky; and in Lewalski's *Writing Women in Jacobean England.* Recent studies are surveyed in *ELR* 18 (1988) and 24 (1994).

THE RESTORATION AND THE EIGHTEENTH CENTURY

In recent decades, historians have placed less emphasis on stories about the ruling classes and their political conflicts and more on the economic and social forces that shape the lives of ordinary people. A good example of this approach is *The Peoples of the British Isles: A New History,* 3 vols., 1992; volume 2, by T. W. Heyck, covers the period from 1688 to 1870. A fuller account is provided by J. R. Jones, *Country and Court: England, 1658–1714,* 1978; W. A. Speck, *Stability and Strife: England, 1714–1760,* 1977; and Ian Christie, *Wars and Revolutions: Britain, 1760–1815,* 1982. Linda Colley, *Britons,* 1992, studies the forging of a new national identity. J. H. Plumb, *England in the Eighteenth Century,* 1950, describes the structure of society, and Roy Porter, *English Society in the Eighteenth Century,* rev. 1990, is a mine of information. John Brewer, *The Pleasures of the Imagination,* 1997, is a wide-ranging history of popular culture. The life and manners of the age are surveyed in *Johnson's England,* 2 vols., ed. A. S. Turberville, 1933; Dorothy Marshall, *English People in the Eighteenth Century,* 1956; R. B. Schwartz, *Daily Life in Johnson's England,* 1983; and Paul Langford, *A Polite and Commercial People,* 1989. *The Birth of a Consumer Society,* 1982, by Neil McKendrick, Brewer, and J. H. Plumb, traces the rise of modern commercialization in the eighteenth century. Useful guides to the historical and cultural contexts of literature include A. R. Humphreys, *The Augustan World,* 1954; Donald Greene, *The Age of Exuberance,* 1970; *The Eighteenth Century,* ed. Pat Rogers, 1978; and James Sambrook, *The Eighteenth Century, 1700–1789,* 2nd ed., 1993.

On the intellectual background of the period, Sir Leslie Stephen, *History of English Thought in the Eighteenth Century,* 2 vols., 1876, remains valuable; so do A. O. Lovejoy, *The Great Chain of Being,* 1942, and *Essays in the History of Ideas,* 1948. Basil Willey, *The Eighteenth Century Background,* 1940, studies ideas about nature, and Keith Thomas, *Man and the Natural World,* 1983, shows the development of a modern sensibility between 1500 and 1800. Gordon Rupp, *Religion in England, 1688–1791,* 1986, is dependable. Volumes 4 to 6 of F. C. Copleston, *History of Philosophy,* 1960, deal with the period from Descartes to Kant; Peter Gay, *The Enlightenment: An Interpretation,* 2 vols., 1969, forcefully defends the philosophers of the Age of Reason. Jürgen Habermas, *The Structural Transformation of the Public Sphere,* 1962, trans. 1989, includes an extremely influential discussion of the British public sphere in the period as a model case. The works of J. G. A. Pocock, especially *Virtue, Commerce, and History,* 1985, have strongly influenced discussions of the period's political, social, and economic thought. J. W. Johnson, *The Formation of English Neo-Classical Thought,* 1967, and J. M. Levine, *The Battle of the Books: History and Literature in the Augustan Age,* 1991, study the ways that writers came to terms with the past. Burton Feldman and R. D. Richardson, *The Rise of Mod-*

ern Mythology 1680–1860, 1972, and Gerald Newman, *The Rise of English Nationalism*, 1987, deal with important new directions of thought. Steven Shapin, *The Scientific Revolution*, 1996, is a brief clear survey. Valuable studies of the influence of scientific ideas include R. F. Jones, *Ancients and Moderns*, 1936; Marjorie Nicolson, *Newton Demands the Muse*, 1946, and *Science and Imagination*, 1956; and W. P. Jones, *The Rhetoric of Science*, 1966. Myra Reynolds, *The Learned Lady in England, 1650–1760*, 1920, still useful, should be supplemented by Sylvia Myers, *The Bluestocking Circle*, 1990. The reflection in eighteenth-century literature of Britain's imperial and colonial enterprises has generated much interest in recent years. Books on this topic include Laura Brown, *The Ends of Empire*, 1993, and Felicity Nussbaum, *Torrid Zones*, 1995, both of which focus on the role of women in colonialist discourses; Srinivas Aravamudan, *Tropicopolitans*, 1999, which presents readings of Behn's *Oroonoko*, Swift's *Gulliver's Travels*, Johnson's *Rasselas*, and Equiano's *Interesting Narrative*; Suvir Kaul, *Poems of Nation, Anthems of Empire*, 2000; and Bridget Orr, *Empire on the English Stage, 1660–1714*, 2001. Sensibility, a set of new ideas and feelings associated especially with women, is the subject of several good books, including Jean Hagstrum, *Sex and Sensibility*, 1980; Janet Todd, *Sensibility: An Introduction*, 1986; John Mullan, *Sentiment and Sociability*, 1988; and G. J. Barker-Benfield, *The Culture of Sensibility*, 1992. Changes in the literary marketplace are illuminated by Pat Rogers, *Grub Street*, 1972; Paula McDowell, *The Women of Grub Street*, 1998; Mark Rose, *Authors and Owners: The Invention of Copyright*, 1993; and Dustin Griffin, *Literary Patronage in England, 1650–1800*, 1996. Martin Price, *To the Palace of Wisdom: Studies in Order and Energy from Dryden to Blake*, 1964; Paul Fussell, *The Rhetorical World of Augustan Humanism*, 1965; W. J. Bate, *The Burden of the Past and the English Poet*, 1970; John Sitter, *Literary Loneliness in Mid-Eighteenth-Century England*, 1982; Howard Weinbrot, *Britannia's Issue: The Rise of British Literature from Dryden to Ossian*, 1993; and Stuart Sherman, *Telling Time: Clocks, Diaries, and English Diurnal Form, 1660–1785*, 1996, are all thoughtful and stimulating studies that relate ideas to literary art.

Good surveys of the literature of the age include George Sherburn, "The Restoration and Eighteenth Century," in *A Literary History of England*, ed. A. C. Baugh, rev. 1967, and *Dryden to Johnson*, ed. Roger Lonsdale, rev. 1987, vol. 4 of the Sphere History of Literature. Far more detailed are three volumes of the *Oxford History of English Literature*: James Sutherland, *English Literature of the Late Seventeenth Century*, 1969; Bonamy Dobrée, *English Literature in the Early Eighteenth Century, 1700–1740*, 1959; and John Butt and Geoffrey Carnall, *English Literature in the Mid-Eighteenth Century*, 1979. On women writers they need to be supplemented by Janet Todd, *A Dictionary of British and American Women Writers, 1660–1800*, 1985.

Among books that deal with a single literary mode, James Sutherland, *A Preface to Eighteenth-Century Poetry*, 1948, is a deft introduction, and Eric Rothstein, *Restoration and Eighteenth-Century Poetry, 1660–1780*, 1981, is a fresh, informative survey. *The Cambridge Companion to Eighteenth-Century Poetry*, ed. John Sitter, 2001, offers a variety of perspectives. Other useful studies include Ian Jack, *Augustan Satire*, 1952; Earl Miner, *The Restoration Mode from Milton to Dryden*, 1974; Rachel Trickett, *The Honest Muse*, 1974; Margaret Doody, *The Daring Muse*, 1985; and Robert Griffin, *Wordsworth's Pope*, 1995. Two anthologies edited by Roger Lonsdale, *The New Oxford Book of Eighteenth Century Verse*, 1984, and *Eighteenth-Century Women Poets*, 1989, have sparked an interest in neglected poems about daily life; Joyce Fullard edited *Eighteenth-Century Women Poets 1660–1800*, 1990; and David Fairer and Christine Gerrard edited an annotated anthology, *Eighteenth-Century Poetry*, 2nd ed., 2004.

On drama, a good introduction is R. W. Bevis, *English Drama: Restoration and Eighteenth Century, 1660–1789*, 1988. Fuller accounts appear in Allardyce Nicoll, *A History of Restoration Drama 1660–1700, A History of Early Eighteenth-Century Drama, 1700–1750*, and *A History of Late Eighteenth-Century Drama, 1750–1800*, rev. 1952; and *The Revels History of Drama in English*, Vol. 5, *1660–1750*, 1976, and Vol. 6, *1750–1880*, 1975. An invaluable store of detailed information is *The London Stage, 1660–1800*, 11 vols., 1960–68, the critical introductions of which have been gathered in five paperback books. Six of the most important plays of the period, together with critical commentary and background material on theaters, staging, and audience, are edited by Scott McMillin in a Norton Critical Edition, *Restoration and Eighteenth-Century Comedy*, 2nd ed., 1997. *The Broadview Anthology of Restoration and Early Eighteenth-Century Drama*, gen. ed. J. Douglas Canfield, 2003, brings together forty-one plays. Two collections, *Restoration Dramatists*, ed. Earl Miner, 1966, and *Restoration Drama*, ed. John Loftis, 1966, provide essays in criticism by various writers; Loftis also analyzed *Comedy and Society from Congreve to Fielding*, 1959. Walter Graham, *English Literary Periodicals*, 1930, is a survey. Letter writing was an important eighteenth-century genre, discussed in *The Familiar Letter in the Eighteenth Century*, ed. Howard Anderson, P. B. Daghlian, and Irvin Ehrenpreis, 1966, and Bruce Redford, *The Converse of the Pen*, 1986. Another important genre, history writing, is examined in Karen

O'Brien, *Narratives of Enlightenment*, 1997. D. A. Stauffer, *English Biography before 1700*, 1930, and *The Art of Biography in Eighteenth-Century England*, 2 vols., 1941, are standard surveys; William H. Epstein, *Recognizing Biography*, 1987, is a challenging theoretical study. Bunyan figures prominently in two books on autobiography: John N. Morris, *Versions of the Self*, 1966, and Felicity Nussbaum, *The Autobiographical Subject*, 1989. Patricia Spacks, *Imagining a Self*, 1976, discusses conceptions of personal identity in eighteenth-century autobiographies and novels.

The Cambridge Companion to the Eighteenth-Century Novel, ed. John Richetti, 1996, is a good general survey. E. A. Baker, *The History of the English Novel*, vols. 3–5, 1930–34, assembles many details. A. D. McKillop, *The Early Masters of English Fiction*, 1956, and Clive Probyn, *English Fiction of the Eighteenth Century, 1700–1789*, 1987, offer good introductions to major novelists. Ian Watt, *The Rise of the Novel*, 1957, an influential study of Defoe, Richardson, and Fielding, set off a long discussion that has been joined by Jane Spencer, *The Rise of the Woman Novelist*, 1986; Michael McKeon, *The Origins of the English Novel*, 1987; Nancy Armstong, *Desire and Domestic Fiction*, 1987; J. Paul Hunter, *Before Novels*, 1990; Homer O. Brown, *Institutions of the English Novel from Defoe to Scott*, 1997; and William B. Warner, *Licensing Entertainment*, 1998. Interesting studies of special aspects of fiction include Lennard Davis, *Factual Fictions*, 1983; Terry Castle, *Masquerade and Civilization*, 1986; John Bender, *Imagining the Penitentiary*, 1987; Carol Kay, *Political Constructions*, 1988; and Catherine Gallagher, *Nobody's Story*, 1994, which has chapters on *Oroonoko* and Frances Burney.

The most comprehensive account of eighteenth-century criticism is vol. 4 of *The Cambridge History of Literary Criticism*, ed. H. B. Nisbet and Claude Rawson, 1997. J. E. Spingarn, *Critical Essays of the Seventeenth Century*, vols. 2 and 3, 1908 (the preface is still useful), and Scott Elledge, *Eighteenth-Century Critical Essays*, 2 vols., 1961, are valuable collections. R. S. Crane's "Neo-Classical Criticism," in *A Dictionary of World Literature*, ed. J. T. Shipley, 1943, has not been surpassed. A survey of major critical movements is provided by James Engell, *Forming the Critical Mind: Dryden to Coleridge*, 1989. René Wellek, *A History of Modern Criticism 1750–1950*, vol. 1, 1955, and W. K. Wimsatt and Cleanth Brooks, *Literary Criticism: A Short History*, 1957, review important issues of theory and aesthetics. Raymond Williams, *Keywords: A Vocabulary of Culture and Society*, 1983, examines the changing meanings of critical terms. A feminist perspective is offered by Marilyn Williamson, *Raising Their Voices: British Women Writers, 1650–1750*, 1990. The issues explored by Samuel H. Monk's classic study, *The Sublime*, 1935, were taken up by many later critics, among them David Morris, *The Religious Sublime*, 1972; Steven Knapp, *Personification and the Sublime*, 1985; and James Noggle, *The Skeptical Sublime*, 2001. The theory of satire has also been a perennial source of interest, most recently in John Sitter, *Arguments of Augustan Wit*, 1991, and Dustin Griffin, *Satire: A Critical Reintroduction*, 1994. Though primarily concerned with Romantic theory, M. H. Abrams, *The Mirror and the Lamp*, 1953, delves deeply into eighteenth-century critical ideas.

The relation of literature to other arts has been the subject of many instructive studies. Jean Hagstrum, *The Sister Arts*, 1958, compares paintings with poems; John Dixon Hunt, *The Figure in the Landscape*, 1977, deals with poetry, painting, and gardening; and Richard Wendorf, *The Elements of Life*, 1990, compares biography with portrait-painting. Lawrence Lipking discusses the first histories of the arts in *The Ordering of the Arts in Eighteenth-Century England*, 1970; Ronald Paulson, *Breaking and Remaking*, 1989, explores aesthetic practice from 1700 to 1820; and Murray Roston analyzes *Changing Perspectives in Literature and the Visual Arts 1650–1820*, 1990. B. Sprague Allen, *Tides of English Taste 1619–1800*, 2 vols., 1937, on architecture, gardening, and decoration, and Sir Kenneth Clark, *The Gothic Revival*, 2nd ed., 1950, on architecture, chronicle significant changes in style.

Good collections of criticism were edited by James L. Clifford, *Eighteenth-Century English Literature: Modern Essays in Criticism*, 1959, and Leopold Damrosch, *Modern Essays on Eighteenth-Century Literature*, 1988. Essays that explore new theoretical approaches are collected by Felicity Nussbaum and Laura Brown, *The New Eighteenth Century*, 1987. *Studies in English Literature* devotes its summer issue to the Restoration and the eighteenth century and includes an article reviewing important work published in the preceding year. Finally, for elaborate bibliographies and reviews of eighteenth-century studies, the student may consult the bibliography of English literature, 1660–1800, that has appeared annually since 1926 in *Philological Quarterly* and, since 1976, in yearly volumes, *The Eighteenth Century: A Current Bibliography*.

Aphra Behn

Janet Todd edited *The Works of Aphra Behn*, 7 vols., 1992–96. The Norton Critical Edition of *Oroonoko*, ed. Joanna Lipking, 1997, includes relevant historical backgrounds and criticism. The paucity of reliable facts about Behn's life prevents any biography from being authoritative, but Maureen Duffy, *The Passionate Shepherdess*, 1977, is worth reading; and Janet Todd, *The Secret Life of Aphra Behn*, 1997, is full of interesting speculations and fresh information. Wylie Sypher, *Guinea's Captive Kings*, 1942, puts *Oroonoko* in the context of antislavery literature. Mary Ann O'Donnell, *Aphra Behn: An Annotated Bibliography*, 1986, is a thorough review of primary and secondary sources through 1985. Jane Spencer, *Aphra Behn's Afterlife*, 2000, explores Behn's cultural influence, and Derek Hughes, *The Theatre of Aphra Behn*, 2001, discusses her plays and theatrical career.

James Boswell

Modern revaluations of Boswell began with the publication of *The Private Papers of James Boswell from Malahide Castle*, ed. Geoffrey Scott and Frederick A. Pottle, 18 vols., 1928–34. Pottle described the history of the papers in *Pride and Negligence*, 1981. A trade edition of Boswell's *Journals*, 14 vols., 1950–89, has valuable introductions and notes. The *Letters*, ed. C. B. Tinker, 2 vols., 1924, need to be supplemented by the recovered *Correspondence of James Boswell*, 1966–97, of which seven volumes have been published. The best edition of the *Life of Johnson* is L. F. Powell's revision of G. B. Hill's edition, 6 vols., 1934–64. A good one-volume edition by R. W. Chapman and J. D. Fleeman, 1982, is available in paperback.

F. A. Pottle, *James Boswell, The Earlier Years, 1740–1769*, 1966, and Frank Brady, *James Boswell, The Later Years, 1769–1795*, 1984, are the two halves of the standard biography, judicious and well informed. Peter Martin wrote a valuable one-volume *Life of James Boswell*, 2000. Pottle, *The Literary Career of James Boswell*, 1929, and Mary Hyde, *The Impossible Friendship: Boswell and Mrs. Thrale*, 1972, are both useful. B. H. Bronson, "Boswell's Boswell," in *Johnson and Boswell*, 1944, is a wise and sympathetic study; J. L. Smith-Dampier, *Who's Who in Boswell?*, 1935, is a helpful guide through the *Life of Johnson* and Adam Sisman, *Boswell's Presumptuous Task*, 2001, explores the making of the *Life*. Greg Clingham edited a collection of essays, *New Light on Boswell*, 1991.

Frances Burney

The *Diary and Letters* were first edited in a truncated version by Charlotte Barrett, Burney's niece, 7 vols., 1842–46. The original texts of *The Journals and Letters of Fanny Burney (Madame d'Arblay), 1791–1840*, 12 vols., were superbly edited by Joyce Hemlow et al., 1972–84. Several volumes of *The Early Journals and Letters of Fanny Burney, 1768–1791*, which will eventually fill ten to twelve volumes, were edited by Lars Troide et al., 1988–2003. There is no standard edition of the novels, but Peter Sabor edited *The Complete Plays of Frances Burney*, 2 vols., 1995. See the Norton Critical Edition of *Evelina*. Biographies include Joyce Hemlow, *The History of Fanny Burney*, 1958; Margaret Doody's critical biography, *Frances Burney: The Life in the Works*, 1988; Janice Thaddeus, *Frances Burney*, 2000; and Claire Harman, *Fanny Burney*, 2001.

William Collins

The *Works* of Collins, which amount to only one slim volume, were well edited by Richard Wendorf and Charles Ryskamp, 1979. Lonsdale's edition (see **Gray**) has copious notes. P. L. Carver, *The Life of a Poet*, 1967, is the fullest biography. Wendorf, *William Collins and Eighteenth-Century English Poetry*, 1981, is a fine critical study.

William Cowper

The *Poems*, 3 vols., was expertly edited by John D. Baird and Charles Ryskamp, 1980–95. James Sambrook's edition of *The Task and Selected Other Poems*, 1994, has useful notes. James King and Ryskamp edited Cowper's *Letters and Prose Writings*, 5 vols., 1979–86, and one volume of *Selected Letters*, 1989. King, *William Cowper: A Biography*, 1986, is the best full life; Ryskamp's fine *William Cowper of the Inner Temple, Esq.*, 1959, ends in 1768. Useful critical studies include Morris Golden, *In Search of Stability: The Poetry of William Cowper*, 1960; Vincent Newey, *Cowper's Poetry*, 1982; Martin Priestman, *Cowper's Task*, 1983; and the last chapter of Donald Davie, *The Eighteenth-Century Hymn in England*, 1993.

John Dryden

James A. Winn's *John Dryden and His World*, 1987, is the best biography. G. R. Noyes's edition of the *Poetical Works*, 2nd ed., 1950, includes a good biographical sketch; and Samuel Johnson's *Life of Dryden* is still worth reading. A fine scholarly edition of the *Works*, launched in 1956, under the general editorship first of E. N. Hooker, then H. T. Swedenberg, and lately Alan Roper, has reached twenty volumes. Keith Walker has edited a useful selected *Works*, 1987. The poems were edited by James Kinsley, 4 vols., 1958, and the essays by W. P. Ker, 2 vols., 1900, and George Watson, 2 vols., 1962. Paul Hammond's new edition of the poems has useful notes; the first two volumes appeared in 1995.

Important modern criticism includes Arthur Hoffman, *John Dryden's Imagery*, 1962; Alan Roper, *Dryden's Poetic Kingdoms*, 1965; and Earl Miner, *Dryden's Poetry*, 1967. David Hopkins, *John Dryden*, 1986, is a good introduction. Steven Zwicker studied *Politics and Language in Dryden's Poetry*, 1984. The standard work on Dryden's philosophical and religious ideas is Phillip Harth, *Contexts of Dryden's Thought*, 1968, and Harth also analyzed the politics of *Absalom and Achitophel* in *Pen for a Party*, 1993. Two analyses are Robert Hume, *Dryden's Criticism*, 1970, and Edward Pechter, *Dryden's Classical Theory of Literature*, 1975. John C. Aden, *The Critical Opinions of John Dryden, A Dictionary*, 1963, compiles his thought under convenient headings. James Winn, *When Beauty Fires the Blood*, 1992, explores the arts in the context of Dryden's works; he also edited *Critical Essays on John Dryden*, 1997.

Olaudah Equiano

A facsimile of the first edition of the *Interesting Narrative* was published by Paul Edwards, 2 vols., 1969. Equiano's later revisions of the *Narrative* and other writings were edited, with useful notes, by Vincent Carretta, 1995. Carretta includes Equiano as well as other eighteenth-century black authors in two good anthologies: *Unchained Voices*, 1996, and *Genius in Bondage*, 2001, edited with Philip Gould. Angelo Costanzo, *Surprizing Narrative: Olaudah Equiano and the Beginnings of Black Autobiography*, 1987; Keith Sandiford, *Measuring the Moment: Strategies of Protest in Eighteenth-Century Afro-English Writing*, 1988; and Peter Fryer, *Staying Power: The History of Black People in Britain*, 1984, place Equiano amid the debates of his time. See also the Norton Critical Edition of *The Narrative*.

Thomas Gray

The poems of Gray, Collins, and Goldsmith were edited, with informative notes, by Roger Lonsdale, 1969. The standard edition of Gray's *Works* remains that of Edmund Gosse, 4 vols., rev. 1902–06; of the *Correspondence*, that of Paget Toynbee and Leonard Whibley, 3 vols., 1935; of the poems, that of H. W. Starr and J. R. Hendrickson, 1966. R. W. Ketton-Cremer, *Thomas Gray*, 1955, is a valuable biography; Robert Mack, *Thomas Gray*, 2000, contains much detail. Among critical studies, Henry Weinfield, *The Poet without a Name: Gray's Elegy and the Problem of History*, 1991, is thoughtful and searching, and B. Eugene McCarthy, *Thomas Gray: The Progress of a Poet*, 1997, is a good general introduction. Suvir Kaul, *Thomas Gray and Literary Authority*, 1992, explores the ideology of Gray's poems; while Robert Gleckner, *Gray Agonistes*, 1997, examines their reflection of his personal relationships. *From Sensibility to Romanticism*, ed. F. W. Hilles and Harold Bloom, 1965, includes studies of the *Elegy* by Ian Jack, B. H. Bronson, and Frank Brady.

Eliza Haywood

Haywood's novels, novellas, and plays have become available in a number of separate editions and collections in recent years, including *Fantomina and Other Works*, ed. Alexander Pettit et al., 2004; *Selected Fiction and Drama of Eliza Haywood*, ed. Paula Backscheider, 1999; and a four-volume edition of *The Selected Works of Eliza Haywood*, ed. by Pettit et al., 2000, which includes her miscellaneous writings and journalism. A pair of Haywood's novellas are placed alongside works by Behn, Delarivier Manley, Mary Davys, and others in *Popular Fiction By Women, 1660–1730*, ed. Backscheider and John Richetti, 1996. An interesting treatment of Haywood's contribution to shaping the generic character of women's writing in the early eighteenth century appears in Ros Ballaster, *Seductive Forms*, 1992, and a number of critical and biographical essays are assembled in *The Passionate Fictions of Eliza Haywood*, ed. Kirsten T. Saxton and Rebecca P. Bocchicchio, 2000.

William Hogarth

The standard, comprehensive critical biography is Ronald Paulson, *Hogarth*, 3 vols., 1991–93. Jenny Uglow, *Hogarth: A Life and a World*, 1997, is perceptive and lively. Paulson edited *Hogarth's Graphic Works*, 2 vols., 1970, as well as *The Analysis of Beauty*, 1998. The paintings are cataloged by R. B. Beckett, *Hogarth*, 1949, and the drawings by A. P. Oppé, *The Drawings of William Hogarth*, 1948. Sean Shesgreen edited *Engravings by Hogarth*, 1973, in a generous and inexpensive format. *Hogarth on High Life*, 1970, illuminates *Marriage A-la-Mode* with the famous eighteenth-century commentaries by Georg Christoph Lichtenberg, trans. and ed. Arthur Wensinger with W. B. Coley. Judy Egerton, *Hogarth's Marriage-à-la-Mode*, 1997, with color plates and commentary, accompanied an exhibition of the series. David Bindman, *Hogarth*, 1981, is a good brief introduction to the art, and Bindman and Scott Wilcox edited *Among the Whores and Thieves*, 1997, a collection of essays on Hogarth and *The Beggar's Opera*.

Samuel Johnson

Others among Johnson's friends besides Boswell wrote of him: notably, Hester Lynch Thrale Piozzi, whose *Anecdotes* (1786) were edited, along with William Shaw's *Anecdotes*, by Arthur Sherbo, 1974; Sir John Hawkins, whose *Life* (1787) was edited and abridged by Bertram H. Davis, 1961; and Frances Burney (Mme d'Arblay), from whose diary C. B. Tinker extracted the Johnsonian passages in *Dr. Johnson and Fanny Burney*, 1911. Pat Rogers, *The Samuel Johnson Encyclopedia*, 1996, is a handy source of information. James L. Clifford, *Young Sam Johnson*, 1955, and *Dictionary Johnson*, 1979, are well-informed studies of the early and middle years that supplement Boswell's rather sketchy account of Johnson's life before their meeting in 1763. There are fine modern biographies by John Wain, 1975, and W. J. Bate, 1977.

The best collected edition of Johnson's *Works* appeared as long ago as 1825. It is being replaced by an excellent scholarly edition, published by Yale, that has been coming out irregularly since 1958. The poems were edited by D. N. Smith and E. L. McAdam, 2nd ed. rev. by J. D. Fleeman, 1974. G. B. Hill's editions of *Johnsonian Miscellanies*, 2 vols., 1897, and *The Lives of the Poets*, 3 vols., 1905, are still worth consulting for their fine notes. Bruce Redford's edition of the *Letters*, 5 vols., 1992–94, is superb. The *Dictionary* is available on CD-ROM, ed. Anne McDermott, 1996.

Robert DeMaria, *The Life of Samuel Johnson*, 1993, and Lawrence Lipking, *Samuel Johnson: The Life of an Author*, 1998, offer critical overviews of Johnson's literary career. Thomas Woodman, *A Preface to Samuel Johnson*, 1993, and *The Cambridge Companion to Samuel Johnson*, ed. Greg Clingham, 1997, are useful guides. Among critical introductions, W. J. Bate, *The Achievement of Samuel Johnson*, 1955, is inspiring, and Paul Fussell, *Samuel Johnson and the Life of Writing*, 1971, is lively. Good specialized studies include W. K. Wimsatt, *The Prose Style of Samuel Johnson*, 1941; Donald J. Greene, *The Politics of Samuel Johnson*, 2nd ed., 1990; Carey McIntosh, *The Choice of Life: Samuel Johnson and the World of Fiction*, 1973; Robert Folkenflik, *Samuel Johnson, Biographer*, 1978; Nicholas Hudson, *Samuel Johnson and Eighteenth-Century Thought*, 1988; and John Cannon, *Samuel Johnson and the Politics of Hanoverian England*, 1994. Joseph E. Brown collected *The Critical Opinions of Samuel Johnson*, 1926. Jean Hagstrum's fine study of *Samuel Johnson's Literary Criticism*, 1952, has been complemented by Leopold Damrosch, *The Uses of Johnson's Criticism*, 1976, and G. F. Parker, *Johnson's Shakespeare*, 1989. David Venturo, *Johnson the Poet*, 1997, is a worthwhile study. DeMaria, *Johnson's Dictionary and the Language of Learning*, 1986, looks at the range of ideas gathered by Johnson; another study is Allen Reddick, *The Making of Johnson's Dictionary, 1746–1773*, rev. 1996. J. L. Clifford and D. J. Greene's survey and bibliography of critical studies, rev. 1970, was updated through 1985 by Greene and J. A. Vance, 1987.

Lady Mary Wortley Montagu

Isobel Grundy's full-scale biography, *Lady Mary Wortley Montagu: Comet of the Enlightenment*, 1999, adds much information to Robert Halsband's elegant *Life of Lady Mary Wortley Montagu*, 1956. Halsband also edited *The Complete Letters*, 3 vols., 1965–67; *Selected Letters*, 1970; and with Grundy, *Essays and Poems and Simplicity, a Comedy*, 2nd ed., 1993. Grundy edited *Romance Writings*, 1996.

Alexander Pope

There is no reliable complete edition of Pope's works. Although defective in many respects, the Victorian edition by Whitwell Elwin and J. W. Courthope, 10 vols., 1871–89, must still be consulted (with caution). The excellent Twickenham Edition of the poems, 11 vols., 1939–67, a cooperative undertaking by several scholars (under John Butt), includes valuable introductory and critical materials and notes. A convenient selection in a single volume, with selected notes, omits the translations of Homer. *The Prose Works* was edited in 2 vols., by Norman Ault, 1936, and Rosemary Cowler, 1986.

Maynard Mack, *Alexander Pope: A Life*, 1986, is a full and sympathetic biography. George Sherburn, *Early Career of Alexander Pope*, 1934, and Mack, *The Garden and the City*, 1969, on Pope's later career, are valuable studies. David Foxon, *Pope and the Early Eighteenth-Century Book Trade*, 1991, and Brean Hammond, *Professional Imaginative Writing in England, 1670–1740*, 1997, treat Pope's concern with the business of publication. Howard Erskine-Hill, *The Social Milieu of Alexander Pope*, 1975, and Valerie Rumbold, *Women's Place in Pope's World*, 1989, are worthwhile. Sherburn's edition of the *Correspondence*, 5 vols., 1956, is standard. R. H. Griffith, *Alexander Pope: A Bibliography*, 2 vols., 1962, is a detailed list of Pope's writings.

David B. Morris, *Alexander Pope: The Genius of Sense*, 1984, offers fine criticism of individual poems. Reuben A. Brower, *Alexander Pope: The Poetry of Allusion*, 1959, is an enlightening study of Pope's lifelong habit of adapting phrases, images, and ideas from earlier poets, especially those of classical antiquity. Much information is gathered up in Robert W. Rogers, *The Major Satires of Alexander Pope*, 1955. Austin Warren, *Alexander Pope as Critic and Humanist*, 1929, is dated but still useful. Aubrey Williams has analyzed *Pope's Dunciad*, 1955, and John Sitter, *The Poetry of Pope's Dunciad*, 1971. Helen Deutsch, *Resemblance and Disgrace*, 1996, treats Pope as a cultural figure; and Blakey Vermeule, *The Party of Humanity*, 2000, examines his poetry in the context of the moral psychology of the period. Several essays on Pope are included in Maynard Mack, *Collected in Himself*, 1982. Mack also edited *Essential Articles for the Study of Alexander Pope*, 1964, and with James Winn, *Pope: Recent Essays*, 1980. *The Enduring Legacy*, ed. G. S. Rousseau and Pat Rogers, 1988, and *Critical Essays on Alexander Pope*, ed. Wallace Jackson and R. Paul Yoder, 1993, collect new essays on Pope, and Brean Hammond has edited *Pope*, 1996, a critical reader.

John Wilmot, Second Earl of Rochester

There are good editions of the complete works, by Frank Ellis, 1994, and Harold Love, 1999, and of the poems, by David Vieth, 1968, and Keith Walker, 1984. Since Vivian de Sola Pinto's biography, *Enthusiast in Wit*, 1962, new source materials have been added by John Adlard, *The Debt to Pleasure*, 1974, and Jeremy Treglown's edition of the *Letters*, 1980. Dustin Griffin, *Satires against Man*, 1973; David Farley-Hills, *Rochester's Poetry*, 1978; and Marianne Thormählen, *Rochester: The Poems in Context*, 1993, are good critical studies. A collection of *Critical Essays*, 1988, was edited by Vieth.

Jonathan Swift

Irvin Ehrenpreis's standard, comprehensive biography, *Swift: The Man, His Works, and the Age*, consists of three volumes: *Mr. Swift and His*

Contemporaries, 1962, *Dr. Swift*, 1967, and *Dean Swift*, 1983. Victoria Glendinning, *Jonathan Swift*, 1998, offers a portrayal of his character. J. A. Downie, *Jonathan Swift, Political Writer*, 1984, and David Nokes, *Jonathan Swift, A Hypocrite Reversed*, 1985, are good introductions to the life and writings. Louis A. Landa, *Swift and the Church of Ireland*, 1954, is a valuable special study.

The standard edition of the poems is by Sir Harold Williams, 2 vols., 1937, rev., 1958. Pat Rogers's edition of Swift's *Complete Poems*, 1983, is reliable and less expensive. Herbert Davis has edited the prose works in fourteen volumes, 1939–68. Swift's *Correspondence* was edited by Williams, 5 vols., 1963–65. Other distinguished editions include Davis, *The Drapier's Letters*, 1935; Williams, *Journal to Stella*, 2 vols., 1948; A. C. Guthkelch and D. Nichol Smith, *A Tale of a Tub*, 2nd ed., 1958; and Frank H. Ellis, *A Discourse of the Contests and Dissentions between the Nobles and the Commons in Athens and Rome*, 1967. For the Norton Critical Editions series, Robert Greenberg and W. B. Piper edited *The Writings of Jonathan Swift*, 1973, and Albert Rivera edited *Gulliver's Travels*, 2001.

Among the abundant critical studies, the student should find especially helpful Ricardo Quintana, *The Mind and Art of Jonathan Swift*, 1936, and *Swift: An Introduction*, 1955. Arthur Case, *Four Essays on Gulliver's Travels*, Herbert Davis, *Jonathan Swift: Essays on his Satire and Other Studies*, 1964; C. J. Rawson, *Gulliver and the Gentle Reader*, 1973; Robert Phiddian, *Swift's Parody*, 1995; and Frank Boyle, *Swift as Nemesis*, 2000, are all useful. Rawson, *God, Gulliver, and Genocide*, 2001, places Swift's obsessions in the context of world-historical catastrophe. After long neglect, Swift's poems have attracted a wealth of criticism; some of the best were collected by David Vieth, *Essential Articles for the study of Jonathan Swift's Poetry*, 1984. Three books by Robert C. Elliott, *The Power of Satire*, 1960, *The Shape of Utopia*, 1970, and *The Literary Persona*, 1982, contain interesting chapters on Swift; so do Edward Said, *The World, the Text, and the Critic*, 1983, and Carol Houlihan Flynn, *The Body in Swift and Defoe*, 1990. Two good collections of essays are *Jonathan Swift: A Critical Anthology*, ed. Denis Donoghue, 1971, and *The Character of Swift's Satire*, ed. C. J. Rawson, 1983.

Literary Terminology*

Using simple technical terms can sharpen our understanding and streamline our discussion of literary works. Some terms, such as the ones in Sections A, B, and C of this appendix, help us address the internal style, form, and structure of works. Other terms, such as those in Section D, provide insight into the material forms in which literary works have been produced.

In analyzing what they called "rhetoric," ancient Greek and Roman writers determined the elements of what we call "style" and "structure." Our literary terms are derived, via medieval and Renaissance intermediaries, from the Greek and Latin sources. In the definitions that follow, the etymology, or root, of the word is given when it helps illuminate the word's current usage.

Most of the examples are drawn from texts in this anthology.

Words **boldfaced** within definitions are themselves defined in this appendix. Some terms are defined within definitions; such words are *italicized.*

A. Style

In literary works the manner *in which something is expressed contributes substantially to its meaning. The manner of a literary work is its "style," the effect of which is its "tone." We often can intuit the tone of a text; the following terms offer a set of concepts by which we can analyze the stylistic features that produce the tone. The groups within this section move from the micro to the macro level internal to works.*

(i) Diction

"Diction," or "lexis" (from, respectively, Latin "dictio" and Greek "lexis," each meaning "word"), designates the actual words used in any utterance—speech, writing, and, for our purposes here, literary works. The choice of words contributes significantly to the style of a given work.

Connotation: To understand connotation, we need to understand **denotation.** While many words can denote the same concept—that is, have the same basic meaning—those words can evoke different associations, or connotations. Contrast, for example, the clinical-sounding term "depression" and the more colorful, musical, even poetic phrase "the blues."

Denotation: A word has a basic, "prosaic" (factual) meaning prior to the associations it connotes (see **connotation**). The word "steed," for example,

* This appendix was devised and compiled by James Simpson with the collaboration of all the editors.

might call to mind a horse fitted with battle gear, to be ridden by a warrior, but its denotation is simply "horse."

Lexical set: Words that habitually recur together (e.g., January, February, March, etc.; or red, white, and blue) form a lexical set.

Register: The register of a word is its stylistic level, which can be distinguished by degree of technicality but also by degree of formality. We choose our words from different registers according to context, that is, audience and/or environment. Thus a chemist in a laboratory will say "sodium chloride," a cook in a kitchen "salt." A formal register designates the kind of language used in polite society (e.g., "Mr. President"), while an informal or colloquial register is used in less formal or more relaxed social situations (e.g., "the boss"). In **classical** and medieval rhetoric, these registers of formality were called *high style* and *low style*. A *middle style* was defined as the style fit for narrative, not drawing attention to itself.

(ii) Rhetorical Figures: Figures of Speech

Literary language often employs patterns perceptible to the eye and/or to the ear. Such patterns are called "figures of speech"; in **classical** *rhetoric they were called* **"schemes"** *(from Greek "schema," meaning "form, figure").*

Alliteration (from Latin "litera," alphabetic letter): the repetition of an initial consonant sound or consonant cluster in consecutive or closely positioned words. This pattern is often an inseparable part of the meter in Germanic languages, where the tonic, or accented **syllable,** is usually the first syllable. Thus all Old English poetry and some varieties of Middle English poetry use alliteration as part of their basic metrical practice. *Sir Gawain and the Green Knight,* line 1: "Sithen the sege and the assaut was sesed at Troye" (see p. 114). Otherwise used for local effects; Stevie Smith, "Pretty," lines 4–5: "And in the pretty pool the pike stalks / He stalks his prey . . ."

Anaphora (Greek "carrying back"): the repetition of words or groups of words at the beginning of consecutive sentences, clauses, or phrases. Blake, "London," lines 5–8: "In every cry of every Man, / In every Infant's cry of fear, / In every voice, in every ban . . ." (see p. 1422); Louise Bennett, "Jamaica Oman," lines 17–20: "Some backa man a push, some side-a / Man a hole him han, / Some a lick sense eena him head, / Some a guide him pon him plan!"

Assonance (Latin "sounding to"): the repetition of identical or near identical stressed vowel sounds in words whose final consonants differ, producing half-rhyme. Tennyson, "The Lady of Shalott," line 100: "His broad clear brow in sunlight glowed" (see p. 1955).

Chiasmus (Greek "crosswise"): the inversion of an already established sequence. This can involve verbal echoes: Pope, "Eloisa to Abelard," line 104, "The crime was common, common be the pain"; or it can be purely a matter of syntactic inversion: Pope, *Epistle to Dr. Arbuthnot,* line 8: "They pierce my thickets, through my grot they glide" (see p. 1164).

Consonance (Latin "sounding with"): the repetition of final consonants in words or stressed syllables whose vowel sounds are different. Herbert, "Easter," line 13: "Consort, both heart and lute . . ."

Homophone (Greek "same sound"): a word that sounds identical to another word but has a different meaning ("bear" / "bare").

Onomatopoeia (Greek "name making"): verbal sounds that imitate and evoke the sounds they denotate. Hopkins, "Binsey Poplars," lines 10–12 (about some felled trees): "O if we but knew what we do / When we delve [dig] or hew— / Hack and rack the growing green!" (see p. 2163).

Rhyme: the repetition of identical vowel sounds in stressed syllables whose initial consonants differ ("dead" / "head"). In poetry, rhyme often links the end of one line with another. *Masculine rhyme:* full rhyme on the final syllable of the line ("decays" / "days"). *Feminine rhyme:* full rhyme on syllables that are followed by unaccented syllables ("fountains" / "mountains"). *Internal rhyme:* full rhyme within a single line; Coleridge, *The Rime of the Ancient Mariner,* line 7: "The guests are met, the feast is set" (see p. 1616). *Rhyme riche:* rhyming on **homophones;** Chaucer, *General Prologue,* lines 17/18: "seeke" / "seke." *Off rhyme* (also known as *half rhyme, near rhyme,* or *slant rhyme*): differs from perfect rhyme in changing the vowel sound and/or the concluding consonants expected of perfect rhyme; Byron, "They say that Hope is Happiness," lines 5–7: "most" / "lost" (see p. 1677). *Pararhyme:* stressed vowel sounds differ but are flanked by identical or similar consonants; Owen, "Miners," lines 9–11: "simmer" / "summer."

(iii) Rhetorical Figures: Figures of Thought

Language can also be patterned conceptually, even outside the rules that normally govern it. Literary language in particular exploits this licensed linguistic irregularity. Synonyms for figures of thought are "trope" (Greek "twisting," referring to the irregularity of use) and "conceit" (Latin "concept," referring to the fact that these figures are perceptible only to the mind). Be careful not to confuse "trope" with "topos" (a common error).

Allegory (Greek "saying otherwise"): saying one thing (the "vehicle" of the allegory) and meaning another (the allegory's "tenor"). Allegories may be momentary aspects of a work, as in **metaphor** ("John is a lion"), or, through extended metaphor, may constitute the basis of narrative, as in Bunyan's *Pilgrim's Progress;* this second meaning is the dominant one. See also **symbol** and **type.**

Antithesis (Greek "placing against"): juxtaposition of opposed terms in clauses or sentences that are next to or near each other; Milton, *Paradise Lost* 1.777–80: "They but now who seemed / In bigness to surpass Earth's giant sons / Now less than smallest dwarfs, in narrow room / Throng numberless" (see p. 743).

Bathos (Greek "depth"): a sudden and sometimes ridiculous descent of tone; Pope, *The Rape of the Lock* 3.157–58: "Not louder shrieks to pitying heaven are cast, / When husbands, or when lapdogs breathe their last" (see p. 1147).

Emblem (Greek "an insertion"): a picture allegorically expressing a moral, or a verbal picture open to such interpretation. Donne, "A Hymn to Christ," lines 1–2: "In what torn ship soever I embark, / That ship shall be my emblem of thy ark."

Euphemism (Greek "sweet saying"): the figure by which something distasteful is described in alternative, less repugnant terms (e.g., "he passed away").

Hyperbole (Greek "throwing over"): overstatement, exaggeration; Marvell, "To His Coy Mistress," lines 11–12: "My vegetable love would grow / Vaster than empires, and more slow" (see p. 677); Auden, "As I Walked Out One Evening," lines 9–12: " 'I'll love you, dear, I'll love you / Till China and Africa meet / And the river jumps over the mountain / And the salmon sing in the street" (see p. 2691).

Irony (Greek "dissimulation"): strictly, a subset of allegory: whereas allegory says one thing and means another, irony says one thing and means its opposite; Byron, *Don Juan* 1.1–2: "I want a hero: an uncommon want, / When every year and month sends forth a new one" (see p. 1691). For an extended example of irony, see Swift's "Modest Proposal."

Litotes (from Greek "smooth"): strictly, understatement by denying the contrary; More, *Utopia*: "differences of no slight import." More loosely, understatement; Swift, "A Tale of a Tub": "Last week I saw a woman flayed, and you will hardly believe how much it altered her person for the worse." Stevie Smith, "Sunt Leones," lines 11–12: "And if the Christians felt a little blue— / Well people being eaten often do."

Metaphor (Greek "carrying across," etymologically parallel to Latin "translation"): the identification or implicit identification of one thing with another with which it is not literally identifiable. Blake, "London," lines 11–12: "And the hapless Soldier's sigh / Runs in blood down Palace walls" (see p. 1423).

Metonymy (Greek "change of name"): using a word to **denote** another concept or other concepts, by virtue of habitual association. Thus "The Press," designating printed news media. Fictional names often work by associations of this kind. A figure closely related to **synecdoche.**

Occupatio (Latin "taking possession"): denying that one will discuss a subject while actually discussing it; also known as "praeteritio" (Latin "passing by"). See Chaucer, *Nun's Priest's Tale,* lines 414–32 (see p. 259).

Oxymoron (Greek "sharp blunt"): conjunction of normally incompatible terms; Milton, *Paradise Lost* 1.63: "darkness visible" (see p. 727). Ramanujan, "Foundlings in the Yukon," line 41: "these infants compact with age."

Paradox (Greek "contrary to received opinion"): an apparent contradiction that requires thought to reveal an inner consistency. Chaucer, "Troilus's Song," line 12: "O sweete harm so quainte."

Periphrasis (Greek "declaring around"): circumlocution; the use of many words to express what could be expressed in few or one; Sidney, *Astrophil and Stella* 39.1–4.

Personification, or prosopopoeia (Greek "person making"): the attribution of human qualities to nonhuman forces or objects; Shakespeare, *King Lear* 3.2.1: "Blow winds and crack your cheeks, rage! Blow!"

Pun: a sometimes irresolvable doubleness of meaning in a single word or expression; Shakespeare, Sonnet 135, line 1: "Whoever hath her wish, thou hast thy *Will*" (see p. 507).

Sarcasm (Greek "flesh tearing"): a wounding remark, often expressed ironically; Boswell, *Life of Johnson*: Johnson [asked if any man of the modern age could have written the **epic** poem *Fingal*] replied, "Yes, Sir, many men, many women, and many children."

Simile (Latin "like"): comparison, usually using the word "like" or "as," of one thing with another so as to produce sometimes surprising analogies. Donne, "The Storm," lines 29–30: "Sooner than you read this line did the gale, / Like shot, not feared till felt, our sails assail." Frequently used, in extended form, in **epic** poetry; Milton, *Paradise Lost* 1.338–46 (see p. 733).

Symbol (Greek "token"): something that stands for something else, and yet seems necessarily to evoke that other thing. Blake, "The Sick Rose," lines 1–8: "O Rose, thou art sick. / The invisible worm / That flies in the night / In the howling storm / Has found out thy bed / Of crimson joy, And his dark secret love / Does thy life destroy" (see p. 1420). In Neoplatonic, and therefore Romantic, theory, to be distinguished from **allegory** thus: whereas allegory involves connections between vehicle and tenor agreed by convention or made explicit, the meanings of a symbol are supposedly inherent to it.

Synecdoche (Greek "to take with something else"): using a part to express the whole, or vice versa; "Donne, "A Hymn to Christ," lines 1–2: "In what torn ship soever I embark / That ship shall be my emblem of thy ark."

Type (Greek "impression, figure"): In Christian allegorical interpretation of the Old Testament, pre-Christian figures were regarded as "types," or foreshadowings, of Christ or the Christian dispensation. *Typology* has been the source of much visual and literary art in which the parallelisms between old and new are extended to nonbiblical figures; thus the virtuous plowman in *Piers Plowman* becomes a type of Christ.

Zeugma (Greek "a yoking"): a syntactic pun whereby the one word is revealed to have more than one sense in the sentence as a whole; Pope, *Rape of the Lock* 3.7–8, in which the word "take" is used in two senses: "Here thou, great Anna! whom three realms obey, / Dost sometimes counsel take—and sometimes tea" (see p. 1144).

(iv) Meter, Rhythm

Verse (from Latin "versus," turned) is distinguished from prose (from Latin "prorsus," straightforward) as a more compressed form of expression, shaped by metrical norms. ***Meter*** *(Greek "measure") refers to the regularly recurring sound pattern of verse lines. The means of producing sound patterns across lines differ in different poetic traditions. Verse may be* ***quantitative****, or determined by the quantities of syllables (set patterns of long and short syllables), as in Latin and Greek poetry. It may be* ***syllabic****, determined by fixed numbers of syllables in the line, as in the verse of Romance languages (e.g., French and Italian). It may be* ***accentual****, determined by the number of accents, or stresses in the line, with variable numbers of syllables, as in Old English and some varieties of Middle English alliterative verse. Or it may be* ***accentual-syllabic****, determined by the numbers of accents, but possessing a regular pattern of stressed and unstressed syllables, so as to produce regular numbers of syllables per line. Since Chaucer, English verse has worked primarily within the many possibilities of accentual-syllabic meter. The unit of meter is the* ***foot****. In English verse the number of feet per line corresponds to the number of accents in a line. For the types and examples of different meters, see* ***monometer, dimeter, trimeter, tetrameter, pentameter****, and* ***hexameter****. In the definitions below, "u" designates one unstressed syllable, and "/" one stressed syllable.*

Rhythm *is not absolutely distinguishable from meter. One way of making a clear distinction between these terms is to say that rhythm (from the Greek "to flow") denotes the patterns of sound within the feet of verse lines and the combination of those feet. Very often a particular meter will raise expectations that a given* *rhythm will be used regularly through a whole line or a whole poem. Thus in English verse the pentameter regularly uses an iambic rhythm. Rhythm, however, is much more fluid than meter, and many lines within the same poem using a single meter will frequently exploit different rhythmic possibilities. For examples of different rhythms, see* **iamb, trochee, anapest, spondee,** *and* **dactyl.**

Accent (synonym "stress"): the special force devoted to the voicing of one syllable in a word over others. In the noun "accent," for example, the stress is on the first syllable.

Alexandrine: in French verse a line of twelve syllables, and, by analogy, in English verse a line of six stresses. See **hexameter.**

Anapest: a three-syllable foot following the rhythmic pattern, in English verse, of two unstressed (uu) syllables followed by one stressed (/). Thus, for example, "Illinois."

Caesura (Latin "cut"): a pause or breathing space within a line of verse, generally occurring between syntactic units; Louise Bennett, "Colonization in Reverse," lines 5–8: "By de hundred, by de tousan, / From country an from town, / By de ship-load, by de plane-load, / Jamaica is Englan boun."

Dactyl (Greek "finger," because of the finger's three joints): a three-syllable foot following the rhythmic pattern, in English verse, of one stressed (/) followed by two unstressed (uu) syllables. Thus, for example, "Oregon."

Dimeter (Greek "two measure"): a two-stress line, rarely used as the meter of whole poems, though used with great frequency in single poems by Skelton, e.g., "The Tunning of Elinour Rumming." Otherwise used for single lines, as in Herbert, "Discipline," line 3: "O my God."

End-stopping: the placement of a complete syntactic unit within a complete metrical pattern; Auden, "In Memory of W. B. Yeats," line 42: "Earth, receive an honoured guest" (see p. 2694). Compare **enjambment.**

Enjambment (French "striding," encroaching): The opposite of **end-stopping,** enjambment occurs when the syntactic unit does not end with the metrical pattern, i.e., when the sense of the line overflows its meter and, therefore, the line break; Auden, "In Memory of W. B. Yeats," lines 44–45: "Let the Irish vessel lie / Emptied of its poetry" (see p. 2694).

Hexameter (Greek "six measure"): The hexameter line (a six-stress line) is the meter of **classical** Latin **epic;** while not imitated in that form for epic verse in English, some instances of the hexameter exist. See, for example, the last line of a Spenserian stanza, *Faerie Queene* 1.1.2: "O help thou my weake wit, and sharpen my dull tong" (p. 370), or Yeats, "The Lake Isle of Innisfree," line 1: "I will arise and go now, and go to Innisfree" (p. 2391).

Hypermetrical (adj.; Greek "over measured"): describes a breaking of the expected metrical pattern by at least one extra syllable.

Iamb: the basic foot of English verse; two syllables following the rhythmic pattern of unstressed (u) followed by stressed (/) and producing a rising effect. Thus, for example, "Vermont."

Monometer (Greek "one measure"): an entire line with just one stress; *Sir Gawain and the Green Knight,* line 15, "wyth (u) wynne (/)" (p. 114).

Pentameter (Greek "five measure"): in English verse, a five-stress line. Between the late fourteenth and the nineteenth centuries, this meter, frequently employing an iambic rhythm, was the basic line of English verse. Chaucer, Shakespeare, Milton, and Wordsworth each, for example, deployed this very flexible line as their primary resource; Milton, *Paradise*

Lost 1.128: "O Prince, O Chief of many thronèd Powers" (see p. 729).

Spondee: a two-syllable foot following the rhythmic pattern, in English verse, of two stressed (//) syllables. Thus, for example, "Utah."

Syllable: the smallest unit of sound in a pronounced word. The syllable that receives the greatest stress is called the *tonic* syllable.

Tetrameter (Greek "four measure"): a line with four stresses. Coleridge, *Christabel*, line 31: "She stole along, she nothing spoke" (see p. 1636).

Trimeter (Greek "three measure"): a line with three stresses. Herbert, "Discipline," line 1: "Throw away thy rod."

Trochee: a two-syllable foot following the pattern, in English verse, of stressed (/) followed by unstressed (u) syllable, producing a falling effect. Thus, for example, "Texas."

(vi) Verse Forms

The terms related to meter and rhythm describe the shape of individual lines. Lines of verse are combined to produce larger groupings, called verse forms. These larger groupings are in the first instance ***stanzas (Italian "rooms")****: groupings of two or more lines, though "stanza" is usually reserved for groupings of at least four lines. Stanzas are often joined by rhyme, often in sequence, where each group shares the same metrical pattern and, when rhymed, rhyme scheme. Stanzas can themselves be arranged into larger groupings. Poets often invent new verse forms, or they may work within established forms, a list of which follows.*

Ballad stanza: usually a **quatrain** in alternating **iambic tetrameter** and **iambic trimeter** lines, rhyming abcb. See "Sir Patrick Spens"; Larkin, "This Be The Verse" (p. 2716).

Ballade: a form consisting usually of three stanzas followed by a four-line envoi (French, "send off"). The last line of the first stanza establishes a **refrain,** which is repeated, or subtly varied, as the last line of each stanza. The form was derived from French medieval poetry; English poets, from the fourteenth to the sixteenth centuries especially, used it with varying stanza forms.

Blank verse: unrhymed **iambic pentameter** lines. Blank verse has no stanzas, but is broken up into uneven units (verse paragraphs) determined by sense rather than form. First devised in English by Henry Howard, Earl of Surrey, in his translation of two books of Virgil's *Aeneid*, this very flexible verse type became the standard form for dramatic poetry in the seventeenth century, as in most of Shakespeare's plays. Milton and Wordsworth, among many others, also used it to create an English equivalent to **classical epic.**

Couplet: in English verse two consecutive, rhyming lines usually containing the same number of stresses. Chaucer first introduced the **iambic pentameter** couplet into English (*Canterbury Tales*); the form was later used in many types of writing, including drama; imitations and translations of **classical epic** (thus *heroic couplet*); essays; and **satire** (see Dryden and Pope). The *distich* (Greek "two lines") is a couplet usually making complete sense; Aemilia Lanyer, *Salve Deus Rex Judaeorum*, lines 5–6: "Read it fair queen, though it defective be, / Your excellence can grace both it and me."

Ottava rima: an eight-line stanza form, rhyming abababcc, using **iambic pentameter;** Yeats, "Sailing to Byzantium" (see p. 2406). Derived from the Italian poet Boccaccio, an eight-line stanza was used by fifteenth-century

English poets for inset passages (e.g., Christ's speech from the Cross in Lydgate's *Testament*, lines 754–897). The form in this rhyme scheme was used in English poetry for long narrative by, for example, Byron (*Don Juan;* see p. 1690).

Quatrain: a stanza of four lines, usually rhyming abcb, abab, or abba. Of many possible examples, see Crashaw, "On the Wounds of Our Crucified Lord."

Refrain: usually a single line repeated as the last line of consecutive stanzas, sometimes with subtly different wording and ideally with subtly different meaning as the poem progresses. See, for example, Wyatt, "Blame not my lute."

Rhyme royal: a stanza form of seven **iambic pentameter** lines, rhyming ababbcc; first introduced by Chaucer and called "royal" because the form was used by James I of Scotland for his *Kingis Quair* in the early fifteenth century.

Sonnet: a form combining a variable number of units of rhymed lines to produce a fourteen-line poem, usually in rhyming **iambic pentameter** lines. In English there are two principal varieties: the Petrarchan sonnet, formed by an octave (an eight-line stanza, often broken into two **quatrains** having the same rhyme scheme, typically abba abba) and a sestet (a six-line stanza, typically cdecde or cdcdcd); and the Shakespearean sonnet, formed by three quatrains (abab cdcd efef) and a **couplet** (gg). The declaration of a sonnet can take a sharp turn, or "volta," often at the decisive formal shift from octave to sestet in the Petrarchan sonnet, or in the final couplet of a Shakespearean sonnet, introducing a trenchant counterstatement. Derived from Italian poetry, and especially from the poetry of Petrarch, the sonnet was first introduced to English poetry by Wyatt, and initially used principally for the expression of unrequited erotic love, though later poets used the form for many other purposes. See Wyatt, "Whoso list to hunt" (p. 350); Sidney, *Astrophil and Stella* (p. 451); Shakespeare, *Sonnets* (p. 497); Wordsworth, "London, 1802" (p. 1549); Heaney, "Clearances" (p. 2798).

Spenserian stanza: the stanza developed by Spenser for *The Faerie Queene*; nine **iambic** lines, the first eight of which are **pentameters,** followed by one **hexameter,** rhyming ababbcbcc. See also, for example, Shelley, *Adonais* (p. 1772), and Keats, *The Eve of St. Agnes* (p. 1830).

Tercet: a stanza or group of three lines, used in larger forms such as **terza rima,** the **Petrarchan sonnet,** and the **villanelle**.

Terza rima: a sequence of rhymed **tercets** linked by rhyme thus: aba bcb cdc, etc. First used extensively by Dante in *The Divine Comedy,* the form was adapted in English **iambic pentameters** by Wyatt and revived in the nineteenth century. See Wyatt, "Mine own John Poins"; Shelley, "Ode to the West Wind" (p. 1743). For modern adaptations see Eliot, lines 78–149 (though unrhymed) of "Little Gidding" (pp. 2634–36); Heaney, "Station Island" (p. 2797); Walcott, *Omeros* (p. 2774).

Triplet: a **tercet** rhyming on the same sound. Pope inserts triplets among heroic **couplets** to emphasize a particular thought; see *Essay on Criticism,* 315–17 (p. 1131).

Villanelle: a fixed form of usually five **tercets** and a **quatrain** employing only two rhyme sounds altogether, rhyming aba for the tercets and abaa for the quatrain, with a complex pattern of two **refrains.** Derived from a French fixed form. Thomas, "Do Not Go Gentle into That Good Night" (p. 2710).

(v) Syntax

Syntax (Greek "ordering with") designates the rules by which sentences are constructed in a given language. Discussion of meter is impossible without some reference to syntax, since the overall effect of a poem is, in part, always the product of a subtle balance of meter and sentence construction. Syntax is also essential to the understanding of prose style, since prose writers, deprived of the full shaping possibilities of meter, rely all the more heavily on syntactic resources. A working command of syntactical practice requires an understanding of the parts of speech (nouns, verbs, adjectives, adverbs, conjunctions, pronouns, prepositions, and interjections), since writers exploit syntactic possibilities by using particular combinations and concentrations of the parts of speech. The list below offers some useful terms for the description of syntactic features of a work.

Apposition: the repetition of elements serving an identical grammatical function in one sentence. The effect of this repetition is to arrest the flow of the sentence, but in doing so to add extra semantic nuance to repeated elements. This is an especially important feature of Old English poetic style. See, for example, Caedmon's Hymn, where the phrases "heaven kingdom's guardian," "the Measurer's might," "his mind-plans," and "the work of the Glory-Father" each serve an identical syntactic function as the direct objects of "praise."

Hyperbaton (Greek "overstepping"): the rearrangement, or inversion, of the expected word order in a sentence or clause. Gray, "Elegy Written in a Country Churchyard," line 38: "If Memory o'er their tomb no trophies raise" (p. 1333). Poets can suspend the expected syntax over many lines, as in the first sentences of the *Canterbury Tales* (p. 170) and of *Paradise Lost* (p. 726).

Hypotaxis, or subordination (respectively Greek and Latin "ordering under"): the subordination, by the use of subordinate clauses, of different elements of a sentence to a single main verb. Milton, *Paradise Lost* 9.513–15: "As when a ship by skillful steersman wrought / Nigh river's mouth or foreland, where the wind / Veers oft, as oft so steers, and shifts her sail; So varied he" (p. 821). The contrary principle to **parataxis.**

Parataxis, or coordination (respectively Greek and Latin "ordering beside"): the coordination, by the use of coordinating conjunctions, of different main clauses in a single sentence. Malory, "Morte Darthur": "So Sir Lancelot departed and took his sword under his arm, and so he walked in his mantel, that noble knight, and put himself in great jeopardy" (p. 303). The opposite principle to **hypotaxis.**

(vii) Point of View

All of the many kinds of writing (see "B. Genre and Mode," below) involve a point of view from which a text is, or seems to be, generated. The presence of such a point of view may be powerful and explicit, as in many novels, or deliberately invisible, as in much drama. In some genres, such as the ***novel****, the narrator does not necessarily tell the story from a position we can predict; that is, the needs of a particular story, not the* ***conventions*** *of the genre, determine the narrator's position. In other genres, the narrator's position is fixed by con-*

vention; in certain kinds of love poetry, for example, the narrating voice is always that of a suffering lover. Not only does the point of view significantly inform the style of a work, but it also informs the structure of that work. Most of the terms below are especially relevant to narrative in either verse or prose, but many also apply to other modes of writing.

Deixis (Greek "pointing"): Every work has, implicitly or explicitly, a "here" and a "now" from which it is narrated. Words that refer to or imply this point from which the voice of the work is projected (such as "here," "there," "this," "that," "now," "then") are examples of deixis, or "deictics." This technique is especially important in drama, where it is used to create a sense of the events happening as the spectator witnesses them.

First-person narration: a narrative in which the voice narrating refers to itself with forms of the first-person pronoun ("I," "me," "my," etc., or possibly "we," "us," "our"), and in which the narrative is determined by the limitations of that voice. Thus Mary Wollstonecraft Shelley, *Frankenstein*.

Frame narrative: Some narratives, particularly collections of narratives, involve a frame narrative that explains the genesis of, and/or gives a perspective on, the main narrative or narratives to follow. Thus Chaucer, *Canterbury Tales;* Mary Wollstonecraft Shelley, *Frankenstein;* or Conrad, *Heart of Darkness*.

Free indirect style: a narratorial voice that manages, without explicit reference, to imply, and often implicitly to comment on, the voice of a **character** in the narrative itself. Virginia Woolf, "A Sketch of the Past," where the voice, although strictly that of the adult narrator, manages to convey the child's manner of perception: "—I begin: the first memory. This was of red and purple flowers on a black background—my mother's dress."

Omniscient narrator (Latin "all-knowing narrator"): a narrator who, in the fiction of the narrative, has complete access to both the deeds and the thoughts of all **characters** in the narrative. Thus Thomas Hardy, "On the Western Circuit."

Order: A story may be told in different orders. A narrator might use the sequence of events as they happened, and thereby follow what **classical** rhetoricians called the *natural order;* alternatively, the narrator might reorder the sequence of events, beginning the narration either in the middle or at the end of the sequence of events, thereby following an *artificial order*. If a narrator begins in the middle of events, he or she is said to begin *in medias res* (Latin "in the middle of the matter"). For a brief discussion of these concepts, see Spenser, *Faerie Queene,* "A Letter of the Authors." Modern narratology makes a related distinction, between *histoire* (French "story") for the natural order that readers mentally reconstruct, and *discours* (French, here "narration") for the narrative as presented.

Plot: the sequence of events in a story as narrated.

Stream of consciousness: usually a **first-person** narrative that seems to give the reader access to the narrator's mind as it perceives or reflects on events, prior to organizing those perceptions into a coherent narrative. Thus (though generated from a **third-person** narrative) Joyce, *Ulysses*, "Lestrygonians" (see p. 2548).

Third-person narration: a narration in which the narrator recounts a narrative of **characters** referred to explicitly or implicitly by third-person pronouns ("he," she," etc.), without the limitation of a **first-person narration.** Thus Johnson, *The History of Rasselas*.

Unities: According to a theory supposedly derived from Aristotle's *Poetics*, the events represented in a play should have unity of time, place, and action: that the play take up no more time than the time of the play, or at most a day; that the space of action should be within a single city; and that there should be no subplot. See Johnson, *The Preface to Shakespeare* (p. 1301).

B. Genre and Mode

The style, structure, and, often, length of a work, when coupled with a certain subject matter, raise expectations that a literary work conforms to a certain **genre** *(French "kind"). Good writers might upset these expectations, but they remain aware of the expectations and thwart them purposefully. Works in different genres may nevertheless participate in the same* **mode**, *a broader category designating the fundamental perspectives governing various genres of writing. For mode, see* **tragic, comic, satiric,** *and* **didactic modes.** *All the other terms in this list refer to more or less specific literary genres. Genres are fluid, sometimes very fluid (e.g., the* **novel***); the word "usually" should be added to almost every statement!*

Animal fable: a short narrative of speaking animals, followed by moralizing comment, written in a low style and gathered into a collection.

Aubade (originally from Spanish "alba," dawn): a lover's dawn song or lyric bewailing the arrival of the day and the necessary separation of the lovers; Donne, "The Sun Rising" (see p. 606). Larkin recasts the genre in "Aubade" (see p. 2716).

Autobiography (Greek "self-life writing"): a narrative of a life written by the subject; Wordsworth, *The Prelude* (see p. 1552). There are subgenres, such as the spiritual autobiography, narrating the author's path to conversion and subsequent spiritual trials, as in Bunyan's *Grace Abounding*.

Beast epic: a continuous, unmoralized narrative, in prose or verse, relating the victories of the wholly unscrupulous but brilliant strategist Reynard the Fox over all adversaries. Chaucer arouses, only to deflate, expectations of the genre in *The Nun's Priest's Tale* (see p. 250).

Biography (Greek "life-writing"): a life as the subject of an extended narrative.

Comedy: a term primarily applied to drama, and derived from ancient drama, in opposition to **tragedy**. Comedy deals with humorously confusing, sometimes ridiculous situations in which the ending is, nevertheless, happy. Shakespeare, *Twelfth Night* (see p. 510).

Comic mode: many genres (e.g., **romance, fabliau, comedy**) involve a happy ending in which justice is done, the ravages of time are arrested, and that which is lost is found. Such genres participate in a comic mode.

Dialogue (Greek "conversation"): Dialogue is a feature of many genres, especially in both the **novel** and drama. As a genre itself, dialogue is used in philosophical traditions especially (most famously in Plato's *Dialogues*), as the representation of a conversation in which a philosophical question is pursued among various speakers.

Didactic mode (Greek "teaching mode"): genres in a didactic mode are designed to instruct or teach, sometimes explicitly (e.g., sermons, philosophical **discourses, georgic**), and sometimes through the medium of fiction (e.g., **animal fable, parable**).

Discourse (Latin "running to and fro"): broadly, any nonfictional speech or writing; as a more specific genre, a philosophical meditation on a set theme. Thus Newman, *The Idea of a University*.

Dramatic monologue (Greek "single speaking"): a poem in which the voice of a historical or fictional **character** speaks, unmediated by any narrator, to an implied though silent audience. See Tennyson, "Ulysses" (p. 1962); Browning, "The Bishop Orders His Tomb" (p. 2059); Eliot, "The Love Song of J. Alfred Prufrock" (p. 2610).

Elegy: In **classical** literature elegy was a form written in elegiac **couplets** (a **hexameter** followed by a **pentameter**) devoted to many possible topics. In Ovidian elegy a lover meditates on the trials of erotic desire (e.g., Ovid's *Amores*). The **sonnet** sequences of both Sidney and Shakespeare exploit this genre, and, while it was still practiced in classical tradition by Donne ("On His Mistress" [see p. 616]), by the later seventeenth century the term came to denote the poetry of loss, especially through the death of a loved person. See Tennyson, *In Memoriam* (p. 1973); Yeats, "In Memory of Major Robert Gregory" (p. 2400); Auden, "In Memory of W. B. Yeats" (p. 2693); Heaney, "Clearances" (p. 2798).

Epic (synonym, *heroic poetry*): an extended narrative poem celebrating martial heroes, invoking divine inspiration, beginning in medias res (see **order**), written in a high style (including the deployment of **epic similes;** on high style, see **register**), and divided into long narrative sequences. Homer's *Iliad* and Virgil's *Aeneid* were the prime models for English writers of epic verse. Thus Milton, *Paradise Lost* (see p. 725); Wordsworth, *The Prelude* (see p. 1552); and Walcott, *Omeros* (see p. 2774). With its precise repertoire of stylistic resources, epic lent itself easily to **parodic** and **burlesque** forms, known as **mock epic;** thus Pope, *The Rape of the Lock* (see p. 1137).

Epigram: a short, pithy poem wittily expressed, often with wounding intent.

Epigraph (Greek "inscription"): any formal statement inscribed on stone; also the brief formulation on a book's title page, or a quotation at the beginning of a poem, introducing the work's themes in the most compressed form possible.

Epistle (Latin "letter"): the letter can be shaped as a literary form, involving an intimate address often between equals. The *Epistles* of Horace provided a model for English writers from the sixteenth century. Thus Wyatt, "Mine own John Poins," or Pope, "Epistle to a Lady." Letters can be shaped to form the matter of an extended fiction, as the eighteenth-century epistolary **novel** (e.g., Samuel Richardson's *Pamela*).

Epitaph: a pithy formulation to be inscribed on a funeral monument.

Epithalamion (Greek "concerning the bridal chamber"): a wedding poem, celebrating the marriage and wishing the couple good fortune. Thus Spenser, *Epithalamion* (see p. 438).

Essay (French "trial, attempt"): an informal philosophical meditation, usually in prose and sometimes in verse. The journalistic periodical essay was developed in the early eighteenth century. Thus Addison and Steele, periodical essays; Pope, *An Essay on Criticism* (see p. 1124).

Fabliau (French "little story," plural *fabliaux*): a short, funny, often bawdy narrative in low style (see **register**) imitated and developed from French models most subtly by Chaucer; see *The Miller's Prologue and Tale* (p. 191).

Farce: a play designed to provoke laughter through the often humiliating antics of stock **characters.**

Georgic (Greek "farming"): Virgil's *Georgics* treat agricultural and occasionally scientific subjects, giving instructions on the proper management of farms. Unlike **pastoral,** which treats the countryside as a place of recreational idleness among shepherds, the georgic treats it as a place of productive labor.

Heroic poetry: see **epic.**

Homily (Greek "discourse"): a sermon, to be preached in church. Writers of literary fiction sometimes exploit the homily, or sermon, as in Chaucer, *The Pardoner's Tale* (see p. 235).

Journal (French "daily"): a diary, or daily record of ephemeral experience, whose perspectives are concentrated on, and limited by, the experiences of single days.

Lai: a short narrative, often characterized by images of great intensity; a French term, and a form practiced by Marie de France (see p. 98).

Legend (Latin "requiring to be read"): a narrative of a celebrated, possibly historical, but mortal **protagonist.** To be distinguished from **myth.** Thus the "Arthurian legend" but the "myth of Proserpine."

Lullaby: a bedtime, sleep-inducing song for children, in simple and regular meter. Adapted by Auden, "Lullaby" (see p. 2690).

Lyric (from Greek "lyre"): Initially meaning a song, "lyric" refers to a short poetic form, without restriction of meter, in which the expression of personal emotion, often by a voice in the first person, is given primacy over narrative sequence. Thus Yeats, "The Wild Swans at Coole" (see p. 2399).

Masque: costly entertainments of the Stuart court, involving dance, song, speech, and elaborate stage effects, in which courtiers themselves participated.

Myth: the narrative of **protagonists** with, or subject to, superhuman powers. A myth expresses some profound foundational truth, often by accounting for the origin of natural phenomena. To be distinguished from **legend.** Thus the "Arthurian legend" but the "myth of Proserpine."

Novel: an extremely flexible genre in both form and subject matter. Usually in prose, giving high priority to narration of events, with a certain expectation of length, novels are preponderantly rooted in a specific, and often complex, social world; sensitive to the realities of material life; and often focused on one **character** or a small circle of central characters. By contrast with chivalric **romance** (the main European narrative genre prior to the novel), novels tend to eschew the marvelous in favor of a recognizable social world and credible action. The novel's openness allows it to participate in all modes, and to be co-opted for a huge variety of subgenres. In English literature the novel dates from the late seventeenth century and has been astonishingly successful in appealing to a huge readership, particularly in the nineteenth and twentieth centuries. The English and Irish tradition of the novel includes, for example, Fielding, Austen, the Brontë sisters, Dickens, George Eliot, Conrad, Woolf, Lawrence, Joyce, to name but a few very great exponents of the genre.

Novella: a short **novel,** often characterized by imagistic intensity. Conrad, *Heart of Darkness* (see p. 2328).

Ode (Greek "song"): a **lyric** poem in elevated, or high style (see **register**), often addressed to a natural force, a person, or an abstract quality. The Pindaric ode in English is made up of **stanzas** of unequal length, while the Horatian ode has stanzas of equal length. For examples of both types, see, respectively, Wordsworth, "Ode: Intimations of Immortality" (p. 1538); and Marvell, "An Horatian Ode" (p. 682), or Keats, "Ode on Melancholy" (p. 1849).

Panegyric: Demonstrative, or epideictic (Greek "showing"), rhetoric was a branch of **classical** rhetoric. Its own two main branches were the rhetoric of praise on the one hand and of vituperation on the other. Panegyric, or eulogy (Greek "sweet speaking"), or encomium (plural *encomia*), is the term used to describe the speeches or writings of praise.

Parable: a simple story designed to provoke, and often accompanied by, **allegorical** interpretation, most famously by Christ as reported in the Gospels.

Pastoral (from Latin "pastor," shepherd): Pastoral is set among shepherds, making often refined **allusion** to other apparently unconnected subjects (sometimes politics) from the potentially idyllic world of highly literary if illiterate shepherds. Pastoral is distinguished from **georgic** by representing recreational rural idleness, whereas the georgic offers instruction on how to manage rural labor. English writers had classical models in the *Idylls* of Theocritus in Greek and Virgil's *Eclogues* in Latin. Pastoral is also called bucolic (from the Greek word for "herdsman").

Romance: From the twelfth to the sixteenth century, the main form of European narrative, in either verse or prose, was that of chivalric romance. Romance, like the later **novel,** is a very fluid genre, but romances are often characterized by (i) a tripartite structure of social integration, followed by disintegration, involving moral tests and often marvelous events, itself the prelude to reintegration in a happy ending, frequently of marriage; (ii) **high-style** diction; (iii) aristocratic social mileux. Thus *Sir Gawain and the Green Knight* (see p. 114); Spenser's (unfinished) *Faerie Queene* (p. 368). The immensely popular, fertile genre was absorbed, in both domesticated and undomesticated form, by the novel. For an adaptation of romance, see Chaucer, *Wife of Bath's Tale* (p. 207).

Satire: In Roman literature (e.g., Juvenal), the communication, in the form of a letter between equals, complaining of the ills of contemporary society. The genre in this form is characterized by a first-person narrator exasperated by social ills; the letter form; a high frequency of contemporary reference; and the use of invective in **low-style** language. Pope practices the genre thus in the *Epistle to Dr. Arbuthnot* (see p. 1163). Wyatt's "Mine own John Poins" draws ultimately on a gentler, Horatian model of the genre.

Satiric mode: Works in a very large variety of genres are devoted to the more or less savage attack on social ills. Thus Swift's travel narrative *Gulliver's Travels* (see p. 974), his **essay** "A Modest Proposal" (p. 1114), Pope's mock-**epic** *The Dunciad*, and Gay's *Beggar's Opera*, to look no further than the eighteenth century, are all within a satiric mode.

Short story: generically similar to, though shorter and more concentrated than, the **novel;** often published as part of a collection. Thus Mansfield, "The Daughters of the Late Colonel."

Topographical poem (Greek "place writing"): a poem devoted to the meditative description of particular places.

Tragedy: a dramatic representation of the fall of kings or nobles, beginning in happiness and ending in catastrophe. Later transferred to other social mileux. The opposite of **comedy.**

Tragic mode: Many genres (**epic** poetry, **legendary** chronicles, **tragedy,** the **novel**) either do or can participate in a tragic mode, by representing the fall of noble **protagonists** and the irreparable ravages of human society and history.

Tragicomedy: a play in which potentially tragic events turn out to have a happy, or **comic,** ending. Thus Shakespeare, *Measure for Measure*.

C. Miscellaneous

Act: the major subdivision of a play, usually divided into **scenes.**

Aesthetics (from Greek, "to feel, apprehend by the senses"): the philosophy of artistic meaning as a distinct mode of apprehending untranslatable truth, defined as an alternative to rational enquiry, which is purely abstract. Developed in the late eighteenth century by the German philosopher Immanuel Kant especially.

Allusion: Literary allusion is a passing but illuminating reference within a literary text to another, well-known text (often biblical or **classical**). Topical allusions are also, of course, common in certain modes, especially **satire.**

Anagnorisis (Greek "recognition"): the moment of **protagonists'** recognition in a narrative, which is also often the moment of moral understanding.

Apostrophe (from Greek "turning away"): an address, often to an absent person, a force, or a quality. For example, a poet makes an apostrophe to a Muse when invoking her for inspiration.

Blazon: strictly, a heraldic shield; in rhetorical usage, a **topos** whereby the individual elements of a beloved's face and body are singled out for **hyperbolic** admiration. Spenser, *Epithalamion*, lines 167–84 (see p. 441). For an inversion of the **topos,** see Shakespeare, Sonnet 130 (p. 507).

Burlesque (French and Italian "mocking"): a work that adopts the **conventions** of a genre with the aim less of comically mocking the genre than of satirically mocking the society so represented (see **satire**). Thus Pope's *Rape of the Lock* (see p. 1136) does not mock **classical epic** so much as contemporary mores.

Canon (Greek "rule"): the group of texts regarded as worthy of special respect or attention by a given institution. Also, the group of texts regarded as definitely having been written by a certain author.

Catastrophe (Greek "overturning"): the decisive turn in **tragedy** by which the plot is resolved and, usually, the **protagonist** dies.

Catharsis (Greek "cleansing"): According to Aristotle, the effect of **tragedy** on its audience, through their experience of pity and terror, was a kind of spiritual cleansing, or catharsis.

Character (Greek "stamp, impression"): a person, personified animal, or other figure represented in a literary work, especially in narrative and drama. The more a character seems to generate the action of a narrative, and the less he or she seems merely to serve a preordained narrative pattern, the "fuller," or more "rounded," a character is said to be. A "stock" character, common particularly in many comic genres, will perform a predictable function in different works of a given genre.

Classical, Classicism, Classic: Each term can be widely applied, but in English literary discourse, "classical" primarily describes the works of either Greek or Roman antiquity. "Classicism" denotes the practice of art forms inspired by classical antiquity, in particular the observance of rhetorical norms of **decorum** and balance, as opposed to following the dictates of untutored inspiration, as in Romanticism. "Classic" denotes an especially famous work within a given **canon.**

Climax (Greek "ladder"): a moment of great intensity and structural change, especially in drama. Also a figure of speech whereby a sequence of verbally linked clauses is made, in which each successive clause is of greater consequence than its predecessor. Bacon, *Of Studies*: "Studies serve for pastimes, for ornaments, and for abilities. Their chief use for pastimes is in privateness and retiring; for ornament, is in discourse; and for ability, is in judgement."

Convention: a repeatedly recurring feature (in either form or content) of works, occurring in combination with other recurring formal features, constitutes a convention of a particular genre.

Decorum (Latin "that which is fitting"): a rhetorical principle whereby each formal aspect of a work should be in keeping with its subject matter and/or audience.

Denouement (French "unknotting"): the point at which a narrative can be resolved and so ended.

Dramatic irony: a feature of narrative and drama, whereby the audience knows that the outcome of an action will be the opposite of that intended by a **character.**

Ecphrasis (Greek "speaking out"): a **topos** whereby a work of visual art is represented in a literary work. Auden, "Musée des Beaux Arts" (see p. 2693).

Exegesis (Greek "leading out"): interpretation, traditionally of the biblical text, but, by transference, of any text.

Exemplum (Latin "example"): an example inserted into a usually nonfictional writing (e.g., sermon or **essay**) to give extra force to an abstract thesis. Thus Johnson's example of "Sober" in his essay "On Idleness."

Hermeneutics (from the Greek god Hermes, messenger between the gods and humankind): the science of interpretation, first formulated as such by the German philosophical theologian Friedrich Schleiermacher in the early nineteenth century.

Imitation: the practice whereby writers strive ideally to reproduce and yet renew the **conventions** of an older form, often derived from **classical** civilization. Such a practice will be praised in periods of classicism (e.g., the eighteenth century) and repudiated in periods dominated by a model of inspiration (e.g., Romanticism).

Parody: a work that uses the **conventions** of a particular genre with the aim of comically mocking a **topos,** a genre, or a particular exponent of a genre. Shakespeare parodies the topos of **blazon** in Sonnet 130 (see p. 507).

Pathetic fallacy: the attribution of sentiment to natural phenomena, as if they were in sympathy with human feelings. Thus Milton, *Lycidas*, lines 146–47: "With cowslips wan that hang the pensive head, / And every flower that sad embroidery wears" (see p. 710). For critique of the practice, see Ruskin (who coined the term), "Of the Pathetic Fallacy," in *Modern Painters.*

Peripeteia (Greek "turning about"): the sudden reversal of fortune (in both directions) in a dramatic work.

Persona (Latin "sound through"): originally the mask worn in the Roman theater to magnify an actor's voice; in literary discourse persona (plural *personae*) refers to the narrator or speaker of a text, by whose voice the author may mask him- or herself. Eliot, "The Love Song of J. Alfred Prufrock" (see p. 2610).

Protagonist (Greek "first actor"): the hero or heroine of a drama or narrative.

Rhetoric: the art of verbal persuasion. **Classical** rhetoricians distinguished three areas of rhetoric: the forensic, to be used in law courts; the deliberative, to be used in political or philosophical deliberations; and the demonstrative, or epideictic, to be used for the purposes of public praise or blame. Rhetorical manuals covered all the skills required of a speaker, from the management of style and structure to delivery. These manuals powerfully influenced the theory of poetics as a separate branch of verbal practice, particularly in the matter of style.

Scene: a subdivision of an **act,** itself a subdivision of a dramatic performance and/or text. The action of a scene usually occurs in one place.

Sensibility (from Latin, "capable of being perceived by the senses"): as a literary term, an eighteenth-century concept derived from moral philosophy that stressed the social importance of fellow feeling and particularly of sympathy in social relations. The concept generated a literature of "sensibility," such as the sentimental **novel** (the most famous of which was Goethe's *Sorrows of the Young Werther* [1774]), or sentimental poetry, such as Cowper's passage on the stricken deer in *The Task.*

Soliloquy (Latin "single speaking"): a **topos** of drama, in which a **character,** alone or thinking to be alone on stage, speaks so as to give the audience access to his or her private thoughts. Thus Viola's soliloquy in Shakespeare, *Twelfth Night* 2.2.17–41 (p. 528).

Sublime: As a concept generating a literary movement, the sublime refers to the realm of experience beyond the measurable, and so beyond the rational, produced especially by the terrors and grandeur of natural phenomena. Derived especially from the first-century Greek treatise *On the Sublime,* sometimes attributed to Longinus, the notion of the sublime was in the later eighteenth century a spur to Romanticism.

Taste (from Italian "touch"): Although medieval monastic traditions used eating and tasting as a metaphor for reading, the concept of taste as a personal ideal to be cultivated by, and applied to, the appreciation and judgment of works of art in general was developed in the eighteenth century.

Topos (Greek "place," plural *topoi*): a commonplace in the content of a given kind of literature. Originally, in **classical** rhetoric, the topoi were tried-and-tested stimuli to literary invention: lists of standard headings under which a subject might be investigated. In medieval narrative poems, for example, it was commonplace to begin with a description of spring. Writers did, of course, render the commonplace uncommon, as in Chaucer's spring scene at the opening of *The Canterbury Tales* (see p. 170).

Tradition (from Latin "passing on"): A literary tradition is whatever is passed on or revived from the past in a single literary culture, or drawn from others to enrich a writer's culture. "Tradition" is fluid in reference, ranging from small to large referents: thus it may refer to a relatively small aspect of texts (e.g., the tradition of **iambic pentameter**), or it may, at the other extreme, refer to the body of texts that constitute a **canon.**

Translation (Latin "carrying across"): the rendering of a text written in one language into another.

Vernacular (from Latin "verna," servant): the language of the people, as distinguished from learned and arcane languages. From the later Middle Ages especially, the "vernacular" languages and literatures of Europe distinguished themselves from the learned languages and literatures of Latin, Greek, and Hebrew.

Wit: Originally a synonym for "reason" in Old and Middle English, "wit" became a literary ideal in the Renaissance as brilliant play of the full range of mental resources. For eighteenth-century writers, the notion necessarily involved pleasing expression, as in Pope's definition of true wit as "Nature to advantage dressed, / What oft was thought, but ne'er so well expressed" (*Essay on Criticism*, lines 297–98; see p. 1130). Romantic theory of the imagination deprived wit of its full range of apprehension, whence the word came to be restricted to its modern sense, as the clever play of mind that produces laughter.

D. Publishing History, Censorship

By the time we read texts in published books, they have already been treated—that is, changed by authors, editors, and printers—in many ways. Although there are differences across history, in each period literary works are subject to pressures of many kinds, which apply before, while, and after an author writes. The pressures might be financial, as in the relations of author and patron; commercial, as in the marketing of books; and legal, as in, during some periods, the negotiation through official and unofficial censorship. In addition, texts in all periods undergo technological processes, as they move from the material forms in which an author produced them to the forms in which they are presented to readers. Some of the terms below designate important material forms in which books were produced, disseminated, and surveyed across the historical span of this anthology. Others designate the skills developed to understand these processes. The anthology's introductions to individual periods discuss the particular forms these phenomena took in different eras.

Bookseller: In England, and particularly in London, commercial bookmaking and -selling enterprises came into being in the early fourteenth century. These were loose organizations of artisans who usually lived in the same neighborhoods (around St. Paul's Cathedral in London). A bookseller or dealer would coordinate the production of hand-copied books for wealthy patrons (see **patronage**), who would order books to be custom-made. After the introduction of **printing** in the late fifteenth century, authors generally sold the rights to their work to booksellers, without any further **royalties.** Booksellers, who often had their own shops, belonged to the **Stationers' Company.** This system lasted into the eighteenth century. In 1710, however, authors were for the first time granted **copyright,** which tipped the commercial balance in their favor, against booksellers.

Censorship: The term applies to any mechanism for restricting what can be published. Historically, the reasons for imposing censorship are heresy, sedition, blasphemy, libel, or obscenity. External censorship is imposed by institutions having legislative sanctions at their disposal. Thus the pre-Reformation Church imposed the Constitutions of Archbishop Arundel of 1409, aimed at repressing the Lollard "heresy." After the Reformation, some key events in the history of censorship are as follows: 1547, when anti-Lollard legislation and legislation made by Henry VIII concerning treason by writing (1534) were abolished; the Licensing Order of 1643, which legislated that works be licensed, through the Stationers' Company, prior to publication; and 1695, when the last such Act stipulating prepublication licensing lapsed. Postpublication censorship continued in different periods for different reasons. Thus, for example, British publication of D. H. Lawrence's *Lady Chatterley's Lover* (1928) was obstructed (though unsuccessfully) in 1960, under the Obscene Publications Act of 1959. Censorship can also be international: although not published in Iran, Salman Rushdie's *Satanic Verses* (1988) was censored in that country, where the leader, Ayatollah Ruhollah Khomeini, proclaimed a fatwa (religious decree) promising the author's execution. Very often censorship is not imposed externally, however: authors or publishers can censor work in anticipation of what will incur the wrath of readers or the penalties of the law. Victorian and Edwardian publishers of **novels,** for example, urged authors to remove potentially offensive material, especially for serial publication in popular magazines.

Codex (Latin "book"): having the format of a book (usually applied to manuscript books), as distinguished originally from the scroll, which was the standard form of written document in ancient Rome.

Copyright: the legal protection afforded to authors for control of their work's publication, in an attempt to ensure due financial reward. Some key dates in the history of copyright in the United Kingdom are as follows: 1710, when a statute gave authors the exclusive right to publish their work for fourteen years, and fourteen years more if the author were still alive when the first term had expired; 1842, when the period of authorial control was extended to forty-two years; and 1911, when the term was extended yet further, to fifty years after the author's death. In 1995 the period of protection was harmonized with the laws in other European countries to be the life of the author plus seventy years. In the United States no works first published before 1923 are in copyright. Works published since 1978 are, as in the United Kingdom, protected for the life of the author plus seventy years.

Copy text: the particular text of a work used by a textual editor as the basis of an edition of that work.

Folio: Books come in different shapes, depending originally on the number of times a standard sheet of paper is folded. One fold produces a large volume, a *folio* book; two folds produce a *quarto,* four an *octavo*, and six a very small *duodecimo*. Generally speaking, the larger the book, the grander and more expensive. Shakespeare's plays were, for example, first printed in quartos, but were gathered into a folio edition in 1623.

Foul papers: versions of a work before an author has produced, if she or he has, a final copy (a "fair copy") with all corrections removed.

Manuscript (Latin, "written by hand"): Any text written physically by hand is a manuscript. Before the introduction of **printing** with moveable type in 1476, all texts in England were produced and reproduced by hand, in manuscript. This is an extremely labor-intensive task, using expensive materials (e.g., animal skins); the cost of books produced thereby was, accordingly, very high. Even after the introduction of printing, many texts continued to be produced in manuscript. This is obviously true of letters, for example, but until the eighteenth century, poetry written within aristocratic circles was often transmitted in manuscript copies.

Paleography (Greek "ancient writing"): the art of deciphering, describing, and dating forms of handwriting.

Patronage (Latin "protector"): Many technological, legal, and commercial supports were necessary before professional authorship became possible. Although some playwrights (e.g., Shakespeare) made a living by writing for the theater, other authors needed, principally, the large-scale reproductive capacities of **printing** and the security of **copyright** to make a living from writing. Before these conditions obtained, many authors had another main occupation, and most authors had to rely on patronage. In different periods, institutions or individuals offered material support, or patronage, to authors. Thus in Anglo-Saxon England, monasteries afforded the conditions of writing to monastic authors. Between the twelfth and the seventeenth centuries, the main source of patronage was the royal court. Authors offered patrons prestige and ideological support in return for financial support. Even as the conditions of professional authorship came into being at the beginning of the eighteenth century, older forms of direct patronage were not altogether displaced until the middle of the century.

Periodical: Whereas journalism, strictly, applies to daily writing (from French "jour," day), periodical writing appears at larger, but still frequent, intervals, characteristically in the form of the **essay.** Periodicals were developed especially in the eighteenth century.

Printing: Printing, or the mechanical reproduction of books using moveable type, was invented in Germany in the mid-fifteenth century by Johannes Gutenberg; it quickly spread throughout Europe. William Caxton brought printing into England from the Low Countries in 1476. Much greater powers of reproduction at much lower prices transformed every aspect of literary culture.

Publisher: the person or company responsible for the commissioning and publicizing of printed matter. In the early period of **printing,** publisher, printer, and bookseller were often the same person. This trend continued in the ascendancy of the **Stationers' Company,** between the middle of the sixteenth and the end of the seventeenth centuries. Toward the end of the seventeenth century, these three functions began to separate, leading to their modern distinctions.

Royalties: an agreed-upon proportion of the price of each copy of a work sold, paid by the publisher to the author, or an agreed-upon fee paid to the playwright for each performance of a play.

Scribe: in **manuscript** culture, the scribe is the copyist who reproduces a text by hand.

Stationers' Company: The Stationers' Company was an English guild incorporating various tradesmen, including printers, publishers, and booksellers, skilled in the production and selling of books. It was formed in 1403, received its royal charter in 1557, and served as a means both of producing and of regulating books. Authors would sell the manuscripts of their books to individual stationers, who incurred the risks and took the profits of producing and selling the books. The stationers entered their rights over given books in the Stationers' Register. They also regulated the book trade and held their monopoly by licensing books and by being empowered to seize unauthorized books and imprison resisters. This system of licensing broke down in the social unrest of the Civil War and Interregnum (1640–60), and it ended in 1695. Even after the end of licensing, the Stationers' Company continued to be an intrinsic part of the **copyright** process, since the 1710 copyright statute directed that copyright had to be registered at Stationers' Hall.

Subscription: An eighteenth-century system of bookselling somewhere between direct **patronage** and impersonal sales. A subscriber paid half the cost of a book before publication and half on delivery. The author received these payments directly. The subscriber's name appeared in the prefatory pages.

Textual criticism: works in all periods often exist in many subtly or not so subtly different forms. This is especially true with regard to manuscript textual reproduction, but it also applies to printed texts. Textual criticism is the art, developed from the fifteenth century in Italy but raised to new levels of sophistication from the eighteenth century, of deciphering different historical states of texts. This art involves the analysis of textual variants, often with the aim of distinguishing authorial from scribal forms.

Geographic Nomenclature

The British Isles refers to the prominent group of islands off the northwest coast of Europe, especially to the two largest, **Great Britain** and **Ireland**. At present these comprise two sovereign states: **the Republic of Ireland**, or **Éire**, and **the United Kingdom of Great Britain and Northern Ireland**—known for short as the **United Kingdom** or the **U.K.** Most of the smaller islands are part of the **U.K.** but a few, like the **Isle of Man** and the tiny **Channel Islands**, are largely independent. The **U.K.** is often loosely referred to as **"Britain"** or **"Great Britain"** and is sometimes called simply, if inaccurately, **"England."** For obvious reasons, the latter usage is rarely heard among the inhabitants of the other countries of the **U.K.—Scotland, Wales,** and **Northern Ireland** (sometimes called **Ulster**). England is by far the most populous part of the kingdom, as well as the seat of its capital, London.

From the first to the fifth century C.E. most of what is now **England** and **Wales** was a province of the Roman Empire called **Britain** (in Latin, **Britannia**). After the fall of Rome, much of the island was invaded and settled by peoples from northern Germany and Denmark speaking what we now call Old English. These peoples are collectively known as the Anglo-Saxons, and the word **England** is related to the first element of their name. By the time of the Norman Conquest (1066) most of the kingdoms founded by the Anglo-Saxons and subsequent Viking invaders had coalesced into the kingdom of **England,** which, in the latter Middle Ages, conquered and largely absorbed the neighboring Celtic kingdom of **Wales.** In 1603 James VI of **Scotland** inherited the island's other throne as James I of **England,** and for the next hundred years—except for the brief period of Puritan rule—**Scotland** (both its English-speaking **Lowlands** and its Gaelic-speaking **Highlands**) and **England** (with **Wales**) were two kingdoms under a single king. In 1707 the Act of Union welded them together as **the United Kingdom of Great Britain. Ireland,** where English rule had begun in the twelfth century and been tightened in the sixteenth, was incorporated by the 1800–1801 Act of Union into **the United Kingdom of Great Britain and Ireland**. With the division of Ireland and the establishment of **the Irish Free State** after World War I, this name was modified to its present form, and in 1949 **the Irish Free State** became **the Republic of Ireland.** In 1999 **Scotland** elected a separate parliament it had relinquished in 1707, and **Wales** elected an assembly it lost in 1409; neither Scotland nor Wales ceased to be part of the **United Kingdom**.

The **British Isles** are further divided into counties, which in **Great Britain** are also known as shires. This word, with its vowel shortened in pronunciation, forms the suffix in the names of many counties, such as **Yorkshire, Wiltshire, Somersetshire**.

The Latin names **Britannia (Britain), Caledonia (Scotland)**, and **Hibernia (Ireland)** are sometimes used in poetic diction; so too is **Britain**'s ancient Celtic name, **Albion**. Because of its accidental resemblance to *albus* (Latin for "white"), **Albion** is especially associated with the chalk cliffs that seem to gird much of the English coast like defensive walls.

The British Empire took its name from **the British Isles** because it was created not only by the **English** but also by the **Irish, Scots,** and **Welsh**, as well as by civilians and servicemen from other constituent countries of the empire. Some of the empire's **overseas colonies**, or **crown colonies**, were populated largely by settlers of European origin and their descendants. These predominantly white **settler colonies**, such as **Canada**, **Australia**, and **New Zealand**, were allowed significant self-government in the nineteenth century and recognized as **dominions** in the early twentieth century.

The **white dominions** became members of **the Commonwealth of Nations**, also called **the Commonwealth, the British Commonwealth**, and **"the Old Commonwealth"** at different times, an association of sovereign states under the symbolic leadership of the British monarch.

Other **overseas colonies** of the empire had mostly indigenous populations (or, in the Caribbean, the descendants of imported slaves, indentured servants, and others). These **colonies** were granted political independence after World War II, later than the **dominions**, and have often been referred to since as **postcolonial** nations. In South and Southeast Asia, **India** and **Pakistan** gained independence in 1947, followed by other countries including **Sri Lanka** (formerly **Ceylon**), **Burma** (now **Myanmar**), **Malaya** (now **Malaysia**), and **Singapore**. In West and East Africa, the **Gold Coast** was decolonized as **Ghana** in 1957, **Nigeria** in 1960, **Sierra Leone** in 1961, **Uganda** in 1962, **Kenya** in 1963, and so forth, while in southern Africa, the white minority government of **South Africa** was already independent in 1931, though majority rule did not come until 1994. In the Caribbean, **Jamaica** and **Trinidad and Tobago** won independence in 1962, followed by **Barbados** in 1966, and other islands of the British West Indies in the 1970s and '80s. Other regions with nations emerging out of British colonial rule included Central America (**British Honduras**, now **Belize**), South America (**British Guiana**, now **Guyana**), the Pacific islands (**Fiji**), and Europe (**Cyprus, Malta**). After decolonization, many of these nations chose to remain within a newly conceived **Commonwealth** and are sometimes referred to as **"New Commonwealth"** countries. Some nations, such as **Ireland, Pakistan**, and **South Africa**, withdrew from the **Commonwealth**, though **South Africa** and **Pakistan** eventually rejoined, and others, such as **Burma** (**Myanmar**), gained independence outside the **Commonwealth**. Britain's last major overseas colony, **Hong Kong**, was returned to Chinese sovereignty in 1997, but while Britain retains only a handful of dependent territories, such as **Bermuda** and **Montserrat**, the scope of the **Commonwealth** remains vast, with 30 percent of the world's population.

British Money

One of the most dramatic changes to the system of British money came in 1971. In the system previously in place, the pound consisted of 20 shillings, each containing 12 pence, making 240 pence to the pound. Since 1971, British money has been calculated on the decimal system, with 100 pence to the pound. Britons' experience of paper money did not change very drastically: as before, 5- and 10-pound notes constitute the majority of bills passing through their hands (in addition, 20- and 50-pound notes have been added). But the shift necessitated a whole new way of thinking about and exchanging coins and marked the demise of the shilling, one of the fundamental units of British monetary history. Many other coins, still frequently encountered in literature, had already passed. These include the groat, worth 4 pence (the word "groat" is often used to signify a trifling sum); the angel (which depicted the archangel Michael triumphing over a dragon), valued at 10 shillings; the mark, worth in its day two-thirds of a pound or 13 shillings 4 pence; and the sovereign, a gold coin initially worth 22 shillings 6 pence, later valued at 1 pound, last circulated in 1932. One prominent older coin, the guinea, was worth a pound and a shilling; though it has not been minted since 1813, a very few quality items or prestige awards (like the purse in a horse race) may still be quoted in guineas. (The table below includes some other well-known, obsolete coins.) Colloquially, a pound was (and is) called a quid; a shilling a bob; sixpence, a tanner; a copper could refer to a penny, a half-penny, or a farthing (¼ penny).

Old Currency	*New Currency*
1 pound note	1 pound coin (or note in Scotland)
10 shilling (half-pound note)	50 pence
5 shilling (crown)	
2½ shilling (half crown)	20 pence
2 shilling (florin)	10 pence
1 shilling	5 pence
6 pence	
2½ pence	1 penny
2 pence	
1 penny	
½ penny	
¼ penny (farthing)	

In recent years, the British government and people have been contemplating and debating a change even greater than the shift to the decimal system. Britain, a member of the European Union, may adopt the EU's common currency, the Euro, and eventually see the pound itself become obsolete. More than many other EU-member countries, Britain has resisted this change: many people strongly identify their country with its rich commercial history and tend to view their currency patriotically as a national symbol.

Even more challenging than sorting out the values of obsolete coins is calculating for any given period the purchasing power of money, which fluctuates over time by its very nature. At the beginning of the twentieth century, 1 pound was worth about 5 American dollars, though those bought three to four times what they now do. Now, the pound buys anywhere from \$1.50 to \$1.90. As difficult as it is to generalize, it is clear that money used to be worth much more than it is currently. In Anglo-Saxon times, the most valuable circulating coin was the silver penny: four would buy a sheep. Beyond long-term inflationary trends, prices varied from times of plenty to those marked by poor harvests; from peacetime to wartime; from the country to the metropolis (life in London has always been very expensive); and wages varied according to the availability of labor (wages rose sharply, for instance, during the devastating Black Death in the fourteenth century). The chart below provides a glimpse of some actual prices of given periods and their changes across time, though all the variables mentioned above prevent them from being definitive. Even from one year to the next, an added tax on gin or tea could drastically raise prices, and a lottery ticket could cost much more the night before the drawing than just a month earlier. Still, the prices quoted below do indicate important trends, such as the disparity of incomes in British society and the costs of basic commodities. In the chart below, the symbol £ is used for pound, s. for shilling, d. for a penny (from Latin *denarius*); a sum would normally be written £2.19.3, i.e., 2 pounds, 19 shillings, 3 pence. (This is Leopold Bloom's budget for the day depicted in Joyce's novel *Ulysses* [1922]; in the new currency, it would be about £2.96.)

circa	1390	1590	1650	1750	1815	1875	1950
food and drink	gallon (8 pints) of ale, 1.5d.	tankard of beer, .5d.	coffee, 1d. a dish	"drunk for a penny, dead drunk for twopence" (gin shop sign in Hogarth print)	ounce of laudanum, 3d.	pint of beer, 3d.	pint of Guinness stout, 11d.
	gallon (8 pints) of wine, 3 to 4d.	pound of beef, 2s. 5d.	chicken, 1s. 4d.	dinner at a steakhouse, 1s.	ham and potato dinner for two, 7s.	dinner in a good hotel, 5s.	pound of beef, 2s. 2d.
	pound of cinnamon, 1 to 3s.	pound of cinnamon, 10s. 6d.	pound of tea, £3 10s.	pound of tea, 16s.	Prince Regent's dinner party for 2000, £12.000	pound of tea, 2s.	dinner on railway car, 7s. 6d.
entertainment	no cost to watch a cycle play	admission to public theater, 1 to 3d.	falcon, £11 5s.	theater tickets, 1 to 5s.	admission to Covent Garden theater, 1 to 7s.	theater tickets, 6d. to 7s.	admission to Old Vic theater, 1s. 6d. to 10s. 6d.
	contributory admission to professional troupe theater	cheap seat in private theater, 6d.	billiard table, £25	admission to Vauxhall Gardens, 1s.	annual subscription to Almack's (exclusive club), 10 guineas	admission to Madam Tussaud's waxworks, 1s.	admission to Odeon cinema, Manchester, 1s. 3d.
	maintenance for royal hounds at Windsor, .75d. a day	"to see a dead Indian" (qtd. in *The Tempest*), 1.25d. (ten "doits")	three-quarter-length portrait painting, £31	lottery ticket, £20 (shares were sold)	Jane Austen's piano, 30 guineas	annual fees at a gentleman's club, 7–10 guineas	tropical fish tank, £4 4s.
reading	cheap romance, 1s.	play quarto, 6d.	pamphlet, 1 to 6d.	issue of *The Gentleman's Magazine*, 6d.	issue of *Edinburgh Review*, 6s.	copy of *The Times*, 3d.	copy of *The Times*, 3d.

circa	1390	1590	1650	1750	1815	1875	1950
	a Latin Bible, 2 to £4	Shakespeare's *First Folio* (1623), £1	student Bible, 6s.	cheap edition of Milton, 2s.	membership in circulating library (3rd class), £1 4s. a year	illustrated edition of *Through the Looking-glass*, 6s.	issue of *Eagle* comics, 4.5d.
	payment for illuminating a liturgical book, £22 9s.	Foxe's *Acts and Monuments*, 24s.	Hobbes's *Leviathan*, 8s.	Johnson's *Dictionary*, folio, 2 vols., £4 10s.	1st edition of Austen's *Pride and Prejudice*, 18s.	1st edition of Trollope's *The Way We Live Now*, 2 vols., £1 1s.	Orwell's *Nineteen Eighty Four*, paperback, 3s. 6d.
transportation	night's supply of hay for horse, 2d.	wherry (whole boat) across Thames, 1d.	day's journey, coach, 10s.	boat across Thames, 4d.	coach ride, outside, 2 to 3d. a mile; inside, 4 to 5d. a mile	15-minute journey in a London cab, 1s. 6d.	London tube fare, about 2d. a mile
	coach, £8	hiring a horse for a day, 12d.	coach horse, £30	coach fare, London to Edinburgh, £4 10s.	palanquin transport in Madras, 5s. a day	railway, 3rd class, London to Plymouth, 18s. 8d. (about 1d. a mile)	petrol, 3s. a gallon
	quality horse, £10	hiring a coach for a day, 10s.	fancy carriage, £170	transport to America, £5	passage, Liverpool to New York, £10	passage to India, 1st class, £50	midsize Austin sedan, £449 plus £188 4s. 2d. tax
clothes	clothing allowance for peasant, 3s. a year	shoes with buckles, 8d.	footman's frieze coat, 15s.	working woman's gown, 6s. 6d.	checked muslin, 7s. per yard	flannel for a cheap petticoat, 1s. 3d. a yard	woman's sun frock, £3 13s. 10d.

circa	1390	1590	1650	1750	1815	1875	1950
	shoes for gentry wearer, 4d.	woman's gloves, £1 5s.	falconer's hat, 10s.	gentleman's suit, £8	hiring a dress-maker for a pelisse, 8s.	overcoat for an Eton school-boy, £1 1s.	tweed sports jacket, £3 16s. 6d.
	hat for gentry wearer, 10d.	fine cloak, £16	black cloth for mourning house-hold of an earl, £100	very fine wig, £30	ladies silk stock-ings, 12s.	set of false teeth, £2 10s.	"Teddy boy" drape suit, £20
labor/incomes	hiring a skilled building worker, 4d. a day	actor's daily wage during playing sea-son, 1s.	agricultural laborer, 6s. 5d. a week	price of boy slave, £32	lowest-paid sailor on Royal Navy ship, 10s. 9d. a month	seasonal agri-cultural laborer, 14s. a week	minimum wage, agricul-tural laborer, £4 14s. per 47-hour week
	wage for profes-sional scribe, £2 3s. 4d. a year + cloak	household servant 2 to £5 a year + food, clothing	tutor to noble-man's children, £30 a year	housemaid's wage, £6 to £8 a year	contributor to *Quarterly Review*, 10 guineas per sheet	housemaid's wage, £10 to £25 a year	shorthand typ-ist, £367 a year
	minimum income to be called gentle-man, £10 a year; for knighthood, 40 to £400	minimum income for eligibility for knighthood, £30 a year	Milton's salary as Secretary of For-eign Tongues, £288 a year	Boswell's allow-ance, £200 a year	minimum income for a "genteel" family, £100 a year	income of the "comfortable" classes, £800 and up a year	middle man-ager's salary, £1,480 a year
	income from land of richest magnates, £3,500 a year	income from land of average earl, £4000 a year	Earl of Bedford's income, £8,000 a year	Duke of Newcas-tle's income, £40,000 a year	Mr. Darcy's income, *Pride and Prejudice*, £10,000	Trollope's income, £4,000 a year	barrister's sal-ary, £2,032 a year

The British Baronage

The English monarchy is in principle hereditary, though at times during the Middle Ages the rules were subject to dispute. In general, authority passes from father to eldest surviving son, from daughters in order of seniority if there is no son, to a brother if there are no children, and in default of direct descendants to collateral lines (cousins, nephews, nieces) in order of closeness. There have been breaks in the order of succession (1066, 1399, 1688), but so far as possible the usurpers have always sought to paper over the break with a legitimate, i.e., hereditary, claim. When a queen succeeds to the throne and takes a husband, he does not become king unless he is in the line of blood succession; rather, he is named prince consort, as Albert was to Victoria. He may father kings, but is not one himself.

The original Saxon nobles were the king's thanes, ealdormen, or earls, who provided the king with military service and counsel in return for booty, gifts, or landed estates. William the Conqueror, arriving from France, where feudalism was fully developed, considerably expanded this group. In addition, as the king distributed the lands of his new kingdom, he also distributed dignities to men who became known collectively as "the baronage." "Baron" in its root meaning signifies simply "man," and barons were the king's men. As the title was common, a distinction was early made between greater and lesser barons, the former gradually assuming loftier and more impressive titles. The first English "duke" was created in 1337; the title of "marquess," or "marquis" (pronounced "markwis"), followed in 1385, and "viscount" ("vyekount") in 1440. Though "earl" is the oldest title of all, an earl now comes between a marquess and a viscount in order of dignity and precedence, and the old term "baron" now designates a rank just below viscount."Baronets" were created in 1611 as a means of raising revenue for the crown (the title could be purchased for about £1000); they are marginal nobility and have never sat in the House of Lords.

Kings and queens are addressed as "Your Majesty," princes and princesses as "Your Highness," the other hereditary nobility as "My Lord" or "Your Lordship." Peers receive their titles either by inheritance (like Lord Byron, the sixth baron of that line) or from the monarch (like Alfred Lord Tennyson, created first Baron Tennyson by Victoria). The children, even of a duke, are commoners unless they are specifically granted some other title or inherit their father's title from him. A peerage can be forfeited by act of attainder, as for example when a lord is convicted of treason; and, when forfeited, or lapsed for lack of a successor, can be bestowed on another family. Thus in 1605 Robert Cecil was made first earl of Salisbury in the third creation, the first creation dating from 1149, the second from 1337, the title having been in abeyance since 1539. Titles descend by right of succession and do not depend on tenure of land; thus, a title does not always indicate where a lord dwells or holds power. Indeed, noble titles do not always refer to a real place at all. At Prince Edward's marriage in 1999, the queen created him earl of Wessex, although the old kingdom of Wessex has had no political existence since the Anglo-Saxon period, and the name was all but forgotten until it was resurrected by Thomas Hardy as the setting of his novels. (This is perhaps but one of many ways in which the world of the aristocracy increasingly resembles the realm of literature.)

The king and queen	(These are all of the royal line.)
Prince and princess	
Duke and duchess	(These may or may not be of the royal line, but are ordinarily remote from the succession.)
Marquess and marchioness	
Earl and countess	
Viscount and viscountess	
Baron and baroness	
Baronet and lady	

Scottish peers sat in the parliament of Scotland, as English peers did in the parliament of England, till at the Act of Union (1707) Scottish peers were granted sixteen seats in the English House of Lords, to be filled by election. (In 1963, all Scottish lords were allowed to sit.) Similarly, Irish peers, when the Irish parliament was abolished in 1801, were granted the right to elect twenty-eight of their number to the House of Lords in Westminster. (Now that the Republic of Ireland is a separate nation, this no longer applies.) Women members (peeresses) were first allowed to sit in the House as nonhereditary Life Peers in 1958 (when that status was created for members of both genders); women first sat by their own hereditary right in 1963. Today the House of Lords still retains some power to influence or delay legislation, but its future is uncertain. In 1999, the hereditary peers (then amounting to 750) were reduced to 92 temporary members elected by their fellow peers. Holders of Life Peerages remain, as do senior bishops of the Church of England and high-court judges (the "Law Lords").

Below the peerage the chief title of honor is "knight." Knighthood, which is not hereditary, is generally a reward for services rendered. A knight (Sir John Black) is addressed, using his first name, as "Sir John"; his wife, using the last name, is "Lady Black"—unless she is the daughter of an earl or nobleman of higher rank, in which case she will be "Lady Arabella." The female equivalent of a knight bears the title of "Dame." Though the word itself comes from the Anglo-Saxon *cniht*, there is some doubt as to whether knighthood amounted to much before the arrival of the Normans. The feudal system required military service as a condition of land tenure, and a man who came to serve his king at the head of an army of tenants required a title of authority and badges of identity—hence the title of knighthood and the coat of arms. During the Crusades, when men were far removed from their land (or even sold it in order to go on crusade), more elaborate forms of fealty sprang up that soon expanded into orders of knighthood. The Templars, Hospitallers, Knights of the Teutonic Order, Knights of Malta, and Knights of the Golden Fleece were but a few of these companionships; not all of them were available at all times in England.

Gradually, with the rise of centralized government and the decline of feudal tenures, military knighthood became obsolete, and the rank largely honorific; sometimes, as under James I, it degenerated into a scheme of the royal government for making money. For hundreds of years after its establishment in the fourteenth century, the Order of the Garter was the only English order of knighthood, an exclusive courtly companionship. Then, during the late seventeenth, the eighteenth, and the nineteenth centuries, a number of additional orders were created, with names such as the Thistle, Saint Patrick, the Bath, Saint Michael and Saint George, plus a number of special Victorian and Indian orders. They retain the terminology, ceremony, and dignity of knighthood, but the military implications are vestigial.

Although the British Empire now belongs to history, appointments to the Order of the British Empire continue to be conferred for services to that empire at home or abroad. Such honors (commonly referred to as "gongs") are granted by the monarch in her New Year's and Birthday lists, but the decisions are now made by the government in power. In recent years there have been efforts to popularize and democratize the dispensation of honors, with recipients including rock stars and actors. But this does not prevent large sectors of British society from regarding both knighthood and the peerage as largely irrelevant to modern life.

The Royal Lines of England and Great Britain

England

SAXONS AND DANES

Egbert, king of Wessex	802–839
Ethelwulf, son of Egbert	839–858
Ethelbald, second son of Ethelwulf	858–860
Ethelbert, third son of Ethelwulf	860–866
Ethelred I, fourth son of Ethelwulf	866–871
Alfred the Great, fifth son of Ethelwulf	871–899
Edward the Elder, son of Alfred	899–924
Athelstan the Glorious, son of Edward	924–940
Edmund I, third son of Edward	940–946
Edred, fourth son of Edward	946–955
Edwy the Fair, son of Edmund	955–959
Edgar the Peaceful, second son of Edmund	959–975
Edward the Martyr, son of Edgar	975–978 (murdered)
Ethelred II, the Unready, second son of Edgar	978–1016
Edmund II, Ironside, son of Ethelred II	1016–1016
Canute the Dane	1016–1035
Harold I, Harefoot, natural son of Canute	1035–1040
Hardecanute, son of Canute	1040–1042
Edward the Confessor, son of Ethelred II	1042–1066
Harold II, brother-in-law of Edward	1066–1066 (died in battle)

HOUSE OF NORMANDY

William I the Conqueror	1066–1087
William II, Rufus, third son of William I	1087–1100 (shot from ambush)
Henry I, Beauclerc, youngest son of William I	1100–1135

HOUSE OF BLOIS

Stephen, son of Adela, daughter of William I	1135–1154

HOUSE OF PLANTAGENET

Henry II, son of Geoffrey Plantagenet by Matilda, daughter of Henry I	1154–1189
Richard I, Coeur de Lion, son of Henry II	1189–1199
John Lackland, son of Henry II	1199–1216
Henry III, son of John	1216–1272
Edward I, Longshanks, son of Henry III	1272–1307
Edward II, son of Edward I	1307–1327 (deposed)
Edward III of Windsor, son of Edward II	1327–1377
Richard II, grandson of Edward III	1377–1399 (deposed)

HOUSE OF LANCASTER

Henry IV, son of John of Gaunt, son of Edward III	1399–1413
Henry V, Prince Hal, son of Henry IV	1413–1422
Henry VI, son of Henry V	1422–1461 (deposed), 1470–1471 (deposed)

HOUSE OF YORK

Edward IV, great-great-grandson of Edward III	1461–1470 (deposed), 1471–1483
Edward V, son of Edward IV	1483–1483 (murdered)
Richard III, Crookback	1483–1485 (died in battle)

HOUSE OF TUDOR

Henry VII, married daughter of Edward IV	1485–1509
Henry VIII, son of Henry VII	1509–1547
Edward VI, son of Henry VIII	1547–1553
Mary I, "Bloody," daughter of Henry VIII	1553–1558
Elizabeth I, daughter of Henry VIII	1558–1603

HOUSE OF STUART

James I (James VI of Scotland)	1603–1625
Charles I, son of James I	1625–1649 (executed)

COMMONWEALTH & PROTECTORATE

Council of State	1649–1653
Oliver Cromwell, Lord Protector	1653–1658
Richard Cromwell, son of Oliver	1658–1660 (resigned)

HOUSE OF STUART (RESTORED)

Charles II, son of Charles I	1660–1685
James II, second son of Charles I	1685–1688

(INTERREGNUM, 11 DECEMBER 1688 TO 13 FEBRUARY 1689)

William III of Orange, by Mary, daughter of Charles I	1689–1701
and Mary II, daughter of James II	–1694
Anne, second daughter of James II	1702–1714

Great Britain

HOUSE OF HANOVER

George I, son of Elector of Hanover and Sophia, granddaughter of James I	1714–1727
George II, son of George I	1727–1760
George III, grandson of George II	1760–1820
George IV, son of George III	1820–1830
William IV, third son of George III	1830–1837
Victoria, daughter of Edward, fourth son of George III	1837–1901

HOUSE OF SAXE-COBURG AND GOTHA

Edward VII, son of Victoria	1901–1910

HOUSE OF WINDSOR (NAME ADOPTED 17 JULY 1917)

George V, second son of Edward VII	1910–1936
Edward VIII, eldest son of George V	1936–1936 (abdicated)
George VI, second son of George V	1936–1952
Elizabeth II, daughter of George VI	1952–

Religions in England

In the sixth century C.E., missionaries from Ireland and the Continent introduced Christianity to the Anglo-Saxons—actually, reintroduced it, since it had briefly flourished in the southern parts of the British Isles during the Roman occupation, and even after the Roman withdrawal had persisted in the Celtic regions of Scotland and Wales. By the time the earliest poems included in the *Norton Anthology* were composed, therefore, the English people had been Christians for hundreds of years; such Anglo-Saxon poems as "The Dream of the Rood" bear witness to their faith. Our knowledge of the religion of pre-Christian Britain is sketchy, but it is likely that vestiges of paganism assimilated into, or coexisted with, the practice of Christianity: fertility rites were incorporated into the celebration of Easter resurrection, rituals commemorating the dead into All-Hallows Eve and All Saints Day, and elements of winter solstice festivals into the celebration of Christmas. In English literature such "folkloric" elements often elicit romantic nostalgia. Geoffrey Chaucer's Wife of Bath looks back to a magical time before the arrival of Christianity in which the land was "fulfilled of fairye." Hundreds of years later, the seventeenth-century writer Robert Herrick honors the amalgamation of Christian and pagan elements in agrarian British culture in such poems as "Corinna's Gone A-Maying" and "The Hock Cart."

Medieval Christianity was fairly uniform across Western Europe—hence called "catholic," or universally shared—and its rituals and expectations, common to the whole community, permeated everyday life. The Catholic Church was also an international power structure. In its hierarchy of pope, cardinals, archbishops, and bishops, it resembled the feudal state, but the church power structure coexisted alongside a separate hierarchy of lay authorities with a theoretically different sphere of social responsibilities. The sharing out of lay and ecclesiastical authority in medieval England was sometimes a source of conflict. Chaucer's pilgrims are on their way to visit the memorial shrine to one victim of such struggle: Thomas a Becket, Archbishop of Canterbury, who opposed the policies of King Henry III, was assassinated on the king's orders in 1120 and later made a saint. As an international organization, the church conducted its business in the universal language of Latin, and thus although statistically in the period the largest segment of literate persons were monks and priests, the clerical contribution to great writing in English was relatively modest. Yet the lay writers of the period reflect the importance of the church as an institution and the pervasiveness of religion in everyday life.

Beginning in 1517 the German monk Martin Luther, in Wittenberg, Germany, openly challenged many aspects of Catholic practice and by 1520 had completely repudiated the authority of the Pope, setting in train the Protestant Reformation. Luther argued that the Roman Catholic Church had strayed far from the pattern of Christianity laid out in scripture. He rejected Catholic doctrines for which no biblical authority was to be found, such as the belief in Purgatory, and translated the Bible into German, on the grounds that the importance of scripture for all Christians made its translation into the vernacular tongue essential. Luther was not the first to advance such views—followers of the Englishman John Wycliffe had translated the Bible in the fourteenth century. But Luther, protected by powerful German rulers, was able to speak out with impunity and convert others to his views, rather than suffer the persecution usually meted out to heretics. Soon other reformers were following in Luther's footsteps: of these, the Swiss Ulrich Zwingli and the French Jean Calvin would be especially influential for English religious thought.

At first England remained staunchly Catholic. Its king, Henry VIII, was so severe to heretics that the Pope awarded him the title "Defender of the Faith," which British monarchs have retained to this day. In 1534, however, Henry rejected the authority of the Pope to prevent his divorce from his queen, Catherine of Aragon, and his marriage to his mistress, Ann Boleyn. In doing so, Henry appropriated to himself ecclesiastical as well as secular authority. Thomas More, author of *Utopia*, was executed for refusing to endorse Henry's right to govern the English church. Over the following six years, Henry consolidated his grip on the ecclesiastical establishment by dissolving the powerful, populous Catholic monasteries and redistributing their massive landholdings to his own lay followers. Yet Henry's church largely retained Catholic doctrine and liturgy. When Henry died and his young son, Edward, came to the throne in 1547, the English church embarked on a more Protestant path, a direction abruptly reversed when Edward died and his older sister Mary, the daughter of Catherine of Aragon, took the throne in 1553 and attempted to reintroduce Roman Catholicism. Mary's reign was also short, however, and her successor, Elizabeth I, the daughter of Ann Boleyn, was a Protestant. Elizabeth attempted to establish a "middle way" Christianity, compromising between Roman Catholic practices and beliefs and reformed ones.

The Church of England, though it laid claim to a national rather than pan-European authority, aspired like its predecessor to be the universal church of all English subjects. It retained the Catholic structure of parishes and dioceses and the Catholic hierarchy of bishops, though the ecclesiastical authority was now the Archbishop of Canterbury and the Church's "Supreme Governor" was the monarch. Yet disagreement and controversy persisted. Some members of the Church of England wanted to retain many of the ritual and liturgical elements of Catholicism. Others, the Puritans, advocated a more thoroughgoing reformation. Most Puritans remained within the Church of England, but a minority, the "Separatists" or "Congregationalists," split from the established church altogether. These dissenters no longer thought of the ideal church as an organization to which everybody belonged; instead, they conceived it as a more exclusive group of likeminded people, one not necessarily attached to a larger body of believers.

In the seventeenth century, the succession of the Scottish king James to the English throne produced another problem. England and Scotland were separate nations, and in the sixteenth century Scotland had developed its own national Presbyterian church, or "kirk," under the leadership of the reformer John Knox. The kirk retained fewer Catholic liturgical elements than did the Church of England, and its authorities, or "presbyters," were elected by assemblies of their fellow clerics, rather than appointed by the king. James I and his son Charles I, especially the latter, wanted to bring the Scottish kirk into conformity with Church of England practices. The Scots violently resisted these efforts, with the collaboration of many English Puritans, in a conflict that eventually developed into the English Civil War in the mid-seventeenth century. The effect of these disputes is visible in the poetry of such writers as John Milton, Robert Herrick, Henry Vaughan, and Thomas Traherne, and in the prose of Thomas Browne, Lucy Hutchinson, and Dorothy Waugh. Just as in the mid-sixteenth century, when a succession of monarchs with different religious commitments destabilized the church, so the seventeenth century endured spiritual whiplash. King Charles I's highly ritualistic Church of England was violently overturned by the Puritan victors in the Civil War—until 1660, after the death of the Puritan leader, Oliver Cromwell, when the Church of England was restored along with the monarchy.

The religious and political upheavals of the seventeenth century produced Christian sects that de-emphasized the ceremony of the established church and rejected as well its top-down authority structure. Some of these groups were ephemeral, but the Baptists (founded in 1608 in Amsterdam by the English expatriate John Smyth) and Quakers, or Society of Friends (founded by George Fox in the 1640s), flourished outside the established church, sometimes despite cruel persecution. John Bunyan, a Baptist, wrote the Christian allegory *Pilgrim's Progress* while in prison. Some dissenters, like the Baptists, shared the reformed reverence for the absolute authority of scripture but interpreted the scriptural texts differently from their fellow Protestants. Others, like the Quakers, favored, even over the authority of the Bible, the "inner light" or voice of individual conscience, which they took to be the working of the Holy Spirit in the lives of individuals.

The Protestant dissenters were not England's only religious minorities. Despite crushing fines and the threat of imprisonment, a minority of Catholics under Elizabeth and James openly refused to give their allegiance to the new church, and others remained secret adherents to the old ways. John Donne was brought up in an ardently Catholic family, and several other writers converted to Catholicism as adults—Ben Jonson for a considerable part of his career, Elizabeth Carey and Richard Crashaw permanently, and at profound personal cost. In the eighteenth century, Catholics remained objects of suspicion as possible agents of sedition, especially after the "Glorious Revolution" in 1688 deposed the Catholic James II in favor of the Protestant William and Mary. Anti-Catholic prejudice affected John Dryden, a Catholic convert, as well as the lifelong Catholic Alexander Pope. By contrast, the English colony of Ireland remained overwhelmingly Roman Catholic, the fervor of its religious commitment at least partly inspired by resistance to English occupation. Starting in the reign of Elizabeth, England shored up its own authority in Ireland by encouraging Protestant immigrants from Scotland to settle in northern Ireland, producing a virulent religious divide the effects of which are still playing out today.

A small community of Jews had moved from France to London after 1066, when the Norman William the Conqueror came to the English throne. Although despised and persecuted by many Christians, they were allowed to remain as moneylenders to the Crown, until the thirteenth century, when the king developed alternative sources of credit. At this point, in 1290, the Jews were expelled from England. In 1655 Oliver Cromwell permitted a few to return, and in the late seventeenth and early eighteenth centuries the Jewish population slowly increased, mainly by immigration from Germany. In the mid-eighteenth century some prominent Jews had their children brought up as Christians so as to facilitate their full integration into English society: thus the nineteenth-century writer and politician Benjamin Disraeli, although he and his father were members of the Church of England, was widely considered a Jew insofar as his ancestry was Jewish.

In the late seventeenth century, as the Church of England reasserted itself, Catholics, Jews, and dissenting Protestants found themselves subject to significant legal restrictions. The Corporation Act, passed in 1661, and the Test Act, passed in 1673, excluded all who refused to take communion in the Church of England from voting, attending university, or working in government or in the professions. Members of religious minorities, as well as Church of England communicants, paid mandatory taxes in support of Church of England ministers and buildings. In 1689 the dissenters gained the right to worship in public, but Jews and Catholics were not permitted to do so.

During the eighteenth century, political, intellectual, and religious history remained closely intertwined. The Church of England came to accommodate a good deal of variety. "Low church" services resembled those of the dissenting Protestant churches, minimizing ritual and emphasizing the sermon; the "high church" retained more elaborate ritual elements, yet its prestige was under attack on several fronts. Many Enlightenment thinkers subjected the Bible to rational critique and found it wanting: the philosopher David Hume, for instance, argued that the "miracles" described therein were more probably lies or errors than real breaches of the laws of nature. Within the Church of England, the "broad church" Latitudinarians welcomed this rationalism, advocating theological openness and an emphasis on ethics rather than dogma. More radically, the Unitarian movement rejected the divinity of Christ while professing to accept his ethical teachings. Taking a different tack, the preacher

John Wesley, founder of Methodism, responded to the rationalists' challenge with a newly fervent call to evangelism and personal discipline; his movement was particularly successful in Wales. Revolutions in America and France at the end of the century generated considerable millenarian excitement and fostered more new religious ideas, often in conjunction with a radical social agenda. Many important writers of the Romantic period were indebted to traditions of protestant dissent: Unitarian and rationalist protestant ideas influenced William Hazlitt, Anna Barbauld, Mary Wollstonecraft, and the young Samuel Taylor Coleridge. William Blake created a highly idiosyncratic poetic mythology loosely indebted to radical strains of Christian mysticism. Others were even more heterodox: Lord Byron and Robert Burns, brought up as Scots Presbyterians, rebelled fiercely, and Percy Shelley's writing of an atheistic pamphlet resulted in his expulsion from Oxford.

Great Britain never erected an American-style "wall of separation" between church and state, but in practice religion and secular affairs grew more and more distinct during the nineteenth century. In consequence, members of religious minorities no longer seemed to pose a threat to the commonweal. A movement to repeal the Test Act failed in the 1790s, but a renewed effort resulted in the extension of the franchise to dissenting Protestants in 1828 and to Catholics in 1829. The numbers of Roman Catholics in England were swelled by immigration from Ireland, but there were also some prominent English adherents. Among writers, the converts John Newman and Gerard Manley Hopkins are especially important. The political participation and social integration of Jews presented a thornier challenge. Lionel de Rothschild, repeatedly elected to represent London in Parliament during the 1840s and 1850s, was not permitted to take his seat there because he refused to take his oath of office "on the true faith of a Christian"; finally, in 1858, the Jewish Disabilities Act allowed him to omit these words. Only in 1871, however, were Oxford and Cambridge opened to non-Anglicans.

Meanwhile geological discoveries and Charles Darwin's evolutionary theories increasingly cast doubt on the literal truth of the Creation story, and close philological analysis of the biblical text suggested that its origins were human rather than divine. By the end of the nineteenth century, many writers were bearing witness to a world in which Christianity no longer seemed fundamentally plausible. In his poetry and prose, Thomas Hardy depicts a world devoid of benevolent providence. Matthew Arnold's poem "Dover Beach" is in part an elegy to lost spiritual assurance, as the "Sea of Faith" goes out like the tide: "But now I only hear / Its melancholy, long, withdrawing roar / Retreating." For Arnold, literature must replace religion as a source of spiritual truth, and intimacy between individuals substitute for the lost communal solidarity of the universal church.

The work of many twentieth-century writers shows the influence of a religious upbringing or a religious conversion in adulthood. T. S. Eliot and W. S. Auden embrace Anglicanism, William Butler Yeats spiritualism. James Joyce repudiates Irish Catholicism but remains obsessed with it. Yet religion, or lack of it, is a matter of individual choice and conscience, not social or legal mandate. In the past fifty years, church attendance has plummeted in Great Britain. Although 71 percent of the population still identified itself as "Christian" on the 2000 census, only about 7 percent of these regularly attend religious services of any denomination. Meanwhile, immigration from former British colonies has swelled the ranks of religions once alien to the British Isles—Muslim, Sikh, Hindu, Buddhist—though the numbers of adherents remain small relative to the total population.

THE UNIVERSE ACCORDING TO PTOLEMY

Ptolemy was a Roman astronomer of Greek descent, born in Egypt during the second century C.E.; for nearly fifteen hundred years after his death his account of the design of the universe was accepted as standard. During that time, the basic pattern underwent many detailed modifications and was fitted out with many astrological and pseudoscientific trappings. But in essence Ptolemy's followers portrayed the earth as the center of the universe, with the sun, planets, and fixed stars set in transparent spheres orbiting around it. In this scheme of things, as modified for Christian usage, Hell was usually placed under the earth's surface at the center of the cosmic globe, while Heaven, the abode of the blessed spirits, was in the outermost, uppermost circle, the empyrean. But in 1543 the Polish astronomer Copernicus proposed an alternative hypothesis—that the earth rotates around the sun, not vice versa; and despite theological opposition, observations with the new telescope and careful mathematical calculations insured ultimate acceptance of the new view.

The map of the Ptolemaic universe below is a simplified version of a diagram in Peter Apian's *Cosmography* (1584). In such a diagram, the Firmament is the sphere that contained the fixed stars; the Crystalline Sphere, which contained no heavenly bodies, is a late innovation, included to explain certain anomalies in the observed movement of the heavenly bodies; and the Prime Mover is the sphere that, itself put into motion by God, imparts rotation around the earth to all the other spheres.

Milton, writing in the mid-seventeenth century, used two universes. The Copernican universe, though he alludes to it, was too large, formless, and unfamiliar to be the setting for the war between Heaven and Hell in *Paradise Lost*. He therefore used the Ptolemaic cosmos, but placed Heaven well outside this smaller earth-centered universe, Hell far beneath it, and assigned the vast middle space to Chaos.

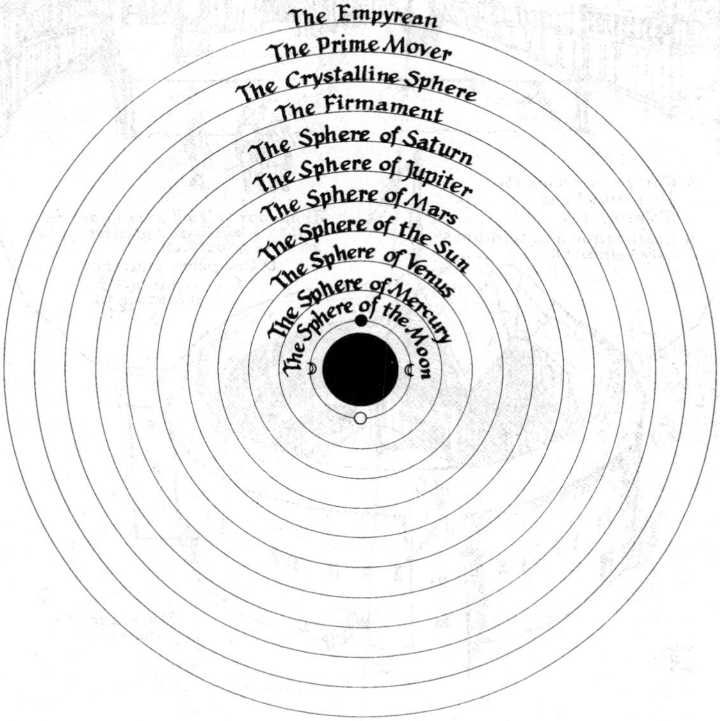

A LONDON PLAYHOUSE OF SHAKESPEARE'S TIME

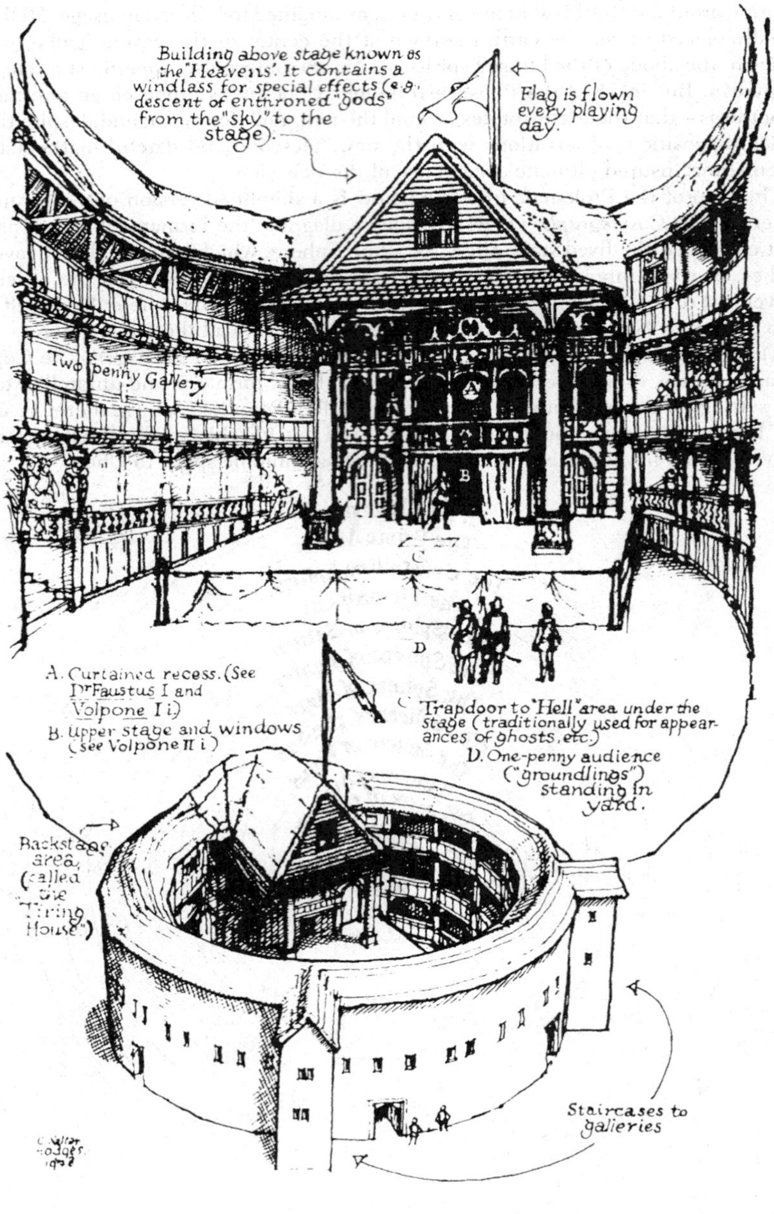

Building above stage known as the "Heavens". It contains a windlass for special effects (e.g. descent of enthroned "gods" from the "sky" to the stage).
Flag is flown every playing day.
Two penny Gallery
B
C
D
A. Curtained recess. (See Dr Faustus I and Volpone I i)
B. Upper stage and windows (see Volpone II i)
C Trapdoor to "Hell" area under the stage (traditionally used for appearances of ghosts, etc.)
D. One-penny audience ("groundlings") standing in yard.
Backstage area, (called the "Tiring House")
Staircases to galleries
C. Walter Hodges 1958

PERMISSIONS ACKNOWLEDGMENTS

Aphra Behn: *The Complete Text of OROONOKO,* edited by Joanna Lipking. Copyright © 1993 by Joanna Lipking and W. W. Norton & Company, Inc. Reprinted by permission of W. W. Norton & Company, Inc.

***Beowulf*:** from BEOWULF, translated by Seamus Heaney. Copyright © 2000 by Seamus Heaney. Used with permission of W. W. Norton & Company, Inc.

Frances Burney: *First Journal Entry* (ca. 800 words), from THE EARLY JOURNALS AND LETTERS OF FANNY BURNEY, VOL. 1, edited by Lars E. Troide (1988). Reprinted by permission of Oxford University Press. *"Down with Her, Burney!"* from THE EARLY JOURNALS AND LETTERS OF FANNY BURNEY, VOL. 3, edited by Lars E. Troide & Stewart J. Cooke. *Mastectomy,* from THE JOURNALS AND LETTERS OF FANNY BURNEY, VOL. 6, edited by Joyce Hemlow. Reprinted with the permission of McGill–Queen's University Press Ltd and Oxford University Press.

Margaret Lucas Cavendish: Extracts from THE BLAZING WORLD are taken from Margaret Cavendish, Duchess of Newcastle, THE DESCRIPTION OF A NEW WORLD CALLED THE BLAZING WORLD AND OTHER WRITINGS, edited by Kate Lilley (London: Pickering & Chatto 1992). Reprinted by permission of the publisher.

Geoffrey Chaucer: All excerpts are from CHAUCER'S POETRY: AN ANTHOLOGY FOR THE MODERN READER, 2nd ed., edited by E. T. Donaldson. Copyright © 1958, 1975 by Scott Foresman and Company. Reprinted by permission of Pearson Educational, Inc.

Queen Elizabeth: *On Monsieur's Departure* from THE POEMS OF QUEEN ELIZABETH I, edited by Leicester Bradner. Copyright © 1964 by Brown University. Reprinted by permission of the University Press of New England. *Letter to Sir Amyas Paulet* from THE LETTERS OF QUEEN ELIZABETH, edited by G. B. Harrison (Cassell, 1935). Reprinted by permission of David Higham Associates. *The Golden Speech* from THE PUBLIC SPEAKING OF QUEEN ELIZABETH: SELECTIONS FROM HER OFFICIAL ADDRESSES, edited by George P. Rice, Jr. (AMS Press, 1966). Reprinted with the permission of AMS Press, Inc.

Thomas Gray: From the manuscript of *Elegy Written in a Country Churchyard.* Transcribed by kind permission of the Provost and Fellows of Eton College.

William Hogarth: *Marriage A-la-Mode,* 1745, Plates 1–6, and *Beggar's Opera,* William Blake's engraving of the Hogarth illustration, 1795, reproduced by permission of the Print Collection, Miriam and Ira D. Wallach Division of Art, Prints and Photographs, The New York Public Library, Astor, Lenox and Tilden Foundations.

Samuel Johnson: Excerpt from the manuscript of *The Vanity of Human Wishes.* Reprinted with permission.

Julian of Norwich: Excerpts reprinted from Julian of Norwich, A BOOK OF SHOWINGS, edited by Edmund Colledge and James Walsh, by permission of the publisher. Copyright © 1978 by the Pontifical Institute of Mediaeval Studies, Toronto.

Margery Kempe: Bibliographical citation excerpts from THE BOOK OF MARGERY KEMPE, Copyright © 1996 by the Board of The Medieval Institute. Reprinted by permission of the publisher & Oxford University Press.

William Langland: Excerpts from PIERS PLOWMAN: AN ALLITERATIVE VERSE TRANSLATION by William Langland, translated by E. Talbot Donaldson. Translation copyright © 1990 by W. W. Norton & Company, Inc. Reprinted by permission of W. W. Norton & Company, Inc.

Marie de France: Translation of LANVAL by Alfred David. Copyright © 2000 by Alfred David. Reprinted with the permission of the translator.

John Milton: Lines from the manuscript of Milton's LYCIDAS. Reprinted with the permission of the Master and Fellows of Trinity College, Cambridge. Excerpts from *Areopagitica* from THE COMPLETE POETRY AND MAJOR PROSE OF MILTON, edited by Merritt Y. Hughes, copyright © 1957. Reprinted by permission of Prentice-Hall, Inc., Upper Saddle River, N.J. Complete text and endnotes From PARADISE LOST: A Norton Critical Edition, Second Edition, by John Milton edited by Scott Elledge. Copyright © 1993, 1975 by W. W. Norton & Company, Inc. Reprinted by permission of W. W. Norton & Company, Inc.

Lady Mary Wortley Montagu: Poems from LADY MARY WORTLEY MONTAGU, ESSAYS AND POEMS, 1977, Revised 1993, edited by R. Halsband and I. Grundy. Reprinted with permission.

Alexander Pope: From the manuscript of AN ESSAY ON MAN, MS Eng 233.21 transcribed by permission of the Houghton Library, Harvard University.

Petrarch: Reprinted by permission of the publisher from PETRARCH'S LYRIC POEMS: THE *RIME SPARSE* AND OTHER LYRICS, translated and edited by Robert M. Durling. Cambridge, Mass.: Harvard University Press, Copyright © 1976 by Robert M. Durling

William Shakespeare: *Twelfth Night,* from THE OXFORD SHAKESPEARE, edited by Stanley Wells and Gary Taylor (1988). Reprinted by permission of Oxford University Press.

Sir Philip Sidney: From THE POEMS OF SIR PHILIP SIDNEY, edited by William A. Ringler, Jr. (1962). Reprinted by permission of Oxford University Press.

Sir Gawain and the Green Knight: Complete text of SIR GAWAIN AND THE GREEN KNIGHT: A NEW VERSE TRANSLATION by Marie Boroff, translator. Copyright © 1967 by W. W. Norton & Company, Inc. Used by permission of W. W. Norton & Company, Inc.

John Wilmot: from THE WORKS OF JOHN WILMOT, EARL OF ROCHESTER edited by Harold Love, copyright © 1999. Reprinted by permission of Oxford University Press.

Lady Mary Wroth: Poems reprinted with the permission of the Louisiana State University Press from THE POEMS OF LADY MARY WROTH, edited, with an introduction and notes, by Josephine A. Roberts. Copyright © 1983 by Louisiana State University Press.

Every effort has been made to contact the copyright holders of each of the selections. Rights holders of any selections not credited should contact W. W. Norton & Company, Inc., 500 Fifth Avenue, New York, NY 10110, in order for a correction to be made in the next reprinting of our work.

Index